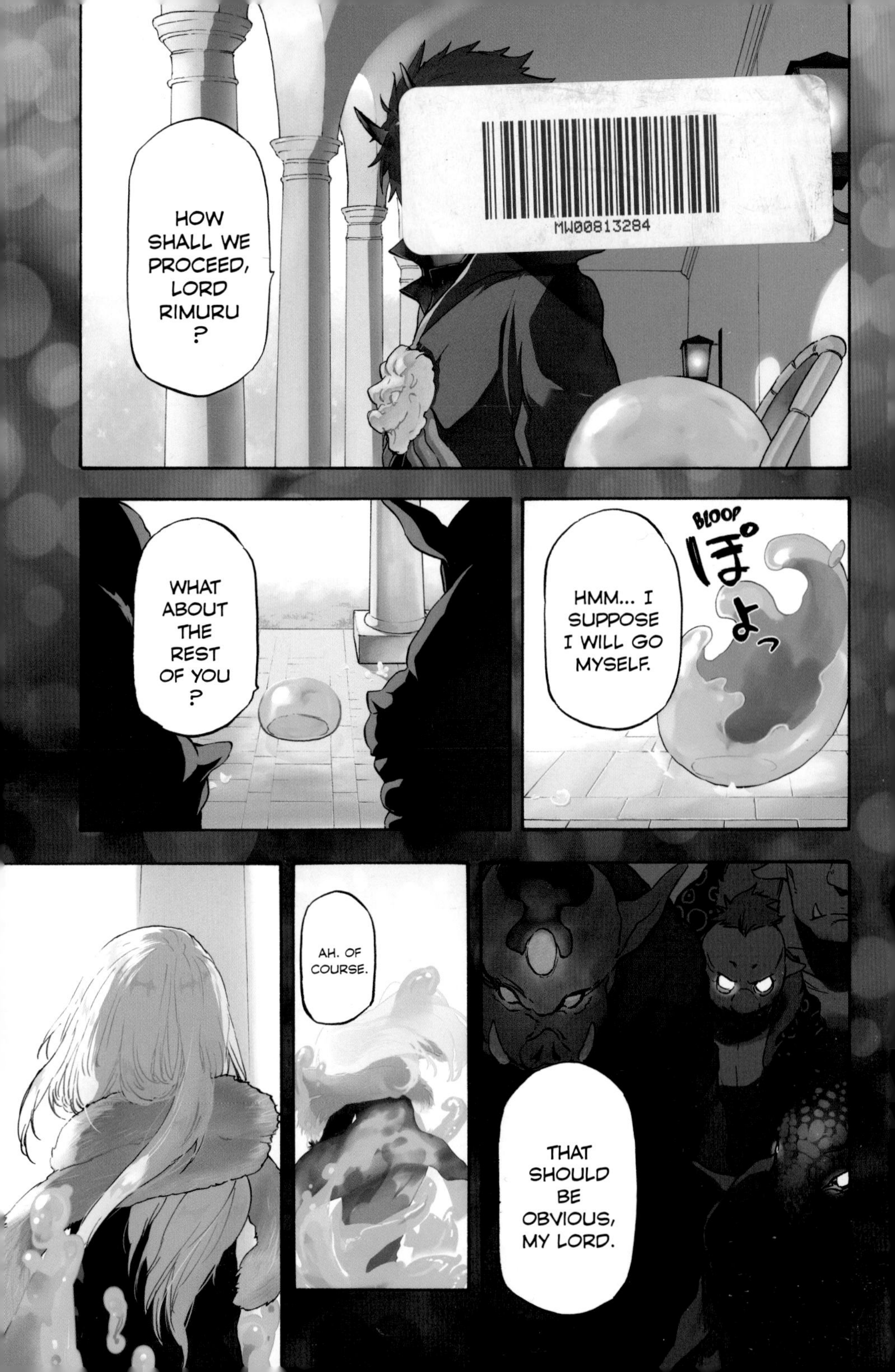
HOW SHALL WE PROCEED, LORD RIMURU?
BLOOP
ぽよっ
HMM... I SUPPOSE I WILL GO MYSELF.
WHAT ABOUT THE REST OF YOU?
THAT SHOULD BE OBVIOUS, MY LORD.
AH. OF COURSE.

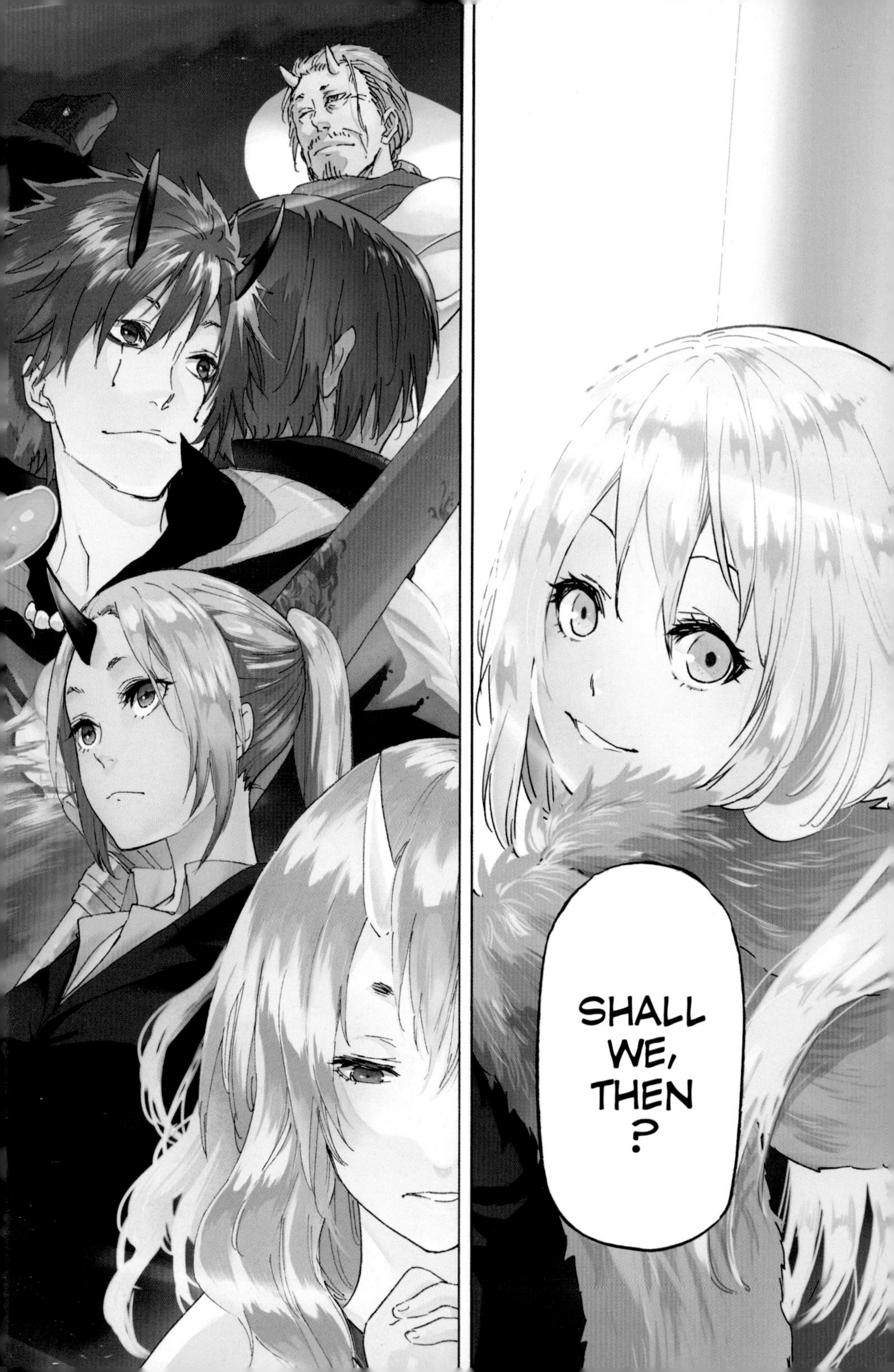
SHALL WE, THEN?

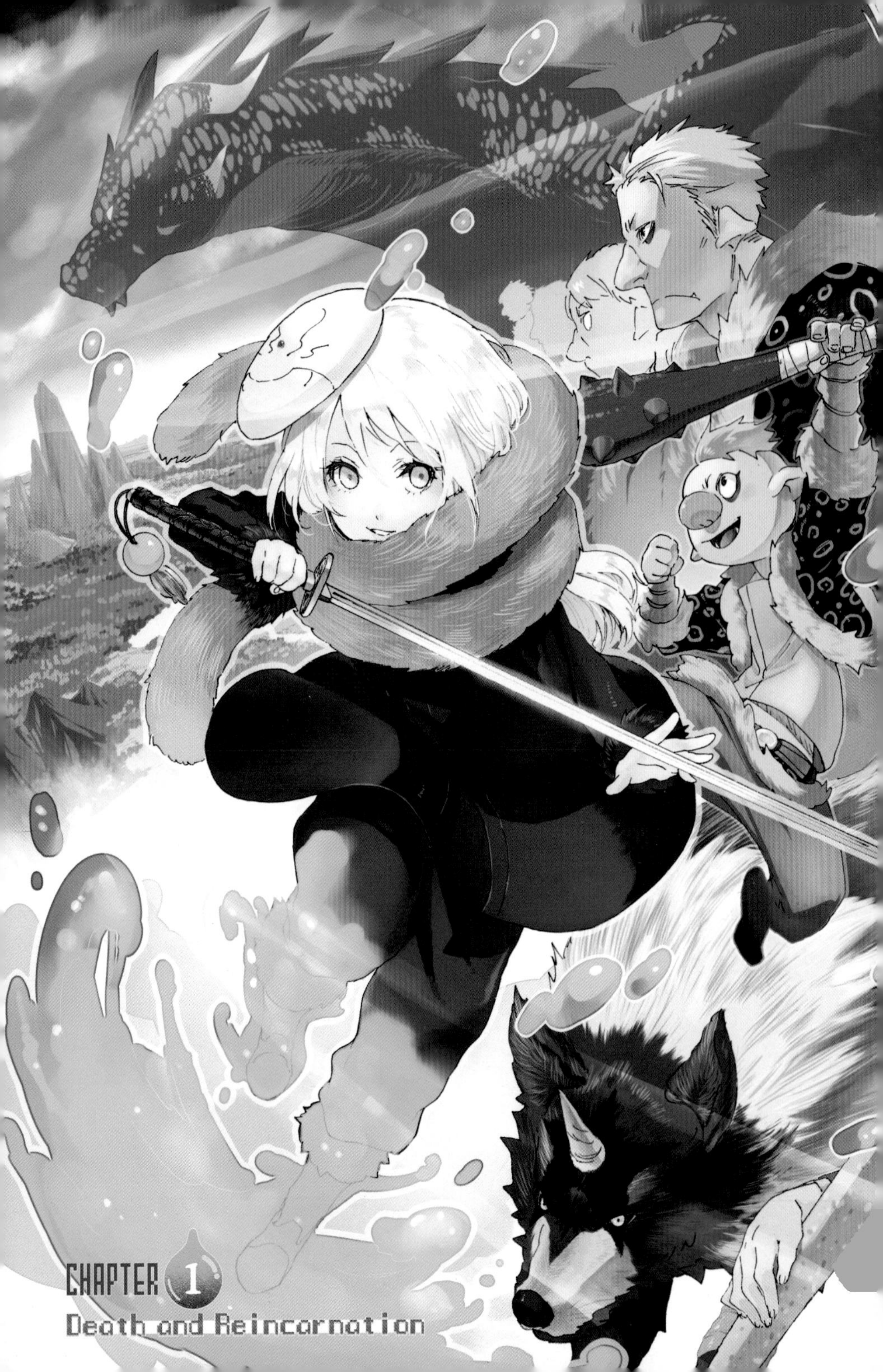
CHAPTER 1
Death and Reincarnation

CONTENTS

THAT TIME I GOT REINCARNATED AS A
SLIME

1

Author : FUSE

Artist : TAIKI KAWAKAMI

Character design : MITZ VAH

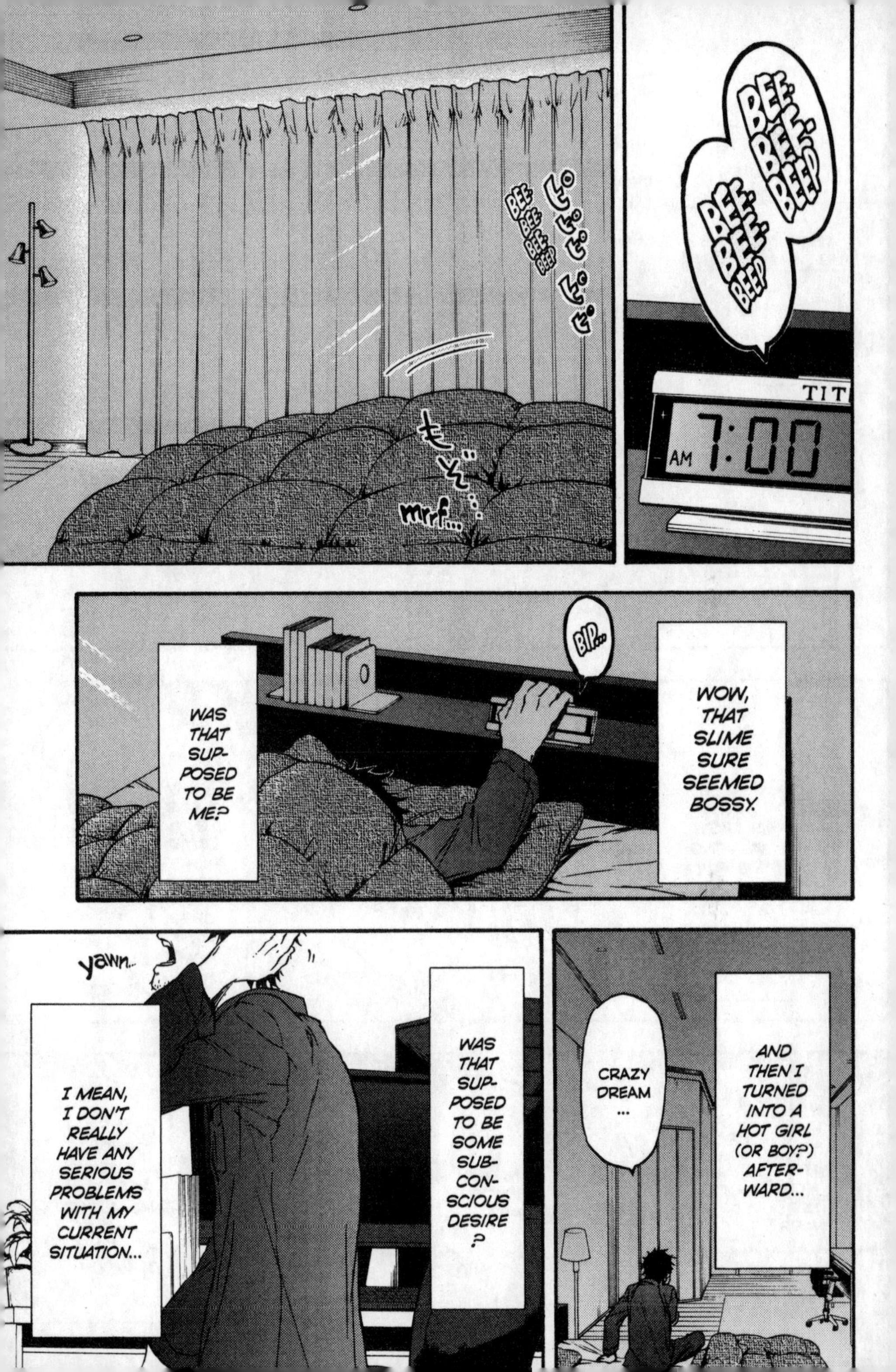
BEE-BEE-BEEP
BEE-BEE-BEEP
BEE BEE BEE BEEP
ぴぴぴぴ
もぞ…
mrrf...
BIP...
WOW, THAT SLIME SURE SEEMED BOSSY.
WAS THAT SUPPOSED TO BE ME?
AND THEN I TURNED INTO A HOT GIRL (OR BOY?) AFTERWARD...
CRAZY DREAM ...
WAS THAT SUPPOSED TO BE SOME SUBCONSCIOUS DESIRE?
yawn...
I MEAN, I DON'T REALLY HAVE ANY SERIOUS PROBLEMS WITH MY CURRENT SITUATION...

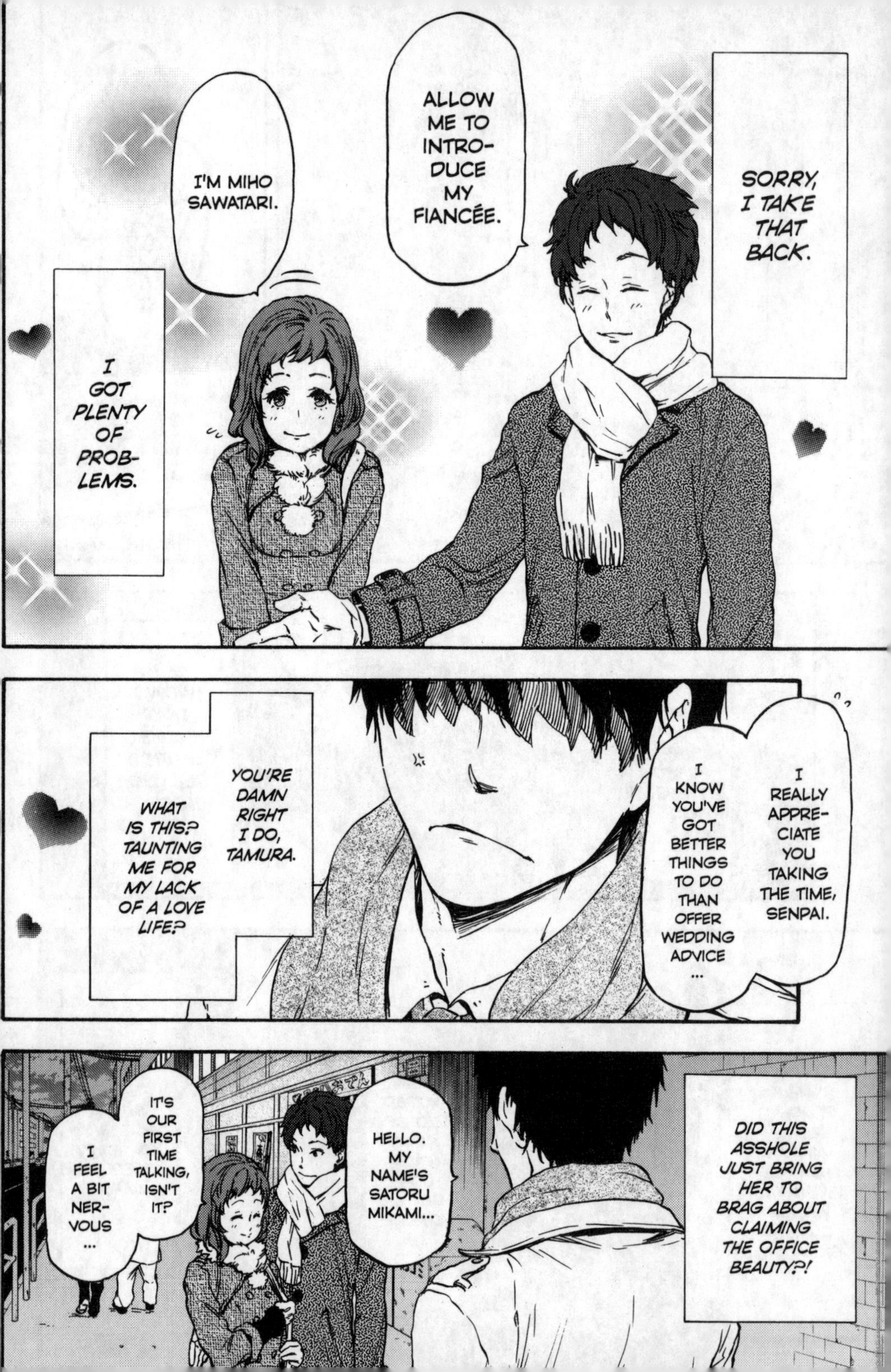
SORRY, I TAKE THAT BACK.
ALLOW ME TO INTRODUCE MY FIANCÉE.
I'M MIHO SAWATARI.
I GOT PLENTY OF PROBLEMS.
I REALLY APPRECIATE YOU TAKING THE TIME, SENPAI.
I KNOW YOU'VE GOT BETTER THINGS TO DO THAN OFFER WEDDING ADVICE...
YOU'RE DAMN RIGHT I DO, TAMURA.
WHAT IS THIS? TAUNTING ME FOR MY LACK OF A LOVE LIFE?
DID THIS ASSHOLE JUST BRING HER TO BRAG ABOUT CLAIMING THE OFFICE BEAUTY?!
HELLO. MY NAME'S SATORU MIKAMI...
IT'S OUR FIRST TIME TALKING, ISN'T IT?
I FEEL A BIT NERVOUS...

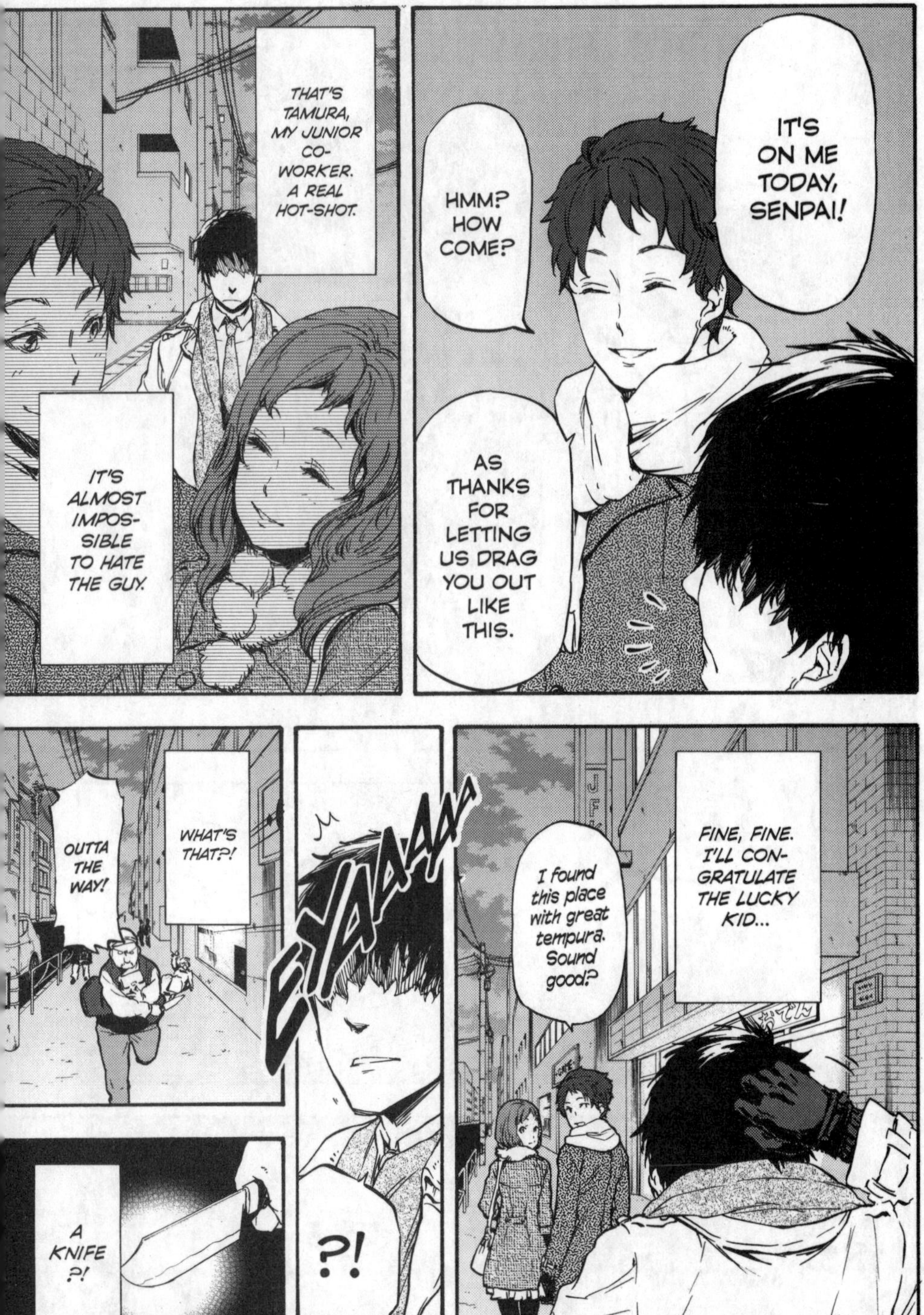
IT'S ON ME TODAY, SENPAI!
HMM? HOW COME?
AS THANKS FOR LETTING US DRAG YOU OUT LIKE THIS.
THAT'S TAMURA, MY JUNIOR CO-WORKER. A REAL HOT-SHOT.
IT'S ALMOST IMPOS-SIBLE TO HATE THE GUY.
FINE, FINE. I'LL CON-GRATULATE THE LUCKY KID...
I found this place with great tempura. Sound good?
EYAAAA
?!
WHAT'S THAT?!
OUTTA THE WAY!
A KNIFE ?!

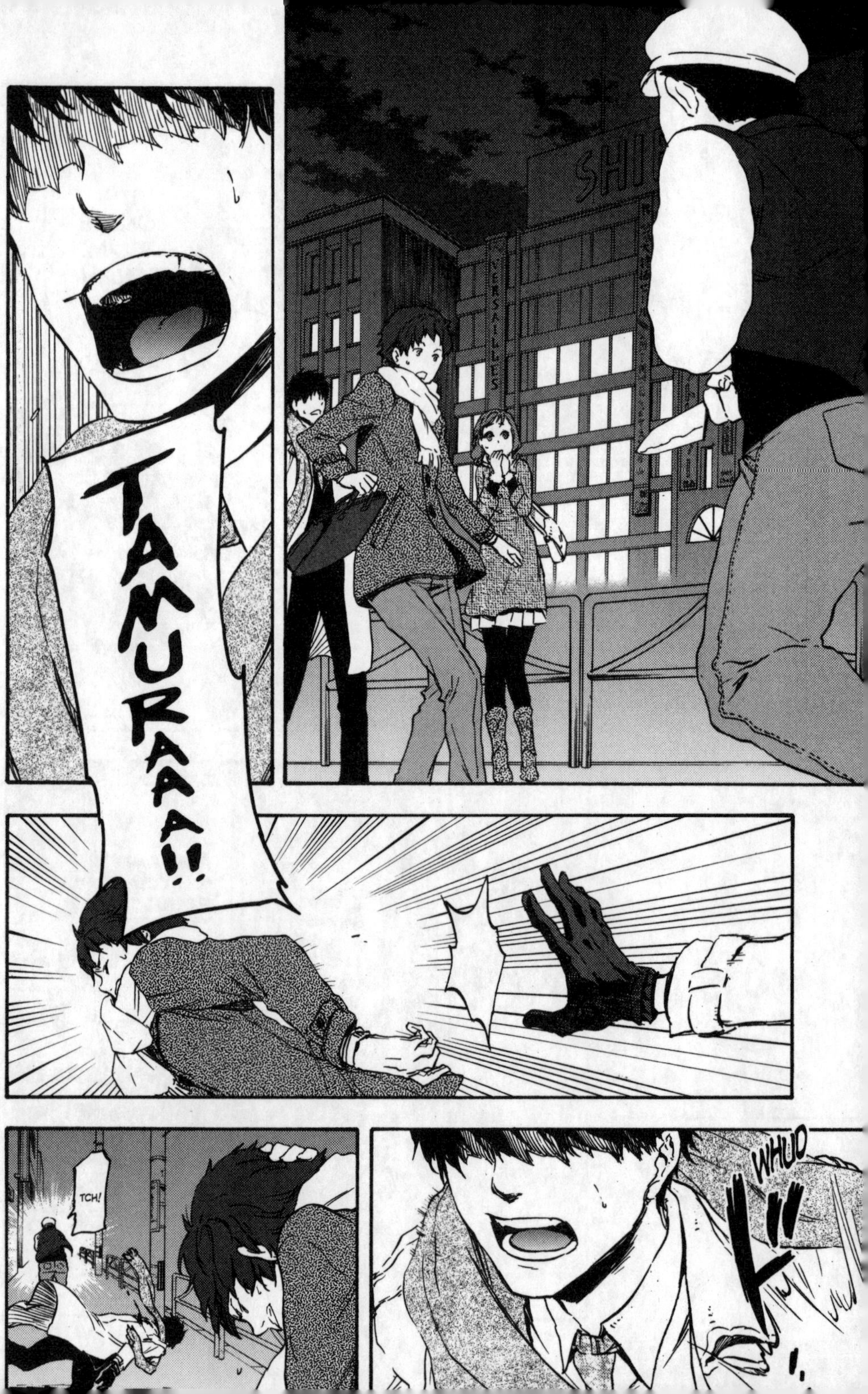
SHI
VERSAILLES
TAMURAAAA!!
WHUD
TCH!

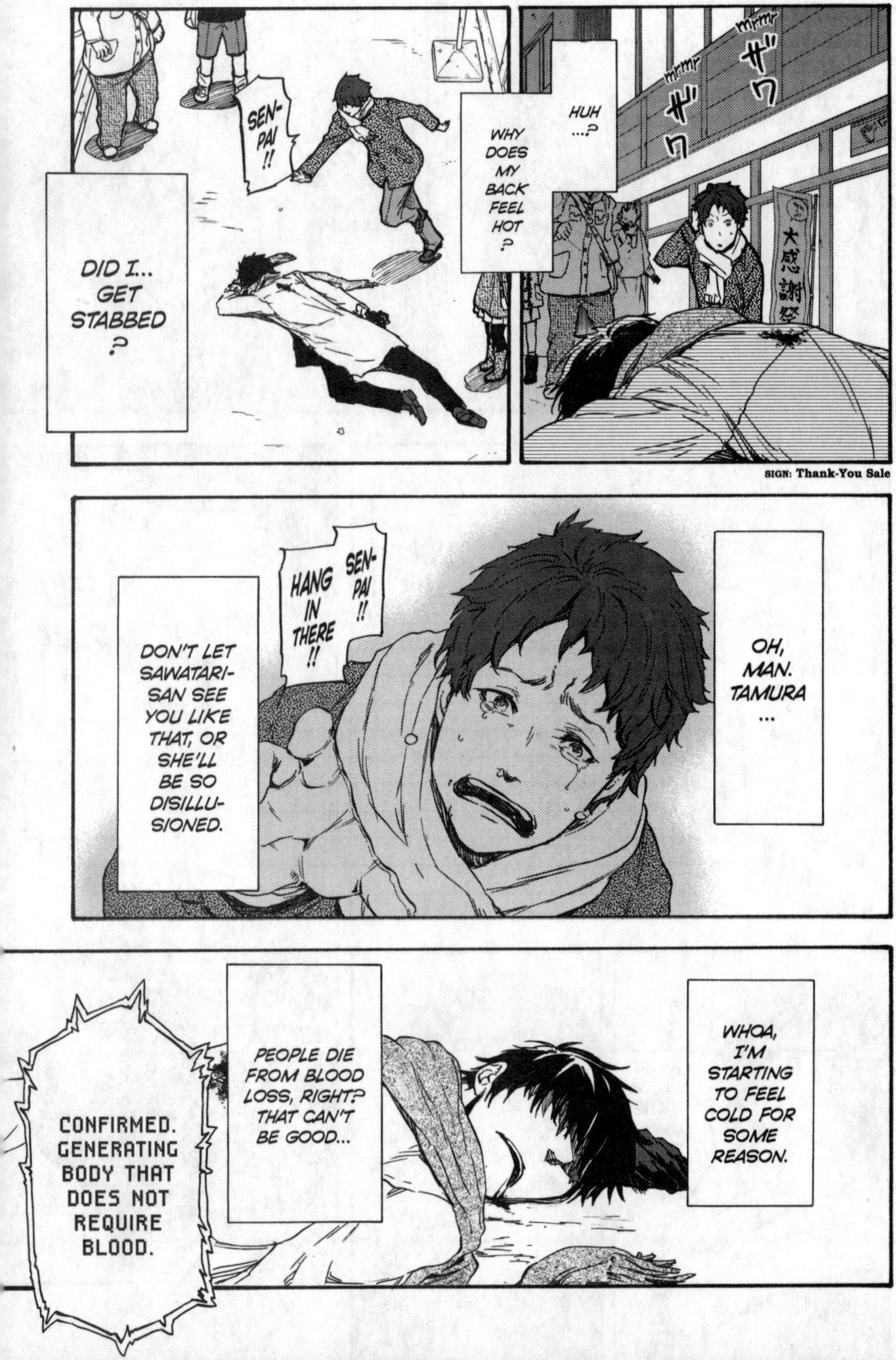
mrmr ザワ
mrmr ザワ
大感謝祭
HUH ...?
WHY DOES MY BACK FEEL HOT?
SEN-PAI!!
DID I... GET STABBED?
OH, MAN. TAMURA...
SEN-PAI!!
HANG IN THERE!!
DON'T LET SAWATARI-SAN SEE YOU LIKE THAT, OR SHE'LL BE SO DISILLUSIONED.
WHOA, I'M STARTING TO FEEL COLD FOR SOME REASON.
PEOPLE DIE FROM BLOOD LOSS, RIGHT? THAT CAN'T BE GOOD...
CONFIRMED. GENERATING BODY THAT DOES NOT REQUIRE BLOOD.

SIGN: Thank-You Sale

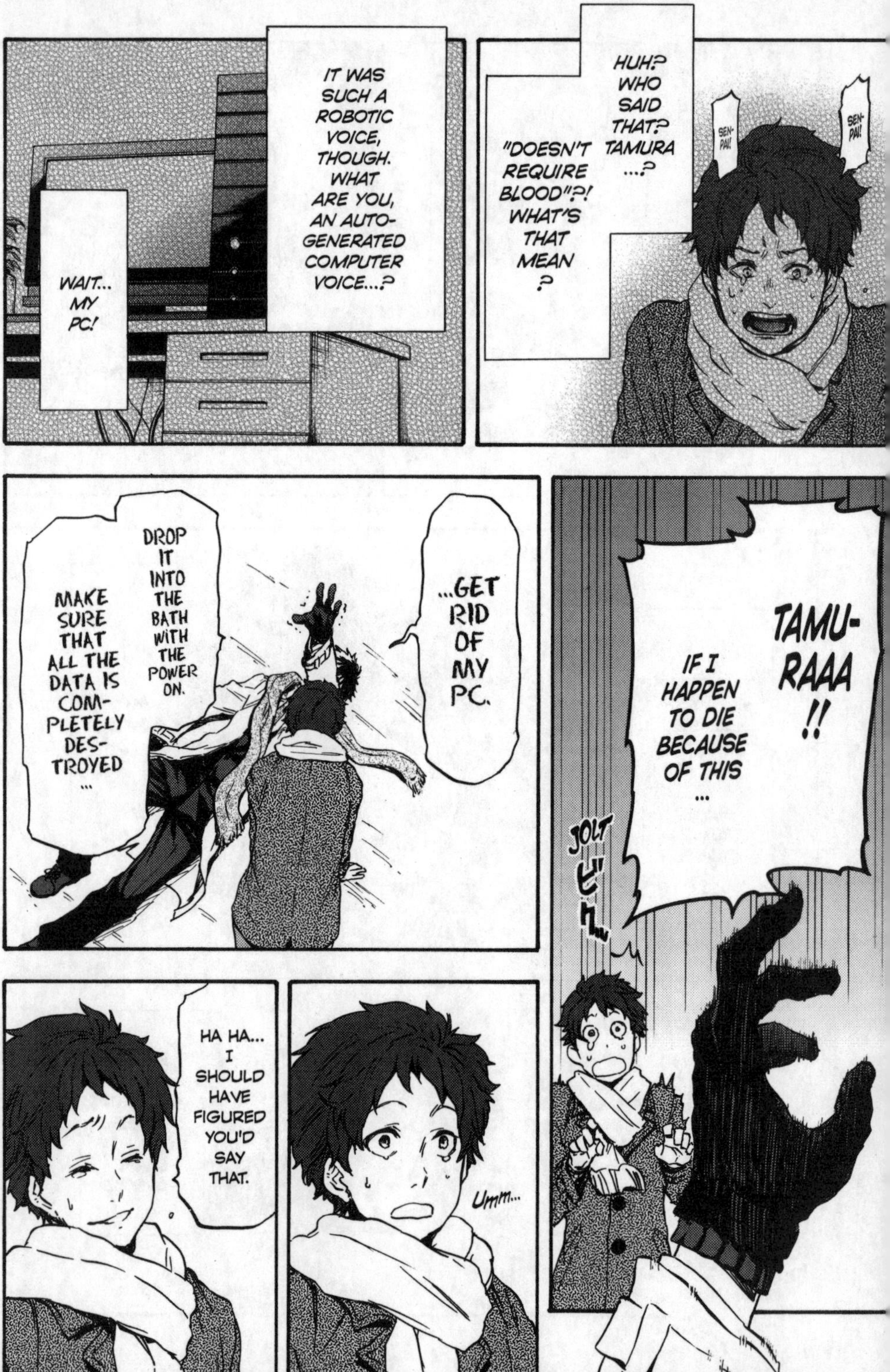
SEN-PAI!
SEN-PAI!
HUH? WHO SAID THAT? TAMURA ...?
"DOESN'T REQUIRE BLOOD"?! WHAT'S THAT MEAN ?
IT WAS SUCH A ROBOTIC VOICE, THOUGH. WHAT ARE YOU, AN AUTO-GENERATED COMPUTER VOICE...?
WAIT... MY PC!
TAMU-RAAA !!
IF I HAPPEN TO DIE BECAUSE OF THIS ...
JOLT
...GET RID OF MY PC.
DROP IT INTO THE BATH WITH THE POWER ON.
MAKE SURE THAT ALL THE DATA IS COMPLETELY DESTROYED ...
Umm...
HA HA... I SHOULD HAVE FIGURED YOU'D SAY THAT.

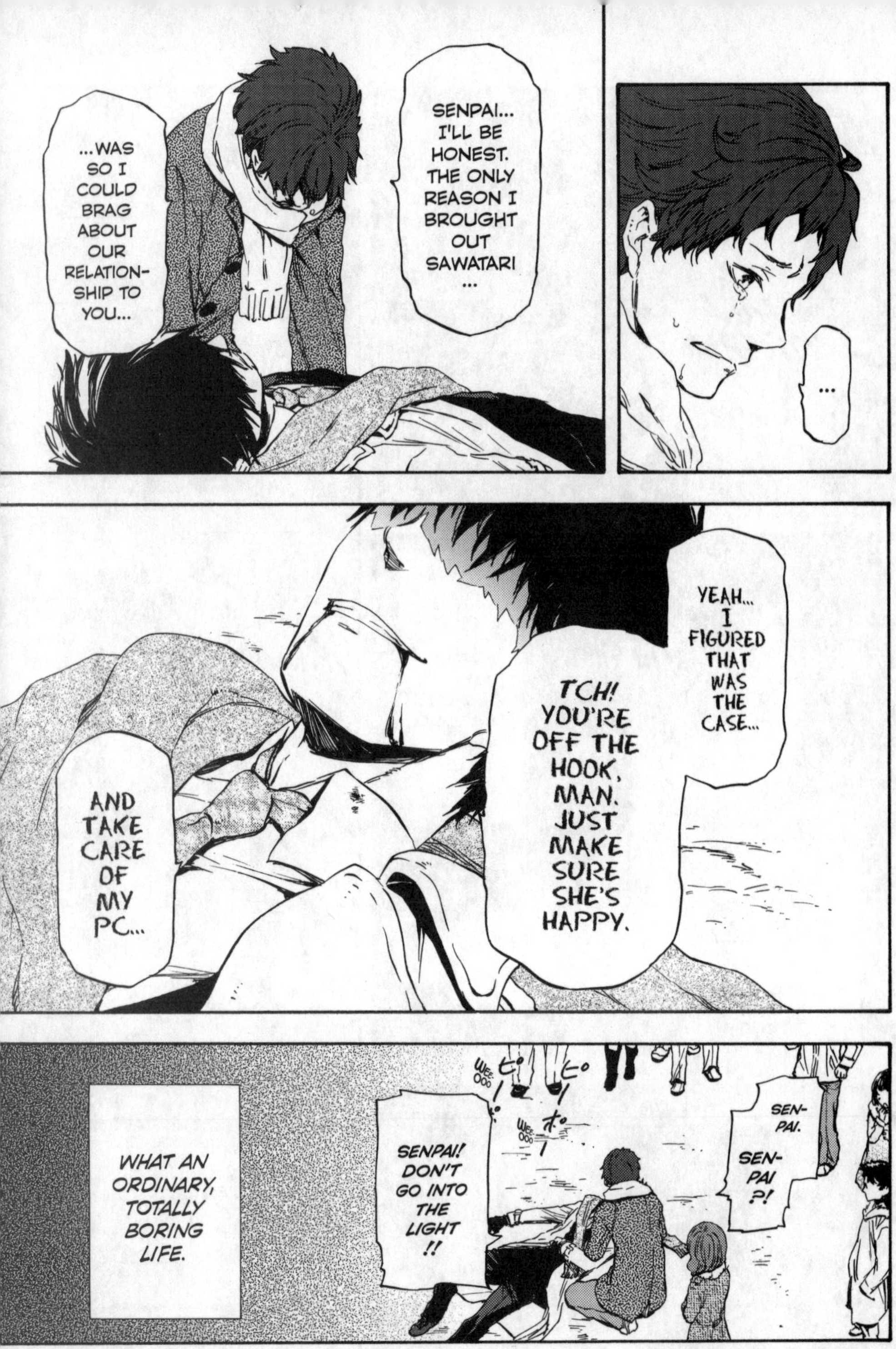
...
SENPAI... I'LL BE HONEST. THE ONLY REASON I BROUGHT OUT SAWATARI ...
...WAS SO I COULD BRAG ABOUT OUR RELATION-SHIP TO YOU...
YEAH... I FIGURED THAT WAS THE CASE...
TCH! YOU'RE OFF THE HOOK, MAN. JUST MAKE SURE SHE'S HAPPY.
AND TAKE CARE OF MY PC...
SEN-PAI.
SEN-PAI ?!
WEE-OOO
WEE-OOO
SENPAI! DON'T GO INTO THE LIGHT !!
WHAT AN ORDINARY, TOTALLY BORING LIFE.

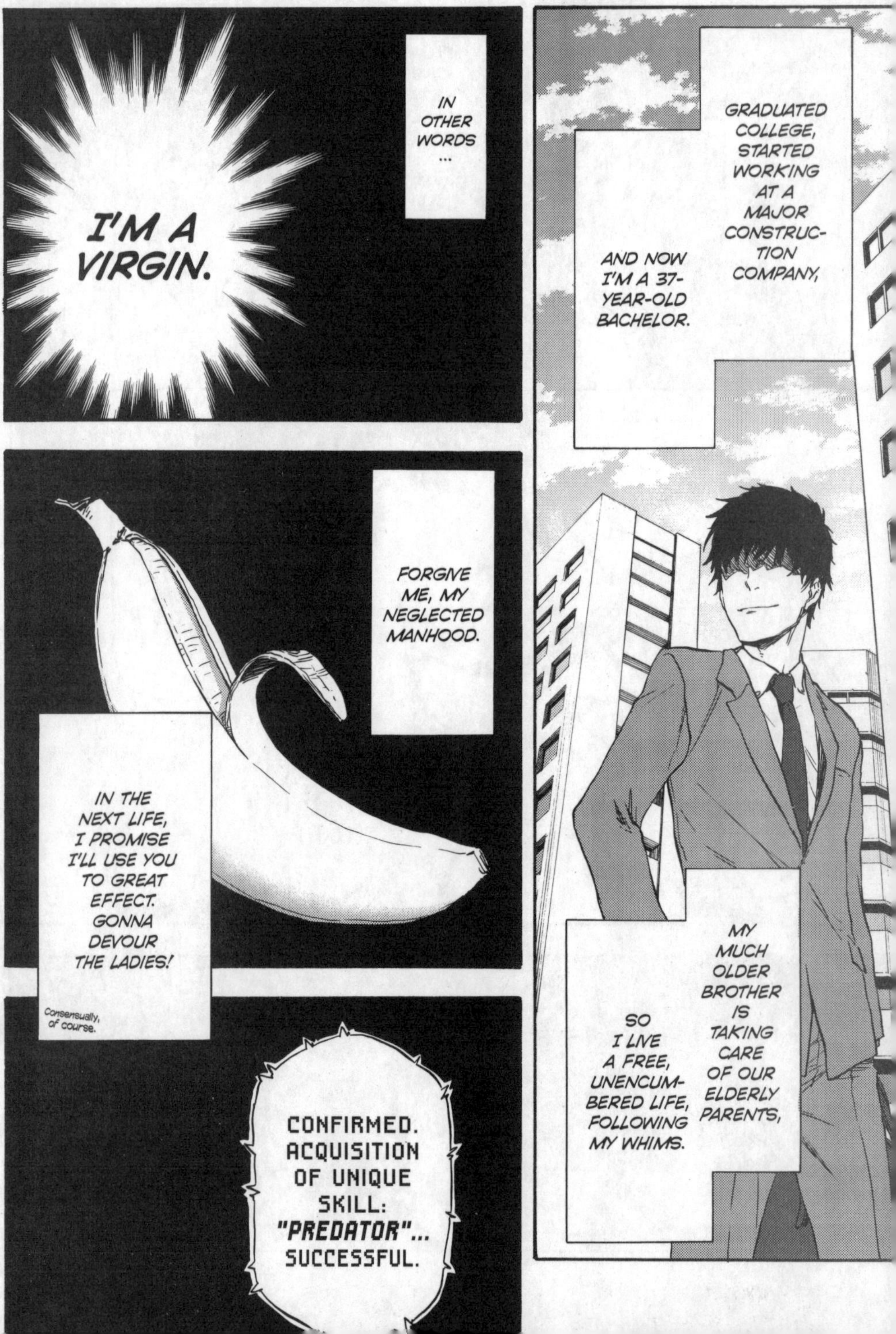
GRADUATED COLLEGE, STARTED WORKING AT A MAJOR CONSTRUCTION COMPANY,
AND NOW I'M A 37-YEAR-OLD BACHELOR.
MY MUCH OLDER BROTHER IS TAKING CARE OF OUR ELDERLY PARENTS,
SO I LIVE A FREE, UNENCUMBERED LIFE, FOLLOWING MY WHIMS.
IN OTHER WORDS...
I'M A VIRGIN.
FORGIVE ME, MY NEGLECTED MANHOOD.
IN THE NEXT LIFE, I PROMISE I'LL USE YOU TO GREAT EFFECT. GONNA DEVOUR THE LADIES!
Consensually, of course.
CONFIRMED. ACQUISITION OF UNIQUE SKILL: "PREDATOR"... SUCCESSFUL.

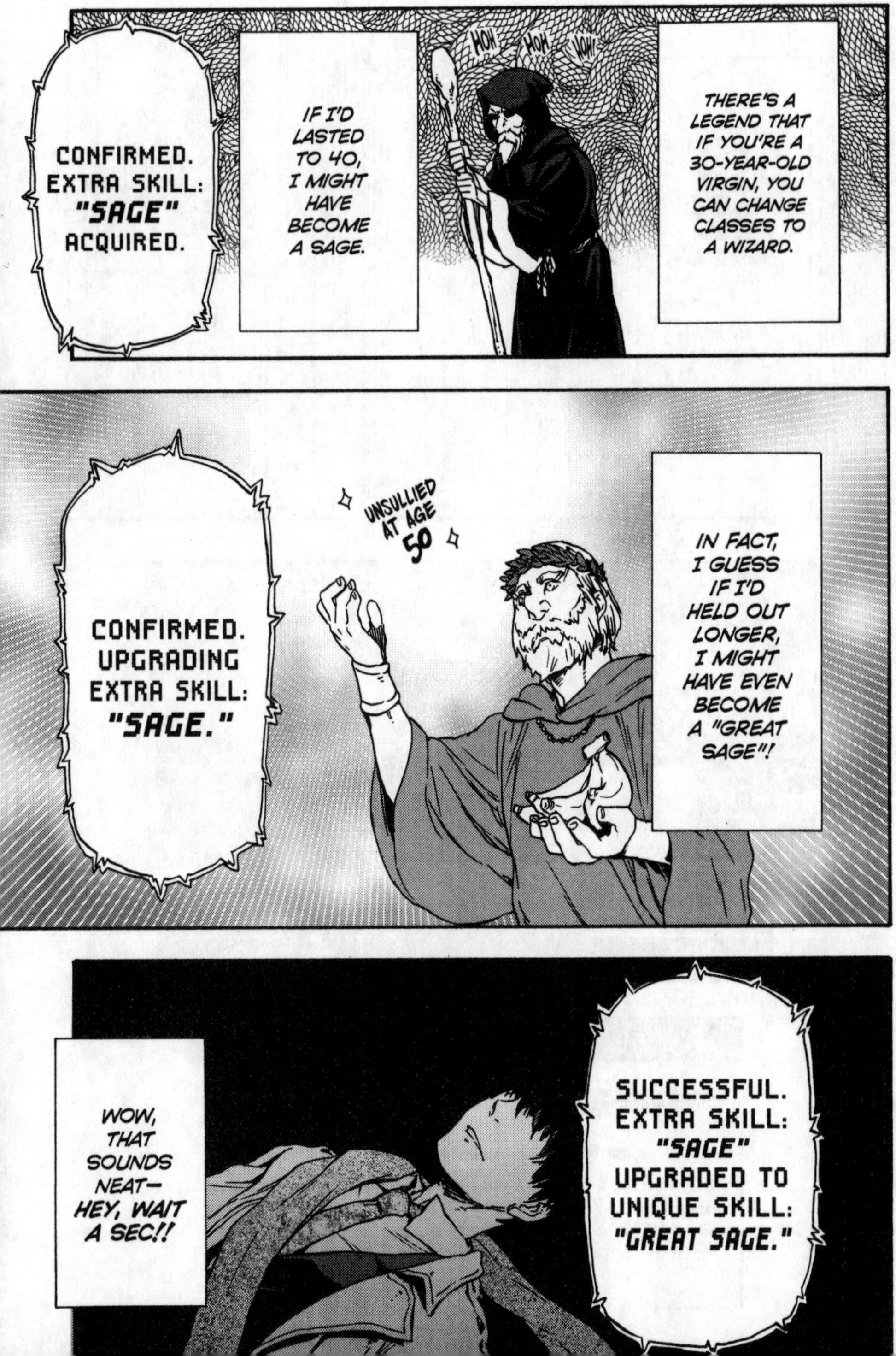
THERE'S A LEGEND THAT IF YOU'RE A 30-YEAR-OLD VIRGIN, YOU CAN CHANGE CLASSES TO A WIZARD.
HOH HOH HOH
IF I'D LASTED TO 40, I MIGHT HAVE BECOME A SAGE.
CONFIRMED. EXTRA SKILL: "SAGE" ACQUIRED.
IN FACT, I GUESS IF I'D HELD OUT LONGER, I MIGHT HAVE EVEN BECOME A "GREAT SAGE"!
UNSULLIED AT AGE 50
CONFIRMED. UPGRADING EXTRA SKILL: "SAGE."
SUCCESSFUL. EXTRA SKILL: "SAGE" UPGRADED TO UNIQUE SKILL: "GREAT SAGE."
WOW, THAT SOUNDS NEAT— HEY, WAIT A SEC!!

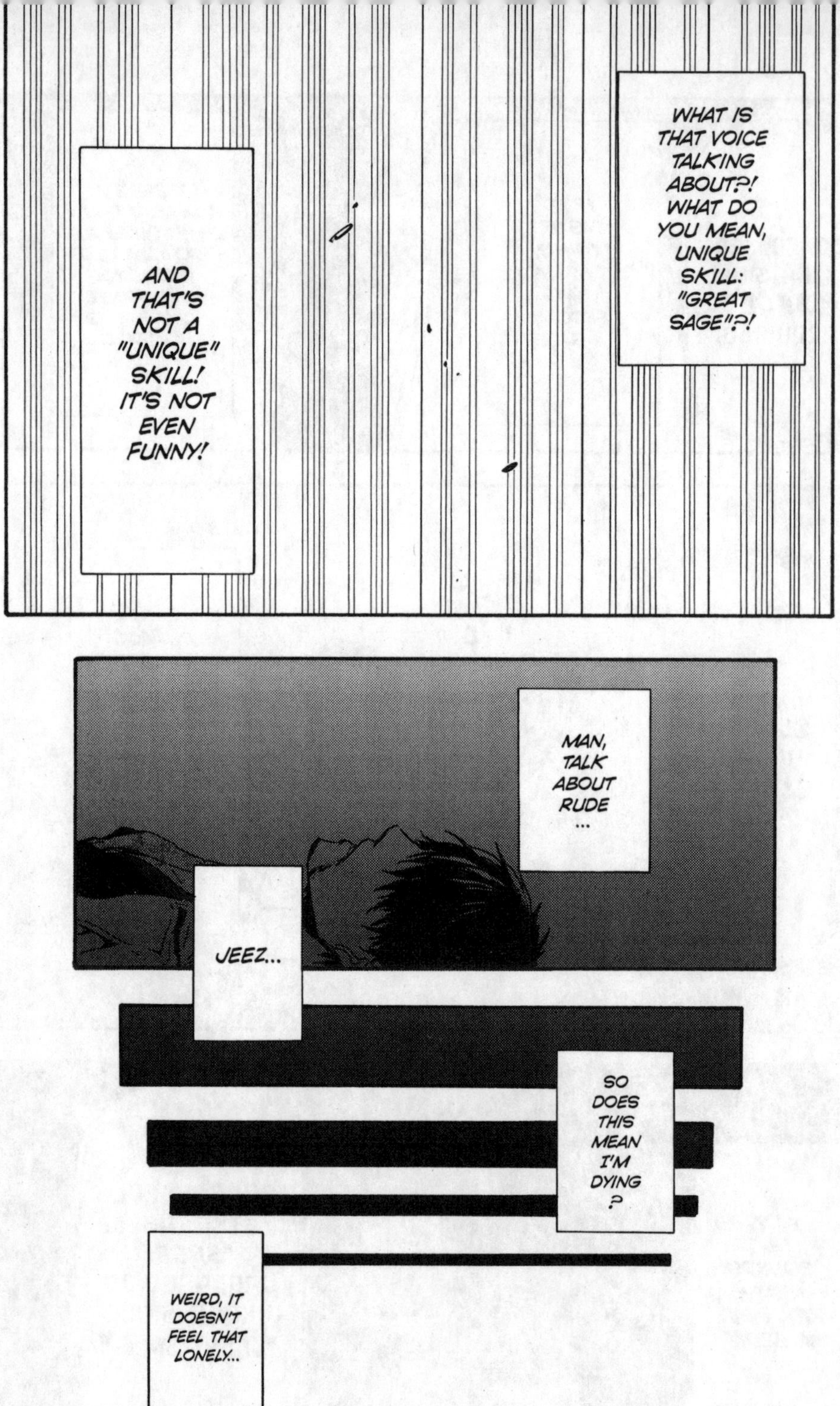
WHAT IS THAT VOICE TALKING ABOUT?! WHAT DO YOU MEAN, UNIQUE SKILL: "GREAT SAGE"?!
AND THAT'S NOT A "UNIQUE" SKILL! IT'S NOT EVEN FUNNY!
MAN, TALK ABOUT RUDE...
JEEZ...
SO DOES THIS MEAN I'M DYING?
WEIRD, IT DOESN'T FEEL THAT LONELY...

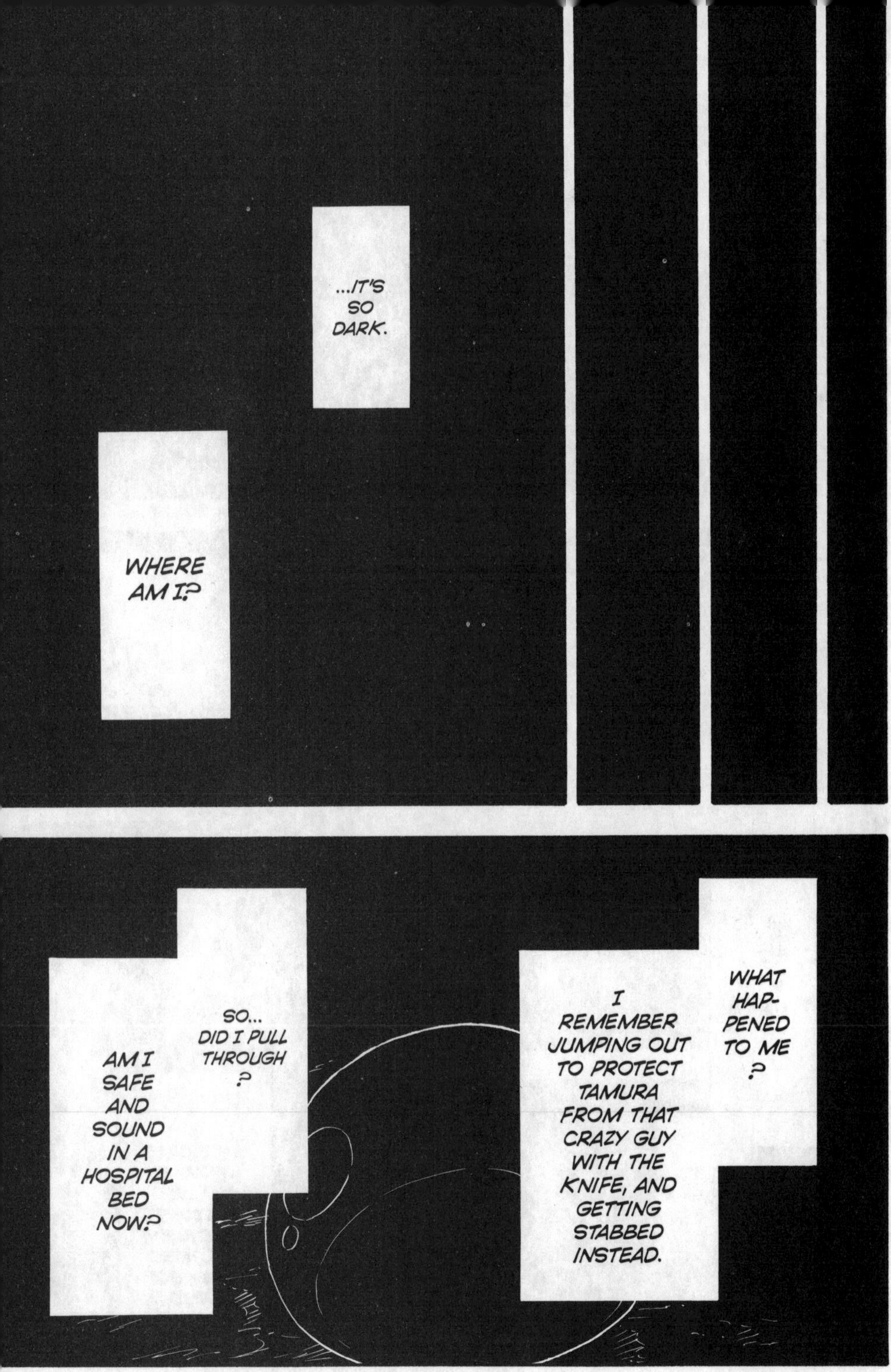
...IT'S SO DARK.
WHERE AM I?
WHAT HAP-PENED TO ME?
I REMEMBER JUMPING OUT TO PROTECT TAMURA FROM THAT CRAZY GUY WITH THE KNIFE, AND GETTING STABBED INSTEAD.
SO... DID I PULL THROUGH?
AM I SAFE AND SOUND IN A HOSPITAL BED NOW?

I CAN'T SEE OR HEAR ANY-THING...
COULD BE AFTER LIGHTS OUT?
ANYWAY, BETTER FIND THE CALL BUTTON...
HUH? WHY WON'T MY LIMBS RESPOND ?!
THAT'S CRAZY. MY ARMS AND LEGS COULDN'T HAVE BEEN AMPUTATED! I ONLY GOT STABBED IN THE BACK...
COULD IT BE THAT...HE SEVERED MY SPINAL CORD AND PARALYZED ME?
NO, NO, NO... ANYTHING BUT THAT!
OH ?!
ズルッ
ZLURP

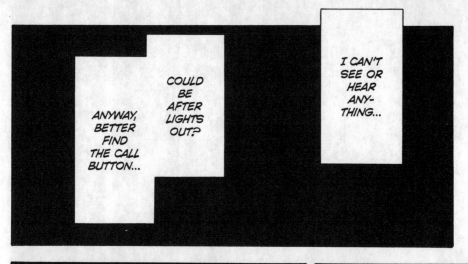

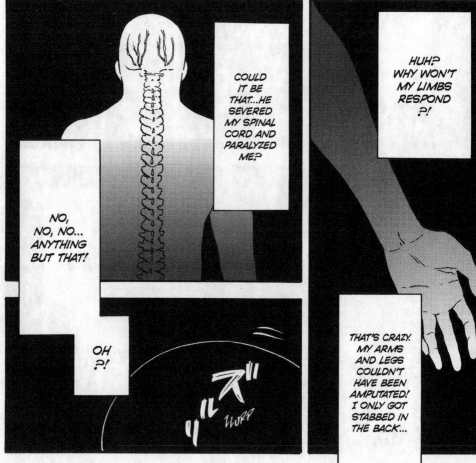

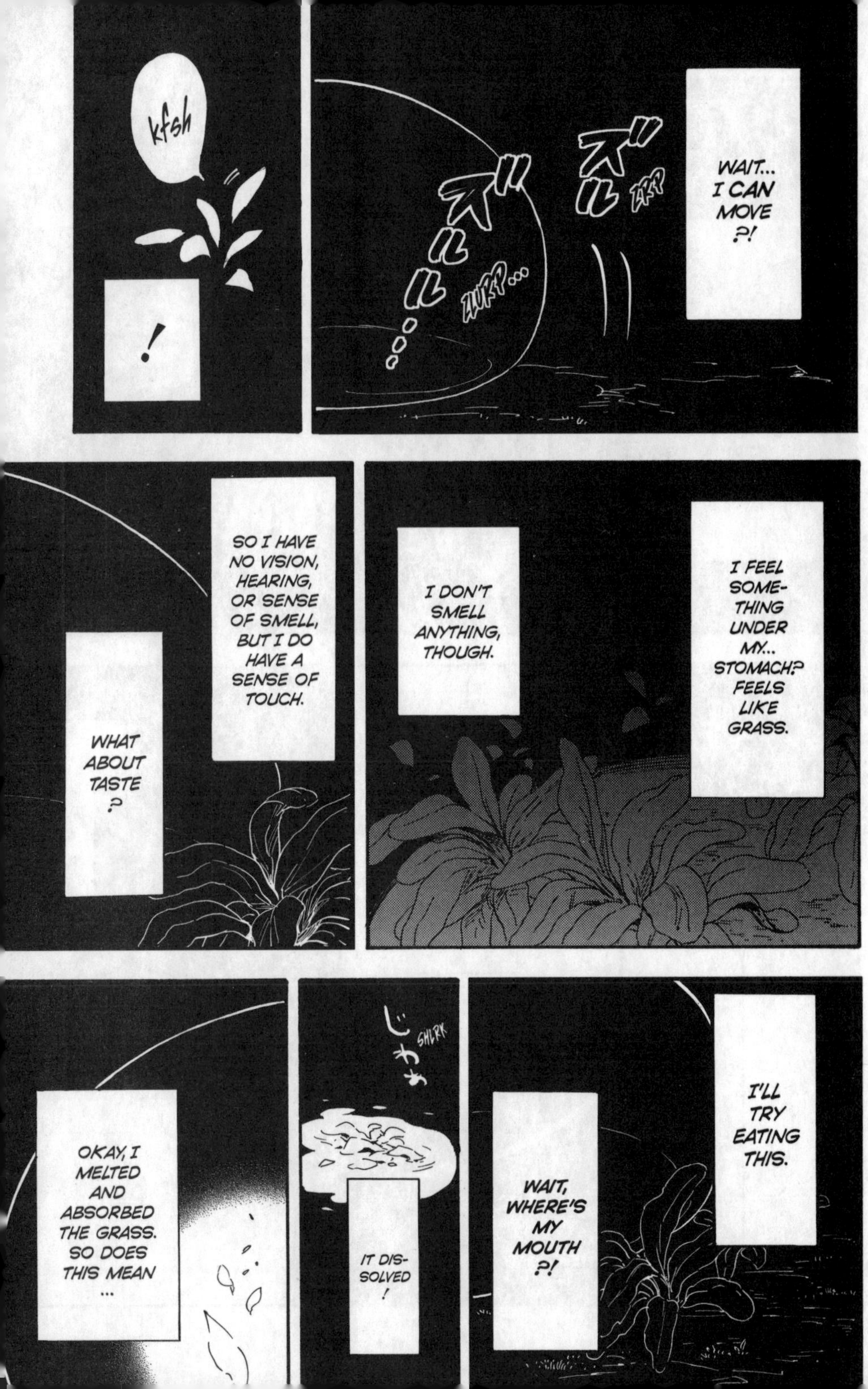
WAIT... I CAN MOVE ?!
ズル
ZRP
ズルル
ZLURP...
kfsh
!
I FEEL SOME-THING UNDER MY... STOMACH? FEELS LIKE GRASS.
I DON'T SMELL ANYTHING, THOUGH.
SO I HAVE NO VISION, HEARING, OR SENSE OF SMELL, BUT I DO HAVE A SENSE OF TOUCH.
WHAT ABOUT TASTE ?
I'LL TRY EATING THIS.
WAIT, WHERE'S MY MOUTH ?!
じわぁ
SHLRK
IT DIS-SOLVED !
OKAY, I MELTED AND ABSORBED THE GRASS. SO DOES THIS MEAN ...

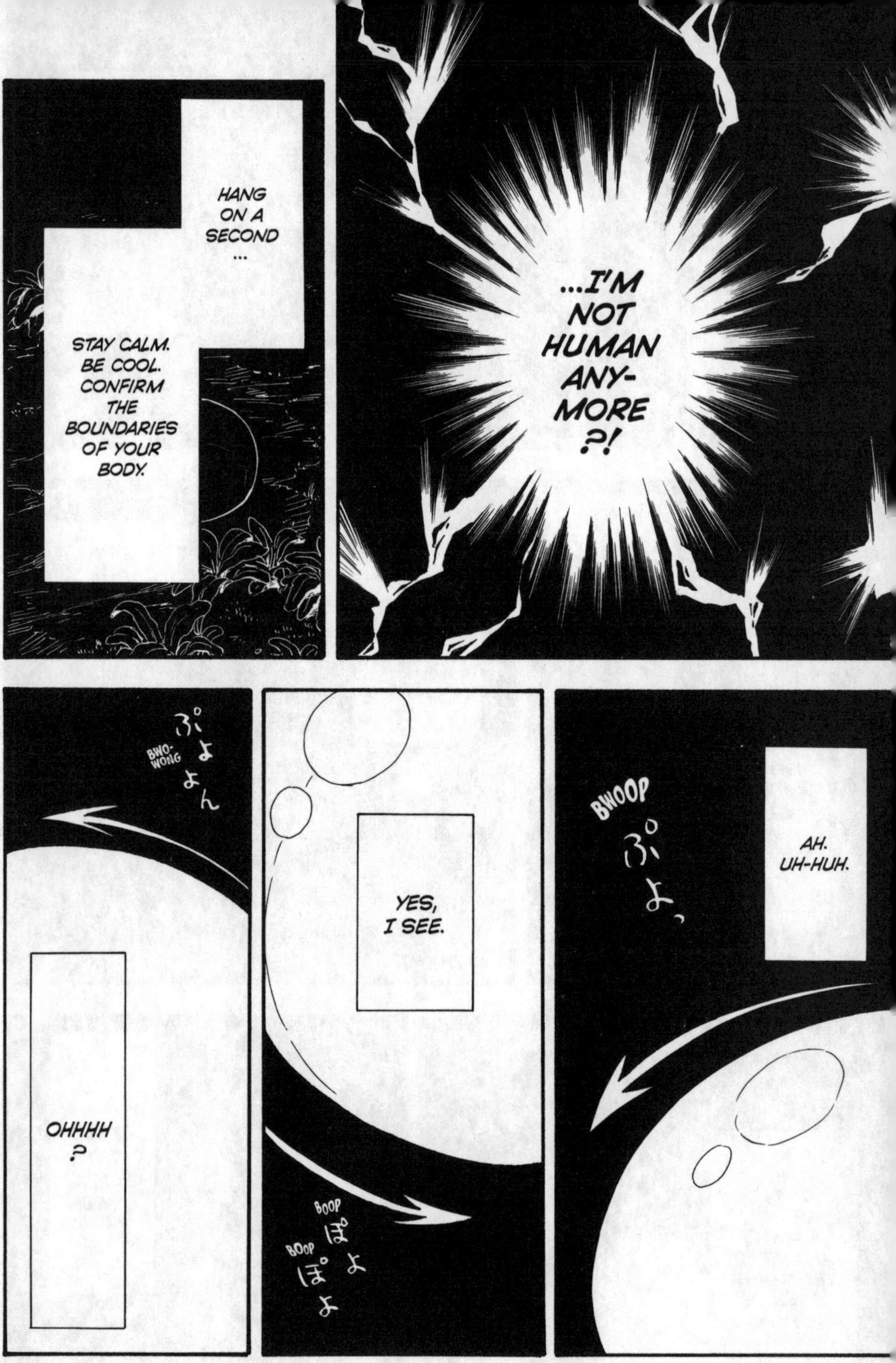
...I'M NOT HUMAN ANYMORE?!
HANG ON A SECOND ...
STAY CALM. BE COOL. CONFIRM THE BOUNDARIES OF YOUR BODY.
AH. UH-HUH.
BWOOP
ぷよ
YES, I SEE.
BOOP
ぽよ
BOOP
ぽよ
ぷよよん
BWO-WONG
OHHHH?

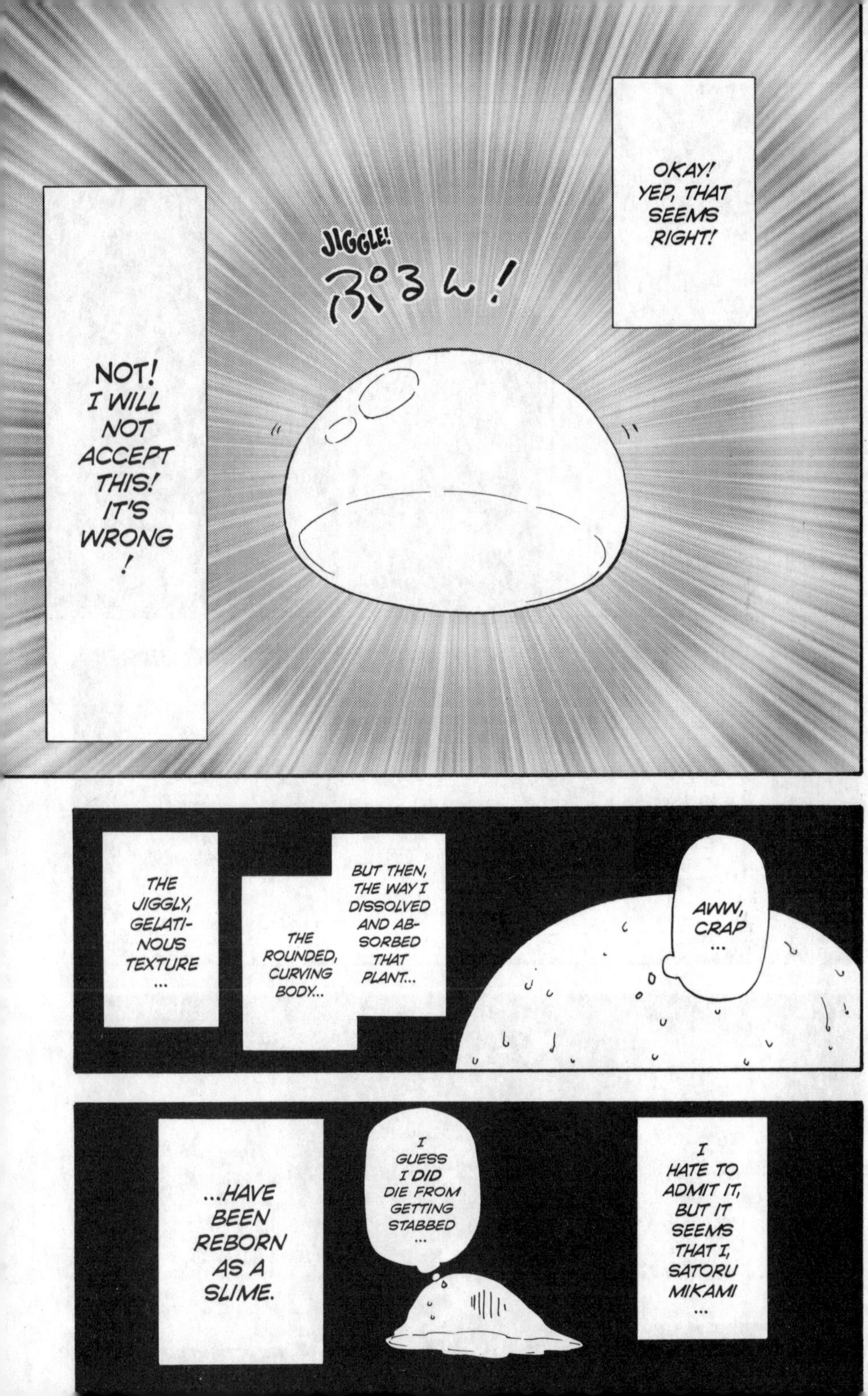
OKAY! YEP, THAT SEEMS RIGHT!
JIGGLE!
ぷるん!
NOT! I WILL NOT ACCEPT THIS! IT'S WRONG!
AWW, CRAP...
BUT THEN, THE WAY I DISSOLVED AND ABSORBED THAT PLANT...
THE ROUNDED, CURVING BODY...
THE JIGGLY, GELATINOUS TEXTURE...
I HATE TO ADMIT IT, BUT IT SEEMS THAT I, SATORU MIKAMI...
I GUESS I DID DIE FROM GETTING STABBED...
...HAVE BEEN REBORN AS A SLIME.

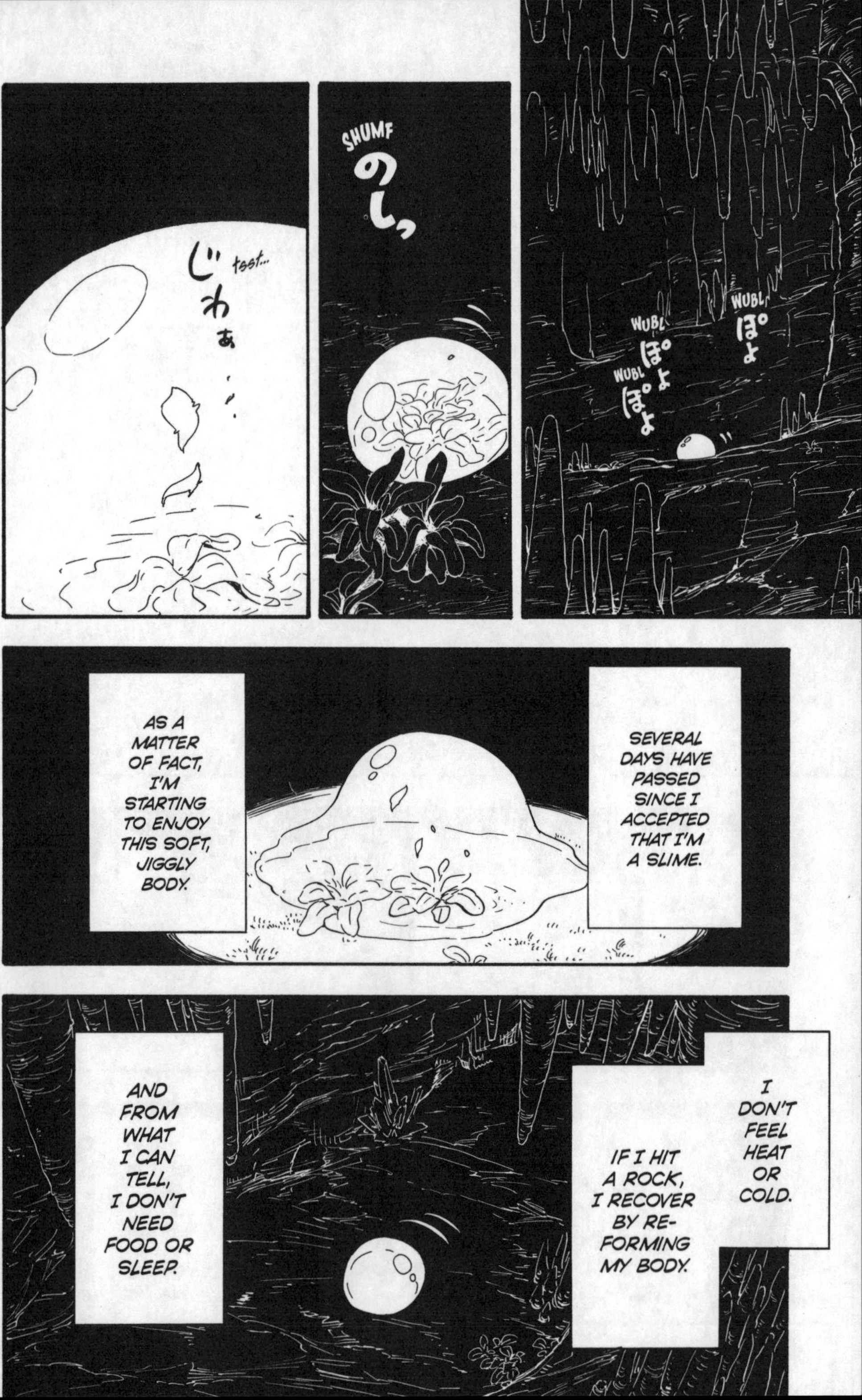
WUBL
ぽよ
WUBL
ぽよ
WUBL
ぽよ
SHUMF
のしっ
tsst...
じわぁ
SEVERAL DAYS HAVE PASSED SINCE I ACCEPTED THAT I'M A SLIME.
AS A MATTER OF FACT, I'M STARTING TO ENJOY THIS SOFT, JIGGLY BODY.
I DON'T FEEL HEAT OR COLD.
IF I HIT A ROCK, I RECOVER BY RE-FORMING MY BODY.
AND FROM WHAT I CAN TELL, I DON'T NEED FOOD OR SLEEP.

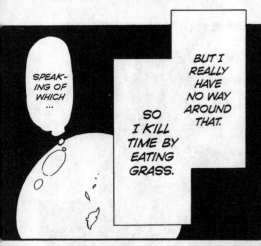

THE ONLY THING IS...
I'M LONELY.
ALONE
ぽつん
BUT I REALLY HAVE NO WAY AROUND THAT.
SO I KILL TIME BY EATING GRASS.
SPEAKING OF WHICH ...
...I DON'T ACTUALLY RECALL TAKING A CRAP AT ANY POINT.
WHERE IS ALL THIS GRASS GOING?
ANSWER: IT IS STORED IN THE STOMACH OF THE USER OF THE UNIQUE SKILL: "PREDATOR."
I GOT A RESPONSE!!
CURRENTLY USING LESS THAN 1% OF FULL CAPACITY.

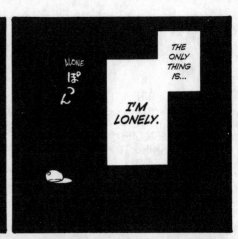

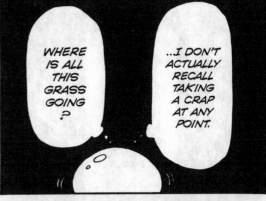

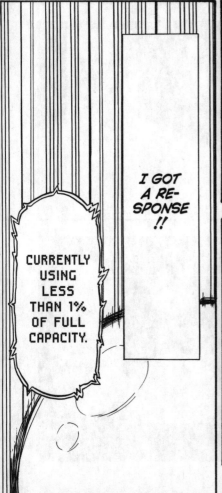

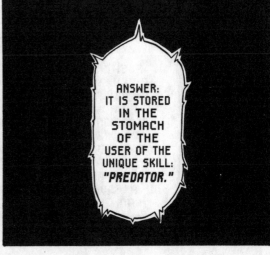

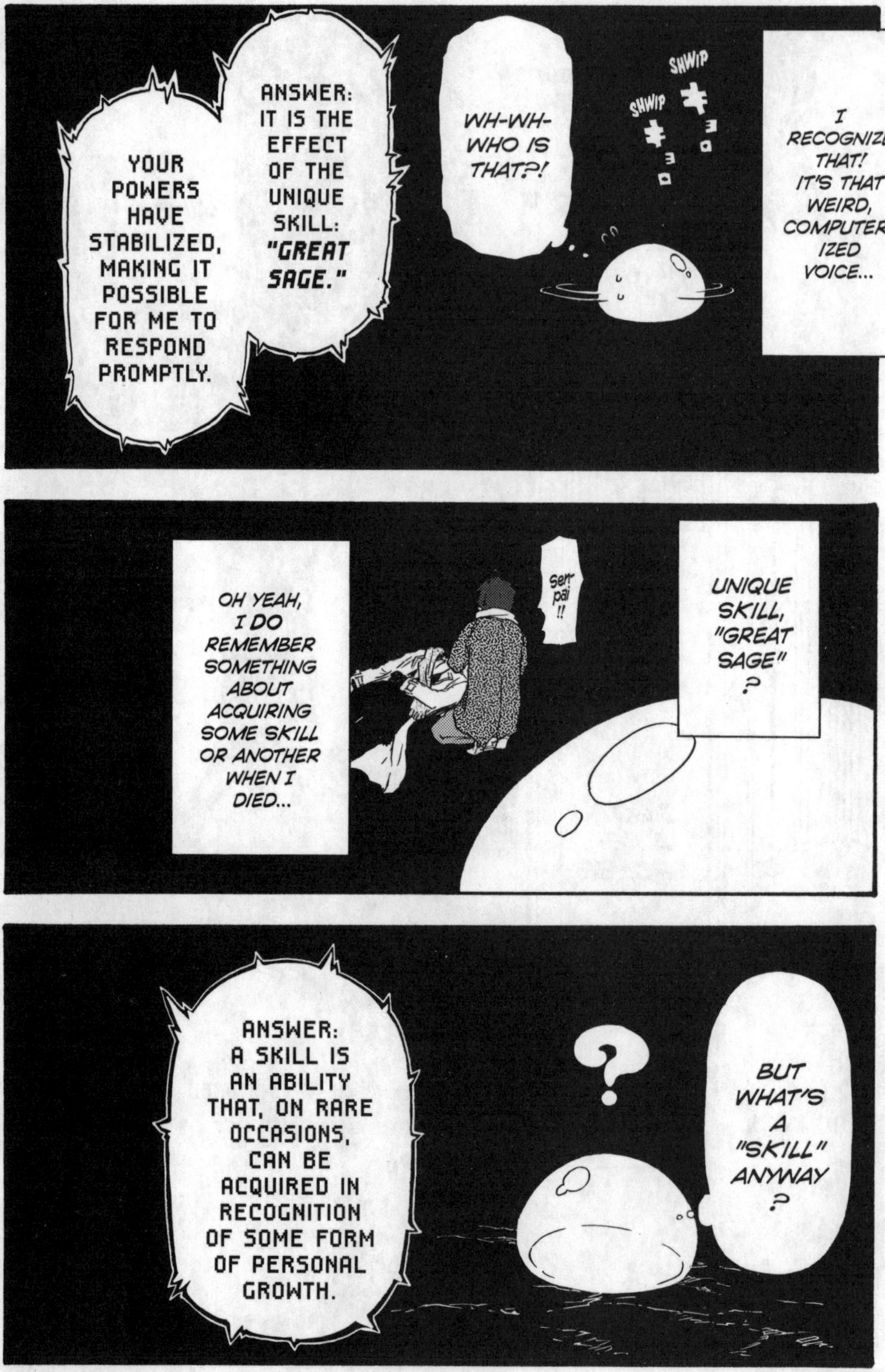
I RECOGNIZE THAT! IT'S THAT WEIRD, COMPUTERIZED VOICE...
SHWIP
SHWIP
WH-WH-WHO IS THAT?!
ANSWER: IT IS THE EFFECT OF THE UNIQUE SKILL: "GREAT SAGE."
YOUR POWERS HAVE STABILIZED, MAKING IT POSSIBLE FOR ME TO RESPOND PROMPTLY.
UNIQUE SKILL, "GREAT SAGE"?
Senpai!!
OH YEAH, I DO REMEMBER SOMETHING ABOUT ACQUIRING SOME SKILL OR ANOTHER WHEN I DIED...
BUT WHAT'S A "SKILL" ANYWAY?
?
ANSWER: A SKILL IS AN ABILITY THAT, ON RARE OCCASIONS, CAN BE ACQUIRED IN RECOGNITION OF SOME FORM OF PERSONAL GROWTH.

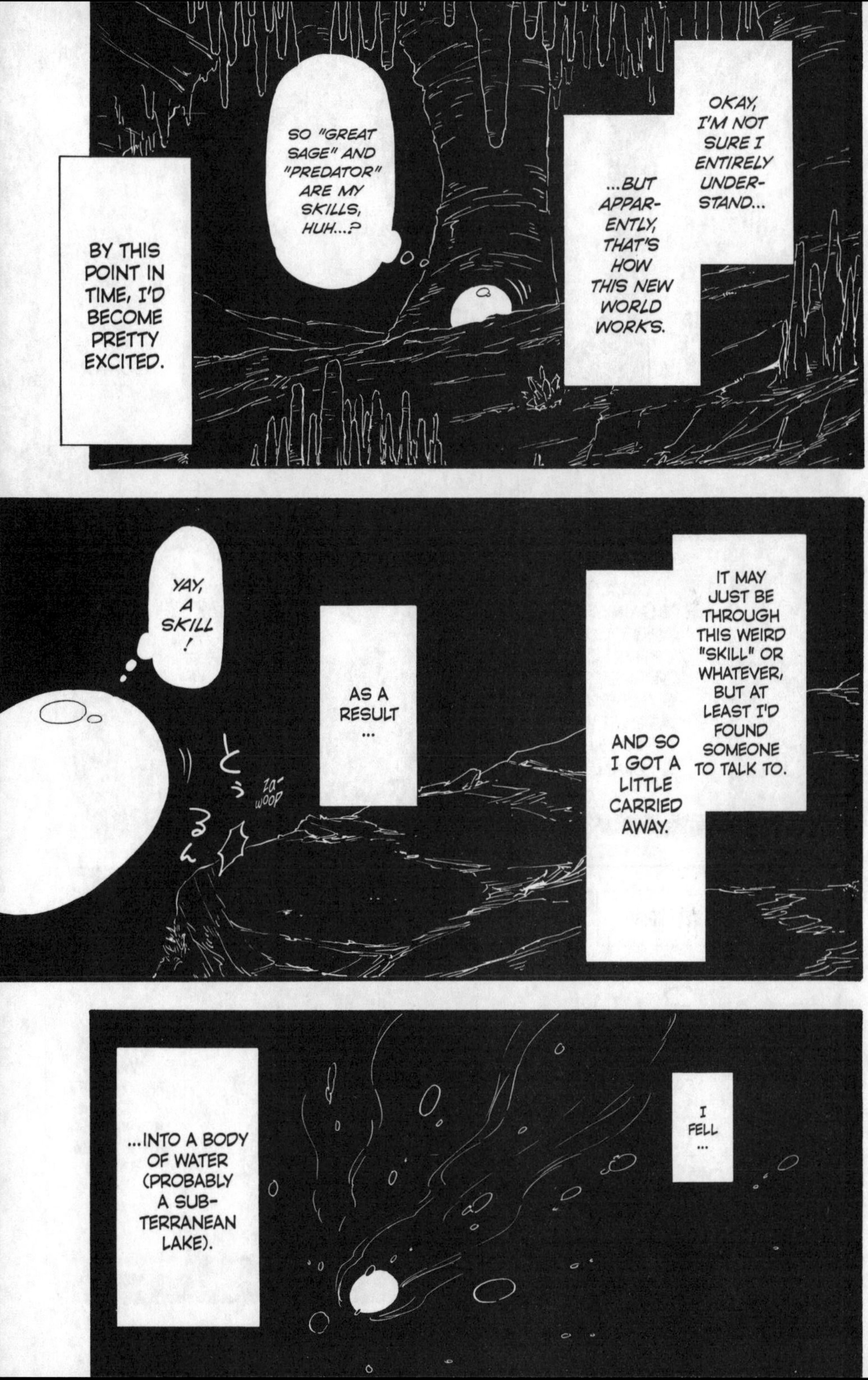
OKAY, I'M NOT SURE I ENTIRELY UNDER-STAND...
...BUT APPAR-ENTLY, THAT'S HOW THIS NEW WORLD WORKS.
SO "GREAT SAGE" AND "PREDATOR" ARE MY SKILLS, HUH...?
BY THIS POINT IN TIME, I'D BECOME PRETTY EXCITED.
IT MAY JUST BE THROUGH THIS WEIRD "SKILL" OR WHATEVER, BUT AT LEAST I'D FOUND SOMEONE TO TALK TO.
AND SO I GOT A LITTLE CARRIED AWAY.
AS A RESULT ...
とぅるん
ZA-WOOP
YAY, A SKILL!
I FELL ...
...INTO A BODY OF WATER (PROBABLY A SUB-TERRANEAN LAKE).

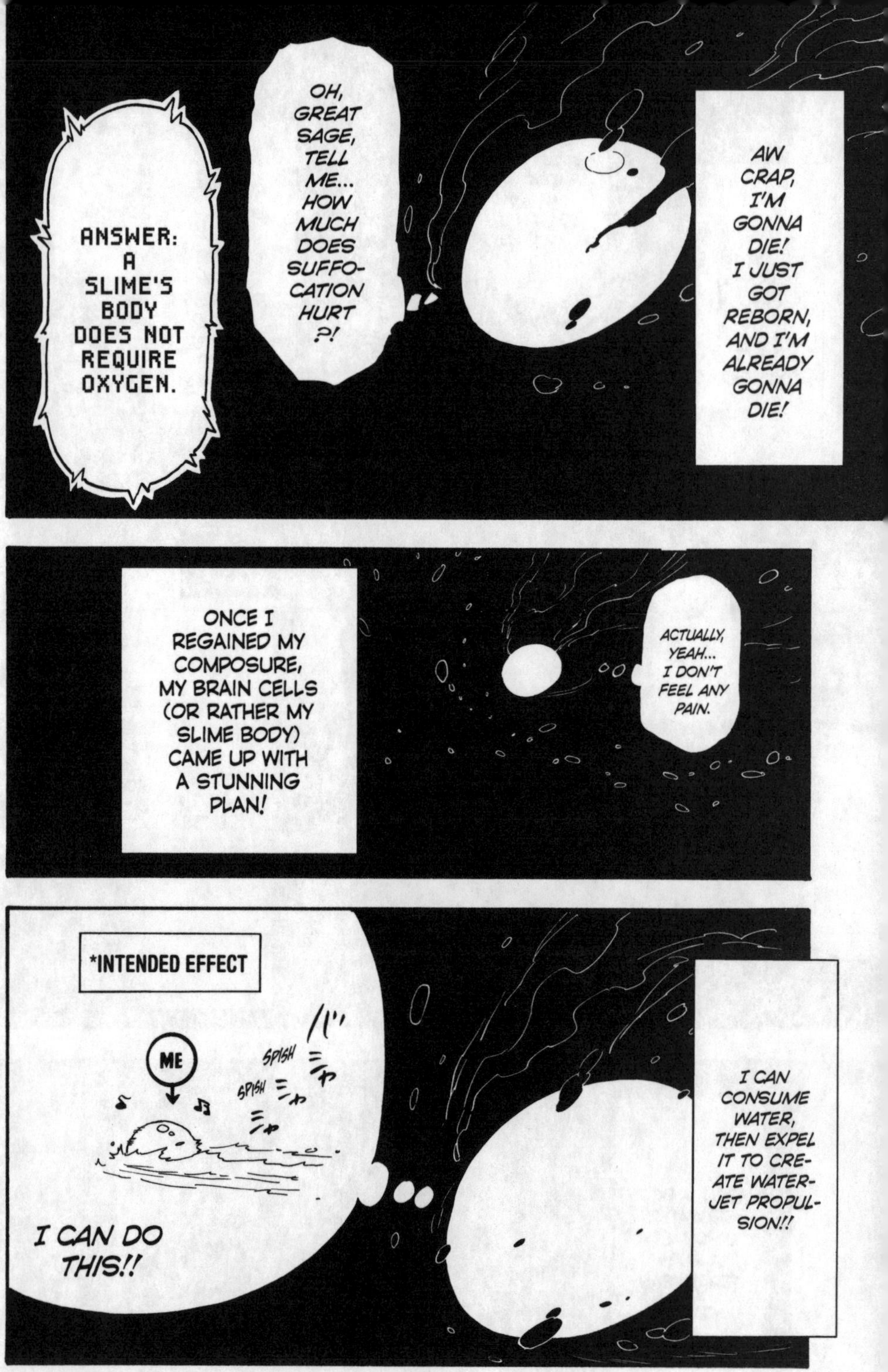
AW CRAP, I'M GONNA DIE! I JUST GOT REBORN, AND I'M ALREADY GONNA DIE!
OH, GREAT SAGE, TELL ME... HOW MUCH DOES SUFFOCATION HURT ?!
ANSWER: A SLIME'S BODY DOES NOT REQUIRE OXYGEN.
ACTUALLY, YEAH... I DON'T FEEL ANY PAIN.
ONCE I REGAINED MY COMPOSURE, MY BRAIN CELLS (OR RATHER MY SLIME BODY) CAME UP WITH A STUNNING PLAN!
I CAN CONSUME WATER, THEN EXPEL IT TO CREATE WATER-JET PROPULSION!!
*INTENDED EFFECT
ME
SPISH
SPISH
I CAN DO THIS!!

BA-ZOOM
SPLAT
ZRLP...
BOI
BOI
BOING
SKILL: "WATER-PRESSURE PROPULSION" ACQUIRED.

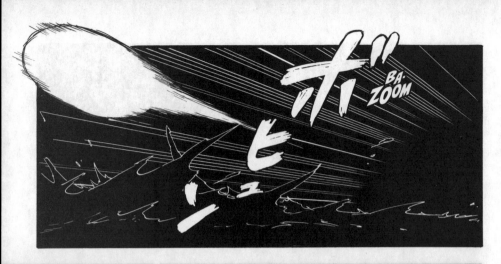

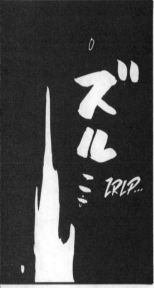

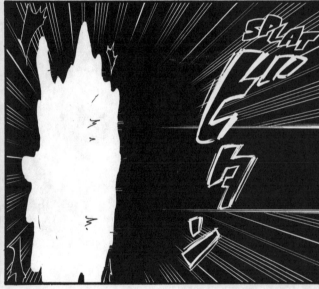

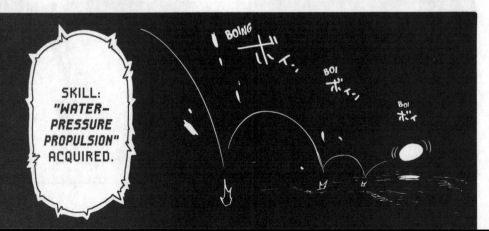

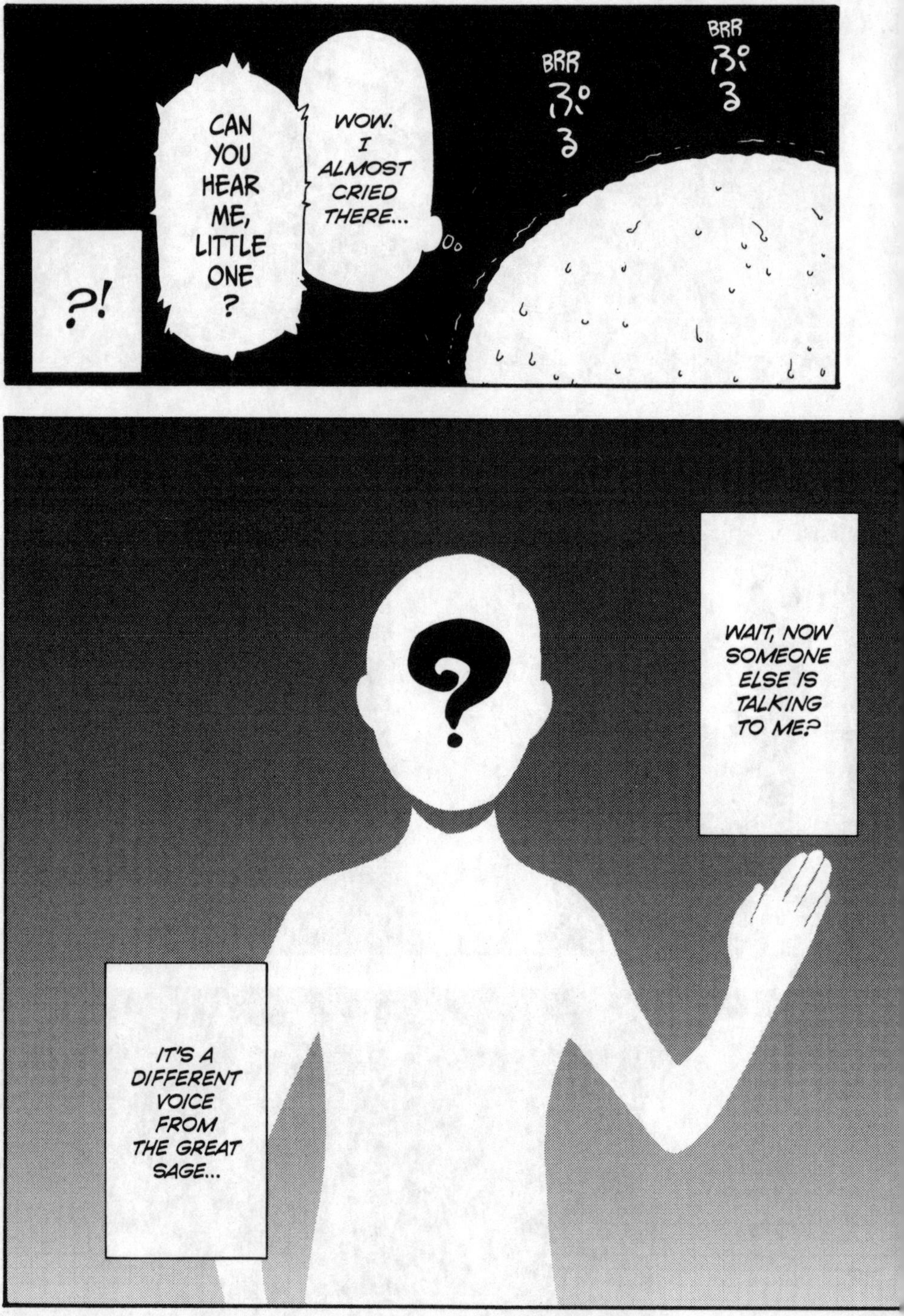
BRR ぷる
BRR ぷる
WOW. I ALMOST CRIED THERE...
CAN YOU HEAR ME, LITTLE ONE?
?!
WAIT, NOW SOMEONE ELSE IS TALKING TO ME?
IT'S A DIFFERENT VOICE FROM THE GREAT SAGE...

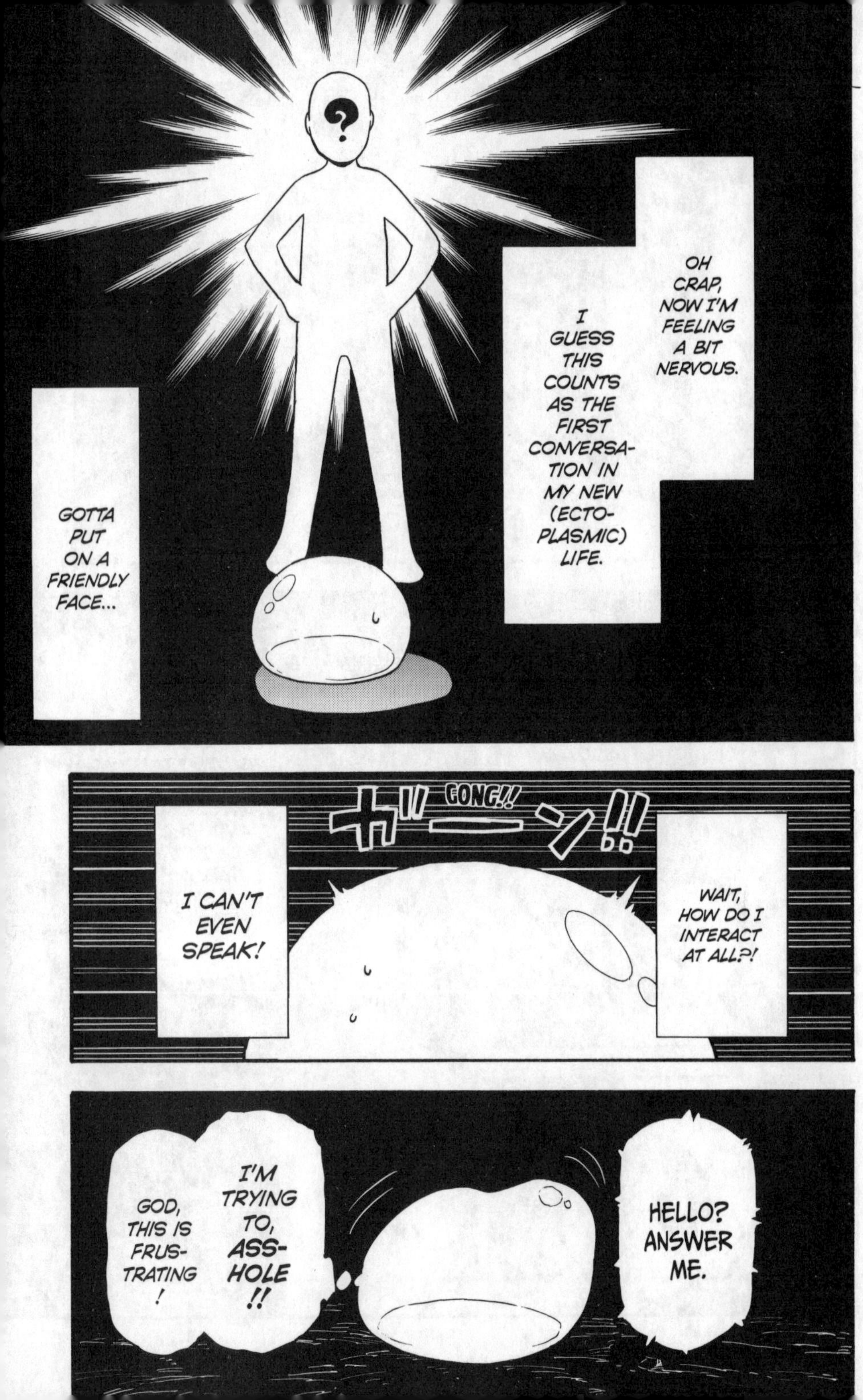
OH CRAP, NOW I'M FEELING A BIT NERVOUS.
I GUESS THIS COUNTS AS THE FIRST CONVERSATION IN MY NEW (ECTOPLASMIC) LIFE.
GOTTA PUT ON A FRIENDLY FACE...
WAIT, HOW DO I INTERACT AT ALL?!
GONG!!
I CAN'T EVEN SPEAK!
HELLO? ANSWER ME.
I'M TRYING TO, ASSHOLE!!
GOD, THIS IS FRUSTRATING!

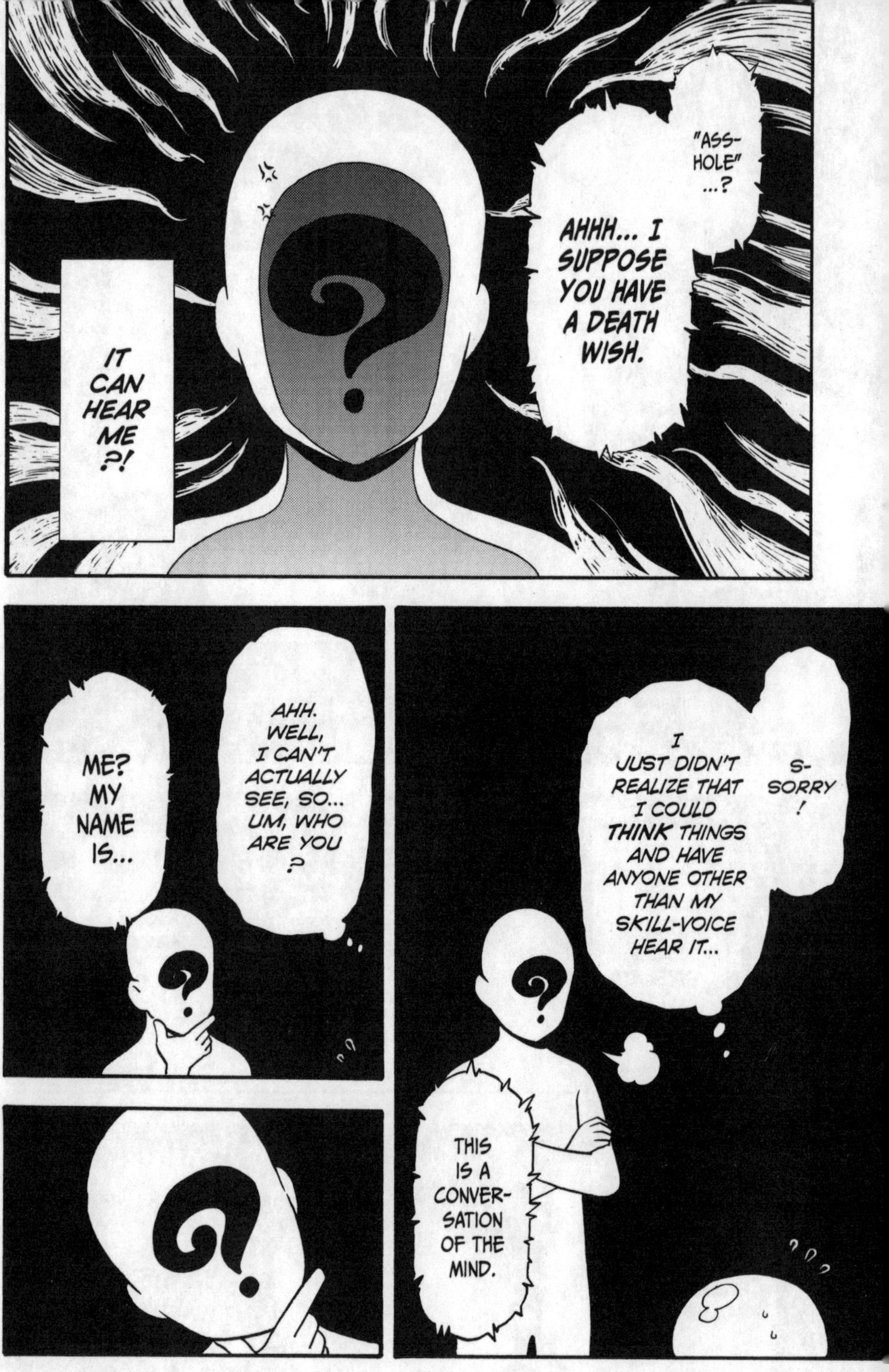
"ASS-HOLE" ...?
AHHH... I SUPPOSE YOU HAVE A DEATH WISH.
IT CAN HEAR ME?!
S-SORRY!
I JUST DIDN'T REALIZE THAT I COULD THINK THINGS AND HAVE ANYONE OTHER THAN MY SKILL-VOICE HEAR IT...
THIS IS A CONVER-SATION OF THE MIND.
AHH. WELL, I CAN'T ACTUALLY SEE, SO... UM, WHO ARE YOU?
ME? MY NAME IS...

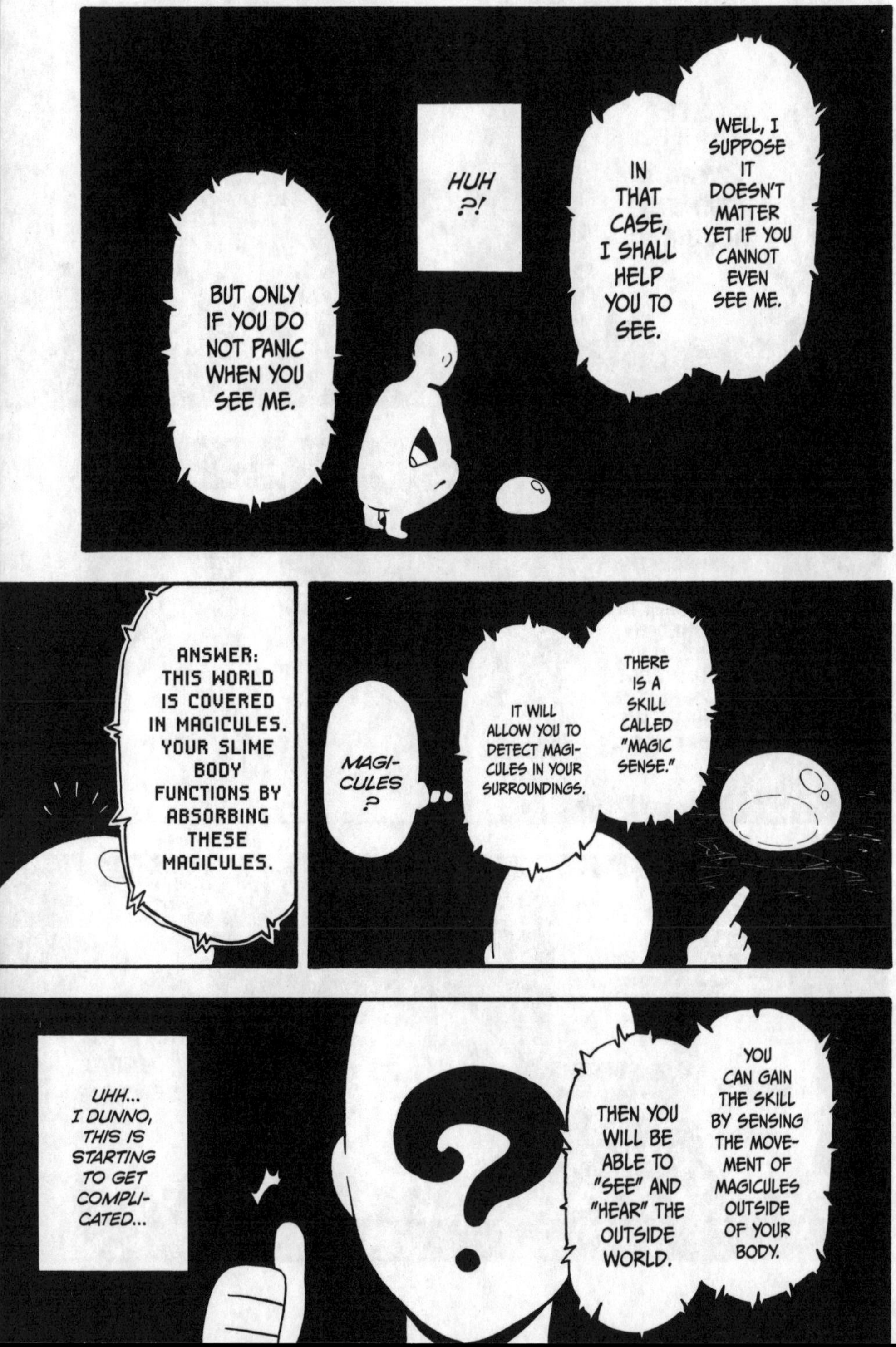

WELL, I SUPPOSE IT DOESN'T MATTER YET IF YOU CANNOT EVEN SEE ME.
IN THAT CASE, I SHALL HELP YOU TO SEE.
HUH?!
BUT ONLY IF YOU DO NOT PANIC WHEN YOU SEE ME.
THERE IS A SKILL CALLED "MAGIC SENSE."
IT WILL ALLOW YOU TO DETECT MAGI-CULES IN YOUR SURROUNDINGS.
MAGI-CULES?
ANSWER: THIS WORLD IS COVERED IN MAGICULES. YOUR SLIME BODY FUNCTIONS BY ABSORBING THESE MAGICULES.
YOU CAN GAIN THE SKILL BY SENSING THE MOVE-MENT OF MAGICULES OUTSIDE OF YOUR BODY.
THEN YOU WILL BE ABLE TO "SEE" AND "HEAR" THE OUTSIDE WORLD.
UHH... I DUNNO, THIS IS STARTING TO GET COMPLI-CATED...

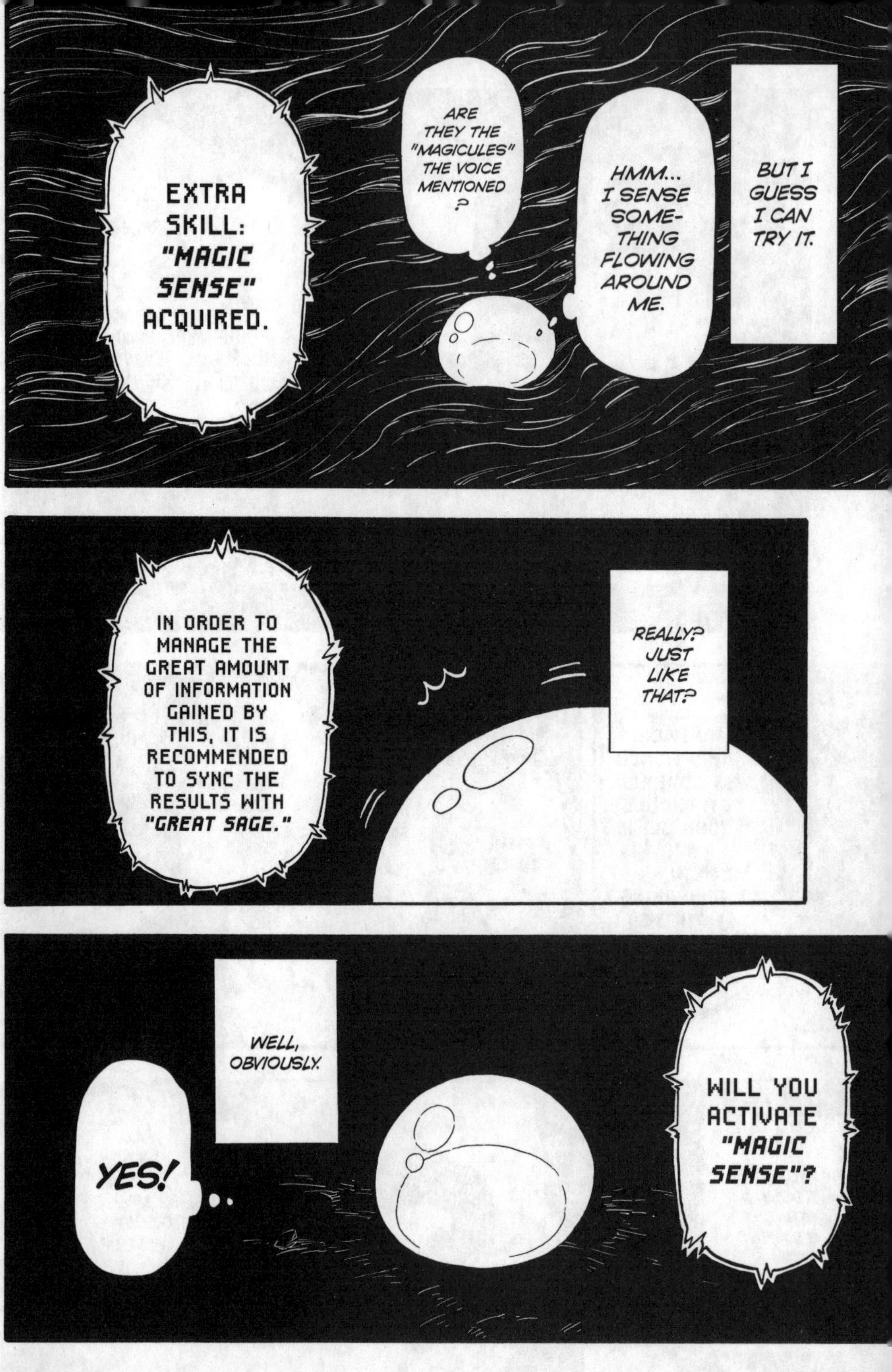
BUT I GUESS I CAN TRY IT.
HMM... I SENSE SOME-THING FLOWING AROUND ME.
ARE THEY THE "MAGICULES" THE VOICE MENTIONED ?
EXTRA SKILL: "MAGIC SENSE" ACQUIRED.
REALLY? JUST LIKE THAT?
IN ORDER TO MANAGE THE GREAT AMOUNT OF INFORMATION GAINED BY THIS, IT IS RECOMMENDED TO SYNC THE RESULTS WITH "GREAT SAGE."
WILL YOU ACTIVATE "MAGIC SENSE"?
WELL, OBVIOUSLY.
YES!

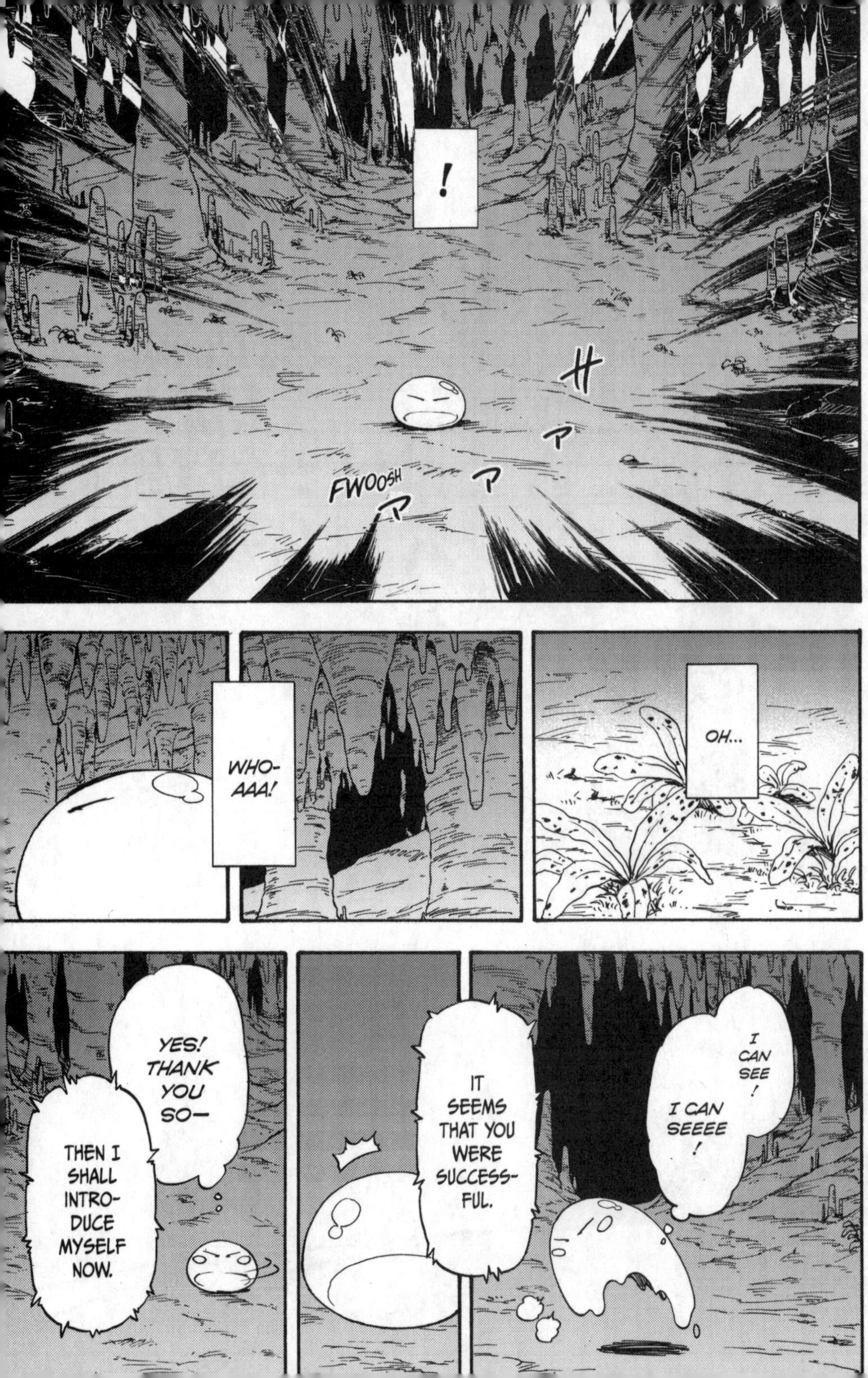
!
FWOOSH
OH...
WHO-AAA!
I CAN SEE! I CAN SEEEE!
IT SEEMS THAT YOU WERE SUCCESSFUL.
YES! THANK YOU SO—
THEN I SHALL INTRODUCE MYSELF NOW.

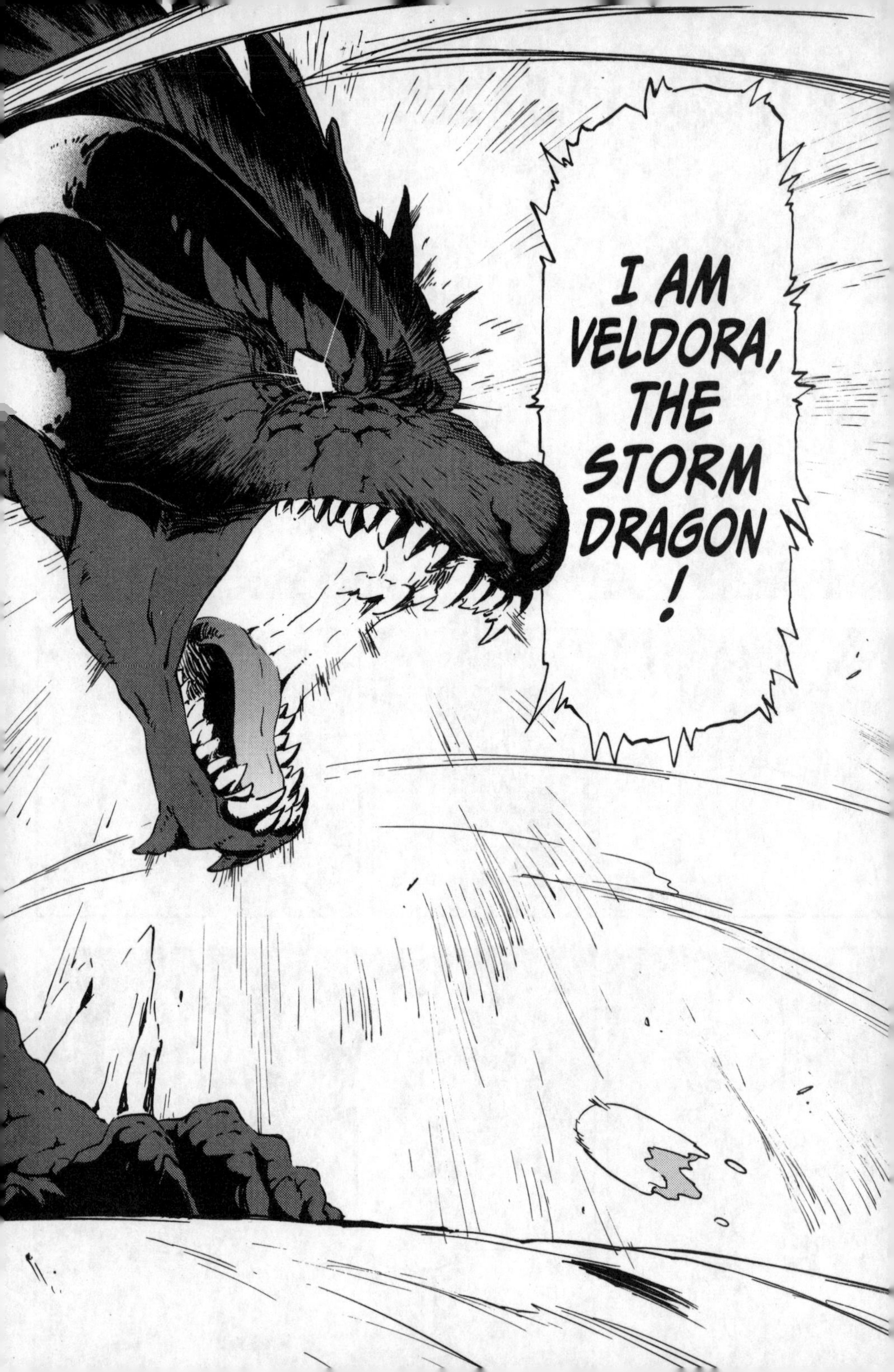
I AM VELDORA, THE STORM DRAGON!

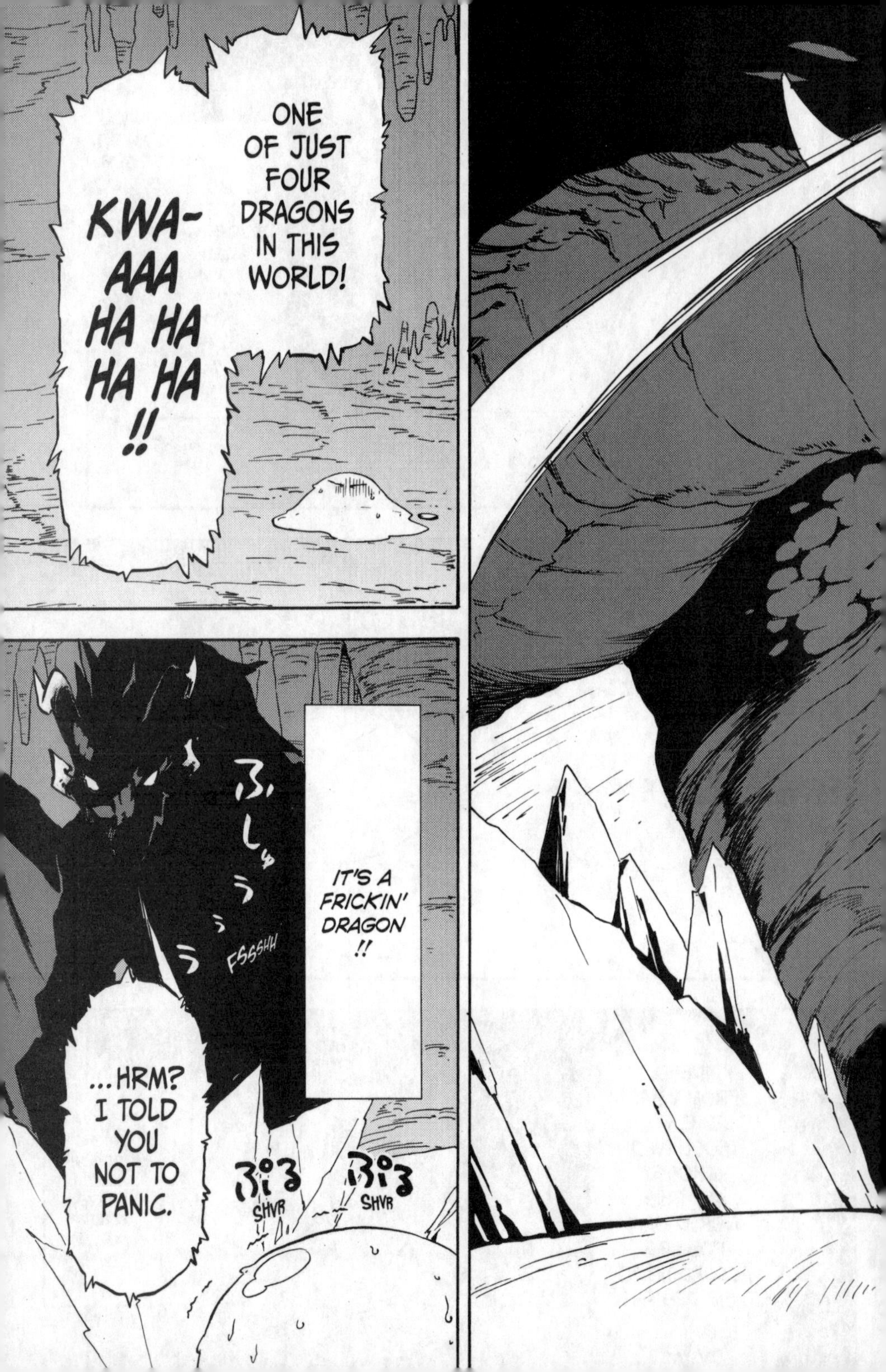

ONE OF JUST FOUR DRAGONS IN THIS WORLD!
KWA-AAA HA HA HA HA!!
IT'S A FRICKIN' DRAGON!!
ふしゅらら
FSSSHH
...HRM? I TOLD YOU NOT TO PANIC.
ぷる
SHVR
ぷる
SHVR

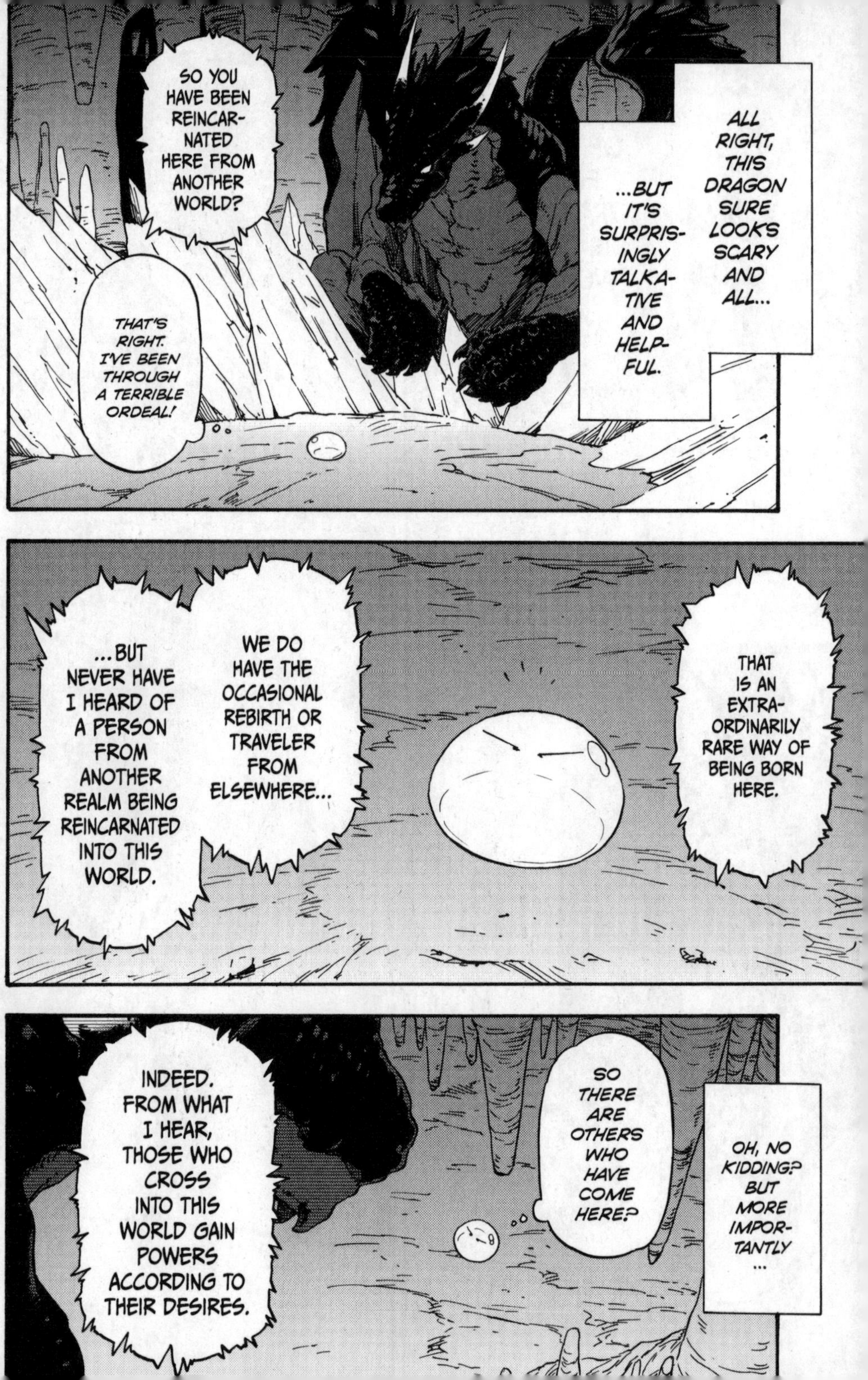
ALL RIGHT, THIS DRAGON SURE LOOKS SCARY AND ALL...
...BUT IT'S SURPRISINGLY TALKATIVE AND HELPFUL.
SO YOU HAVE BEEN REINCARNATED HERE FROM ANOTHER WORLD?
THAT'S RIGHT. I'VE BEEN THROUGH A TERRIBLE ORDEAL!
THAT IS AN EXTRAORDINARILY RARE WAY OF BEING BORN HERE.
WE DO HAVE THE OCCASIONAL REBIRTH OR TRAVELER FROM ELSEWHERE...
...BUT NEVER HAVE I HEARD OF A PERSON FROM ANOTHER REALM BEING REINCARNATED INTO THIS WORLD.
OH, NO KIDDING? BUT MORE IMPORTANTLY...
SO THERE ARE OTHERS WHO HAVE COME HERE?
INDEED. FROM WHAT I HEAR, THOSE WHO CROSS INTO THIS WORLD GAIN POWERS ACCORDING TO THEIR DESIRES.

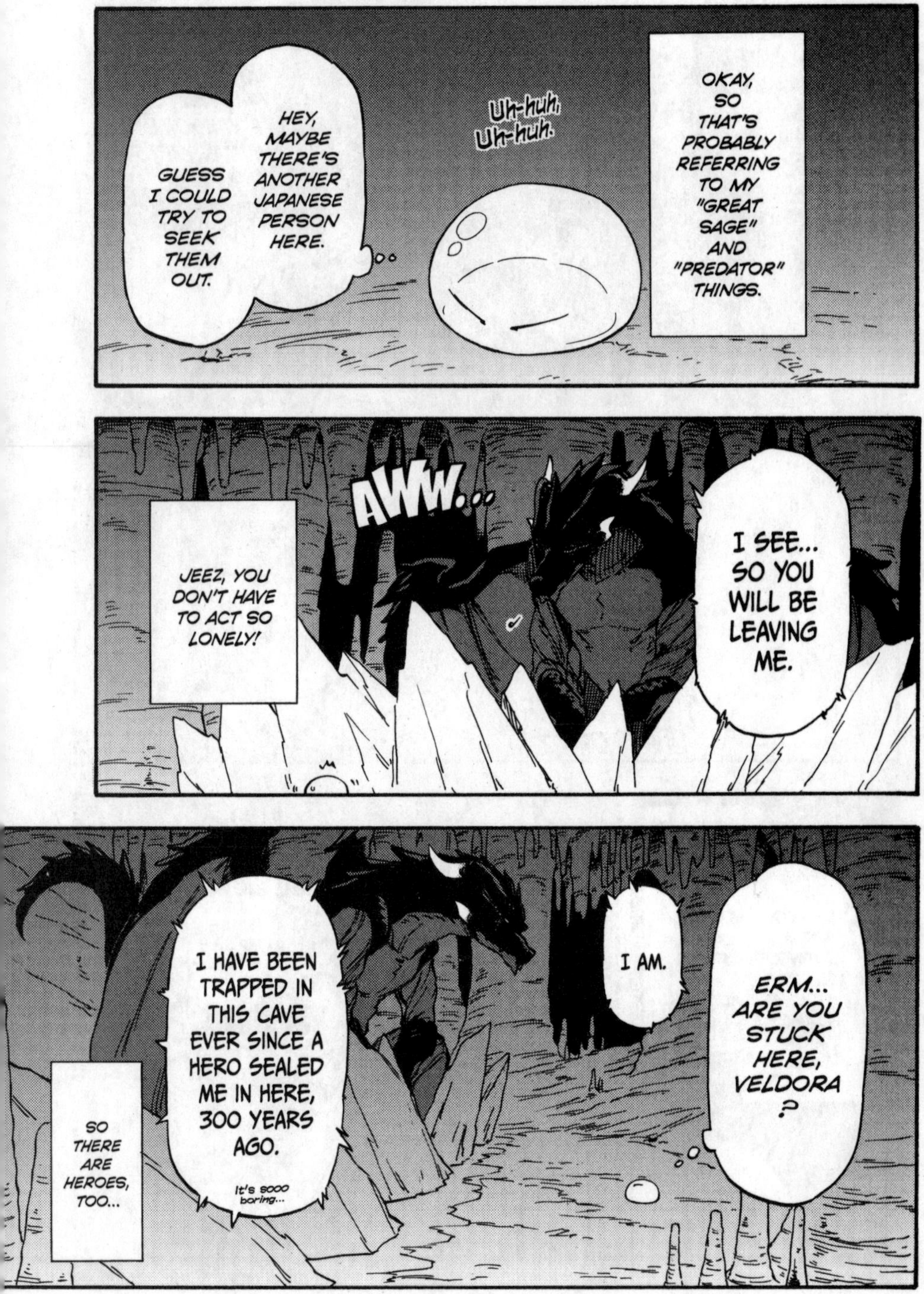
OKAY, SO THAT'S PROBABLY REFERRING TO MY "GREAT SAGE" AND "PREDATOR" THINGS.
Uh-huh, Uh-huh.
HEY, MAYBE THERE'S ANOTHER JAPANESE PERSON HERE.
GUESS I COULD TRY TO SEEK THEM OUT.
I SEE... SO YOU WILL BE LEAVING ME.
AWW...
JEEZ, YOU DON'T HAVE TO ACT SO LONELY!
ERM... ARE YOU STUCK HERE, VELDORA?
I AM.
I HAVE BEEN TRAPPED IN THIS CAVE EVER SINCE A HERO SEALED ME IN HERE, 300 YEARS AGO.
It's sooo boring...
SO THERE ARE HEROES, TOO...

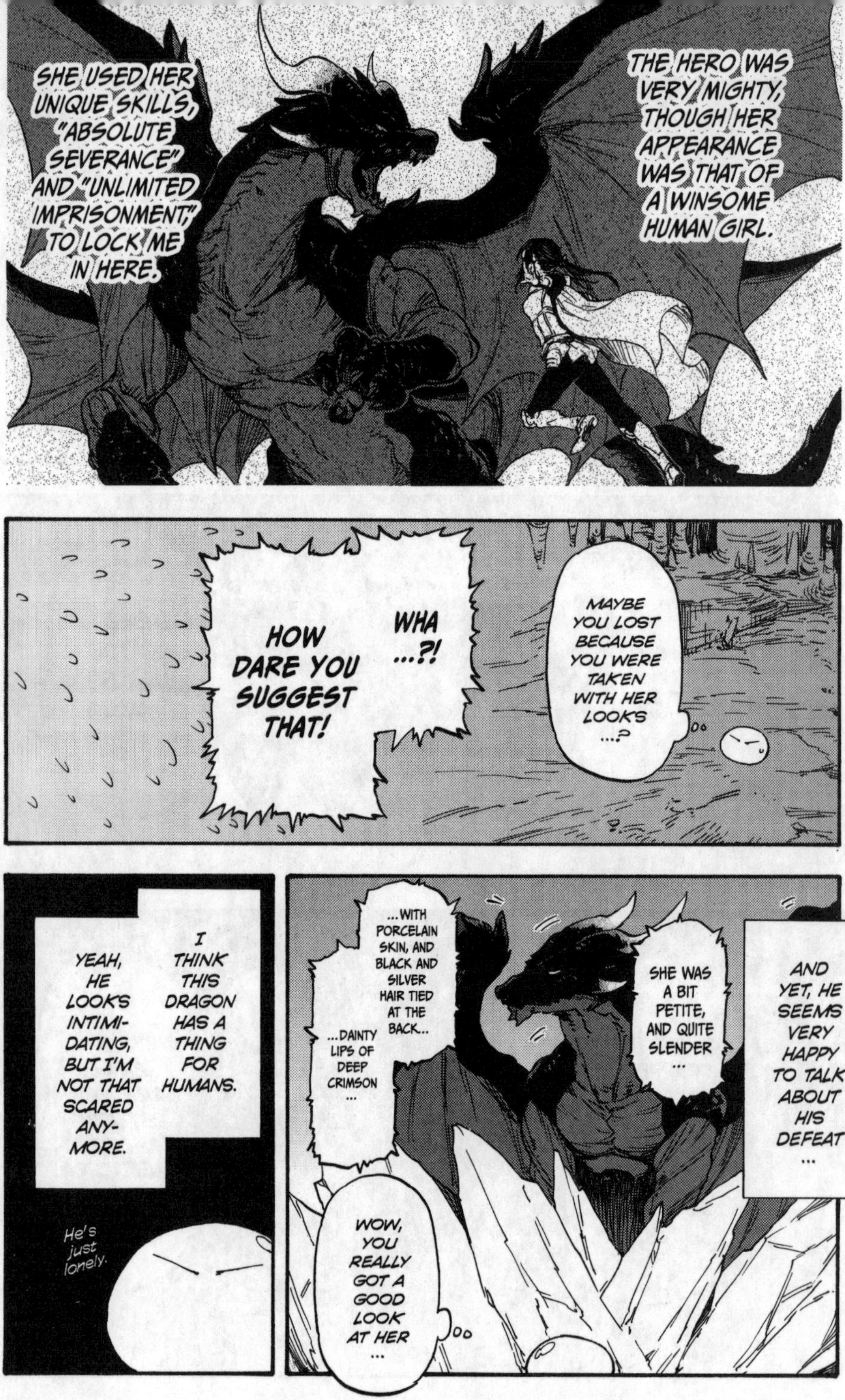
THE HERO WAS VERY MIGHTY, THOUGH HER APPEARANCE WAS THAT OF A WINSOME HUMAN GIRL.
SHE USED HER UNIQUE SKILLS, "ABSOLUTE SEVERANCE" AND "UNLIMITED IMPRISONMENT," TO LOCK ME IN HERE.
MAYBE YOU LOST BECAUSE YOU WERE TAKEN WITH HER LOOKS ...?
WHA ...?!
HOW DARE YOU SUGGEST THAT!
AND YET, HE SEEMS VERY HAPPY TO TALK ABOUT HIS DEFEAT ...
SHE WAS A BIT PETITE, AND QUITE SLENDER ...
...WITH PORCELAIN SKIN, AND BLACK AND SILVER HAIR TIED AT THE BACK...
...DAINTY LIPS OF DEEP CRIMSON ...
WOW, YOU REALLY GOT A GOOD LOOK AT HER ...
I THINK THIS DRAGON HAS A THING FOR HUMANS.
YEAH, HE LOOKS INTIMIDATING, BUT I'M NOT THAT SCARED ANYMORE.
He's just lonely.

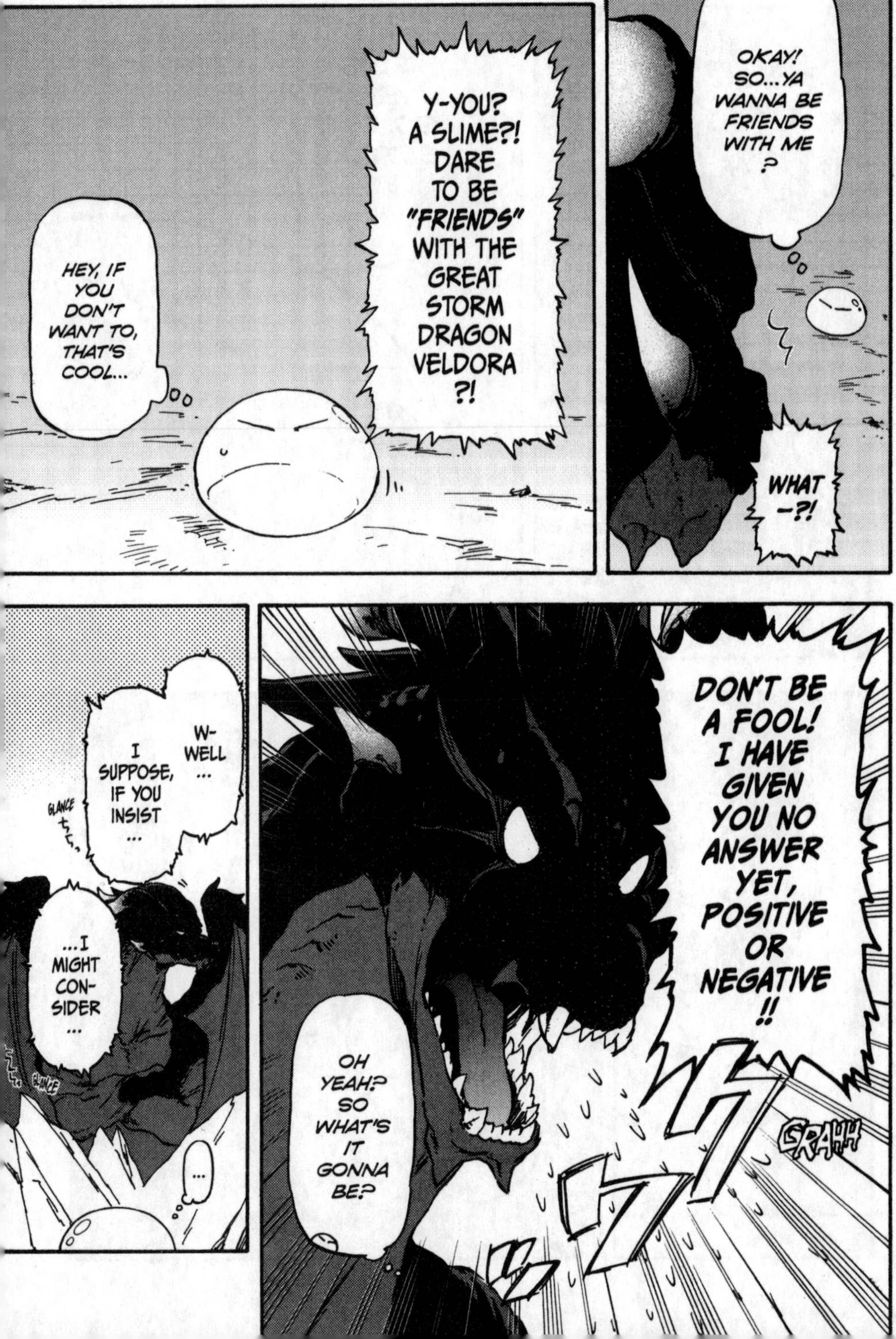
OKAY! SO...YA WANNA BE FRIENDS WITH ME?
WHAT-?!
Y-YOU? A SLIME?! DARE TO BE "FRIENDS" WITH THE GREAT STORM DRAGON VELDORA?!
HEY, IF YOU DON'T WANT TO, THAT'S COOL...
DON'T BE A FOOL! I HAVE GIVEN YOU NO ANSWER YET, POSITIVE OR NEGATIVE!!
GRAHH
OH YEAH? SO WHAT'S IT GONNA BE?
W-WELL...
I SUPPOSE, IF YOU INSIST...
GLANCE
...I MIGHT CONSIDER...
GLANCE
...

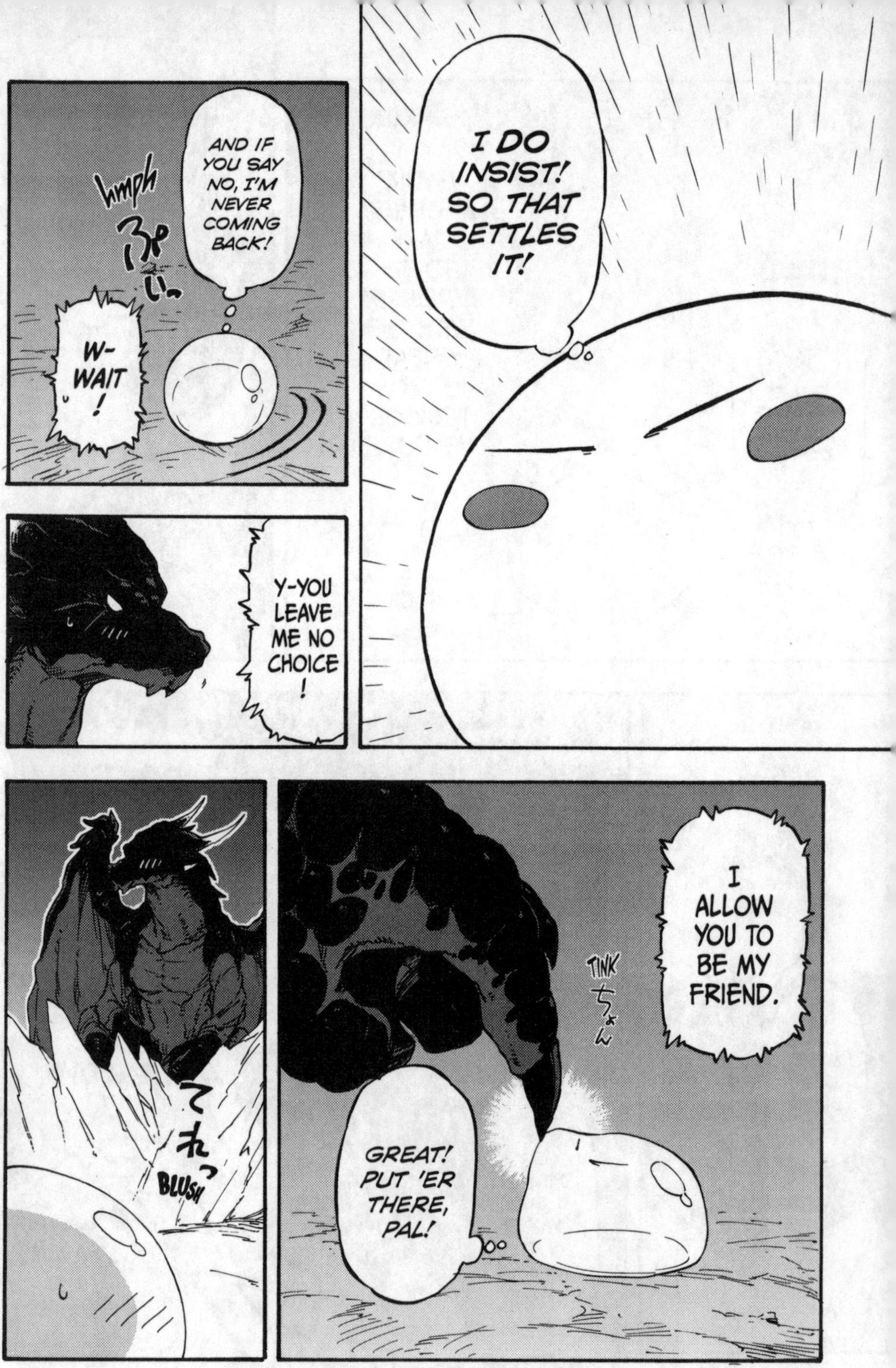
I DO INSIST! SO THAT SETTLES IT!
AND IF YOU SAY NO, I'M NEVER COMING BACK!
hmph
ぷいっ
W-WAIT!
Y-YOU LEAVE ME NO CHOICE!
I ALLOW YOU TO BE MY FRIEND.
TINK
ちょん
GREAT! PUT 'ER THERE, PAL!
てれっ
BLUSH

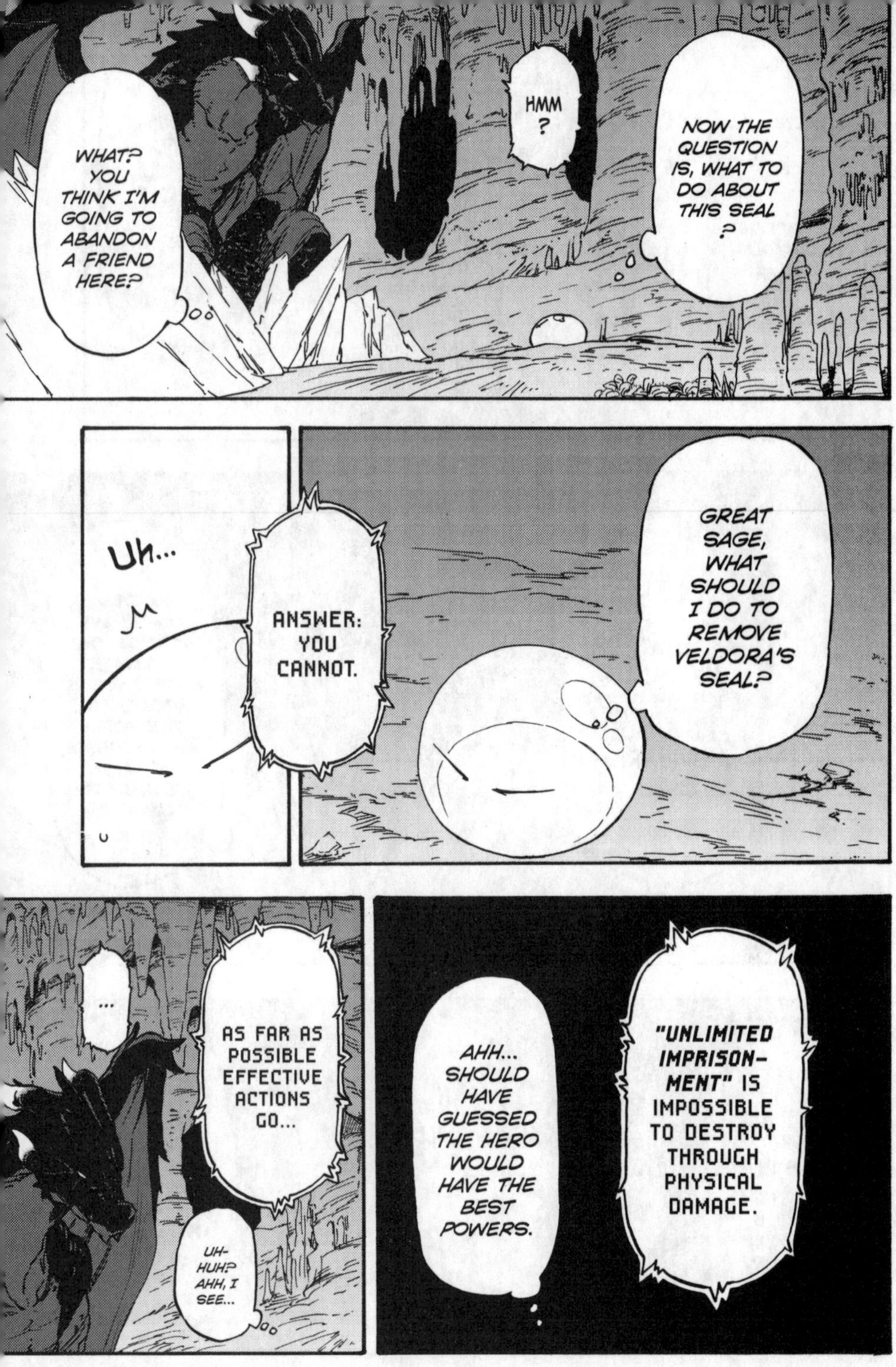

NOW THE QUESTION IS, WHAT TO DO ABOUT THIS SEAL?
HMM?
WHAT? YOU THINK I'M GOING TO ABANDON A FRIEND HERE?
GREAT SAGE, WHAT SHOULD I DO TO REMOVE VELDORA'S SEAL?
ANSWER: YOU CANNOT.
Uh...
"UNLIMITED IMPRISONMENT" IS IMPOSSIBLE TO DESTROY THROUGH PHYSICAL DAMAGE.
AHH... SHOULD HAVE GUESSED THE HERO WOULD HAVE THE BEST POWERS.
AS FAR AS POSSIBLE EFFECTIVE ACTIONS GO...
...
UH-HUH? AHH, I SEE...

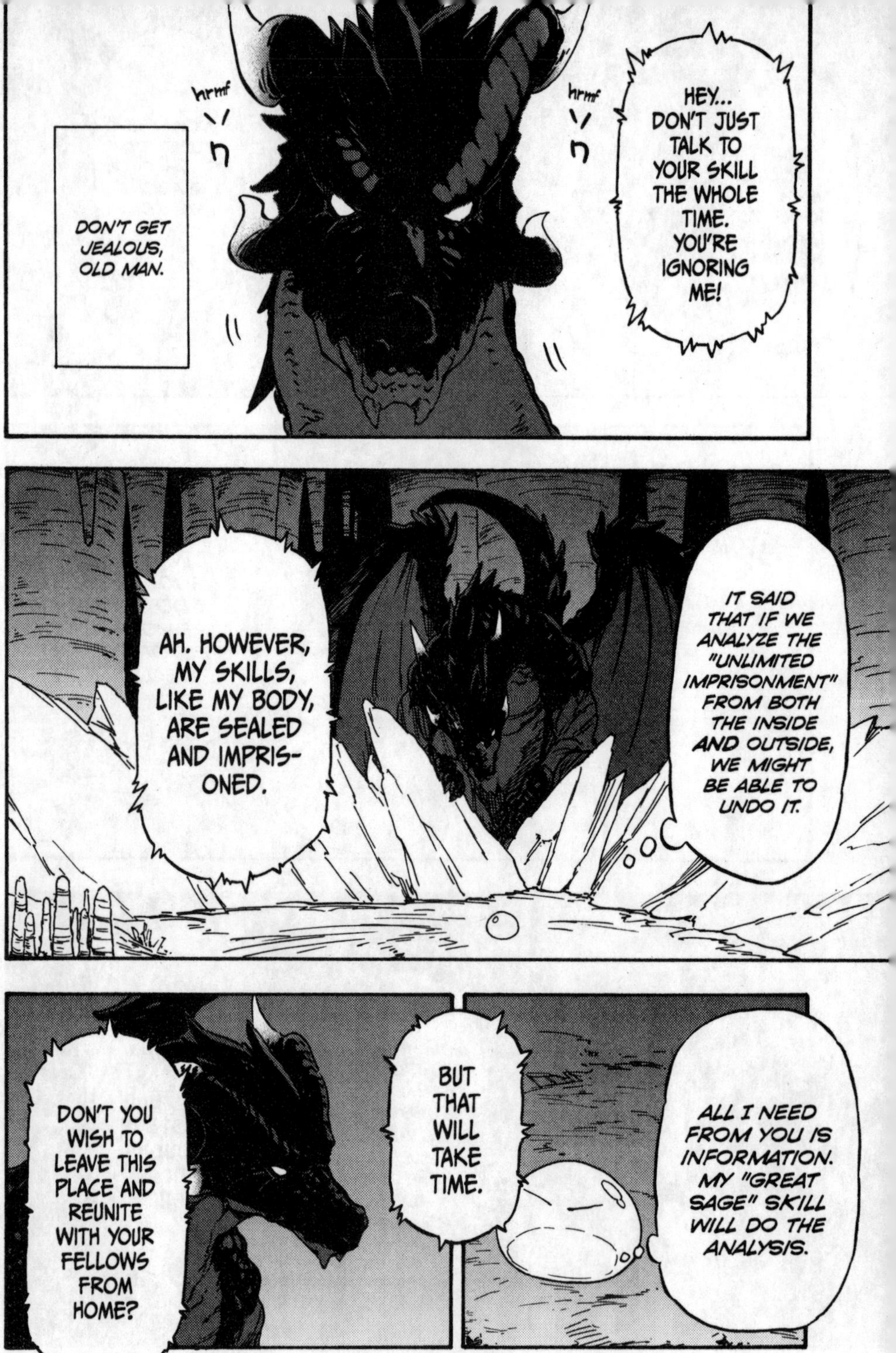
HEY... DON'T JUST TALK TO YOUR SKILL THE WHOLE TIME. YOU'RE IGNORING ME!
hrmf
hrmf
DON'T GET JEALOUS, OLD MAN.
IT SAID THAT IF WE ANALYZE THE "UNLIMITED IMPRISONMENT" FROM BOTH THE INSIDE AND OUTSIDE, WE MIGHT BE ABLE TO UNDO IT.
AH. HOWEVER, MY SKILLS, LIKE MY BODY, ARE SEALED AND IMPRIS-ONED.
ALL I NEED FROM YOU IS INFORMATION. MY "GREAT SAGE" SKILL WILL DO THE ANALYSIS.
BUT THAT WILL TAKE TIME.
DON'T YOU WISH TO LEAVE THIS PLACE AND REUNITE WITH YOUR FELLOWS FROM HOME?

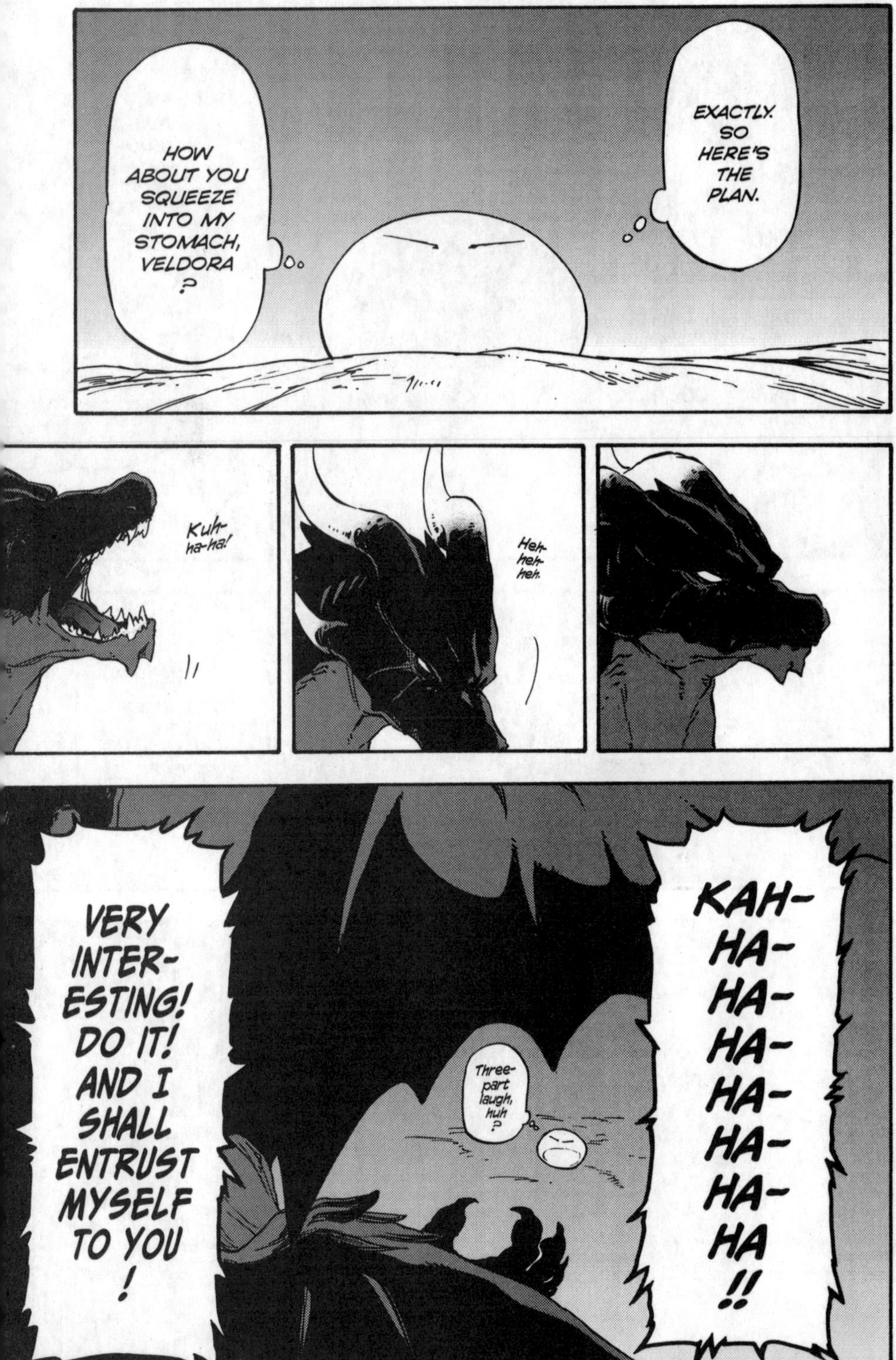
EXACTLY. SO HERE'S THE PLAN.
HOW ABOUT YOU SQUEEZE INTO MY STOMACH, VELDORA?
Heh-heh-heh.
Kuh-ha-ha!
KAH-HA-HA-HA-HA-HA-HA-HA!!
Three-part laugh, huh?
VERY INTER-ESTING! DO IT! AND I SHALL ENTRUST MYSELF TO YOU!

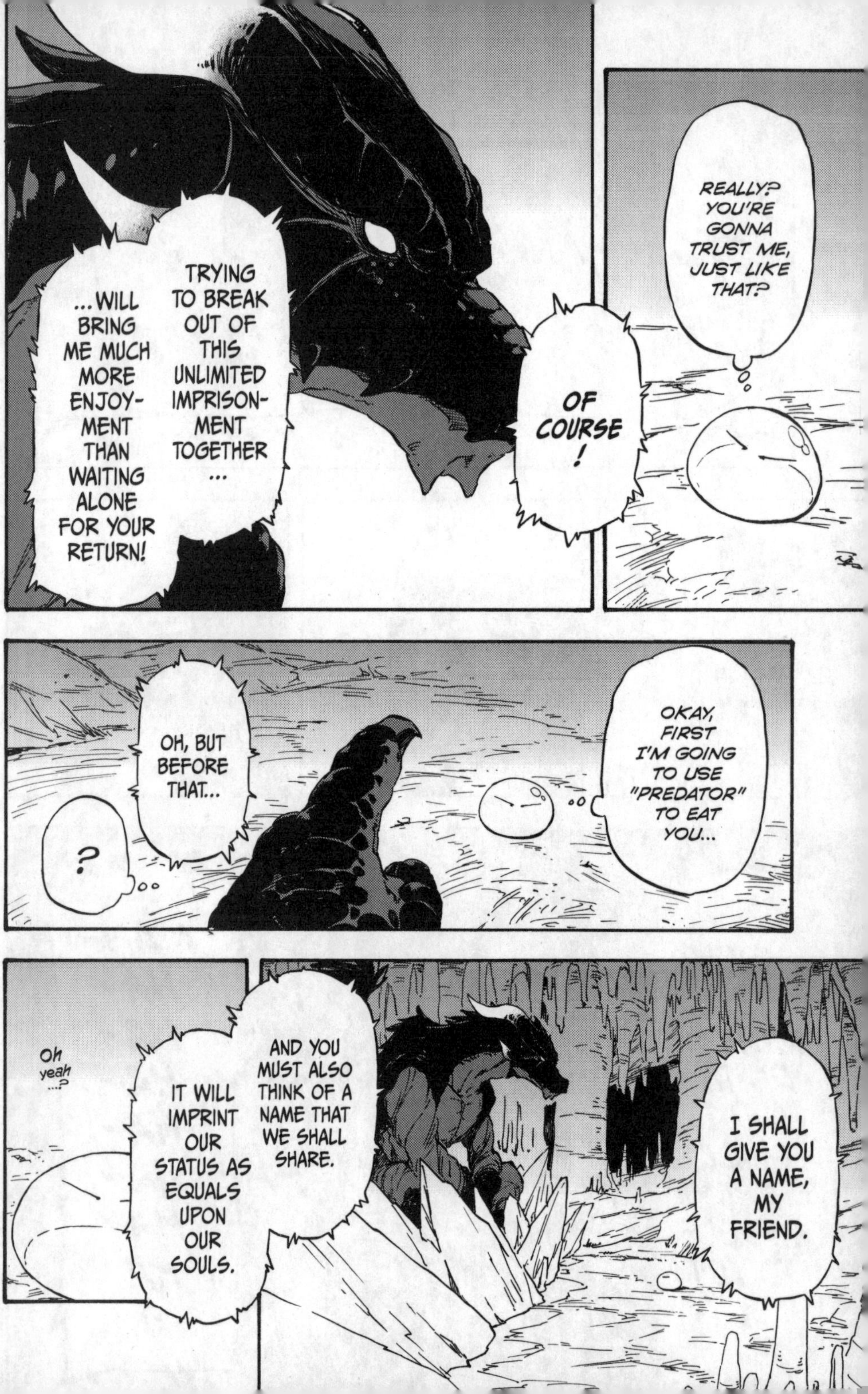
REALLY? YOU'RE GONNA TRUST ME, JUST LIKE THAT?
OF COURSE!
TRYING TO BREAK OUT OF THIS UNLIMITED IMPRISONMENT TOGETHER...
...WILL BRING ME MUCH MORE ENJOYMENT THAN WAITING ALONE FOR YOUR RETURN!
OKAY, FIRST I'M GOING TO USE "PREDATOR" TO EAT YOU...
OH, BUT BEFORE THAT...
?
I SHALL GIVE YOU A NAME, MY FRIEND.
AND YOU MUST ALSO THINK OF A NAME THAT WE SHALL SHARE.
IT WILL IMPRINT OUR STATUS AS EQUALS UPON OUR SOULS.
Oh yeah...?

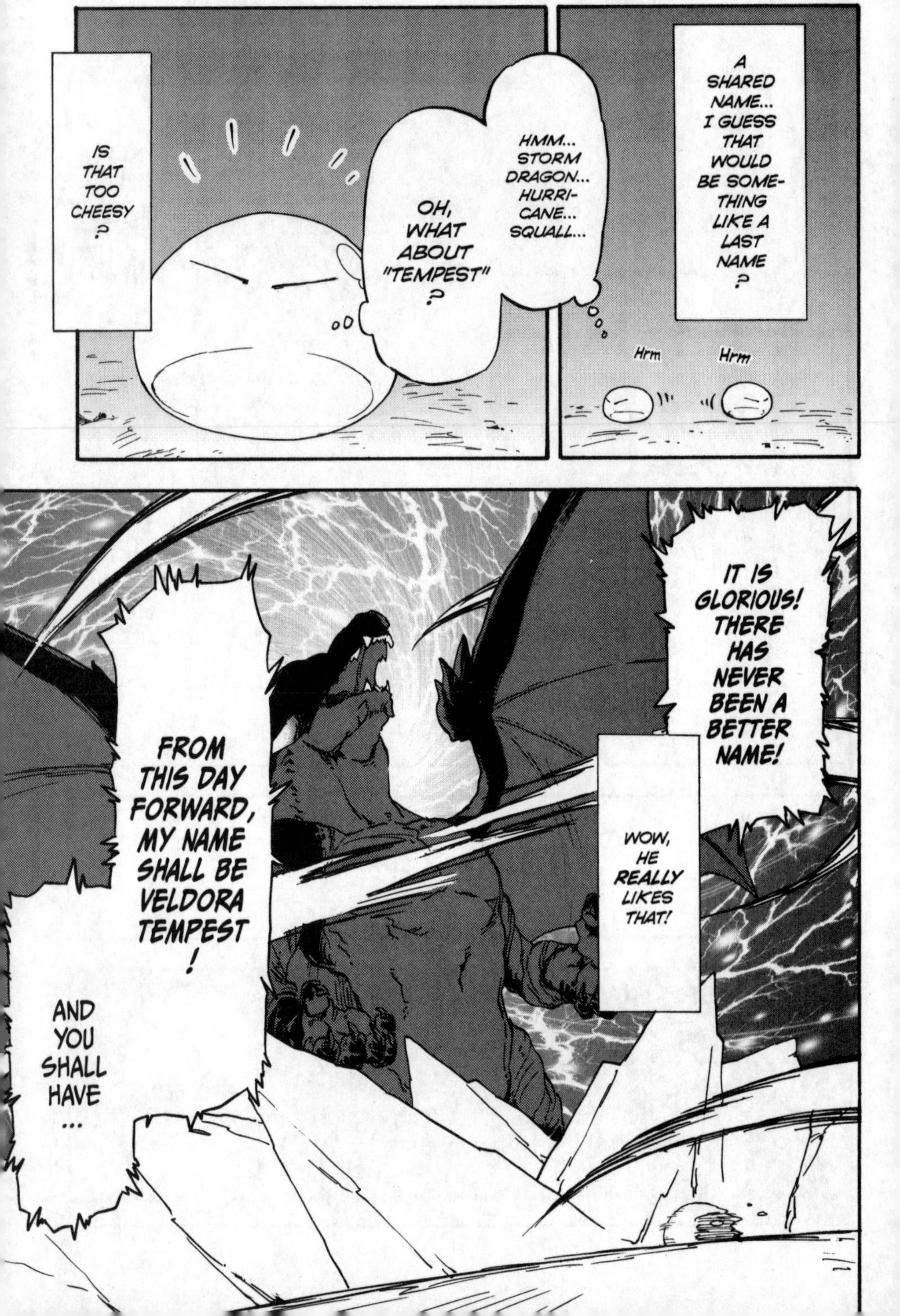
A SHARED NAME... I GUESS THAT WOULD BE SOMETHING LIKE A LAST NAME?
HMM... STORM DRAGON... HURRICANE... SQUALL...
Hrm
Hrm
OH, WHAT ABOUT "TEMPEST"?
IS THAT TOO CHEESY?
IT IS GLORIOUS! THERE HAS NEVER BEEN A BETTER NAME!
WOW, HE REALLY LIKES THAT!
FROM THIS DAY FORWARD, MY NAME SHALL BE VELDORA TEMPEST!
AND YOU SHALL HAVE...

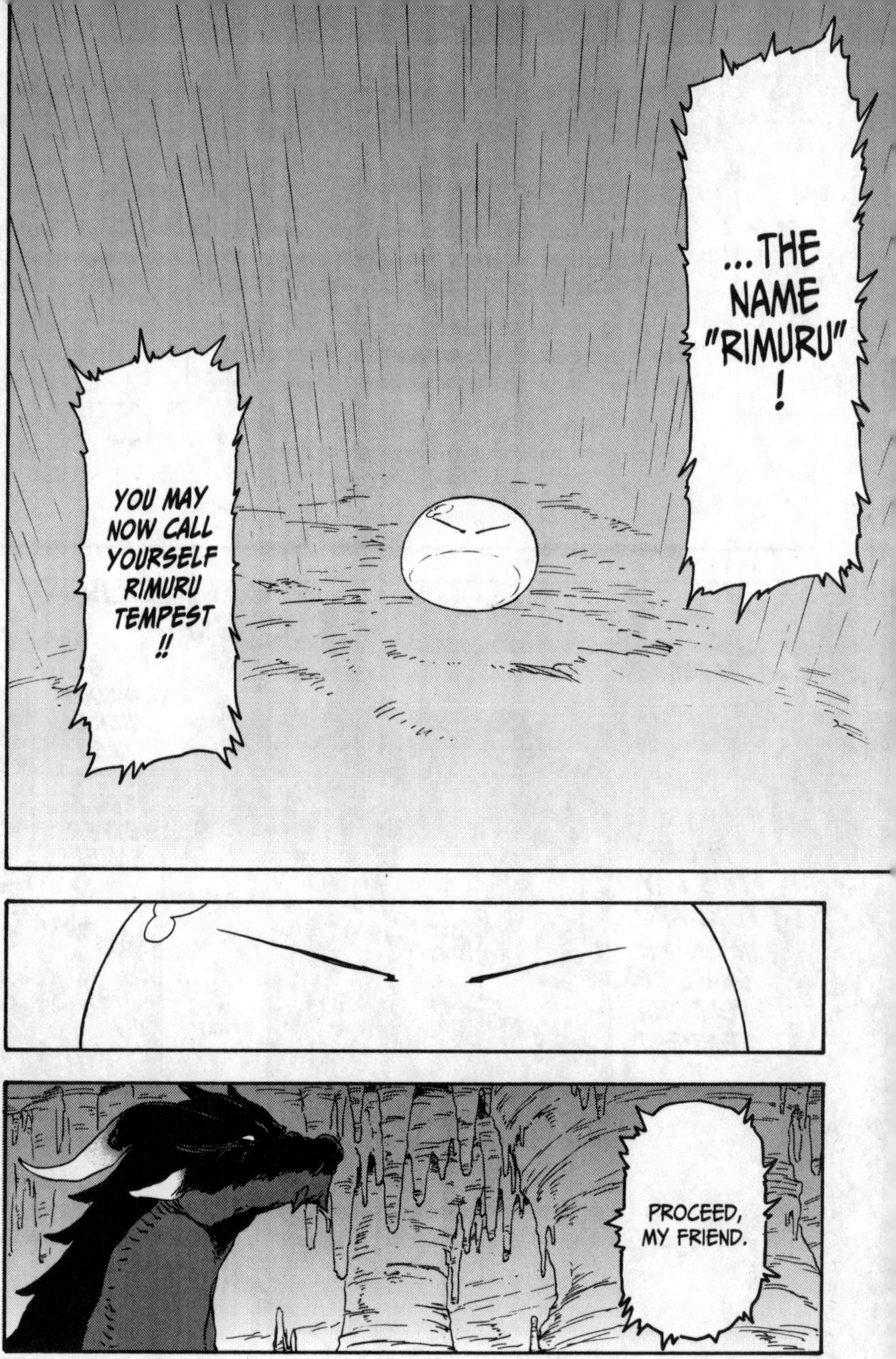
...THE NAME "RIMURU"!
YOU MAY NOW CALL YOURSELF RIMURU TEMPEST!!
PROCEED, MY FRIEND.

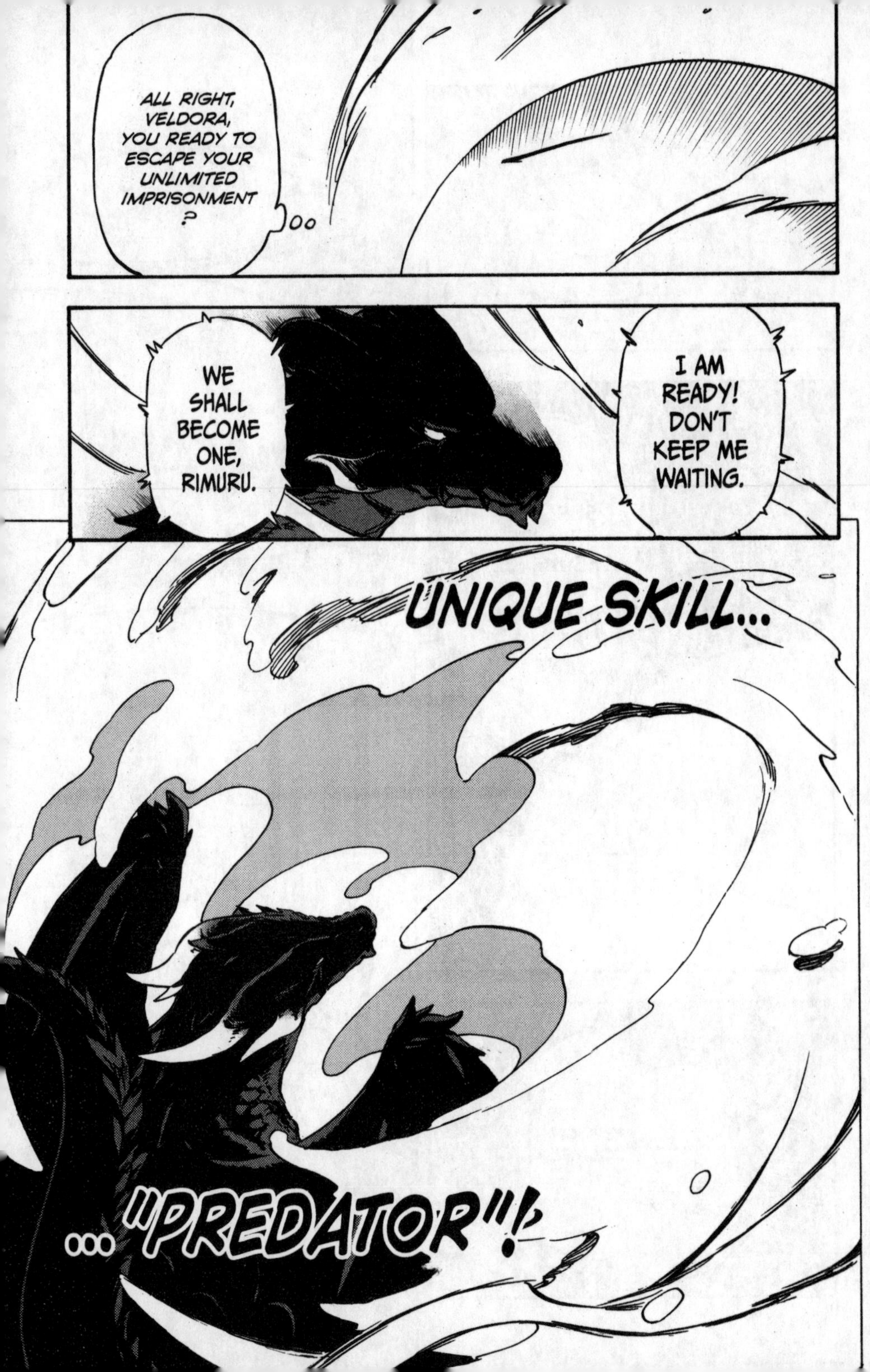
ALL RIGHT, VELDORA, YOU READY TO ESCAPE YOUR UNLIMITED IMPRISONMENT ?
I AM READY! DON'T KEEP ME WAITING.
WE SHALL BECOME ONE, RIMURU.
UNIQUE SKILL...
..."PREDATOR"!

SHALL I
ANALYZE
THE UNIQUE
SKILL:
"UNLIMITED
IMPRISON-
MENT"?

TAKE IT
AWAY,
GREAT
SAGE!

YES, OF
COURSE
!

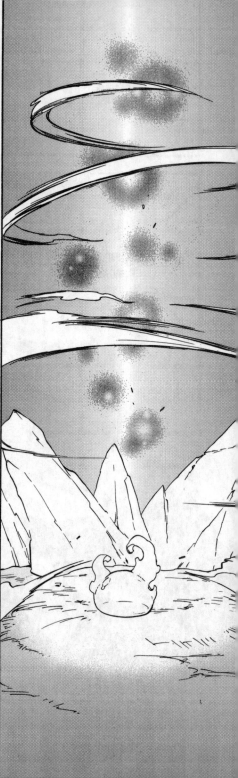

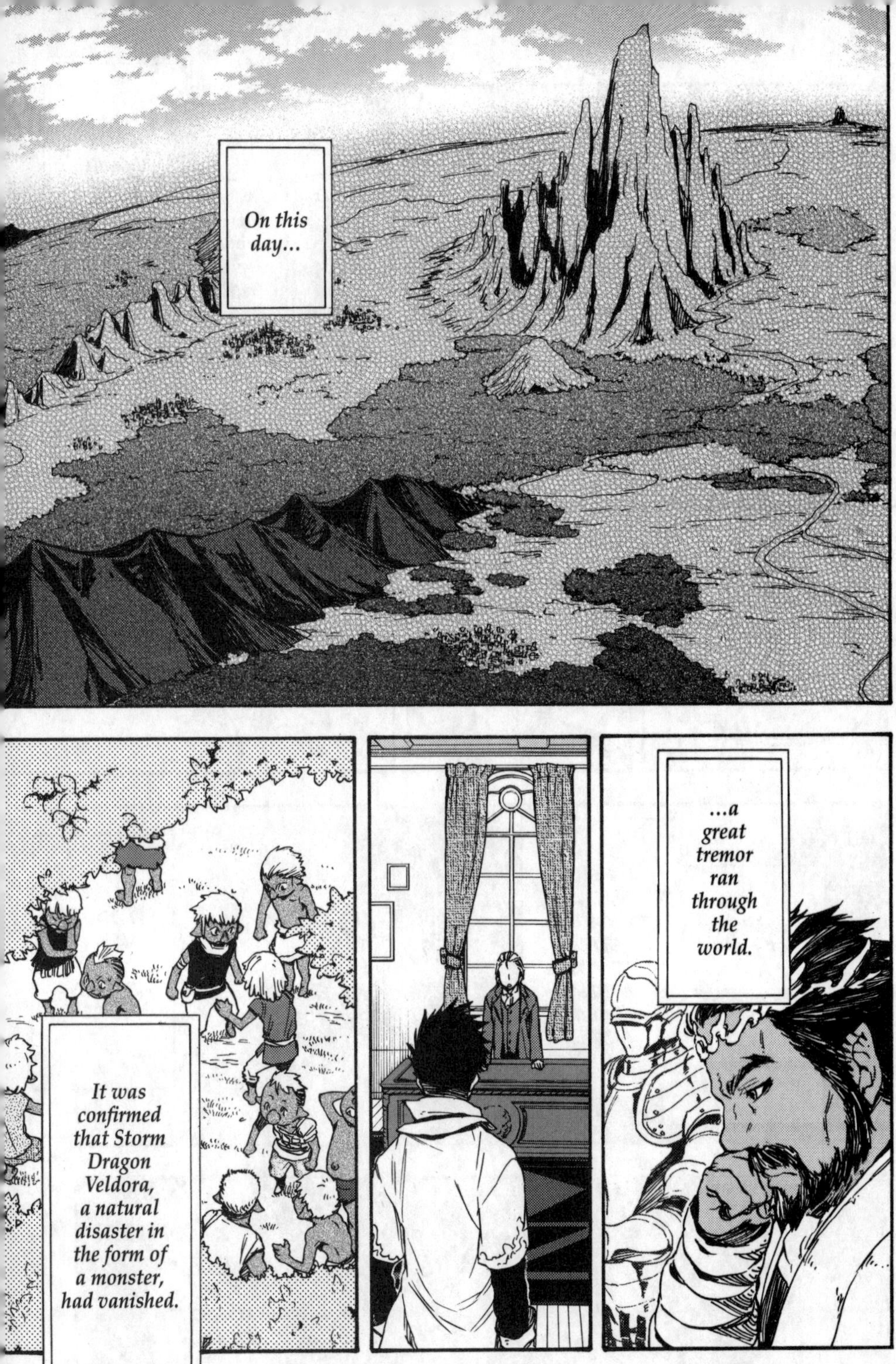
On this day...
...a great tremor ran through the world.
It was confirmed that Storm Dragon Veldora, a natural disaster in the form of a monster, had vanished.

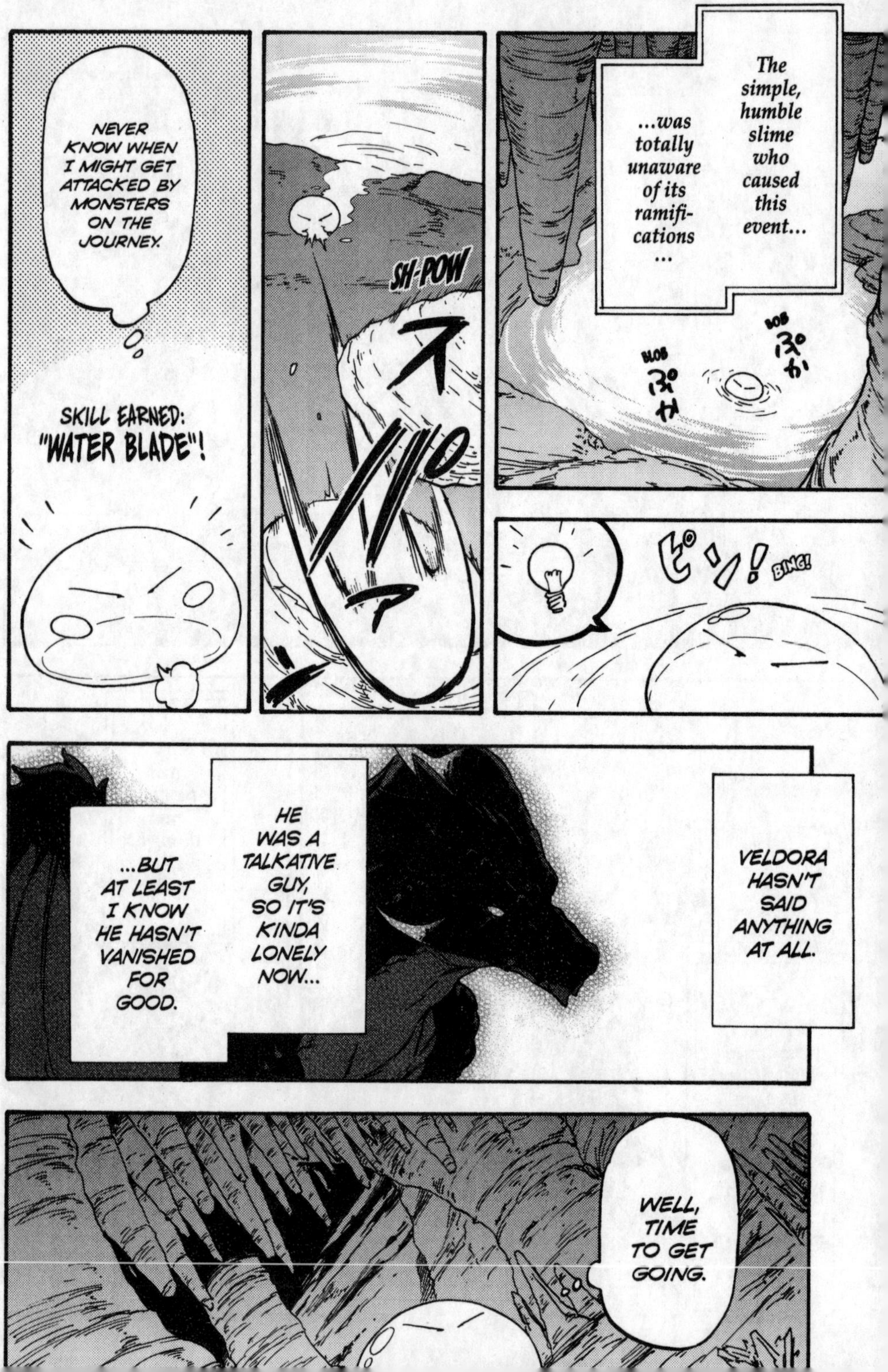
The simple, humble slime who caused this event...
...was totally unaware of its ramifications ...
BLOB
BLOB
BING!
SH-POW
NEVER KNOW WHEN I MIGHT GET ATTACKED BY MONSTERS ON THE JOURNEY.
SKILL EARNED: "WATER BLADE"!
VELDORA HASN'T SAID ANYTHING AT ALL.
HE WAS A TALKATIVE GUY, SO IT'S KINDA LONELY NOW...
...BUT AT LEAST I KNOW HE HASN'T VANISHED FOR GOOD.
WELL, TIME TO GET GOING.

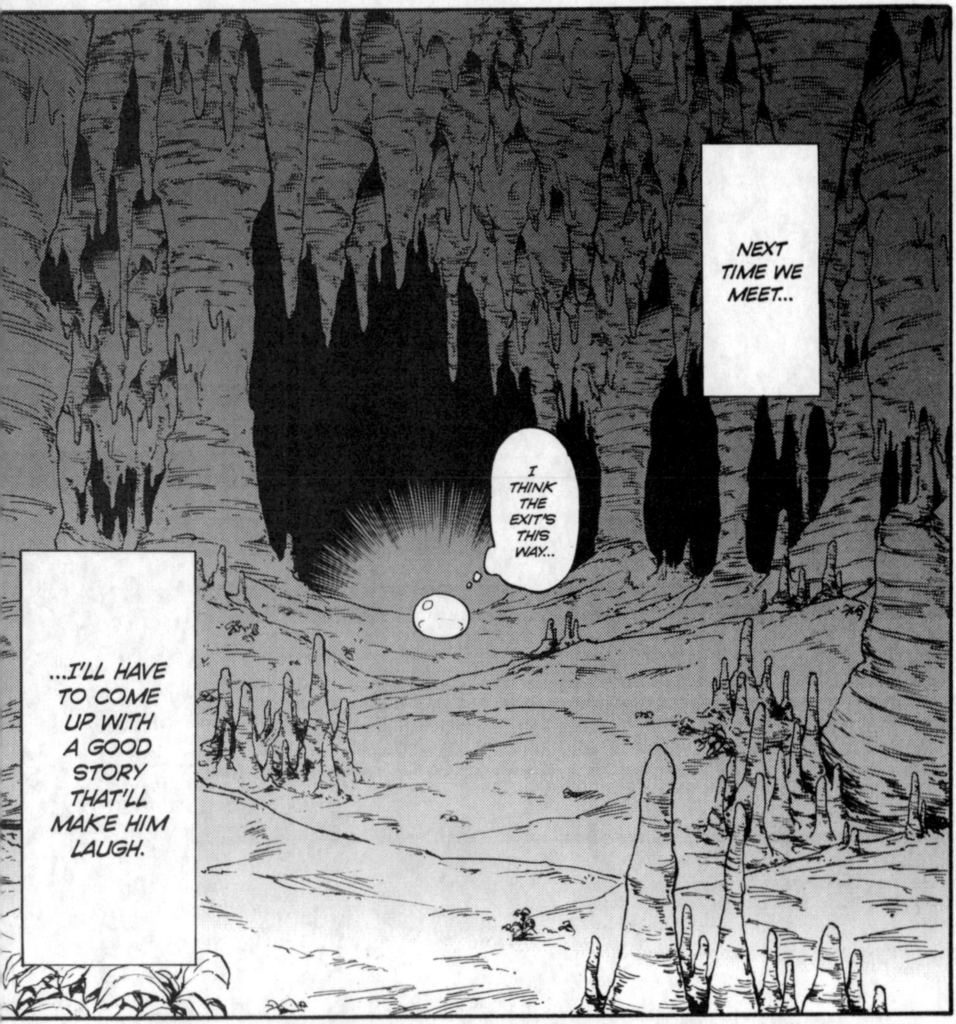
NEXT TIME WE MEET...
I THINK THE EXIT'S THIS WAY...
...I'LL HAVE TO COME UP WITH A GOOD STORY THAT'LL MAKE HIM LAUGH.

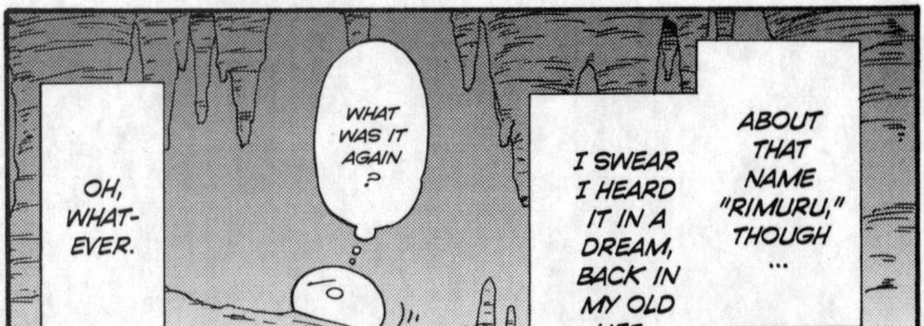
ABOUT THAT NAME "RIMURU," THOUGH ...
I SWEAR I HEARD IT IN A DREAM, BACK IN MY OLD LIFE...
WHAT WAS IT AGAIN ?
OH, WHAT-EVER.

OOH, I FOUND A METAL ORE.

DOWN THE HATCH!

MLOB

OKAY...

GULP

THIS DOOR'S BLOCKING MY PATH.

HOW SHOULD I OPEN IT?

I COULD USE "WATER BLADE" TO CUT IT...

...OR "PREDATOR" TO DEVOUR IT.

Assuming that will even work.

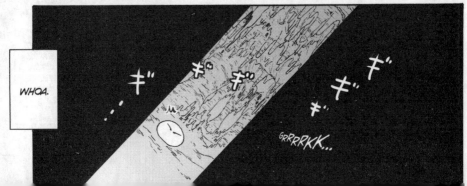

WHOA.

GRRRRKK...

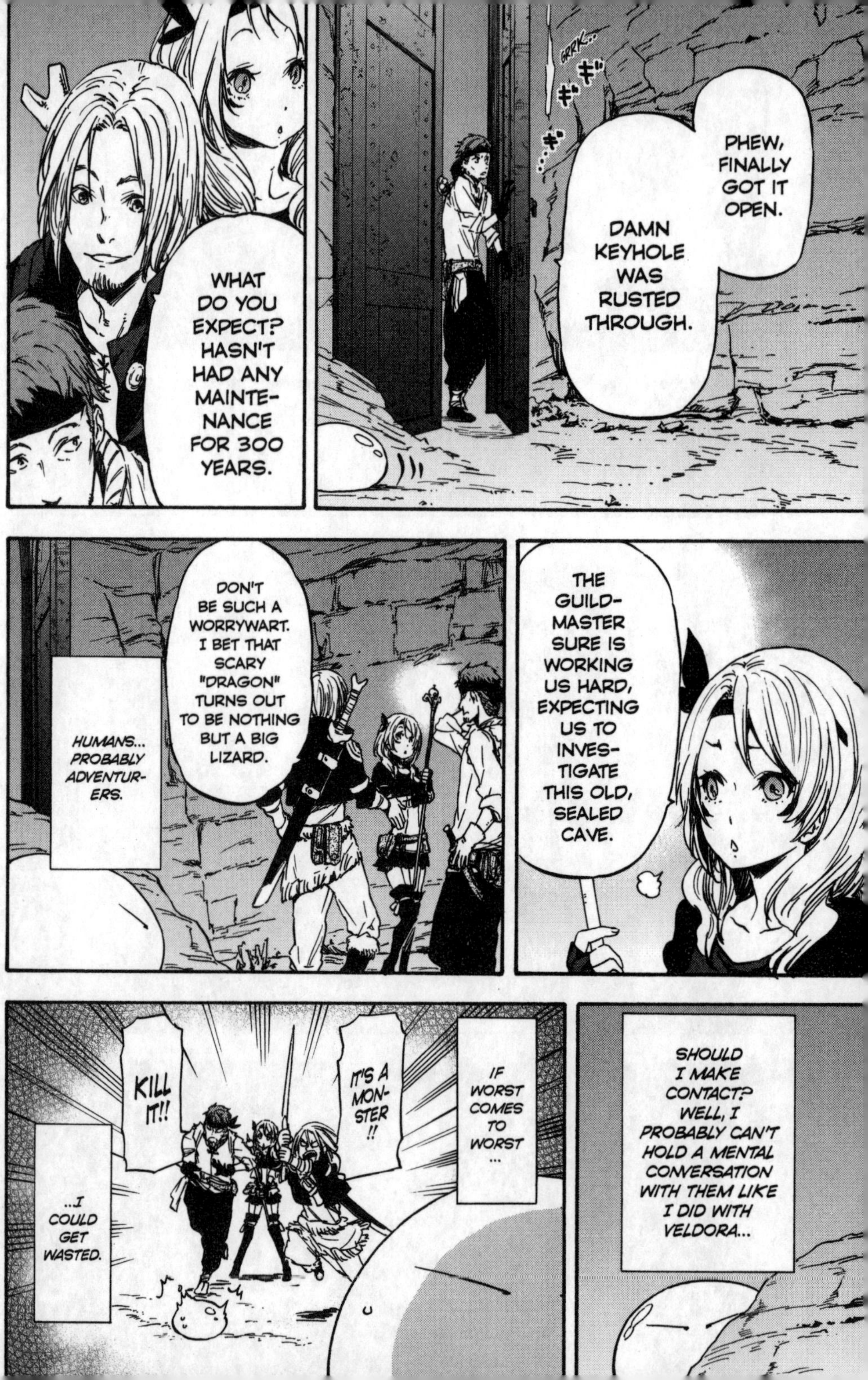
GRRK...
ギ ギ ギ
PHEW, FINALLY GOT IT OPEN.
DAMN KEYHOLE WAS RUSTED THROUGH.
WHAT DO YOU EXPECT? HASN'T HAD ANY MAINTE-NANCE FOR 300 YEARS.
THE GUILD-MASTER SURE IS WORKING US HARD, EXPECTING US TO INVES-TIGATE THIS OLD, SEALED CAVE.
DON'T BE SUCH A WORRYWART. I BET THAT SCARY "DRAGON" TURNS OUT TO BE NOTHING BUT A BIG LIZARD.
HUMANS... PROBABLY ADVENTUR-ERS.
SHOULD I MAKE CONTACT? WELL, I PROBABLY CAN'T HOLD A MENTAL CONVERSATION WITH THEM LIKE I DID WITH VELDORA...
IF WORST COMES TO WORST...
IT'S A MON-STER!!
KILL IT!!
...I COULD GET WASTED.

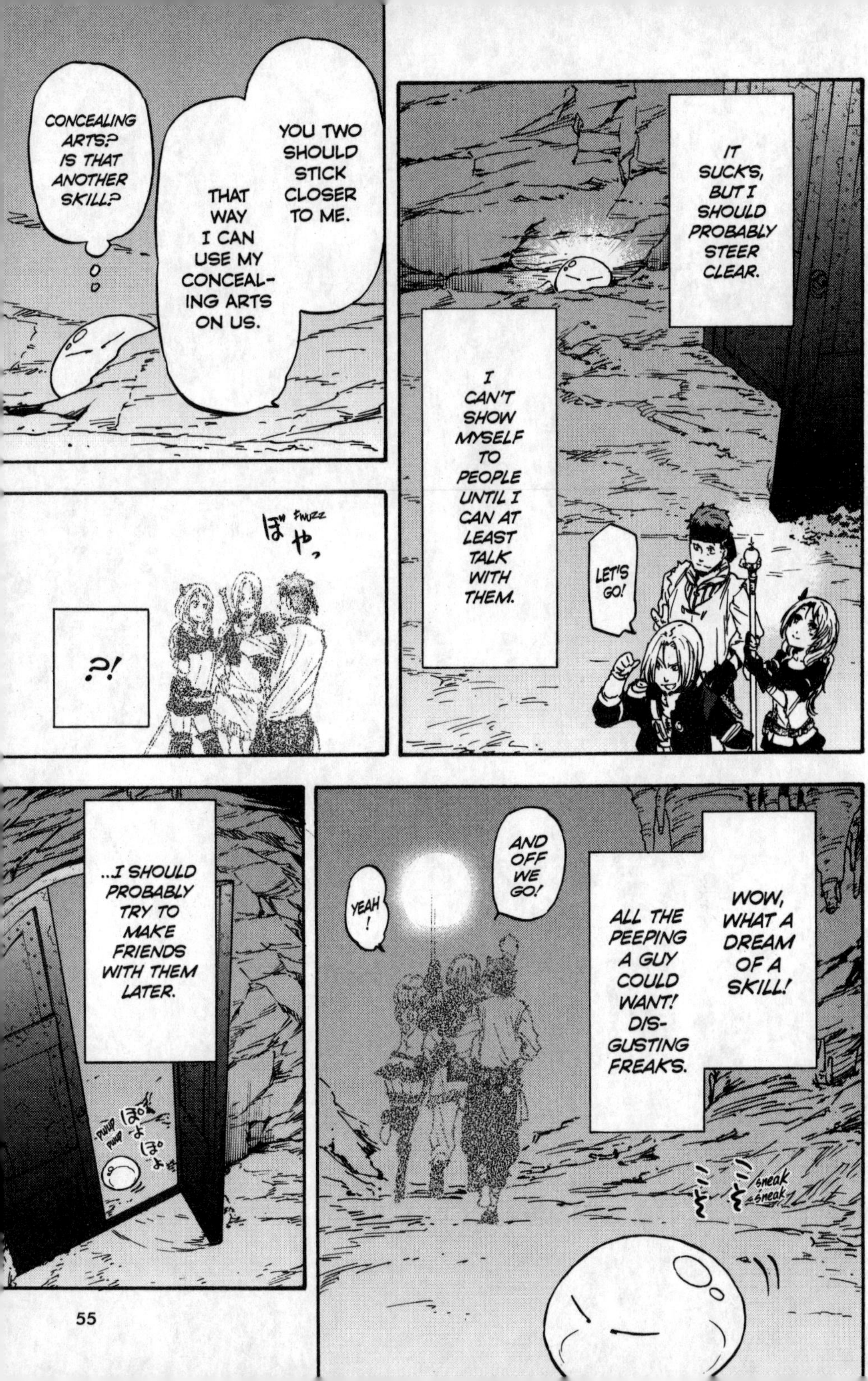
IT SUCKS, BUT I SHOULD PROBABLY STEER CLEAR.
I CAN'T SHOW MYSELF TO PEOPLE UNTIL I CAN AT LEAST TALK WITH THEM.
LET'S GO!
YOU TWO SHOULD STICK CLOSER TO ME.
THAT WAY I CAN USE MY CONCEAL-ING ARTS ON US.
CONCEALING ARTS? IS THAT ANOTHER SKILL?
ぼやっ
Fwuzz
?!
WOW, WHAT A DREAM OF A SKILL!
ALL THE PEEPING A GUY COULD WANT! DIS-GUSTING FREAKS.
AND OFF WE GO!
YEAH!
sneak sneak
...I SHOULD PROBABLY TRY TO MAKE FRIENDS WITH THEM LATER.
ぽよぽよ
pwup pwup

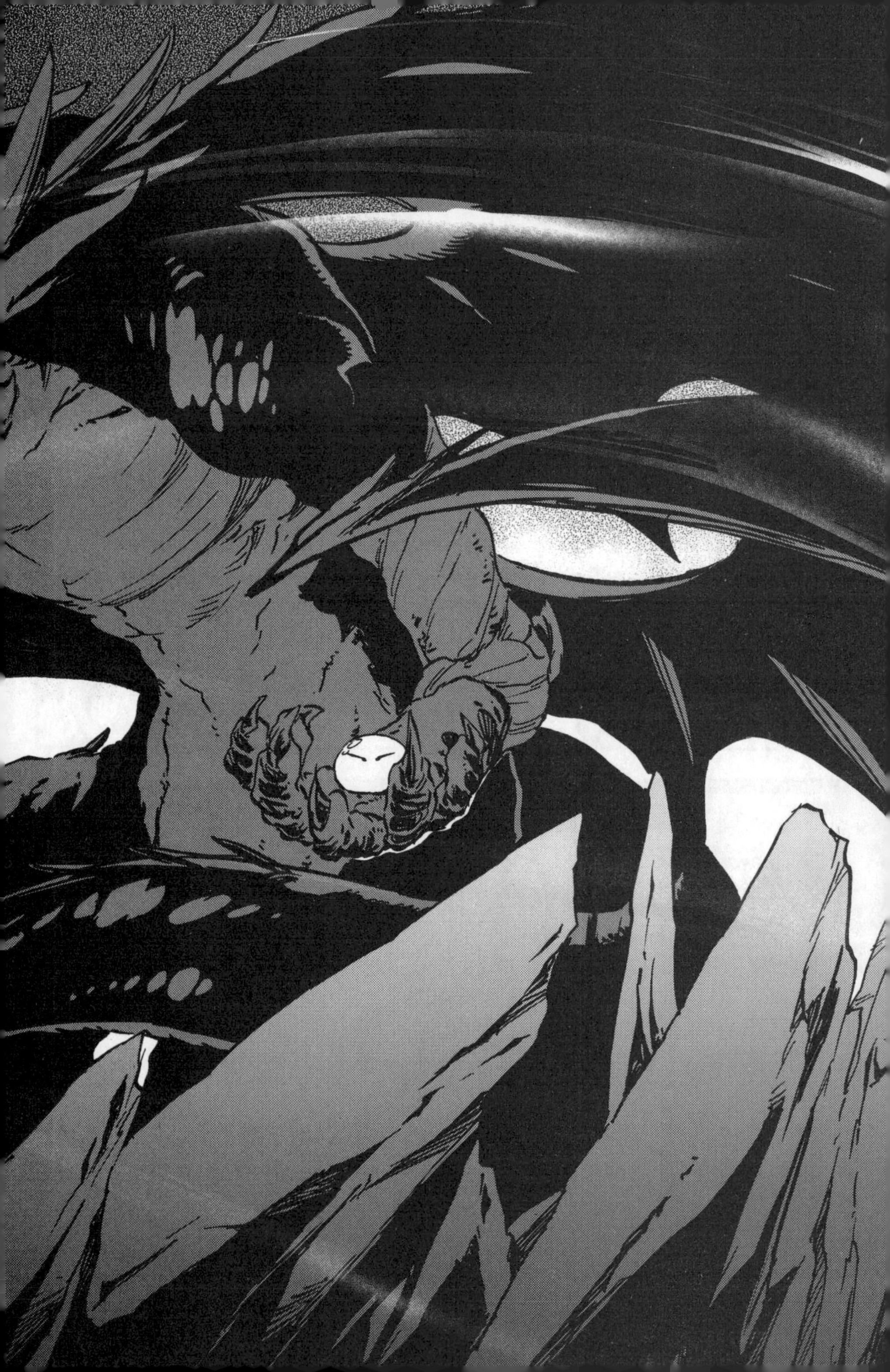

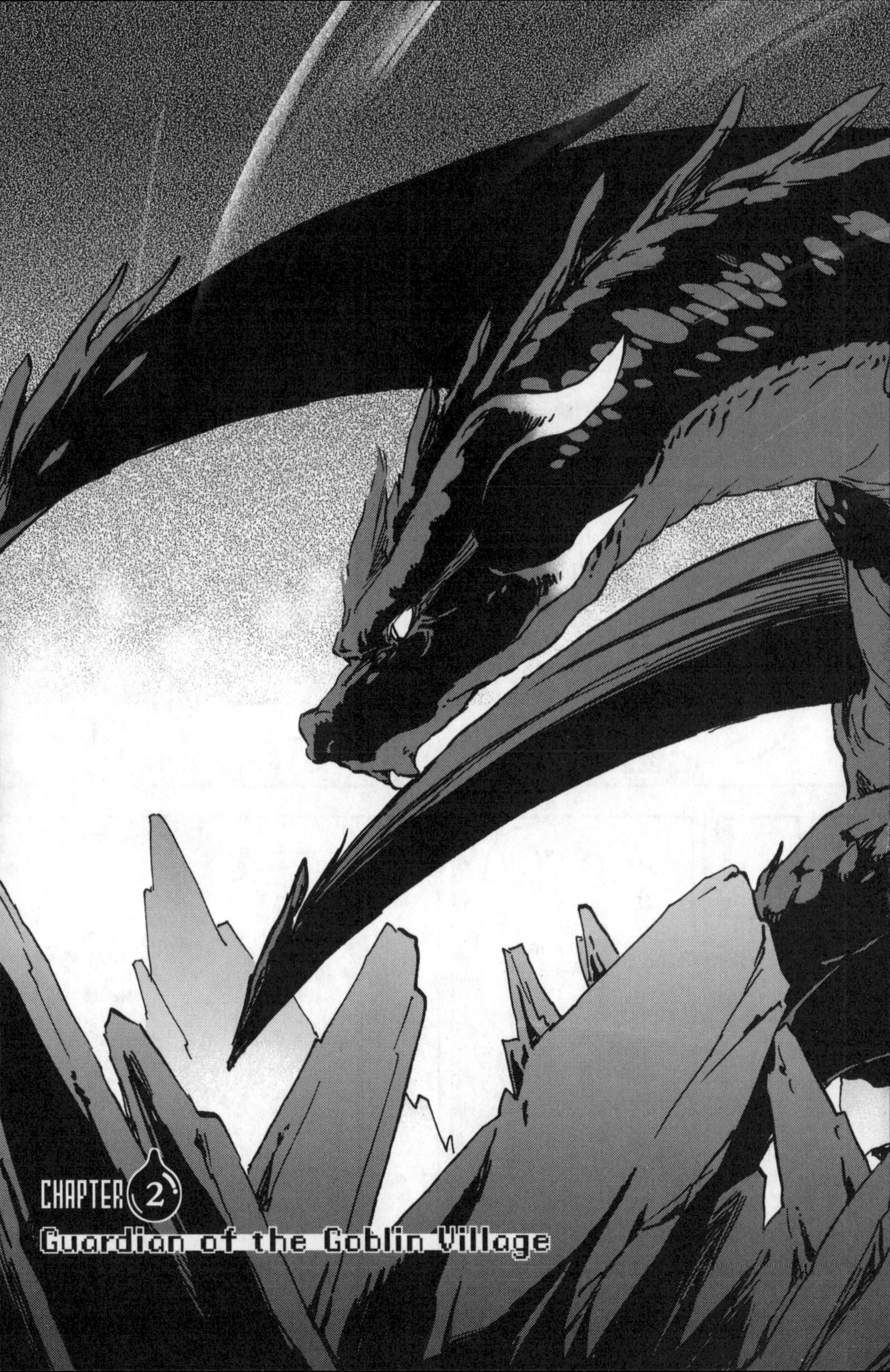
CHAPTER 2
Guardian of the Goblin Village

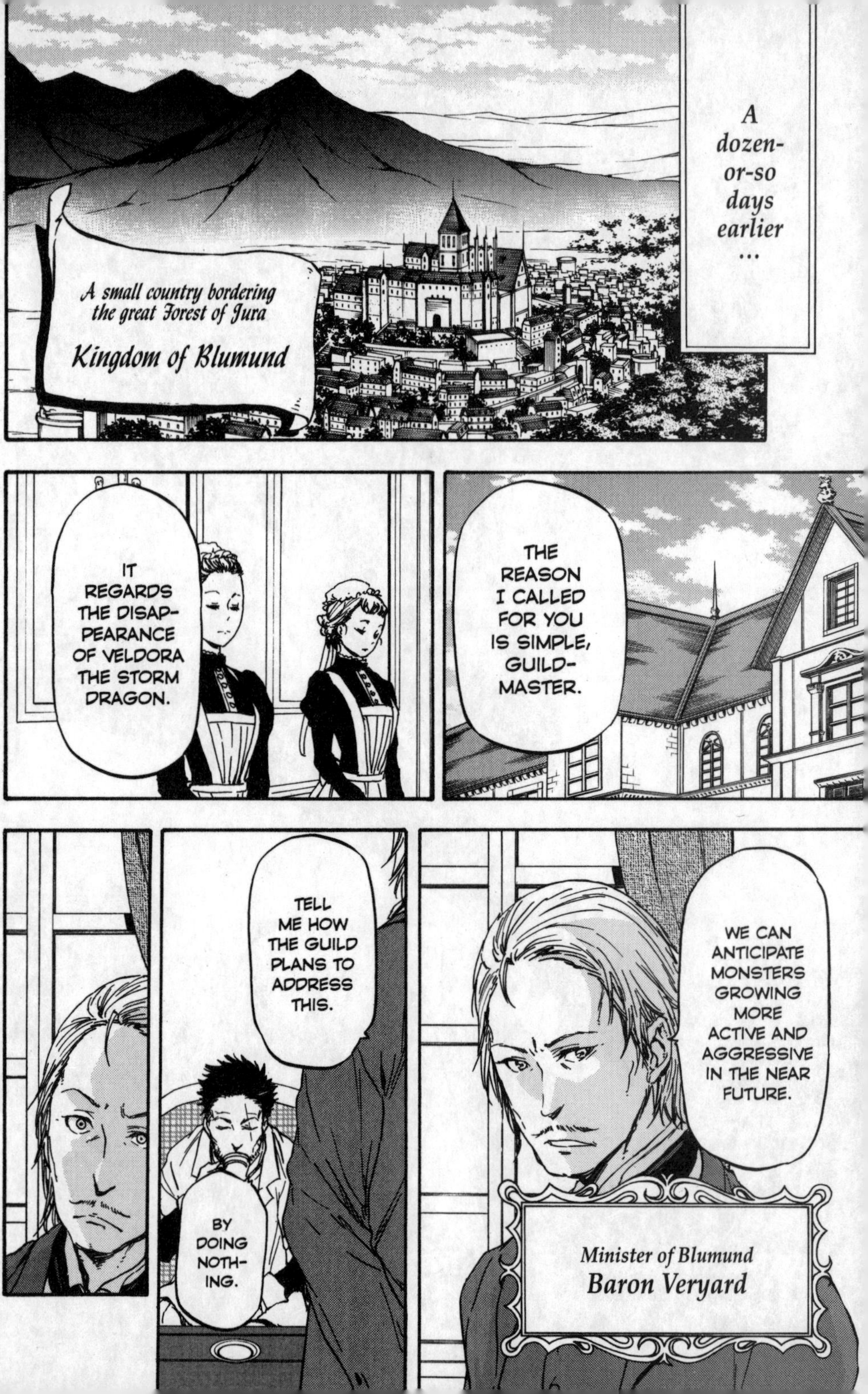
A dozen-or-so days earlier …
A small country bordering the great Forest of Jura
Kingdom of Blumund
THE REASON I CALLED FOR YOU IS SIMPLE, GUILDMASTER.
IT REGARDS THE DISAPPEARANCE OF VELDORA THE STORM DRAGON.
WE CAN ANTICIPATE MONSTERS GROWING MORE ACTIVE AND AGGRESSIVE IN THE NEAR FUTURE.
Minister of Blumund
Baron Veryard
TELL ME HOW THE GUILD PLANS TO ADDRESS THIS.
BY DOING NOTHING.

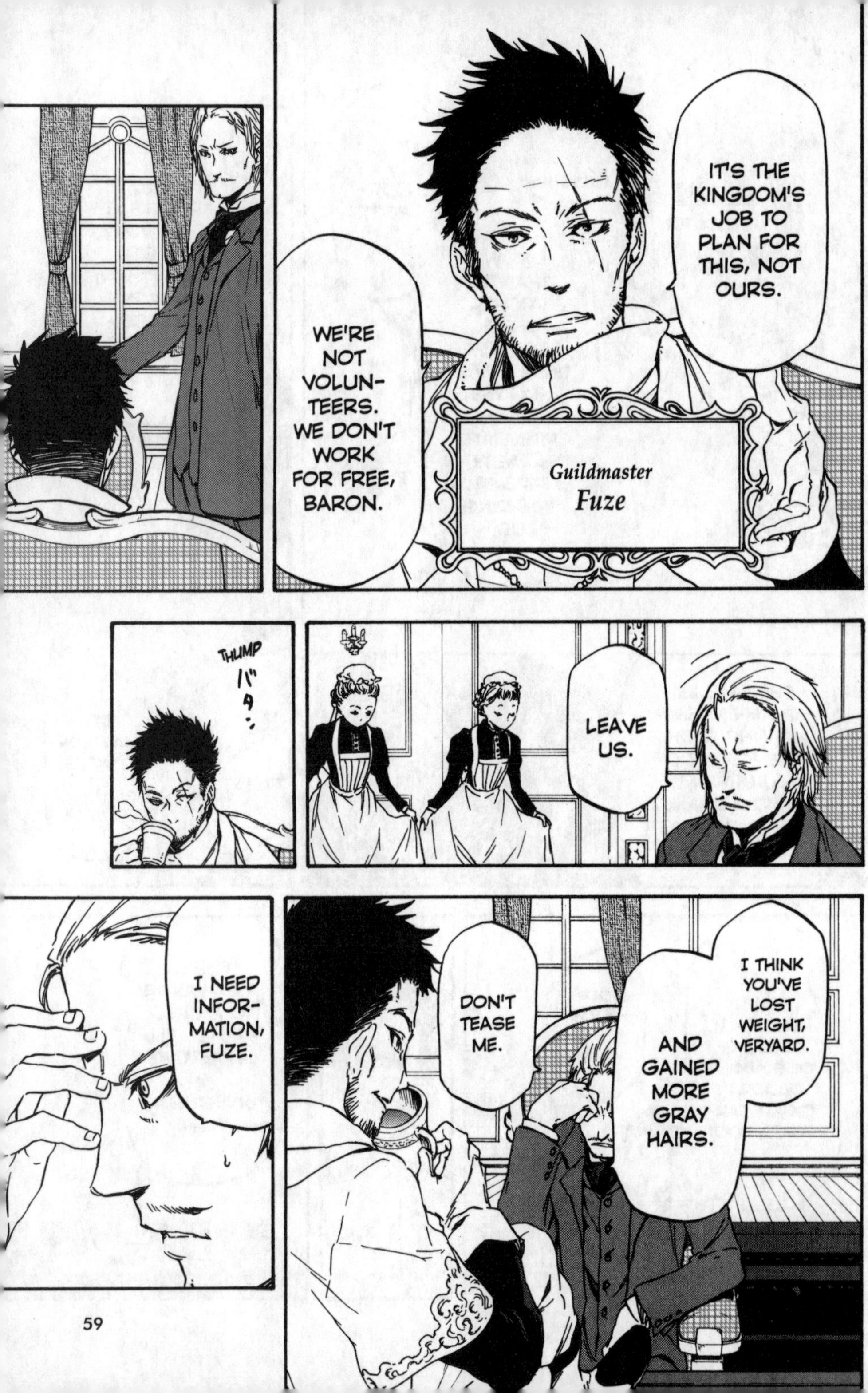
IT'S THE KINGDOM'S JOB TO PLAN FOR THIS, NOT OURS.
WE'RE NOT VOLUNTEERS. WE DON'T WORK FOR FREE, BARON.
Guildmaster
Fuze
LEAVE US.
THUMP
バタン
I THINK YOU'VE LOST WEIGHT, VERYARD.
AND GAINED MORE GRAY HAIRS.
DON'T TEASE ME.
I NEED INFORMATION, FUZE.

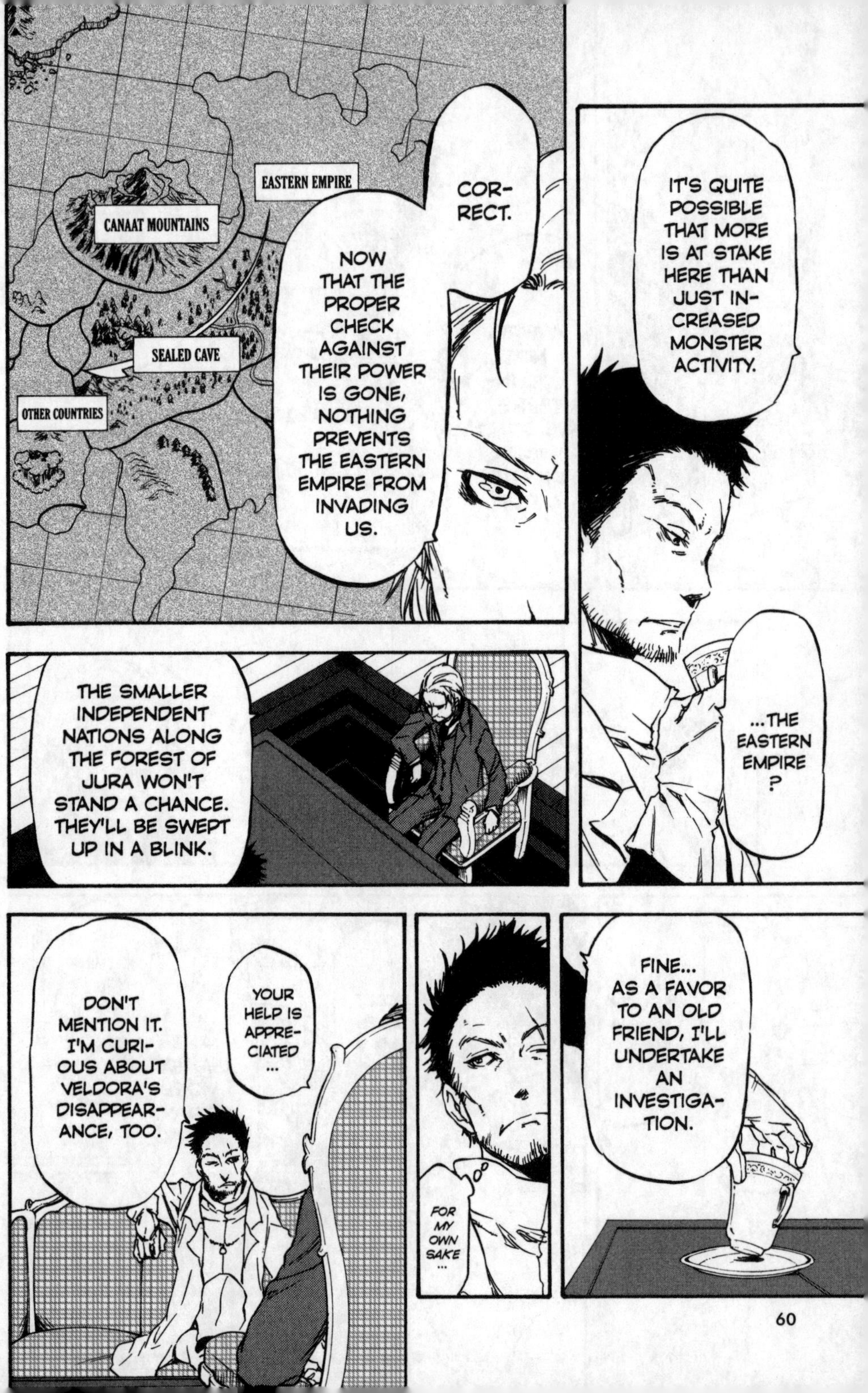
IT'S QUITE POSSIBLE THAT MORE IS AT STAKE HERE THAN JUST INCREASED MONSTER ACTIVITY.
...THE EASTERN EMPIRE?
CORRECT.
NOW THAT THE PROPER CHECK AGAINST THEIR POWER IS GONE, NOTHING PREVENTS THE EASTERN EMPIRE FROM INVADING US.
EASTERN EMPIRE
CANAAT MOUNTAINS
SEALED CAVE
OTHER COUNTRIES
THE SMALLER INDEPENDENT NATIONS ALONG THE FOREST OF JURA WON'T STAND A CHANCE. THEY'LL BE SWEPT UP IN A BLINK.
FINE... AS A FAVOR TO AN OLD FRIEND, I'LL UNDERTAKE AN INVESTIGATION.
FOR MY OWN SAKE...
YOUR HELP IS APPRECIATED...
DON'T MENTION IT. I'M CURIOUS ABOUT VELDORA'S DISAPPEARANCE, TOO.

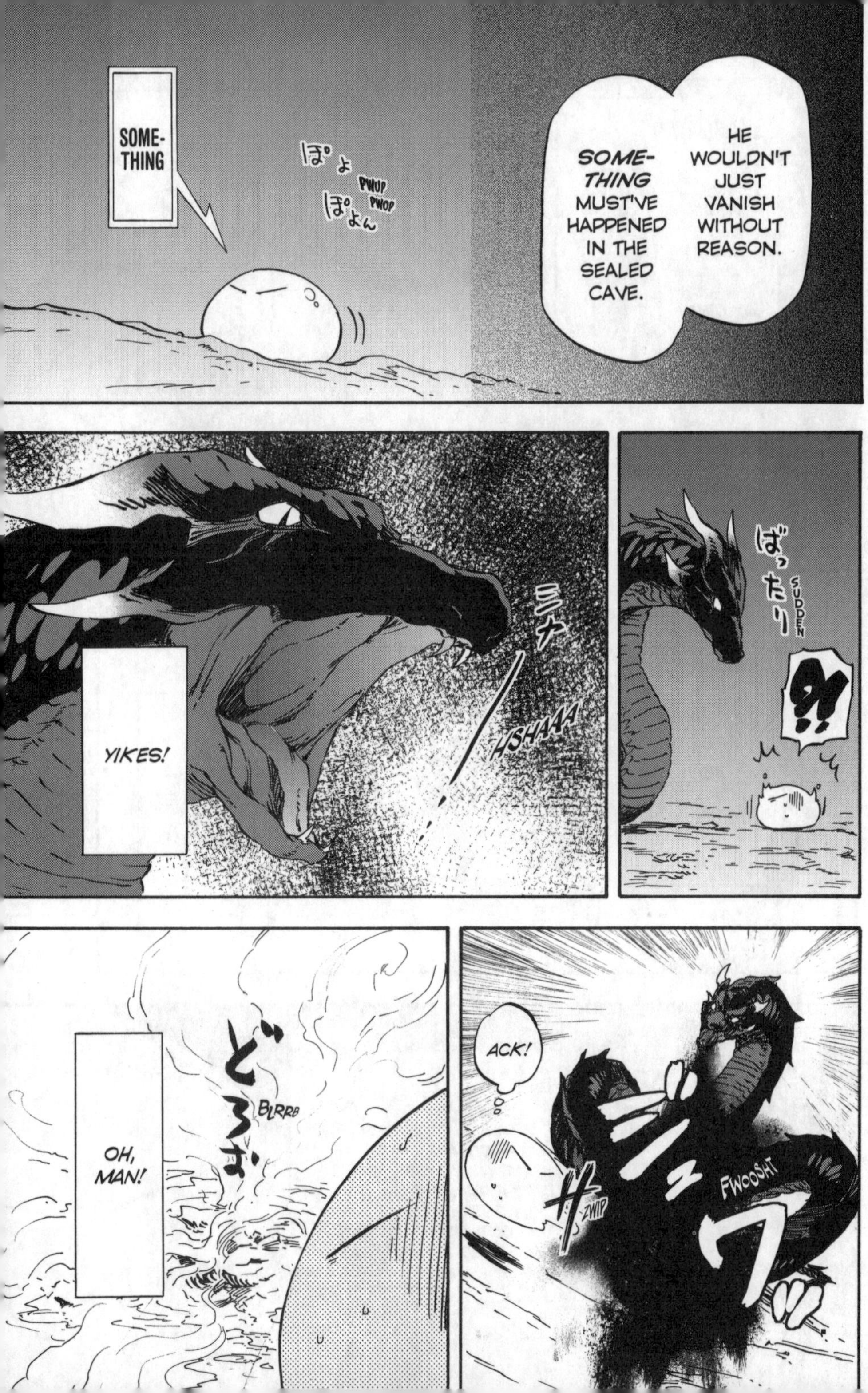
HE WOULDN'T JUST VANISH WITHOUT REASON.
SOMETHING MUST'VE HAPPENED IN THE SEALED CAVE.
ぽよ PWUP
ぽよん PWOP
SOMETHING
ばったり SUDDEN
?!
HSHAAA
YIKES!
ACK!
シュワ FWOOSH
ZWIP
どろぉ BLRRB
OH, MAN!

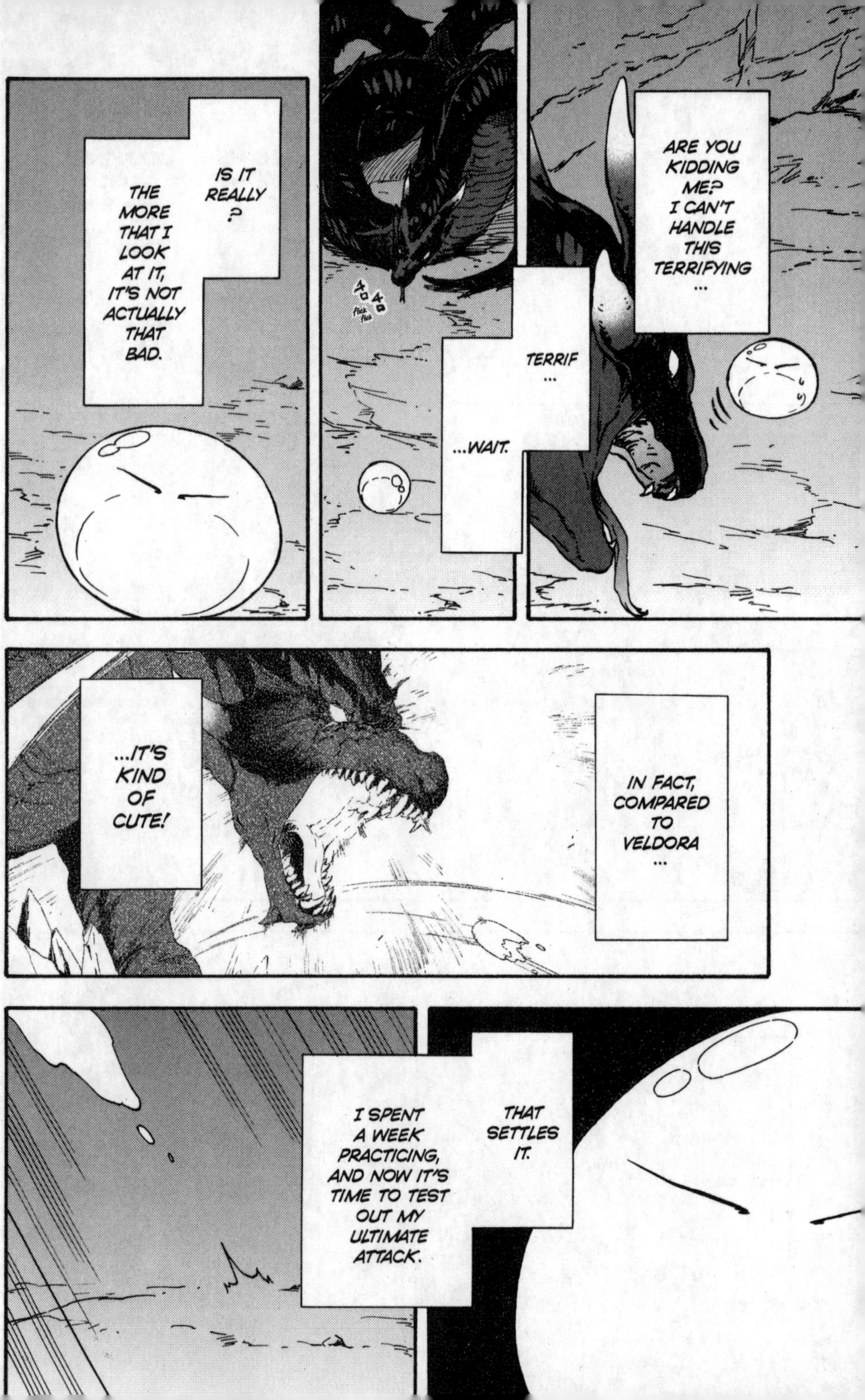
ARE YOU KIDDING ME? I CAN'T HANDLE THIS TERRIFYING ...
TERRIF ...
...WAIT.
flick flick
IS IT REALLY ?
THE MORE THAT I LOOK AT IT, IT'S NOT ACTUALLY THAT BAD.
IN FACT, COMPARED TO VELDORA ...
...IT'S KIND OF CUTE!
THAT SETTLES IT.
I SPENT A WEEK PRACTICING, AND NOW IT'S TIME TO TEST OUT MY ULTIMATE ATTACK.

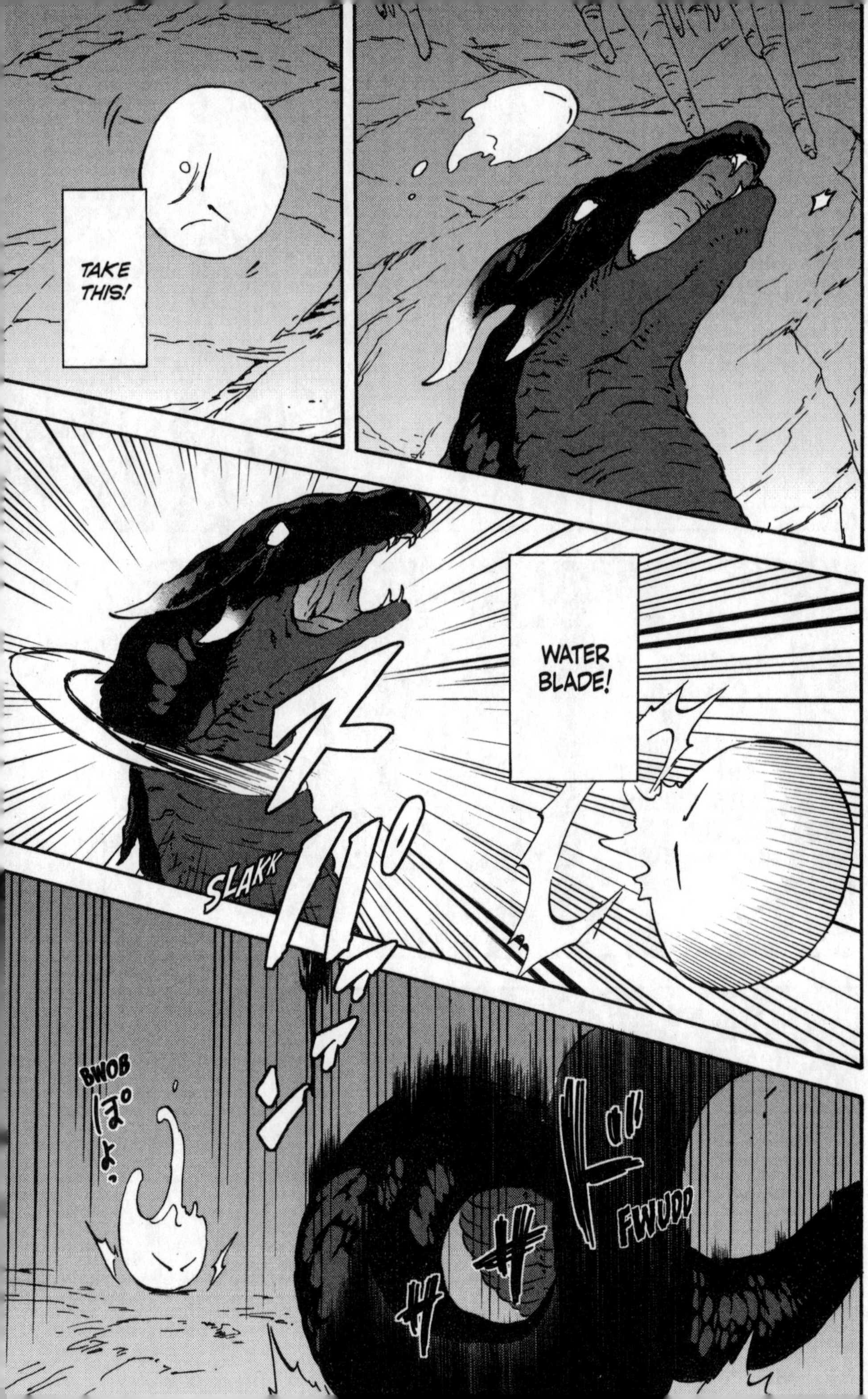
TAKE THIS!
WATER BLADE!
SLAKK
FWUDD
BWOB
ぽよ。

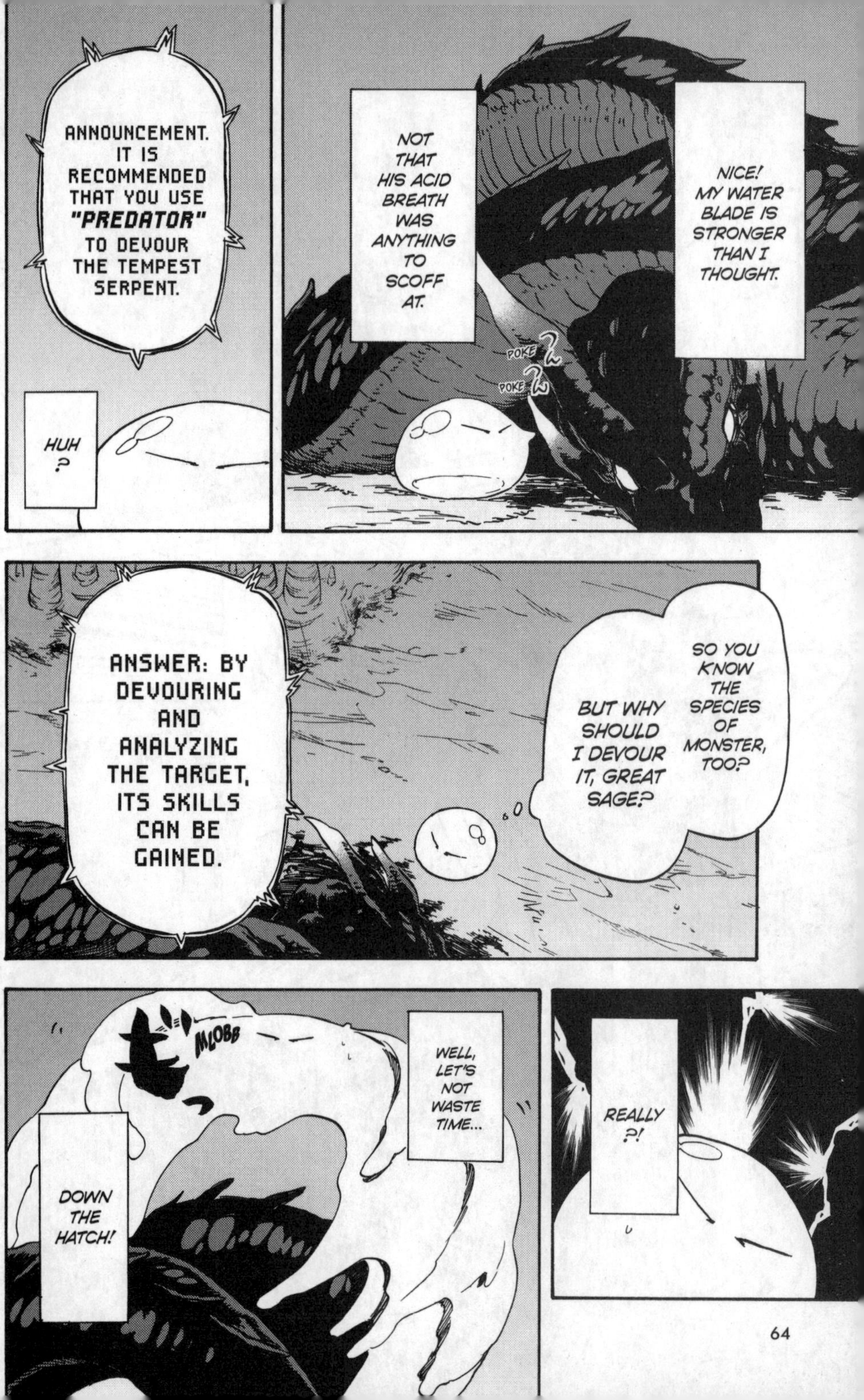
NICE! MY WATER BLADE IS STRONGER THAN I THOUGHT.
NOT THAT HIS ACID BREATH WAS ANYTHING TO SCOFF AT.
POKE
POKE
ANNOUNCEMENT. IT IS RECOMMENDED THAT YOU USE "PREDATOR" TO DEVOUR THE TEMPEST SERPENT.
HUH?
SO YOU KNOW THE SPECIES OF MONSTER, TOO?
BUT WHY SHOULD I DEVOUR IT, GREAT SAGE?
ANSWER: BY DEVOURING AND ANALYZING THE TARGET, ITS SKILLS CAN BE GAINED.
REALLY?!
WELL, LET'S NOT WASTE TIME...
MLOBB
DOWN THE HATCH!

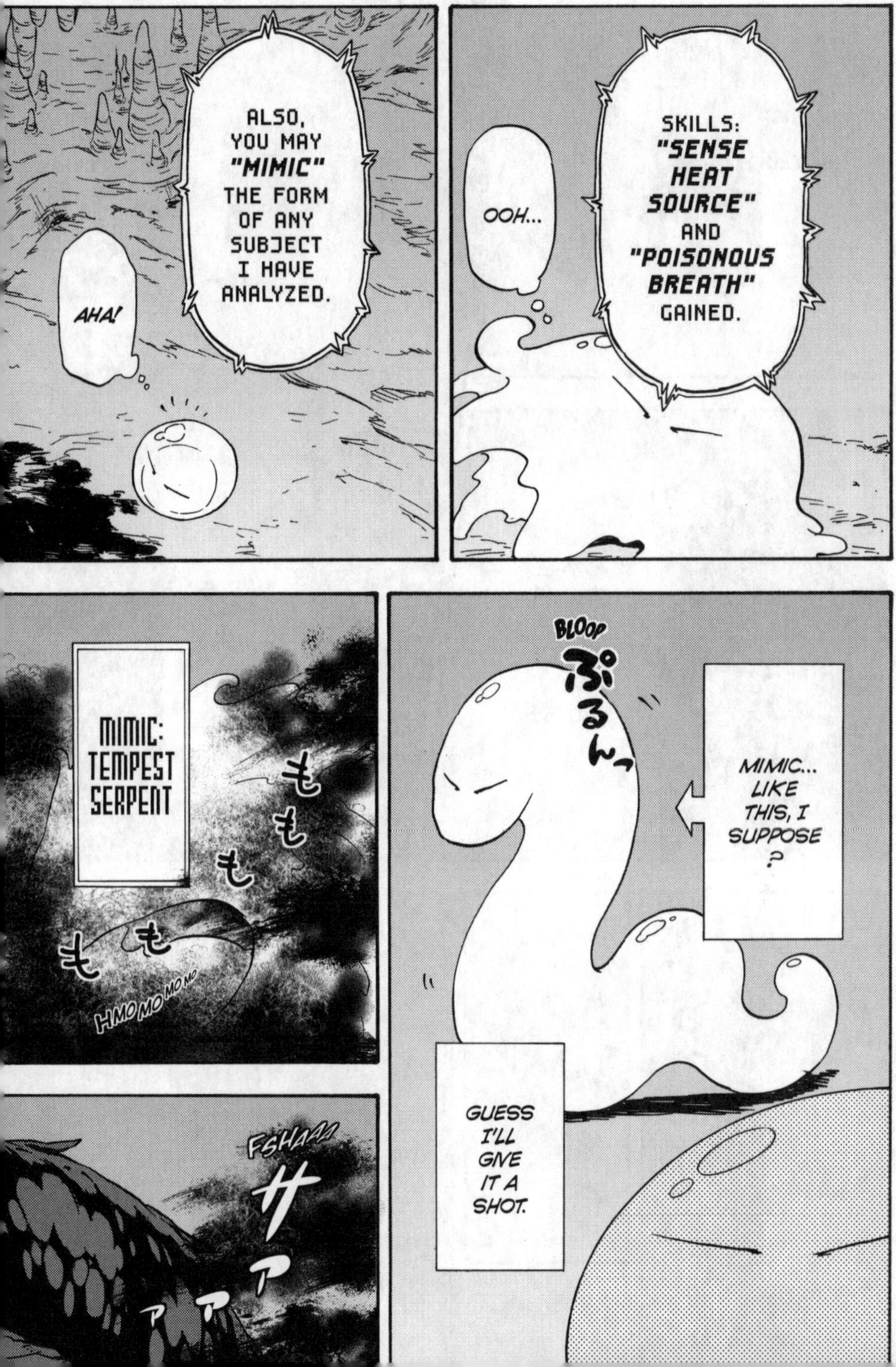
SKILLS: "SENSE HEAT SOURCE" AND "POISONOUS BREATH" GAINED.
OOH...
ALSO, YOU MAY "MIMIC" THE FORM OF ANY SUBJECT I HAVE ANALYZED.
AHA!
BLOOP
ぷるん
MIMIC... LIKE THIS, I SUPPOSE?
GUESS I'LL GIVE IT A SHOT.
MIMIC: TEMPEST SERPENT
ももももも
HMO MO MO MO
FSHAAA
サアアア

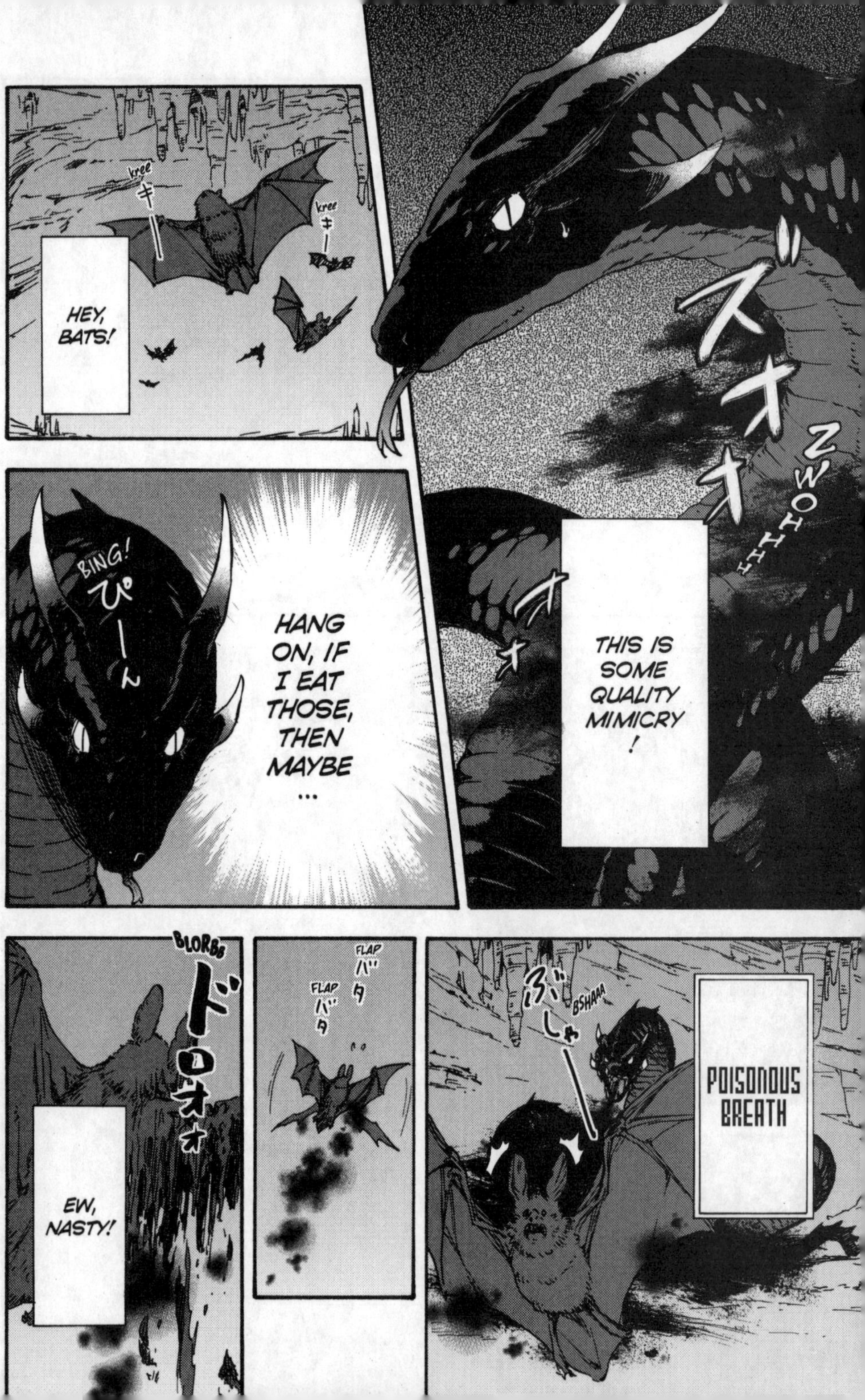
ZWOHHHH
THIS IS SOME QUALITY MIMICRY!
kree
キー
kree
キー
HEY, BATS!
BING!
ぴーん
HANG ON, IF I EAT THOSE, THEN MAYBE...
BSHAAA
ぶしゃー
POISONOUS BREATH
FLAP
バタ
FLAP
バタ
BLORBB
ドロォォ
EW, NASTY!

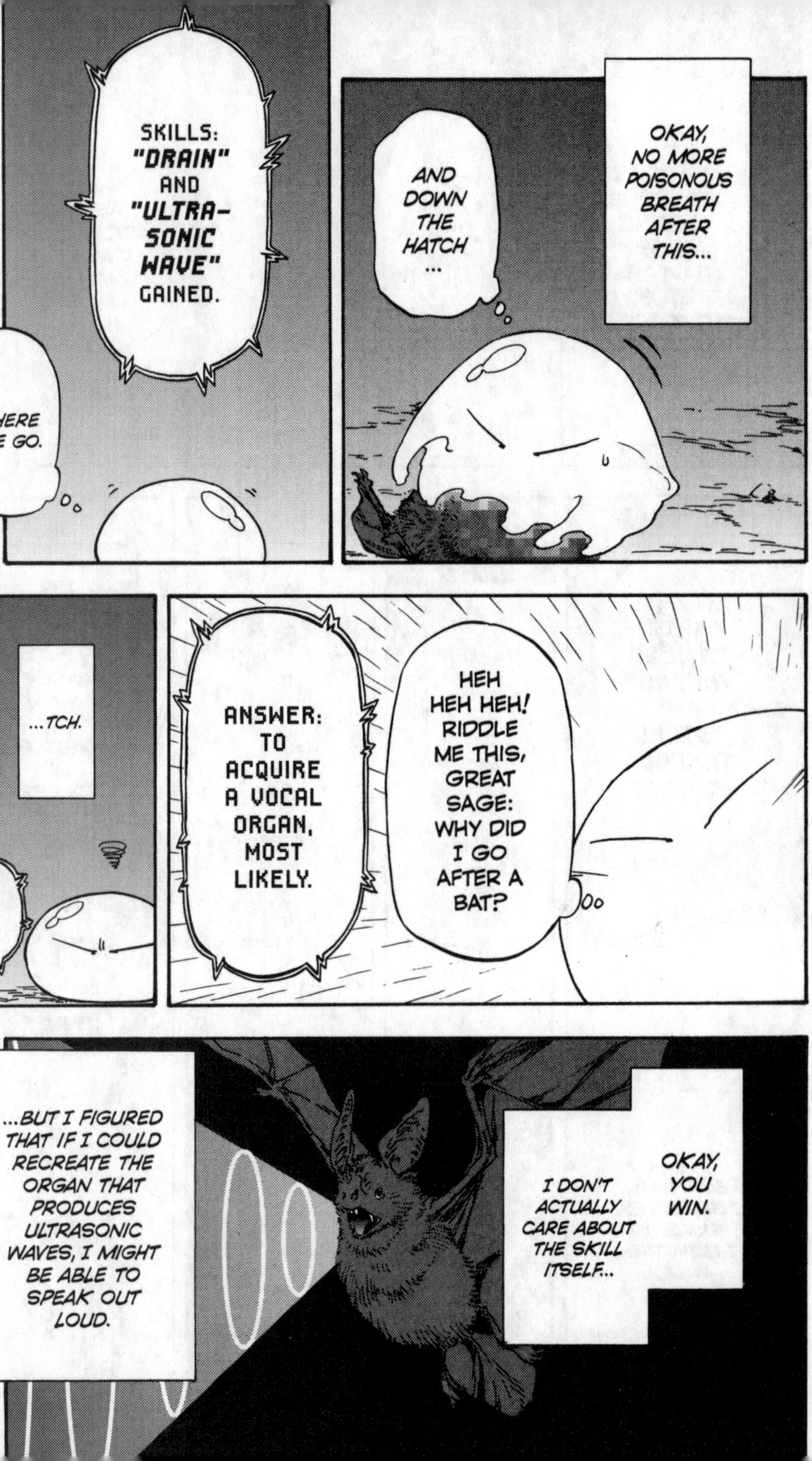
OKAY, NO MORE POISONOUS BREATH AFTER THIS...
AND DOWN THE HATCH ...
SKILLS: "DRAIN" AND "ULTRA-SONIC WAVE" GAINED.
THERE WE GO.
HEH HEH HEH! RIDDLE ME THIS, GREAT SAGE: WHY DID I GO AFTER A BAT?
ANSWER: TO ACQUIRE A VOCAL ORGAN, MOST LIKELY.
...TCH.
?
OKAY, YOU WIN.
I DON'T ACTUALLY CARE ABOUT THE SKILL ITSELF...
...BUT I FIGURED THAT IF I COULD RECREATE THE ORGAN THAT PRODUCES ULTRASONIC WAVES, I MIGHT BE ABLE TO SPEAK OUT LOUD.

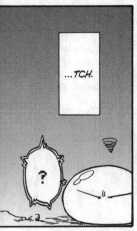

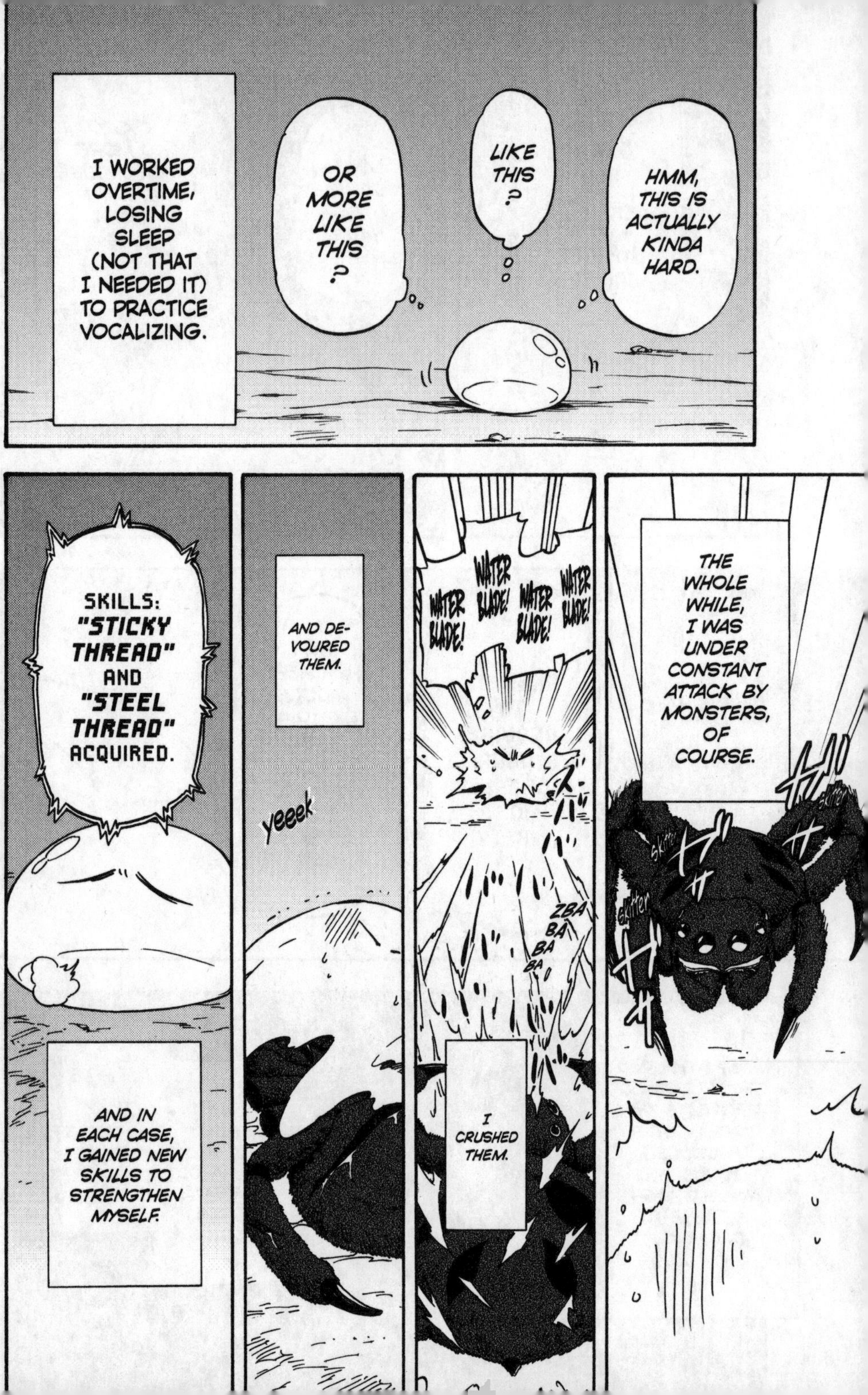

HMM, THIS IS ACTUALLY KINDA HARD.
LIKE THIS?
OR MORE LIKE THIS?
I WORKED OVERTIME, LOSING SLEEP (NOT THAT I NEEDED IT) TO PRACTICE VOCALIZING.
THE WHOLE WHILE, I WAS UNDER CONSTANT ATTACK BY MONSTERS, OF COURSE.
skitter
skitter
skitter
WATER BLADE!
WATER BLADE!
WATER BLADE!
WATER BLADE!
ZBA BA BA BA
I CRUSHED THEM.
AND DE-VOURED THEM.
yeeek
SKILLS: "STICKY THREAD" AND "STEEL THREAD" ACQUIRED.
AND IN EACH CASE, I GAINED NEW SKILLS TO STRENGTHEN MYSELF.

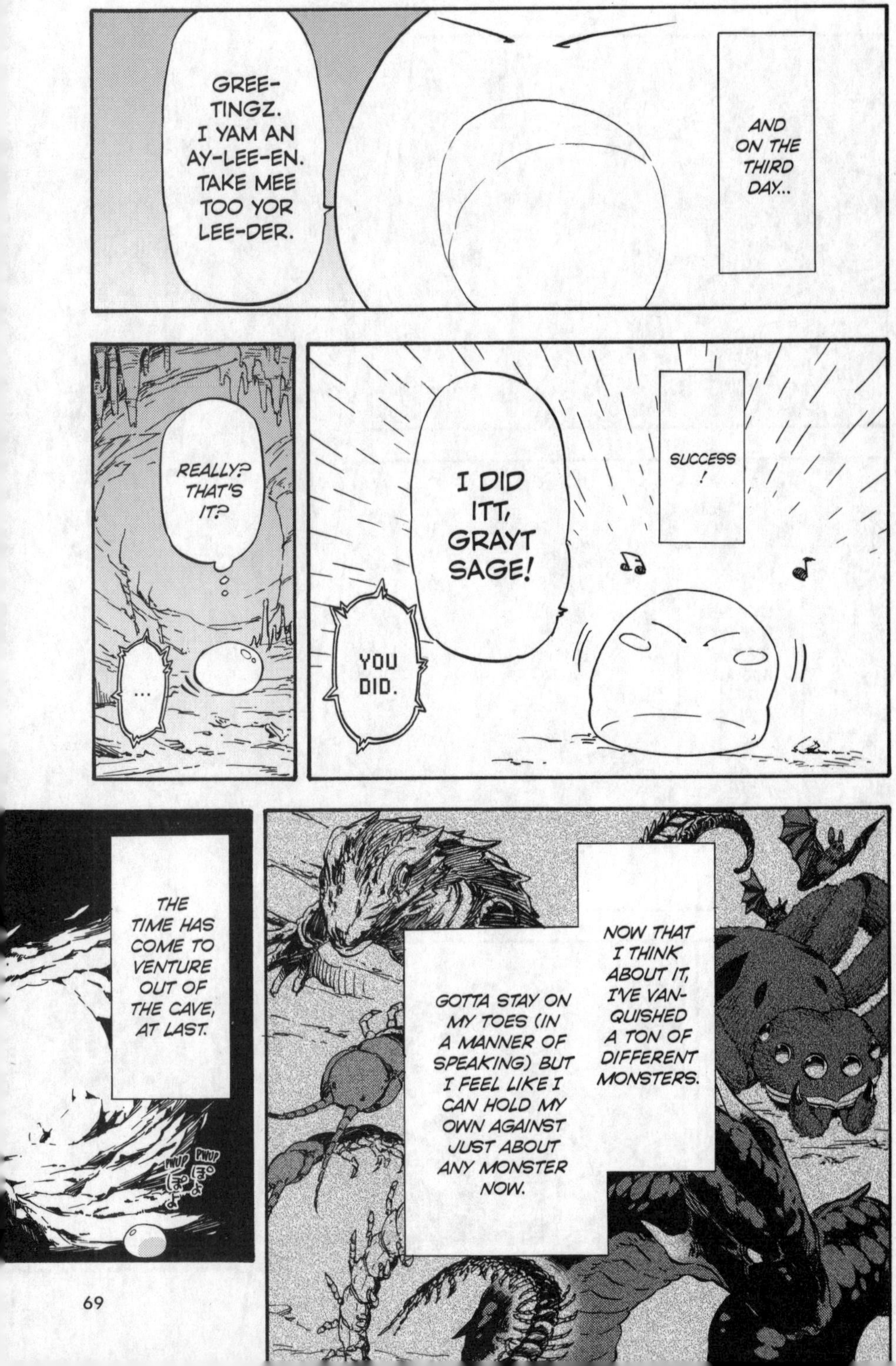
AND ON THE THIRD DAY...
GREE-TINGZ. I YAM AN AY-LEE-EN. TAKE MEE TOO YOR LEE-DER.
SUCCESS!
I DID ITT, GRAYT SAGE!
YOU DID.
REALLY? THAT'S IT?
...
NOW THAT I THINK ABOUT IT, I'VE VAN-QUISHED A TON OF DIFFERENT MONSTERS.
GOTTA STAY ON MY TOES (IN A MANNER OF SPEAKING) BUT I FEEL LIKE I CAN HOLD MY OWN AGAINST JUST ABOUT ANY MONSTER NOW.
THE TIME HAS COME TO VENTURE OUT OF THE CAVE, AT LAST.
PWUP PWUP

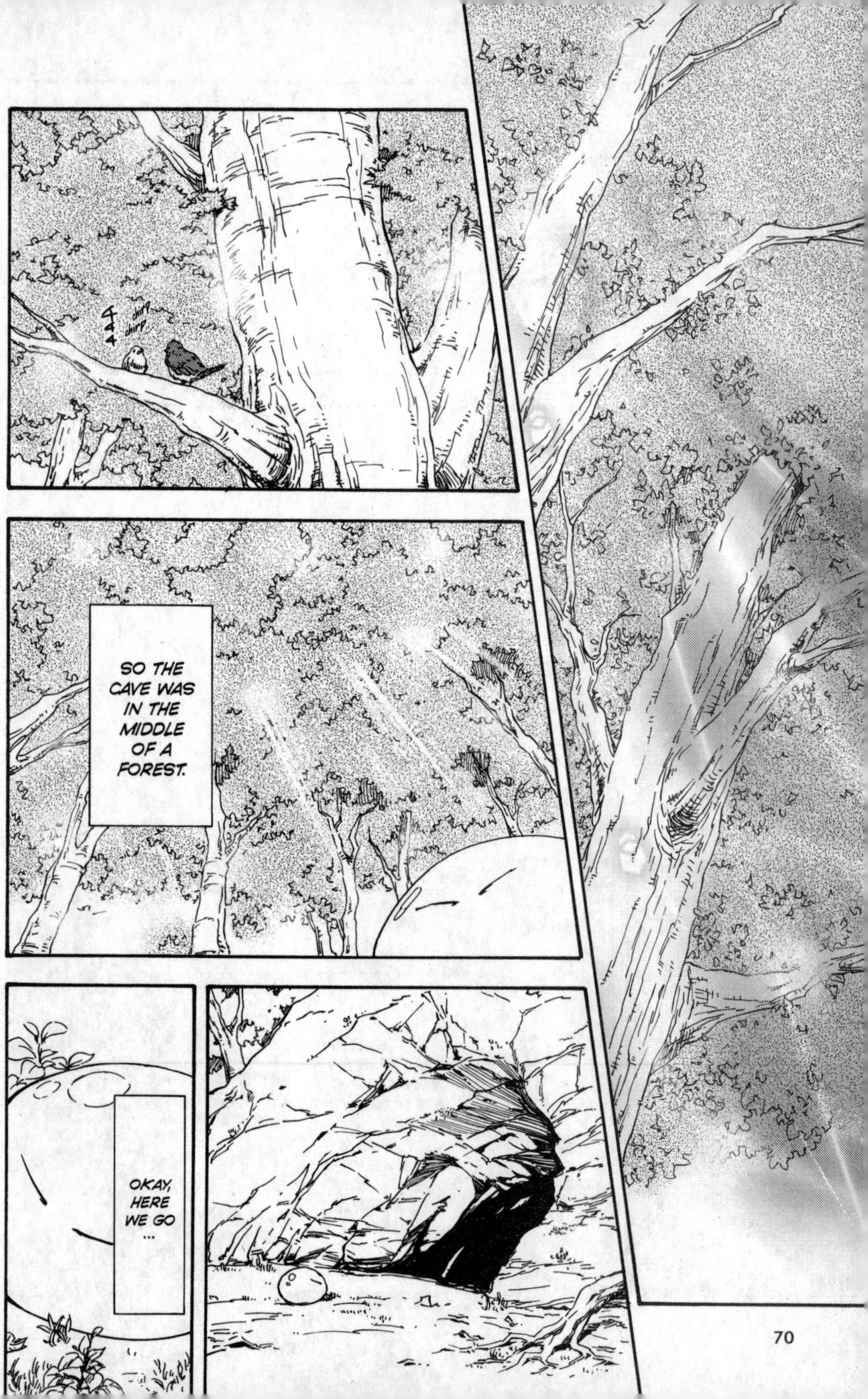
チチチ
chirp chirp
SO THE CAVE WAS IN THE MIDDLE OF A FOREST.
OKAY, HERE WE GO ...

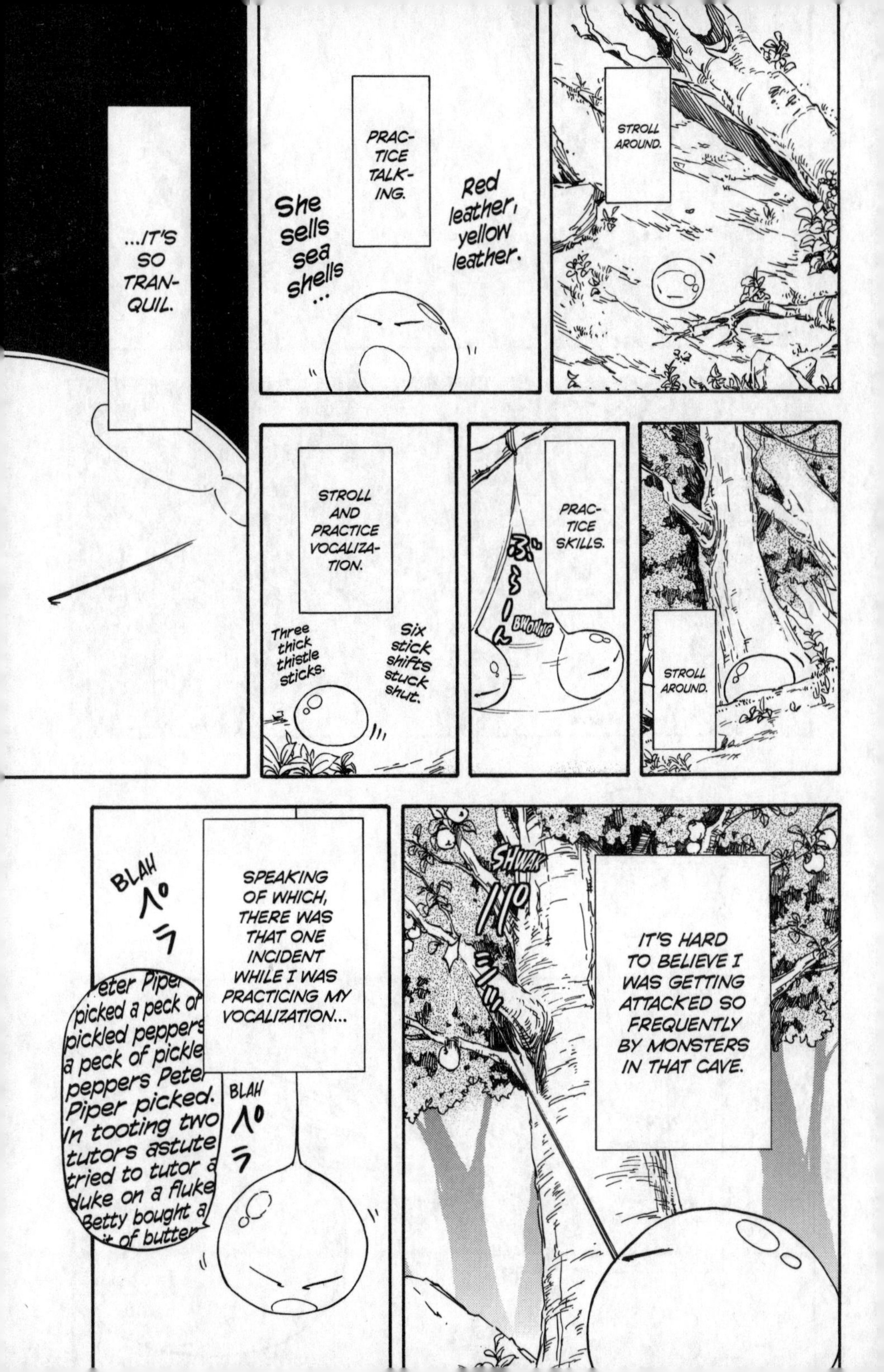
STROLL AROUND.
PRACTICE TALKING.
Red leather, yellow leather.
She sells sea shells...
STROLL AROUND.
PRACTICE SKILLS.
ぶ〜ん
BWONNG
STROLL AND PRACTICE VOCALIZATION.
Six stick shifts stuck shut.
Three thick thistle sticks.
...IT'S SO TRANQUIL.
SHWAK
IT'S HARD TO BELIEVE I WAS GETTING ATTACKED SO FREQUENTLY BY MONSTERS IN THAT CAVE.
SPEAKING OF WHICH, THERE WAS THAT ONE INCIDENT WHILE I WAS PRACTICING MY VOCALIZATION...
BLAH
へら
eter Piper picked a peck of pickled peppers a peck of pickle peppers Peter Piper picked. In tooting two tutors astute tried to tutor a duke on a fluke Betty bought a it of butter
BLAH
へら

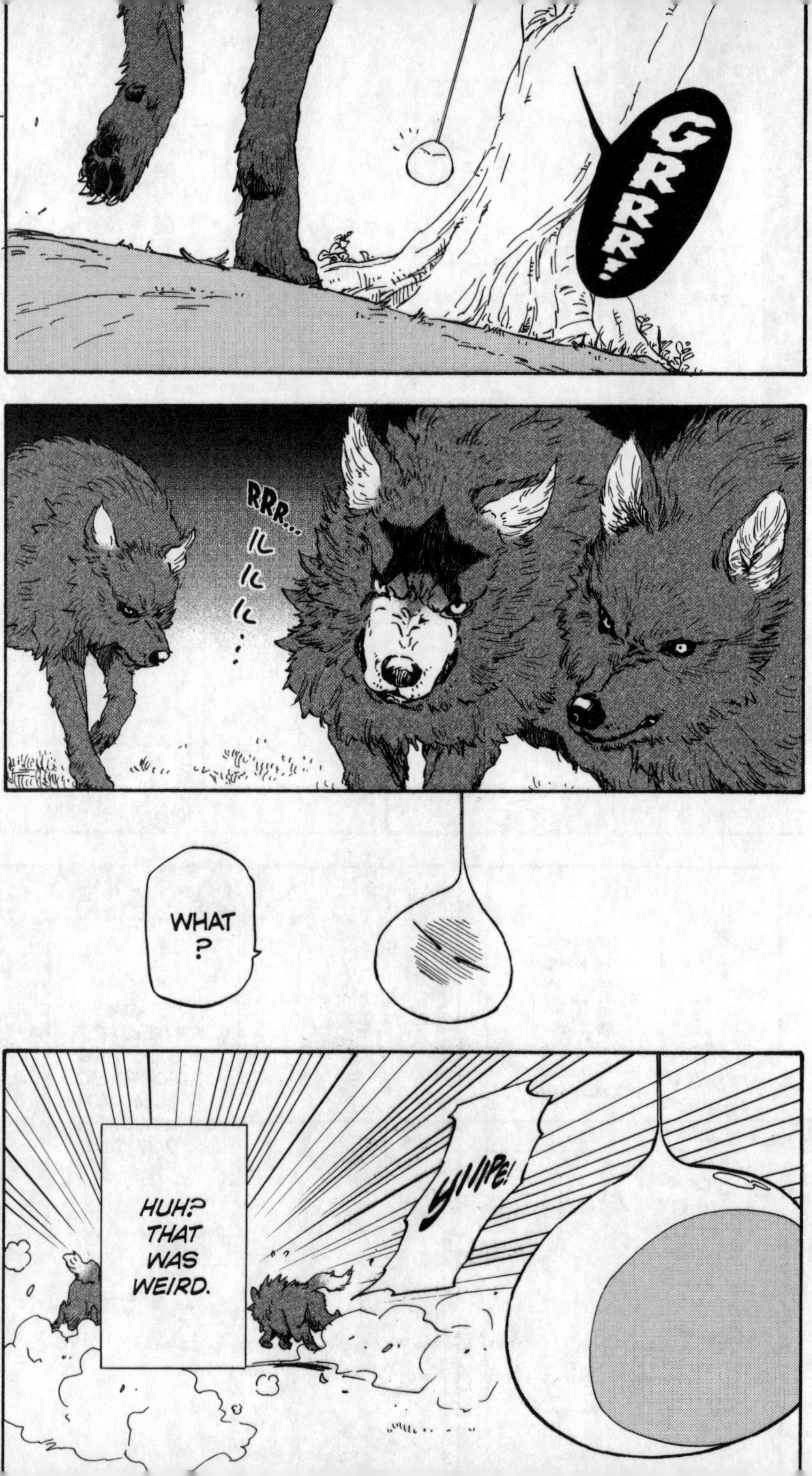
GRRR!
RRR... ルルル...
WHAT?
SWIPE!
HUH? THAT WAS WEIRD.

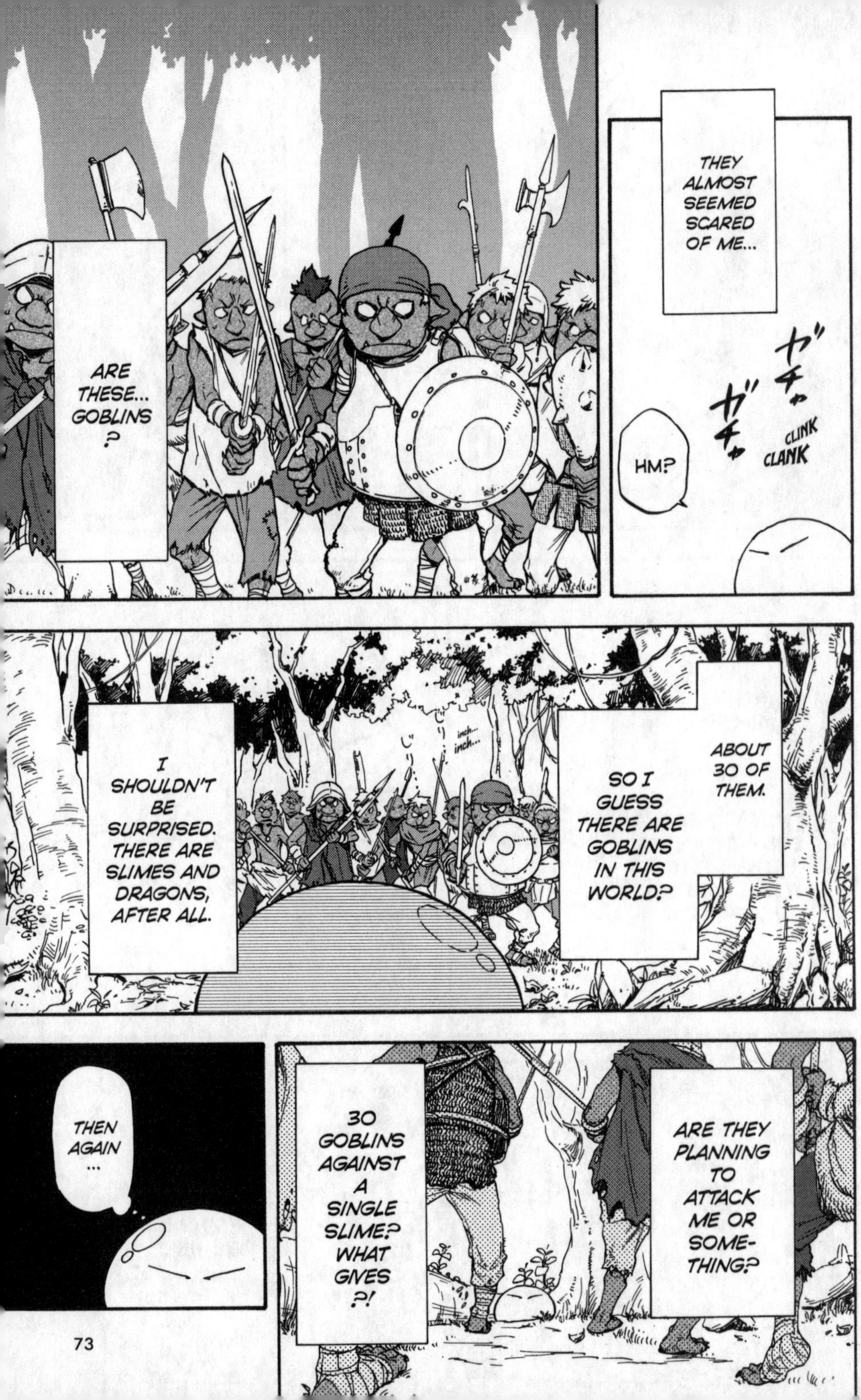
THEY ALMOST SEEMED SCARED OF ME...
ガチャ
ガチャ
CLINK CLANK
HM?
ARE THESE... GOBLINS?
ABOUT 30 OF THEM.
SO I GUESS THERE ARE GOBLINS IN THIS WORLD?
inch... inch...
I SHOULDN'T BE SURPRISED. THERE ARE SLIMES AND DRAGONS, AFTER ALL.
ARE THEY PLANNING TO ATTACK ME OR SOME-THING?
30 GOBLINS AGAINST A SINGLE SLIME? WHAT GIVES?!
THEN AGAIN...

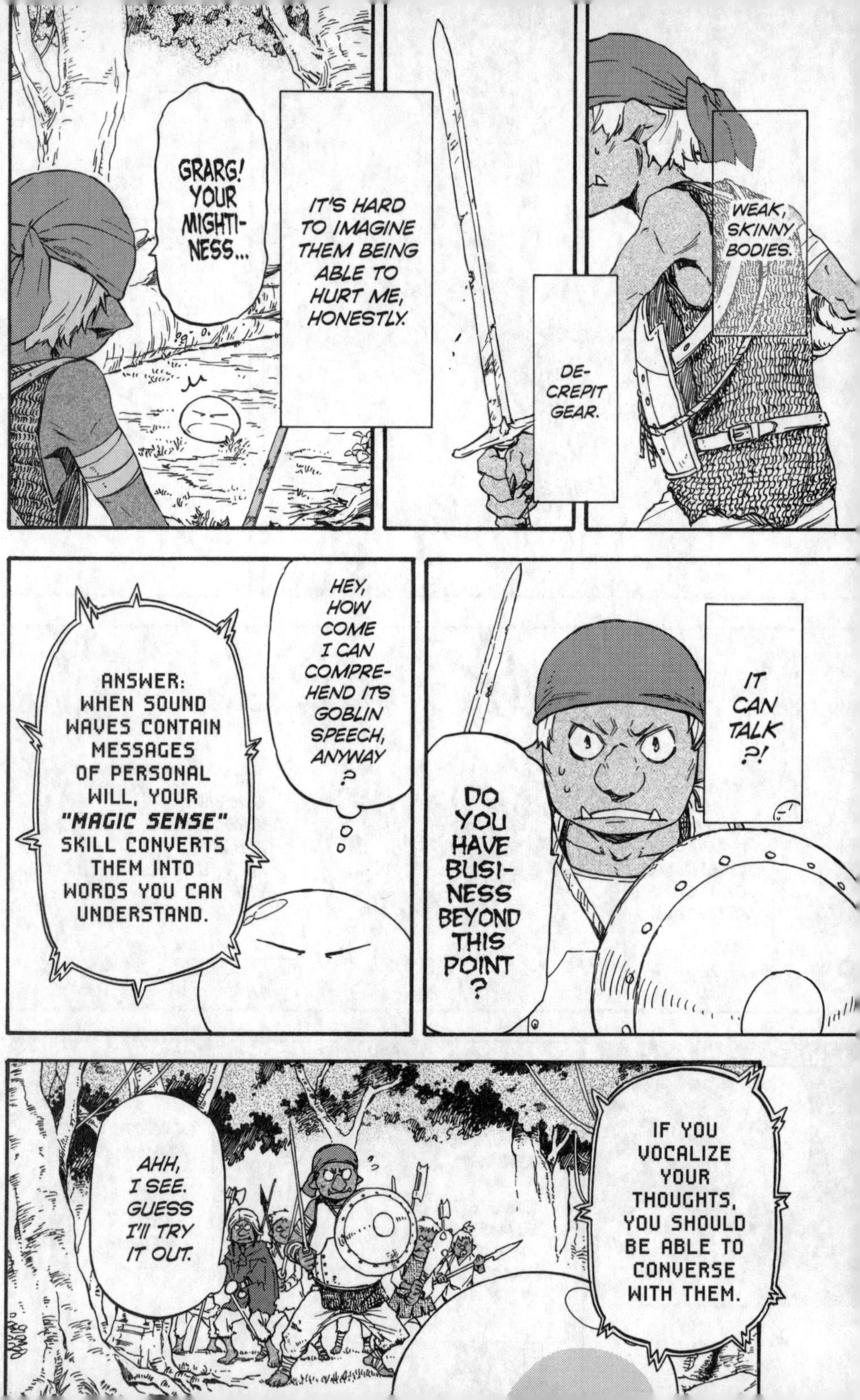
WEAK, SKINNY BODIES.
DE-CREPIT GEAR.
IT'S HARD TO IMAGINE THEM BEING ABLE TO HURT ME, HONESTLY.
GRARG! YOUR MIGHTI-NESS...
IT CAN TALK?!
DO YOU HAVE BUSI-NESS BEYOND THIS POINT?
HEY, HOW COME I CAN COMPRE-HEND ITS GOBLIN SPEECH, ANYWAY?
ANSWER: WHEN SOUND WAVES CONTAIN MESSAGES OF PERSONAL WILL, YOUR "MAGIC SENSE" SKILL CONVERTS THEM INTO WORDS YOU CAN UNDERSTAND.
IF YOU VOCALIZE YOUR THOUGHTS, YOU SHOULD BE ABLE TO CONVERSE WITH THEM.
AHH, I SEE. GUESS I'll TRY IT OUT.

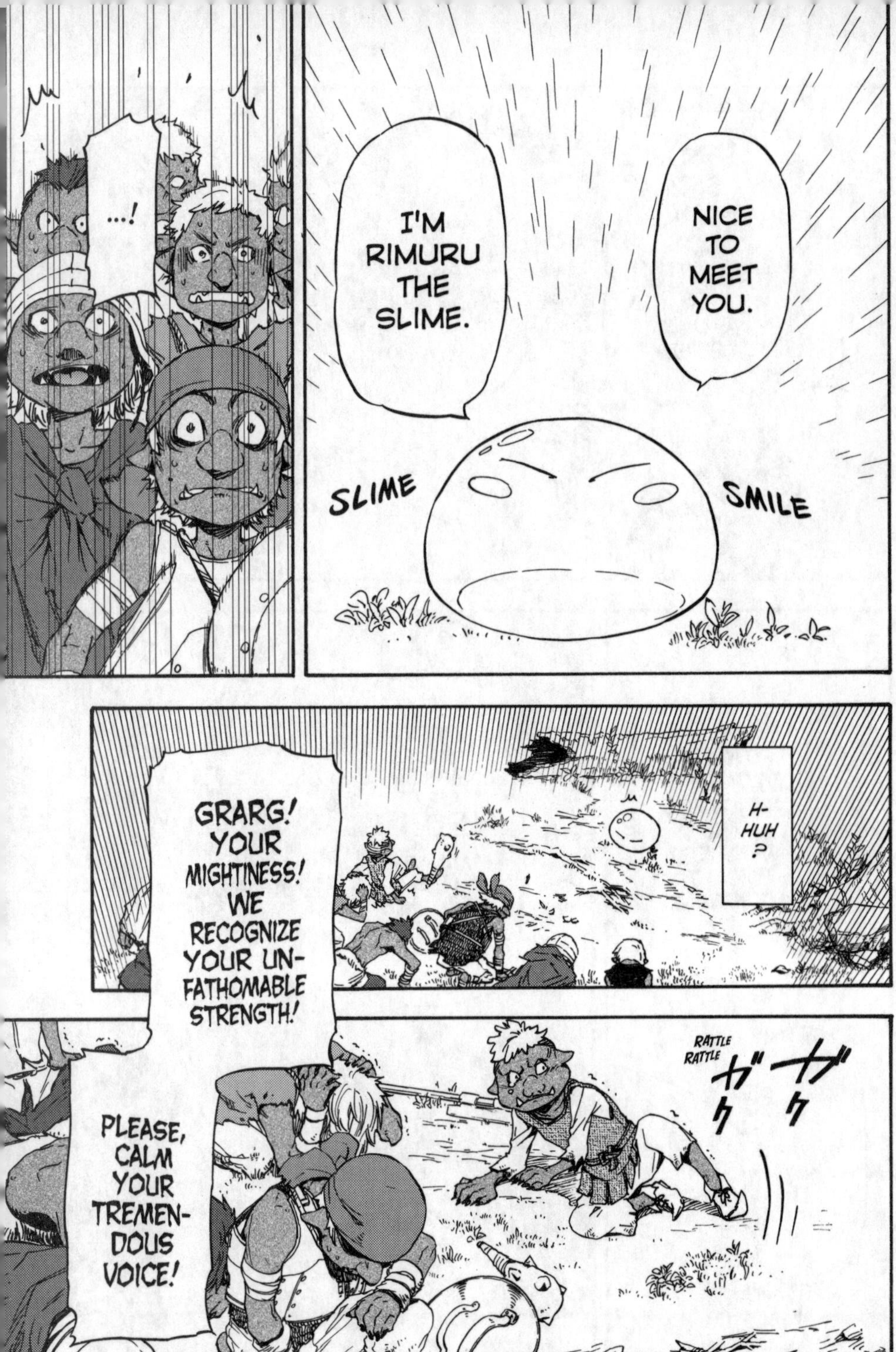
NICE TO MEET YOU.
I'M RIMURU THE SLIME.
SMILE
SLIME
...!
H-HUH?
GRARG! YOUR MIGHTINESS! WE RECOGNIZE YOUR UN-FATHOMABLE STRENGTH!
RATTLE RATTLE
ガクガク
PLEASE, CALM YOUR TREMEN-DOUS VOICE!

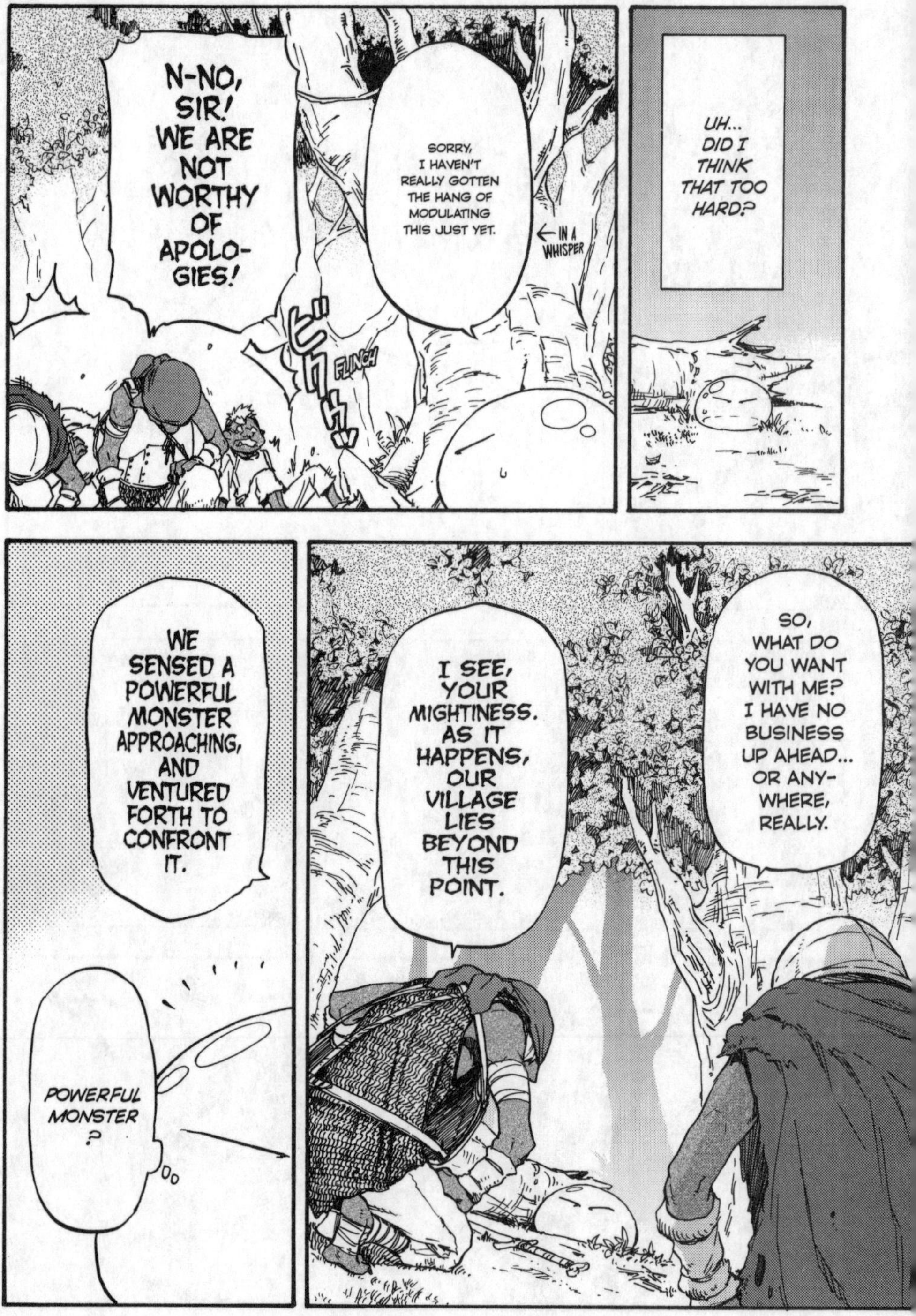
UH... DID I THINK THAT TOO HARD?
SORRY, I HAVEN'T REALLY GOTTEN THE HANG OF MODULATING THIS JUST YET.
← IN A WHISPER
N-NO, SIR! WE ARE NOT WORTHY OF APOLOGIES!
FLINCH
SO, WHAT DO YOU WANT WITH ME? I HAVE NO BUSINESS UP AHEAD... OR ANY-WHERE, REALLY.
I SEE, YOUR MIGHTINESS. AS IT HAPPENS, OUR VILLAGE LIES BEYOND THIS POINT.
WE SENSED A POWERFUL MONSTER APPROACHING, AND VENTURED FORTH TO CONFRONT IT.
POWERFUL MONSTER ?

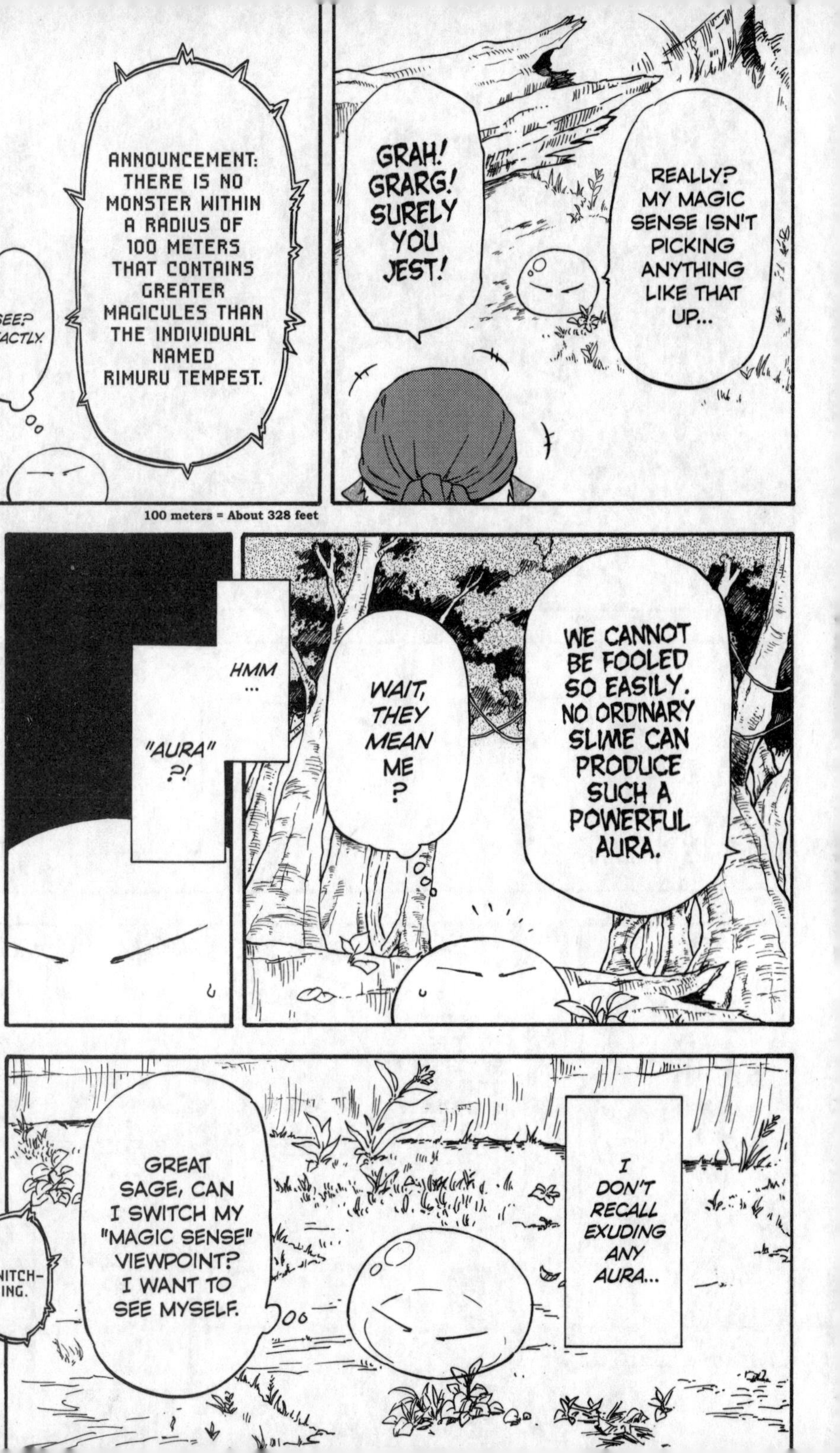
REALLY? MY MAGIC SENSE ISN'T PICKING ANYTHING LIKE THAT UP...
GRAH! GRARG! SURELY YOU JEST!
ANNOUNCEMENT: THERE IS NO MONSTER WITHIN A RADIUS OF 100 METERS THAT CONTAINS GREATER MAGICULES THAN THE INDIVIDUAL NAMED RIMURU TEMPEST.
SEE? EXACTLY.
WE CANNOT BE FOOLED SO EASILY. NO ORDINARY SLIME CAN PRODUCE SUCH A POWERFUL AURA.
WAIT, THEY MEAN ME?
HMM...
"AURA"?!
I DON'T RECALL EXUDING ANY AURA...
GREAT SAGE, CAN I SWITCH MY "MAGIC SENSE" VIEWPOINT? I WANT TO SEE MYSELF.
SWITCHING.

100 meters = About 328 feet

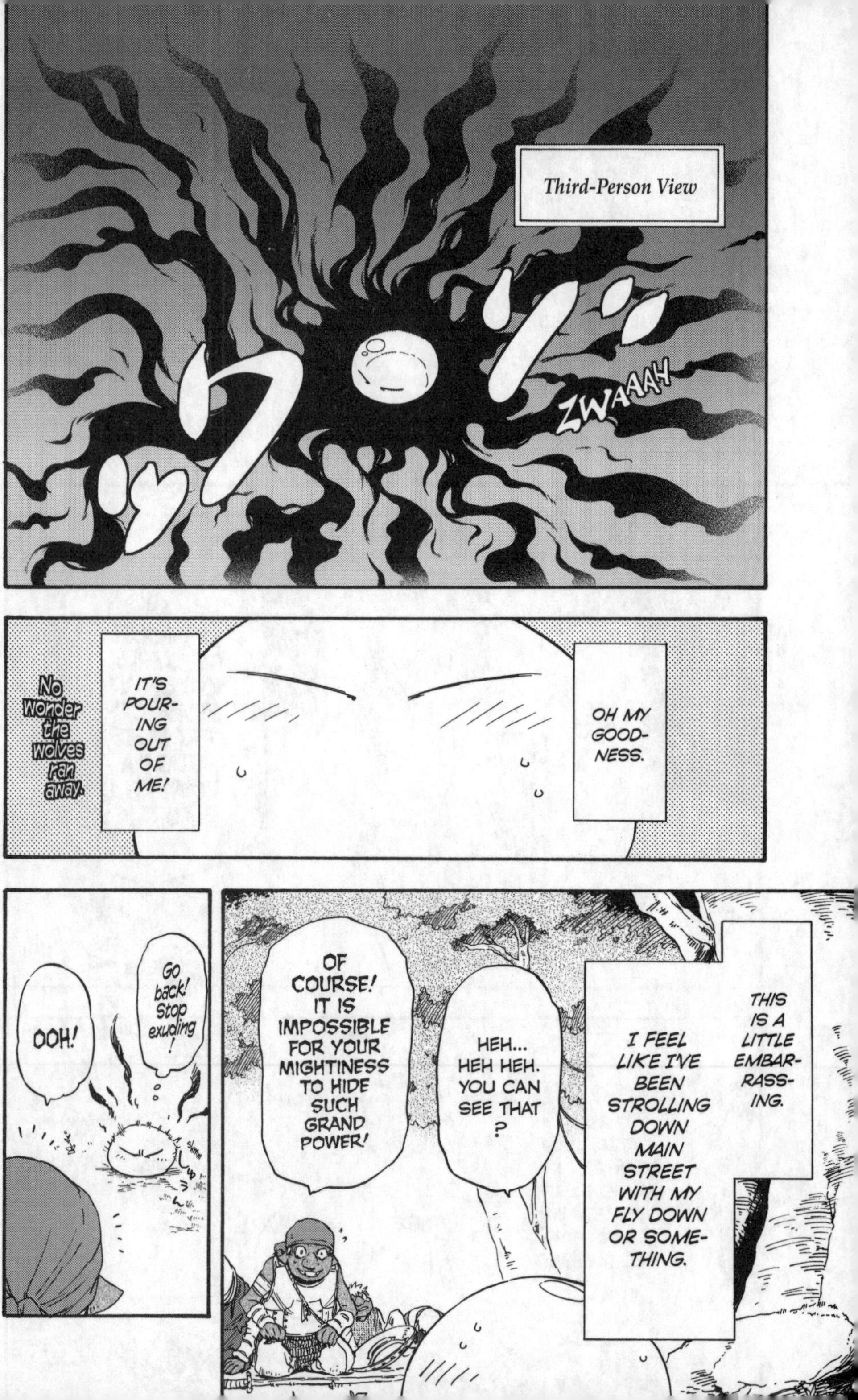
Third-Person View
ZWAAAH
OH MY GOODNESS.
IT'S POURING OUT OF ME!
No wonder the wolves ran away.
THIS IS A LITTLE EMBARRASSING.
I FEEL LIKE I'VE BEEN STROLLING DOWN MAIN STREET WITH MY FLY DOWN OR SOMETHING.
HEH... HEH HEH. YOU CAN SEE THAT?
OF COURSE! IT IS IMPOSSIBLE FOR YOUR MIGHTINESS TO HIDE SUCH GRAND POWER!
Go back! Stop exuding!
OOH!

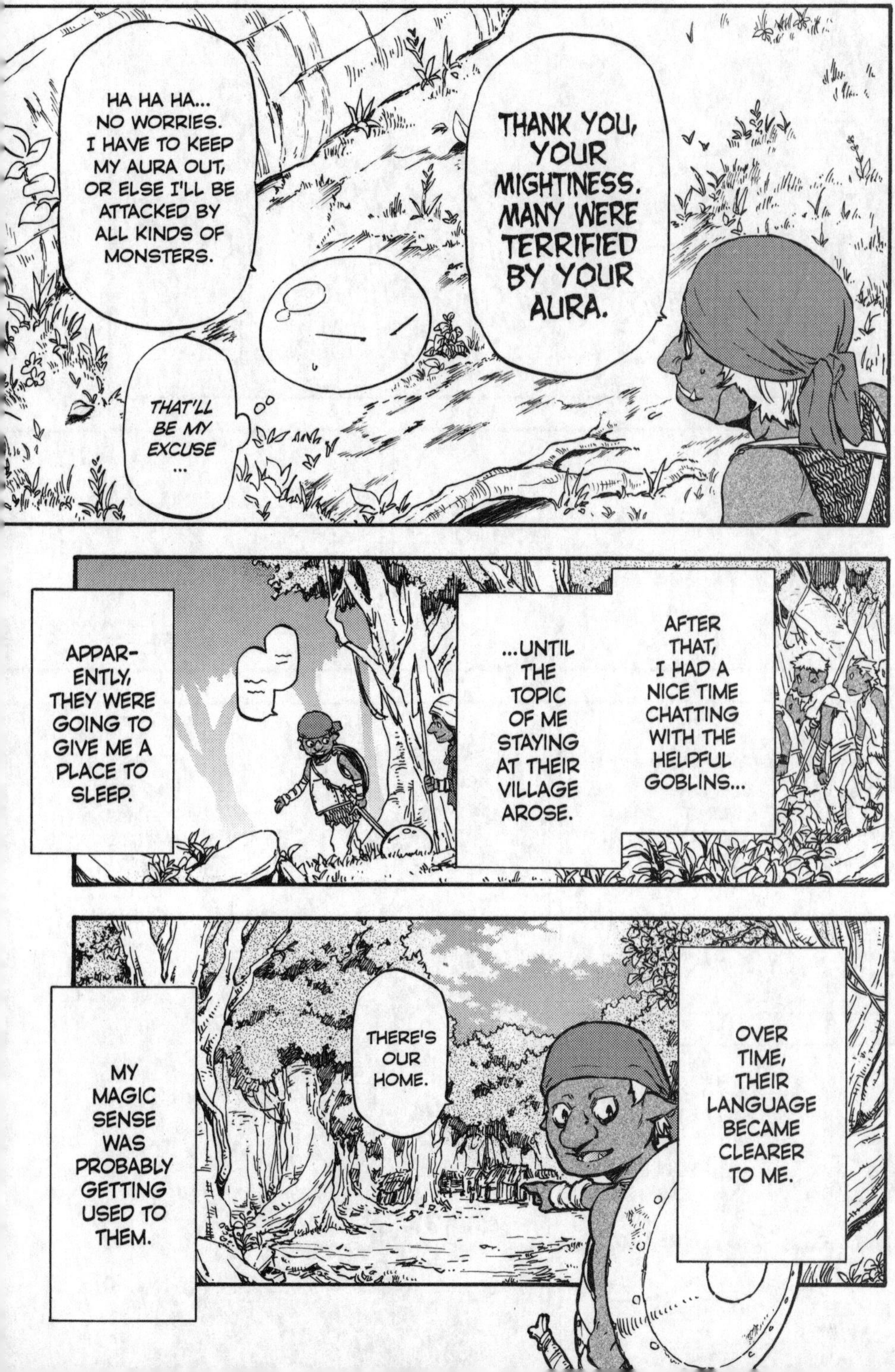
THANK YOU, YOUR MIGHTINESS. MANY WERE TERRIFIED BY YOUR AURA.
HA HA HA... NO WORRIES. I HAVE TO KEEP MY AURA OUT, OR ELSE I'LL BE ATTACKED BY ALL KINDS OF MONSTERS.
THAT'LL BE MY EXCUSE ...
AFTER THAT, I HAD A NICE TIME CHATTING WITH THE HELPFUL GOBLINS...
...UNTIL THE TOPIC OF ME STAYING AT THEIR VILLAGE AROSE.
APPAR-ENTLY, THEY WERE GOING TO GIVE ME A PLACE TO SLEEP.
OVER TIME, THEIR LANGUAGE BECAME CLEARER TO ME.
THERE'S OUR HOME.
MY MAGIC SENSE WAS PROBABLY GETTING USED TO THEM.

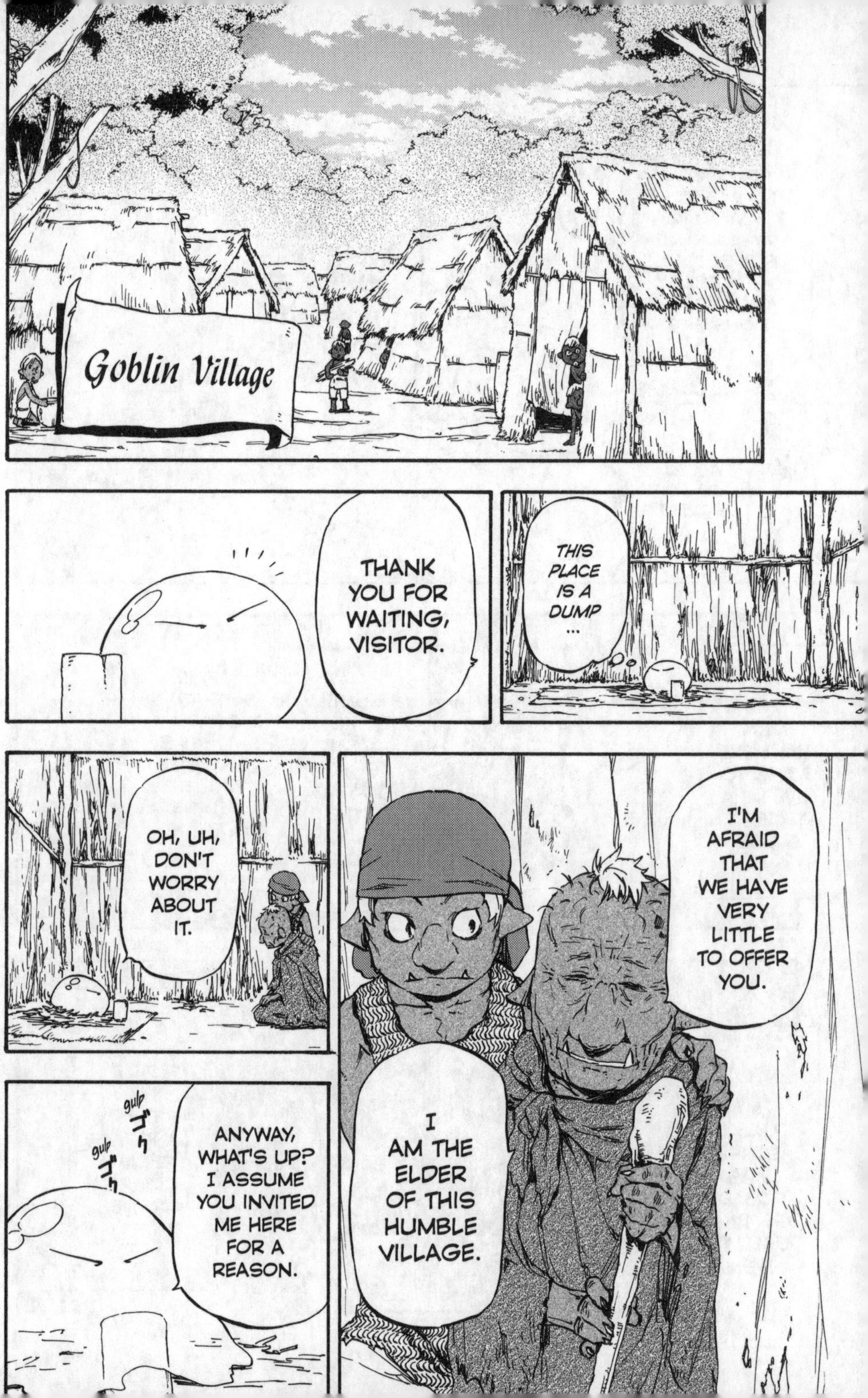
Goblin Village
THIS PLACE IS A DUMP...
THANK YOU FOR WAITING, VISITOR.
I'M AFRAID THAT WE HAVE VERY LITTLE TO OFFER YOU.
I AM THE ELDER OF THIS HUMBLE VILLAGE.
OH, UH, DON'T WORRY ABOUT IT.
gulp ゴク
gulp ゴク
ANYWAY, WHAT'S UP? I ASSUME YOU INVITED ME HERE FOR A REASON.

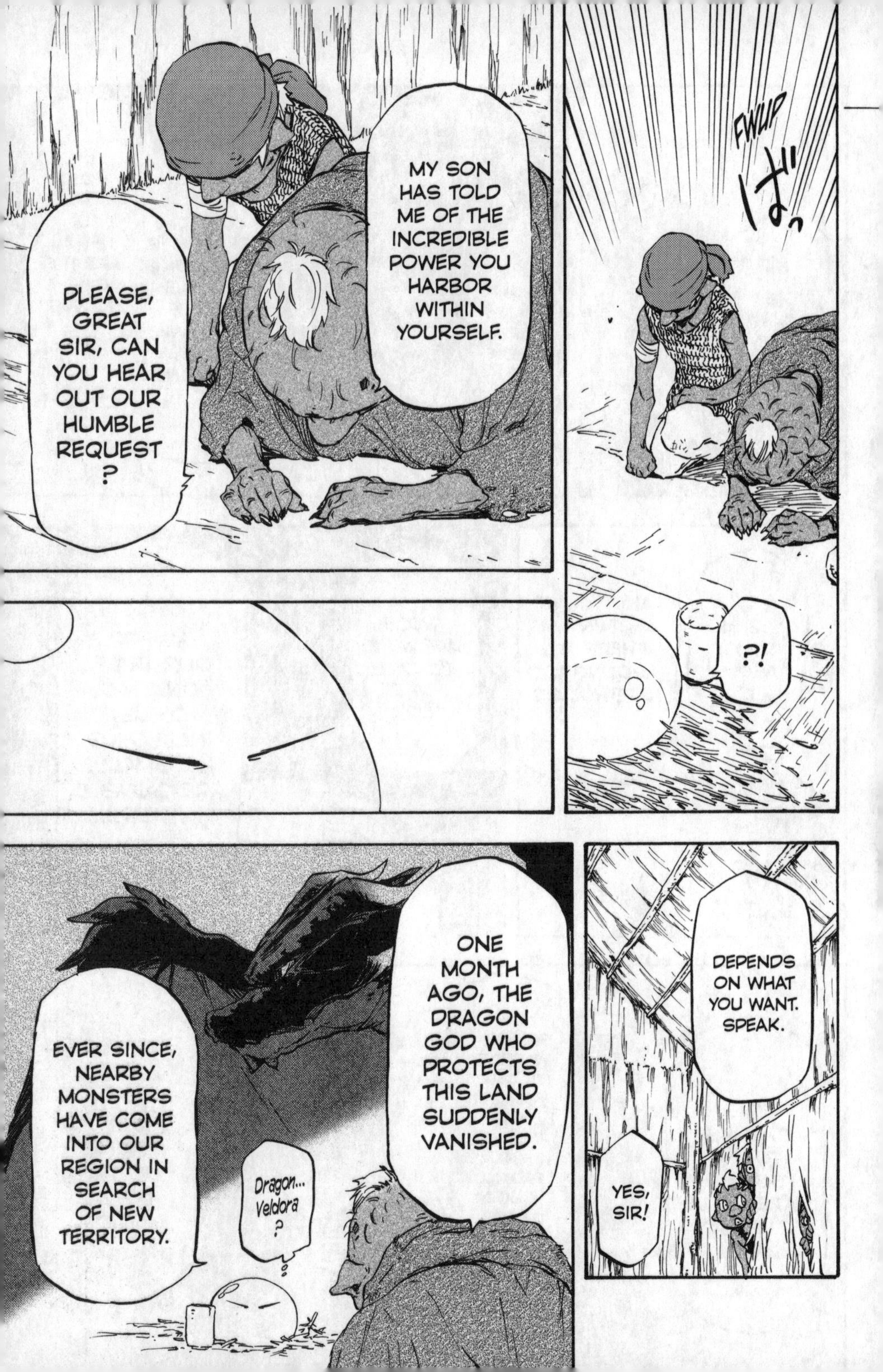
FWUP
ばっ
?!
MY SON HAS TOLD ME OF THE INCREDIBLE POWER YOU HARBOR WITHIN YOURSELF.
PLEASE, GREAT SIR, CAN YOU HEAR OUT OUR HUMBLE REQUEST?
DEPENDS ON WHAT YOU WANT. SPEAK.
YES, SIR!
ONE MONTH AGO, THE DRAGON GOD WHO PROTECTS THIS LAND SUDDENLY VANISHED.
EVER SINCE, NEARBY MONSTERS HAVE COME INTO OUR REGION IN SEARCH OF NEW TERRITORY.
Dragon... Veldora?

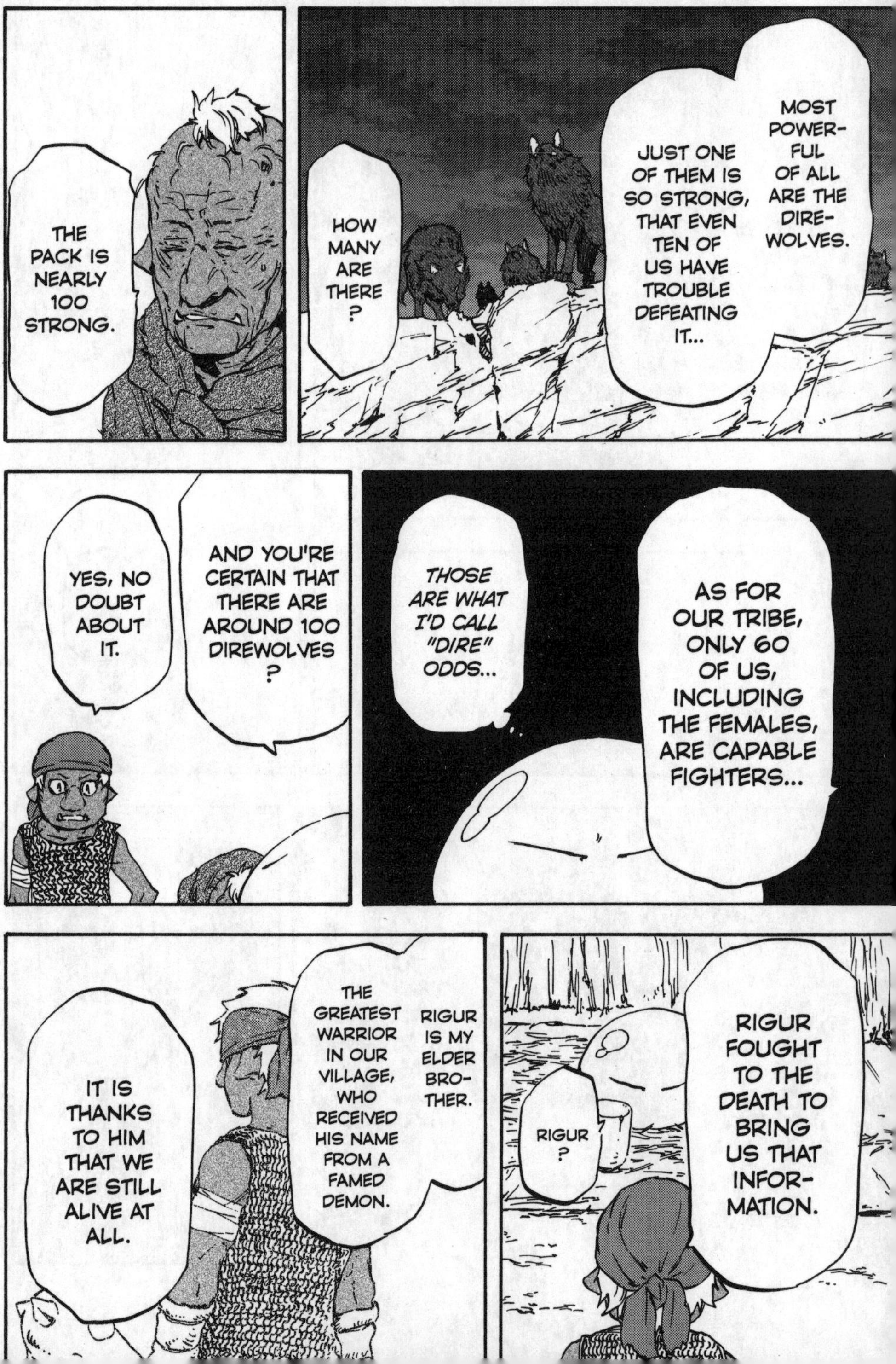
MOST POWERFUL OF ALL ARE THE DIREWOLVES.
JUST ONE OF THEM IS SO STRONG, THAT EVEN TEN OF US HAVE TROUBLE DEFEATING IT...
HOW MANY ARE THERE?
THE PACK IS NEARLY 100 STRONG.
AS FOR OUR TRIBE, ONLY 60 OF US, INCLUDING THE FEMALES, ARE CAPABLE FIGHTERS...
THOSE ARE WHAT I'D CALL "DIRE" ODDS...
AND YOU'RE CERTAIN THAT THERE ARE AROUND 100 DIREWOLVES?
YES, NO DOUBT ABOUT IT.
RIGUR FOUGHT TO THE DEATH TO BRING US THAT INFORMATION.
RIGUR?
RIGUR IS MY ELDER BROTHER.
THE GREATEST WARRIOR IN OUR VILLAGE, WHO RECEIVED HIS NAME FROM A FAMED DEMON.
IT IS THANKS TO HIM THAT WE ARE STILL ALIVE AT ALL.

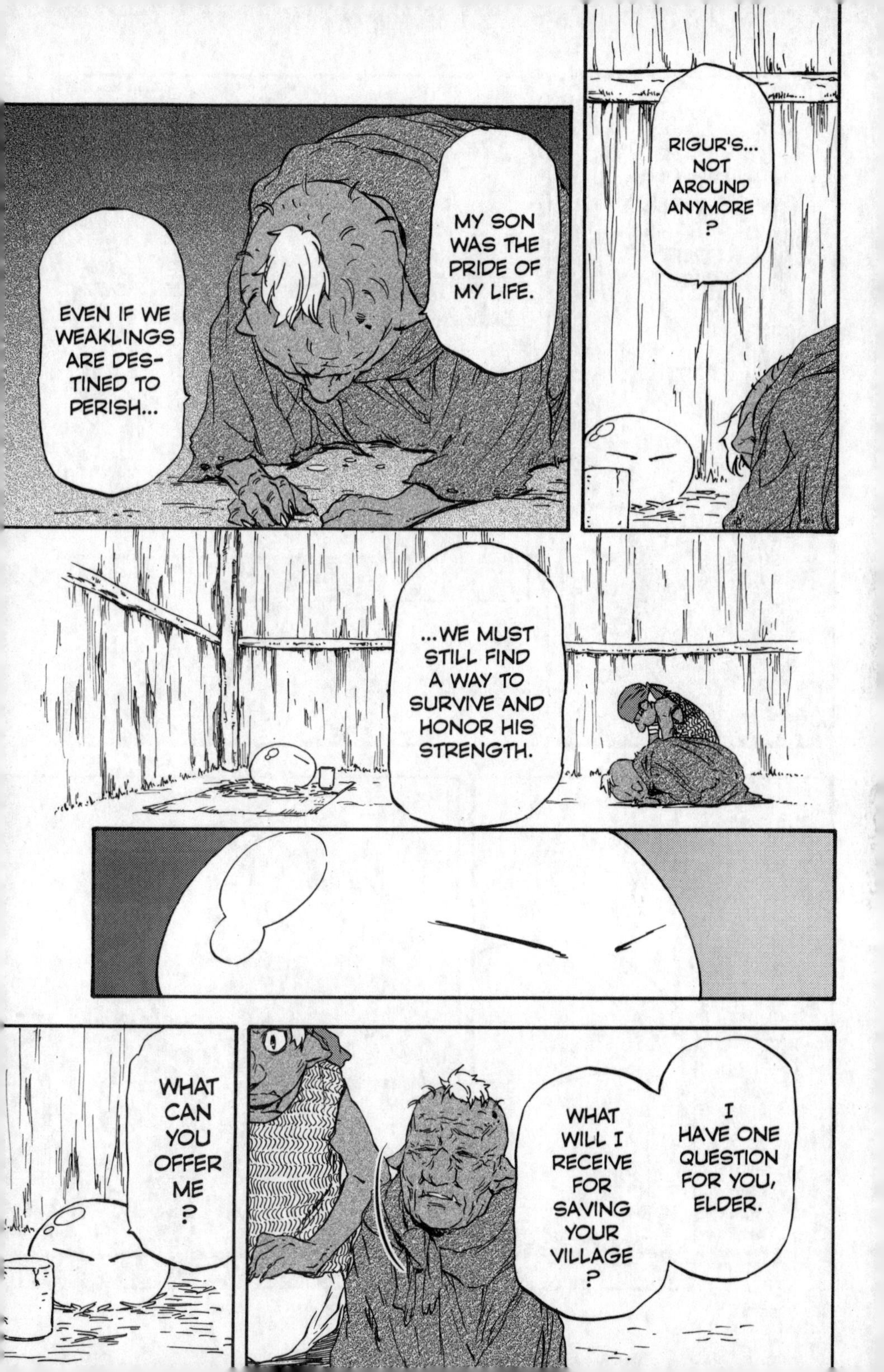
RIGUR'S... NOT AROUND ANYMORE ?
MY SON WAS THE PRIDE OF MY LIFE.
EVEN IF WE WEAKLINGS ARE DES-TINED TO PERISH...
...WE MUST STILL FIND A WAY TO SURVIVE AND HONOR HIS STRENGTH.
I HAVE ONE QUESTION FOR YOU, ELDER.
WHAT WILL I RECEIVE FOR SAVING YOUR VILLAGE ?
WHAT CAN YOU OFFER ME ?

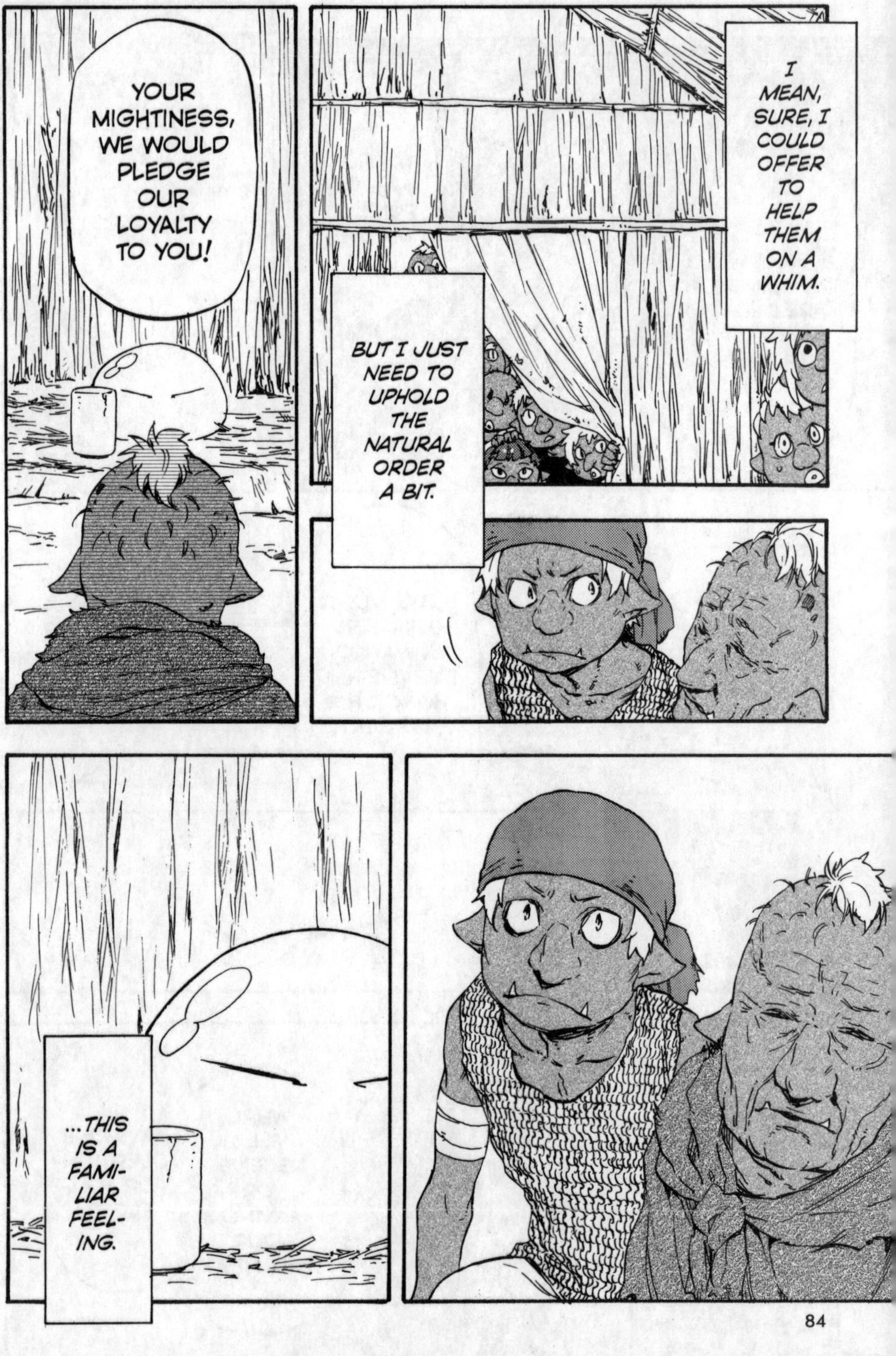
I MEAN, SURE, I COULD OFFER TO HELP THEM ON A WHIM.
BUT I JUST NEED TO UPHOLD THE NATURAL ORDER A BIT.
YOUR MIGHTINESS, WE WOULD PLEDGE OUR LOYALTY TO YOU!
...THIS IS A FAMILIAR FEELING.

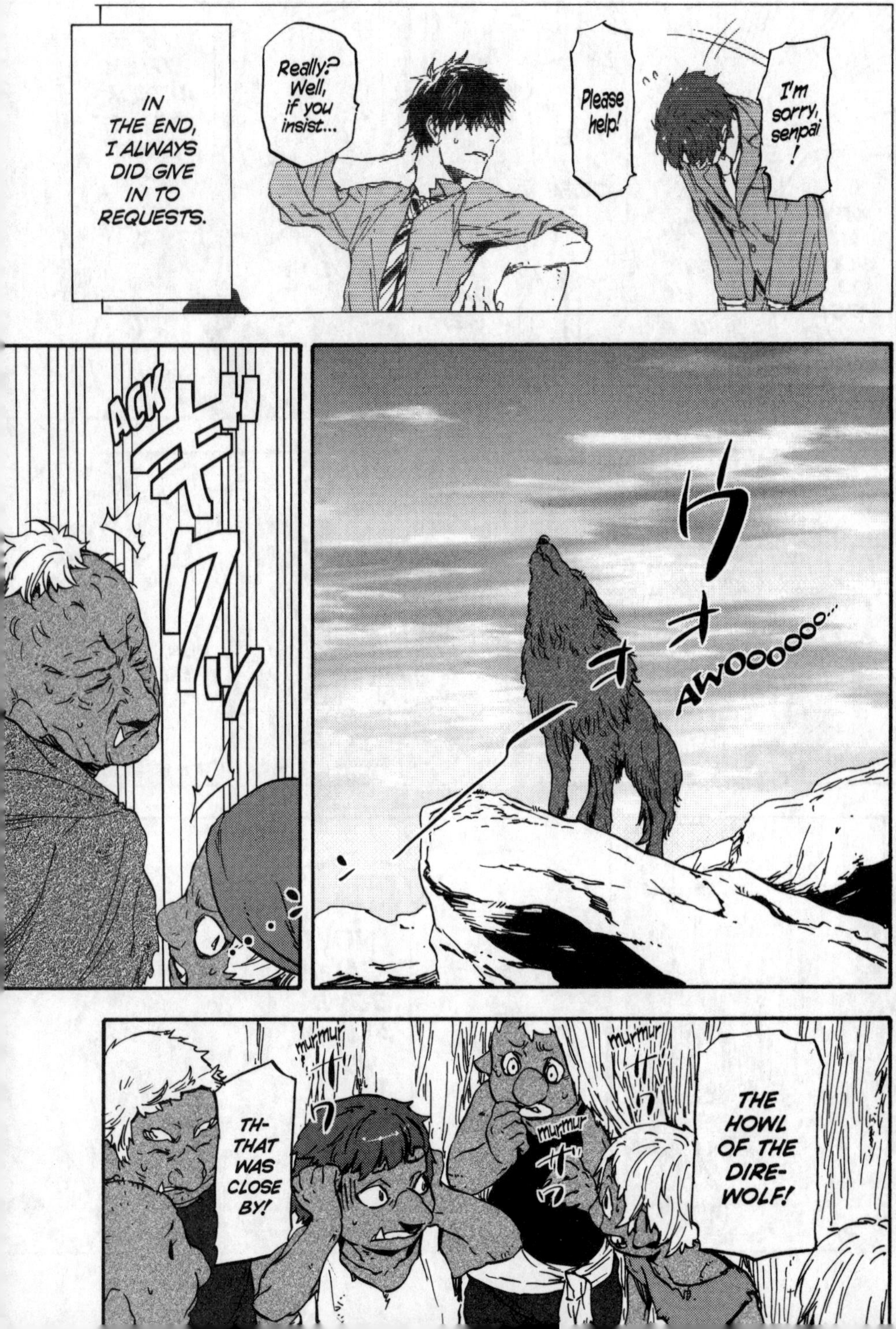
I'm sorry, senpai!
Please help!
Really? Well, if you insist...
IN THE END, I ALWAYS DID GIVE IN TO REQUESTS.
AWOOOOOO...
ACK
THE HOWL OF THE DIRE-WOLF!
murmur
murmur
murmur
TH-THAT WAS CLOSE BY!

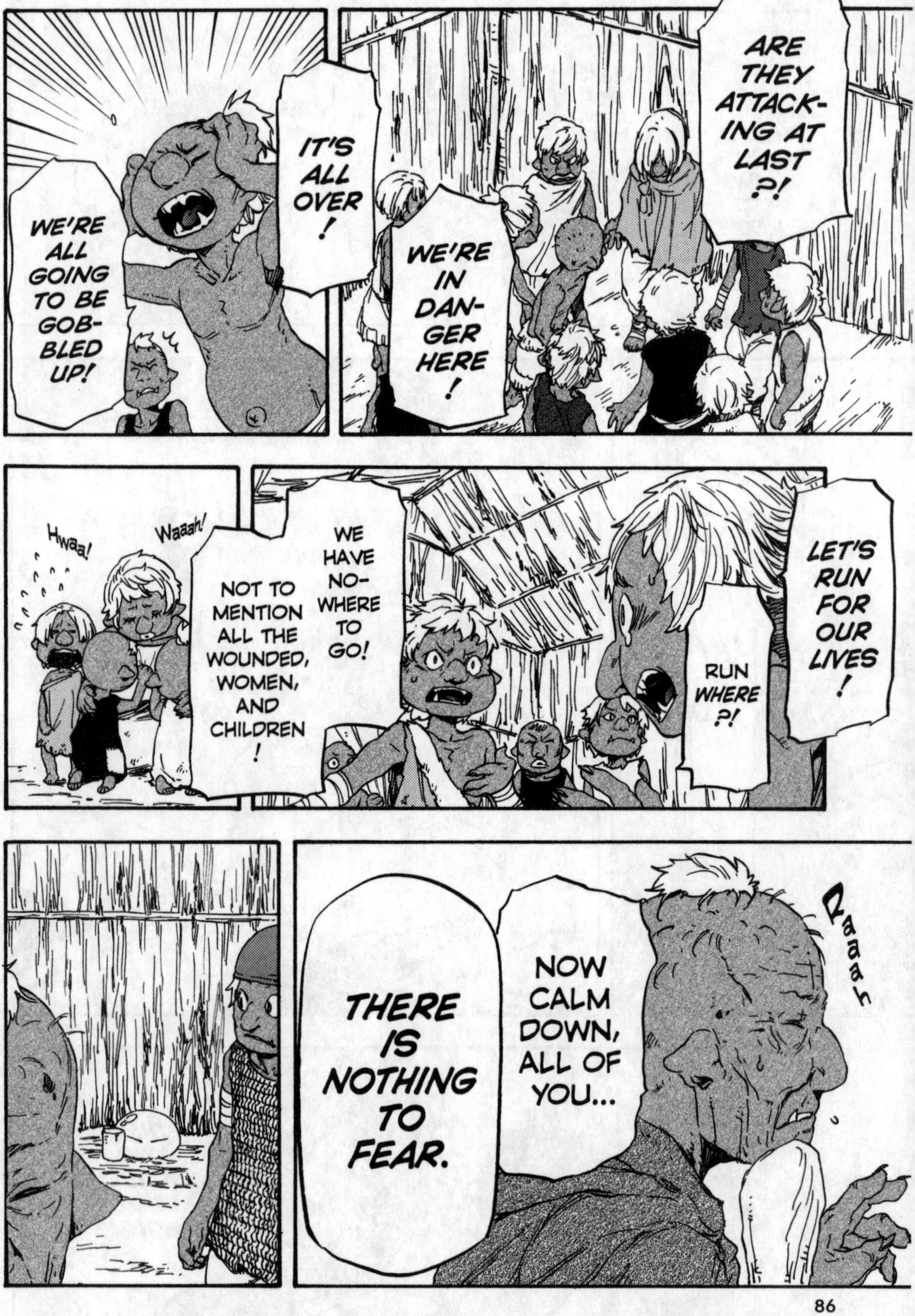
ARE THEY ATTACKING AT LAST?!
IT'S ALL OVER!
WE'RE IN DANGER HERE!
WE'RE ALL GOING TO BE GOBBLED UP!
LET'S RUN FOR OUR LIVES!
RUN WHERE?!
WE HAVE NOWHERE TO GO!
NOT TO MENTION ALL THE WOUNDED, WOMEN, AND CHILDREN!
Waaah!
Hwaa!
Raaah
NOW CALM DOWN, ALL OF YOU...
THERE IS NOTHING TO FEAR.

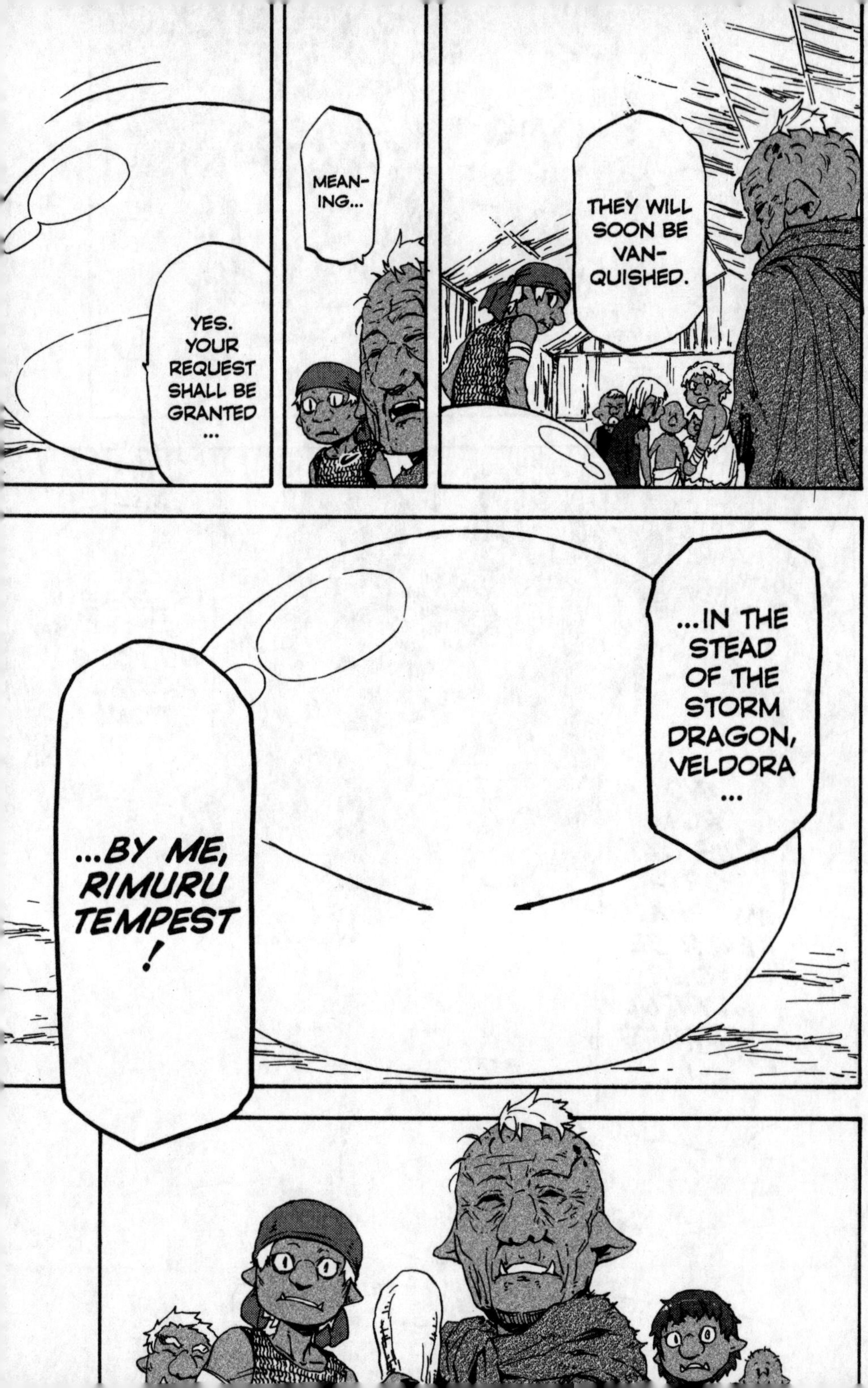
THEY WILL SOON BE VAN-QUISHED.
MEAN-ING...
YES. YOUR REQUEST SHALL BE GRANTED ...
...IN THE STEAD OF THE STORM DRAGON, VELDORA ...
...BY ME, RIMURU TEMPEST!

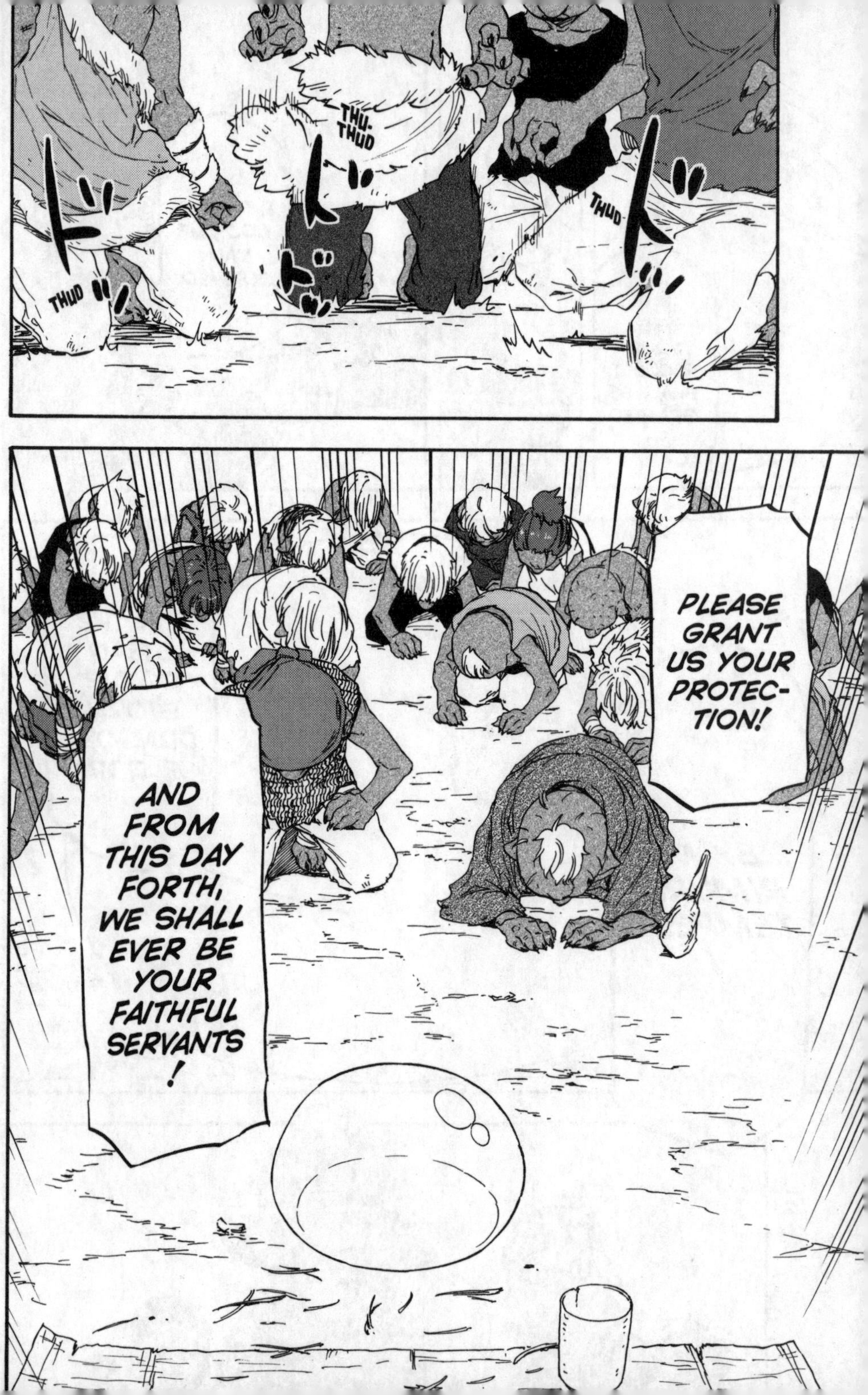
THUD
THU-THUD
THUD
PLEASE GRANT US YOUR PROTECTION!
AND FROM THIS DAY FORTH, WE SHALL EVER BE YOUR FAITHFUL SERVANTS!

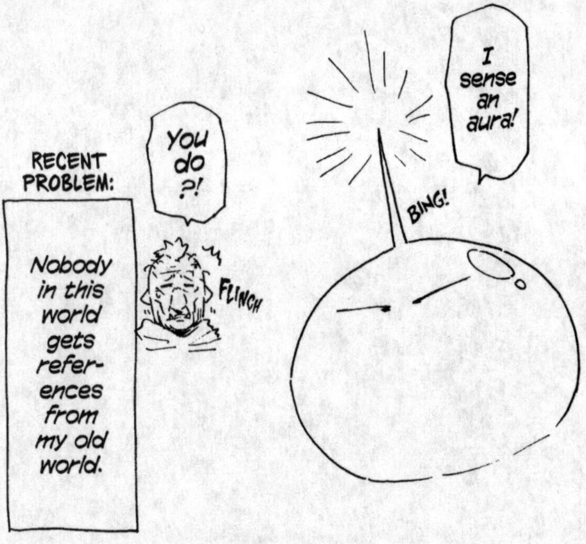

I sense an aura!
BING!
You do?!
FLINCH
RECENT PROBLEM:
Nobody in this world gets references from my old world.

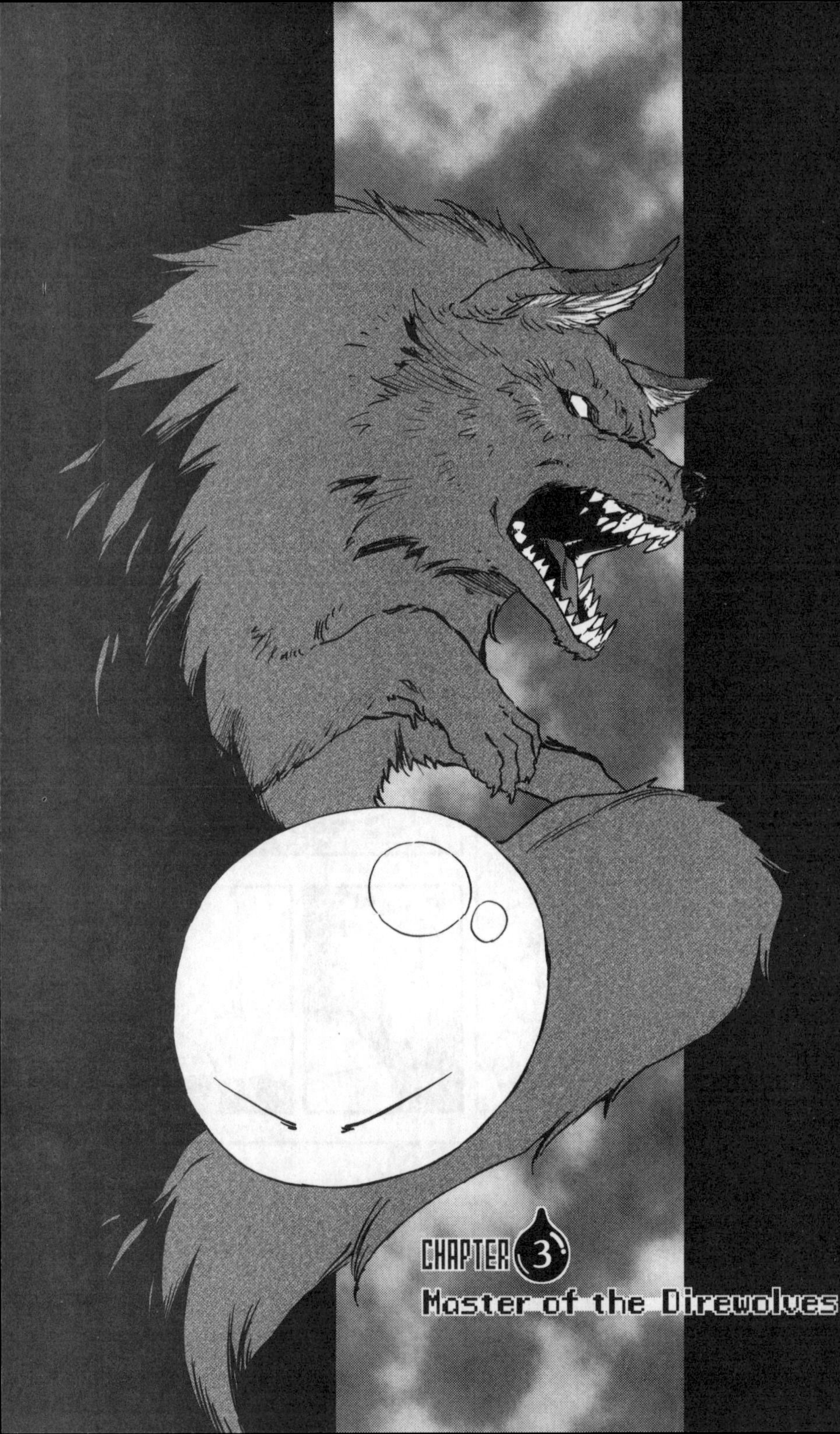
CHAPTER 3
Master of the Direwolves

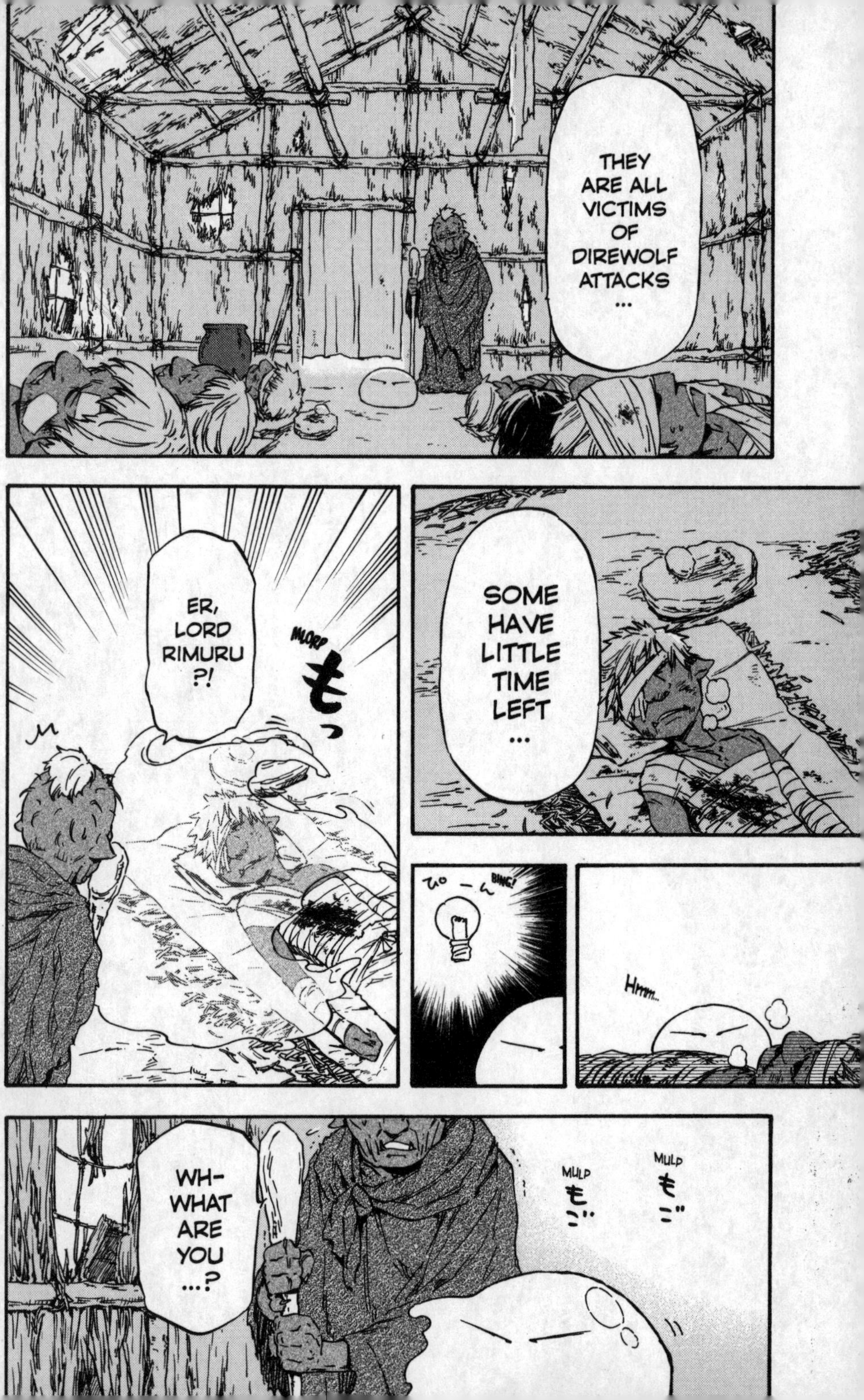

THEY ARE ALL VICTIMS OF DIREWOLF ATTACKS...
SOME HAVE LITTLE TIME LEFT...
Hmm..
BING!
MLORP
もっ
ER, LORD RIMURU?!
MULP
もご
MULP
もご
WH-WHAT ARE YOU...?

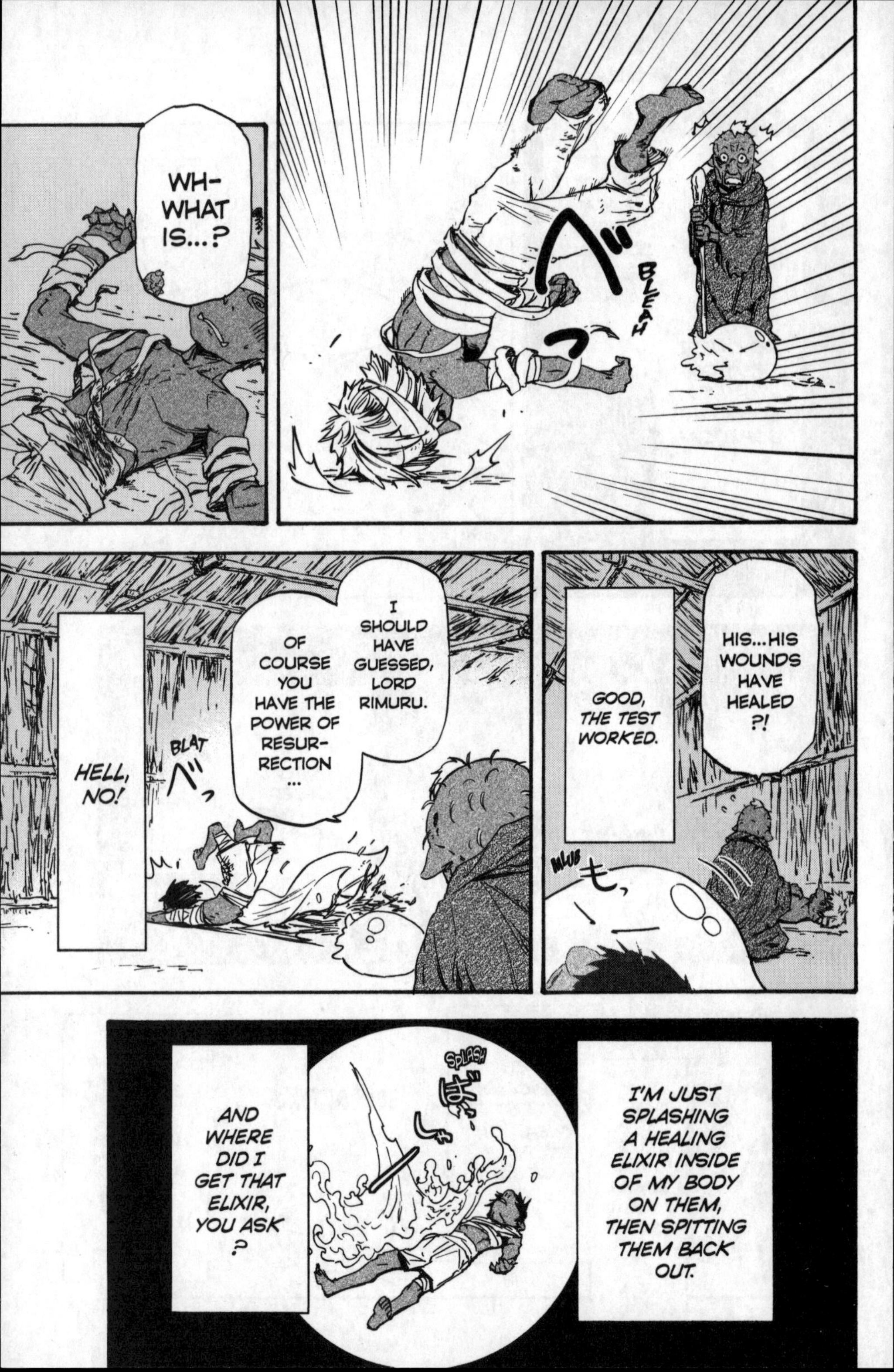

BLEAH
WH- WHAT IS...?
HIS...HIS WOUNDS HAVE HEALED ?!
GOOD, THE TEST WORKED.
MUB
I SHOULD HAVE GUESSED, LORD RIMURU.
OF COURSE YOU HAVE THE POWER OF RESURRECTION ...
BLAT
HELL, NO!
I'M JUST SPLASHING A HEALING ELIXIR INSIDE OF MY BODY ON THEM, THEN SPITTING THEM BACK OUT.
SPLASH
AND WHERE DID I GET THAT ELIXIR, YOU ASK ?

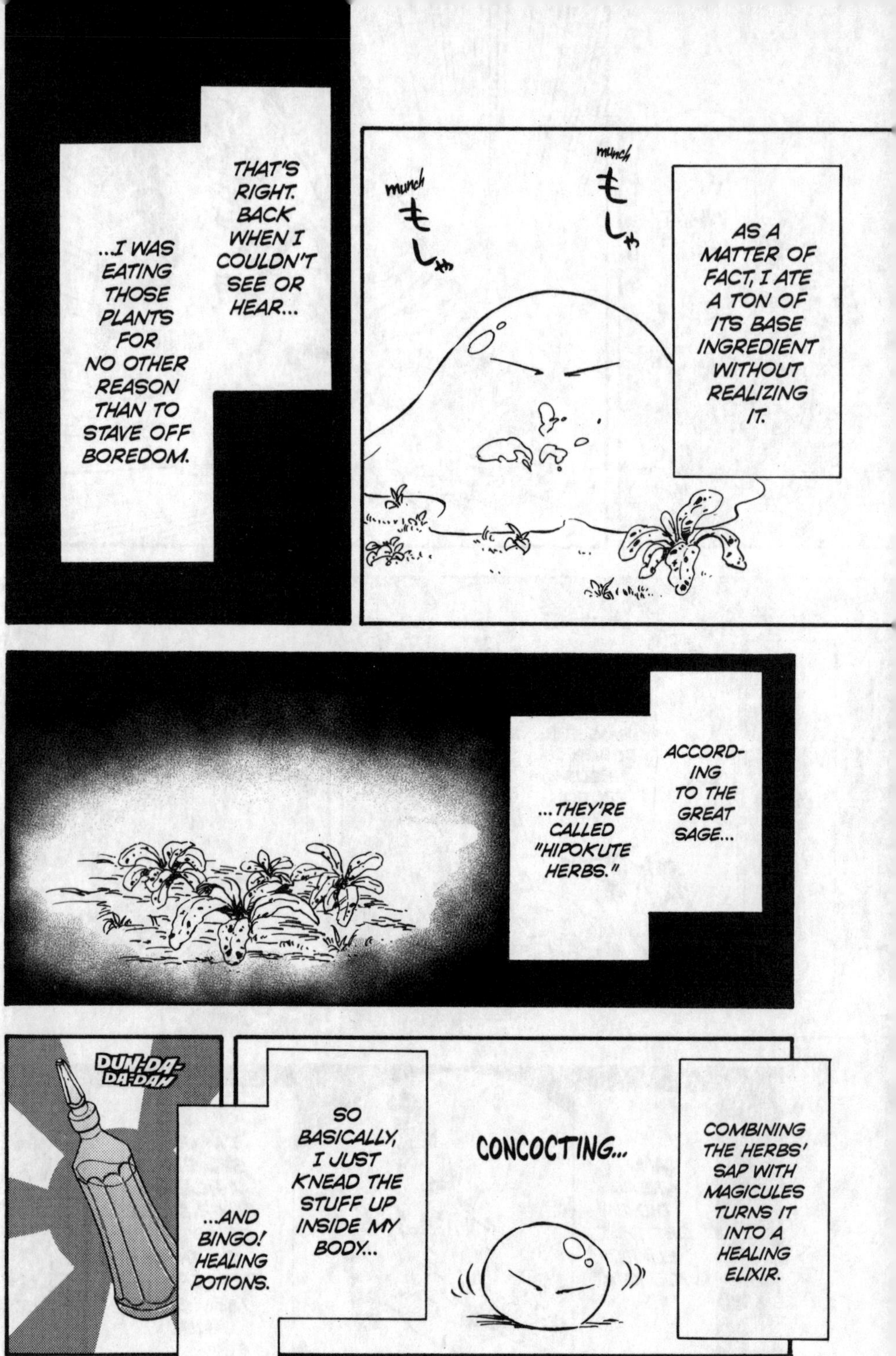
munch
もしゃ
munch
もしゃ
AS A MATTER OF FACT, I ATE A TON OF ITS BASE INGREDIENT WITHOUT REALIZING IT.
THAT'S RIGHT. BACK WHEN I COULDN'T SEE OR HEAR...
...I WAS EATING THOSE PLANTS FOR NO OTHER REASON THAN TO STAVE OFF BOREDOM.
ACCORDING TO THE GREAT SAGE...
...THEY'RE CALLED "HIPOKUTE HERBS."
COMBINING THE HERBS' SAP WITH MAGICULES TURNS IT INTO A HEALING ELIXIR.
CONCOCTING...
SO BASICALLY, I JUST KNEAD THE STUFF UP INSIDE MY BODY...
...AND BINGO! HEALING POTIONS.
DUN-DA-DA-DAH

*Bottle not included

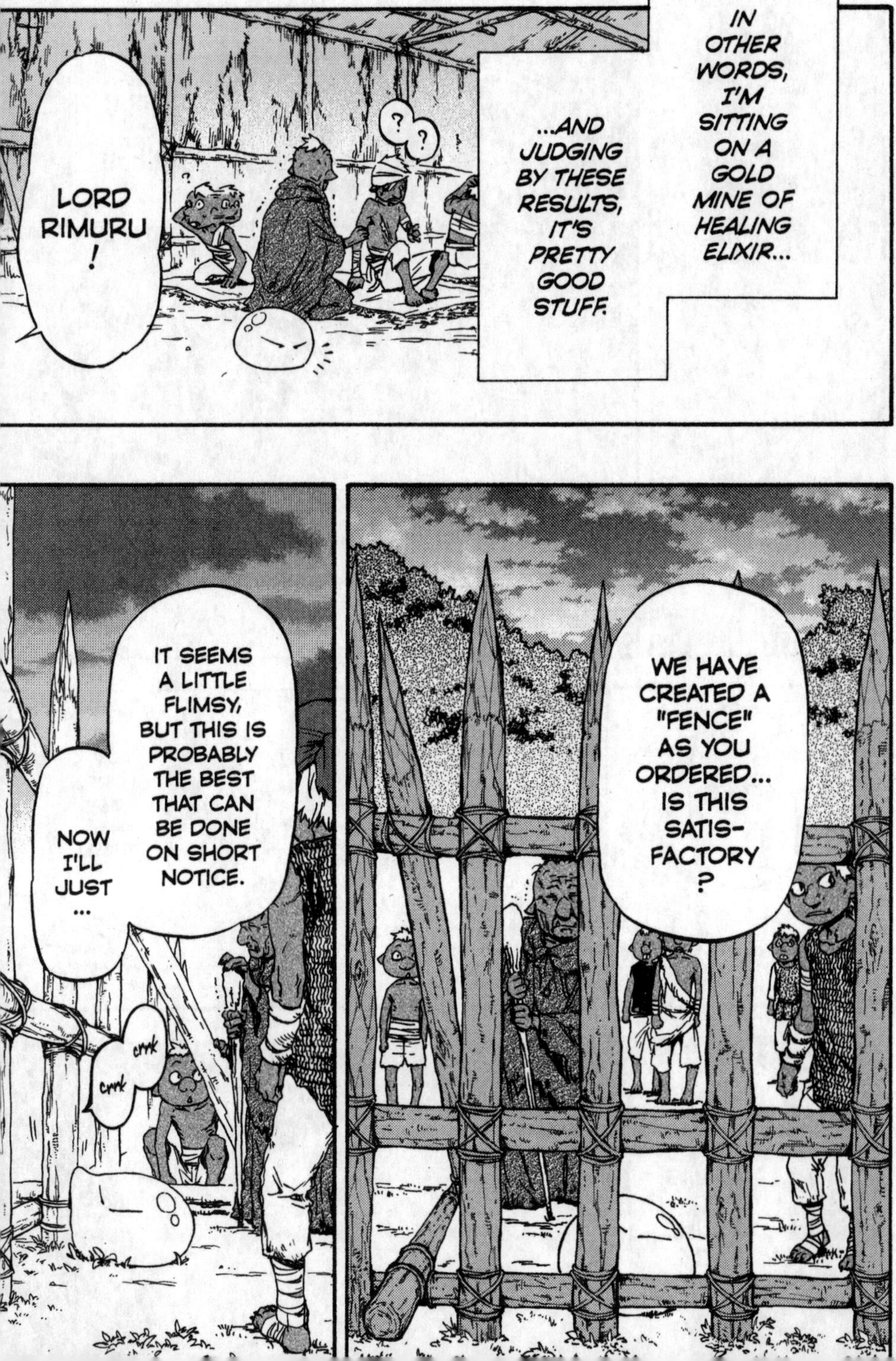
IN OTHER WORDS, I'M SITTING ON A GOLD MINE OF HEALING ELIXIR...
...AND JUDGING BY THESE RESULTS, IT'S PRETTY GOOD STUFF.
? ?
LORD RIMURU!
WE HAVE CREATED A "FENCE" AS YOU ORDERED... IS THIS SATIS-FACTORY?
IT SEEMS A LITTLE FLIMSY, BUT THIS IS PROBABLY THE BEST THAT CAN BE DONE ON SHORT NOTICE.
NOW I'LL JUST ...
crrk
crrk

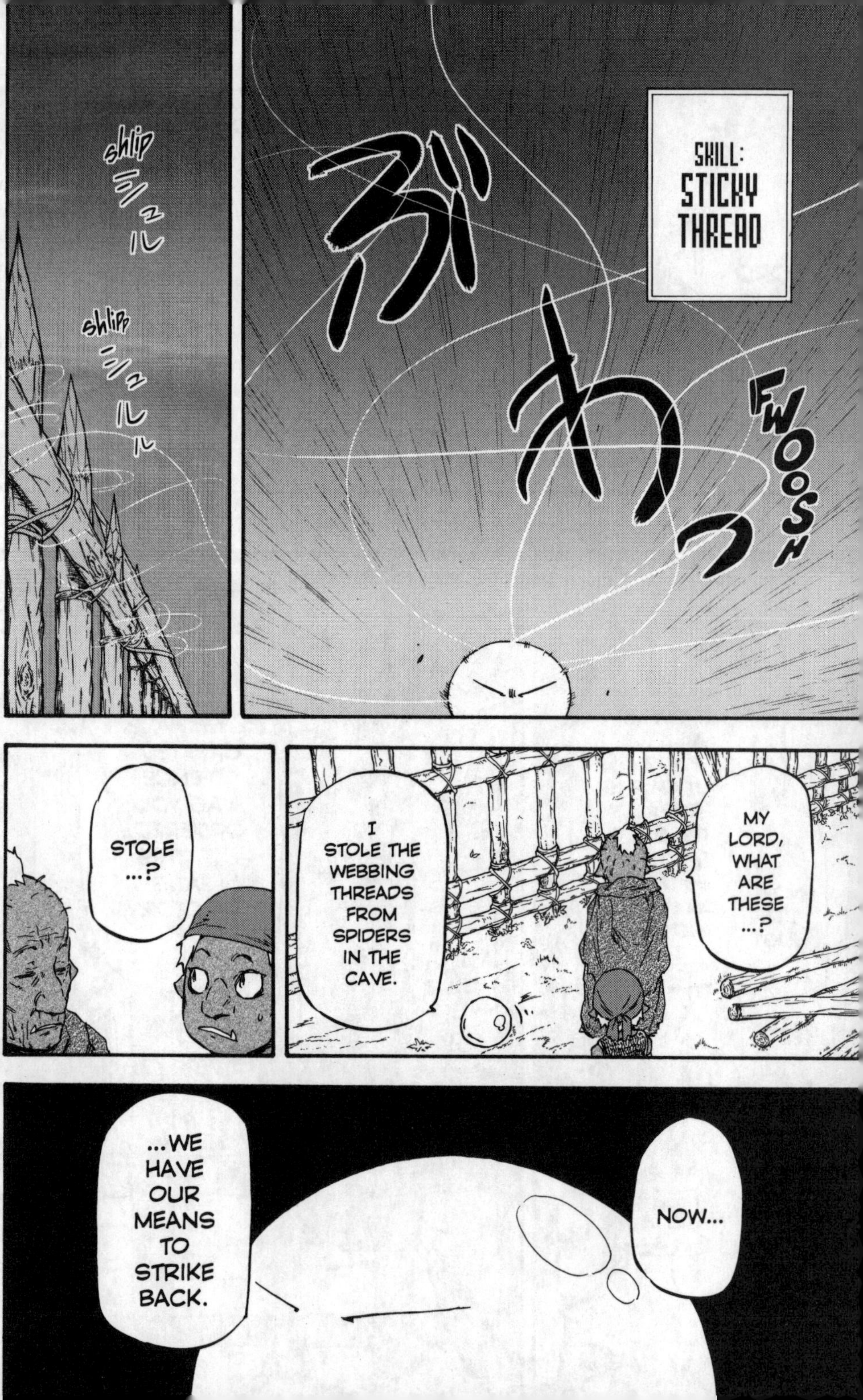
SKILL: STICKY THREAD
ぶわっ
FWOOSH
shlip
シュル
shlipp
シュルル
MY LORD, WHAT ARE THESE ...?
I STOLE THE WEBBING THREADS FROM SPIDERS IN THE CAVE.
STOLE ...?
NOW...
...WE HAVE OUR MEANS TO STRIKE BACK.

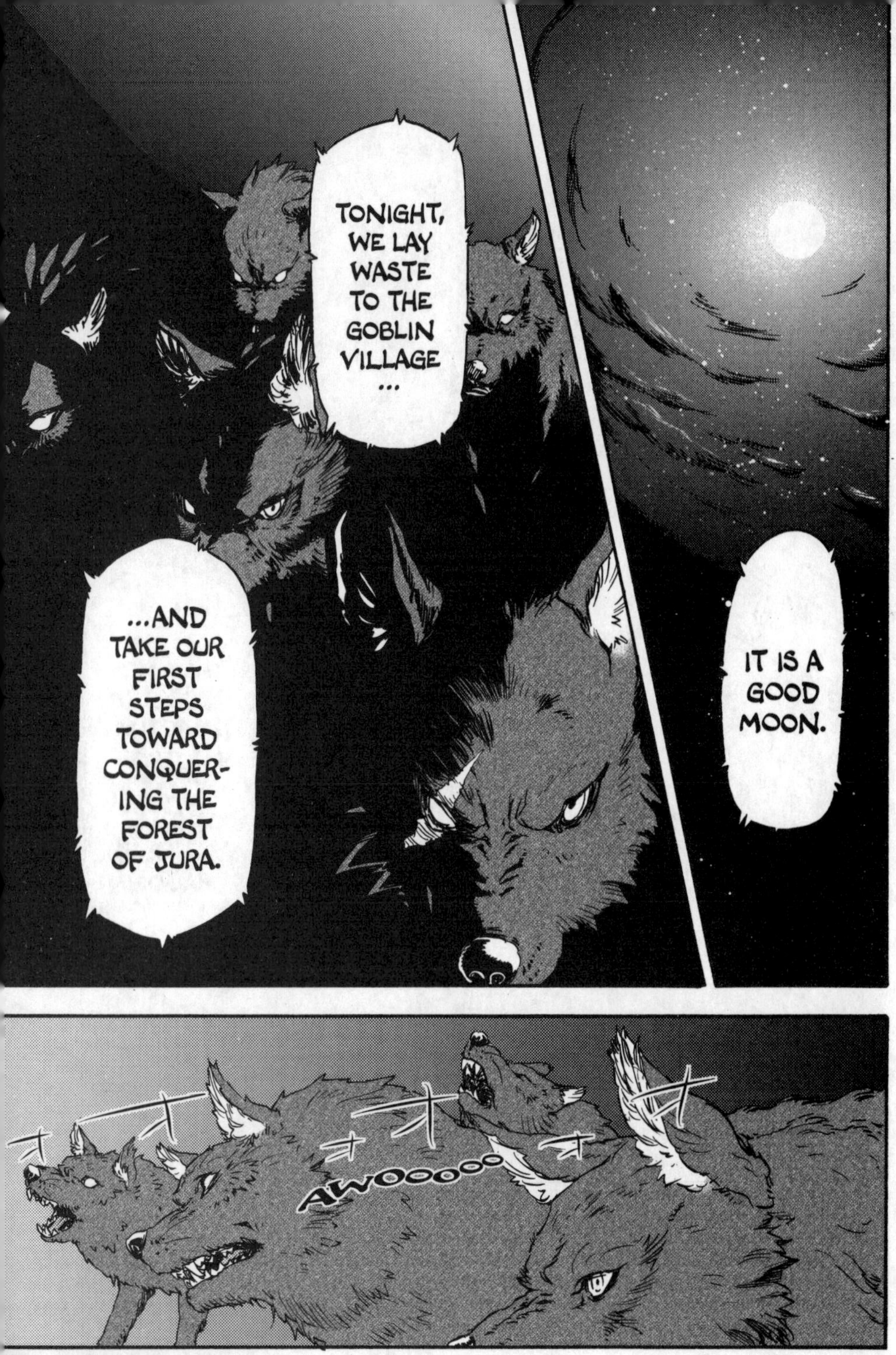
IT IS A GOOD MOON.
TONIGHT, WE LAY WASTE TO THE GOBLIN VILLAGE ...
...AND TAKE OUR FIRST STEPS TOWARD CONQUER-ING THE FOREST OF JURA.
AWOOOOOO

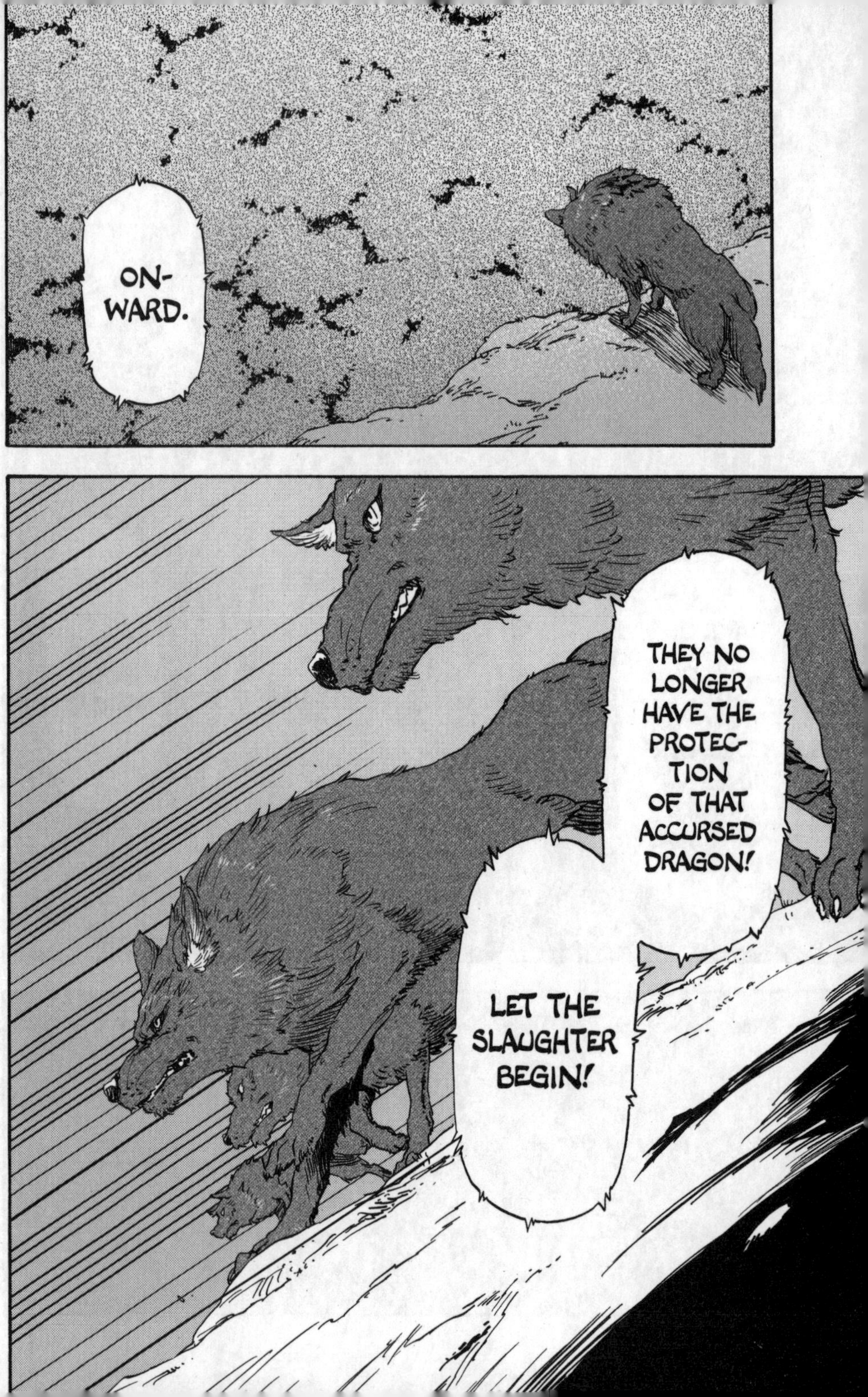
ON-WARD.
THEY NO LONGER HAVE THE PROTEC-TION OF THAT ACCURSED DRAGON!
LET THE SLAUGHTER BEGIN!

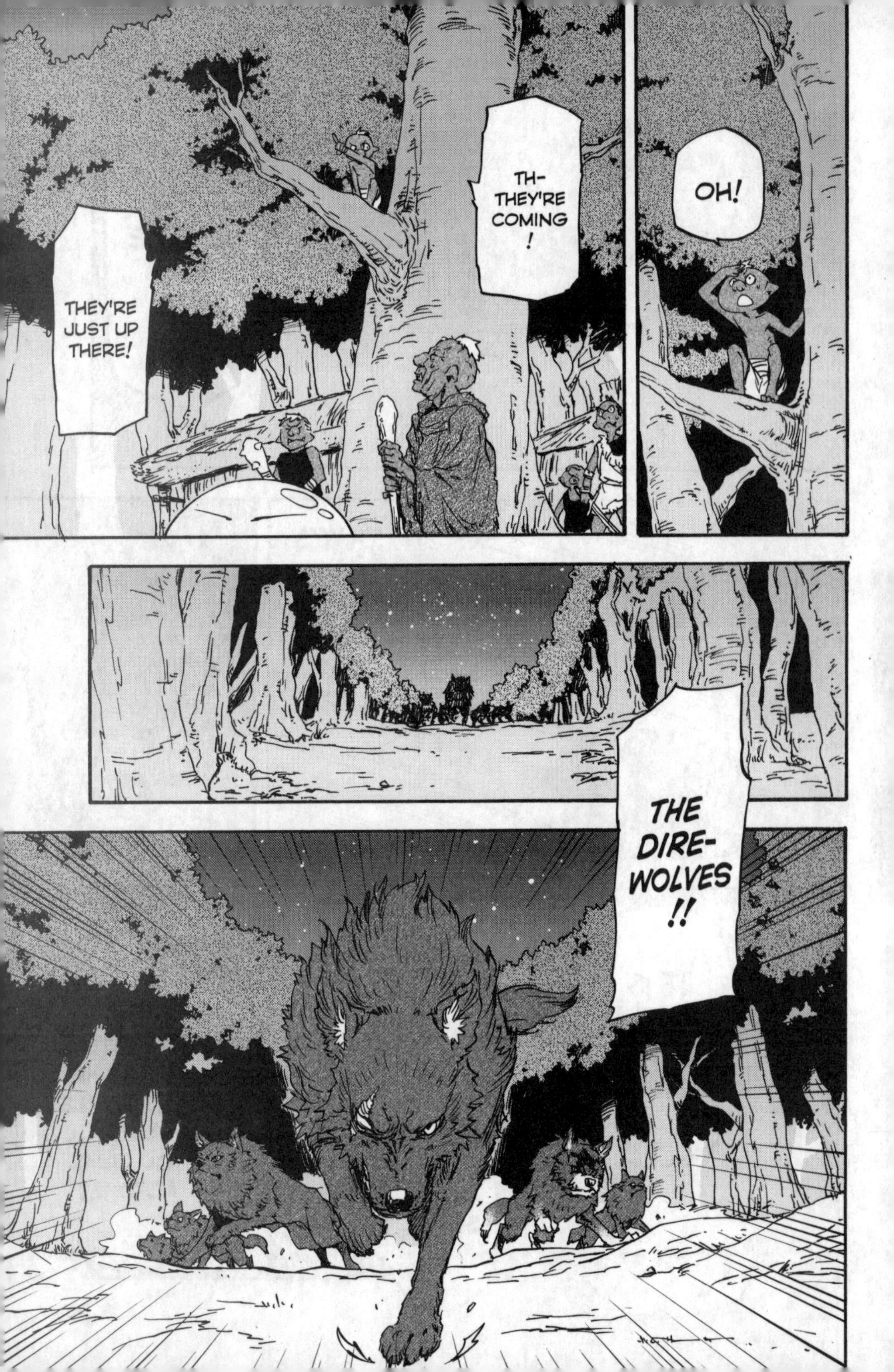
OH!
TH-THEY'RE COMING!
THEY'RE JUST UP THERE!
THE DIRE-WOLVES!!

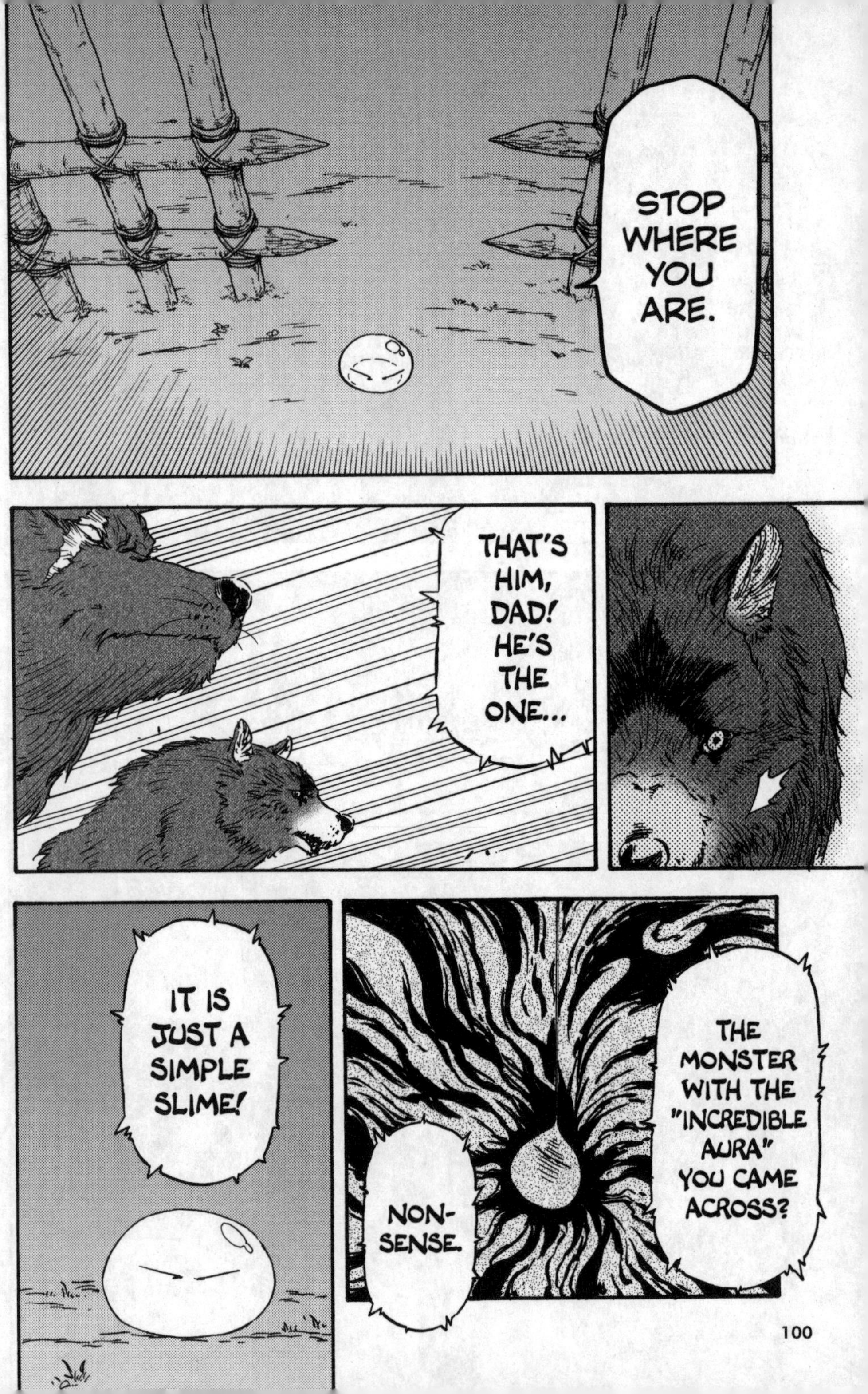
STOP WHERE YOU ARE.
THAT'S HIM, DAD! HE'S THE ONE...
THE MONSTER WITH THE "INCREDIBLE AURA" YOU CAME ACROSS?
NON-SENSE.
IT IS JUST A SIMPLE SLIME!

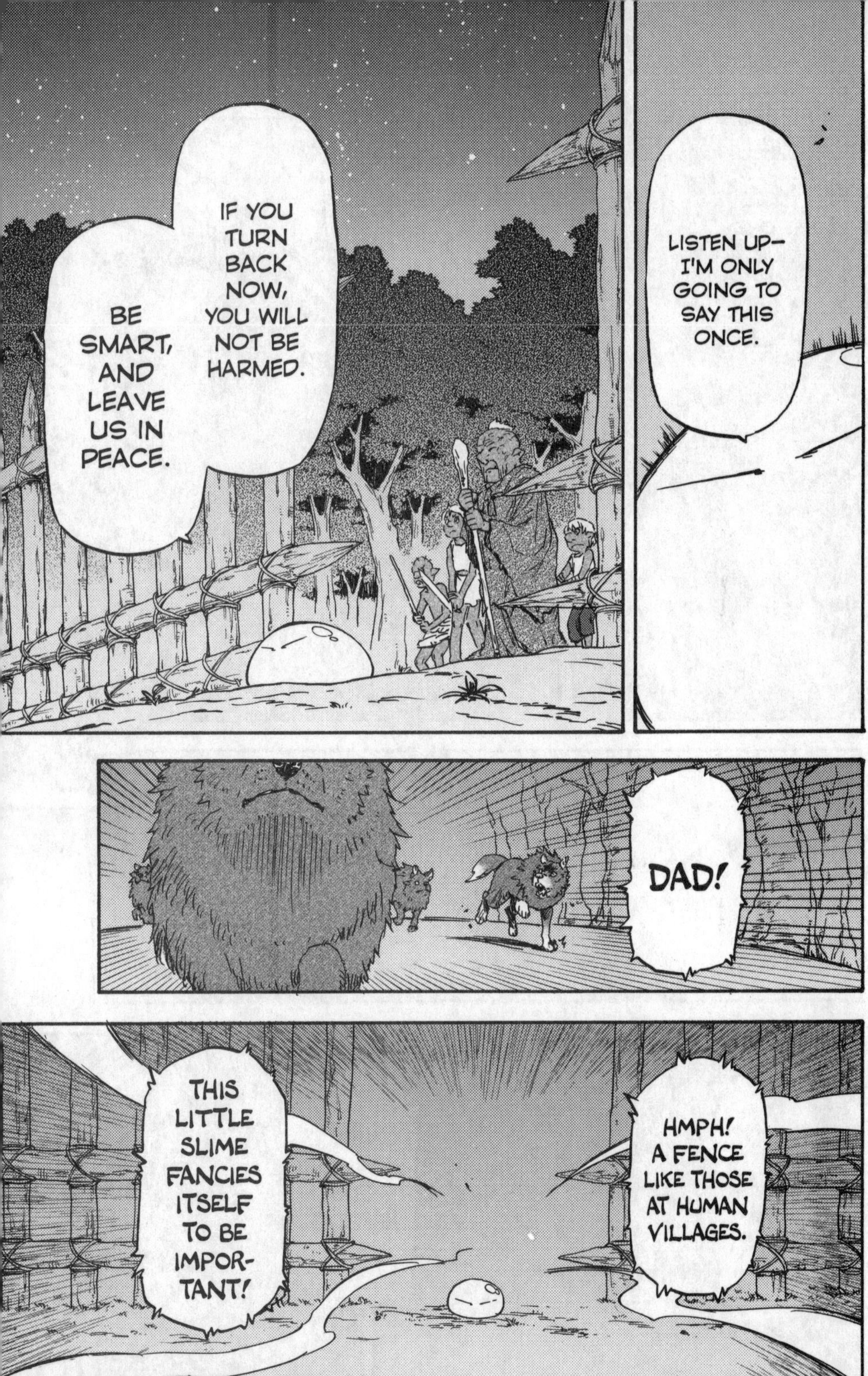
LISTEN UP— I'M ONLY GOING TO SAY THIS ONCE.
IF YOU TURN BACK NOW, YOU WILL NOT BE HARMED.
BE SMART, AND LEAVE US IN PEACE.
DAD!
HMPH! A FENCE LIKE THOSE AT HUMAN VILLAGES.
THIS LITTLE SLIME FANCIES ITSELF TO BE IMPORTANT!

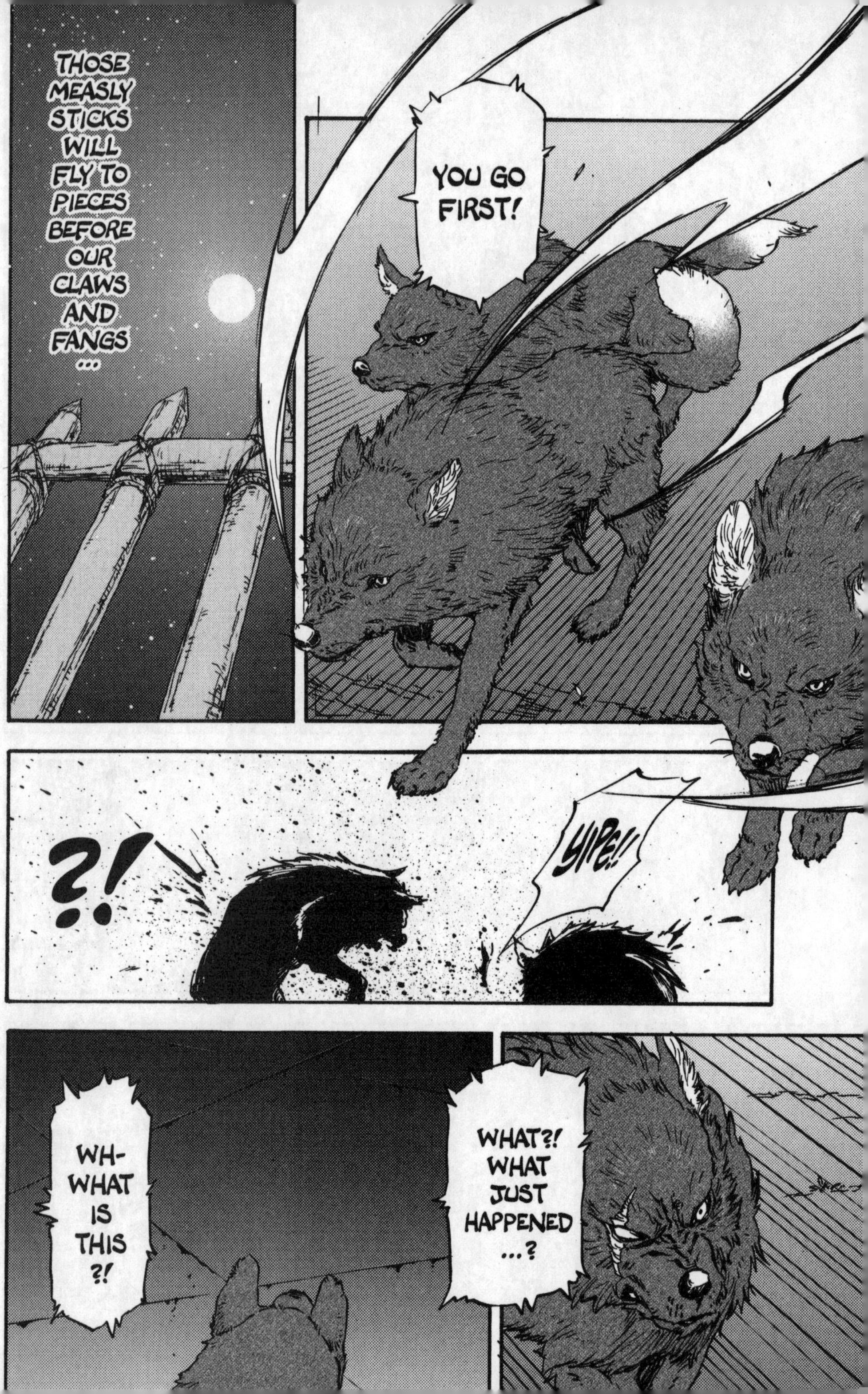
YOU GO FIRST!
THOSE MEASLY STICKS WILL FLY TO PIECES BEFORE OUR CLAWS AND FANGS...
YIPE!!
?!
WHAT?! WHAT JUST HAPPENED...?
WH-WHAT IS THIS?!

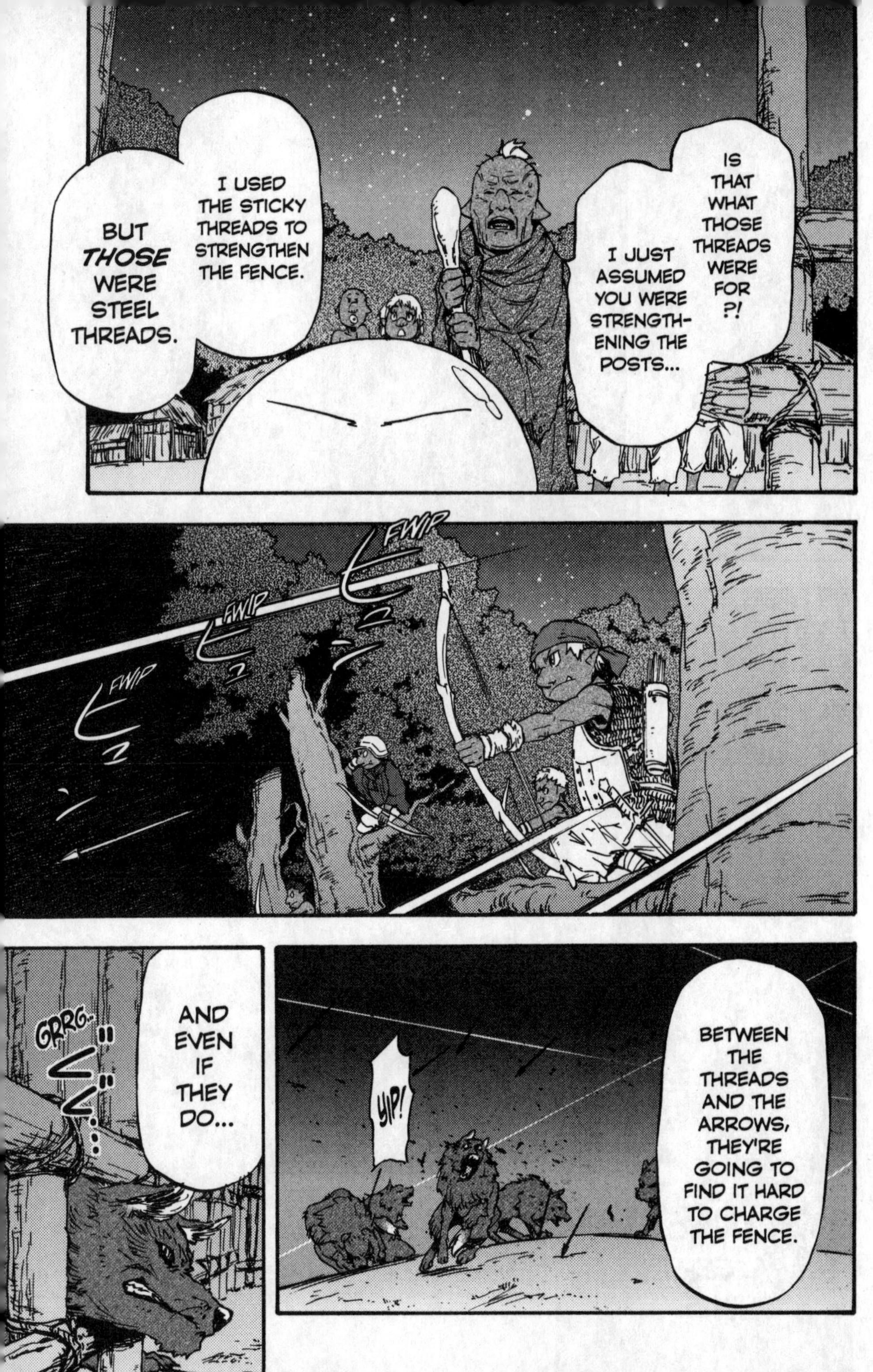
IS THAT WHAT THOSE THREADS WERE FOR ?!
I JUST ASSUMED YOU WERE STRENGTH-ENING THE POSTS...
I USED THE STICKY THREADS TO STRENGTHEN THE FENCE.
BUT *THOSE* WERE STEEL THREADS.
FWIP
FWIP
FWIP
BETWEEN THE THREADS AND THE ARROWS, THEY'RE GOING TO FIND IT HARD TO CHARGE THE FENCE.
YIP!
AND EVEN IF THEY DO...
GRRG...

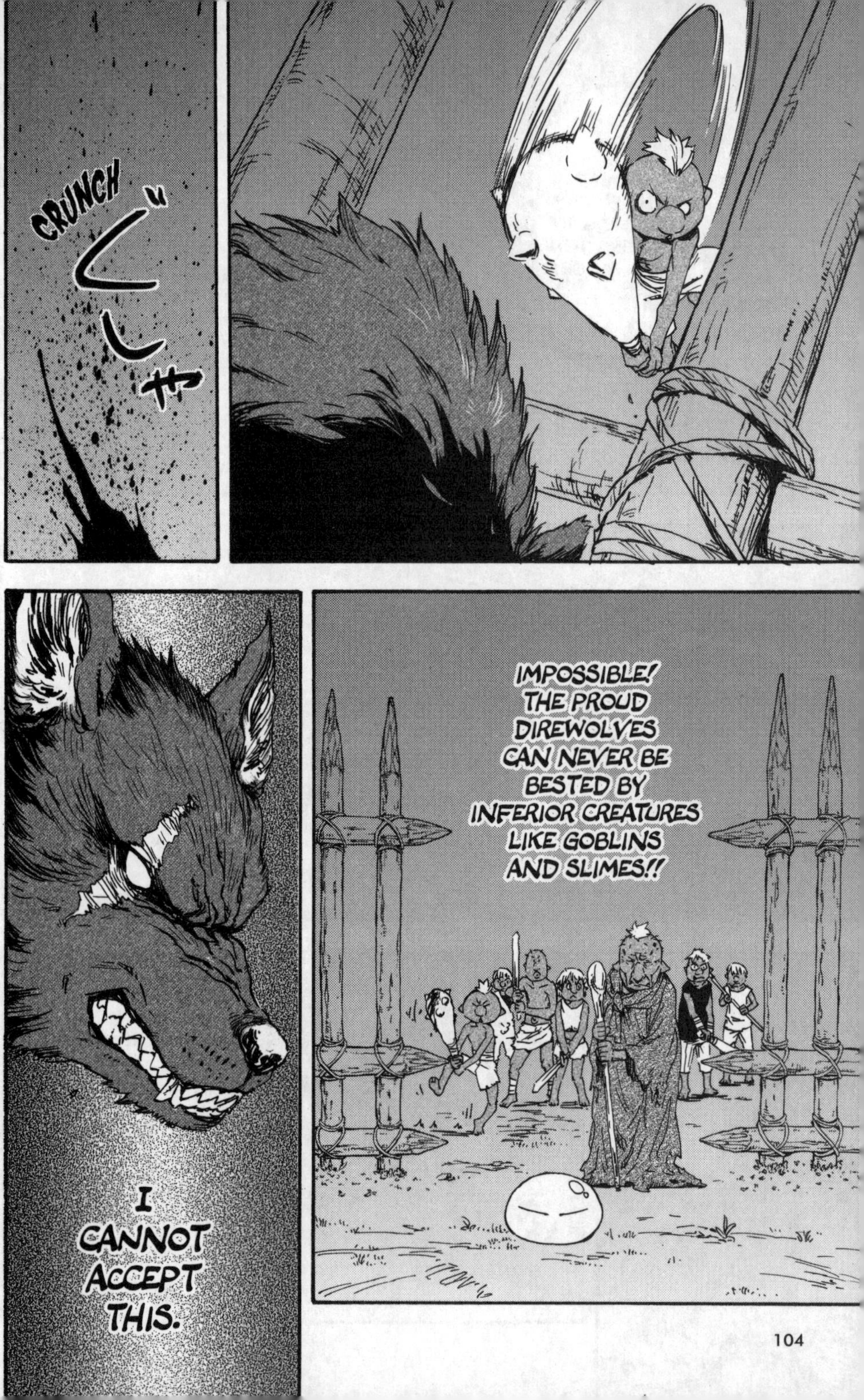
CRUNCH
くしゃ
IMPOSSIBLE! THE PROUD DIREWOLVES CAN NEVER BE BESTED BY INFERIOR CREATURES LIKE GOBLINS AND SLIMES!!
I CANNOT ACCEPT THIS.

DAD ?!

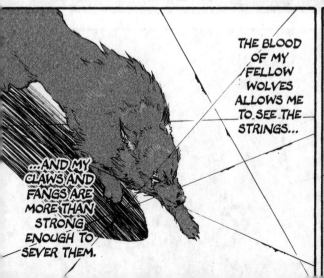

THE BLOOD OF MY FELLOW WOLVES ALLOWS ME TO SEE THE STRINGS...

...AND MY CLAWS AND FANGS ARE MORE THAN STRONG ENOUGH TO SEVER THEM.

MERE TRICKS.

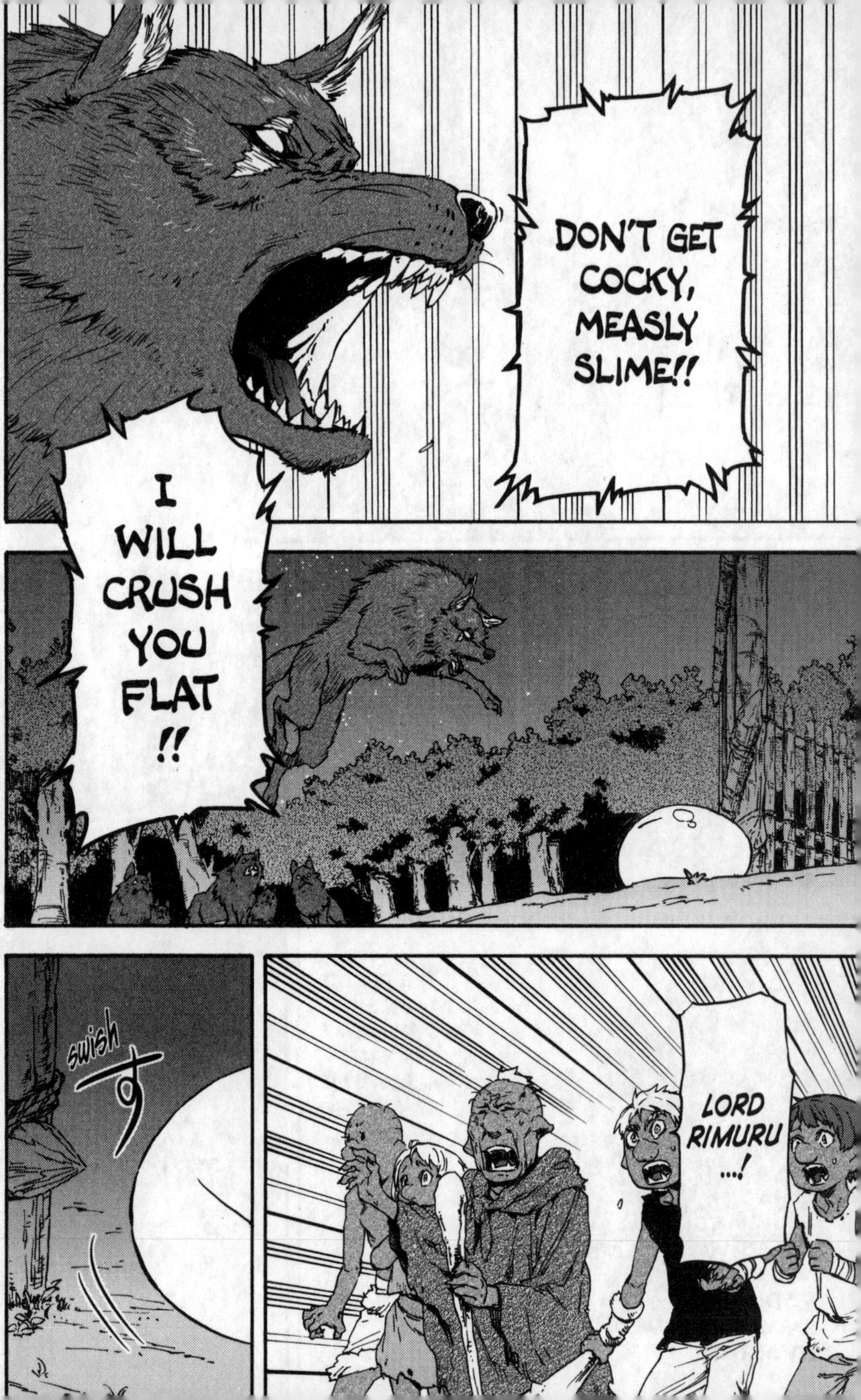
DON'T GET COCKY, MEASLY SLIME!!
I WILL CRUSH YOU FLAT!!
LORD RIMURU...!
swish
す

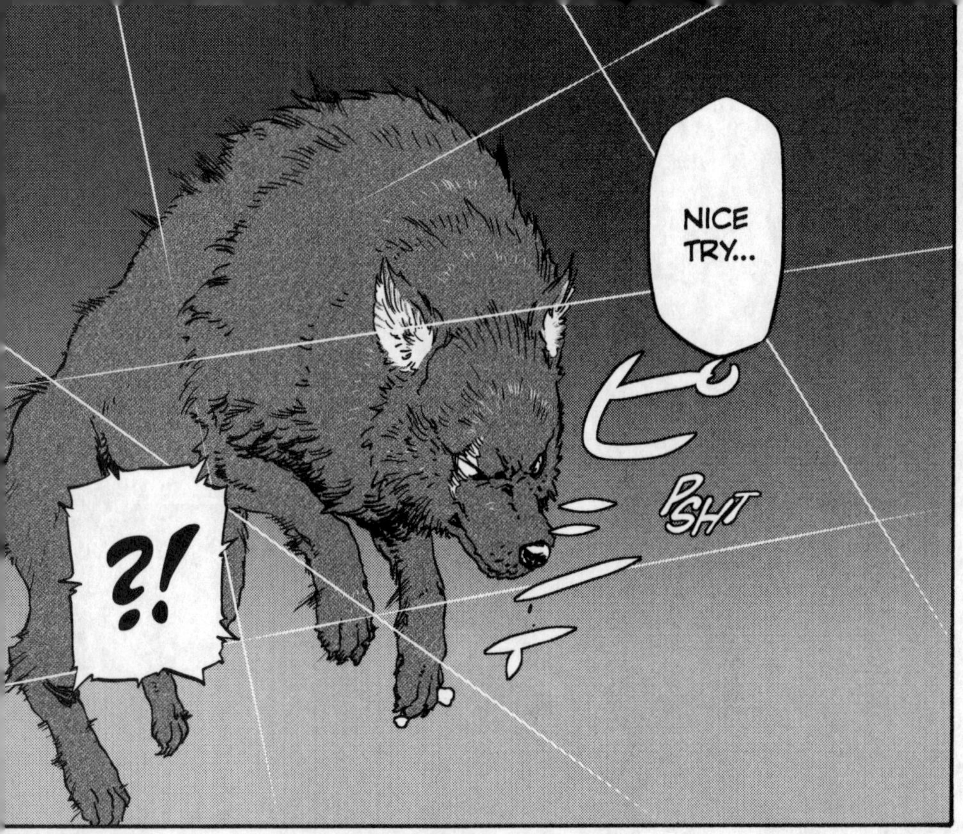
NICE TRY...
PSHT
?!

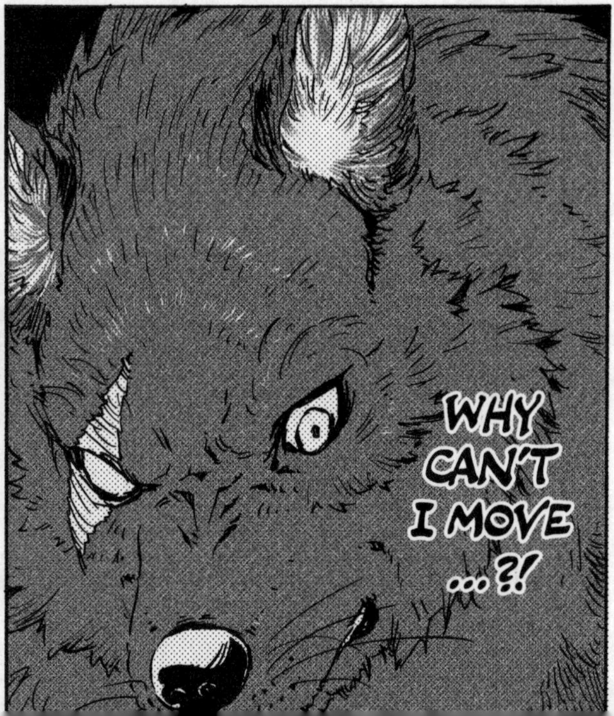
WHY CAN'T I MOVE ...?!

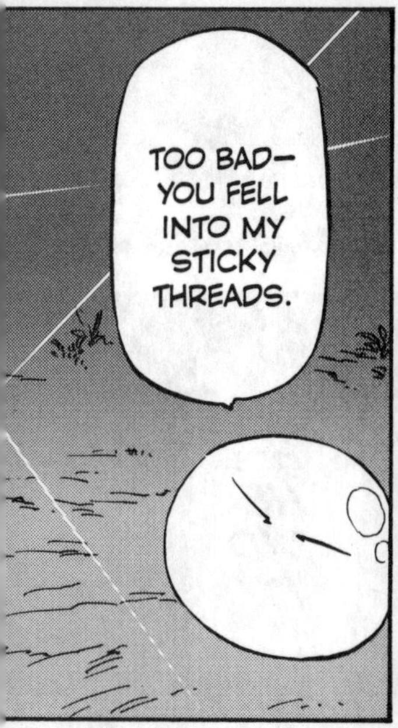
TOO BAD— YOU FELL INTO MY STICKY THREADS.

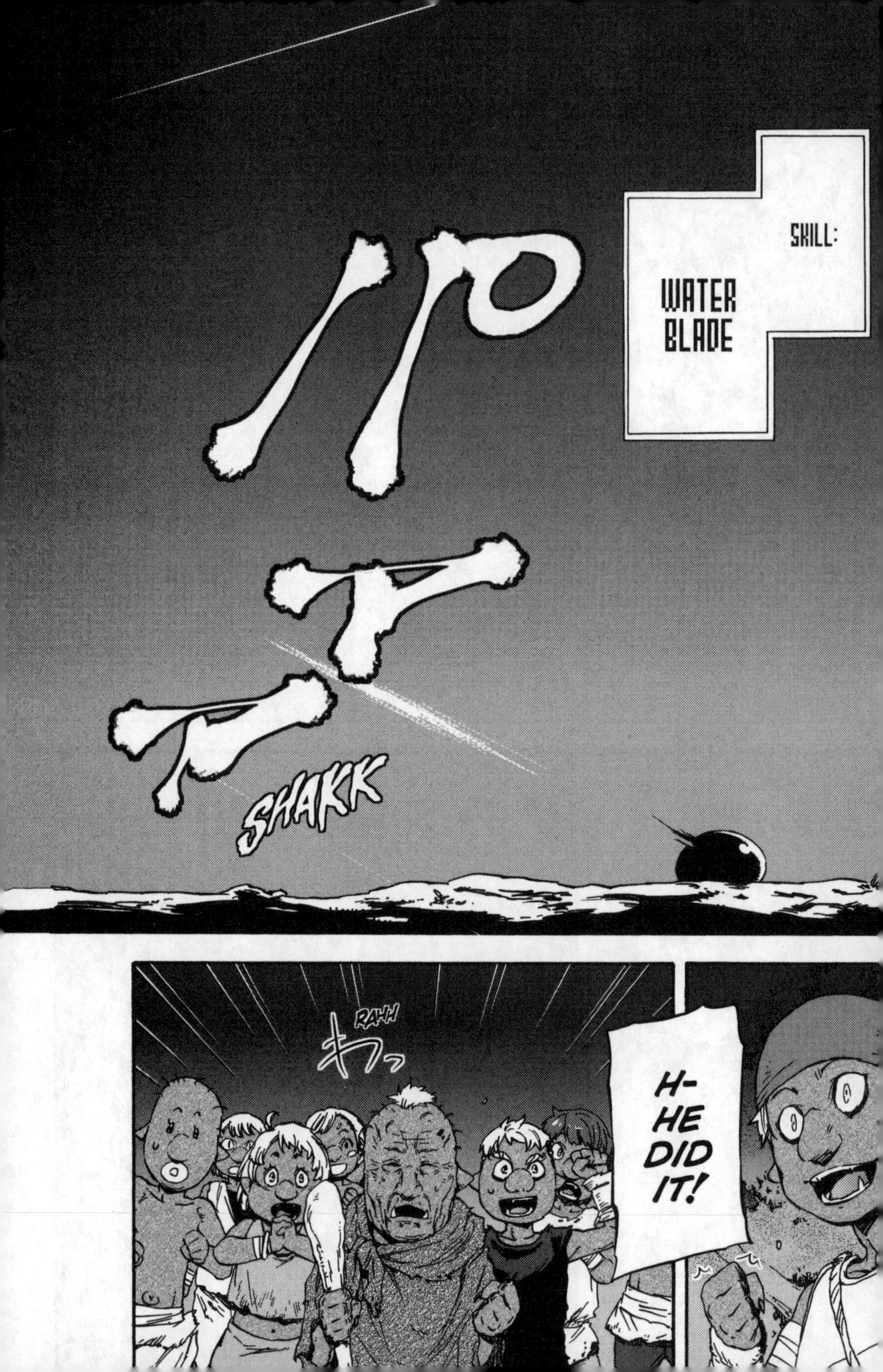
SKILL:
WATER BLADE
パァァ
SHAKK
H- HE DID IT!
RAHH
わっ

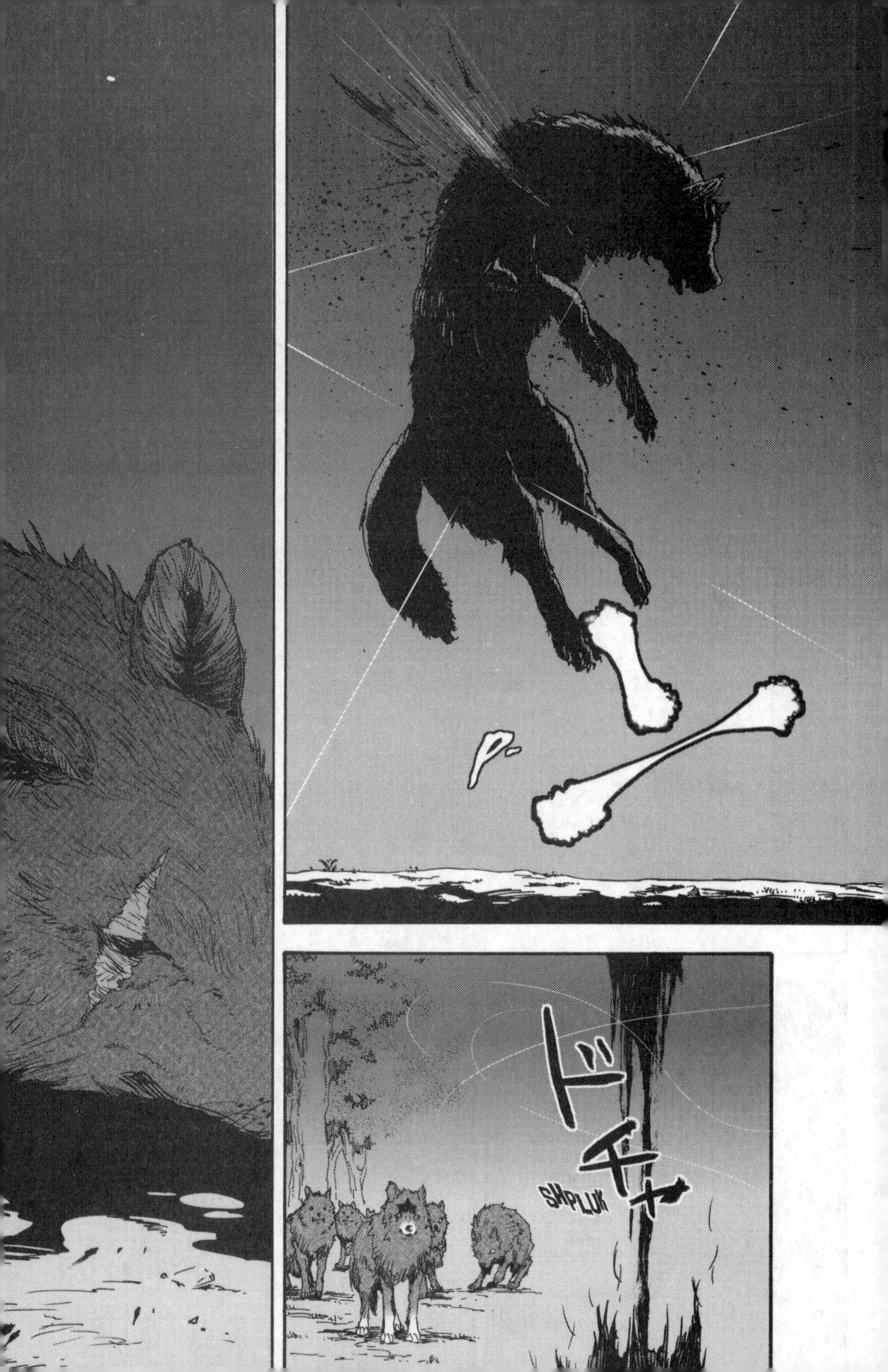
ドチャ
SHPLUK

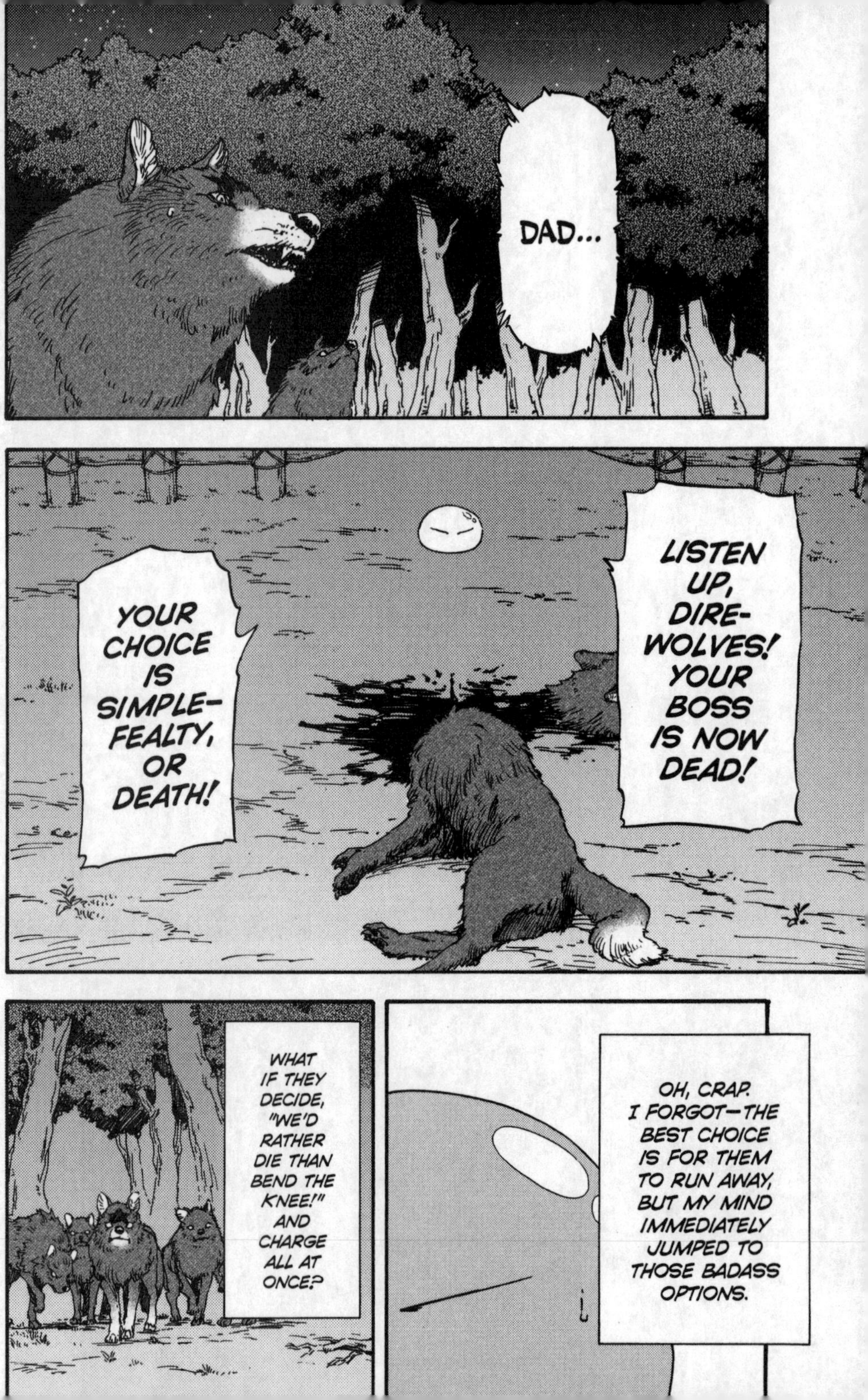
DAD...
LISTEN UP, DIRE-WOLVES! YOUR BOSS IS NOW DEAD!
YOUR CHOICE IS SIMPLE-FEALTY, OR DEATH!
OH, CRAP. I FORGOT—THE BEST CHOICE IS FOR THEM TO RUN AWAY, BUT MY MIND IMMEDIATELY JUMPED TO THOSE BADASS OPTIONS.
WHAT IF THEY DECIDE, "WE'D RATHER DIE THAN BEND THE KNEE!" AND CHARGE ALL AT ONCE?

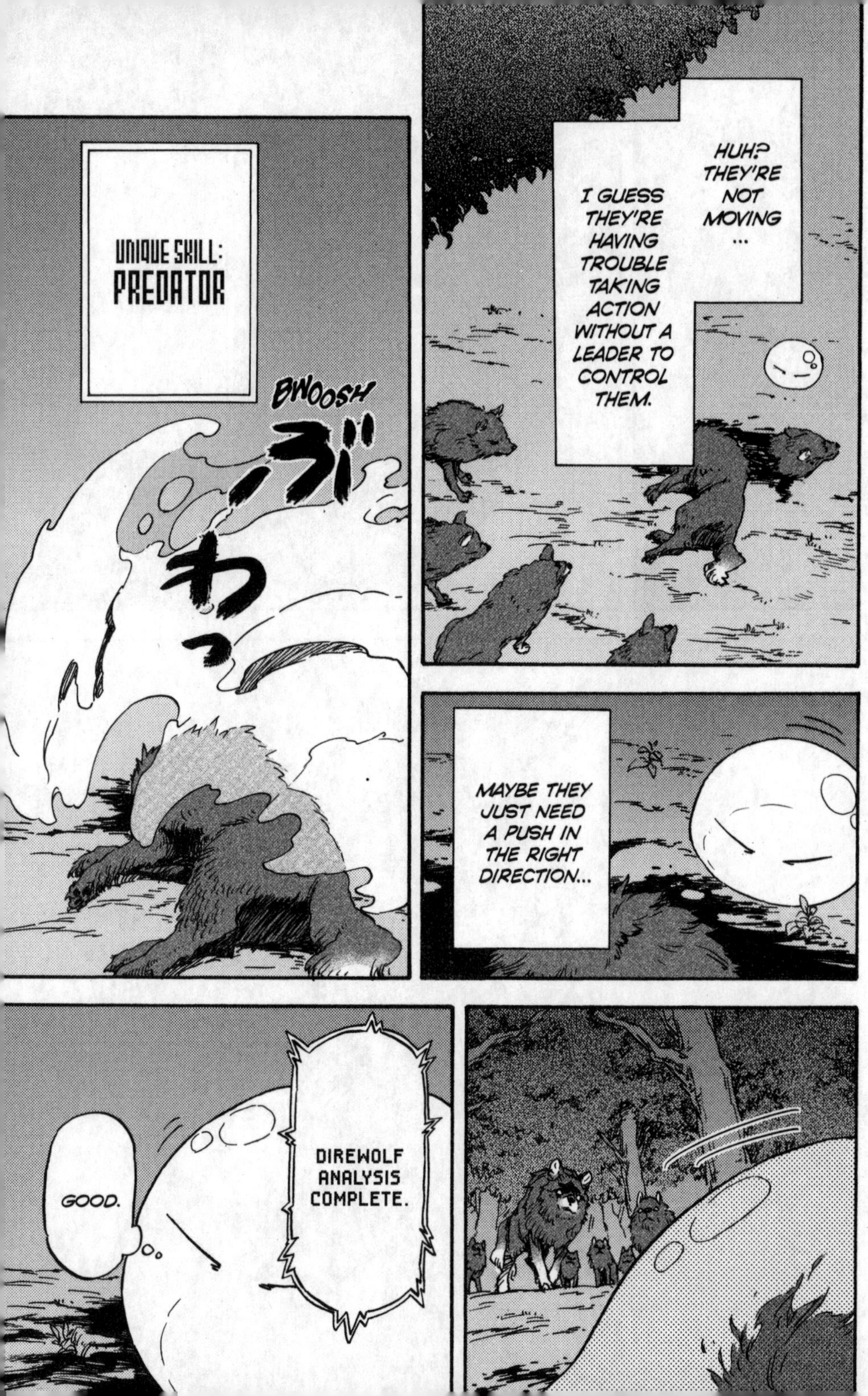
HUH? THEY'RE NOT MOVING...
I GUESS THEY'RE HAVING TROUBLE TAKING ACTION WITHOUT A LEADER TO CONTROL THEM.
MAYBE THEY JUST NEED A PUSH IN THE RIGHT DIRECTION...
UNIQUE SKILL: PREDATOR
BWOOSH
ぶわっ
DIREWOLF ANALYSIS COMPLETE.
GOOD.

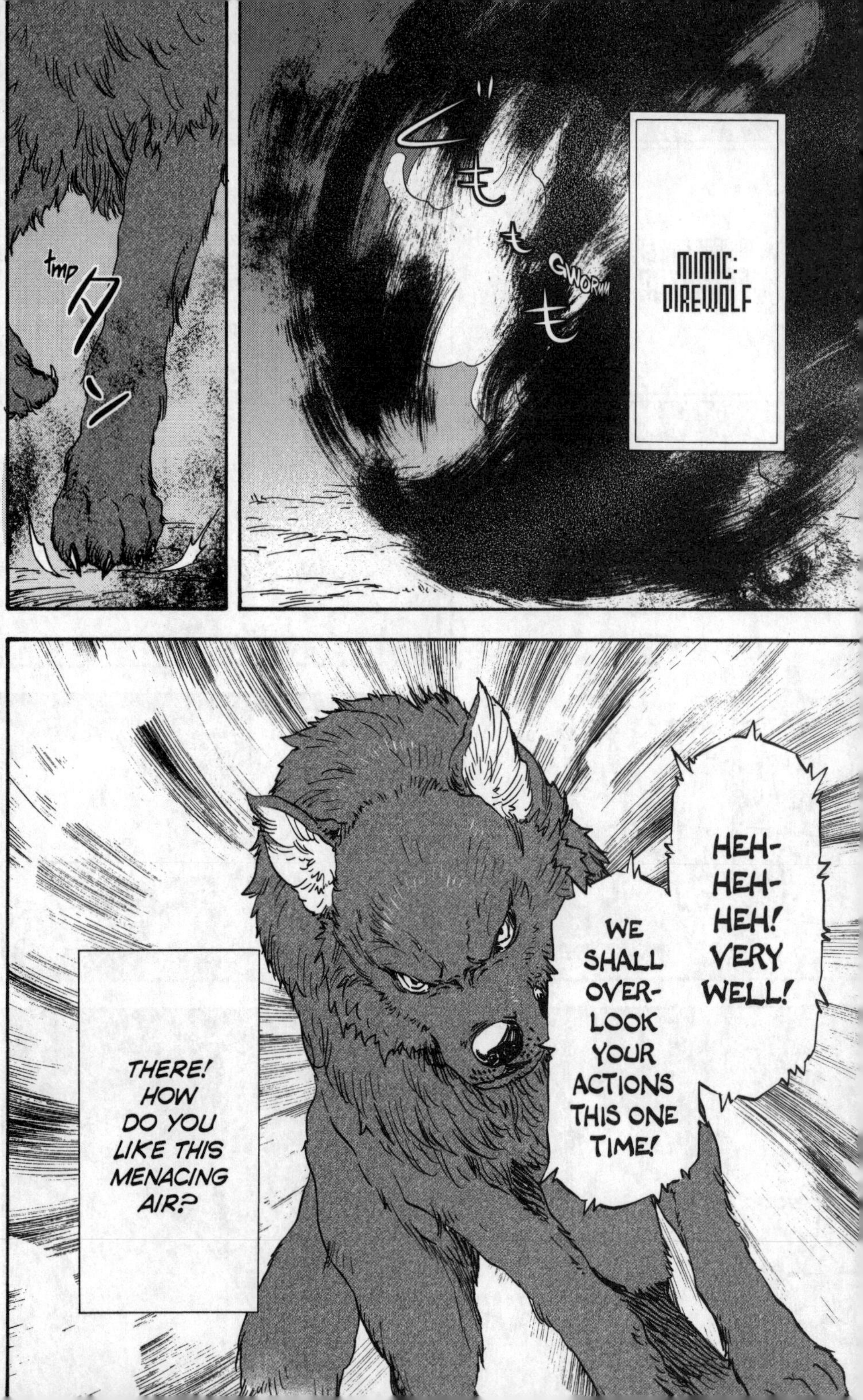
MIMIC: DIREWOLF
GWOR
tmp
HEH-HEH-HEH! VERY WELL!
WE SHALL OVER-LOOK YOUR ACTIONS THIS ONE TIME!
THERE! HOW DO YOU LIKE THIS MENACING AIR?

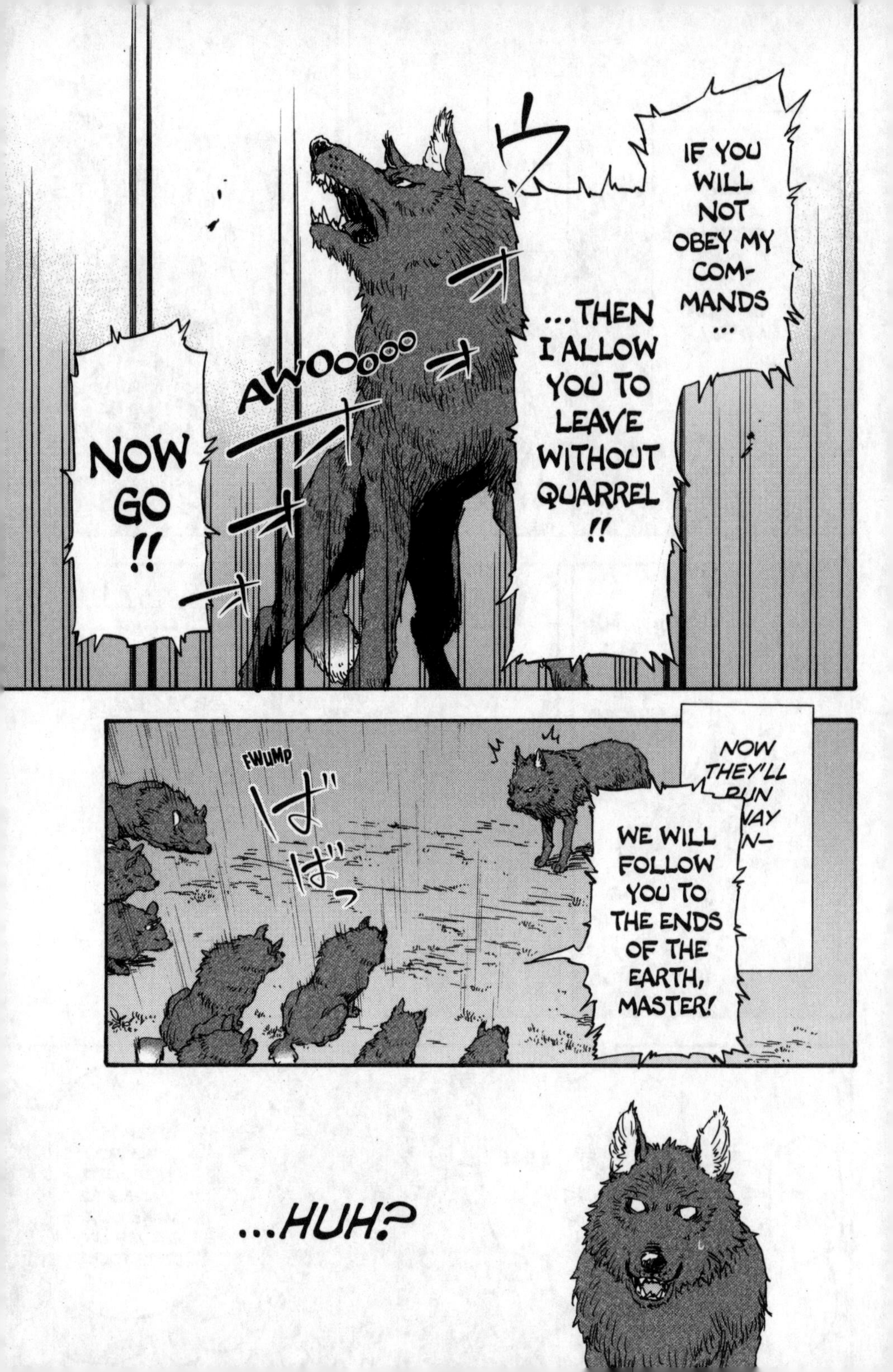
IF YOU WILL NOT OBEY MY COMMANDS ...
...THEN I ALLOW YOU TO LEAVE WITHOUT QUARREL!!
AWOOOOO
NOW GO!!
NOW THEY'LL
WE WILL FOLLOW YOU TO THE ENDS OF THE EARTH, MASTER!
FWUMP
...HUH?

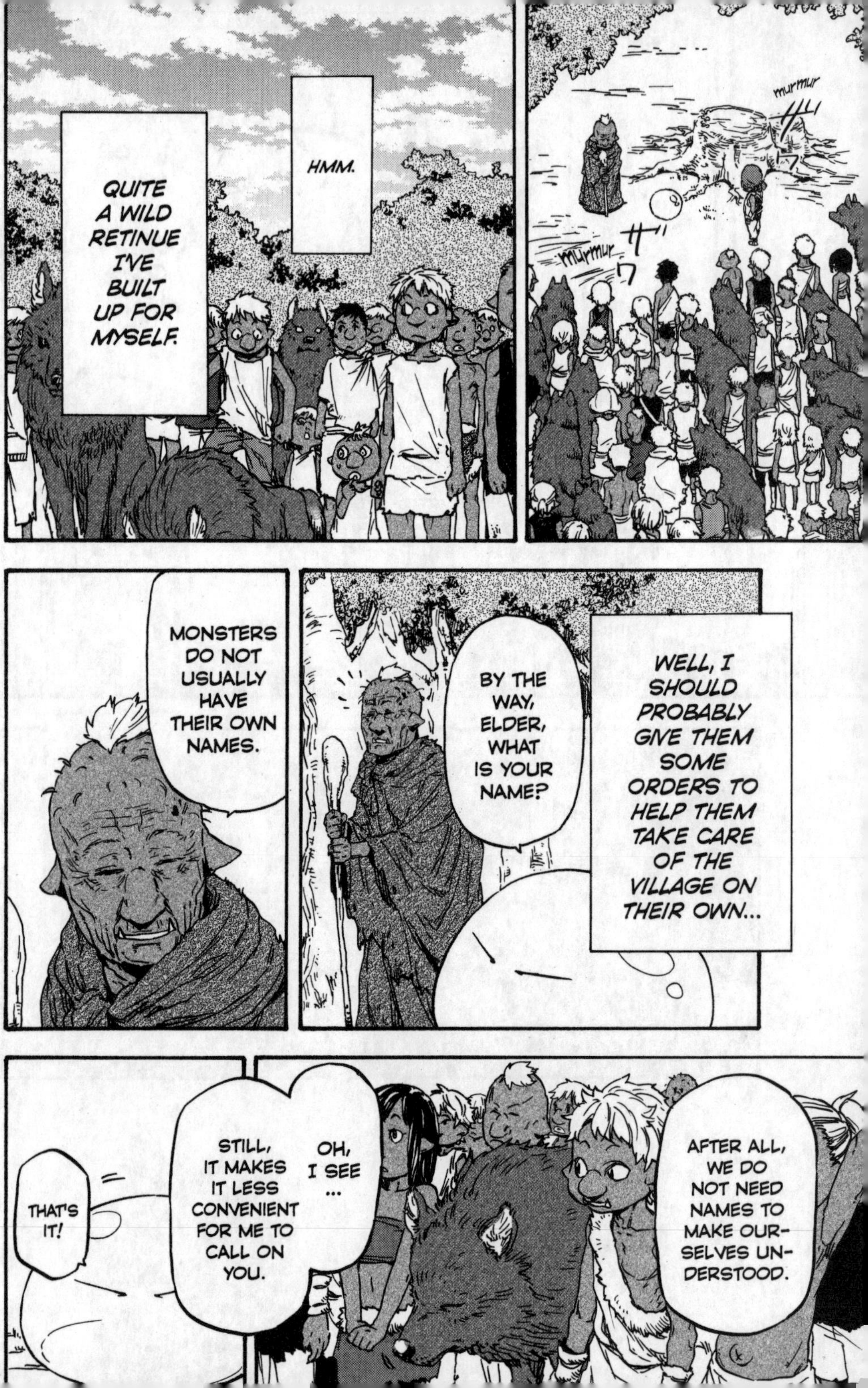
murmur
murmur
HMM.
QUITE A WILD RETINUE I'VE BUILT UP FOR MYSELF.
WELL, I SHOULD PROBABLY GIVE THEM SOME ORDERS TO HELP THEM TAKE CARE OF THE VILLAGE ON THEIR OWN...
BY THE WAY, ELDER, WHAT IS YOUR NAME?
MONSTERS DO NOT USUALLY HAVE THEIR OWN NAMES.
AFTER ALL, WE DO NOT NEED NAMES TO MAKE OURSELVES UNDERSTOOD.
OH, I SEE ...
STILL, IT MAKES IT LESS CONVENIENT FOR ME TO CALL ON YOU.
THAT'S IT!

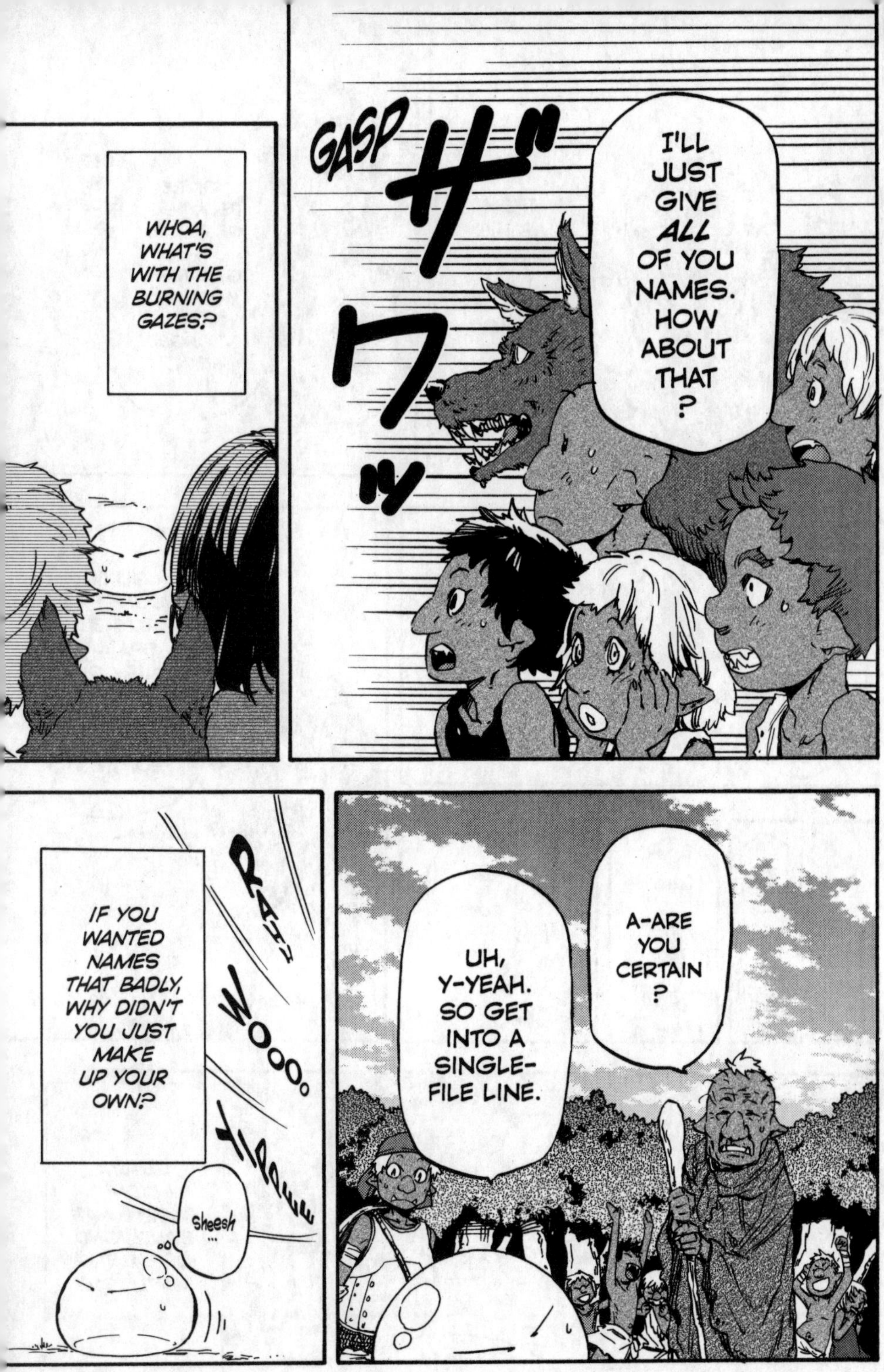
GASP
ザワッ
I'LL JUST GIVE ALL OF YOU NAMES. HOW ABOUT THAT?
WHOA, WHAT'S WITH THE BURNING GAZES?
A-ARE YOU CERTAIN?
UH, Y-YEAH. SO GET INTO A SINGLE-FILE LINE.
IF YOU WANTED NAMES THAT BADLY, WHY DIDN'T YOU JUST MAKE UP YOUR OWN?
RAHH
WOOOO
Sheesh...

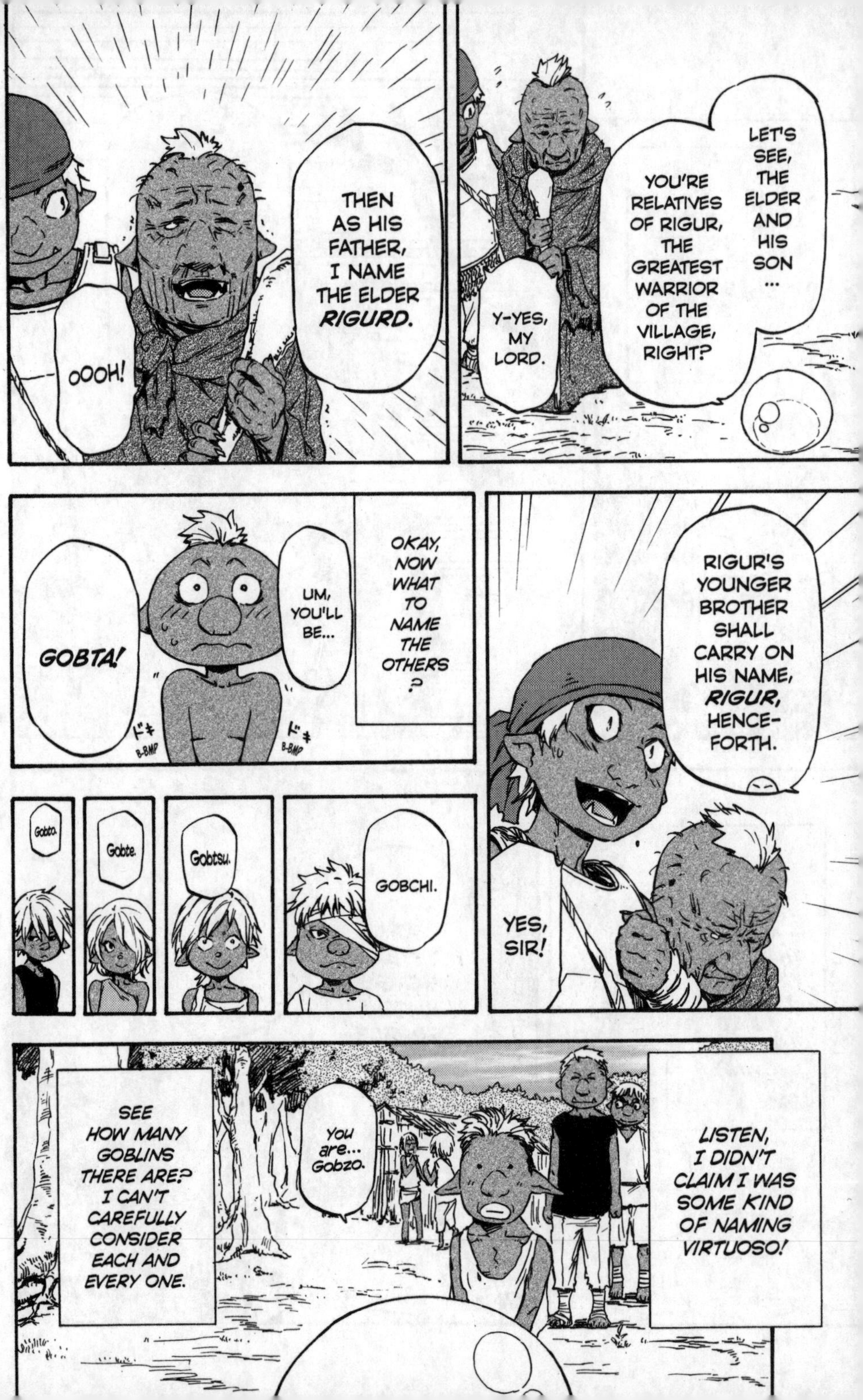
LET'S SEE, THE ELDER AND HIS SON ...
YOU'RE RELATIVES OF RIGUR, THE GREATEST WARRIOR OF THE VILLAGE, RIGHT?
Y-YES, MY LORD.
THEN AS HIS FATHER, I NAME THE ELDER *RIGURD*.
OOOH!
RIGUR'S YOUNGER BROTHER SHALL CARRY ON HIS NAME, *RIGUR*, HENCE-FORTH.
YES, SIR!
OKAY, NOW WHAT TO NAME THE OTHERS?
UM, YOU'LL BE...
GOBTA!
ドキ B-BMP
ドキ B-BMP
GOBCHI.
Gobtsu.
Gobte.
Gobto.
LISTEN, I DIDN'T CLAIM I WAS SOME KIND OF NAMING VIRTUOSO!
You are... Gobzo.
SEE HOW MANY GOBLINS THERE ARE? I CAN'T CAREFULLY CONSIDER EACH AND EVERY ONE.

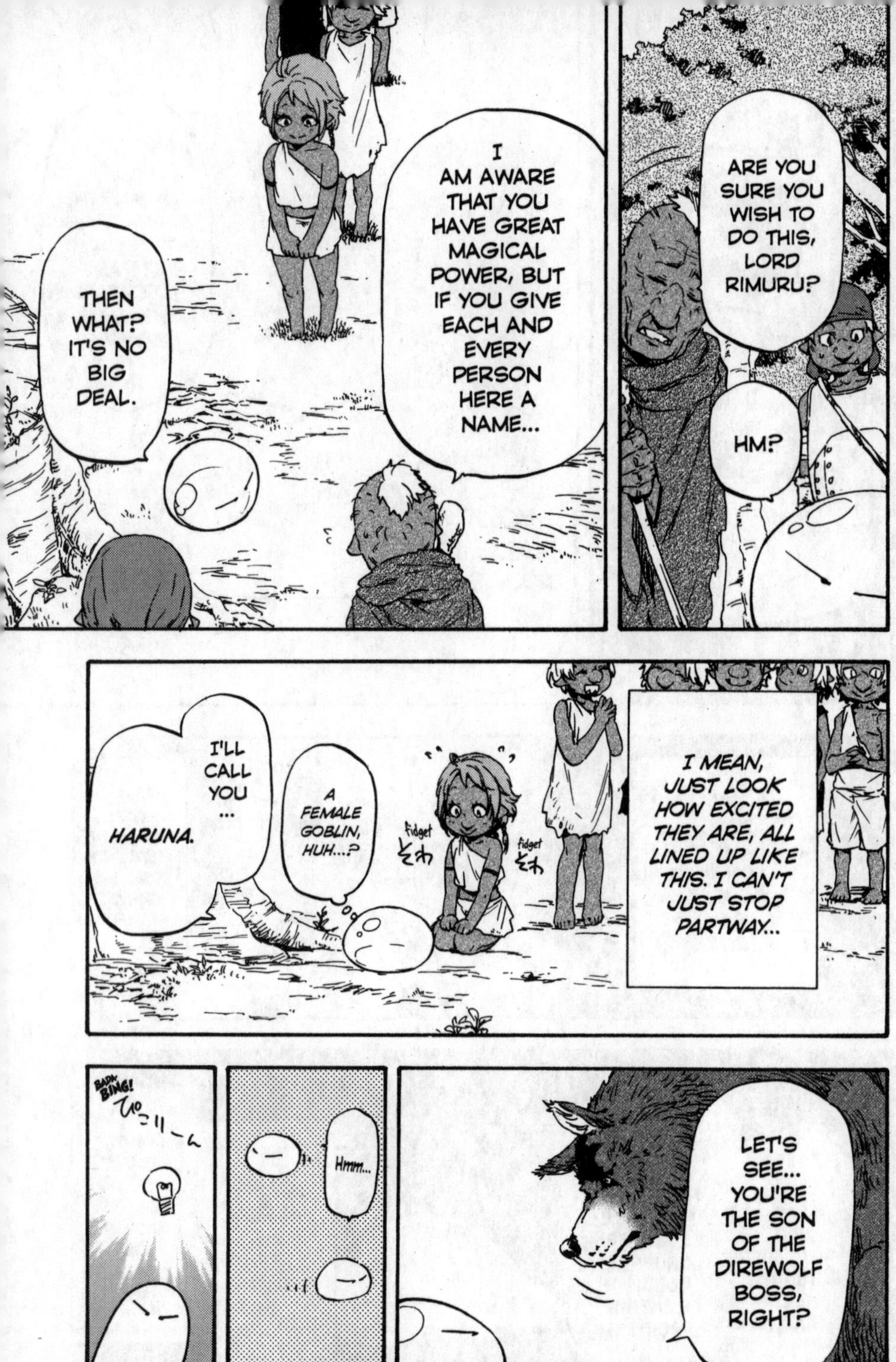
ARE YOU SURE YOU WISH TO DO THIS, LORD RIMURU?
HM?
I AM AWARE THAT YOU HAVE GREAT MAGICAL POWER, BUT IF YOU GIVE EACH AND EVERY PERSON HERE A NAME...
THEN WHAT? IT'S NO BIG DEAL.
I MEAN, JUST LOOK HOW EXCITED THEY ARE, ALL LINED UP LIKE THIS. I CAN'T JUST STOP PARTWAY...
fidget
そわ
fidget
そわ
A FEMALE GOBLIN, HUH...?
I'LL CALL YOU ... HARUNA.
LET'S SEE... YOU'RE THE SON OF THE DIREWOLF BOSS, RIGHT?
Hmm...
BADA-BING!

Now Loading

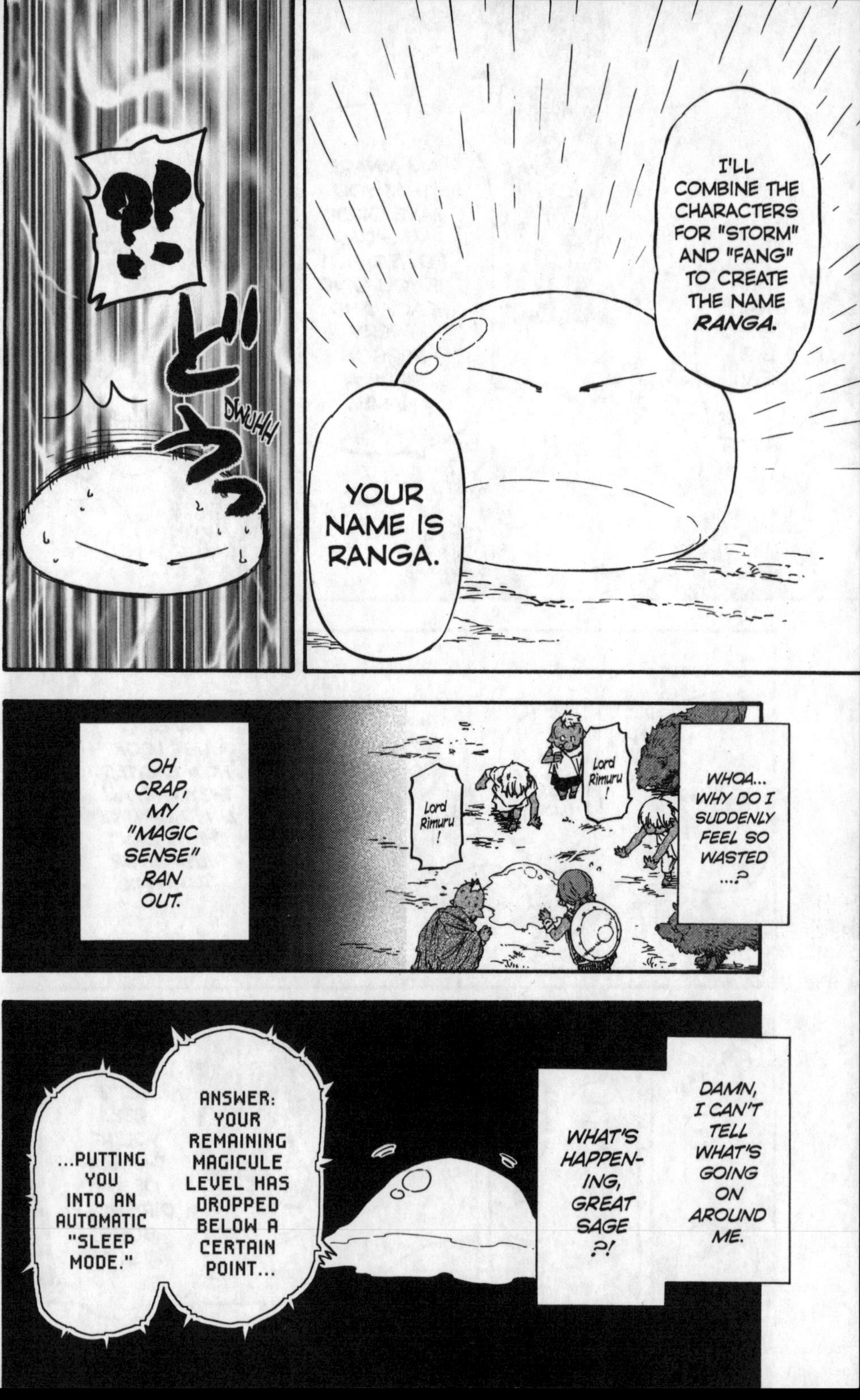

I'LL COMBINE THE CHARACTERS FOR "STORM" AND "FANG" TO CREATE THE NAME *RANGA.*
YOUR NAME IS RANGA.
?!
DWUHH
WHOA... WHY DO I SUDDENLY FEEL SO WASTED ...?
Lord Rimuru!
Lord Rimuru!
OH CRAP, MY "MAGIC SENSE" RAN OUT.
DAMN, I CAN'T TELL WHAT'S GOING ON AROUND ME.
WHAT'S HAPPEN-ING, GREAT SAGE?!
ANSWER: YOUR REMAINING MAGICULE LEVEL HAS DROPPED BELOW A CERTAIN POINT...
...PUTTING YOU INTO AN AUTOMATIC "SLEEP MODE."

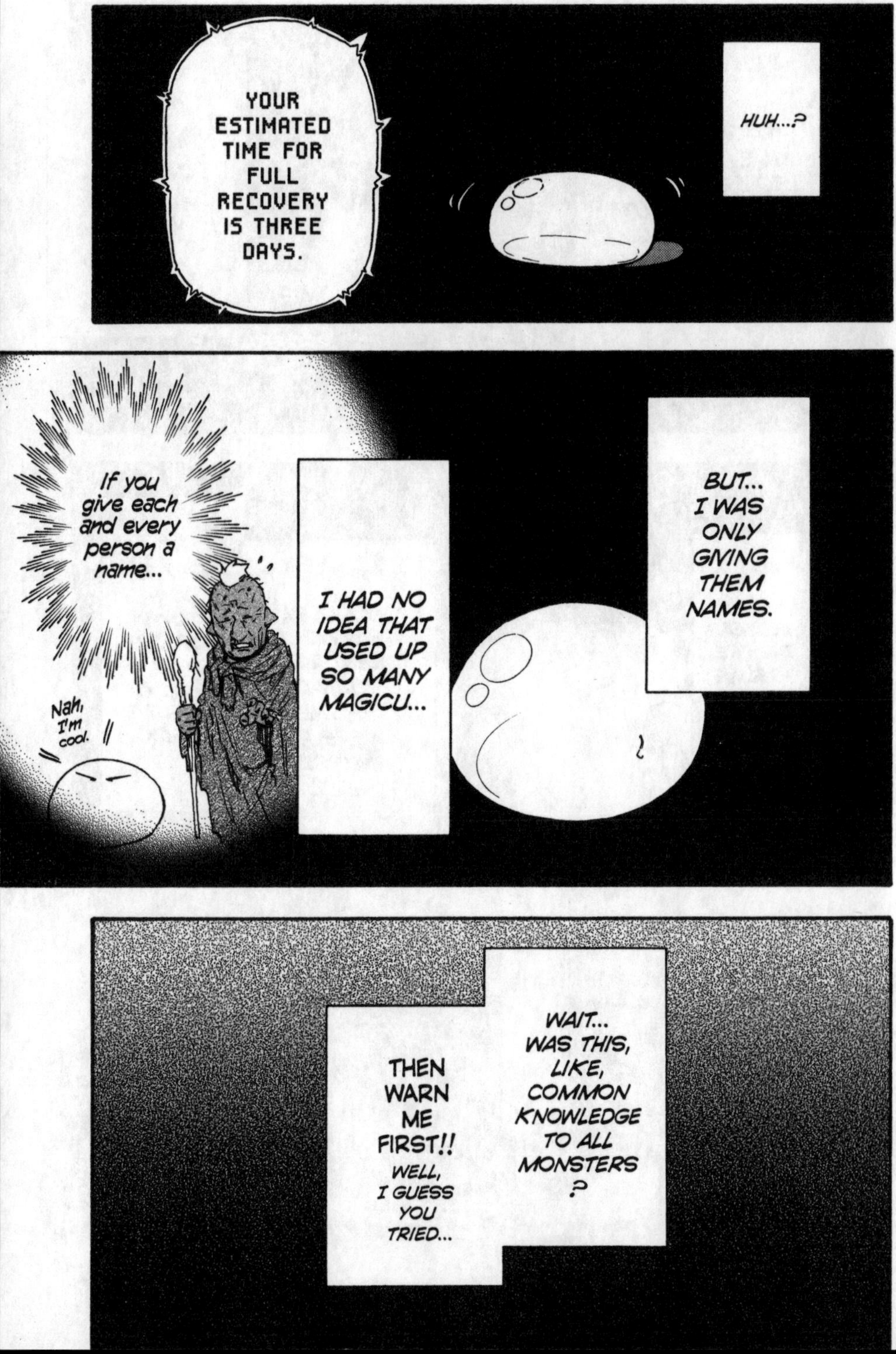
HUH...?
YOUR ESTIMATED TIME FOR FULL RECOVERY IS THREE DAYS.
BUT... I WAS ONLY GIVING THEM NAMES.
I HAD NO IDEA THAT USED UP SO MANY MAGICU...
If you give each and every person a name...
Nah, I'm cool.
WAIT... WAS THIS, LIKE, COMMON KNOWLEDGE TO ALL MONSTERS?
THEN WARN ME FIRST!!
WELL, I GUESS YOU TRIED...

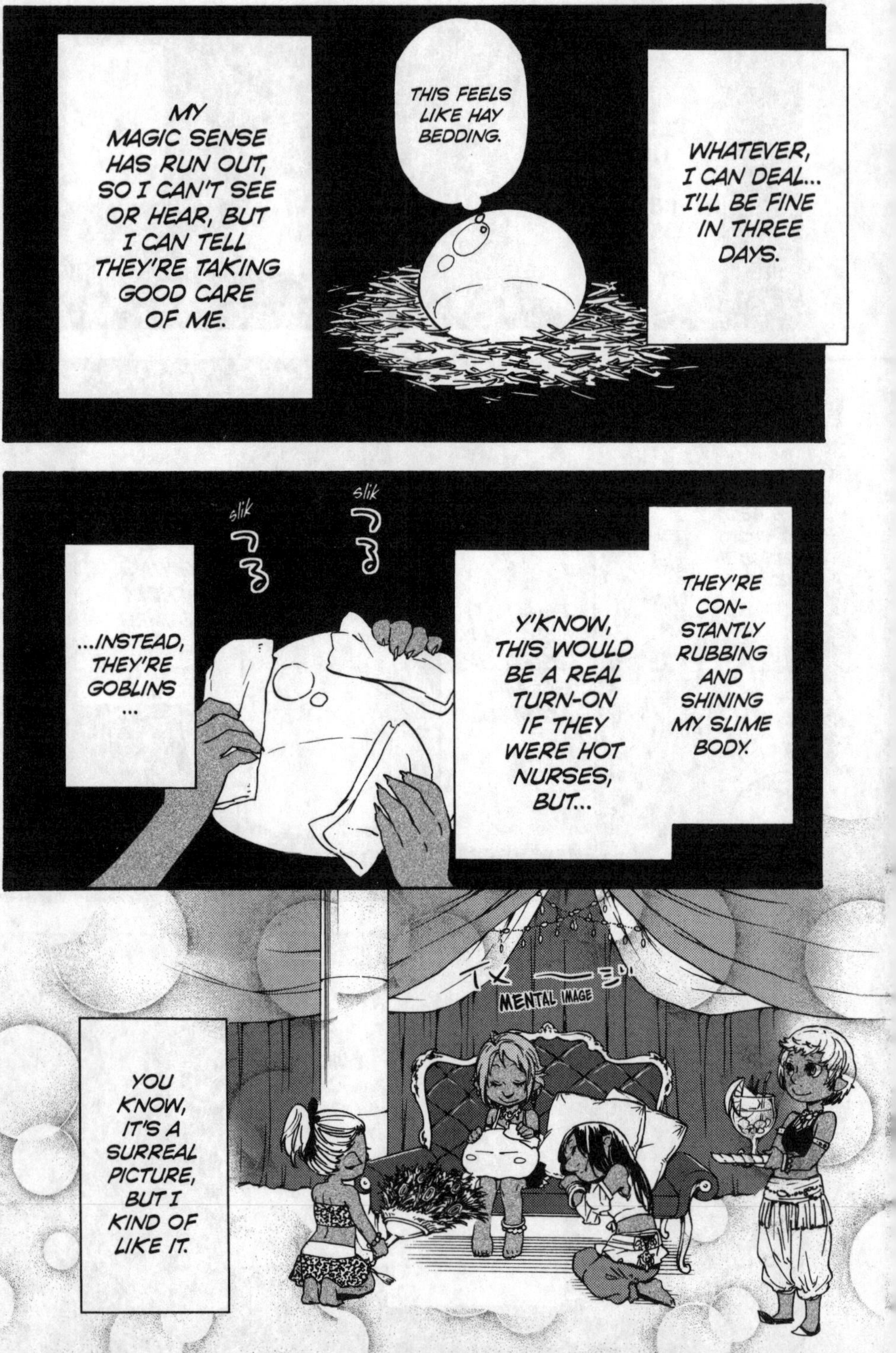
WHATEVER, I CAN DEAL... I'LL BE FINE IN THREE DAYS.
THIS FEELS LIKE HAY BEDDING.
MY MAGIC SENSE HAS RUN OUT, SO I CAN'T SEE OR HEAR, BUT I CAN TELL THEY'RE TAKING GOOD CARE OF ME.
THEY'RE CON-STANTLY RUBBING AND SHINING MY SLIME BODY.
Y'KNOW, THIS WOULD BE A REAL TURN-ON IF THEY WERE HOT NURSES, BUT...
slik
slik
...INSTEAD, THEY'RE GOBLINS ...
MENTAL IMAGE
YOU KNOW, IT'S A SURREAL PICTURE, BUT I KIND OF LIKE IT.

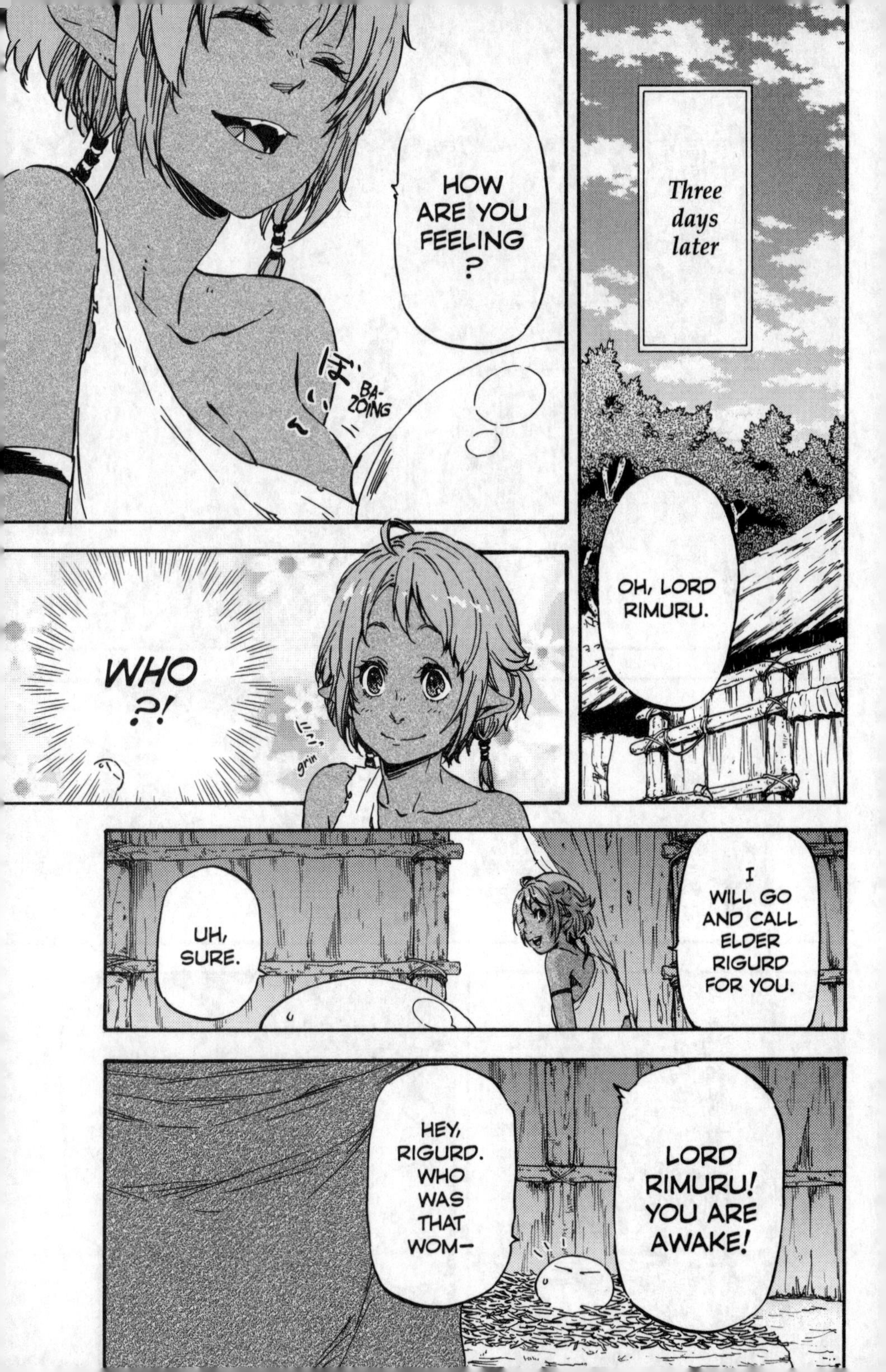
Three days later
OH, LORD RIMURU.
HOW ARE YOU FEELING?
BA-ZOING
WHO?!
grin
I WILL GO AND CALL ELDER RIGURD FOR YOU.
UH, SURE.
LORD RIMURU! YOU ARE AWAKE!
HEY, RIGURD. WHO WAS THAT WOM—

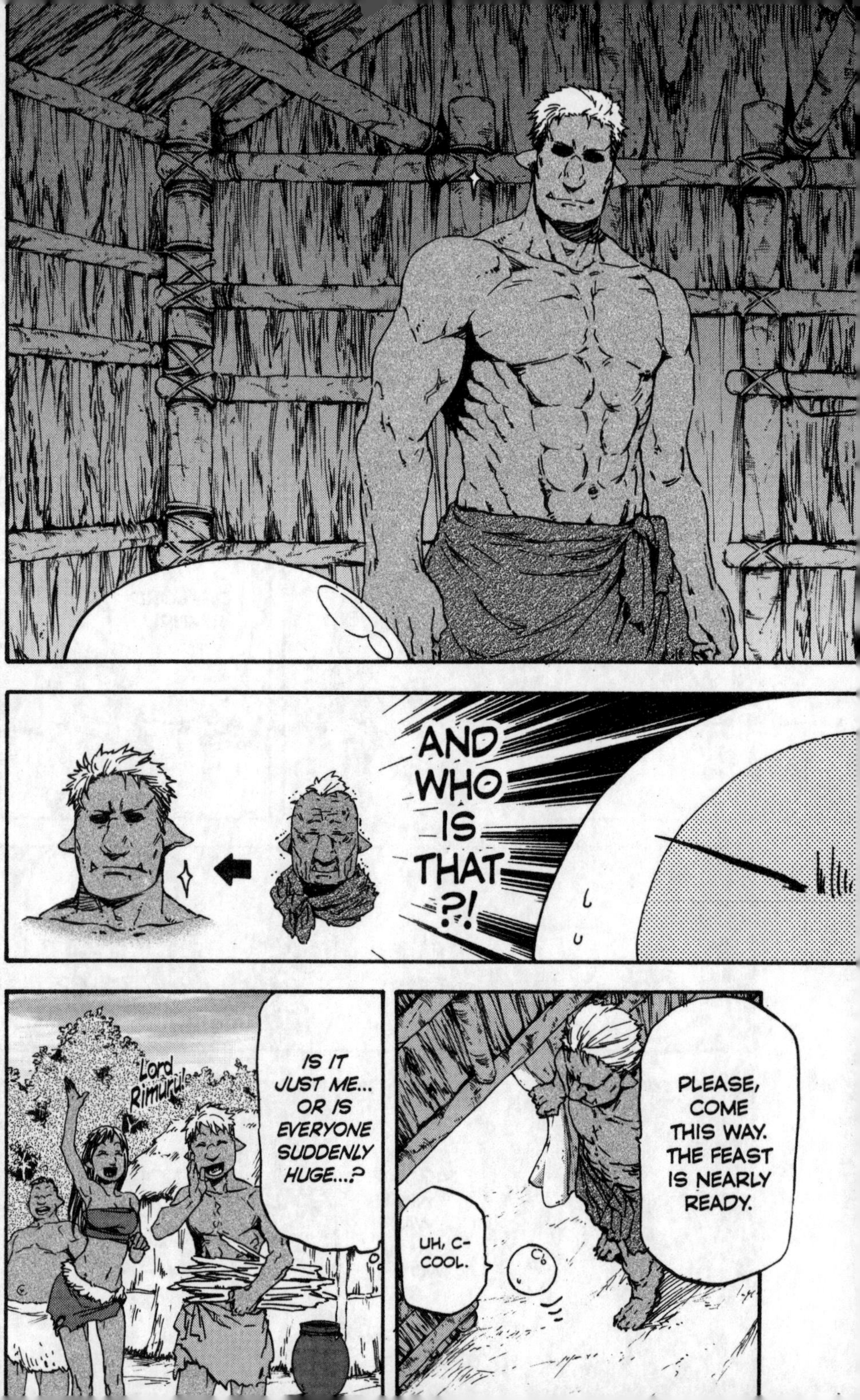
AND WHO IS THAT?!
PLEASE, COME THIS WAY. THE FEAST IS NEARLY READY.
UH, C-COOL.
IS IT JUST ME... OR IS EVERYONE SUDDENLY HUGE...?
Lord Rimuru!

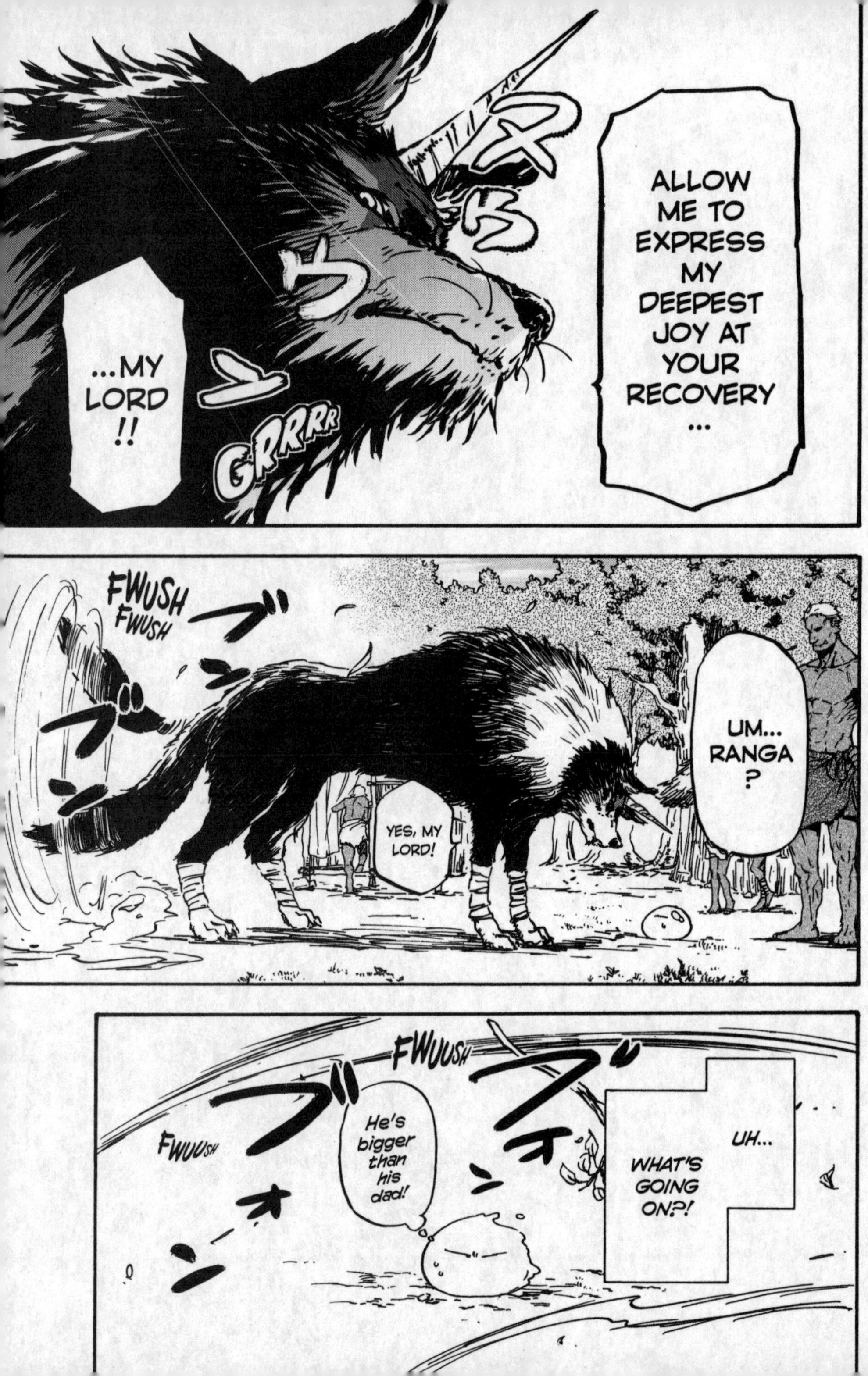
ALLOW ME TO EXPRESS MY DEEPEST JOY AT YOUR RECOVERY ...
...MY LORD !!
GRRRR
UM... RANGA ?
YES, MY LORD!
FWUSH FWUSH
UH... WHAT'S GOING ON?!
FWUUSH
He's bigger than his dad!
FWUUSH

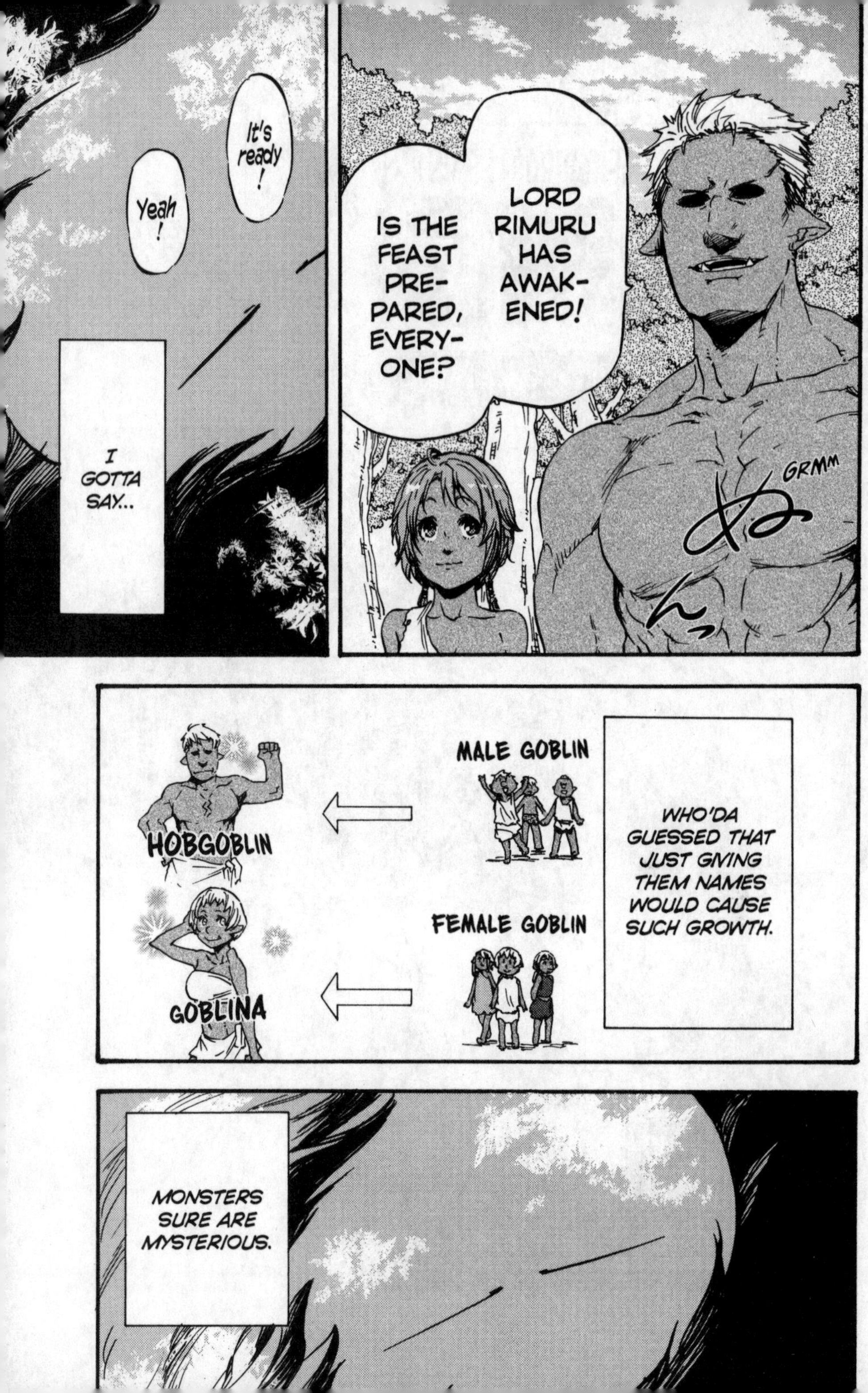
LORD RIMURU HAS AWAKENED!
IS THE FEAST PREPARED, EVERYONE?
GRMM
It's ready!
Yeah!
I GOTTA SAY...
WHO'DA GUESSED THAT JUST GIVING THEM NAMES WOULD CAUSE SUCH GROWTH.
MALE GOBLIN
HOBGOBLIN
FEMALE GOBLIN
GOBLINA
MONSTERS SURE ARE MYSTERIOUS.

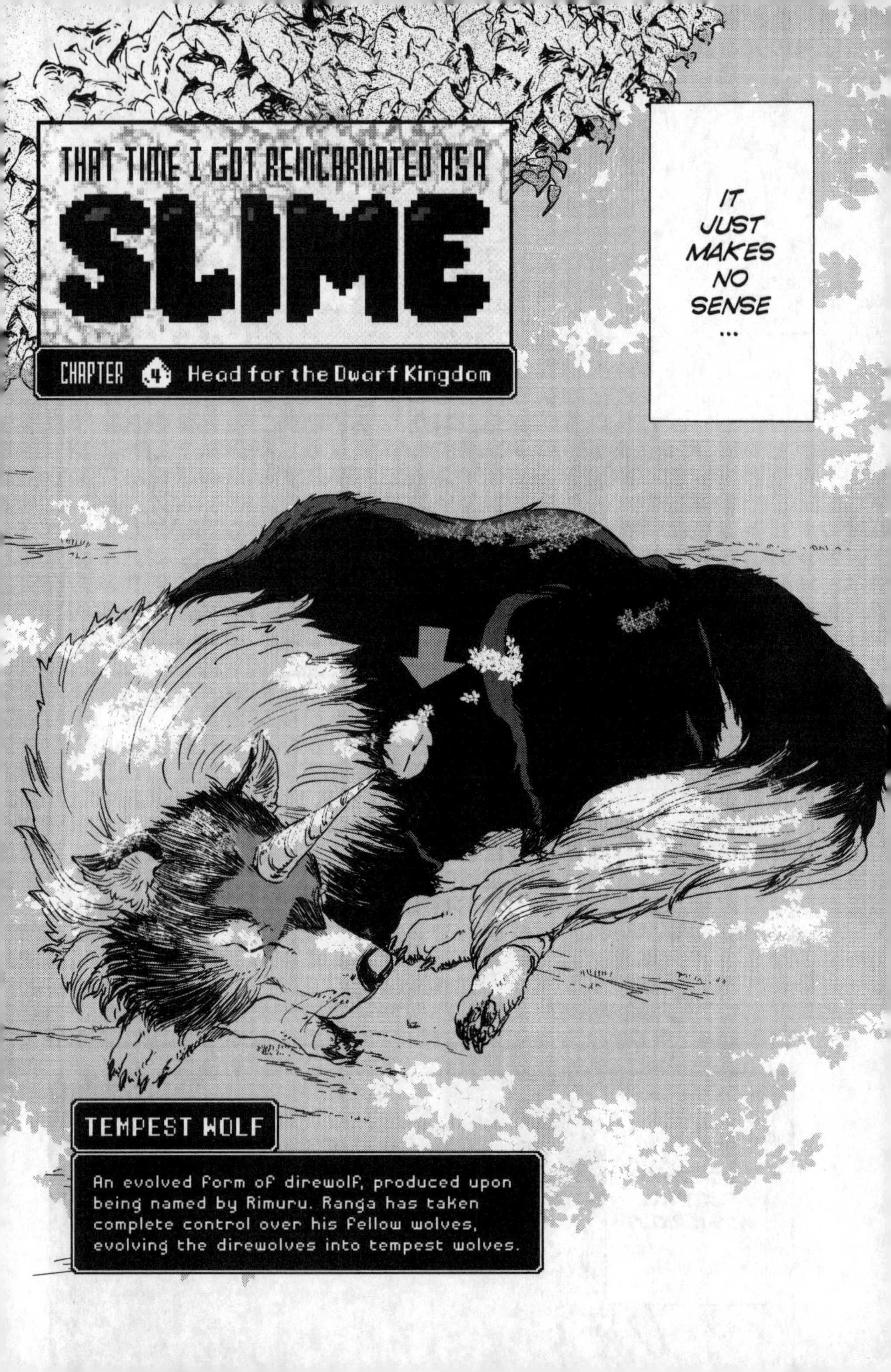
IT JUST MAKES NO SENSE ...
THAT TIME I GOT REINCARNATED AS A
SLIME
CHAPTER 4 Head for the Dwarf Kingdom
TEMPEST WOLF
An evolved form of direwolf, produced upon being named by Rimuru. Ranga has taken complete control over his fellow wolves, evolving the direwolves into tempest wolves.

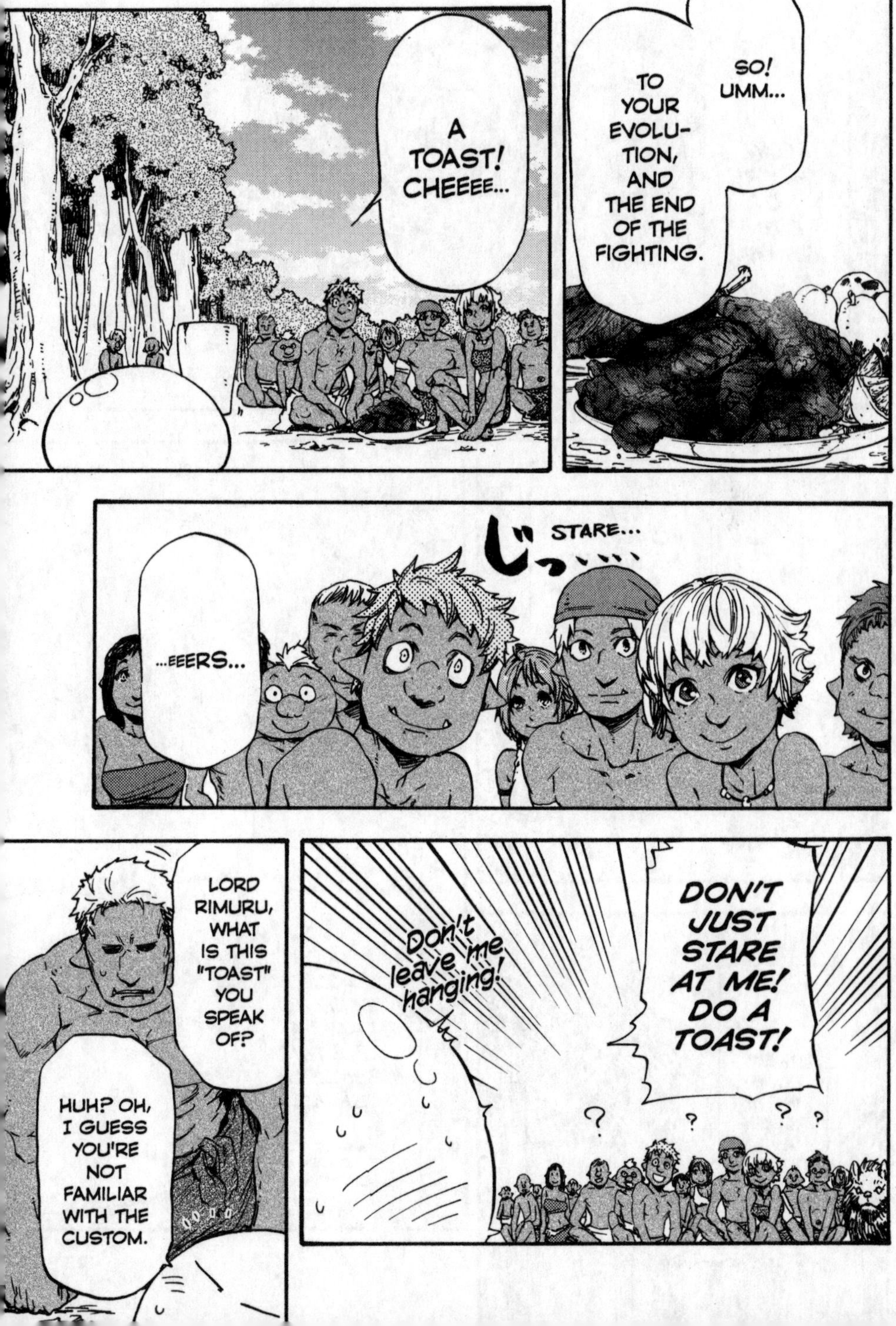
SO! UMM...
TO YOUR EVOLUTION, AND THE END OF THE FIGHTING.
A TOAST! CHEEEEE...
じーっ
STARE...
...EEERS...
DON'T JUST STARE AT ME! DO A TOAST!
Don't leave me hanging!
LORD RIMURU, WHAT IS THIS "TOAST" YOU SPEAK OF?
HUH? OH, I GUESS YOU'RE NOT FAMILIAR WITH THE CUSTOM.

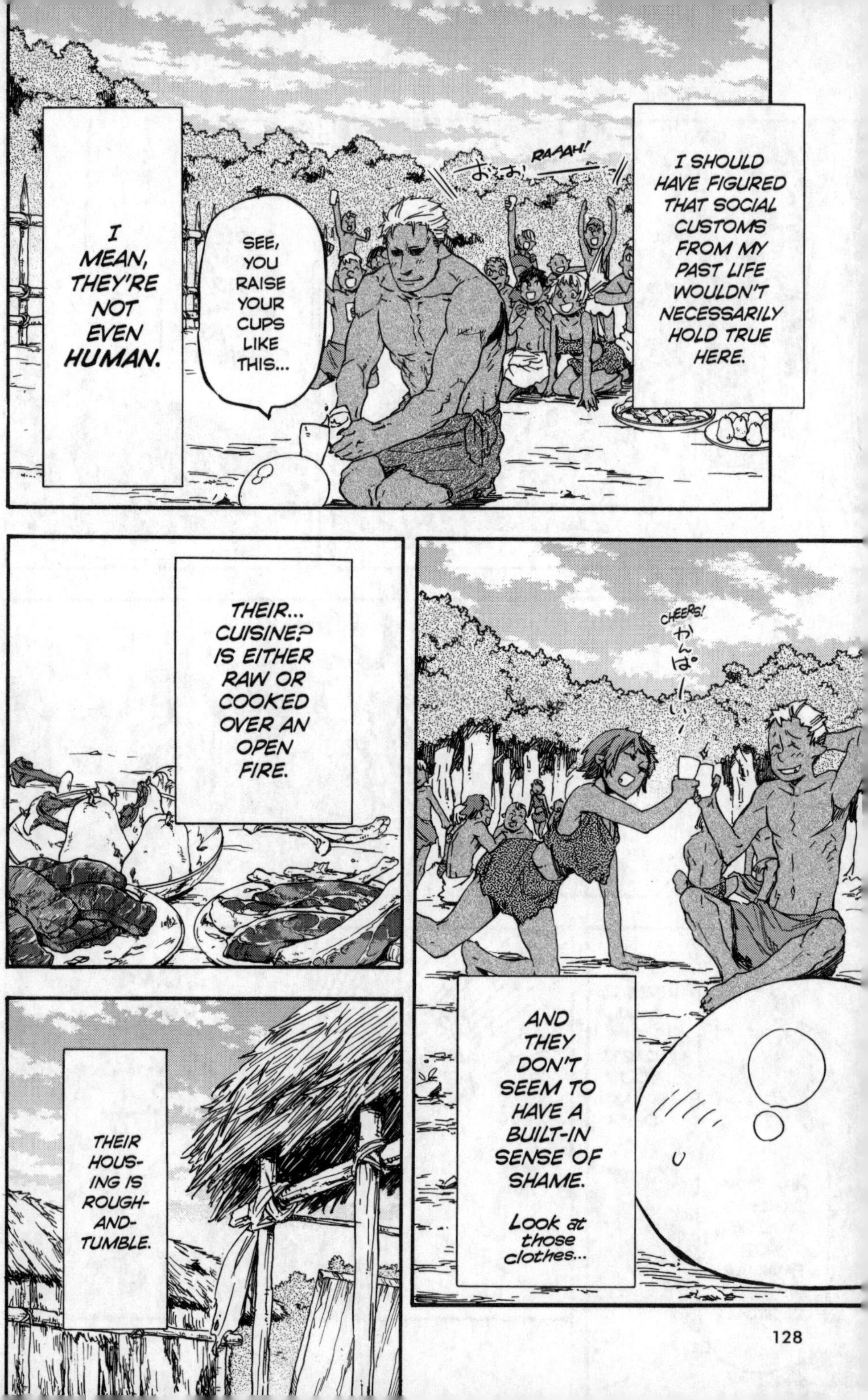
I SHOULD HAVE FIGURED THAT SOCIAL CUSTOMS FROM MY PAST LIFE WOULDN'T NECESSARILY HOLD TRUE HERE.
RAAAH!
SEE, YOU RAISE YOUR CUPS LIKE THIS...
I MEAN, THEY'RE NOT EVEN HUMAN.
CHEERS!
かんぱーい!
AND THEY DON'T SEEM TO HAVE A BUILT-IN SENSE OF SHAME.
Look at those clothes...
THEIR... CUISINE? IS EITHER RAW OR COOKED OVER AN OPEN FIRE.
THEIR HOUSING IS ROUGH-AND-TUMBLE.

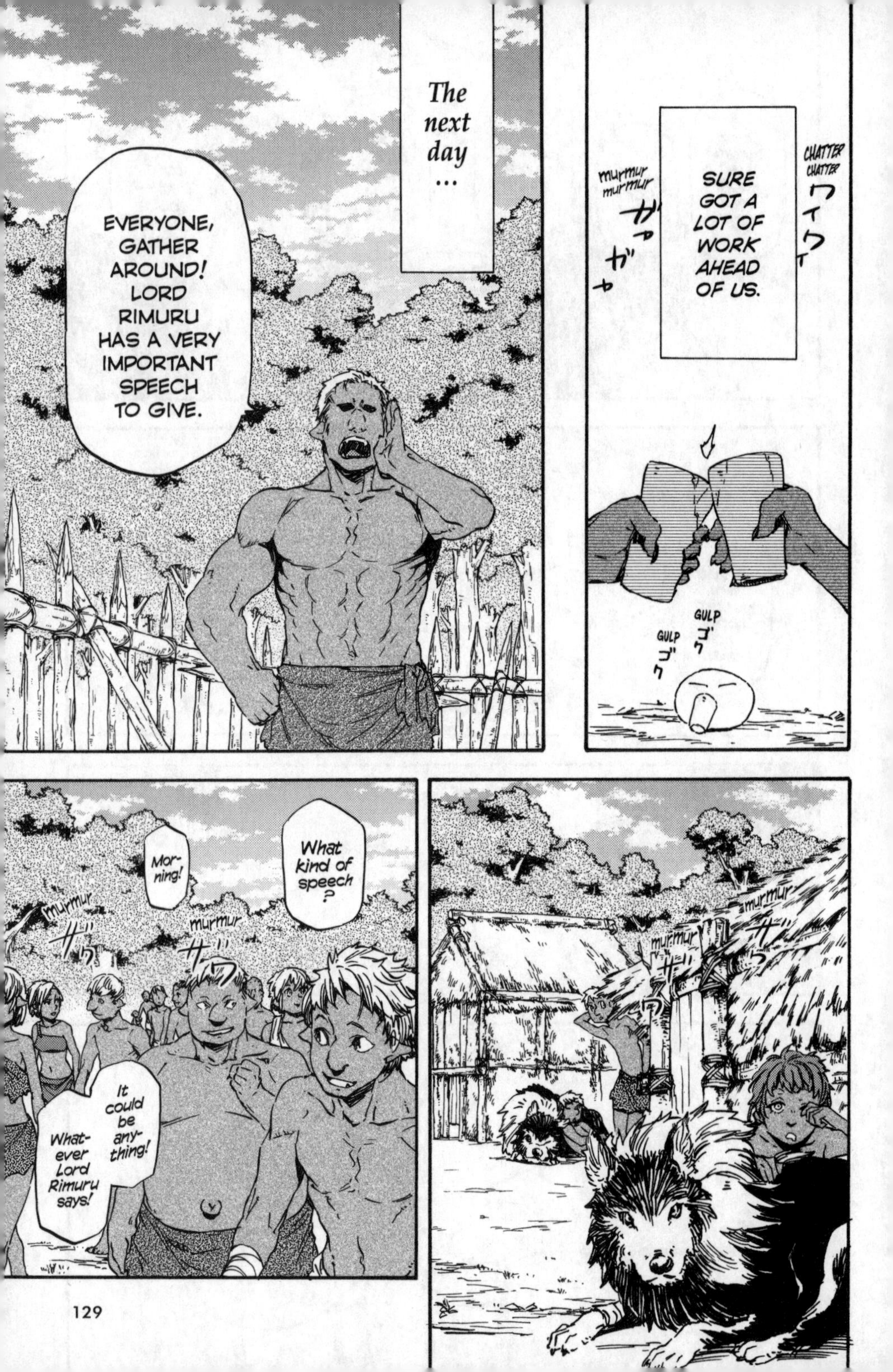
CHATTER CHATTER
murmur murmur
SURE GOT A LOT OF WORK AHEAD OF US.
GULP GULP
The next day ...
EVERYONE, GATHER AROUND! LORD RIMURU HAS A VERY IMPORTANT SPEECH TO GIVE.
murmur
murmur
What kind of speech?
Mor-ning!
murmur
murmur
It could be any-thing!
What-ever Lord Rimuru says!

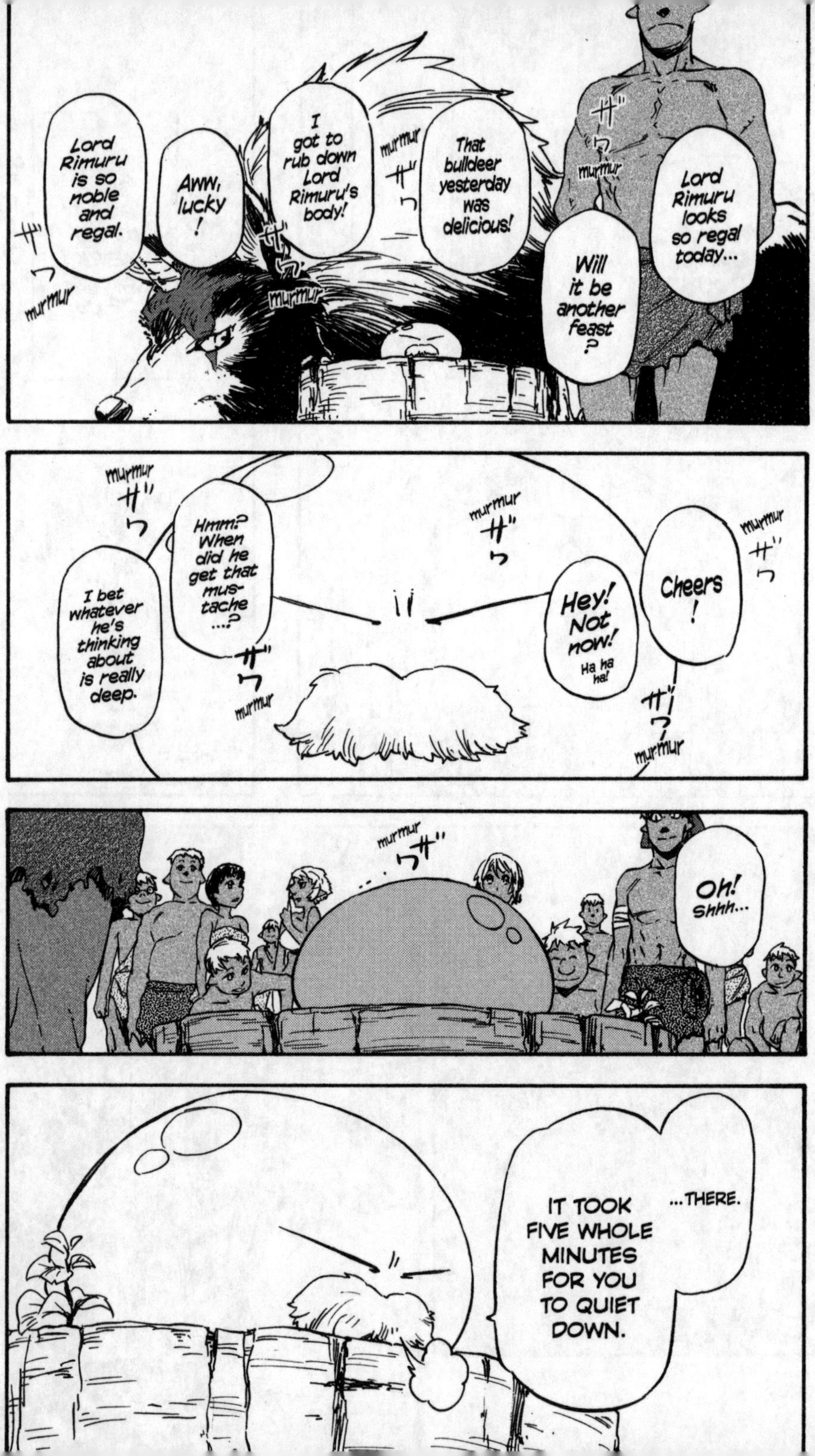
Lord Rimuru looks so regal today...
murmur
Will it be another feast?
That bulldeer yesterday was delicious!
murmur
I got to rub down Lord Rimuru's body!
murmur
Aww, lucky!
Lord Rimuru is so noble and regal.
murmur
murmur
Cheers!
murmur
Hey! Not now!
Ha ha ha!
murmur
murmur
Hmm? When did he get that mus-tache...?
murmur
I bet whatever he's thinking about is really deep.
Oh! Shhh...
murmur
...There.
It took five whole minutes for you to quiet down.

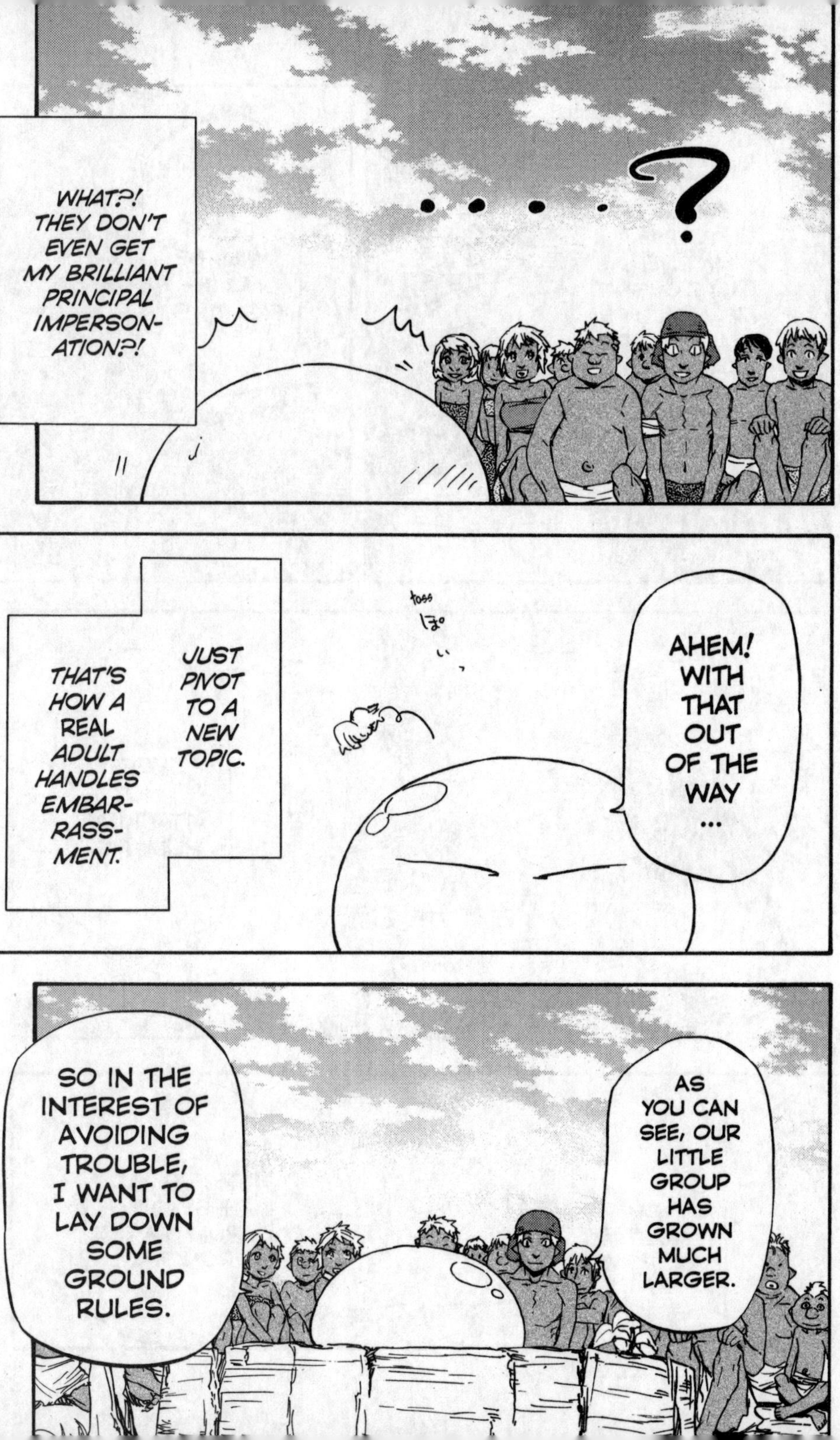
...?
WHAT?! THEY DON'T EVEN GET MY BRILLIANT PRINCIPAL IMPERSONATION?!
AHEM! WITH THAT OUT OF THE WAY...
toss
ぽ
JUST PIVOT TO A NEW TOPIC.
THAT'S HOW A REAL ADULT HANDLES EMBARRASSMENT.
AS YOU CAN SEE, OUR LITTLE GROUP HAS GROWN MUCH LARGER.
SO IN THE INTEREST OF AVOIDING TROUBLE, I WANT TO LAY DOWN SOME GROUND RULES.

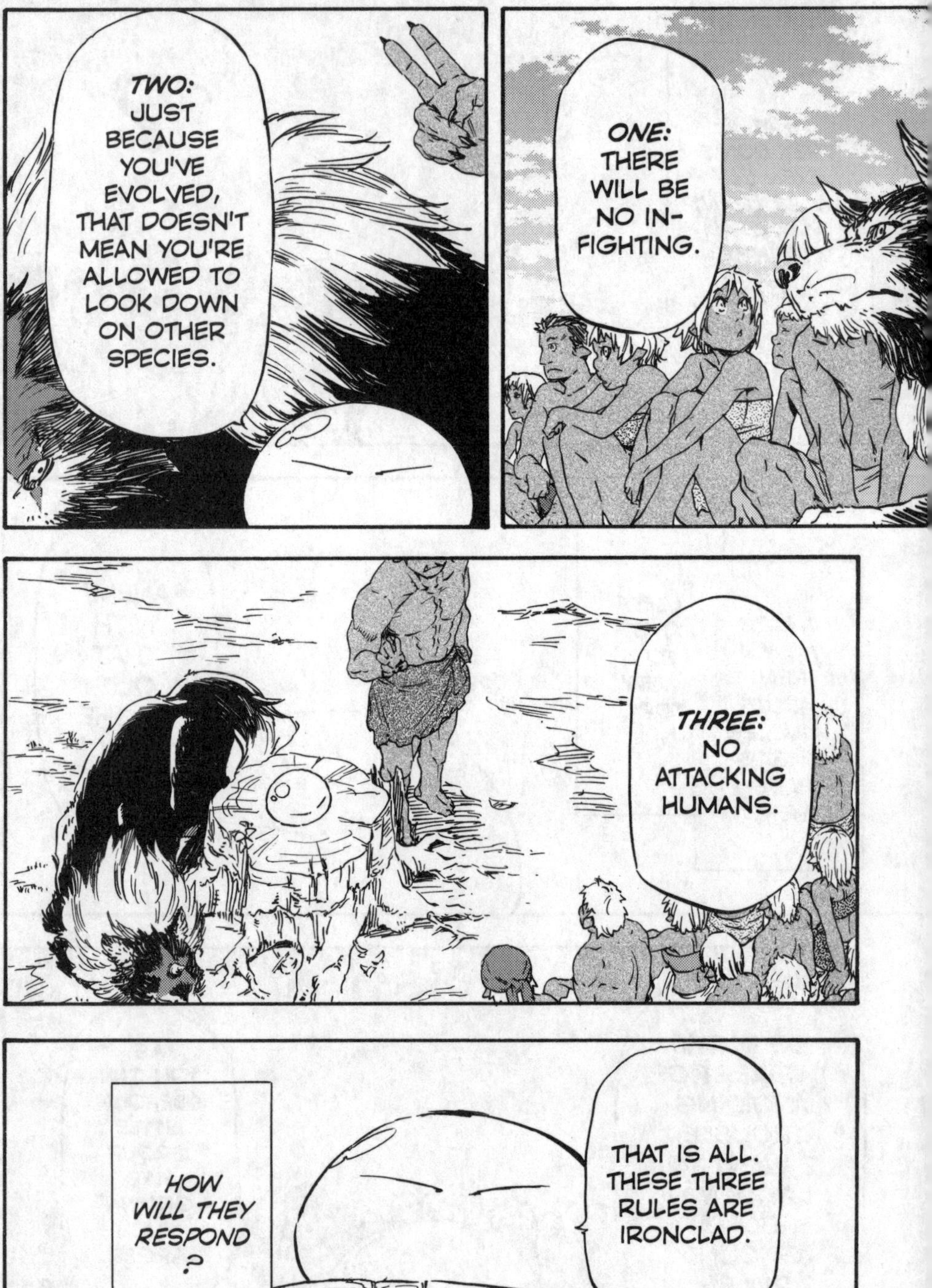
ONE: THERE WILL BE NO IN-FIGHTING.
TWO: JUST BECAUSE YOU'VE EVOLVED, THAT DOESN'T MEAN YOU'RE ALLOWED TO LOOK DOWN ON OTHER SPECIES.
THREE: NO ATTACKING HUMANS.
THAT IS ALL. THESE THREE RULES ARE IRONCLAD.
HOW WILL THEY RESPOND?

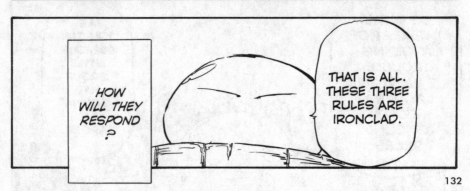

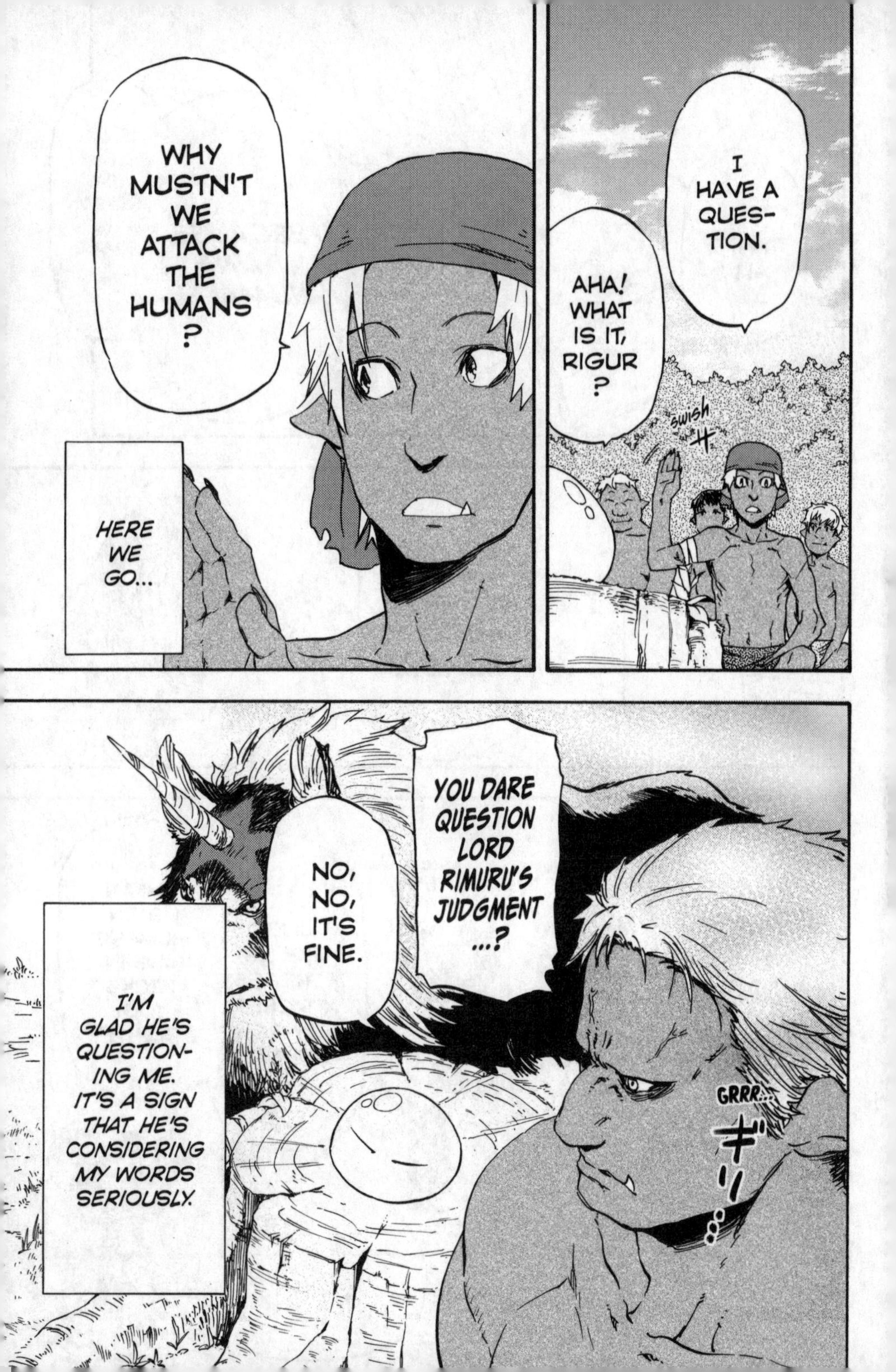

I HAVE A QUESTION.
AHA! WHAT IS IT, RIGUR?
swish
WHY MUSTN'T WE ATTACK THE HUMANS?
HERE WE GO...
YOU DARE QUESTION LORD RIMURU'S JUDGMENT ...?
NO, NO, IT'S FINE.
GRRR...
ギリ…
I'M GLAD HE'S QUESTIONING ME. IT'S A SIGN THAT HE'S CONSIDERING MY WORDS SERIOUSLY.

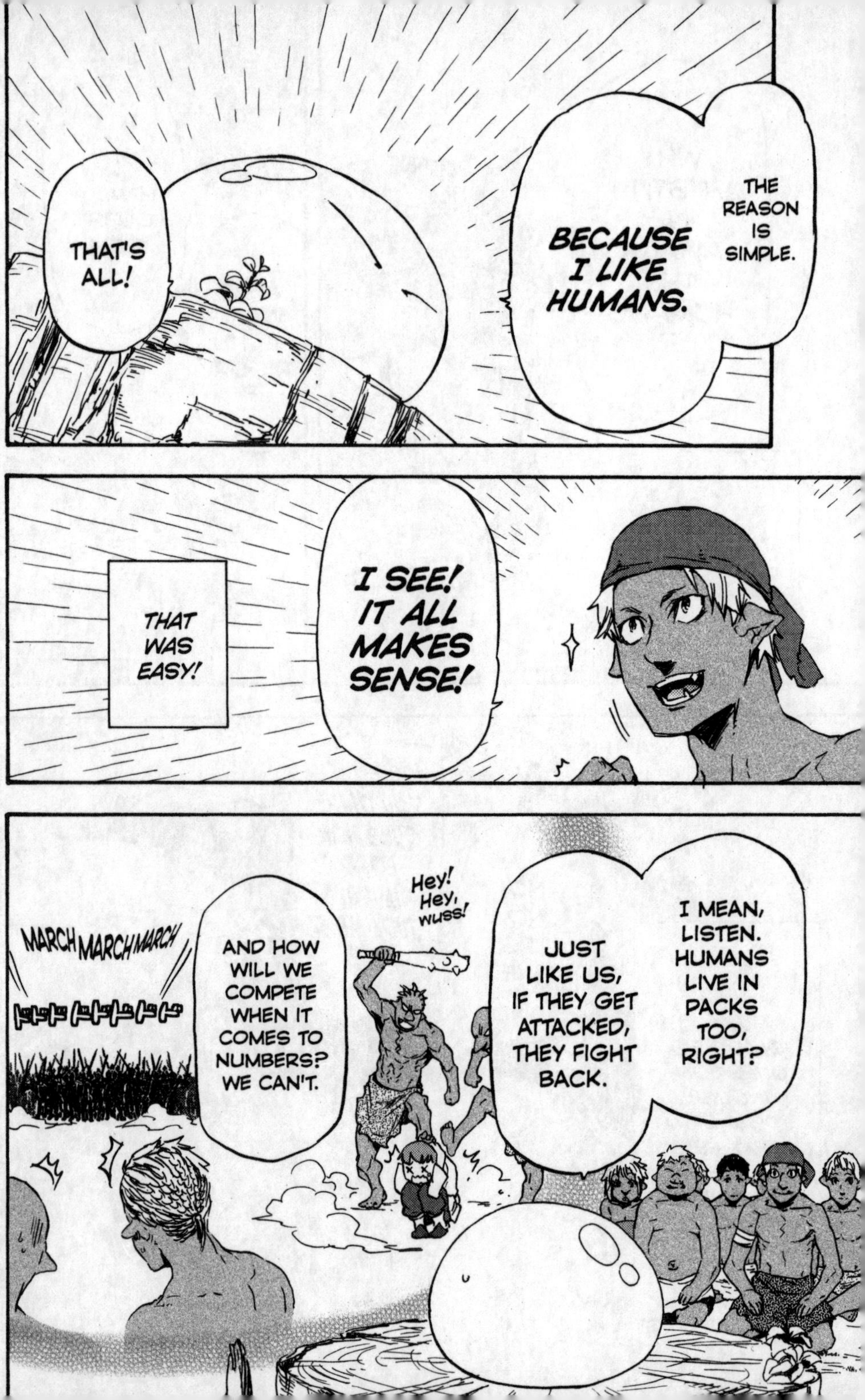
THE REASON IS SIMPLE.
BECAUSE I LIKE HUMANS.
THAT'S ALL!
I SEE! IT ALL MAKES SENSE!
THAT WAS EASY!
I MEAN, LISTEN. HUMANS LIVE IN PACKS TOO, RIGHT?
JUST LIKE US, IF THEY GET ATTACKED, THEY FIGHT BACK.
Hey! Hey, wuss!
AND HOW WILL WE COMPETE WHEN IT COMES TO NUMBERS? WE CAN'T.
MARCH MARCH MARCH

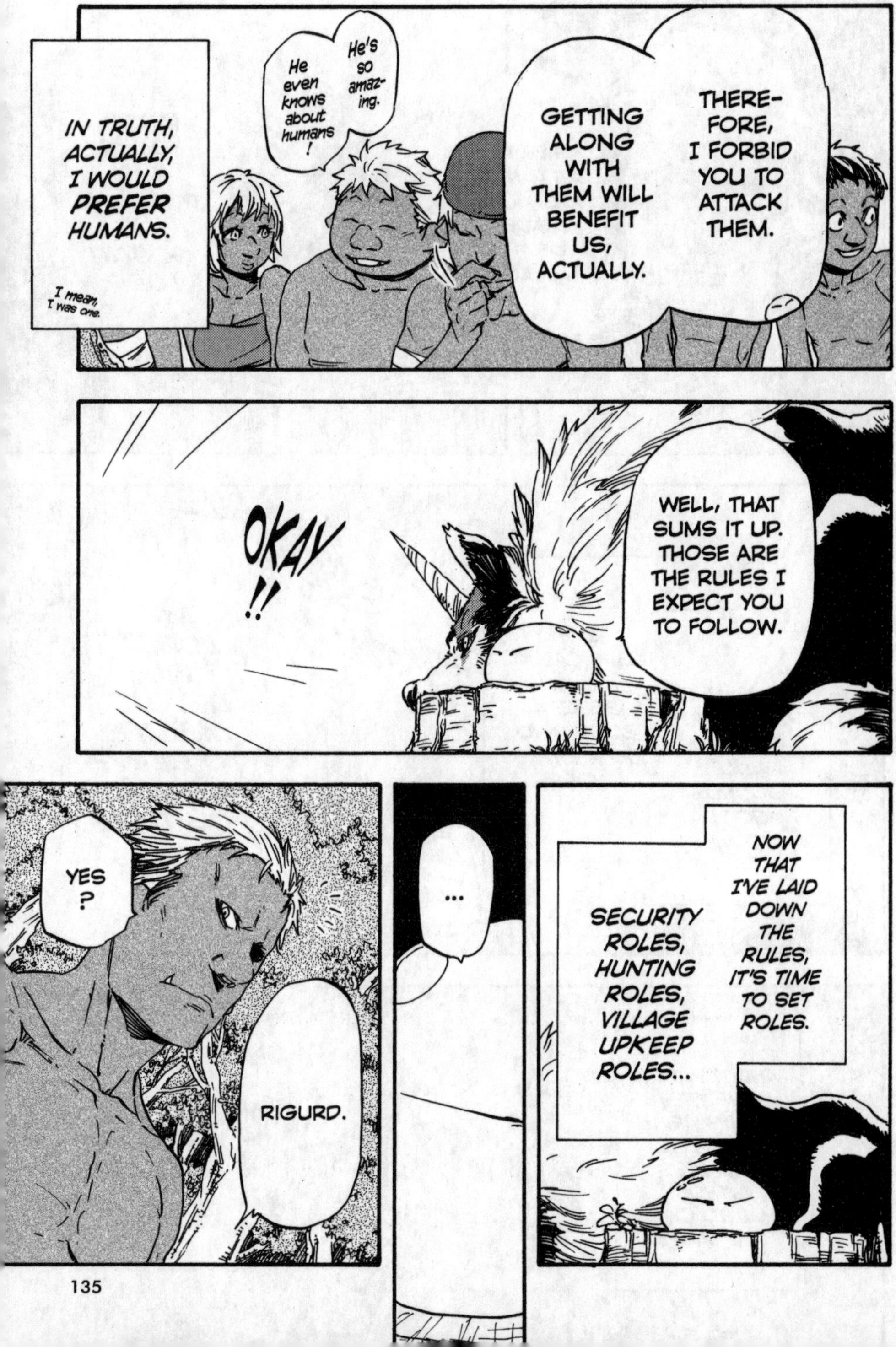

GETTING ALONG WITH THEM WILL BENEFIT US, ACTUALLY.
THEREFORE, I FORBID YOU TO ATTACK THEM.
He's so amazing.
He even knows about humans!
IN TRUTH, ACTUALLY, I WOULD PREFER HUMANS.
I mean, I was one.
WELL, THAT SUMS IT UP. THOSE ARE THE RULES I EXPECT YOU TO FOLLOW.
OKAY!!
NOW THAT I'VE LAID DOWN THE RULES, IT'S TIME TO SET ROLES.
SECURITY ROLES, HUNTING ROLES, VILLAGE UPKEEP ROLES...
...
RIGURD.
YES?

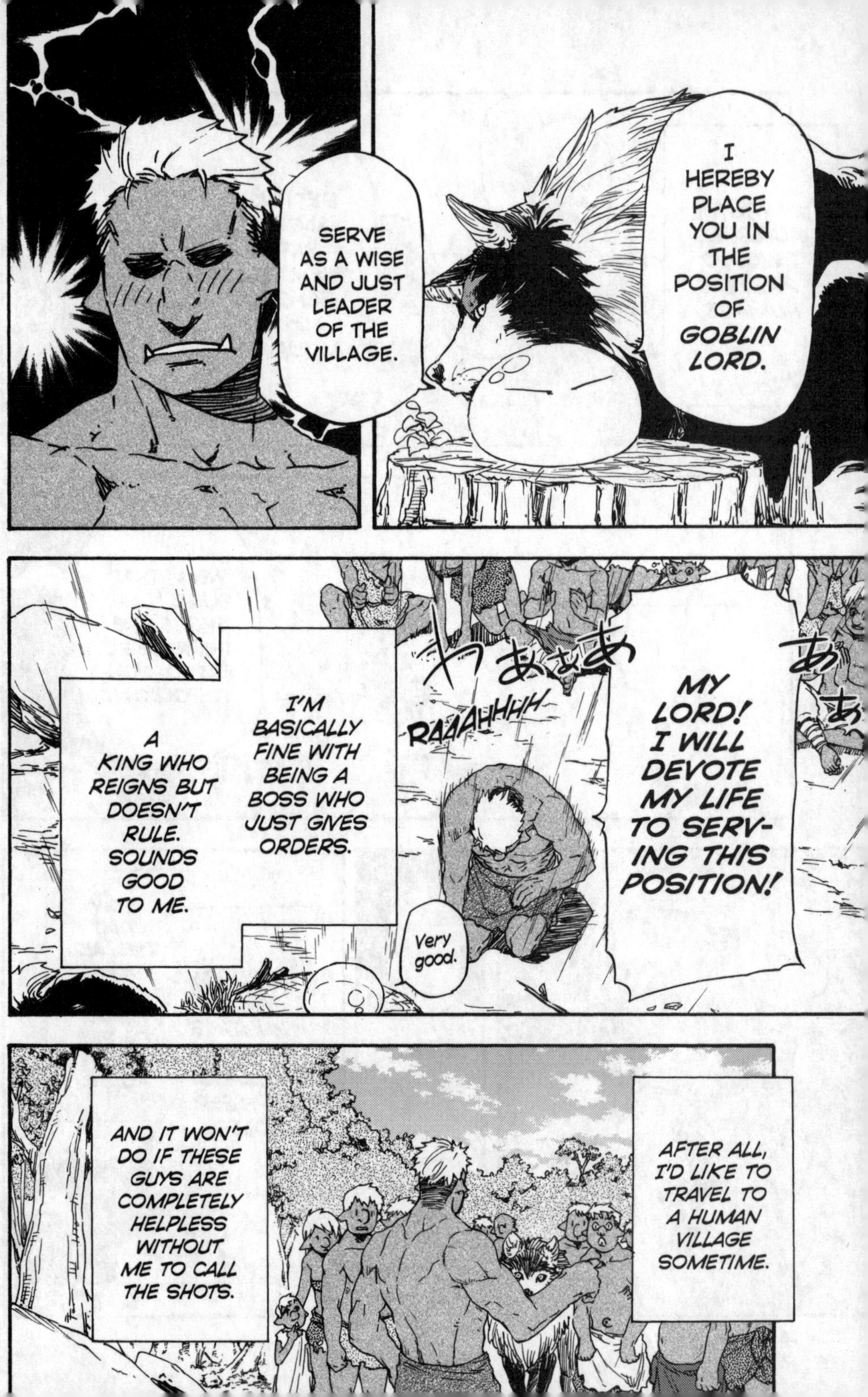
I HEREBY PLACE YOU IN THE POSITION OF GOBLIN LORD.
SERVE AS A WISE AND JUST LEADER OF THE VILLAGE.
MY LORD! I WILL DEVOTE MY LIFE TO SERVING THIS POSITION!
RAAAHHHH
Very good.
I'M BASICALLY FINE WITH BEING A BOSS WHO JUST GIVES ORDERS.
A KING WHO REIGNS BUT DOESN'T RULE. SOUNDS GOOD TO ME.
AFTER ALL, I'D LIKE TO TRAVEL TO A HUMAN VILLAGE SOMETIME.
AND IT WON'T DO IF THESE GUYS ARE COMPLETELY HELPLESS WITHOUT ME TO CALL THE SHOTS.

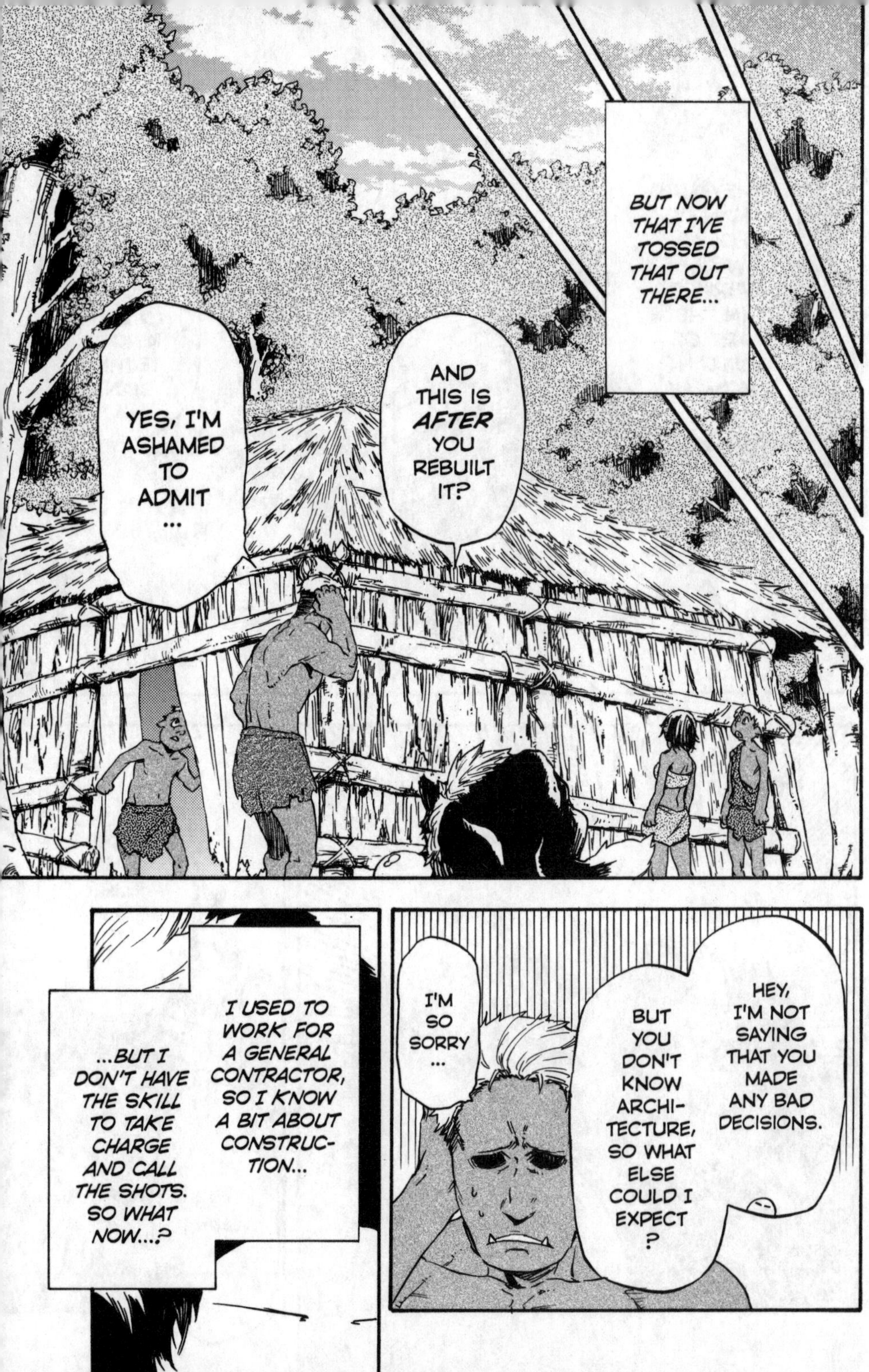
BUT NOW THAT I'VE TOSSED THAT OUT THERE...
AND THIS IS *AFTER* YOU REBUILT IT?
YES, I'M ASHAMED TO ADMIT...
HEY, I'M NOT SAYING THAT YOU MADE ANY BAD DECISIONS.
BUT YOU DON'T KNOW ARCHI-TECTURE, SO WHAT ELSE COULD I EXPECT?
I'M SO SORRY...
I USED TO WORK FOR A GENERAL CONTRACTOR, SO I KNOW A BIT ABOUT CONSTRUC-TION...
...BUT I DON'T HAVE THE SKILL TO TAKE CHARGE AND CALL THE SHOTS. SO WHAT NOW...?

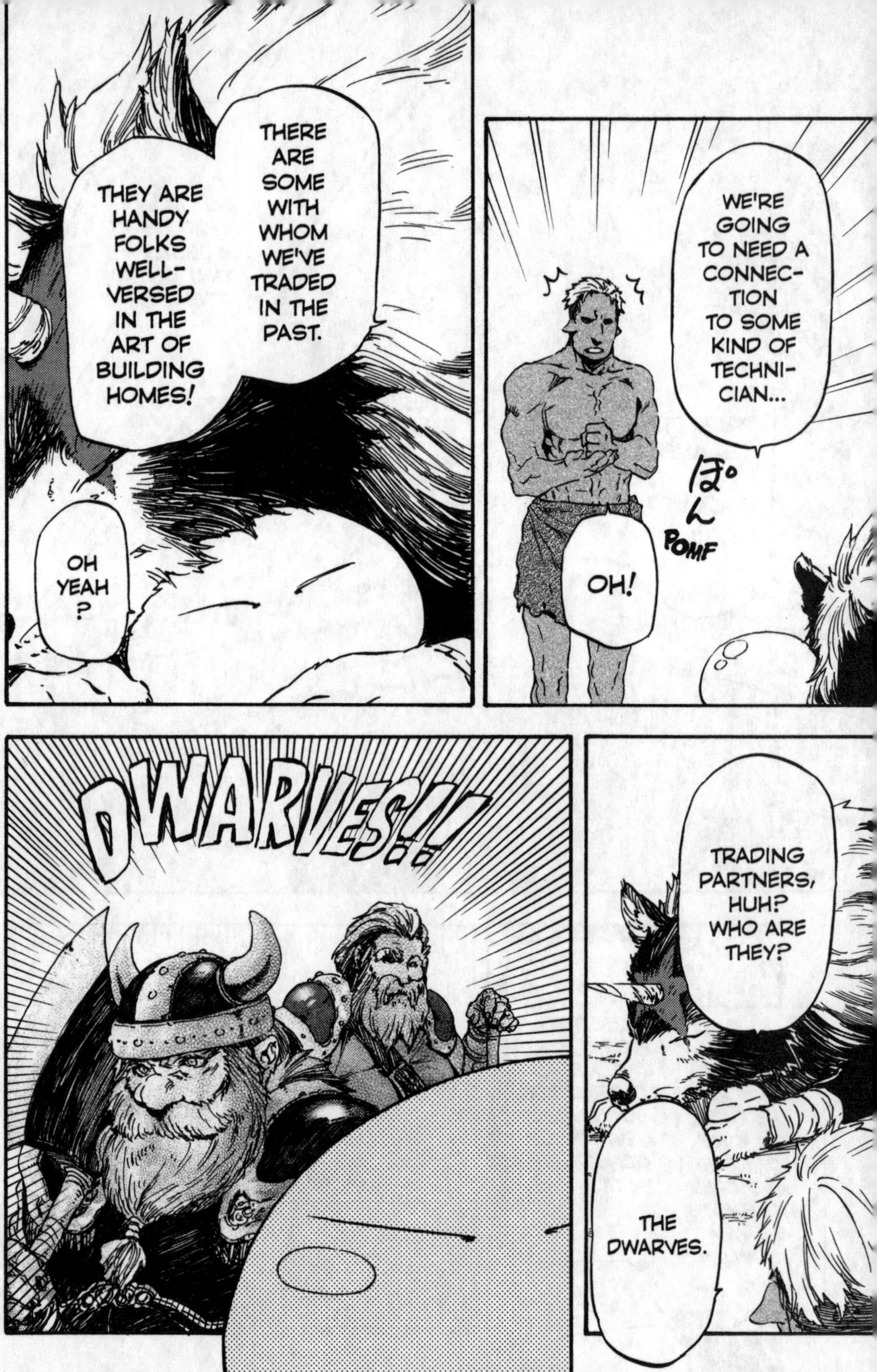
WE'RE GOING TO NEED A CONNECTION TO SOME KIND OF TECHNICIAN...
ぽん
POMF
OH!
THERE ARE SOME WITH WHOM WE'VE TRADED IN THE PAST.
THEY ARE HANDY FOLKS WELL-VERSED IN THE ART OF BUILDING HOMES!
OH YEAH?
TRADING PARTNERS, HUH? WHO ARE THEY?
THE DWARVES.
DWARVES!!

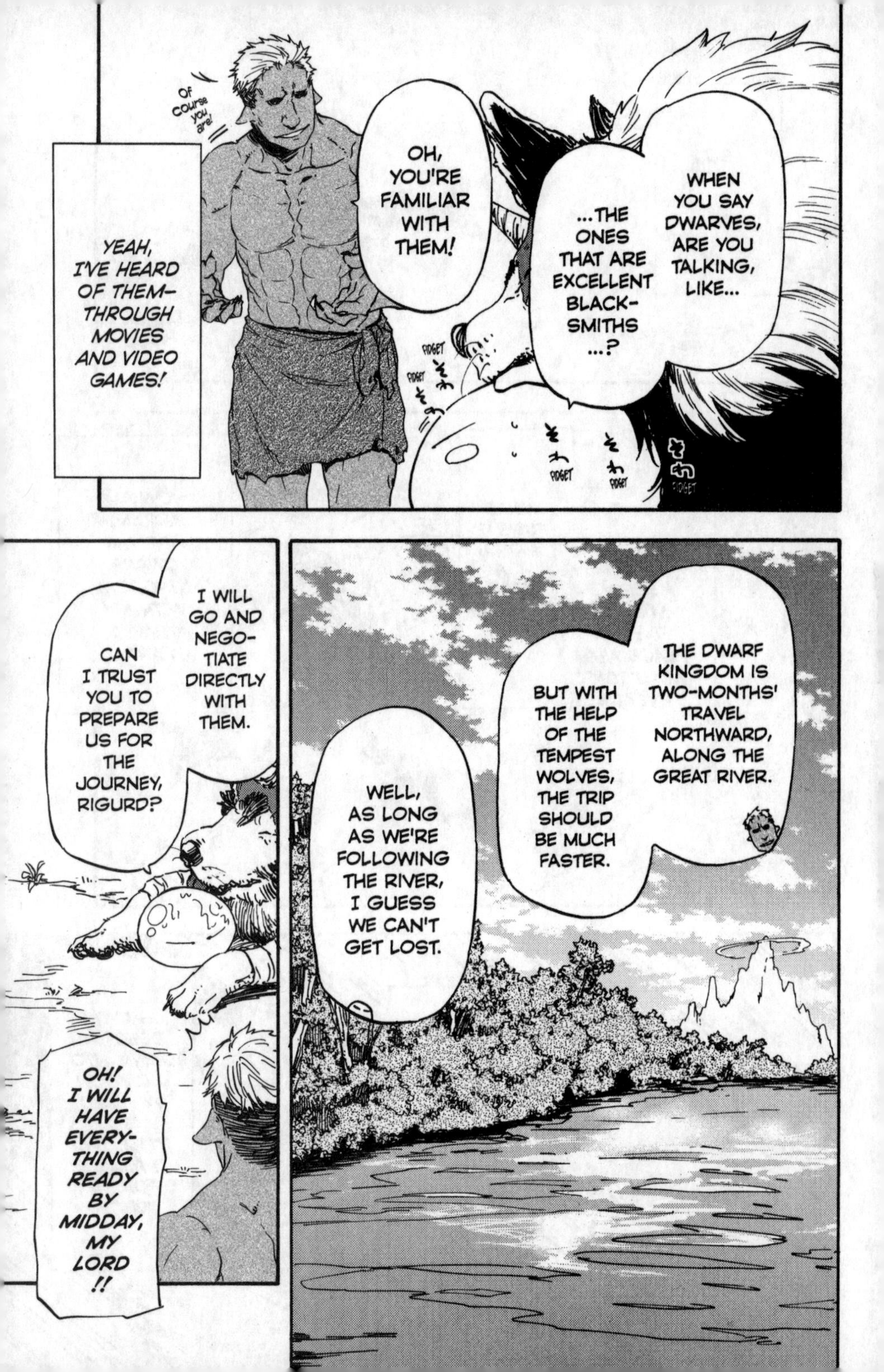

WHEN YOU SAY DWARVES, ARE YOU TALKING, LIKE...
...THE ONES THAT ARE EXCELLENT BLACK-SMITHS ...?
そわ FIDGET
そわ FIDGET
そわ FIDGET
そわ FIDGET
そわ FIDGET
OH, YOU'RE FAMILIAR WITH THEM!
Of course you are!
YEAH, I'VE HEARD OF THEM—THROUGH MOVIES AND VIDEO GAMES!
THE DWARF KINGDOM IS TWO-MONTHS' TRAVEL NORTHWARD, ALONG THE GREAT RIVER.
BUT WITH THE HELP OF THE TEMPEST WOLVES, THE TRIP SHOULD BE MUCH FASTER.
WELL, AS LONG AS WE'RE FOLLOWING THE RIVER, I GUESS WE CAN'T GET LOST.
I WILL GO AND NEGO-TIATE DIRECTLY WITH THEM.
CAN I TRUST YOU TO PREPARE US FOR THE JOURNEY, RIGURD?
OH! I WILL HAVE EVERY-THING READY BY MIDDAY, MY LORD !!

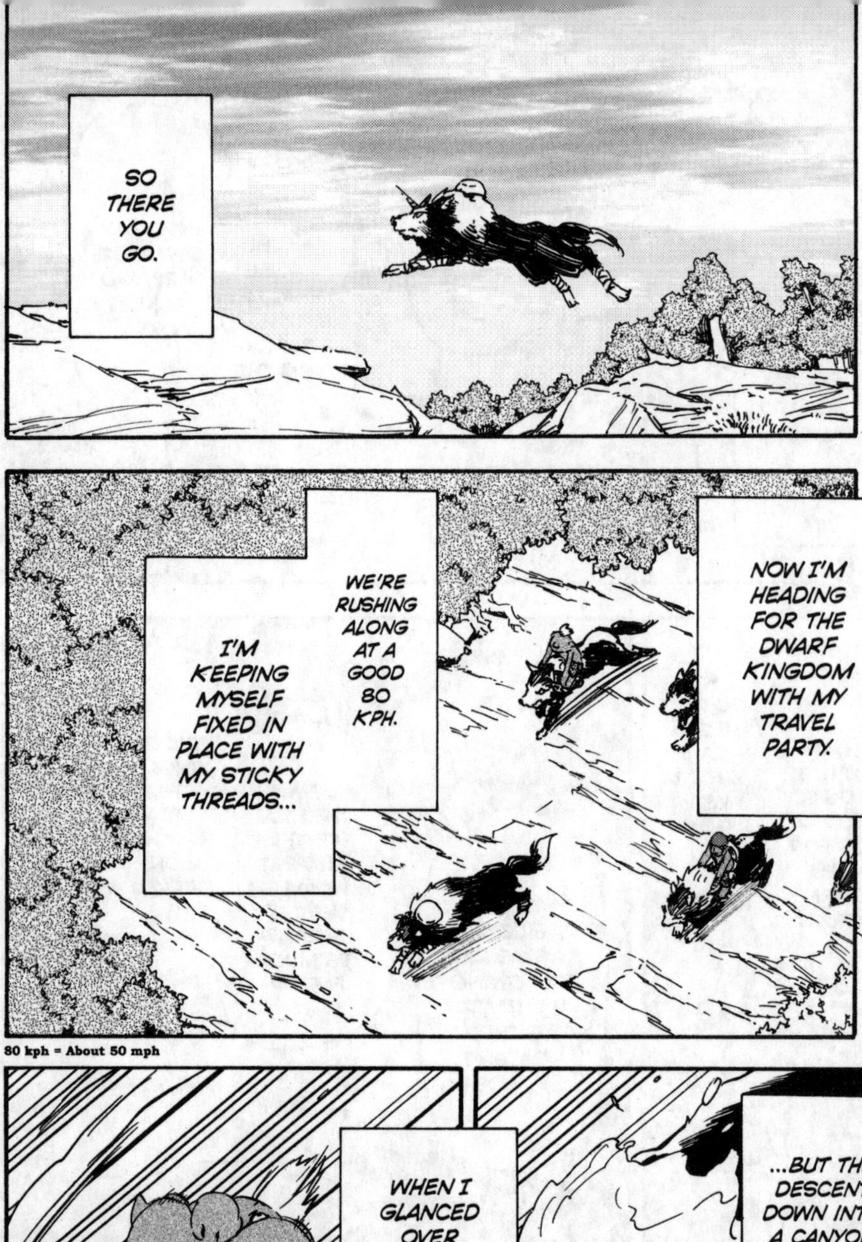
SO THERE YOU GO.
NOW I'M HEADING FOR THE DWARF KINGDOM WITH MY TRAVEL PARTY.
WE'RE RUSHING ALONG AT A GOOD 80 KPH.
I'M KEEPING MYSELF FIXED IN PLACE WITH MY STICKY THREADS...

80 kph = About 50 mph

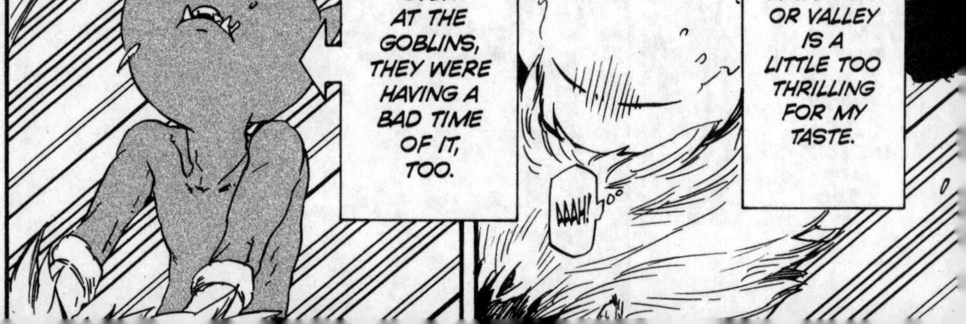
...BUT THE DESCENT DOWN INTO A CANYON OR VALLEY IS A LITTLE TOO THRILLING FOR MY TASTE.
AAAH!
WHEN I GLANCED OVER AT THE GOBLINS, THEY WERE HAVING A BAD TIME OF IT, TOO.

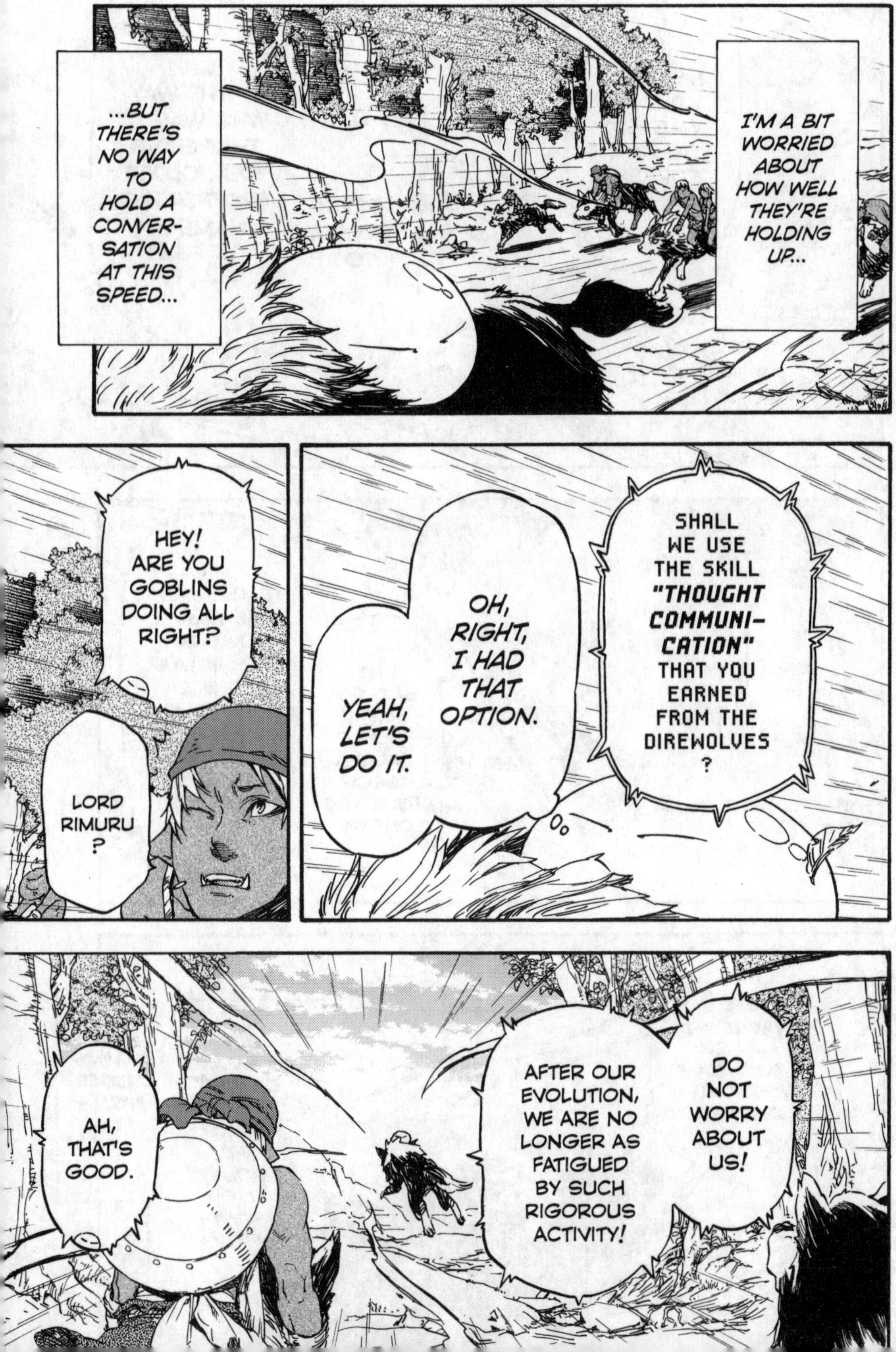
I'M A BIT WORRIED ABOUT HOW WELL THEY'RE HOLDING UP...
...BUT THERE'S NO WAY TO HOLD A CONVER-SATION AT THIS SPEED...
SHALL WE USE THE SKILL "THOUGHT COMMUNI-CATION" THAT YOU EARNED FROM THE DIREWOLVES?
OH, RIGHT, I HAD THAT OPTION.
YEAH, LET'S DO IT.
HEY! ARE YOU GOBLINS DOING ALL RIGHT?
LORD RIMURU?
DO NOT WORRY ABOUT US!
AFTER OUR EVOLUTION, WE ARE NO LONGER AS FATIGUED BY SUCH RIGOROUS ACTIVITY!
AH, THAT'S GOOD.

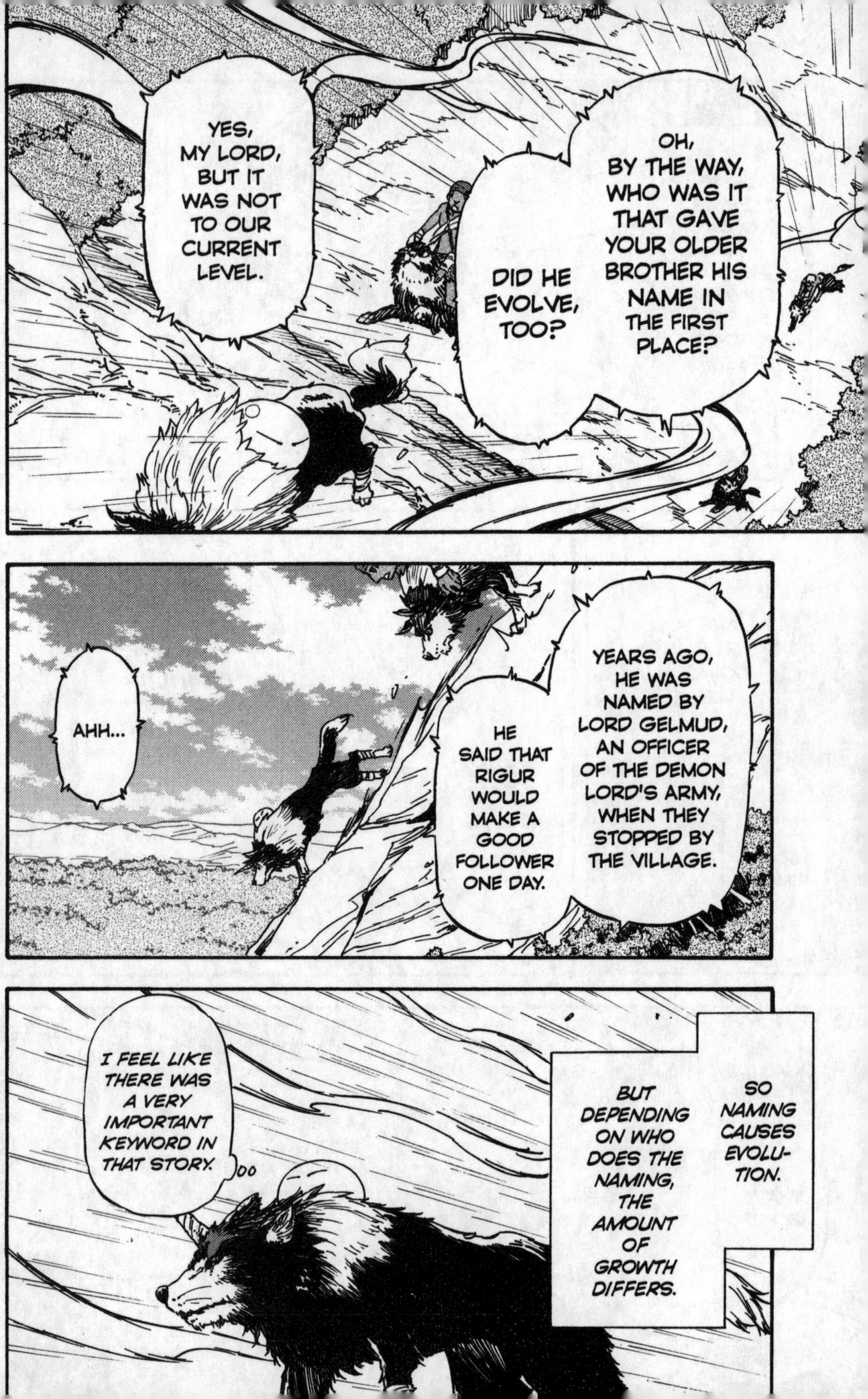
OH, BY THE WAY, WHO WAS IT THAT GAVE YOUR OLDER BROTHER HIS NAME IN THE FIRST PLACE?
DID HE EVOLVE, TOO?
YES, MY LORD, BUT IT WAS NOT TO OUR CURRENT LEVEL.
YEARS AGO, HE WAS NAMED BY LORD GELMUD, AN OFFICER OF THE DEMON LORD'S ARMY, WHEN THEY STOPPED BY THE VILLAGE.
HE SAID THAT RIGUR WOULD MAKE A GOOD FOLLOWER ONE DAY.
AHH...
SO NAMING CAUSES EVOLU-TION.
BUT DEPENDING ON WHO DOES THE NAMING, THE AMOUNT OF GROWTH DIFFERS.
I FEEL LIKE THERE WAS A VERY IMPORTANT KEYWORD IN THAT STORY.

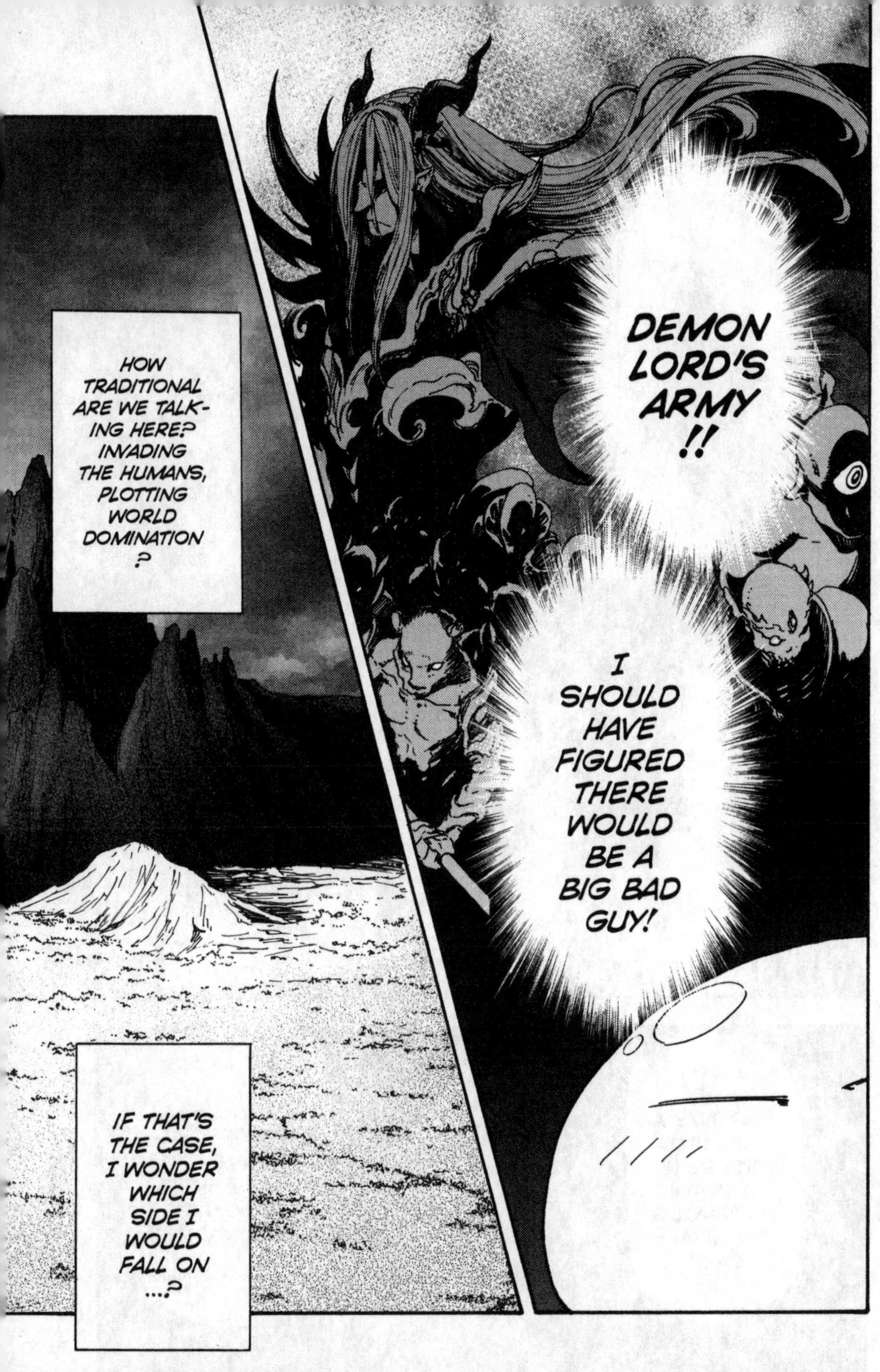
DEMON LORD'S ARMY !!
I SHOULD HAVE FIGURED THERE WOULD BE A BIG BAD GUY!
HOW TRADITIONAL ARE WE TALK-ING HERE? INVADING THE HUMANS, PLOTTING WORLD DOMINATION ?
IF THAT'S THE CASE, I WONDER WHICH SIDE I WOULD FALL ON ...?

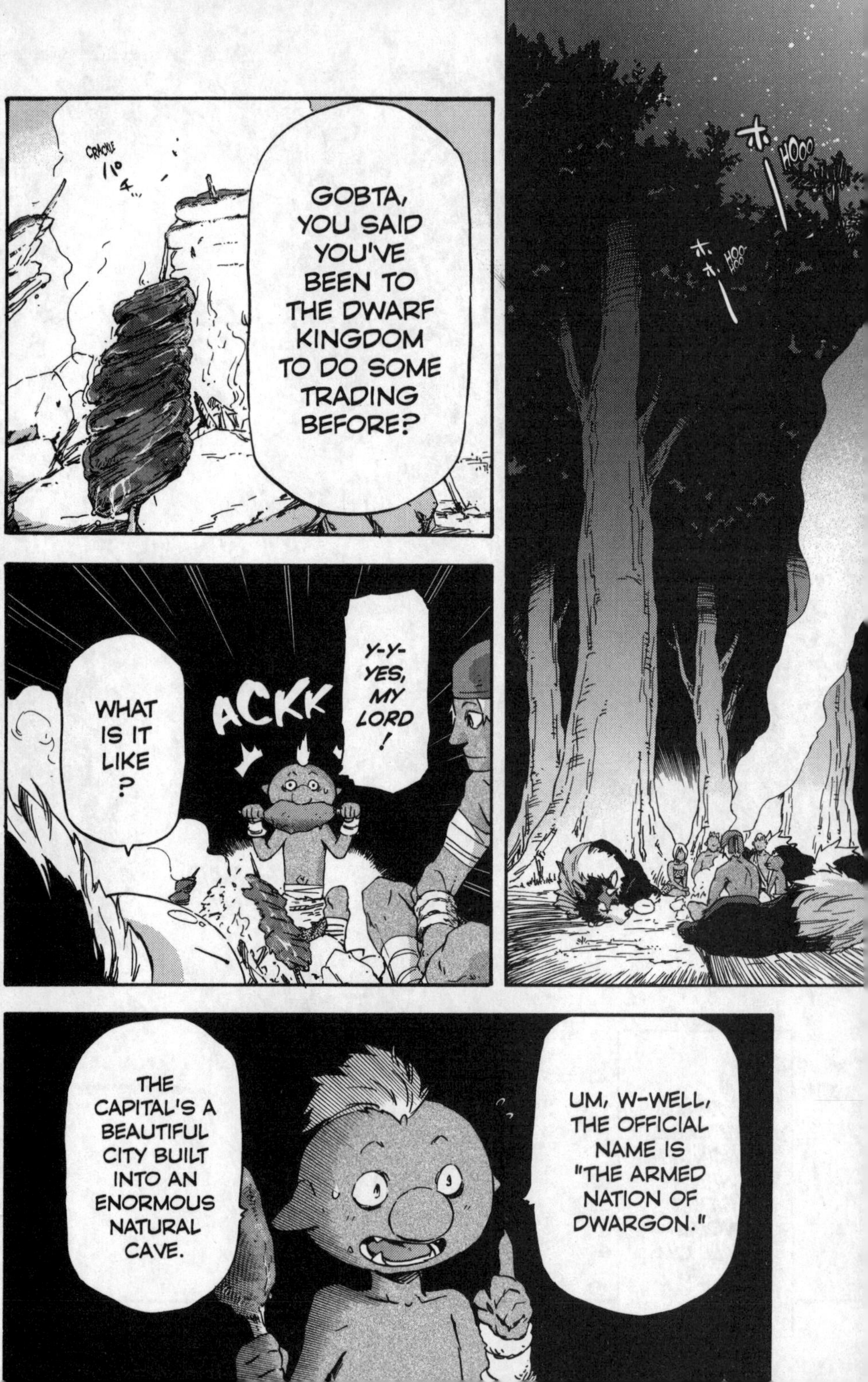
HOOO
HOO-HOO
CRACKLE
GOBTA, YOU SAID YOU'VE BEEN TO THE DWARF KINGDOM TO DO SOME TRADING BEFORE?
Y-Y-YES, MY LORD!
ACKK
WHAT IS IT LIKE?
UM, W-WELL, THE OFFICIAL NAME IS "THE ARMED NATION OF DWARGON."
THE CAPITAL'S A BEAUTIFUL CITY BUILT INTO AN ENORMOUS NATURAL CAVE.

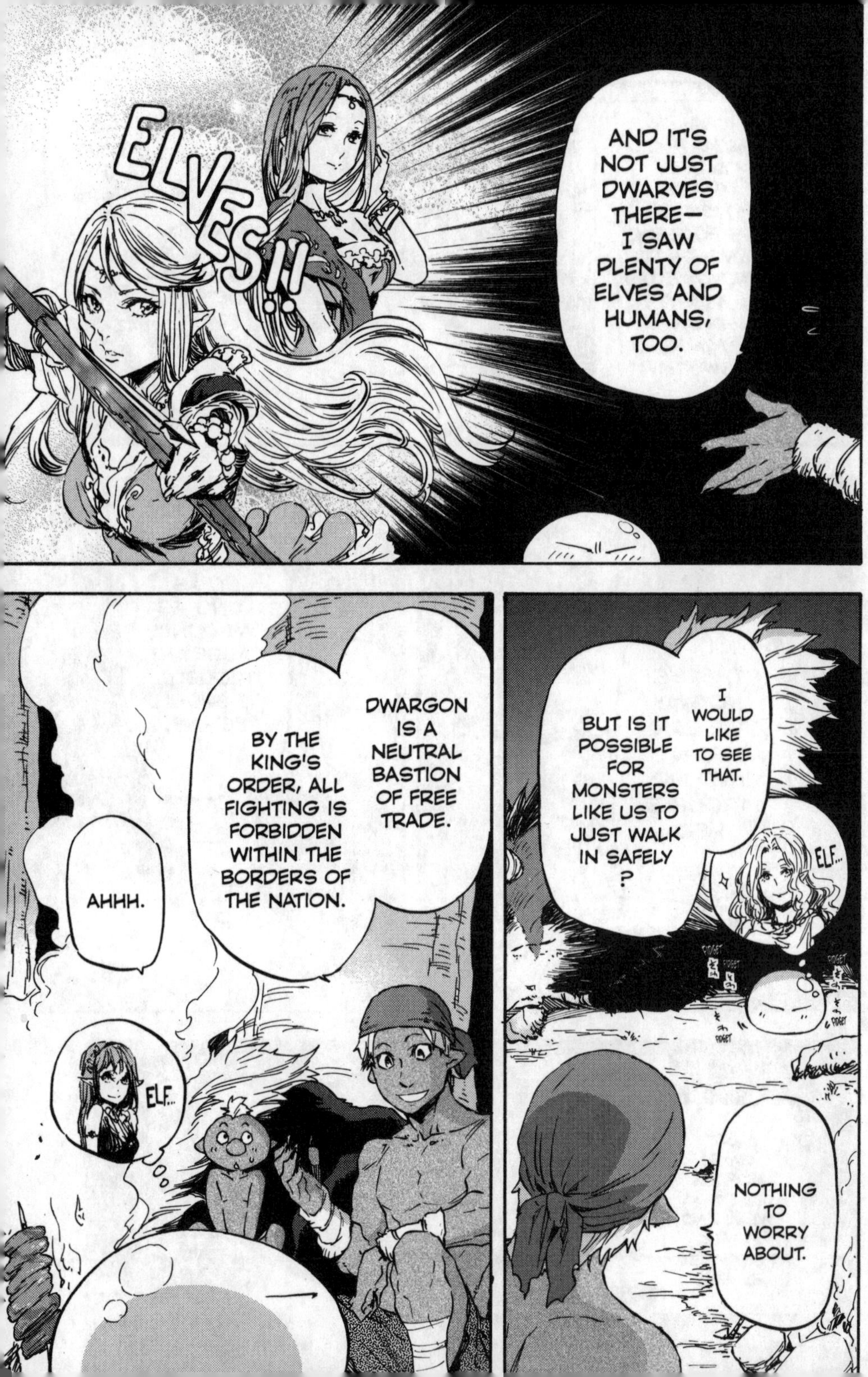
AND IT'S NOT JUST DWARVES THERE— I SAW PLENTY OF ELVES AND HUMANS, TOO.
ELVES!!
I WOULD LIKE TO SEE THAT.
BUT IS IT POSSIBLE FOR MONSTERS LIKE US TO JUST WALK IN SAFELY?
ELF...
FIDGET FIDGET
FIDGET FIDGET
NOTHING TO WORRY ABOUT.
DWARGON IS A NEUTRAL BASTION OF FREE TRADE.
BY THE KING'S ORDER, ALL FIGHTING IS FORBIDDEN WITHIN THE BORDERS OF THE NATION.
AHHH.
ELF...

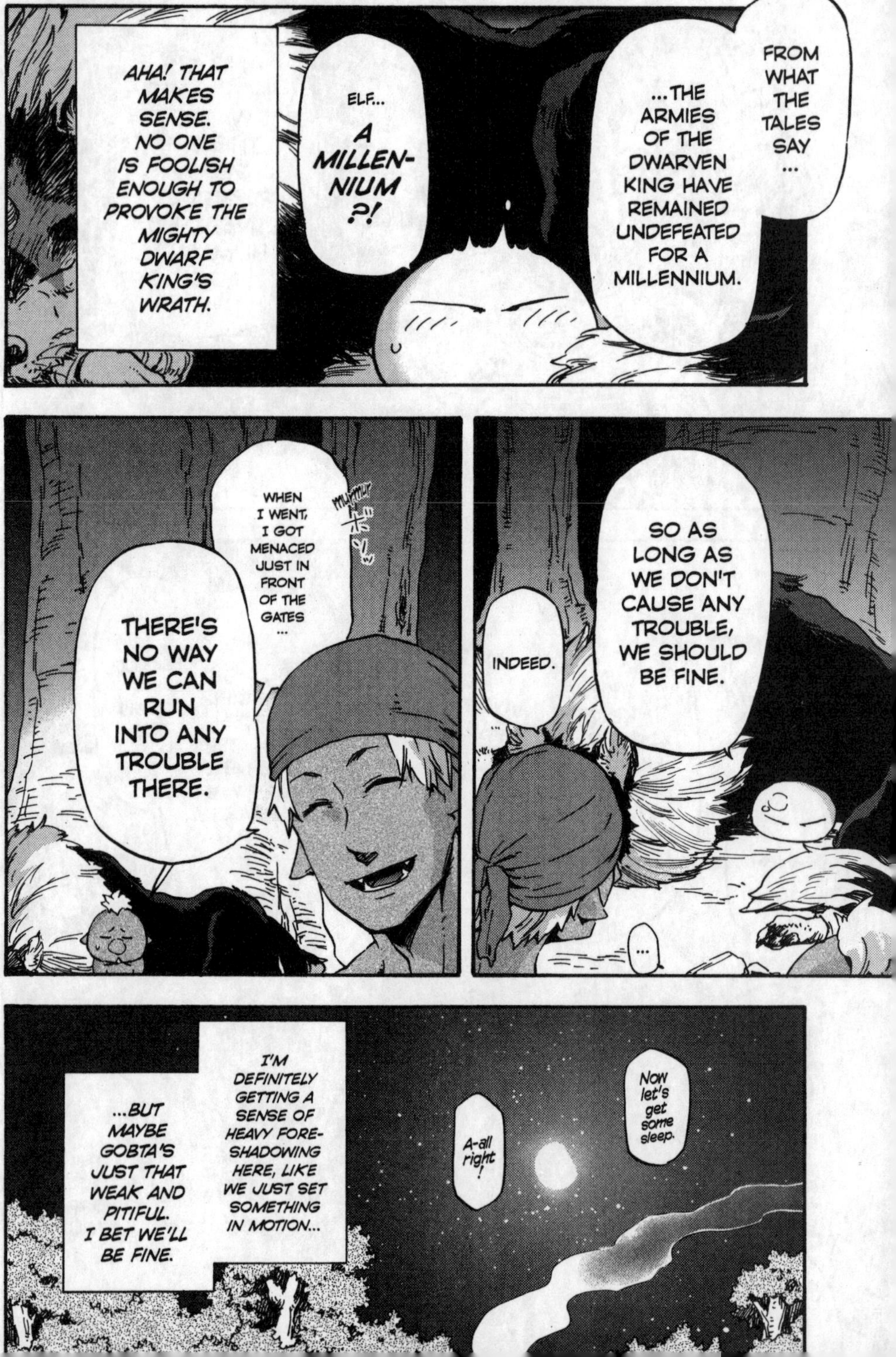
FROM WHAT THE TALES SAY ...
...THE ARMIES OF THE DWARVEN KING HAVE REMAINED UNDEFEATED FOR A MILLENNIUM.
ELF... A MILLENNIUM?!
AHA! THAT MAKES SENSE. NO ONE IS FOOLISH ENOUGH TO PROVOKE THE MIGHTY DWARF KING'S WRATH.
SO AS LONG AS WE DON'T CAUSE ANY TROUBLE, WE SHOULD BE FINE.
INDEED.
...
...
WHEN I WENT, I GOT MENACED JUST IN FRONT OF THE GATES ...
THERE'S NO WAY WE CAN RUN INTO ANY TROUBLE THERE.
Now let's get some sleep.
A-all right!
I'M DEFINITELY GETTING A SENSE OF HEAVY FORE-SHADOWING HERE, LIKE WE JUST SET SOMETHING IN MOTION...
...BUT MAYBE GOBTA'S JUST THAT WEAK AND PITIFUL. I BET WE'LL BE FINE.

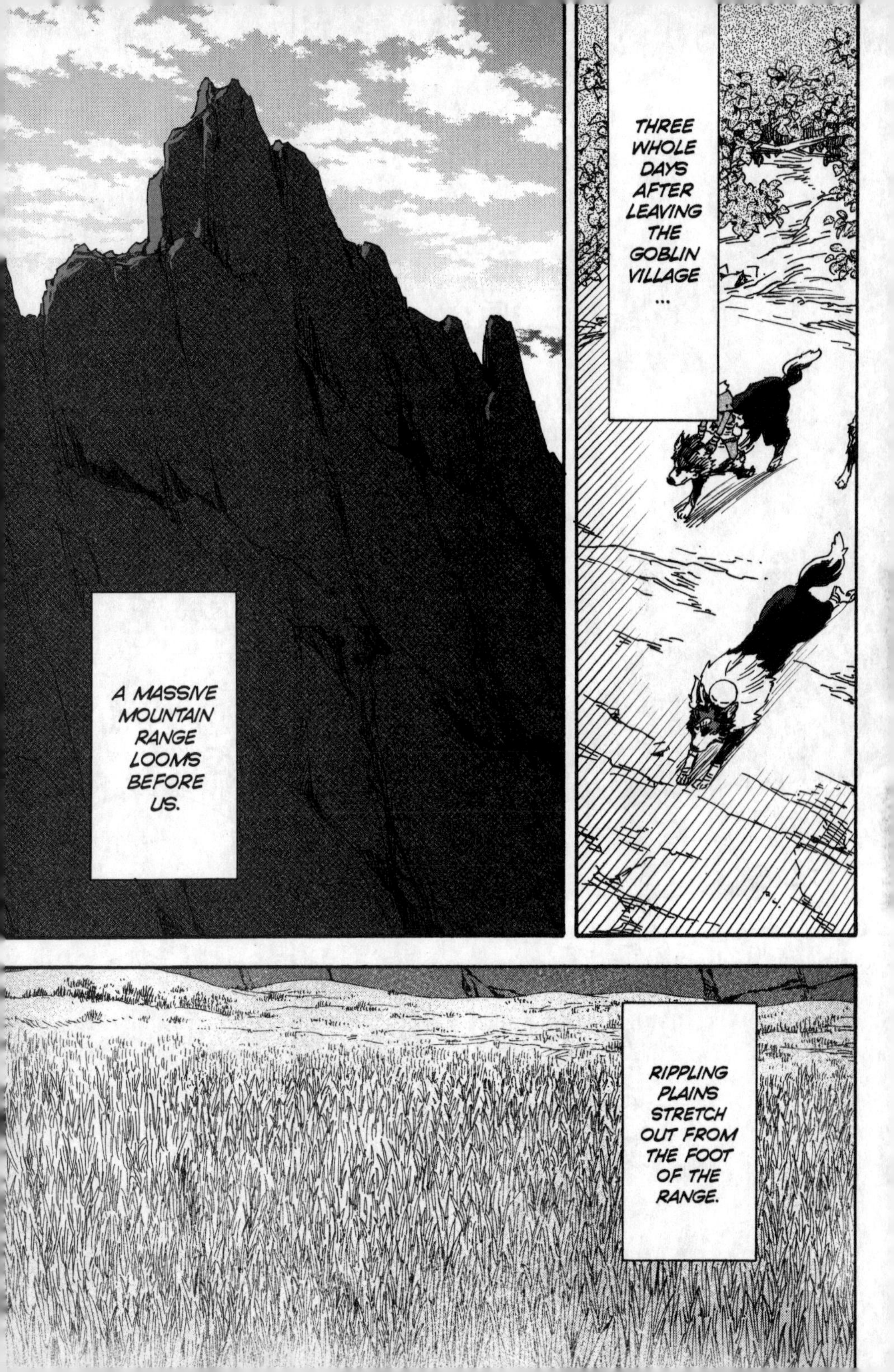
THREE WHOLE DAYS AFTER LEAVING THE GOBLIN VILLAGE...
A MASSIVE MOUNTAIN RANGE LOOMS BEFORE US.
RIPPLING PLAINS STRETCH OUT FROM THE FOOT OF THE RANGE.

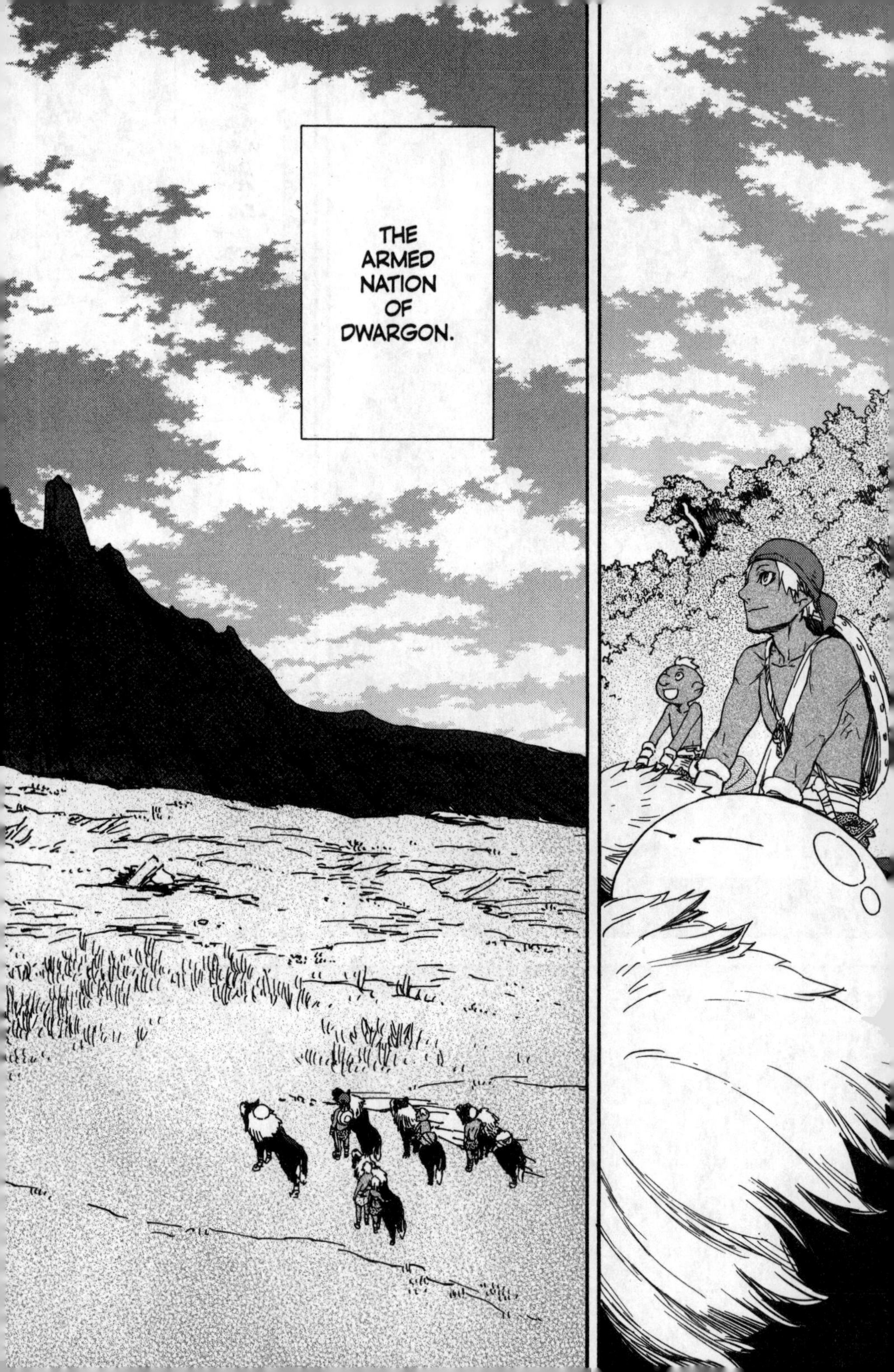
THE ARMED NATION OF DWARGON.

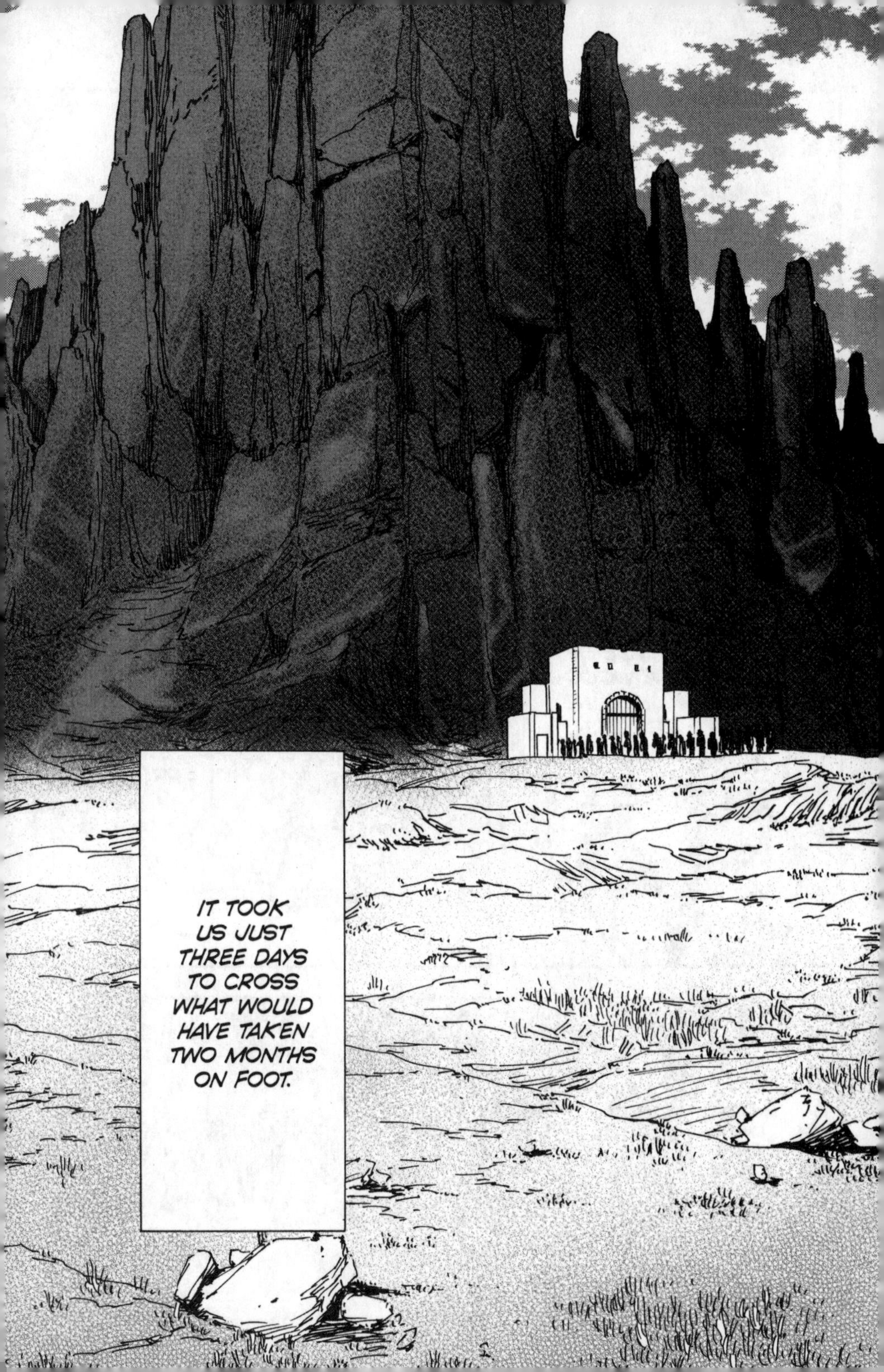
IT TOOK US JUST THREE DAYS TO CROSS WHAT WOULD HAVE TAKEN TWO MONTHS ON FOOT.

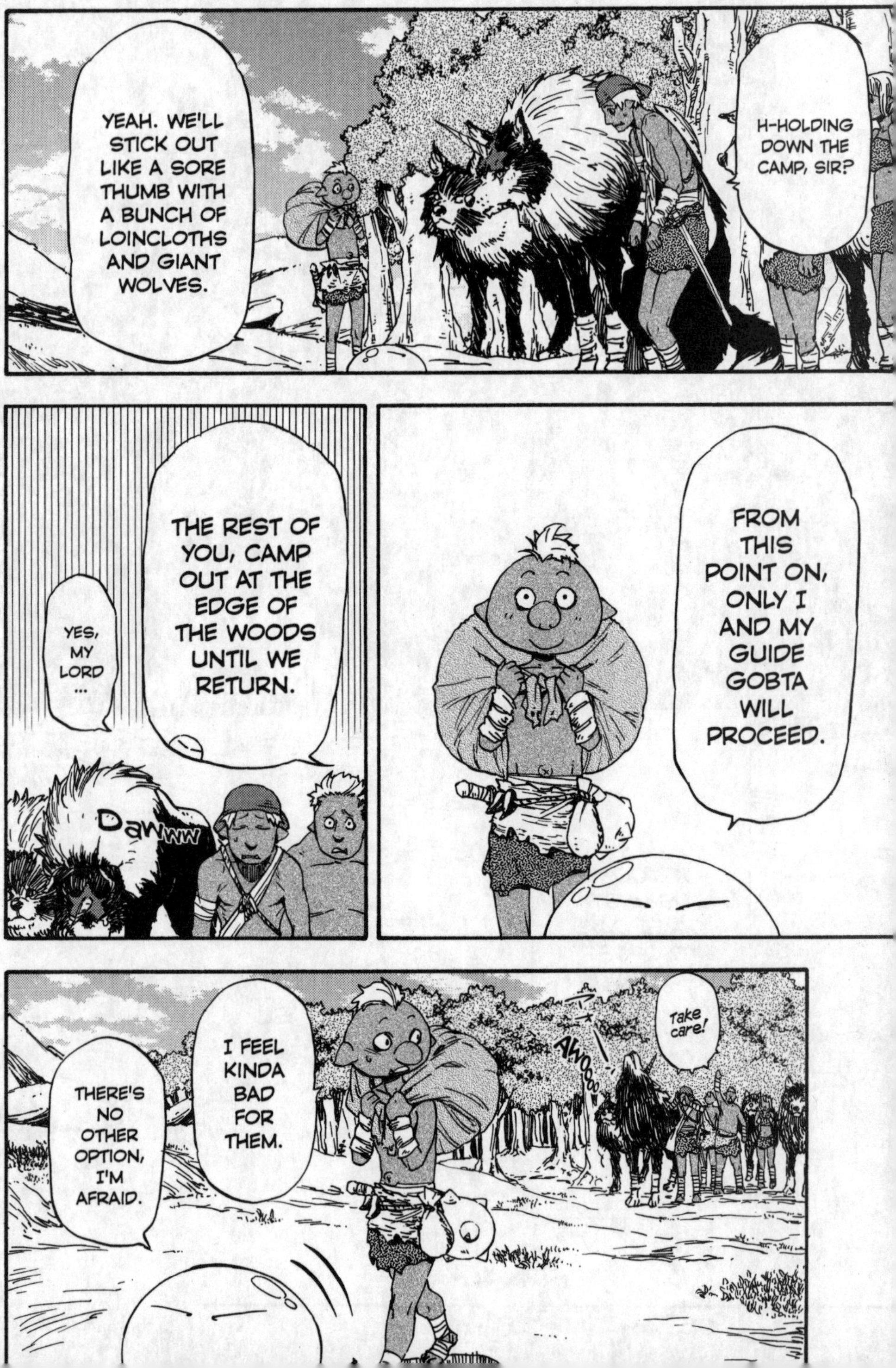
H-HOLDING DOWN THE CAMP, SIR?
YEAH. WE'LL STICK OUT LIKE A SORE THUMB WITH A BUNCH OF LOINCLOTHS AND GIANT WOLVES.
FROM THIS POINT ON, ONLY I AND MY GUIDE GOBTA WILL PROCEED.
THE REST OF YOU, CAMP OUT AT THE EDGE OF THE WOODS UNTIL WE RETURN.
YES, MY LORD ...
Dawww
Take care!
AWOOO
I FEEL KINDA BAD FOR THEM.
THERE'S NO OTHER OPTION, I'M AFRAID.

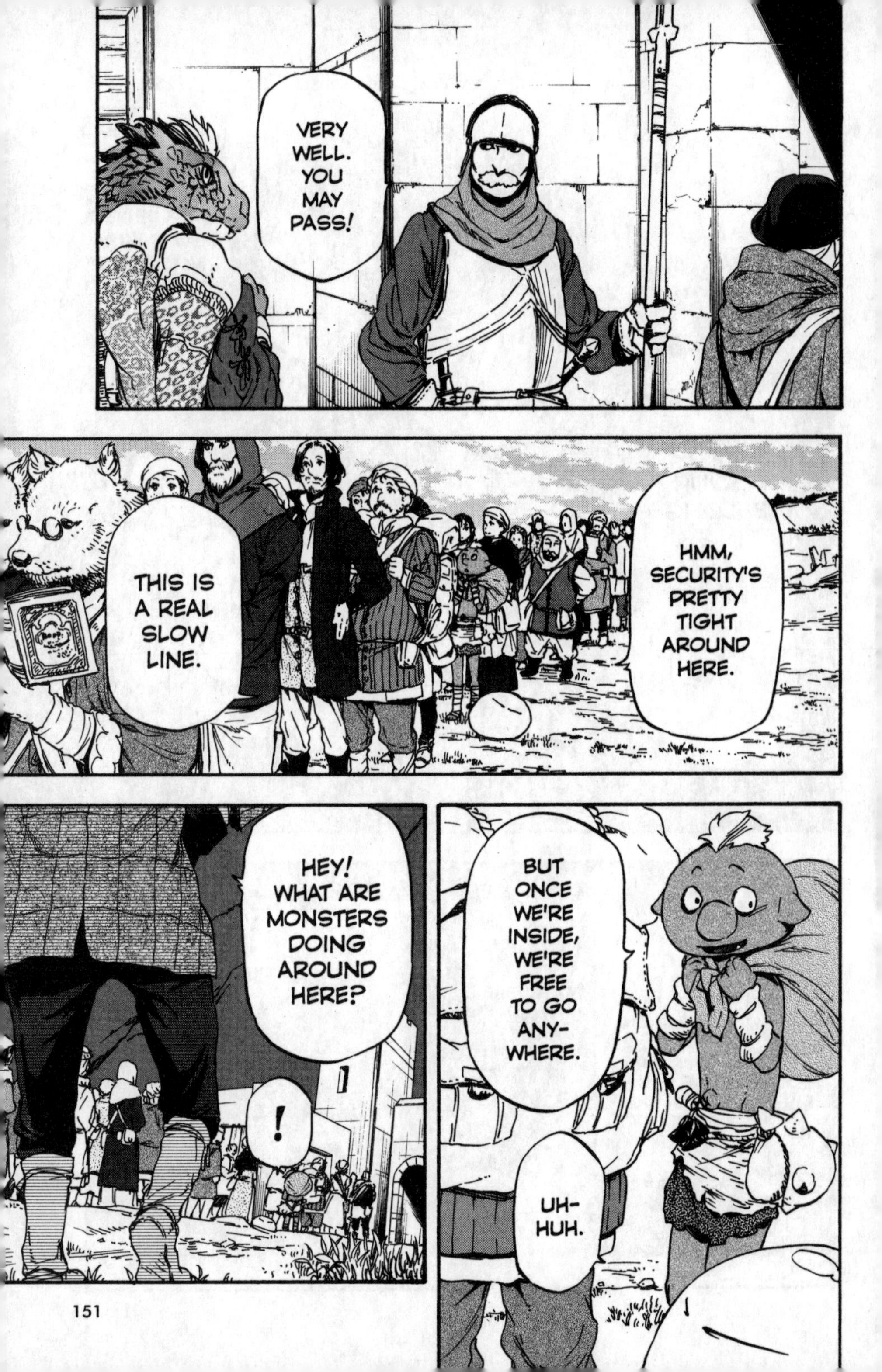
VERY WELL. YOU MAY PASS!
HMM, SECURITY'S PRETTY TIGHT AROUND HERE.
THIS IS A REAL SLOW LINE.
BUT ONCE WE'RE INSIDE, WE'RE FREE TO GO ANY-WHERE.
UH-HUH.
HEY! WHAT ARE MONSTERS DOING AROUND HERE?
!

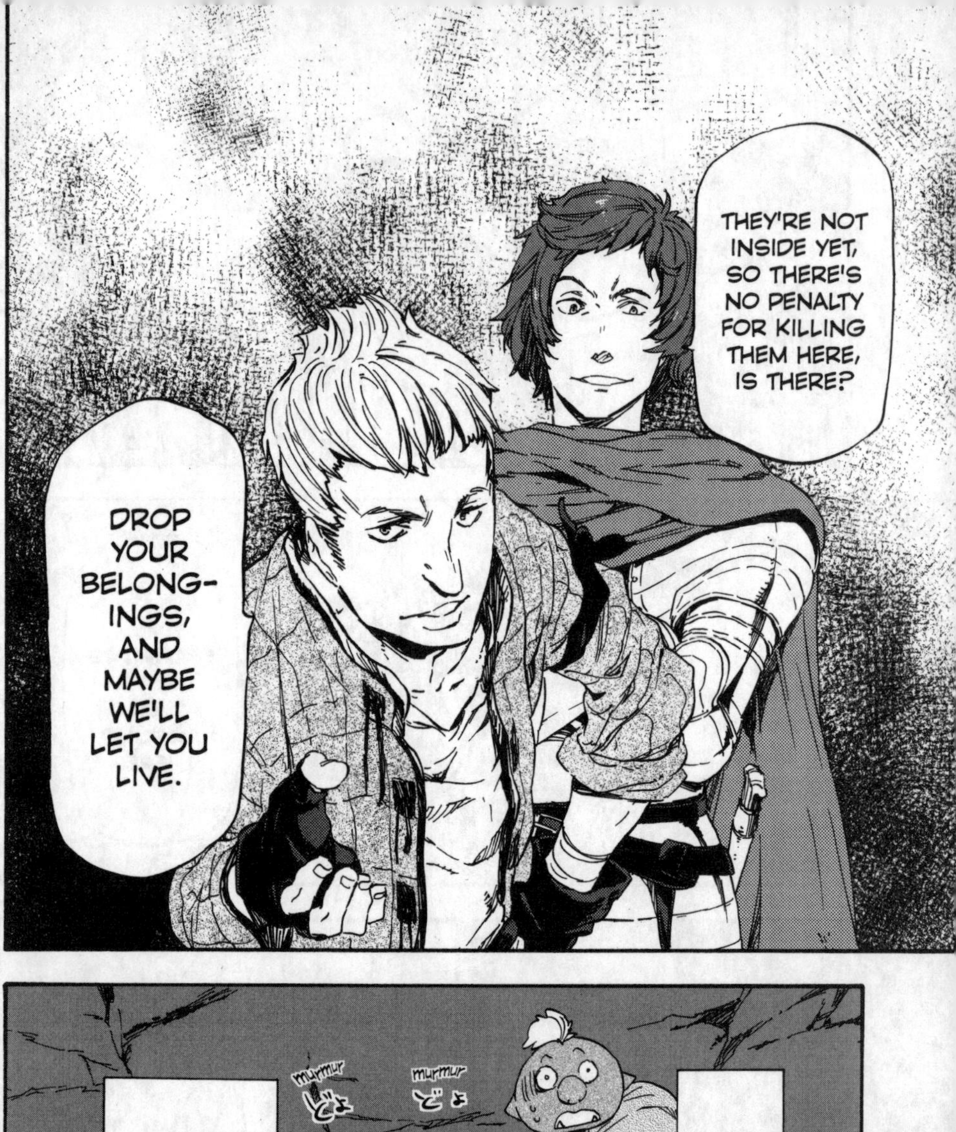
THEY'RE NOT INSIDE YET, SO THERE'S NO PENALTY FOR KILLING THEM HERE, IS THERE?
DROP YOUR BELONG-INGS, AND MAYBE WE'LL LET YOU LIVE.

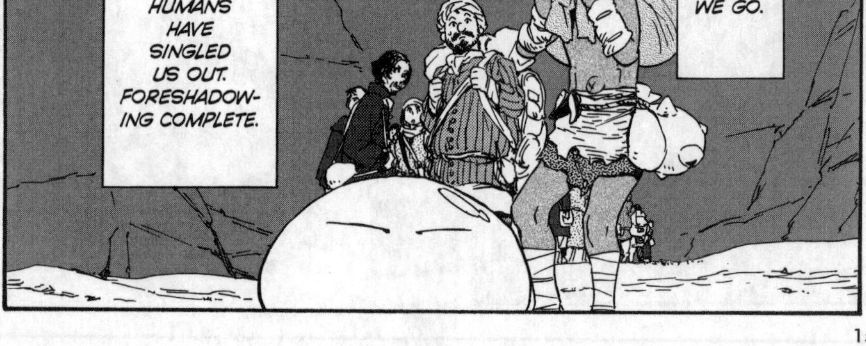
THERE WE GO.
murmur
どよ
murmur
どよ
THE HUMANS HAVE SINGLED US OUT. FORESHADOW-ING COMPLETE.

GOBTA.

Why does he look basically the same as before his evolution ....?

My growth was more of the symbolic type!!

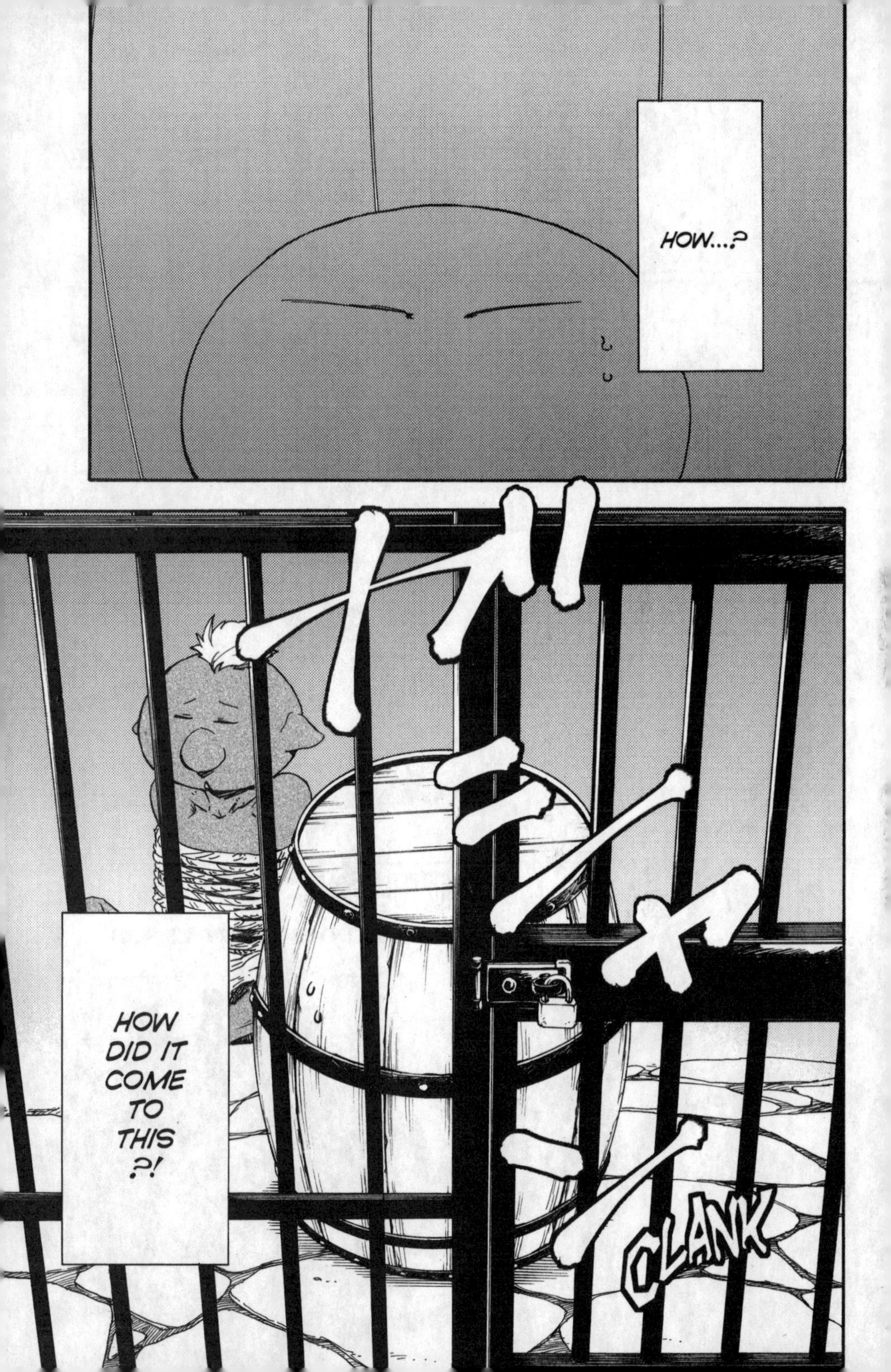
HOW...?
HOW DID IT COME TO THIS?!
CLANK

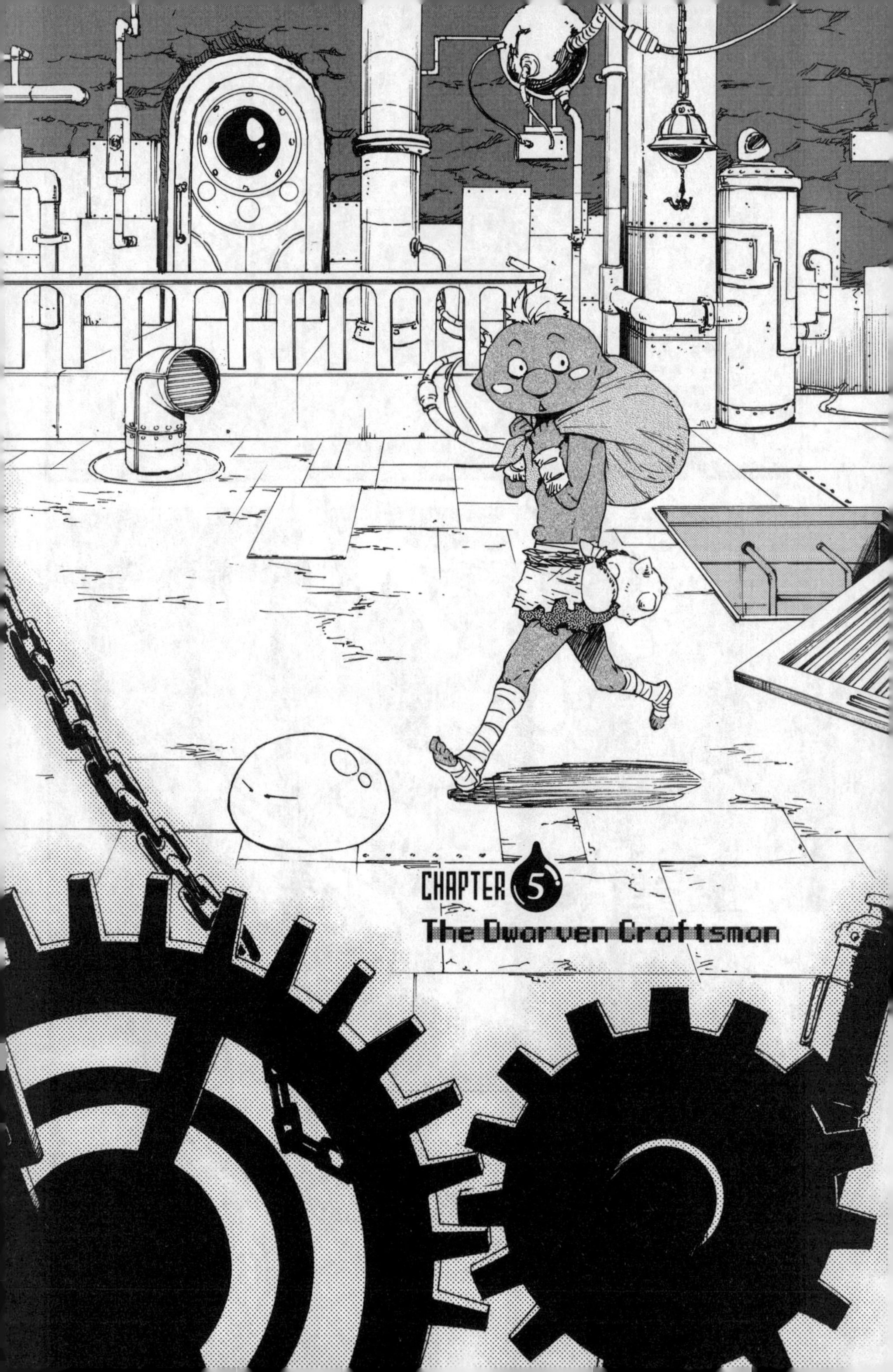
CHAPTER 5
The Dwarven Craftsman

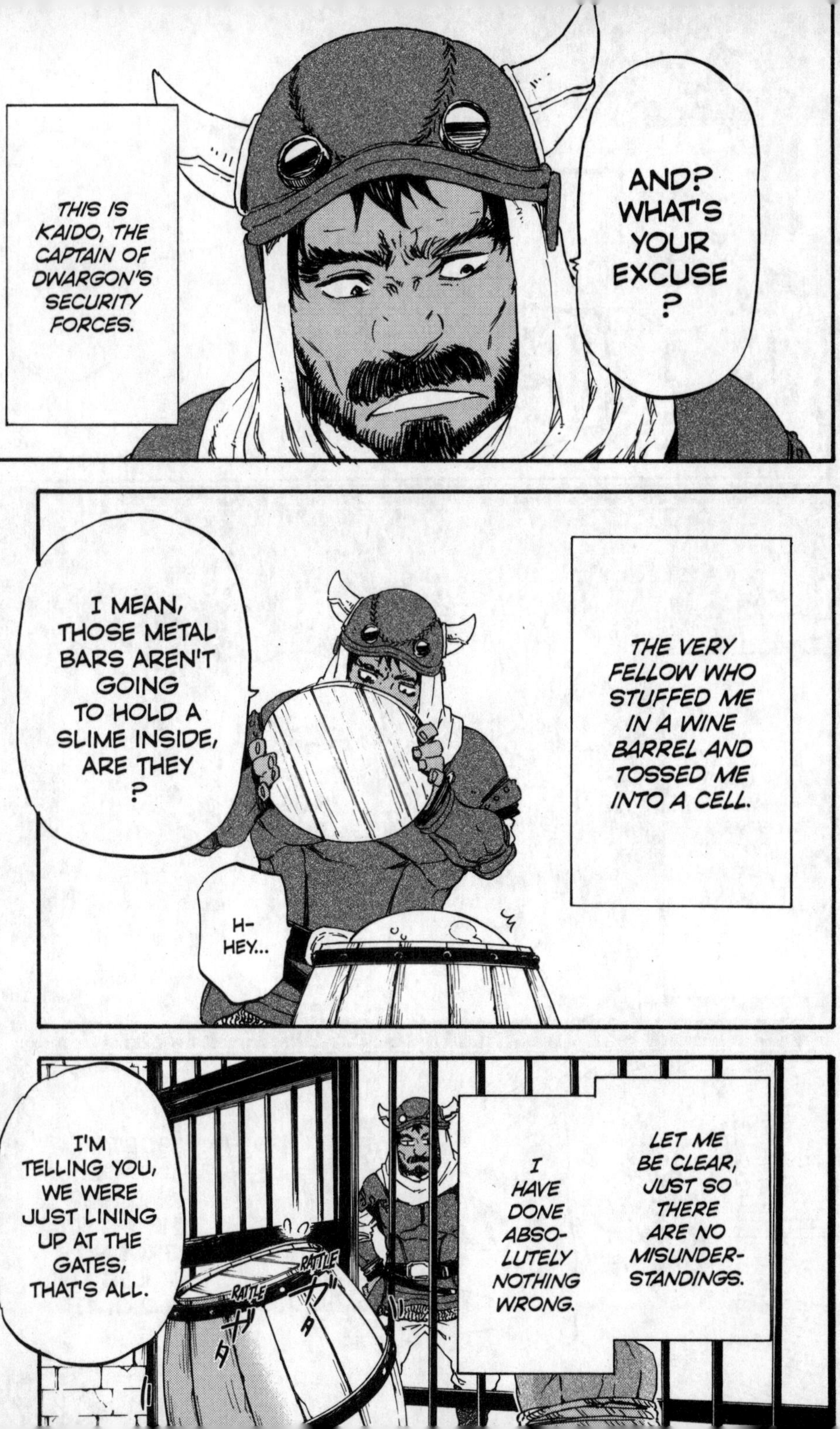
AND? WHAT'S YOUR EXCUSE?
THIS IS KAIDO, THE CAPTAIN OF DWARGON'S SECURITY FORCES.
THE VERY FELLOW WHO STUFFED ME IN A WINE BARREL AND TOSSED ME INTO A CELL.
I MEAN, THOSE METAL BARS AREN'T GOING TO HOLD A SLIME INSIDE, ARE THEY?
H-HEY...
LET ME BE CLEAR, JUST SO THERE ARE NO MISUNDERSTANDINGS.
I HAVE DONE ABSOLUTELY NOTHING WRONG.
RATTLE
RATTLE
I'M TELLING YOU, WE WERE JUST LINING UP AT THE GATES, THAT'S ALL.

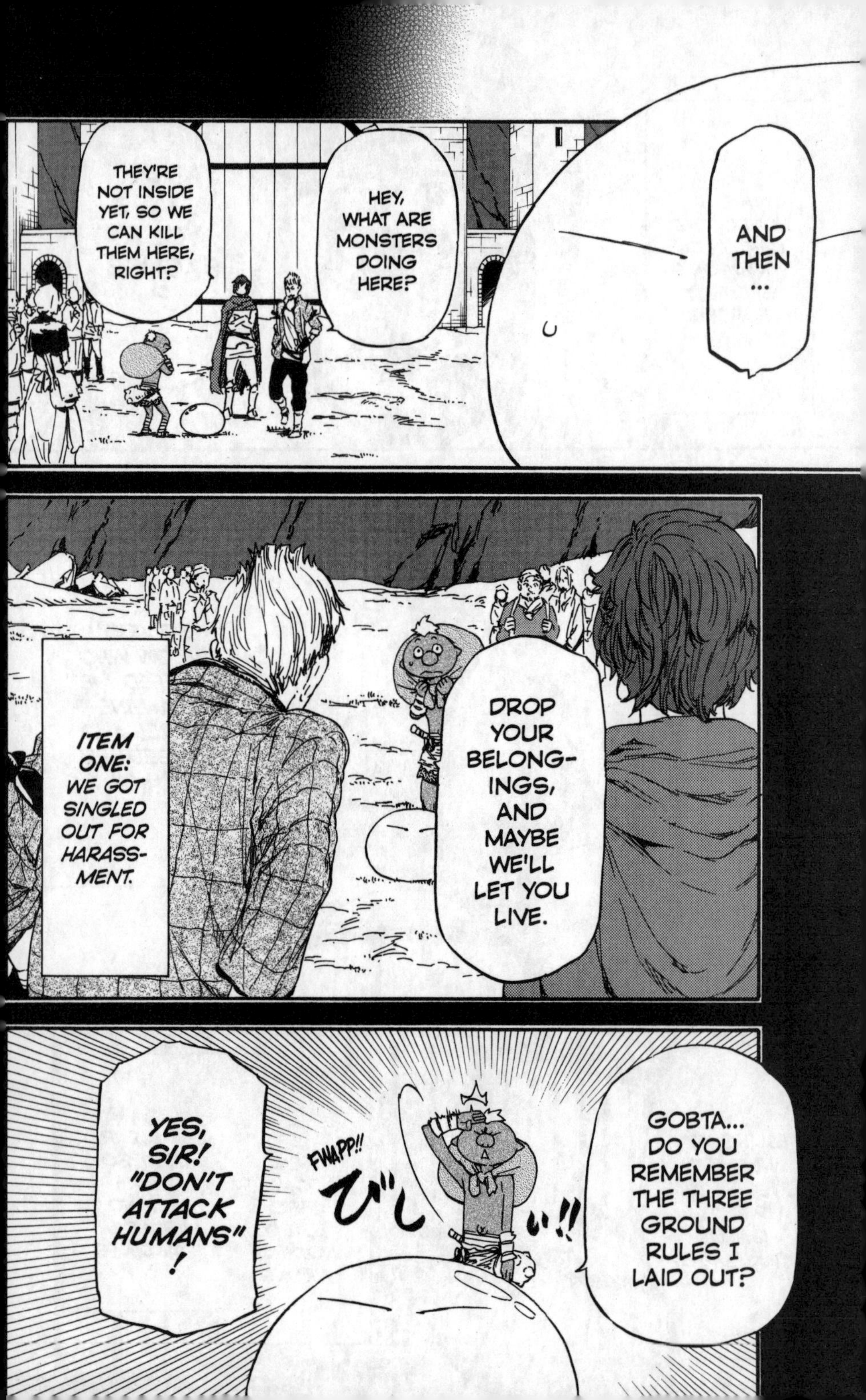
AND THEN...
HEY, WHAT ARE MONSTERS DOING HERE?
THEY'RE NOT INSIDE YET, SO WE CAN KILL THEM HERE, RIGHT?
DROP YOUR BELONG-INGS, AND MAYBE WE'LL LET YOU LIVE.
ITEM ONE: WE GOT SINGLED OUT FOR HARASS-MENT.
GOBTA... DO YOU REMEMBER THE THREE GROUND RULES I LAID OUT?
FWAPP!!
びしぃ!!
YES, SIR! "DON'T ATTACK HUMANS"!

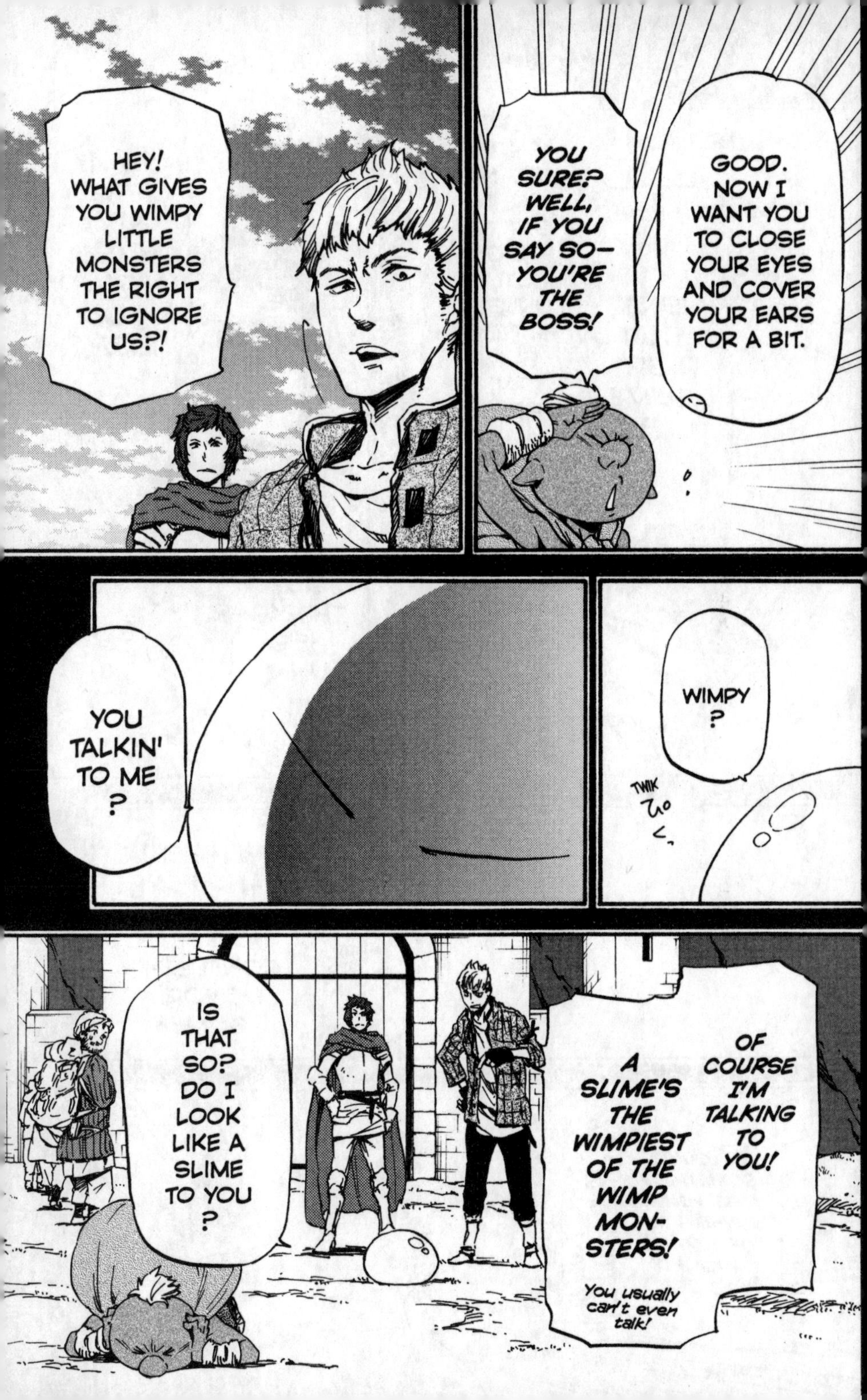
GOOD. NOW I WANT YOU TO CLOSE YOUR EYES AND COVER YOUR EARS FOR A BIT.
YOU SURE? WELL, IF YOU SAY SO—YOU'RE THE BOSS!
HEY! WHAT GIVES YOU WIMPY LITTLE MONSTERS THE RIGHT TO IGNORE US?!
WIMPY?
TWIK
YOU TALKIN' TO ME?
OF COURSE I'M TALKING TO YOU!
A SLIME'S THE WIMPIEST OF THE WIMP MONSTERS!
You usually can't even talk!
IS THAT SO? DO I LOOK LIKE A SLIME TO YOU?

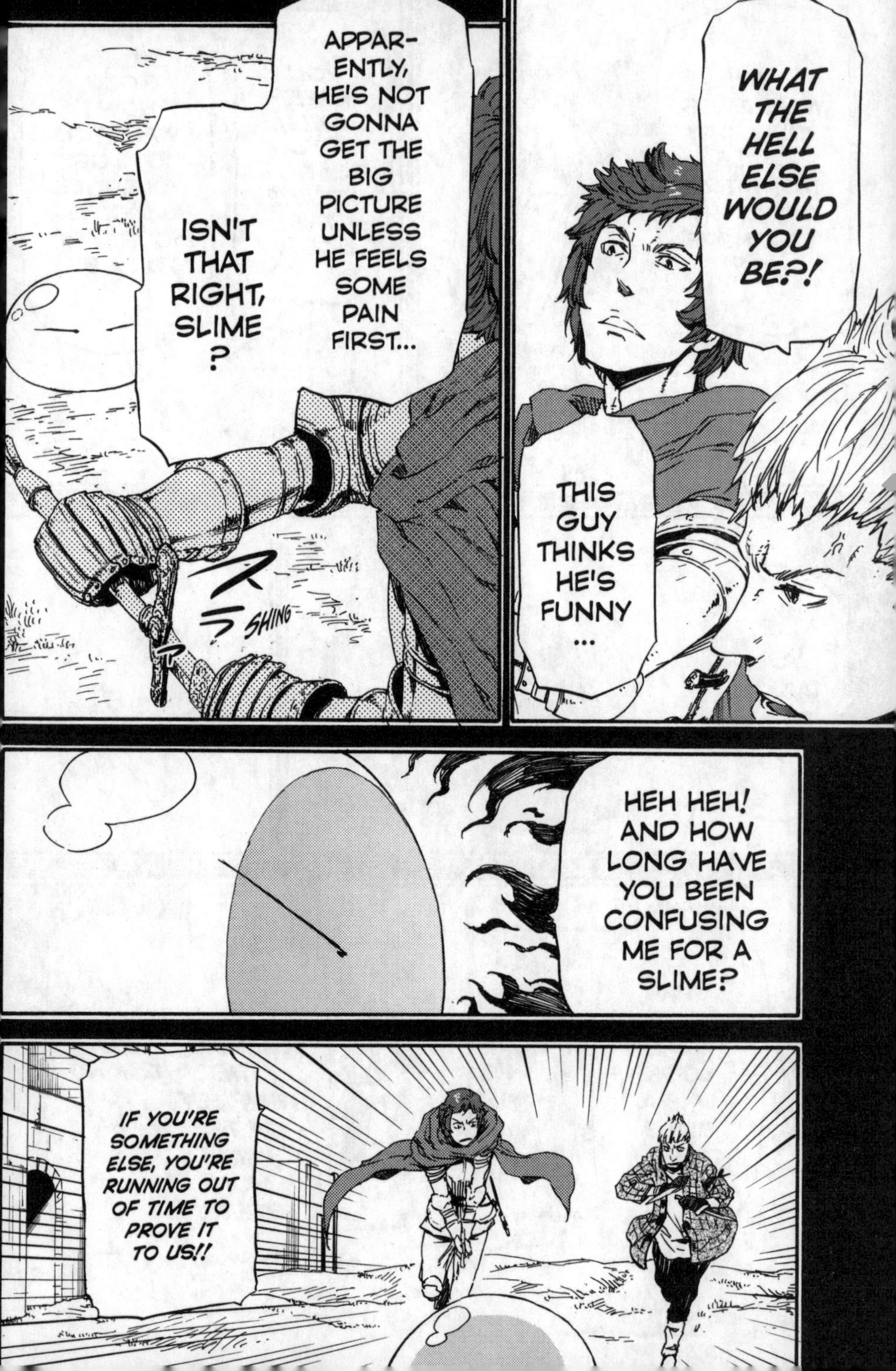
WHAT THE HELL ELSE WOULD YOU BE?!
THIS GUY THINKS HE'S FUNNY...
APPARENTLY, HE'S NOT GONNA GET THE BIG PICTURE UNLESS HE FEELS SOME PAIN FIRST...
ISN'T THAT RIGHT, SLIME?
SHING
HEH HEH! AND HOW LONG HAVE YOU BEEN CONFUSING ME FOR A SLIME?
IF YOU'RE SOMETHING ELSE, YOU'RE RUNNING OUT OF TIME TO PROVE IT TO US!!

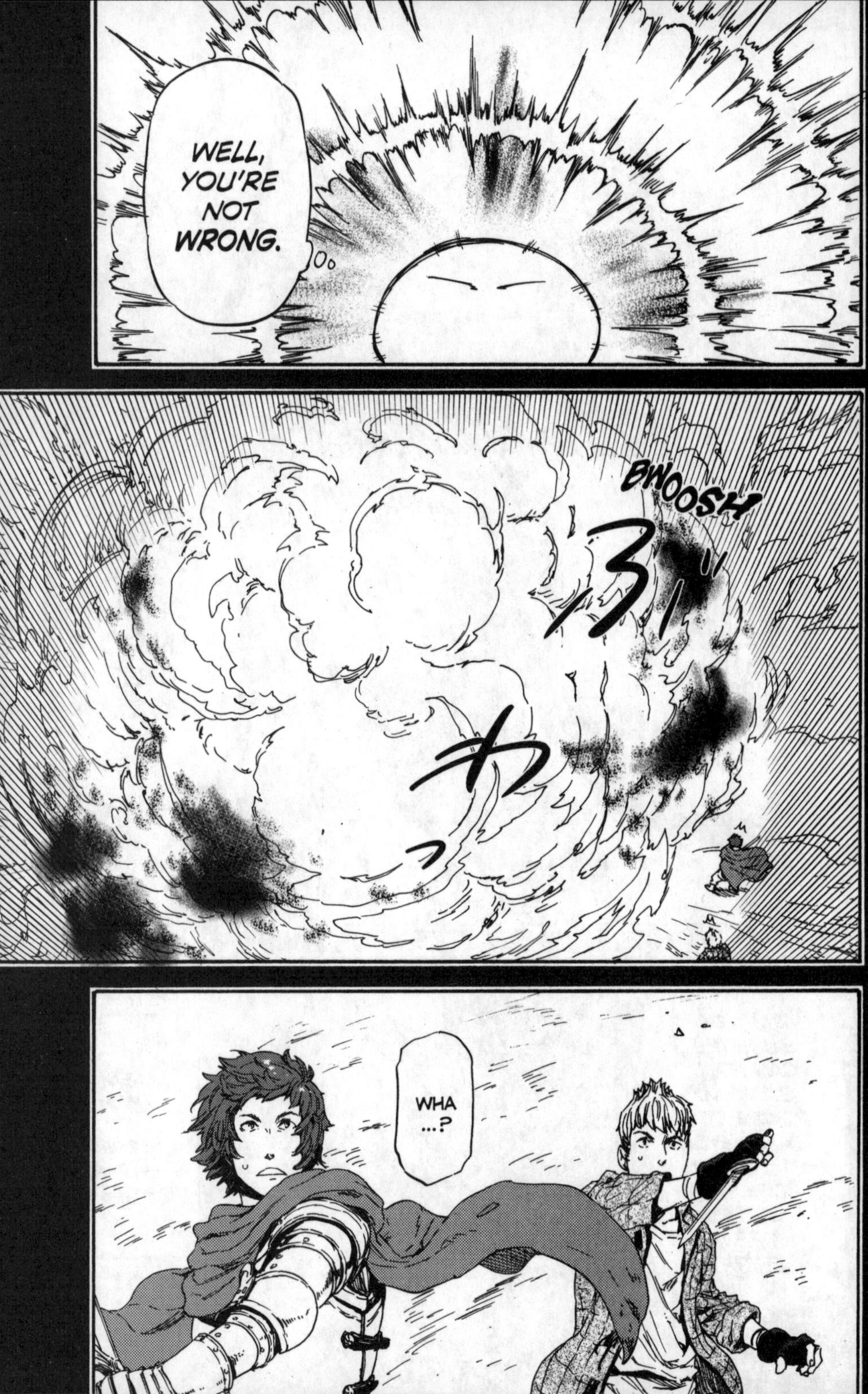
WELL, YOU'RE NOT WRONG.
BWOOSH
WHA ...?

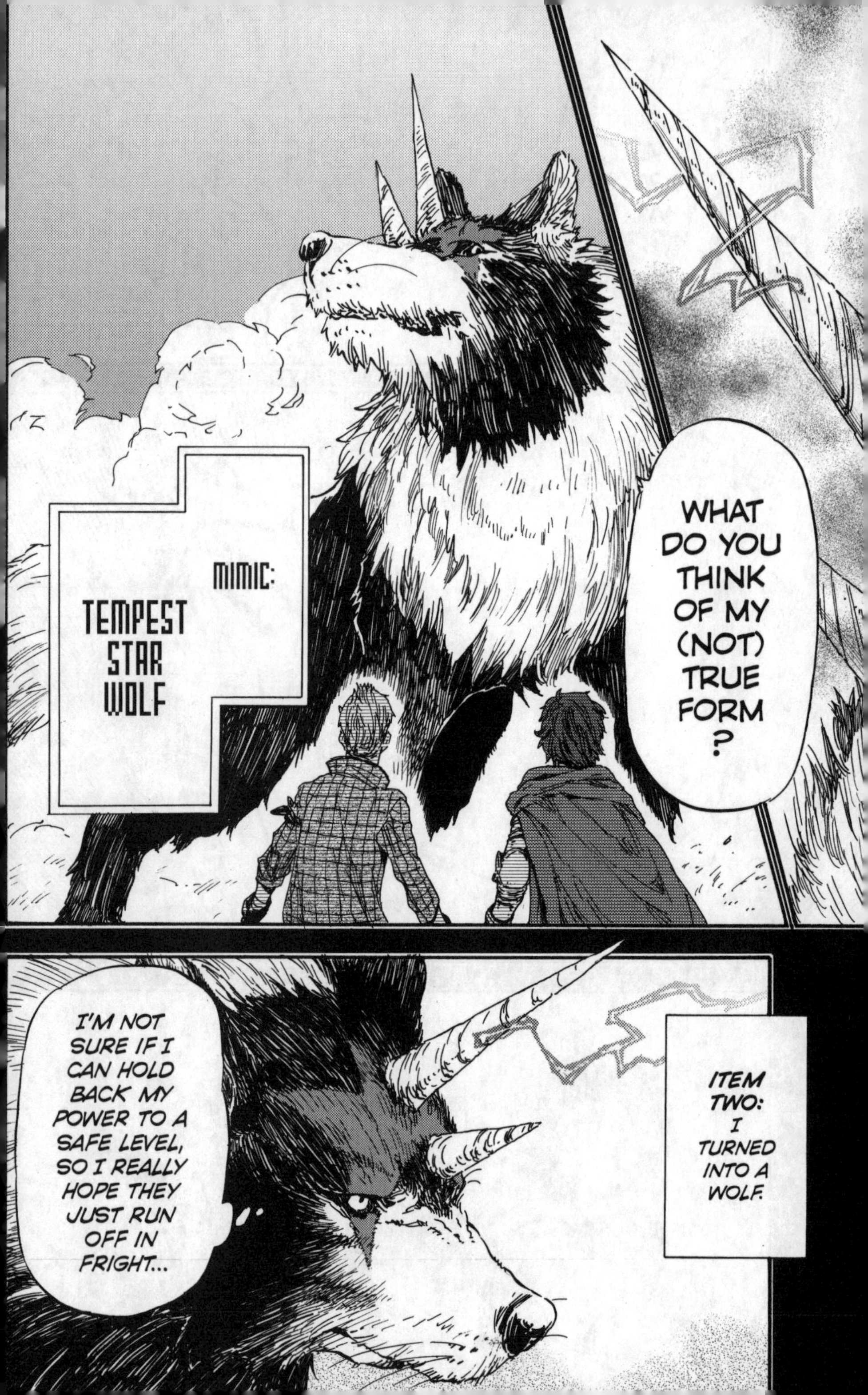
WHAT DO YOU THINK OF MY (NOT) TRUE FORM?
MIMIC: TEMPEST STAR WOLF
ITEM TWO: I TURNED INTO A WOLF.
I'M NOT SURE IF I CAN HOLD BACK MY POWER TO A SAFE LEVEL, SO I REALLY HOPE THEY JUST RUN OFF IN FRIGHT...

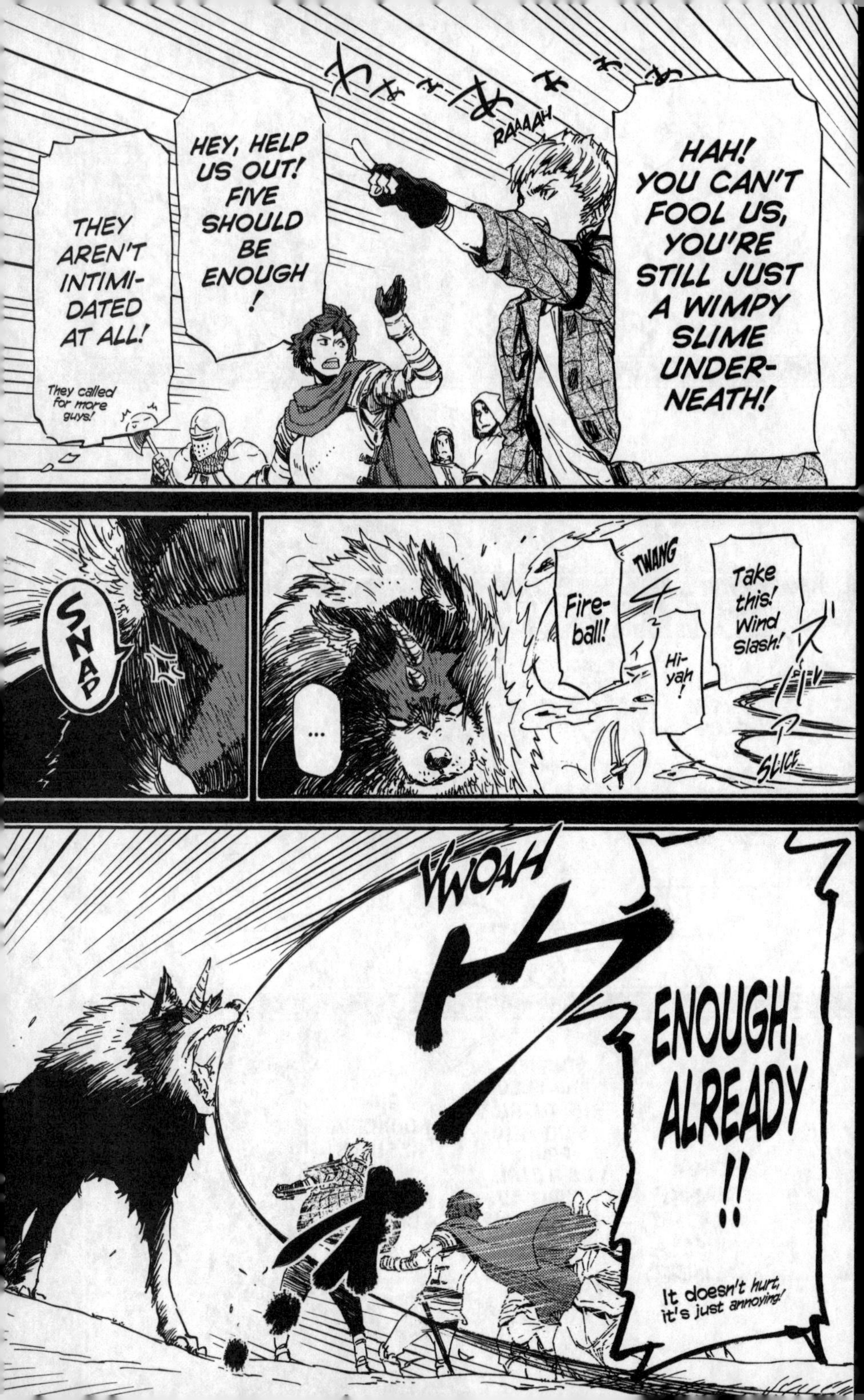
RAAAAH
HAH! YOU CAN'T FOOL US, YOU'RE STILL JUST A WIMPY SLIME UNDER-NEATH!
HEY, HELP US OUT! FIVE SHOULD BE ENOUGH!
THEY AREN'T INTIMI-DATED AT ALL!
They called for more guys!
Take this! Wind Slash!
SLICE
Hi-yah!
TWANG
Fire-ball!
...
SNAP
ENOUGH, ALREADY!!
VWOAH
It doesn't hurt, it's just annoying!

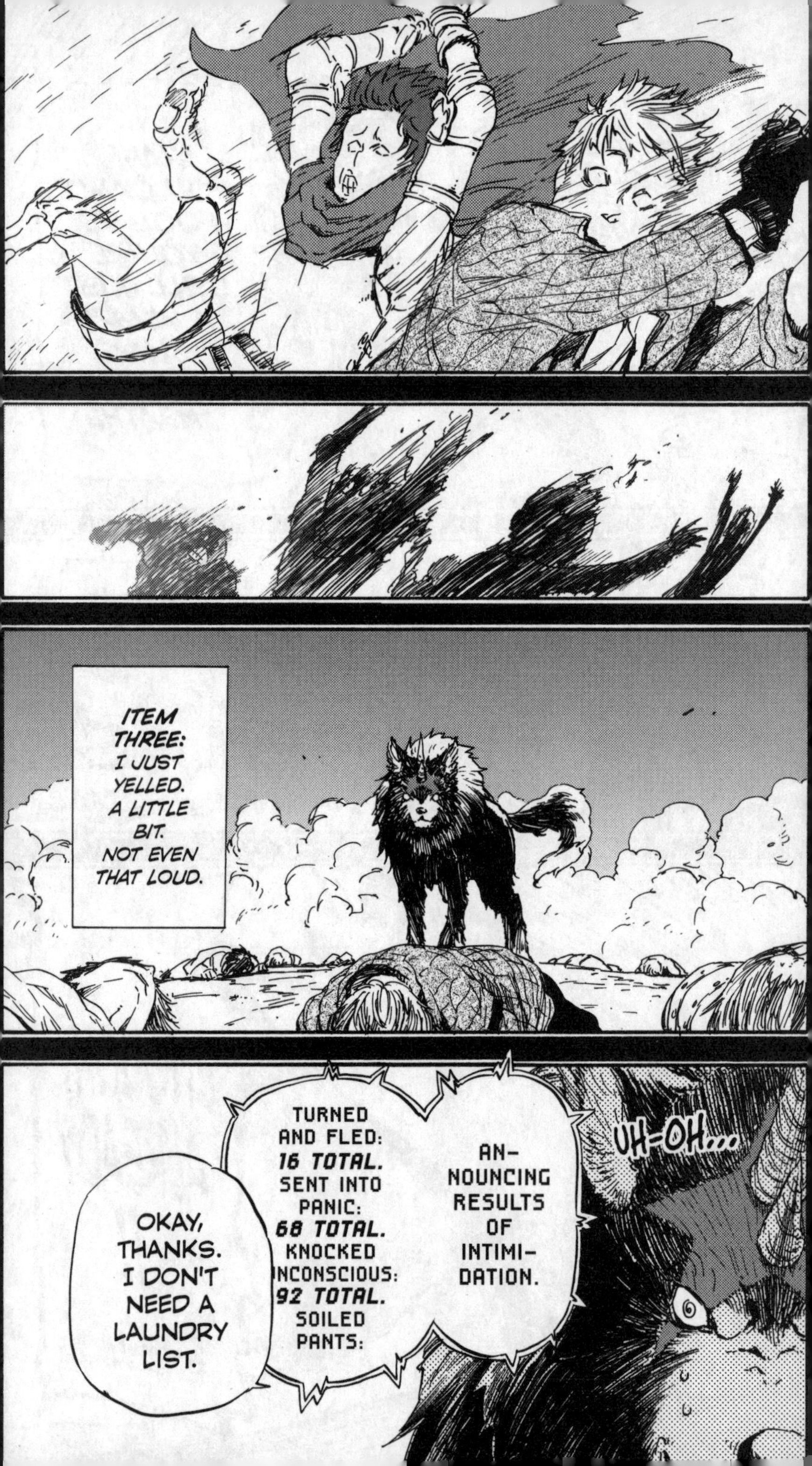
ITEM THREE: I JUST YELLED. A LITTLE BIT. NOT EVEN THAT LOUD.
UH-OH...
AN-NOUNCING RESULTS OF INTIMI-DATION.
TURNED AND FLED: 16 TOTAL. SENT INTO PANIC: 68 TOTAL. KNOCKED UNCONSCIOUS: 92 TOTAL. SOILED PANTS:
OKAY, THANKS. I DON'T NEED A LAUNDRY LIST.

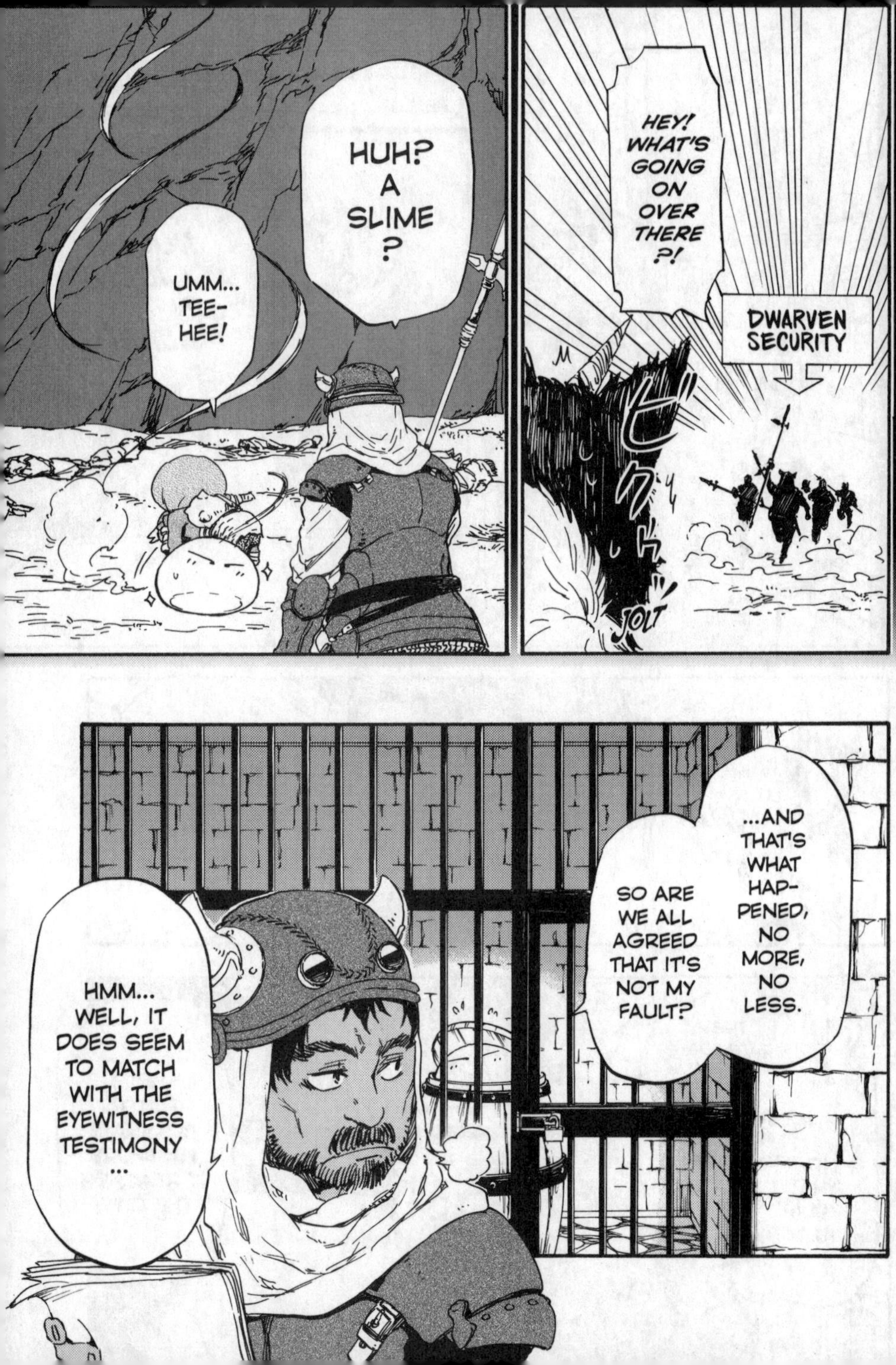
HEY! WHAT'S GOING ON OVER THERE?!
DWARVEN SECURITY
ビクッ
JOLT
HUH? A SLIME?
UMM... TEE-HEE!
...AND THAT'S WHAT HAPPENED, NO MORE, NO LESS.
SO ARE WE ALL AGREED THAT IT'S NOT MY FAULT?
HMM... WELL, IT DOES SEEM TO MATCH WITH THE EYEWITNESS TESTIMONY...

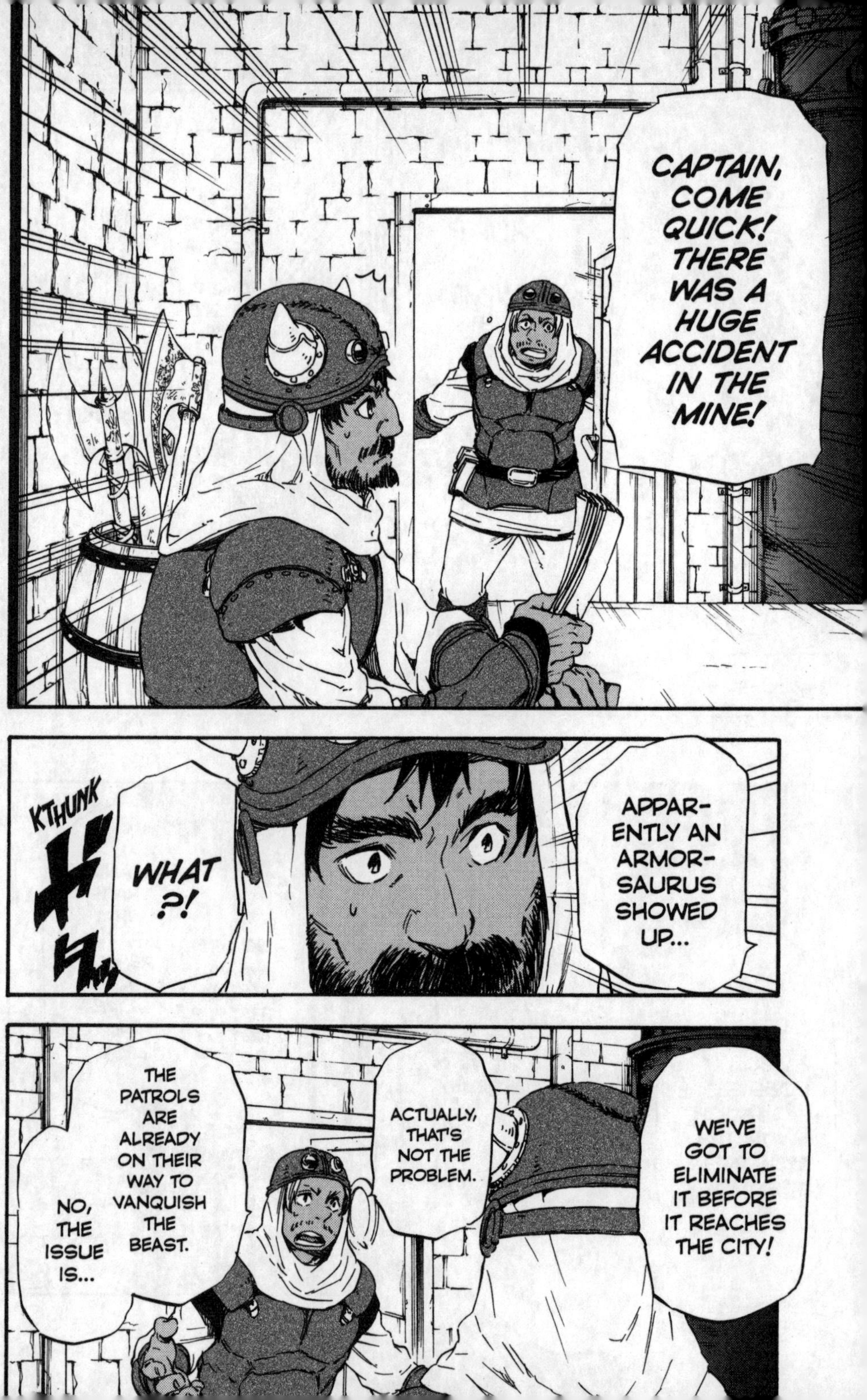
CAPTAIN, COME QUICK! THERE WAS A HUGE ACCIDENT IN THE MINE!
APPAR-ENTLY AN ARMOR-SAURUS SHOWED UP...
WHAT?!
KTHUNK
WE'VE GOT TO ELIMINATE IT BEFORE IT REACHES THE CITY!
ACTUALLY, THAT'S NOT THE PROBLEM.
THE PATROLS ARE ALREADY ON THEIR WAY TO VANQUISH THE BEAST.
NO, THE ISSUE IS...

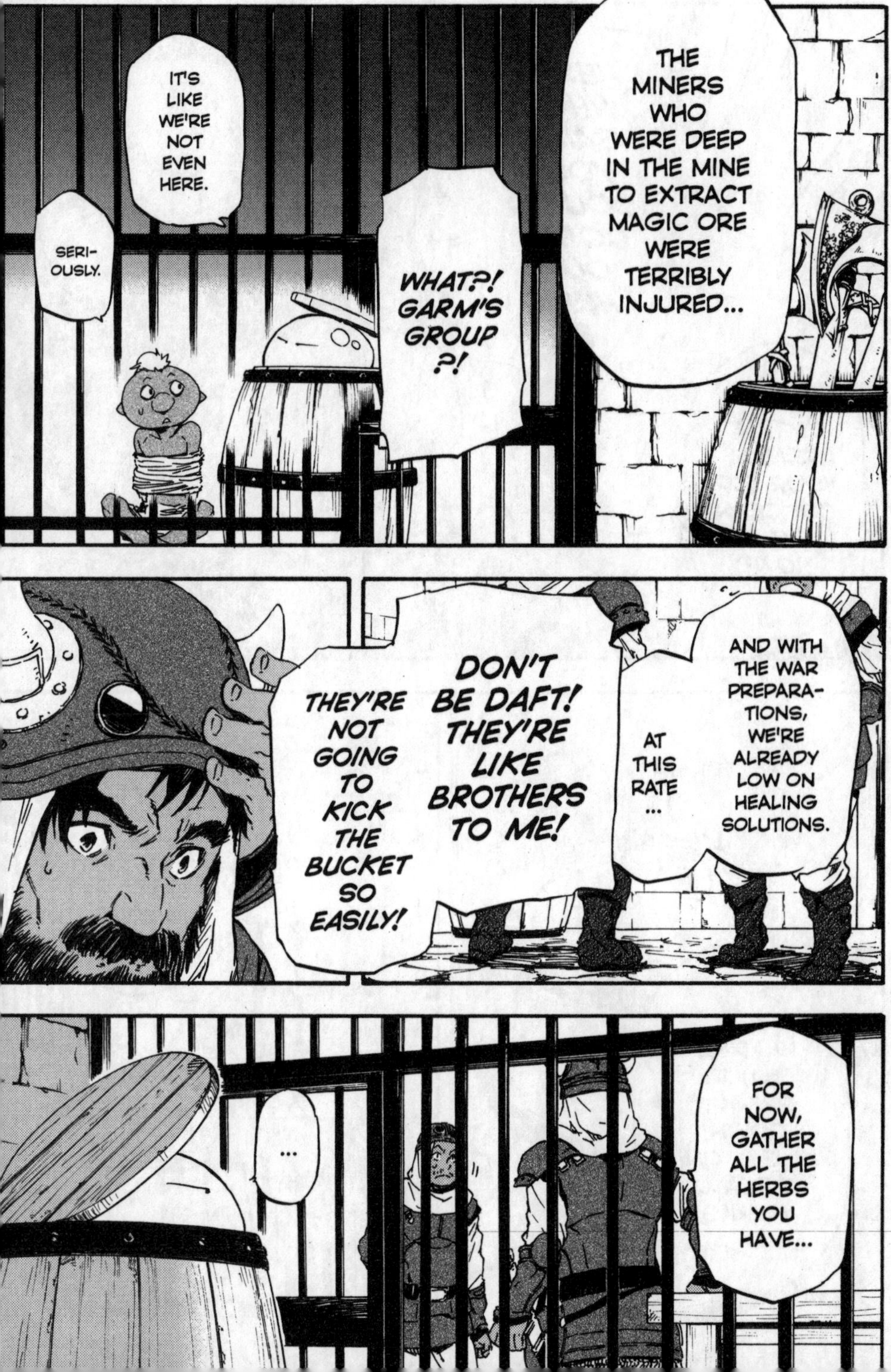
THE MINERS WHO WERE DEEP IN THE MINE TO EXTRACT MAGIC ORE WERE TERRIBLY INJURED...
WHAT?! GARM'S GROUP?!
IT'S LIKE WE'RE NOT EVEN HERE.
SERI-OUSLY.
AND WITH THE WAR PREPARA-TIONS, WE'RE ALREADY LOW ON HEALING SOLUTIONS.
AT THIS RATE...
DON'T BE DAFT! THEY'RE LIKE BROTHERS TO ME!
THEY'RE NOT GOING TO KICK THE BUCKET SO EASILY!
FOR NOW, GATHER ALL THE HERBS YOU HAVE...
...

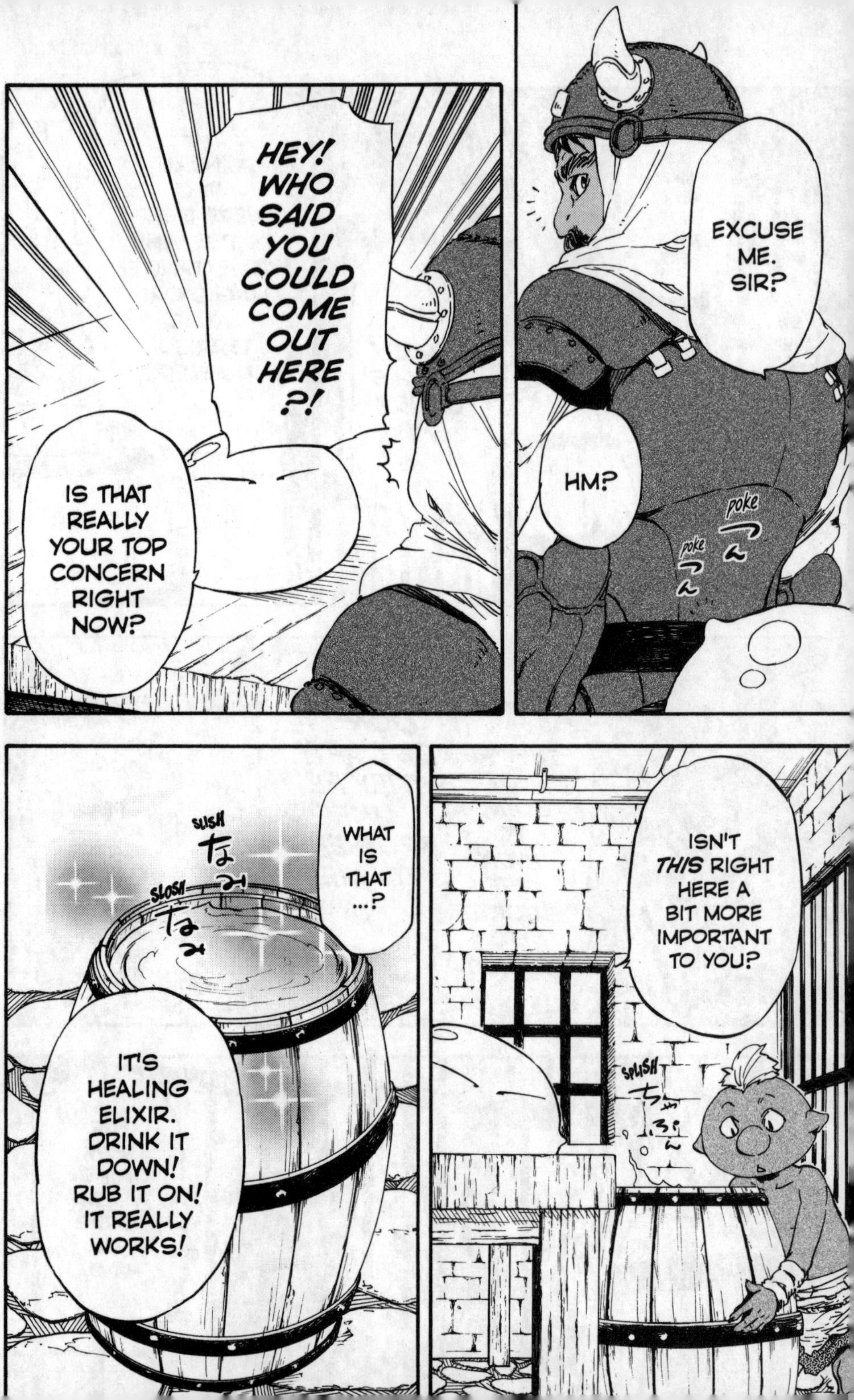
EXCUSE ME. SIR?
HM?
poke つん
poke つん
HEY! WHO SAID YOU COULD COME OUT HERE?!
IS THAT REALLY YOUR TOP CONCERN RIGHT NOW?
ISN'T *THIS* RIGHT HERE A BIT MORE IMPORTANT TO YOU?
SPLISH
WHAT IS THAT ...?
SLISH なみ
SLOSH なみ
IT'S HEALING ELIXIR. DRINK IT DOWN! RUB IT ON! IT REALLY WORKS!

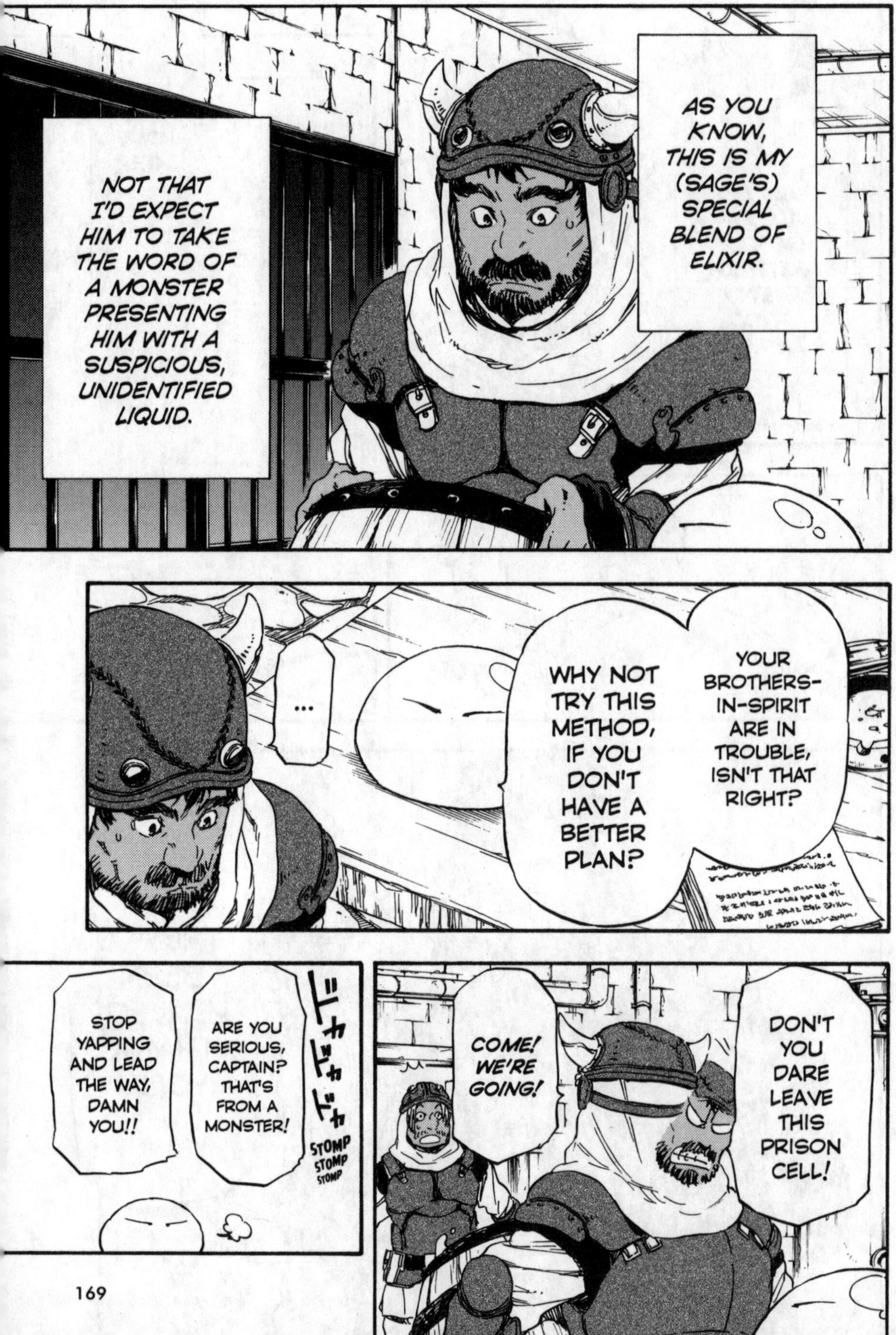
AS YOU KNOW, THIS IS MY (SAGE'S) SPECIAL BLEND OF ELIXIR.
NOT THAT I'D EXPECT HIM TO TAKE THE WORD OF A MONSTER PRESENTING HIM WITH A SUSPICIOUS, UNIDENTIFIED LIQUID.
YOUR BROTHERS-IN-SPIRIT ARE IN TROUBLE, ISN'T THAT RIGHT?
WHY NOT TRY THIS METHOD, IF YOU DON'T HAVE A BETTER PLAN?
...
DON'T YOU DARE LEAVE THIS PRISON CELL!
COME! WE'RE GOING!
STOMP STOMP STOMP
ARE YOU SERIOUS, CAPTAIN? THAT'S FROM A MONSTER!
STOP YAPPING AND LEAD THE WAY, DAMN YOU!!

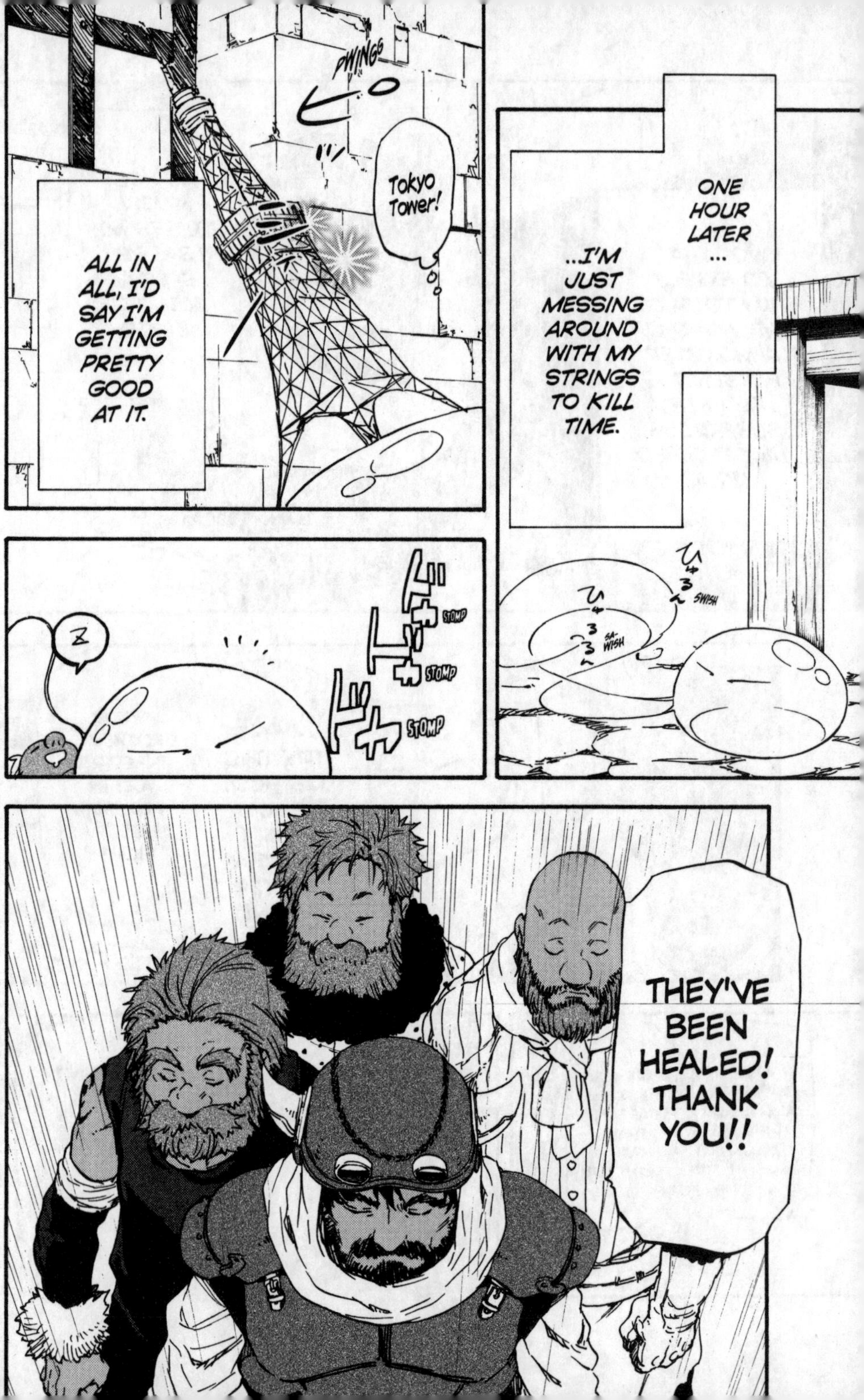

ONE HOUR LATER...
...I'M JUST MESSING AROUND WITH MY STRINGS TO KILL TIME.
SWISH
SA-WISH
PWINGS
Tokyo Tower!
ALL IN ALL, I'D SAY I'M GETTING PRETTY GOOD AT IT.
STOMP
STOMP
STOMP
Z
THEY'VE BEEN HEALED! THANK YOU!!

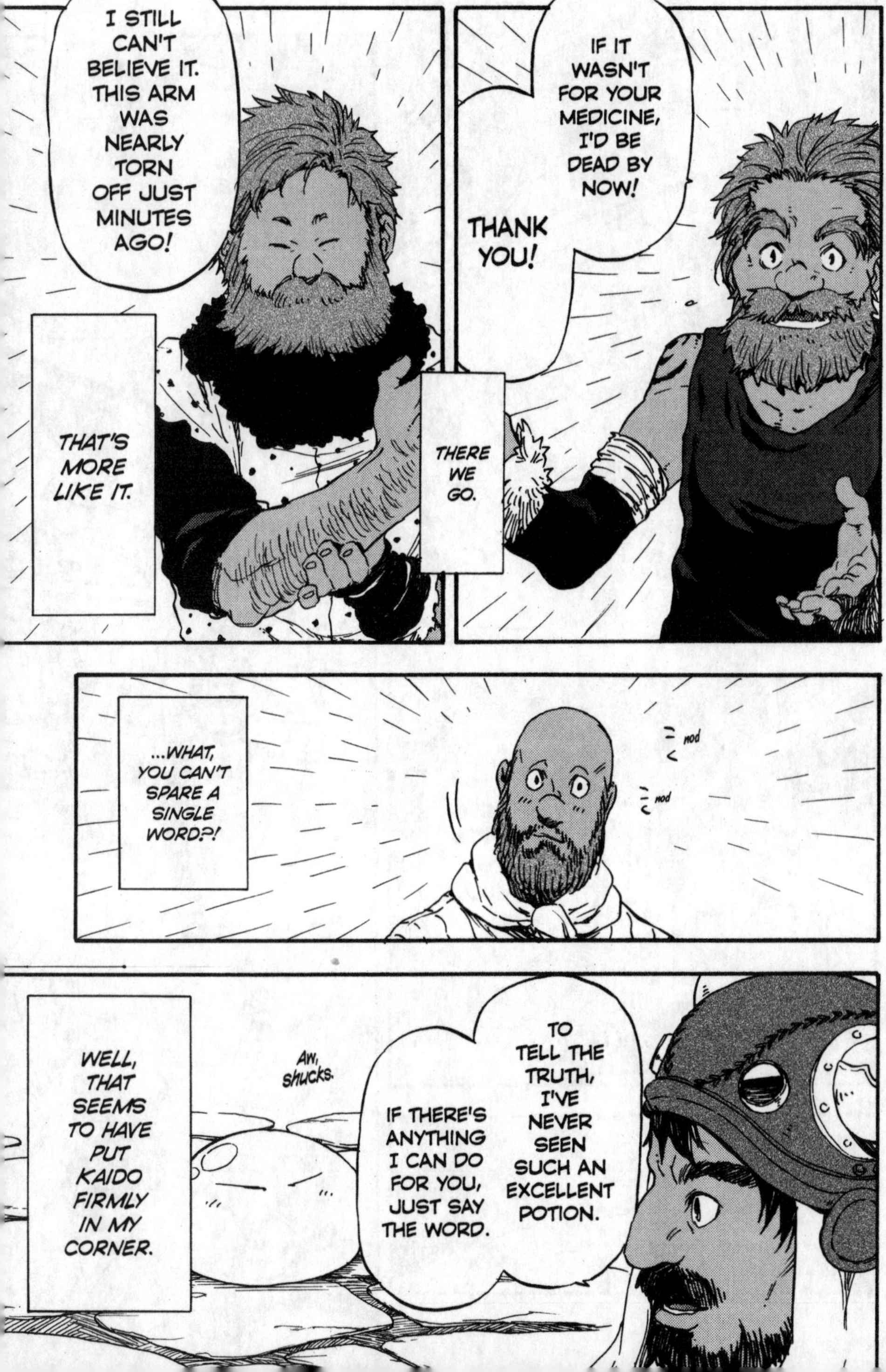
IF IT WASN'T FOR YOUR MEDICINE, I'D BE DEAD BY NOW!
THANK YOU!
THERE WE GO.
I STILL CAN'T BELIEVE IT. THIS ARM WAS NEARLY TORN OFF JUST MINUTES AGO!
THAT'S MORE LIKE IT.
nod
nod
...WHAT, YOU CAN'T SPARE A SINGLE WORD?!
TO TELL THE TRUTH, I'VE NEVER SEEN SUCH AN EXCELLENT POTION.
IF THERE'S ANYTHING I CAN DO FOR YOU, JUST SAY THE WORD.
Aw, shucks.
WELL, THAT SEEMS TO HAVE PUT KAIDO FIRMLY IN MY CORNER.

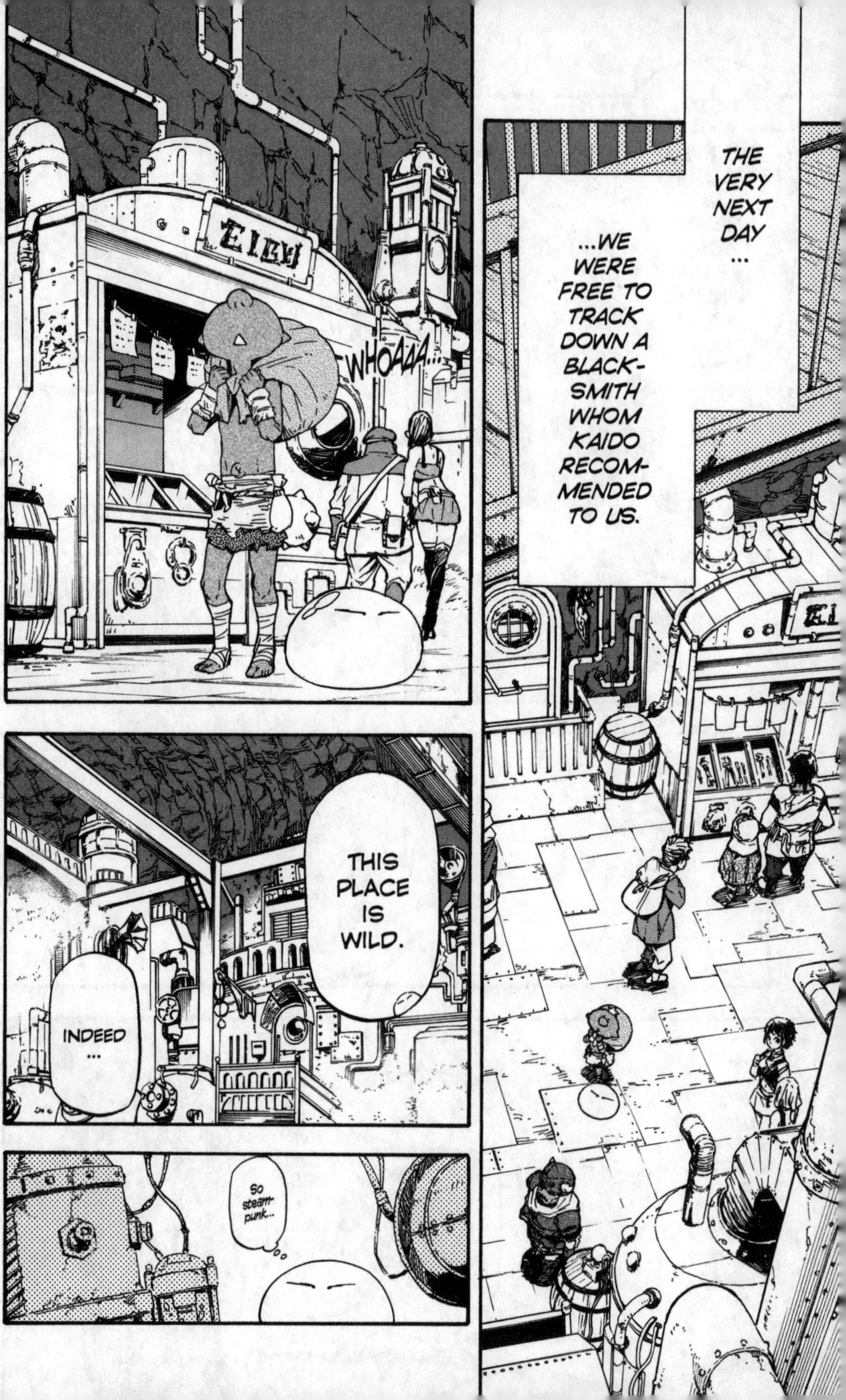
THE VERY NEXT DAY...
...WE WERE FREE TO TRACK DOWN A BLACKSMITH WHOM KAIDO RECOMMENDED TO US.
WHOAAA...
THIS PLACE IS WILD.
INDEED...
So steampunk...

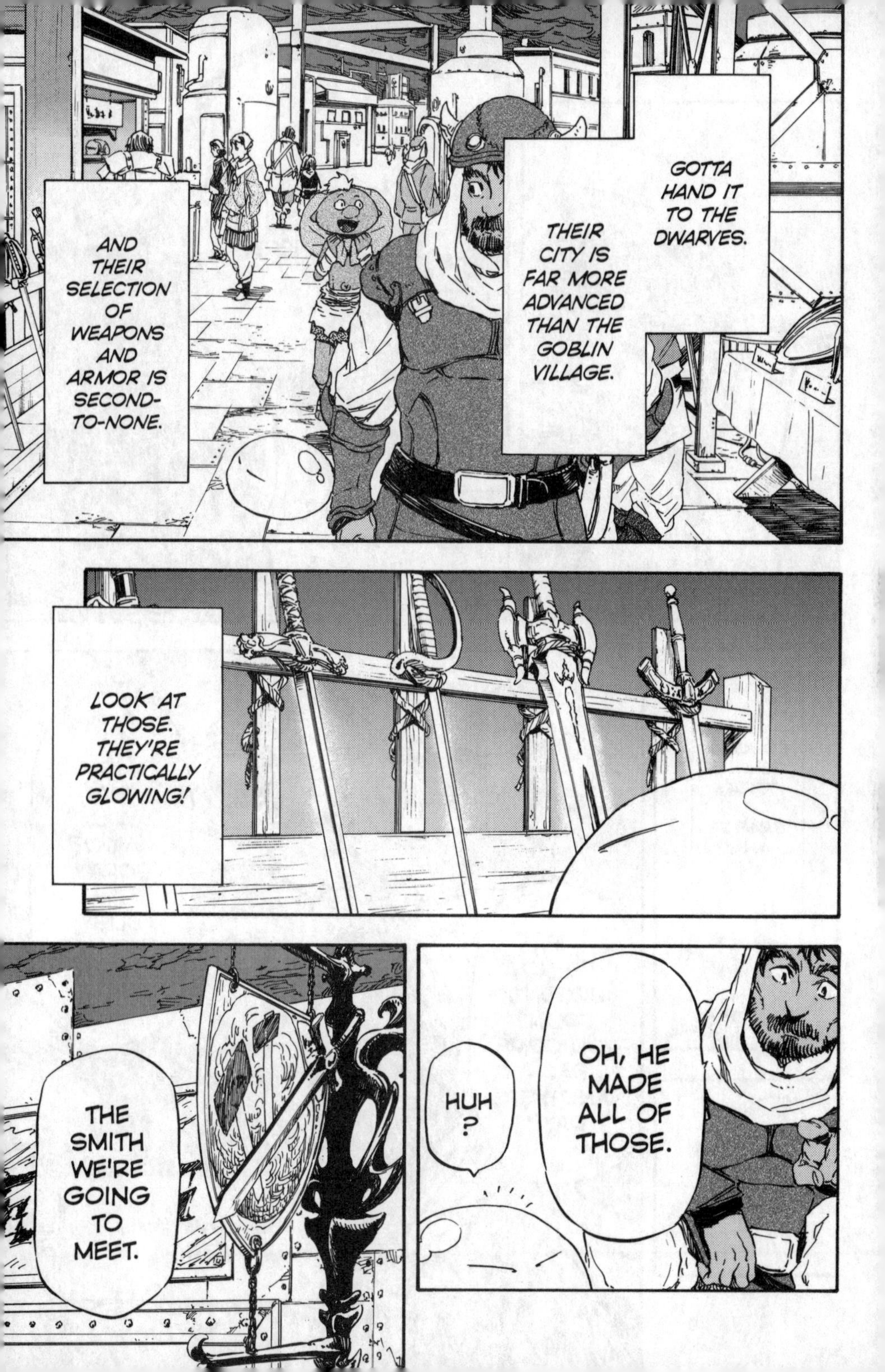
GOTTA HAND IT TO THE DWARVES.
THEIR CITY IS FAR MORE ADVANCED THAN THE GOBLIN VILLAGE.
AND THEIR SELECTION OF WEAPONS AND ARMOR IS SECOND-TO-NONE.
LOOK AT THOSE. THEY'RE PRACTICALLY GLOWING!
OH, HE MADE ALL OF THOSE.
HUH?
THE SMITH WE'RE GOING TO MEET.

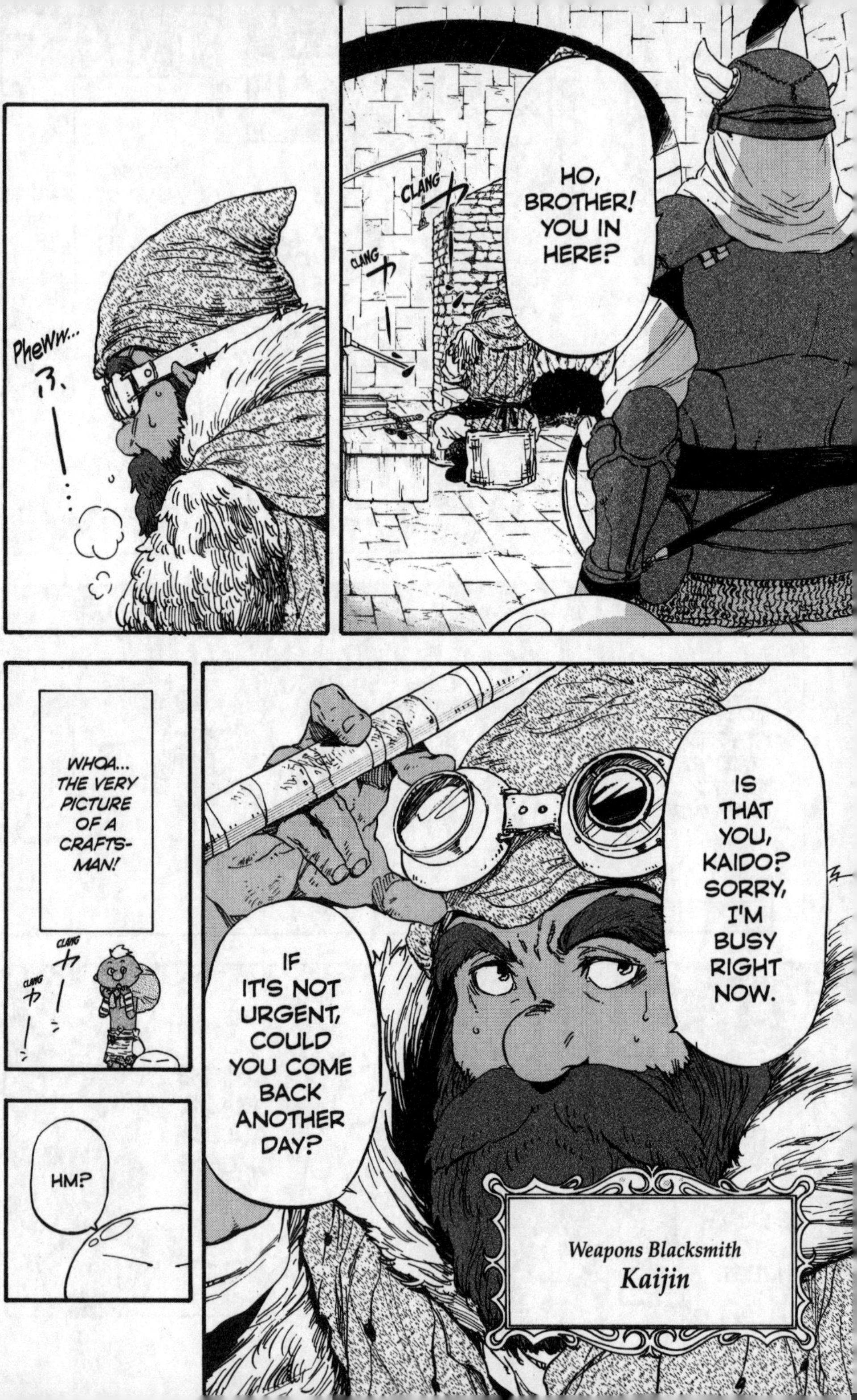
HO, BROTHER! YOU IN HERE?
CLANG カ
CLANG カ
Pheww... ふ...
IS THAT YOU, KAIDO? SORRY, I'M BUSY RIGHT NOW.
IF IT'S NOT URGENT, COULD YOU COME BACK ANOTHER DAY?
Weapons Blacksmith
Kaijin
WHOA... THE VERY PICTURE OF A CRAFTS-MAN!
CLANG カ
CLANG カ
HM?

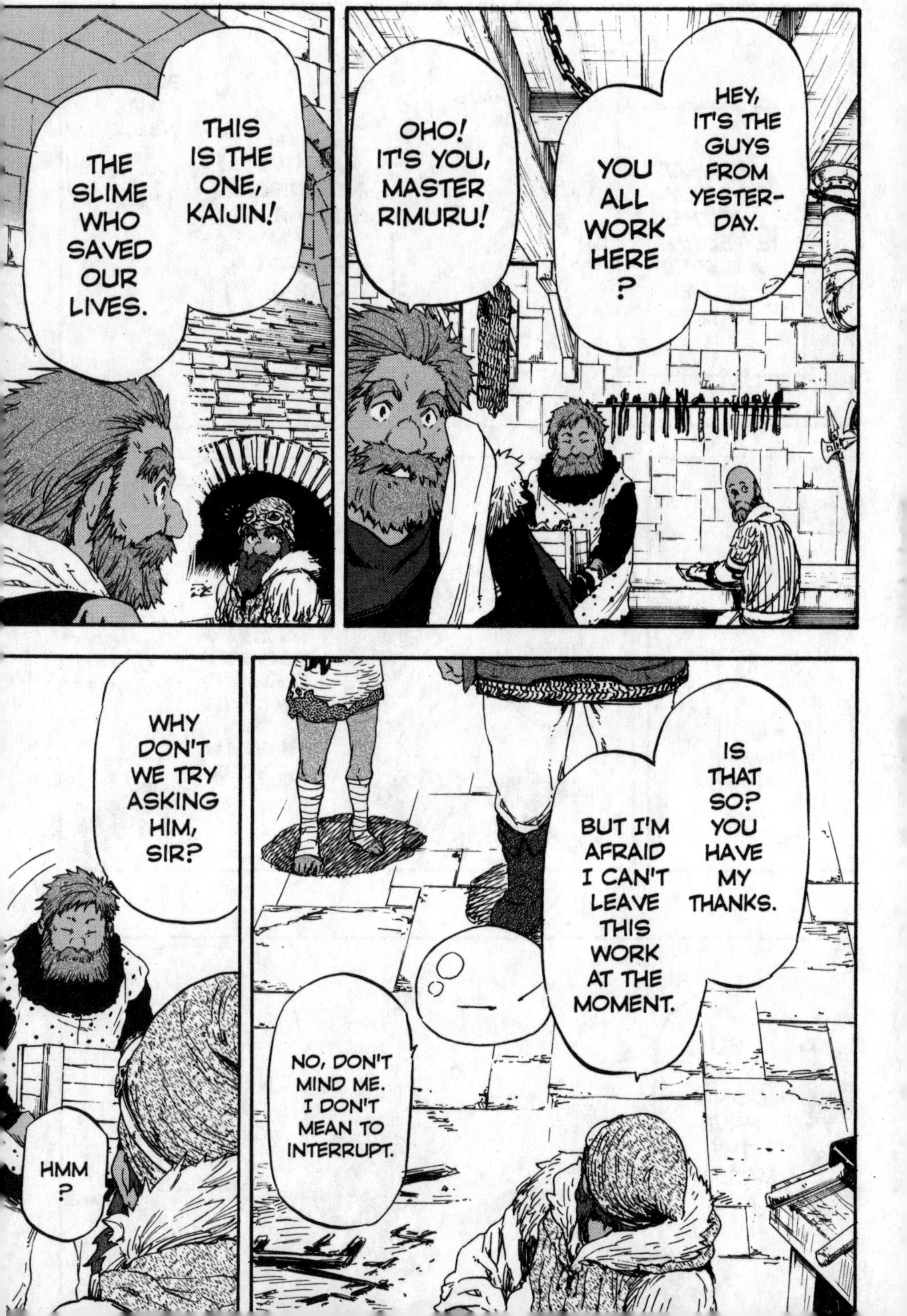
HEY, IT'S THE GUYS FROM YESTER-DAY.
YOU ALL WORK HERE?
OHO! IT'S YOU, MASTER RIMURU!
THIS IS THE ONE, KAIJIN!
THE SLIME WHO SAVED OUR LIVES.
IS THAT SO? YOU HAVE MY THANKS.
BUT I'M AFRAID I CAN'T LEAVE THIS WORK AT THE MOMENT.
NO, DON'T MIND ME. I DON'T MEAN TO INTERRUPT.
WHY DON'T WE TRY ASKING HIM, SIR?
HMM?

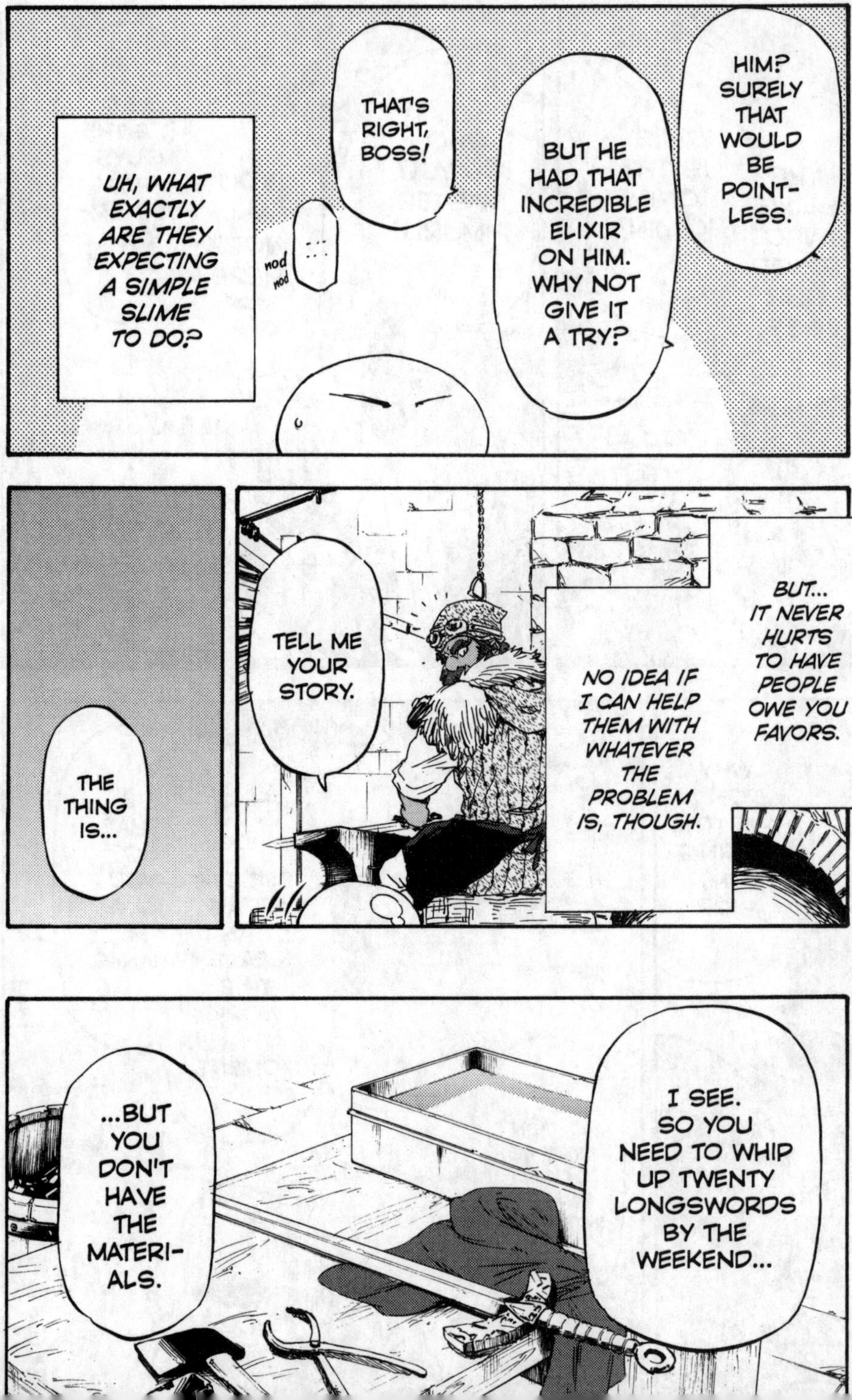
HIM? SURELY THAT WOULD BE POINT-LESS.
BUT HE HAD THAT INCREDIBLE ELIXIR ON HIM. WHY NOT GIVE IT A TRY?
THAT'S RIGHT, BOSS!
......
nod nod
UH, WHAT EXACTLY ARE THEY EXPECTING A SIMPLE SLIME TO DO?
BUT... IT NEVER HURTS TO HAVE PEOPLE OWE YOU FAVORS.
NO IDEA IF I CAN HELP THEM WITH WHATEVER THE PROBLEM IS, THOUGH.
TELL ME YOUR STORY.
THE THING IS...
I SEE. SO YOU NEED TO WHIP UP TWENTY LONGSWORDS BY THE WEEKEND...
...BUT YOU DON'T HAVE THE MATERI-ALS.

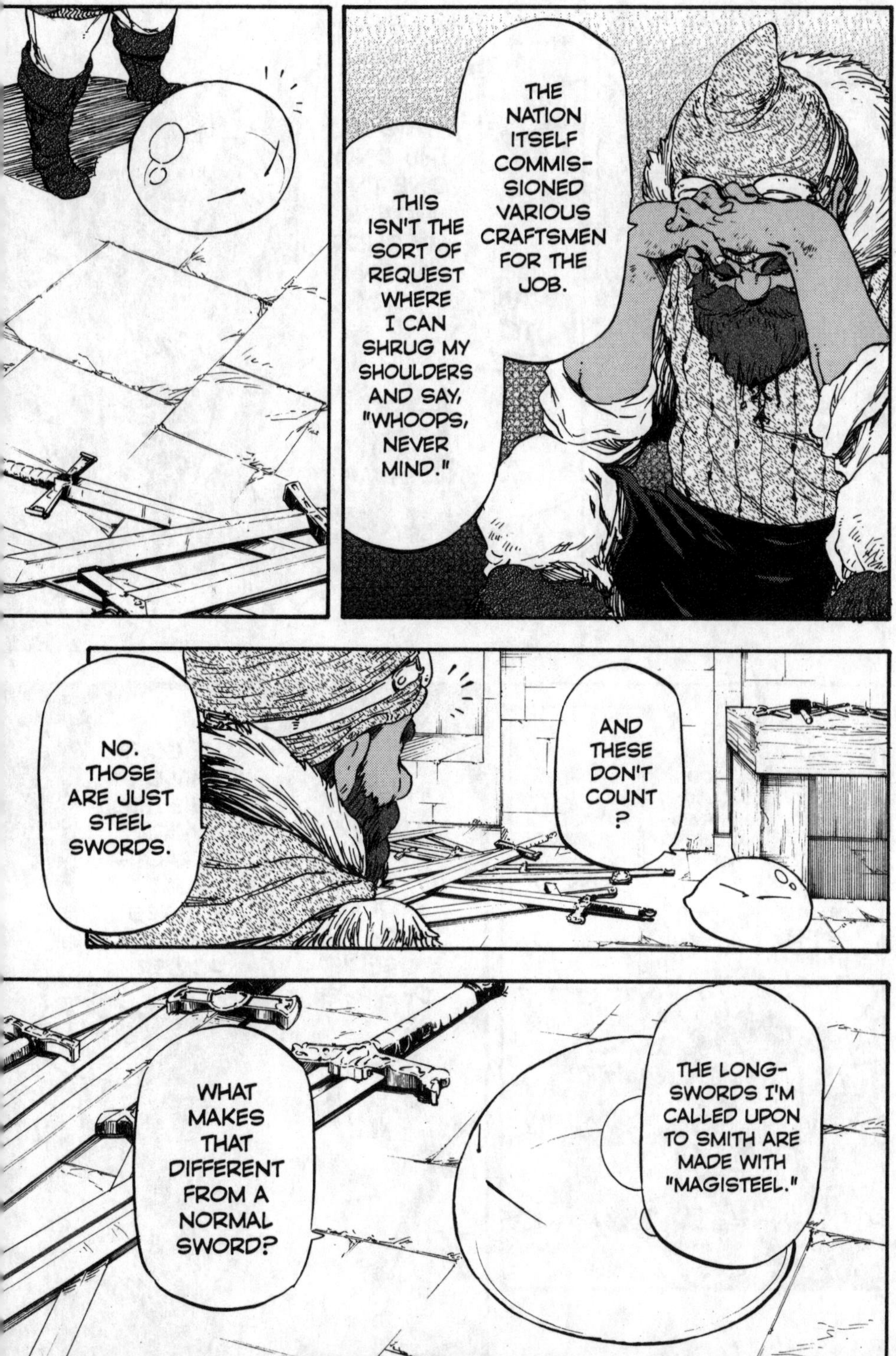
THE NATION ITSELF COMMISSIONED VARIOUS CRAFTSMEN FOR THE JOB.
THIS ISN'T THE SORT OF REQUEST WHERE I CAN SHRUG MY SHOULDERS AND SAY, "WHOOPS, NEVER MIND."
AND THESE DON'T COUNT?
NO. THOSE ARE JUST STEEL SWORDS.
THE LONG-SWORDS I'M CALLED UPON TO SMITH ARE MADE WITH "MAGISTEEL."
WHAT MAKES THAT DIFFERENT FROM A NORMAL SWORD?

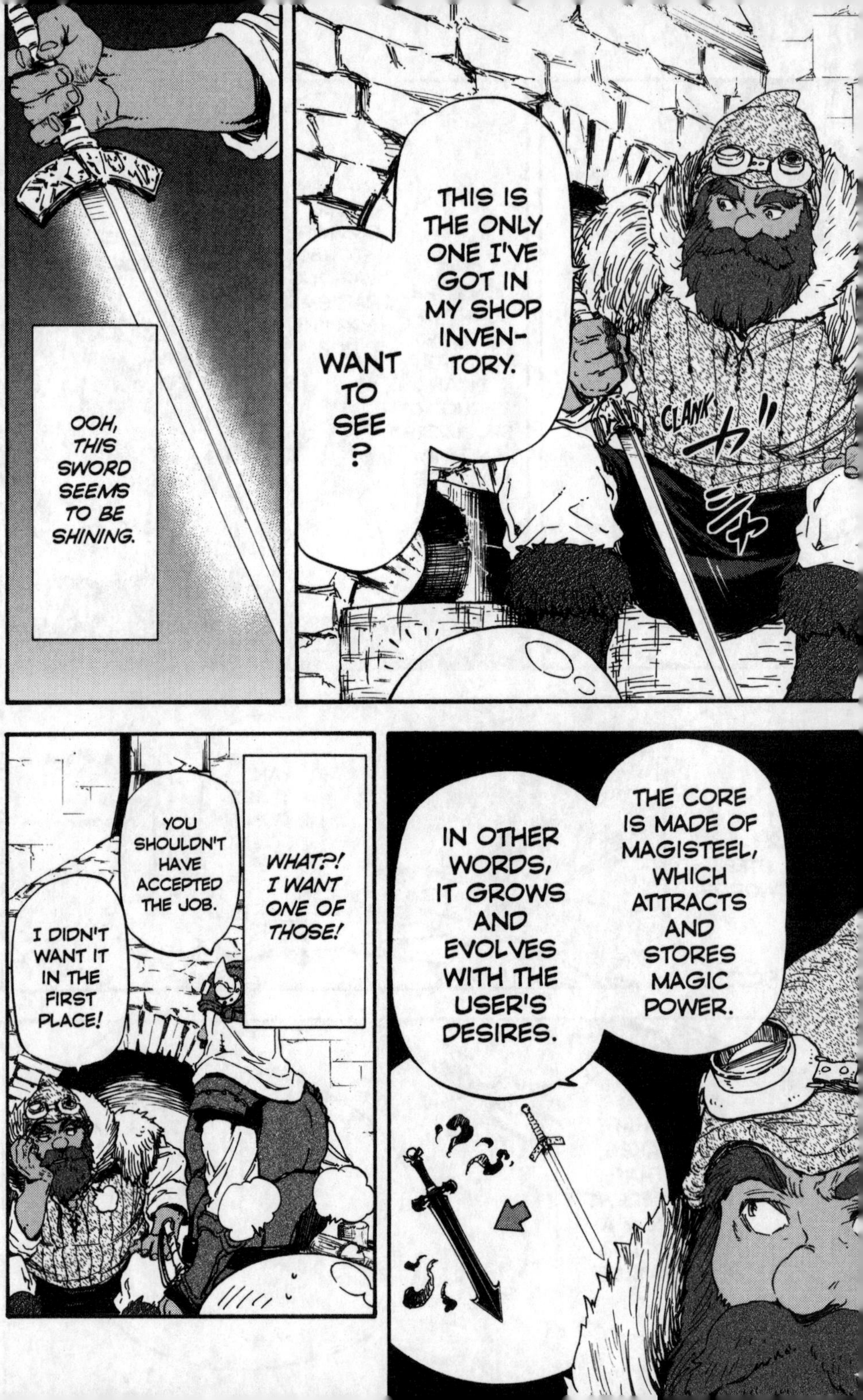
THIS IS THE ONLY ONE I'VE GOT IN MY SHOP INVENTORY.
WANT TO SEE?
CLANK
OOH, THIS SWORD SEEMS TO BE SHINING.
THE CORE IS MADE OF MAGISTEEL, WHICH ATTRACTS AND STORES MAGIC POWER.
IN OTHER WORDS, IT GROWS AND EVOLVES WITH THE USER'S DESIRES.
WHAT?! I WANT ONE OF THOSE!
YOU SHOULDN'T HAVE ACCEPTED THE JOB.
I DIDN'T WANT IT IN THE FIRST PLACE!

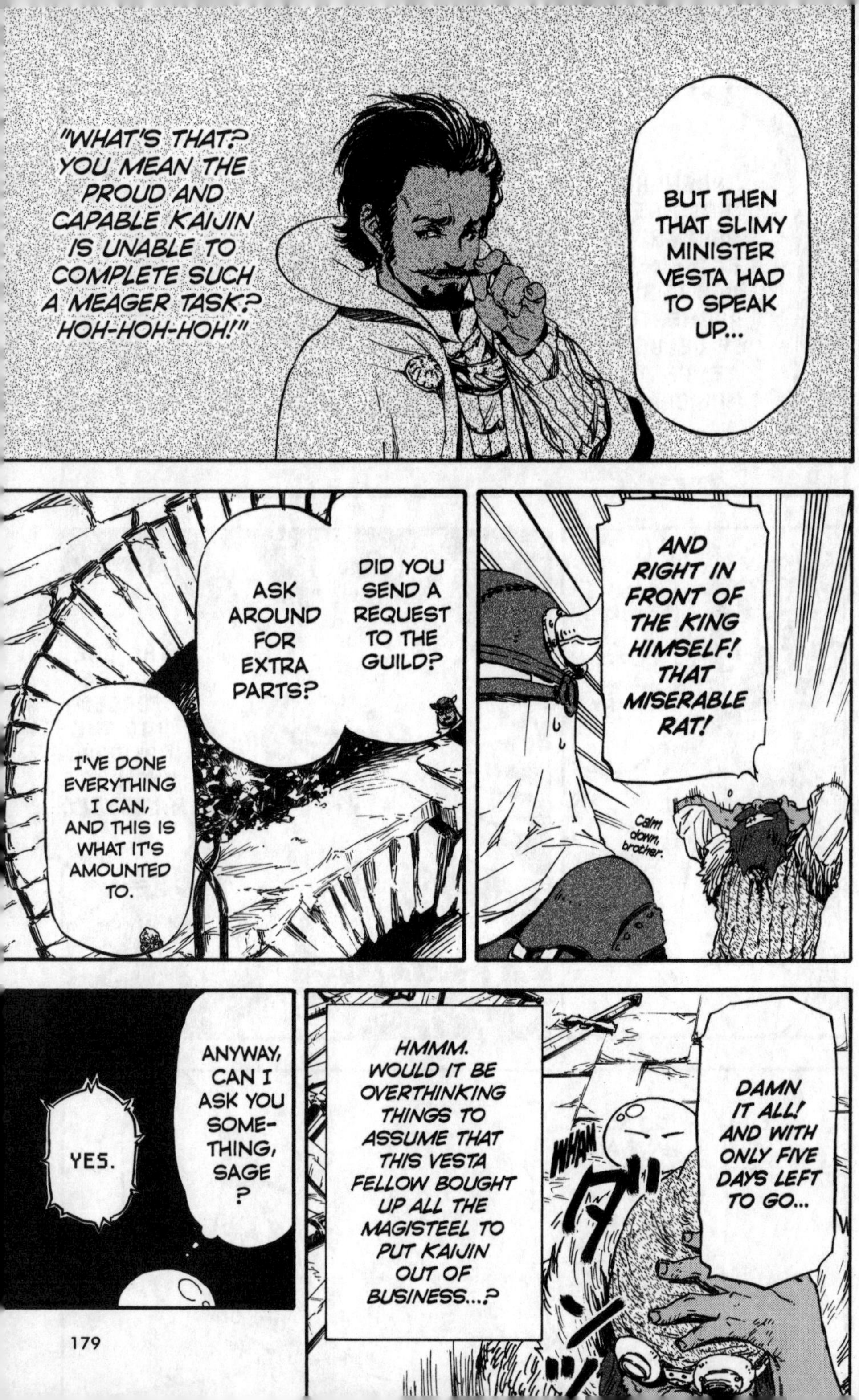
BUT THEN THAT SLIMY MINISTER VESTA HAD TO SPEAK UP...
"WHAT'S THAT? YOU MEAN THE PROUD AND CAPABLE KAIJIN IS UNABLE TO COMPLETE SUCH A MEAGER TASK? HOH-HOH-HOH!"
AND RIGHT IN FRONT OF THE KING HIMSELF! THAT MISERABLE RAT!
Calm down, brother.
DID YOU SEND A REQUEST TO THE GUILD?
ASK AROUND FOR EXTRA PARTS?
I'VE DONE EVERYTHING I CAN, AND THIS IS WHAT IT'S AMOUNTED TO.
DAMN IT ALL! AND WITH ONLY FIVE DAYS LEFT TO GO...
WHAM
HMMM. WOULD IT BE OVERTHINKING THINGS TO ASSUME THAT THIS VESTA FELLOW BOUGHT UP ALL THE MAGISTEEL TO PUT KAIJIN OUT OF BUSINESS...?
ANYWAY, CAN I ASK YOU SOME-THING, SAGE?
YES.

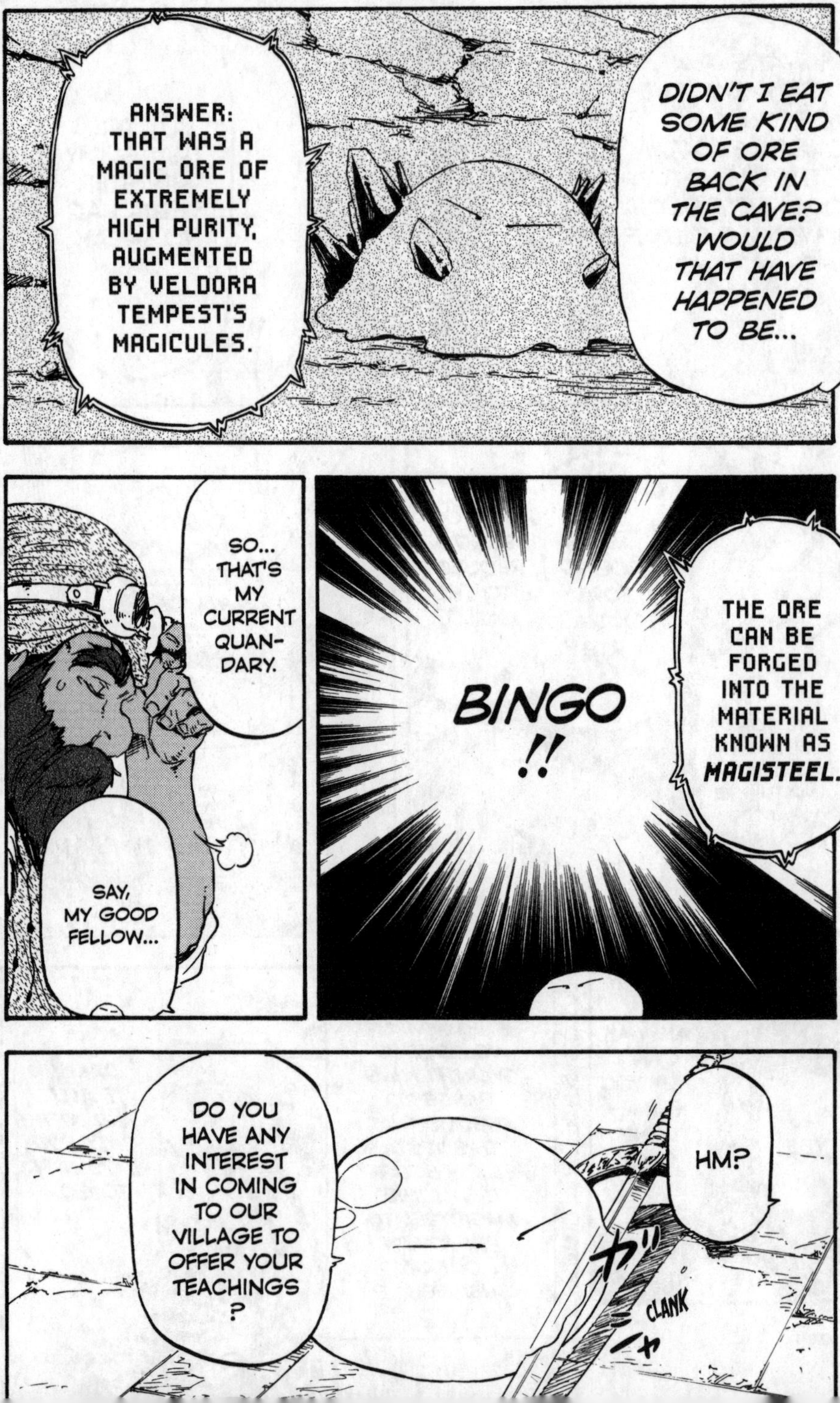
DIDN'T I EAT SOME KIND OF ORE BACK IN THE CAVE? WOULD THAT HAVE HAPPENED TO BE...
ANSWER: THAT WAS A MAGIC ORE OF EXTREMELY HIGH PURITY, AUGMENTED BY VELDORA TEMPEST'S MAGICULES.
THE ORE CAN BE FORGED INTO THE MATERIAL KNOWN AS **MAGISTEEL.**
BINGO !!
SO... THAT'S MY CURRENT QUAN-DARY.
SAY, MY GOOD FELLOW...
HM?
DO YOU HAVE ANY INTEREST IN COMING TO OUR VILLAGE TO OFFER YOUR TEACHINGS ?
CLANK

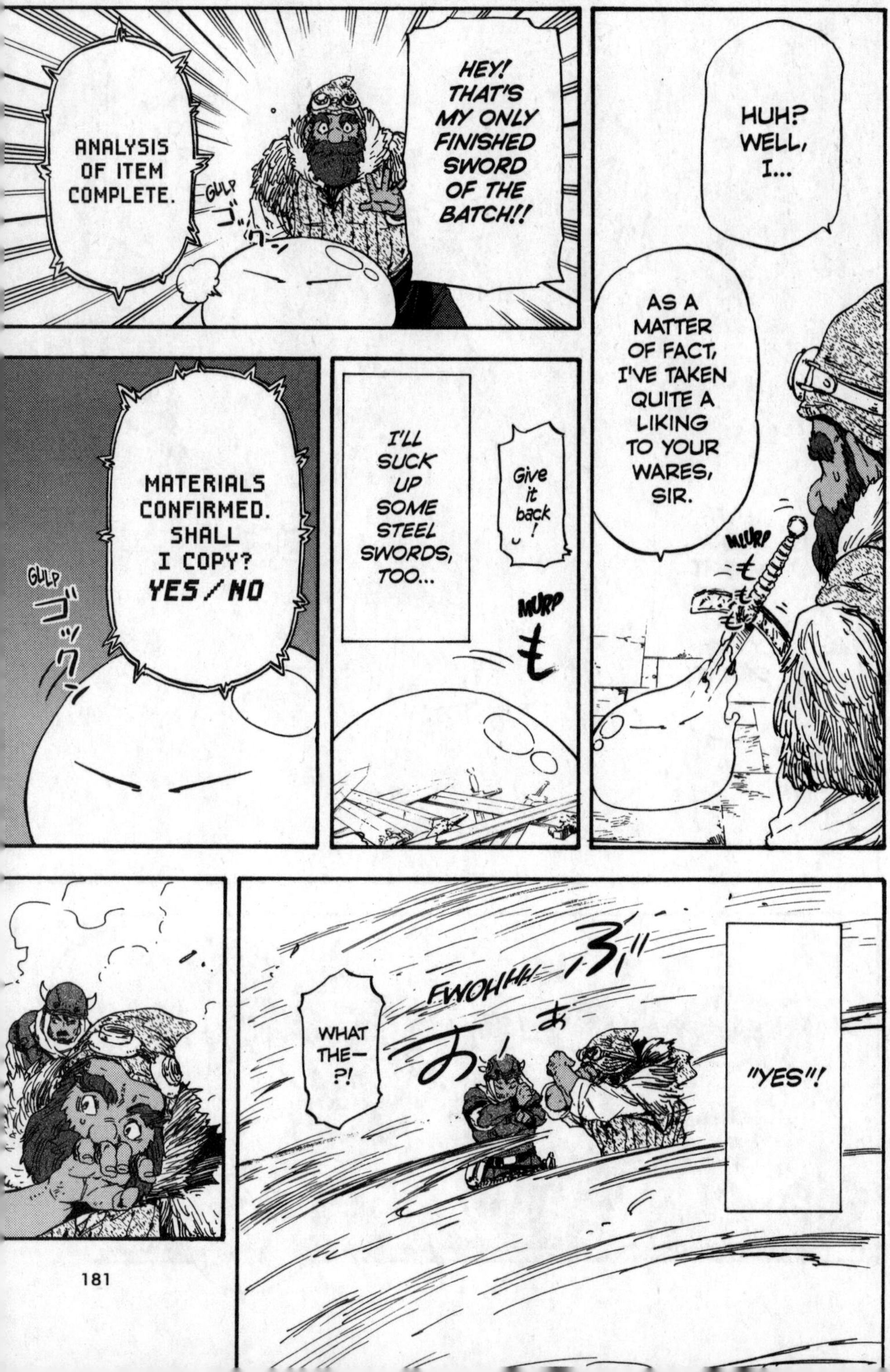
HUH? WELL, I...
AS A MATTER OF FACT, I'VE TAKEN QUITE A LIKING TO YOUR WARES, SIR.
MURP
HEY! THAT'S MY ONLY FINISHED SWORD OF THE BATCH!!
ANALYSIS OF ITEM COMPLETE.
GULP
Give it back!
I'LL SUCK UP SOME STEEL SWORDS, TOO...
MURP
も
MATERIALS CONFIRMED. SHALL I COPY? YES / NO
GULP
"YES"!
FWOHHH
あ
WHAT THE—?!
お

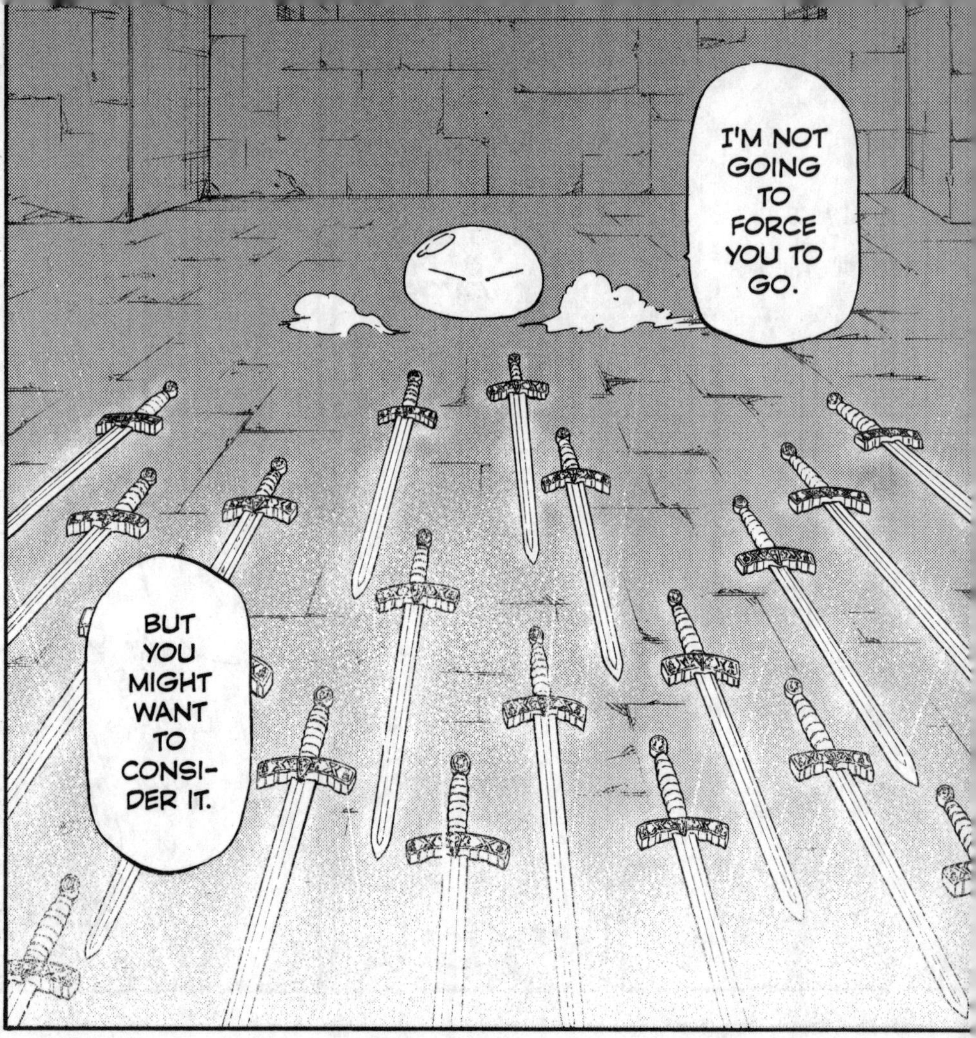
I'M NOT GOING TO FORCE YOU TO GO.
BUT YOU MIGHT WANT TO CONSI-DER IT.

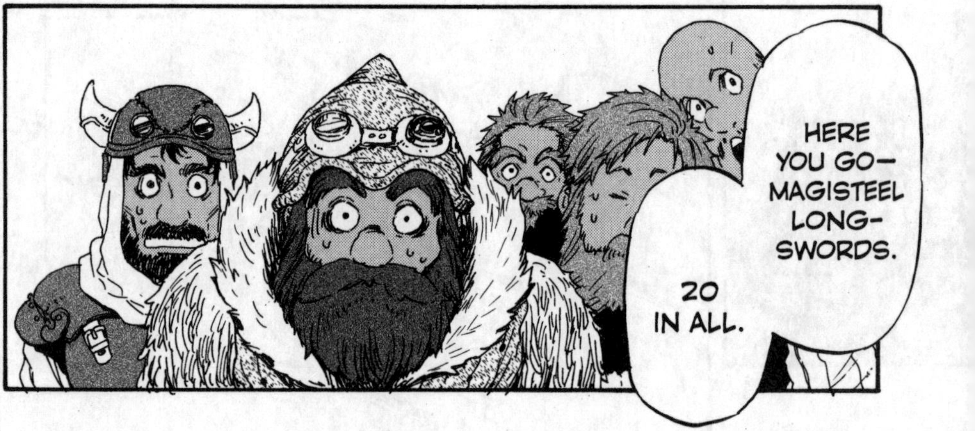
HERE YOU GO—MAGISTEEL LONG-SWORDS.
20 IN ALL.

I
shall
protect
this
village
until
Lord
Rimuru
returns
!!

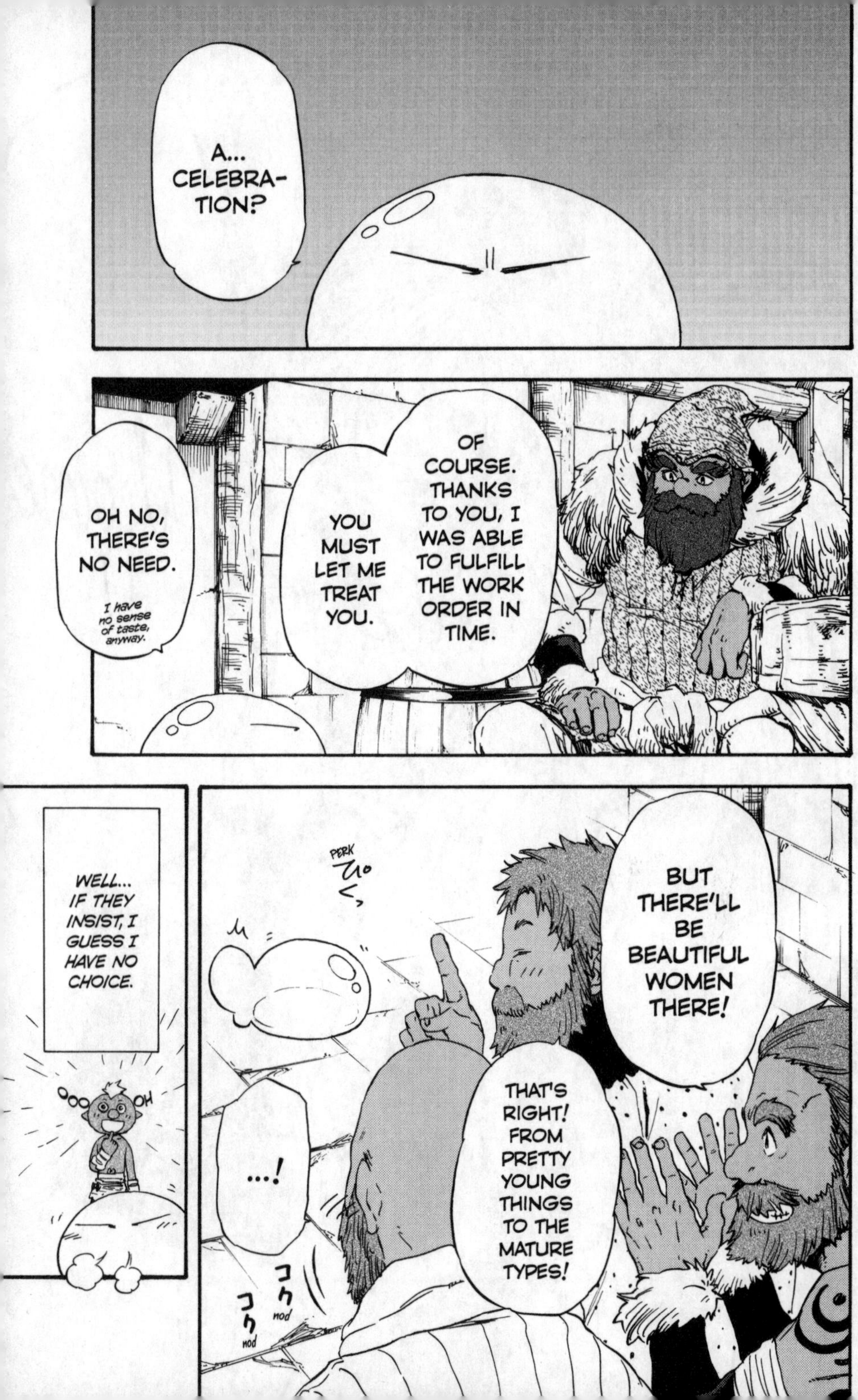
A... CELEBRATION?
OF COURSE. THANKS TO YOU, I WAS ABLE TO FULFILL THE WORK ORDER IN TIME.
YOU MUST LET ME TREAT YOU.
OH NO, THERE'S NO NEED.
I have no sense of taste, anyway.
PERK
BUT THERE'LL BE BEAUTIFUL WOMEN THERE!
THAT'S RIGHT! FROM PRETTY YOUNG THINGS TO THE MATURE TYPES!
...!
nod
nod
WELL... IF THEY INSIST, I GUESS I HAVE NO CHOICE.
OOOOH

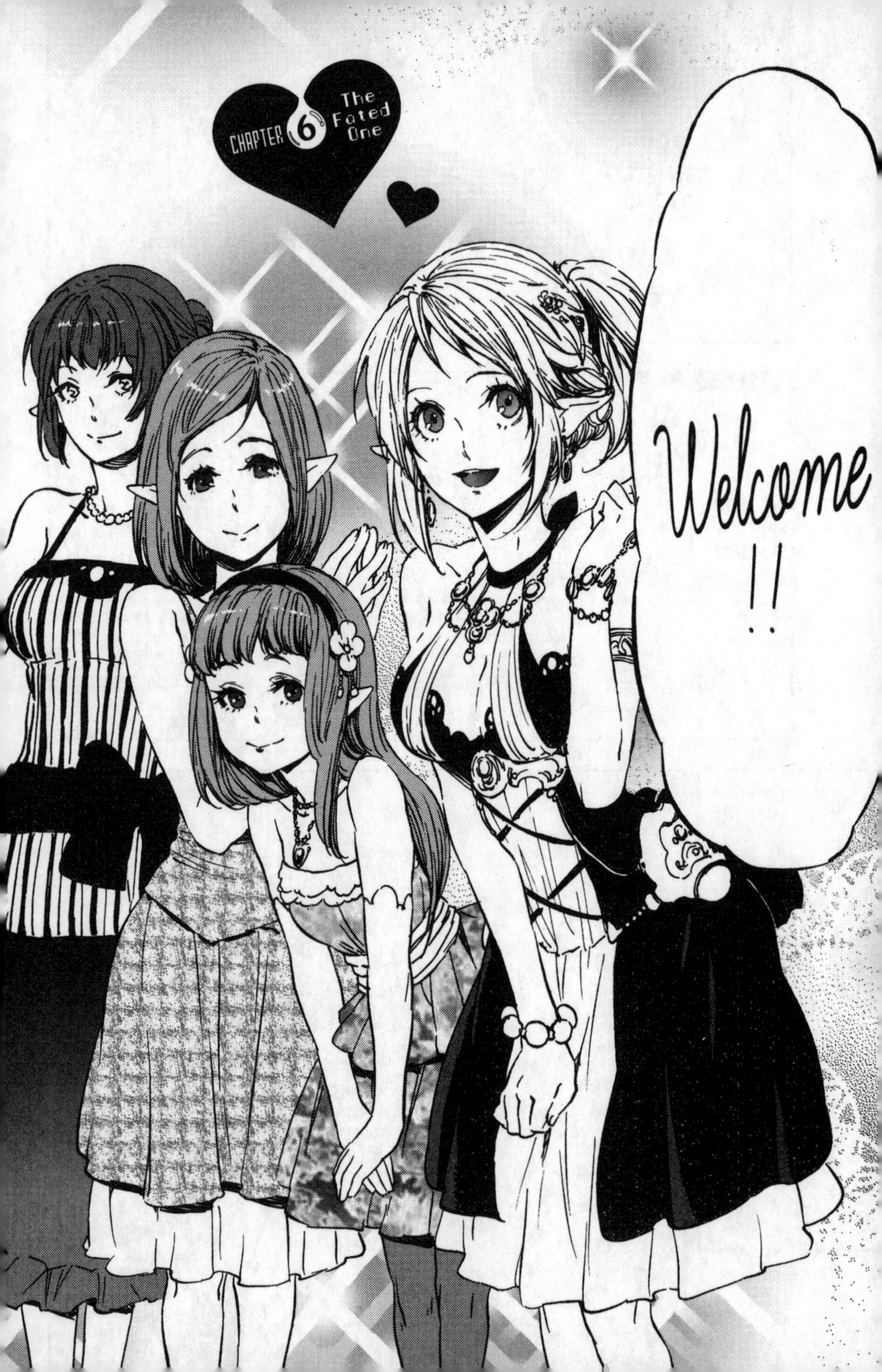
CHAPTER 6 The Fated One
Welcome!!

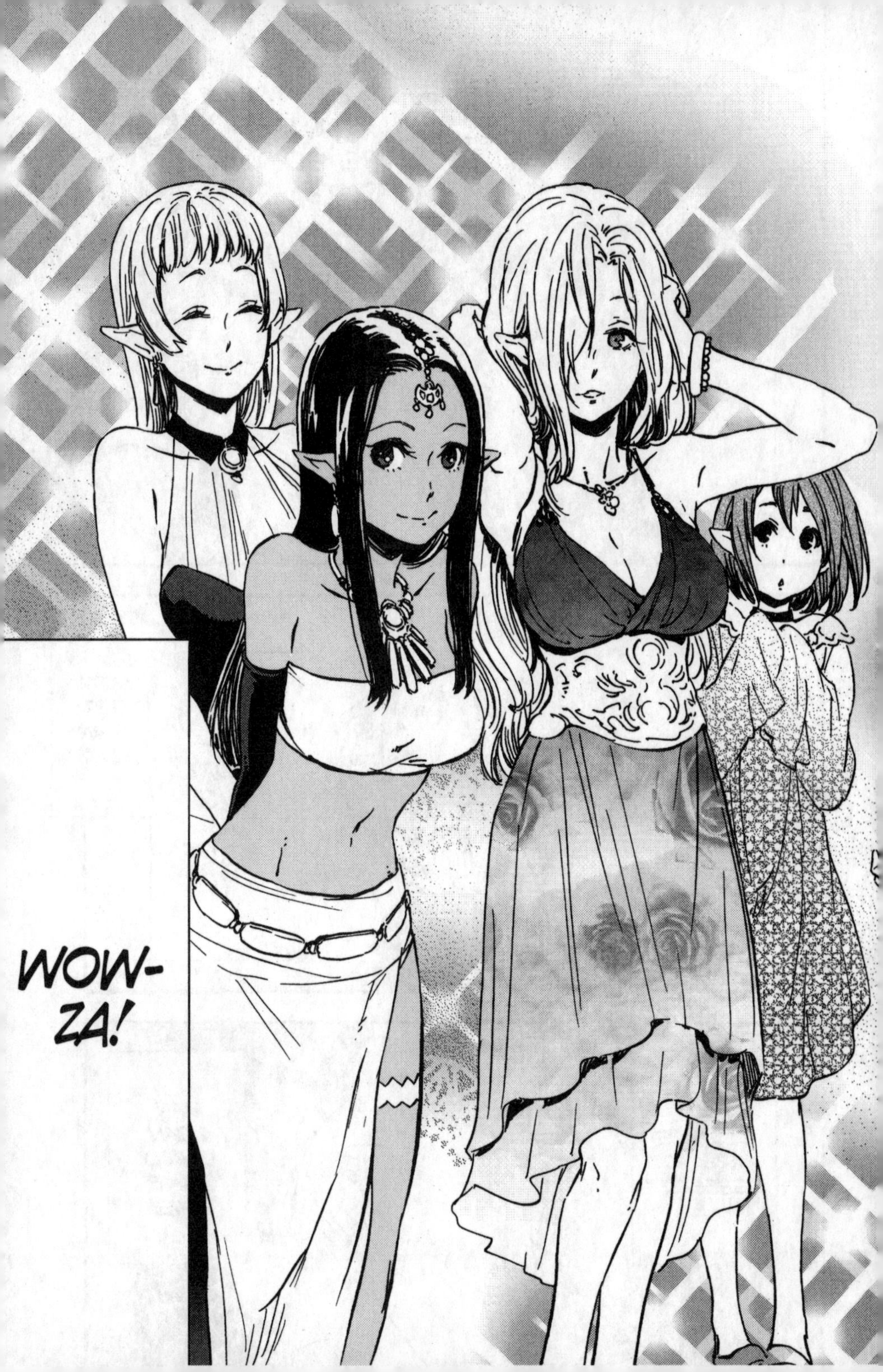
WOW-
ZA!

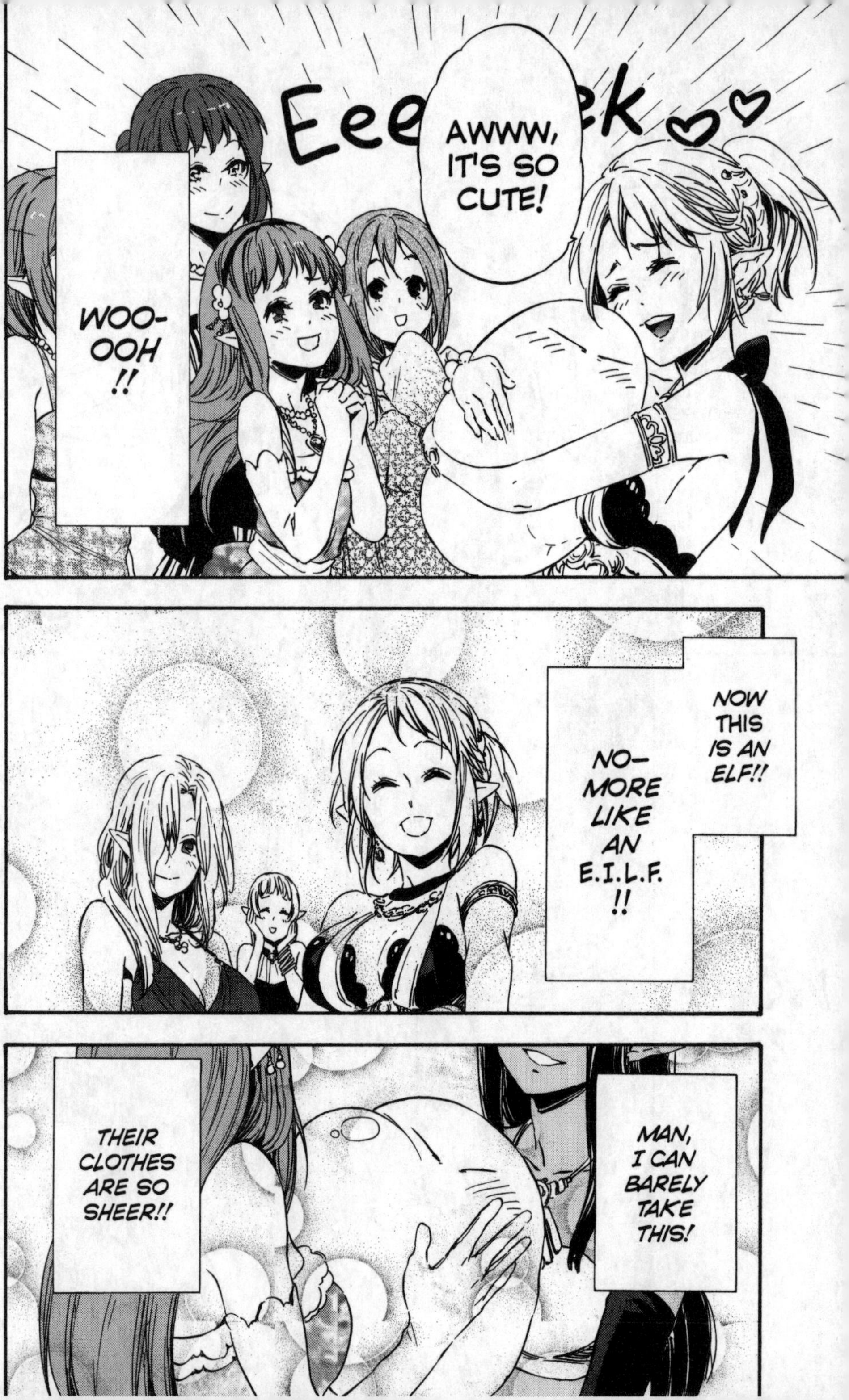
Eee ek
AWWW, IT'S SO CUTE!
WOO-OOH!!
NOW THIS IS AN ELF!!
NO—MORE LIKE AN E.I.L.F.!!
MAN, I CAN BARELY TAKE THIS!
THEIR CLOTHES ARE SO SHEER!!

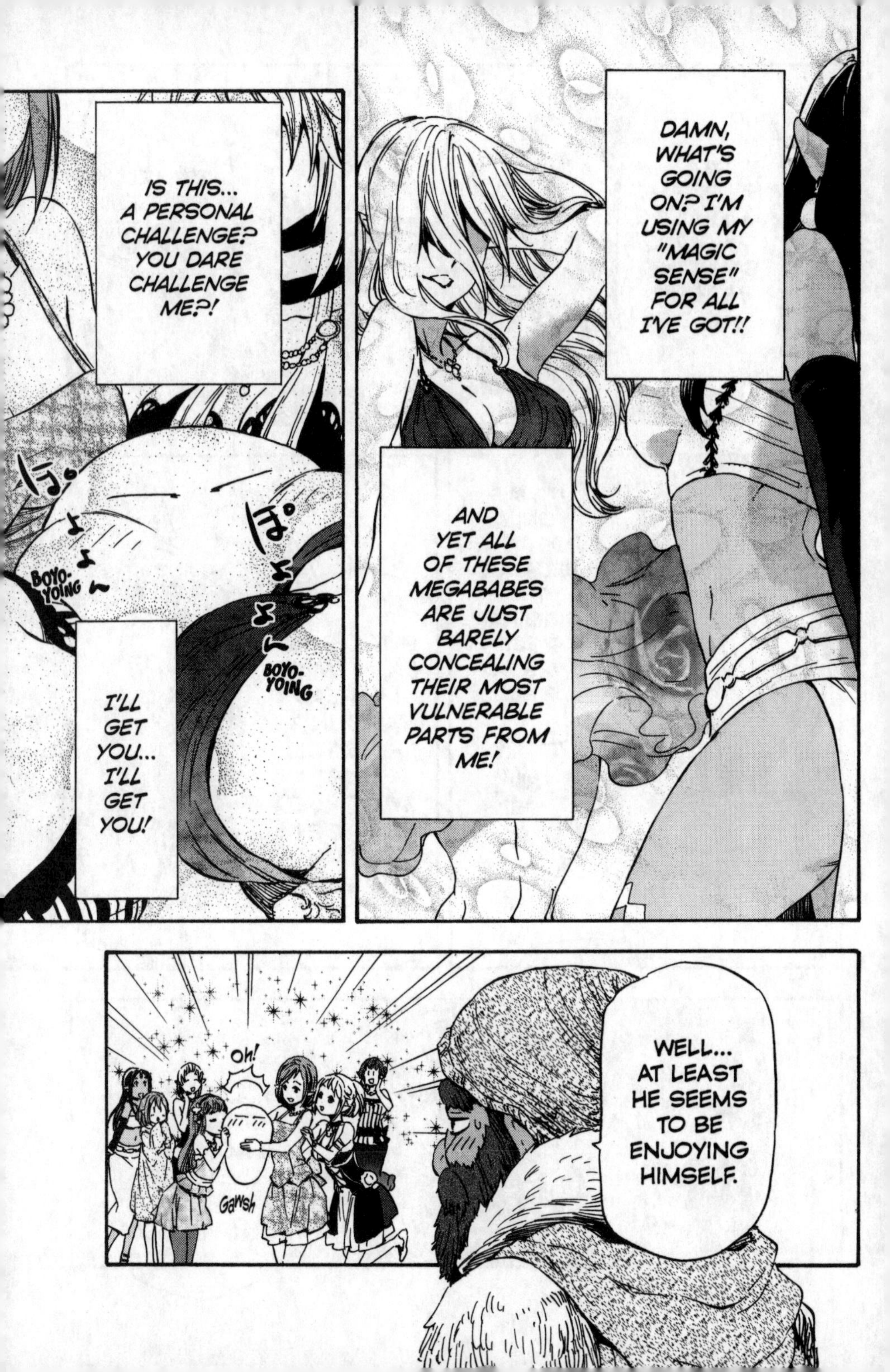
DAMN, WHAT'S GOING ON? I'M USING MY "MAGIC SENSE" FOR ALL I'VE GOT!!
AND YET ALL OF THESE MEGABABES ARE JUST BARELY CONCEALING THEIR MOST VULNERABLE PARTS FROM ME!
IS THIS... A PERSONAL CHALLENGE? YOU DARE CHALLENGE ME?!
BOYO-YOING
BOYO-YOING
I'LL GET YOU... I'LL GET YOU!
WELL... AT LEAST HE SEEMS TO BE ENJOYING HIMSELF.
Oh!
Gawsh

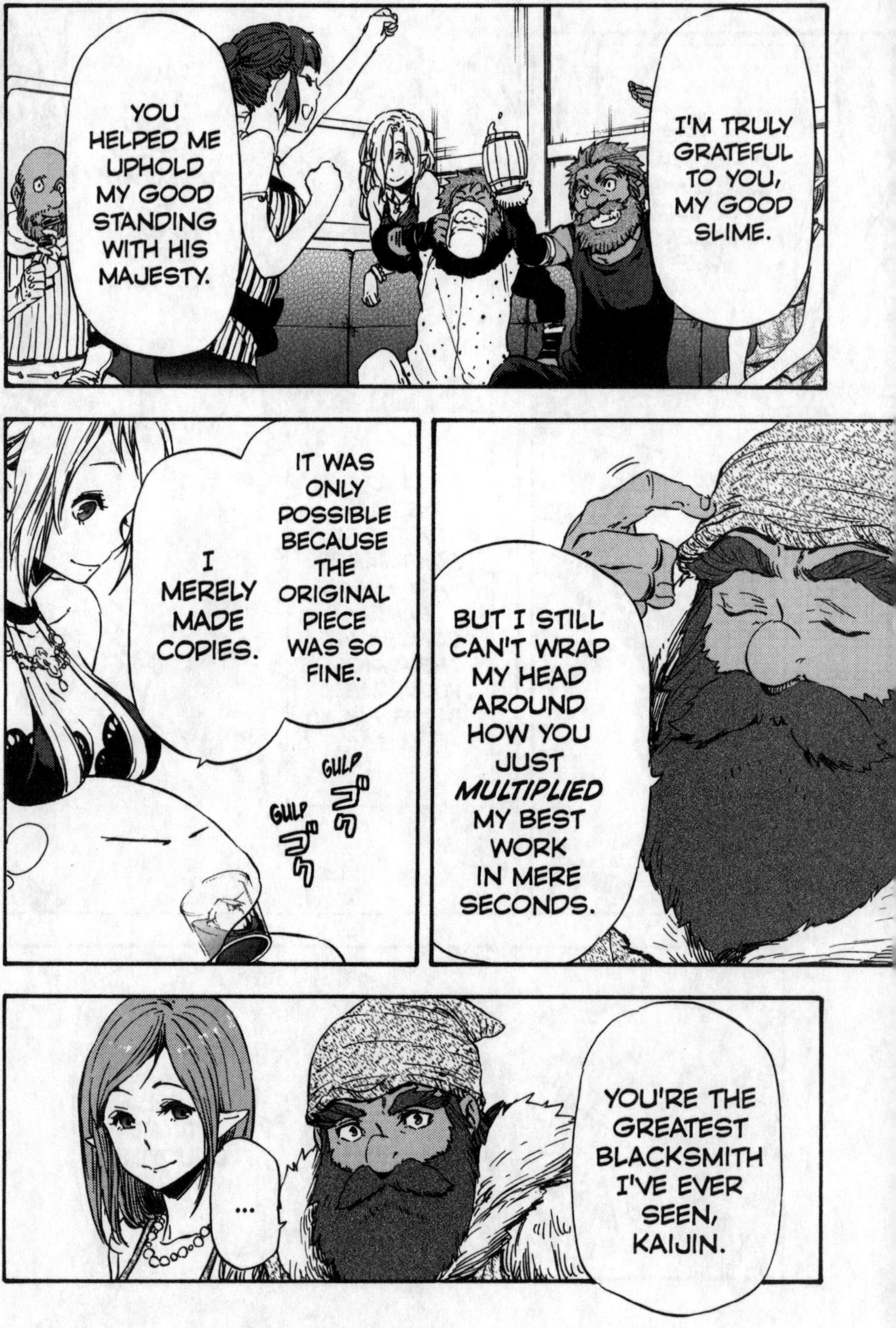
I'M TRULY GRATEFUL TO YOU, MY GOOD SLIME.
YOU HELPED ME UPHOLD MY GOOD STANDING WITH HIS MAJESTY.
BUT I STILL CAN'T WRAP MY HEAD AROUND HOW YOU JUST *MULTIPLIED* MY BEST WORK IN MERE SECONDS.
I MERELY MADE COPIES. IT WAS ONLY POSSIBLE BECAUSE THE ORIGINAL PIECE WAS SO FINE.
GULP
GULP
YOU'RE THE GREATEST BLACKSMITH I'VE EVER SEEN, KAIJIN.
...

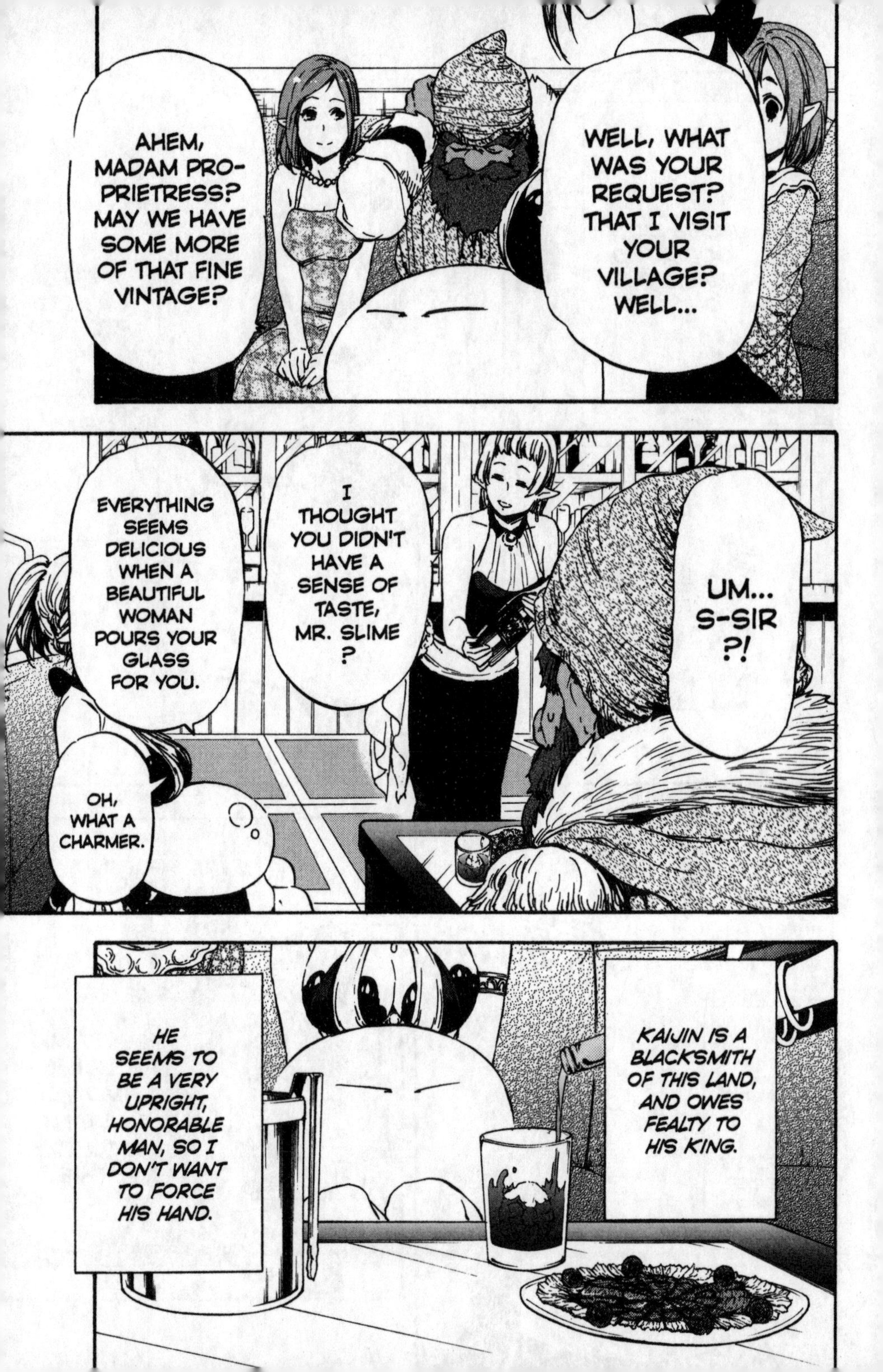
WELL, WHAT WAS YOUR REQUEST? THAT I VISIT YOUR VILLAGE? WELL...
AHEM, MADAM PRO-PRIETRESS? MAY WE HAVE SOME MORE OF THAT FINE VINTAGE?
UM... S-SIR ?!
I THOUGHT YOU DIDN'T HAVE A SENSE OF TASTE, MR. SLIME ?
EVERYTHING SEEMS DELICIOUS WHEN A BEAUTIFUL WOMAN POURS YOUR GLASS FOR YOU.
OH, WHAT A CHARMER.
KAIJIN IS A BLACKSMITH OF THIS LAND, AND OWES FEALTY TO HIS KING.
HE SEEMS TO BE A VERY UPRIGHT, HONORABLE MAN, SO I DON'T WANT TO FORCE HIS HAND.

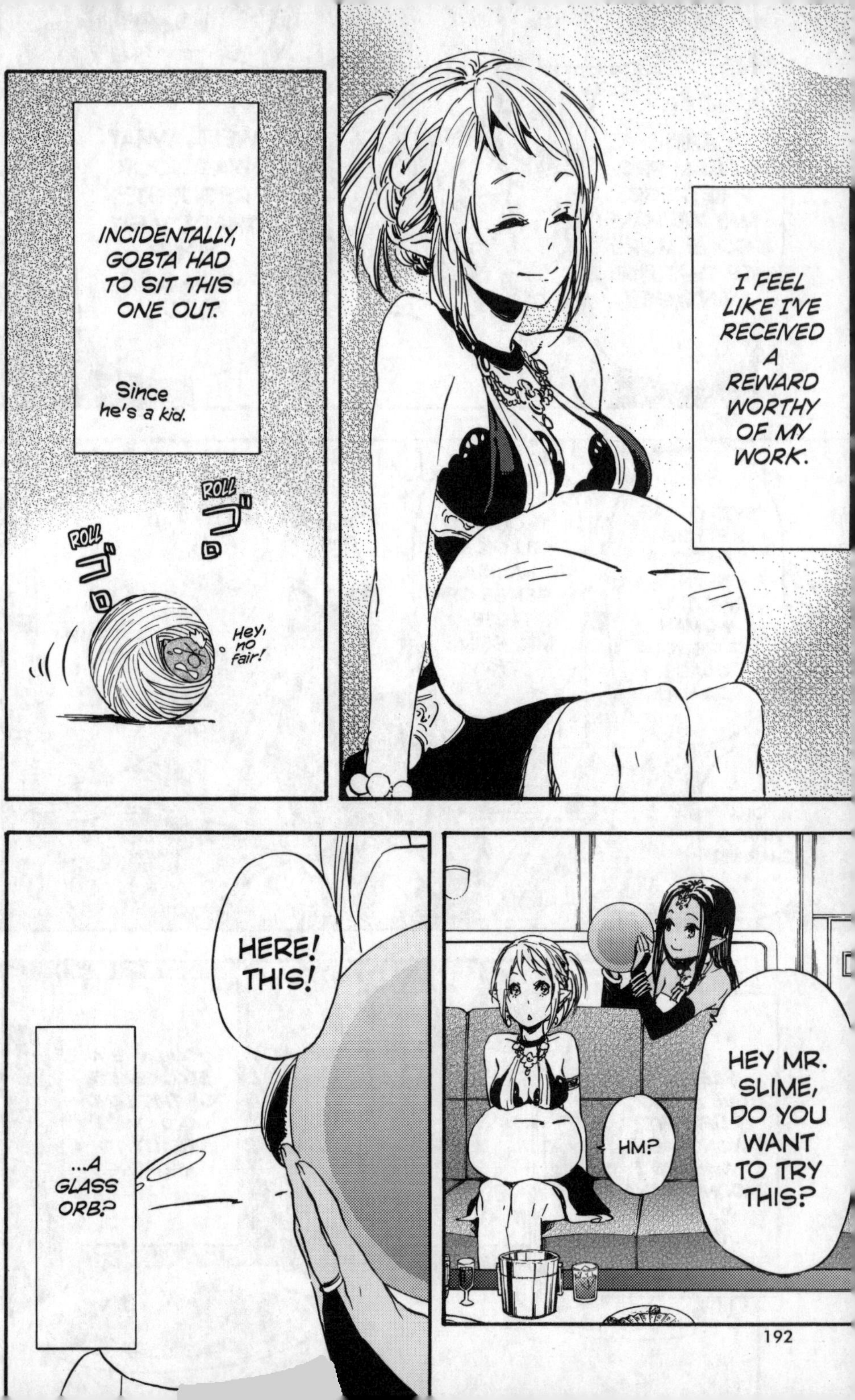
I FEEL LIKE I'VE RECEIVED A REWARD WORTHY OF MY WORK.
INCIDENTALLY, GOBTA HAD TO SIT THIS ONE OUT.
Since he's a kid.
ROLL
ROLL
Hey, no fair!
HEY MR. SLIME, DO YOU WANT TO TRY THIS?
HM?
HERE! THIS!
...A GLASS ORB?

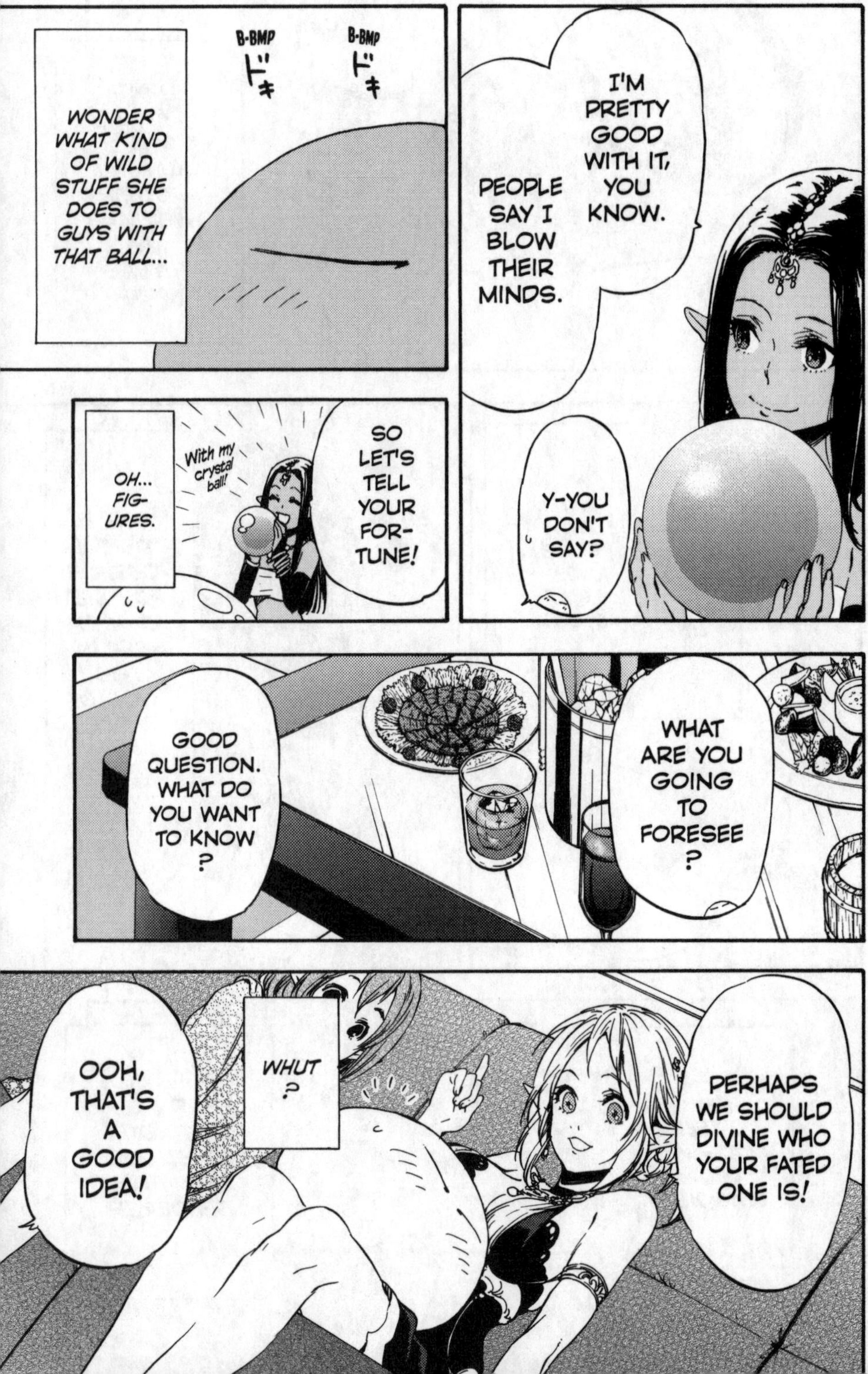
I'M PRETTY GOOD WITH IT, YOU KNOW.
PEOPLE SAY I BLOW THEIR MINDS.
Y-YOU DON'T SAY?
B-BMP ドキ
B-BMP ドキ
WONDER WHAT KIND OF WILD STUFF SHE DOES TO GUYS WITH THAT BALL...
SO LET'S TELL YOUR FOR-TUNE!
With my crystal ball!
OH... FIG-URES.
WHAT ARE YOU GOING TO FORESEE ?
GOOD QUESTION. WHAT DO YOU WANT TO KNOW ?
PERHAPS WE SHOULD DIVINE WHO YOUR FATED ONE IS!
WHUT ?
OOH, THAT'S A GOOD IDEA!

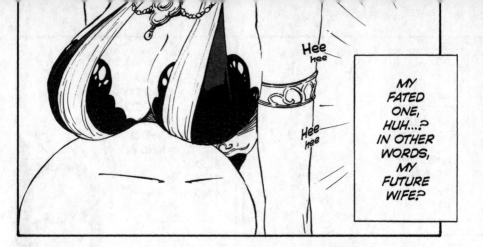

MY FATED ONE, HUH...? IN OTHER WORDS, MY FUTURE WIFE?
Hee hee
Hee hee
IS IT EVEN POSSIBLE FOR ME TO GET A WIFE IN THIS WORLD ?!
Satoru-san ♡
NO, WAIT... I'M A SLIME NOW, SO I GUESS...
...IT WOULD BE MORE LIKE THIS?
Rimuru-saan! ♡
All pink or whatever
ON THAT NOTE, DO SLIMES EVEN HAVE GENDERS?
NYORRRP
HOW DO THEY MULTIPLY? CELL DIVISION?

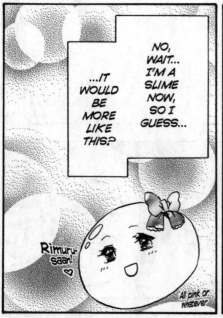

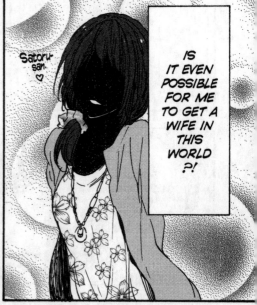

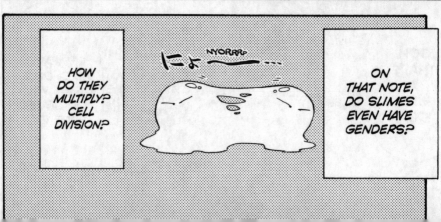

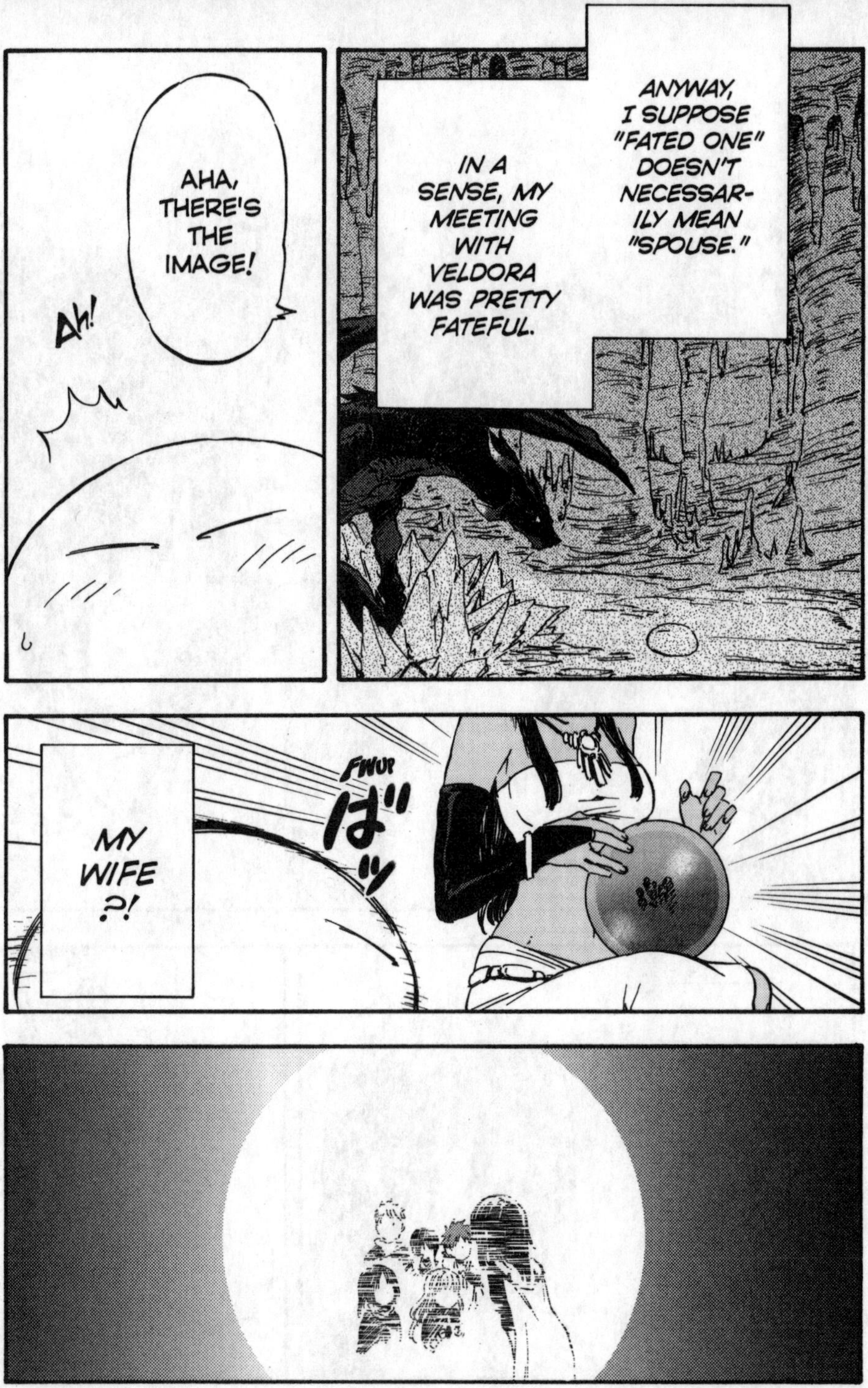
ANYWAY, I SUPPOSE "FATED ONE" DOESN'T NECESSARILY MEAN "SPOUSE."
IN A SENSE, MY MEETING WITH VELDORA WAS PRETTY FATEFUL.
AHA, THERE'S THE IMAGE!
Ah!
FWUP
ばッ
MY WIFE ?!

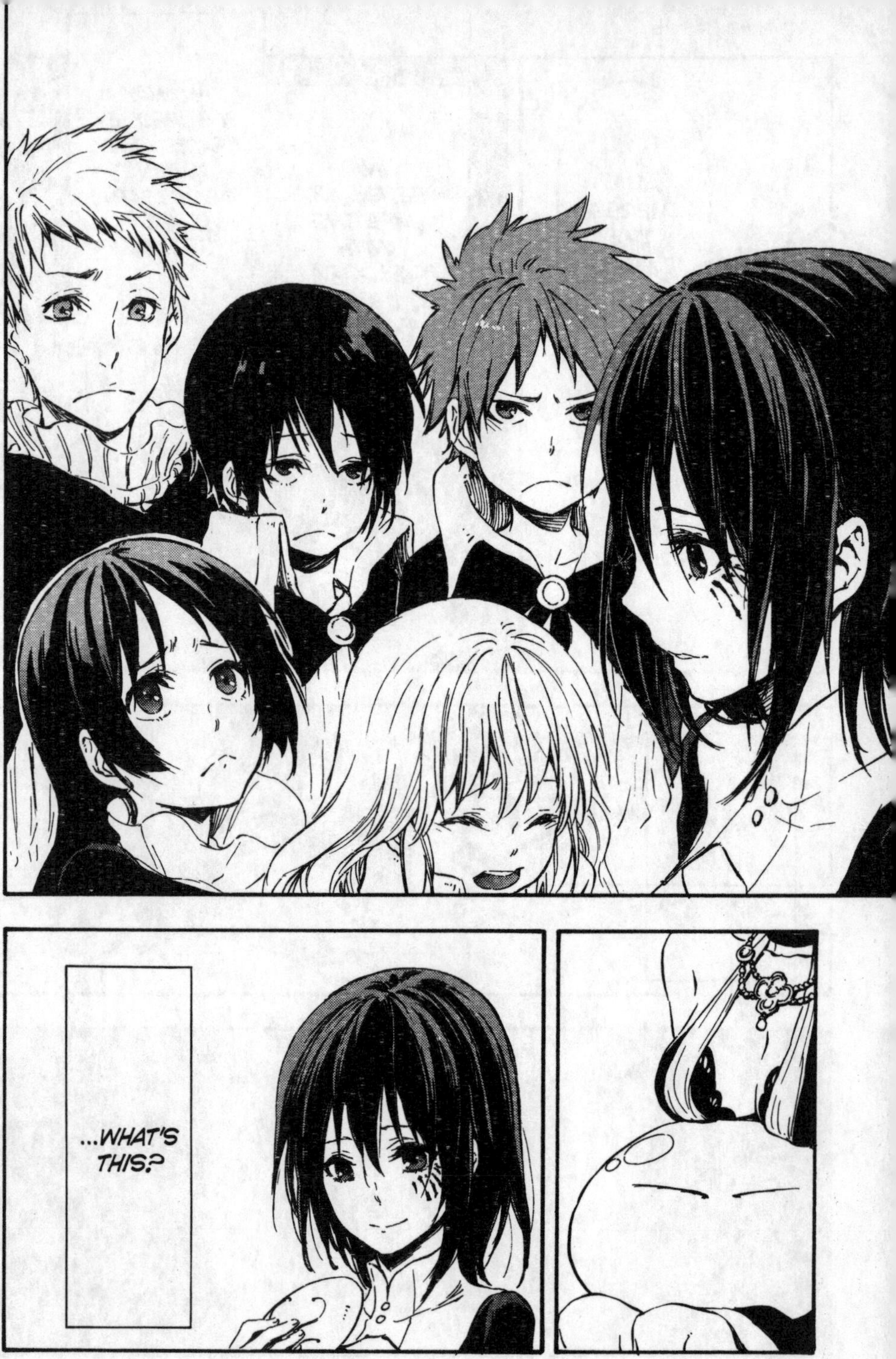
...WHAT'S
THIS?

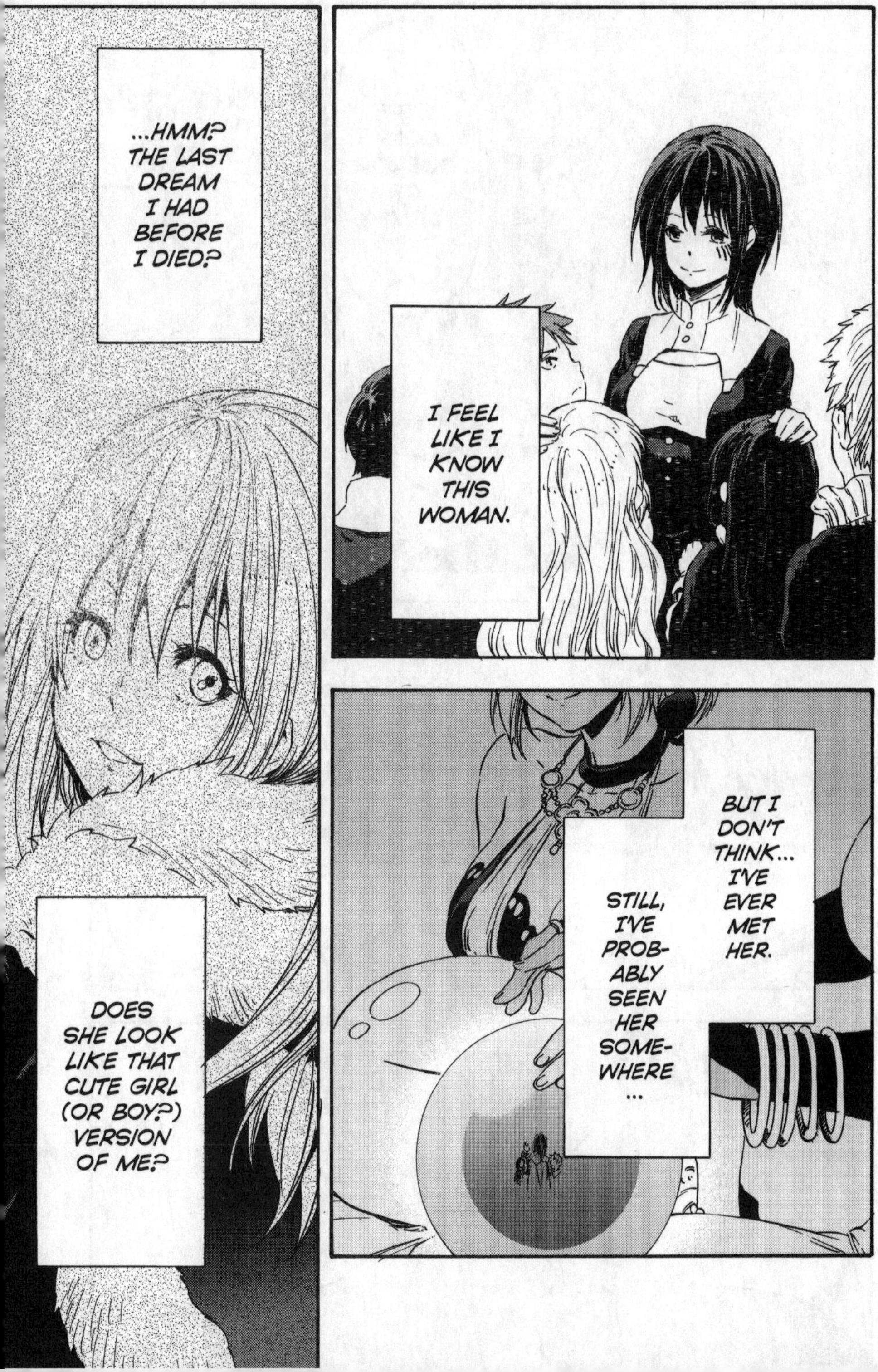
I FEEL LIKE I KNOW THIS WOMAN.
BUT I DON'T THINK... I'VE EVER MET HER.
STILL, I'VE PROBABLY SEEN HER SOMEWHERE...
...HMM? THE LAST DREAM I HAD BEFORE I DIED?
DOES SHE LOOK LIKE THAT CUTE GIRL (OR BOY?) VERSION OF ME?

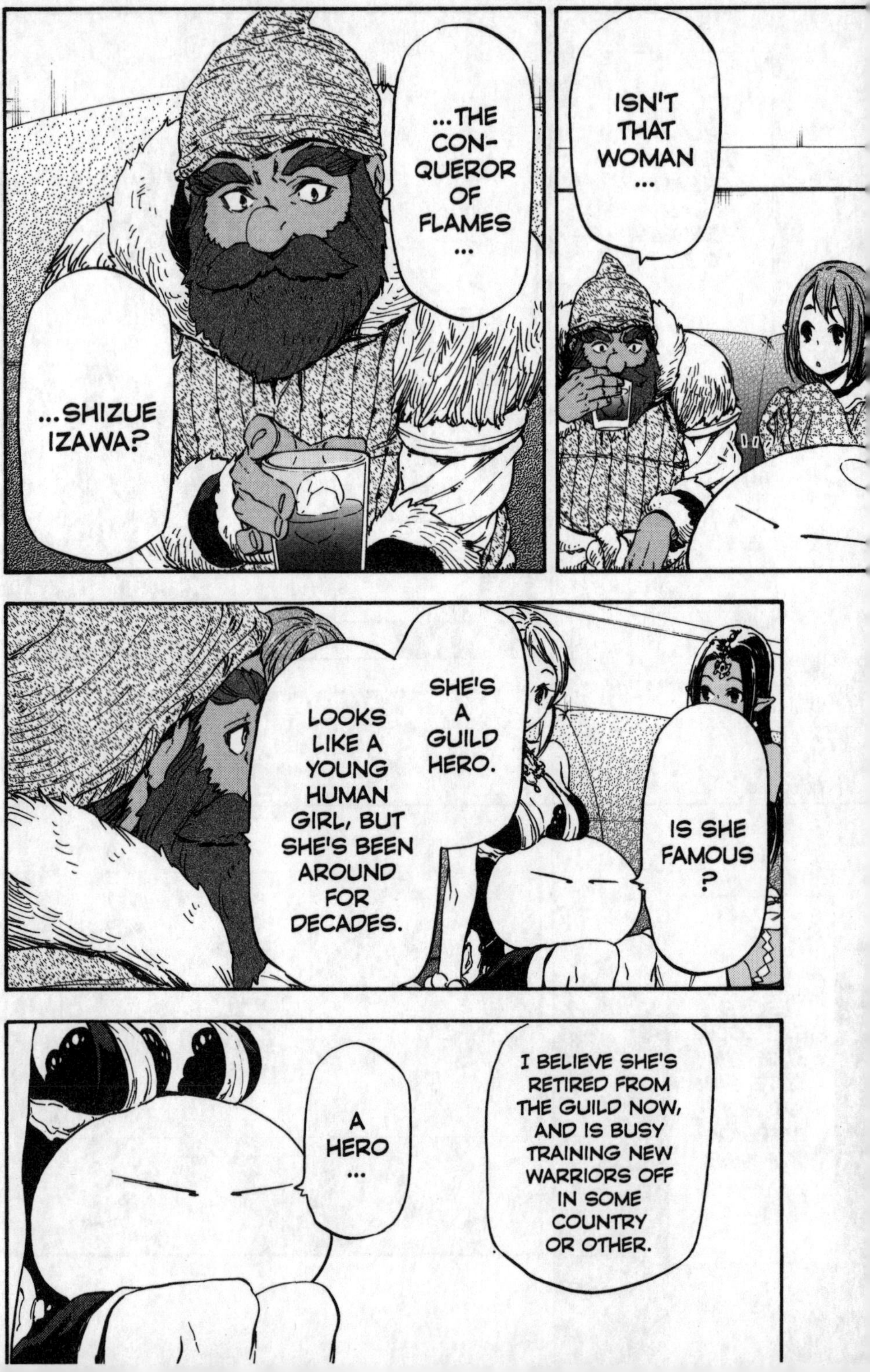
ISN'T THAT WOMAN ...
...THE CON-QUEROR OF FLAMES ...
...SHIZUE IZAWA?
IS SHE FAMOUS ?
SHE'S A GUILD HERO.
LOOKS LIKE A YOUNG HUMAN GIRL, BUT SHE'S BEEN AROUND FOR DECADES.
I BELIEVE SHE'S RETIRED FROM THE GUILD NOW, AND IS BUSY TRAINING NEW WARRIORS OFF IN SOME COUNTRY OR OTHER.
A HERO ...

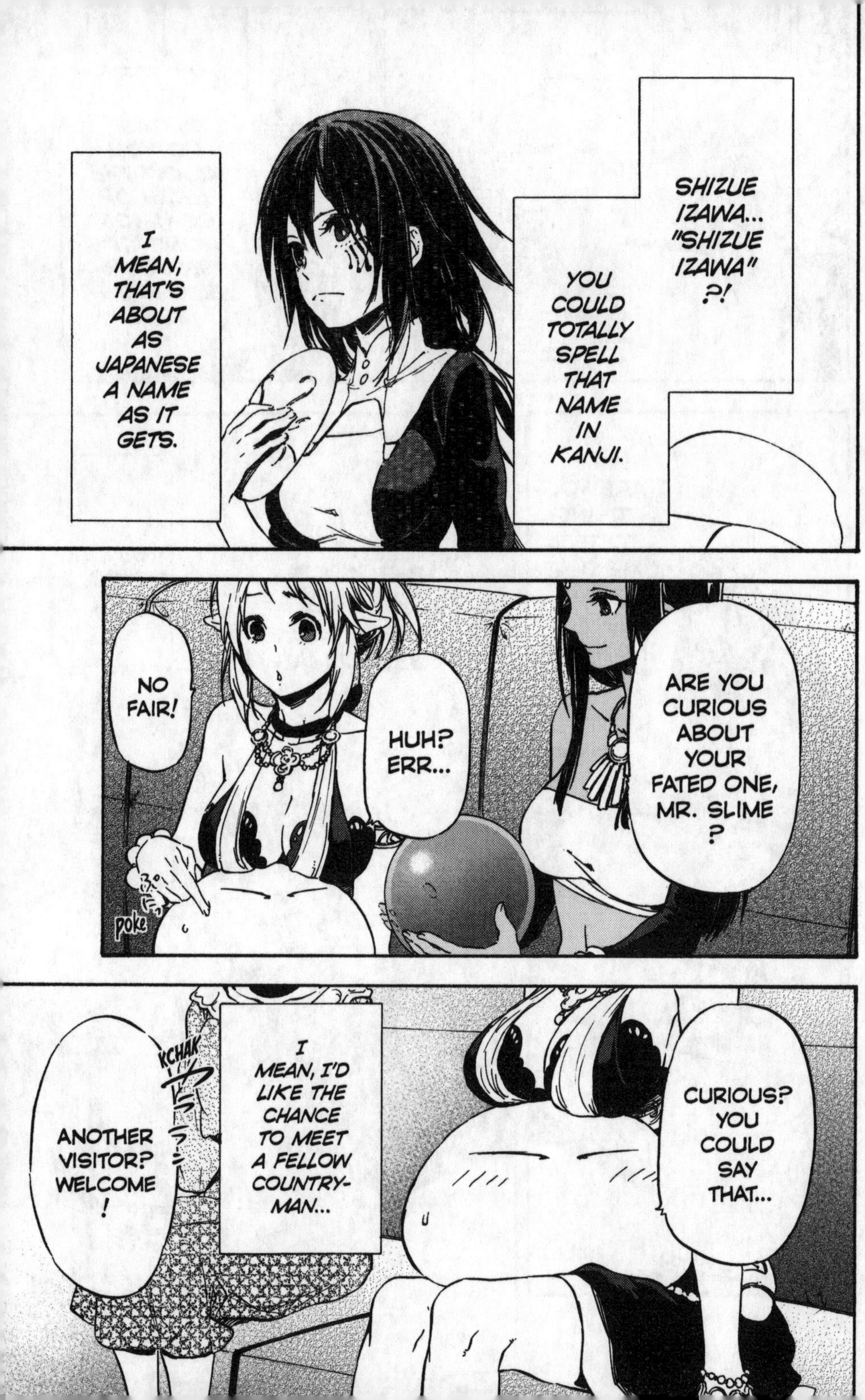
SHIZUE IZAWA... "SHIZUE IZAWA" ?!
YOU COULD TOTALLY SPELL THAT NAME IN KANJI.
I MEAN, THAT'S ABOUT AS JAPANESE A NAME AS IT GETS.
ARE YOU CURIOUS ABOUT YOUR FATED ONE, MR. SLIME ?
HUH? ERR...
NO FAIR!
poke
CURIOUS? YOU COULD SAY THAT...
I MEAN, I'D LIKE THE CHANCE TO MEET A FELLOW COUNTRY-MAN...
KCHAK
ANOTHER VISITOR? WELCOME !

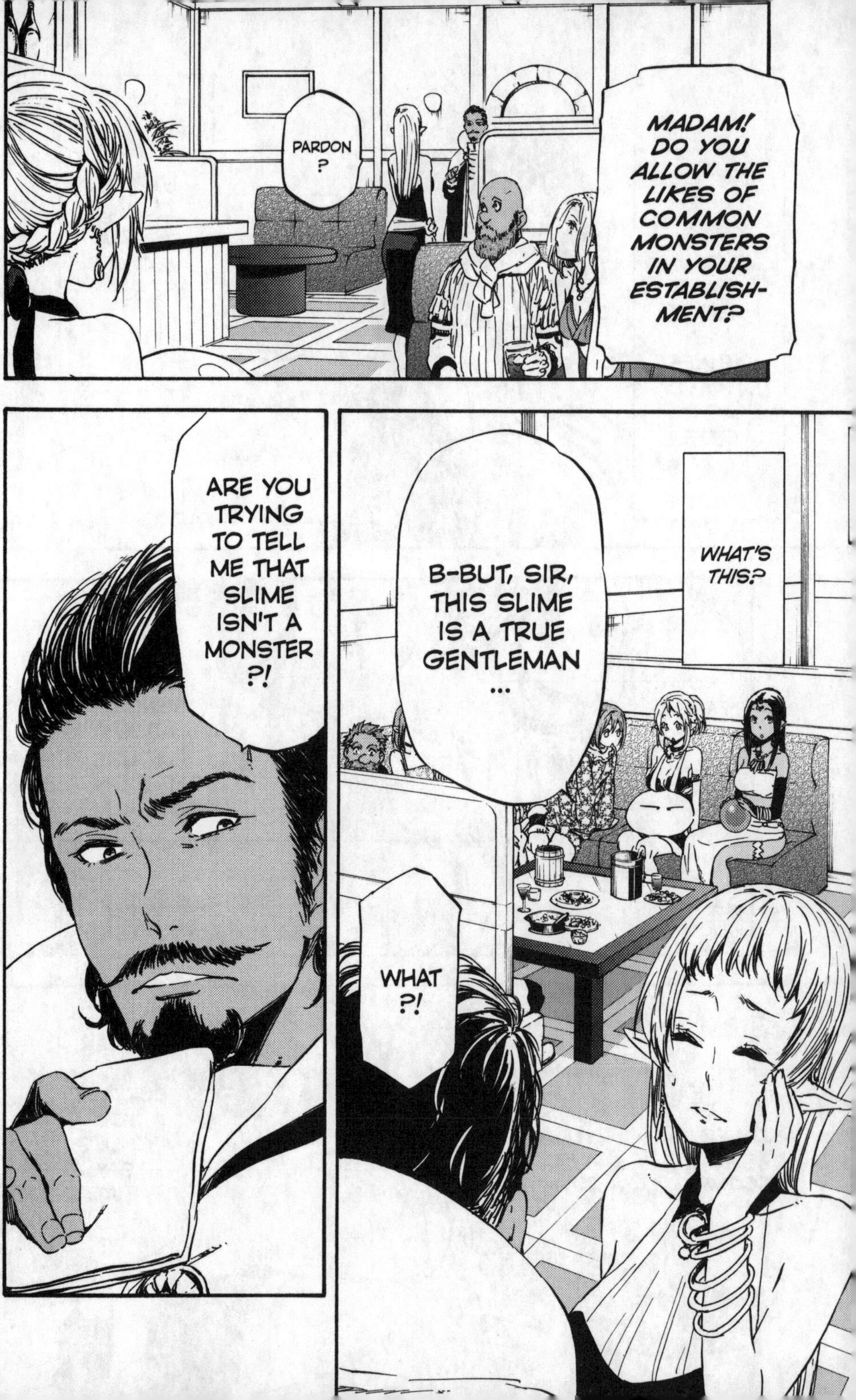
MADAM! DO YOU ALLOW THE LIKES OF COMMON MONSTERS IN YOUR ESTABLISH-MENT?
PARDON ?
WHAT'S THIS?
B-BUT, SIR, THIS SLIME IS A TRUE GENTLEMAN ...
WHAT ?!
ARE YOU TRYING TO TELL ME THAT SLIME ISN'T A MONSTER ?!

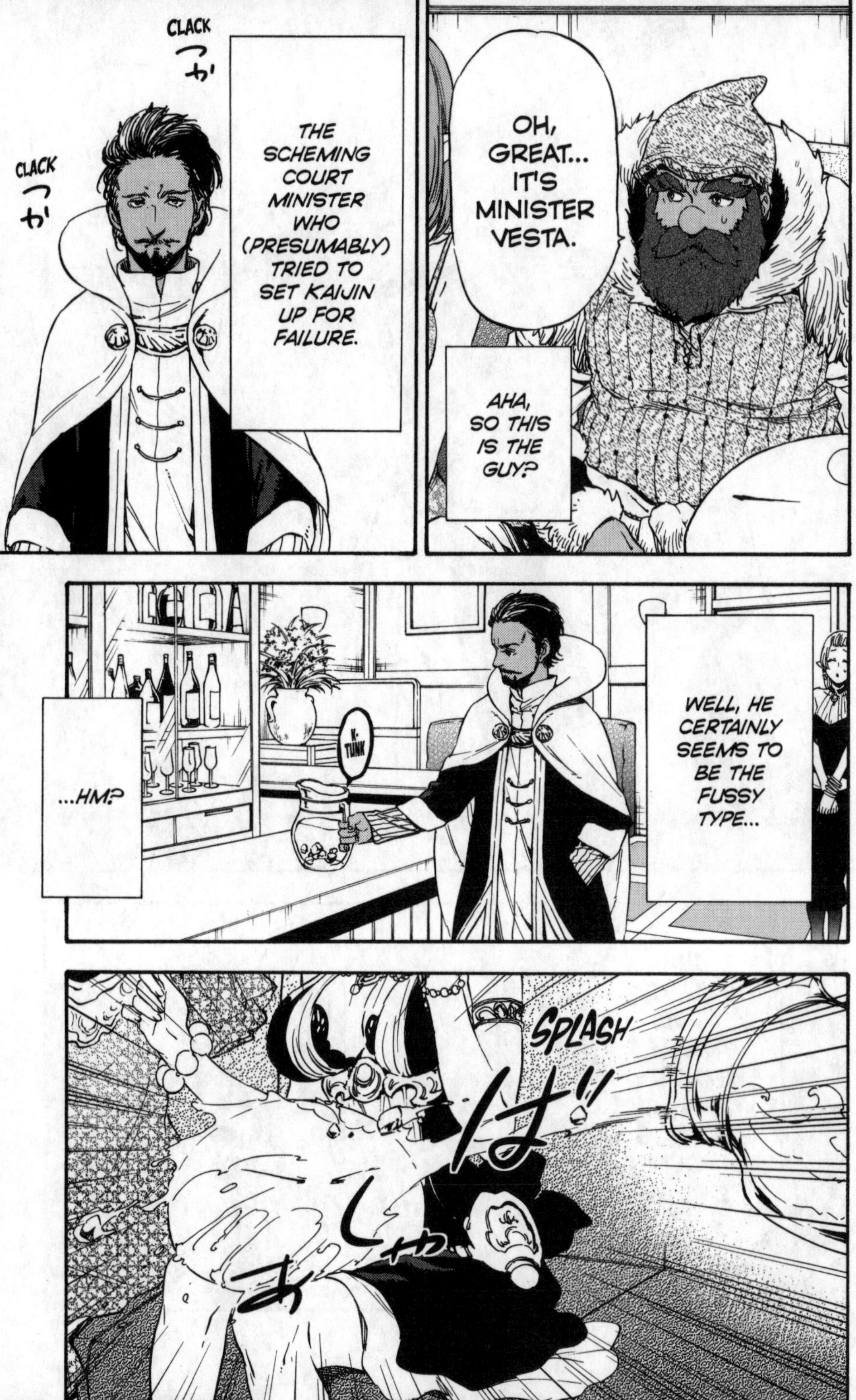
OH, GREAT... IT'S MINISTER VESTA.
AHA, SO THIS IS THE GUY?
CLACK
つか
CLACK
つか
THE SCHEMING COURT MINISTER WHO (PRESUMABLY) TRIED TO SET KAIJIN UP FOR FAILURE.
WELL, HE CERTAINLY SEEMS TO BE THE FUSSY TYPE...
K-TUNK
...HM?
SPLASH

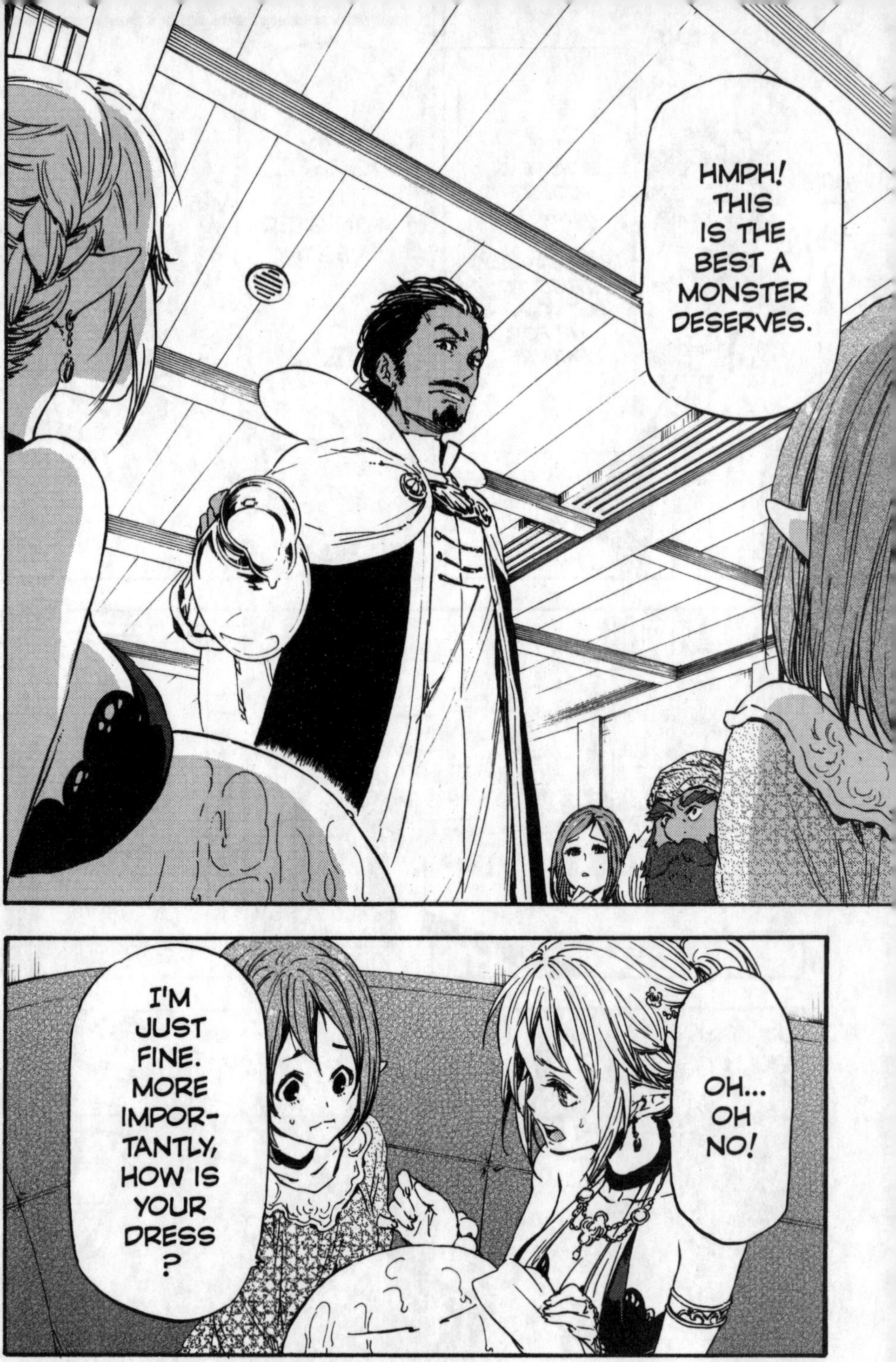
HMPH! THIS IS THE BEST A MONSTER DESERVES.
OH... OH NO!
I'M JUST FINE. MORE IMPOR-TANTLY, HOW IS YOUR DRESS?

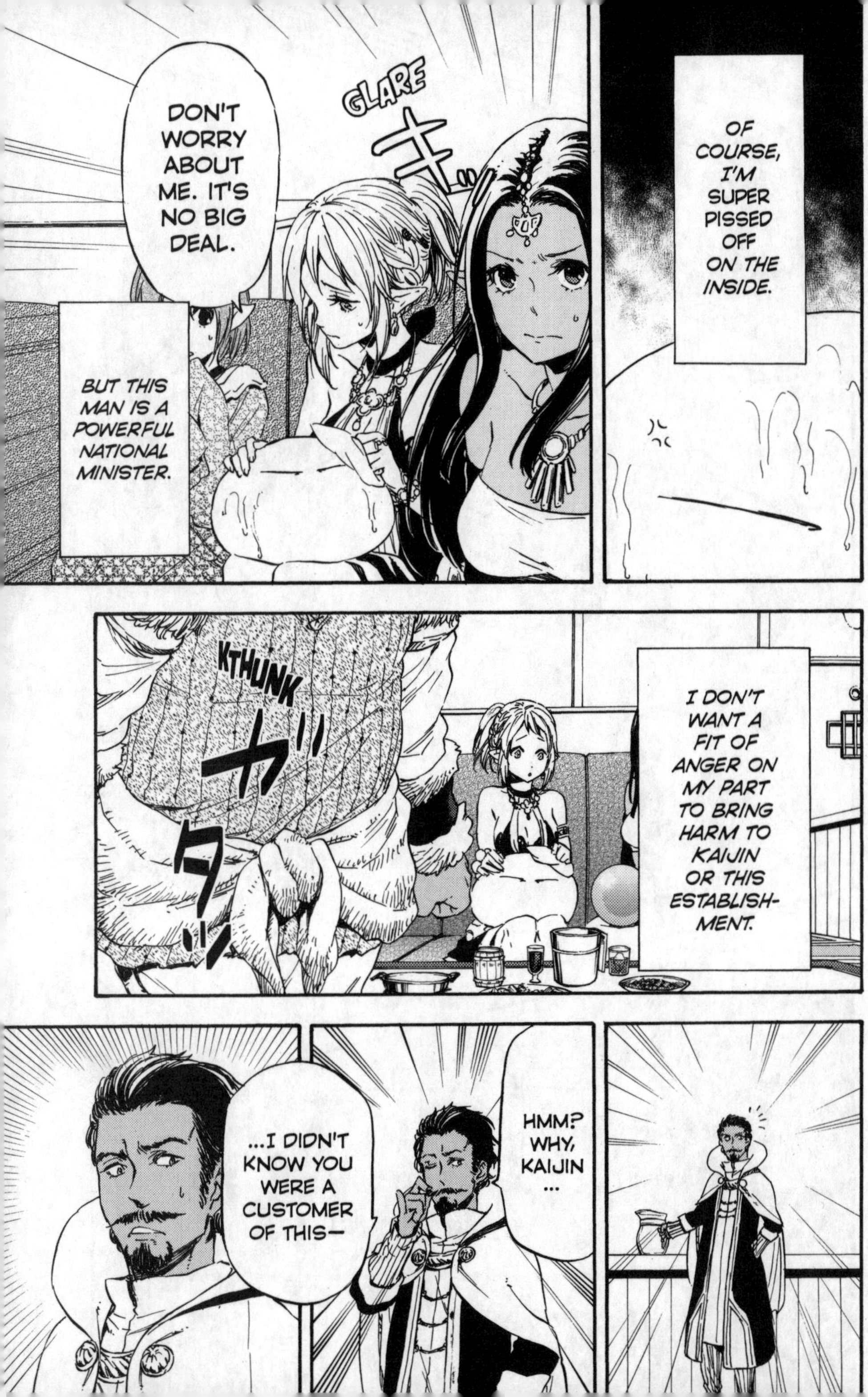
OF COURSE, I'M SUPER PISSED OFF ON THE INSIDE.
GLARE
DON'T WORRY ABOUT ME. IT'S NO BIG DEAL.
BUT THIS MAN IS A POWERFUL NATIONAL MINISTER.
I DON'T WANT A FIT OF ANGER ON MY PART TO BRING HARM TO KAIJIN OR THIS ESTABLISHMENT.
KTHUNK
HMM? WHY, KAIJIN ...
...I DIDN'T KNOW YOU WERE A CUSTOMER OF THIS—

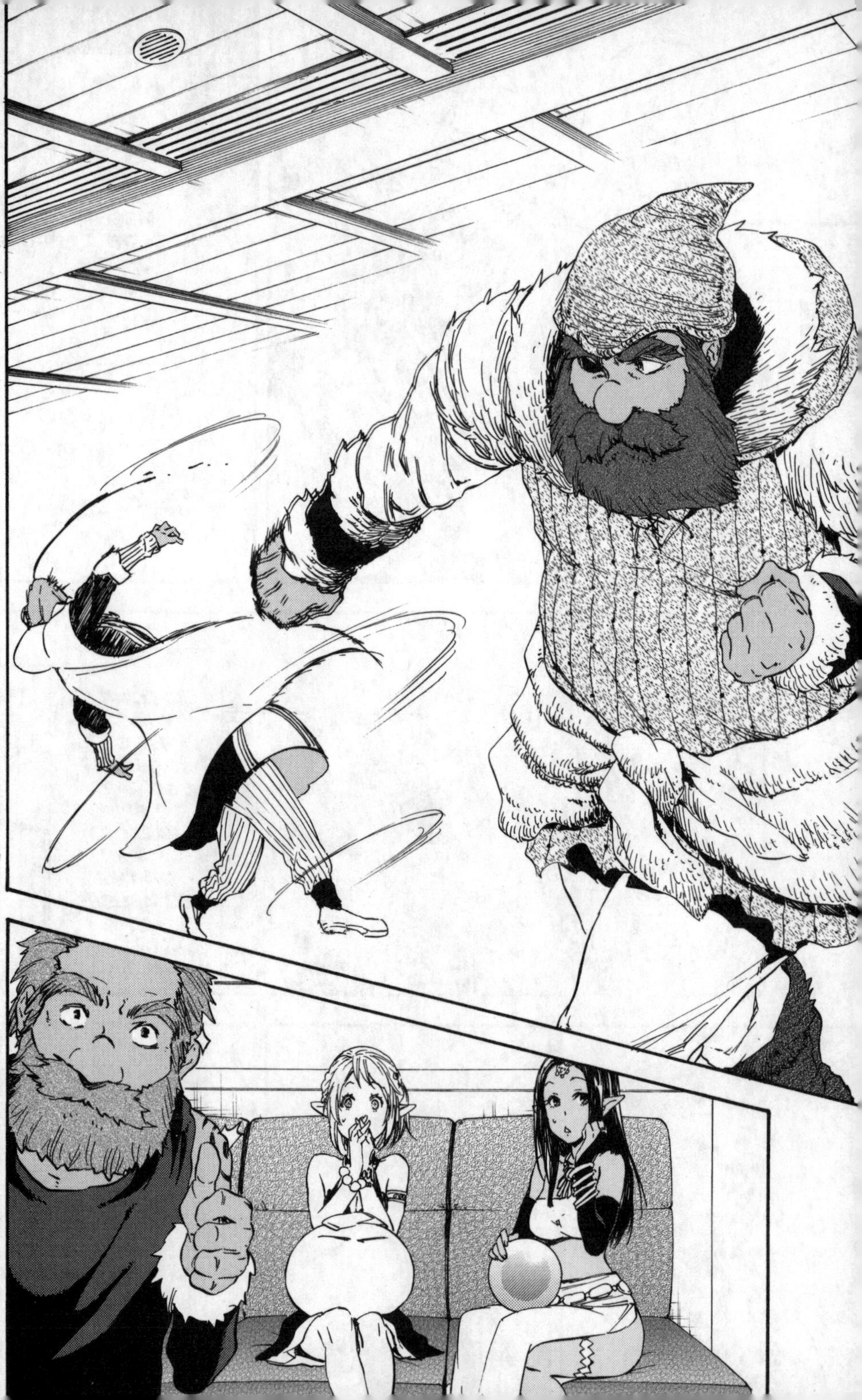

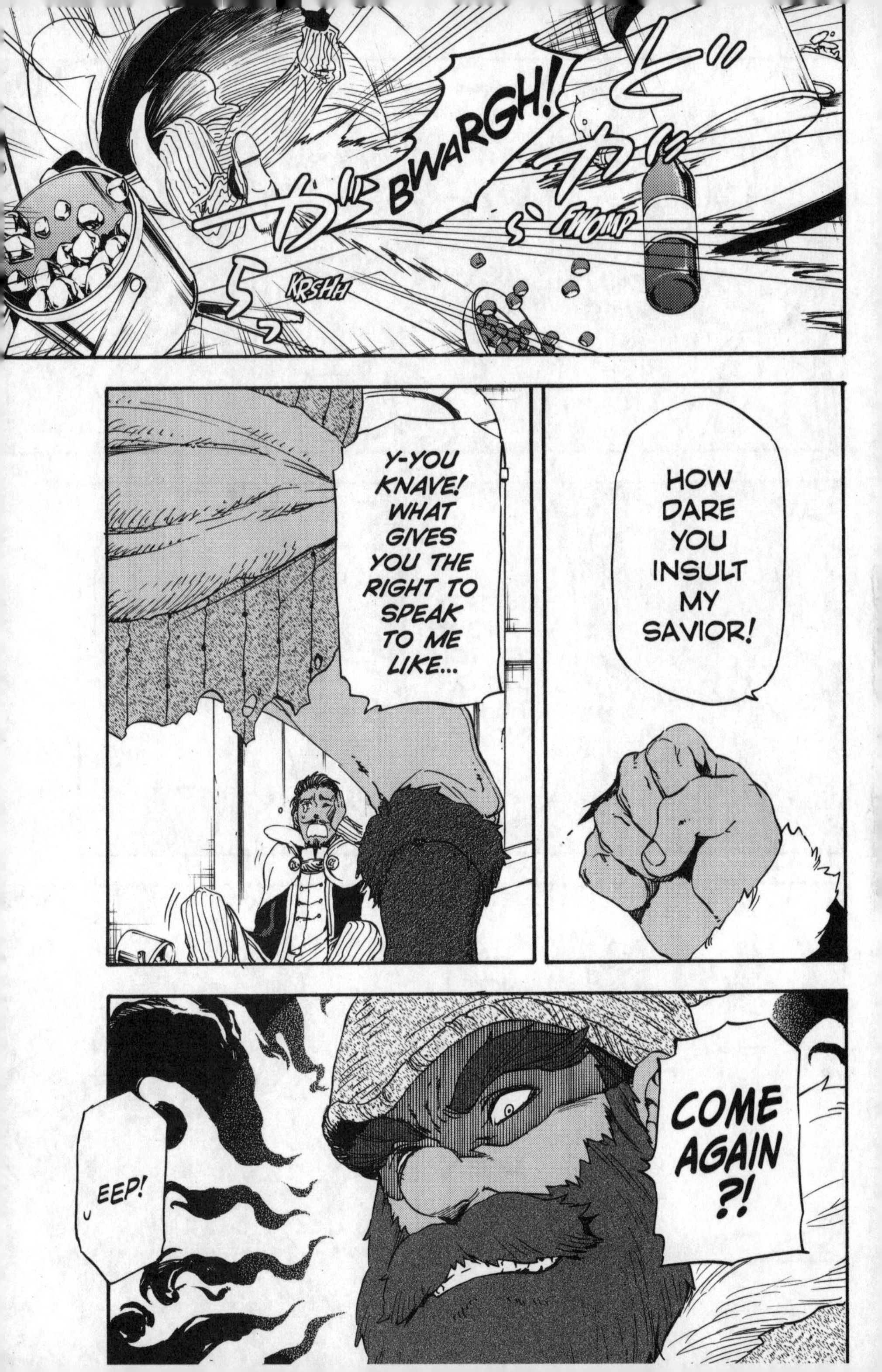
BWARGH!!
FWOMP
KRSHH
HOW DARE YOU INSULT MY SAVIOR!
Y-YOU KNAVE! WHAT GIVES YOU THE RIGHT TO SPEAK TO ME LIKE...
COME AGAIN?!
EEP!

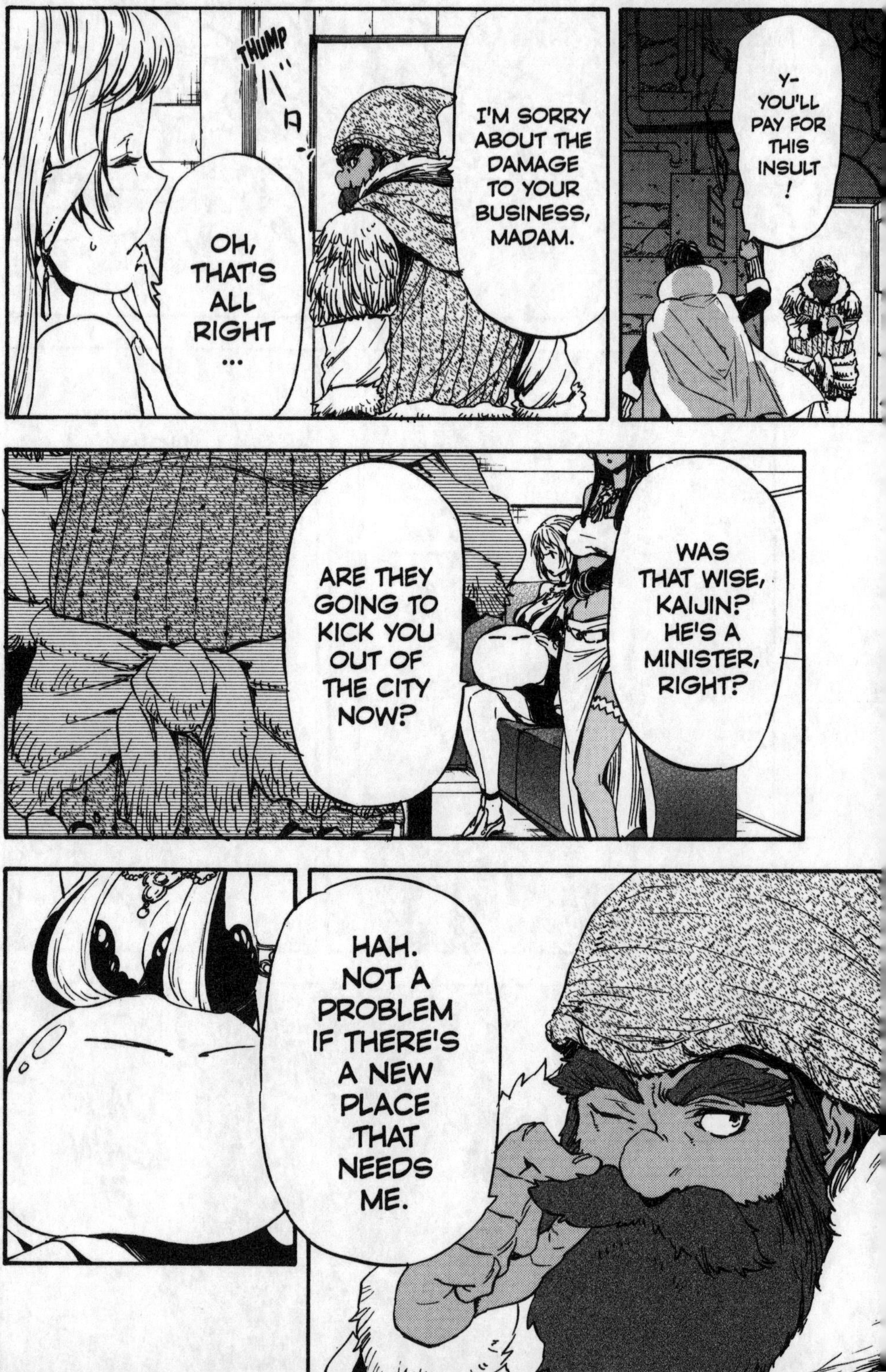
Y-YOU'LL PAY FOR THIS INSULT!
I'M SORRY ABOUT THE DAMAGE TO YOUR BUSINESS, MADAM.
THUMP
OH, THAT'S ALL RIGHT...
WAS THAT WISE, KAIJIN? HE'S A MINISTER, RIGHT?
ARE THEY GOING TO KICK YOU OUT OF THE CITY NOW?
HAH. NOT A PROBLEM IF THERE'S A NEW PLACE THAT NEEDS ME.

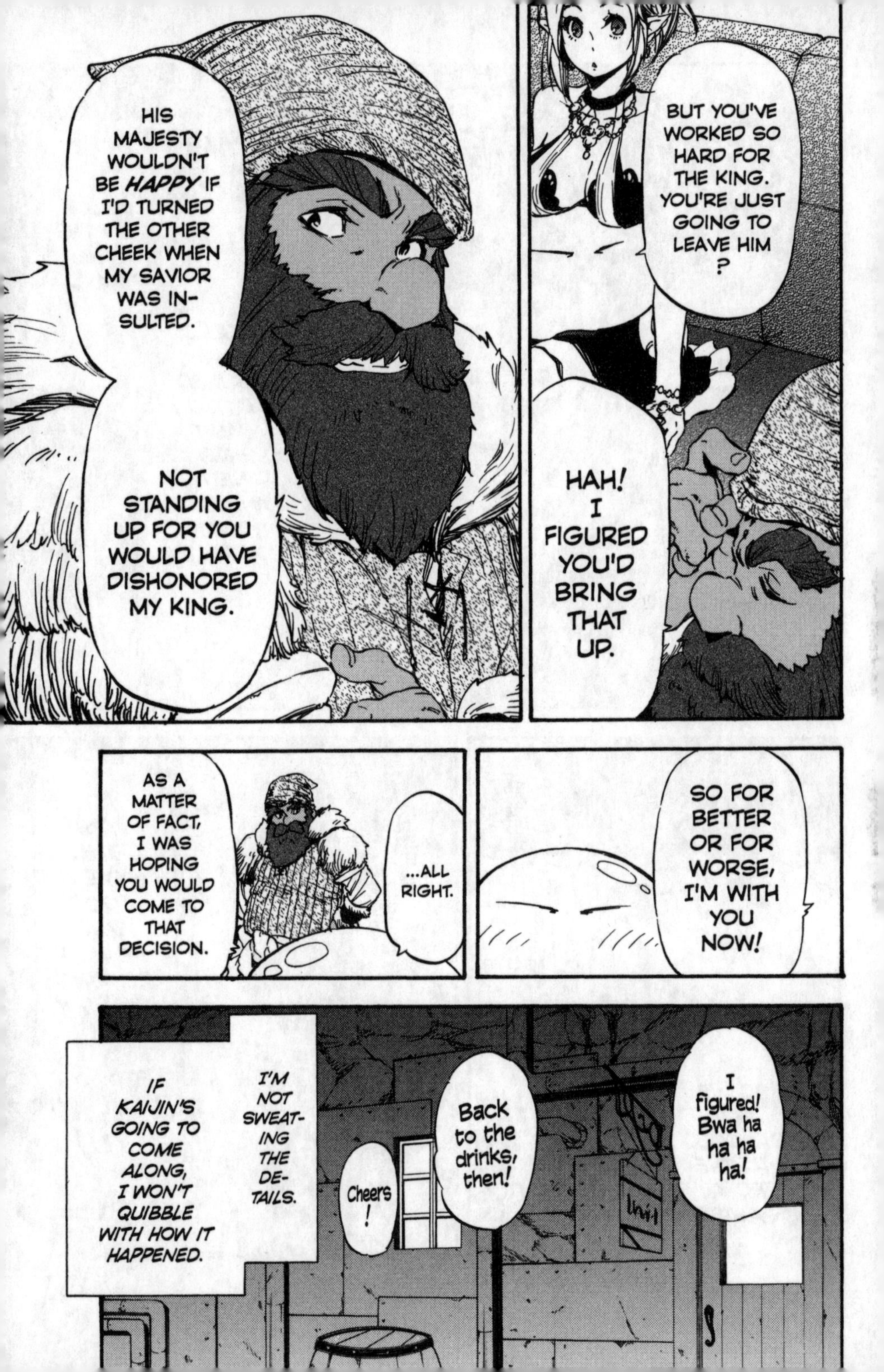
BUT YOU'VE WORKED SO HARD FOR THE KING. YOU'RE JUST GOING TO LEAVE HIM?
HAH! I FIGURED YOU'D BRING THAT UP.
HIS MAJESTY WOULDN'T BE *HAPPY* IF I'D TURNED THE OTHER CHEEK WHEN MY SAVIOR WAS IN-SULTED.
NOT STANDING UP FOR YOU WOULD HAVE DISHONORED MY KING.
SO FOR BETTER OR FOR WORSE, I'M WITH YOU NOW!
...ALL RIGHT.
AS A MATTER OF FACT, I WAS HOPING YOU WOULD COME TO THAT DECISION.
I figured! Bwa ha ha ha ha!
Back to the drinks, then!
Cheers!
I'M NOT SWEAT-ING THE DE-TAILS.
IF KAIJIN'S GOING TO COME ALONG, I WON'T QUIBBLE WITH HOW IT HAPPENED.

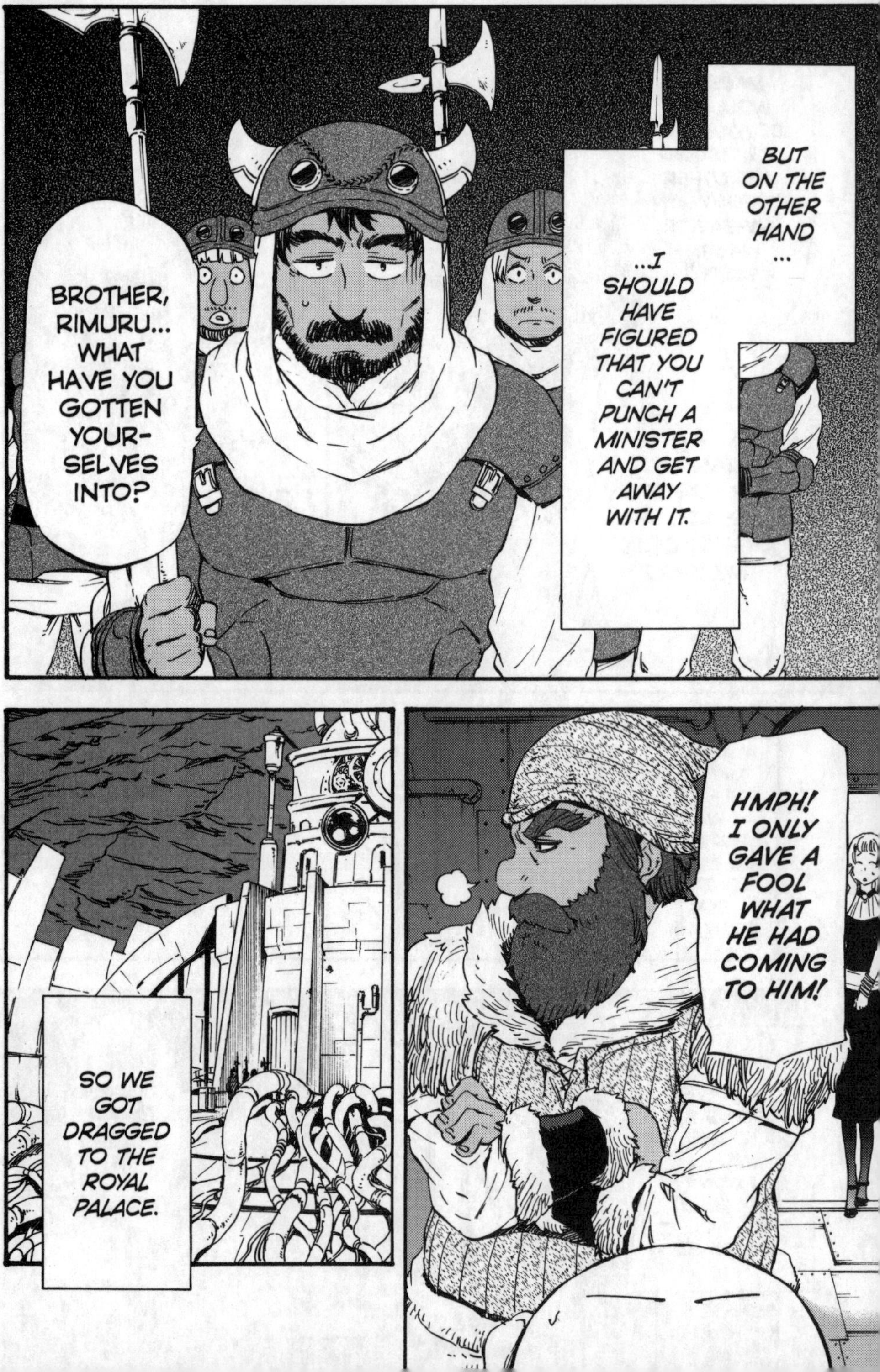
BUT ON THE OTHER HAND ...
...I SHOULD HAVE FIGURED THAT YOU CAN'T PUNCH A MINISTER AND GET AWAY WITH IT.
BROTHER, RIMURU... WHAT HAVE YOU GOTTEN YOUR-SELVES INTO?
HMPH! I ONLY GAVE A FOOL WHAT HE HAD COMING TO HIM!
SO WE GOT DRAGGED TO THE ROYAL PALACE.

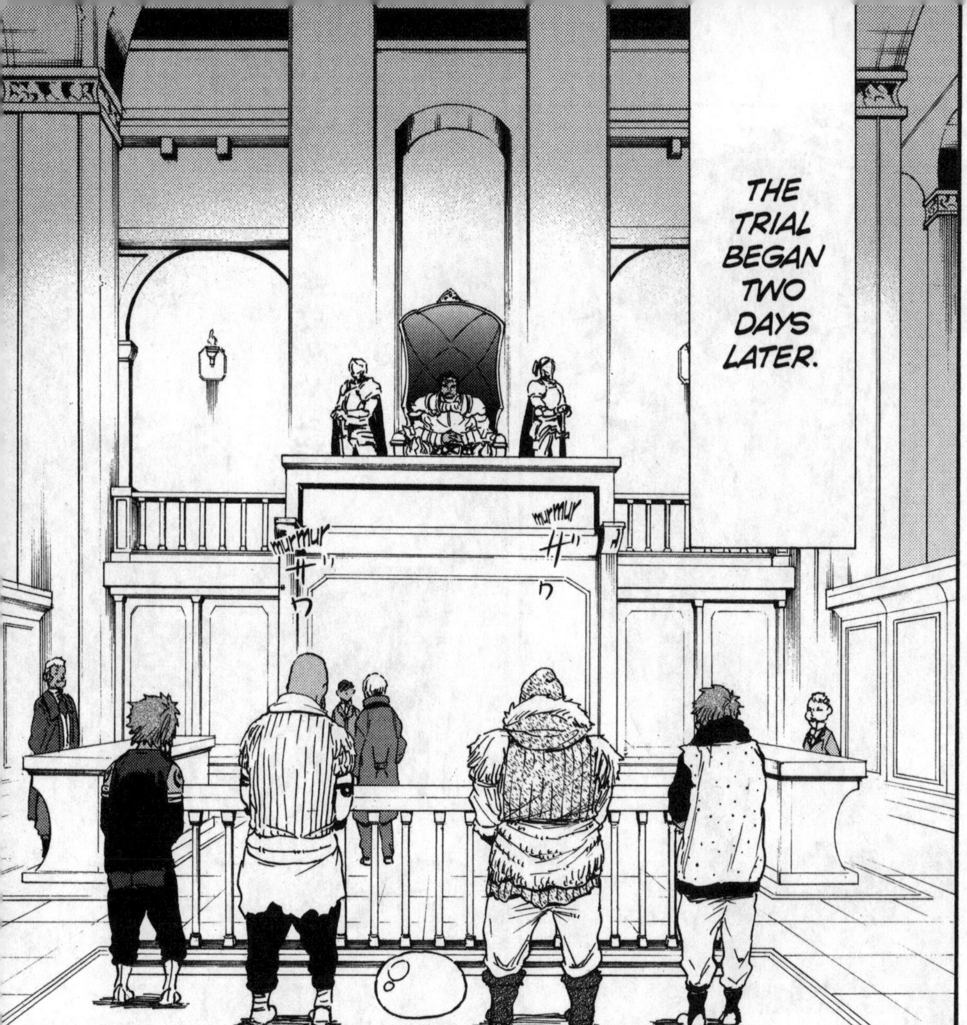
THE TRIAL BEGAN TWO DAYS LATER.
murmur
murmur

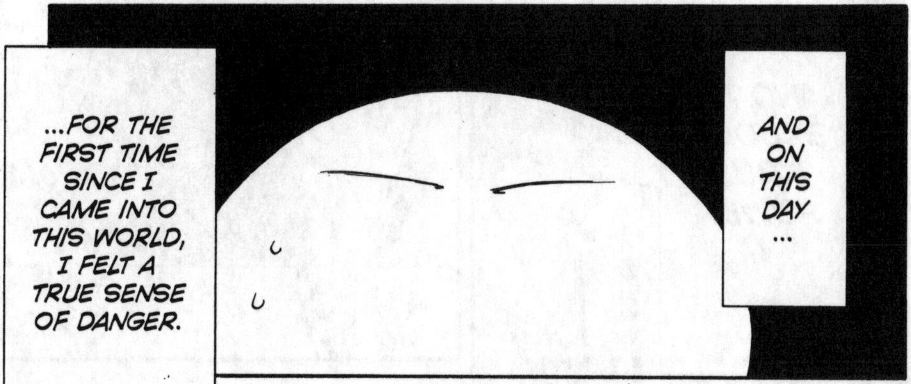
AND ON THIS DAY...
...FOR THE FIRST TIME SINCE I CAME INTO THIS WORLD, I FELT A TRUE SENSE OF DANGER.

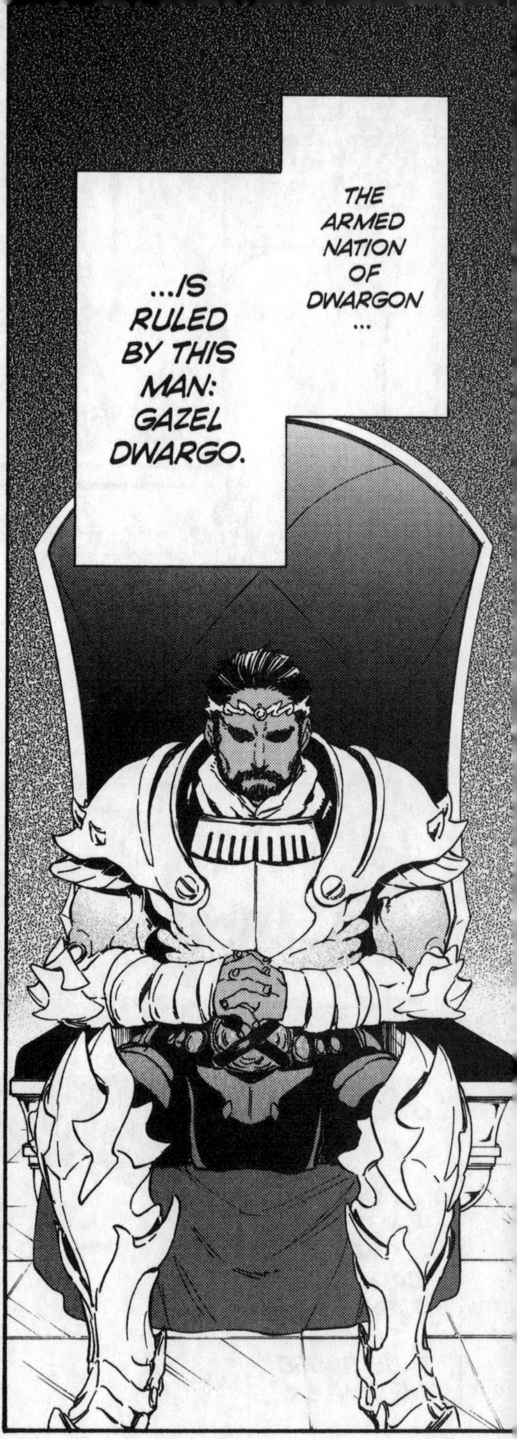
THE ARMED NATION OF DWARGON ...
...IS RULED BY THIS MAN: GAZEL DWARGO.
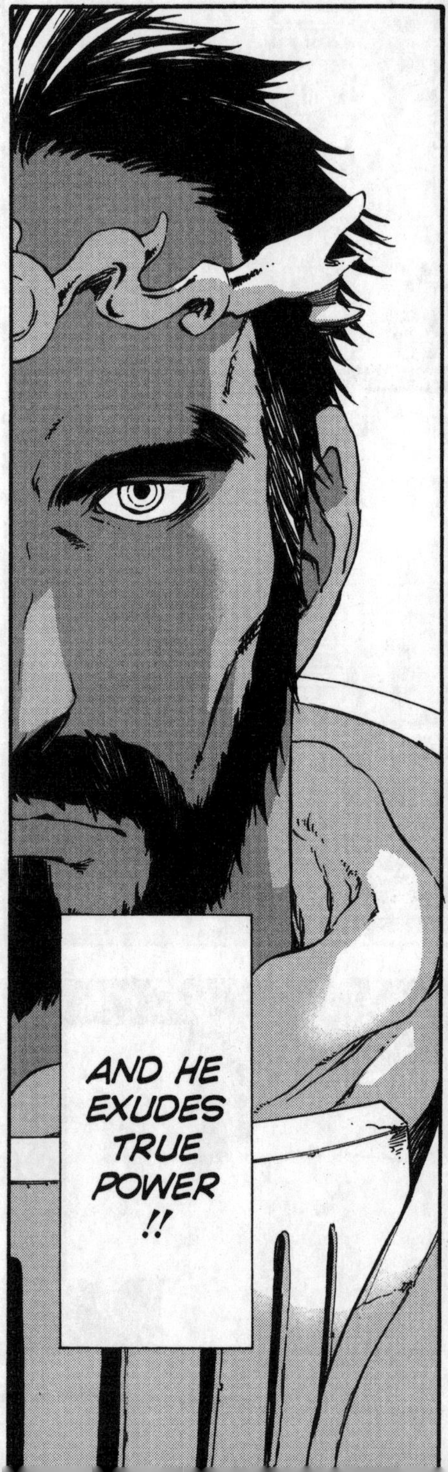
AND HE EXUDES TRUE POWER !!

Reincarnate
in Volume 2?

→YES

NO

Bonus Short Story

Veldora's Slime Observation Journal
~THE FATEFUL MEETING~

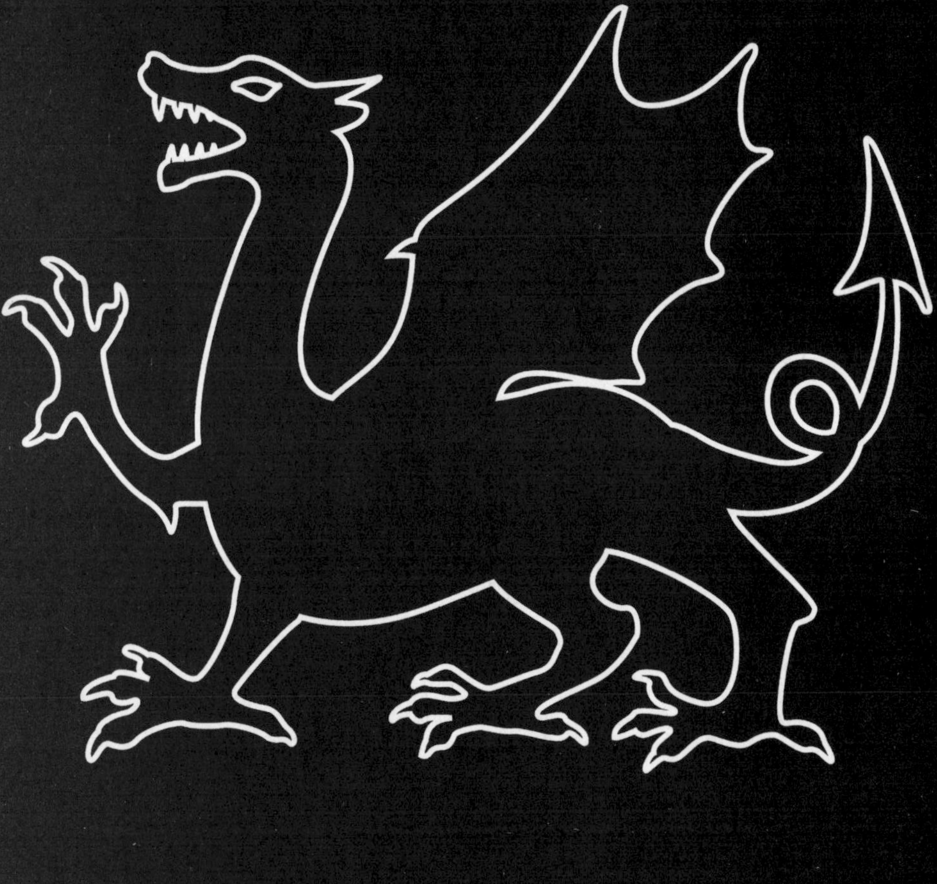

Veldora's Slime Observation Journal
~THE FATEFUL MEETING~

◆DEATH AND REINCARNATION◆

Hello there. It's me, Veldora.

What? What do you mean, you don't know me?

Kwaaa ha ha hah! Your jokes are very amusing. Surely you are not ignorant of the great Storm Dragon, one of the most powerful beings in the entire world. On the other hand, I am currently nothing more than a prisoner. For eons I have been sealed away by this infernal "Unlimited Imprisonment," and am thus unable to escape. In fact, I recall a moment 300 years ago…
………
……
…

Porcelain skin. Dainty lips of deep crimson. Black-and-silver hair, tied into one tail. Not that tall, really. The petite stature and slender figure leads me to assume that the individual was female. Her eyes were hidden by a mask, but it could not hide their beauty.

A *hero*.

Her presence was so dazzling that my eyes could not help but follow her. Of course, it goes without saying that I was not charmed by this beauty. We fought one-on-one in fair contest, and I lost. It would be a lie to claim that I was not chagrined by my defeat. But strangely, I bore her no enmity. Was it because the girl was totally unafraid of me, and challenged me without any sign of emotion?

If anything, the presence of this hero has provoked within me not hatred, but an intense interest in people. How disappointing that she was indifferent to all but turning turned her blade upon me.

I wish that we could have spoken more. I fought as my spirit willed, and lived as my spirit willed. There were some who offered their opinions to me, but I did not offer them my ears in return. I had been invincible, and believed that I had the right to do as I pleased.

But then I lost. It was not my first defeat, but I cannot recall ever losing as thoroughly as I had in that moment. My arrogance in assuming that I was utterly unstoppable had been shattered, and came to a sudden, spectacular end at her hands. I was so impressed that I hoped to battle her again once I was freed from my prison.

But sadly, human lives are short. Assuming the hero was of human birth, my desire shall never come true, I fear. So as I sit in my prison, I have found a surprising, new side of myself—a self-reflective one.
....
......
...

However! 300 years is too long a time. Simply put, I am bored. Within a few more centuries, or perhaps not even that long, I would have been unable to maintain my existence, and would then reincarnate. When a dragon perishes, it always returns elsewhere. Had it happened, my identity would be lost, replaced with a different individual's...but I did not mourn this fact. On the contrary, I was looking forward to it. The unchanging boredom was so crushing that I welcomed my coming oblivion.

Such was my state until that clever little slime appeared before me.

Hurtling towards me with bursting energy, the slime brazenly slammed into me. I was stunned, to be honest. If I do say so myself, my aura is rich and powerful, with a tremendous magical density. It is for these reasons that very few can stand in my presence. Even in my imprisoned state, lower monsters are totally unable to approach me. Even a higher-level monster would find it difficult to touch a being of such pure energy as myself.

Intrigued, I decided I would speak to the creature. Perhaps it had no higher intelligence or will, or was too newly born to understand, but I was not concerned with these possibilities. All I wanted was something to stave off my boredom. But I had a feeling. A feeling that this encounter would bring something much greater. I knew that it had something in store for me. So with this unflinching, unerring premonition in hand, I decided to parlay with the slime.

"Can you hear me, little one?" I asked, directly into its mind.

To my delight, it reacted. The slime's mind was fiercely conflicted. That was enough to show that it had a will of its own. Next, I needed to converse.

"Hello? Answer me," I said, feeling excited.

Those who are as powerful as I am can learn to read the thoughts of beings in their presence, to an extent. Although limited to the surface level, it can be quite useful. As I had not spoken with another soul in a very long time, I decided to read the slime's thoughts without waiting for an answer, and...

"I'm trying to, asshole!!"

Why, I ought to crush that measly slime!!
Asshole! It dares call me an asshole?!

I was outraged. And let me tell you, it is no mean feat to anger one as patient as I. In fact, I was so taken aback that I almost felt admiration at the courage of this tiny creature to refer to a great dragon as—and I quote—an "asshole."

After this, I was able to successfully converse with the slime, and taught it the Extra Skill, "Magic Sense" as a means to make up for its lack of sight and hearing. The slime was a very quick learner, and it gained the skill for its own use in just minutes.

By my estimation, this slime was already an A-Rank monster, going by the scale often used by humans. As it had been likely birthed from the incredible magic field surrounding me, this is perhaps not such a surprise. And its quick mastery of the Magic Sense Skill is no mystery, either.

I thought that it would be overcome with gratitude when it saw me, but instead, it was terrified. The plucky little thing quickly overcame its fear, however.

That part was a little annoying, but I could overlook it. Speaking with the slime, I found it to be extraordinarily intelligent. This would be impossible for a freshly-born monster, so it must have been memory from its previous life.

Such things do happen on rare occasion, so on its own, this would not be a major shock. But I soon learned that there was more to this slime's story.

What an extraordinary twist! In fact, it was a human from another world that was reincarnated as a slime here. This was truly a remarkable combination of events. Even my Unique Skill, "Inquirer" —which allows me to consult a record of the world's events—was unable to find another example of this particular coincidence. This slime was clearly far more fascinating than I first realized. I was instantly intrigued.

Just then, it asked, "Ya wanna be friends with me?"

I couldn't believe my ears. A humble slime? And yet, I had never known a "friend" before this point. Plenty of enemies, however…

Not that it matters now. The slime looked like it was going to cry if I didn't agree to be friends with it. It was begging and pleading.

Naturally, with my generous and understanding nature, I granted its request. I didn't want it to start crying, of course. What a handful that little slime was.

And so, I gave the slime the name of Rimuru, and it became my closest, inseparable friend. This was the meeting of Veldora Tempest and Rimuru Tempest, and the beginning of our journey together.

◆GUARDIAN OF THE GOBLIN VILLAGE◆

Placing my full trust in Rimuru, I am now contained within his stomach. For the most part, he has rather ridiculous skills. To his good fortune, he was born with the Unique Skill, "Predator."

When traveling from another world to this one, one will die without the proper aptitude. Or in other words, with aptitude one gains tremendous magical energy and great strength. Most of these people use that energy to gain a power they desire—a Unique Skill. We call such individuals "Otherworlders." Like them, Rimuru gained his powers when he was reborn into this world.

I do not know what he wished for, but he clearly gained a most fortuitous skill, indeed. On the other hand, Rimuru is so lackadaisical that it seems he may not fathom what a rare power it is that he possesses. I find this situation to be quite humorous, and have thus chosen to hold my tongue. *Hah hah hah!*

But that will explain how it is that I am observing the world through Rimuru's eyes.

What do you mean, "That doesn't explain anything"?

I am a great and mighty dragon, you fool! Naturally, my Unique Skill, "Inquirer" interfaces with our shared name, gleaning the information for my sake—and other such details that I don't need to explain to you. Why would I waste my time with that, rather than just breaking my Unlimited Imprisonment?

You fool!! Boredom is a deadly affliction—it can easily kill those with no interest or joy in their lives. I am no different. Even with my invincible might, the span of 300 years was enough to drive me to despondence and resignation. But I will not make that mistake again.

I have found a fascinating figure, and we have become fast friends. Now I shall share my days with him, and enjoy this world to its fullest! My mind is made up. And thus this is not a waste of time, you buffoon. It is crucial!

Oh?! Rimuru just defeated the most powerful Tempest Serpent in the cave, has he? The beast had grown and transformed due to my mighty aura, until it was worthy of being called the guardian of this cave. The humans would classify it as A-Rank, meaning that it is quite strong...and yet, it fell in just one blow.

Rimuru is very mighty indeed, though he knows it not. Still, he is no more than a pitiful worm to me. *Kwaaaaah ha ha hah!*

And while I laugh, Rimuru continues his progress through the cave. Along the way, he preys upon monsters, stealing their skills. He shut off his Magic Sense to close his eyes as he ate, thanking his lucky stars that he does not have a sense of taste.

Actually, he is not using his Predator Skill properly. He doesn't need to literally eat the target, just touch and corrode it...but this is no matter to me. All I can do is watch, not speak, so there is no way for me to correct his behavior. And watching is certainly enjoyable enough on its own.

There he goes again. Right as he consumed a C+-Rank Giant Bat, something fascinating happened. I assumed that he would take its skills like usual, but this time, he also stole the monster's bodily functions. He found a most novel use for the hypnotic "Ultrasonic Wave" ability. Rimuru used the skill to re-create just the sound-emitting organ alone, and improved it to create a speaking voice. Truly a clever bit of insight. Surely, if he can come up with that, he could also re-create a monster's tongue and enjoy the sense of taste for his meals—but he hasn't come up with that idea yet. He's probably just forgotten about the concept, as he has no sense of hunger.
What a clever, yet forgetful little slime.

Apparently, he's done enough within the cave to satisfy his curiosity about his powers, as Rimuru has decided to leave now. Is he being cowardly, or just careful? I cannot determine the answer.

Rimuru seems to be very cautious in certain ways, and yet bold and fearless in others. Like just now. He is surrounded by pitiful little goblins, and unsure of what to do. I would have slaughtered them all by now, but Rimuru thinks differently.

After a brief conversation, he hides his own aura! There's just a bit leaking out now; only to the level of an ultra-low monster. I would have assumed that the goblins would take advantage of him...but then things took a startling turn.

The goblins have sworn loyalty to him in exchange for his help. I have absolutely no idea why this is happening. I have no personal experience dealing with monsters so inferior to me. They would be unable to survive even my presence. And as a conqueror of this mortal plane, I certainly would never have considered it proper to lower myself to their standards... Yet Rimuru chose to do so without hesitation. And unlike me, he is no longer alone because of it.

Could I have been wrong? I do not regret any of my choices in life, but perhaps I could have chosen a different way for myself. Such was the sobering effect of Rimuru's actions.

◆MASTER OF THE DIREWOLVES◆

Well, Rimuru has taken on the duty of defending the village, and his first action was to heal the wounded. It seems he crafted a high-purity healing elixir from the Hipokute herbs that grew in abundance thanks to my aura. But he only just reincarnated into this world. How can he possess such acute knowledge already? Then again, he did seem to be conversing with someone else when I first met him. Perhaps it was...

Even with my Inquirer Skill, I cannot scry into the depths of Rimuru's mind. Perhaps Predator is not the only Unique Skill that he possesses. Predator is not a skill capable of performing an analysis on the Unlimited Imprisonment which holds me captive. I suppose I must assume that he holds some other, more secret ability. But wait...

When we first met, he was talking to his own skill then. And...what did he call it, again? It certainly wasn't Predator. Rimuru knew what that skill was, at the very least, but I couldn't hear it.

Was I being obstructed from hearing it? That would make sense. It is unheard of for a skill to act independently in order to sabotage another's senses. That Rimuru is a crafty one indeed to fool a dragon! Yes, I see now. I thought he was careless, but he is far more cautious than I ever dreamed. Endlessly fascinating, this Rimuru.

His bold plan for the goblins involved tearing down their worthless shanty huts and constructing a defensive fence of the sort humans build. Rimuru helped craft the fence using sticky thread he gained from a B-Rank Black Spider. With the help of steel thread, he strengthened the fence and set a trap.

It was a crafty trap, and an ingenious use of materials... When I tried to sense Rimuru's surface thoughts, it turned out the idea came from things that he called "manga" and "novels." He merely combined traps he had seen before, and " — —" helped him optimize it. But what is this " — —"? It seems that it sensed I was listening in, and prevented me from scrying. Just as I thought, Rimuru possesses some hidden skill I am not familiar with. I find it rather cruel of him to keep secrets from me, his closest confidant.

But setting that aside—manga and novels? These things are most curious. I also sensed the related terms "movies" and "anime." My curiosity is piqued mightily. This will require some investigation.

To that end, I spared some of my Inquirer resources that were busy trying to unlock my Unlimited Imprisonment and attempted to connect with Rimuru's surface memory. I found some resistance again, but I did my best in the service of my intellectual curiosity. To my delight, I succeeded in unlocking a portion of his surface memory. As a side effect, this made it a smoother process for Rimuru and I to share information, which suits my purposes anyway. As Rimuru would say, "I planned for that to happen."

What I found was a treasure trove of details. A wonderful mountain of information. The story was written in the language of another world, but studying and learning language is child's play to me. I treat it like solving a puzzle.

What's this? "And thus, the boy would become king"?

Simply fascinating. The protagonist enjoys the guidance of a tactician so brilliant, it is as if he can read the minds of the enemy forces. This story features a kind of sorcery, but not the vivid effects of magic spells. Therefore, there is no mass-slaughter through magic, and the main form of conflict is tactical battle. This is the ideal type of knowledge for our current situation.

Ah yes, I see. It is through knowledge from such writings that Rimuru is able to handle the wolves in the clever way he does. Based on the state of battle, I can see that the wolves fell into his trap, and are being soundly beaten by the inferior goblins.

If Rimuru himself bothered to fight, he could have easily destroyed the wolves on his own, but instead he chose to have the weaker goblins do the work—and the reason was clear. By forcing them to fight, he provides them with confidence and experience. That becomes trust in Rimuru, and binds them closer together.

So, this is all according to Rimuru's plan, is it? He seems to have some level of ability to see what magic or skills an opponent wields.

The ability to change his tactics depending on the foe makes him quite the expert tactician.

I cannot rest on my laurels. I must consume more of this information and gain greater wisdom.

Later, I was enjoying a fascinating story composed of a combination of images and text, when something unexpected occurred. I suddenly felt weak.

"What happened?" I wondered, focusing on Rimuru's senses, and found that he was speaking to the goblins and wolves, one by one.

What does he think he's...? I nearly doubted my own eyes, but the unthinkable was coming true. To my utter shock, Rimuru was foolish enough to give each and every individual a name. I screamed, "What are you doing?!" but of course, he could not hear me.

The naming of a monster is not at all like that of a human. The act is a kind of contract that binds the two parties closer than even a parent and child. This act is never undertaken without a deep trust. Unless the relationship between the two is one of shared power, such as the bond between Rimuru and I, the danger is too great to risk.

For one thing, the act of giving a name is the bestowing of one's power upon a trusted subordinate. It inevitably lowers one's own strength, so even the ultra-powerful such as I only attempt the act in extremely rare circumstances.

Now this fool Rimuru comes along and decides to use up not just his own magical energy, but my stockpile as well, merely to give the monsters names. Even my benevolence has its limits.

I hastily attempted to block his actions, but the smoothness of our information sharing made that quite difficult. Was this outcome part of his plan when he allowed me greater access to his mind?! I had thought I was getting the best of him, but ultimately I only fell into his trap. The devious slime.

Still, I will not be defeated. I did what I needed to in order to stop the outflow of magic energy. This continued until Rimuru eventually went into sleep mode.

◆HEAD FOR THE DWARF KINGDOM◆

When Rimuru awoke, the monsters had evolved.

That was no surprise. After all, he stole my own magical energy to name them. I suppose that it is pointless to complain at this stage, but it could mean that my freedom from Unlimited Imprisonment is delayed.

What did you say? "Stop reading manga and get back to my analysis"?

Kwaaaaa ha ha hah! Do not bother yourself with my affairs. Even if that should cause my efforts to be delayed, it makes little difference. But this train of thought does not further my own ends, thus I shall conclude it.

Back to observing Rimuru.

He claims that he will even find a way to co-exist peacefully with the humans. That is good. I have an interest in humans, and have wanted to visit one of their towns for myself. I could never do so as a dragon without inciting a battle, but through Rimuru, even I may have the chance to interact with humanity. Only once I am free of this infernal Unlimited Imprisonment, however.

It seems they had decided to rebuild the village they tore down in the first place. I read Rimuru's surface thoughts as usual, and found that he was planning to construct a home that he found pleasant and enjoyable.

This is, of course, a very self-centered line of thought, but I have no quarrel with it. One who cannot enjoy his own life cannot make others happy.

On the other hand, observing Rimuru has taught me that one must not only pursue one's own happiness, as I once did. In order for one to live happily, everyone must be happy. I never bothered with lesser beings, and it seems that was a mistake.

Now the goblins have evolved into hobgoblins, with greater intelligence and active wills. Perhaps Rimuru is correct, and they will develop culture and arts, bringing enjoyment to their lives.

The buds of possibility are to be cultivated, not plucked. Another fine lesson learned in the short time that I have been with Rimuru.

It seems we are heading to the Dwarf Kingdom now. The wind is bracing from our position on the back of a racing wolf. I can fly through the air faster than sound, so I have never experienced what it means to run on the surface. I have now learned that because the ground is so close, it passes by very quickly.

The experience was more thrilling than I expected.

◆THE DWARVEN CRAFTSMAN◆

No sooner had we arrived at the Dwarf Kingdom than we ran into trouble. The humans are infamous for being unable to measure their foes' true strength, and some were foolish enough to interfere with us.

I have been similarly challenged by them in my time, and am well familiar with their lack of foresight. ...Then again, I suppose I cannot fault them for seeing a mere lowly slime and jumping to conclusions.

It seems the interlopers are adventurers, and no pushovers at that. Rimuru transformed into a Tempest Star Wolf hoping to scare them away, but they took his attempt as a bluff. This reveals the shallowness of their thinking.

An ordinary slime has no intelligence at all, much less the ability to transform. They ought to have been wary, yet the fools assumed no danger to themselves. I suppose that I was the only one who was undeceived by his appearance and could see through to his true nature.

Rimuru roared at the adventurers, and they received their just desserts, fleeing in terror. Some of the onlookers even voided their bodily waste, creating an embarrassing spectacle that was certain to bring them public shame.

Kwaaa ha ha ha! I bellowed—and no sooner had I started than our group was arrested. There is no end to the entertainment. Do you wish to kill me with laughter, Rimuru?

The group tried to play the fool to the authorities, but it did not work, of course. Rimuru attempted no further resistance, and they were tossed into a cell.

Naturally, being a slime, he could easily escape, but then what would become of his goblin companion? Rimuru seems unfazed by any of this, so I expect he has a plan to deal with it.

But does he really? I am not certain myself, but surely he must. He has an oddly powerful streak of luck, so as usual, some element or another will conspire to—

"Captain, big trouble! There was a huge accident in the mine!"

There, you see? While the guards panic, Rimuru busies himself with producing a healing draught for them. Clearly he intends to prove that he is no enemy to the dwarven people.

What a well-prepared slime he is! I must take notes on his ability to get by in the world.

So it came to pass that Rimuru was released from prison.

Not only that, but the captain of the guard has now promised to introduce us to a craftsman. Such good fortune that Rimuru is blessed with!

A grand view of the Dwarf Kingdom. It is my first visit, I will admit. I have viewed human settlements, but only from above. My dragon body was far too large to settle down among them for a proper visit. And the dwarves live in a natural fortress built into a massive cave within the Canaat Mountains. It is perfectly obvious why I could never fit into such a place.

To my surprise, the city was full of fascinating and entertaining sights and items. If I could use my unique Inquirer skill on these items to appraise them, I might learn how such things are meant to be used. Sadly, seeing and touching are two very different things.

Oh, how I curse my imprisoned body! Why could I not have found an interest in these things sooner? I am stunned at my own stupidity. During my reign as a Storm Dragon, I only found pleasure in conquest and terror. But as the saying goes, I was but a big frog in a small pond.

The world is vast. Experiencing the wonder of such novel sights has filled me with a powerful resolve—to gain my freedom and explore this world on my own two legs.

◆THE FATED ONE◆

Today, I experienced a "party" for the first time in my life. Rimuru's aid to the troubled dwarven craftsman was repaid with an invitation to celebrate.

Through some unknown means, likely another hidden skill, Rimuru managed to create copies of a mighty sword. I am unsure whether he truly means to keep his abilities a secret. Rimuru is so open about them that nobody is able to bring any accusations against him. I find myself in agreement with this tactic. When one considers that Rimuru can do anything, it all begins to make a kind of sense.

As for this "party," it is a bracing event. I have long had a curiosity about human food. Especially their spirits. I've heard of such things in stories, and always wanted the opportunity to sample them for myself. But with my enormous body, I could never have succeeded in drinking liquor, and thus the sensation is unknown to me. Now that the opportunity arises, I must certainly take it.

And now I realize that I had forgotten Rimuru possesses no sense of taste. Damn it all!

Meanwhile, Rimuru himself claims that "everything seems delicious when a beautiful woman pours your glass for you."

Easy to say when the women are fawning over you!

What good is a friend who forgets about you and only seeks his own enjoyment? So I warned him: grow yourself a tongue right this instant! A demand which never left the realm of mere thought, hurled into the void...

Envying Rimuru will earn me nothing. In a sense, he is unaware that I am watching at all, so sadly, I must abandon my hopes. But I will keep this place in mind. On the day of my revival, I shall return! Like Rimuru, I will glory in being fawned upon by these women.

I have been a fool until now. It feels much better to be revered than to be feared. I must exhibit my strength in an admirable manner, and gain the respect of all. The hobgoblins whom Rimuru named are the perfect start—he was quite clever and forward-thinking in this regard.

Rimuru is exceedingly skilled at blending among peoples. At this very moment, he has made himself the center of attention in this establishment, receiving some kind of divination.

Apparently, the figure that flashed across the crystal ball is Rimuru's "fated one." It seems to be a beautiful woman, albeit with a burn scar across her face. Something about her is vaguely reminiscent of the Hero. Perhaps they share some distant connection. But that is a discussion for another time.

What must one do to become well-liked? I wish to get along with others as Rimuru does.

This is all a waste of my time. I must read through more reference materials, and study dashing and attractive gestures and quotations.

Hmm? What's all the commotion about?

Just as I was readying myself for a good study session, some kind of scuffle arose. Is Rimuru accursed in some manner, that extraordinary events should follow him wherever he goes?

As soon as I take my attention away from him, something occurs. Of course, something occurs even when I *am* paying attention, so the cause surely does not lie with me.

In this latest bit of trouble, it seems a slender man threw water upon Rimuru, and claimed, most insultingly, "This is the best a monster deserves."

This man acts with purpose. He came to this place for the express purpose of causing trouble, and casting aspersions on Rimuru.

So what happens now?

I would turn the man into ash, of course, but how will Rimuru react? Out of curiosity, I read his surface thoughts, and found that he wishes to avoid conflict.

The man seemed to be a senior official of this nation, meaning that killing him would have significant consequences. This would not influence me in any way, of course. Why would he hesitate?

What's this? If such trouble arises, we will never be able to return to this place?! That is a dire consequence indeed!

What will happen, then? Shall we simply grin and bear it?

For the first time in ages, I am flustered. For one as mighty as I to feel such panic over so trivial a matter would have been unthinkable in the old days. No one who knows me would believe it possible. But now I am learning. When pleasures grow, sometimes patience is required in order to preserve them.

Such inconvenient and annoying rules society creates for us! But without these rules, I suppose such pleasures would be impossible. I feel as though I have learned another valuable lesson.

Just then, the dwarf who owed Rimuru his livelihood stood up. To my surprise, this dwarf named Kaijin walked over to the official and punched the hateful man.

I couldn't help but cheer. Yes, it was satisfying to watch. But more importantly, Kaijin struck that blow for my good friend Rimuru.

Surely, this is an act worthy of celebration. I've come to understand that it is more infuriating for one's friend to be insulted than to be the object of derision yourself. Life has become one surprise after another since I came to know Rimuru. I am satisfied that the choice I made on that day was the correct one.

Alas, it seems that Kaijin's actions did indeed cause trouble.Rimuru's group was once again arrested and locked in chains. This time, the stakes are more dire.

The dwarven king—Gazel Dwargo.

I can sense that Rimuru feels danger. But of course he does. This is no ordinary man he faces. Even Rimuru cannot get the better of him.

I must admit that I am eager to see how my slime friend reacts now.

To be reincarnated in Volume 2!

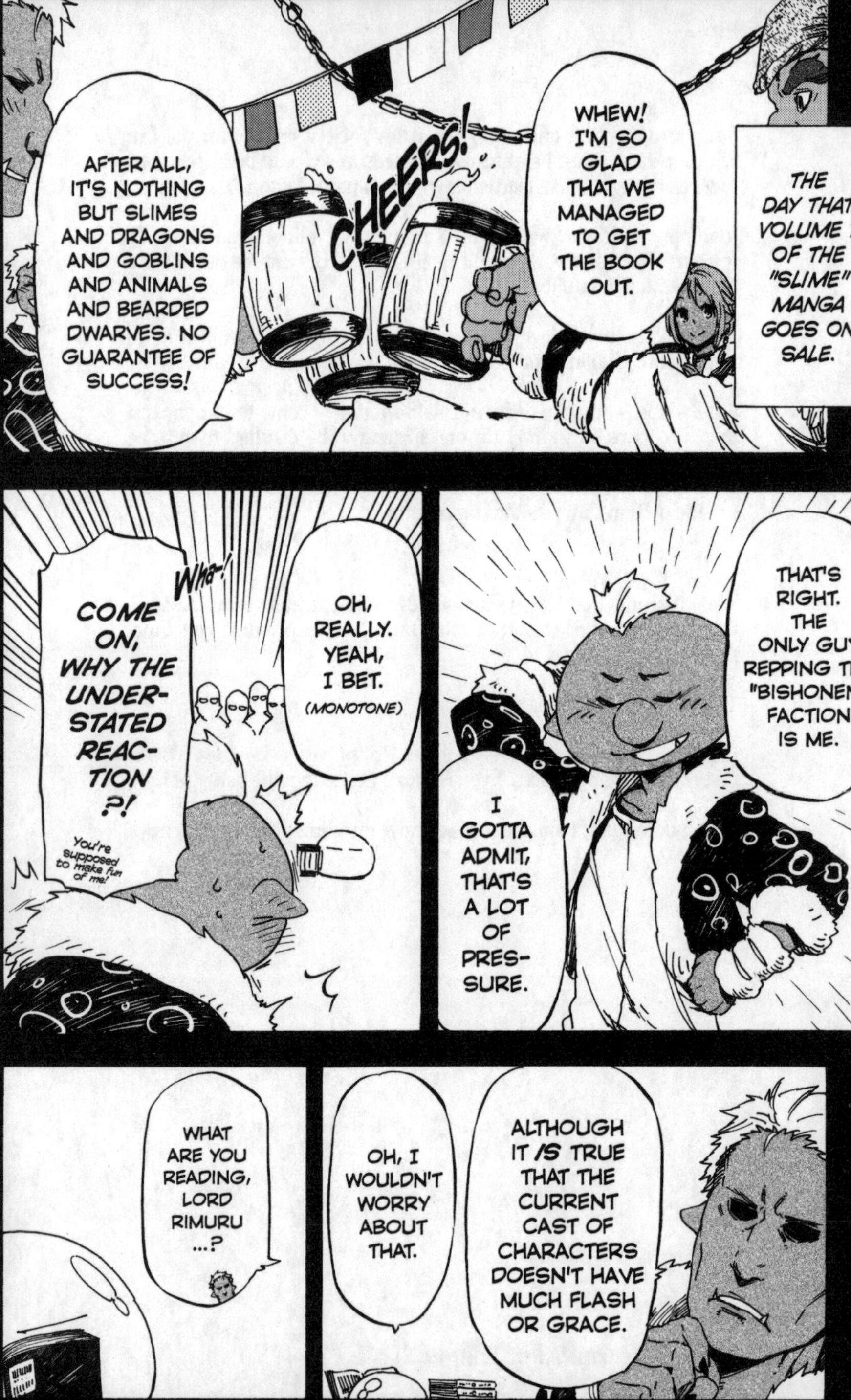
THE DAY THAT VOLUME 1 OF THE "SLIME" MANGA GOES ON SALE.
WHEW! I'M SO GLAD THAT WE MANAGED TO GET THE BOOK OUT.
CHEERS!
AFTER ALL, IT'S NOTHING BUT SLIMES AND DRAGONS AND GOBLINS AND ANIMALS AND BEARDED DWARVES. NO GUARANTEE OF SUCCESS!
THAT'S RIGHT. THE ONLY GUY REPPING THE "BISHONEN" FACTION IS ME.
I GOTTA ADMIT, THAT'S A LOT OF PRES-SURE.
OH, REALLY. YEAH, I BET. (MONOTONE)
Wha-!
COME ON, WHY THE UNDER-STATED REAC-TION ?!
You're supposed to make fun of me!
ALTHOUGH IT IS TRUE THAT THE CURRENT CAST OF CHARACTERS DOESN'T HAVE MUCH FLASH OR GRACE.
OH, I WOULDN'T WORRY ABOUT THAT.
WHAT ARE YOU READING, LORD RIMURU ...?

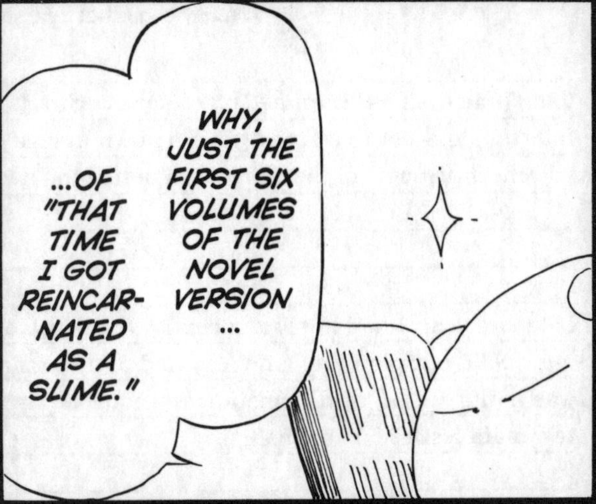
WHY, JUST THE FIRST SIX VOLUMES OF THE NOVEL VERSION ...
...OF "THAT TIME I GOT REINCARNATED AS A SLIME."

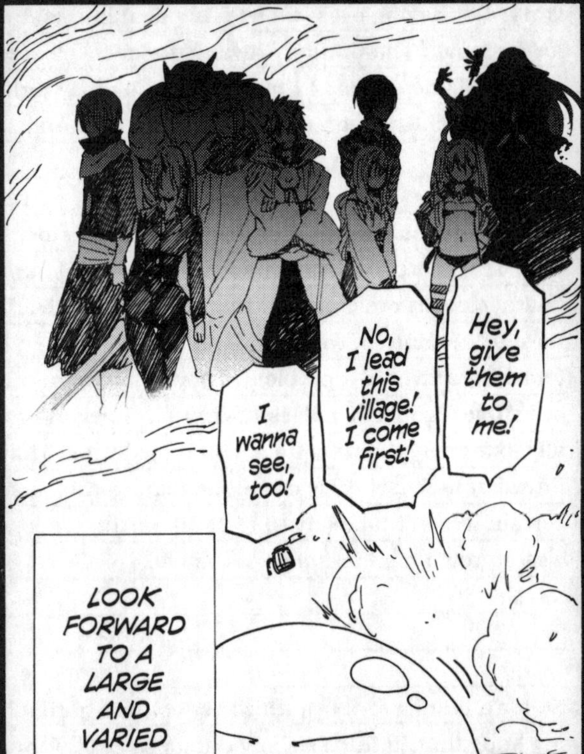
Hey, give them to me!
No, I lead this village! I come first!
I wanna see, too!
LOOK FORWARD TO A LARGE AND VARIED CAST TO COME!

LIST OF ACKNOWLEDGMENTS

AUTHOR:

Fuse-sensei

ASSISTANTS:

Taku Arao-san

Akoron-san

Takuya Nishida-san

Muraichi-san

Hino-san

Daiki Haraguchi-san

Shigemi Kudo-san

Akiko Takahashi-san

Everyone at the editorial department

And You!!

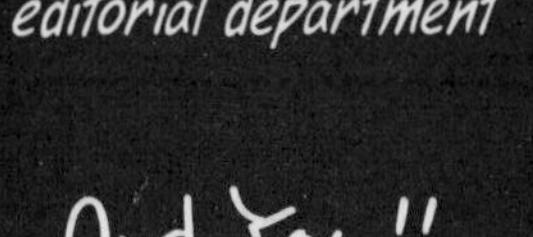

AFTERWORD

from the author, Fuse

That Time I Got Reincarnated as a Slime began its life as a novel on the Internet, and now it's actually got its own manga adaptation! So I thought I'd reflect on some of the challenges of turning it into a visual format...

◇◇◇

Late last year, I had my first meeting with Kawakami-sensei. At this meeting we did our planning, and also had to do signings for a giveaway, which was a difficult set of circumstances—not that I'm complaining.We settled on two main issues for the manga.

The first problem was the protagonist's sense of vision at the start of the story. Not having eyes wasn't a big deal in a text novel, but it's a major issue for a manga. Thankfully, Kawakami-sensei cleared that hurdle with flying colors! His depiction of the senses unfolding worked wonders. It's the exact sort of touch that can only be done in the manga format, and never in a novel.

The other problem was that the start of the story features very few characters. Yes, there are monsters, of course, but you just don't see any human characters. In other words, there's no female lead! It's quite possible not to have a "heroine" in the traditional sense, but not having any female characters whatsoever is a problem. There's no beauty in the manga. All we have are slimes, goblins, wolves, dwarves... I began to worry: is this story actually extremely unsuited to a visual medium?! Thankfully, the cute way that Kawakami-sensei drew our slime managed to assuage my fears a bit. I'm certain it won't take any time at all for the readers to forget that our hero was a grown man in his previous life...

◇◇◇

So for a manga for boys, this first volume hardly had any cute girls. It's my hope that Rimuru's slimy cuteness got us through that difficulty. Nothing would make me happier than for you to continue following along with Rimuru's adventures. And with that, my afterword is finished. Please check out the next volume of *That Time I Got Reincarnated as a Slime!!*

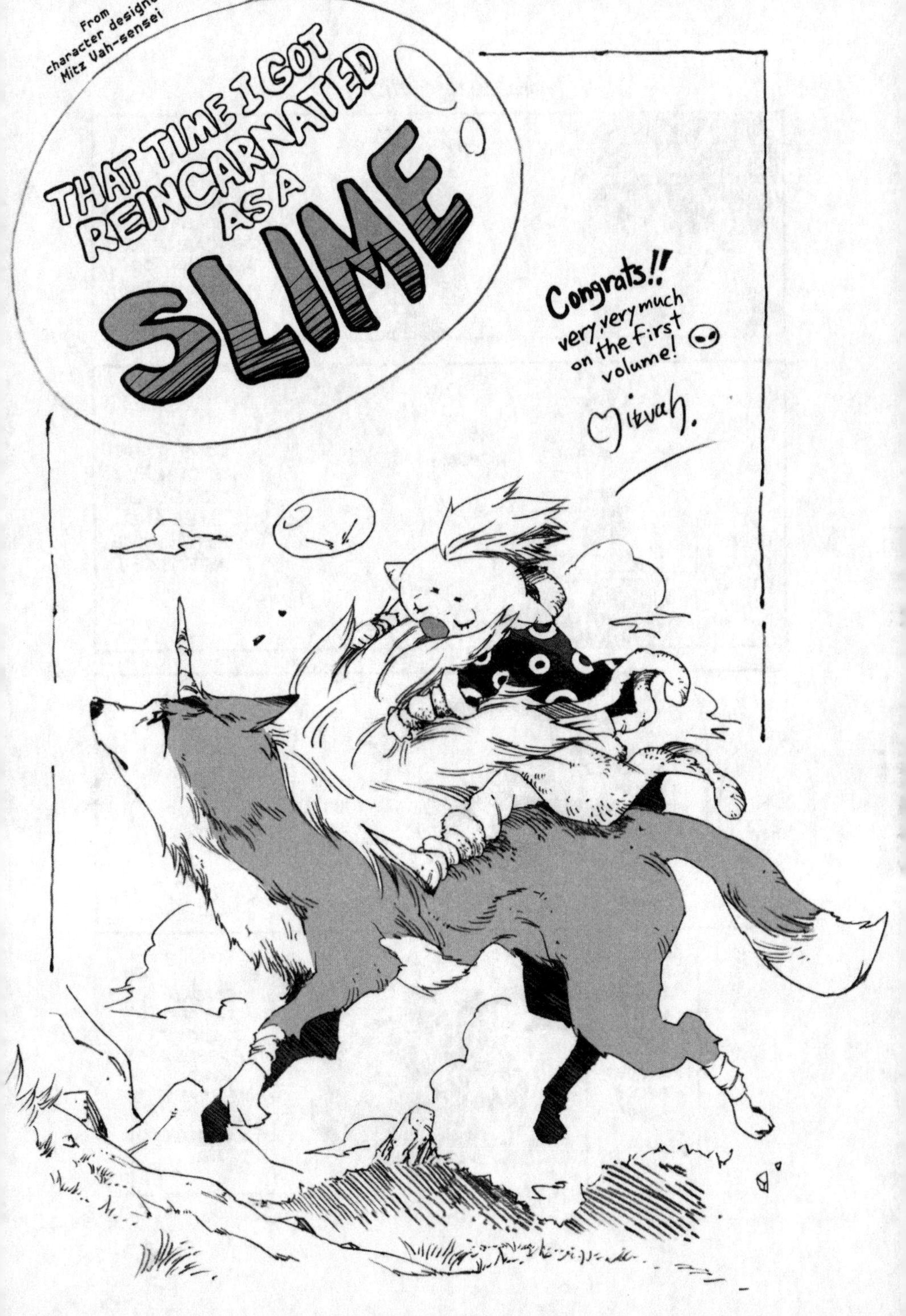
From character designer Mitz Vah-sensei
THAT TIME I GOT REINCARNATED AS A SLIME
Congrats!! very, very much on the first volume!
Mitzvah.

Typical Conversation

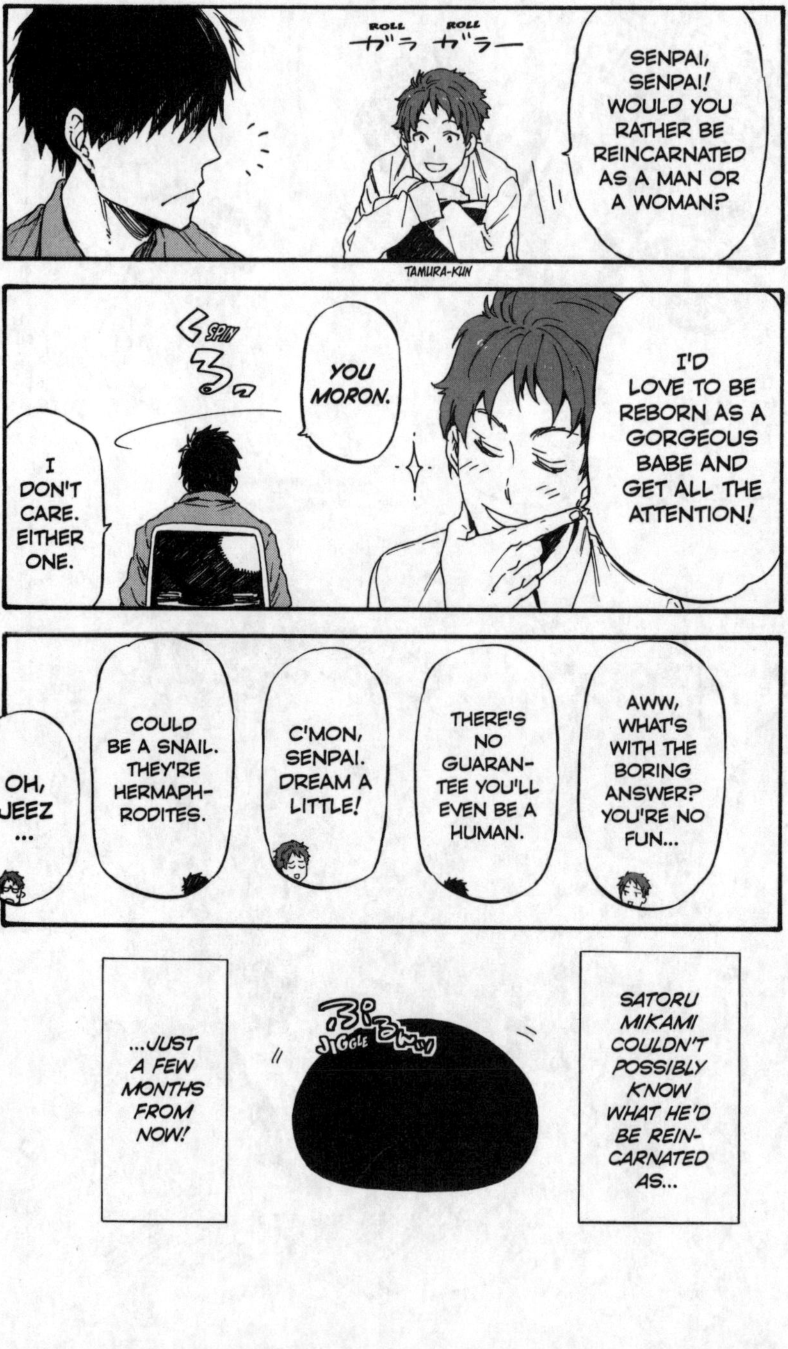
ROLL ROLL
ガラ ガラー
SENPAI, SENPAI! WOULD YOU RATHER BE REINCARNATED AS A MAN OR A WOMAN?
TAMURA-KUN
I'D LOVE TO BE REBORN AS A GORGEOUS BABE AND GET ALL THE ATTENTION!
YOU MORON.
SPIN
I DON'T CARE. EITHER ONE.
AWW, WHAT'S WITH THE BORING ANSWER? YOU'RE NO FUN...
THERE'S NO GUARANTEE YOU'LL EVEN BE A HUMAN.
C'MON, SENPAI. DREAM A LITTLE!
COULD BE A SNAIL. THEY'RE HERMAPHRODITES.
OH, JEEZ...
SATORU MIKAMI COULDN'T POSSIBLY KNOW WHAT HE'D BE REINCARNATED AS...
JIGGLE
...JUST A FEW MONTHS FROM NOW!

Hiding among the
sweet mochi

TRANSLATION NOTES

KITARO

page 89

I sense an aura!
BING!
You do?!
FLINCH
RECENT PROBLEM:
Nobody in this world gets refer-ences from my old world.

Rimuru is referring to the famous character Kitaro (of *GeGeGe no Kitaro* fame) developed by Shigeru Mizuki. Kitaro is a boy with both human and *yokai* heritage—*yokai* being the catch-all term for traditional folklore creatures of Japan. In his adventures to create peace between humans and *yokai*, Kitaro utilizes a number of special abilities, one of which is a "*yokai* sense" in which his hair acts as an antenna that picks up supernatural signals. When he senses *yokai*, Kitaro claims that he feels *yoki*, which could be translated as "*yokai* presence" or "otherworldly spirit." In this story, the term "aura" is written with the kanji characters for *yoki*, allowing Rimuru to make this Kitaro joke.

GOBLIN NAMES

page 116

Gobtsu.
Gobte.

It's not just that these names all sound similar—it's that Rimuru is literally taking "gob" (from goblin) and running through the letters of the Japanese alphabet one after the other. Japanese characters (known as *kana*) are grouped together so that a consonant sound is then followed by a vowel, with each "row" having five kana for the five vowels. So the *ta* (or "t") row goes, in order: *ta, chi, tsu, te, to*. The other consonants (as we would call them) in the Japanese language follow a similar pattern: *ka, ki, ku, ke, ko; sa, shi, su, se, so*, etc.

"AND THUS, THE BOY WOULD BECOME KING"

page 220

> would say, "I planned for that to happen."
>
> What I found was a treasure trove of details. A wonderful of information. The story was written in the language world, but studying and learning language is child's pla treat it like solving a puzzle.
>
> What's this? "And thus, the boy would become king"?
>
> Simply fascinating. The protagonist enjoys the guidance cian so brilliant, it is as if he can read the minds of the e es. This story features a kind of sorcery, but not the vivi magic spells. Therefore, there is no mass-slaughter throu and the main form of conflict is tactical battle. This is the of knowledge for our current situation.

This and part of the text that follows in Veldora's musings are references to the *Heroic Legend of Arslan*, a series of novels by Yoshiki Tanaka that has also been adapted into manga and anime. The most current rendition of the series in manga form is currently being published by Kodansha and is illustrated by Hiromu Arakawa of *Fullmetal Alchemist* fame. The series follows the adventures of young prince Arslan of Pars, whose world is shattered when his country is defeated by a rival kingdom. He sets out on a journey to gather forces to reclaim his land, and along the way, picks up a crew of talented characters, including the brilliant tactician, Narsus. *The Heroic Legend of Arslan* is set in a fantasy world that appears to be inspired by the medieval Middle East. As Veldora points out, magic exists in Arslan's world, but it is limited, and not as powerful as it would be in an RPG-based world like that of *That Time I Got Reincarnated as a Slime*.

The award-winning manga about what happens inside you!

"Far more entertaining than it ought to be... what kid doesn't want to think that every time they sneeze a torpedo shoots out their nose?"
—Anime News Network

Strep throat! Hay fever! Influenza! The world is a dangerous place for a red blood cell just trying to get her deliveries finished. Fortunately, she's not alone…she's got a whole human body's worth of cells ready to help out! The mysterious white blood cells, the buff and brash killer T cells, even the cute little platelets— everyone's got to come together if they want to keep you healthy!

Cells at Work!

はたらく細胞

By Akane Shimizu

A new
series
from the
creator
of *Soul
Eater*, the
megahit
manga and
anime seen
on Toonami!

"Fun and lively...
a great start!"
-Adventures in
Poor Taste

FIRE FORCE

By Atsushi Ohkubo

The city of Tokyo is plagued by a deadly phenomenon: spontaneous human combustion! Luckily, a special team is there to quench the inferno: The Fire Force! The fire soldiers at Special Fire Cathedral 8 are about to get a unique addition. Enter Shinra, a boy who possesses the power to run at the speed of a rocket, leaving behind the famous "devil's footprints" (and destroying his shoes in the process). Can Shinra and his colleagues discover the source of this strange epidemic before the city burns to ashes?

Japan's most powerful spirit medium delves into the ghost world's greatest mysteries!

Story by Kyo Shirodaira, famed author of mystery fiction and creator of *Spiral*, *Blast of Tempest*, and *The Record of a Fallen Vampire*.

Both touched by spirits called yôkai, Kotoko and Kurô have gained unique superhuman powers. But to gain her powers Kotoko has given up an eye and a leg, and Kurô's personal life is in shambles. So when Kotoko suggests they team up to deal with renegades from the spirit world, Kurô doesn't have many other choices, but Kotoko might just have a few ulterior motives...

IN/SPECTRE

STORY BY **KYO SHIRODAIRA**
ART BY **CHASHIBA KATASE**

HAPPINESS

—— ハピネス ——

By Shuzo Oshimi

From the creator of *The Flowers of Evil*

Nothing interesting is happening in Makoto Ozaki's first year of high school. His life is a series of quiet humiliations: low-grade bullies, unreliable friends, and the constant frustration of his adolescent lust. But one night, a pale, thin girl knocks him to the ground in an alley and offers him a choice. Now everything is different. Daylight is searingly bright. Food tastes awful. And worse than anything is the terrible, consuming thirst...

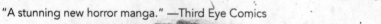

Praise for Shuzo Oshimi's *The Flowers of Evil*

"A shockingly readable story that vividly—one might even say queasily—evokes the fear and confusion of discovering one's own sexuality. Recommended." —The Manga Critic

"A page-turning tale of sordid middle school blackmail." —Otaku USA Magazine

"A stunning new horror manga." —Third Eye Comics

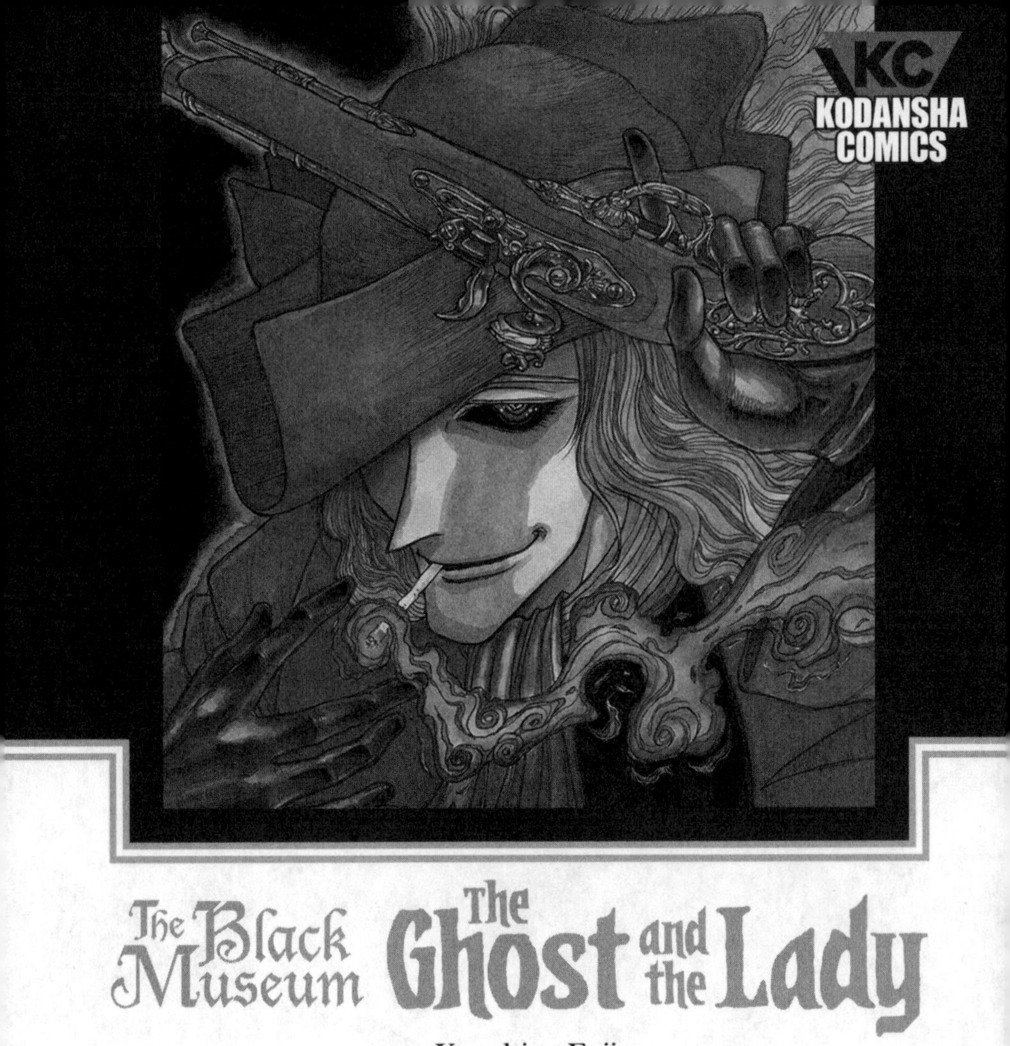
KC
KODANSHA COMICS

The Black Museum The Ghost and the Lady

By Kazuhiro Fujita

Deep in Scotland Yard in London sits an evidence room dedicated to the greatest mysteries of British history. In this "Black Museum" sits a misshapen hunk of lead—two bullets fused together—the key to a wartime encounter between Florence Nightingale, the mother of modern nursing, and a supernatural Man in Grey. This story is unknown to most scholars of history, but a special guest of the museum will tell the tale of The Ghost and the Lady...

Praise for Kazuhiro Fujita's *Ushio and Tora*

"A charming revival that combines a classic look with modern depth and pacing... **Essential viewing both for curmudgeons and new fans alike.**" — Anime News Network

"**GREAT!** The first episode of Ushio and Tora captures the essence of '90s anime." — IGN

New action series from Hiroyuki Takei, creator of the classic shonen franchise Shaman King!

In medieval Japan, a bell hanging on the collar is a sign that a cat has a master. Norachiyo's bell hangs from his katana sheath, but he is nonetheless a stray — a ronin. This one-eyed cat samurai travels across a dishonest world, cutting through pretense and deception with his blade.

NeKogaHara

STRAY CAT SAMURAI

By

Hiroyuki Takei

Based on the critically acclaimed classic horror manga

The first new *Parasyte* manga in over 20 years!

NEO ParaSyte f

BY ASUMIKO NAKAMURA, EMA TOYAMA, MIKI RINNO, LALAKO KOJIMA, KAORI YUKI, BANKO KUZE, YUUKI OBATA, KASHIO, YUI KUROE, ASIA WATANABE, MIKIMAKI, HIKARU SURUGA, HAJIME SHINJO, RENJURO KINDAICHI, AND YURI NARUSHIMA

A collection of chilling new *Parasyte* stories from Japan's top shojo artists!

Parasites: shape-shifting aliens whose only purpose is to assimilate with and consume the human race... but do these monsters have a different side? A parasite becomes a prince to save his romance-obsessed female host from a dangerous stalker. Another hosts a cooking show, in which the real monsters are revealed. These and 13 more stories, from some of the greatest shojo manga artists alive today, together make up a chilling, funny, and entertaining tribute to one of manga's horror classics!

KC KODANSHA COMICS

A Kodansha Comics Trade Paperback Original.

Published in the United States by Kodansha Comics,
an imprint of Kodansha USA Publishing, LLC, New York.

Publication rights for this English edition arranged through Kodansha Ltd., Tokyo.

First published in Japan in 2015 by Kodansha Ltd., Tokyo, as *Tensei Shitara Suraimu Datta Ken*.

ISBN 978-1-63236-506-4

Printed in the United States of America.

www.kodanshacomics.com

13th Printing

Translation: Stephen Paul
Lettering: Evan Hayden
Editing: Ajani Oloye
Kodansha Comics edition cover design: Phil Balsman

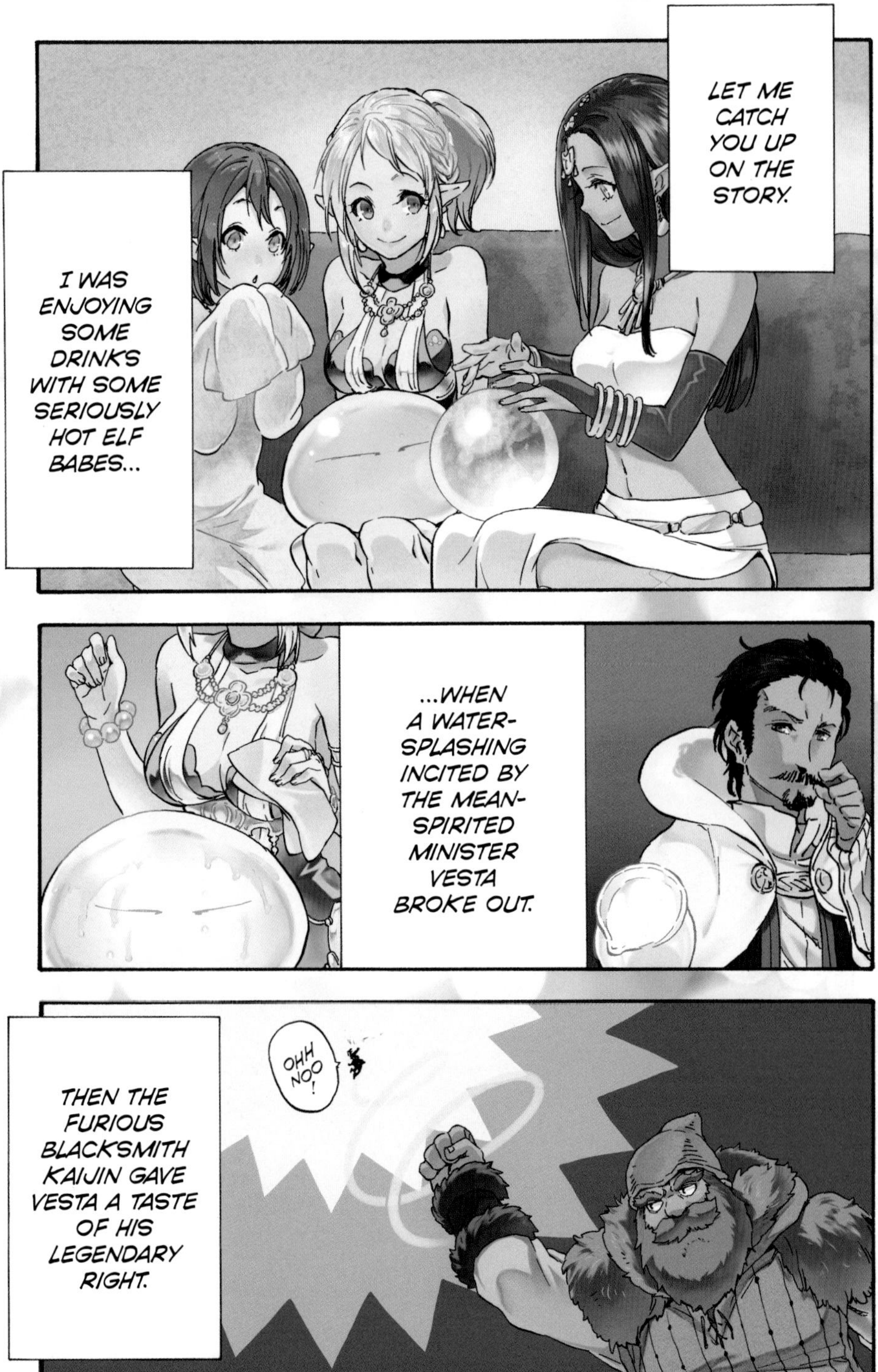
LET ME CATCH YOU UP ON THE STORY.
I WAS ENJOYING SOME DRINKS WITH SOME SERIOUSLY HOT ELF BABES...
...WHEN A WATER-SPLASHING INCITED BY THE MEAN-SPIRITED MINISTER VESTA BROKE OUT.
OHH NOO!
THEN THE FURIOUS BLACKSMITH KAIJIN GAVE VESTA A TASTE OF HIS LEGENDARY RIGHT.

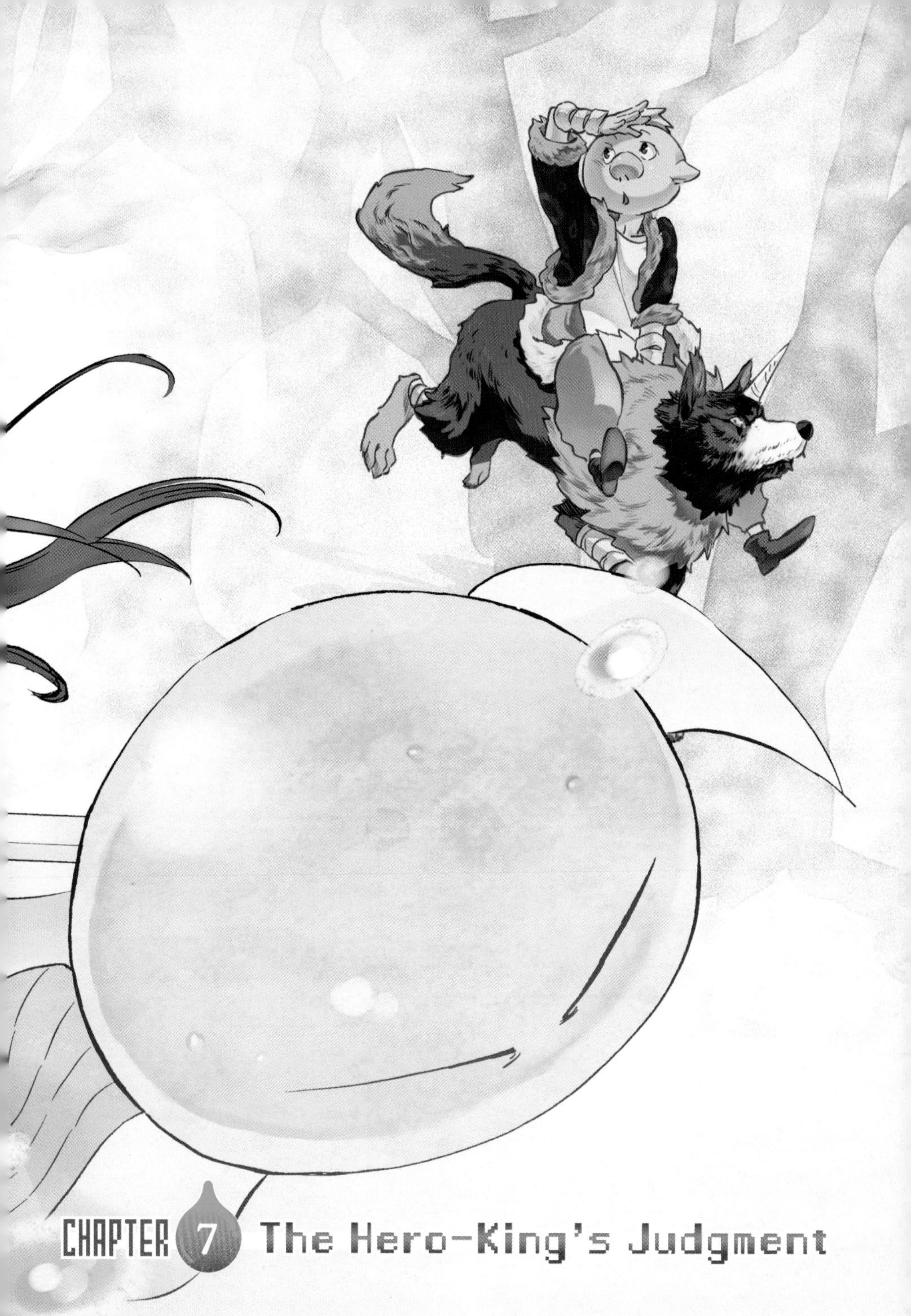

CHAPTER 7 The Hero-King's Judgment

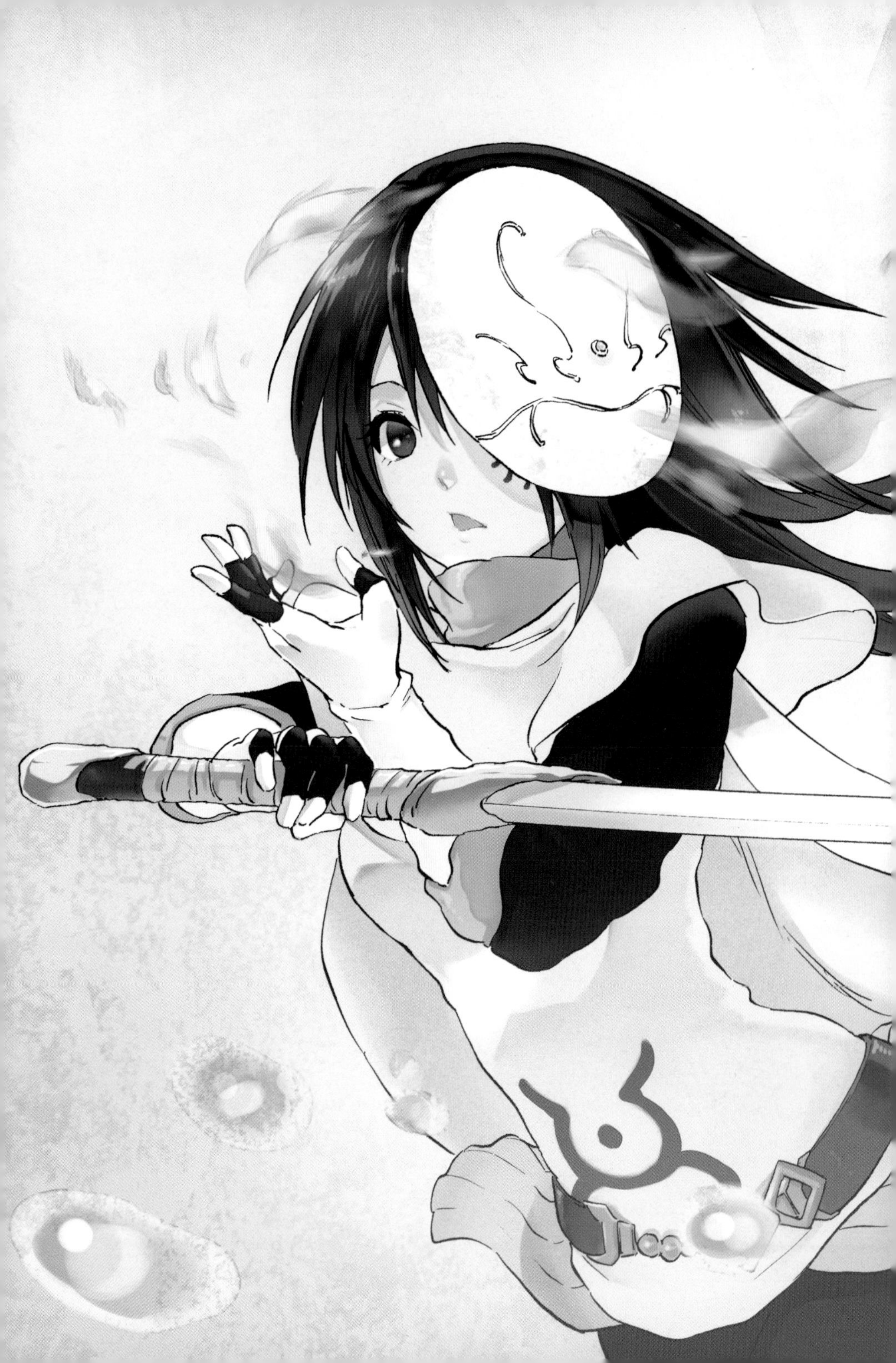

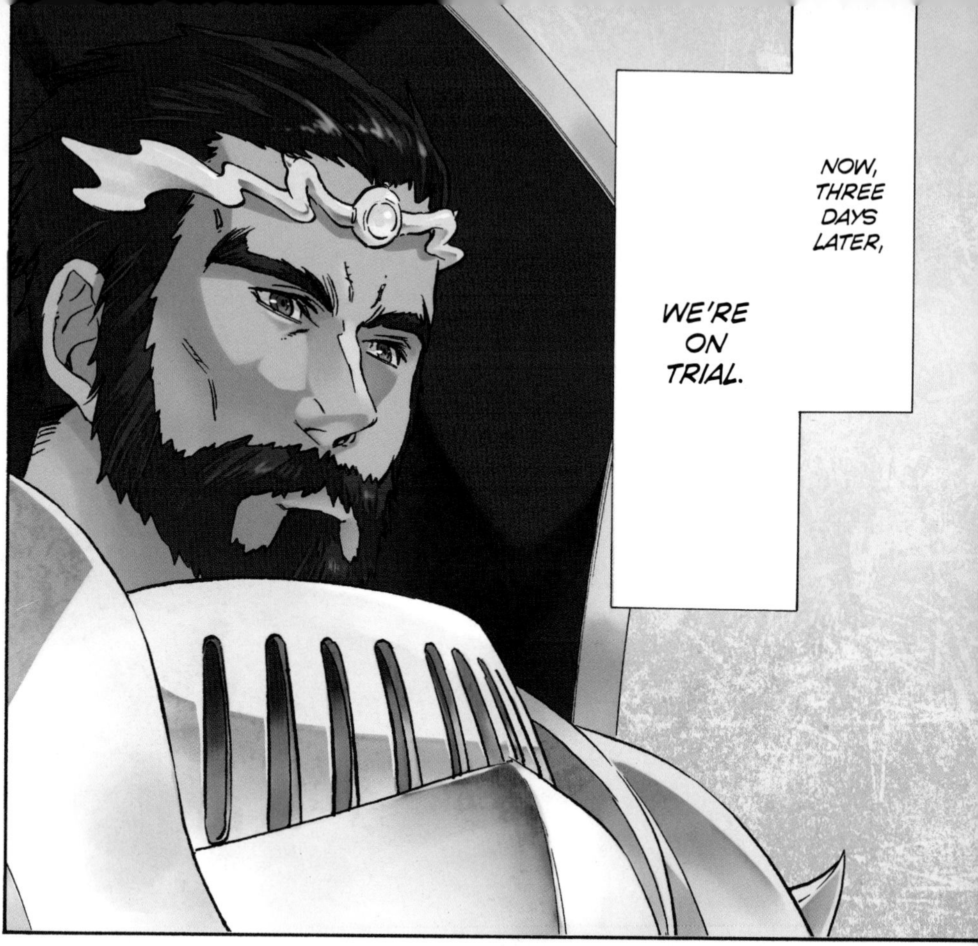
NOW, THREE DAYS LATER,
WE'RE ON TRIAL.

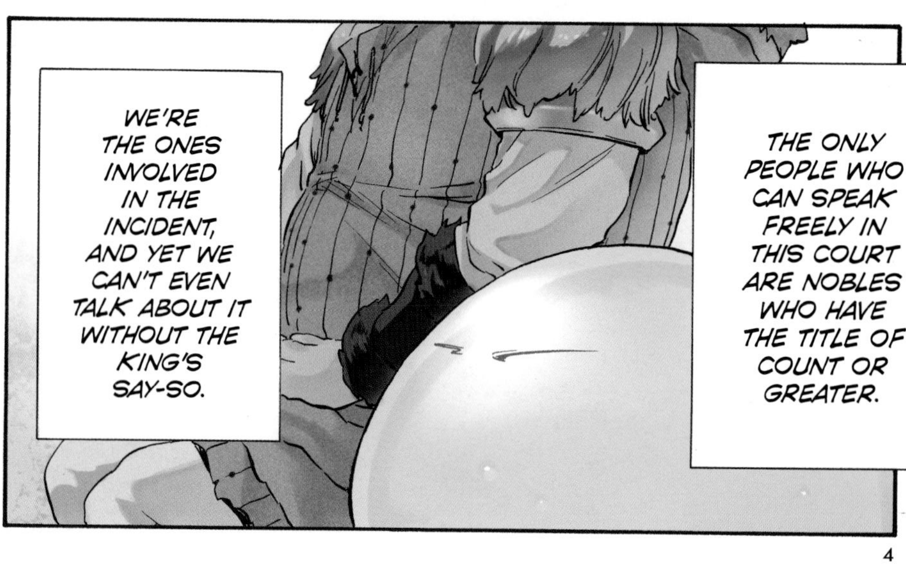
THE ONLY PEOPLE WHO CAN SPEAK FREELY IN THIS COURT ARE NOBLES WHO HAVE THE TITLE OF COUNT OR GREATER.
WE'RE THE ONES INVOLVED IN THE INCIDENT, AND YET WE CAN'T EVEN TALK ABOUT IT WITHOUT THE KING'S SAY-SO.

THAT TIME I GOT REINCARNATED AS A

SLIME

2

Author: FUSE

Artist: TAIKI KAWAKAMI

Character design: MITZ VAH

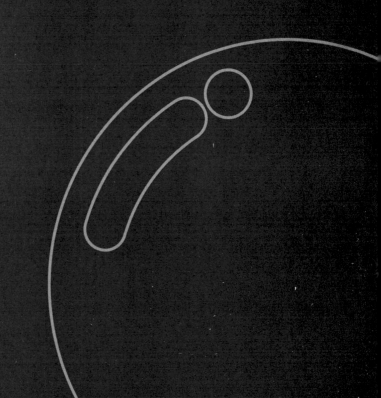

CONTENTS

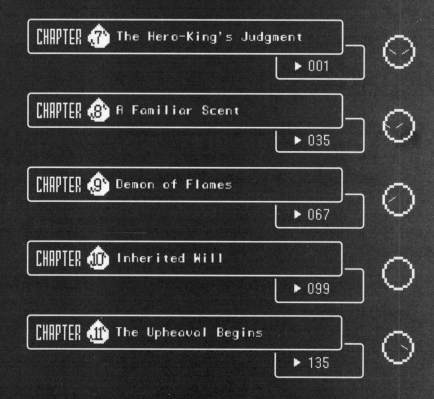

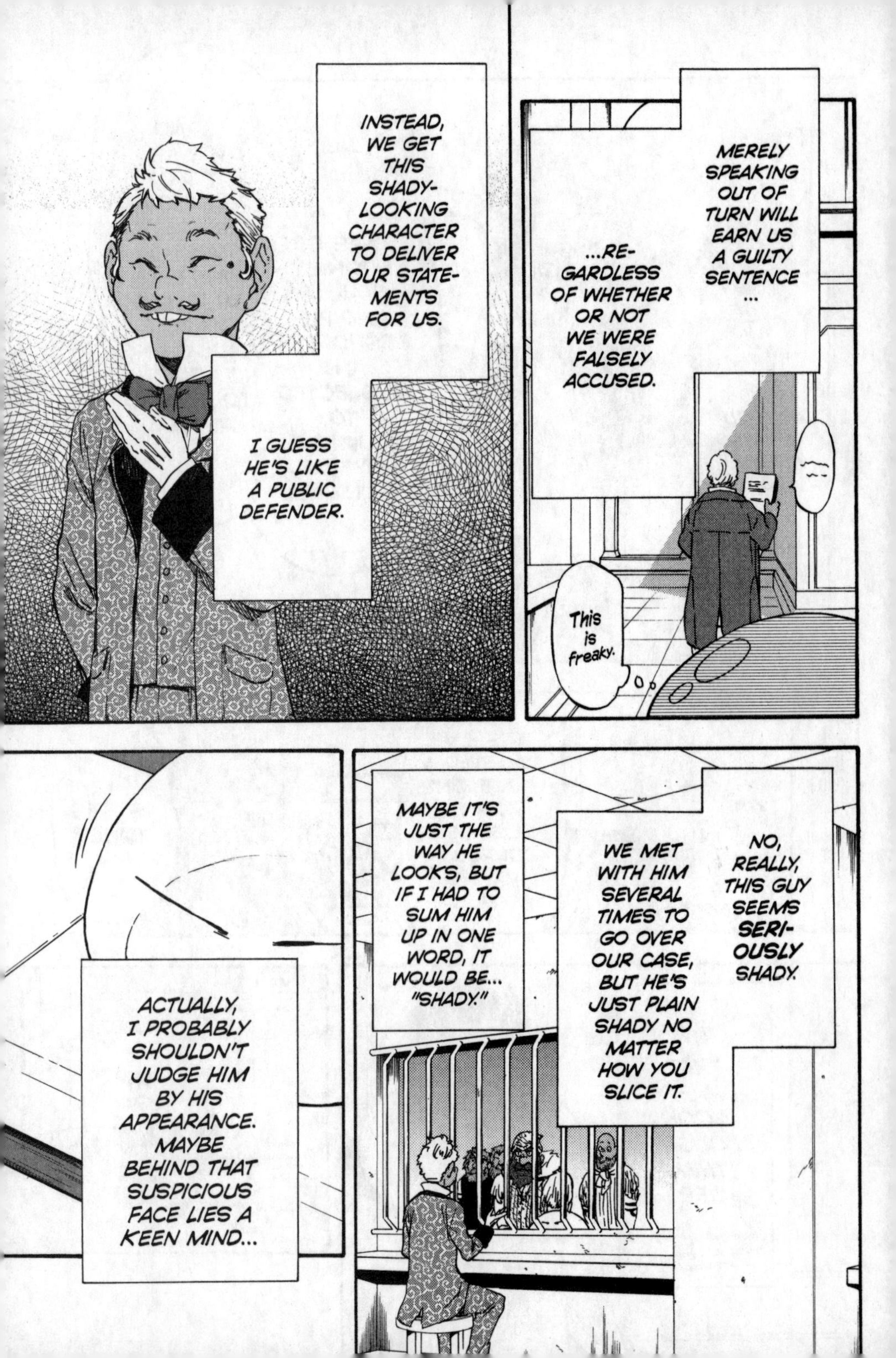
MERELY SPEAKING OUT OF TURN WILL EARN US A GUILTY SENTENCE ...
...RE-GARDLESS OF WHETHER OR NOT WE WERE FALSELY ACCUSED.
This is freaky.
INSTEAD, WE GET THIS SHADY-LOOKING CHARACTER TO DELIVER OUR STATE-MENTS FOR US.
I GUESS HE'S LIKE A PUBLIC DEFENDER.
NO, REALLY, THIS GUY SEEMS SERI-OUSLY SHADY.
WE MET WITH HIM SEVERAL TIMES TO GO OVER OUR CASE, BUT HE'S JUST PLAIN SHADY NO MATTER HOW YOU SLICE IT.
MAYBE IT'S JUST THE WAY HE LOOKS, BUT IF I HAD TO SUM HIM UP IN ONE WORD, IT WOULD BE... "SHADY."
ACTUALLY, I PROBABLY SHOULDN'T JUDGE HIM BY HIS APPEARANCE. MAYBE BEHIND THAT SUSPICIOUS FACE LIES A KEEN MIND...

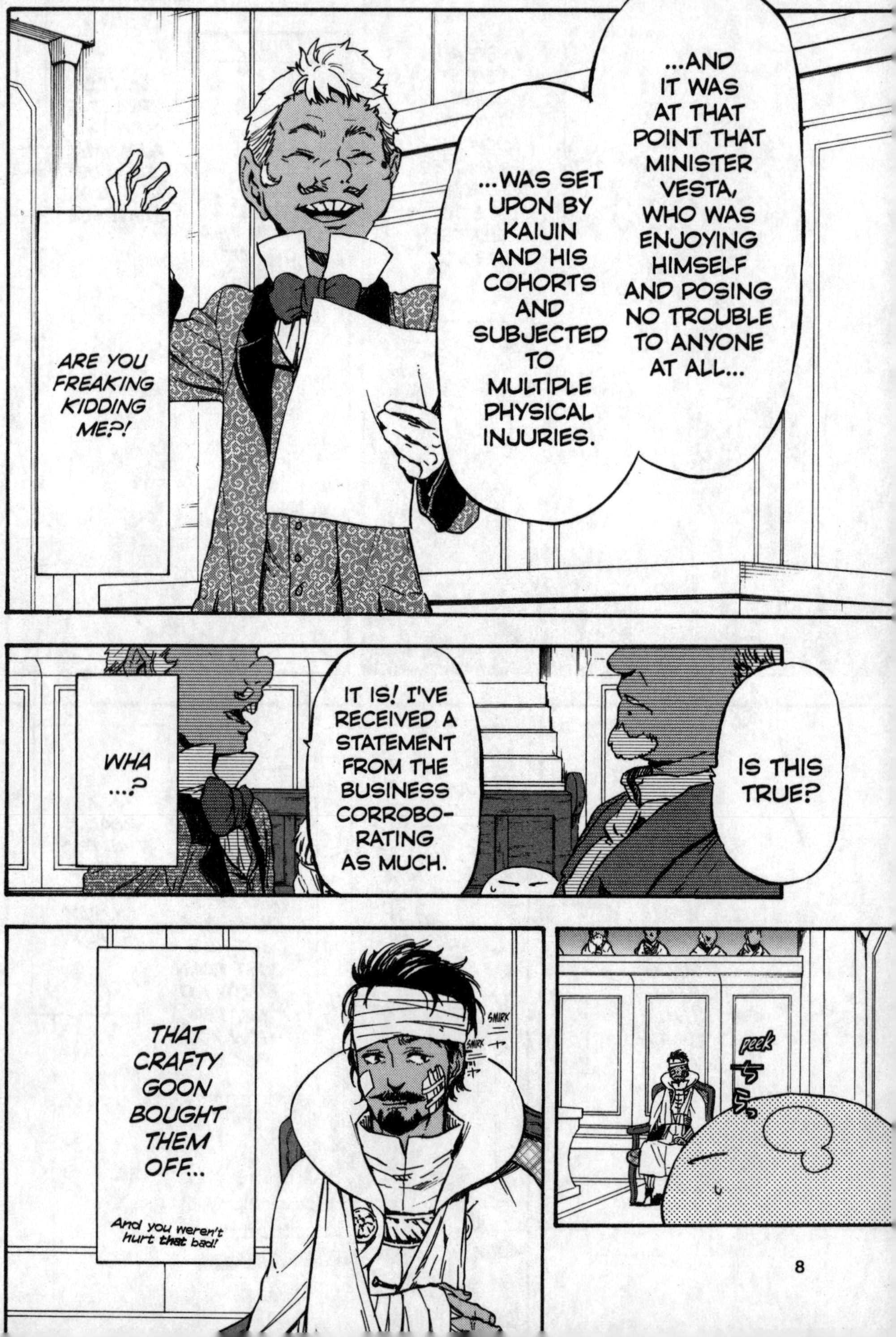
...AND IT WAS AT THAT POINT THAT MINISTER VESTA, WHO WAS ENJOYING HIMSELF AND POSING NO TROUBLE TO ANYONE AT ALL...
...WAS SET UPON BY KAIJIN AND HIS COHORTS AND SUBJECTED TO MULTIPLE PHYSICAL INJURIES.
ARE YOU FREAKING KIDDING ME?!
IS THIS TRUE?
IT IS! I'VE RECEIVED A STATEMENT FROM THE BUSINESS CORROBO-RATING AS MUCH.
WHA ...?
peek
ちら
SMIRK
SMIRK
THAT CRAFTY GOON BOUGHT THEM OFF...
And you weren't hurt that bad!

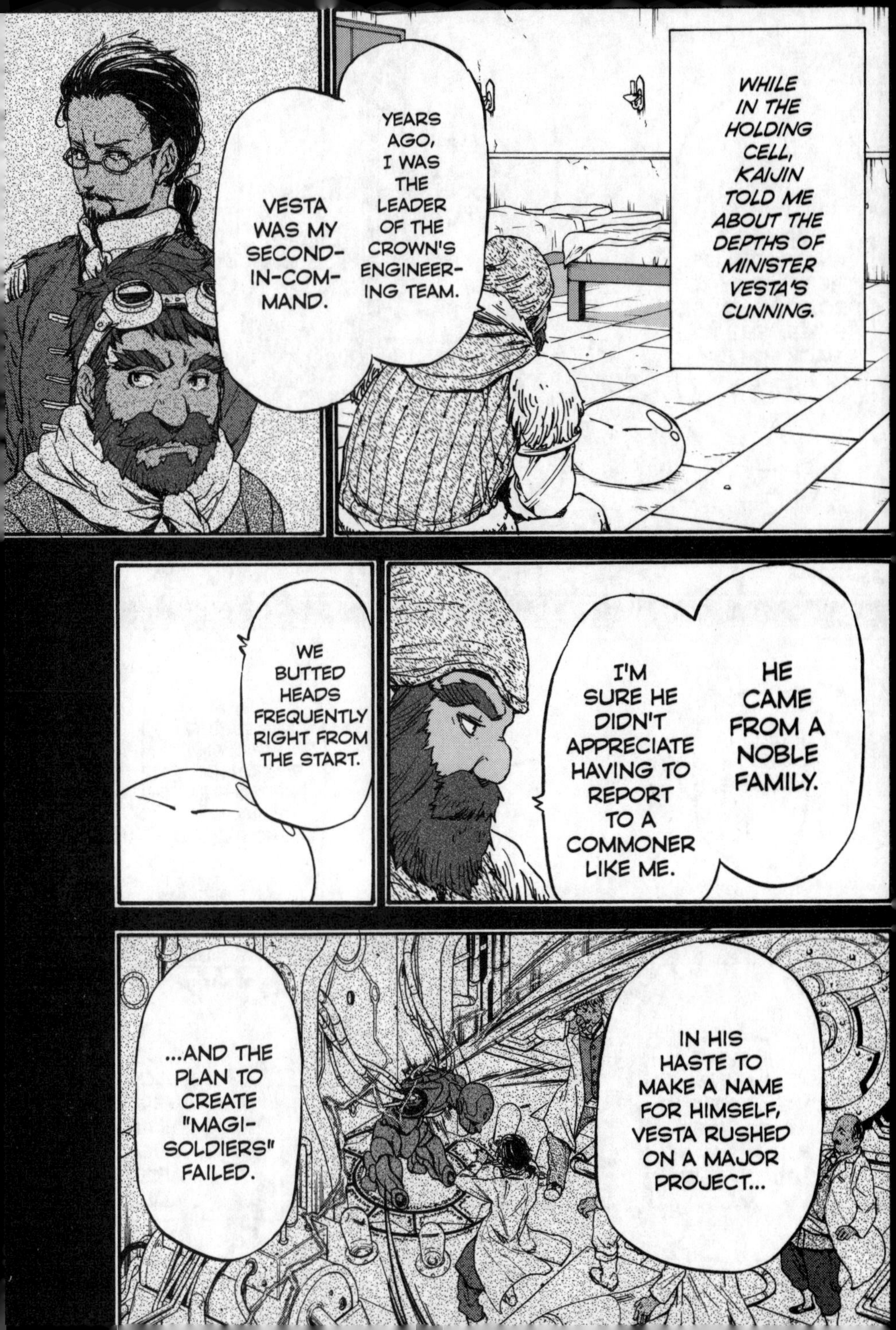
WHILE IN THE HOLDING CELL, KAIJIN TOLD ME ABOUT THE DEPTHS OF MINISTER VESTA'S CUNNING.
YEARS AGO, I WAS THE LEADER OF THE CROWN'S ENGINEER-ING TEAM.
VESTA WAS MY SECOND-IN-COM-MAND.
HE CAME FROM A NOBLE FAMILY.
I'M SURE HE DIDN'T APPRECIATE HAVING TO REPORT TO A COMMONER LIKE ME.
WE BUTTED HEADS FREQUENTLY RIGHT FROM THE START.
IN HIS HASTE TO MAKE A NAME FOR HIMSELF, VESTA RUSHED ON A MAJOR PROJECT...
...AND THE PLAN TO CREATE "MAGI-SOLDIERS" FAILED.

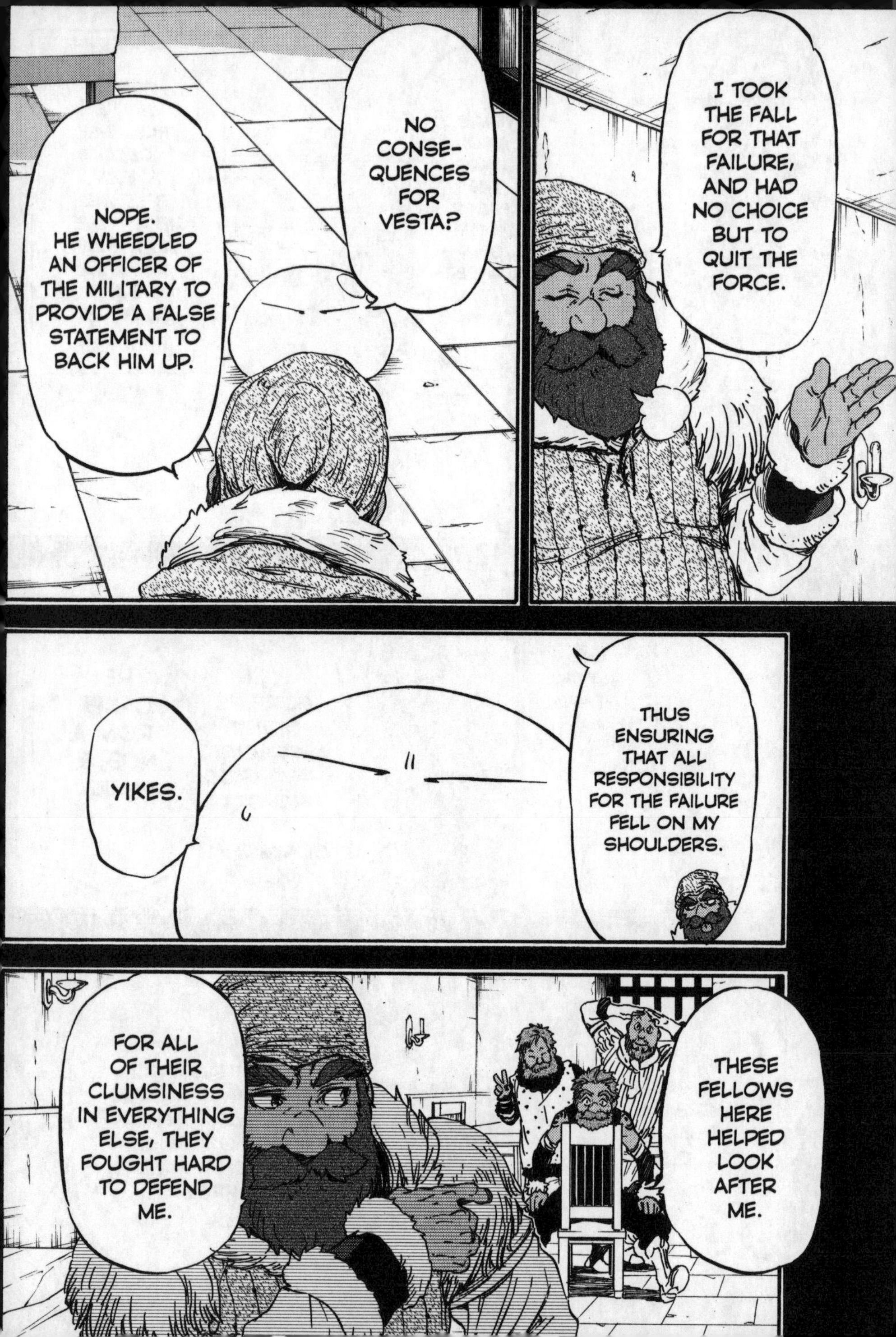
I TOOK THE FALL FOR THAT FAILURE, AND HAD NO CHOICE BUT TO QUIT THE FORCE.
NO CONSEQUENCES FOR VESTA?
NOPE. HE WHEEDLED AN OFFICER OF THE MILITARY TO PROVIDE A FALSE STATEMENT TO BACK HIM UP.
THUS ENSURING THAT ALL RESPONSIBILITY FOR THE FAILURE FELL ON MY SHOULDERS.
YIKES.
THESE FELLOWS HERE HELPED LOOK AFTER ME.
FOR ALL OF THEIR CLUMSINESS IN EVERYTHING ELSE, THEY FOUGHT HARD TO DEFEND ME.

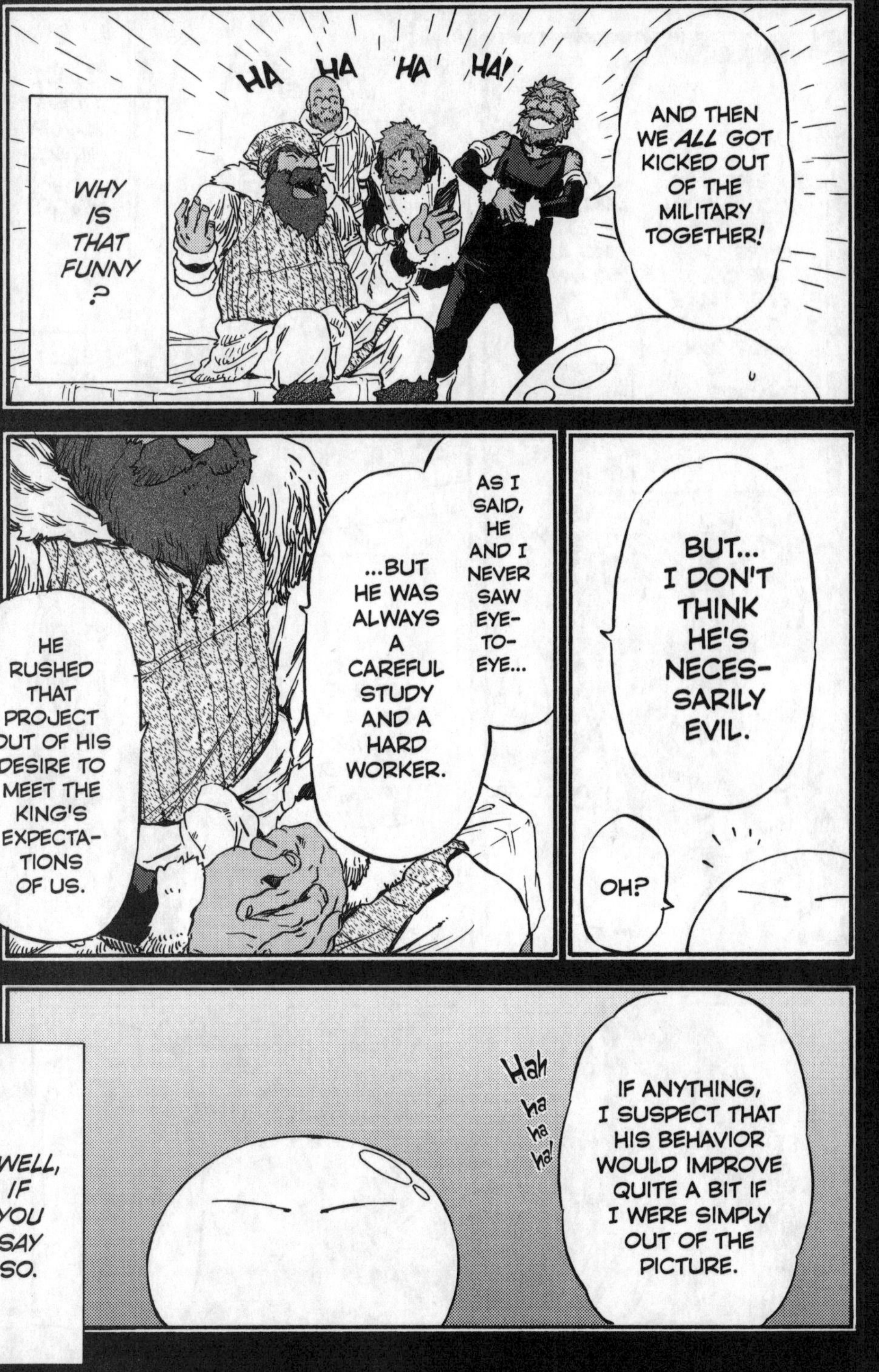
AND THEN WE ALL GOT KICKED OUT OF THE MILITARY TOGETHER!
HA HA HA HA!
WHY IS THAT FUNNY?
BUT... I DON'T THINK HE'S NECES-SARILY EVIL.
OH?
AS I SAID, HE AND I NEVER SAW EYE-TO-EYE...
...BUT HE WAS ALWAYS A CAREFUL STUDY AND A HARD WORKER.
HE RUSHED THAT PROJECT OUT OF HIS DESIRE TO MEET THE KING'S EXPECTA-TIONS OF US.
IF ANYTHING, I SUSPECT THAT HIS BEHAVIOR WOULD IMPROVE QUITE A BIT IF I WERE SIMPLY OUT OF THE PICTURE.
Hah ha ha ha!
...WELL, IF YOU SAY SO.

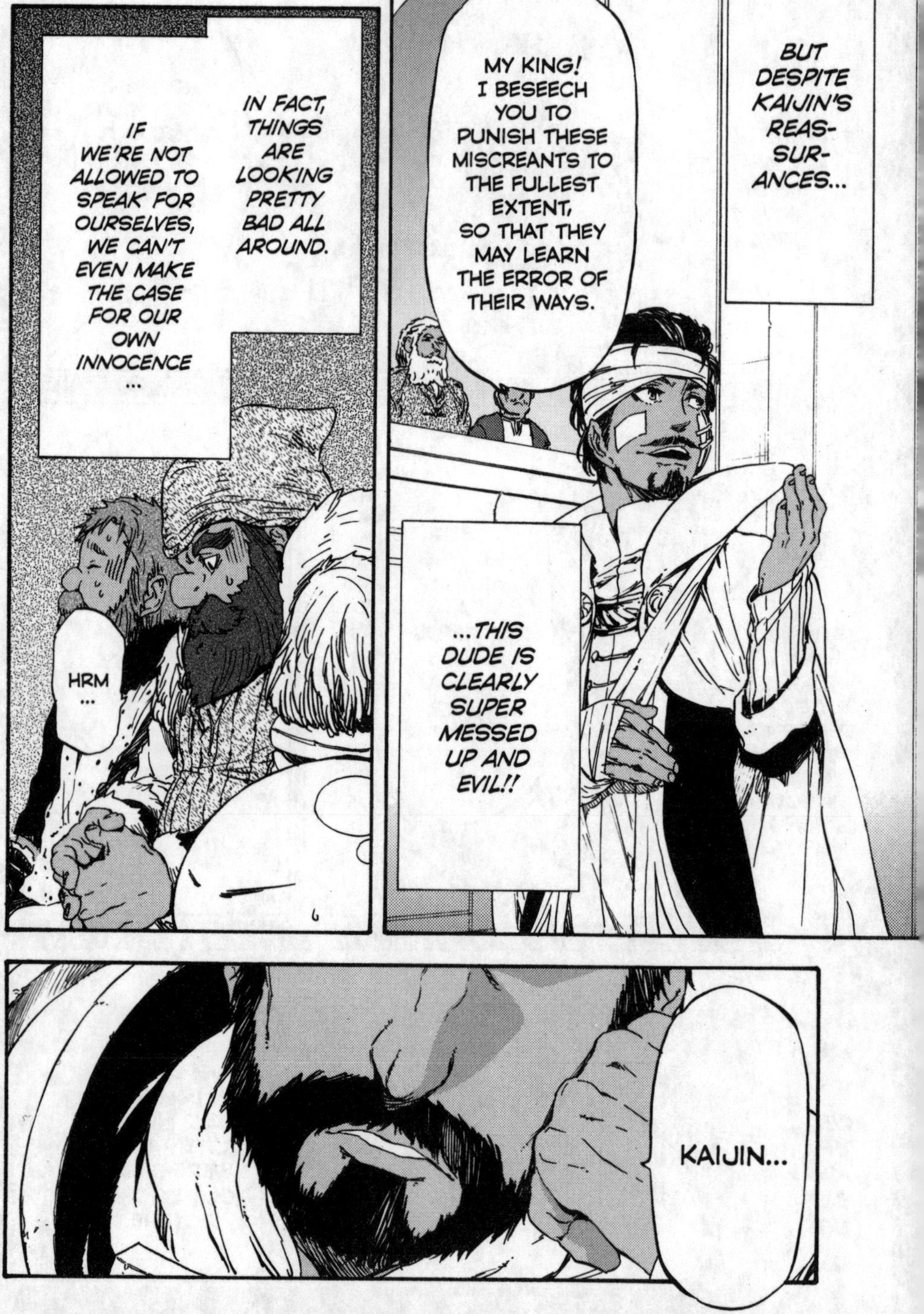
BUT DESPITE KAIJIN'S REAS-SUR-ANCES...
MY KING! I BESEECH YOU TO PUNISH THESE MISCREANTS TO THE FULLEST EXTENT, SO THAT THEY MAY LEARN THE ERROR OF THEIR WAYS.
...THIS DUDE IS CLEARLY SUPER MESSED UP AND EVIL!!
IN FACT, THINGS ARE LOOKING PRETTY BAD ALL AROUND.
IF WE'RE NOT ALLOWED TO SPEAK FOR OURSELVES, WE CAN'T EVEN MAKE THE CASE FOR OUR OWN INNOCENCE ...
HRM ...
KAIJIN...

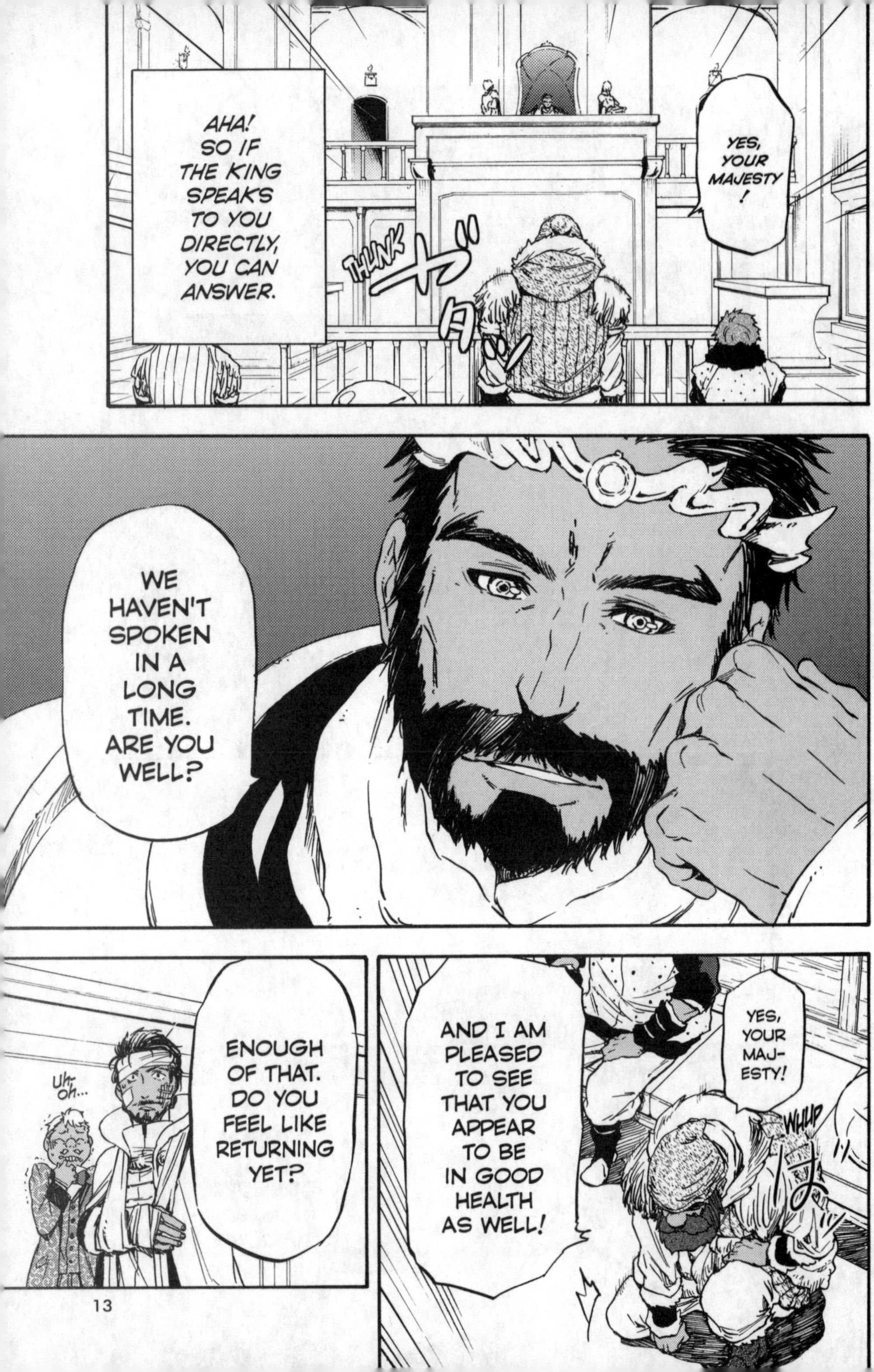
YES, YOUR MAJESTY!
THUNK
AHA! SO IF THE KING SPEAKS TO YOU DIRECTLY, YOU CAN ANSWER.
WE HAVEN'T SPOKEN IN A LONG TIME. ARE YOU WELL?
YES, YOUR MAJ-ESTY!
WHUP
AND I AM PLEASED TO SEE THAT YOU APPEAR TO BE IN GOOD HEALTH AS WELL!
ENOUGH OF THAT. DO YOU FEEL LIKE RETURNING YET?
uh-oh...

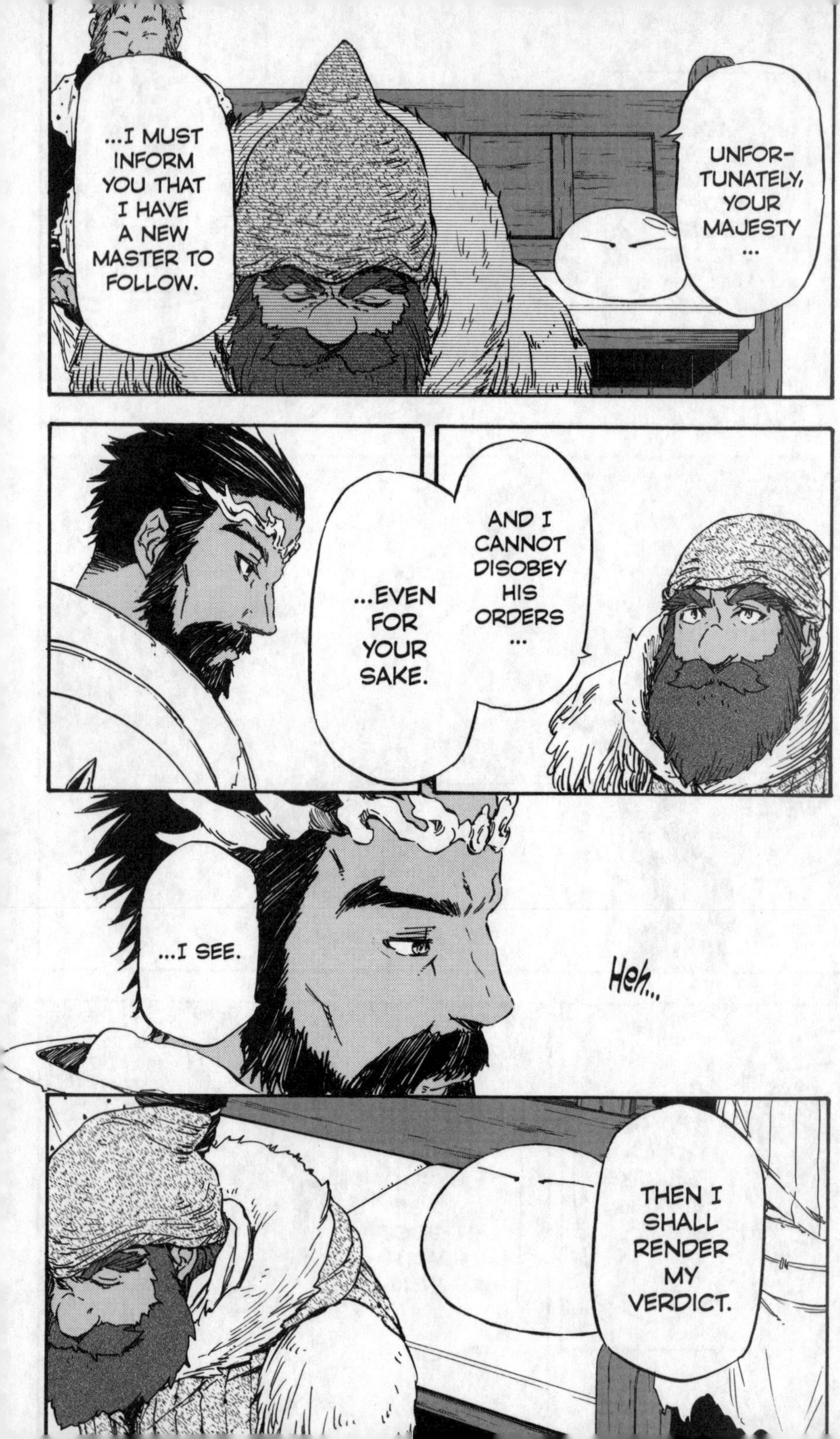
UNFOR-TUNATELY, YOUR MAJESTY ...
...I MUST INFORM YOU THAT I HAVE A NEW MASTER TO FOLLOW.
AND I CANNOT DISOBEY HIS ORDERS ...
...EVEN FOR YOUR SAKE.
Heh...
...I SEE.
THEN I SHALL RENDER MY VERDICT.

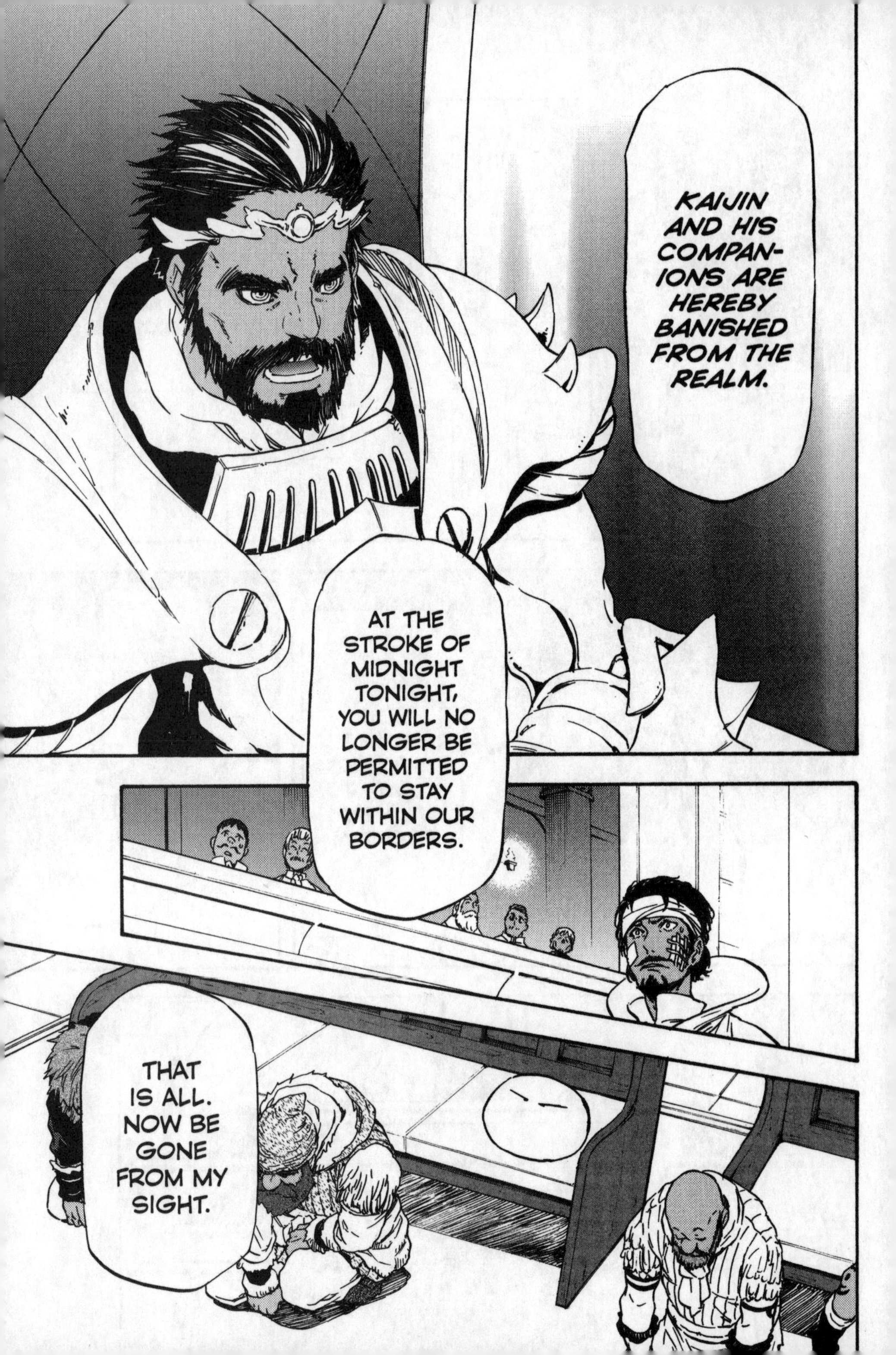
KAIJIN AND HIS COMPANIONS ARE HEREBY BANISHED FROM THE REALM.
AT THE STROKE OF MIDNIGHT TONIGHT, YOU WILL NO LONGER BE PERMITTED TO STAY WITHIN OUR BORDERS.
THAT IS ALL. NOW BE GONE FROM MY SIGHT.

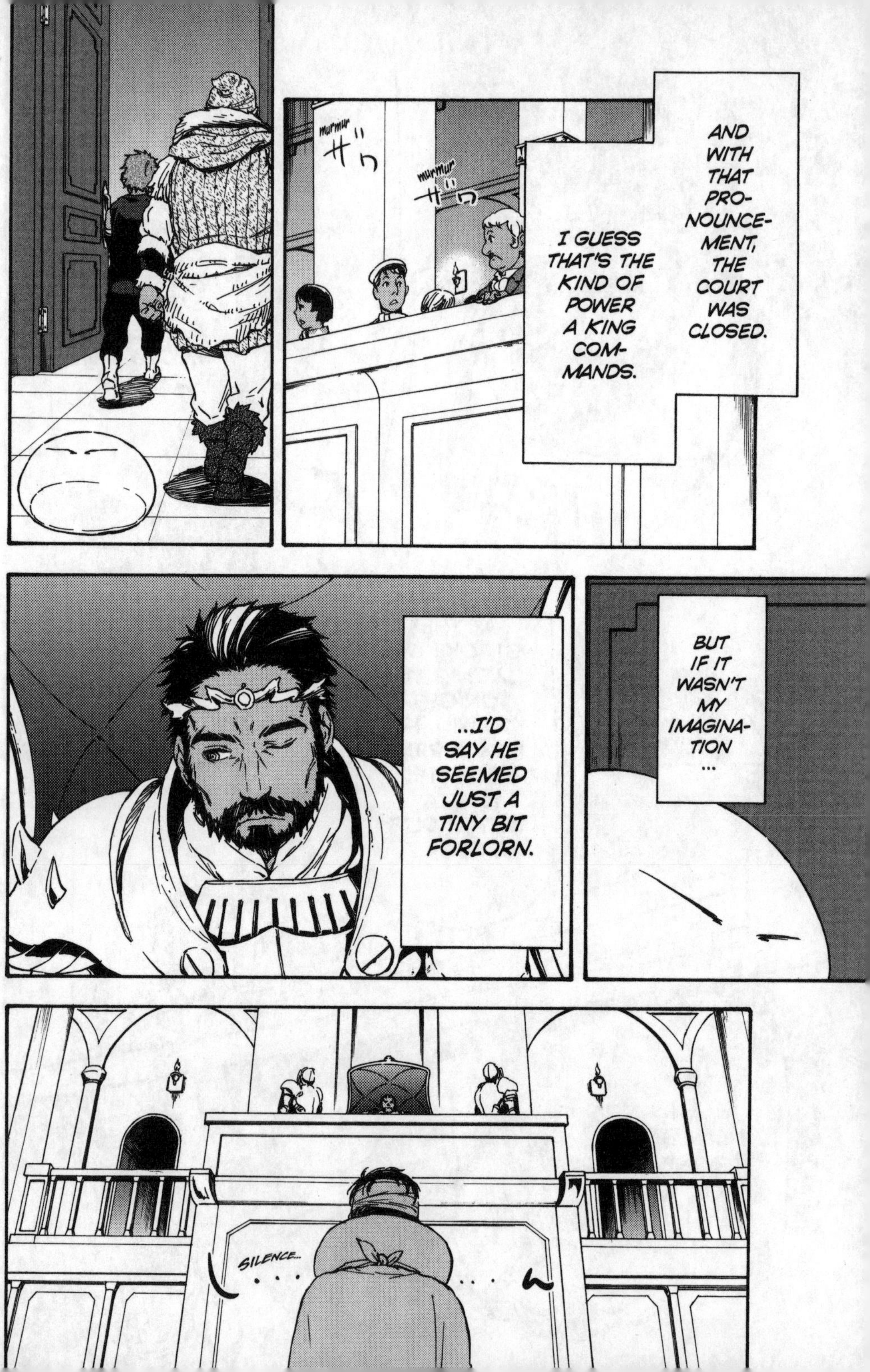
murmur
ザワ
murmur
ザワ
AND WITH THAT PRONOUNCEMENT, THE COURT WAS CLOSED.
I GUESS THAT'S THE KIND OF POWER A KING COMMANDS.
BUT IF IT WASN'T MY IMAGINATION...
...I'D SAY HE SEEMED JUST A TINY BIT FORLORN.
SILENCE...

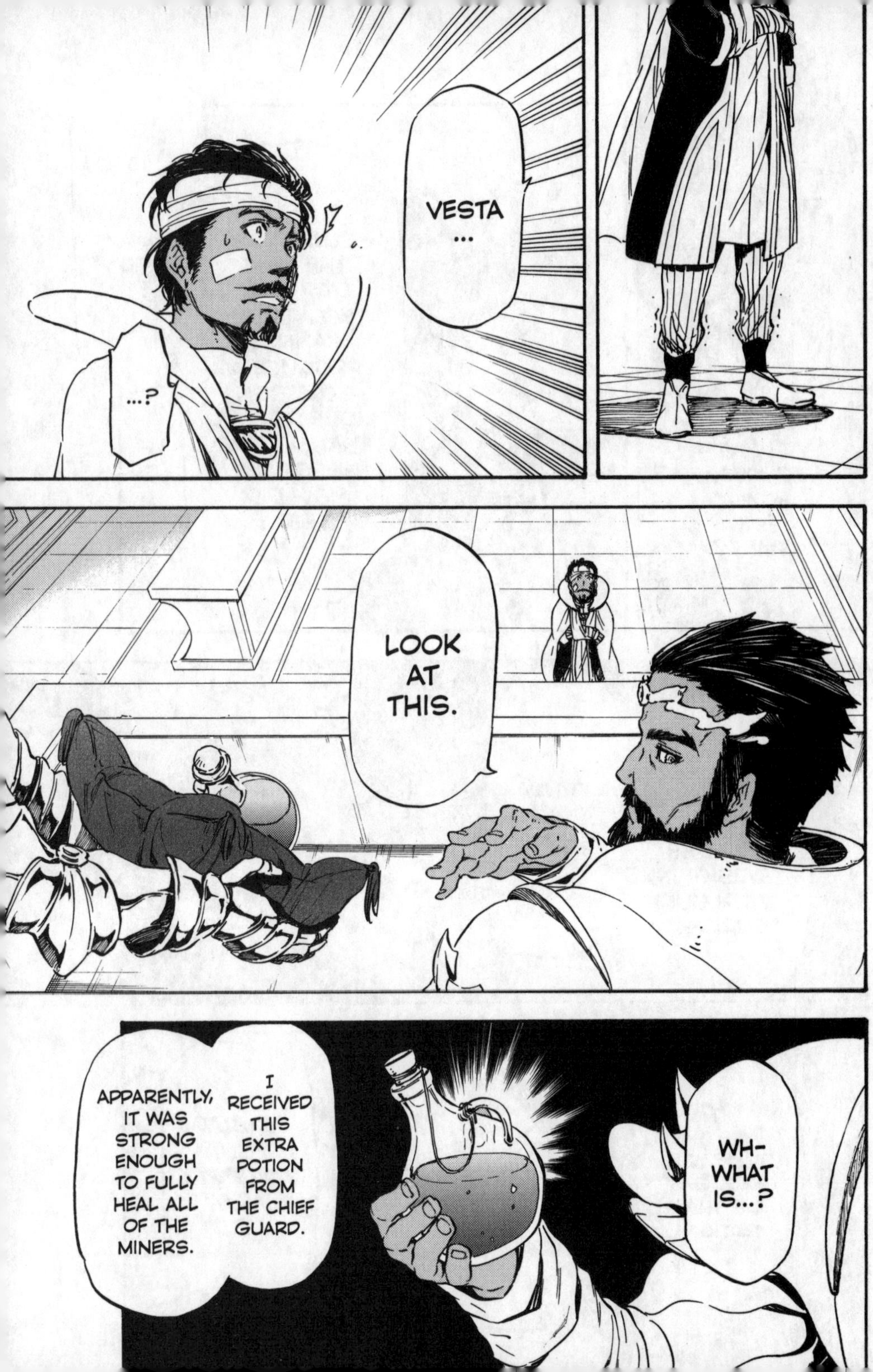
VESTA ...
...?
LOOK AT THIS.
WH- WHAT IS...?
I RECEIVED THIS EXTRA POTION FROM THE CHIEF GUARD.
APPARENTLY, IT WAS STRONG ENOUGH TO FULLY HEAL ALL OF THE MINERS.

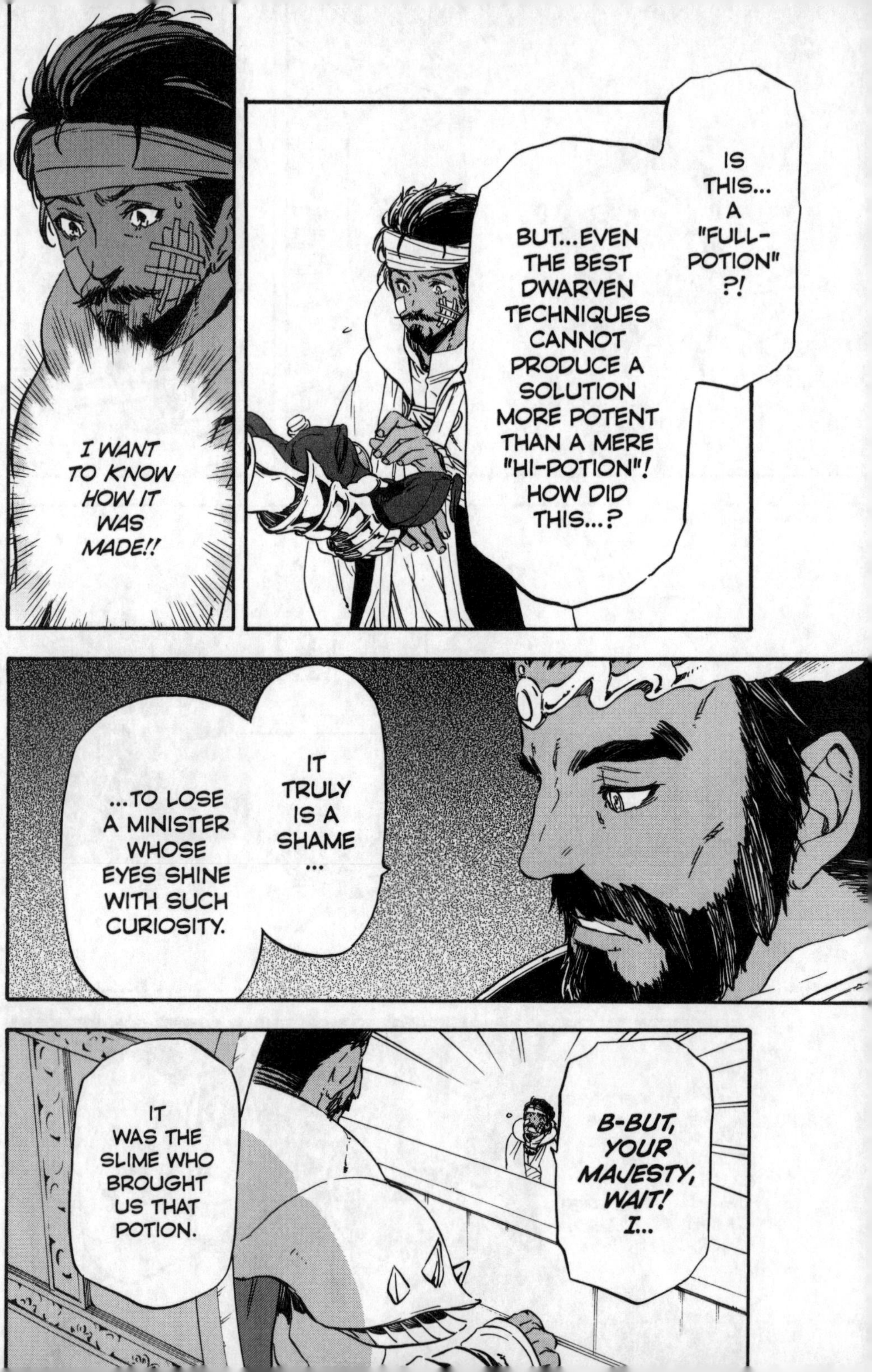
IS THIS... A "FULL-POTION"?!
BUT...EVEN THE BEST DWARVEN TECHNIQUES CANNOT PRODUCE A SOLUTION MORE POTENT THAN A MERE "HI-POTION"! HOW DID THIS...?
I WANT TO KNOW HOW IT WAS MADE!!
IT TRULY IS A SHAME...
...TO LOSE A MINISTER WHOSE EYES SHINE WITH SUCH CURIOSITY.
B-BUT, YOUR MAJESTY, WAIT! I...
IT WAS THE SLIME WHO BROUGHT US THAT POTION.

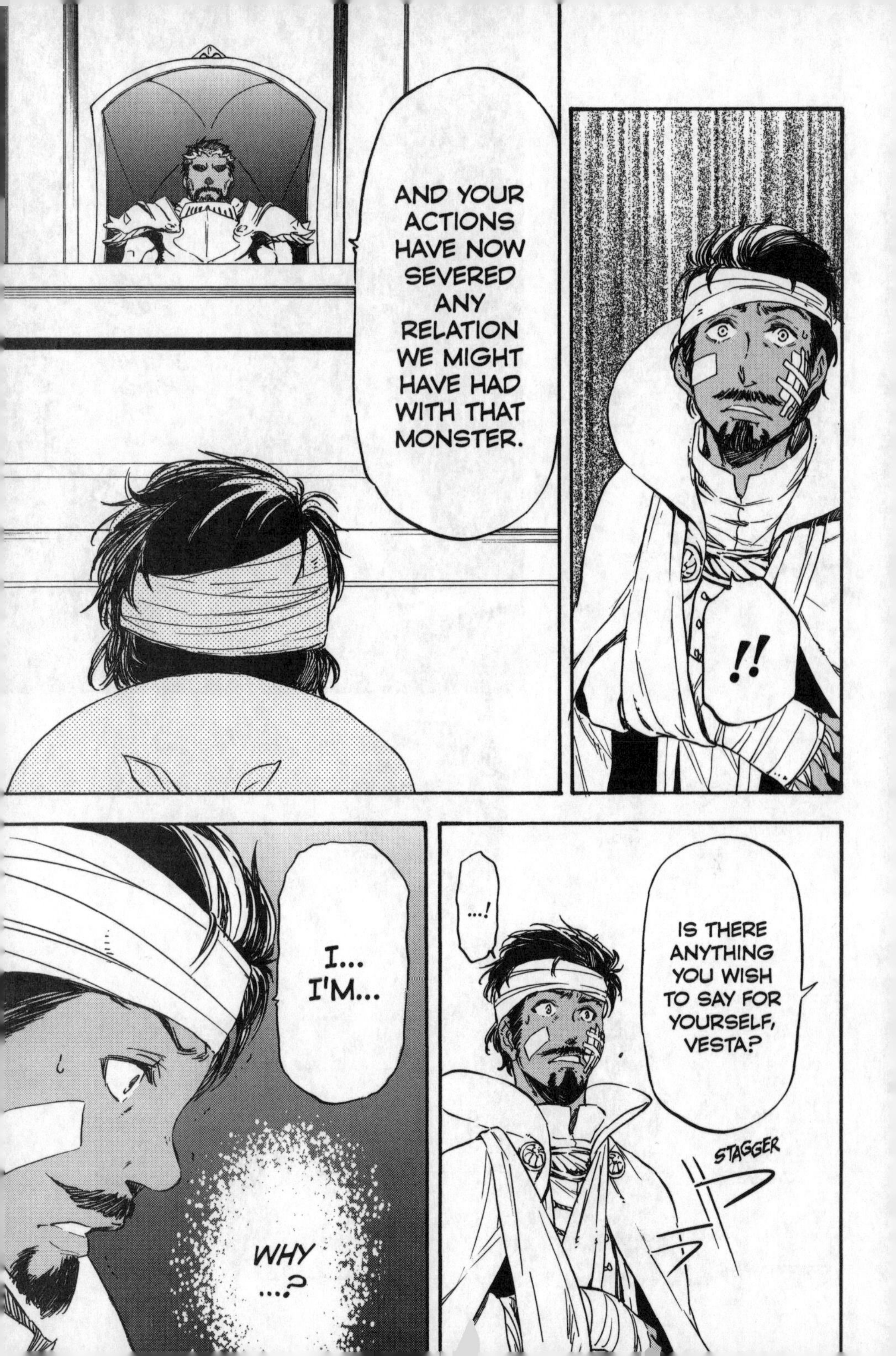

AND YOUR ACTIONS HAVE NOW SEVERED ANY RELATION WE MIGHT HAVE HAD WITH THAT MONSTER.
!!
IS THERE ANYTHING YOU WISH TO SAY FOR YOURSELF, VESTA?
...!
STAGGER
I... I'M...
WHY ...?

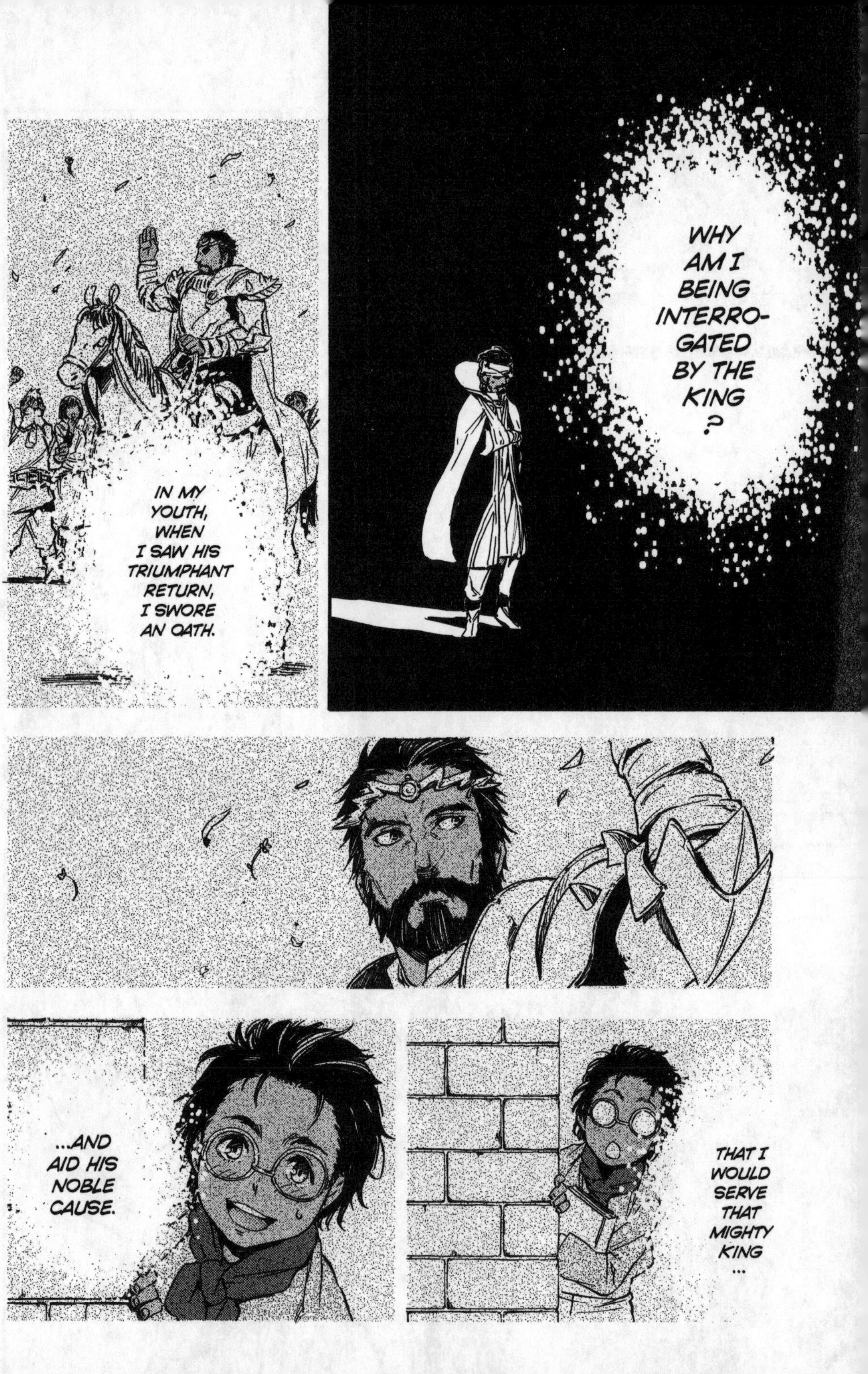
WHY AM I BEING INTERRO-GATED BY THE KING ?
IN MY YOUTH, WHEN I SAW HIS TRIUMPHANT RETURN, I SWORE AN OATH.
THAT I WOULD SERVE THAT MIGHTY KING ...
...AND AID HIS NOBLE CAUSE.

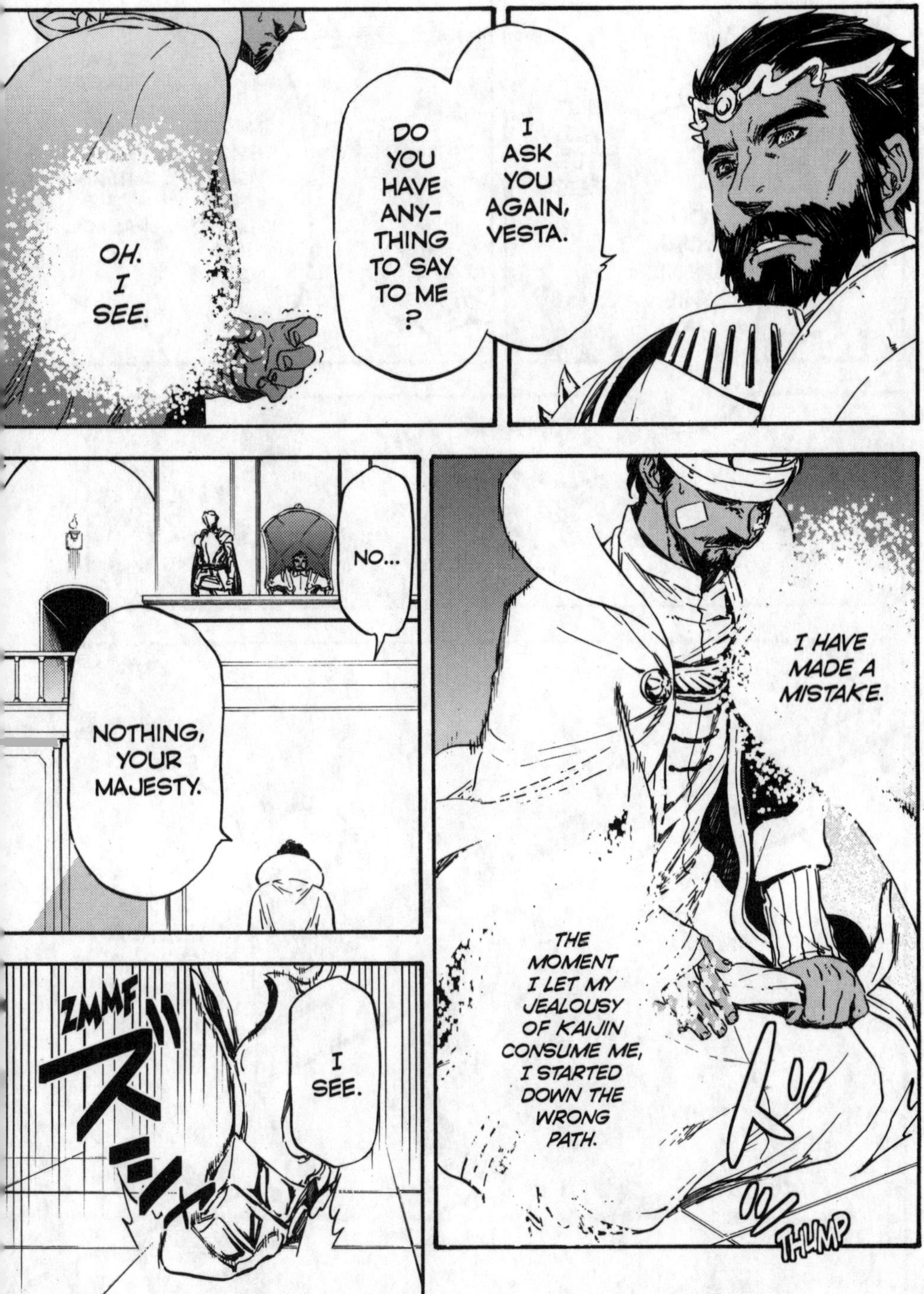
I ASK YOU AGAIN, VESTA.
DO YOU HAVE ANYTHING TO SAY TO ME?
OH. I SEE.
I HAVE MADE A MISTAKE.
THE MOMENT I LET MY JEALOUSY OF KAIJIN CONSUME ME, I STARTED DOWN THE WRONG PATH.
THUMP
NO...
NOTHING, YOUR MAJESTY.
I SEE.
ZMMF

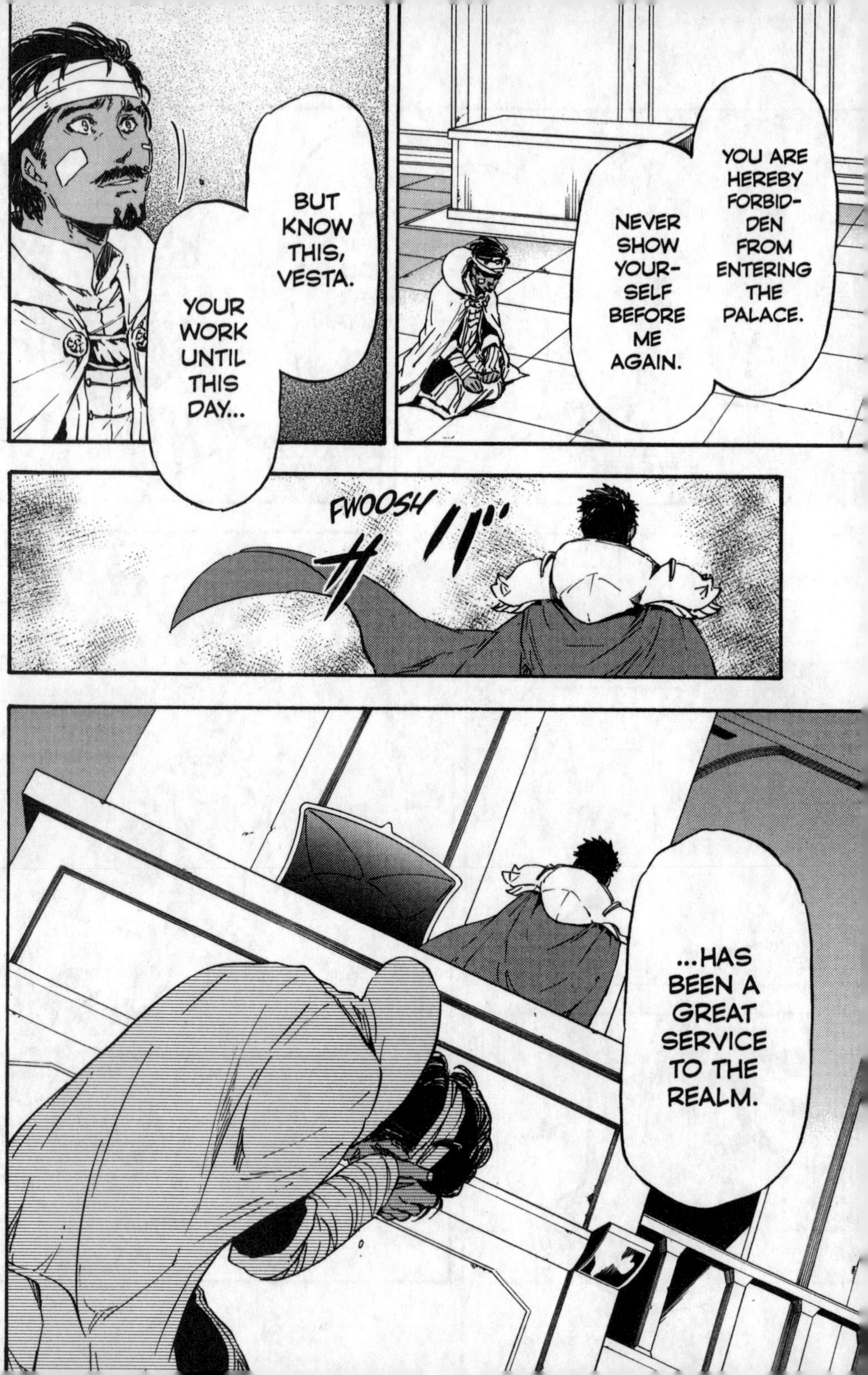
YOU ARE HEREBY FORBIDDEN FROM ENTERING THE PALACE.
NEVER SHOW YOURSELF BEFORE ME AGAIN.
BUT KNOW THIS, VESTA.
YOUR WORK UNTIL THIS DAY...
FWOOSH
...HAS BEEN A GREAT SERVICE TO THE REALM.

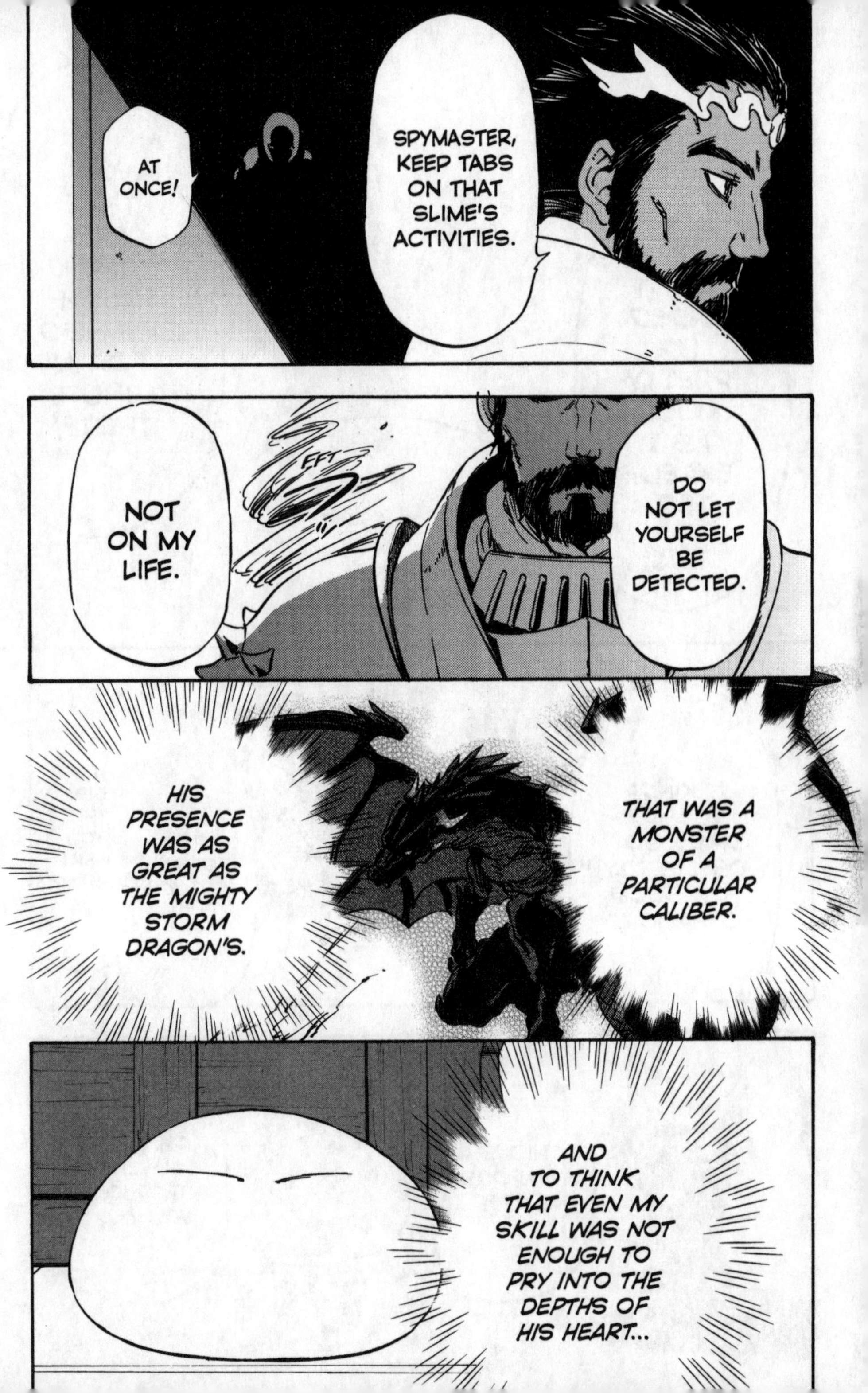
SPYMASTER, KEEP TABS ON THAT SLIME'S ACTIVITIES.
AT ONCE!
DO NOT LET YOURSELF BE DETECTED.
FFT
NOT ON MY LIFE.
THAT WAS A MONSTER OF A PARTICULAR CALIBER.
HIS PRESENCE WAS AS GREAT AS THE MIGHTY STORM DRAGON'S.
AND TO THINK THAT EVEN MY SKILL WAS NOT ENOUGH TO PRY INTO THE DEPTHS OF HIS HEART...

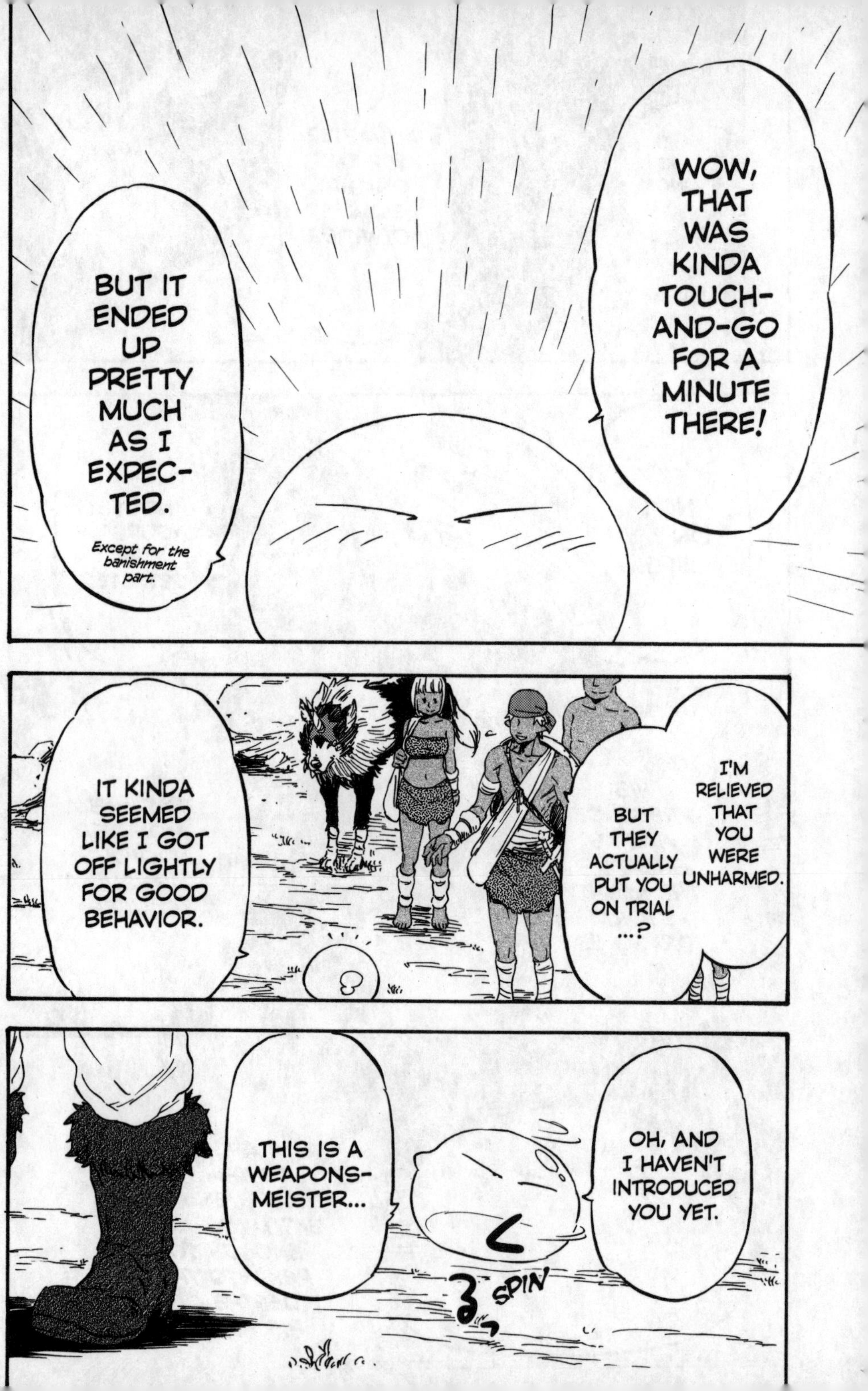
WOW, THAT WAS KINDA TOUCH-AND-GO FOR A MINUTE THERE!
BUT IT ENDED UP PRETTY MUCH AS I EXPECTED.
Except for the banishment part.
I'M RELIEVED THAT YOU WERE UNHARMED.
BUT THEY ACTUALLY PUT YOU ON TRIAL ...?
IT KINDA SEEMED LIKE I GOT OFF LIGHTLY FOR GOOD BEHAVIOR.
OH, AND I HAVEN'T INTRODUCED YOU YET.
SPIN
THIS IS A WEAPONS-MEISTER...

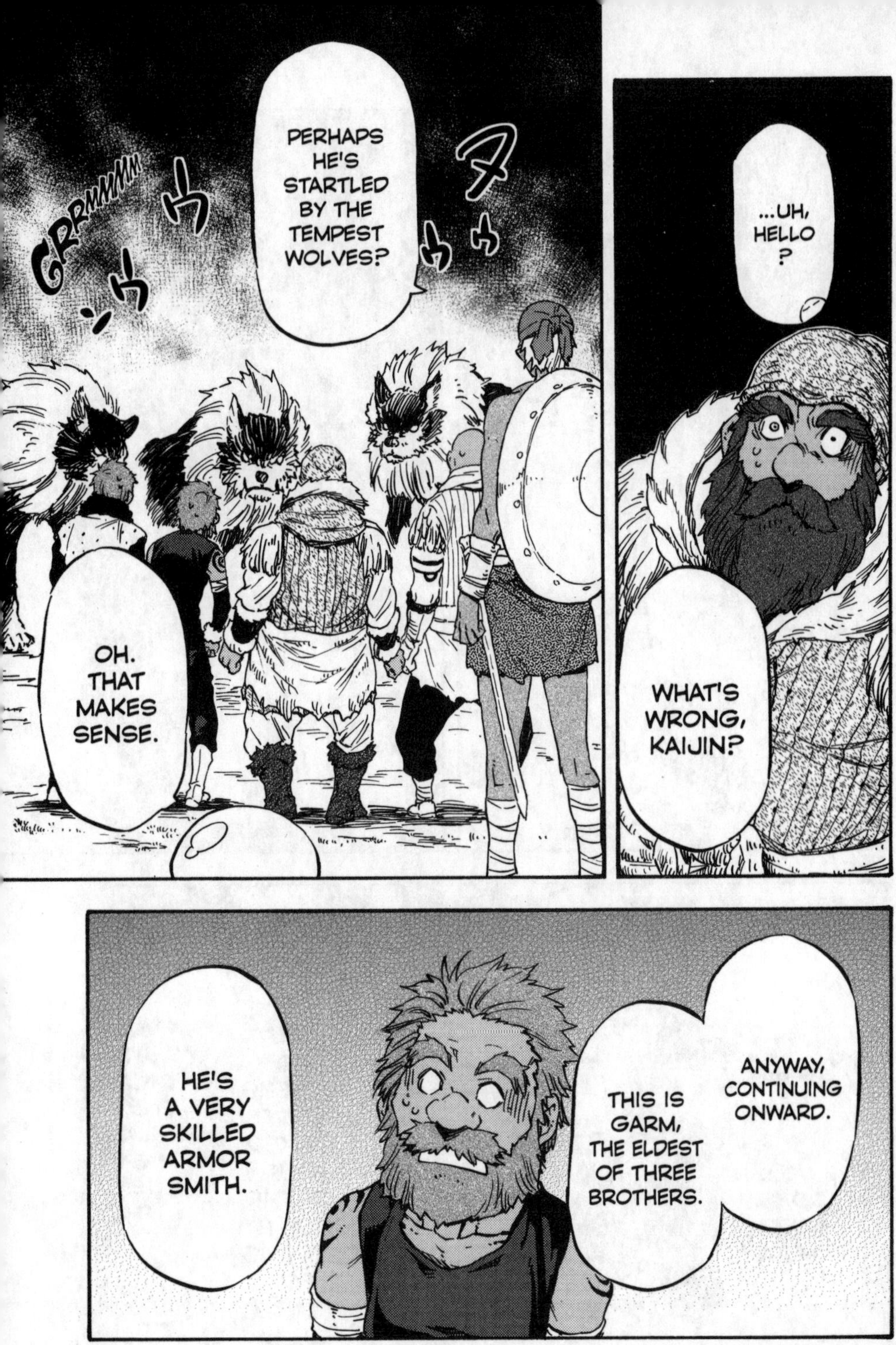
...UH, HELLO?
WHAT'S WRONG, KAIJIN?
PERHAPS HE'S STARTLED BY THE TEMPEST WOLVES?
GRRMMMM
OH. THAT MAKES SENSE.
ANYWAY, CONTINUING ONWARD.
THIS IS GARM, THE ELDEST OF THREE BROTHERS.
HE'S A VERY SKILLED ARMOR SMITH.

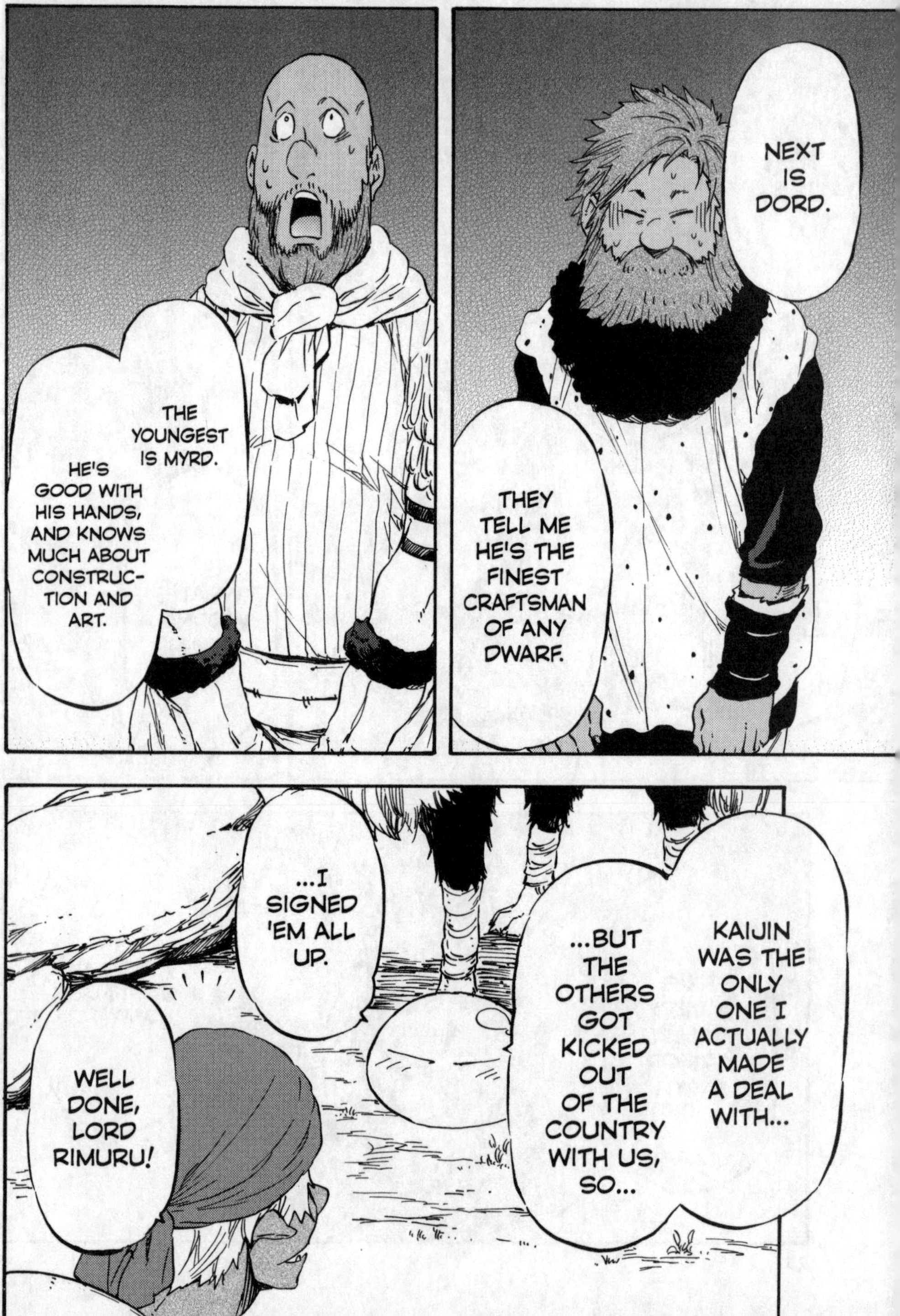
NEXT IS DORD.
THEY TELL ME HE'S THE FINEST CRAFTSMAN OF ANY DWARF.
THE YOUNGEST IS MYRD.
HE'S GOOD WITH HIS HANDS, AND KNOWS MUCH ABOUT CONSTRUC-TION AND ART.
KAIJIN WAS THE ONLY ONE I ACTUALLY MADE A DEAL WITH...
...BUT THE OTHERS GOT KICKED OUT OF THE COUNTRY WITH US, SO...
...I SIGNED 'EM ALL UP.
WELL DONE, LORD RIMURU!

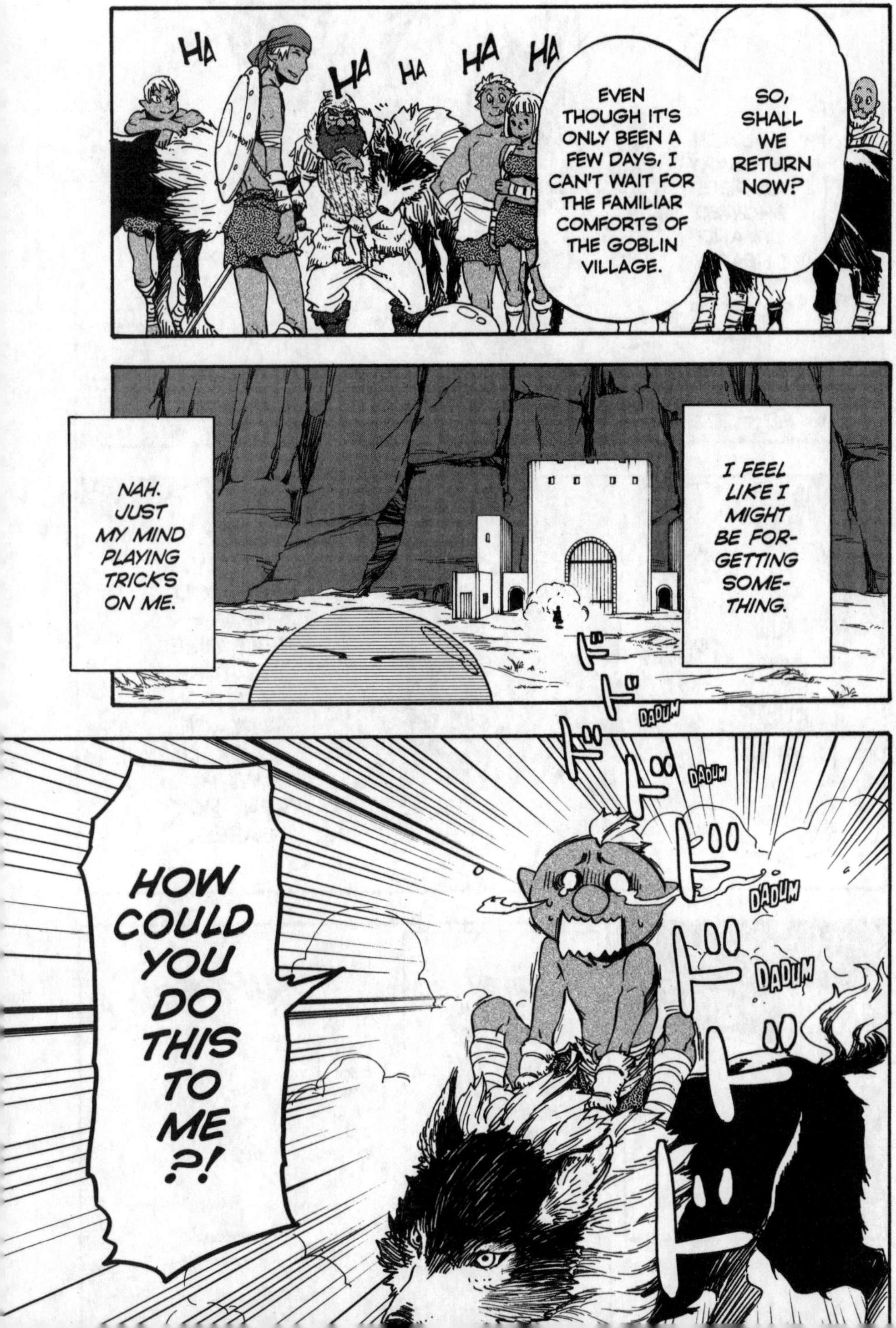
SO, SHALL WE RETURN NOW?
EVEN THOUGH IT'S ONLY BEEN A FEW DAYS, I CAN'T WAIT FOR THE FAMILIAR COMFORTS OF THE GOBLIN VILLAGE.
HA HA HA HA HA
I FEEL LIKE I MIGHT BE FOR-GETTING SOME-THING.
NAH. JUST MY MIND PLAYING TRICKS ON ME.
DADUM
DADUM
DADUM
DADUM
HOW COULD YOU DO THIS TO ME?!

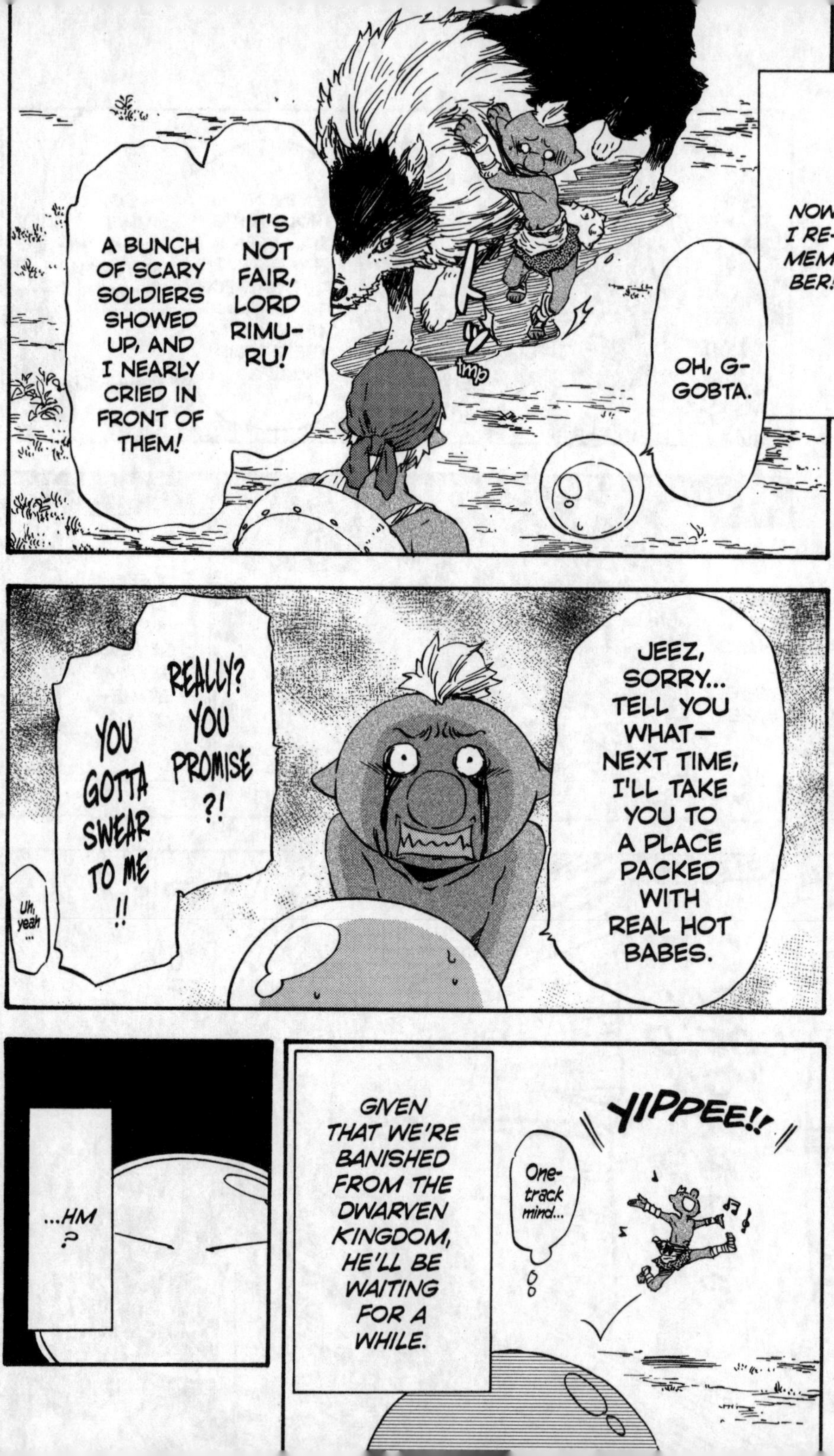
NOW I REMEMBER!
OH, G-GOBTA.
IT'S NOT FAIR, LORD RIMURU!
A BUNCH OF SCARY SOLDIERS SHOWED UP, AND I NEARLY CRIED IN FRONT OF THEM!
tmp
JEEZ, SORRY... TELL YOU WHAT— NEXT TIME, I'LL TAKE YOU TO A PLACE PACKED WITH REAL HOT BABES.
REALLY? YOU PROMISE?!
YOU GOTTA SWEAR TO ME!!
Uh, yeah...
YIPPEE!!
One-track mind...
GIVEN THAT WE'RE BANISHED FROM THE DWARVEN KINGDOM, HE'LL BE WAITING FOR A WHILE.
...HM?

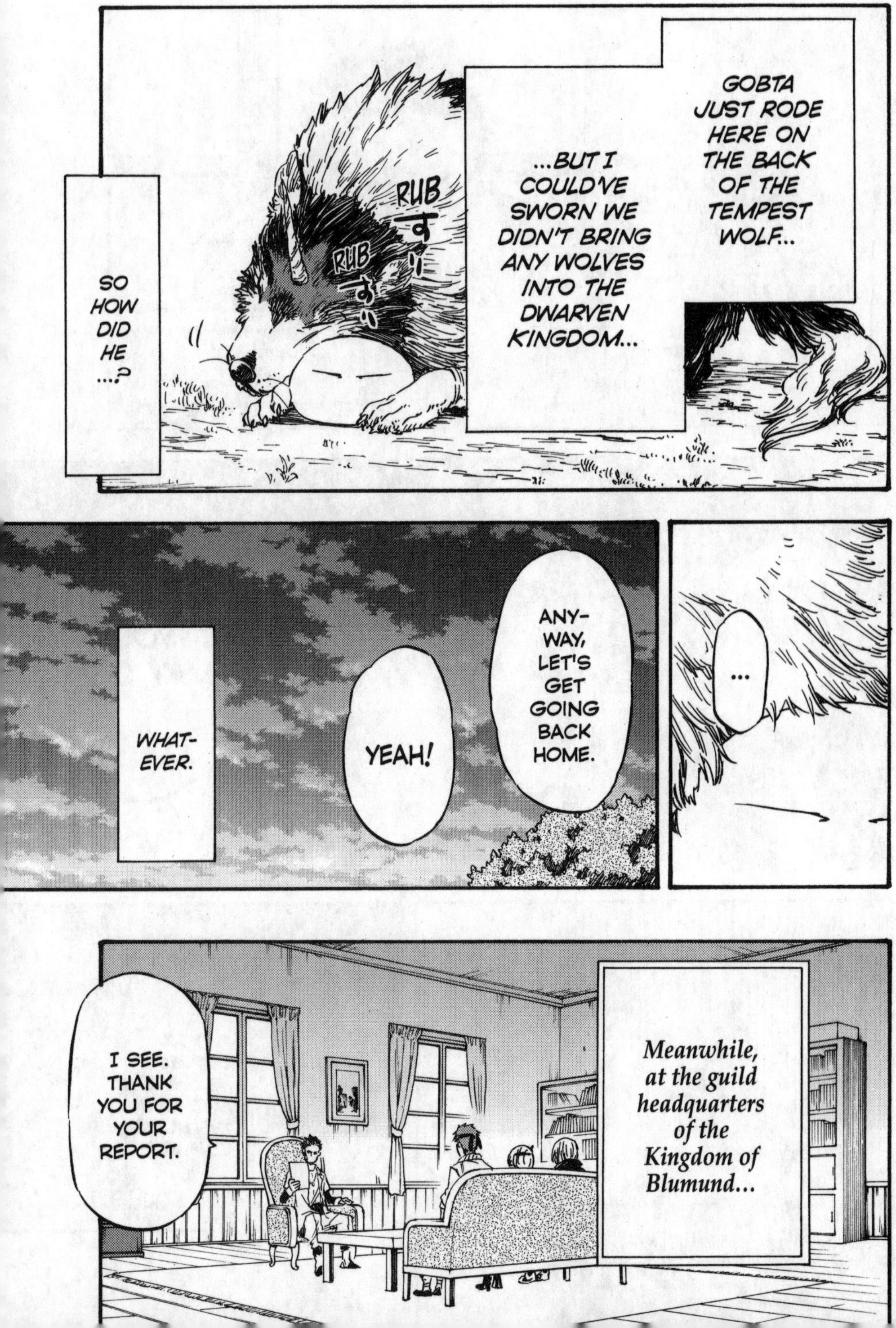
GOBTA JUST RODE HERE ON THE BACK OF THE TEMPEST WOLF...
...BUT I COULD'VE SWORN WE DIDN'T BRING ANY WOLVES INTO THE DWARVEN KINGDOM...
RUB すり
RUB すり
SO HOW DID HE ...?
...
ANY-WAY, LET'S GET GOING BACK HOME.
YEAH!
WHAT-EVER.
Meanwhile, at the guild headquarters of the Kingdom of Blumund...
I SEE. THANK YOU FOR YOUR REPORT.

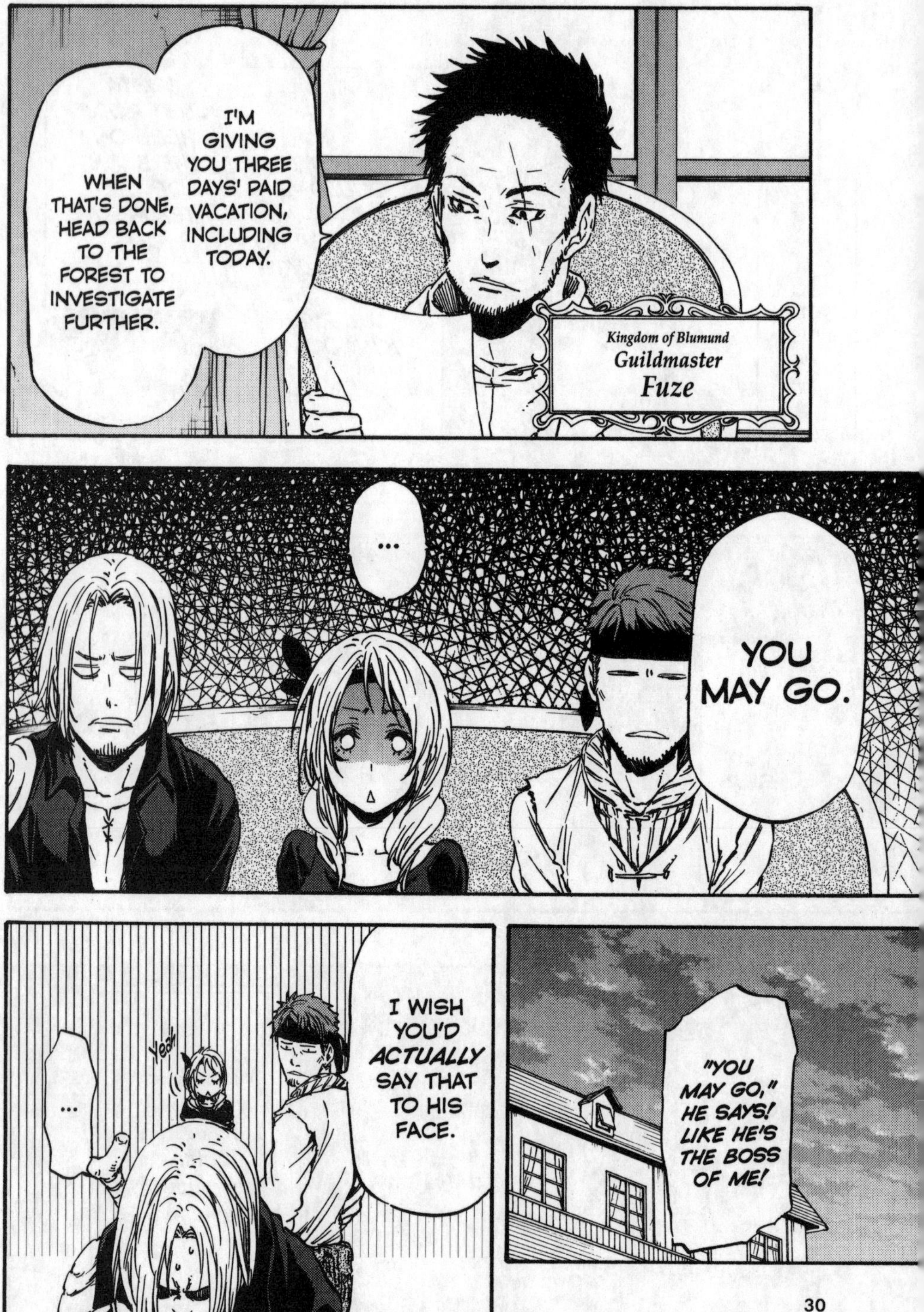
Kingdom of Blumund
Guildmaster
Fuze
I'M GIVING YOU THREE DAYS' PAID VACATION, INCLUDING TODAY.
WHEN THAT'S DONE, HEAD BACK TO THE FOREST TO INVESTIGATE FURTHER.
YOU MAY GO.
...
"YOU MAY GO," HE SAYS! LIKE HE'S THE BOSS OF ME!
I WISH YOU'D *ACTUALLY* SAY THAT TO HIS FACE.
Yeah
...

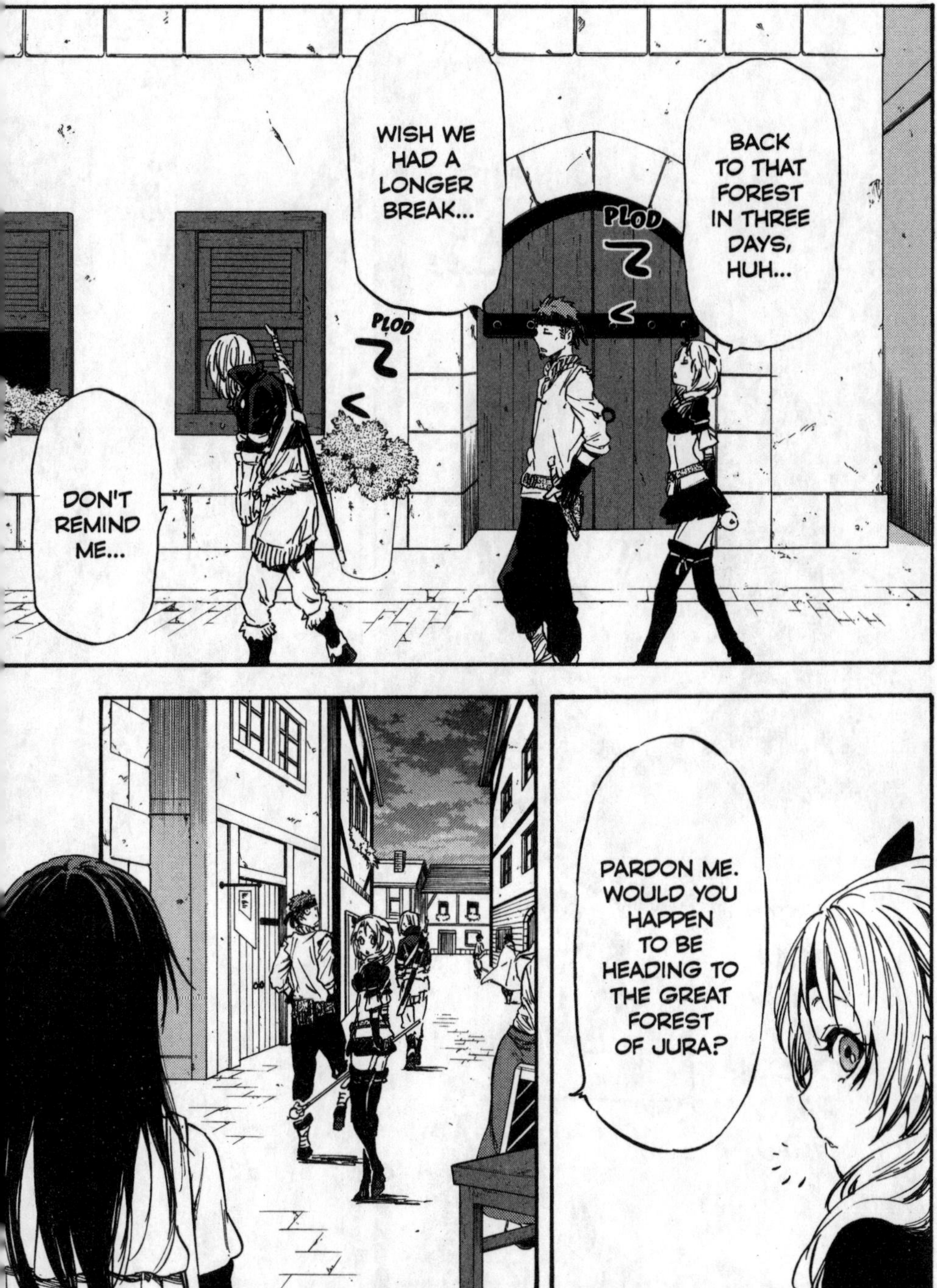
BACK TO THAT FOREST IN THREE DAYS, HUH...
PLOD
WISH WE HAD A LONGER BREAK...
PLOD
DON'T REMIND ME...
PARDON ME. WOULD YOU HAPPEN TO BE HEADING TO THE GREAT FOREST OF JURA?

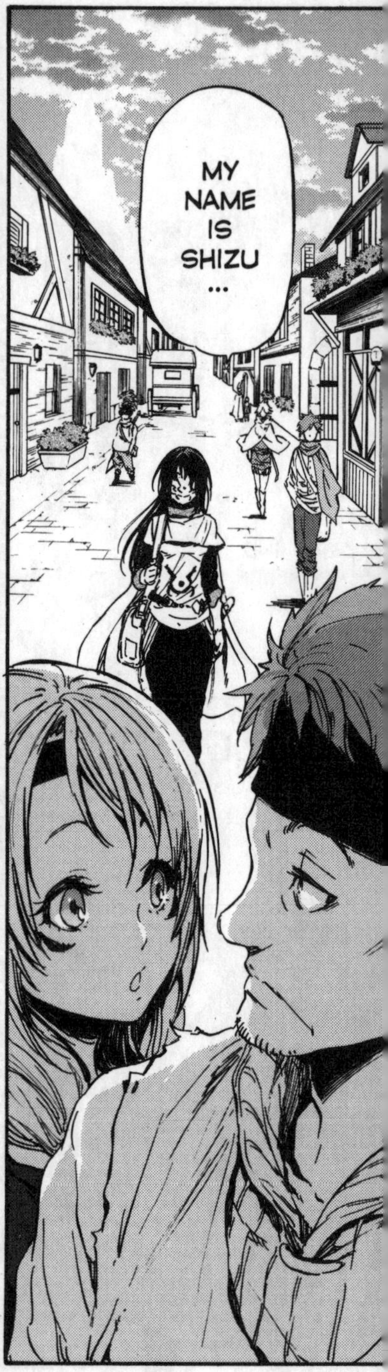
MY NAME IS SHIZU ...
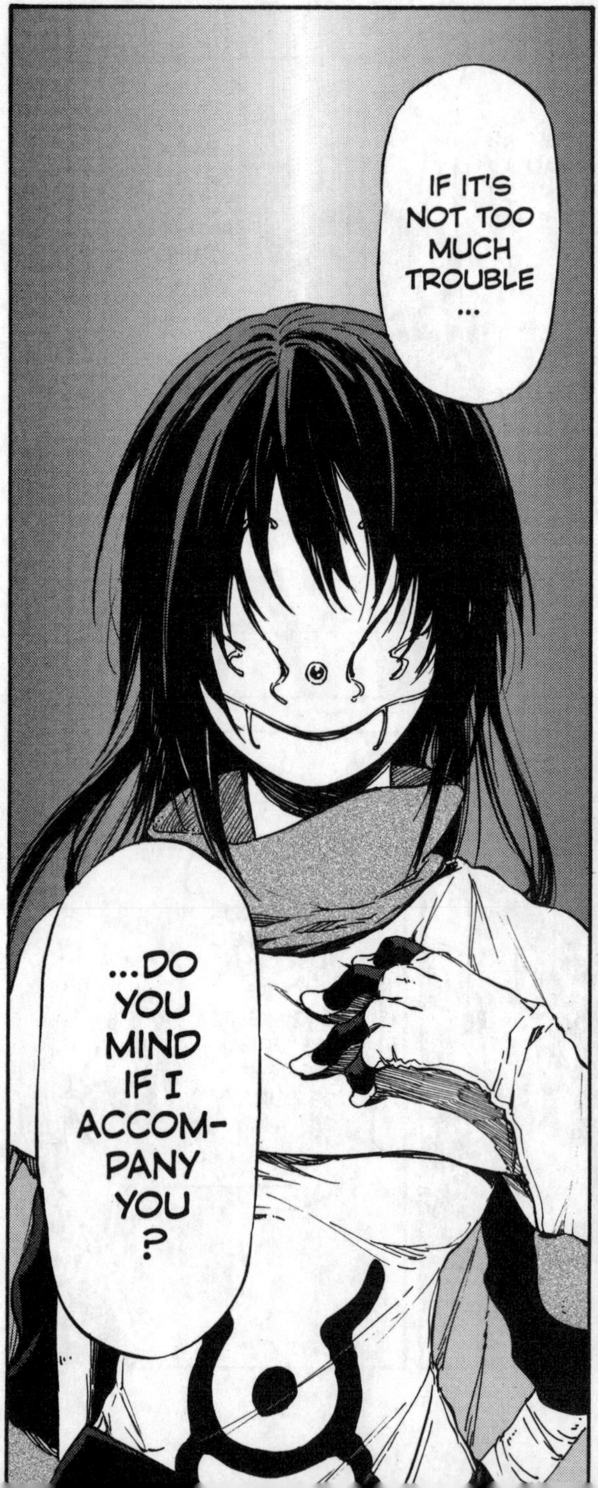
IF IT'S NOT TOO MUCH TROUBLE ...
...DO YOU MIND IF I ACCOM-PANY YOU ?

YOUNG VESTA
WAS MORE OF A
BABYFACE THAN
EXPECTED

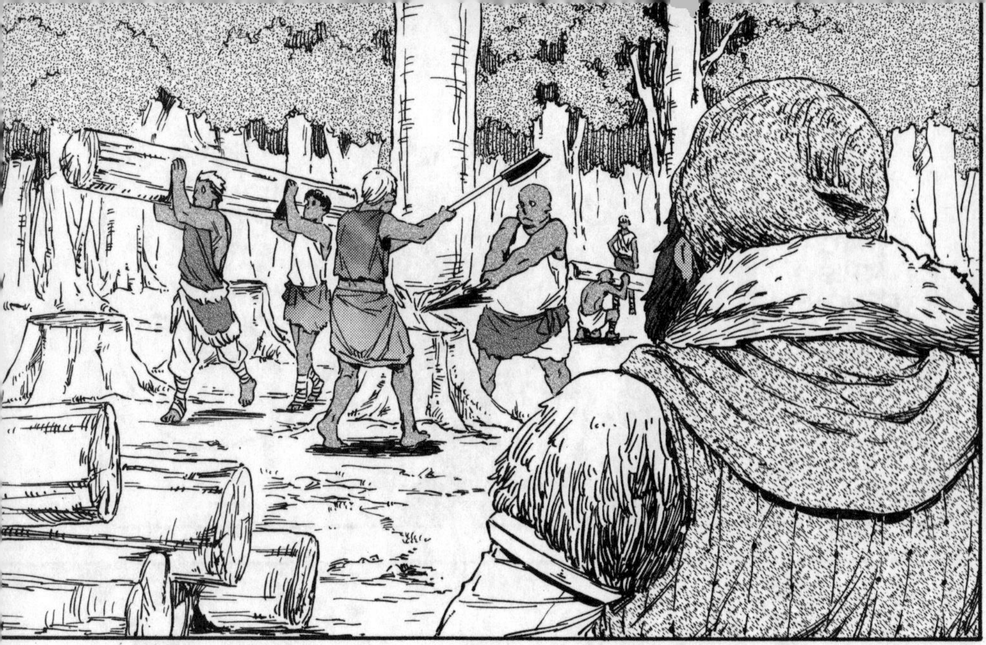

CHAPTER 8 A Familiar Scent

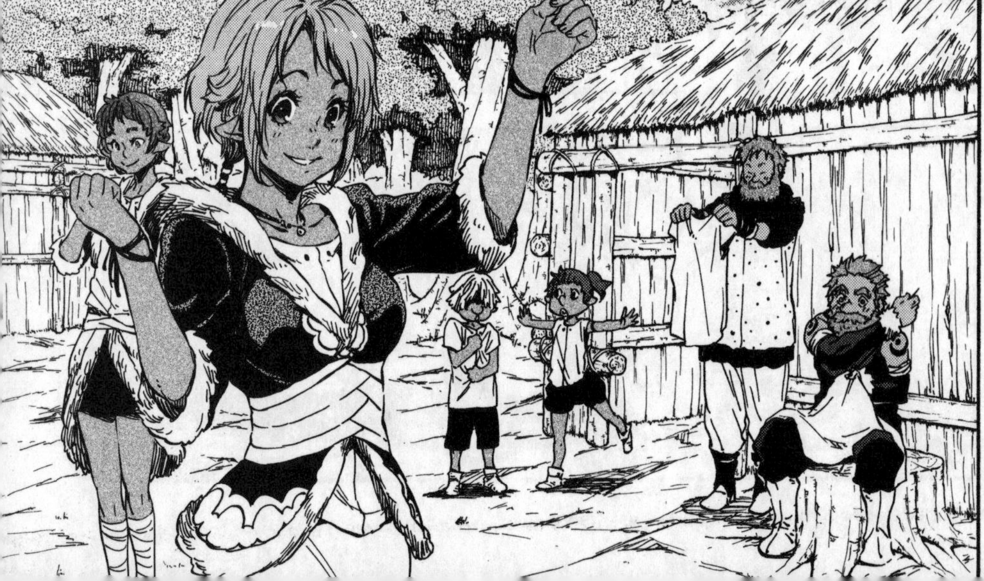

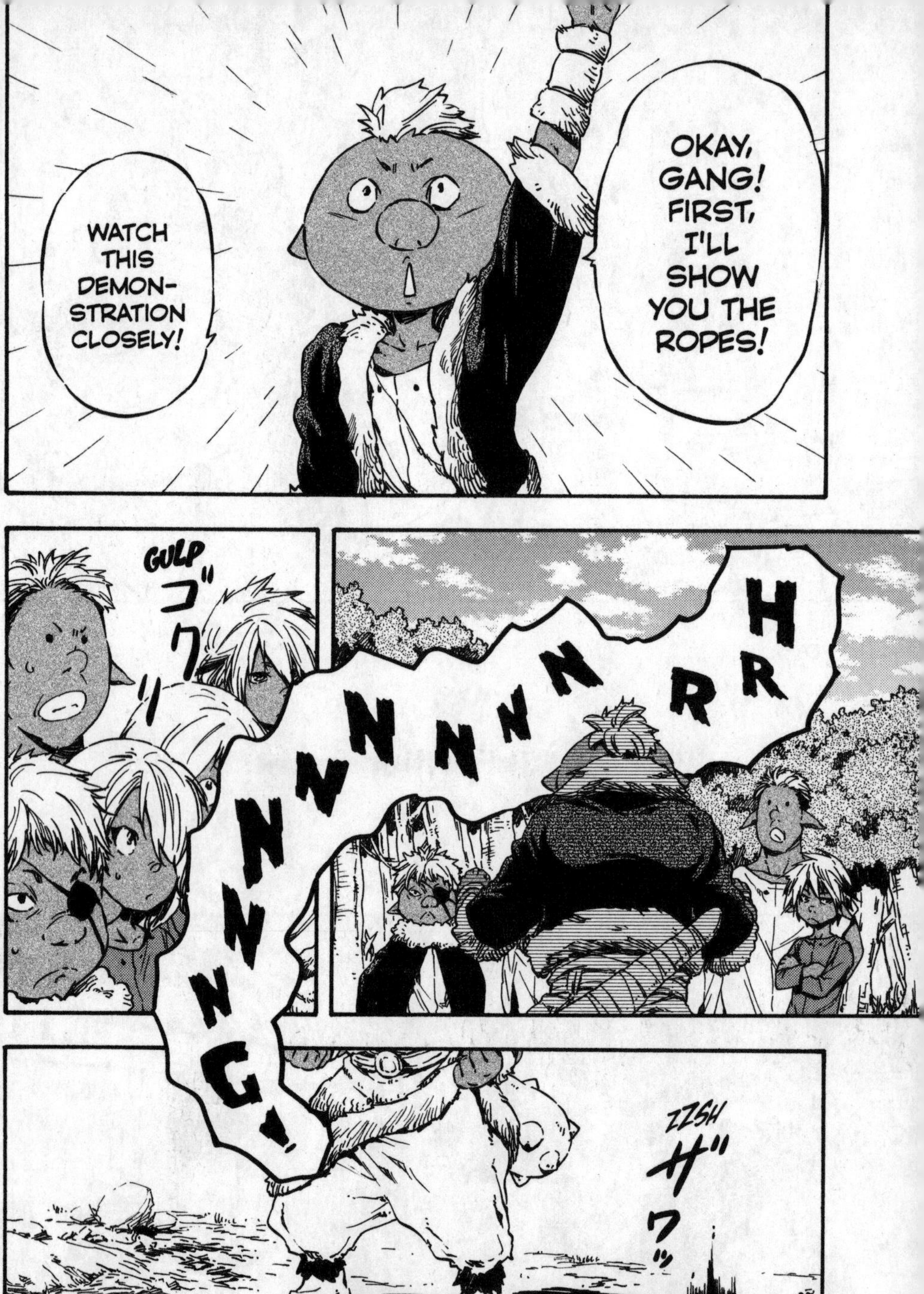
OKAY, GANG! FIRST, I'LL SHOW YOU THE ROPES!
WATCH THIS DEMON-STRATION CLOSELY!
HRRNNNNNNNNNG!
GULP
ゴクリ
ZZSH
ザワッ

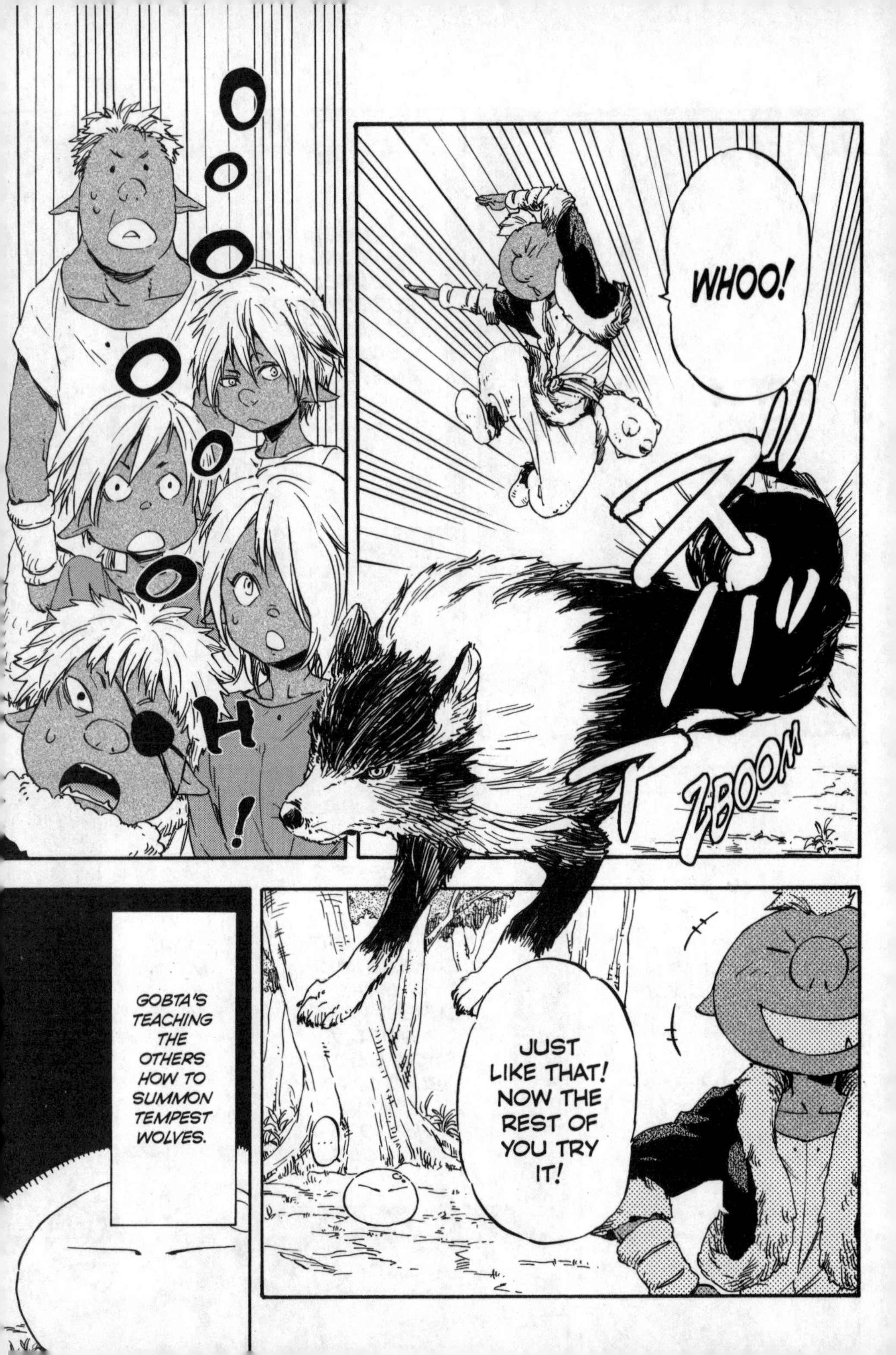
WHOO!
ZBOOM
OOOOOOOH!
JUST LIKE THAT! NOW THE REST OF YOU TRY IT!
GOBTA'S TEACHING THE OTHERS HOW TO SUMMON TEMPEST WOLVES.

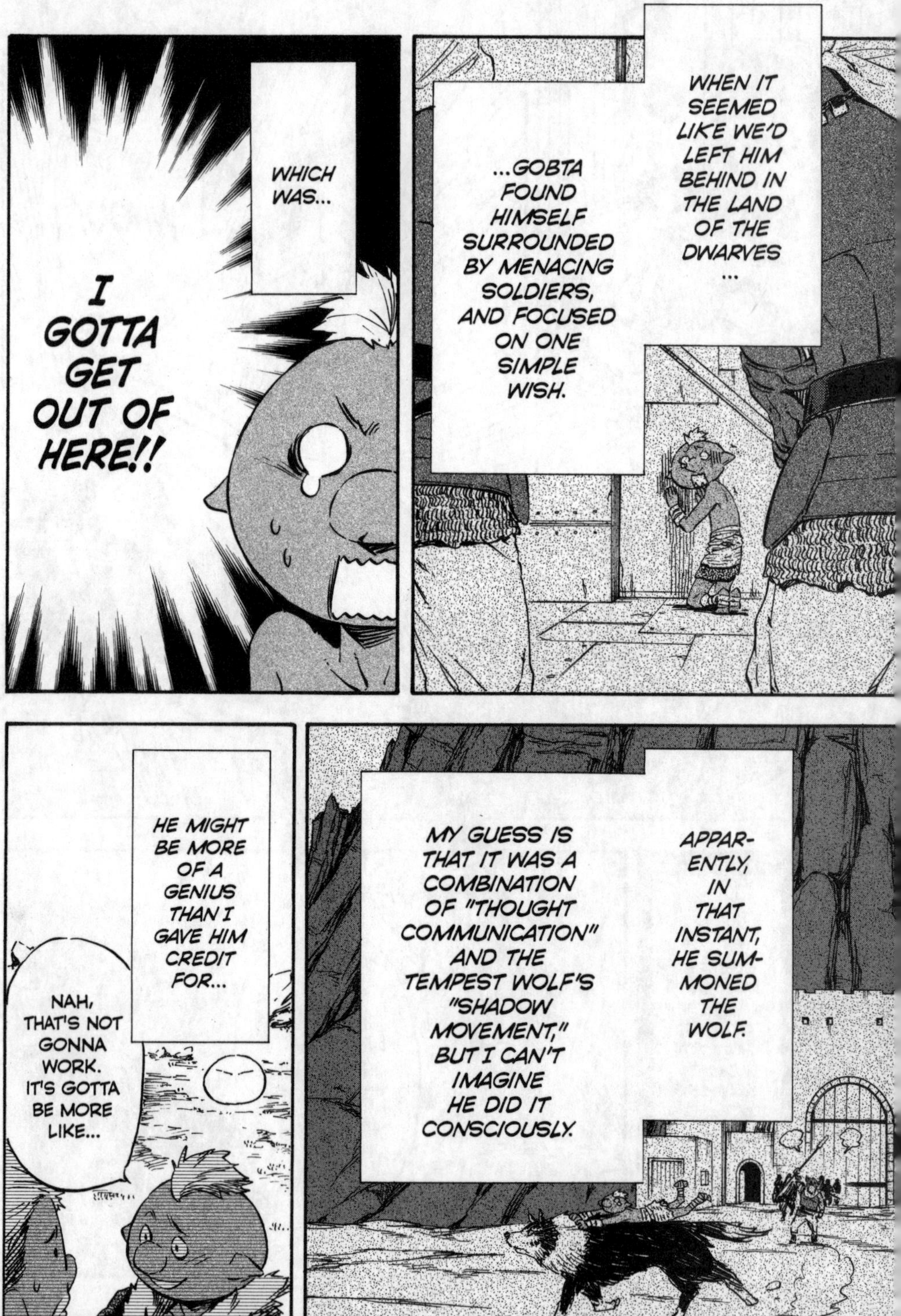
WHEN IT SEEMED LIKE WE'D LEFT HIM BEHIND IN THE LAND OF THE DWARVES ...
...GOBTA FOUND HIMSELF SURROUNDED BY MENACING SOLDIERS, AND FOCUSED ON ONE SIMPLE WISH.
WHICH WAS...
I GOTTA GET OUT OF HERE!!
APPAR-ENTLY, IN THAT INSTANT, HE SUM-MONED THE WOLF.
MY GUESS IS THAT IT WAS A COMBINATION OF "THOUGHT COMMUNICATION" AND THE TEMPEST WOLF'S "SHADOW MOVEMENT," BUT I CAN'T IMAGINE HE DID IT CONSCIOUSLY.
HE MIGHT BE MORE OF A GENIUS THAN I GAVE HIM CREDIT FOR...
NAH, THAT'S NOT GONNA WORK. IT'S GOTTA BE MORE LIKE...

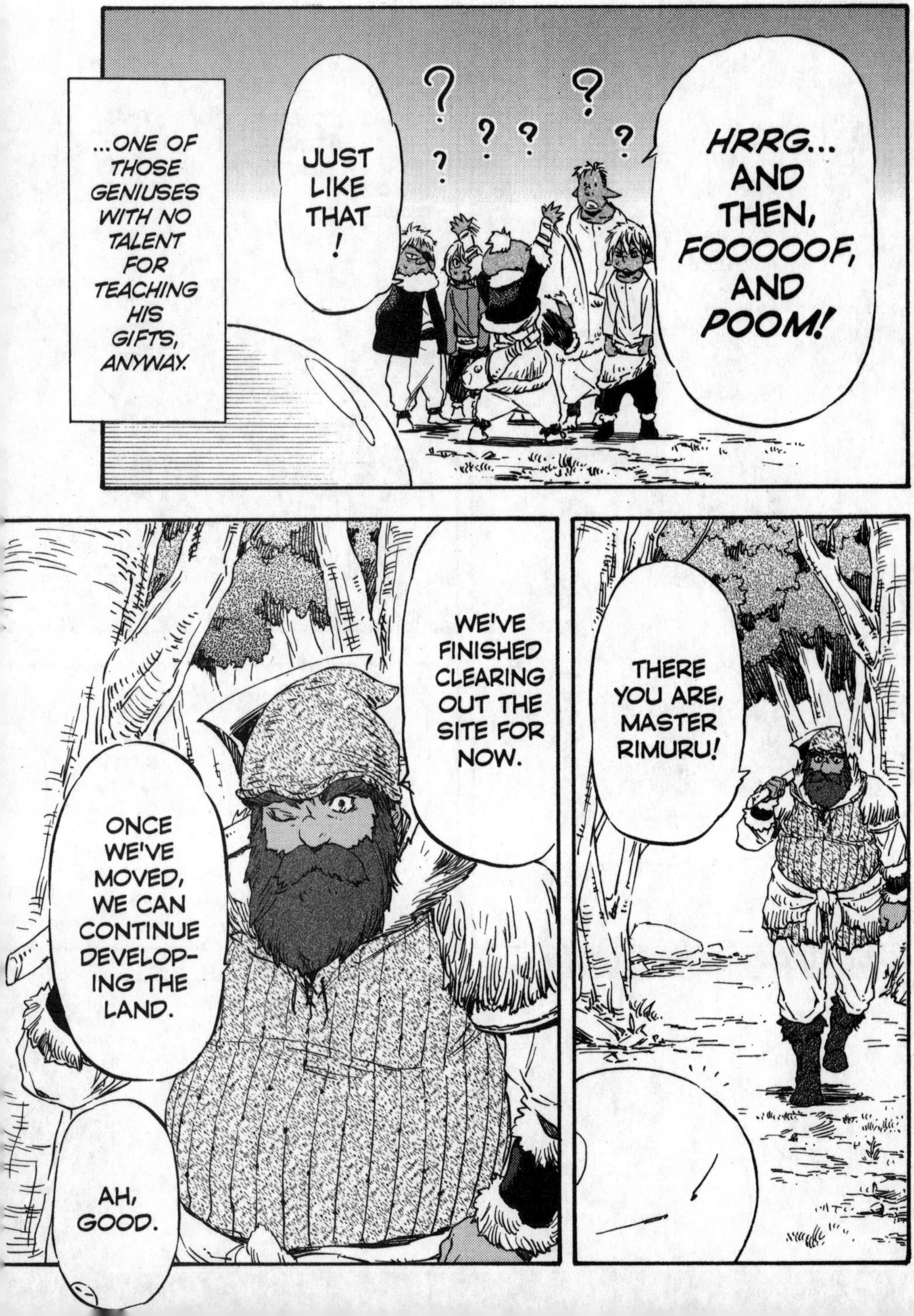
HRRG... AND THEN, FOOOOOF, AND POOM!
JUST LIKE THAT!
...ONE OF THOSE GENIUSES WITH NO TALENT FOR TEACHING HIS GIFTS, ANYWAY.
THERE YOU ARE, MASTER RIMURU!
WE'VE FINISHED CLEARING OUT THE SITE FOR NOW.
ONCE WE'VE MOVED, WE CAN CONTINUE DEVELOP-ING THE LAND.
AH, GOOD.

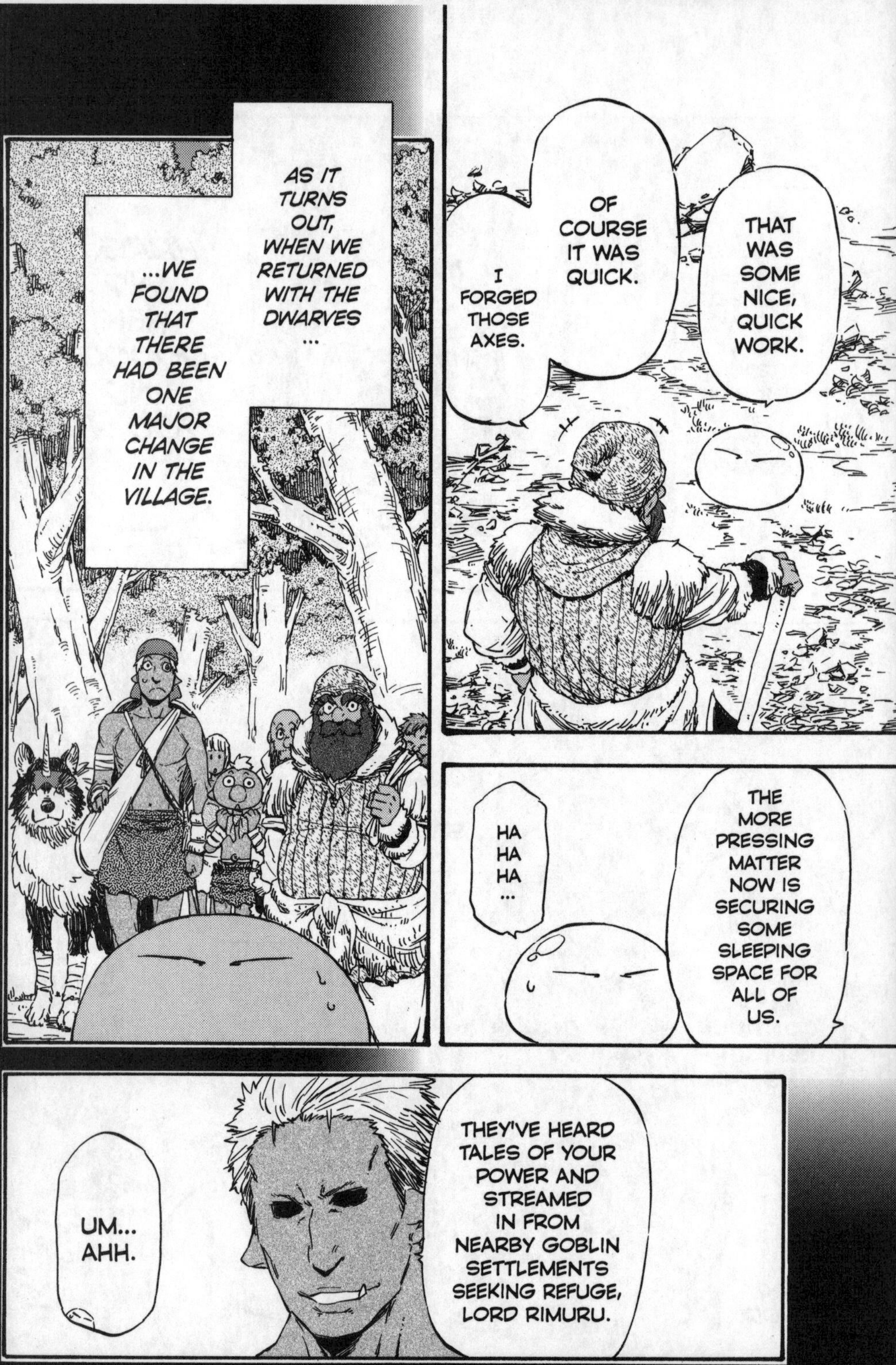
THAT WAS SOME NICE, QUICK WORK.
OF COURSE IT WAS QUICK. I FORGED THOSE AXES.
THE MORE PRESSING MATTER NOW IS SECURING SOME SLEEPING SPACE FOR ALL OF US.
HA HA HA ...
AS IT TURNS OUT, WHEN WE RETURNED WITH THE DWARVES ...
...WE FOUND THAT THERE HAD BEEN ONE MAJOR CHANGE IN THE VILLAGE.
THEY'VE HEARD TALES OF YOUR POWER AND STREAMED IN FROM NEARBY GOBLIN SETTLEMENTS SEEKING REFUGE, LORD RIMURU.
UM... AHH.

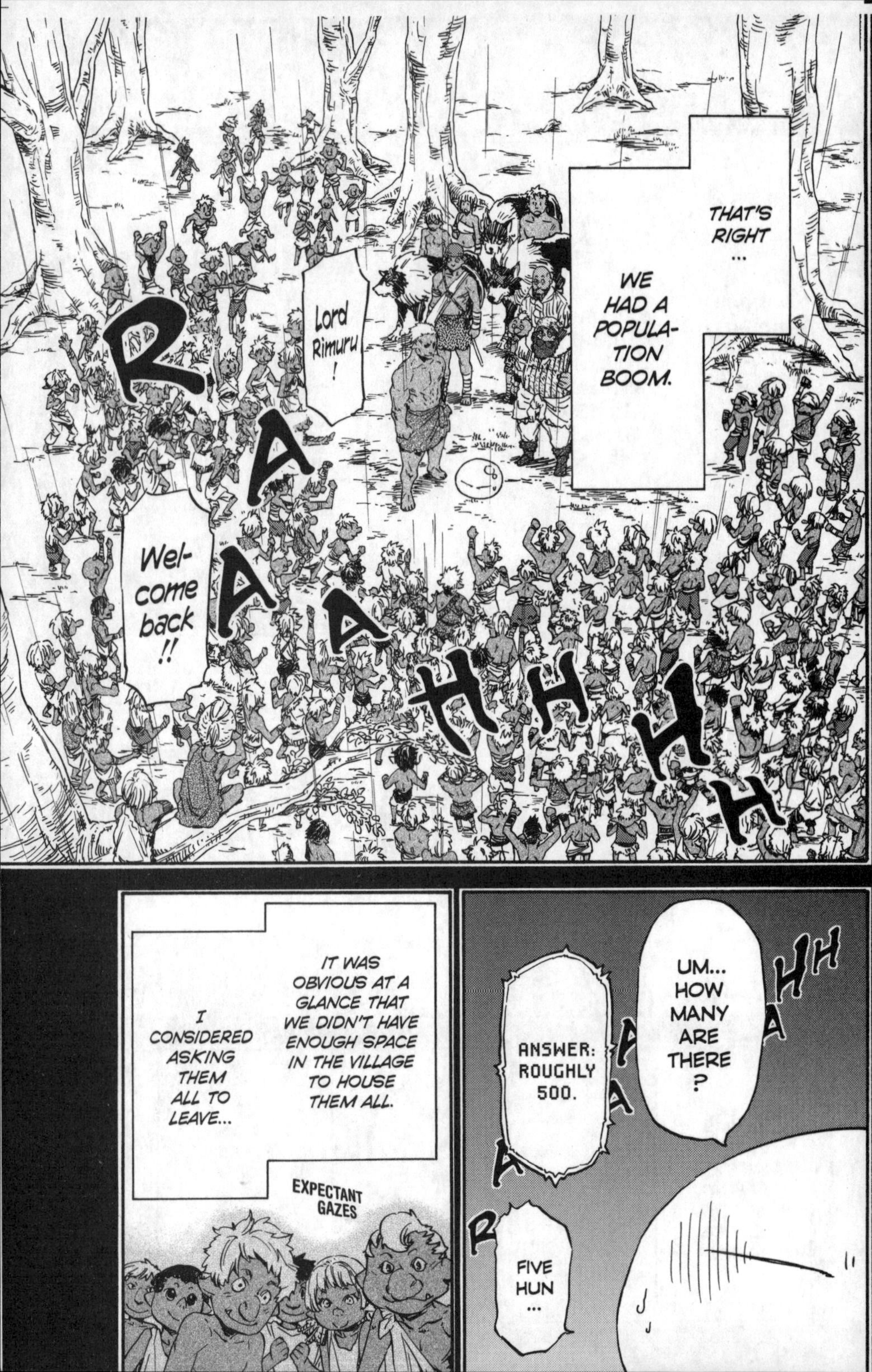
THAT'S RIGHT ...
WE HAD A POPULATION BOOM.
Lord Rimuru!
RAAAHHHH
Welcome back!!
UM... HOW MANY ARE THERE?
ANSWER: ROUGHLY 500.
RAAAHH
FIVE HUN ...
IT WAS OBVIOUS AT A GLANCE THAT WE DIDN'T HAVE ENOUGH SPACE IN THE VILLAGE TO HOUSE THEM ALL.
I CONSIDERED ASKING THEM ALL TO LEAVE...
EXPECTANT GAZES

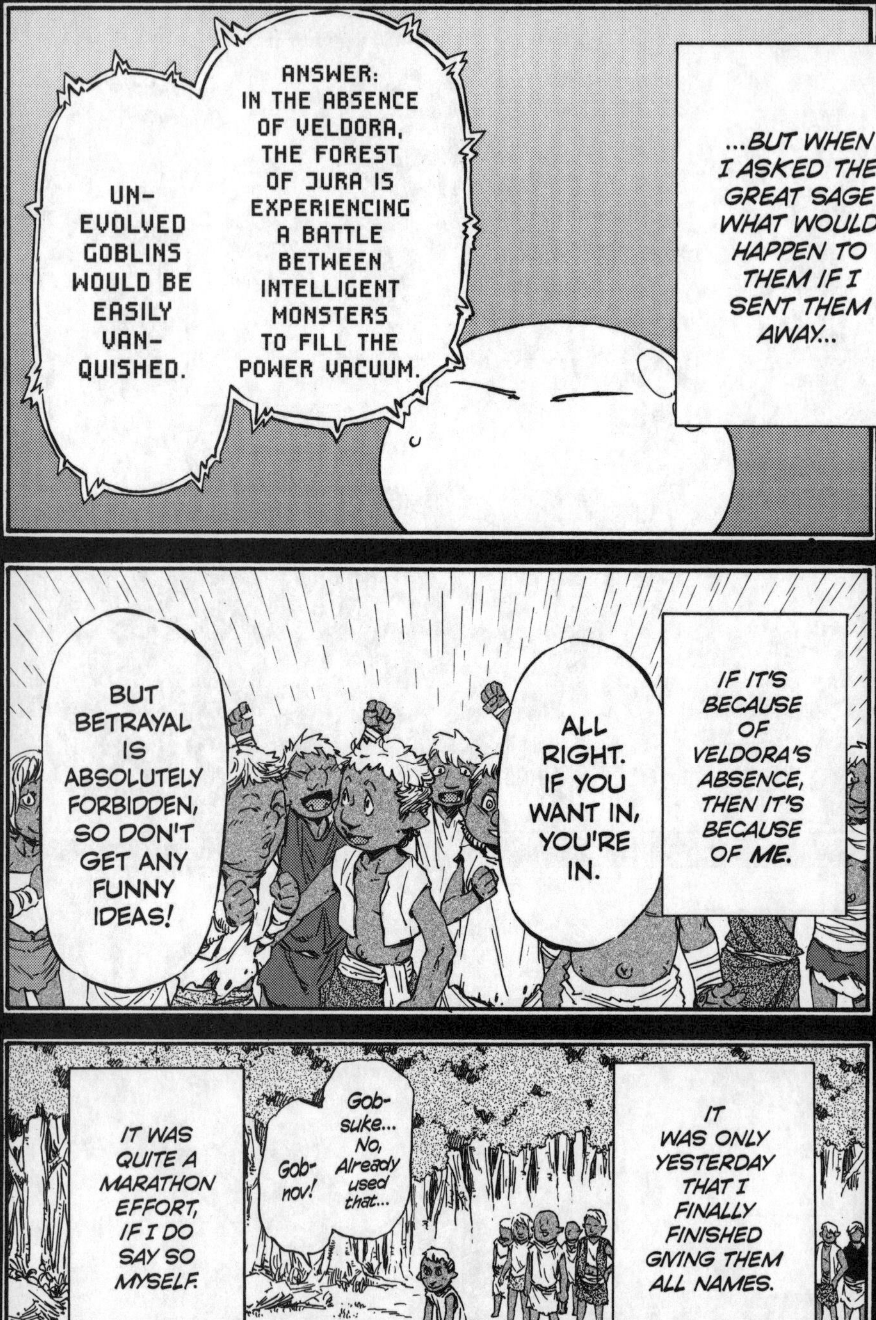
...BUT WHEN I ASKED THE GREAT SAGE WHAT WOULD HAPPEN TO THEM IF I SENT THEM AWAY...
ANSWER: IN THE ABSENCE OF VELDORA, THE FOREST OF JURA IS EXPERIENCING A BATTLE BETWEEN INTELLIGENT MONSTERS TO FILL THE POWER VACUUM.
UN-EVOLVED GOBLINS WOULD BE EASILY VAN-QUISHED.
IF IT'S BECAUSE OF VELDORA'S ABSENCE, THEN IT'S BECAUSE OF ME.
ALL RIGHT. IF YOU WANT IN, YOU'RE IN.
BUT BETRAYAL IS ABSOLUTELY FORBIDDEN, SO DON'T GET ANY FUNNY IDEAS!
IT WAS ONLY YESTERDAY THAT I FINALLY FINISHED GIVING THEM ALL NAMES.
Gob-suke... No, Already used that...
Gob-nov!
IT WAS QUITE A MARATHON EFFORT, IF I DO SAY SO MYSELF.

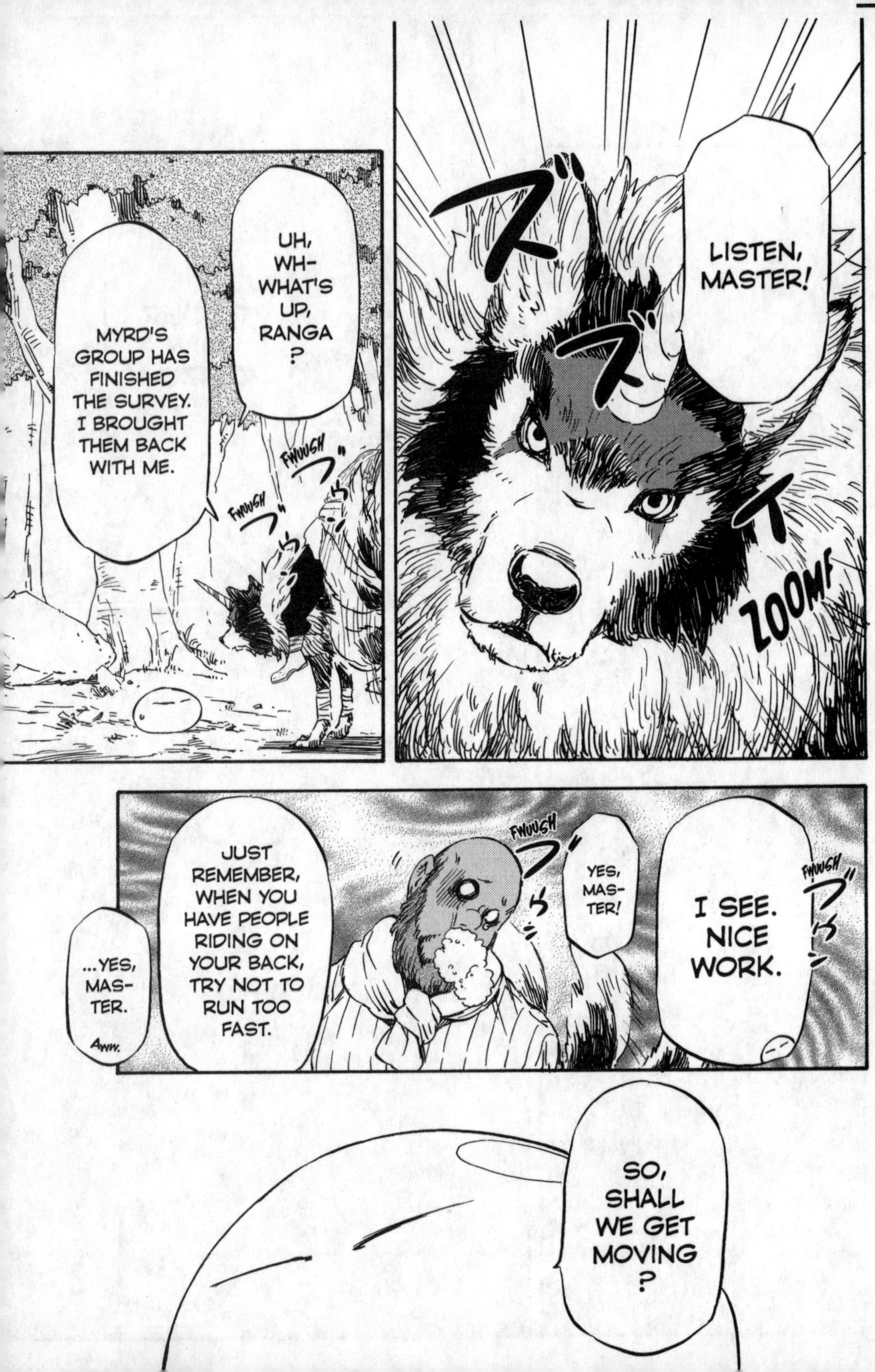
LISTEN, MASTER!
ZOOMF
UH, WH- WHAT'S UP, RANGA?
MYRD'S GROUP HAS FINISHED THE SURVEY. I BROUGHT THEM BACK WITH ME.
FWUUSH
FWUUSH
FWUUSH
I SEE. NICE WORK.
FWUUSH
YES, MAS- TER!
JUST REMEMBER, WHEN YOU HAVE PEOPLE RIDING ON YOUR BACK, TRY NOT TO RUN TOO FAST.
...YES, MAS- TER.
AWW.
SO, SHALL WE GET MOVING?

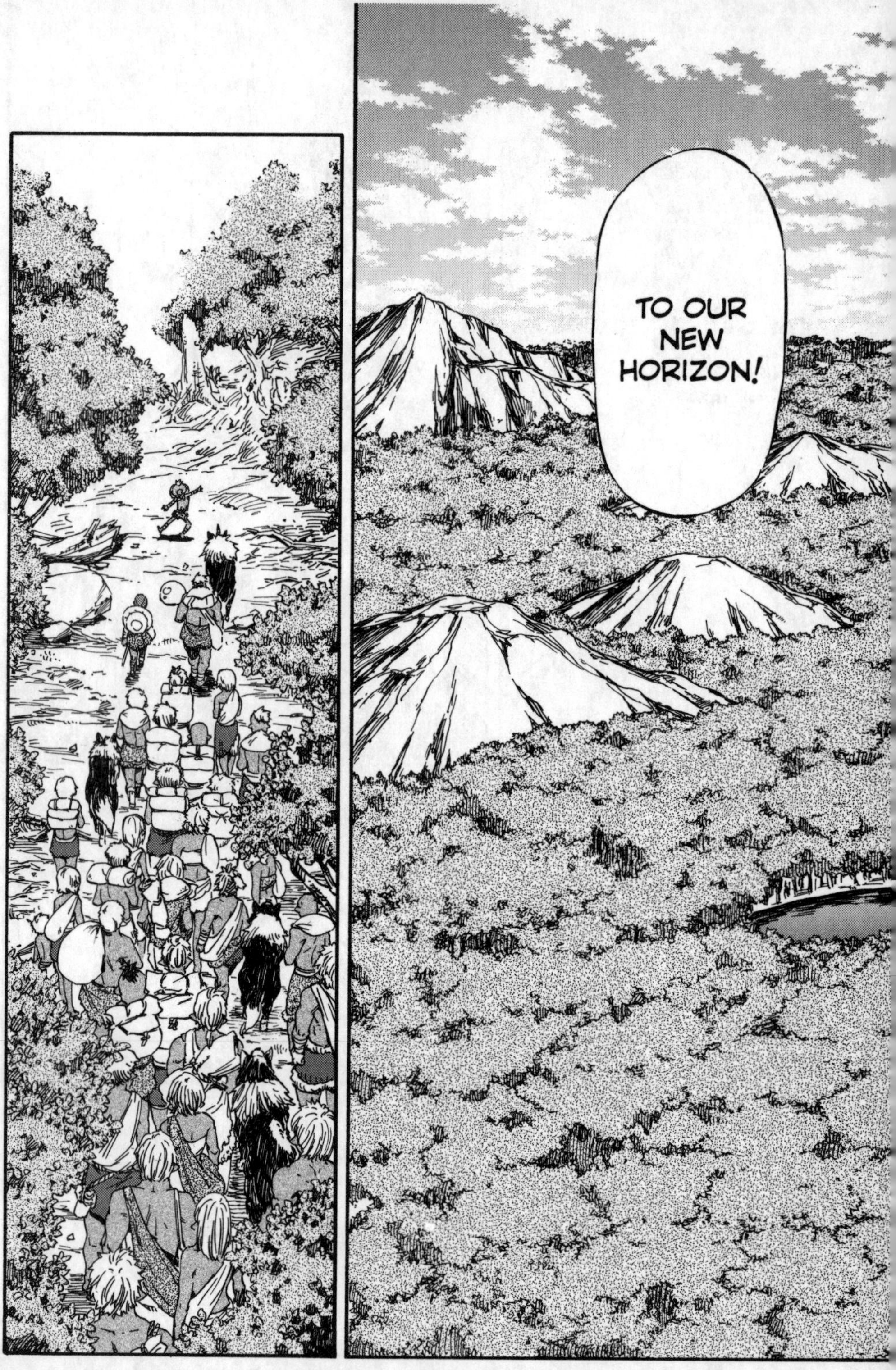
TO OUR NEW HORIZON!

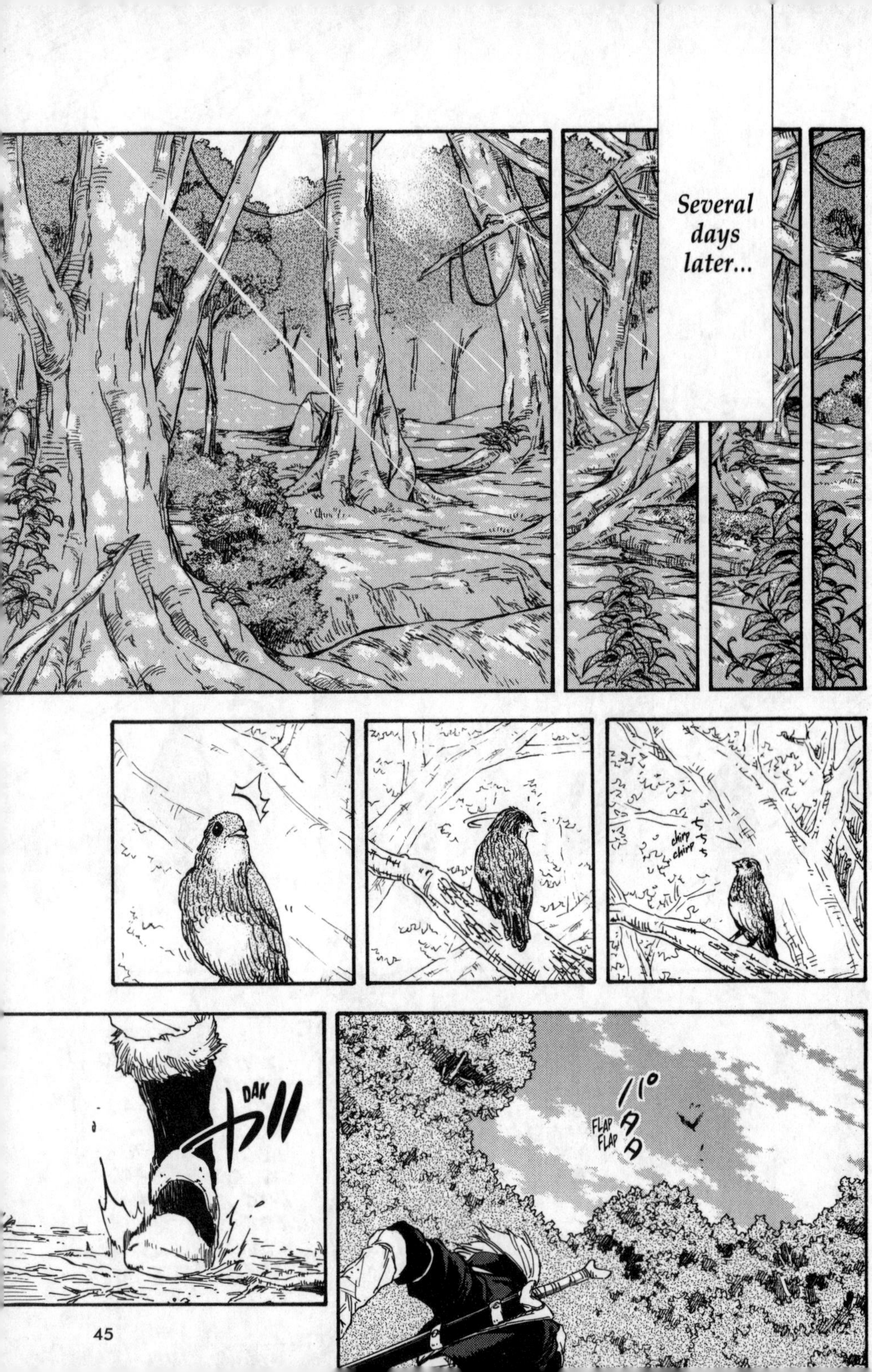
Several days later...
chirp chirp
FLAP FLAP
DAK

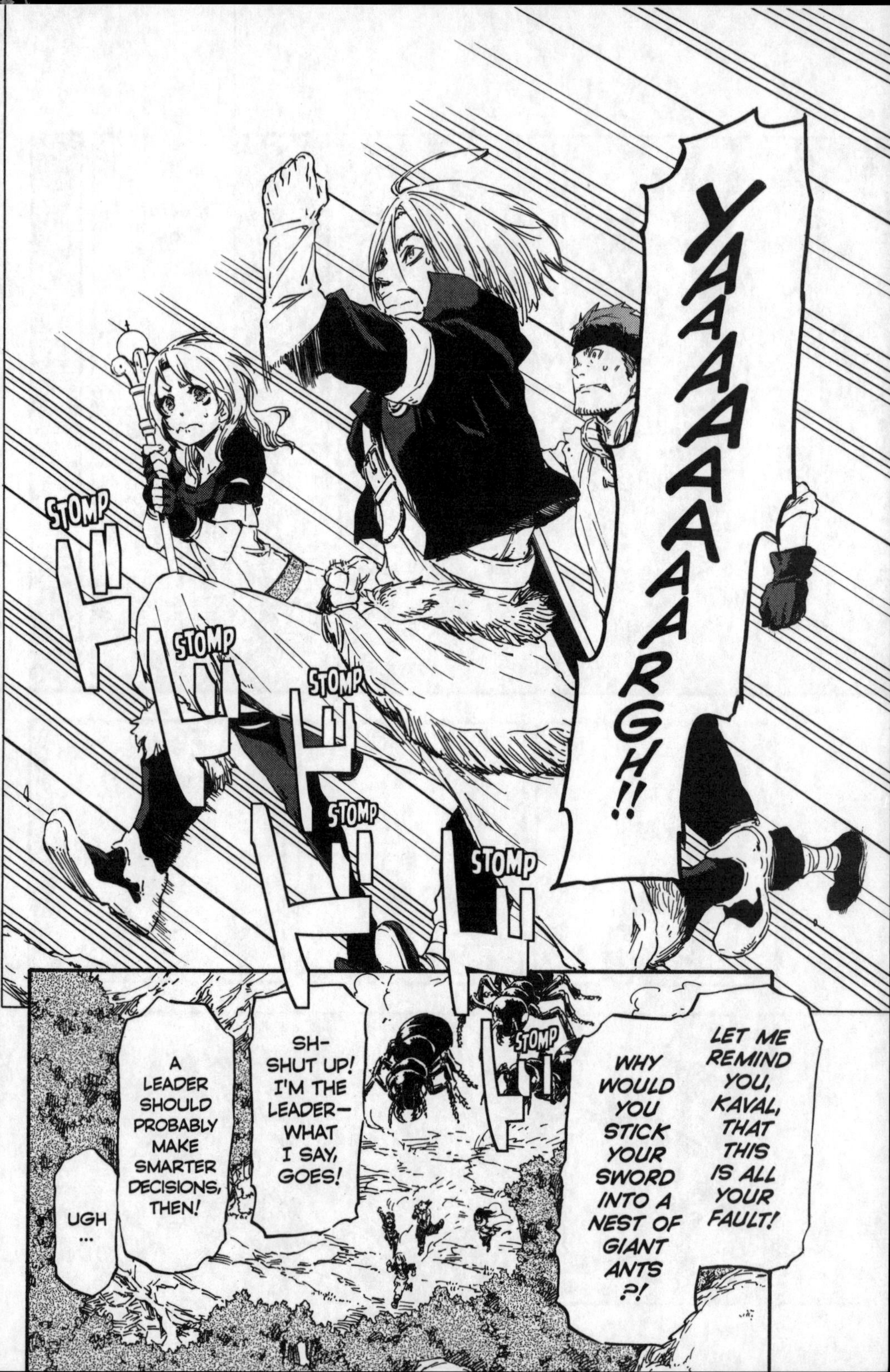
YAAAAAAAARGH!!
STOMP
STOMP
STOMP
STOMP
STOMP
STOMP
LET ME REMIND YOU, KAVAL, THAT THIS IS ALL YOUR FAULT!
WHY WOULD YOU STICK YOUR SWORD INTO A NEST OF GIANT ANTS?!
SH- SHUT UP! I'M THE LEADER— WHAT I SAY, GOES!
A LEADER SHOULD PROBABLY MAKE SMARTER DECISIONS, THEN!
UGH ...

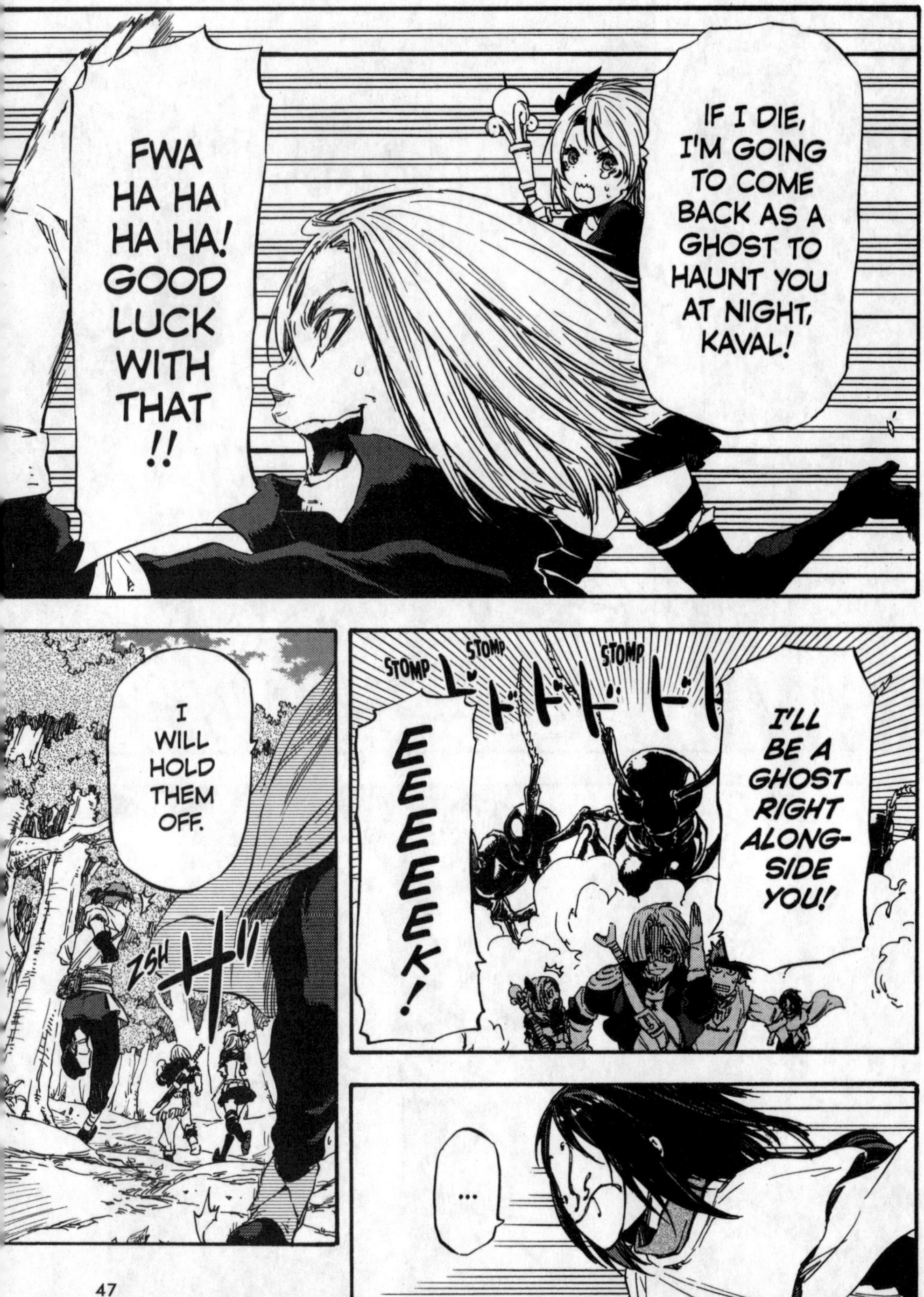
IF I DIE, I'M GOING TO COME BACK AS A GHOST TO HAUNT YOU AT NIGHT, KAVAL!
FWA HA HA HA HA! GOOD LUCK WITH THAT!!
STOMP
STOMP
STOMP
I'LL BE A GHOST RIGHT ALONG-SIDE YOU!
EEEEEEK!
...
I WILL HOLD THEM OFF.
ZSH

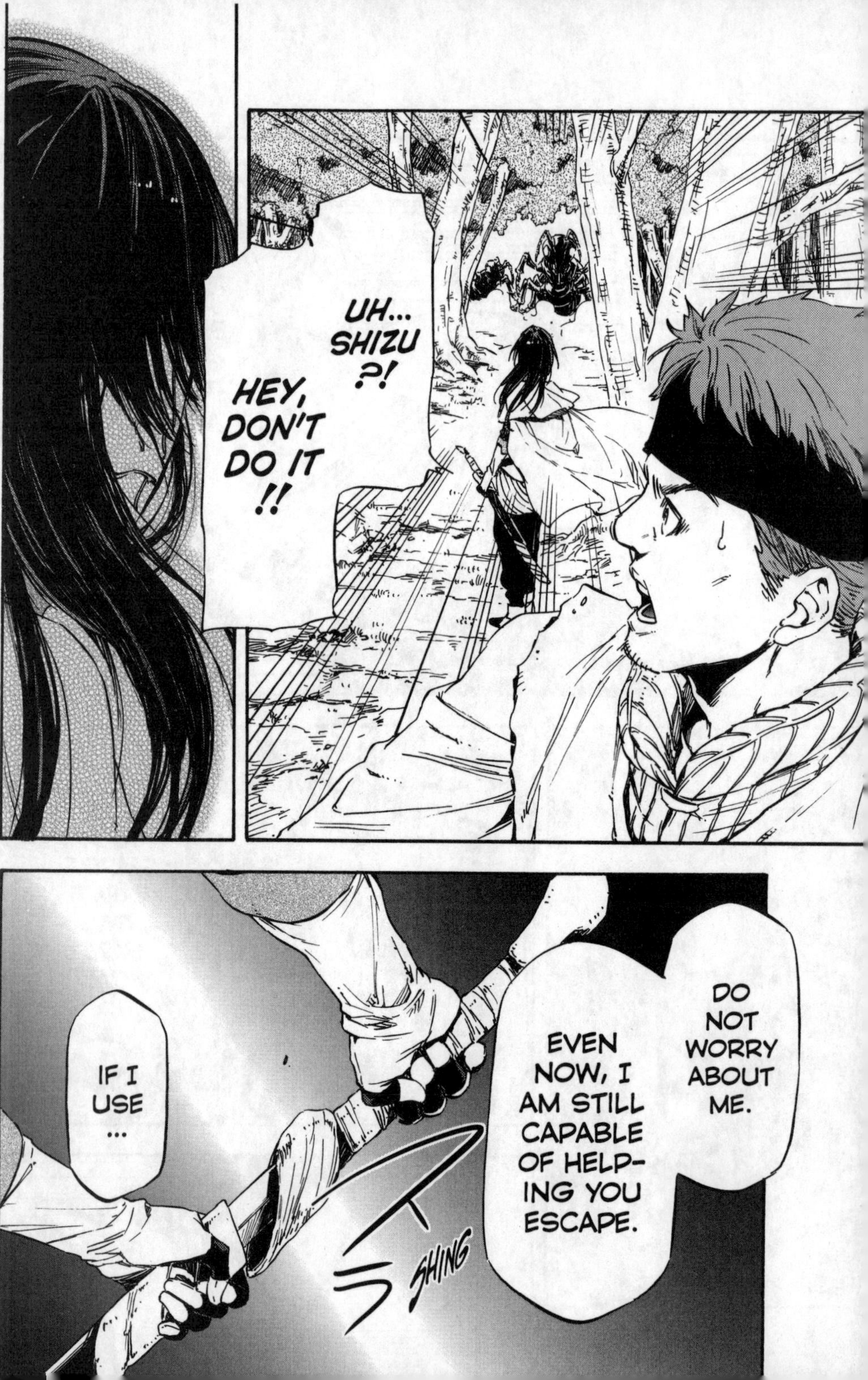
UH... SHIZU?!
HEY, DON'T DO IT!!
DO NOT WORRY ABOUT ME.
EVEN NOW, I AM STILL CAPABLE OF HELPING YOU ESCAPE.
SHING
IF I USE...

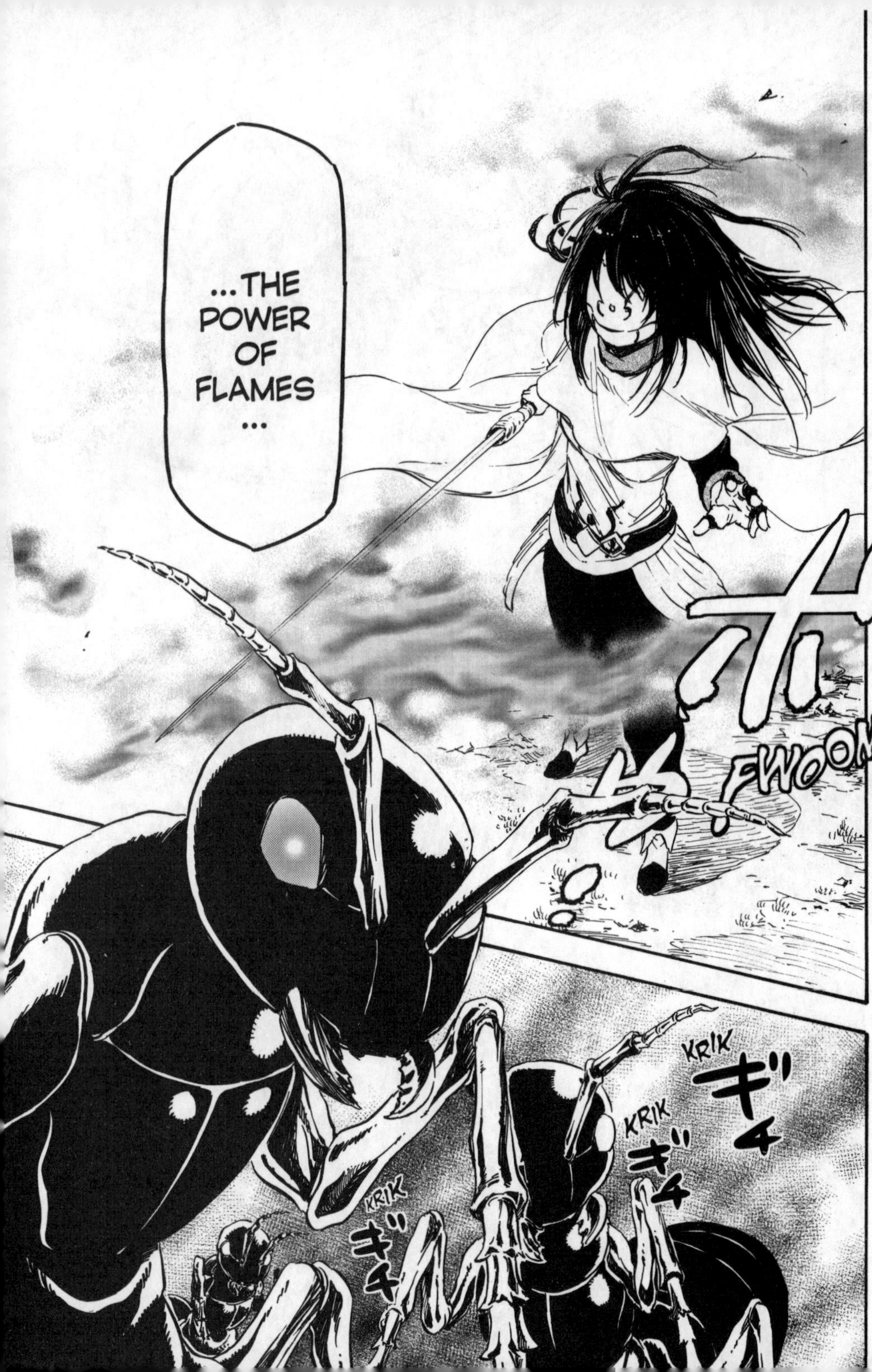
...THE POWER OF FLAMES ...
FWOOM...
KRIK
KRIK
KRIK

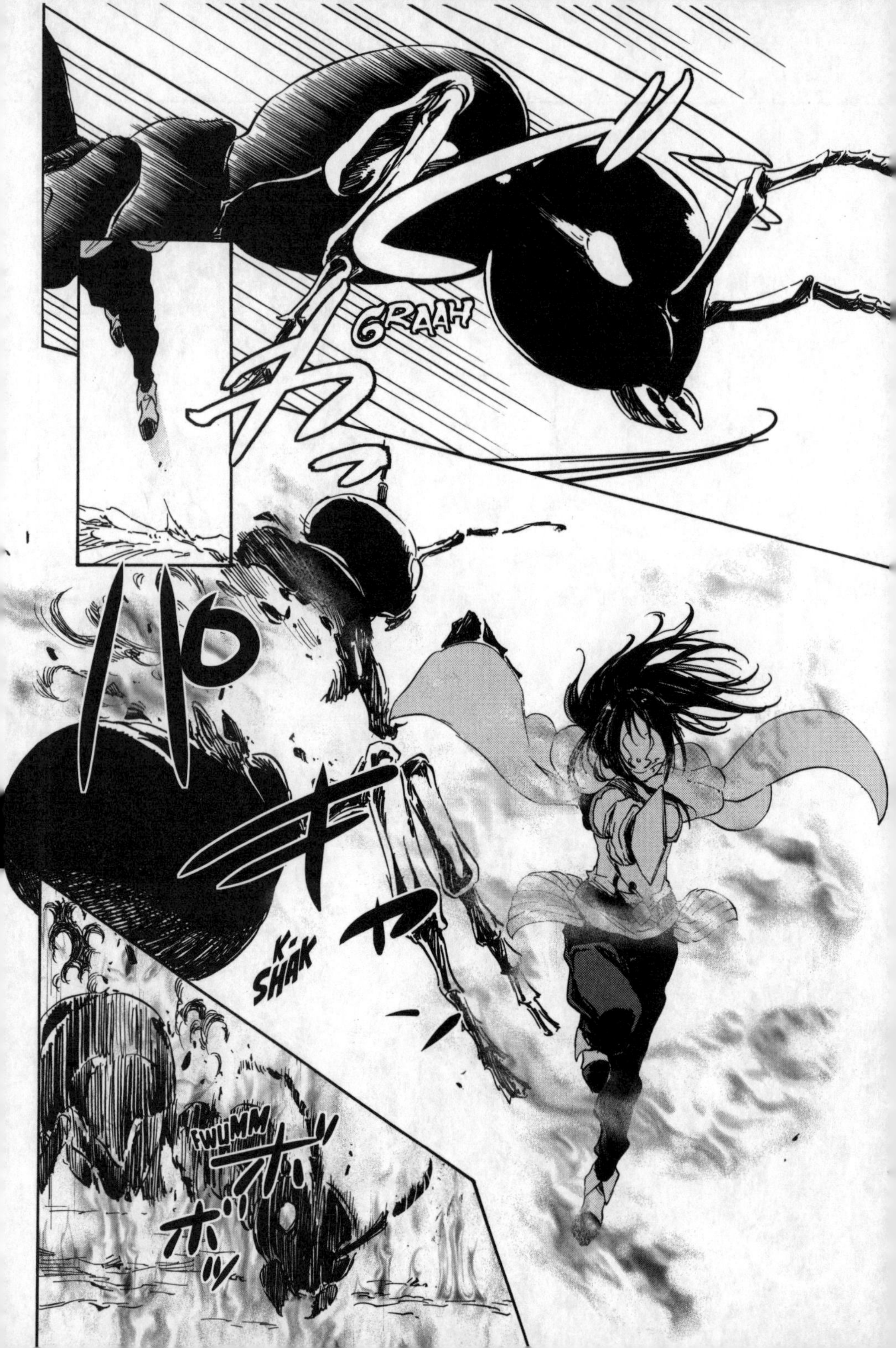
GRAAH
K-SHAK
FWUMM

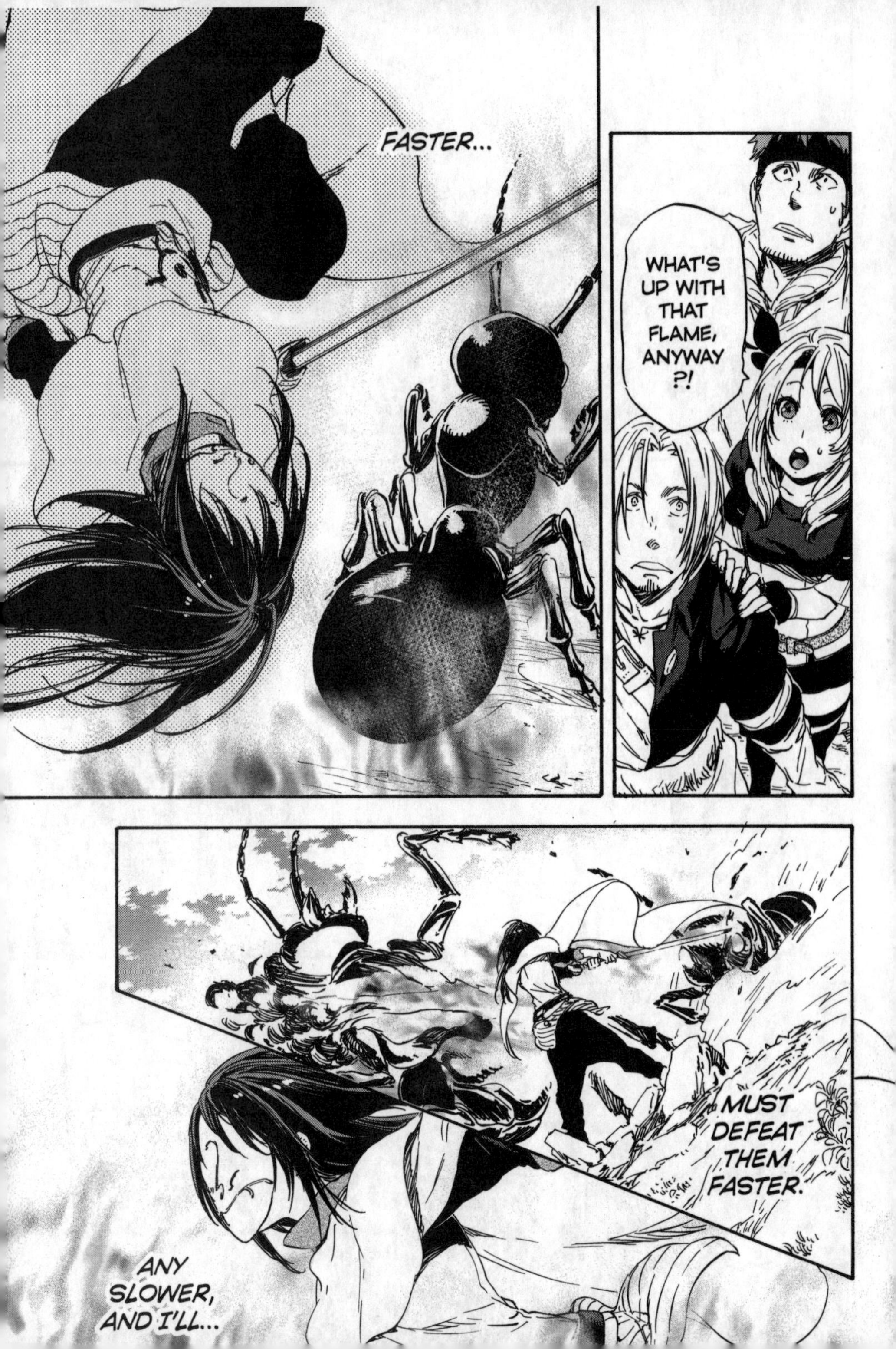
WHAT'S UP WITH THAT FLAME, ANYWAY?!
FASTER...
MUST DEFEAT THEM FASTER.
ANY SLOWER, AND I'LL...

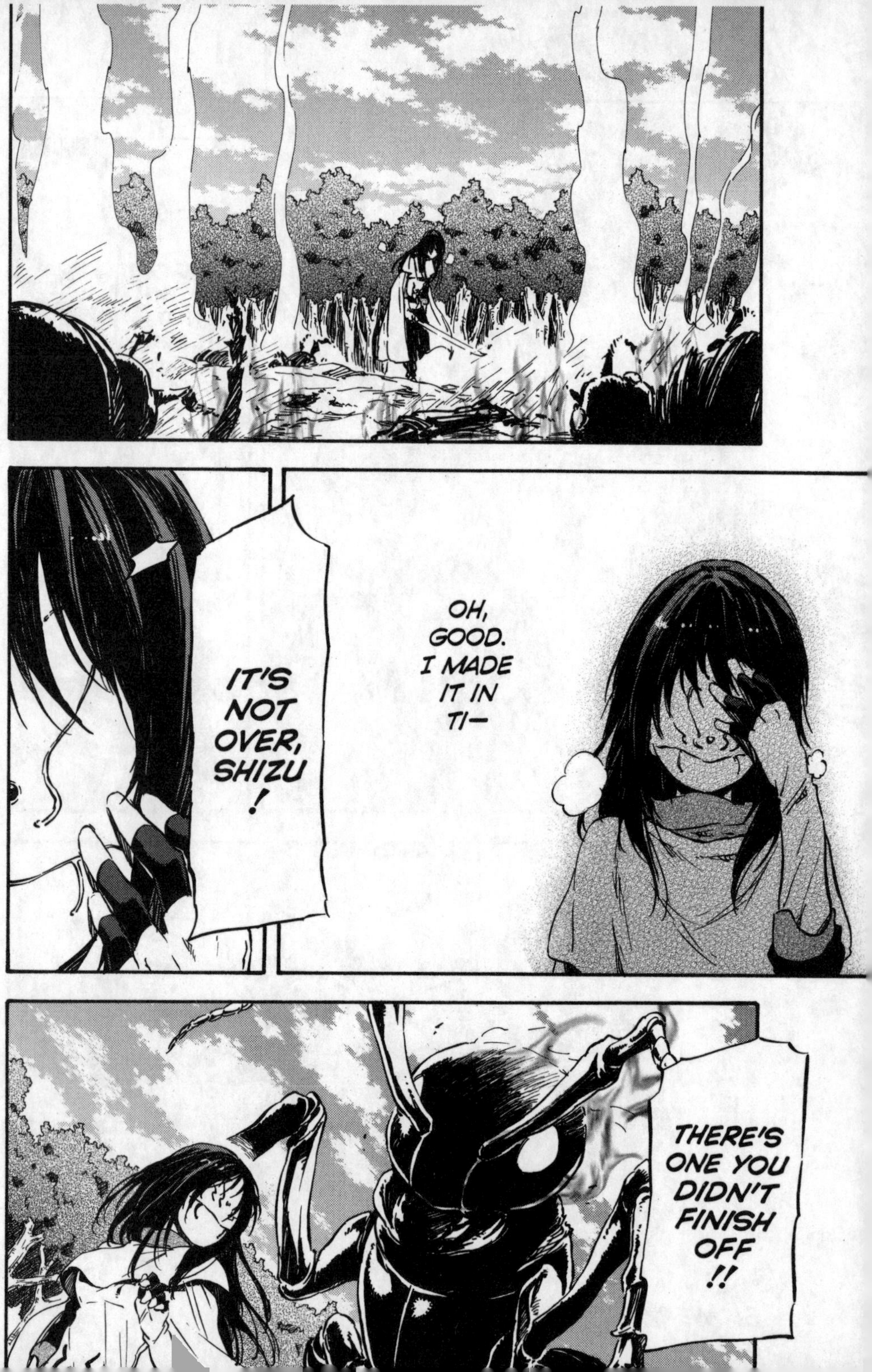
OH, GOOD. I MADE IT IN TI—
IT'S NOT OVER, SHIZU!
THERE'S ONE YOU DIDN'T FINISH OFF!!

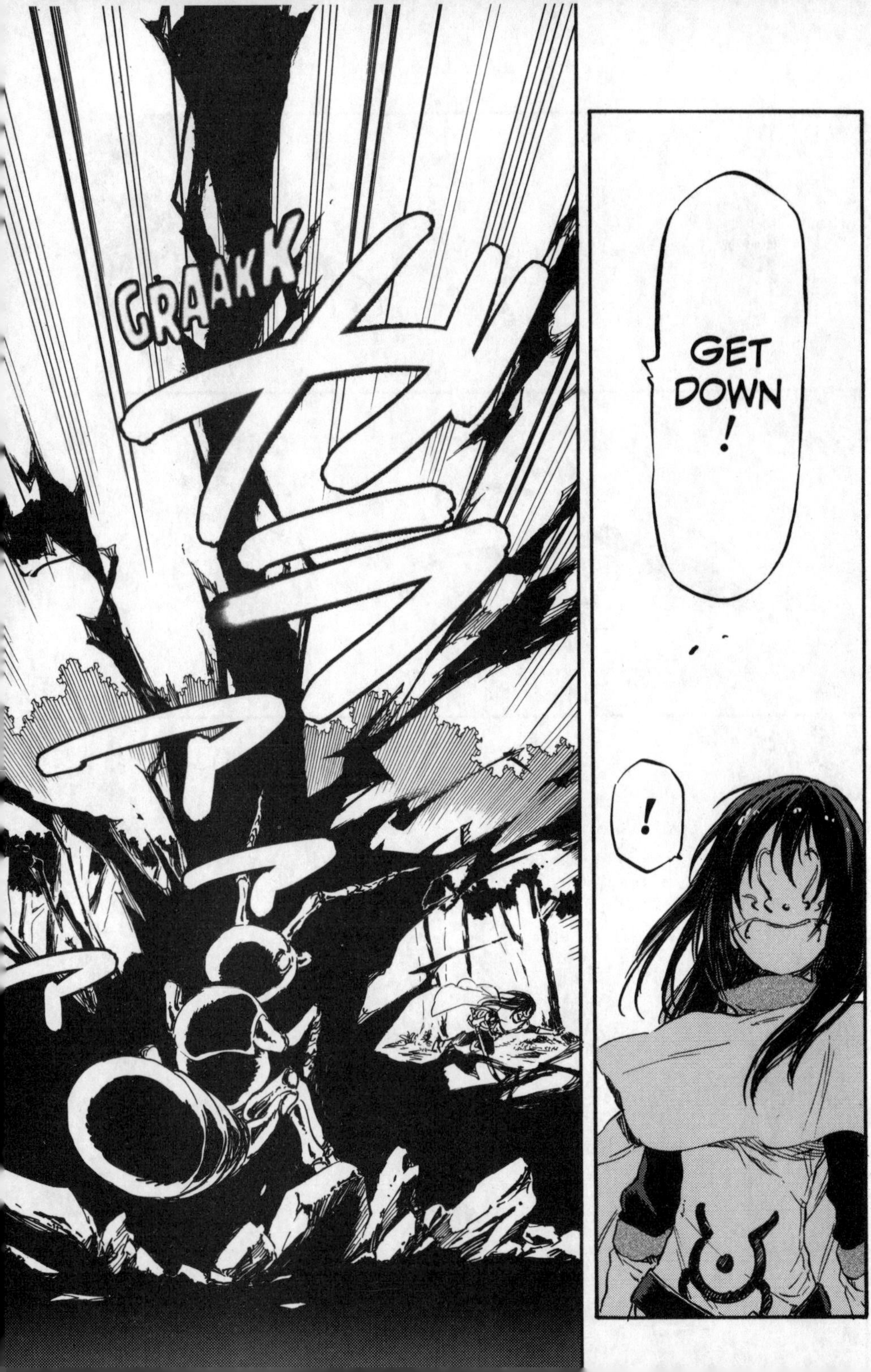
GET DOWN !
!
GRAAKK

CLACK
CLANG

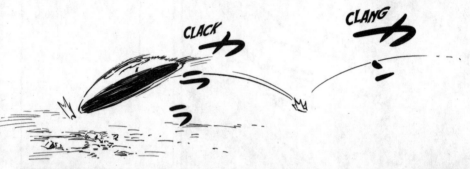

PUFF
PUFF

SHIZU, YOU ALL RIGHT ?!

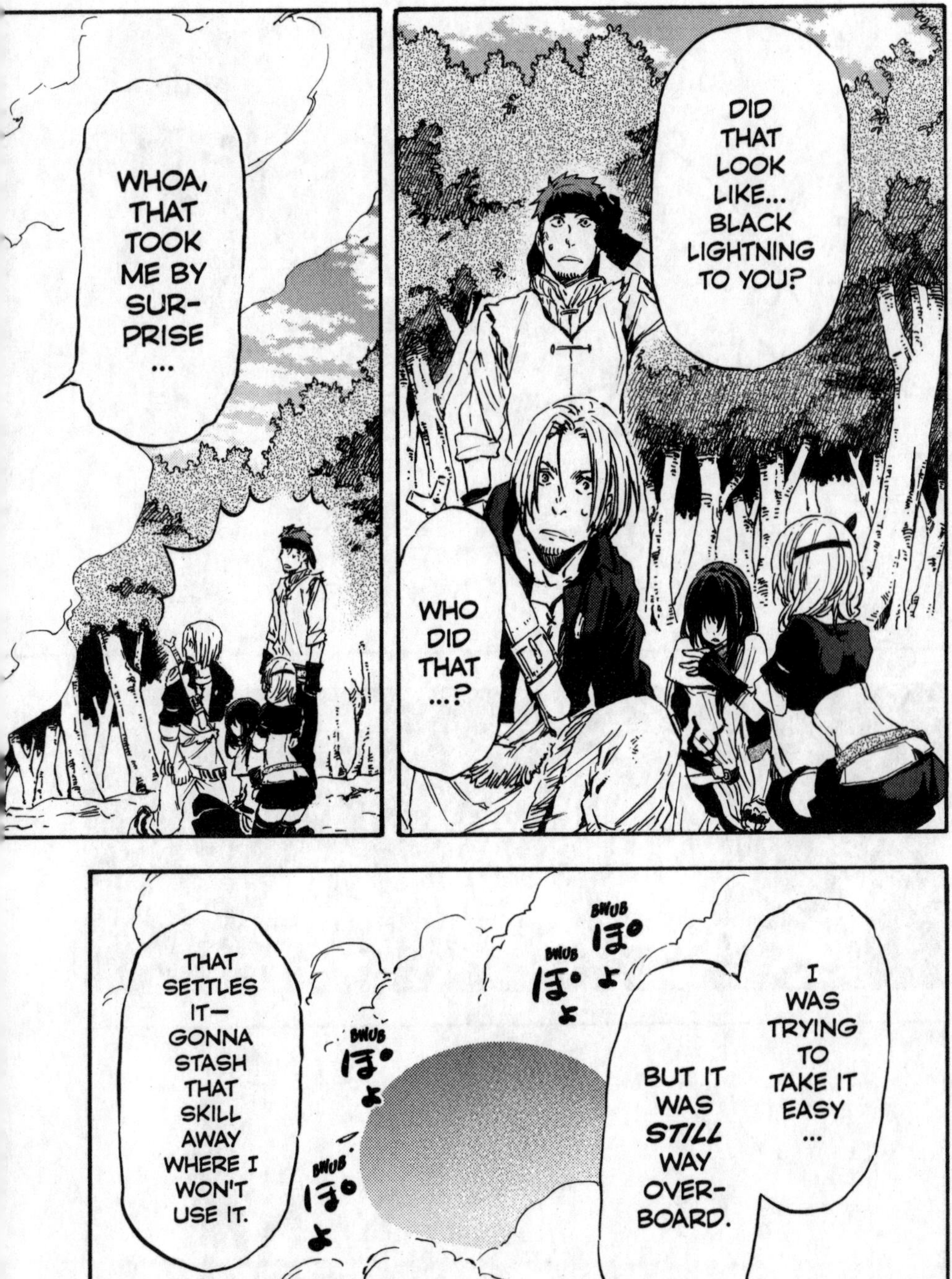
DID THAT LOOK LIKE... BLACK LIGHTNING TO YOU?
WHO DID THAT ...?
WHOA, THAT TOOK ME BY SUR-PRISE ...
I WAS TRYING TO TAKE IT EASY ...
BUT IT WAS *STILL* WAY OVER-BOARD.
BWUB ぽよ
BWUB ぽよ
BWUB ぽよ
BWUB ぽよ
THAT SETTLES IT— GONNA STASH THAT SKILL AWAY WHERE I WON'T USE IT.

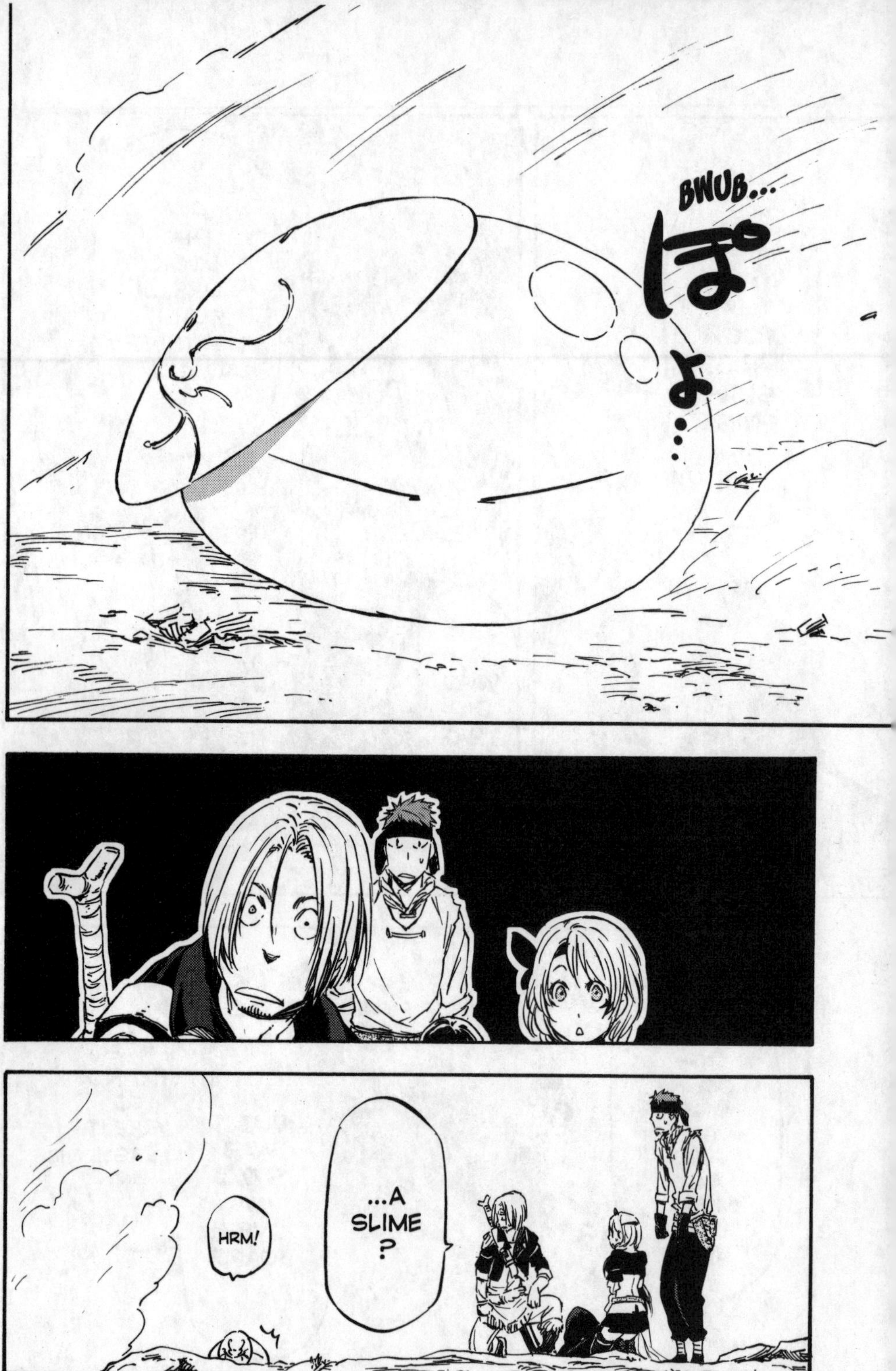
BWUB...
ぽよ...
...A SLIME?
HRM!

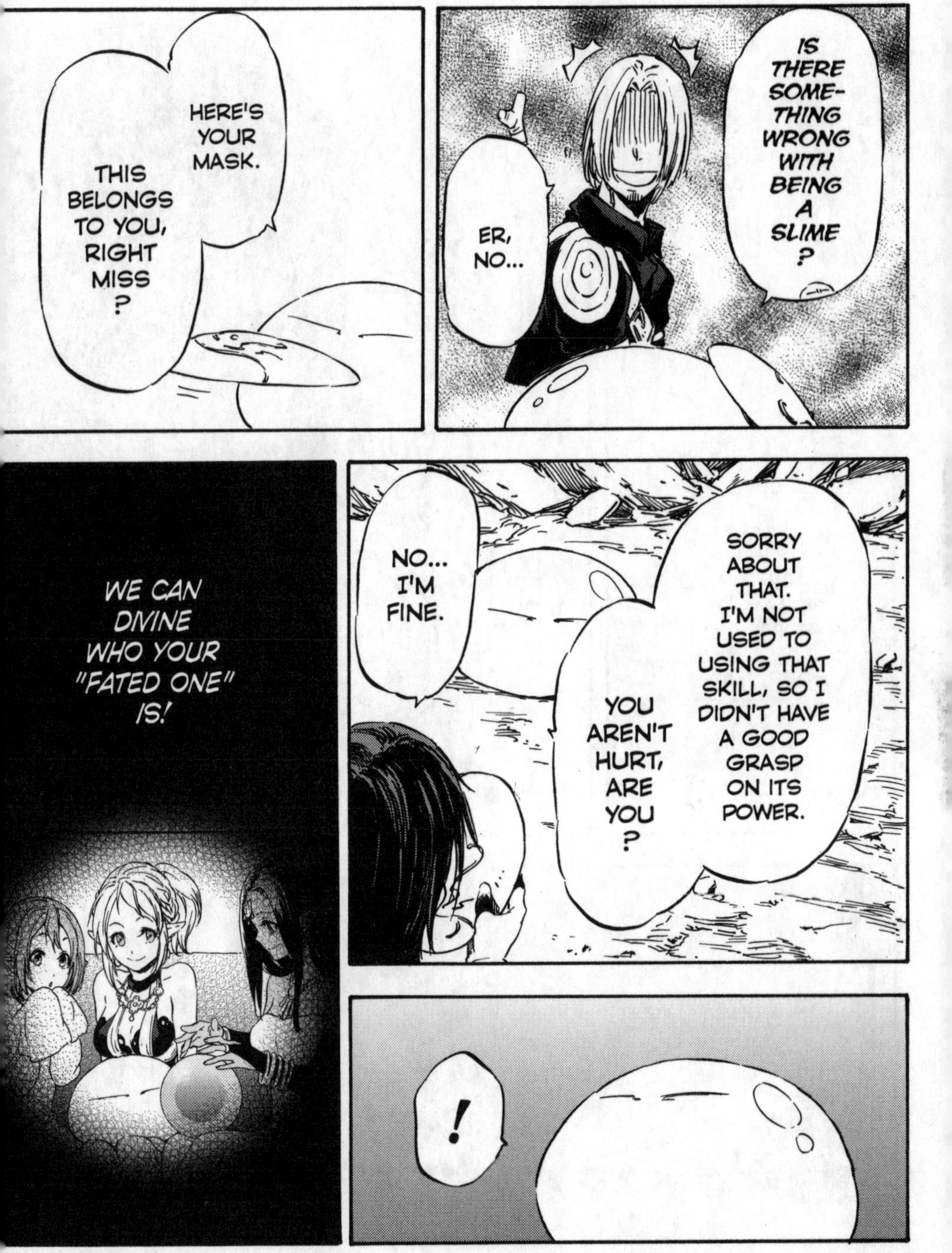
IS THERE SOMETHING WRONG WITH BEING A SLIME?
ER, NO...
HERE'S YOUR MASK.
THIS BELONGS TO YOU, RIGHT MISS?
SORRY ABOUT THAT. I'M NOT USED TO USING THAT SKILL, SO I DIDN'T HAVE A GOOD GRASP ON ITS POWER.
YOU AREN'T HURT, ARE YOU?
NO... I'M FINE.
!
WE CAN DIVINE WHO YOUR "FATED ONE" IS!

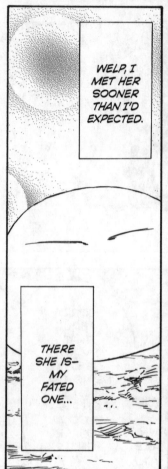

WELP, I MET HER SOONER THAN I'D EXPECTED.

THERE SHE IS— MY FATED ONE...

YOU SAVED ME.

THANK YOU.

UGHHH ...

THUMP

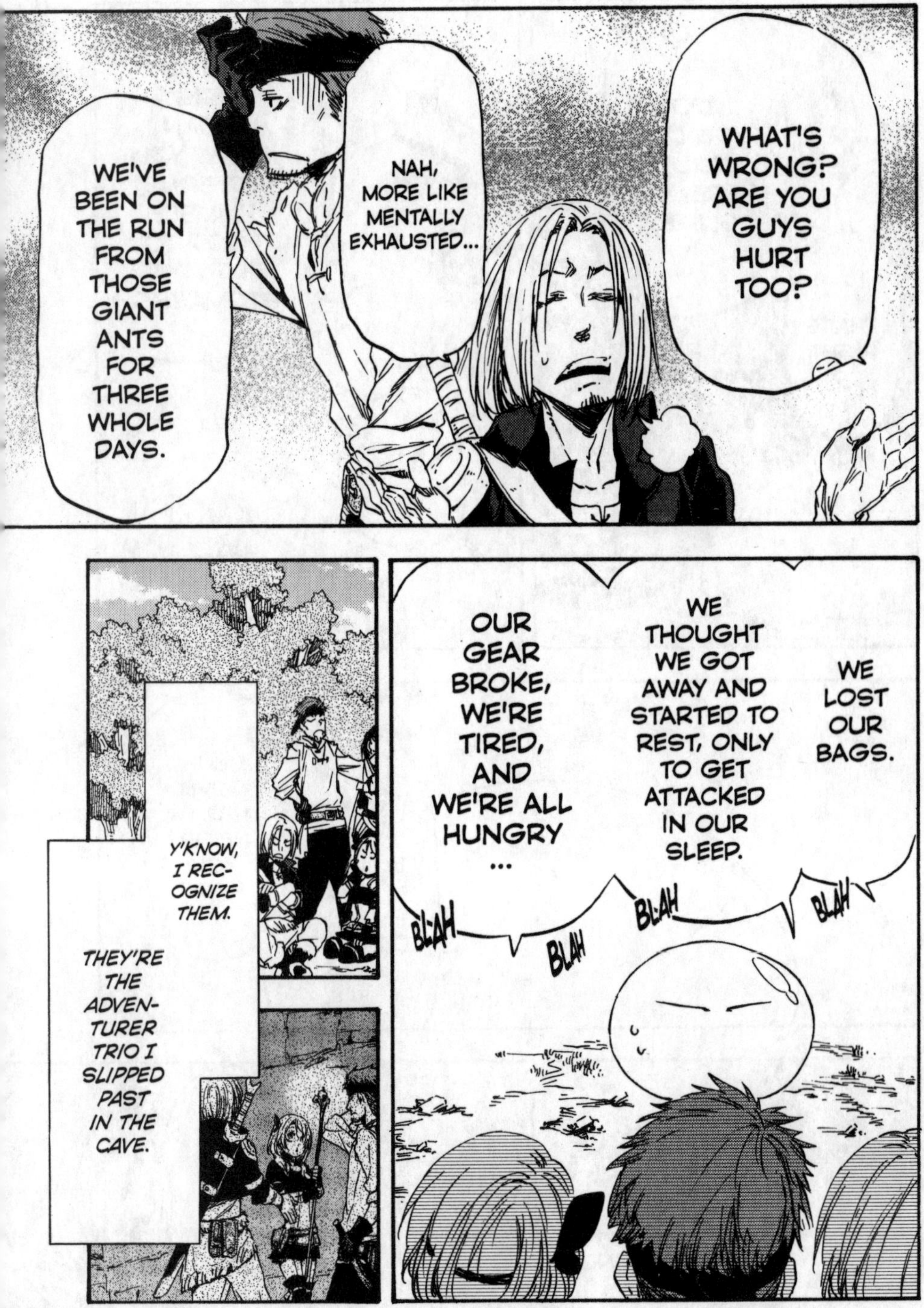
WHAT'S WRONG? ARE YOU GUYS HURT TOO?
NAH, MORE LIKE MENTALLY EXHAUSTED...
WE'VE BEEN ON THE RUN FROM THOSE GIANT ANTS FOR THREE WHOLE DAYS.
WE LOST OUR BAGS.
WE THOUGHT WE GOT AWAY AND STARTED TO REST, ONLY TO GET ATTACKED IN OUR SLEEP.
OUR GEAR BROKE, WE'RE TIRED, AND WE'RE ALL HUNGRY ...
BLAH
BLAH
BLAH
BLAH
Y'KNOW, I RECOGNIZE THEM.
THEY'RE THE ADVENTURER TRIO I SLIPPED PAST IN THE CAVE.

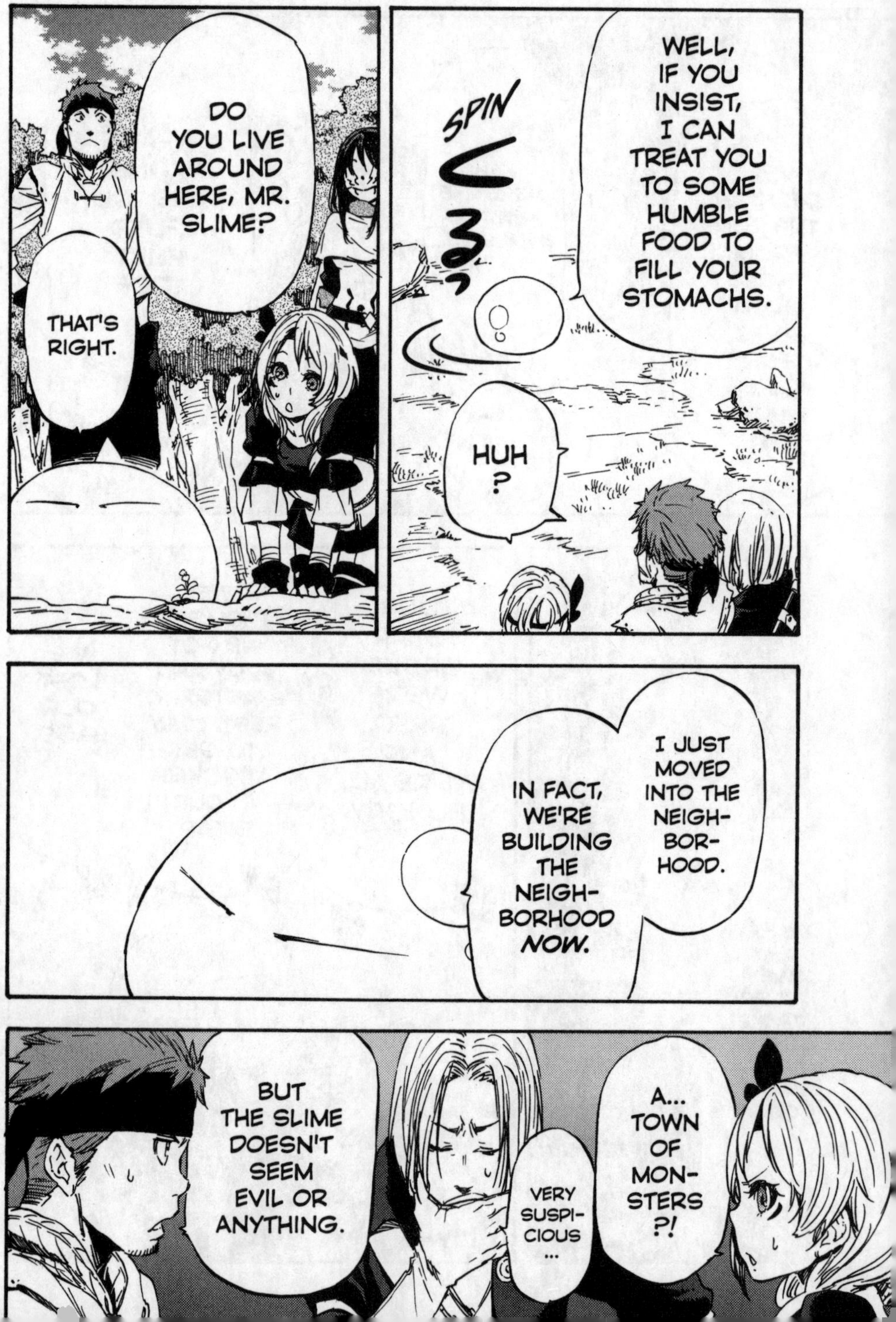

WELL, IF YOU INSIST, I CAN TREAT YOU TO SOME HUMBLE FOOD TO FILL YOUR STOMACHS.
SPIN
HUH?
DO YOU LIVE AROUND HERE, MR. SLIME?
THAT'S RIGHT.
I JUST MOVED INTO THE NEIGH-BOR-HOOD.
IN FACT, WE'RE BUILDING THE NEIGH-BORHOOD *NOW*.
A... TOWN OF MON-STERS?!
VERY SUSPI-CIOUS...
BUT THE SLIME DOESN'T SEEM EVIL OR ANYTHING.

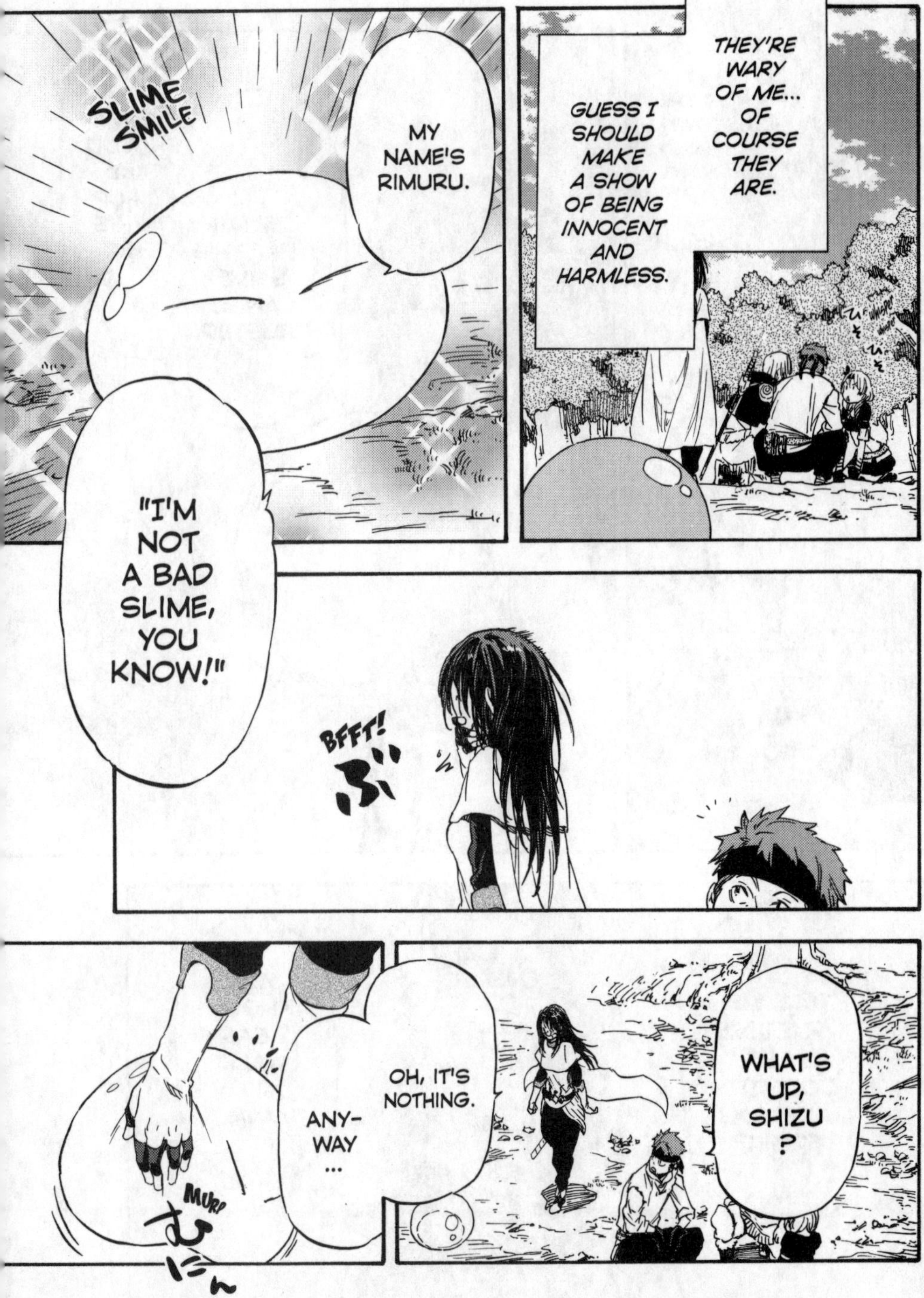

THEY'RE WARY OF ME... OF COURSE THEY ARE.
GUESS I SHOULD MAKE A SHOW OF BEING INNOCENT AND HARMLESS.
SLIME SMILE
MY NAME'S RIMURU.
"I'M NOT A BAD SLIME, YOU KNOW!"
BFFT!
ぶ
WHAT'S UP, SHIZU?
OH, IT'S NOTHING.
ANY-WAY ...

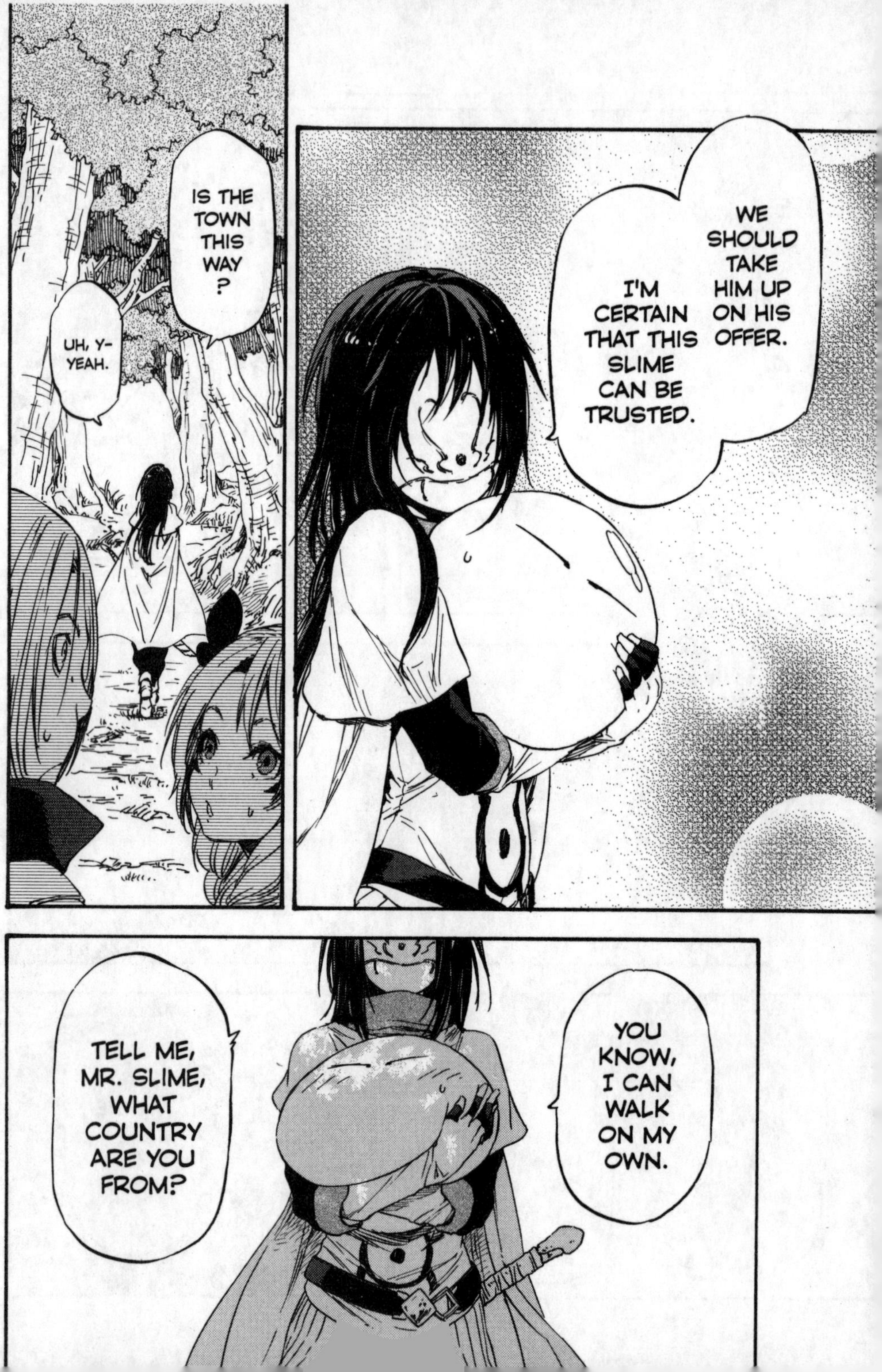
WE SHOULD TAKE HIM UP ON HIS OFFER.
I'M CERTAIN THAT THIS SLIME CAN BE TRUSTED.
IS THE TOWN THIS WAY ?
UH, Y-YEAH.
YOU KNOW, I CAN WALK ON MY OWN.
TELL ME, MR. SLIME, WHAT COUNTRY ARE YOU FROM?

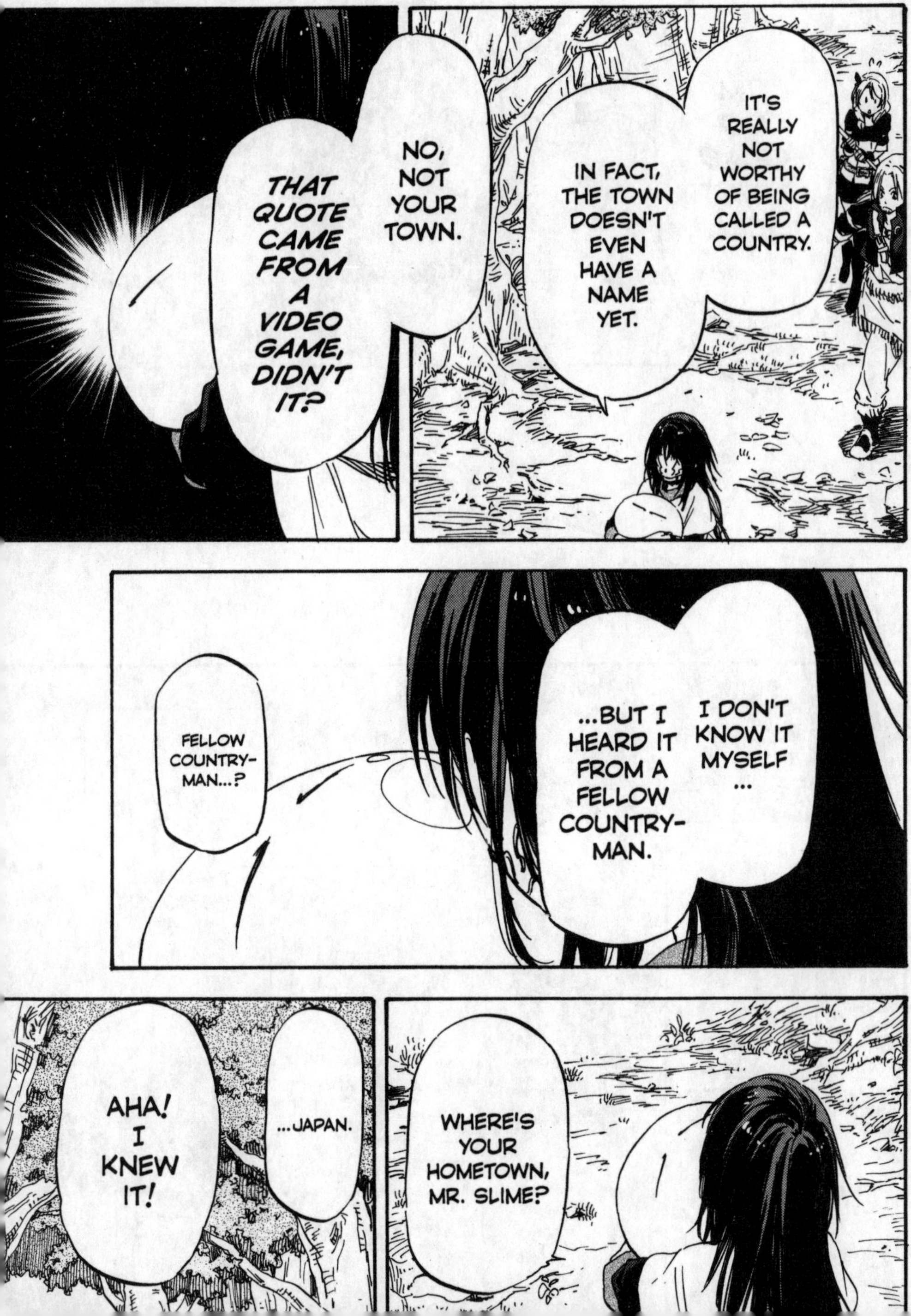
IT'S REALLY NOT WORTHY OF BEING CALLED A COUNTRY.
IN FACT, THE TOWN DOESN'T EVEN HAVE A NAME YET.
NO, NOT YOUR TOWN.
THAT QUOTE CAME FROM A VIDEO GAME, DIDN'T IT?
I DON'T KNOW IT MYSELF...
...BUT I HEARD IT FROM A FELLOW COUNTRYMAN.
FELLOW COUNTRYMAN...?
WHERE'S YOUR HOMETOWN, MR. SLIME?
...JAPAN.
AHA! I KNEW IT!

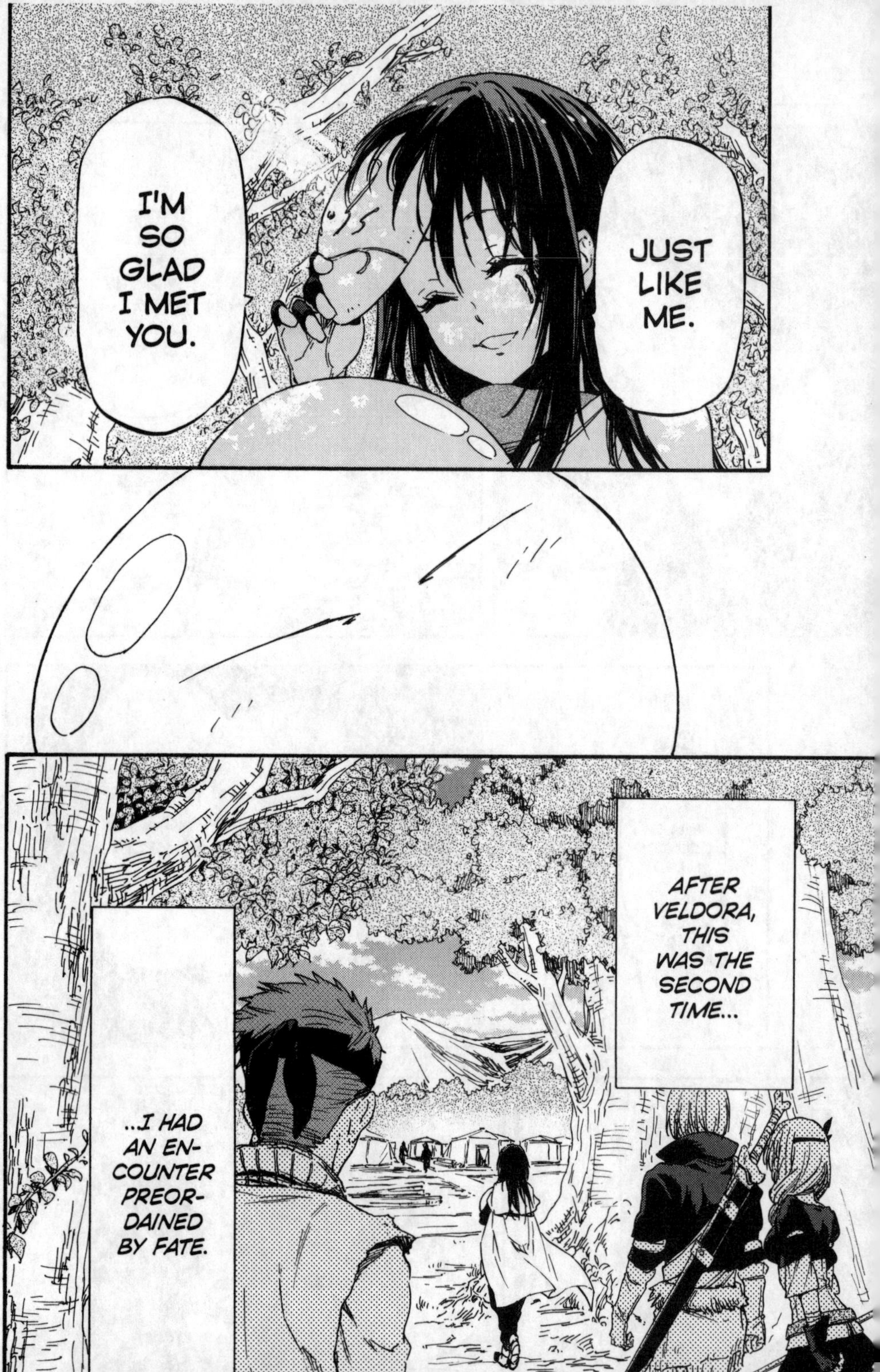
JUST LIKE ME.
I'M SO GLAD I MET YOU.
AFTER VELDORA, THIS WAS THE SECOND TIME...
...I HAD AN EN-COUNTER PREOR-DAINED BY FATE.

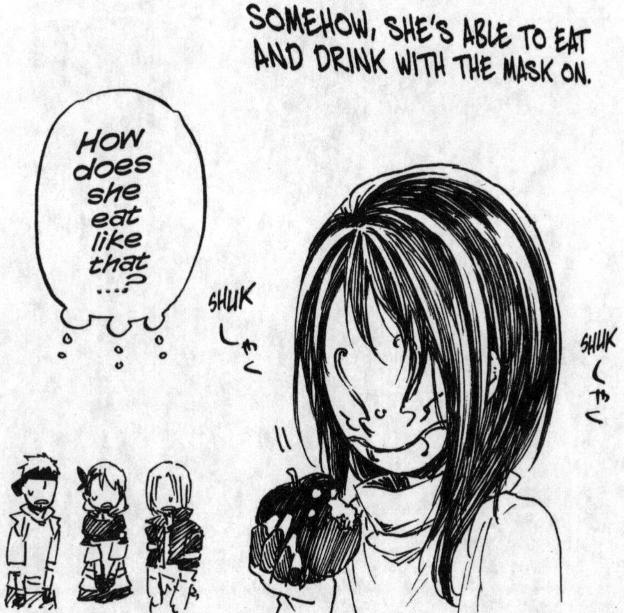
SOMEHOW, SHE'S ABLE TO EAT AND DRINK WITH THE MASK ON.
SHUK
しゃく
SHUK
しゃく
How does she eat like that ....?

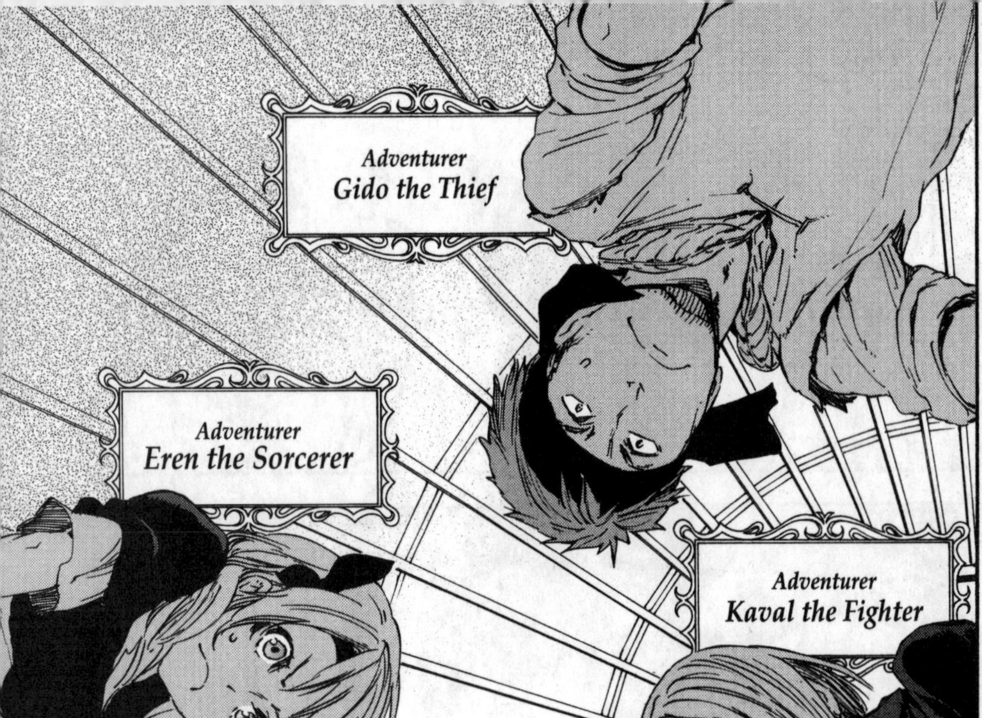
Adventurer
Gido the Thief
Adventurer
Kaval the Fighter
Adventurer
Eren the Sorcerer
CHAPTER 9 Demon of Flames

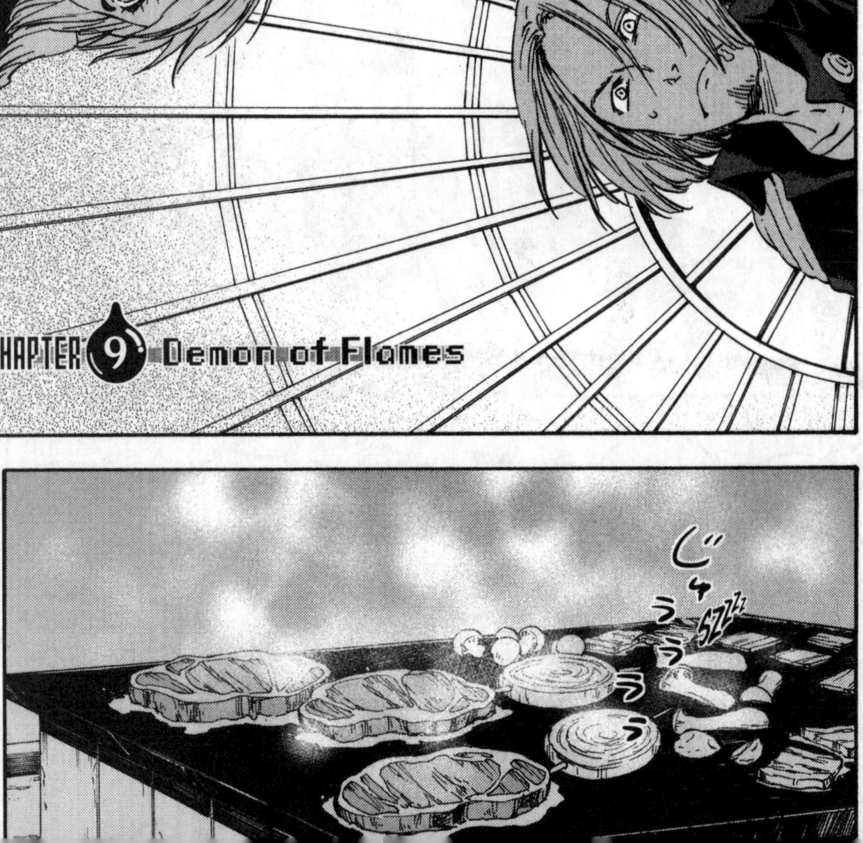
じゅうううう
SZZZZ

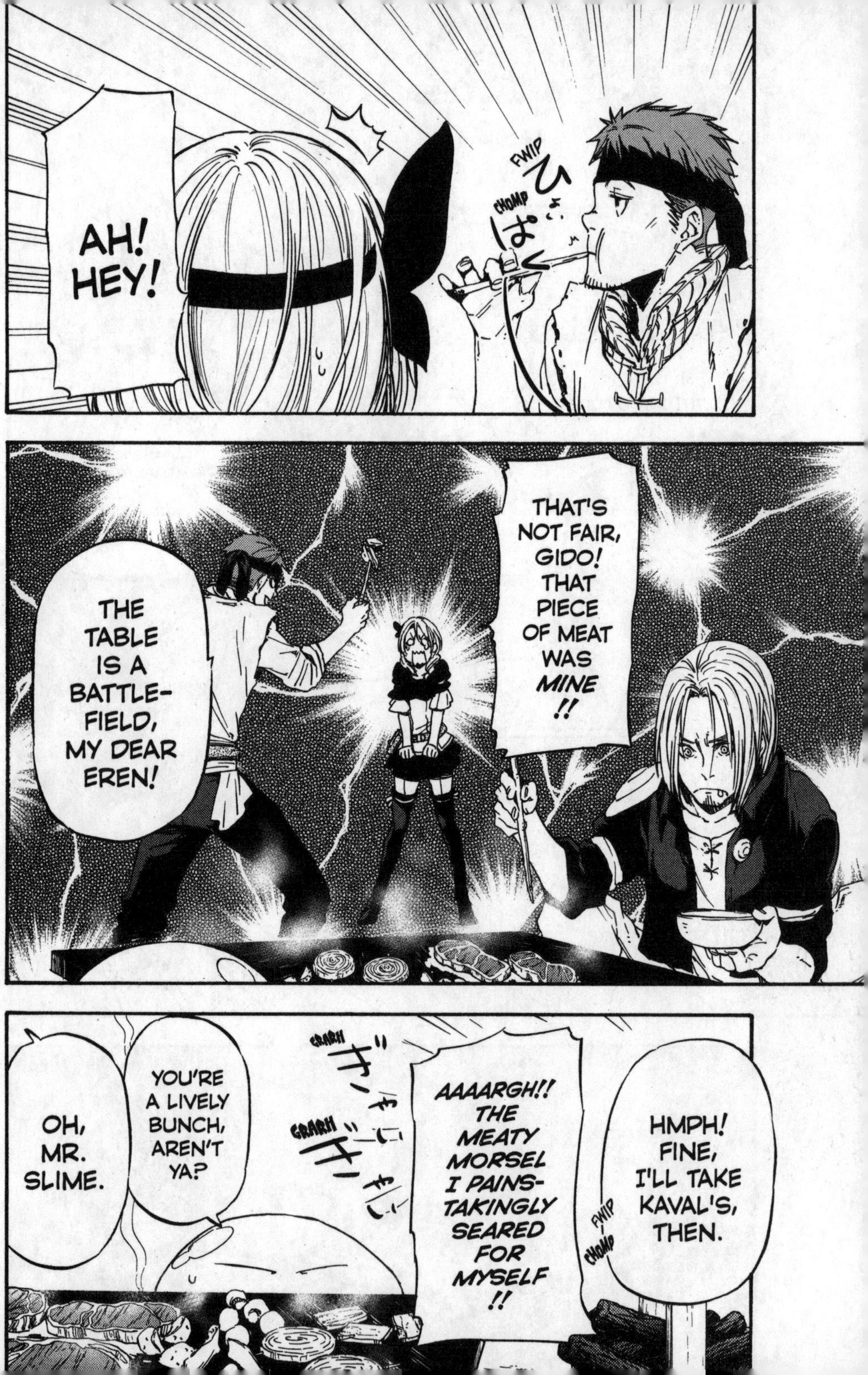
FWIP ひょい
CHOMP ぱく
AH! HEY!
THAT'S NOT FAIR, GIDO! THAT PIECE OF MEAT WAS *MINE*!!
THE TABLE IS A BATTLE-FIELD, MY DEAR EREN!
HMPH! FINE, I'LL TAKE KAVAL'S, THEN.
FWIP
CHOMP
AAAARGH!! THE MEATY MORSEL I PAINS-TAKINGLY SEARED FOR MYSELF!!
GRAAH
GRAAH
YOU'RE A LIVELY BUNCH, AREN'T YA?
OH, MR. SLIME.

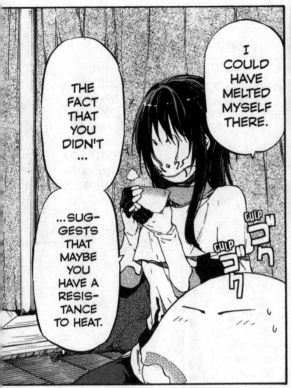

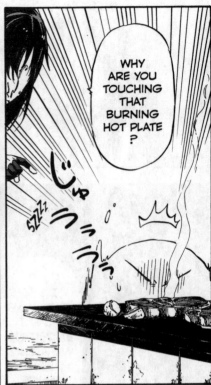

WHY ARE YOU TOUCHING THAT BURNING HOT PLATE?
じゅううう
SZZZZ
I COULD HAVE MELTED MYSELF THERE.
THE FACT THAT YOU DIDN'T...
...SUG-GESTS THAT MAYBE YOU HAVE A RESIS-TANCE TO HEAT.
GULP
ゴク
GULP
ゴク
RESIS-TANCE?
THOSE WHO PASS HERE FROM ANOTHER WORLD ARE GRANTED THE KIND OF POWER THAT THEY YEARNED FOR.
SOME-TIMES THEY'RE SKILLS, SOME-TIMES THEY'RE RESIS-TANCES.

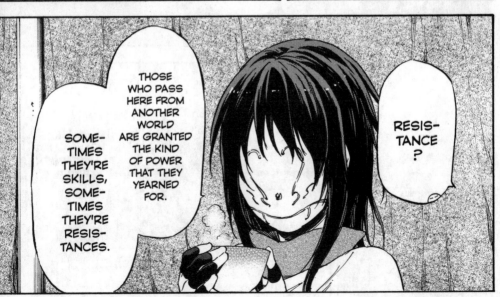

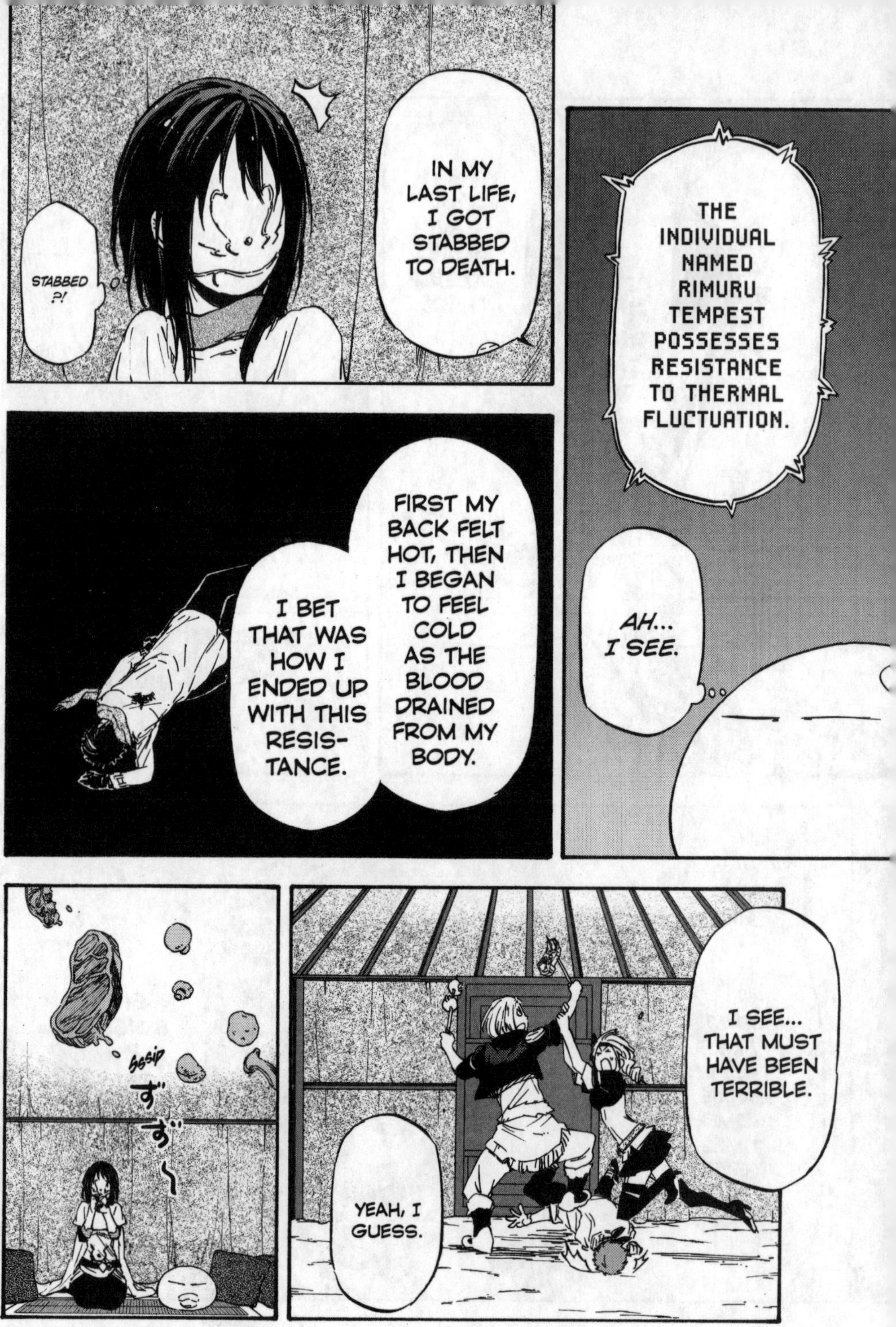
IN MY LAST LIFE, I GOT STABBED TO DEATH.
STABBED ?!
FIRST MY BACK FELT HOT, THEN I BEGAN TO FEEL COLD AS THE BLOOD DRAINED FROM MY BODY.
I BET THAT WAS HOW I ENDED UP WITH THIS RESIS-TANCE.
THE INDIVIDUAL NAMED RIMURU TEMPEST POSSESSES RESISTANCE TO THERMAL FLUCTUATION.
AH... I SEE.
I SEE... THAT MUST HAVE BEEN TERRIBLE.
YEAH, I GUESS.
SSSIP
ずず~

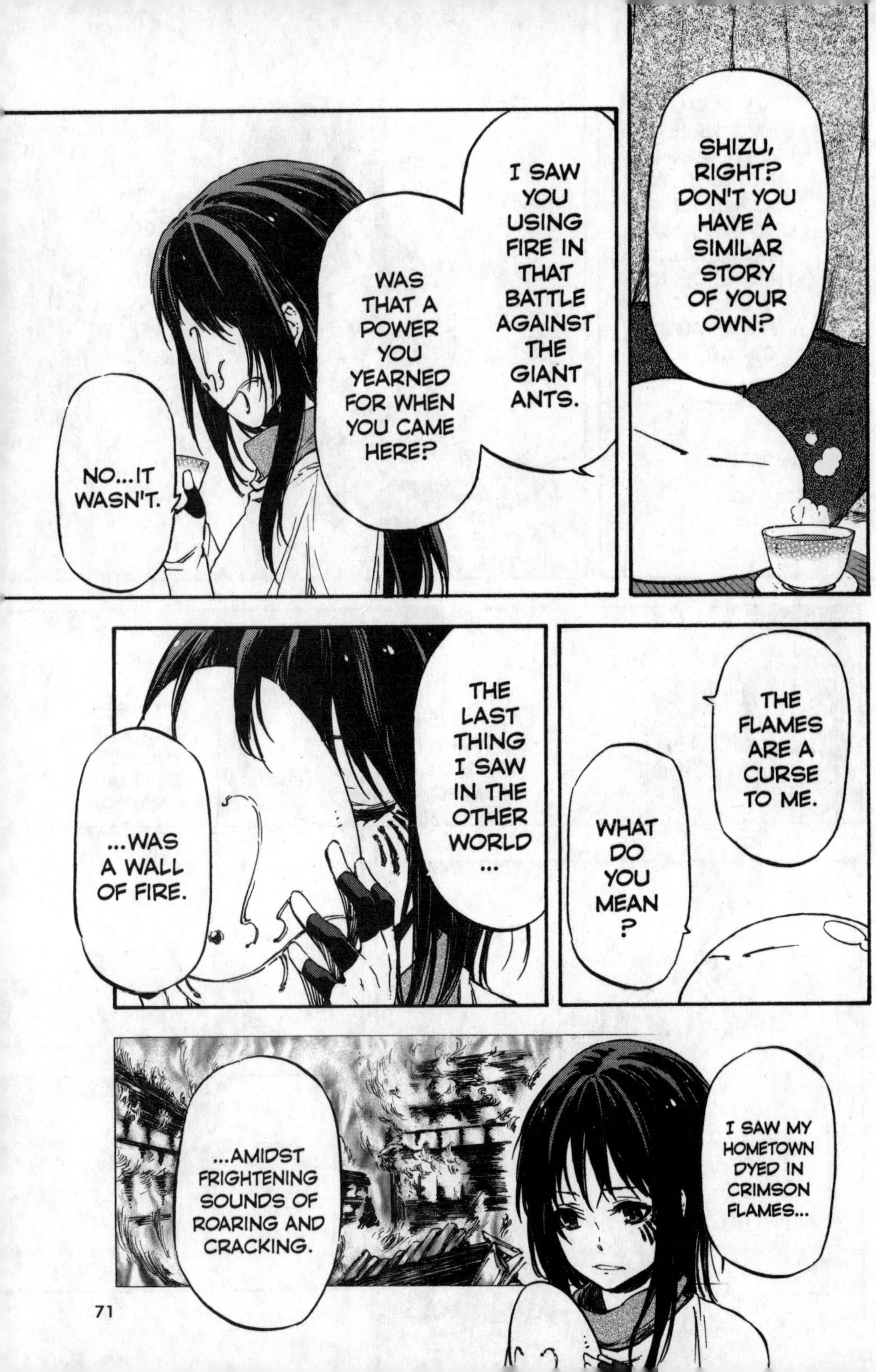
SHIZU, RIGHT? DON'T YOU HAVE A SIMILAR STORY OF YOUR OWN?
I SAW YOU USING FIRE IN THAT BATTLE AGAINST THE GIANT ANTS.
WAS THAT A POWER YOU YEARNED FOR WHEN YOU CAME HERE?
NO...IT WASN'T.
THE FLAMES ARE A CURSE TO ME.
WHAT DO YOU MEAN?
THE LAST THING I SAW IN THE OTHER WORLD...
...WAS A WALL OF FIRE.
I SAW MY HOMETOWN DYED IN CRIMSON FLAMES...
...AMIDST FRIGHTENING SOUNDS OF ROARING AND CRACKING.

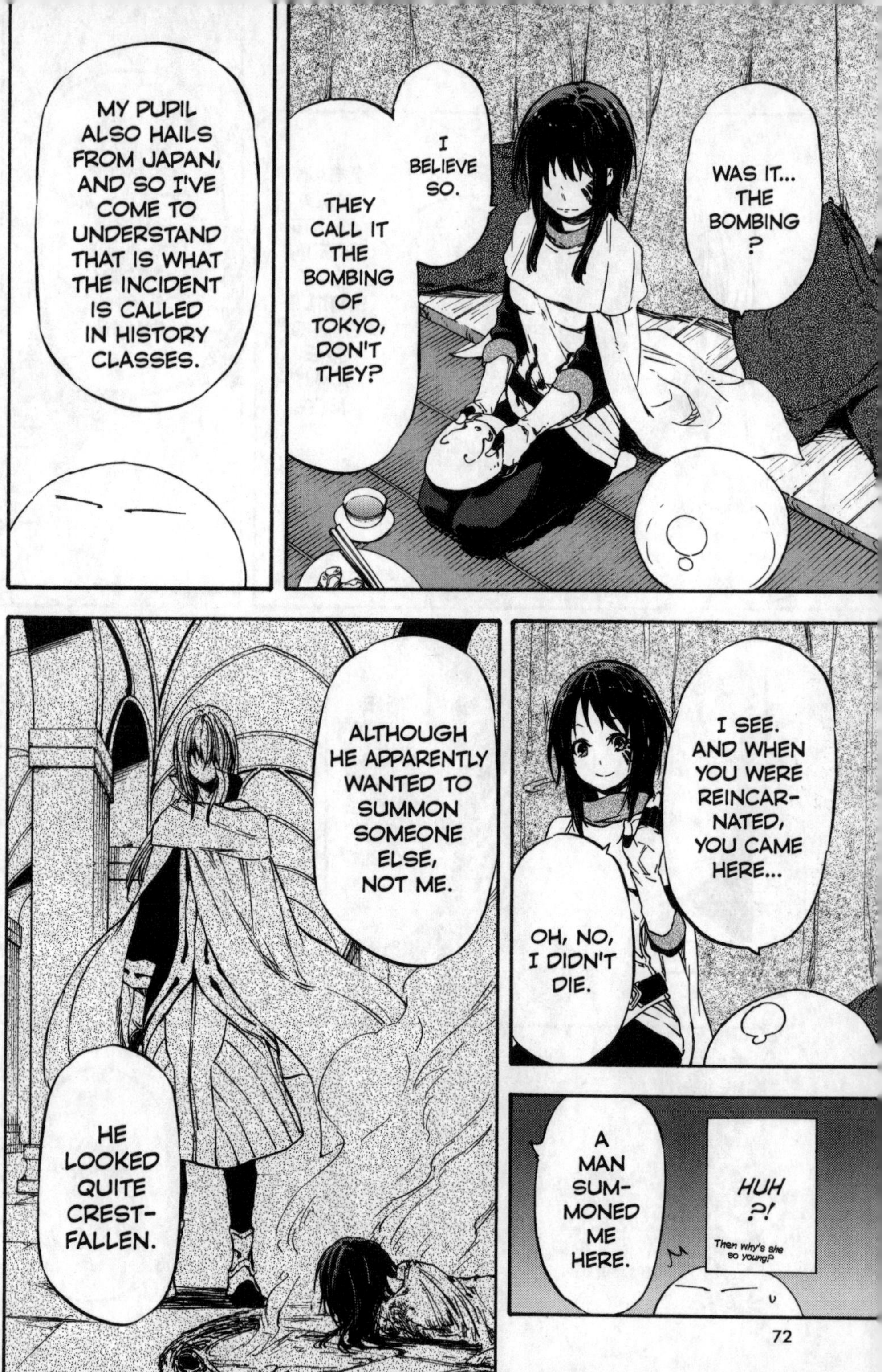
WAS IT... THE BOMBING?
I BELIEVE SO.
THEY CALL IT THE BOMBING OF TOKYO, DON'T THEY?
MY PUPIL ALSO HAILS FROM JAPAN, AND SO I'VE COME TO UNDERSTAND THAT IS WHAT THE INCIDENT IS CALLED IN HISTORY CLASSES.
I SEE. AND WHEN YOU WERE REINCAR-NATED, YOU CAME HERE...
OH, NO, I DIDN'T DIE.
A MAN SUM-MONED ME HERE.
HUH?!
Then why's she so young?
ALTHOUGH HE APPARENTLY WANTED TO SUMMON SOMEONE ELSE, NOT ME.
HE LOOKED QUITE CREST-FALLEN.

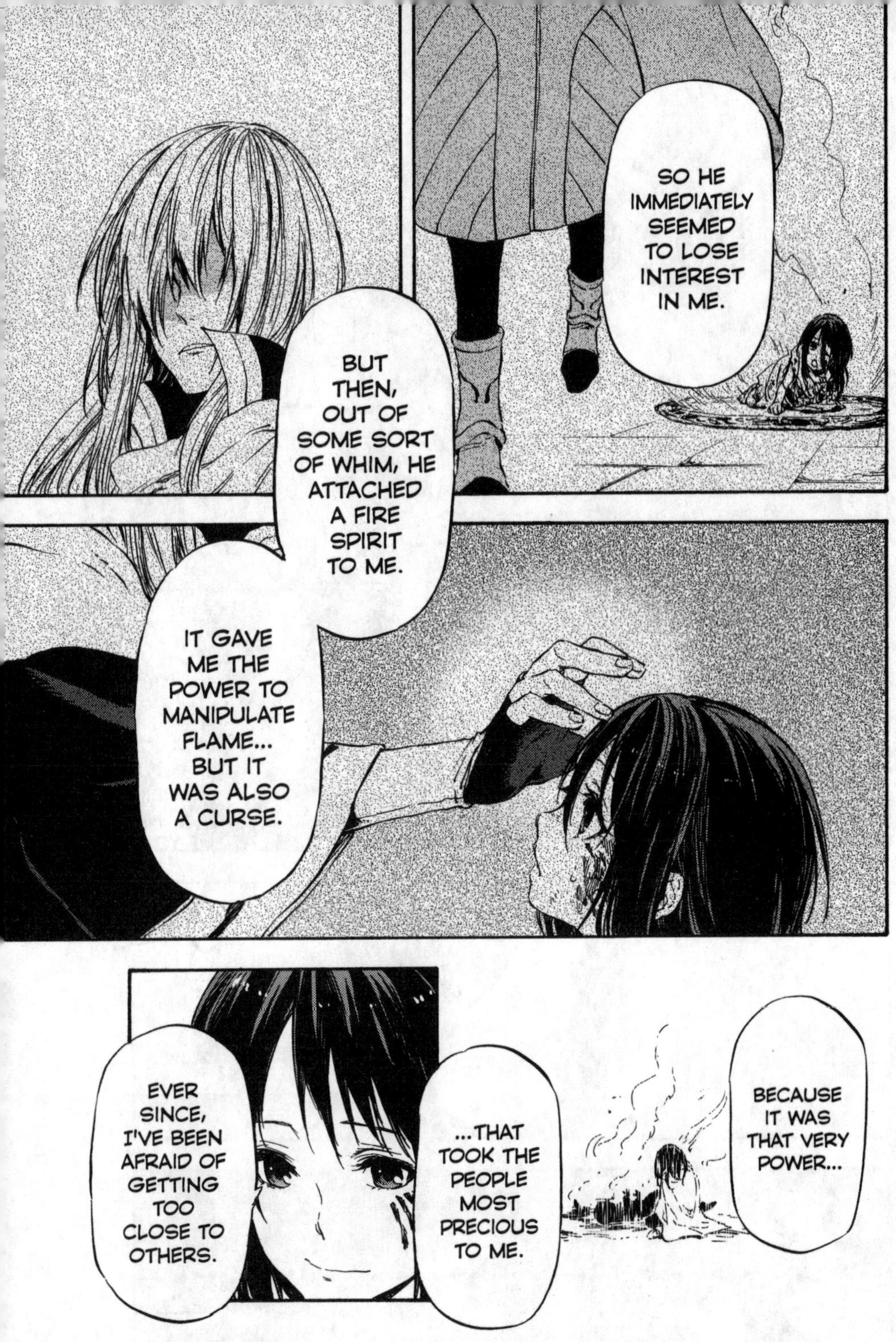
SO HE IMMEDIATELY SEEMED TO LOSE INTEREST IN ME.
BUT THEN, OUT OF SOME SORT OF WHIM, HE ATTACHED A FIRE SPIRIT TO ME.
IT GAVE ME THE POWER TO MANIPULATE FLAME... BUT IT WAS ALSO A CURSE.
BECAUSE IT WAS THAT VERY POWER...
...THAT TOOK THE PEOPLE MOST PRECIOUS TO ME.
EVER SINCE, I'VE BEEN AFRAID OF GETTING TOO CLOSE TO OTHERS.

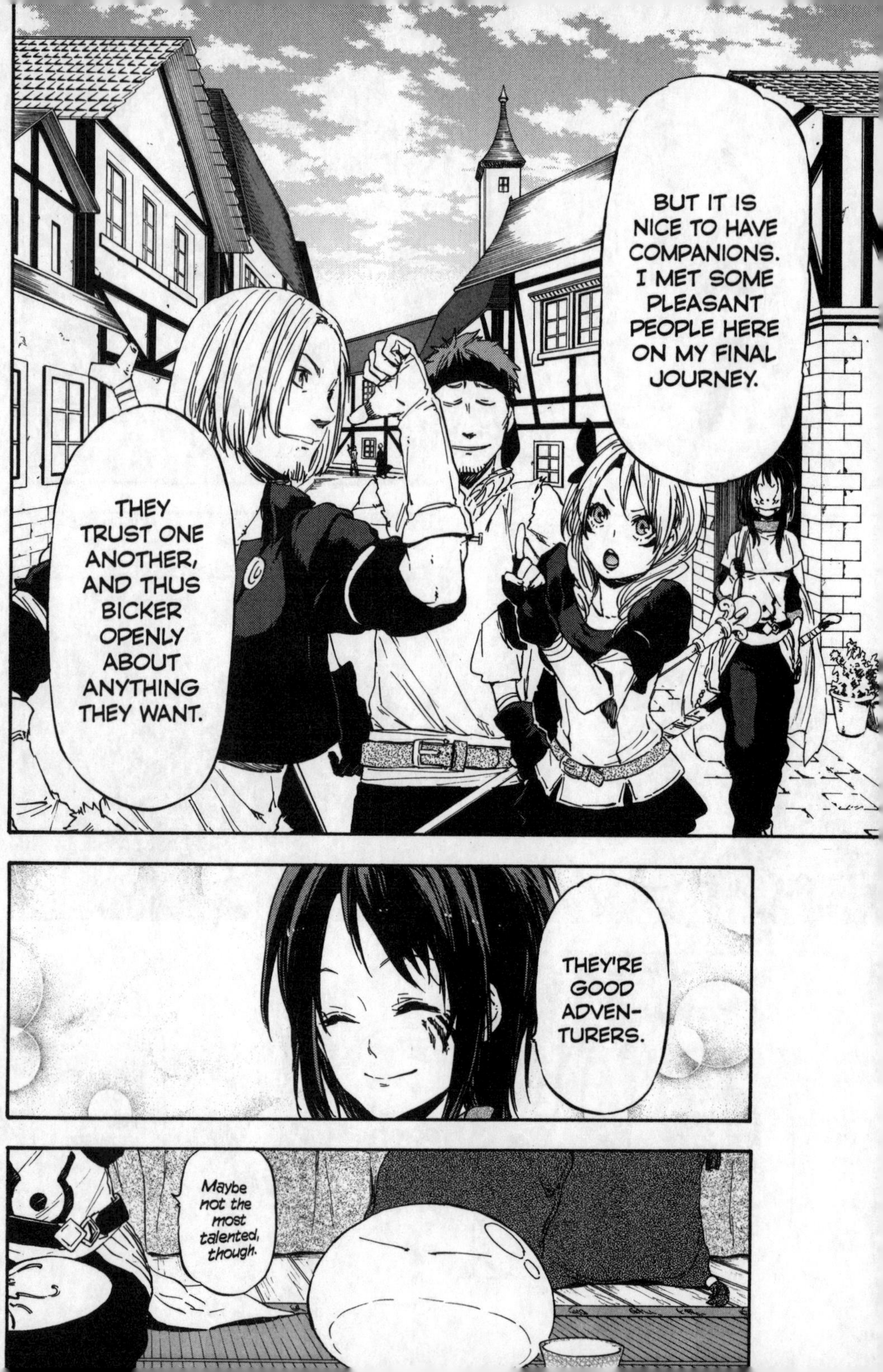
BUT IT IS NICE TO HAVE COMPANIONS. I MET SOME PLEASANT PEOPLE HERE ON MY FINAL JOURNEY.
THEY TRUST ONE ANOTHER, AND THUS BICKER OPENLY ABOUT ANYTHING THEY WANT.
THEY'RE GOOD ADVEN-TURERS.
Maybe not the most talented, though.

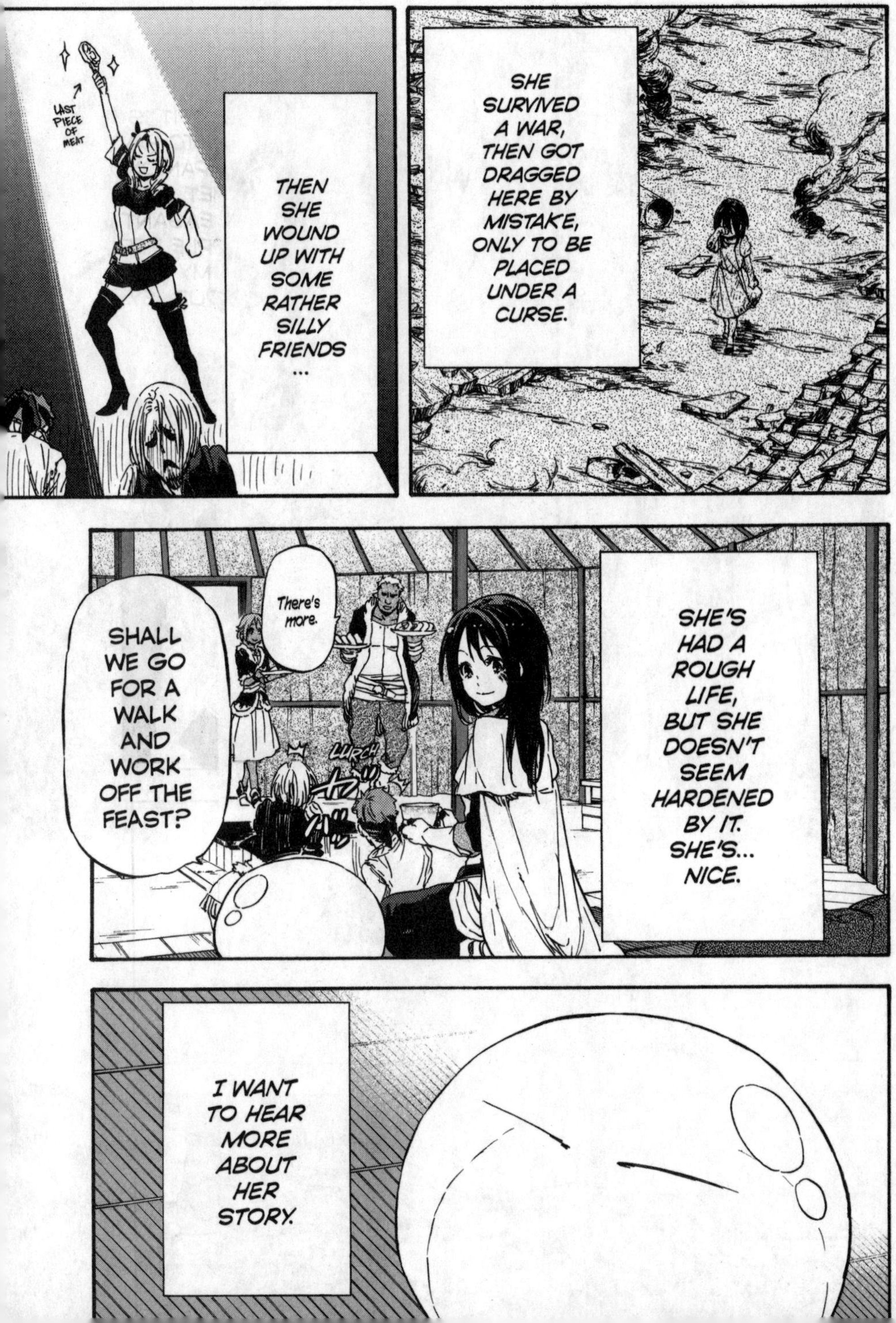
SHE SURVIVED A WAR, THEN GOT DRAGGED HERE BY MISTAKE, ONLY TO BE PLACED UNDER A CURSE.
LAST PIECE OF MEAT
THEN SHE WOUND UP WITH SOME RATHER SILLY FRIENDS...
SHE'S HAD A ROUGH LIFE, BUT SHE DOESN'T SEEM HARDENED BY IT. SHE'S... NICE.
There's more.
LURCH
SHALL WE GO FOR A WALK AND WORK OFF THE FEAST?
I WANT TO HEAR MORE ABOUT HER STORY.

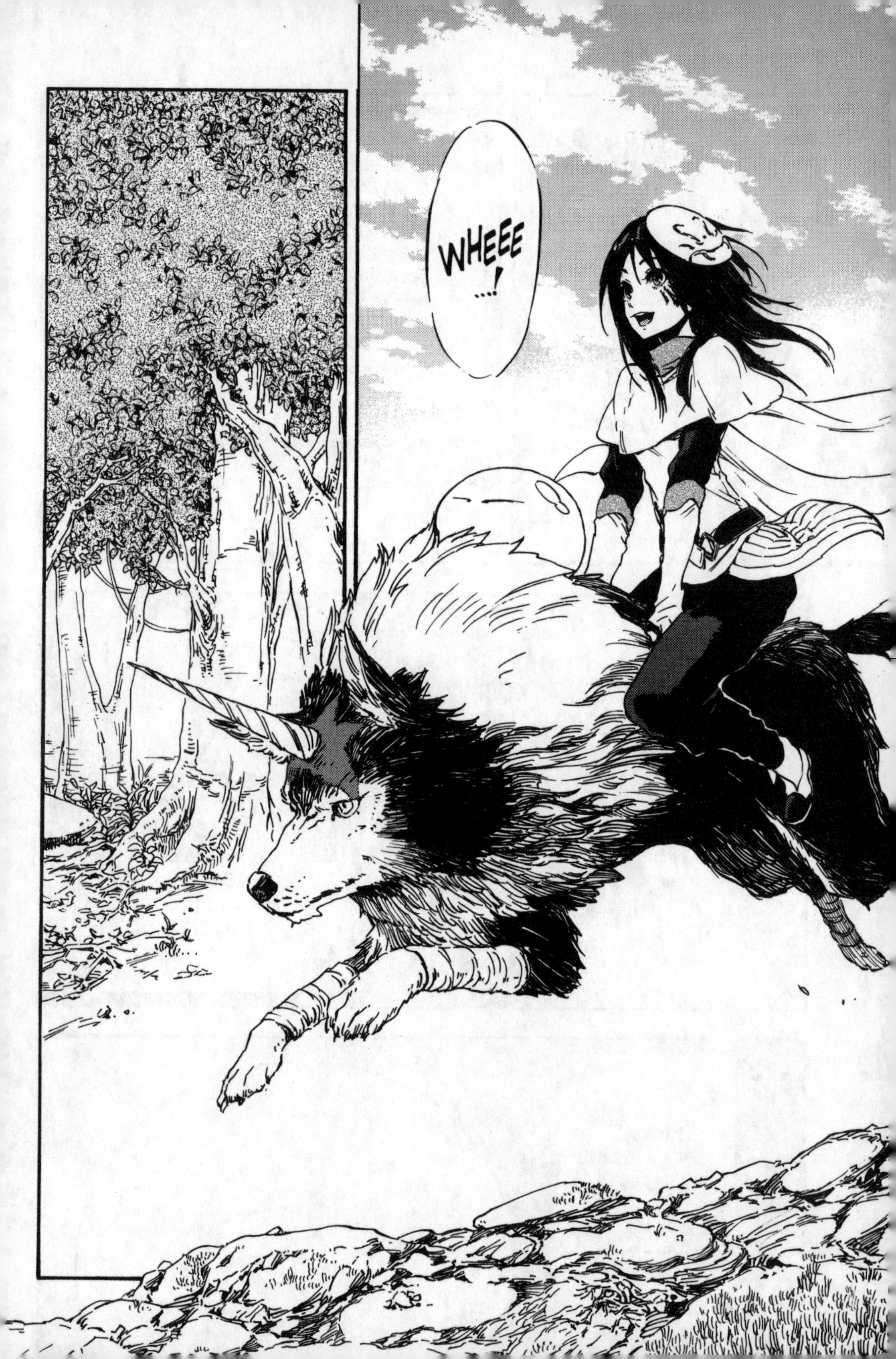
WHEEE
...!

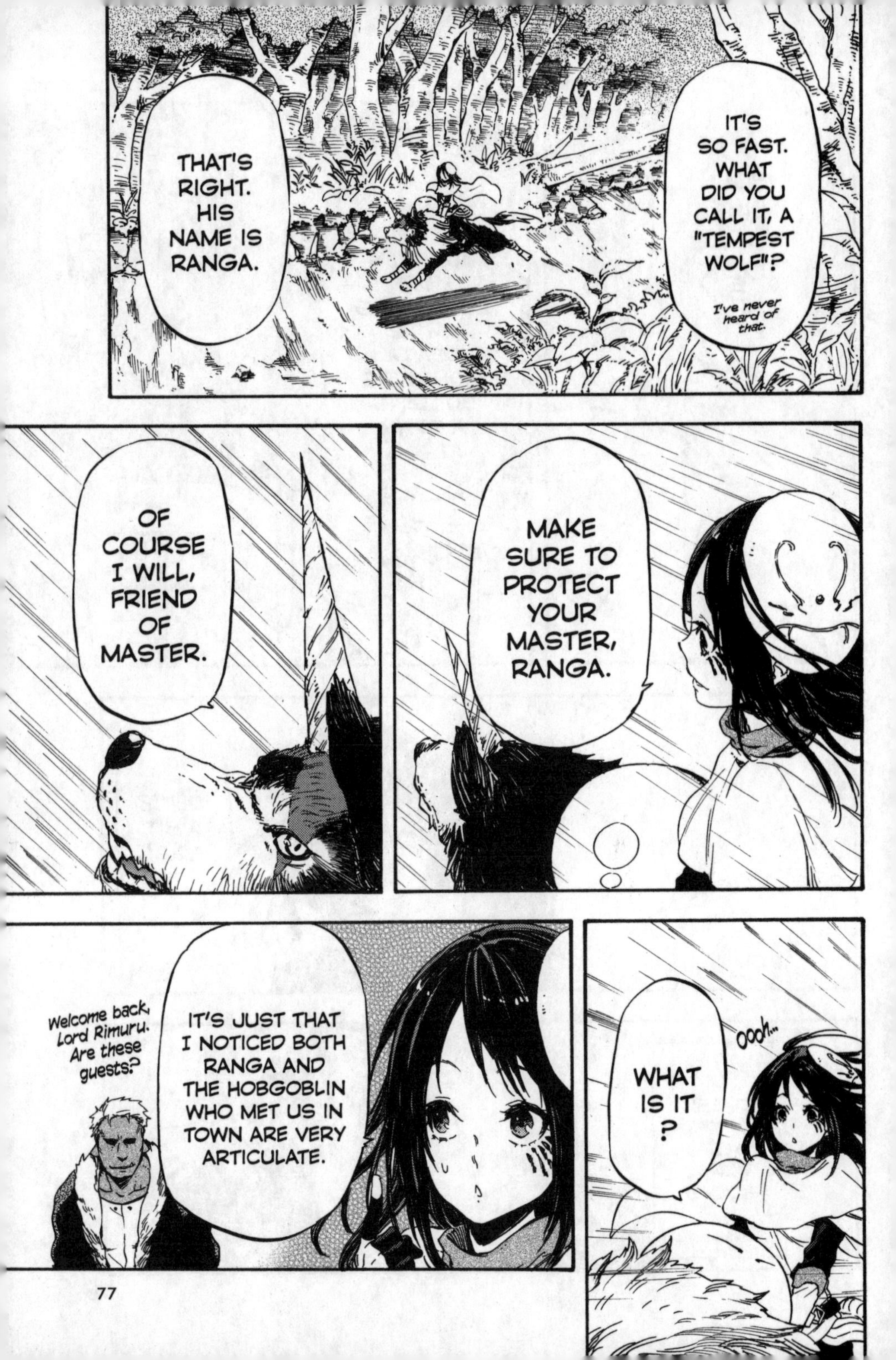

IT'S SO FAST. WHAT DID YOU CALL IT, A "TEMPEST WOLF"?
I've never heard of that.
THAT'S RIGHT. HIS NAME IS RANGA.
MAKE SURE TO PROTECT YOUR MASTER, RANGA.
OF COURSE I WILL, FRIEND OF MASTER.
Oooh...
WHAT IS IT ?
IT'S JUST THAT I NOTICED BOTH RANGA AND THE HOBGOBLIN WHO MET US IN TOWN ARE VERY ARTICULATE.
Welcome back, Lord Rimuru. Are these guests?

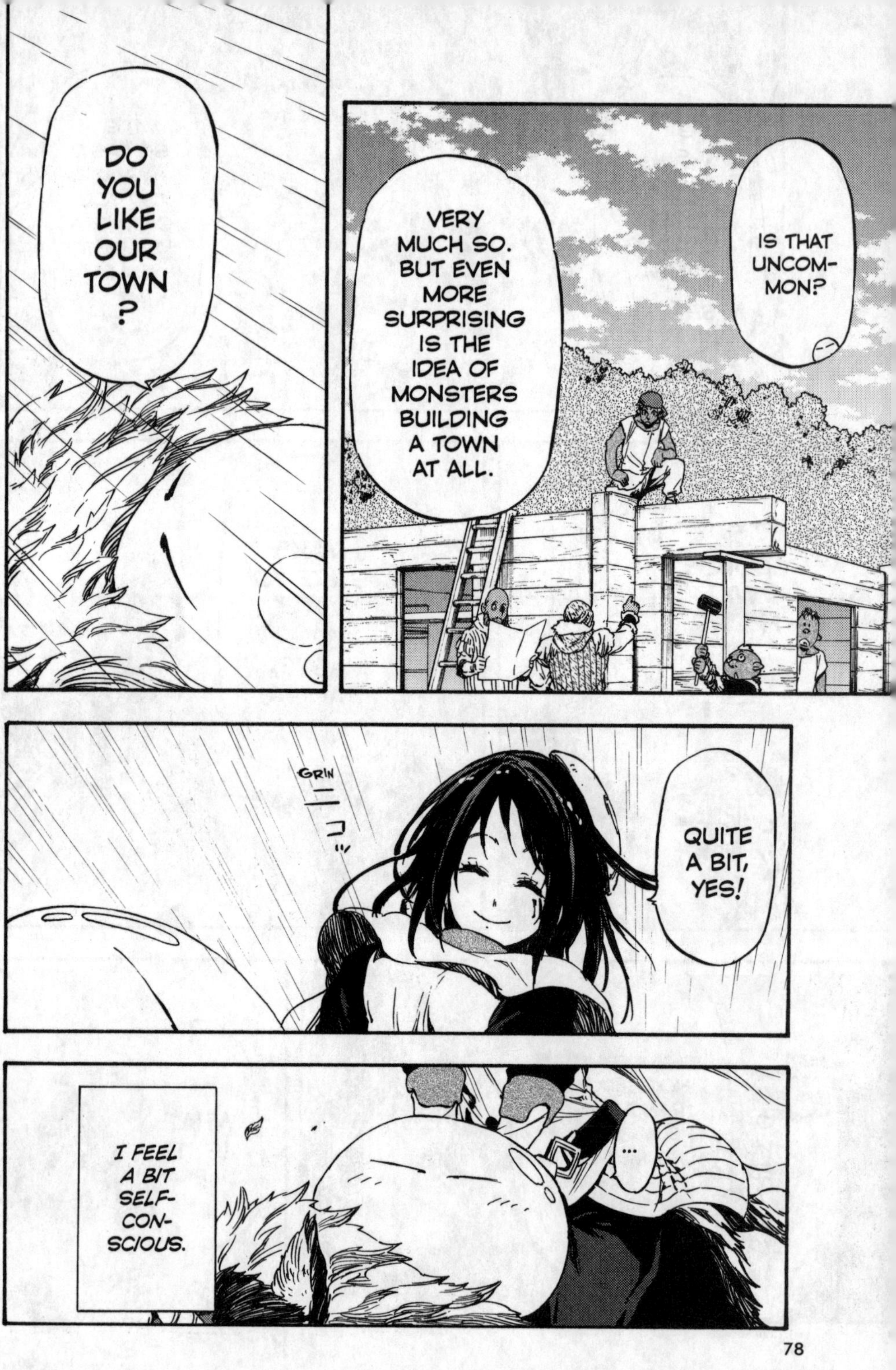
DO YOU LIKE OUR TOWN?
VERY MUCH SO. BUT EVEN MORE SURPRISING IS THE IDEA OF MONSTERS BUILDING A TOWN AT ALL.
IS THAT UNCOMMON?
GRIN
QUITE A BIT, YES!
...
I FEEL A BIT SELF-CONSCIOUS.

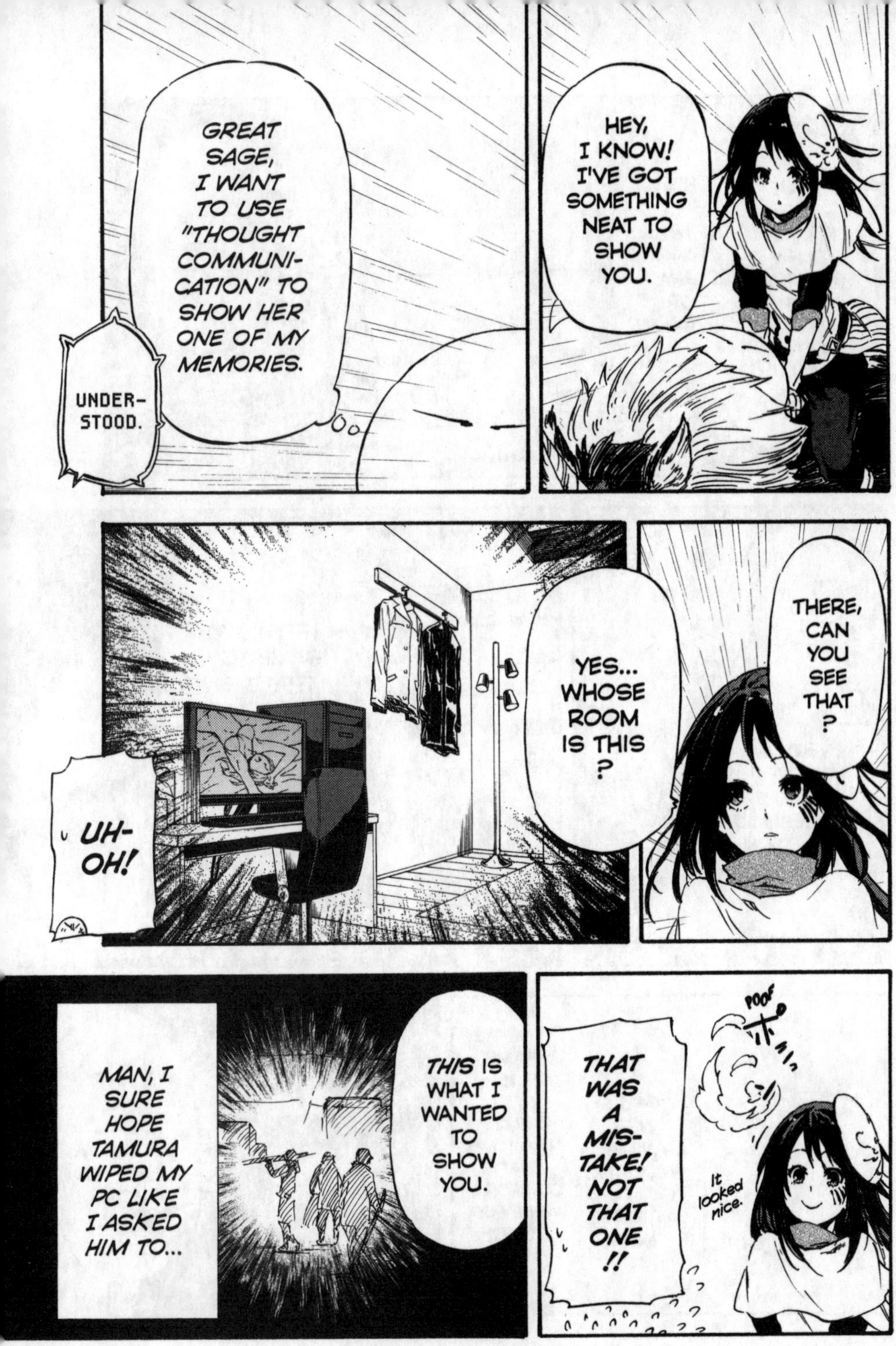
HEY, I KNOW! I'VE GOT SOMETHING NEAT TO SHOW YOU.
GREAT SAGE, I WANT TO USE "THOUGHT COMMUNICATION" TO SHOW HER ONE OF MY MEMORIES.
UNDER-STOOD.
THERE, CAN YOU SEE THAT?
YES... WHOSE ROOM IS THIS?
UH-OH!
POOF
THAT WAS A MIS-TAKE! NOT THAT ONE!!
It looked nice.
THIS IS WHAT I WANTED TO SHOW YOU.
MAN, I SURE HOPE TAMURA WIPED MY PC LIKE I ASKED HIM TO...

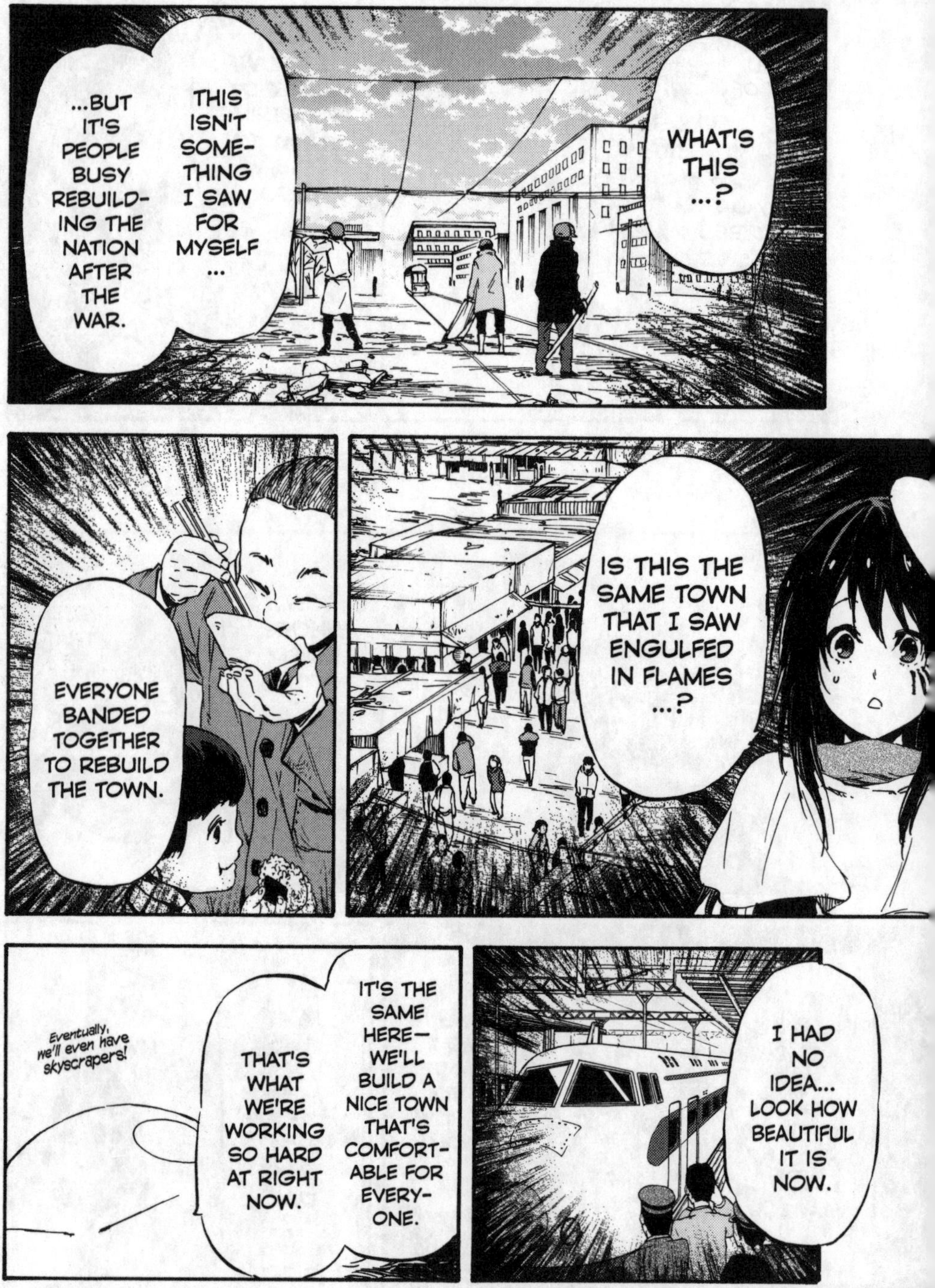
WHAT'S THIS ...?
THIS ISN'T SOMETHING I SAW FOR MYSELF ...
...BUT IT'S PEOPLE BUSY REBUILDING THE NATION AFTER THE WAR.
IS THIS THE SAME TOWN THAT I SAW ENGULFED IN FLAMES ...?
EVERYONE BANDED TOGETHER TO REBUILD THE TOWN.
I HAD NO IDEA... LOOK HOW BEAUTIFUL IT IS NOW.
IT'S THE SAME HERE— WE'LL BUILD A NICE TOWN THAT'S COMFORTABLE FOR EVERYONE.
THAT'S WHAT WE'RE WORKING SO HARD AT RIGHT NOW.
Eventually, we'll even have skyscrapers!

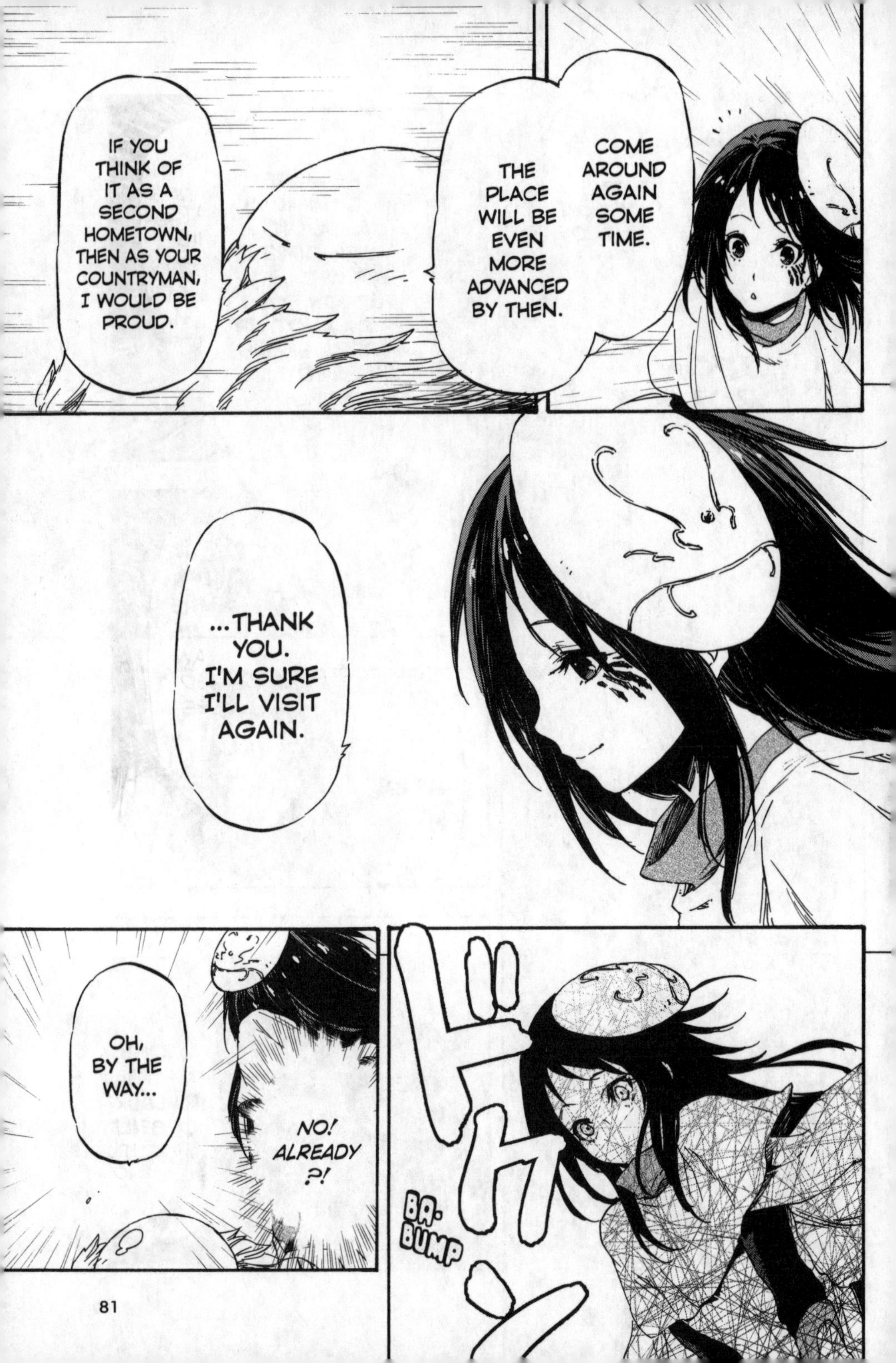
COME AROUND AGAIN SOME TIME.
THE PLACE WILL BE EVEN MORE ADVANCED BY THEN.
IF YOU THINK OF IT AS A SECOND HOMETOWN, THEN AS YOUR COUNTRYMAN, I WOULD BE PROUD.
...THANK YOU. I'M SURE I'LL VISIT AGAIN.
BA-BUMP
OH, BY THE WAY...
NO! ALREADY?!

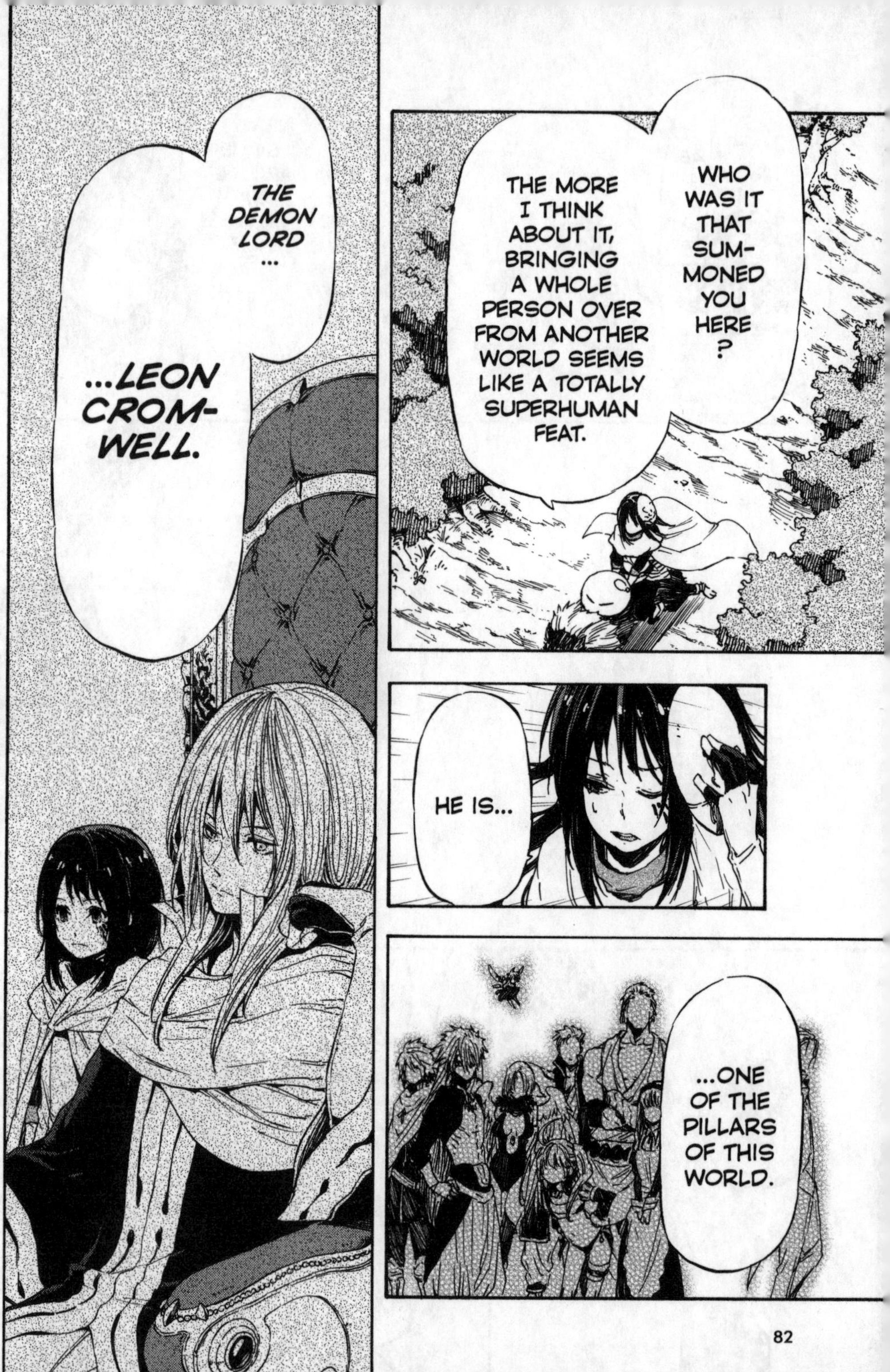
WHO WAS IT THAT SUMMONED YOU HERE?
THE MORE I THINK ABOUT IT, BRINGING A WHOLE PERSON OVER FROM ANOTHER WORLD SEEMS LIKE A TOTALLY SUPERHUMAN FEAT.
HE IS...
...ONE OF THE PILLARS OF THIS WORLD.
THE DEMON LORD...
...LEON CROMWELL.

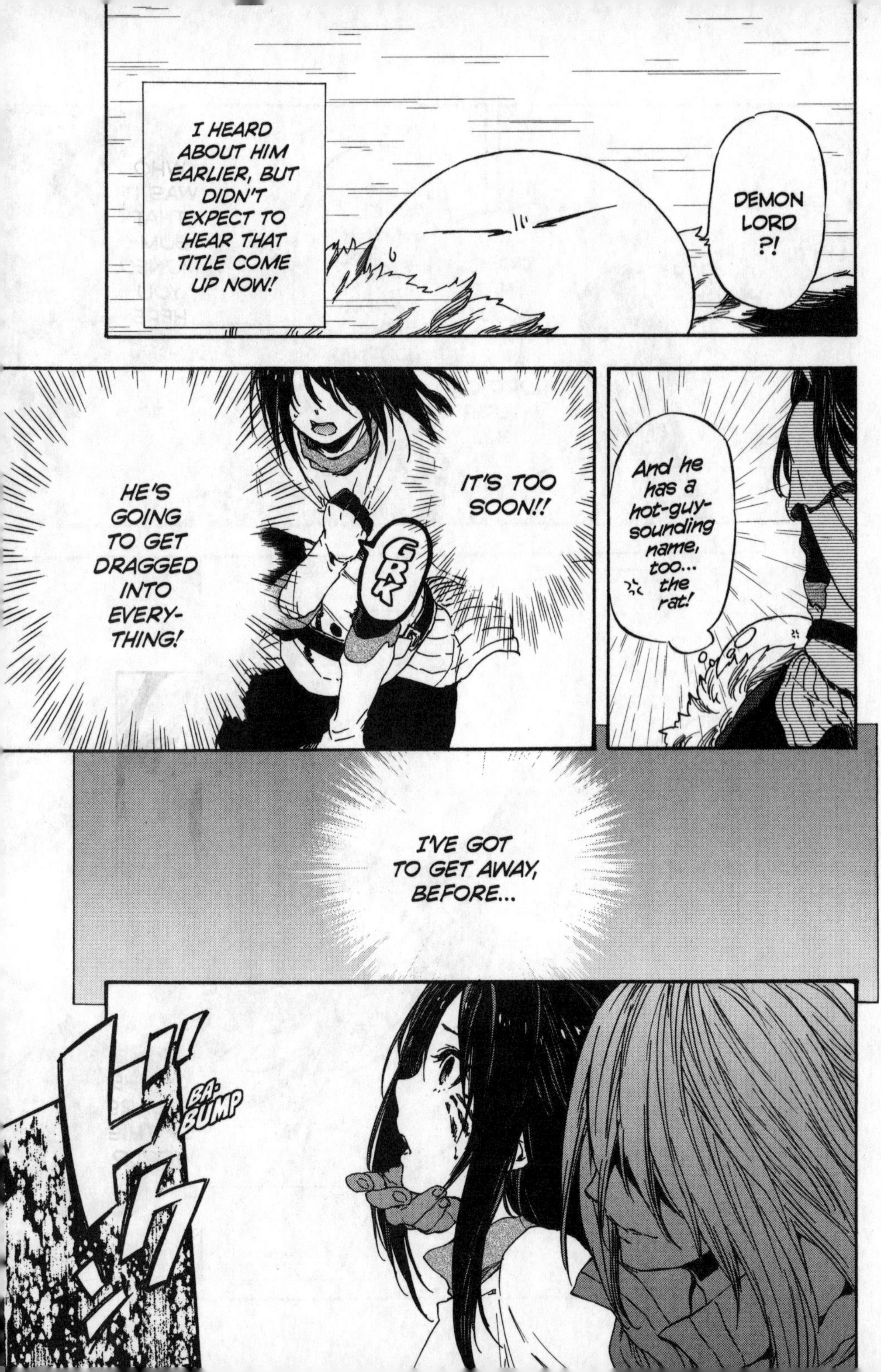
DEMON LORD ?!
I HEARD ABOUT HIM EARLIER, BUT DIDN'T EXPECT TO HEAR THAT TITLE COME UP NOW!
And he has a hot-guy-sounding name, too... the rat!
IT'S TOO SOON!!
GRK
HE'S GOING TO GET DRAGGED INTO EVERYTHING!
I'VE GOT TO GET AWAY, BEFORE...
BA-BUMP

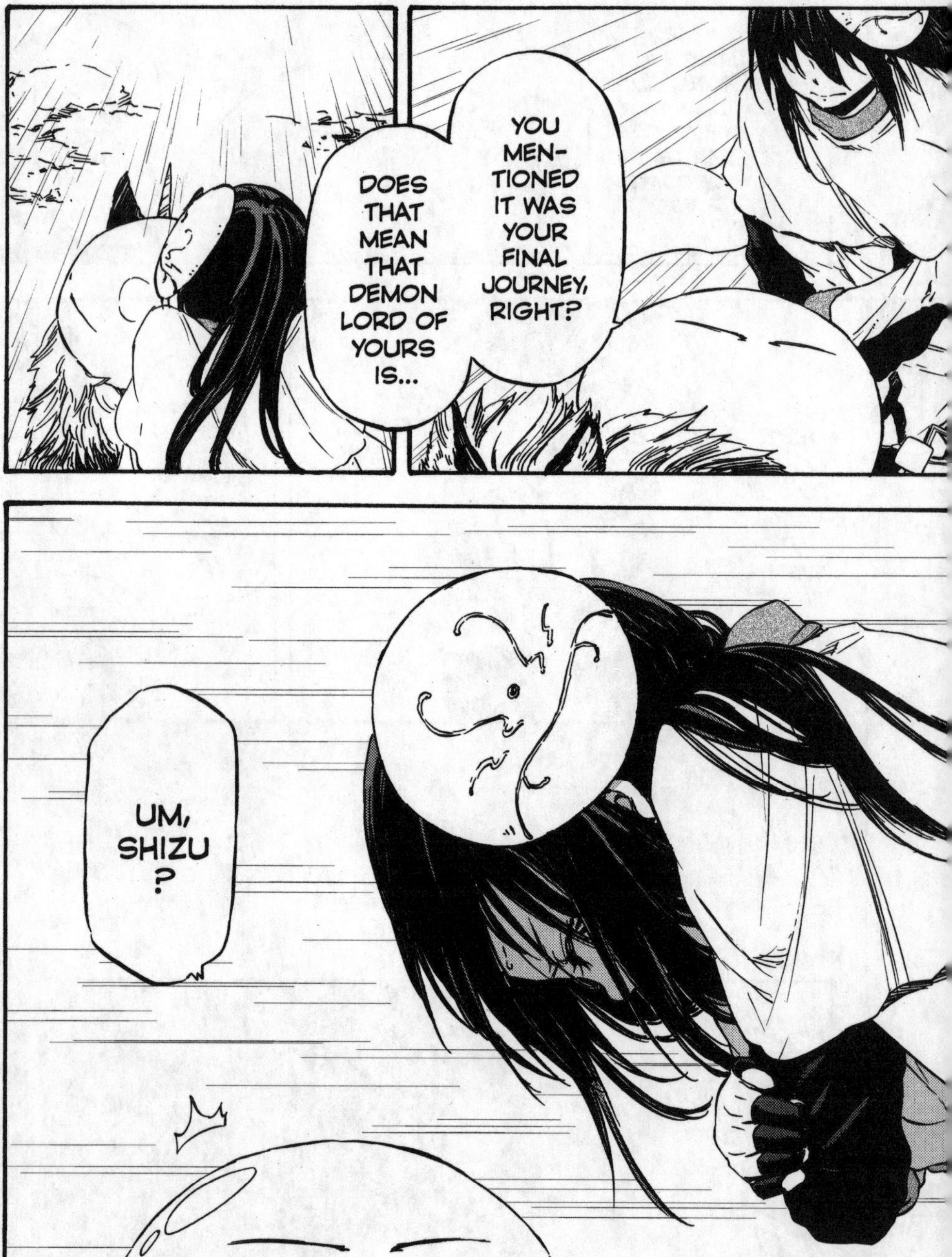
YOU MENTIONED IT WAS YOUR FINAL JOURNEY, RIGHT?
DOES THAT MEAN THAT DEMON LORD OF YOURS IS...
UM, SHIZU?

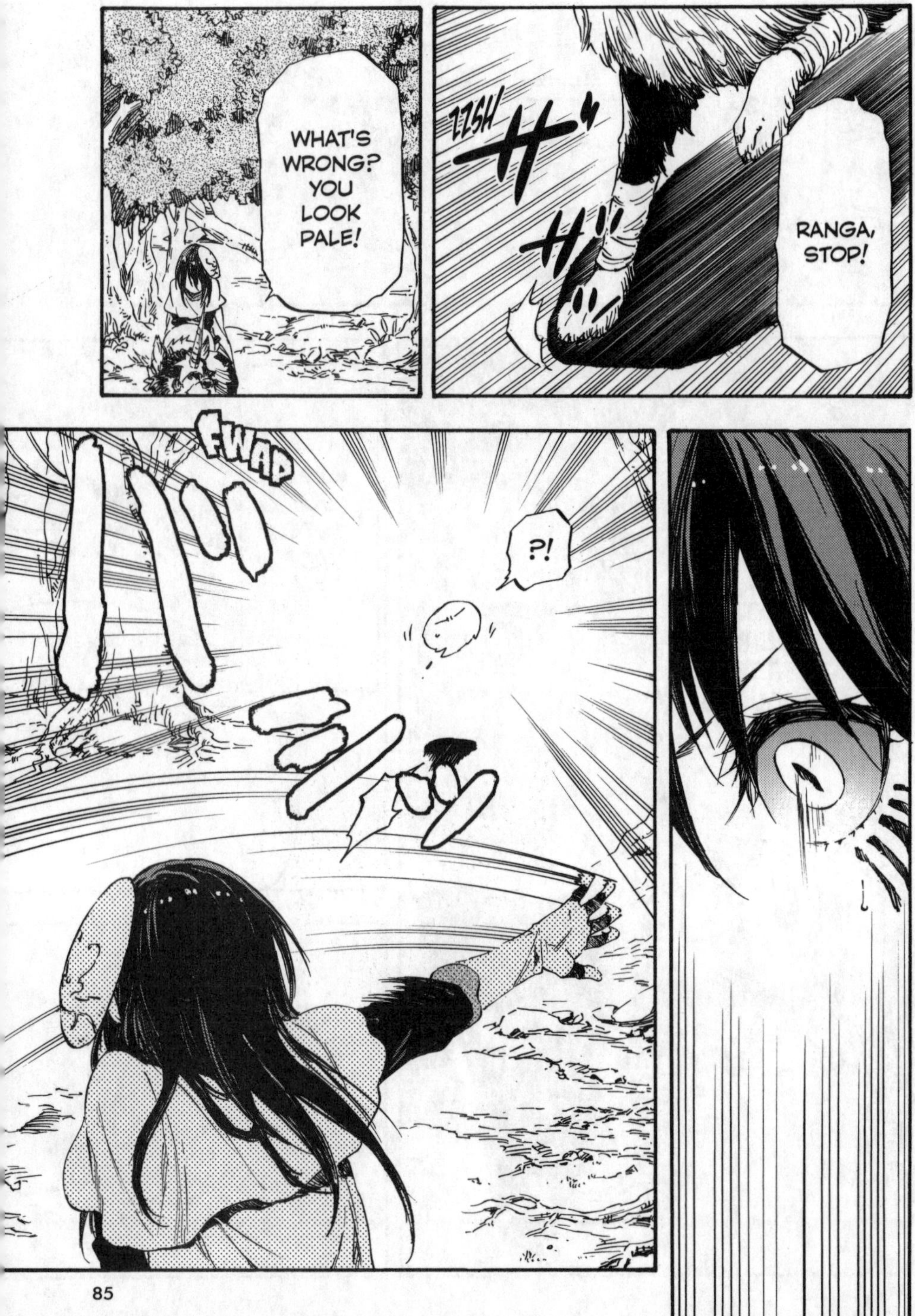
ZZSH
RANGA, STOP!
WHAT'S WRONG? YOU LOOK PALE!
FWAP
?!

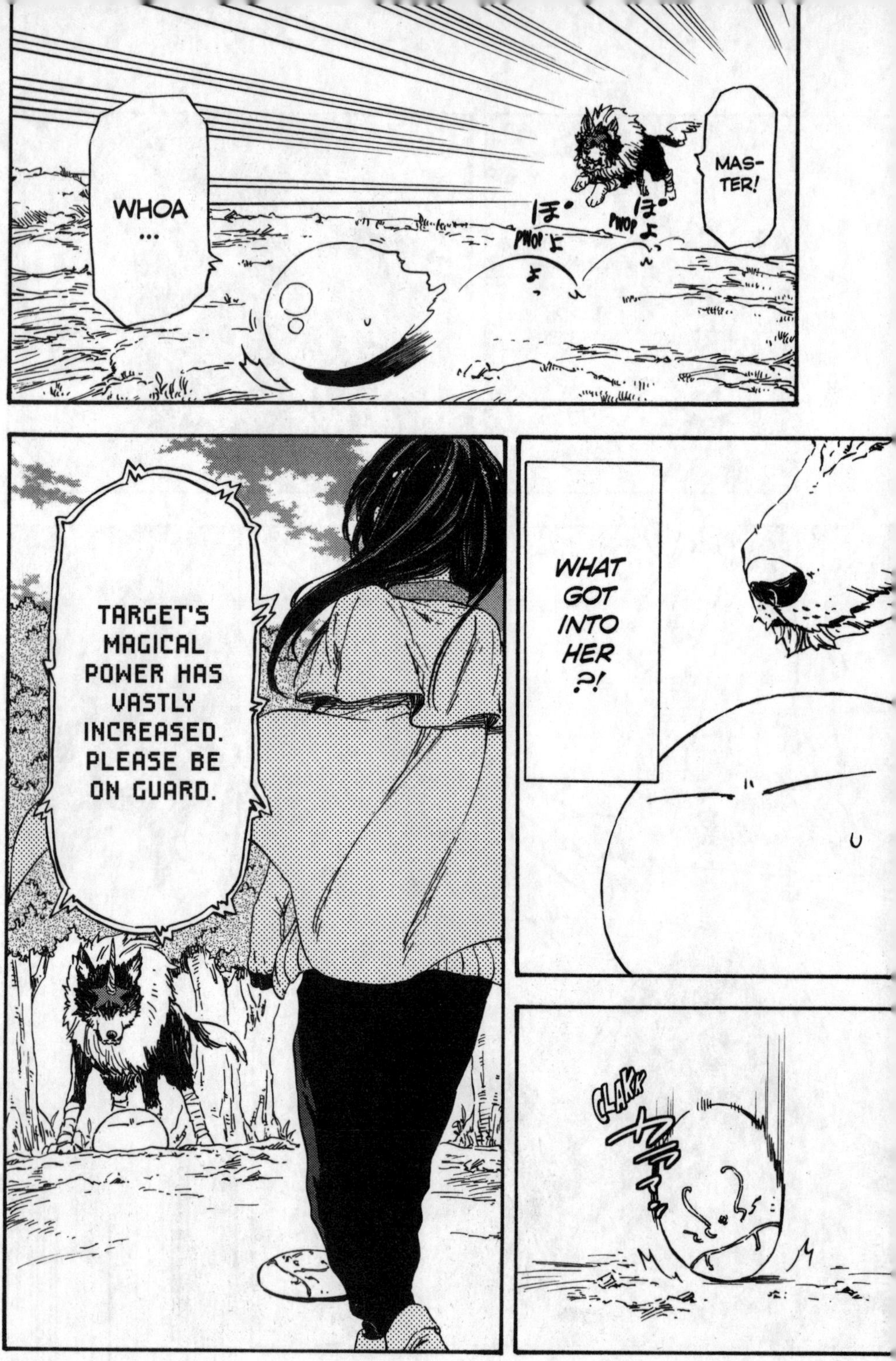
MAS-TER!
PWOP
PWOP
WHOA ...
WHAT GOT INTO HER?!
CLAKK
TARGET'S MAGICAL POWER HAS VASTLY INCREASED. PLEASE BE ON GUARD.

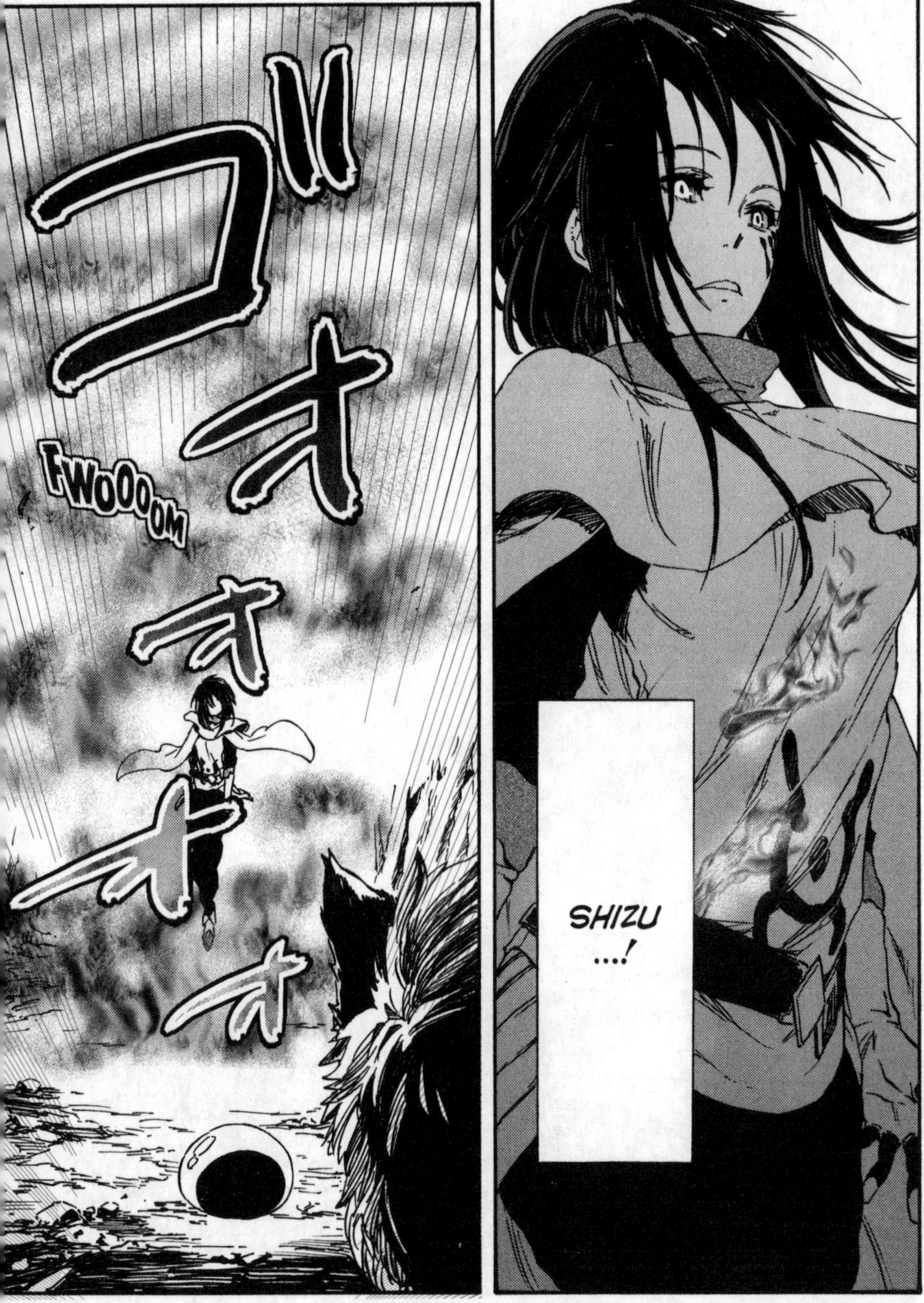
SHIZU
...!
ゴオォォォ
FWOOOOOM

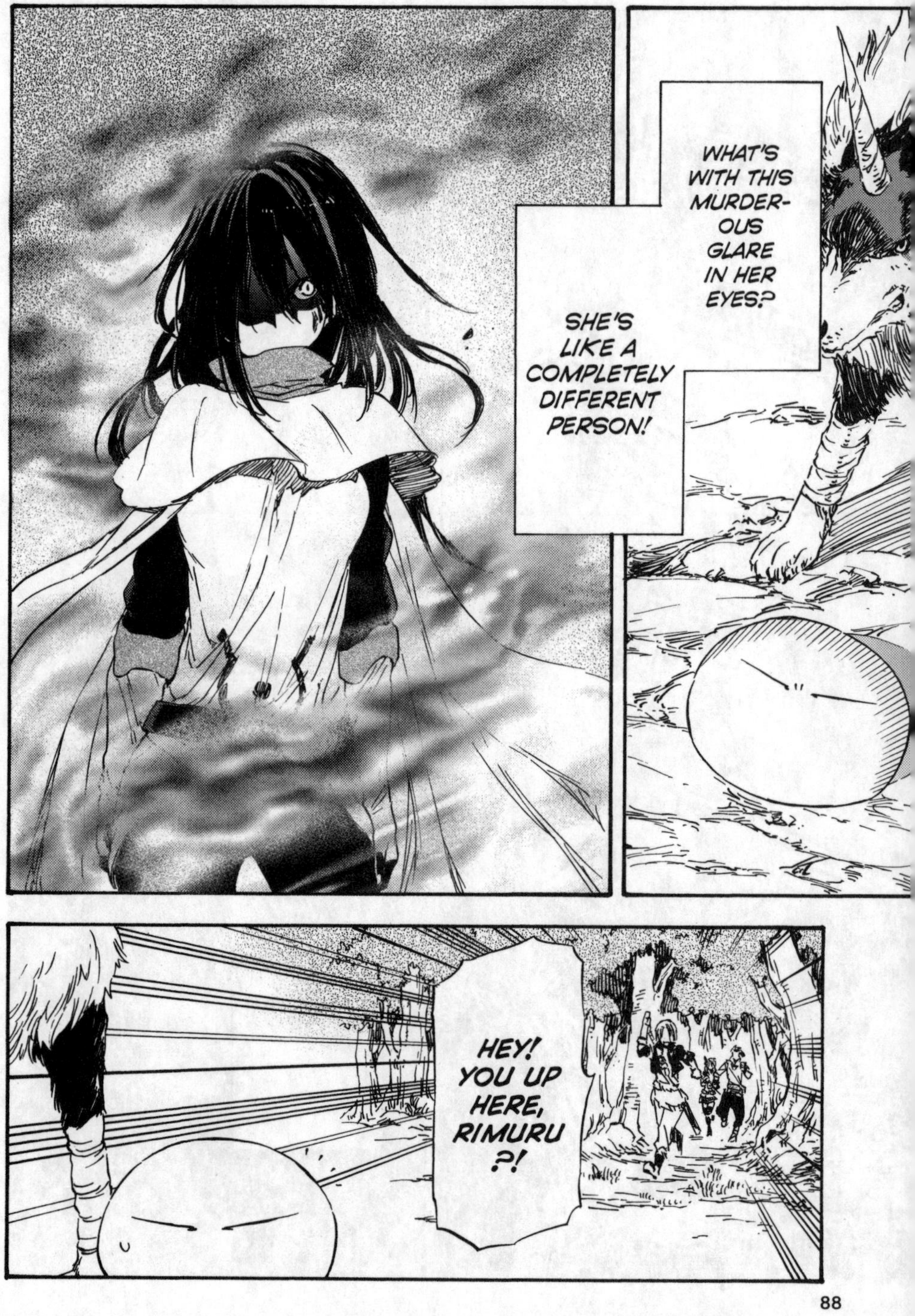
WHAT'S WITH THIS MURDER-OUS GLARE IN HER EYES?
SHE'S LIKE A COMPLETELY DIFFERENT PERSON!
HEY! YOU UP HERE, RIMURU ?!

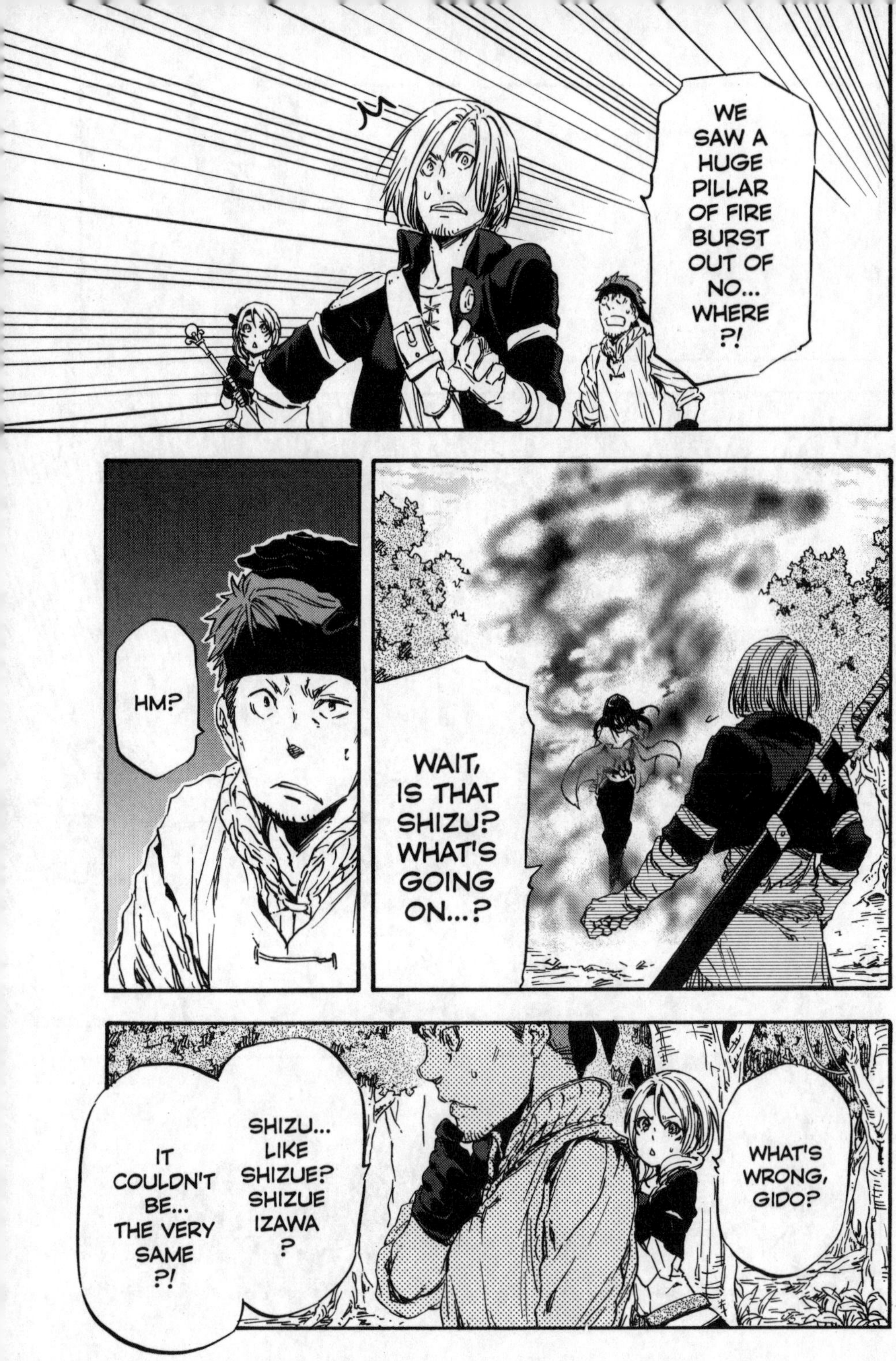
WE SAW A HUGE PILLAR OF FIRE BURST OUT OF NO... WHERE ?!
WAIT, IS THAT SHIZU? WHAT'S GOING ON...?
HM?
WHAT'S WRONG, GIDO?
SHIZU... LIKE SHIZUE? SHIZUE IZAWA ?
IT COULDN'T BE... THE VERY SAME ?!

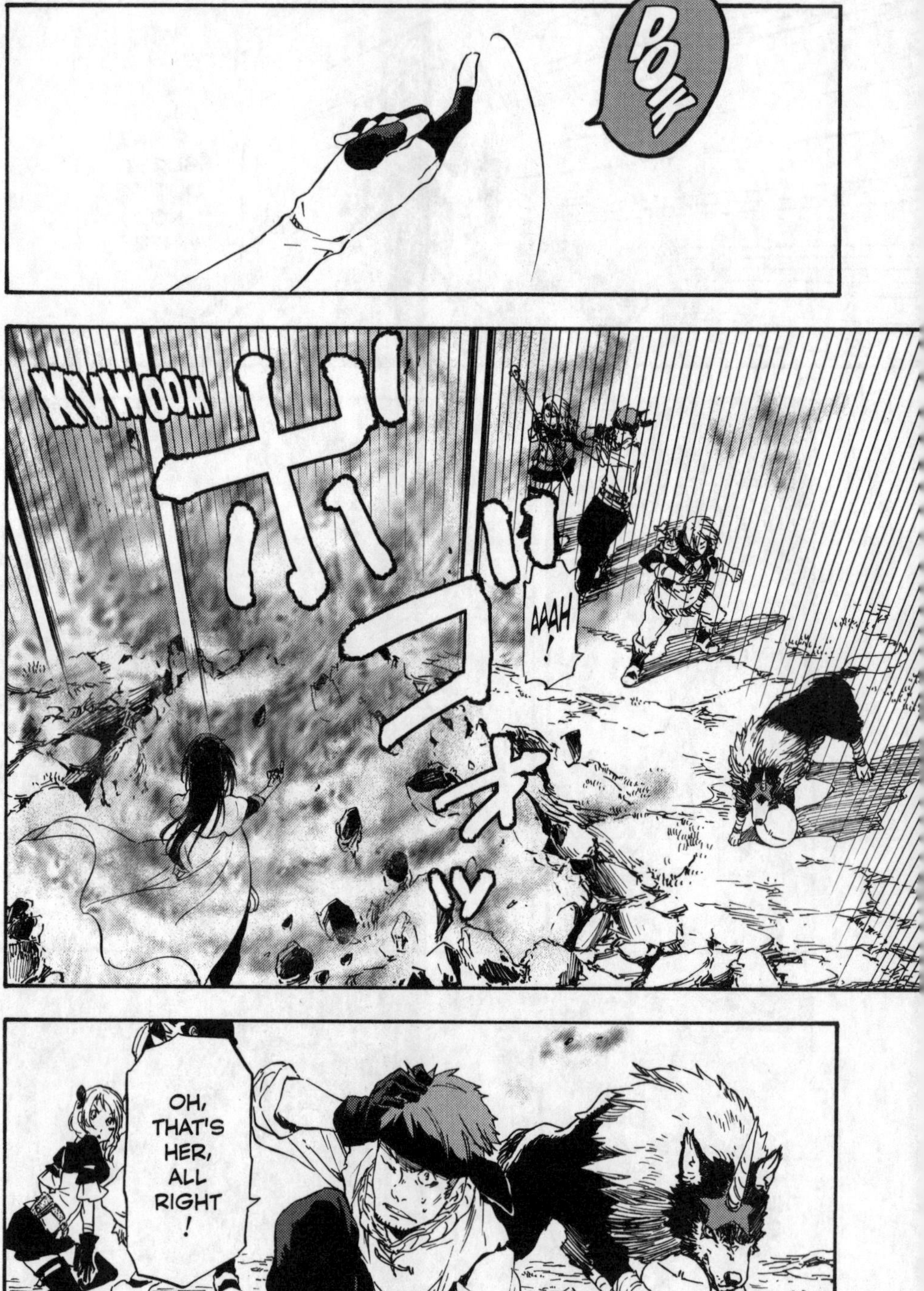
POIK
KVWOOM
AAAH!
OH, THAT'S HER, ALL RIGHT!

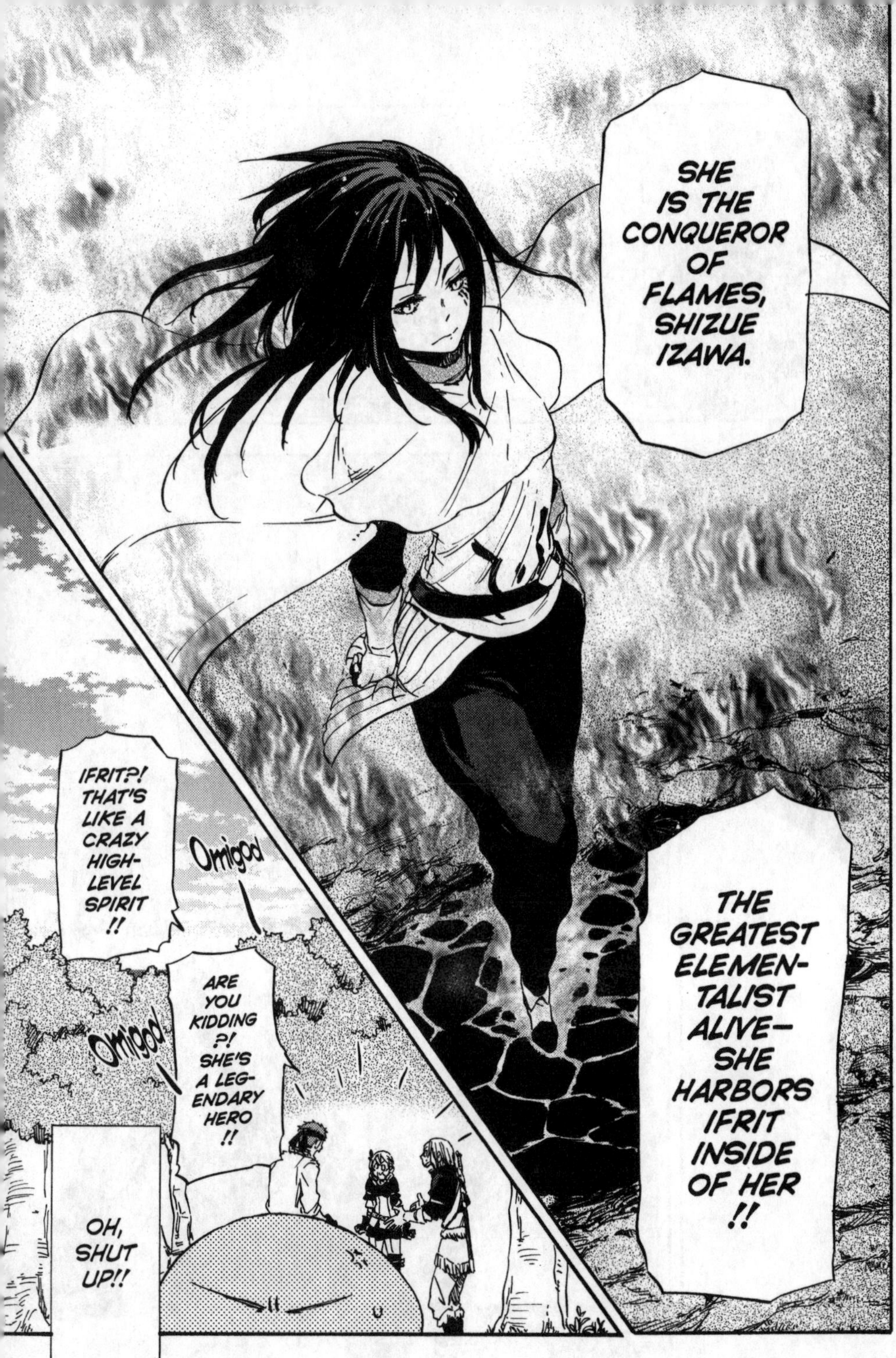
SHE IS THE CONQUEROR OF FLAMES, SHIZUE IZAWA.
THE GREATEST ELEMEN-TALIST ALIVE—SHE HARBORS IFRIT INSIDE OF HER !!
IFRIT?! THAT'S LIKE A CRAZY HIGH-LEVEL SPIRIT !!
Omigod
ARE YOU KIDDING ?! SHE'S A LEG-ENDARY HERO !!
Omigod
OH, SHUT UP!!

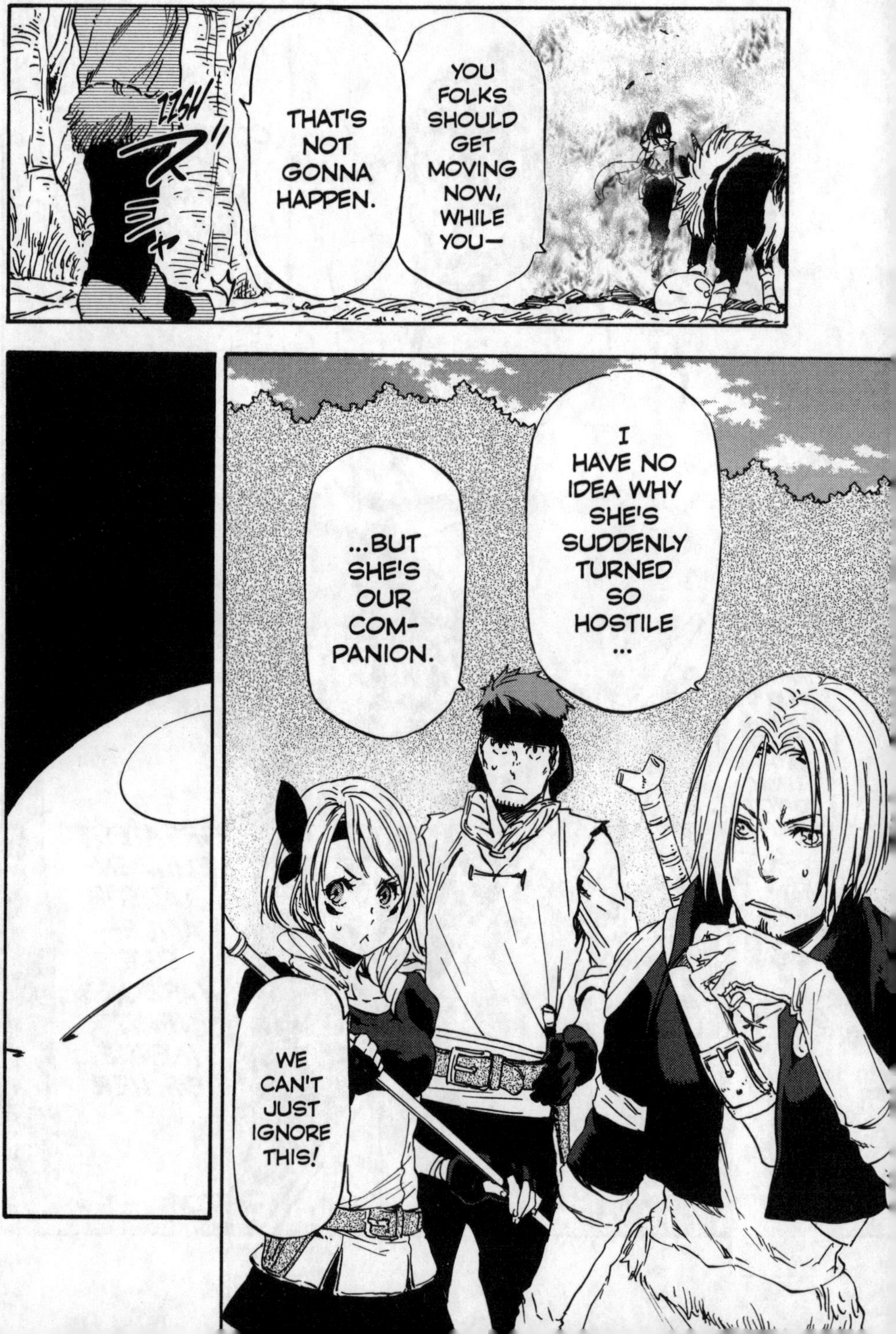
ZZSH
YOU FOLKS SHOULD GET MOVING NOW, WHILE YOU—
THAT'S NOT GONNA HAPPEN.
I HAVE NO IDEA WHY SHE'S SUDDENLY TURNED SO HOSTILE ...
...BUT SHE'S OUR COM- PANION.
WE CAN'T JUST IGNORE THIS!

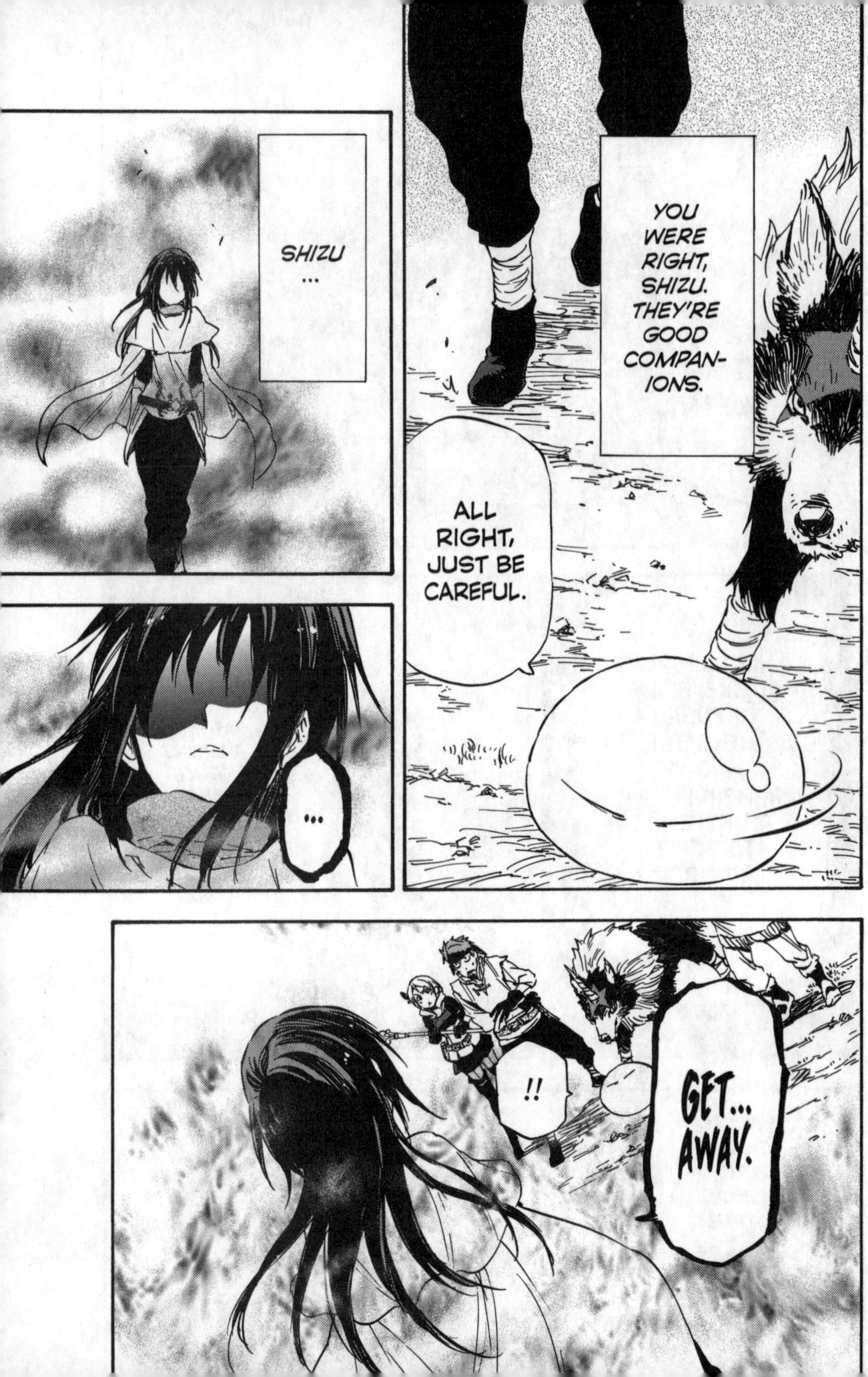
YOU WERE RIGHT, SHIZU. THEY'RE GOOD COMPANIONS.
ALL RIGHT, JUST BE CAREFUL.
SHIZU ...
...
GET... AWAY.
!!

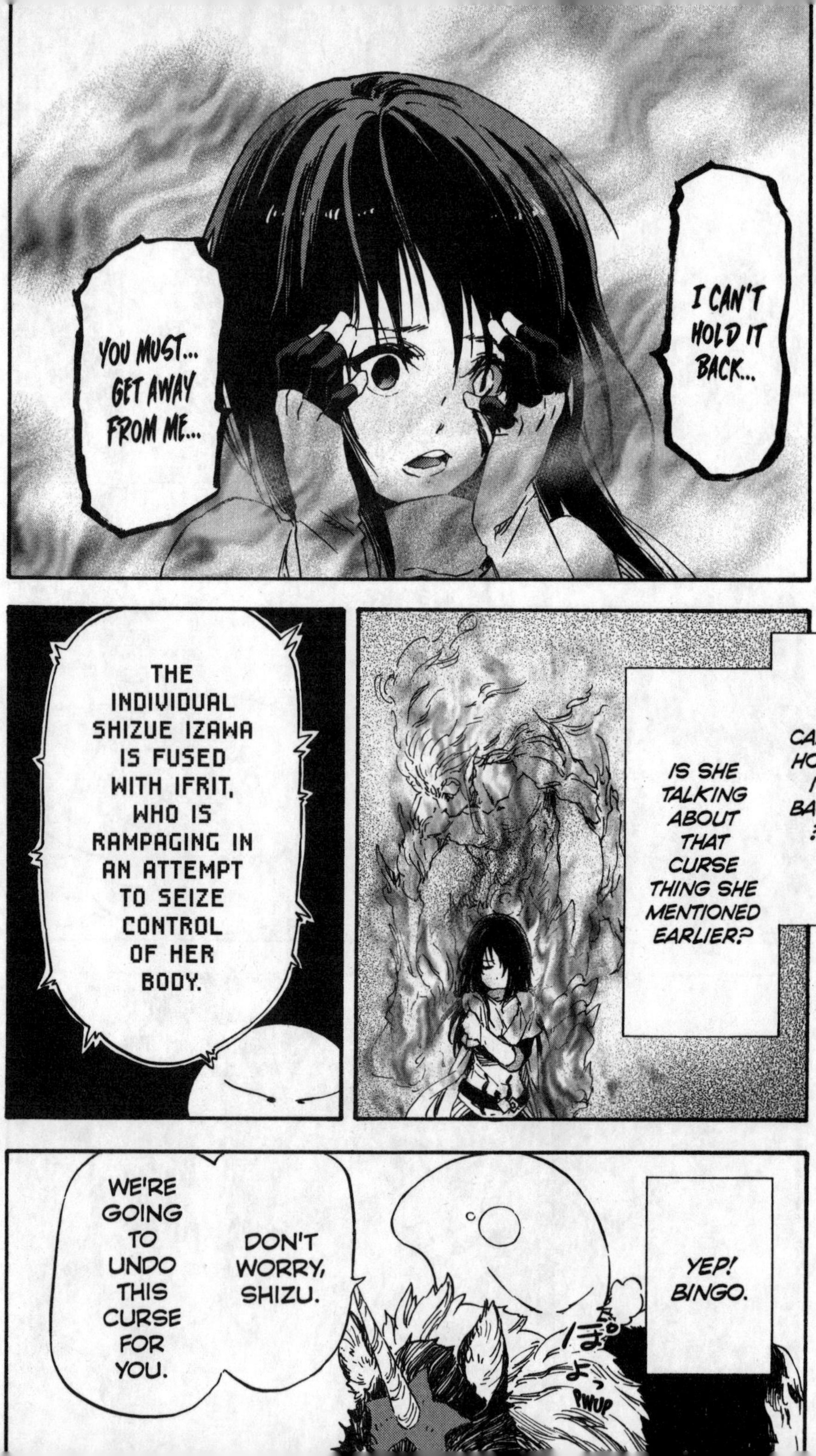
I CAN'T HOLD IT BACK...
YOU MUST... GET AWAY FROM ME...
CAN'T HOLD IT BACK?
IS SHE TALKING ABOUT THAT CURSE THING SHE MENTIONED EARLIER?
THE INDIVIDUAL SHIZUE IZAWA IS FUSED WITH IFRIT, WHO IS RAMPAGING IN AN ATTEMPT TO SEIZE CONTROL OF HER BODY.
YEP! BINGO.
ぽよっ
PWUP
DON'T WORRY, SHIZU.
WE'RE GOING TO UNDO THIS CURSE FOR YOU.

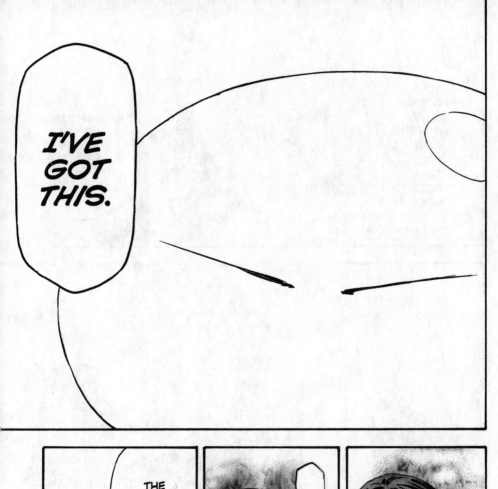

I'VE GOT THIS.

THE CONDITIONS FOR VICTORY ARE: SUBDUING IFRIT, AND RESCUING SHIZU.

Please...

he...

p

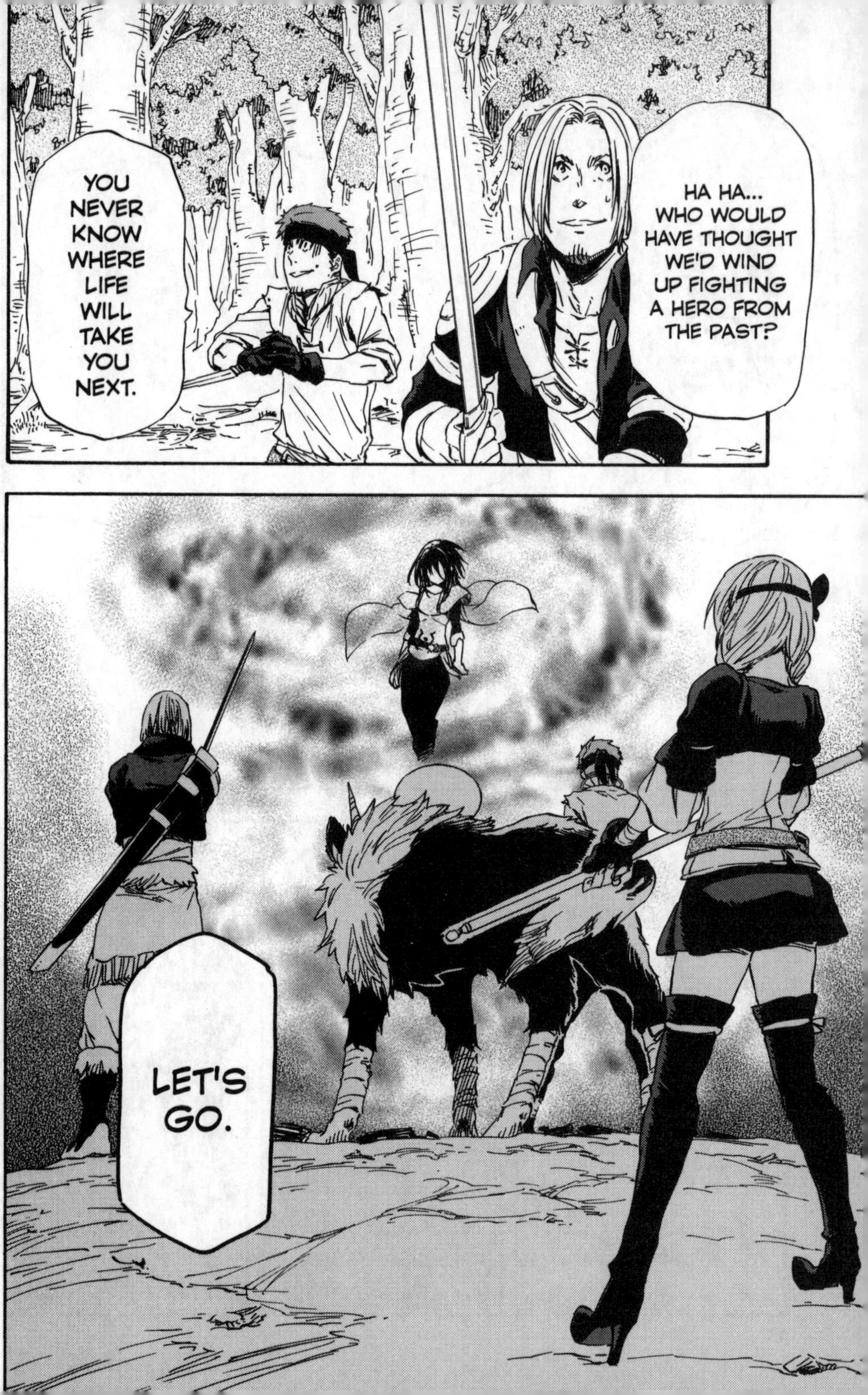
HA HA... WHO WOULD HAVE THOUGHT WE'D WIND UP FIGHTING A HERO FROM THE PAST?
YOU NEVER KNOW WHERE LIFE WILL TAKE YOU NEXT.
LET'S GO.

AFTER THE YAKINIKU PARTY

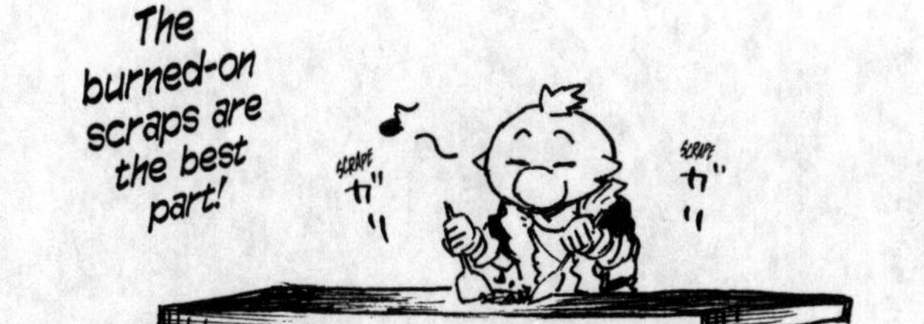
The burned-on scraps are the best part!
SCRAPE
ガリ
SCRAPE
ガリ

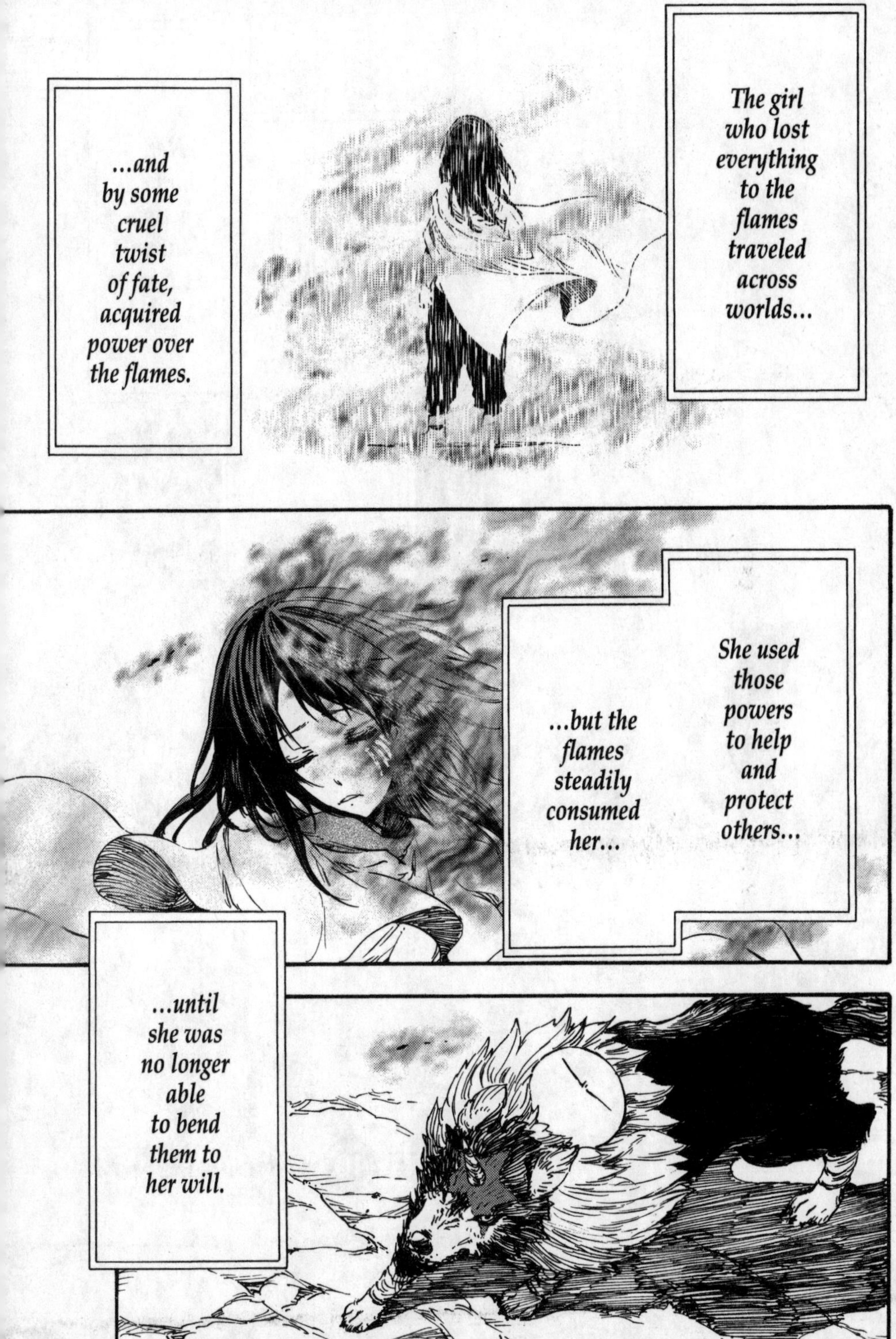
The girl who lost everything to the flames traveled across worlds...
...and by some cruel twist of fate, acquired power over the flames.
She used those powers to help and protect others...
...but the flames steadily consumed her...
...until she was no longer able to bend them to her will.

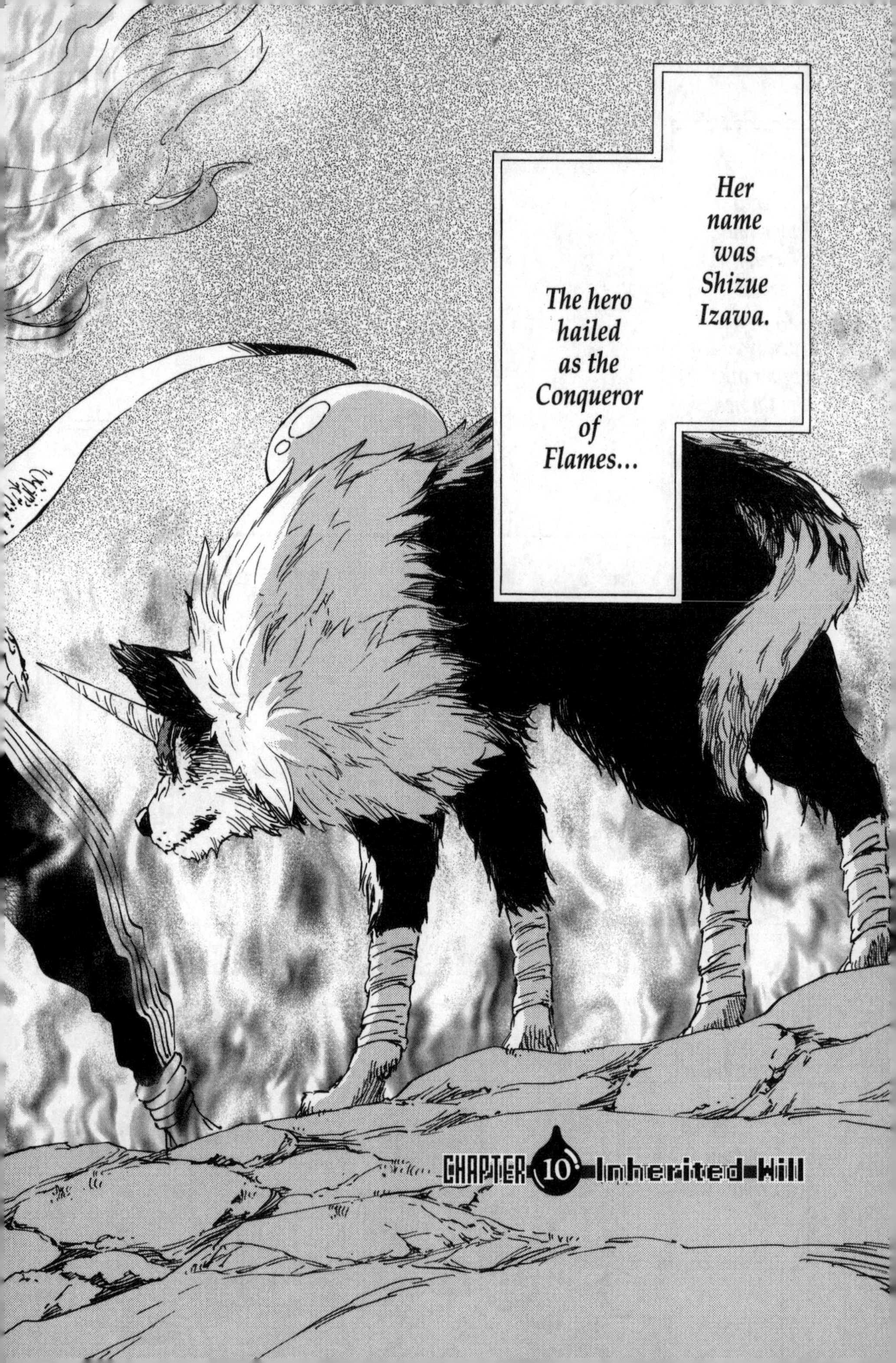
Her name was Shizue Izawa.
The hero hailed as the Conqueror of Flames...
CHAPTER 10 Inherited Will

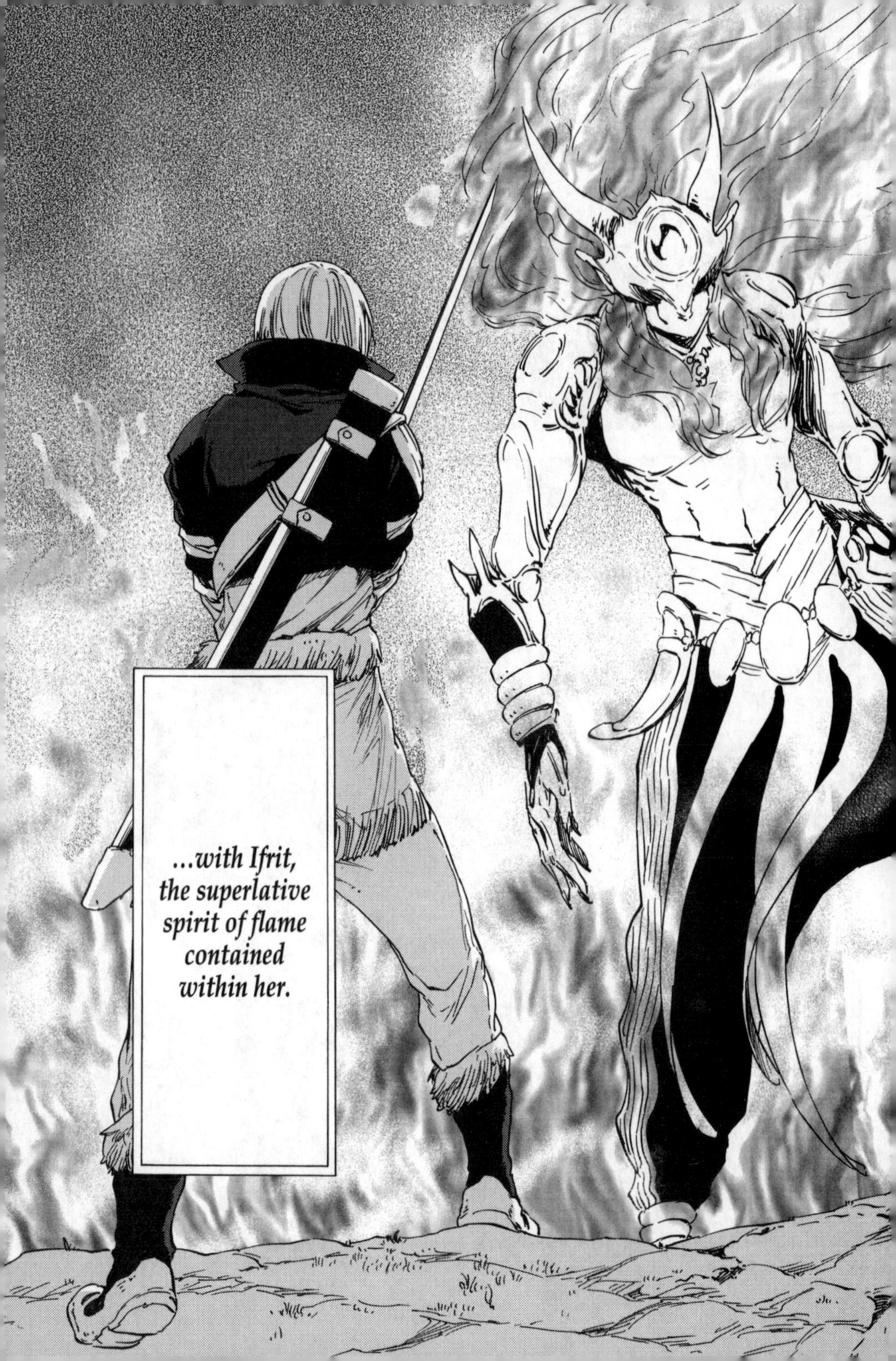
...with Ifrit, the superlative spirit of flame contained within her.

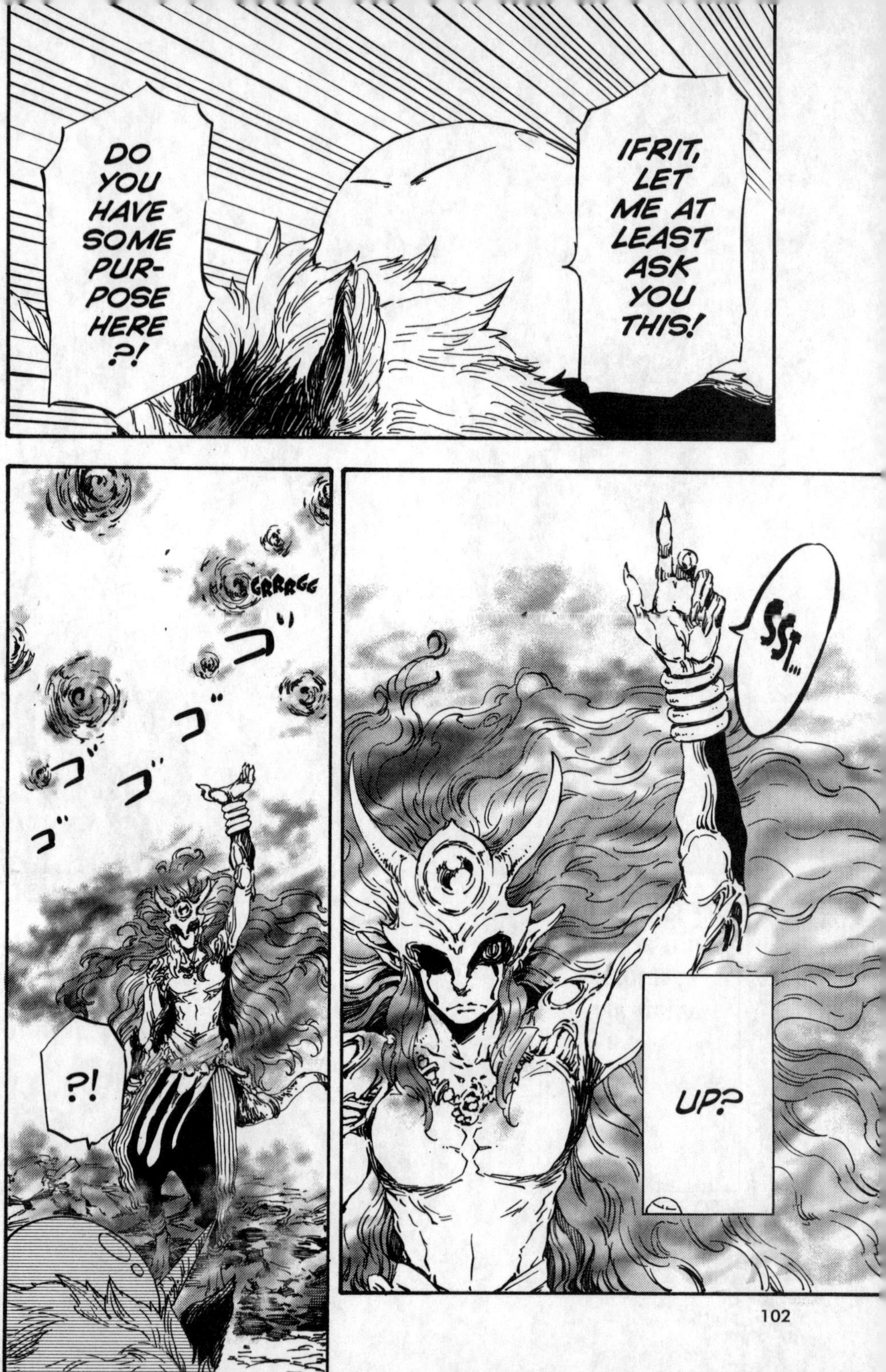
IFRIT, LET ME AT LEAST ASK YOU THIS!
DO YOU HAVE SOME PUR-POSE HERE?!
SST...
UP?
GRRRGG
ゴゴゴゴ
?!

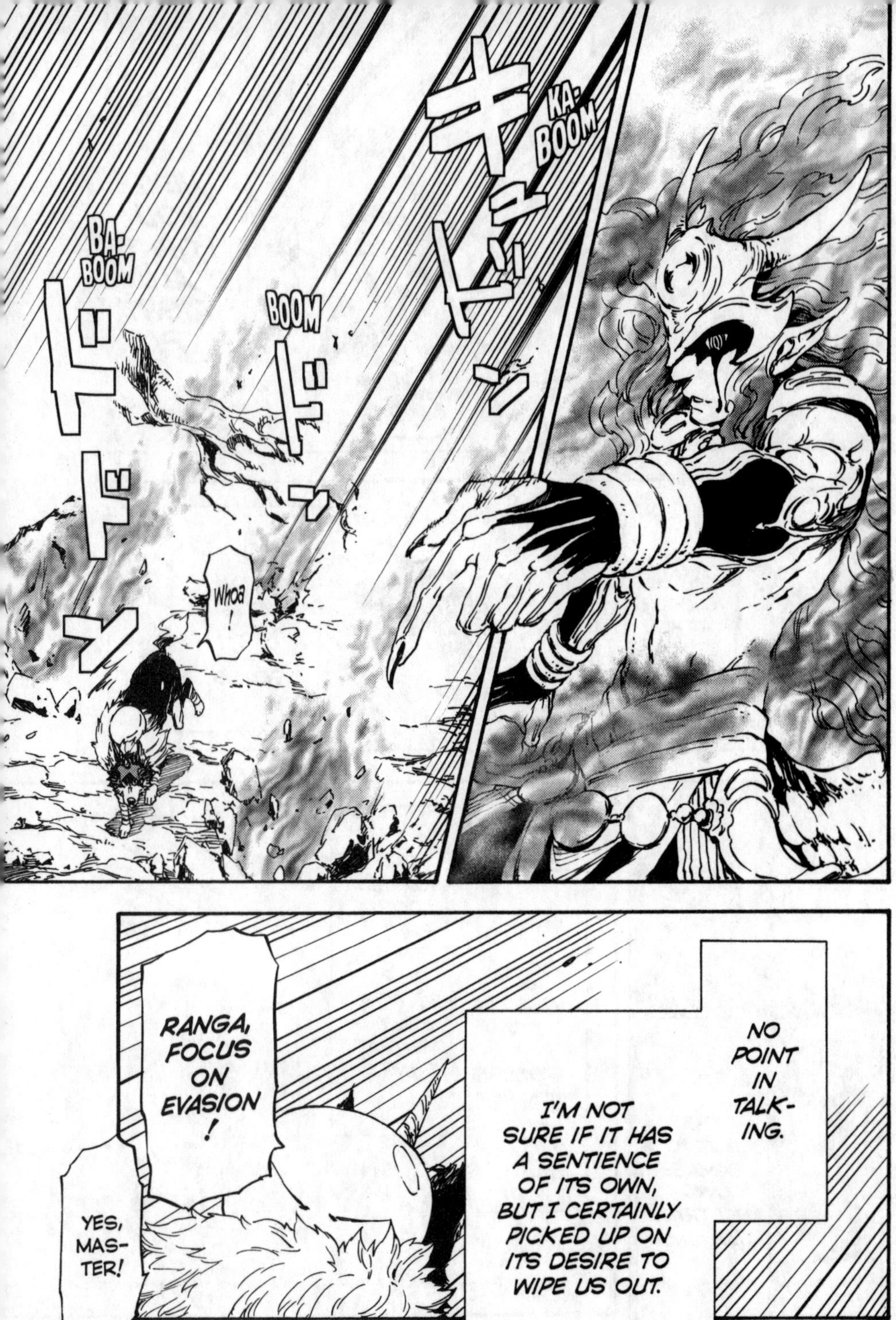
KA-BOOM
BOOM
BA-BOOM
Whoa!
NO POINT IN TALKING.
I'M NOT SURE IF IT HAS A SENTIENCE OF ITS OWN, BUT I CERTAINLY PICKED UP ON ITS DESIRE TO WIPE US OUT.
RANGA, FOCUS ON EVASION!
YES, MASTER!

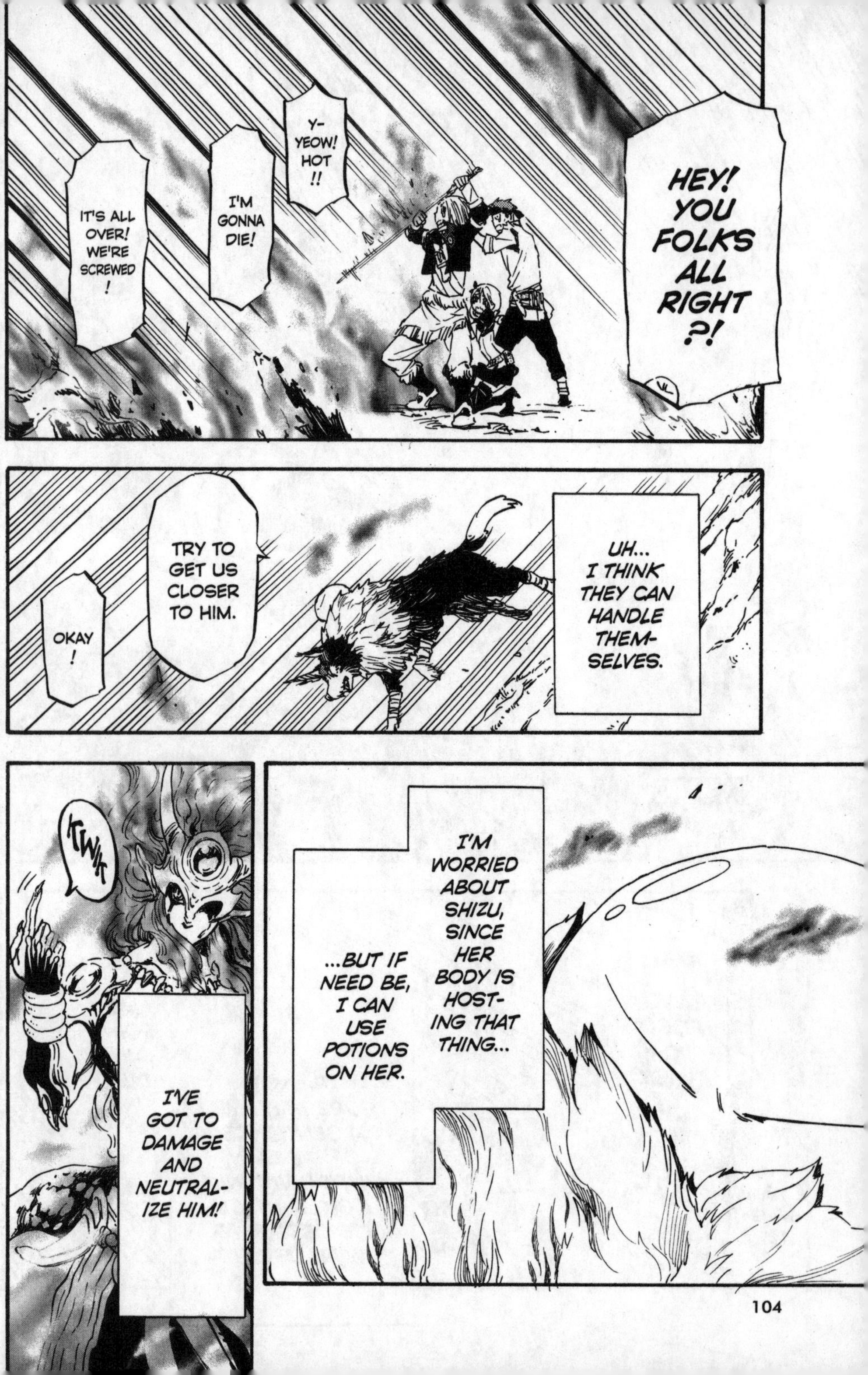

HEY! YOU FOLKS ALL RIGHT?!
Y-YEOW! HOT!!
I'M GONNA DIE!
IT'S ALL OVER! WE'RE SCREWED!
UH... I THINK THEY CAN HANDLE THEMSELVES.
TRY TO GET US CLOSER TO HIM.
OKAY!
I'M WORRIED ABOUT SHIZU, SINCE HER BODY IS HOSTING THAT THING...
...BUT IF NEED BE, I CAN USE POTIONS ON HER.
KWIK
I'VE GOT TO DAMAGE AND NEUTRALIZE HIM!

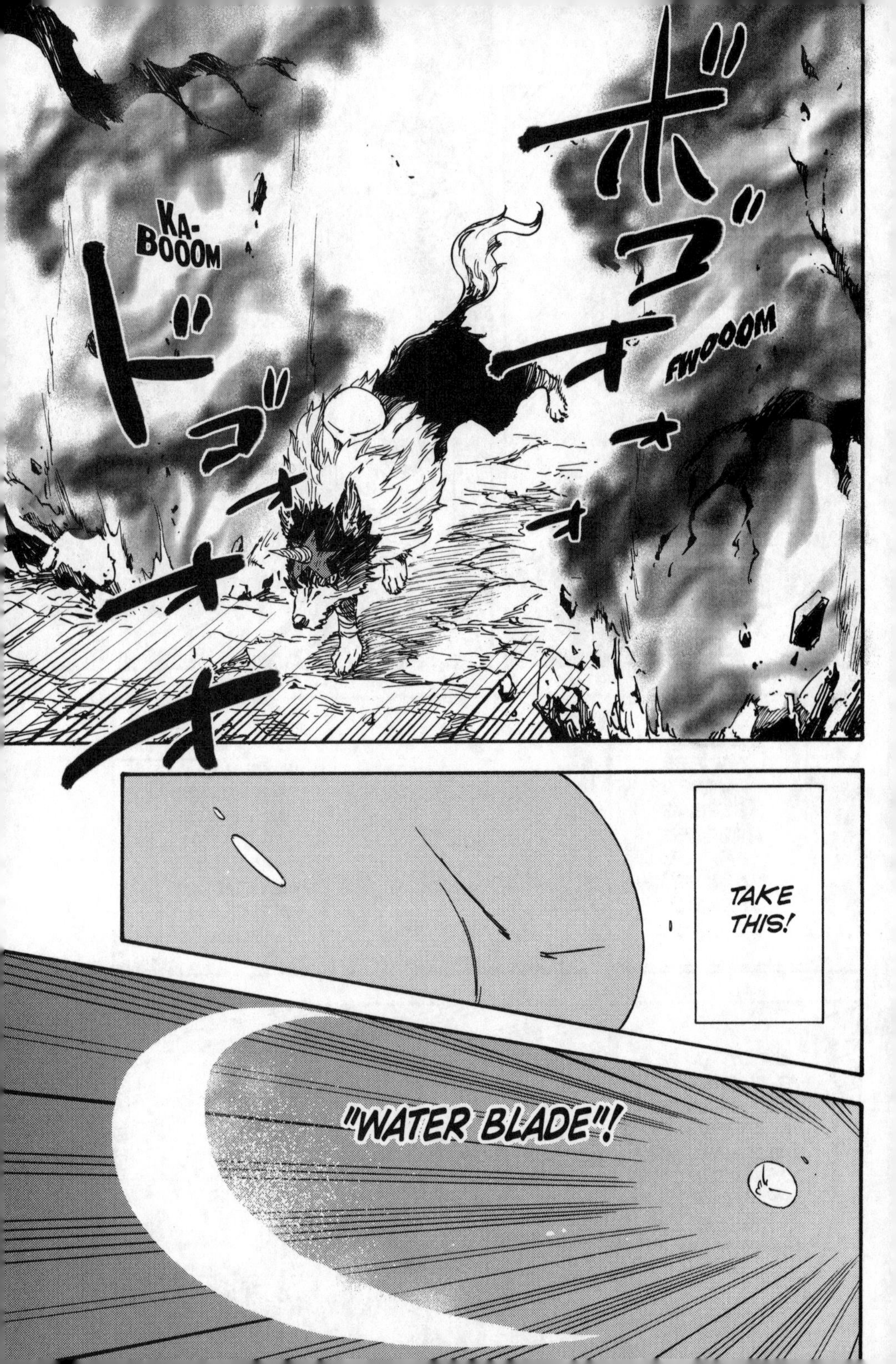

FWOOOM
KA-BOOOM
TAKE THIS!
"WATER BLADE"!

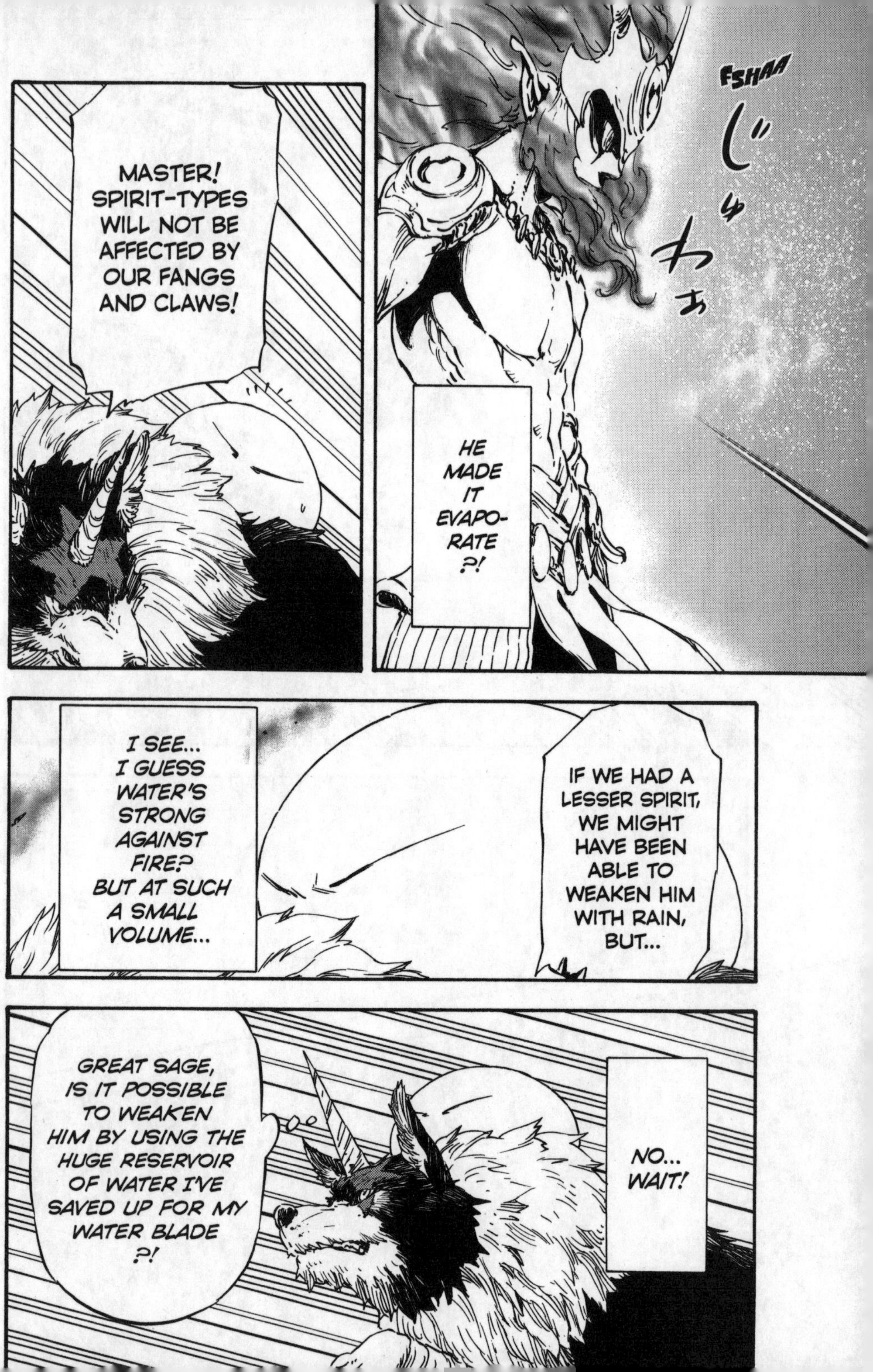
FSHAA
じゅわぁ
HE MADE IT EVAPORATE ?!
MASTER! SPIRIT-TYPES WILL NOT BE AFFECTED BY OUR FANGS AND CLAWS!
IF WE HAD A LESSER SPIRIT, WE MIGHT HAVE BEEN ABLE TO WEAKEN HIM WITH RAIN, BUT...
I SEE... I GUESS WATER'S STRONG AGAINST FIRE? BUT AT SUCH A SMALL VOLUME...
NO... WAIT!
GREAT SAGE, IS IT POSSIBLE TO WEAKEN HIM BY USING THE HUGE RESERVOIR OF WATER I'VE SAVED UP FOR MY WATER BLADE ?!

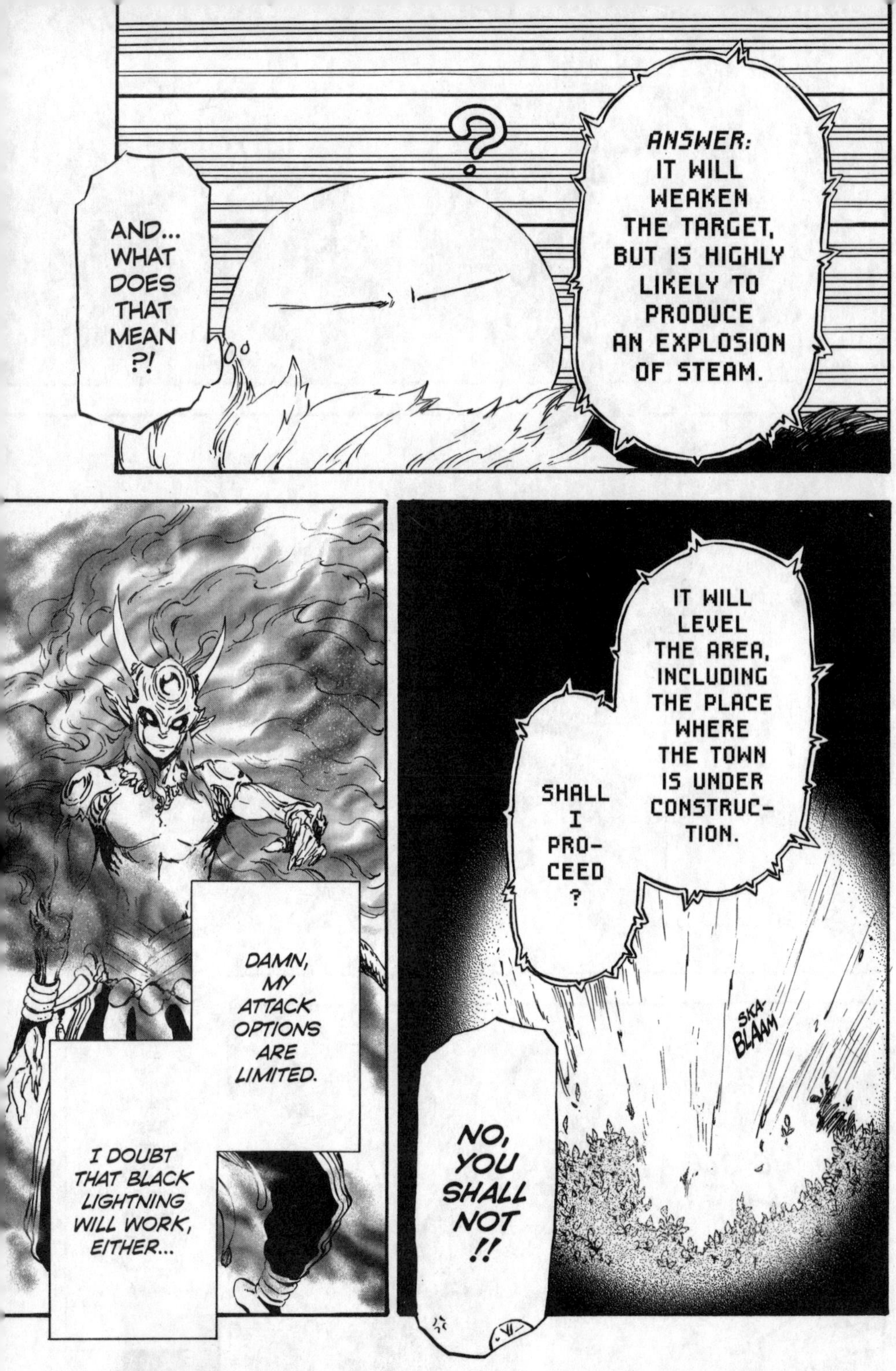

ANSWER: IT WILL WEAKEN THE TARGET, BUT IS HIGHLY LIKELY TO PRODUCE AN EXPLOSION OF STEAM.
AND... WHAT DOES THAT MEAN?!
IT WILL LEVEL THE AREA, INCLUDING THE PLACE WHERE THE TOWN IS UNDER CONSTRUCTION.
SHALL I PROCEED?
SKA-BLAAM
NO, YOU SHALL NOT!!
DAMN, MY ATTACK OPTIONS ARE LIMITED.
I DOUBT THAT BLACK LIGHTNING WILL WORK, EITHER...

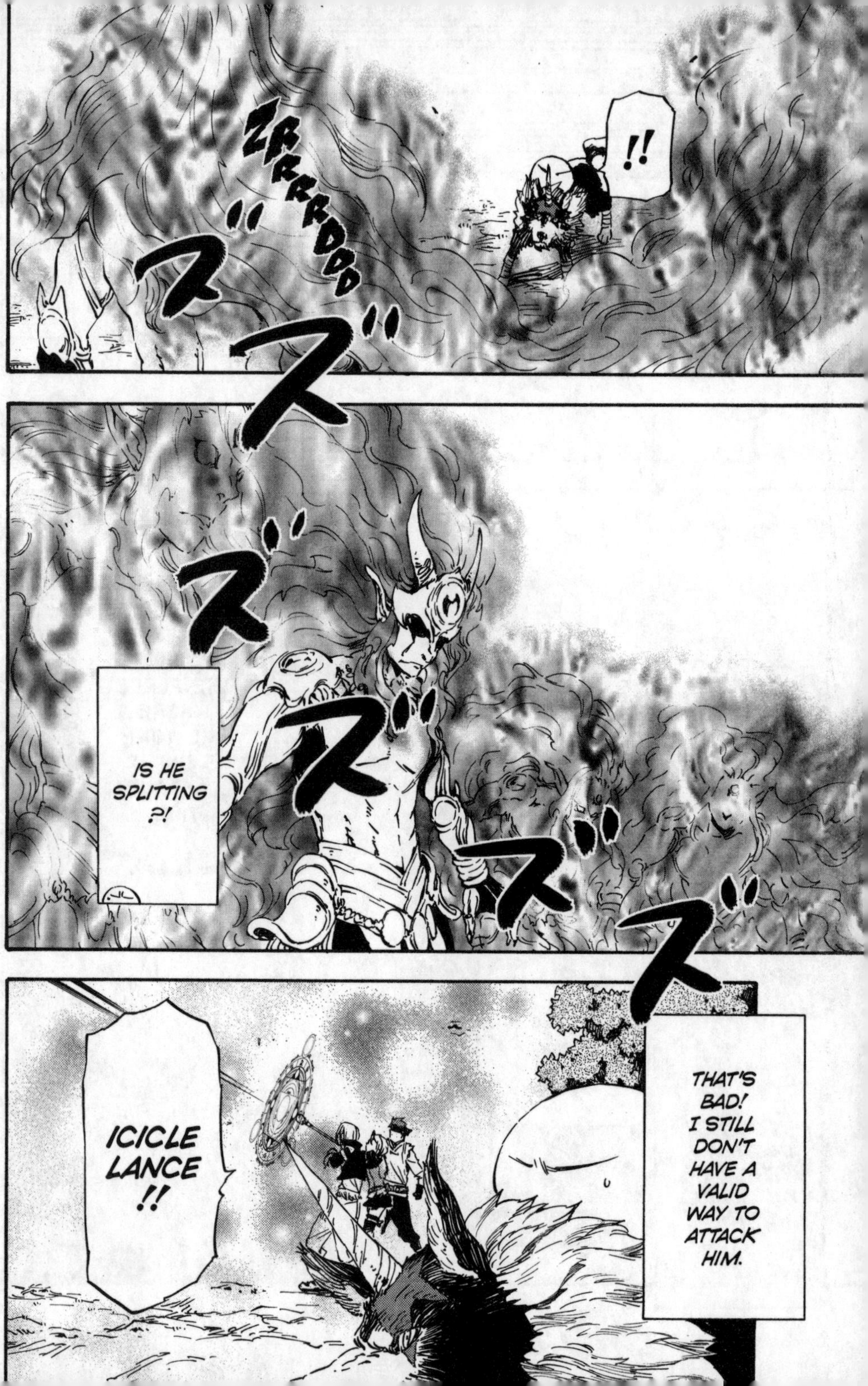
!!
ZRRRRDDD
IS HE SPLITTING ?!
THAT'S BAD! I STILL DON'T HAVE A VALID WAY TO ATTACK HIM.
ICICLE LANCE !!

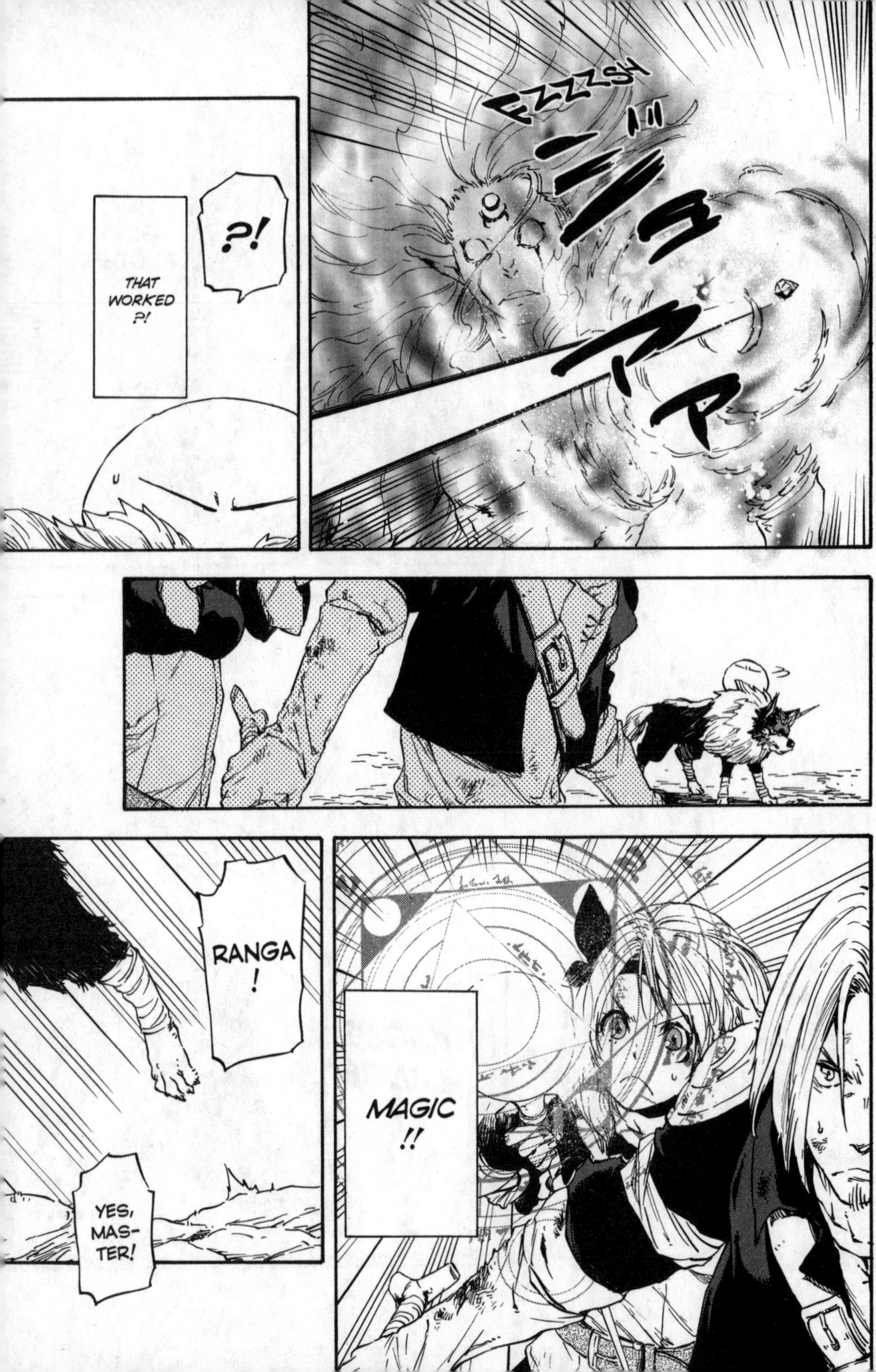
FZZZSH
?!
THAT WORKED?!
MAGIC!!
RANGA!
YES, MASTER!

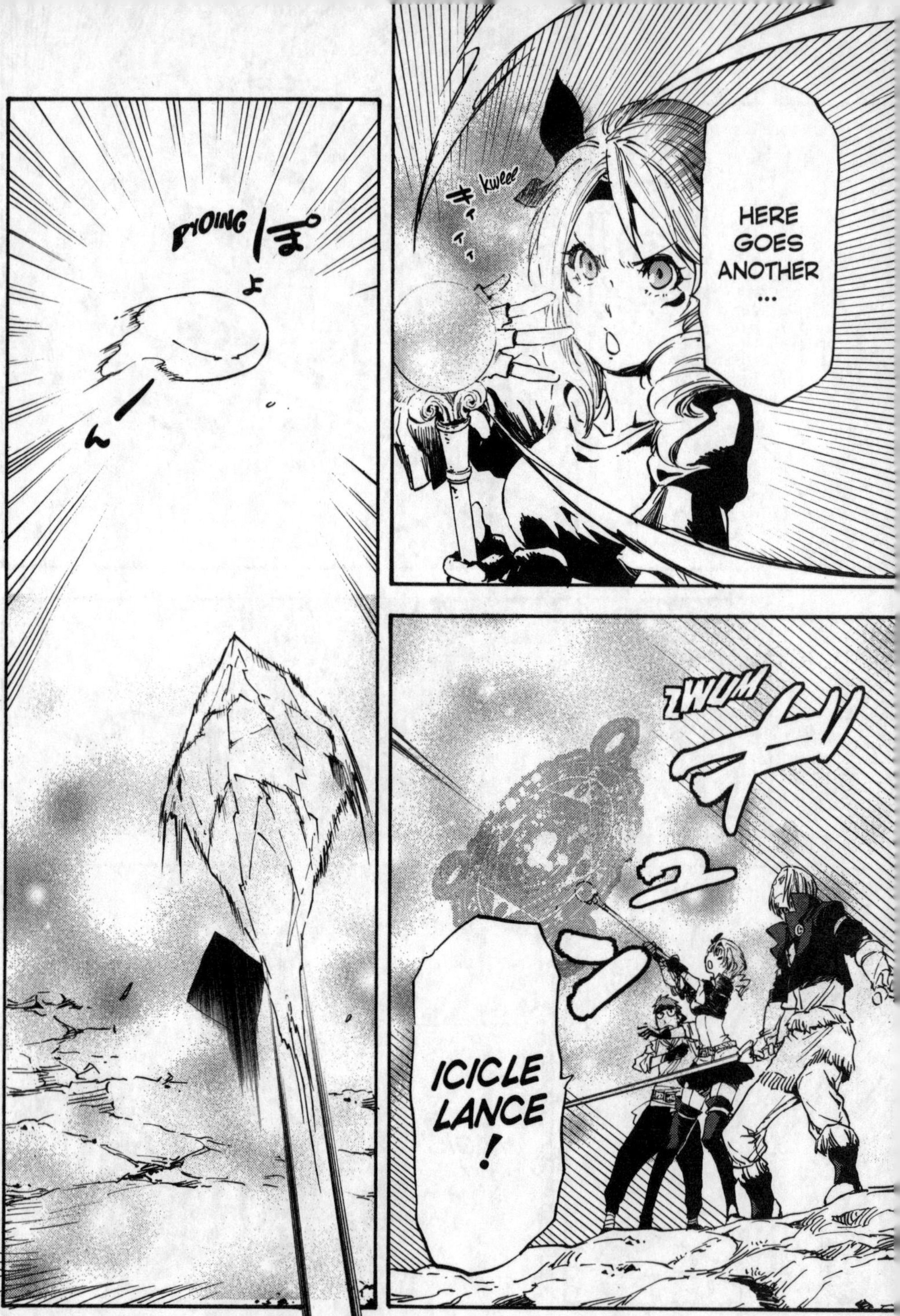
HERE GOES ANOTHER ...
kweee
キィィィ
ZWUM
ICICLE LANCE!
PYOING
ぽよーん

ACK!

WAIT! RIMURU, NO!

WHAAA?! WHAT HAPPENED TO MY SPELL?!

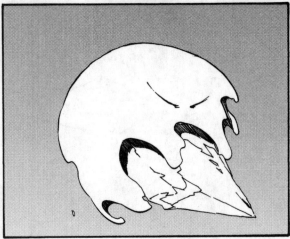

PWOOP

SWOOP

SORRY, I'LL EXPLAIN LATER.

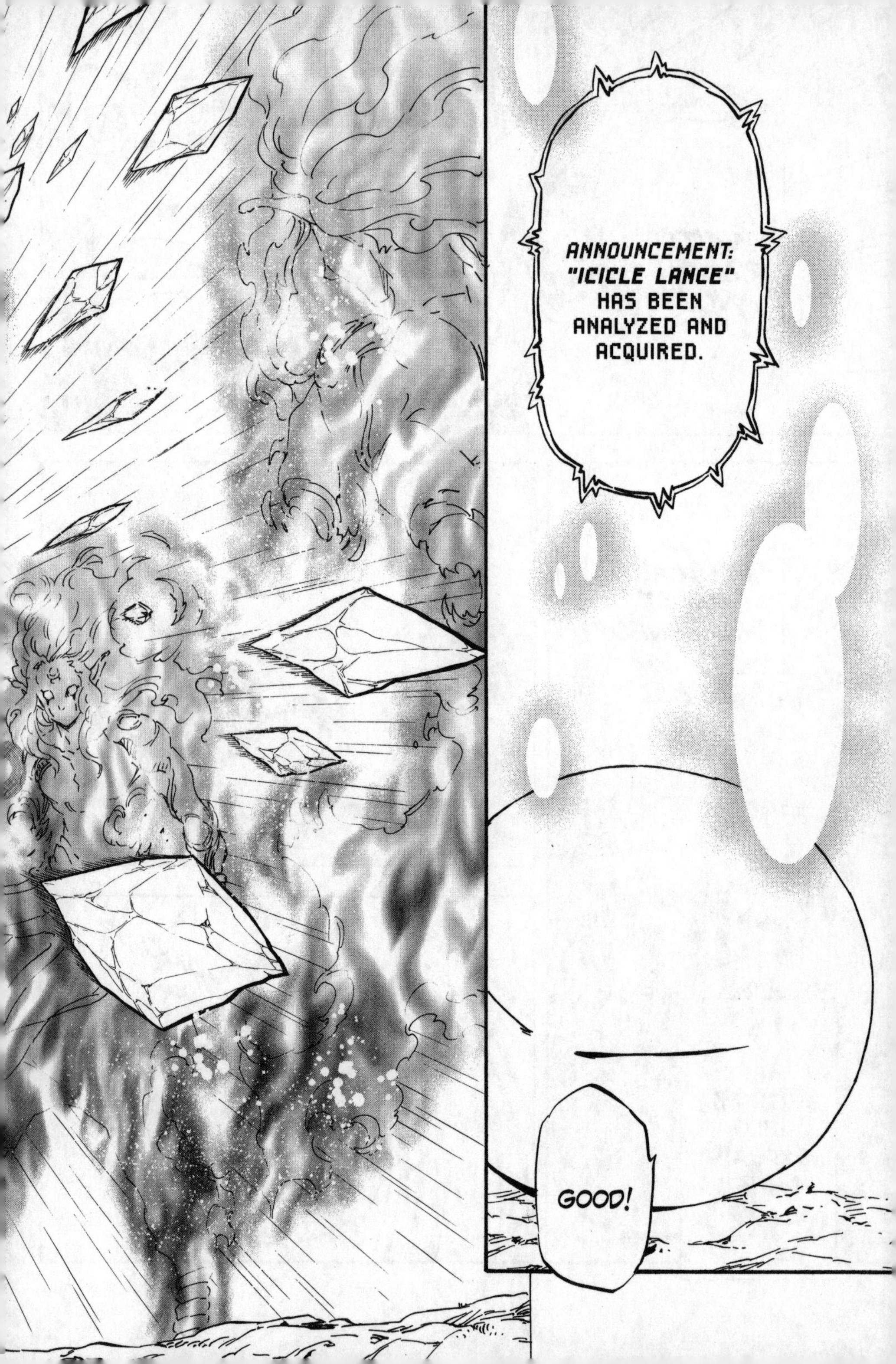
ANNOUNCEMENT: "ICICLE LANCE" HAS BEEN ANALYZED AND ACQUIRED.
GOOD!

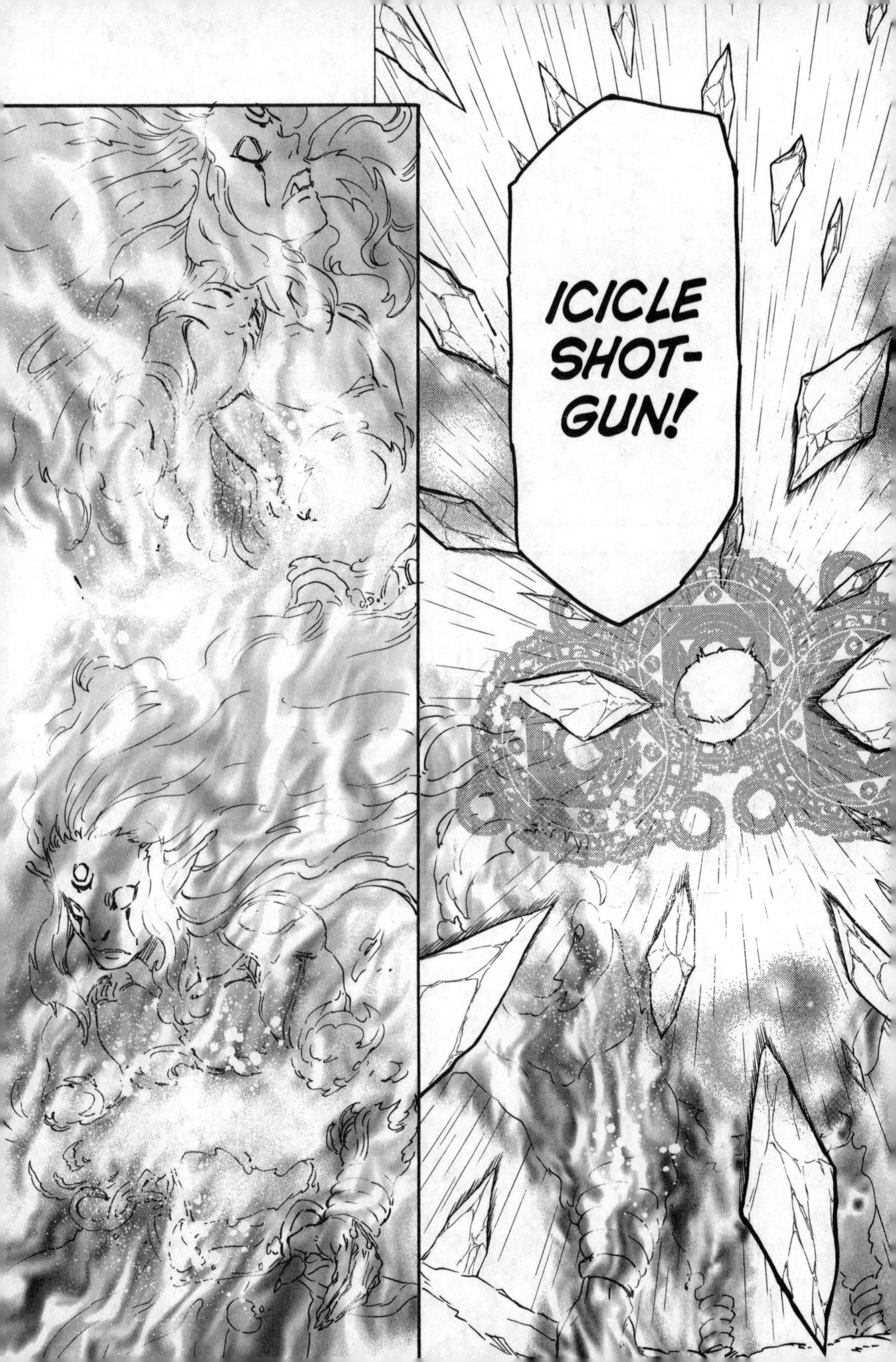
ICICLE SHOT-GUN!

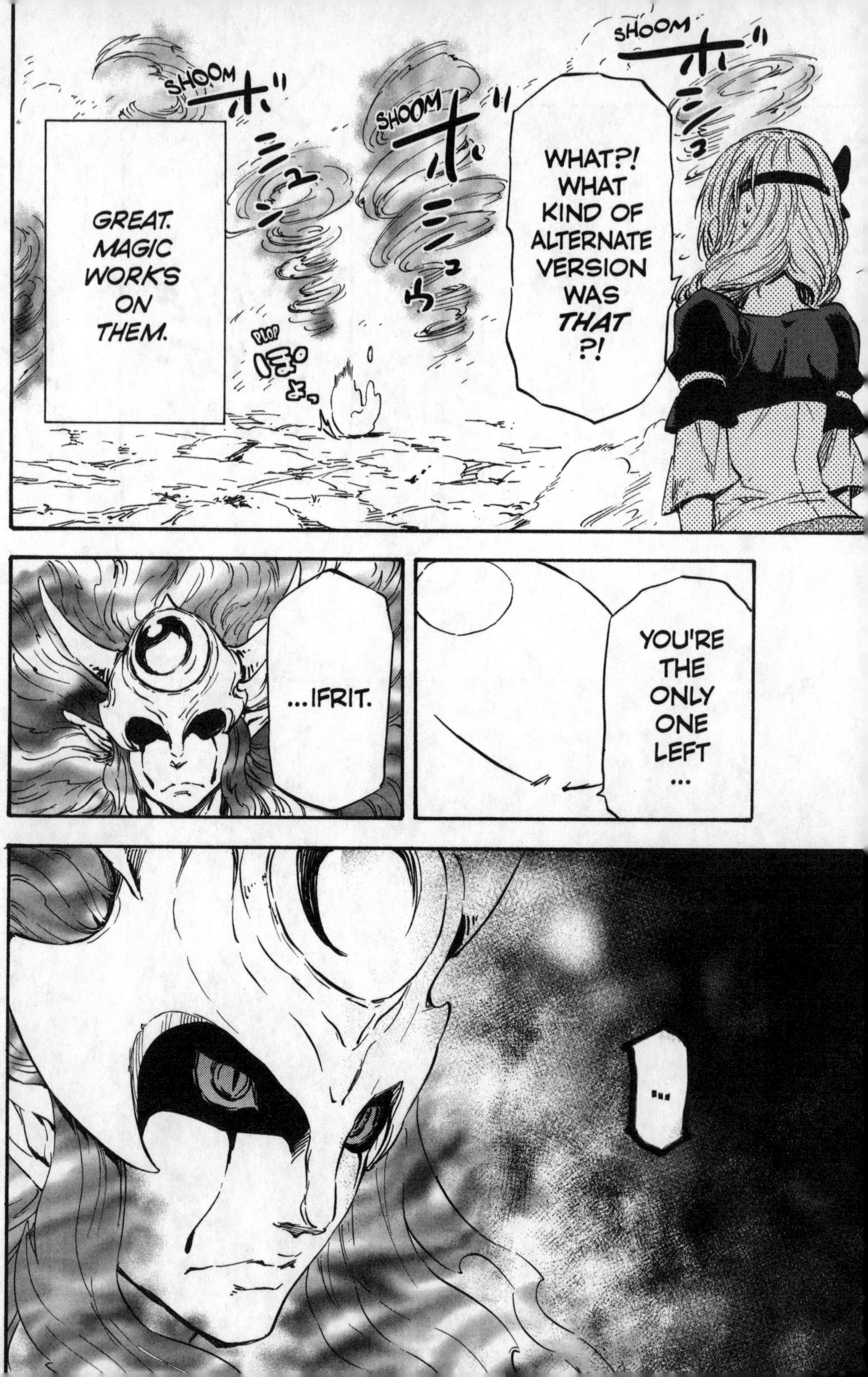
SHOOM
WHAT?! WHAT KIND OF ALTERNATE VERSION WAS THAT?!
SHOOM
SHOOM
PLOP
GREAT. MAGIC WORKS ON THEM.
YOU'RE THE ONLY ONE LEFT...
...IFRIT.
...

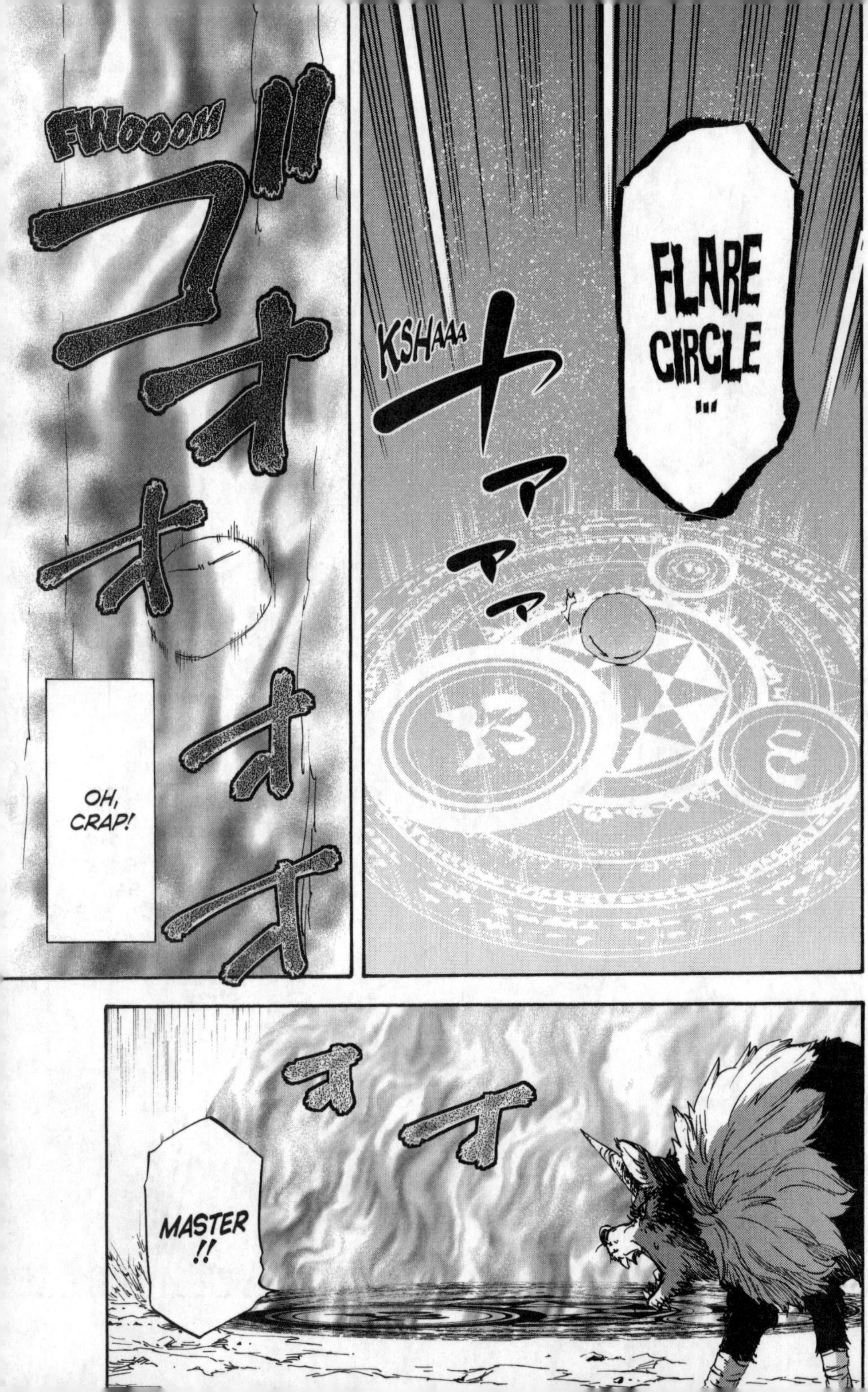
FLARE CIRCLE ...
KSHAAA
FWOOOM
OH, CRAP!
MASTER !!

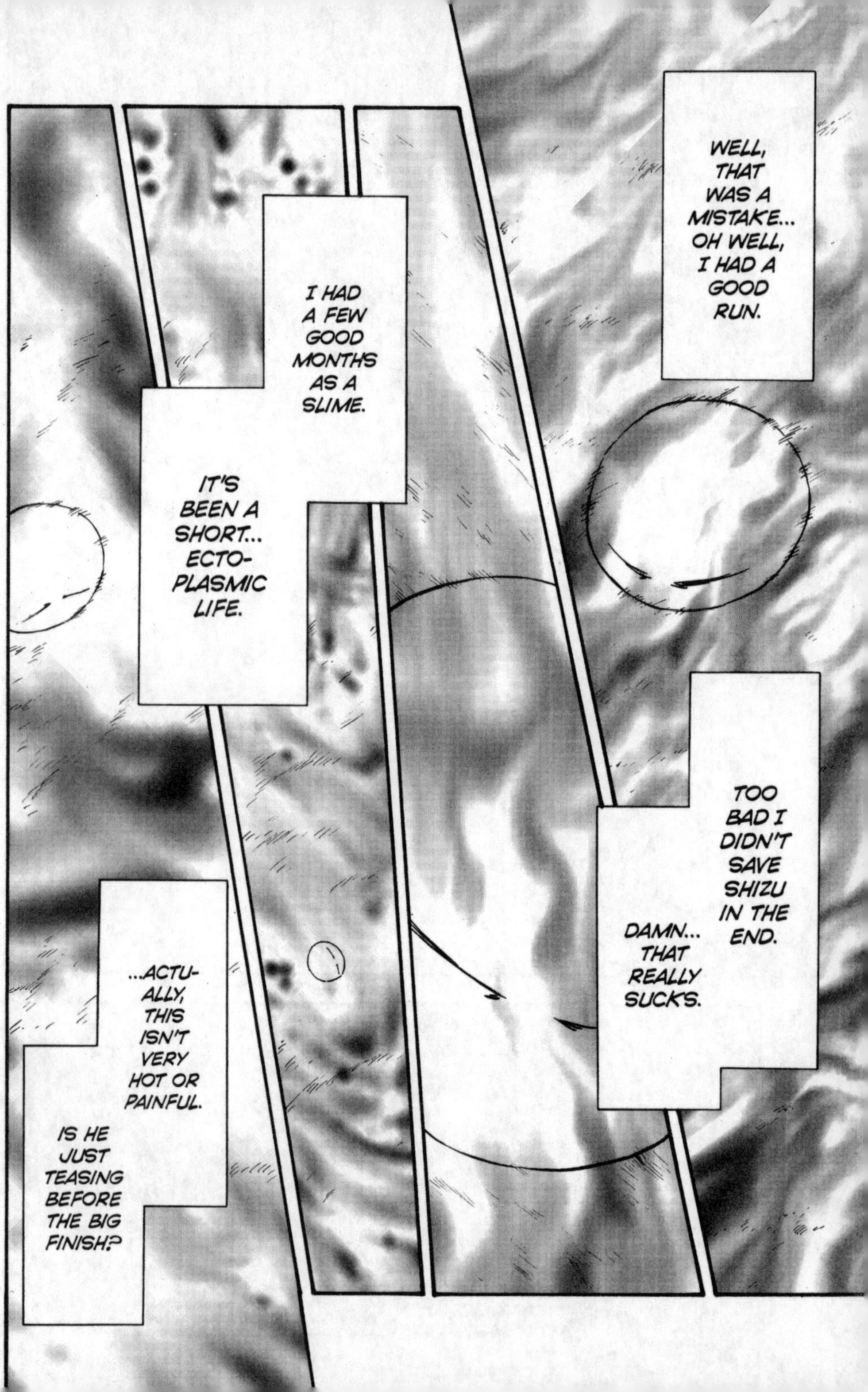
WELL, THAT WAS A MISTAKE... OH WELL, I HAD A GOOD RUN.
TOO BAD I DIDN'T SAVE SHIZU IN THE END.
DAMN... THAT REALLY SUCKS.
I HAD A FEW GOOD MONTHS AS A SLIME.
IT'S BEEN A SHORT... ECTO-PLASMIC LIFE.
...ACTU-ALLY, THIS ISN'T VERY HOT OR PAINFUL.
IS HE JUST TEASING BEFORE THE BIG FINISH?

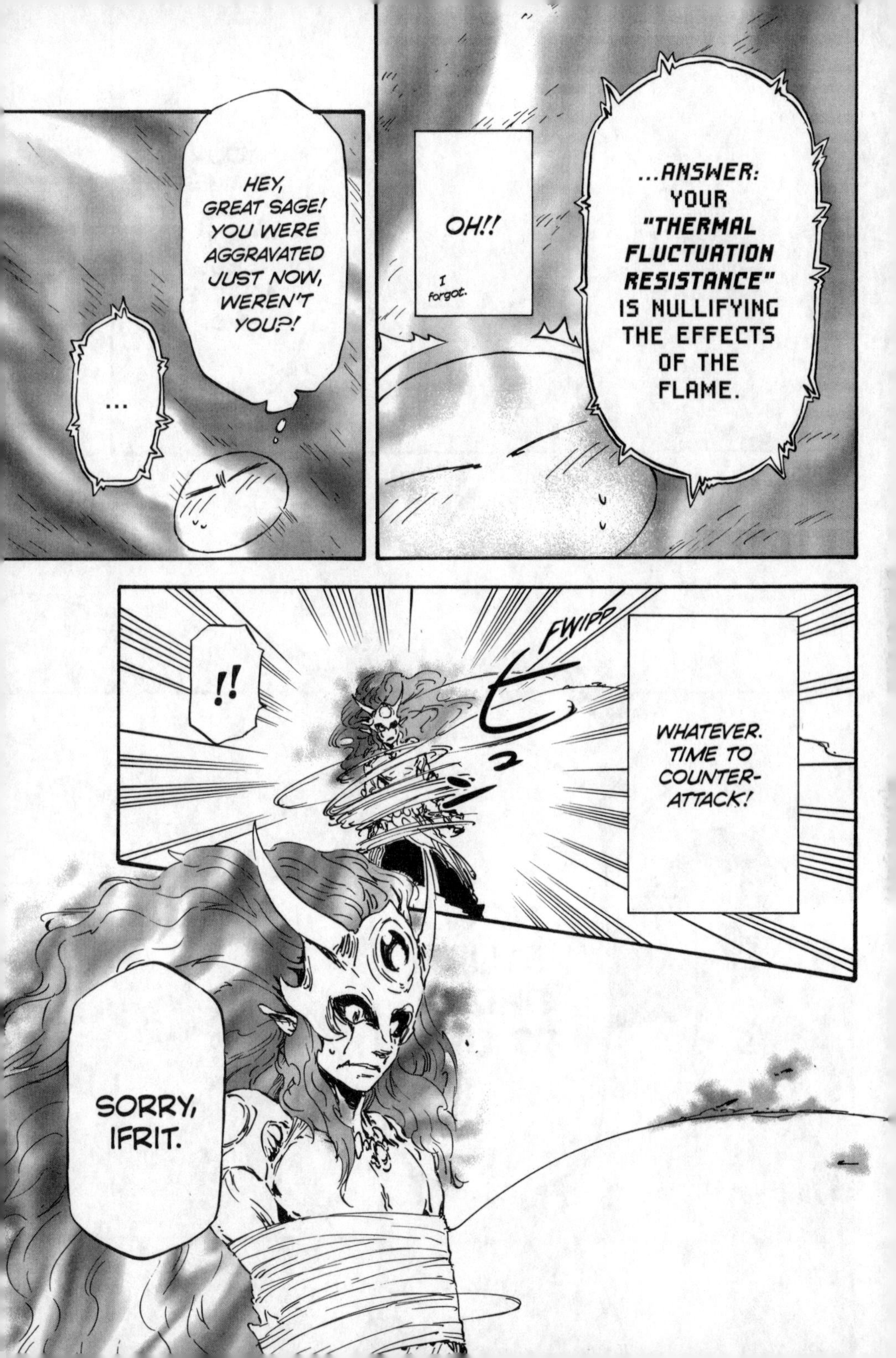
...ANSWER: YOUR "THERMAL FLUCTUATION RESISTANCE" IS NULLIFYING THE EFFECTS OF THE FLAME.
OH!!
I forgot.
HEY, GREAT SAGE! YOU WERE AGGRAVATED JUST NOW, WEREN'T YOU?!
...
WHATEVER. TIME TO COUNTER-ATTACK!
FWIPP
!!
SORRY, IFRIT.

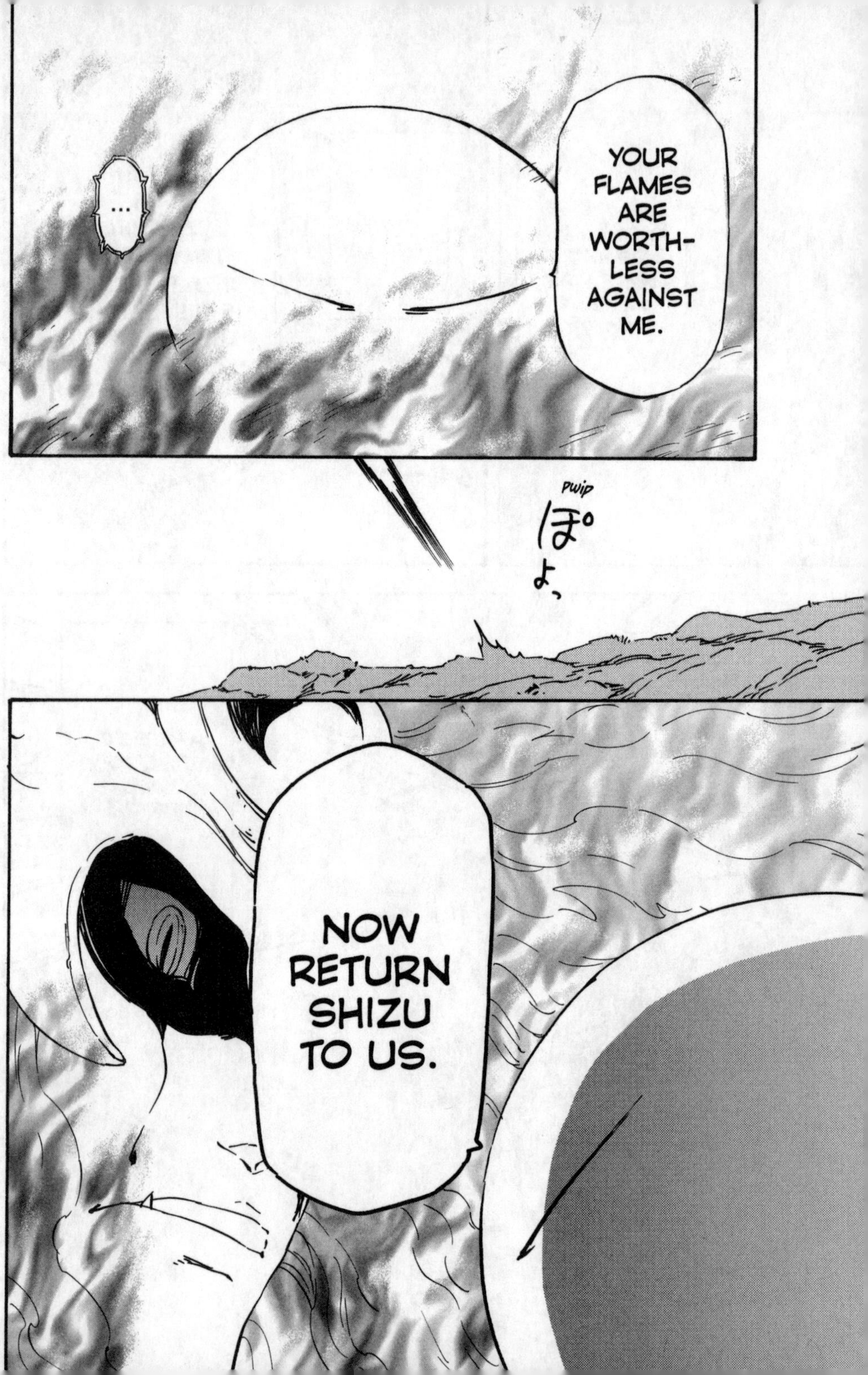
YOUR FLAMES ARE WORTH-LESS AGAINST ME.
...
PWIP
ぽよ
NOW RETURN SHIZU TO US.

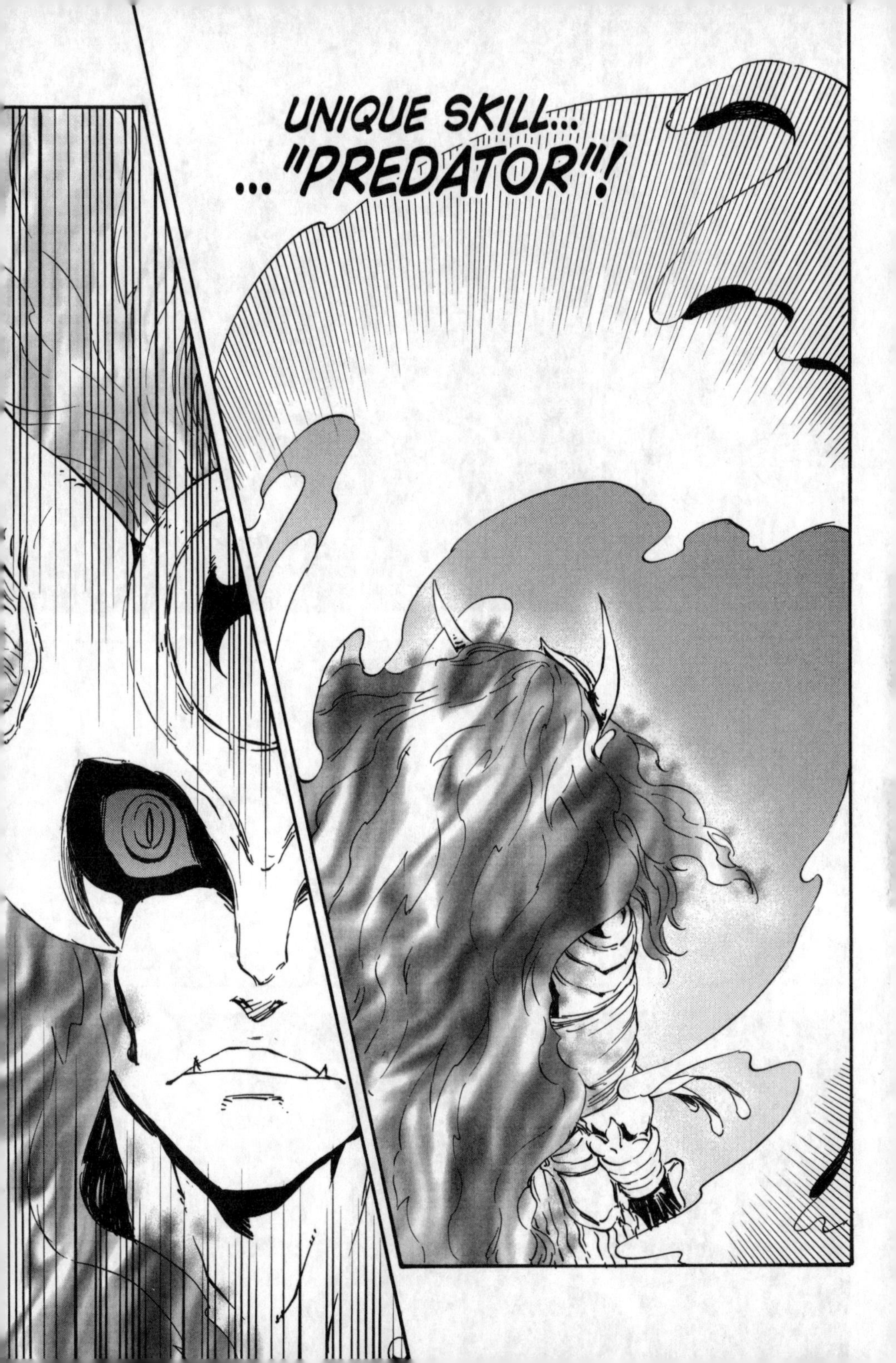
UNIQUE SKILL...
..."PREDATOR"!

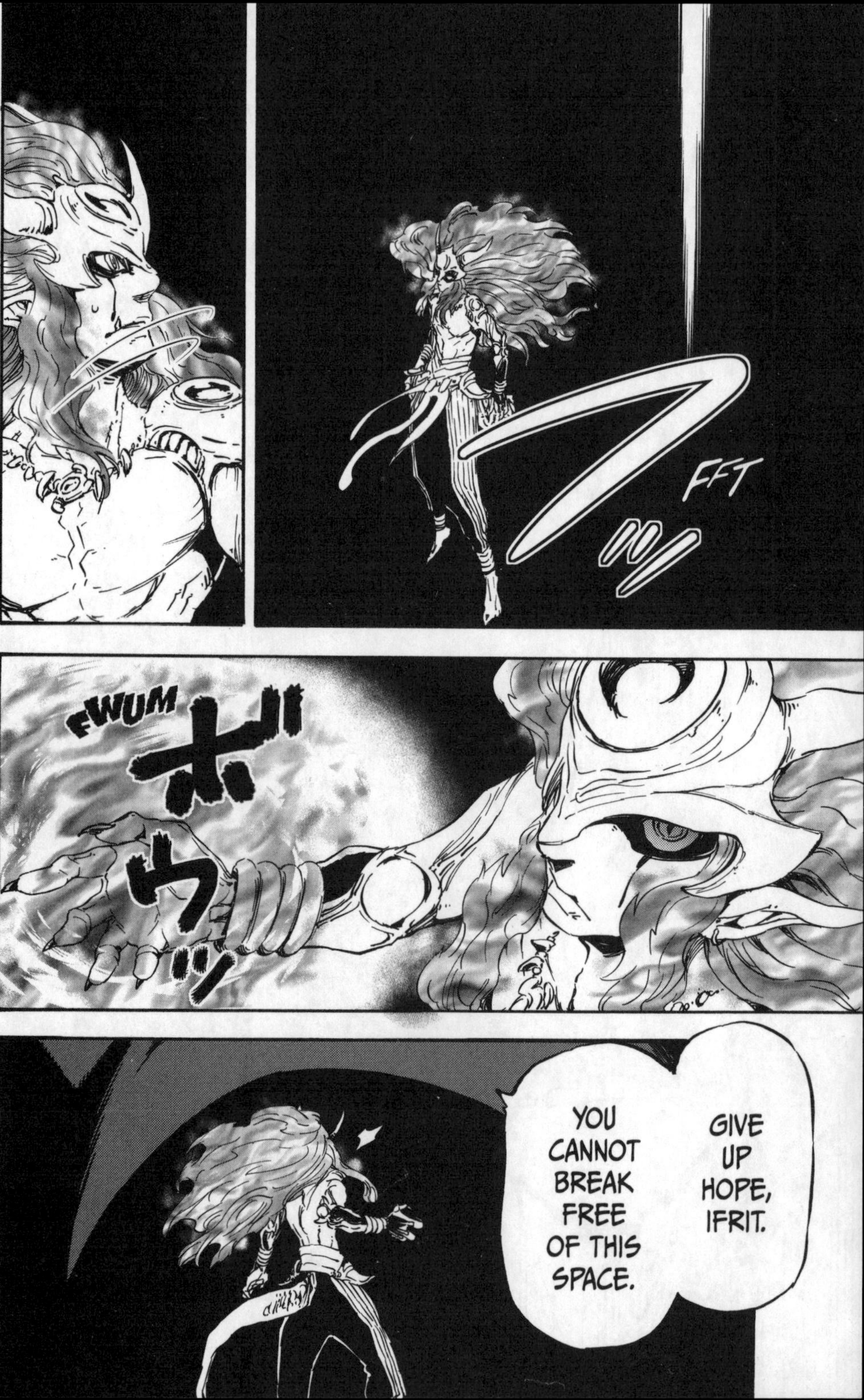
FFT
FWUM
YOU CANNOT BREAK FREE OF THIS SPACE.
GIVE UP HOPE, IFRIT.

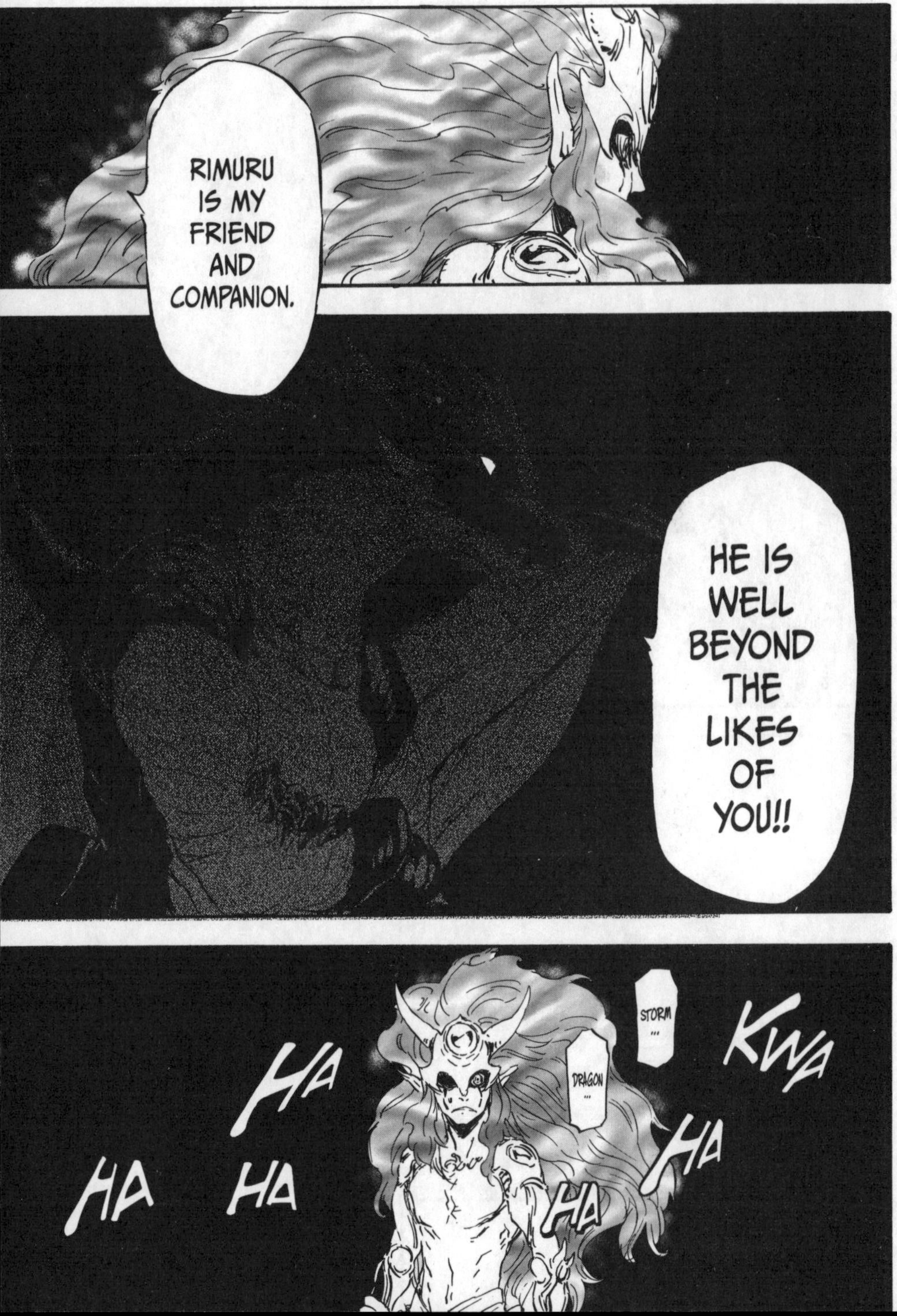
RIMURU IS MY FRIEND AND COMPANION.
HE IS WELL BEYOND THE LIKES OF YOU!!
STORM ...
KWA
DRAGON ...
HA
HA
HA
HA
HA

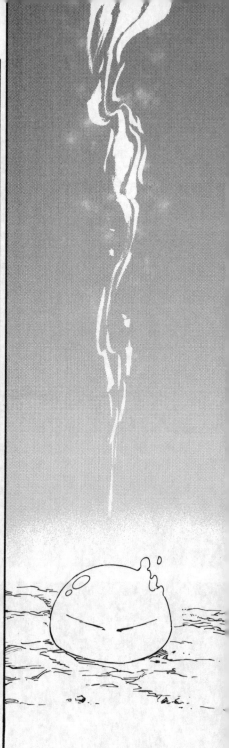

PLOP...
ぽ
よ...

THANK YOU...

...MR. SLIME.

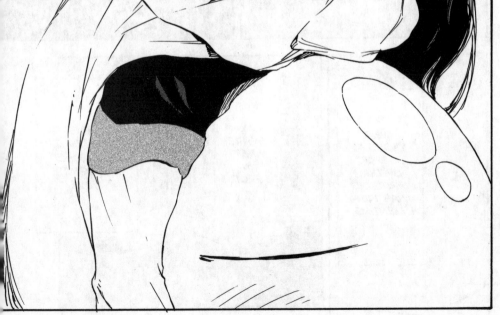

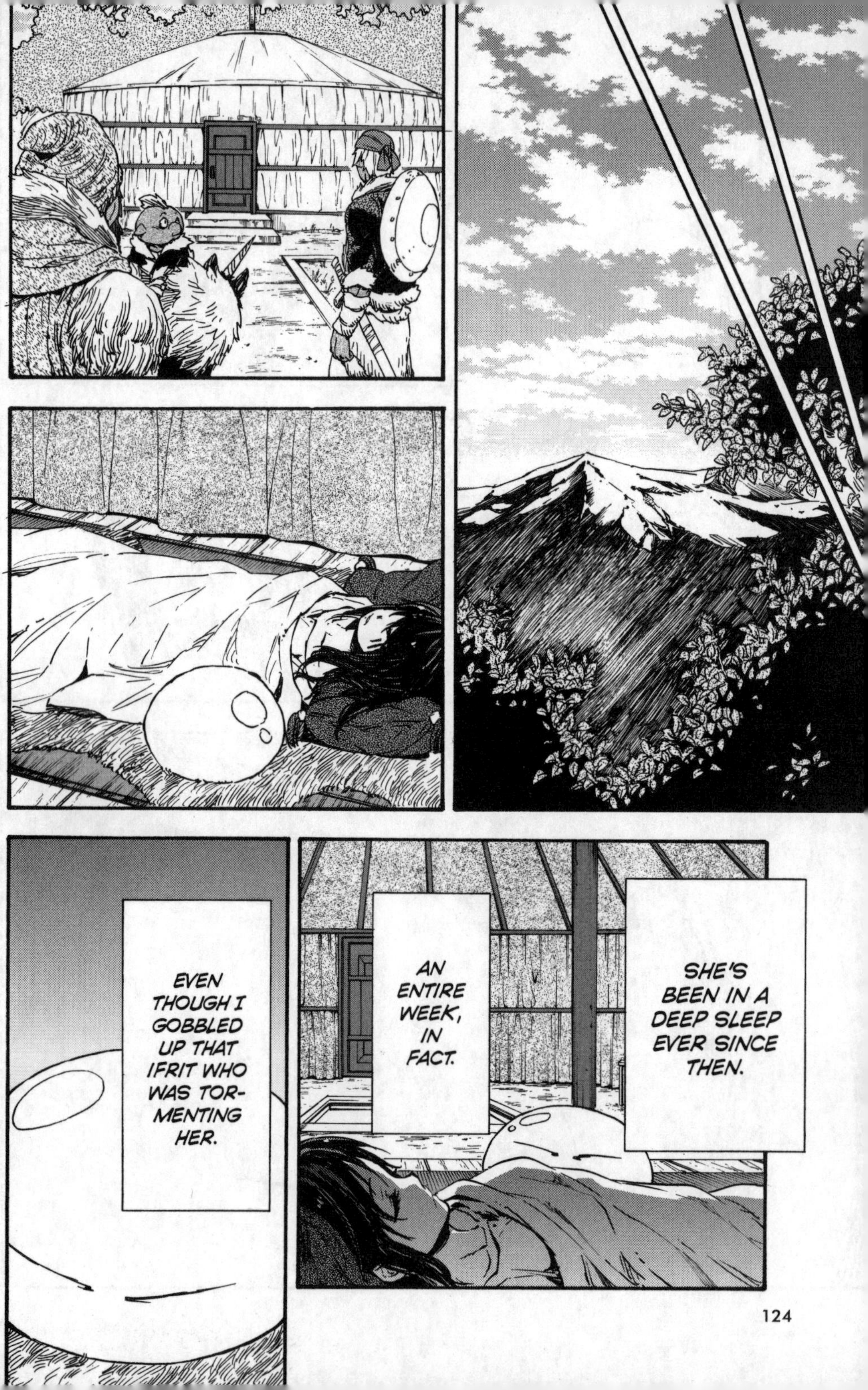
SHE'S BEEN IN A DEEP SLEEP EVER SINCE THEN.
AN ENTIRE WEEK, IN FACT.
EVEN THOUGH I GOBBLED UP THAT IFRIT WHO WAS TORMENTING HER.

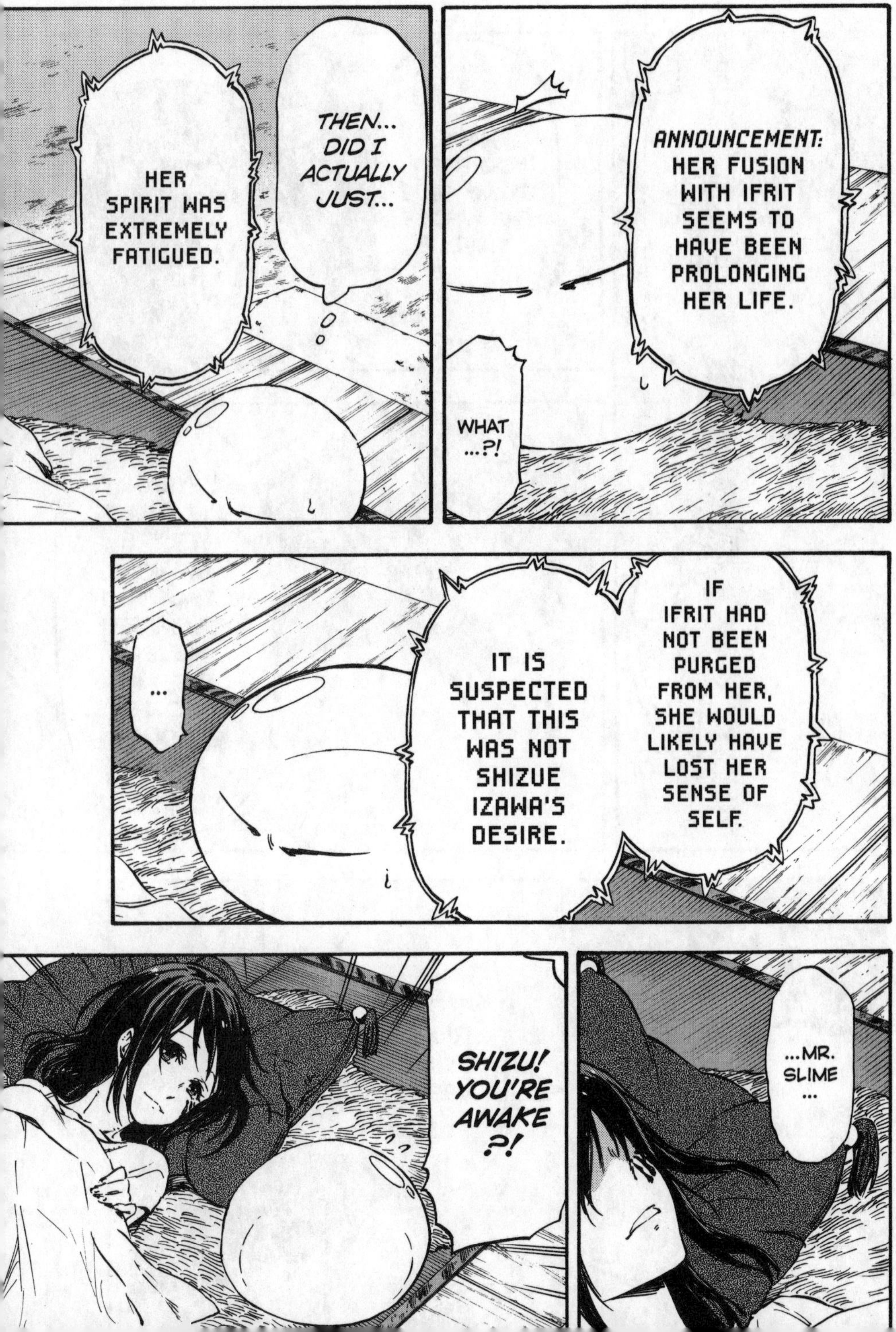
ANNOUNCEMENT: HER FUSION WITH IFRIT SEEMS TO HAVE BEEN PROLONGING HER LIFE.
WHAT ...?!
THEN... DID I ACTUALLY JUST...
HER SPIRIT WAS EXTREMELY FATIGUED.
IF IFRIT HAD NOT BEEN PURGED FROM HER, SHE WOULD LIKELY HAVE LOST HER SENSE OF SELF.
IT IS SUSPECTED THAT THIS WAS NOT SHIZUE IZAWA'S DESIRE.
...
...MR. SLIME ...
SHIZU! YOU'RE AWAKE ?!

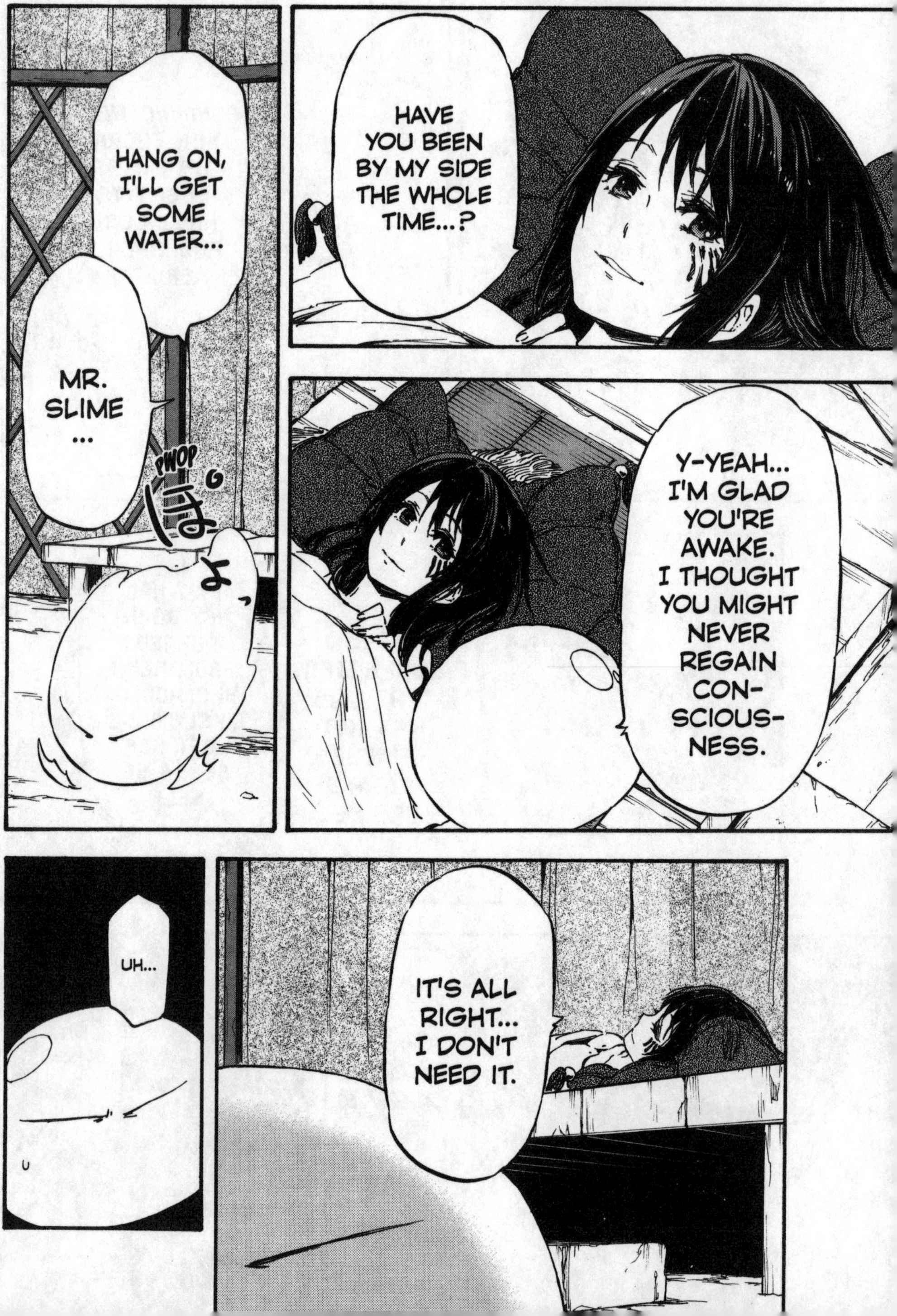
HAVE YOU BEEN BY MY SIDE THE WHOLE TIME...?
Y-YEAH... I'M GLAD YOU'RE AWAKE. I THOUGHT YOU MIGHT NEVER REGAIN CON-SCIOUS-NESS.
HANG ON, I'LL GET SOME WATER...
MR. SLIME ...
PWOP
ぽよ
IT'S ALL RIGHT... I DON'T NEED IT.
UH...

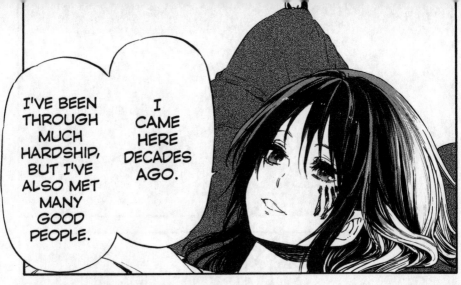

I CAME HERE DECADES AGO.
I'VE BEEN THROUGH MUCH HARDSHIP, BUT I'VE ALSO MET MANY GOOD PEOPLE.
AND AT THE VERY END... I HAD A MIRACULOUS ENCOUNTER.
I DIDN'T GET TO DO EVERYTHING I WANTED IN LIFE...
...BUT I'VE LIVED LONG ENOUGH.

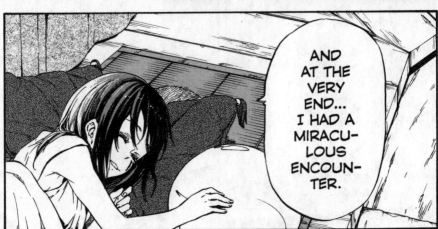

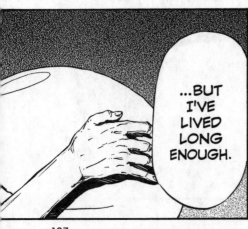

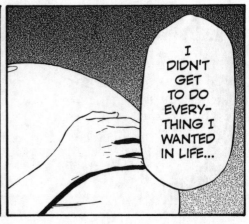

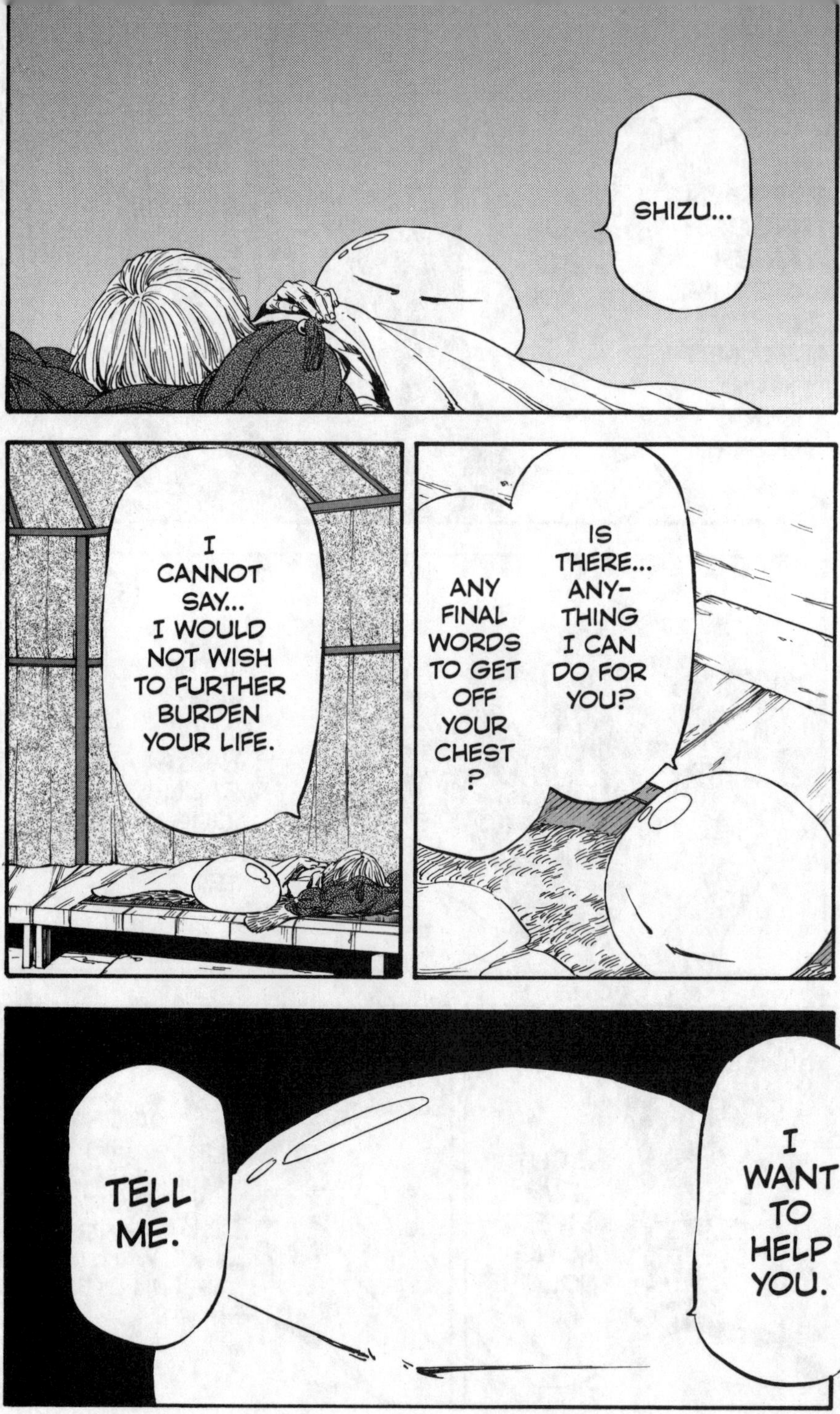
SHIZU...
IS THERE... ANYTHING I CAN DO FOR YOU?
ANY FINAL WORDS TO GET OFF YOUR CHEST?
I CANNOT SAY... I WOULD NOT WISH TO FURTHER BURDEN YOUR LIFE.
I WANT TO HELP YOU.
TELL ME.

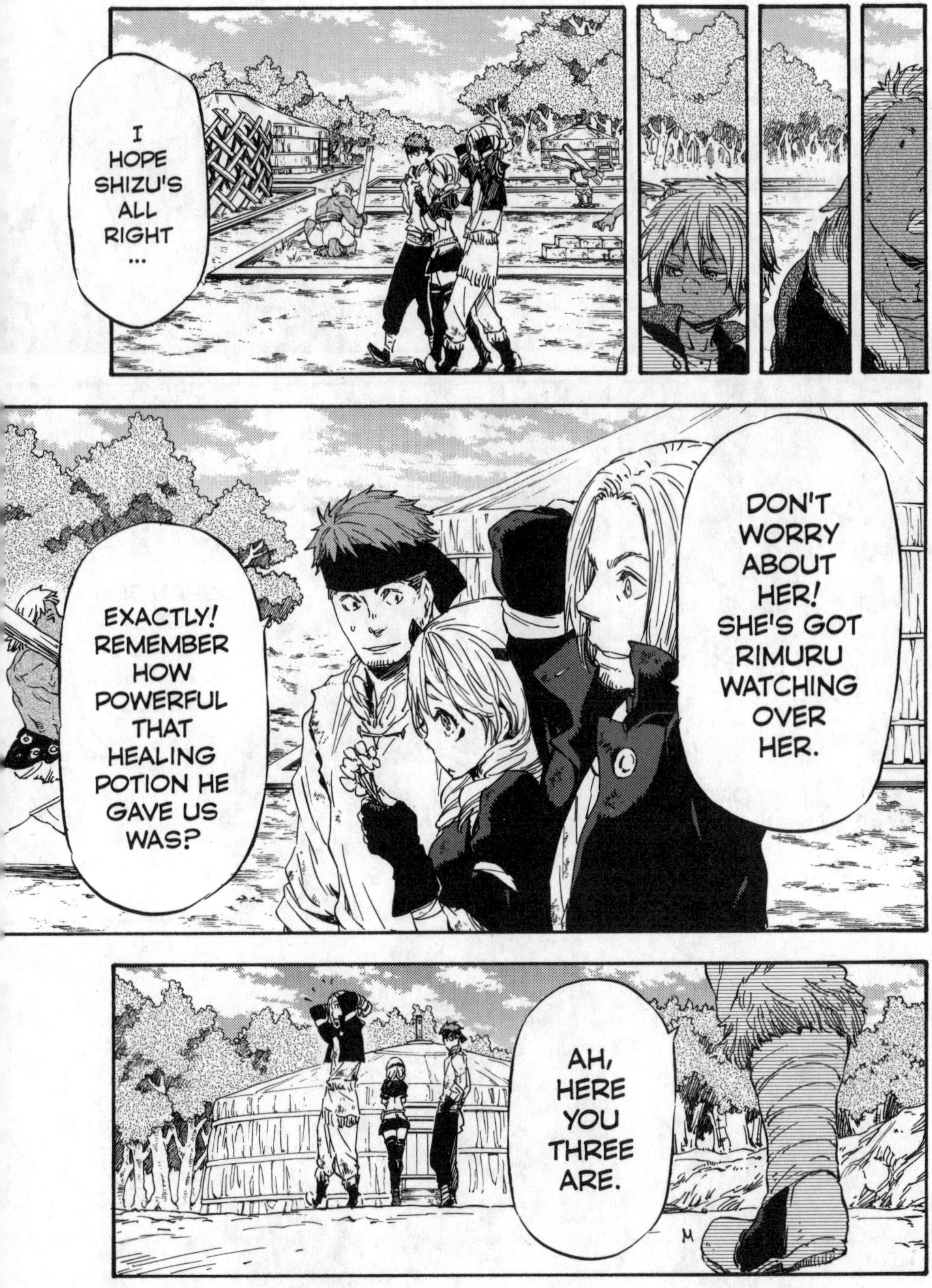
I HOPE SHIZU'S ALL RIGHT...
DON'T WORRY ABOUT HER! SHE'S GOT RIMURU WATCHING OVER HER.
EXACTLY! REMEMBER HOW POWERFUL THAT HEALING POTION HE GAVE US WAS?
AH, HERE YOU THREE ARE.

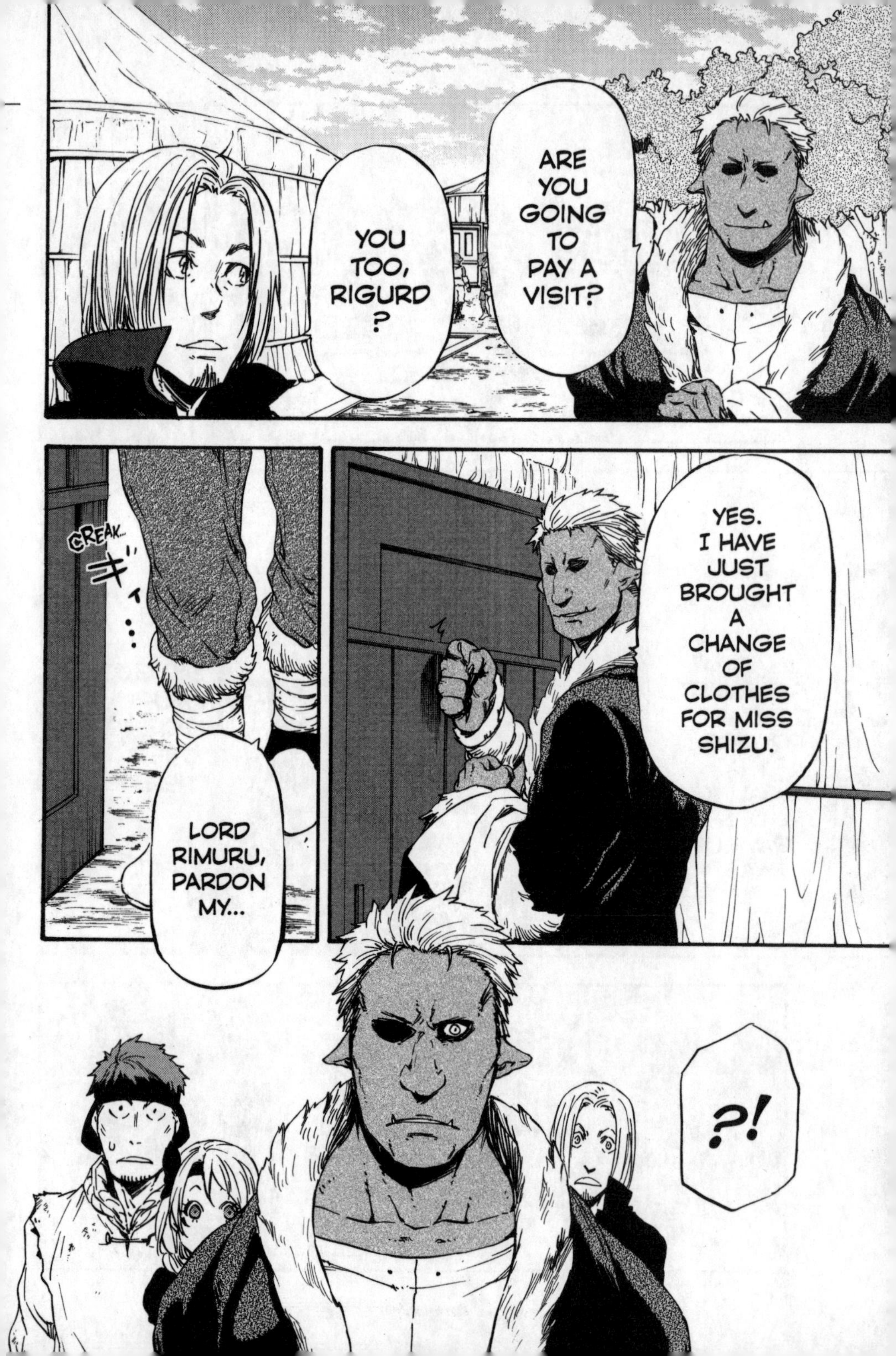
ARE YOU GOING TO PAY A VISIT?
YOU TOO, RIGURD?
YES. I HAVE JUST BROUGHT A CHANGE OF CLOTHES FOR MISS SHIZU.
CREAK...
ギィ…
LORD RIMURU, PARDON MY...
?!

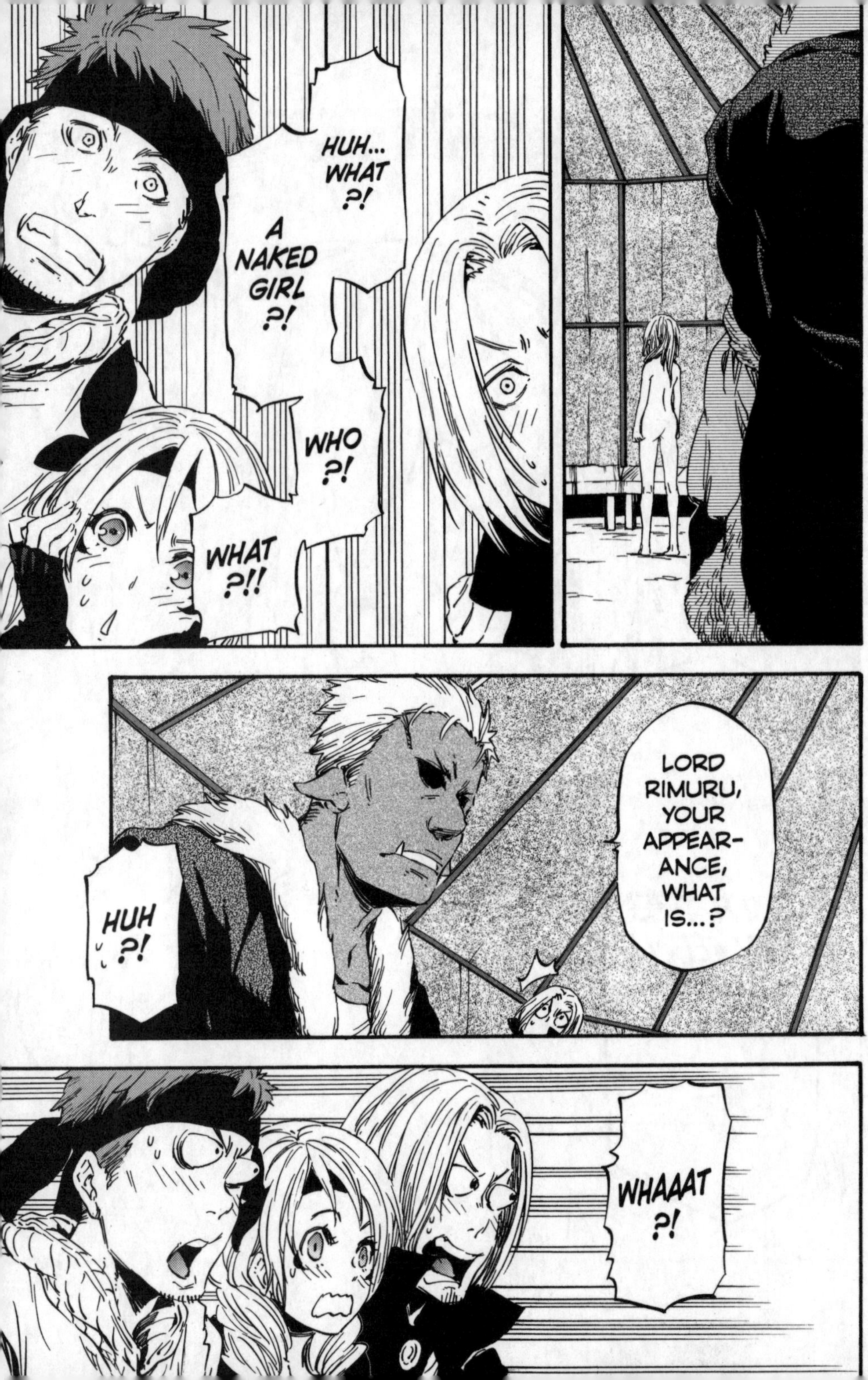
HUH... WHAT ?!
A NAKED GIRL ?!
WHO ?!
WHAT ?!!
LORD RIMURU, YOUR APPEARANCE, WHAT IS...?
HUH ?!
WHAAAT ?!

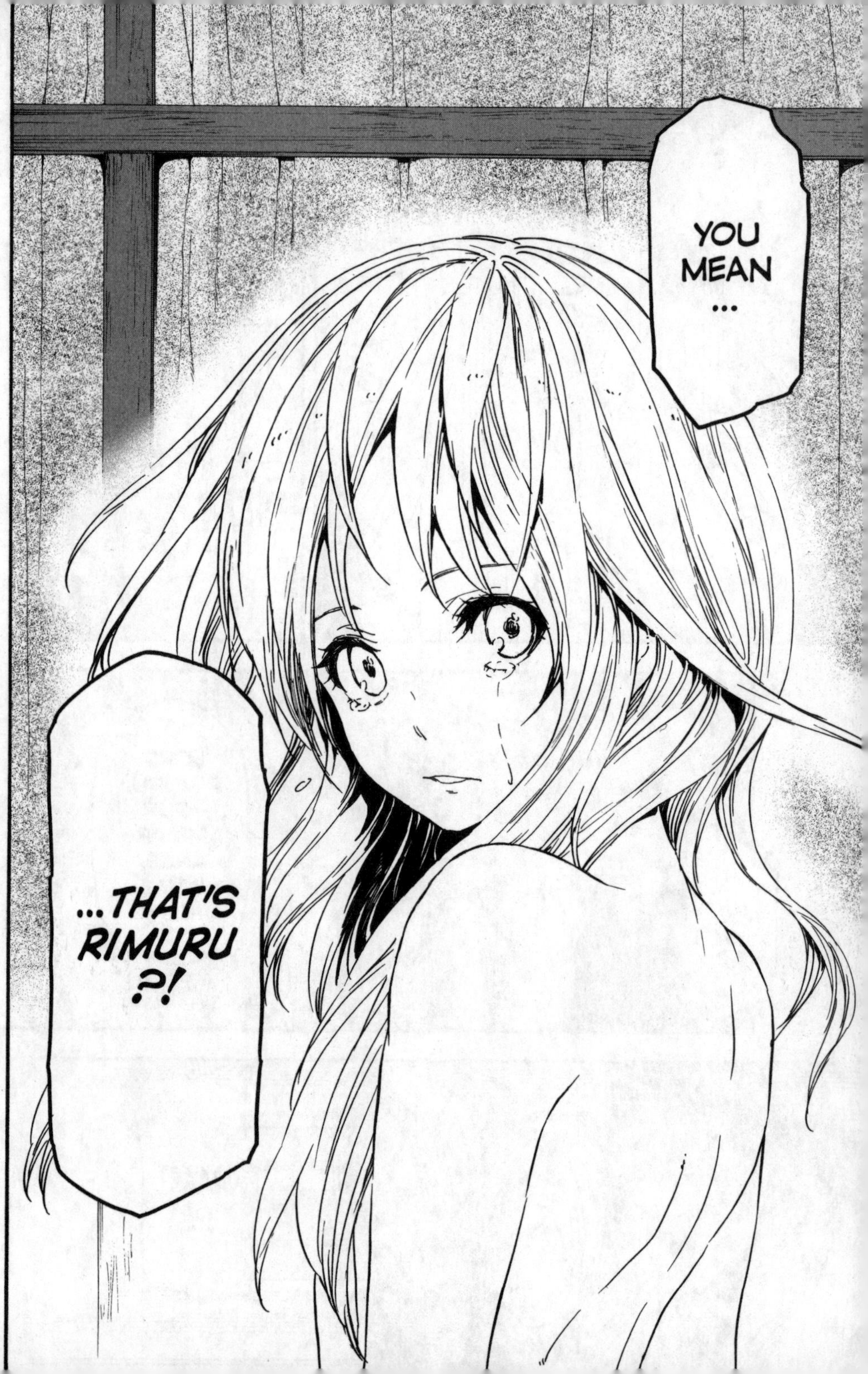
YOU MEAN ...
...THAT'S RIMURU ?!

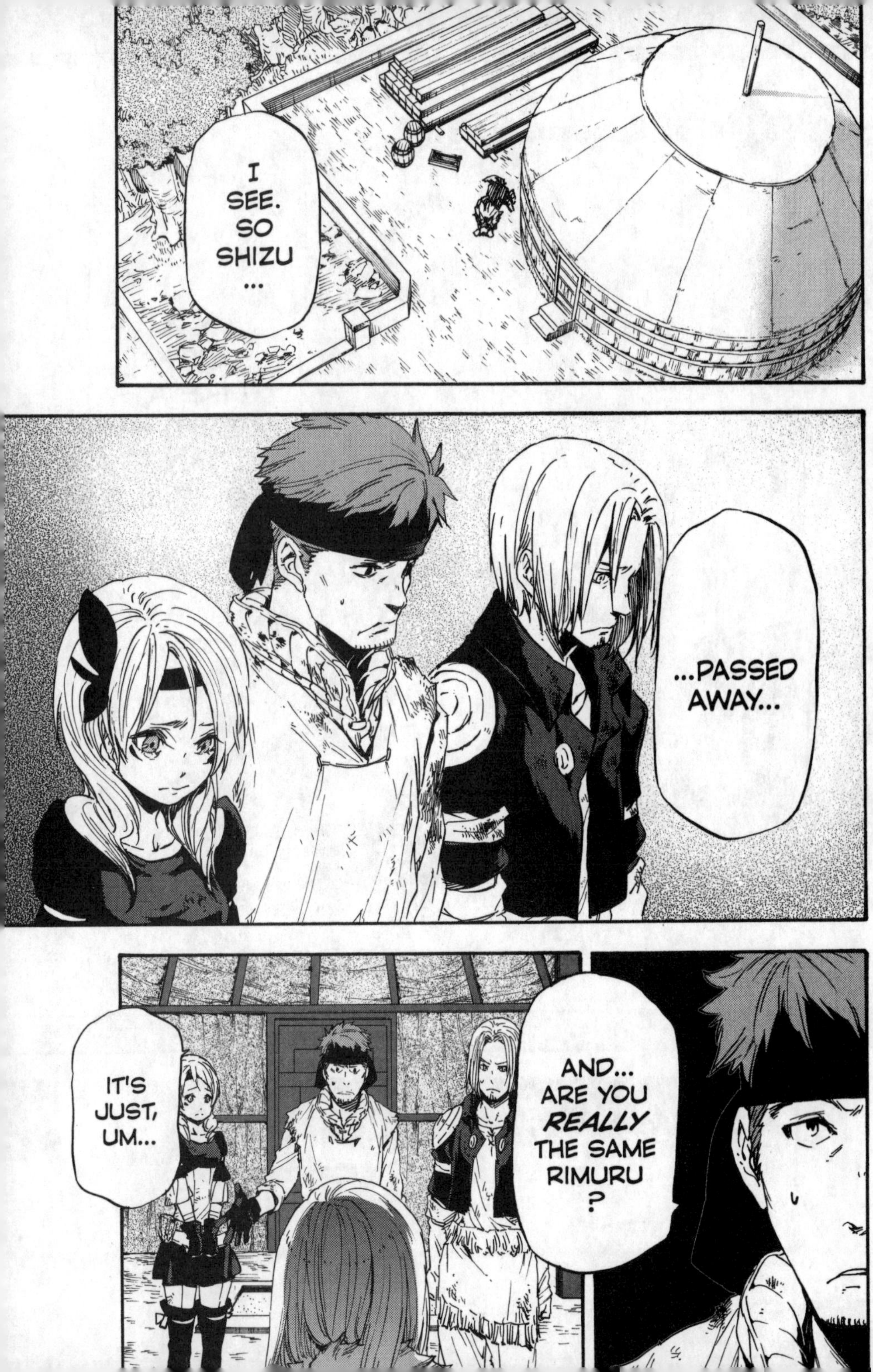
I SEE. SO SHIZU ...
...PASSED AWAY...
AND... ARE YOU *REALLY* THE SAME RIMURU ?
IT'S JUST, UM...

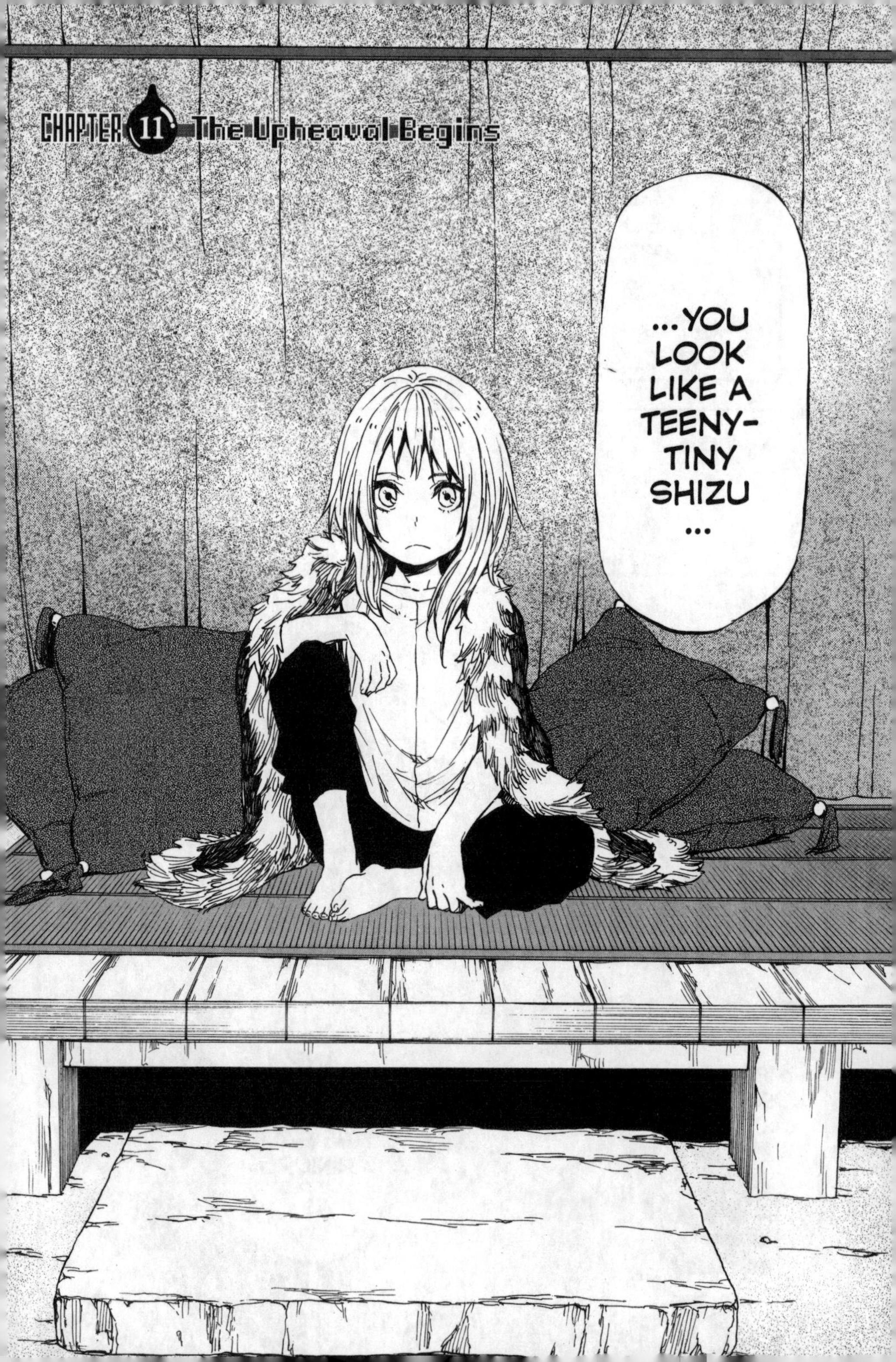
CHAPTER 11 The Upheaval Begins
...YOU LOOK LIKE A TEENY-TINY SHIZU ...

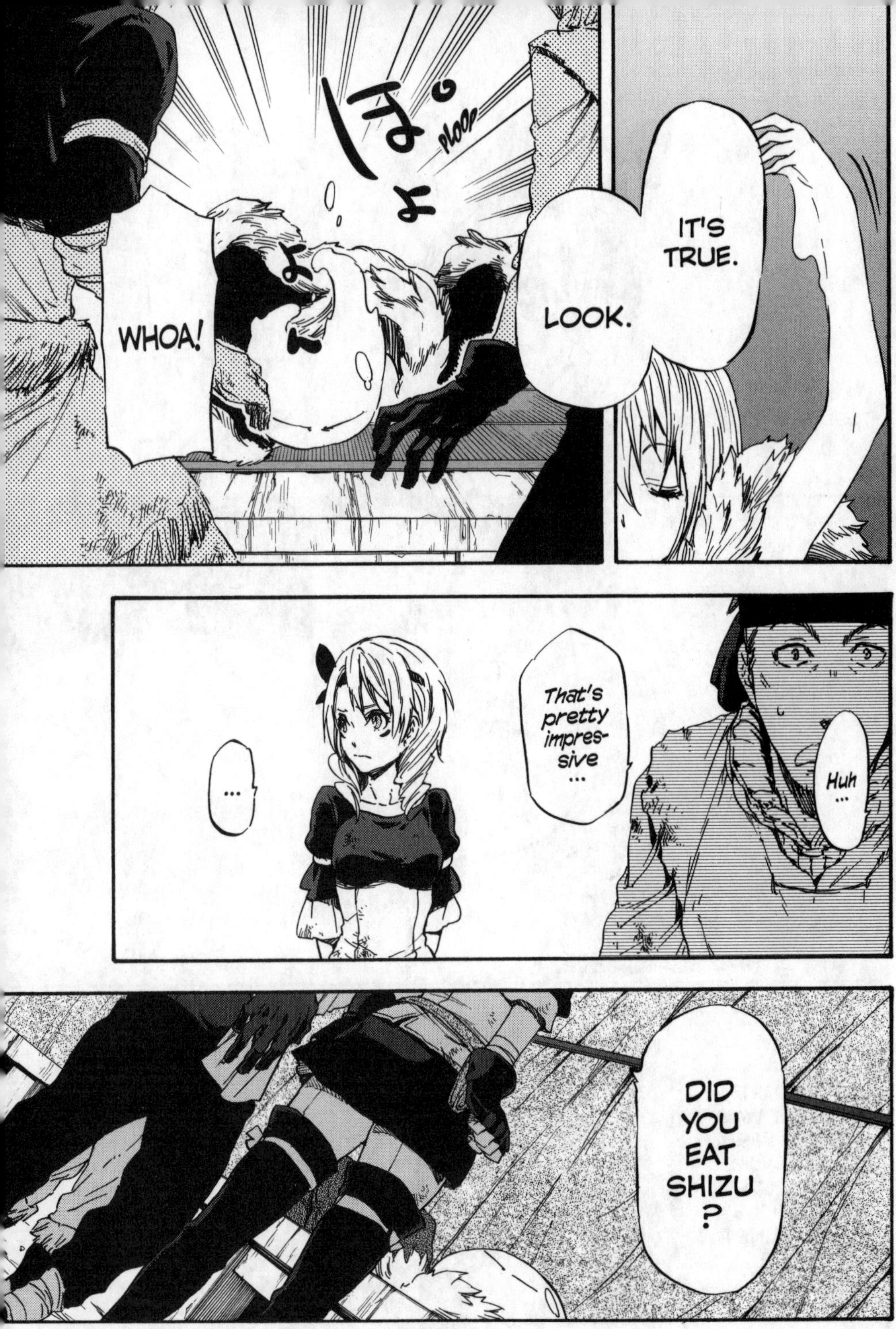
IT'S TRUE.
LOOK.
ぽよ
PLOOP
WHOA!
Huh ...
That's pretty impres-sive ...
...
DID YOU EAT SHIZU ?

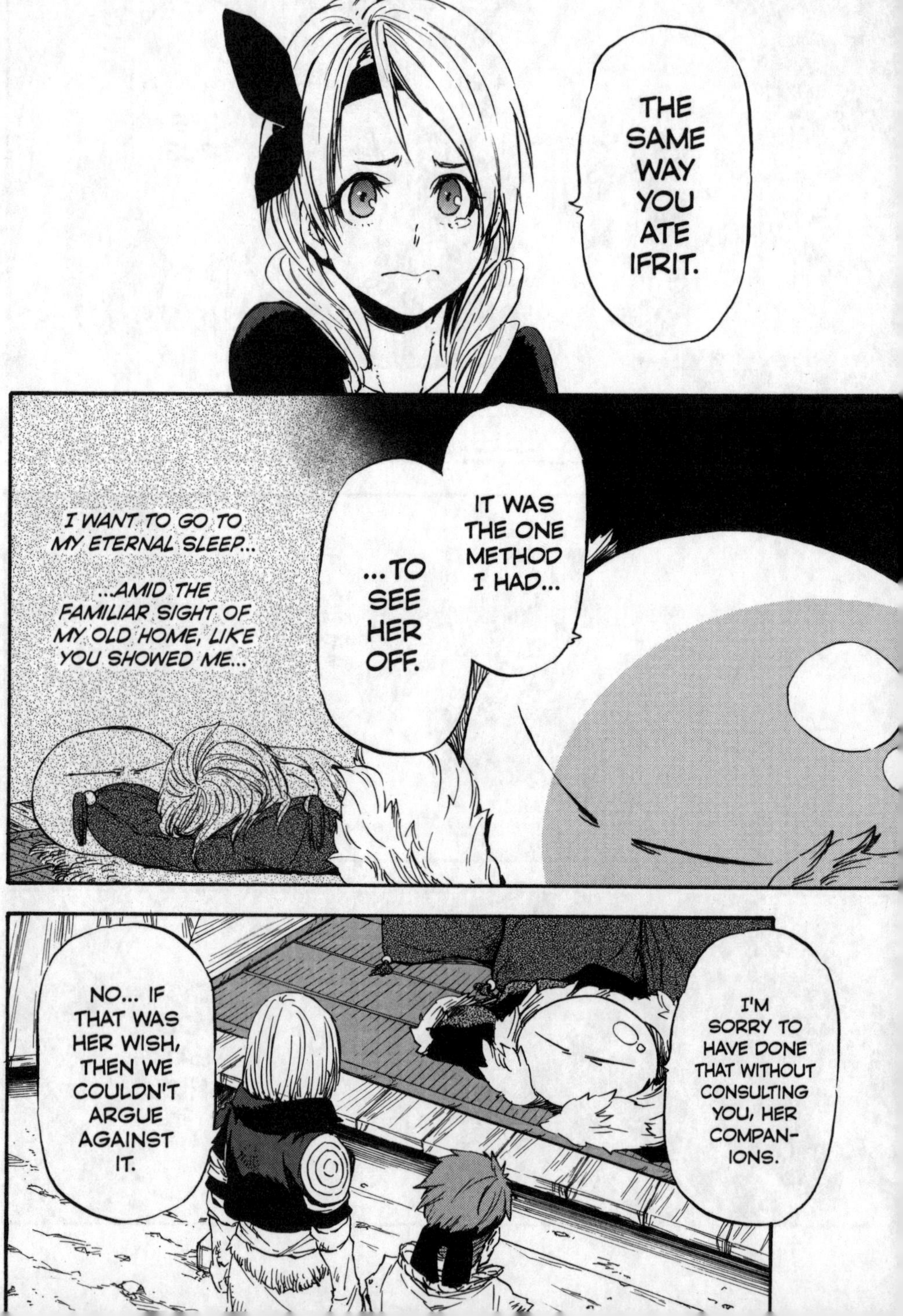
THE SAME WAY YOU ATE IFRIT.
IT WAS THE ONE METHOD I HAD...
...TO SEE HER OFF.
I WANT TO GO TO MY ETERNAL SLEEP...
...AMID THE FAMILIAR SIGHT OF MY OLD HOME, LIKE YOU SHOWED ME...
I'M SORRY TO HAVE DONE THAT WITHOUT CONSULTING YOU, HER COMPANIONS.
NO... IF THAT WAS HER WISH, THEN WE COULDN'T ARGUE AGAINST IT.

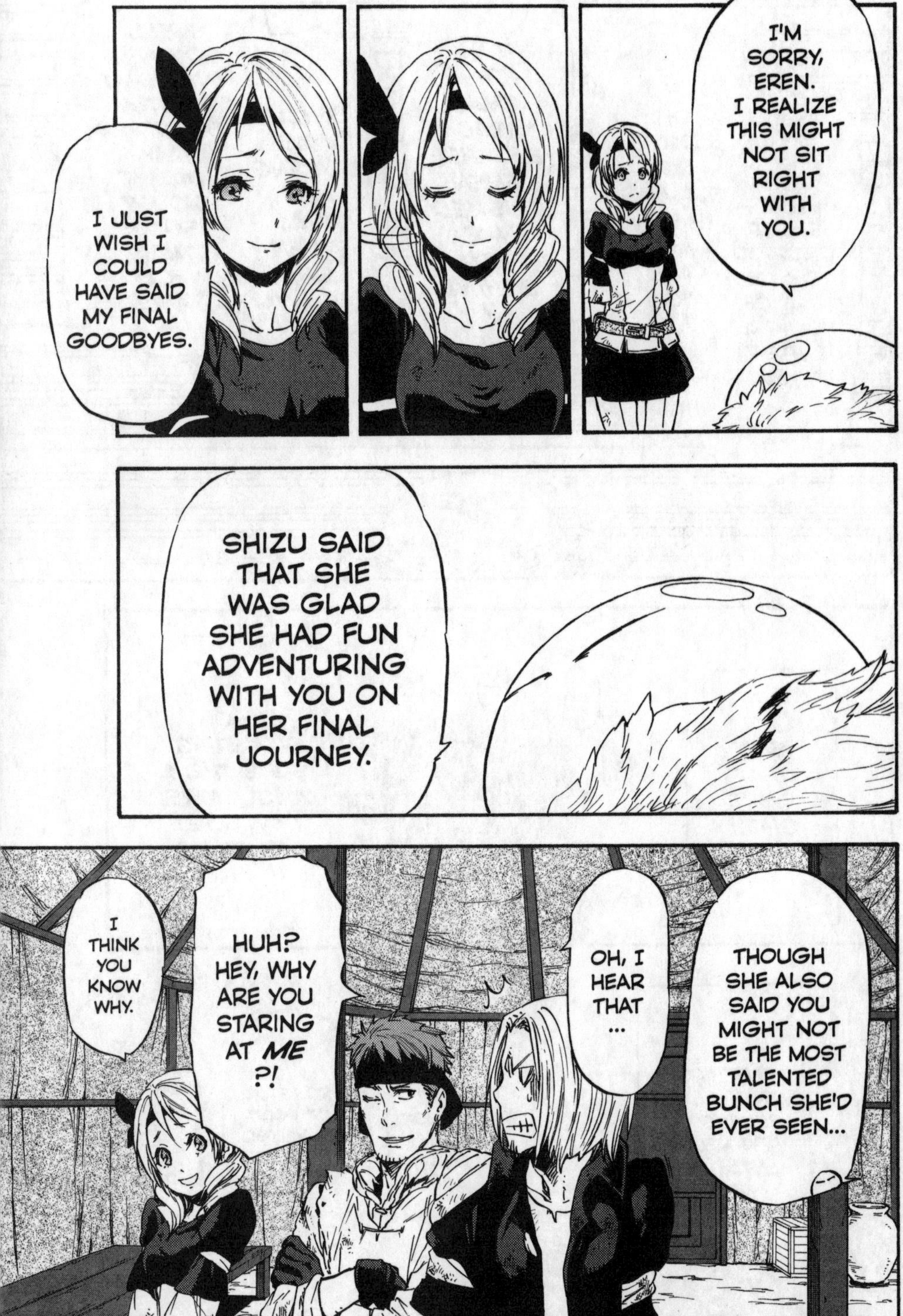
I'M SORRY, EREN. I REALIZE THIS MIGHT NOT SIT RIGHT WITH YOU.
I JUST WISH I COULD HAVE SAID MY FINAL GOODBYES.
SHIZU SAID THAT SHE WAS GLAD SHE HAD FUN ADVENTURING WITH YOU ON HER FINAL JOURNEY.
THOUGH SHE ALSO SAID YOU MIGHT NOT BE THE MOST TALENTED BUNCH SHE'D EVER SEEN...
OH, I HEAR THAT ...
HUH? HEY, WHY ARE YOU STARING AT *ME*?!
I THINK YOU KNOW WHY.

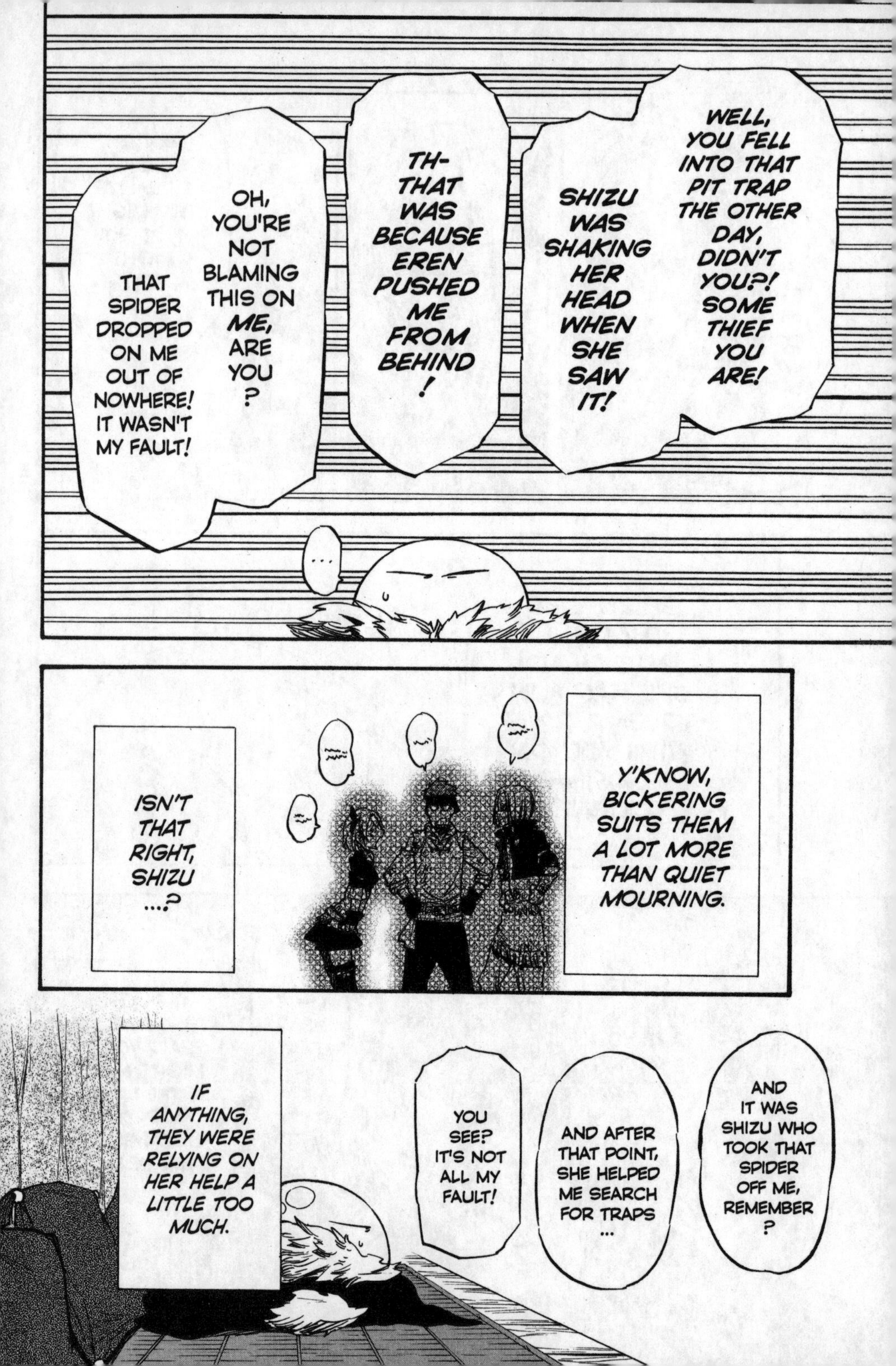
WELL, YOU FELL INTO THAT PIT TRAP THE OTHER DAY, DIDN'T YOU?! SOME THIEF YOU ARE!
SHIZU WAS SHAKING HER HEAD WHEN SHE SAW IT!
TH-THAT WAS BECAUSE EREN PUSHED ME FROM BEHIND!
OH, YOU'RE NOT BLAMING THIS ON ME, ARE YOU?
THAT SPIDER DROPPED ON ME OUT OF NOWHERE! IT WASN'T MY FAULT!
...
Y'KNOW, BICKERING SUITS THEM A LOT MORE THAN QUIET MOURNING.
ISN'T THAT RIGHT, SHIZU ...?
AND IT WAS SHIZU WHO TOOK THAT SPIDER OFF ME, REMEMBER?
AND AFTER THAT POINT, SHE HELPED ME SEARCH FOR TRAPS ...
YOU SEE? IT'S NOT ALL MY FAULT!
IF ANYTHING, THEY WERE RELYING ON HER HELP A LITTLE TOO MUCH.

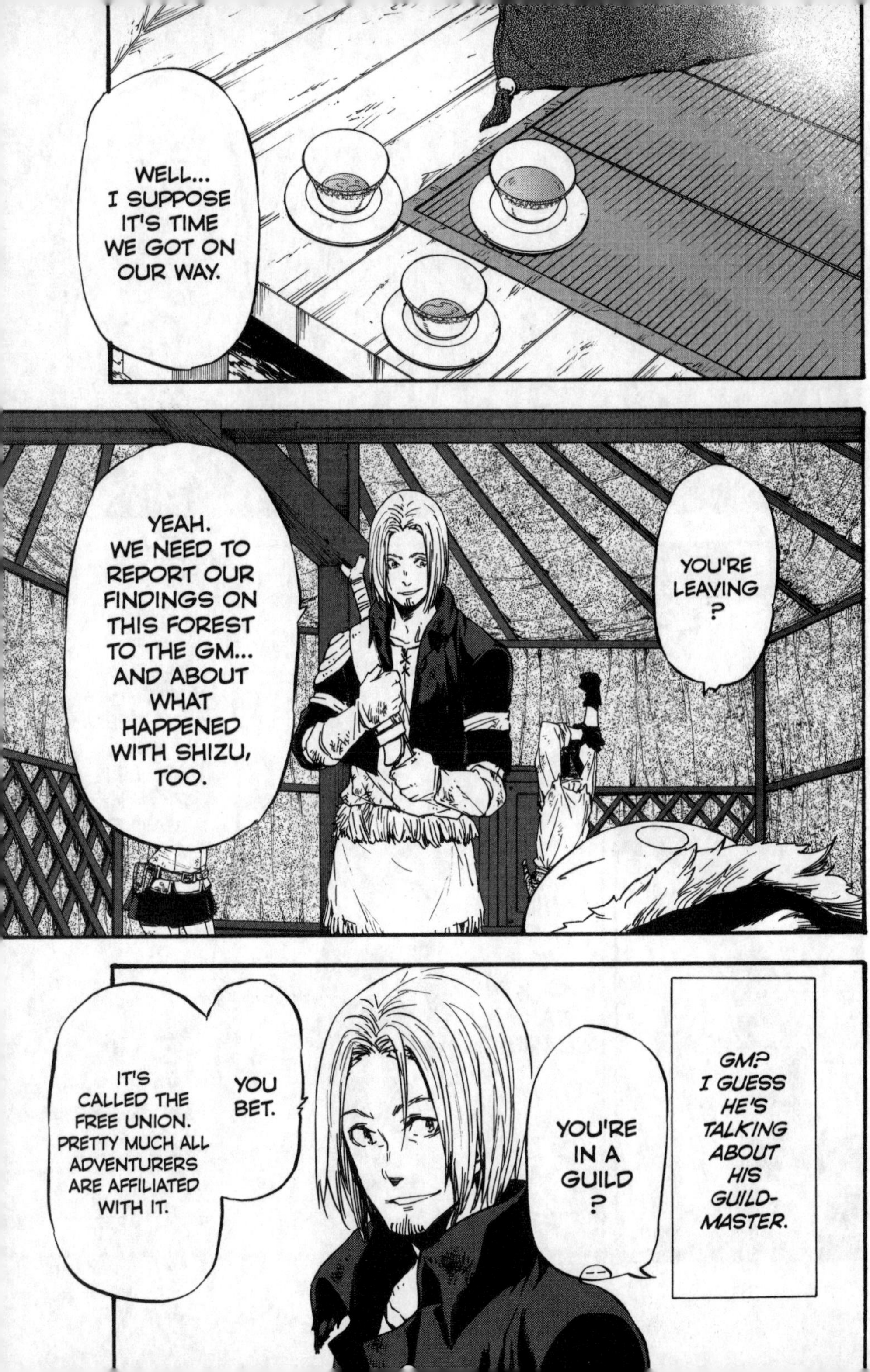
WELL... I SUPPOSE IT'S TIME WE GOT ON OUR WAY.
YOU'RE LEAVING?
YEAH. WE NEED TO REPORT OUR FINDINGS ON THIS FOREST TO THE GM... AND ABOUT WHAT HAPPENED WITH SHIZU, TOO.
GM? I GUESS HE'S TALKING ABOUT HIS GUILD-MASTER.
YOU'RE IN A GUILD?
YOU BET.
IT'S CALLED THE FREE UNION. PRETTY MUCH ALL ADVENTURERS ARE AFFILIATED WITH IT.

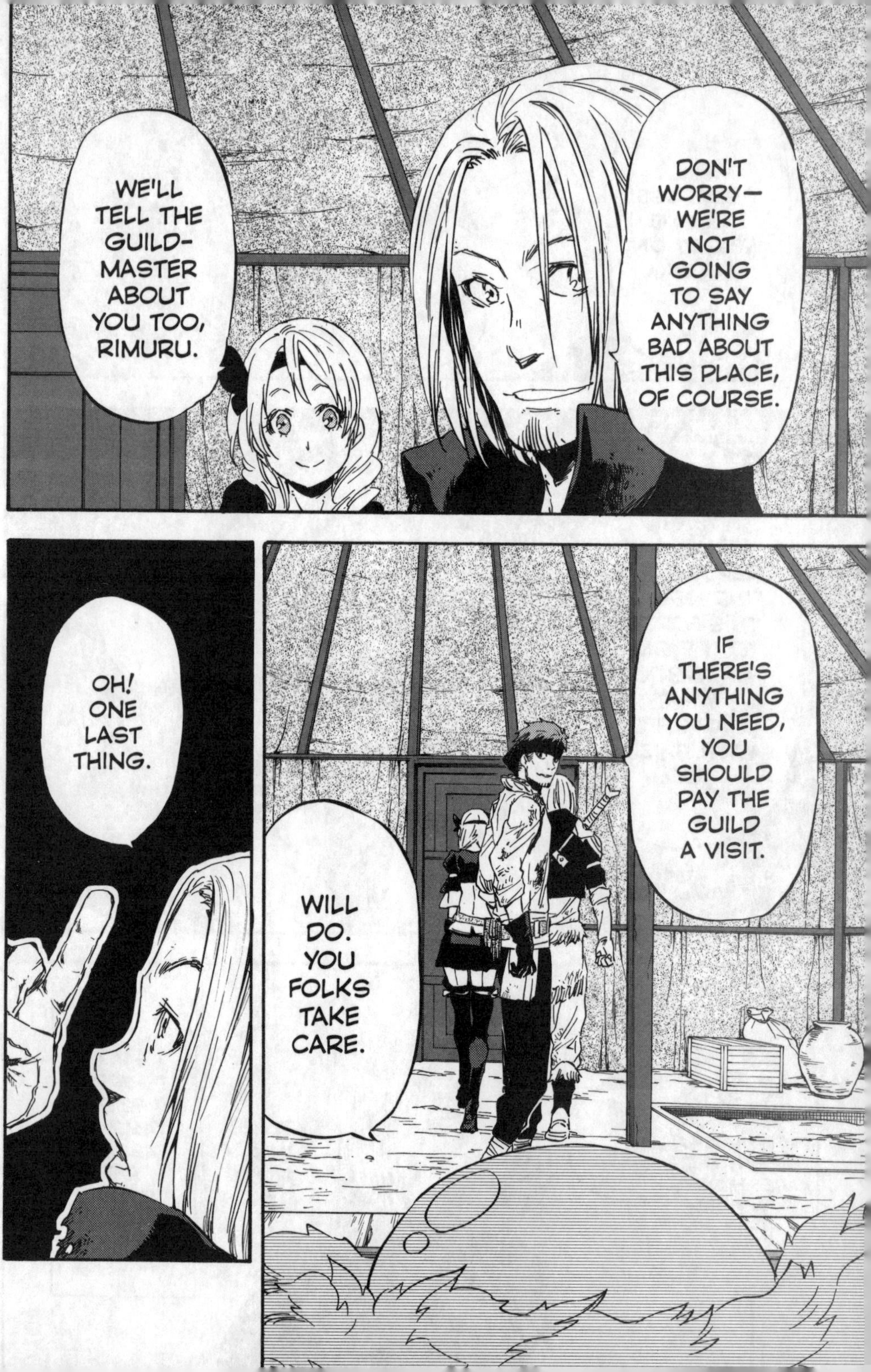
DON'T WORRY—WE'RE NOT GOING TO SAY ANYTHING BAD ABOUT THIS PLACE, OF COURSE.
WE'LL TELL THE GUILD-MASTER ABOUT YOU TOO, RIMURU.
IF THERE'S ANYTHING YOU NEED, YOU SHOULD PAY THE GUILD A VISIT.
WILL DO. YOU FOLKS TAKE CARE.
OH! ONE LAST THING.

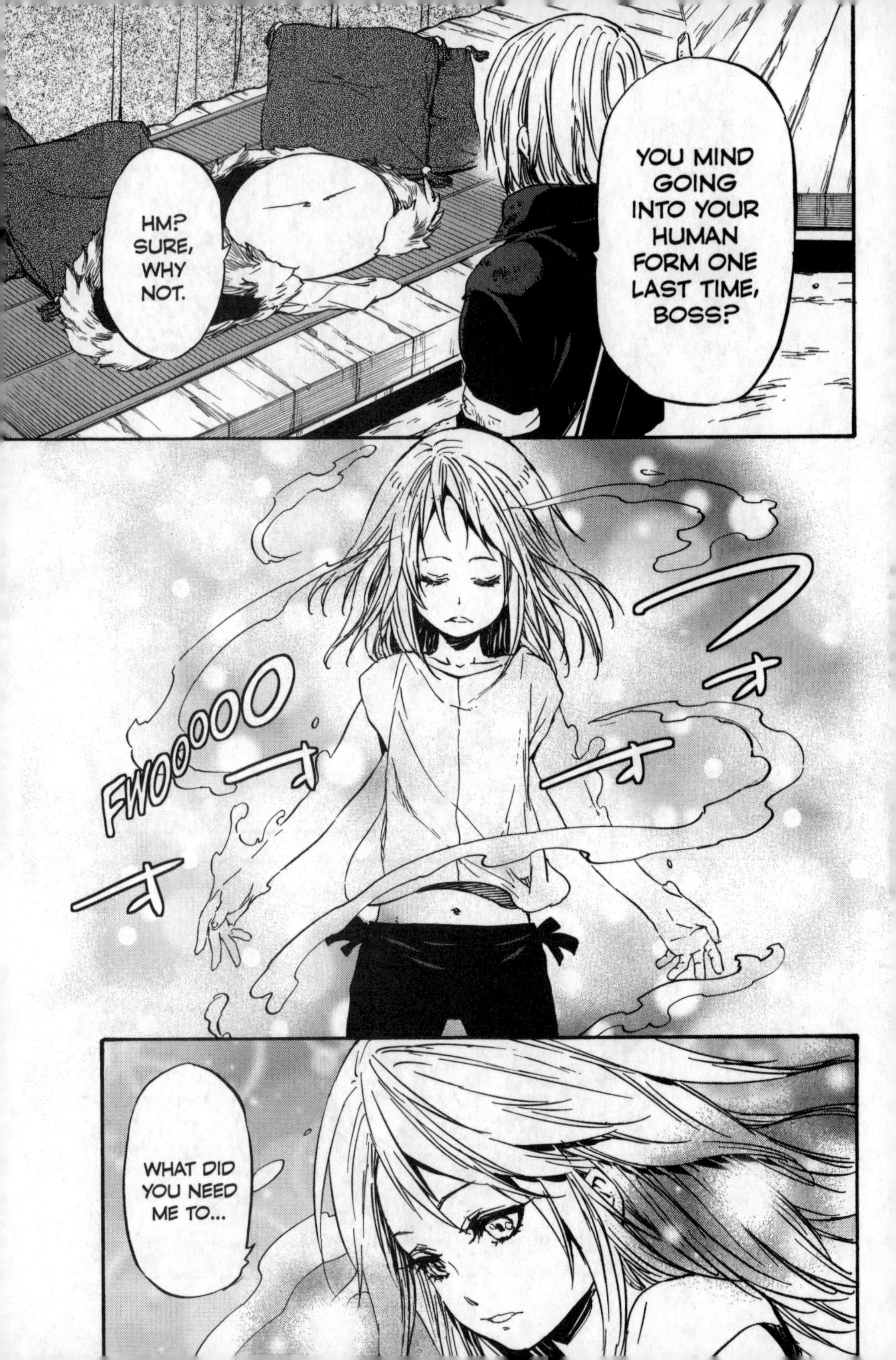
YOU MIND GOING INTO YOUR HUMAN FORM ONE LAST TIME, BOSS?
HM? SURE, WHY NOT.
FWOOOOO
WHAT DID YOU NEED ME TO...

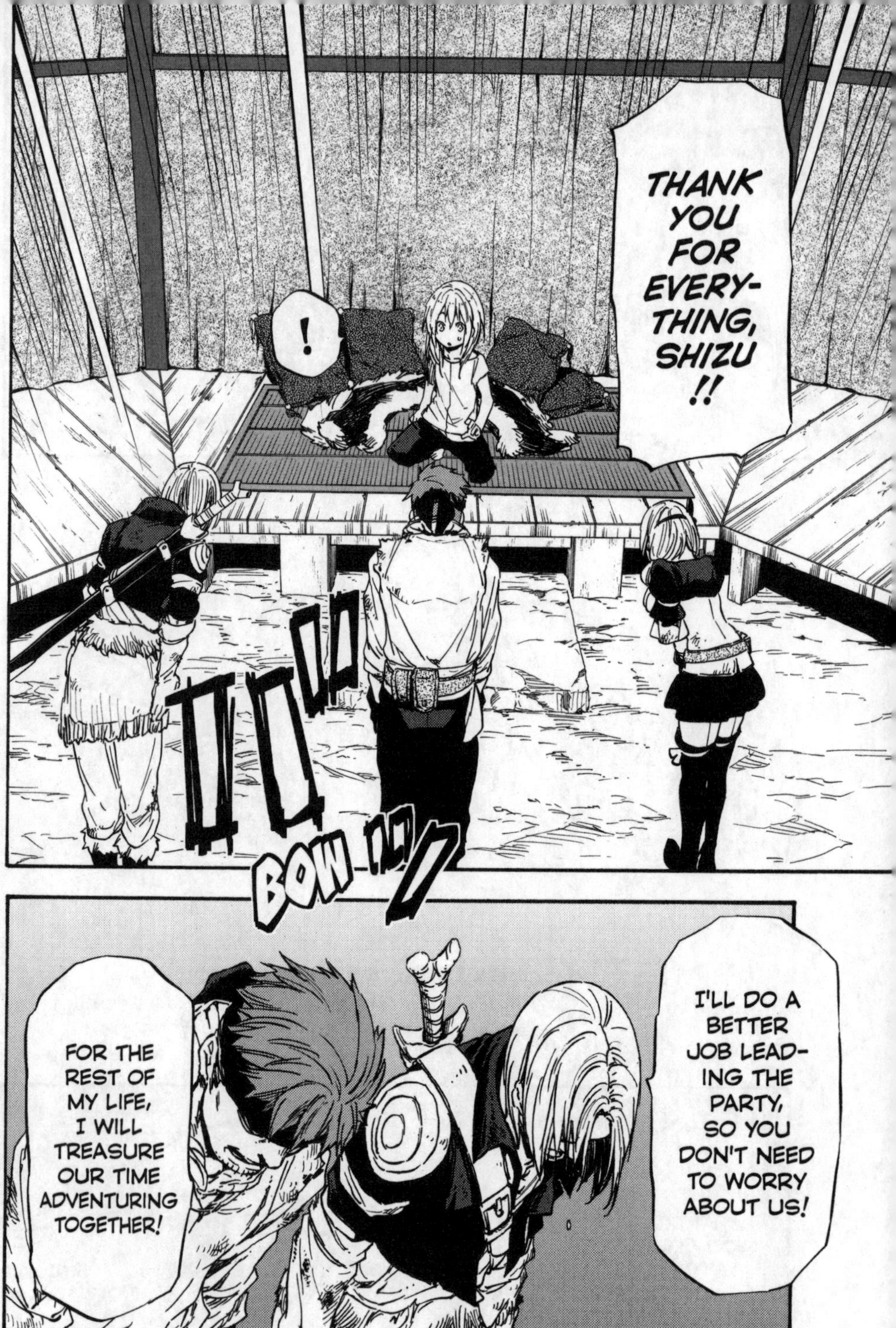
THANK YOU FOR EVERY-THING, SHIZU!!
!
BOW
I'LL DO A BETTER JOB LEAD-ING THE PARTY, SO YOU DON'T NEED TO WORRY ABOUT US!
FOR THE REST OF MY LIFE, I WILL TREASURE OUR TIME ADVENTURING TOGETHER!

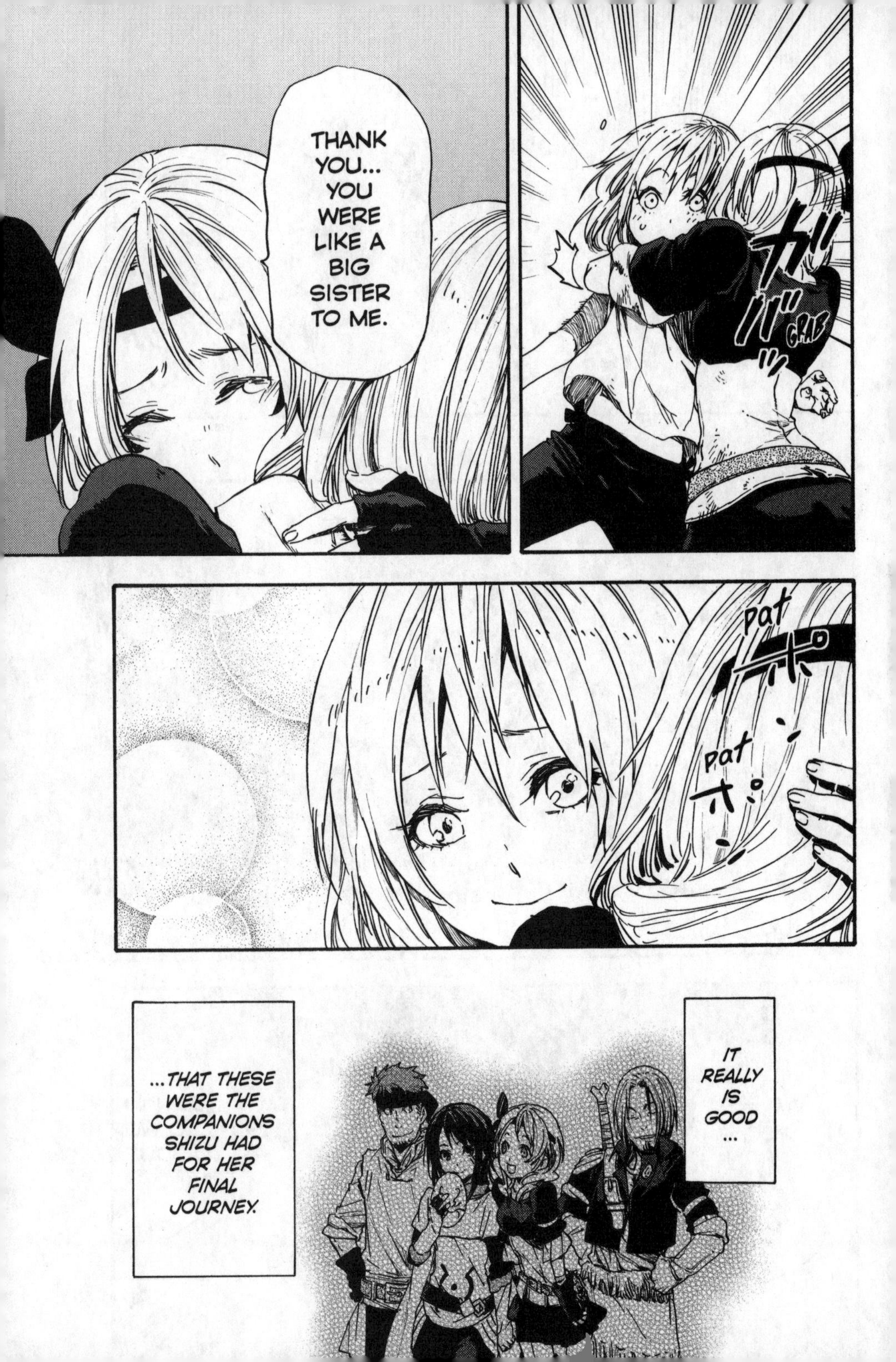
GRAB
THANK YOU... YOU WERE LIKE A BIG SISTER TO ME.
Pat
Pat
IT REALLY IS GOOD ...
...THAT THESE WERE THE COMPANIONS SHIZU HAD FOR HER FINAL JOURNEY.

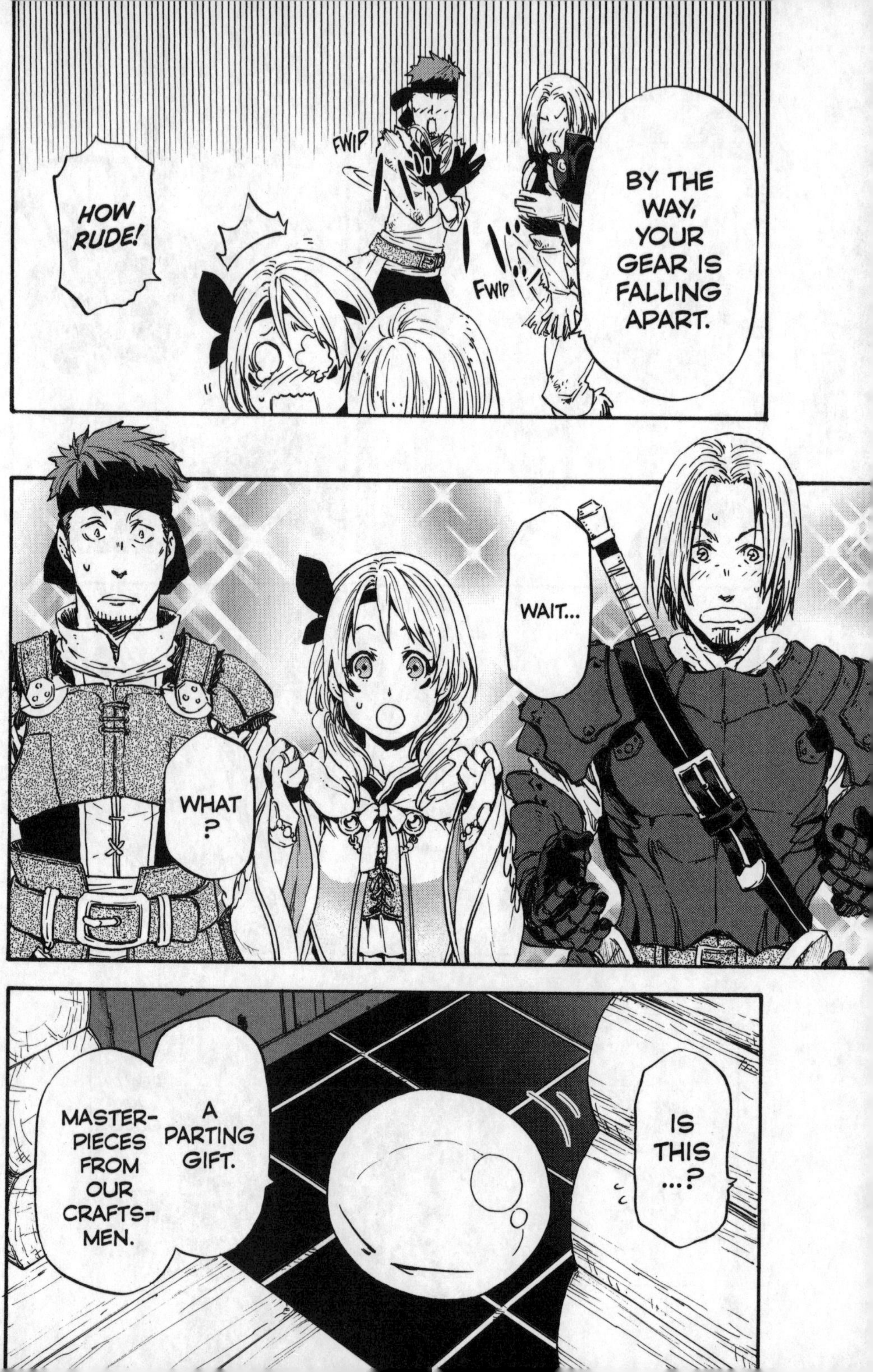
BY THE WAY, YOUR GEAR IS FALLING APART.
FWIP
FWIP
HOW RUDE!
WAIT...
WHAT?
IS THIS ...?
A PARTING GIFT.
MASTER-PIECES FROM OUR CRAFTS-MEN.

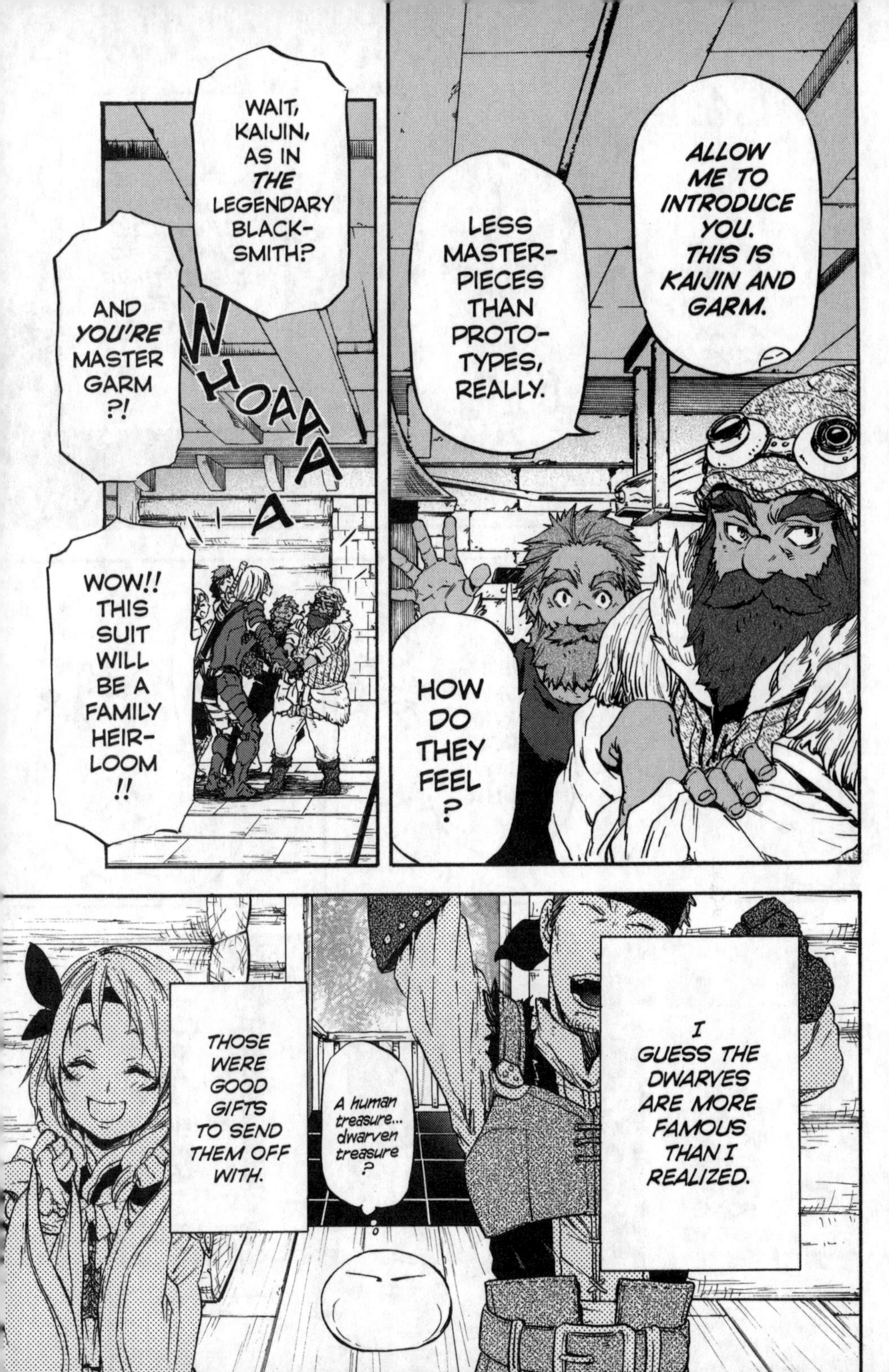
ALLOW ME TO INTRODUCE YOU. THIS IS KAIJIN AND GARM.
LESS MASTERPIECES THAN PROTOTYPES, REALLY.
HOW DO THEY FEEL?
WAIT, KAIJIN, AS IN THE LEGENDARY BLACKSMITH?
AND YOU'RE MASTER GARM?!
WHOAAAA
WOW!! THIS SUIT WILL BE A FAMILY HEIRLOOM!!
I GUESS THE DWARVES ARE MORE FAMOUS THAN I REALIZED.
A human treasure... dwarven treasure?
THOSE WERE GOOD GIFTS TO SEND THEM OFF WITH.

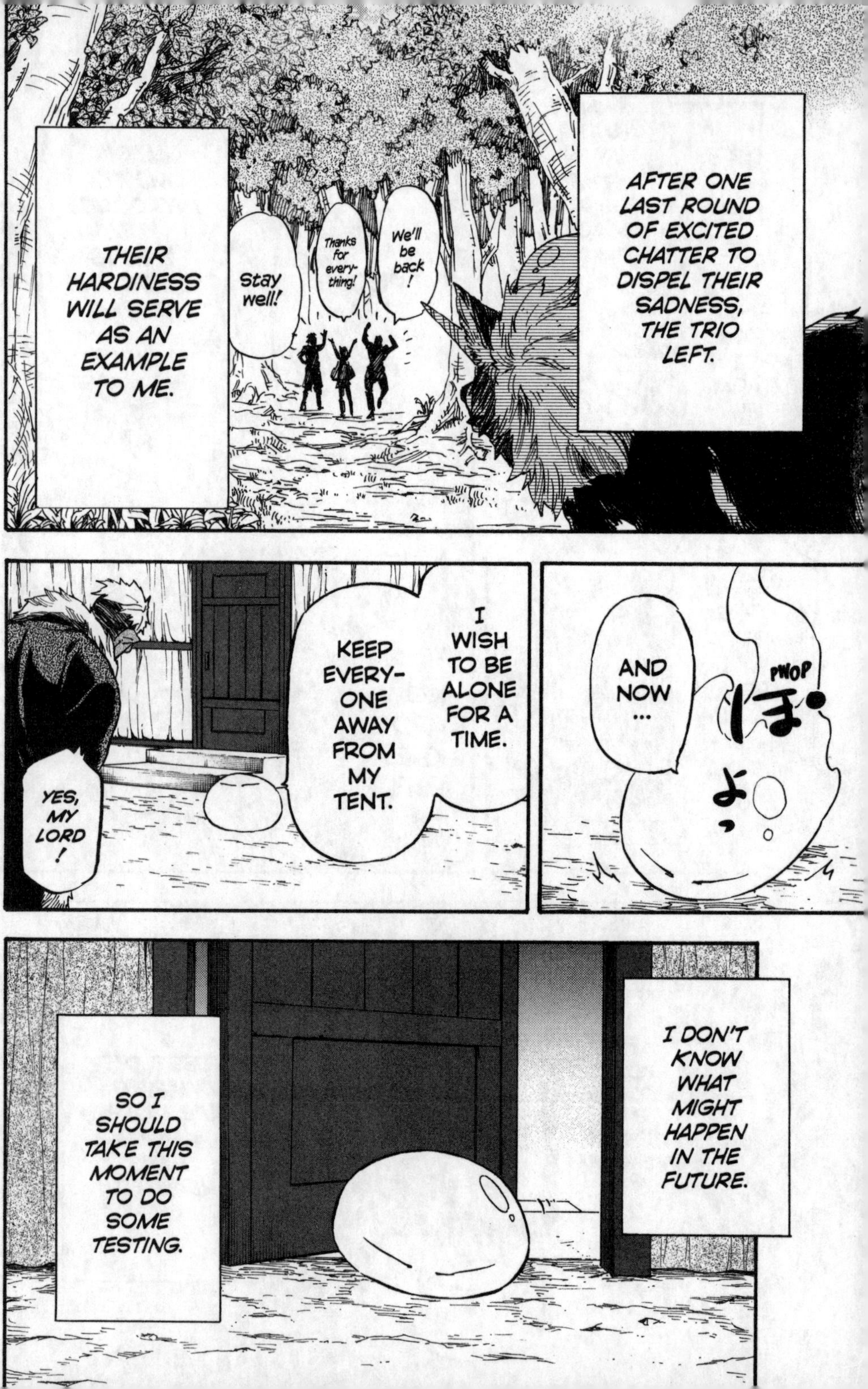
AFTER ONE LAST ROUND OF EXCITED CHATTER TO DISPEL THEIR SADNESS, THE TRIO LEFT.
We'll be back!
Thanks for every-thing!
Stay well!
THEIR HARDINESS WILL SERVE AS AN EXAMPLE TO ME.
AND NOW...
PWOP
ぽよっ
I WISH TO BE ALONE FOR A TIME.
KEEP EVERY-ONE AWAY FROM MY TENT.
YES, MY LORD!
I DON'T KNOW WHAT MIGHT HAPPEN IN THE FUTURE.
SO I SHOULD TAKE THIS MOMENT TO DO SOME TESTING.

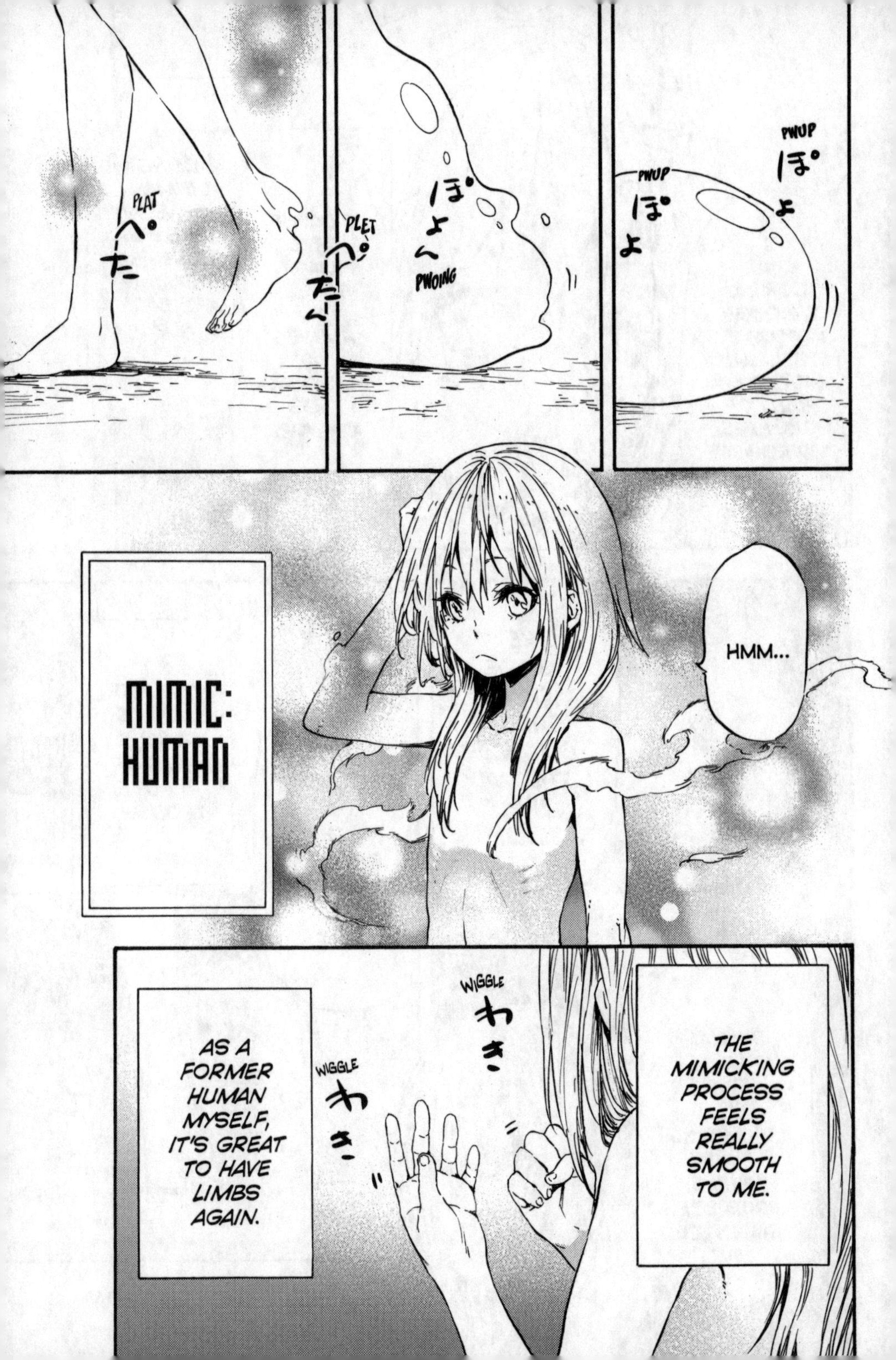
PWUP
ぽよ
PWUP
ぽよ
ぽよん
PWOING
PLET
ぺたん
PLAT
ぺた
HMM...
MIMIC: HUMAN
THE MIMICKING PROCESS FEELS REALLY SMOOTH TO ME.
WIGGLE
わき
WIGGLE
わき
AS A FORMER HUMAN MYSELF, IT'S GREAT TO HAVE LIMBS AGAIN.

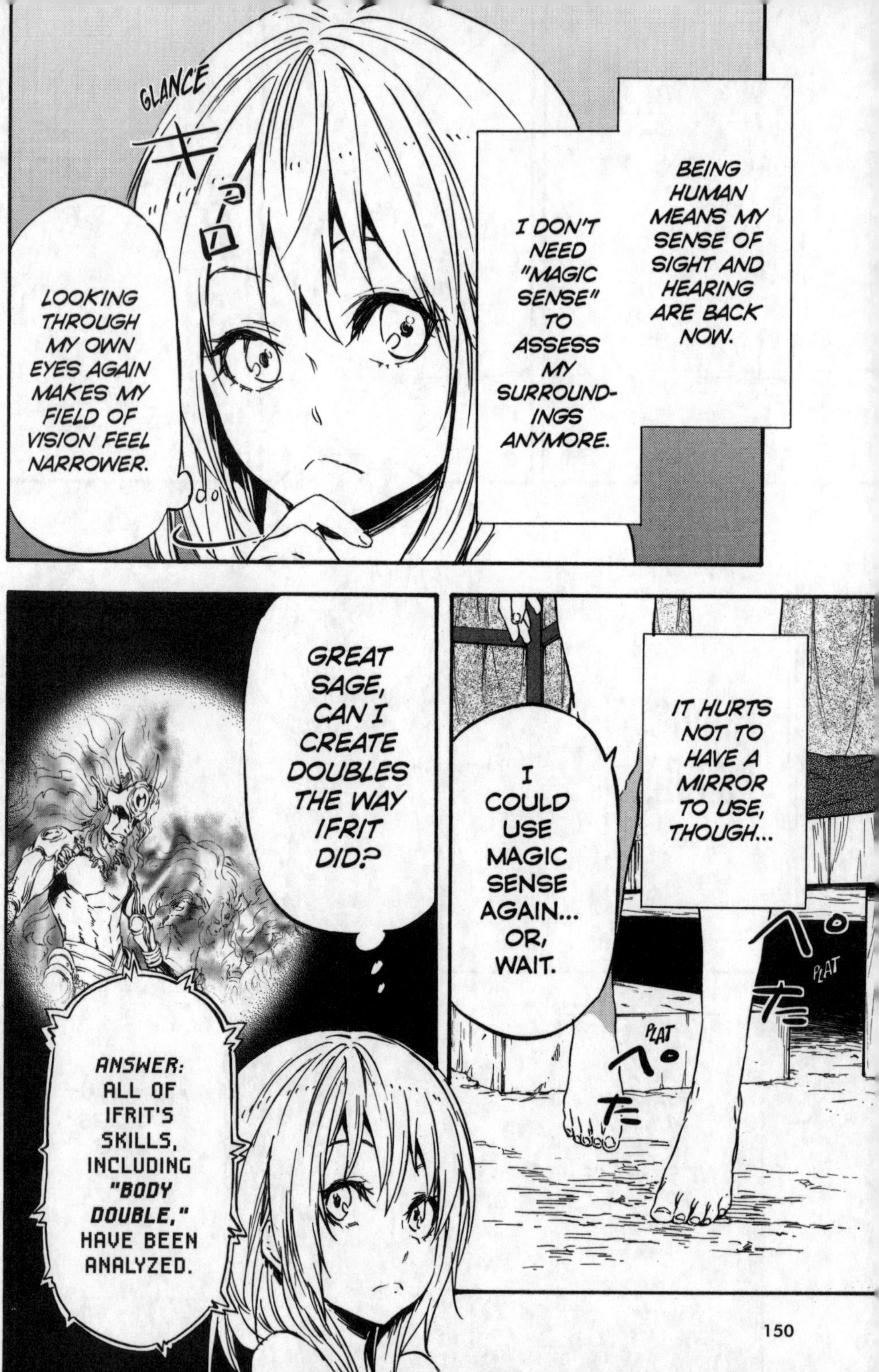
BEING HUMAN MEANS MY SENSE OF SIGHT AND HEARING ARE BACK NOW.
I DON'T NEED "MAGIC SENSE" TO ASSESS MY SURROUNDINGS ANYMORE.
GLANCE
LOOKING THROUGH MY OWN EYES AGAIN MAKES MY FIELD OF VISION FEEL NARROWER.
IT HURTS NOT TO HAVE A MIRROR TO USE, THOUGH...
I COULD USE MAGIC SENSE AGAIN... OR, WAIT.
PLAT
PLAT
GREAT SAGE, CAN I CREATE DOUBLES THE WAY IFRIT DID?
ANSWER: ALL OF IFRIT'S SKILLS, INCLUDING "BODY DOUBLE," HAVE BEEN ANALYZED.

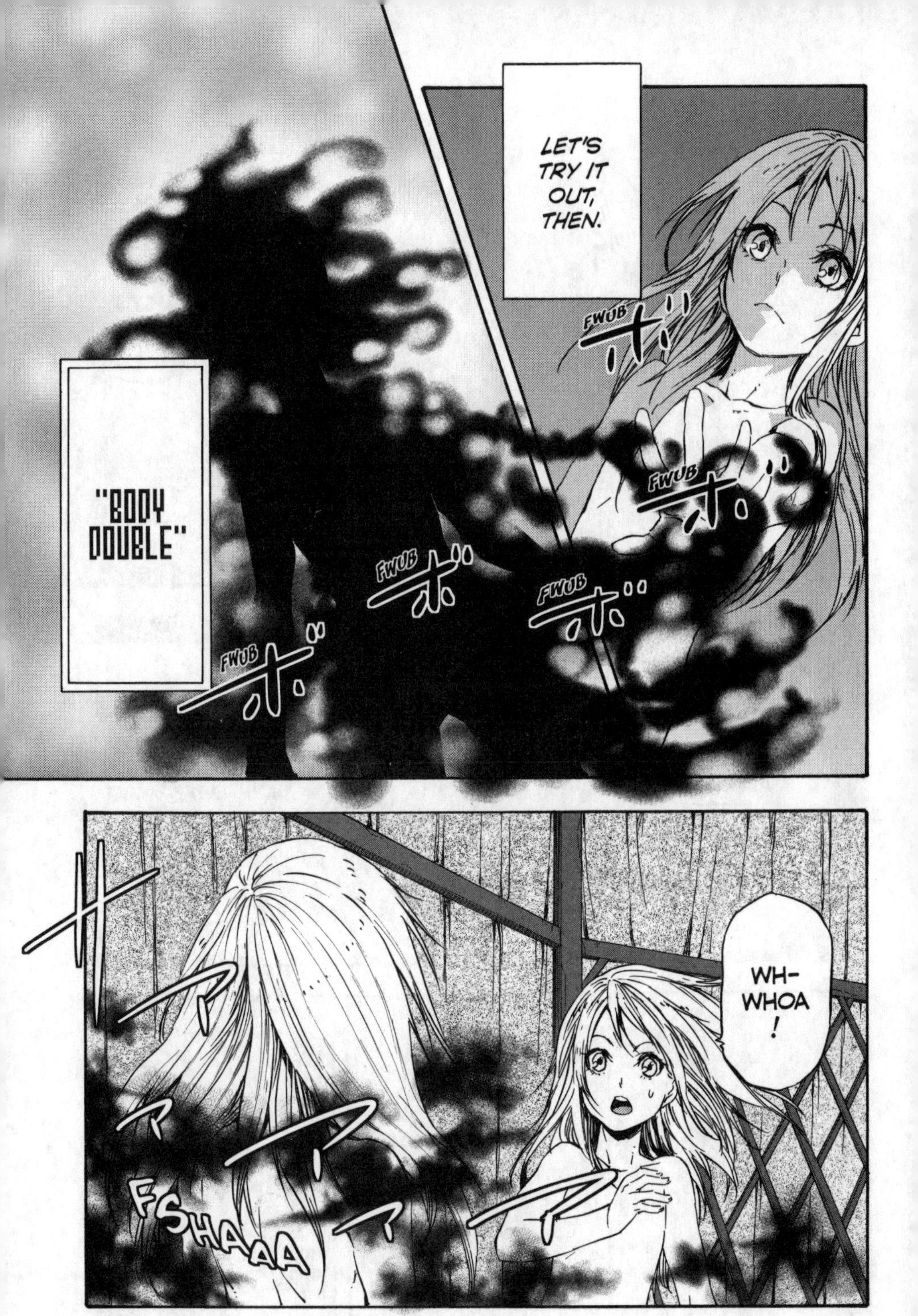
LET'S TRY IT OUT, THEN.
FWUB
FWUB
FWUB
FWUB
FWUB
"BODY DOUBLE"
WH-WHOA!
FSHAAA

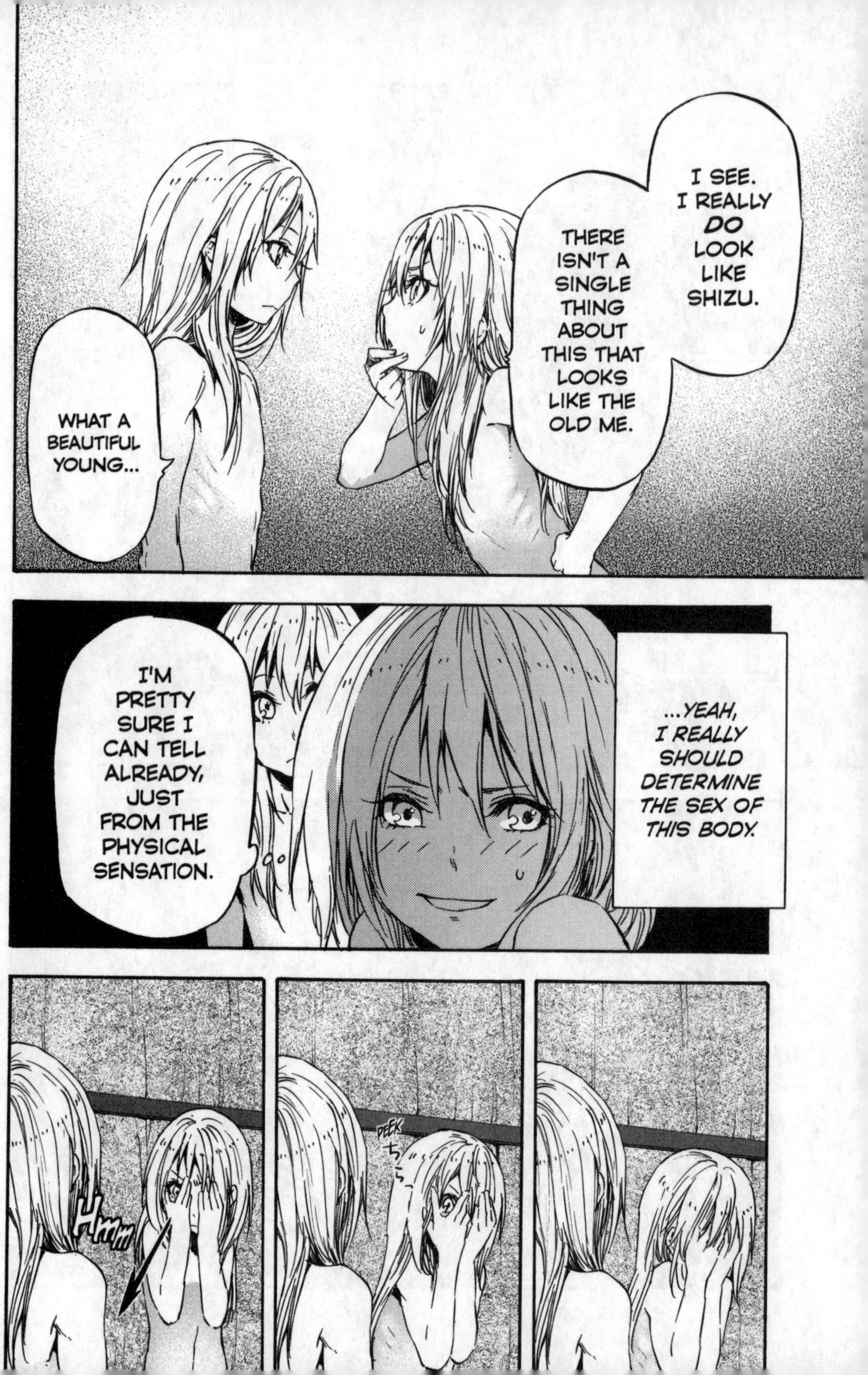
I SEE. I REALLY DO LOOK LIKE SHIZU.
THERE ISN'T A SINGLE THING ABOUT THIS THAT LOOKS LIKE THE OLD ME.
WHAT A BEAUTIFUL YOUNG...
...YEAH, I REALLY SHOULD DETERMINE THE SEX OF THIS BODY.
I'M PRETTY SURE I CAN TELL ALREADY, JUST FROM THE PHYSICAL SENSATION.
PEEK
Hmm

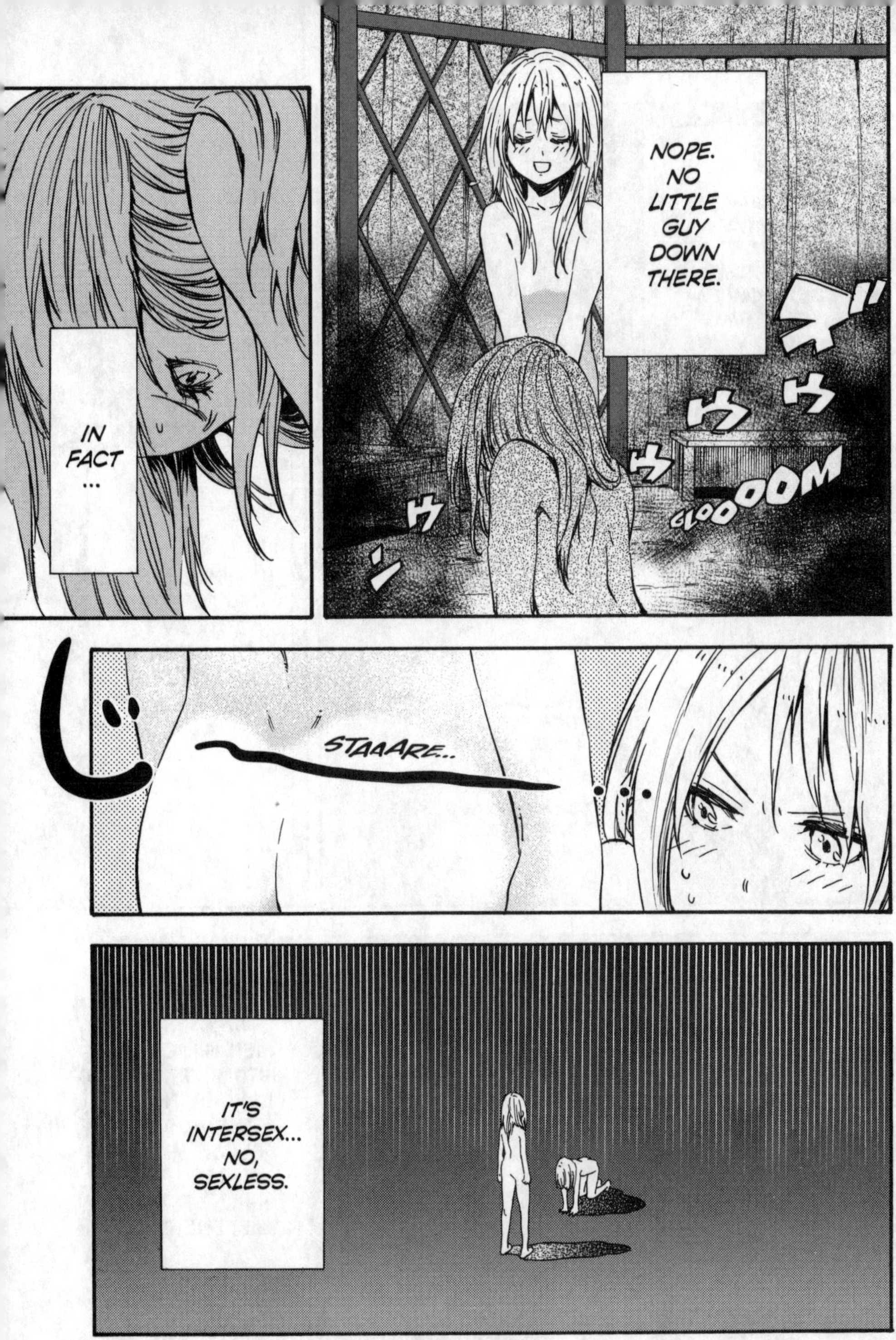
NOPE. NO LITTLE GUY DOWN THERE.
ズゥゥゥゥン
GLOOOOM
IN FACT ...
じ
STAAARE...
IT'S INTERSEX... NO, SEXLESS.

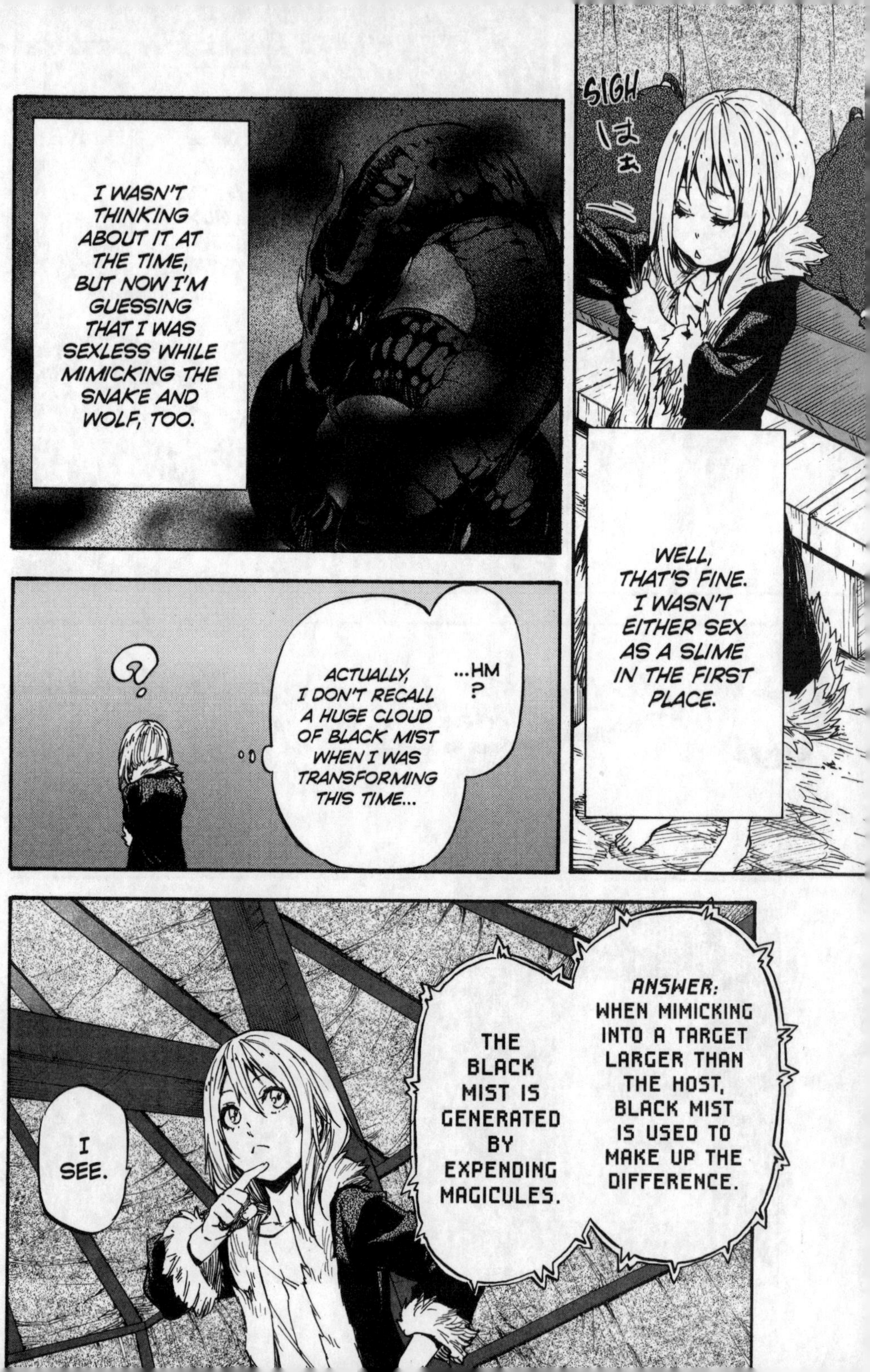
SIGH
はぁ~
WELL, THAT'S FINE. I WASN'T EITHER SEX AS A SLIME IN THE FIRST PLACE.
I WASN'T THINKING ABOUT IT AT THE TIME, BUT NOW I'M GUESSING THAT I WAS SEXLESS WHILE MIMICKING THE SNAKE AND WOLF, TOO.
...HM?
ACTUALLY, I DON'T RECALL A HUGE CLOUD OF BLACK MIST WHEN I WAS TRANSFORMING THIS TIME...
?
ANSWER: WHEN MIMICKING INTO A TARGET LARGER THAN THE HOST, BLACK MIST IS USED TO MAKE UP THE DIFFERENCE.
THE BLACK MIST IS GENERATED BY EXPENDING MAGICULES.
I SEE.

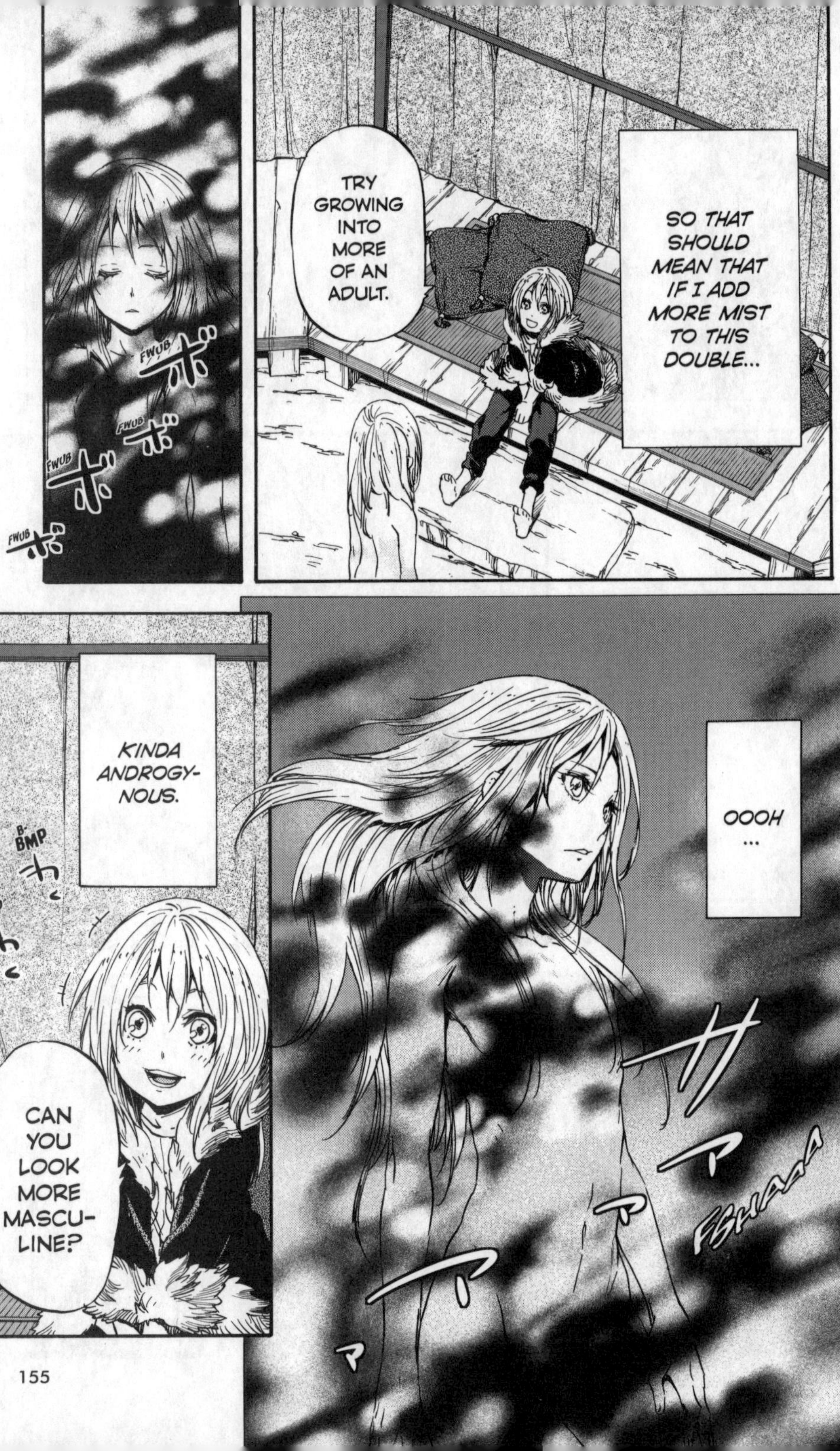
SO THAT SHOULD MEAN THAT IF I ADD MORE MIST TO THIS DOUBLE...
TRY GROWING INTO MORE OF AN ADULT.
FWUB
FWUB
FWUB
FWUB
OOOH ...
FSHAAA
KINDA ANDROGY- NOUS.
B-BMP
B-BMP
CAN YOU LOOK MORE MASCU- LINE?

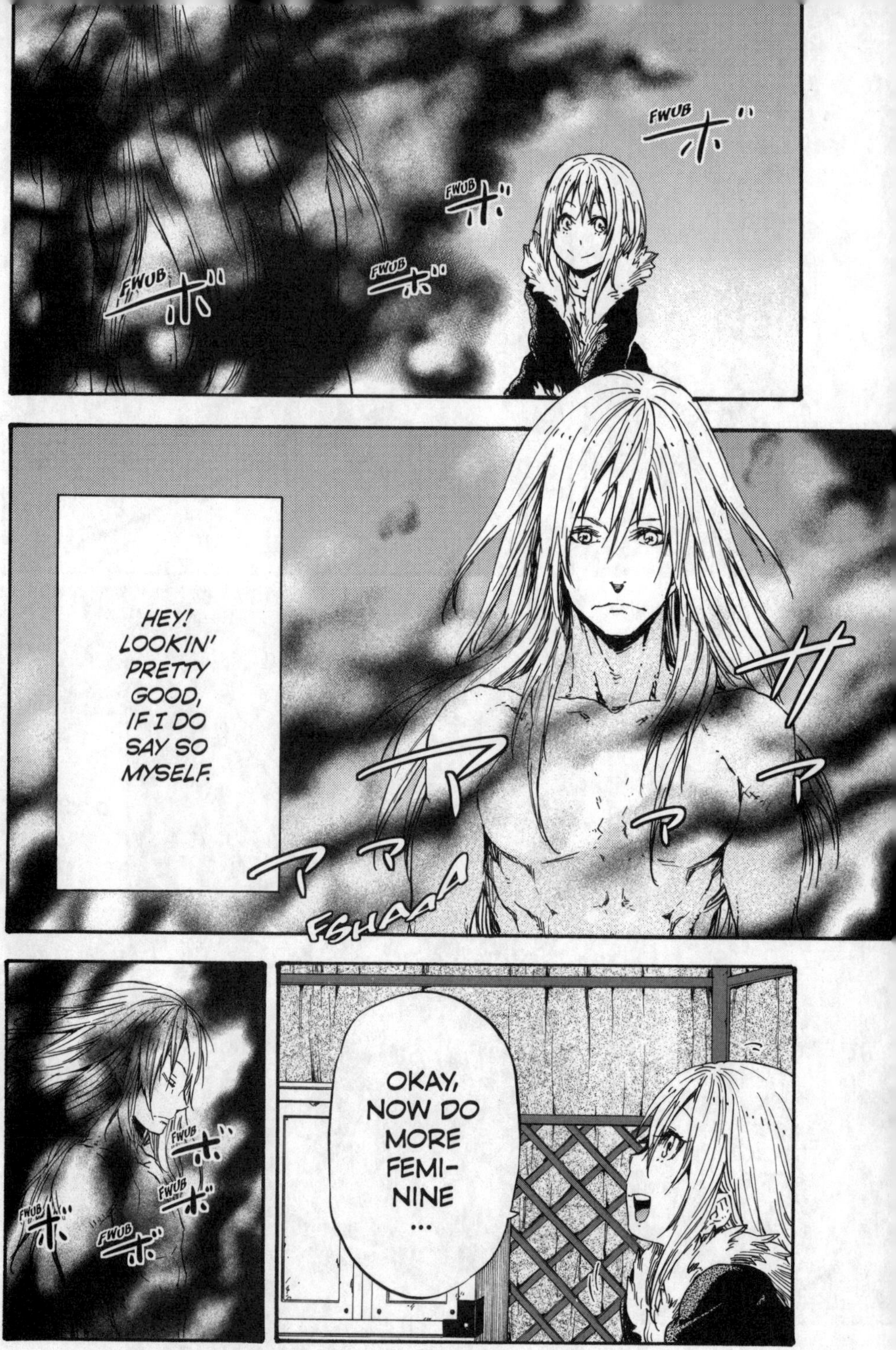
FWUB
FWUB
FWUB
FWUB
HEY! LOOKIN' PRETTY GOOD, IF I DO SAY SO MYSELF.
FSHAAA
OKAY, NOW DO MORE FEMI-NINE ...
FWUB
FWUB
FWUB
FWUB

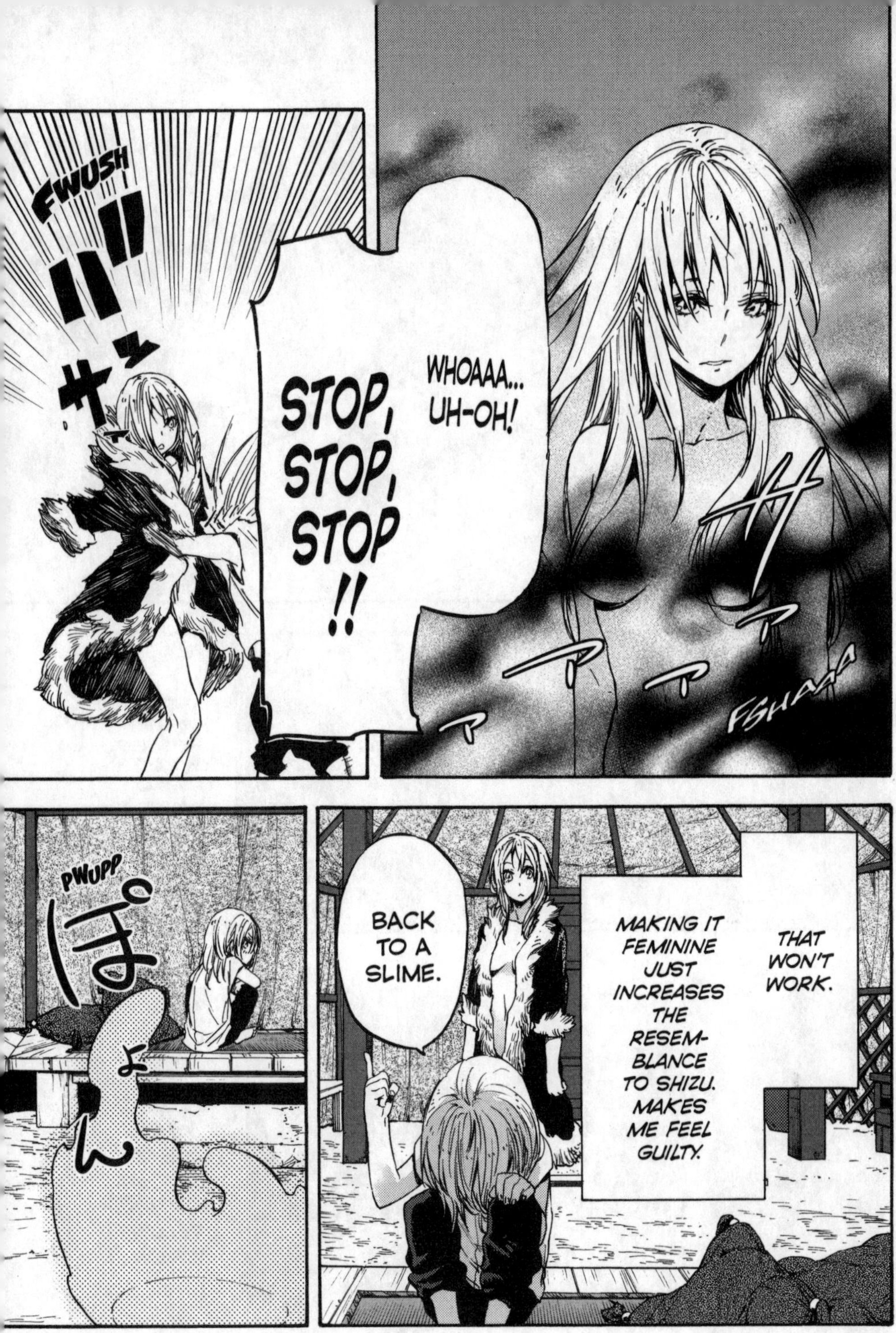
WHOAAA... UH-OH!
STOP, STOP, STOP!!
FSHAAA
FWUSH
THAT WON'T WORK.
MAKING IT FEMININE JUST INCREASES THE RESEMBLANCE TO SHIZU. MAKES ME FEEL GUILTY.
BACK TO A SLIME.
PWUPP

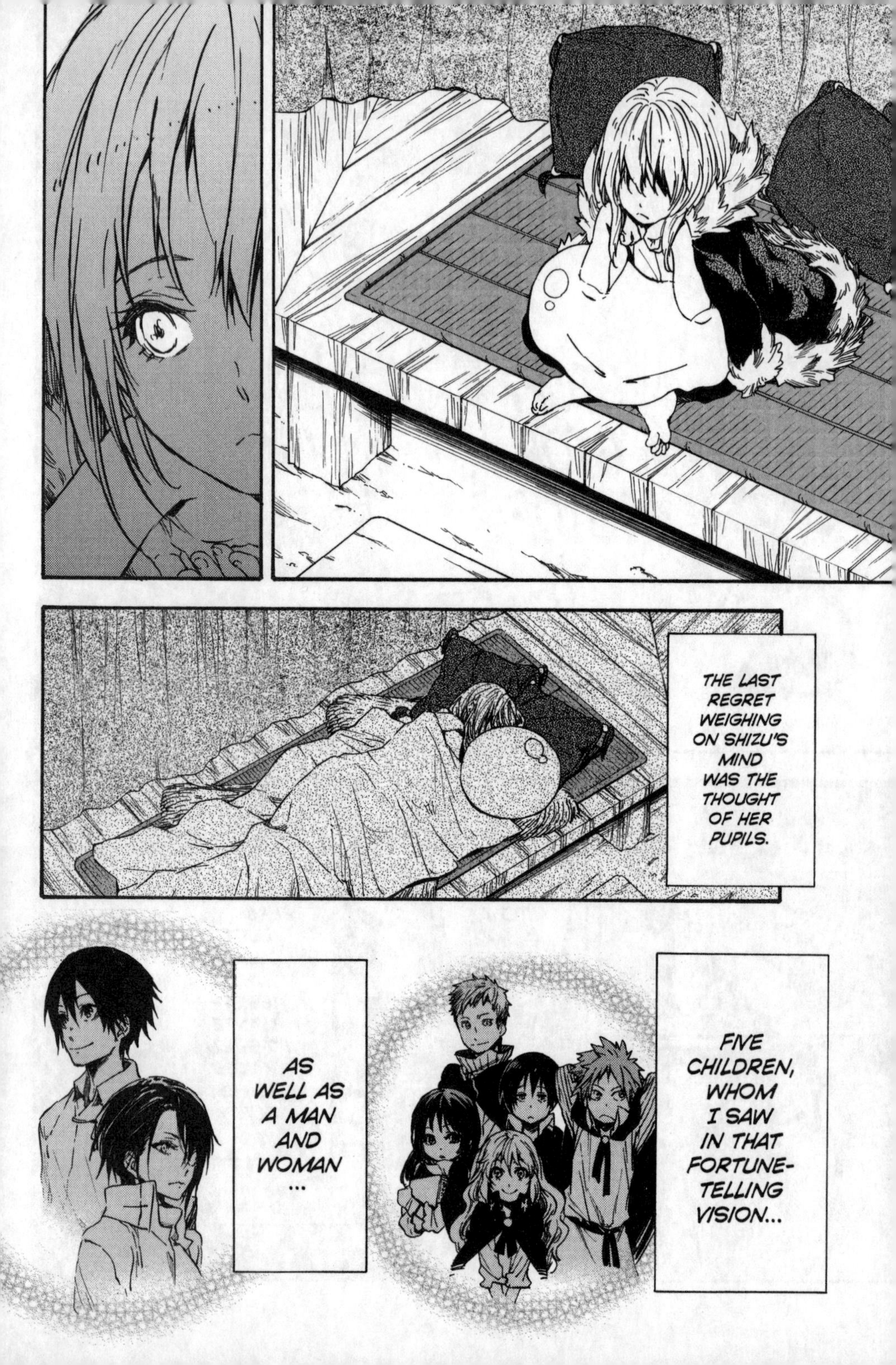
THE LAST REGRET WEIGHING ON SHIZU'S MIND WAS THE THOUGHT OF HER PUPILS.
FIVE CHILDREN, WHOM I SAW IN THAT FORTUNE-TELLING VISION...
AS WELL AS A MAN AND WOMAN ...

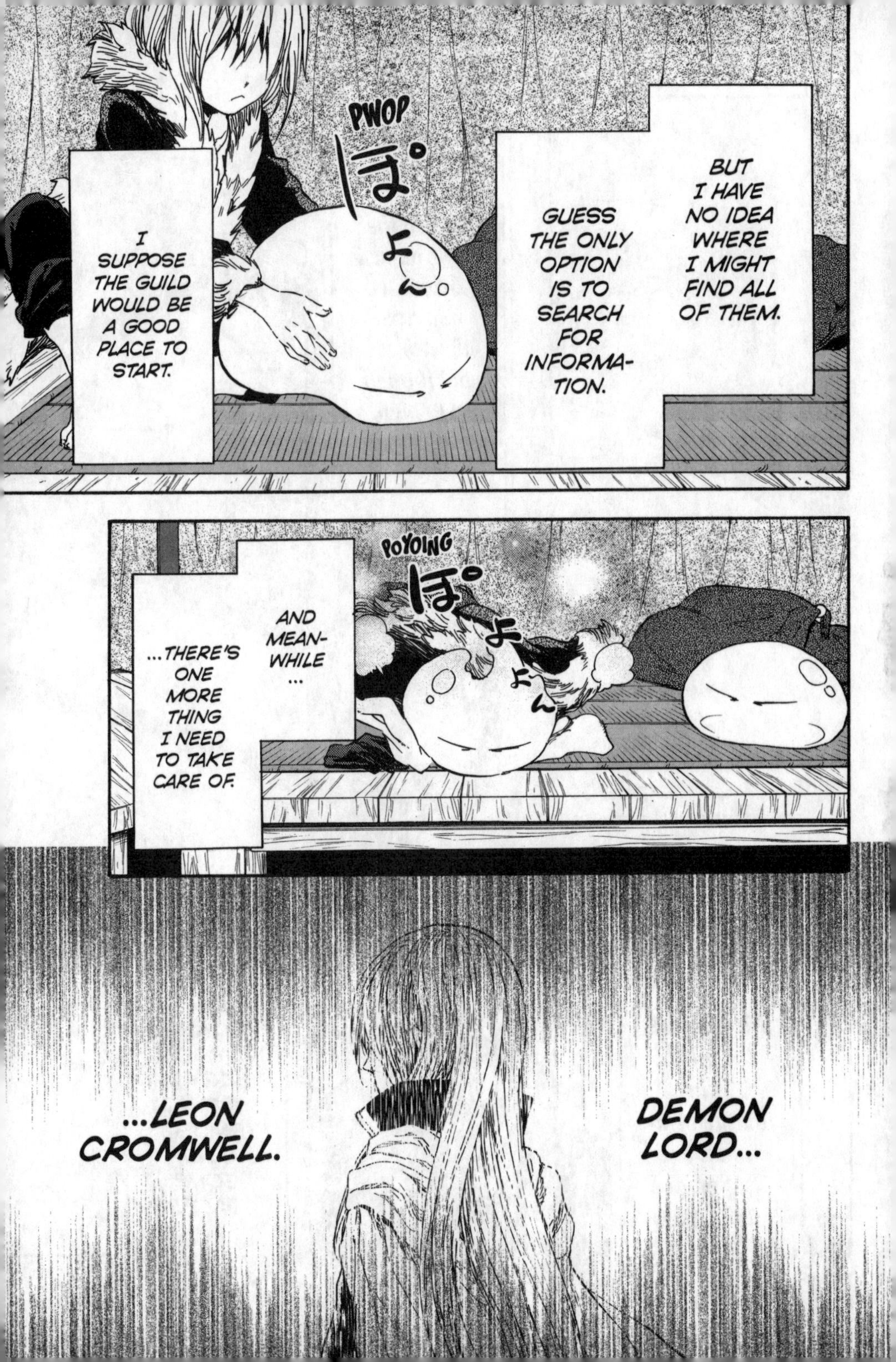
BUT I HAVE NO IDEA WHERE I MIGHT FIND ALL OF THEM.
GUESS THE ONLY OPTION IS TO SEARCH FOR INFORMATION.
PWOP
ぽよん
I SUPPOSE THE GUILD WOULD BE A GOOD PLACE TO START.
POYOING
ぽよん
AND MEANWHILE...
...THERE'S ONE MORE THING I NEED TO TAKE CARE OF.
DEMON LORD...
...LEON CROMWELL.

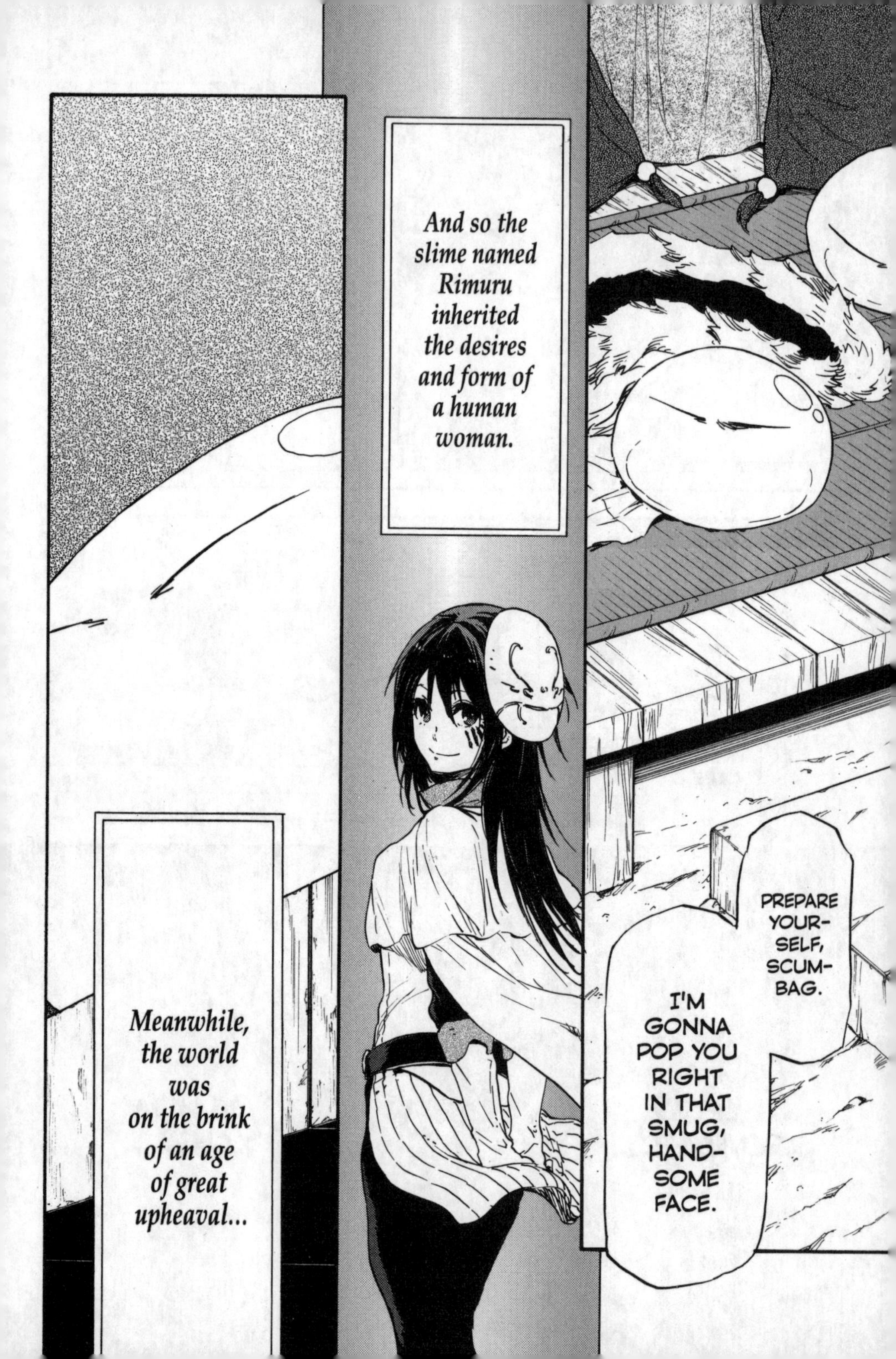
PREPARE YOURSELF, SCUMBAG.
I'M GONNA POP YOU RIGHT IN THAT SMUG, HANDSOME FACE.
And so the slime named Rimuru inherited the desires and form of a human woman.
Meanwhile, the world was on the brink of an age of great upheaval...

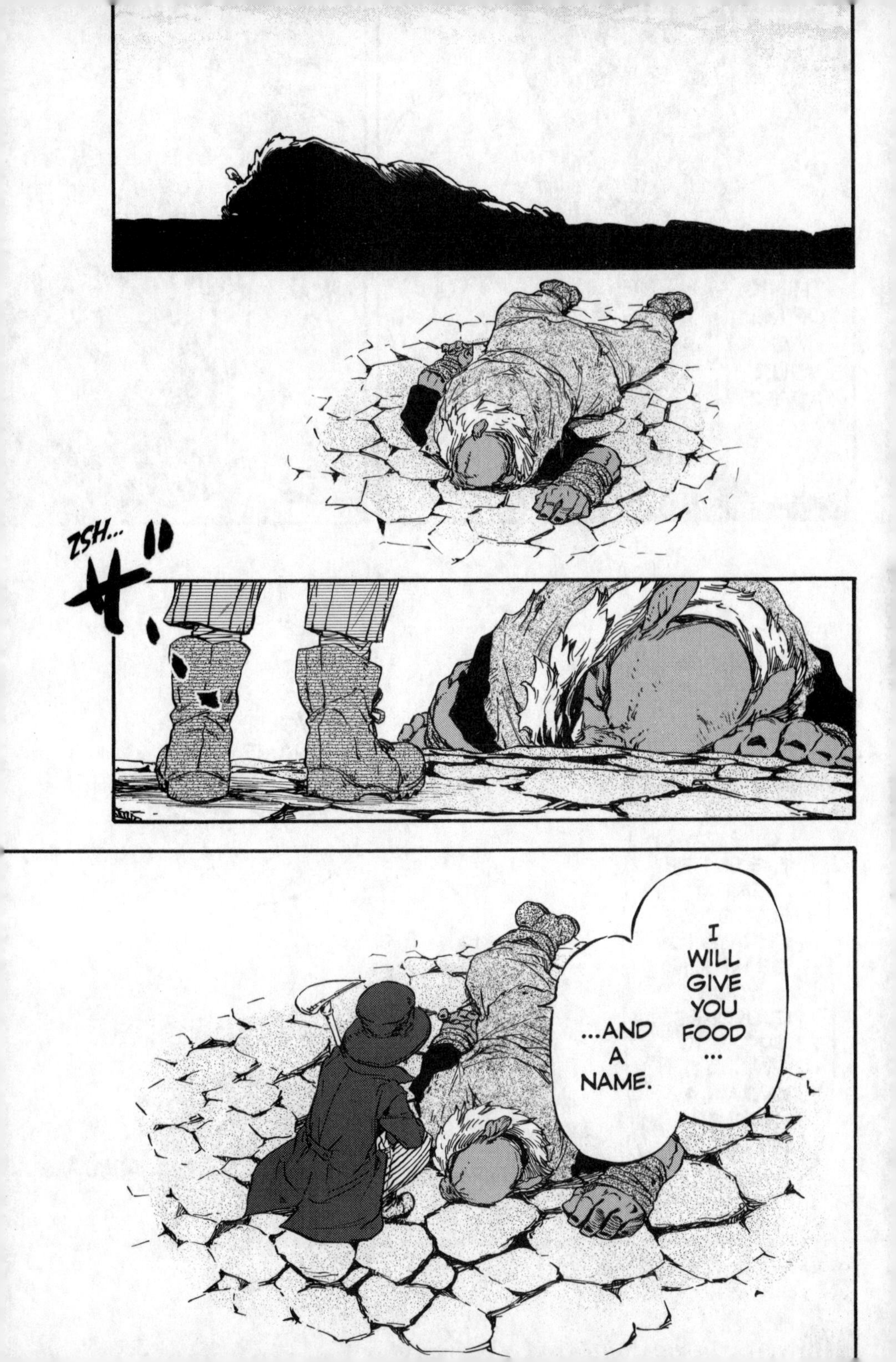
ZSH...
I WILL GIVE YOU FOOD ...
...AND A NAME.

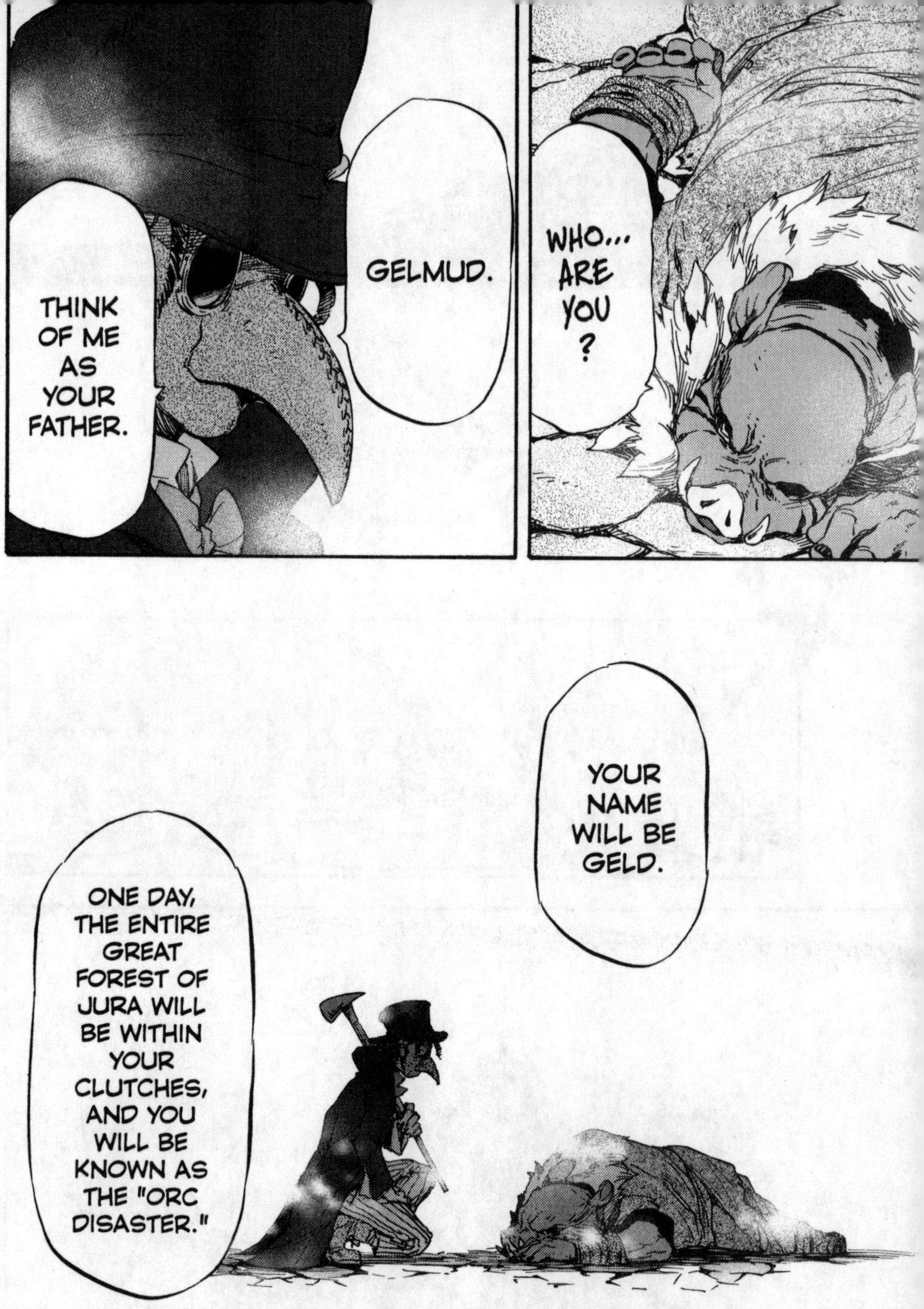
WHO... ARE YOU?
GELMUD.
THINK OF ME AS YOUR FATHER.
YOUR NAME WILL BE GELD.
ONE DAY, THE ENTIRE GREAT FOREST OF JURA WILL BE WITHIN YOUR CLUTCHES, AND YOU WILL BE KNOWN AS THE "ORC DISASTER."

```
Reincarnate
in Volume 3?

  →YES

   NO
```

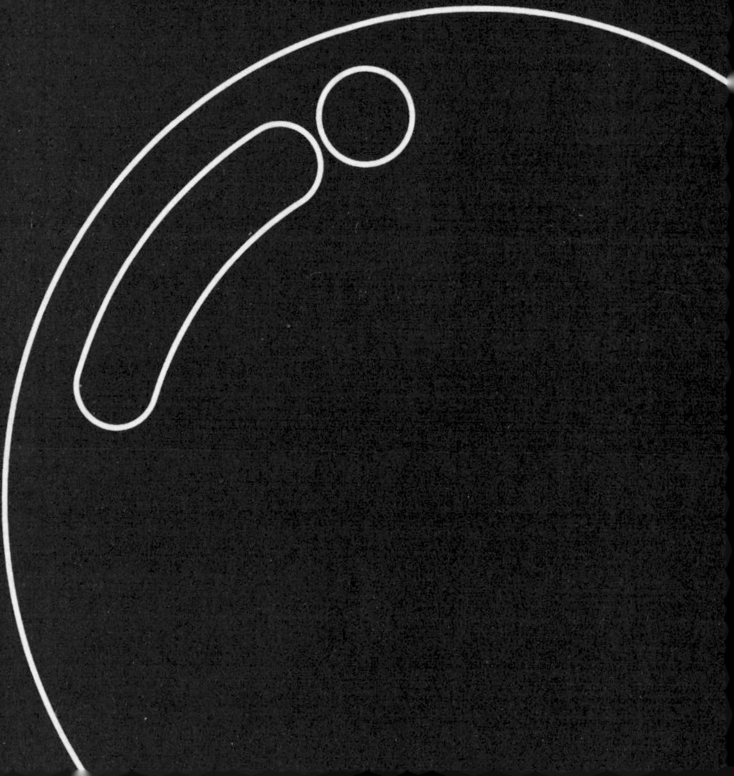

Bonus
Short Story

Veldora's Slime Observation Journal
~STUNNING DEVELOPMENTS~

Veldora's Slime Observation Journal
~STUNNING DEVELOPMENTS~

◆THE HERO-KING'S JUDGMENT◆

The trial began.

Excitement coursed through me as I waited and watched. A suspect-looking man begins to explain things on his own. Rimuru is content to remain calm and quiet for now, so I realize that perhaps my expectations were off-base.

The entire group is groveling before the mighty dwarf king. However, as all those before the king bow their heads in fealty, Rimiru alone has been standing proud and upright. It seems that they do not realize from his appearance that he is not bowing in the least. While his words are polite, he maintains his same proud, challenging attitude. Given that he is the equal to one such as me, that is only natural.

I will need him to continue to maintain our proud status, but it seems that might prove difficult. A curious facet of human society is that strength alone is not enough to solve all matters. This instance is a good example of that.

I would have assumed that those involved would have beaten one another in an effort to establish dominance. But for some reason, they intend to determine the winner and loser through words alone.

But what if one of the parties is lying?

As if in answer, the man appointed to argue Rimuru's case acts to betray them. They must have known from the very start that he was a tricky and untrustworthy fellow... And yet they allowed him to bring them to ruin. I would have engaged in some minor rampaging to silence his lying tongue.

Human society is such a vexing thing. I had thought that my recent studies would have granted me some understanding of its ways. However, this incident proves that I have still more to learn. I must search out a more detailed text on the matter.

And yet it seems that Rimuru's choice was correct this time. If he had started a fight, he would not stand a chance against that man— that...Gazel Dwargo fellow. He is apparently the sovereign of this dwarven kingdom, but his power seems to transcend that of the humanoid peoples.

Of course, he is no match for the hero who sealed me away in my prison, but I might admit that is he is at least worthy of standing in my presence. In fact, the way he looked at us, it appeared that he could see right through Rimuru.

"Interference with deep psyche detected. Attempt rebuffed."

There, you see? Even such a natural action from Gazel was capable of penetrating to Rimuru's deep psyche. Rimuru didn't seem to realize it, but I could tell that this Gazel fellow was capable of reading minds.

Regardless of the kind of skill he used, it is clear enough that this bodes ill. This is the very reason that Rimuru cannot best the man.

But perhaps it is not Gazel's capabilities that I should be worried about but Rimuru's. At first, I thought it a trick of my own imagination, but it seems that Rimuru's skill had activated on its own, without his input. This skill did not activate when Gazel read Rimuru's surface thoughts, but it did prevent him from interacting with his deep psyche.

I found my own attempts to connect to his deep memories blocked in the past—could it have been the same process?

Is it autonomous?!

No, that would be silly. My mind is getting carried away, I imagine. I have never heard of such a skill, nor do I believe it exists. No powers can take effect without the intentional bidding of the user.

Then how to explain this? Unless—but, wait...

Rimuru is too cautious for any other explanation. He must have anticipated such an outcome and ordered this skill of his to autonomously guard against any contact. Doubtless he sensed Gazel probing his surface thoughts, and ordered for his subliminal defense systems to act autonomously.

Kwaaaa ha ha ha! I very nearly fell victim to Rimuru's deceptions, myself. But it is his fault for seeming so thoughtless. Actually, upon closer examination, he does appear rather thoughtful. It is strange that the more one comes to know Rimuru, the more capable he seems.

And just as he expected, Gazel is taken aback. He is confused that he could easily read the surface thoughts, but not peer into the depths. Moreover, the surface of Rimuru's mind shows no signs of awareness that Gazel is reading his thoughts. No wonder the man was confused.

But this was Rimuru's trap. He knew that he could not win through prowess alone, and thus lured the other into a battle of wits. Now Gazel is totally unaware that he has been taken in by Rimuru's scheme.

A manga text contained this piece of wisdom: "To fool your enemies, first fool your friends." I was not fooled, of course, but Gazel is now beset by paranoia. Gazel must have recognized Rimuru as a slime who, though he appears easy to defeat, hides a great and powerful mind, and so released him and his companions. Thus, Rimuru passed safely through the dangers of the trial.

I am quite impressed by his skill.

Rimuru left the dwarven kingdom and rejoined his fellows at the entrance to the forest. Then he explained the series of events to them and concluded that, "It ended up pretty much as expected."

I knew it. He holds everything in the palm of his hand. What a formidable slime.

Strength cannot be measured solely by might, it seems. It is clear to me now that being able to manipulate others to join your side is another form of strength. Those he has bent to his will understand it as well. They all accept and agree with Rimuru's words. And now we have four dwarves among our group.

Just as Rimuru began to journey back to his forest dwelling, a young whelp charged from behind, lamenting, "How could you do this to me?!" I recognized him as the one Rimuru named Gobta.

Rimuru appeared to have forgotten him, but he hid this fact well, promising to take the lad to a business full of beautiful women in the future—yet I found this strange. The group had just been banished from the dwarven kingdom—could it be that Rimuru was simply lying? After all, I had wished to see such a place for myself, so we must address this situation. I suppose I shall have to trust Rimuru to come up with a plan to meet these beautiful women again by the time I have recovered my powers. The thought of this brings me excitement and joy.

◆ A FAMILIAR SCENT ◆

With the addition of the dwarves, Rimuru's village quickly became a bustling town. Garments of wild animal pelts are being assembled and distributed to all. And the dwarves taught their techniques to the hobgoblins. This is, I have no doubt, on Rimuru's orders.

Plans are also underway to cut down trees for the wood to construct new dwellings. How I lament that I am unable to take part in the excitement of progress, imprisoned as I am. Watching Gobta show off his pitiful skills made me itch to unleash my truly impressive tricks for all to admire.

Perhaps I should start thinking of a fantastic new finishing move to demonstrate when I am freed. With that in mind, I tore through more and more holy manga texts for inspiration.

Gwuaaaah?!

Suddenly, I felt a terrible loss of strength. To my dismay, I found that Rimuru hadn't learned his lesson from the last round of naming monsters, and was doing it again. I figuratively cradled my head in my hands at his seeming folly.

He already failed at this once. Why would he attempt it again...? And there is a truly daunting number of subjects awaiting him— five hundred in all. Again, I was forced to desperately brace myself against the outward flow of energy, when...

"Announcement. Total level of magical energy required to complete task has been successfully calculated. Your assistance is requested to ensure safety until the calculated value is reached."

What's this?!

Despite being locked inside the "Unlimited Imprisonment," the voice spoke directly to me! How is such a thing possible...?

"Answer: By using 'Words of the World,' successful communication of will is possible."

What nonsense is this?! I am sealed from the world, in an "alternate space," and yet this message can reach me from the outside...?

No, wait. Now I recall that in order to decipher Rimuru's knowledge, I made the process of sharing information smoother. I suppose that would make it possible to communicate in a way through information alone.

Because Rimuru has not learned how to read my knowledge, it is difficult to make my will known to him. On the other hand, it is possible for me to understand his desires. In other words, Rimuru is aware that I am reading his thoughts, and utilizing that to his ends— the devious runt.

I suppose I must offer some begrudging respect to the fact that he thought to make use of "Words of the World" as a means to express his will to me. That idea never occurred to me, and I had not thought it possible. Regardless of the means by which it came about, the fact remains that it happened.

Come to think of it, I glossed over something that I should be grappling with. What is this "safety until the calculated value is reached" nonsense? Surely it can't mean...

"Answer: The data collected during the previous experience has helped to improve the safety factor. The amount of magical energy available to use without risking the loss of maximum energy value is estimated to be..."

So that skill was collecting data during the last naming round? I don't know whether to call it overly cautious or just plain shrewd...

But enough of this! I believe you. I believe you already! My friend Rimuru has placed his trust in me. I must meet that level of trust. And so I steeled myself for the consequences and allowed him to borrow my energy.

As part of my promise to help, I expected to suffer some loss of power. Naming is a dangerous act, and there is no guarantee that the energy expended in the process will ever fully return. In fact, I have never heard of such an outcome... But my concerns turned out to be unnecessary. As Rimuru said, my magical energy stores returned to their full value.

As a consequence, however, he was once more forced into a three-day hibernation. Perhaps he should realize that his helpful personality ought to have limits. Common sense would tell him that naming five hundred individuals is simply madness. Strange as it is for me to lecture about common sense, Rimuru's recklessness makes even one such as me seem almost rational.

In fact, perhaps I was the rational type all along. Perhaps it is the views of the rest of the world that are excessively dramatized. I let these thoughts entertain me as I settled back to recover my energy.

With the naming finished and a large addition to the village population, Rimuru and his brain trust are considering moving the settlement. They are surveying the lands near the cave in which I was sealed. They've cut down a number of trees and opened up a sizable plot of land to use.

With Rimuru's new servants, and the evolution from goblins to hobgoblins, the group's physical abilities are much higher than before. The work proceeds quicker than I thought possible. As for Rimuru himself...he appears absorbed in developing various new techniques.

I am itching to test out some new spectacular moves of my own—how does he have all the luck?! Alas, all I can do is grumble and complain to myself.

Oh, it seems that he has discovered something. Are those...humans?

Four adventurers, under attack by a nest of giant ants. Rimuru being Rimuru, he has of course decided to help them.

No, wait! That's "Black Lightning"...

But my warning did not reach Rimuru. Despite his attempt to limit the power as much as possible, the Black Lightning spell possesses devastating force. The bolt lashed out faster than sound and obliterated its target. His skill exhibited a power and effectiveness many times that of ordinary magic; it had heavy shades of the dark lightning that is a feature of my Tempest Magic.

Lightning is powerful on its own—with my influence, it was bound to be a deadly assault—certainly not suited for such puny threats. That adventurer woman was sure to die, which seemed a pity. However, to my surprise, she was not caught in the blast; she had evaded one of the most powerful spells in existence.

Kwaaa ha ha ha! This is why I find humans so entertaining.

The woman could very well be the equal of Gazel the Dwarf King.

On short notice yet again, Rimuru has somehow managed to unexpectedly acquaint himself with an extraordinary figure. I continued my observation from within Rimuru, more convinced than ever that his exploits must be seen to be believed.

◆DEMON OF FLAMES◆

Meat sizzles as it cooks atop a rectangular sheet of metal.

I'd wondered what this sheet would be used for when Rimuru ordered it fashioned. Lacking any handles, it seemed rather too awkward to be a shield. And yet, to use such a thing for this! A most satisfying resolution to my curiosity.

This was my first encounter with the concept of "teppanyaki."

The adventurers Rimuru saved are now cooking strips of meat on the hot plate. I've never eaten it—in fact, I have no need to eat at all—but it does look quite delicious. Even Rimuru is looking at the humans with envy.

He doesn't seem to realize that his body is touching the burning plate, because it isn't hurting him. Apparently the slime has a resistance to heat.

"The individual named Rimuru Tempest possesses resistance to thermal fluctuation."

So my suspicions were correct. But how did he acquire "Thermal Fluctuation Resistance" from being stabbed in the back? I do not understand. It makes no sense.

I would understand "Piercing Resistance", but one does not gain resistance to thermal fluctuation from being stabbed. The woman with him hears his explanation and accepts it at face value, showing her own keen mind. Even I, sagacious as I am, cannot follow the thread of logic.

Apparently, the woman hails from the same world from which Rimuru came. But unlike Rimuru, she is a complete "otherworlder" who made the transition in her own flesh. She was summoned here, in fact. And yet, summoning requires a grand ritual with many arcane requirements, and from the way she describes it, she was summoned by a lone individual.

Whoever it is, that summoner must be mighty, indeed.

I had a hunch about this woman; the stench of trouble seemed to hang thick and heavy around her. And my hunch was soon proven correct. The summoner who brought her here is one of the very pillars of the world: the Demon Lord, Leon Cromwell. However, I do not know this Lord Leon.

Some neophyte who appeared during the time that I was sealed in that cave, perhaps? One as powerful as I am can maintain knowledge of the world's power balance, even from behind a magical seal. With my Unique Skill "Inquirer," I can collect information even while confined by the hero's "Unlimited Imprisonment" curse. But sadly, its powers are not infinite.

The best I could manage was an infrequent influx of limited amounts of information. Ultimately, there was little I could do about this. Even a top-level being such as a demon lord could not be monitored on an individual basis.

However, if he is a recent arrival to the world, then he surely cannot be that great of a threat. Compared to those frequent foes of mine, such as the giants and that lady vampire, a newborn demon lord is but a trifle.

That reminds me of the time I destroyed the city built by the vampiress. She was absolutely livid about it, and I think I might understand a sliver of that emotion now. The sight of Rimuru happily creating a town with his hobgoblin and dwarf companions made me realize that I, too, would be furious if it were all torn down. Perhaps my past actions were unkind. I might even consider an apology, if I should run into her again.

But back to the topic of the Demon Lord, Leon. The part that concerns me is his summoning of this woman. Gathering hardy warriors and expanding territory has been a common strategy of all demon lords throughout time. Like Rimuru, some of them named their subjects, though never with such abandon, considering the risk of permanent power loss.

Instead, the most common tactic is to conscript powerful demons to do their bidding. I dare say none of them ever thought of summoning otherworlders before. From what I recall, the crossing over infuses the body with a great rush of magicules. Most die in the process, but those who survive receive a great influx of power to their souls, which is then shaped according to their desires. Just as the woman named Shizu explained.

There is no difference between one who crosses out of coincidence, and one who crosses in a summons. The problem is that when one is summoned by means of a ritual, absolute obedience can be etched into the target's soul.

Naturally, that depends on the intention of the summoner. Assuming it is a success, the ritual is typically undertaken in the hopes of gaining a faithful and powerful servant. This is common to demon lords in particular, and yet I do not sense such compulsion from Shizu's soul.

If only I weren't behind this seal, I could analyze the situation in more detail… But if my suspicion is correct, then why would Demon Lord Leon have summoned her? If he was not seeking a follower, then what…

Hrm?!

I was shaken from my thoughts as I felt a tremendous aura bloom. It was coming from right next to Rimuru—from that Shizu woman. And this presence is burning with fierce flames—the presence of a higher-order flame spirit!

As I recognized this, Shizu tossed Rimuru aside.

No, she did not do so of her own volition. The spirit within her is controlling her.

What a surprising level of synchronization! And even in the face of such power, Shizu has the strength of will to defy the spirit's command. I suspect that she was able to hold back the inferno raging within her to allow Rimuru to escape.

The barbecue-eating adventurers have noticed something is wrong and come to investigate. They're all staring at Shizu in shock. One of them even says, "She is the Conqueror of Flames, Shizue Izawa. The greatest elementalist alive—she harbors Ifrit inside of her!!"

Ifrit is considered a threat to humanity, I believe. His menace has been categorized as a "calamity," or a "special A-Rank threat," or some such. In his current state, Rimuru will likely not fare well against a being whose power transcends that of even a greater demon.

What? Me?

Do not associate me with such puny beings. I am known as a "catastrophe": the greatest of all menaces. I am of the most powerful rank of all beings; Special S-Rank.

Kwaaaa ha ha ha! But despite my bold and haughty laughter, I am currently helpless. So I have no choice but to stay put and observe the battle for now.

◆INHERITED WILL◆

The battle has commenced.

I can see that Ifrit's status as a superior flame spirit is well earned. He wields fire with such skill that he might as well be made from fire himself. But the biggest shock was the trio of adventurers. Ifrit's each and every attack is on the level of a Fireball spell, yet they persist in the fight. It seems there is more to them than meets the eye. Rimuru must have determined the same, because he is leaving them to their own devices and focusing directly on Ifrit.

Rimuru's first attempt was a Water Blade—a poor choice. He wants to damage and neutralize Ifrit, which is wise, but Water Blade will do nothing. It merely fizzled and dissipated in an instant. It is a high-velocity spray of magicule-infused water, and thus possesses a severing effect. It is, therefore, a physical attack power.

But an elemental is a spiritual being, and is essentially immune to physical attacks. Adding spin might increase its power, but none of that will have any effect. Even if Ifrit hadn't evaporated the Water Blade with his heat, the attack itself would have done nothing.

Rimuru seems to have learned his lesson. I can feel him running through a rapid sequence of questions and answers inside his mind in search of a new plan. Conferring with one's own skill is a fascinating fighting style.

"Icicle Lance!" shouts the woman adventurer, while Rimuru considers his next move. Ahh, most impressive. That seems to have done the trick against Ifrit's body doubles. Sadly, even hundreds of such attacks would not finish the fight if they do not hit the main body...

"Here goes another..." That's Eren, I believe her name was? She should have known it was pointless, but she prepared another attack on Ifrit. Her companions are backing her up, placing all their hopes on this meager chance. Their boldness is admirable. Weak though they may be, I enjoy the attitude of these humans.

Suddenly, Rimuru launches into an unthinkable action. He actually rushes forward to protect Ifrit, taking the full brunt of Eren's Icicle Lance.

What is he thinking…?

But in the next moment, Rimuru shouts, "Icicle Shotgun!" and sprays out the Icicle Lance as countless blades. Even I was stunned at this development. Rimuru didn't know magic, as far as I was aware, so he must have acquired the skill in that moment.

The spray of ice wiped out all of the Ifrit copies. This is utter madness.

Ever since the beginning, when my efforts to interface had first been blocked, I knew that Rimuru's skills were highly suited to strategy and analysis. But after this, I must admit that his ability to analyze is at least the equal of my "Inquirer" skill, if not greater.

Simply stunning. He instantly analyzed the Icicle Lance and made it his own, even though his resources have been divided for the purposes of unlocking my prison. It is impossible not to be amazed.

He owns "Predator," which can devour anything, and some other, mystery skill that can analyze and reuse anything he absorbs…

Wait. Is it just me…or is this an extraordinarily convenient pairing of Unique Skills to have?! The synergistic capabilities of such a pair are unfathomable. I cannot imagine its limits.

Ifrit seems to have realized this as well. His expression has changed, and now he brings out his best attack to force a conclusion.

"Flare Circle…" The widest-area flame attack, perhaps to prevent his prey from escaping. But this was a poor choice. It won't work on Rimu—

"Oh, well…I had a good run."

What?! For whatever reason, Rimuru seems to believe that he's lost. *What nonsense!* I wish I could lecture him directly and remind him that he has Thermal Fluctuation Resistance.

If it were a concentrated, individual heat attack on Rimuru, he might have suffered damage. With enough accumulated damage, he might even be defeated. But Ifrit's choice of attack was dispersed over a wide range. An attack that an ordinary being might not survive, but which is meaningless with Rimuru's resistance.

This was the reason for your failure, Ifrit. And Rimuru eventually realized it.

"Sorry, Ifrit. Your flames are worthless against me," he said cockily.

A bold statement from one who was panicked just moments ago. That was when Ifrit made his fatal mistake. He let Rimuru's words rattle him, and paused. Rimuru seized on the opportunity, sealing the spirit's fate.

His Unique Skill, "Predator," ushered Ifrit into my little domain. I believe he was meant to be isolated in his own space, but I was able to probe outward with my thoughts and draw him closer. A forceful method, perhaps, but there is no other way that I can have this conversation partner.

"Storm...Dragon..."

Ifrit was shocked to see me. And now, I have gained a new playmate in my stomach prison.

◆THE UPHEAVAL BEGINS◆

While I played with Ifrit, Rimuru finished his farewells with the woman named Shizu. And in the time that I was looking away, he learned how to take human form.

How regrettable! Why must I divert my attention at such a pivotal moment? Perhaps my failing lies in my obsession with the game "shogi" that I found in Rimuru's memory and challenged Ifrit to...

"Please don't blame me for that, Storm Dragon..."
"I told you to call me Veldora."

Ifrit is a most stubborn fool. Apparently he was ill-suited to his bodily host, the woman named Shizue.

Not in terms of synchronization, but in terms of their nature, you might say. Ifrit worshipped the Demon Lord Leon. Shizue, meanwhile, held a deep-seated grudge against him.

Of course these two would not find common purpose. It was Shizue's skill that kept Ifrit's power bottled up. That speaks to the source of her weakness. She was unable to take full advantage of Ifrit's mighty powers. If she had been able to share her mind with the spirit's, her abilities would have far surpassed such limitations. And I doubt she would have reached the end of her life at this moment...

But because she was not more adept, Rimuru has now inherited Shizue's will and gained her appearance for his own. I suppose it was simply a matter of fate.

The three adventurers happily receive new test equipment from the dwarven smiths as they take their leave. It may seem heartless of them to rush off so promptly, but that is the way of things.

The world is a cruel place, and those with the strength to survive must set their sights on the future, not the past. One must have the strength to accept the life and death of others in order to survive. That applies to Rimuru as well.

He might seem to have gifted them the equipment out of generosity, but there is keen calculation behind it. It seems he has chosen this course of action out of a desire to build a friendly relationship with the humans.

I agree with his plan. Now that I have gained an interest in the ways of the human world, I do not oppose Rimuru in this. And now, his new, human form has endowed him with an array of new abilities. In all honesty, I am jealous. I wish to take human form and frolic amongst them, too.

I am a spiritual being, so I can take any form I wish...but I have never tested it until now. There's no telling if it will go well or not. I am unsure.

I suppose I can just leave the human transforming to Rimuru. That unfathomable slime is a creature of endless delights. No doubt he has some idea in mind.

I then sat back and waited, allowing my mind to run wild with possibilities.

To be reincarnated in Volume 3!

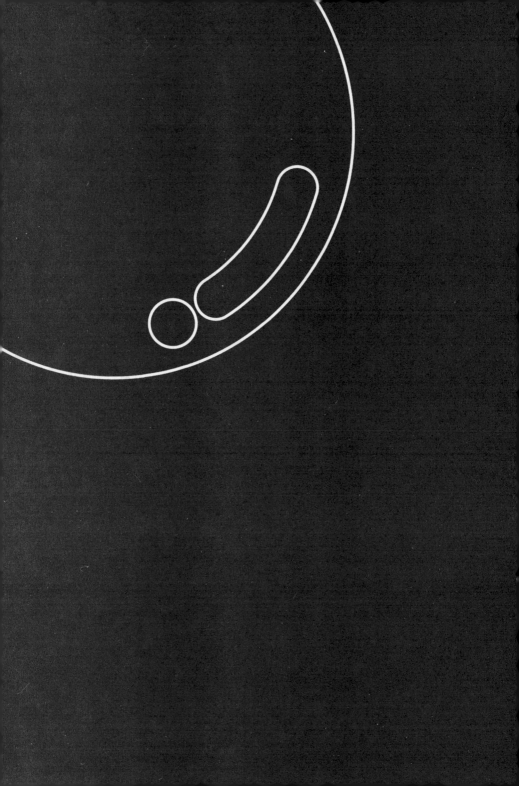

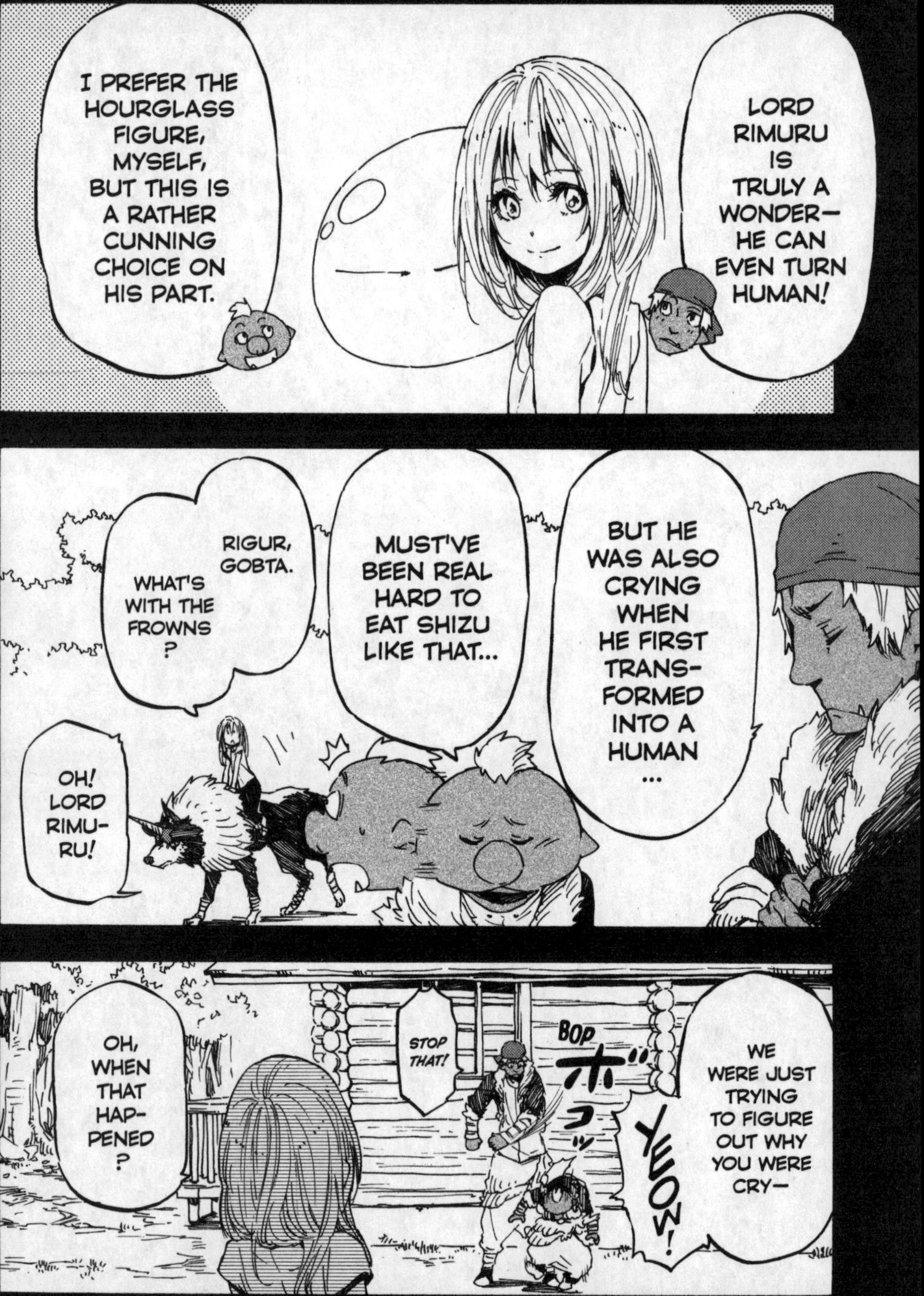
LORD RIMURU IS TRULY A WONDER— HE CAN EVEN TURN HUMAN!
I PREFER THE HOURGLASS FIGURE, MYSELF, BUT THIS IS A RATHER CUNNING CHOICE ON HIS PART.
BUT HE WAS ALSO CRYING WHEN HE FIRST TRANS-FORMED INTO A HUMAN...
MUST'VE BEEN REAL HARD TO EAT SHIZU LIKE THAT...
RIGUR, GOBTA.
WHAT'S WITH THE FROWNS?
OH! LORD RIMU-RU!
WE WERE JUST TRYING TO FIGURE OUT WHY YOU WERE CRY—
YEOW!
BOP
STOP THAT!
OH, WHEN THAT HAP-PENED?

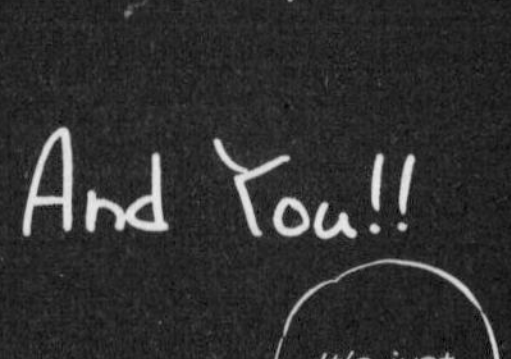

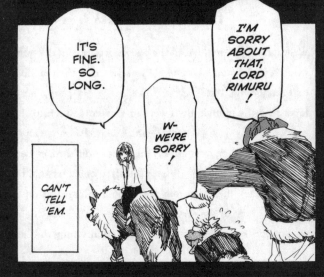

I'M SORRY ABOUT THAT, LORD RIMURU!
W-WE'RE SORRY!
IT'S FINE. SO LONG.
CAN'T TELL 'EM.
HURRY. JUST RUN.
YES, MASTER...
sniff
I CAN'T TELL THEM THE SORROW I FELT WHEN I FINALLY GOT A HUMAN BODY AGAIN, AND LEARNED MY LITTLE GUY DIDN'T COME WITH IT...

*Please take this as an "extra" little story.

LIST OF ACKNOWLEDGMENTS

AUTHOR:
Fuse-sensei

ASSISTANTS:
Taku Arao-san
Takuya Nishida-san
Muraichi-san
Hino-san
Daiki Haraguchi-san
Kiritani-sensei

Congrats on your series!!

Everyone at the editorial department

And You!!

It's just easier to stay in this form.

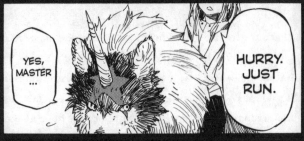

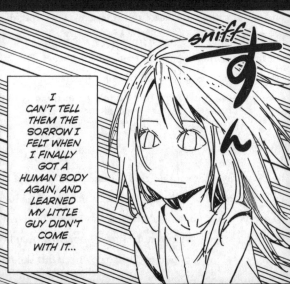

AFTERWORD from the author, Fuse

Well, well, we've made it to the second volume of the manga adaptation of *That Time I Got Reincarnated as a Slime!* I was afraid of the reaction for Volume 1, given that it had no heroine, but I'm glad to see that most people accepted it. It seems like some folks read the manga, then were interested enough to check out the online and print versions of my original novels, which is just wonderful! As those who have read both can tell you, there are actually significant differences between the online and print editions. If those can be different despite being written by the same person (that would be me), then naturally the manga will also be different. There are alterations here and there to the sequence of events and other fine details. Don't think of them as a major issue, though. Just laugh off anything that seems odd.

"The online version is just a rough plot!!"

That's the excuse I often tell myself. Sure, the major movements should be the same, but it's fine for the little details to change! At our very first planning meeting, I told Kawakami-sensei that it's perfectly fine to draw things as you see fit, up to a point. We do have significant meetings before every chapter, however! The print version is the fundamental base we start with, but my hope as the creator is for the manga and novel to be distinctly different things. My role in the manga adaptation, as the story creator, is simply to ensure that there aren't jarring discrepancies. Not so that the stories are exactly the same, but perhaps to preserve the feel of the novel in a different medium. As long as you readers don't react like, "This is all wrong!" then I consider it a success. There will be enjoyable features of the manga version that aren't in the novels, so I just hope that I don't get in the way of that.

So that's my afterword for this volume. I really had a lot of fun rereading this book and spotting all of Kawakami-sensei's little original touches. It's too bad that I can't go overboard in gushing about the end result, or else it'll sound like I'm singing my own praises! Now that Rimuru has a human form at last, the story's about to get into the real meat of things. Please do check out the next volume of *That Time I Got Reincarnated as a Slime!!*

From character designer Mitz Vah-sensei

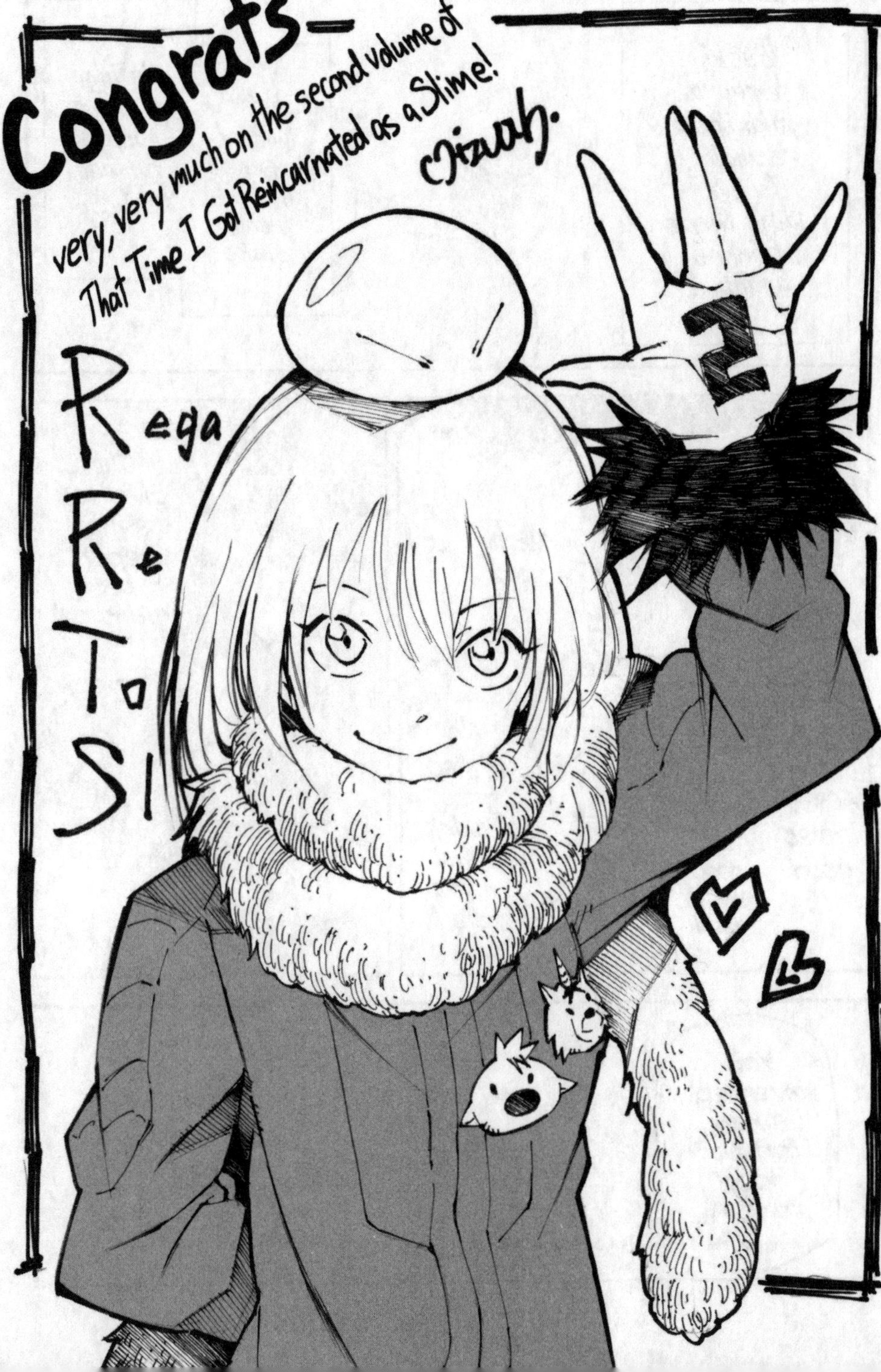
Congrats—
very, very much on the second volume of
That Time I Got Reincarnated as a Slime!
Rega
Re
To
Sl
2

「MEAL REPORT」

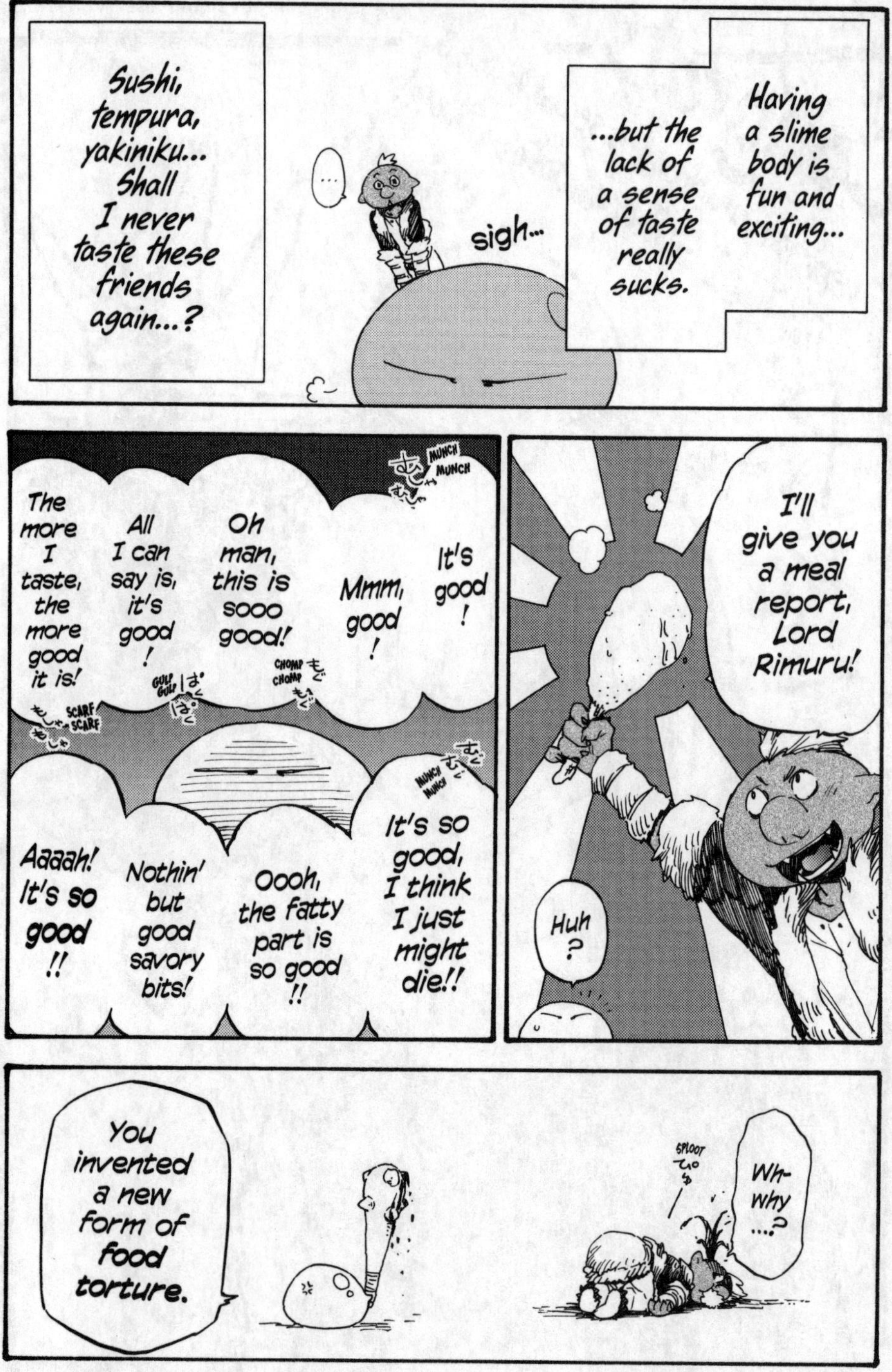
Having a slime body is fun and exciting...
...but the lack of a sense of taste really sucks.
sigh...
...
Sushi, tempura, yakiniku... Shall I never taste these friends again...?
I'll give you a meal report, Lord Rimuru!
Huh?
MUNCH MUNCH
It's good!
Mmm, good!
Oh man, this is sooo good!
CHOMP CHOMP
All I can say is, it's good!
GULP GULP
The more I taste, the more good it is!
SCARF SCARF
MUNCH MUNCH
It's so good, I think I just might die!!
Oooh, the fatty part is so good!!
Nothin' but good savory bits!
Aaaah! It's so good!!
SPLOOT
Wh-why...?
You invented a new form of food torture.

The "Three Brothers" theory.

TRANSLATION
NOTES

"I'M NOT A BAD SLIME, YOU KNOW!"

page 61

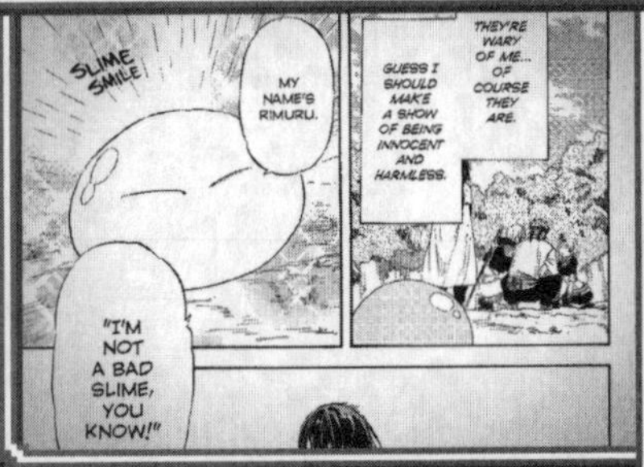
THEY'RE WARY OF ME... OF COURSE THEY ARE.
GUESS I SHOULD MAKE A SHOW OF BEING INNOCENT AND HARMLESS.
MY NAME'S RIMURU.
SLIME SMILE
"I'M NOT A BAD SLIME, YOU KNOW!"

Though it may not be obvious at first, the quotation marks in Rimuru's speech are a sign that he's quoting a line from something else—in this case, it's a well-known bit of dialogue from the *Dragon Quest* RPG series, in which the cute and largely harmless blue slimes are an iconic foe, the easiest in the game. Over time, it's become a bit of a staple for the games in the series to feature an NPC (non-player character, as opposed to a generic enemy) slime who can be conversed with, rather than fought. The first line of dialogue the slime says will always be something along the lines of, "Don't be mean to me. I'm not a bad slime, you know!"

YAKINIKU

page 97

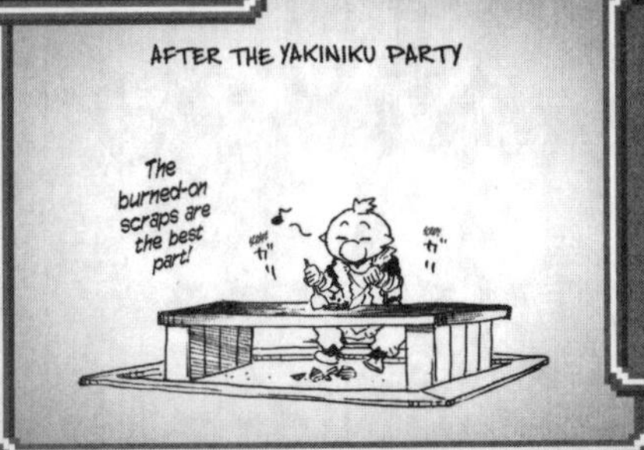
AFTER THE YAKINIKU PARTY
The burned-on scraps are the best part!

The Japanese name for grilled meat, which is often styled "Korean BBQ" in English. While yakiniku is usually done over a grilled surface, the *teppanyaki* style is also popular, as seen here: a flat metal surface like a griddle that cooks more evenly. Many Western *teppanyaki* restaurants feature cooks who put on flashy presentations, but the key to any good *yakiniku* party is placing the pieces of meat yourself and watching them cook until they're just right.

Three Brothers

page 185

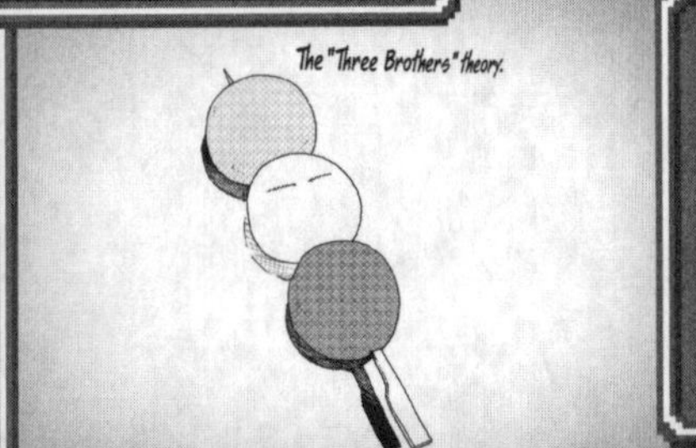
The "Three Brothers" theory.

A reference to the ultra-popular "Dango San-Kyôdai" song, meaning "Three Dango Brothers." Dango are little cakes made with rice flour, similar to mochi, and typically served on skewers. The Dango song originated on an NHK children's program and exploded in popularity around the turn of the millennium. The song's lyrics imagine that the three dango on the skewer are brothers with their own personalities. Appropriately, the song itself was a tango.

The Black Museum The Ghost and the Lady

By Kazuhiro Fujita

Deep in Scotland Yard in London sits an evidence room dedicated to the greatest mysteries of British history. In this "Black Museum" sits a misshapen hunk of lead—two bullets fused together—the key to a wartime encounter between Florence Nightingale, the mother of modern nursing, and a supernatural Man in Grey. This story is unknown to most scholars of history, but a special guest of the museum will tell the tale of The Ghost and the Lady...

Praise for Kazuhiro Fujita's *Ushio and Tora*

"A charming revival that combines a classic look with modern depth and pacing... **Essential viewing both for curmudgeons and new fans alike.**" — Anime News Network

"**GREAT!** The first episode of Ushio and Tora captures the essence of '90s anime." — IGN

A new series from the creator of *Soul Eater*, the megahit manga and anime seen on Toonami!

"Fun and lively... a great start!"
-Adventures in Poor Taste

FIRE FORCE

By Atsushi Ohkubo

The city of Tokyo is plagued by a deadly phenomenon: spontaneous human combustion! Luckily, a special team is there to quench the inferno: The Fire Force! The fire soldiers at Special Fire Cathedral 8 are about to get a unique addition. Enter Shinra, a boy who possesses the power to run at the speed of a rocket, leaving behind the famous "devil's footprints" (and destroying his shoes in the process). Can Shinra and his colleagues discover the source of this strange epidemic before the city burns to ashes?

The award-winning manga about what happens inside you!

"Far more entertaining than it ought to be... what kid doesn't want to think that every time they sneeze a torpedo shoots out their nose?"
–Anime News Network

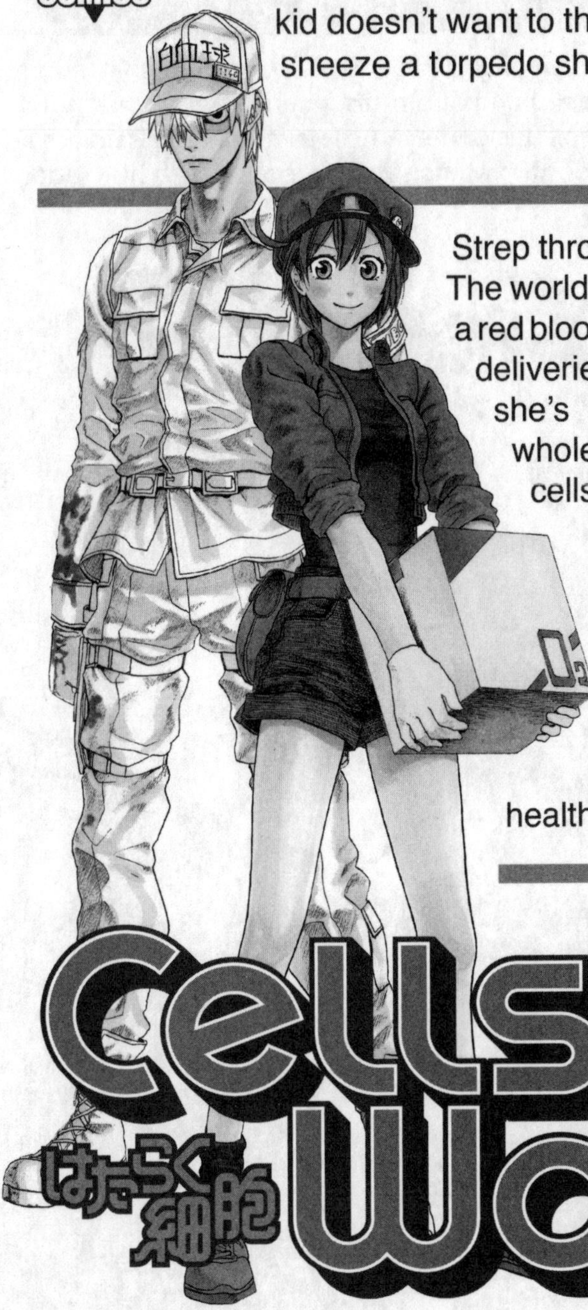

Strep throat! Hay fever! Influenza! The world is a dangerous place for a red blood cell just trying to get her deliveries finished. Fortunately, she's not alone…she's got a whole human body's worth of cells ready to help out! The mysterious white blood cells, the buff and brash killer T cells, even the cute little platelets— everyone's got to come together if they want to keep you healthy!

Cells at Work!

はたらく細胞

By Akane Shimizu

New action series from Hiroyuki Takei, creator of the classic shonen franchise Shaman King!

In medieval Japan, a bell hanging on the collar is a sign that a cat has a master. Norachiyo's bell hangs from his katana sheath, but he is nonetheless a stray — a ronin. This one-eyed cat samurai travels across a dishonest world, cutting through pretense and deception with his blade.

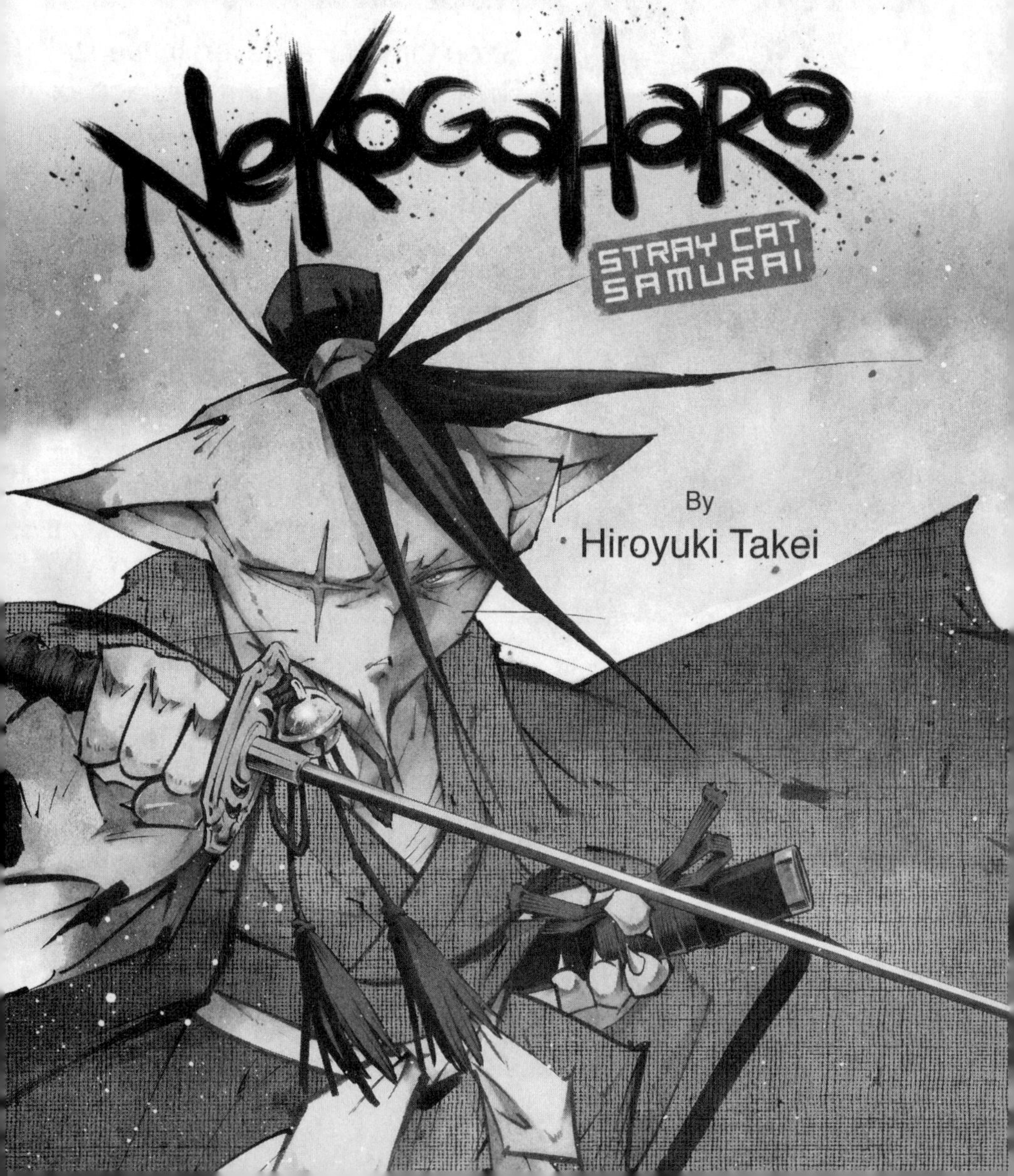
NekoGaHara
STRAY CAT SAMURAI
By
Hiroyuki Takei

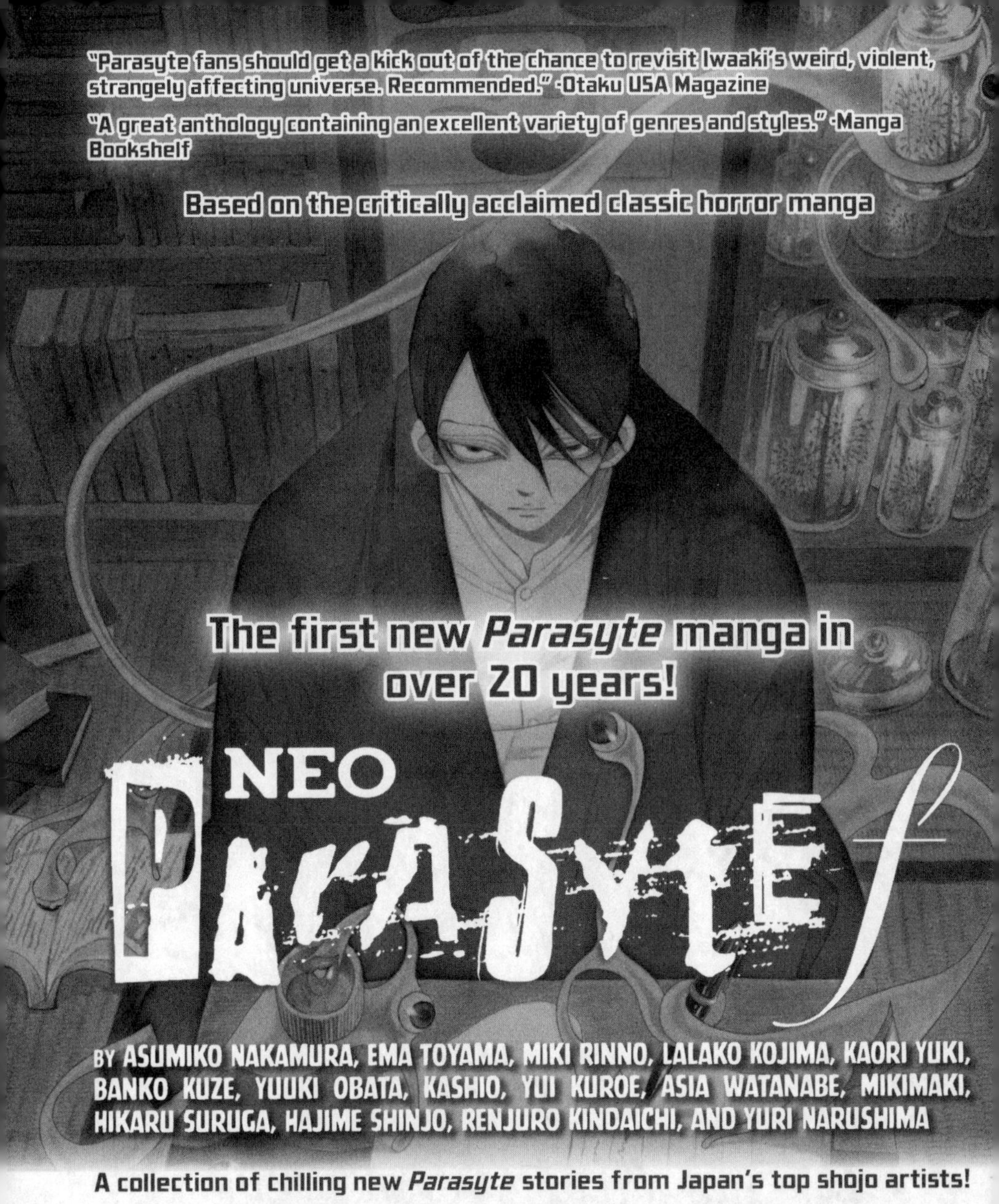
"Parasyte fans should get a kick out of the chance to revisit Iwaaki's weird, violent, strangely affecting universe. Recommended." -Otaku USA Magazine
"A great anthology containing an excellent variety of genres and styles." -Manga Bookshelf
Based on the critically acclaimed classic horror manga
The first new *Parasyte* manga in over 20 years!
NEO PARASYTE f
BY ASUMIKO NAKAMURA, EMA TOYAMA, MIKI RINNO, LALAKO KOJIMA, KAORI YUKI, BANKO KUZE, YUUKI OBATA, KASHIO, YUI KUROE, ASIA WATANABE, MIKIMAKI, HIKARU SURUGA, HAJIME SHINJO, RENJURO KINDAICHI, AND YURI NARUSHIMA

A collection of chilling new *Parasyte* stories from Japan's top shojo artists!

Parasites: shape-shifting aliens whose only purpose is to assimilate with and consume the human race... but do these monsters have a different side? A parasite becomes a prince to save his romance-obsessed female host from a dangerous stalker. Another hosts a cooking show, in which the real monsters are revealed. These and 13 more stories, from some of the greatest shojo manga artists alive today, together make up a chilling, funny, and entertaining tribute to one of manga's horror classics!

KC KODANSHA COMICS

Having lost his wife, high school teacher Kōhei Inuzuka is doing his best to raise his young daughter Tsumugi as a single father. He's pretty bad at cooking and doesn't have a huge appetite to begin with, but chance brings his little family together with one of his students, the lonely Kotori. The three of them are anything but comfortable in the kitchen, but the healing power of home cooking might just work on their grieving hearts.

"This season's number-one feel-good anime!" —Anime News Network

"A beautifully-drawn story about comfort food and family and grief. Recommended." —Otaku USA Magazine

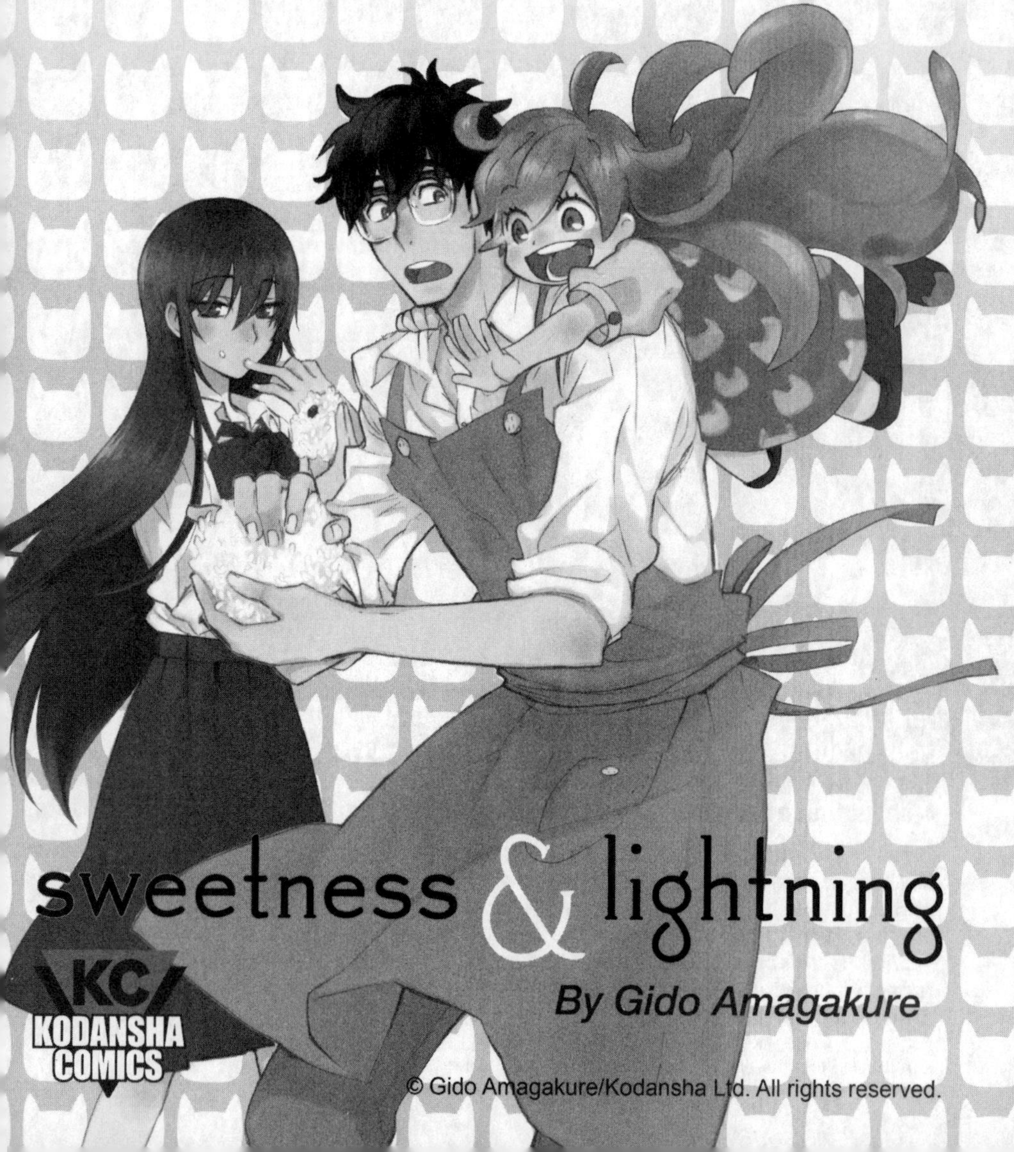

sweetness & lightning

By Gido Amagakure

KC KODANSHA COMICS

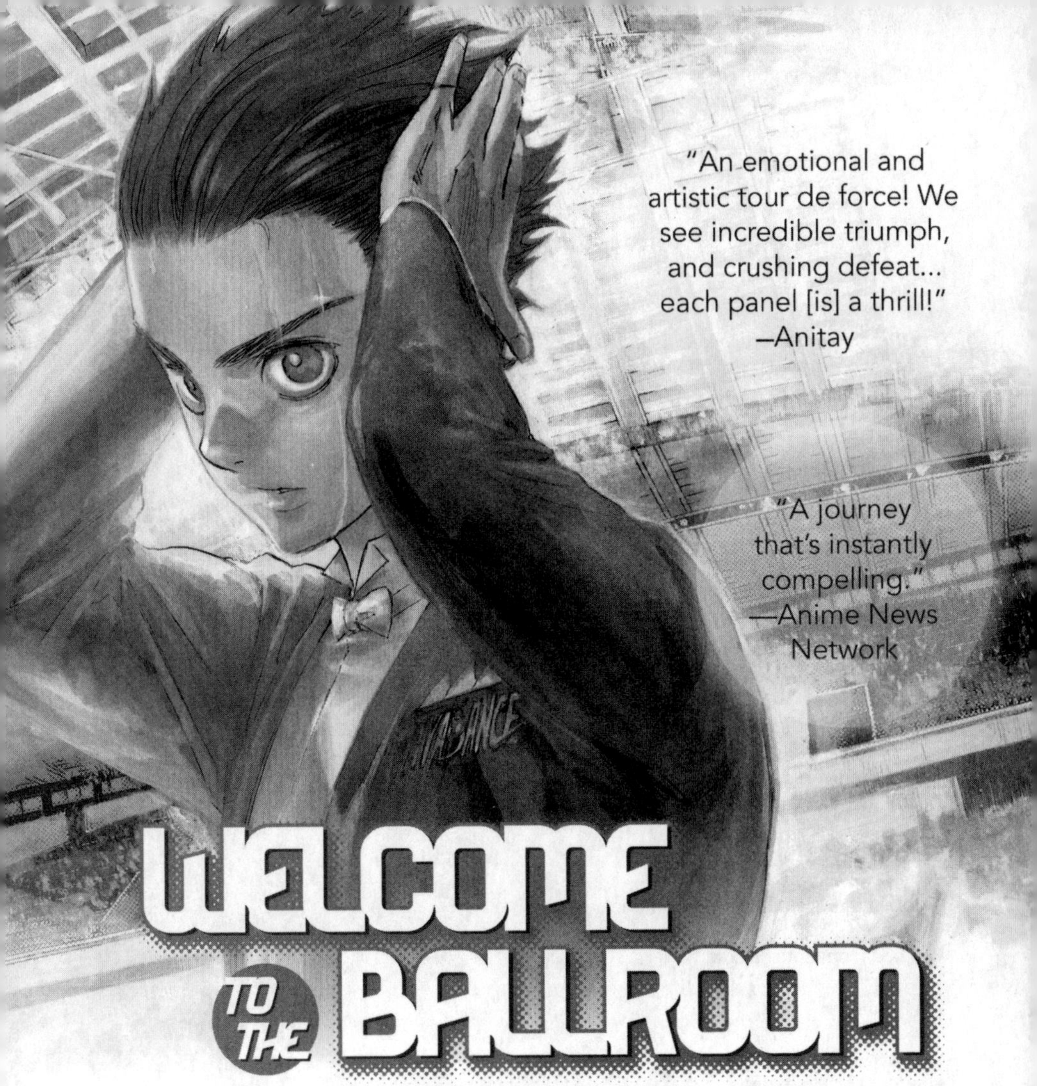
"An emotional and artistic tour de force! We see incredible triumph, and crushing defeat... each panel [is] a thrill!"
—Anitay
"A journey that's instantly compelling."
—Anime News Network
WELCOME TO THE BALLROOM

By Tomo Takeuchi

Feckless high school student Tatara Fujita wants to be good at something—anything. Unfortunately, he's about as average as a slouchy teen can be. The local bullies know this, and make it a habit to hit him up for cash, but all that changes when the debonair Kaname Sengoku sends them packing. Sengoku's not the neighborhood watch, though. He's a professional ballroom dancer. And once Tatara Fujita gets pulled into the world of ballroom, his life will never be the same.

KC KODANSHA COMICS

A Kodansha Comics Trade Paperback Original.

Published in the United States by Kodansha Comics,
an imprint of Kodansha USA Publishing, LLC, New York.

Publication rights for this English edition arranged through Kodansha Ltd., Tokyo.

First published in Japan in 2016 by Kodansha Ltd., Tokyo, as *Tensei Shitara Suraimu Datta Ken* volume 2.

ISBN 978-1-63236-507-1

Printed in the United States of America.

www.kodanshacomics.com

12th Printing

Translation: Stephen Paul
Lettering: Evan Hayden
Editing: Ajani Oloye
Kodansha Comics edition cover design: Phil Balsman

THAT TIME I GOT REINCARNATED AS A SLIME 3

Author: FUSE
Artist: TAIKI KAWAKAMI
Character design: MITZ VAH

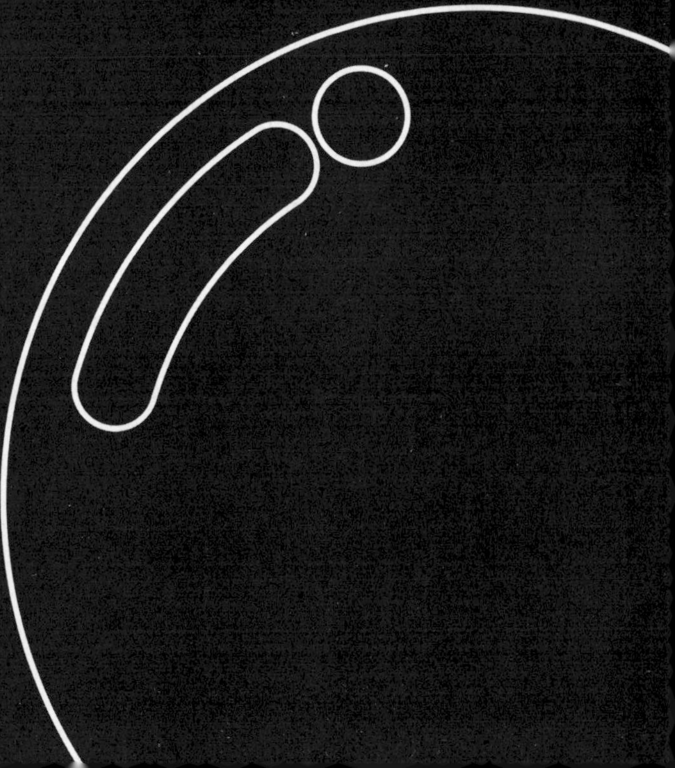

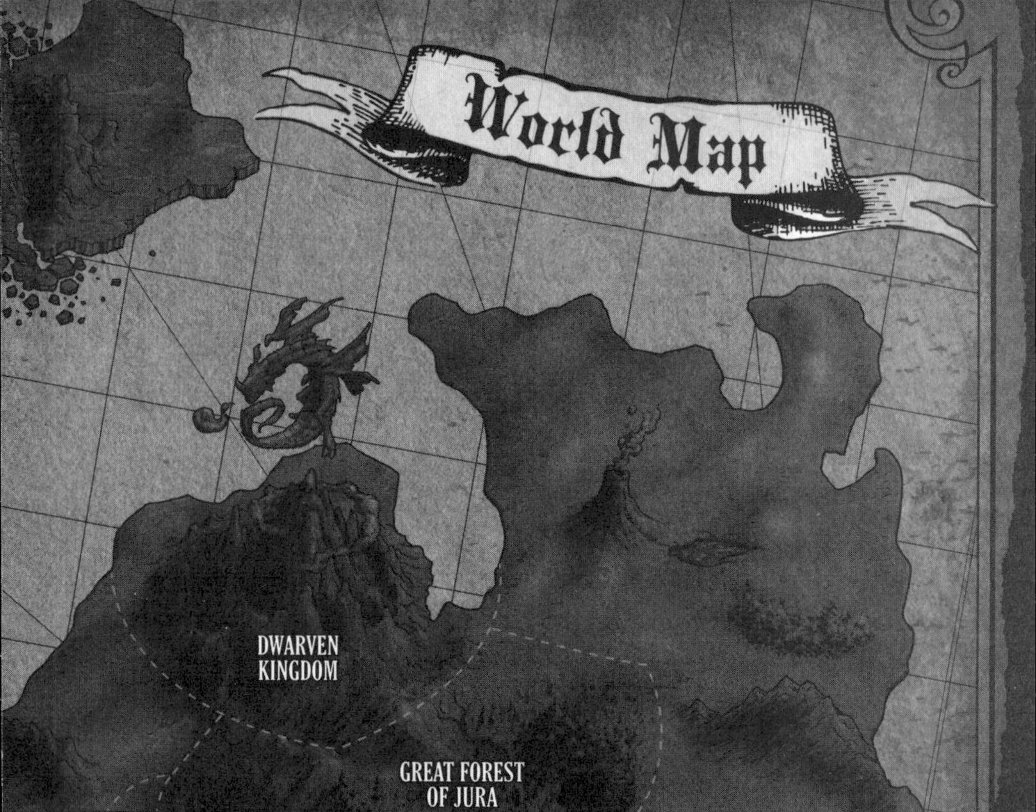
World Map
DWARVEN KINGDOM
GREAT FOREST OF JURA
KINGDOM OF BLUMUND
SEALED CAVE

PLOT SUMMARY

For the first time since he was reincarnated into this other world, Rimuru met someone from his homeland, Shizue Izawa. She was an all-powerful Elementalist and known as the "Conqueror of Flames," because she bore the spirit of Ifrit within her. But then Ifrit rebelled, attempting to seize control of her body. Rimuru battled the fire spirit to quell him, and after a dire battle, he devoured Ifrit. Shizue had her body back, but because the flame spirit had been keeping her alive, she grew weaker by the moment, until...
After Shizue's passing, Rimuru inherited her desires and appearance, and found himself on the path to a new goal. ▼

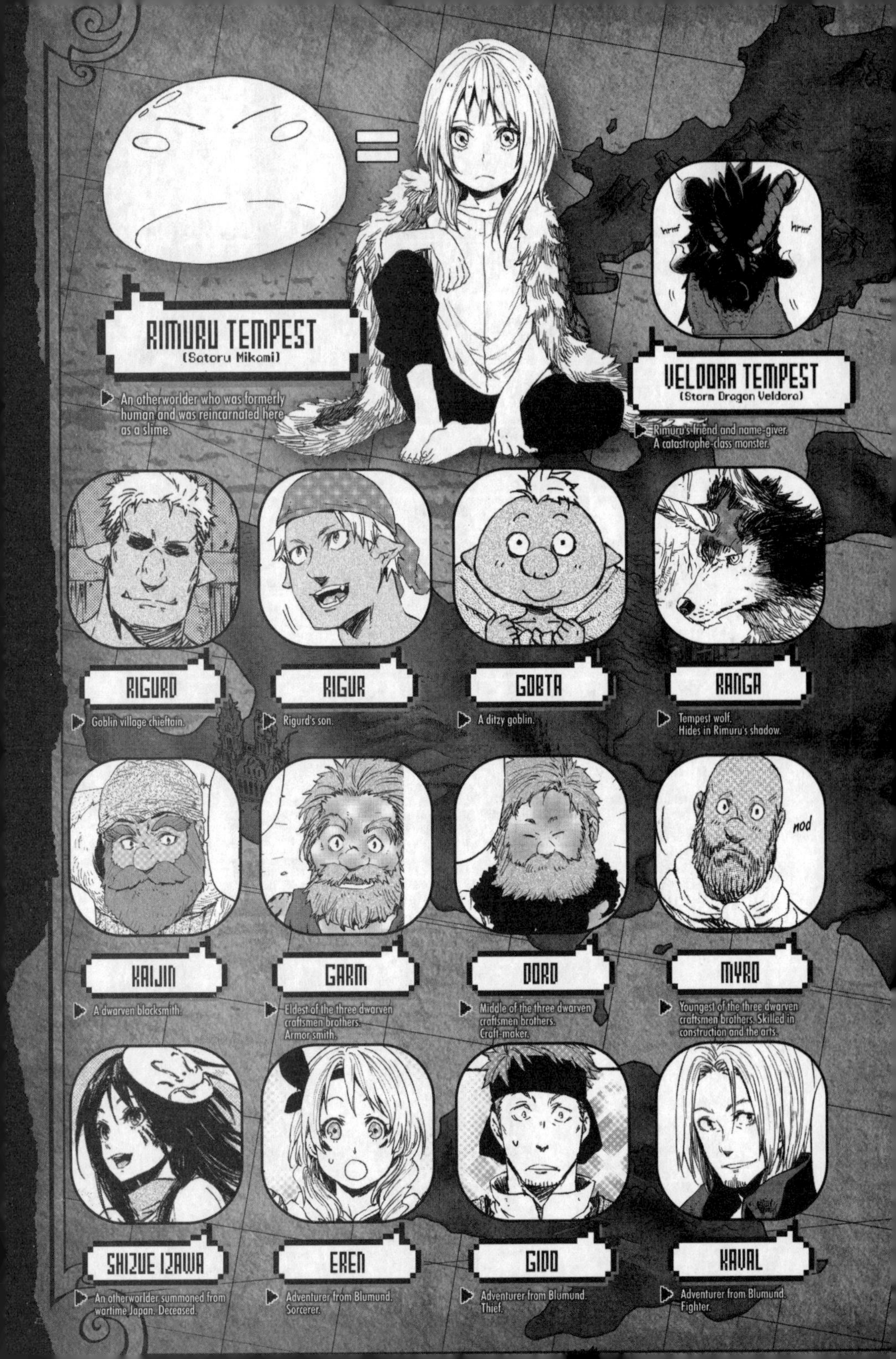
RIMURU TEMPEST
(Satoru Mikami)
An otherworlder who was formerly human and was reincarnated here as a slime.
hrmf
hrmf
VELDORA TEMPEST
(Storm Dragon Veldora)
Rimuru's friend and name-giver. A catastrophe-class monster.
RIGURD
Goblin village chieftain.
RIGUR
Rigurd's son.
GOBTA
A ditzy goblin.
RANGA
Tempest wolf. Hides in Rimuru's shadow.
KAIJIN
A dwarven blacksmith.
GARM
Eldest of the three dwarven craftsmen brothers. Armor smith.
DORD
Middle of the three dwarven craftsmen brothers. Craft-maker.
nod
MYRD
Youngest of the three dwarven craftsmen brothers. Skilled in construction and the arts.
SHIZUE IZAWA
An otherworlder summoned from wartime Japan. Deceased.
EREN
Adventurer from Blumund. Sorcerer.
GIDO
Adventurer from Blumund. Thief.
KAVAL
Adventurer from Blumund. Fighter.

CONTENTS

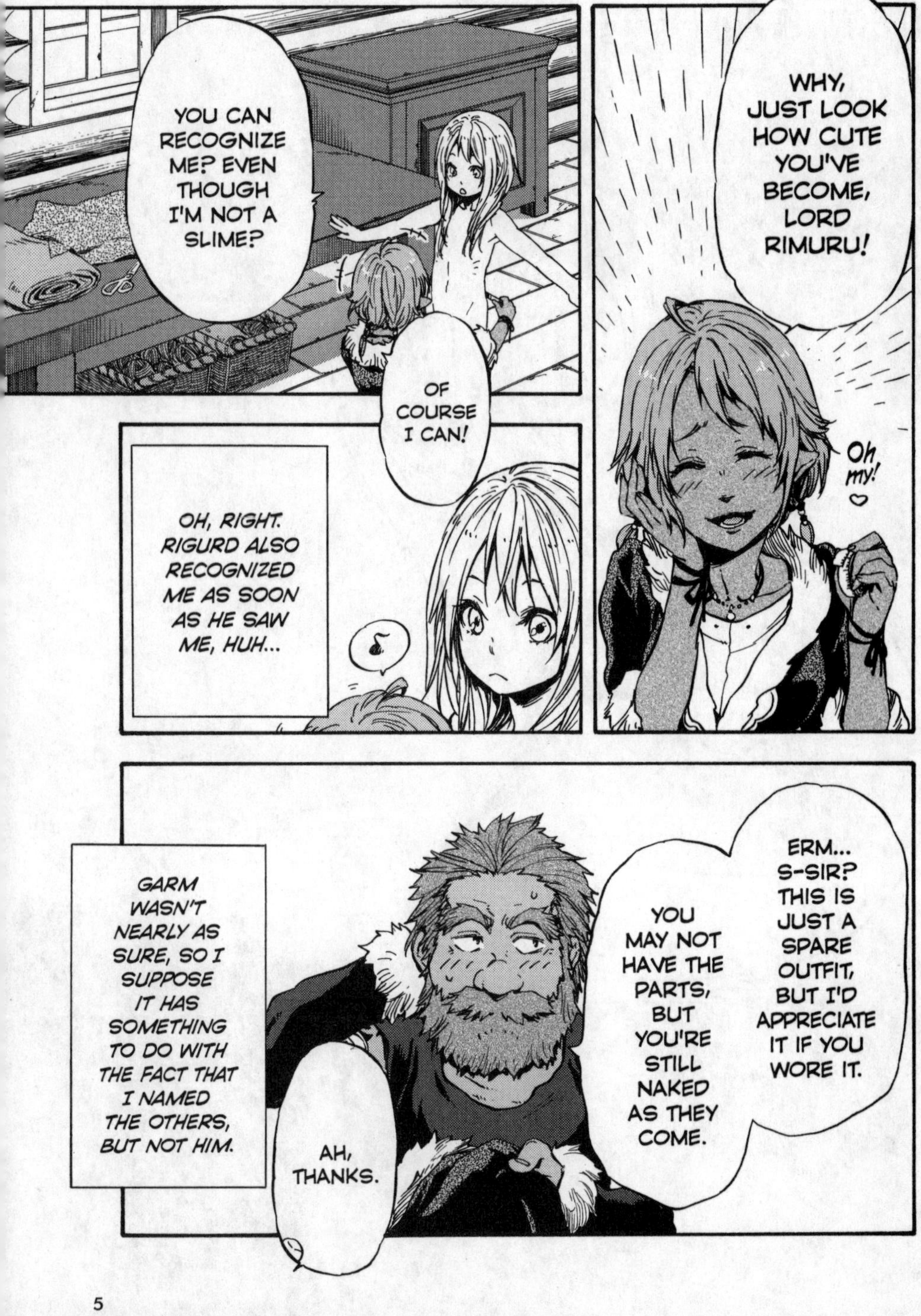
WHY, JUST LOOK HOW CUTE YOU'VE BECOME, LORD RIMURU!
Oh my! ♡
YOU CAN RECOGNIZE ME? EVEN THOUGH I'M NOT A SLIME?
OF COURSE I CAN!
OH, RIGHT. RIGURD ALSO RECOGNIZED ME AS SOON AS HE SAW ME, HUH...
ERM... S-SIR? THIS IS JUST A SPARE OUTFIT, BUT I'D APPRECIATE IT IF YOU WORE IT.
YOU MAY NOT HAVE THE PARTS, BUT YOU'RE STILL NAKED AS THEY COME.
GARM WASN'T NEARLY AS SURE, SO I SUPPOSE IT HAS SOMETHING TO DO WITH THE FACT THAT I NAMED THE OTHERS, BUT NOT HIM.
AH, THANKS.

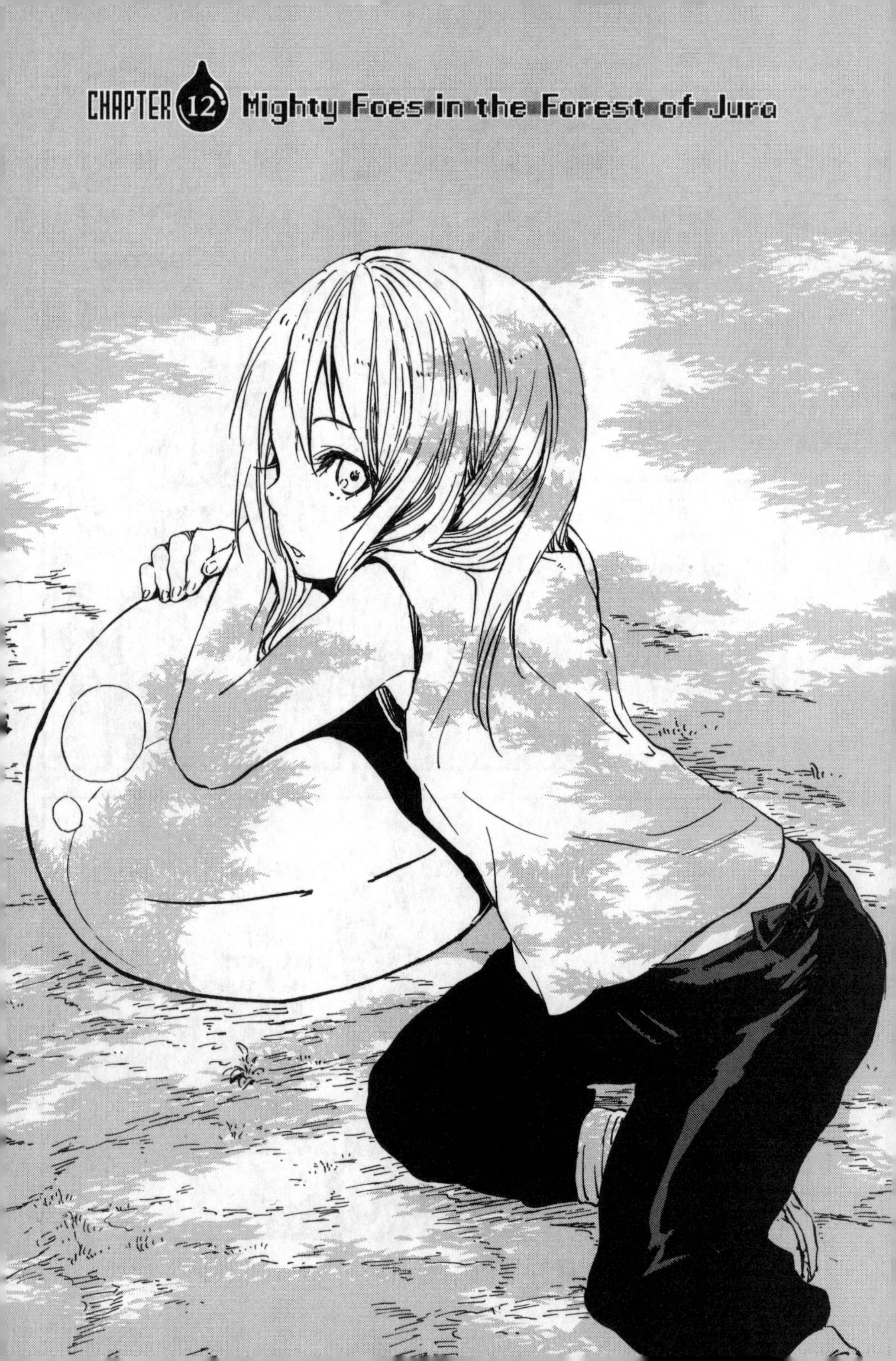
CHAPTER 12 Mighty Foes in the Forest of Jura

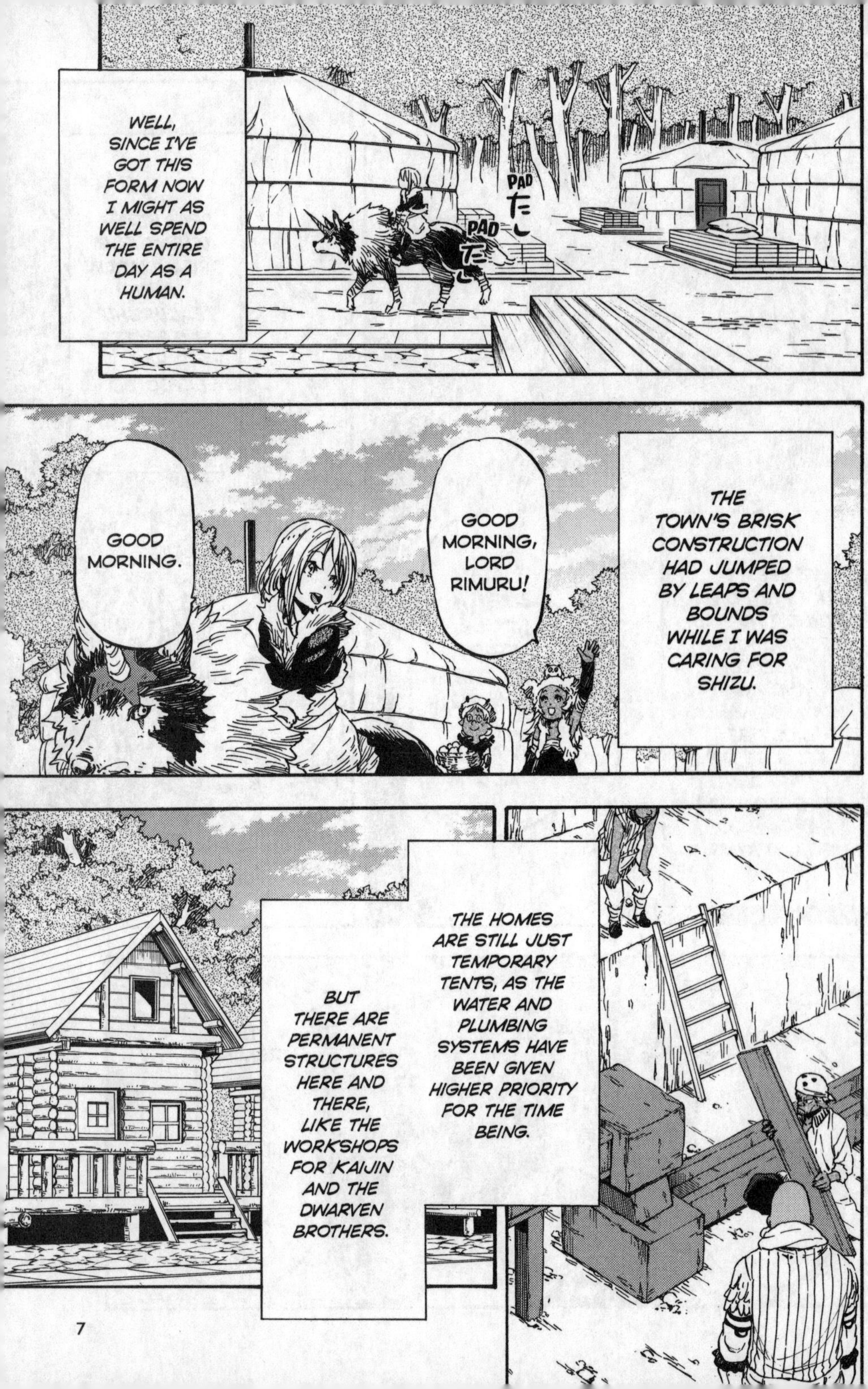
WELL, SINCE I'VE GOT THIS FORM NOW I MIGHT AS WELL SPEND THE ENTIRE DAY AS A HUMAN.
PAD たし
PAD たし
THE TOWN'S BRISK CONSTRUCTION HAD JUMPED BY LEAPS AND BOUNDS WHILE I WAS CARING FOR SHIZU.
GOOD MORNING, LORD RIMURU!
GOOD MORNING.
THE HOMES ARE STILL JUST TEMPORARY TENTS, AS THE WATER AND PLUMBING SYSTEMS HAVE BEEN GIVEN HIGHER PRIORITY FOR THE TIME BEING.
BUT THERE ARE PERMANENT STRUCTURES HERE AND THERE, LIKE THE WORKSHOPS FOR KAIJIN AND THE DWARVEN BROTHERS.

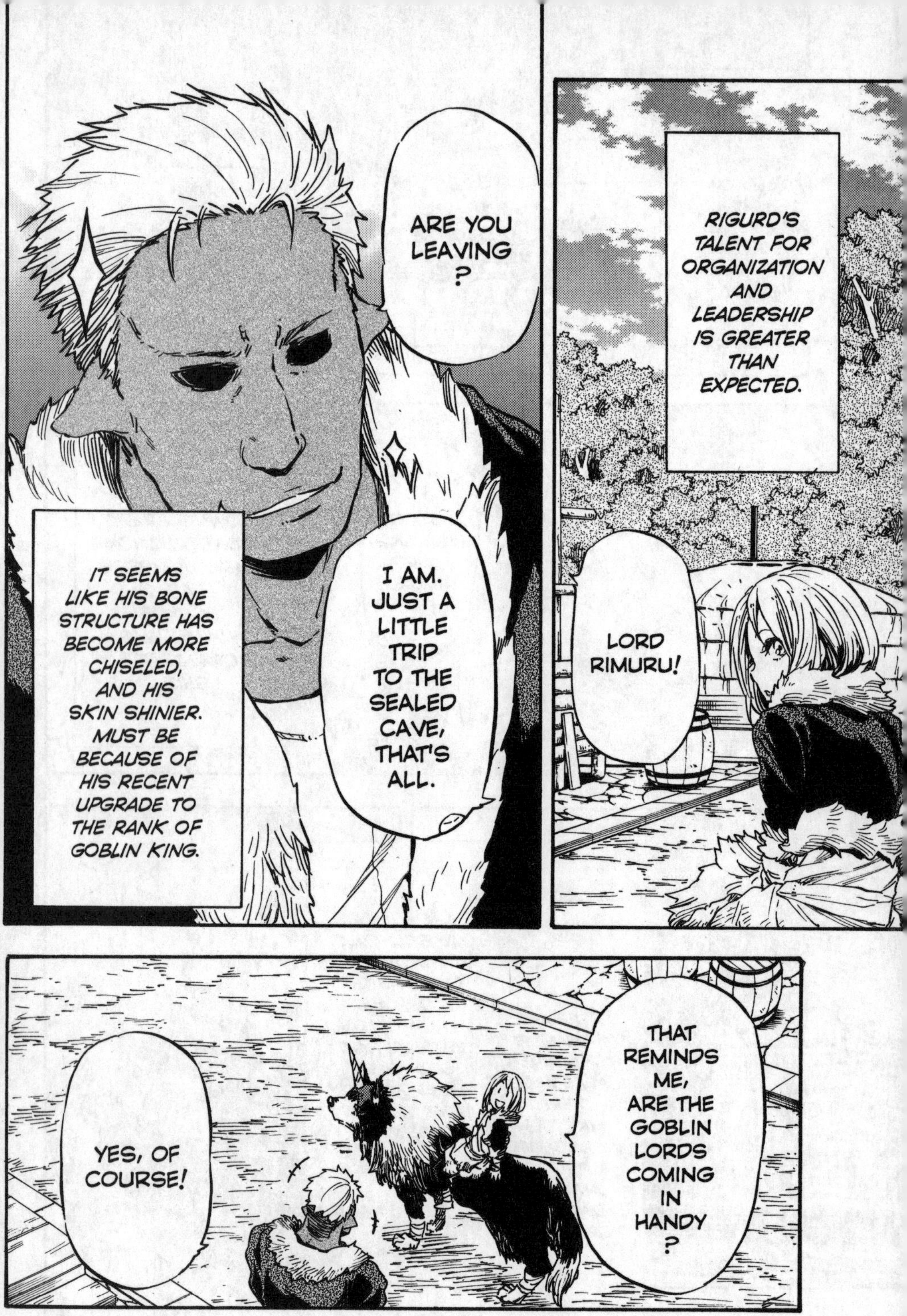

RIGURD'S TALENT FOR ORGANIZATION AND LEADERSHIP IS GREATER THAN EXPECTED.
LORD RIMURU!
ARE YOU LEAVING?
I AM. JUST A LITTLE TRIP TO THE SEALED CAVE, THAT'S ALL.
IT SEEMS LIKE HIS BONE STRUCTURE HAS BECOME MORE CHISELED, AND HIS SKIN SHINIER. MUST BE BECAUSE OF HIS RECENT UPGRADE TO THE RANK OF GOBLIN KING.
THAT REMINDS ME, ARE THE GOBLIN LORDS COMING IN HANDY?
YES, OF COURSE!

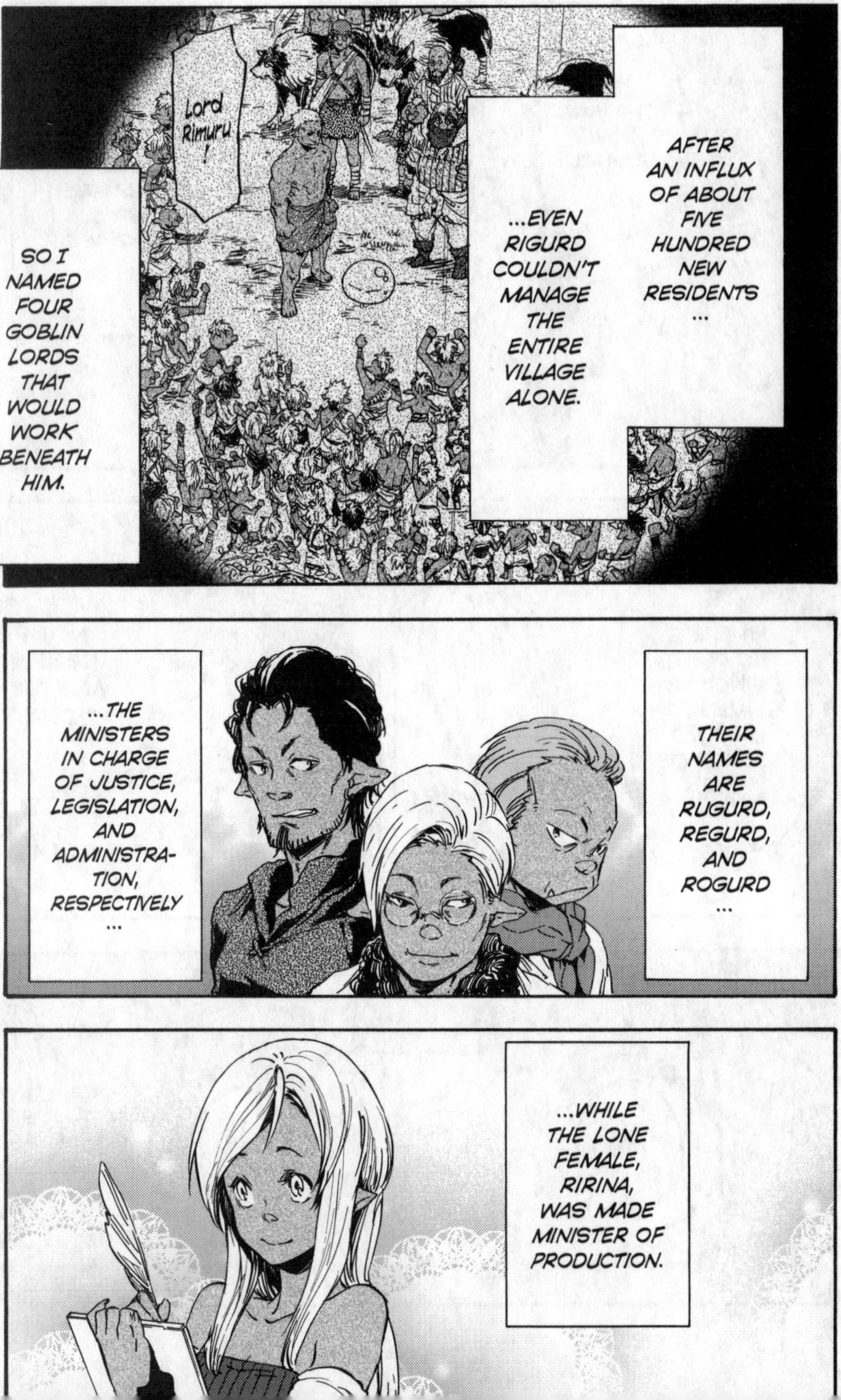
AFTER AN INFLUX OF ABOUT FIVE HUNDRED NEW RESIDENTS...
...EVEN RIGURD COULDN'T MANAGE THE ENTIRE VILLAGE ALONE.
Lord Rimuru!
SO I NAMED FOUR GOBLIN LORDS THAT WOULD WORK BENEATH HIM.
THEIR NAMES ARE RUGURD, REGURD, AND ROGURD...
...THE MINISTERS IN CHARGE OF JUSTICE, LEGISLATION, AND ADMINISTRATION, RESPECTIVELY...
...WHILE THE LONE FEMALE, RIRINA, WAS MADE MINISTER OF PRODUCTION.

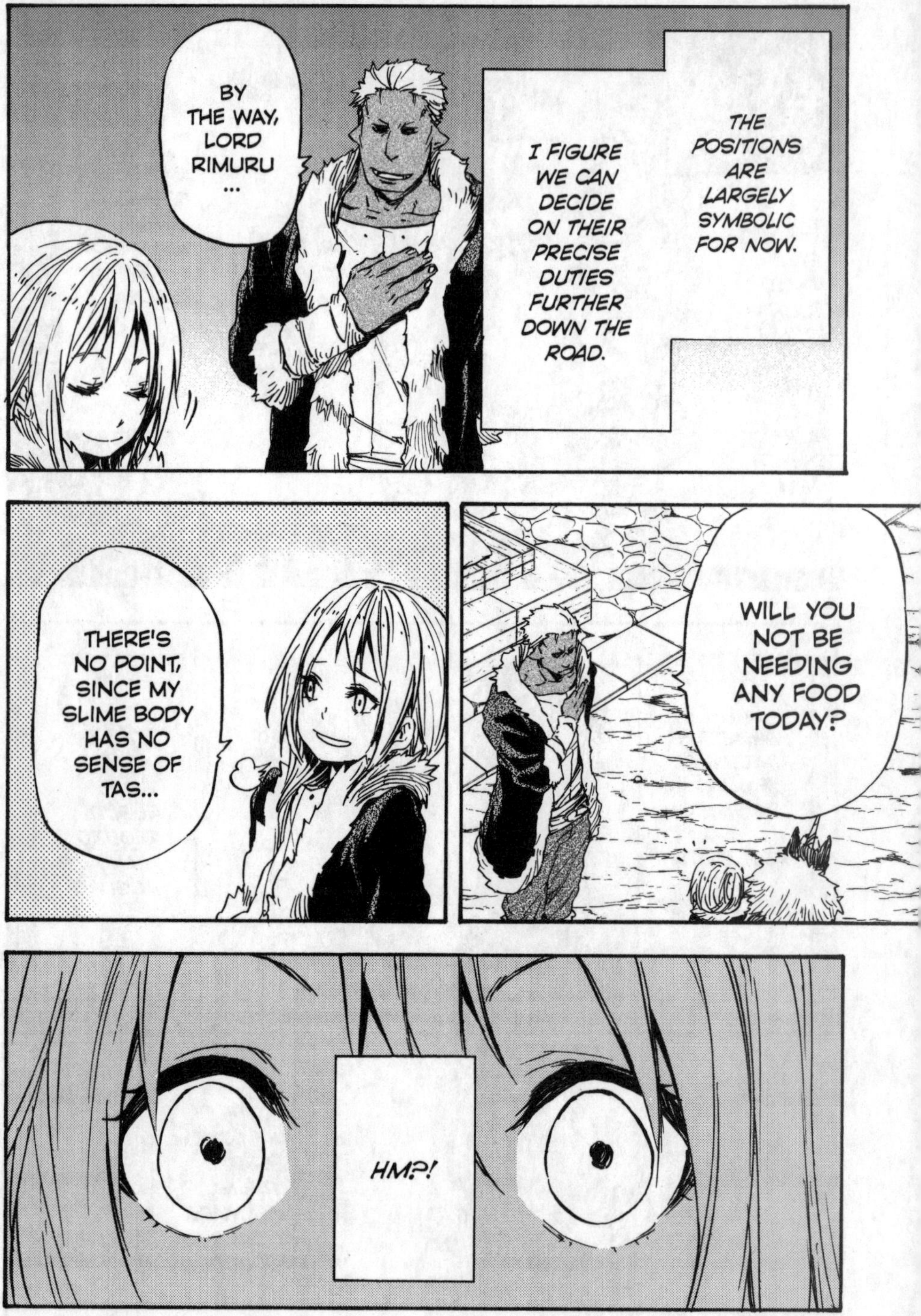
THE POSITIONS ARE LARGELY SYMBOLIC FOR NOW.
I FIGURE WE CAN DECIDE ON THEIR PRECISE DUTIES FURTHER DOWN THE ROAD.
BY THE WAY, LORD RIMURU ...
WILL YOU NOT BE NEEDING ANY FOOD TODAY?
THERE'S NO POINT, SINCE MY SLIME BODY HAS NO SENSE OF TAS...
HM?!

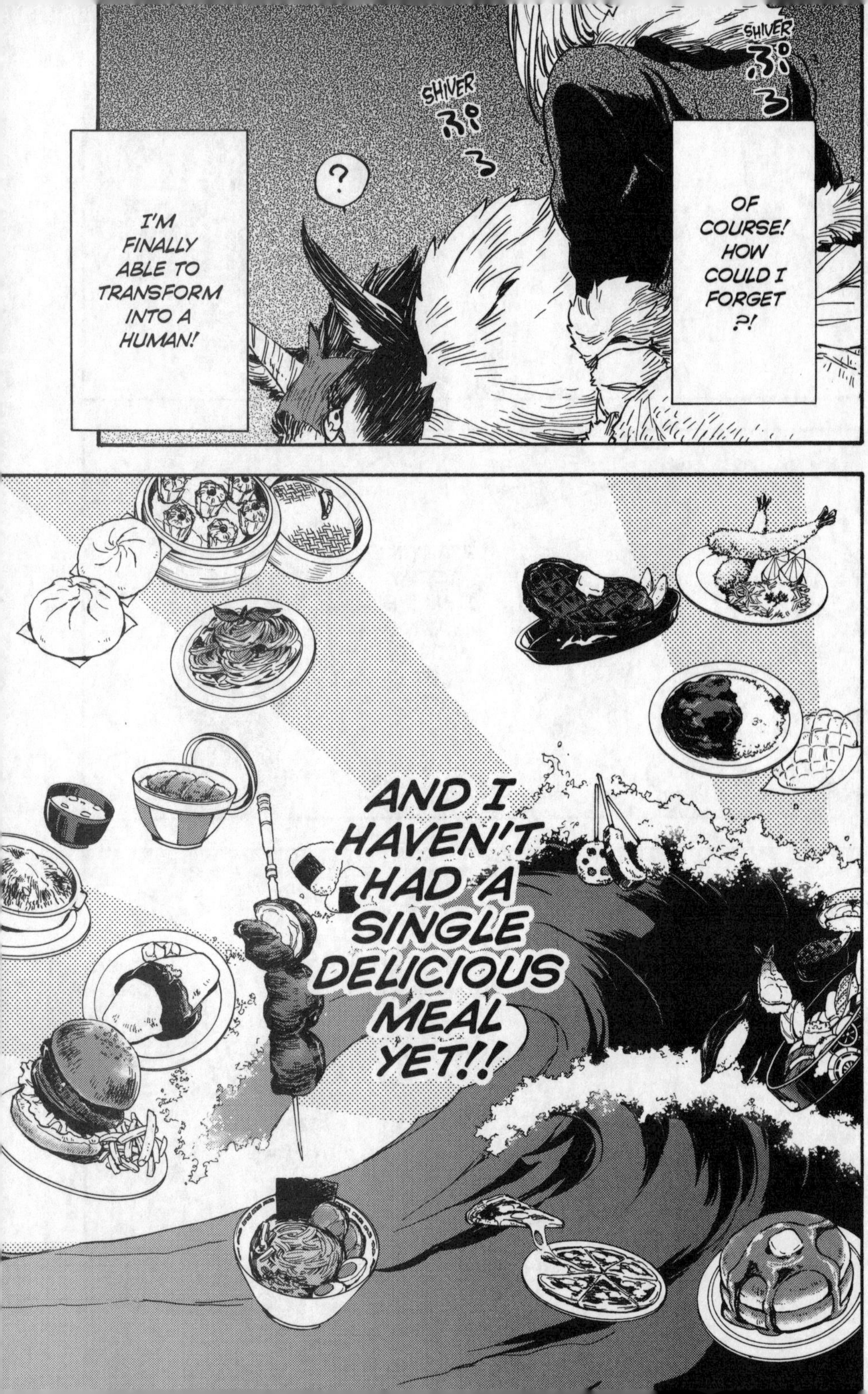
OF COURSE! HOW COULD I FORGET ?!
SHIVER
ぷる
SHIVER
ぷる
?
I'M FINALLY ABLE TO TRANSFORM INTO A HUMAN!
AND I HAVEN'T HAD A SINGLE DELICIOUS MEAL YET!!

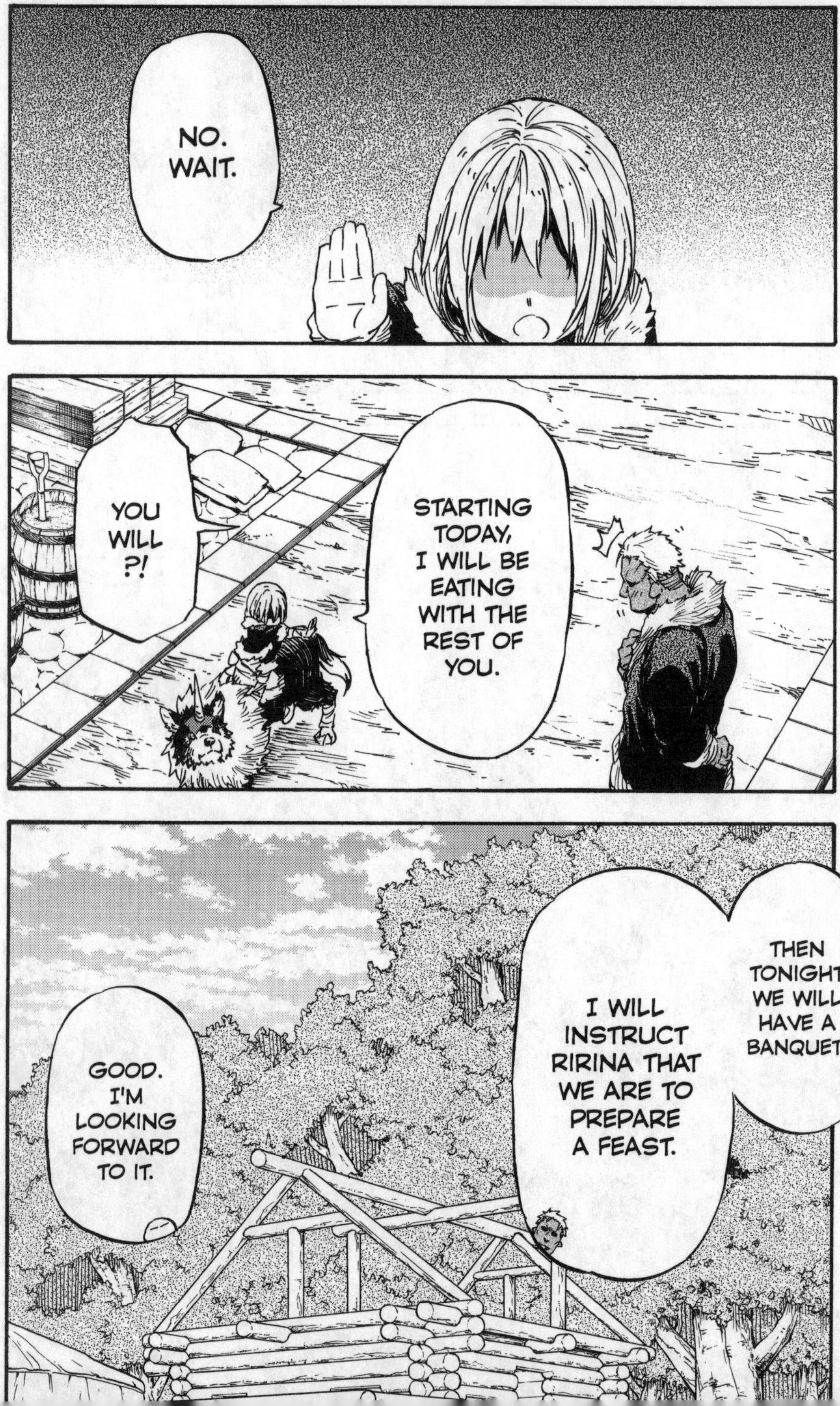
NO. WAIT.
STARTING TODAY, I WILL BE EATING WITH THE REST OF YOU.
YOU WILL ?!
THEN TONIGHT WE WILL HAVE A BANQUET.
I WILL INSTRUCT RIRINA THAT WE ARE TO PREPARE A FEAST.
GOOD. I'M LOOKING FORWARD TO IT.

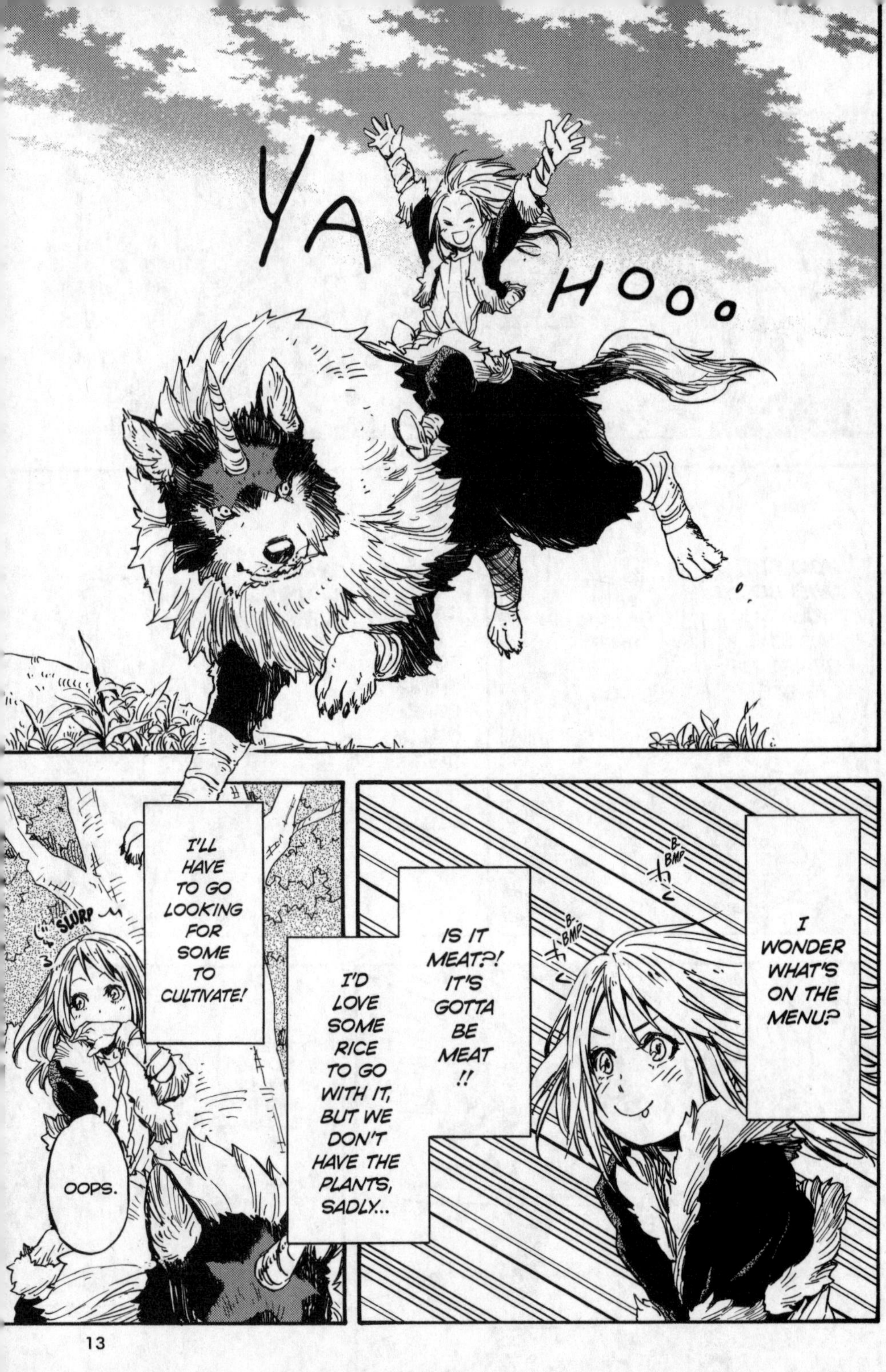
YAHOOO
I WONDER WHAT'S ON THE MENU?
B-BMP
B-BMP
IS IT MEAT?! IT'S GOTTA BE MEAT!!
I'D LOVE SOME RICE TO GO WITH IT, BUT WE DON'T HAVE THE PLANTS, SADLY...
I'LL HAVE TO GO LOOKING FOR SOME TO CULTIVATE!
SLURP
OOPS.

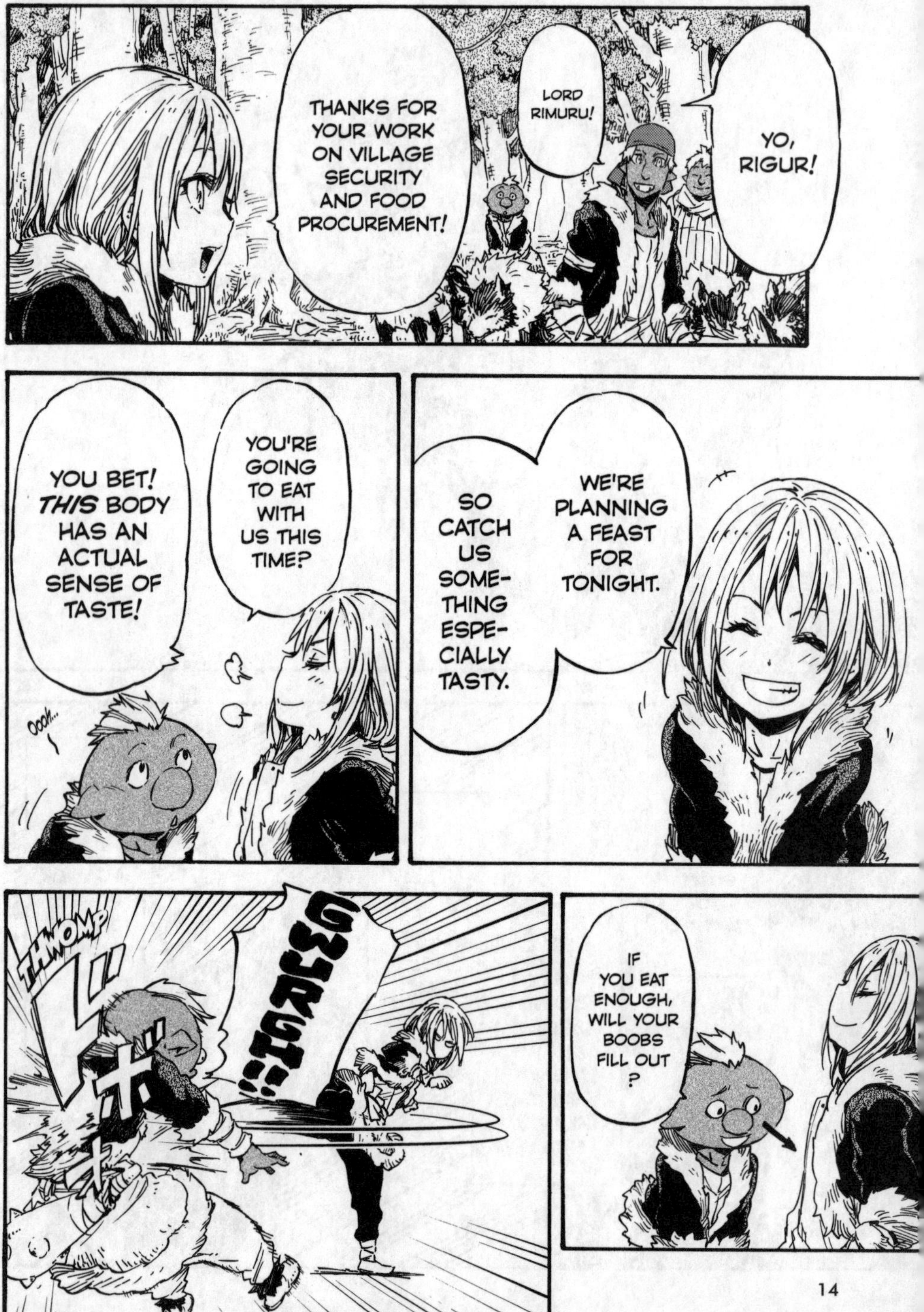
YO, RIGUR!
LORD RIMURU!
THANKS FOR YOUR WORK ON VILLAGE SECURITY AND FOOD PROCUREMENT!
WE'RE PLANNING A FEAST FOR TONIGHT.
SO CATCH US SOMETHING ESPECIALLY TASTY.
YOU'RE GOING TO EAT WITH US THIS TIME?
YOU BET! *THIS* BODY HAS AN ACTUAL SENSE OF TASTE!
Oooh...
IF YOU EAT ENOUGH, WILL YOUR BOOBS FILL OUT ?
GWURGH!!
THWOMP

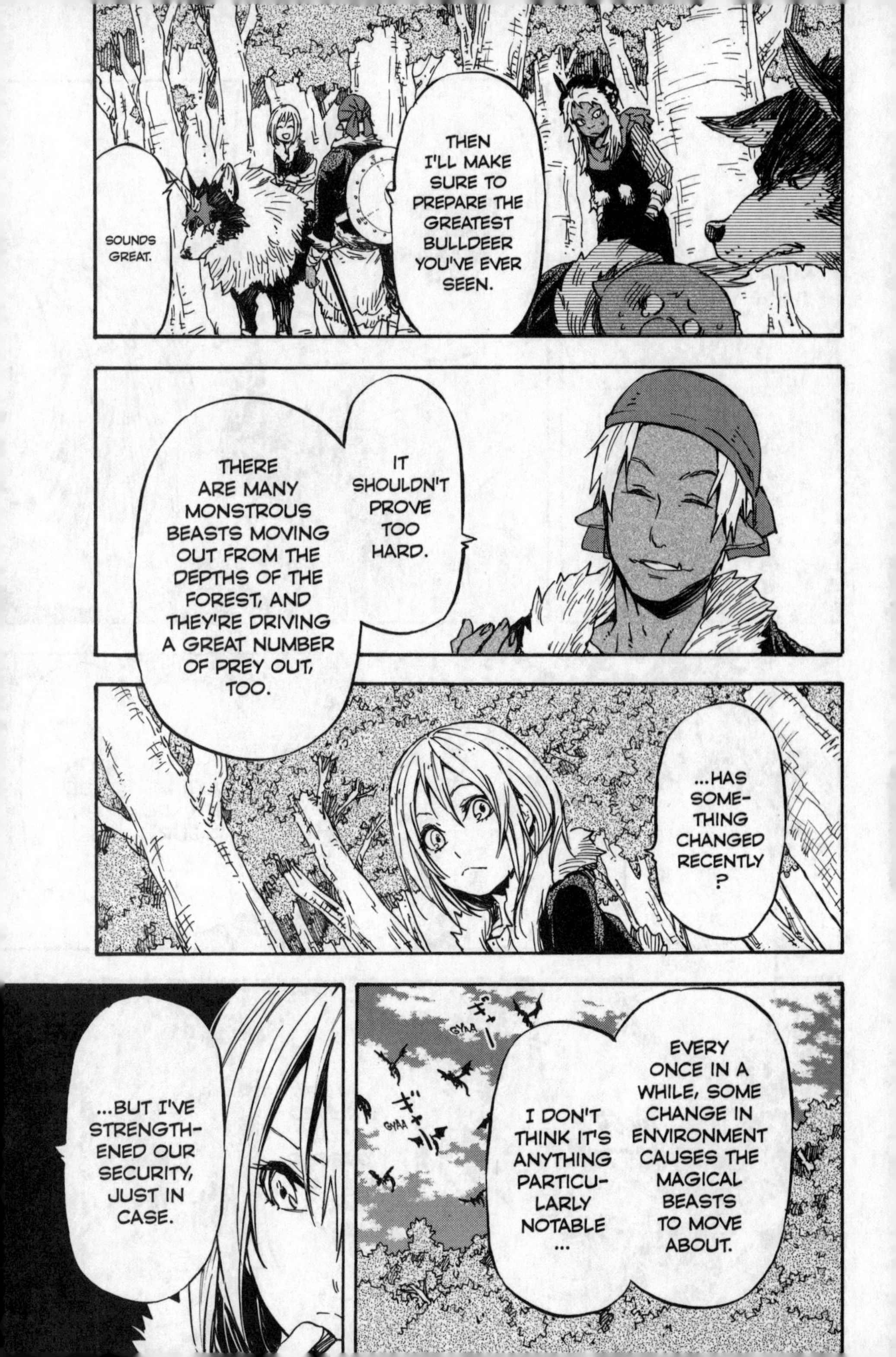
THEN I'LL MAKE SURE TO PREPARE THE GREATEST BULLDEER YOU'VE EVER SEEN.
SOUNDS GREAT.
IT SHOULDN'T PROVE TOO HARD.
THERE ARE MANY MONSTROUS BEASTS MOVING OUT FROM THE DEPTHS OF THE FOREST, AND THEY'RE DRIVING A GREAT NUMBER OF PREY OUT, TOO.
...HAS SOME-THING CHANGED RECENTLY?
GYAA
GYAA
EVERY ONCE IN A WHILE, SOME CHANGE IN ENVIRONMENT CAUSES THE MAGICAL BEASTS TO MOVE ABOUT.
I DON'T THINK IT'S ANYTHING PARTICU-LARLY NOTABLE...
...BUT I'VE STRENGTH-ENED OUR SECURITY, JUST IN CASE.

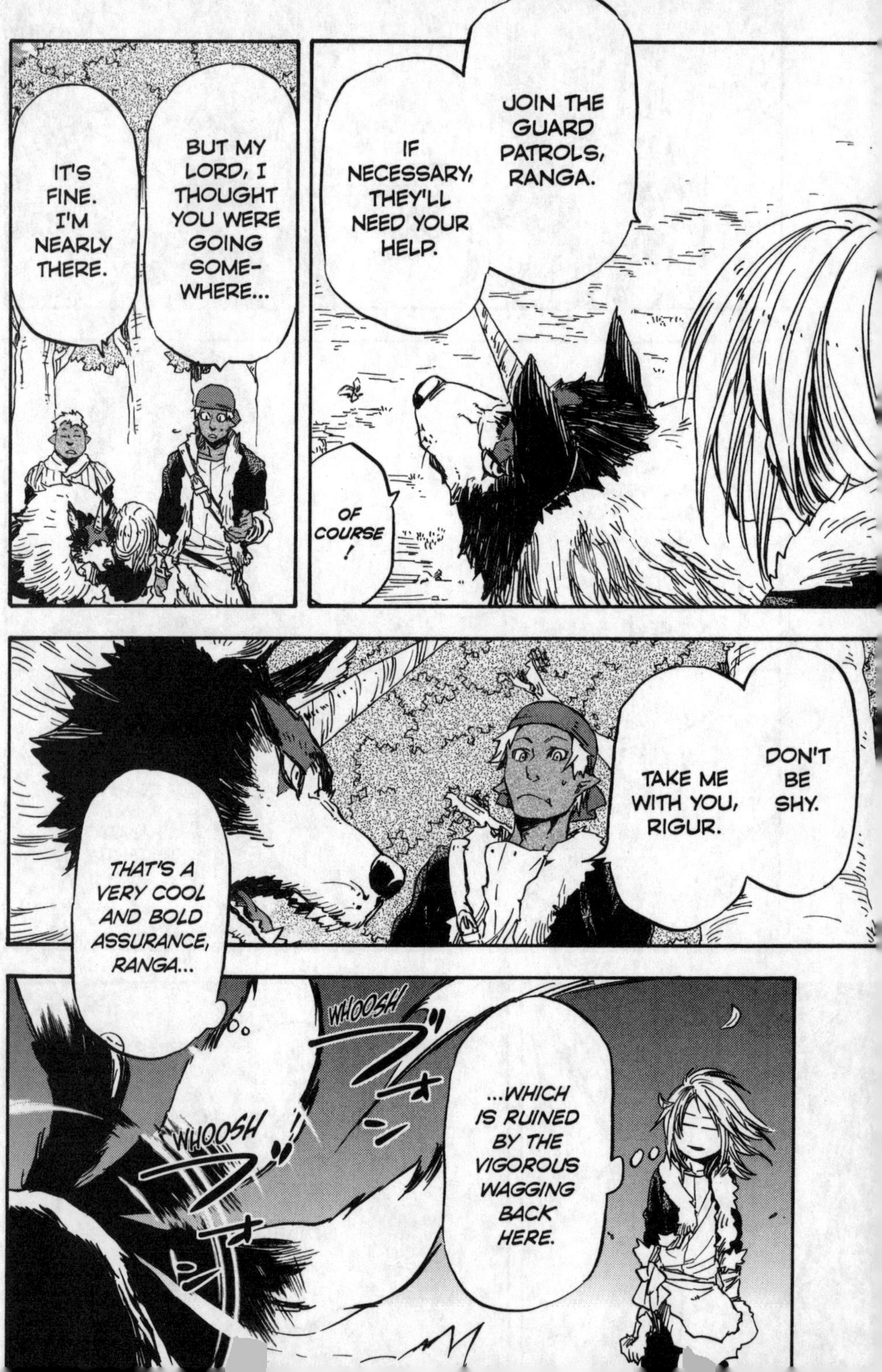
JOIN THE GUARD PATROLS, RANGA.
IF NECESSARY, THEY'LL NEED YOUR HELP.
OF COURSE!
BUT MY LORD, I THOUGHT YOU WERE GOING SOME-WHERE...
IT'S FINE. I'M NEARLY THERE.
DON'T BE SHY.
TAKE ME WITH YOU, RIGUR.
THAT'S A VERY COOL AND BOLD ASSURANCE, RANGA...
...WHICH IS RUINED BY THE VIGOROUS WAGGING BACK HERE.
WHOOSH
WHOOSH

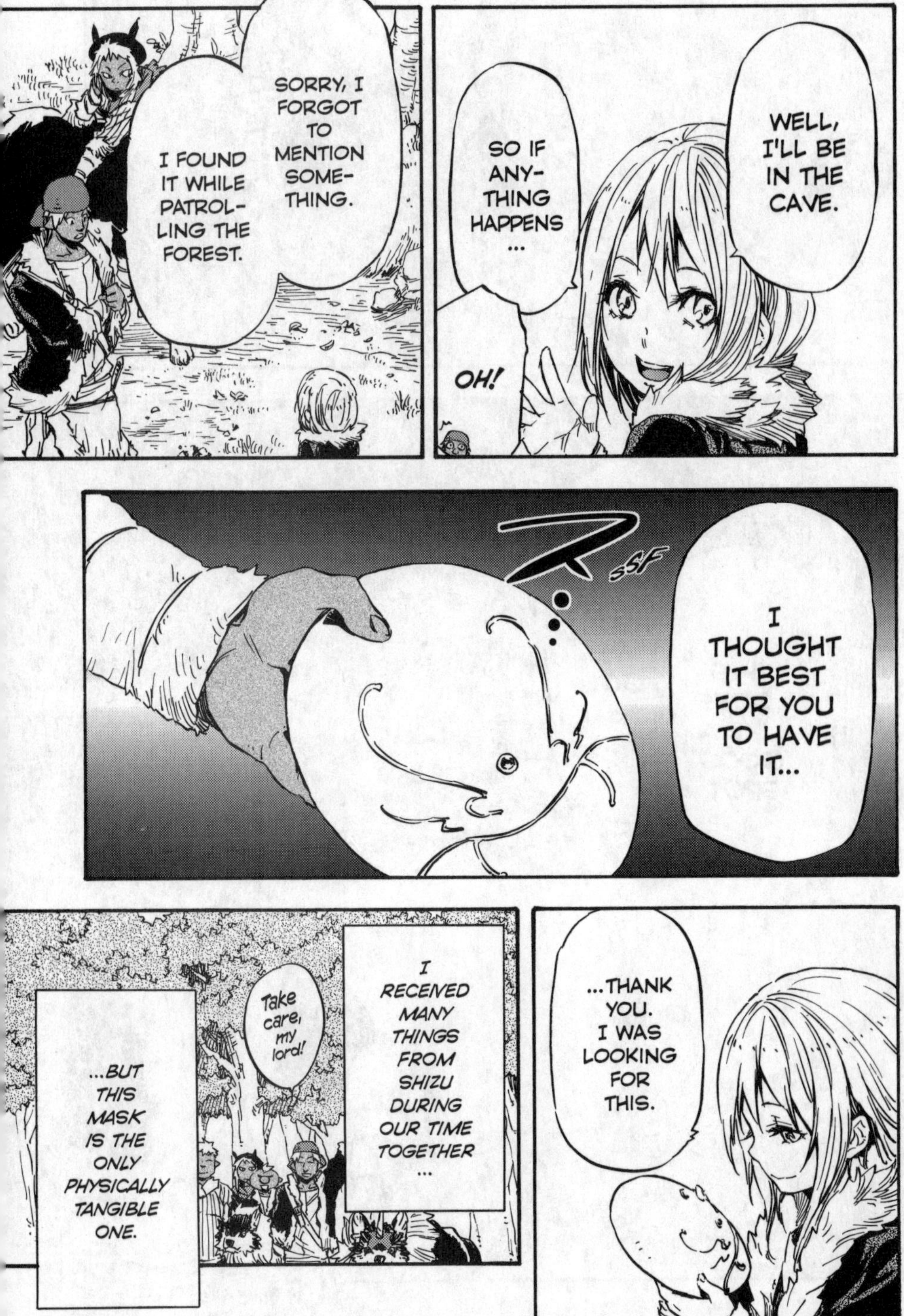
WELL, I'LL BE IN THE CAVE.
SO IF ANYTHING HAPPENS ...
OH!
SORRY, I FORGOT TO MENTION SOMETHING.
I FOUND IT WHILE PATROLLING THE FOREST.
SSF
I THOUGHT IT BEST FOR YOU TO HAVE IT...
...THANK YOU. I WAS LOOKING FOR THIS.
I RECEIVED MANY THINGS FROM SHIZU DURING OUR TIME TOGETHER ...
Take care, my lord!
...BUT THIS MASK IS THE ONLY PHYSICALLY TANGIBLE ONE.

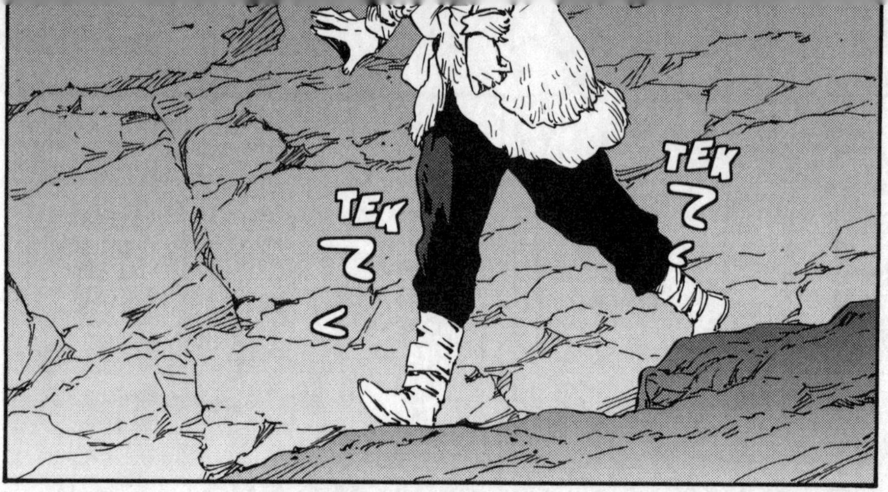
TEK
TEK
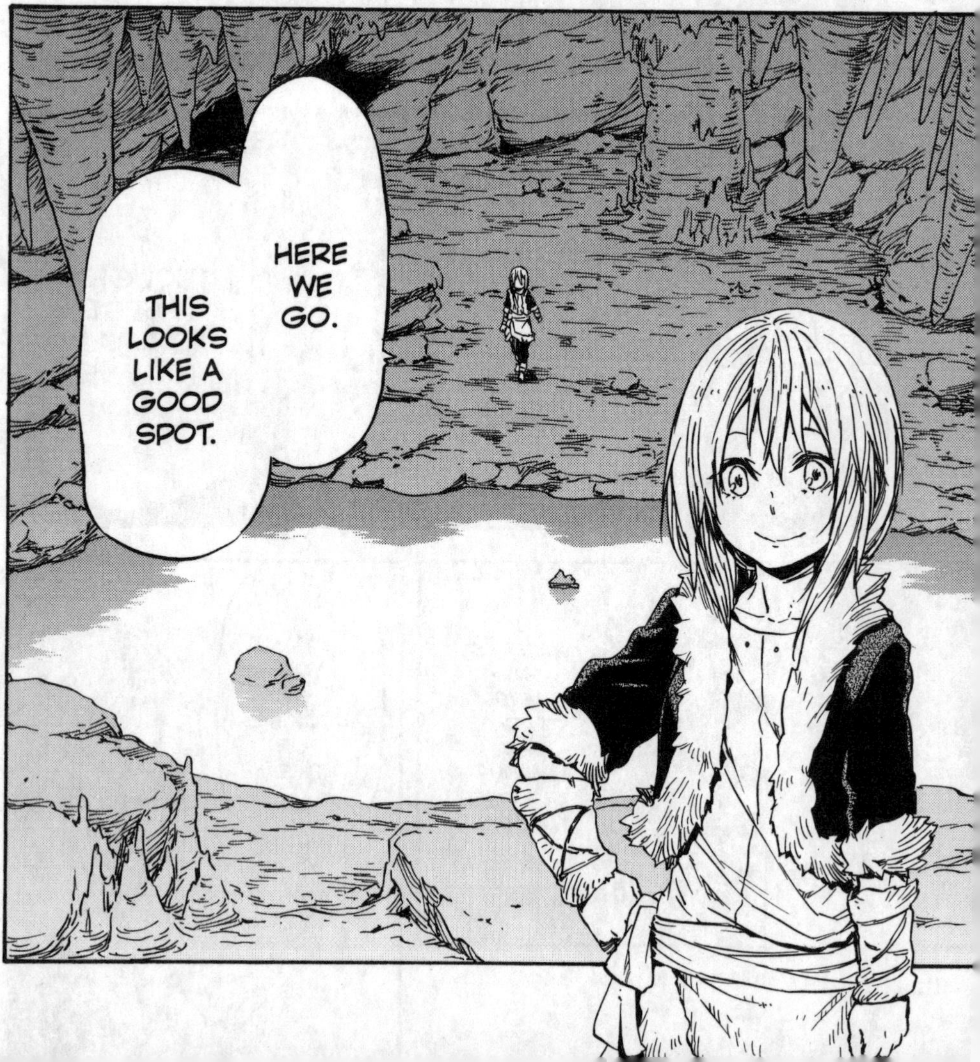
HERE WE GO.
THIS LOOKS LIKE A GOOD SPOT.

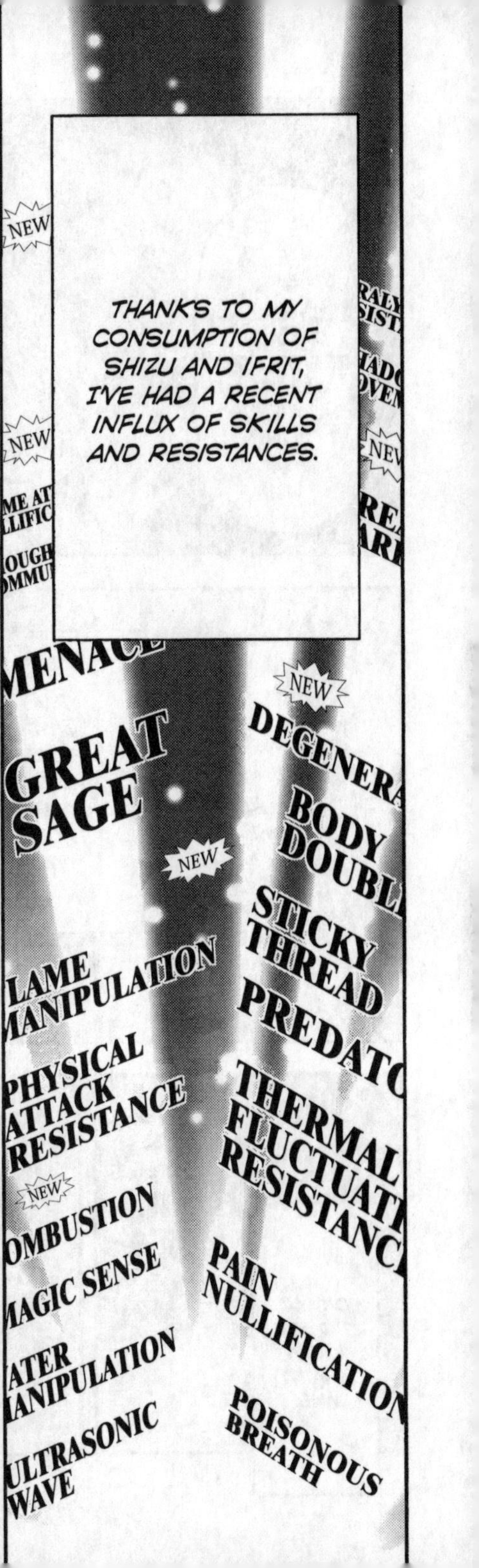
THANKS TO MY CONSUMPTION OF SHIZU AND IFRIT, I'VE HAD A RECENT INFLUX OF SKILLS AND RESISTANCES.
NEW
NEW
NEW
NEW
NEW
NEW
GREAT SAGE
STICKY THREAD
PHYSICAL ATTACK RESISTANCE
MAGIC SENSE
PAIN NULLIFICATION
ULTRASONIC WAVE
POISONOUS BREATH

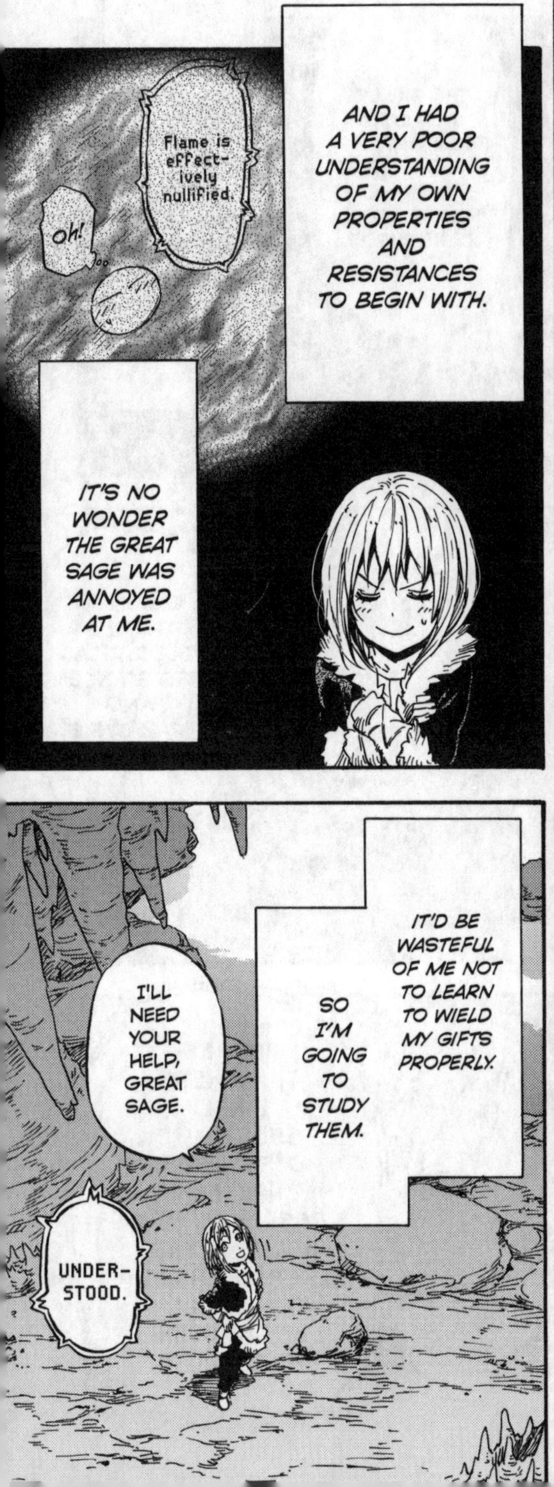
AND I HAD A VERY POOR UNDERSTANDING OF MY OWN PROPERTIES AND RESISTANCES TO BEGIN WITH.
Flame is effect-ively nullified.
Oh!
IT'S NO WONDER THE GREAT SAGE WAS ANNOYED AT ME.
IT'D BE WASTEFUL OF ME NOT TO LEARN TO WIELD MY GIFTS PROPERLY.
SO I'M GOING TO STUDY THEM.
I'LL NEED YOUR HELP, GREAT SAGE.
UNDER-STOOD.

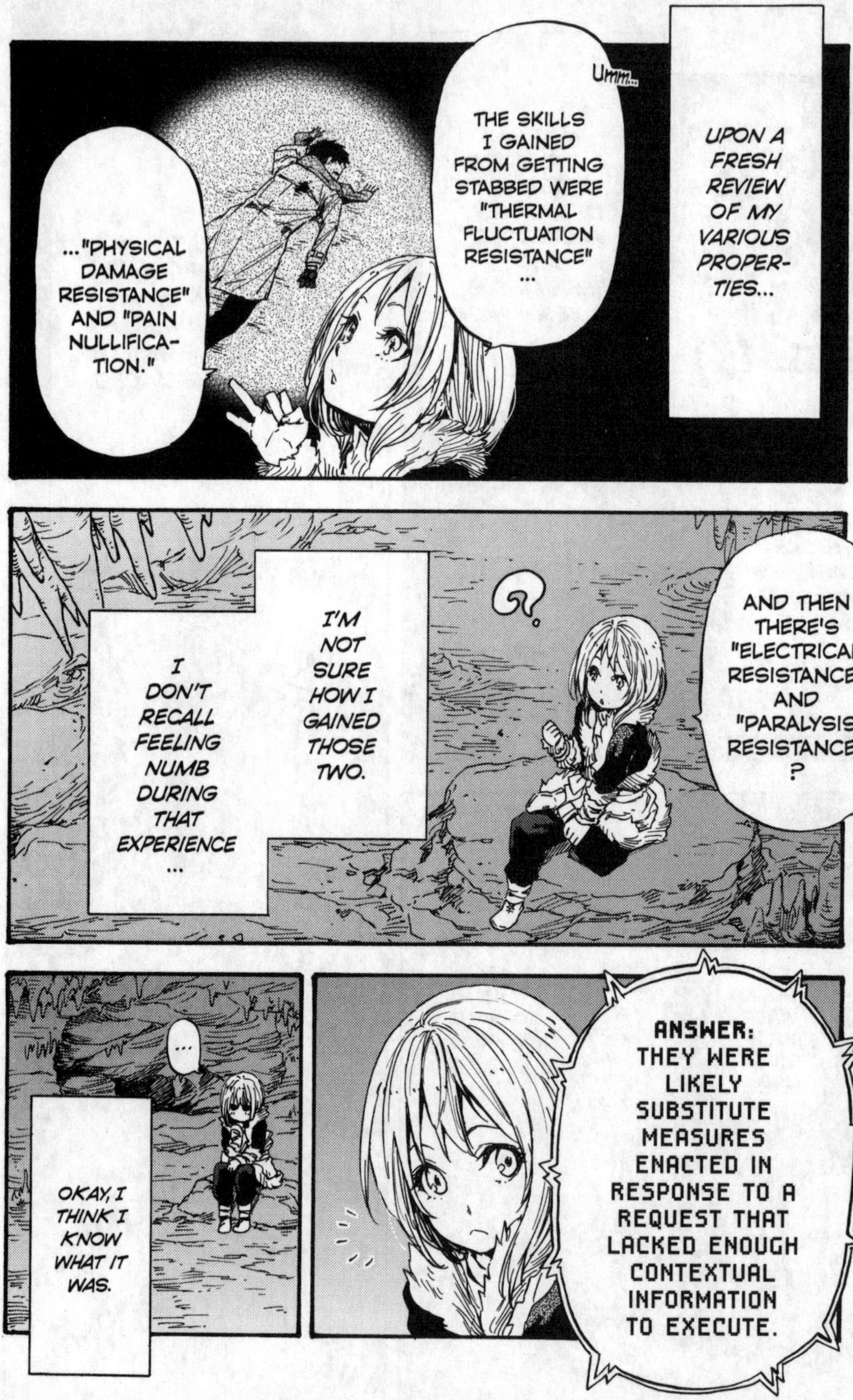
UPON A FRESH REVIEW OF MY VARIOUS PROPERTIES...
Umm...
THE SKILLS I GAINED FROM GETTING STABBED WERE "THERMAL FLUCTUATION RESISTANCE" ...
..."PHYSICAL DAMAGE RESISTANCE" AND "PAIN NULLIFICATION."
AND THEN THERE'S "ELECTRICAL RESISTANCE" AND "PARALYSIS RESISTANCE" ?
I'M NOT SURE HOW I GAINED THOSE TWO.
I DON'T RECALL FEELING NUMB DURING THAT EXPERIENCE ...
ANSWER: THEY WERE LIKELY SUBSTITUTE MEASURES ENACTED IN RESPONSE TO A REQUEST THAT LACKED ENOUGH CONTEXTUAL INFORMATION TO EXECUTE.
...
OKAY, I THINK I KNOW WHAT IT WAS.

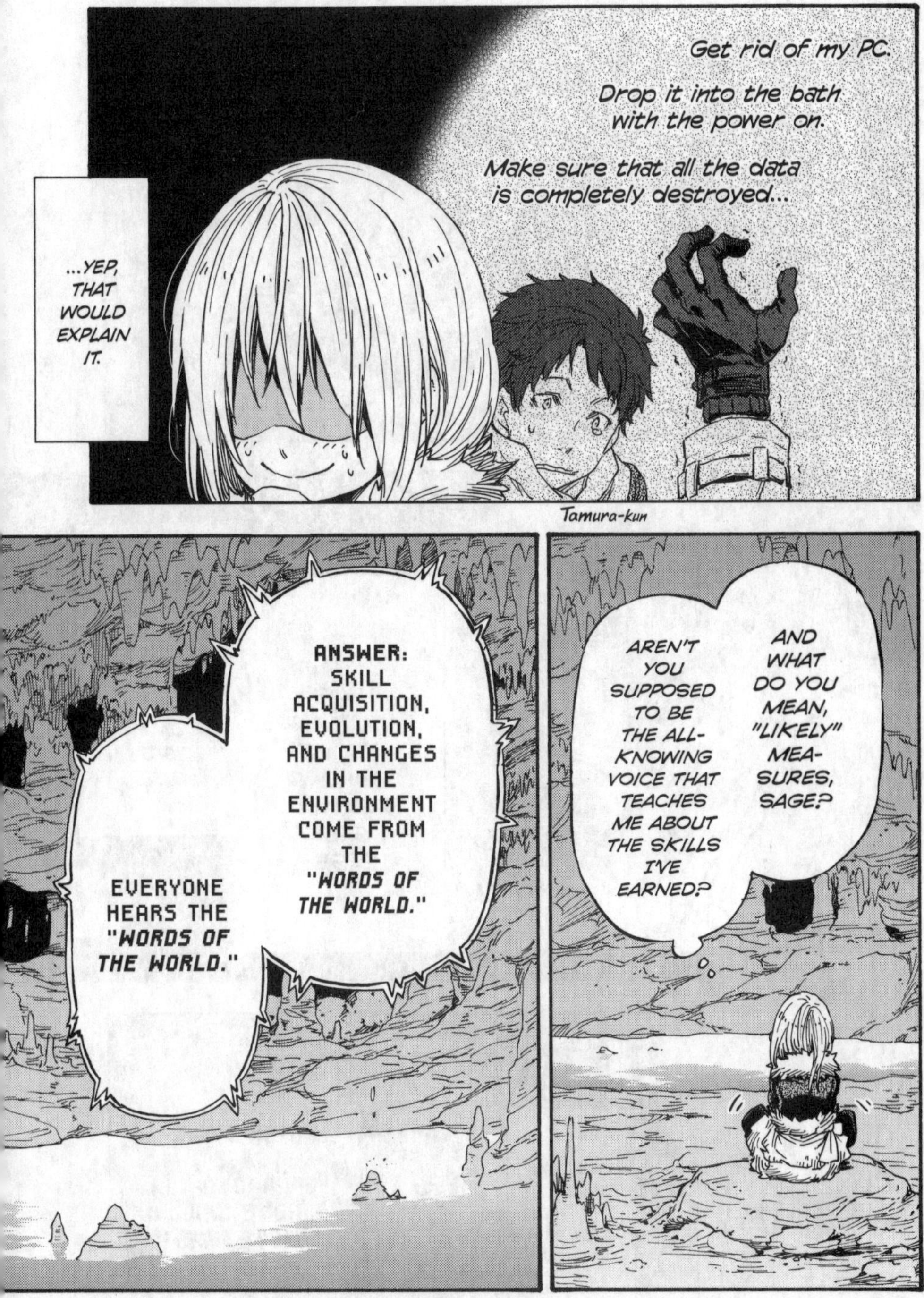

Get rid of my PC.
Drop it into the bath with the power on.
Make sure that all the data is completely destroyed...
...YEP, THAT WOULD EXPLAIN IT.
Tamura-kun
AREN'T YOU SUPPOSED TO BE THE ALL-KNOWING VOICE THAT TEACHES ME ABOUT THE SKILLS I'VE EARNED? AND WHAT DO YOU MEAN, "LIKELY" MEASURES, SAGE?
ANSWER: SKILL ACQUISITION, EVOLUTION, AND CHANGES IN THE ENVIRONMENT COME FROM THE "WORDS OF THE WORLD."
EVERYONE HEARS THE "WORDS OF THE WORLD."

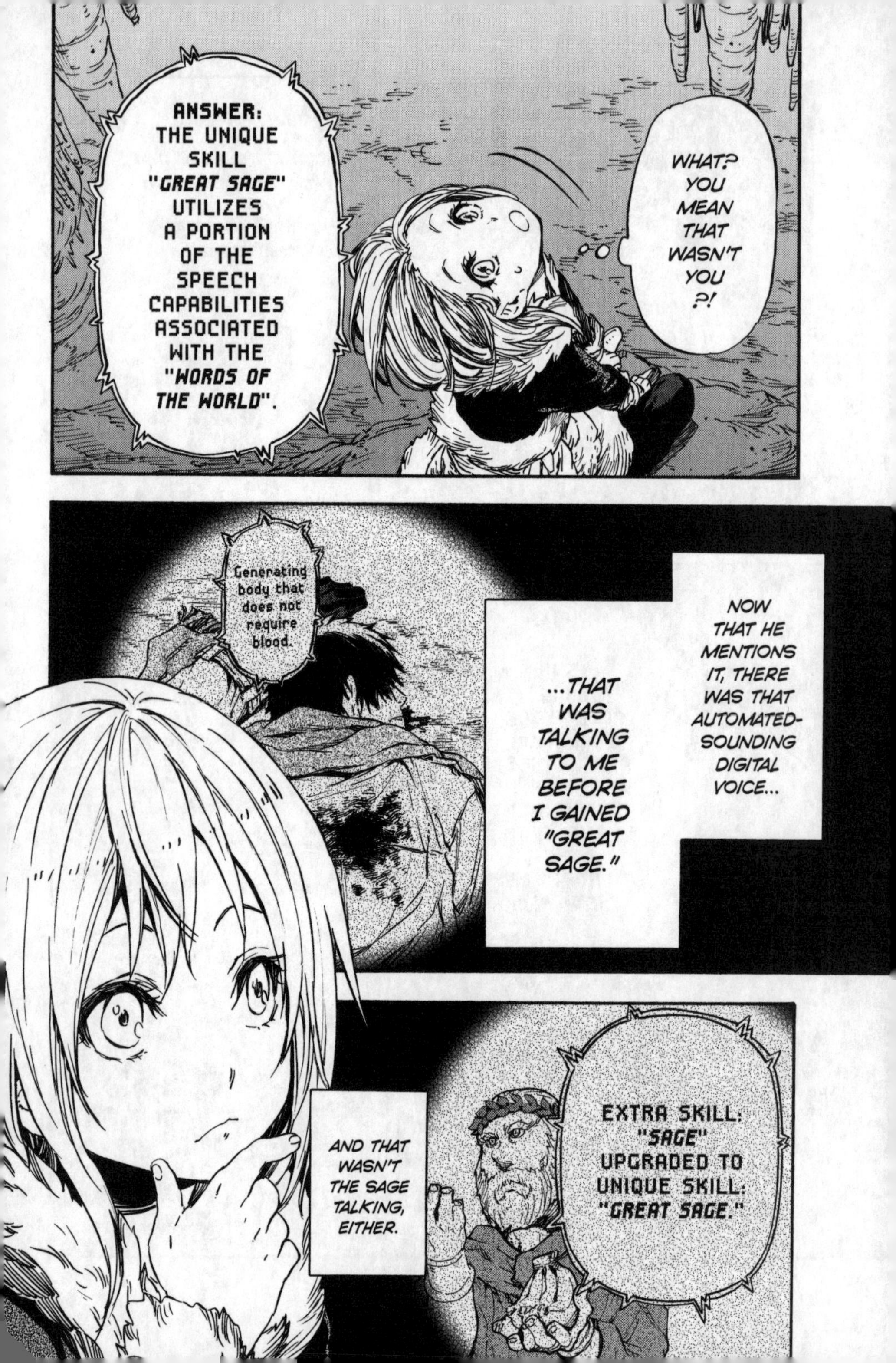
WHAT? YOU MEAN THAT WASN'T YOU ?!
ANSWER: THE UNIQUE SKILL "GREAT SAGE" UTILIZES A PORTION OF THE SPEECH CAPABILITIES ASSOCIATED WITH THE "WORDS OF THE WORLD".
NOW THAT HE MENTIONS IT, THERE WAS THAT AUTOMATED-SOUNDING DIGITAL VOICE...
...THAT WAS TALKING TO ME BEFORE I GAINED "GREAT SAGE."
Generating body that does not require blood.
EXTRA SKILL: "SAGE" UPGRADED TO UNIQUE SKILL: "GREAT SAGE."
AND THAT WASN'T THE SAGE TALKING, EITHER.

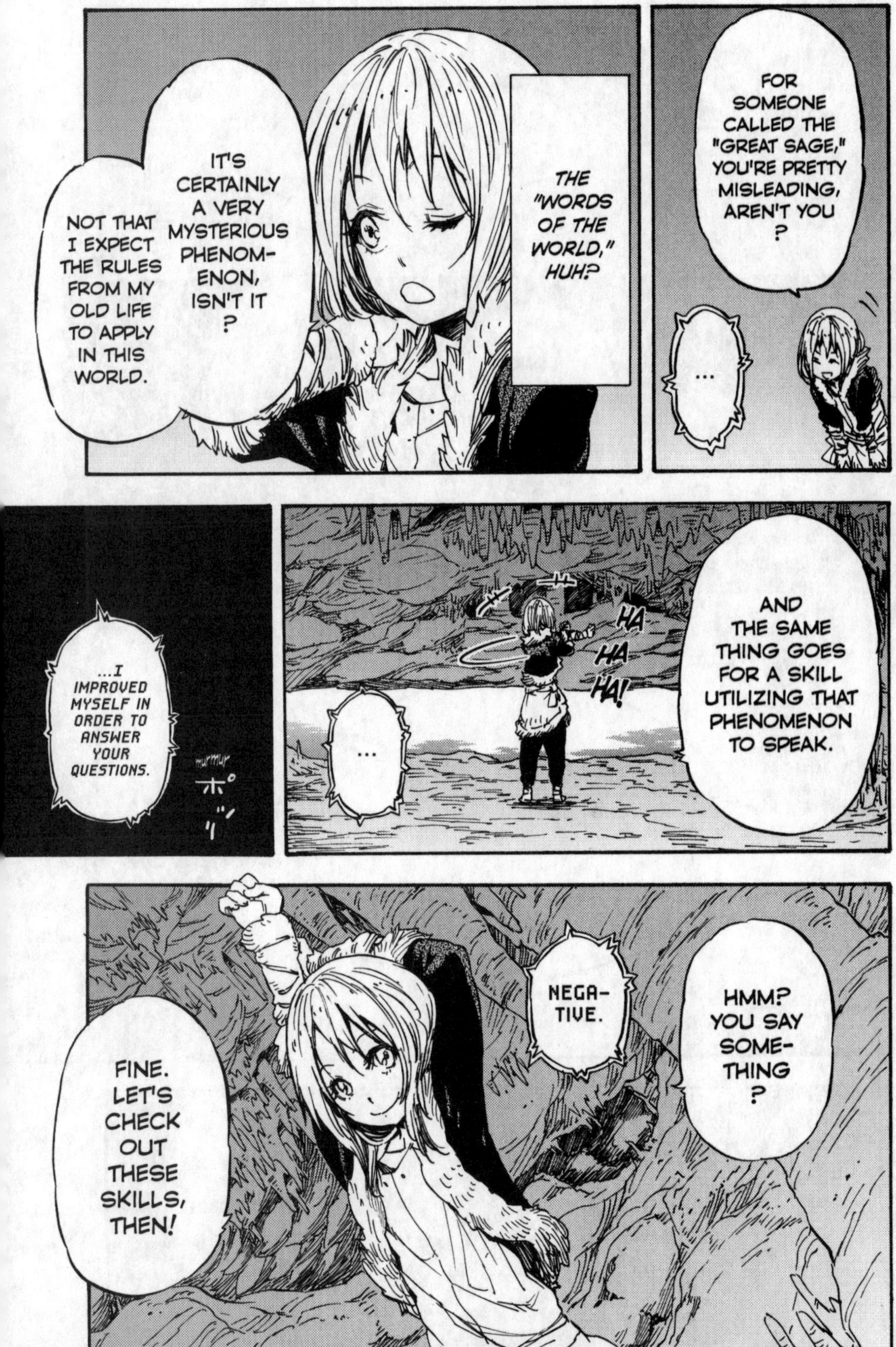
FOR SOMEONE CALLED THE "GREAT SAGE," YOU'RE PRETTY MISLEADING, AREN'T YOU?
...
THE "WORDS OF THE WORLD," HUH?
IT'S CERTAINLY A VERY MYSTERIOUS PHENOMENON, ISN'T IT?
NOT THAT I EXPECT THE RULES FROM MY OLD LIFE TO APPLY IN THIS WORLD.
AND THE SAME THING GOES FOR A SKILL UTILIZING THAT PHENOMENON TO SPEAK.
HA HA HA!
...
murmur
ポツリ
...I IMPROVED MYSELF IN ORDER TO ANSWER YOUR QUESTIONS.
HMM? YOU SAY SOMETHING?
NEGATIVE.
FINE. LET'S CHECK OUT THESE SKILLS, THEN!

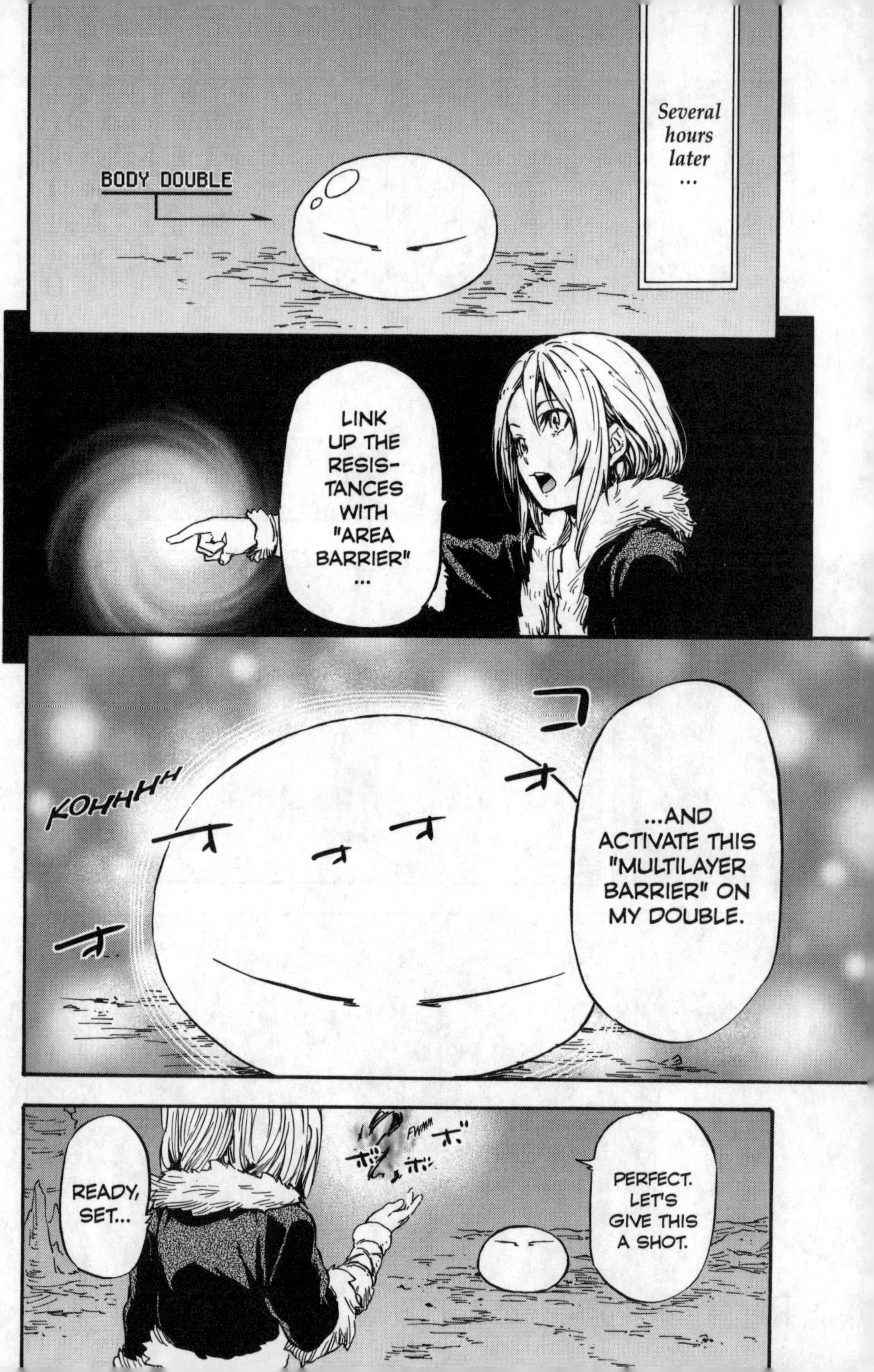
Several hours later ...
BODY DOUBLE
LINK UP THE RESISTANCES WITH "AREA BARRIER" ...
コオオオオオ
...AND ACTIVATE THIS "MULTILAYER BARRIER" ON MY DOUBLE.
KOHHHH
PERFECT. LET'S GIVE THIS A SHOT.
FWMM
ボボボ
READY, SET...

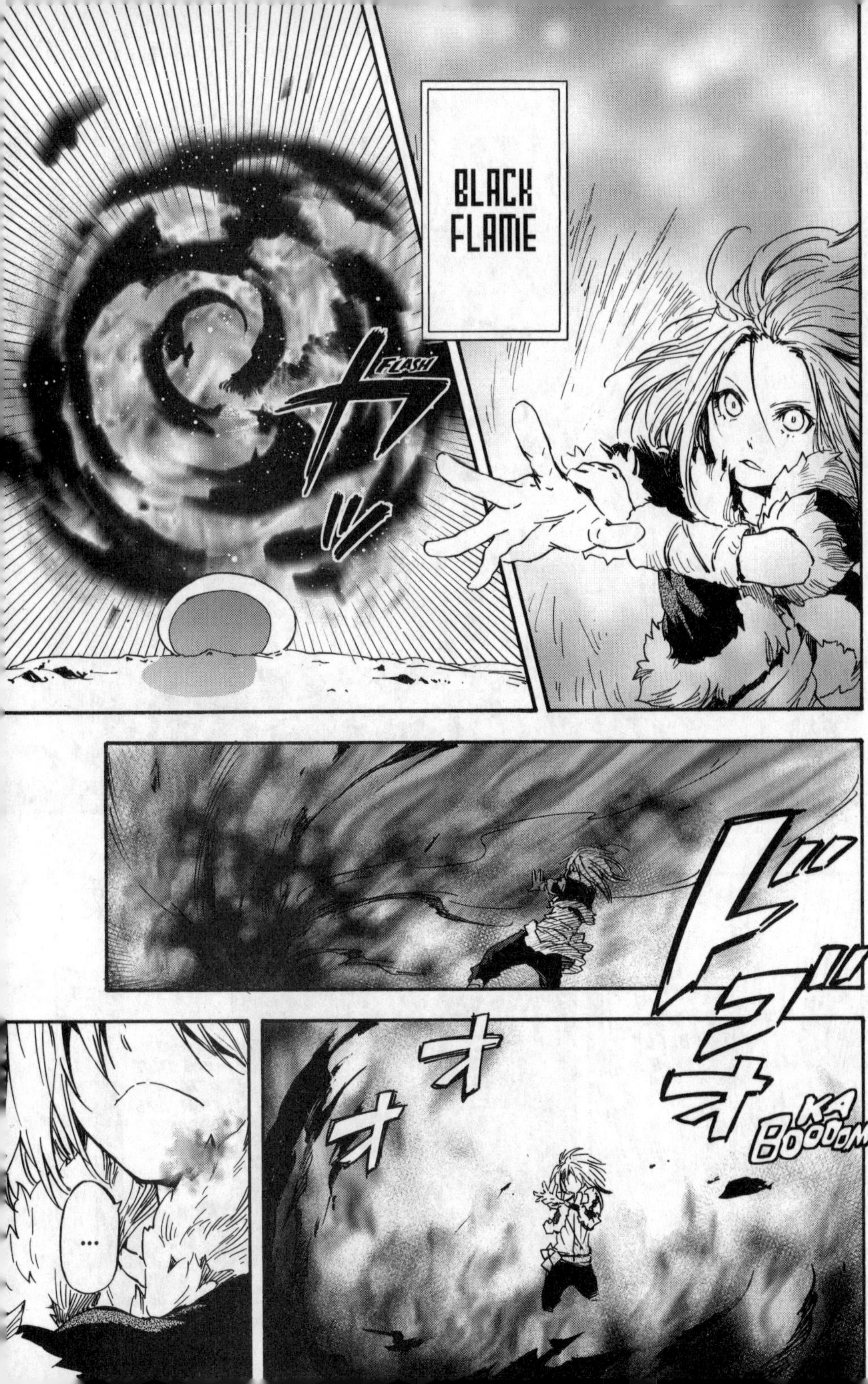
BLACK FLAME
FLASH
KA BOOOOM
...

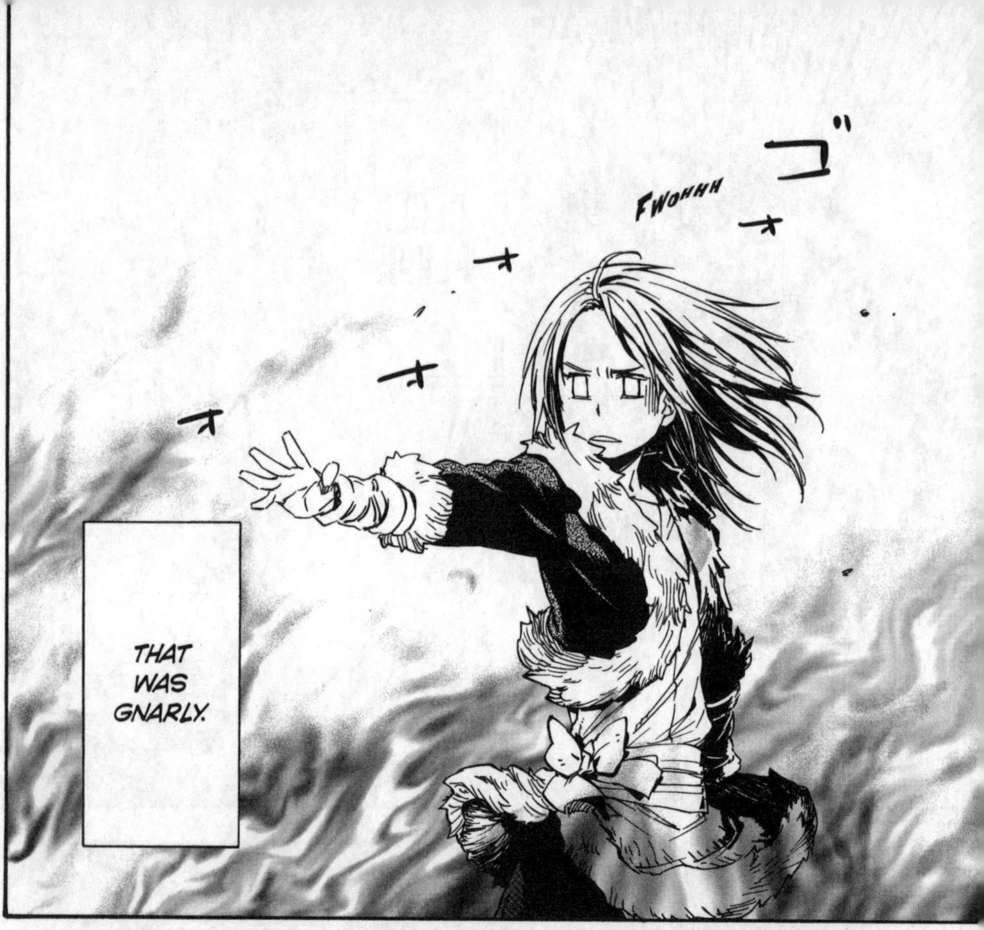
ゴオオオオ
FWOHHH
THAT WAS GNARLY.

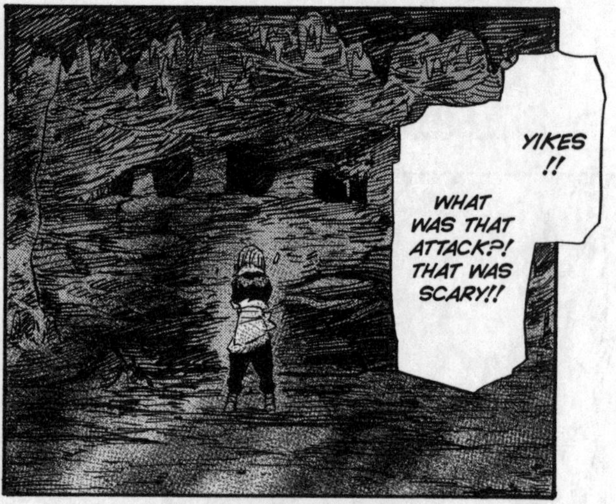
YIKES!!
WHAT WAS THAT ATTACK?! THAT WAS SCARY!!

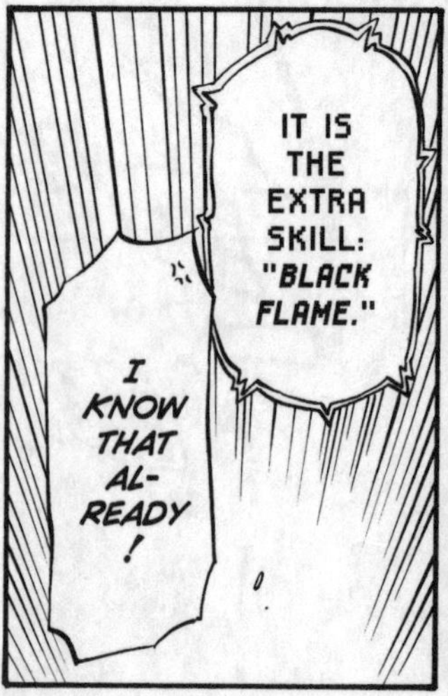
IT IS THE EXTRA SKILL: "BLACK FLAME."
I KNOW THAT AL-READY!

*He extinguished the flame with Predator.

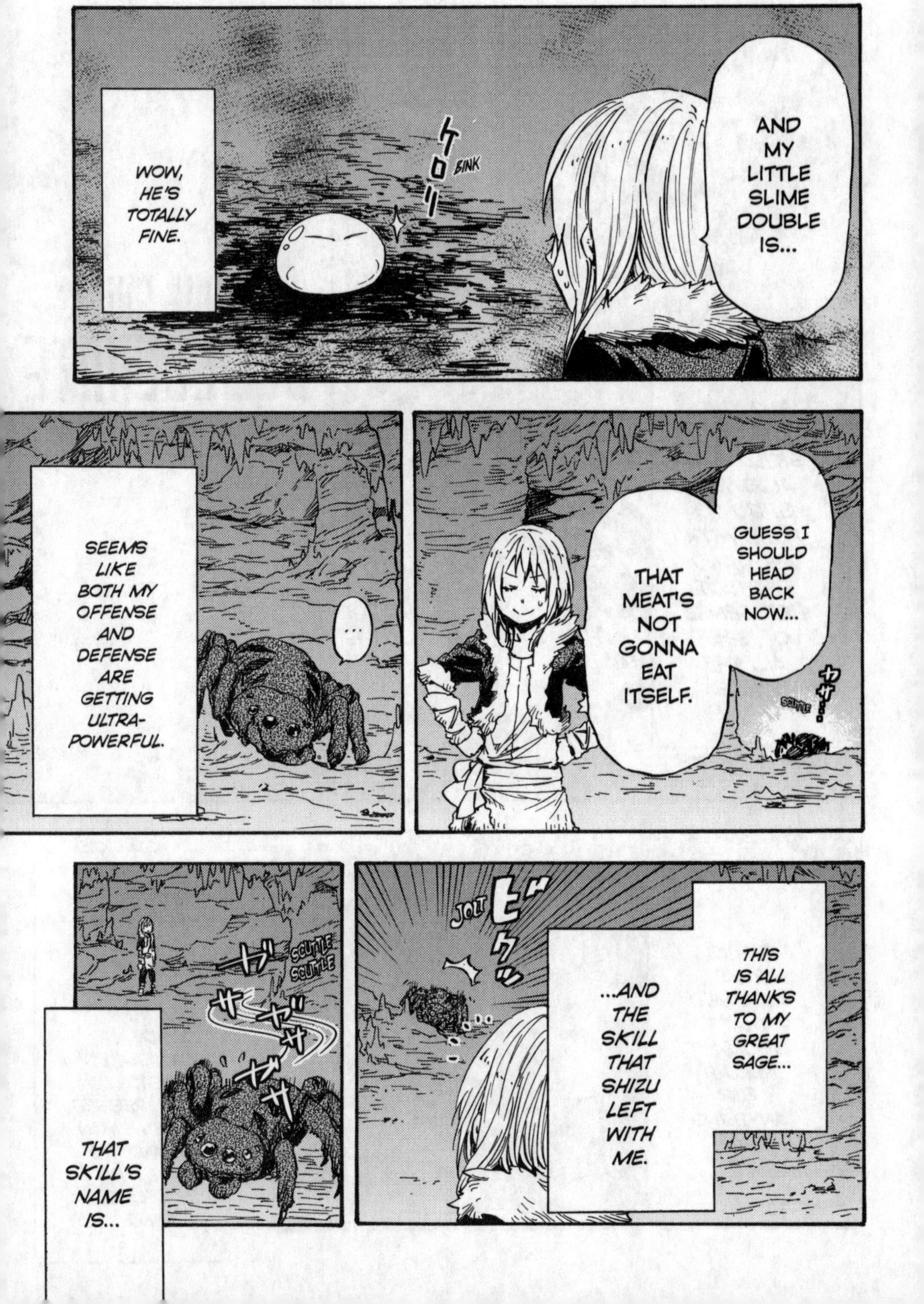
AND MY LITTLE SLIME DOUBLE IS...
ケロリ
BINK
WOW, HE'S TOTALLY FINE.
GUESS I SHOULD HEAD BACK NOW...
THAT MEAT'S NOT GONNA EAT ITSELF.
SCUTTLE
...
SEEMS LIKE BOTH MY OFFENSE AND DEFENSE ARE GETTING ULTRA-POWERFUL.
JOLT
ビクッ
THIS IS ALL THANKS TO MY GREAT SAGE...
...AND THE SKILL THAT SHIZU LEFT WITH ME.
SCUTTLE SCUTTLE
THAT SKILL'S NAME IS...

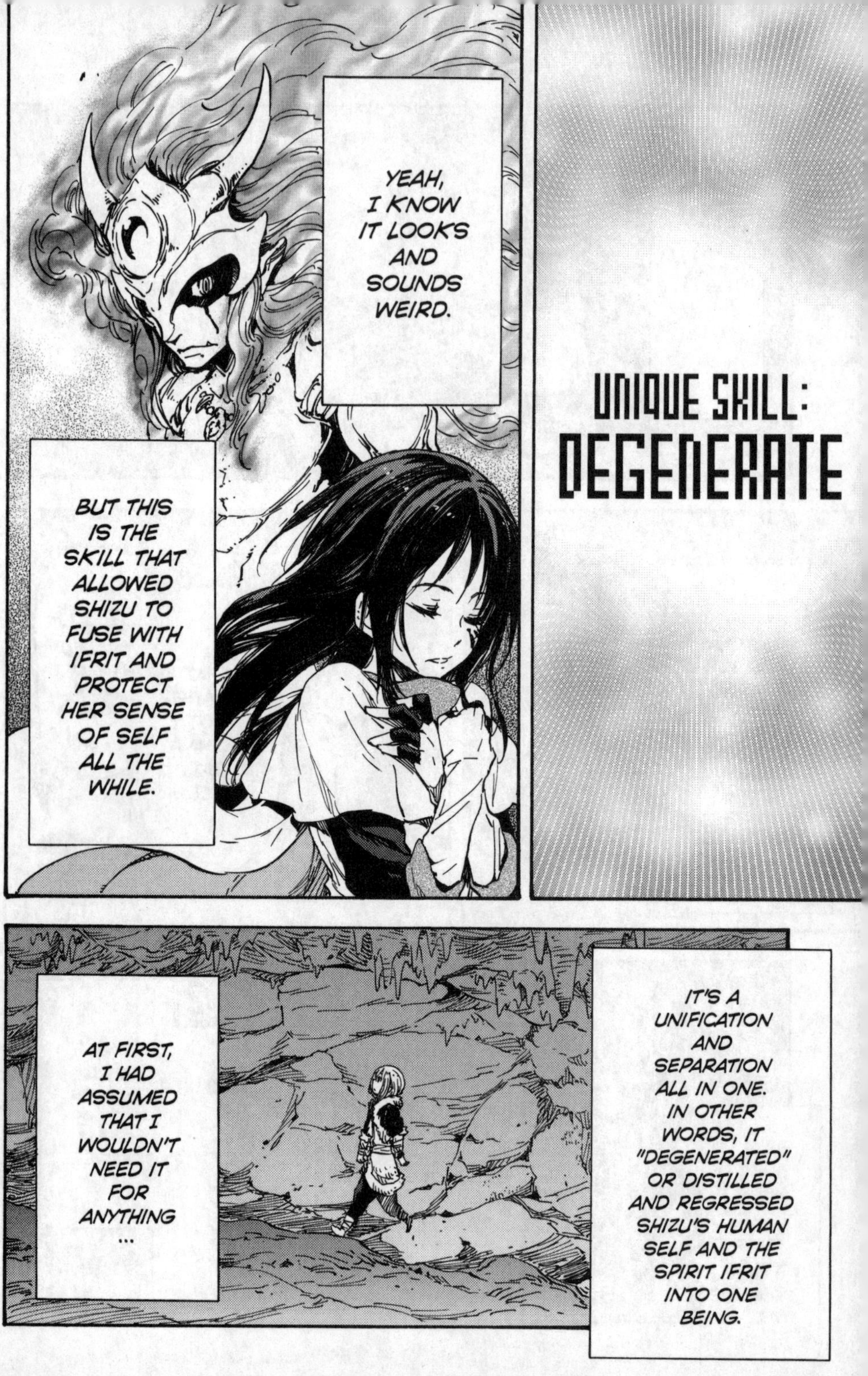
UNIQUE SKILL:
DEGENERATE
YEAH, I KNOW IT LOOKS AND SOUNDS WEIRD.
BUT THIS IS THE SKILL THAT ALLOWED SHIZU TO FUSE WITH IFRIT AND PROTECT HER SENSE OF SELF ALL THE WHILE.
IT'S A UNIFICATION AND SEPARATION ALL IN ONE. IN OTHER WORDS, IT "DEGENERATED" OR DISTILLED AND REGRESSED SHIZU'S HUMAN SELF AND THE SPIRIT IFRIT INTO ONE BEING.
AT FIRST, I HAD ASSUMED THAT I WOULDN'T NEED IT FOR ANYTHING...

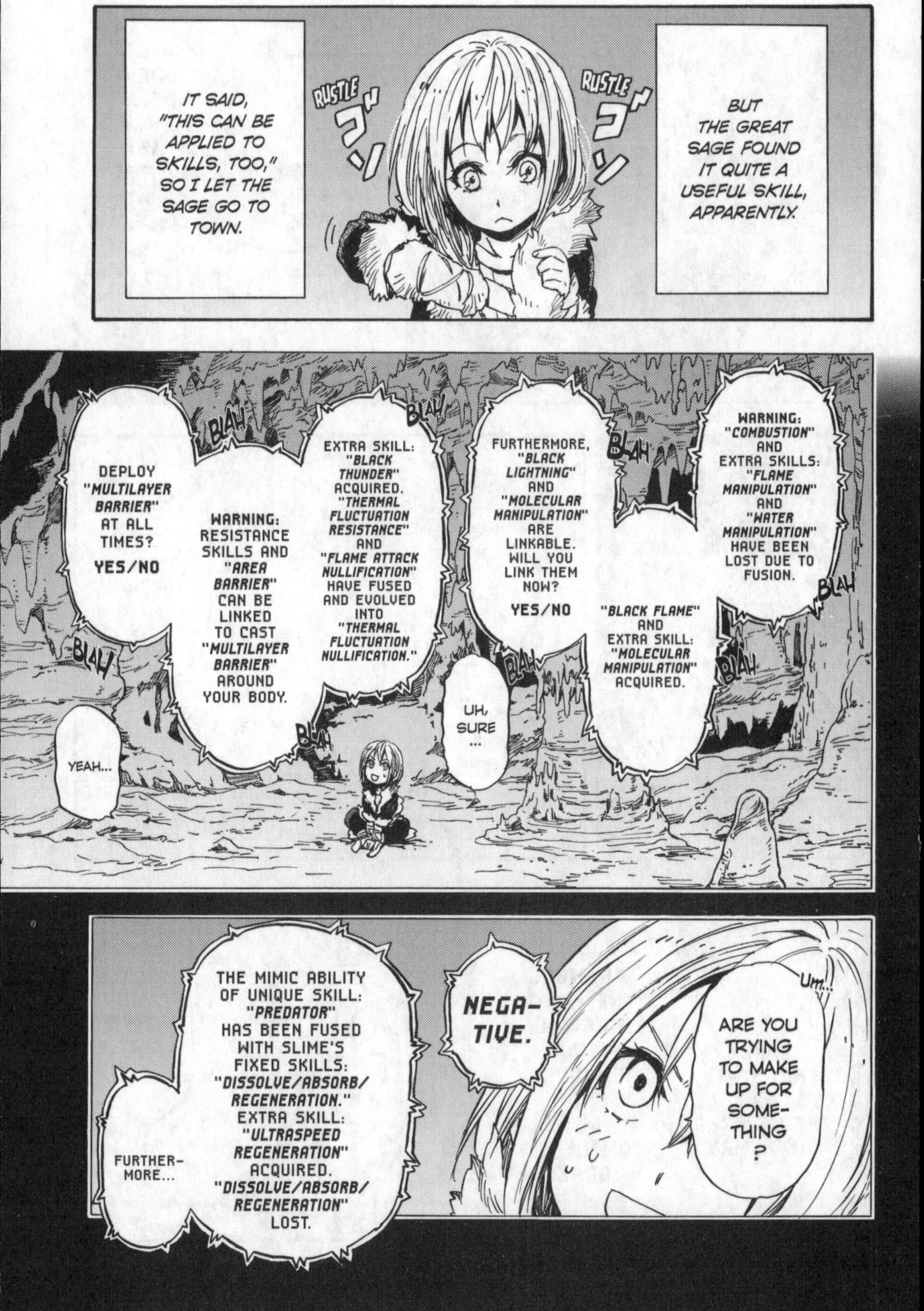
BUT THE GREAT SAGE FOUND IT QUITE A USEFUL SKILL, APPARENTLY.
RUSTLE
RUSTLE
IT SAID, "THIS CAN BE APPLIED TO SKILLS, TOO," SO I LET THE SAGE GO TO TOWN.
WARNING: "COMBUSTION" AND EXTRA SKILLS: "FLAME MANIPULATION" AND "WATER MANIPULATION" HAVE BEEN LOST DUE TO FUSION.
BLAH
BLAH
"BLACK FLAME" AND EXTRA SKILL: "MOLECULAR MANIPULATION" ACQUIRED.
BLAH
FURTHERMORE, "BLACK LIGHTNING" AND "MOLECULAR MANIPULATION" ARE LINKABLE. WILL YOU LINK THEM NOW?
YES/NO
BLAH
UH, SURE...
BLAH
EXTRA SKILL: "BLACK THUNDER" ACQUIRED. "THERMAL FLUCTUATION RESISTANCE" AND "FLAME ATTACK NULLIFICATION" HAVE FUSED AND EVOLVED INTO "THERMAL FLUCTUATION NULLIFICATION."
BLAH
WARNING: RESISTANCE SKILLS AND "AREA BARRIER" CAN BE LINKED TO CAST "MULTILAYER BARRIER" AROUND YOUR BODY.
BLAH
DEPLOY "MULTILAYER BARRIER" AT ALL TIMES?
YES/NO
BLAH
YEAH...
UM...
ARE YOU TRYING TO MAKE UP FOR SOME-THING?
NEGA-TIVE.
THE MIMIC ABILITY OF UNIQUE SKILL: "PREDATOR" HAS BEEN FUSED WITH SLIME'S FIXED SKILLS: "DISSOLVE/ABSORB/REGENERATION." EXTRA SKILL: "ULTRASPEED REGENERATION" ACQUIRED. "DISSOLVE/ABSORB/REGENERATION" LOST.
FURTHER-MORE...

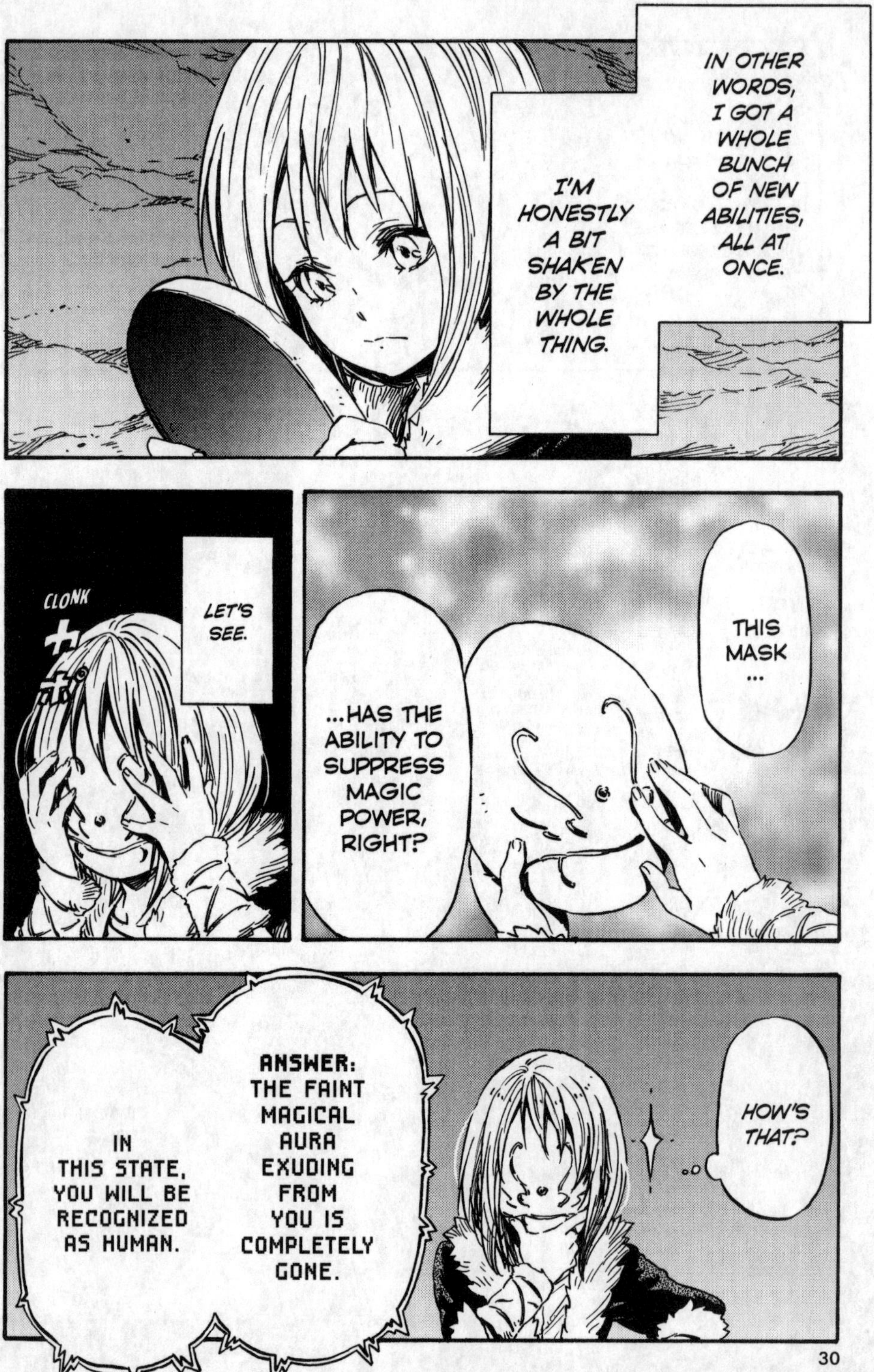
IN OTHER WORDS, I GOT A WHOLE BUNCH OF NEW ABILITIES, ALL AT ONCE.
I'M HONESTLY A BIT SHAKEN BY THE WHOLE THING.
THIS MASK...
...HAS THE ABILITY TO SUPPRESS MAGIC POWER, RIGHT?
LET'S SEE.
CLONK
HOW'S THAT?
ANSWER: THE FAINT MAGICAL AURA EXUDING FROM YOU IS COMPLETELY GONE.
IN THIS STATE, YOU WILL BE RECOGNIZED AS HUMAN.

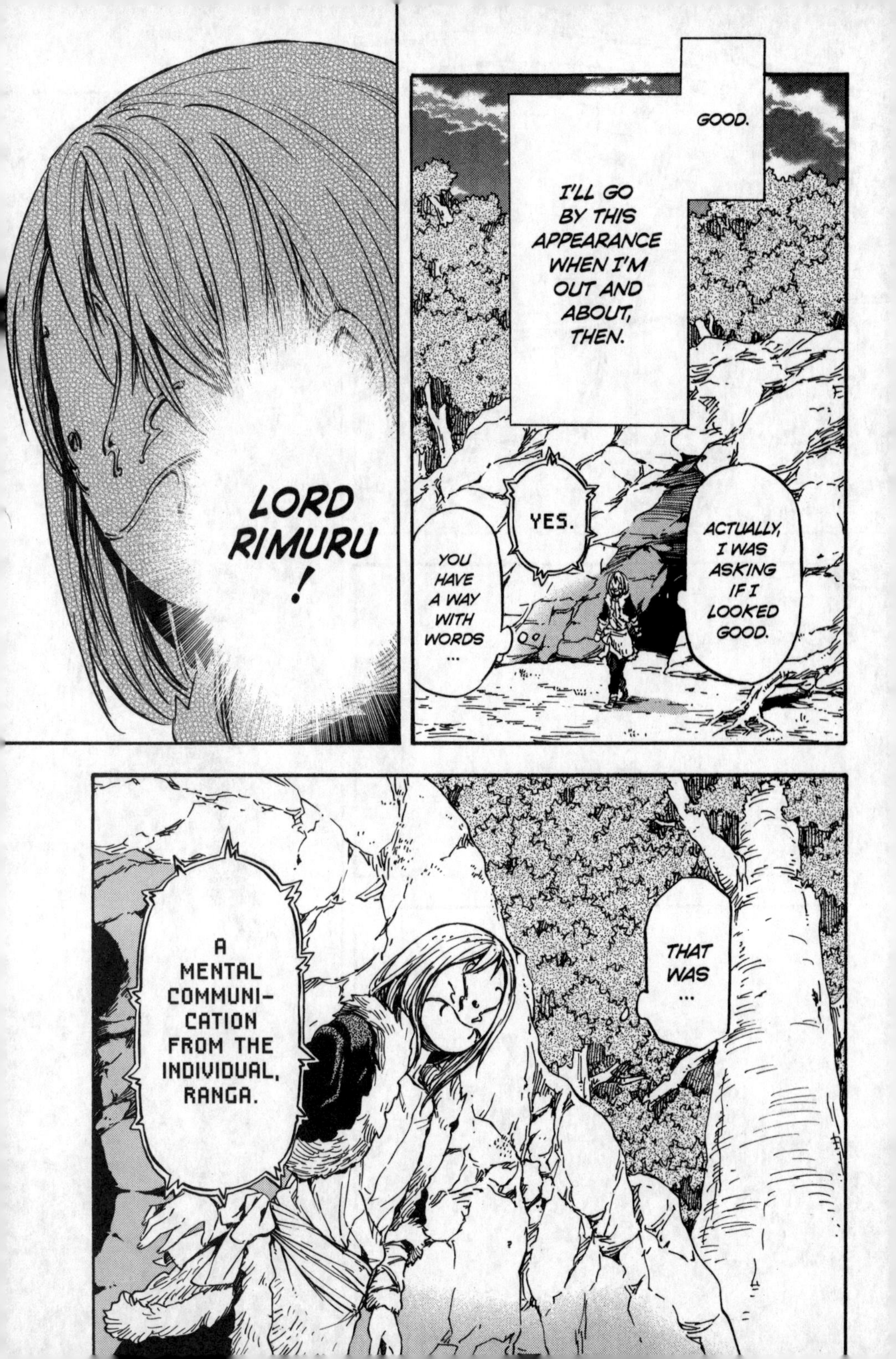
GOOD.
I'LL GO BY THIS APPEARANCE WHEN I'M OUT AND ABOUT, THEN.
ACTUALLY, I WAS ASKING IF I LOOKED GOOD.
YES.
YOU HAVE A WAY WITH WORDS ...
LORD RIMURU!
THAT WAS ...
A MENTAL COMMUNI-CATION FROM THE INDIVIDUAL, RANGA.

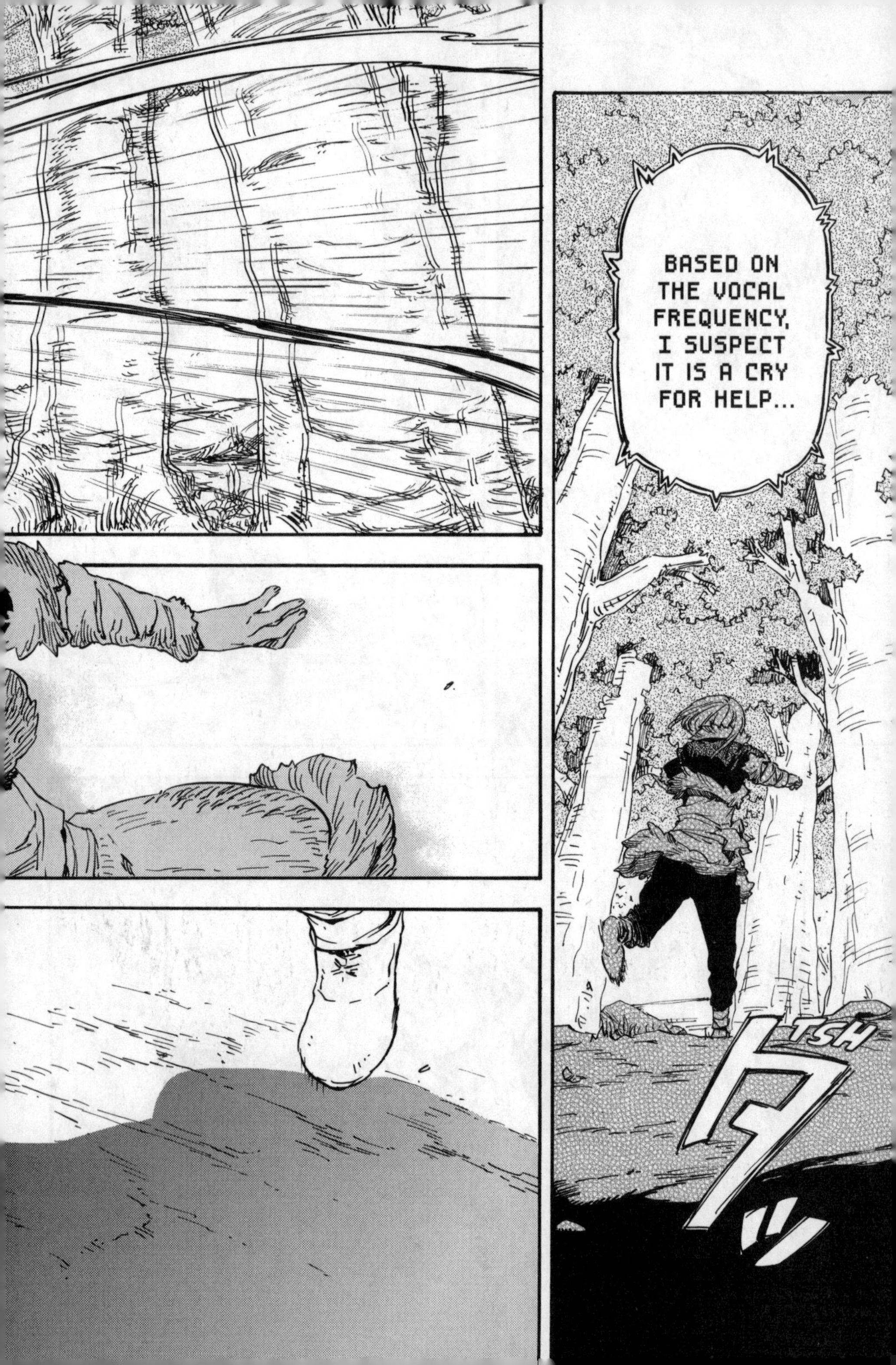
BASED ON THE VOCAL FREQUENCY, I SUSPECT IT IS A CRY FOR HELP...
TSH
トッ

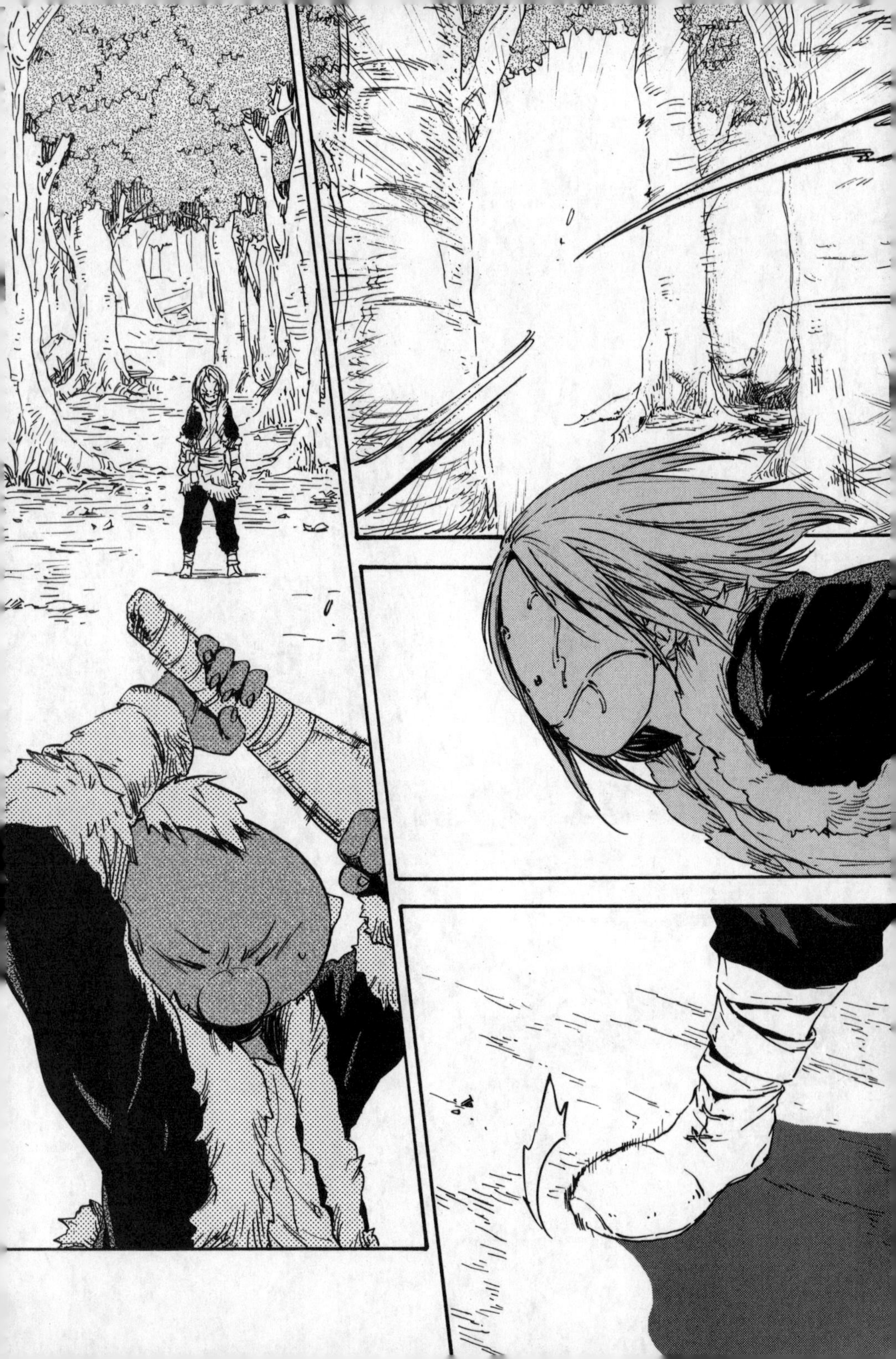

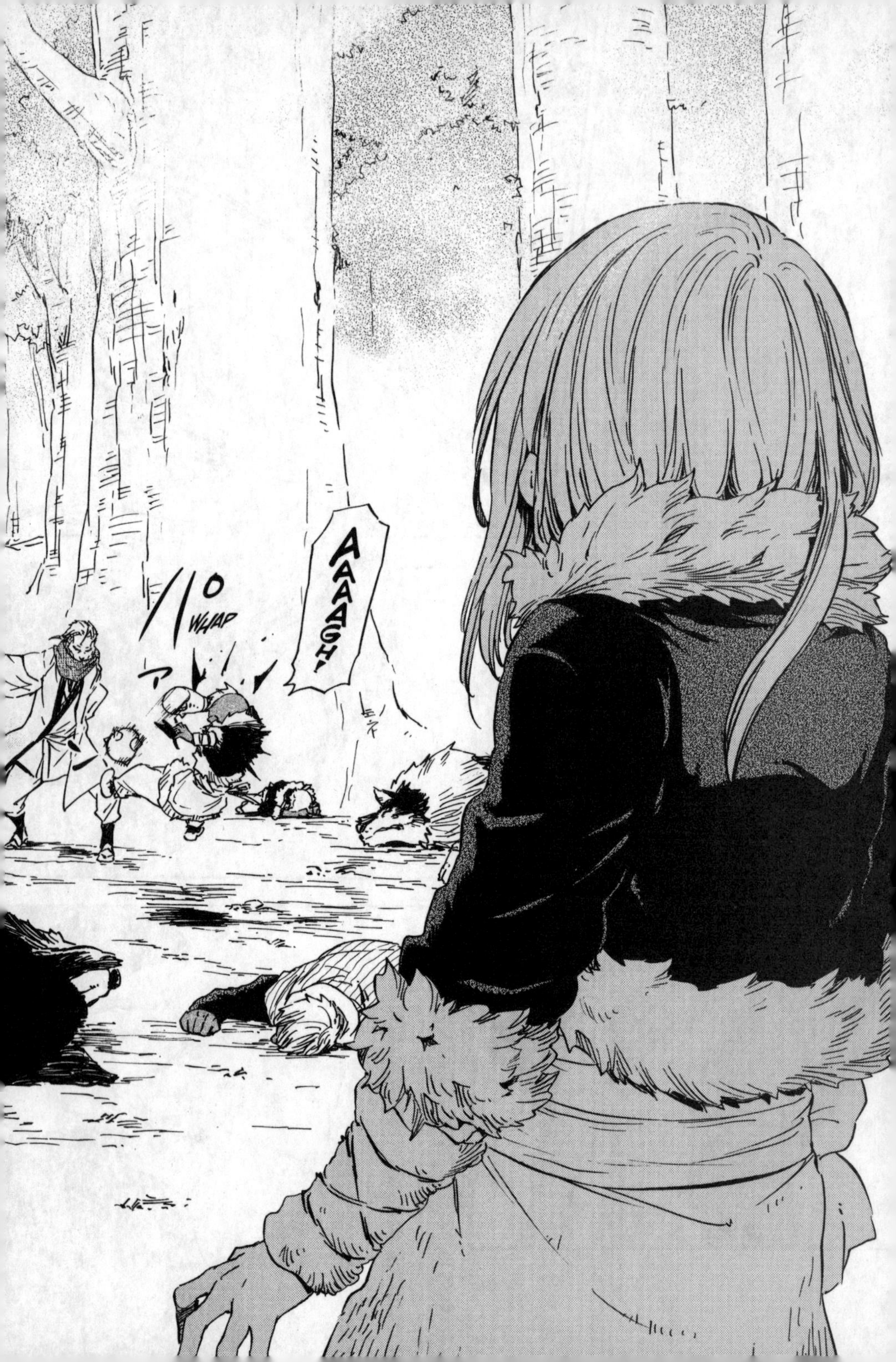
AAAAGH!
WHAP
ア

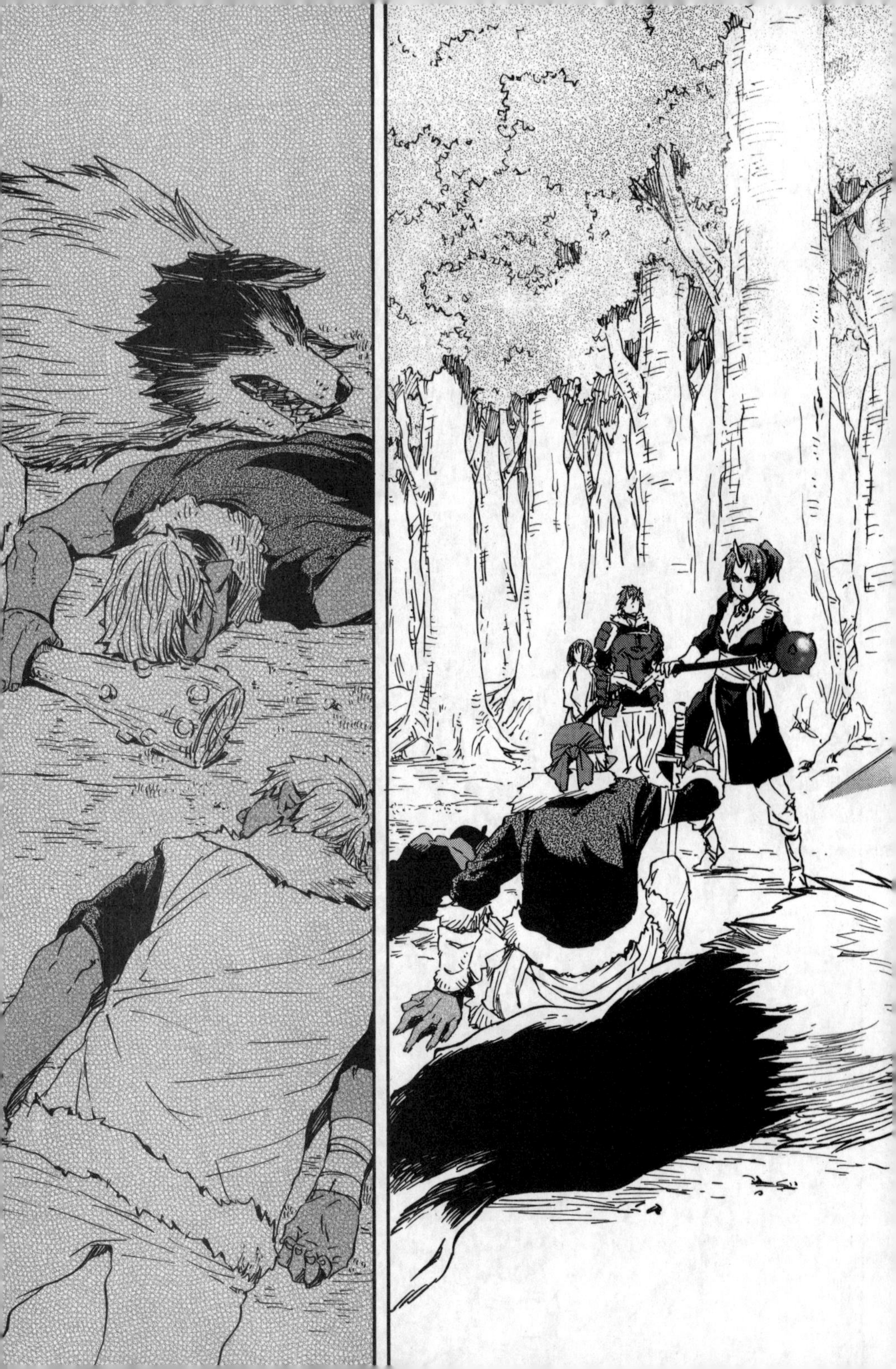

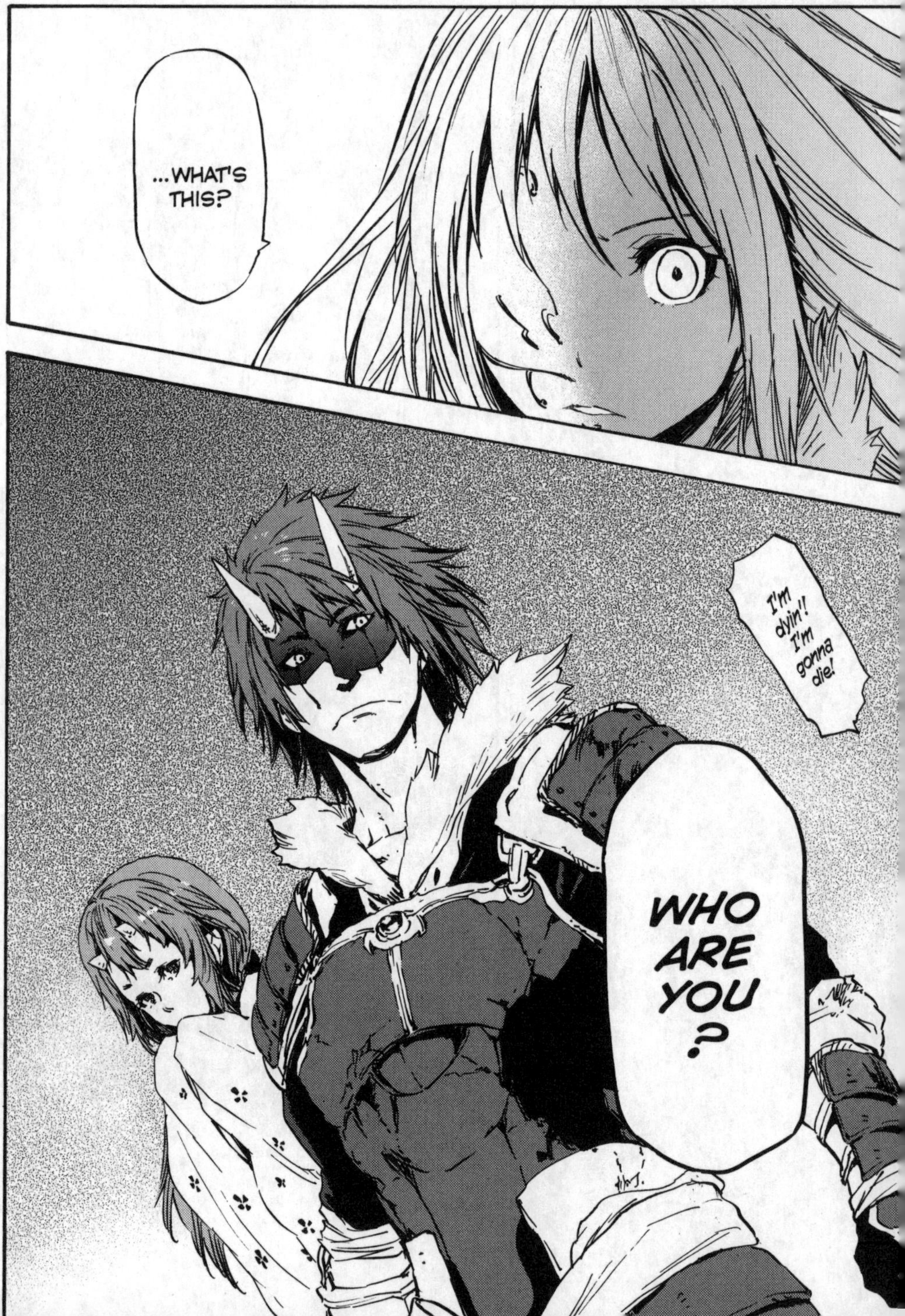
...WHAT'S THIS?
I'm dyin'! I'm gonna die!
WHO ARE YOU?

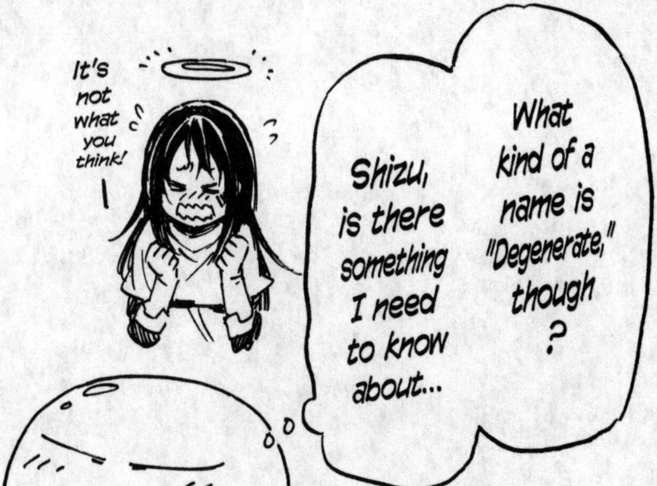
What kind of a name is "Degenerate," though?
Shizu, is there something I need to know about...
It's not what you think!

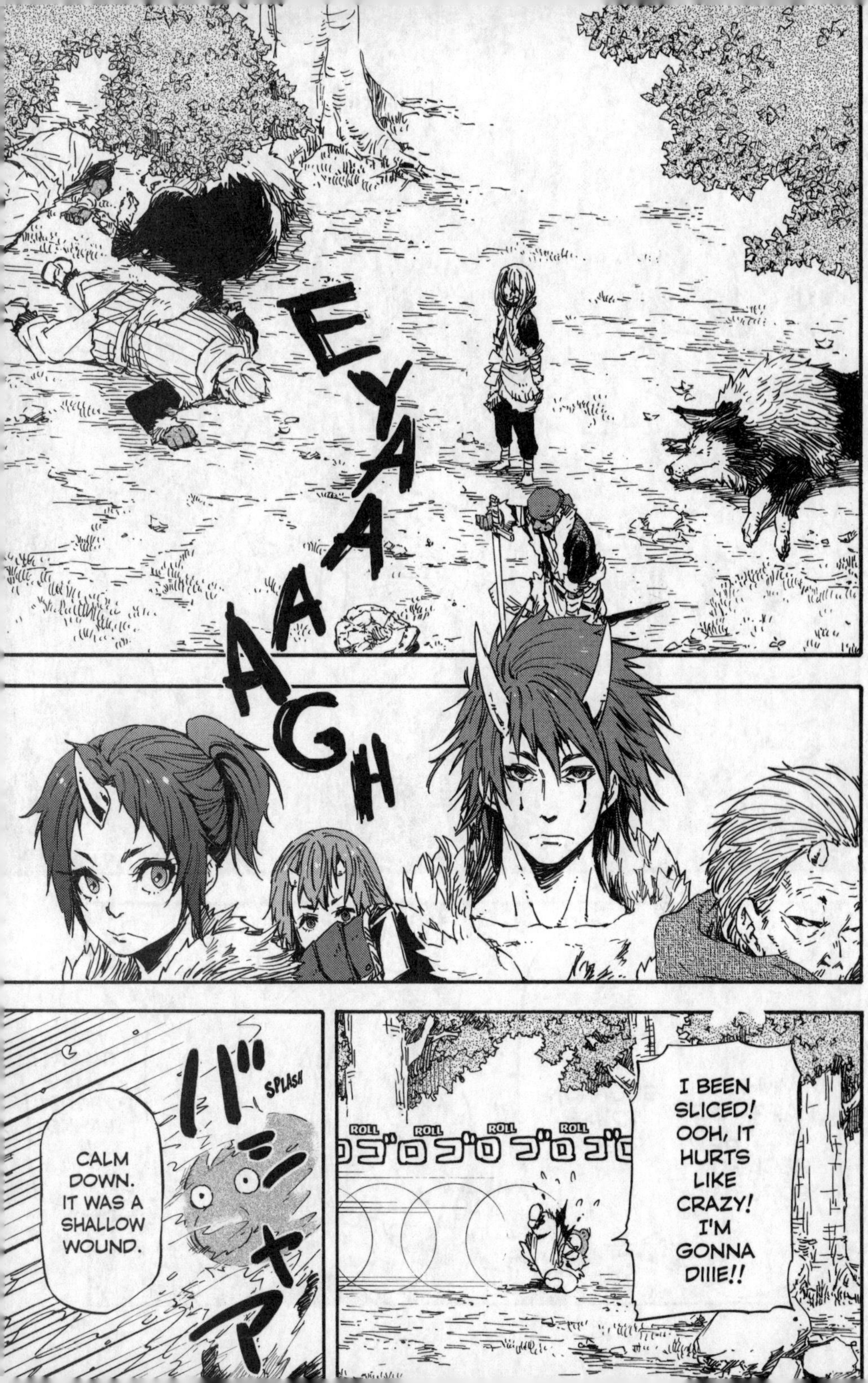
EYAAAAGH
ROLL ROLL ROLL ROLL
ゴロゴロゴロゴロ
I BEEN SLICED! OOH, IT HURTS LIKE CRAZY! I'M GONNA DIIIE!!
SPLASH
バシャア
CALM DOWN. IT WAS A SHALLOW WOUND.

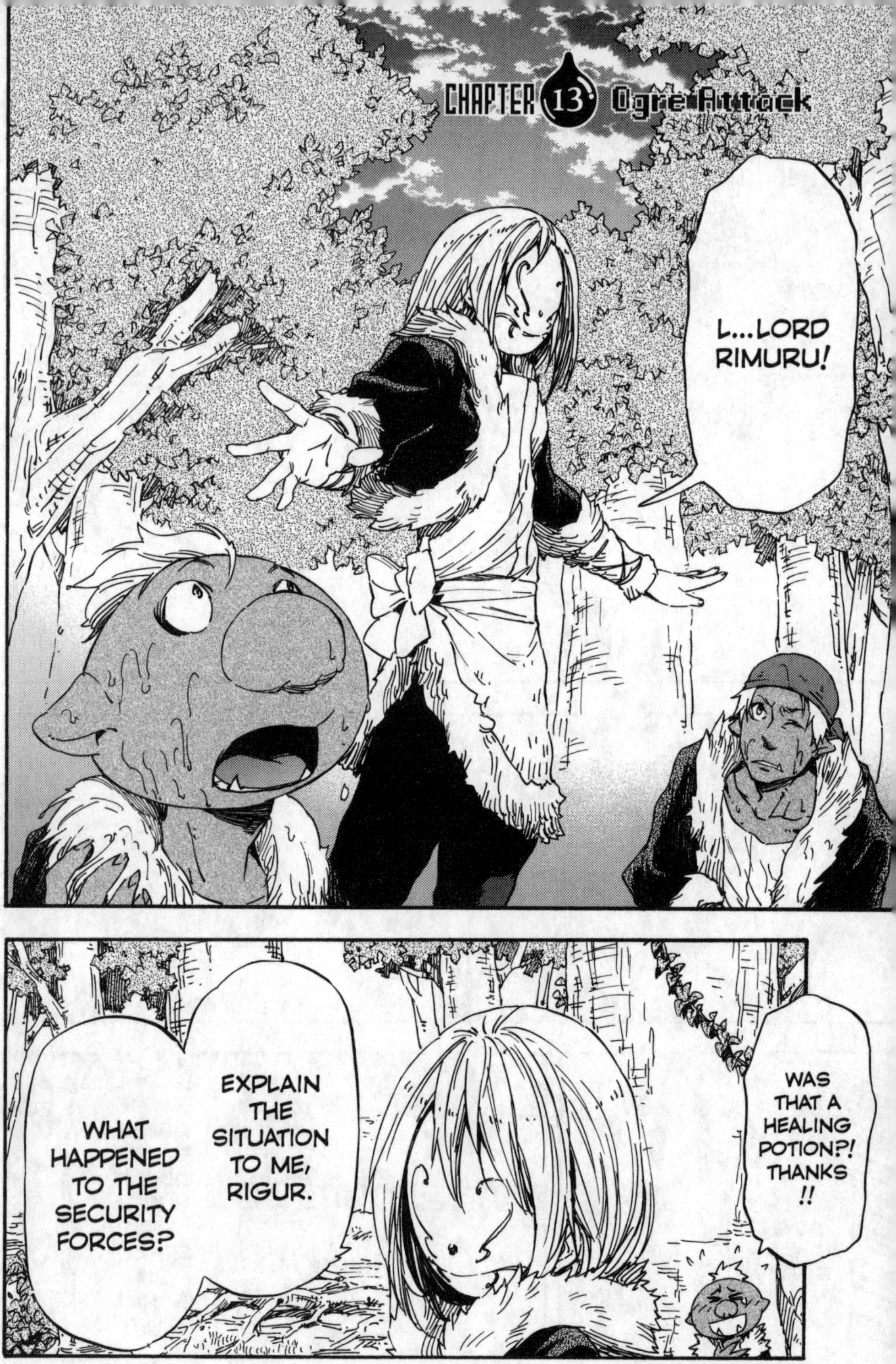
CHAPTER 13 Ogre Attack
L...LORD RIMURU!
WAS THAT A HEALING POTION?! THANKS !!
EXPLAIN THE SITUATION TO ME, RIGUR.
WHAT HAPPENED TO THE SECURITY FORCES?

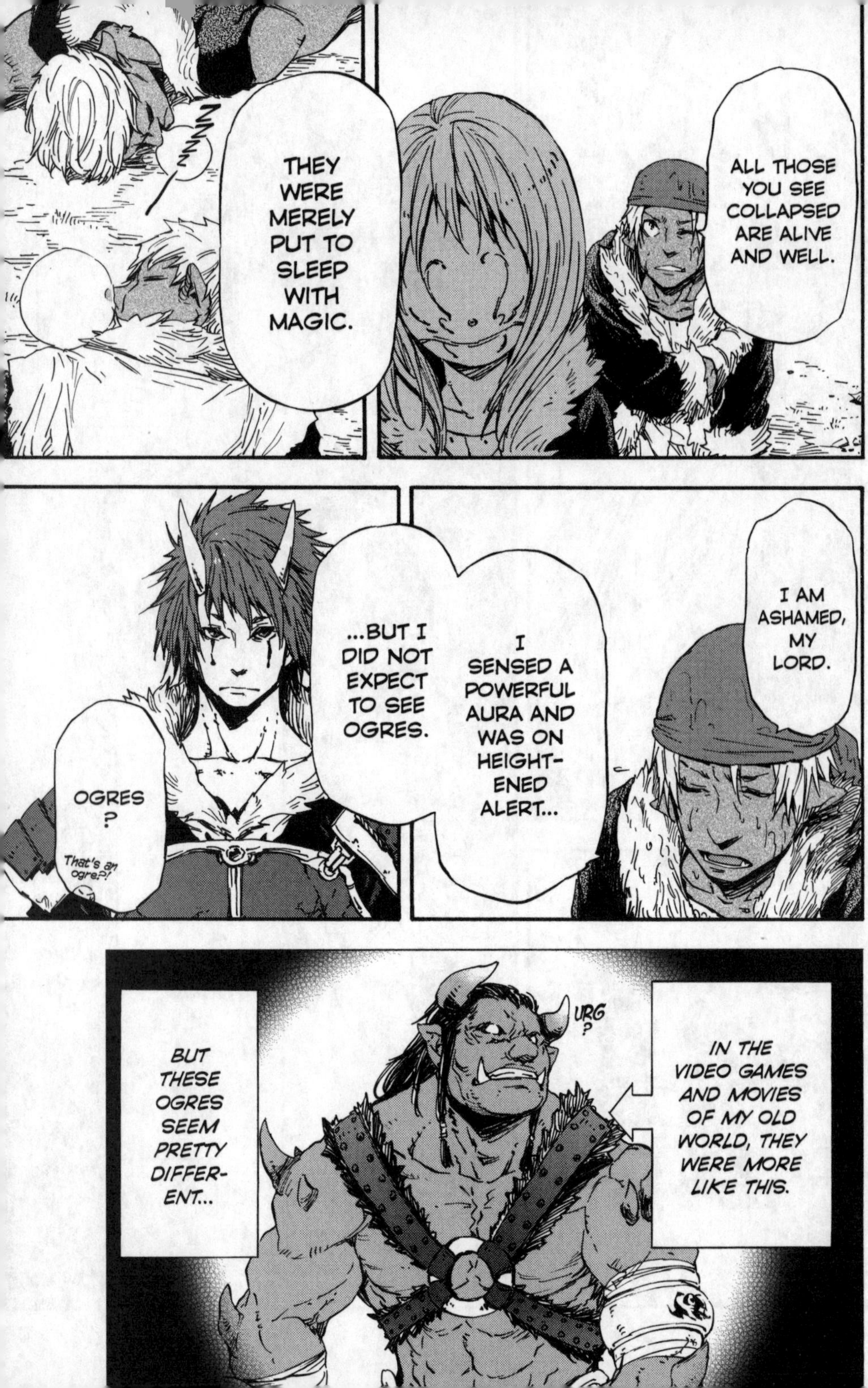
ALL THOSE YOU SEE COLLAPSED ARE ALIVE AND WELL.
THEY WERE MERELY PUT TO SLEEP WITH MAGIC.
ZZZZ
I AM ASHAMED, MY LORD.
I SENSED A POWERFUL AURA AND WAS ON HEIGHT-ENED ALERT...
...BUT I DID NOT EXPECT TO SEE OGRES.
OGRES ?
That's an ogre?!
IN THE VIDEO GAMES AND MOVIES OF MY OLD WORLD, THEY WERE MORE LIKE THIS.
URG ?
BUT THESE OGRES SEEM PRETTY DIFFER-ENT...

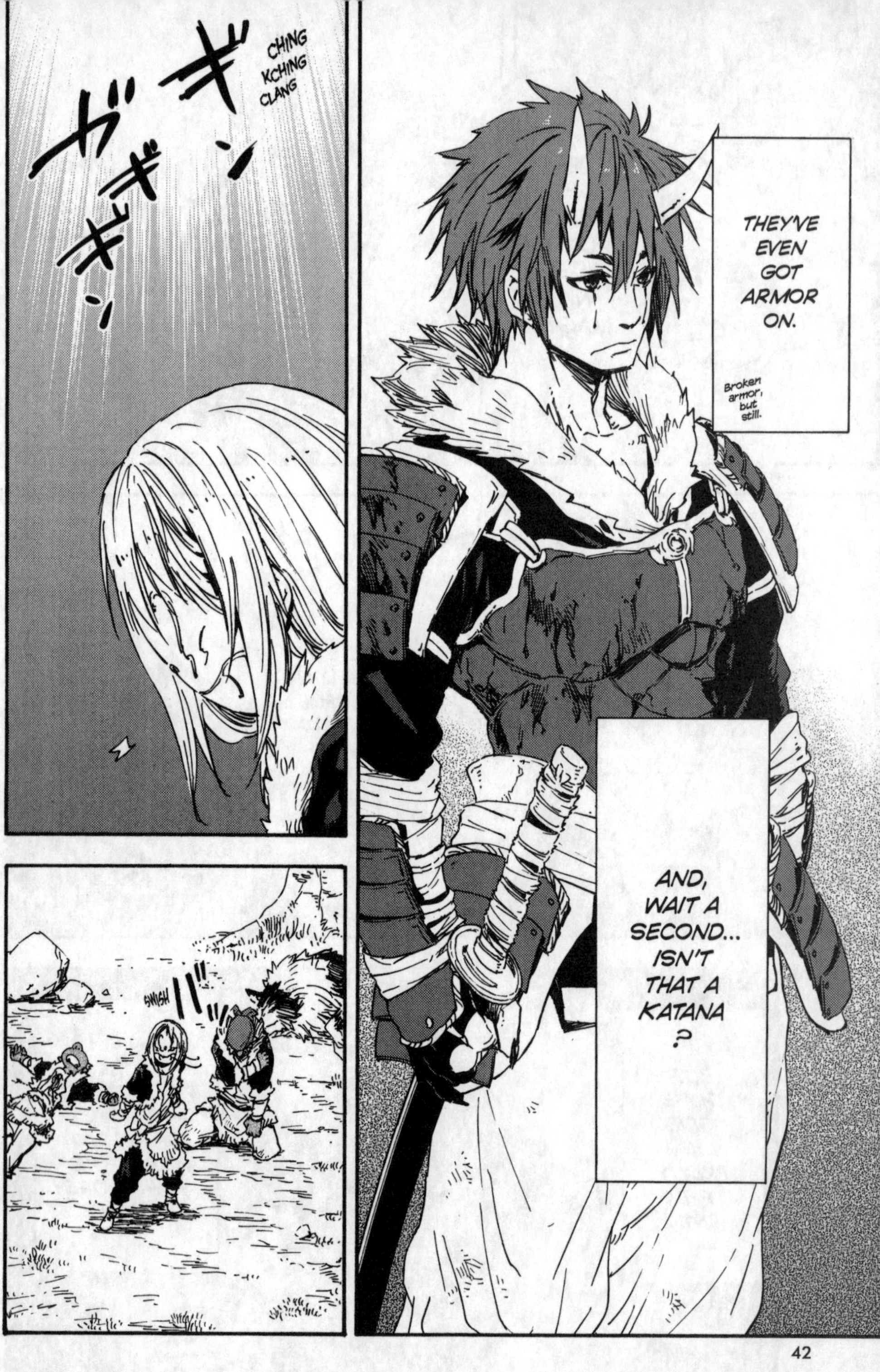
THEY'VE EVEN GOT ARMOR ON.
Broken armor, but still.
AND, WAIT A SECOND... ISN'T THAT A KATANA?
ギン
ガギギギン
CHING KCHING CLANG
SWISH

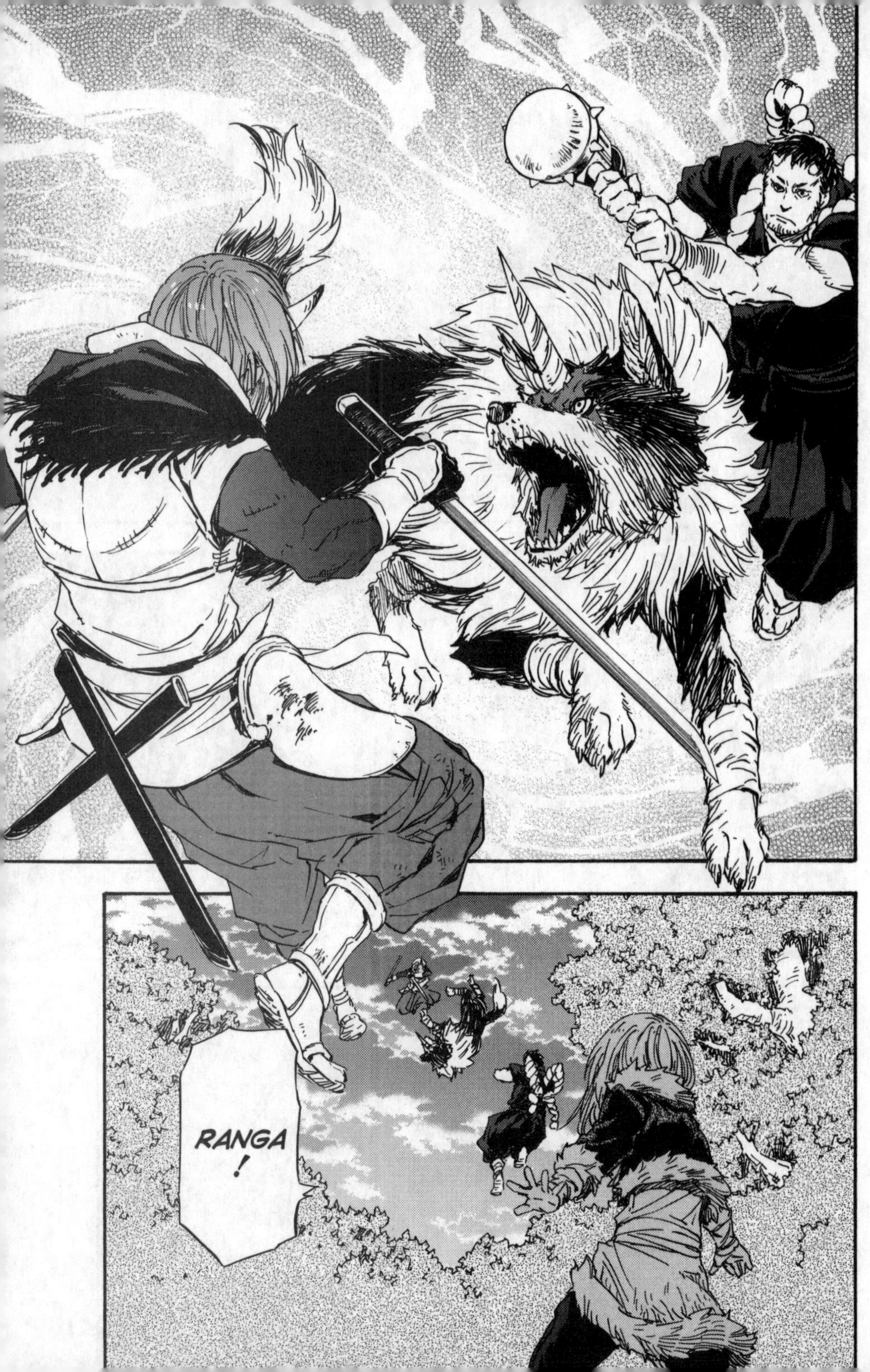
RANGA!

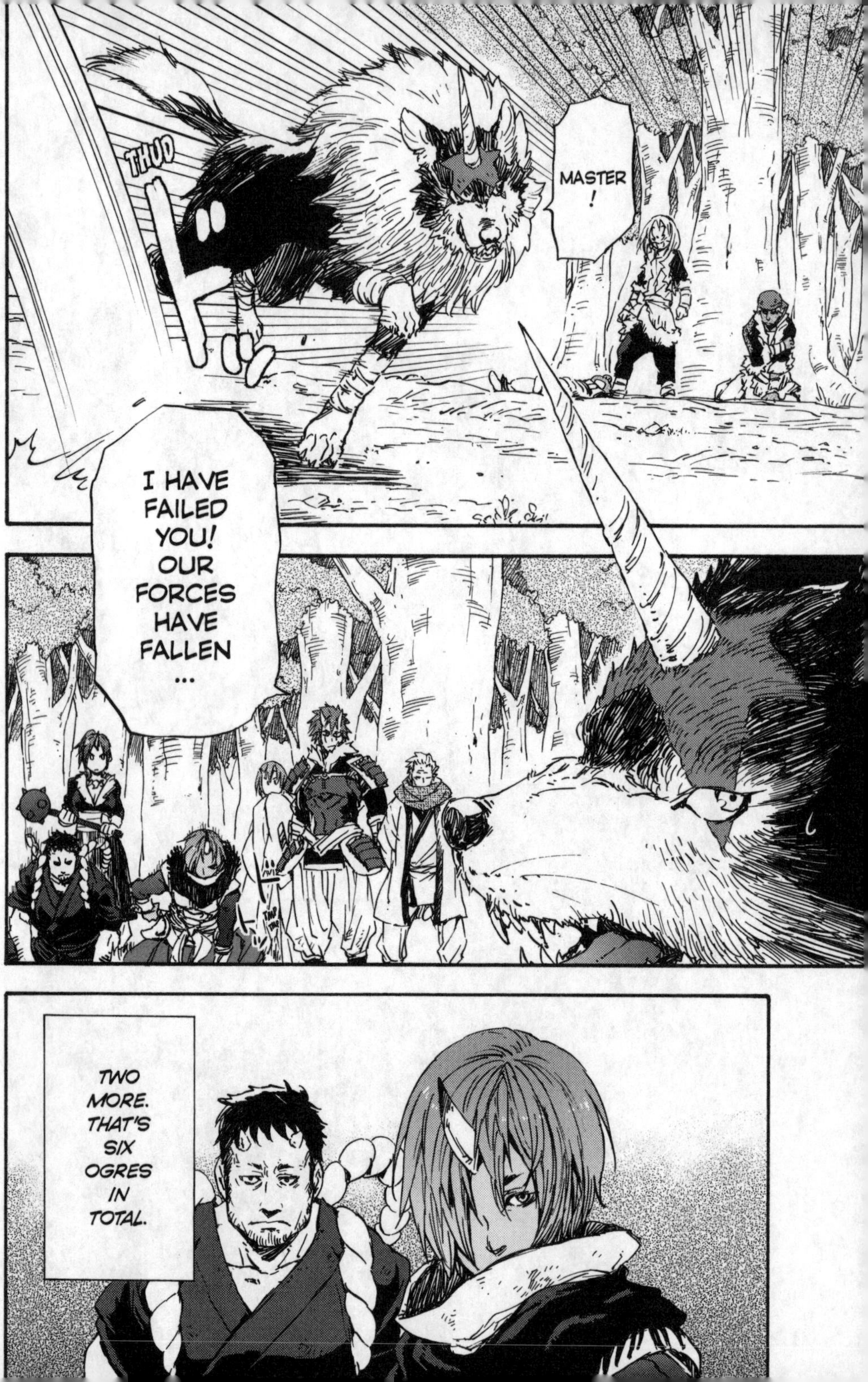
MASTER!
THUD
I HAVE FAILED YOU! OUR FORCES HAVE FALLEN...
TWO MORE. THAT'S SIX OGRES IN TOTAL.

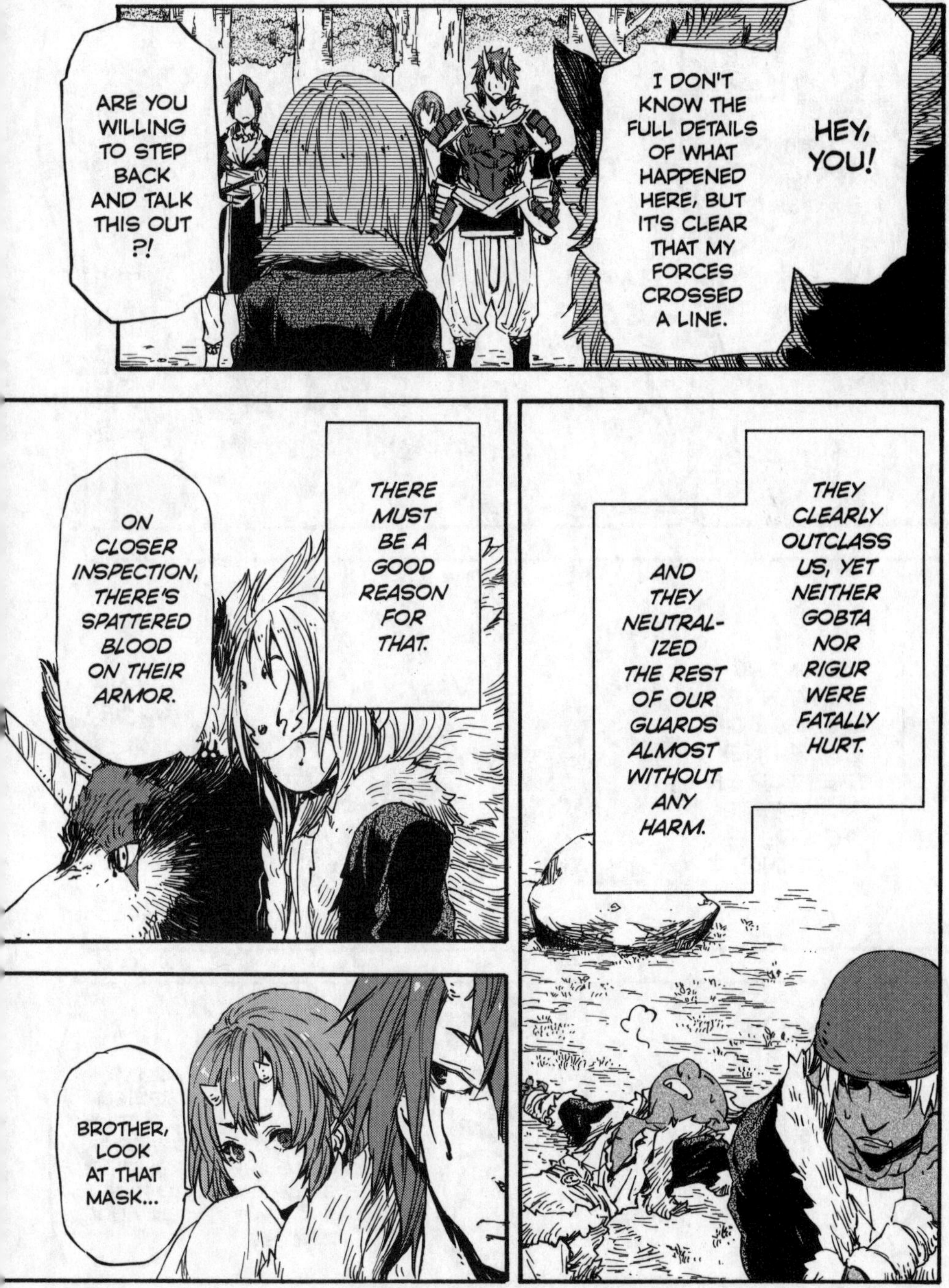
HEY, YOU!
I DON'T KNOW THE FULL DETAILS OF WHAT HAPPENED HERE, BUT IT'S CLEAR THAT MY FORCES CROSSED A LINE.
ARE YOU WILLING TO STEP BACK AND TALK THIS OUT ?!
THEY CLEARLY OUTCLASS US, YET NEITHER GOBTA NOR RIGUR WERE FATALLY HURT.
AND THEY NEUTRAL-IZED THE REST OF OUR GUARDS ALMOST WITHOUT ANY HARM.
THERE MUST BE A GOOD REASON FOR THAT.
ON CLOSER INSPECTION, THERE'S SPATTERED BLOOD ON THEIR ARMOR.
BROTHER, LOOK AT THAT MASK...

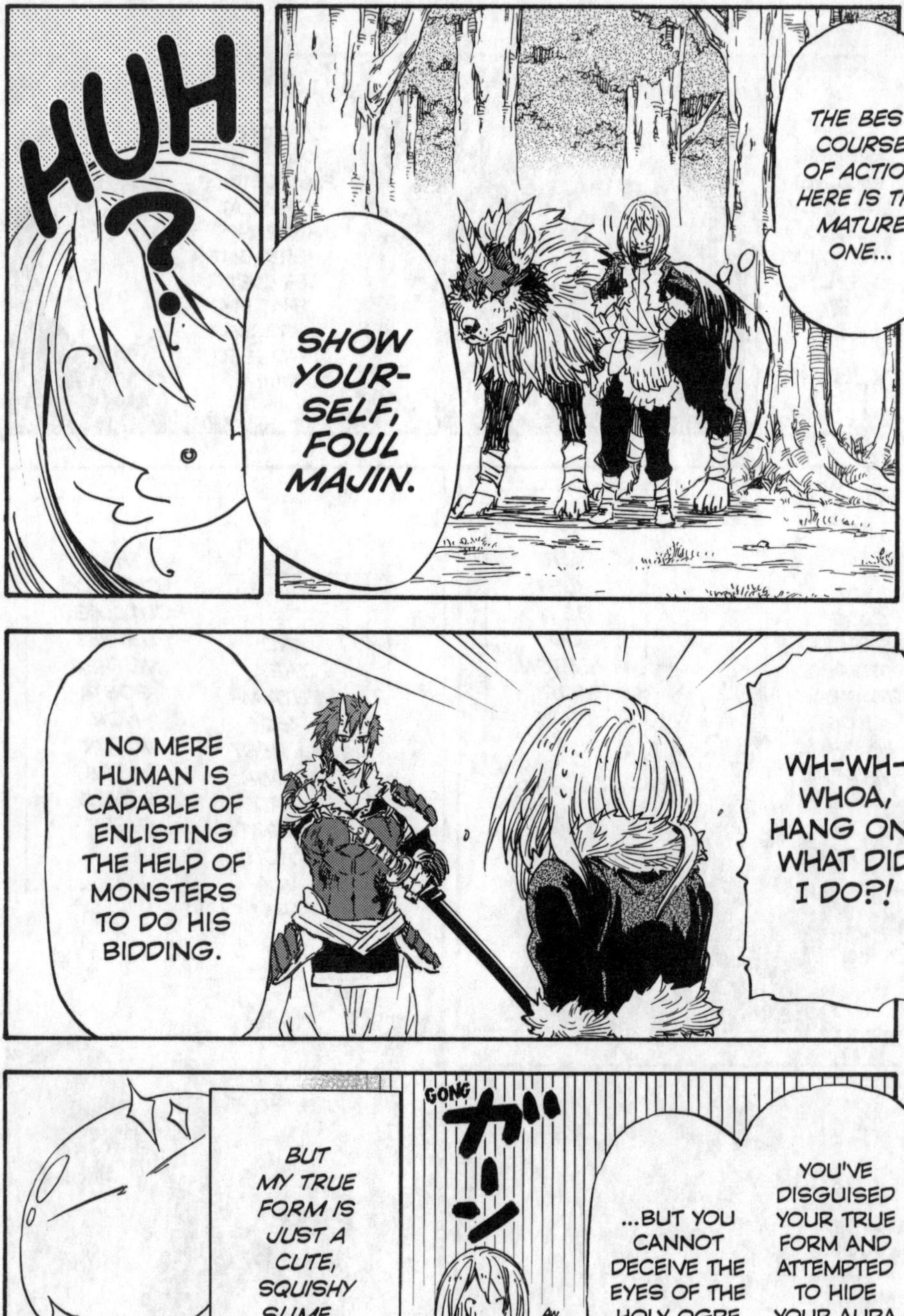
THE BEST COURSE OF ACTION HERE IS THE MATURE ONE...
SHOW YOURSELF, FOUL MAJIN.
HUH?
WH-WH-WHOA, HANG ON! WHAT DID I DO?!
NO MERE HUMAN IS CAPABLE OF ENLISTING THE HELP OF MONSTERS TO DO HIS BIDDING.
YOU'VE DISGUISED YOUR TRUE FORM AND ATTEMPTED TO HIDE YOUR AURA ...
...BUT YOU CANNOT DECEIVE THE EYES OF THE HOLY OGRE PRINCESS.
GONG
AW, man...
BUT MY TRUE FORM IS JUST A CUTE, SQUISHY SLIME...

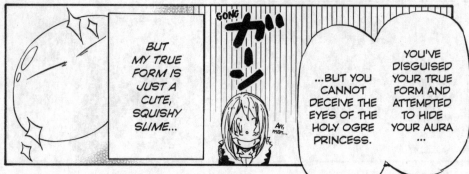

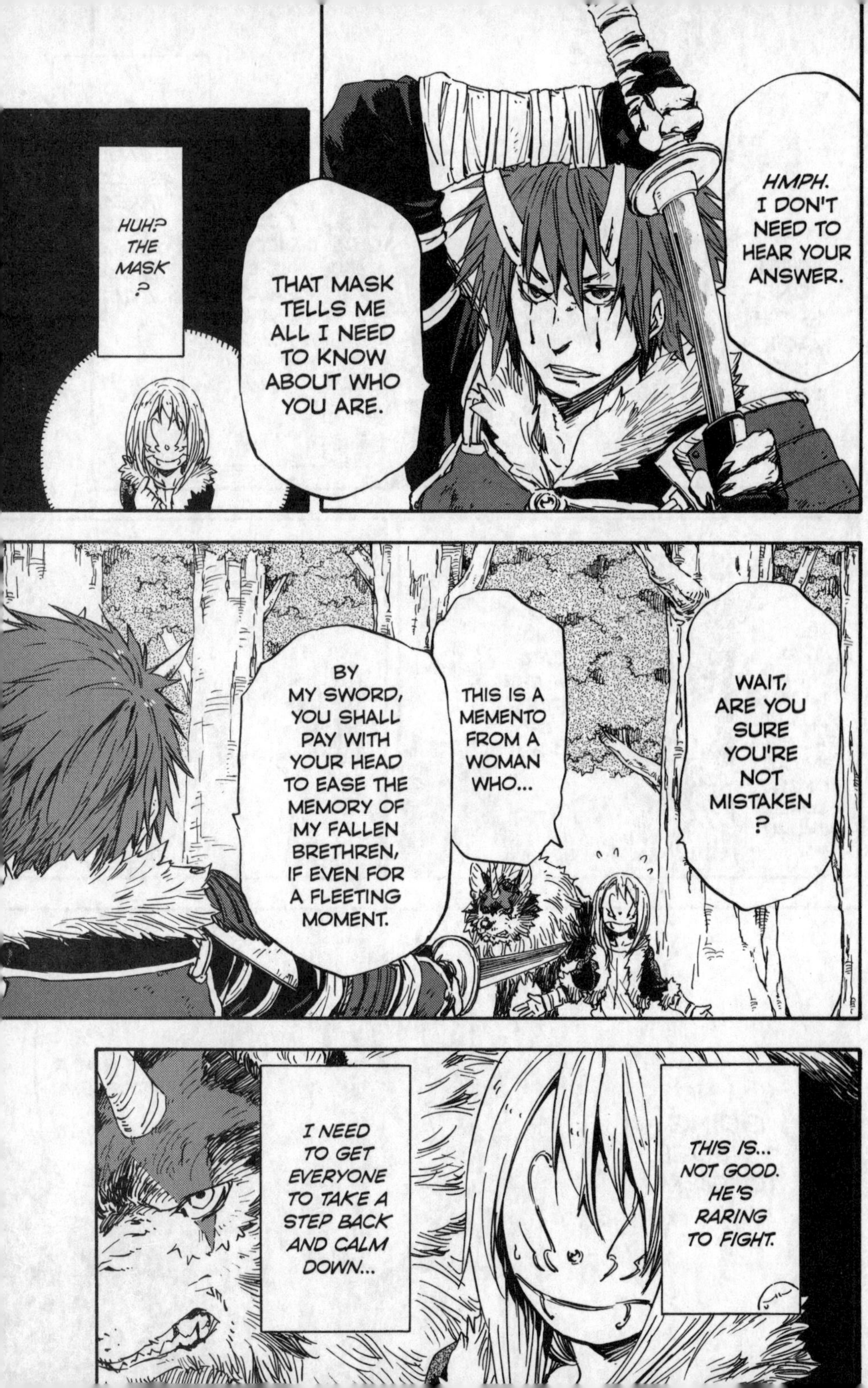
HMPH. I DON'T NEED TO HEAR YOUR ANSWER.
THAT MASK TELLS ME ALL I NEED TO KNOW ABOUT WHO YOU ARE.
HUH? THE MASK?
WAIT, ARE YOU SURE YOU'RE NOT MISTAKEN?
THIS IS A MEMENTO FROM A WOMAN WHO...
BY MY SWORD, YOU SHALL PAY WITH YOUR HEAD TO EASE THE MEMORY OF MY FALLEN BRETHREN, IF EVEN FOR A FLEETING MOMENT.
THIS IS... NOT GOOD. HE'S RARING TO FIGHT.
I NEED TO GET EVERYONE TO TAKE A STEP BACK AND CALM DOWN...

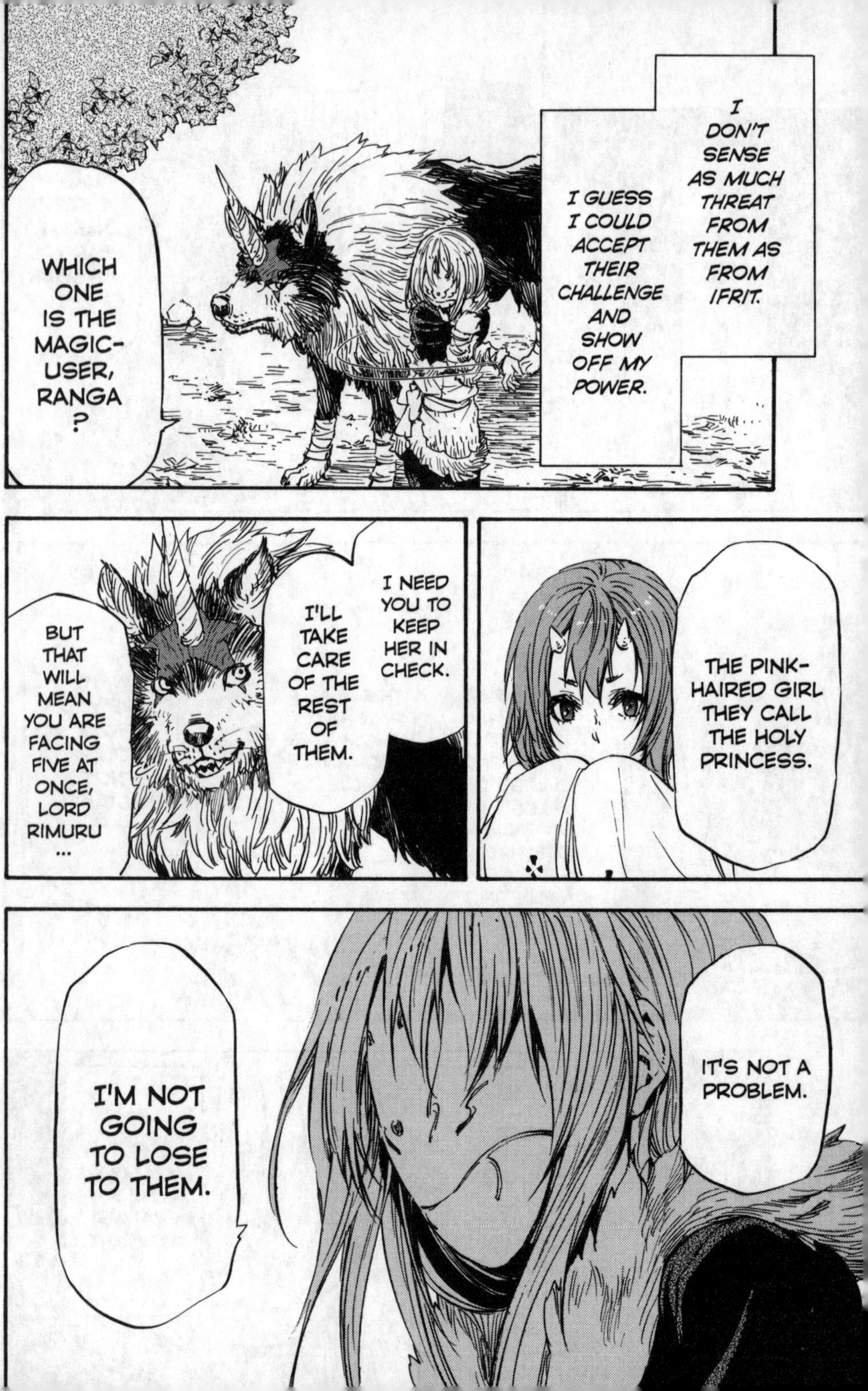
I DON'T SENSE AS MUCH THREAT FROM THEM AS FROM IFRIT.
I GUESS I COULD ACCEPT THEIR CHALLENGE AND SHOW OFF MY POWER.
WHICH ONE IS THE MAGIC-USER, RANGA?
THE PINK-HAIRED GIRL THEY CALL THE HOLY PRINCESS.
I NEED YOU TO KEEP HER IN CHECK.
I'LL TAKE CARE OF THE REST OF THEM.
BUT THAT WILL MEAN YOU ARE FACING FIVE AT ONCE, LORD RIMURU...
IT'S NOT A PROBLEM.
I'M NOT GOING TO LOSE TO THEM.

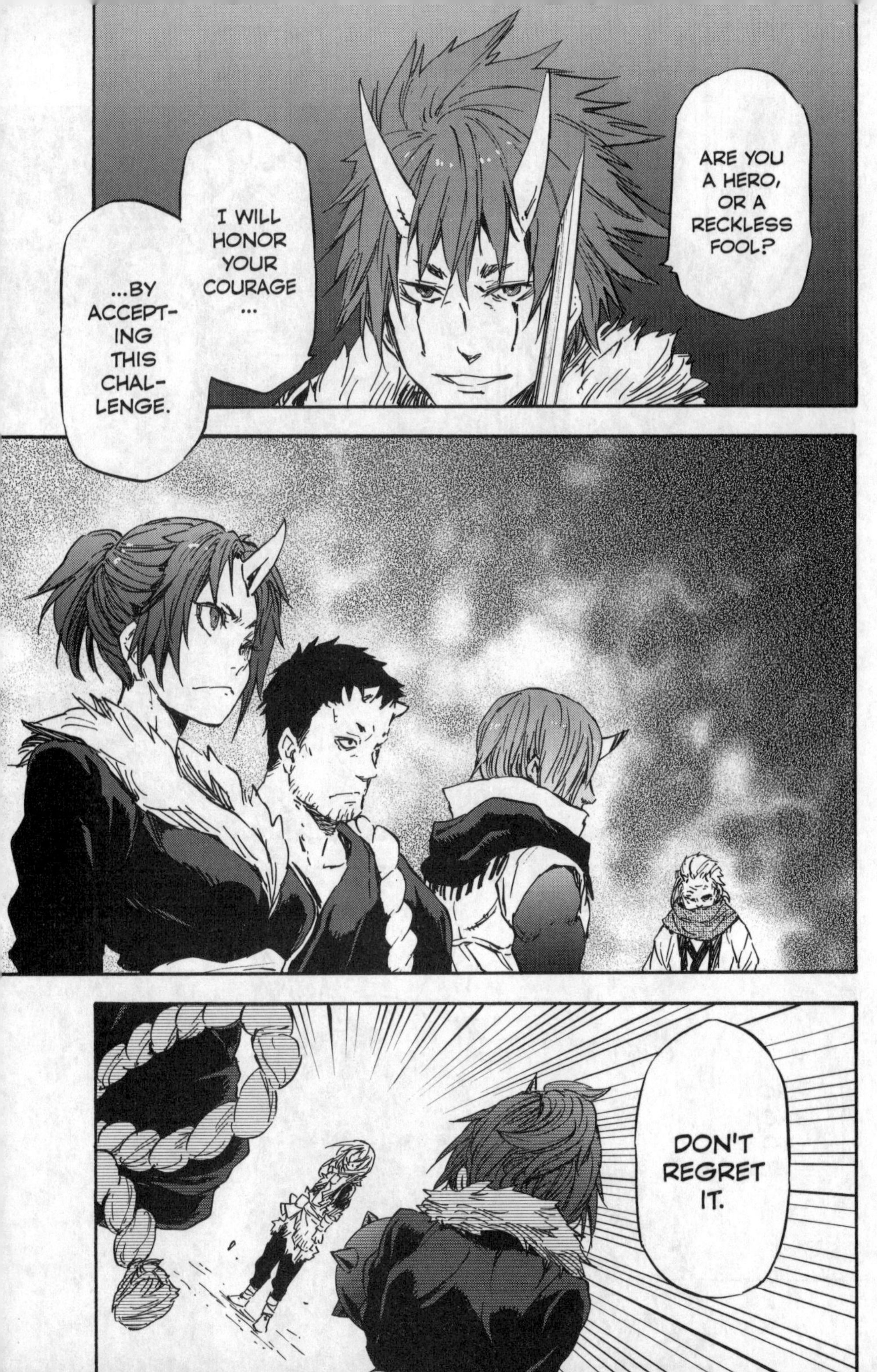
ARE YOU A HERO, OR A RECKLESS FOOL?
I WILL HONOR YOUR COURAGE ...
...BY ACCEPTING THIS CHALLENGE.
DON'T REGRET IT.

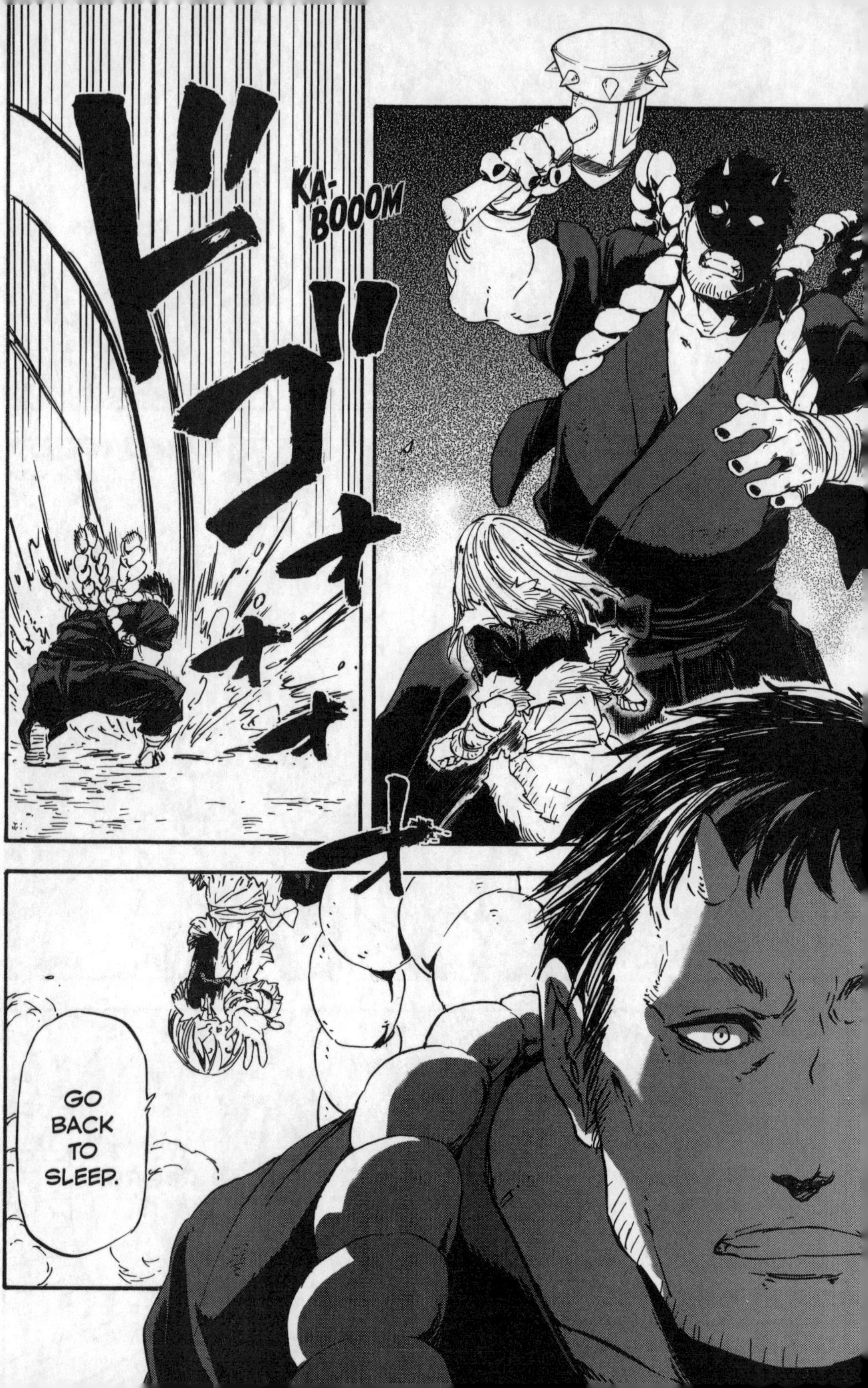

ドゴオオオオ
KA-BOOOM
GO BACK TO SLEEP.

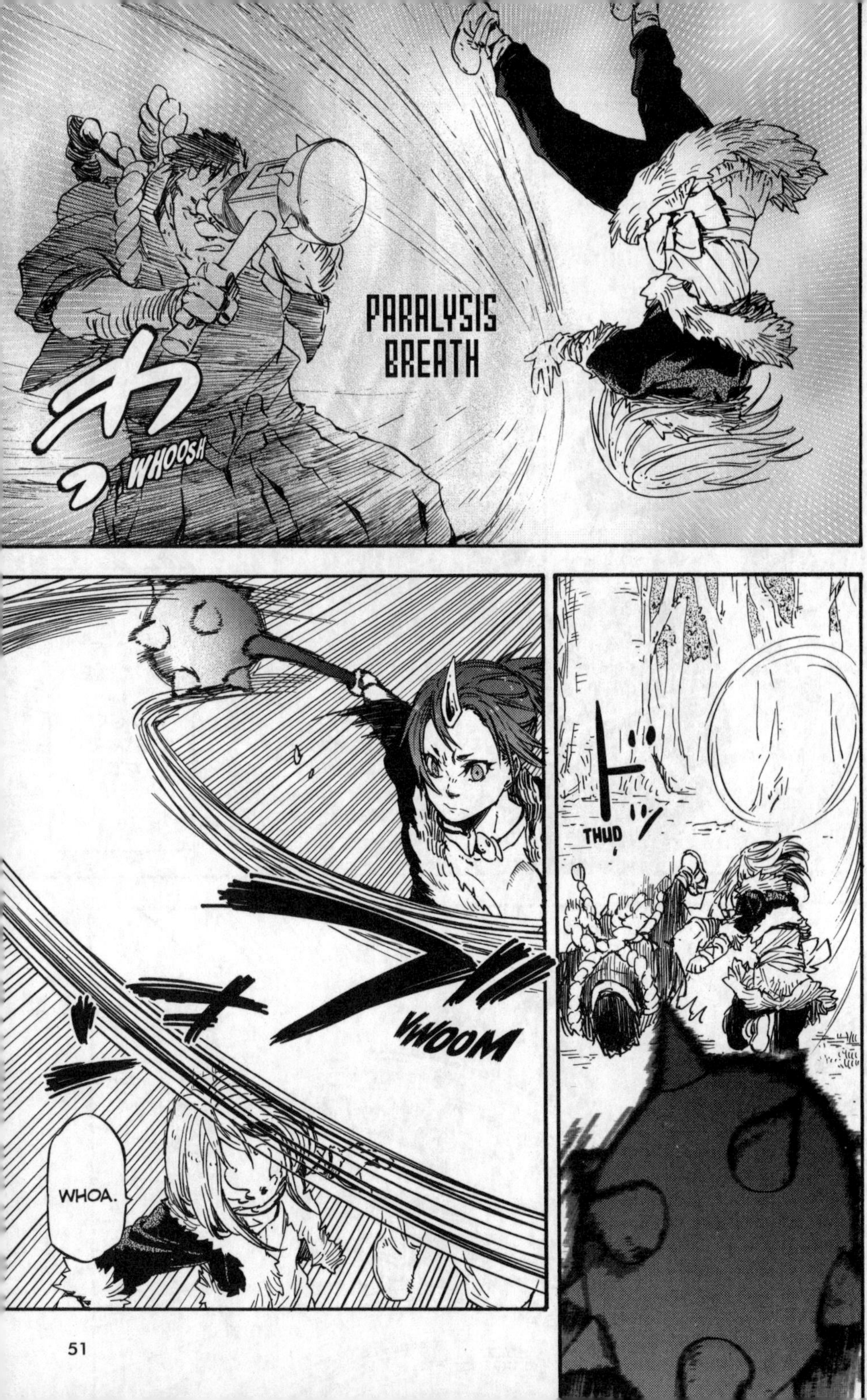
PARALYSIS BREATH
WHOOSH
THUD
VWOOM
WHOA.

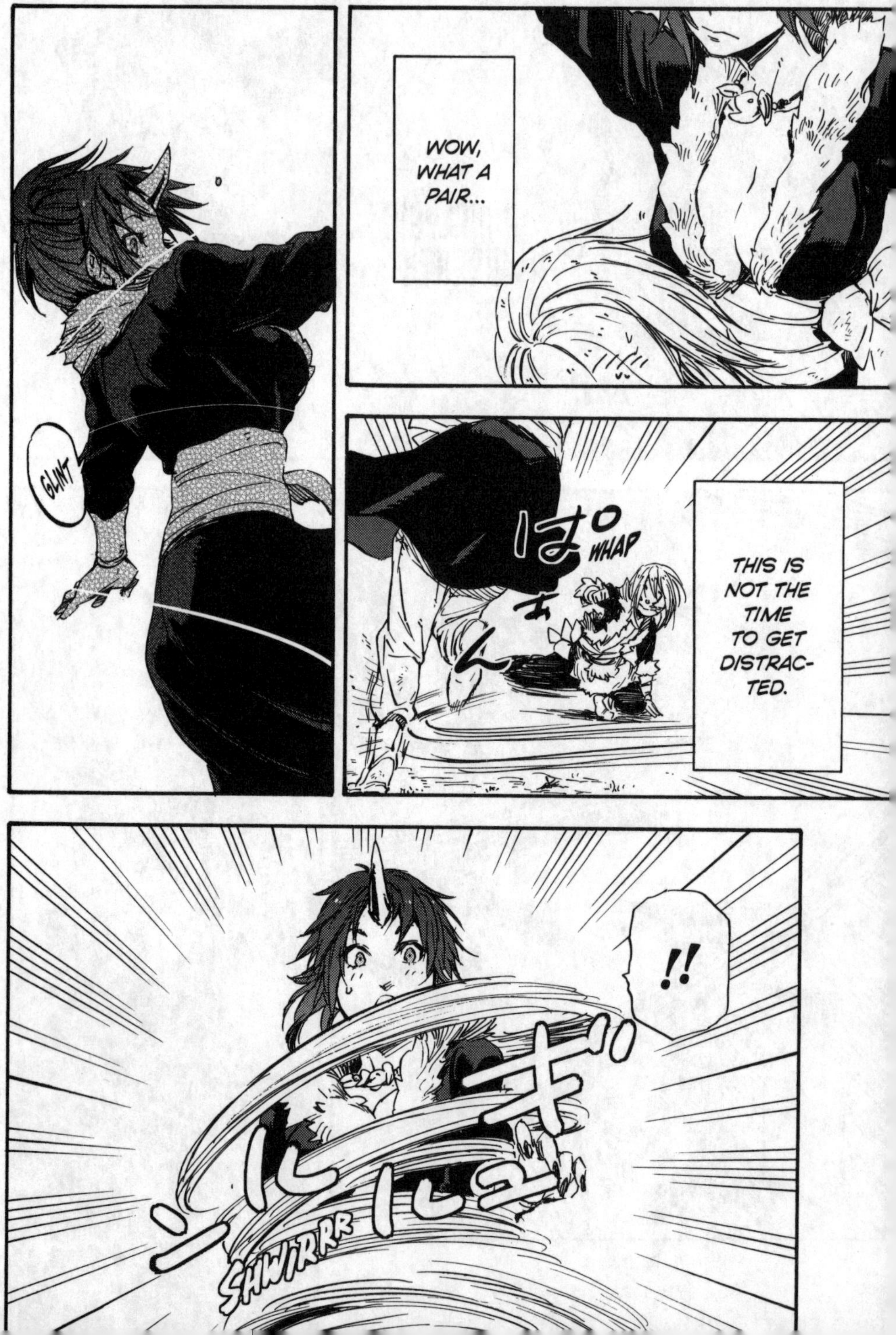
WOW, WHAT A PAIR...
WHAP
THIS IS NOT THE TIME TO GET DISTRACTED.
GLINT
!!
SHWIRRR

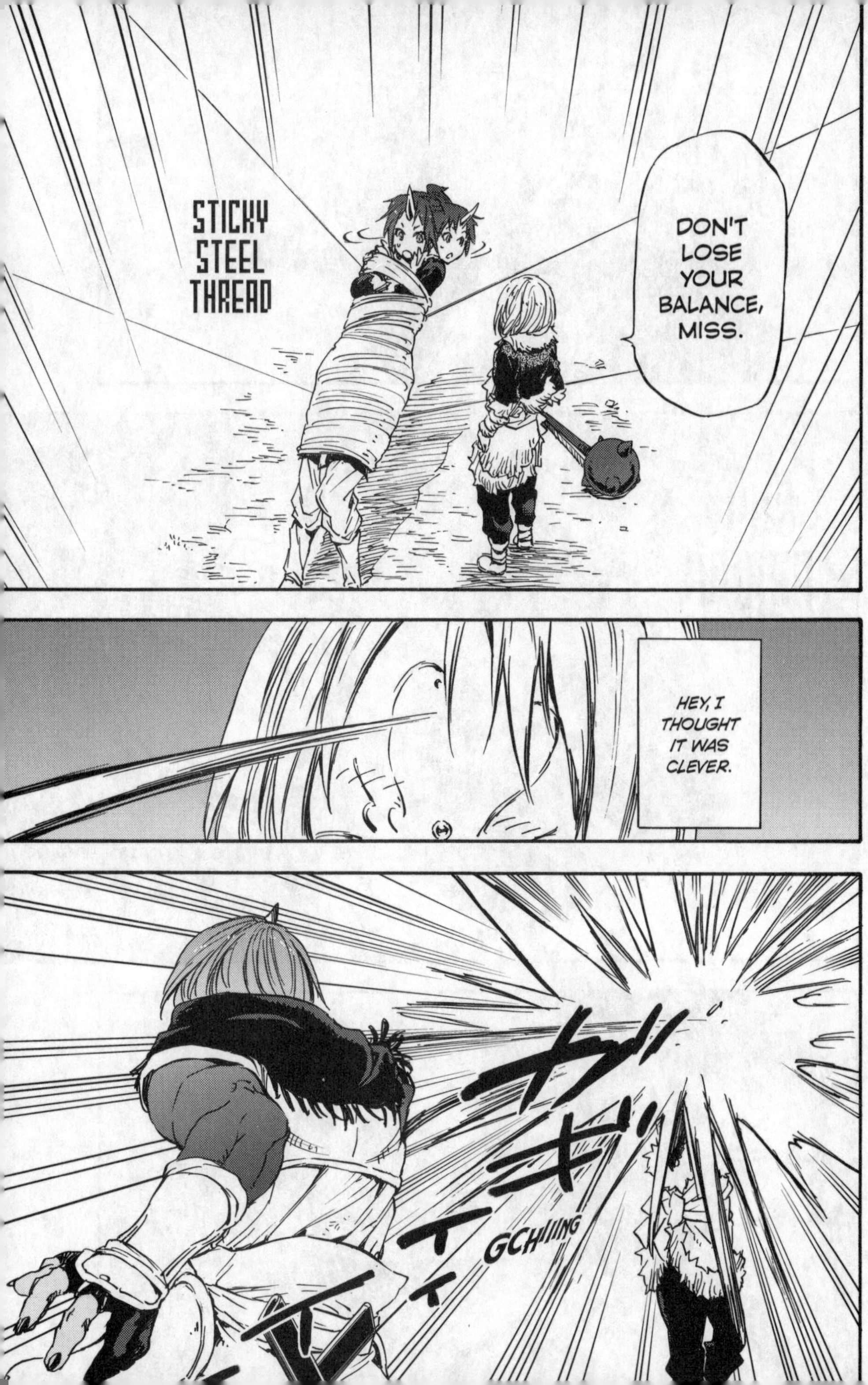
DON'T LOSE YOUR BALANCE, MISS.
STICKY STEEL THREAD
HEY, I THOUGHT IT WAS CLEVER.
GCHIIING

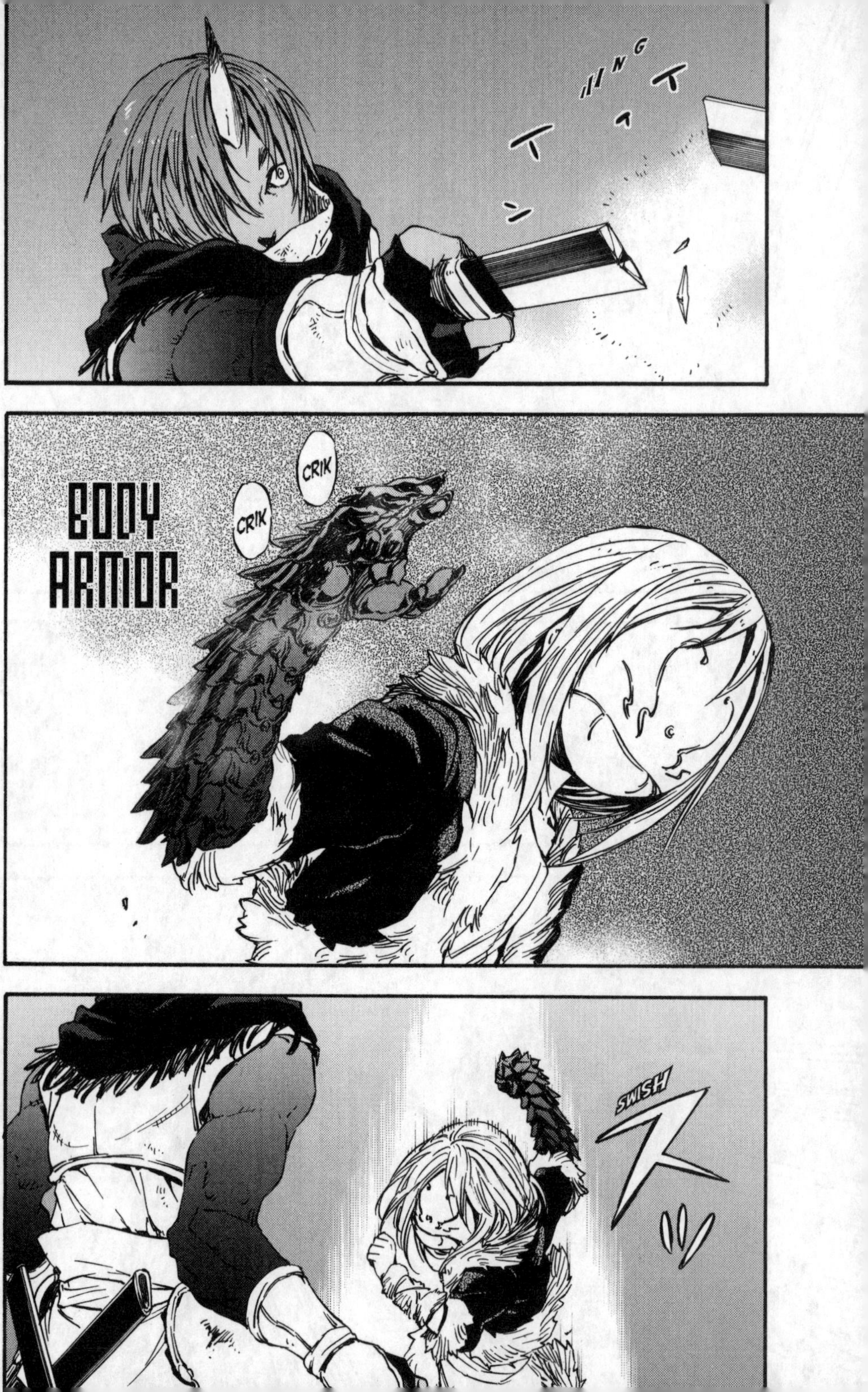
IIING
BODY ARMOR
CRIK
CRIK
SWISH

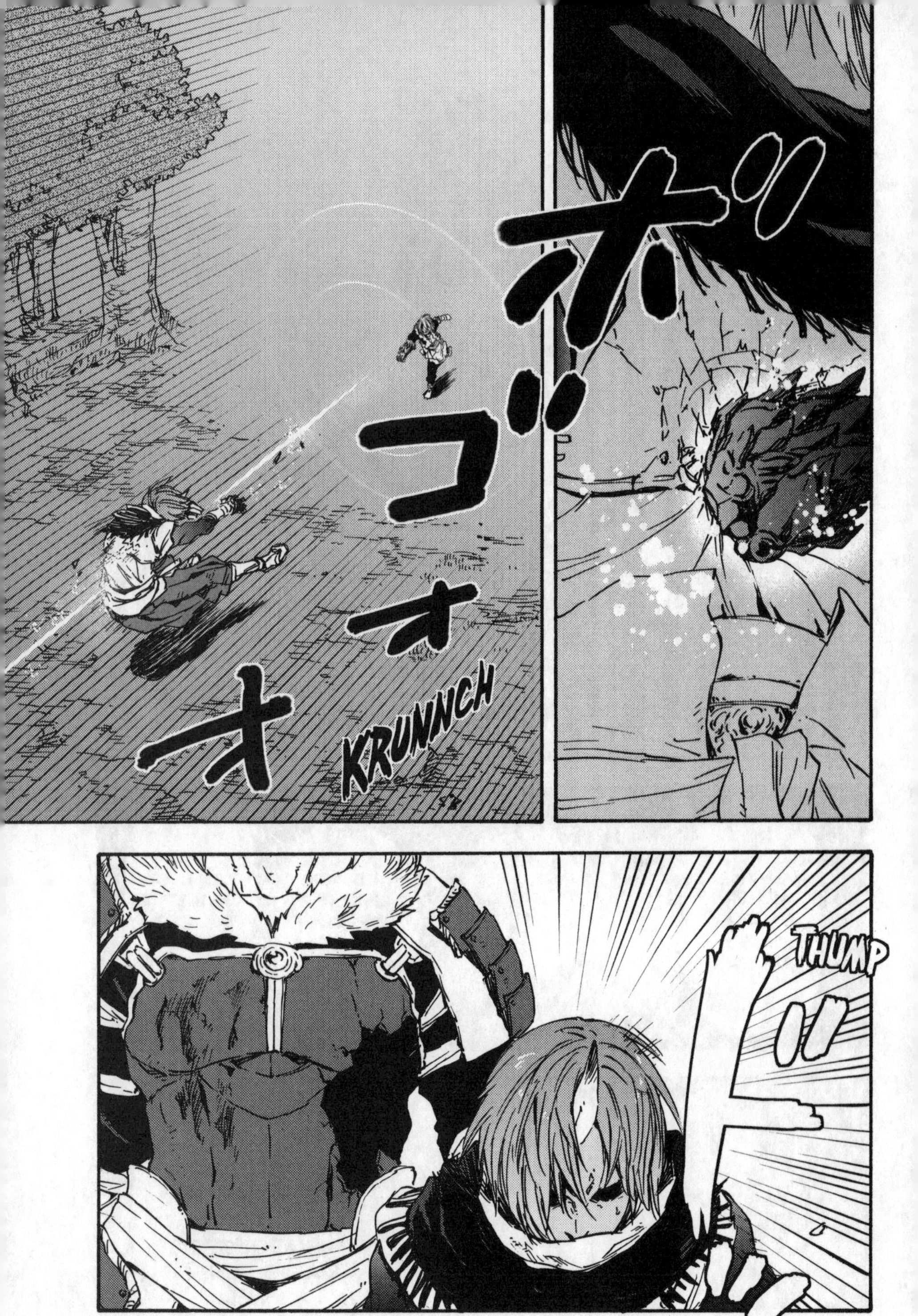
ズ
ゴォォ
KRUNNCH
THUMP
ド

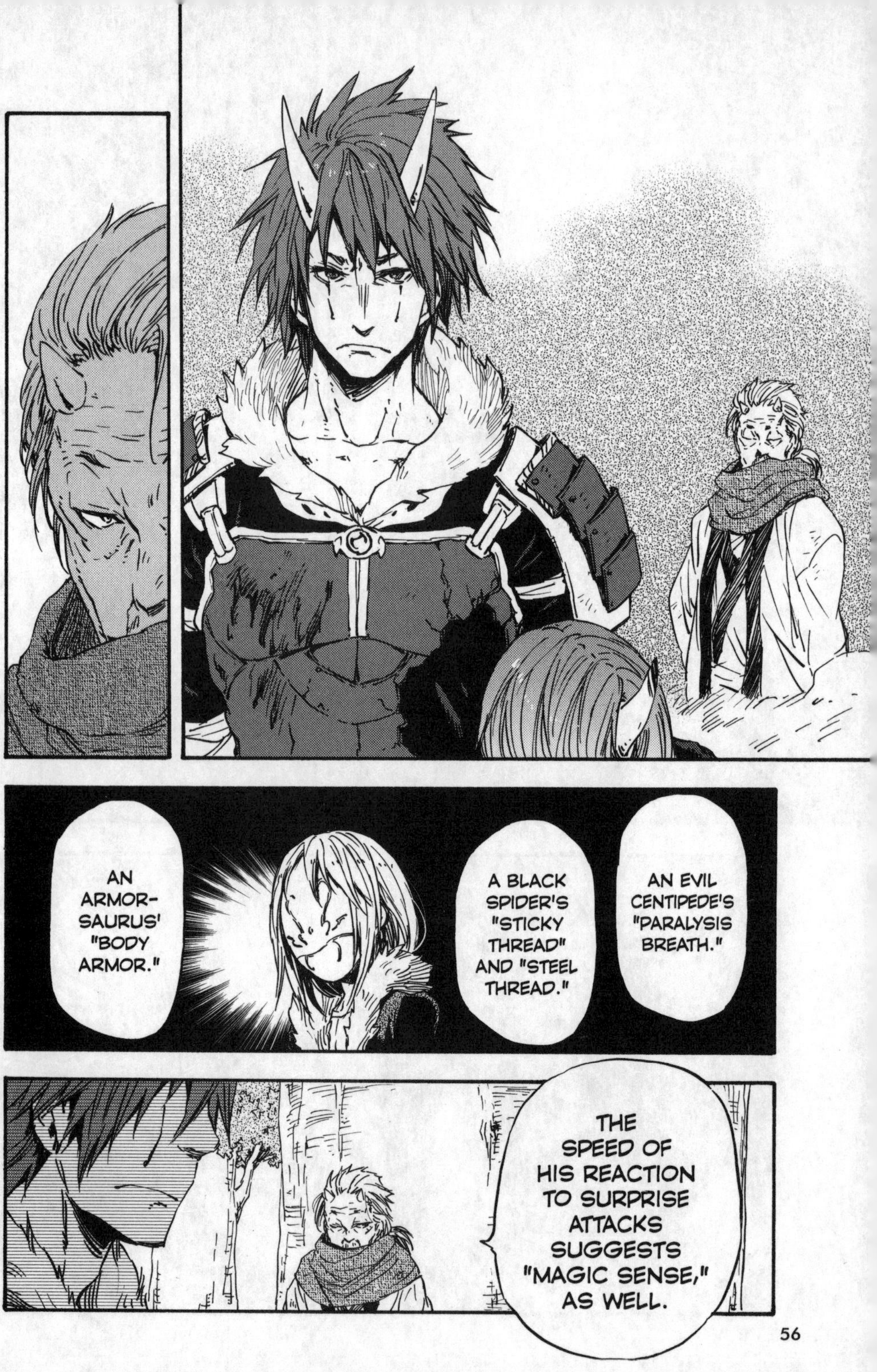

AN EVIL CENTIPEDE'S "PARALYSIS BREATH."
A BLACK SPIDER'S "STICKY THREAD" AND "STEEL THREAD."
AN ARMOR-SAURUS' "BODY ARMOR."
THE SPEED OF HIS REACTION TO SURPRISE ATTACKS SUGGESTS "MAGIC SENSE," AS WELL.

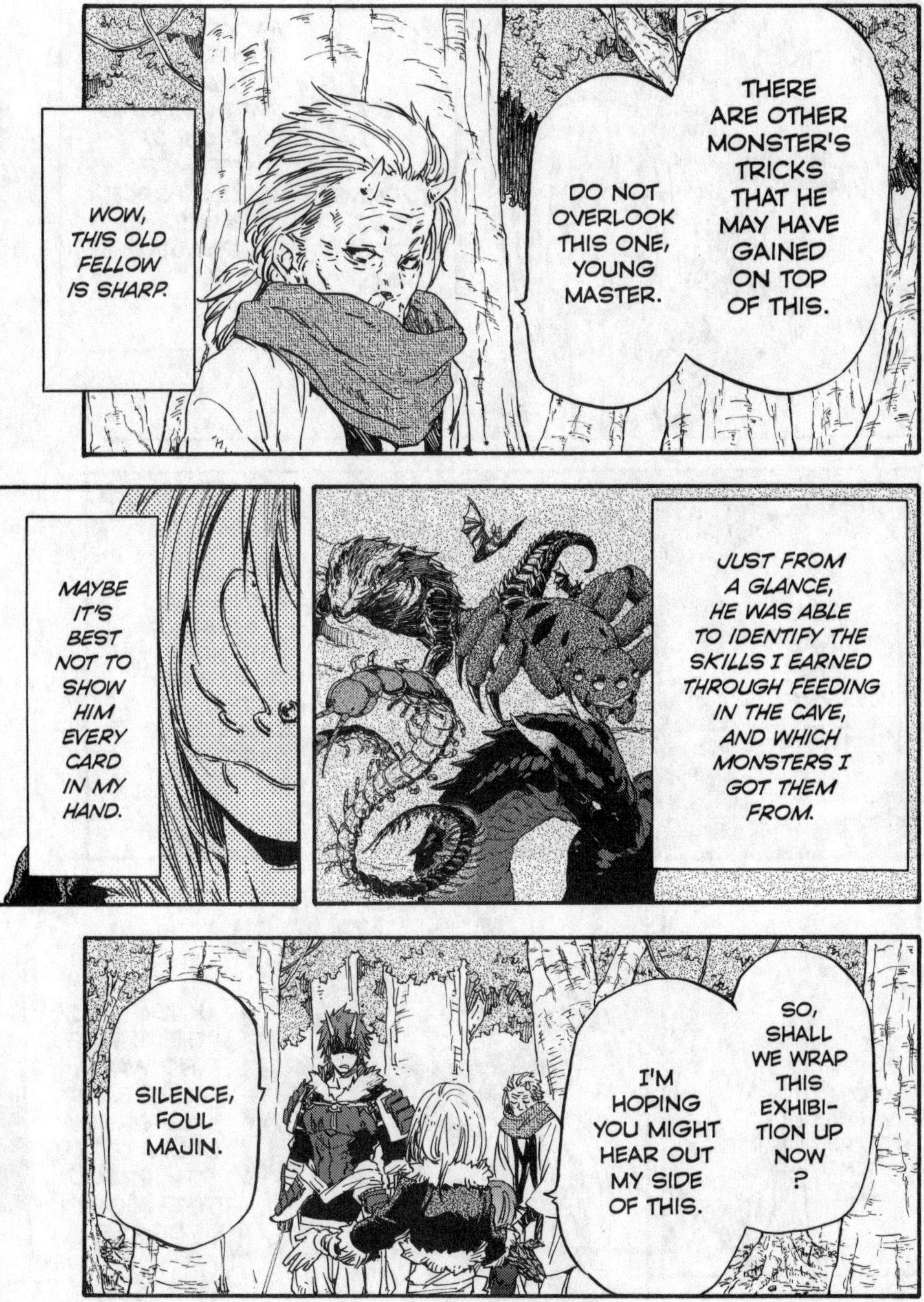
DO NOT OVERLOOK THIS ONE, YOUNG MASTER.
THERE ARE OTHER MONSTER'S TRICKS THAT HE MAY HAVE GAINED ON TOP OF THIS.
WOW, THIS OLD FELLOW IS SHARP.
JUST FROM A GLANCE, HE WAS ABLE TO IDENTIFY THE SKILLS I EARNED THROUGH FEEDING IN THE CAVE, AND WHICH MONSTERS I GOT THEM FROM.
MAYBE IT'S BEST NOT TO SHOW HIM EVERY CARD IN MY HAND.
I'M HOPING YOU MIGHT HEAR OUT MY SIDE OF THIS.
SO, SHALL WE WRAP THIS EXHIBITION UP NOW?
SILENCE, FOUL MAJIN.

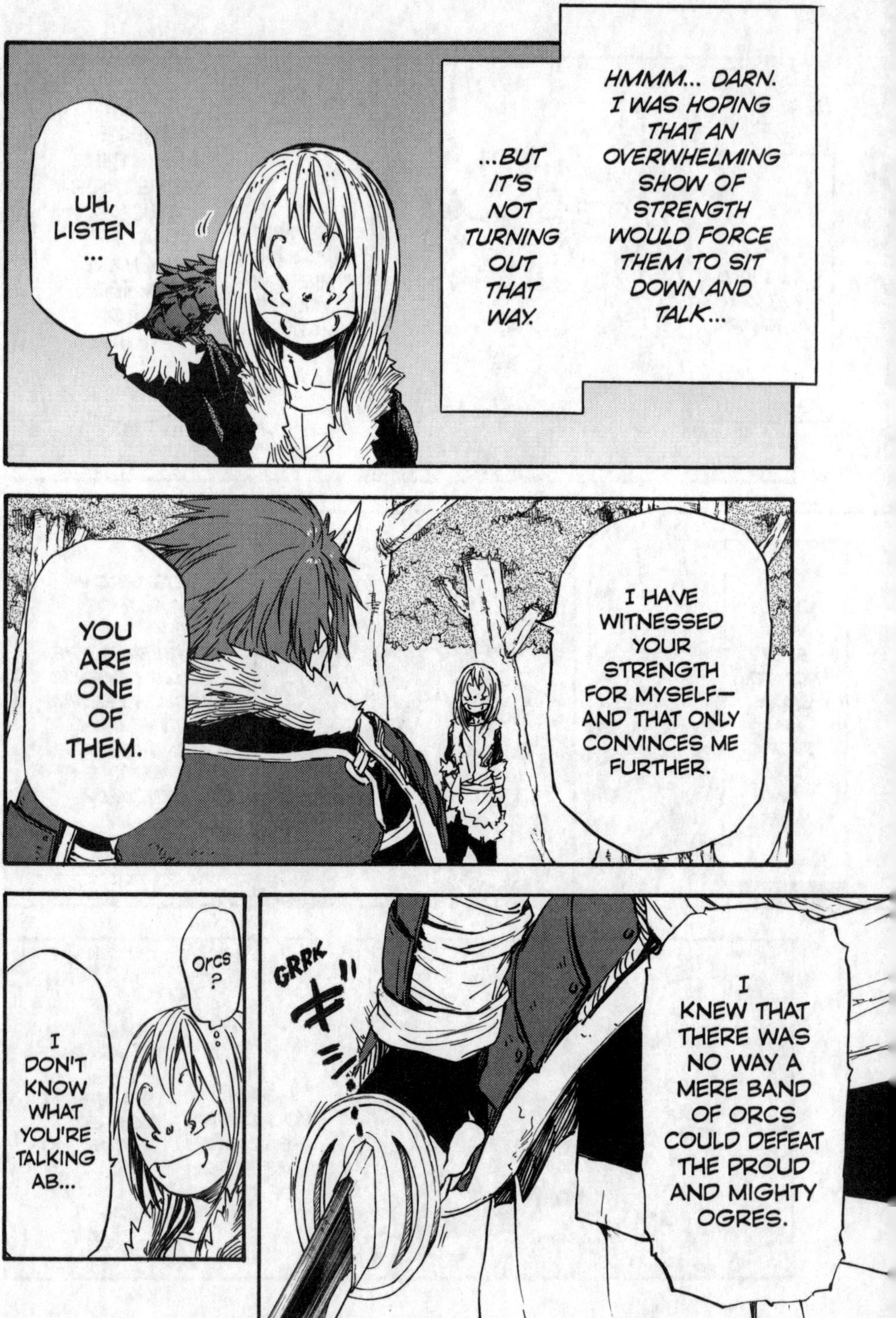
HMMM... DARN. I WAS HOPING THAT AN OVERWHELMING SHOW OF STRENGTH WOULD FORCE THEM TO SIT DOWN AND TALK...
...BUT IT'S NOT TURNING OUT THAT WAY.
UH, LISTEN ...
I HAVE WITNESSED YOUR STRENGTH FOR MYSELF— AND THAT ONLY CONVINCES ME FURTHER.
YOU ARE ONE OF THEM.
I KNEW THAT THERE WAS NO WAY A MERE BAND OF ORCS COULD DEFEAT THE PROUD AND MIGHTY OGRES.
GRRK
Orcs?
I DON'T KNOW WHAT YOU'RE TALKING AB...

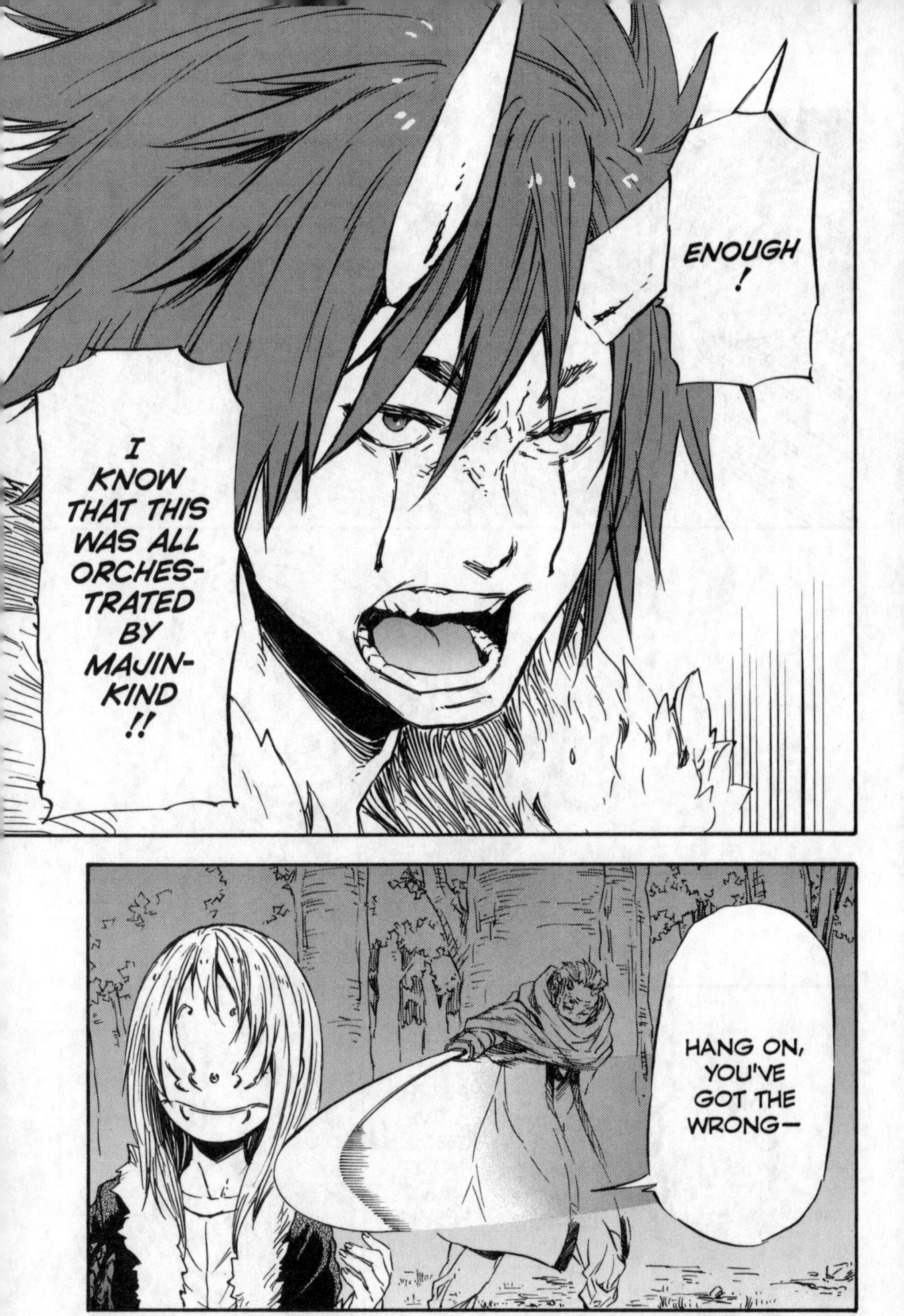
ENOUGH!
I KNOW THAT THIS WAS ALL ORCHES-TRATED BY MAJIN-KIND!!
HANG ON, YOU'VE GOT THE WRONG—

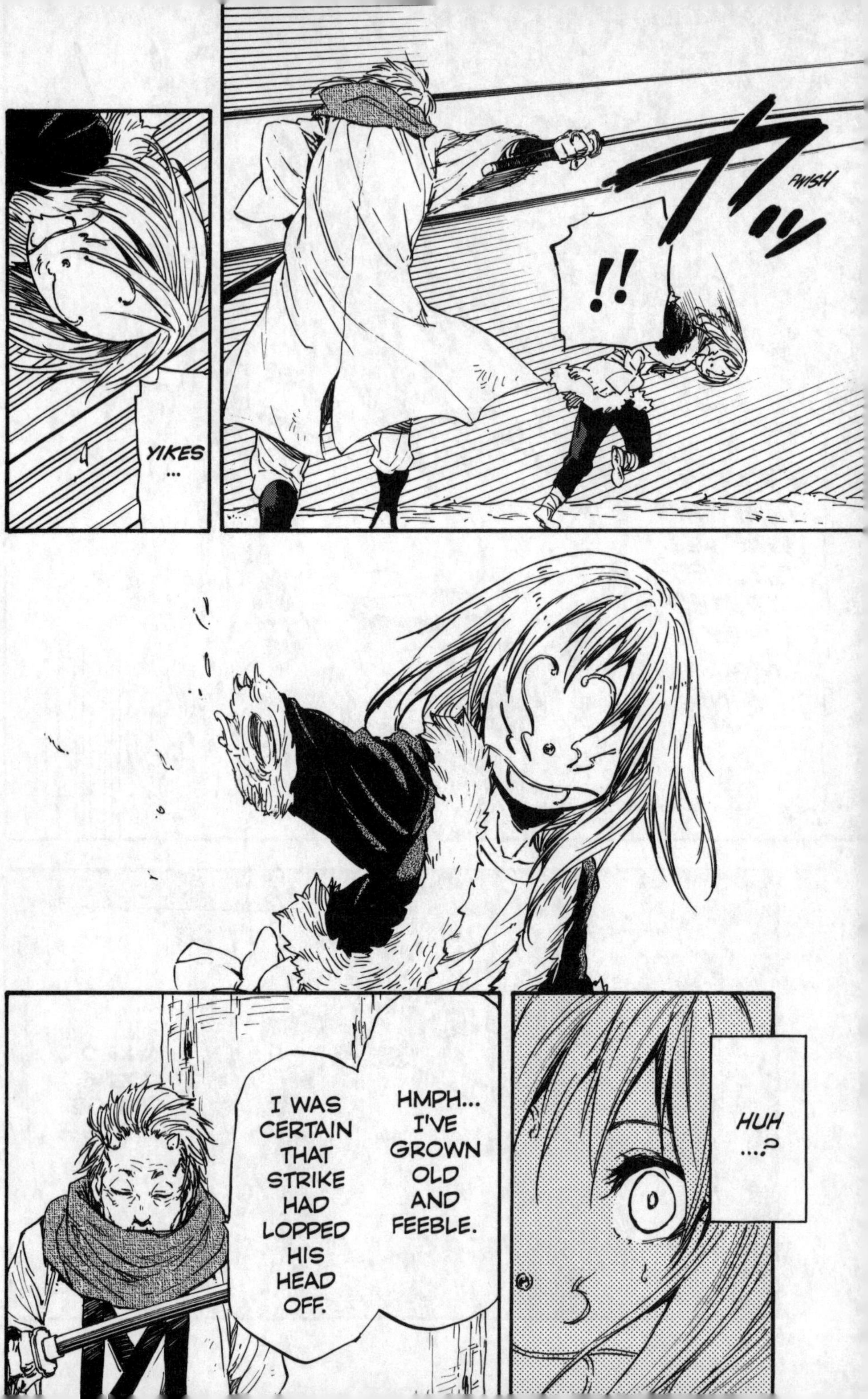
FWISH
!!
YIKES...
HUH...?
HMPH... I'VE GROWN OLD AND FEEBLE.
I WAS CERTAIN THAT STRIKE HAD LOPPED HIS HEAD OFF.

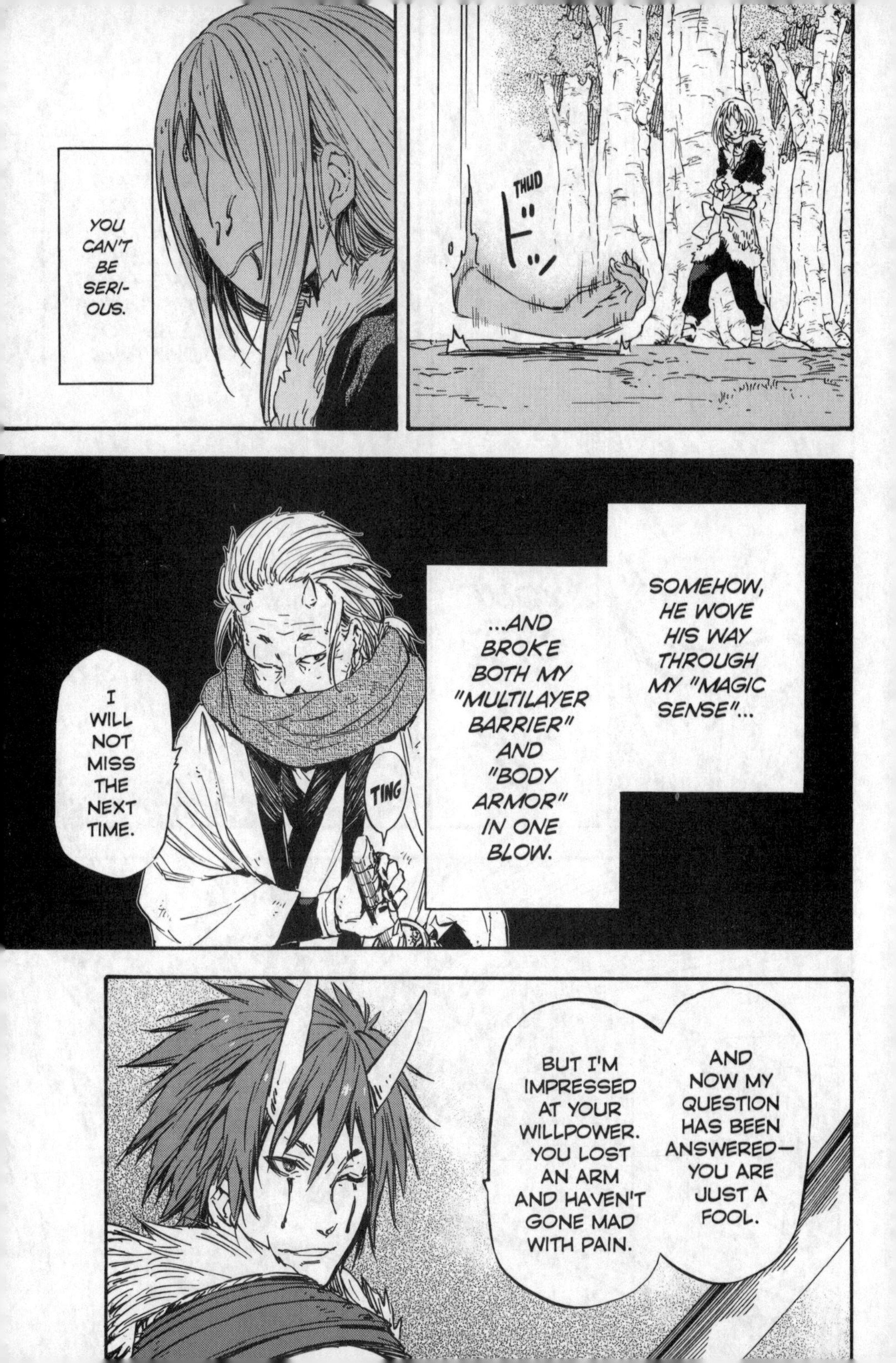
THUD
YOU CAN'T BE SERIOUS.
SOMEHOW, HE WOVE HIS WAY THROUGH MY "MAGIC SENSE"...
...AND BROKE BOTH MY "MULTILAYER BARRIER" AND "BODY ARMOR" IN ONE BLOW.
TING
I WILL NOT MISS THE NEXT TIME.
AND NOW MY QUESTION HAS BEEN ANSWERED— YOU ARE JUST A FOOL.
BUT I'M IMPRESSED AT YOUR WILLPOWER. YOU LOST AN ARM AND HAVEN'T GONE MAD WITH PAIN.

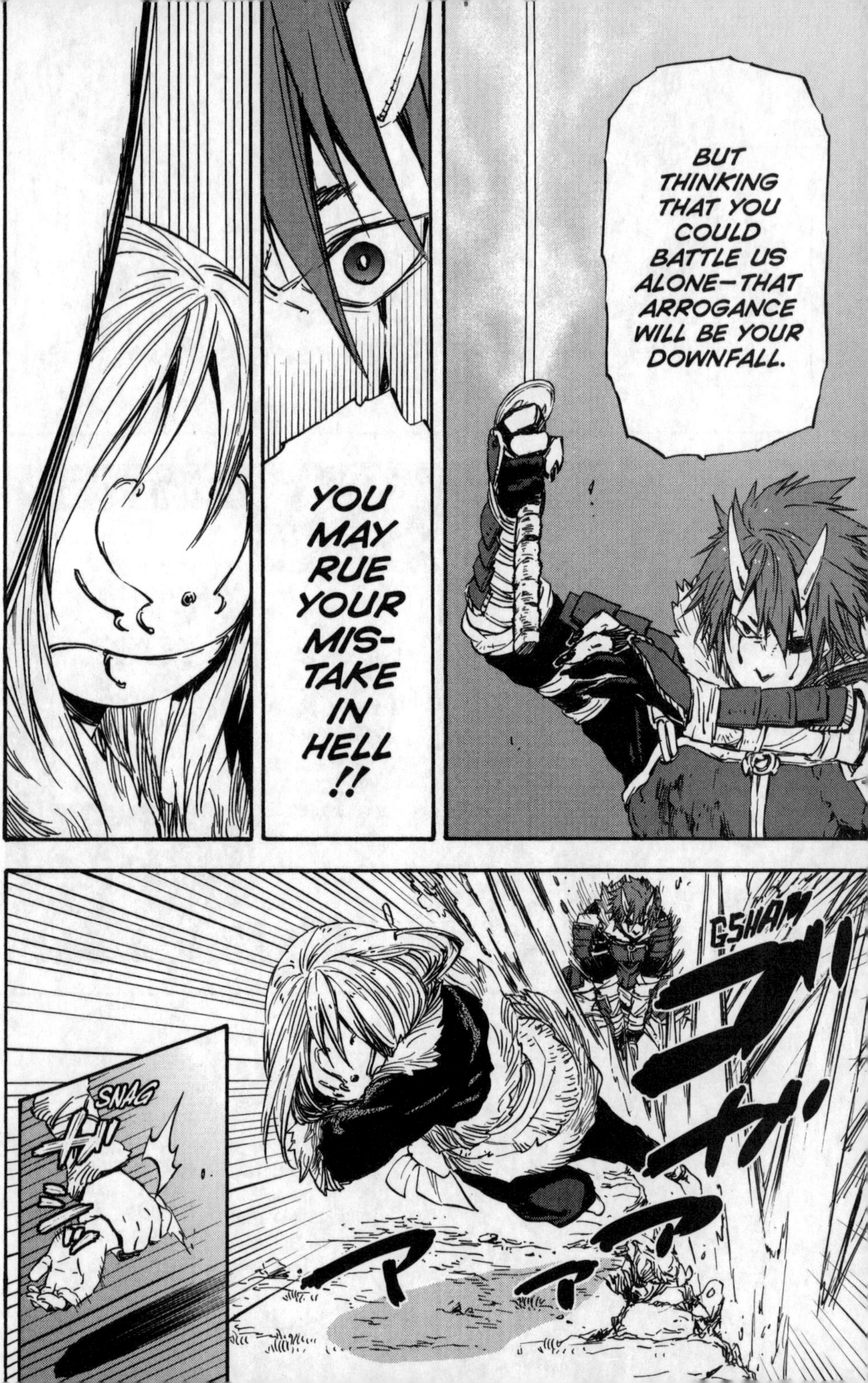
BUT THINKING THAT YOU COULD BATTLE US ALONE—THAT ARROGANCE WILL BE YOUR DOWNFALL.
YOU MAY RUE YOUR MIS-TAKE IN HELL!!
GSHAM
SNAG

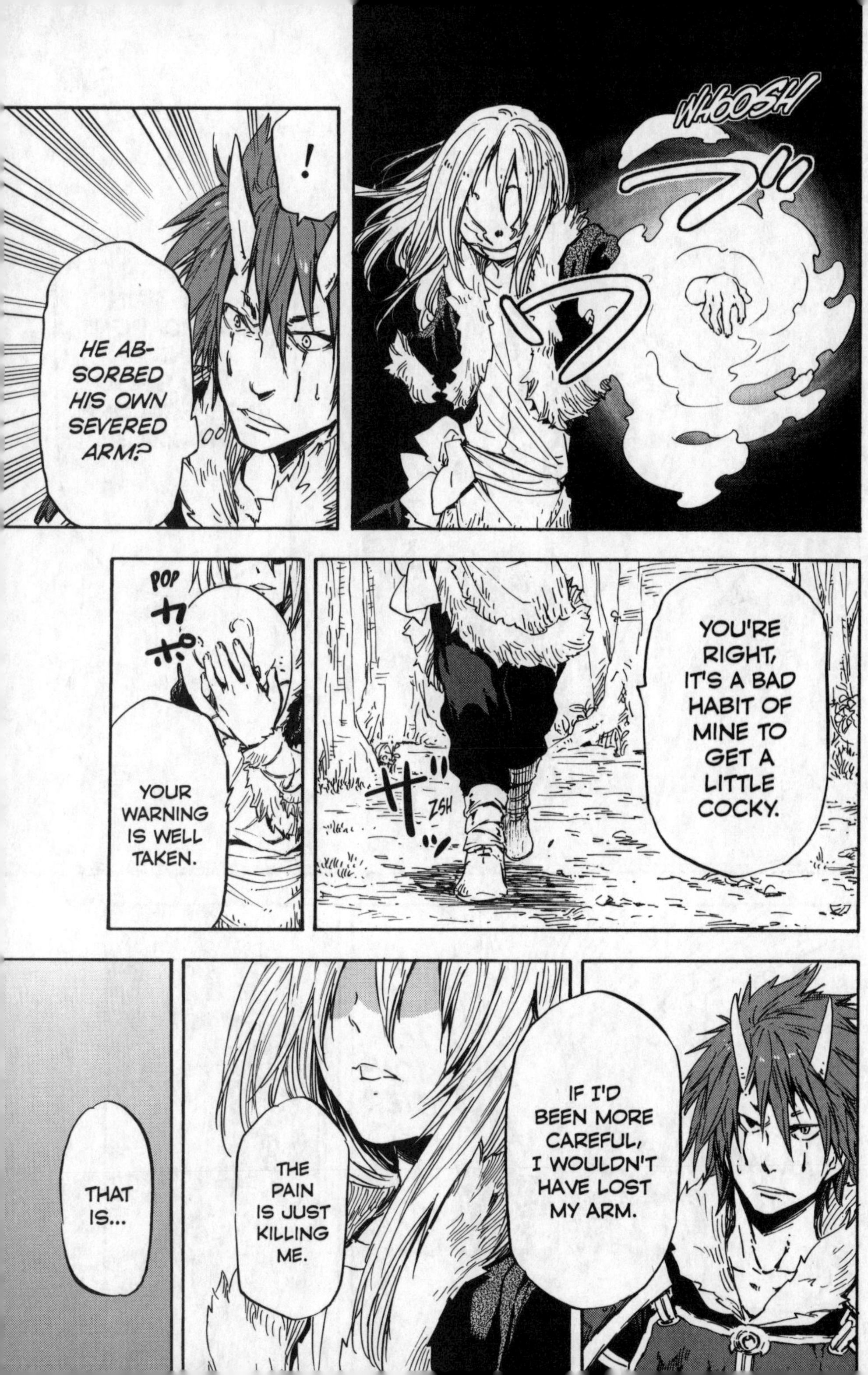
WHOOSH
!
HE ABSORBED HIS OWN SEVERED ARM?
YOU'RE RIGHT, IT'S A BAD HABIT OF MINE TO GET A LITTLE COCKY.
ZSH
POP
YOUR WARNING IS WELL TAKEN.
IF I'D BEEN MORE CAREFUL, I WOULDN'T HAVE LOST MY ARM.
THE PAIN IS JUST KILLING ME.
THAT IS...

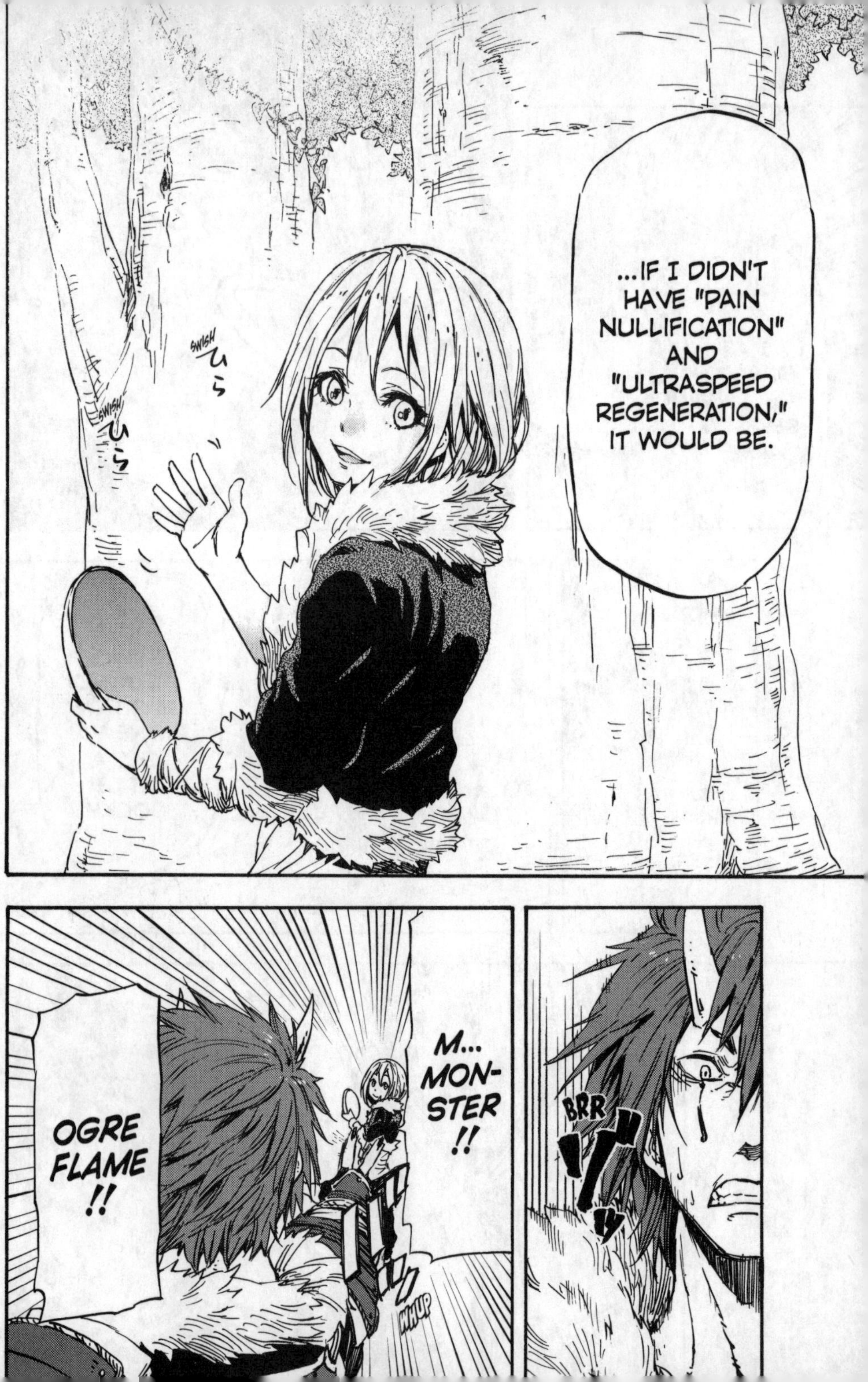

...IF I DIDN'T HAVE "PAIN NULLIFICATION" AND "ULTRASPEED REGENERATION," IT WOULD BE.
SWISH
ひら
SWISH
ひら
BRR
M... MON-STER !!
WHUP
OGRE FLAME !!

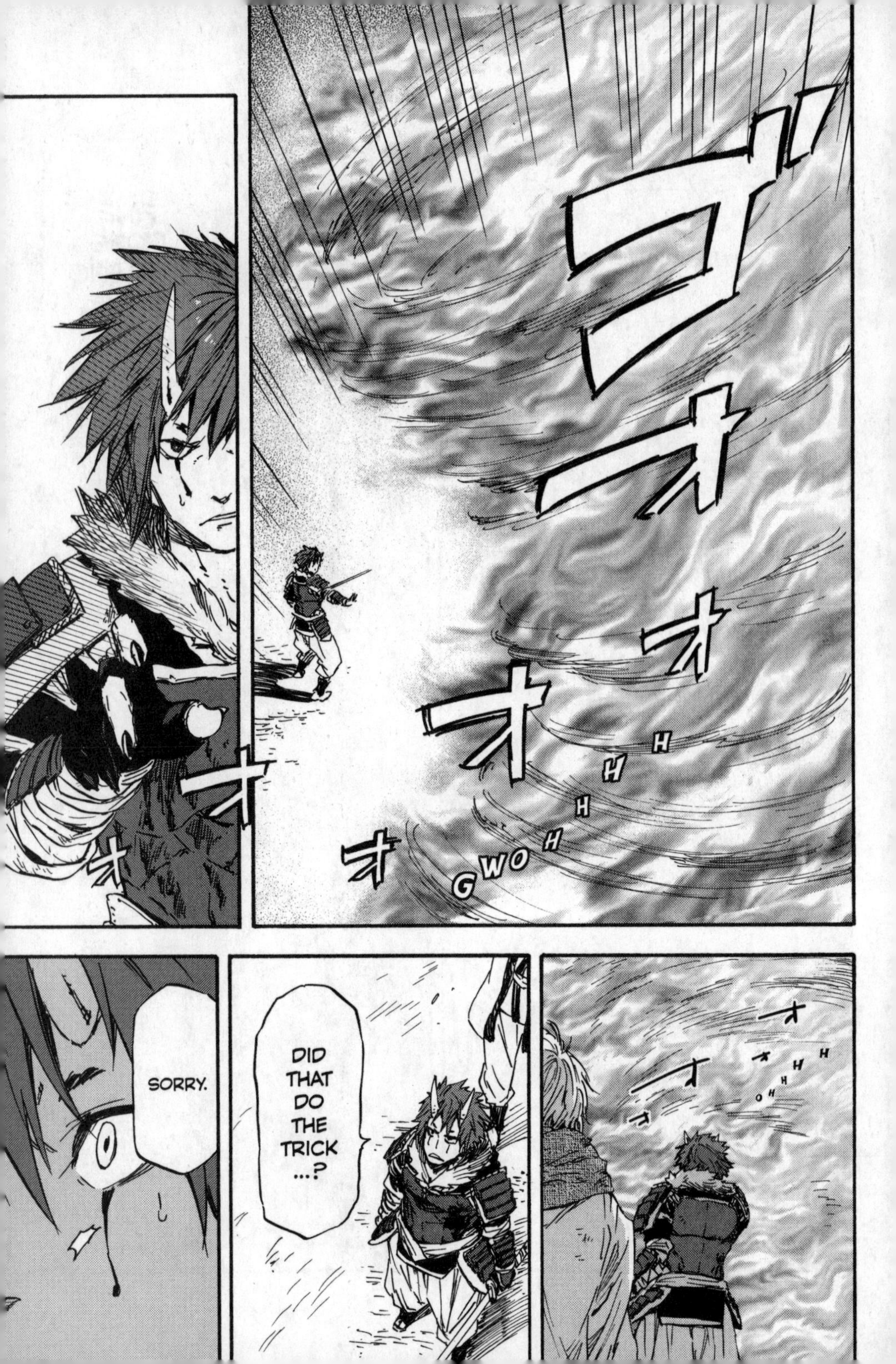
GWOHHHH
OHHHH
DID THAT DO THE TRICK ...?
SORRY.

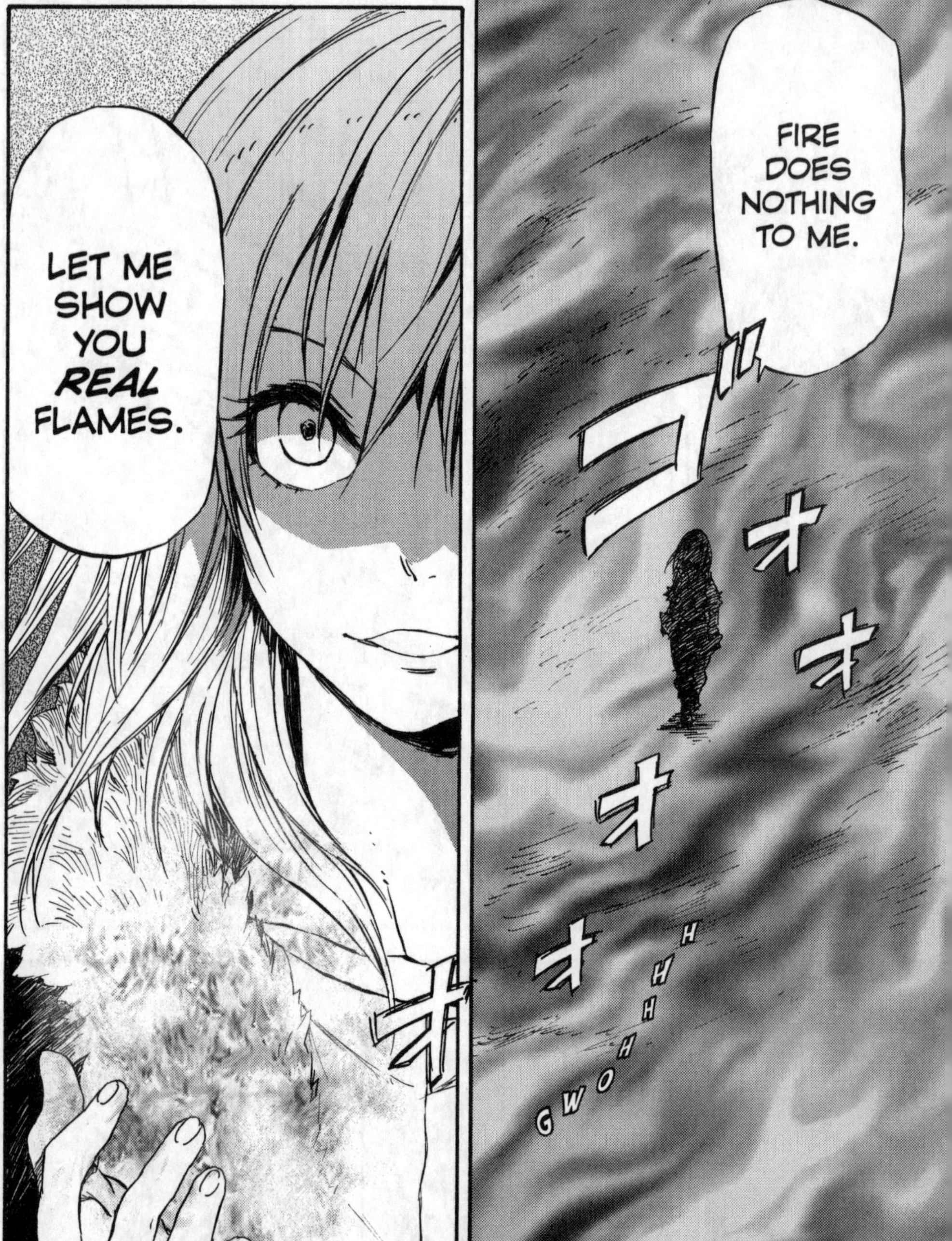
FIRE DOES NOTHING TO ME.
ゴオオオオオ
GWOHHHHH
LET ME SHOW YOU *REAL* FLAMES.

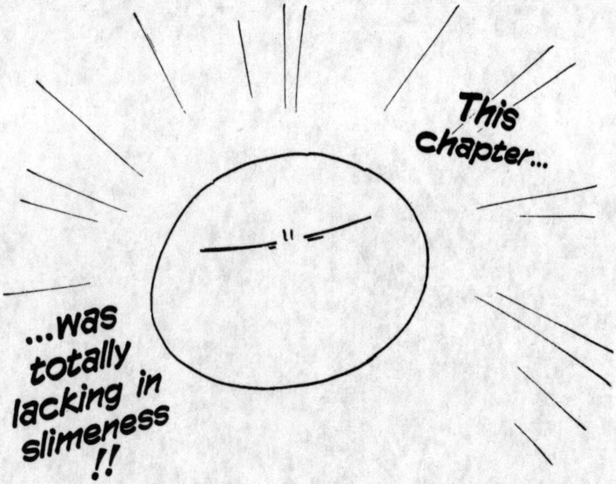
This chapter...
...was totally lacking in slimeness!!

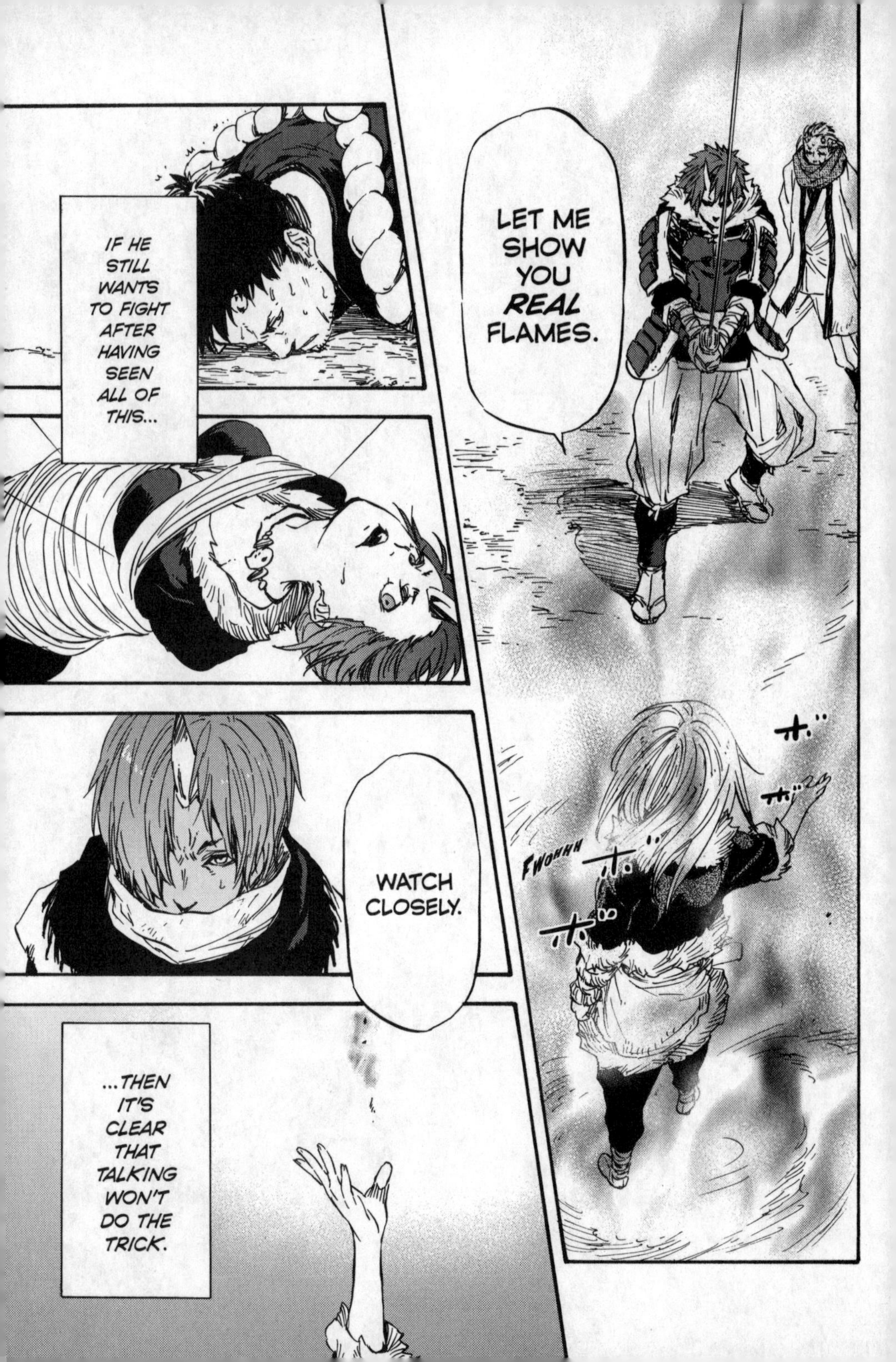
LET ME SHOW YOU *REAL* FLAMES.
FWOHHH
IF HE STILL WANTS TO FIGHT AFTER HAVING SEEN ALL OF THIS...
WATCH CLOSELY.
...THEN IT'S CLEAR THAT TALKING WON'T DO THE TRICK.

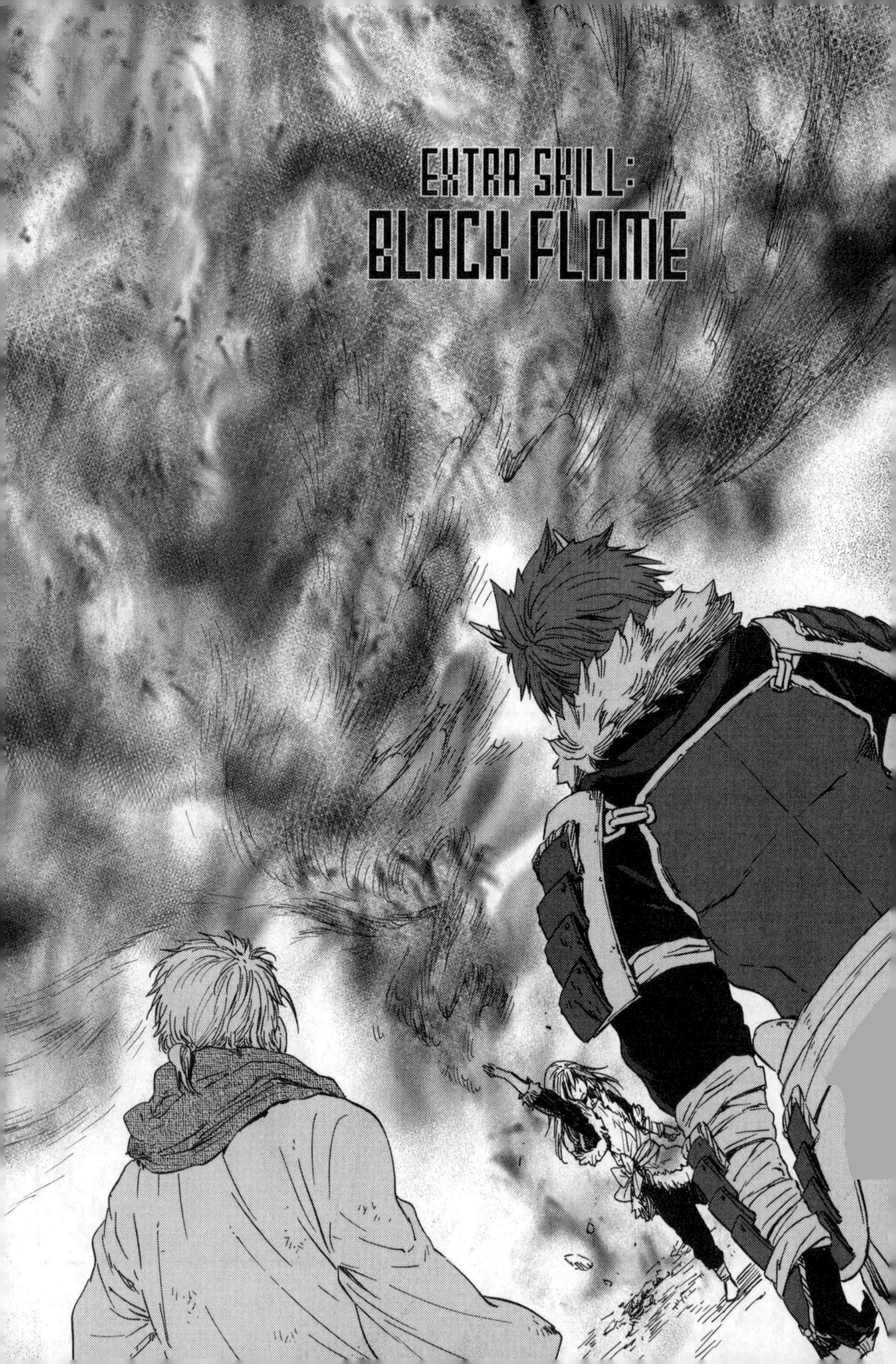
EXTRA SKILL:
BLACK FLAME

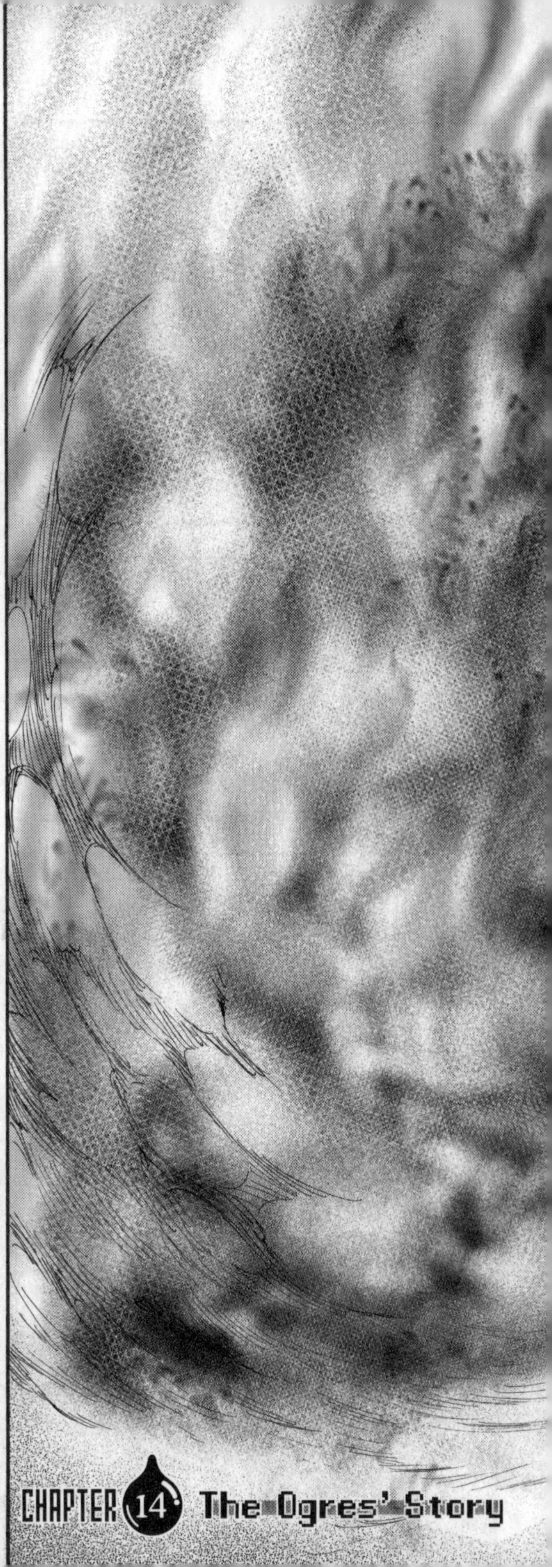
CHAPTER 14 The Ogres' Story
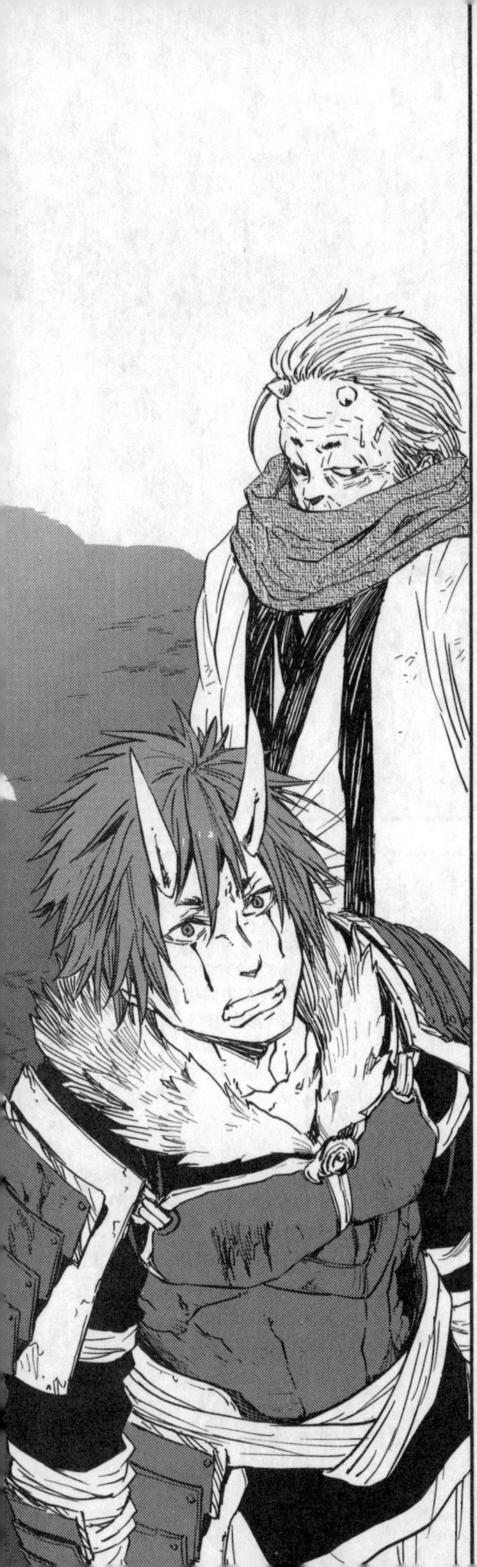

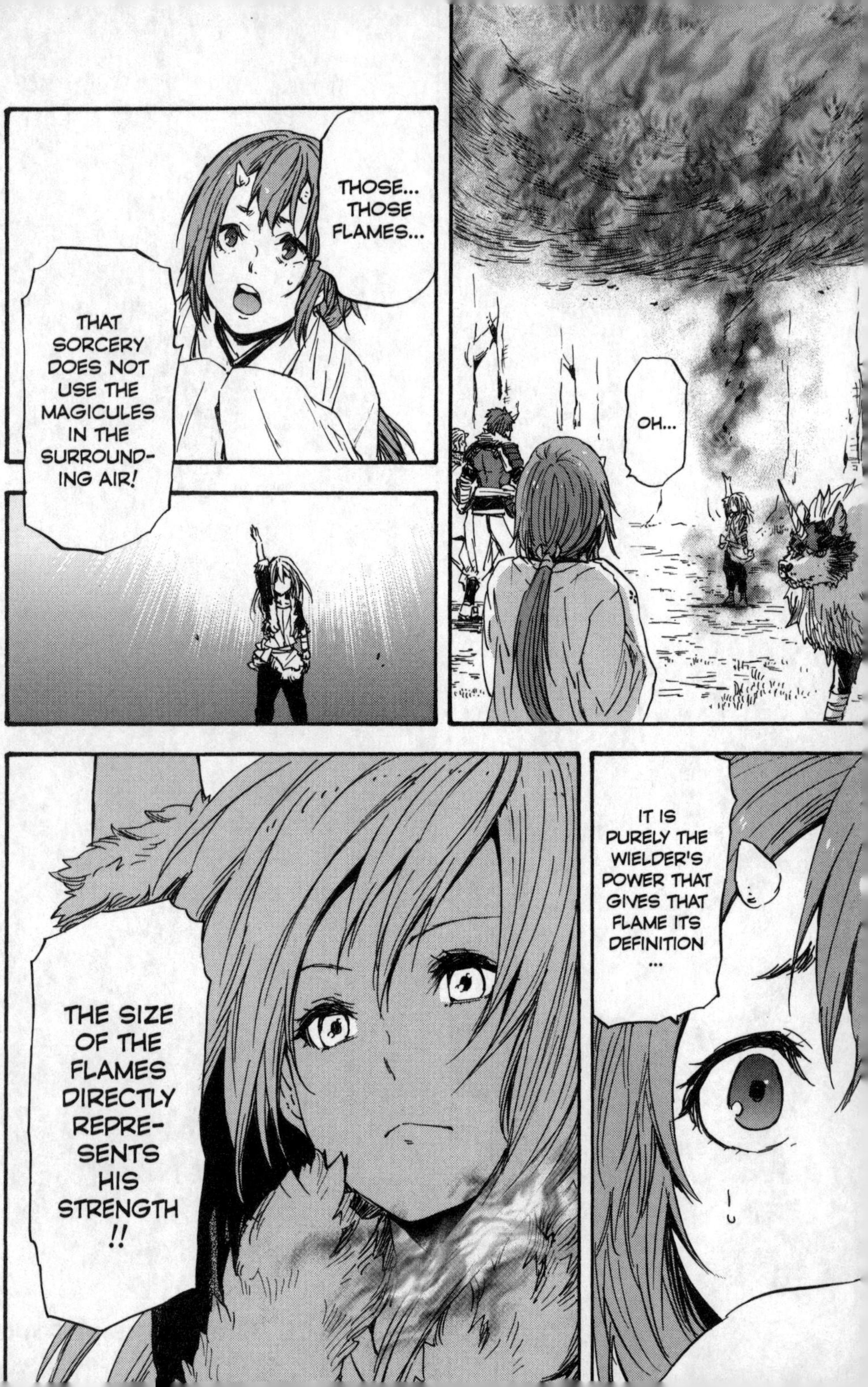
OH...
THOSE... THOSE FLAMES...
THAT SORCERY DOES NOT USE THE MAGICULES IN THE SURROUNDING AIR!
IT IS PURELY THE WIELDER'S POWER THAT GIVES THAT FLAME ITS DEFINITION...
THE SIZE OF THE FLAMES DIRECTLY REPRESENTS HIS STRENGTH!!

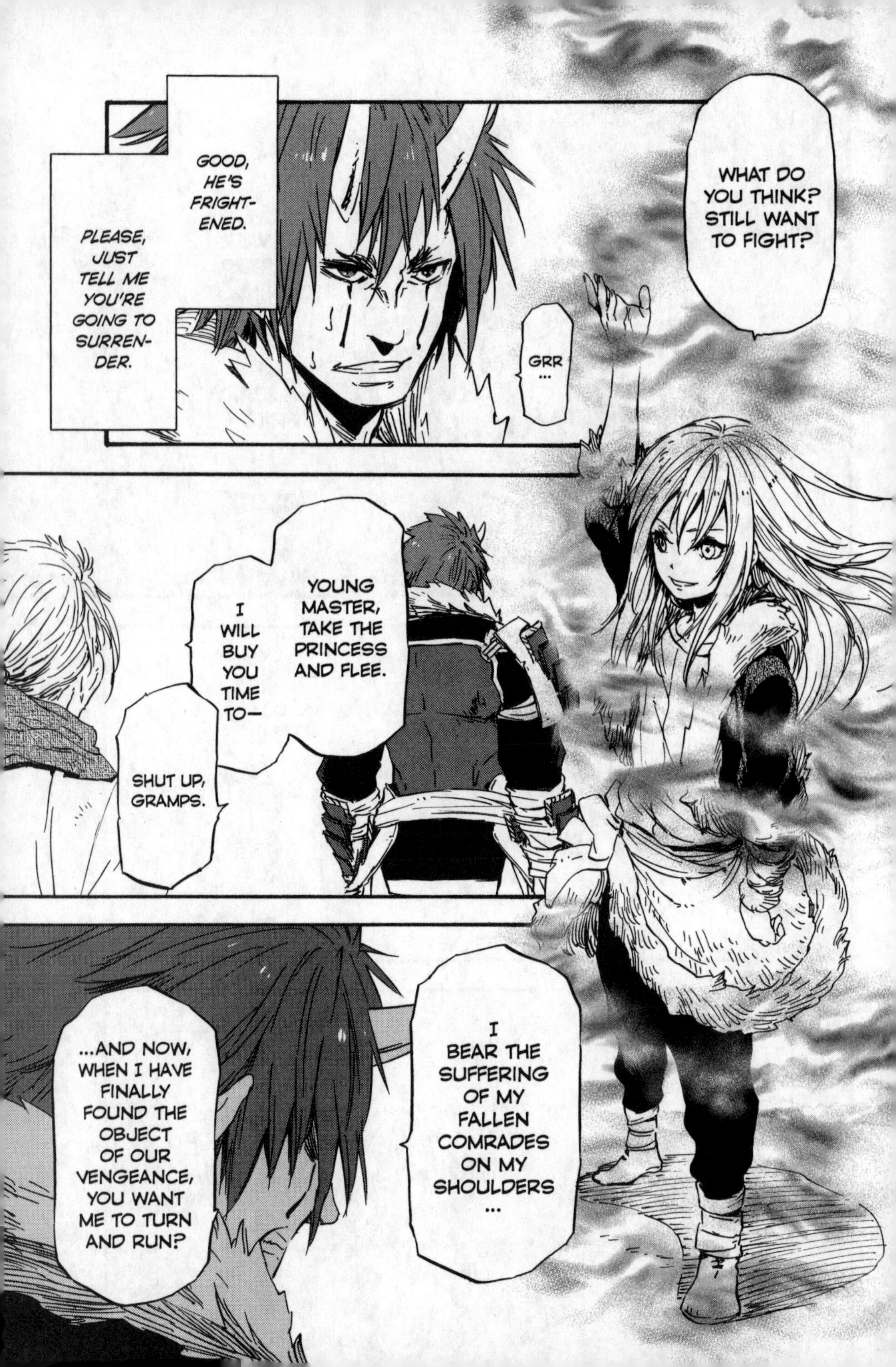
WHAT DO YOU THINK? STILL WANT TO FIGHT?
GRR...
GOOD, HE'S FRIGHT-ENED.
PLEASE, JUST TELL ME YOU'RE GOING TO SURREN-DER.
YOUNG MASTER, TAKE THE PRINCESS AND FLEE.
I WILL BUY YOU TIME TO—
SHUT UP, GRAMPS.
I BEAR THE SUFFERING OF MY FALLEN COMRADES ON MY SHOULDERS...
...AND NOW, WHEN I HAVE FINALLY FOUND THE OBJECT OF OUR VENGEANCE, YOU WANT ME TO TURN AND RUN?

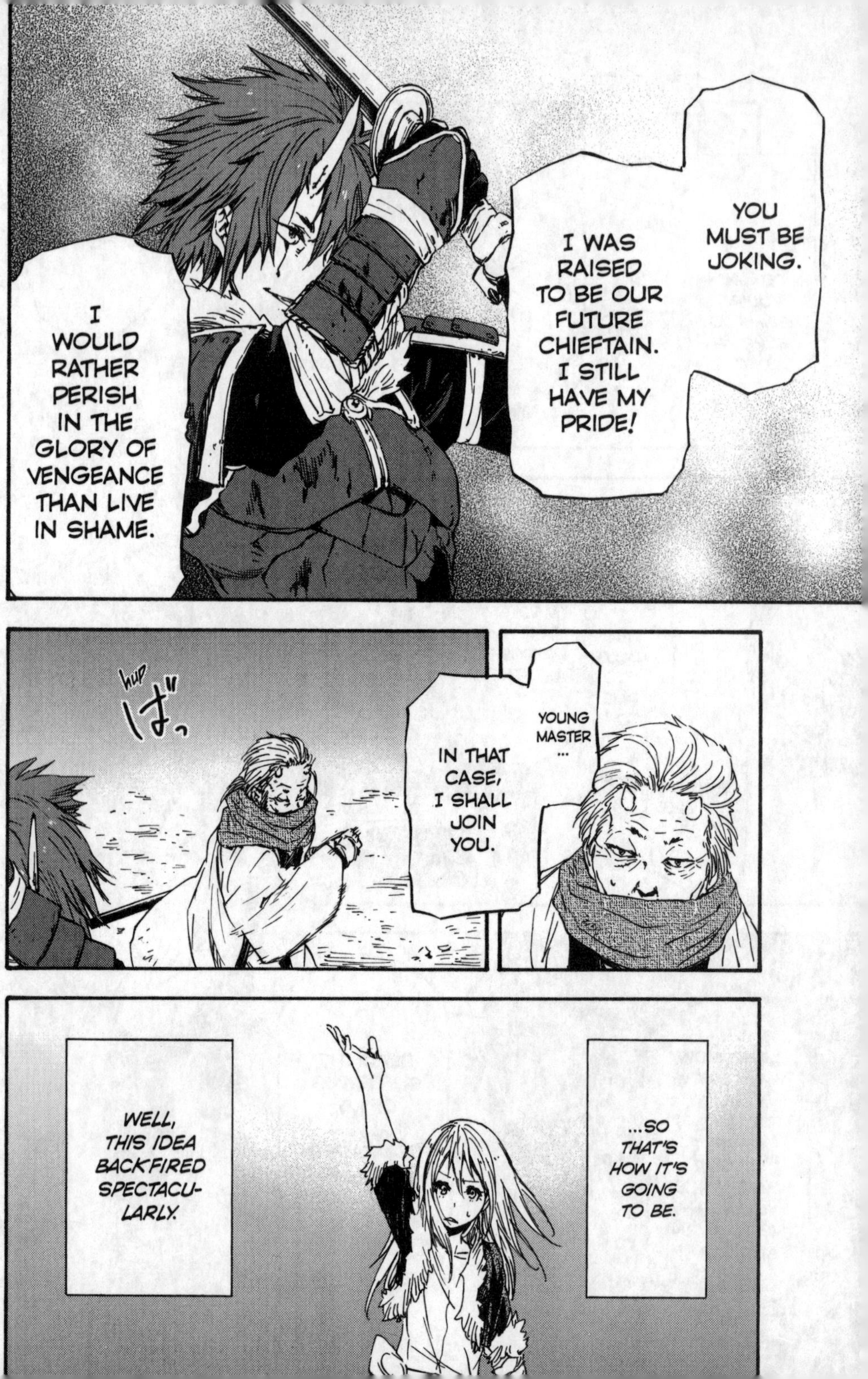
YOU MUST BE JOKING.
I WAS RAISED TO BE OUR FUTURE CHIEFTAIN. I STILL HAVE MY PRIDE!
I WOULD RATHER PERISH IN THE GLORY OF VENGEANCE THAN LIVE IN SHAME.
YOUNG MASTER ...
IN THAT CASE, I SHALL JOIN YOU.
hup
ばっ
...SO THAT'S HOW IT'S GOING TO BE.
WELL, THIS IDEA BACKFIRED SPECTACU-LARLY.

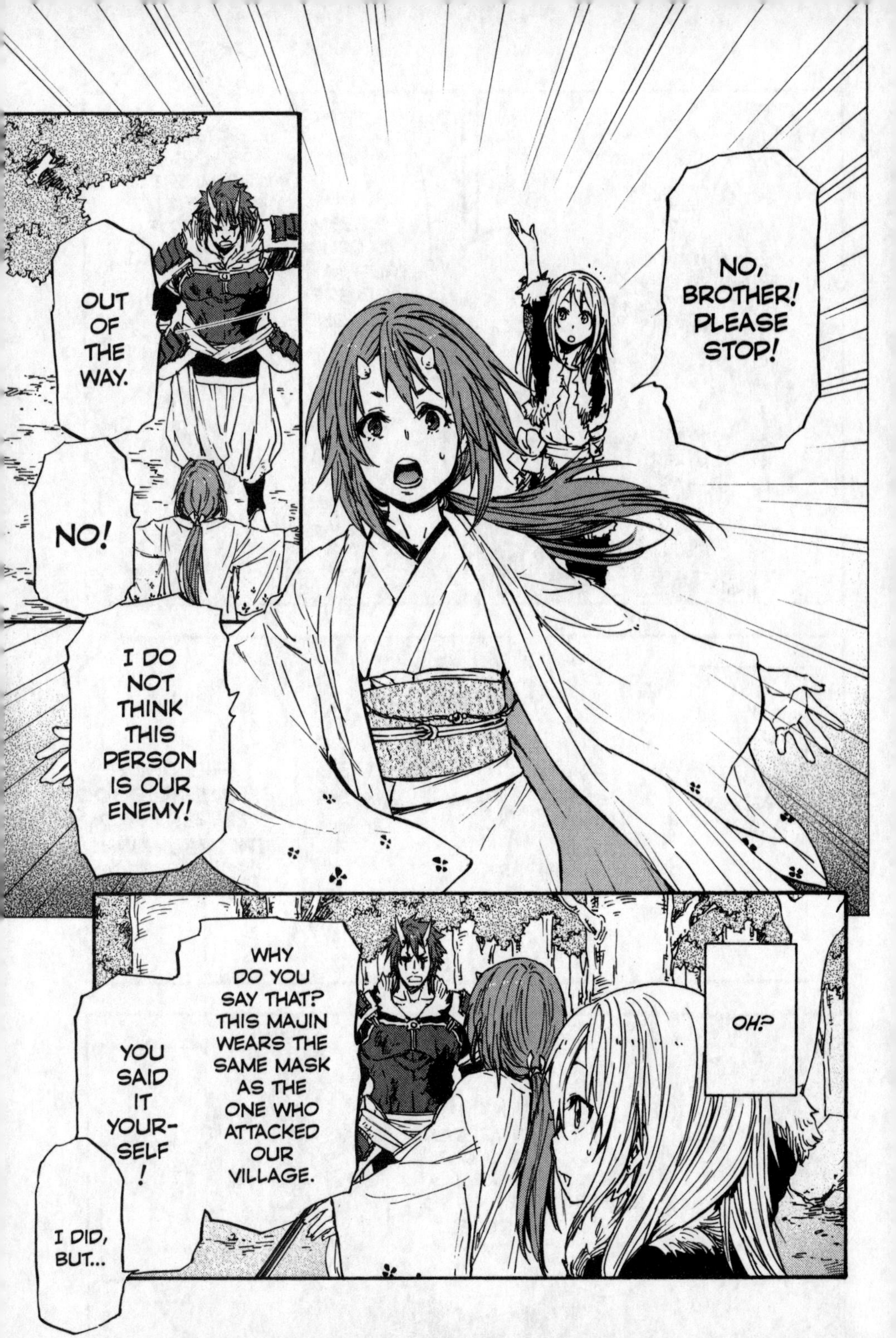
NO, BROTHER! PLEASE STOP!
OUT OF THE WAY.
NO!
I DO NOT THINK THIS PERSON IS OUR ENEMY!
OH?
WHY DO YOU SAY THAT? THIS MAJIN WEARS THE SAME MASK AS THE ONE WHO ATTACKED OUR VILLAGE.
YOU SAID IT YOURSELF!
I DID, BUT...

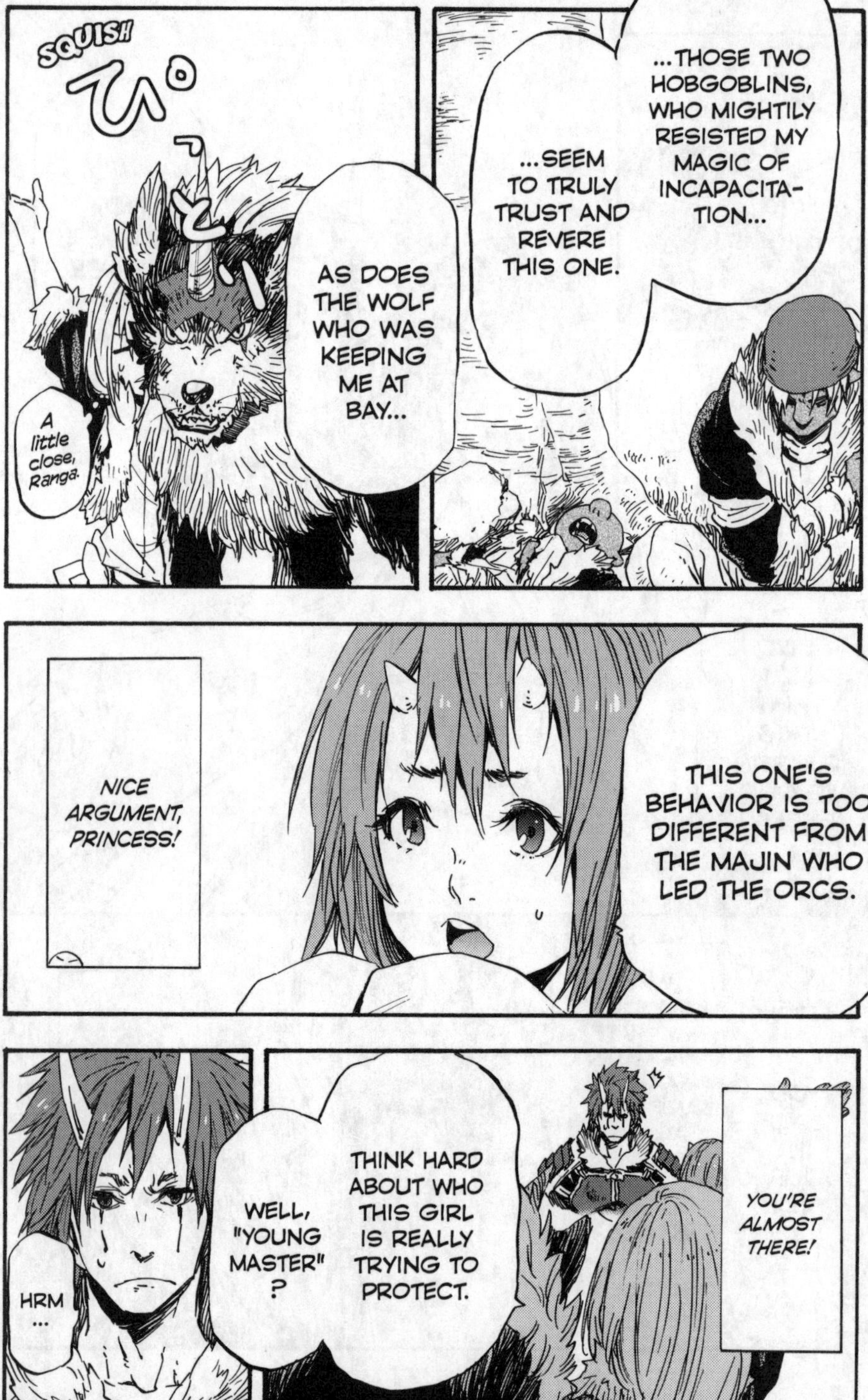
...THOSE TWO HOBGOBLINS, WHO MIGHTILY RESISTED MY MAGIC OF INCAPACITATION...
...SEEM TO TRULY TRUST AND REVERE THIS ONE.
SQUISH
AS DOES THE WOLF WHO WAS KEEPING ME AT BAY...
A little close, Ranga.
THIS ONE'S BEHAVIOR IS TOO DIFFERENT FROM THE MAJIN WHO LED THE ORCS.
NICE ARGUMENT, PRINCESS!
YOU'RE ALMOST THERE!
THINK HARD ABOUT WHO THIS GIRL IS REALLY TRYING TO PROTECT.
WELL, "YOUNG MASTER"?
HRM...

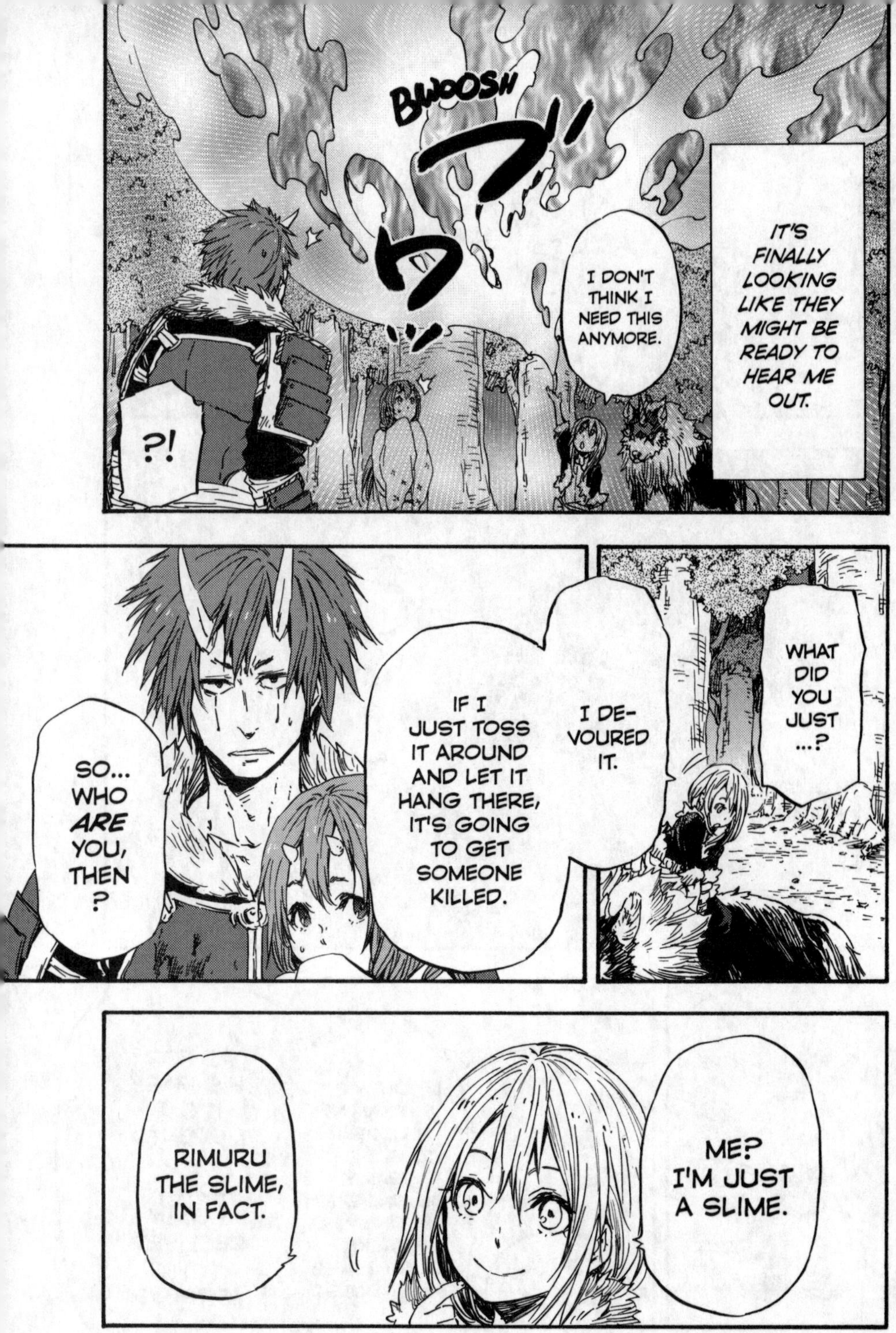
IT'S FINALLY LOOKING LIKE THEY MIGHT BE READY TO HEAR ME OUT.
I DON'T THINK I NEED THIS ANYMORE.
BWOOSH
?!
WHAT DID YOU JUST ...?
I DE-VOURED IT.
IF I JUST TOSS IT AROUND AND LET IT HANG THERE, IT'S GOING TO GET SOMEONE KILLED.
SO... WHO ARE YOU, THEN?
ME? I'M JUST A SLIME.
RIMURU THE SLIME, IN FACT.

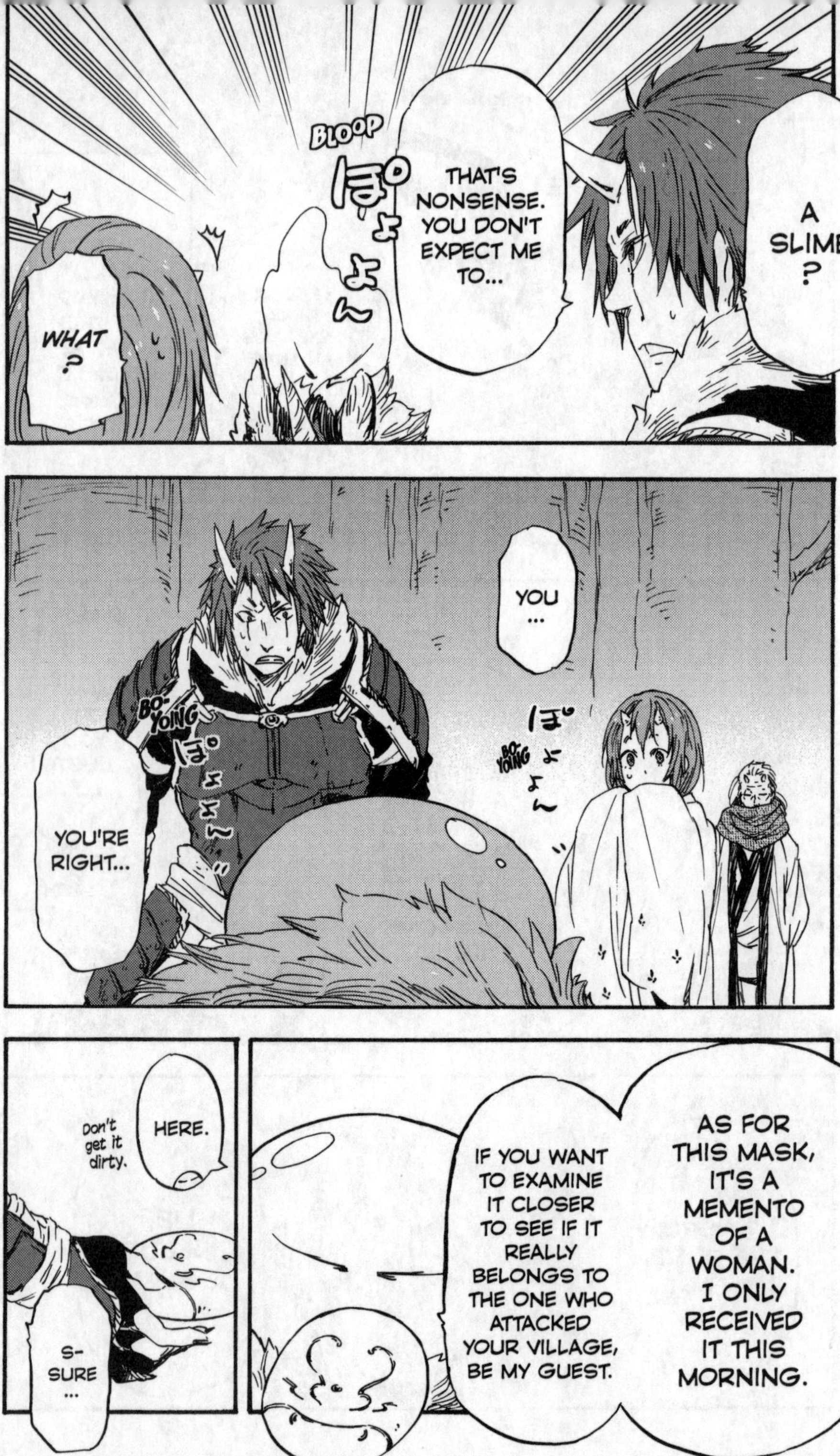
A SLIME?
THAT'S NONSENSE. YOU DON'T EXPECT ME TO...
BLOOP
ぽよよん
WHAT?
YOU...
BO-YOING
ぽよよん
BO-YOING
ぽよよん~
YOU'RE RIGHT...
AS FOR THIS MASK, IT'S A MEMENTO OF A WOMAN. I ONLY RECEIVED IT THIS MORNING.
IF YOU WANT TO EXAMINE IT CLOSER TO SEE IF IT REALLY BELONGS TO THE ONE WHO ATTACKED YOUR VILLAGE, BE MY GUEST.
HERE.
Don't get it dirty.
S-SURE...

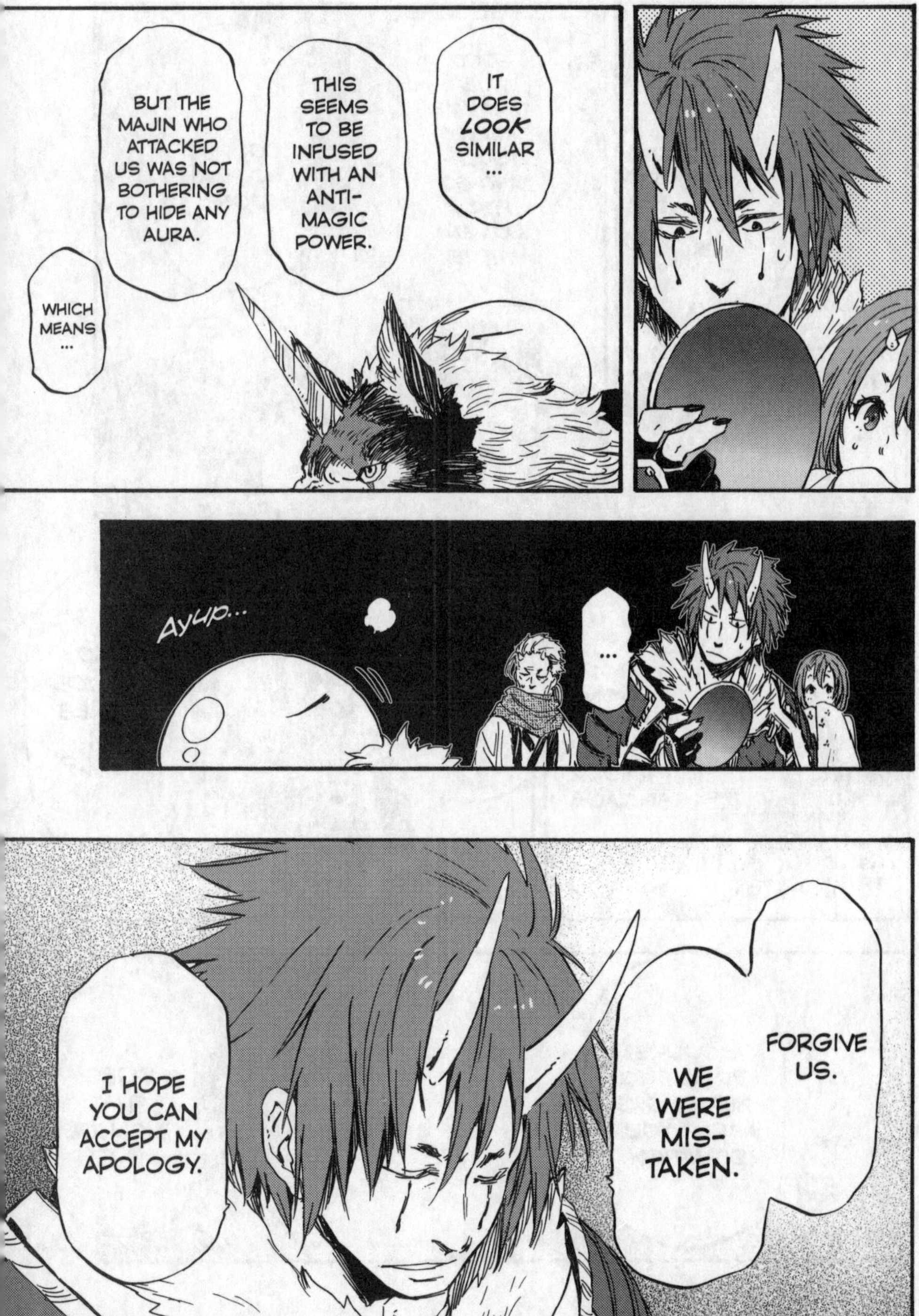
IT DOES *LOOK* SIMILAR ...
THIS SEEMS TO BE INFUSED WITH AN ANTI-MAGIC POWER.
BUT THE MAJIN WHO ATTACKED US WAS NOT BOTHERING TO HIDE ANY AURA.
WHICH MEANS ...
...
Ayup...
FORGIVE US.
WE WERE MIS-TAKEN.
I HOPE YOU CAN ACCEPT MY APOLOGY.

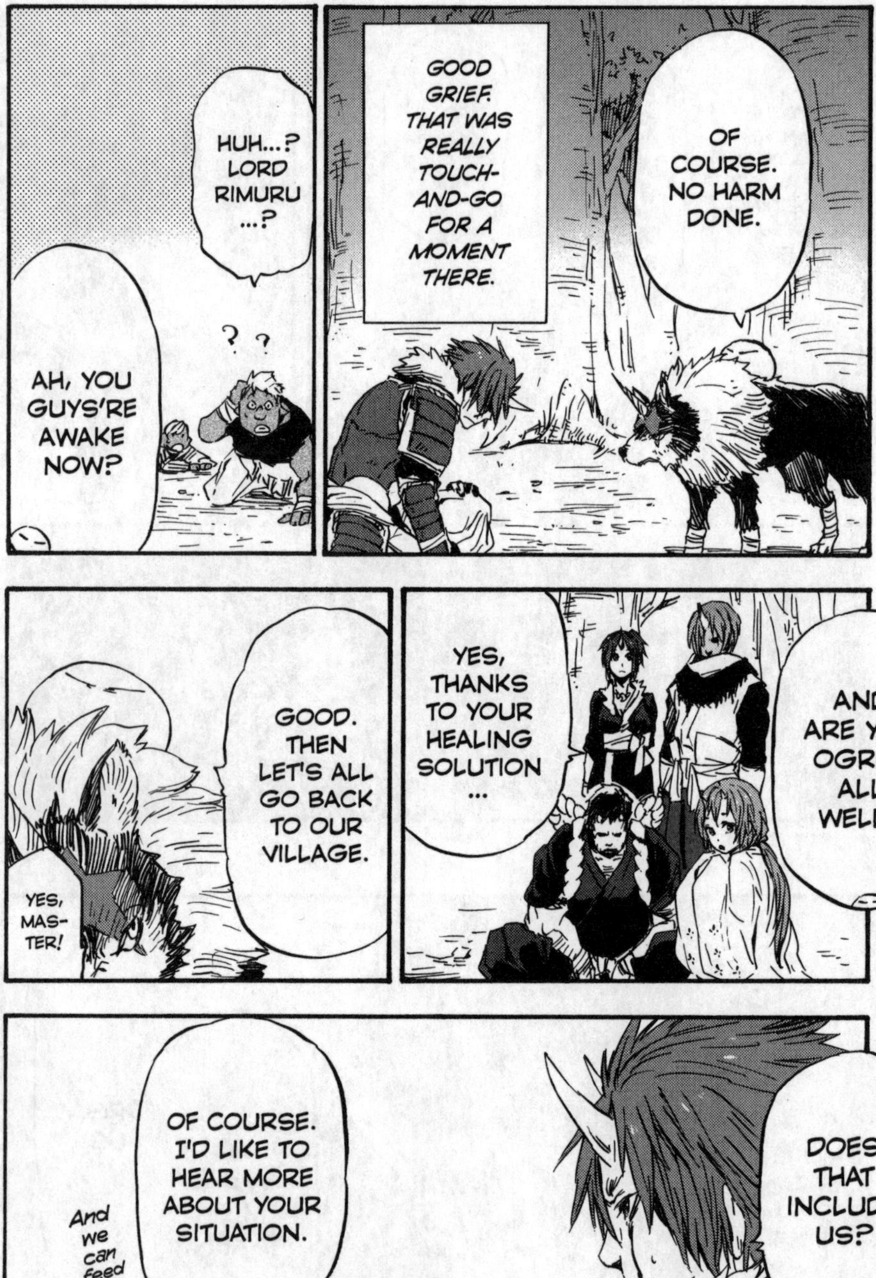
OF COURSE. NO HARM DONE.
GOOD GRIEF. THAT WAS REALLY TOUCH-AND-GO FOR A MOMENT THERE.
HUH...? LORD RIMURU ...?
AH, YOU GUYS'RE AWAKE NOW?
AND ARE YOU OGRES ALL WELL?
YES, THANKS TO YOUR HEALING SOLUTION ...
GOOD. THEN LET'S ALL GO BACK TO OUR VILLAGE.
YES, MASTER!
DOES THAT INCLUDE US?
OF COURSE. I'D LIKE TO HEAR MORE ABOUT YOUR SITUATION.
And we can feed you.

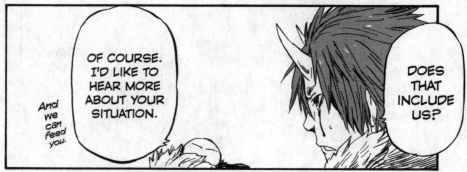

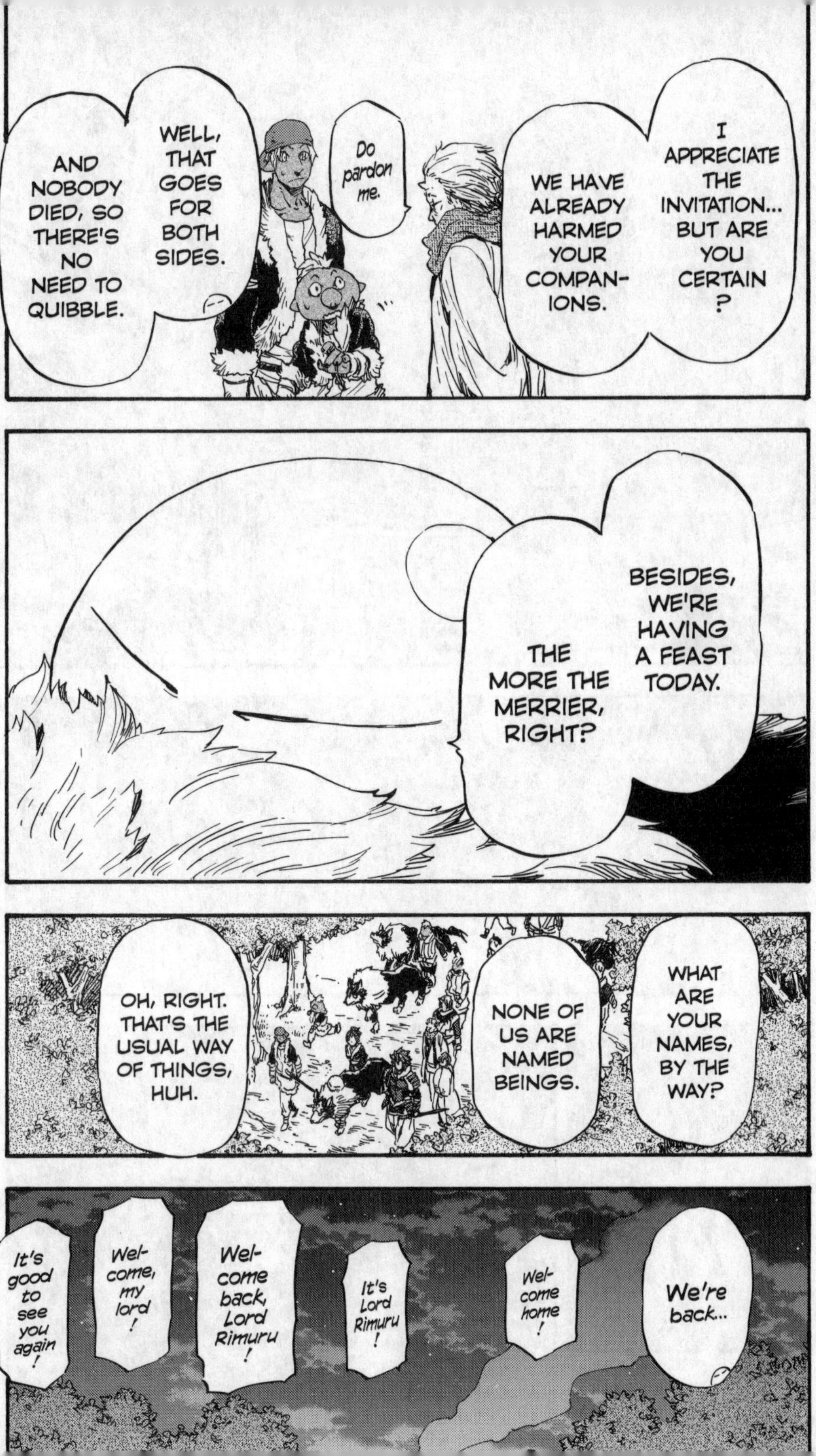
I APPRECIATE THE INVITATION... BUT ARE YOU CERTAIN?
WE HAVE ALREADY HARMED YOUR COMPANIONS.
Do pardon me.
WELL, THAT GOES FOR BOTH SIDES.
AND NOBODY DIED, SO THERE'S NO NEED TO QUIBBLE.
BESIDES, WE'RE HAVING A FEAST TODAY.
THE MORE THE MERRIER, RIGHT?
WHAT ARE YOUR NAMES, BY THE WAY?
NONE OF US ARE NAMED BEINGS.
OH, RIGHT. THAT'S THE USUAL WAY OF THINGS, HUH.
We're back...
Welcome home!
It's Lord Rimuru!
Welcome back, Lord Rimuru!
Welcome, my lord!
It's good to see you again!

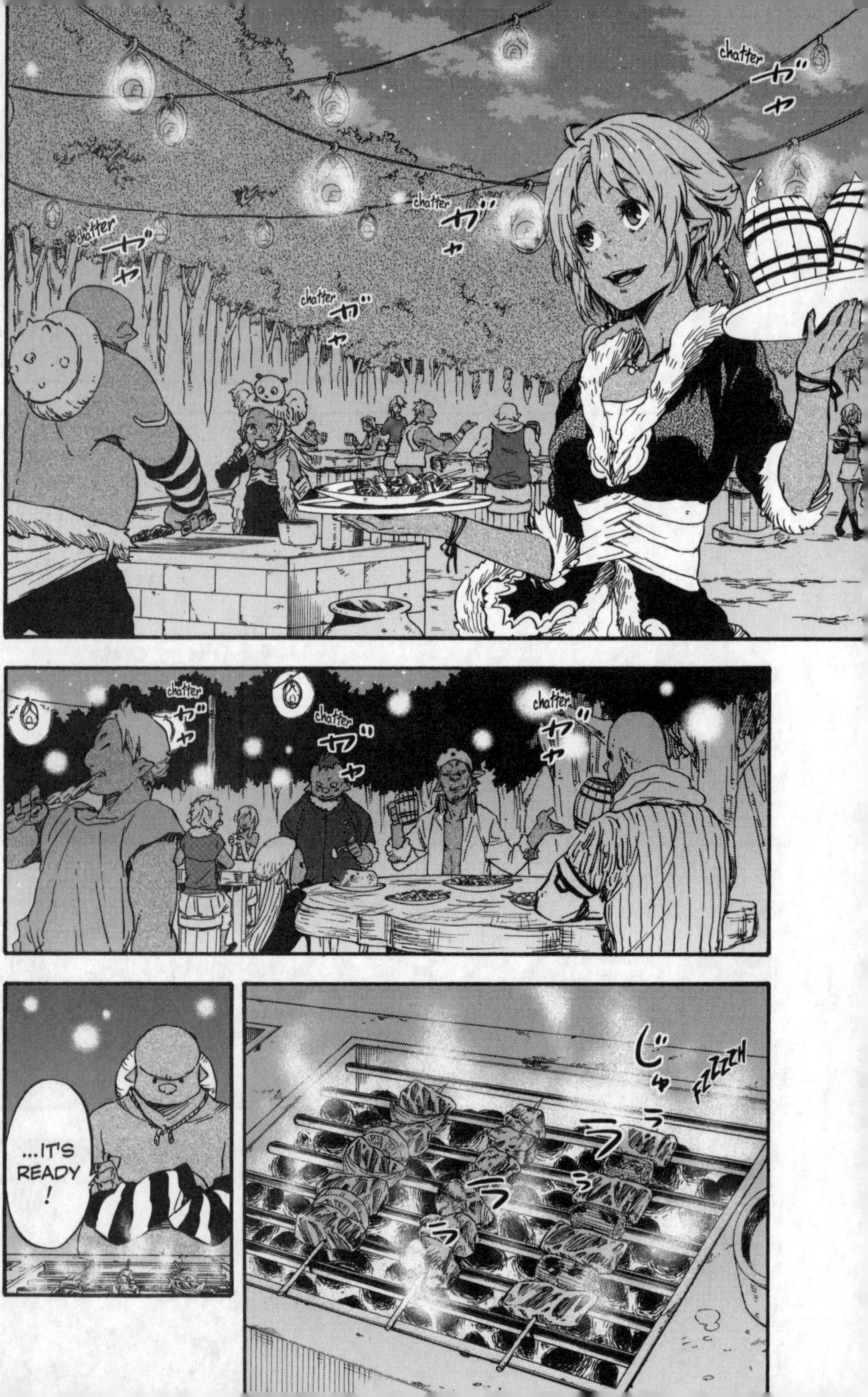
chatter
ガヤ
chatter
ガヤ
chatter
ガヤ
chatter
ガヤ
chatter
ガヤ
chatter
ガヤ
chatter
ガヤ
じゅ
FZZZZH
...IT'S READY!

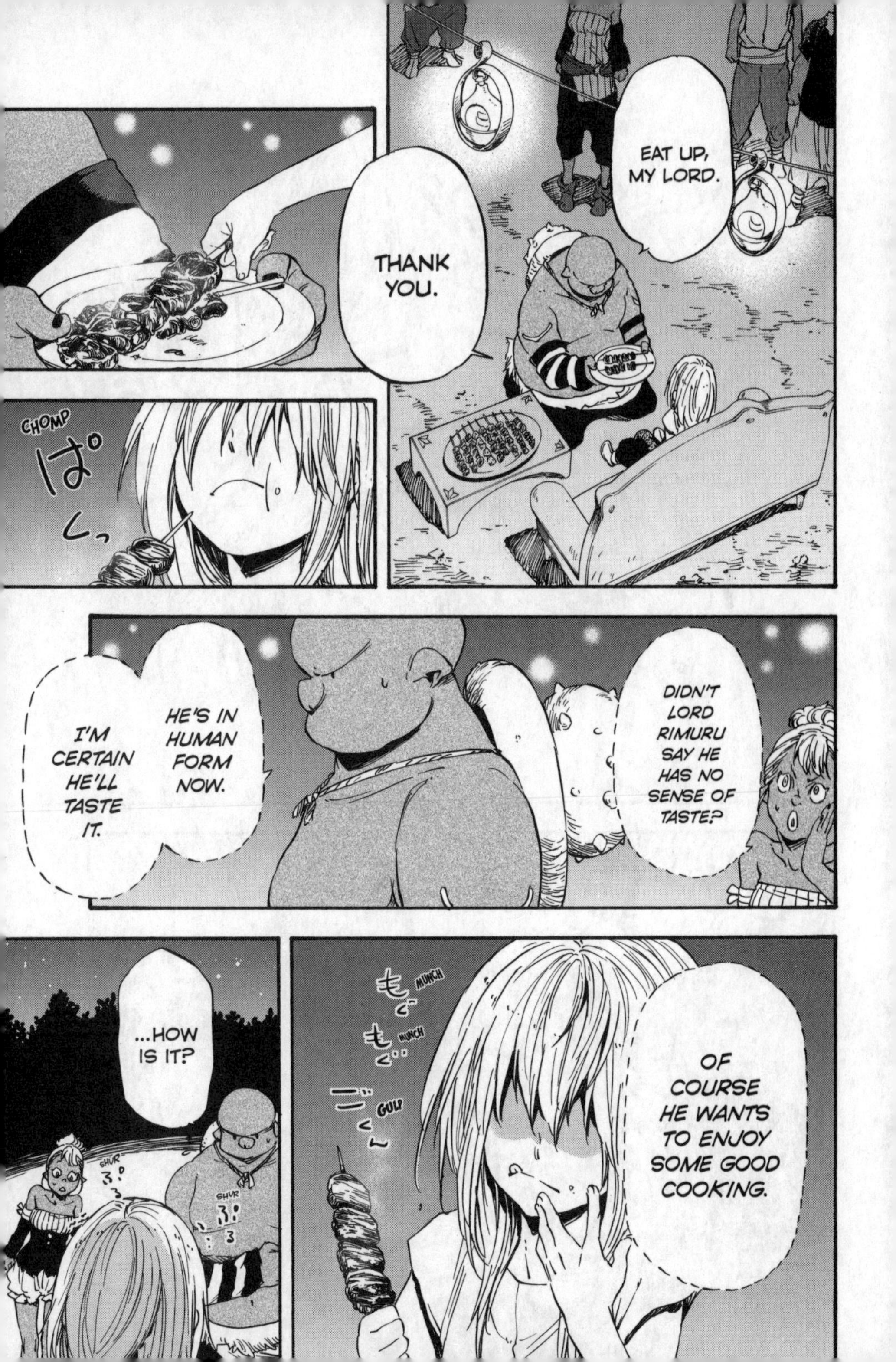
EAT UP, MY LORD.
THANK YOU.
CHOMP
ぱくっ
DIDN'T LORD RIMURU SAY HE HAS NO SENSE OF TASTE?
HE'S IN HUMAN FORM NOW.
I'M CERTAIN HE'LL TASTE IT.
もぐ MUNCH
もぐ MUNCH
ごくん GULP
OF COURSE HE WANTS TO ENJOY SOME GOOD COOKING.
...HOW IS IT?
SHUR
SHUR

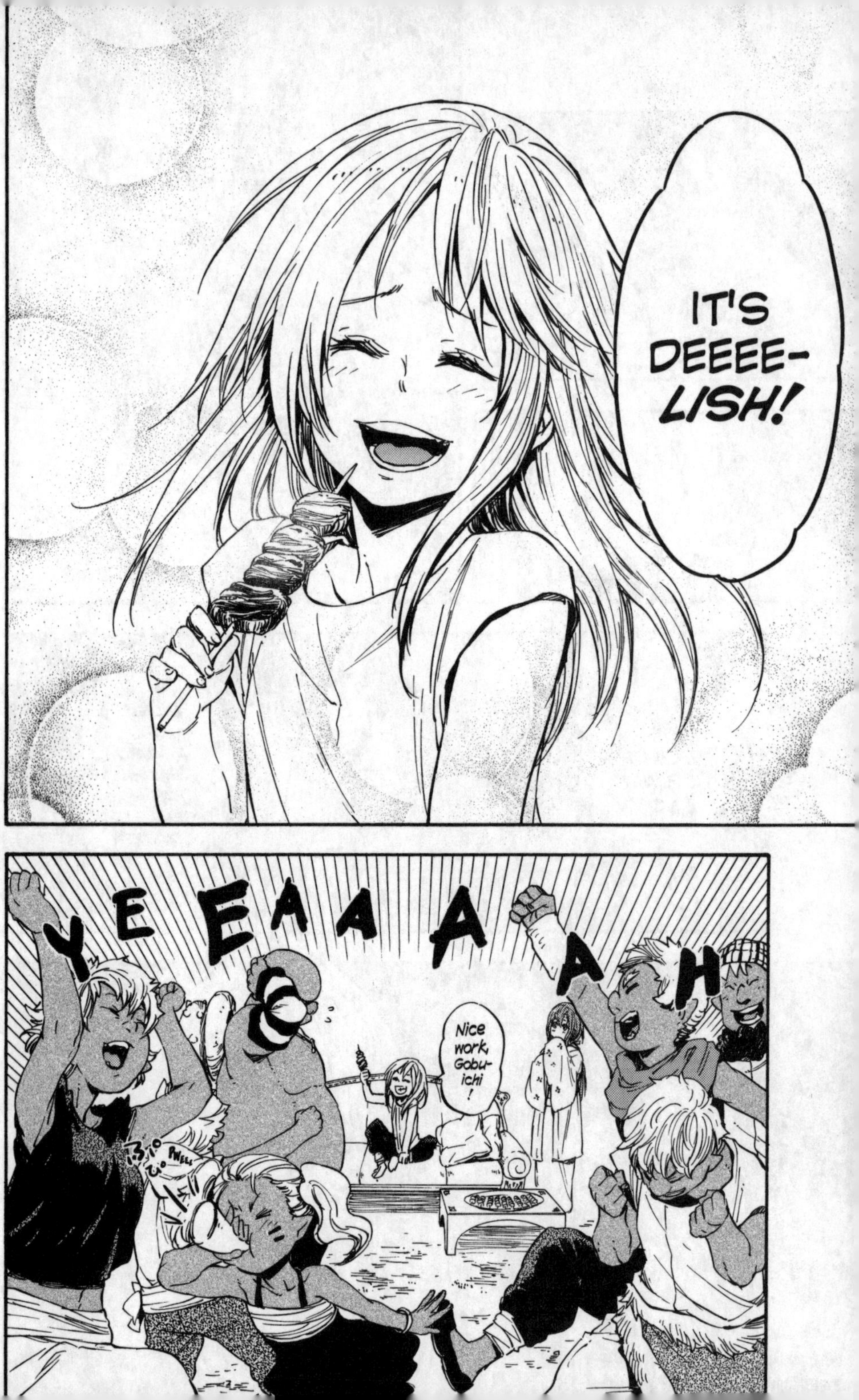
IT'S DEEEE-LISH!
YEAAAAH
Nice work, Gobu-ichi!

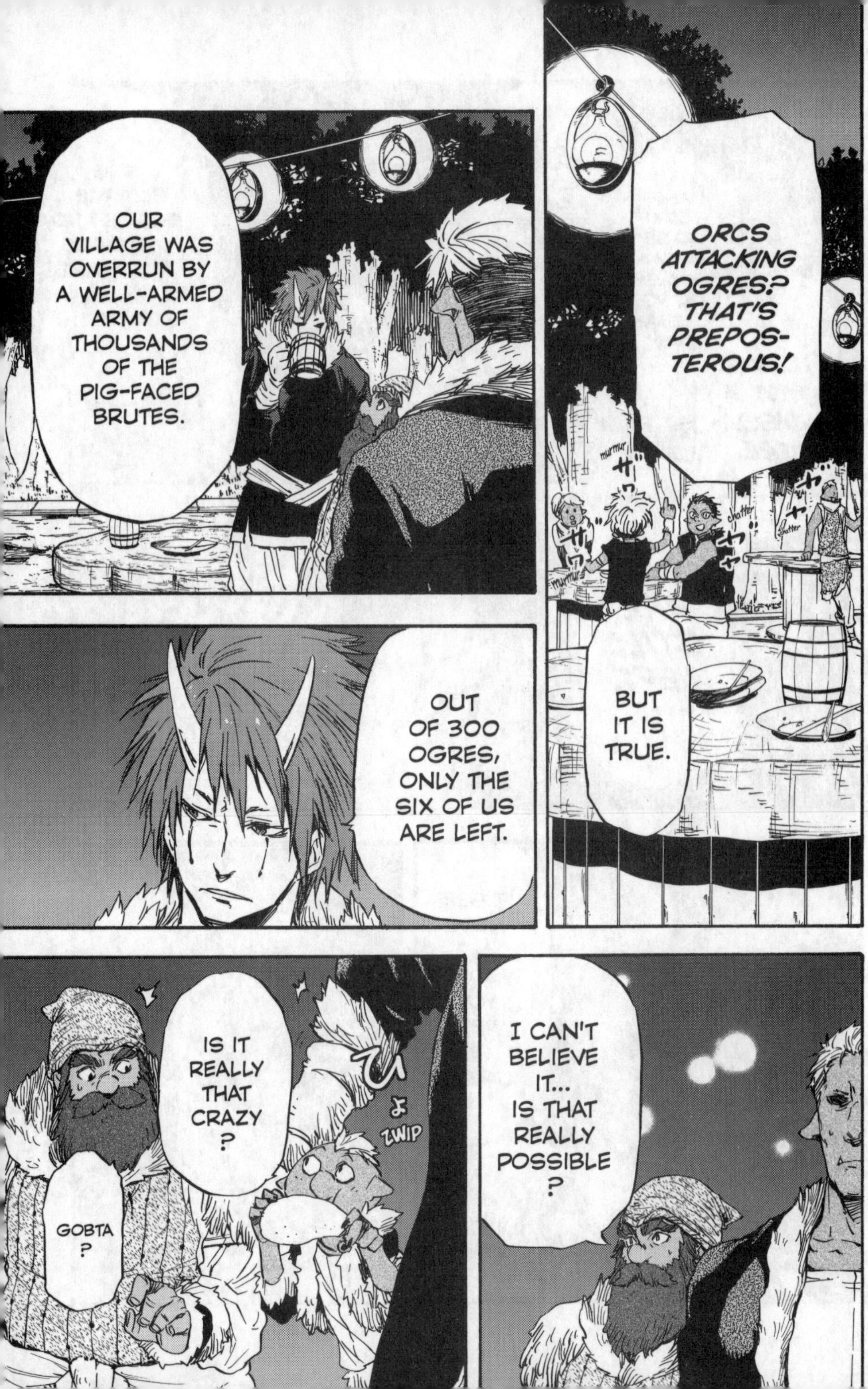
ORCS ATTACKING OGRES? THAT'S PREPOS-TEROUS!
murmur
chatter
chatter
murmur
BUT IT IS TRUE.
OUR VILLAGE WAS OVERRUN BY A WELL-ARMED ARMY OF THOUSANDS OF THE PIG-FACED BRUTES.
OUT OF 300 OGRES, ONLY THE SIX OF US ARE LEFT.
I CAN'T BELIEVE IT... IS THAT REALLY POSSIBLE?
IS IT REALLY THAT CRAZY?
ZWIP
GOBTA?

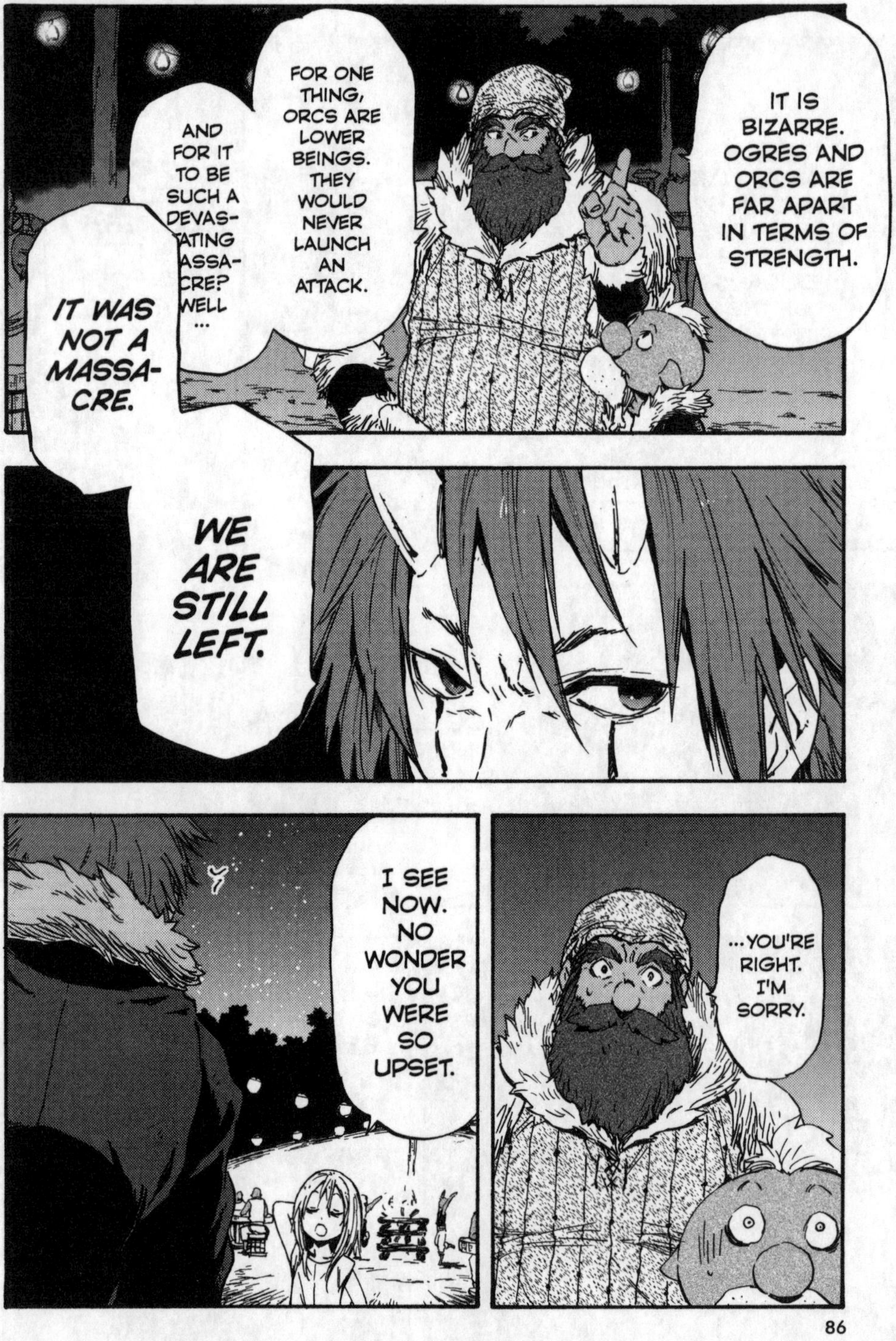
IT IS BIZARRE. OGRES AND ORCS ARE FAR APART IN TERMS OF STRENGTH.
FOR ONE THING, ORCS ARE LOWER BEINGS. THEY WOULD NEVER LAUNCH AN ATTACK.
AND FOR IT TO BE SUCH A DEVASTATING MASSACRE? WELL ...
IT WAS NOT A MASSACRE.
WE ARE STILL LEFT.
...YOU'RE RIGHT. I'M SORRY.
I SEE NOW. NO WONDER YOU WERE SO UPSET.

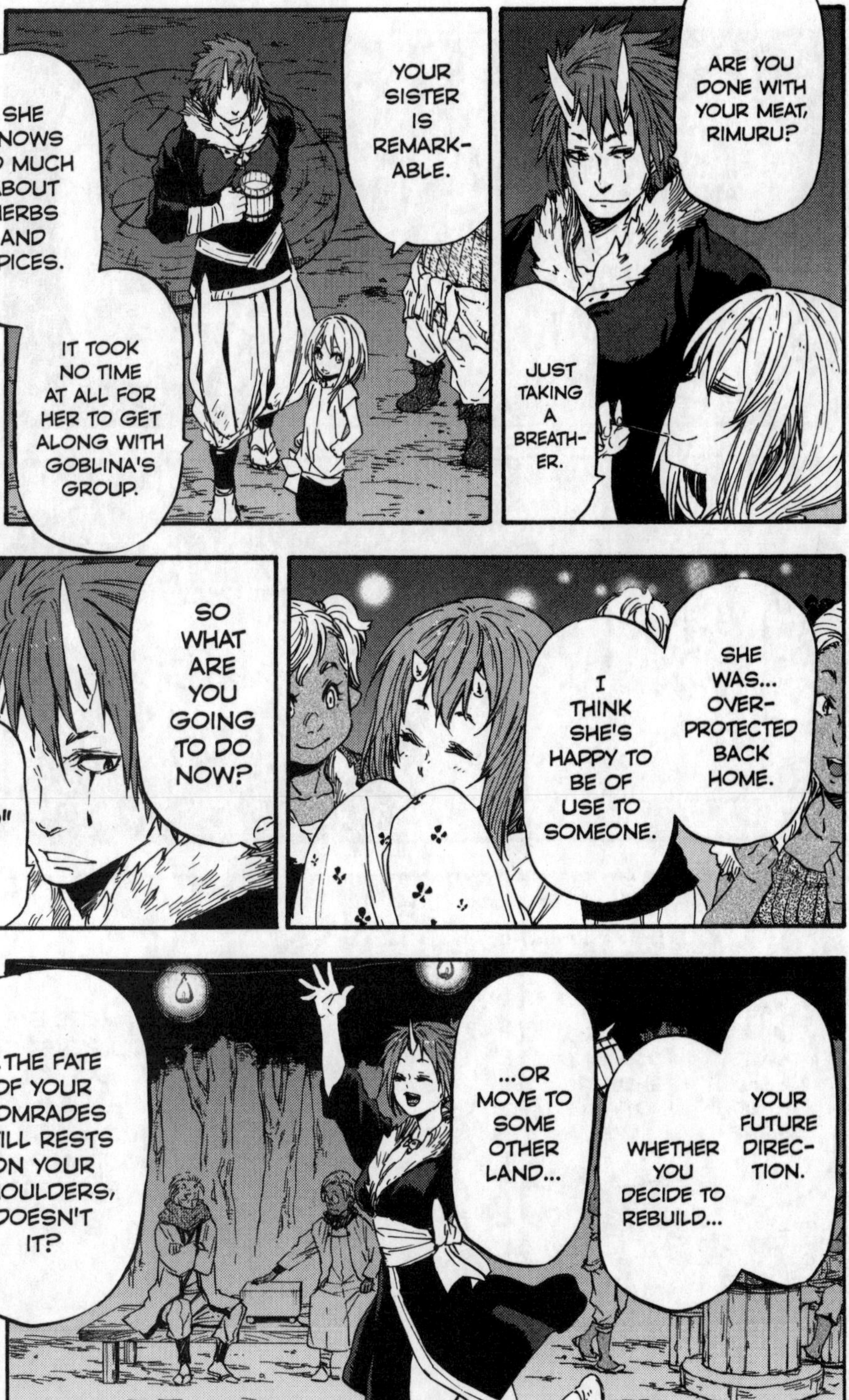
ARE YOU DONE WITH YOUR MEAT, RIMURU?
JUST TAKING A BREATHER.
YOUR SISTER IS REMARKABLE.
SHE KNOWS SO MUCH ABOUT HERBS AND SPICES.
IT TOOK NO TIME AT ALL FOR HER TO GET ALONG WITH GOBLINA'S GROUP.
SHE WAS... OVER-PROTECTED BACK HOME.
I THINK SHE'S HAPPY TO BE OF USE TO SOMEONE.
SO WHAT ARE YOU GOING TO DO NOW?
"DO"?
YOUR FUTURE DIRECTION.
WHETHER YOU DECIDE TO REBUILD...
...OR MOVE TO SOME OTHER LAND...
...THE FATE OF YOUR COMRADES STILL RESTS ON YOUR SHOULDERS, DOESN'T IT?

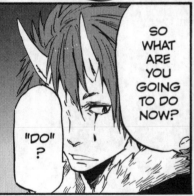

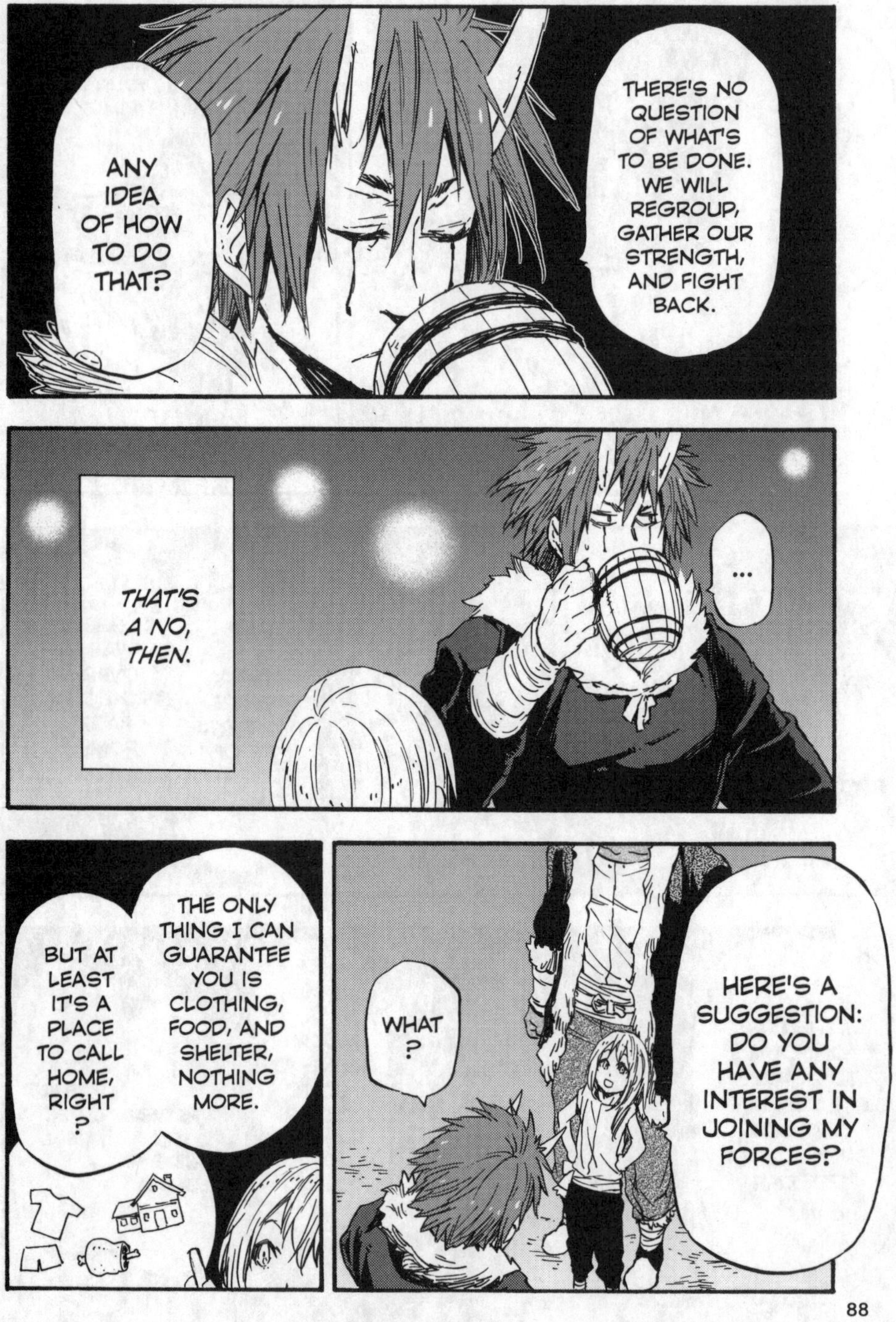
THERE'S NO QUESTION OF WHAT'S TO BE DONE. WE WILL REGROUP, GATHER OUR STRENGTH, AND FIGHT BACK.
ANY IDEA OF HOW TO DO THAT?
...
THAT'S A NO, THEN.
HERE'S A SUGGESTION: DO YOU HAVE ANY INTEREST IN JOINING MY FORCES?
WHAT?
THE ONLY THING I CAN GUARANTEE YOU IS CLOTHING, FOOD, AND SHELTER, NOTHING MORE.
BUT AT LEAST IT'S A PLACE TO CALL HOME, RIGHT?

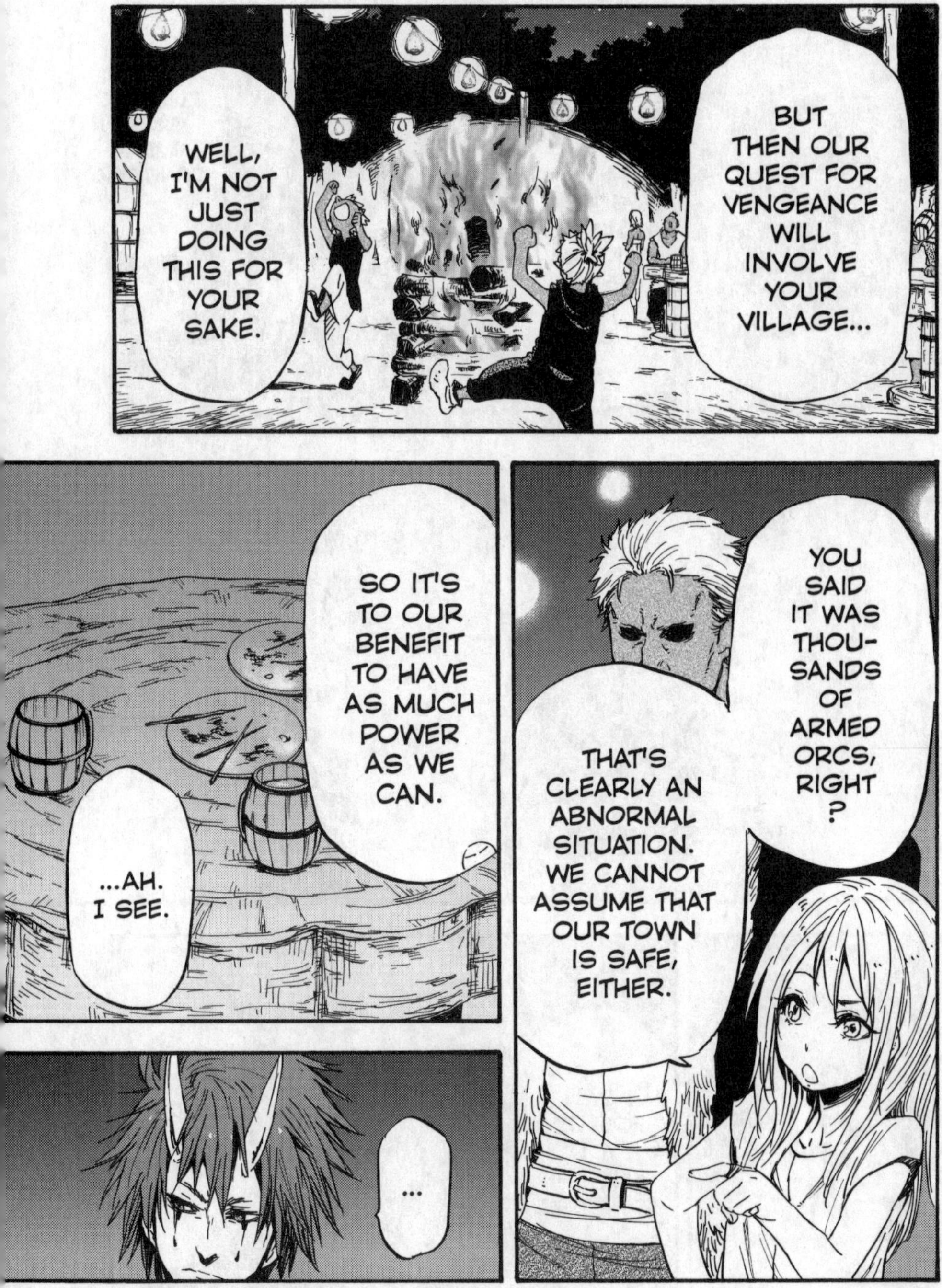
BUT THEN OUR QUEST FOR VENGEANCE WILL INVOLVE YOUR VILLAGE...
WELL, I'M NOT JUST DOING THIS FOR YOUR SAKE.
YOU SAID IT WAS THOU-SANDS OF ARMED ORCS, RIGHT?
THAT'S CLEARLY AN ABNORMAL SITUATION. WE CANNOT ASSUME THAT OUR TOWN IS SAFE, EITHER.
SO IT'S TO OUR BENEFIT TO HAVE AS MUCH POWER AS WE CAN.
...AH. I SEE.
...

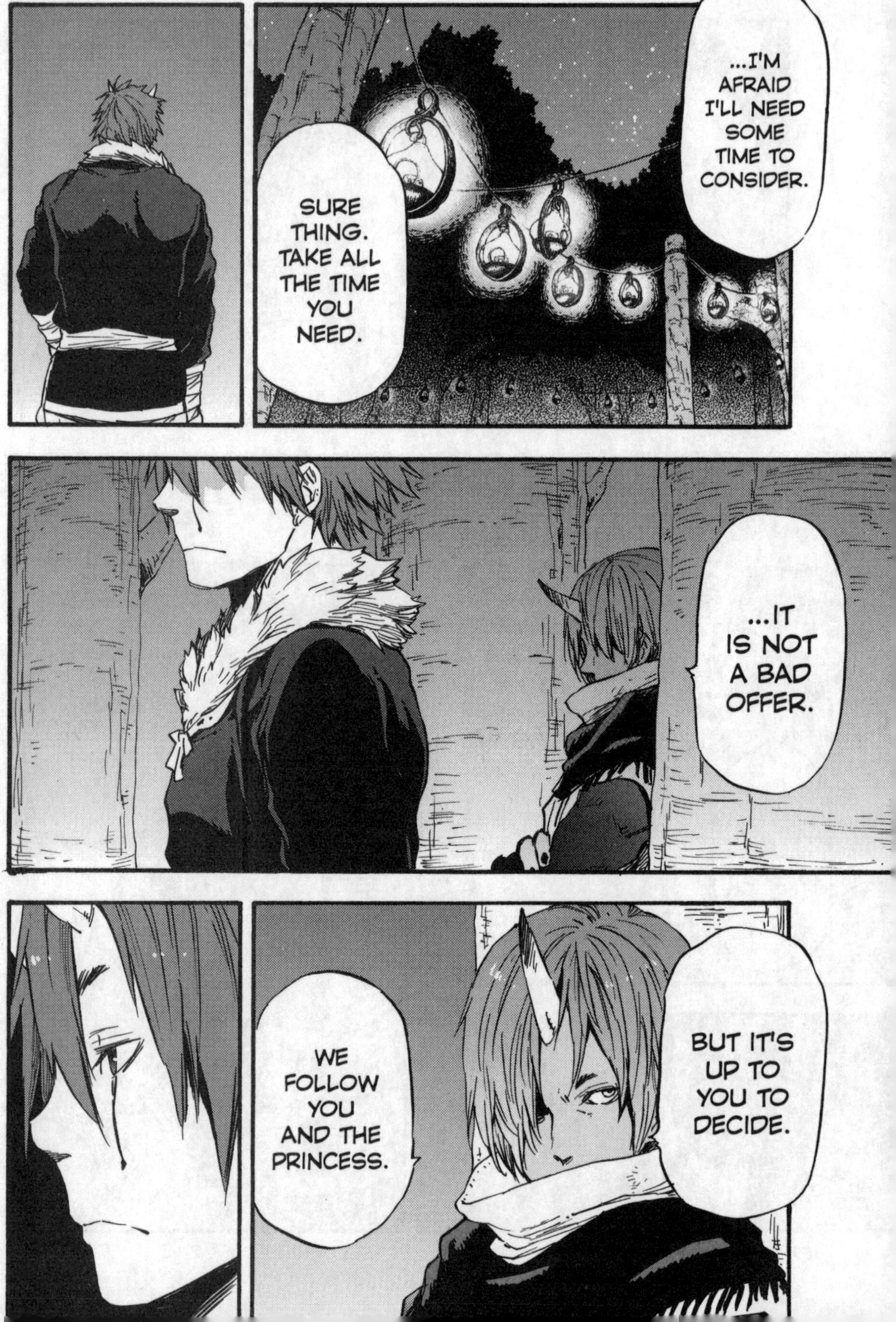
...I'M AFRAID I'LL NEED SOME TIME TO CONSIDER.
SURE THING. TAKE ALL THE TIME YOU NEED.
...IT IS NOT A BAD OFFER.
BUT IT'S UP TO YOU TO DECIDE.
WE FOLLOW YOU AND THE PRINCESS.

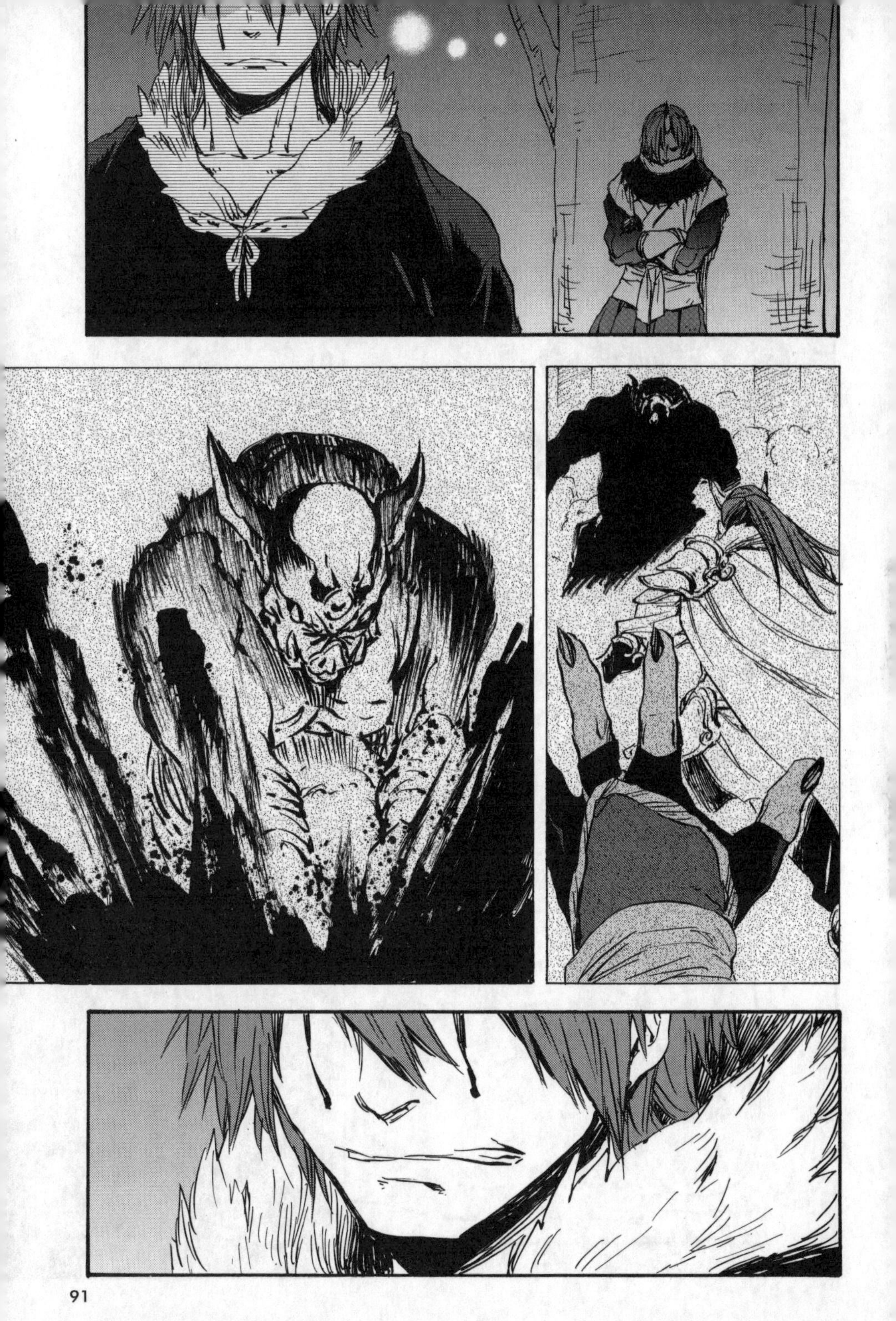

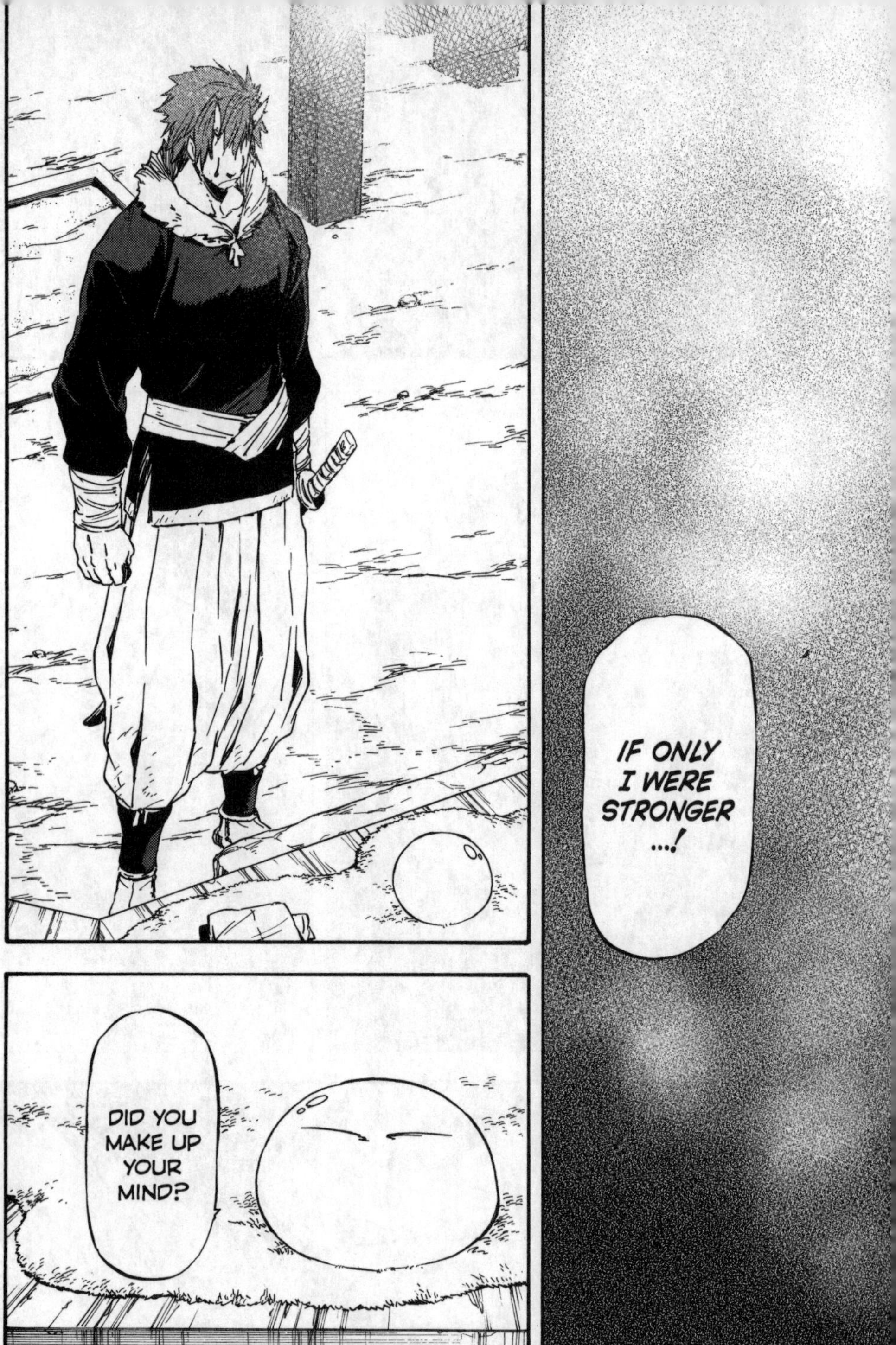
IF ONLY I WERE STRONGER ...!
DID YOU MAKE UP YOUR MIND?

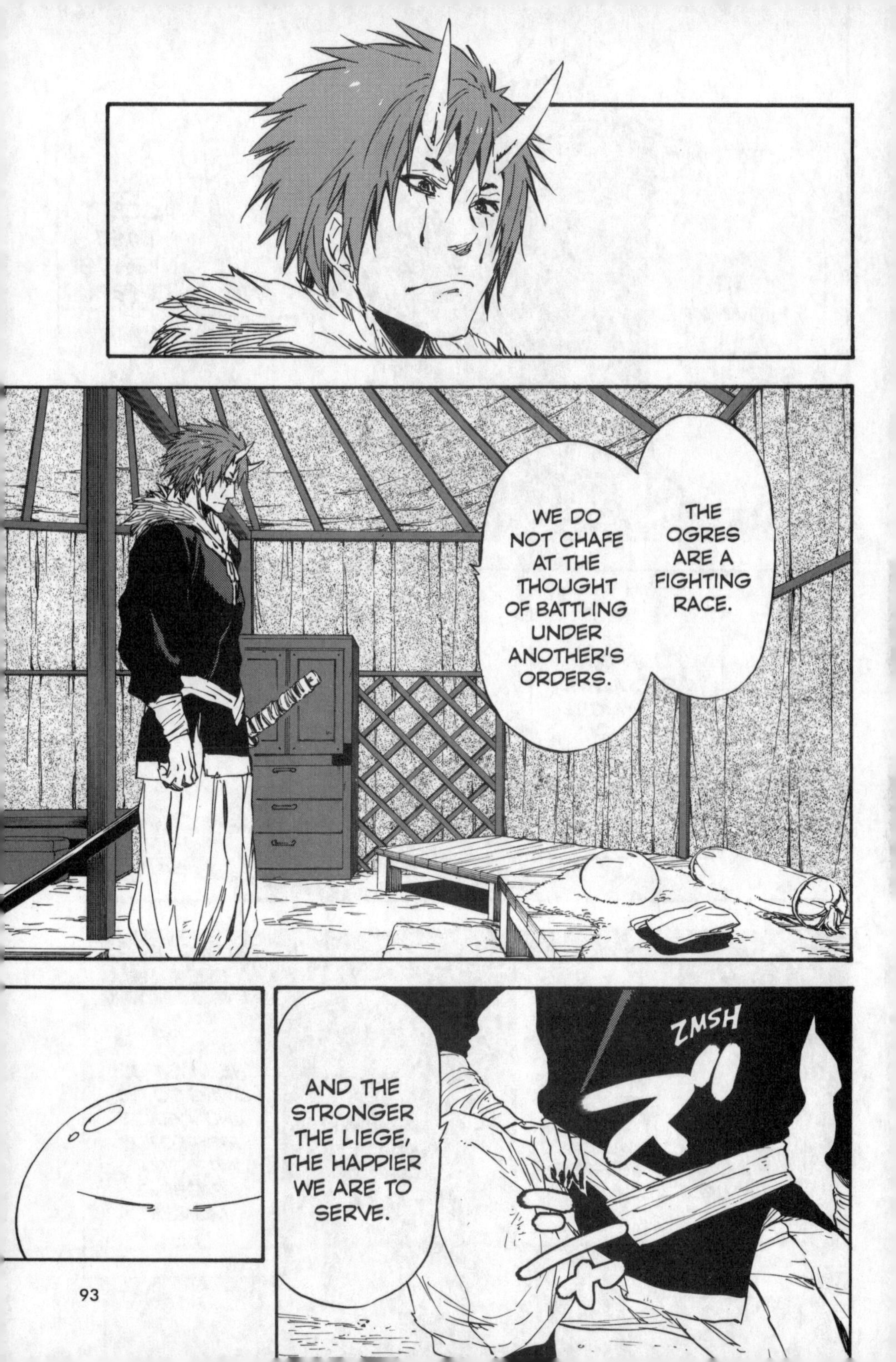
THE OGRES ARE A FIGHTING RACE.
WE DO NOT CHAFE AT THE THOUGHT OF BATTLING UNDER ANOTHER'S ORDERS.
ZMSH
AND THE STRONGER THE LIEGE, THE HAPPIER WE ARE TO SERVE.

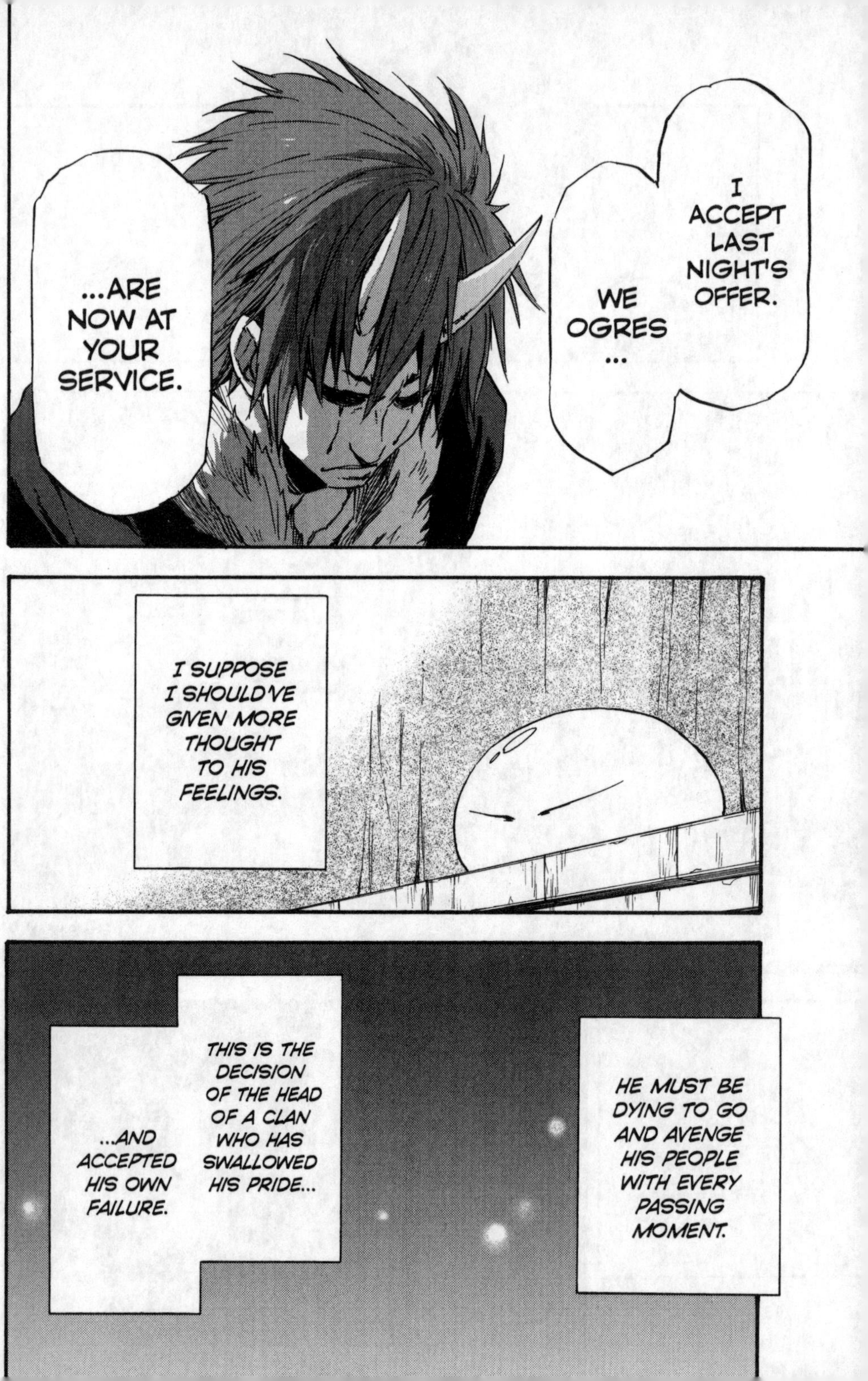
I ACCEPT LAST NIGHT'S OFFER.
WE OGRES ...
...ARE NOW AT YOUR SERVICE.
I SUPPOSE I SHOULD'VE GIVEN MORE THOUGHT TO HIS FEELINGS.
HE MUST BE DYING TO GO AND AVENGE HIS PEOPLE WITH EVERY PASSING MOMENT.
THIS IS THE DECISION OF THE HEAD OF A CLAN WHO HAS SWALLOWED HIS PRIDE...
...AND ACCEPTED HIS OWN FAILURE.

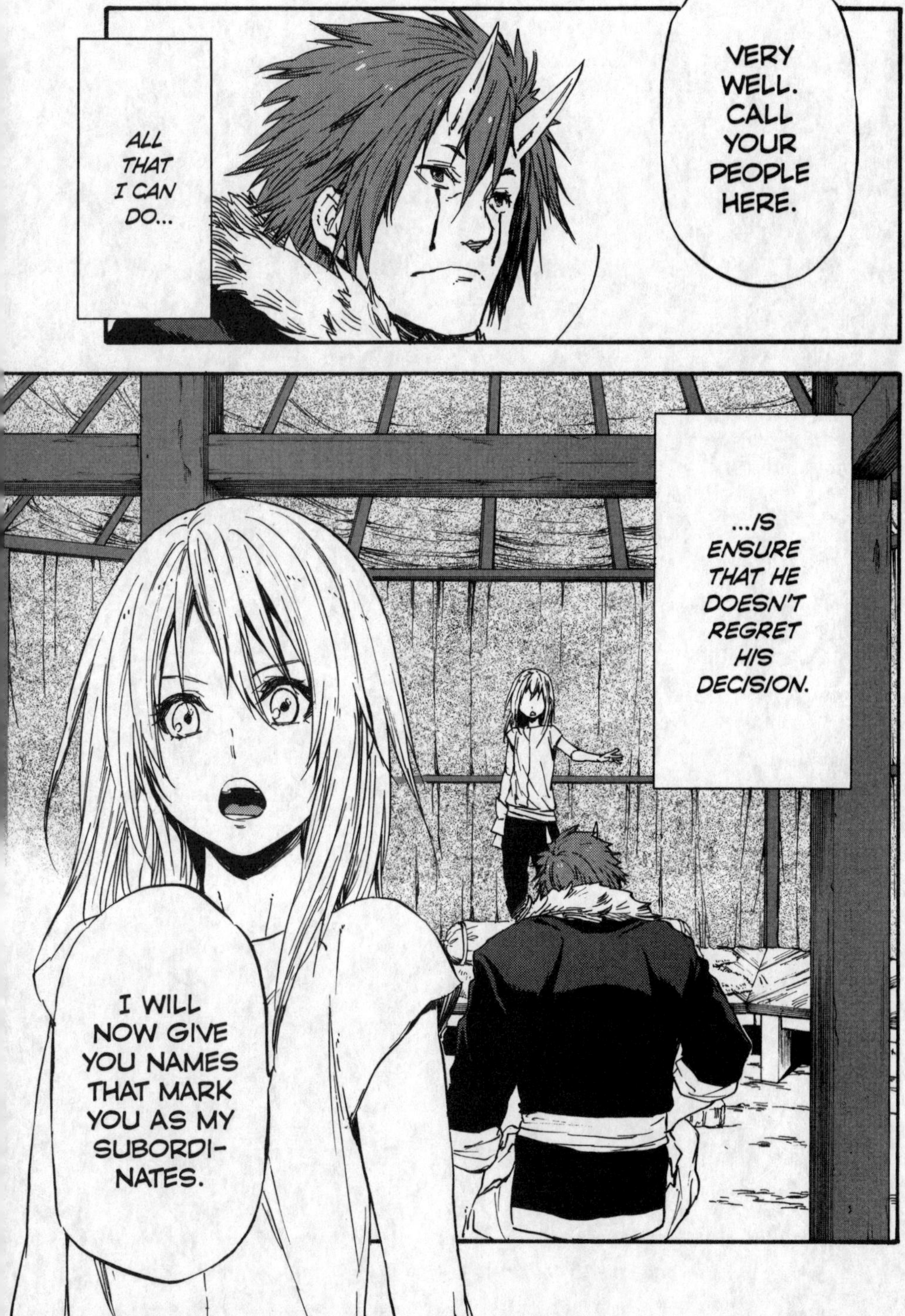
VERY WELL. CALL YOUR PEOPLE HERE.
ALL THAT I CAN DO...
...IS ENSURE THAT HE DOESN'T REGRET HIS DECISION.
I WILL NOW GIVE YOU NAMES THAT MARK YOU AS MY SUBORDI-NATES.

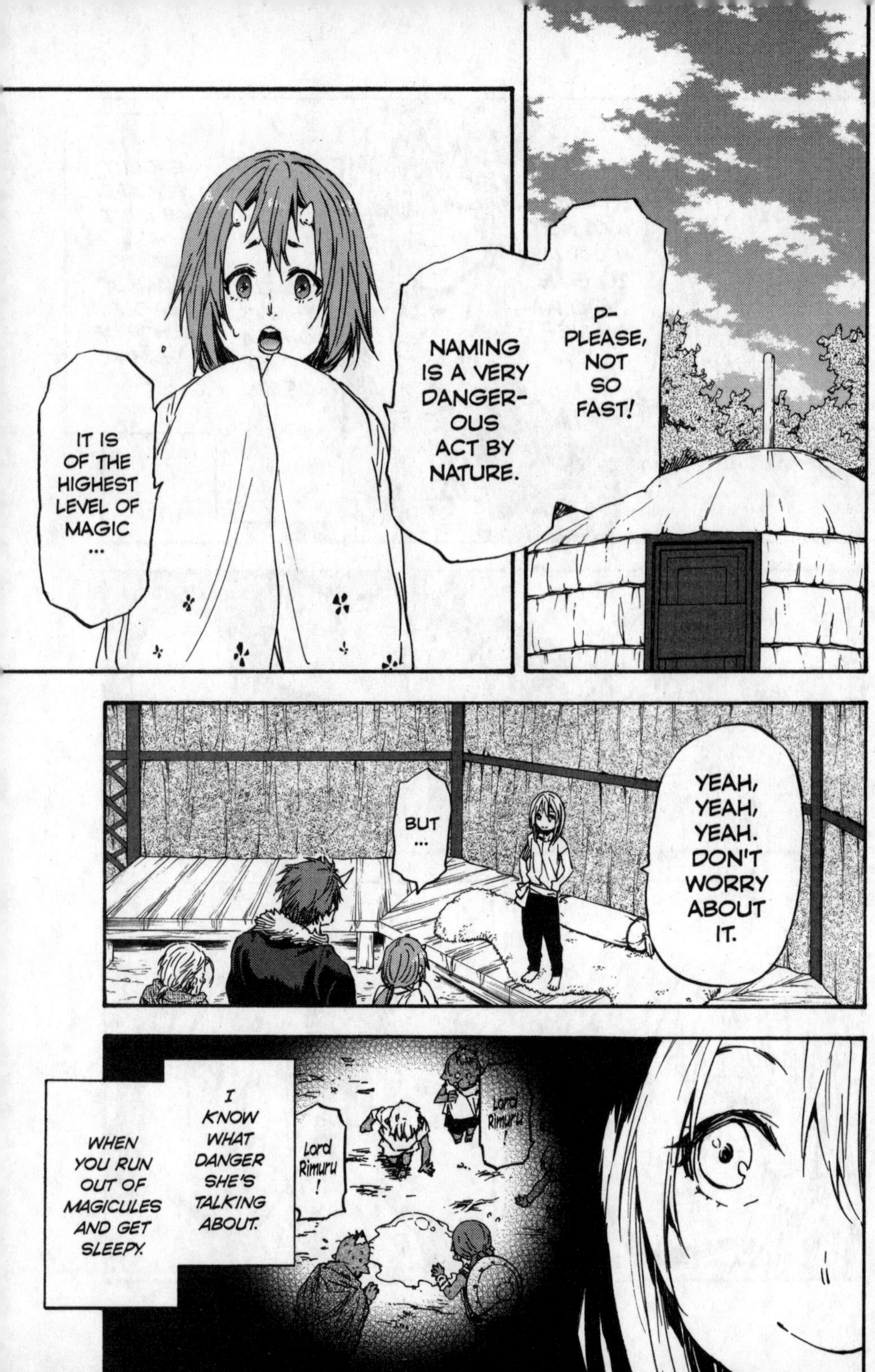
P-PLEASE, NOT SO FAST!
NAMING IS A VERY DANGEROUS ACT BY NATURE.
IT IS OF THE HIGHEST LEVEL OF MAGIC ...
YEAH, YEAH, YEAH. DON'T WORRY ABOUT IT.
BUT ...
I KNOW WHAT DANGER SHE'S TALKING ABOUT.
Lord Rimuru!
Lord Rimuru!
WHEN YOU RUN OUT OF MAGICULES AND GET SLEEPY.

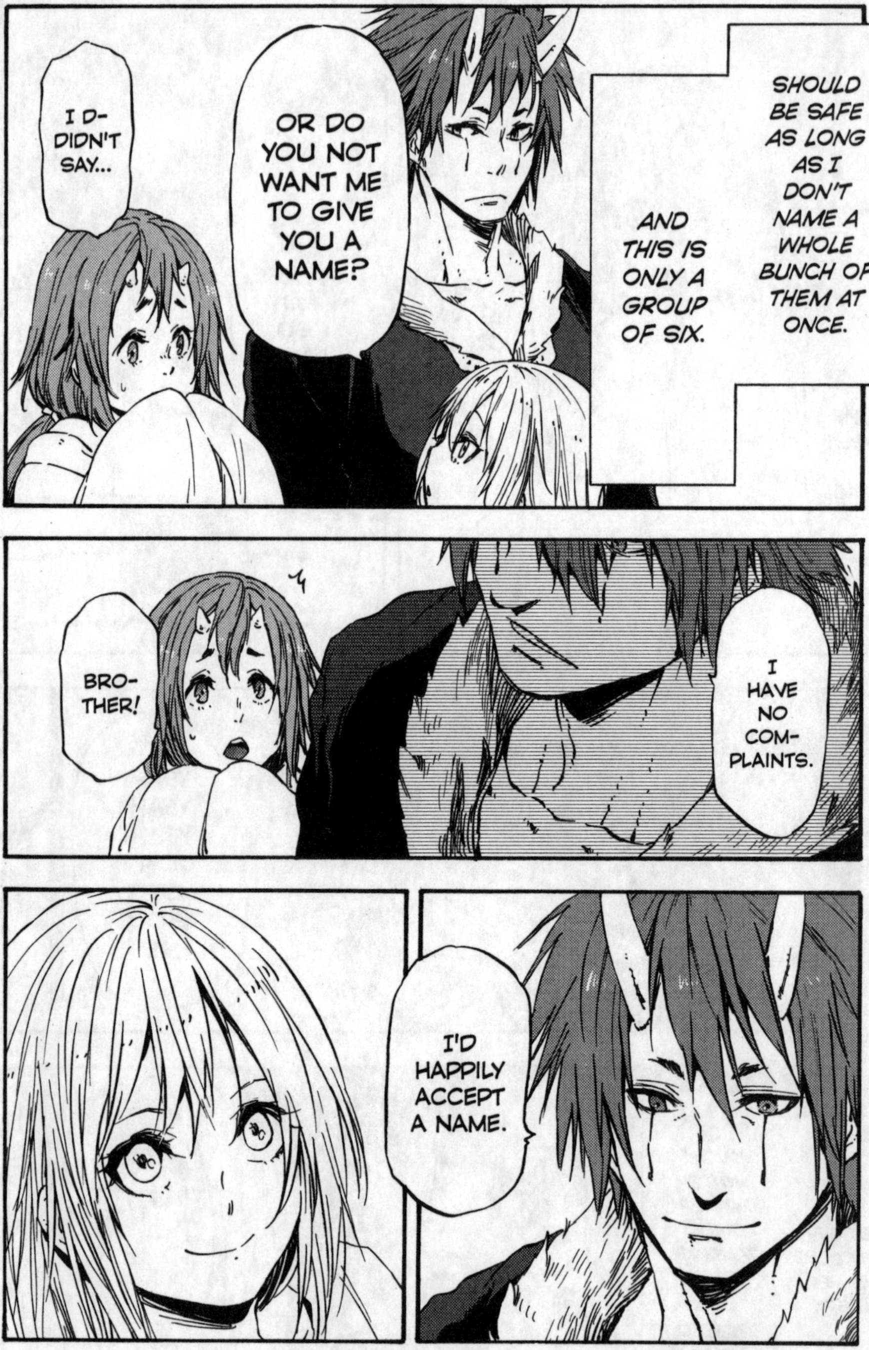

SHOULD BE SAFE AS LONG AS I DON'T NAME A WHOLE BUNCH OF THEM AT ONCE.
AND THIS IS ONLY A GROUP OF SIX.
OR DO YOU NOT WANT ME TO GIVE YOU A NAME?
I D-DIDN'T SAY...
I HAVE NO COM-PLAINTS.
BRO-THER!
I'D HAPPILY ACCEPT A NAME.

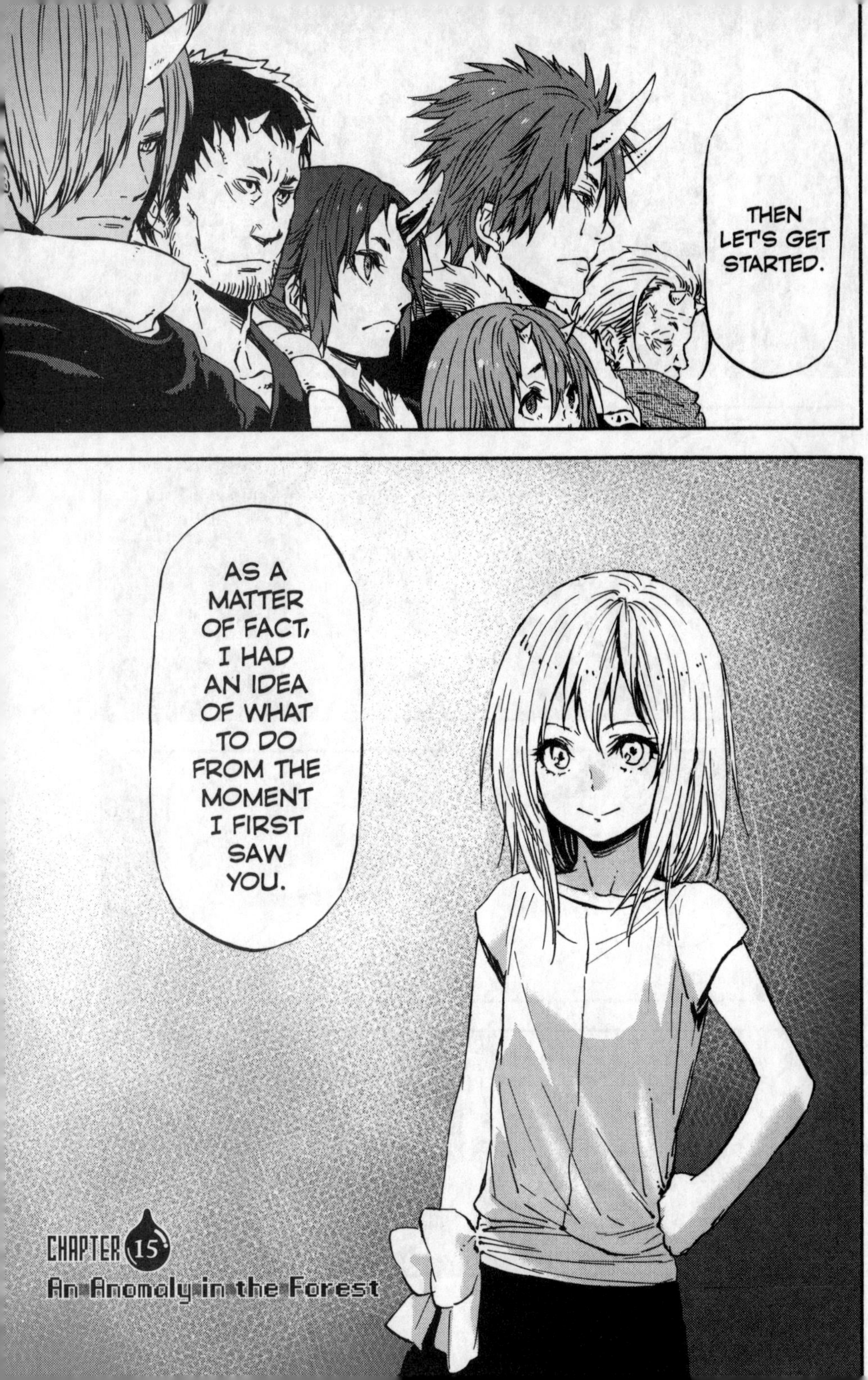
THEN LET'S GET STARTED.
AS A MATTER OF FACT, I HAD AN IDEA OF WHAT TO DO FROM THE MOMENT I FIRST SAW YOU.
CHAPTER 15
An Anomaly in the Forest

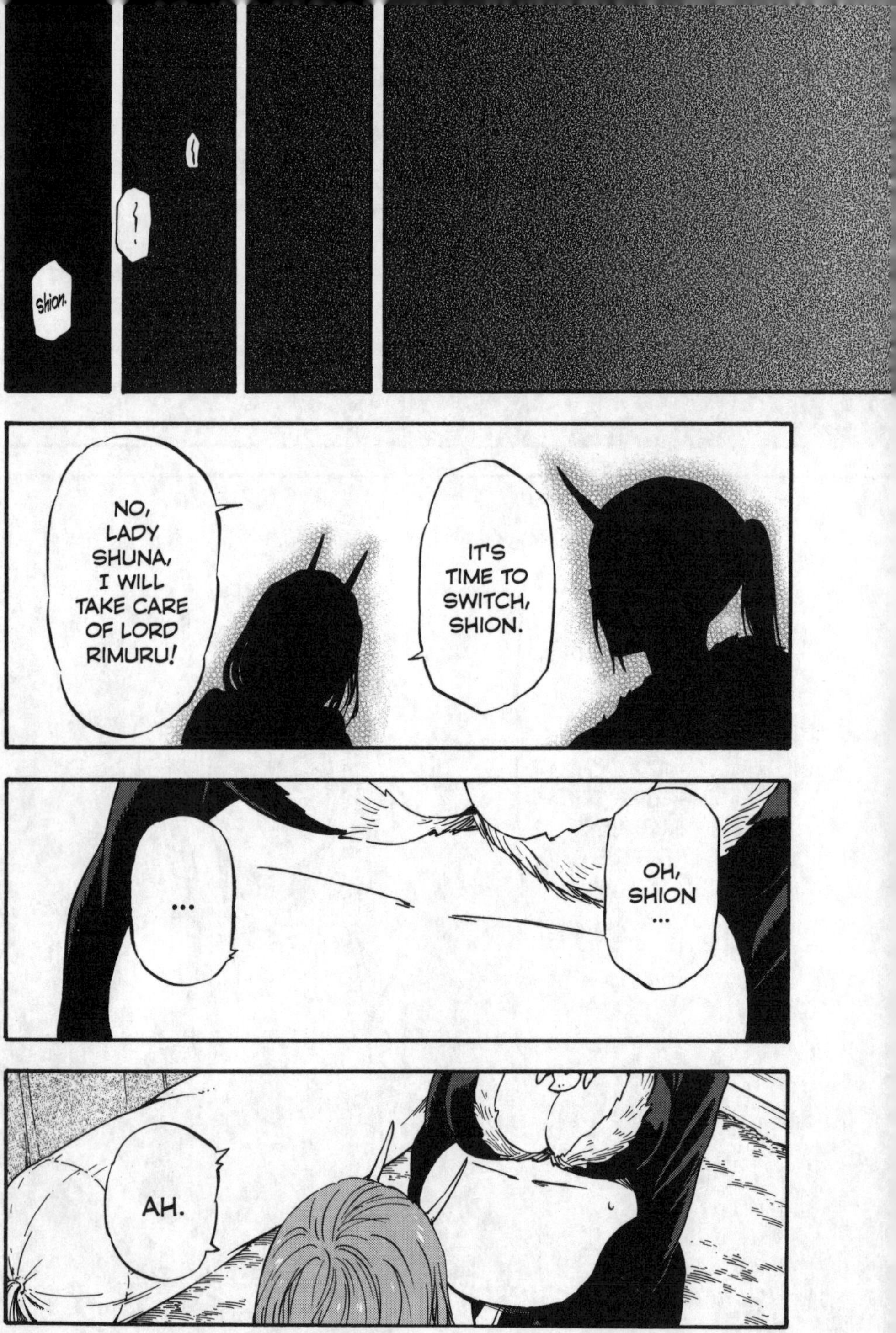
!
?!
Shion.
IT'S TIME TO SWITCH, SHION.
NO, LADY SHUNA, I WILL TAKE CARE OF LORD RIMURU!
OH, SHION ...
...
AH.

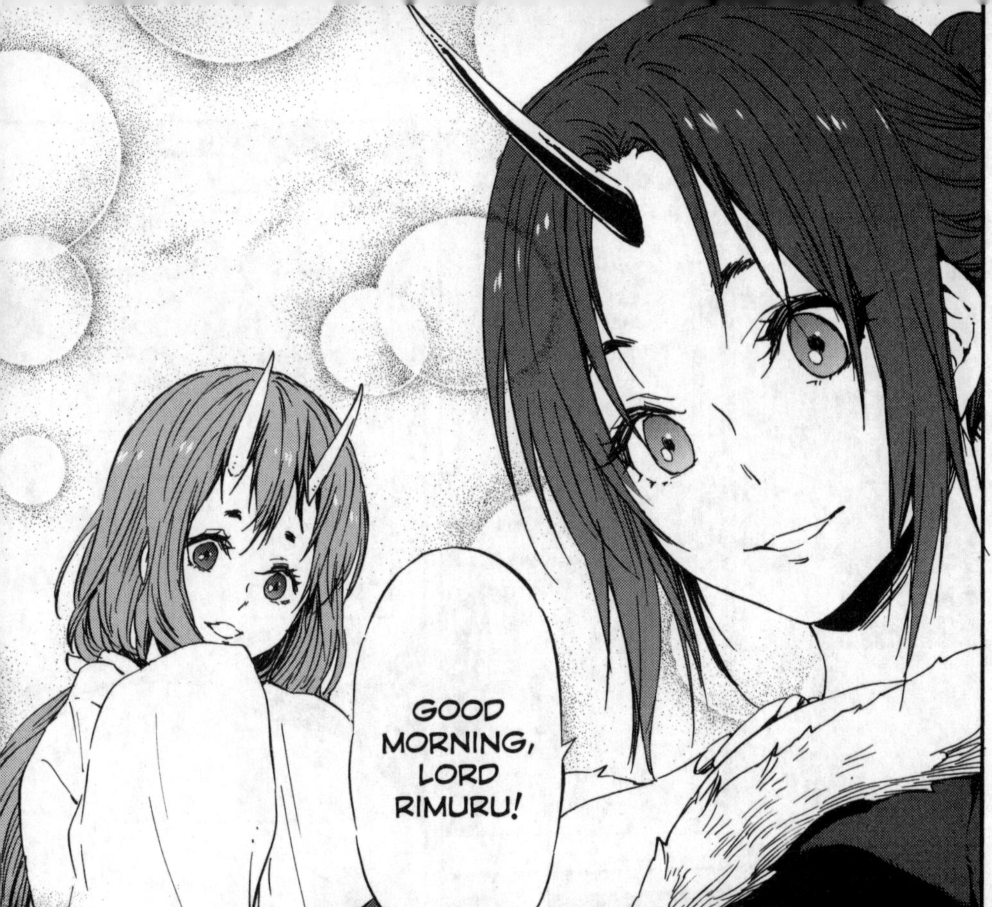
GOOD MORNING, LORD RIMURU!

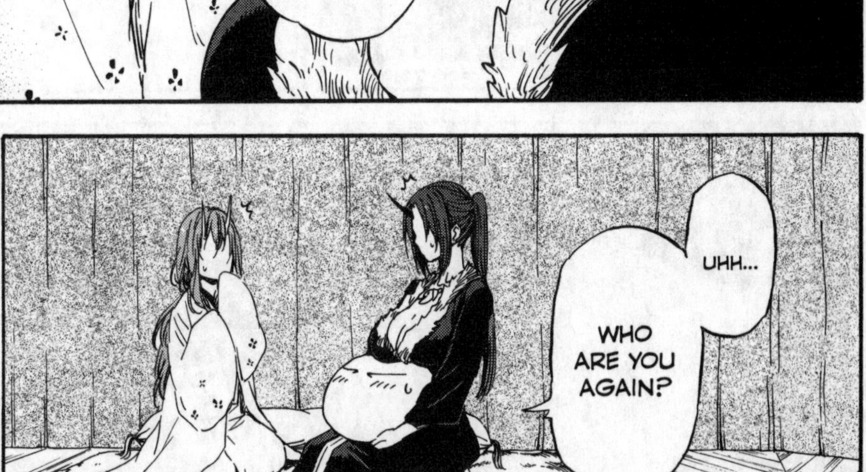
UHH...
WHO ARE YOU AGAIN?

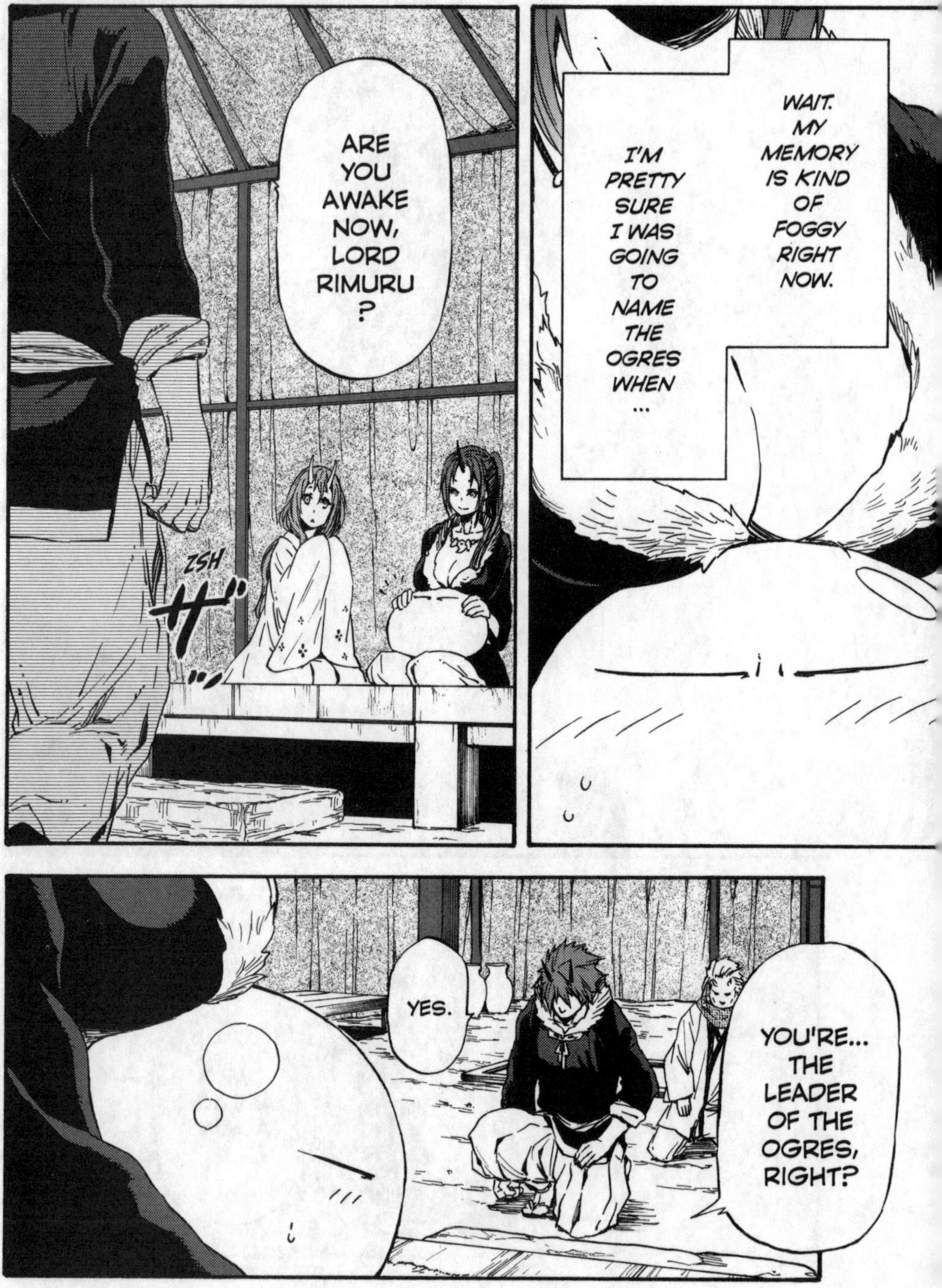
WAIT. MY MEMORY IS KIND OF FOGGY RIGHT NOW.
I'M PRETTY SURE I WAS GOING TO NAME THE OGRES WHEN ...
ZSH
ARE YOU AWAKE NOW, LORD RIMURU?
YOU'RE... THE LEADER OF THE OGRES, RIGHT?
YES.

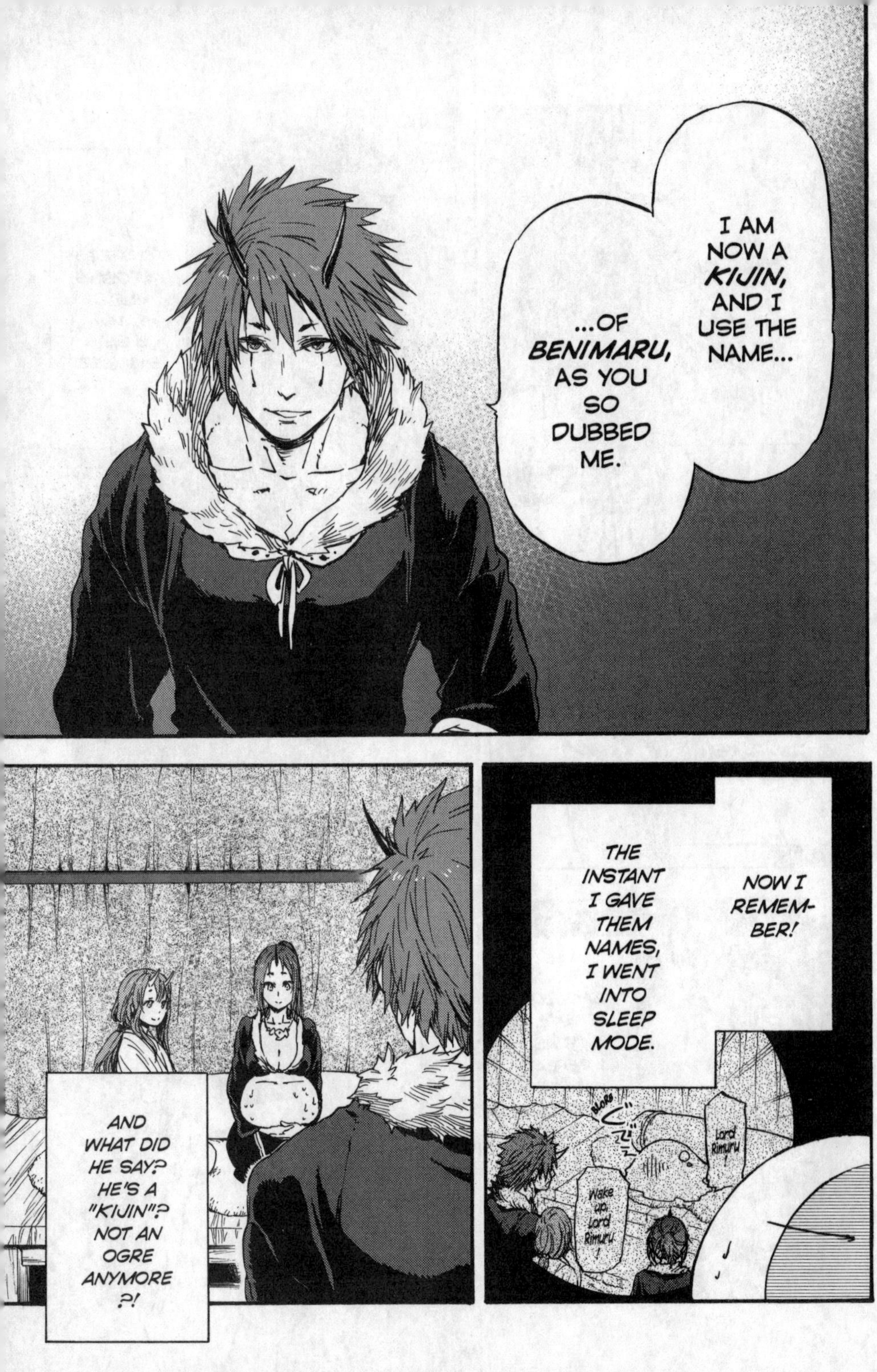

I AM NOW A KIJIN, AND I USE THE NAME...
...OF BENIMARU, AS YOU SO DUBBED ME.
NOW I REMEMBER!
THE INSTANT I GAVE THEM NAMES, I WENT INTO SLEEP MODE.
Lord Rimuru!
Wake up, Lord Rimuru!
AND WHAT DID HE SAY? HE'S A "KIJIN"? NOT AN OGRE ANYMORE?!

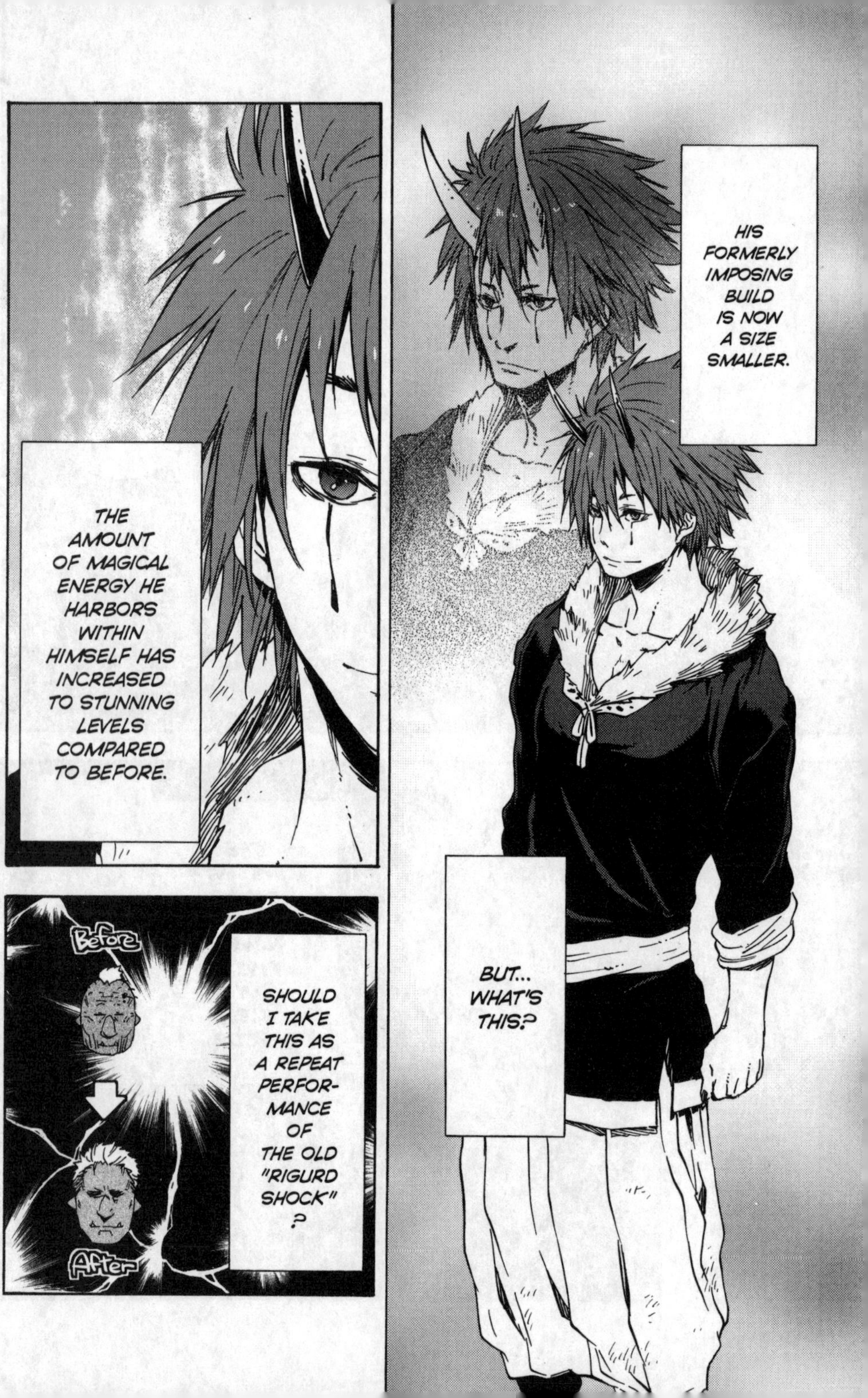
HIS FORMERLY IMPOSING BUILD IS NOW A SIZE SMALLER.
BUT... WHAT'S THIS?
THE AMOUNT OF MAGICAL ENERGY HE HARBORS WITHIN HIMSELF HAS INCREASED TO STUNNING LEVELS COMPARED TO BEFORE.
SHOULD I TAKE THIS AS A REPEAT PERFORMANCE OF THE OLD "RIGURD SHOCK"?
Before
After

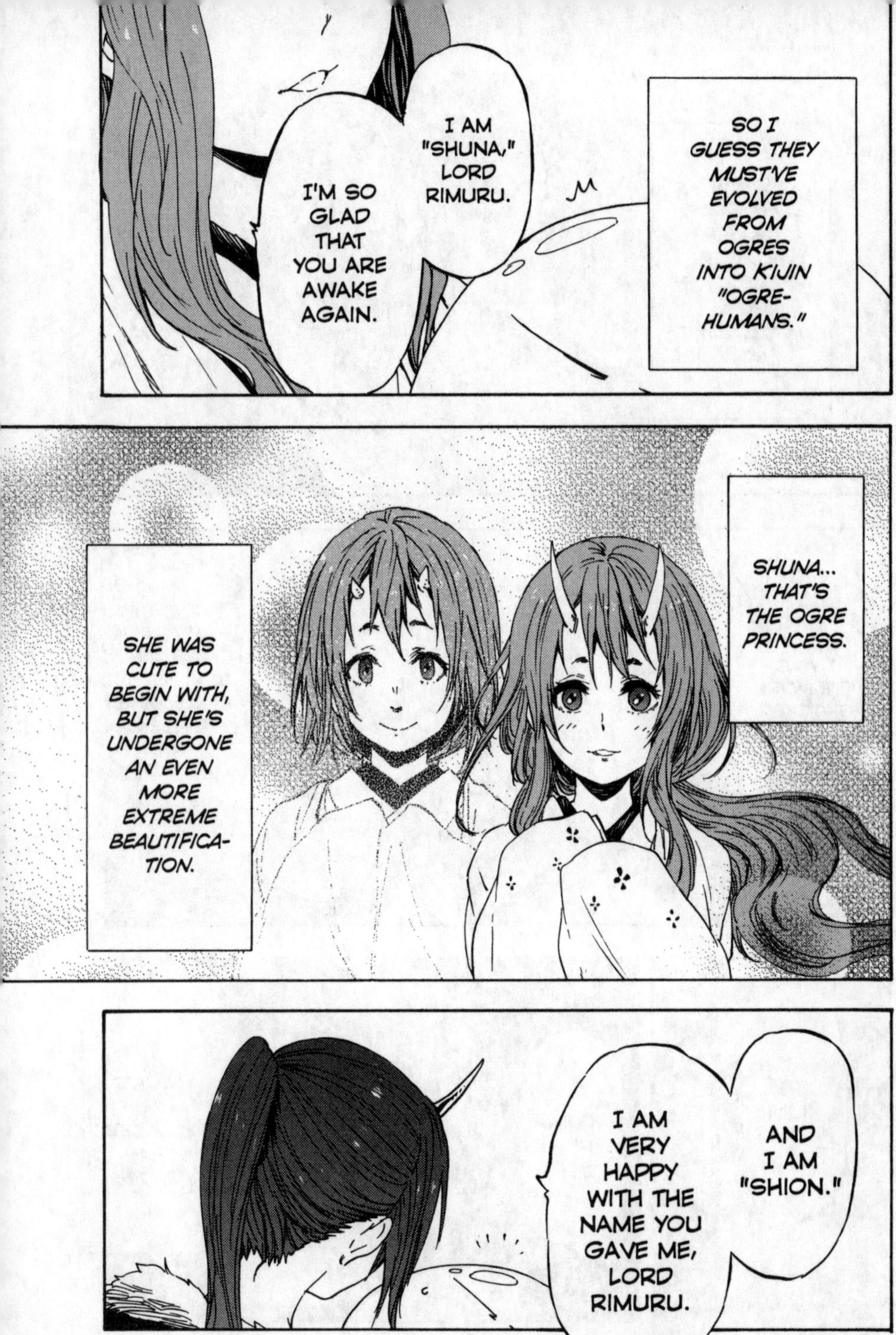
SO I GUESS THEY MUST'VE EVOLVED FROM OGRES INTO KIJIN "OGRE-HUMANS."
I AM "SHUNA," LORD RIMURU.
I'M SO GLAD THAT YOU ARE AWAKE AGAIN.
SHUNA... THAT'S THE OGRE PRINCESS.
SHE WAS CUTE TO BEGIN WITH, BUT SHE'S UNDERGONE AN EVEN MORE EXTREME BEAUTIFICA-TION.
AND I AM "SHION."
I AM VERY HAPPY WITH THE NAME YOU GAVE ME, LORD RIMURU.

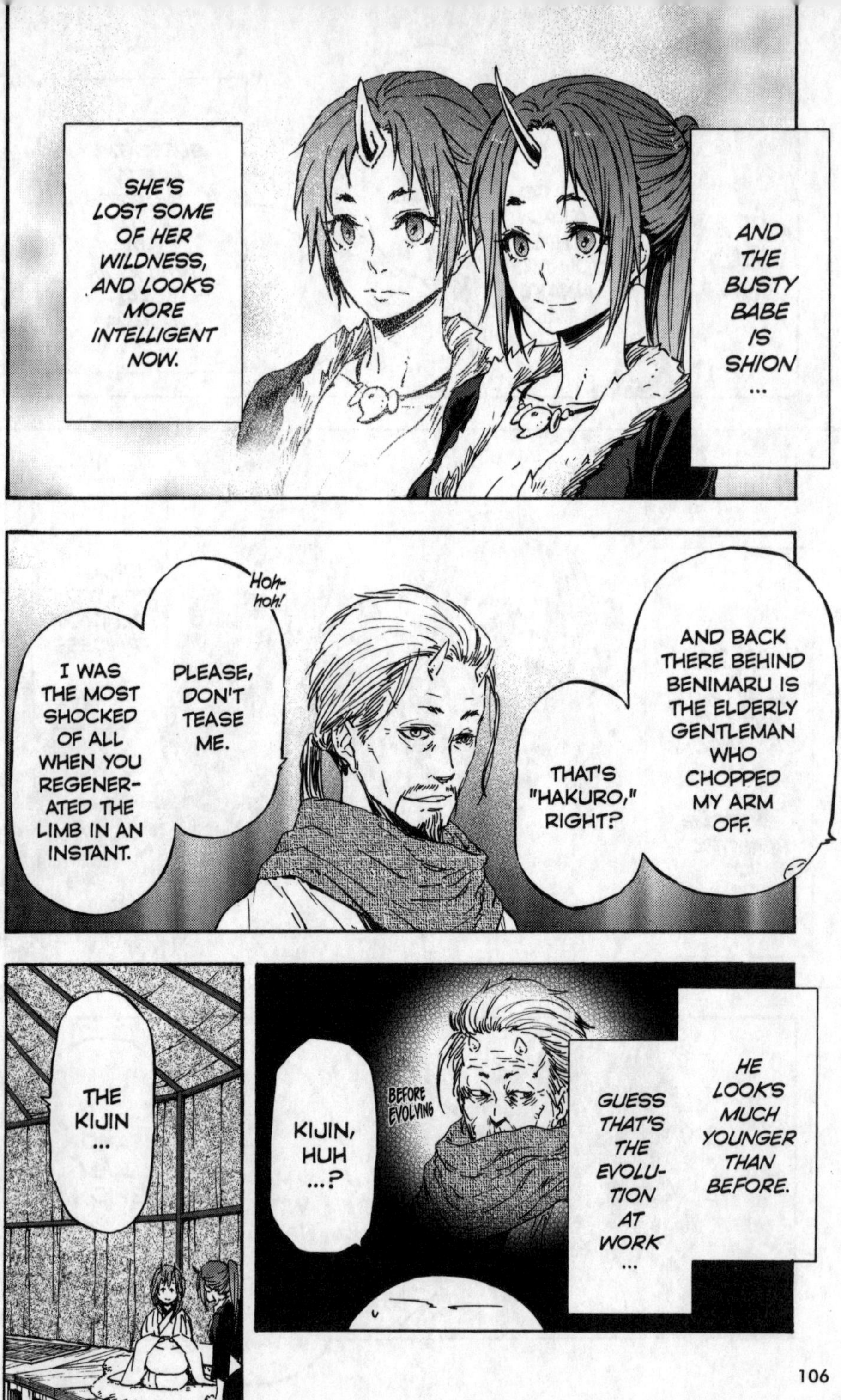
AND THE BUSTY BABE IS SHION ...
SHE'S LOST SOME OF HER WILDNESS, AND LOOKS MORE INTELLIGENT NOW.
AND BACK THERE BEHIND BENIMARU IS THE ELDERLY GENTLEMAN WHO CHOPPED MY ARM OFF.
THAT'S "HAKURO," RIGHT?
Hoh-hoh!
PLEASE, DON'T TEASE ME.
I WAS THE MOST SHOCKED OF ALL WHEN YOU REGENERATED THE LIMB IN AN INSTANT.
HE LOOKS MUCH YOUNGER THAN BEFORE.
GUESS THAT'S THE EVOLUTION AT WORK ...
BEFORE EVOLVING
KIJIN, HUH ...?
THE KIJIN ...

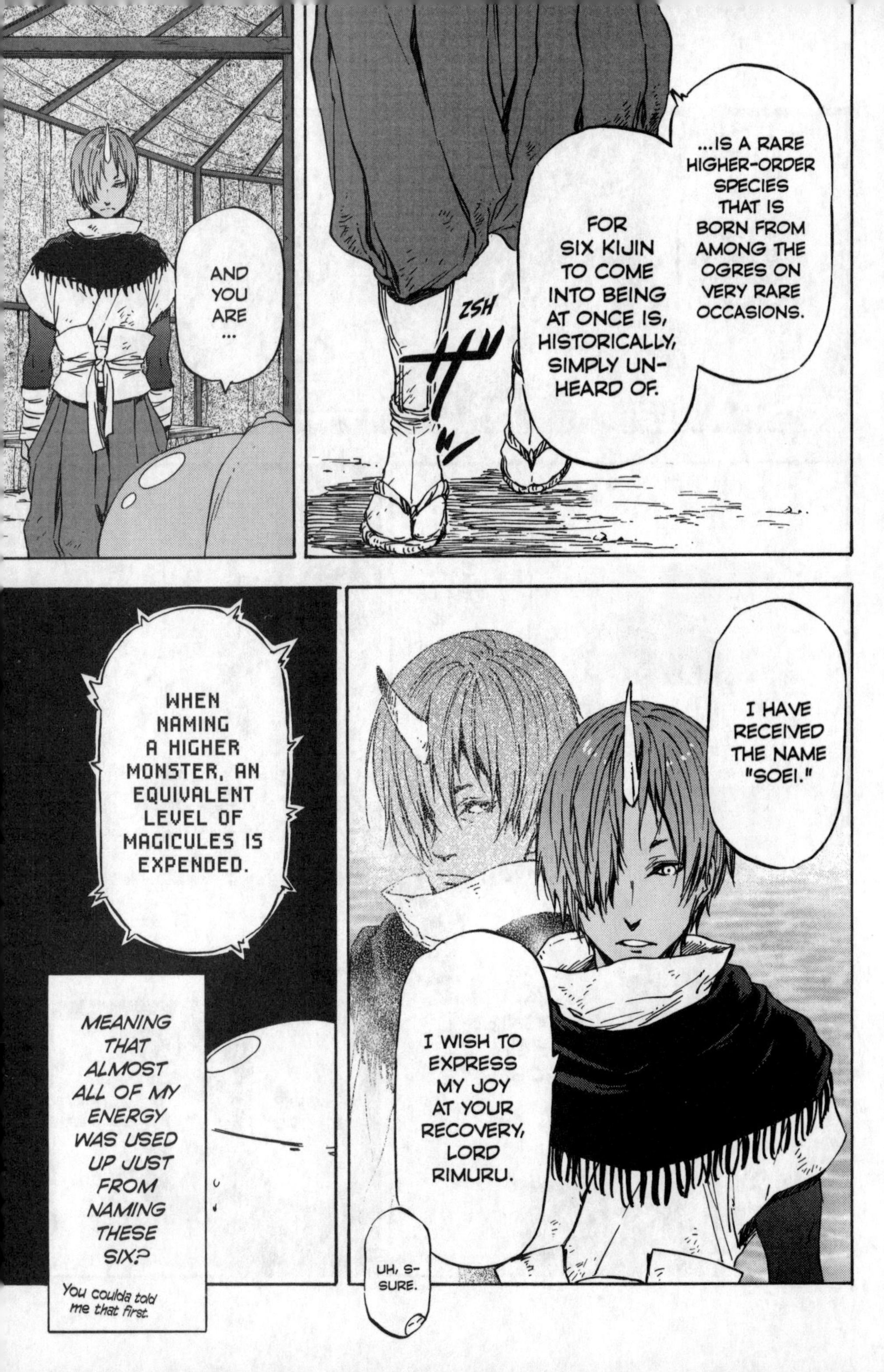
...IS A RARE HIGHER-ORDER SPECIES THAT IS BORN FROM AMONG THE OGRES ON VERY RARE OCCASIONS.
FOR SIX KIJIN TO COME INTO BEING AT ONCE IS, HISTORICALLY, SIMPLY UN-HEARD OF.
ZSH
AND YOU ARE...
I HAVE RECEIVED THE NAME "SOEI."
I WISH TO EXPRESS MY JOY AT YOUR RECOVERY, LORD RIMURU.
UH, S-SURE.
WHEN NAMING A HIGHER MONSTER, AN EQUIVALENT LEVEL OF MAGICULES IS EXPENDED.
MEANING THAT ALMOST ALL OF MY ENERGY WAS USED UP JUST FROM NAMING THESE SIX?
You coulda told me that first.

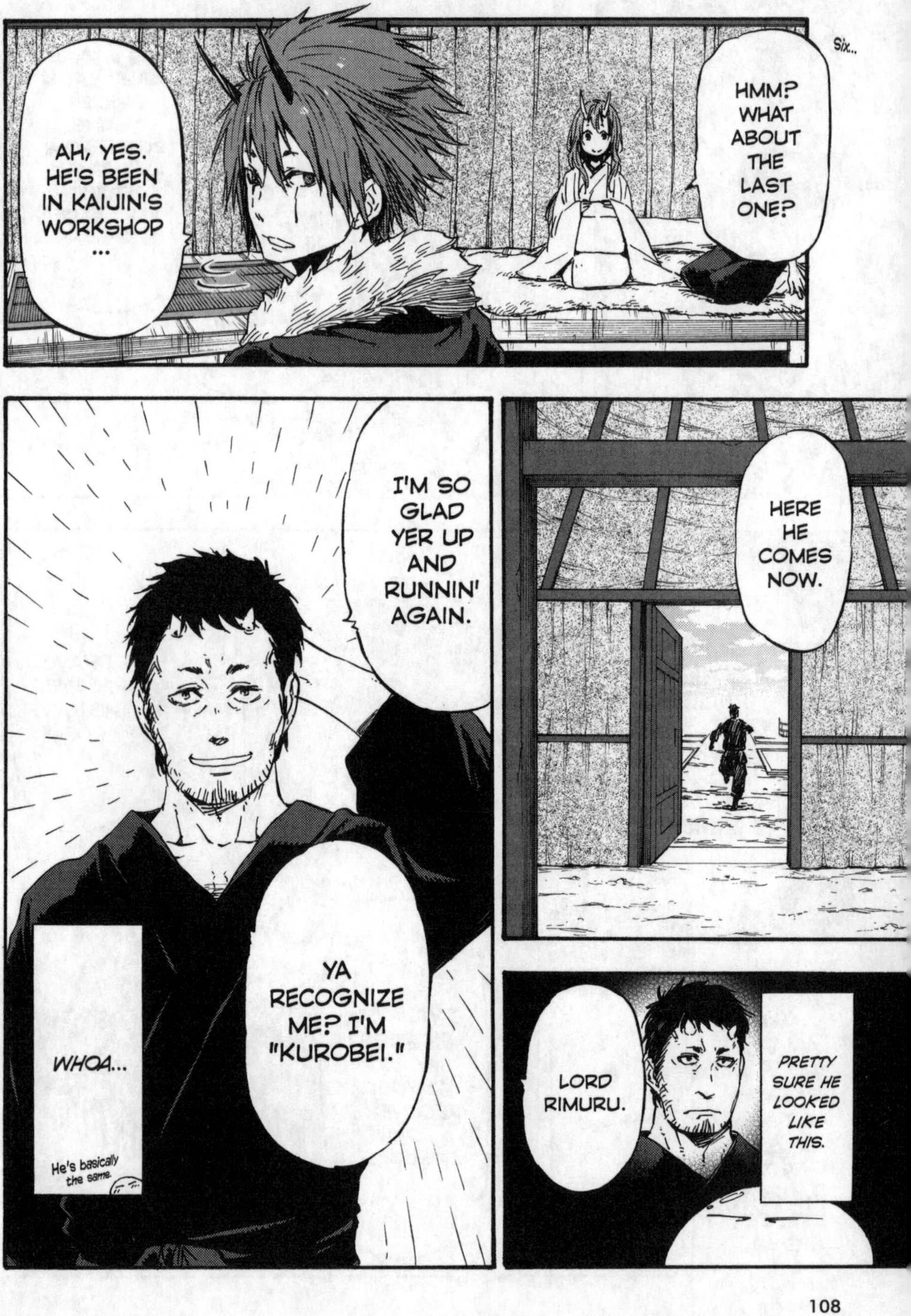
Six...
HMM? WHAT ABOUT THE LAST ONE?
AH, YES. HE'S BEEN IN KAIJIN'S WORKSHOP ...
HERE HE COMES NOW.
PRETTY SURE HE LOOKED LIKE THIS.
LORD RIMURU.
I'M SO GLAD YER UP AND RUNNIN' AGAIN.
YA RECOGNIZE ME? I'M "KUROBEI."
WHOA...
He's basically the same.

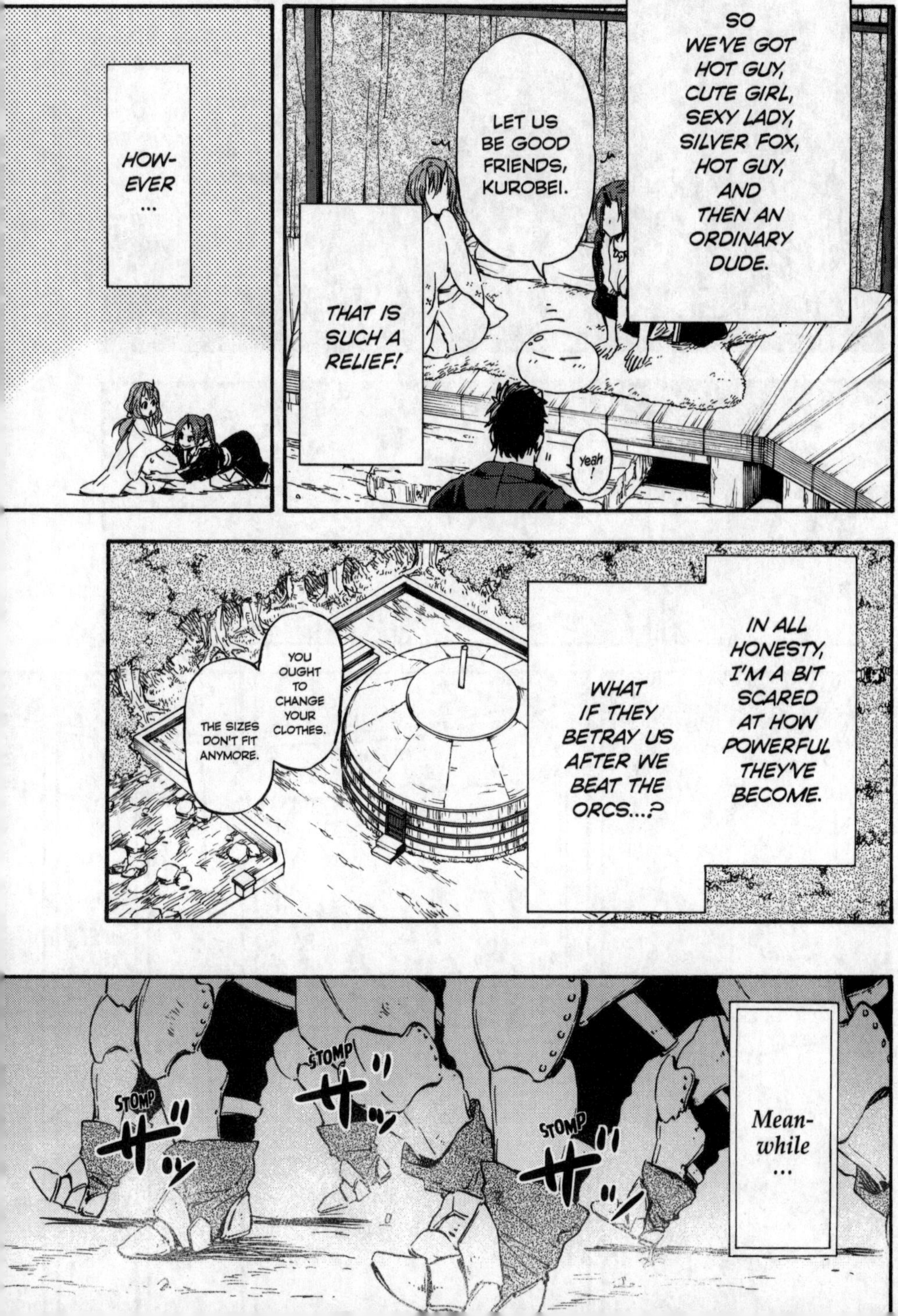
SO WE'VE GOT HOT GUY, CUTE GIRL, SEXY LADY, SILVER FOX, HOT GUY, AND THEN AN ORDINARY DUDE.
LET US BE GOOD FRIENDS, KUROBEI.
THAT IS SUCH A RELIEF!
Yeah!
HOW-EVER ...
IN ALL HONESTY, I'M A BIT SCARED AT HOW POWERFUL THEY'VE BECOME.
WHAT IF THEY BETRAY US AFTER WE BEAT THE ORCS...?
YOU OUGHT TO CHANGE YOUR CLOTHES.
THE SIZES DON'T FIT ANYMORE.
Mean-while ...
STOMP
STOMP
STOMP

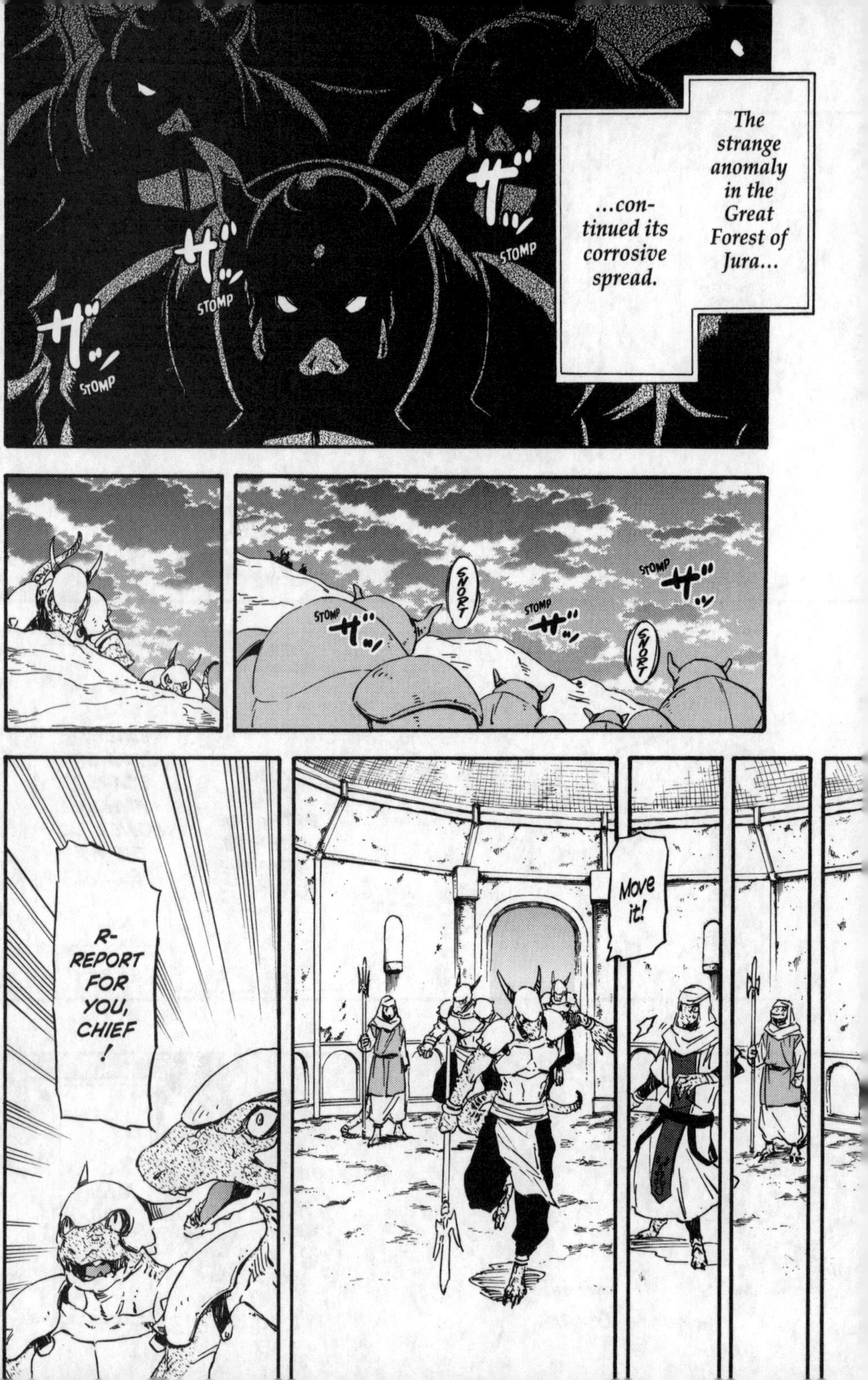
The strange anomaly in the Great Forest of Jura...
...con-tinued its corrosive spread.
ザッ STOMP
ザッ STOMP
ザッ STOMP
ザッ STOMP
SNORT
ザッ STOMP
SNORT
ザッ STOMP
Move it!
R-REPORT FOR YOU, CHIEF!

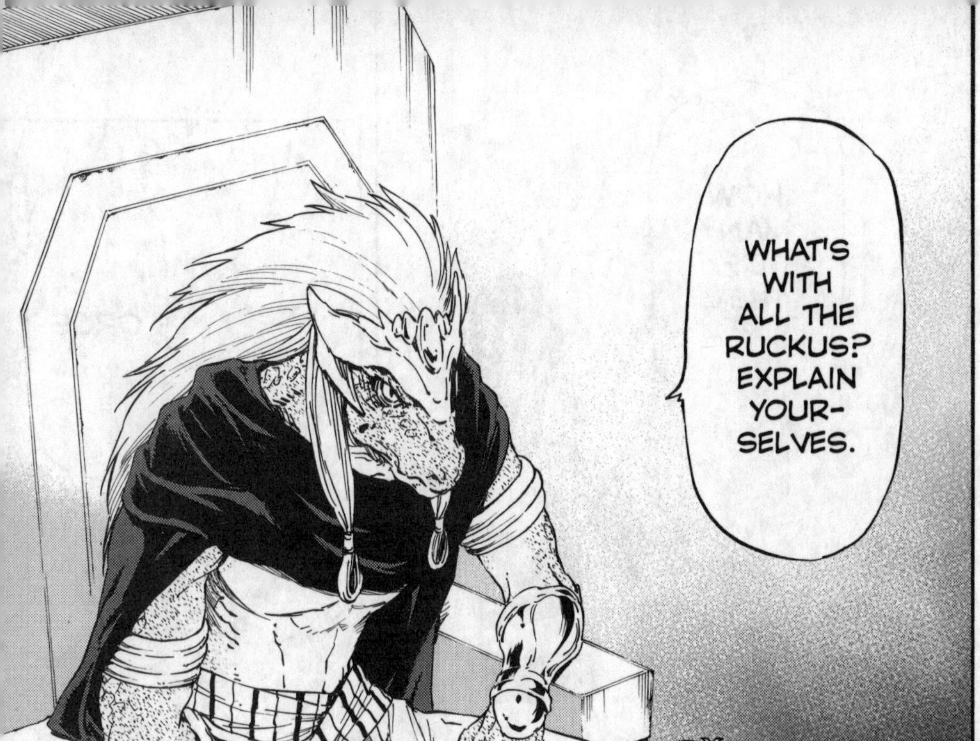
WHAT'S WITH ALL THE RUCKUS? EXPLAIN YOUR-SELVES.
Lizardman Chieftain
Unnamed
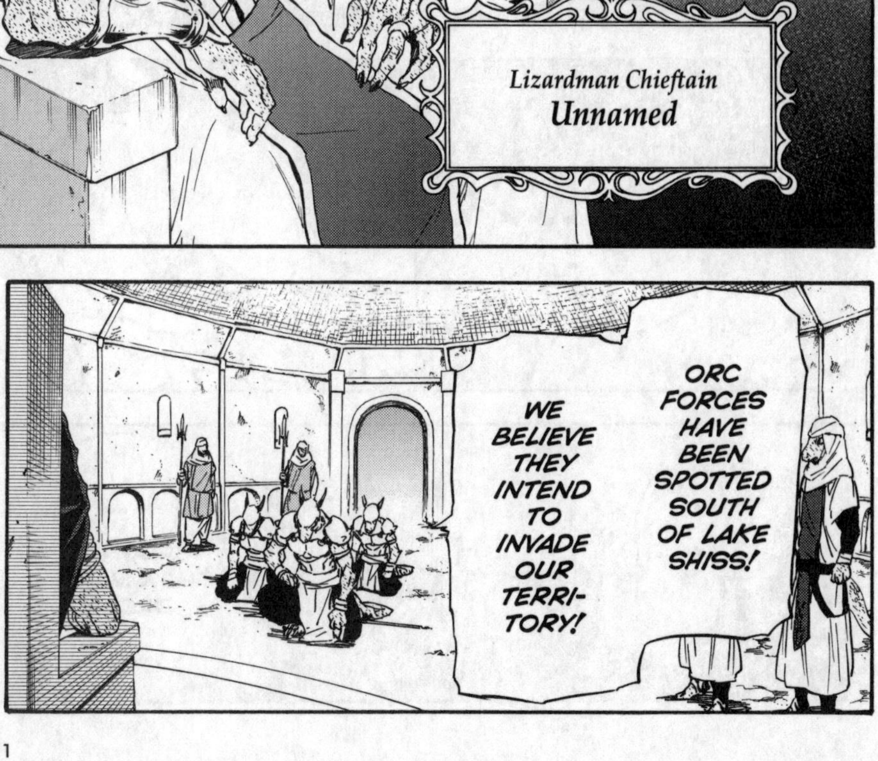
ORC FORCES HAVE BEEN SPOTTED SOUTH OF LAKE SHISS!
WE BELIEVE THEY INTEND TO INVADE OUR TERRI-TORY!

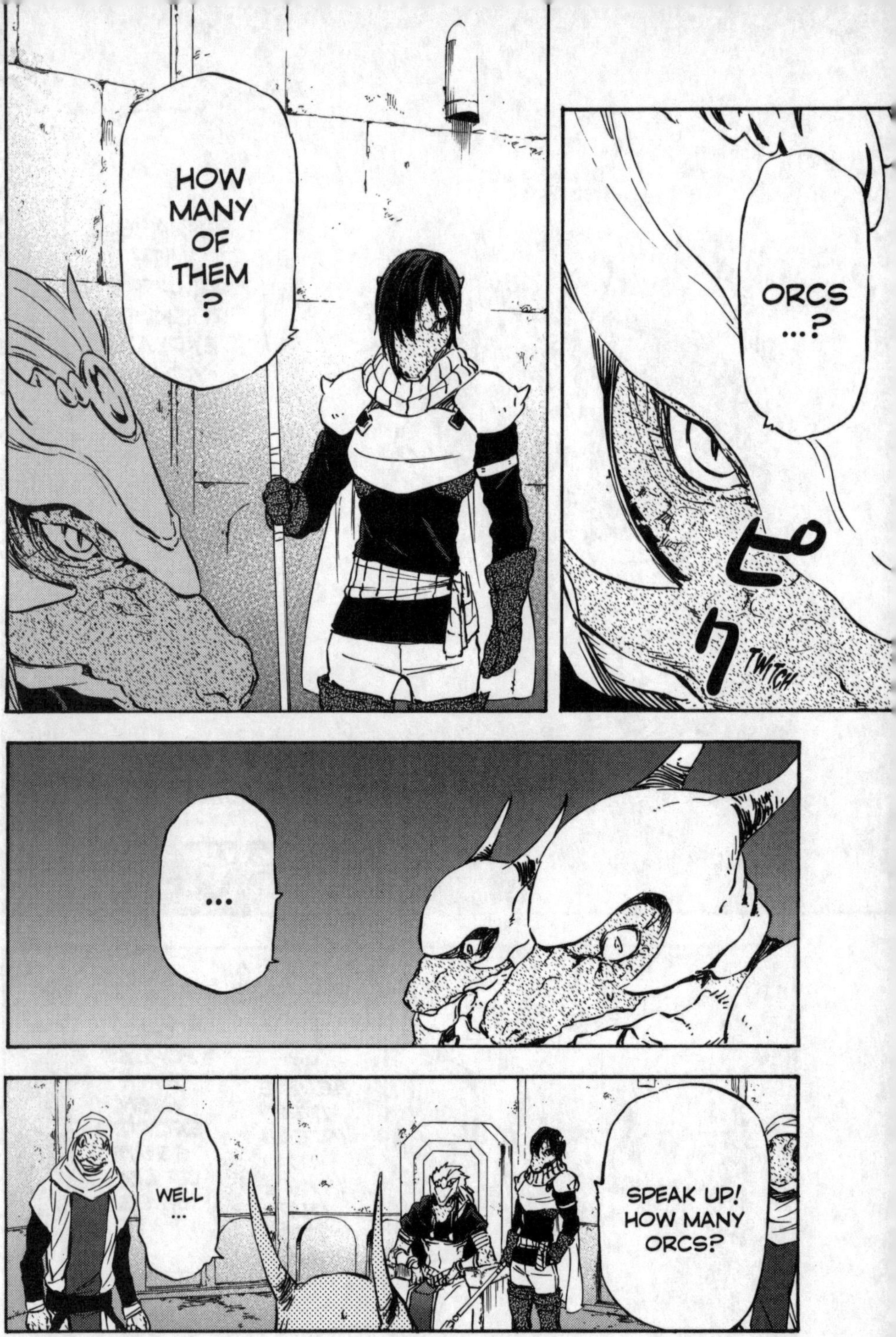
ORCS ...?
ピク
TWITCH
HOW MANY OF THEM ?
...
SPEAK UP! HOW MANY ORCS?
WELL ...

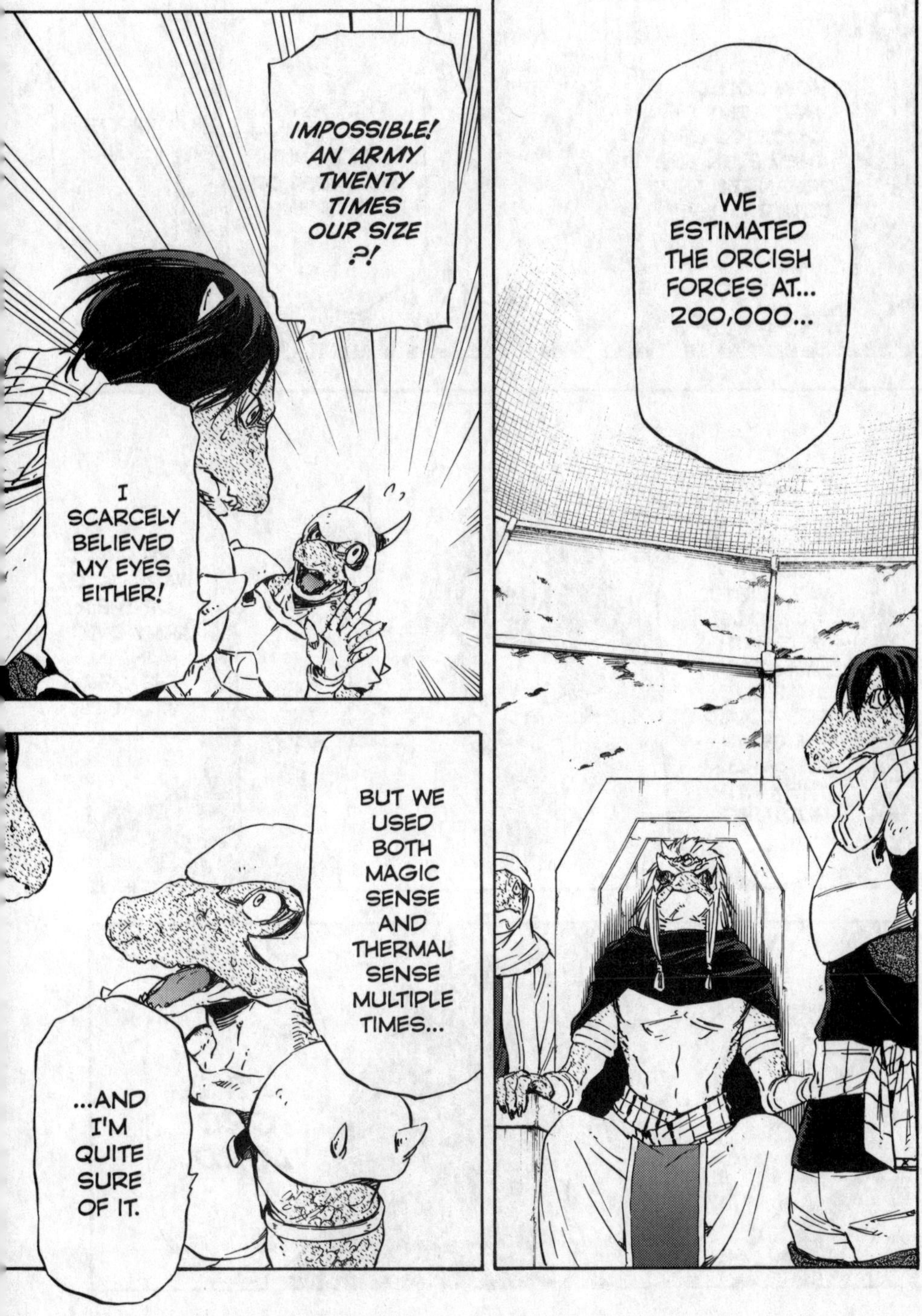
WE ESTIMATED THE ORCISH FORCES AT... 200,000...
IMPOSSIBLE! AN ARMY TWENTY TIMES OUR SIZE ?!
I SCARCELY BELIEVED MY EYES EITHER!
BUT WE USED BOTH MAGIC SENSE AND THERMAL SENSE MULTIPLE TIMES...
...AND I'M QUITE SURE OF IT.

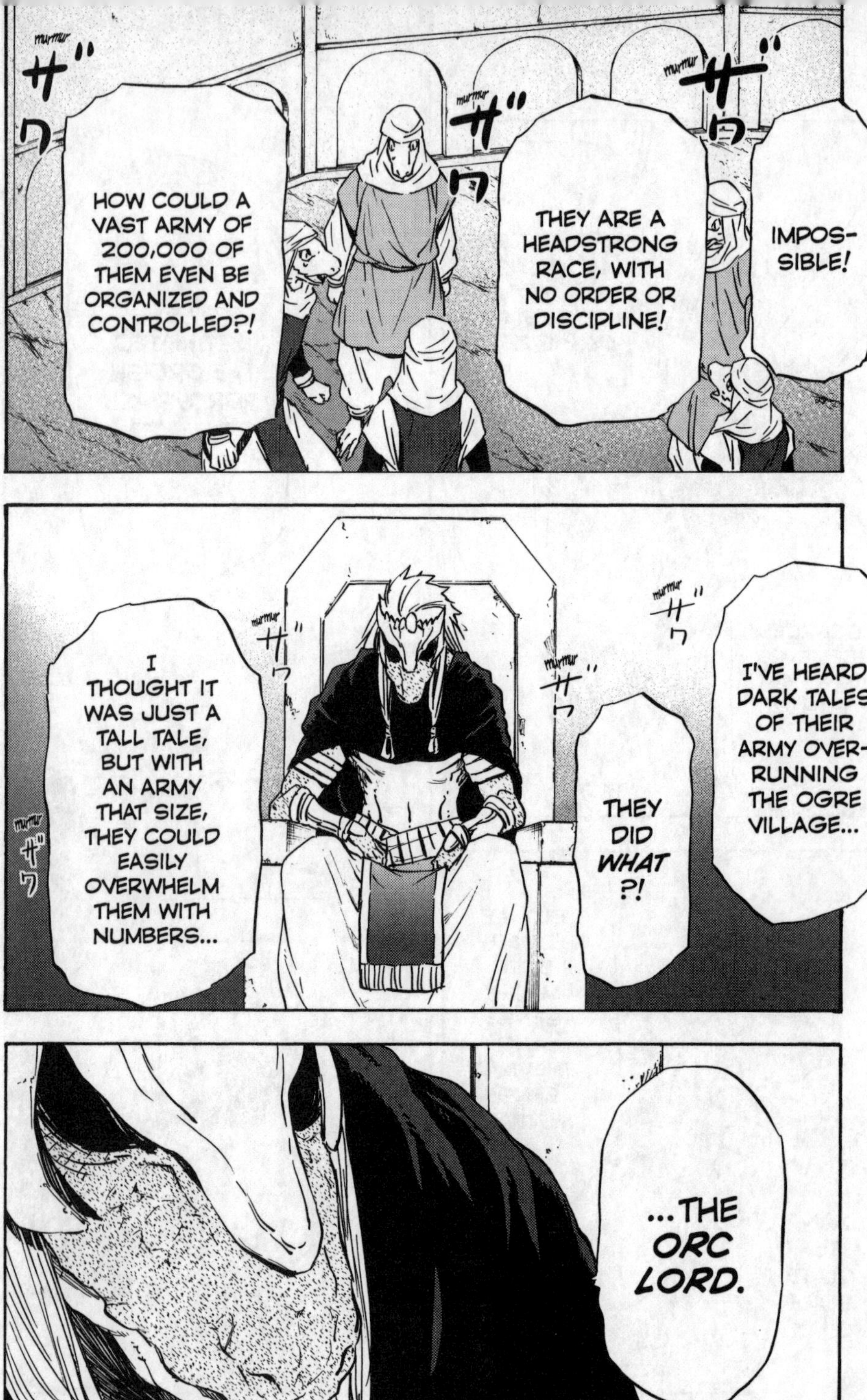

murmur ザワ
IMPOSSIBLE!
murmur ザワ
THEY ARE A HEADSTRONG RACE, WITH NO ORDER OR DISCIPLINE!
murmur ザワ
HOW COULD A VAST ARMY OF 200,000 OF THEM EVEN BE ORGANIZED AND CONTROLLED?!
murmur ザワ
I'VE HEARD DARK TALES OF THEIR ARMY OVER-RUNNING THE OGRE VILLAGE...
murmur ザワ
THEY DID WHAT?!
murmur ザワ
I THOUGHT IT WAS JUST A TALL TALE, BUT WITH AN ARMY THAT SIZE, THEY COULD EASILY OVERWHELM THEM WITH NUMBERS...
murmur ザワ
...THE ORC LORD.

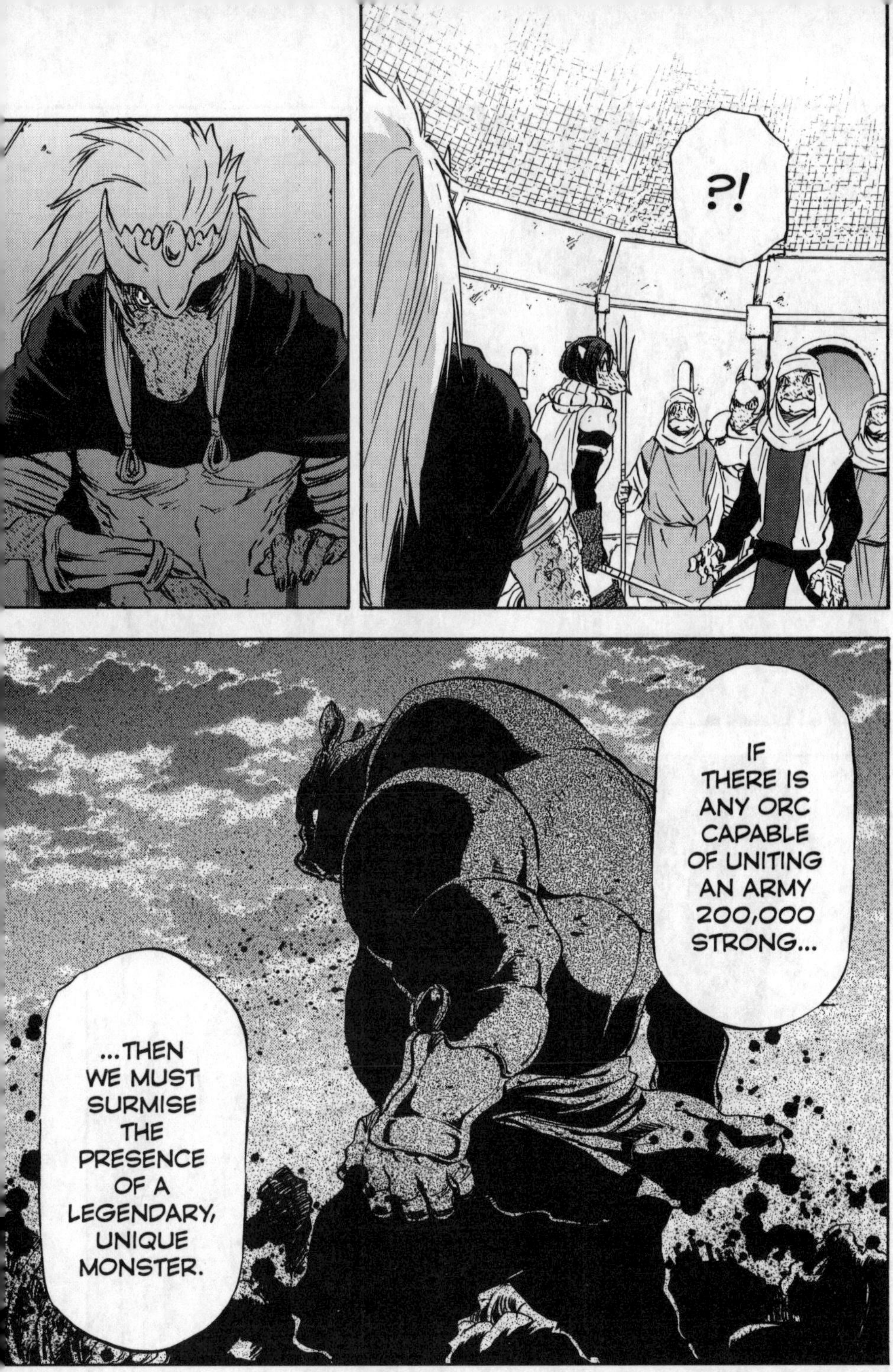
?!
IF THERE IS ANY ORC CAPABLE OF UNITING AN ARMY 200,000 STRONG...
...THEN WE MUST SURMISE THE PRESENCE OF A LEGENDARY, UNIQUE MONSTER.

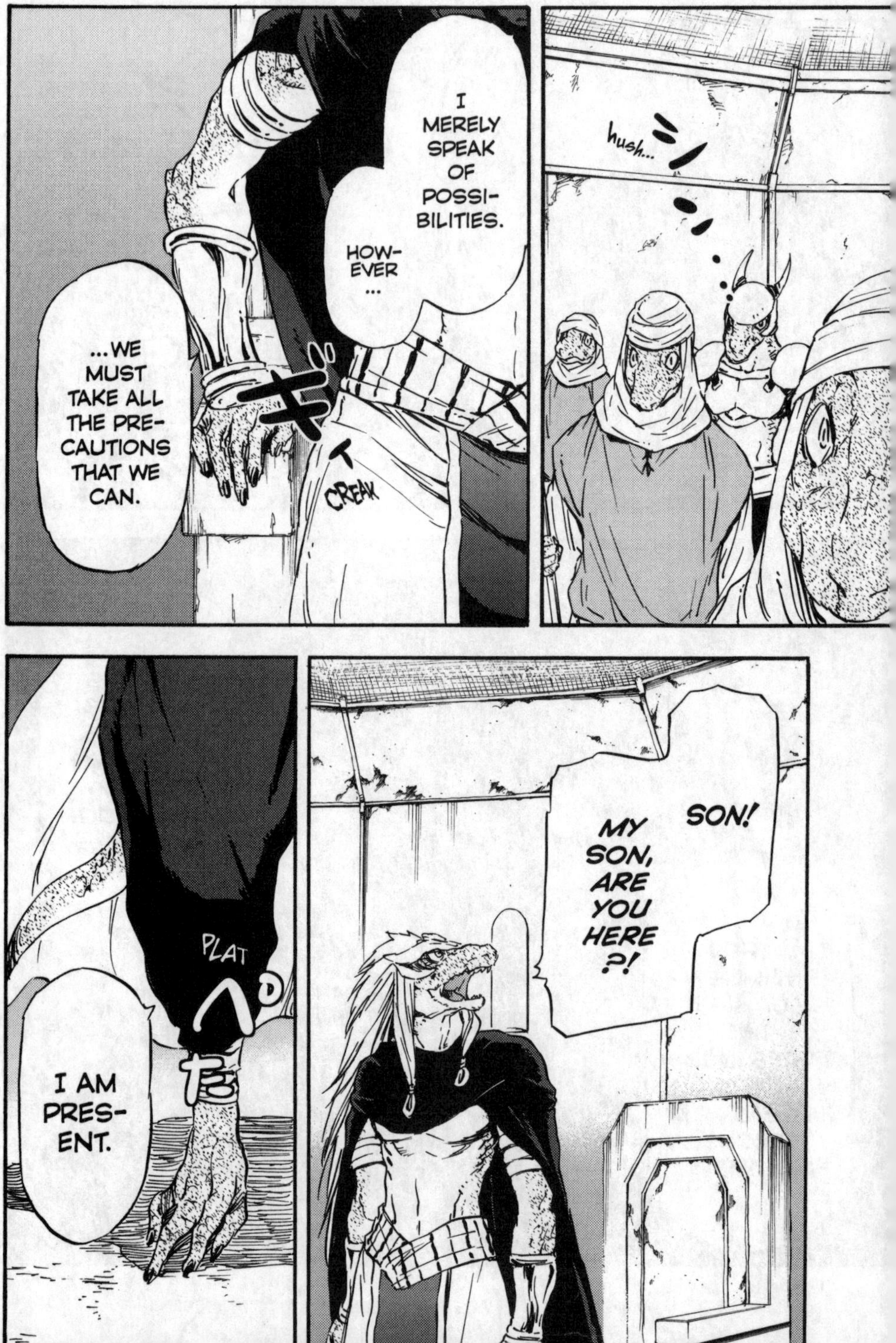
hush...
I MERELY SPEAK OF POSSI-BILITIES.
HOW-EVER ...
...WE MUST TAKE ALL THE PRE-CAUTIONS THAT WE CAN.
CREAK
SON!
MY SON, ARE YOU HERE?!
PLAT
I AM PRES-ENT.

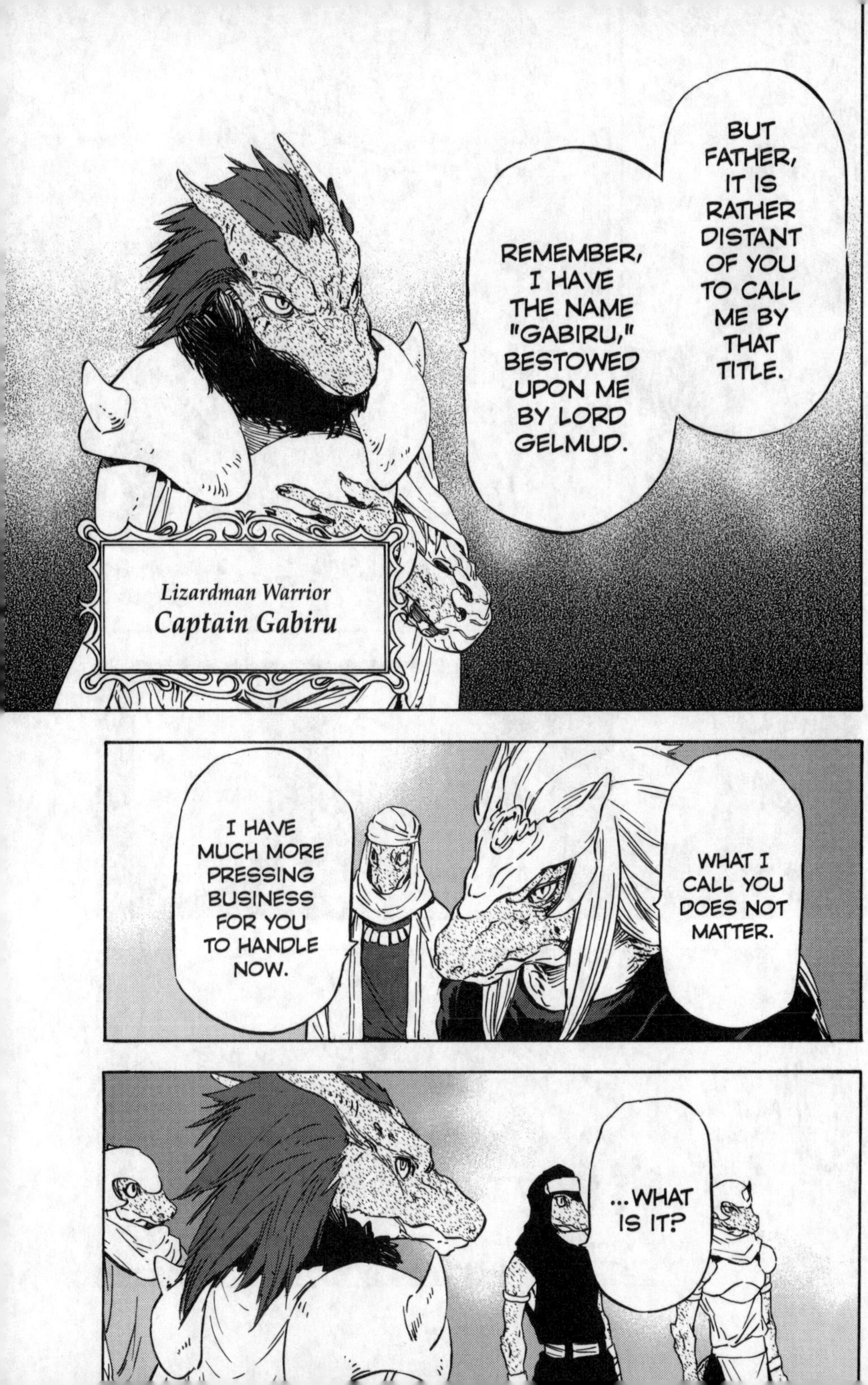
BUT FATHER, IT IS RATHER DISTANT OF YOU TO CALL ME BY THAT TITLE.
REMEMBER, I HAVE THE NAME "GABIRU," BESTOWED UPON ME BY LORD GELMUD.
Lizardman Warrior
Captain Gabiru
WHAT I CALL YOU DOES NOT MATTER.
I HAVE MUCH MORE PRESSING BUSINESS FOR YOU TO HANDLE NOW.
...WHAT IS IT?

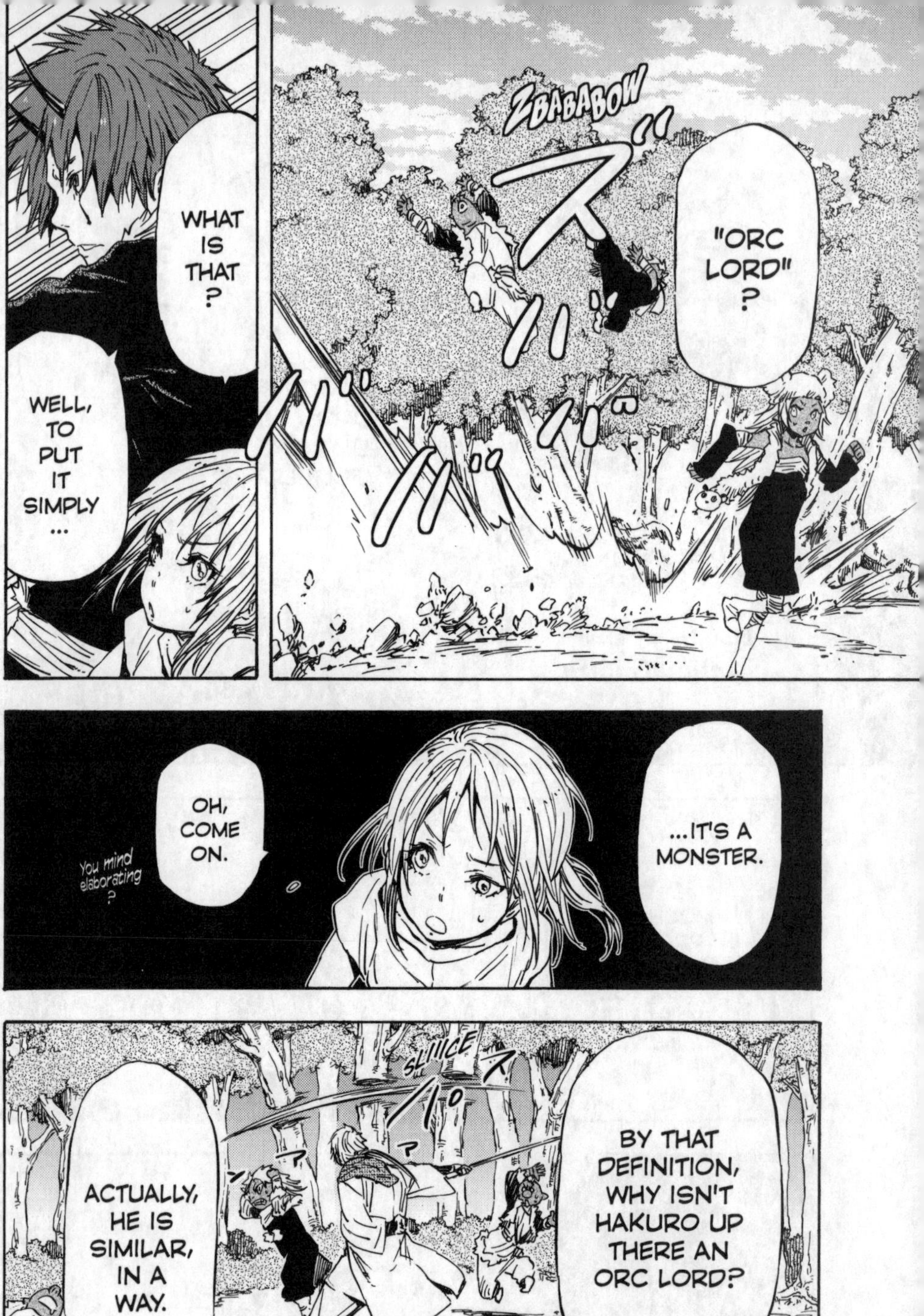
ZBABABOW
"ORC LORD"?
WHAT IS THAT?
WELL, TO PUT IT SIMPLY...
...IT'S A MONSTER.
OH, COME ON.
You mind elaborating?
SLIIICE
BY THAT DEFINITION, WHY ISN'T HAKURO UP THERE AN ORC LORD?
ACTUALLY, HE IS SIMILAR, IN A WAY.

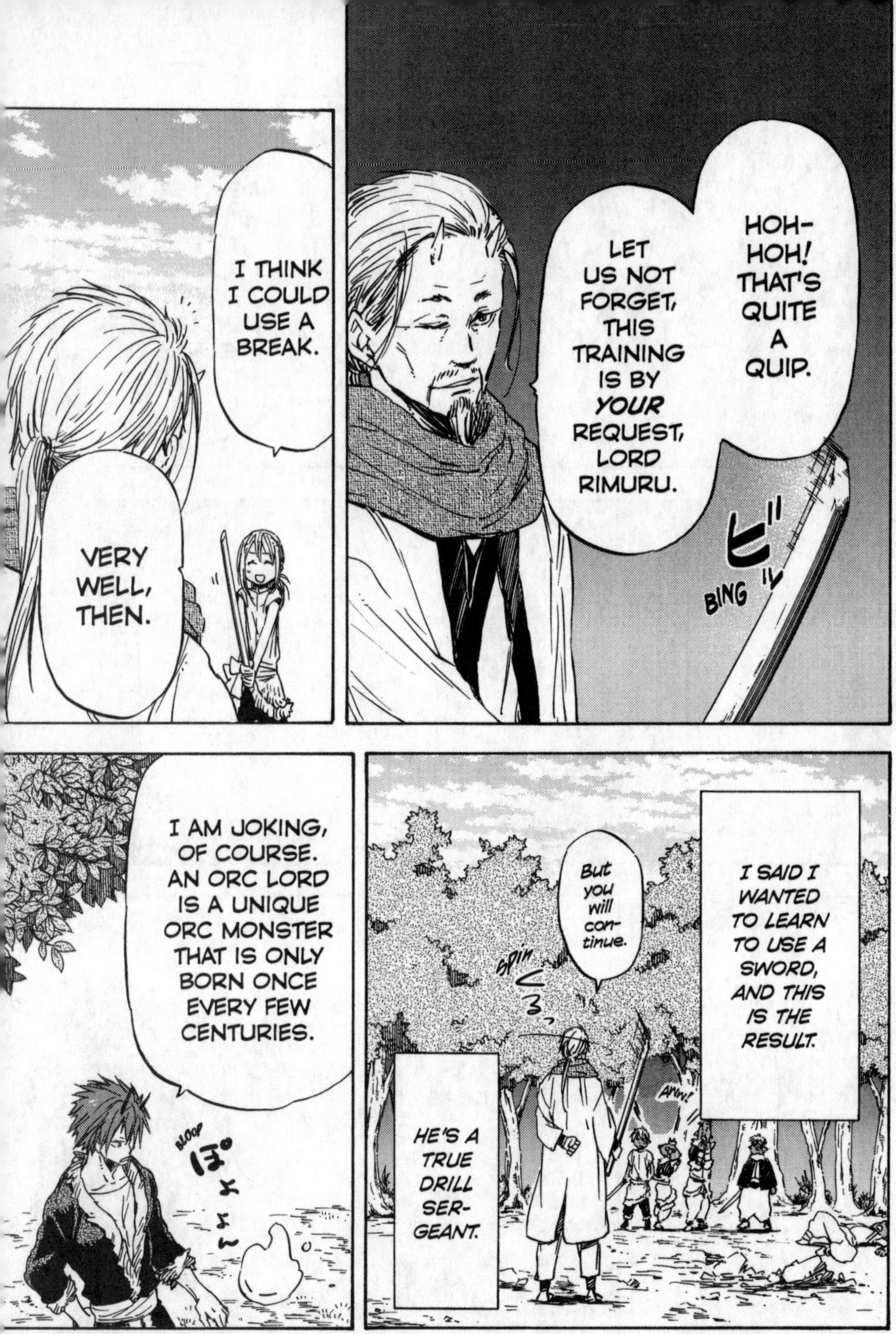
HOH-HOH! THAT'S QUITE A QUIP.
LET US NOT FORGET, THIS TRAINING IS BY *YOUR* REQUEST, LORD RIMURU.
BING
I THINK I COULD USE A BREAK.
VERY WELL, THEN.
I SAID I WANTED TO LEARN TO USE A SWORD, AND THIS IS THE RESULT.
But you will continue.
SPIN
AWW!
HE'S A TRUE DRILL SERGEANT.
I AM JOKING, OF COURSE. AN ORC LORD IS A UNIQUE ORC MONSTER THAT IS ONLY BORN ONCE EVERY FEW CENTURIES.
BLOOP

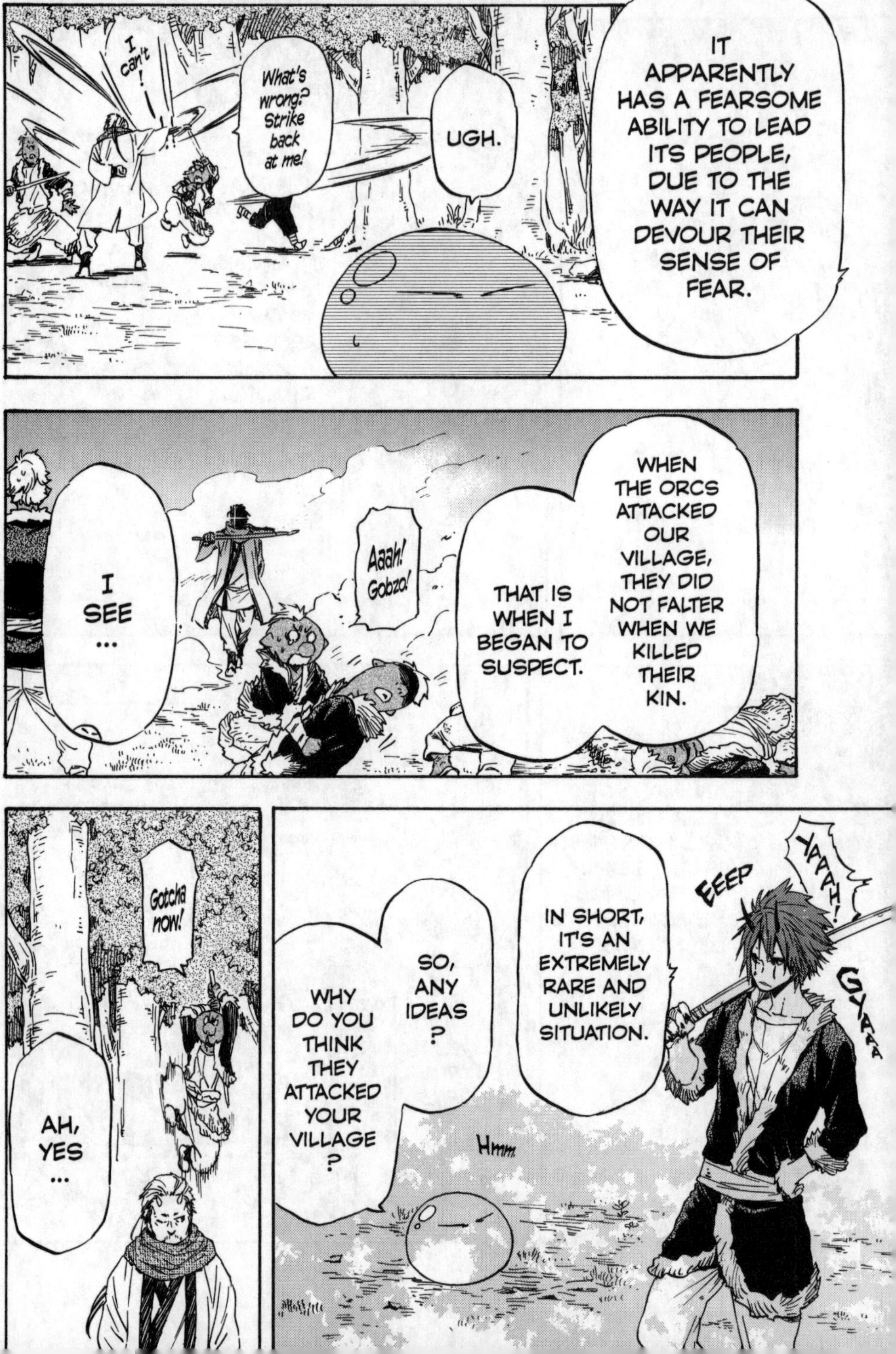
IT APPARENTLY HAS A FEARSOME ABILITY TO LEAD ITS PEOPLE, DUE TO THE WAY IT CAN DEVOUR THEIR SENSE OF FEAR.
UGH.
What's wrong? Strike back at me!
I can't!
WHEN THE ORCS ATTACKED OUR VILLAGE, THEY DID NOT FALTER WHEN WE KILLED THEIR KIN.
THAT IS WHEN I BEGAN TO SUSPECT.
Aaah! Gobzo!
I SEE...
YAAAH!
EEEP
IN SHORT, IT'S AN EXTREMELY RARE AND UNLIKELY SITUATION.
GYAAA
SO, ANY IDEAS?
WHY DO YOU THINK THEY ATTACKED YOUR VILLAGE?
Hmm
Gotcha now!
AH, YES...

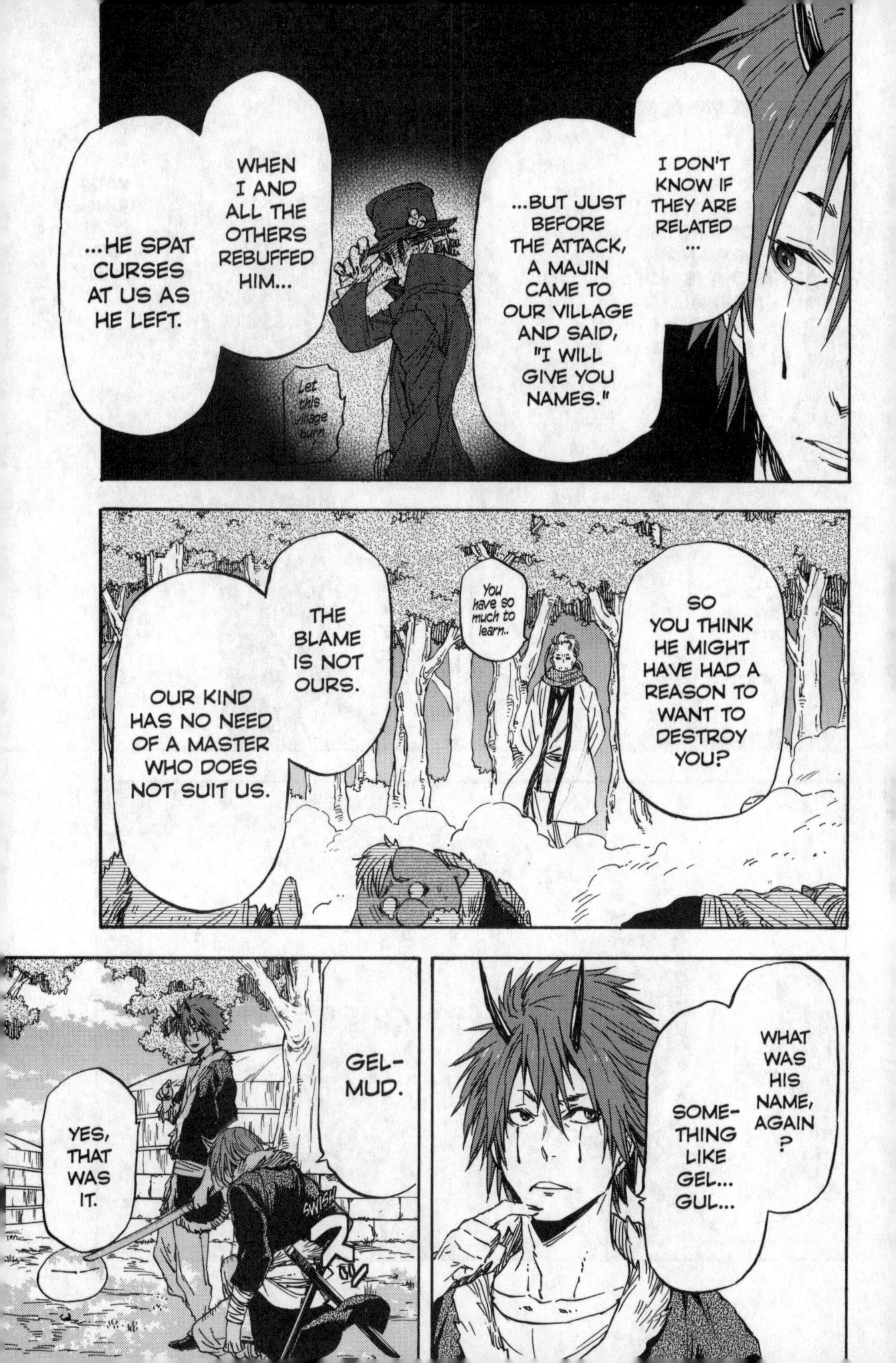
I DON'T KNOW IF THEY ARE RELATED...
...BUT JUST BEFORE THE ATTACK, A MAJIN CAME TO OUR VILLAGE AND SAID, "I WILL GIVE YOU NAMES."
WHEN I AND ALL THE OTHERS REBUFFED HIM...
Let this village burn!
...HE SPAT CURSES AT US AS HE LEFT.
SO YOU THINK HE MIGHT HAVE HAD A REASON TO WANT TO DESTROY YOU?
You have so much to learn..
THE BLAME IS NOT OURS.
OUR KIND HAS NO NEED OF A MASTER WHO DOES NOT SUIT US.
WHAT WAS HIS NAME, AGAIN?
SOME-THING LIKE GEL... GUL...
GEL-MUD.
YES, THAT WAS IT.
SWISH

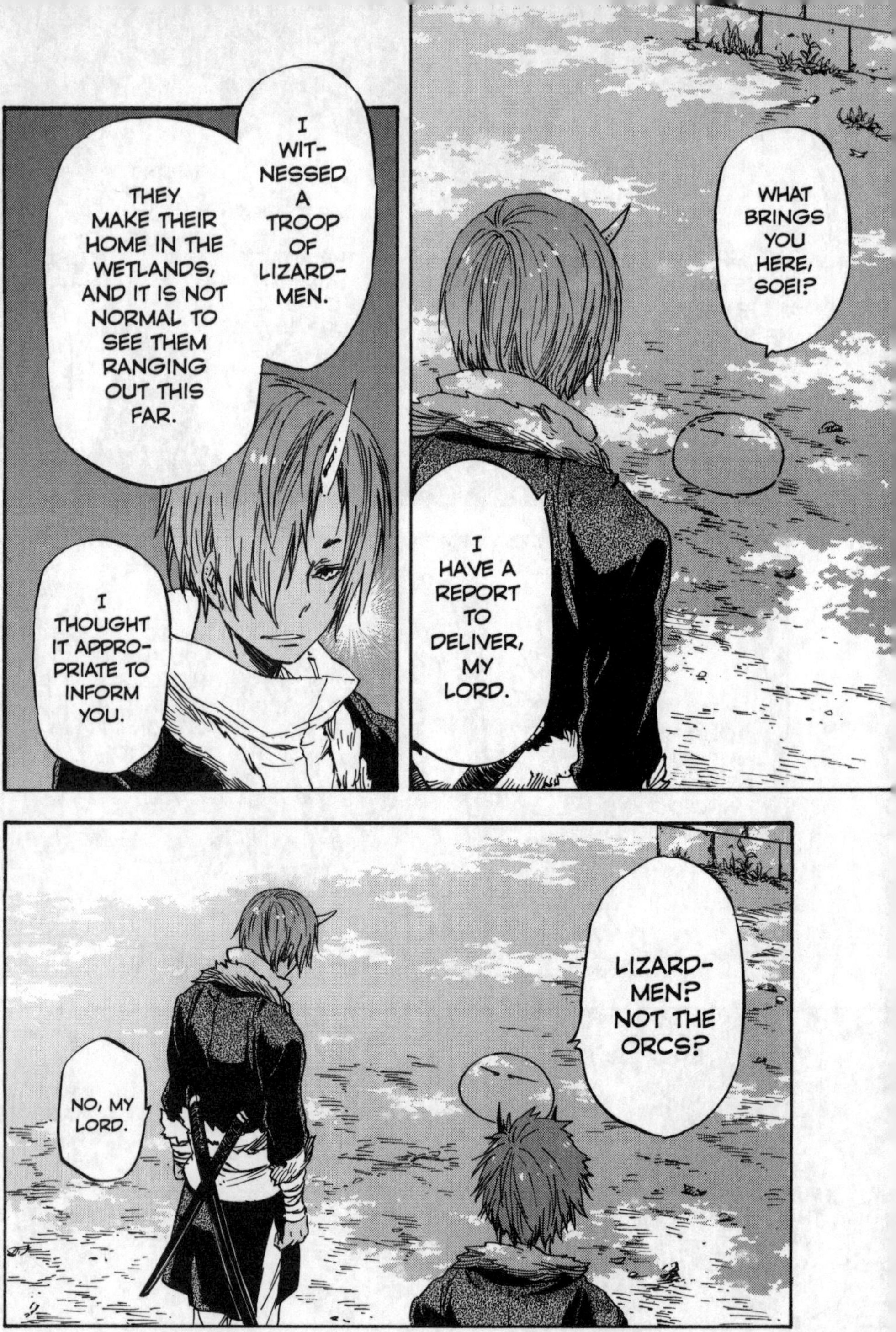
WHAT BRINGS YOU HERE, SOEI?
I HAVE A REPORT TO DELIVER, MY LORD.
I WIT-NESSED A TROOP OF LIZARD-MEN.
THEY MAKE THEIR HOME IN THE WETLANDS, AND IT IS NOT NORMAL TO SEE THEM RANGING OUT THIS FAR.
I THOUGHT IT APPRO-PRIATE TO INFORM YOU.
LIZARD-MEN? NOT THE ORCS?
NO, MY LORD.

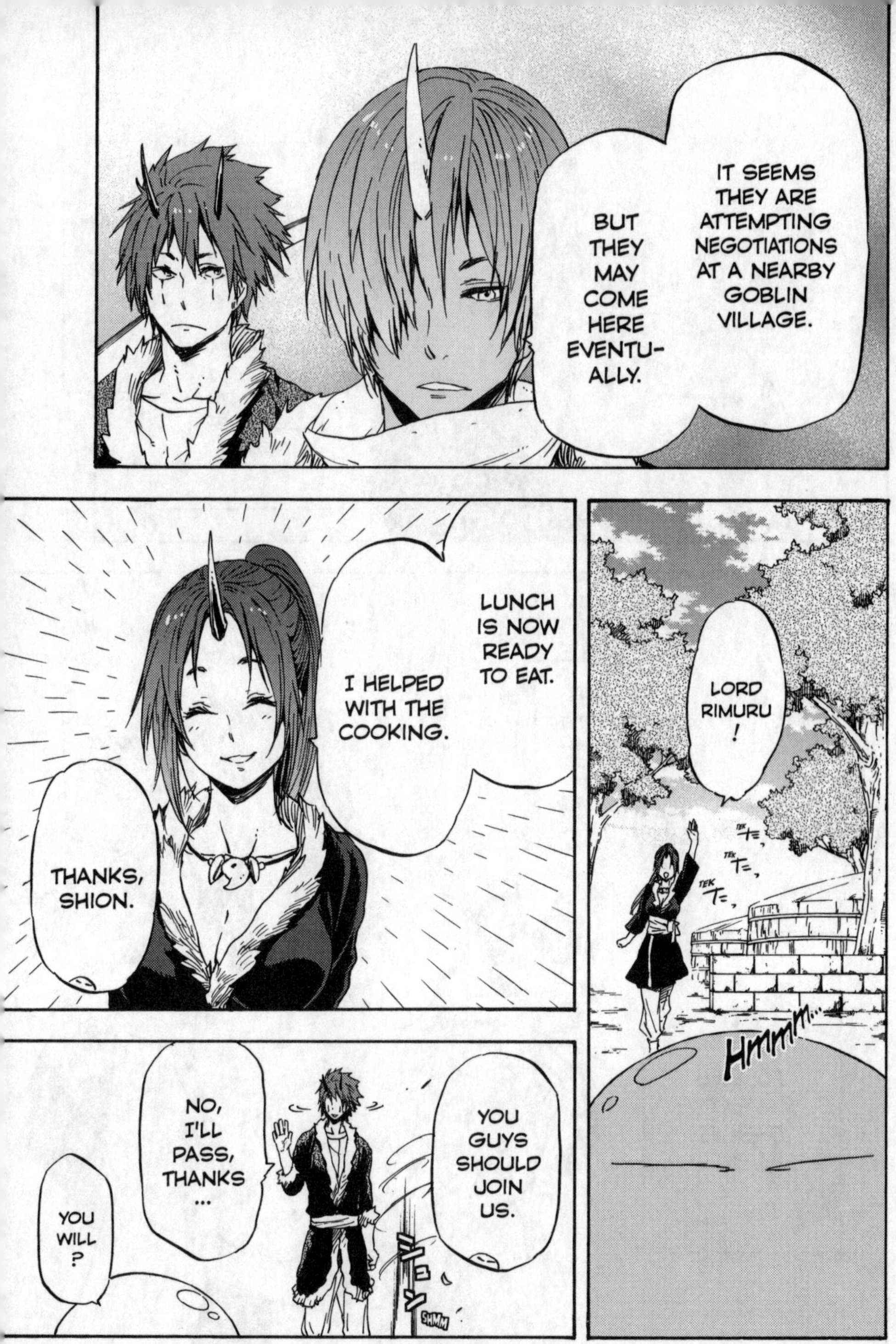

IT SEEMS THEY ARE ATTEMPTING NEGOTIATIONS AT A NEARBY GOBLIN VILLAGE.
BUT THEY MAY COME HERE EVENTU-ALLY.
LORD RIMURU!
TEK
TEK
TEK
Hmmm...
LUNCH IS NOW READY TO EAT.
I HELPED WITH THE COOKING.
THANKS, SHION.
YOU GUYS SHOULD JOIN US.
SHMM
NO, I'LL PASS, THANKS...
YOU WILL?

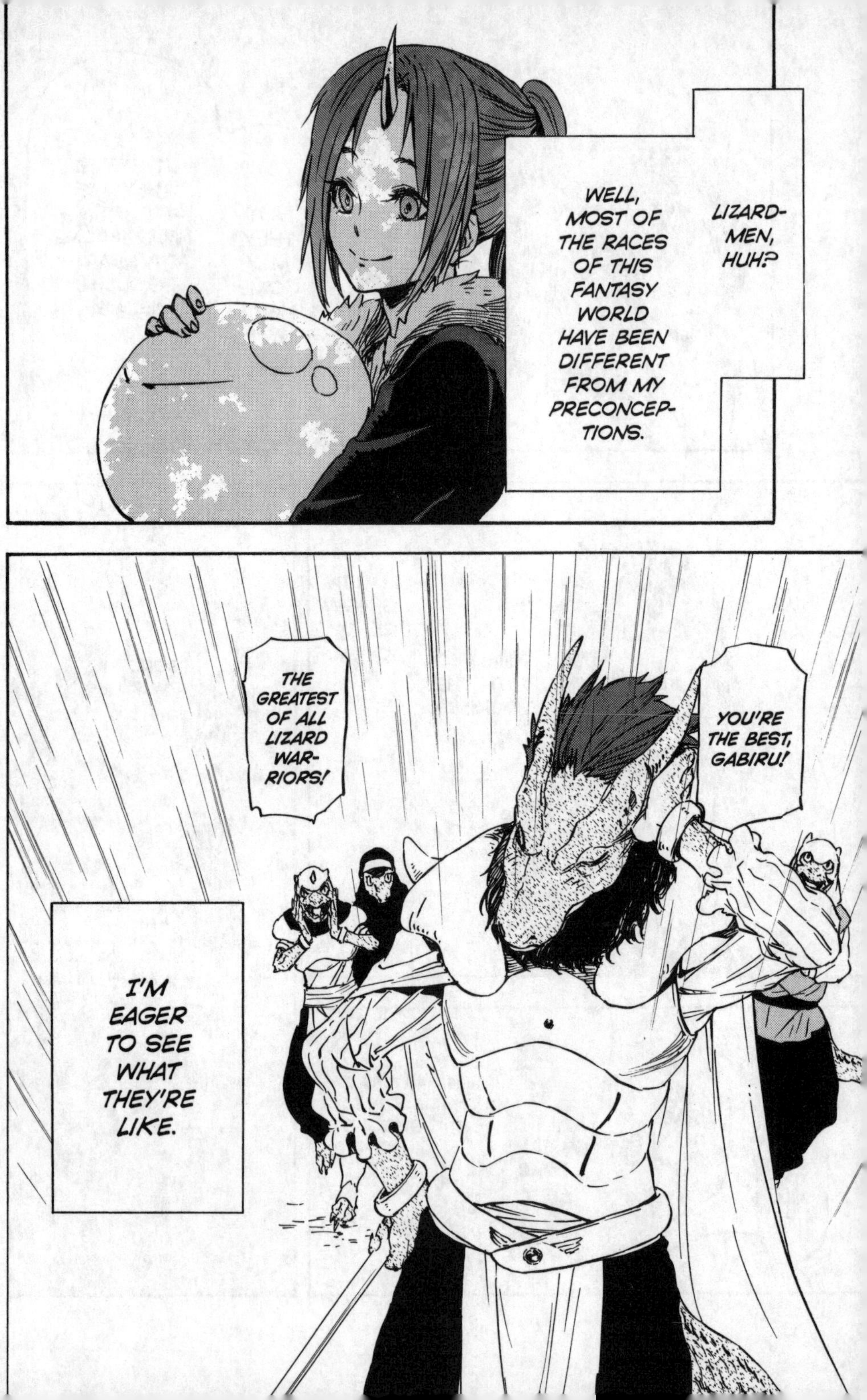
LIZARD-MEN, HUH?
WELL, MOST OF THE RACES OF THIS FANTASY WORLD HAVE BEEN DIFFERENT FROM MY PRECONCEPTIONS.
YOU'RE THE BEST, GABIRU!
THE GREATEST OF ALL LIZARD WARRIORS!
I'M EAGER TO SEE WHAT THEY'RE LIKE.

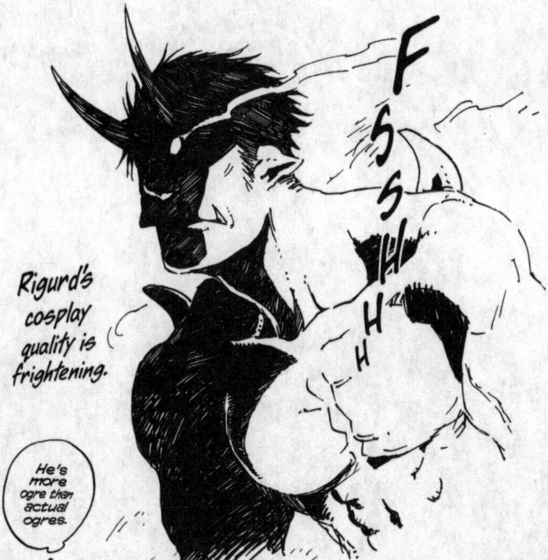
FSSHHH
Rigurd's cosplay quality is frightening.
He's more ogre than actual ogres.

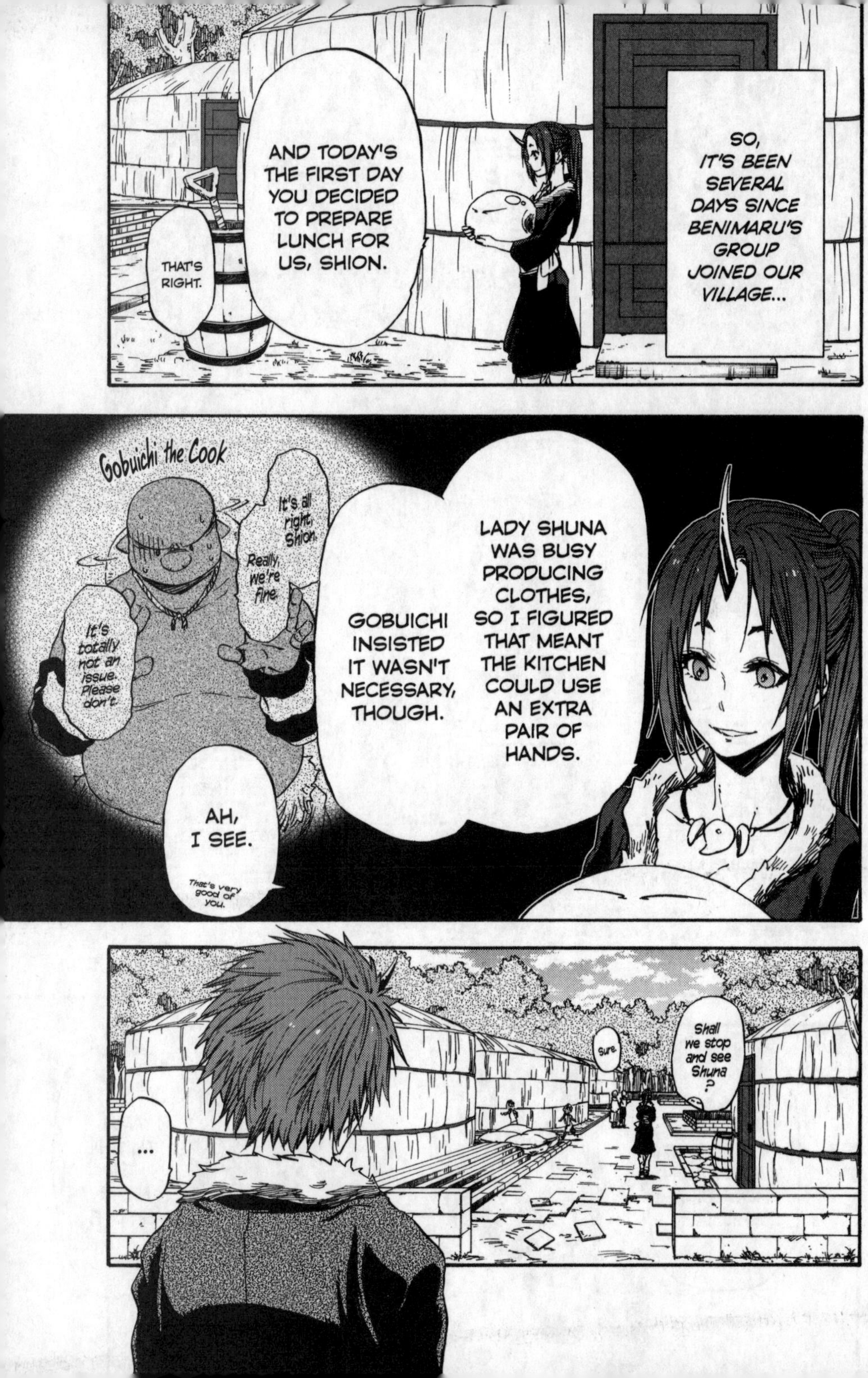
SO, IT'S BEEN SEVERAL DAYS SINCE BENIMARU'S GROUP JOINED OUR VILLAGE...
AND TODAY'S THE FIRST DAY YOU DECIDED TO PREPARE LUNCH FOR US, SHION.
THAT'S RIGHT.
LADY SHUNA WAS BUSY PRODUCING CLOTHES, SO I FIGURED THAT MEANT THE KITCHEN COULD USE AN EXTRA PAIR OF HANDS.
GOBUICHI INSISTED IT WASN'T NECESSARY, THOUGH.
Gobuichi the Cook
It's all right, Shion.
Really, we're fine.
It's totally not an issue. Please don't.
AH, I SEE.
That's very good of you.
Shall we stop and see Shuna?
Sure.
...

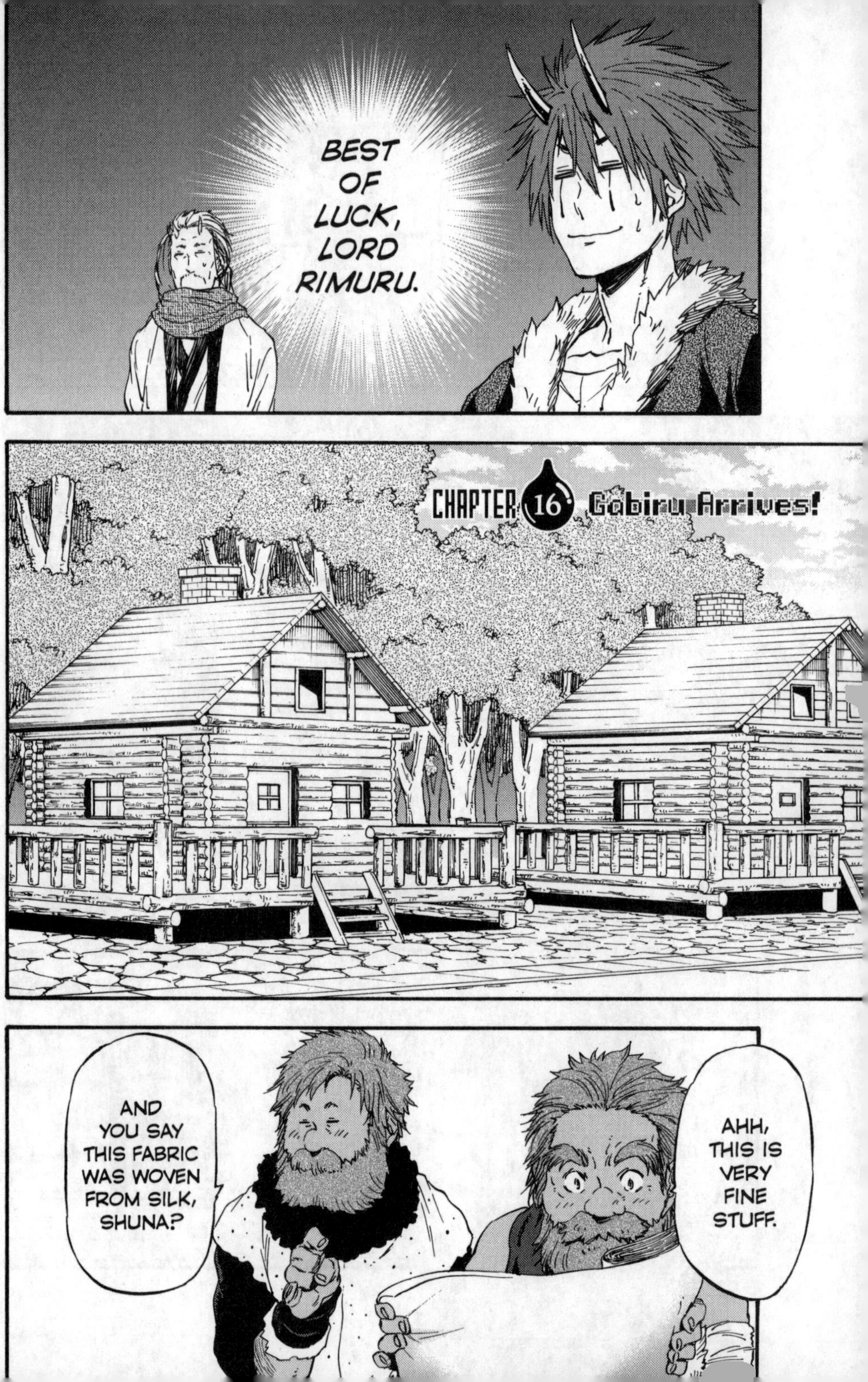
BEST OF LUCK, LORD RIMURU.
CHAPTER 16 Gabiru Arrives!
AHH, THIS IS VERY FINE STUFF.
AND YOU SAY THIS FABRIC WAS WOVEN FROM SILK, SHUNA?

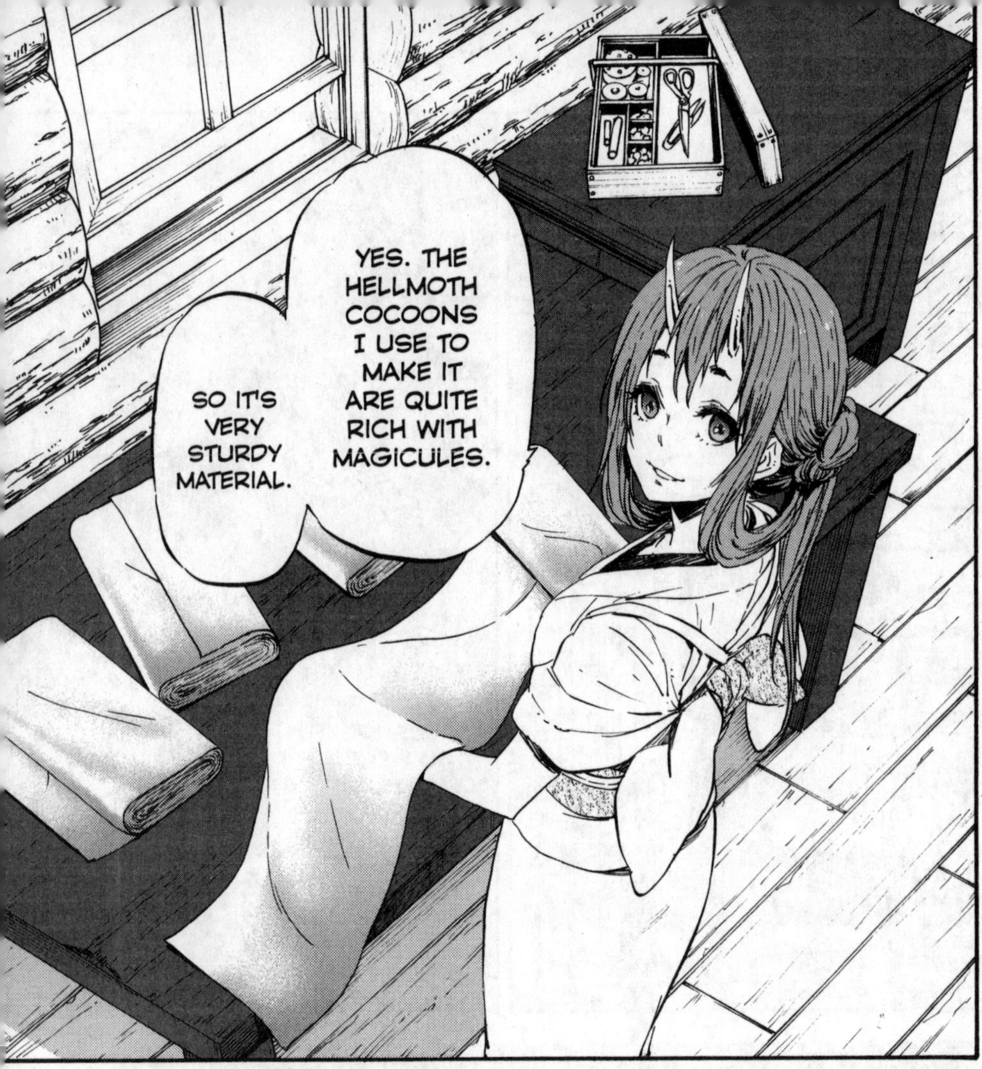
YES. THE HELLMOTH COCOONS I USE TO MAKE IT ARE QUITE RICH WITH MAGICULES.
SO IT'S VERY STURDY MATERIAL.

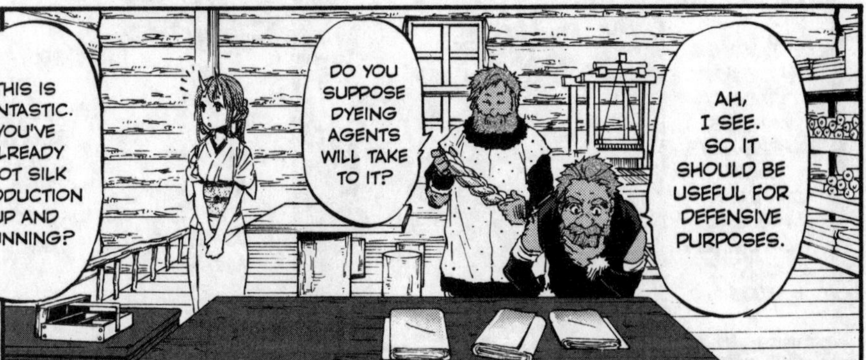
AH, I SEE. SO IT SHOULD BE USEFUL FOR DEFENSIVE PURPOSES.
DO YOU SUPPOSE DYEING AGENTS WILL TAKE TO IT?
THIS IS FANTASTIC. YOU'VE ALREADY GOT SILK PRODUCTION UP AND RUNNING?

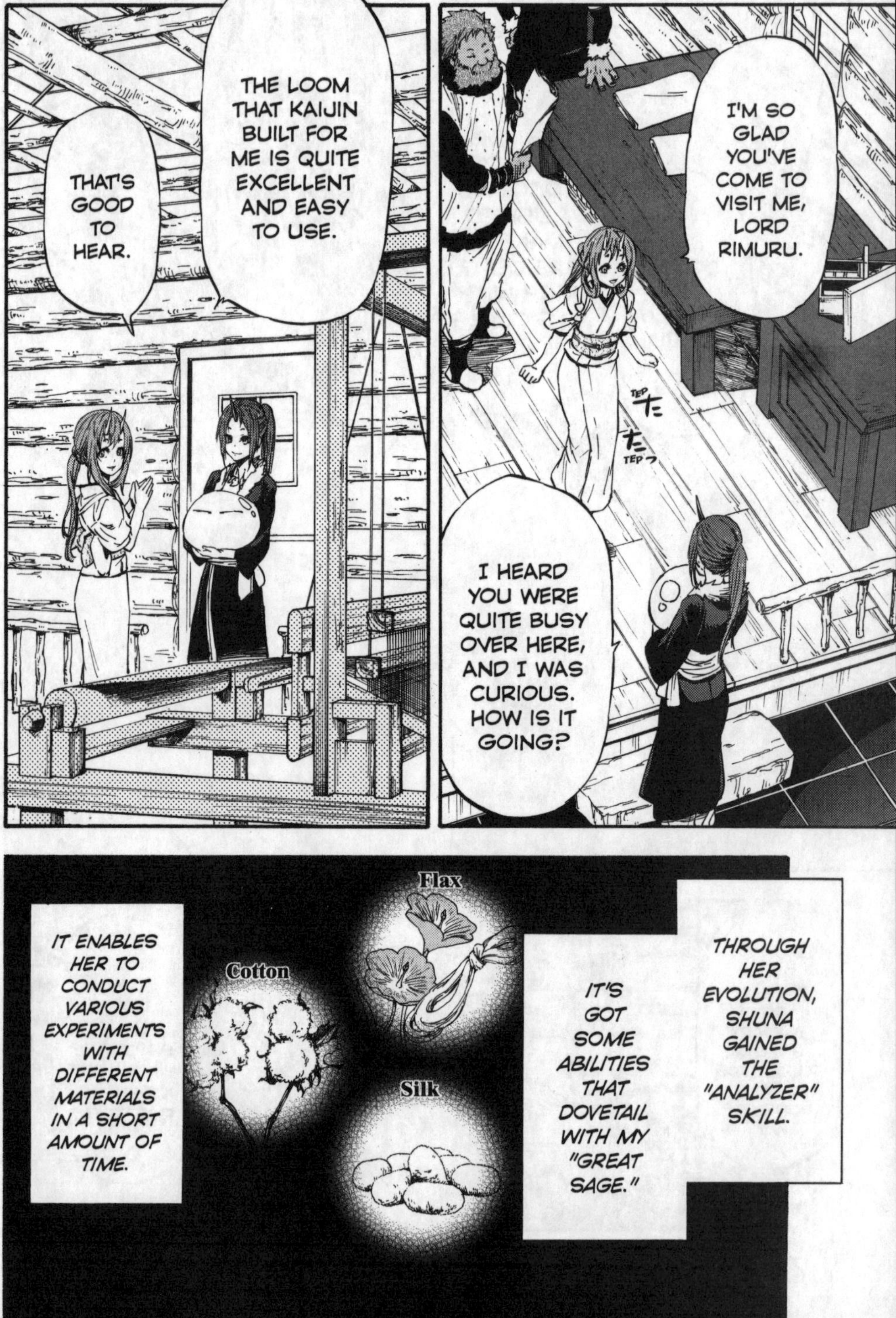
I'M SO GLAD YOU'VE COME TO VISIT ME, LORD RIMURU.
TEP TEP
I HEARD YOU WERE QUITE BUSY OVER HERE, AND I WAS CURIOUS. HOW IS IT GOING?
THE LOOM THAT KAIJIN BUILT FOR ME IS QUITE EXCELLENT AND EASY TO USE.
THAT'S GOOD TO HEAR.
THROUGH HER EVOLUTION, SHUNA GAINED THE "ANALYZER" SKILL.
IT'S GOT SOME ABILITIES THAT DOVETAIL WITH MY "GREAT SAGE."
Flax
Cotton
Silk
IT ENABLES HER TO CONDUCT VARIOUS EXPERIMENTS WITH DIFFERENT MATERIALS IN A SHORT AMOUNT OF TIME.

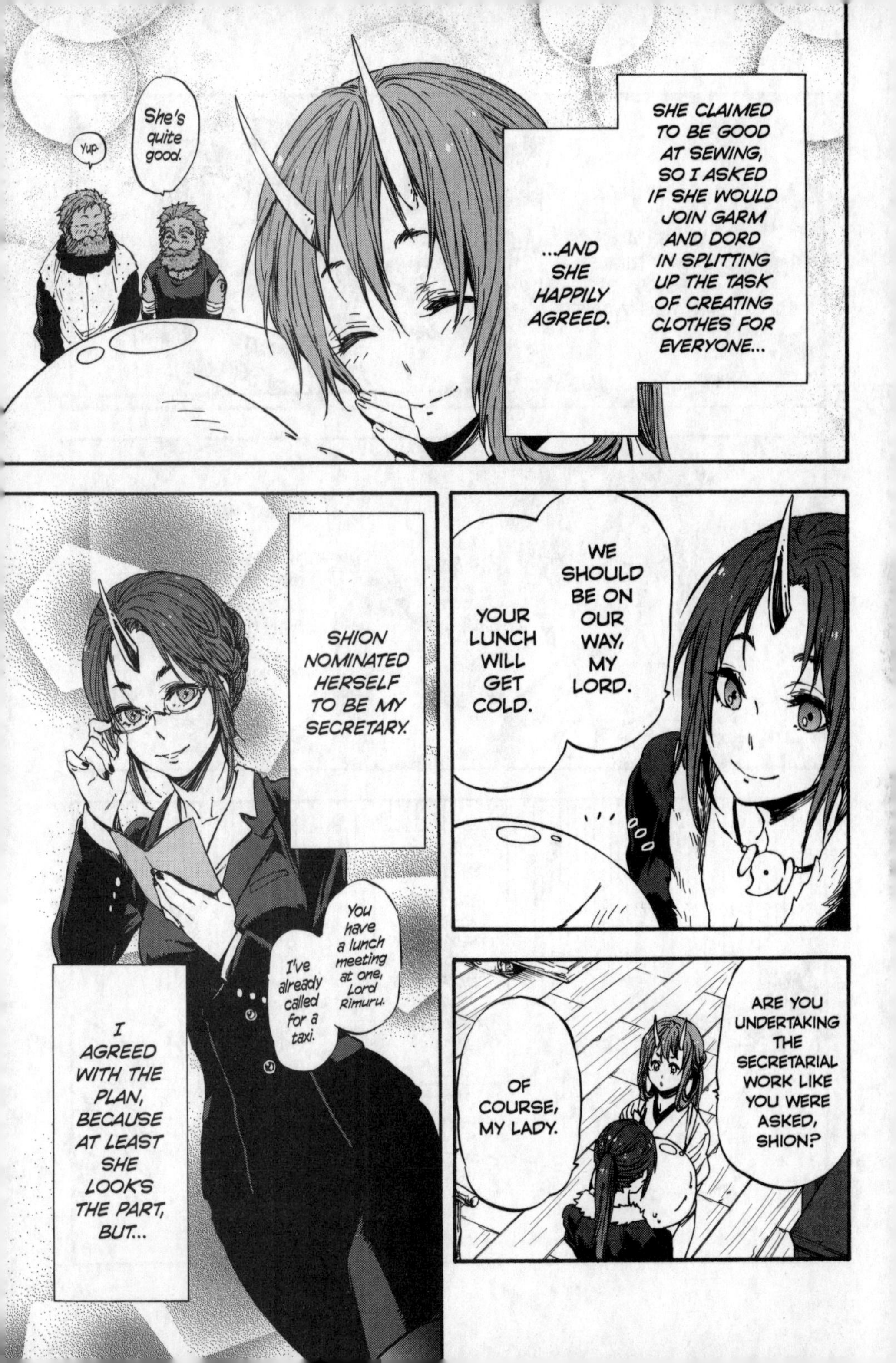
SHE CLAIMED TO BE GOOD AT SEWING, SO I ASKED IF SHE WOULD JOIN GARM AND DORD IN SPLITTING UP THE TASK OF CREATING CLOTHES FOR EVERYONE...
...AND SHE HAPPILY AGREED.
She's quite good.
Yup.
WE SHOULD BE ON OUR WAY, MY LORD.
YOUR LUNCH WILL GET COLD.
ARE YOU UNDERTAKING THE SECRETARIAL WORK LIKE YOU WERE ASKED, SHION?
OF COURSE, MY LADY.
SHION NOMINATED HERSELF TO BE MY SECRETARY.
You have a lunch meeting at one, Lord Rimuru.
I've already called for a taxi.
I AGREED WITH THE PLAN, BECAUSE AT LEAST SHE LOOKS THE PART, BUT...

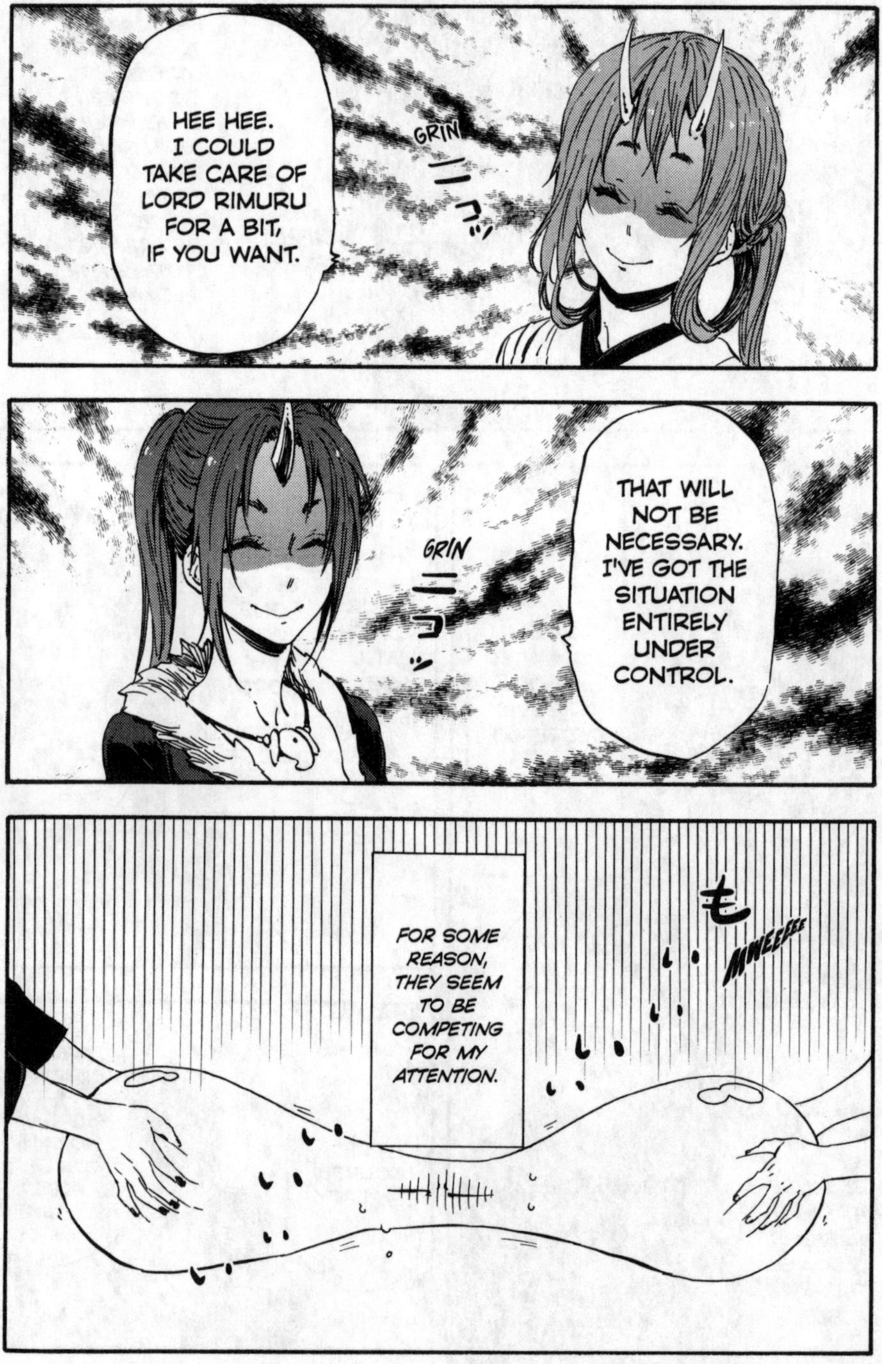
HEE HEE. I COULD TAKE CARE OF LORD RIMURU FOR A BIT, IF YOU WANT.
GRIN
THAT WILL NOT BE NECESSARY. I'VE GOT THE SITUATION ENTIRELY UNDER CONTROL.
GRIN
FOR SOME REASON, THEY SEEM TO BE COMPETING FOR MY ATTENTION.
MWEEEEE

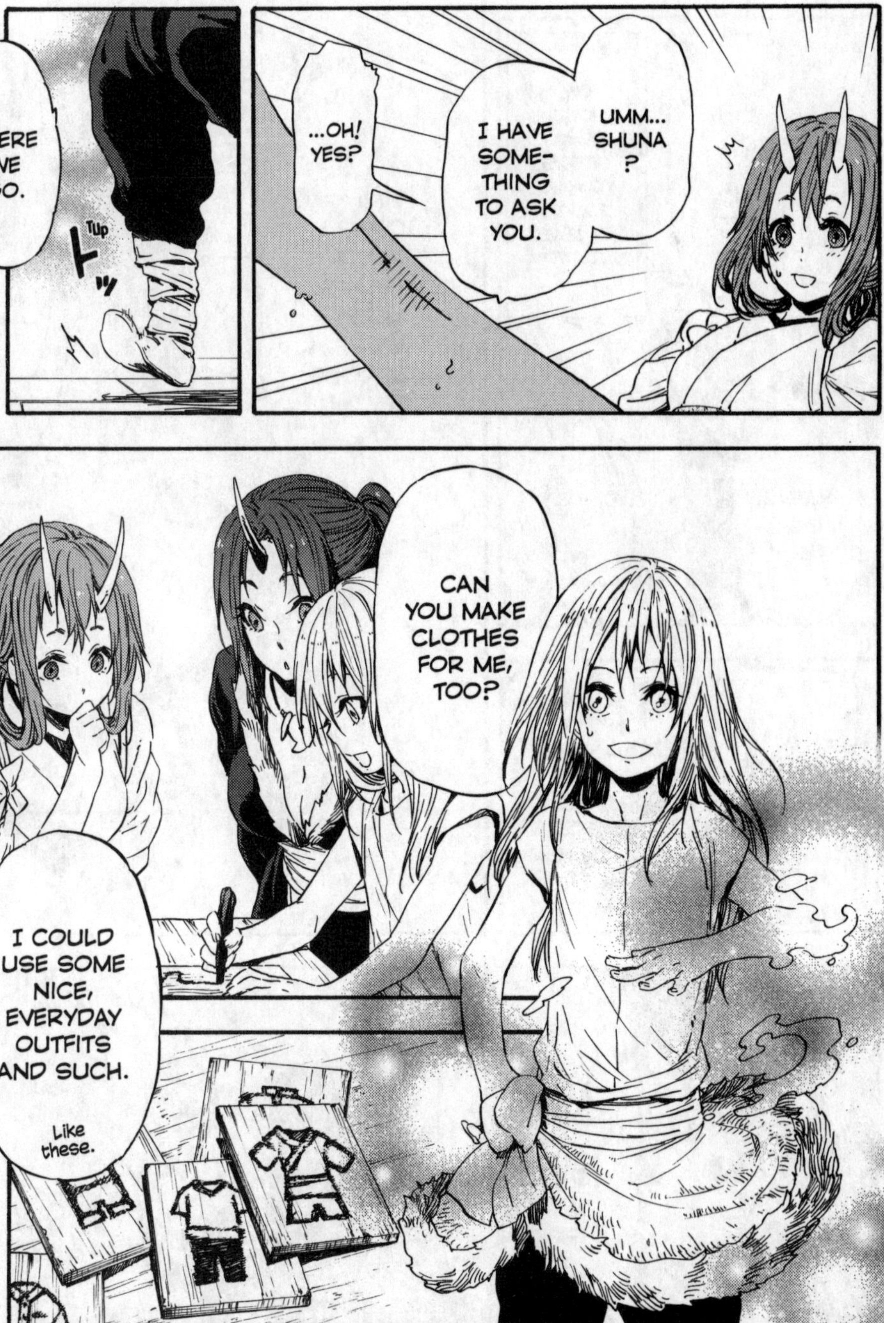
UMM... SHUNA?
I HAVE SOMETHING TO ASK YOU.
...OH! YES?
THERE WE GO.
Tup
CAN YOU MAKE CLOTHES FOR ME, TOO?
I COULD USE SOME NICE, EVERYDAY OUTFITS AND SUCH.
Like these.

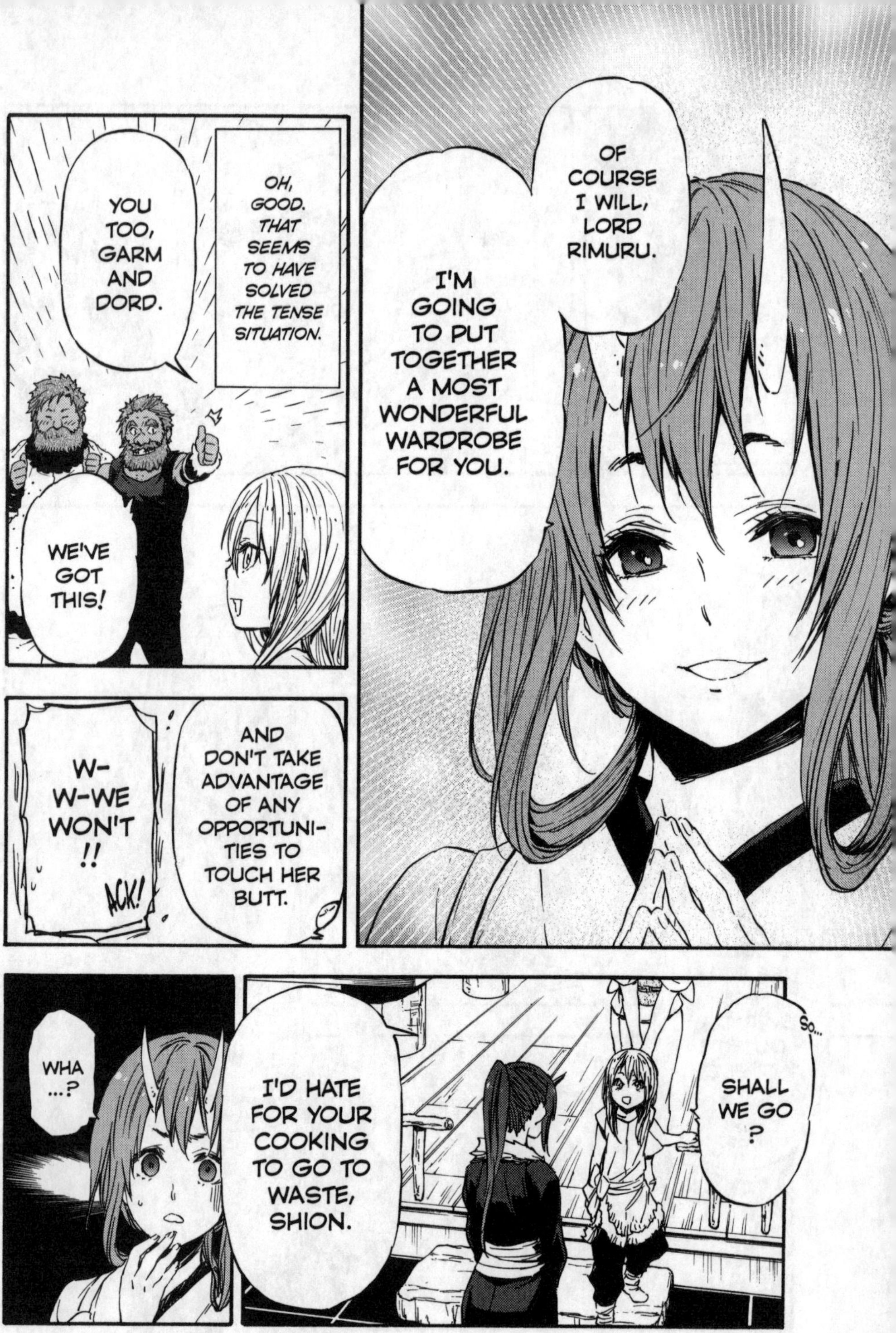
OF COURSE I WILL, LORD RIMURU.
I'M GOING TO PUT TOGETHER A MOST WONDERFUL WARDROBE FOR YOU.
OH, GOOD. THAT SEEMS TO HAVE SOLVED THE TENSE SITUATION.
YOU TOO, GARM AND DORD.
WE'VE GOT THIS!
AND DON'T TAKE ADVANTAGE OF ANY OPPORTUNITIES TO TOUCH HER BUTT.
W-W-WE WON'T!!
ACK!
So...
SHALL WE GO?
I'D HATE FOR YOUR COOKING TO GO TO WASTE, SHION.
WHA...?

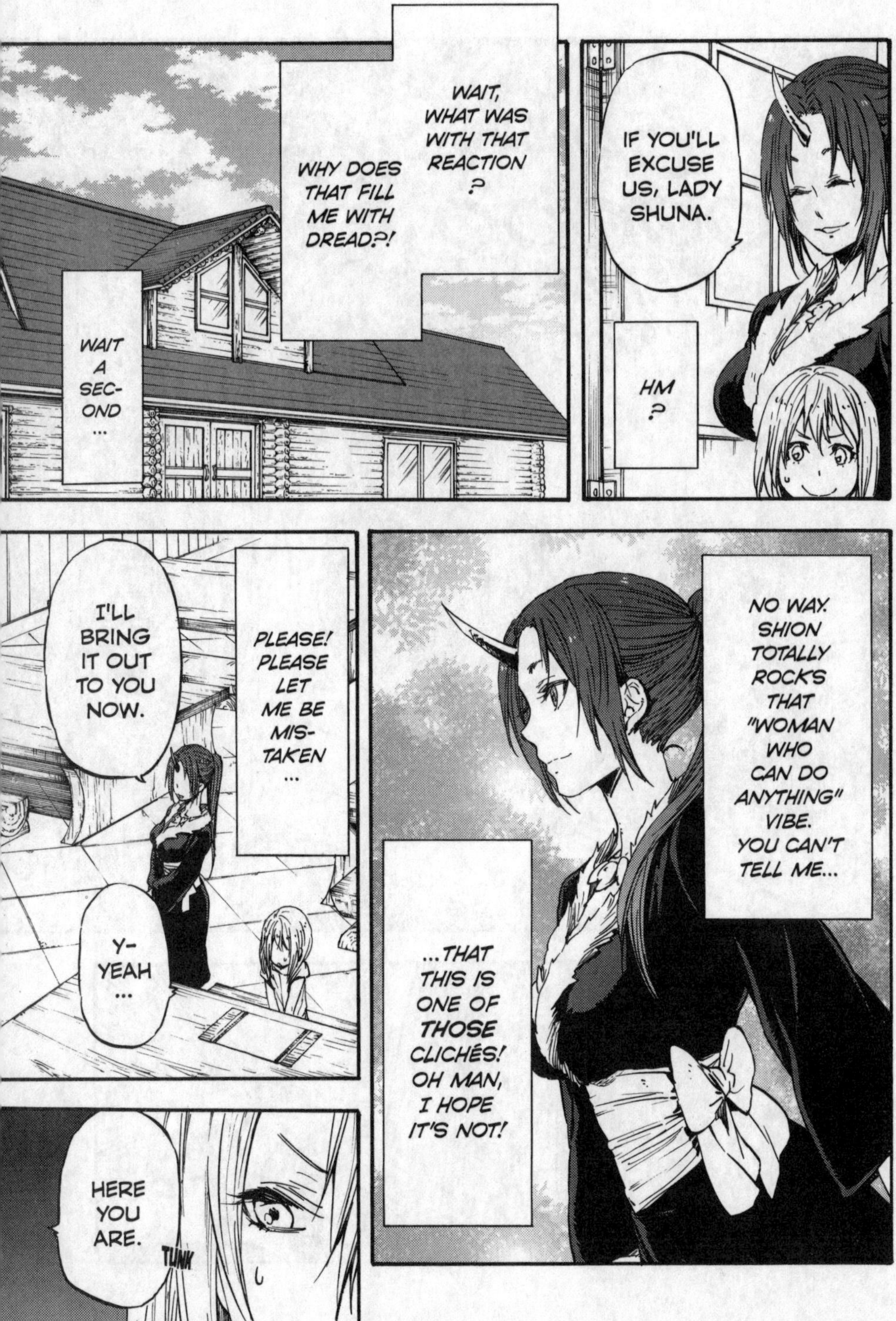

IF YOU'LL EXCUSE US, LADY SHUNA.
HM?
WAIT, WHAT WAS WITH THAT REACTION?
WHY DOES THAT FILL ME WITH DREAD?!
WAIT A SEC-OND...
NO WAY. SHION TOTALLY ROCKS THAT "WOMAN WHO CAN DO ANYTHING" VIBE. YOU CAN'T TELL ME...
...THAT THIS IS ONE OF THOSE CLICHÉS! OH MAN, I HOPE IT'S NOT!
PLEASE! PLEASE LET ME BE MIS-TAKEN...
I'LL BRING IT OUT TO YOU NOW.
Y-YEAH...
HERE YOU ARE.
TUNK

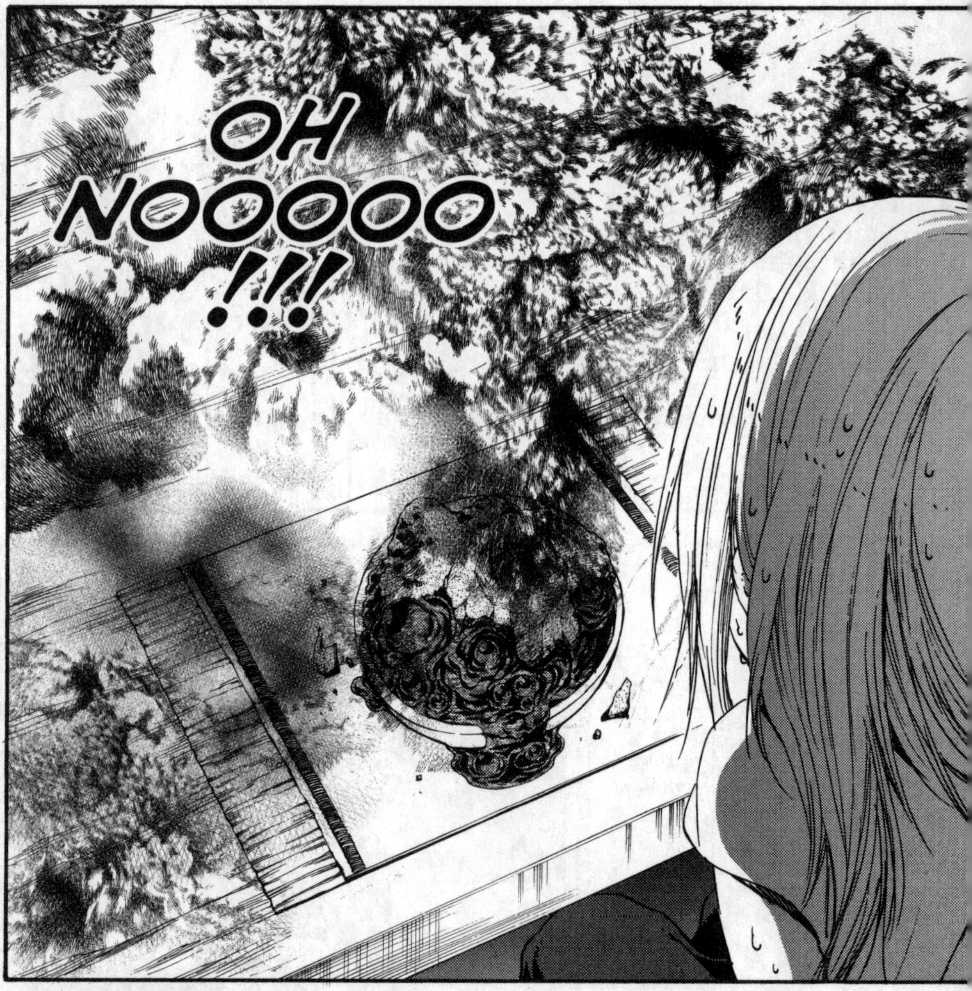
OH NOOOOO!!!
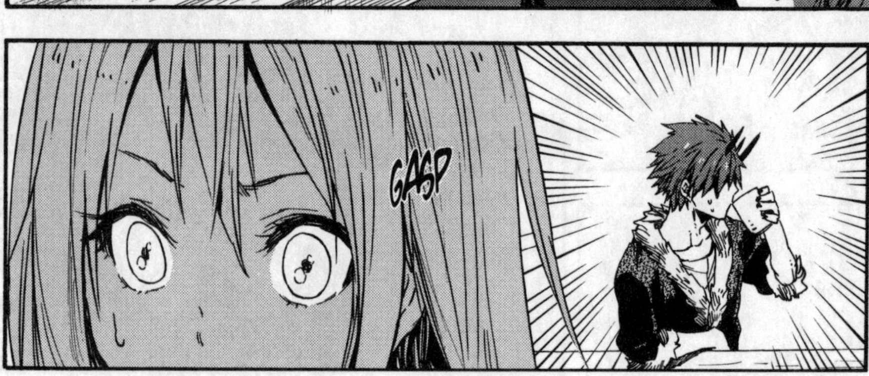
GASP

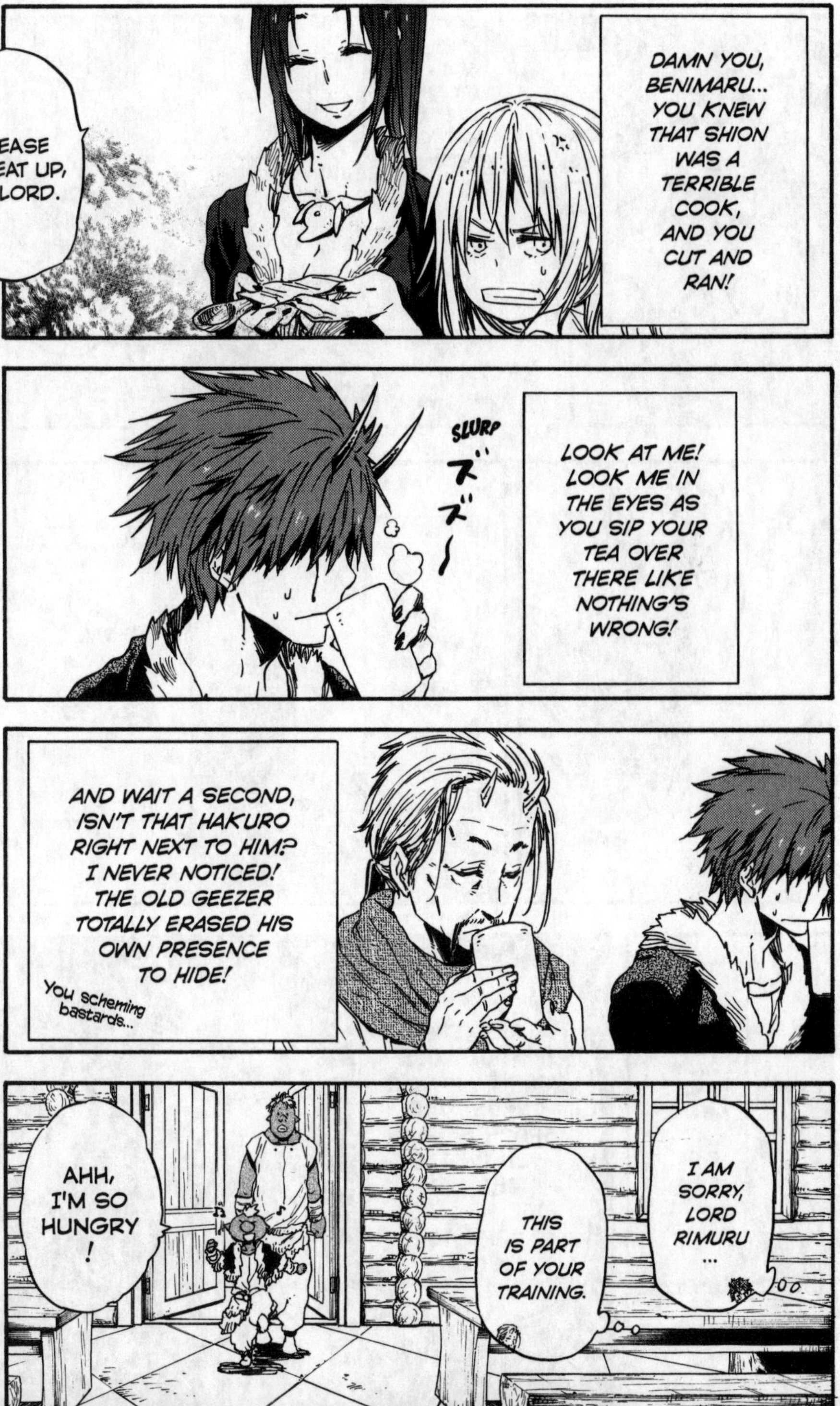
DAMN YOU, BENIMARU... YOU KNEW THAT SHION WAS A TERRIBLE COOK, AND YOU CUT AND RAN!
PLEASE DO EAT UP, MY LORD.
LOOK AT ME! LOOK ME IN THE EYES AS YOU SIP YOUR TEA OVER THERE LIKE NOTHING'S WRONG!
SLURP
ズズー
AND WAIT A SECOND, ISN'T THAT HAKURO RIGHT NEXT TO HIM? I NEVER NOTICED! THE OLD GEEZER TOTALLY ERASED HIS OWN PRESENCE TO HIDE!
You scheming bastards...
I AM SORRY, LORD RIMURU...
THIS IS PART OF YOUR TRAINING.
AHH, I'M SO HUNGRY!

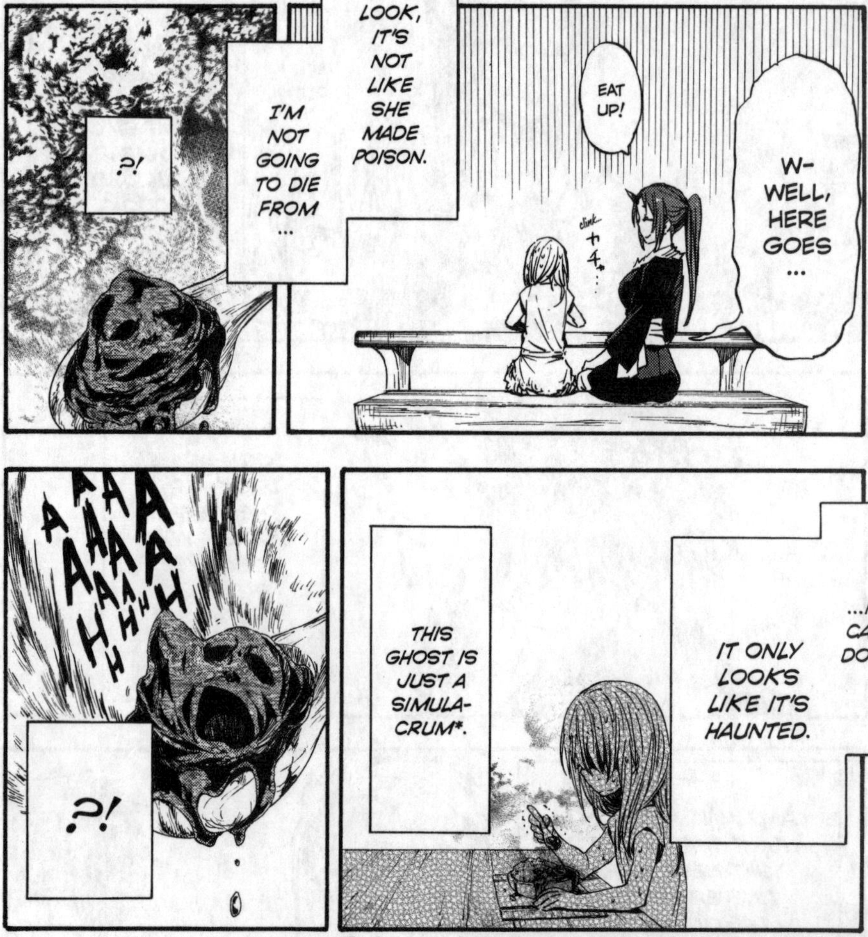
EAT UP!
W-WELL, HERE GOES...
clink
LOOK, IT'S NOT LIKE SHE MADE POISON.
I'M NOT GOING TO DIE FROM...
?!
...NO. CALM DOWN.
IT ONLY LOOKS LIKE IT'S HAUNTED.
THIS GHOST IS JUST A SIMULA-CRUM*.
AAAAAAAAAAAHHHHHH
?!

*The phenomenon of seeing things as visual symbols, such as three dots looking like a face.

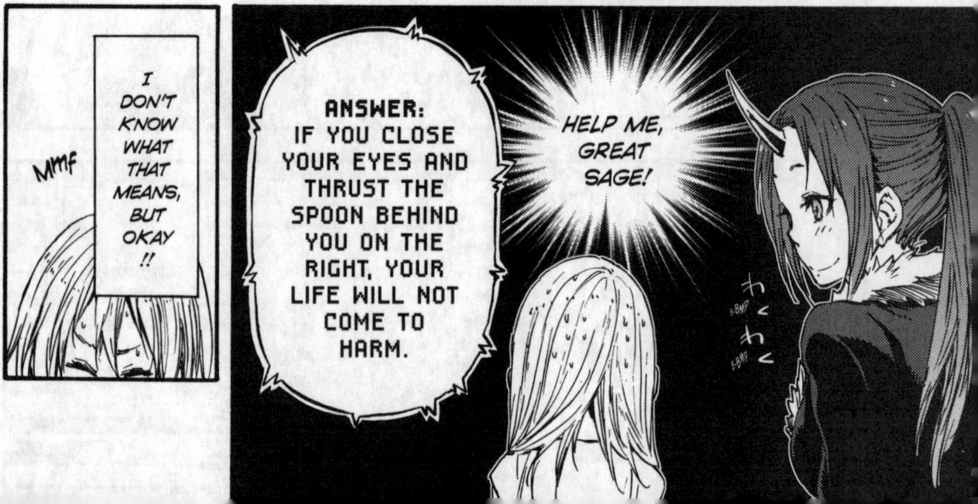
HELP ME, GREAT SAGE!
ANSWER: IF YOU CLOSE YOUR EYES AND THRUST THE SPOON BEHIND YOU ON THE RIGHT, YOUR LIFE WILL NOT COME TO HARM.
BBMP
BBMP
MMF
I DON'T KNOW WHAT THAT MEANS, BUT OKAY!!

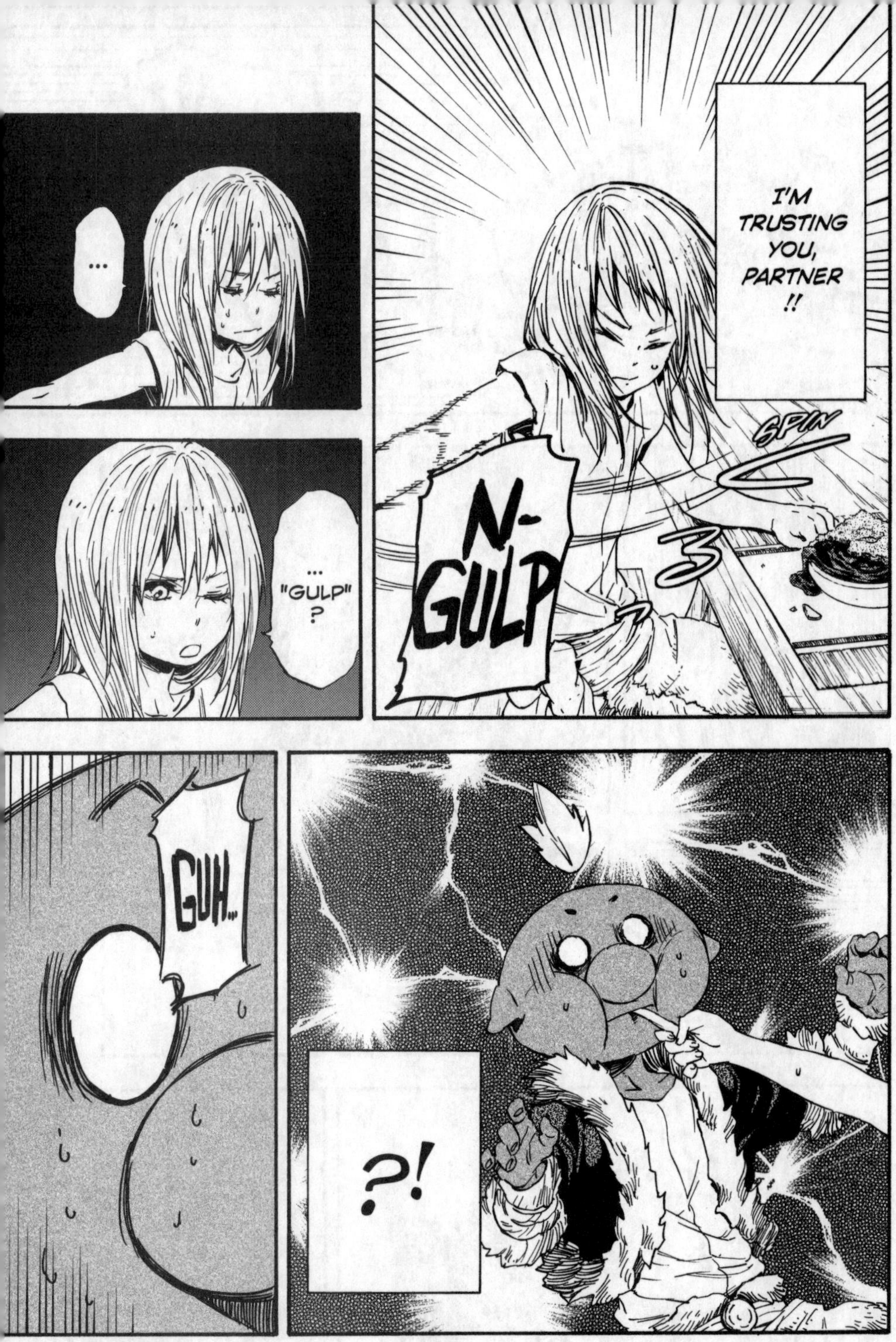
I'M TRUSTING YOU, PARTNER !!
SPIN
N-GULP
...
... "GULP" ?
?!
GUH...

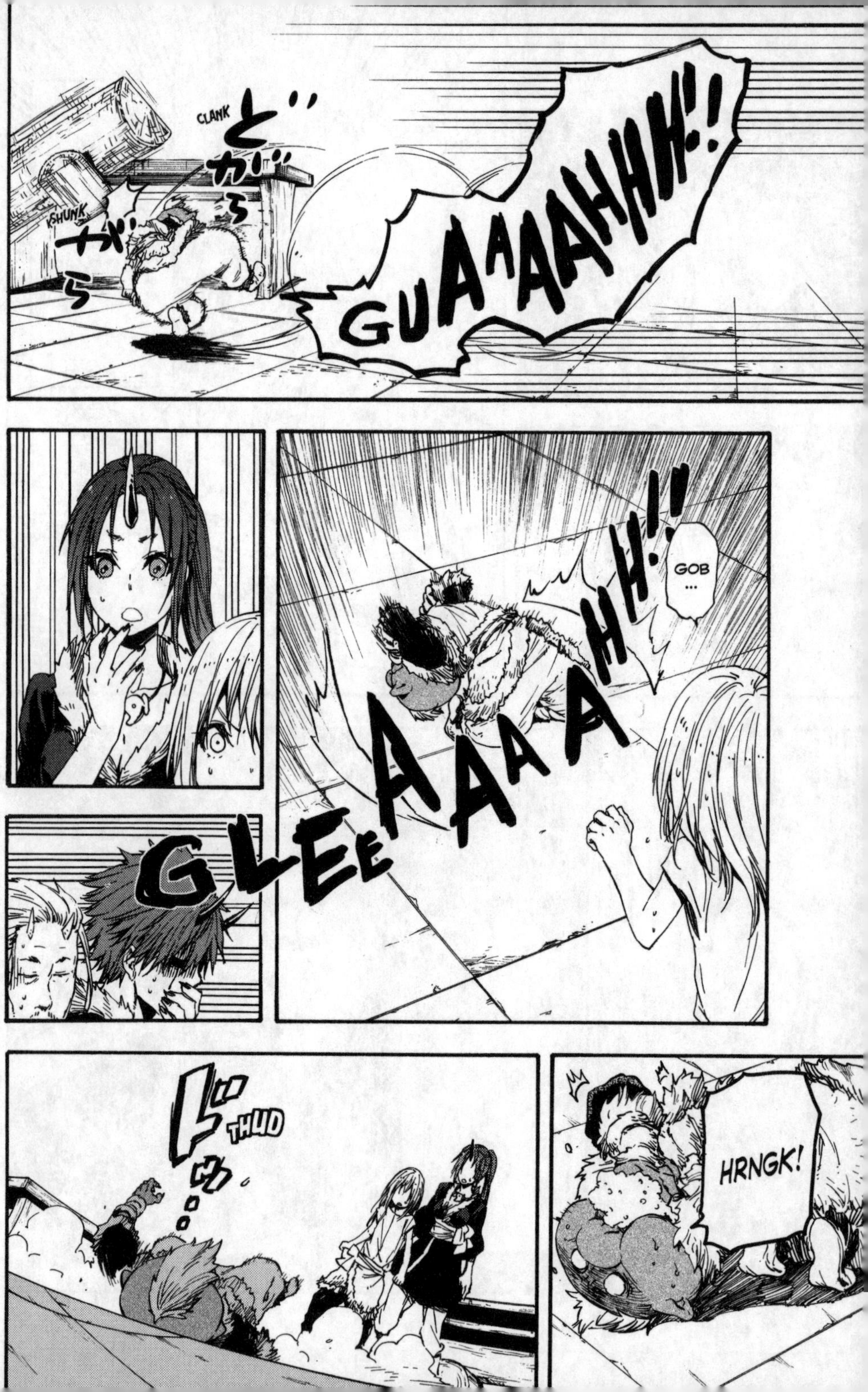
CLANK
SHUNK
GUAAAAAHHHH!!
GOB ...
GLEEAAAAAHH!!
HRNGK!
THUD

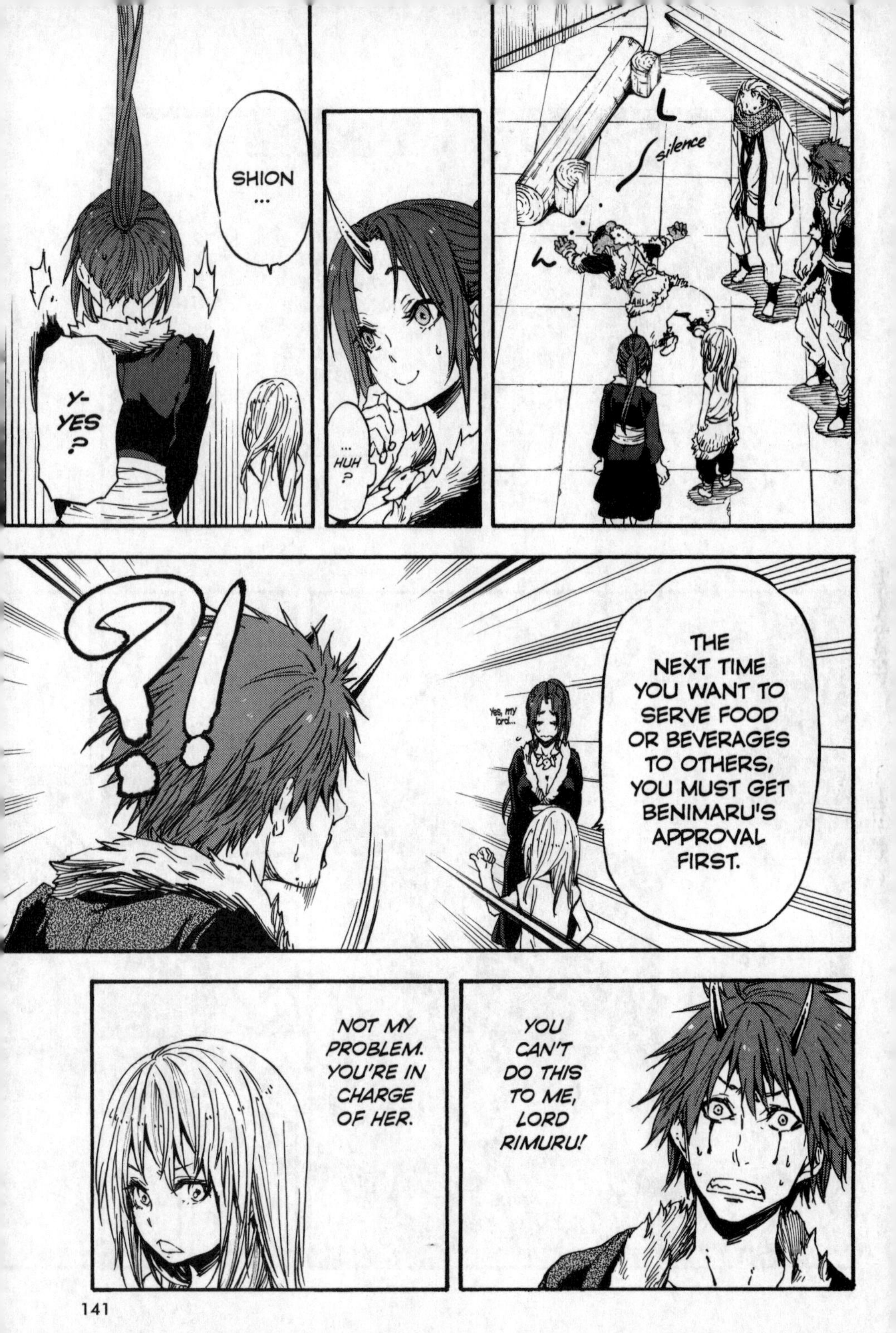
silence
SHION ...
... HUH ?
Y- YES ?
THE NEXT TIME YOU WANT TO SERVE FOOD OR BEVERAGES TO OTHERS, YOU MUST GET BENIMARU'S APPROVAL FIRST.
Yes, my lord...
YOU CAN'T DO THIS TO ME, LORD RIMURU!
NOT MY PROBLEM. YOU'RE IN CHARGE OF HER.

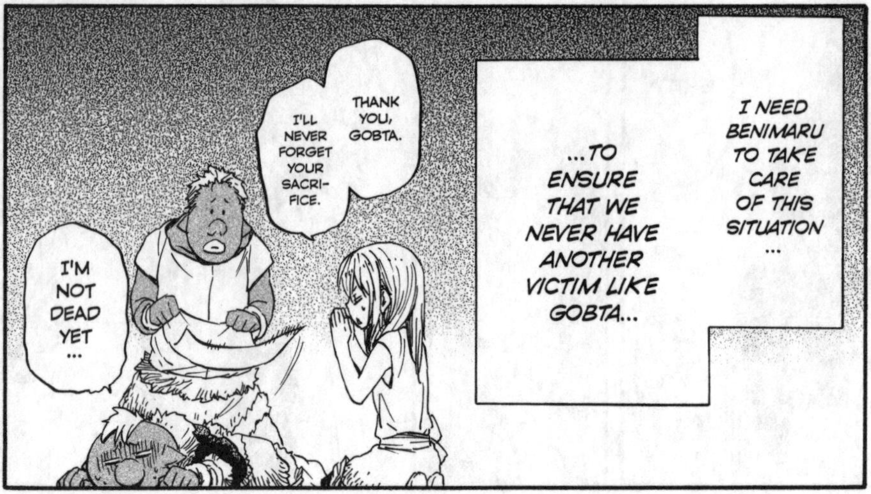
I NEED BENIMARU TO TAKE CARE OF THIS SITUATION ...
...TO ENSURE THAT WE NEVER HAVE ANOTHER VICTIM LIKE GOBTA...
THANK YOU, GOBTA.
I'LL NEVER FORGET YOUR SACRI-FICE.
I'M NOT DEAD YET ...

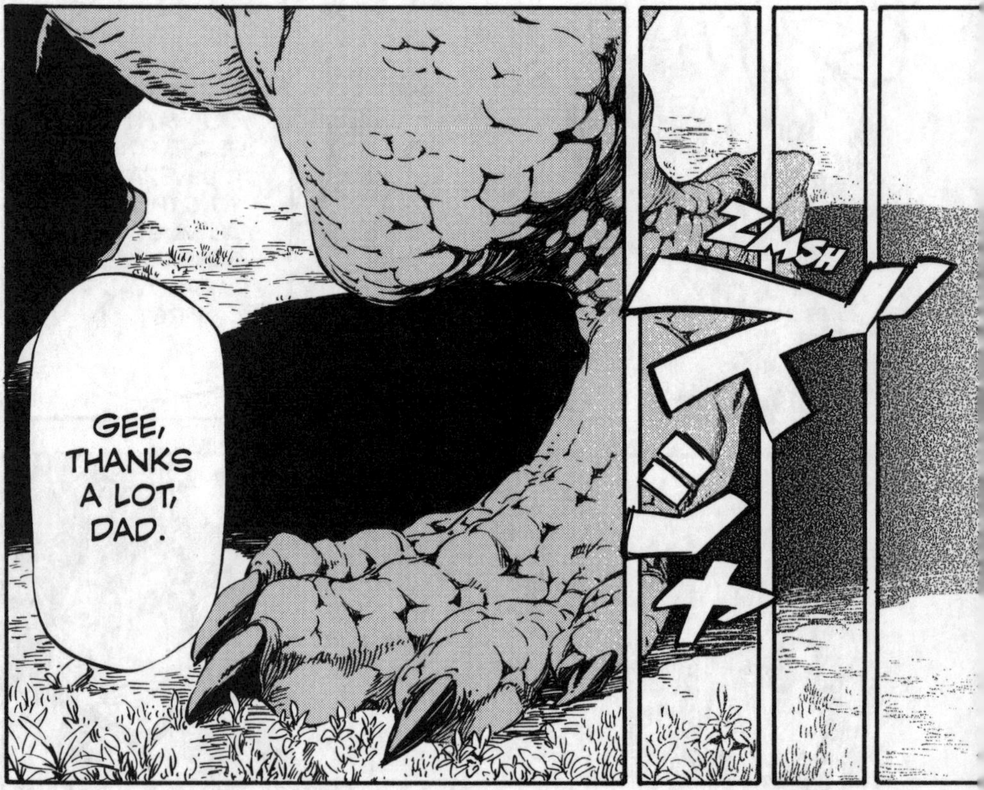
ZMSH
GEE, THANKS A LOT, DAD.

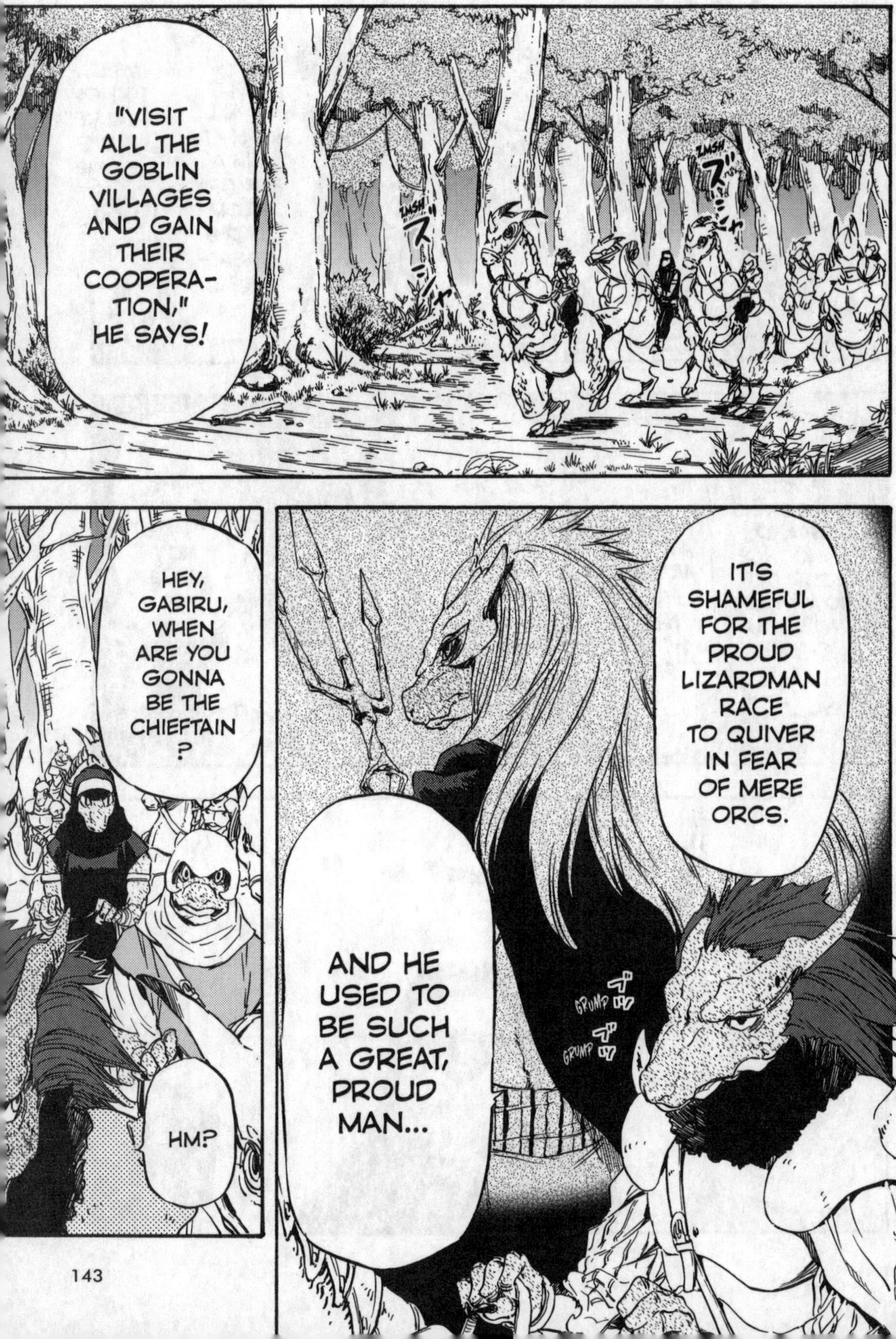
"VISIT ALL THE GOBLIN VILLAGES AND GAIN THEIR COOPERATION," HE SAYS!
ZMSH
ZMSH
IT'S SHAMEFUL FOR THE PROUD LIZARDMAN RACE TO QUIVER IN FEAR OF MERE ORCS.
AND HE USED TO BE SUCH A GREAT, PROUD MAN...
GRUMP
GRUMP
HEY, GABIRU, WHEN ARE YOU GONNA BE THE CHIEFTAIN?
HM?

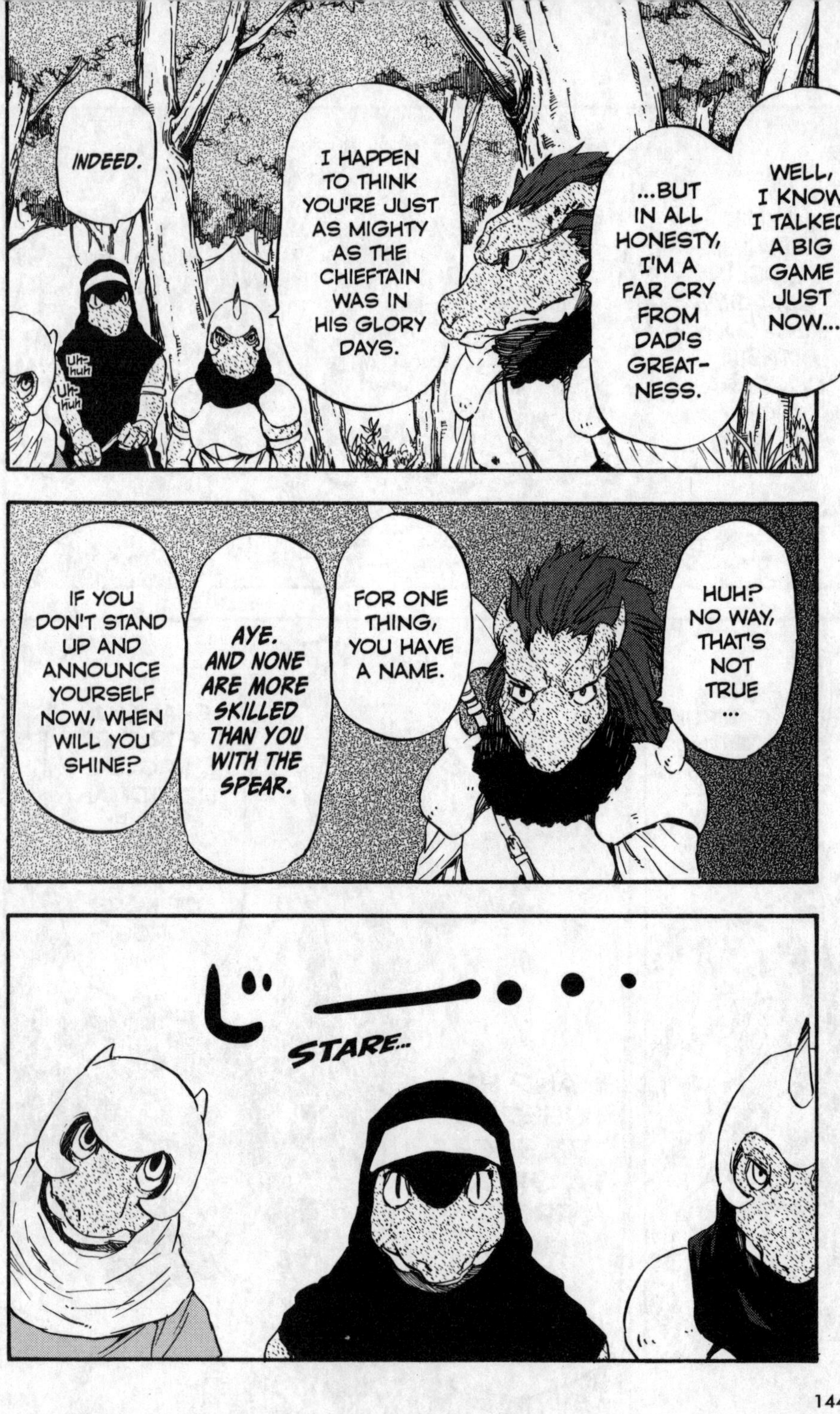
WELL, I KNOW I TALKED A BIG GAME JUST NOW...
...BUT IN ALL HONESTY, I'M A FAR CRY FROM DAD'S GREAT-NESS.
I HAPPEN TO THINK YOU'RE JUST AS MIGHTY AS THE CHIEFTAIN WAS IN HIS GLORY DAYS.
INDEED.
Uh-huh
Uh-huh
HUH? NO WAY, THAT'S NOT TRUE ...
FOR ONE THING, YOU HAVE A NAME.
AYE. AND NONE ARE MORE SKILLED THAN YOU WITH THE SPEAR.
IF YOU DON'T STAND UP AND ANNOUNCE YOURSELF NOW, WHEN WILL YOU SHINE?
じー・・・
STARE...

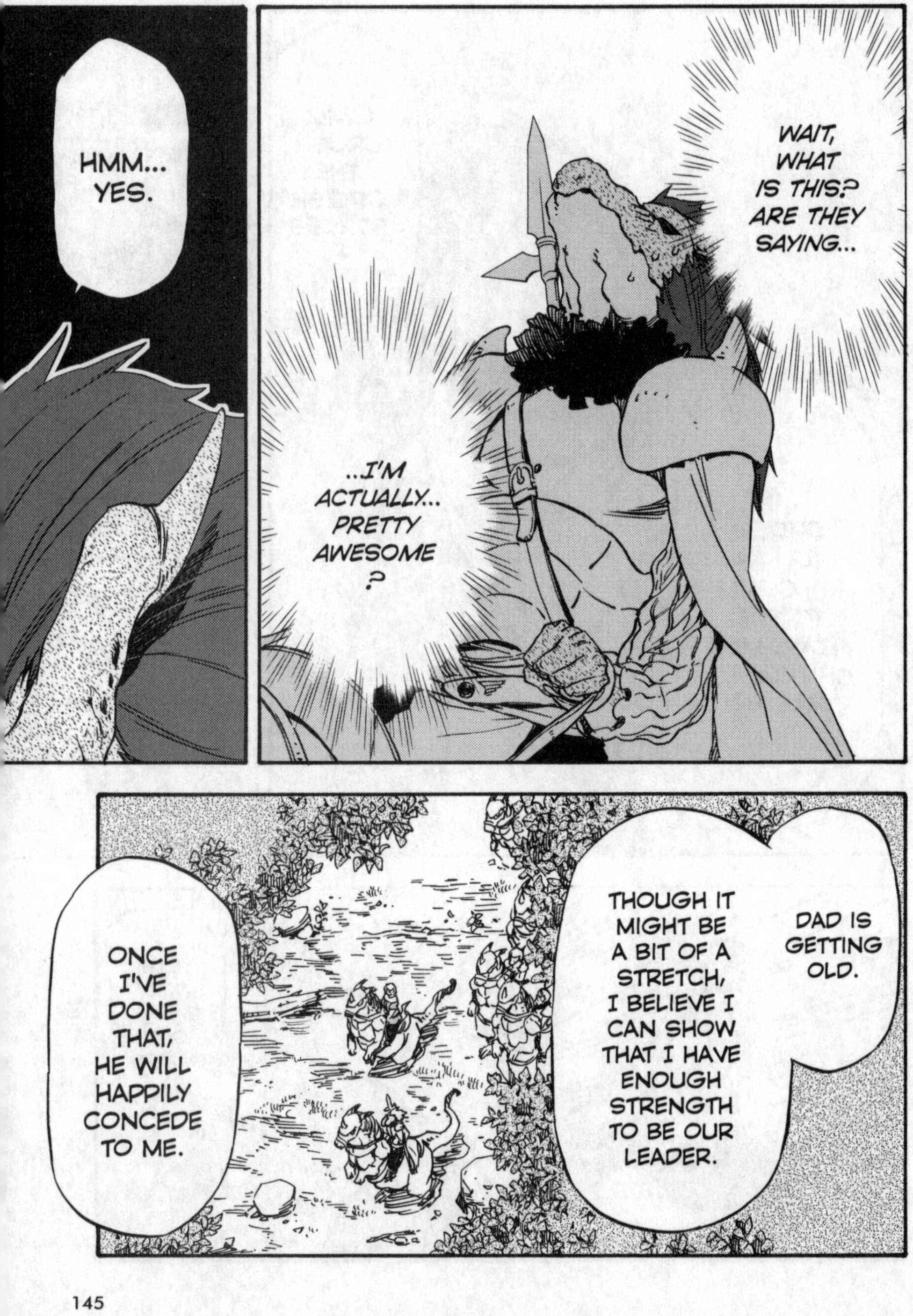
WAIT, WHAT IS THIS? ARE THEY SAYING...
...I'M ACTUALLY... PRETTY AWESOME?
HMM... YES.
DAD IS GETTING OLD.
THOUGH IT MIGHT BE A BIT OF A STRETCH, I BELIEVE I CAN SHOW THAT I HAVE ENOUGH STRENGTH TO BE OUR LEADER.
ONCE I'VE DONE THAT, HE WILL HAPPILY CONCEDE TO ME.

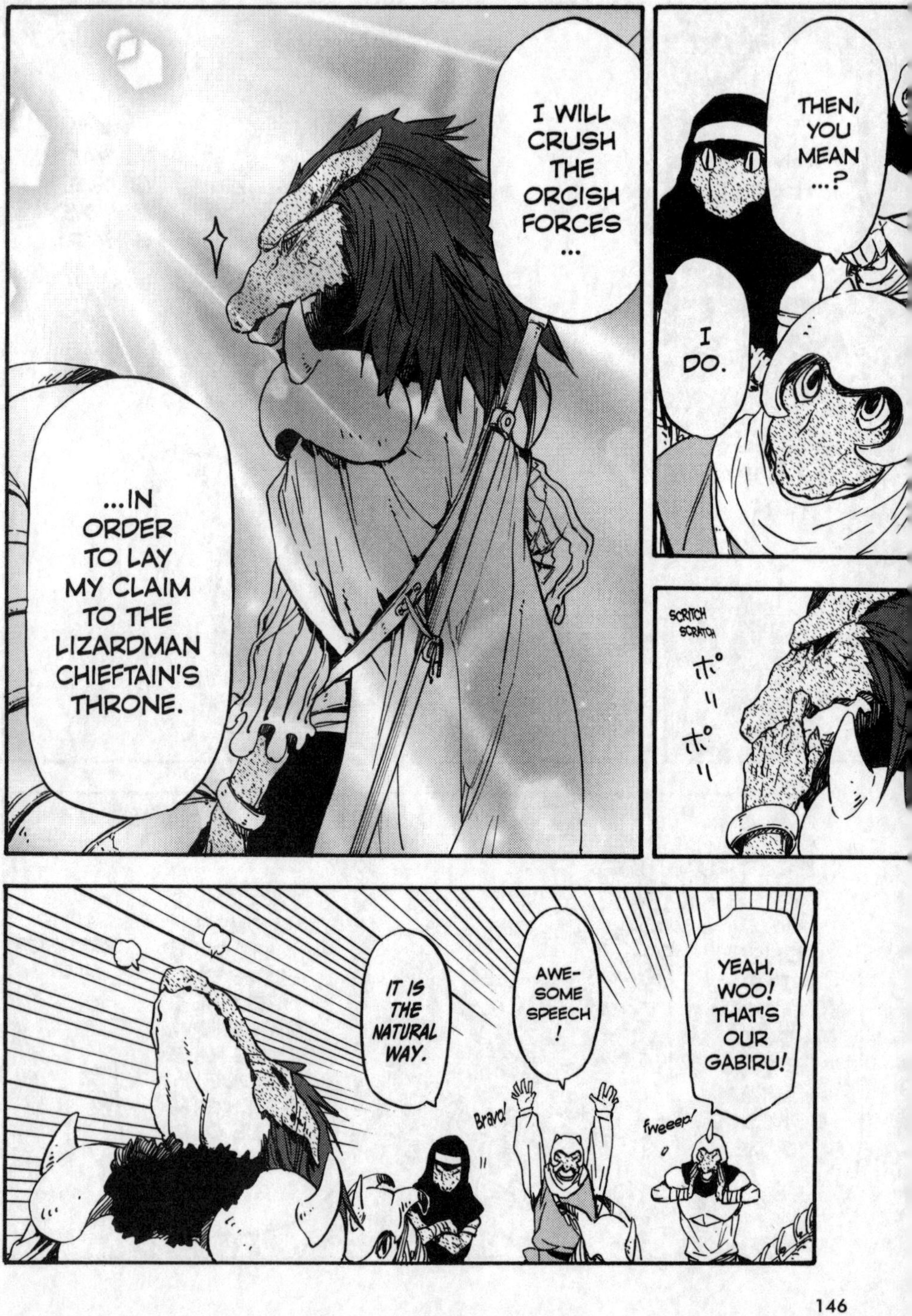
THEN, YOU MEAN ...?
I DO.
SCRITCH SCRATCH
ポリポリ
I WILL CRUSH THE ORCISH FORCES ...
...IN ORDER TO LAY MY CLAIM TO THE LIZARDMAN CHIEFTAIN'S THRONE.
YEAH, WOO! THAT'S OUR GABIRU!
fweeep!
AWE-SOME SPEECH!
Bravo!
IT IS THE NATURAL WAY.

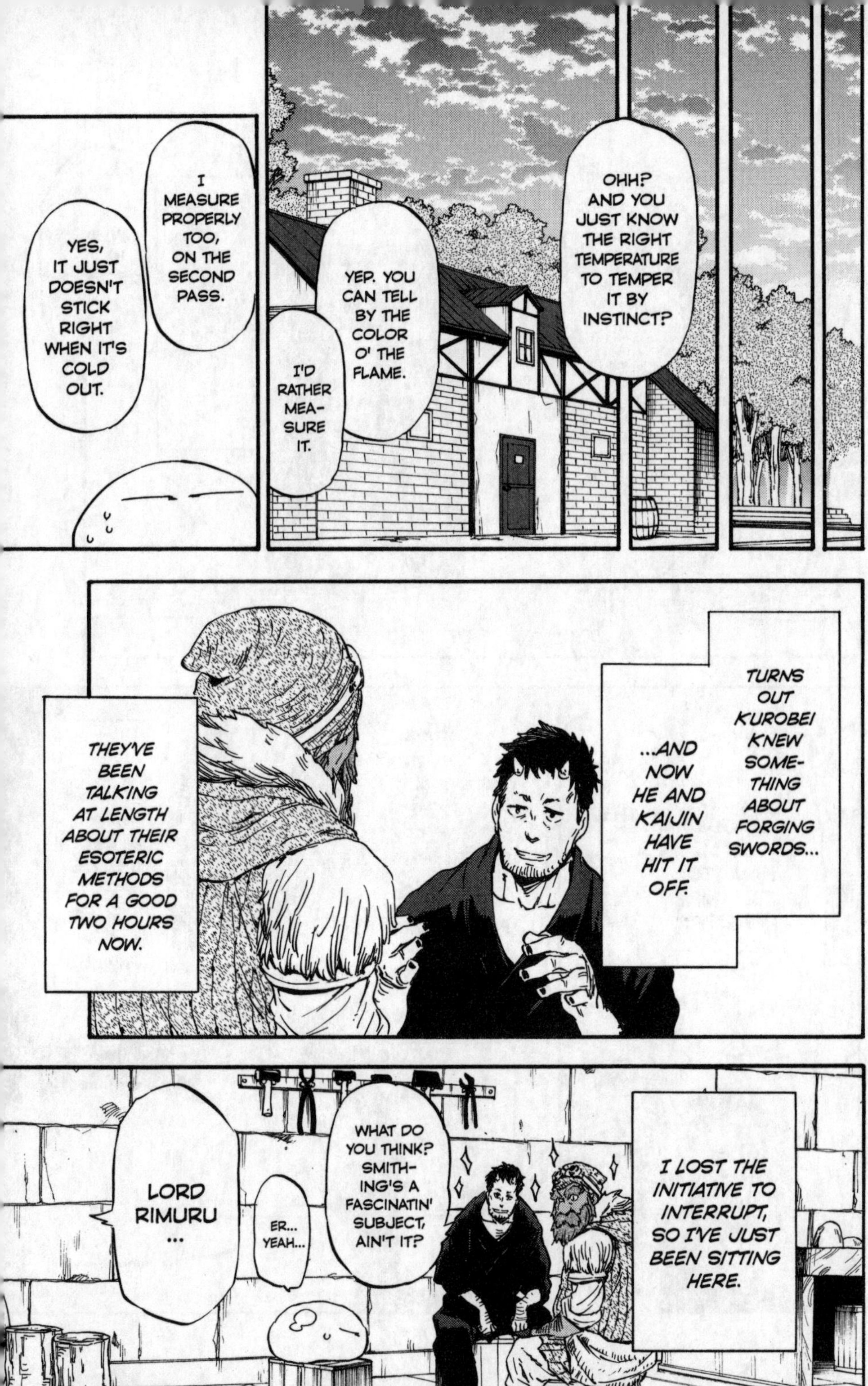
OHH? AND YOU JUST KNOW THE RIGHT TEMPERATURE TO TEMPER IT BY INSTINCT?
YEP. YOU CAN TELL BY THE COLOR O' THE FLAME.
I'D RATHER MEA-SURE IT.
I MEASURE PROPERLY TOO, ON THE SECOND PASS.
YES, IT JUST DOESN'T STICK RIGHT WHEN IT'S COLD OUT.
TURNS OUT KUROBEI KNEW SOME-THING ABOUT FORGING SWORDS...
...AND NOW HE AND KAIJIN HAVE HIT IT OFF.
THEY'VE BEEN TALKING AT LENGTH ABOUT THEIR ESOTERIC METHODS FOR A GOOD TWO HOURS NOW.
I LOST THE INITIATIVE TO INTERRUPT, SO I'VE JUST BEEN SITTING HERE.
WHAT DO YOU THINK? SMITH-ING'S A FASCINATIN' SUBJECT, AIN'T IT?
ER... YEAH...
LORD RIMURU...

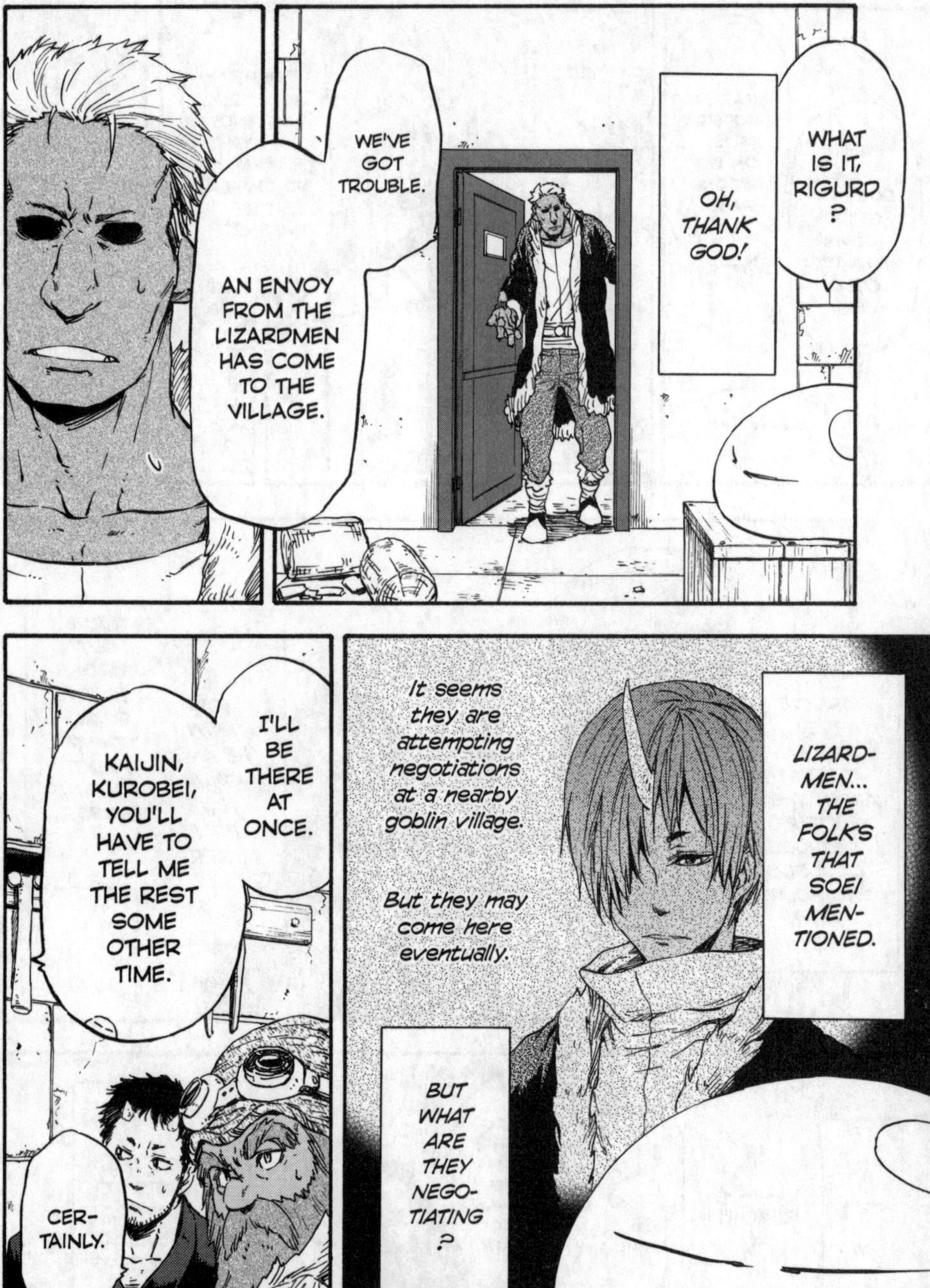
WHAT IS IT, RIGURD?
OH, THANK GOD!
WE'VE GOT TROUBLE.
AN ENVOY FROM THE LIZARDMEN HAS COME TO THE VILLAGE.
LIZARD-MEN... THE FOLKS THAT SOEI MEN-TIONED.
It seems they are attempting negotiations at a nearby goblin village.
But they may come here eventually.
BUT WHAT ARE THEY NEGO-TIATING?
I'LL BE THERE AT ONCE.
KAIJIN, KUROBEI, YOU'LL HAVE TO TELL ME THE REST SOME OTHER TIME.
CER-TAINLY.

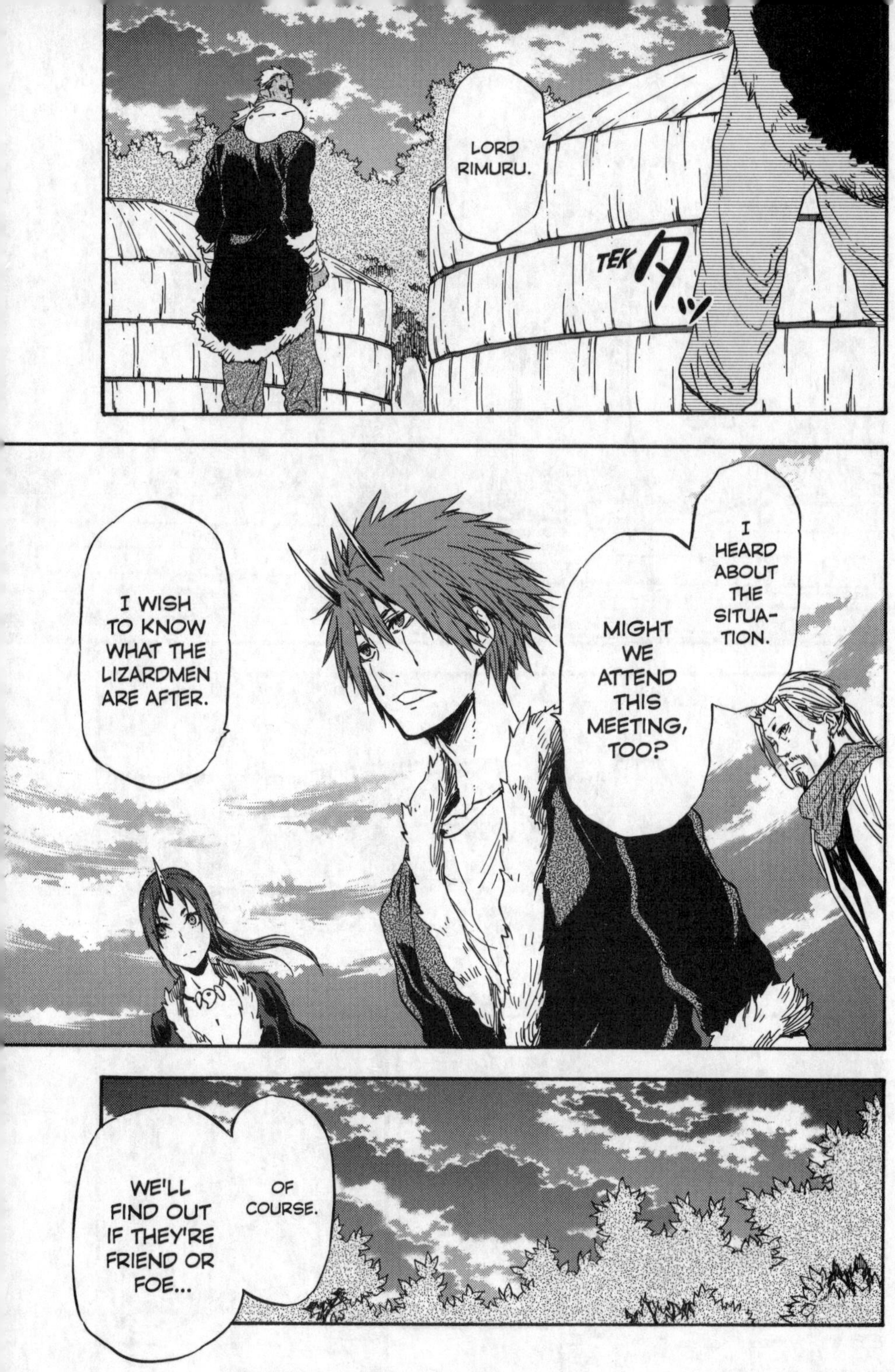
LORD RIMURU.
TEK タッ
I HEARD ABOUT THE SITUA-TION.
MIGHT WE ATTEND THIS MEETING, TOO?
I WISH TO KNOW WHAT THE LIZARDMEN ARE AFTER.
OF COURSE.
WE'LL FIND OUT IF THEY'RE FRIEND OR FOE...

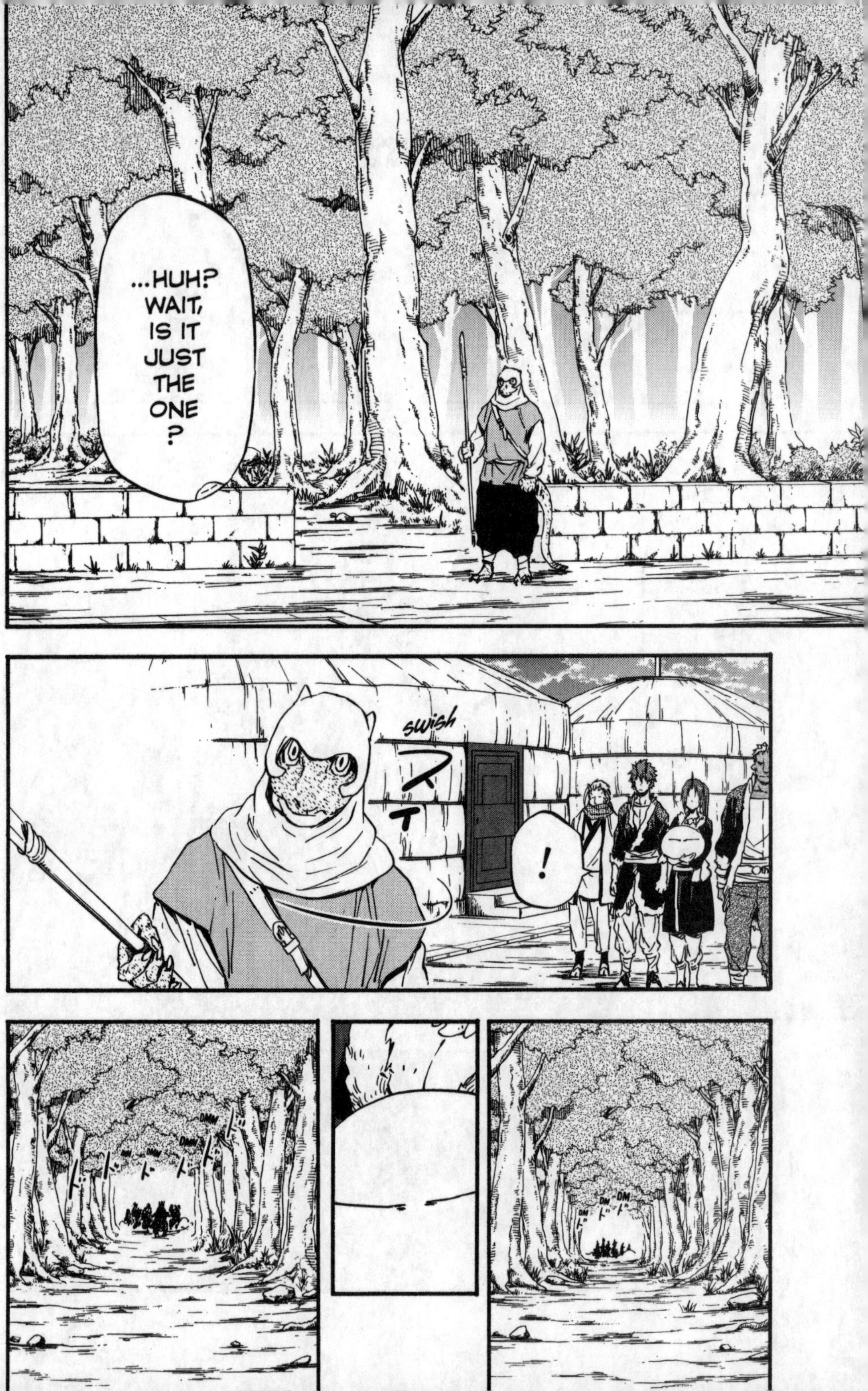
...HUH? WAIT, IS IT JUST THE ONE ?
swish
スッ
!
DM ド DM ド
DMM ド DMM ド DMM ド DMM ド

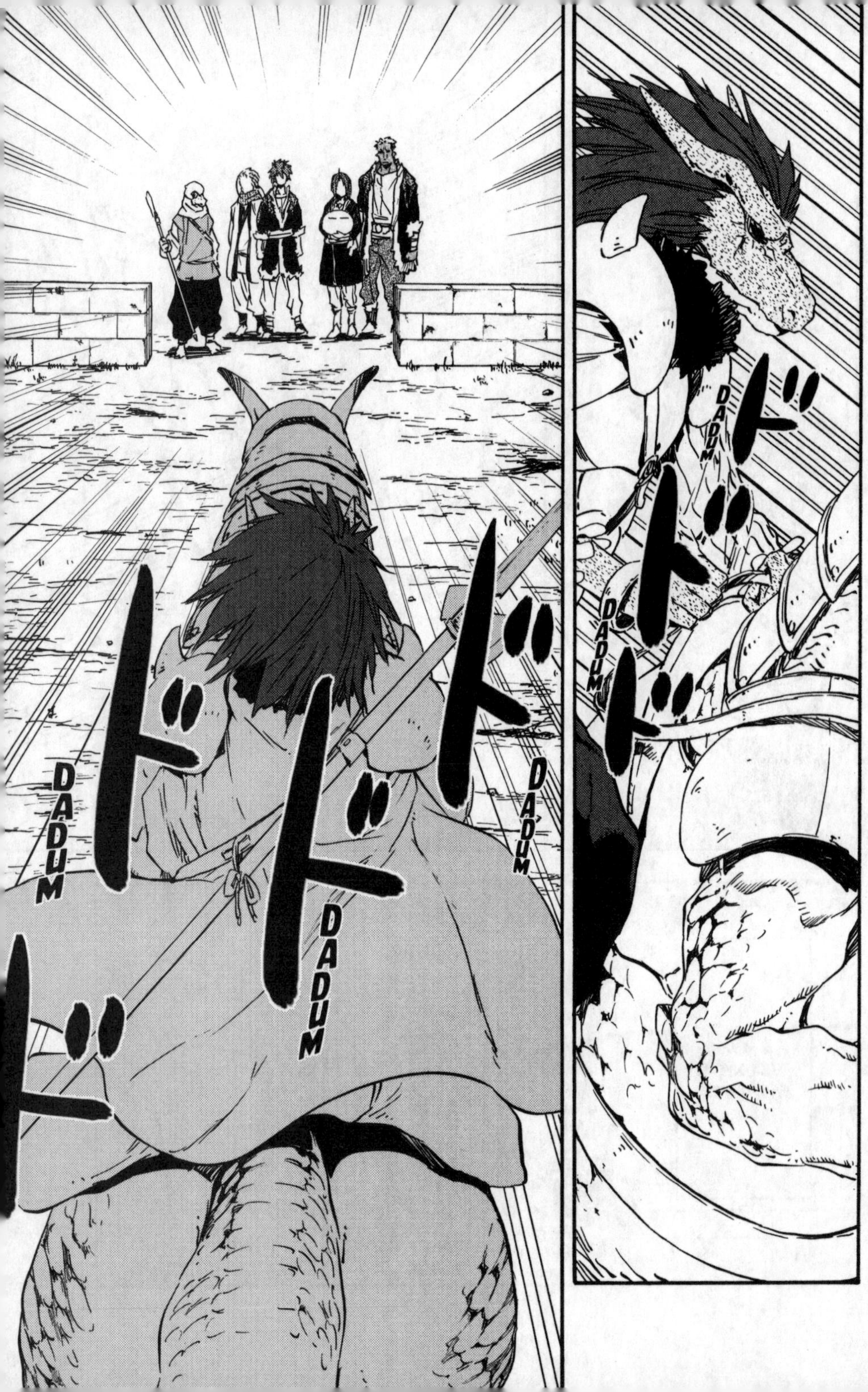
ドドド
DADUM
DADUM
ドドドド
DADUM
DADUM
DADUM

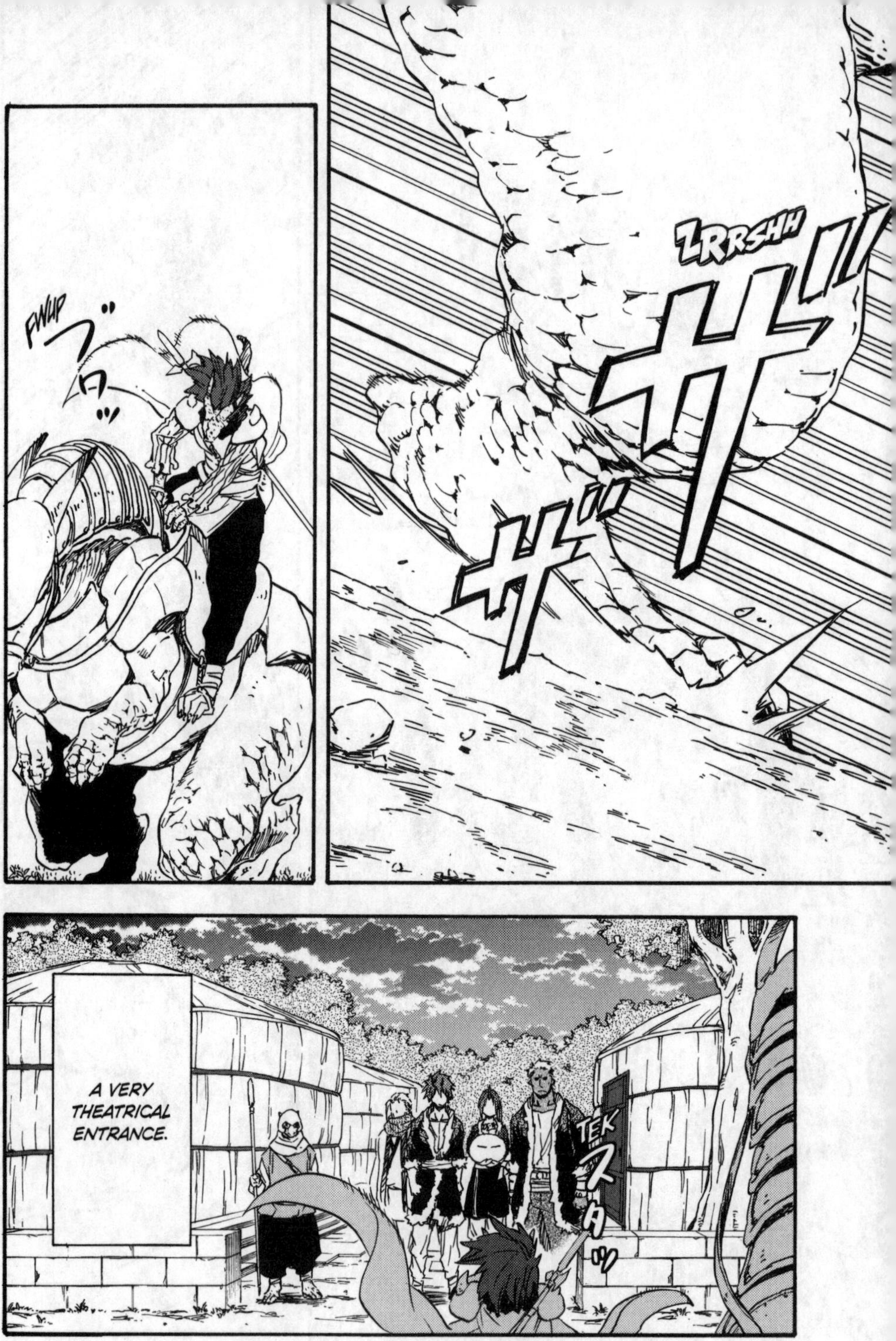
ZRRSHH
ザザ
FWUP
ブワッ
A VERY THEATRICAL ENTRANCE.
TEK
スタッ

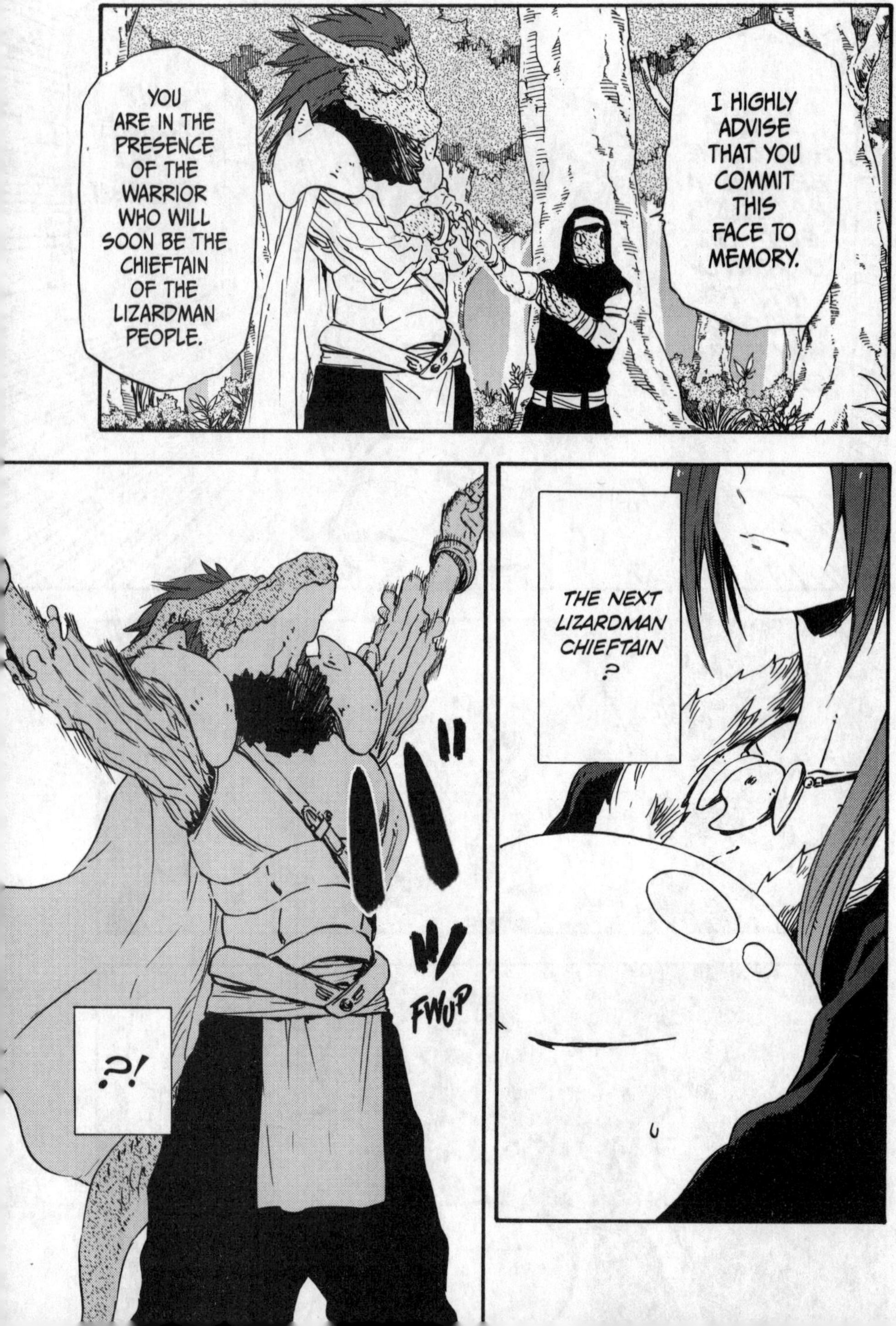
I HIGHLY ADVISE THAT YOU COMMIT THIS FACE TO MEMORY.
YOU ARE IN THE PRESENCE OF THE WARRIOR WHO WILL SOON BE THE CHIEFTAIN OF THE LIZARDMAN PEOPLE.
THE NEXT LIZARDMAN CHIEFTAIN ?
FWUP
?!

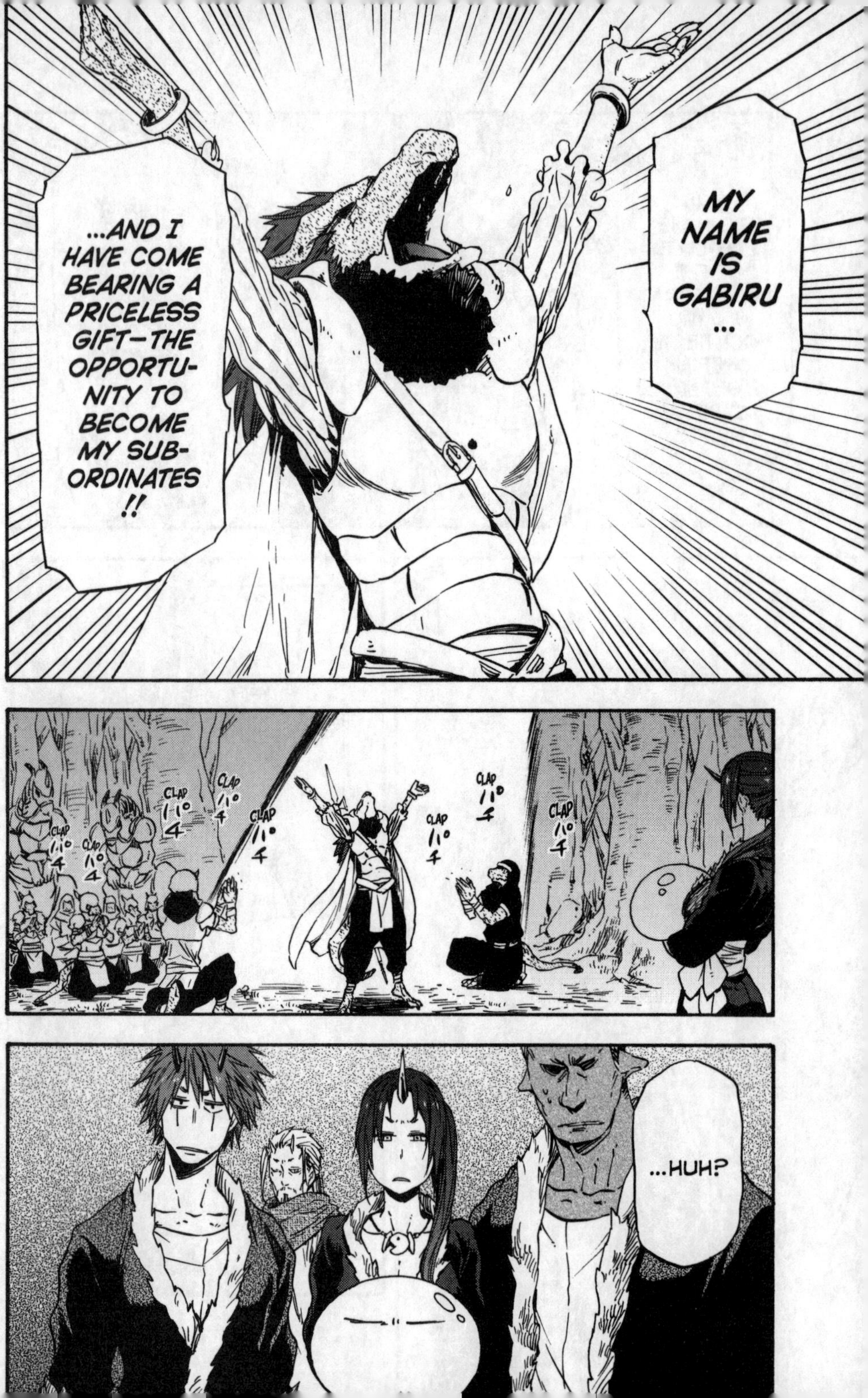
MY NAME IS GABIRU...
...AND I HAVE COME BEARING A PRICELESS GIFT—THE OPPORTUNITY TO BECOME MY SUBORDINATES!!
CLAP
CLAP
CLAP
CLAP
CLAP
CLAP
CLAP
...HUH?

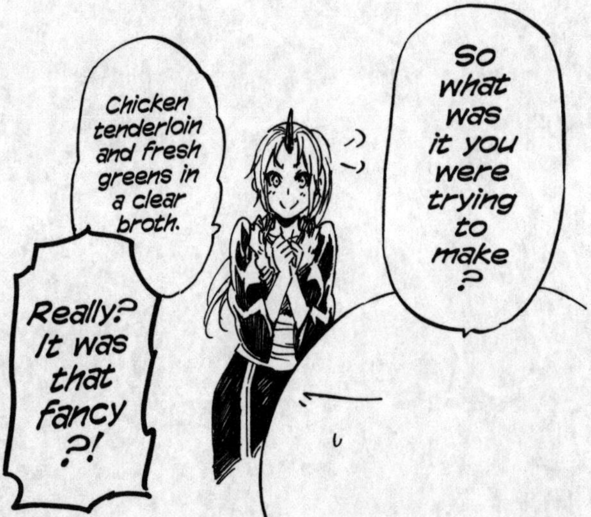
So what was it you were trying to make?
Chicken tenderloin and fresh greens in a clear broth.
Really? It was that fancy?!

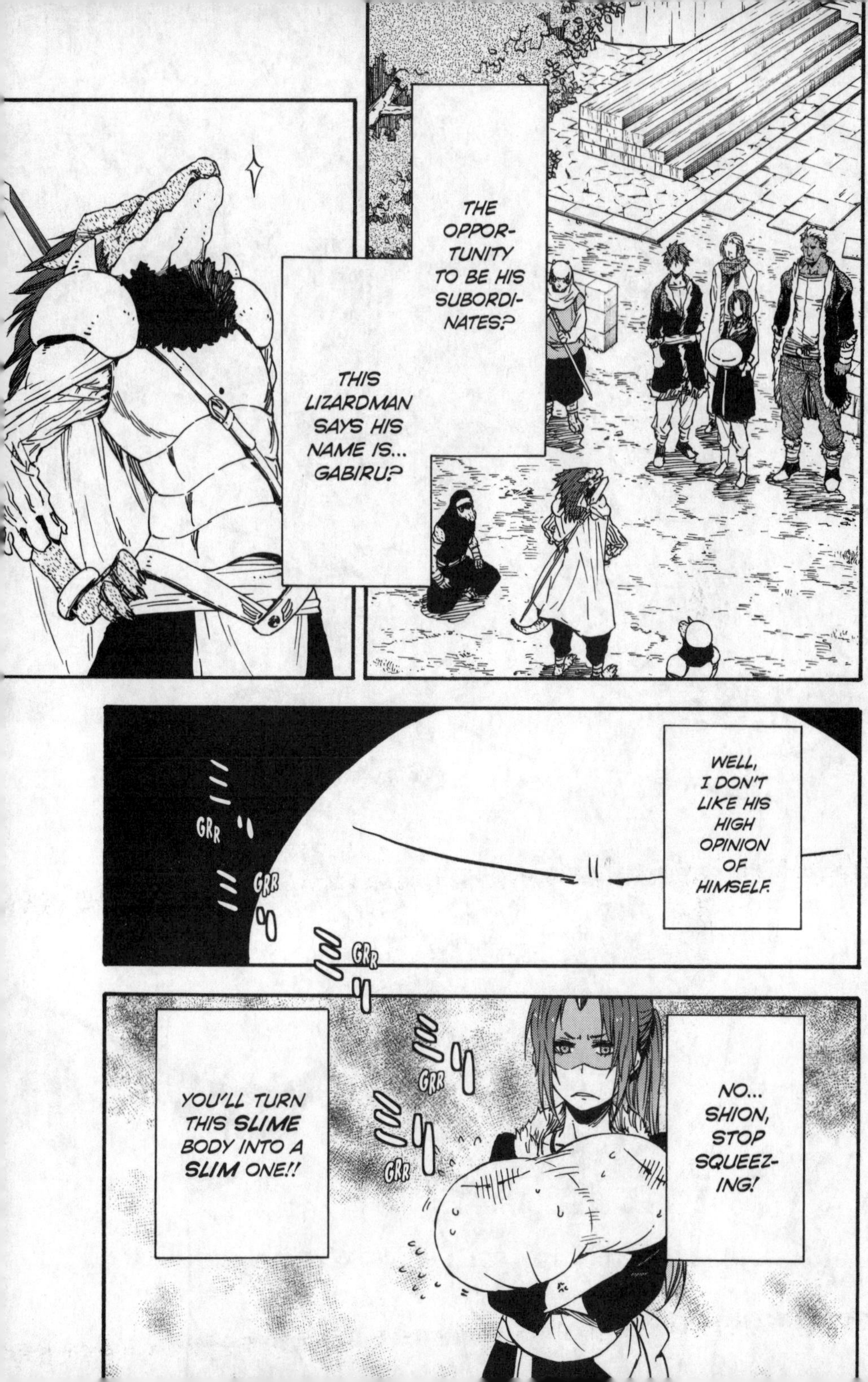

THE OPPORTUNITY TO BE HIS SUBORDINATES?
THIS LIZARDMAN SAYS HIS NAME IS... GABIRU?
WELL, I DON'T LIKE HIS HIGH OPINION OF HIMSELF.
GRR
GRR
GRR
NO... SHION, STOP SQUEEZING!
GRR
GRR
YOU'LL TURN THIS SLIME BODY INTO A SLIM ONE!!

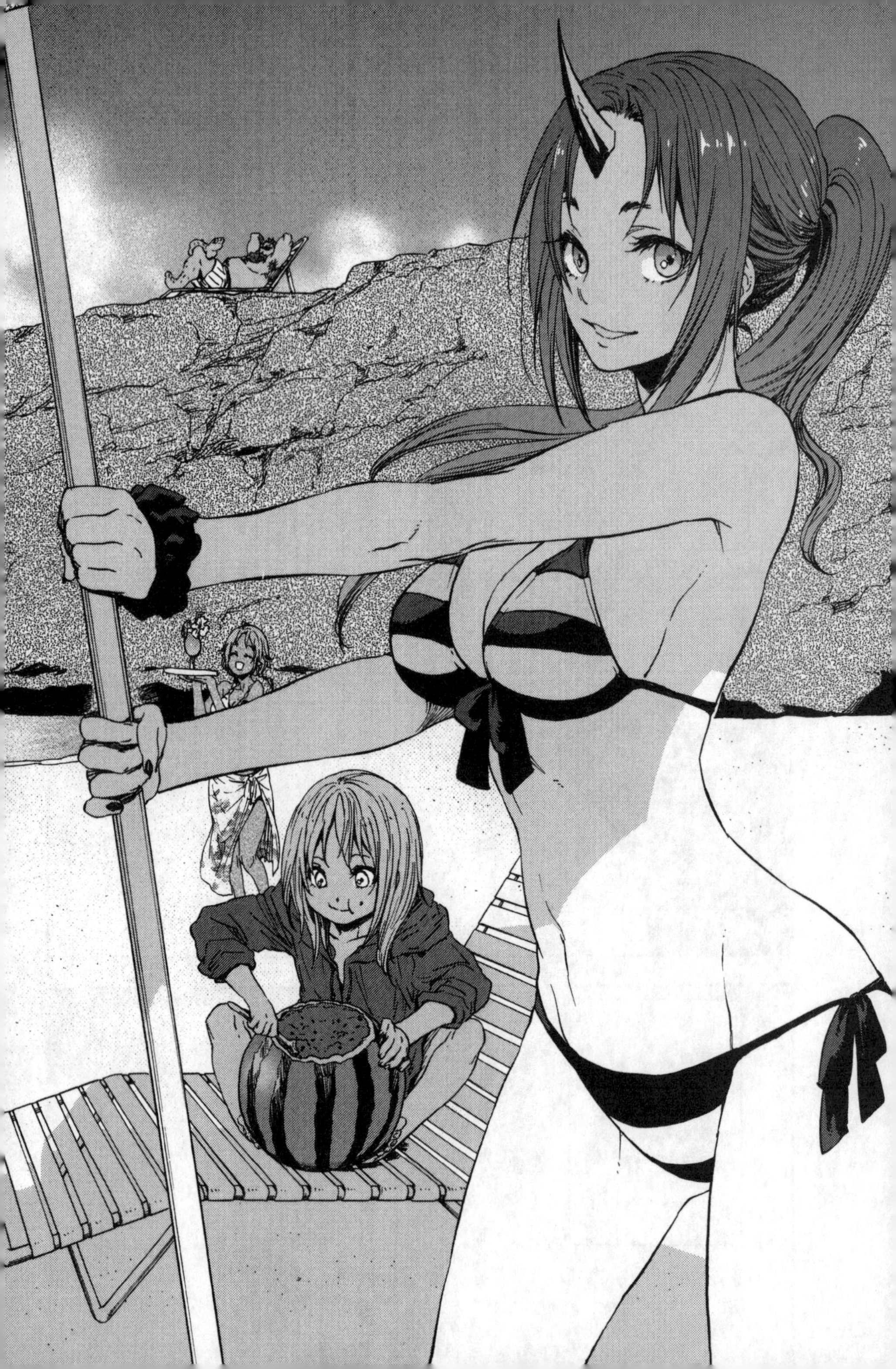

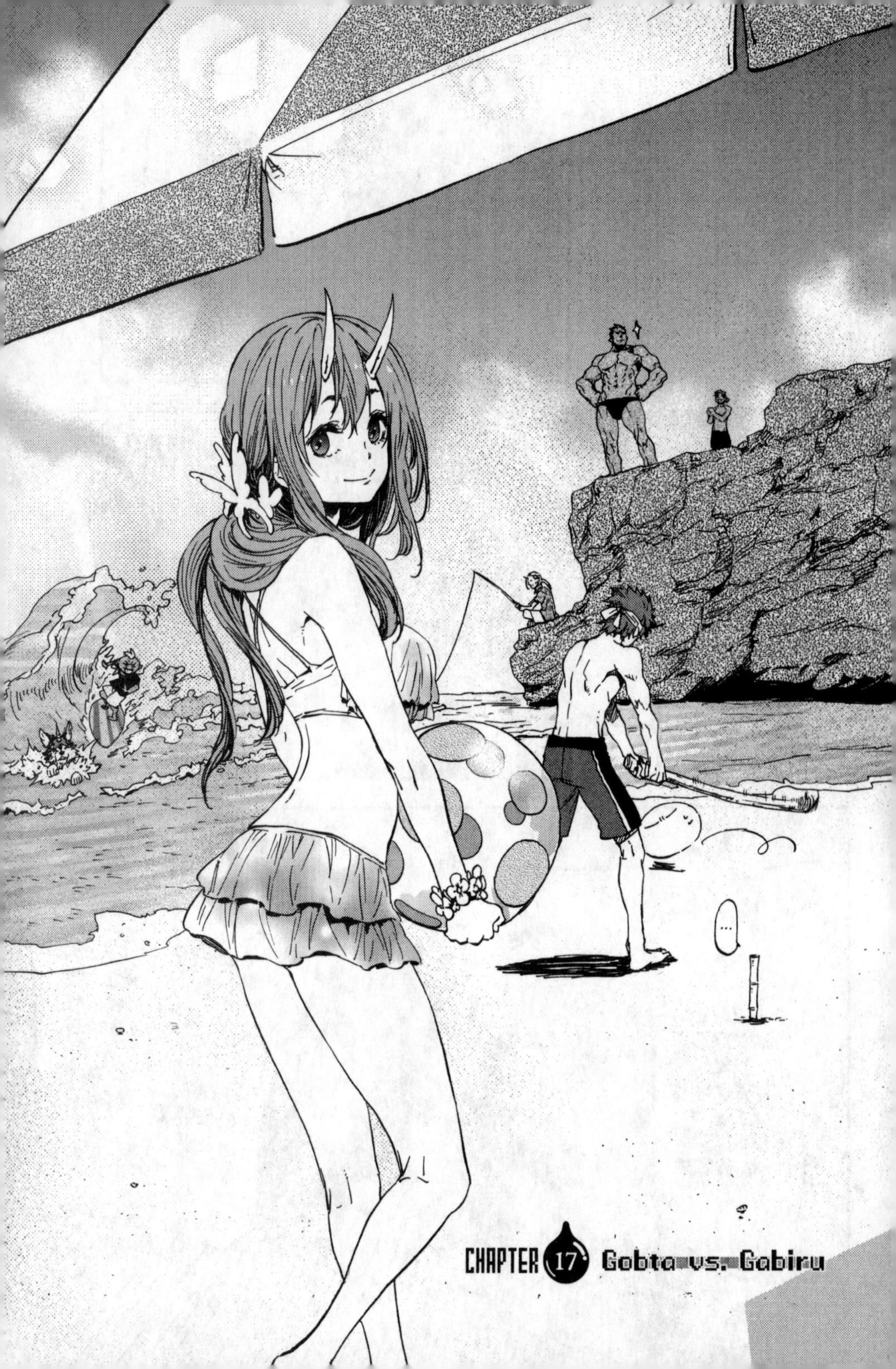
...
CHAPTER 17 Gobta vs. Gabiru

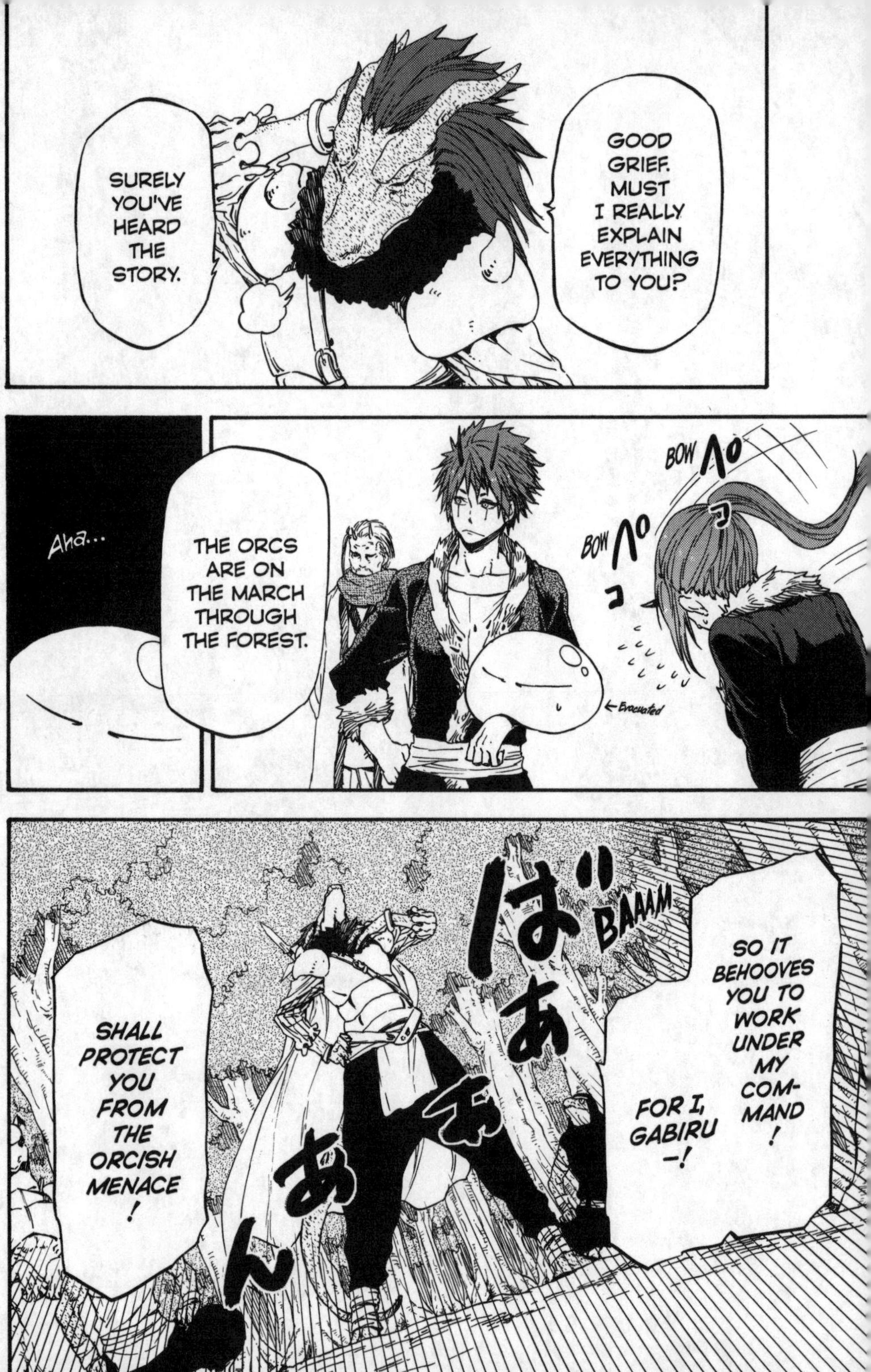
GOOD GRIEF. MUST I REALLY EXPLAIN EVERYTHING TO YOU?
SURELY YOU'VE HEARD THE STORY.
BOW
BOW
THE ORCS ARE ON THE MARCH THROUGH THE FOREST.
← Evacuated
Aha...
SO IT BEHOOVES YOU TO WORK UNDER MY COM-MAND!
BAAAM
FOR I, GABIRU—!
SHALL PROTECT YOU FROM THE ORCISH MENACE!

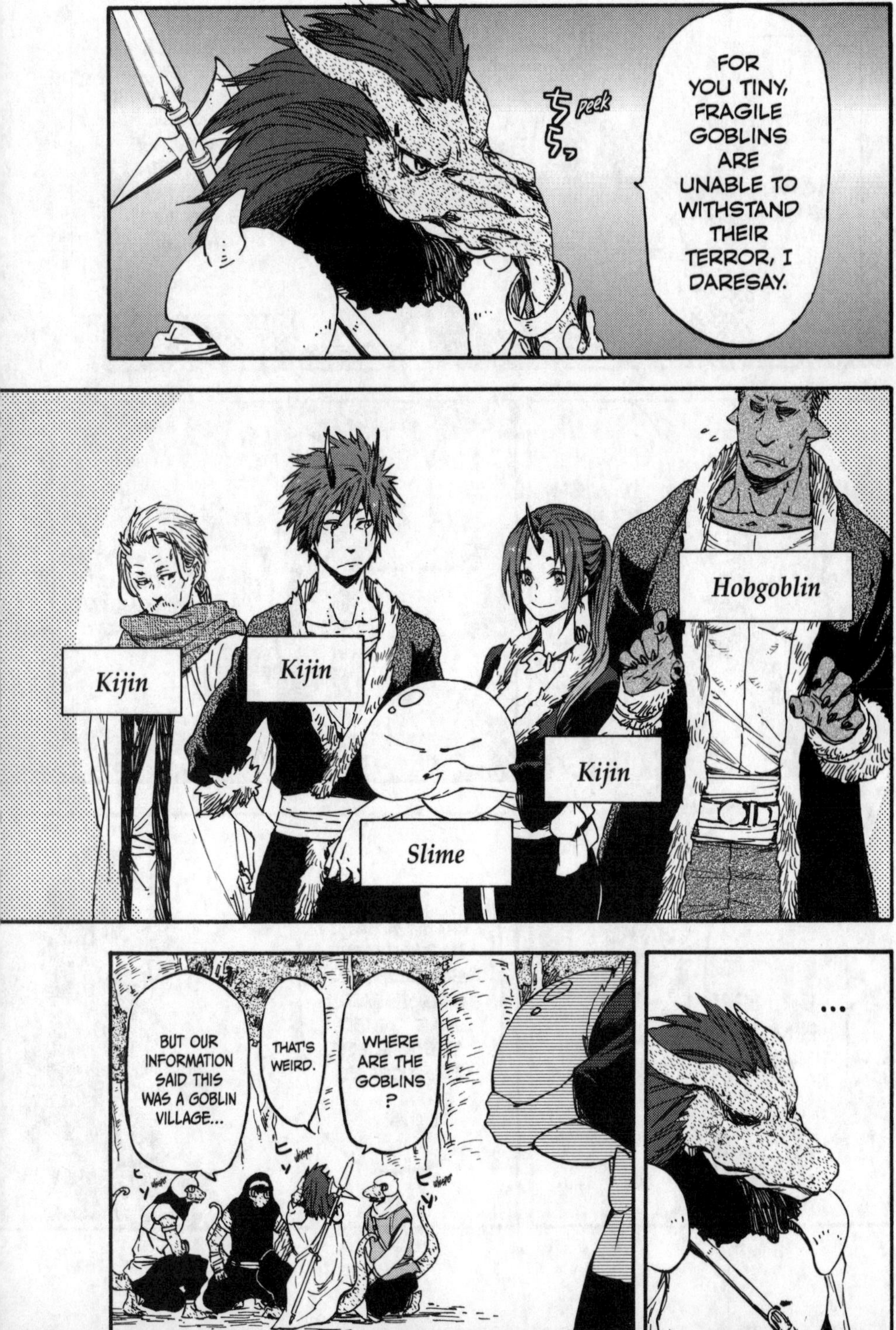
FOR YOU TINY, FRAGILE GOBLINS ARE UNABLE TO WITHSTAND THEIR TERROR, I DARESAY.
ちらっ peek
Hobgoblin
Kijin
Slime
Kijin
Kijin
...
WHERE ARE THE GOBLINS?
THAT'S WEIRD.
BUT OUR INFORMATION SAID THIS WAS A GOBLIN VILLAGE...

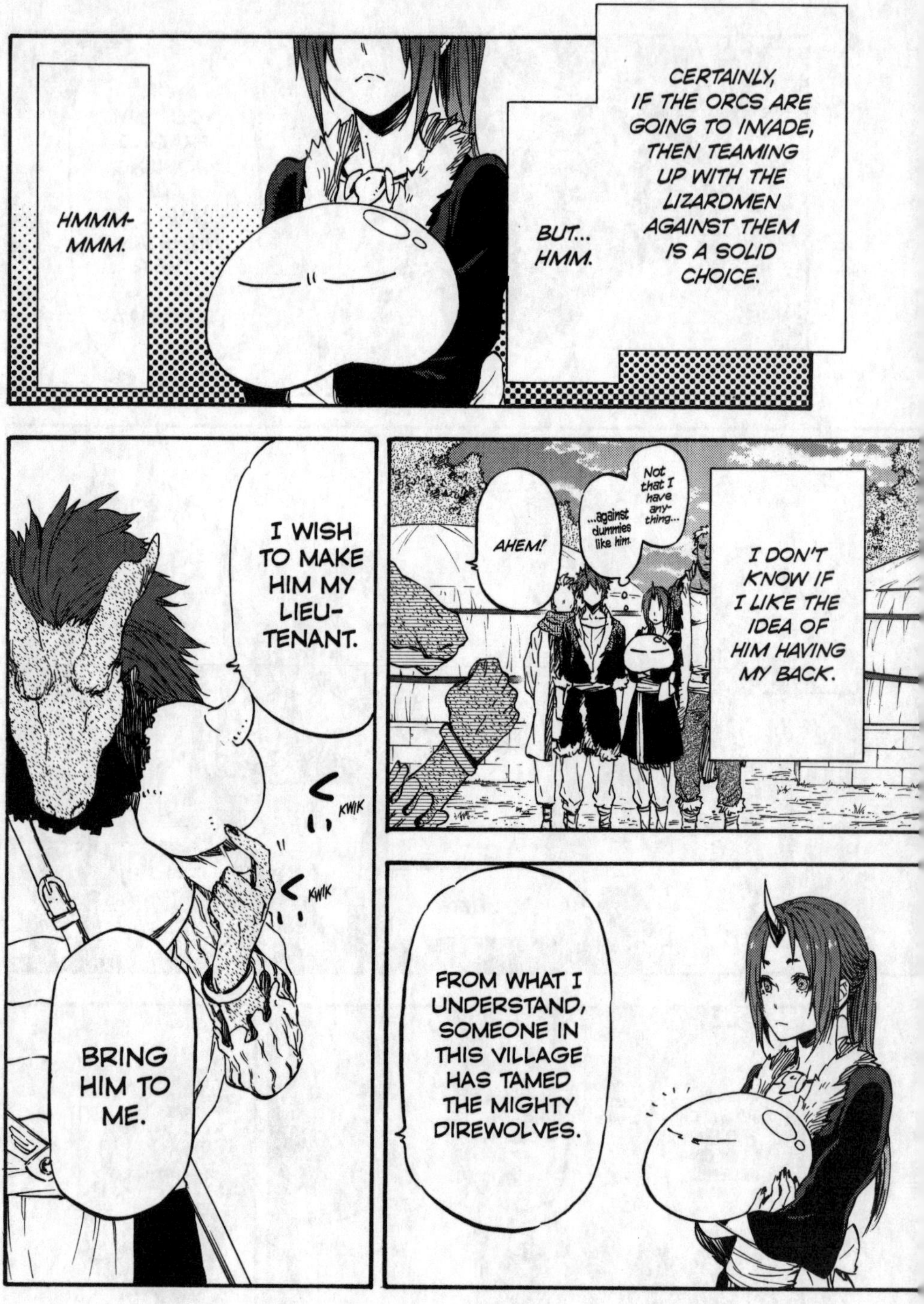
CERTAINLY, IF THE ORCS ARE GOING TO INVADE, THEN TEAMING UP WITH THE LIZARDMEN AGAINST THEM IS A SOLID CHOICE.
BUT... HMM.
HMMM-MMM.
I DON'T KNOW IF I LIKE THE IDEA OF HIM HAVING MY BACK.
Not that I have anything...
...against dummies like him.
AHEM!
FROM WHAT I UNDERSTAND, SOMEONE IN THIS VILLAGE HAS TAMED THE MIGHTY DIREWOLVES.
I WISH TO MAKE HIM MY LIEU-TENANT.
KWIK
KWIK
BRING HIM TO ME.

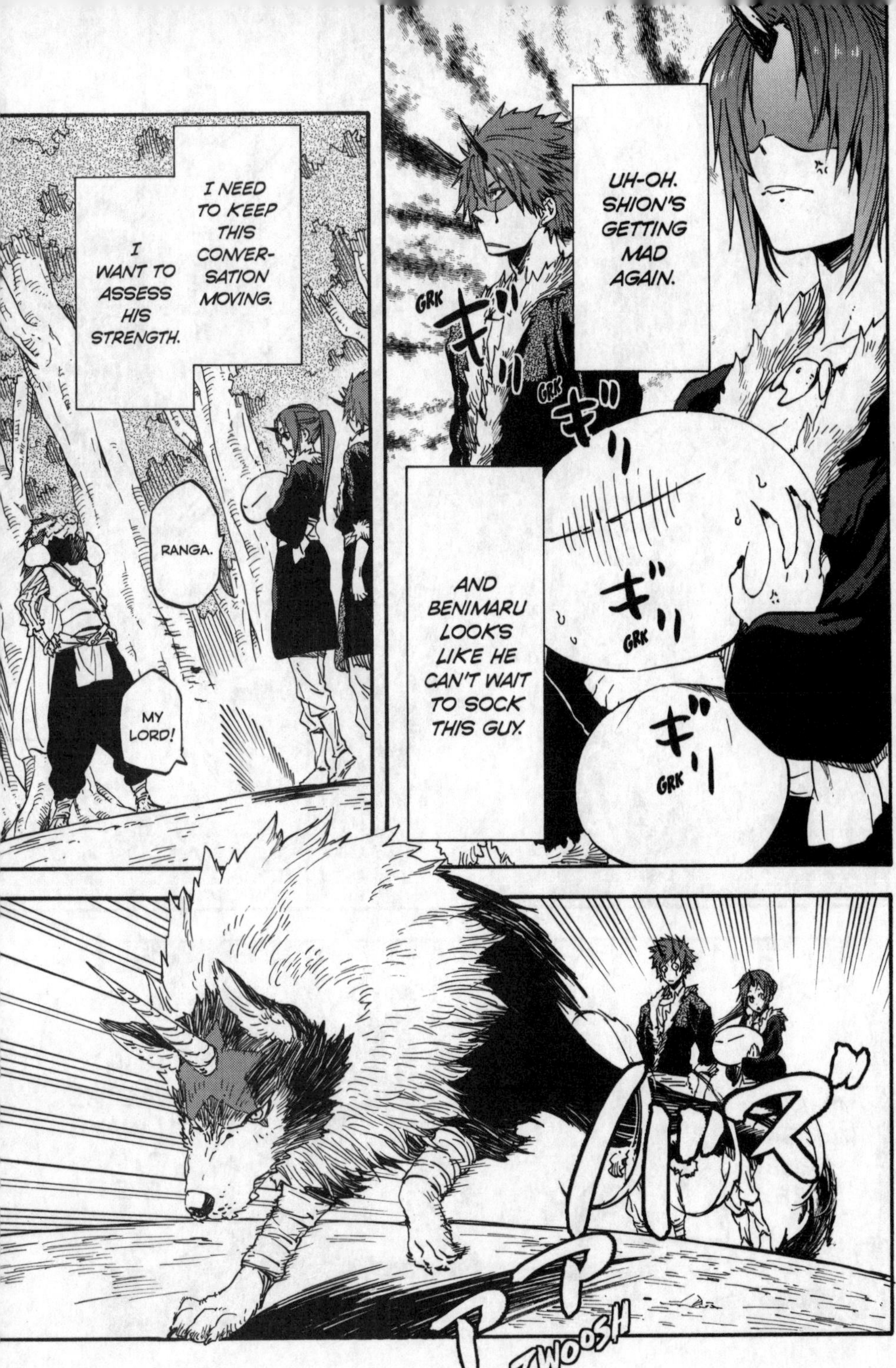
UH-OH. SHION'S GETTING MAD AGAIN.
GRK
GRK
GRK
GRK
AND BENIMARU LOOKS LIKE HE CAN'T WAIT TO SOCK THIS GUY.
I NEED TO KEEP THIS CONVER-SATION MOVING.
I WANT TO ASSESS HIS STRENGTH.
RANGA.
MY LORD!
ZWOOSH

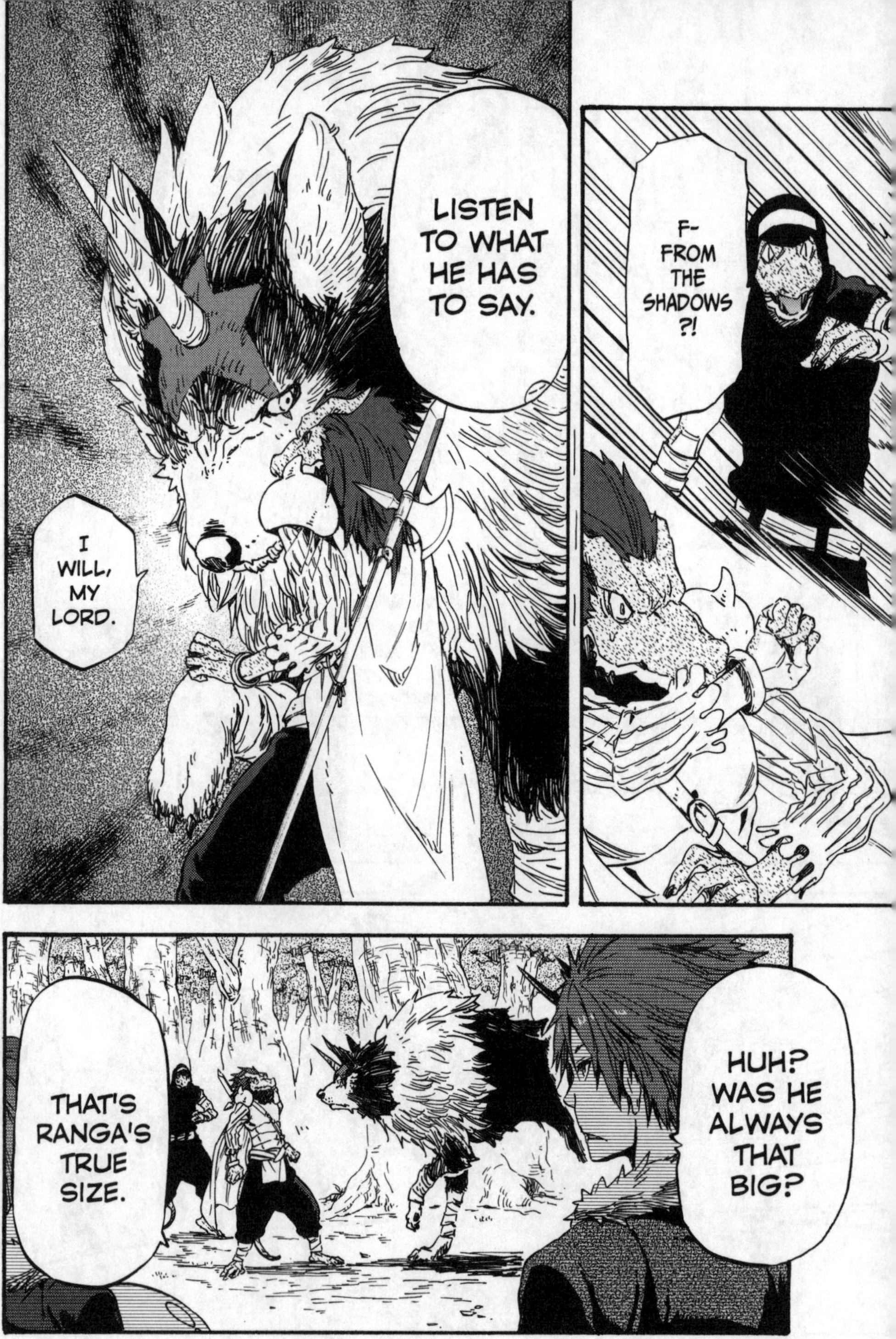
F- FROM THE SHADOWS ?!
LISTEN TO WHAT HE HAS TO SAY.
I WILL, MY LORD.
HUH? WAS HE ALWAYS THAT BIG?
THAT'S RANGA'S TRUE SIZE.

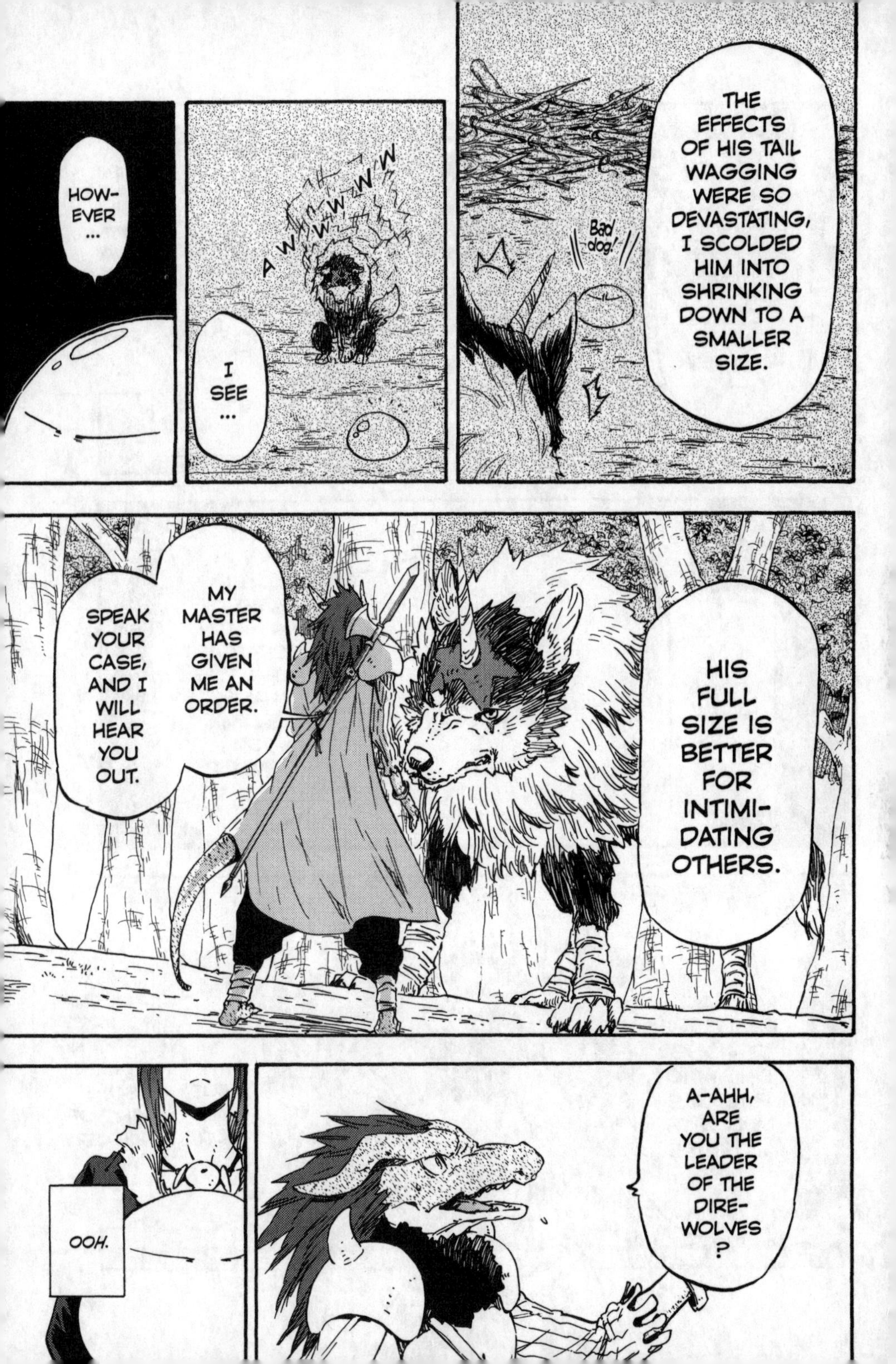
THE EFFECTS OF HIS TAIL WAGGING WERE SO DEVASTATING, I SCOLDED HIM INTO SHRINKING DOWN TO A SMALLER SIZE.
Bad dog!
AWWWWWW
I SEE...
HOW-EVER...
HIS FULL SIZE IS BETTER FOR INTIMI-DATING OTHERS.
MY MASTER HAS GIVEN ME AN ORDER.
SPEAK YOUR CASE, AND I WILL HEAR YOU OUT.
A-AHH, ARE YOU THE LEADER OF THE DIRE-WOLVES?
OOH.

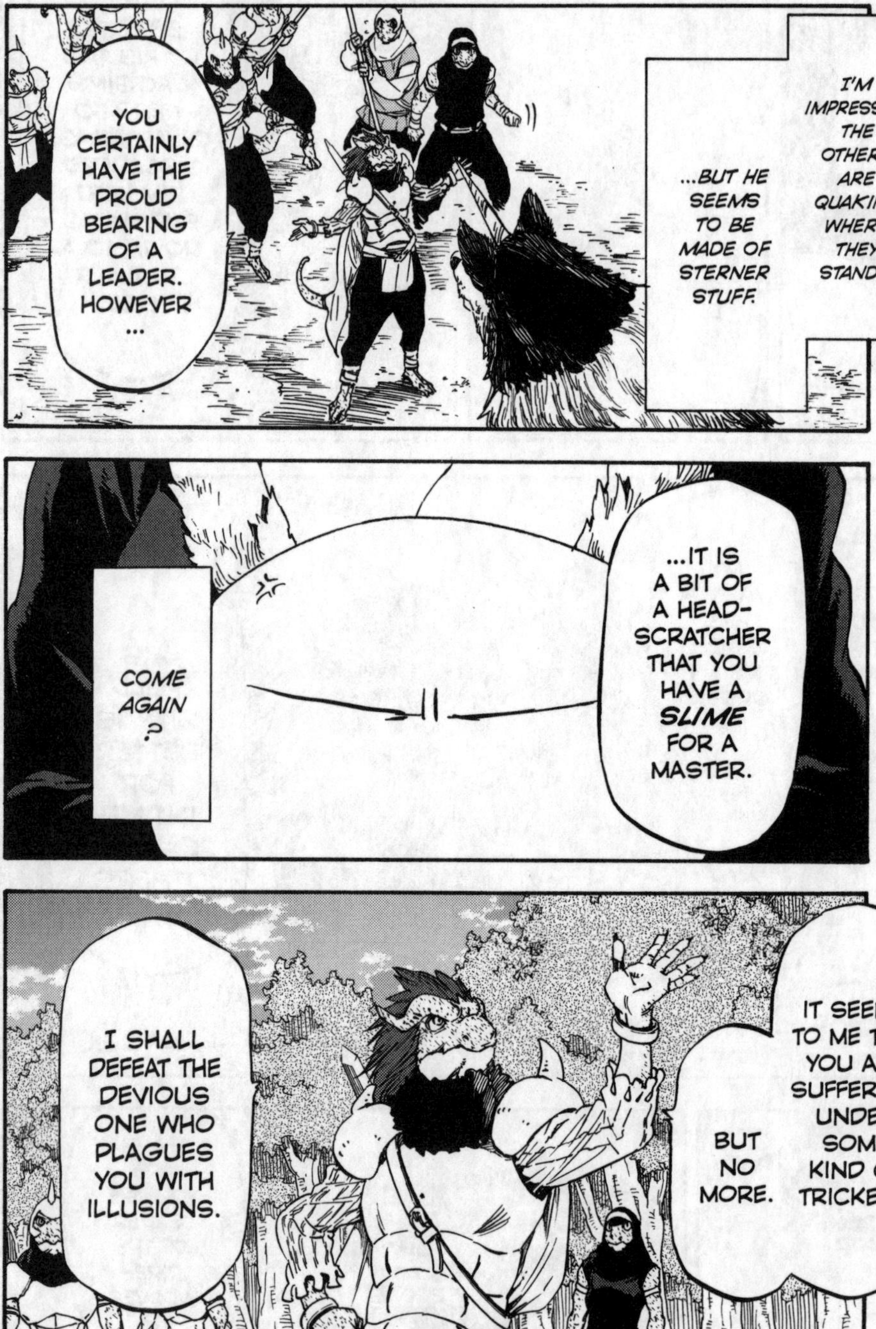
I'M IMPRESSED. THE OTHERS ARE QUAKING WHERE THEY STAND...
...BUT HE SEEMS TO BE MADE OF STERNER STUFF.
YOU CERTAINLY HAVE THE PROUD BEARING OF A LEADER. HOWEVER ...
...IT IS A BIT OF A HEAD-SCRATCHER THAT YOU HAVE A SLIME FOR A MASTER.
COME AGAIN ?
IT SEEMS TO ME THAT YOU ARE SUFFERING UNDER SOME KIND OF TRICKERY.
BUT NO MORE.
I SHALL DEFEAT THE DEVIOUS ONE WHO PLAGUES YOU WITH ILLUSIONS.

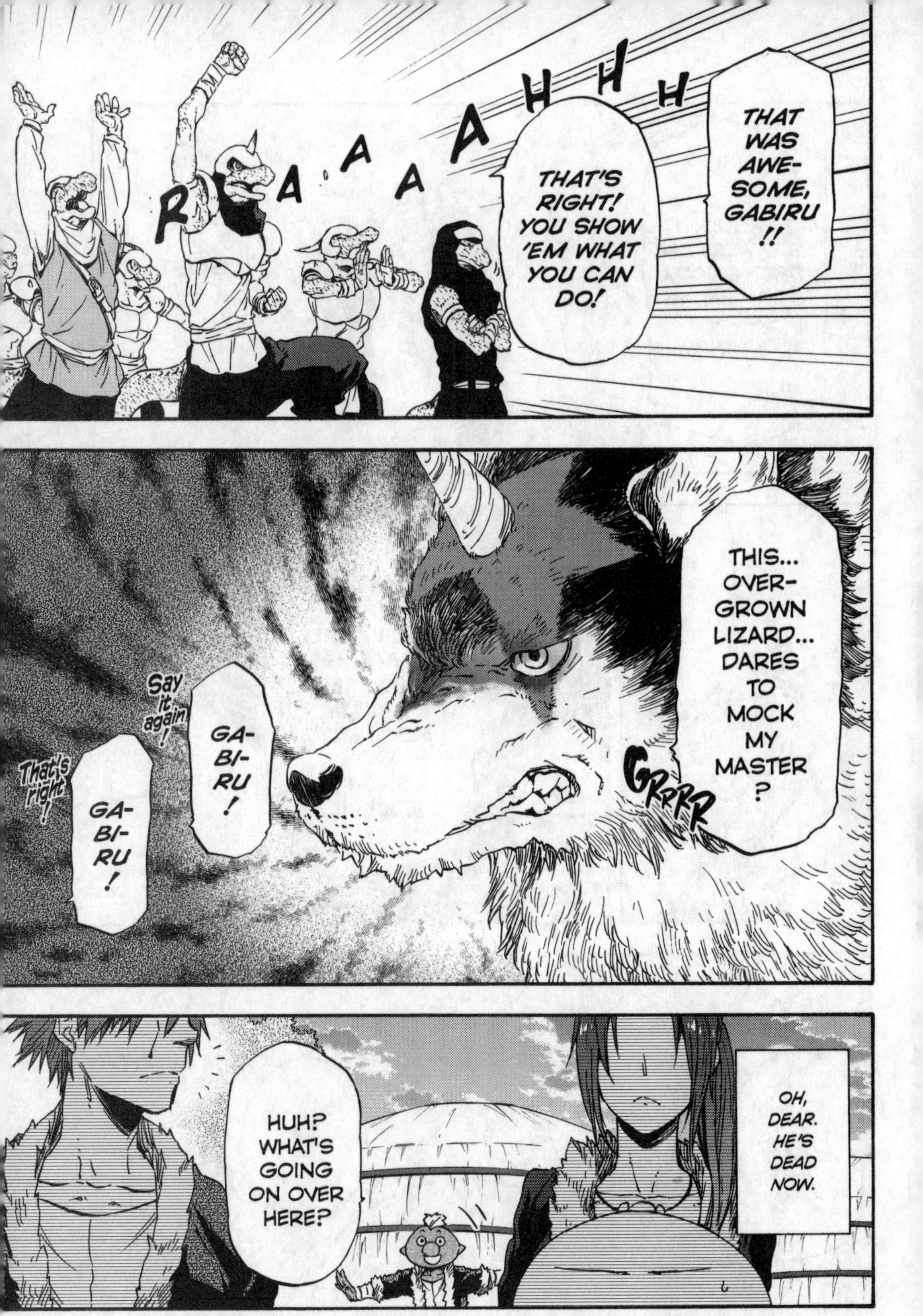
THAT WAS AWE-SOME, GABIRU!!
THAT'S RIGHT! YOU SHOW 'EM WHAT YOU CAN DO!
RAAAAHHH
THIS... OVER-GROWN LIZARD... DARES TO MOCK MY MASTER?
GRRRR
GA-BI-RU!
Say it again!
GA-BI-RU!
That's right!
OH, DEAR. HE'S DEAD NOW.
HUH? WHAT'S GOING ON OVER HERE?

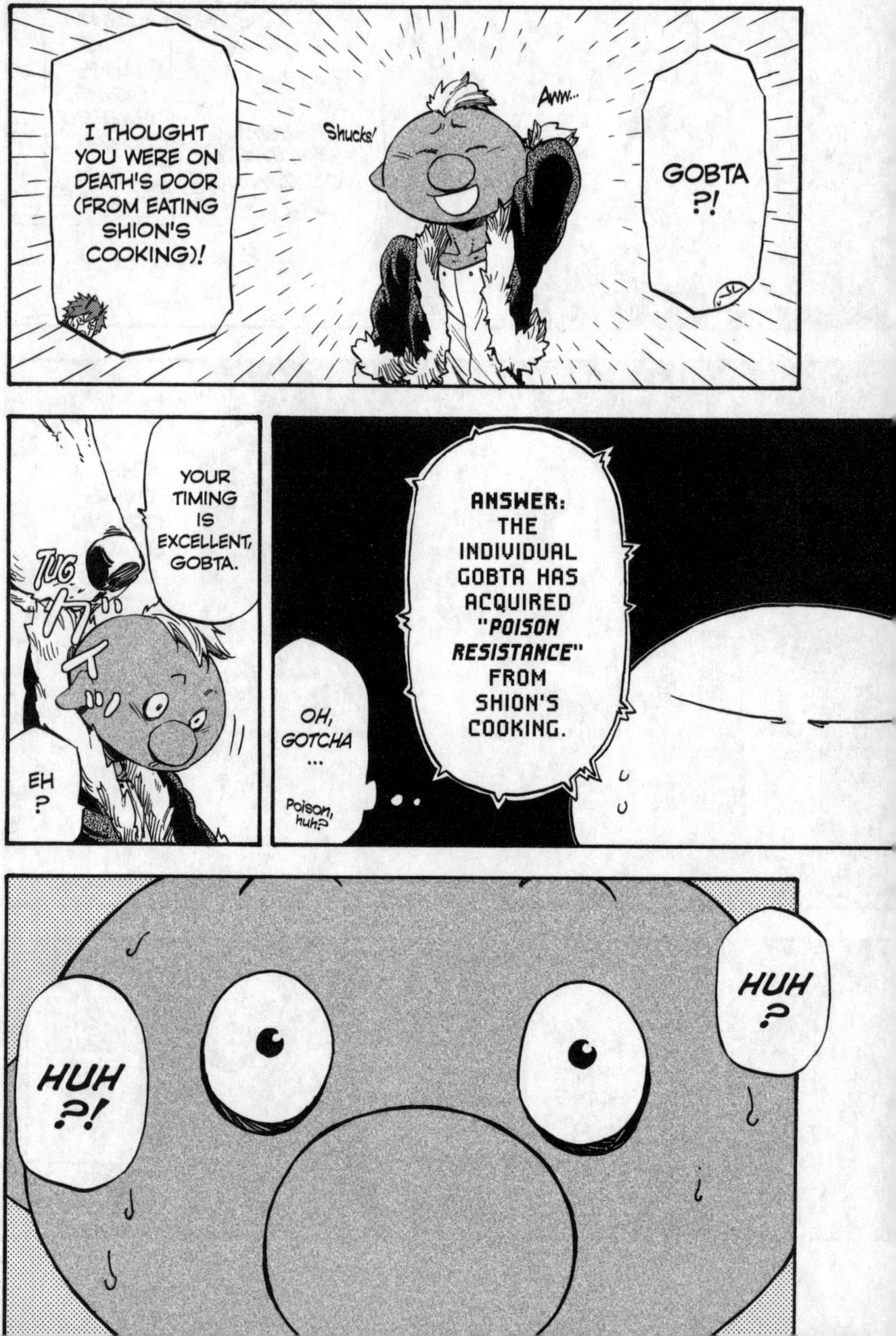
GOBTA ?!
Aww...
Shucks!
I THOUGHT YOU WERE ON DEATH'S DOOR (FROM EATING SHION'S COOKING)!
ANSWER: THE INDIVIDUAL GOBTA HAS ACQUIRED "POISON RESISTANCE" FROM SHION'S COOKING.
OH, GOTCHA...
Poison, huh?
YOUR TIMING IS EXCELLENT, GOBTA.
TUG
EH?
HUH?
HUH?!

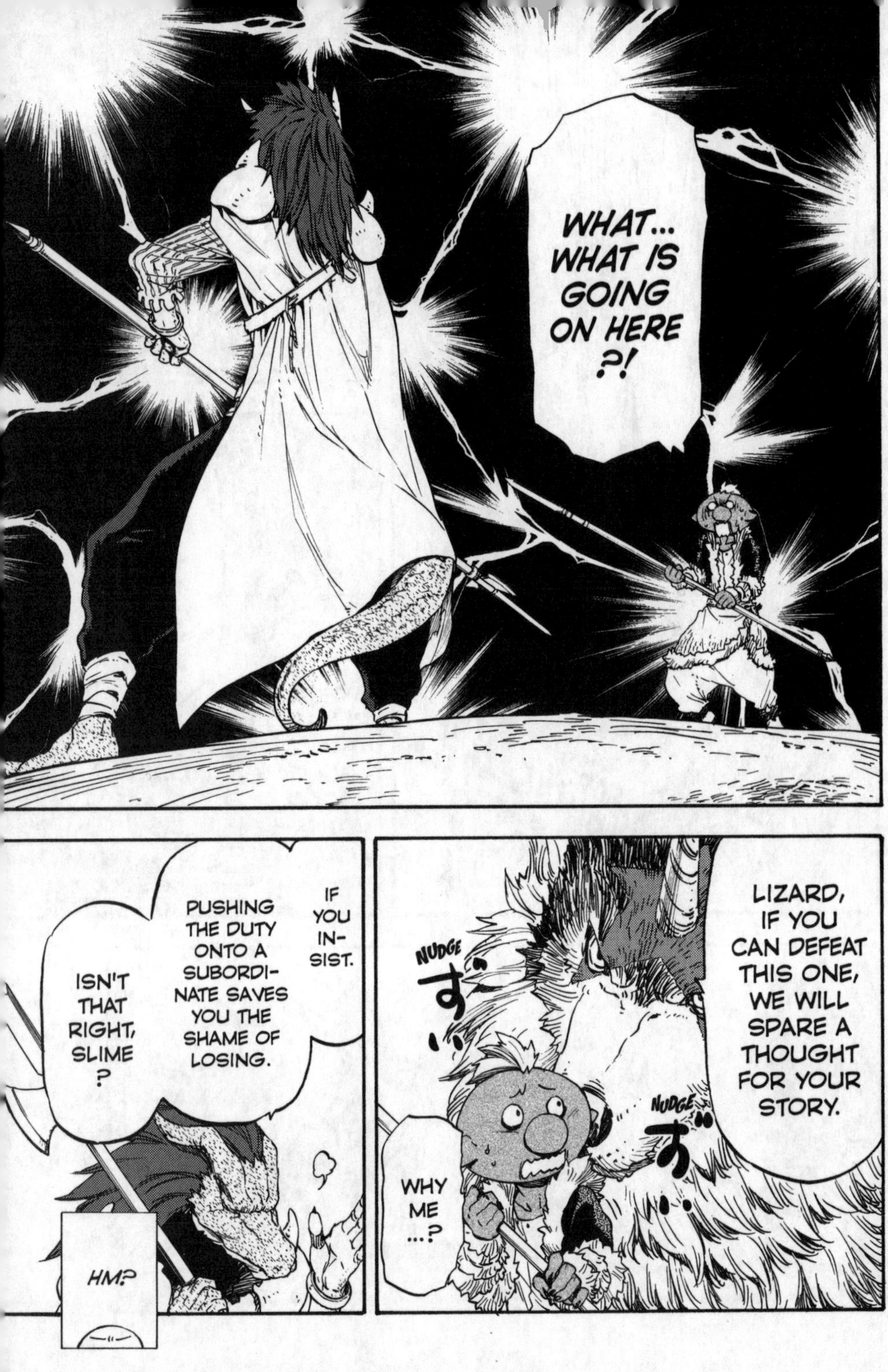
WHAT... WHAT IS GOING ON HERE ?!
LIZARD, IF YOU CAN DEFEAT THIS ONE, WE WILL SPARE A THOUGHT FOR YOUR STORY.
NUDGE
すい
NUDGE
お...
WHY ME ...?
IF YOU IN-SIST.
PUSHING THE DUTY ONTO A SUBORDI-NATE SAVES YOU THE SHAME OF LOSING.
ISN'T THAT RIGHT, SLIME ?
HM?

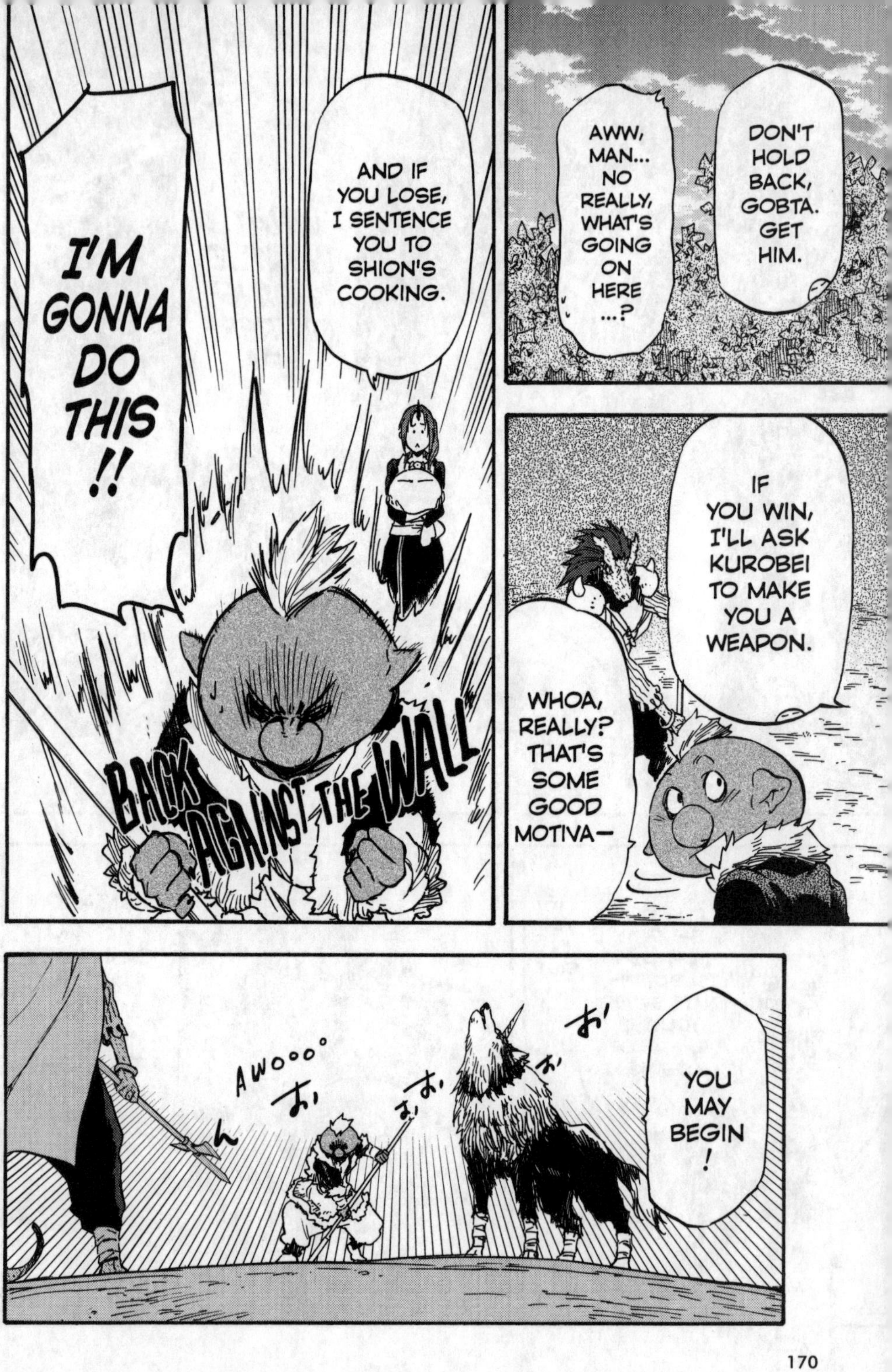
DON'T HOLD BACK, GOBTA. GET HIM.
AWW, MAN... NO REALLY, WHAT'S GOING ON HERE ...?
IF YOU WIN, I'LL ASK KUROBEI TO MAKE YOU A WEAPON.
WHOA, REALLY? THAT'S SOME GOOD MOTIVA—
AND IF YOU LOSE, I SENTENCE YOU TO SHION'S COOKING.
I'M GONNA DO THIS!!
BACK AGAINST THE WALL
YOU MAY BEGIN!
AWOOO

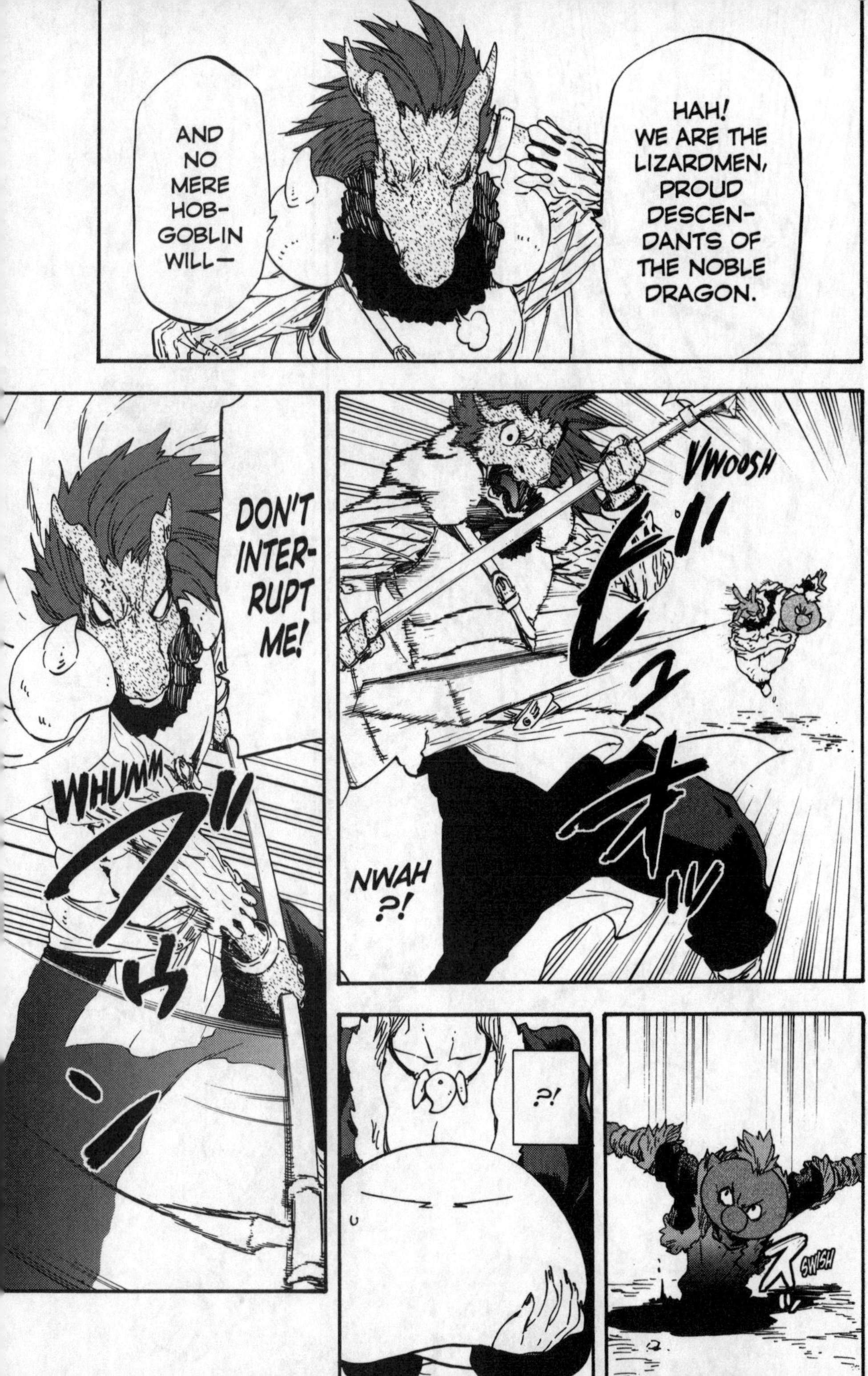
HAH! WE ARE THE LIZARDMEN, PROUD DESCEN-DANTS OF THE NOBLE DRAGON.
AND NO MERE HOB-GOBLIN WILL—
VWOOSH
NWAH ?!
DON'T INTER-RUPT ME!
WHUMM
SWISH
?!

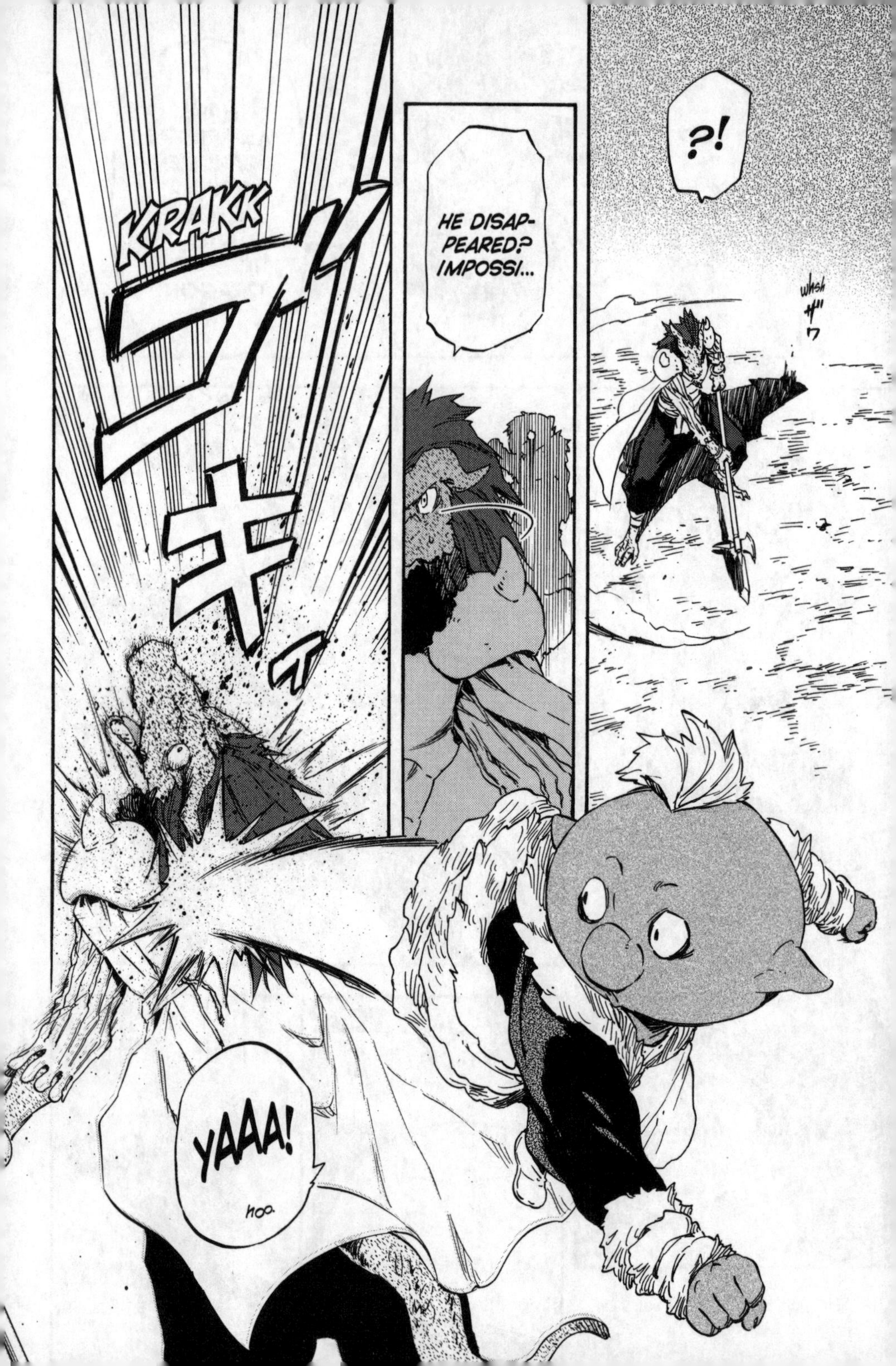
?!
whsh
HE DISAP-PEARED? IMPOSSI...
KRAKK
YAAA!
hoo.

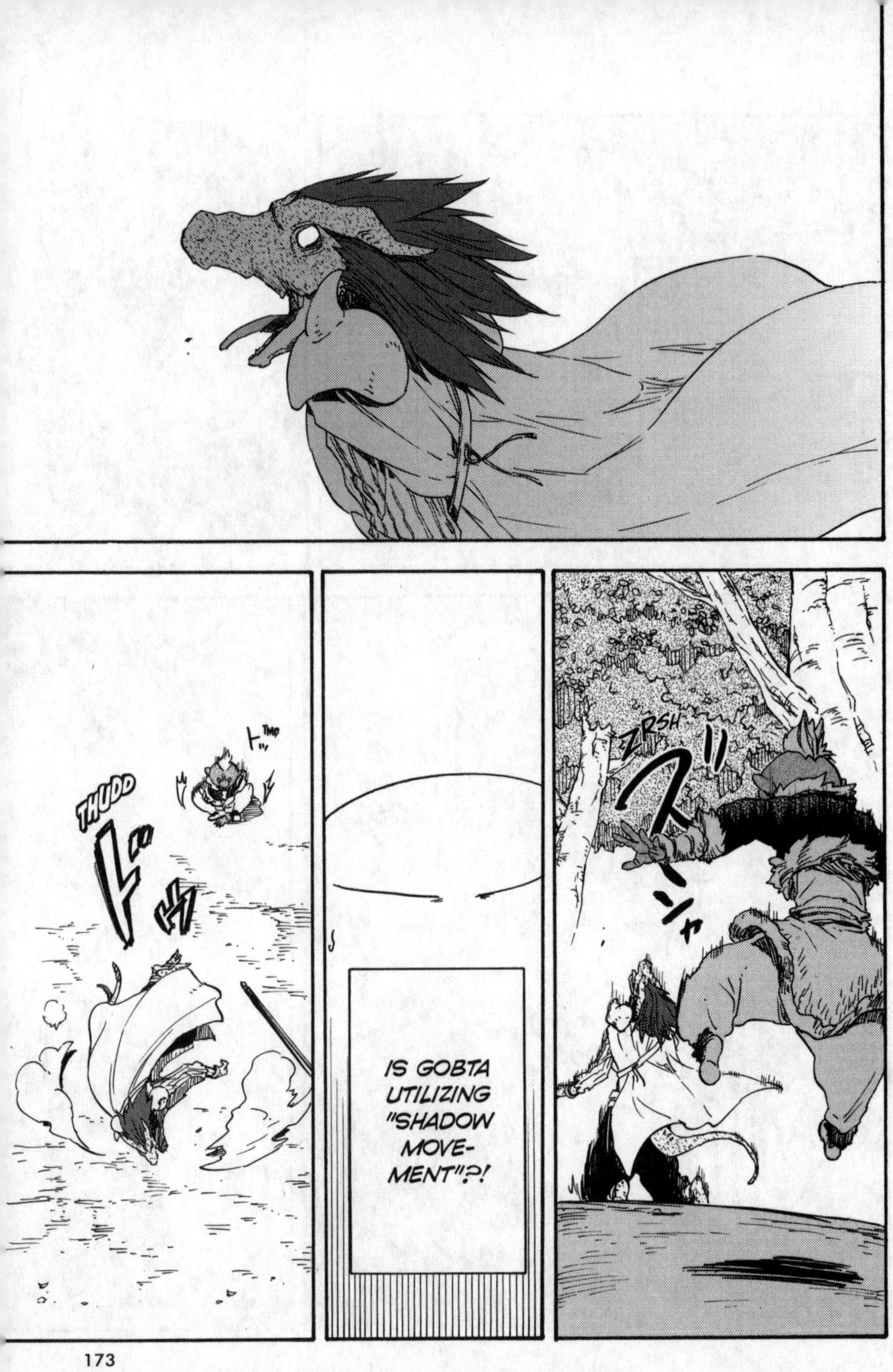

ZRSH
IS GOBTA UTILIZING "SHADOW MOVEMENT"?!
TMP
THUDD

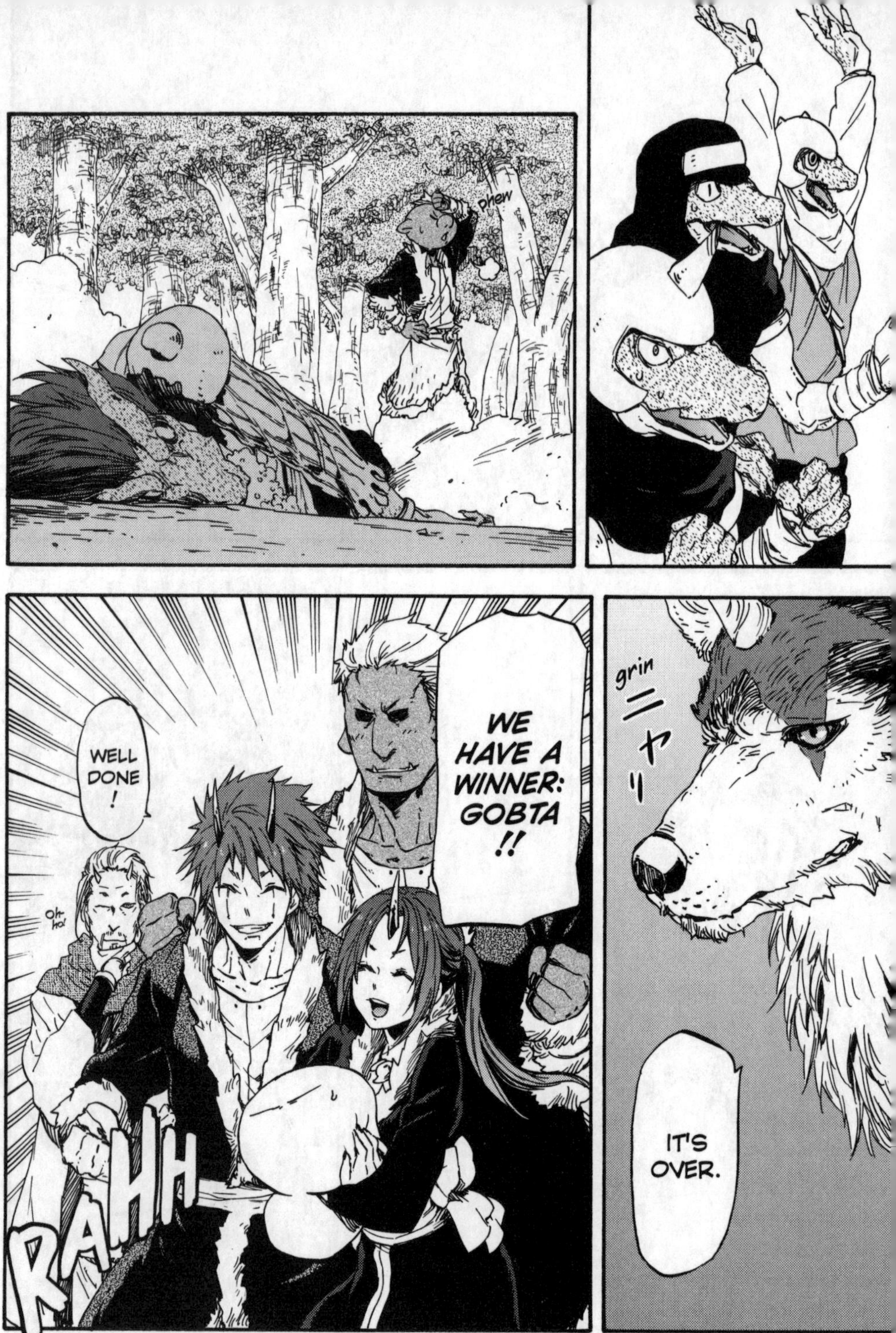
phew
grin
ニヤリ
IT'S OVER.
WE HAVE A WINNER: GOBTA!!
WELL DONE!
Oh-ho!
RAHH

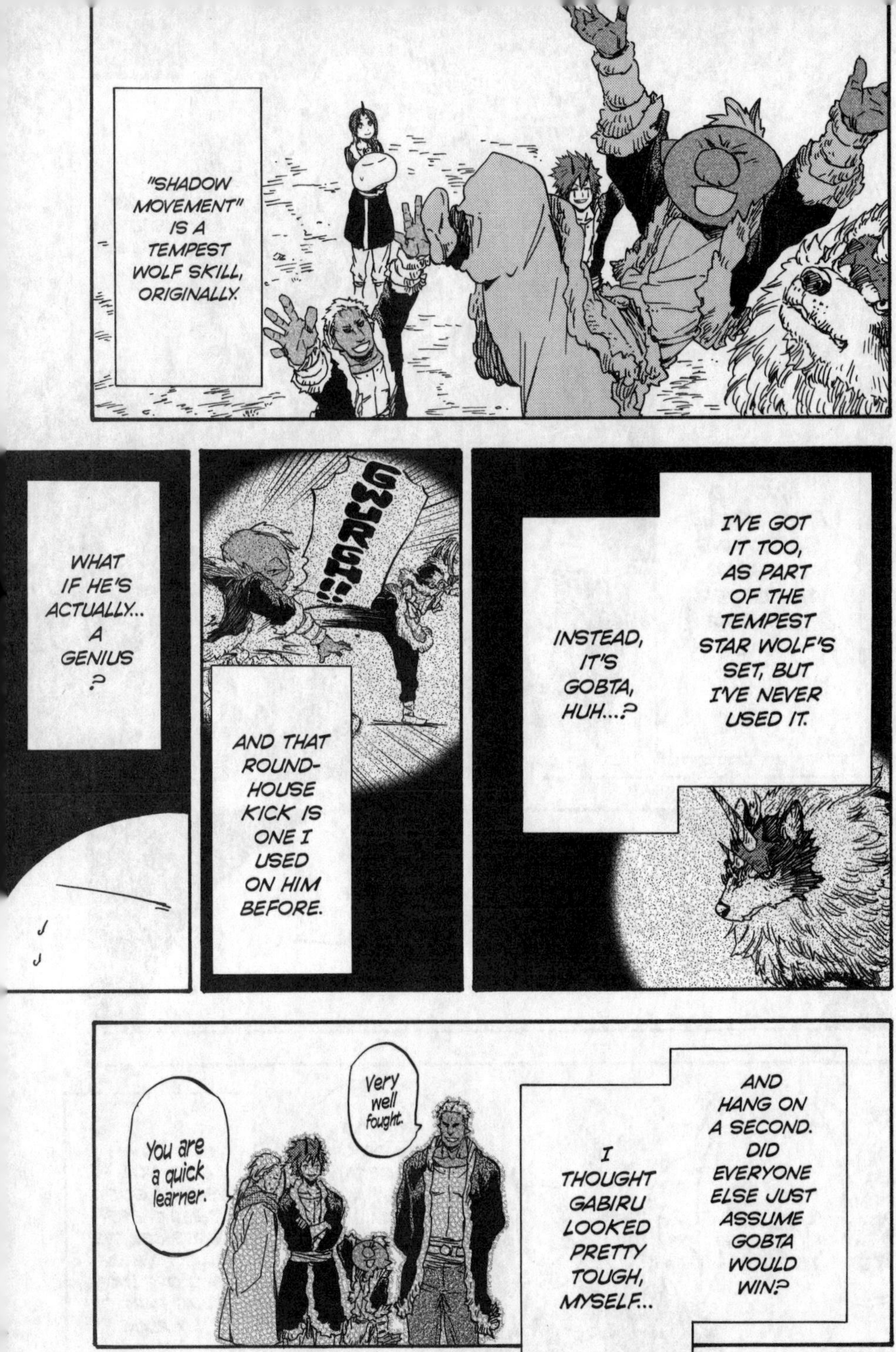
"SHADOW MOVEMENT" IS A TEMPEST WOLF SKILL, ORIGINALLY.
I'VE GOT IT TOO, AS PART OF THE TEMPEST STAR WOLF'S SET, BUT I'VE NEVER USED IT.
INSTEAD, IT'S GOBTA, HUH...?
GWURGH!!
AND THAT ROUND-HOUSE KICK IS ONE I USED ON HIM BEFORE.
WHAT IF HE'S ACTUALLY... A GENIUS?
AND HANG ON A SECOND. DID EVERYONE ELSE JUST ASSUME GOBTA WOULD WIN?
I THOUGHT GABIRU LOOKED PRETTY TOUGH, MYSELF...
Very well fought.
You are a quick learner.

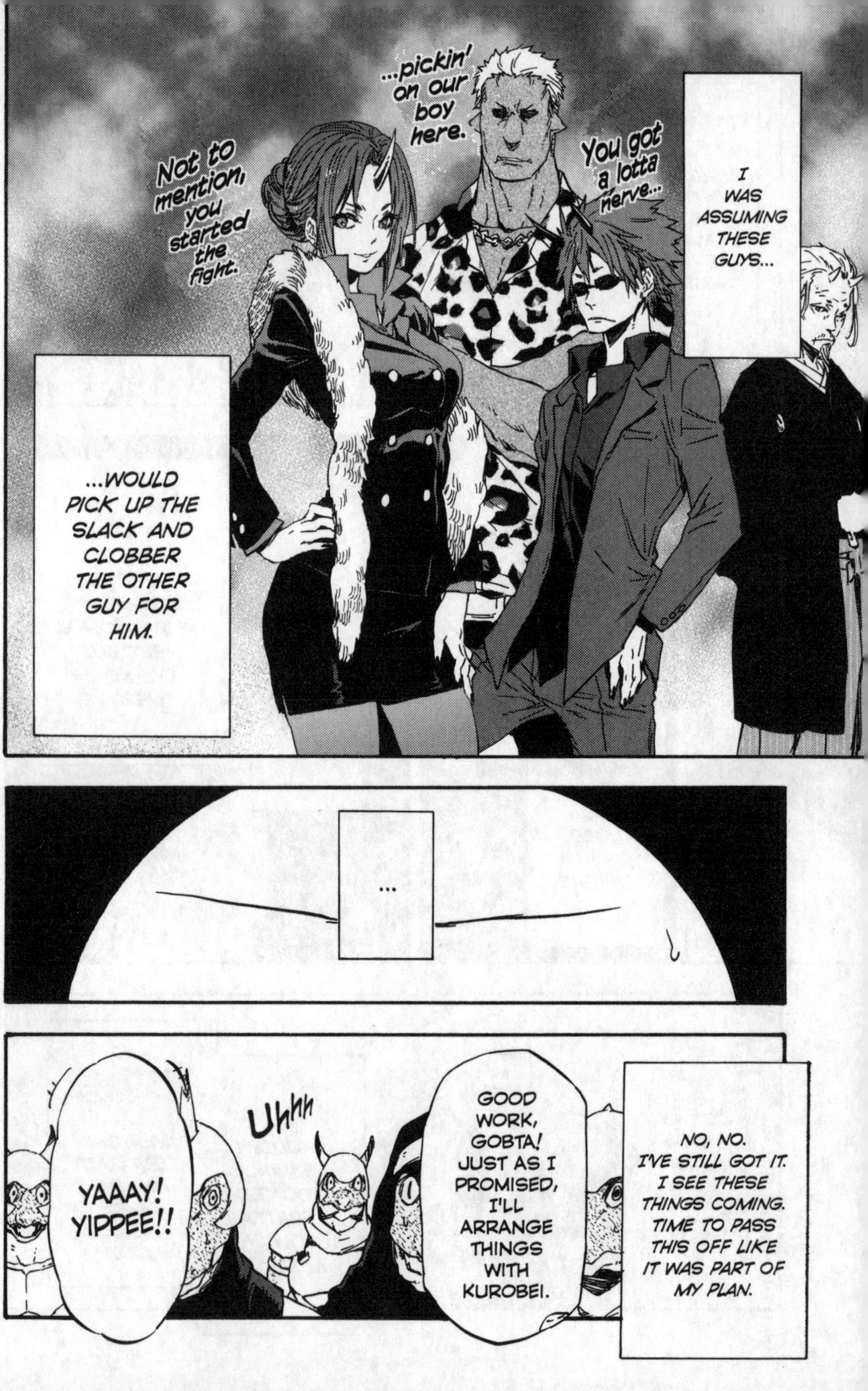

I WAS ASSUMING THESE GUYS...
You got a lotta nerve...
...pickin' on our boy here.
Not to mention, you started the fight.
...WOULD PICK UP THE SLACK AND CLOBBER THE OTHER GUY FOR HIM.
...
NO, NO. I'VE STILL GOT IT. I SEE THESE THINGS COMING. TIME TO PASS THIS OFF LIKE IT WAS PART OF MY PLAN.
GOOD WORK, GOBTA! JUST AS I PROMISED, I'LL ARRANGE THINGS WITH KUROBEI.
Uhhh
YAAAY! YIPPEE!!

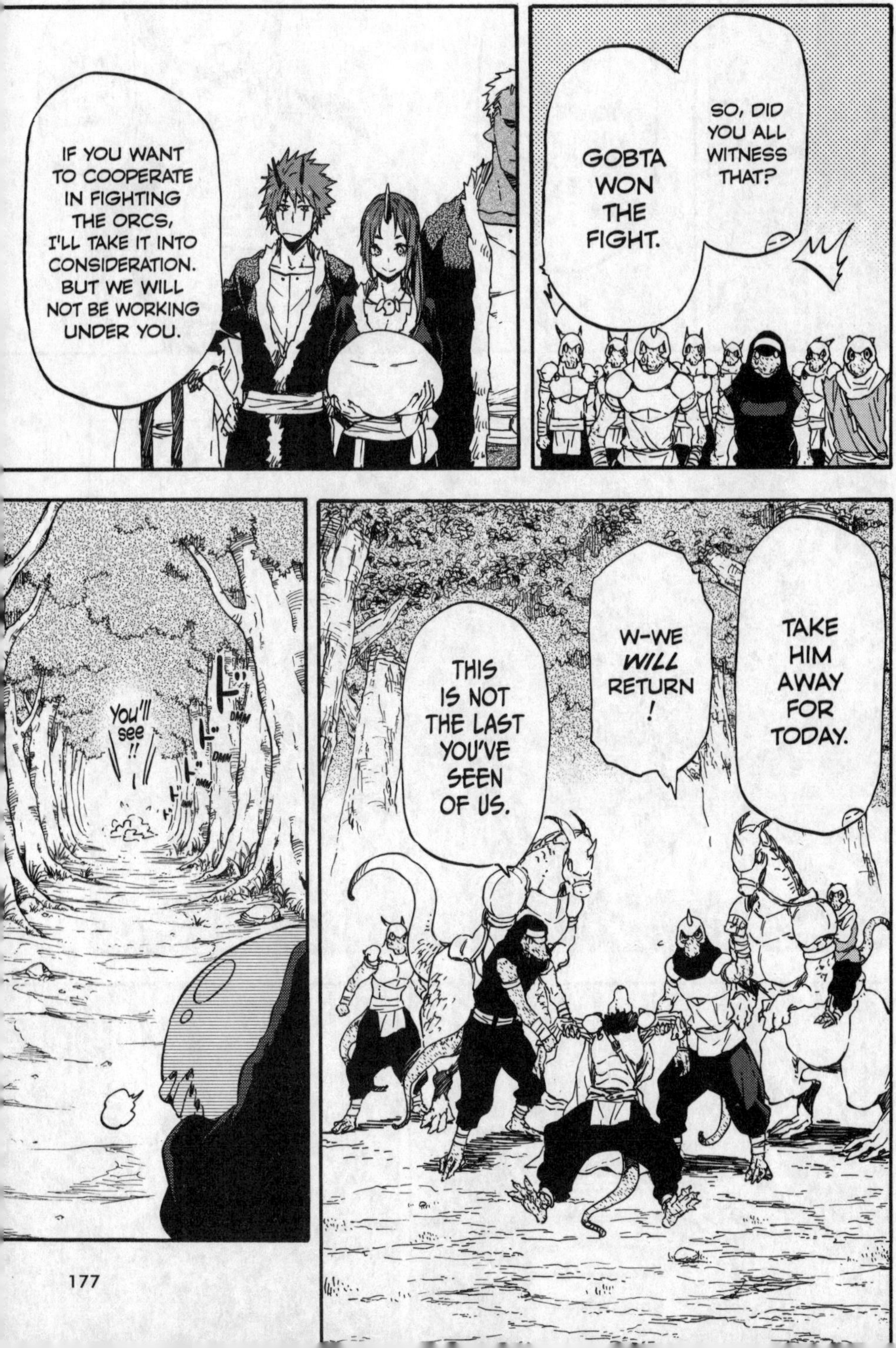
SO, DID YOU ALL WITNESS THAT?
GOBTA WON THE FIGHT.
IF YOU WANT TO COOPERATE IN FIGHTING THE ORCS, I'LL TAKE IT INTO CONSIDERATION. BUT WE WILL NOT BE WORKING UNDER YOU.
TAKE HIM AWAY FOR TODAY.
W-WE *WILL* RETURN!
THIS IS NOT THE LAST YOU'VE SEEN OF US.
You'll see!!
DMM
DMM
DMM

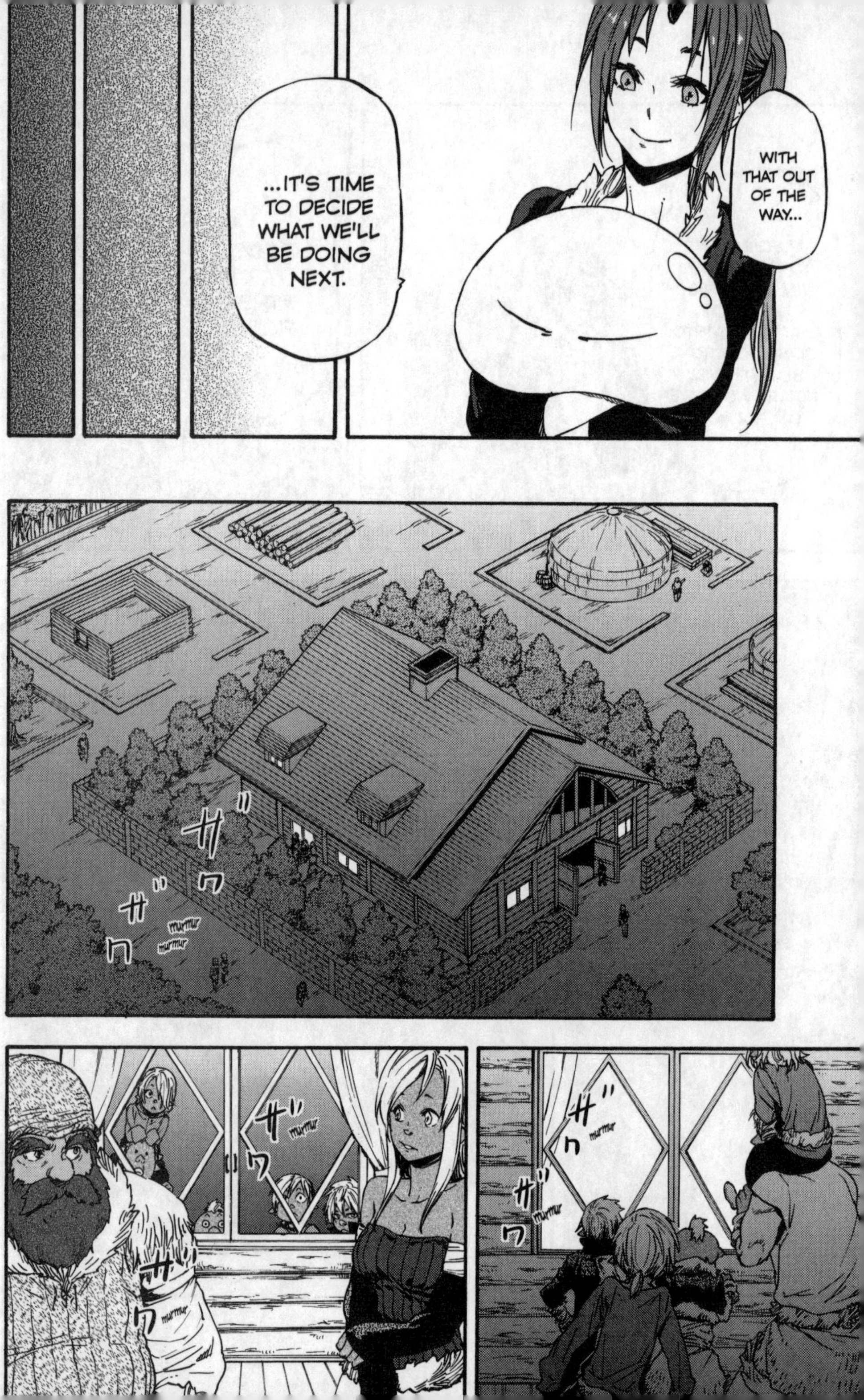
WITH THAT OUT OF THE WAY...
...IT'S TIME TO DECIDE WHAT WE'LL BE DOING NEXT.
ザワ
ザワ
murmur
murmur
ザワ
murmur
ザワ
murmur
ザワ
murmur
ザワ
murmur

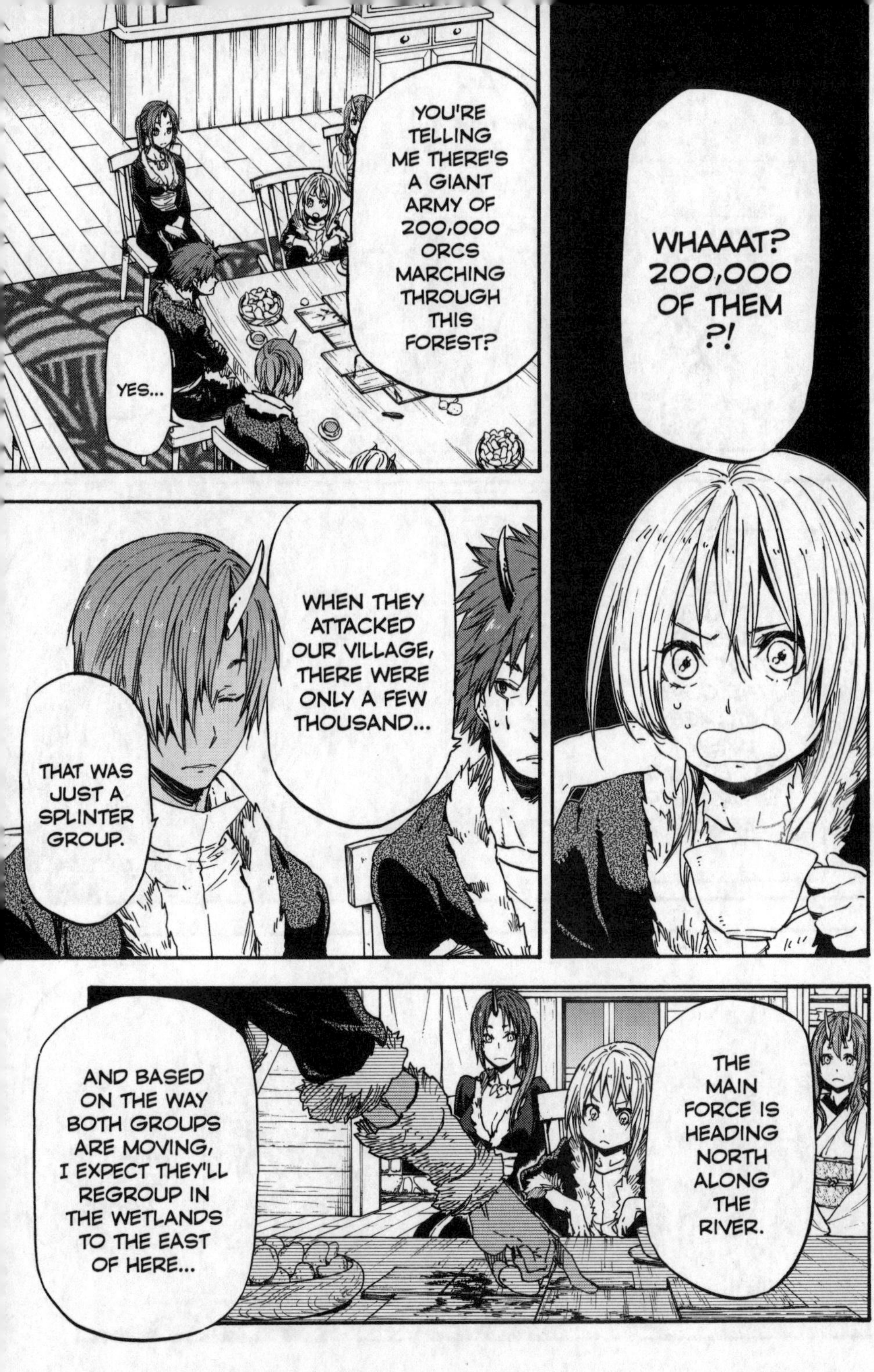
WHAAAT? 200,000 OF THEM ?!
YOU'RE TELLING ME THERE'S A GIANT ARMY OF 200,000 ORCS MARCHING THROUGH THIS FOREST?
YES...
WHEN THEY ATTACKED OUR VILLAGE, THERE WERE ONLY A FEW THOUSAND...
THAT WAS JUST A SPLINTER GROUP.
THE MAIN FORCE IS HEADING NORTH ALONG THE RIVER.
AND BASED ON THE WAY BOTH GROUPS ARE MOVING, I EXPECT THEY'LL REGROUP IN THE WETLANDS TO THE EAST OF HERE...

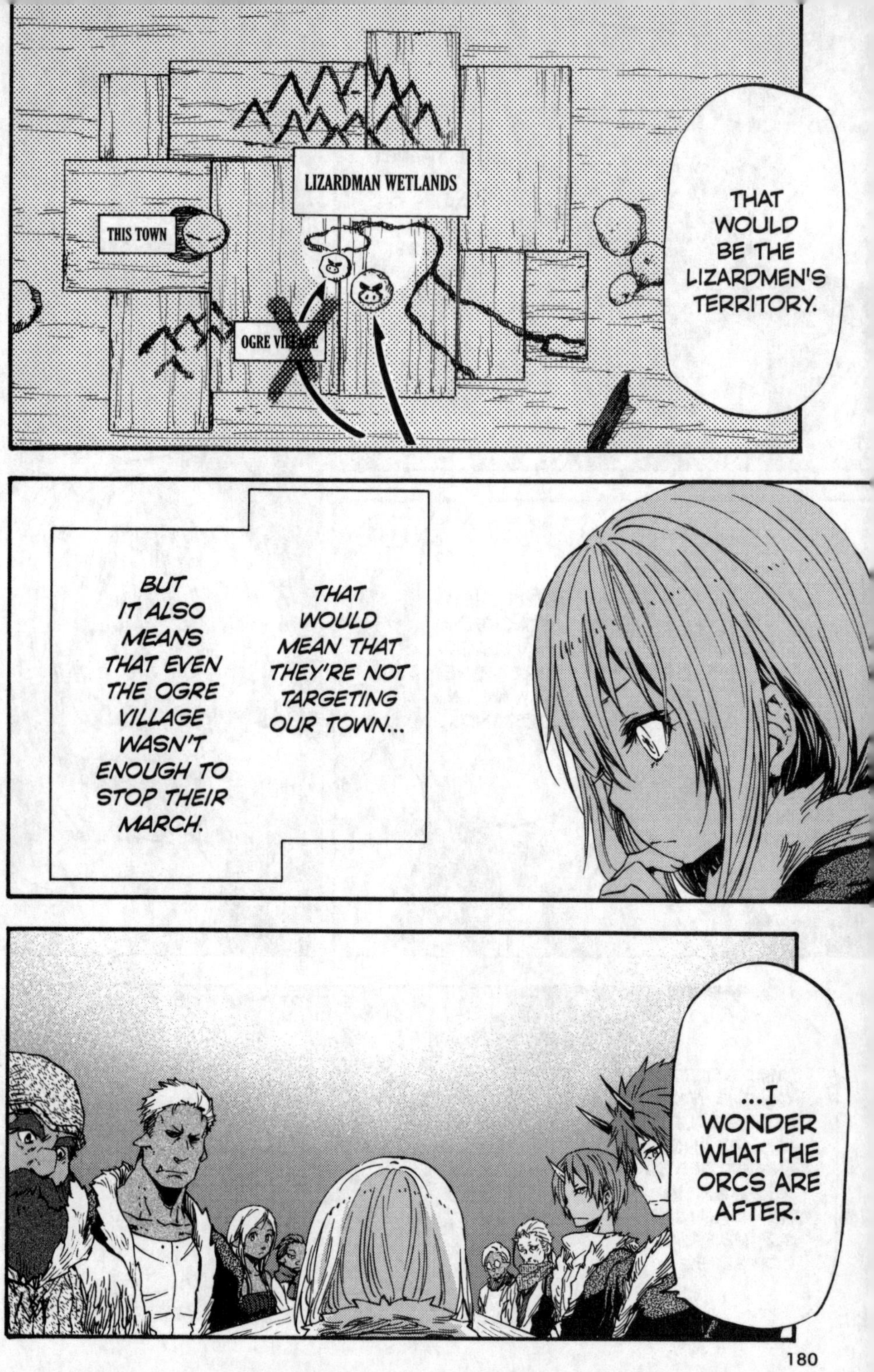
LIZARDMAN WETLANDS
THIS TOWN
THAT WOULD BE THE LIZARDMEN'S TERRITORY.
THAT WOULD MEAN THAT THEY'RE NOT TARGETING OUR TOWN...
BUT IT ALSO MEANS THAT EVEN THE OGRE VILLAGE WASN'T ENOUGH TO STOP THEIR MARCH.
...I WONDER WHAT THE ORCS ARE AFTER.

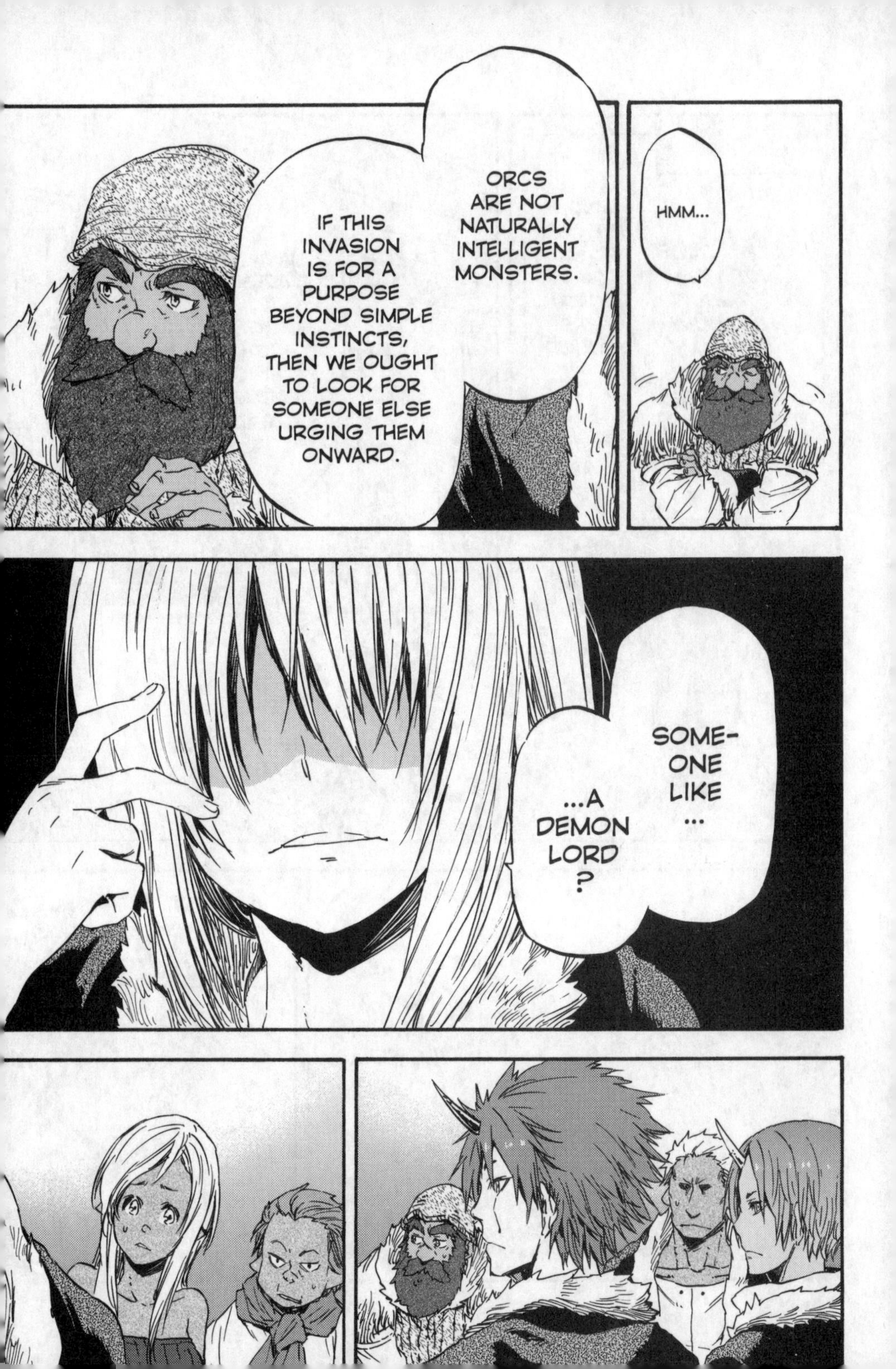
HMM...
ORCS ARE NOT NATURALLY INTELLIGENT MONSTERS.
IF THIS INVASION IS FOR A PURPOSE BEYOND SIMPLE INSTINCTS, THEN WE OUGHT TO LOOK FOR SOMEONE ELSE URGING THEM ONWARD.
SOME-ONE LIKE ...
...A DEMON LORD ?

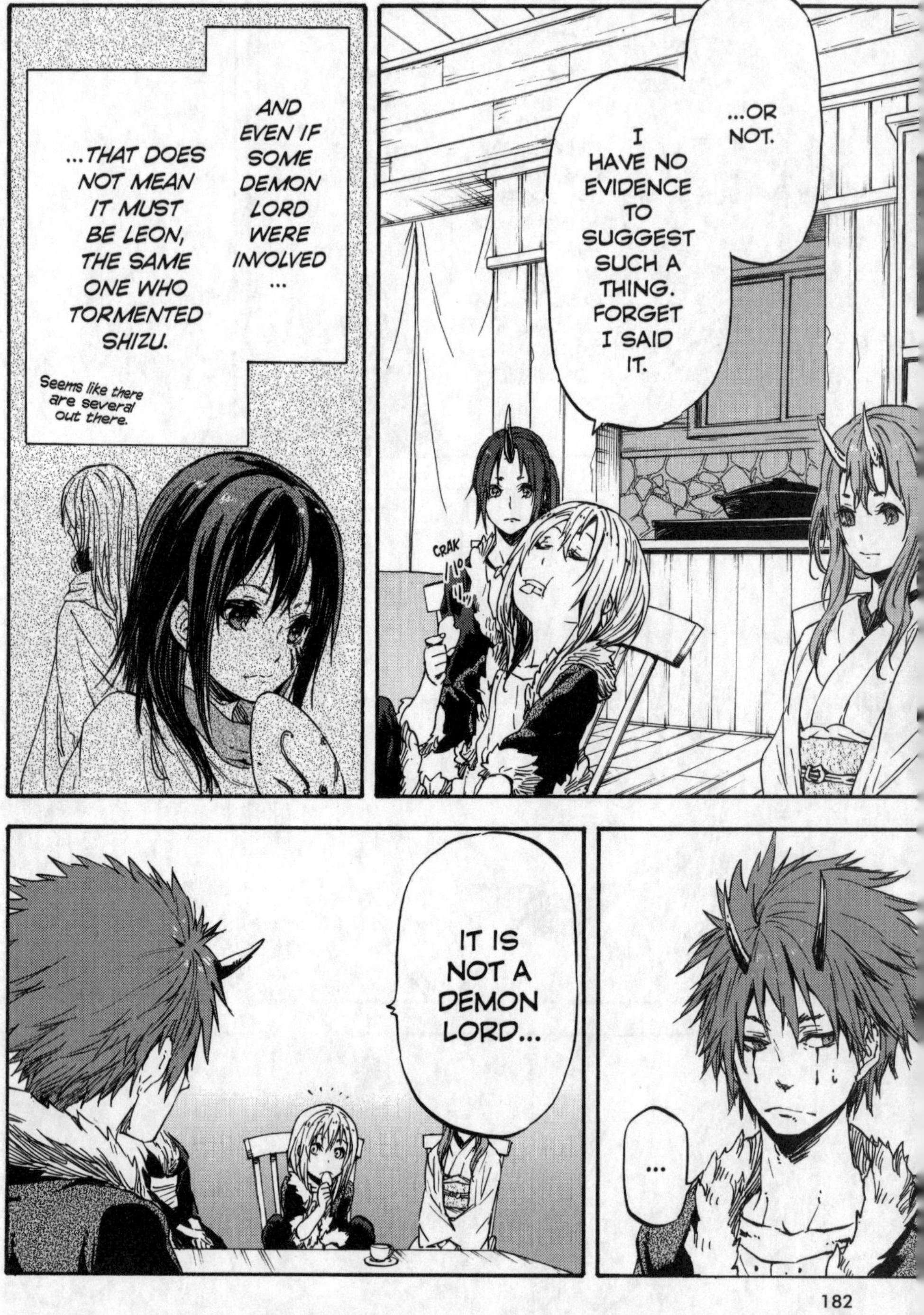
...OR NOT.
I HAVE NO EVIDENCE TO SUGGEST SUCH A THING. FORGET I SAID IT.
CRAK
AND EVEN IF SOME DEMON LORD WERE INVOLVED ...
...THAT DOES NOT MEAN IT MUST BE LEON, THE SAME ONE WHO TORMENTED SHIZU.
Seems like there are several out there.
...
IT IS NOT A DEMON LORD...

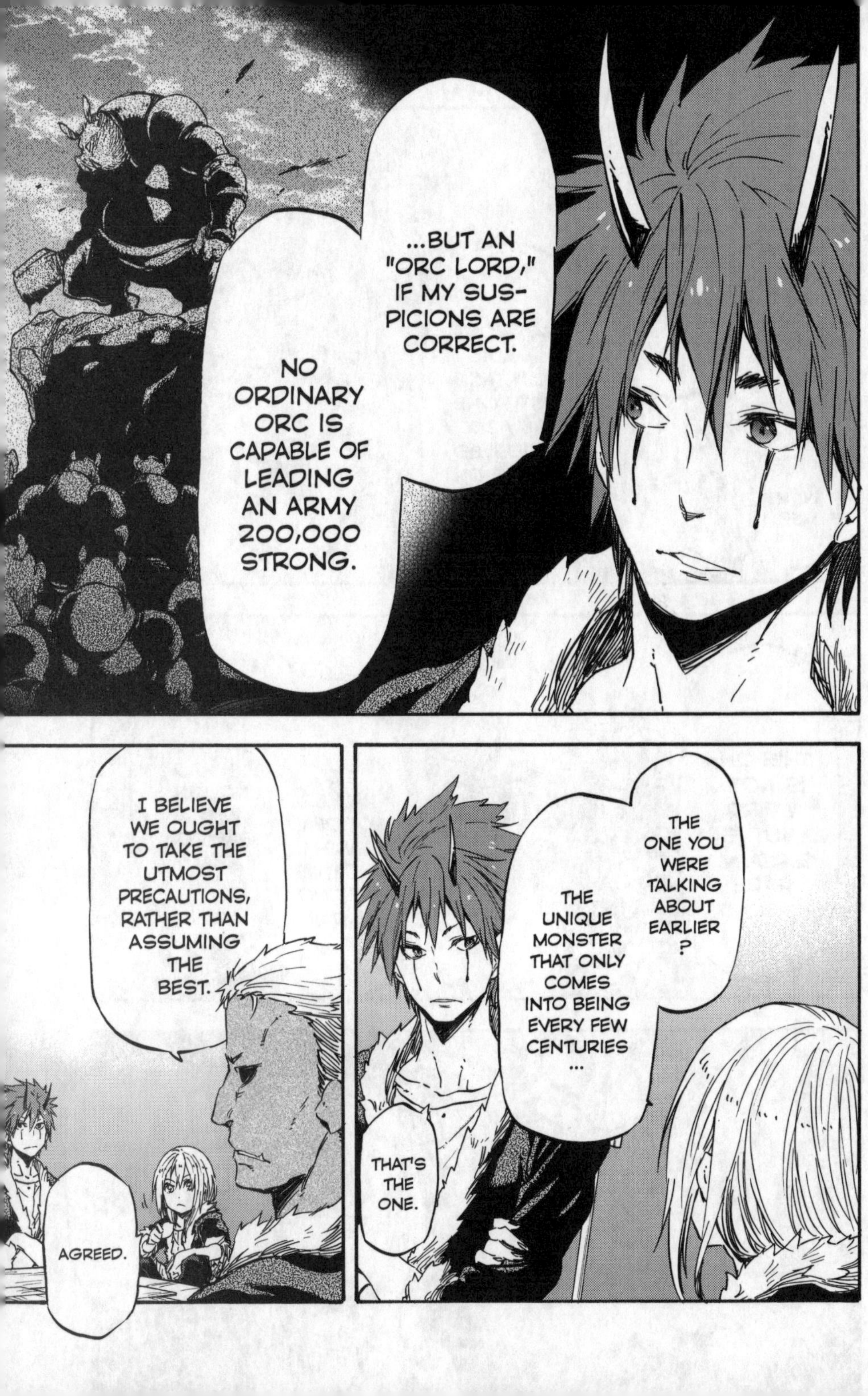
NO ORDINARY ORC IS CAPABLE OF LEADING AN ARMY 200,000 STRONG.
...BUT AN "ORC LORD," IF MY SUSPICIONS ARE CORRECT.
THE ONE YOU WERE TALKING ABOUT EARLIER?
THE UNIQUE MONSTER THAT ONLY COMES INTO BEING EVERY FEW CENTURIES...
THAT'S THE ONE.
I BELIEVE WE OUGHT TO TAKE THE UTMOST PRECAUTIONS, RATHER THAN ASSUMING THE BEST.
AGREED.

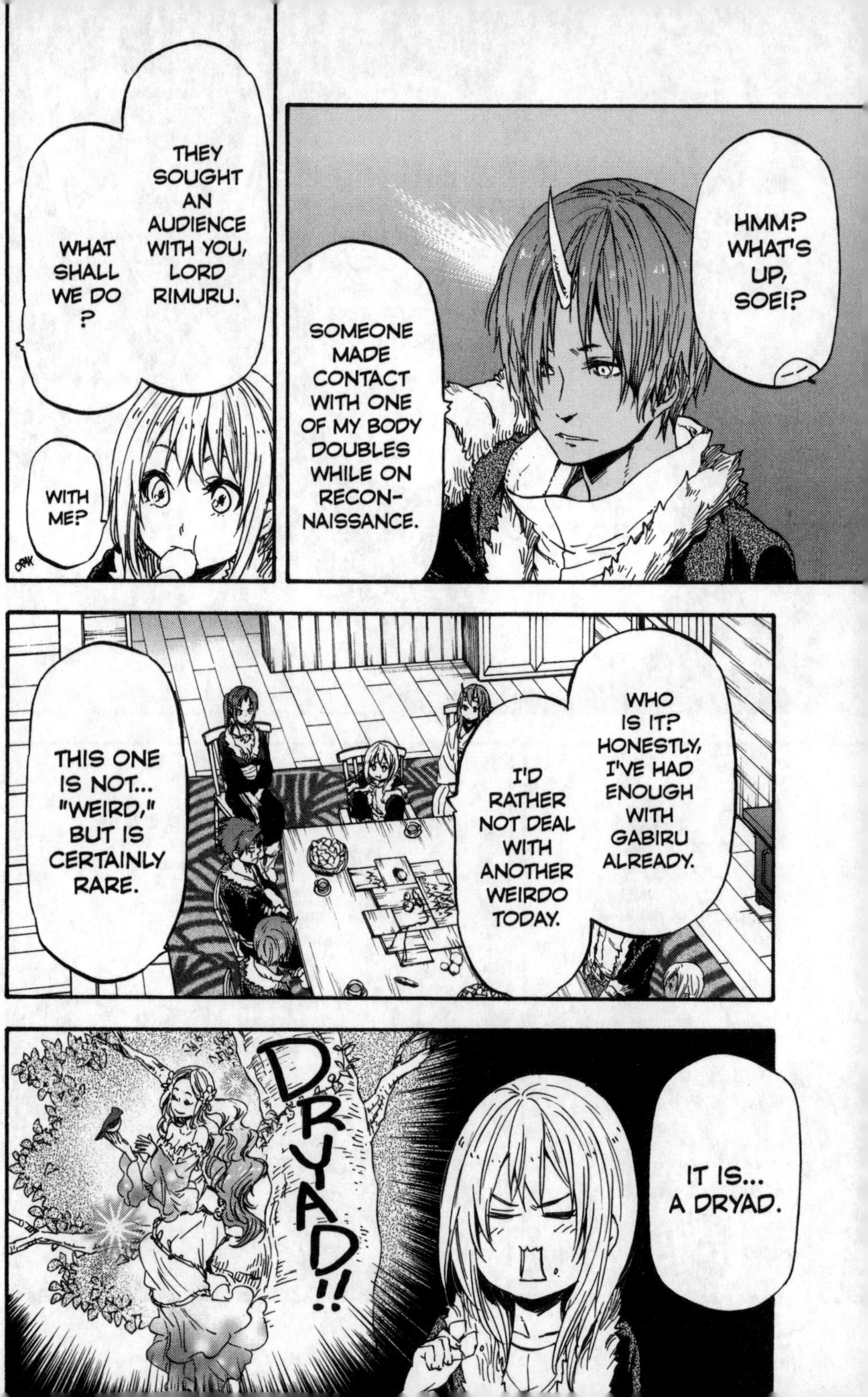
HMM? WHAT'S UP, SOEI?
SOMEONE MADE CONTACT WITH ONE OF MY BODY DOUBLES WHILE ON RECON-NAISSANCE.
THEY SOUGHT AN AUDIENCE WITH YOU, LORD RIMURU.
WHAT SHALL WE DO ?
WITH ME?
WHO IS IT? HONESTLY, I'VE HAD ENOUGH WITH GABIRU ALREADY.
I'D RATHER NOT DEAL WITH ANOTHER WEIRDO TODAY.
THIS ONE IS NOT... "WEIRD," BUT IS CERTAINLY RARE.
IT IS... A DRYAD.
DRYAD!!

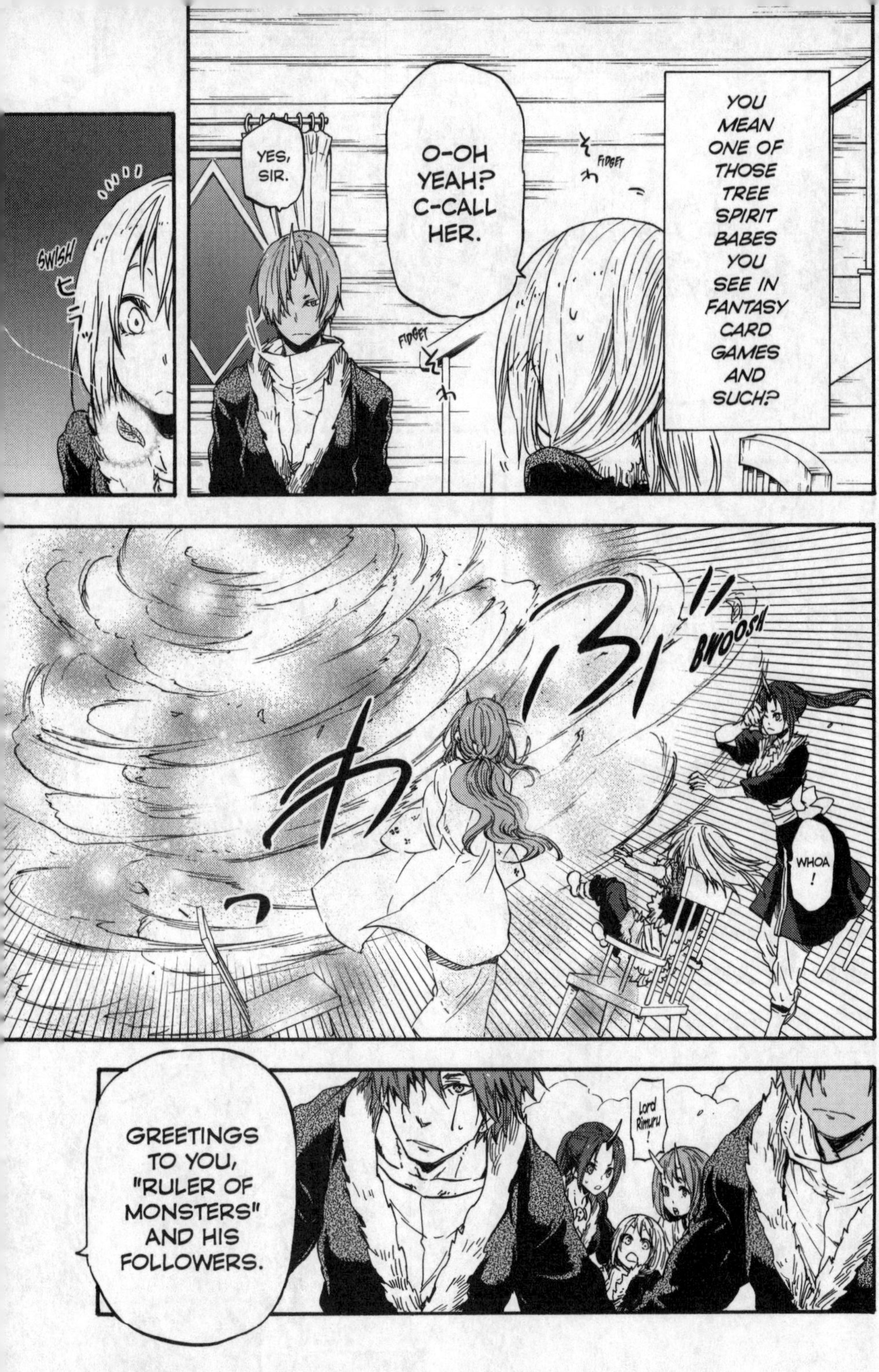
YOU MEAN ONE OF THOSE TREE SPIRIT BABES YOU SEE IN FANTASY CARD GAMES AND SUCH?
FIDGET
O-OH YEAH? C-CALL HER.
FIDGET
YES, SIR.
SWISH
BWOOSH
WHOA!
Lord Rimuru!
GREETINGS TO YOU, "RULER OF MONSTERS" AND HIS FOLLOWERS.

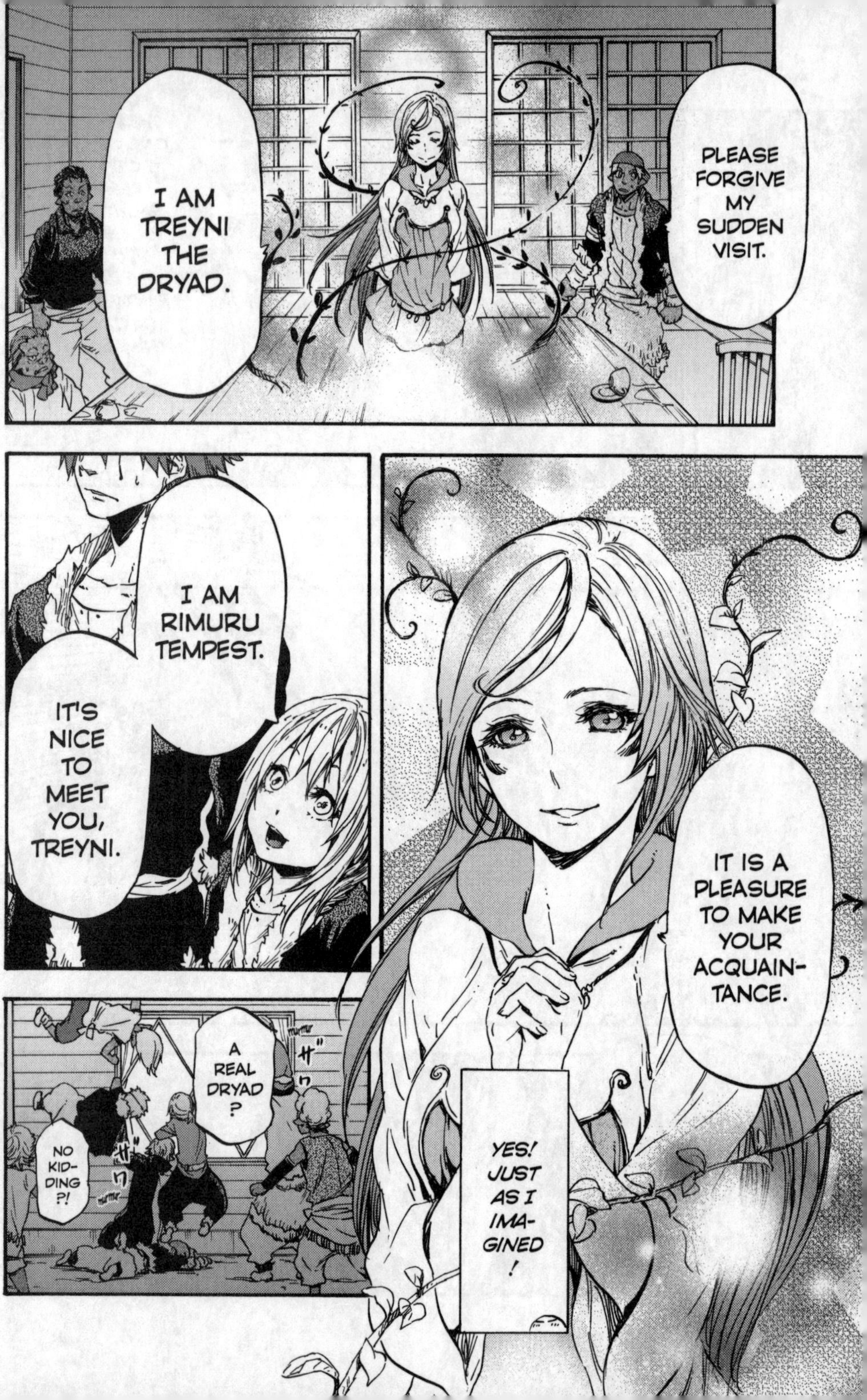
PLEASE FORGIVE MY SUDDEN VISIT.
I AM TREYNI THE DRYAD.
IT IS A PLEASURE TO MAKE YOUR ACQUAIN-TANCE.
YES! JUST AS I IMA-GINED!
I AM RIMURU TEMPEST.
IT'S NICE TO MEET YOU, TREYNI.
A REAL DRYAD?
NO KID-DING?!

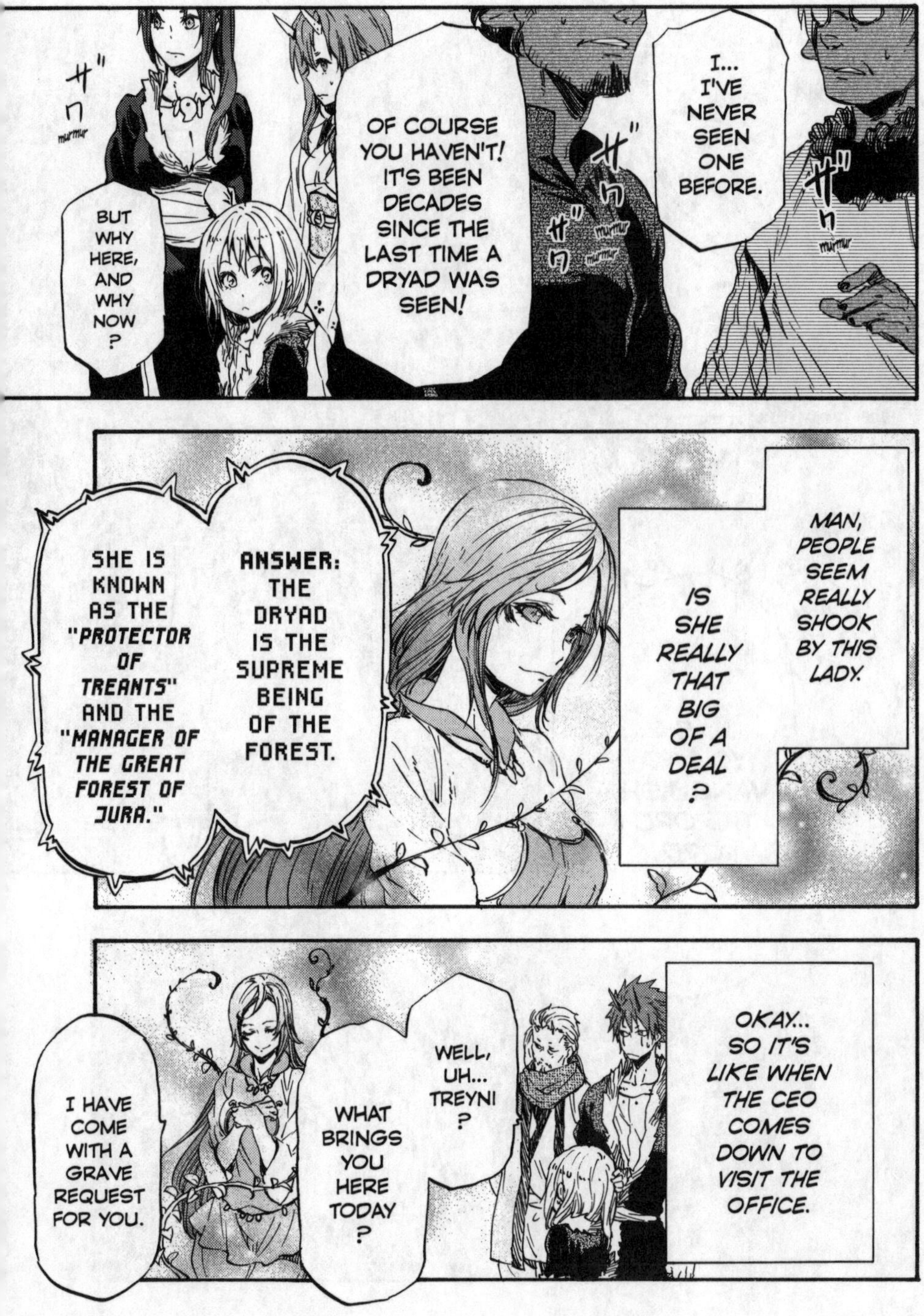
I... I'VE NEVER SEEN ONE BEFORE.
ザワ murmur
ザワ murmur
OF COURSE YOU HAVEN'T! IT'S BEEN DECADES SINCE THE LAST TIME A DRYAD WAS SEEN!
ザワ murmur
BUT WHY HERE, AND WHY NOW?
MAN, PEOPLE SEEM REALLY SHOOK BY THIS LADY.
IS SHE REALLY THAT BIG OF A DEAL?
ANSWER: THE DRYAD IS THE SUPREME BEING OF THE FOREST.
SHE IS KNOWN AS THE "PROTECTOR OF TREANTS" AND THE "MANAGER OF THE GREAT FOREST OF JURA."
OKAY... SO IT'S LIKE WHEN THE CEO COMES DOWN TO VISIT THE OFFICE.
WELL, UH... TREYNI?
WHAT BRINGS YOU HERE TODAY?
I HAVE COME WITH A GRAVE REQUEST FOR YOU.

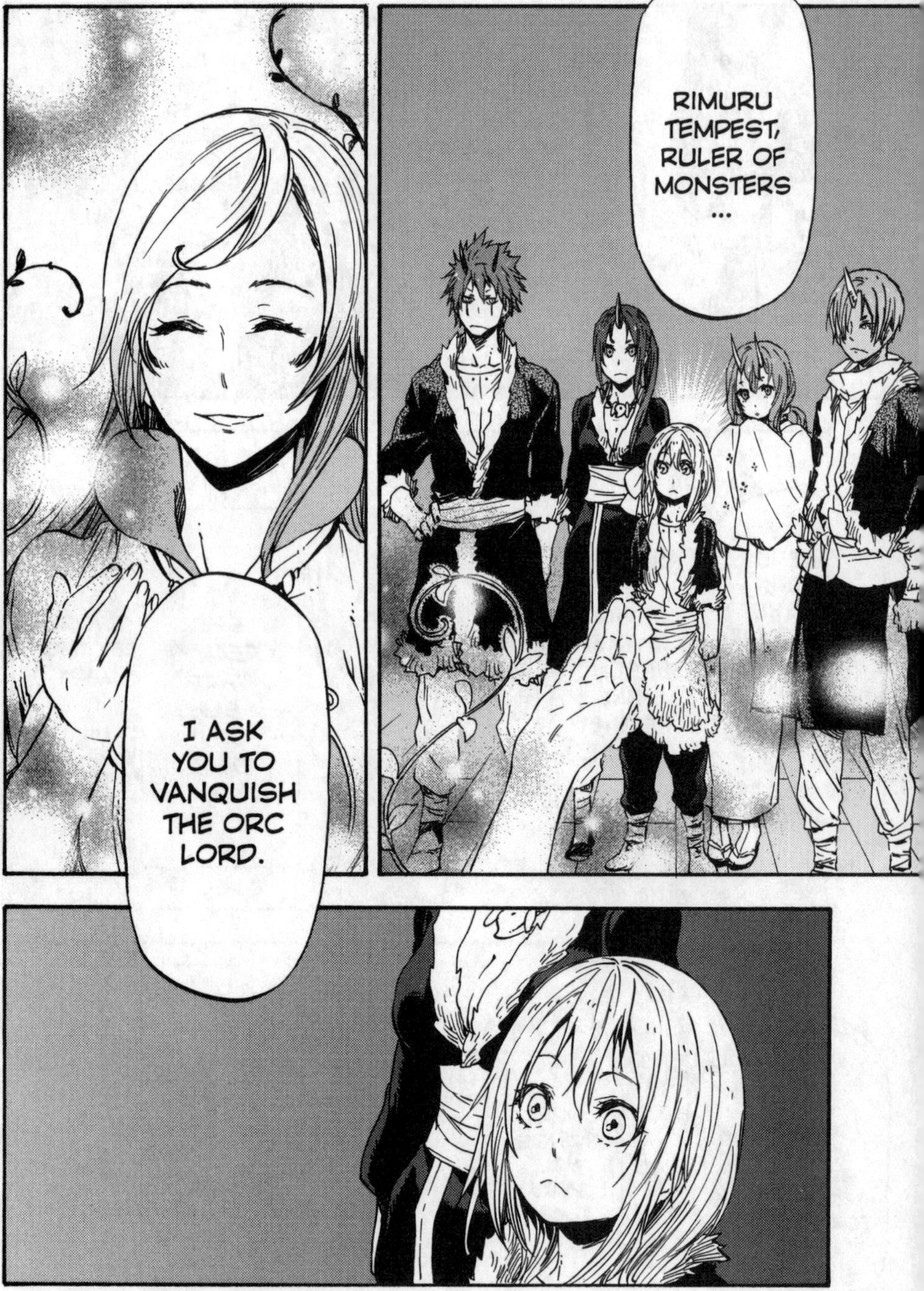
RIMURU TEMPEST, RULER OF MONSTERS ...
I ASK YOU TO VANQUISH THE ORC LORD.

Reincarnate
in Volume 4?

→YES

NO

Bonus
Short Story

Veldora's Slime Observation Journal
~STUNNING DEVELOPMENTS~

Veldora's Slime Observation Journal
~STUNNING DEVELOPMENTS~

◆MIGHTY FOES IN THE FOREST OF JURA◆

Click. Clack.

Sounds that should be impossible in a space of nothing but darkness. Yes, this is all in the imagination.

With my mental fortitude alone, I conjured a board for the game known as *shogi*, at which Ifrit and I were locked in a battle of wits. True to his nature as a higher-order spirit, Ifrit learned the game quickly. He followed my example and produced the appropriate clicking sounds as he moved his pieces.

This is proper. The little details go a long way to sell the presentation.

Satisfied, I decided to cast my gaze outside.

Now that Rimuru had a human form to use, he was more attentive to his clothing. Under his influence, the monsters began to enjoy the concept of fashion. There were even shops dedicated to crafting and arranging monster pelts to wear.

There were also places for large groups to gather and eat, and even a meeting hall for the purpose of facilitating conversation. Much had changed in the town. And this was not the end of the building process. From what I could observe through Rimuru's sight, the dwarf craftsmen he recruited to the village were at the center of the improvements to its core facilities.

Rimuru was making use of the "Edo-period water and plumbing" system I found in his knowledge banks. Through some property I am not aware of, it seems that maintaining clean surroundings will prevent disease in the townsfolk. Or does it simply lower the breeding rate of pathogens?

In any case, if Rimuru thinks it important, then surely it must be. The dwellings themselves are still rudimentary, but they are putting the emphasis on little, unseen things. It is a wonder to me. All I can say is that bustling activity is a wonderful thing.

"By the way, Lord Rimuru...will you not be needing any food today?" Rigurd, the steward of the entire town, asked me—I mean, asked Rimuru.

Like me, Rimuru does not require food, so I assumed that he would decline today, as with every other day. But then he said, "Starting today, I will be eating with the rest of you."

So, Rimuru thinks that he will enjoy all the delights of food for himself! The food that he could not taste with his monster senses is no longer an issue now that he has human form. Very clever of Rimuru to realize this. I shall not mention the fact that he was human for several days before he came to this decision.

Click.

"That is check, Master Veldora."

Whaaat?!

N-no, just a moment. Take that move back. This is unbelievable. While I was busy observing the outside world, Ifrit has turned the game to his advantage.

Grrrrr...

In that case...

"S-so, you've learned the ropes, I see. But you've got much left to understand, my apprentice," I cautioned, moving back my promoted bishop to take Ifrit's silver general.

How very dangerous—I nearly made a terrible mistake.

"Excellent move, Master Veldora. Clearly I was too early to press the attack. But I have learned the standard practices of the game, so the outcome is still in flux," said Ifrit, who had just memorized the rules. When did he get so advanced that he could lecture me about common play styles?

In all of our games until now, I easily had my way with Ifrit. Every single one. It was the foremost reason that I was so focused on our competition...but then Rimuru gained the ability to take human form, so I decided to pay attention to the outside, to ensure that I couldn't be caught unawares again.

Now I learn that Ifrit has been utilizing these moments to study on his own! The crafty spirit. This is the benefit of regular hard work.

On the outside, Rimuru is practicing the skills he's earned. In a sense, I suppose this bears some similarity to learning the rules of a game. It is absolutely crucial to understand what one can and cannot do.

When one is as powerful as I, this knowledge comes naturally, but Rimuru and Ifrit cannot help but be less advanced. Rimuru is so foolish that he completely forgot about his "Thermal Fluctuation Resistance" when fighting Ifrit. No wonder he requires time to study like this...

But as a great and mighty being, I never test my own power. I simply live in the moment at all times. It is the root of my beliefs.

"Kwa ha ha ha! Bold words...but if you let the rules and standards define you, you will never be a true competitor!!"

Who cares about hard work? It is totally unnecessary, I proudly declared. And yet—

"Actually, the standard moves are one thing, but one must surely follow the rules," said Ifrit, immediately contradicting my opinion.

...What a saucy little spirit. I hate to admit that I cannot rebut his argument.

Based on the vocal frequency, I suspect it is a cry for help...

Hmm?!

"It sounds as though there's an emergency, Master Veldora."

"Indeed. We have more important matters than this little argument," I said, to which Ifrit agreed. We then turned our attention outward.

And by doing this, I cleverly ensured that the question of our little competition would remain unsettled.

◆OGRE ATTACK◆

So, what happened?

There was a group of six ogres facing Rimuru.

The hobgoblins Rimuru named had tried to swarm them as a pack, and still lost. They can't be blamed for that. It is inevitable that the weak fall to the strong. It is an ironclad rule of the world.

Now Rimuru is giving one of the wailing hobgoblins some healing ointment. He made it back before the worst could happen, it seems.

"All those you see collapsed are alive and well. They were merely put to sleep with magic," said Rigur, the son of Rigurd.

That is a relief. Who better to worship my splendor than Rimuru's companions and followers? I shall hear no praises of my name if they are dead.

So...ogres. Rimuru's mental image of them is strange. Yes, there are some ogres like crude, unintelligent beasts. But these ones, armed and working in a group, are the dangerous sort. Especially with a magic-user among them. The hobgoblins are higher Class-C beings, so of course they would not be a match.

Clang, clang, clang, ring the sounds of battle.

The fighting continues with Rimuru's pet against the ogres. I think its name is...Ranga? He is handling two ogres at once, and holding his ground. His effective resistance against magic has made the beast rather powerful. But this does not matter. Now that Rimuru is here, the ogres are finished.

"After how easily he crushed the Ifrit and absorbed its power, Rimuru has nothing to fear from a rabble of six ogres!!"

"Umm…could you at least not say that right in front of me…?"

Hmm? I suppose I didn't realize that I'd spoken out loud. How silly of me. I got a little carried away.

"Very well, I will be more careful from now on. Kwaaaa ha ha ha!!"

I am, if nothing else, a mature dragon, and I recognize where I have gone wrong.

"I'd appreciate it…" said the Ifrit. For whatever reason, it seemed annoyed, even though I did it the favor of showing contrition. It makes no sense. I do not understand…but it is no matter. The outcome of Rimuru's battle is of more interest to me now.

"It seems the battle is afoot!"

The ogres spurned Rimuru's offer of peace. There is clearly more to their story, but it was the ogres who struck first. Rimuru must be furious at their aggression—actually…he is…not?

He would win in a straightforward fight, but a moment of carelessness might result in injury, I suppose. As a being of ultimate power, I have never been careless. It is why I have never lost a…Why am I talking about this?

Rimuru left the ogres' magic-wielding holy princess to Ranga, and now faces the other five of them alone. He means to display his overwhelming strength to subdue them without slaughter.

In my opinion, Rimuru is far too soft. If he fought to kill, he could vaporize all six of them in a single instant…but he does seem to enjoy fussing over the little details instead.

It's not a problem. "I'm not going to lose to them," Rimuru claimed. Of course not! I will not accept that my friend could fall in combat to anyone. But I digress. Whatever his plan, I will enjoy observing the results.

The ogres have not yet noticed the full extent of his power. Monsters recognize the difference in strength between themselves and others by the relative size of their magical energy. It is an instinctual process; they detect the aura that exudes from others. But due to Rimuru's mysterious mask, his aura is completely shut off. It seems the ogres are vastly underestimating him as a result. But even then, the situation is precarious.

These ogres appear intelligent, and think much as humans do. Therefore, they will fight not based on animal instinct, but experience and disciplined technique. Humankind, which is physically inferior, develops techniques through an amalgamation of experience, which are then passed on to others. In time, they produce individuals who are capable of besting even mighty monsters. If the physically powerful ogres have learned to build on their techniques, it will be difficult to gauge their true power through levels of magical energy alone.

Rimuru understands that too, of course. It is why he carefully observes how they act first, before he makes his move.

Ah, the black-haired one strikes. He swung a massive hammer down upon Rimuru. It is a mighty swing, but slow. This will hardly be sufficient to bring down Rimuru.

As I expected, he quickly dodges the swing and emits "Paralysis Breath" from his palm to neutralize the black-haired ogre.

Without pause, a purple-haired female now bears down on him from behind. But Rimuru is not worried, as evidenced by his appreciation for her chest. Why does a larger size delight him so? I do not understand this, and shall have to ask Rimuru about it in the future.

In no time at all, Rimuru trussed the woman up with "Sticky Steel Thread." But the black-haired one and the purple-haired one were just decoys. While they were grabbing attention with their attacks, the blue-haired ogre prepared to strike.

However—Rimuru blocks this blade by powering his arm with "Body Armor." That skill came from the Armorsaurus, but he made it his own. Utilizing it to protect a single part of the body at a time is a rather striking and inspired choice. Between that and the "Paralysis Breath," he's learned to transform his slime body into nearly anything he desires. I am truly impressed by this fight.

And I was not the only one. The eldest of the ogres was watching the fate of the previous three closely, and he brilliantly named each of the skills that Rimuru deployed, along with their sources. It is clear that he possesses "Magic Sense," too. And for an ogre, his aura is suspiciously shielded...

Perhaps this ogre elder is actually the most troublesome of them all—even more so than the holy princess? My instinct was proven correct. Instantly, the elder got behind Rimuru, and severed his arm.

I am a genius. Once again, I am impressed with my own brilliance, but I suppose this is not the best time to reflect on it.

It is stunning to see what a physically gifted ogre can do once paired with a level of skill that surpasses others. This means nothing to transcendent beings such as myself, however. And neither does it bother Rimuru. If the ogre had been in the prime of his youth, it might have been a tougher fight, but we shall never know. With "Pain Nullification" and "Ultraspeed Regeneration," a simple slicing attack does nothing to Rimuru.

"M...monster!!" cries the younger leader of the ogres. How rude.

Hurry up, Rimuru! Cast aside these boorish guests once and for all!!

◆THE OGRES' STORY◆

The young leader of the ogres produces an illusory magic known as Ogre Flame. Of course, Rimuru already withstood the flames of Ifrit; this trick means nothing to him. He promptly nullifies its effects, completely stunning the ogres. Next he shows them up by using "Black Flame" with my power behind it. In Rimuru's hands, it has about the power of an Extra Skill, but its might increases with the amount of energy placed into it. In a sense, this technique could even surpass magic spells or Unique Skills.

At last, the ogres seem to understand the threat posed by their opponent.

"That sorcery does not use the magicules in the surrounding air!" the holy ogre princess said, and she was correct. Much magic is performed by using the magicules in the air as a source of energy—human magic is like this. It takes longer to perform, but minimizes the strain upon the body. However, gathering those magicules takes time. And the length will depend upon the density of said airborne magicules.

It seems they've invented "magistones," which are produced by processing magicrystals taken from monsters, that aid in the execution of magic…but the items have not made it into widespread use.

Great works of magic require huge amounts of energy and vast sums of time. It consumes one's willpower as well, so it is customary to gather multiple casters and a healthy supply of magistones.

This is the limit of the human body. But monster skills use only one's own magical energy. It saves the time to collect magicules, enabling the user to attack very quickly by comparison. This has its own problem, of course.

Many monsters are essentially constructs of magical energy. I possess an infinite source of energy, of course, but the smaller creatures are limited to a number of uses of any skill. Overuse may pose a threat to their very existence, so most seem to save them as a last resort.

Each way has its strengths and drawbacks, so debating which is "better" is a fruitless exercise. There is also spiritual magic, which involves borrowing the power of contracted spirits. The best strategy is thus to utilize whichever best suits the situation.

Now, as for Rimuru…the Black Fire he just used looks impressive, but he is actually holding back quite a bit. No need to be concerned with his energy levels. And if he had fought his hardest from the start, there would be no more ogres, anyway. After witnessing his power, they understand this too. Their continued defiance is a sign that they have resigned themselves to death—a pointless one.

"No, Brother! Please stop!"

To my surprise, it was the ogre princess who stepped in. Her pleading must have worked, because the leader of the ogres promptly apologizes to Rimuru. In fact, his change of heart was so honest and true that I had to reassess my opinion of the ogres.

I must admit that this leaves me feeling conflicted. If it had been me, I would have eliminated the ogres immediately. But that would have left me unable to come to an understanding with them in this way.

Perhaps this is why Rimuru always seeks to find an accord with those he meets. Success likely depends on the creature, but identifying which ones are willing to see eye-to-eye must be difficult, indeed.

At any rate, Rimuru's diagnosis of the situation was correct. Moments ago, they were enemies, but now they are carrying on and making merry at a feast. It is no fun only to watch. I wish to be released into the outside world soon.

Once the merriment was over, Rimuru set about to recruiting the ogres. What in the world is he thinking—no, this is Rimuru I speak of. No doubt he has some deep, fathomless idea in mind.

The ogres claim that a horde of thousands of orcs might invade. Rimuru understands that this could spell disaster for our fledgling village. But that is not all there is to the story. He wonders if there is anything he can do for these ogres he only just met. It is naïve—the height of naïveté. And yet, for some reason I cannot dislike the idea.

After much thought, the young leader of the ogres chose to follow Rimuru. And in turn, he decided to give them names. Such a dreary pain all of this is. But for some reason, I felt a twinge of excitement that it might be my turn to help once again.

◆ AN ANOMALY IN THE FOREST ◆

Ah, yes. I knew that I was right. Rimuru thought that he could handle just six of them, but he was not prepared for the toll of naming a higher race.

"Siphoning as much energy as possible."

After the last time, I received back every bit of the energy that I lent him. I have no doubts about Rimuru's character. Go ahead and take all that you need. I offered him as much of my energy as required.

❖

He is merciless. Rimuru stole my energy without a twinkling of consideration for me. He drew upon the very limits of his own magical energy for the purpose of naming the ogres.

The result is that he went back into sleep mode again. I should have known. Since I could not sense the outside world anymore, I started devising a new game, which I have been formulating since Rimuru gained a human body. And now, in this little cage of a world, I have created a copied form out of pure imagination.

It is a creation of pure thought, and not physical. But with the strict boundaries of this internal world, there is no fear of it multiplying out of control. That is, in fact, the very condition that makes it possible.

Yes! I have finally gained my own human form!!

"Master Veldora, what in the world are you doing...?"

"Kwaaa ha ha ha! Can't you see, Ifrit? Now that I have my own human form, there is only one thing to do!"

"...And that is?"

"It is obvious. Now we may learn the ways of human techniques!!" I said to Ifrit.

As seen in the ogres, the addition of a high experience "level" to superior physical attributes will lead to unfathomable power. The ogre elder certainly managed to fool Rimuru. That is a good example of fighting potential being more than simple numerical ability values.

"You don't intend to fight me here, do you?"

"Of course I do. Do not worry—it is not actual battle, just a facsimile. And having your conceptual self destroyed isn't the same as death, is it?"

"O-only for you, Master Veldora! I'm not—"

Ifrit is screaming about something or other, but it doesn't matter. Probably just fussing about some trivial detail, like always.

"Ready to begin?"

"A-are you listening to—?"

Spare no quarter! I struck a pose and unleashed a kick on Ifrit. It was a technique I learned from my holy manga texts, a kick attack that darted and changed course in midair like a dragon in flight.

This technique is impossible with the moving parts of the human body, but I can make it work in practical combat. To my great entertainment, Ifrit looked stunned, and desperately prepared to defend against it.

"I keep trying to tell you, if you destroy me, I will be obliterated for good! Besides, I have never engaged in martial combat to begin with!!" the Ifrit wailed pathetically.

I have never engaged in martial combat, either. Why else would I be trying to learn it now? If he vanishes from here, he can just reappear somewhere else again. Such a needless worrywart he is.

"Here goes some more!"

"Wh-wh-whaaa—?!"

I tried out all the moves I could imagine. Then I selected those that seemed useful, in order to work on them further. The holy manga texts were not always accurate in their depictions; some of the techniques turned out to be nonsense. Crossing my limbs did not produce any vacuum waves, and no matter how I tried, I could not break down the target's natural resistance with my first blow and destroy it entirely with the second.

But I suppose such things happen. At any rate, I brought many of these techniques into practical use. It is the birth of the Veldora-Style Killing Arts!! An ultra-practical style of physical combat based around blows. Now it is my mission in life to spread these lessons.

"Um, c-can we stop now?" gasped Ifrit, who was in tatters for some reason. The light was gone from his eyes.

Was he all right? I am not a demon, so of course I had mercy.

"Absolutely," I said kindly.

"I will wait for you to recover before I resume the beating."

But for some reason, the Ifrit simply passed right out. Ah, of course! He wants to heal himself that much faster in order to continue my lessons. Most excellent.

And that was how my secret training began.

When Rimuru awoke, the ogres had evolved into kijin.

Ahh, yes. I can see that the tremendous energy I gave him went to good use. No doubt Rimuru intended to strengthen his forces with this move. They mean nothing to a being such as myself, but I have no doubt these kijin will be a fearsome threat to the piddling creatures of the Jura Forest. Their young leader is Benimaru: the "red circle."
His sister, the holy princess, is Shuna: the "crimson leaf."
The most troublesome of them is Hakuro: the "white elder."

And the other three are Soei the blue shadow, Shion the purple garden and Kurobei the black guard.

They do not have as much magical energy as Ifrit, but in total power, they are all at least Class-A beings. And all of them (to different degrees) have grown by leaps and bounds compared to their pre-evolution forms.

The elder Hakuro is particularly striking. His energy level is not quite so impressive, but he has gained so much youth that his speed is nearly unrecognizable. Even before evolving, he was fast enough to fool Rimuru. At this point, he might even be stronger than the slime.

No, that would be silly. None of his attacks would have an effect on Rimuru, so there would be no resolution to the fight, if that were the case.

"Witness the way that Hakuro moves, Ifrit."

"It is impressive. And now I understand his style. He pauses for an instant in order to fool the opponent's attempt to anticipate his attack."

"Exactly. He allows his foe to time his own speed, then alters it. A very advanced combat art."

"It's hard to understand when simply watching from afar, but I bet it's very confusing if you experience it in person."

"It would seem as though he disappeared from sight. Even Rimuru felt that way, so unless his opponent was significantly more powerful, it would be difficult to stop that veteran warrior."

I do not care for the topic of this orc lord, or whatever it is that was troubling Rimuru. I just want to observe Hakuro more closely. I have a feeling that I will need to study him in order to bring my Veldora-Style Killing Arts to a greater level of perfection.

◆GABIRU ARRIVES!◆

Today Rimuru had an arrangement to receive his own set of clothes.

I am jealous. Absolutely seething with jealousy. Surely he has not forgotten clothes for me as well, now that I have a human form at last…but I suppose an imaginary body does not need clothes.

I would hope that Rimuru produces a body for me soon. I must remember to request a human one when the occasion presents itself.

While I busied myself with these happy, anticipatory thoughts, Rimuru headed for the dining hall to enjoy his lunch. The former ogre known as Shion cooked it just for him, apparently.

Harrumph! My jealousy knows no bounds.

Once again, he is allowed to indulge in the delicacies of the outside world, while I stew here in my frustration...but... what seems to be the matter? What is this?! My super-intuition tells me that this food is not to be trusted!

And my suspicions were proven correct. Rimuru sensed that something was amiss with Shion's meal as well. Quite the unexpected little trap.

So, how does Rimuru plan to squeak through this one...? I feel as though I've learned a valuable lesson today. I always assumed that cooking was delicious, no matter the circumstances—but I see now that I was wrong.

"Ifrit, you fused with the woman Shizue and lived with her for decades, correct? Tell me straight. Was cooked food not always splendid?"

"I couldn't say. I am an elemental with no need for food, and no interest beyond that, so my knowledge in that regard is completely lacking..."

Well, the Ifrit was useless. What good is he?

"You are an utterly boring clod. Why did you even fuse with a human, then?"

"I was following my summoner's orders. It wasn't for the purpose of excitement."

"The Demon Lord Leon? I always thought that was strange. You are a spirit; why do you revere a wicked demon? There's no need to owe such an obligation to him if he's not a hero..."

Angels, demons, spirits. The trianglular relationship between spiritual beings is written into the very laws of this world. While some might develop their own identities, and escape the rules that bound them, they rarely stray far from their innate nature.

The spirits are meant to guard and serve heroes, which means that they are naturally opposed to demon lords, the enemies of those heroes. But that is merely the general view of things. Given their independent nature, spirits are really more neutral than anything, and it is not impossible that one might cooperate with a demon lord instead. It is just that Ifrit's relationship seems more extreme than is the norm.

"Oh!" Ifrit gasped. I glanced outside, and saw that for some reason, Gobta had Rimuru's spoon in his mouth.

"What happened?"

"It would seem that Rimuru predicted the movements of the hobgoblin named Gobta, and used him as a sacrificial shield…"

My word…

Never let it be said that Rimuru is not a fearsome fellow. He sacrificed his own faithful follower without a second thought. And yet, that quick thinking seems to have saved him from peril in this instance.

◆GOBTA VS. GABIRU◆

A strange lizardman called Gabiru has arrived. He wants Rimuru's entire retinue to become his own army, which is entirely foolish.

This orc army is of no concern to us. Ahh, but it is frustrating. I would be able to lay them to waste in but a moment. But I digress.

Rimuru's group does not find Gabiru's antics amusing, either. Like me, they are incensed. Rimuru just sent his pet Ranga forth. It seems he wants the wolf to deal with this lizardman. It is clearly overkill. All of the lizardmen put together could not hope to stop Ranga alone.

"That was awesome, Gabiru!"

"You show 'em what you can do!"

The lizardmen are egging this fool on, and it is working wonders. He clearly cannot fairly assess his strength against his opponent's. Ranga will tear the creature to shreds, just as Rimuru and his cohorts expect. But this is no fun to watch.

—And just now, Gobta, who had almost died earlier, passed by. He has been recruited to fight in Ranga's stead. Does this make him lucky, or unlucky? In straightforward strength, he falls far short of Gabiru. Hakuro has been training the hobgoblin lately, and I must admit he's gained some levels... but I cannot believe he is capable of handling Gabiru. We are speaking of a Class-C monster against a high Class-B. The discrepancy is stark.

And yet, my expectations were far off the mark. Spurred on by the carrot of reward and the stick of punishment, Gobta fought like his life depended on it. He showed skill I have never seen from him before. In fact, at times he resembled his teacher, Hakuro. And not only that—he put together a brilliant plan with careful calculation.

I am stunned by his brilliance. Varying speeds, feints, and a surefire finisher. These things are easy to describe, but much more difficult to execute—but Gobta pulled it off.

He threw a spear to distract Gabiru, then used "Shadow Movement" to swing behind him. While Gabiru looked about in confusion for his foe, Gobta unleashed a round-house kick to the head.

Much of this was due to Gabiru's overconfidence and under-estimation of his opponent, but it must be said that Gobta's training most certainly paid off.

This. This is why I decided to raise my own "level," if you will. There is plenty of time before my release, so I might as well master the Veldora-style Killing Arts in anticipation of that moment. And on the occasion of my release, I shall teach Gobta the Veldora Killing Arts as well. That shall be a heady dream that tickles my mind as the eventual day draws closer.

But as for the lizardman Gabiru, his end was far too pathetic. He claims to be a distant descendent of the great dragons? A side-splitter!

"Gabiru does indeed possess some draconic elements, but amongst us dragons there are none as arrogant and self-obsessed as he!!"

"Huh?"

"What was that, Ifrit? Did you have something to say?"
"N-no, nothing…"

For some reason, Ifrit reacted to my words. He seemed to have something on his mind, but he would not speak it aloud.

After the arrival of Gabiru, the town was in quite an uproar. The matter of the orc invasion was looking more and more likely. And then, the former ogre named Soei brought back more accurate information.

I happen to know an applicable quote to this situation: "He who controls the information, controls the outcome!"

Ha ha ha…how brilliant Rimuru is. He has not been reading his manga tomes for nothing.

Soei reported that an army of 200,000 orcs is on the march. Whether that many, or ten times that number, they would stand no chance against me. But it seems that the situation is more serious to Rimuru and his followers. They argue over the influence of some demon lord, or the appearance of an orc lord, and so on.

Just then, another being appeared seeking an audience with Rimuru.

It was the dryad that I left to manage the Great Forest of Jura for me. I protected her once in the distant past, and she has felt a debt to me ever since.

The dryad's name is Treyni. She had other sisters before, but is here alone now. No doubt the others are busy elsewhere in the forest, attempting to calm the uproar.

But for some reason, Rimuru is more interested in meeting the dryad. It seems to be providing him with excitement. He is too at ease in this situation, I feel. Is this not a dire emergency for their village? It is not my concern, but it should be theirs.

Meanwhile, Treyni delivered a request with a fetching smile. "I ask you to vanquish the orc lord."

And how will Rimuru respond? No matter the answer, I am certain that it will entertain me!

To be reincarnated in Volume 4!

THE MYSTERY OF TRADITIONAL DRESS

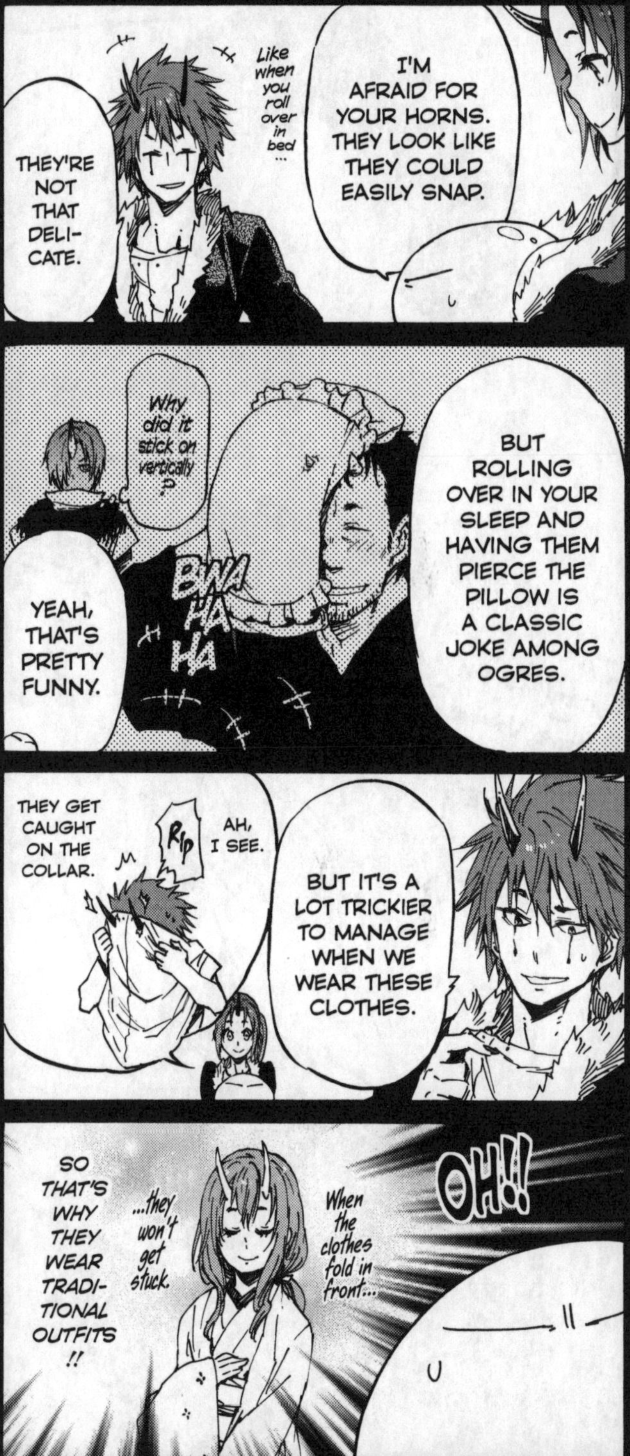
I'M AFRAID FOR YOUR HORNS. THEY LOOK LIKE THEY COULD EASILY SNAP.
Like when you roll over in bed...
THEY'RE NOT THAT DELI-CATE.
BUT ROLLING OVER IN YOUR SLEEP AND HAVING THEM PIERCE THE PILLOW IS A CLASSIC JOKE AMONG OGRES.
Why did it stick on vertically?
BWA HA HA
YEAH, THAT'S PRETTY FUNNY.
BUT IT'S A LOT TRICKIER TO MANAGE WHEN WE WEAR THESE CLOTHES.
AH, I SEE.
RIP
THEY GET CAUGHT ON THE COLLAR.
OH!!
When the clothes fold in front...
...they won't get stuck.
SO THAT'S WHY THEY WEAR TRADI-TIONAL OUTFITS!!

LIST OF ACKNOWLEDGMENTS

AUTHOR:
Fuse-sensei

ASSISTANTS:
Takuya Nishida-san
Muraichi-san
Hino-san
Daiki Haraguchi-san
Kiritani-sensei
Sachi Kohinata-sensei
Taku Arao-sensei

Everyone at the editorial department

And You!!

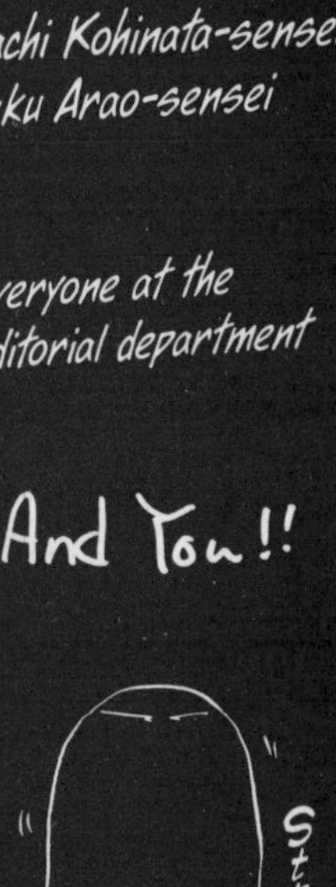

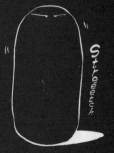

From character designer Mitz Vah-sensei

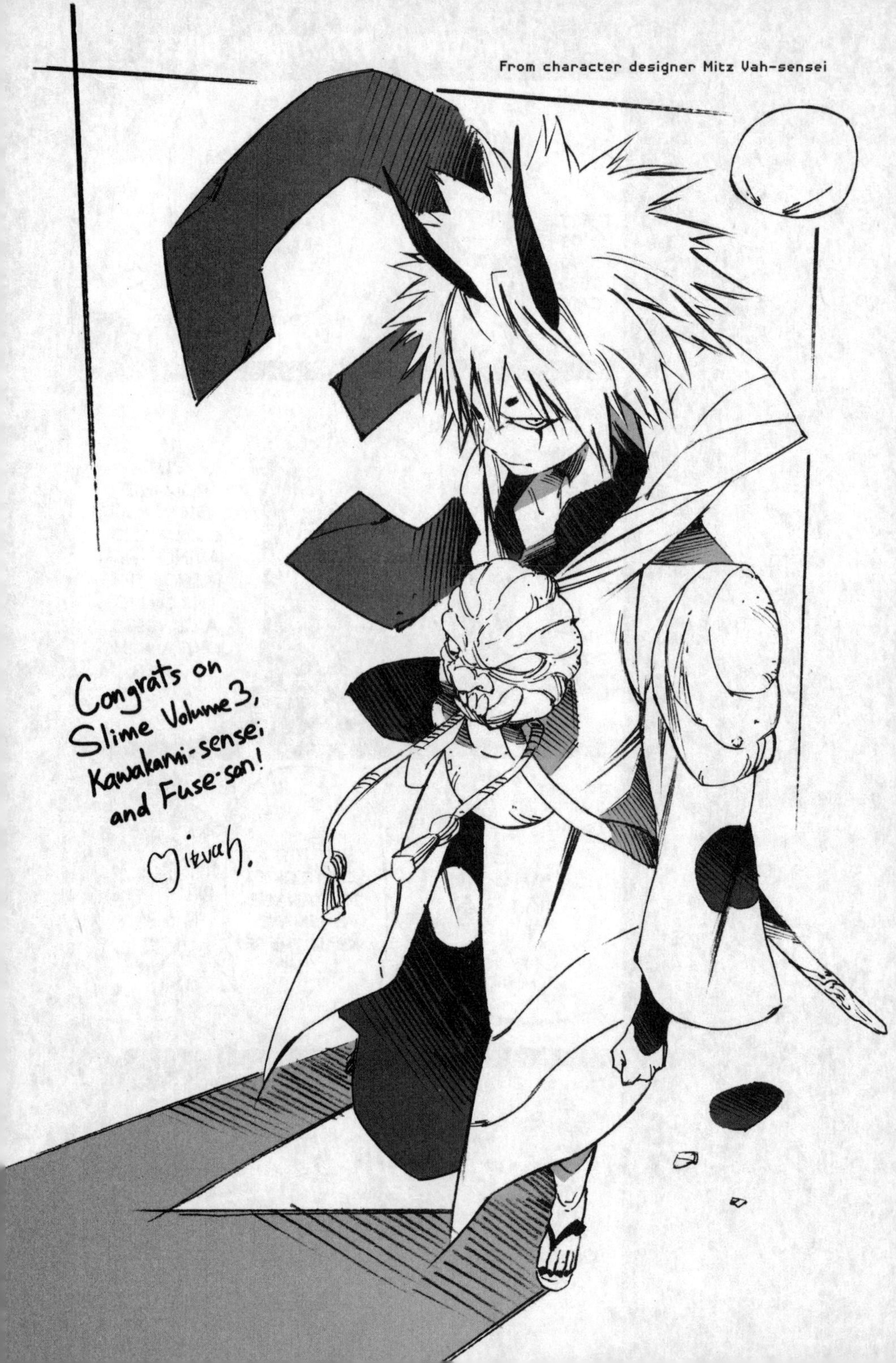
Congrats on Slime Volume 3, Kawakami-sensei and Fuse-san!
Mitzvah.

Black and White

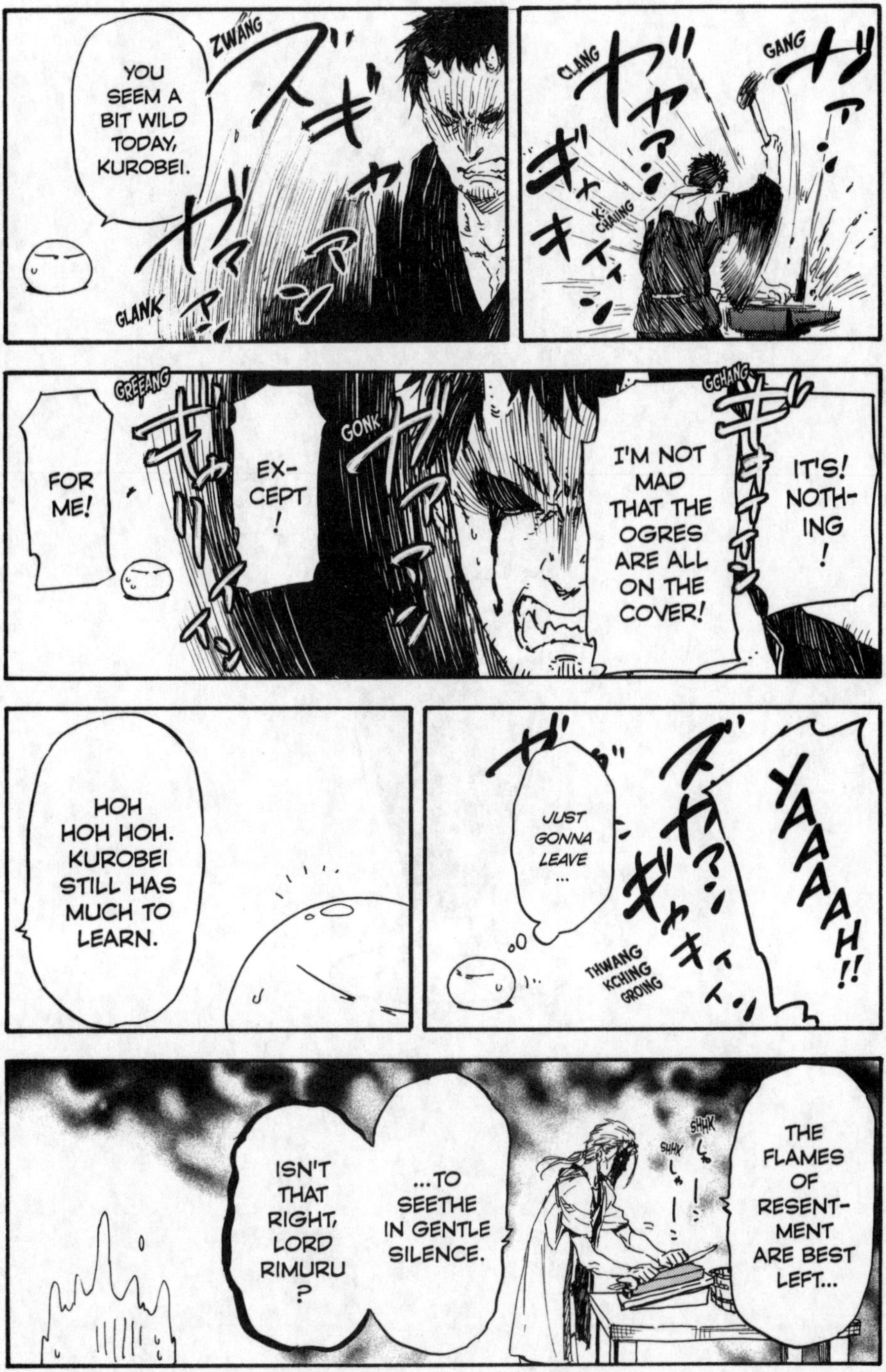

CLANG
GANG
K-CHAIING
ZWANG
YOU SEEM A BIT WILD TODAY, KUROBEI.
GLANK
GCHANG
IT'S! NOTHING!
I'M NOT MAD THAT THE OGRES ARE ALL ON THE COVER!
GONK
EXCEPT!
GREEANG
FOR ME!
YAAAAAH!!
THWANG KCHING GROING
JUST GONNA LEAVE...
HOH HOH HOH. KUROBEI STILL HAS MUCH TO LEARN.
THE FLAMES OF RESENTMENT ARE BEST LEFT...
SHHK
SHHK
...TO SEETHE IN GENTLE SILENCE.
ISN'T THAT RIGHT, LORD RIMURU?

Melon
Slime
Soda

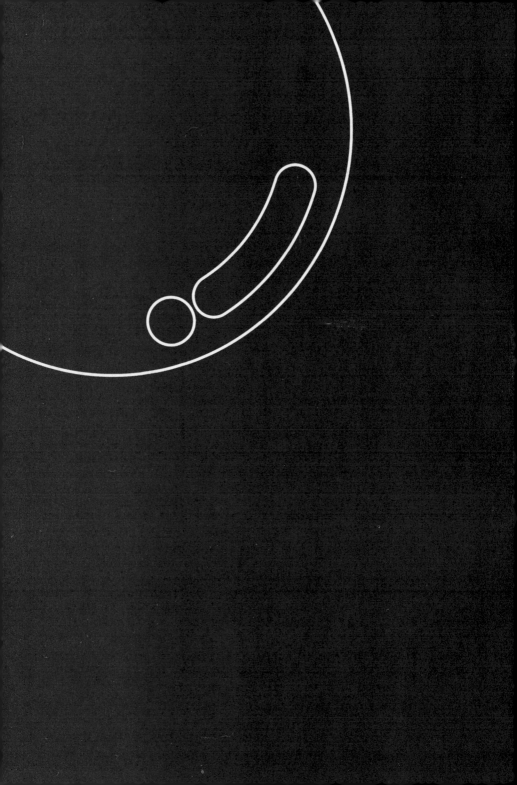

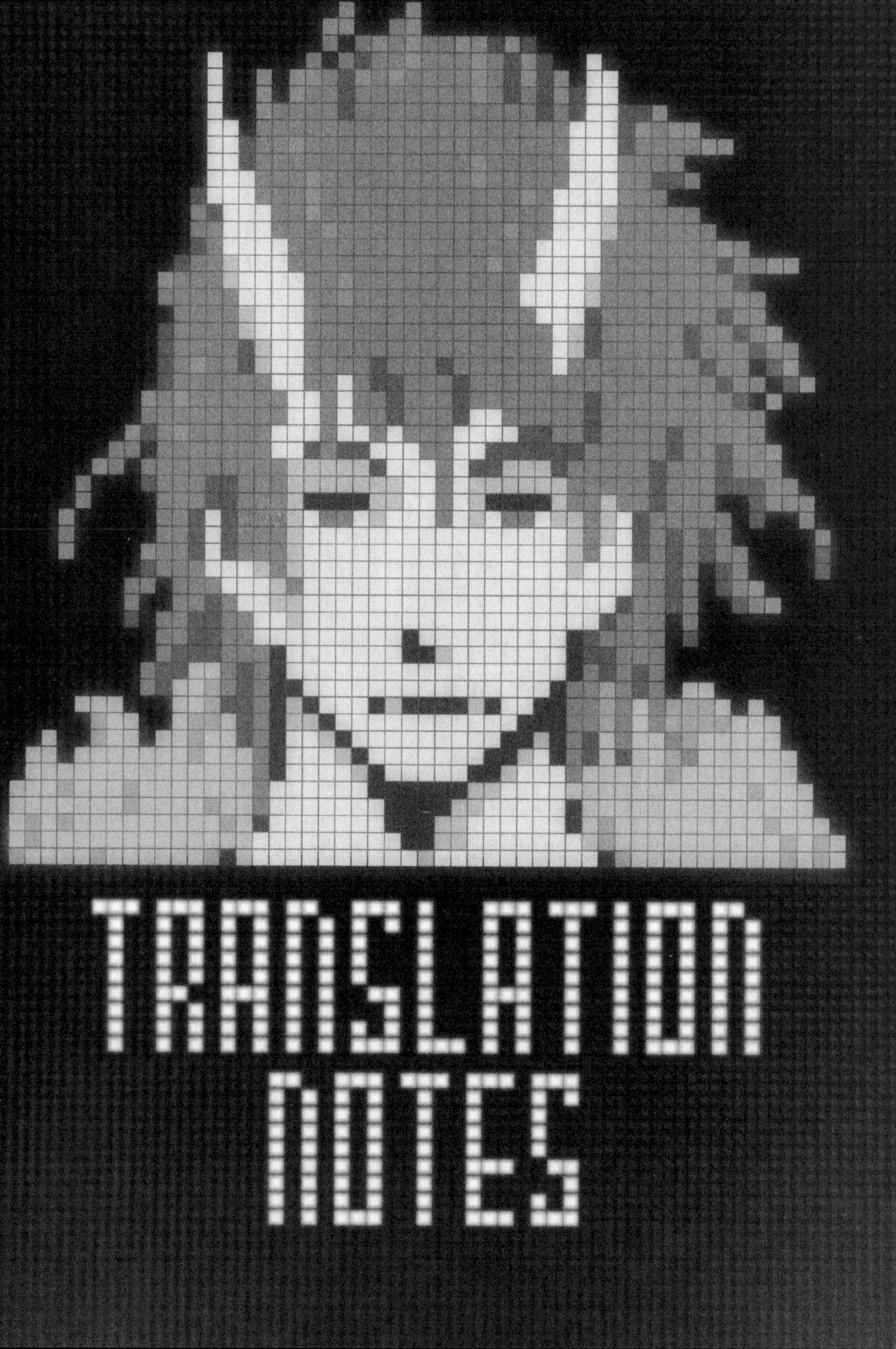

TRANSLATION NOTES

OGRES

THEY'VE EVEN GOT ARMOR ON.

Broken armor, but still.

As the protagonist notes, this depiction of "ogres" is distinguished by a more humanlike design and traditional Japanese style of dress. This, combined with the kanji used to help define their name in Japanese (which is pronounced ôga or "ogre"), suggests that they're meant to be seen like oni, the biggest and most fearsome of Japanese folklore monsters. Indeed, the most common English translation of oni is "ogre."

MAJIN

THE COU OF A HERE MAT ON

SHOW YOUR- SELF, FOUL MAJIN.

Unlike many of the terms for the fantasy races of this world (e.g. dwarves, elves, goblins), this word is not originally West- ern in origin, but Japanese. The kanji mean "wicked/magical" and "person," and they refer to a being who is human-like but also possesses a magical nature. In real-life mythology, the term majin is most often used in Japan to refer to beings such as the Indian asura or the Arabian jinn or "genie." A famous example of the word in fiction would be Majin Boo from Dragon Ball.

KIJIN

I AM NOW A KIJIN, AND I USE THE NAME...

...OF BENIMARU, AS YOU SO DUBBED ME.

This term is similar in construction to majin, except that the kanji mean "ogre (oni)" and "person." The previous kanji for when the characters were presented as ogres were "large" and "ogre (oni)" instead. This would suggest that evolving has made them more humanlike.

EVERY SLIME'S GOTTA START SOMEWHERE...

TENSEI SHITARA SLIME DATTA KEN volume 1 © Fuse / Mitz Vah
All rights reserved.

Wanna learn more about Rimuru's adventures?

Go back to the source with the original light novel from author Fuse and illustrator Mitz Vah!

That Time I Got Reincarnated as a SLIME 1

Out in stores now from Yen On!

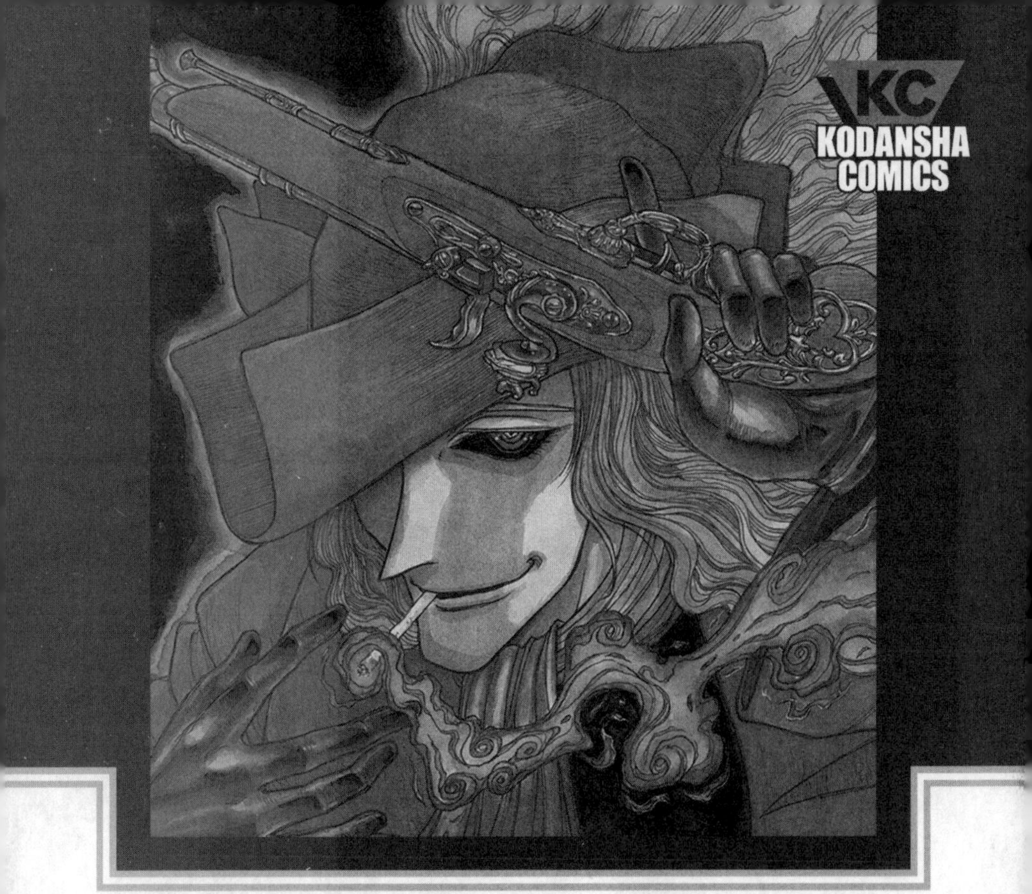
KC
KODANSHA
COMICS

The Black Museum: The Ghost and the Lady

By Kazuhiro Fujita

Deep in Scotland Yard in London sits an evidence room dedicated to the greatest mysteries of British history. In this "Black Museum" sits a misshapen hunk of lead–two bullets fused together–the key to a wartime encounter between Florence Nightingale, the mother of modern nursing, and a supernatural Man in Grey. This story is unknown to most scholars of history, but a special guest of the museum will tell the tale of The Ghost and the Lady...

Praise for Kazuhiro Fujita's *Ushio and Tora*

"A charming revival that combines a classic look with modern depth and pacing... **Essential viewing both for curmudgeons and new fans alike.**" — Anime News Network

"**GREAT!** The first episode of Ushio and Tora captures the essence of '90s anime." — IGN

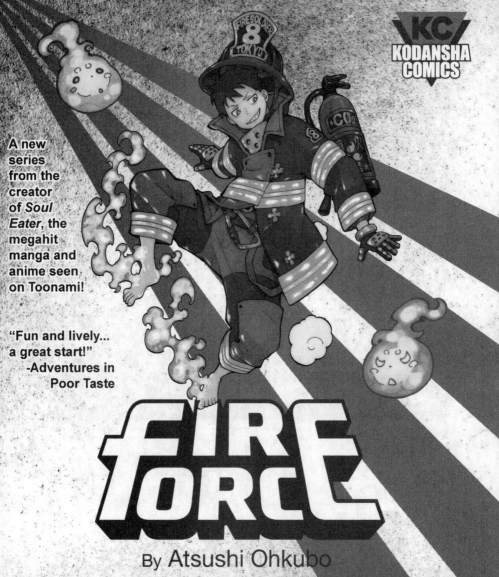

A new series from the creator of *Soul Eater*, the megahit manga and anime seen on Toonami!

"Fun and lively... a great start!"
-Adventures in Poor Taste

FIRE FORCE

By Atsushi Ohkubo

The city of Tokyo is plagued by a deadly phenomenon: spontaneous human combustion! Luckily, a special team is there to quench the inferno: The Fire Force! The fire soldiers at Special Fire Cathedral 8 are about to get a unique addition. Enter Shinra, a boy who possesses the power to run at the speed of a rocket, leaving behind the famous "devil's footprints" (and destroying his shoes in the process). Can Shinra and his colleagues discover the source of this strange epidemic before the city burns to ashes?

The award-winning manga about what happens inside you!

"Far more entertaining than it ought to be... what kid doesn't want to think that every time they sneeze a torpedo shoots out their nose?"
—Anime News Network

Strep throat! Hay fever! Influenza! The world is a dangerous place for a red blood cell just trying to get her deliveries finished. Fortunately, she's not alone...she's got a whole human body's worth of cells ready to help out! The mysterious white blood cells, the buff and brash killer T cells, even the cute little platelets— everyone's got to come together if they want to keep you healthy!

Cells at Work!

By Akane Shimizu

KODANSHA COMICS

New action series from Hiroyuki Takei, creator of the classic shonen franchise Shaman King!

In medieval Japan, a bell hanging on the collar is a sign that a cat has a master. Norachiyo's bell hangs from his katana sheath, but he is nonetheless a stray — a ronin. This one-eyed cat samurai travels across a dishonest world, cutting through pretense and deception with his blade.

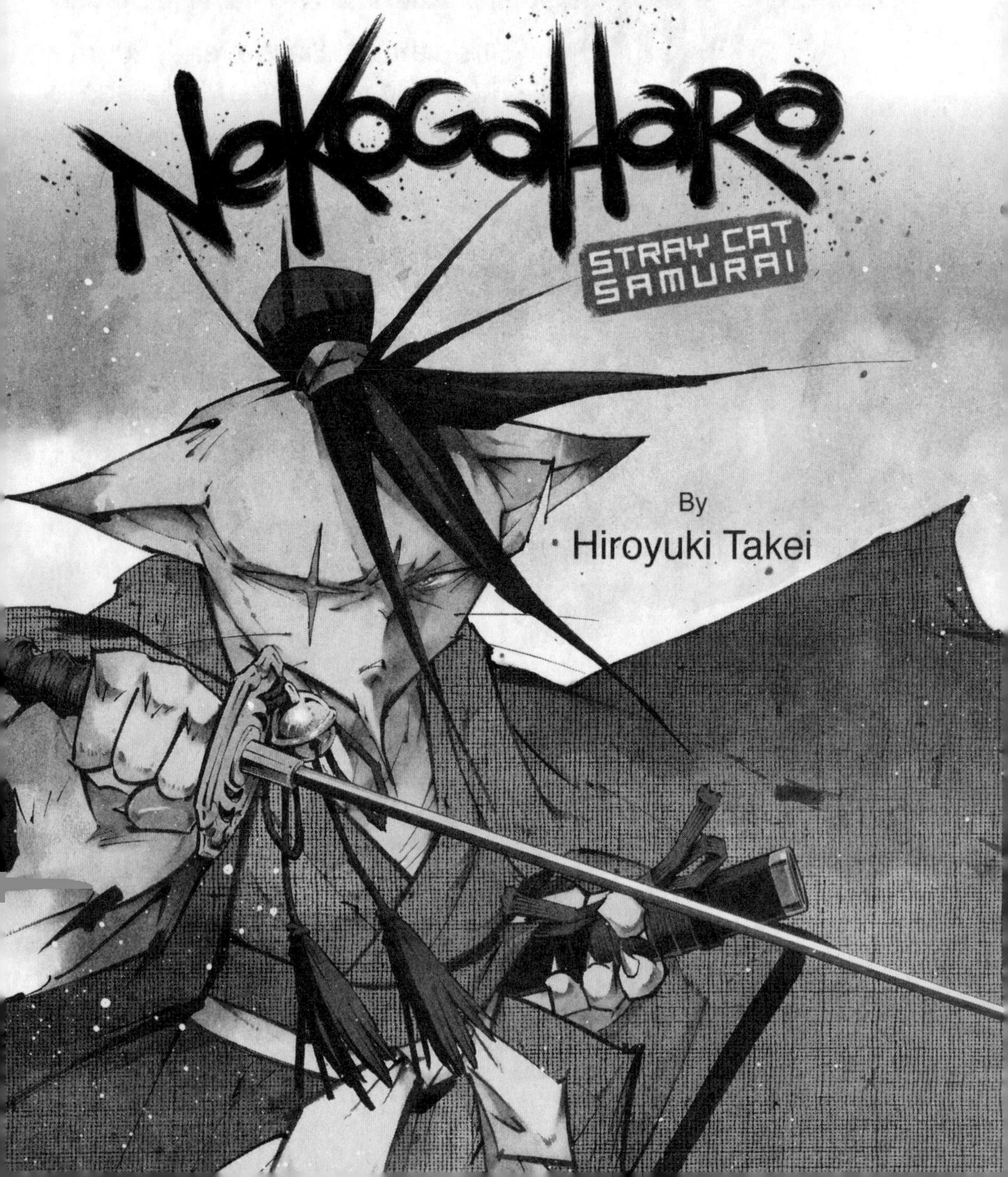
NEKOGAHARA
STRAY CAT SAMURAI
By
Hiroyuki Takei

Based on the critically acclaimed classic horror manga

The first new *Parasyte* manga in over 20 years!

NEO PARASYTE f

BY ASUMIKO NAKAMURA, EMA TOYAMA, MIKI RINNO, LALAKO KOJIMA, KAORI YUKI, BANKO KUZE, YUUKI OBATA, KASHIO, YUI KUROE, ASIA WATANABE, MIKIMAKI, HIKARU SURUGA, HAJIME SHINJO, RENJURO KINDAICHI, AND YURI NARUSHIMA

A collection of chilling new *Parasyte* stories from Japan's top shojo artists!

Parasites: shape-shifting aliens whose only purpose is to assimilate with and consume the human race... but do these monsters have a different side? A parasite becomes a prince to save his romance-obsessed female host from a dangerous stalker. Another hosts a cooking show, in which the real monsters are revealed. These and 13 more stories, from some of the greatest shojo manga artists alive today, together make up a chilling, funny, and entertaining tribute to one of manga's horror classics!

KC KODANSHA COMICS

That Time I Got Reincarnated as a Slime volume 3 is a work of fiction. Names, characters, places, and incidents are the products of the author's imagination or are used fictitiously. Any resemblance to actual events, locales, or persons, living or dead, is entirely coincidental.

A Kodansha Comics Trade Paperback Original.

Published in the United States by Kodansha Comics,
an imprint of Kodansha USA Publishing, LLC, New York.

Publication rights for this English edition arranged through Kodansha Ltd., Tokyo.

First published in Japan in 2016 by Kodansha Ltd., Tokyo, as *Tensei Shitara Suraimu Datta Ken* volume 3.

ISBN 978-1-63236-508-8

Printed in the United States of America.

www.kodansha.us

8th Printing

Translation: Stephen Paul
Lettering: Evan Hayden
Editing: Ajani Oloye
Kodansha Comics edition cover design: Phil Balsman

THAT TIME I GOT REINCARNATED AS A
SLIME
4

Author: FUSE

Artist: TAIKI KAWAKAMI

Character design: MITZ VAH

World Map

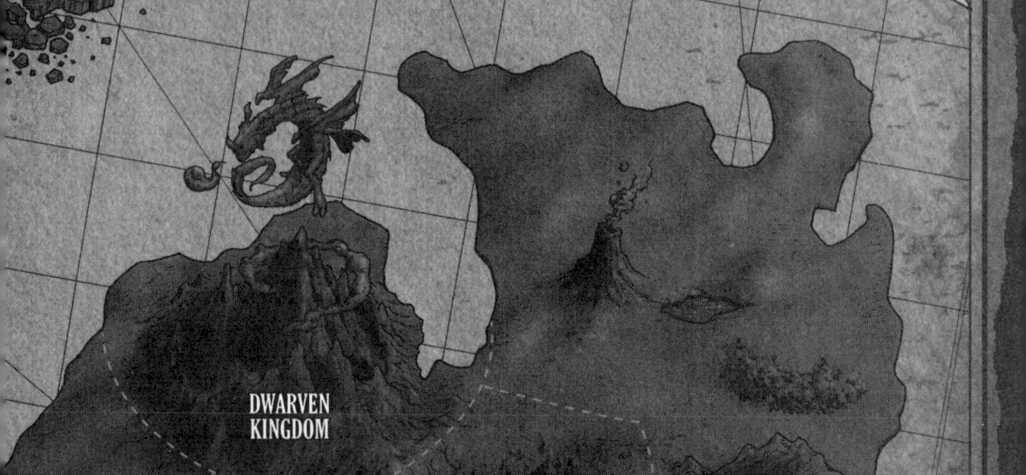
DWARVEN KINGDOM
GREAT FOREST OF JURA
KINGDOM OF BLUMUND
SEALED CAVE

PLOT SUMMARY

The ogres lost many of their brethren when their village was attacked by a masked majin leading an army of orcs. While seeking their revenge, they attacked Rimuru, believing him to be that masked majin. However, Rimuru was able to clear up the mistake and recruit them to his cause. Soon after, it was revealed that the orcs' next target would be the wetlands, home to the lizardmen. While the various monster races worked on plans to defend against an army of 200,000, a dryad claiming to be the protector of the forest showed up in Rimuru's camp, asking him to vanquish the orc lord.

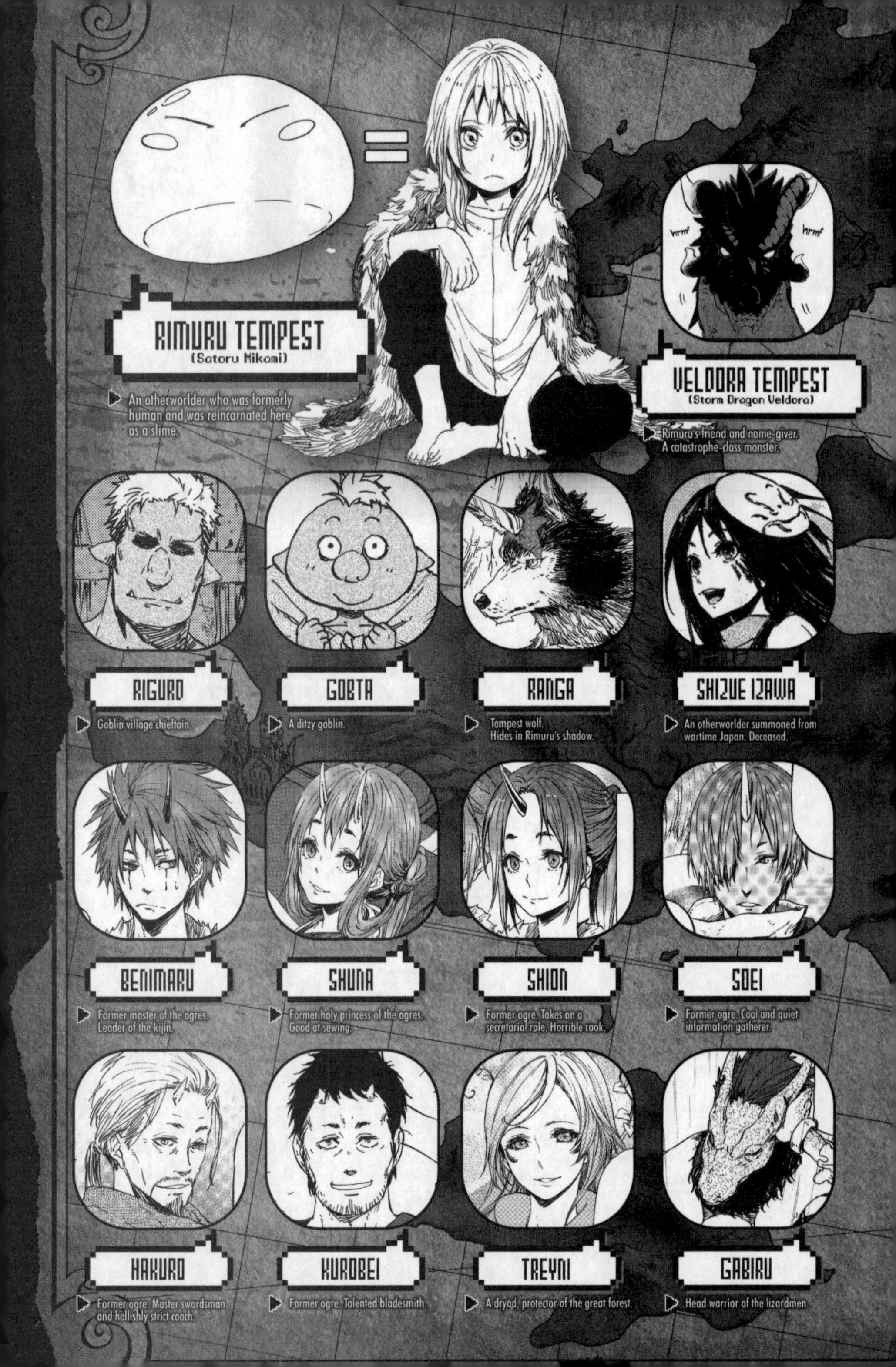
RIMURU TEMPEST
(Satoru Mikami)
An otherworlder who was formerly human and was reincarnated here as a slime.
hrmf
hrmf
VELDORA TEMPEST
(Storm Dragon Veldora)
Rimuru's friend and name-giver. A catastrophe-class monster.
RIGURD
Goblin village chieftain.
GOBTA
A ditzy goblin.
RANGA
Tempest wolf. Hides in Rimuru's shadow.
SHIZUE IZAWA
An otherworlder summoned from wartime Japan. Deceased.
BENIMARU
Former master of the ogres. Leader of the kijin.
SHUNA
Former holy princess of the ogres. Good at sewing.
SHION
Former ogre. Takes on a secretarial role. Horrible cook.
SOEI
Former ogre. Cool and quiet information gatherer.
HAKURO
Former ogre. Master swordsman and hellishly strict coach.
KUROBEI
Former ogre. Talented bladesmith.
TREYNI
A dryad, protector of the great forest.
GABIRU
Head warrior of the lizardmen.

CONTENTS

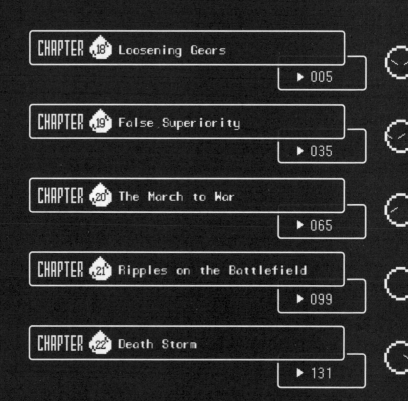

BONUS SHORT STORY

Veldora's Slime Observation Journal

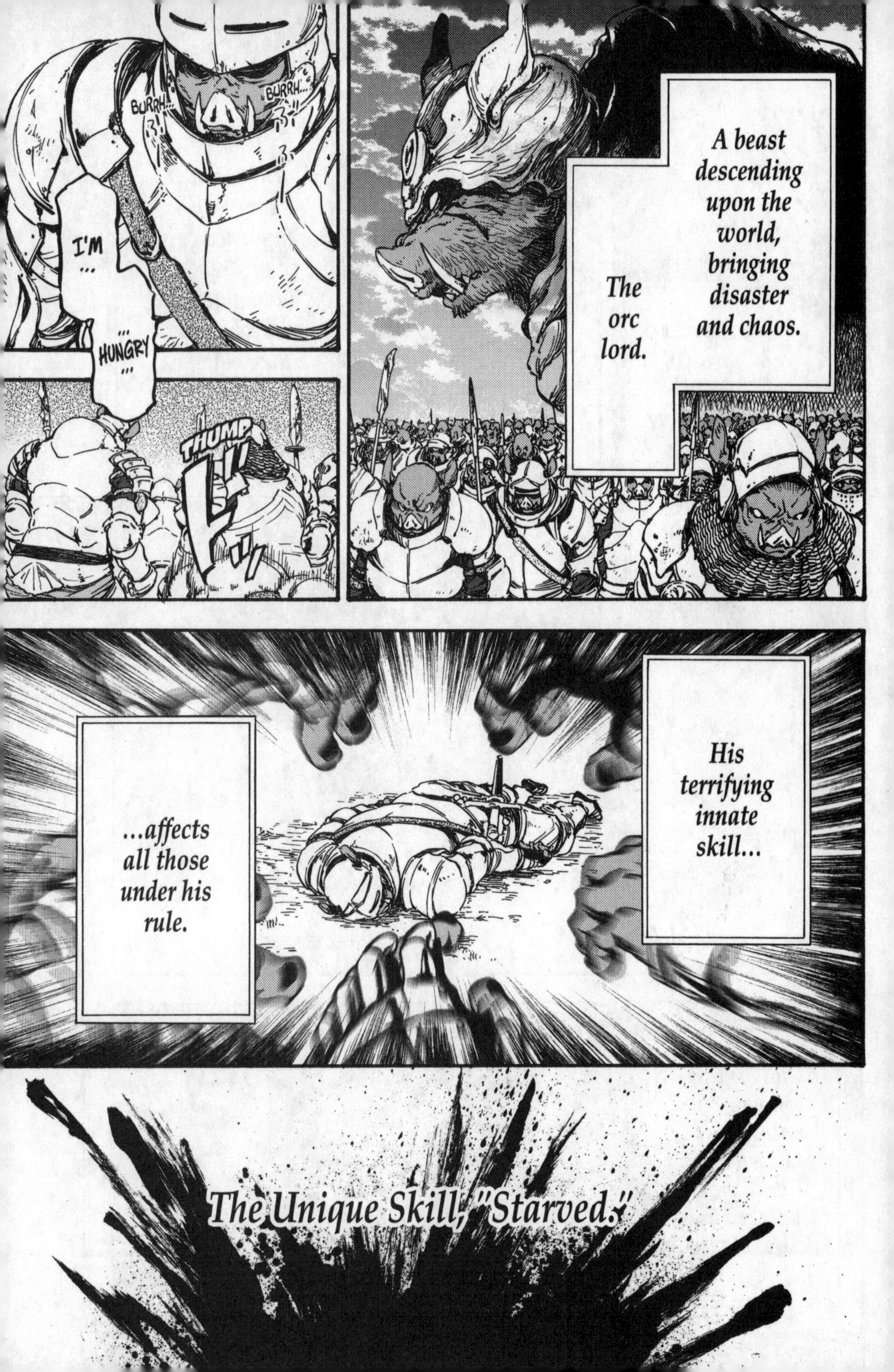
A beast descending upon the world, bringing disaster and chaos.
The orc lord.
BURRH...
BURRH...
I'M ...
... HUNGRY ...
THUMP
His terrifying innate skill...
...affects all those under his rule.
The Unique Skill, "Starved."

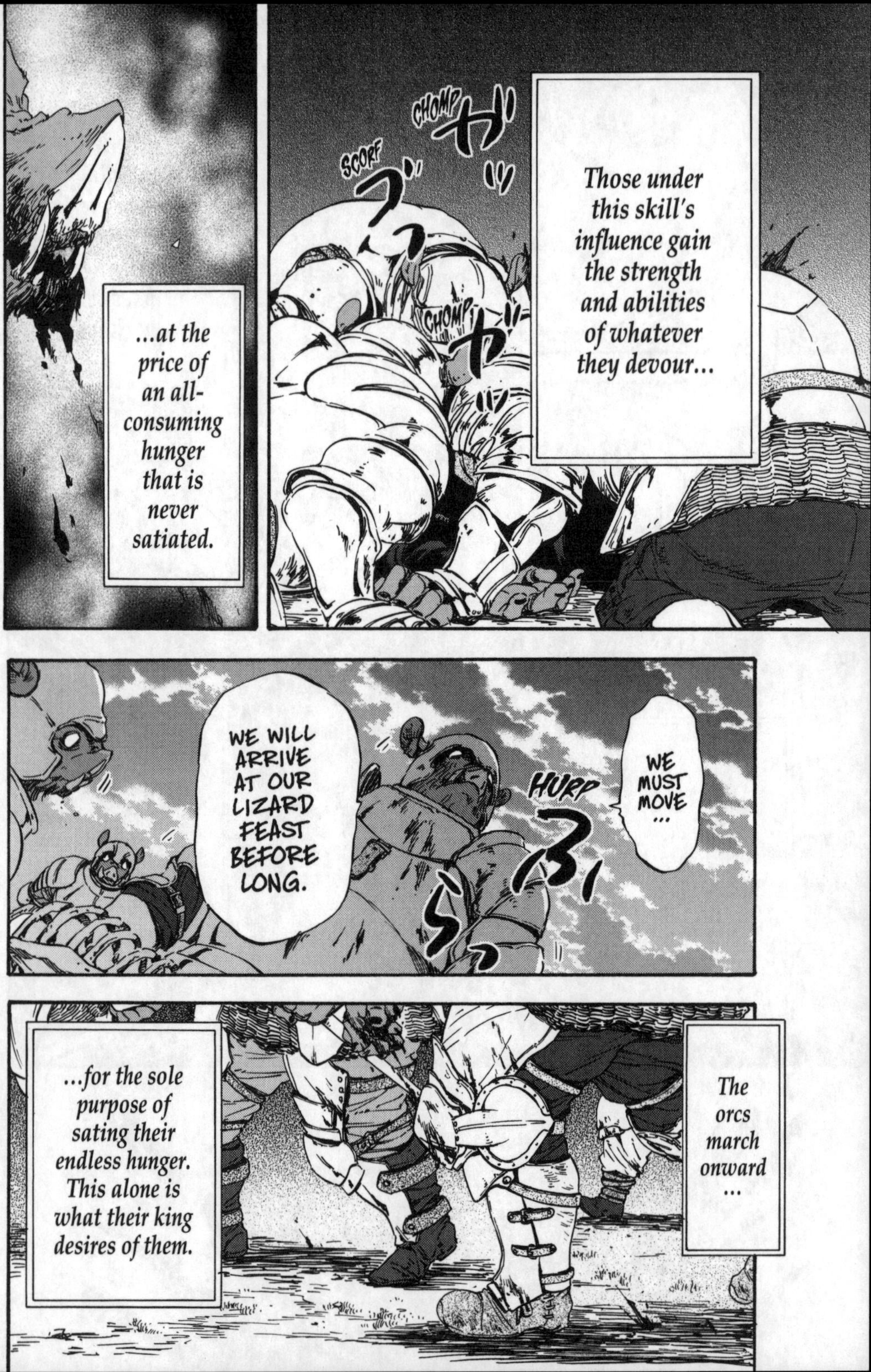
Those under this skill's influence gain the strength and abilities of whatever they devour...
CHOMP
SCORF
CHOMP
...at the price of an all-consuming hunger that is never satiated.
WE MUST MOVE ...
HURP
WE WILL ARRIVE AT OUR LIZARD FEAST BEFORE LONG.
The orcs march onward ...
...for the sole purpose of sating their endless hunger. This alone is what their king desires of them.

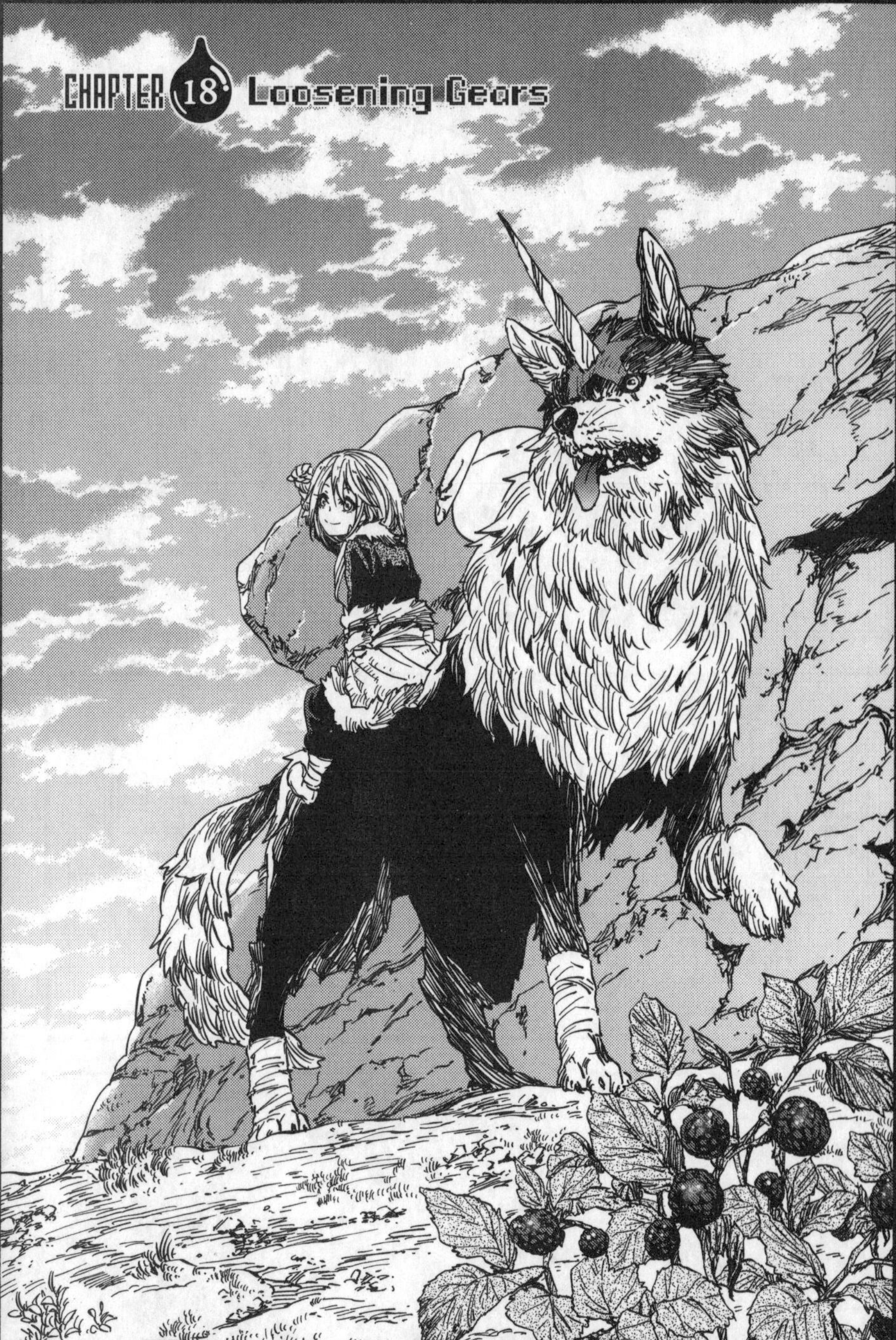
CHAPTER 18 Loosening Gears

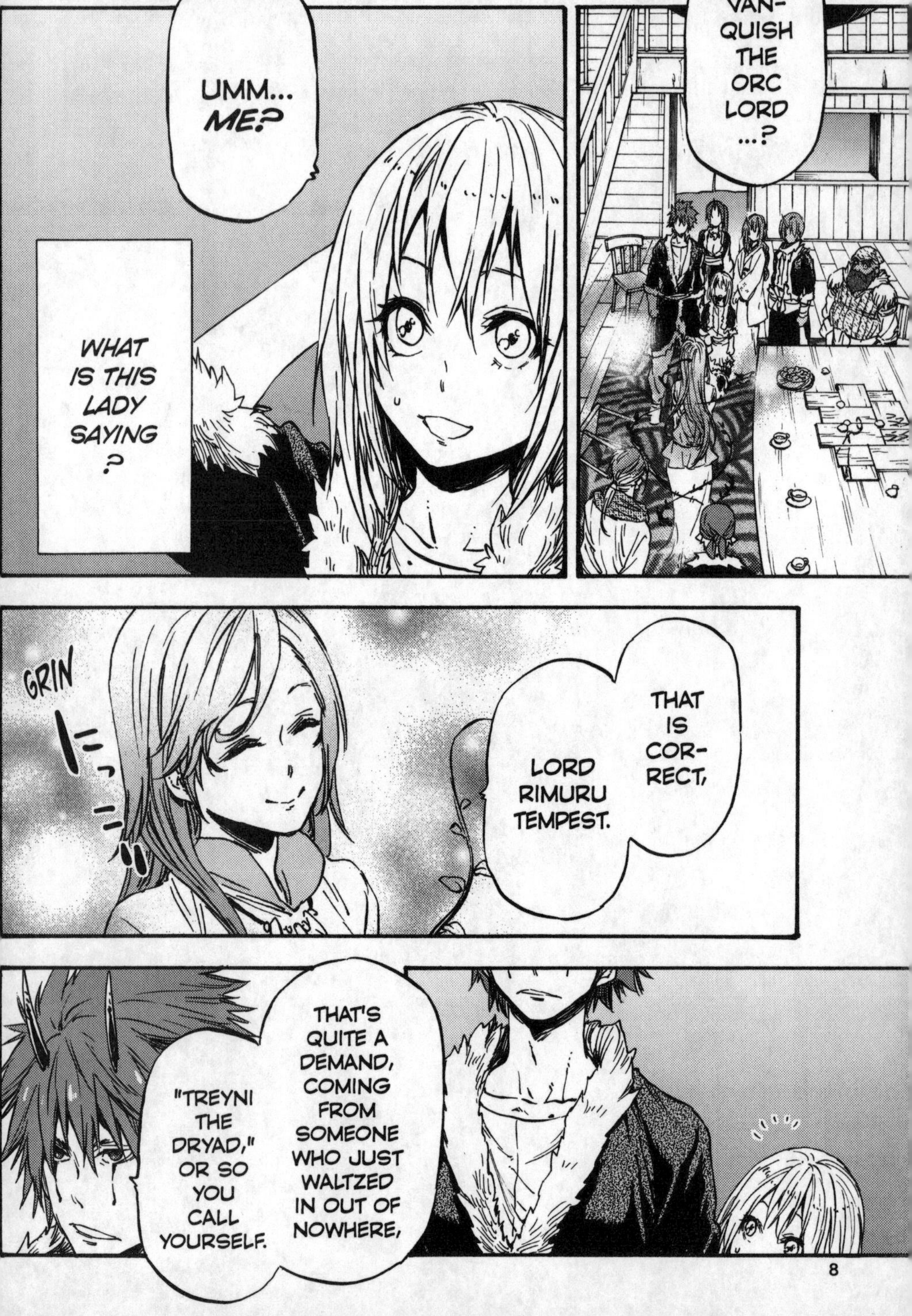
VAN-QUISH THE ORC LORD ...?
UMM... *ME?*
WHAT IS THIS LADY SAYING?
GRIN
THAT IS COR-RECT, LORD RIMURU TEMPEST.
THAT'S QUITE A DEMAND, COMING FROM SOMEONE WHO JUST WALTZED IN OUT OF NOWHERE,
"TREYNI THE DRYAD," OR SO YOU CALL YOURSELF.

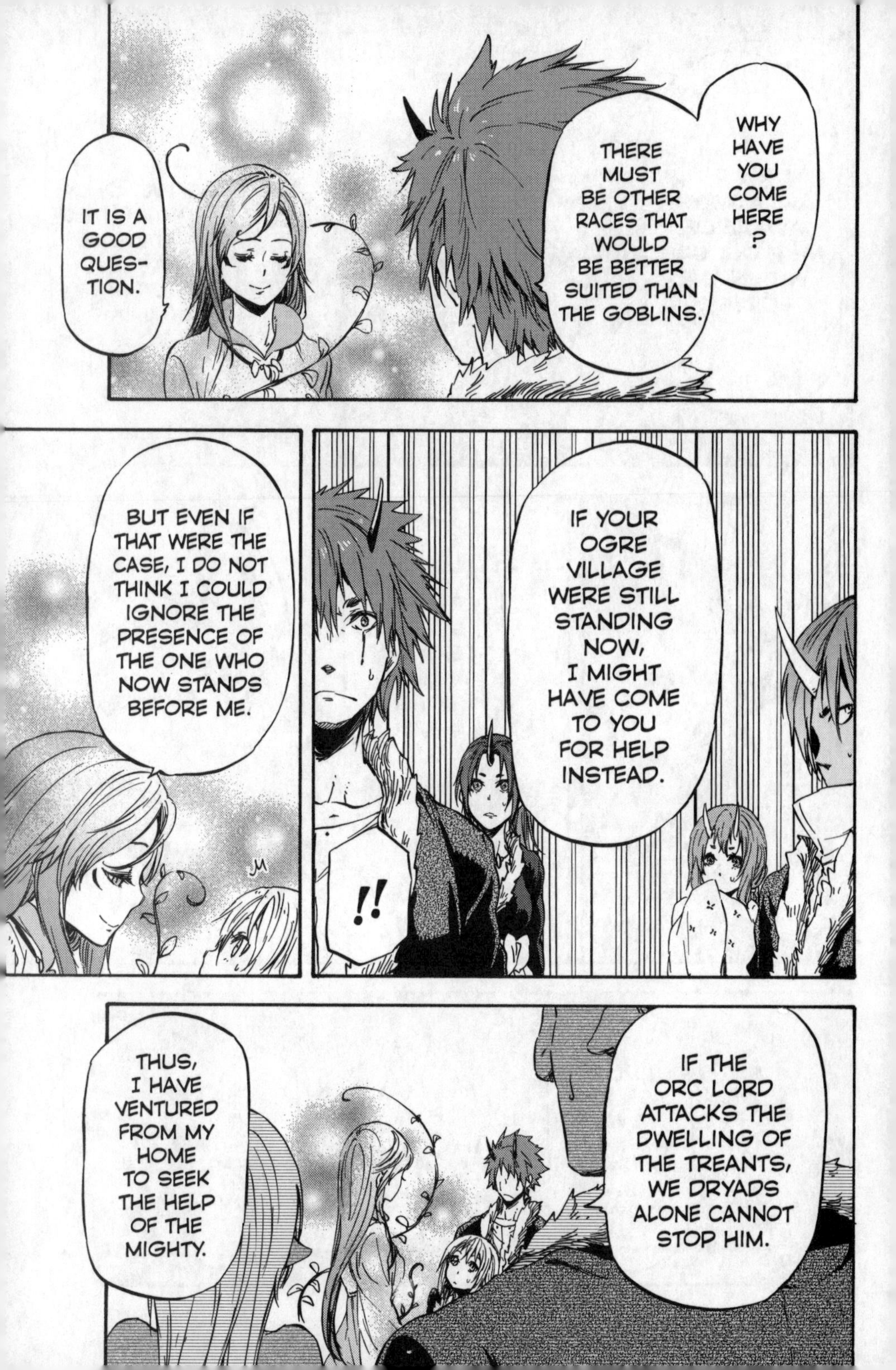

WHY HAVE YOU COME HERE?
THERE MUST BE OTHER RACES THAT WOULD BE BETTER SUITED THAN THE GOBLINS.
IT IS A GOOD QUES-TION.
IF YOUR OGRE VILLAGE WERE STILL STANDING NOW, I MIGHT HAVE COME TO YOU FOR HELP INSTEAD.
!!
BUT EVEN IF THAT WERE THE CASE, I DO NOT THINK I COULD IGNORE THE PRESENCE OF THE ONE WHO NOW STANDS BEFORE ME.
IF THE ORC LORD ATTACKS THE DWELLING OF THE TREANTS, WE DRYADS ALONE CANNOT STOP HIM.
THUS, I HAVE VENTURED FROM MY HOME TO SEEK THE HELP OF THE MIGHTY.

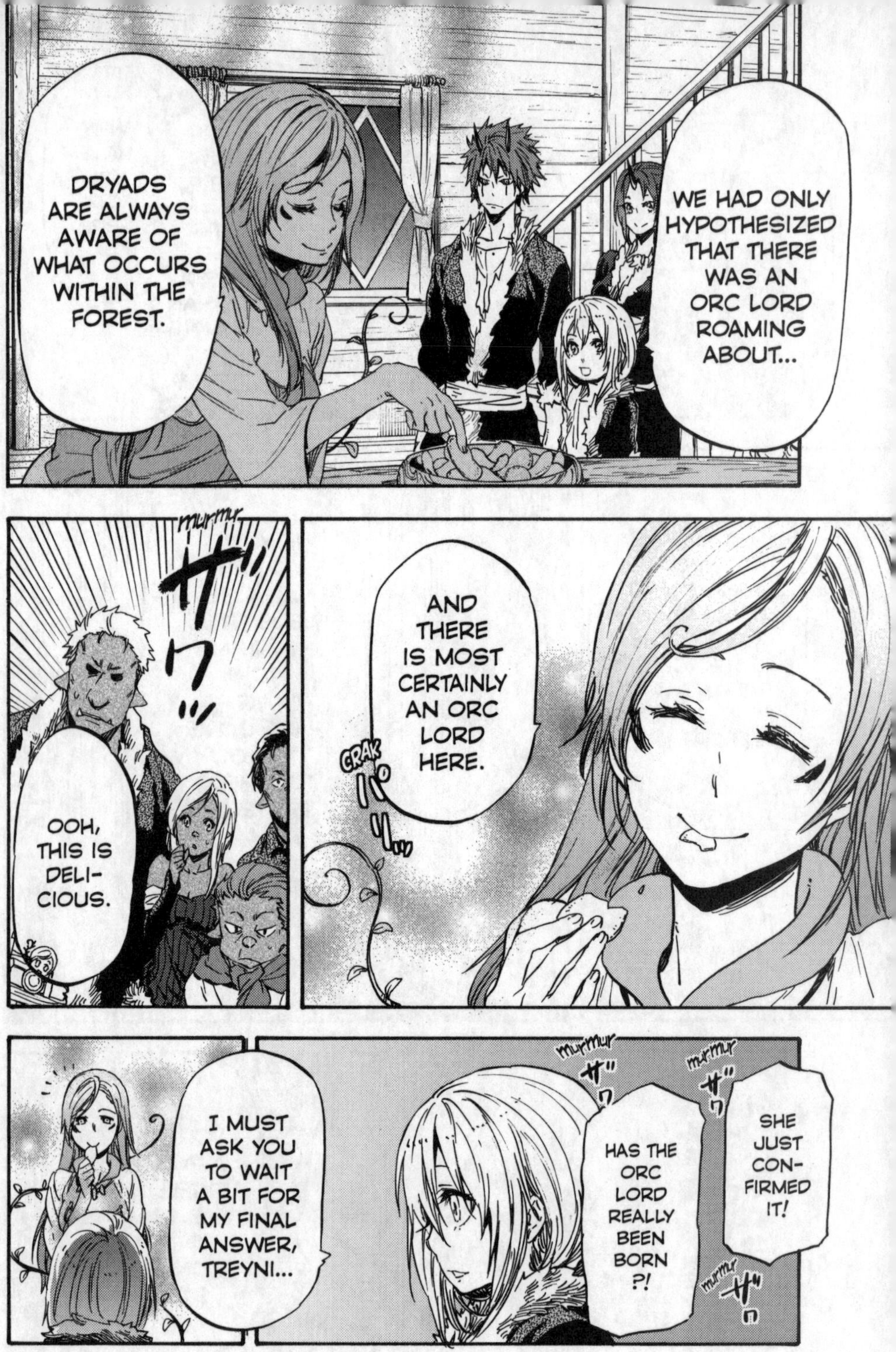
WE HAD ONLY HYPOTHESIZED THAT THERE WAS AN ORC LORD ROAMING ABOUT...
DRYADS ARE ALWAYS AWARE OF WHAT OCCURS WITHIN THE FOREST.
AND THERE IS MOST CERTAINLY AN ORC LORD HERE.
CRAK
murmur
OOH, THIS IS DELICIOUS.
murmur
murmur
SHE JUST CON-FIRMED IT!
HAS THE ORC LORD REALLY BEEN BORN?!
murmur
I MUST ASK YOU TO WAIT A BIT FOR MY FINAL ANSWER, TREYNI...

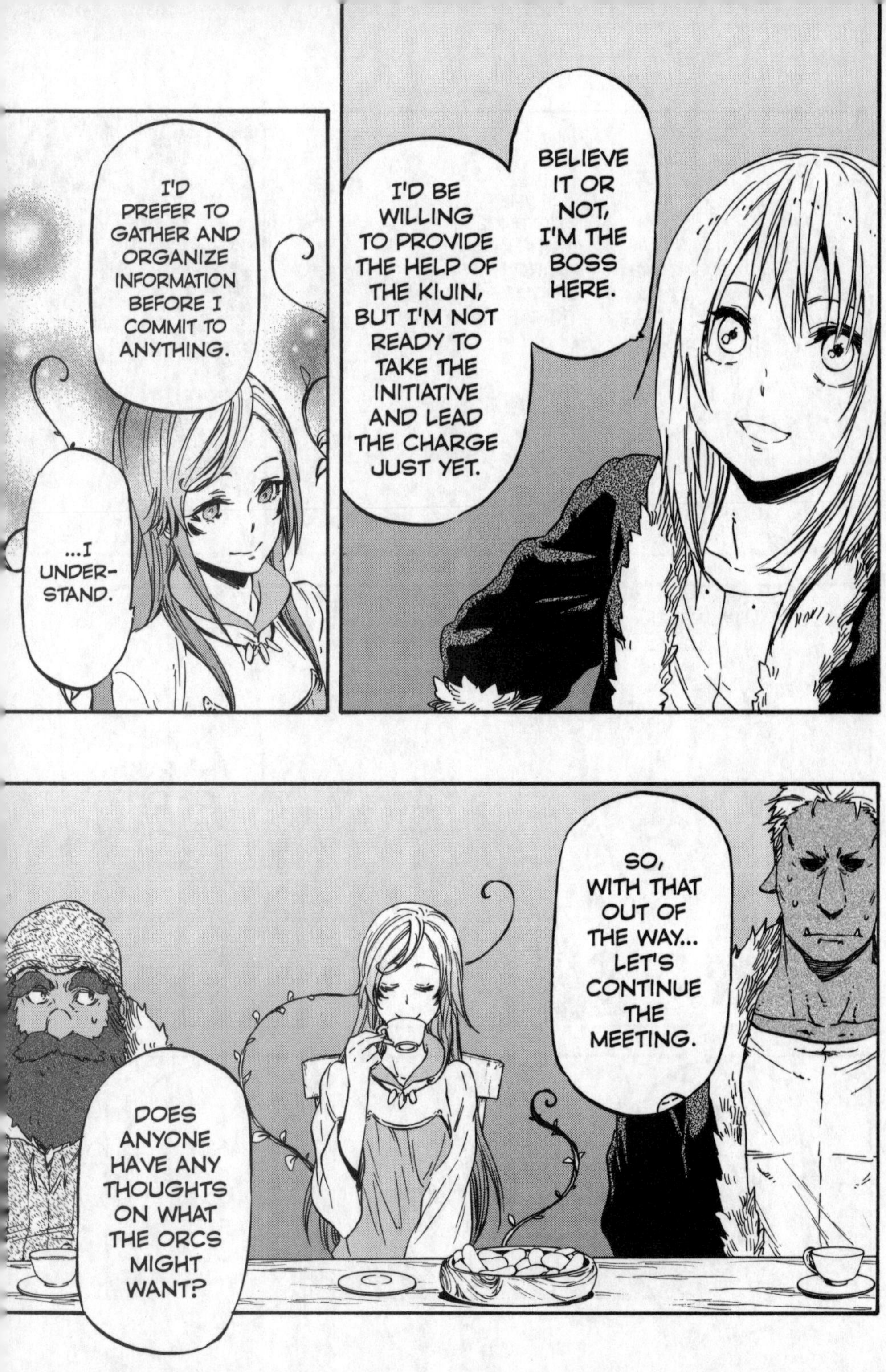
BELIEVE IT OR NOT, I'M THE BOSS HERE.
I'D BE WILLING TO PROVIDE THE HELP OF THE KIJIN, BUT I'M NOT READY TO TAKE THE INITIATIVE AND LEAD THE CHARGE JUST YET.
I'D PREFER TO GATHER AND ORGANIZE INFORMATION BEFORE I COMMIT TO ANYTHING.
...I UNDER-STAND.
SO, WITH THAT OUT OF THE WAY... LET'S CONTINUE THE MEETING.
DOES ANYONE HAVE ANY THOUGHTS ON WHAT THE ORCS MIGHT WANT?

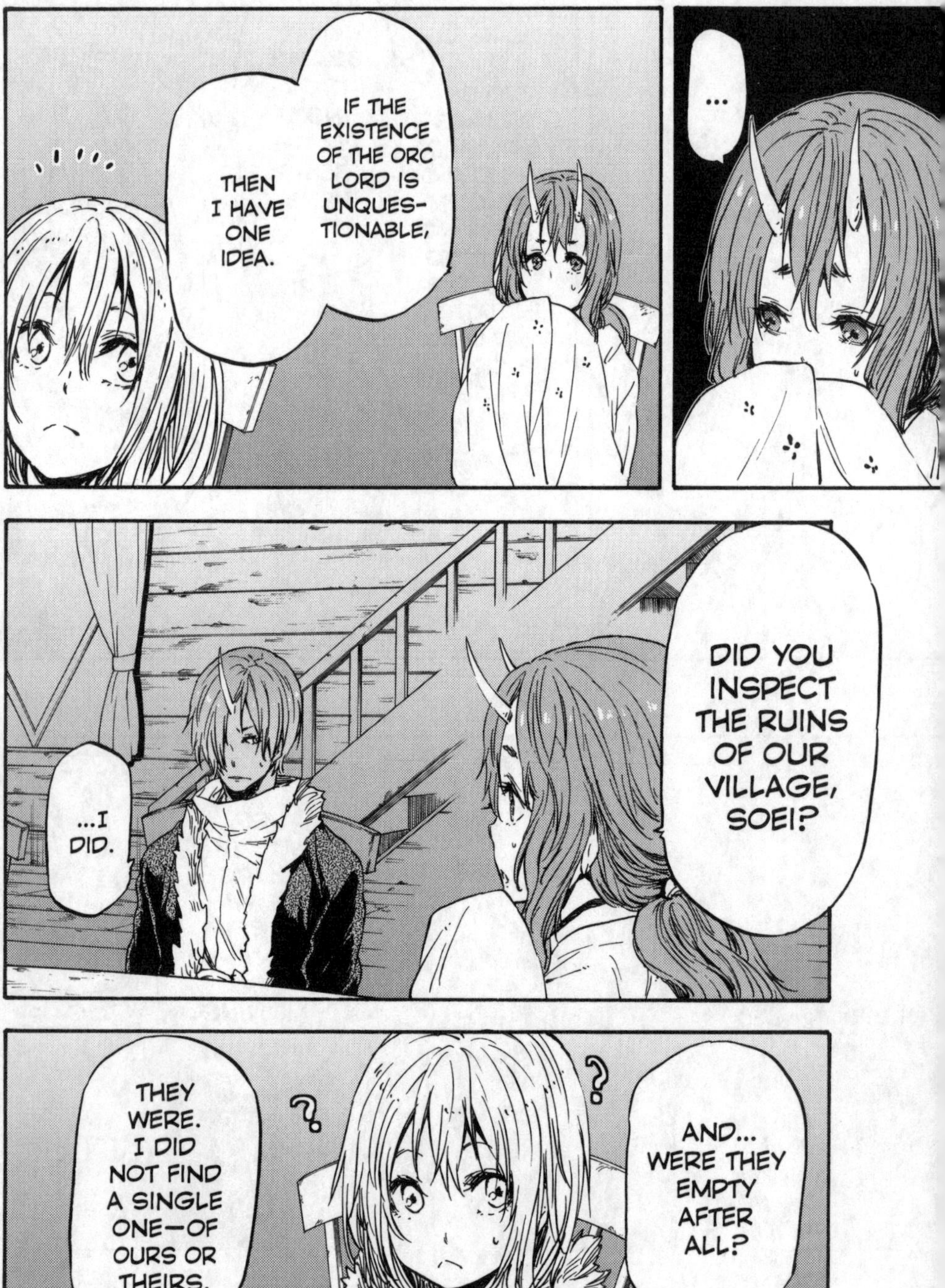
...
IF THE EXISTENCE OF THE ORC LORD IS UNQUESTIONABLE,
THEN I HAVE ONE IDEA.
DID YOU INSPECT THE RUINS OF OUR VILLAGE, SOEI?
...I DID.
AND... WERE THEY EMPTY AFTER ALL?
THEY WERE. I DID NOT FIND A SINGLE ONE—OF OURS OR THEIRS.

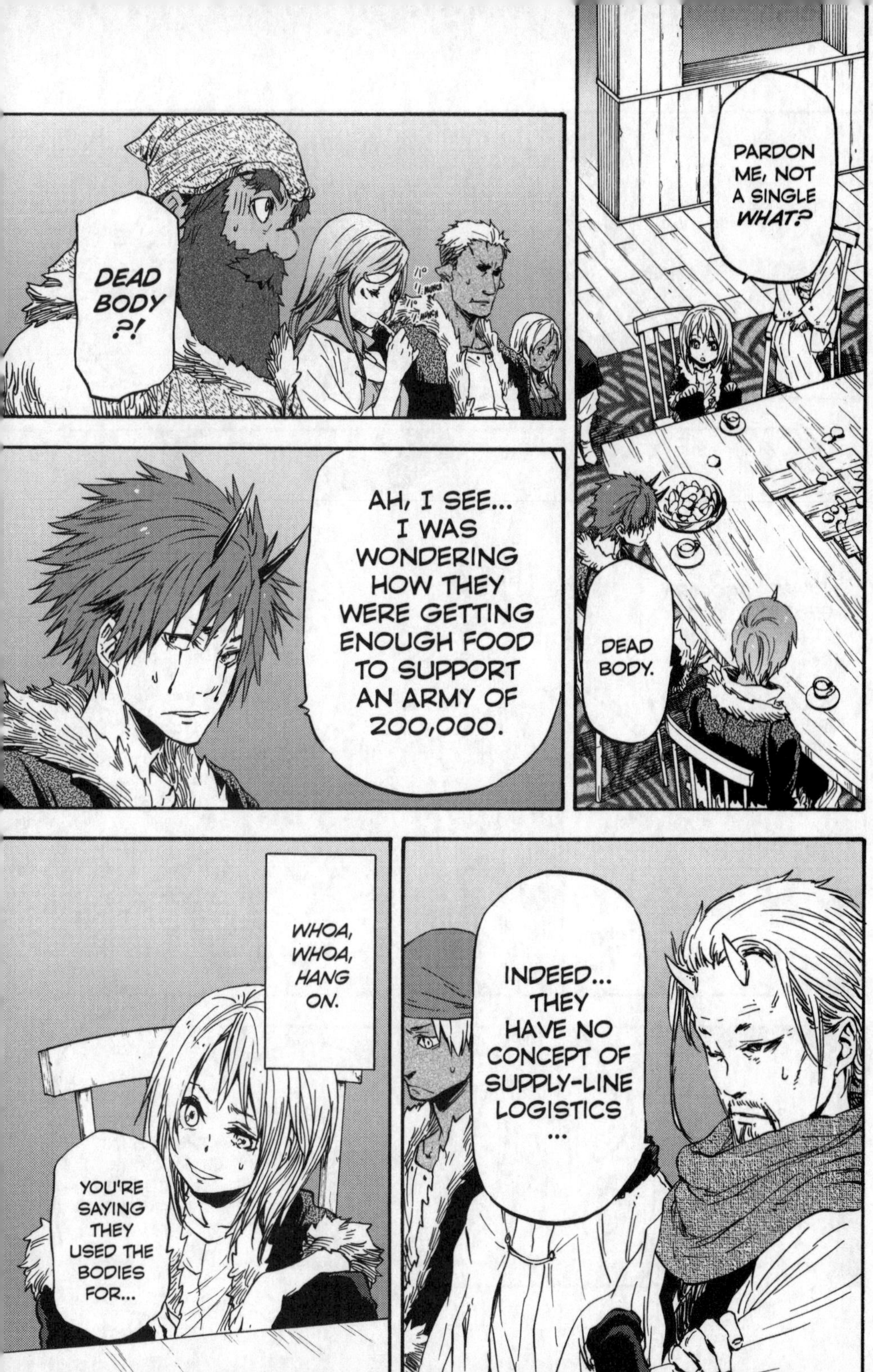
PARDON ME, NOT A SINGLE *WHAT?*
DEAD BODY.
DEAD BODY ?!
AH, I SEE... I WAS WONDERING HOW THEY WERE GETTING ENOUGH FOOD TO SUPPORT AN ARMY OF 200,000.
INDEED... THEY HAVE NO CONCEPT OF SUPPLY-LINE LOGISTICS ...
WHOA, WHOA, HANG ON.
YOU'RE SAYING THEY USED THE BODIES FOR...

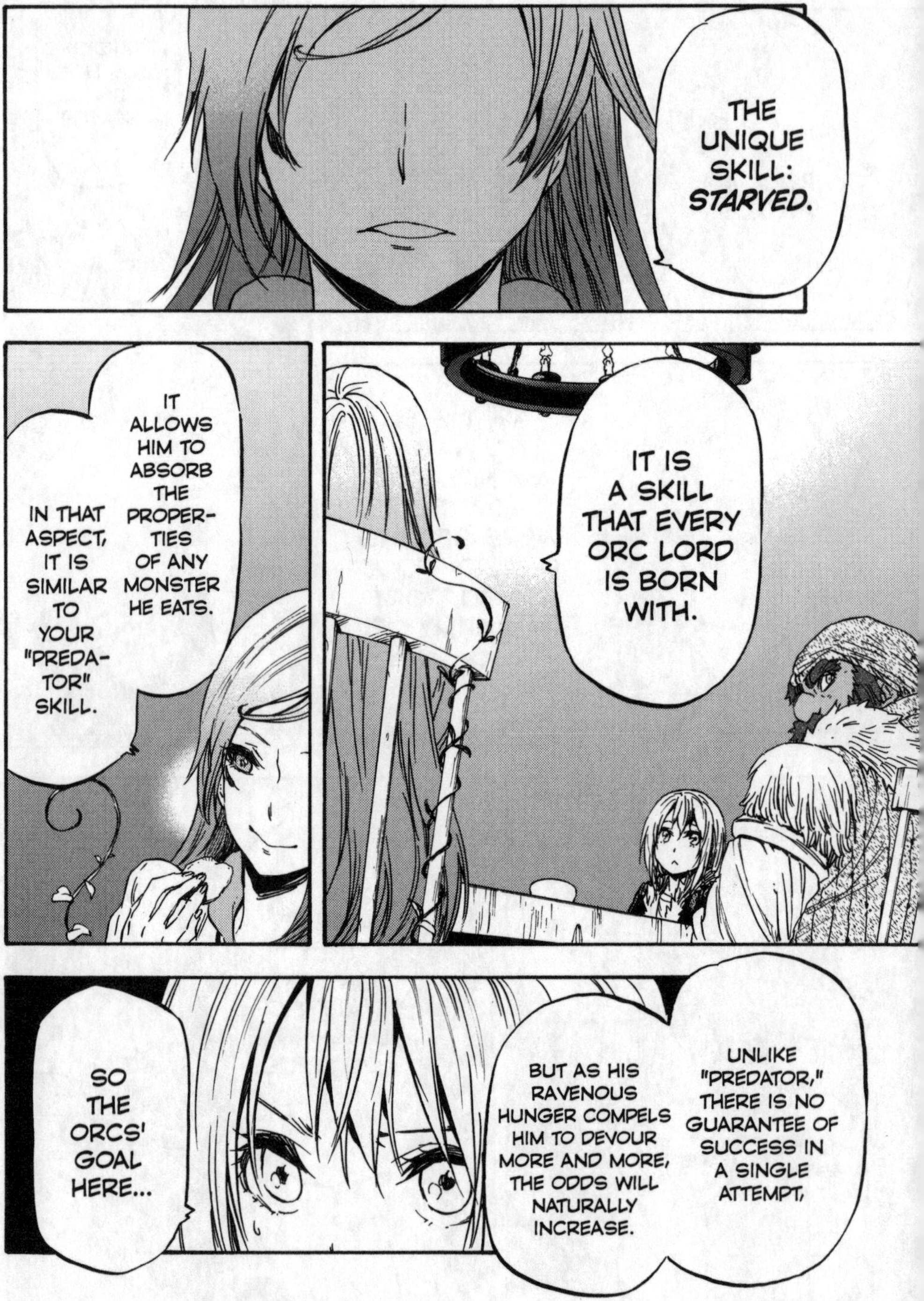

THE UNIQUE SKILL: *STARVED.*
IT IS A SKILL THAT EVERY ORC LORD IS BORN WITH.
IT ALLOWS HIM TO ABSORB THE PROPERTIES OF ANY MONSTER HE EATS.
IN THAT ASPECT, IT IS SIMILAR TO YOUR "PREDATOR" SKILL.
UNLIKE "PREDATOR," THERE IS NO GUARANTEE OF SUCCESS IN A SINGLE ATTEMPT,
BUT AS HIS RAVENOUS HUNGER COMPELS HIM TO DEVOUR MORE AND MORE, THE ODDS WILL NATURALLY INCREASE.
SO THE ORCS' GOAL HERE...

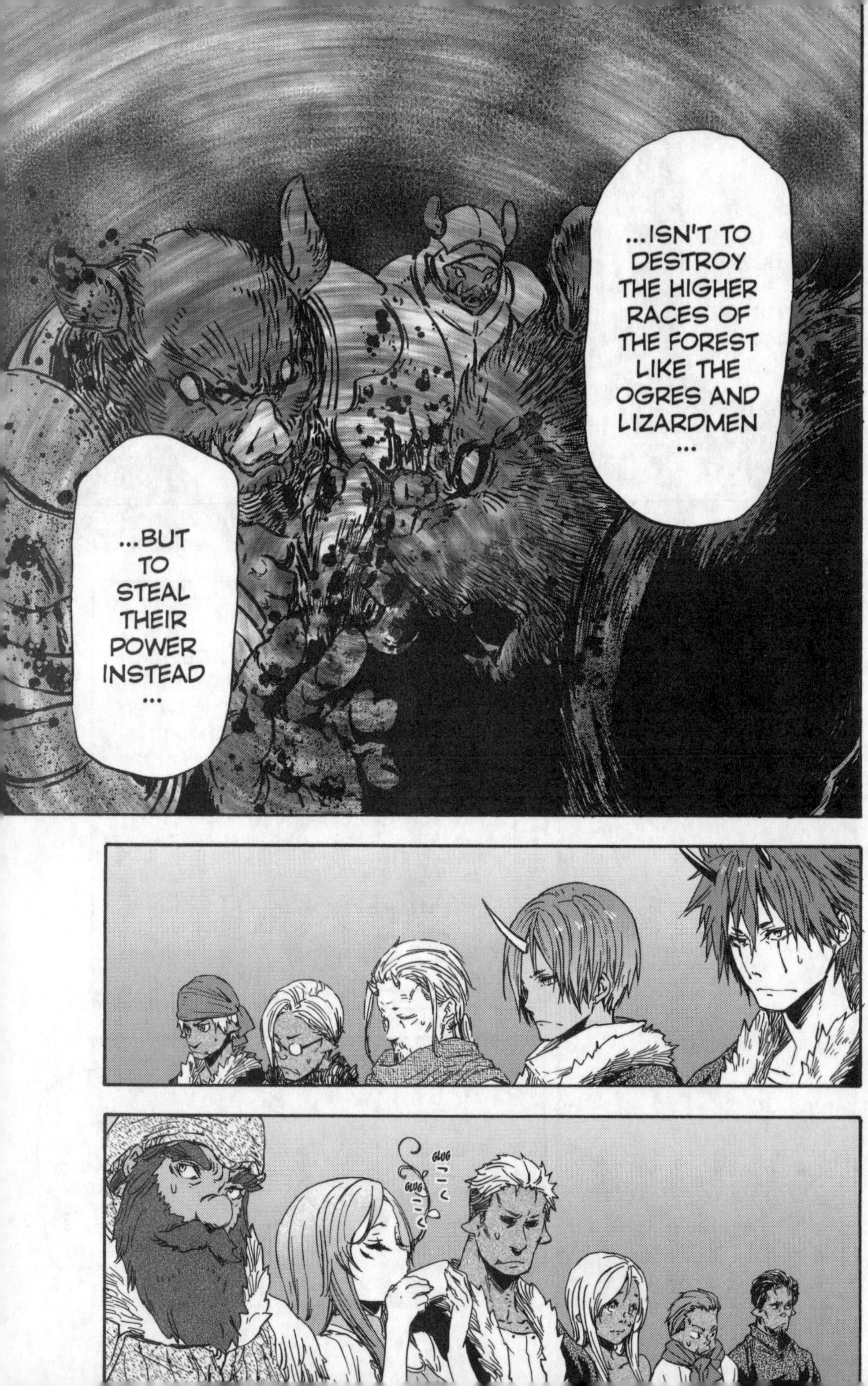
...ISN'T TO DESTROY THE HIGHER RACES OF THE FOREST LIKE THE OGRES AND LIZARDMEN ...
...BUT TO STEAL THEIR POWER INSTEAD ...
GLUG
GLUG

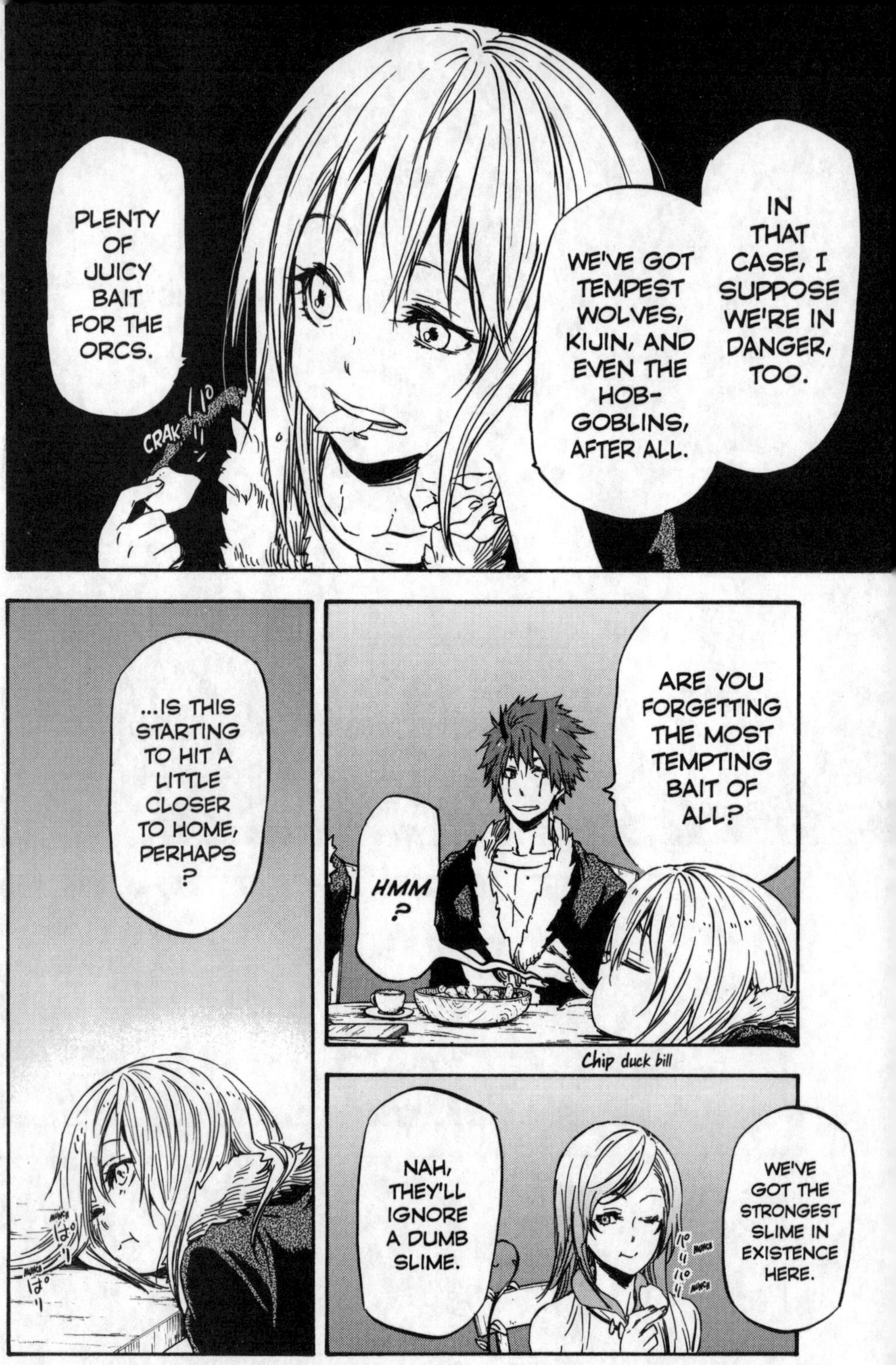
IN THAT CASE, I SUPPOSE WE'RE IN DANGER, TOO.
WE'VE GOT TEMPEST WOLVES, KIJIN, AND EVEN THE HOB-GOBLINS, AFTER ALL.
PLENTY OF JUICY BAIT FOR THE ORCS.
CRAK
ARE YOU FORGETTING THE MOST TEMPTING BAIT OF ALL?
HMM?
Chip duck bill
WE'VE GOT THE STRONGEST SLIME IN EXISTENCE HERE.
NAH, THEY'LL IGNORE A DUMB SLIME.
...IS THIS STARTING TO HIT A LITTLE CLOSER TO HOME, PERHAPS?

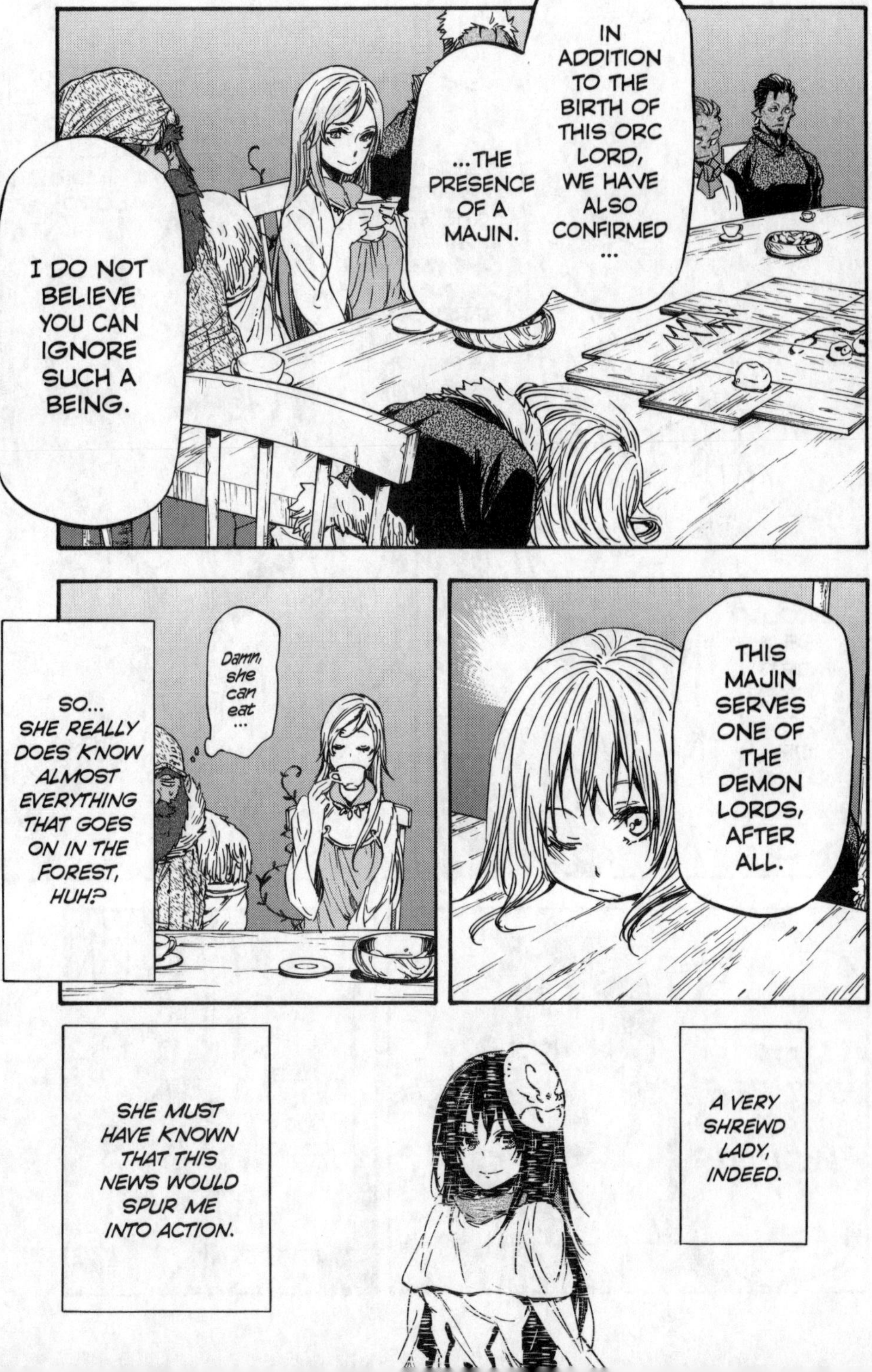
IN ADDITION TO THE BIRTH OF THIS ORC LORD, WE HAVE ALSO CONFIRMED ...
...THE PRESENCE OF A MAJIN.
I DO NOT BELIEVE YOU CAN IGNORE SUCH A BEING.
THIS MAJIN SERVES ONE OF THE DEMON LORDS, AFTER ALL.
Damn, she can eat ...
SO... SHE REALLY DOES KNOW ALMOST EVERYTHING THAT GOES ON IN THE FOREST, HUH?
A VERY SHREWD LADY, INDEED.
SHE MUST HAVE KNOWN THAT THIS NEWS WOULD SPUR ME INTO ACTION.

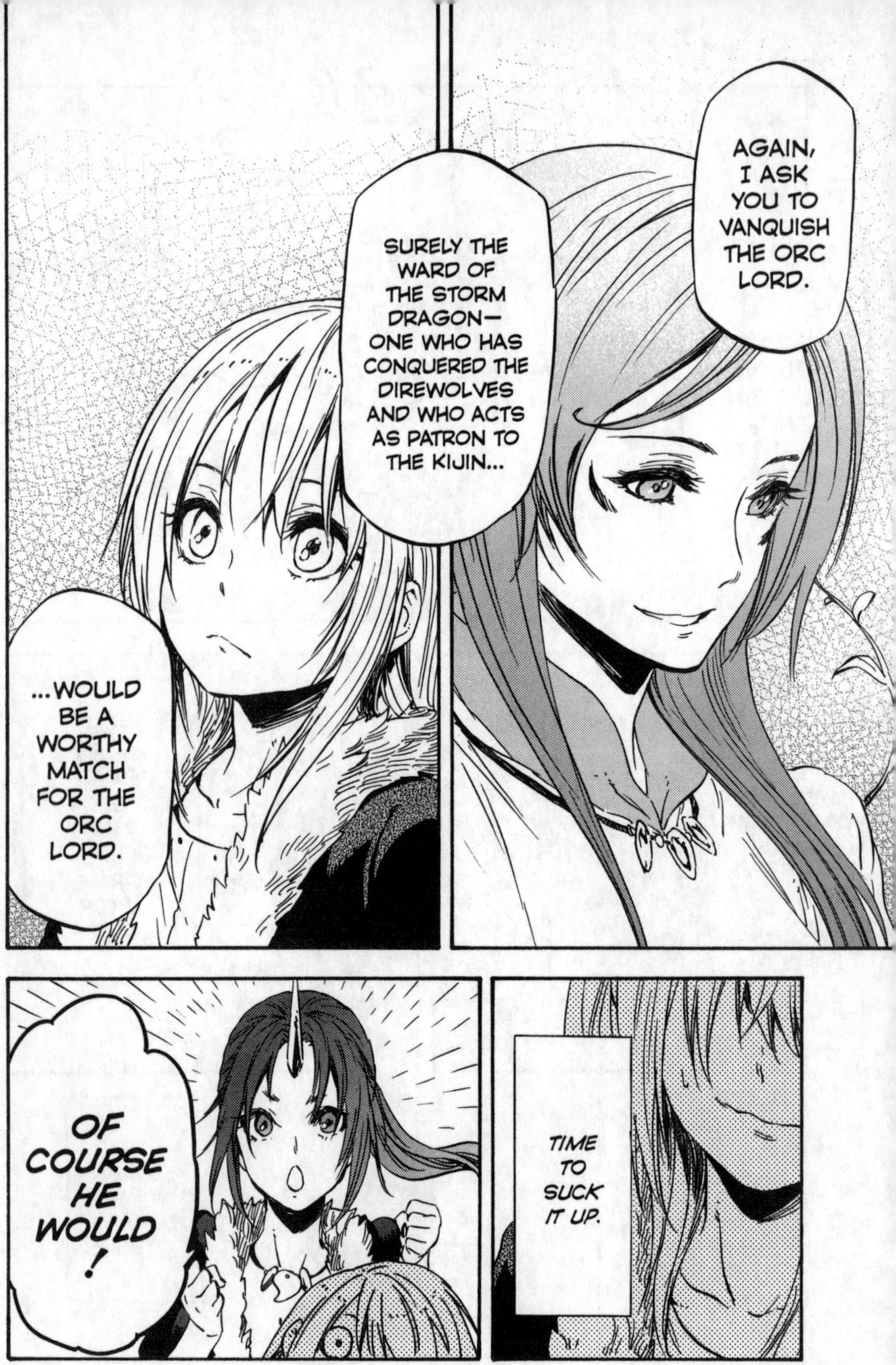
AGAIN, I ASK YOU TO VANQUISH THE ORC LORD.
SURELY THE WARD OF THE STORM DRAGON— ONE WHO HAS CONQUERED THE DIREWOLVES AND WHO ACTS AS PATRON TO THE KIJIN...
...WOULD BE A WORTHY MATCH FOR THE ORC LORD.
TIME TO SUCK IT UP.
OF COURSE HE WOULD!

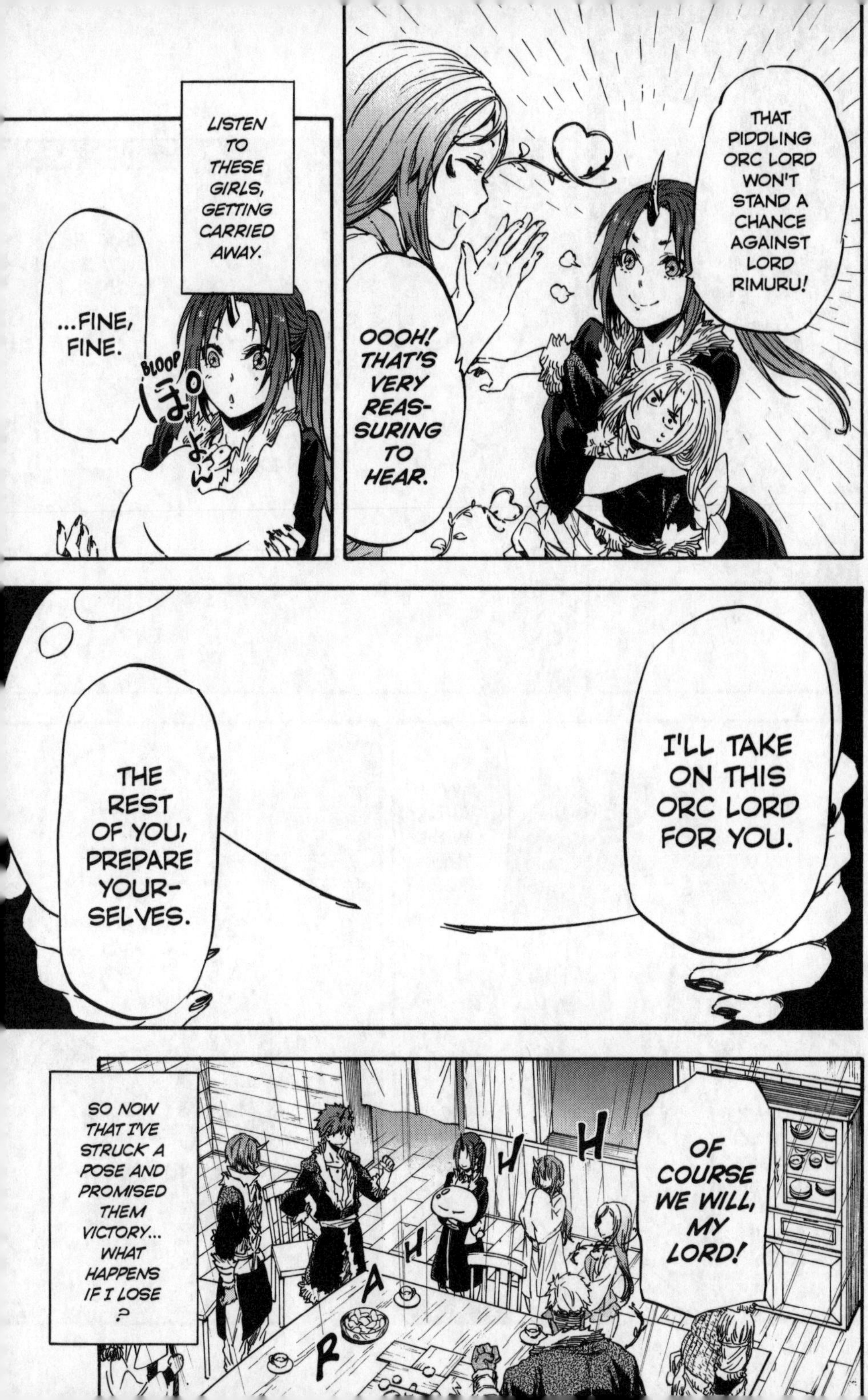
THAT PIDDLING ORC LORD WON'T STAND A CHANCE AGAINST LORD RIMURU!
OOOH! THAT'S VERY REAS-SURING TO HEAR.
LISTEN TO THESE GIRLS, GETTING CARRIED AWAY.
...FINE, FINE.
BLOOP
ぽよん
I'LL TAKE ON THIS ORC LORD FOR YOU.
THE REST OF YOU, PREPARE YOUR-SELVES.
OF COURSE WE WILL, MY LORD!
RAHHH
SO NOW THAT I'VE STRUCK A POSE AND PROMISED THEM VICTORY... WHAT HAPPENS IF I LOSE?

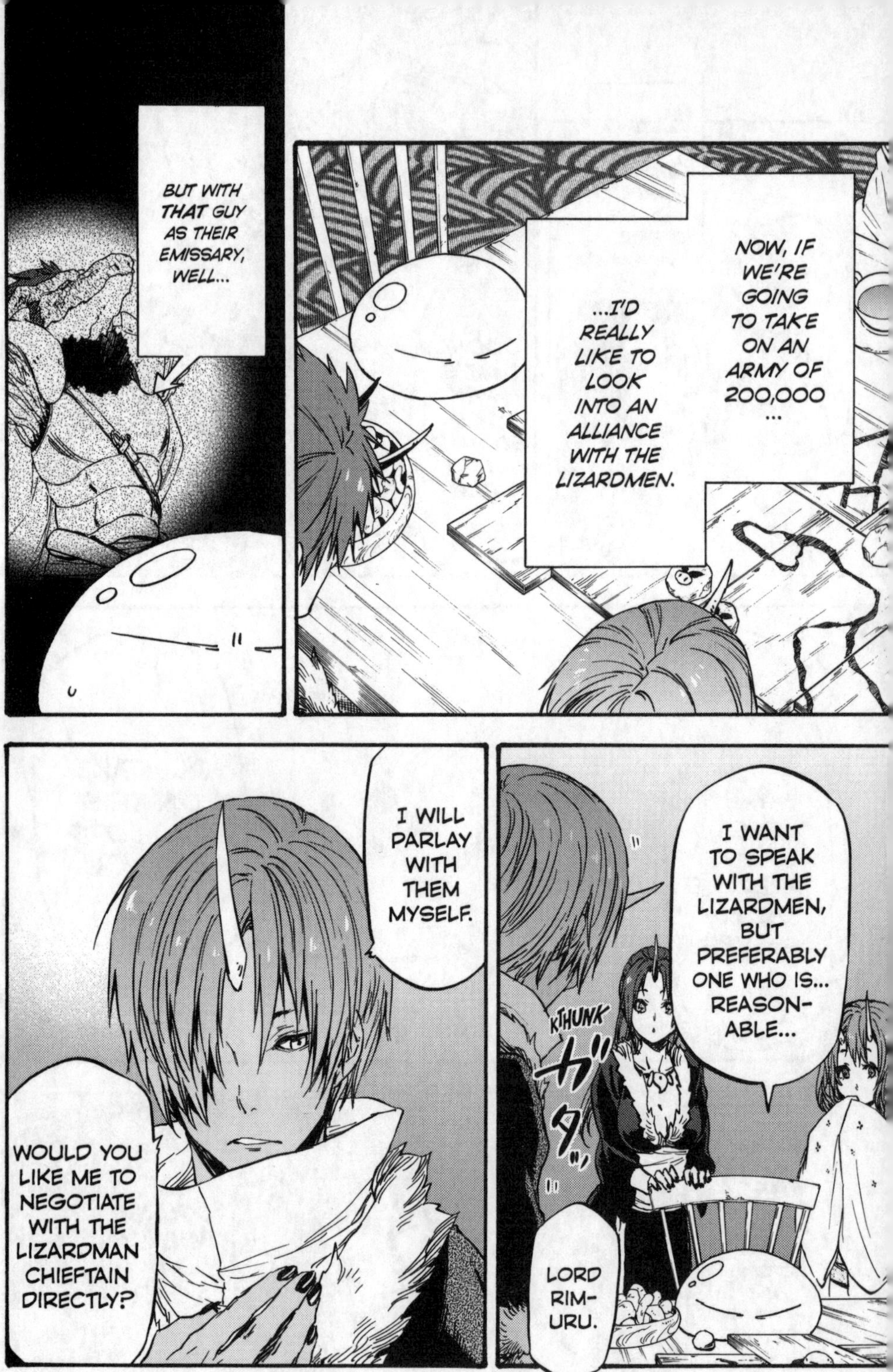
NOW, IF WE'RE GOING TO TAKE ON AN ARMY OF 200,000 ...
...I'D REALLY LIKE TO LOOK INTO AN ALLIANCE WITH THE LIZARDMEN.
BUT WITH THAT GUY AS THEIR EMISSARY, WELL...
I WANT TO SPEAK WITH THE LIZARDMEN, BUT PREFERABLY ONE WHO IS... REASONABLE...
KTHUNK
LORD RIMURU.
I WILL PARLAY WITH THEM MYSELF.
WOULD YOU LIKE ME TO NEGOTIATE WITH THE LIZARDMAN CHIEFTAIN DIRECTLY?

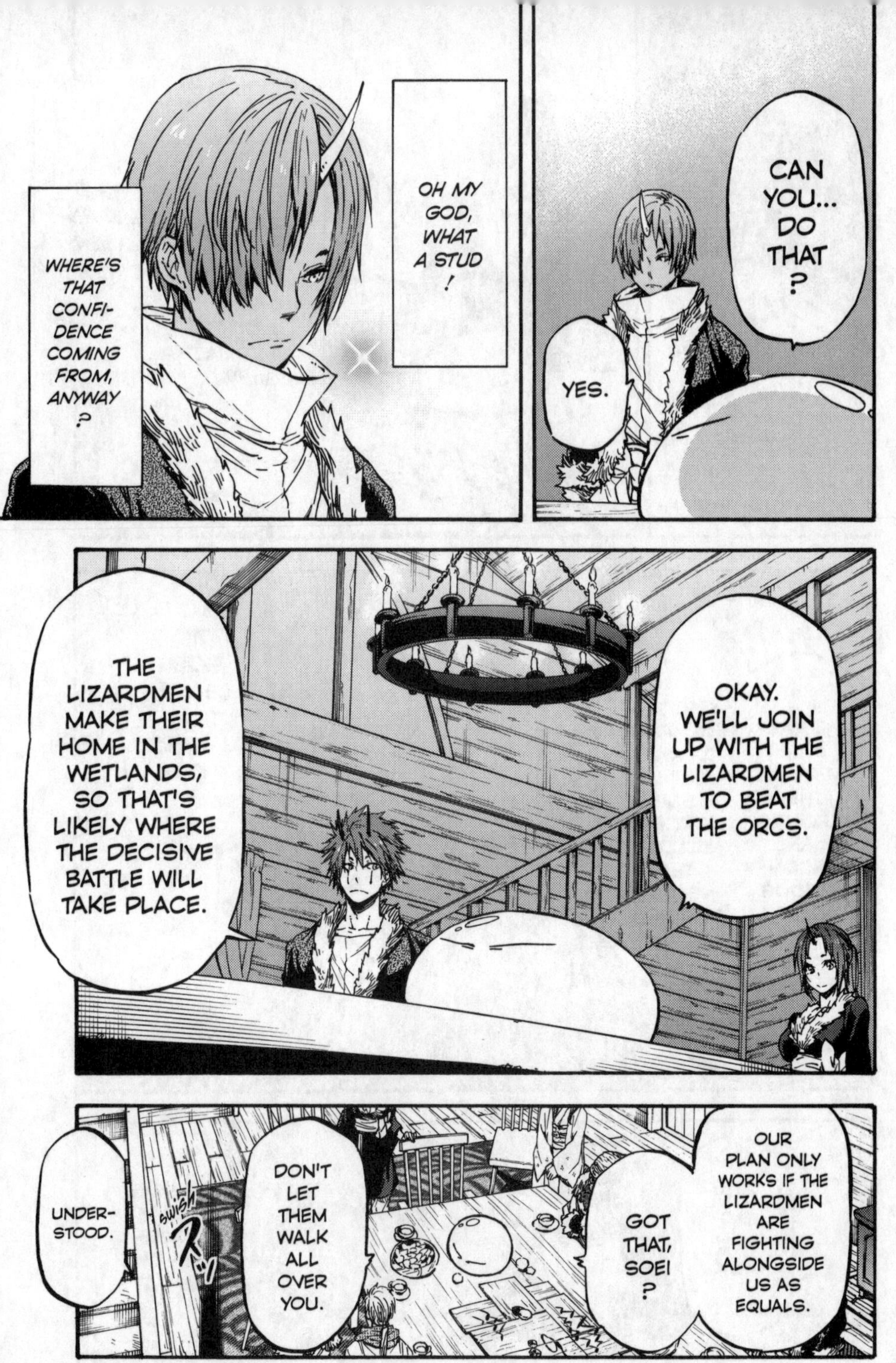
CAN YOU... DO THAT?
YES.
OH MY GOD, WHAT A STUD!
WHERE'S THAT CONFIDENCE COMING FROM, ANYWAY?
OKAY. WE'LL JOIN UP WITH THE LIZARDMEN TO BEAT THE ORCS.
THE LIZARDMEN MAKE THEIR HOME IN THE WETLANDS, SO THAT'S LIKELY WHERE THE DECISIVE BATTLE WILL TAKE PLACE.
OUR PLAN ONLY WORKS IF THE LIZARDMEN ARE FIGHTING ALONGSIDE US AS EQUALS.
GOT THAT, SOEI?
DON'T LET THEM WALK ALL OVER YOU.
SWISH
UNDERSTOOD.

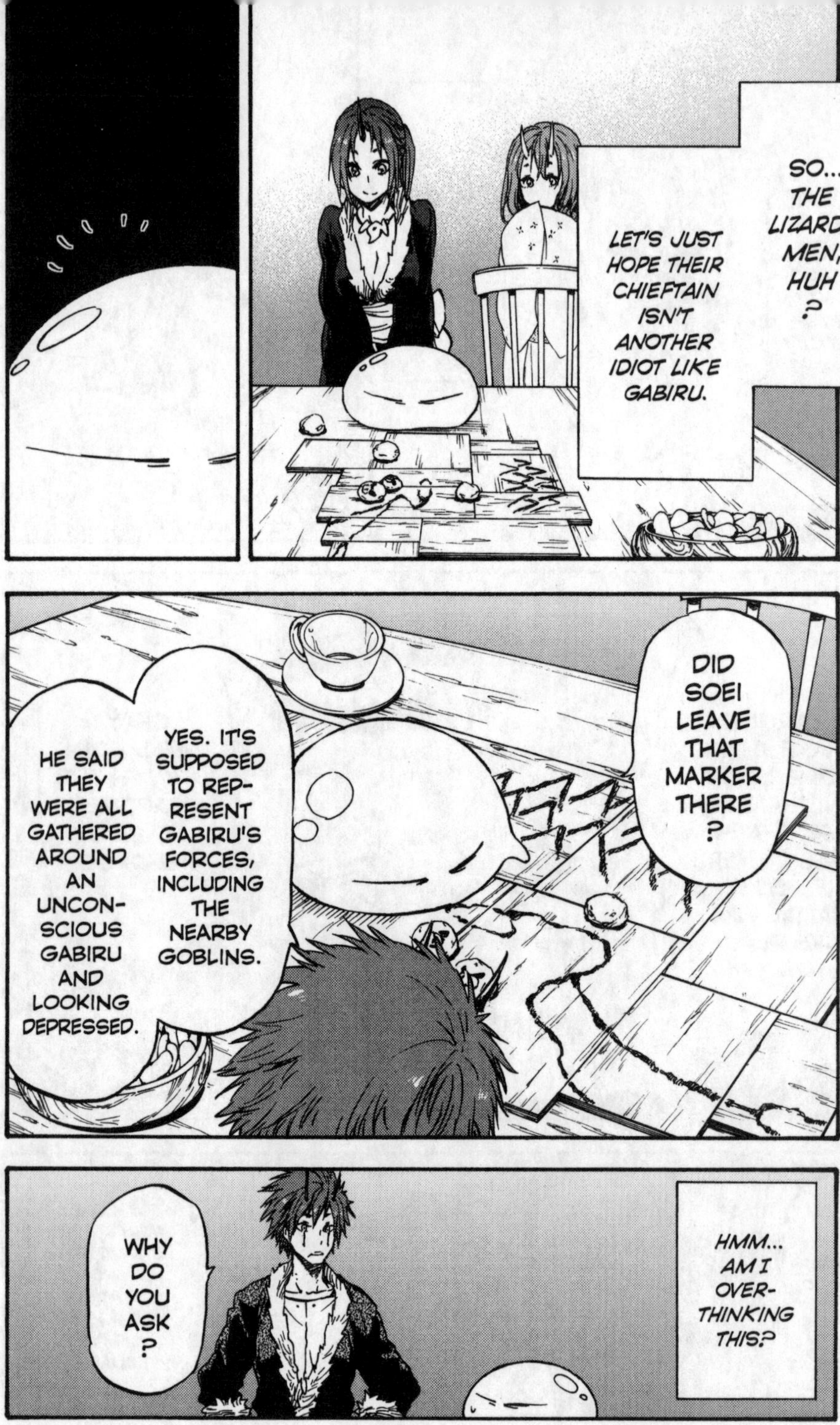
SO... THE LIZARD-MEN, HUH?
LET'S JUST HOPE THEIR CHIEFTAIN ISN'T ANOTHER IDIOT LIKE GABIRU.
DID SOEI LEAVE THAT MARKER THERE?
YES. IT'S SUPPOSED TO REP-RESENT GABIRU'S FORCES, INCLUDING THE NEARBY GOBLINS.
HE SAID THEY WERE ALL GATHERED AROUND AN UNCON-SCIOUS GABIRU AND LOOKING DEPRESSED.
HMM... AM I OVER-THINKING THIS?
WHY DO YOU ASK?

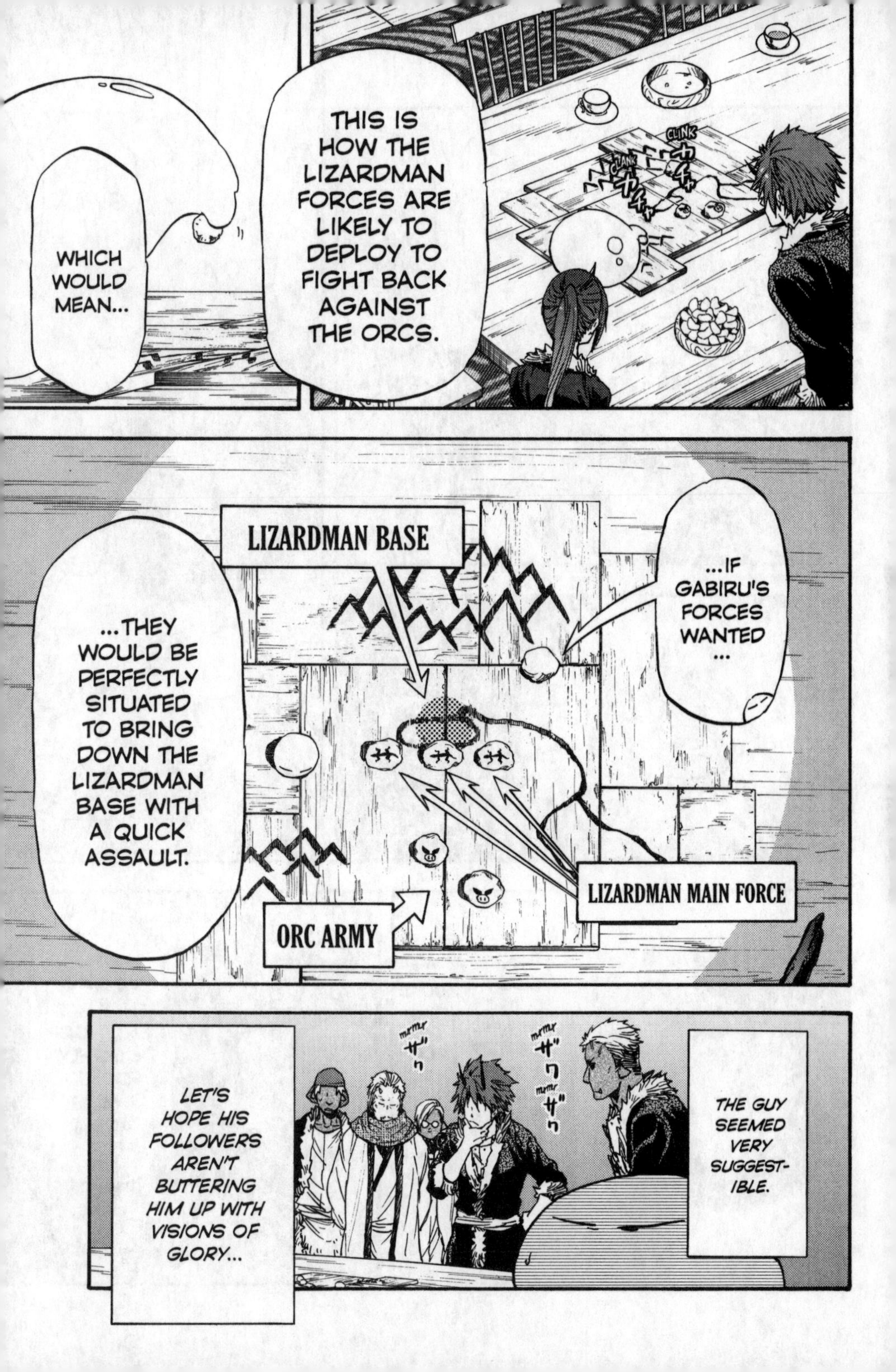

CLINK
CLANK
THIS IS HOW THE LIZARDMAN FORCES ARE LIKELY TO DEPLOY TO FIGHT BACK AGAINST THE ORCS.
WHICH WOULD MEAN...
...IF GABIRU'S FORCES WANTED ...
LIZARDMAN BASE
LIZARDMAN MAIN FORCE
ORC ARMY
...THEY WOULD BE PERFECTLY SITUATED TO BRING DOWN THE LIZARDMAN BASE WITH A QUICK ASSAULT.
THE GUY SEEMED VERY SUGGEST-IBLE.
mrmr
mrmr
mrmr
LET'S HOPE HIS FOLLOWERS AREN'T BUTTERING HIM UP WITH VISIONS OF GLORY...

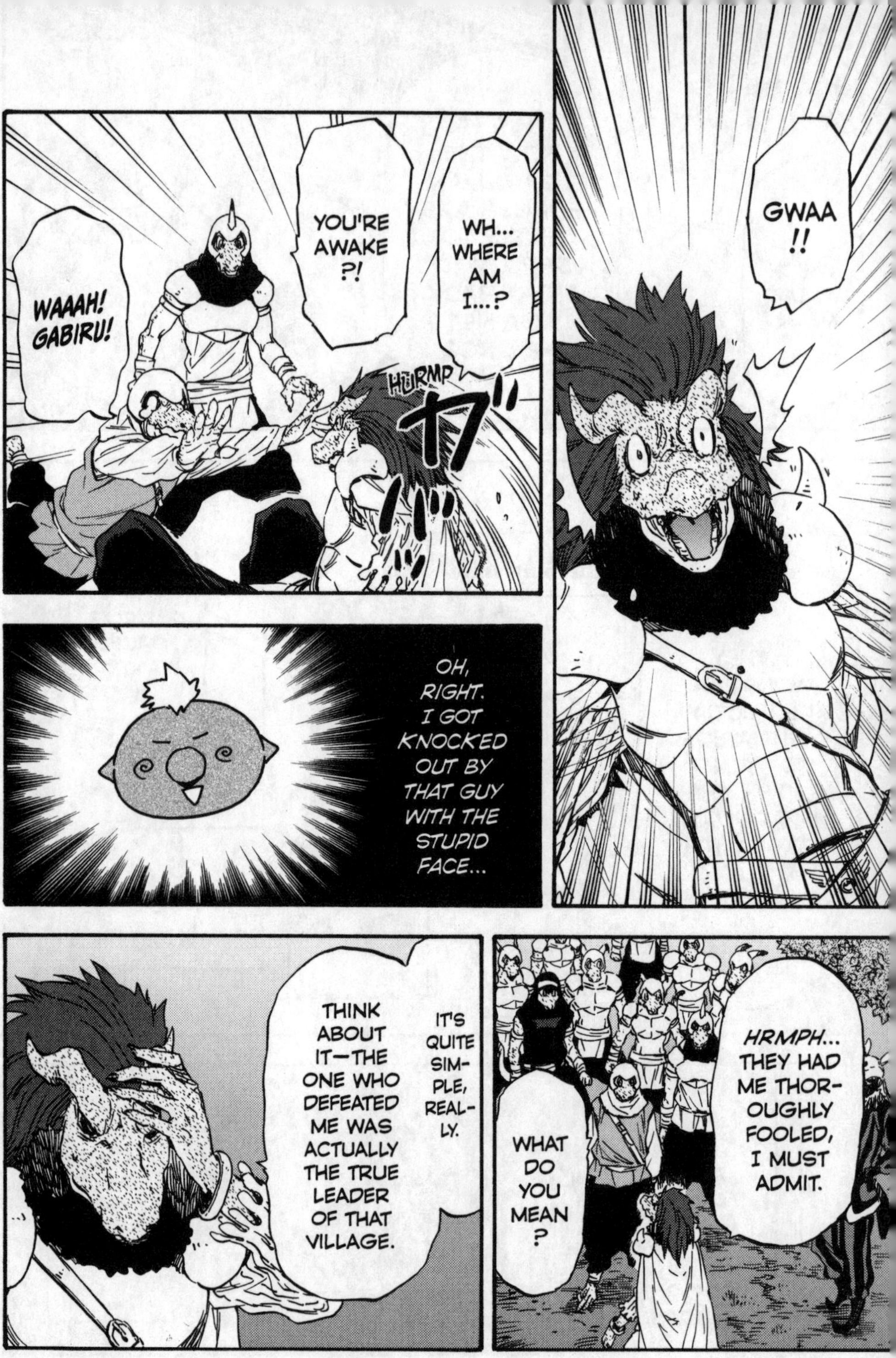
GWAA!!
WH... WHERE AM I...?
YOU'RE AWAKE?!
WAAAH! GABIRU!
HURMP
OH, RIGHT. I GOT KNOCKED OUT BY THAT GUY WITH THE STUPID FACE...
HRMPH... THEY HAD ME THOROUGHLY FOOLED, I MUST ADMIT.
WHAT DO YOU MEAN?
IT'S QUITE SIMPLE, REALLY.
THINK ABOUT IT—THE ONE WHO DEFEATED ME WAS ACTUALLY THE TRUE LEADER OF THAT VILLAGE.

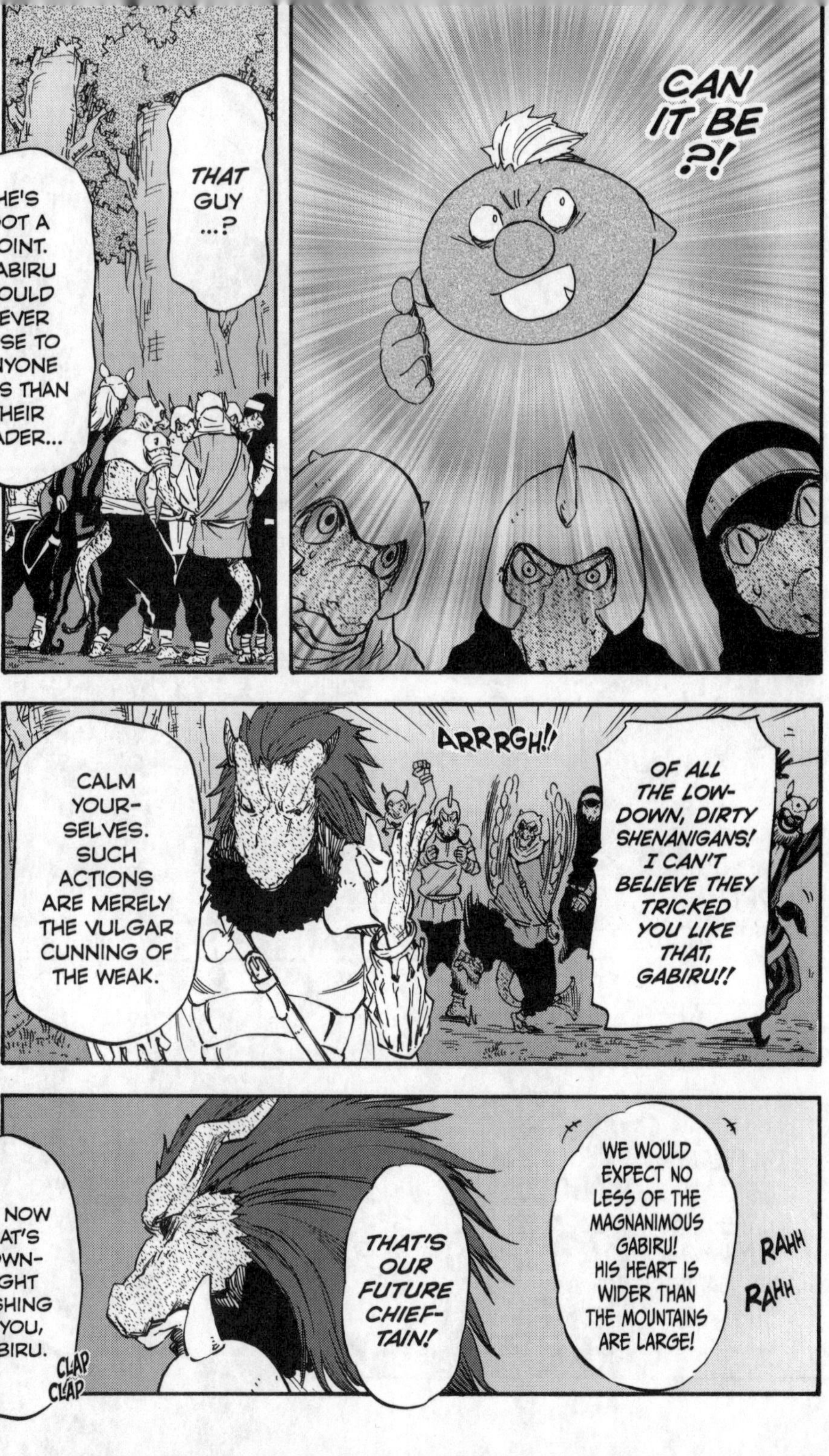
CAN IT BE ?!
THAT GUY ...?
HE'S GOT A POINT. GABIRU WOULD NEVER LOSE TO ANYONE LESS THAN THEIR LEADER...
OF ALL THE LOW-DOWN, DIRTY SHENANIGANS! I CAN'T BELIEVE THEY TRICKED YOU LIKE THAT, GABIRU!!
ARRRGH!!
CALM YOUR-SELVES. SUCH ACTIONS ARE MERELY THE VULGAR CUNNING OF THE WEAK.
RAHH RAHH
WE WOULD EXPECT NO LESS OF THE MAGNANIMOUS GABIRU! HIS HEART IS WIDER THAN THE MOUNTAINS ARE LARGE!
THAT'S OUR FUTURE CHIEF-TAIN!
MY, NOW THAT'S DOWN-RIGHT DASHING O' YOU, GABIRU.
CLAP CLAP

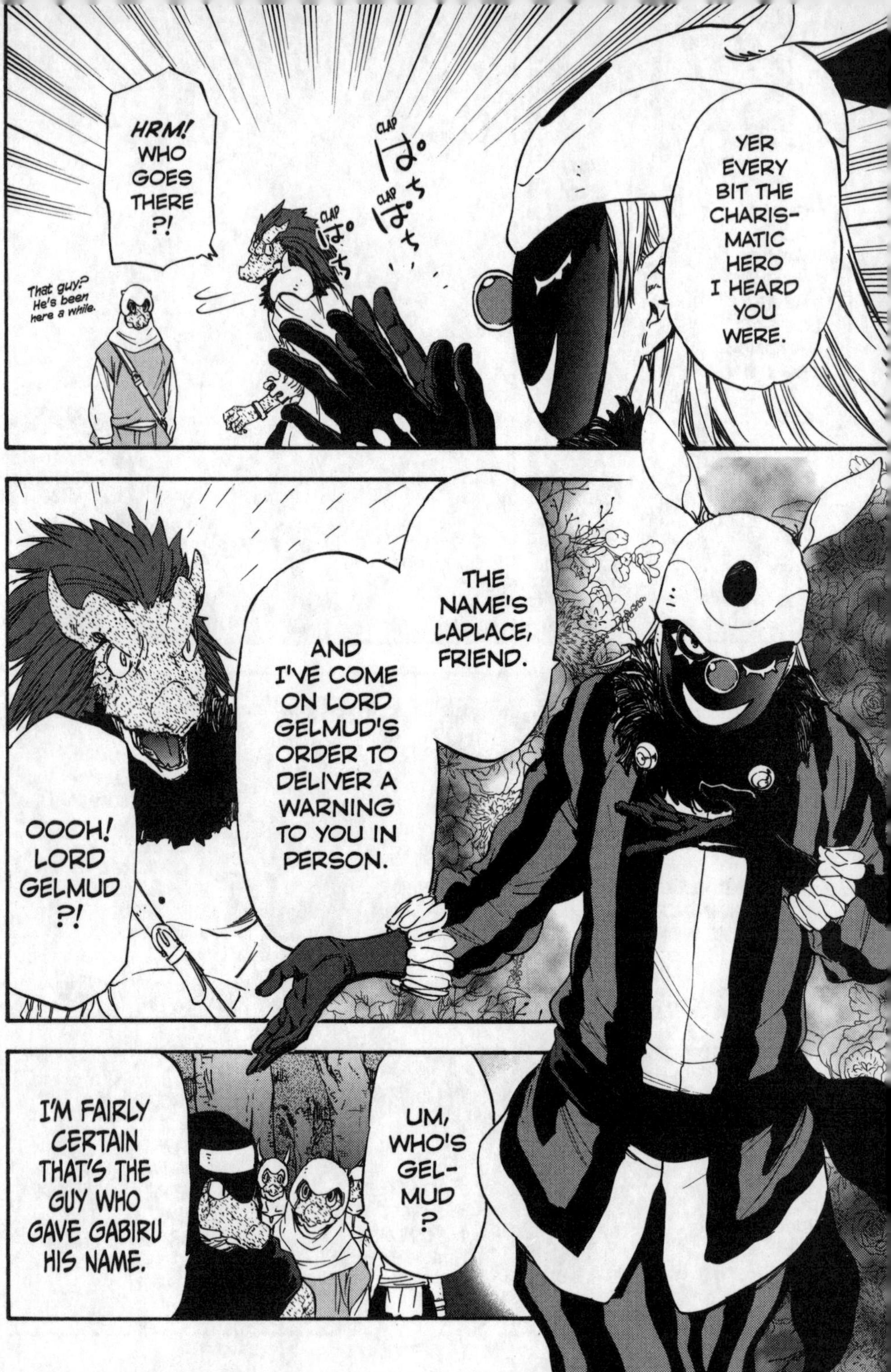
YER EVERY BIT THE CHARIS-MATIC HERO I HEARD YOU WERE.
CLAP ぱち
CLAP ぱち
CLAP ぱち
HRM! WHO GOES THERE?!
That guy? He's been here a while.
THE NAME'S LAPLACE, FRIEND.
AND I'VE COME ON LORD GELMUD'S ORDER TO DELIVER A WARNING TO YOU IN PERSON.
OOOH! LORD GELMUD?!
UM, WHO'S GEL-MUD?
I'M FAIRLY CERTAIN THAT'S THE GUY WHO GAVE GABIRU HIS NAME.

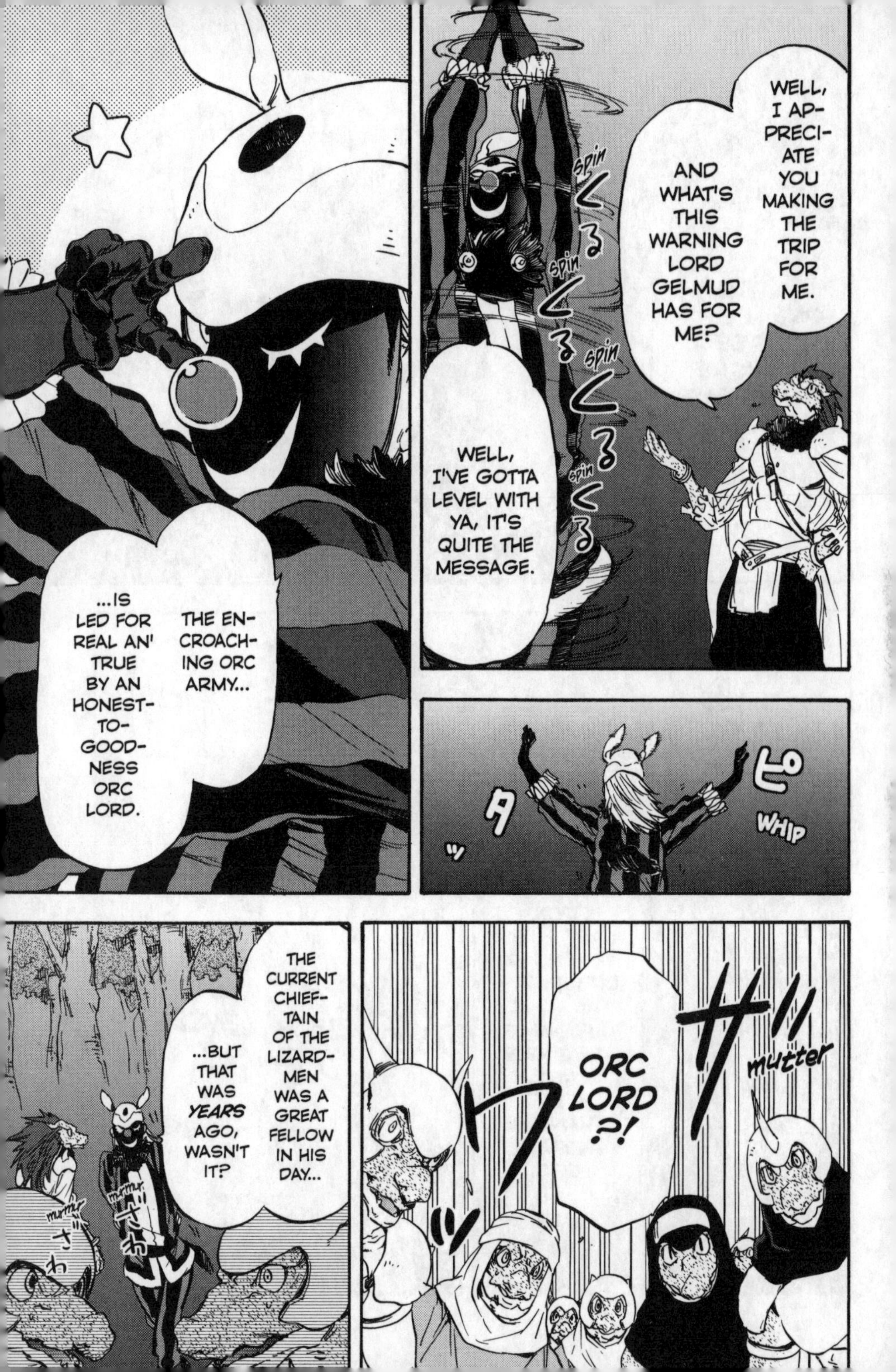

WELL, I APPRECIATE YOU MAKING THE TRIP FOR ME.
AND WHAT'S THIS WARNING LORD GELMUD HAS FOR ME?
spin spin spin spin
WELL, I'VE GOTTA LEVEL WITH YA, IT'S QUITE THE MESSAGE.
WHIP
THE ENCROACHING ORC ARMY...
...IS LED FOR REAL AN' TRUE BY AN HONEST-TO-GOODNESS ORC LORD.
mutter
ORC LORD?!
THE CURRENT CHIEFTAIN OF THE LIZARDMEN WAS A GREAT FELLOW IN HIS DAY...
...BUT THAT WAS YEARS AGO, WASN'T IT?
murmur murmur

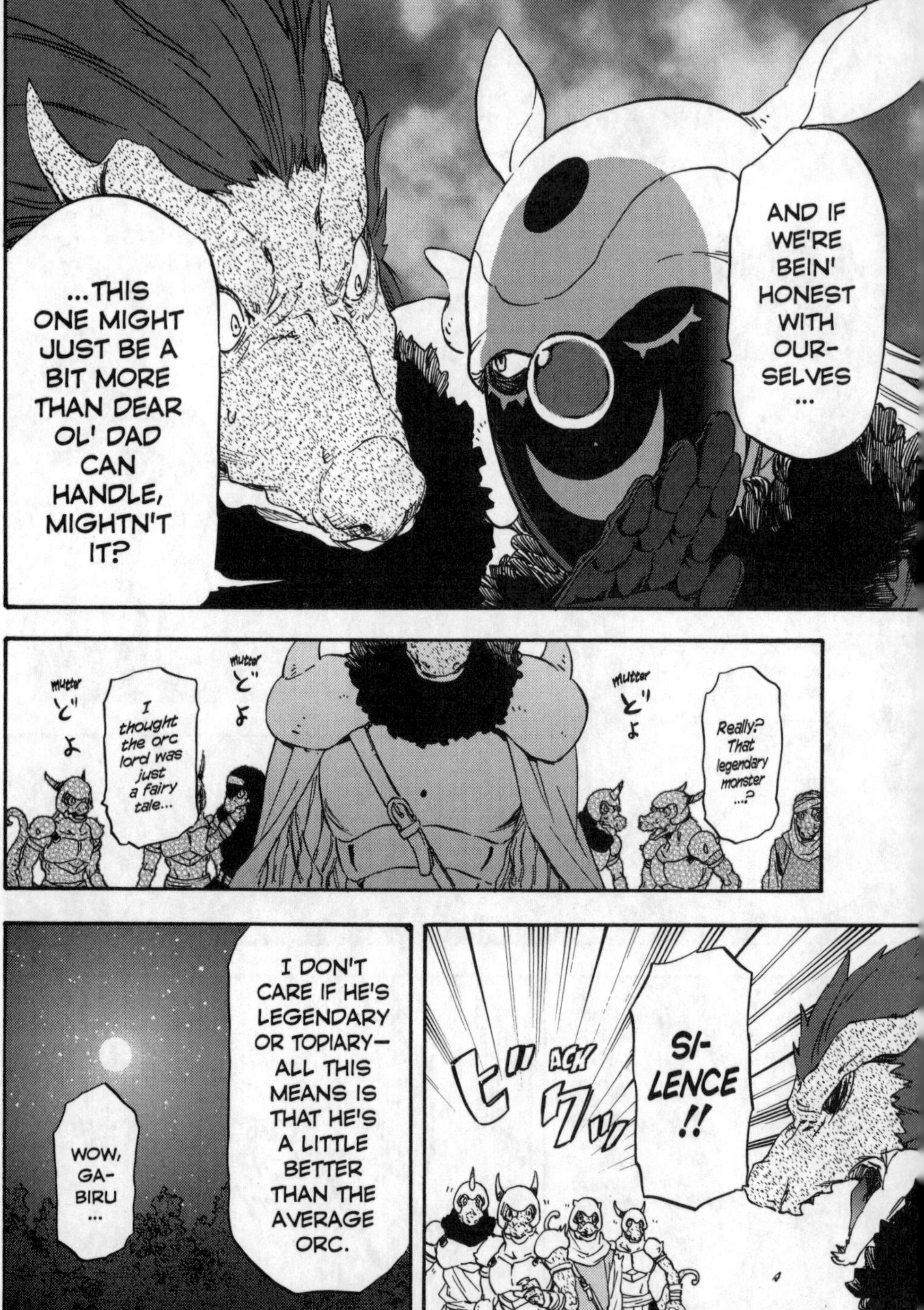
AND IF WE'RE BEIN' HONEST WITH OUR-SELVES...
...THIS ONE MIGHT JUST BE A BIT MORE THAN DEAR OL' DAD CAN HANDLE, MIGHTN'T IT?
mutter どよ
Really? That legendary monster...?
mutter どよ
mutter どよ
I thought the orc lord was just a fairy tale...
SI-LENCE!!
ACK
I DON'T CARE IF HE'S LEGENDARY OR TOPIARY—ALL THIS MEANS IS THAT HE'S A LITTLE BETTER THAN THE AVERAGE ORC.
WOW, GA-BIRU...

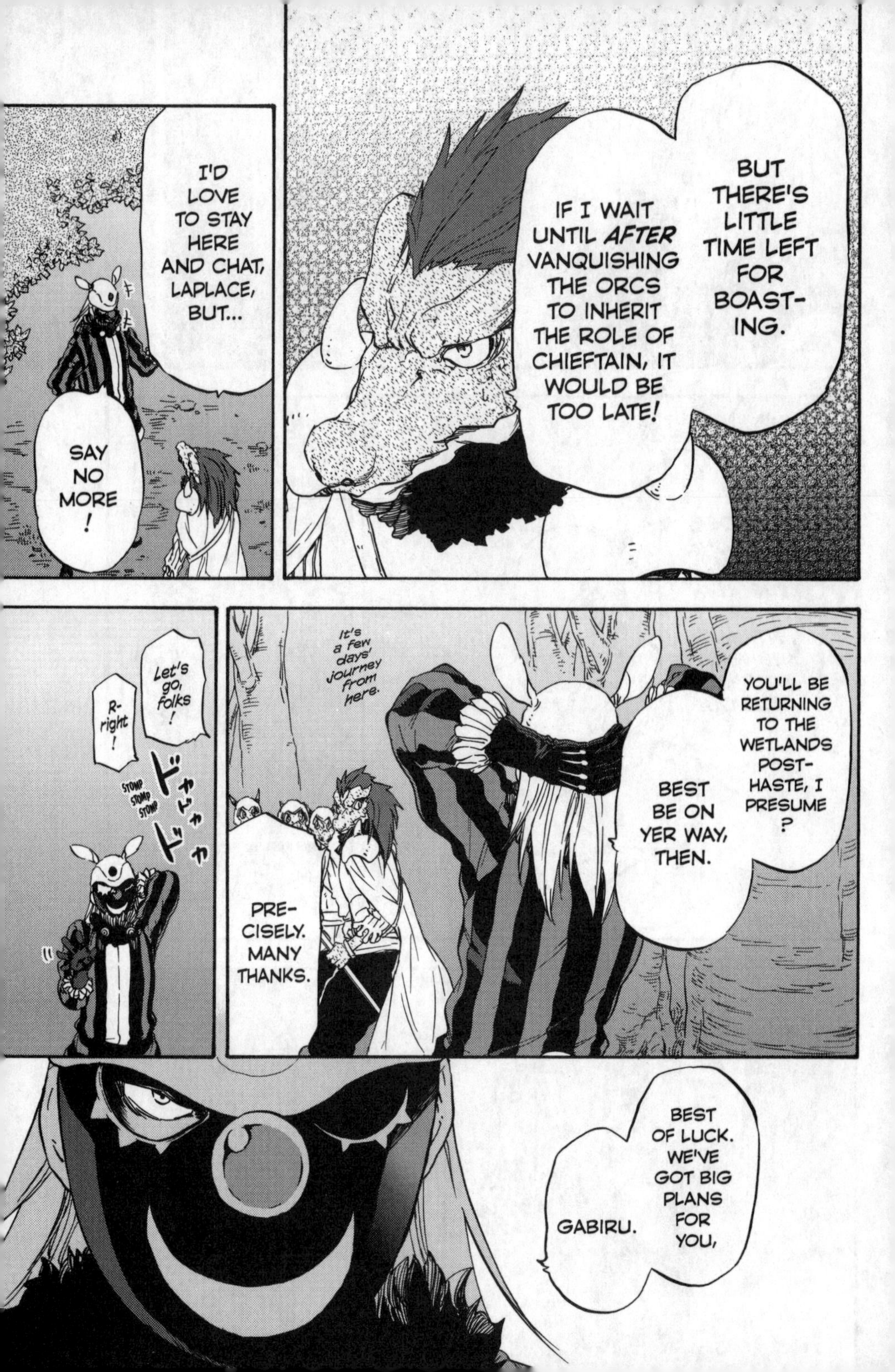
BUT THERE'S LITTLE TIME LEFT FOR BOASTING.
IF I WAIT UNTIL *AFTER* VANQUISHING THE ORCS TO INHERIT THE ROLE OF CHIEFTAIN, IT WOULD BE TOO LATE!
I'D LOVE TO STAY HERE AND CHAT, LAPLACE, BUT...
SAY NO MORE!
YOU'LL BE RETURNING TO THE WETLANDS POST-HASTE, I PRESUME?
BEST BE ON YER WAY, THEN.
It's a few days' journey from here.
PRECISELY. MANY THANKS.
Let's go, folks!
R-right!
STOMP STOMP STOMP
BEST OF LUCK. WE'VE GOT BIG PLANS FOR YOU,
GABIRU.

CHIEF... CHIEF!

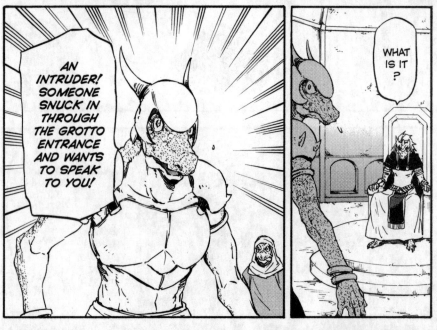

AN INTRUDER! SOMEONE SNUCK IN THROUGH THE GROTTO ENTRANCE AND WANTS TO SPEAK TO YOU!

WHAT IS IT?

UH, WHAT?!

VERY WELL. BRING THEM IN.

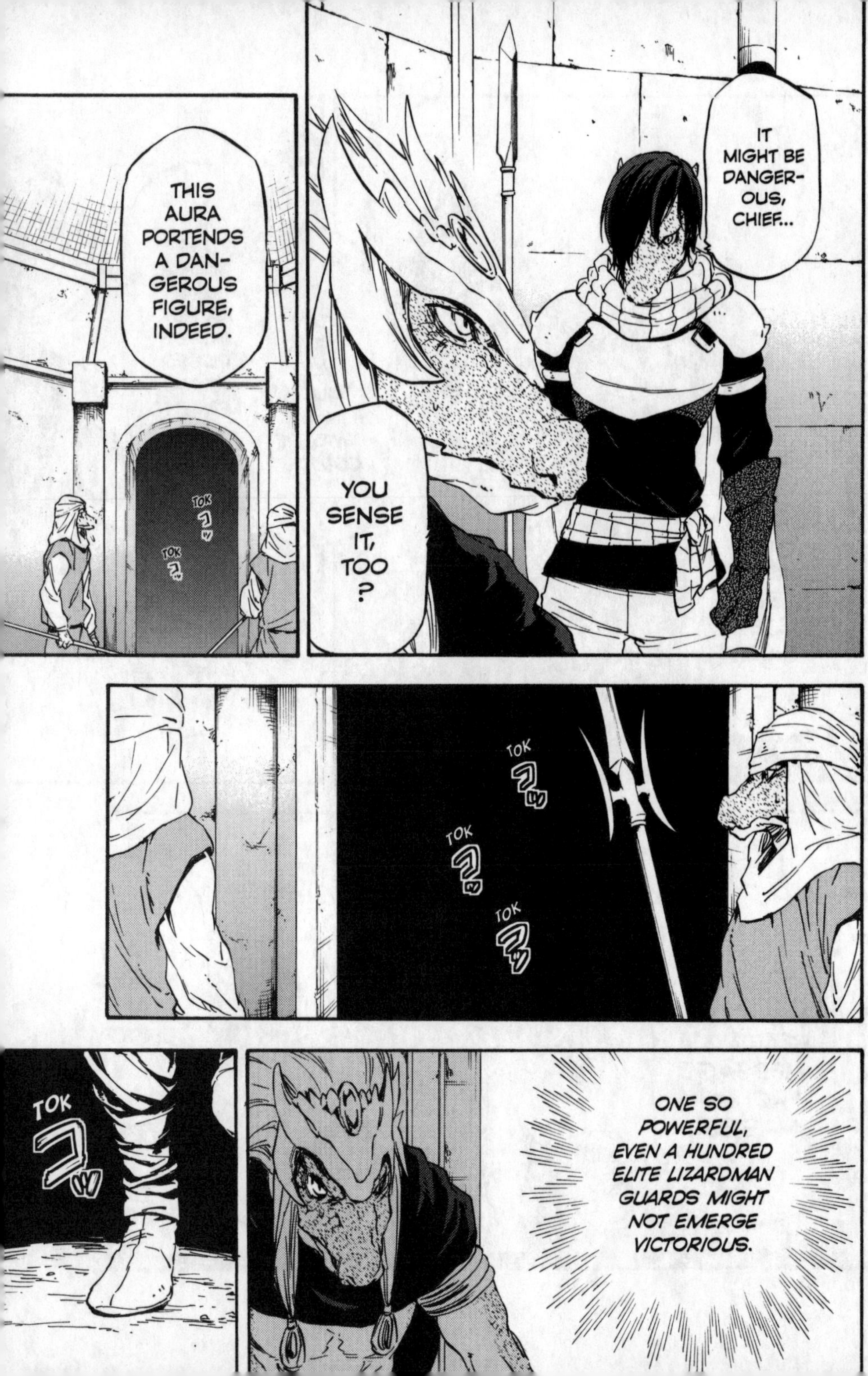
IT MIGHT BE DANGER-OUS, CHIEF...
YOU SENSE IT, TOO ?
THIS AURA PORTENDS A DAN-GEROUS FIGURE, INDEED.
TOK
TOK
TOK
TOK
TOK
ONE SO POWERFUL, EVEN A HUNDRED ELITE LIZARDMAN GUARDS MIGHT NOT EMERGE VICTORIOUS.
TOK

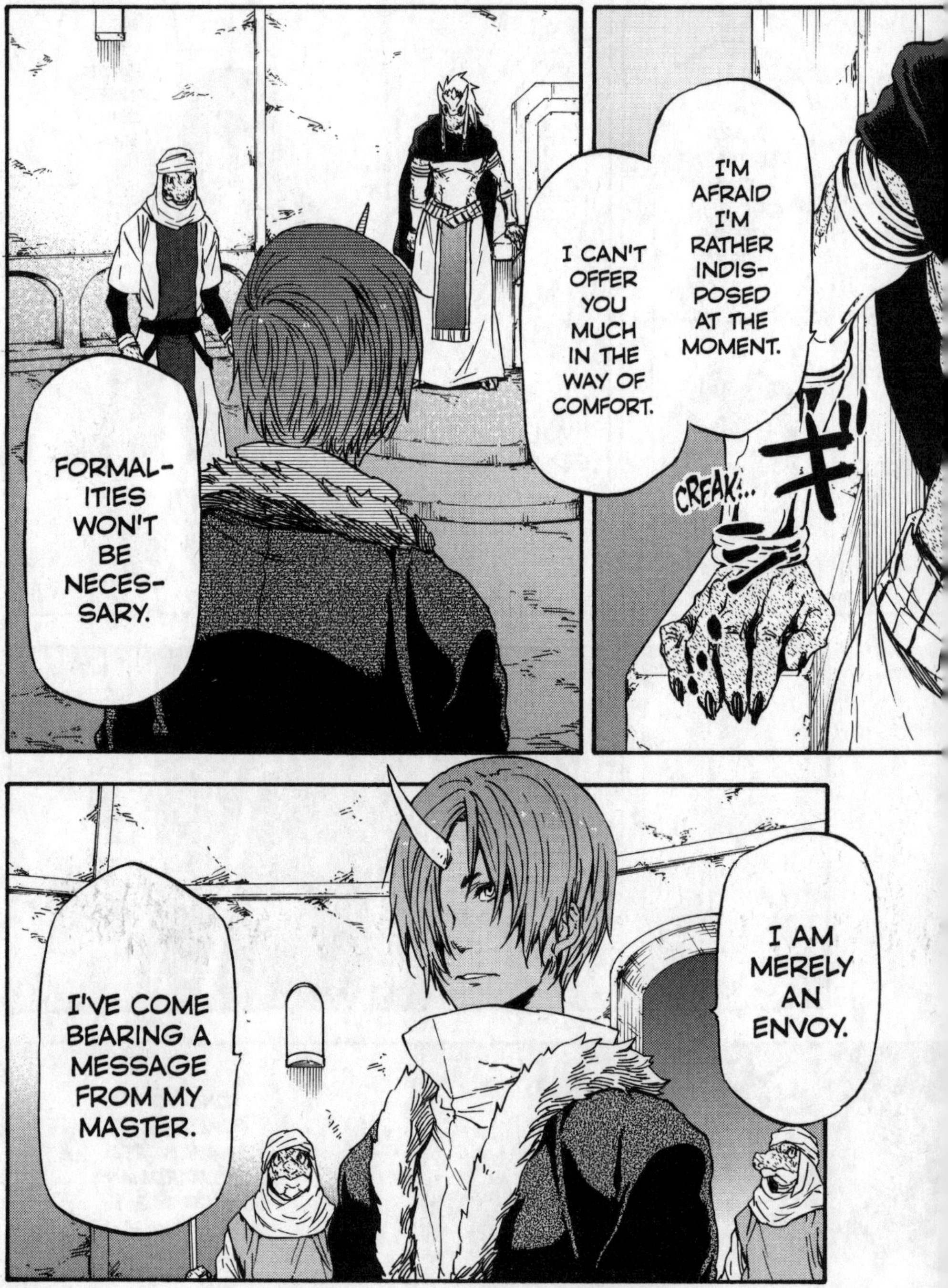
I'M AFRAID I'M RATHER INDIS-POSED AT THE MOMENT.
I CAN'T OFFER YOU MUCH IN THE WAY OF COMFORT.
CREAK...
FORMAL-ITIES WON'T BE NECES-SARY.
I AM MERELY AN ENVOY.
I'VE COME BEARING A MESSAGE FROM MY MASTER.

Imitation potato chips.
Lightly salted.

Oooh!

I could really go for some seaweed-sprinkled and consommé flavored chips next.

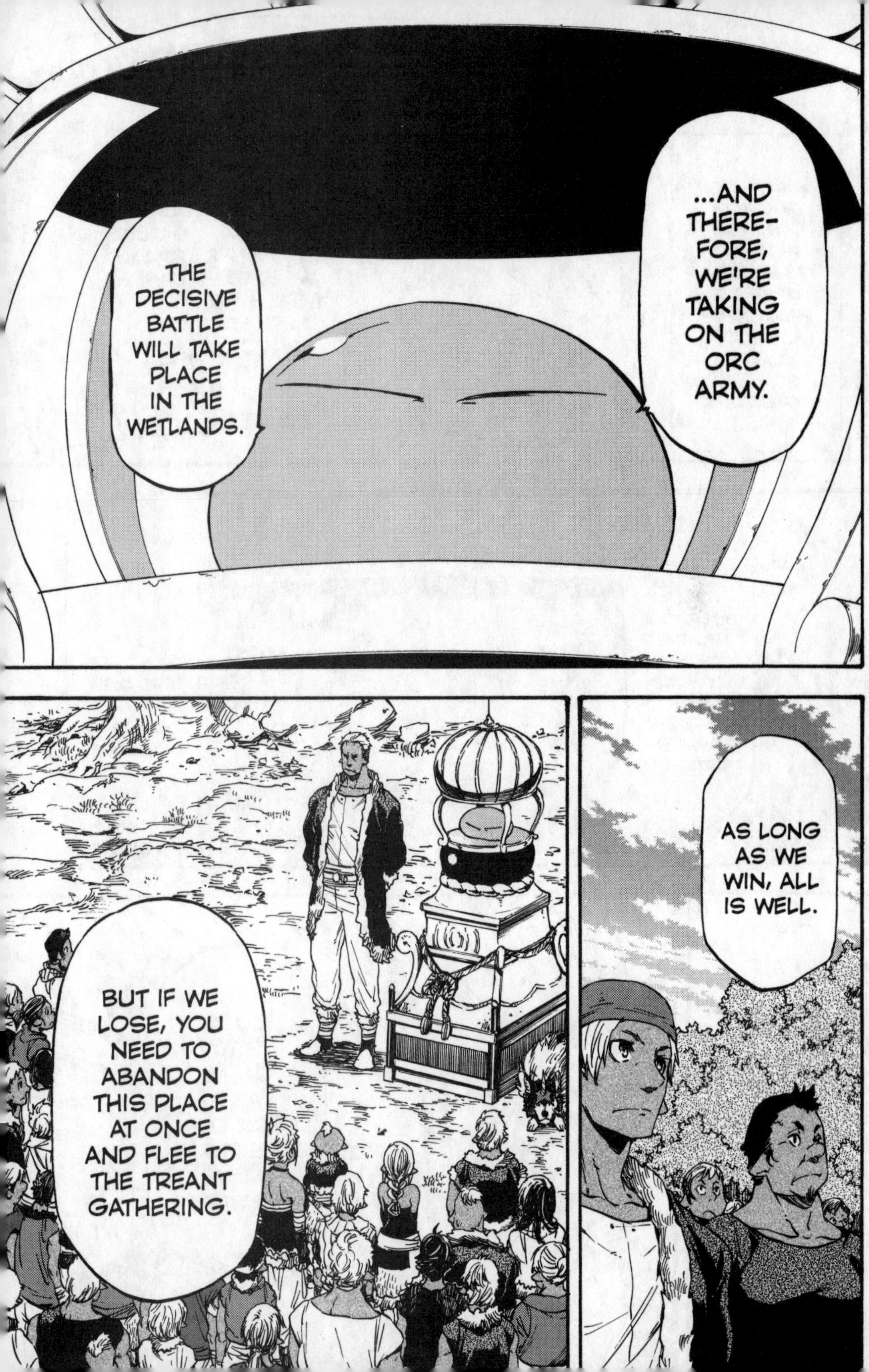
...AND THERE-FORE, WE'RE TAKING ON THE ORC ARMY.
THE DECISIVE BATTLE WILL TAKE PLACE IN THE WETLANDS.
AS LONG AS WE WIN, ALL IS WELL.
BUT IF WE LOSE, YOU NEED TO ABANDON THIS PLACE AT ONCE AND FLEE TO THE TREANT GATHERING.

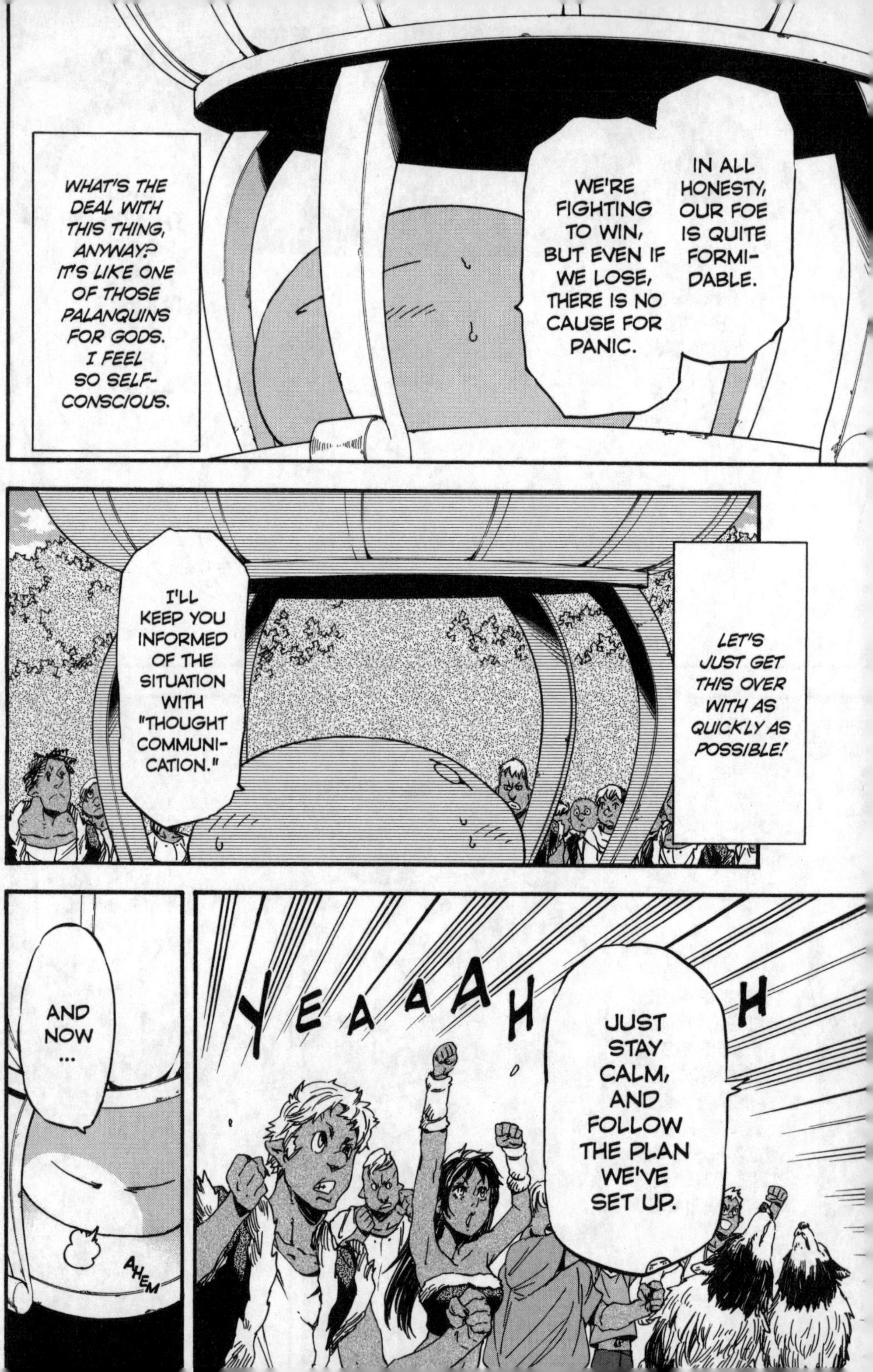
IN ALL HONESTY, OUR FOE IS QUITE FORMIDABLE.
WE'RE FIGHTING TO WIN, BUT EVEN IF WE LOSE, THERE IS NO CAUSE FOR PANIC.
WHAT'S THE DEAL WITH THIS THING, ANYWAY? IT'S LIKE ONE OF THOSE PALANQUINS FOR GODS. I FEEL SO SELF-CONSCIOUS.
LET'S JUST GET THIS OVER WITH AS QUICKLY AS POSSIBLE!
I'LL KEEP YOU INFORMED OF THE SITUATION WITH "THOUGHT COMMUNICATION."
YEAAAAHH
JUST STAY CALM, AND FOLLOW THE PLAN WE'VE SET UP.
AND NOW ...
AHEM

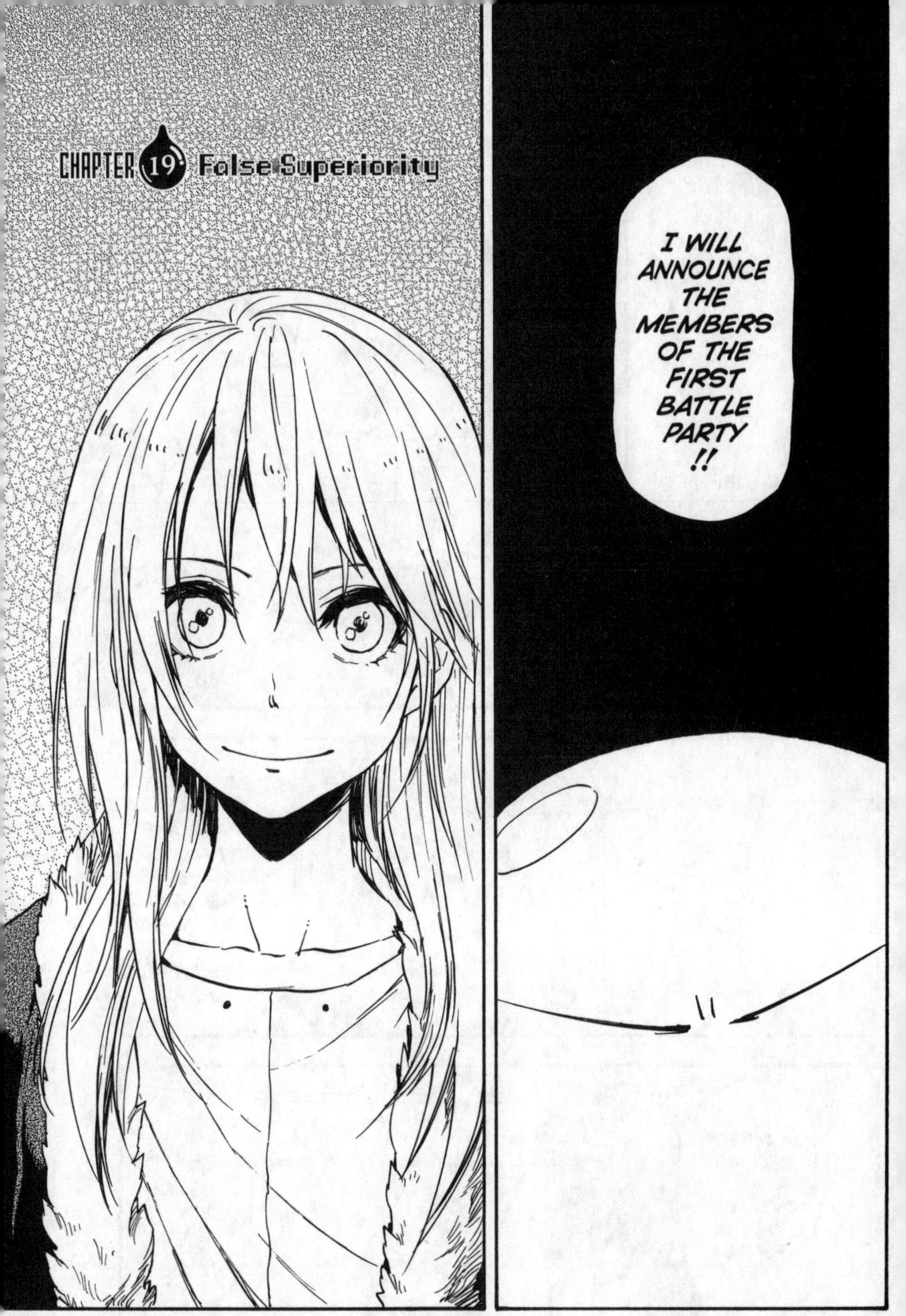
I WILL ANNOUNCE THE MEMBERS OF THE FIRST BATTLE PARTY!!
CHAPTER 19 False Superiority

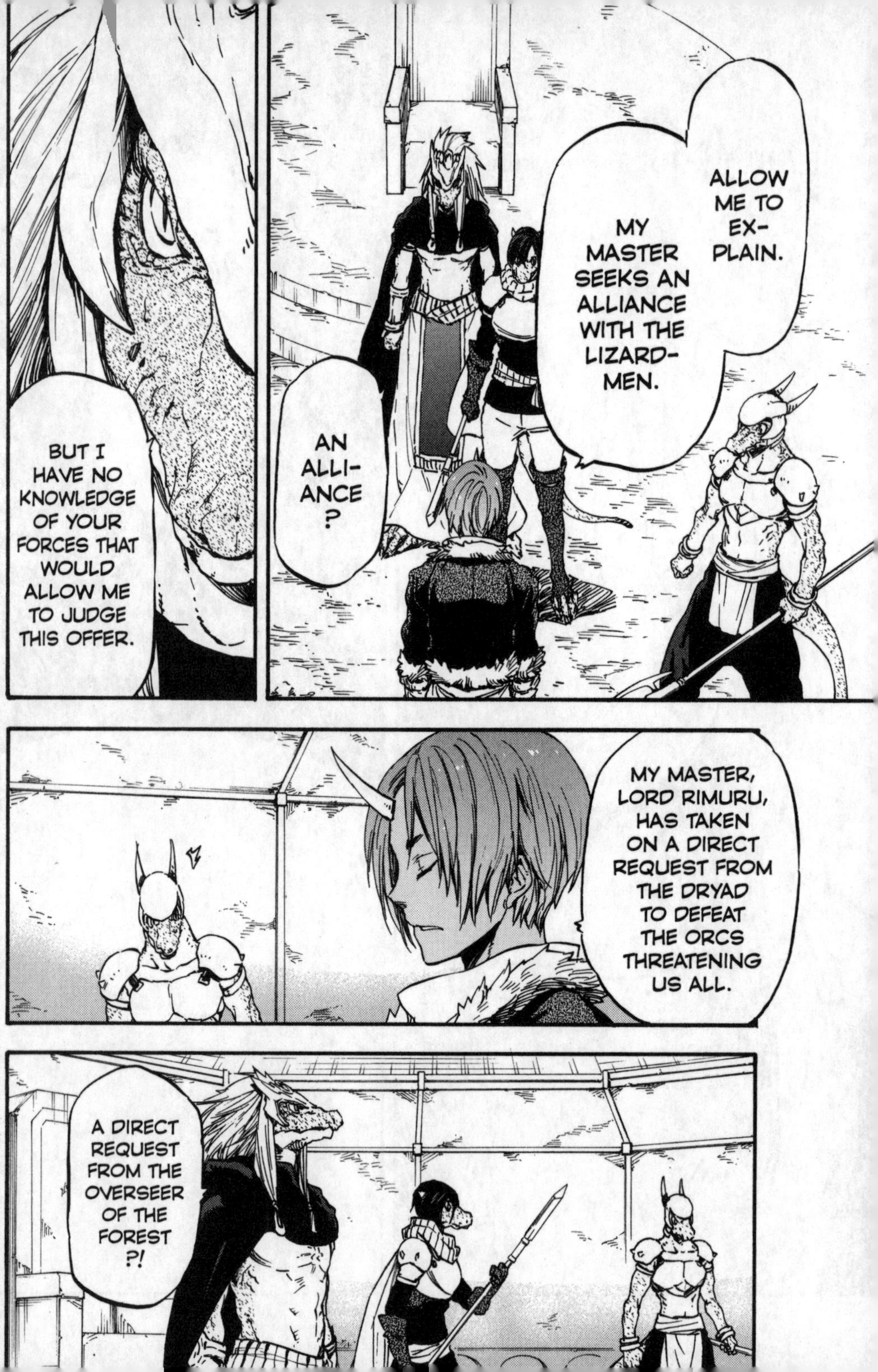
ALLOW ME TO EX-PLAIN.
MY MASTER SEEKS AN ALLIANCE WITH THE LIZARD-MEN.
AN ALLI-ANCE?
BUT I HAVE NO KNOWLEDGE OF YOUR FORCES THAT WOULD ALLOW ME TO JUDGE THIS OFFER.
MY MASTER, LORD RIMURU, HAS TAKEN ON A DIRECT REQUEST FROM THE DRYAD TO DEFEAT THE ORCS THREATENING US ALL.
A DIRECT REQUEST FROM THE OVERSEER OF THE FOREST?!

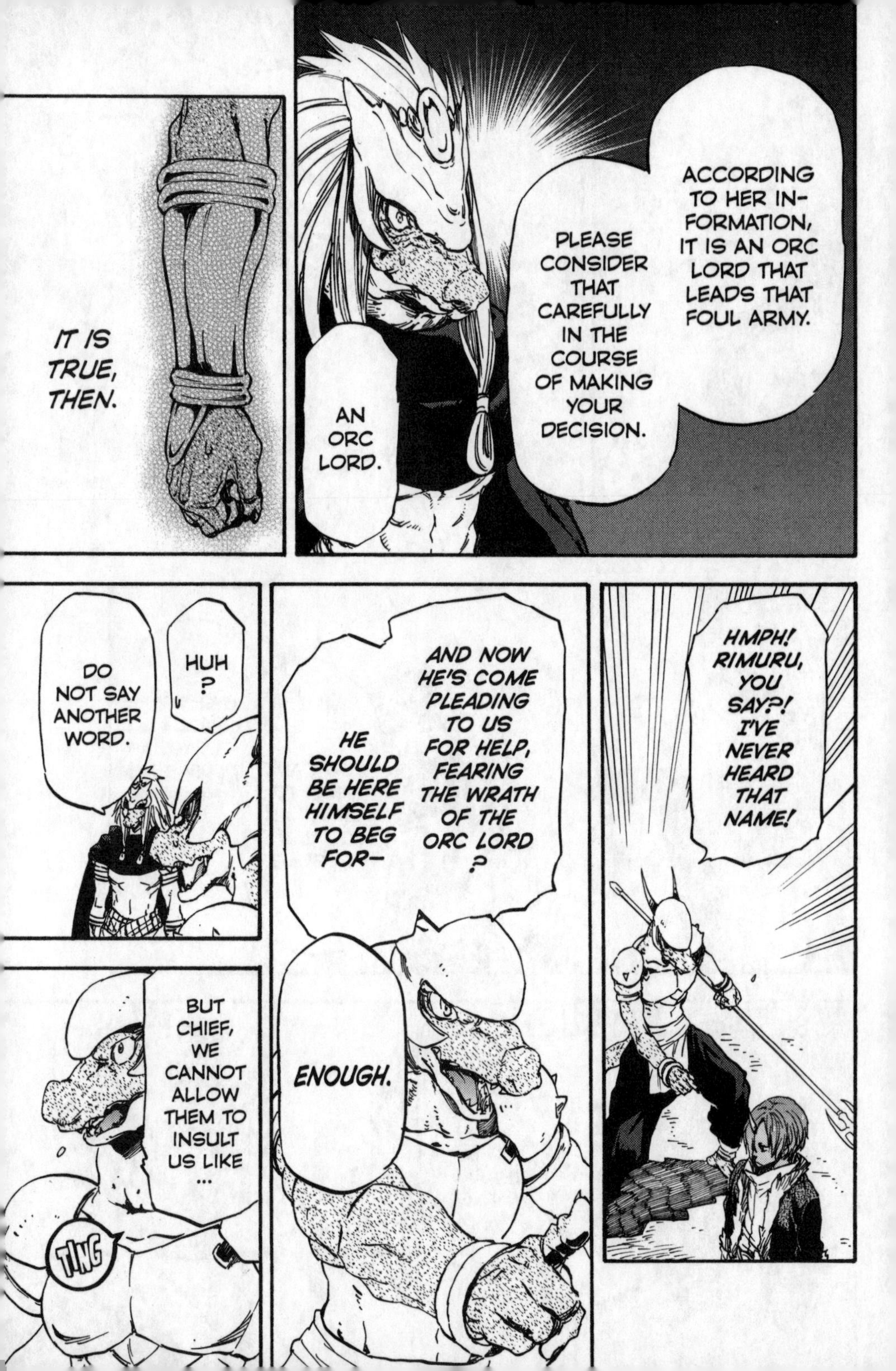
ACCORDING TO HER IN-FORMATION, IT IS AN ORC LORD THAT LEADS THAT FOUL ARMY.
PLEASE CONSIDER THAT CAREFULLY IN THE COURSE OF MAKING YOUR DECISION.
AN ORC LORD.
IT IS TRUE, THEN.
HMPH! RIMURU, YOU SAY?! I'VE NEVER HEARD THAT NAME!
AND NOW HE'S COME PLEADING TO US FOR HELP, FEARING THE WRATH OF THE ORC LORD?
HE SHOULD BE HERE HIMSELF TO BEG FOR—
ENOUGH.
HUH?
DO NOT SAY ANOTHER WORD.
BUT CHIEF, WE CANNOT ALLOW THEM TO INSULT US LIKE ...
TING

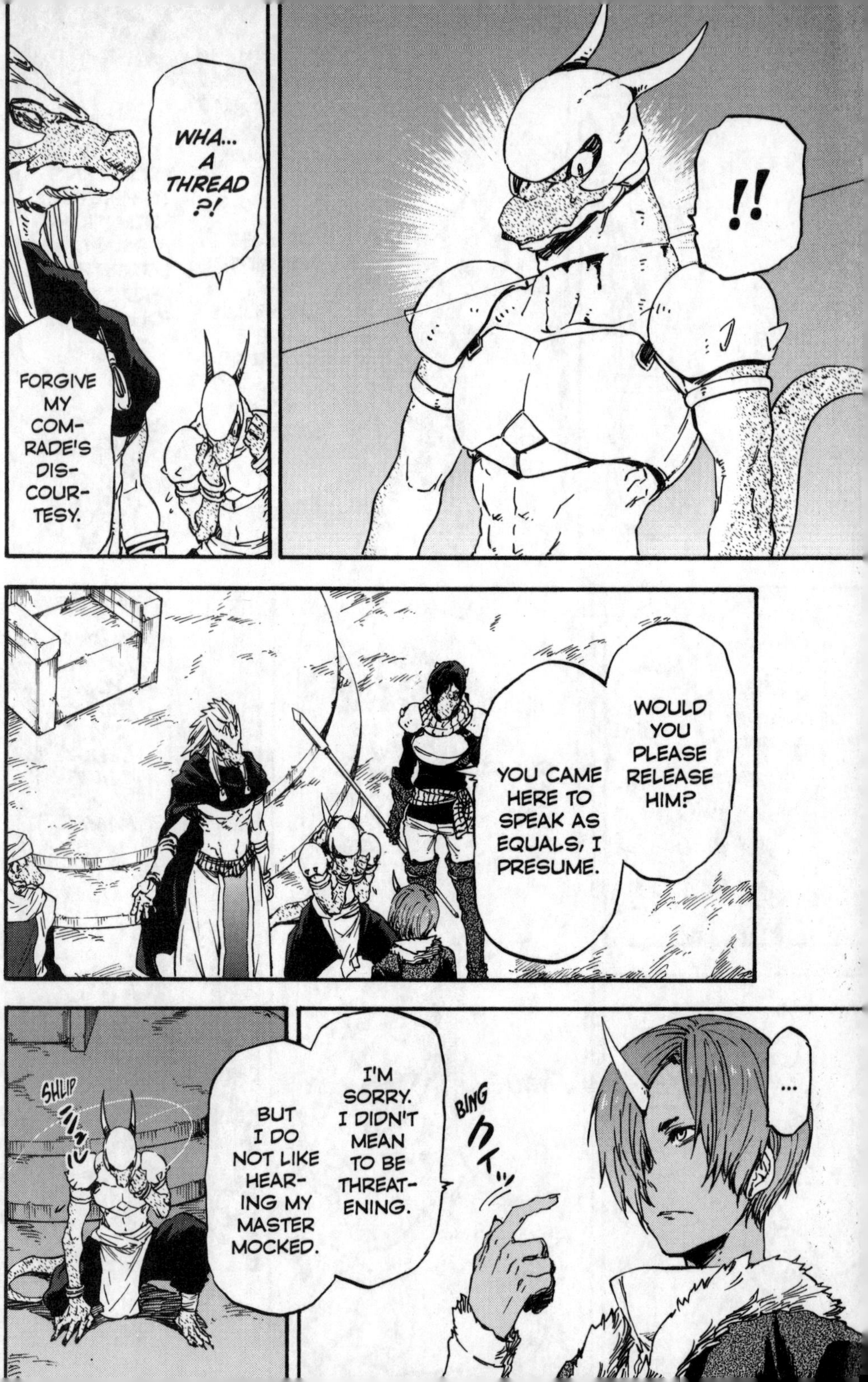
!!
WHA... A THREAD ?!
FORGIVE MY COMRADE'S DISCOURTESY.
WOULD YOU PLEASE RELEASE HIM?
YOU CAME HERE TO SPEAK AS EQUALS, I PRESUME.
...
BING
I'M SORRY. I DIDN'T MEAN TO BE THREATENING.
BUT I DO NOT LIKE HEARING MY MASTER MOCKED.
SHLIP

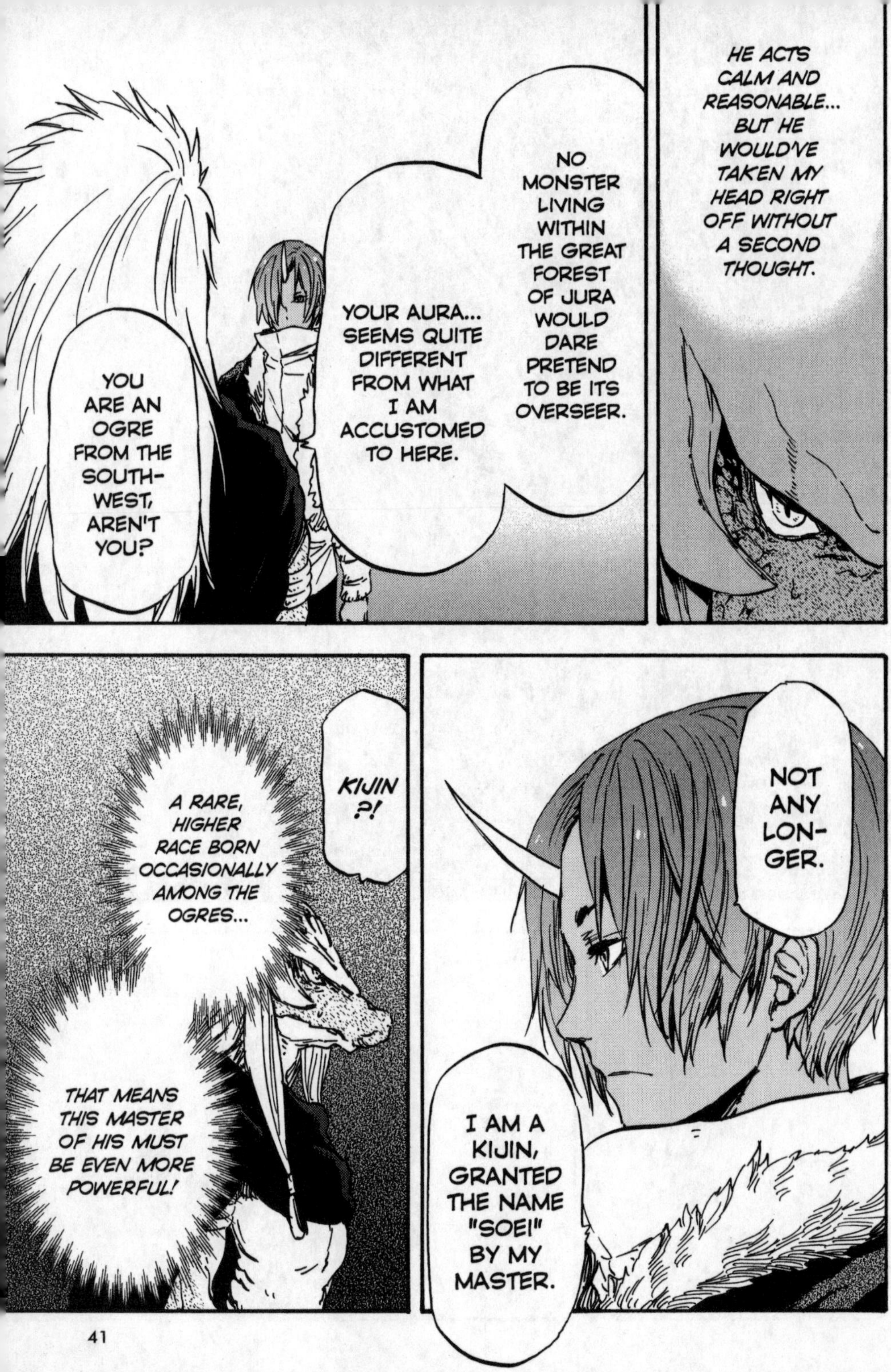
HE ACTS CALM AND REASONABLE... BUT HE WOULD'VE TAKEN MY HEAD RIGHT OFF WITHOUT A SECOND THOUGHT.
NO MONSTER LIVING WITHIN THE GREAT FOREST OF JURA WOULD DARE PRETEND TO BE ITS OVERSEER.
YOUR AURA... SEEMS QUITE DIFFERENT FROM WHAT I AM ACCUSTOMED TO HERE.
YOU ARE AN OGRE FROM THE SOUTH-WEST, AREN'T YOU?
NOT ANY LON-GER.
I AM A KIJIN, GRANTED THE NAME "SOEI" BY MY MASTER.
KIJIN ?!
A RARE, HIGHER RACE BORN OCCASIONALLY AMONG THE OGRES...
THAT MEANS THIS MASTER OF HIS MUST BE EVEN MORE POWERFUL!

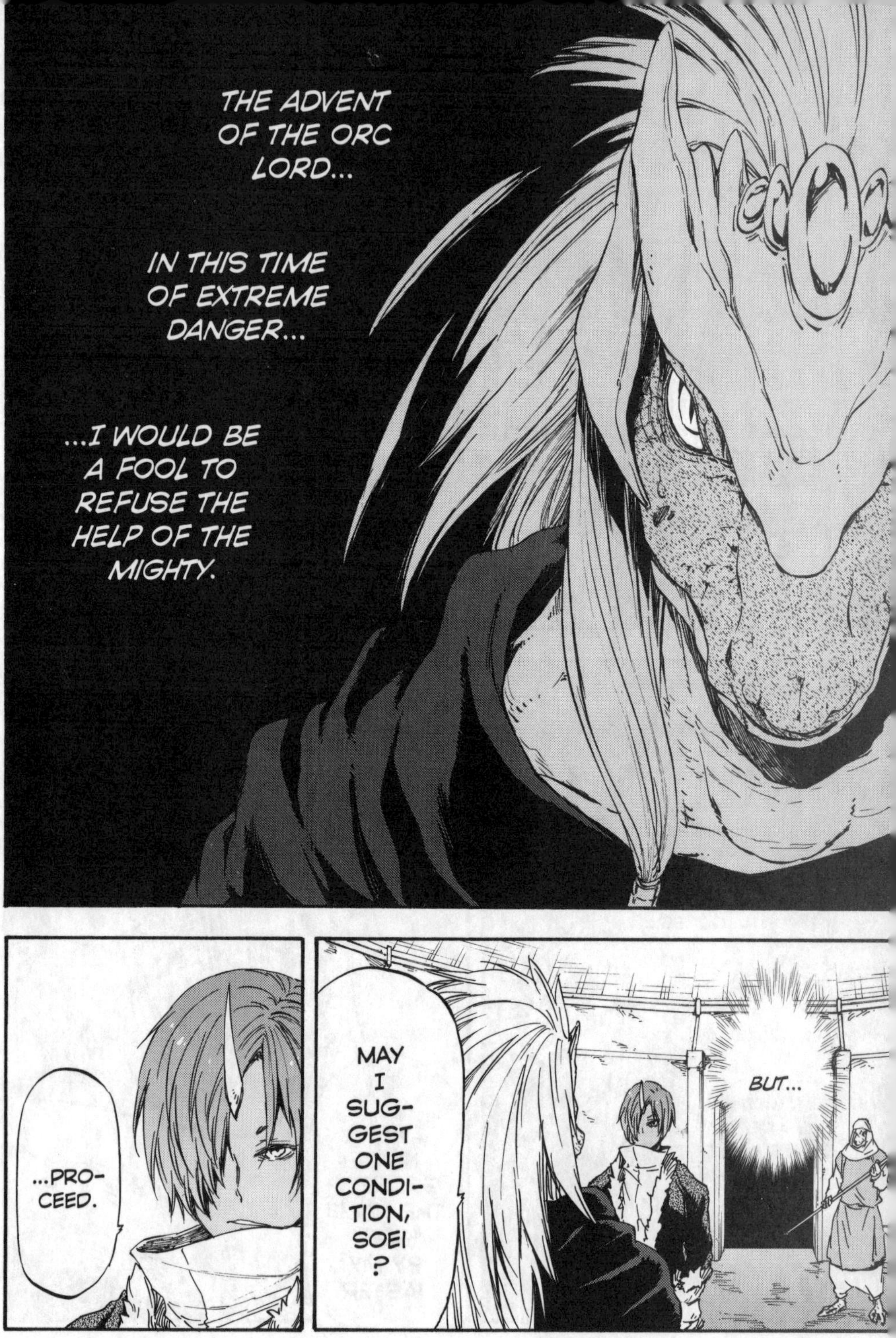
THE ADVENT OF THE ORC LORD...
IN THIS TIME OF EXTREME DANGER...
...I WOULD BE A FOOL TO REFUSE THE HELP OF THE MIGHTY.
BUT...
MAY I SUG-GEST ONE CONDI-TION, SOEI?
...PRO-CEED.

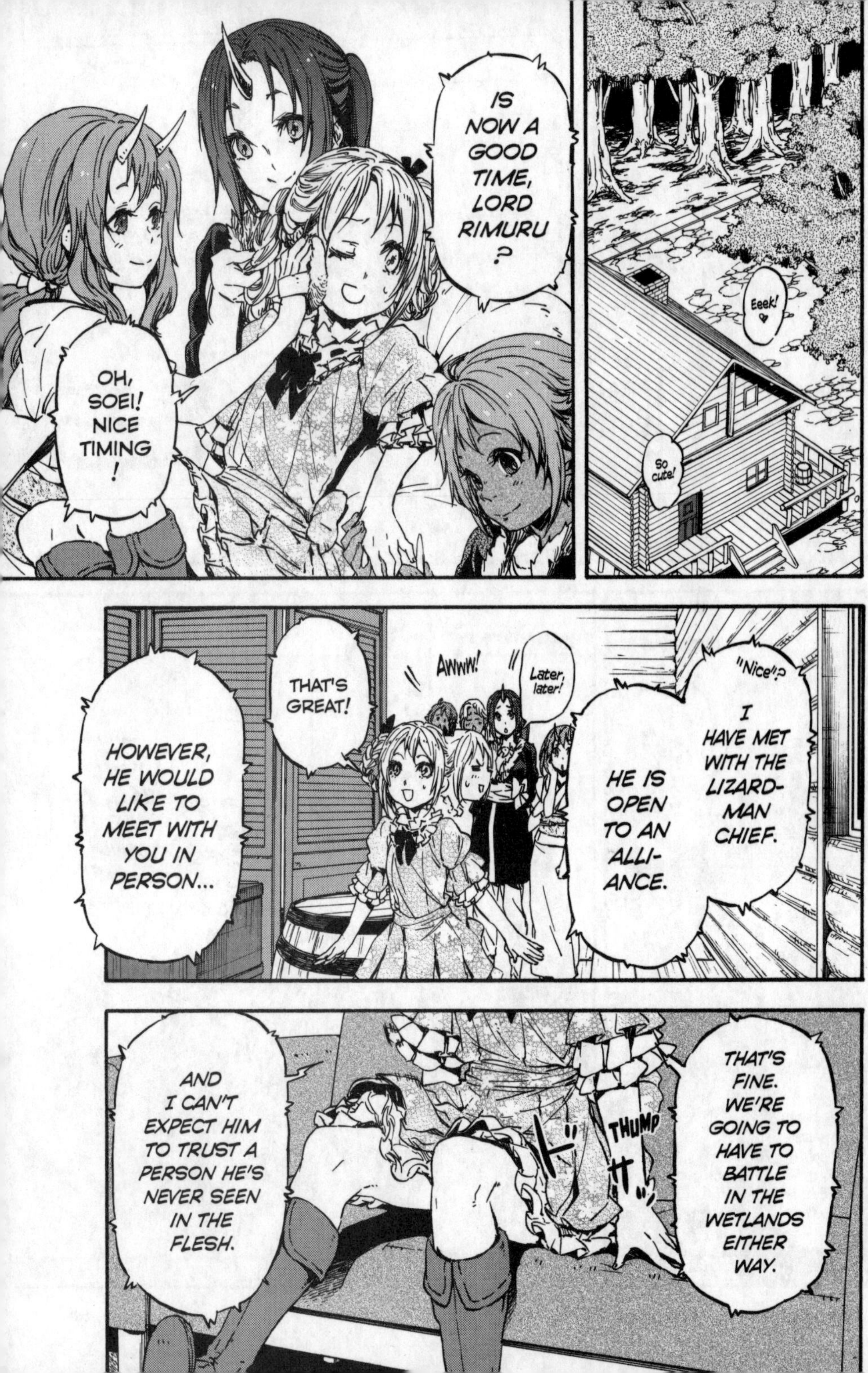
Eeek! ♥
So cute!
IS NOW A GOOD TIME, LORD RIMURU?
OH, SOEI! NICE TIMING!
"Nice"?
I HAVE MET WITH THE LIZARD-MAN CHIEF.
HE IS OPEN TO AN ALLI-ANCE.
Later, later!
AWWW!
THAT'S GREAT!
HOWEVER, HE WOULD LIKE TO MEET WITH YOU IN PERSON...
THAT'S FINE. WE'RE GOING TO HAVE TO BATTLE IN THE WETLANDS EITHER WAY.
THUMP
AND I CAN'T EXPECT HIM TO TRUST A PERSON HE'S NEVER SEEN IN THE FLESH.

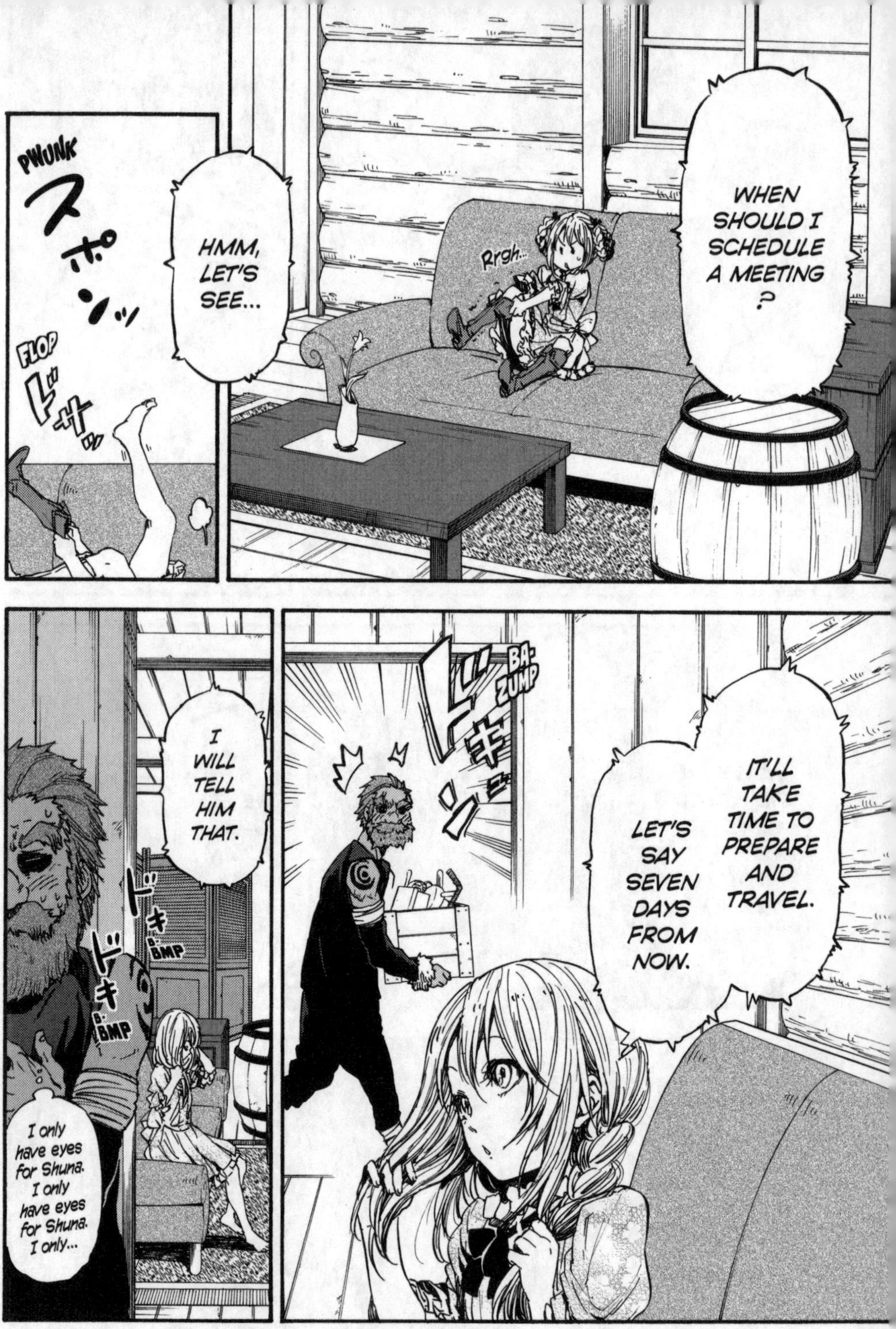

WHEN SHOULD I SCHEDULE A MEETING?
Rrgh...
HMM, LET'S SEE...
PWUNK
スポンッ
FLOP
ドサッ
IT'LL TAKE TIME TO PREPARE AND TRAVEL.
LET'S SAY SEVEN DAYS FROM NOW.
BA-ZUMP
ドキーン
I WILL TELL HIM THAT.
ドキ
B-BMP
ドキ
B-BMP
I only have eyes for Shuna. I only have eyes for Shuna. I only...

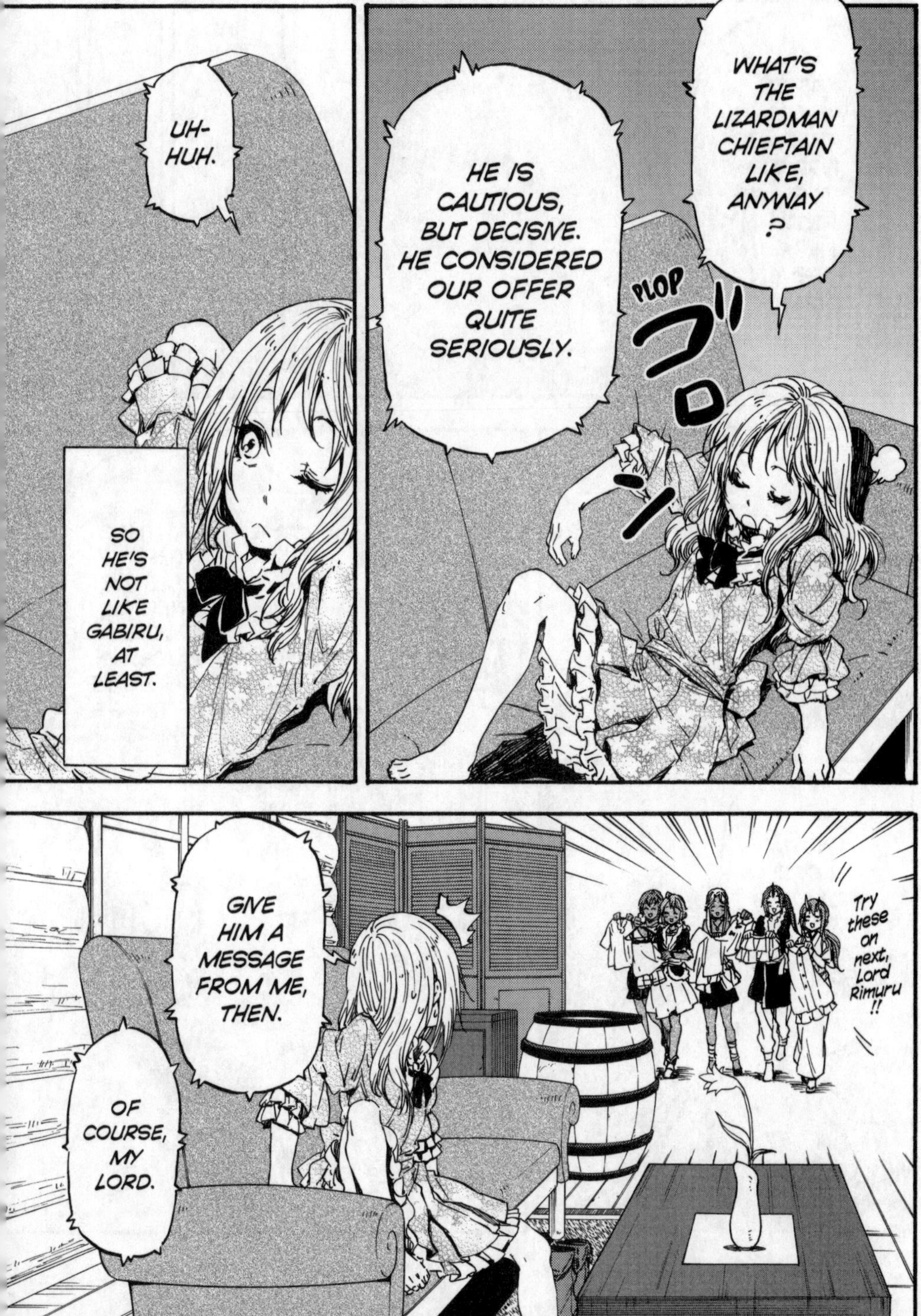
WHAT'S THE LIZARDMAN CHIEFTAIN LIKE, ANYWAY?
PLOP
HE IS CAUTIOUS, BUT DECISIVE. HE CONSIDERED OUR OFFER QUITE SERIOUSLY.
UH-HUH.
SO HE'S NOT LIKE GABIRU, AT LEAST.
Try these on next, Lord Rimuru!!
GIVE HIM A MESSAGE FROM ME, THEN.
OF COURSE, MY LORD.

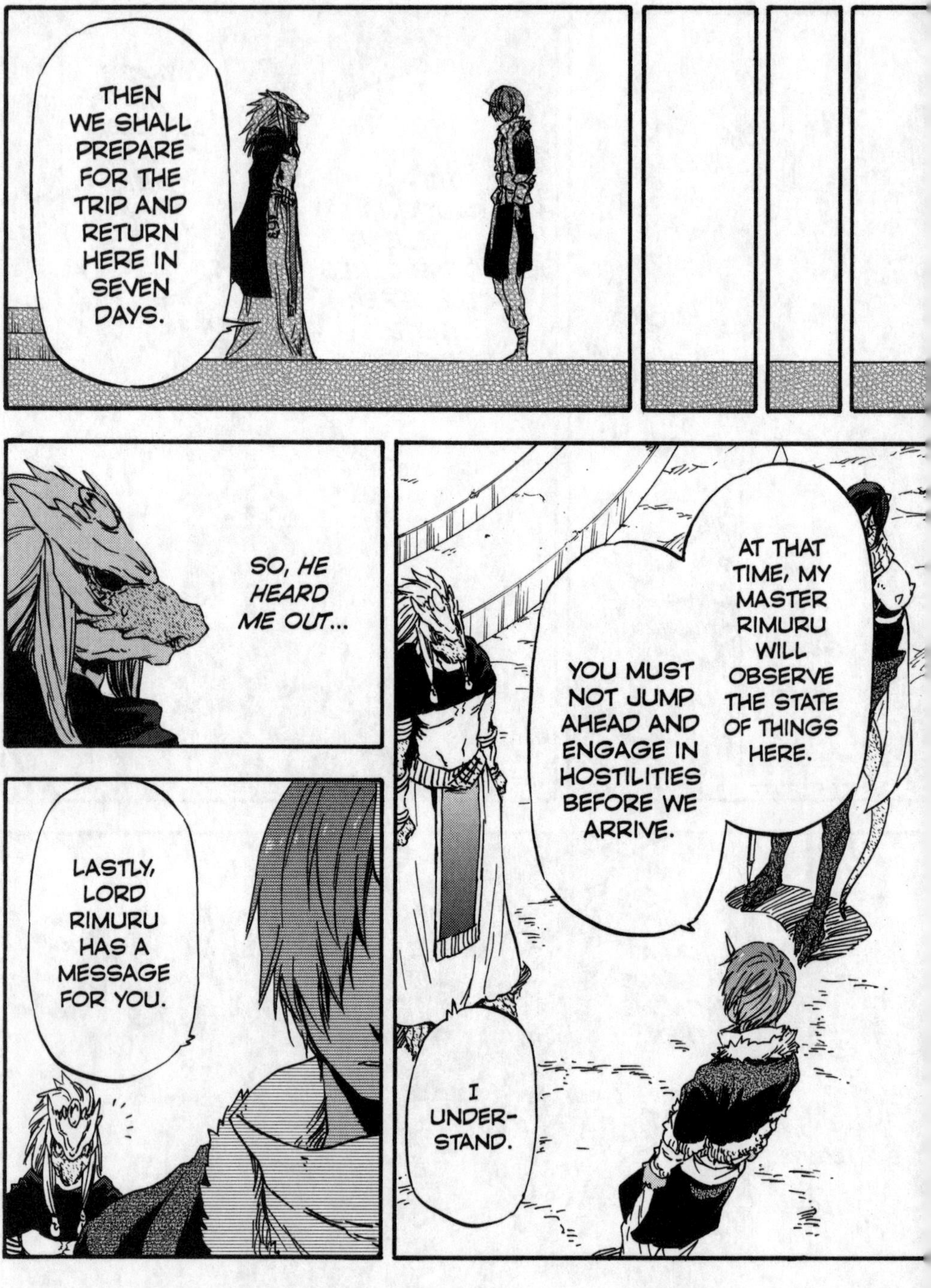
THEN WE SHALL PREPARE FOR THE TRIP AND RETURN HERE IN SEVEN DAYS.
SO, HE HEARD ME OUT...
LASTLY, LORD RIMURU HAS A MESSAGE FOR YOU.
AT THAT TIME, MY MASTER RIMURU WILL OBSERVE THE STATE OF THINGS HERE.
YOU MUST NOT JUMP AHEAD AND ENGAGE IN HOSTILITIES BEFORE WE ARRIVE.
I UNDER-STAND.

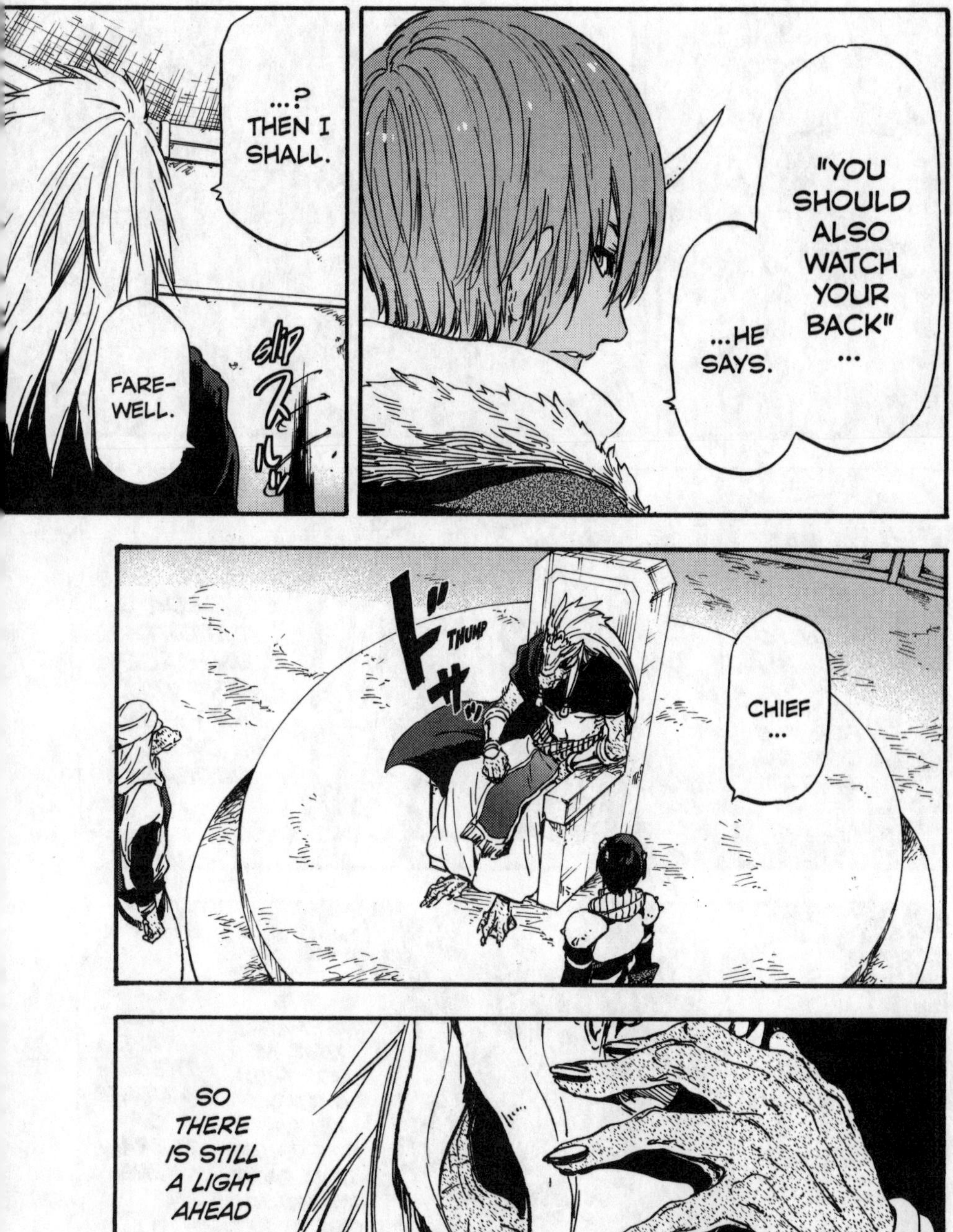
"YOU SHOULD ALSO WATCH YOUR BACK" ...
...HE SAYS.
...? THEN I SHALL.
slip
FARE-WELL.
THUMP
CHIEF ...
SO THERE IS STILL A LIGHT AHEAD ...

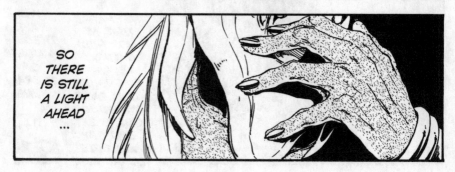

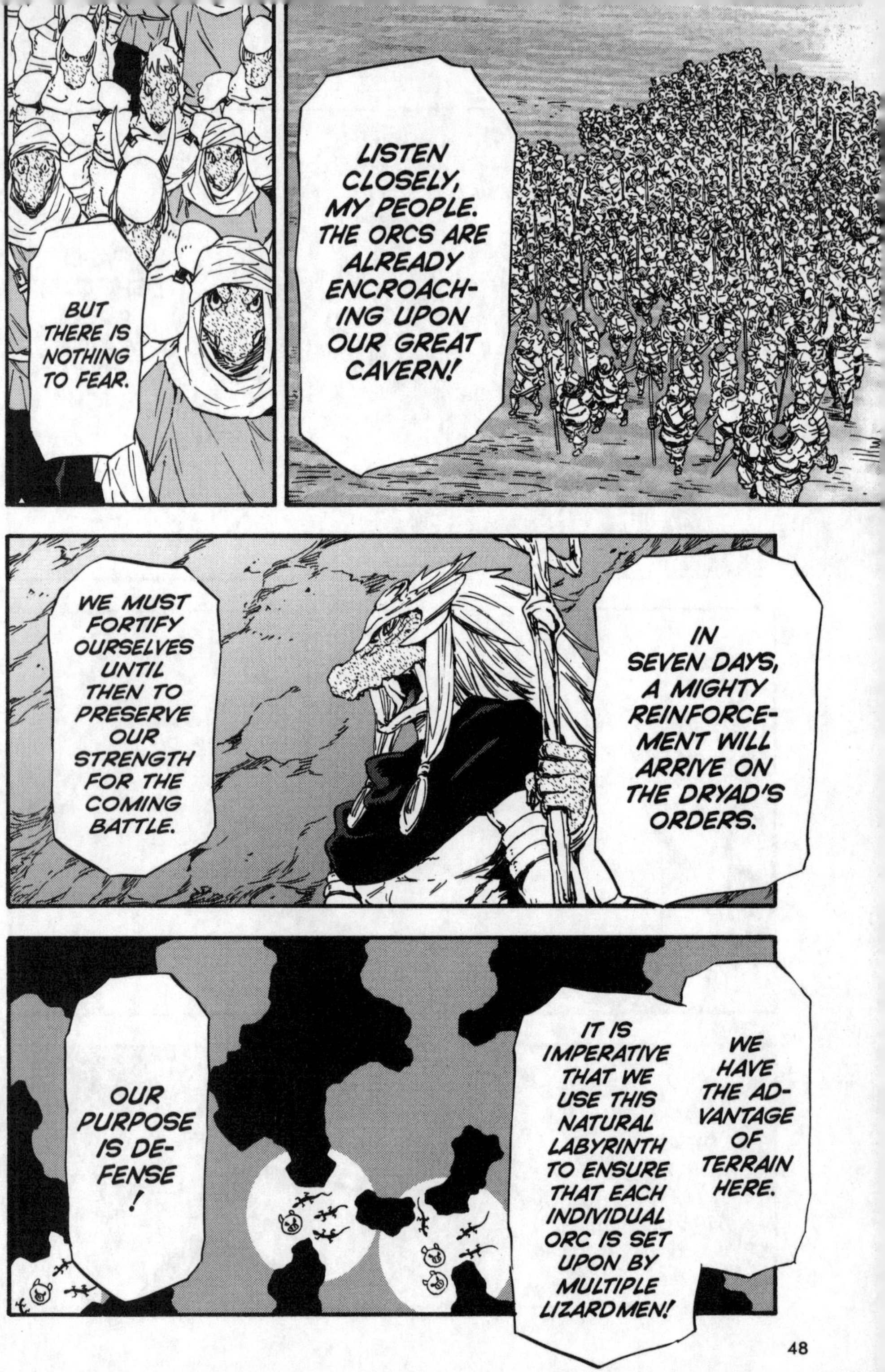
LISTEN CLOSELY, MY PEOPLE. THE ORCS ARE ALREADY ENCROACH-ING UPON OUR GREAT CAVERN!
BUT THERE IS NOTHING TO FEAR.
IN SEVEN DAYS, A MIGHTY REINFORCE-MENT WILL ARRIVE ON THE DRYAD'S ORDERS.
WE MUST FORTIFY OURSELVES UNTIL THEN TO PRESERVE OUR STRENGTH FOR THE COMING BATTLE.
WE HAVE THE AD-VANTAGE OF TERRAIN HERE.
IT IS IMPERATIVE THAT WE USE THIS NATURAL LABYRINTH TO ENSURE THAT EACH INDIVIDUAL ORC IS SET UPON BY MULTIPLE LIZARDMEN!
OUR PURPOSE IS DE-FENSE!

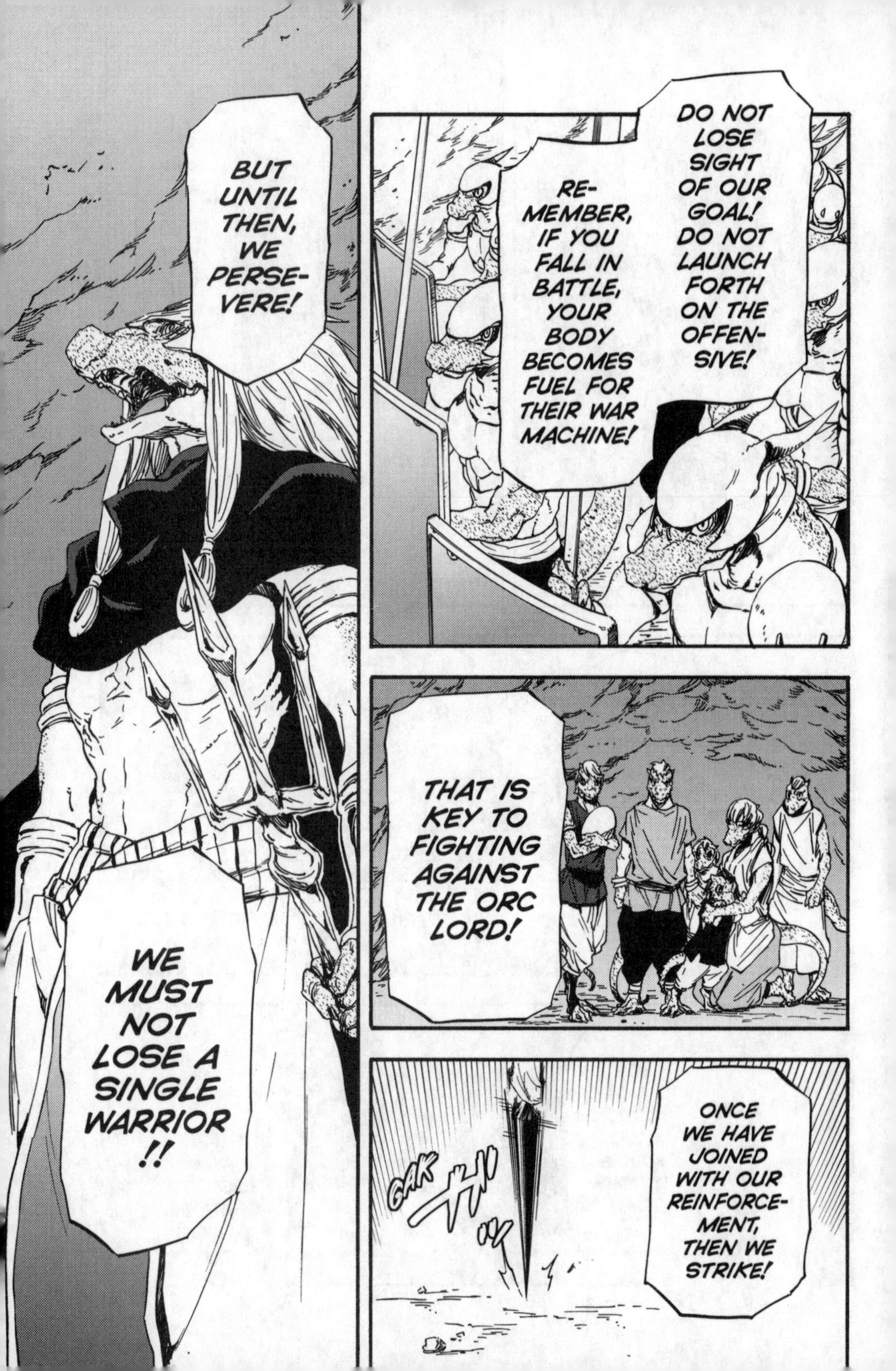
DO NOT LOSE SIGHT OF OUR GOAL! DO NOT LAUNCH FORTH ON THE OFFEN-SIVE!
RE-MEMBER, IF YOU FALL IN BATTLE, YOUR BODY BECOMES FUEL FOR THEIR WAR MACHINE!
THAT IS KEY TO FIGHTING AGAINST THE ORC LORD!
ONCE WE HAVE JOINED WITH OUR REINFORCE-MENT, THEN WE STRIKE!
GAK
BUT UNTIL THEN, WE PERSE-VERE!
WE MUST NOT LOSE A SINGLE WARRIOR !!

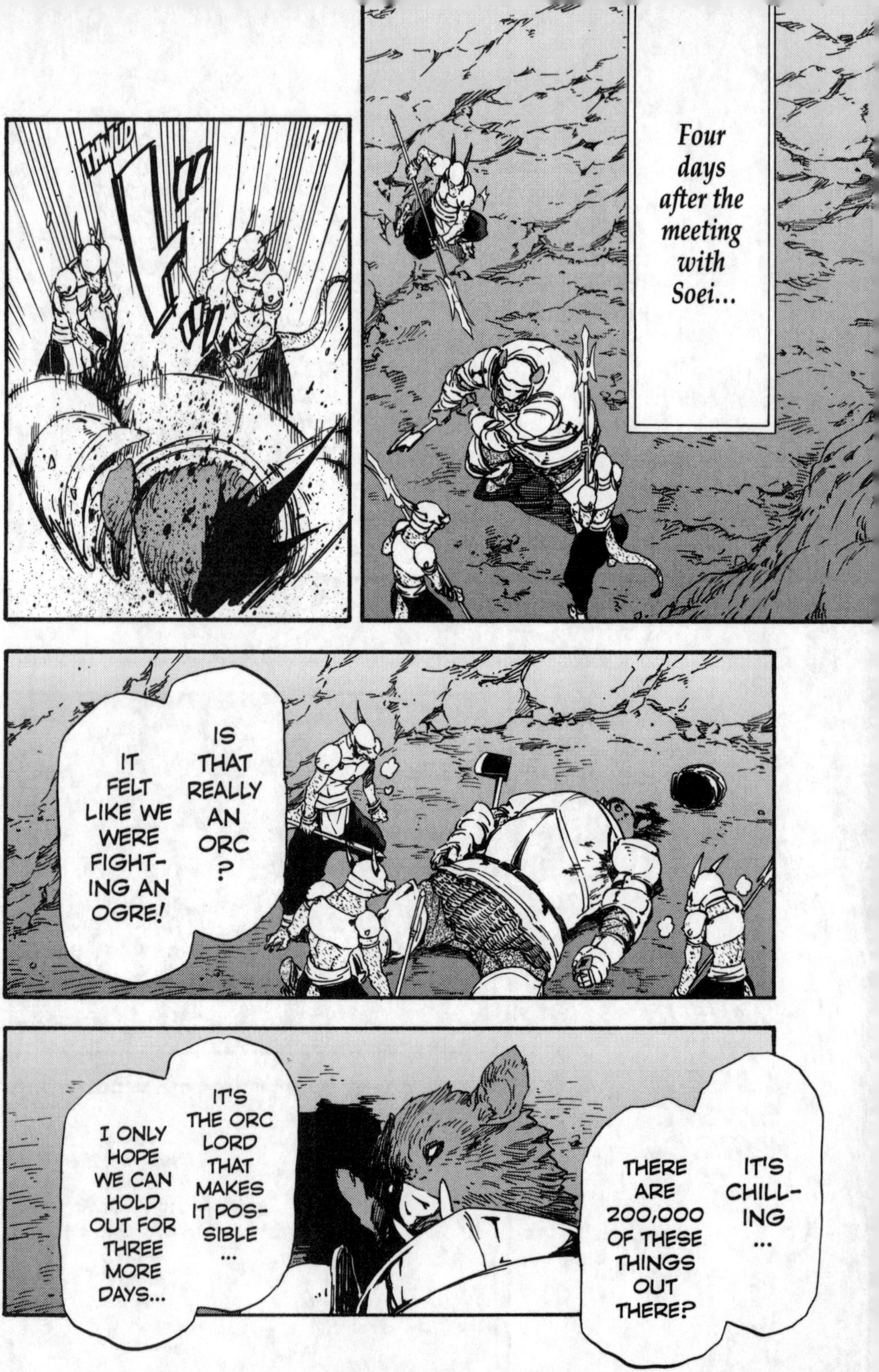
Four days after the meeting with Soei...
THWUD
IS THAT REALLY AN ORC?
IT FELT LIKE WE WERE FIGHTING AN OGRE!
IT'S CHILLING...
THERE ARE 200,000 OF THESE THINGS OUT THERE?
IT'S THE ORC LORD THAT MAKES IT POSSIBLE...
I ONLY HOPE WE CAN HOLD OUT FOR THREE MORE DAYS...

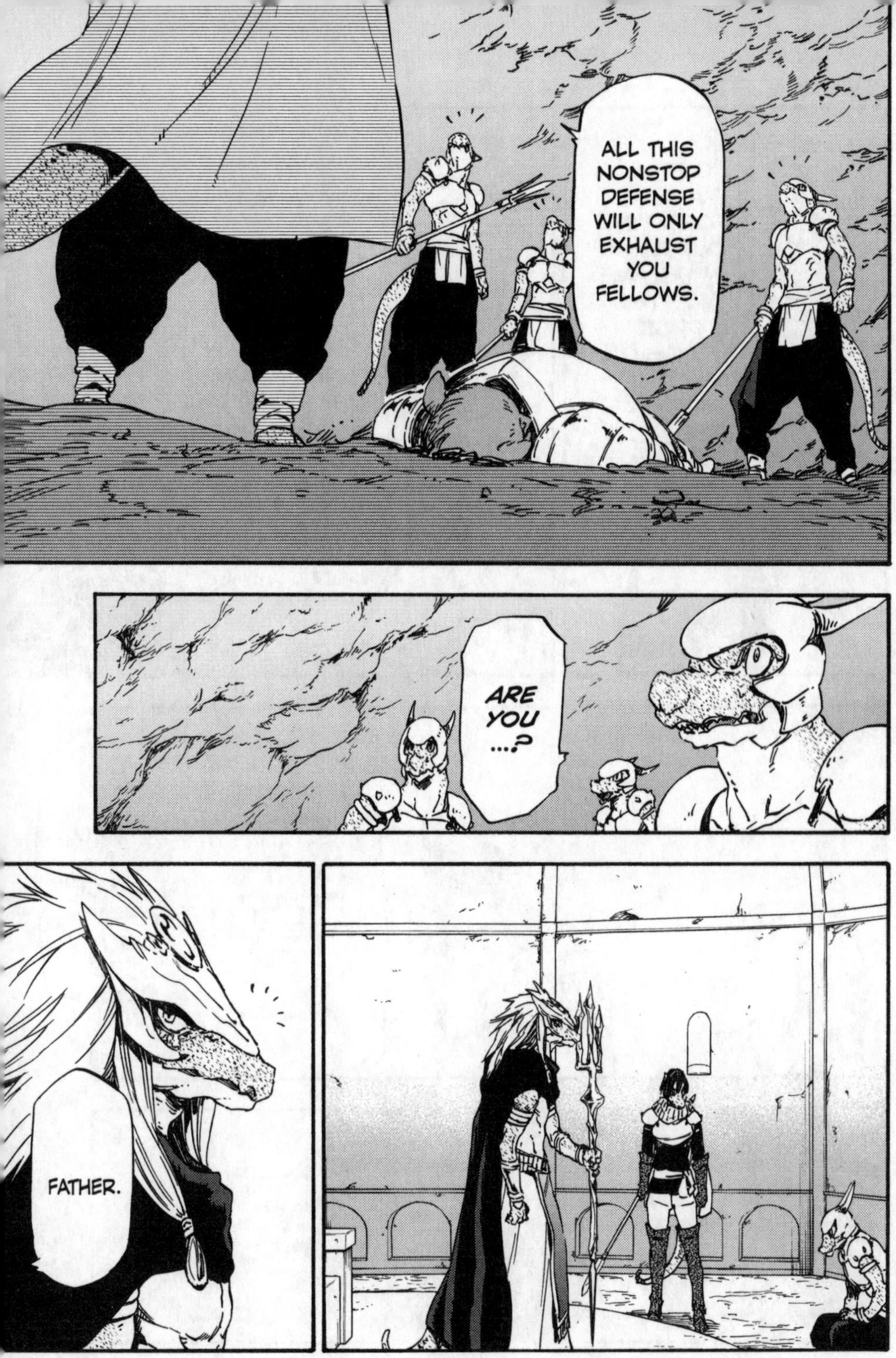
ALL THIS NONSTOP DEFENSE WILL ONLY EXHAUST YOU FELLOWS.
ARE YOU ...?
FATHER.

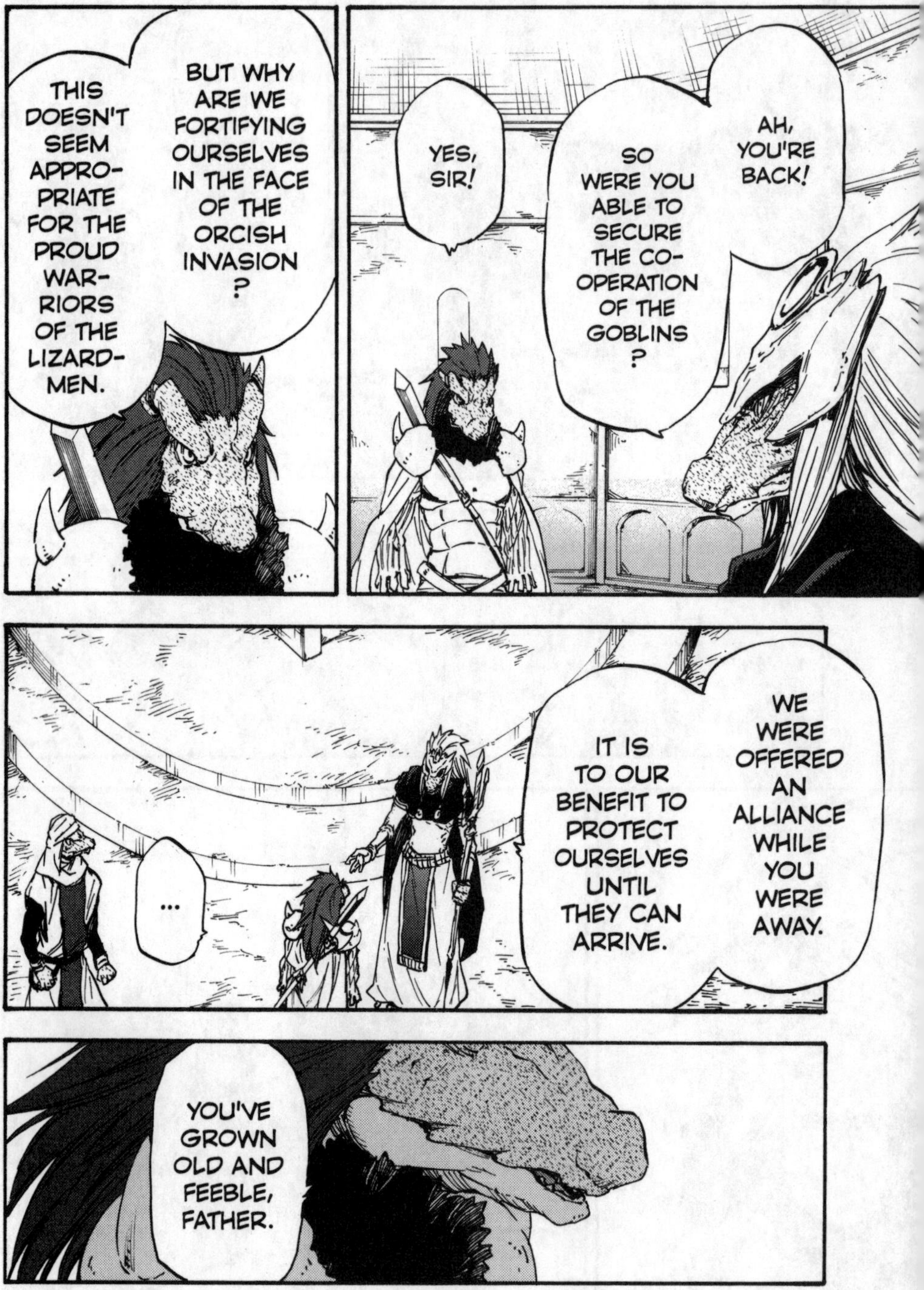
AH, YOU'RE BACK!
SO WERE YOU ABLE TO SECURE THE CO-OPERATION OF THE GOBLINS?
YES, SIR!
BUT WHY ARE WE FORTIFYING OURSELVES IN THE FACE OF THE ORCISH INVASION?
THIS DOESN'T SEEM APPROPRIATE FOR THE PROUD WARRIORS OF THE LIZARDMEN.
WE WERE OFFERED AN ALLIANCE WHILE YOU WERE AWAY.
IT IS TO OUR BENEFIT TO PROTECT OURSELVES UNTIL THEY CAN ARRIVE.
...
YOU'VE GROWN OLD AND FEEBLE, FATHER.

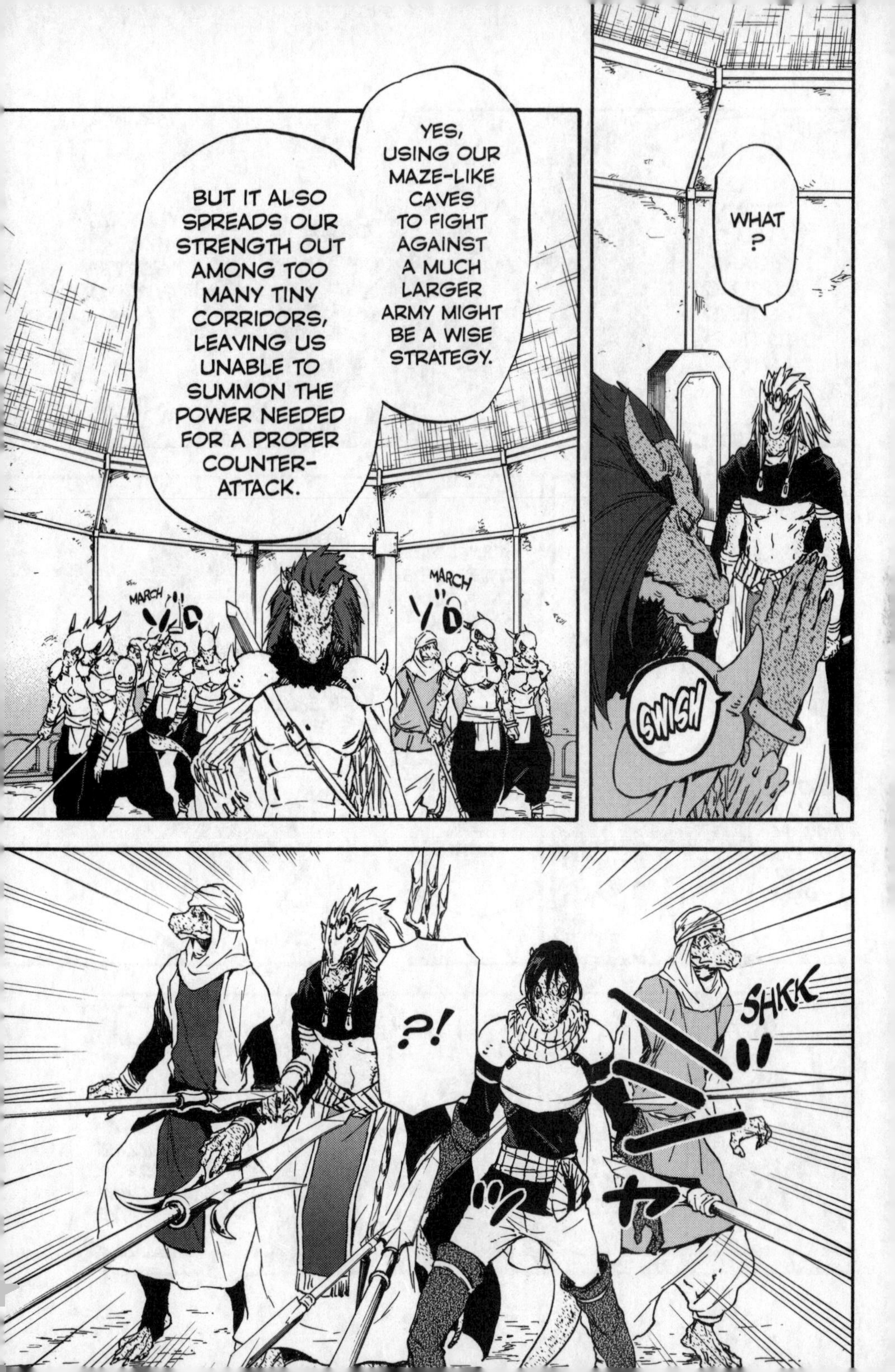
WHAT?
SWISH
YES, USING OUR MAZE-LIKE CAVES TO FIGHT AGAINST A MUCH LARGER ARMY MIGHT BE A WISE STRATEGY.
BUT IT ALSO SPREADS OUR STRENGTH OUT AMONG TOO MANY TINY CORRIDORS, LEAVING US UNABLE TO SUMMON THE POWER NEEDED FOR A PROPER COUNTER-ATTACK.
MARCH
MARCH
SHKK
?!

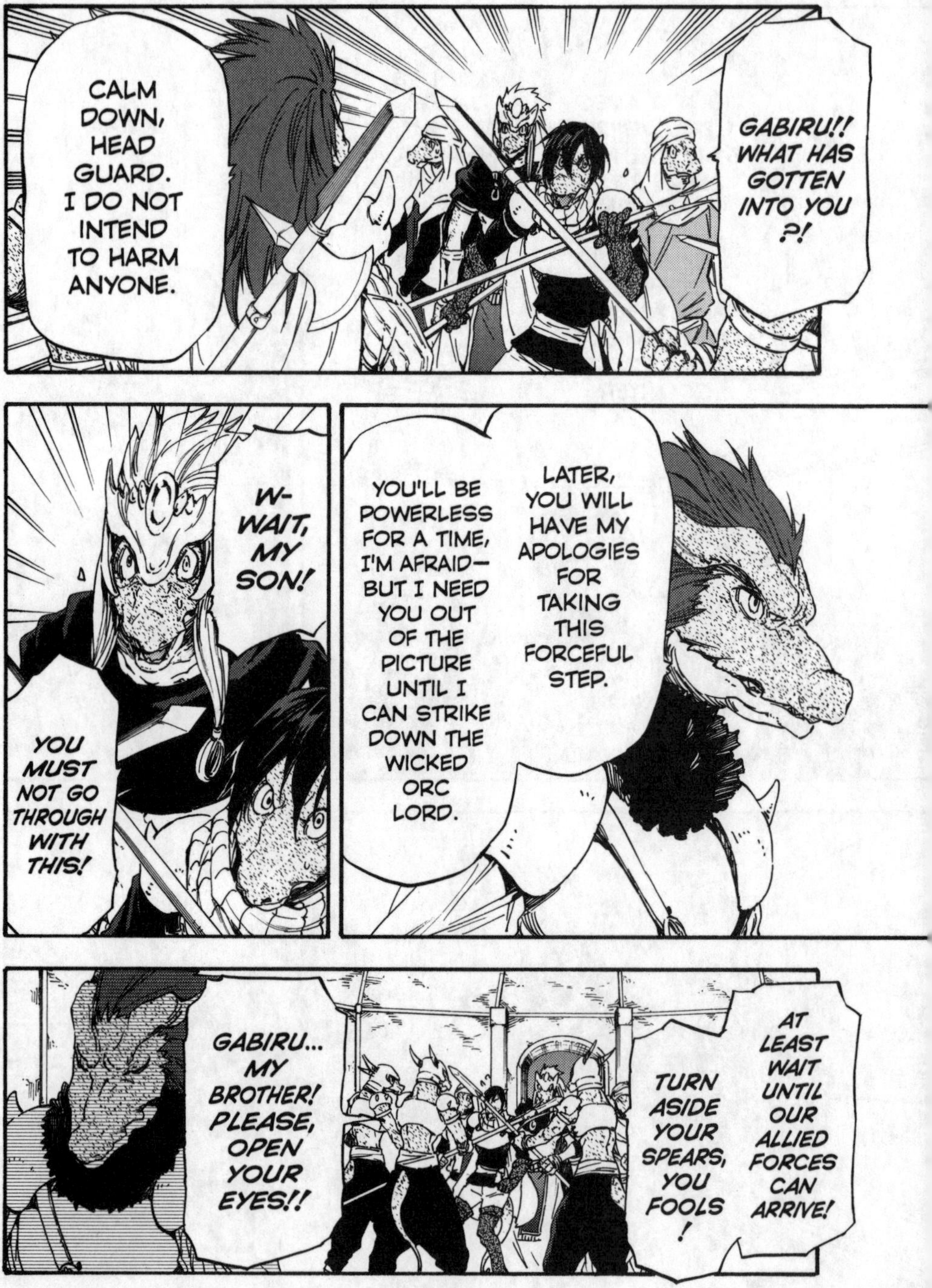
GABIRU!! WHAT HAS GOTTEN INTO YOU?!
CALM DOWN, HEAD GUARD. I DO NOT INTEND TO HARM ANYONE.
LATER, YOU WILL HAVE MY APOLOGIES FOR TAKING THIS FORCEFUL STEP.
YOU'LL BE POWERLESS FOR A TIME, I'M AFRAID— BUT I NEED YOU OUT OF THE PICTURE UNTIL I CAN STRIKE DOWN THE WICKED ORC LORD.
W-WAIT, MY SON!
YOU MUST NOT GO THROUGH WITH THIS!
AT LEAST WAIT UNTIL OUR ALLIED FORCES CAN ARRIVE!
TURN ASIDE YOUR SPEARS, YOU FOOLS!
GABIRU... MY BROTHER! PLEASE, OPEN YOUR EYES!!

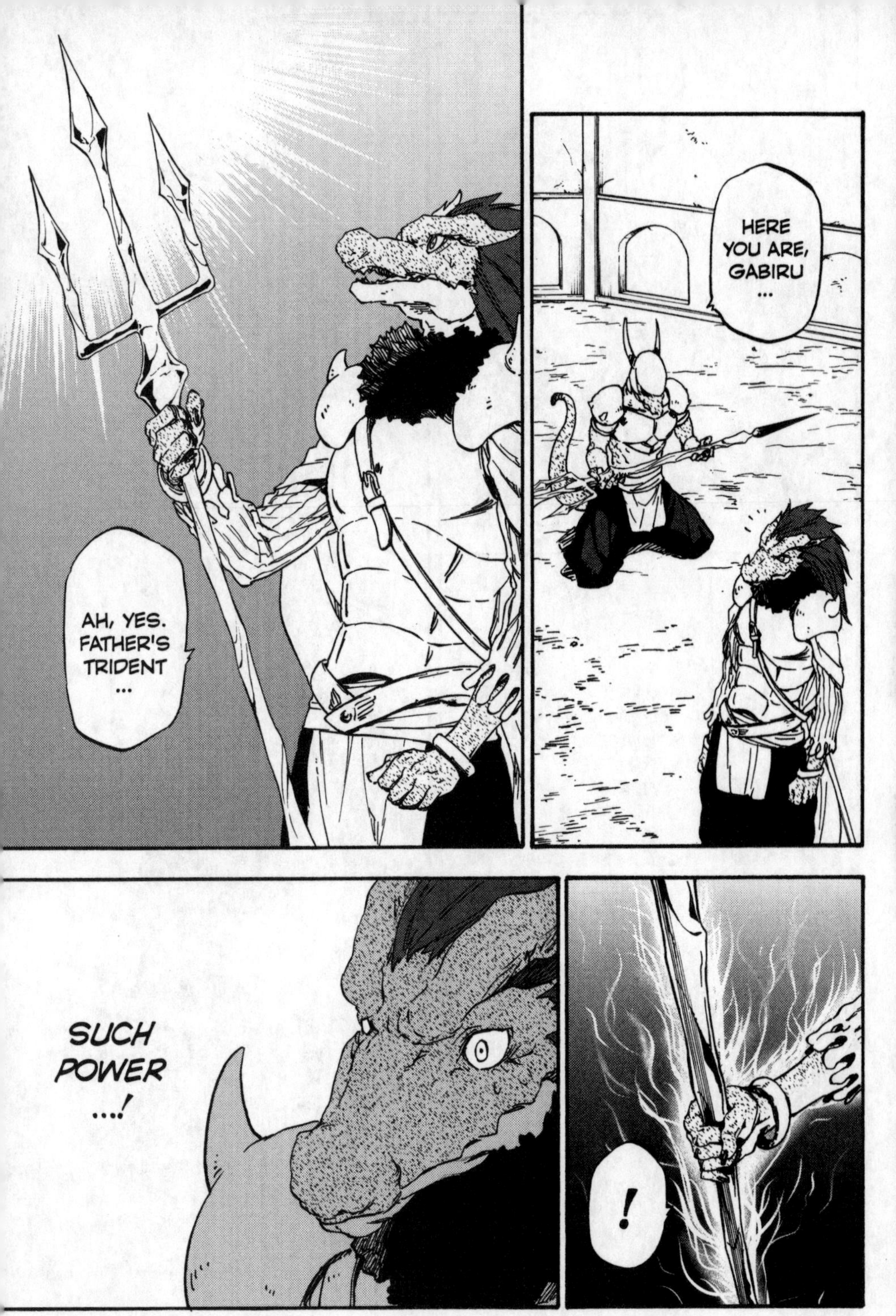
HERE YOU ARE, GABIRU ...
AH, YES. FATHER'S TRIDENT ...
!
SUCH POWER ...!

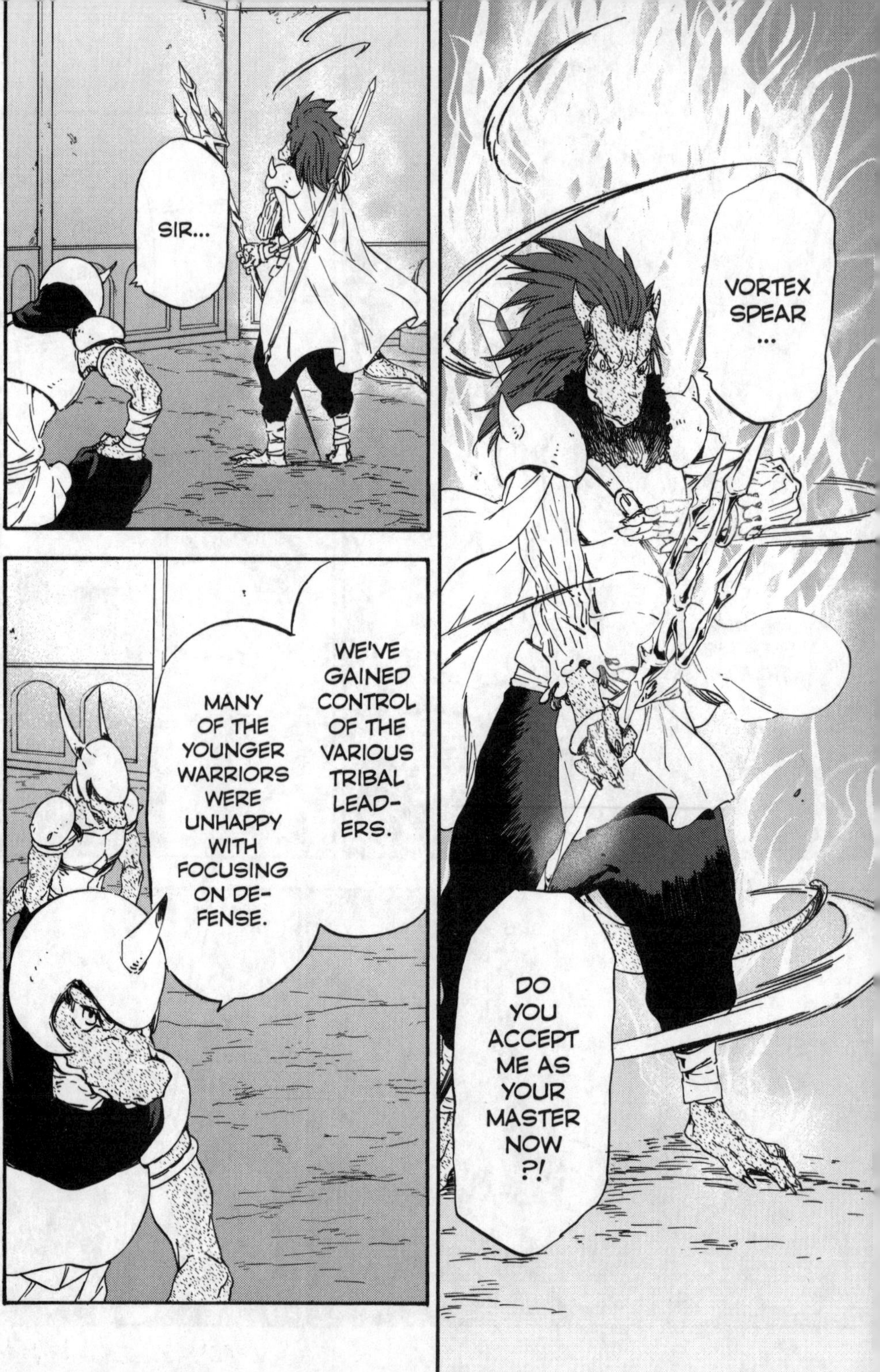
VORTEX SPEAR ...
DO YOU ACCEPT ME AS YOUR MASTER NOW?!
SIR...
WE'VE GAINED CONTROL OF THE VARIOUS TRIBAL LEADERS.
MANY OF THE YOUNGER WARRIORS WERE UNHAPPY WITH FOCUSING ON DEFENSE.

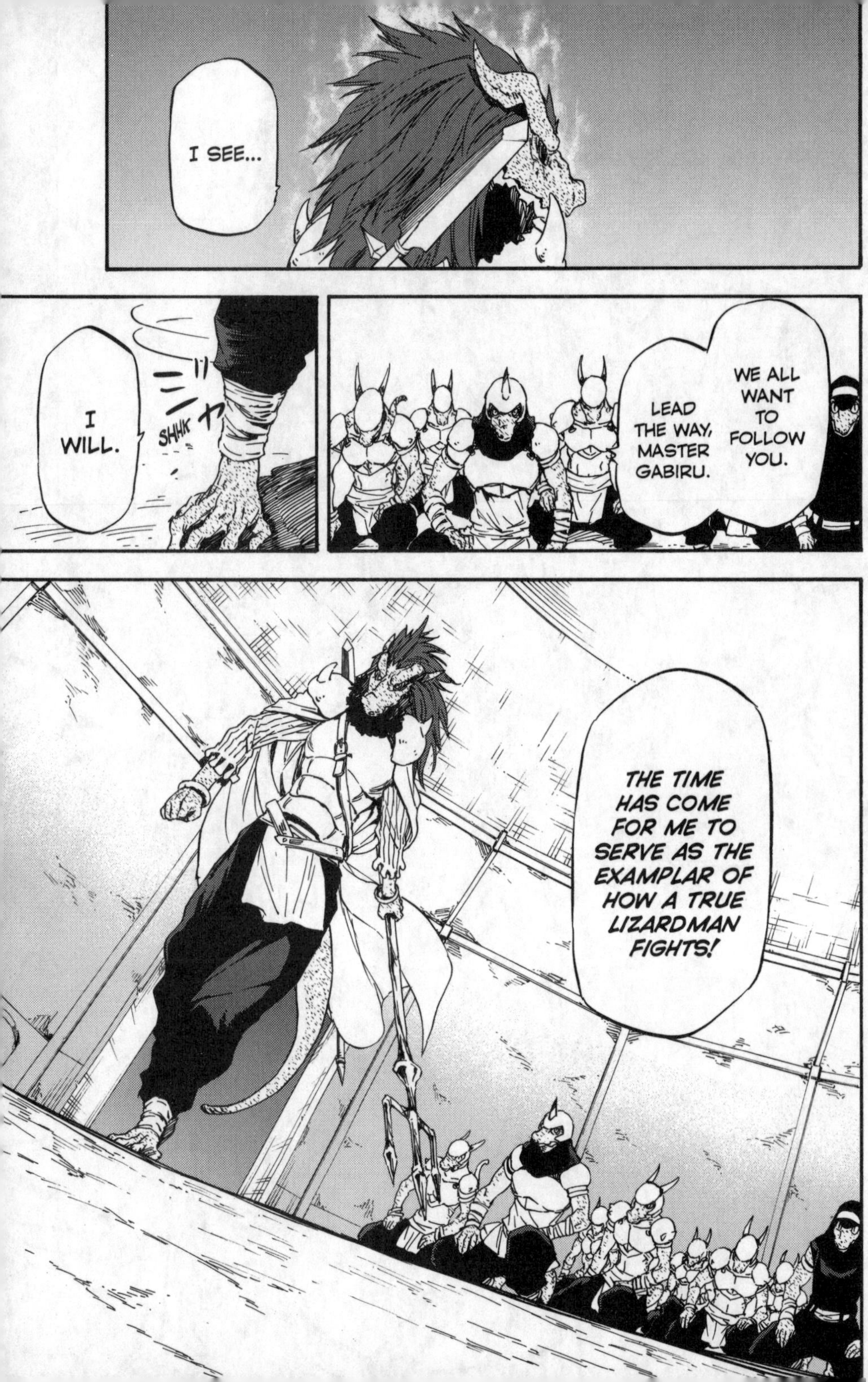
I SEE...
WE ALL WANT TO FOLLOW YOU. LEAD THE WAY, MASTER GABIRU.
SHHK
I WILL.
THE TIME HAS COME FOR ME TO SERVE AS THE EXAMPLAR OF HOW A TRUE LIZARDMAN FIGHTS!

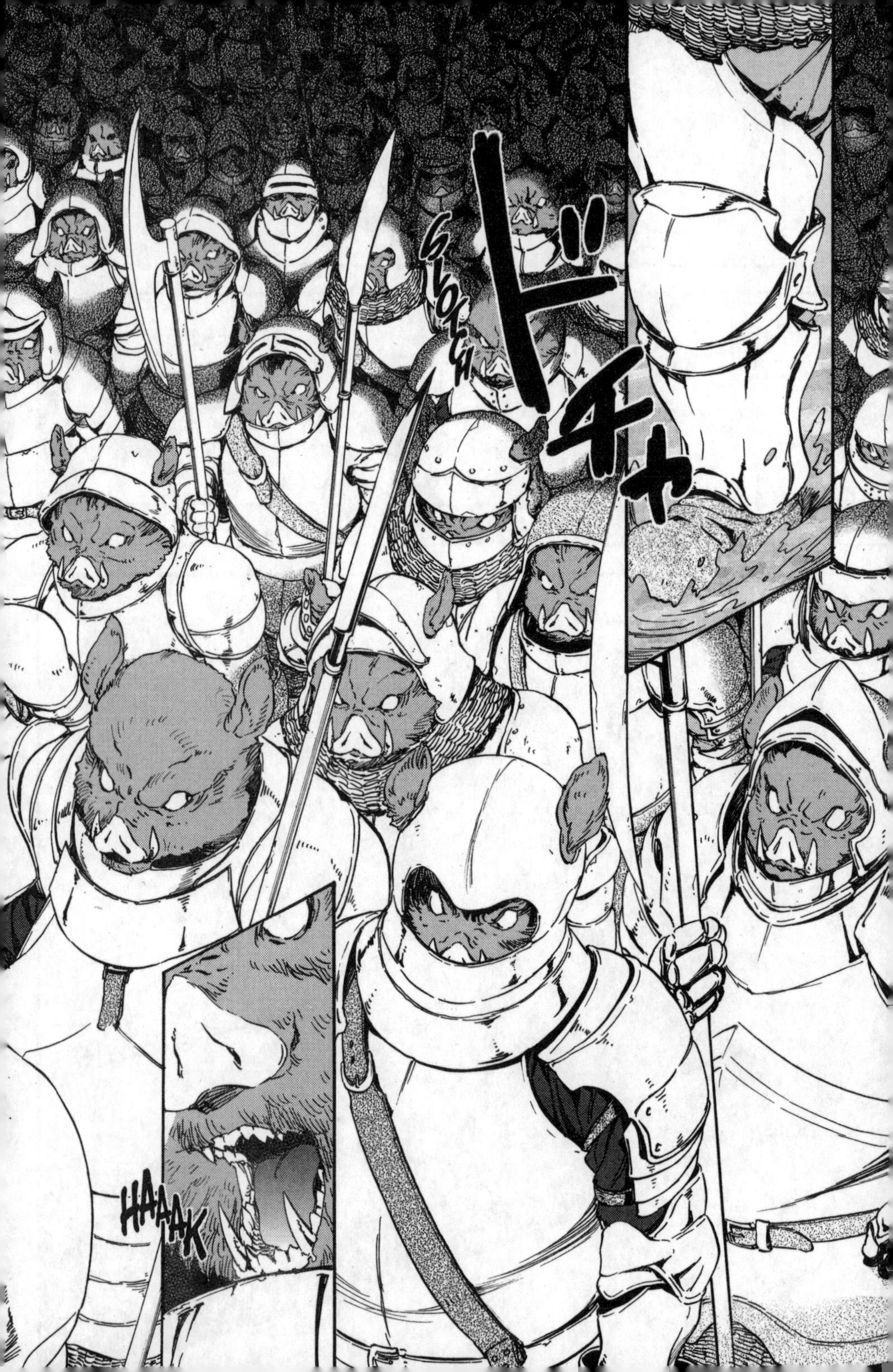

ドチャ
SLOTCH
HAAAK

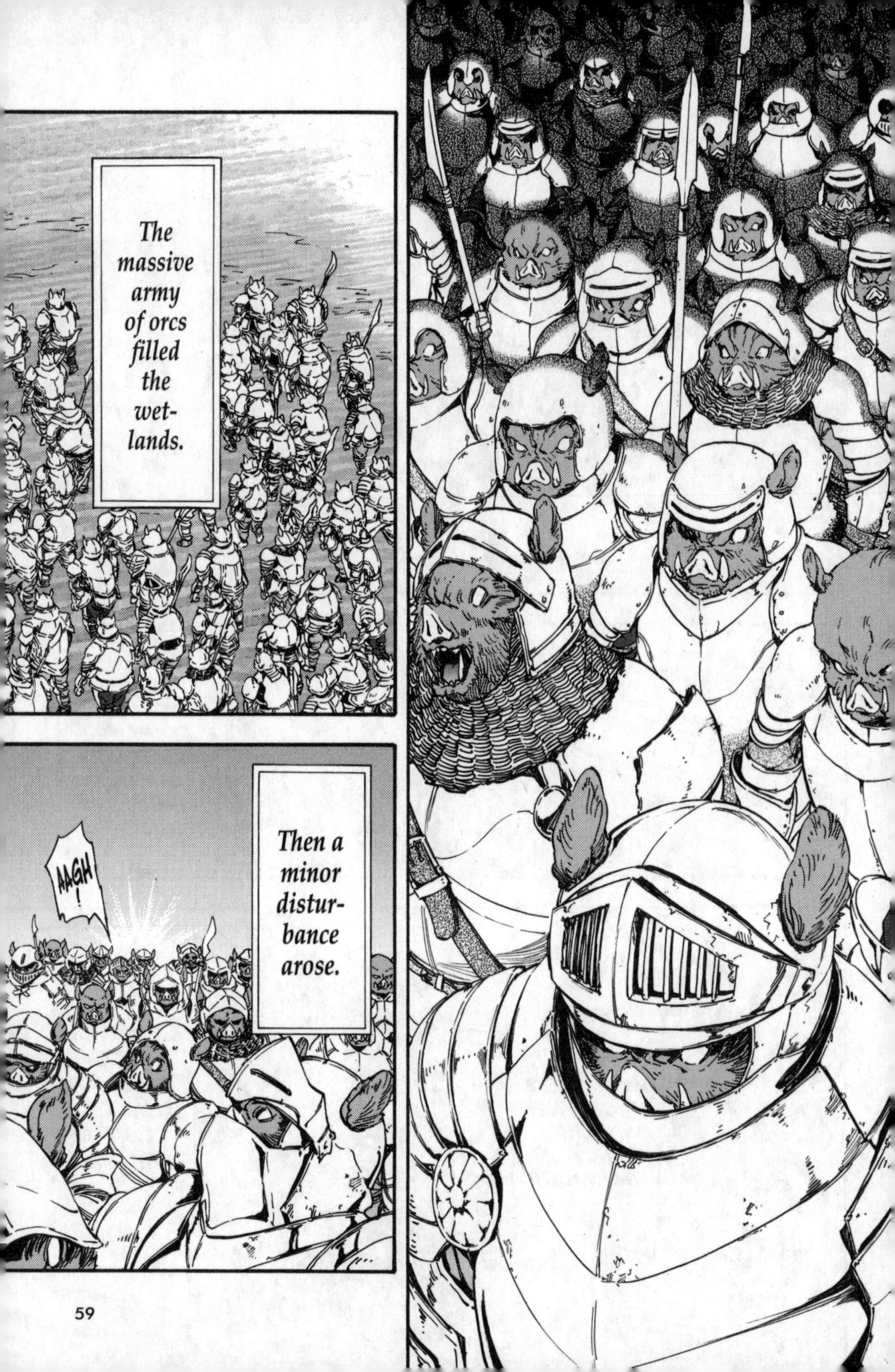
The massive army of orcs filled the wet-lands.
Then a minor distur-bance arose.
AAGH!

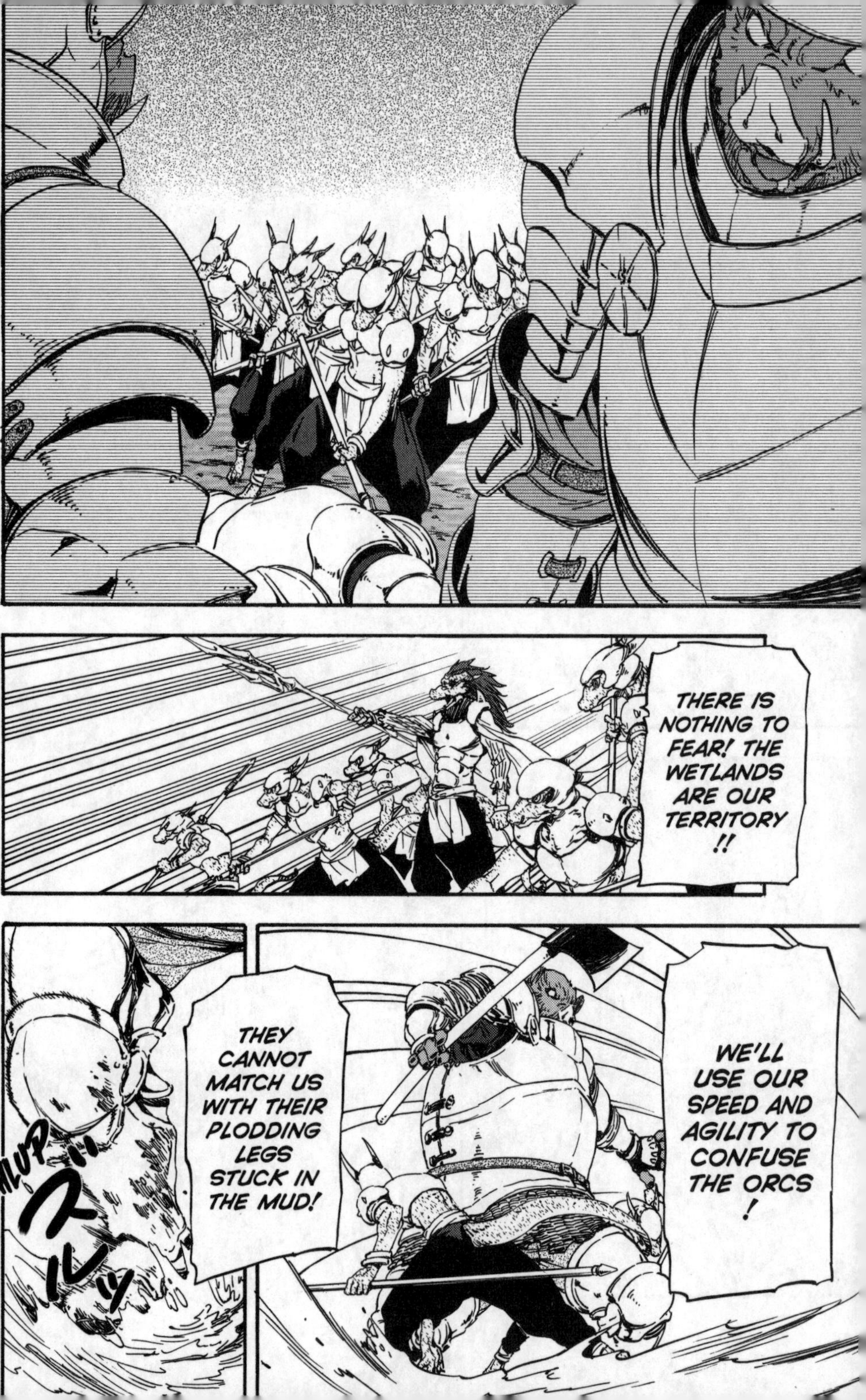

THERE IS NOTHING TO FEAR! THE WETLANDS ARE OUR TERRITORY!!
WE'LL USE OUR SPEED AND AGILITY TO CONFUSE THE ORCS!
THEY CANNOT MATCH US WITH THEIR PLODDING LEGS STUCK IN THE MUD!
SHLUP

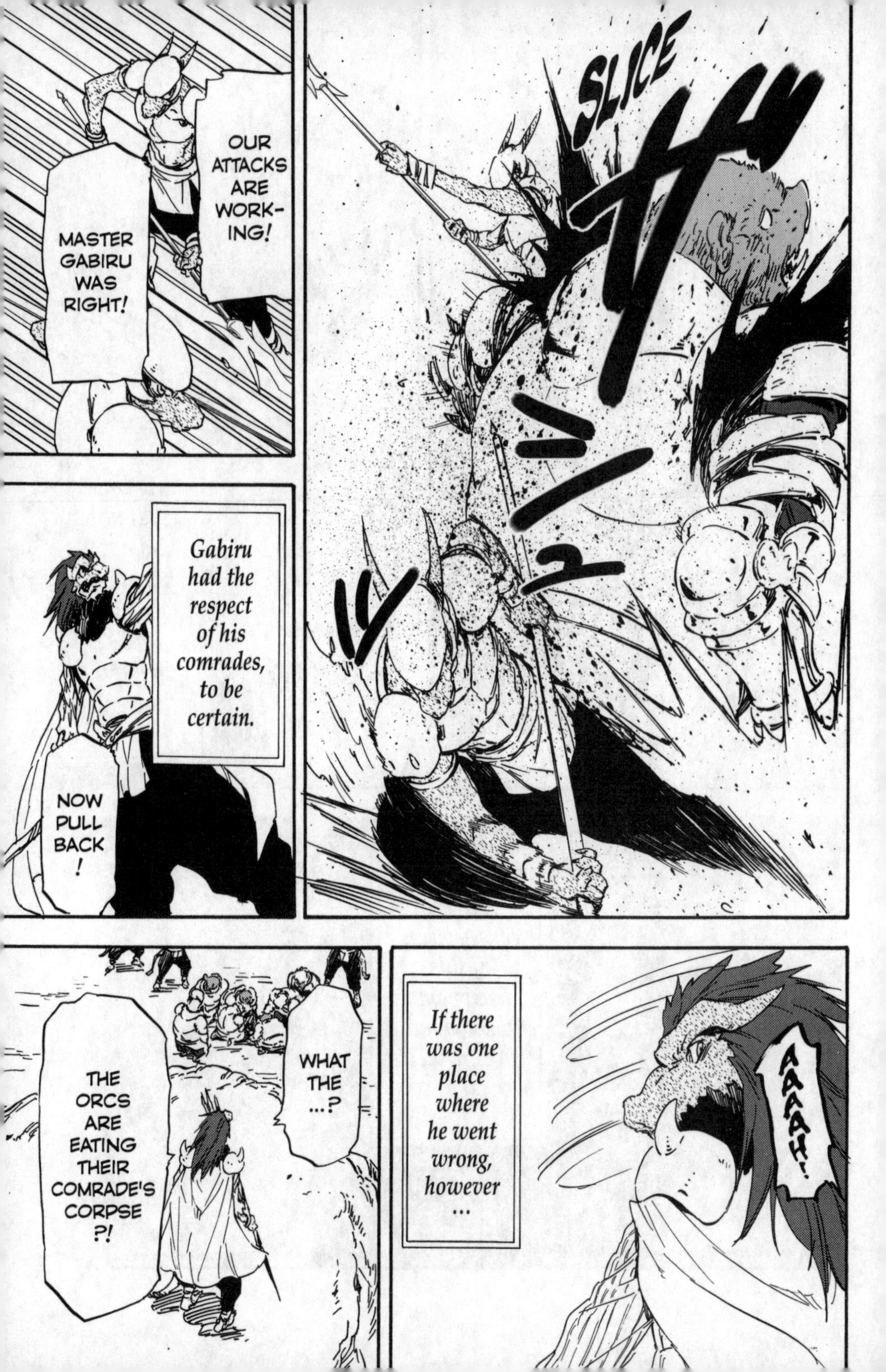
SLICE
OUR ATTACKS ARE WORKING!
MASTER GABIRU WAS RIGHT!
Gabiru had the respect of his comrades, to be certain.
NOW PULL BACK!
If there was one place where he went wrong, however…
AAAAH!
WHAT THE …?
THE ORCS ARE EATING THEIR COMRADE'S CORPSE ?!

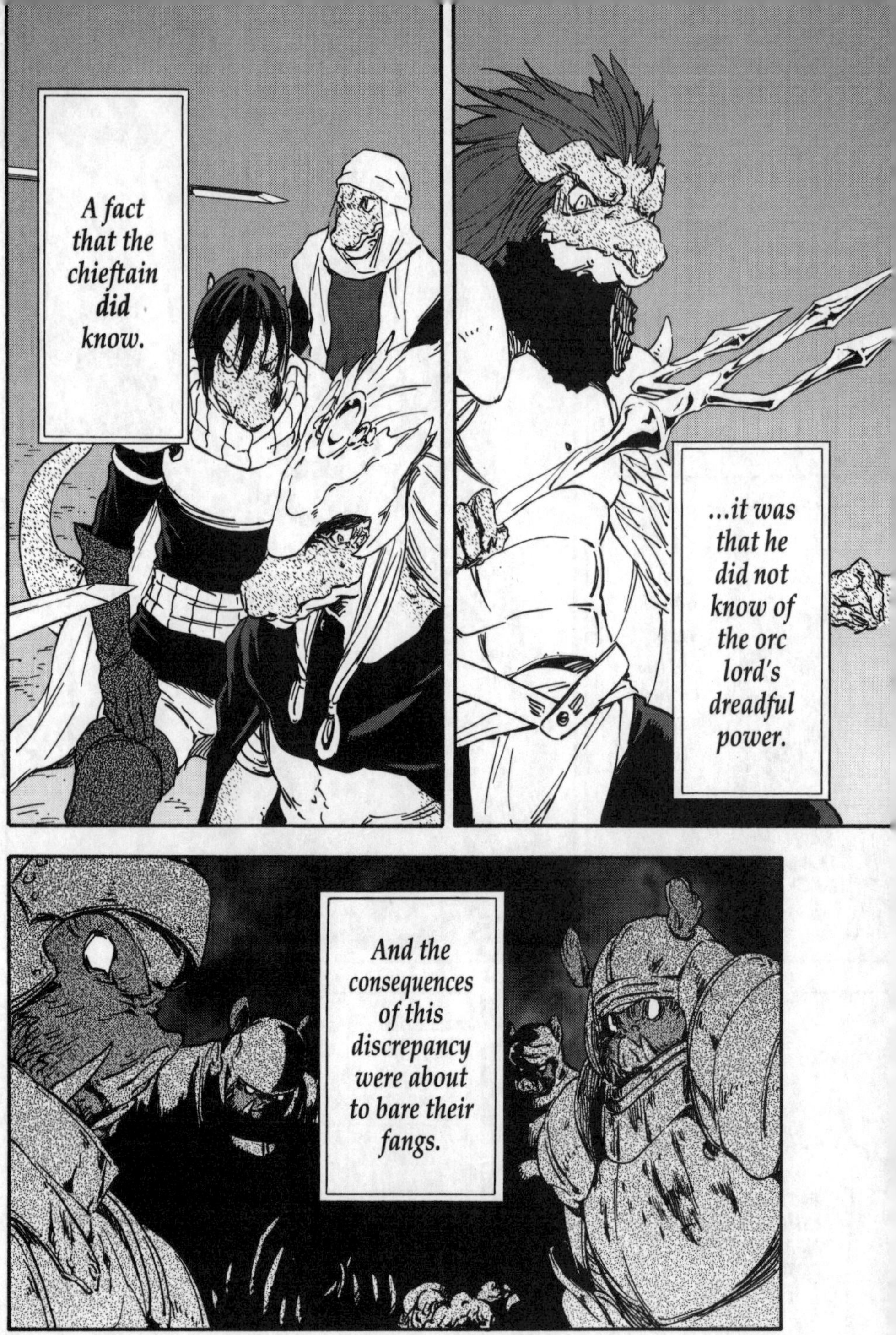
...it was that he did not know of the orc lord's dreadful power.
A fact that the chieftain did know.
And the consequences of this discrepancy were about to bare their fangs.

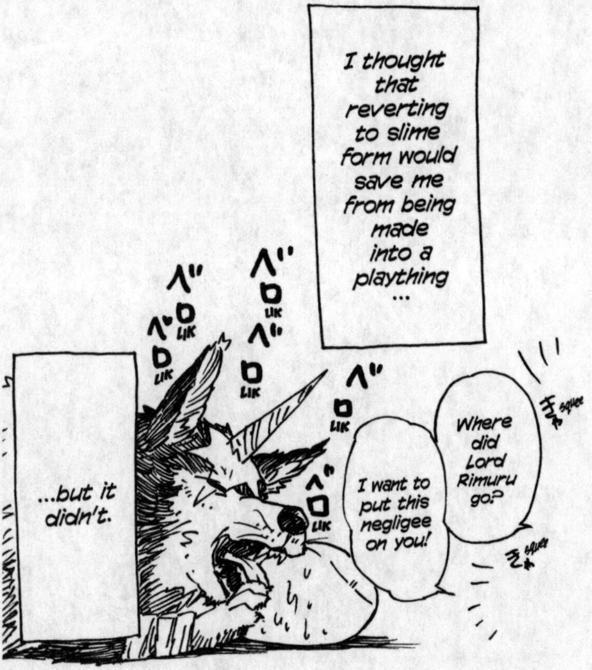
I thought that reverting to slime form would save me from being made into a plaything...
Where did Lord Rimuru go?
I want to put this negligee on you!
ベロ LIK
ベロ LIK
ベロ LIK
ベロ LIK
ベロ LIK
ベロ LIK
...but it didn't.

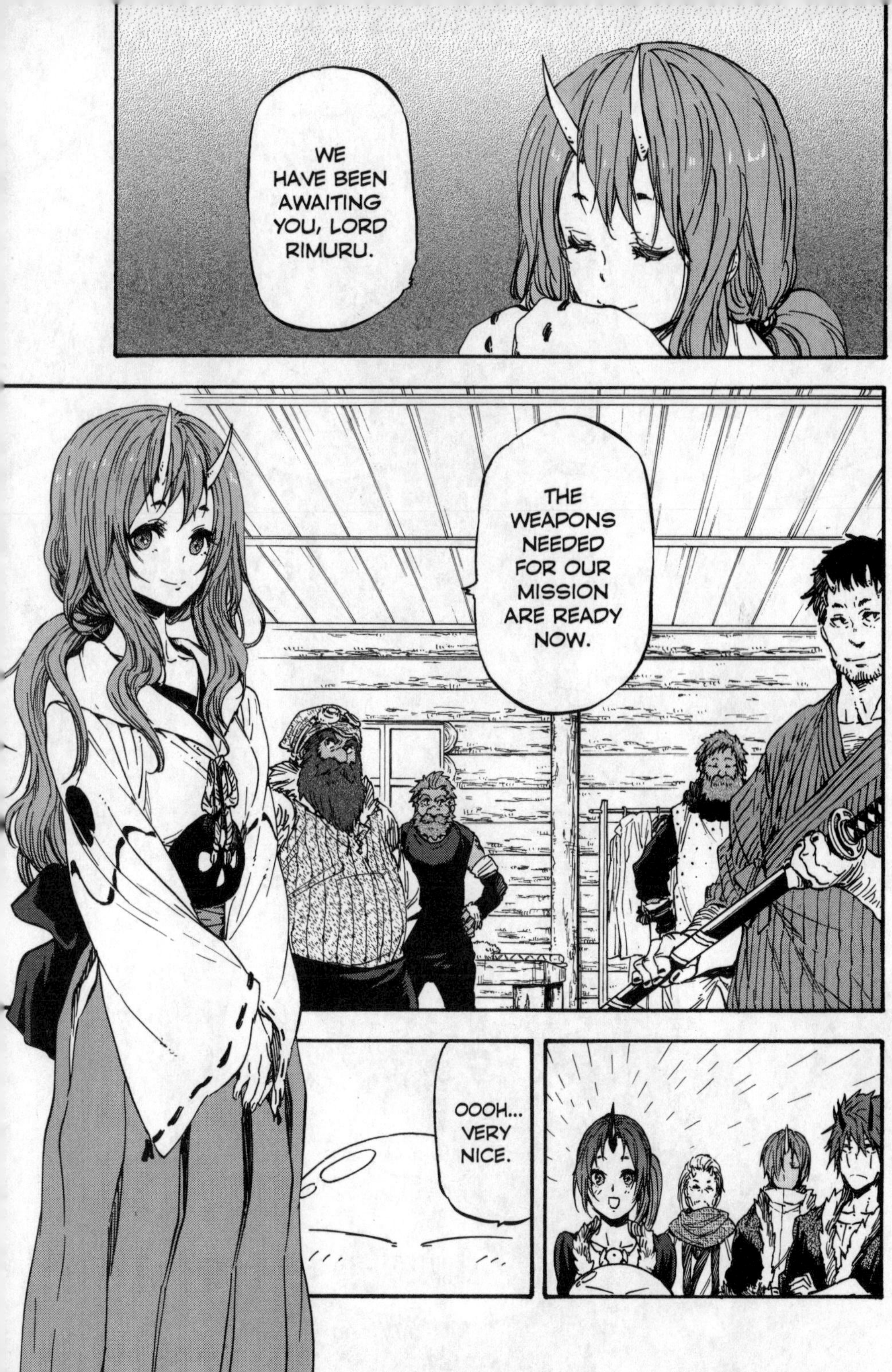
WE HAVE BEEN AWAITING YOU, LORD RIMURU.
THE WEAPONS NEEDED FOR OUR MISSION ARE READY NOW.
OOOH... VERY NICE.

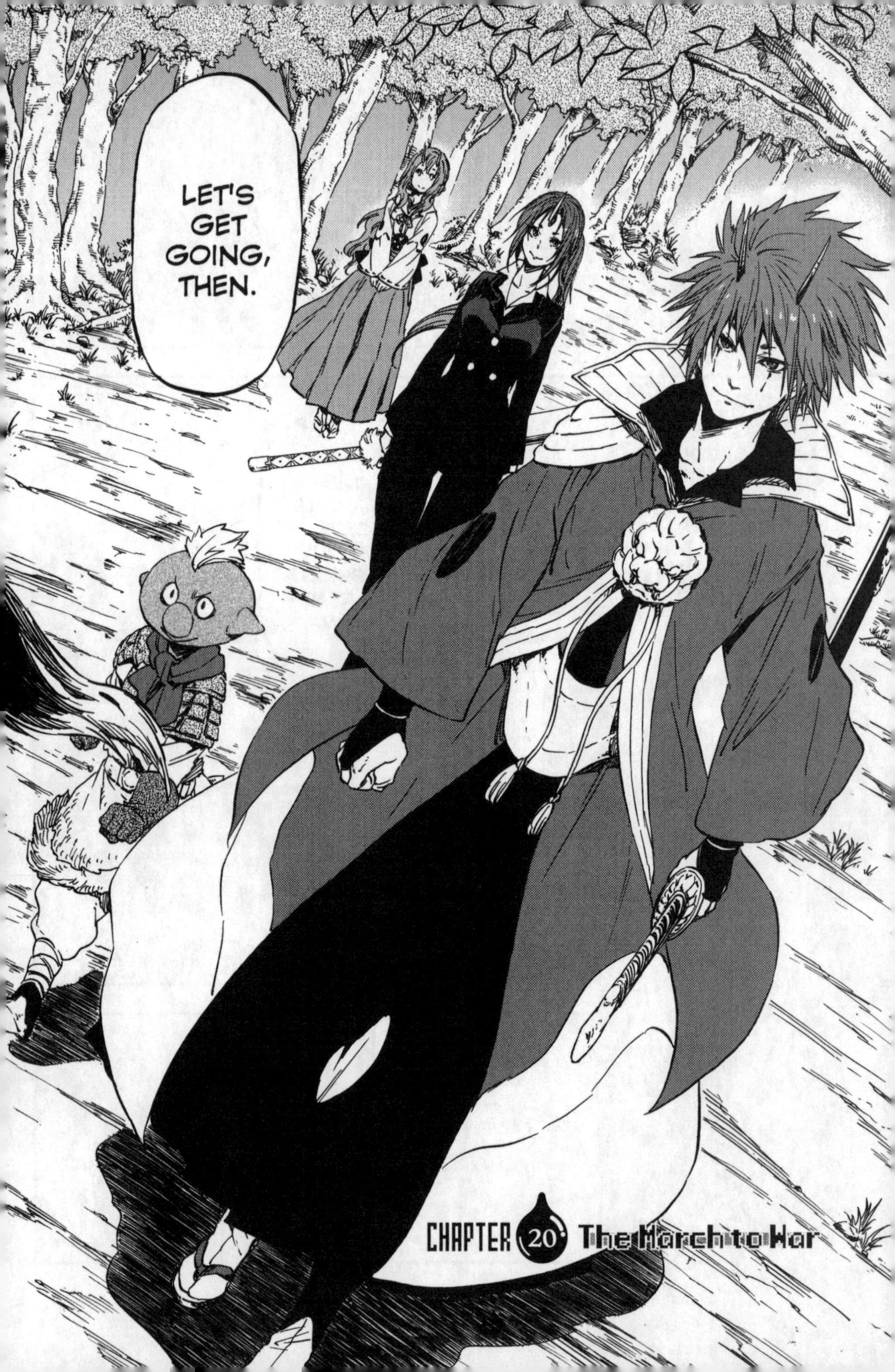
LET'S GET GOING, THEN.
CHAPTER 20 The March to War

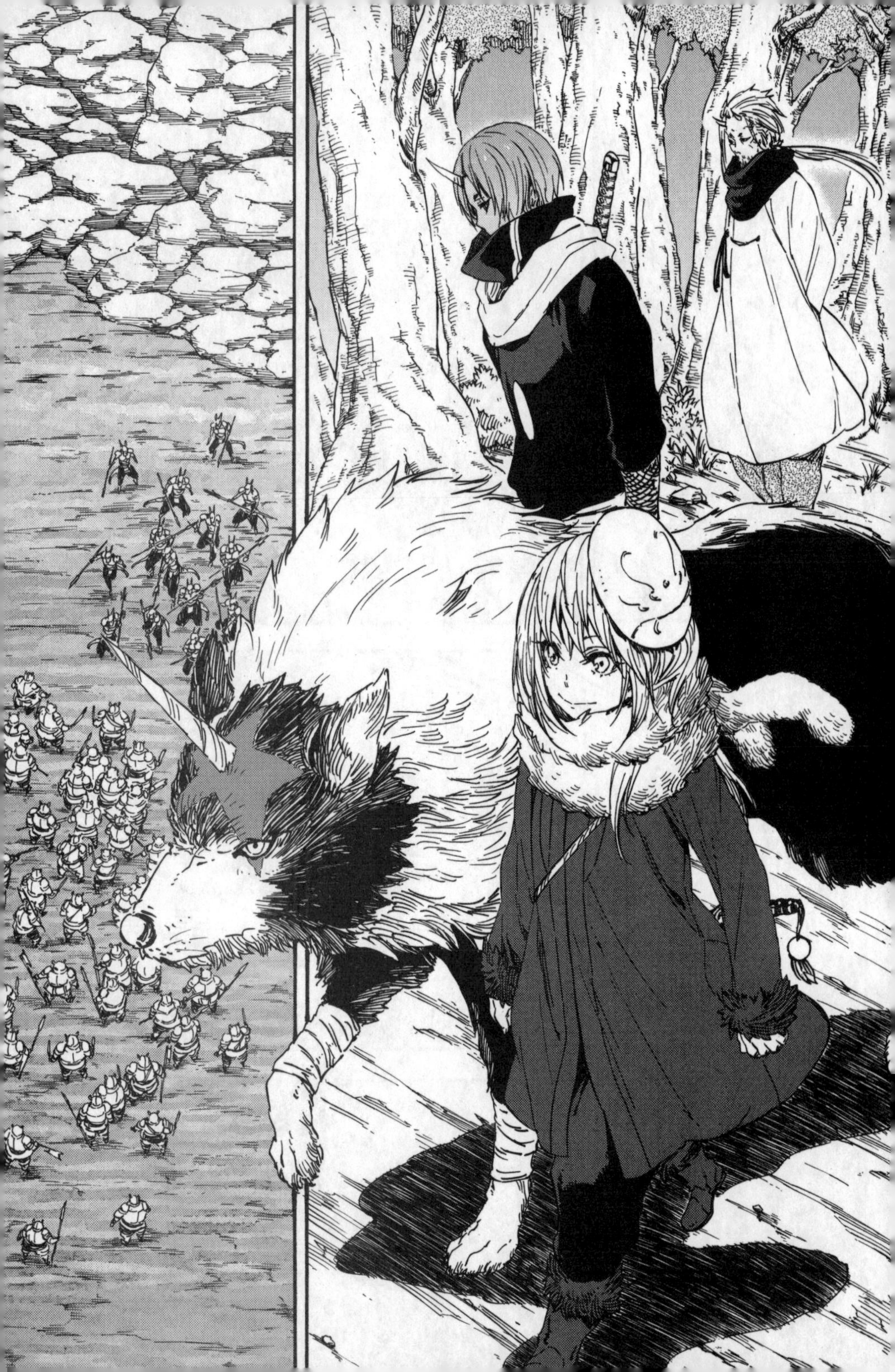

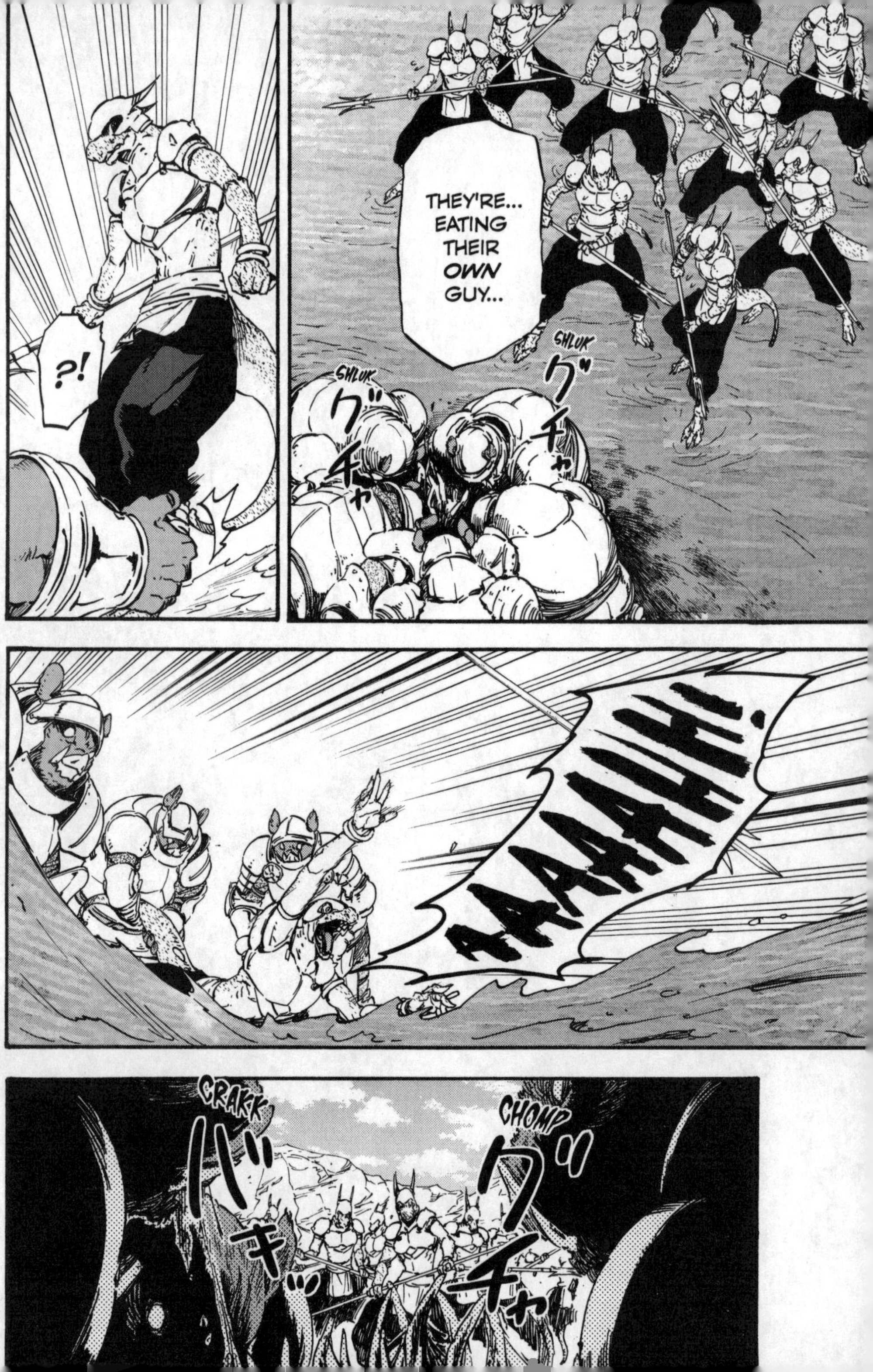
THEY'RE... EATING THEIR *OWN* GUY...
SHLUK
グチャ
SHLUK
グチャ
?!
AAAAHH!!
CHOMP
グチャ
CRAKK
バキッ

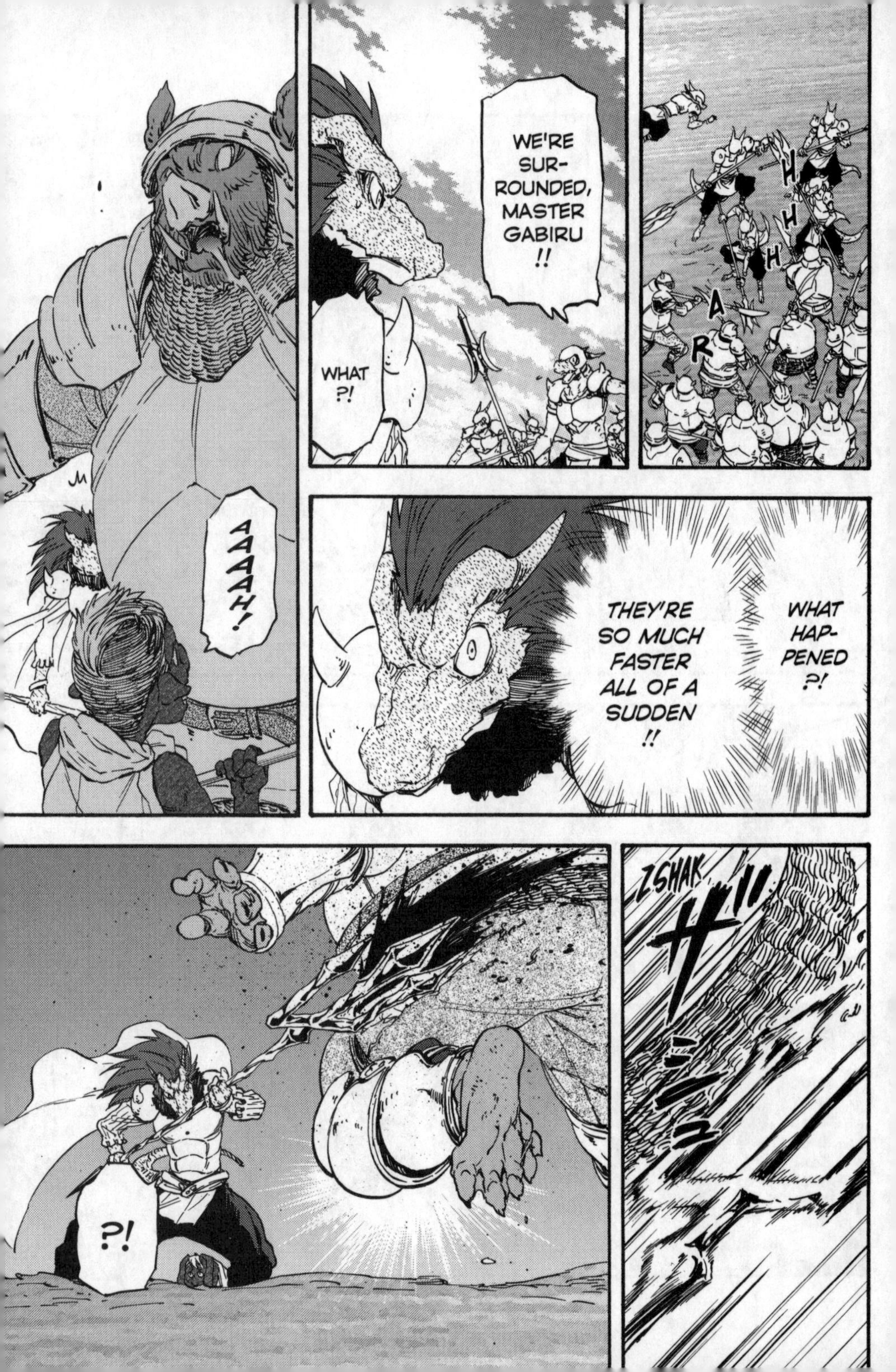
RAHHH
WE'RE SURROUNDED, MASTER GABIRU!!
WHAT?!
WHAT HAPPENED?!
THEY'RE SO MUCH FASTER ALL OF A SUDDEN!!
AAAAH!
ZSHAK!!
?!

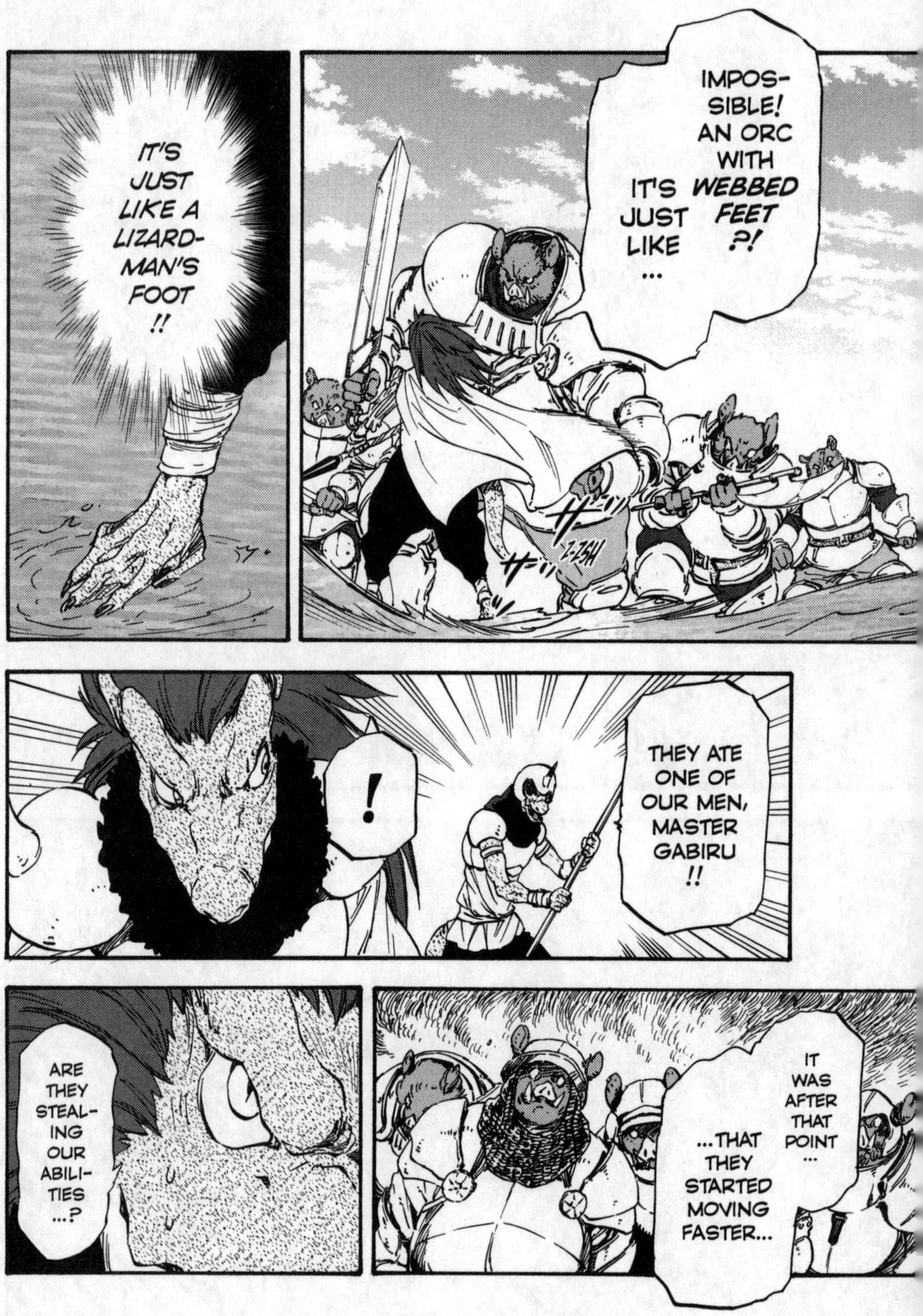
IMPOSSIBLE! AN ORC WITH WEBBED FEET?!
IT'S JUST LIKE ...
Z-ZSH
IT'S JUST LIKE A LIZARD-MAN'S FOOT!!
THEY ATE ONE OF OUR MEN, MASTER GABIRU!!
!
IT WAS AFTER THAT POINT ...
...THAT THEY STARTED MOVING FASTER...
ARE THEY STEALING OUR ABILITIES ...?

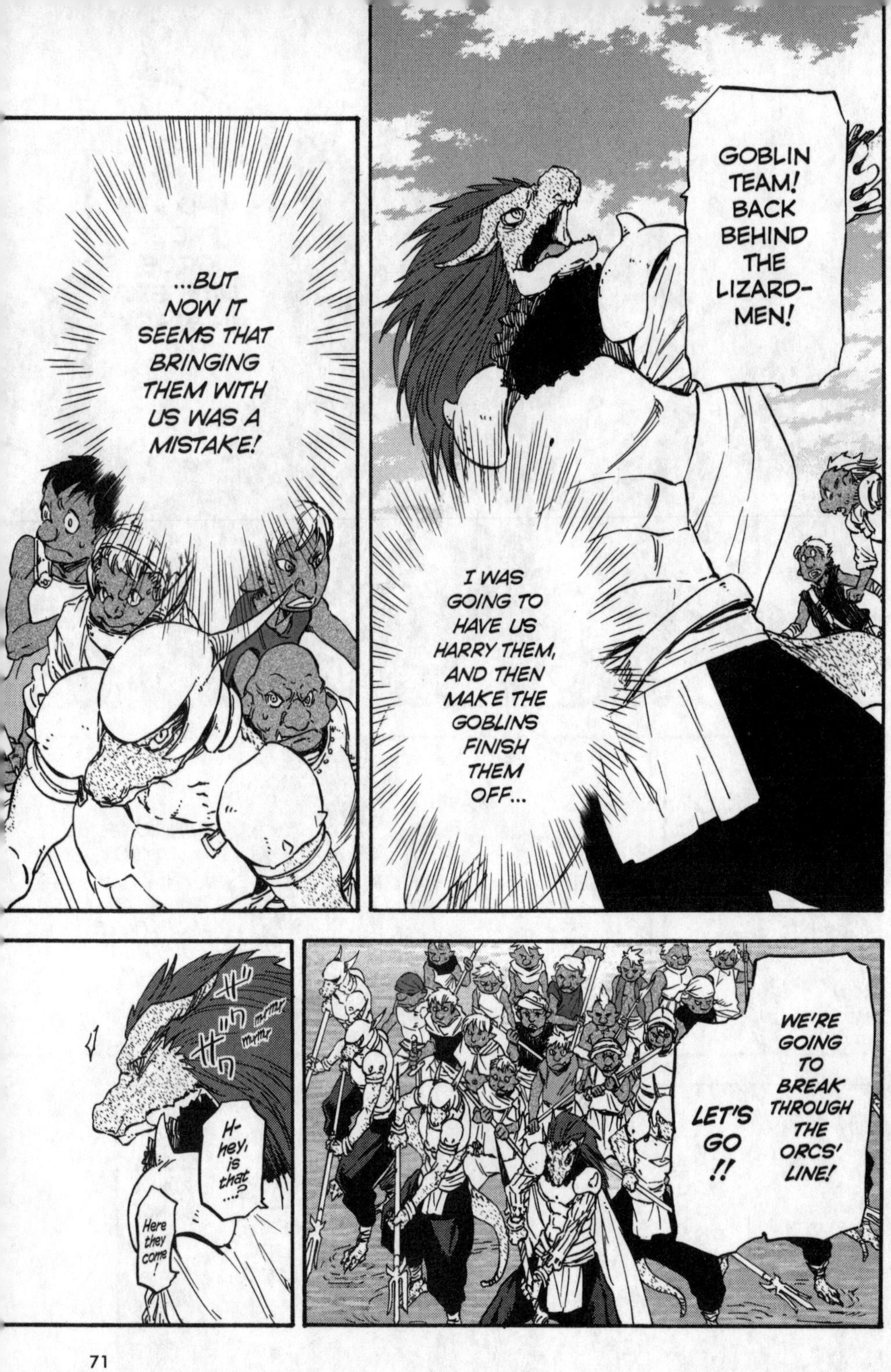
GOBLIN TEAM! BACK BEHIND THE LIZARD-MEN!
I WAS GOING TO HAVE US HARRY THEM, AND THEN MAKE THE GOBLINS FINISH THEM OFF...
...BUT NOW IT SEEMS THAT BRINGING THEM WITH US WAS A MISTAKE!
WE'RE GOING TO BREAK THROUGH THE ORCS' LINE!
LET'S GO!!
mrmr mrmr
H-hey, is that...?
Here they come!

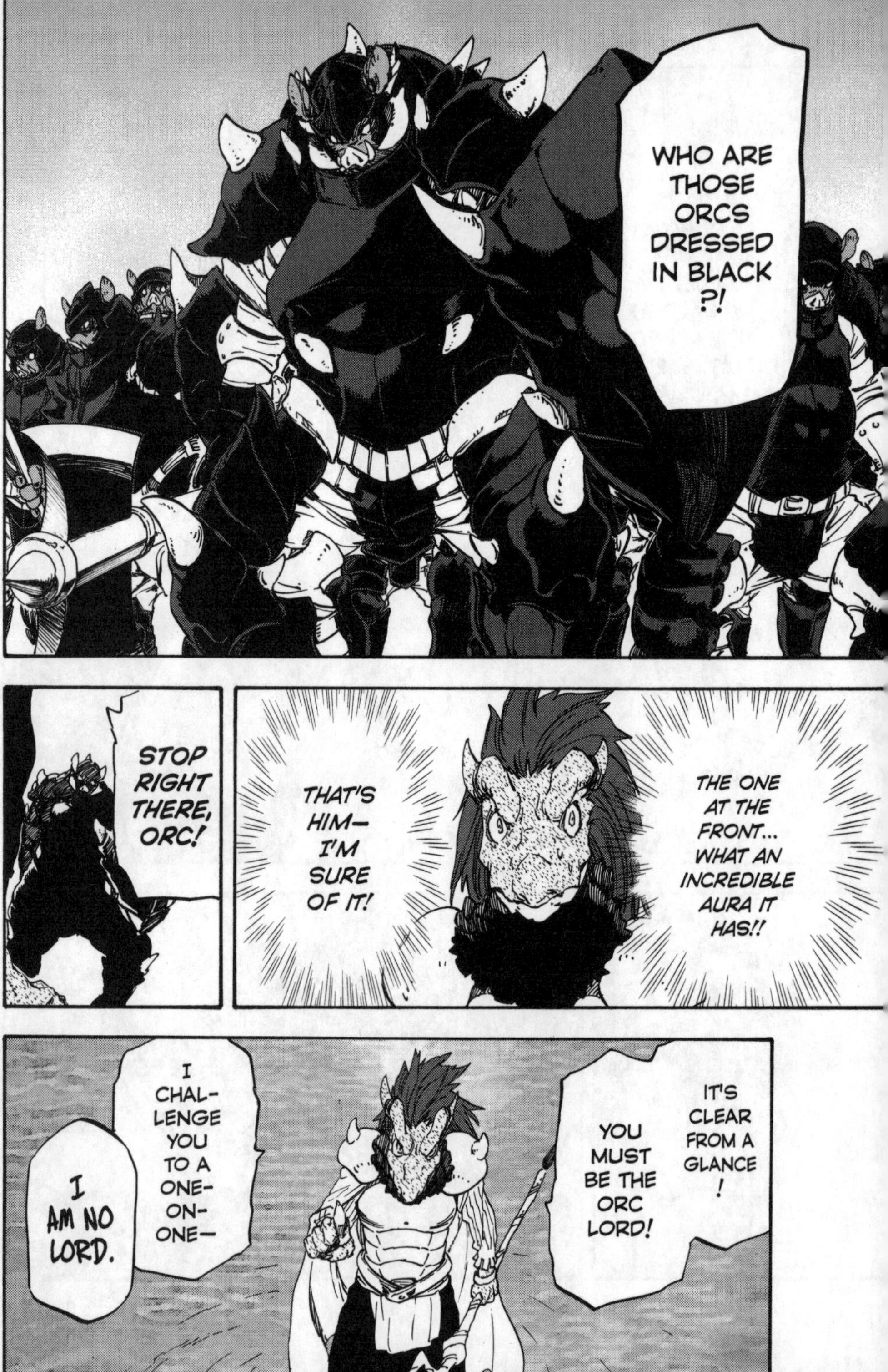
WHO ARE THOSE ORCS DRESSED IN BLACK?!
THE ONE AT THE FRONT... WHAT AN INCREDIBLE AURA IT HAS!!
THAT'S HIM— I'M SURE OF IT!
STOP RIGHT THERE, ORC!
IT'S CLEAR FROM A GLANCE!
YOU MUST BE THE ORC LORD!
I CHALLENGE YOU TO A ONE-ON-ONE—
I AM NO LORD.

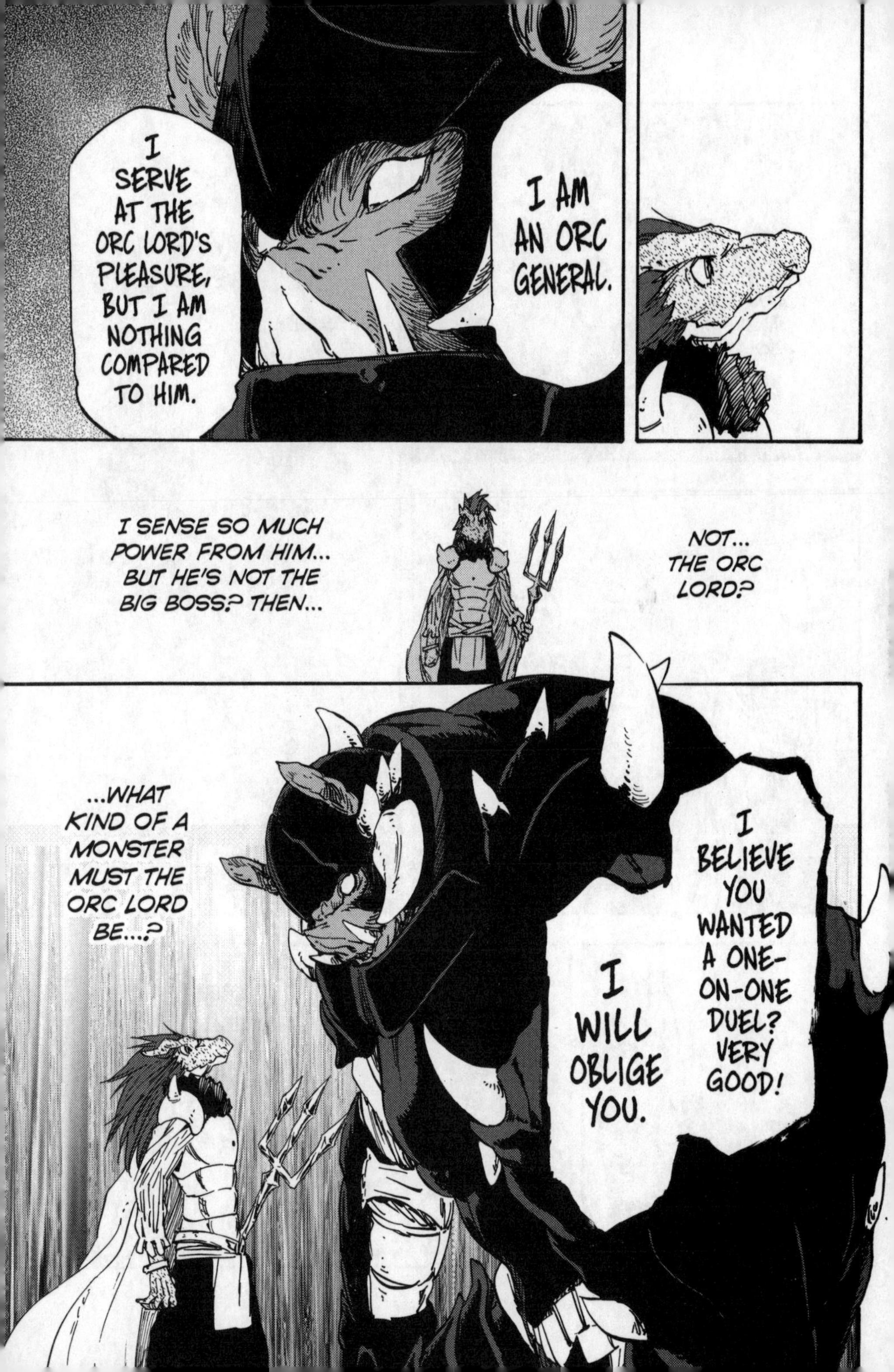
I AM AN ORC GENERAL.
I SERVE AT THE ORC LORD'S PLEASURE, BUT I AM NOTHING COMPARED TO HIM.
NOT... THE ORC LORD?
I SENSE SO MUCH POWER FROM HIM... BUT HE'S NOT THE BIG BOSS? THEN...
I BELIEVE YOU WANTED A ONE-ON-ONE DUEL? VERY GOOD!
I WILL OBLIGE YOU.
...WHAT KIND OF A MONSTER MUST THE ORC LORD BE...?

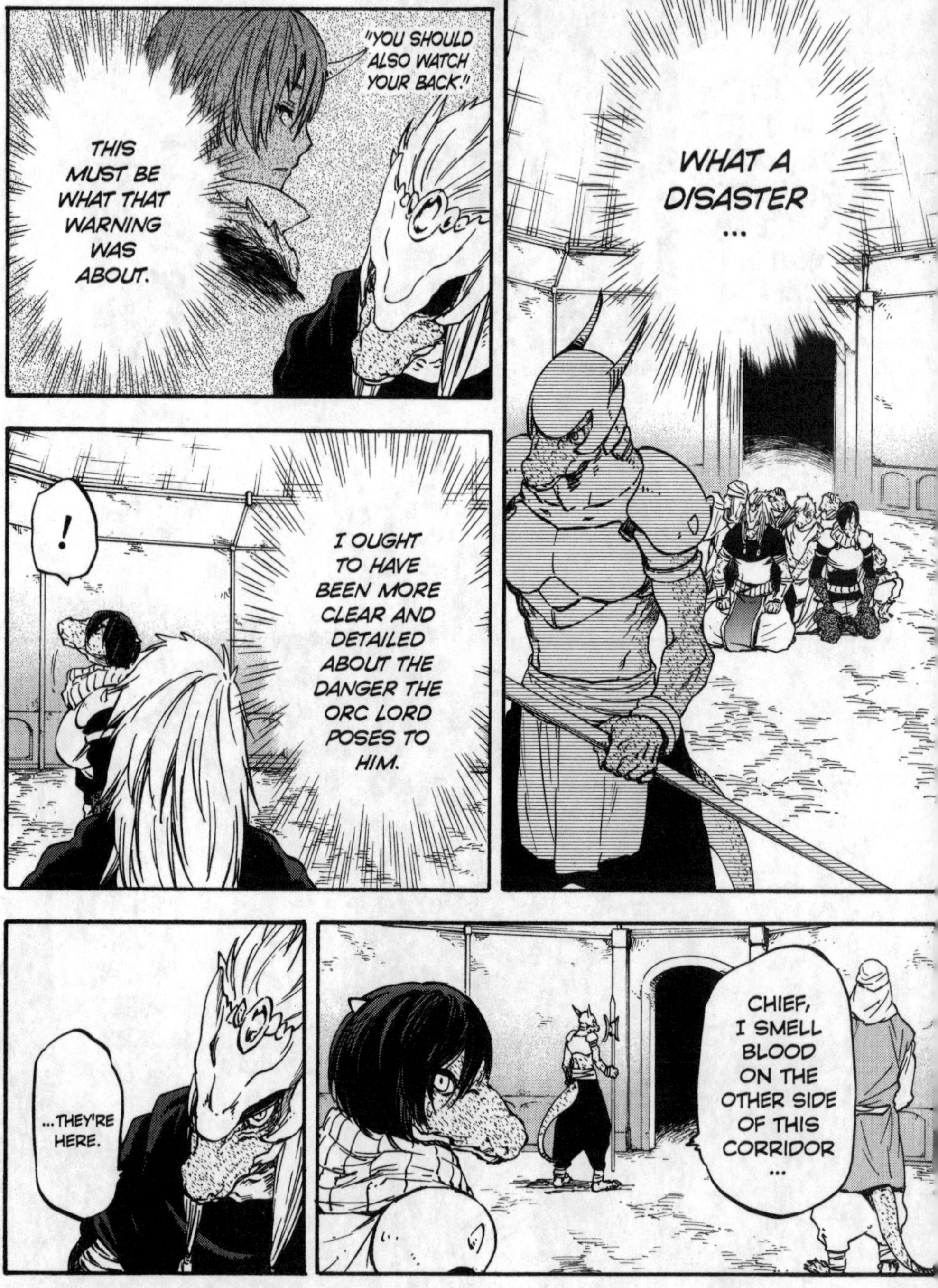
WHAT A DISASTER ...
"YOU SHOULD ALSO WATCH YOUR BACK."
THIS MUST BE WHAT THAT WARNING WAS ABOUT.
I OUGHT TO HAVE BEEN MORE CLEAR AND DETAILED ABOUT THE DANGER THE ORC LORD POSES TO HIM.
!
CHIEF, I SMELL BLOOD ON THE OTHER SIDE OF THIS CORRIDOR ...
...THEY'RE HERE.

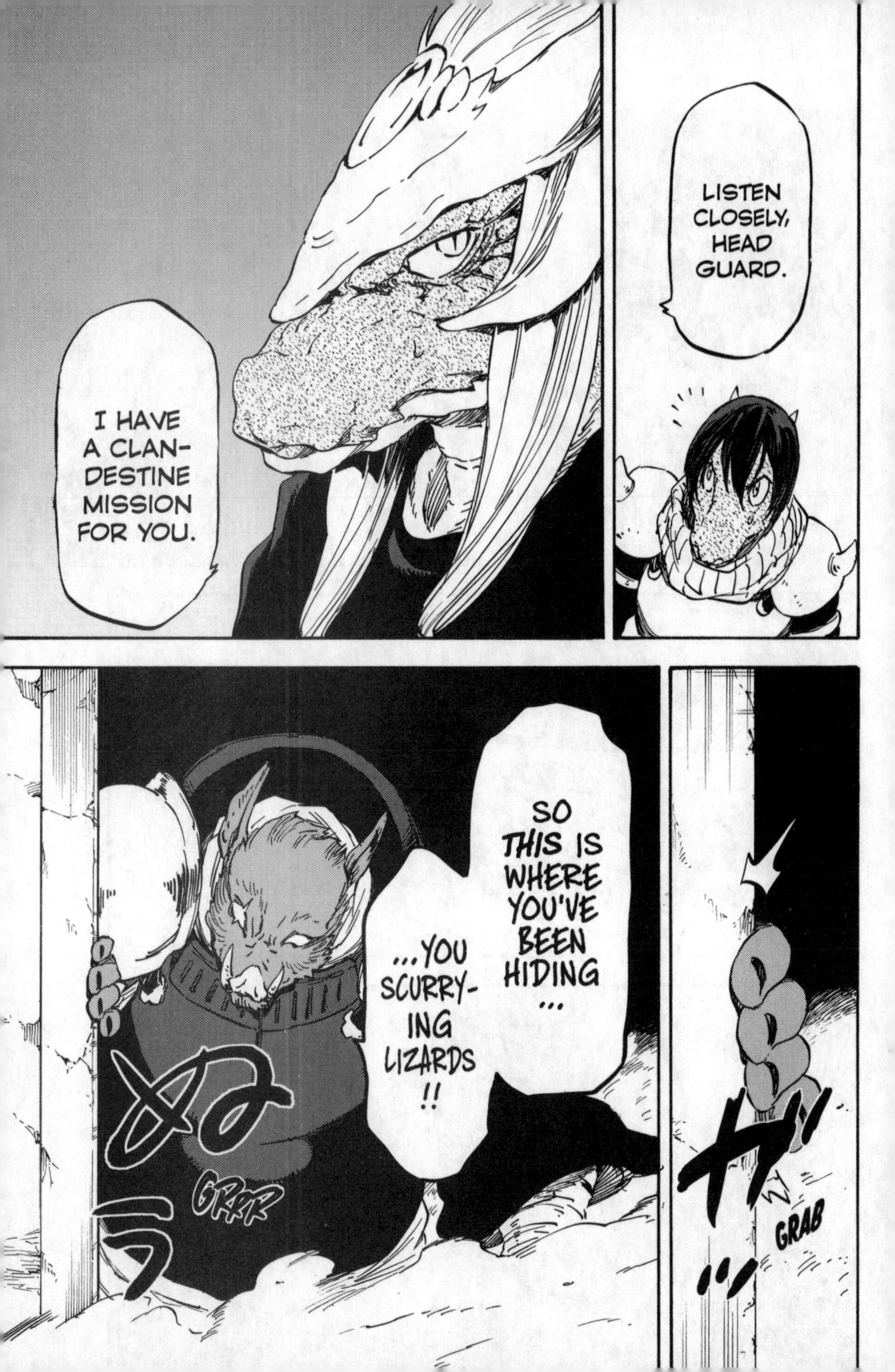
LISTEN CLOSELY, HEAD GUARD.
I HAVE A CLAN-DESTINE MISSION FOR YOU.
GRAB
SO THIS IS WHERE YOU'VE BEEN HIDING...
...YOU SCURRY-ING LIZARDS!!
GRRR

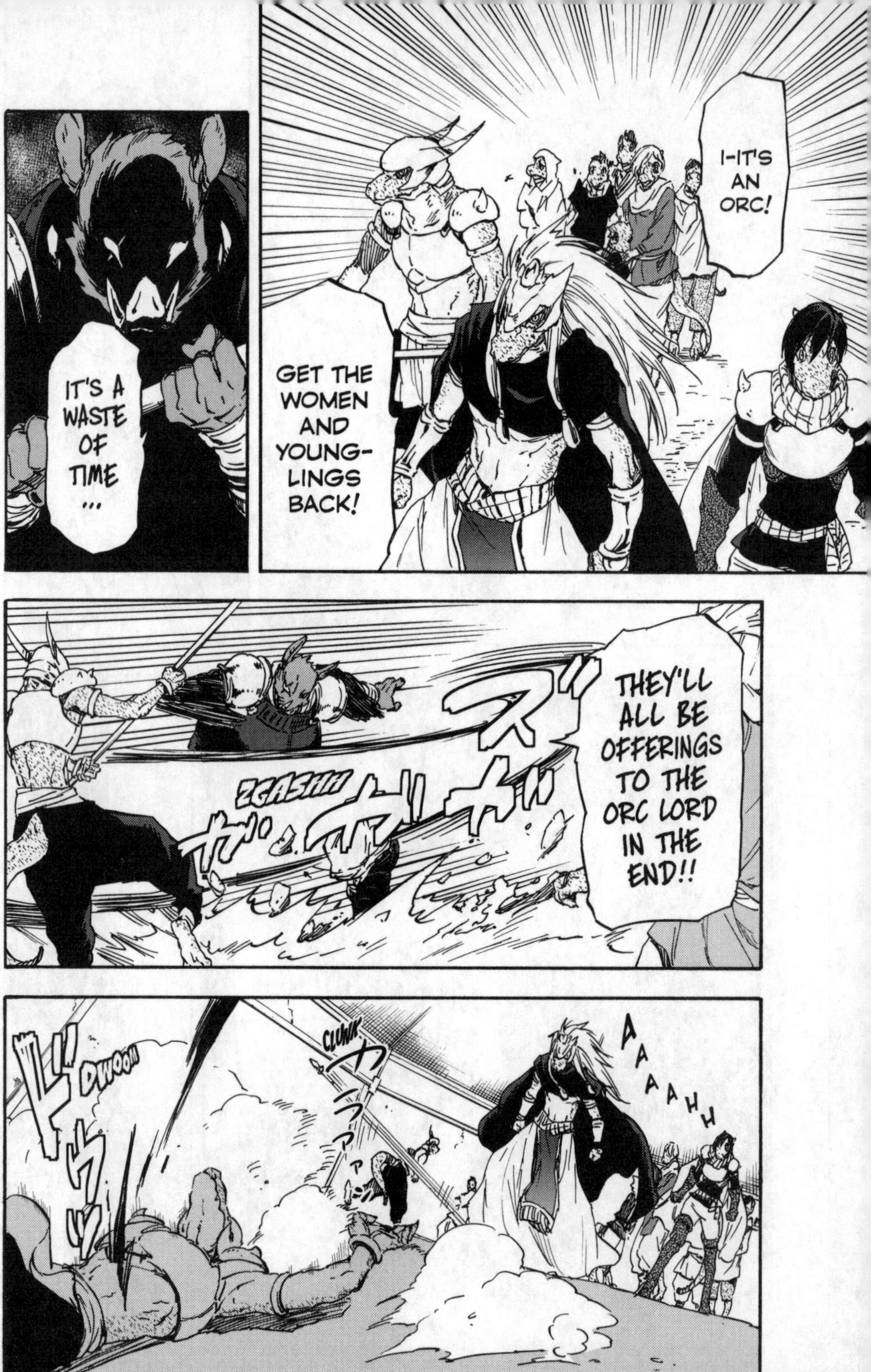
I-IT'S AN ORC!
GET THE WOMEN AND YOUNG-LINGS BACK!
IT'S A WASTE OF TIME ...
THEY'LL ALL BE OFFERINGS TO THE ORC LORD IN THE END!!
ZGASHH
AAAAAHH
CLUNK
DWOOM

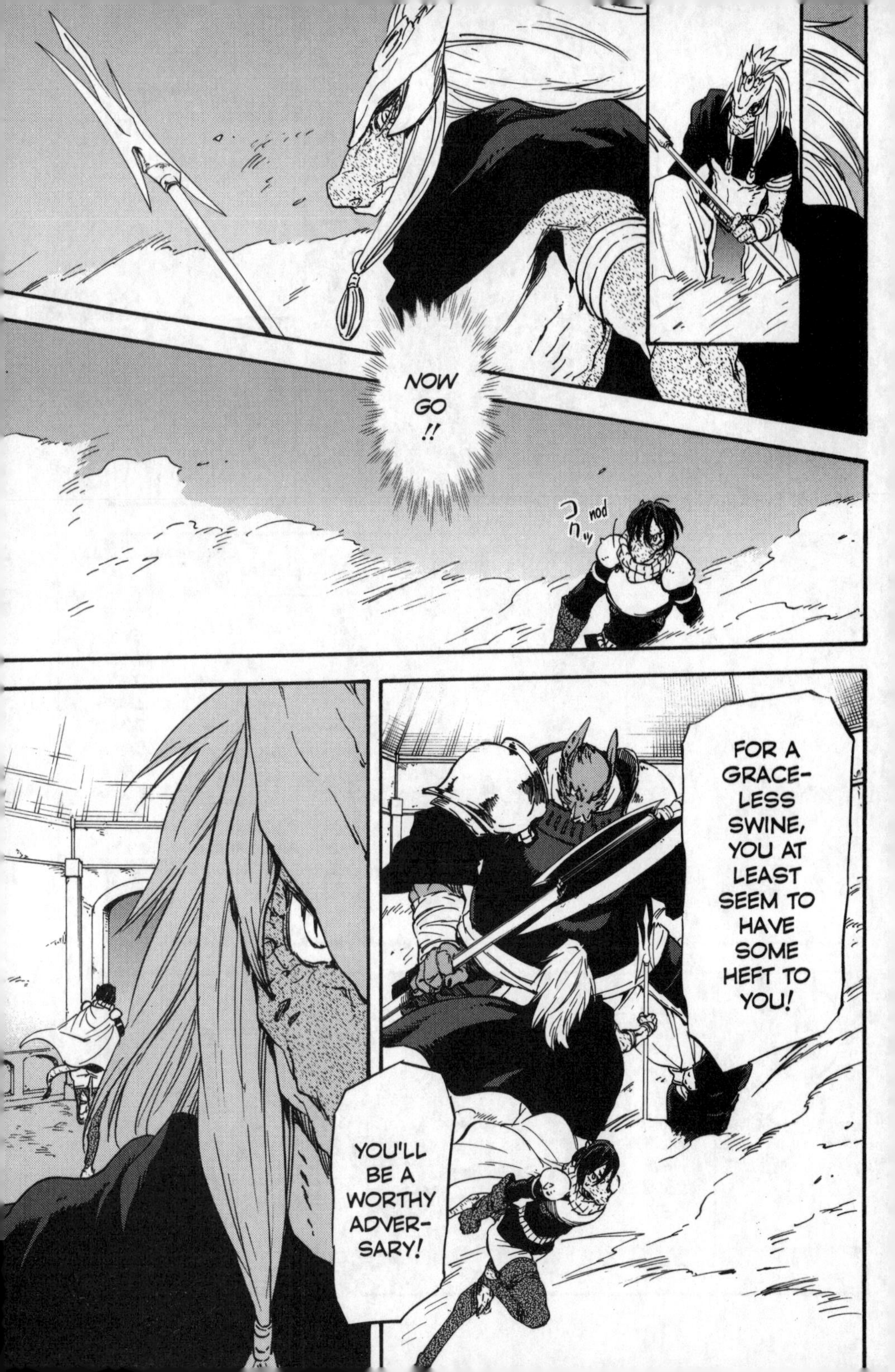
NOW GO !!
コクッ
nod
FOR A GRACE-LESS SWINE, YOU AT LEAST SEEM TO HAVE SOME HEFT TO YOU!
YOU'LL BE A WORTHY ADVER-SARY!

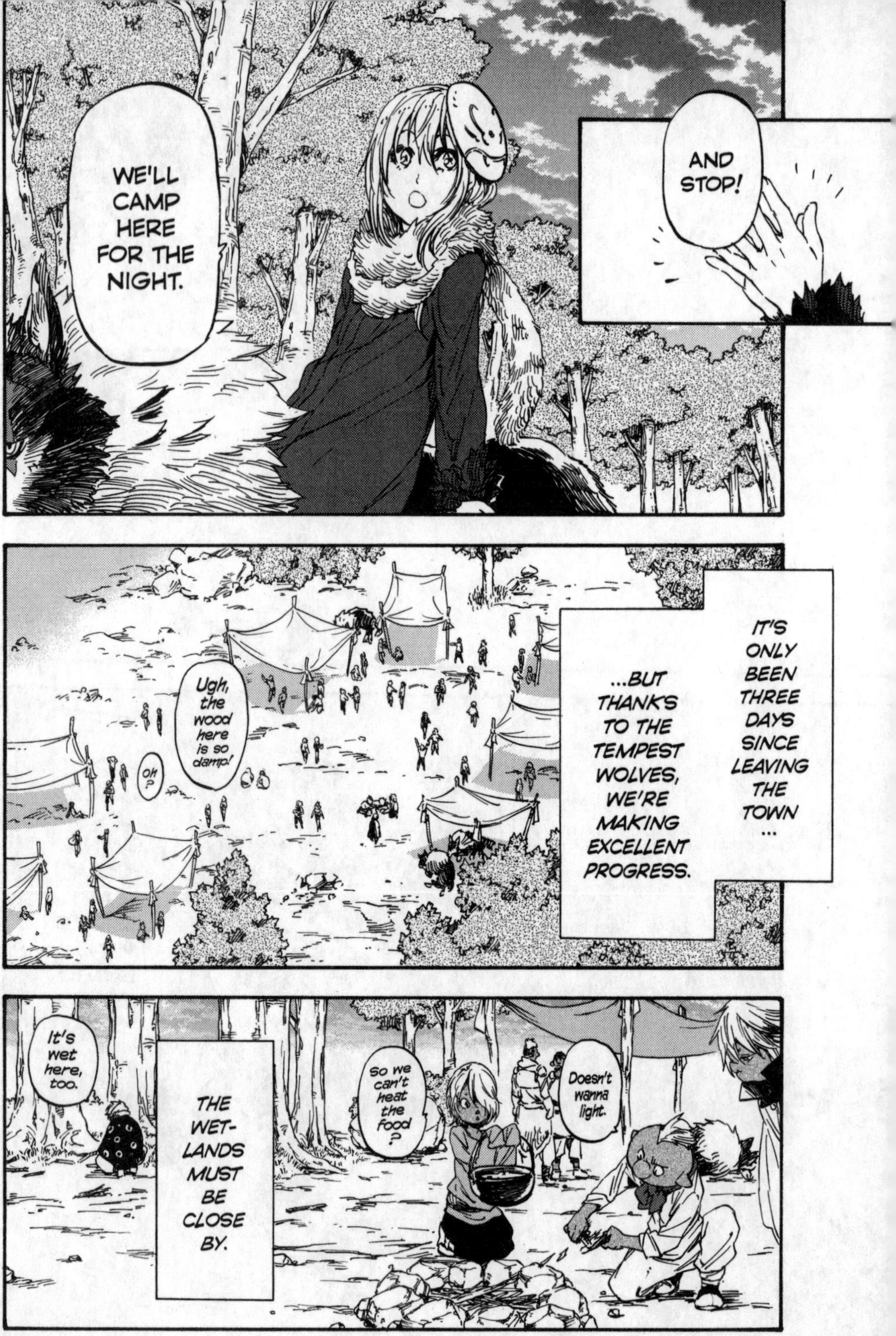
AND STOP!
WE'LL CAMP HERE FOR THE NIGHT.
IT'S ONLY BEEN THREE DAYS SINCE LEAVING THE TOWN ...
...BUT THANKS TO THE TEMPEST WOLVES, WE'RE MAKING EXCELLENT PROGRESS.
Ugh, the wood here is so damp!
Oh?
Doesn't wanna light.
So we can't heat the food?
THE WET-LANDS MUST BE CLOSE BY.
It's wet here, too.

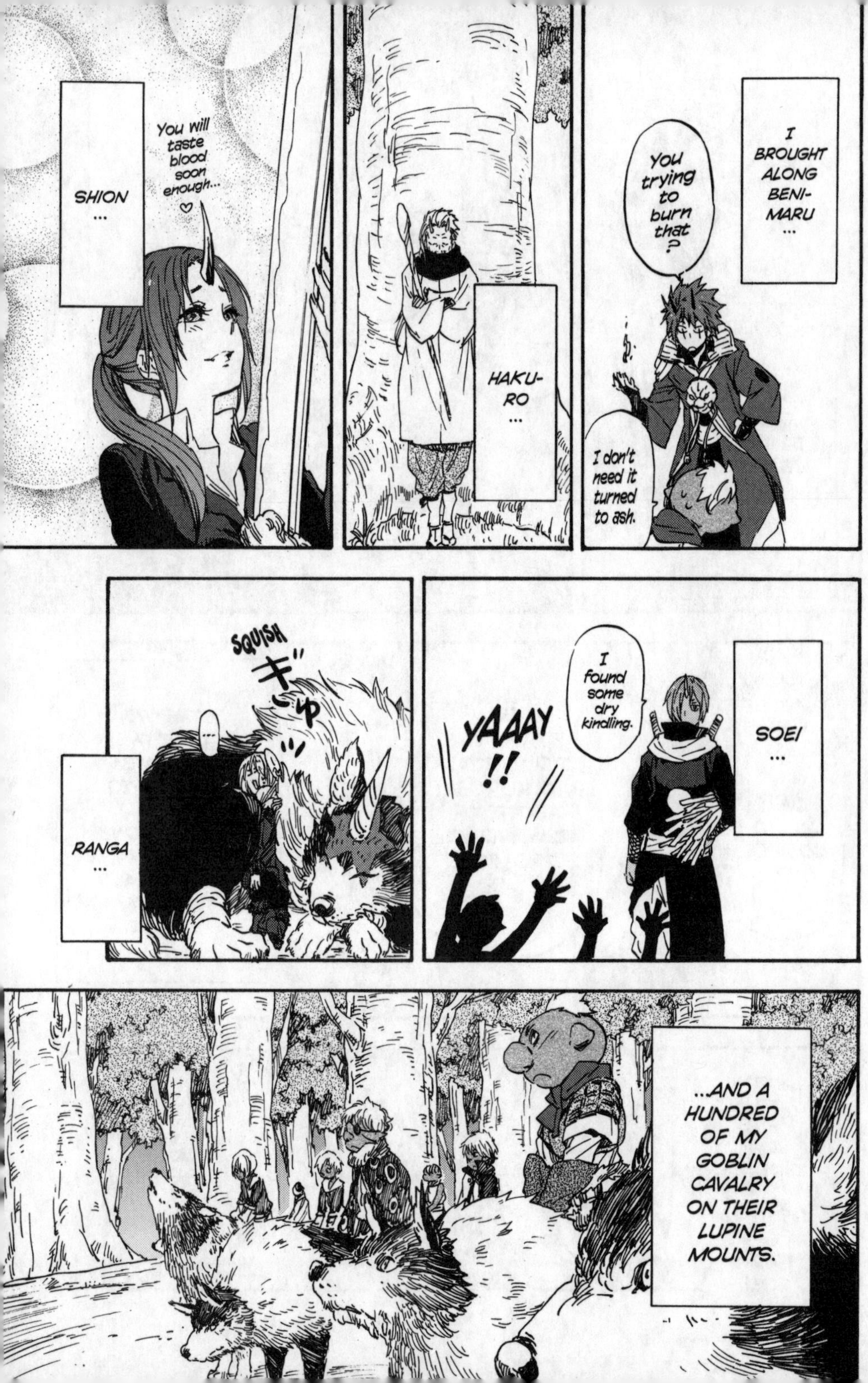
I BROUGHT ALONG BENI-MARU ...
You trying to burn that?
I don't need it turned to ash.
HAKU-RO ...
SHION ...
You will taste blood soon enough... ♡
SOEI ...
I found some dry kindling.
YAAAY !!
SQUISH
...
RANGA ...
...AND A HUNDRED OF MY GOBLIN CAVALRY ON THEIR LUPINE MOUNTS.

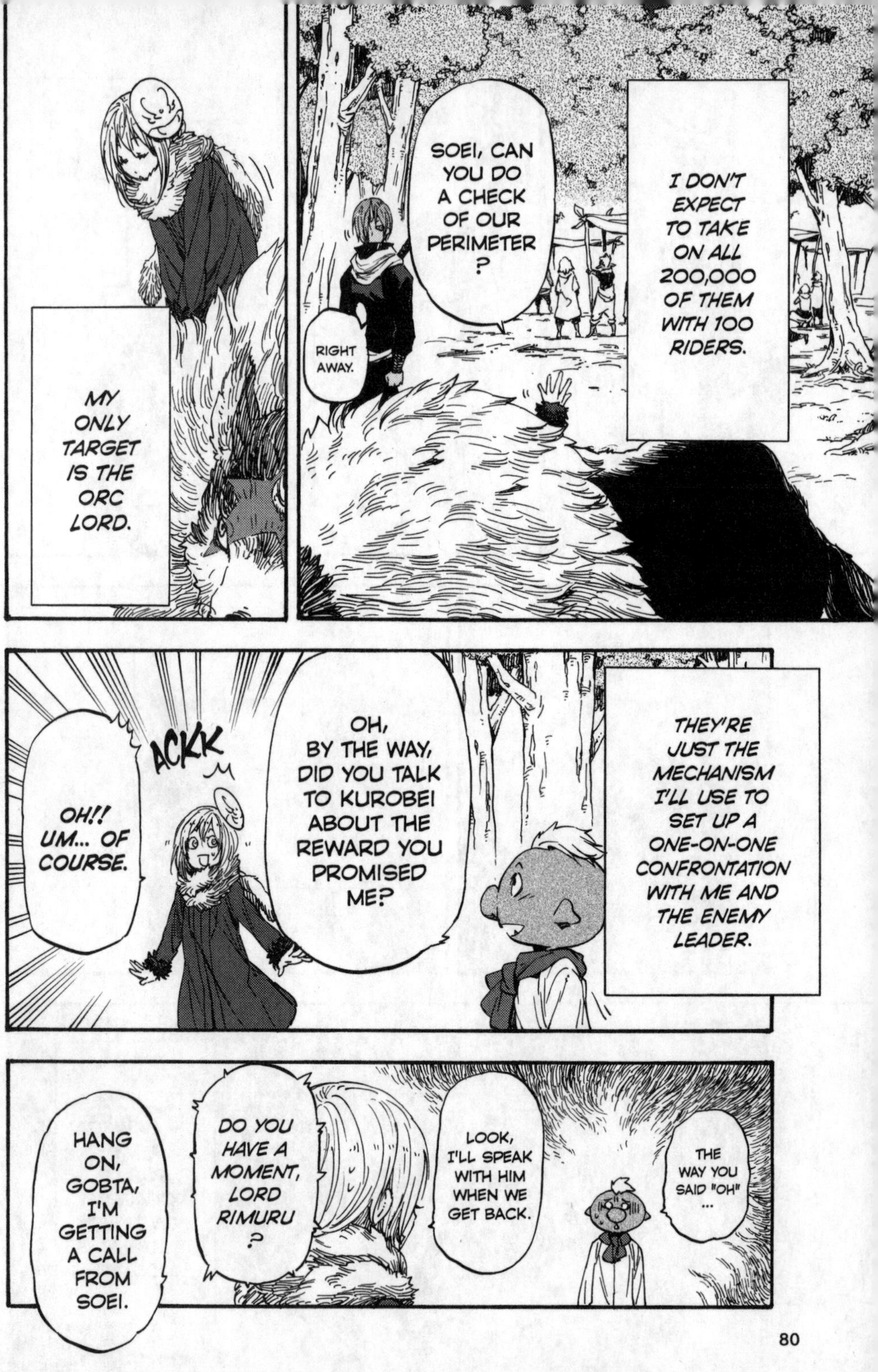
I DON'T EXPECT TO TAKE ON ALL 200,000 OF THEM WITH 100 RIDERS.
SOEI, CAN YOU DO A CHECK OF OUR PERIMETER?
RIGHT AWAY.
MY ONLY TARGET IS THE ORC LORD.
THEY'RE JUST THE MECHANISM I'LL USE TO SET UP A ONE-ON-ONE CONFRONTATION WITH ME AND THE ENEMY LEADER.
OH, BY THE WAY, DID YOU TALK TO KUROBEI ABOUT THE REWARD YOU PROMISED ME?
ACKK
OH!! UM... OF COURSE.
THE WAY YOU SAID "OH"...
LOOK, I'LL SPEAK WITH HIM WHEN WE GET BACK.
DO YOU HAVE A MOMENT, LORD RIMURU?
HANG ON, GOBTA, I'M GETTING A CALL FROM SOEI.

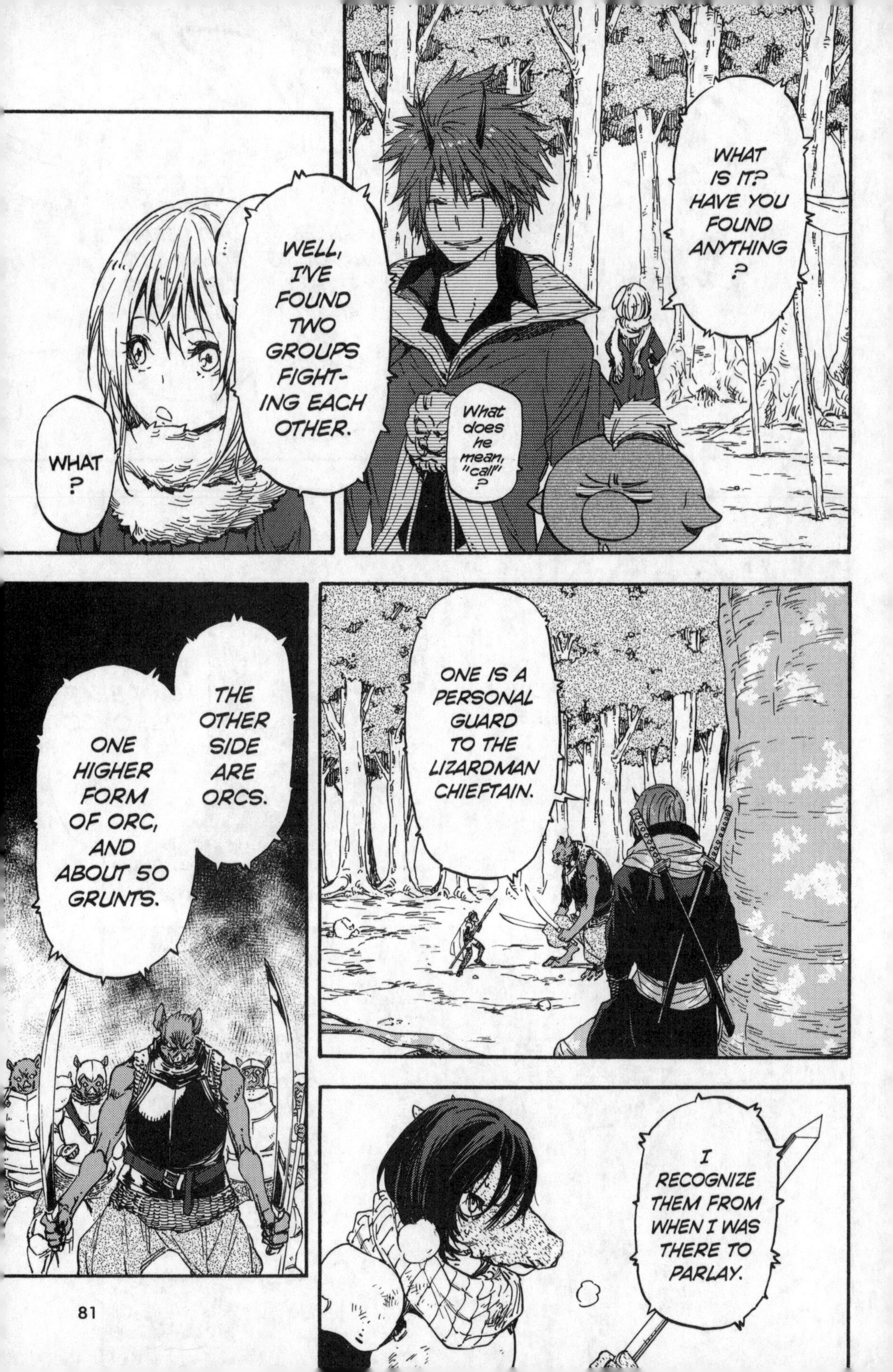
WHAT IS IT? HAVE YOU FOUND ANYTHING?
WELL, I'VE FOUND TWO GROUPS FIGHT-ING EACH OTHER.
What does he mean, "call"?
WHAT?
ONE IS A PERSONAL GUARD TO THE LIZARDMAN CHIEFTAIN.
I RECOGNIZE THEM FROM WHEN I WAS THERE TO PARLAY.
THE OTHER SIDE ARE ORCS.
ONE HIGHER FORM OF ORC, AND ABOUT 50 GRUNTS.

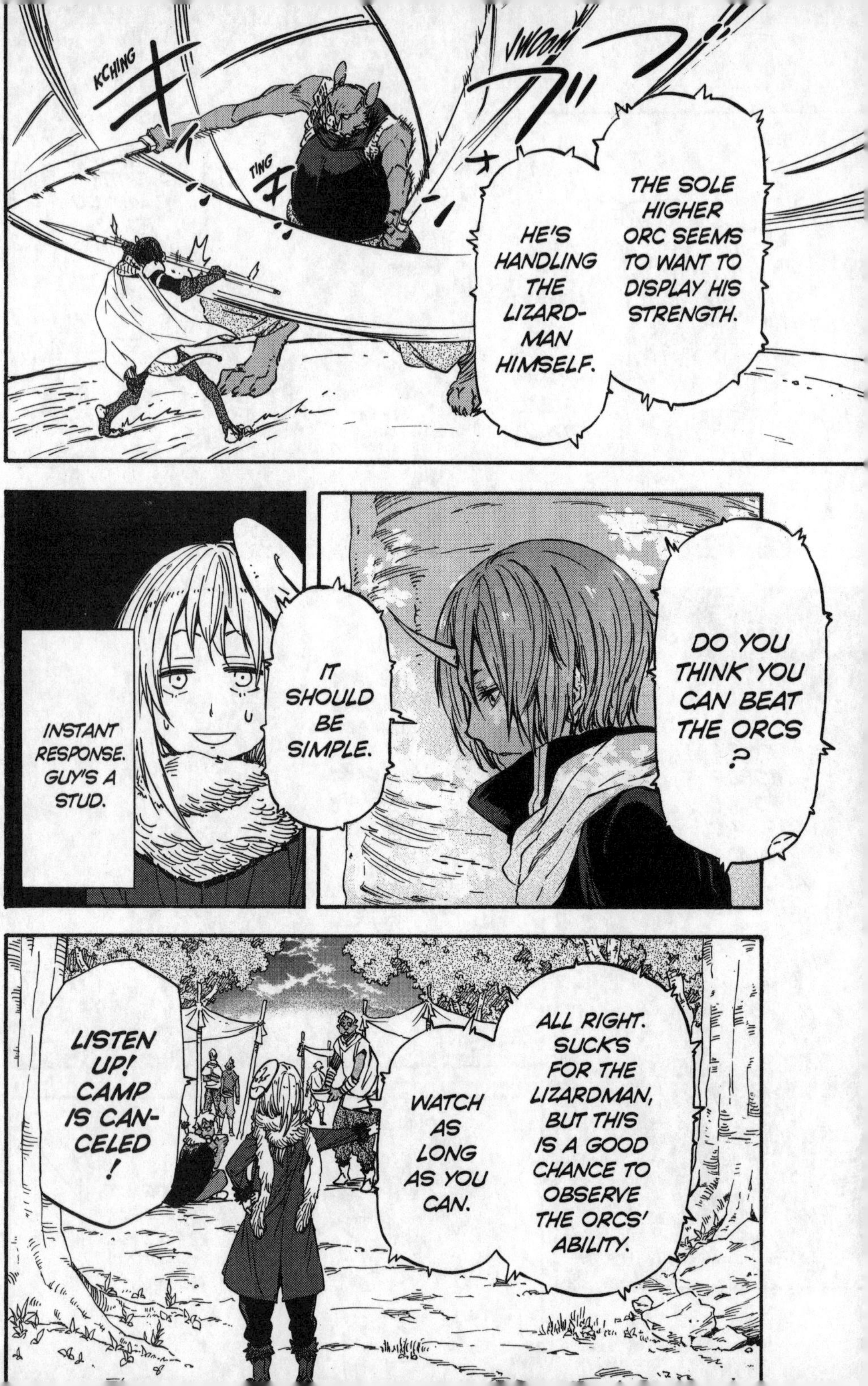
VWOOM
KCHING
TING
THE SOLE HIGHER ORC SEEMS TO WANT TO DISPLAY HIS STRENGTH.
HE'S HANDLING THE LIZARDMAN HIMSELF.
DO YOU THINK YOU CAN BEAT THE ORCS?
IT SHOULD BE SIMPLE.
INSTANT RESPONSE. GUY'S A STUD.
ALL RIGHT. SUCKS FOR THE LIZARDMAN, BUT THIS IS A GOOD CHANCE TO OBSERVE THE ORCS' ABILITY.
WATCH AS LONG AS YOU CAN.
LISTEN UP! CAMP IS CANCELED!

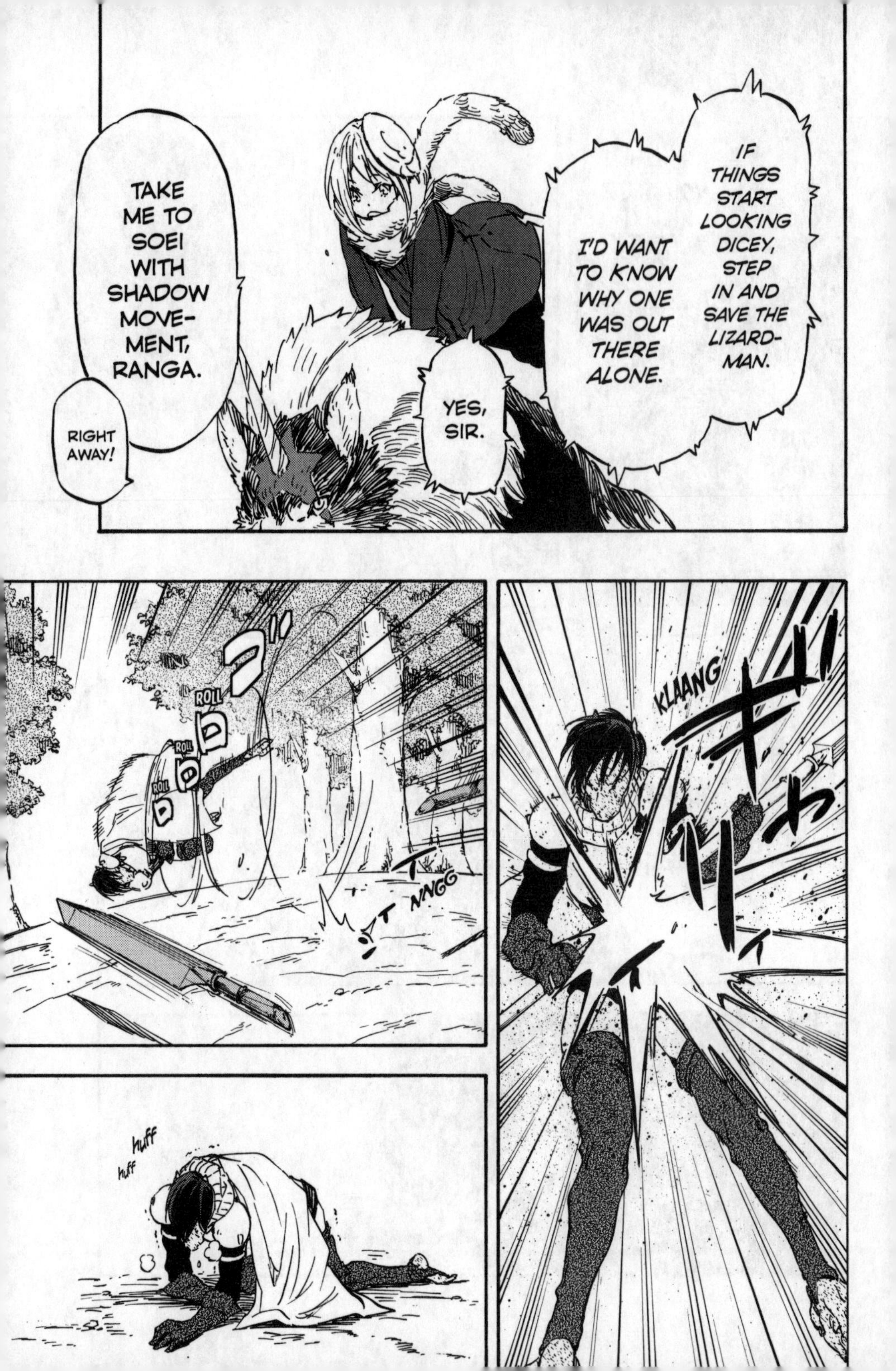
IF THINGS START LOOKING DICEY, STEP IN AND SAVE THE LIZARD-MAN.
I'D WANT TO KNOW WHY ONE WAS OUT THERE ALONE.
YES, SIR.
TAKE ME TO SOEI WITH SHADOW MOVE-MENT, RANGA.
RIGHT AWAY!
KLAANG
ROLL
ROLL
ROLL
TNNGG
huff
huff

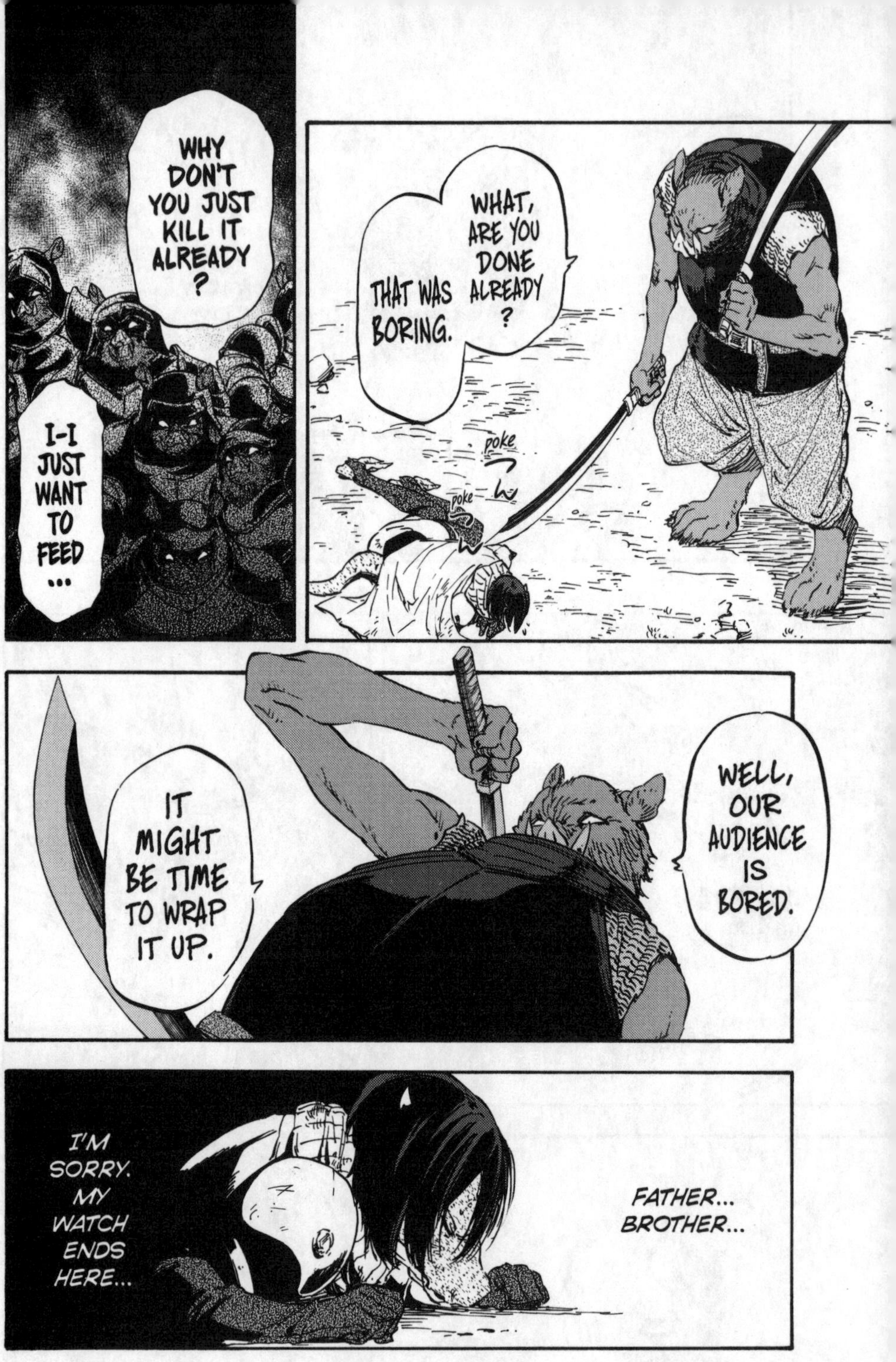
WHAT, ARE YOU DONE ALREADY?
THAT WAS BORING.
poke
poke
WHY DON'T YOU JUST KILL IT ALREADY?
I-I JUST WANT TO FEED...
WELL, OUR AUDIENCE IS BORED.
IT MIGHT BE TIME TO WRAP IT UP.
FATHER... BROTHER...
I'M SORRY. MY WATCH ENDS HERE...

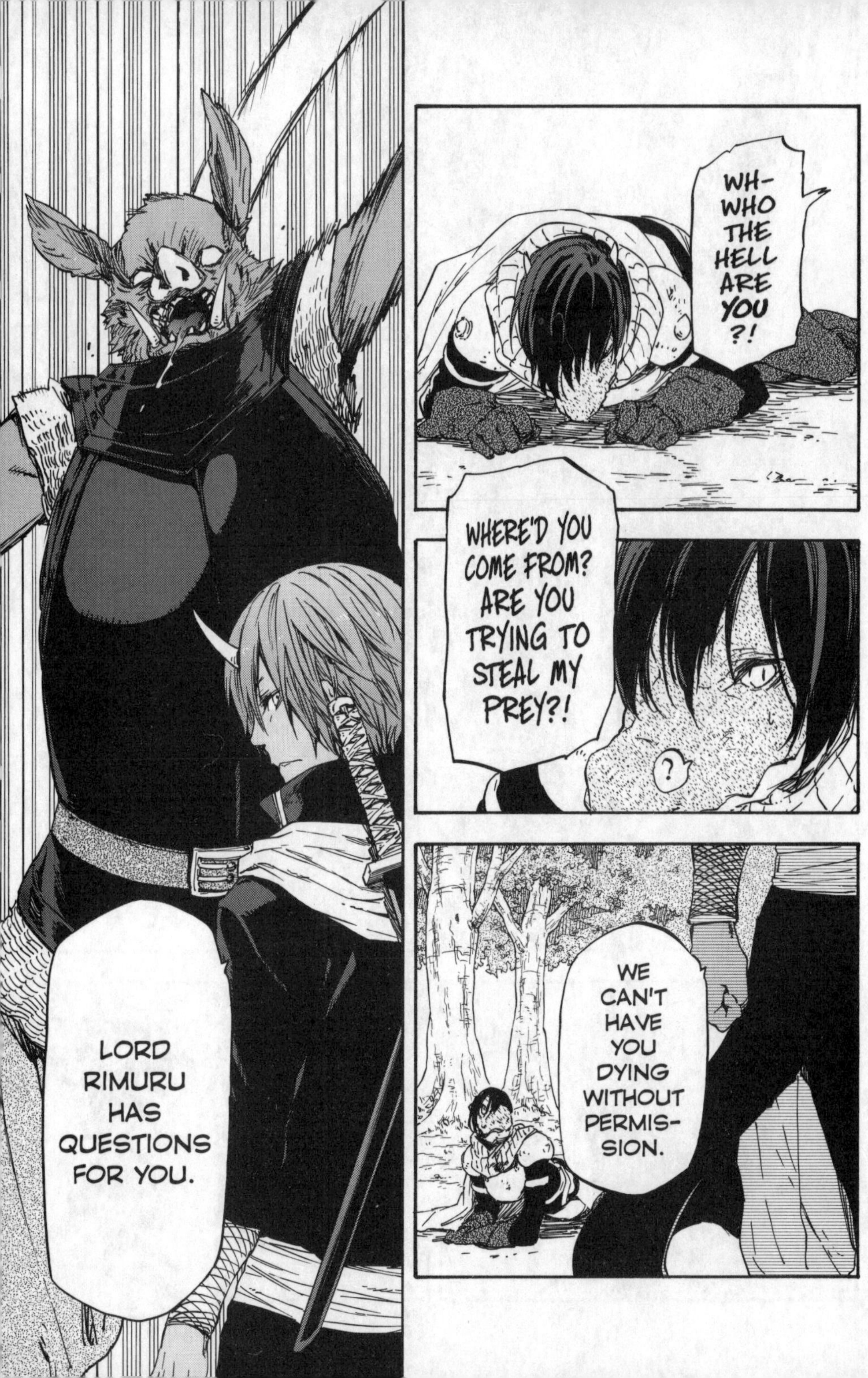
WH-WHO THE HELL ARE YOU?!
WHERE'D YOU COME FROM? ARE YOU TRYING TO STEAL MY PREY?!
?
WE CAN'T HAVE YOU DYING WITHOUT PERMIS-SION.
LORD RIMURU HAS QUESTIONS FOR YOU.

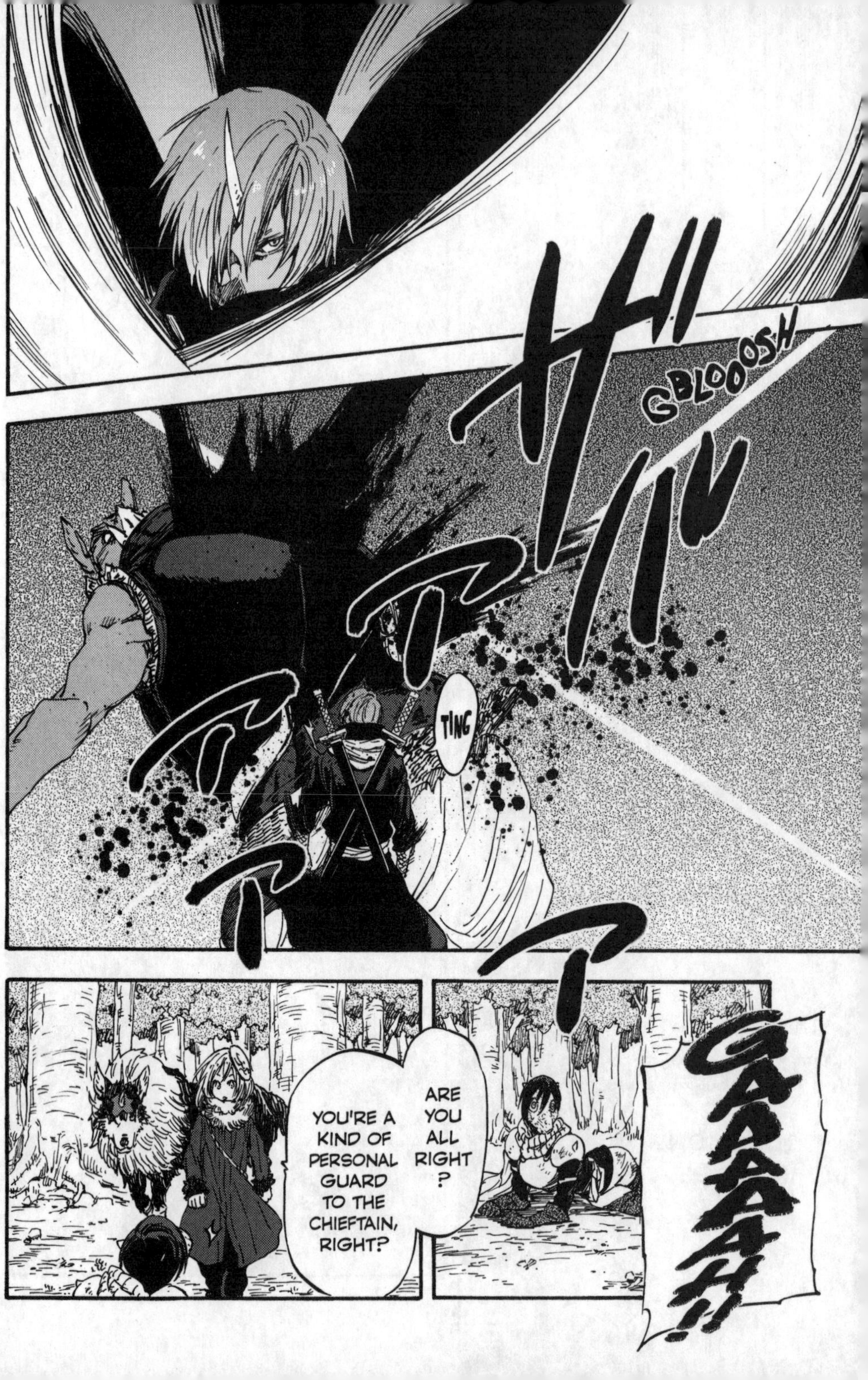
GBLOOOSH
TING
GAAAAH!!
ARE YOU ALL RIGHT?
YOU'RE A KIND OF PERSONAL GUARD TO THE CHIEFTAIN, RIGHT?

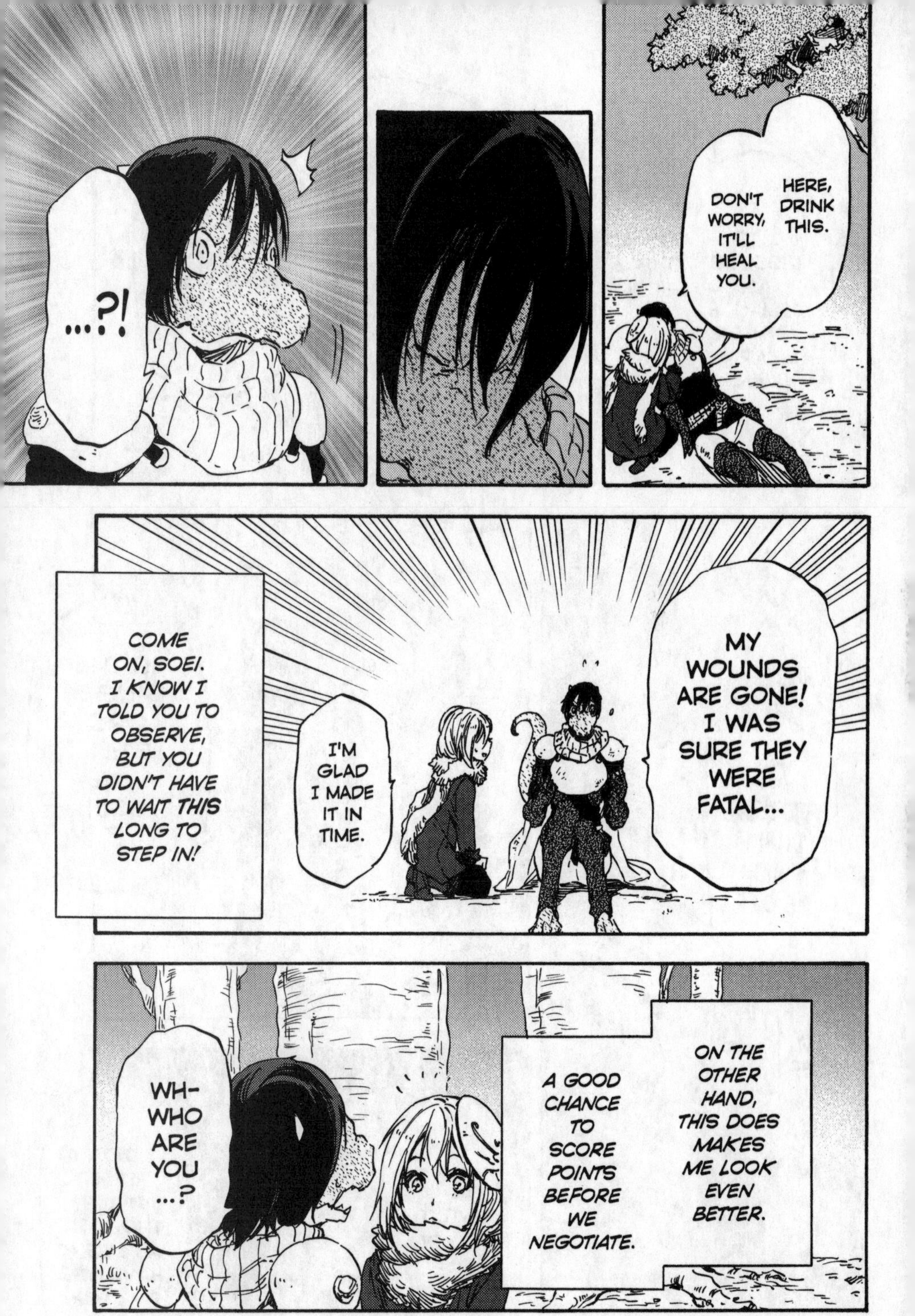
HERE, DRINK THIS.
DON'T WORRY, IT'LL HEAL YOU.
...?!
MY WOUNDS ARE GONE! I WAS SURE THEY WERE FATAL...
I'M GLAD I MADE IT IN TIME.
COME ON, SOEI. I KNOW I TOLD YOU TO OBSERVE, BUT YOU DIDN'T HAVE TO WAIT THIS LONG TO STEP IN!
ON THE OTHER HAND, THIS DOES MAKES ME LOOK EVEN BETTER.
A GOOD CHANCE TO SCORE POINTS BEFORE WE NEGOTIATE.
WH-WHO ARE YOU...?

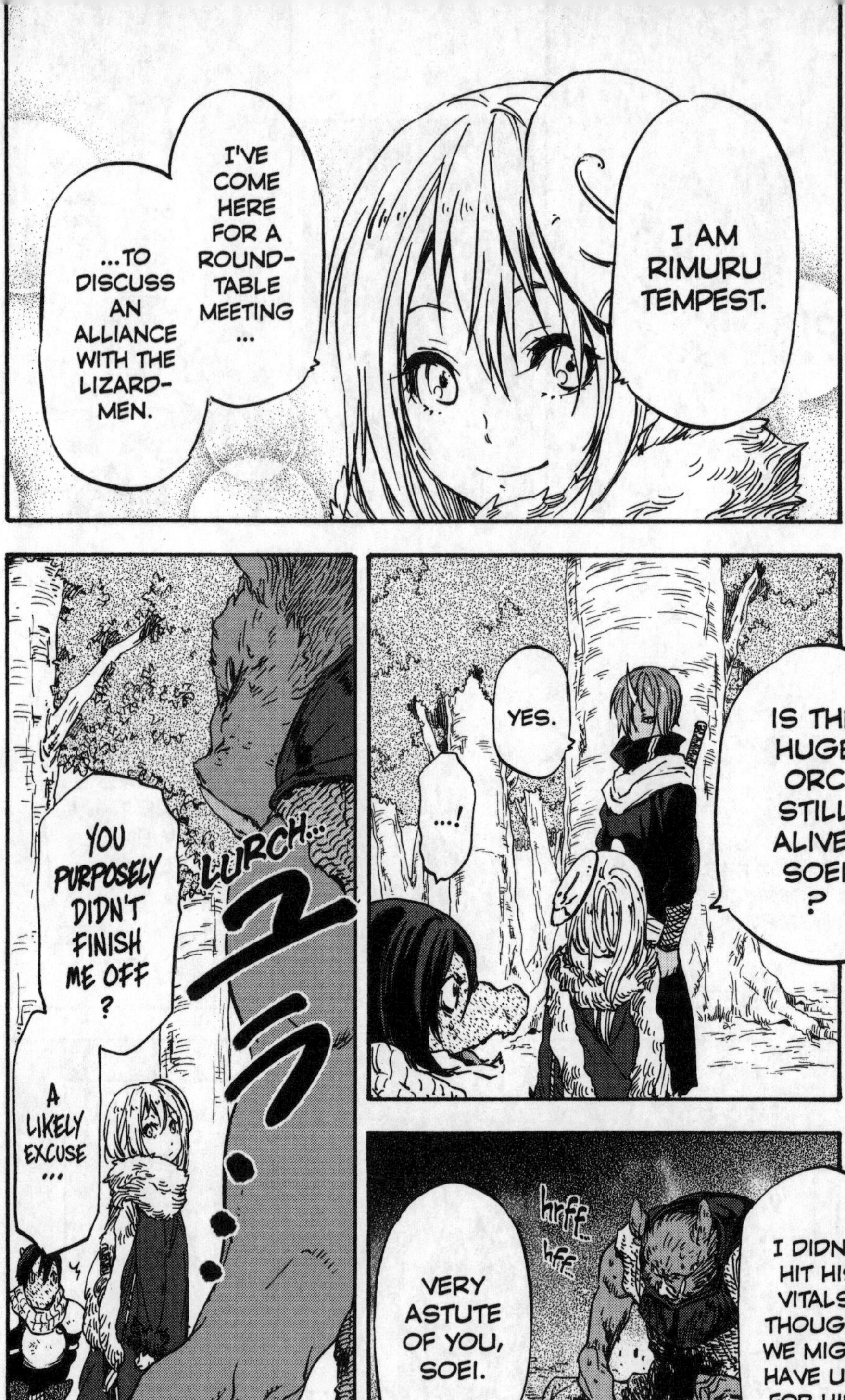
I AM RIMURU TEMPEST.
I'VE COME HERE FOR A ROUND-TABLE MEETING ...
...TO DISCUSS AN ALLIANCE WITH THE LIZARDMEN.
IS THE HUGE ORC STILL ALIVE, SOEI?
YES.
...!
I DIDN'T HIT HIS VITALS. THOUGHT WE MIGHT HAVE USE FOR HIM.
hrff... hff...
VERY ASTUTE OF YOU, SOEI.
LURCH...
YOU PURPOSELY DIDN'T FINISH ME OFF?
A LIKELY EXCUSE...

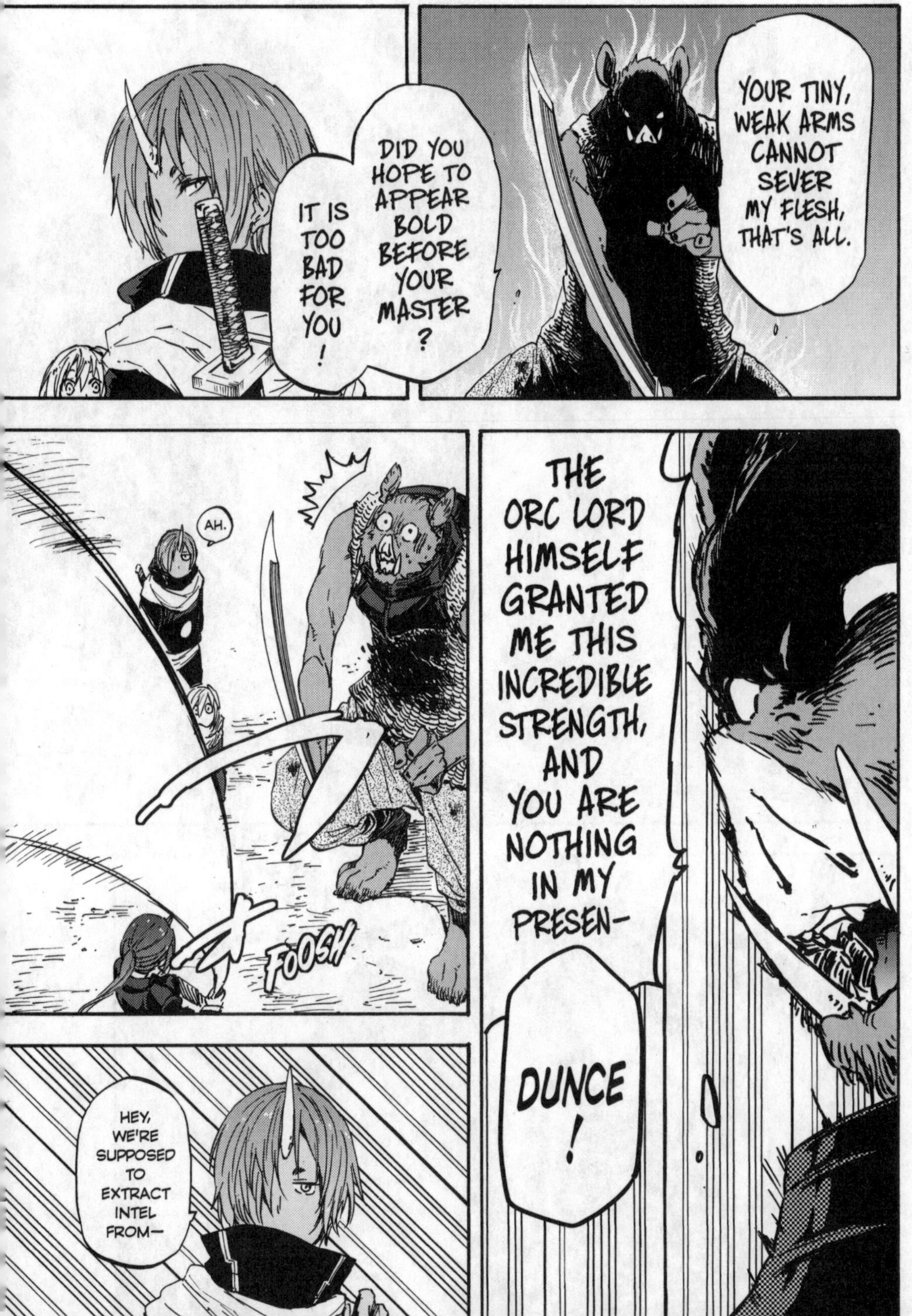
YOUR TINY, WEAK ARMS CANNOT SEVER MY FLESH, THAT'S ALL.
DID YOU HOPE TO APPEAR BOLD BEFORE YOUR MASTER?
IT IS TOO BAD FOR YOU!
THE ORC LORD HIMSELF GRANTED ME THIS INCREDIBLE STRENGTH, AND YOU ARE NOTHING IN MY PRESEN-
DUNCE!
AH.
FOOSH
HEY, WE'RE SUPPOSED TO EXTRACT INTEL FROM—

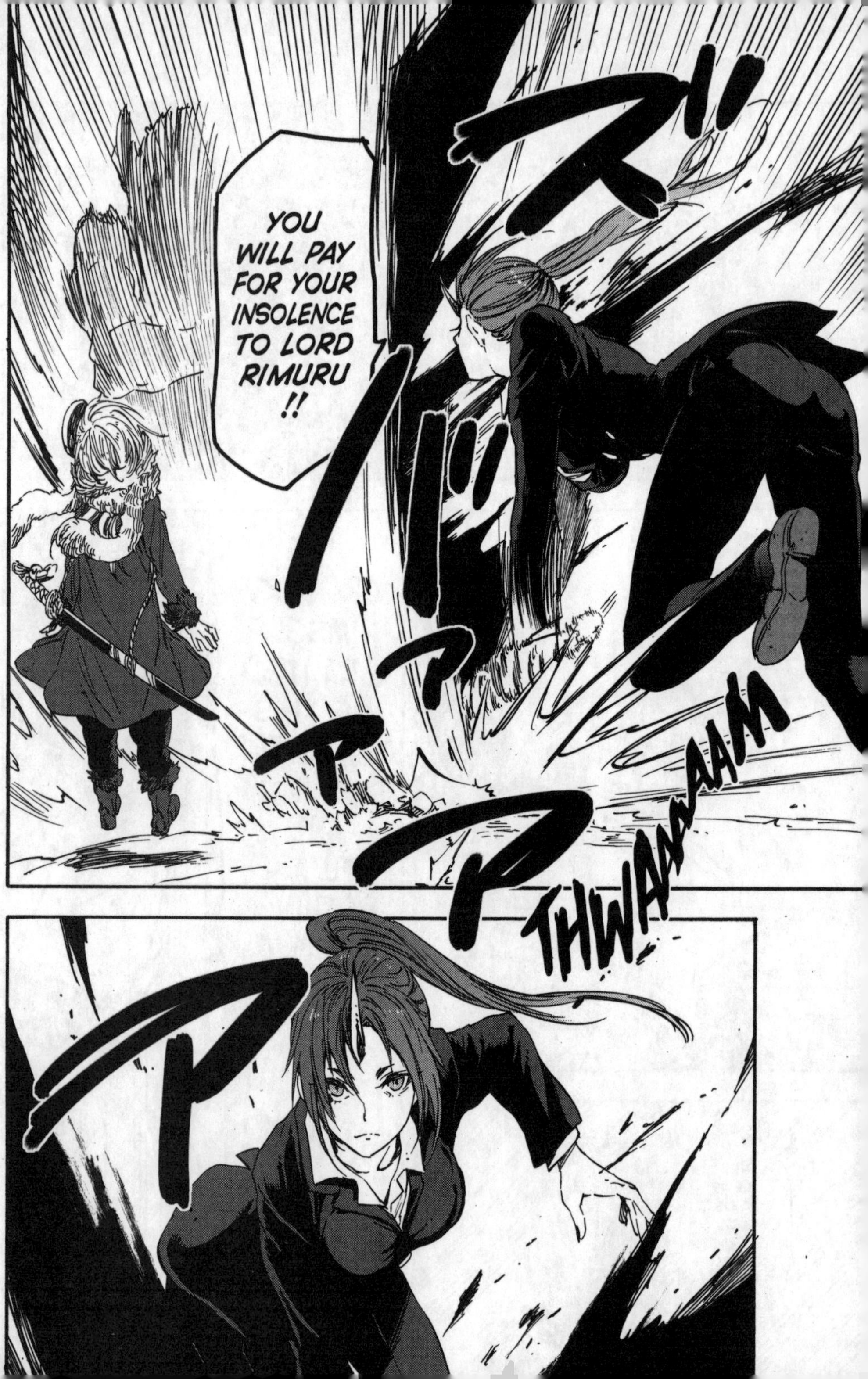
YOU WILL PAY FOR YOUR INSOLENCE TO LORD RIMURU !!
THWAAAAAM

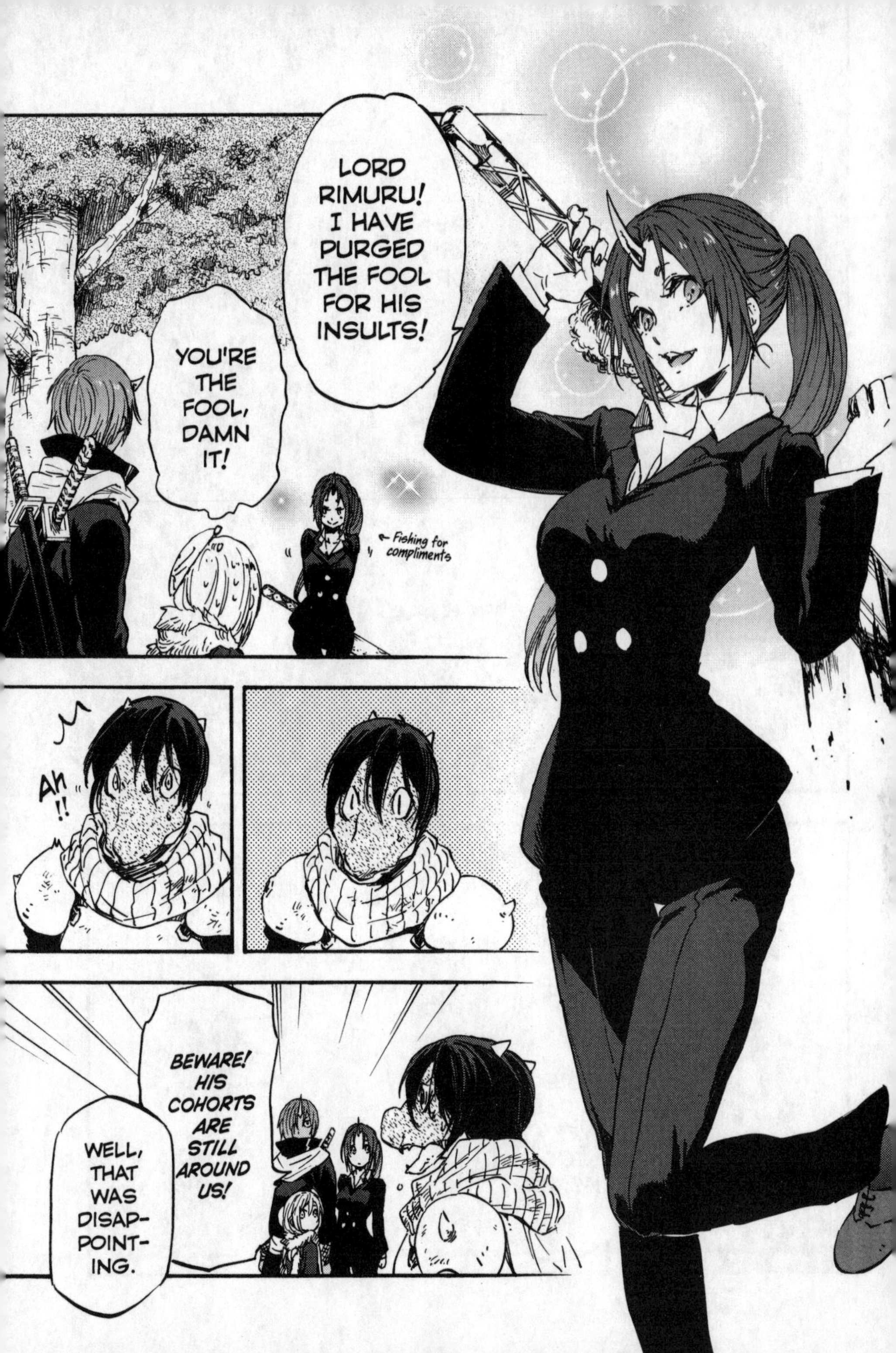
LORD RIMURU! I HAVE PURGED THE FOOL FOR HIS INSULTS!
YOU'RE THE FOOL, DAMN IT!
Fishing for compliments
Ah!!
BEWARE! HIS COHORTS ARE STILL AROUND US!
WELL, THAT WAS DISAP-POINT-ING.

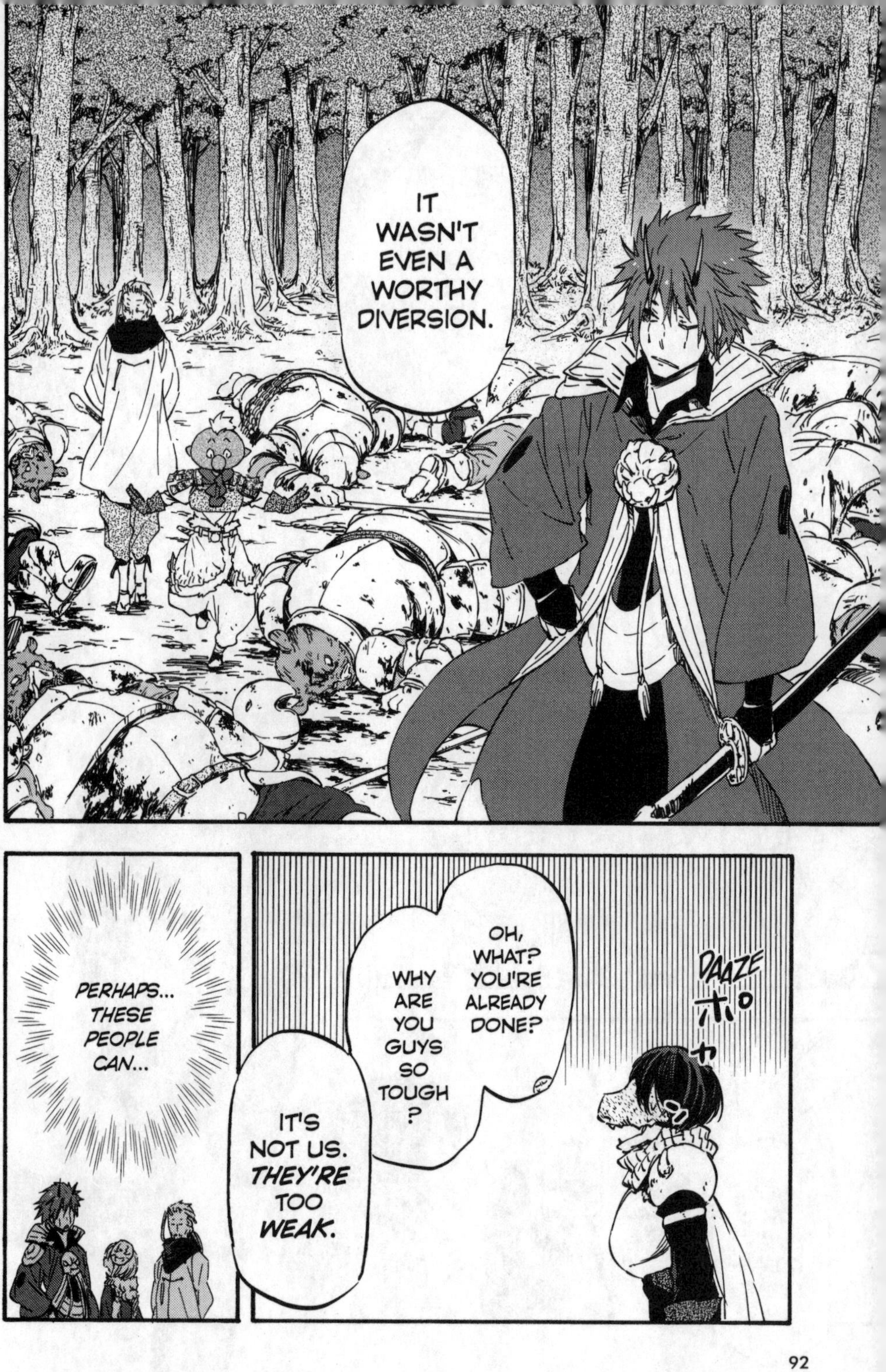
IT WASN'T EVEN A WORTHY DIVERSION.
DAAZE
OH, WHAT? YOU'RE ALREADY DONE?
WHY ARE YOU GUYS SO TOUGH ?
IT'S NOT US. *THEY'RE* TOO *WEAK*.
PERHAPS... THESE PEOPLE CAN...

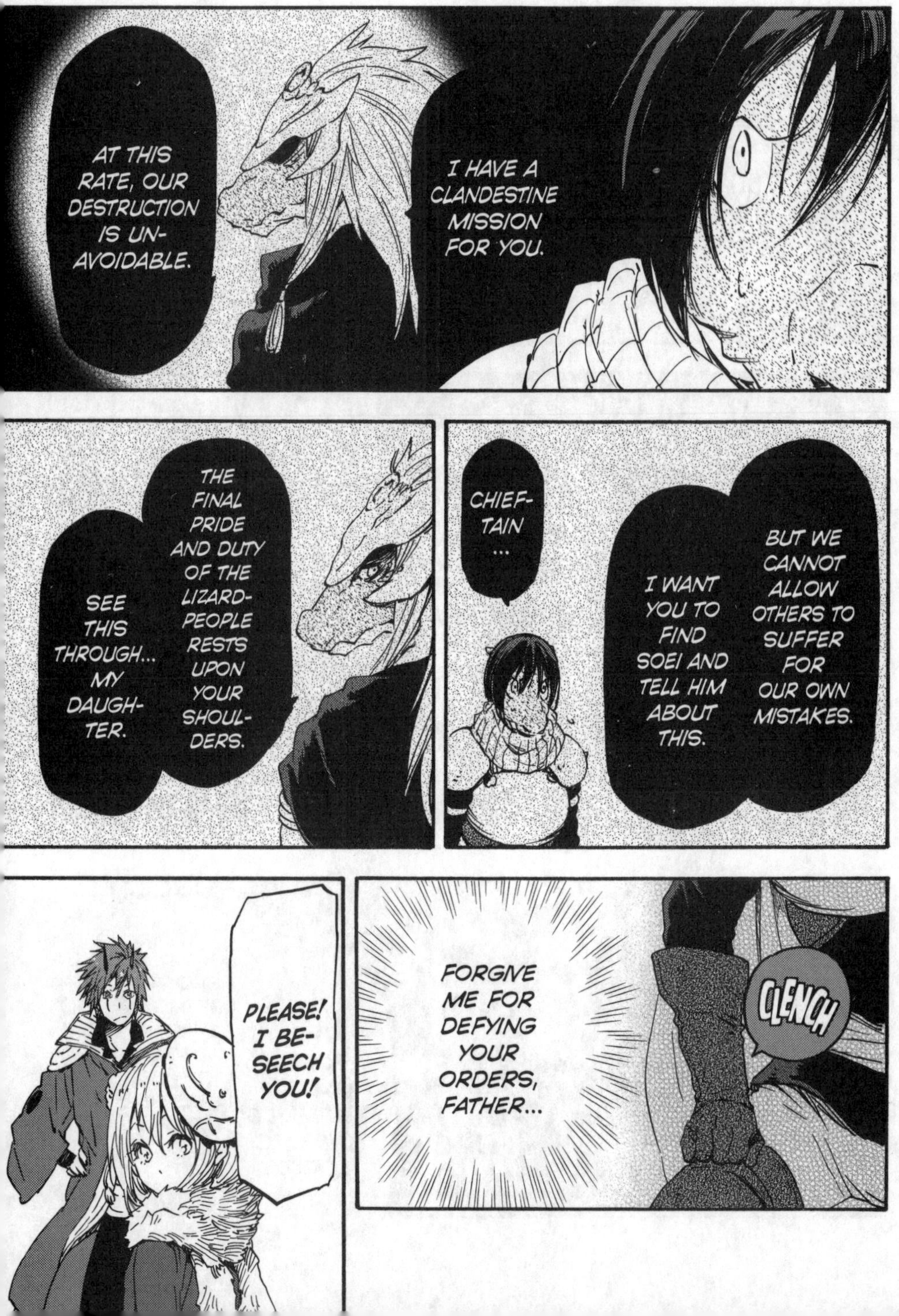
I HAVE A CLANDESTINE MISSION FOR YOU.
AT THIS RATE, OUR DESTRUCTION IS UN-AVOIDABLE.
BUT WE CANNOT ALLOW OTHERS TO SUFFER FOR OUR OWN MISTAKES.
I WANT YOU TO FIND SOEI AND TELL HIM ABOUT THIS.
CHIEF-TAIN ...
THE FINAL PRIDE AND DUTY OF THE LIZARD-PEOPLE RESTS UPON YOUR SHOUL-DERS.
SEE THIS THROUGH... MY DAUGH-TER.
CLENCH
FORGIVE ME FOR DEFYING YOUR ORDERS, FATHER...
PLEASE! I BE-SEECH YOU!

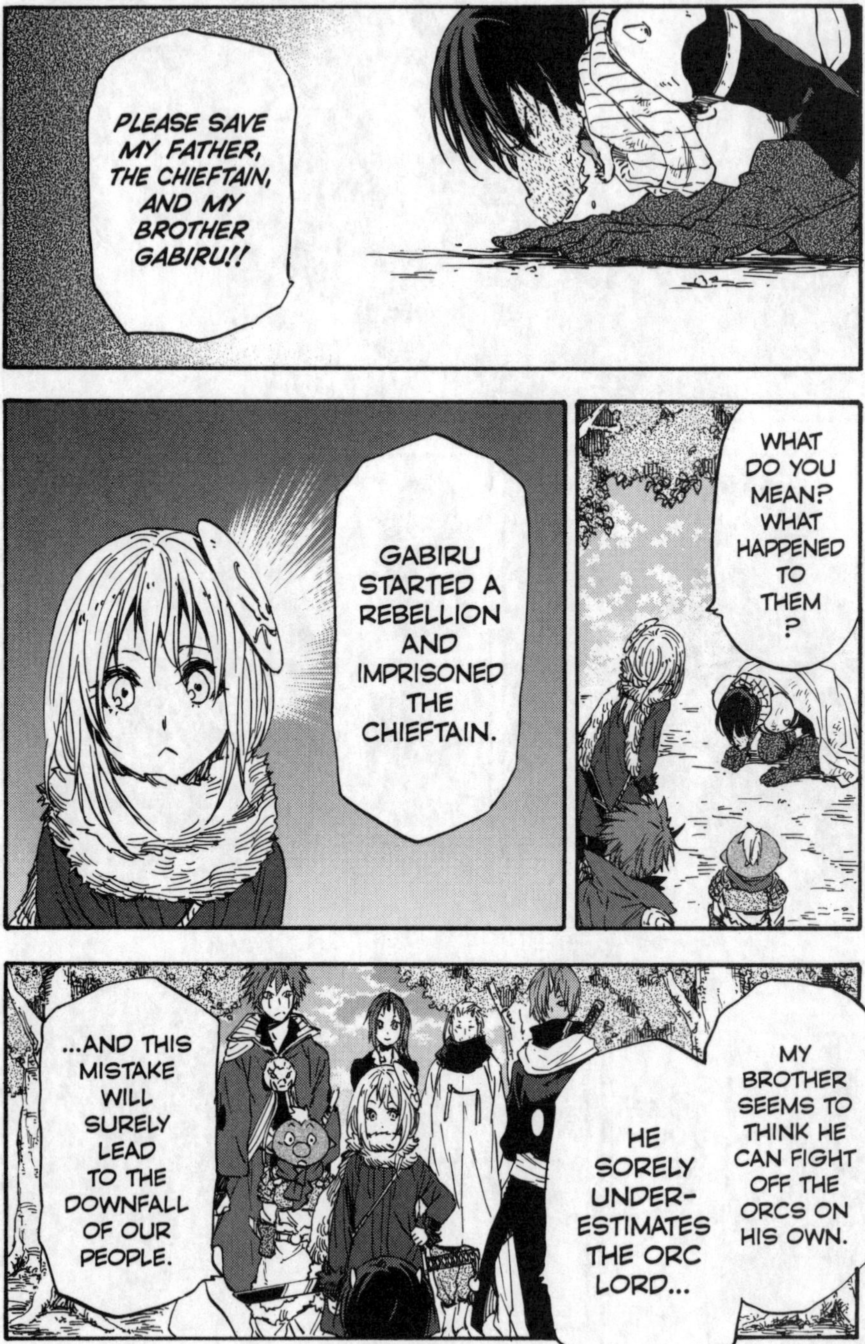
PLEASE SAVE MY FATHER, THE CHIEFTAIN, AND MY BROTHER GABIRU!!
WHAT DO YOU MEAN? WHAT HAPPENED TO THEM?
GABIRU STARTED A REBELLION AND IMPRISONED THE CHIEFTAIN.
MY BROTHER SEEMS TO THINK HE CAN FIGHT OFF THE ORCS ON HIS OWN.
HE SORELY UNDER-ESTIMATES THE ORC LORD...
...AND THIS MISTAKE WILL SURELY LEAD TO THE DOWNFALL OF OUR PEOPLE.

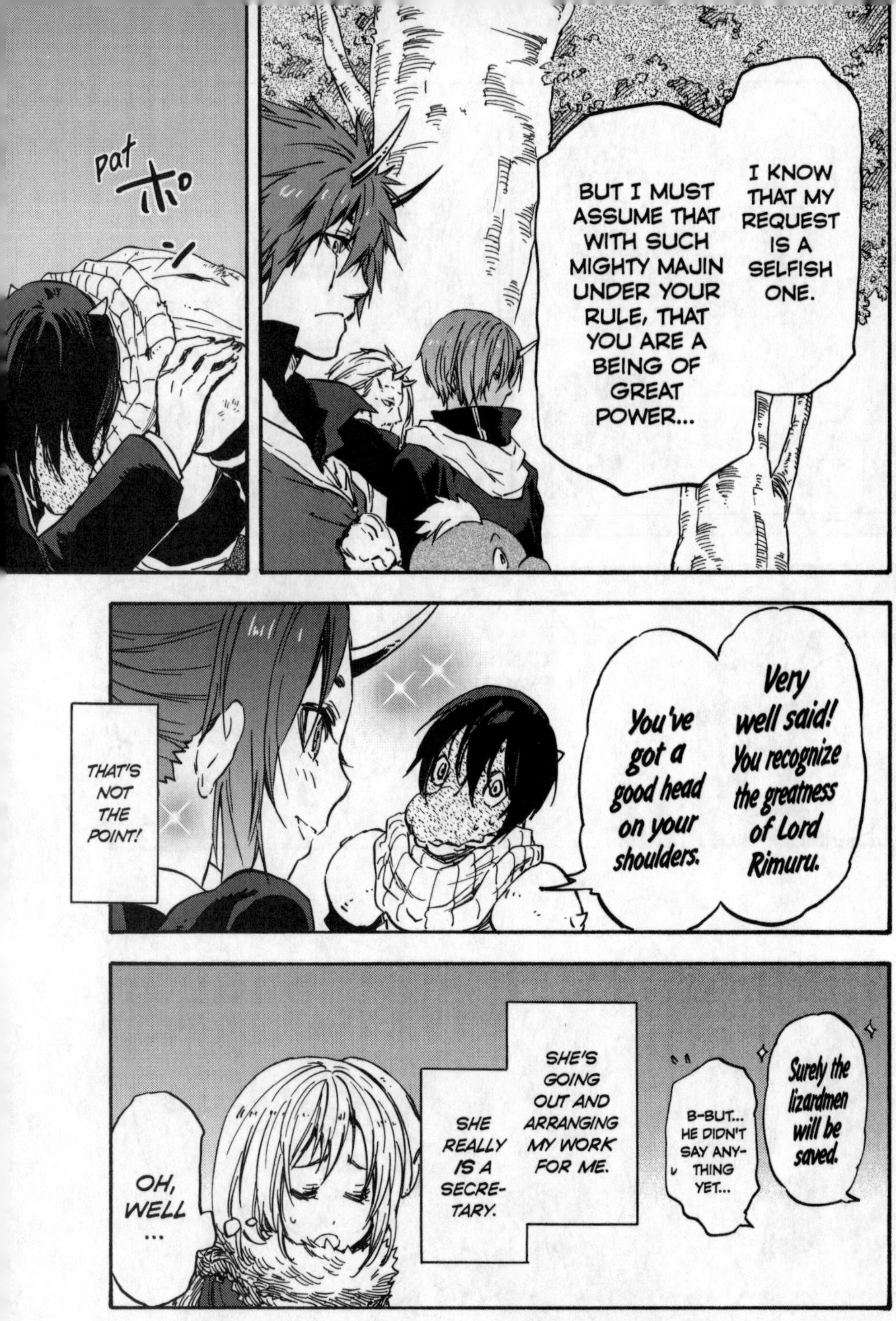
I KNOW THAT MY REQUEST IS A SELFISH ONE.
BUT I MUST ASSUME THAT WITH SUCH MIGHTY MAJIN UNDER YOUR RULE, THAT YOU ARE A BEING OF GREAT POWER...
pat
Very well said! You recognize the greatness of Lord Rimuru.
You've got a good head on your shoulders.
THAT'S NOT THE POINT!
Surely the lizardmen will be saved.
B-BUT... HE DIDN'T SAY ANY-THING YET...
SHE'S GOING OUT AND ARRANGING MY WORK FOR ME.
SHE REALLY IS A SECRE-TARY.
OH, WELL ...

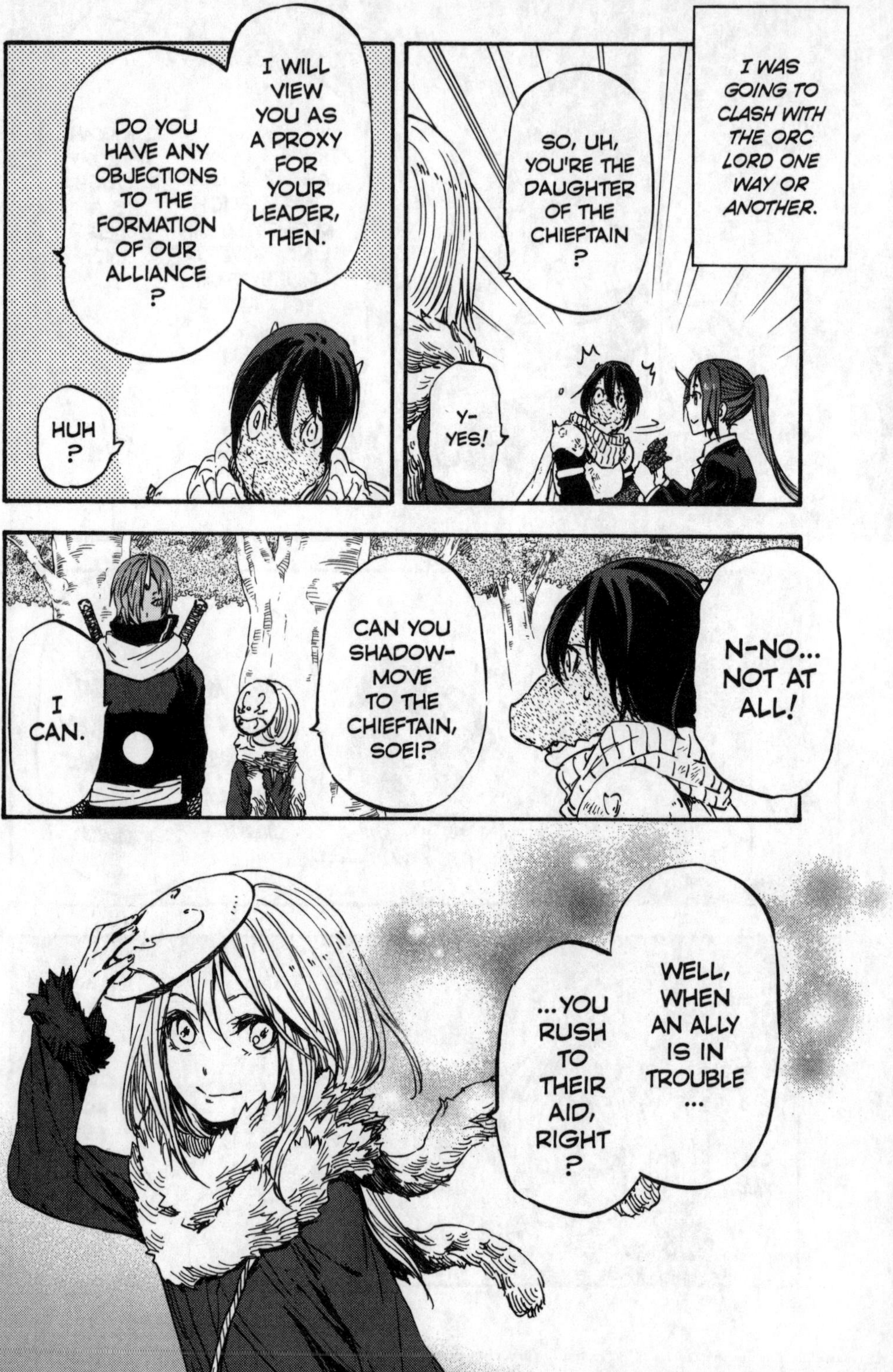
I WAS GOING TO CLASH WITH THE ORC LORD ONE WAY OR ANOTHER.
SO, UH, YOU'RE THE DAUGHTER OF THE CHIEFTAIN?
Y-YES!
I WILL VIEW YOU AS A PROXY FOR YOUR LEADER, THEN.
DO YOU HAVE ANY OBJECTIONS TO THE FORMATION OF OUR ALLIANCE?
HUH?
N-NO... NOT AT ALL!
CAN YOU SHADOW-MOVE TO THE CHIEFTAIN, SOEI?
I CAN.
WELL, WHEN AN ALLY IS IN TROUBLE...
...YOU RUSH TO THEIR AID, RIGHT?

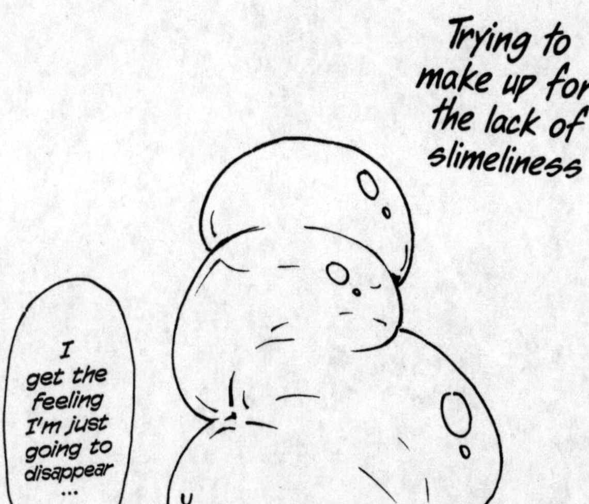
Trying to make up for the lack of slimeliness
I get the feeling I'm just going to disappear ...

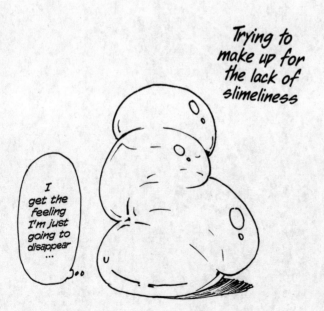

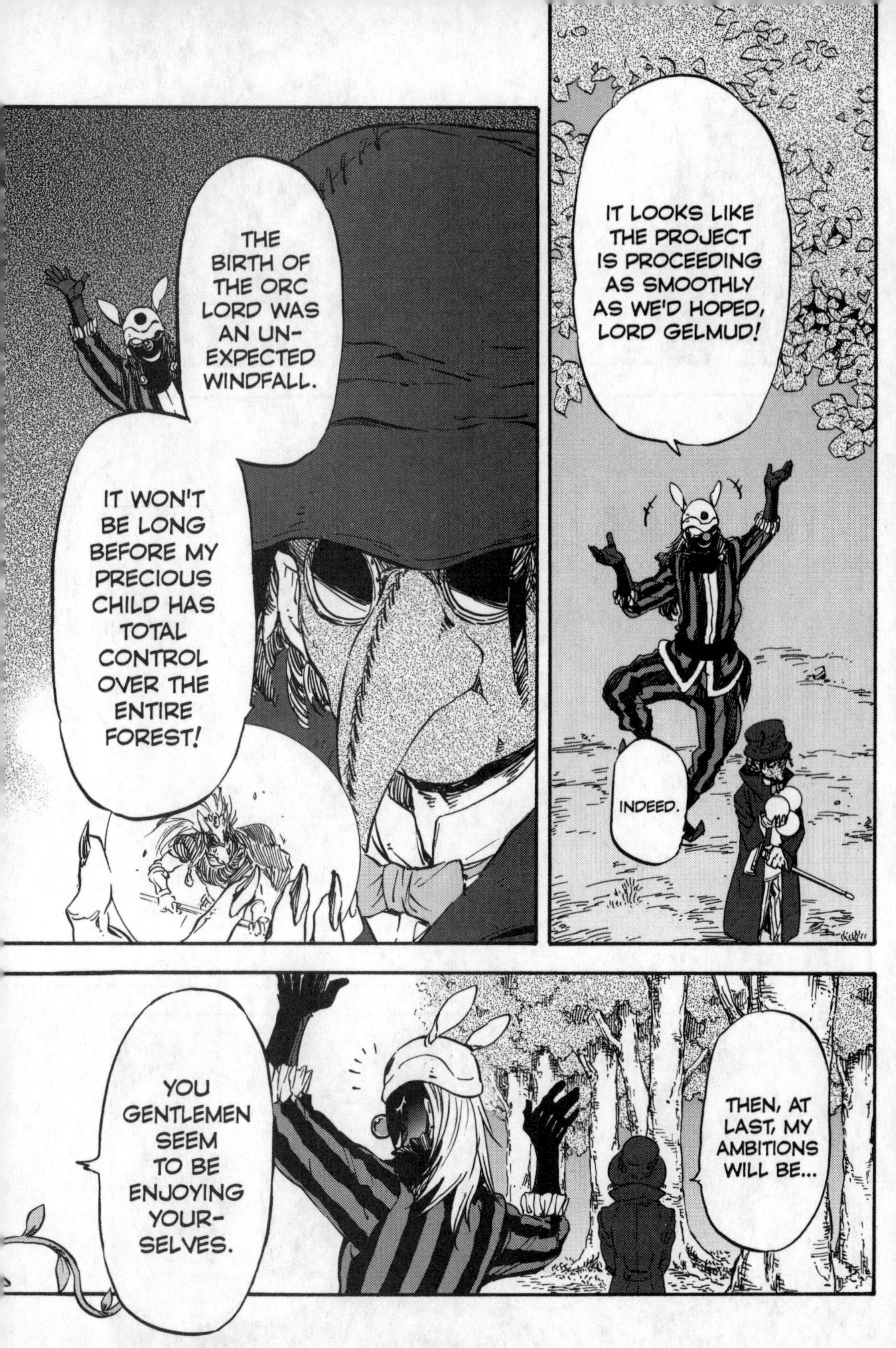
IT LOOKS LIKE THE PROJECT IS PROCEEDING AS SMOOTHLY AS WE'D HOPED, LORD GELMUD!
INDEED.
THE BIRTH OF THE ORC LORD WAS AN UN-EXPECTED WINDFALL.
IT WON'T BE LONG BEFORE MY PRECIOUS CHILD HAS TOTAL CONTROL OVER THE ENTIRE FOREST!
THEN, AT LAST, MY AMBITIONS WILL BE...
YOU GENTLEMEN SEEM TO BE ENJOYING YOUR-SELVES.

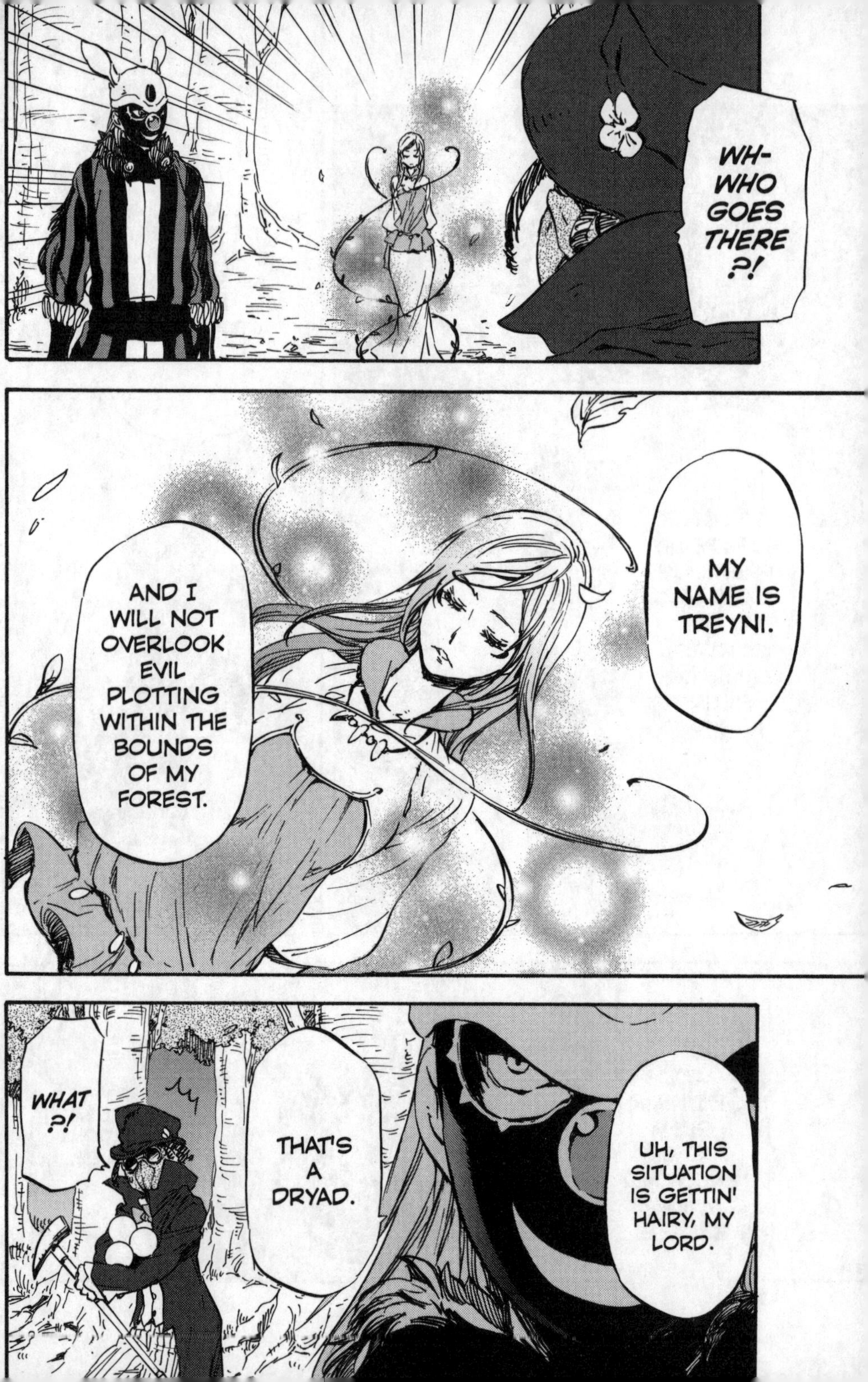
WH- WHO GOES THERE ?!
MY NAME IS TREYNI.
AND I WILL NOT OVERLOOK EVIL PLOTTING WITHIN THE BOUNDS OF MY FOREST.
UH, THIS SITUATION IS GETTIN' HAIRY, MY LORD.
THAT'S A DRYAD.
WHAT ?!

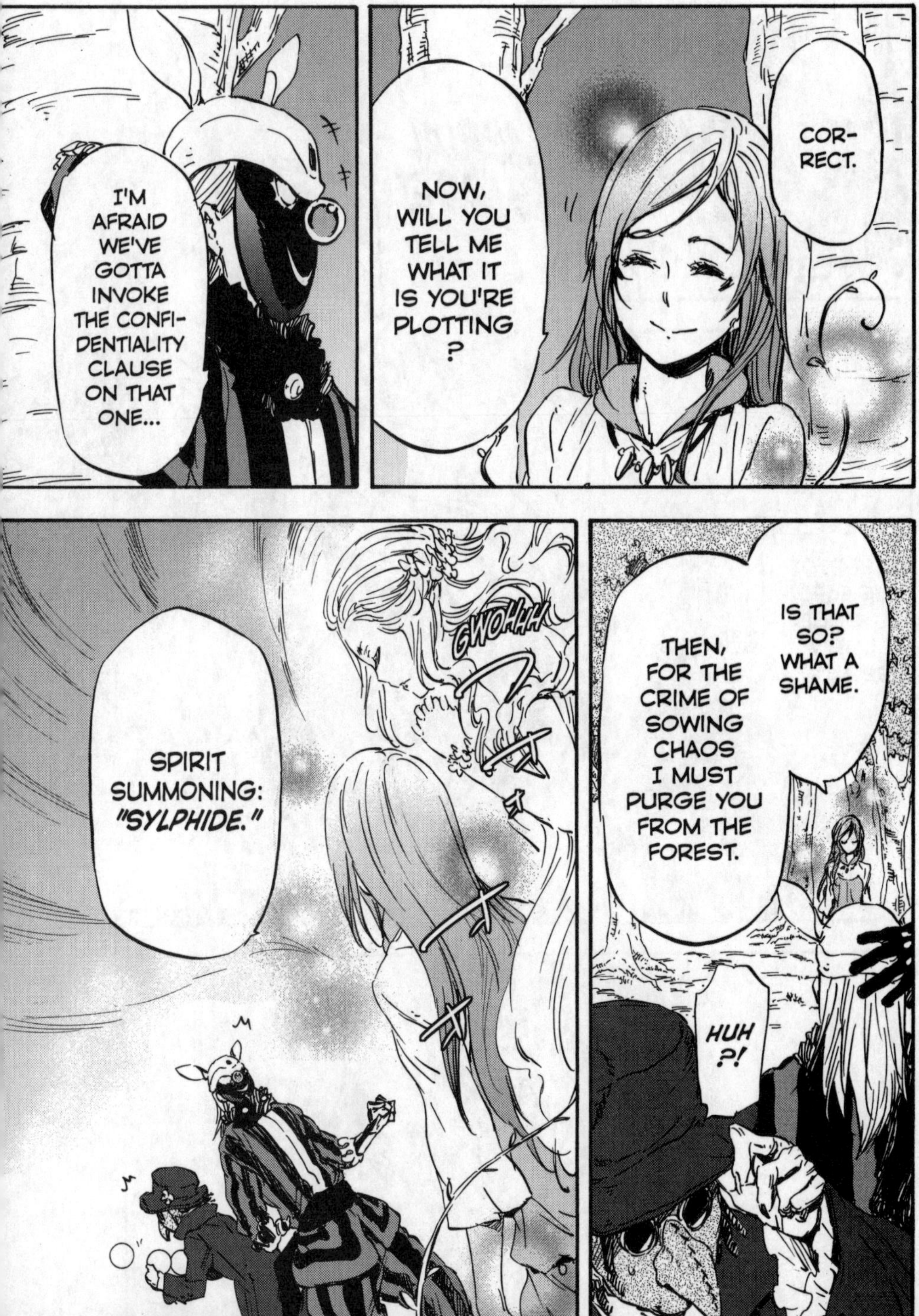

CORRECT.
NOW, WILL YOU TELL ME WHAT IT IS YOU'RE PLOTTING?
I'M AFRAID WE'VE GOTTA INVOKE THE CONFIDENTIALITY CLAUSE ON THAT ONE...
IS THAT SO? WHAT A SHAME.
THEN, FOR THE CRIME OF SOWING CHAOS I MUST PURGE YOU FROM THE FOREST.
HUH?!
GWOHHH
SPIRIT SUMMONING: "SYLPHIDE."

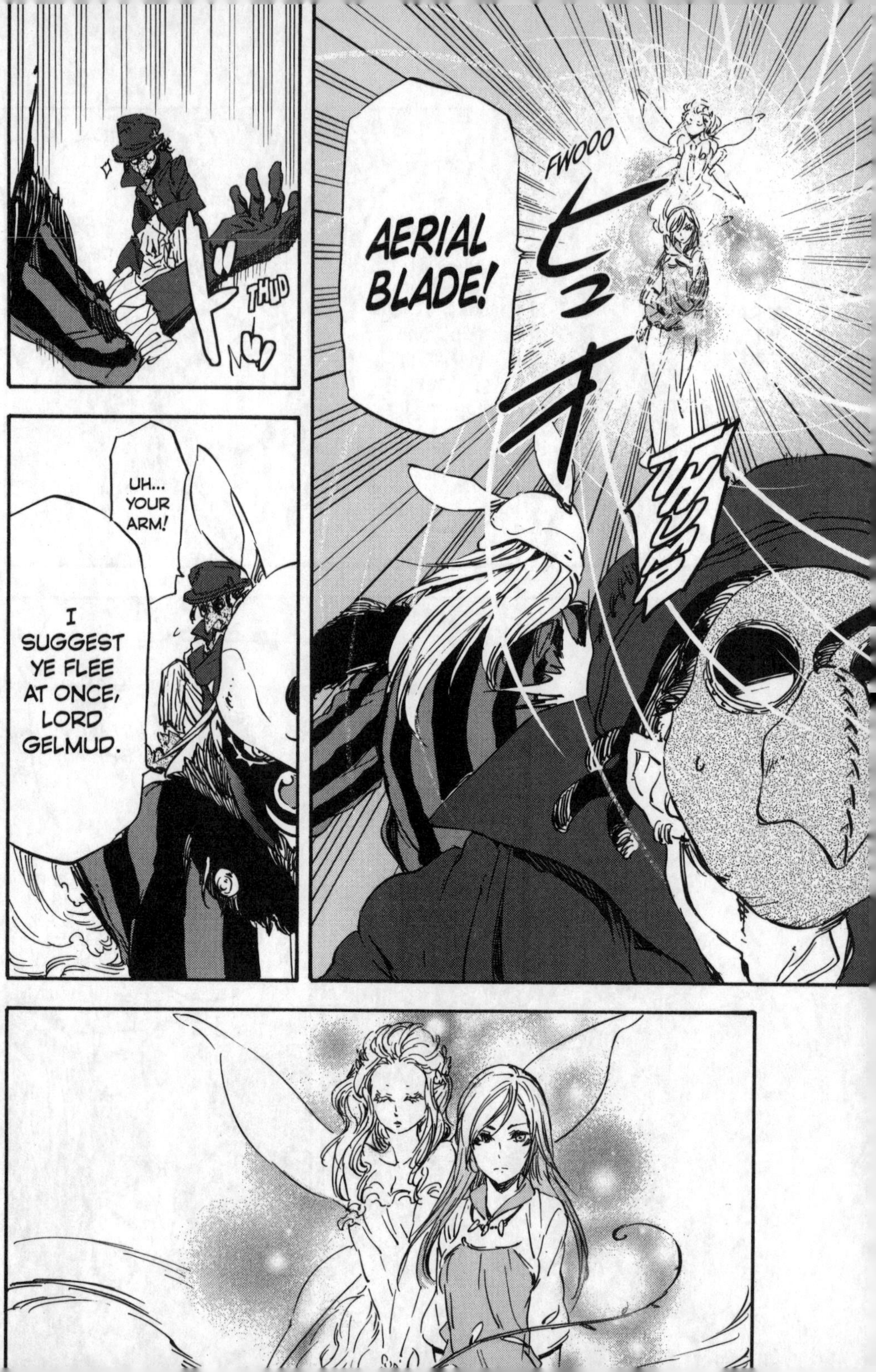
AERIAL BLADE!
FWOOO
THUMP
THUD
UH... YOUR ARM!
I SUGGEST YE FLEE AT ONCE, LORD GELMUD.

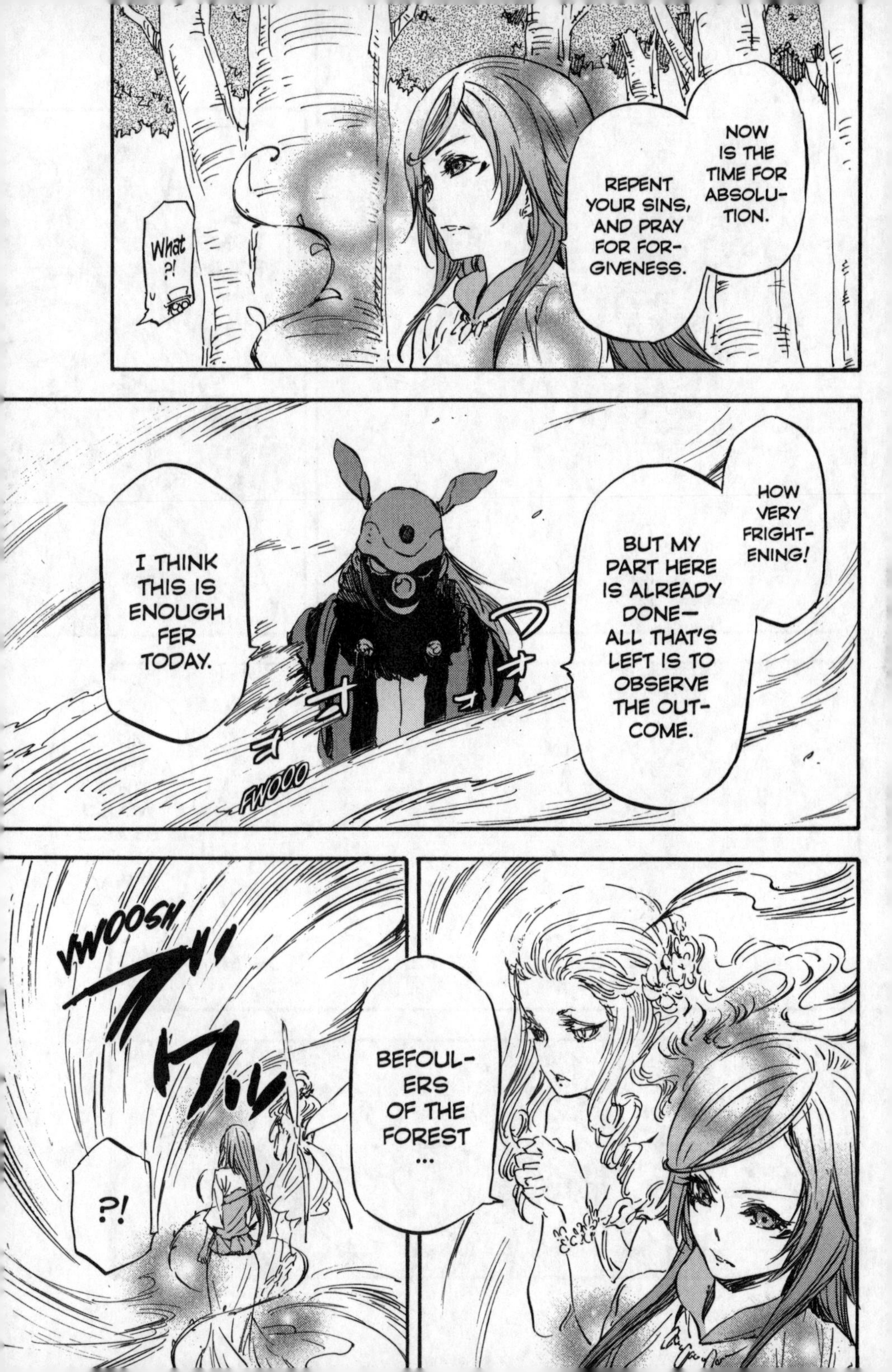
NOW IS THE TIME FOR ABSOLUTION.
REPENT YOUR SINS, AND PRAY FOR FORGIVENESS.
What ?!
HOW VERY FRIGHTENING!
BUT MY PART HERE IS ALREADY DONE— ALL THAT'S LEFT IS TO OBSERVE THE OUTCOME.
FWOOO
I THINK THIS IS ENOUGH FER TODAY.
BEFOULERS OF THE FOREST ...
VWOOSH
?!

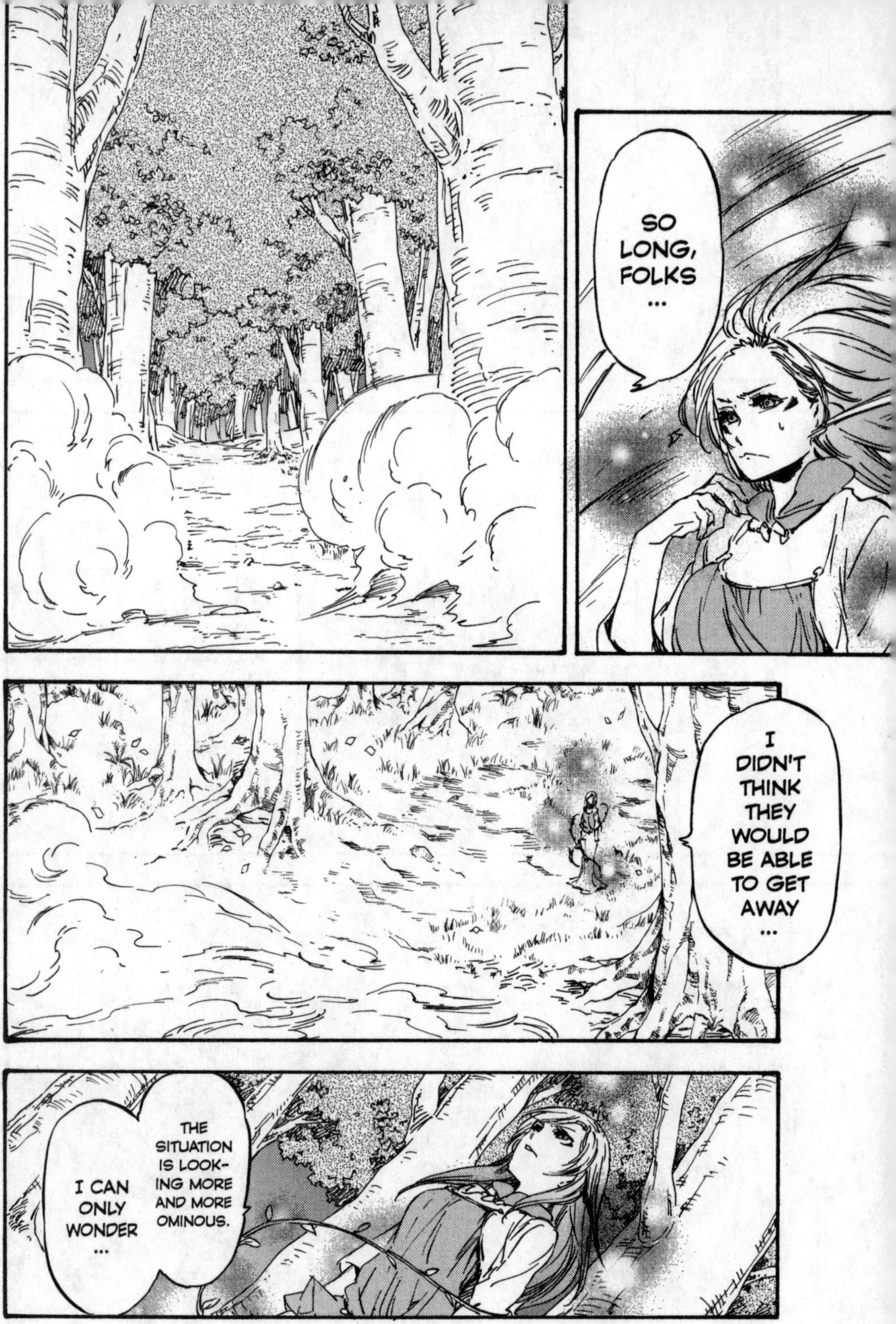
SO LONG, FOLKS ...
I DIDN'T THINK THEY WOULD BE ABLE TO GET AWAY ...
THE SITUATION IS LOOKING MORE AND MORE OMINOUS.
I CAN ONLY WONDER ...

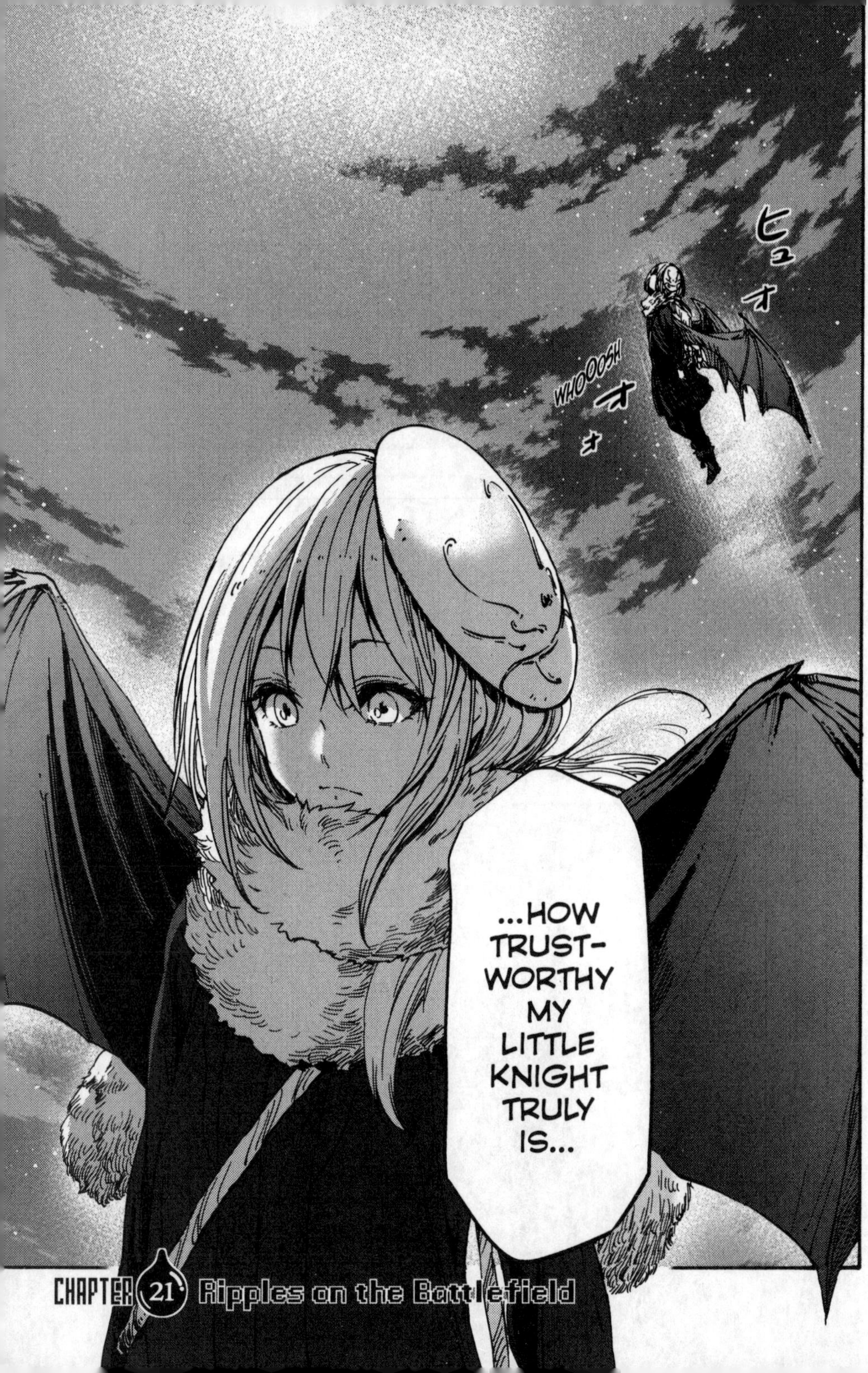
ヒュオオォ
WHOOOSH
...HOW TRUST-WORTHY MY LITTLE KNIGHT TRULY IS...

CHAPTER 21 Ripples on the Battlefield

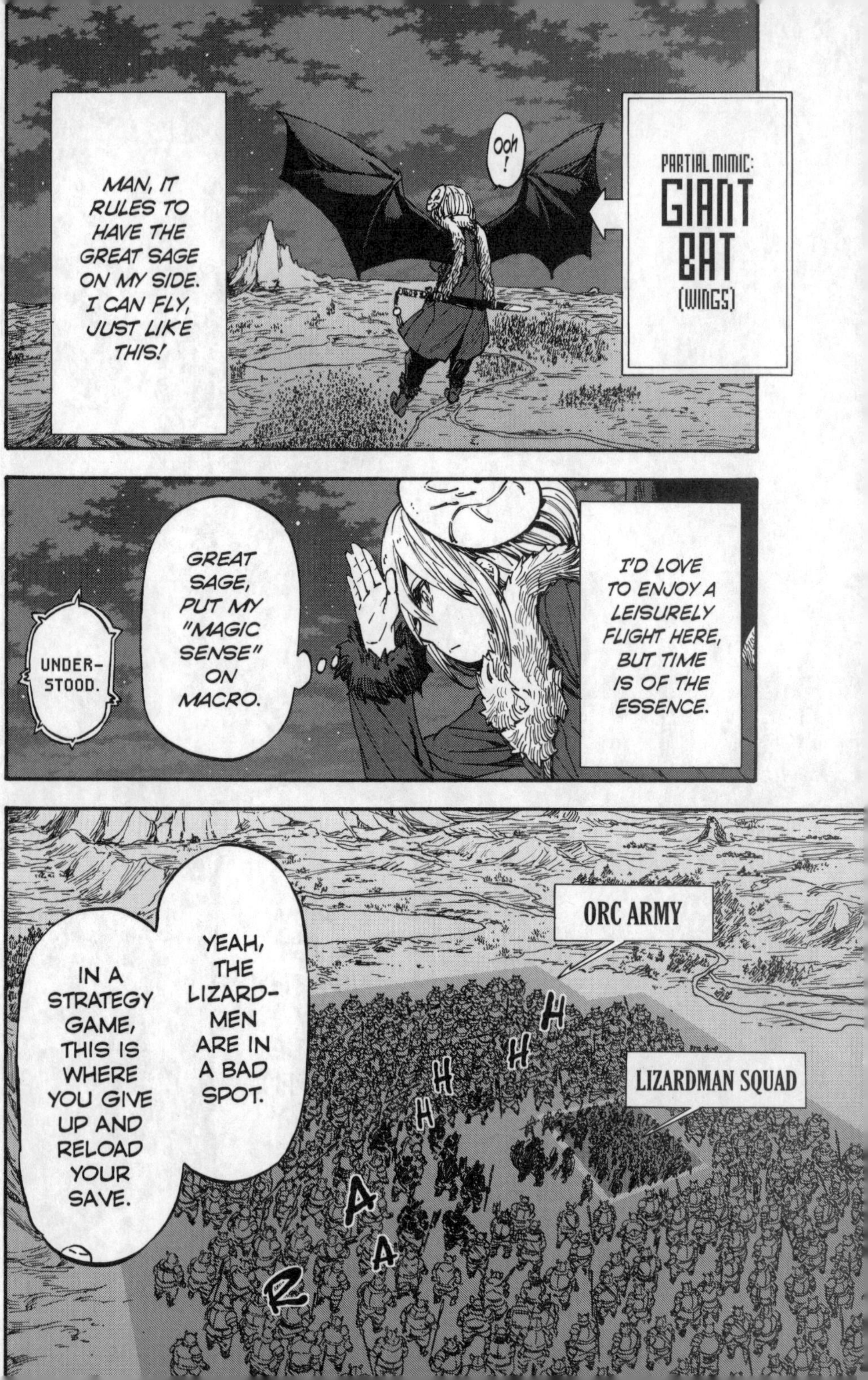
PARTIAL MIMIC: GIANT BAT (WINGS)
Ooh!
MAN, IT RULES TO HAVE THE GREAT SAGE ON MY SIDE. I CAN FLY, JUST LIKE THIS!
I'D LOVE TO ENJOY A LEISURELY FLIGHT HERE, BUT TIME IS OF THE ESSENCE.
GREAT SAGE, PUT MY "MAGIC SENSE" ON MACRO.
UNDER-STOOD.
ORC ARMY
LIZARDMAN SQUAD
RAAHHHH
YEAH, THE LIZARD-MEN ARE IN A BAD SPOT.
IN A STRATEGY GAME, THIS IS WHERE YOU GIVE UP AND RELOAD YOUR SAVE.

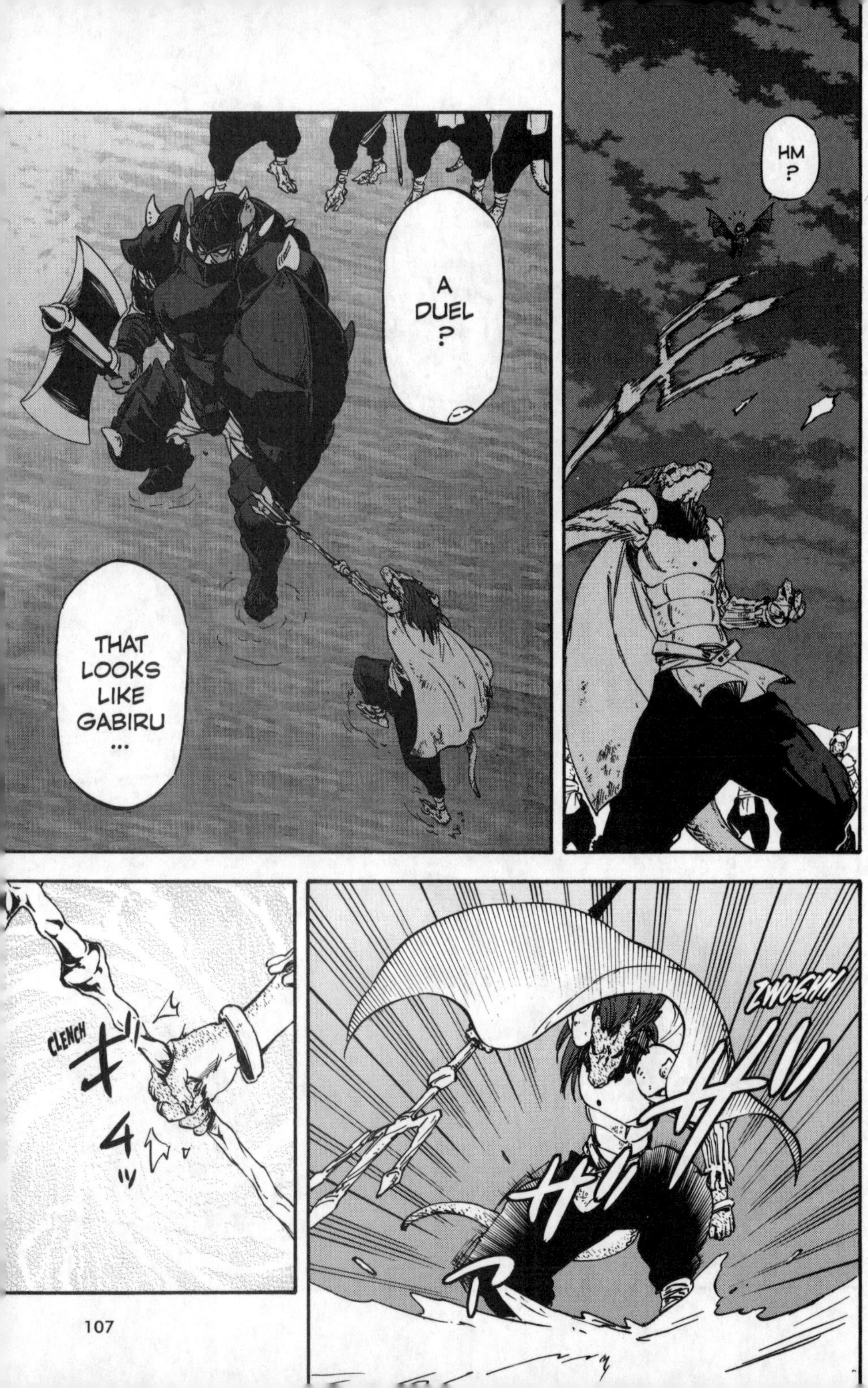
HM?
A DUEL?
THAT LOOKS LIKE GABIRU...
ZWOSHH
CLENCH

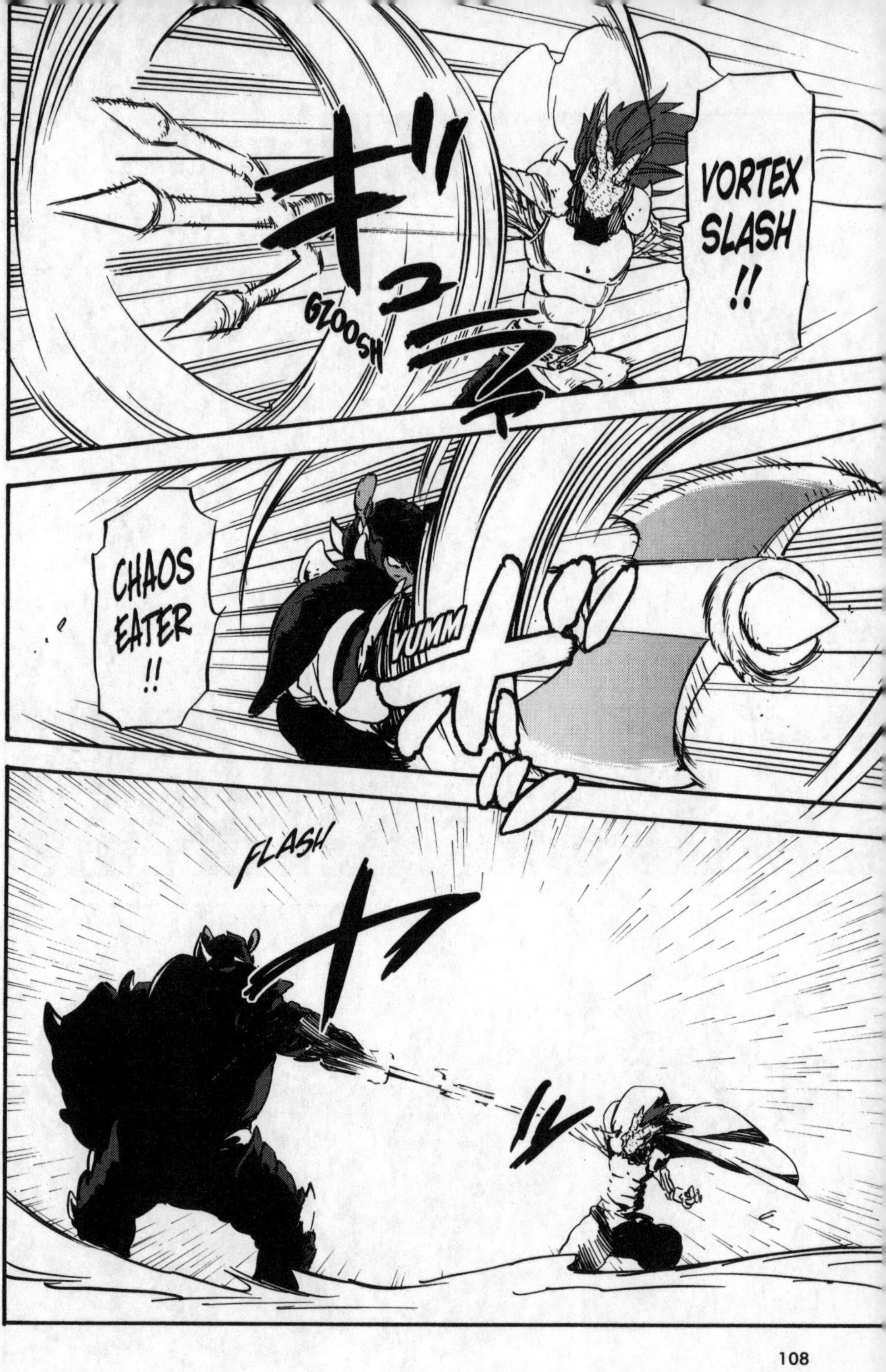
VORTEX SLASH !!
GZOOSH
VUMM
CHAOS EATER !!
FLASH

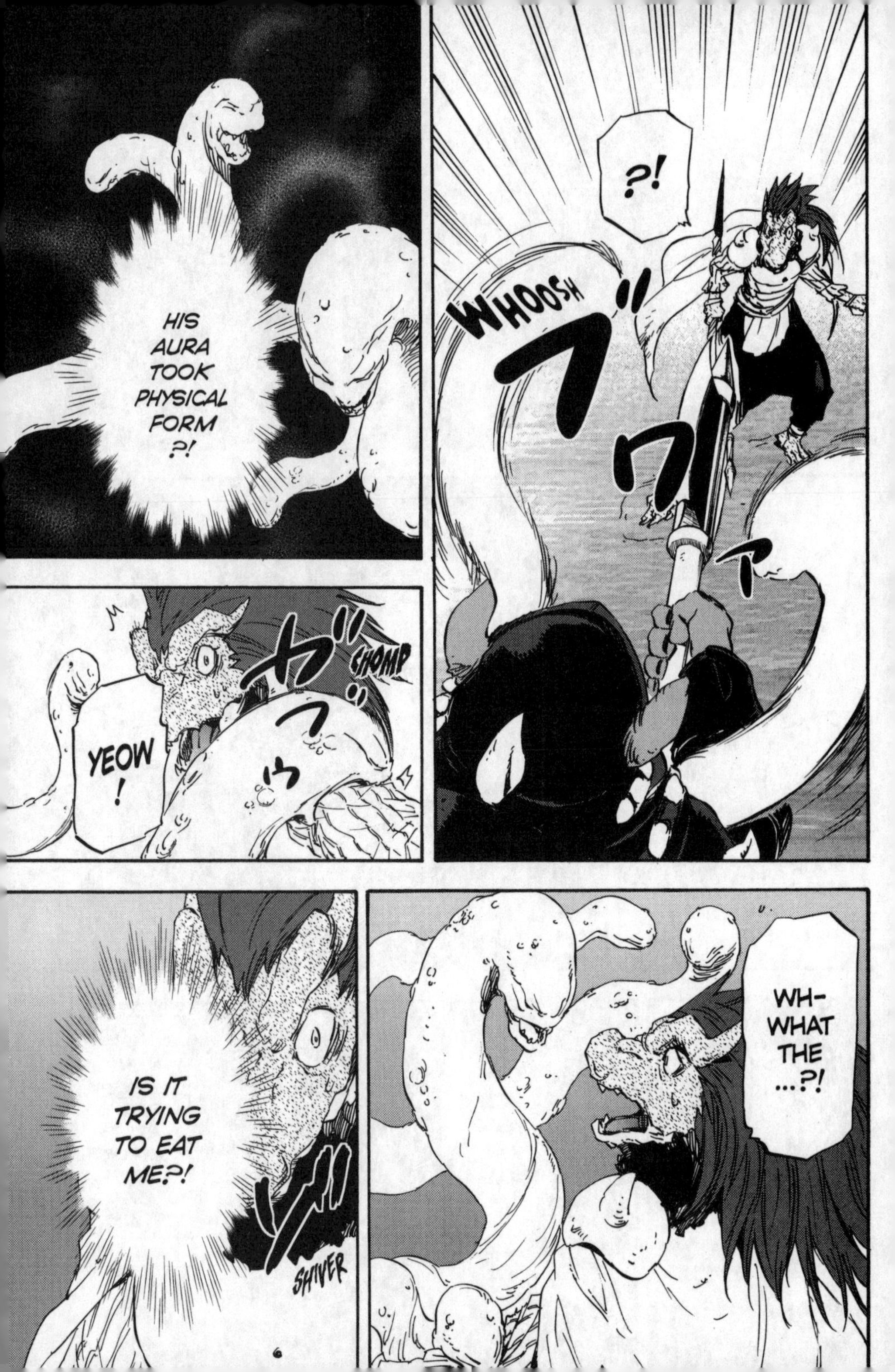
?!
WHOOSH
HIS AURA TOOK PHYSICAL FORM?!
CHOMP
YEOW!
WH-WHAT THE...?!
IS IT TRYING TO EAT ME?!
SHIVER

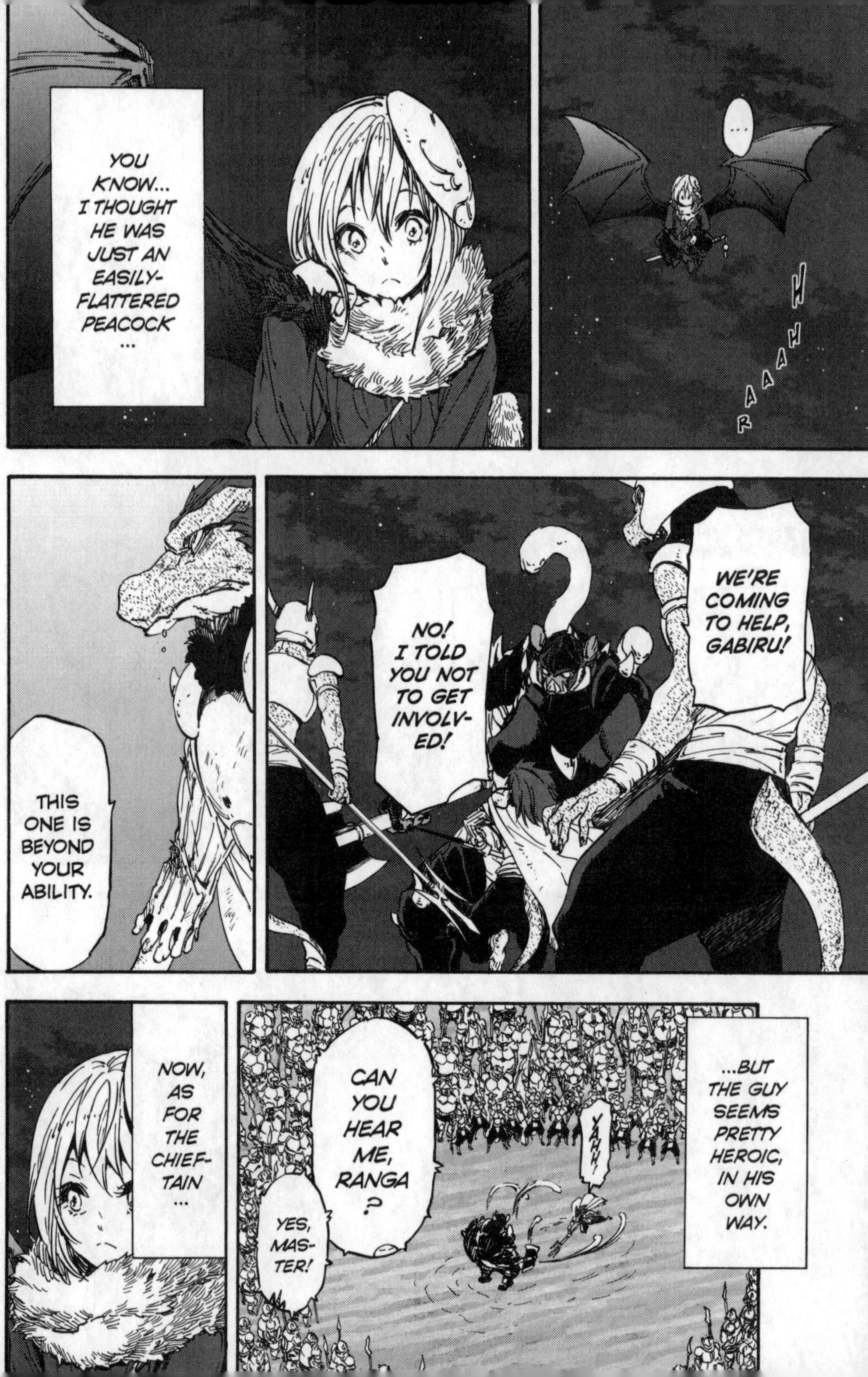
...
RAAAAHH
YOU KNOW... I THOUGHT HE WAS JUST AN EASILY-FLATTERED PEACOCK...
WE'RE COMING TO HELP, GABIRU!
NO! I TOLD YOU NOT TO GET INVOLVED!
THIS ONE IS BEYOND YOUR ABILITY.
...BUT THE GUY SEEMS PRETTY HEROIC, IN HIS OWN WAY.
YAHH!
CAN YOU HEAR ME, RANGA?
YES, MASTER!
NOW, AS FOR THE CHIEFTAIN...

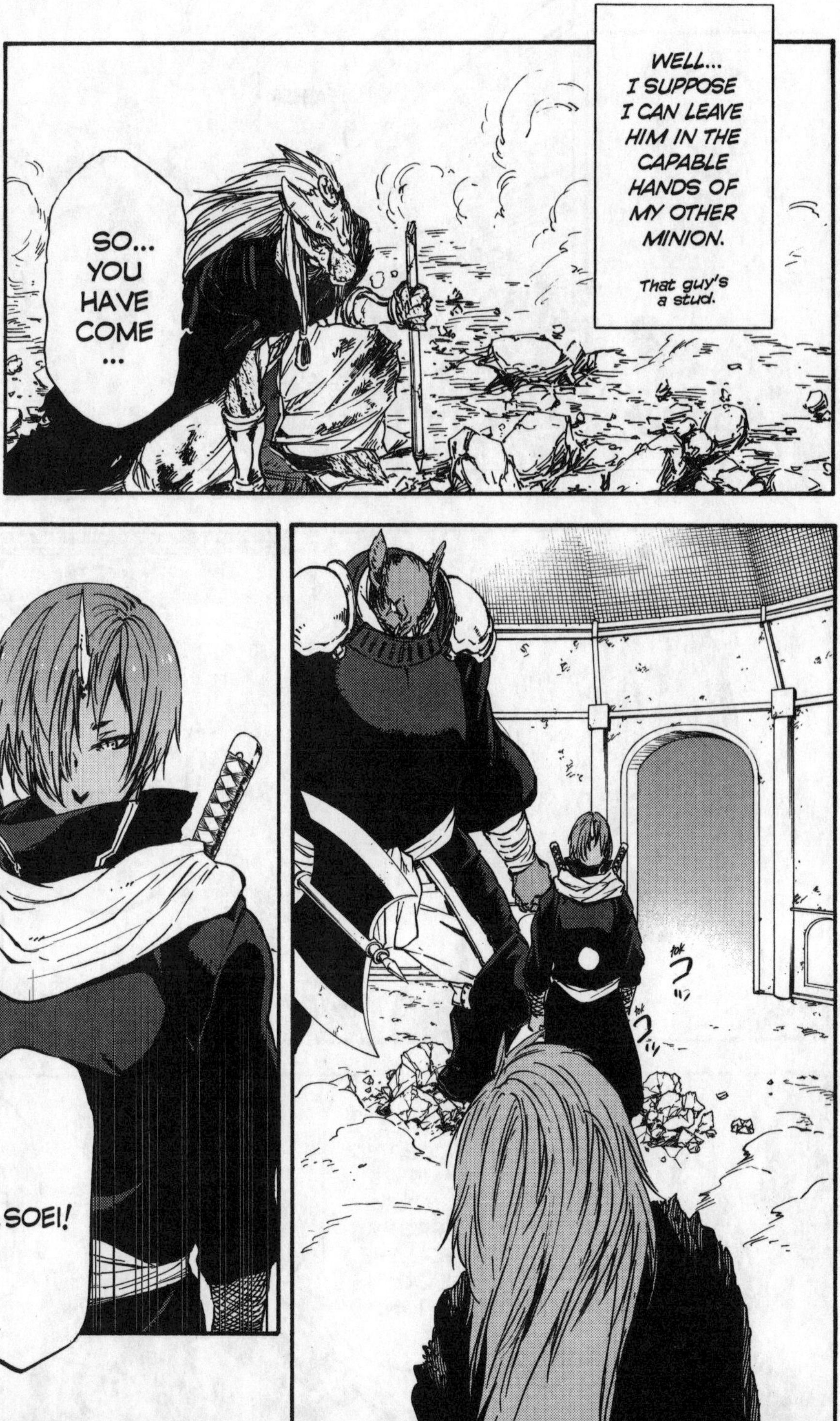
WELL... I SUPPOSE I CAN LEAVE HIM IN THE CAPABLE HANDS OF MY OTHER MINION.
That guy's a stud.
SO... YOU HAVE COME...
tok
tok
...SOEI!

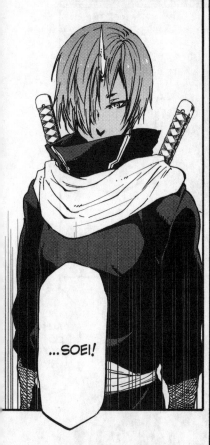

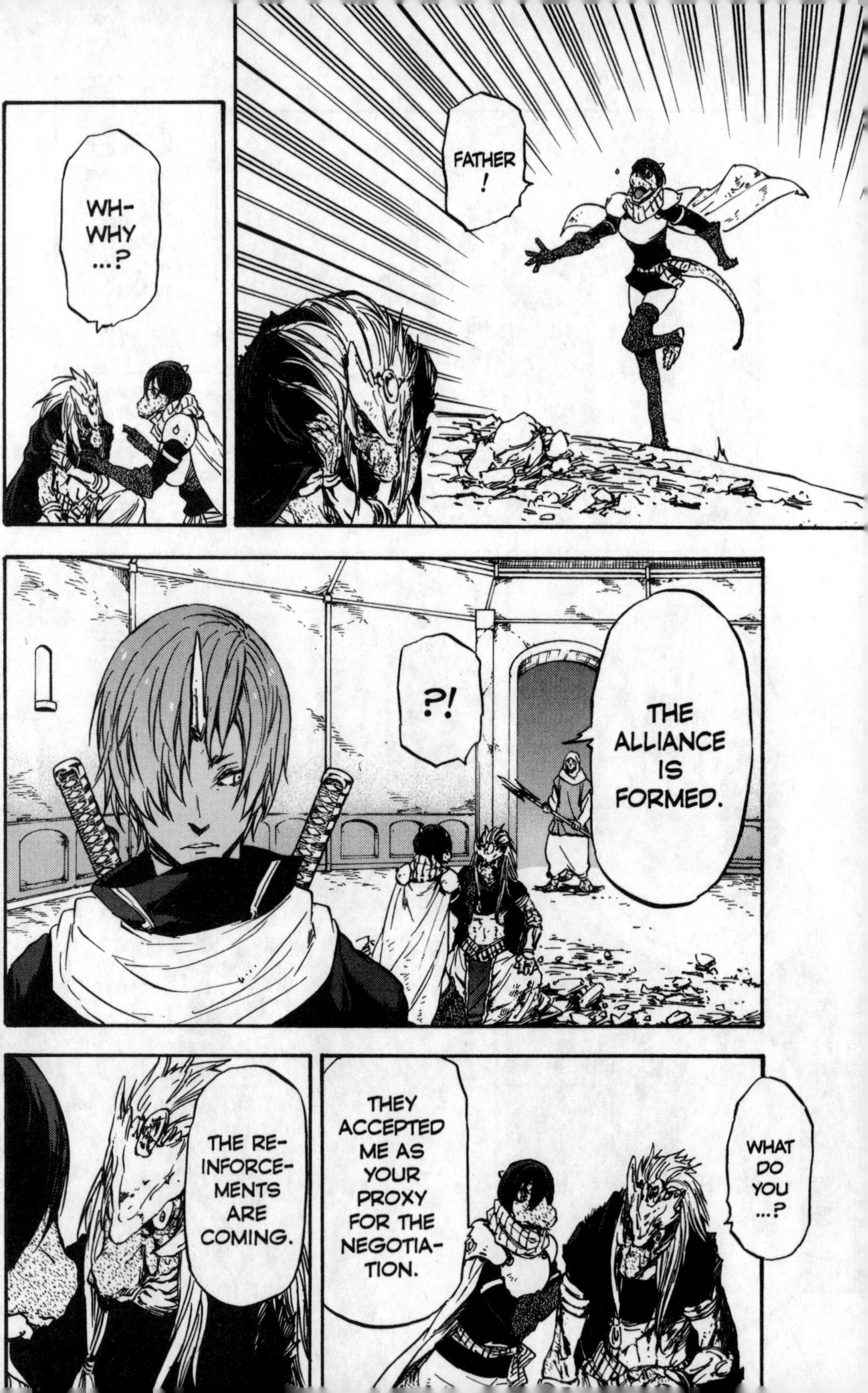
FATHER!
WH-WHY ...?
THE ALLIANCE IS FORMED.
?!
WHAT DO YOU ...?
THEY ACCEPTED ME AS YOUR PROXY FOR THE NEGOTIATION.
THE RE-INFORCEMENTS ARE COMING.

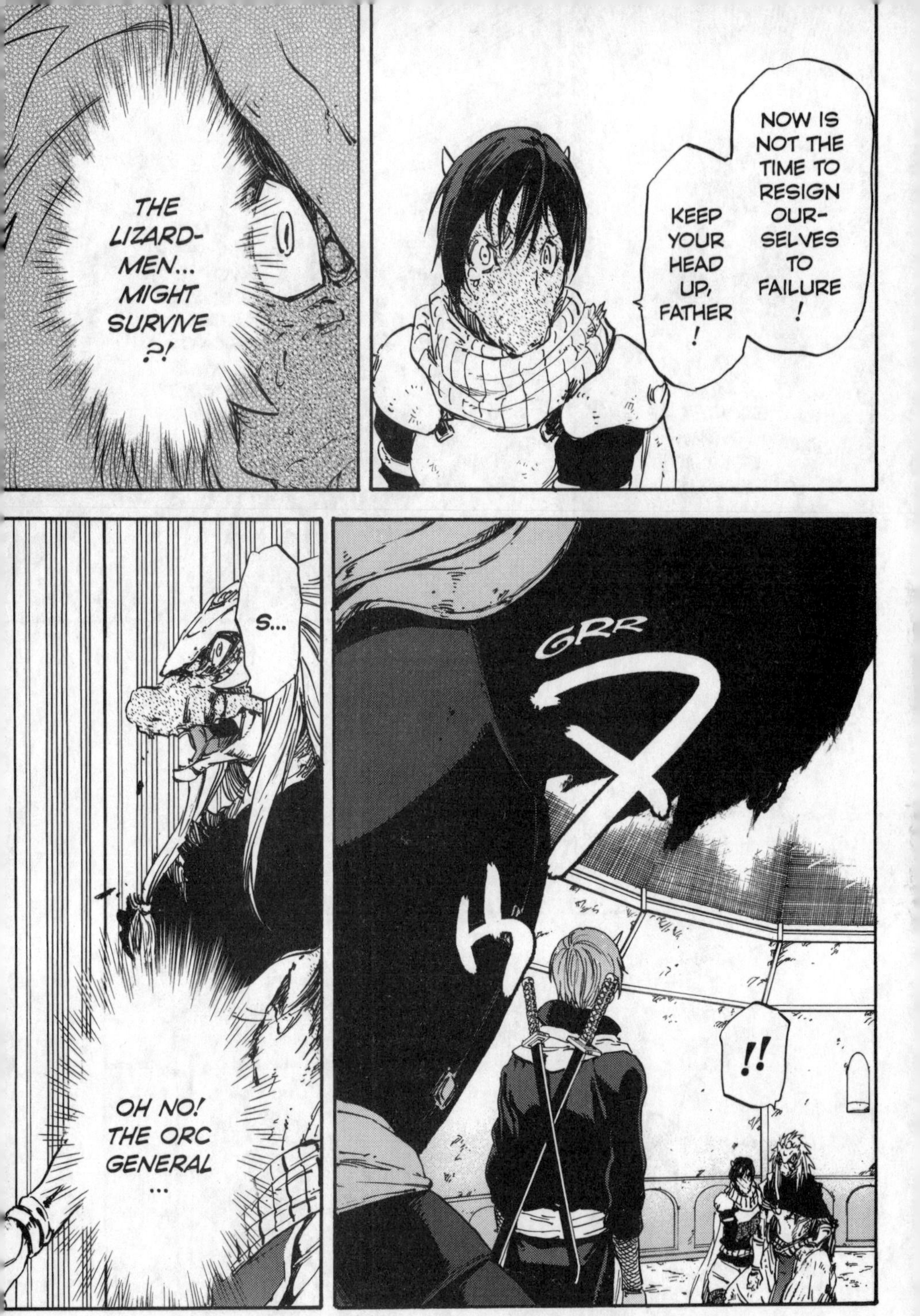
NOW IS NOT THE TIME TO RESIGN OURSELVES TO FAILURE!
KEEP YOUR HEAD UP, FATHER!
THE LIZARDMEN... MIGHT SURVIVE?!
GRR
!!
S...
OH NO! THE ORC GENERAL...

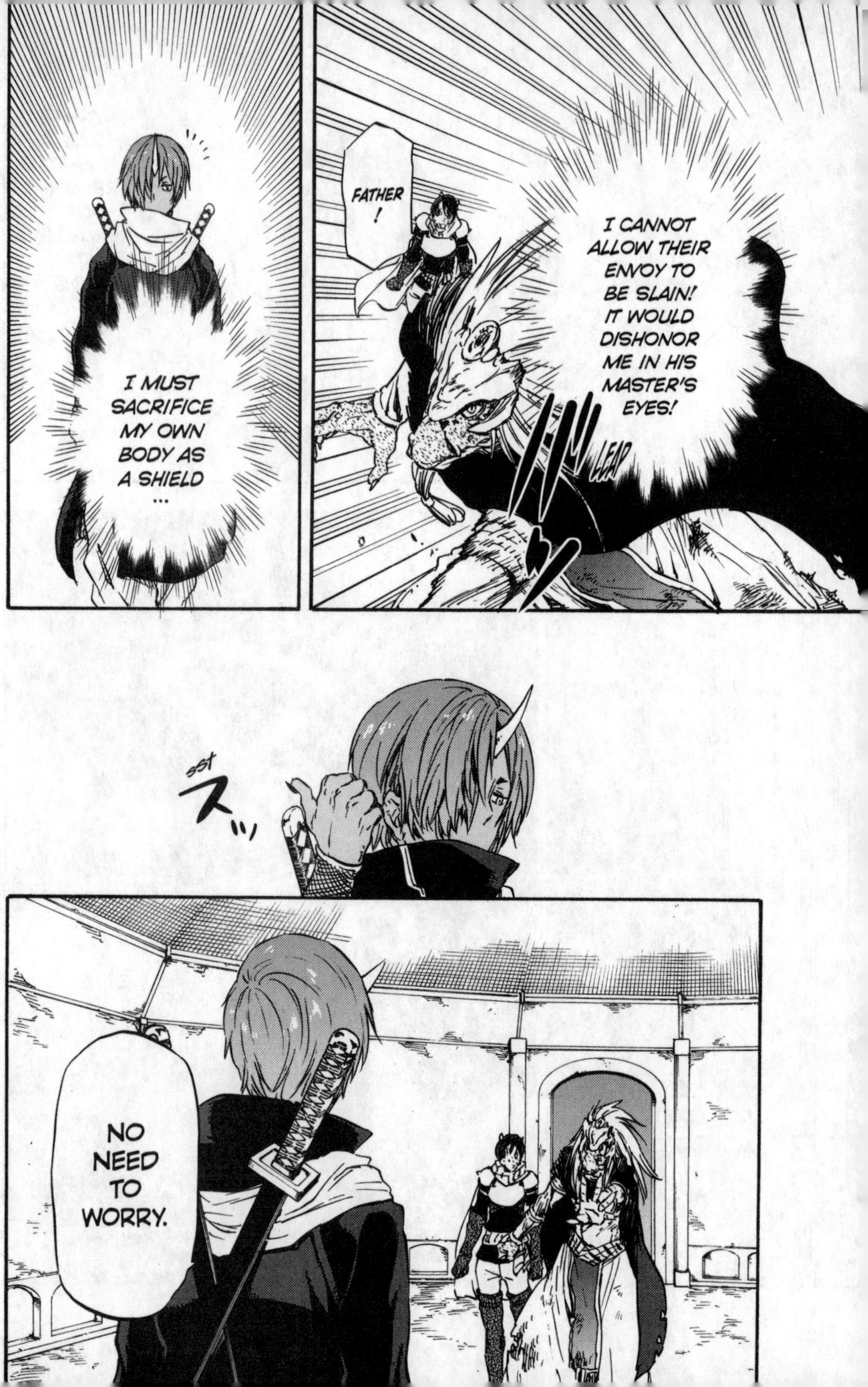
I CANNOT ALLOW THEIR ENVOY TO BE SLAIN! IT WOULD DISHONOR ME IN HIS MASTER'S EYES!
FATHER!
LEAP
I MUST SACRIFICE MY OWN BODY AS A SHIELD ...
SST
NO NEED TO WORRY.

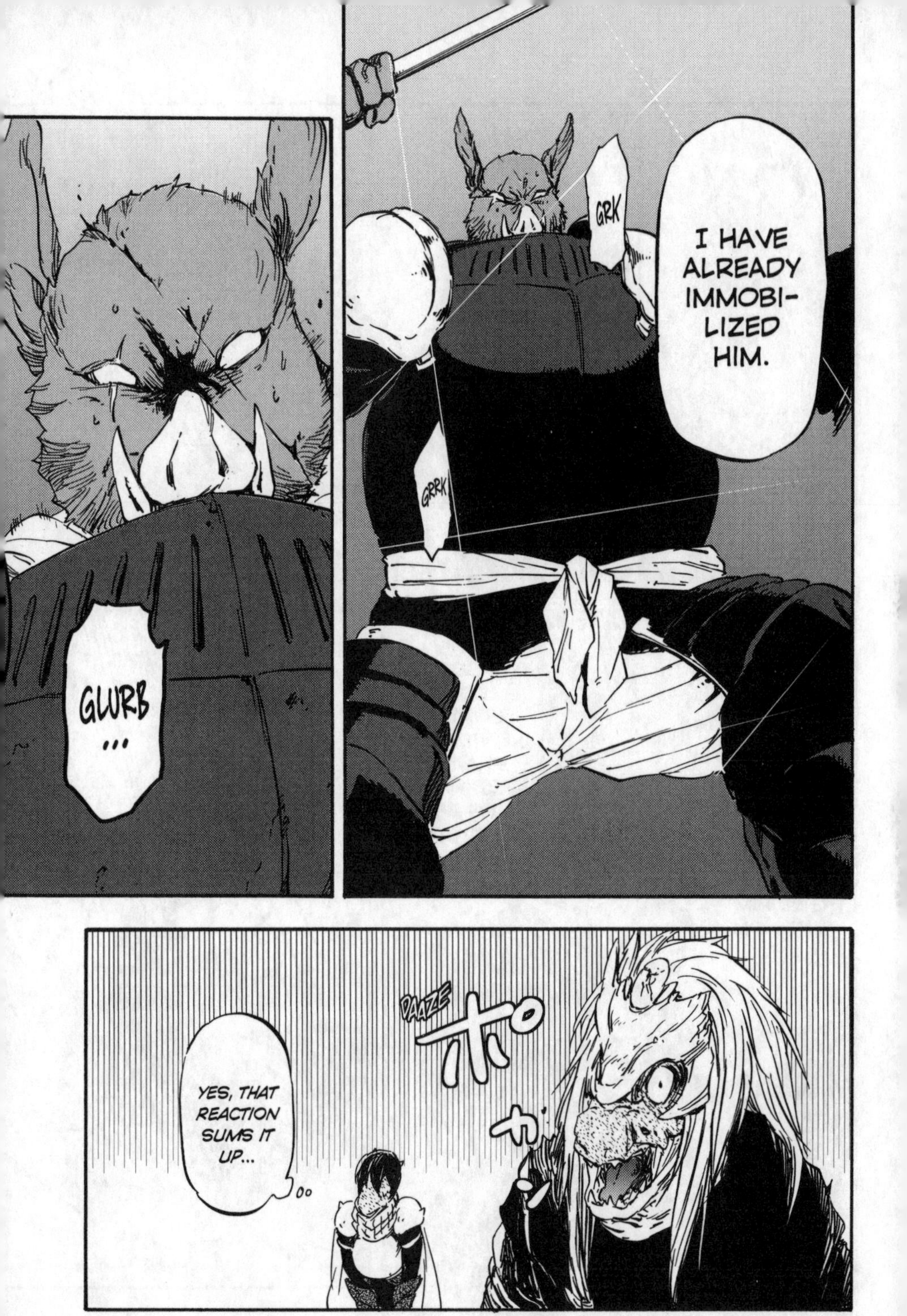
GRK
I HAVE ALREADY IMMOBI-LIZED HIM.
GRRK
GLURB ...
DAAZE
ポ
YES, THAT REACTION SUMS IT UP...

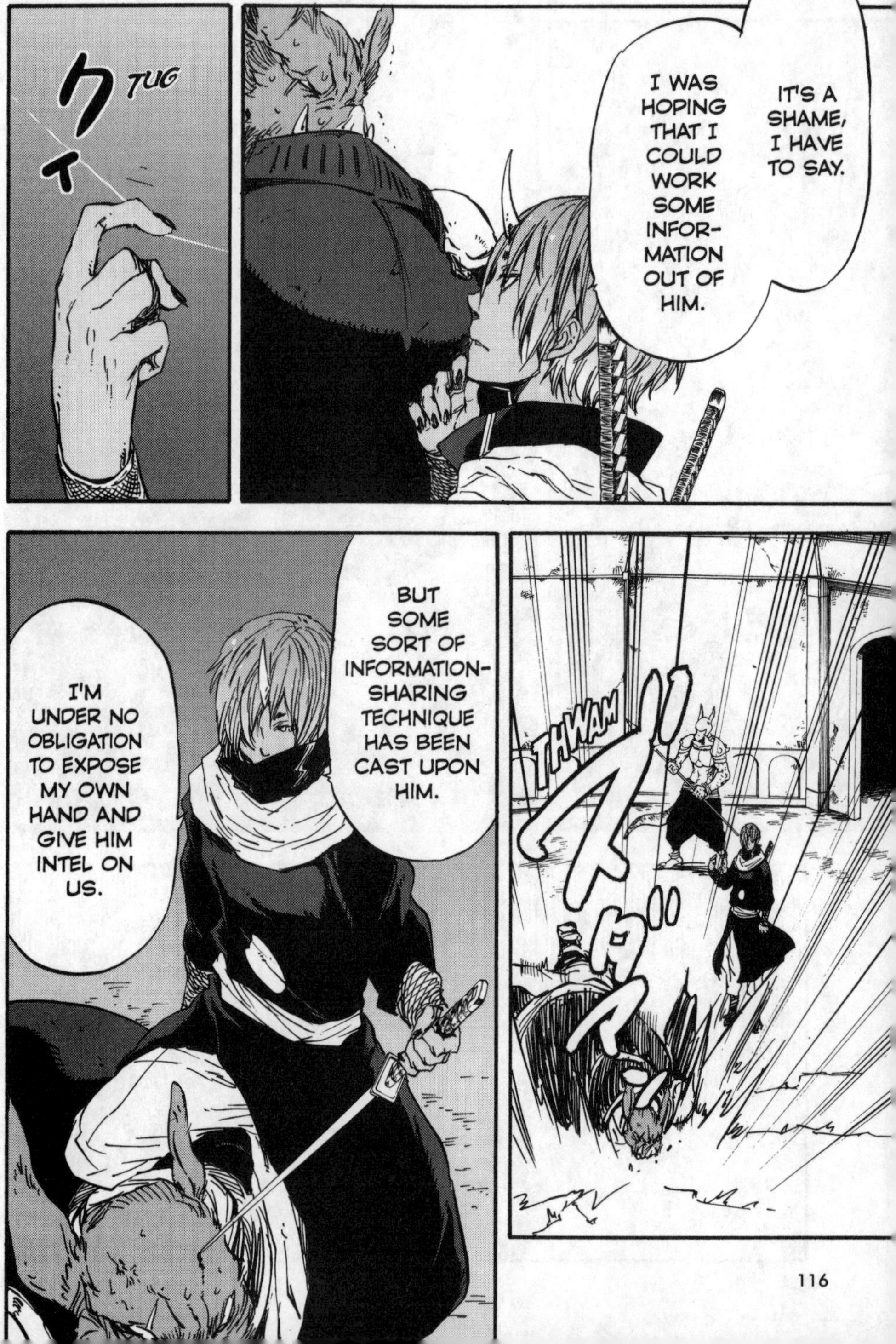
IT'S A SHAME, I HAVE TO SAY.
I WAS HOPING THAT I COULD WORK SOME INFORMATION OUT OF HIM.
TUG
THWAM
BUT SOME SORT OF INFORMATION-SHARING TECHNIQUE HAS BEEN CAST UPON HIM.
I'M UNDER NO OBLIGATION TO EXPOSE MY OWN HAND AND GIVE HIM INTEL ON US.

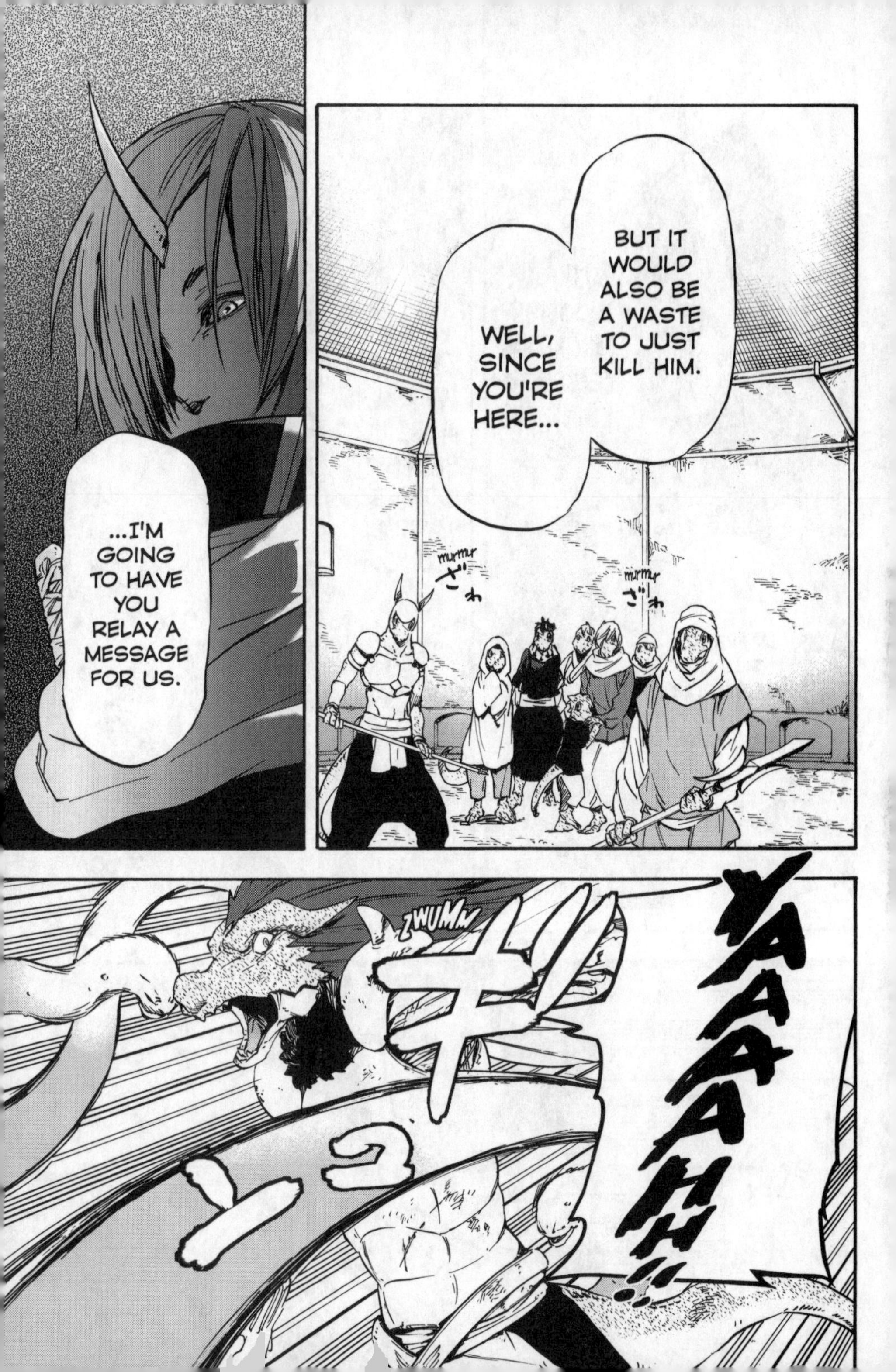
BUT IT WOULD ALSO BE A WASTE TO JUST KILL HIM.
WELL, SINCE YOU'RE HERE...
murmur ざわ
murmur ざわ
...I'M GOING TO HAVE YOU RELAY A MESSAGE FOR US.
YAAAAHH!!!
ZWUMM

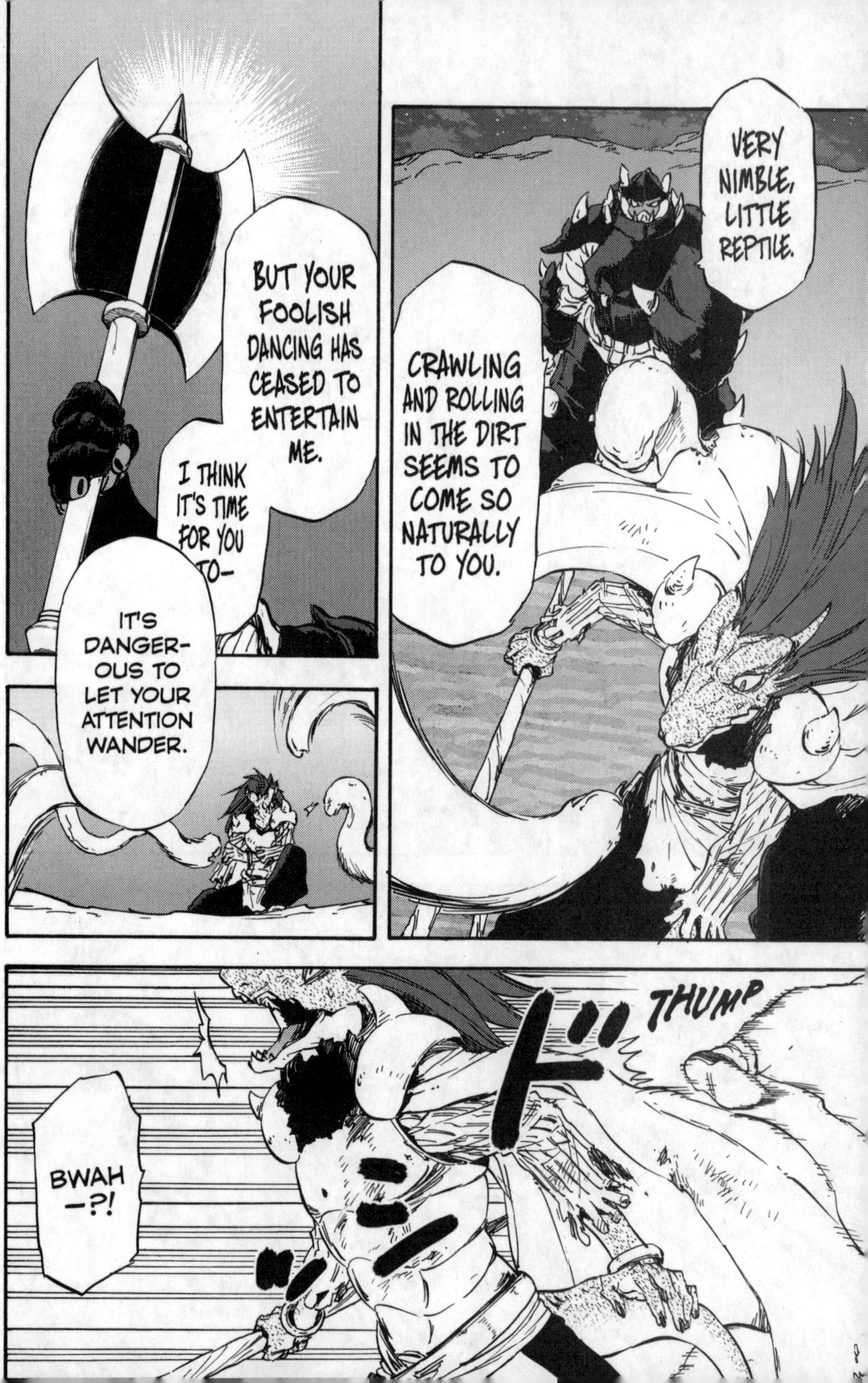
VERY NIMBLE, LITTLE REPTILE.
CRAWLING AND ROLLING IN THE DIRT SEEMS TO COME SO NATURALLY TO YOU.
BUT YOUR FOOLISH DANCING HAS CEASED TO ENTERTAIN ME.
I THINK IT'S TIME FOR YOU TO—
IT'S DANGER-OUS TO LET YOUR ATTENTION WANDER.
THUMP
BWAH—?!

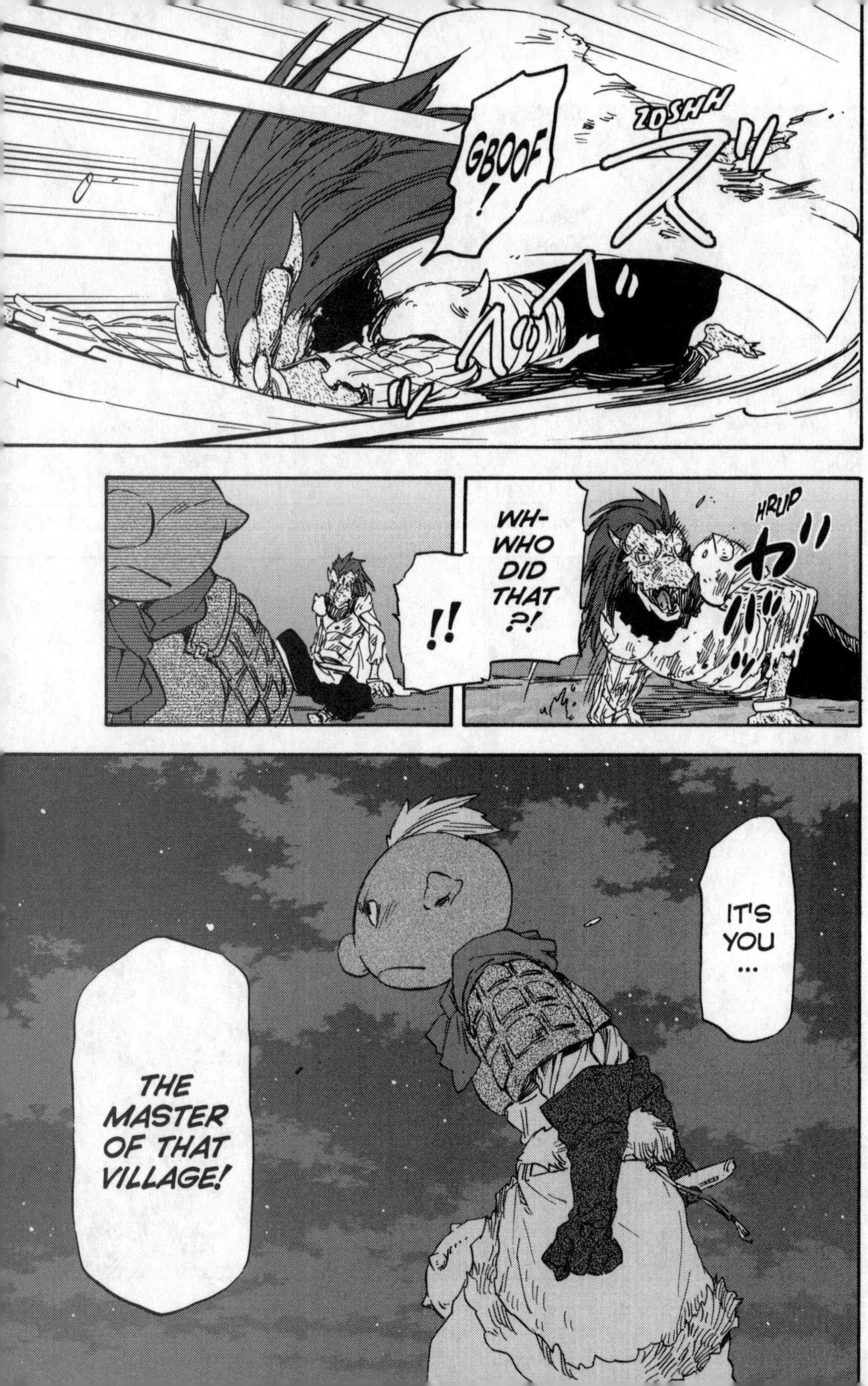
ZOSHH
GBOOF!
HRUP
WH- WHO DID THAT?!
!!
IT'S YOU ...
THE MASTER OF THAT VILLAGE!

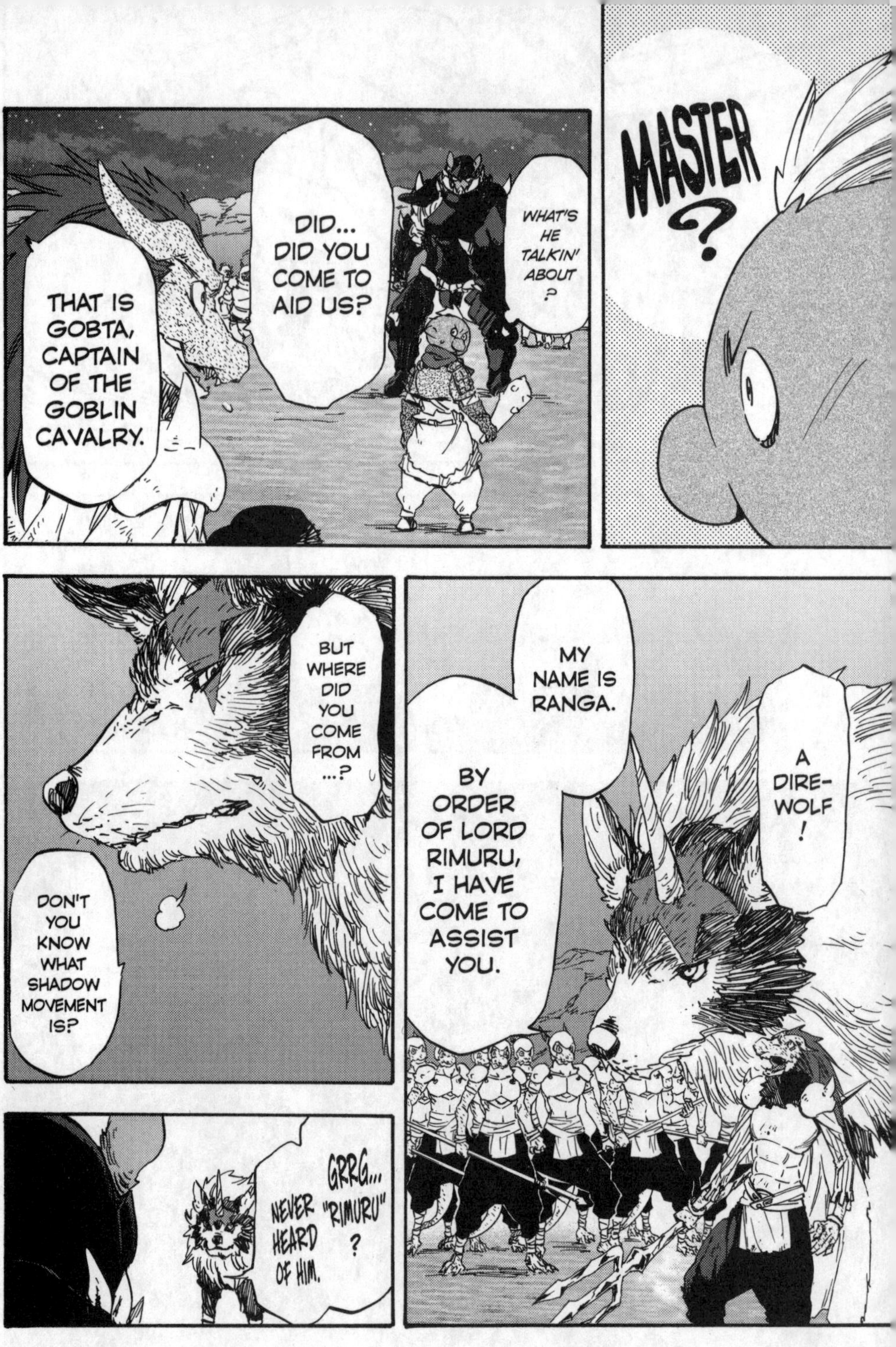
MASTER?
WHAT'S HE TALKIN' ABOUT?
DID... DID YOU COME TO AID US?
THAT IS GOBTA, CAPTAIN OF THE GOBLIN CAVALRY.
A DIRE-WOLF!
MY NAME IS RANGA.
BY ORDER OF LORD RIMURU, I HAVE COME TO ASSIST YOU.
BUT WHERE DID YOU COME FROM...?
DON'T YOU KNOW WHAT SHADOW MOVEMENT IS?
GRRG... "RIMURU"?
NEVER HEARD OF HIM.

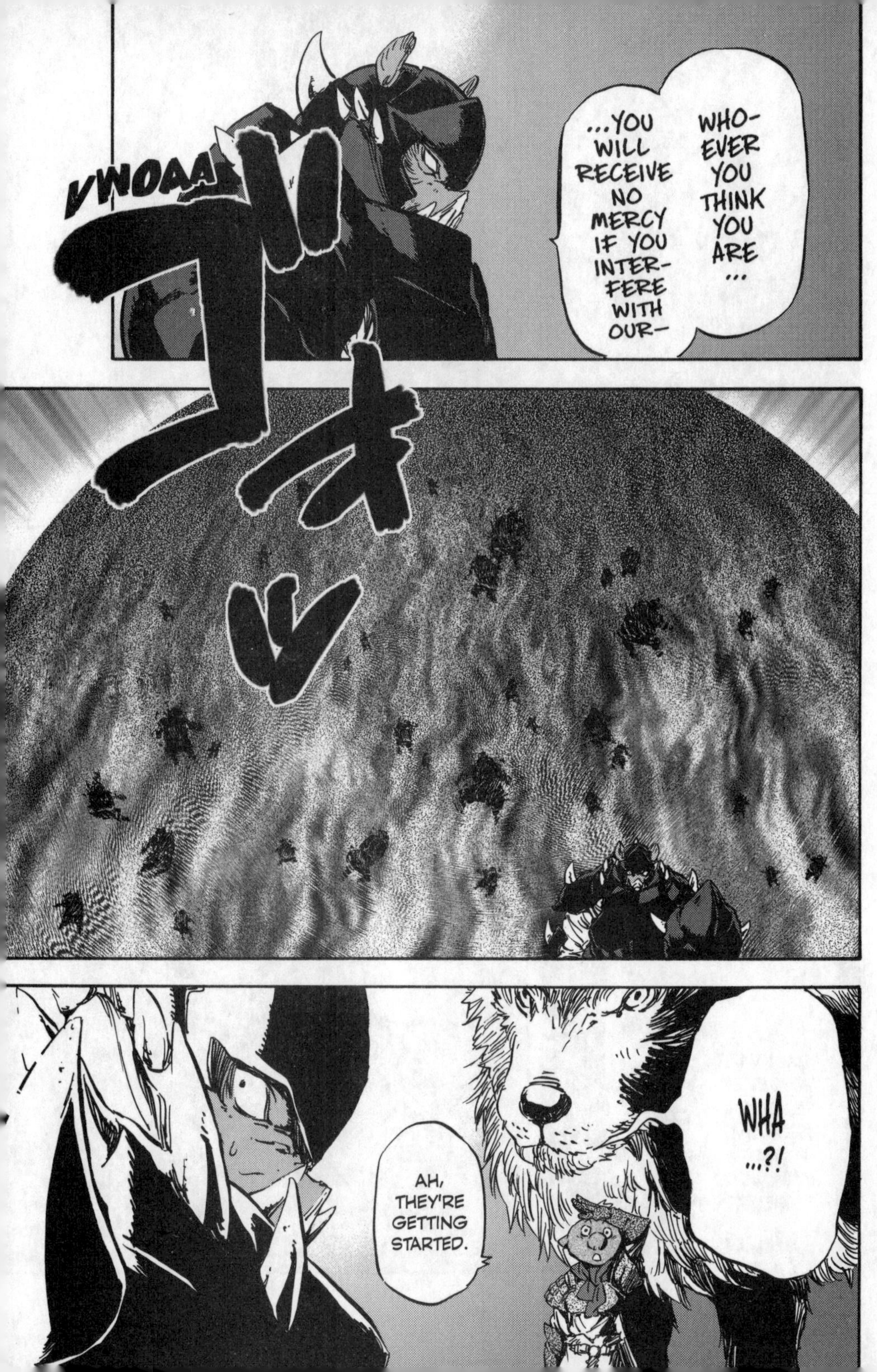
WHO-EVER YOU THINK YOU ARE...
...YOU WILL RECEIVE NO MERCY IF YOU INTER-FERE WITH OUR-
VWOAA
ゴォッ
WHA...?!
AH, THEY'RE GETTING STARTED.

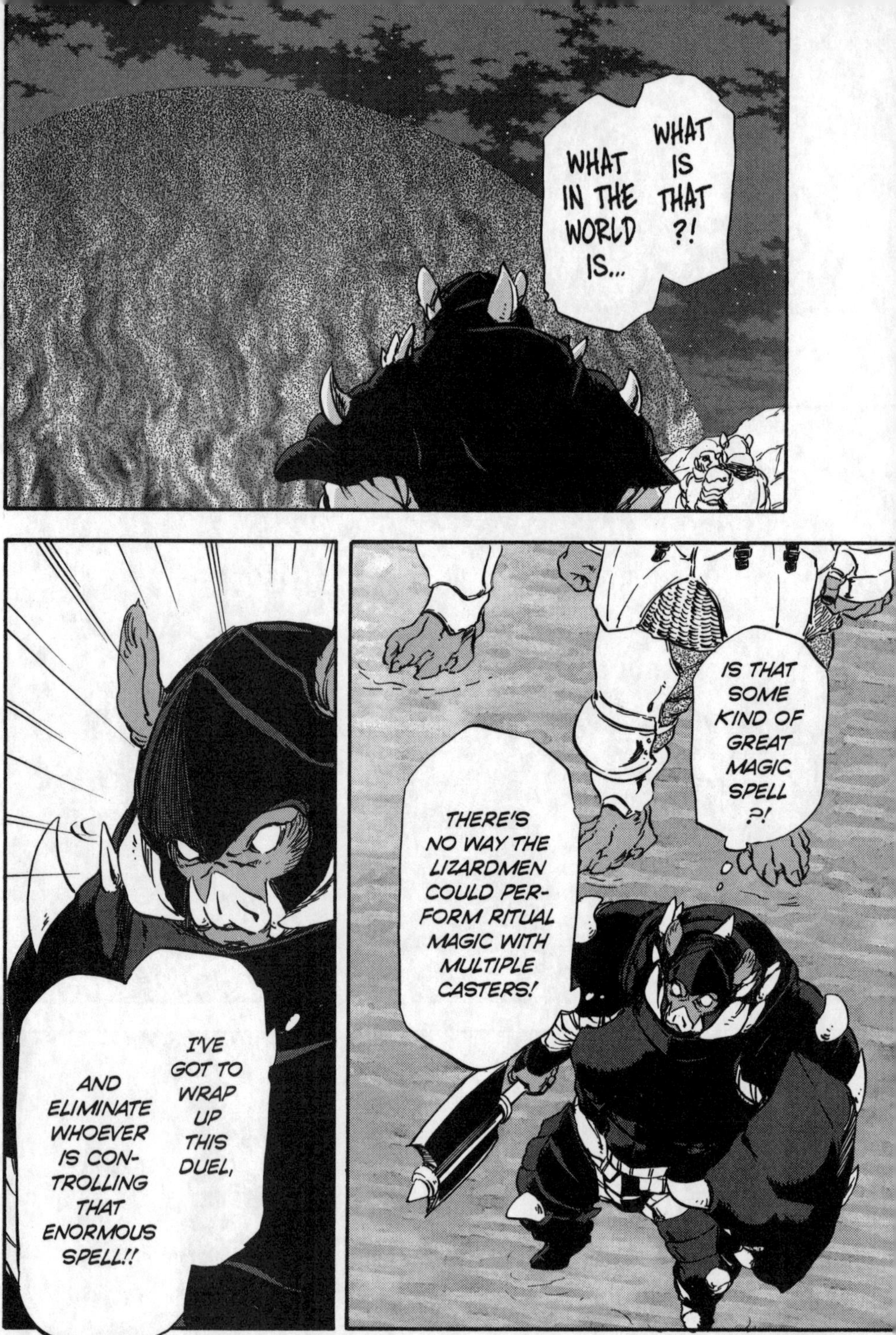
WHAT IS THAT ?!
WHAT IN THE WORLD IS...
IS THAT SOME KIND OF GREAT MAGIC SPELL ?!
THERE'S NO WAY THE LIZARDMEN COULD PER-FORM RITUAL MAGIC WITH MULTIPLE CASTERS!
I'VE GOT TO WRAP UP THIS DUEL,
AND ELIMINATE WHOEVER IS CON-TROLLING THAT ENORMOUS SPELL!!

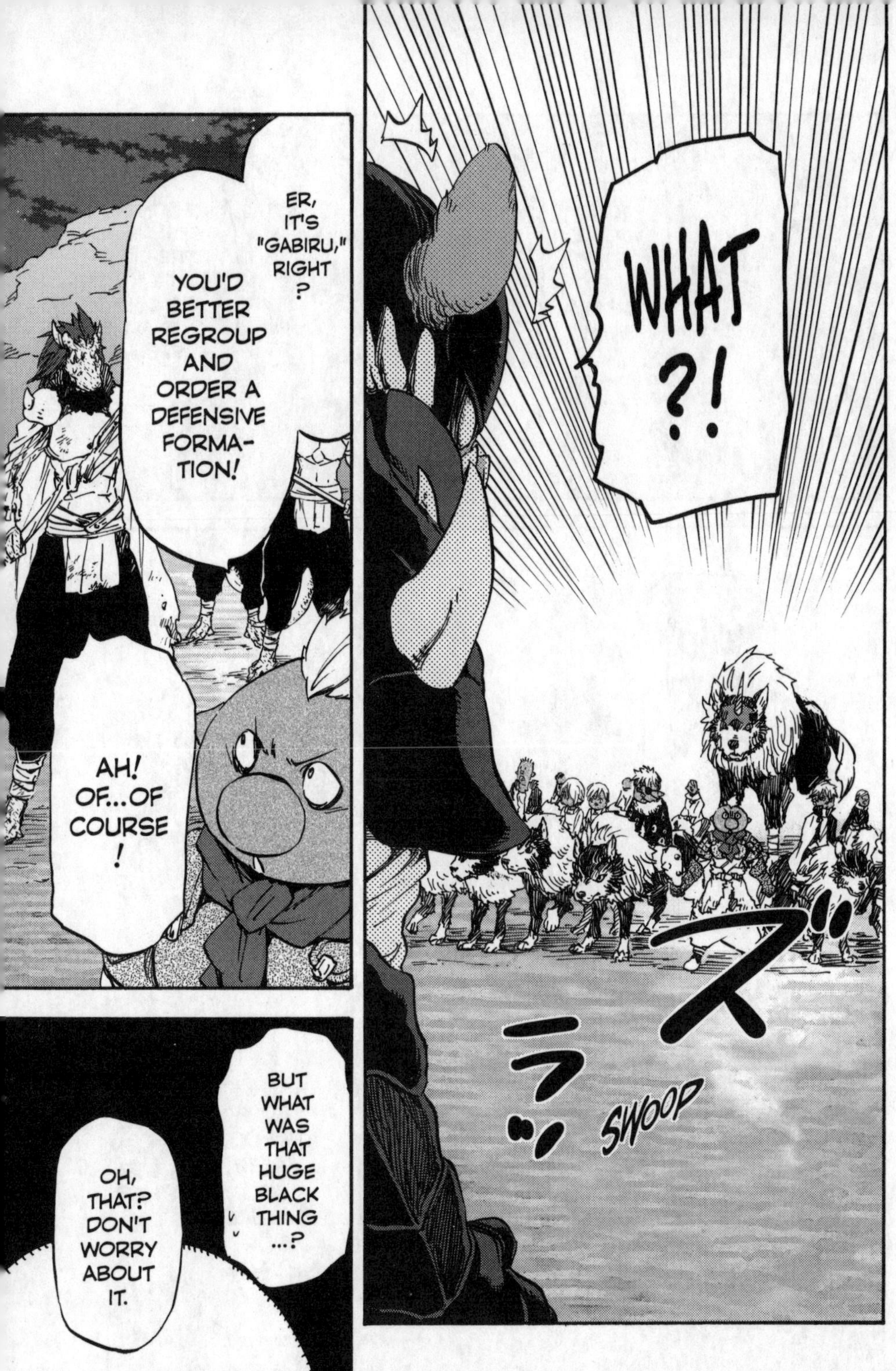
WHAT?!
SWOOP
ER, IT'S "GABIRU," RIGHT?
YOU'D BETTER REGROUP AND ORDER A DEFENSIVE FORMATION!
AH! OF...OF COURSE!
BUT WHAT WAS THAT HUGE BLACK THING...?
OH, THAT? DON'T WORRY ABOUT IT.

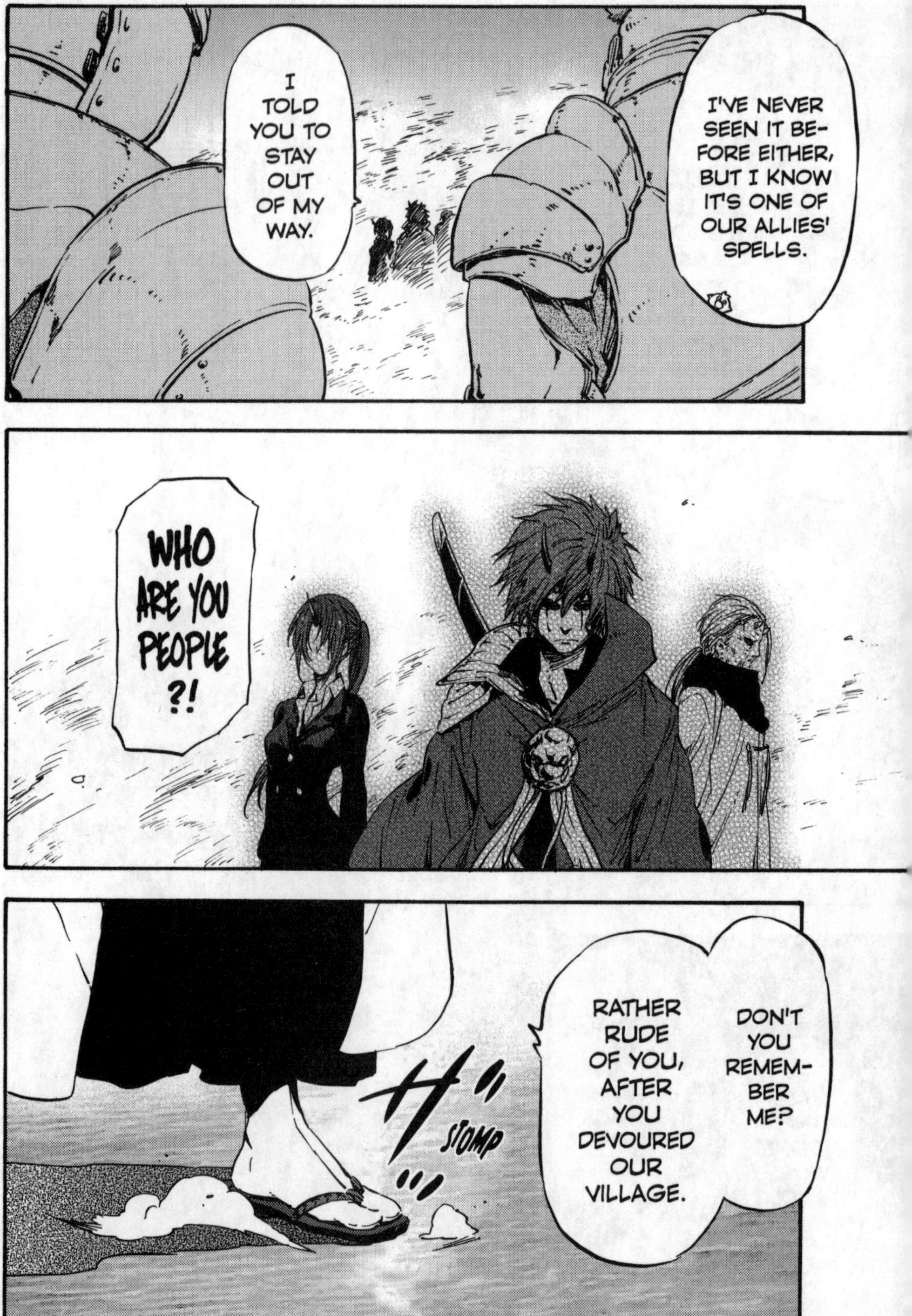
I'VE NEVER SEEN IT BEFORE EITHER, BUT I KNOW IT'S ONE OF OUR ALLIES' SPELLS.
I TOLD YOU TO STAY OUT OF MY WAY.
WHO ARE YOU PEOPLE?!
DON'T YOU REMEMBER ME?
RATHER RUDE OF YOU, AFTER YOU DEVOURED OUR VILLAGE.
STOMP

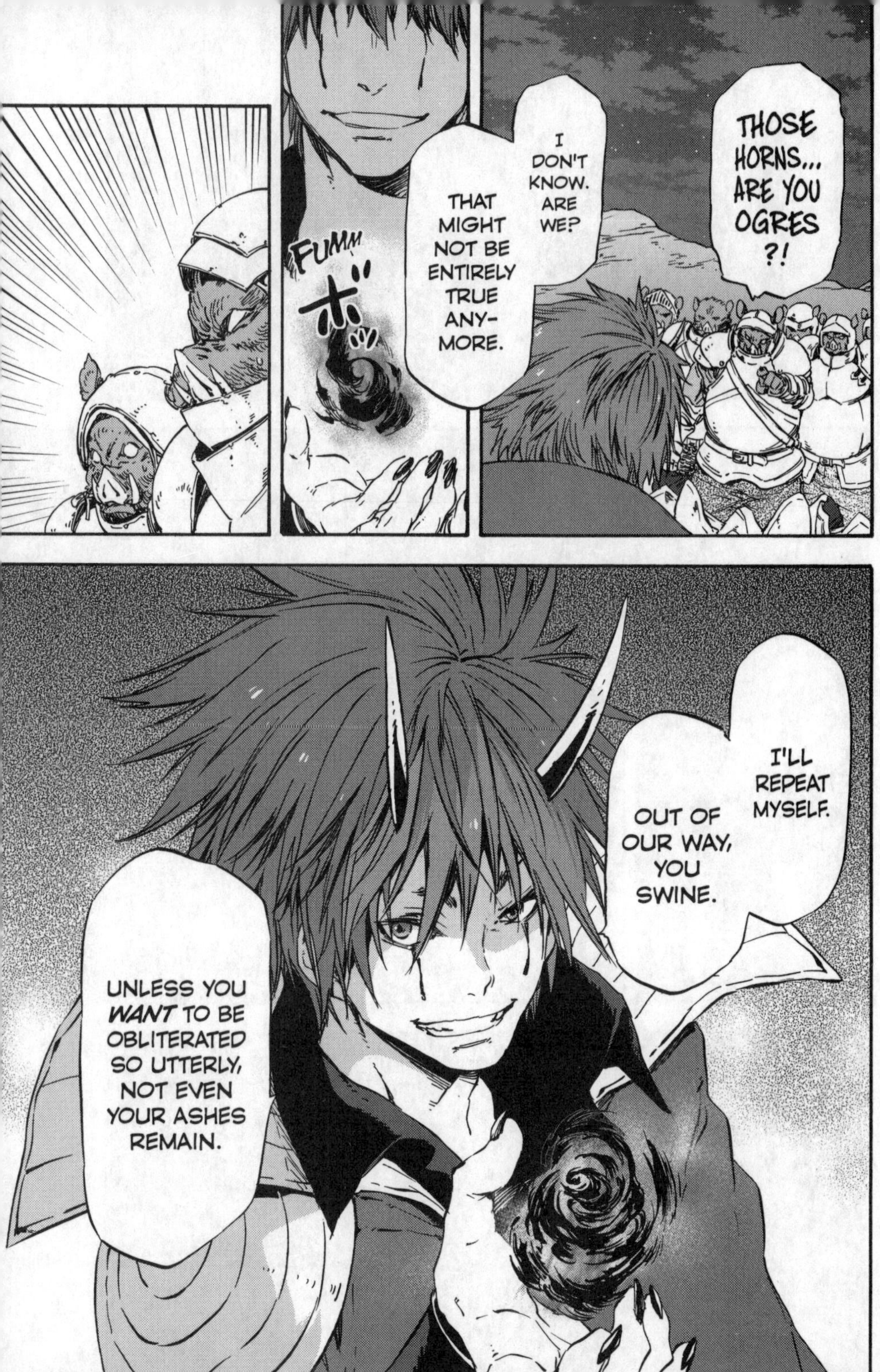
THOSE HORNS... ARE YOU OGRES ?!
I DON'T KNOW. ARE WE?
THAT MIGHT NOT BE ENTIRELY TRUE ANY-MORE.
FUMM
ボッ
I'LL REPEAT MYSELF.
OUT OF OUR WAY, YOU SWINE.
UNLESS YOU *WANT* TO BE OBLITERATED SO UTTERLY, NOT EVEN YOUR ASHES REMAIN.

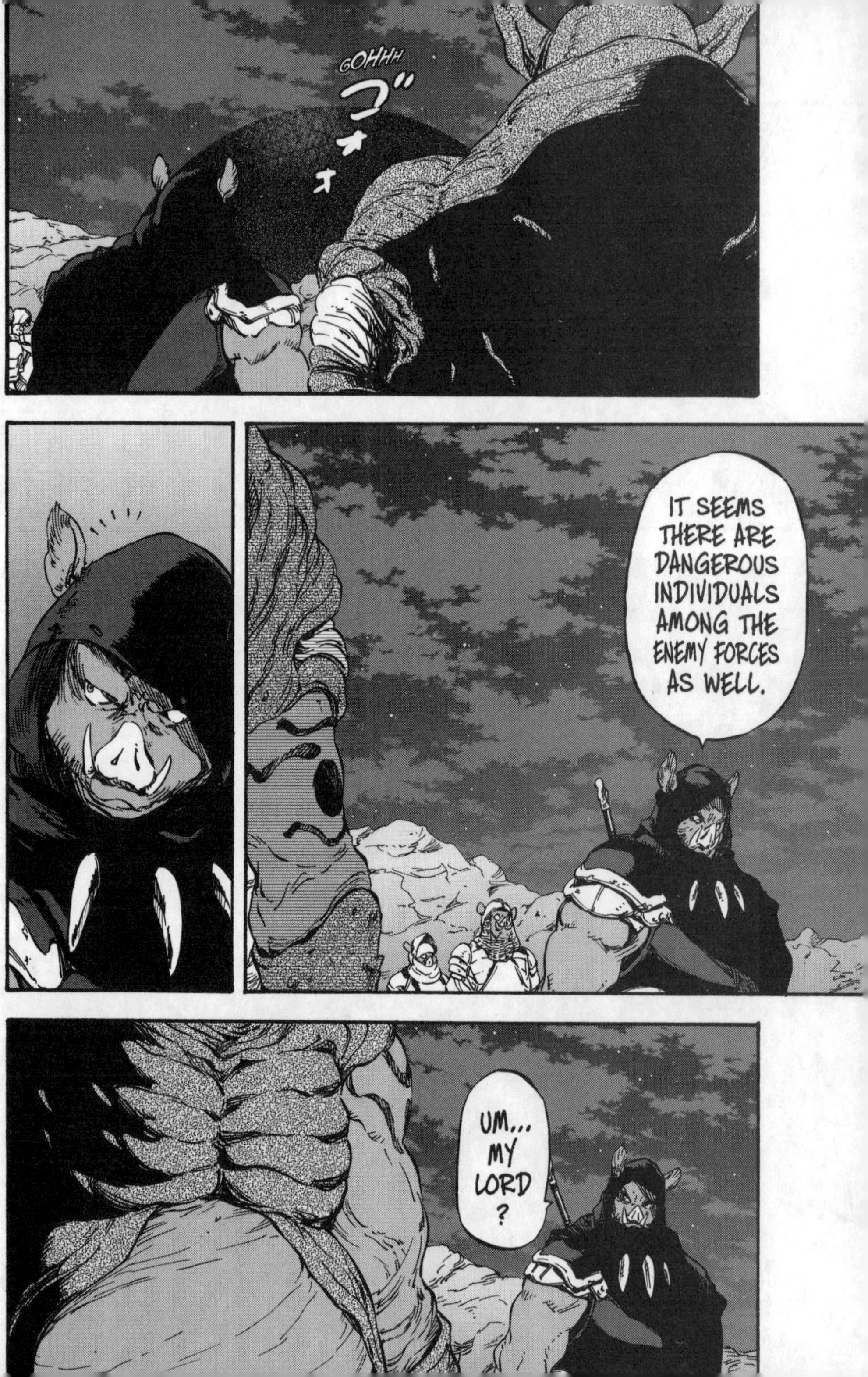
GOHHH
ゴオオ
IT SEEMS THERE ARE DANGEROUS INDIVIDUALS AMONG THE ENEMY FORCES AS WELL.
UM... MY LORD ?

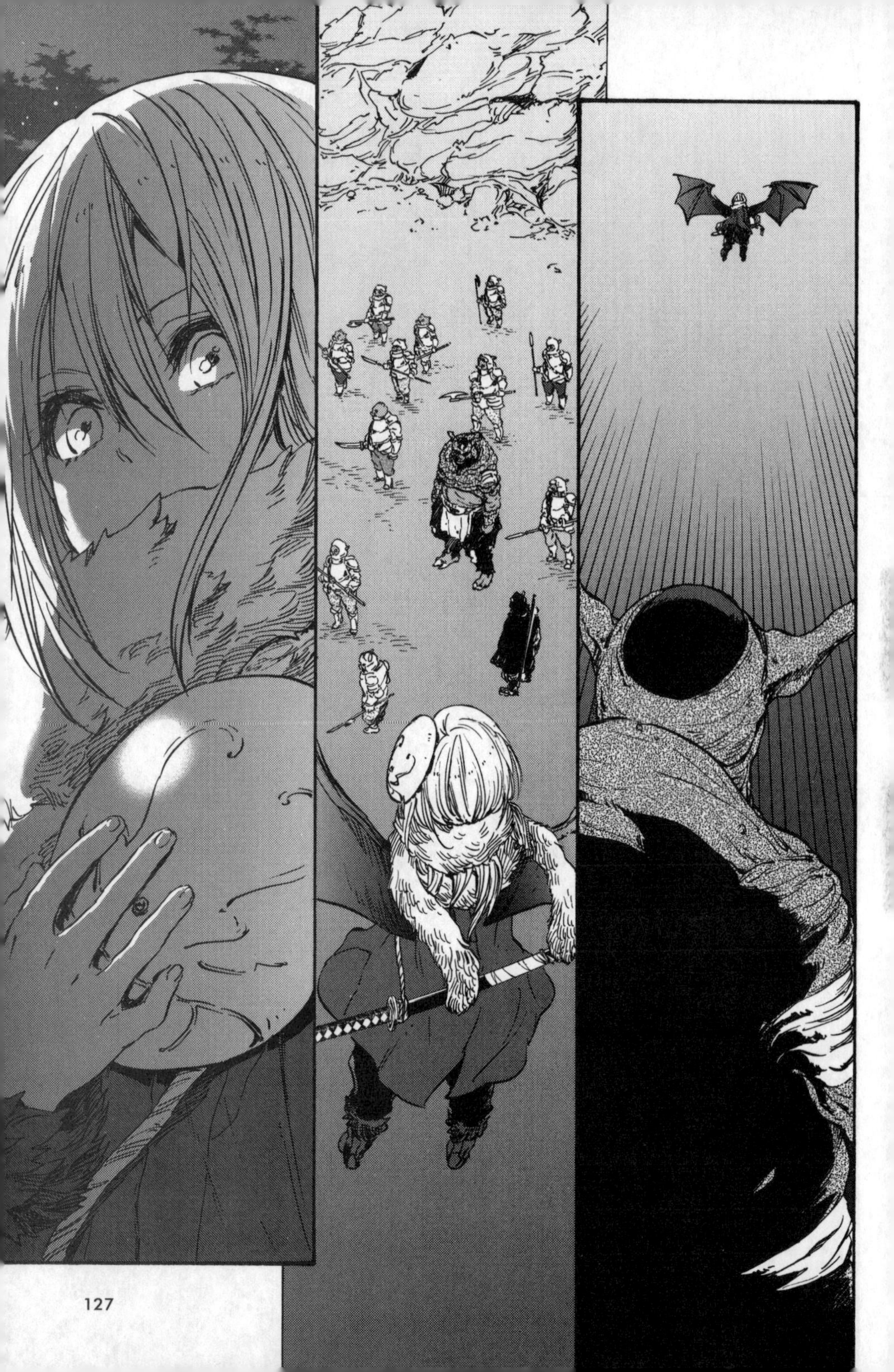

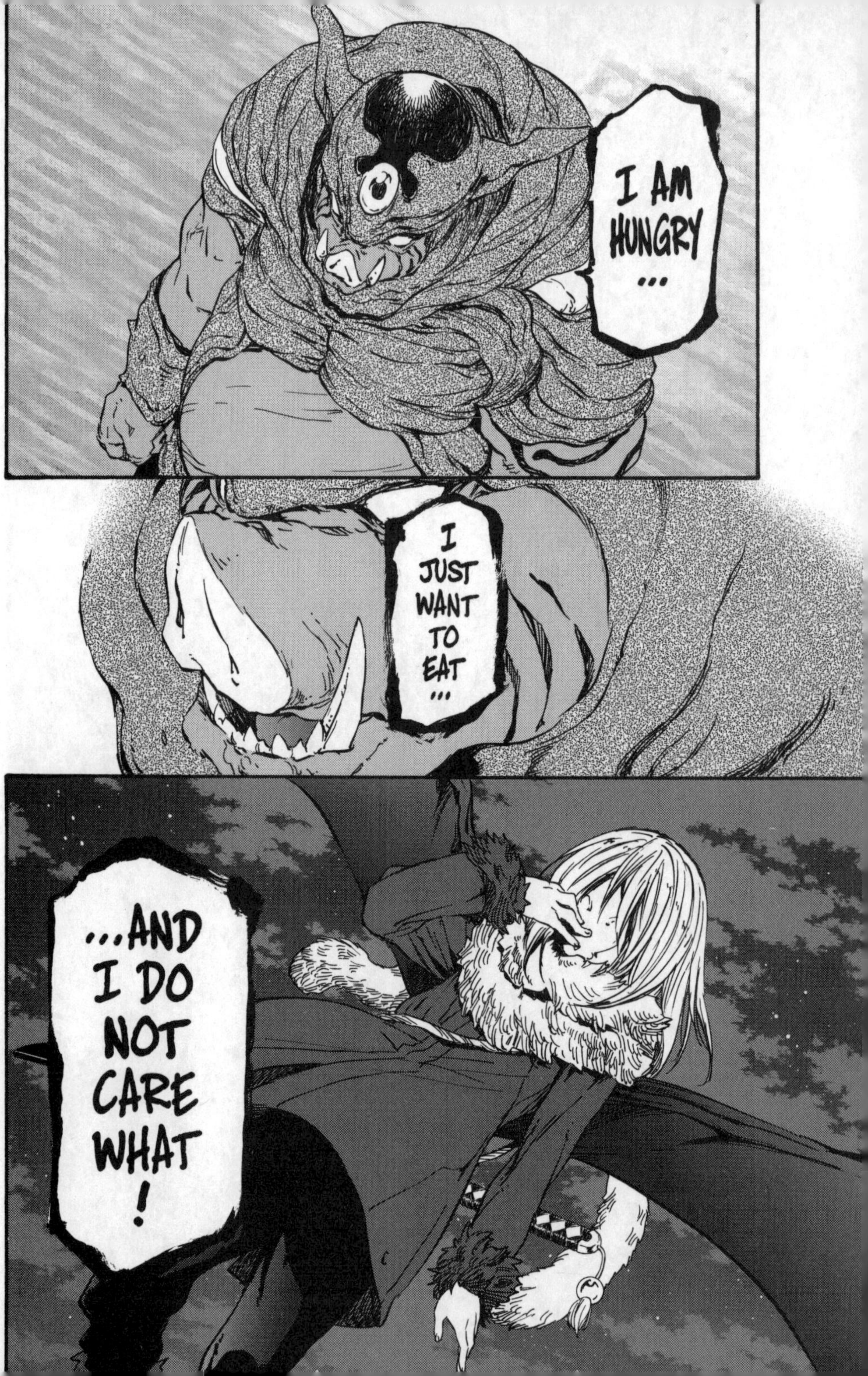
I AM HUNGRY ...
I JUST WANT TO EAT ...
...AND I DO NOT CARE WHAT!

If he just mimics the wings while in slime form...

...he turns into this cute little beastie.

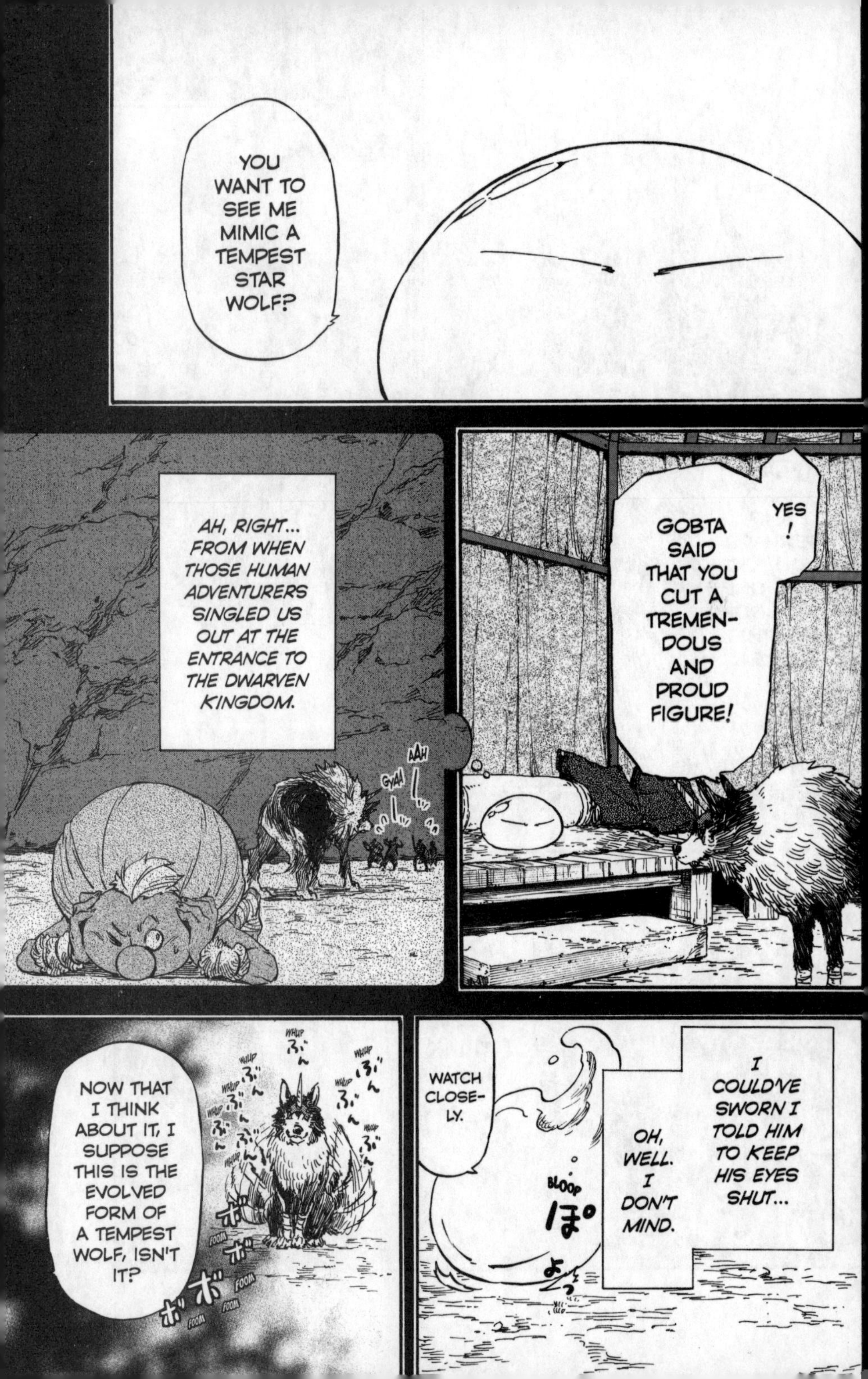
YOU WANT TO SEE ME MIMIC A TEMPEST STAR WOLF?
YES!
GOBTA SAID THAT YOU CUT A TREMENDOUS AND PROUD FIGURE!
AH, RIGHT... FROM WHEN THOSE HUMAN ADVENTURERS SINGLED US OUT AT THE ENTRANCE TO THE DWARVEN KINGDOM.
AAH
GYAA
I COULD'VE SWORN I TOLD HIM TO KEEP HIS EYES SHUT...
OH, WELL. I DON'T MIND.
WATCH CLOSE-LY.
BLOOP
ぽ
よっ
NOW THAT I THINK ABOUT IT, I SUPPOSE THIS IS THE EVOLVED FORM OF A TEMPEST WOLF, ISN'T IT?
WHUP
ぶん
FOOM
ボ

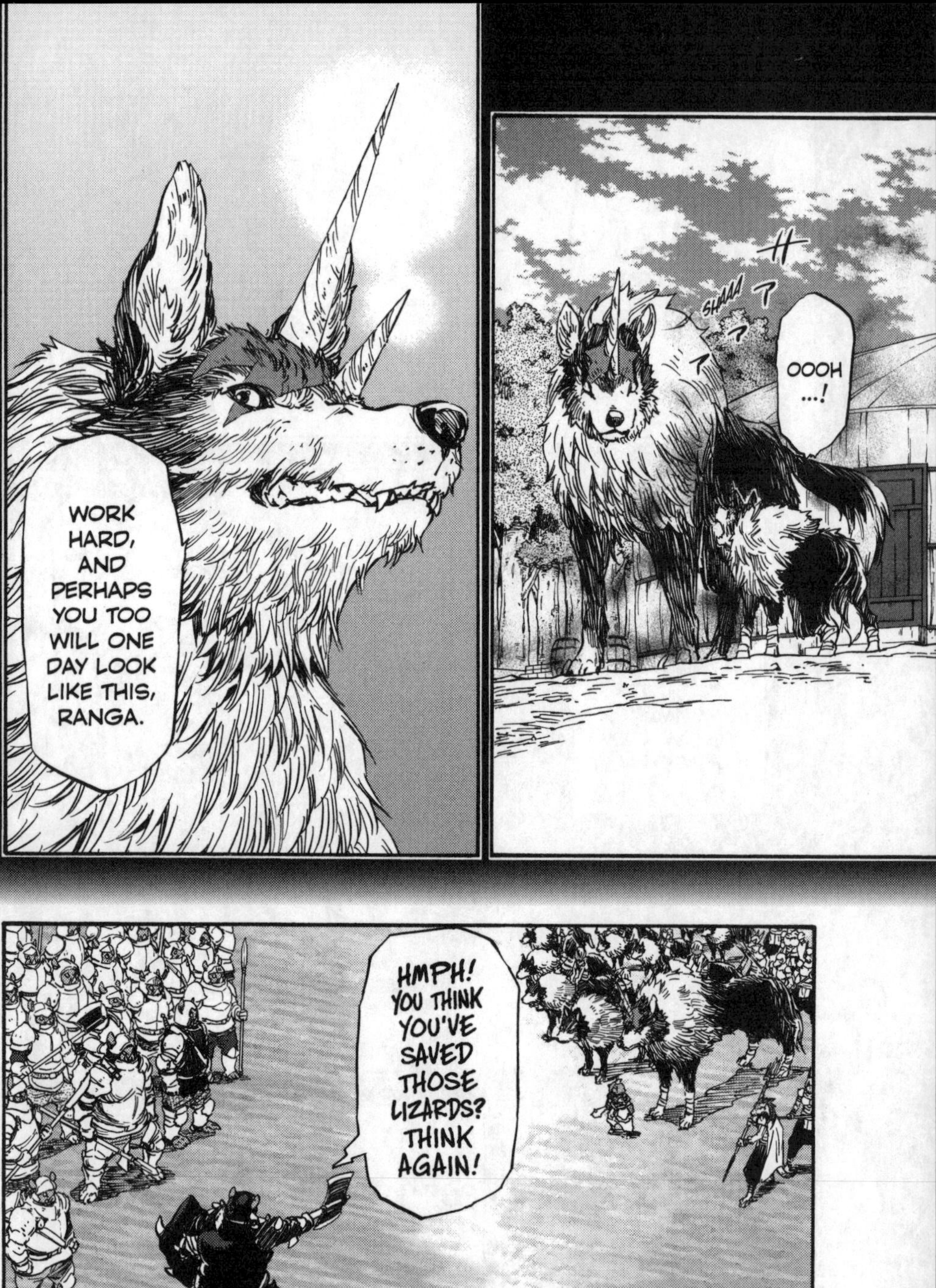
SHAAA
OOOH ...!
WORK HARD, AND PERHAPS YOU TOO WILL ONE DAY LOOK LIKE THIS, RANGA.
HMPH! YOU THINK YOU'VE SAVED THOSE LIZARDS? THINK AGAIN!

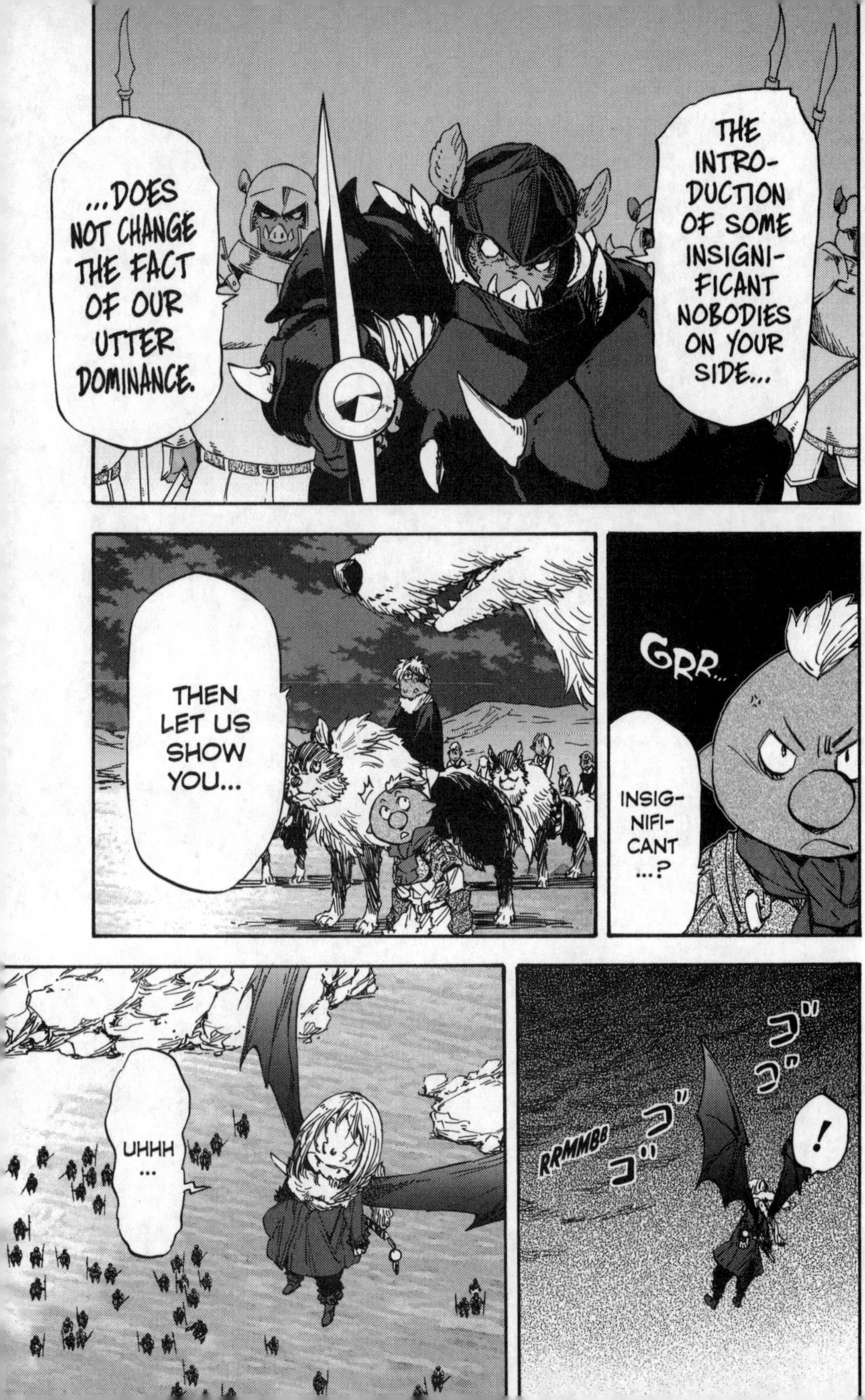
THE INTRO-DUCTION OF SOME INSIGNI-FICANT NOBODIES ON YOUR SIDE...
...DOES NOT CHANGE THE FACT OF OUR UTTER DOMINANCE.
GRR...
INSIG-NIFI-CANT ...?
THEN LET US SHOW YOU...
ゴゴゴゴ
RRMMBB
!
UHHH ...

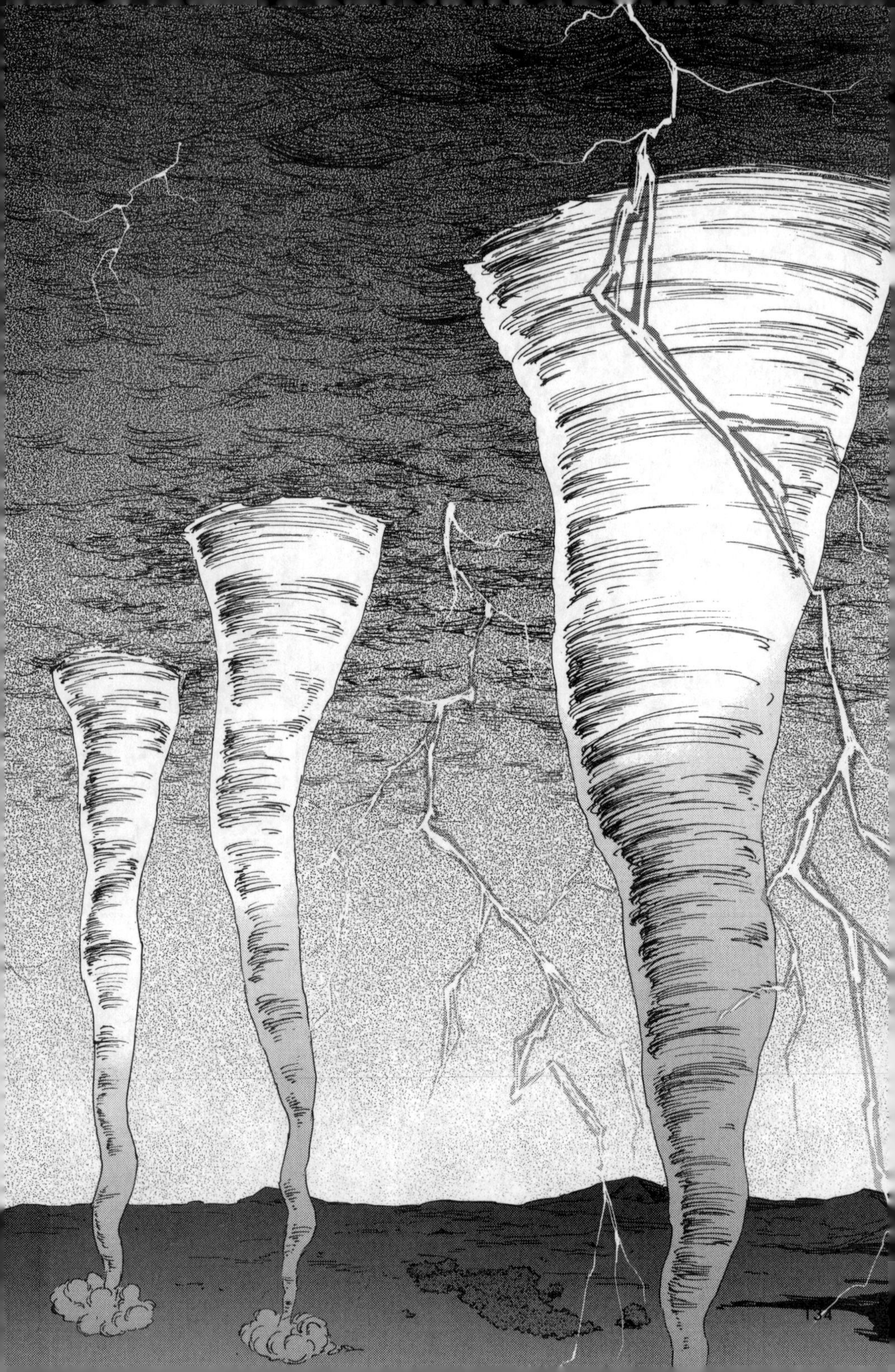

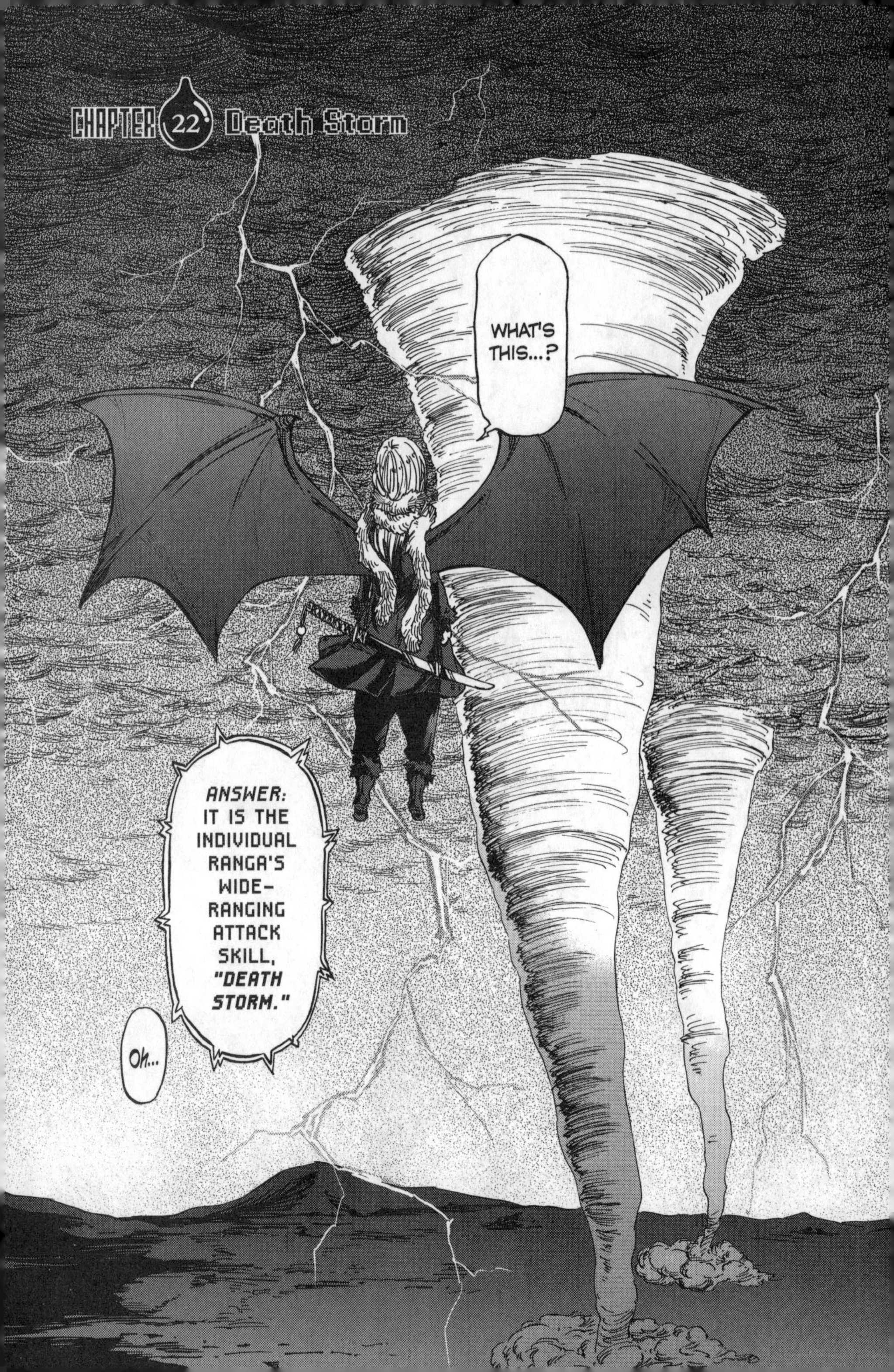
CHAPTER 22 Death Storm
WHAT'S THIS...?
ANSWER: IT IS THE INDIVIDUAL RANGA'S WIDE-RANGING ATTACK SKILL, "DEATH STORM."
Oh...

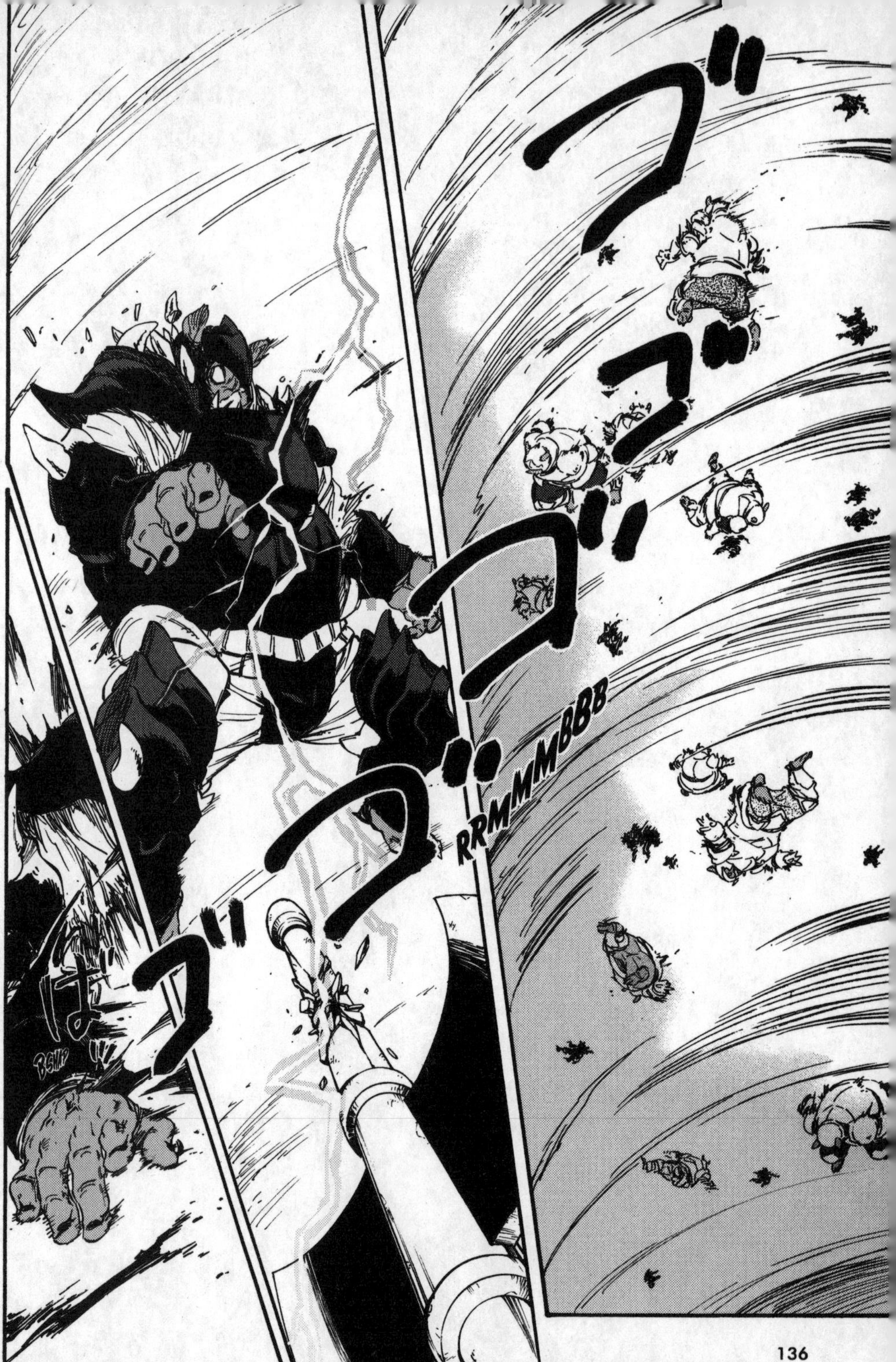

ゴゴゴゴゴ
RRMMMMBBB
ばっ!!
BSHP

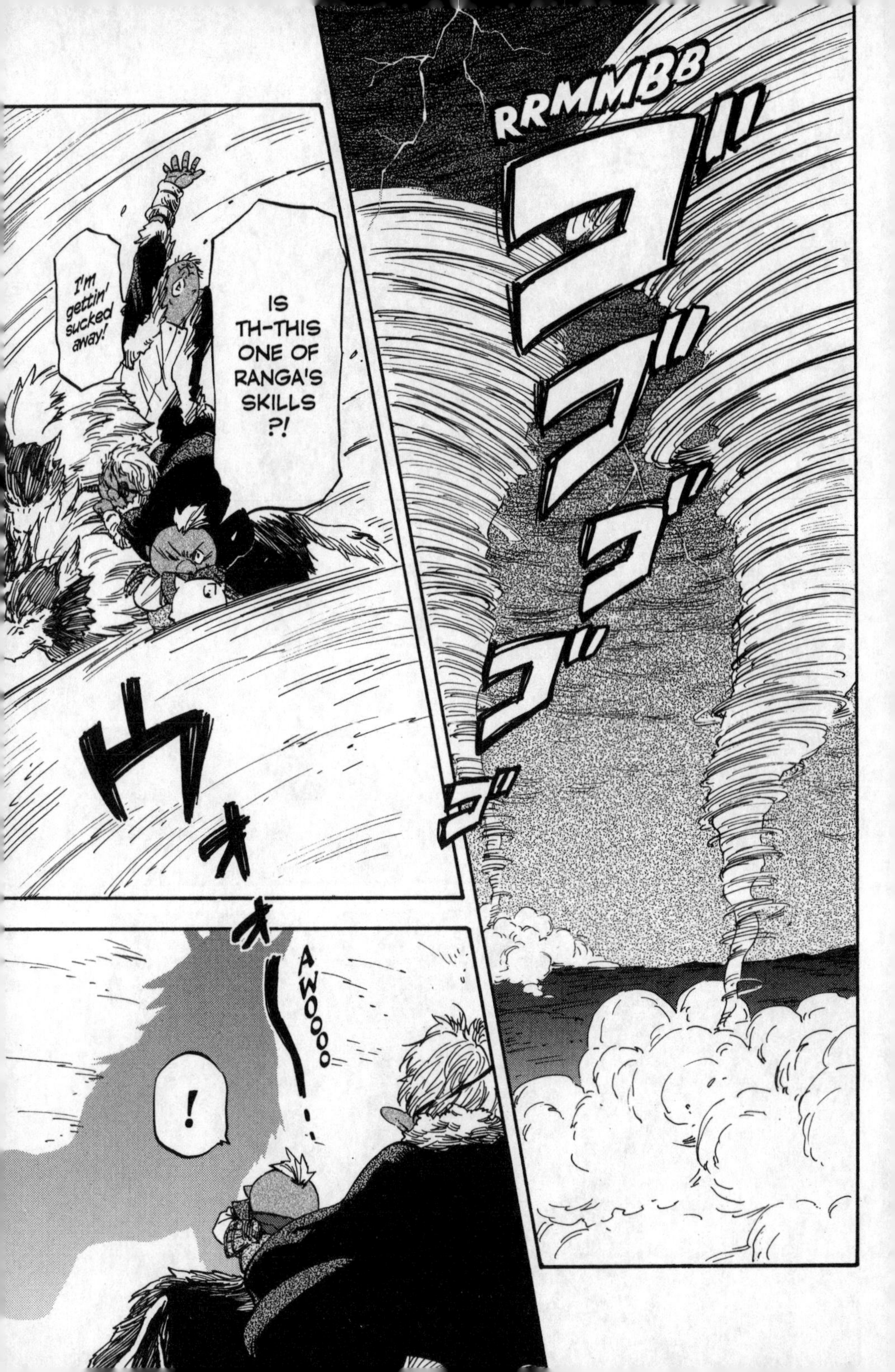
RRMMBB
IS TH-THIS ONE OF RANGA'S SKILLS?!
I'm gettin' sucked away!
AWOOOO
!

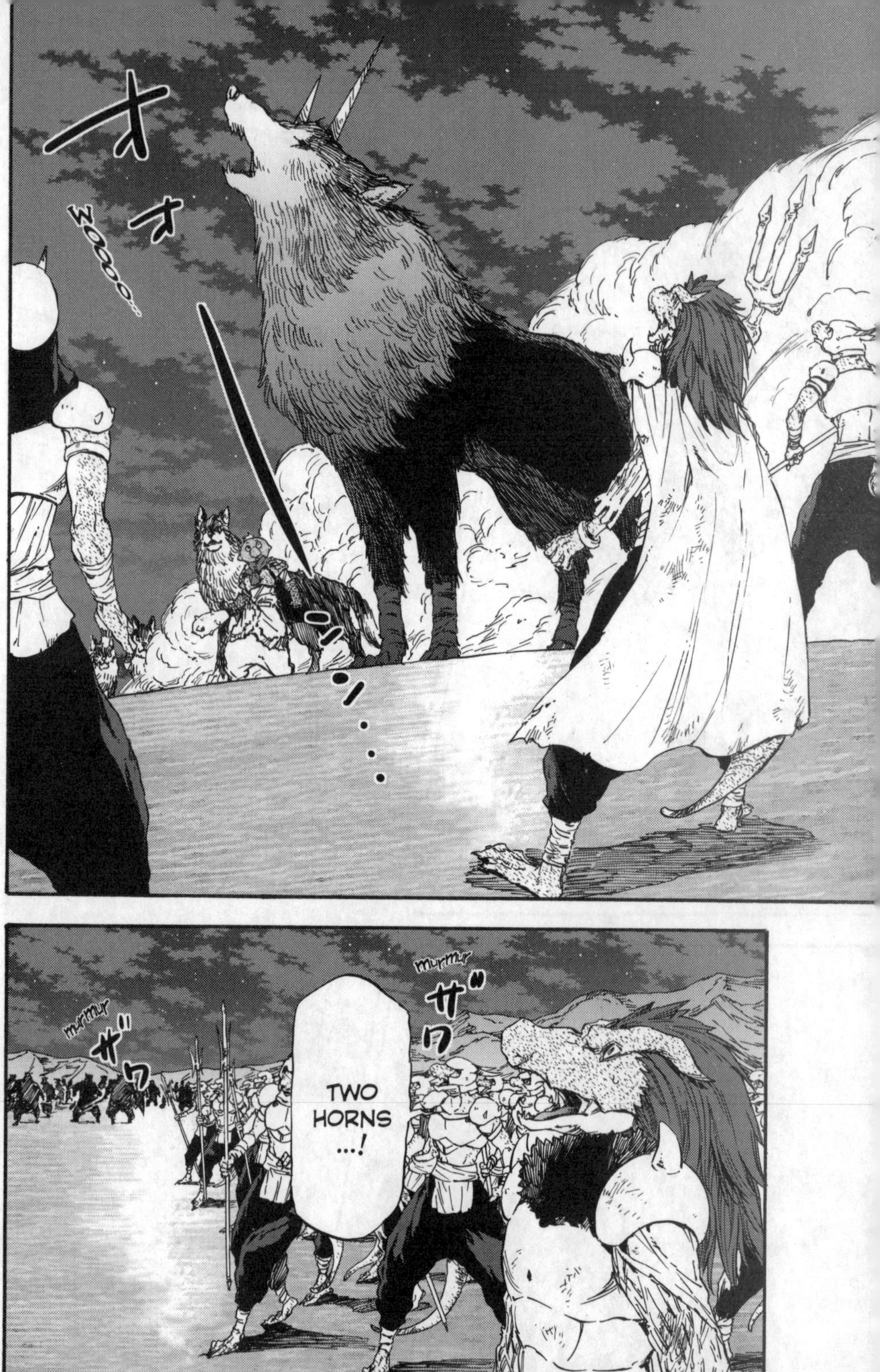
オオ
WOOOO...
murmur
ザワ
TWO HORNS ...!
murmur
ザワ

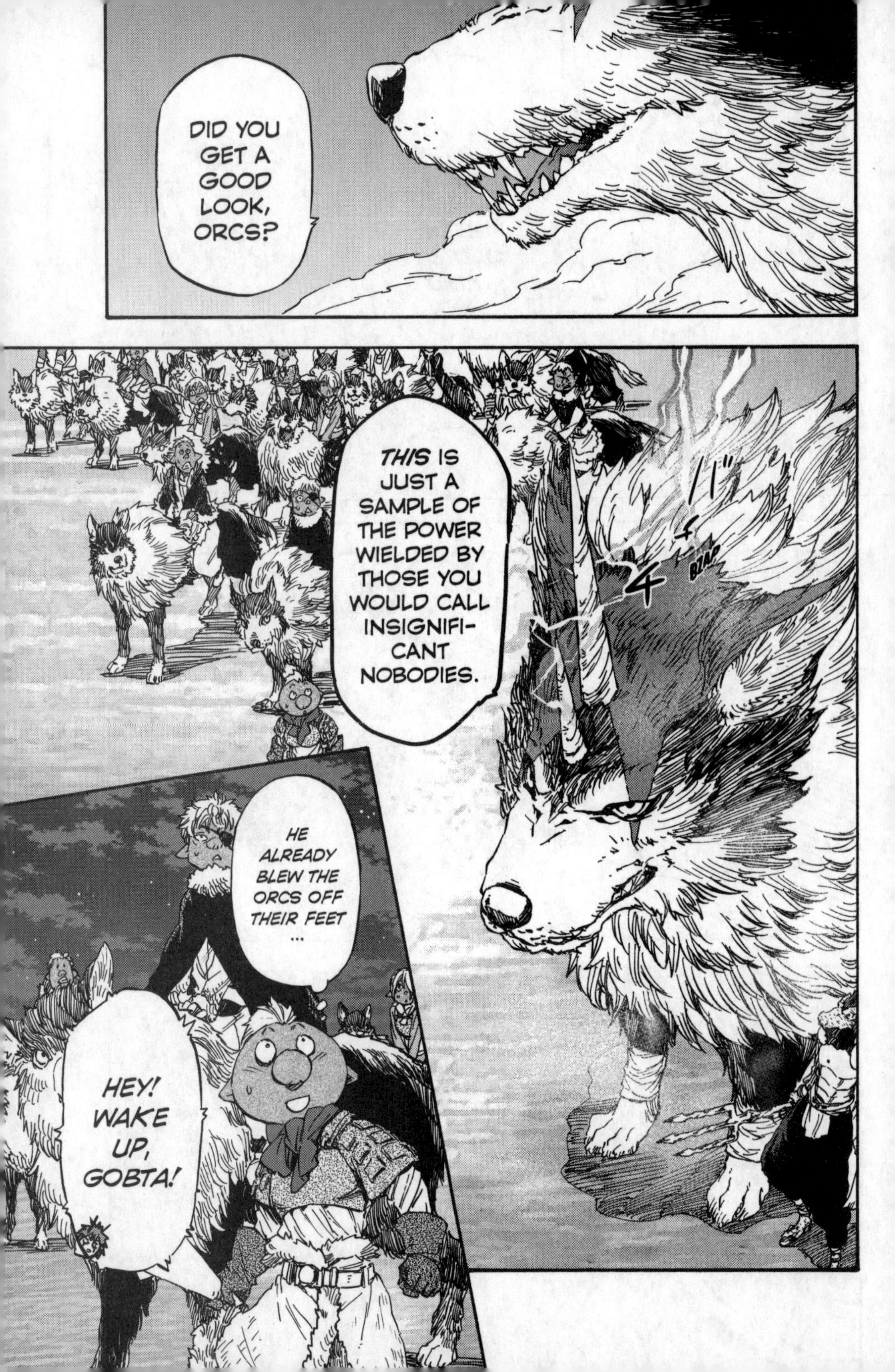
DID YOU GET A GOOD LOOK, ORCS?
THIS IS JUST A SAMPLE OF THE POWER WIELDED BY THOSE YOU WOULD CALL INSIGNIFI-CANT NOBODIES.
BZAP
HE ALREADY BLEW THE ORCS OFF THEIR FEET ...
HEY! WAKE UP, GOBTA!

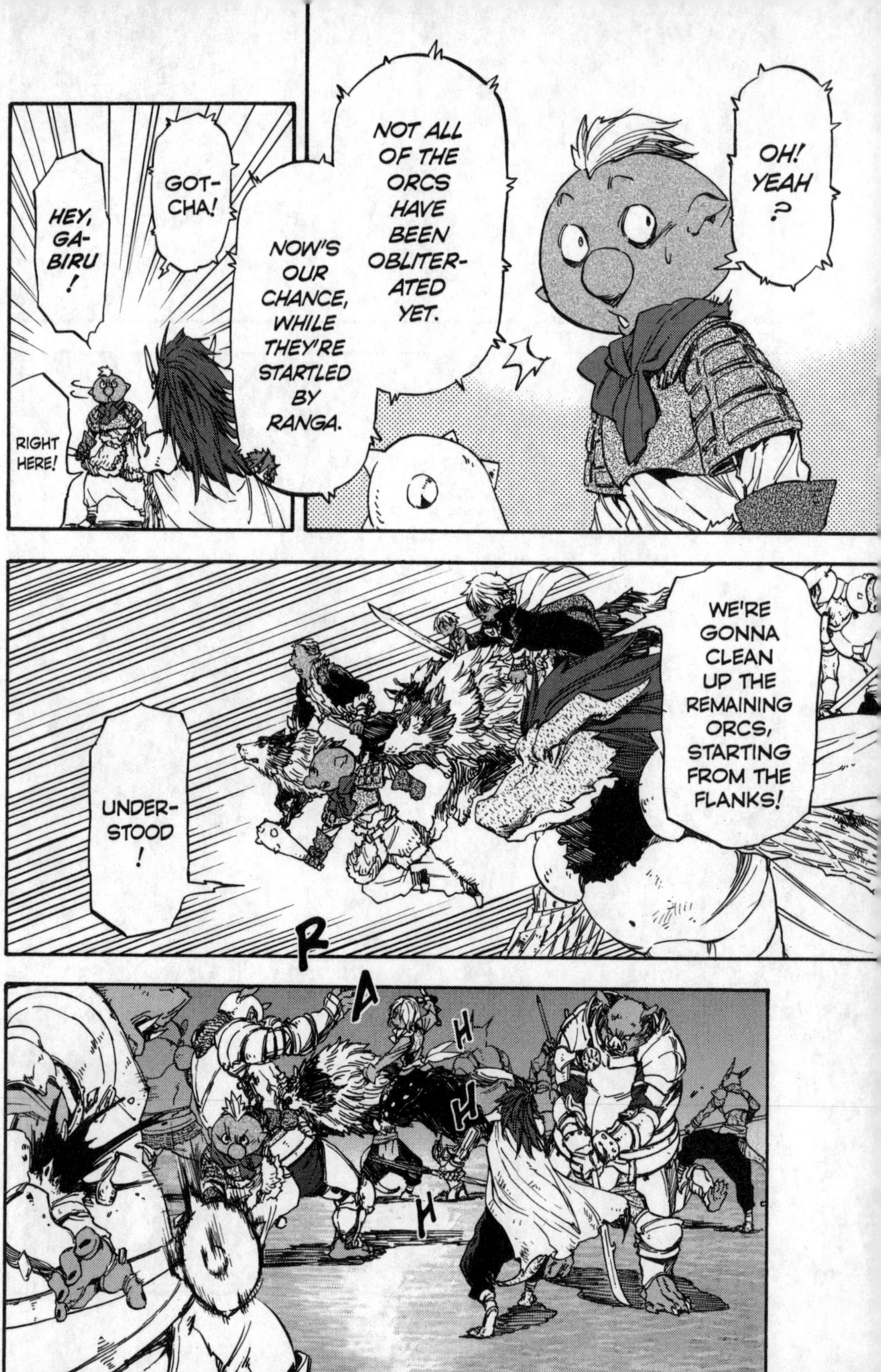
OH! YEAH?
NOT ALL OF THE ORCS HAVE BEEN OBLITERATED YET.
NOW'S OUR CHANCE, WHILE THEY'RE STARTLED BY RANGA.
GOT-CHA!
HEY, GA-BIRU!
RIGHT HERE!
WE'RE GONNA CLEAN UP THE REMAINING ORCS, STARTING FROM THE FLANKS!
UNDER-STOOD!
RAHHH

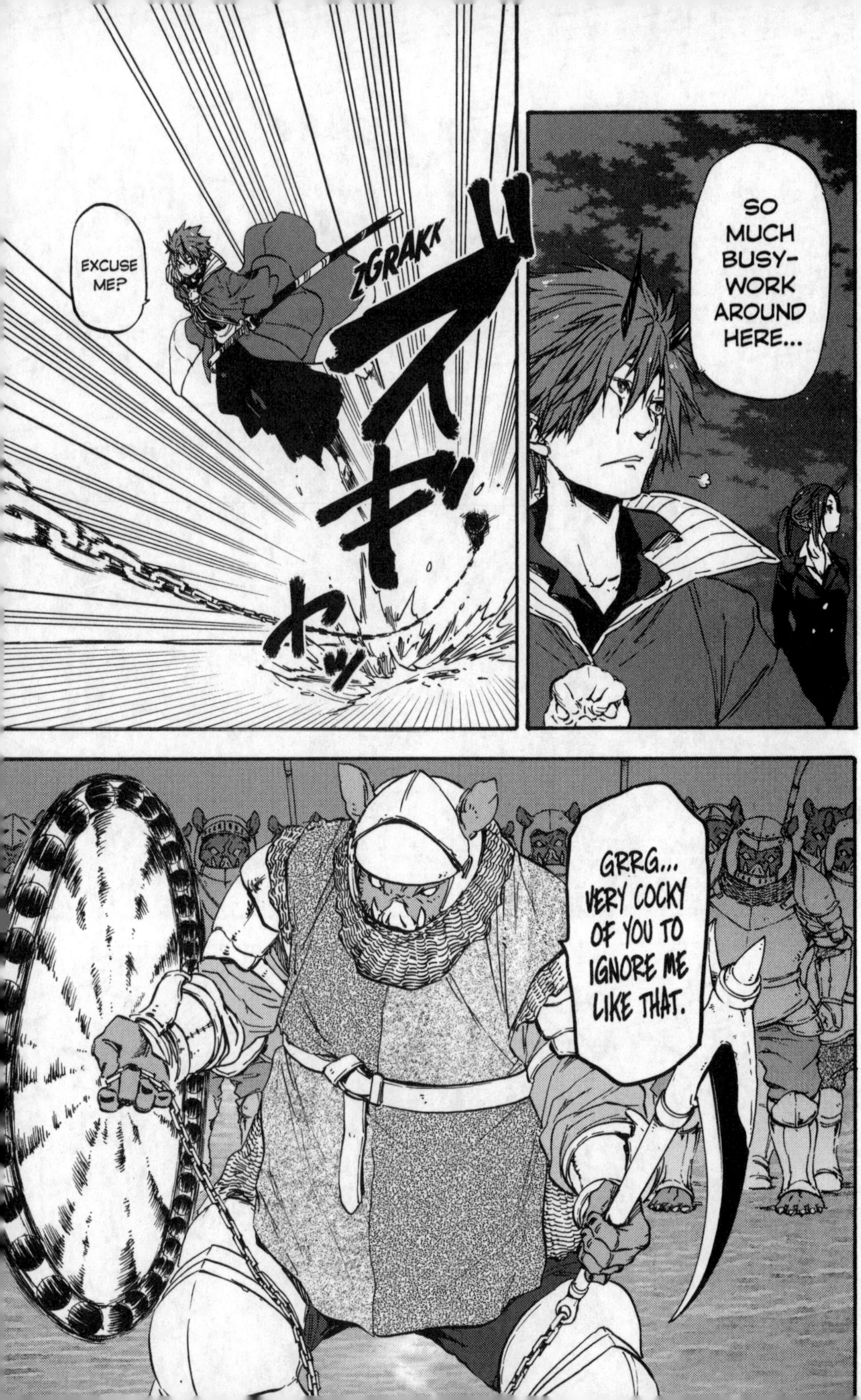
SO MUCH BUSY-WORK AROUND HERE...
ZGRAKK
EXCUSE ME?
GRRG... VERY COCKY OF YOU TO IGNORE ME LIKE THAT.

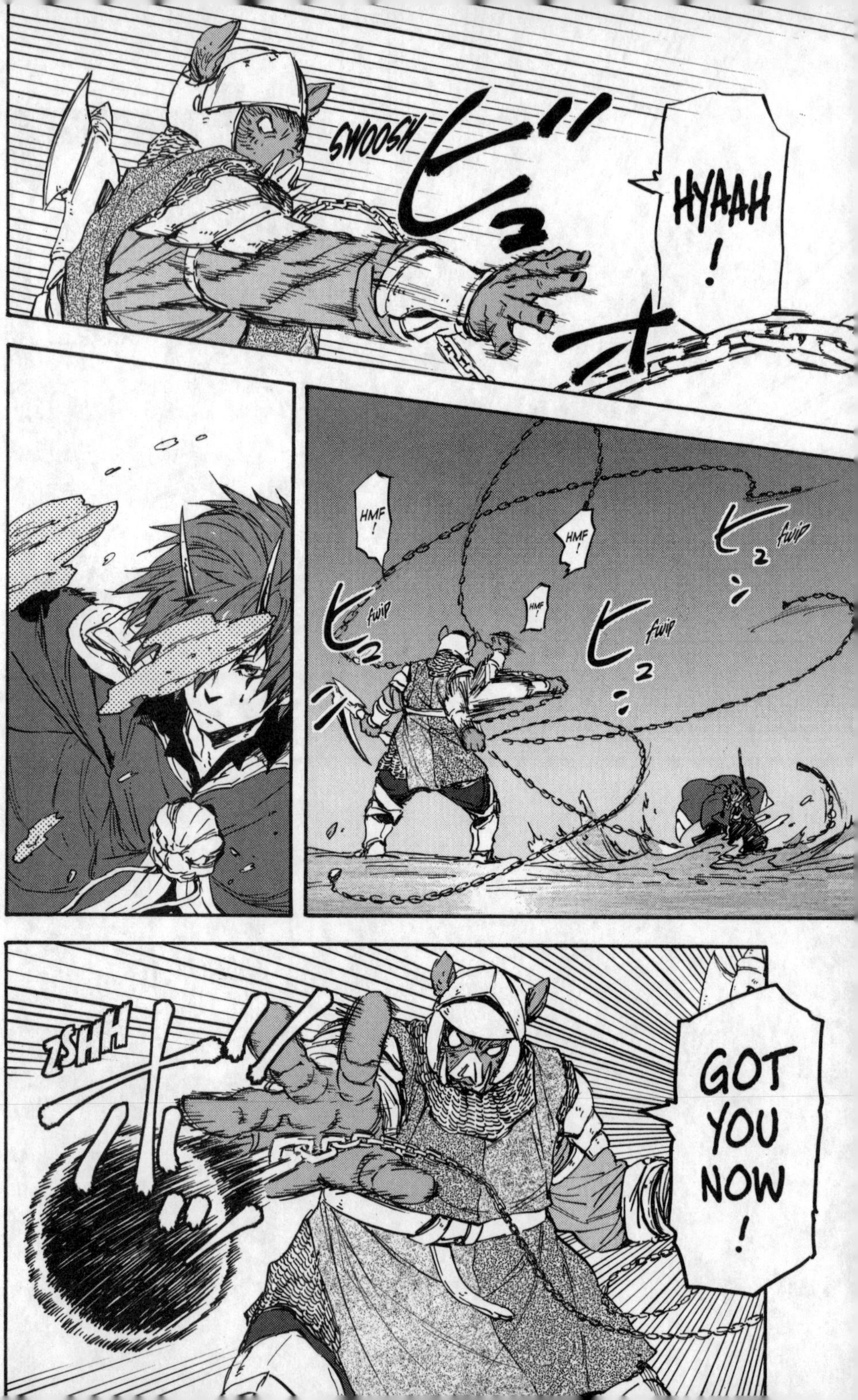
HYAAH!
SWOOSH
fwip
HMF!
fwip
HMF!
HMF!
fwip
GOT YOU NOW!
ZSHH

GRK...

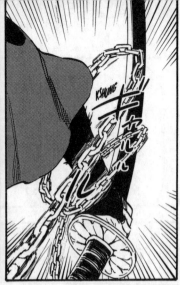

KSHUNG

FWUU!

YEOW!

THERE CAN BE NO ESCAPE NOW.

JANGLE

L- LET GO...

?!

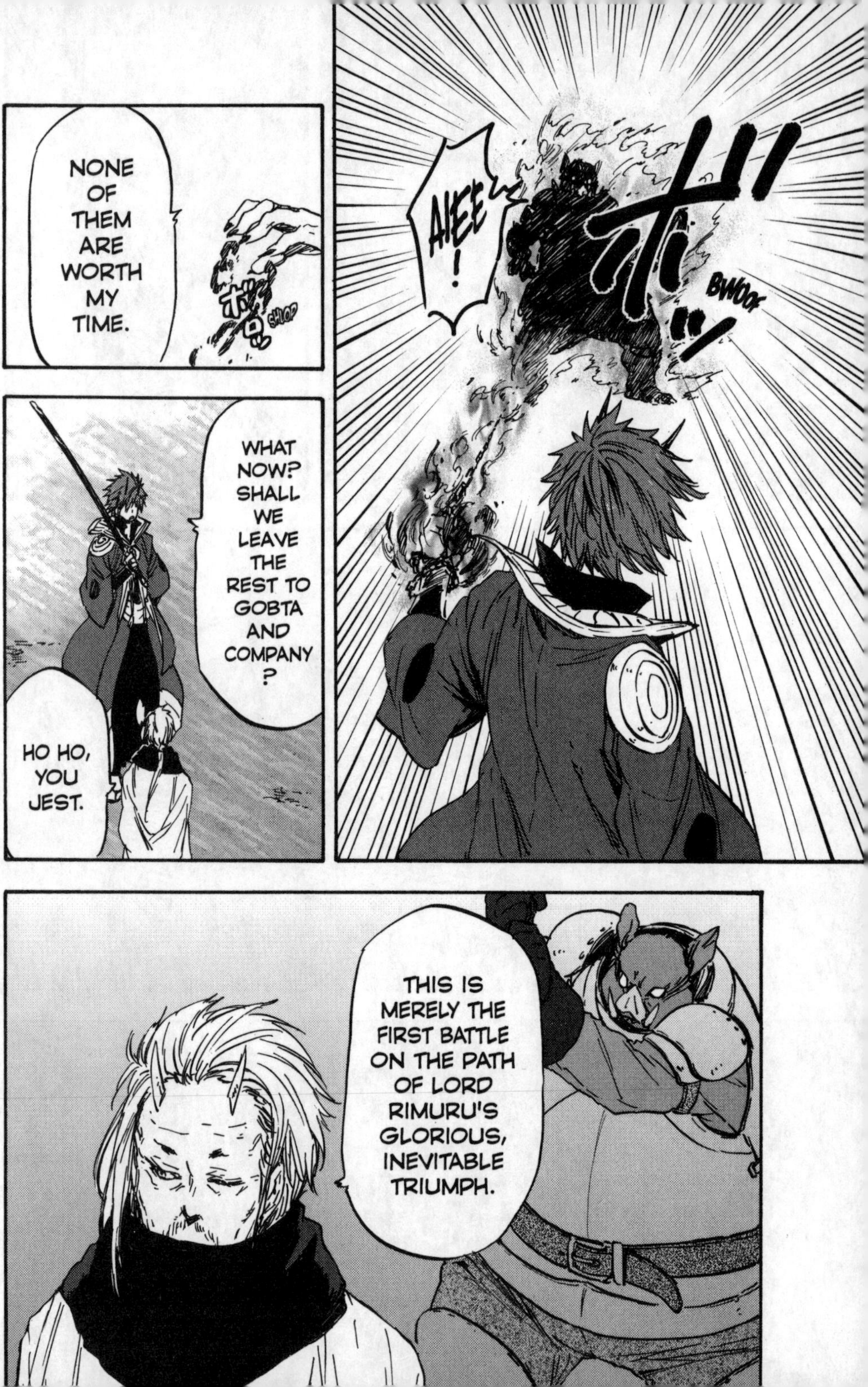
AIEE!
BWOOF
NONE OF THEM ARE WORTH MY TIME.
SHLOP
WHAT NOW? SHALL WE LEAVE THE REST TO GOBTA AND COMPANY?
HO HO, YOU JEST.
THIS IS MERELY THE FIRST BATTLE ON THE PATH OF LORD RIMURU'S GLORIOUS, INEVITABLE TRIUMPH.

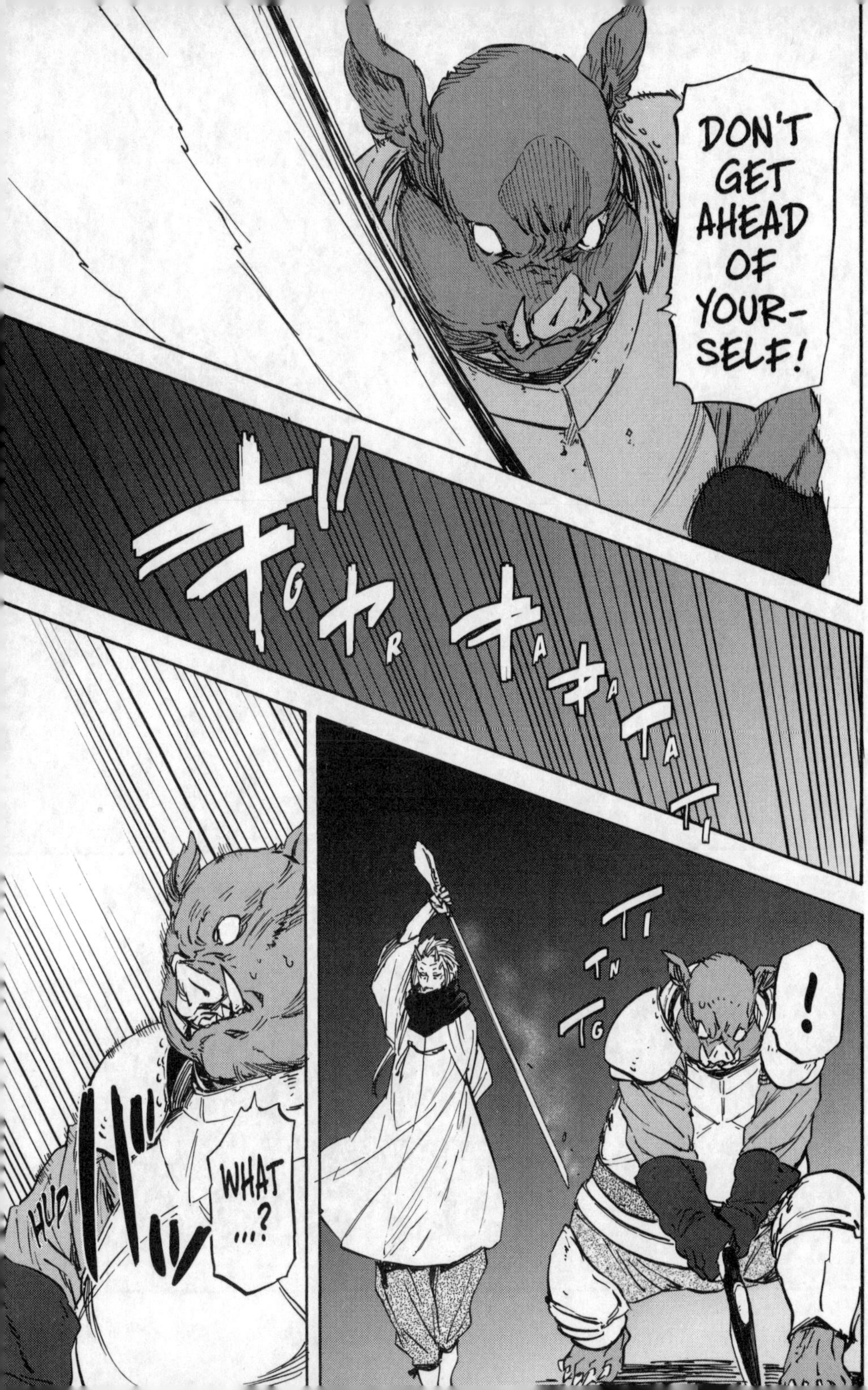
DON'T GET AHEAD OF YOUR-SELF!
G R A A A TI
TI TN TG
!
HUD
WHAT ...?

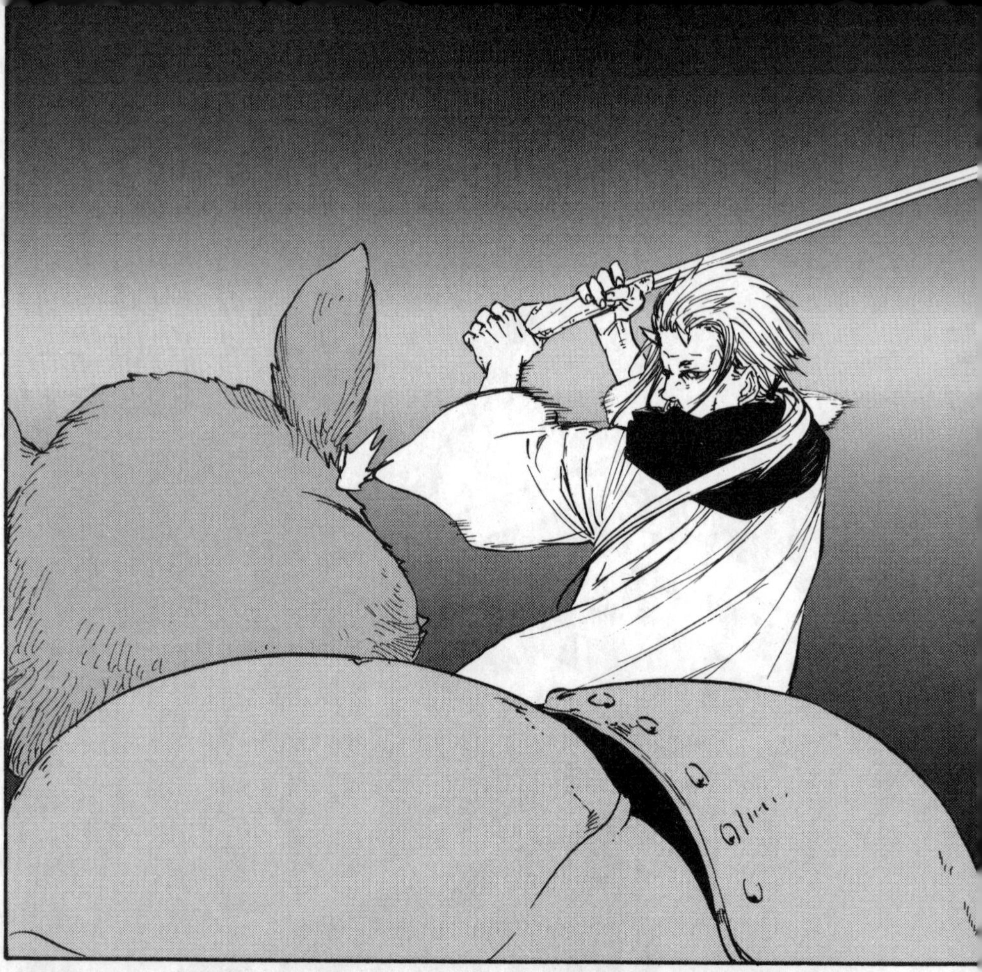

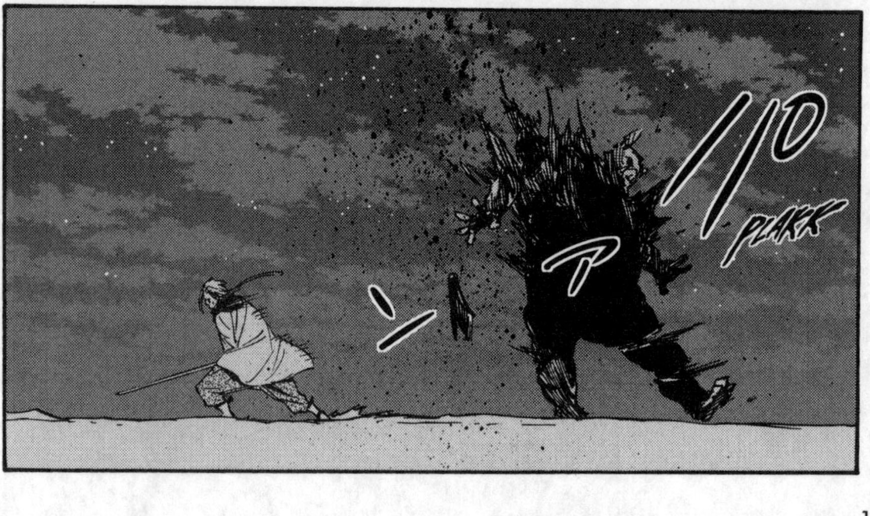
パァン
PLAKK

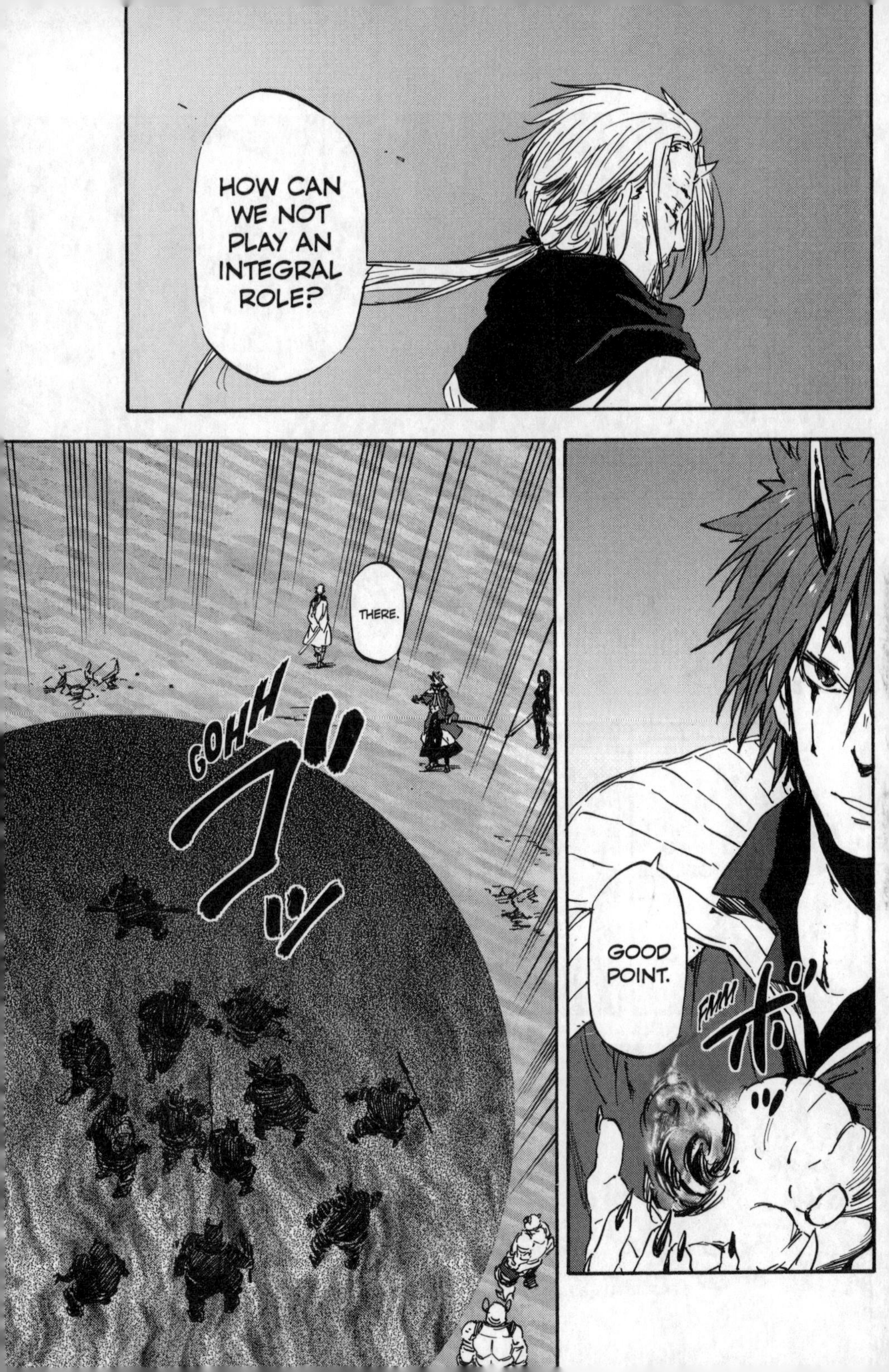
HOW CAN WE NOT PLAY AN INTEGRAL ROLE?
GOOD POINT.
FMM
ボッ
THERE.
GOHH
ゴッ

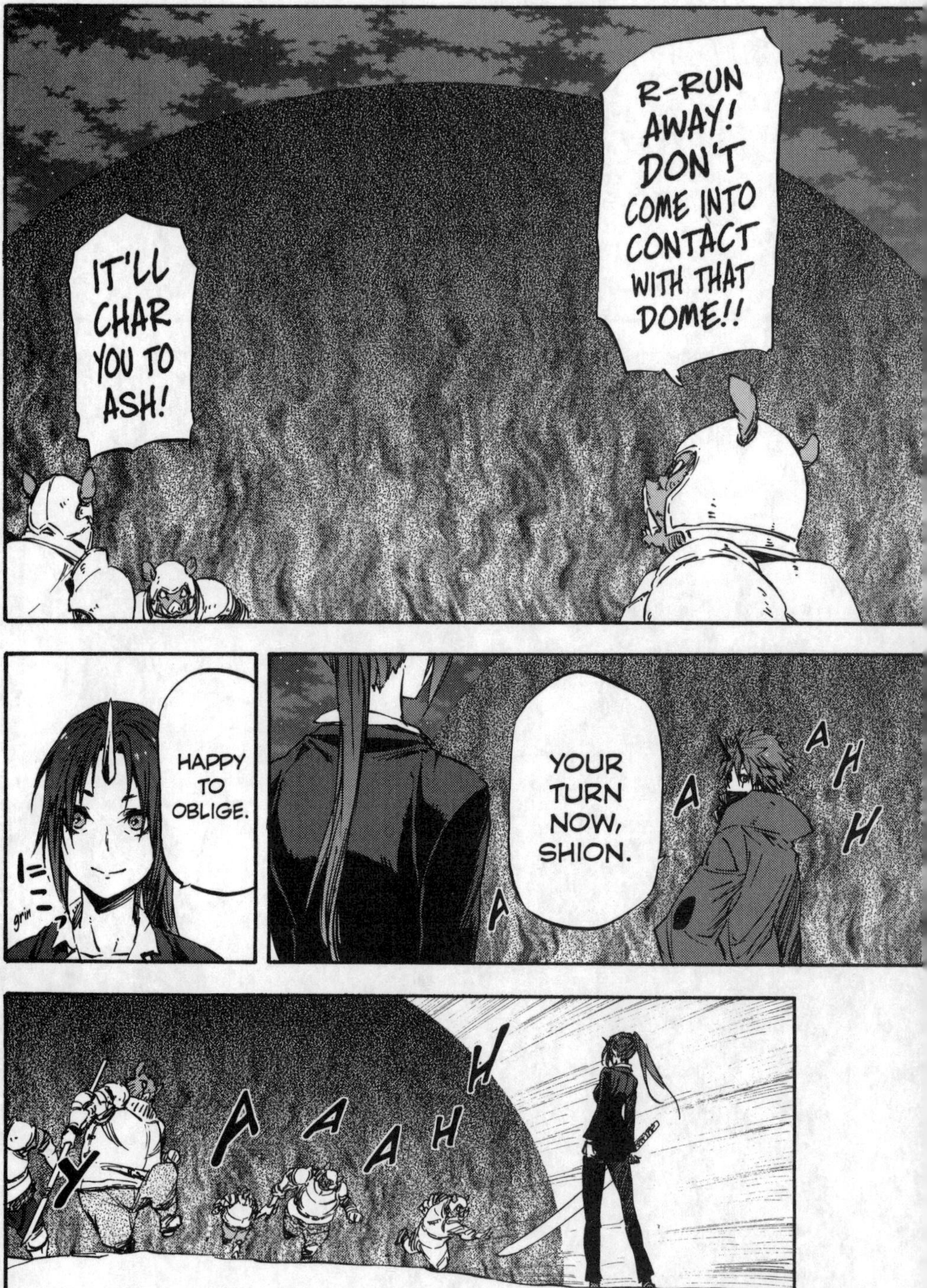
R-RUN AWAY! DON'T COME INTO CONTACT WITH THAT DOME!!
IT'LL CHAR YOU TO ASH!
AAAHH
YOUR TURN NOW, SHION.
A
HAPPY TO OBLIGE.
grin
YAAAAHH

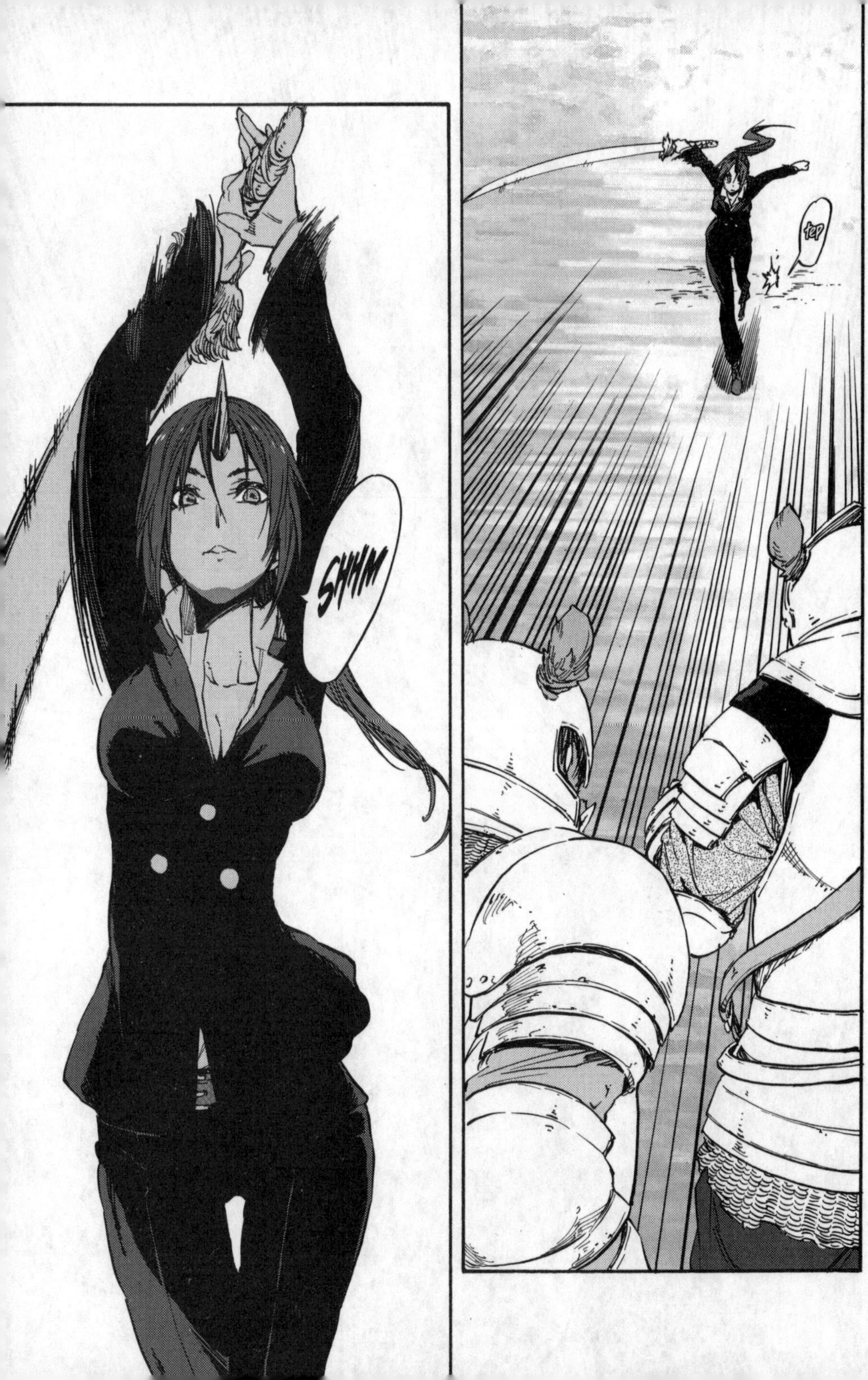
tep
SHHM

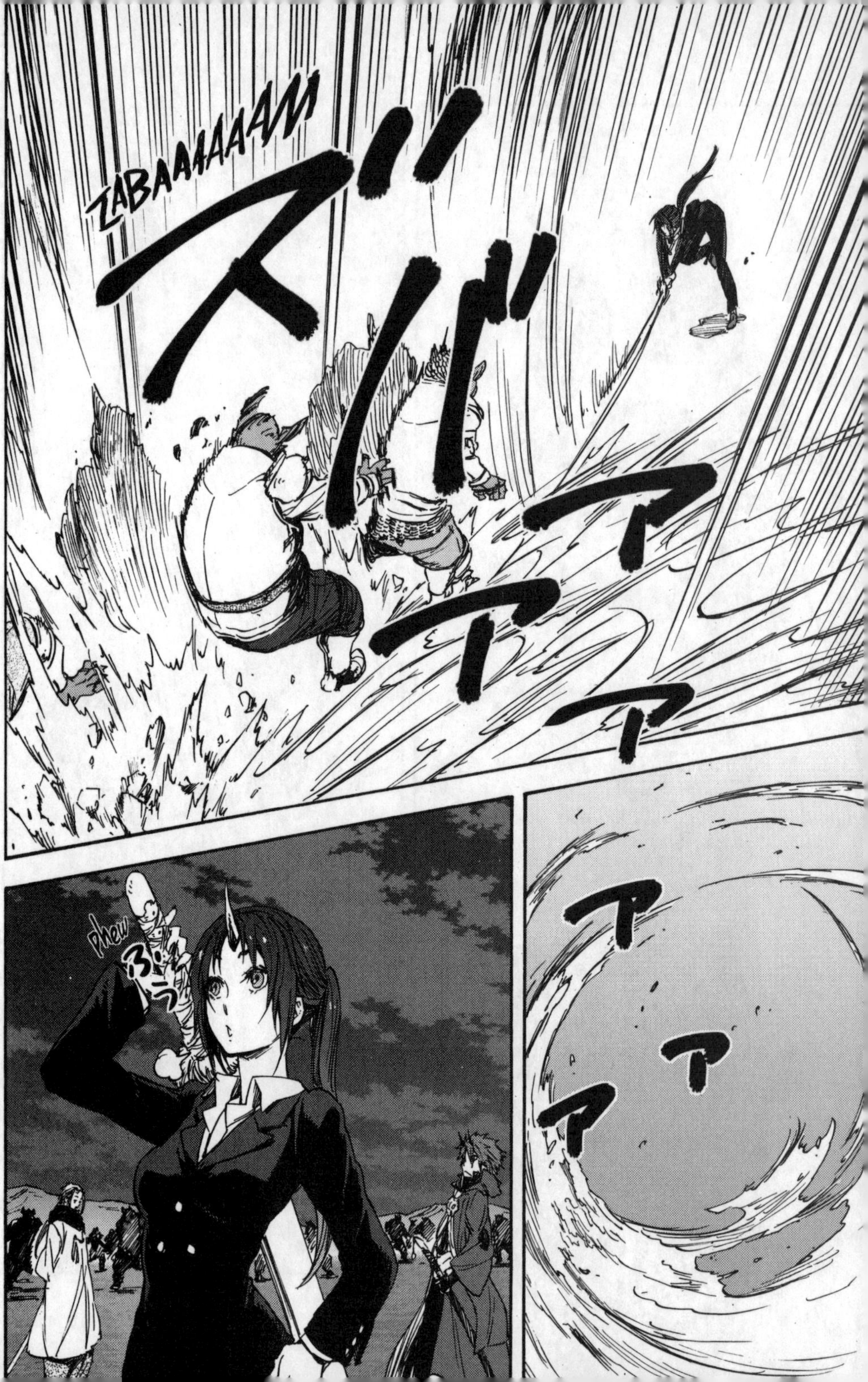
ZABAAAAAAM
ズバアアア
アアア
phew
ふぅ

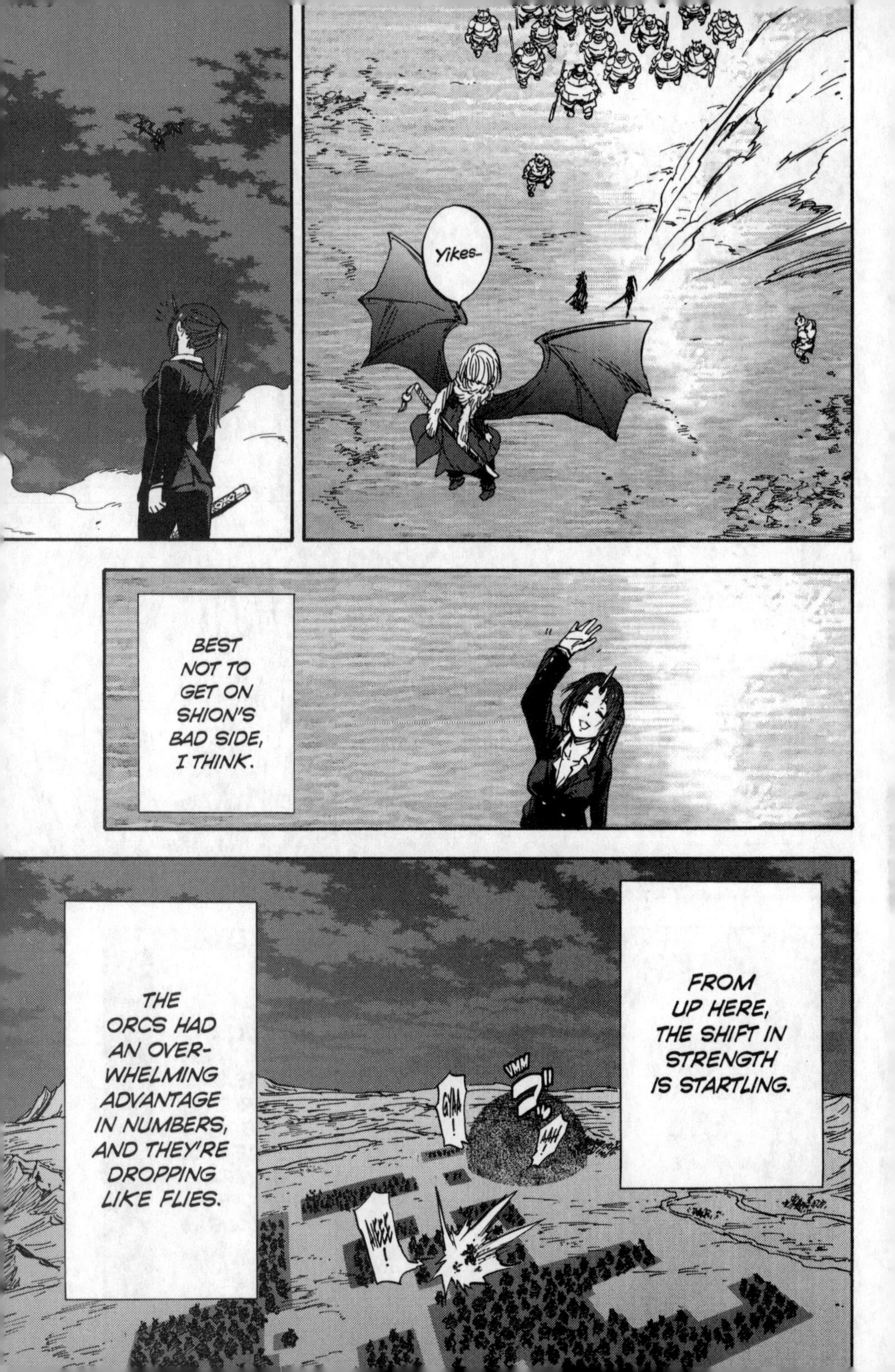
Yikes...
BEST NOT TO GET ON SHION'S BAD SIDE, I THINK.
FROM UP HERE, THE SHIFT IN STRENGTH IS STARTLING.
THE ORCS HAD AN OVER-WHELMING ADVANTAGE IN NUMBERS, AND THEY'RE DROPPING LIKE FLIES.
VMM
GYAA!
AAH!
AIEEE!

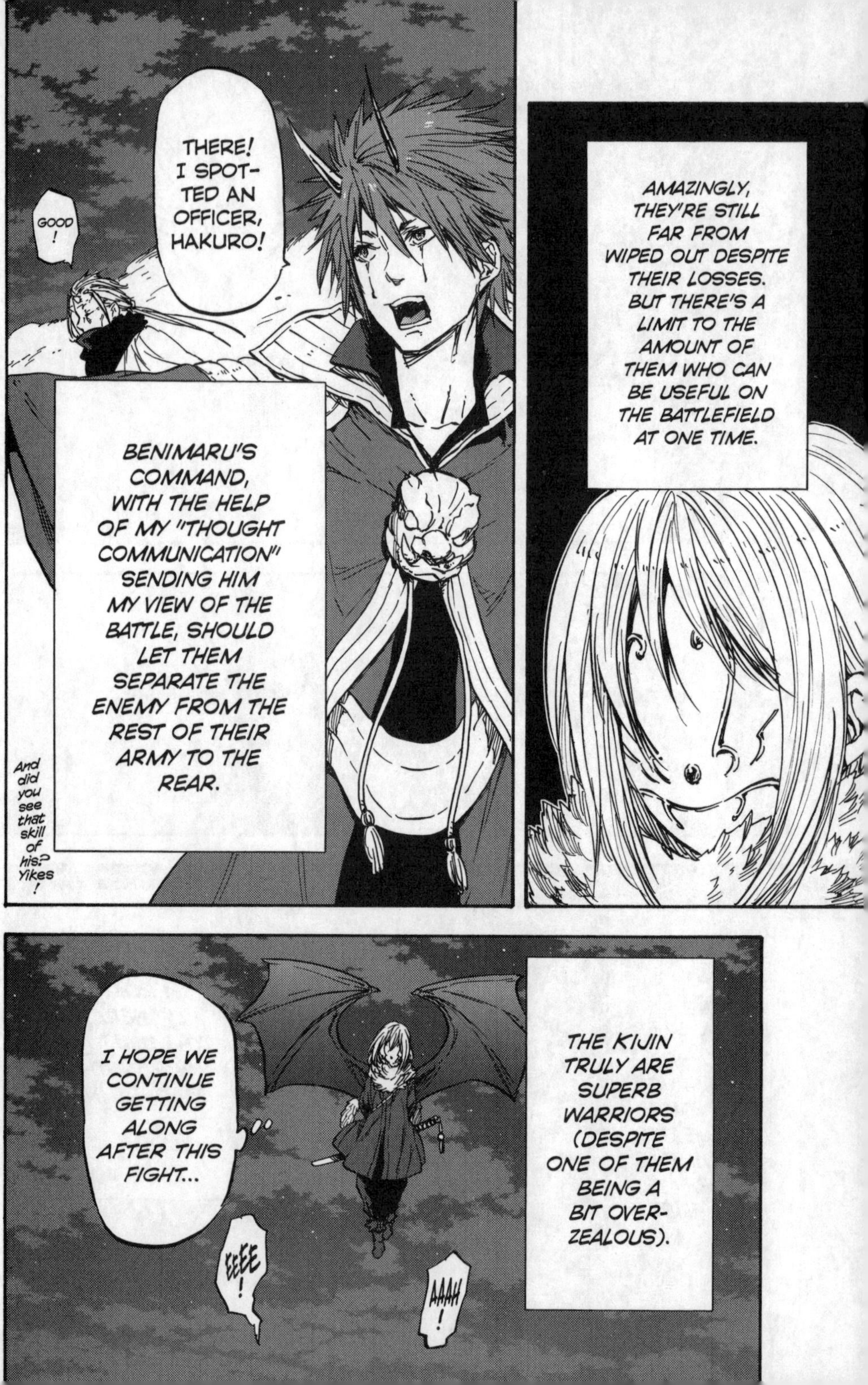

AMAZINGLY, THEY'RE STILL FAR FROM WIPED OUT DESPITE THEIR LOSSES. BUT THERE'S A LIMIT TO THE AMOUNT OF THEM WHO CAN BE USEFUL ON THE BATTLEFIELD AT ONE TIME.
THERE! I SPOTTED AN OFFICER, HAKURO!
GOOD!
BENIMARU'S COMMAND, WITH THE HELP OF MY "THOUGHT COMMUNICATION" SENDING HIM MY VIEW OF THE BATTLE, SHOULD LET THEM SEPARATE THE ENEMY FROM THE REST OF THEIR ARMY TO THE REAR.
And did you see that skill of his? Yikes!
THE KIJIN TRULY ARE SUPERB WARRIORS (DESPITE ONE OF THEM BEING A BIT OVER-ZEALOUS).
I HOPE WE CONTINUE GETTING ALONG AFTER THIS FIGHT...
AAAH!
EEEE!

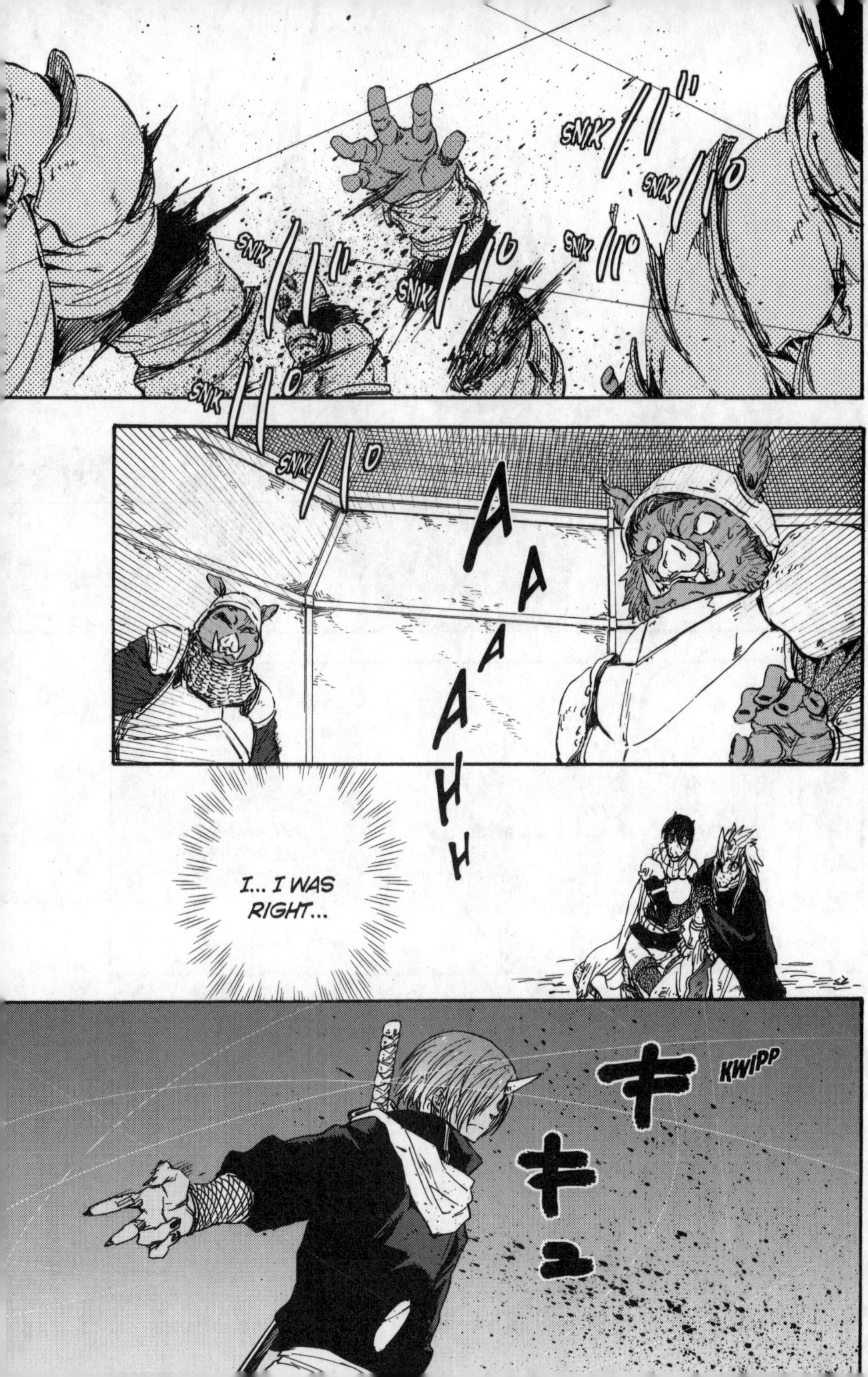
SNK
SNK
SNK
SNK
SNK
SNK
SNK
AAAAHH
I... I WAS RIGHT...
KWIPP
キキュ

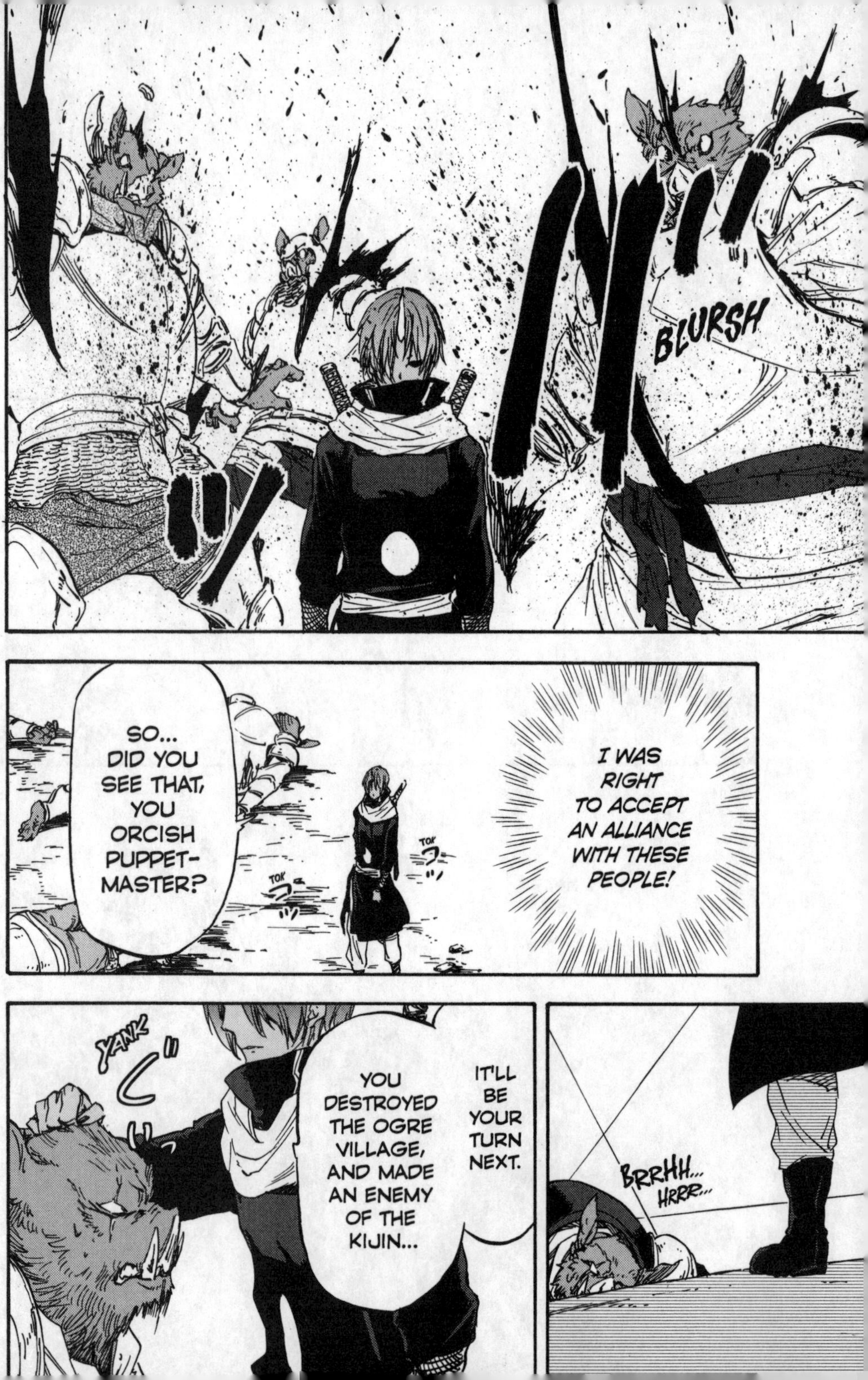
BLURSH
I WAS RIGHT TO ACCEPT AN ALLIANCE WITH THESE PEOPLE!
TOK
TOK
SO... DID YOU SEE THAT, YOU ORCISH PUPPET-MASTER?
BRRHH... HRRR...
IT'LL BE YOUR TURN NEXT.
YOU DESTROYED THE OGRE VILLAGE, AND MADE AN ENEMY OF THE KIJIN...
YANK

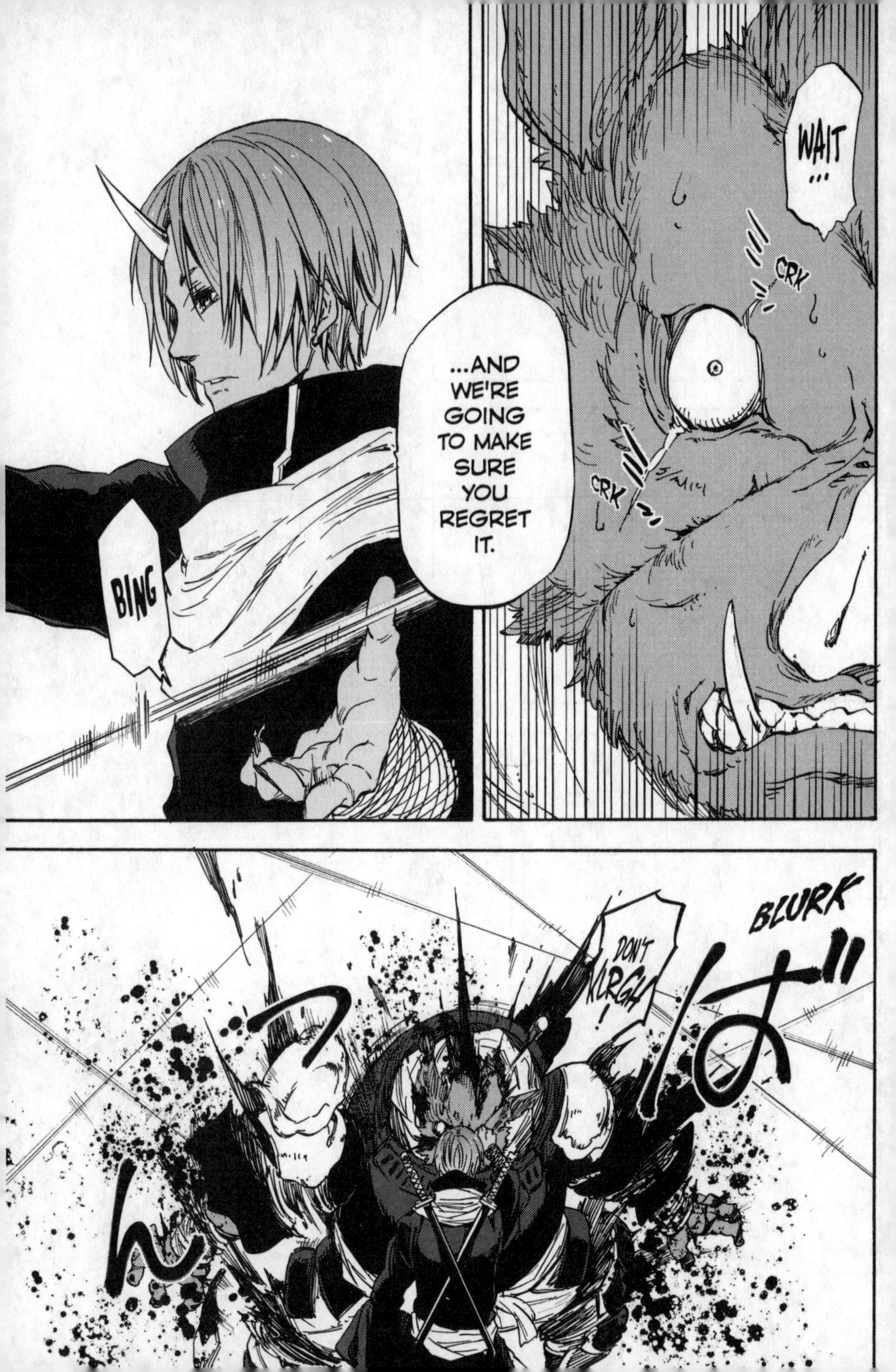
WAIT ...
CRK
CRK
...AND WE'RE GOING TO MAKE SURE YOU REGRET IT.
BING
BLURK
DON'T KURGH!

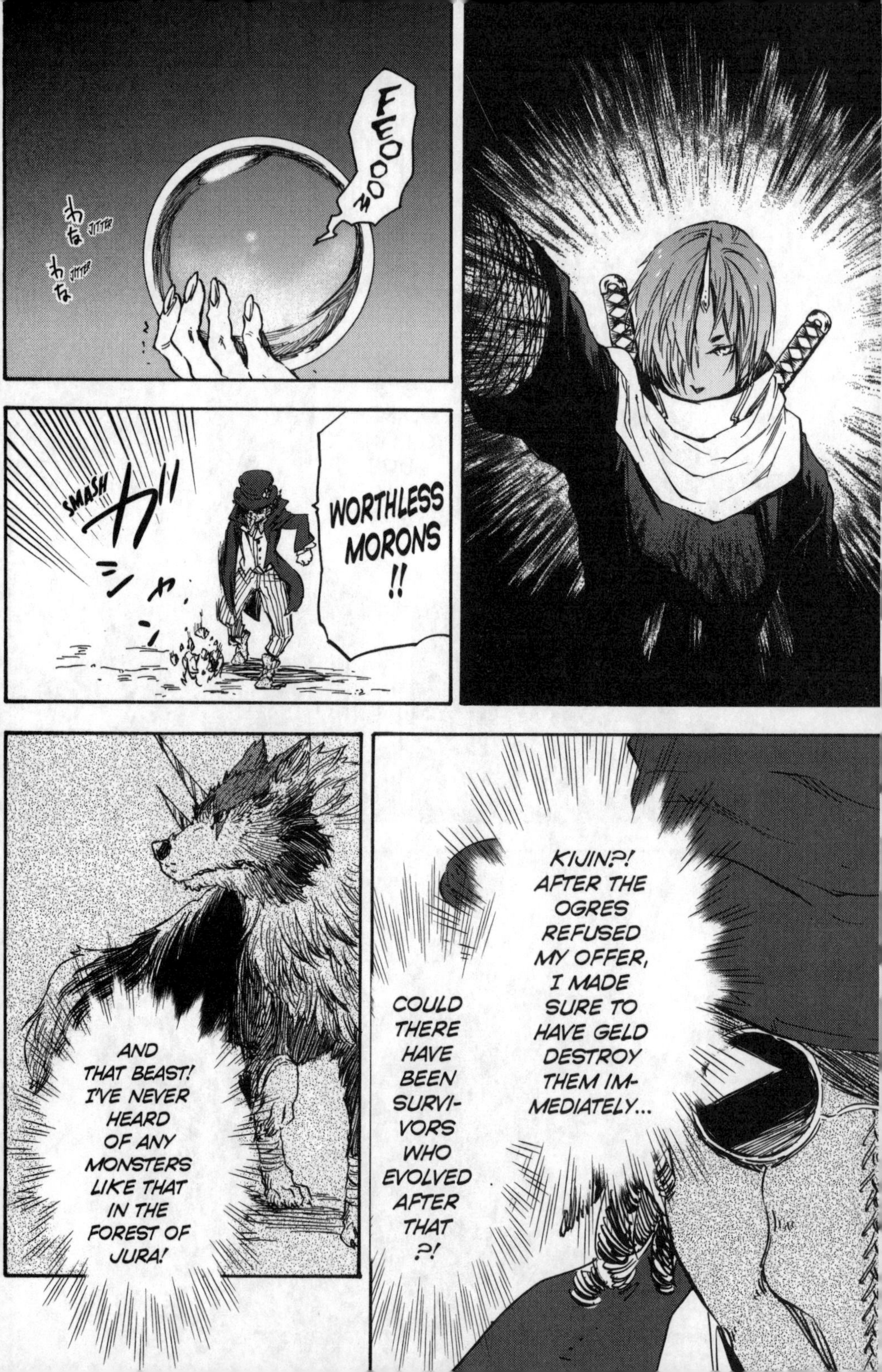
FEOOOOM
わなわな JITTER
わなわな JITTER
WORTHLESS MORONS!!
SMASH
ガッ
シャン
KIJIN?! AFTER THE OGRES REFUSED MY OFFER, I MADE SURE TO HAVE GELD DESTROY THEM IMMEDIATELY...
COULD THERE HAVE BEEN SURVIVORS WHO EVOLVED AFTER THAT?!
AND THAT BEAST! I'VE NEVER HEARD OF ANY MONSTERS LIKE THAT IN THE FOREST OF JURA!

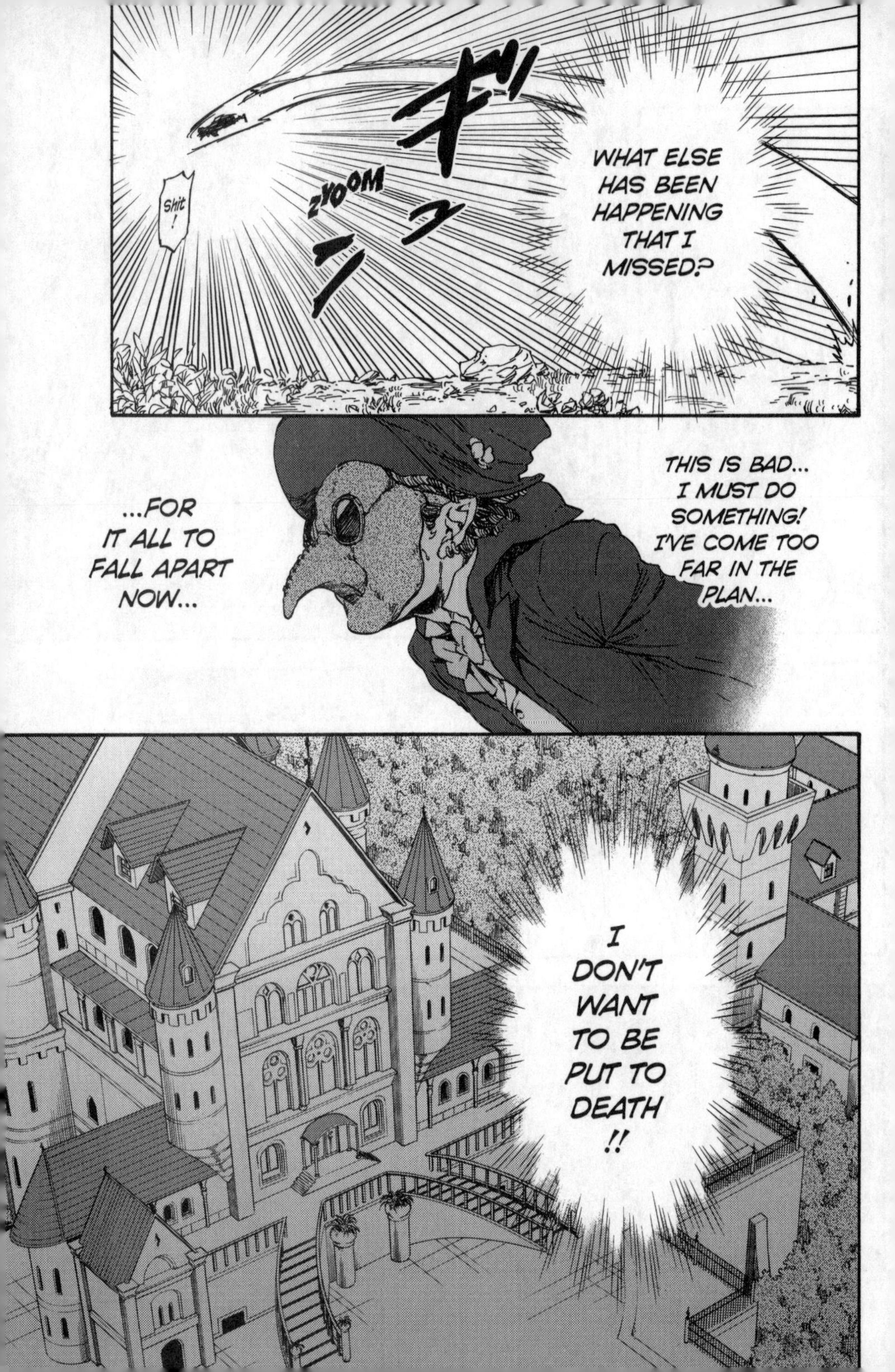
WHAT ELSE HAS BEEN HAPPENING THAT I MISSED?
ZYOOM
Shit!
THIS IS BAD... I MUST DO SOMETHING! I'VE COME TOO FAR IN THE PLAN...
...FOR IT ALL TO FALL APART NOW...
I DON'T WANT TO BE PUT TO DEATH!!

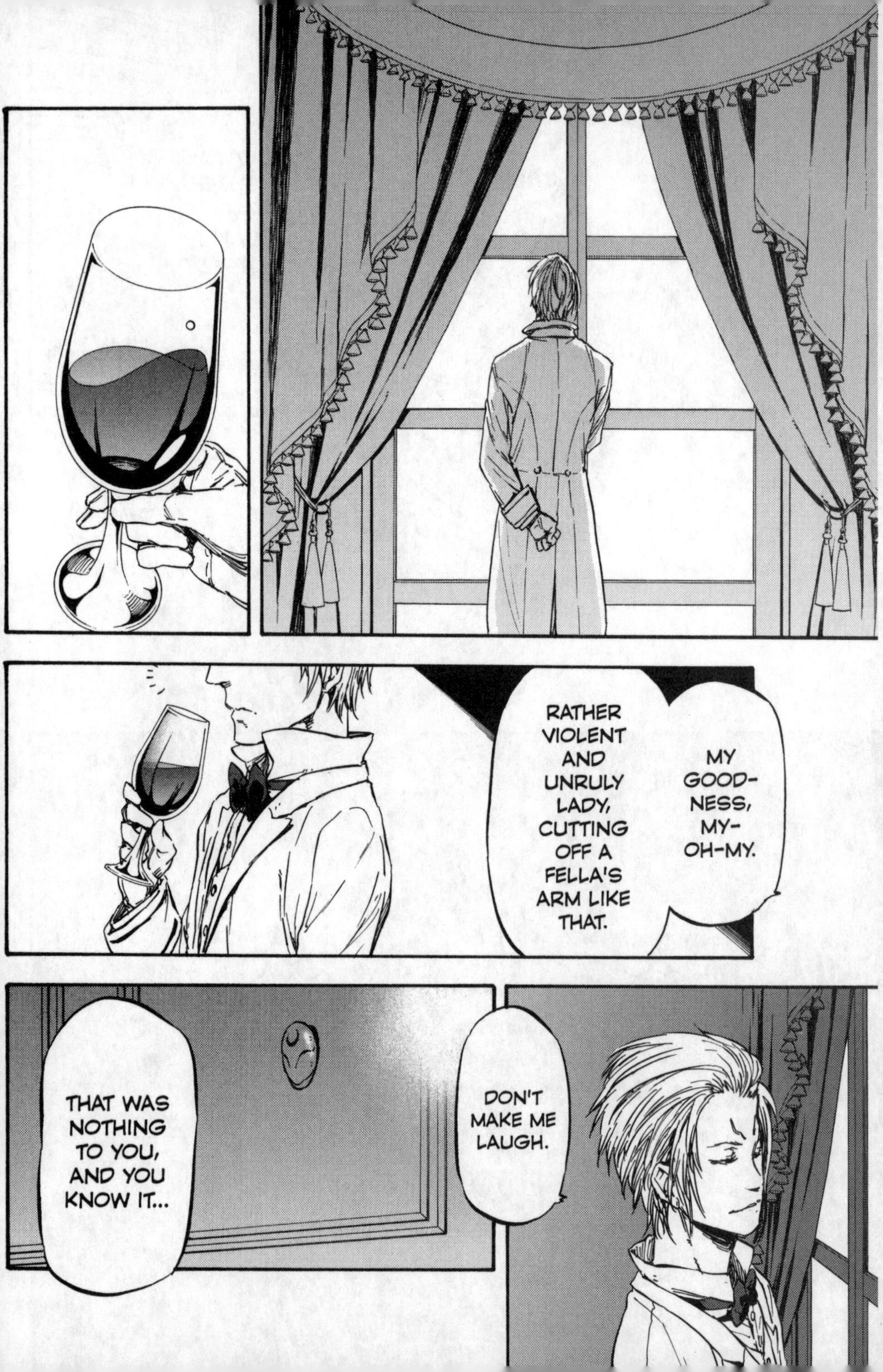
MY GOODNESS, MY-OH-MY.
RATHER VIOLENT AND UNRULY LADY, CUTTING OFF A FELLA'S ARM LIKE THAT.
DON'T MAKE ME LAUGH.
THAT WAS NOTHING TO YOU, AND YOU KNOW IT...

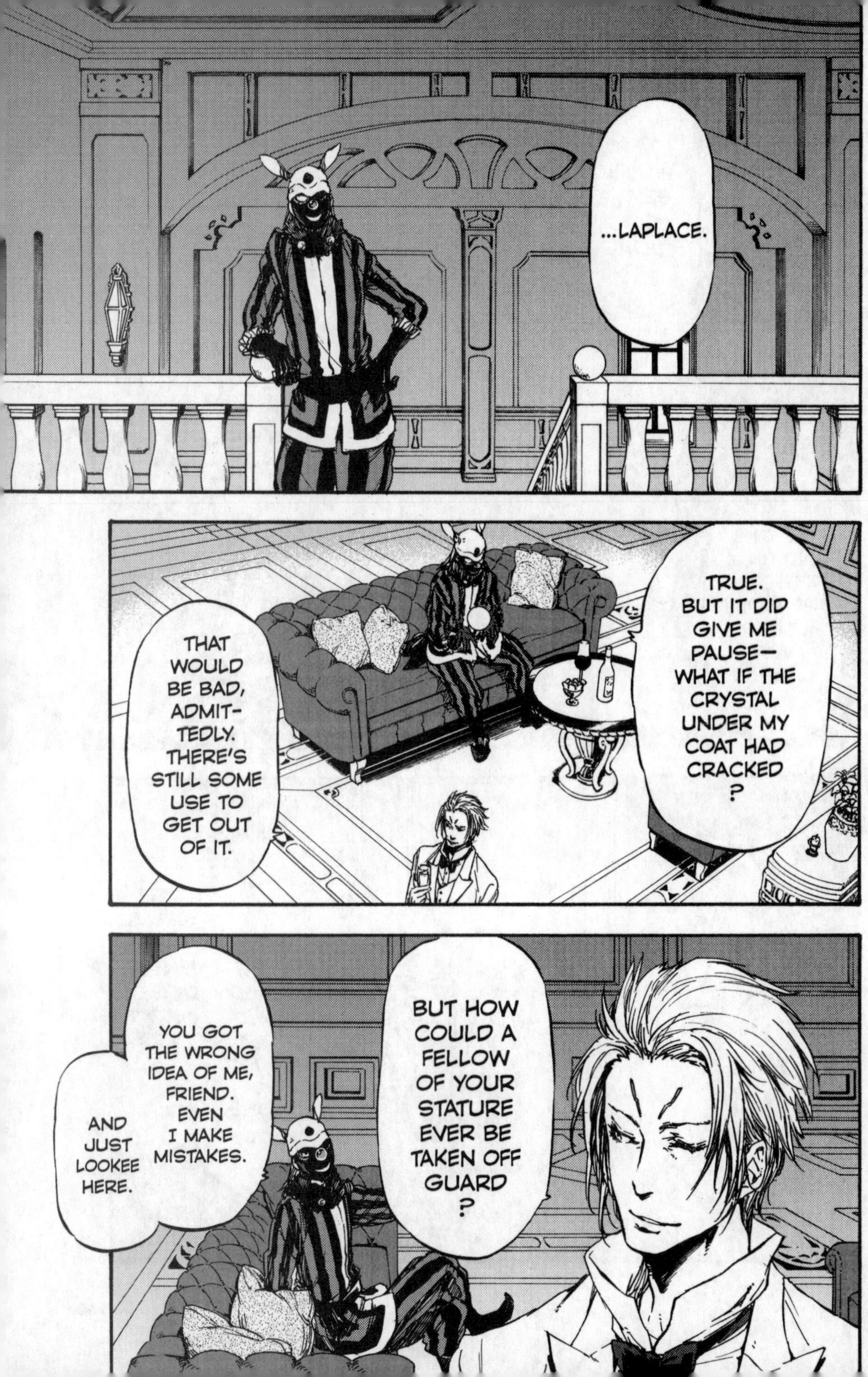
...LAPLACE.
TRUE. BUT IT DID GIVE ME PAUSE— WHAT IF THE CRYSTAL UNDER MY COAT HAD CRACKED?
THAT WOULD BE BAD, ADMITTEDLY. THERE'S STILL SOME USE TO GET OUT OF IT.
BUT HOW COULD A FELLOW OF YOUR STATURE EVER BE TAKEN OFF GUARD?
YOU GOT THE WRONG IDEA OF ME, FRIEND. EVEN I MAKE MISTAKES.
AND JUST LOOKEE HERE.

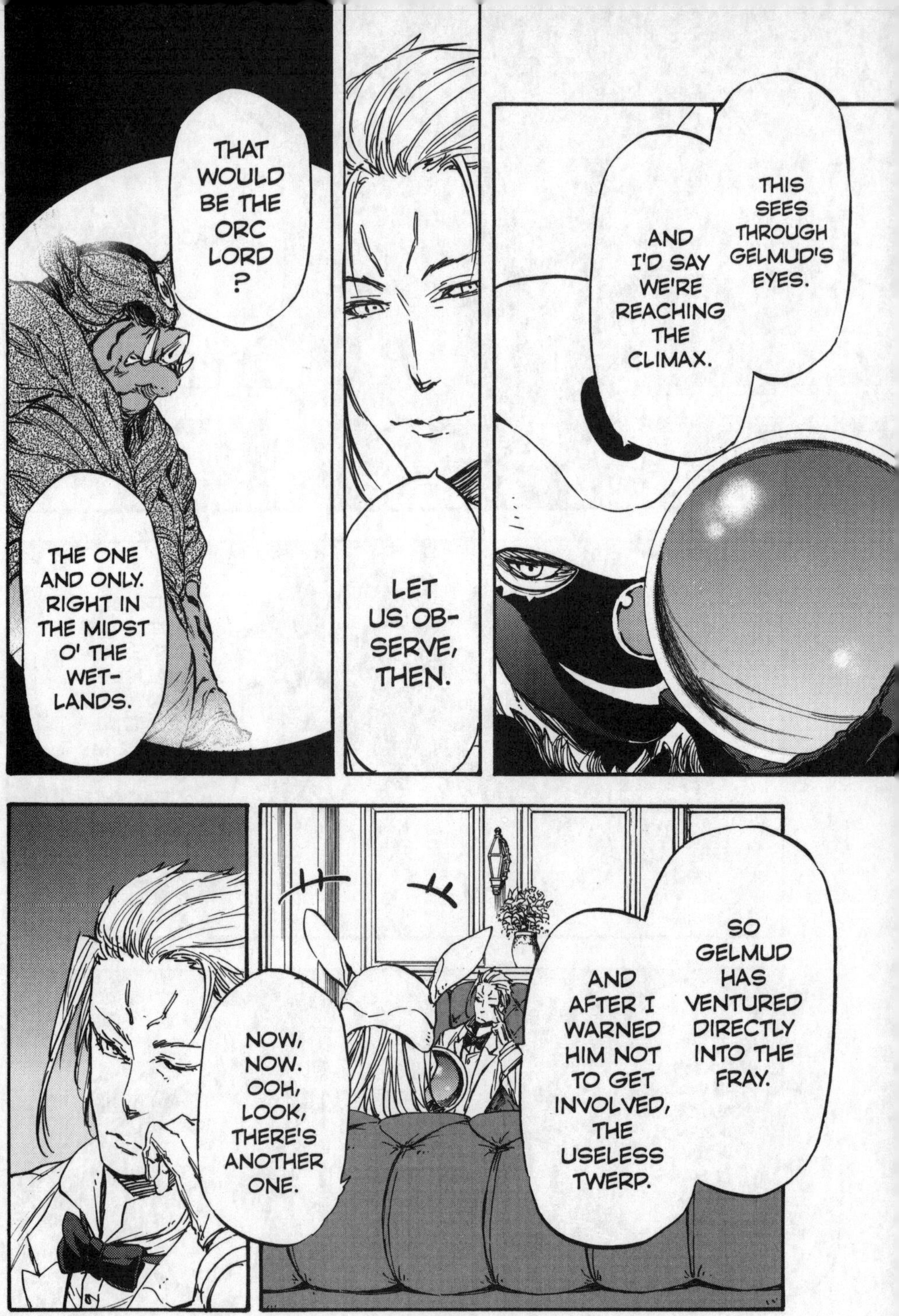
THIS SEES THROUGH GELMUD'S EYES.
AND I'D SAY WE'RE REACHING THE CLIMAX.
LET US OB-SERVE, THEN.
THAT WOULD BE THE ORC LORD?
THE ONE AND ONLY. RIGHT IN THE MIDST O' THE WET-LANDS.
SO GELMUD HAS VENTURED DIRECTLY INTO THE FRAY.
AND AFTER I WARNED HIM NOT TO GET INVOLVED, THE USELESS TWERP.
NOW, NOW. OOH, LOOK, THERE'S ANOTHER ONE.

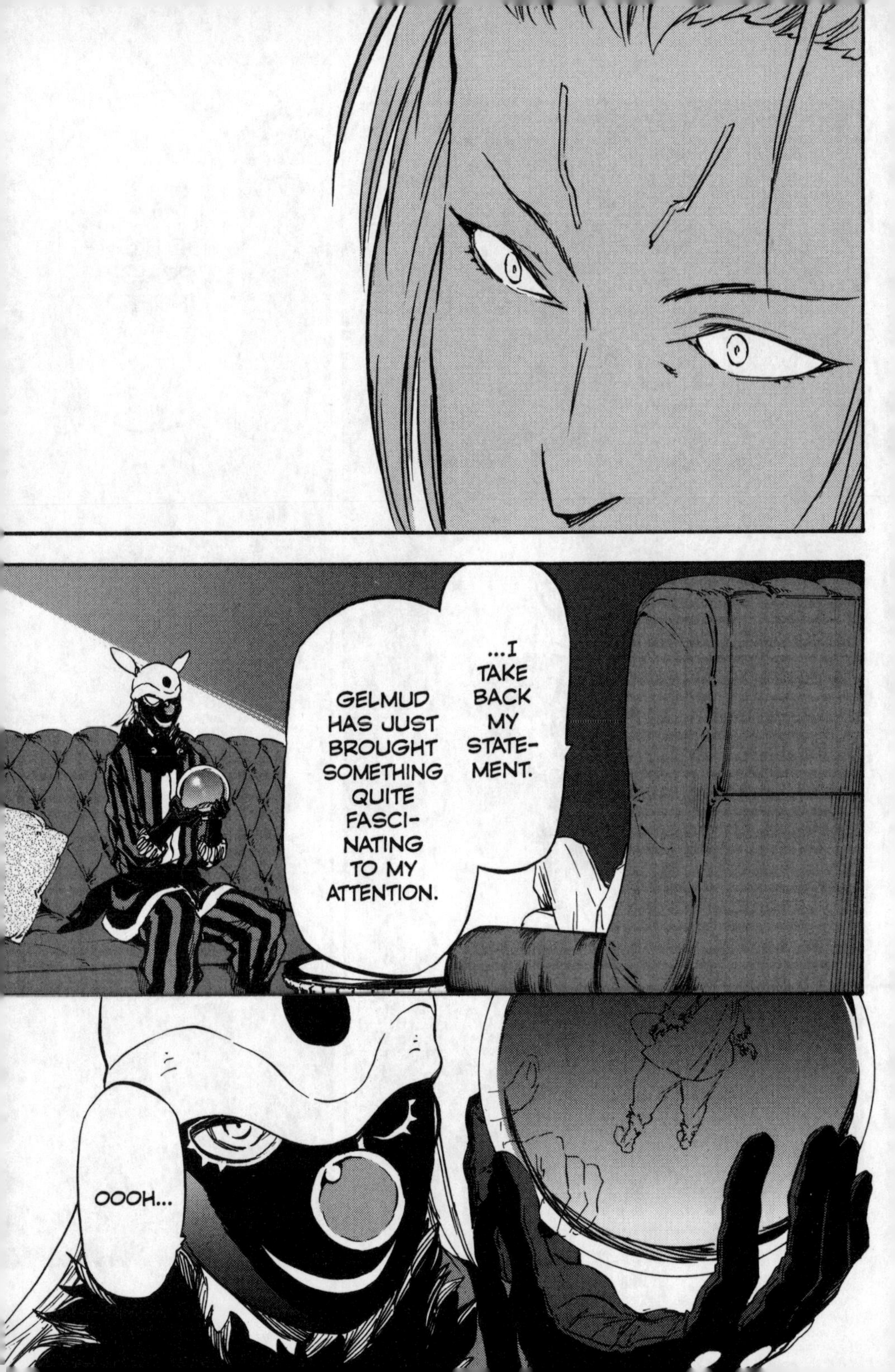
...I TAKE BACK MY STATEMENT.
GELMUD HAS JUST BROUGHT SOMETHING QUITE FASCINATING TO MY ATTENTION.
OOOH...

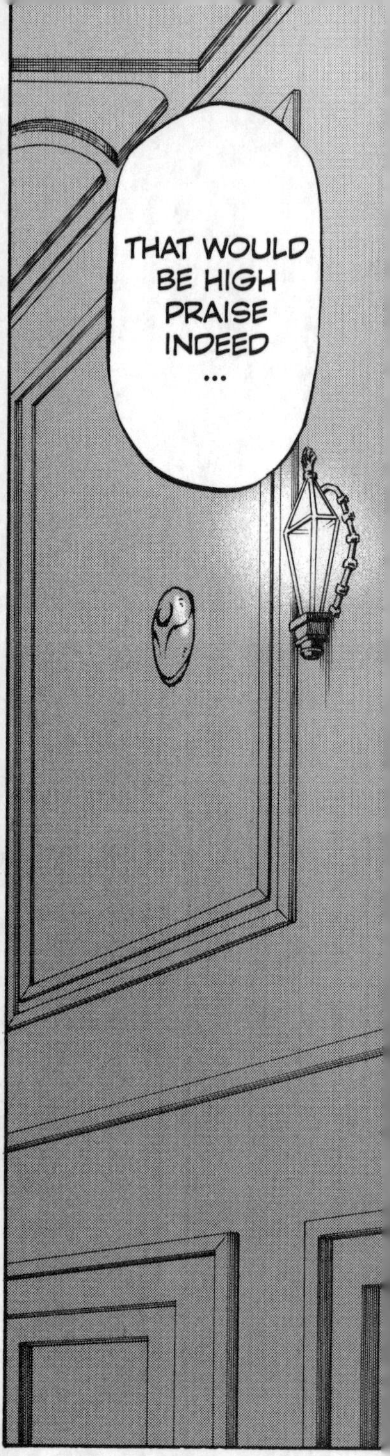
THAT WOULD BE HIGH PRAISE INDEED ...

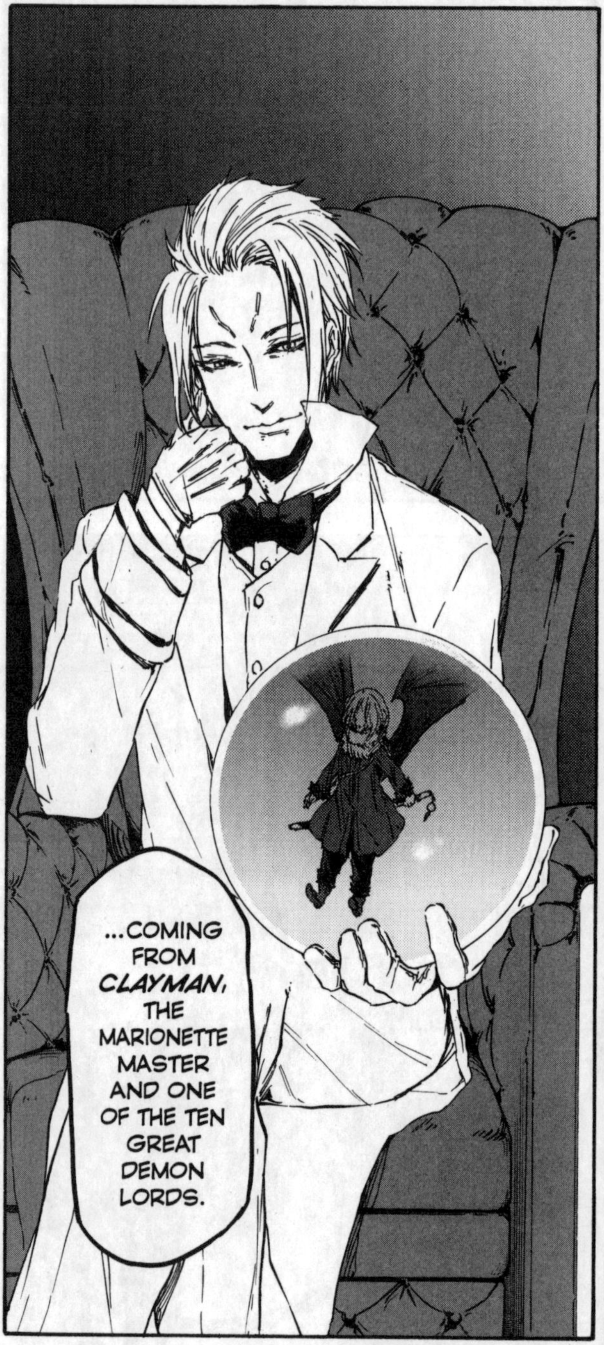
...COMING FROM CLAYMAN, THE MARIONETTE MASTER AND ONE OF THE TEN GREAT DEMON LORDS.

```
Reincarnate
in Volume 5?

  →YES

   NO
```

Bonus
Short Story

Veldora's Slime Observation Journal
~STUNNING DEVELOPMENTS~

Veldora's Slime Observation Journal
~PITCHED BATTLE~

◆LOOSENING GEARS◆

So, the dryad Treyni has requested that Rimuru vanquish the orc lord.

Hrmm…

Her request was rather bold, but I have no doubt that her situation is dire. She pretends to be confident and in control, but she cannot deceive me. There is panic within her.

While she may not look like much, Treyni is actually an elite monster who watches over the Great Forest of Jura. She is capable of handling most threats to the forest on her own, and she would never rely on the strength of others for help.

A dire situation indeed, then.

"That's quite a demand, coming from someone who just waltzed in out of nowhere, Treyni the Dryad, or so you call yourself," said the red-haired one. Benimaru, I believe.

He seems upset that she was asking for help from goblins, one of the weaker races. His suspicion is reasonable, but it is also misplaced.

Treyni is acting with great conviction. She understands that Rimuru is the strongest being in the forest. Dryads have special abilities that allow them to maintain awareness of any location where there is grass or trees. Therefore, they cannot be deceived within the forest of Jura. A being of great magical energy was born within the forest, so they would naturally be keeping tabs on him.

They also saw his battle with Benimaru's group—and Rimuru's treatment of them afterward. It would be obvious from that conversation that Rimuru is a soft and sympathetic fellow. What better pawn than one with both great power, and an inability to allow others to suffer? This is why Treyni came straight to Rimuru.

If the orc lord attacks the treant settlement, the dryads alone would be unable to stop him, she said. I have no doubt that she is sincere in this regard, but her true intentions lie elsewhere.

She is testing Rimuru. After my disappearance, Jura has had no protector. This latest disaster is a natural result. And now she is hoping to choose a new protector, one who will ensure that such an incident does not arise again.

In my case, I was not so much a diligent protector, but rather an unholy terror to those I disliked. That did succeed in stabilizing the forest—and to monsters, might makes right.

Such thoughts must certainly have been in the back of Treyni's mind during the negotiations. To my surprise, Rimuru only offered to consider her request. I had anticipated him accepting without a second thought, but I was mistaken.

The presence of the orc lord is certain. Defeat him, and the problem is solved. It seems simple enough to me. Then my strength would be clear to all, and I would bask in their admiration. The perfect plan.

But Rimuru is strangely cautious. Upon glancing through his thoughts, I found that he was concerned about damage to his townspeople. Hmph, quite a bother. He could handle the situation on his own, but protecting the weak at the same time will naturally limit his options.

This weight of responsibility is requisite for the showers of admiration to come later—I suppose I must admit that I was oversimplifying the matter. So what is he to do? I must be patient and see how this meeting unfolds.

The conversation moved to the orcs' goal—a rather tricky matter. It seems that the biggest problem is the overall strength of their army, numbering two hundred thousand.

The kijin named Hakuro said, "Indeed... They have no concept of supply-line logistics."

Logistics? *I* have no concept of supply-line logistics!!

"Ifrit, what is logistics?"

"I don't know, either. There are no 'logistics' in the rules to shogi," said Ifrit, holding the rules for shogi, which had quickly become his favorite book.

Shogi is merely a game, of course. I cannot blame it for not containing this abstract concept. More interesting to me was Ifrit's fascination with the game. If I gave him a manual of battle strategy, would he then turn into a master tactician? I decided to tap into Rimuru's deep memory banks.

Now that I have become accustomed to manga and novels, finding the text I seek is a simple matter.

My target: the dictionary.

Thankfully, Rimuru's memory is organized so neatly that I promptly succeeded in finding the desired knowledge.

Lo-gis-tics (n.): the management and transportation of military personnel, weapons, and supplies behind a fighting force. Also, the acquisition and maintenance of supply lines. The three primary elements of logistics are supply, transport, and management. Logistical methods are broadly divided into self-sufficiency, field procurement, and supply bases.

Ahh, yes, I see. My considerable wisdom has grown once again.

"Kwaaa ha ha ha! You have much to learn yet, Ifrit! Logistics is defined as the management and transportation of..."
I repeated my new knowledge to Ifrit.

"B-brilliant! You are so wise, Master Veldora. I am stunned at the depth of your knowledge and intelligence."

"No doubt you are, and rightly so. Read this, and you yourself may scratch the surface of my intellect!!"

"Oh, thank you. I will strive to follow your example, Master Veldora!"

I am pleased at Ifrit's earnest obedience. Now I have delegated all of the boring and complex study to him, so that I might focus more purely on entertainment.

❖

The orcs' intentions have been revealed. It seems that they have the unique skill "Starved," which they are using to steal the abilities of a wide variety of races and species. Upon reflection, I do recall that the previous orc lord had the same ability.

It was a human who vanquished that lord, for one very simple reason. "Starved" can take the unique characteristics and skills of monsters, but it cannot take arts gained through experience and effort. In that sense, his focus on monsters is logical. He wants to devour all the monsters in the forest and take control of it...

If he does, it will surely lead to the birth of a new demon lord. And lurking behind the orc lord's efforts, there might be majin plotting and sneaking about.

It is clear to me—the reek of danger and intrigue. Make your decision swiftly, Rimuru!

After all, if left unchecked, this situation could cause harm to those who are meant to one day worship me! Stem the bleeding and stop the orc lord before my reputation suffers further losses!!
But my lament did not reach Rimuru's ears. To my humiliation, it was the purple-haired Shion who gave Rimuru encouragement.

"That piddling orc lord won't stand a chance against Lord Rimuru!" she claimed.

I agree!

At last, Rimuru seemed chagrined. "I'll take on this orc lord for you. The rest of you, prepare yourselves for that," he proclaimed.

Orc lord, you are done for.

I sat back proudly, relieved that my town would be safe from harm now.

◆FALSE SUPERIORITY◆

What is that?! It is splendid!

Rimuru sits upon a most magnificent seat. Sure, it is strangely shaped, but it is unfair that he should have all the glory for himself.

Is this what they call a divine palanquin?

Rimuru seems embarrassed by it, but I think it is perfect. When I am fully recovered, I shall have one for myself.

Rimuru's group is busy preparing for battle. Ifrit is hard at work, reading books on military strategy from writers of all places and eras. And I have nothing to do.

I am exceedingly bored.

"It is so boring, Ifrit."

"Not for me. I am studying—"

"And bored. Yes?"

"...Yes. It is as you say, Master Veldora."

What a surprise! Ifrit was just as bored as me? He should have said something. What an odd and reserved fellow.

"Kwaa ha ha ha! In that case, we ought to determine how you have grown. What say you to another game?" I said, referring to shogi.

A pleased Ifrit rushed about, setting up the game. I seem to recall that I had thrown up my hands and prevented the end of our last game—I was merely feeling under the weather that day.

What? "How can you be under the weather if there is no weather in there"?

Don't be preposterous. Of course there is weather!

I would never lose otherwise, so logic would dictate that if I was about to lose, it was because there was weather, and I was under it!

So *this* time I will attempt to challenge him for real.

....
......
...

S-something is wrong. Something is very wrong!

I started this game with all the confidence of a champion, but things are proceeding very poorly for me.

"That is check, Master Veldora."

"Wh-what nonsense it this?!" I cried, and smoothly moved my gold general to dispatch the encroaching knight.

How do you like that?! Now I have neutralized your—

"Then I'll just take your rook."

Gwaaaah!! Impossible! How is this possible?! My precious and powerful rook, taken in an act of merciless cruelty by Ifrit's bishop!! Curses! Curses!

I fell right into Ifrit's trap… It is not fair. Such sly and devious trickery.

I have no choice. I was hoping not to need to do this…

"Ifrit, you have made admirable strides. Out of respect to you, I shall show you my ultimate technique!" I cried, and flipped over my king.

Written on it were the characters for "emperor."

"Wh-what is that…?" Ifrit gasped.

"Kwaaa ha ha ha!" I bellowed, pleased with myself. "This is the true, final form of my king. An emperor is allowed to move twice!"

"Huh?! But there's no piece called…nothing in the rules that say…"

"You fool! Would one as proud and great as I bend the knee to someone else's rules?!"

"—?!" Ifrit simply gaped, unable to hide his shock. And I cannot blame him! It is the proper reaction to his contact with my noble greatness.

"No, no," he stammered, "it could not be something so childish. It just couldn't. No doubt Master Veldora has some very deep and profound reason for it…"

"Yes. Hold your head high, Ifrit. Now begins the true match!" I announced.

And thus my counterattack began.

◆THE MARCH TO WAR◆

The tables had turned, and much for the better.

Confident that the situation was in my favor, I decided to check in on Rimuru. The last time I had seen him, he was wearing frilly, many-layered clothes. I did not find them terribly beautiful. I prefer bold and striking outfits, myself.

This time, he and the kijin were dressed in much better clothes. Not only were they more pleasing to the eye, they were high in defensive power too.

"Look at them, Ifrit. Is it fair for them to boast of such finery?"

"Hmm... No matter how I put you into check, you can escape with two moves, so..."

"Are you listening to me?"

"Huh? Oh! Forgive me, Master. I was focused on the game."

Hah! He was so taken aback at my devastating momentum that he didn't have time to look outside, either. But I cannot blame him— my emperor piece is unstoppable.

As long as I have the emperor, I am undefeated. But enough about that.

"You should learn from my example and be more cautious. See? Rimuru and his cohorts have new equipment."

"Oh, you're right. They must have come from the dwarves and that kijin named Kurobei. They've even improved their clothes in subtle ways. Such a fascinating fellow, that Rimuru," Ifrit said, impressed.

I can see what makes him a higher-order elemental. His eye for detail regarding their armor marks him as the sort worthy of following in the Demon Lord Leon's army.

"And what do you think? Can they tackle that vast army of orcs with just their little group?" I asked deviously.

In fact, I had no doubt of Rimuru's victory. No collection of inferior C-Rank and D-Rank monsters would bear a threat to a powerful majin of A-Rank or higher, no matter how many of them there were. By my estimation, those evolved kijin have an energy amount that puts them beyond A-Rank. They cannot possibly be bested by mere orcs.

So how will Ifrit respond? He has been reading those strategy manuals I gave to him. If his way of thinking is stubbornly tied down to numbers alone, he may not yet be worthy of the position of my tactician...

"Lord Rimuru would be victorious, of course. What Treyni the dryad is truly concerned about is the majin lurking behind this threat. Even Demon Lord Leon has been vexed by their machinations."

"Ohh?"

That Ifrit is sharper than I gave him credit for. Intrigued, I bade him continue his explanation.

"In a sense, you can think of the orc army as a lure. Without your presence in the forest, Master Veldora, these might be the movements of people who would seize control of it for their own ends."

"Are you sure you're not overthinking this?"

"Perhaps. But it's quite within the realm of possibility, in my opinion. I can certainly think of some demon lords who enjoy crafty skullduggery of this sort," Ifrit admitted, his expression sour. I could sense that he had undergone some bitter experiences when he worked under Leon.

"Then if the orc army is nothing but a feint, you think they are incapable of triumphing over Rimuru's squad?"

"That is correct. In terms of shogi, Lord Rimuru and his companions would be gold and silver generals, rooks, and bishops—all powerful pieces. But the vast majority of the orc army are pawns. Perhaps a handful of silver generals. Unless their king were to turn into an 'emperor,' it is a war that Lord Rimuru cannot help but win," Ifrit claimed.

In a sense, I agreed with him. But Ifrit, is that not a storytelling "flag," as the terminology goes? In the novels that I read, it was common for such overly-obvious developments to be flipped on their heads...but I digress.

"You have learned much. Your explanation was very thorough," I said.

"Thank you! I am honored, Master."

This Ifrit is going places, I sense. Rimuru has many followers, but I have none. I never considered this to be a failing before this point, but now it strikes me as a bit of a shame. It might be interesting to continue honing Ifrit's mind and bring him on board as my strategist.

"In that case, Master Veldora, may I ask for one thing?"

"I am feeling generous. Ask away," I said magnanimously. A master must distribute rewards as well.

"I would like to play another game with modified rules."

"Hmm?"

"Please allow me to use the 'emperor' piece, as you do."

"W-well..."

"I am simply incapable of matching you as it is. I would appreciate the opportunity to receive training in it."

"Ah, yes. Indeed..."

Damn it all! This has backfired spectacularly! However...

"Very well. I shall show you the ropes."

Escape is not an option for the great Veldora. For I have learned something today: there is no defeat for an emperor. And neither is there for me.

Never retreat! Never grovel! Never look back!! I will accept the Ifrit's challenge!! There is no time to watch Rimuru leave for battle now. This situation demands my complete attention.

Ifrit's gaze pains me. His reverence for me is obvious, a silent pressure reminding me that I must live up to his expectations. As he set about, preparing a new game, I was filled with a newfound determination not to lose.

Just then, I glanced out at Rimuru.

"Very well said! You've recognized the greatness of Lord Rimuru.

You've got a good head on your shoulders," said Shion, Rimuru's secretary, as she brought him more work.

I had never considered it before, but perhaps Rimuru was feeing the same sensation that I am right now. Being forced to live up to the expectations of others can be such a weight upon the heart.

"When an ally is in trouble you rush to their aid, right?"

Simply incredible. On the inside, Rimuru was shaken by this, but he showed no signs of it to the outside world. And in the meantime, I could not help but wonder: if he would do that for an ally, why has he not yet saved me, his dearest friend?

◆RIPPLES ON THE BATTLEFIELD◆

"Yeah, the lizardmen are in a bad spot. In a strategy game, this is where you give up and reload your save," Rimuru muttered. Remarkably enough, it was an accurate description of my own situation.

"That is check, Master Veldora!"

Grrr. Ifrit knows no mercy in his brutal forays into my territory. It is simply the height of unfairness that a king piece should move twice. What moron decided to make that a rule?!

Elsewhere, Gabiru the lizardman was locked in a desperate duel. But I had no attention to spare for him. I was too busy maneuvering my pieces to stave off the Ifrit's fiendish attack.

Meanwhile, as though he had plenty of time to spare, Ifrit said, "Look at that, Master Veldora. That man named Benimaru seems to have inherited my flames."

Shut up! I do not have time for this nonsense!

But I will not deny a measure of curiosity, so I gave it a glance. As Ifrit said, Benimaru was in the process of unleashing a devastating skill.

"Ahh. He is also making use of my Black Flames. It seems this is an advanced skill that Benimaru crafted himself, not one that just anyone can wield."

"Indeed. At his energy level, it would be difficult to produce the same amount of heat as I can. He would need to combine it with a few different skills to create this effect."

That is correct. I suspect it is a combination of Ifrit's "Flame Manipulation," my "Black Flames," and his own "Ogre Flames." In addition, he is utilizing a space-limiting skill. All in all, a very impressive display.

Answer: Correct. That is the wide-range conflagration attack "Hell Flare," developed by the individual named Benimaru.

"Hell Flare," eh? It will have no effect on me or Ifrit, but your average monster will not stand a chance against it. The kijin named Benimaru is tremendously advanced to make such a skill his own.

Now it seems Gobta has gone to assist that Gabiru fellow. Gabiru might be a clown, but he's displayed manly valor by taking a blow for his followers. Rimuru doesn't want to simply abandon him, and I agree with that sentiment.

Gobta might not be much, but he has Ranga with him. The orcs don't stand a chance.

The battle is reaching its climax.

Normally this is where I would watch with delight. But now my heart is heavy. Surely I need not elaborate on the reason…

I glanced down at the board, where my defeat was writ large.

There is no other choice. Now is the time for me to re-allot the mental resources spent on "Inquiring" my imprisonment seal to find the formula that will guide me to victory!

Warning: Usage denied.

Wha—?!

Curse you, Rimuru. You saw my attempt coming?!

I am willing to undo my prison later if it will mean winning this contest. But Rimuru does not seem to want this outcome. I won't deny that I would like to be returned to power soon, but…

But a dragon cannot be a loser.

Answer: You have earned this outcome. You altered the established and accepted rules of shogi for your own selfish purposes. You ought to have been satisfied with the legal advantage of first move instead.

I've been scolded. Why, it seems that Rimuru is furious that I changed the rules.

Still, I want to win.

Dignity? I would rather have victory. I have lived a long, long time, and I may never have been more fixated on a victory than this one.

It's not like I have never tasted defeat. As with my battle against the hero, when I knew I did not stand a chance, I abandoned my struggle. The dragons are unstoppable; if we die, we eventually return to life.

But shogi is different. And not just shogi—all the games contained within Rimuru's mind. The contestants engage in competition on equal footing, no matter their backgrounds.

In this game, I have engaged perhaps too deeply. My desire to avoid defeat led me to cheat, which my opponent has now utilized back against me. Rimuru is correct: I have earned this.

Regardless, I have decided that the best way for me to make up for my mistake is to win anyway.

❖

—At last, Rimuru heard my plea.

Suggestion: Utilize proxy calculation? YES/NO

I could sense a kind of exasperated resignation from the offer, which I happily accepted.

I knew that Rimuru was my friend.

◆DEATH STORM◆

The showdown between me and the Ifrit is reaching a pitched finale. Meanwhile, Rimuru's followers are closing in on a conclusion to their battle.

Most eye-catching of them all is Benimaru, with his "Hell Flare" ability. Also impressive is Rimuru's pet, the wolf Ranga. He summoned several whirlwinds that shoot bolts of electricity as they carve through the orcs.

Is that a combination of the Extra Skill "Wind Manipulation" and my "Black Lightning"?

Answer: It is the area attack technique "Death Storm" developed by the individual named Ranga.

"Death Storm," then. It reminds me of an inferior version of my "Storm of Destruction." Perhaps because he hides in Rimuru's shadow, and basks in his magicules? It is a rather strange evolutionary path he has taken.

Ranga's current species is Tempest Star Wolf. Frankly, it is a mighty beast. Anyone utilizing such a powerful area attack is easily over A-Rank. Such wide-range, tactically decisive attacks consume a tremendous amount of energy. This is the wall that must be scaled to transcend the A-Rank tier.

It is exceedingly difficult to reach these heights, but the rewards are great. Like Benimaru and Ranga, tremendous powers come along with it. But without a proper level of skill and experience, such riches are wasted.

The majin mentioned in Rimuru's earlier strategy meeting would likely be A-Rank as well. Anyone called a majin is a worthy foe, so you can bet they will be at least at this level.

As for me? I am special, of course. Ifrit has much going for him as well, too. Only the elite officers of the demon lords would be his equal.

Rimuru might be intelligent, but he is unlearned in this regard. He is overly cautious, not realizing that the orc lord is not truly such a fearsome enemy. If he truly enlisted all of those thousands and thousands of orcs, that might speak to a certain greatness...but I do not doubt Rimuru's coming victory in the least.

The real problem will be the number of orcs. 200,000 will mean a considerable expenditure of stamina before we even reach the important ones.

But with the hard work of those following Rimuru to clear the way...

It has been planned out, I'm sure. Rimuru is floating up in the sky, and even making time to give me advice. He's got this all worked out.

I must give up and admit that in these situations, I am no match for him.

Benimaru, Ranga, Hakuro, Shion. Even the scrambling of little Gobta has succeeded in tilting the battle to Rimuru's favor. At this rate, the Orc Lord does himself no favors by standing back to watch.

In the meantime, my battle against Ifrit is also nearing its conclusion.

"It c-can't be... At this rate..."

Ifrit is panicking. I do not blame him. I can scarcely believe it myself.

Next move will be check.

I carelessly set my pieces, guiding and luring Ifrit's emperor into the corner...where two lances and my rook have it trapped.

The key to all of this: the weakest piece of all, the one I had never taken seriously.

A pawn.

"This is check, Ifrit."

At Rimuru's advice, I moved my pawn one square forward. My infiltration into enemy territory was complete. I flipped the piece over, making it a promoted pawn.

"Impossible..."

Even with two moves, his emperor has no escape.

"That is checkmate! I am victorious," I declared.

"I...I give," Ifrit said, stunned. "Even under these circumstances, victory is impossible for me... Master Veldora, you did this to teach me the importance of never giving up, didn't you?"

What?

It seems Ifrit has misunderstood our competition in a rather complimentary way. I must take advantage of this.

"That is indeed correct."

"I should have known... I am ashamed of my own shallowness. No matter what, I will never give up, and swear to always pursue victory to the bitter end!"

What a melodramatic fellow. Still, I cannot deny that this was a fortunate conclusion to the game.

"That is what I wanted to hear from you. It was worth enacting that preposterous rule to teach you this. We no longer have any need for the emperor piece."

"I didn't realize that's what you intended," Ifrit said, impressed.

Very good. I have completely fooled him, and now Ifrit has even more respect for me than before. All is well.

Once again, it all comes back to Rimuru.

He impresses me every time, and this is no exception. Even outside, the battle's triumph is nigh.

And then...

...

Hmm?

Is there still some trouble to address?

Rimuru is looking ahead to the orc lord, who seems rather insignificant to me...

Is it possible that, like my own promoted pawn, the orc lord has jumped in stature?!

No, I am merely overthinking it. But one never knows what might happen on the battlefield.

And as a wise master himself, Rimuru would never let his guard down for this reason.

Very well. I must witness the conclusion of this great battle!!

To be reincarnated in Volume 5!

MAYBE ON TWO LEGS

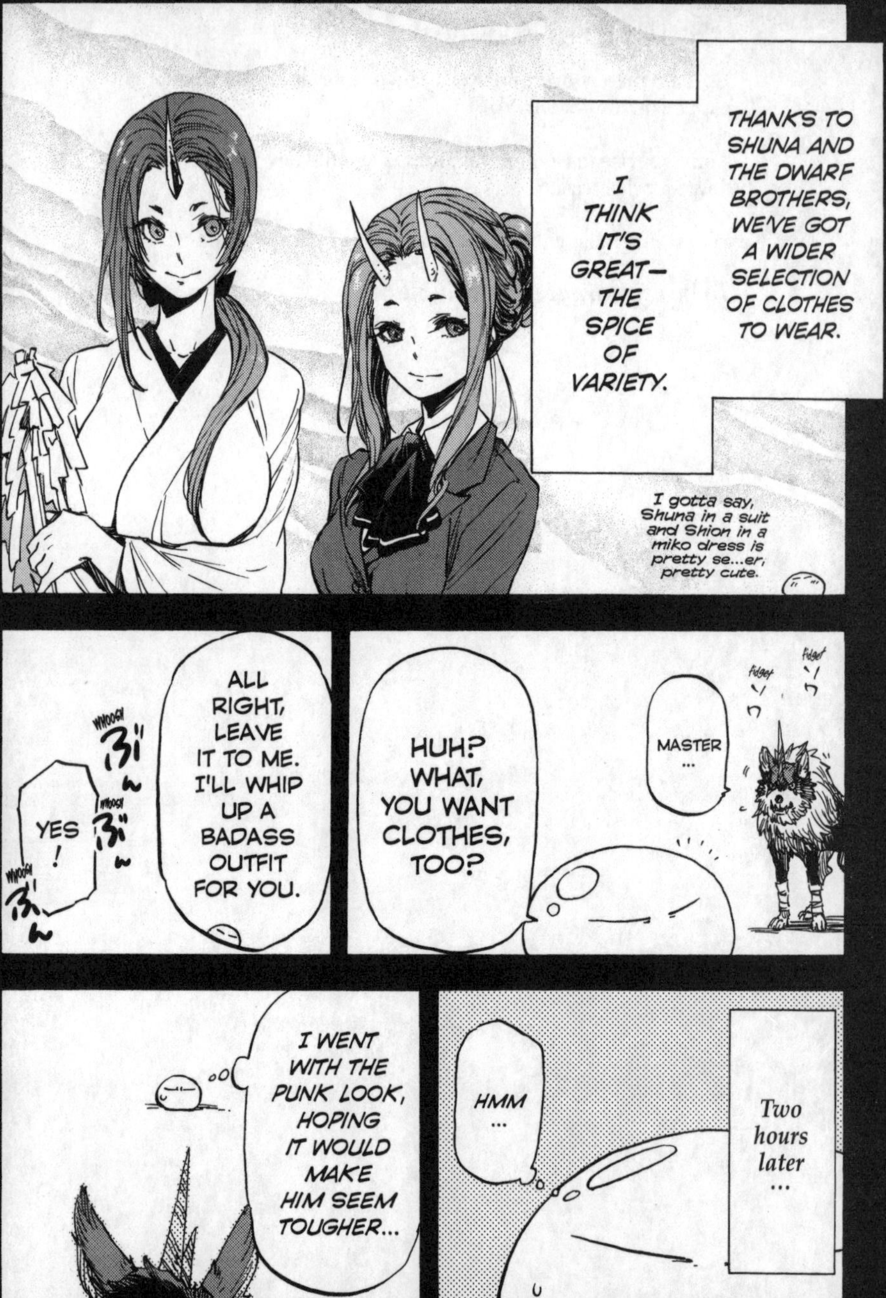
THANKS TO SHUNA AND THE DWARF BROTHERS, WE'VE GOT A WIDER SELECTION OF CLOTHES TO WEAR.
I THINK IT'S GREAT—THE SPICE OF VARIETY.
I gotta say, Shuna in a suit and Shion in a miko dress is pretty se...er, pretty cute.
fidget ソワ
fidget ソワ
MASTER ...
HUH? WHAT, YOU WANT CLOTHES, TOO?
ALL RIGHT, LEAVE IT TO ME. I'LL WHIP UP A BADASS OUTFIT FOR YOU.
WHOOSH ぶん
WHOOSH ぶん
YES!
WHOOSH ぶん
Two hours later ...
HMM ...
I WENT WITH THE PUNK LOOK, HOPING IT WOULD MAKE HIM SEEM TOUGHER...

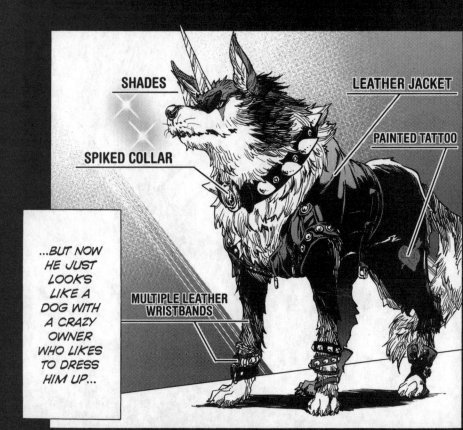

LEATHER JACKET
PAINTED TATTOO
SHADES
SPIKED COLLAR
MULTIPLE LEATHER WRISTBANDS
...BUT NOW HE JUST LOOKS LIKE A DOG WITH A CRAZY OWNER WHO LIKES TO DRESS HIM UP...

IN CONCLUSION...
NEVER MIND.
GONG
...NOTHING'S FIERCER THAN BEING IN THE BUFF.

LIST OF ACKNOWLEDGMENTS

AUTHOR:
Fuse-sensei

AUTHOR:
Mitz Vah-sensei

ASSISTANTS:
Takuya Nishida-san Muraichi-san Hino-san Daiki Haraguchi-san

I just ran into a wild slime...

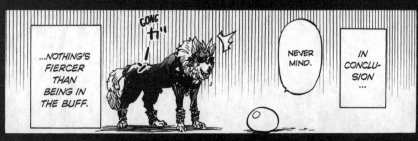

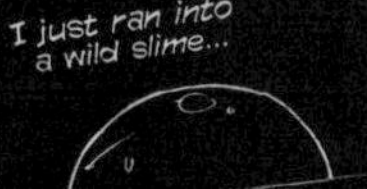

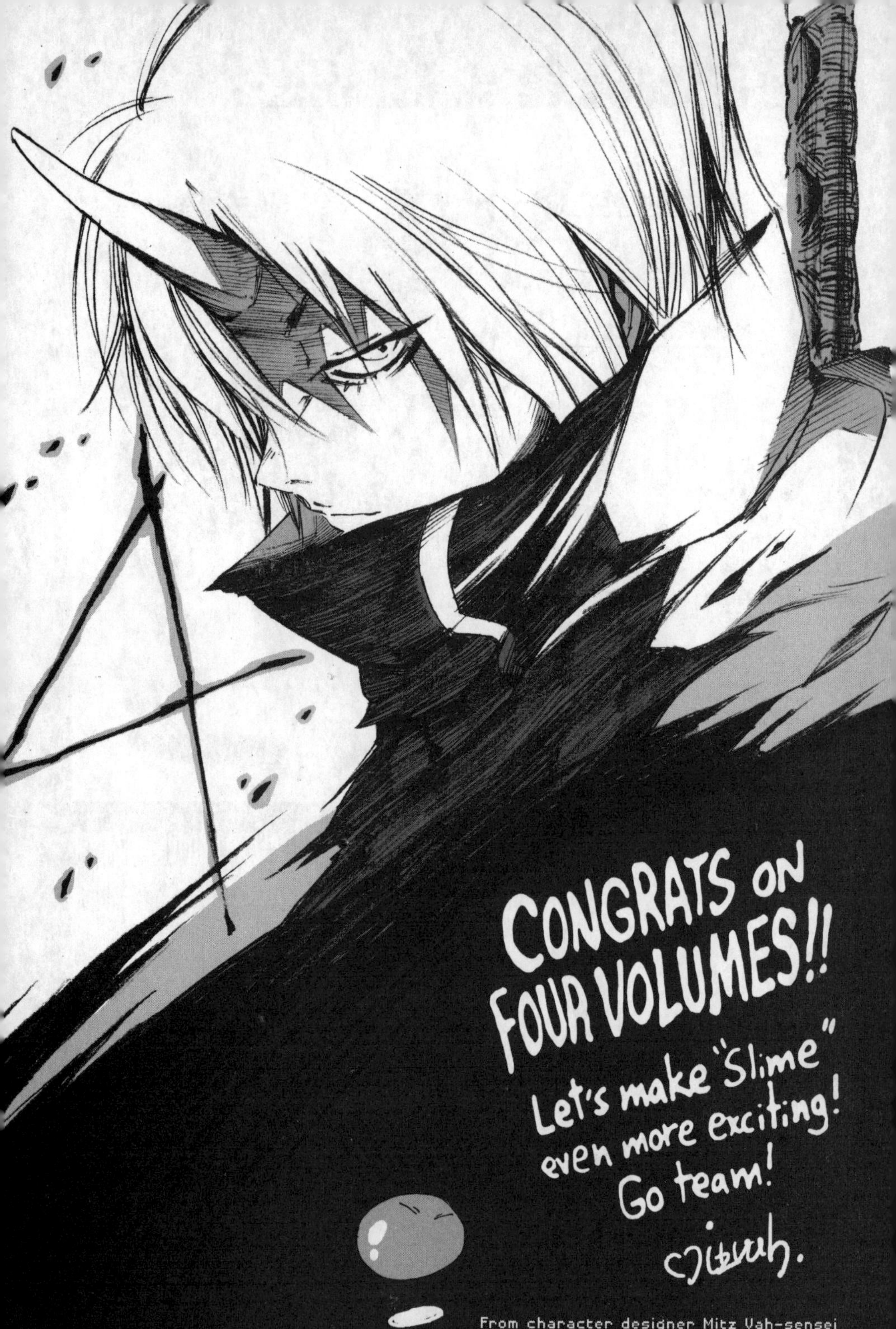
CONGRATS ON FOUR VOLUMES!!
Let's make "Slime" even more exciting! Go team!
From character designer Mitz Vah-sensei

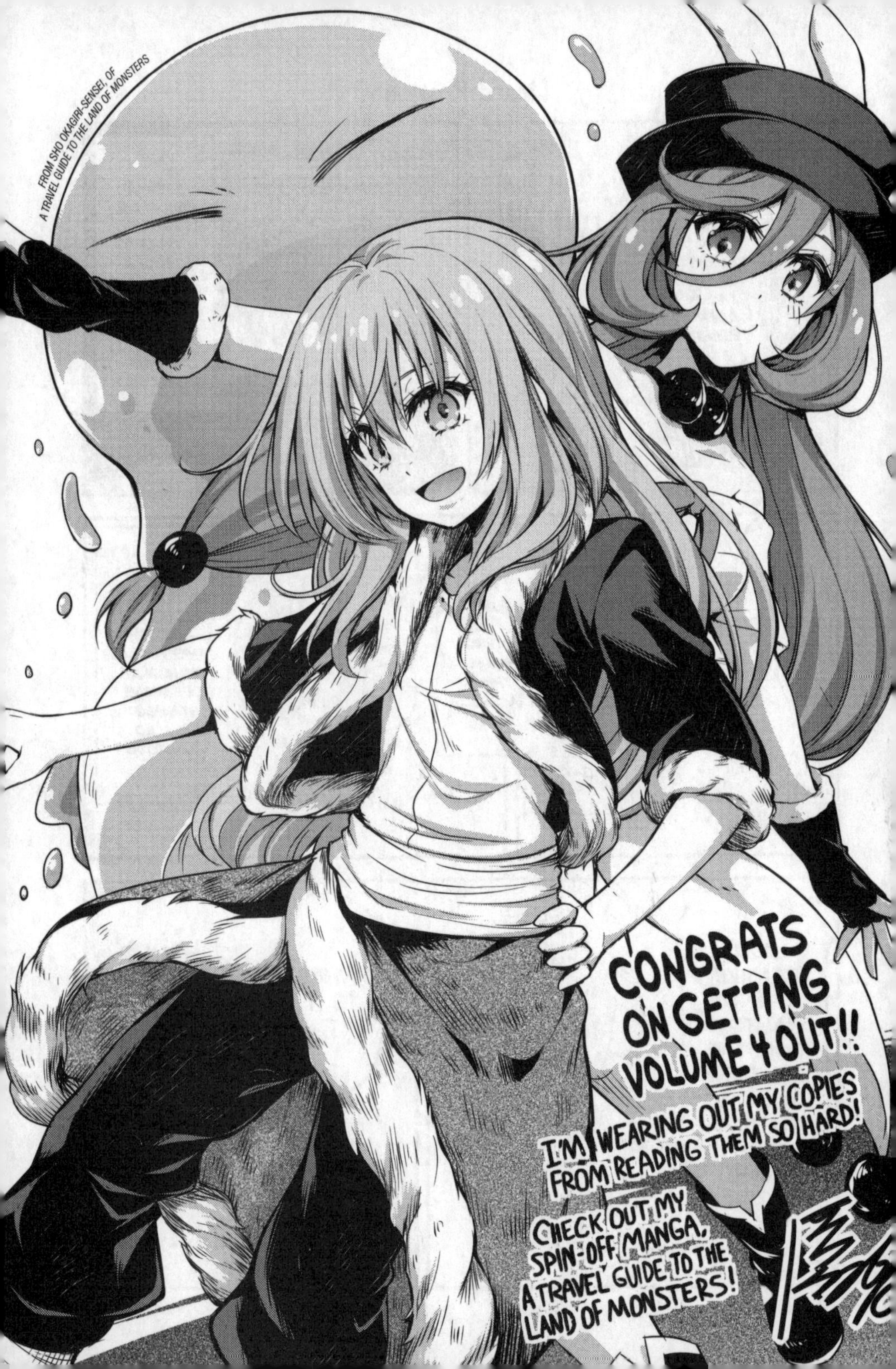
FROM SHO OKAGIRI-SENSEI, OF
A TRAVEL GUIDE TO THE LAND OF MONSTERS
CONGRATS ON GETTING VOLUME 4 OUT!!
I'M WEARING OUT MY COPIES FROM READING THEM SO HARD!
CHECK OUT MY SPIN-OFF MANGA, A TRAVEL GUIDE TO THE LAND OF MONSTERS!

Lizard Problems

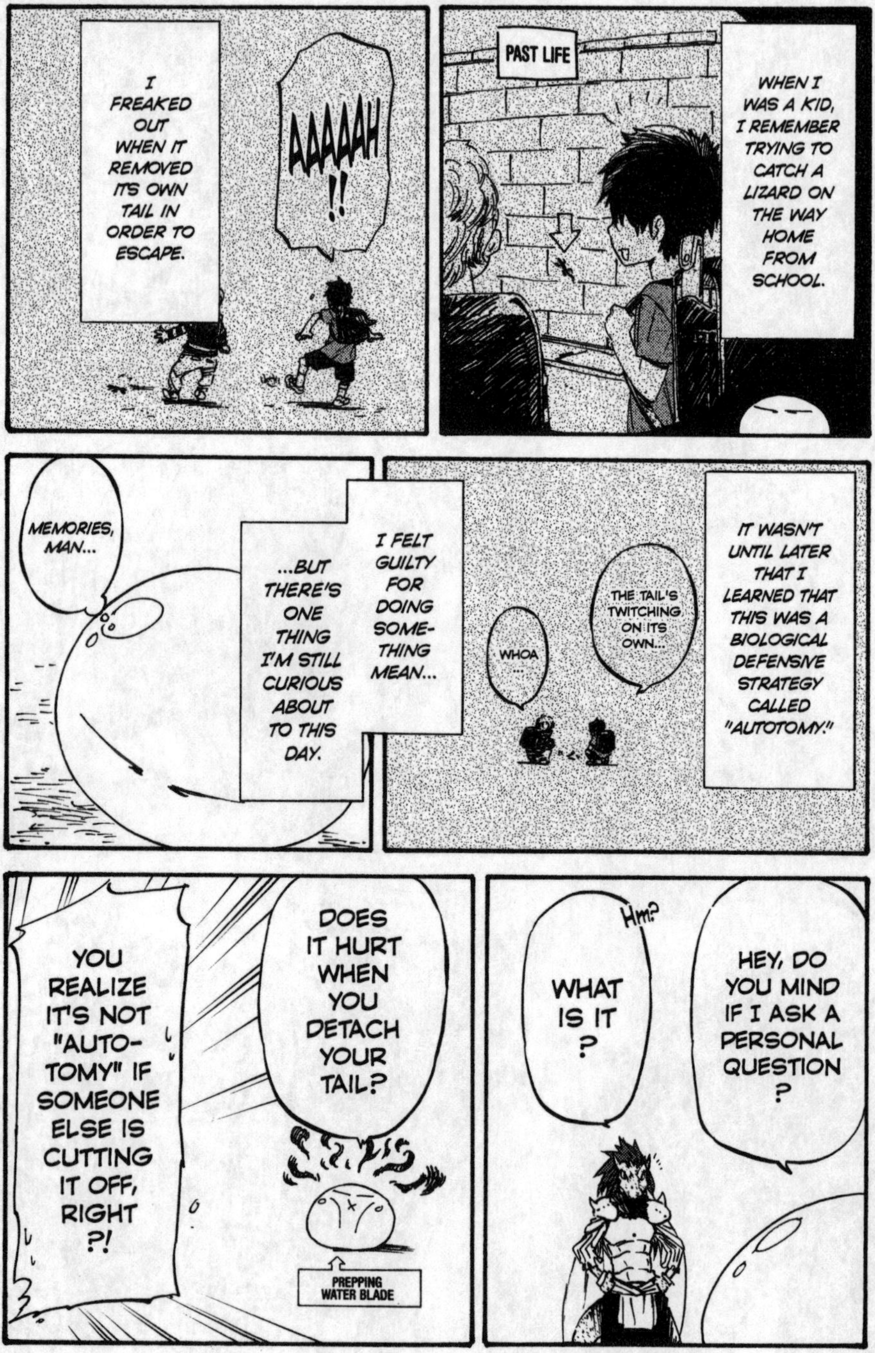
PAST LIFE
WHEN I WAS A KID, I REMEMBER TRYING TO CATCH A LIZARD ON THE WAY HOME FROM SCHOOL.
I FREAKED OUT WHEN IT REMOVED ITS OWN TAIL IN ORDER TO ESCAPE.
AAAAAH!!
IT WASN'T UNTIL LATER THAT I LEARNED THAT THIS WAS A BIOLOGICAL DEFENSIVE STRATEGY CALLED "AUTOTOMY."
THE TAIL'S TWITCHING ON ITS OWN...
WHOA...
I FELT GUILTY FOR DOING SOMETHING MEAN...
...BUT THERE'S ONE THING I'M STILL CURIOUS ABOUT TO THIS DAY.
MEMORIES, MAN...
HEY, DO YOU MIND IF I ASK A PERSONAL QUESTION?
Hm?
WHAT IS IT?
DOES IT HURT WHEN YOU DETACH YOUR TAIL?
PREPPING WATER BLADE
YOU REALIZE IT'S NOT "AUTOTOMY" IF SOMEONE ELSE IS CUTTING IT OFF, RIGHT?!

Rimuru Natto

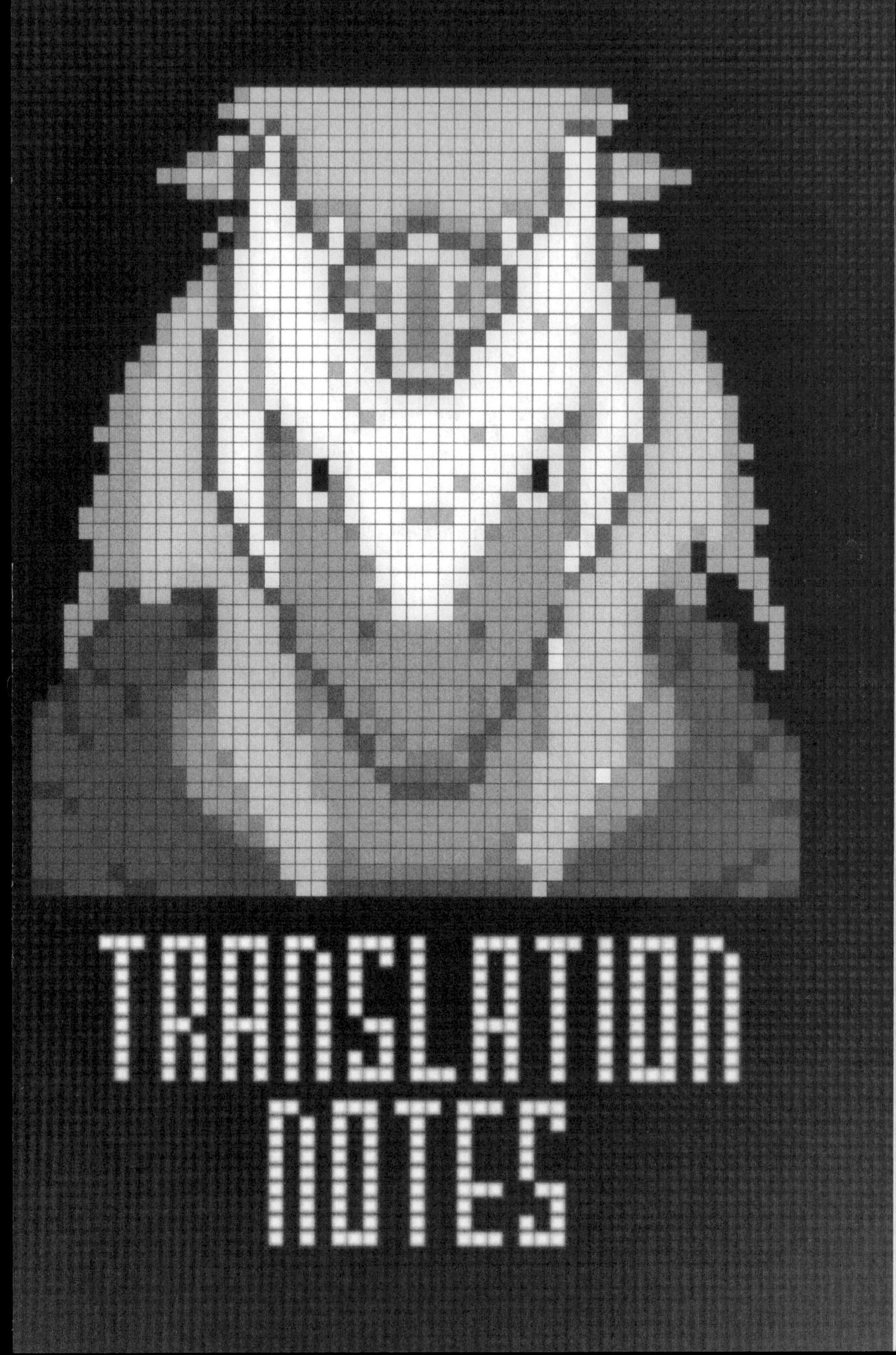

TRANSLATION NOTES

POTATO CHIPS

page 33

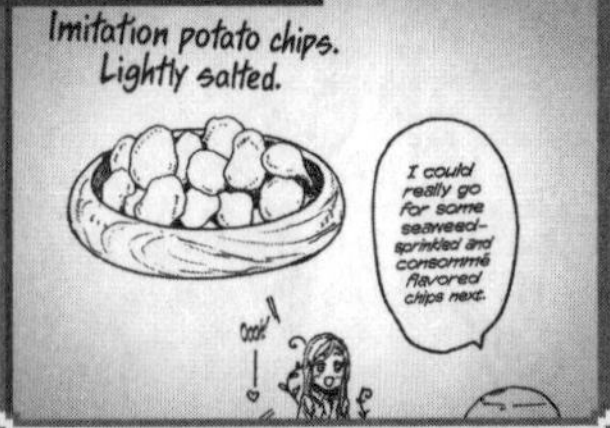
Imitation potato chips. Lightly salted.
I could really go for some seaweed-sprinkled and consommé flavored chips next.

One of the more entertaining facets of Japan's food culture for those from the West is the uniquely Japanese take on things like junk food and candy. Potato chips are one type of food that is commonly sold in a variety of savory flavors familiar to the Japanese and exotic to Westerners. This includes seaweed and salt, wasabi, shrimp, fish roe (*mentaiko*), and consommé flavor, which is a rich and creamy beef bouillon taste.

SHOGI

page 168

Shogi is merely a game, of course. I cannot blame it for not c
ing this abstract concept. More interesting to me was Ifrit's fa
tion with the game. If I gave him a manual of battle strategy,
he then turn into a master tactician? I decided to tap into Rim
deep memory banks.

Now that I have become accustomed to manga and novels, fi
the text I seek is a simple matter.

My target: the dictionary.

Thankfully, Rimuru's memory is organized so neatly that I promptly succeeded in finding the desired knowledge.

Lo·gis·tics (n.): the management and transportation of military pe

A Japanese variation within the family of chess games. It is somewhat more complex than basic chess; rather than sixteen pieces per player on an 8x8 board, shogi features twenty pieces per player on a 9x9 board, with a wider variety of pieces as well. Unlike the ornamental pieces of chess, shogi pieces are all the same shape, with *kanji* indicating the type. They are all double-sided, as every piece in the game can be promoted (and thus flipped over) by reaching a certain row of enemy territory. Captured pieces can be replayed on the board by the taker. Victory via checking the opponent's king into checkmate works the same way as in chess.

NEVER RETREAT! NEVER GROVEL! NEVER LOOK BACK!

page 174

re is no defeat for an e

Never retreat! Never grovel! Never look bac
Ifrit's challenge!! There is no time to watch I
now. This situation demands my complete a

Ifrit's gaze pains me. His reverence for me is
pressure reminding me that I must live up t
he set about, preparing a new game, I was f
determination not to lose.

A famous quote from the character Souther of *Fist of the North Star*.

NATTO

page 187

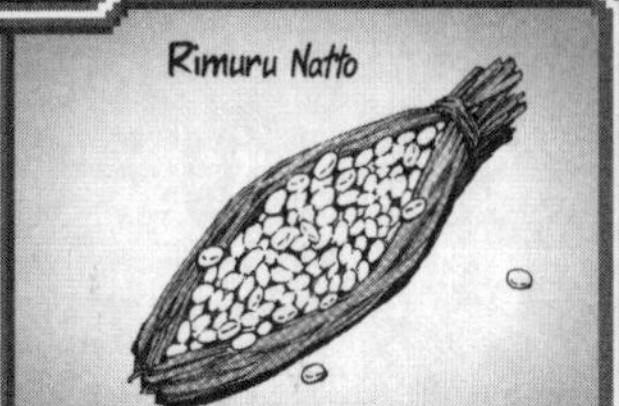
Rimuru Natto

A traditional Japanese food of fermented soybeans, usually eaten over rice. The soybeans were traditionally fermented within husks of rice straw, which naturally contains the proper bacteria for the process. The fermentation gives it a very strong, pungent smell and slimy/sticky texture that many find off-putting, although it is considered to have significant health benefits as well. The original caption referred to 'Rimurukinase,' a play on the enzyme 'nattokinase,' (which is not technically a kinase but a different kind of enzyme) which is a byproduct of the Bacillus *natto* fermentation process. This enzyme is also extracted and sold in pills for its health benefits, primarily as a blood thinner to reduce the danger of blood clots in people with high blood pressure.

EVERY SLIME'S GOTTA START SOMEWHERE...

TENSEI SHITARA SLIME DATTA KEN volume 1 © Fuse / Mitz Vah
All rights reserved.

Wanna learn more about Rimuru's adventures?

Go back to the source with the original light novel from author Fuse and illustrator Mitz Vah!

That **Time I Got Reincarnated as a SLIME ①**

Out in stores now from Yen On!

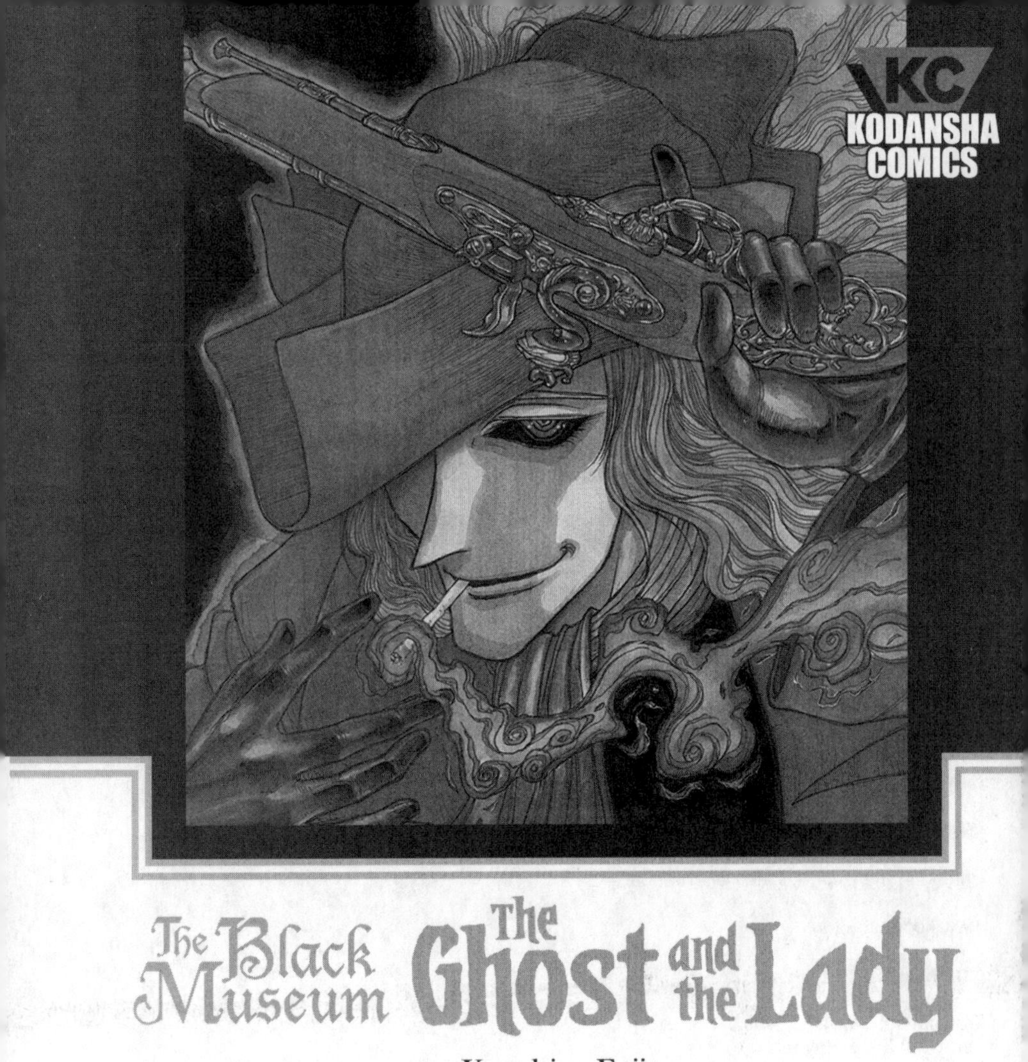

KODANSHA COMICS

The Black Museum
The Ghost and the Lady

By Kazuhiro Fujita

Deep in Scotland Yard in London sits an evidence room dedicated to the greatest mysteries of British history. In this "Black Museum" sits a misshapen hunk of lead—two bullets fused together—the key to a wartime encounter between Florence Nightingale, the mother of modern nursing, and a supernatural Man in Grey. This story is unknown to most scholars of history, but a special guest of the museum will tell the tale of The Ghost and the Lady...

Praise for Kazuhiro Fujita's *Ushio and Tora*

"A charming revival that combines a classic look with modern depth and pacing... **Essential viewing both for curmudgeons and new fans alike.**" — Anime News Network

"**GREAT!** The first episode of Ushio and Tora captures the essence of '90s anime." — IGN

A Kodansha Comics Trade Paperback Original.

Published in the United States by Kodansha Comics,
an imprint of Kodansha USA Publishing, LLC, New York.

Publication rights for this English edition arranged through Kodansha Ltd., Tokyo.

First published in Japan in 2017 by Kodansha Ltd., Tokyo, as *Tensei Shitara Suraimu Datta Ken* volume 4.

ISBN 978-1-63236-638-2

Printed in the United States of America.

www.kodansha.us

8th Printing

Translation: Stephen Paul
Lettering: Evan Hayden
Editing: Ajani Oloye
Kodansha Comics edition cover design: Phil Balsman

THAT TIME I GOT REINCARNATED AS A
SLIME

5

Author: FUSE

Artist: TAIKI KAWAKAMI

Character design: MITZ VAH

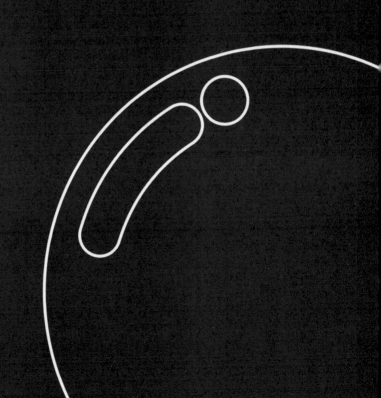

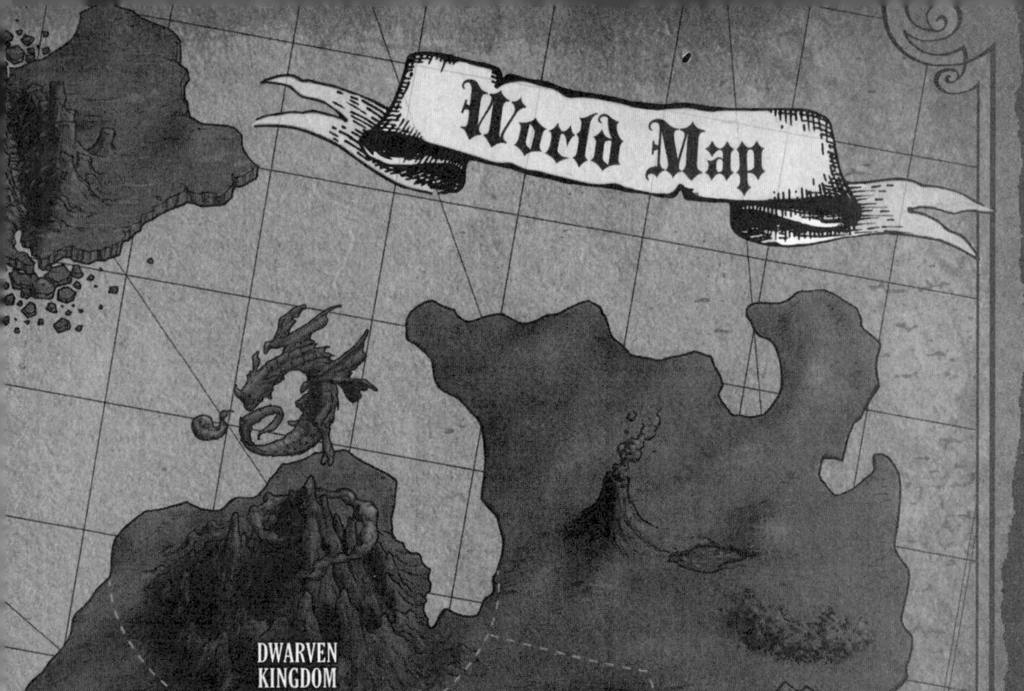
World Map
DWARVEN KINGDOM
GREAT FOREST OF JURA
KINGDOM OF BLUMUND
SEALED CAVE

PLOT SUMMARY

The orc lord and his army of 200,000 threaten the Great Forest of Jura. Rimuru had hoped to join forces with the lizardmen of the swamp to fight this menace, but Gabiru the lizardman, underestimating the orc lord's threat, stages a rebellion that accidentally plunges the lizardmen into the threat of extinction. Only the timely arrival of Rimuru's band saves them. The tide is turned against the orcs thanks to the help of Benimaru and the other kijin. This is when the mastermind behind the orcs, Gelmud the majin, takes the field... ▼

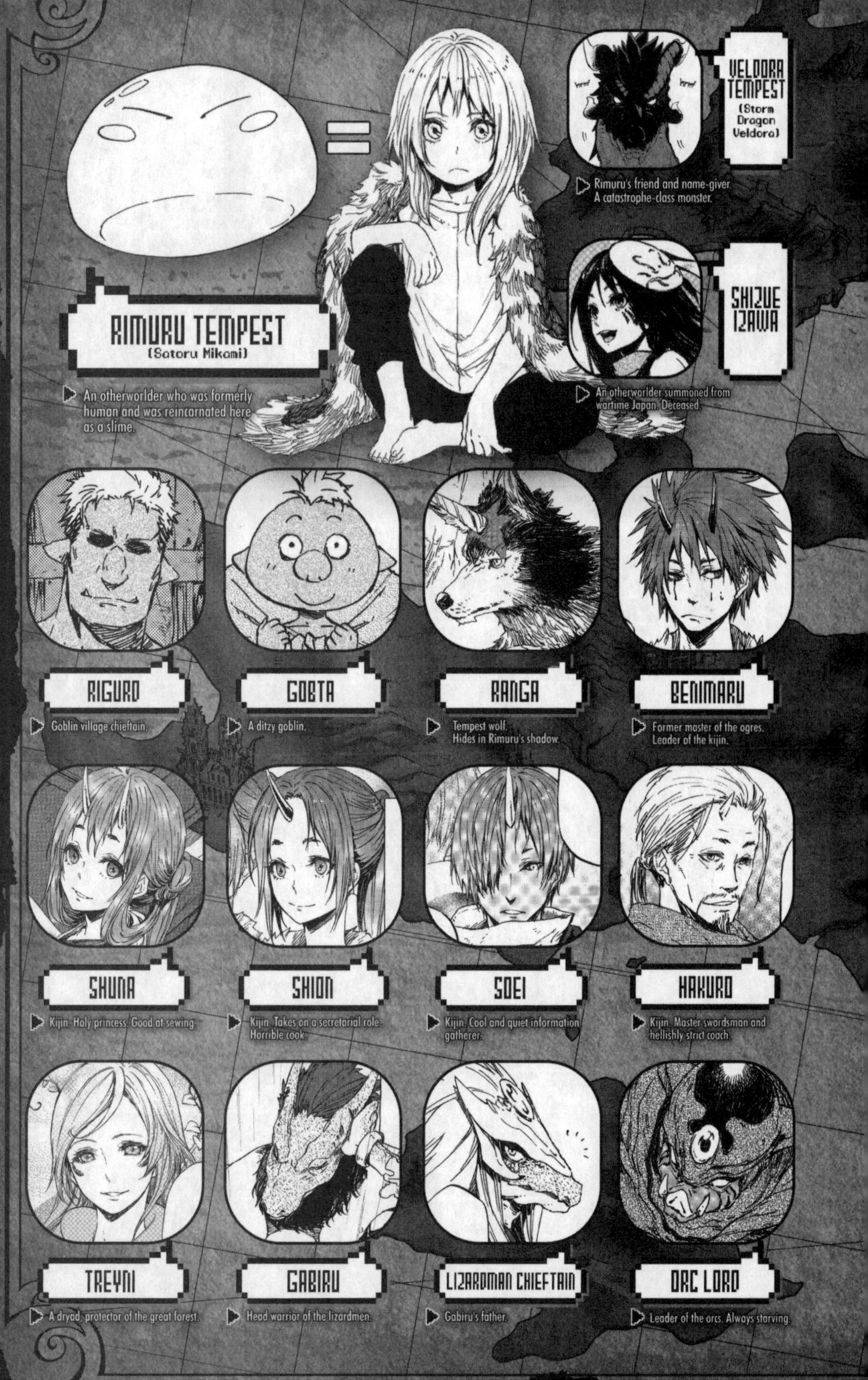

RIMURU TEMPEST
(Satoru Mikami)
An otherworlder who was formerly human and was reincarnated here as a slime.
VELDORA TEMPEST
(Storm Dragon Veldora)
Rimuru's friend and name-giver. A catastrophe-class monster.
SHIZUE IZAWA
An otherworlder summoned from wartime Japan. Deceased.
RIGURD
Goblin village chieftain.
GOBTA
A ditzy goblin.
RANGA
Tempest wolf. Hides in Rimuru's shadow.
BENIMARU
Former master of the ogres. Leader of the kijin.
SHUNA
Kijin. Holy princess. Good at sewing.
SHION
Kijin. Takes on a secretarial role. Horrible cook.
SOEI
Kijin. Cool and quiet information gatherer.
HAKURO
Kijin. Master swordsman and hellishly strict coach.
TREYNI
A dryad, protector of the great forest.
GABIRU
Head warrior of the lizardmen.
LIZARDMAN CHIEFTAIN
Gabiru's father.
ORC LORD
Leader of the orcs. Always starving.

CONTENTS

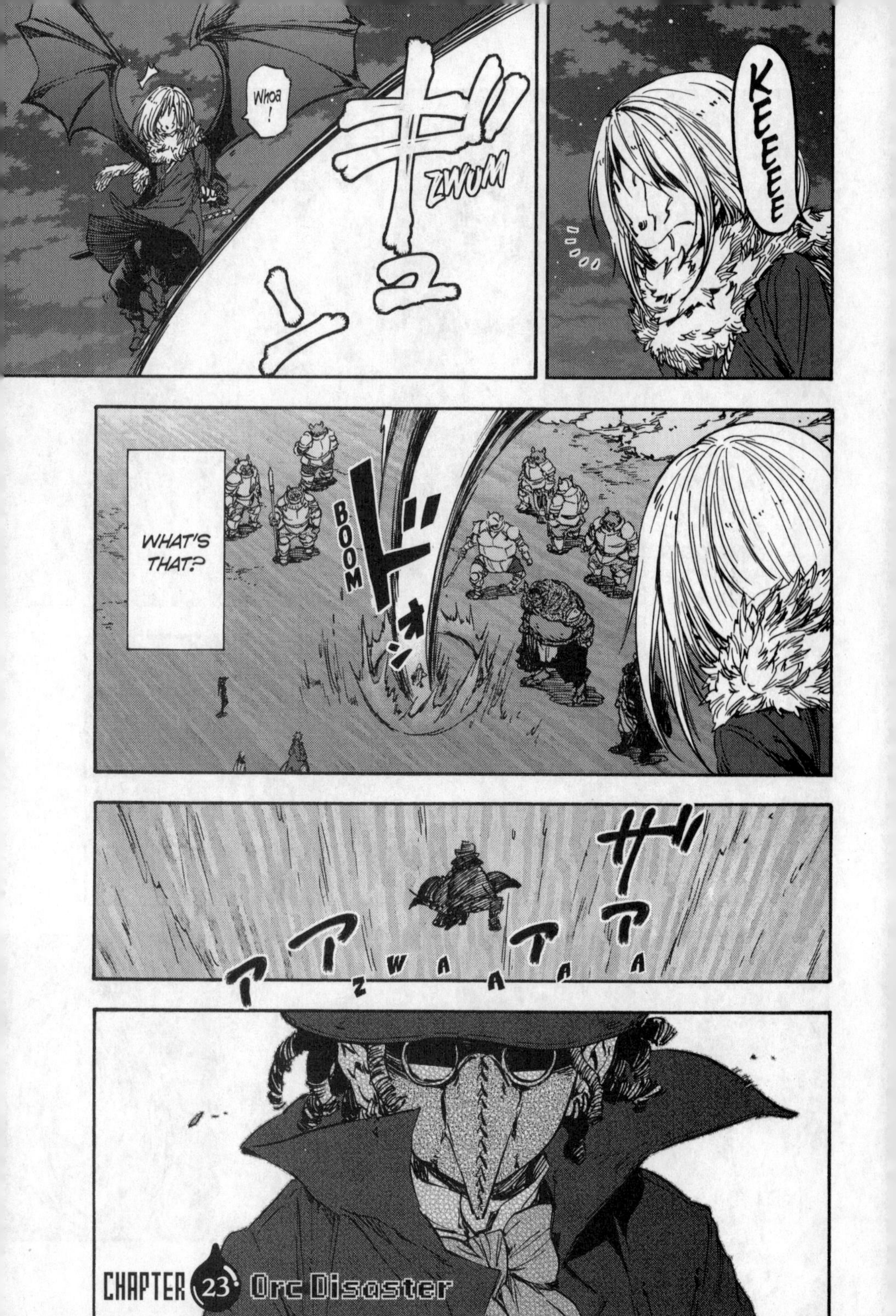
KEEEEE
Whoa!
ZWUM
WHAT'S THAT?
BOOM
ZWAAAA
CHAPTER 23 Orc Disaster

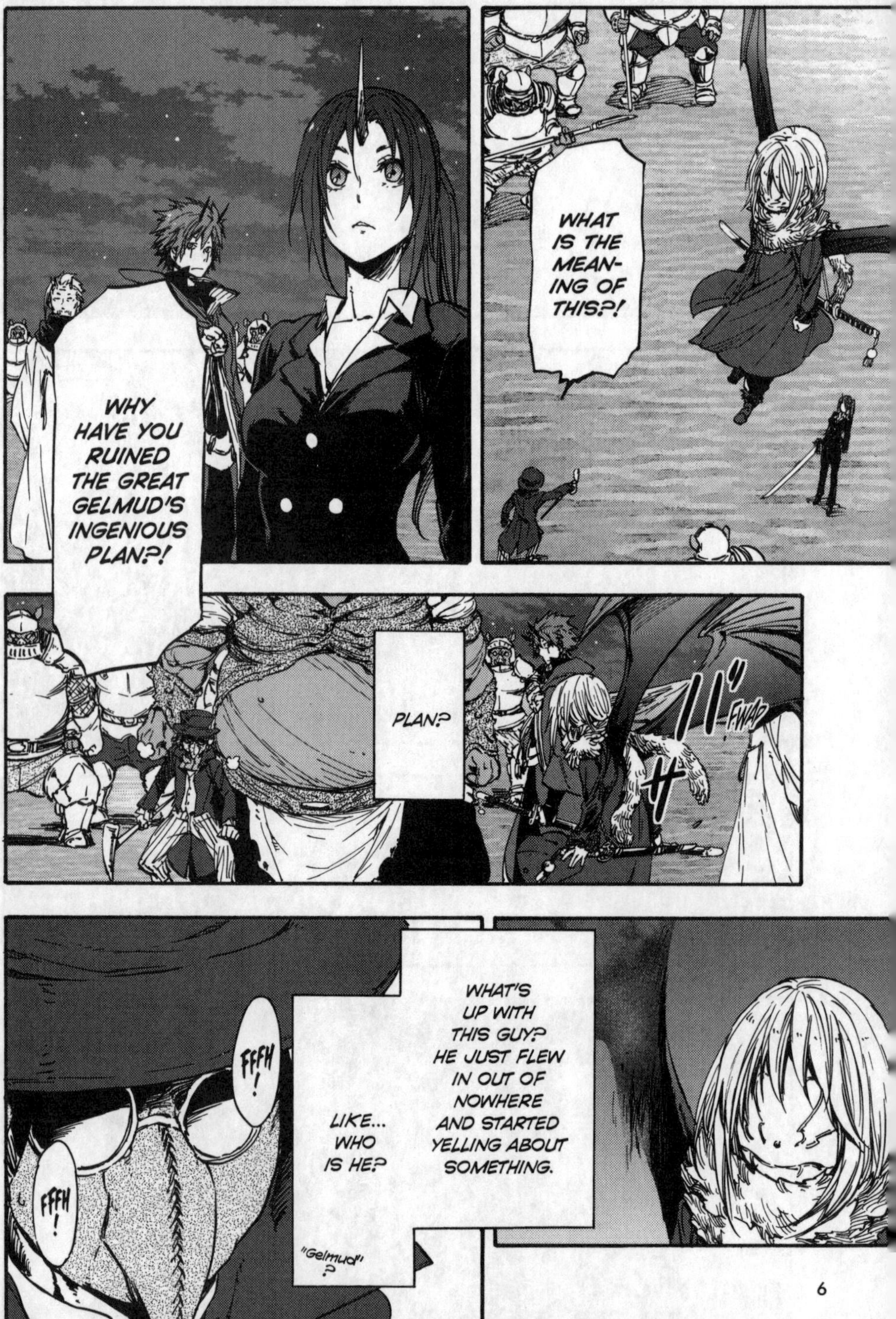
WHAT IS THE MEANING OF THIS?!
WHY HAVE YOU RUINED THE GREAT GELMUD'S INGENIOUS PLAN?!
FWAP
PLAN?
WHAT'S UP WITH THIS GUY? HE JUST FLEW IN OUT OF NOWHERE AND STARTED YELLING ABOUT SOMETHING.
LIKE... WHO IS HE?
FFFH!
FFFH!
"Gelmud"?

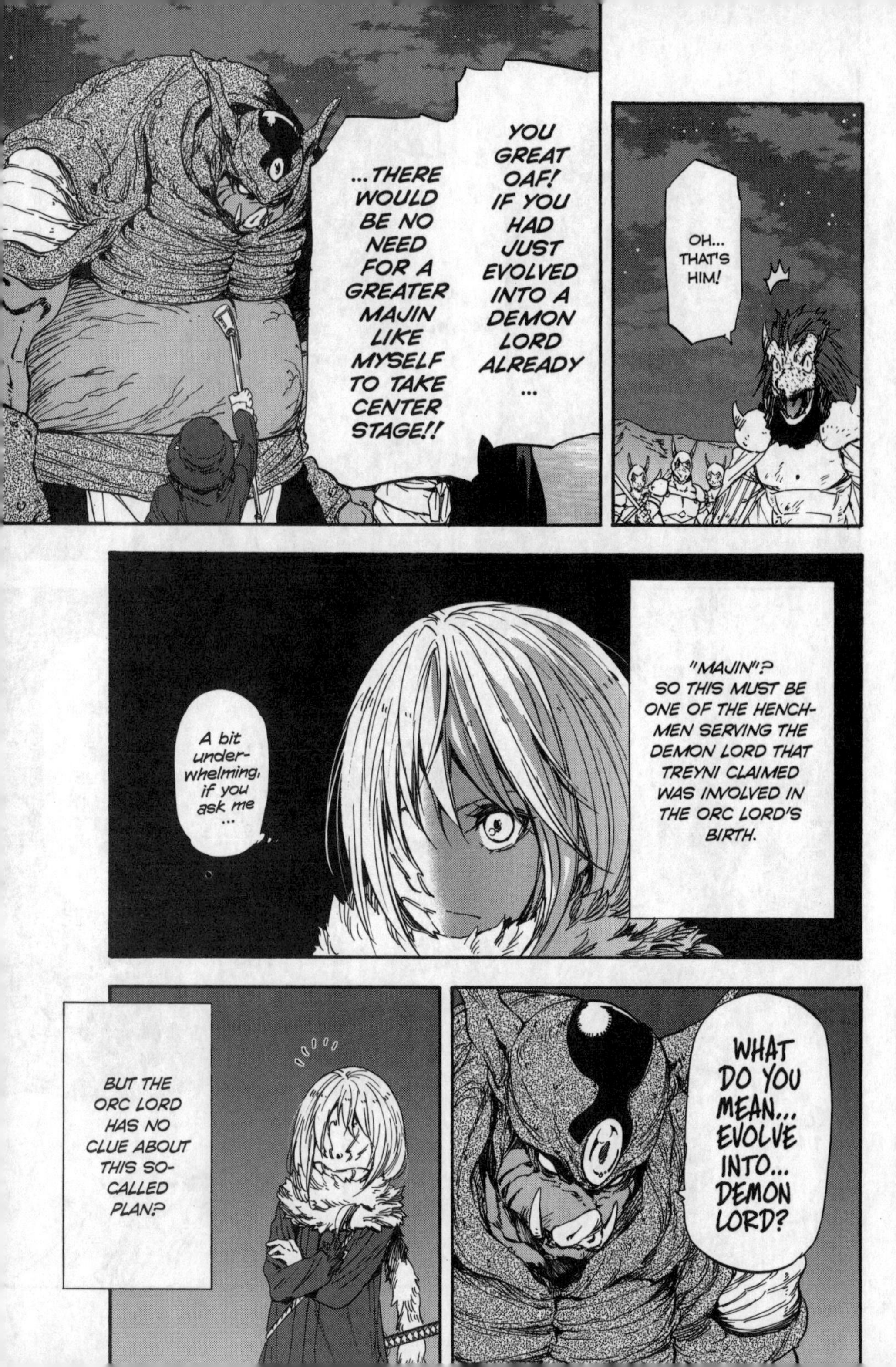
OH... THAT'S HIM!
YOU GREAT OAF! IF YOU HAD JUST EVOLVED INTO A DEMON LORD ALREADY...
...THERE WOULD BE NO NEED FOR A GREATER MAJIN LIKE MYSELF TO TAKE CENTER STAGE!!
"MAJIN"? SO THIS MUST BE ONE OF THE HENCH-MEN SERVING THE DEMON LORD THAT TREYNI CLAIMED WAS INVOLVED IN THE ORC LORD'S BIRTH.
A bit under-whelming, if you ask me...
WHAT DO YOU MEAN... EVOLVE INTO... DEMON LORD?
BUT THE ORC LORD HAS NO CLUE ABOUT THIS SO-CALLED PLAN?

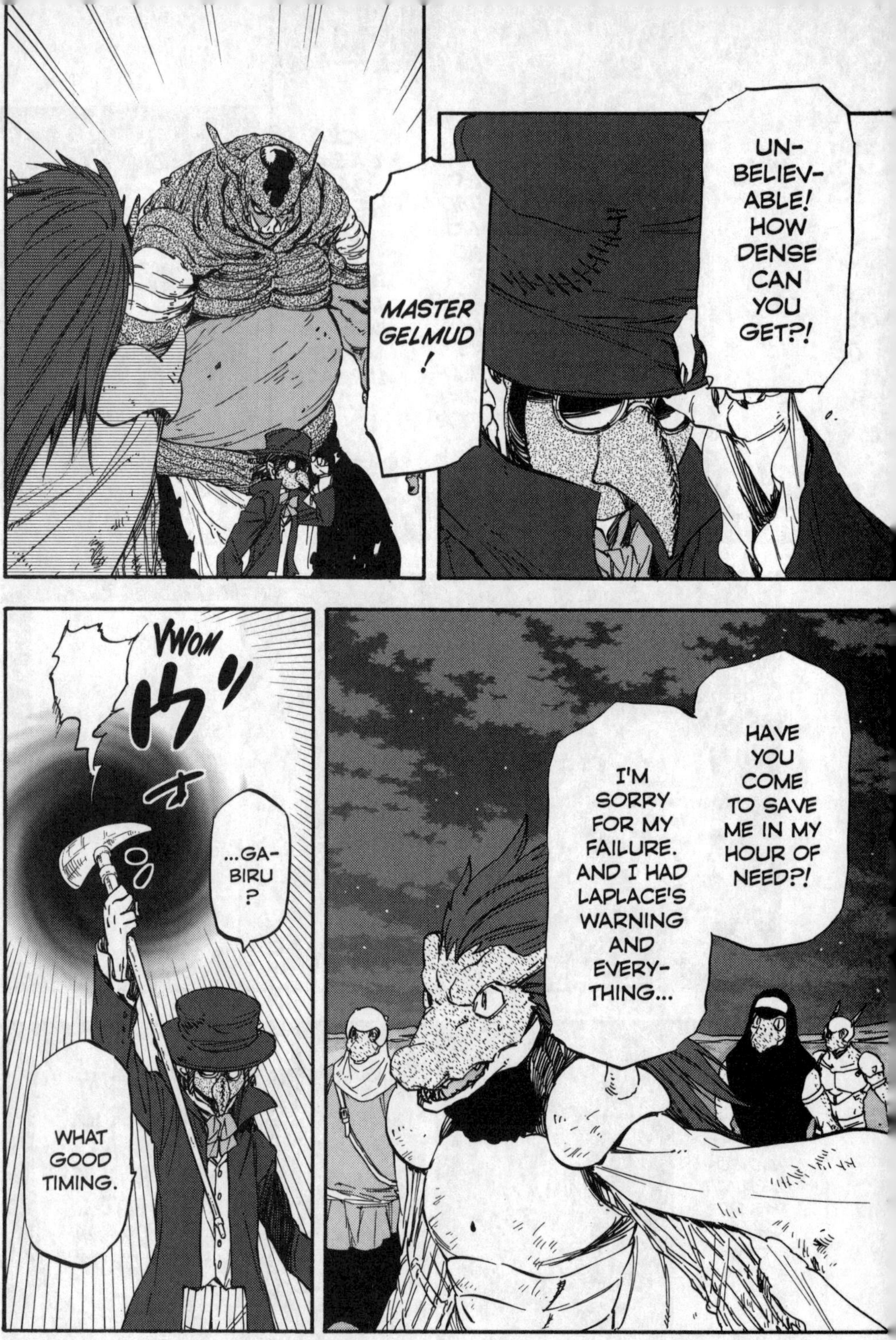
UN-BELIEVABLE! HOW DENSE CAN YOU GET?!
MASTER GELMUD!
HAVE YOU COME TO SAVE ME IN MY HOUR OF NEED?!
I'M SORRY FOR MY FAILURE. AND I HAD LAPLACE'S WARNING AND EVERYTHING...
VWOM
...GABIRU?
WHAT GOOD TIMING.

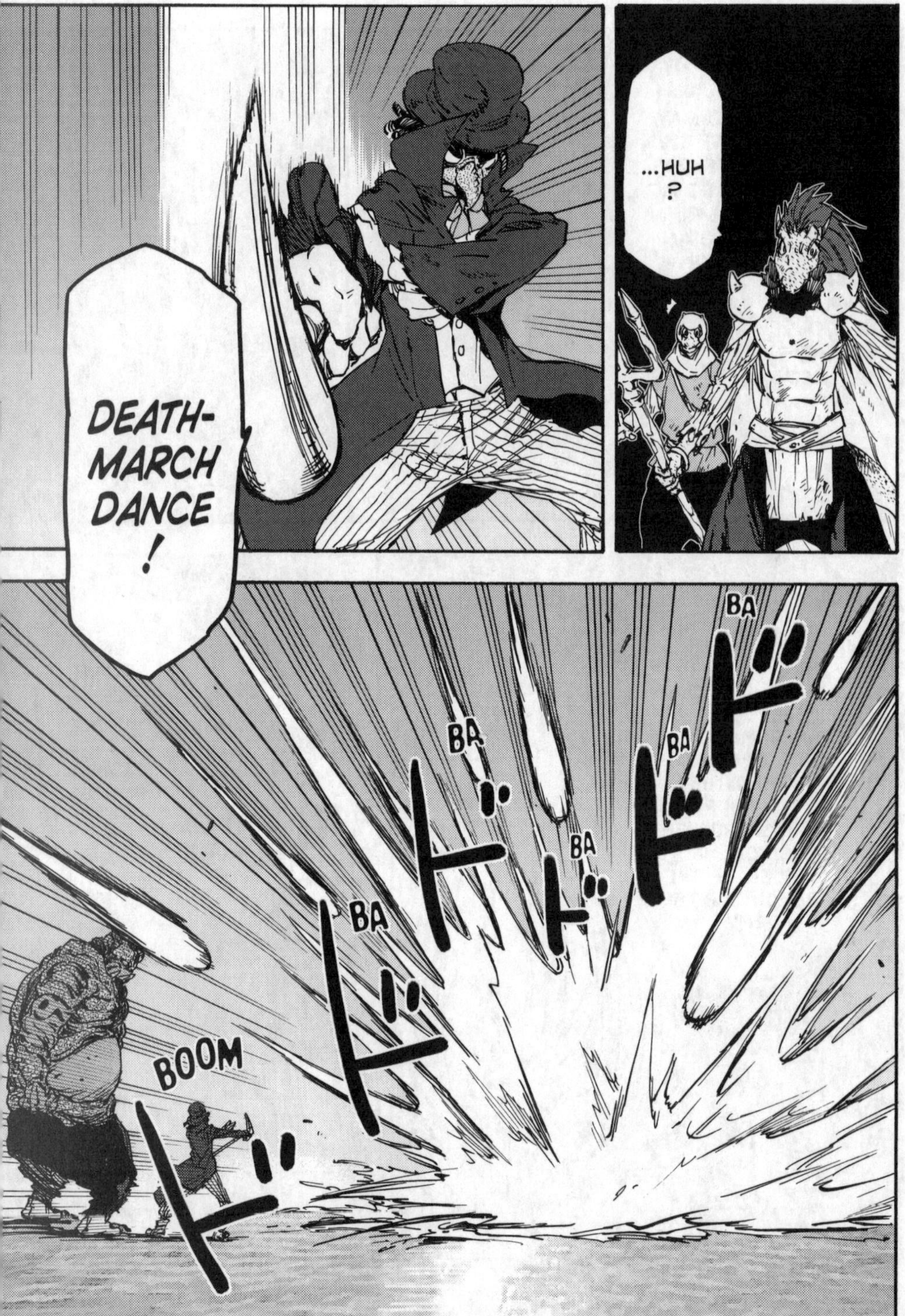
...HUH
?
DEATH-
MARCH
DANCE
!
BA
BA
BA
BA
BA
BOOM

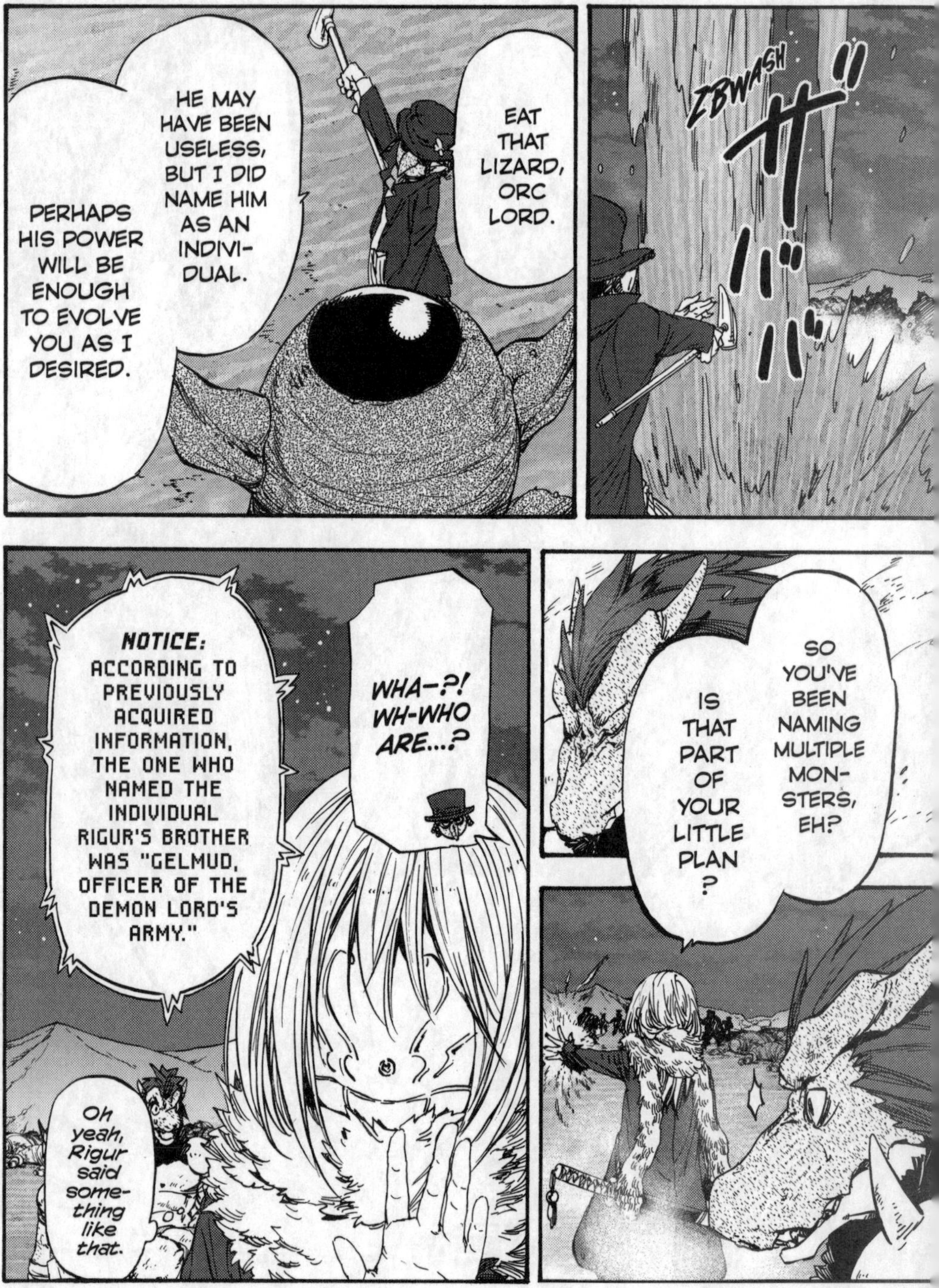
ZBWASH!!
EAT THAT LIZARD, ORC LORD.
HE MAY HAVE BEEN USELESS, BUT I DID NAME HIM AS AN INDIVIDUAL.
PERHAPS HIS POWER WILL BE ENOUGH TO EVOLVE YOU AS I DESIRED.
SO YOU'VE BEEN NAMING MULTIPLE MONSTERS, EH?
IS THAT PART OF YOUR LITTLE PLAN?
WHA-?! WH-WHO ARE...?
NOTICE: ACCORDING TO PREVIOUSLY ACQUIRED INFORMATION, THE ONE WHO NAMED THE INDIVIDUAL RIGUR'S BROTHER WAS "GELMUD, OFFICER OF THE DEMON LORD'S ARMY."
Oh yeah, Rigur said something like that.

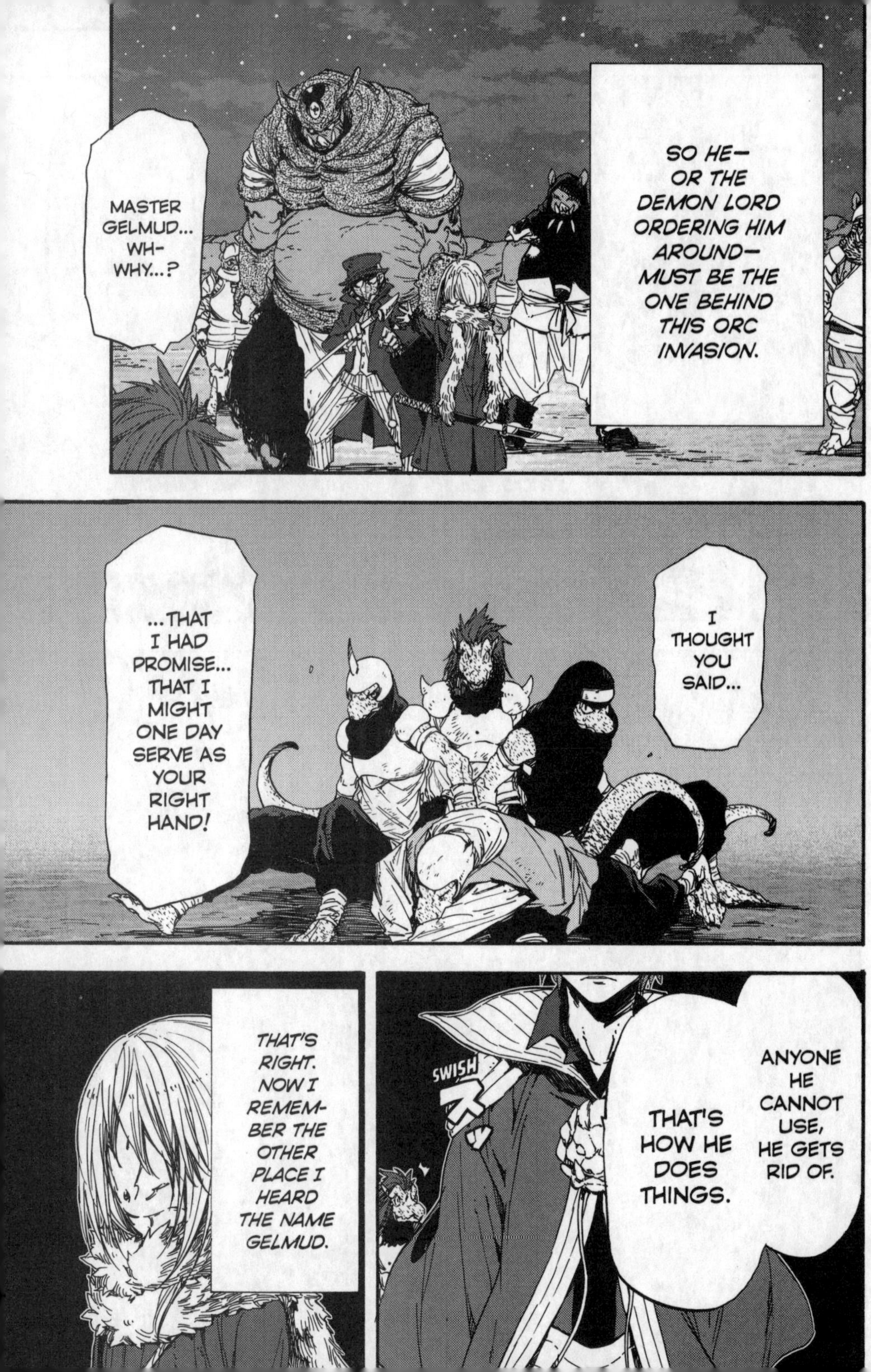
SO HE— OR THE DEMON LORD ORDERING HIM AROUND— MUST BE THE ONE BEHIND THIS ORC INVASION.
MASTER GELMUD... WH- WHY...?
I THOUGHT YOU SAID...
...THAT I HAD PROMISE... THAT I MIGHT ONE DAY SERVE AS YOUR RIGHT HAND!
ANYONE HE CANNOT USE, HE GETS RID OF.
THAT'S HOW HE DOES THINGS.
SWISH
THAT'S RIGHT. NOW I REMEMBER THE OTHER PLACE I HEARD THE NAME GELMUD.

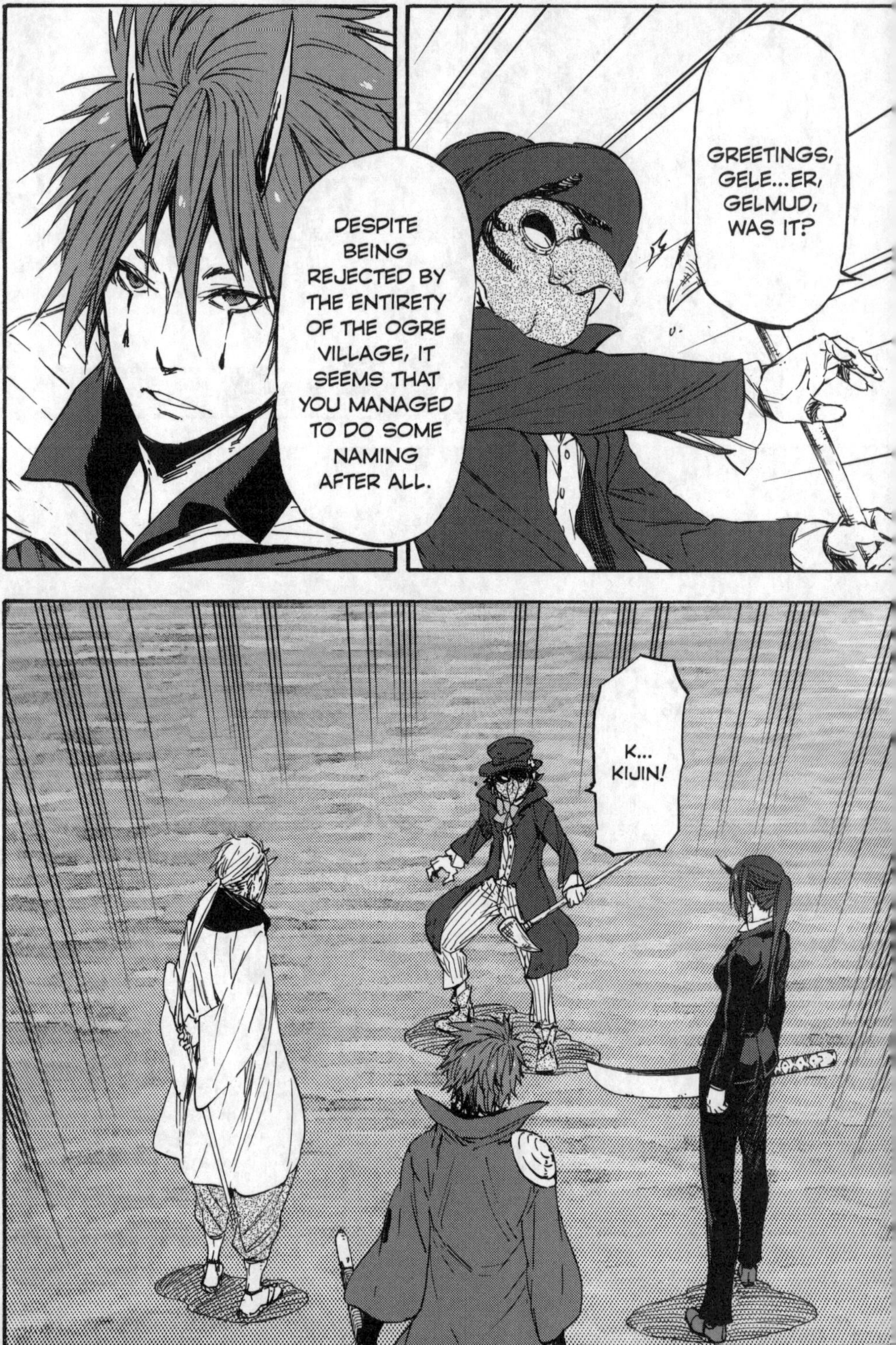
GREETINGS, GELE...ER, GELMUD, WAS IT?
DESPITE BEING REJECTED BY THE ENTIRETY OF THE OGRE VILLAGE, IT SEEMS THAT YOU MANAGED TO DO SOME NAMING AFTER ALL.
K... KIJIN!

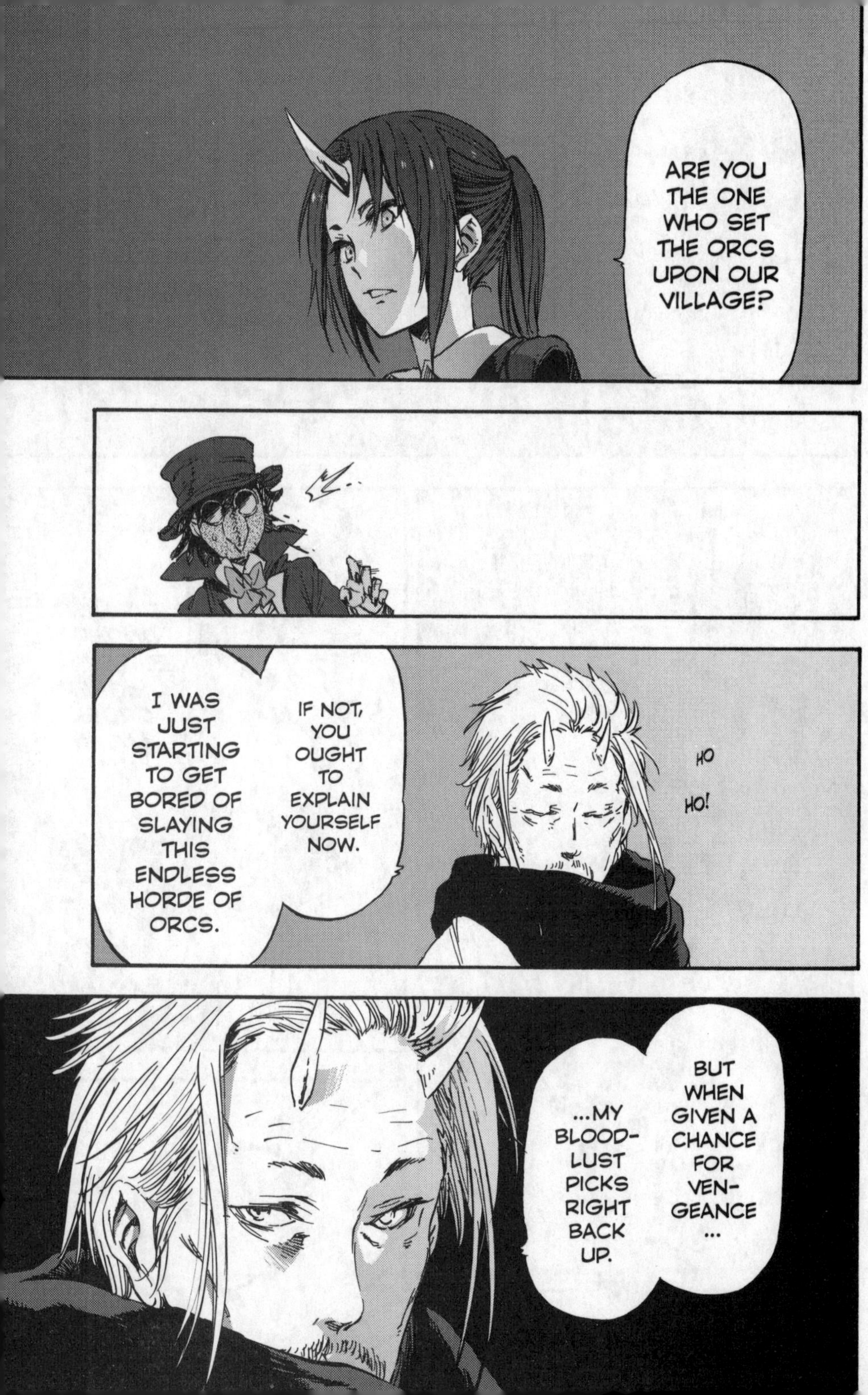
ARE YOU THE ONE WHO SET THE ORCS UPON OUR VILLAGE?
HO HO!
IF NOT, YOU OUGHT TO EXPLAIN YOURSELF NOW.
I WAS JUST STARTING TO GET BORED OF SLAYING THIS ENDLESS HORDE OF ORCS.
BUT WHEN GIVEN A CHANCE FOR VEN-GEANCE...
...MY BLOOD-LUST PICKS RIGHT BACK UP.

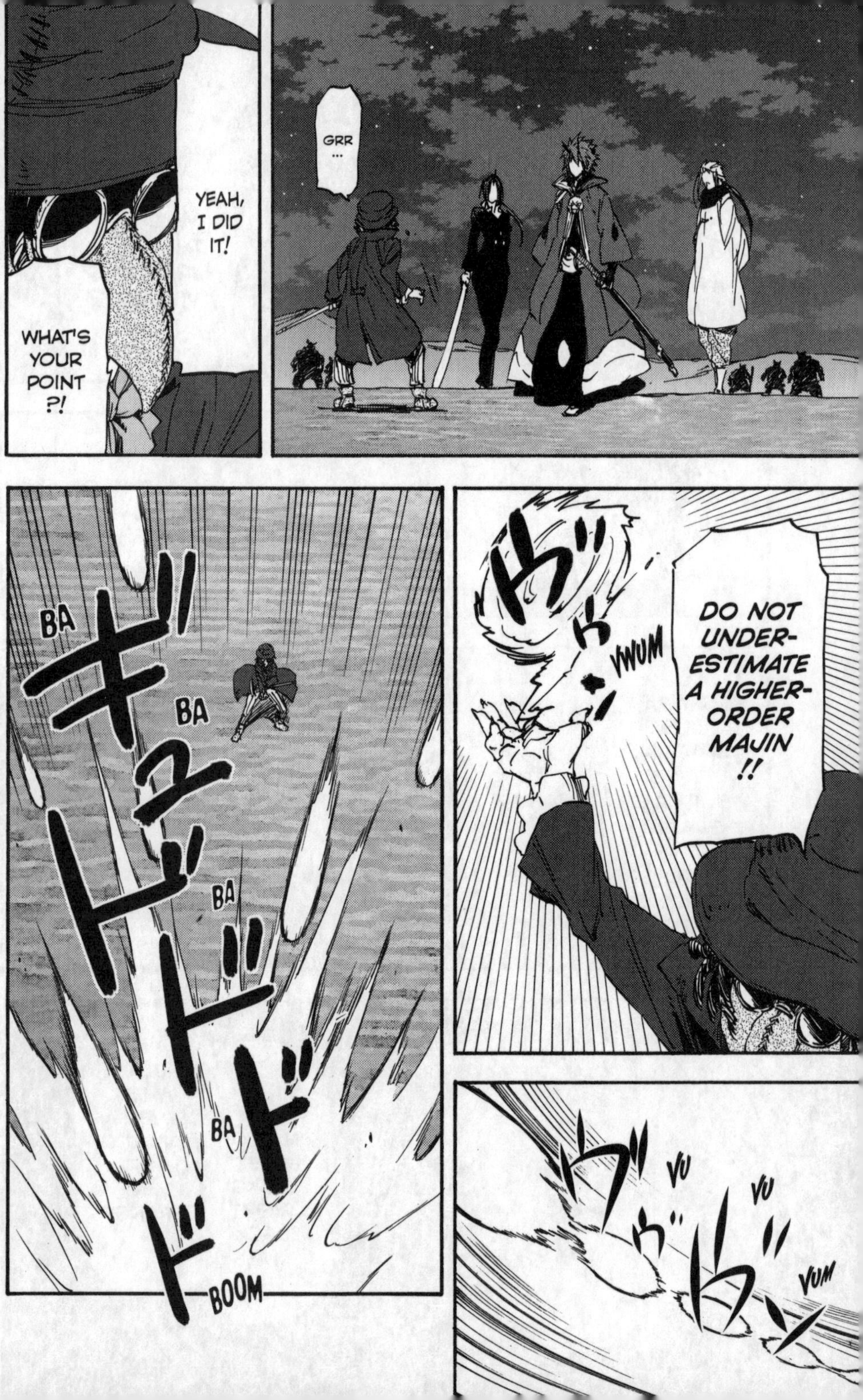
GRR ...
YEAH, I DID IT!
WHAT'S YOUR POINT ?!
VWUM
DO NOT UNDER-ESTIMATE A HIGHER-ORDER MAJIN !!
VU
VU
VUM
BA
BA
BA
BA
BOOM

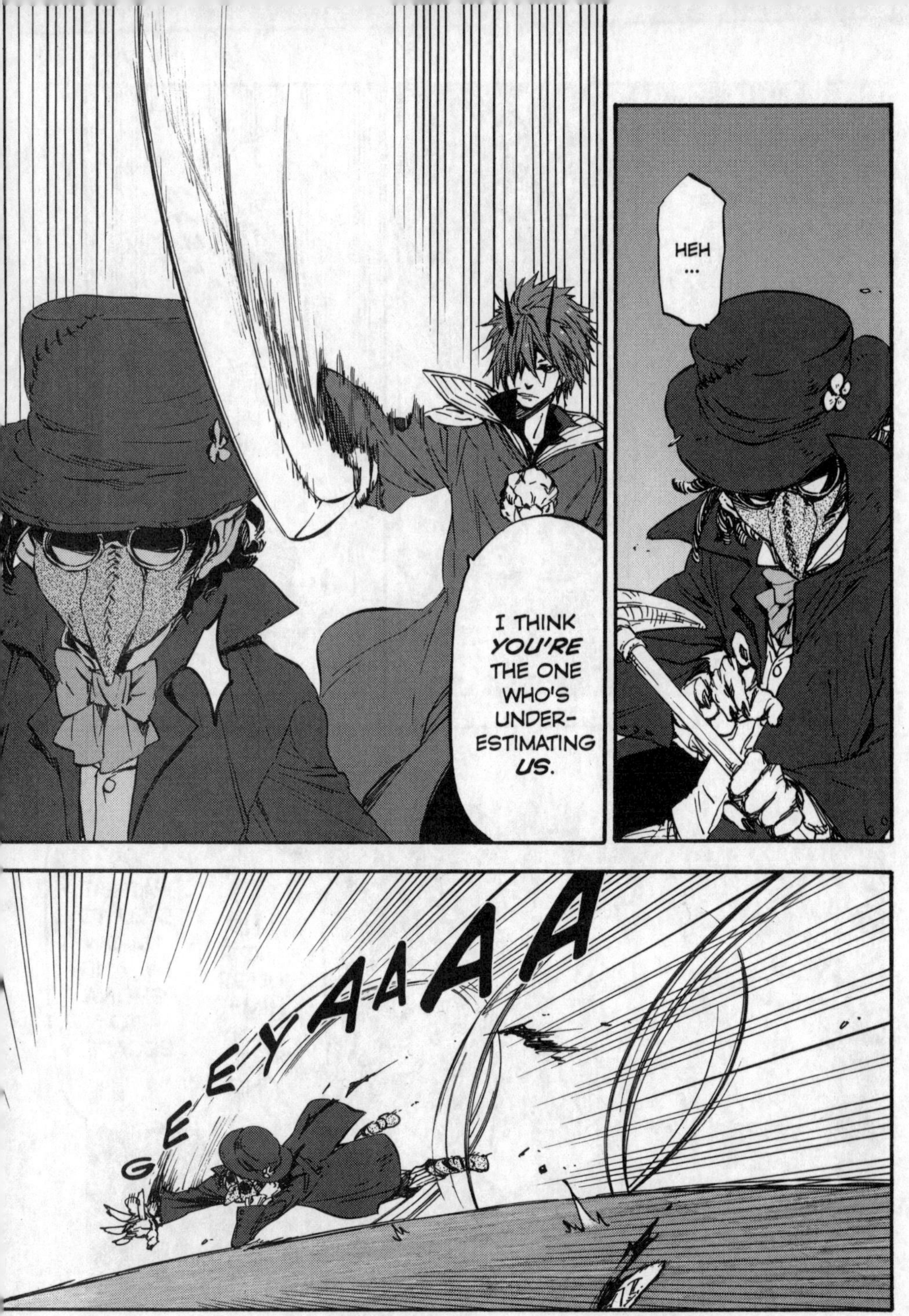
HEH ...
I THINK *YOU'RE* THE ONE WHO'S UNDER-ESTIMATING *US*.
GEEYAAAAA

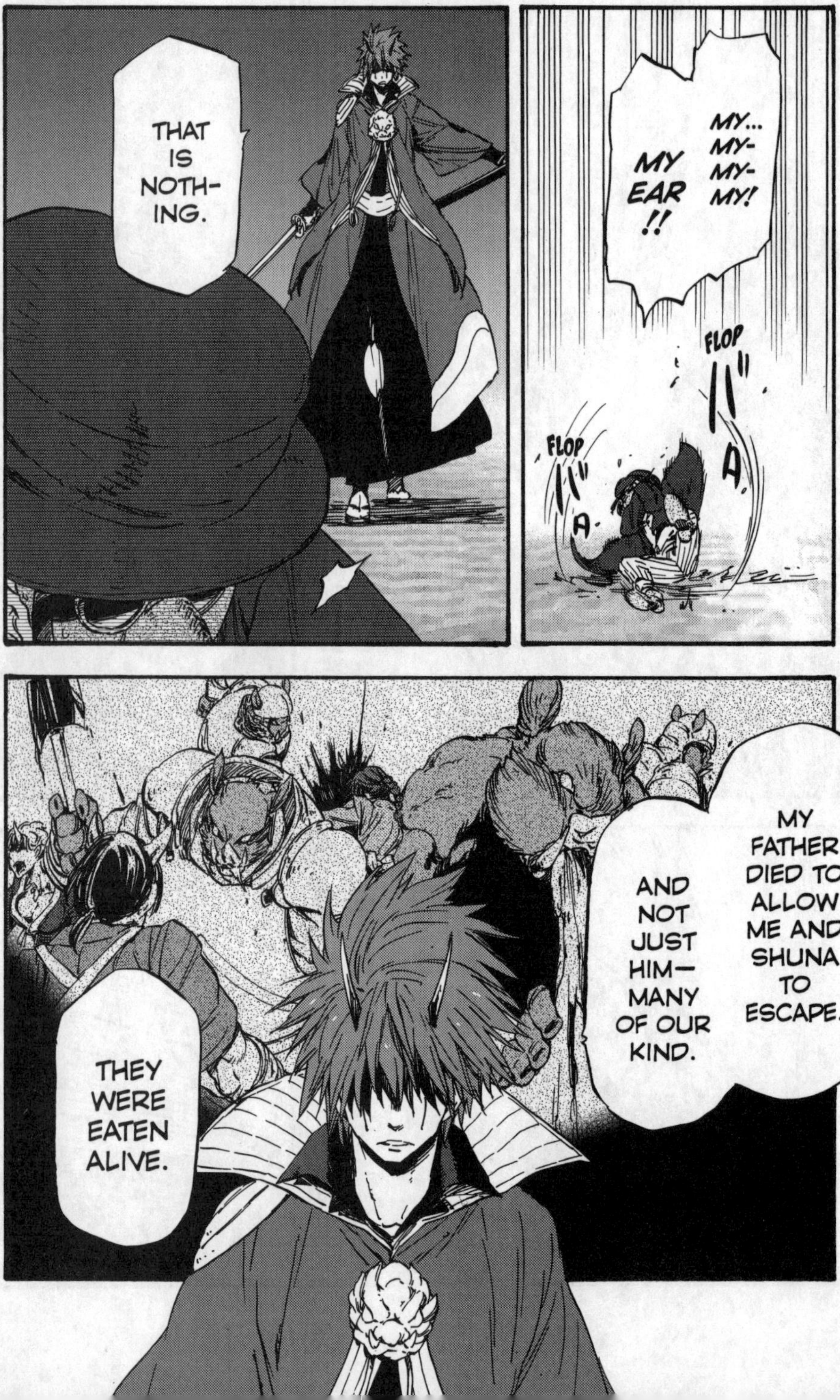
MY... MY-MY-MY! MY EAR!!
FLOP
A
FLOP
A
THAT IS NOTHING.
MY FATHER DIED TO ALLOW ME AND SHUNA TO ESCAPE.
AND NOT JUST HIM—MANY OF OUR KIND.
THEY WERE EATEN ALIVE.

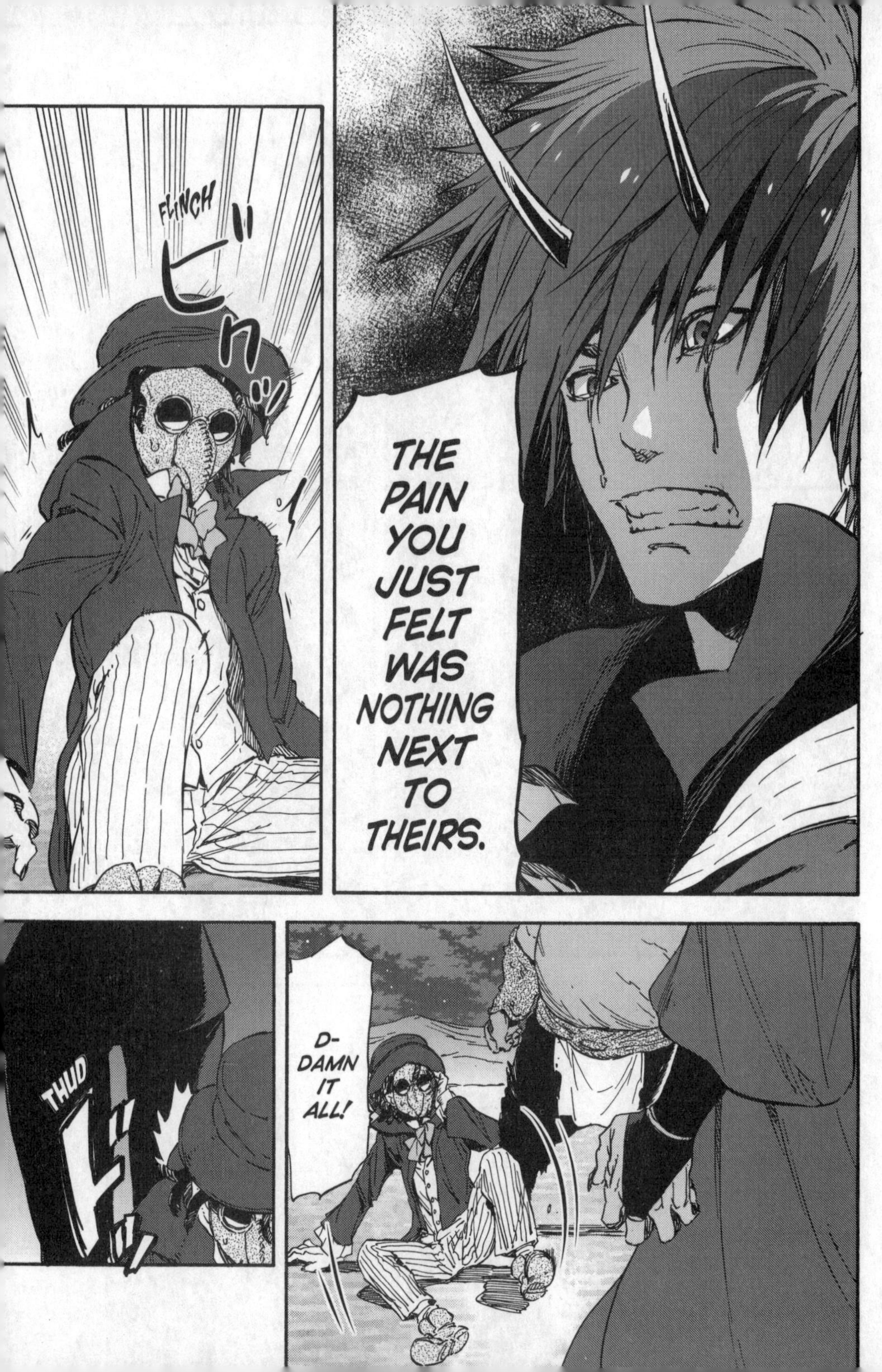
THE PAIN YOU JUST FELT WAS NOTHING NEXT TO THEIRS.
FLINCH
D-DAMN IT ALL!
THUD

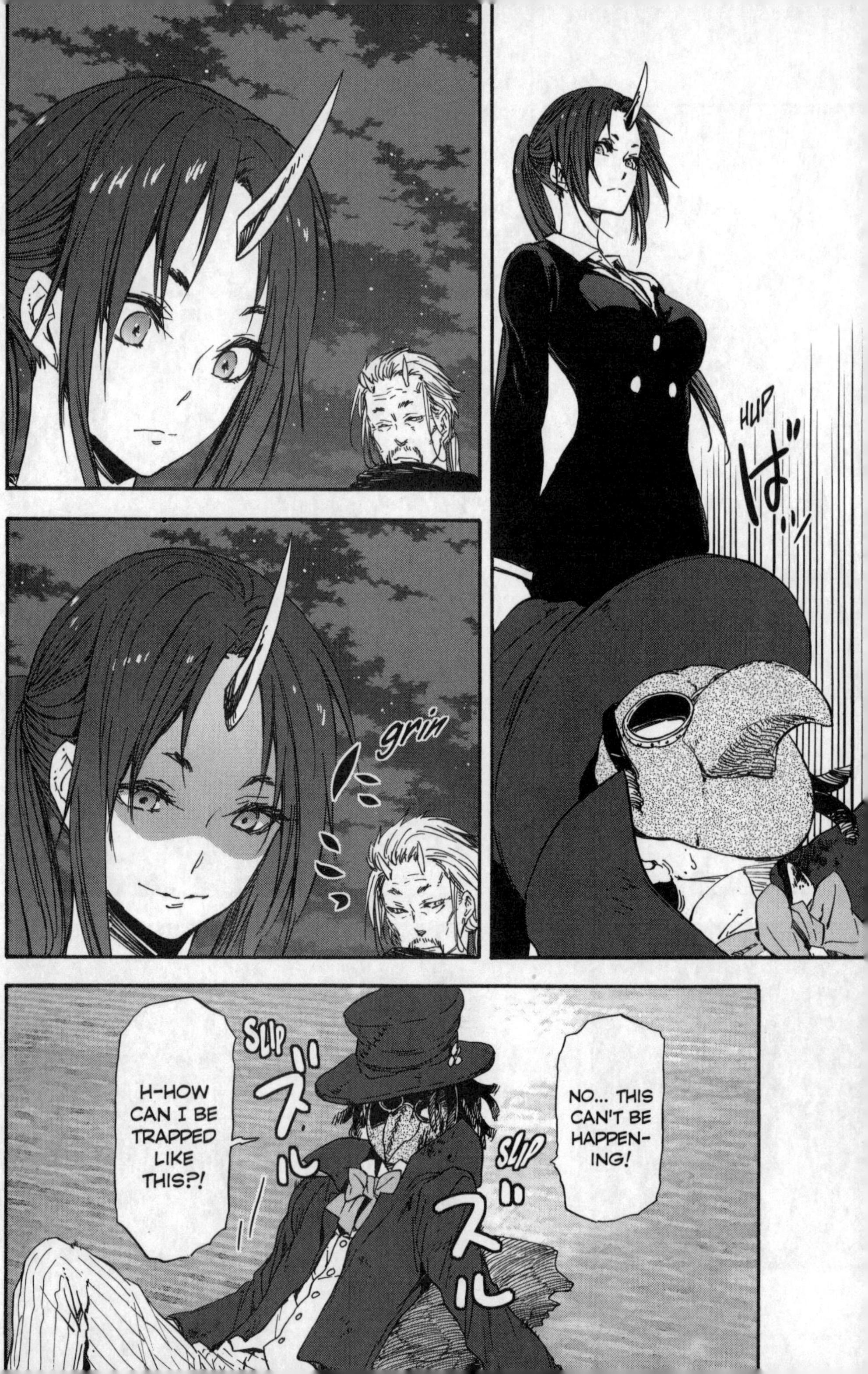

HUP
grin
NO... THIS CAN'T BE HAPPEN-ING!
SLIP
SLIP
H-HOW CAN I BE TRAPPED LIKE THIS?!

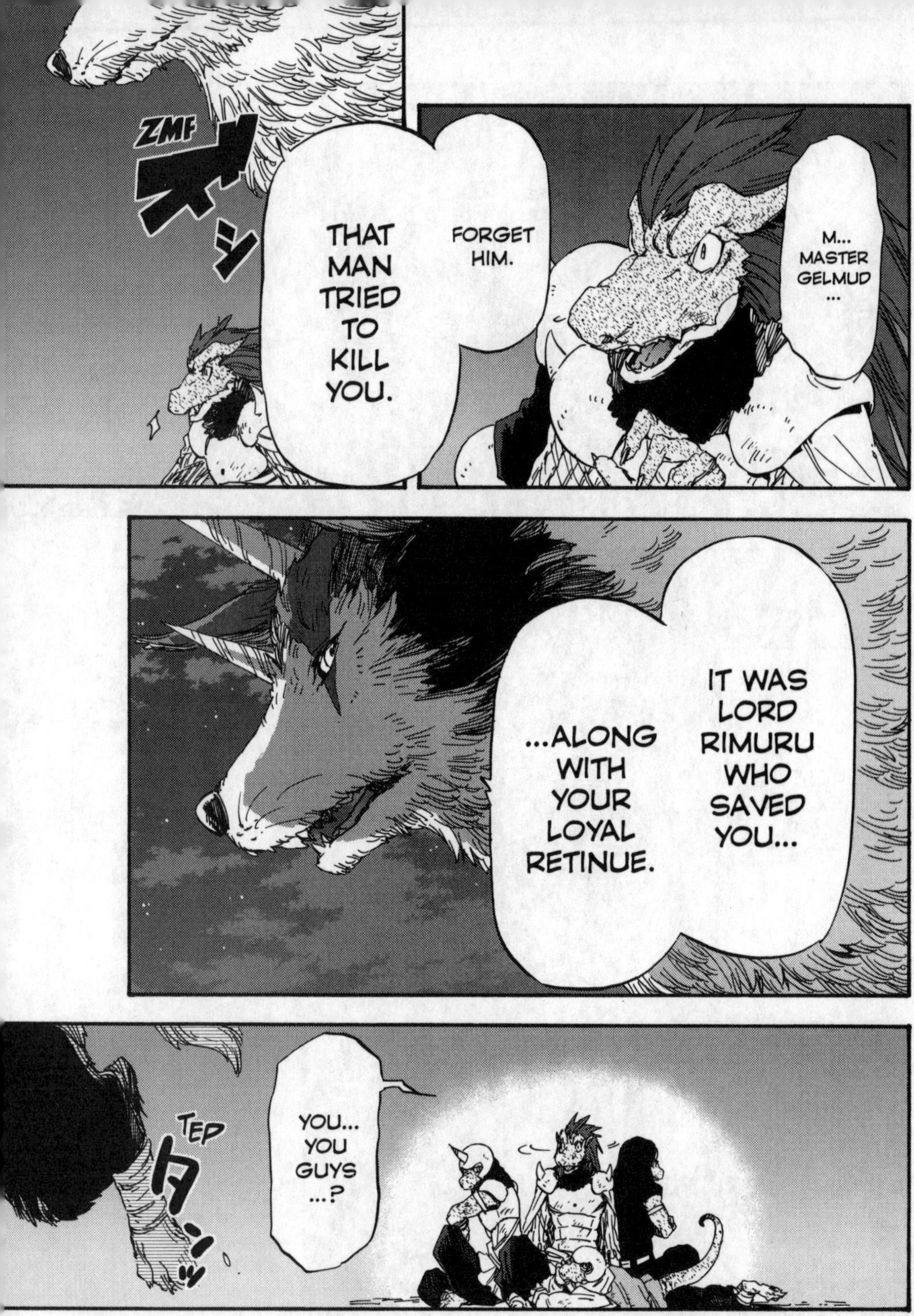
M... MASTER GELMUD ...
FORGET HIM.
THAT MAN TRIED TO KILL YOU.
ZMF
IT WAS LORD RIMURU WHO SAVED YOU...
...ALONG WITH YOUR LOYAL RETINUE.
YOU... YOU GUYS ...?
TEP

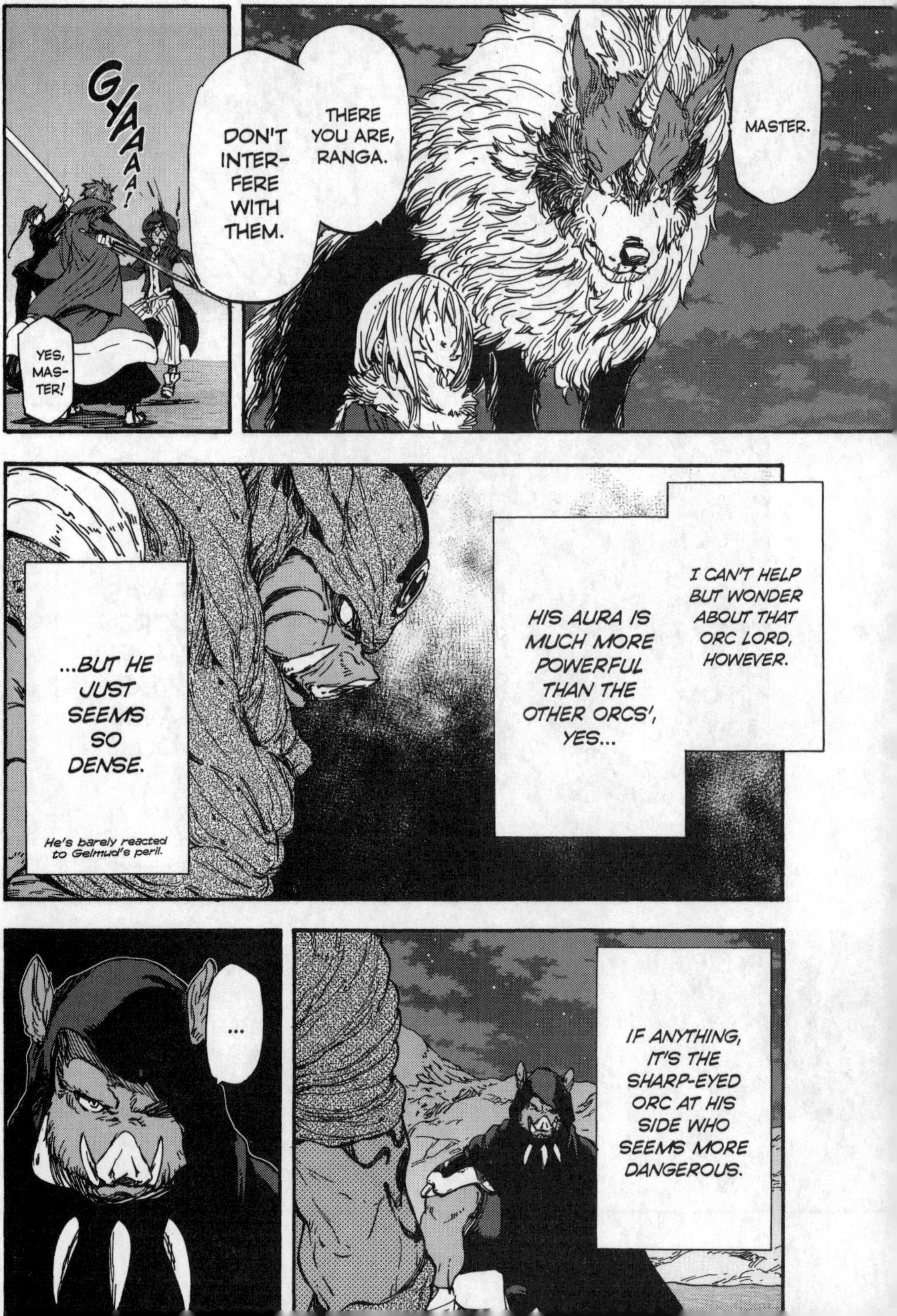
MASTER.
THERE YOU ARE, RANGA.
DON'T INTERFERE WITH THEM.
GYAAAAA!
YES, MASTER!
I CAN'T HELP BUT WONDER ABOUT THAT ORC LORD, HOWEVER.
HIS AURA IS MUCH MORE POWERFUL THAN THE OTHER ORCS', YES...
...BUT HE JUST SEEMS SO DENSE.
He's barely reacted to Gelmud's peril.
IF ANYTHING, IT'S THE SHARP-EYED ORC AT HIS SIDE WHO SEEMS MORE DANGEROUS.
...

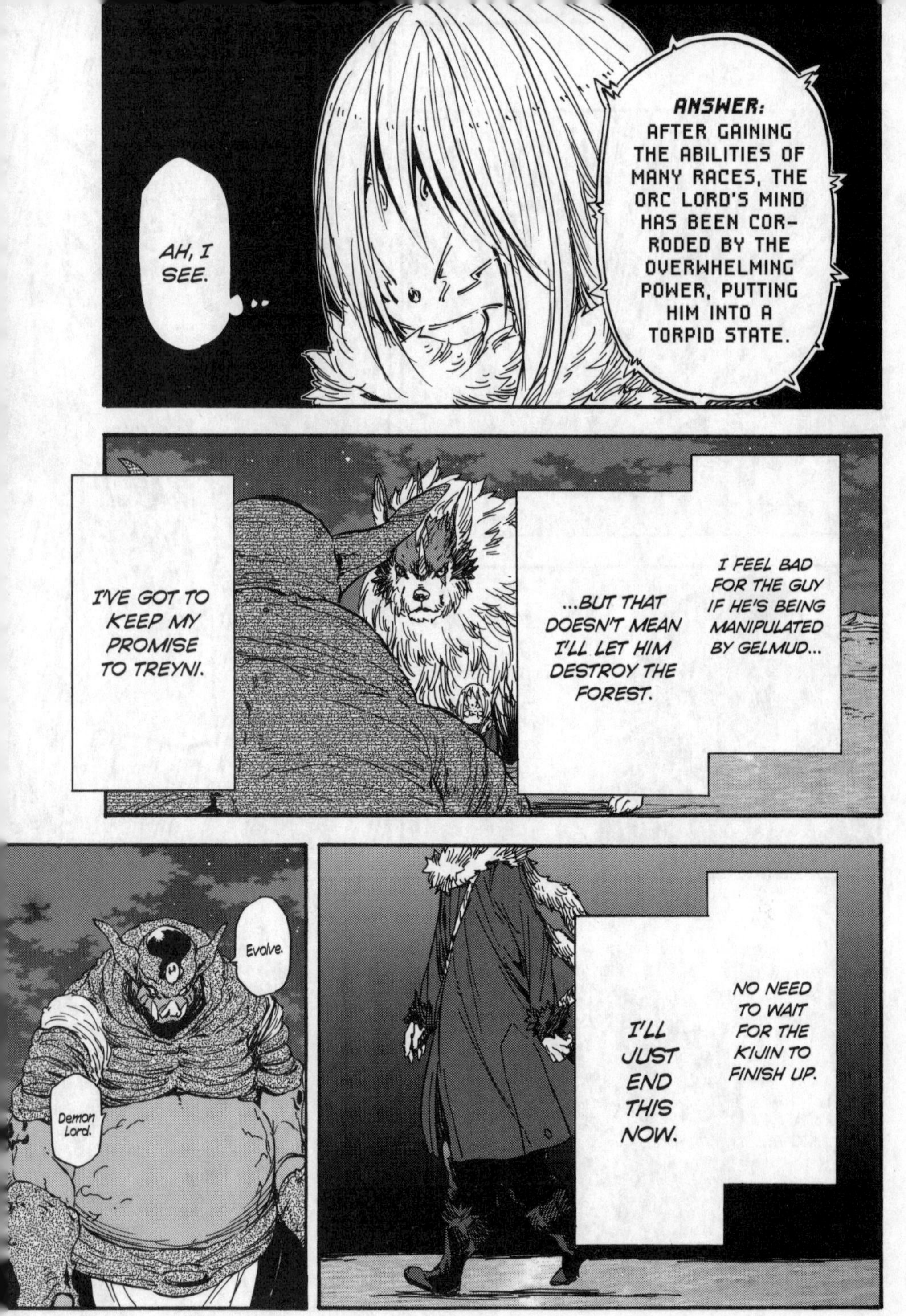
ANSWER: AFTER GAINING THE ABILITIES OF MANY RACES, THE ORC LORD'S MIND HAS BEEN COR-RODED BY THE OVERWHELMING POWER, PUTTING HIM INTO A TORPID STATE.
AH, I SEE.
I FEEL BAD FOR THE GUY IF HE'S BEING MANIPULATED BY GELMUD...
...BUT THAT DOESN'T MEAN I'LL LET HIM DESTROY THE FOREST.
I'VE GOT TO KEEP MY PROMISE TO TREYNI.
NO NEED TO WAIT FOR THE KIJIN TO FINISH UP.
I'LL JUST END THIS NOW.
Evolve.
Demon Lord.

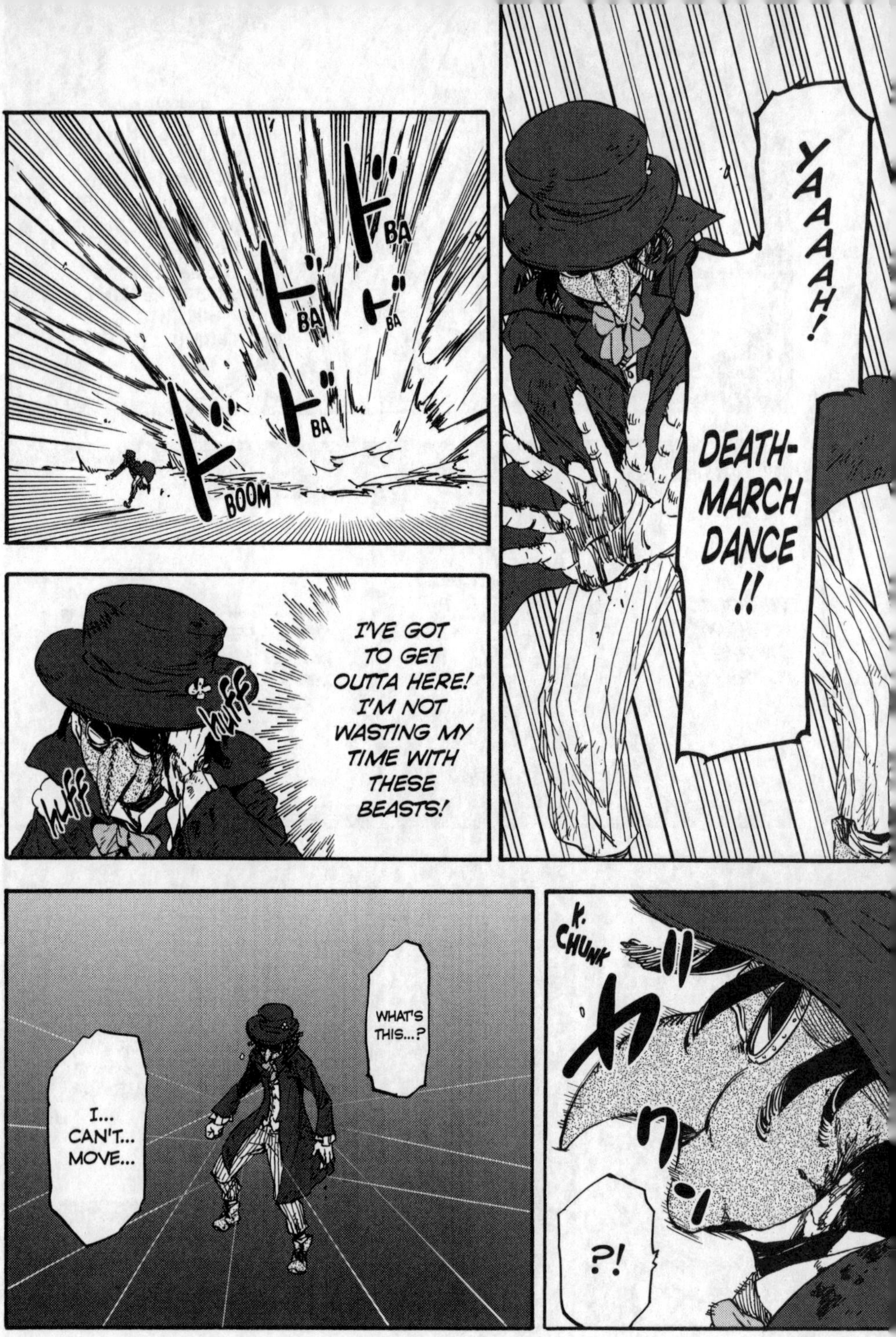
YAAAAAH!
DEATH-MARCH DANCE!!
BA
BA
BA
BA
BOOM
huff
huff
I'VE GOT TO GET OUTTA HERE! I'M NOT WASTING MY TIME WITH THESE BEASTS!
K-CHUNK
?!
WHAT'S THIS...?
I... CAN'T... MOVE...

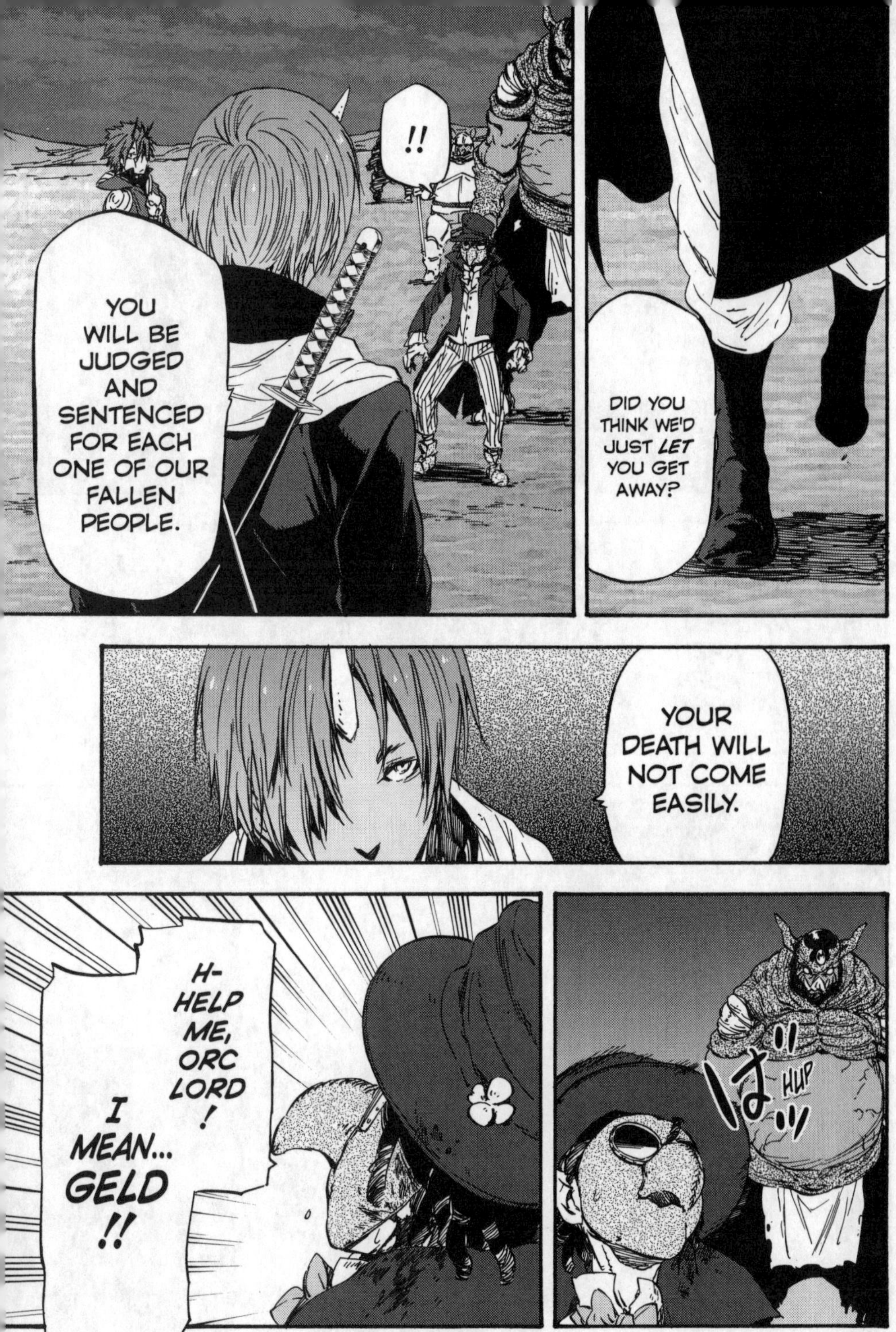
DID YOU THINK WE'D JUST *LET* YOU GET AWAY?
!!
YOU WILL BE JUDGED AND SENTENCED FOR EACH ONE OF OUR FALLEN PEOPLE.
YOUR DEATH WILL NOT COME EASILY.
はッ
HUP
H-HELP ME, ORC LORD!
I MEAN... GELD!!

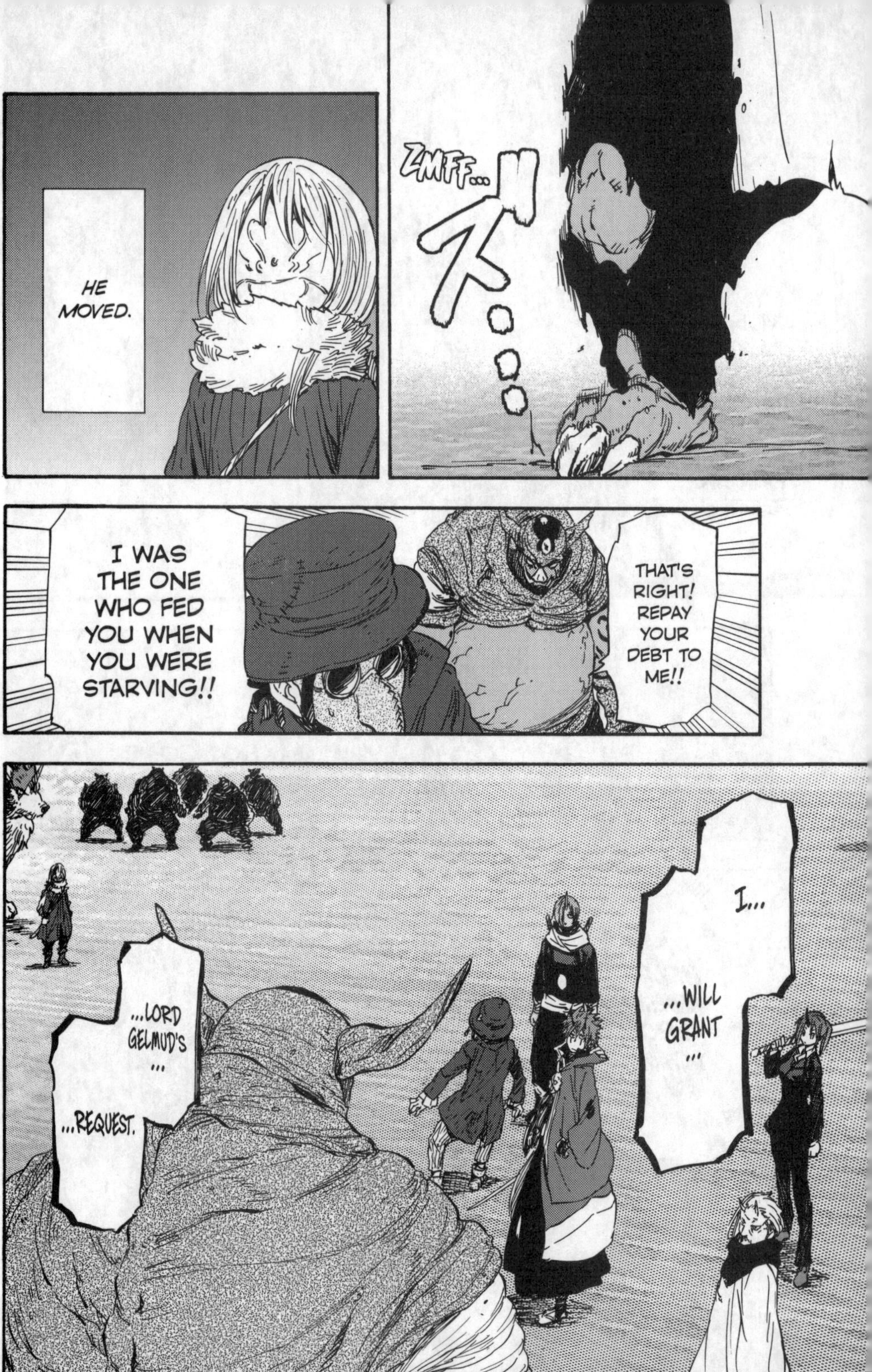
ZMFF...
HE MOVED.
THAT'S RIGHT! REPAY YOUR DEBT TO ME!!
I WAS THE ONE WHO FED YOU WHEN YOU WERE STARVING!!
I...
...WILL GRANT ...
...LORD GELMUD'S ...
...REQUEST.

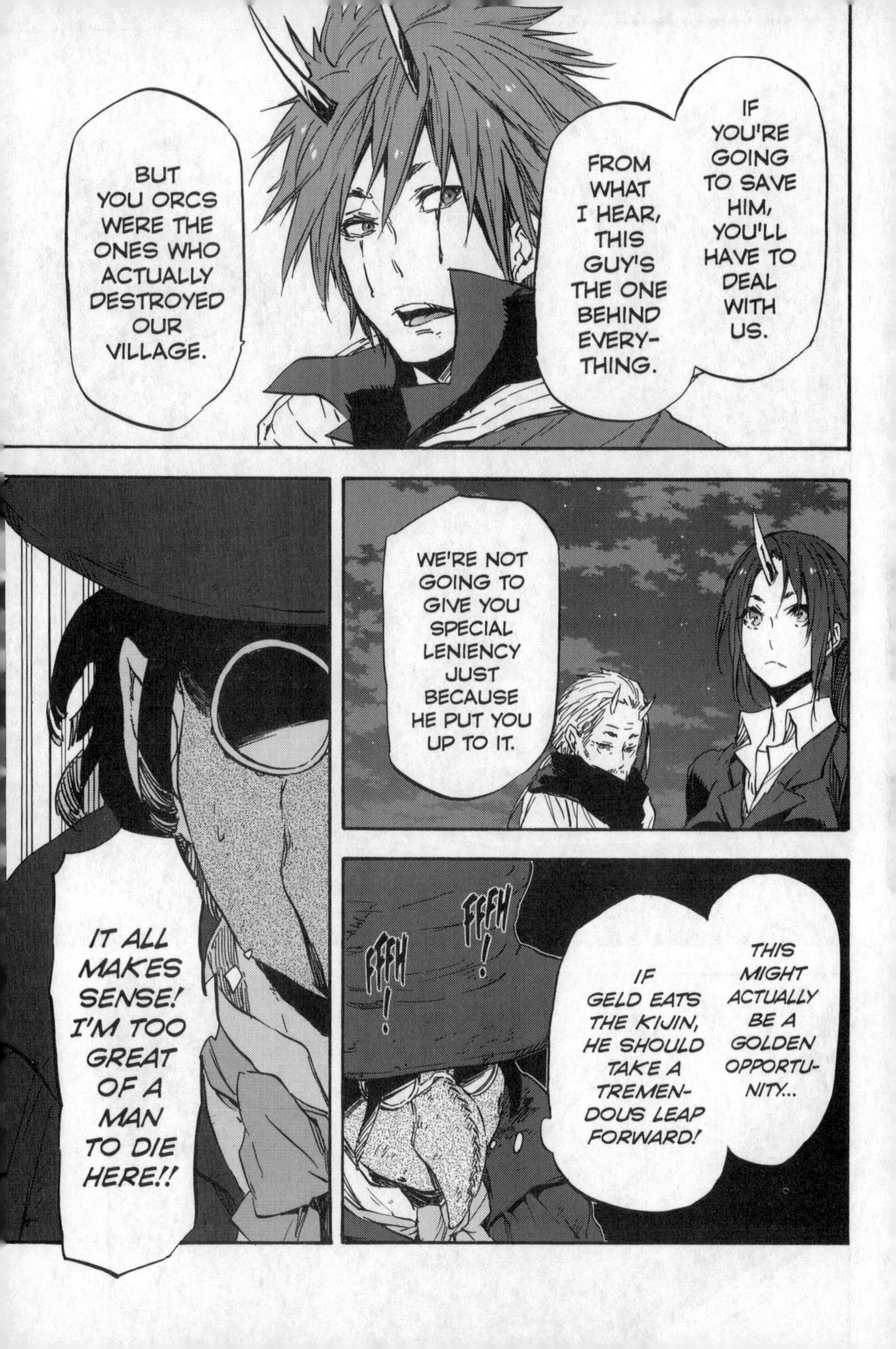
IF YOU'RE GOING TO SAVE HIM, YOU'LL HAVE TO DEAL WITH US.
FROM WHAT I HEAR, THIS GUY'S THE ONE BEHIND EVERYTHING.
BUT YOU ORCS WERE THE ONES WHO ACTUALLY DESTROYED OUR VILLAGE.
WE'RE NOT GOING TO GIVE YOU SPECIAL LENIENCY JUST BECAUSE HE PUT YOU UP TO IT.
FFFH!
FFFH!
THIS MIGHT ACTUALLY BE A GOLDEN OPPORTUNITY...
IF GELD EATS THE KIJIN, HE SHOULD TAKE A TREMENDOUS LEAP FORWARD!
IT ALL MAKES SENSE! I'M TOO GREAT OF A MAN TO DIE HERE!!

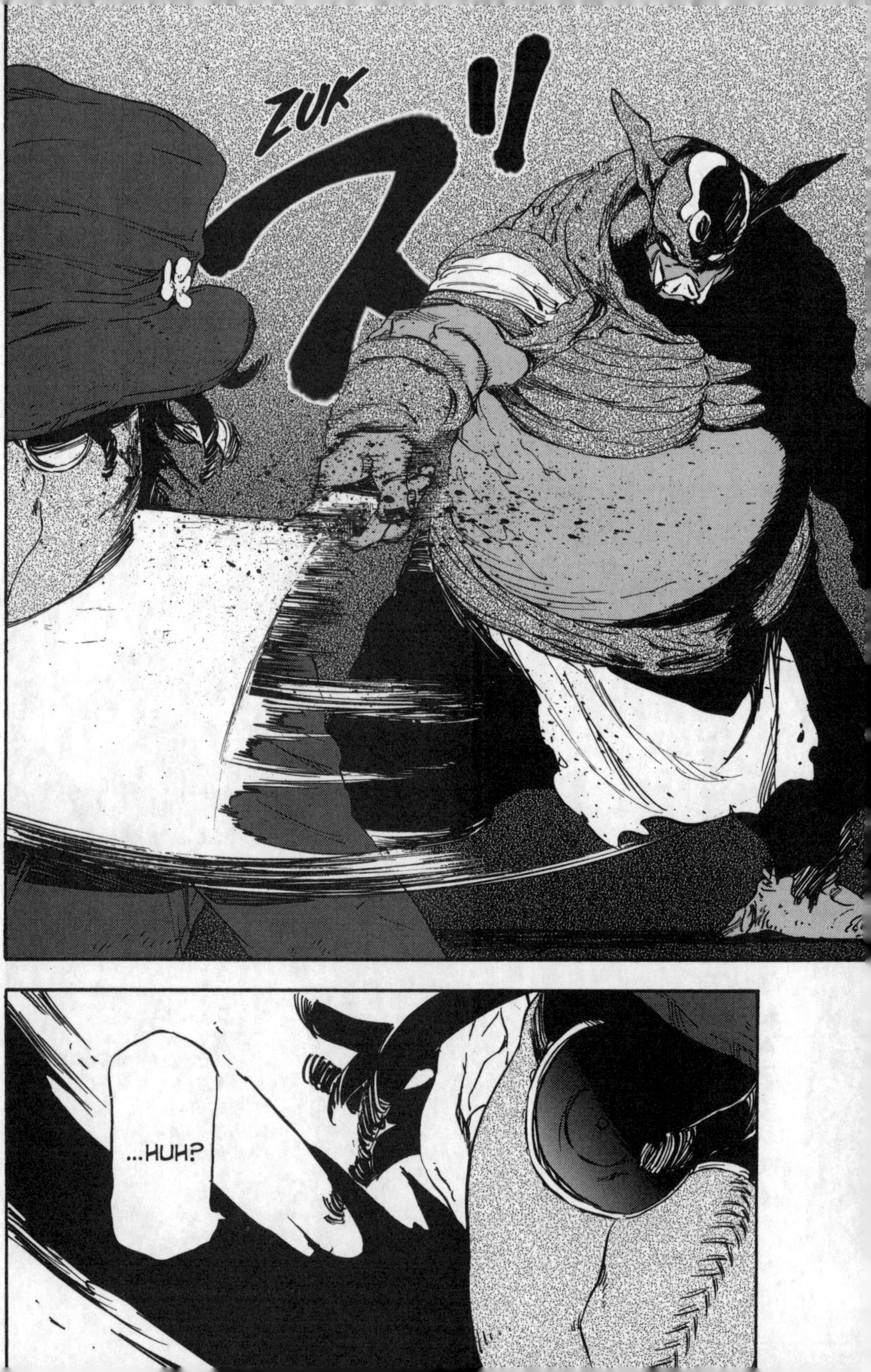
ZUK
...HUH?

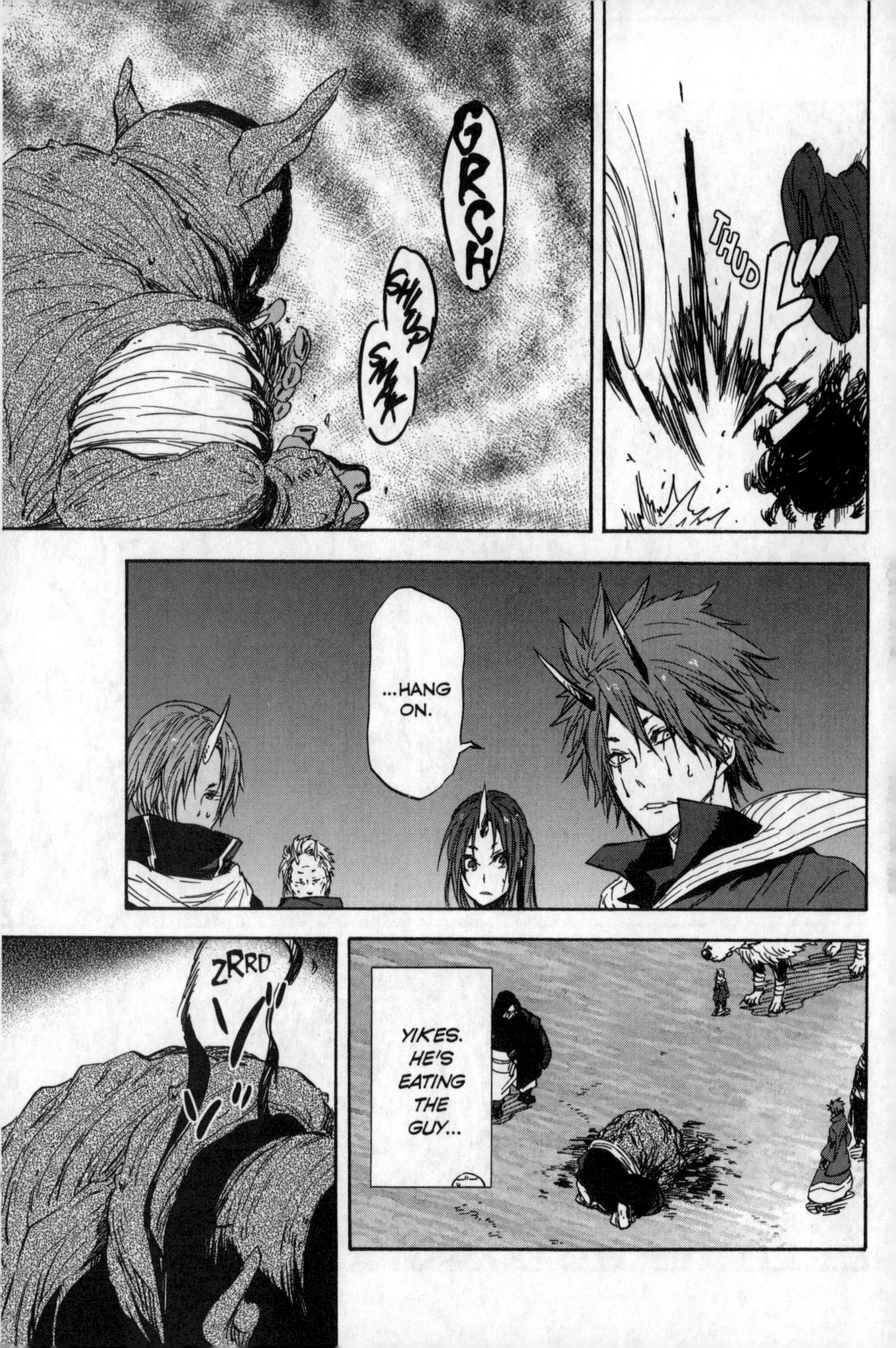
THUD
GRCH
SHLUP
SMAK
...HANG ON.
YIKES. HE'S EATING THE GUY...
ZRRD

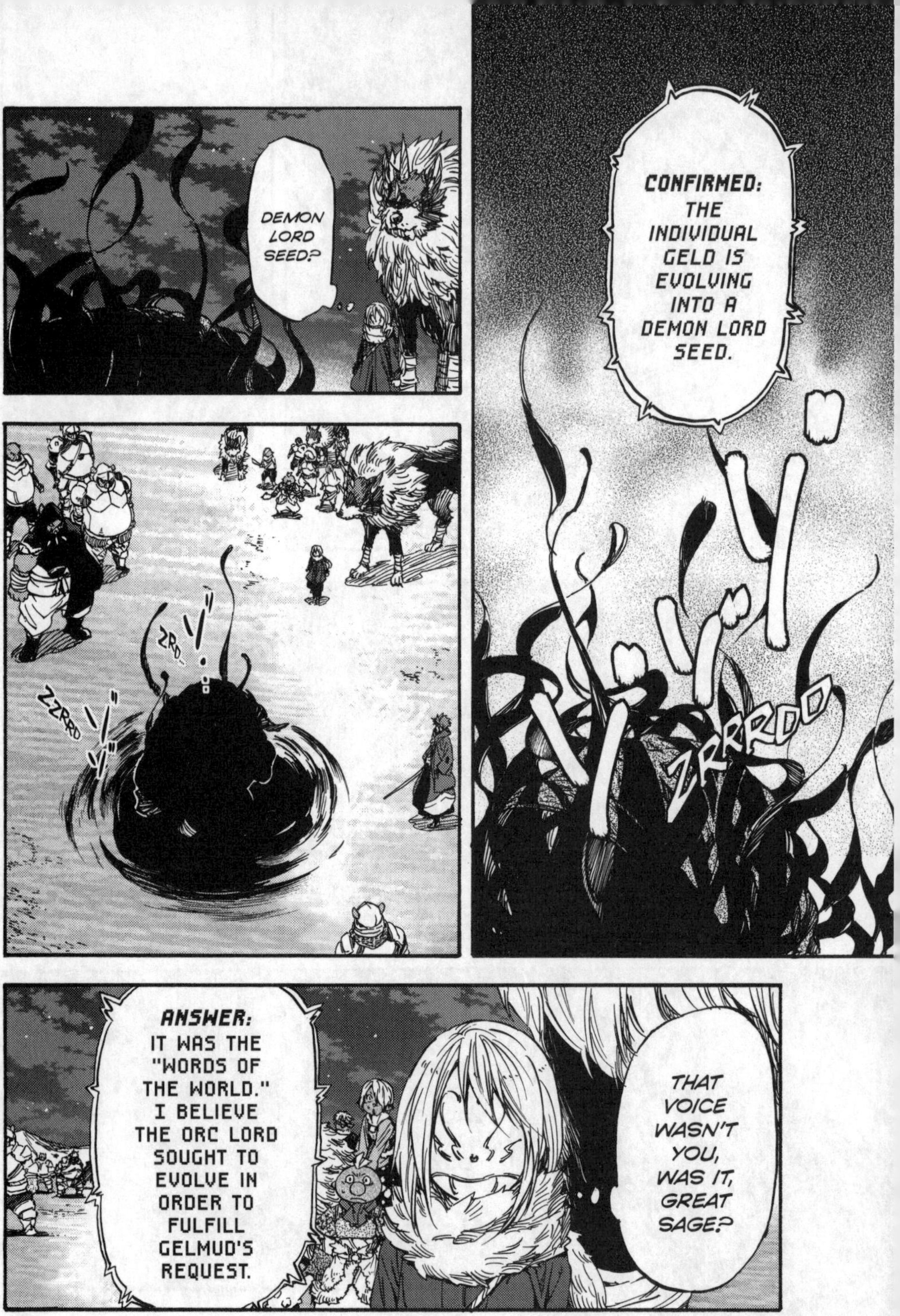
CONFIRMED: THE INDIVIDUAL GELD IS EVOLVING INTO A DEMON LORD SEED.
ZRRRDO
DEMON LORD SEED?
ZRD...
Z-ZRRD
THAT VOICE WASN'T YOU, WAS IT, GREAT SAGE?
ANSWER: IT WAS THE "WORDS OF THE WORLD." I BELIEVE THE ORC LORD SOUGHT TO EVOLVE IN ORDER TO FULFILL GELMUD'S REQUEST.

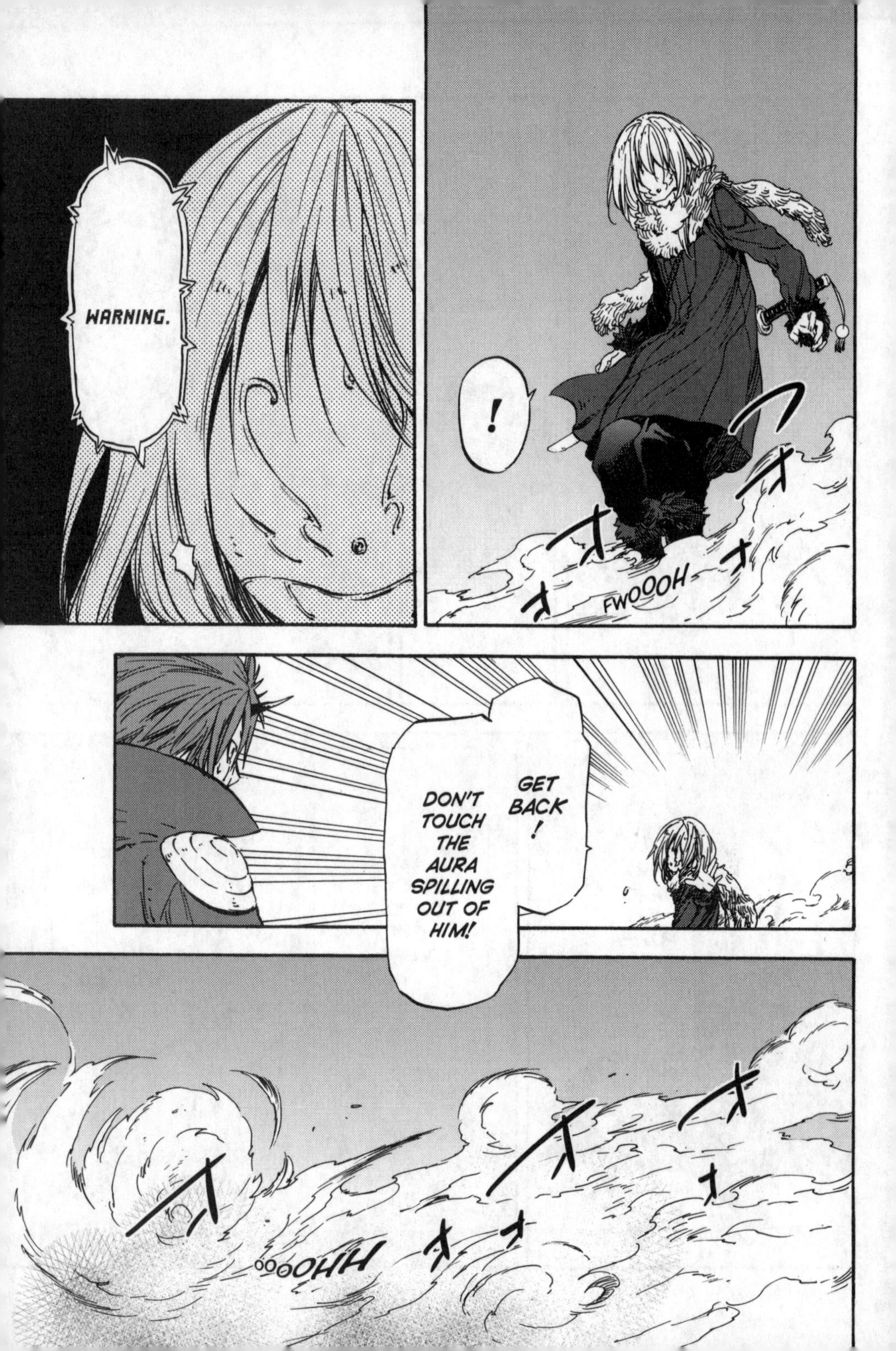
!
FWOOOH
WARNING.
GET BACK!
DON'T TOUCH THE AURA SPILLING OUT OF HIM!
oooOOHH

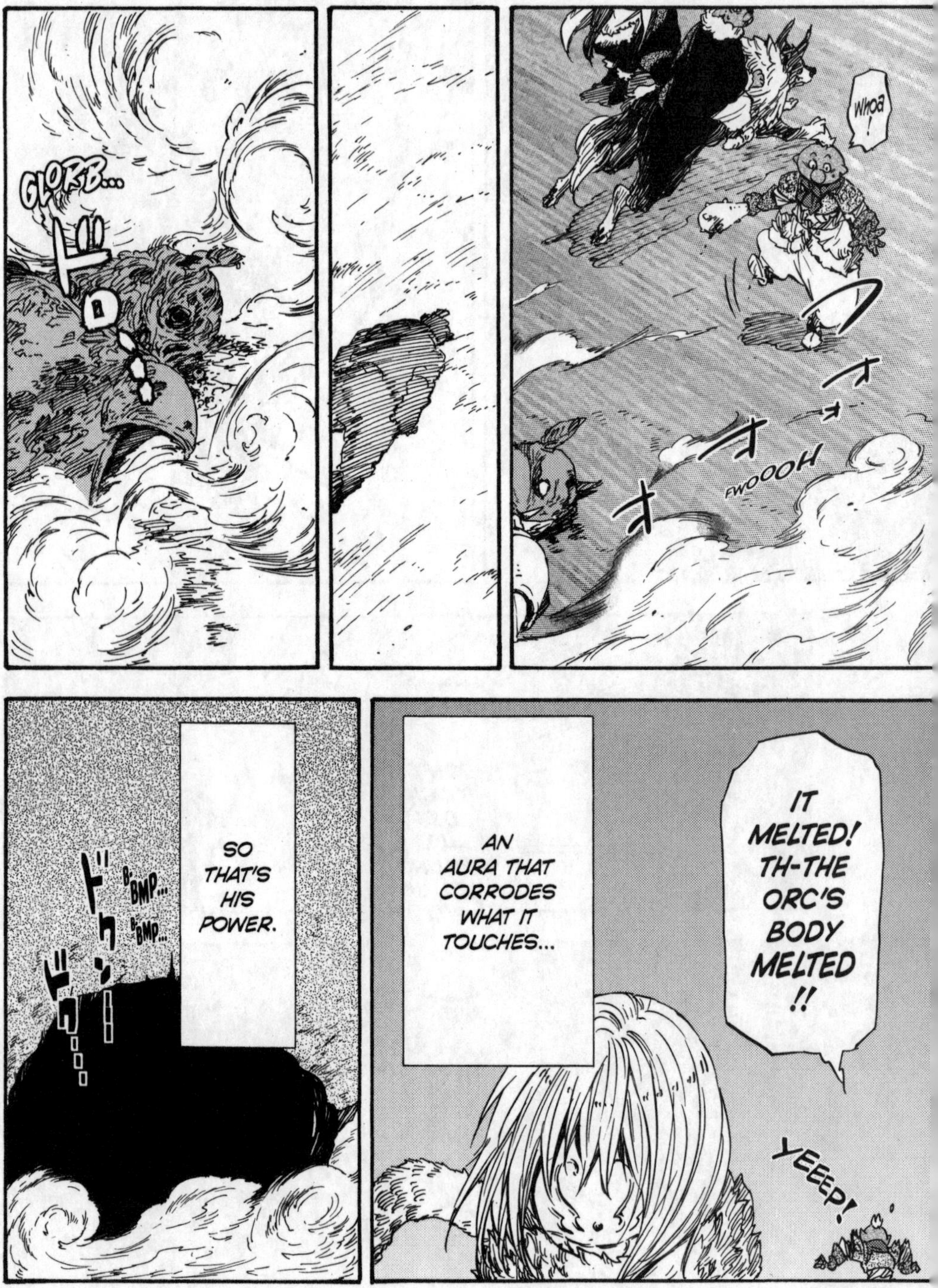
Whoa!
FWOOOH
GLORB...
IT MELTED! TH-THE ORC'S BODY MELTED!!
AN AURA THAT CORRODES WHAT IT TOUCHES...
YEEEP!
SO THAT'S HIS POWER.
B-BMP...
B-BMP...

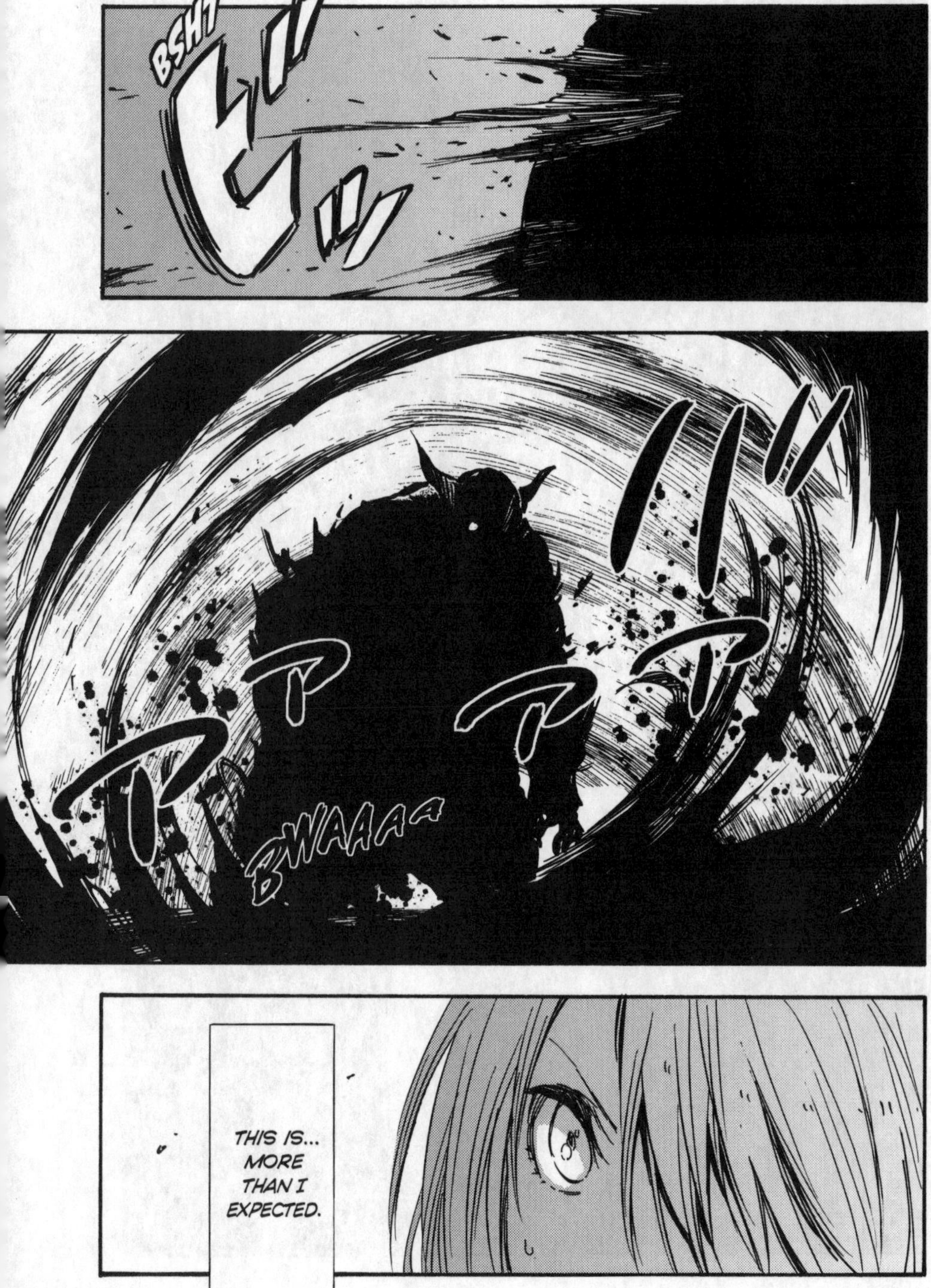
BSHT
BWAAAA
THIS IS... MORE THAN I EXPECTED.

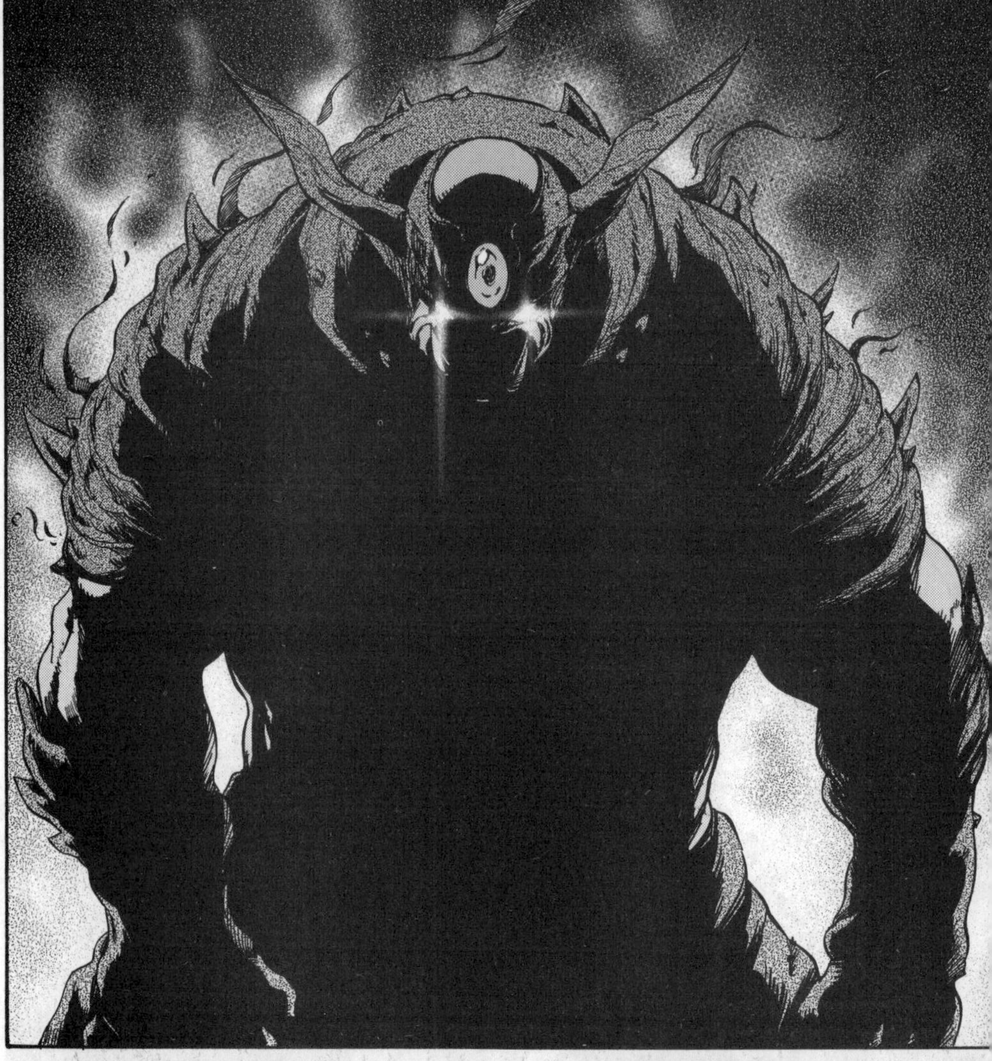
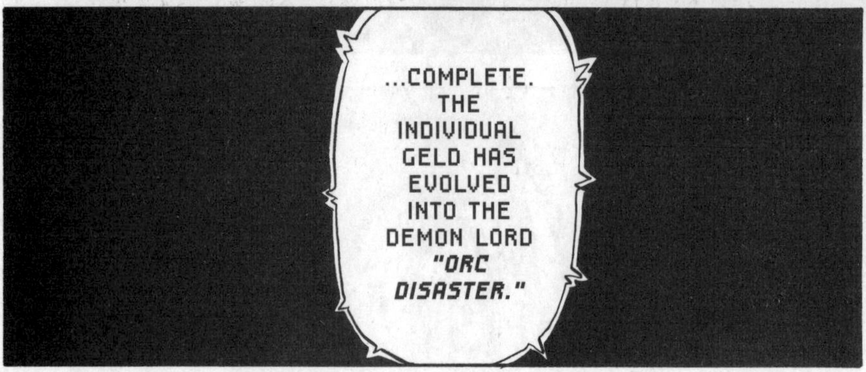
...COMPLETE. THE INDIVIDUAL GELD HAS EVOLVED INTO THE DEMON LORD "ORC DISASTER."

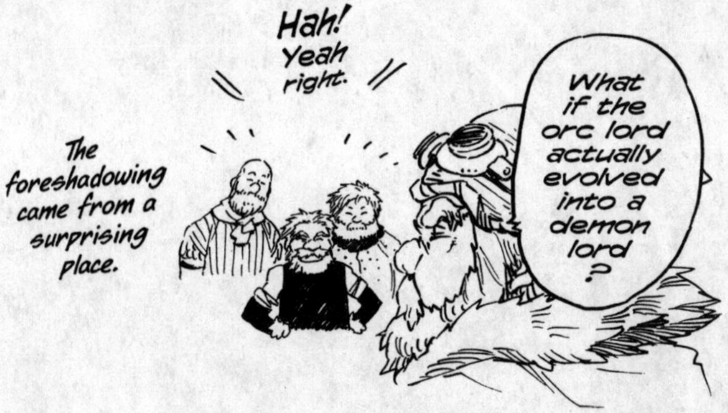
What if the orc lord actually evolved into a demon lord?
Hah! Yeah right.
The foreshadowing came from a surprising place.

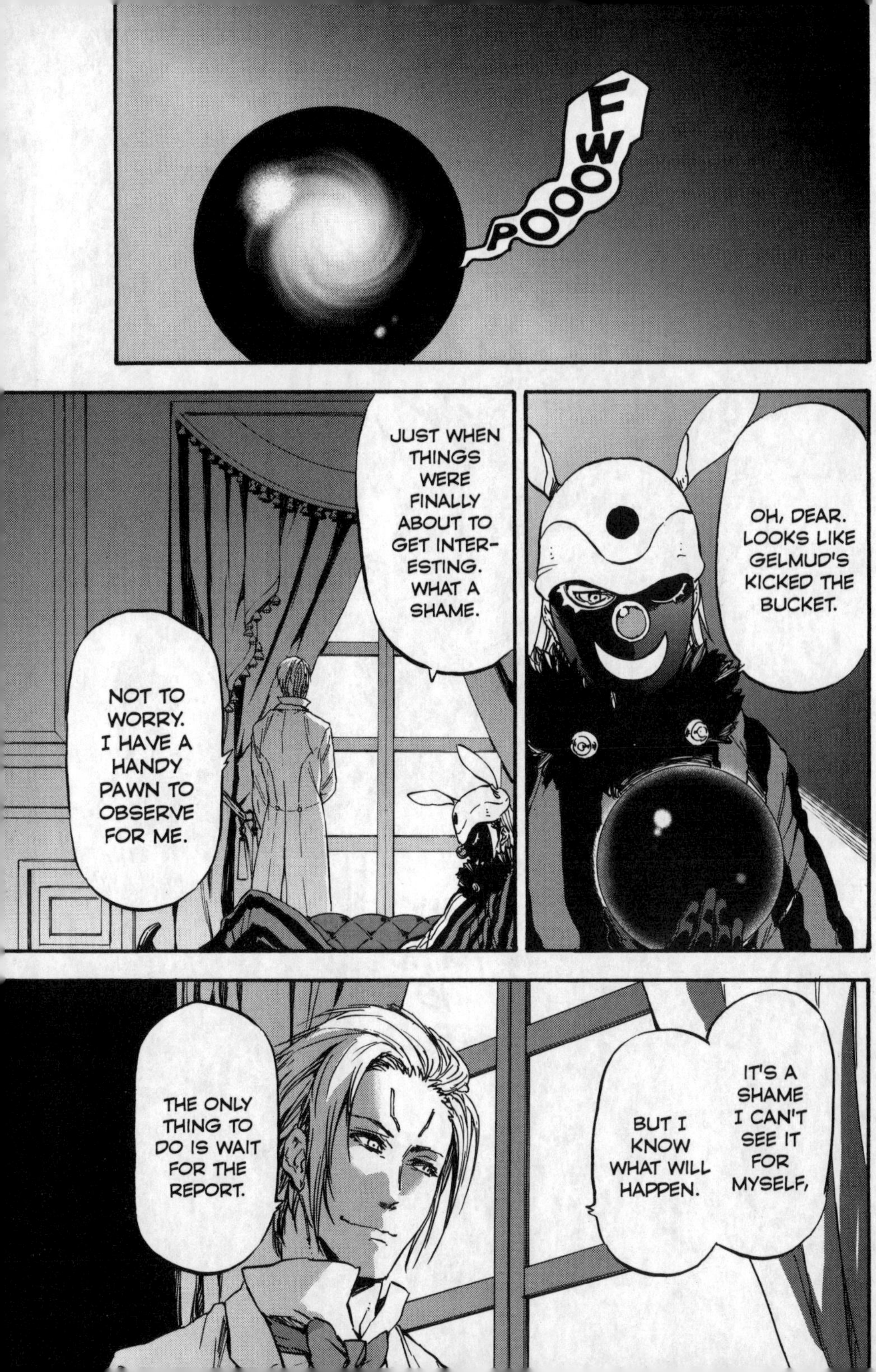
FWOOOP
OH, DEAR. LOOKS LIKE GELMUD'S KICKED THE BUCKET.
JUST WHEN THINGS WERE FINALLY ABOUT TO GET INTER-ESTING. WHAT A SHAME.
NOT TO WORRY. I HAVE A HANDY PAWN TO OBSERVE FOR ME.
IT'S A SHAME I CAN'T SEE IT FOR MYSELF,
BUT I KNOW WHAT WILL HAPPEN.
THE ONLY THING TO DO IS WAIT FOR THE REPORT.

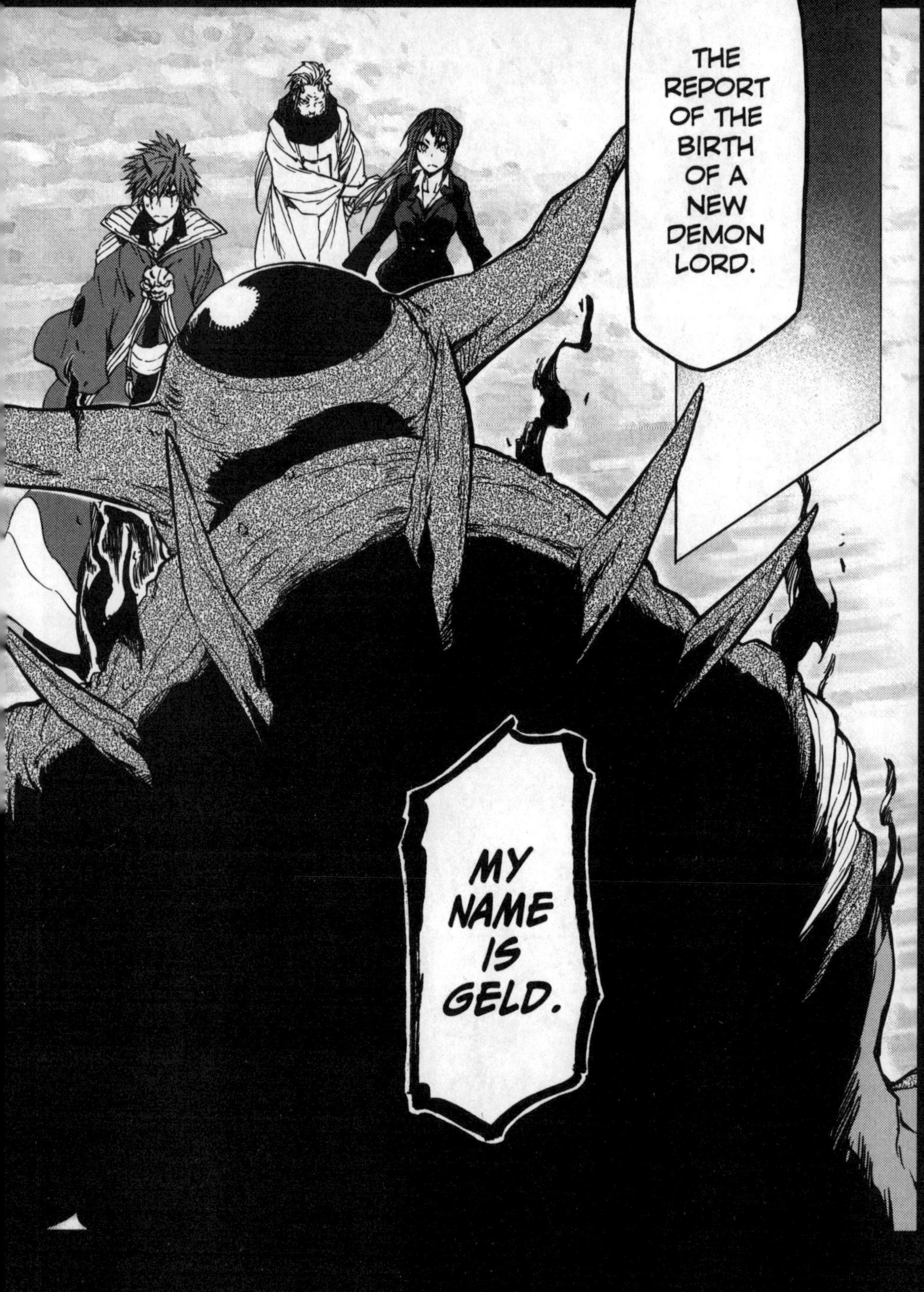
THE REPORT OF THE BIRTH OF A NEW DEMON LORD.
MY NAME IS GELD.

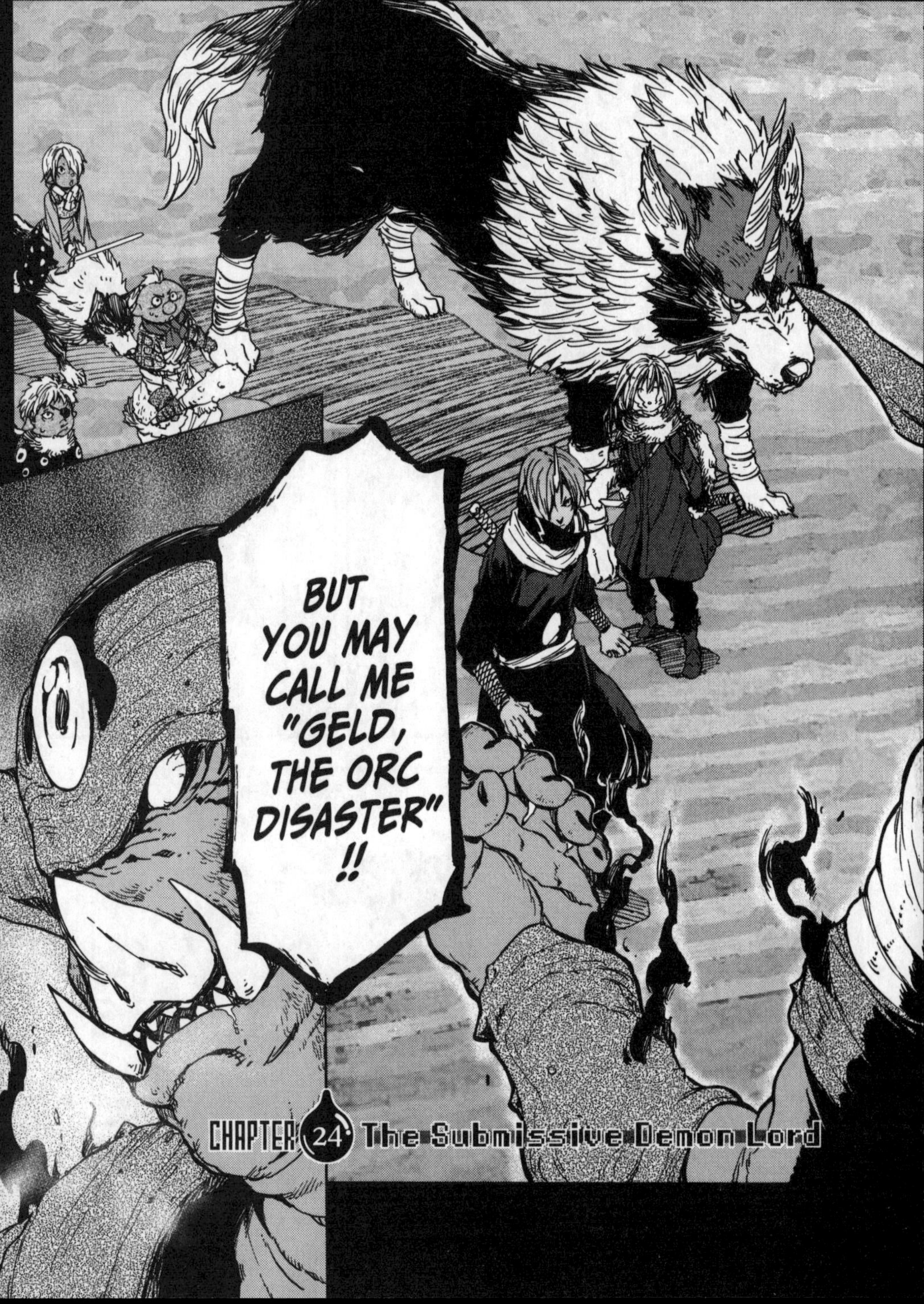
BUT YOU MAY CALL ME "GELD, THE ORC DISASTER" !!
CHAPTER 24 The Submissive Demon Lord

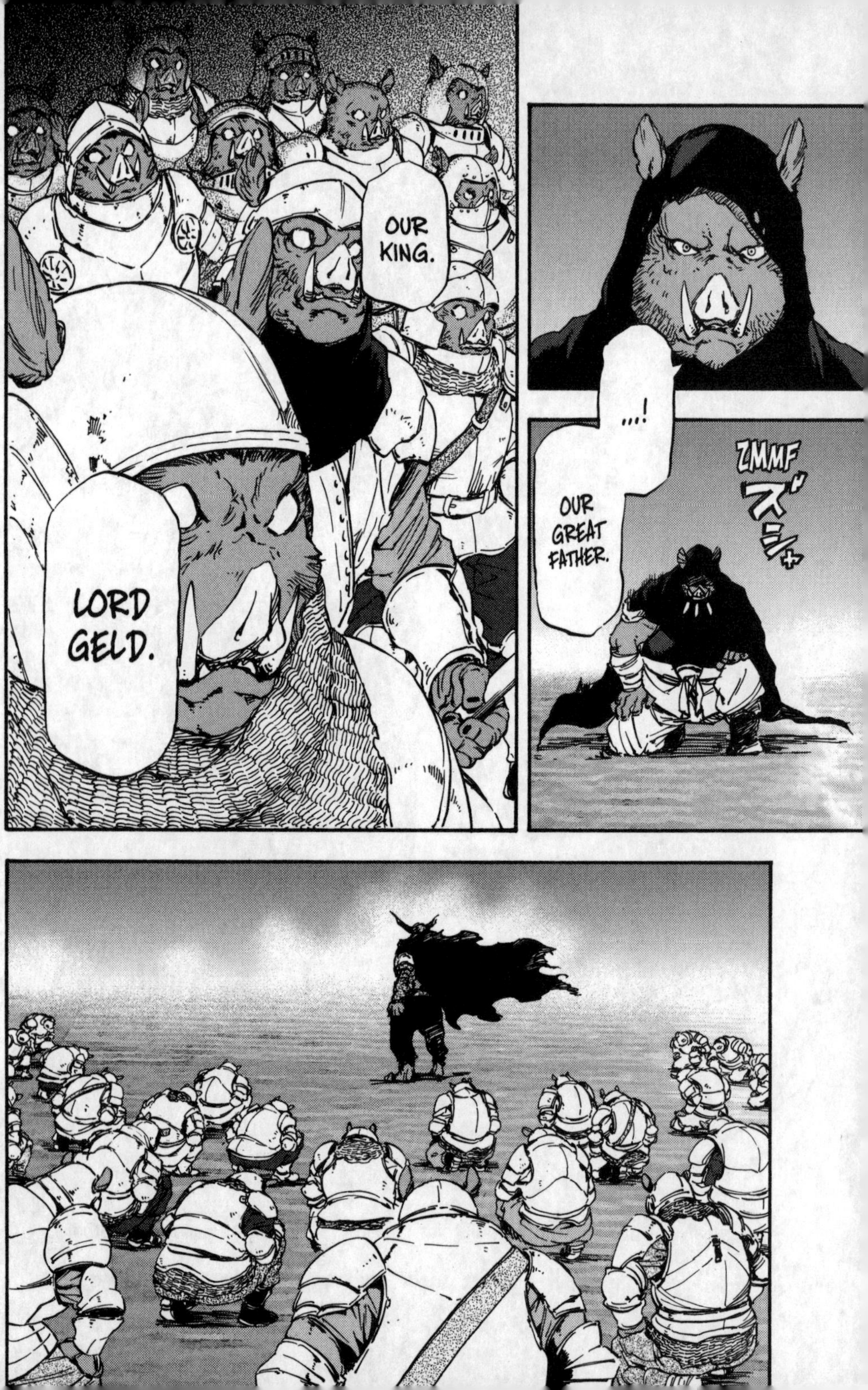
...!
OUR GREAT FATHER.
ZMMF
ズシャ
OUR KING.
LORD GELD.

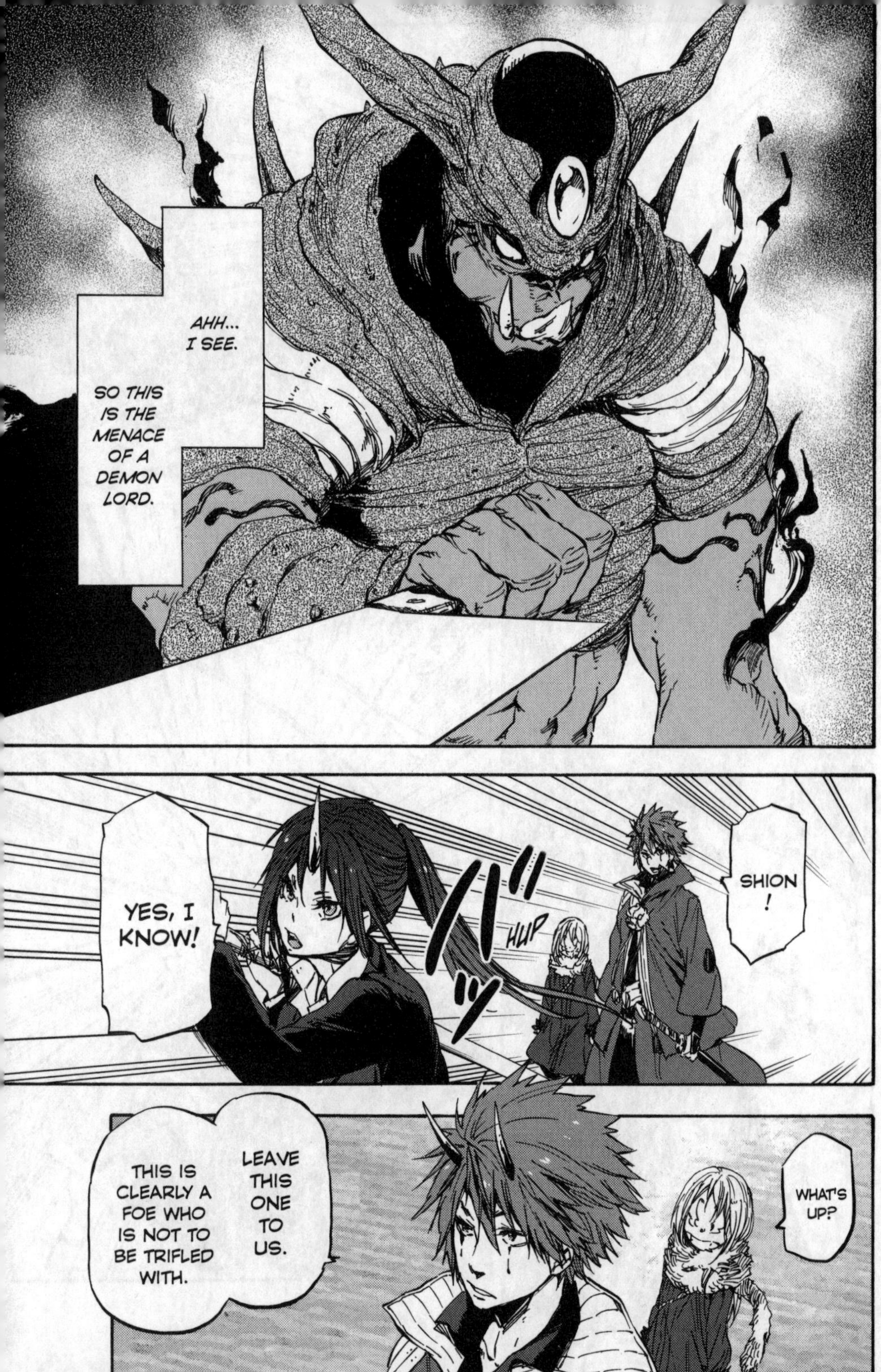
AHH... I SEE.
SO THIS IS THE MENACE OF A DEMON LORD.
SHION!
HUP
YES, I KNOW!
WHAT'S UP?
LEAVE THIS ONE TO US.
THIS IS CLEARLY A FOE WHO IS NOT TO BE TRIFLED WITH.

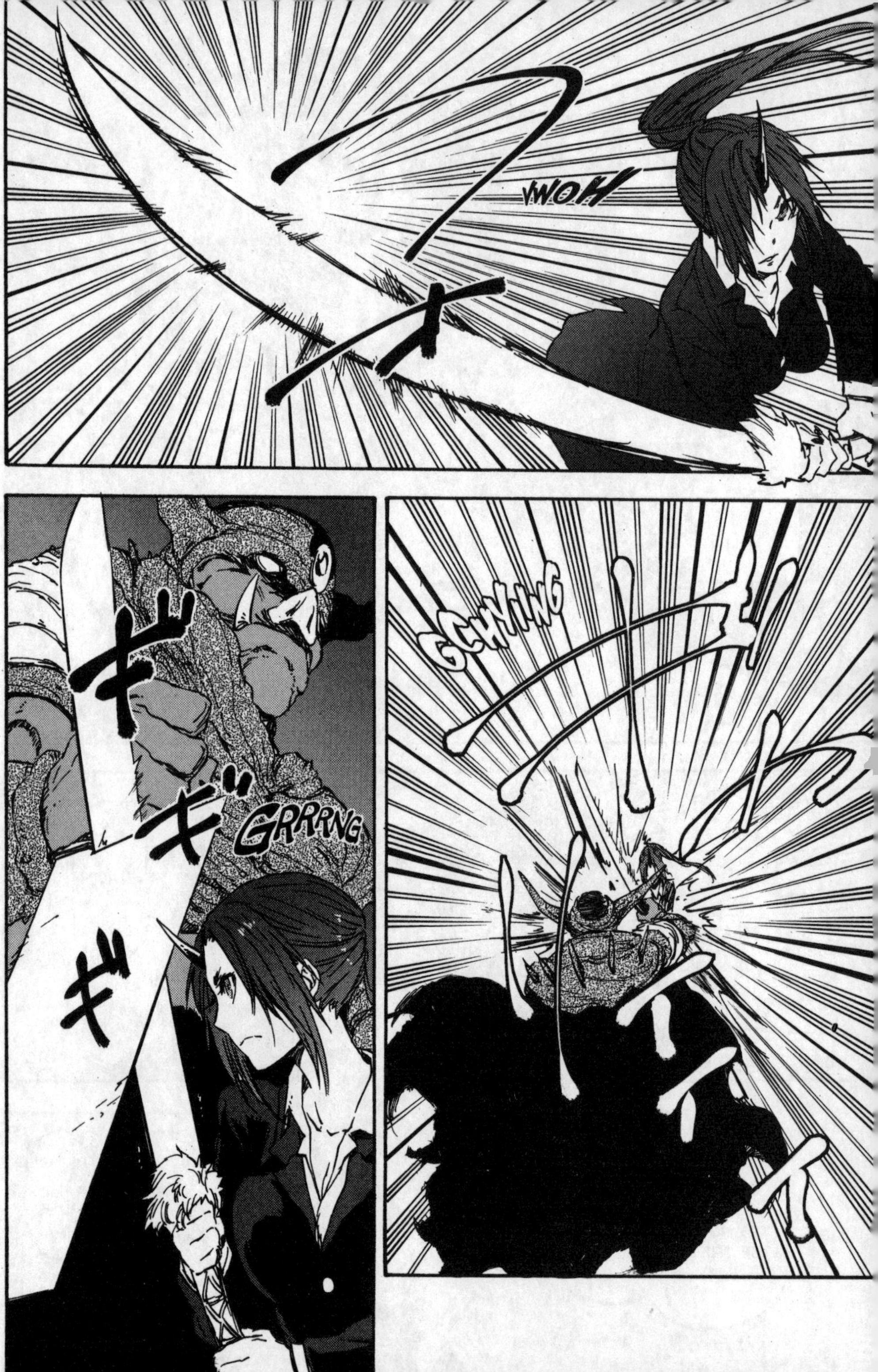
VWOH
GCHYING
ギ
ギ
GRRRNG
ギ

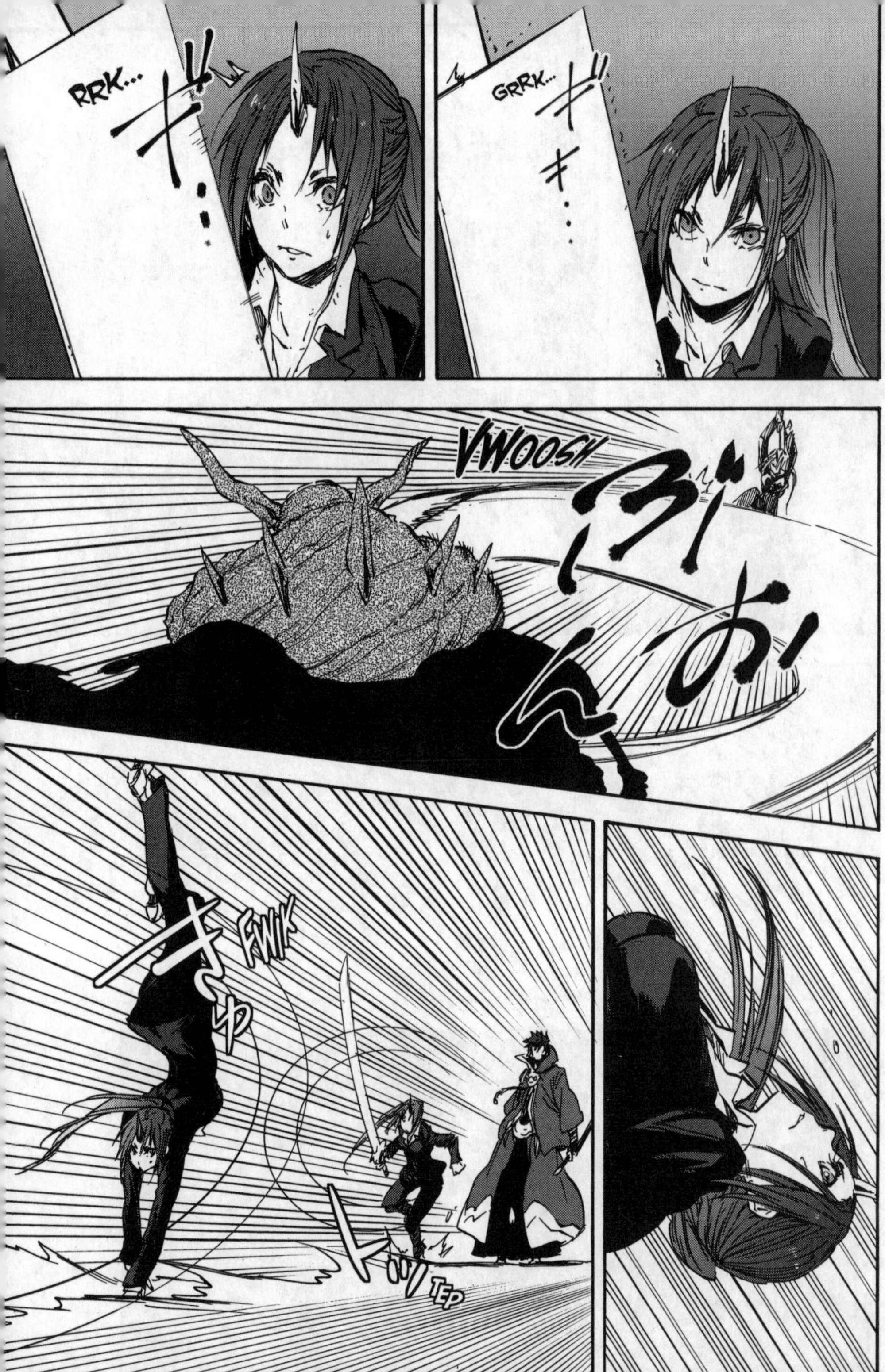
GRRK...
RRK...
VWOOSH
FWIK
TEP

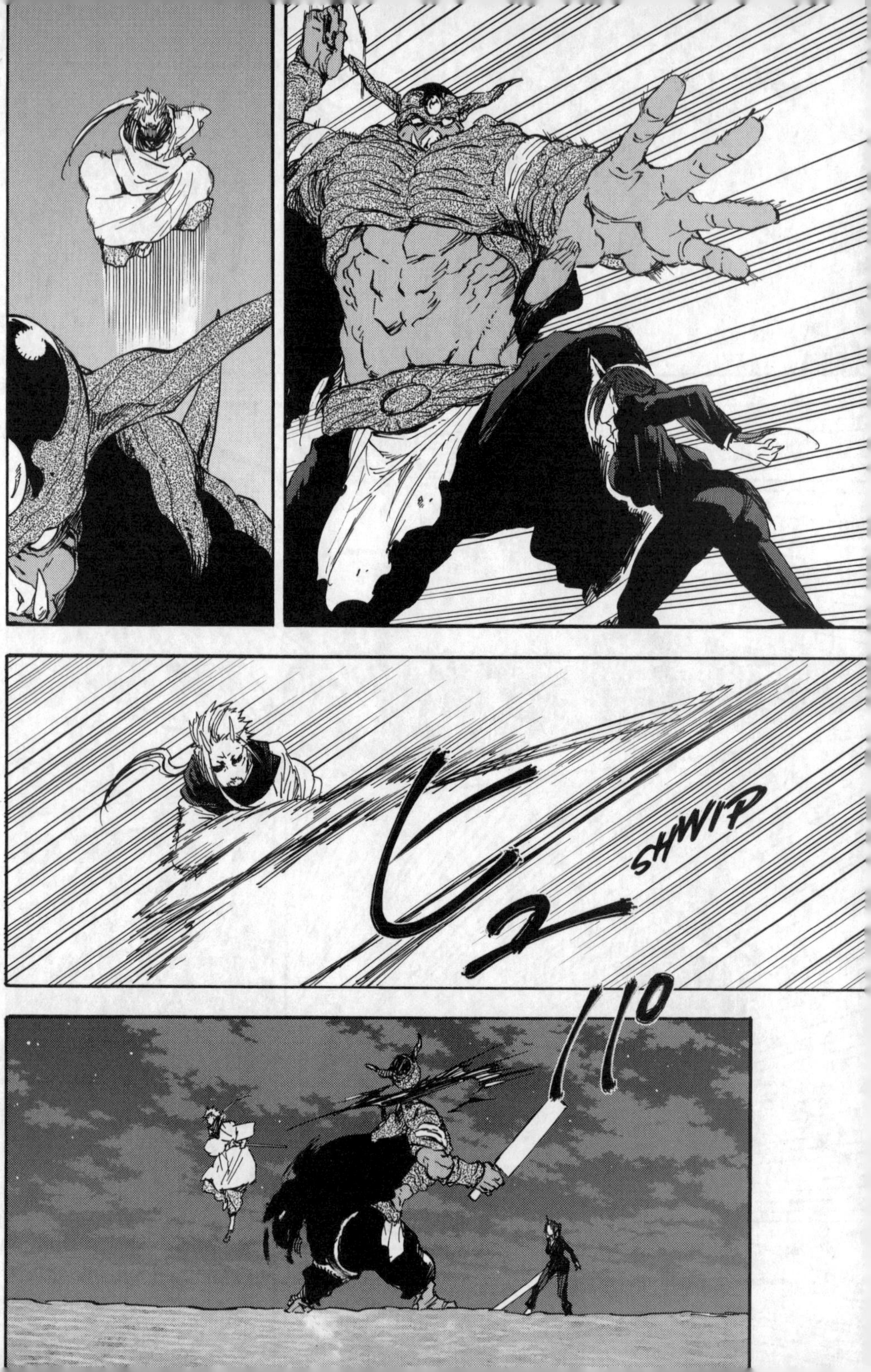
SHWIP

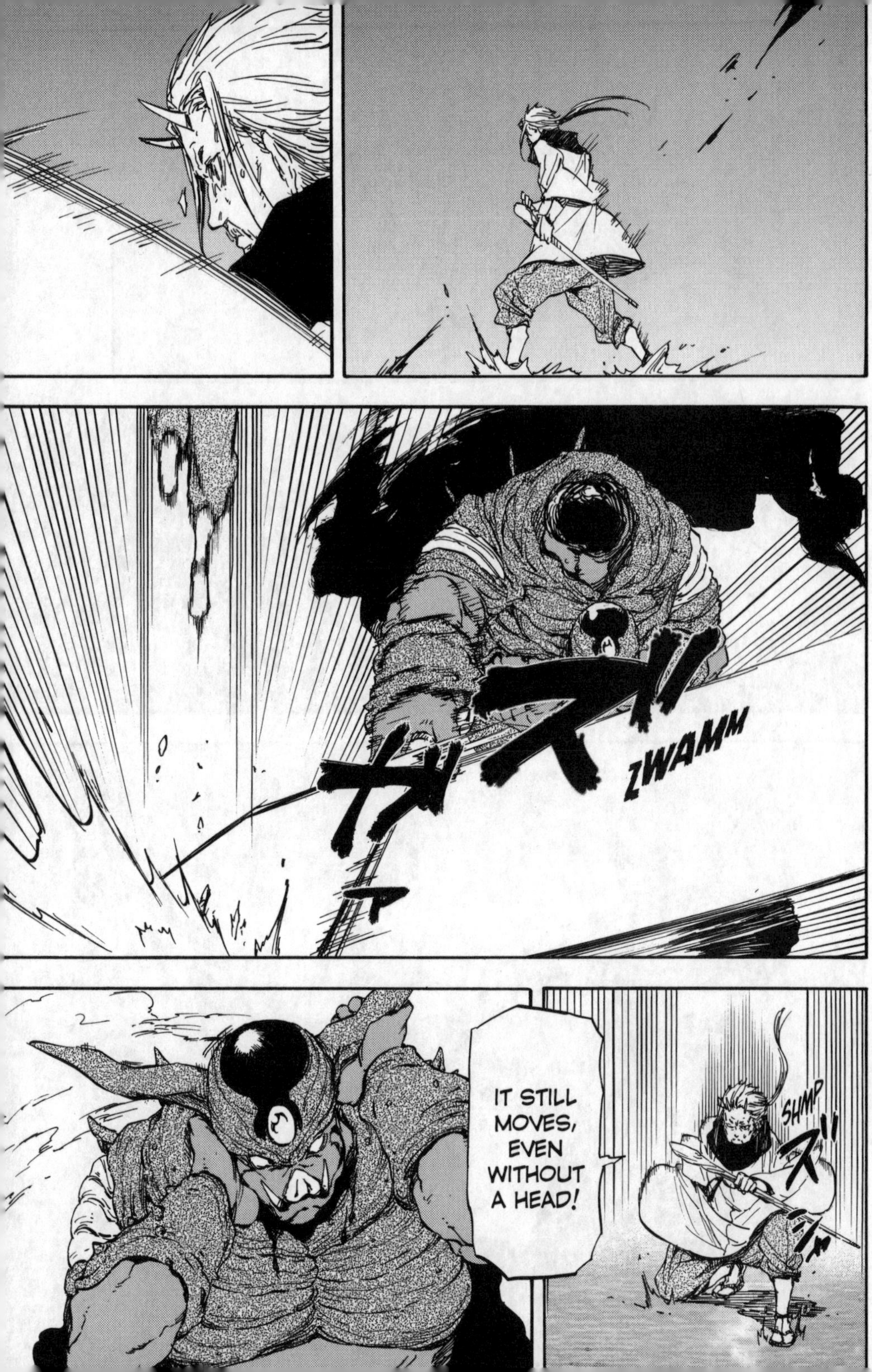
ZWAMM
SHMP
IT STILL MOVES, EVEN WITHOUT A HEAD!

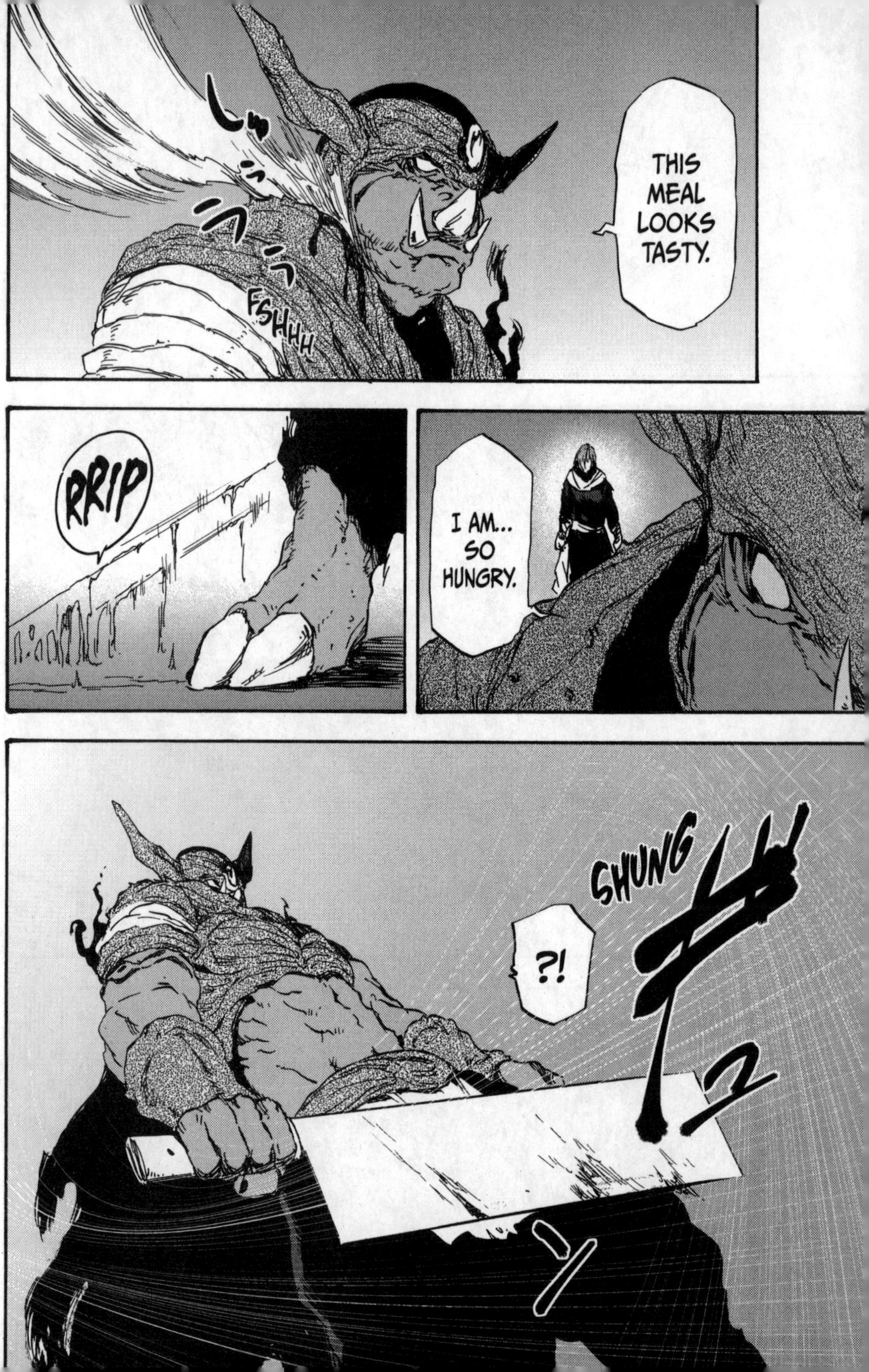
THIS MEAL LOOKS TASTY.
FSHHH
I AM... SO HUNGRY.
RRIP
SHUNG
?!

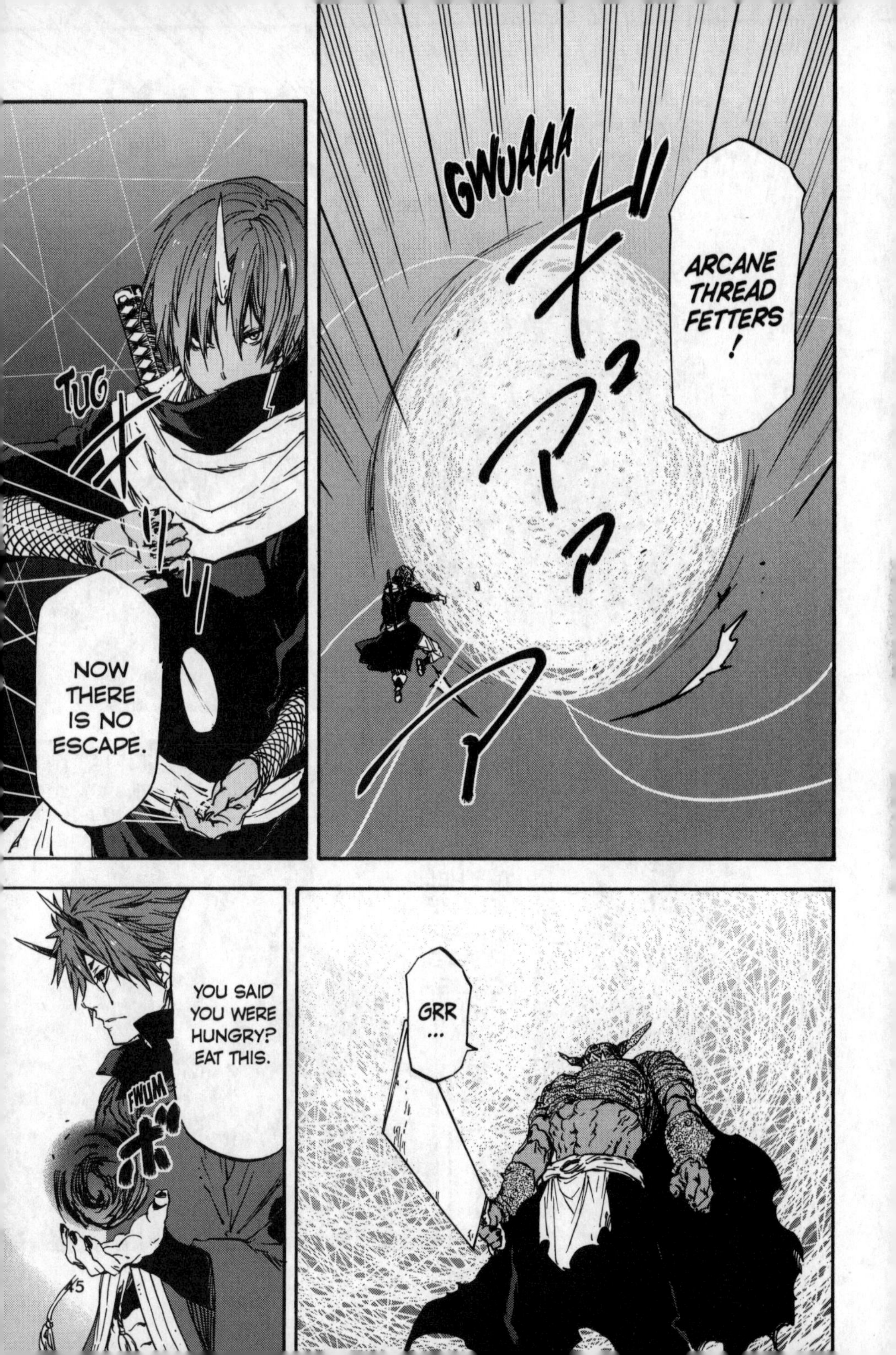
GWUAAA
ARCANE THREAD FETTERS!
TUG
NOW THERE IS NO ESCAPE.
GRR ...
YOU SAID YOU WERE HUNGRY? EAT THIS.
FWUM

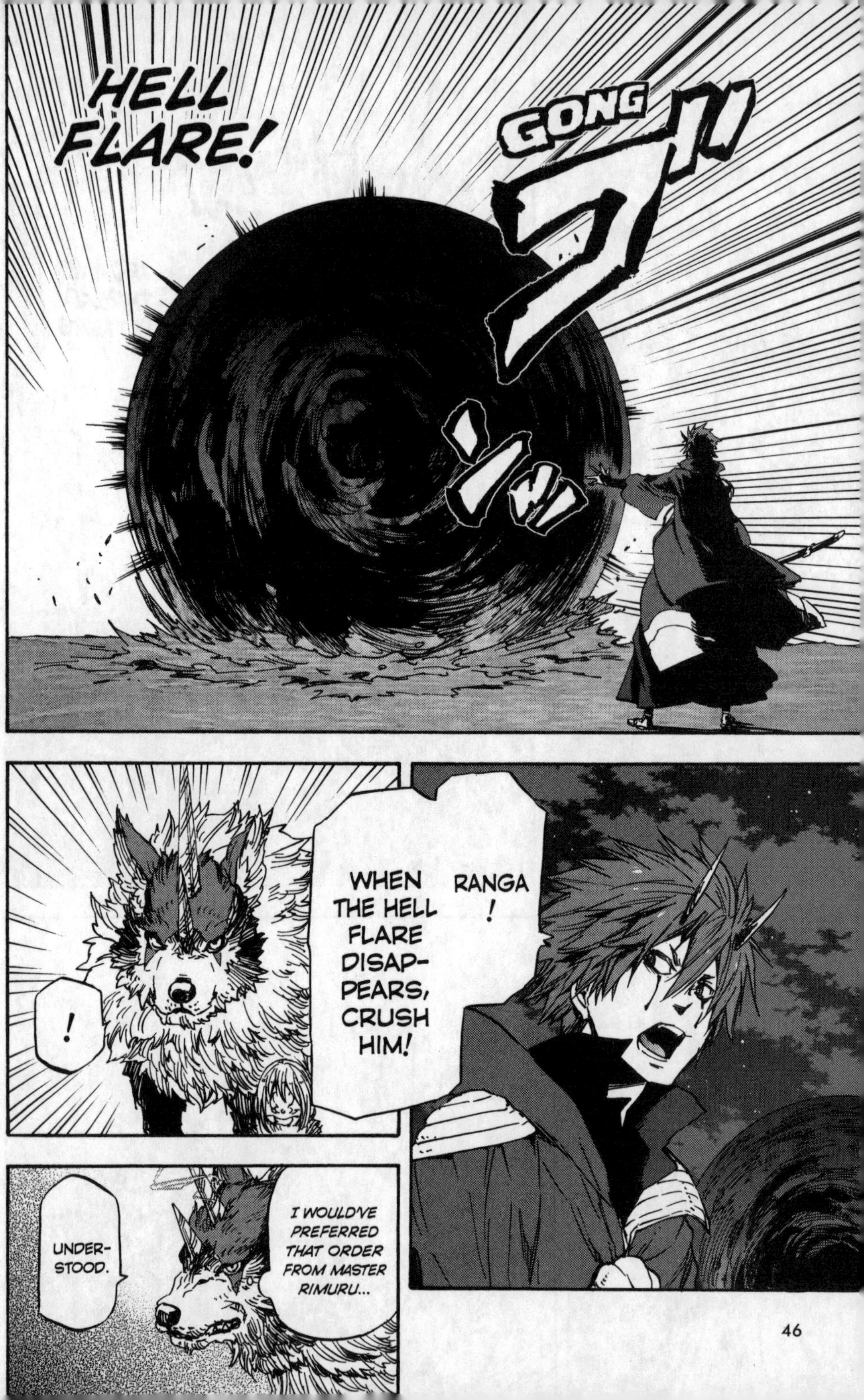
GONG
HELL FLARE!
RANGA!
WHEN THE HELL FLARE DISAPPEARS, CRUSH HIM!
!
I WOULD'VE PREFERRED THAT ORDER FROM MASTER RIMURU...
UNDERSTOOD.

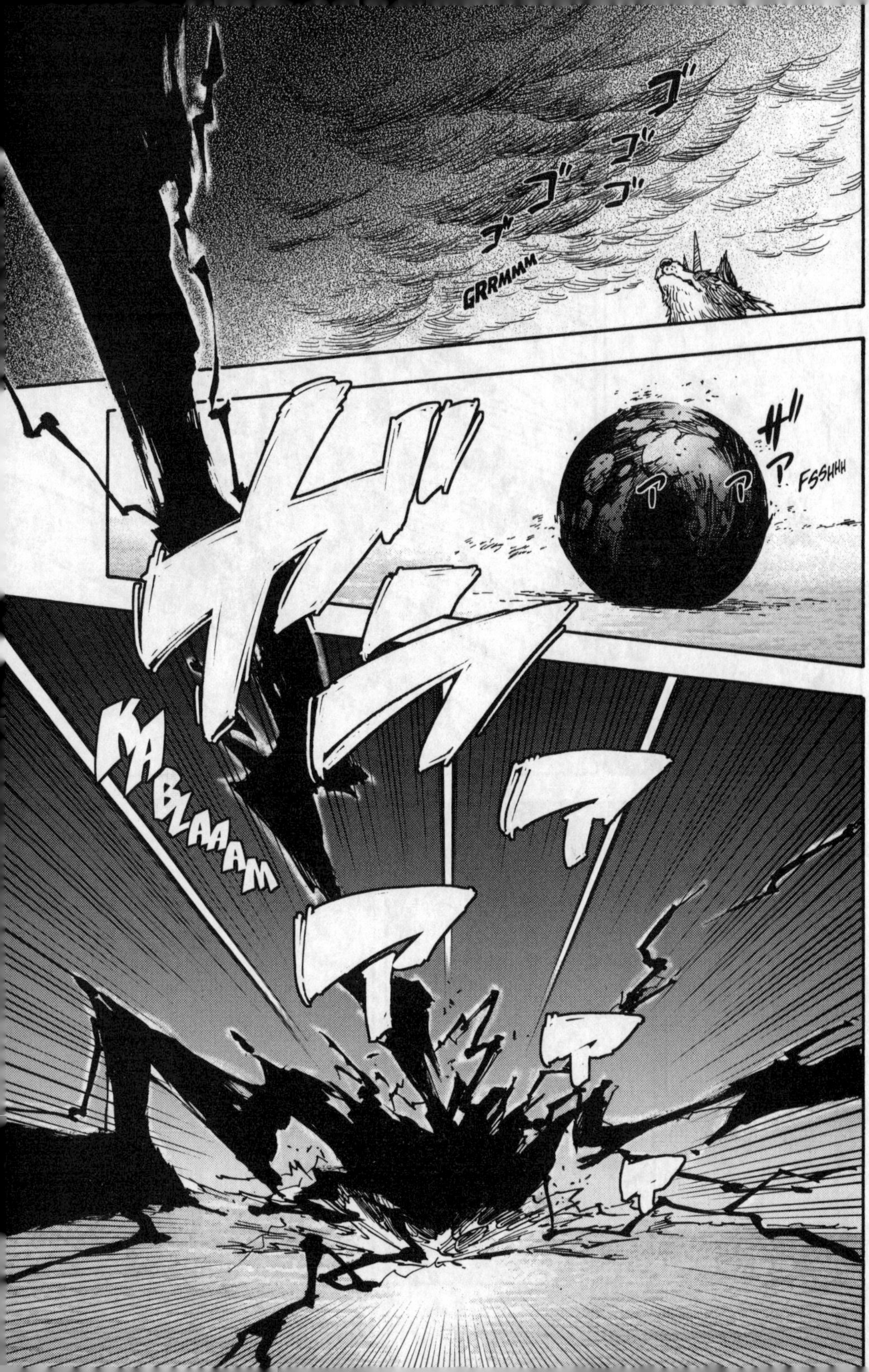
GRRMMM
FSSHHH
KABLAAAAM

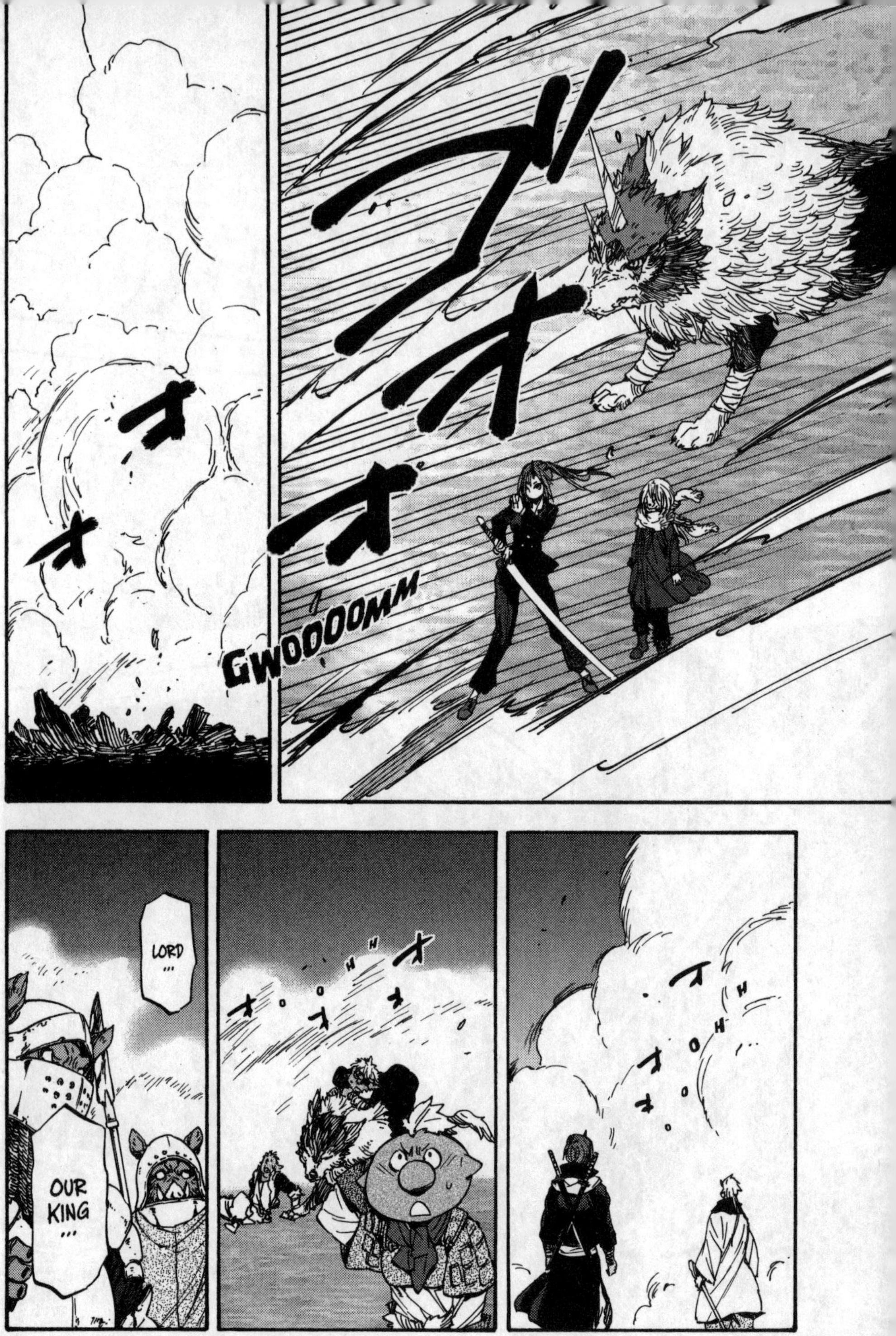
GWOOOOMM
LORD ...
OUR KING ...

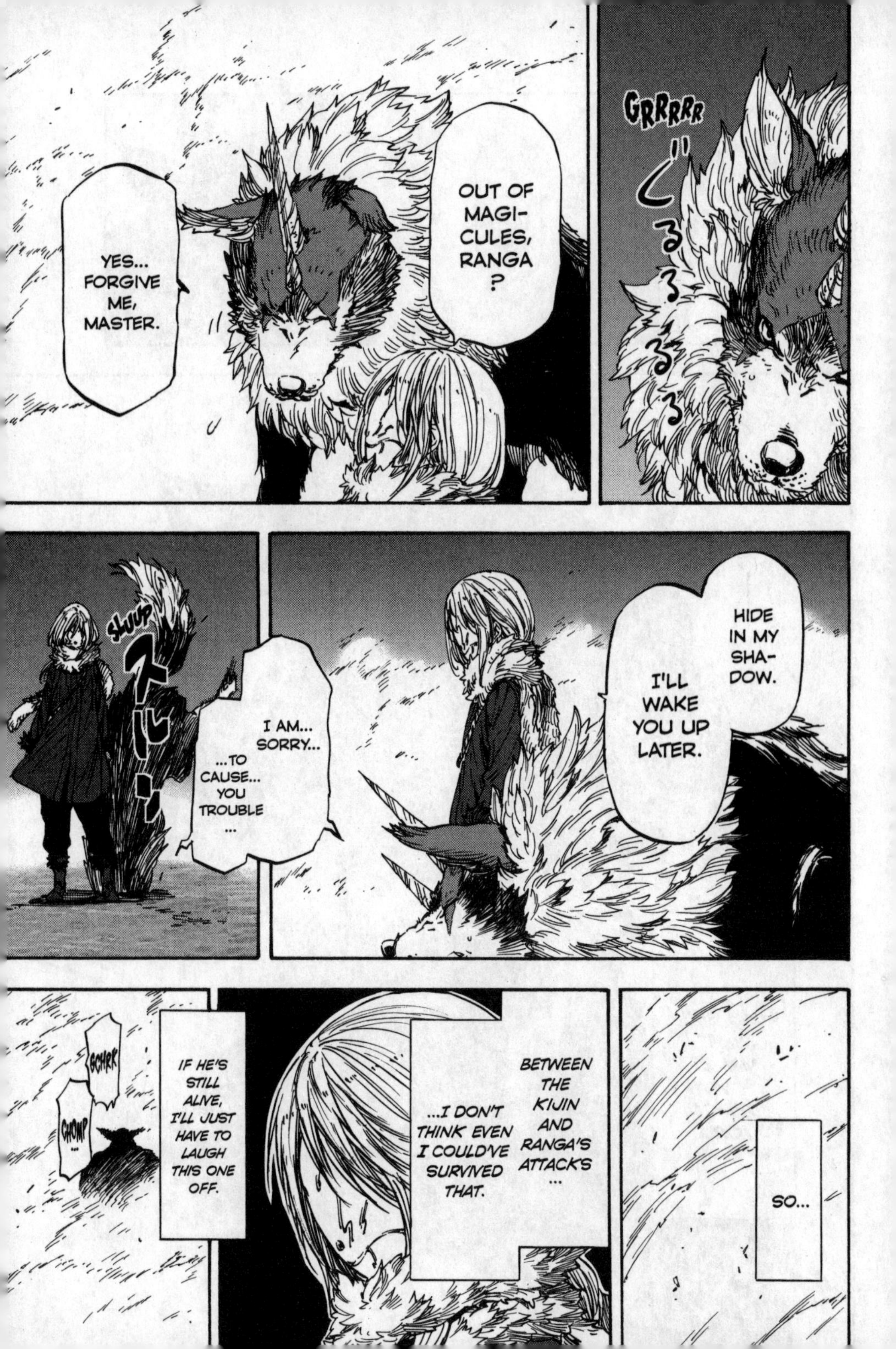

GRRRRR
ぐるるる
OUT OF MAGI-CULES, RANGA?
YES... FORGIVE ME, MASTER.
HIDE IN MY SHA-DOW.
I'LL WAKE YOU UP LATER.
I AM... SORRY...
...TO CAUSE... YOU TROUBLE ...
SLUUP
SO...
BETWEEN THE KIJIN AND RANGA'S ATTACKS ...
...I DON'T THINK EVEN I COULD'VE SURVIVED THAT.
IF HE'S STILL ALIVE, I'LL JUST HAVE TO LAUGH THIS ONE OFF.
GCHRK
CHOMP ...

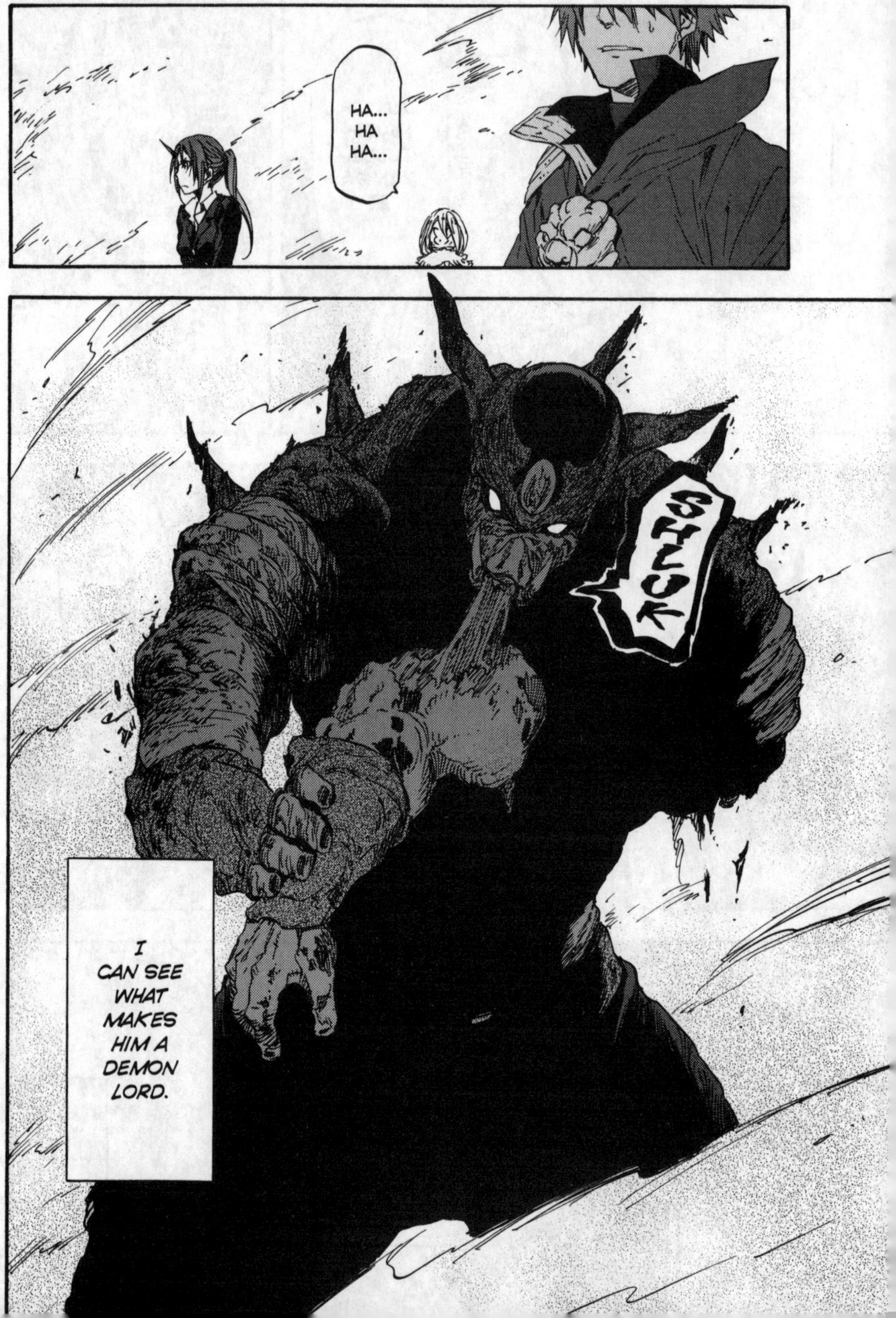
HA... HA HA...
SHLUK
I CAN SEE WHAT MAKES HIM A DEMON LORD.

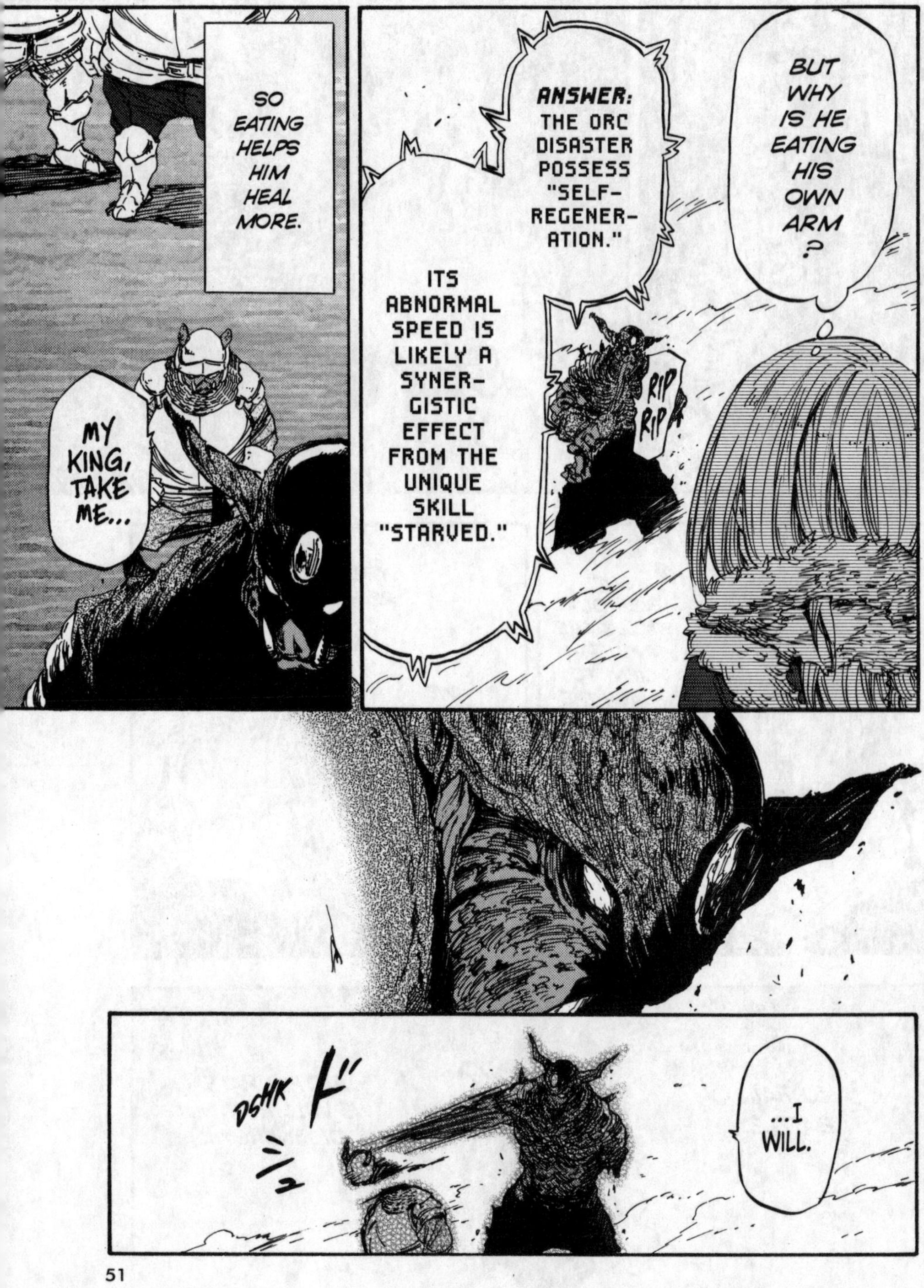
BUT WHY IS HE EATING HIS OWN ARM?
ANSWER: THE ORC DISASTER POSSESS "SELF-REGENERATION."
RIP RIP
ITS ABNORMAL SPEED IS LIKELY A SYNERGISTIC EFFECT FROM THE UNIQUE SKILL "STARVED."
SO EATING HELPS HIM HEAL MORE.
MY KING, TAKE ME...
...I WILL.
ド
DSHK

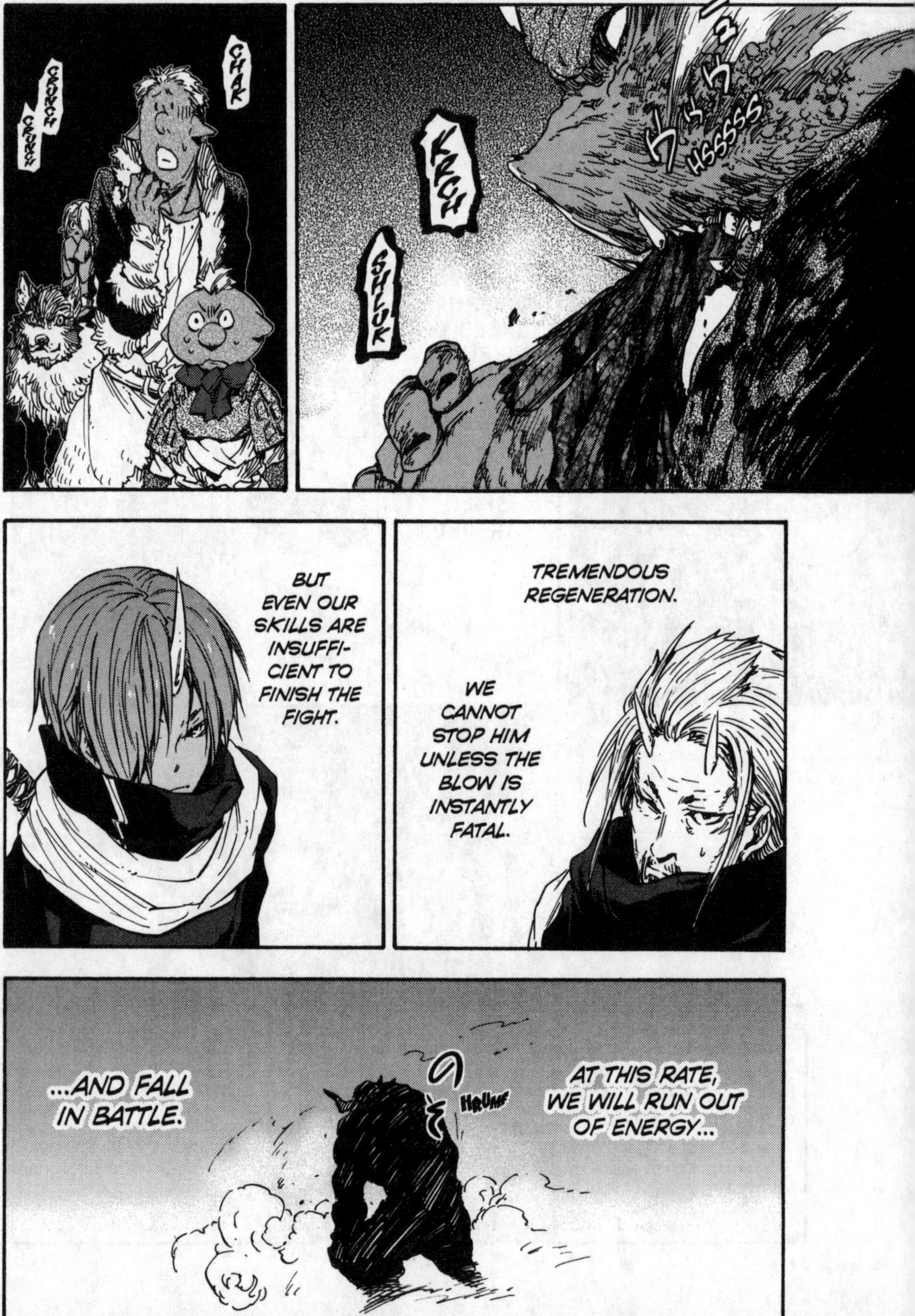
HSSSSS
KRCH
SHLUK
CHAK
CRUNCH
CRUNCH
TREMENDOUS REGENERATION.
WE CANNOT STOP HIM UNLESS THE BLOW IS INSTANTLY FATAL.
BUT EVEN OUR SKILLS ARE INSUFFI- CIENT TO FINISH THE FIGHT.
AT THIS RATE, WE WILL RUN OUT OF ENERGY...
HRUMF
...AND FALL IN BATTLE.

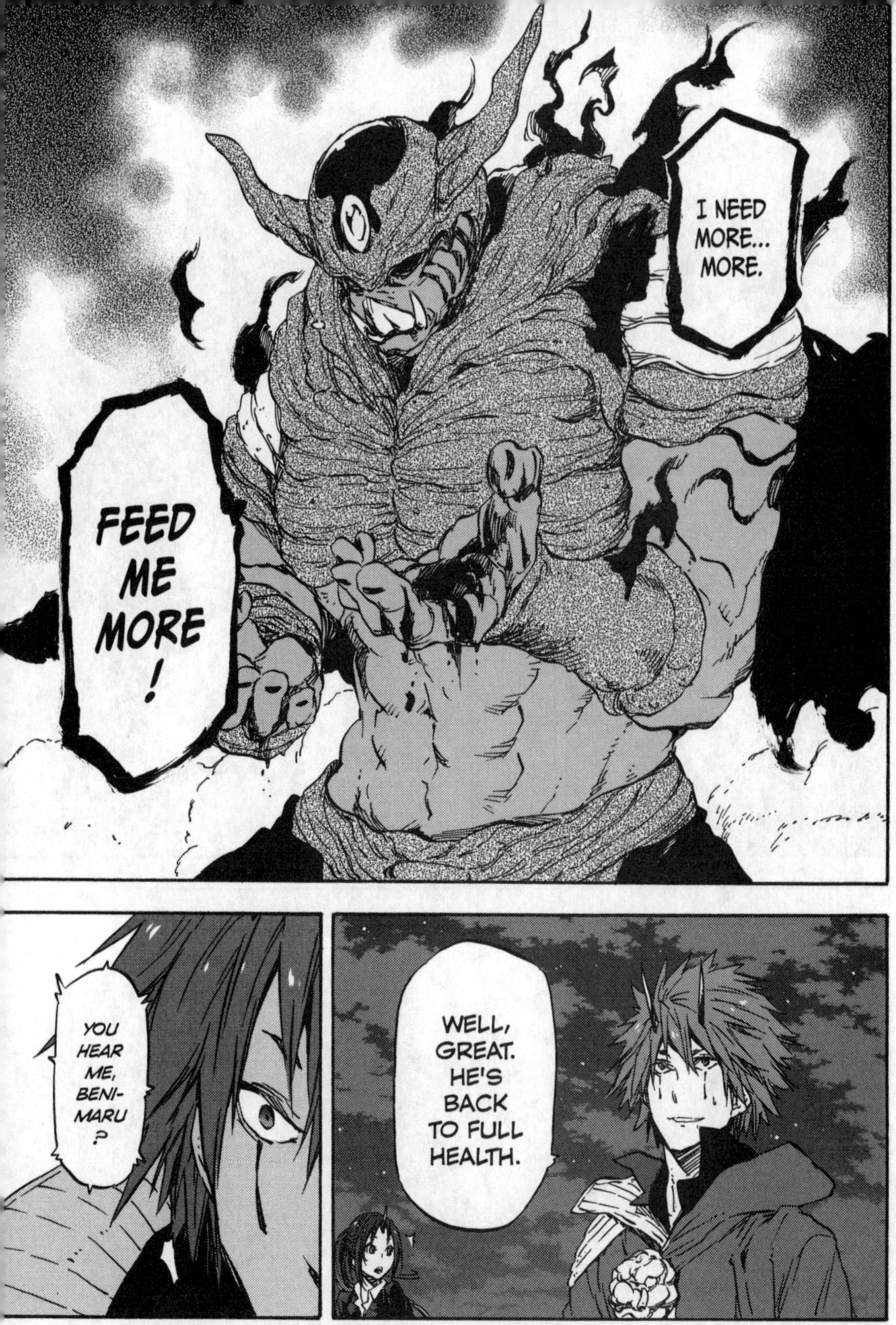
I NEED MORE... MORE.
FEED ME MORE!
WELL, GREAT. HE'S BACK TO FULL HEALTH.
YOU HEAR ME, BENI-MARU?

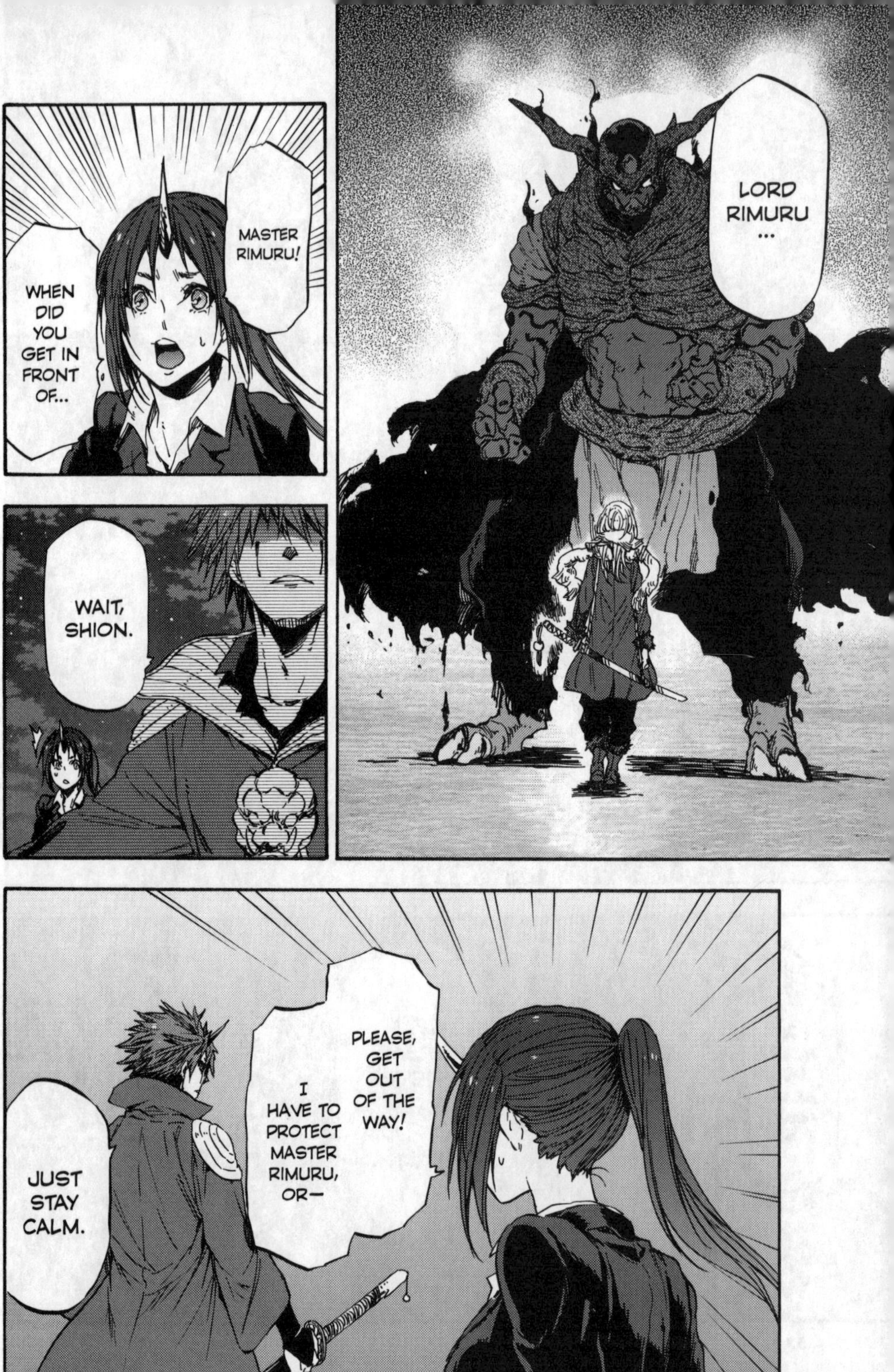
LORD RIMURU...
MASTER RIMURU!
WHEN DID YOU GET IN FRONT OF...
WAIT, SHION.
PLEASE, GET OUT OF THE WAY!
I HAVE TO PROTECT MASTER RIMURU, OR—
JUST STAY CALM.

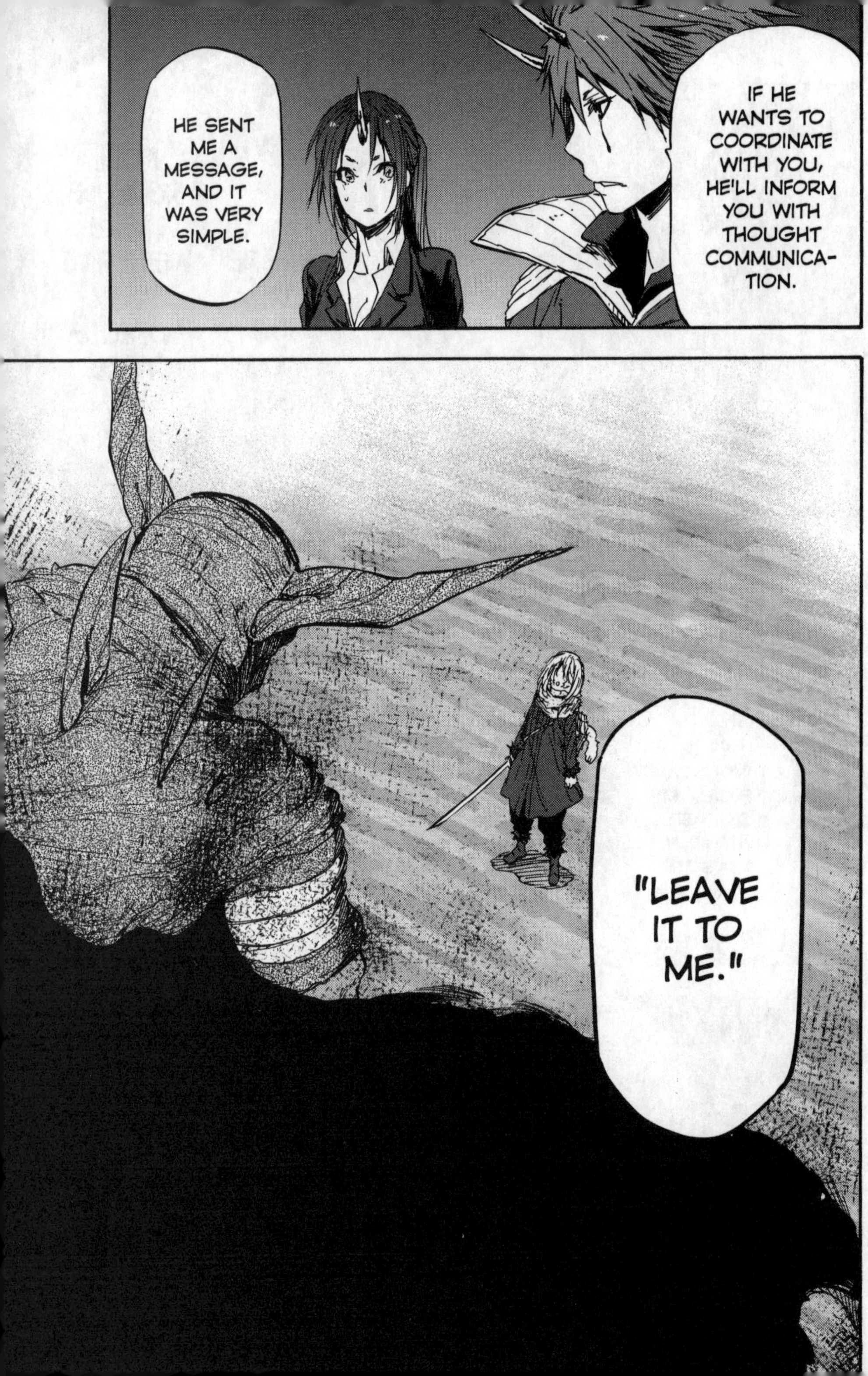
IF HE WANTS TO COORDINATE WITH YOU, HE'LL INFORM YOU WITH THOUGHT COMMUNICA-TION.
HE SENT ME A MESSAGE, AND IT WAS VERY SIMPLE.
"LEAVE IT TO ME."

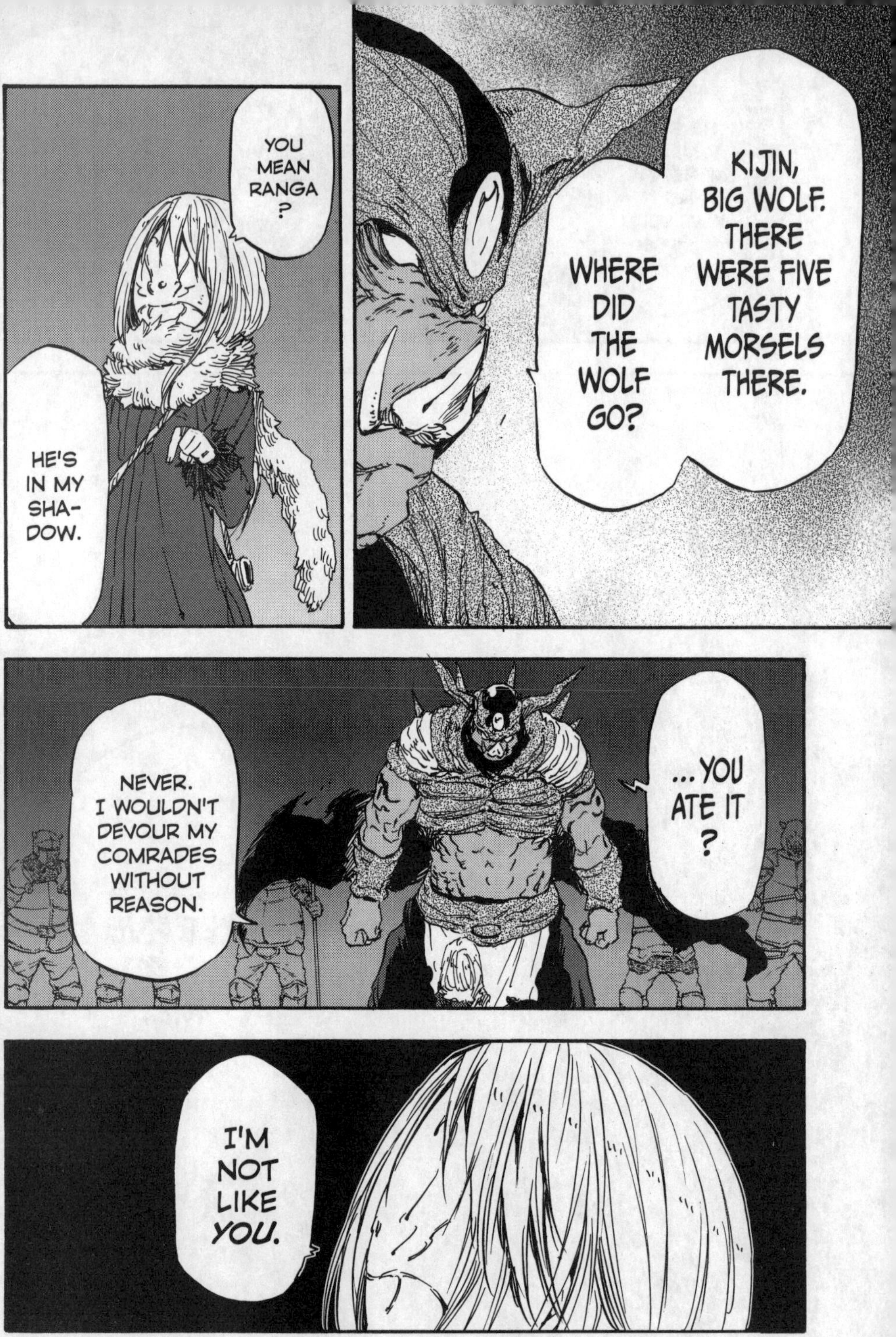
KIJIN, BIG WOLF. THERE WERE FIVE TASTY MORSELS THERE.
WHERE DID THE WOLF GO?
YOU MEAN RANGA?
HE'S IN MY SHADOW.
...YOU ATE IT?
NEVER. I WOULDN'T DEVOUR MY COMRADES WITHOUT REASON.
I'M NOT LIKE *YOU*.

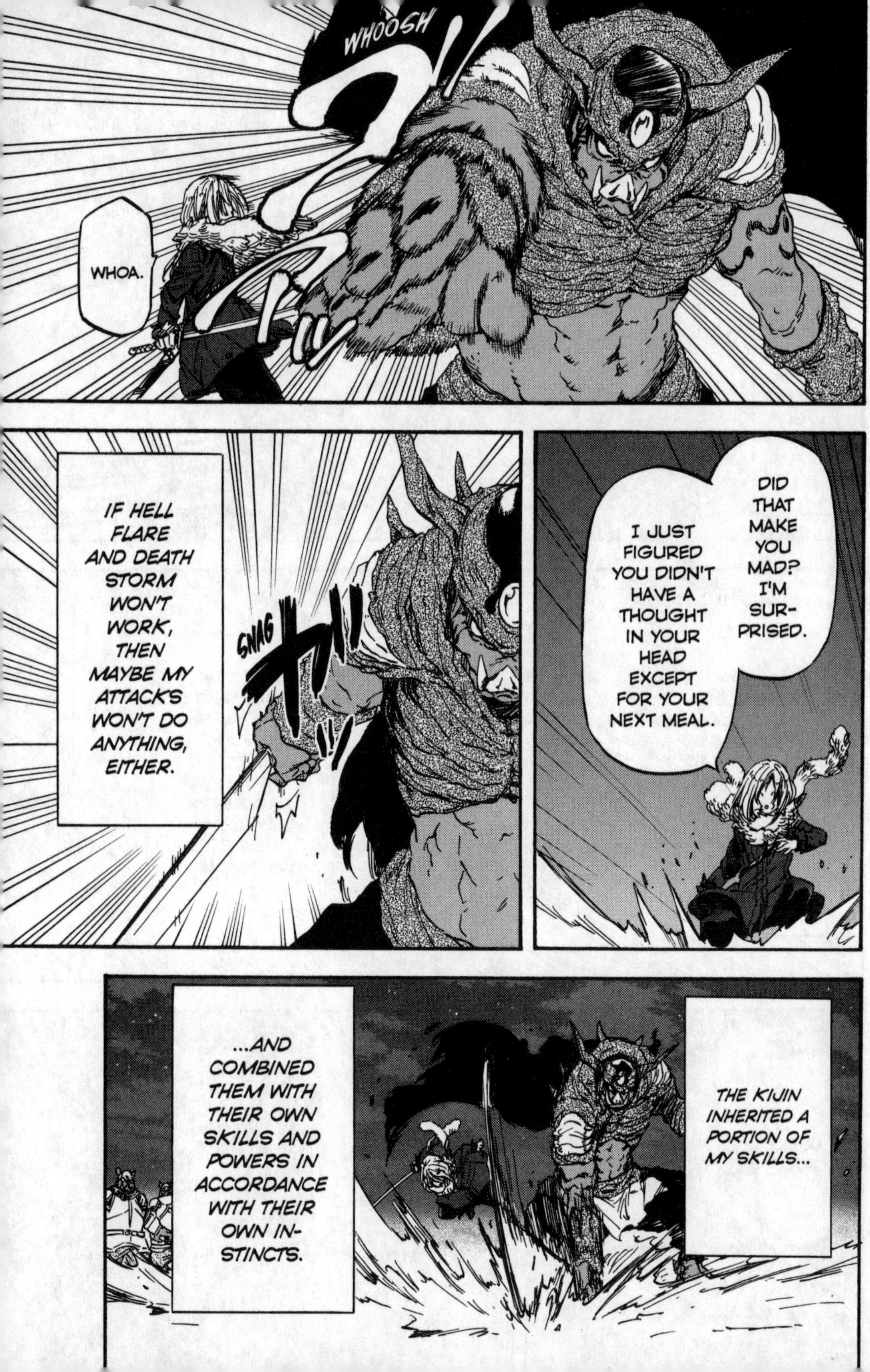
WHOOSH
WHOA.
DID THAT MAKE YOU MAD? I'M SUR-PRISED.
I JUST FIGURED YOU DIDN'T HAVE A THOUGHT IN YOUR HEAD EXCEPT FOR YOUR NEXT MEAL.
IF HELL FLARE AND DEATH STORM WON'T WORK, THEN MAYBE MY ATTACKS WON'T DO ANYTHING, EITHER.
SNAG
THE KIJIN INHERITED A PORTION OF MY SKILLS...
...AND COMBINED THEM WITH THEIR OWN SKILLS AND POWERS IN ACCORDANCE WITH THEIR OWN IN-STINCTS.

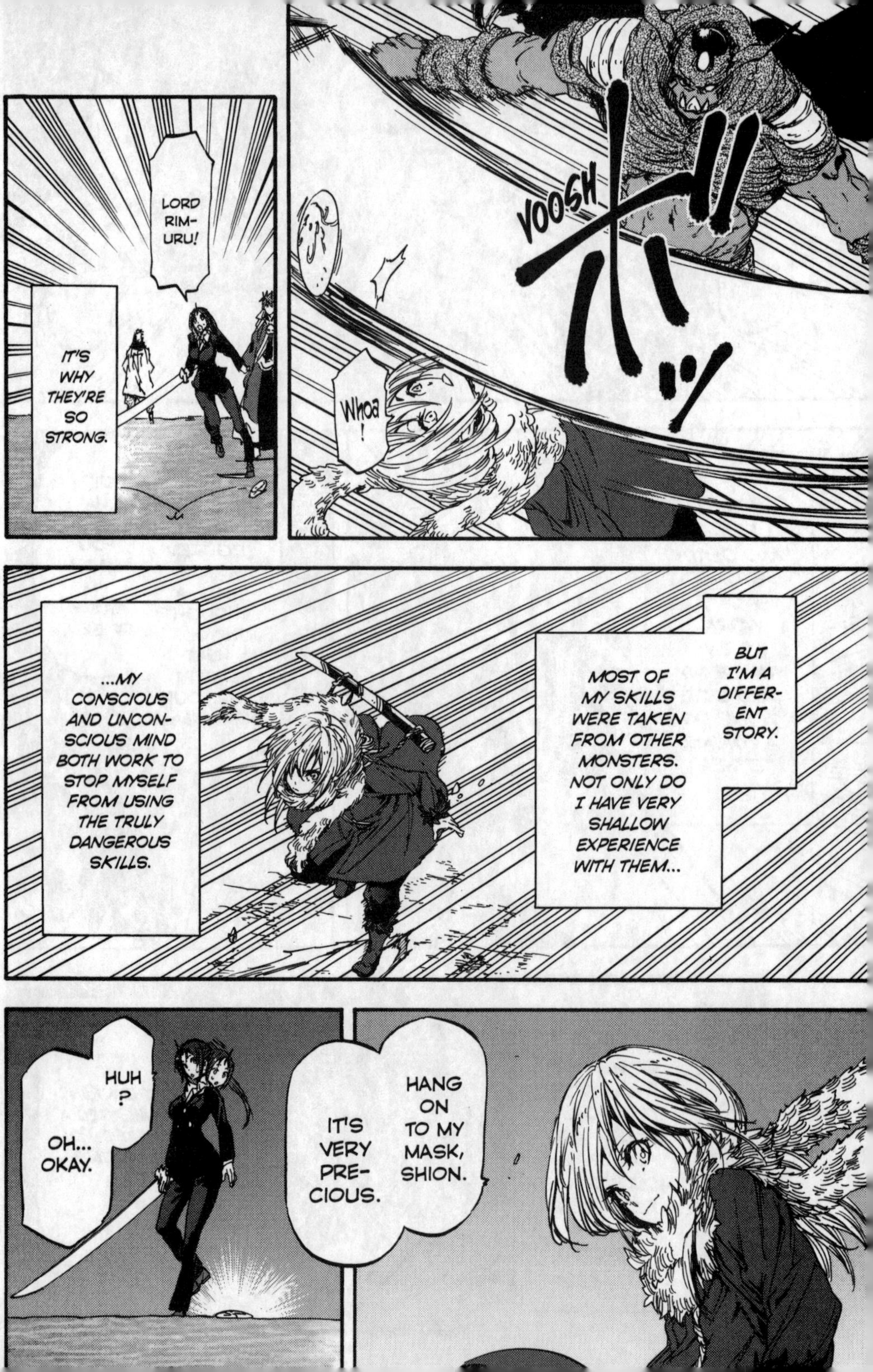
VOOSH
Whoa!
LORD RIM-URU!
IT'S WHY THEY'RE SO STRONG.
BUT I'M A DIFFERENT STORY.
MOST OF MY SKILLS WERE TAKEN FROM OTHER MONSTERS. NOT ONLY DO I HAVE VERY SHALLOW EXPERIENCE WITH THEM...
...MY CONSCIOUS AND UNCONSCIOUS MIND BOTH WORK TO STOP MYSELF FROM USING THE TRULY DANGEROUS SKILLS.
HANG ON TO MY MASK, SHION.
IT'S VERY PRECIOUS.
HUH?
OH... OKAY.

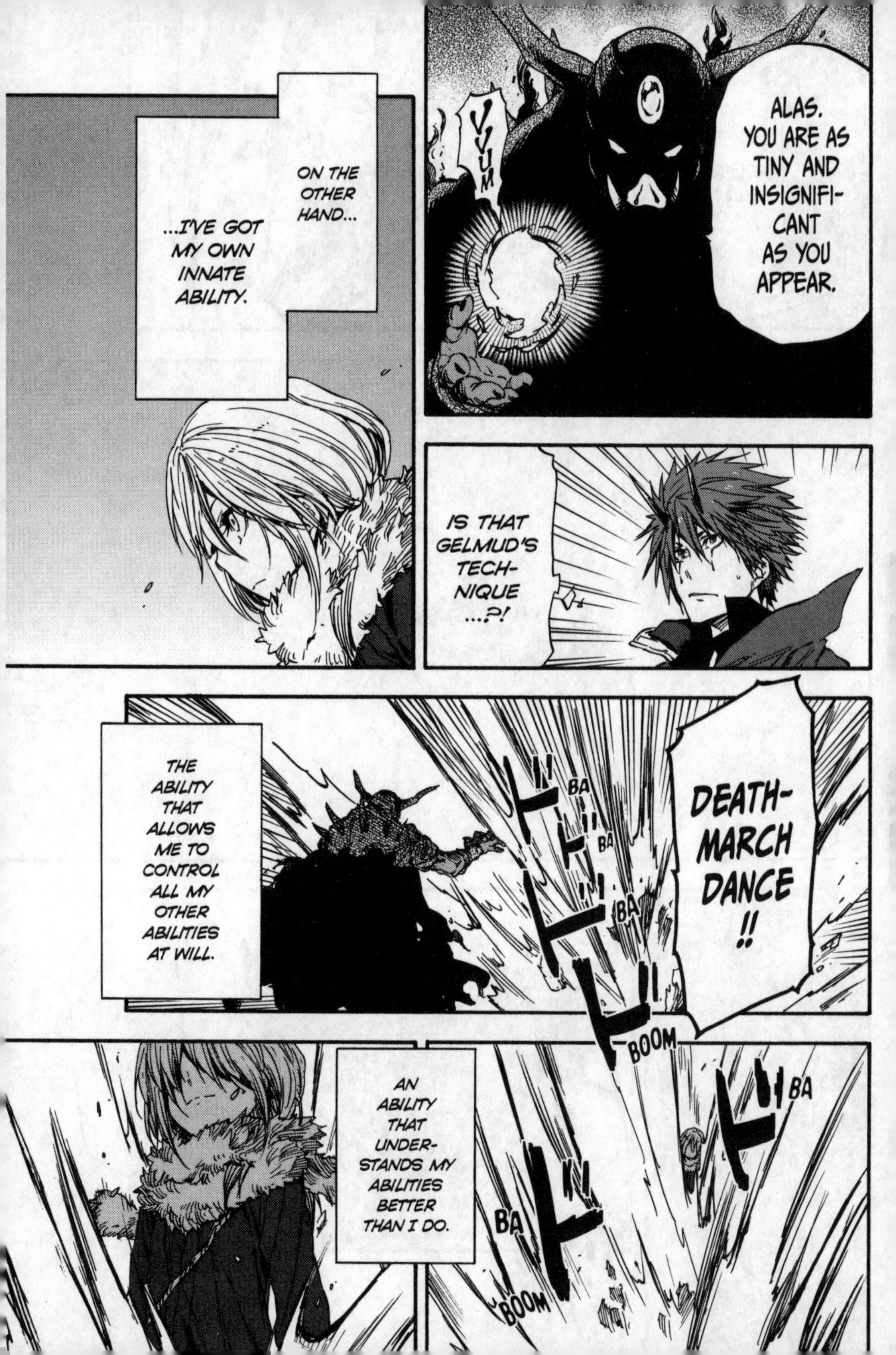
VVUM
ALAS. YOU ARE AS TINY AND INSIGNIFI- CANT AS YOU APPEAR.
IS THAT GELMUD'S TECH- NIQUE ...?!
ON THE OTHER HAND...
...I'VE GOT MY OWN INNATE ABILITY.
DEATH- MARCH DANCE !!
BA
BA
BA
THE ABILITY THAT ALLOWS ME TO CONTROL ALL MY OTHER ABILITIES AT WILL.
BOOM
BA
BA
BOOM
AN ABILITY THAT UNDER- STANDS MY ABILITIES BETTER THAN I DO.

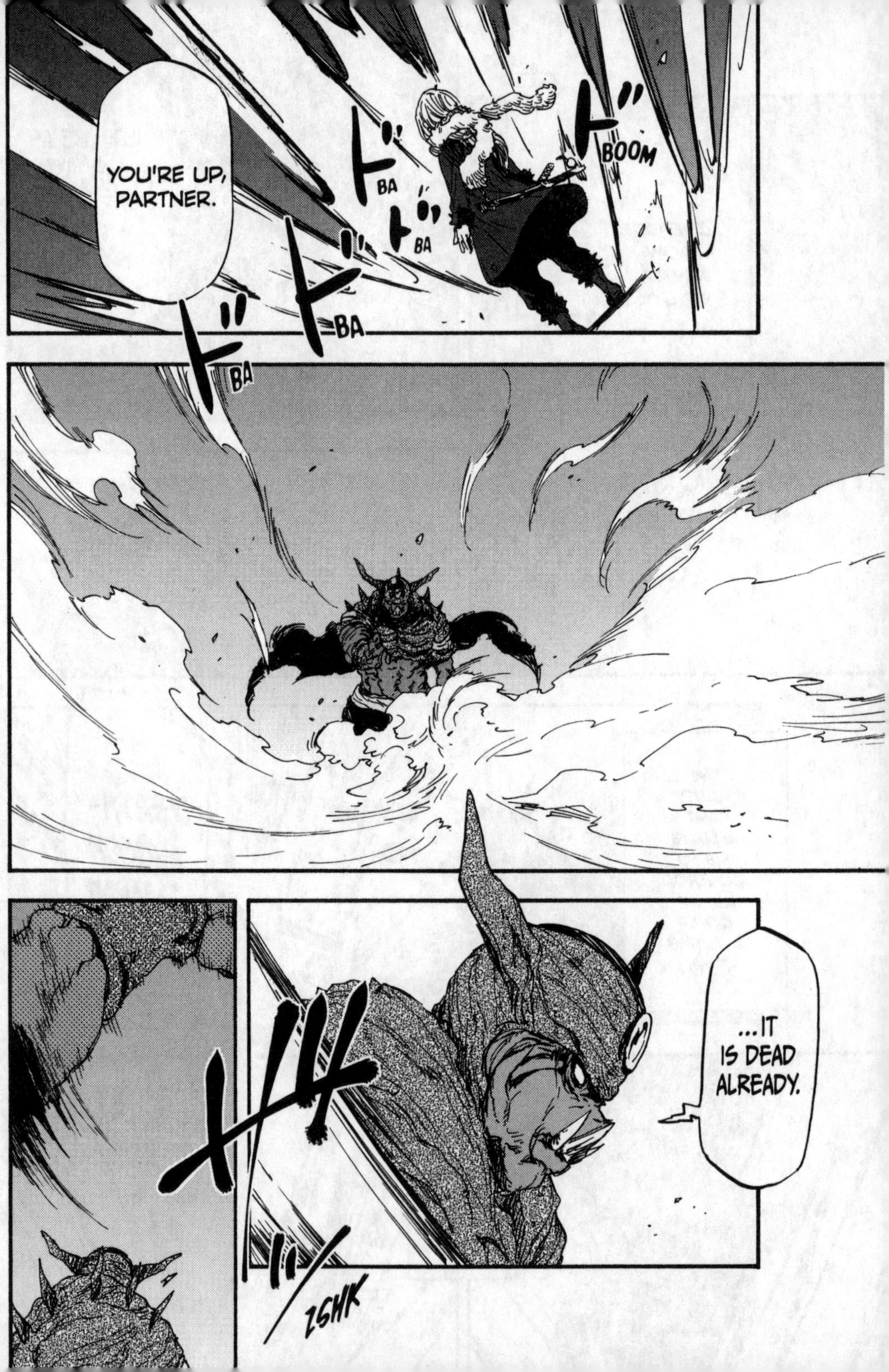
BOOM
BA
BA
YOU'RE UP, PARTNER.
BA
BA
...IT IS DEAD ALREADY.
ZSHK

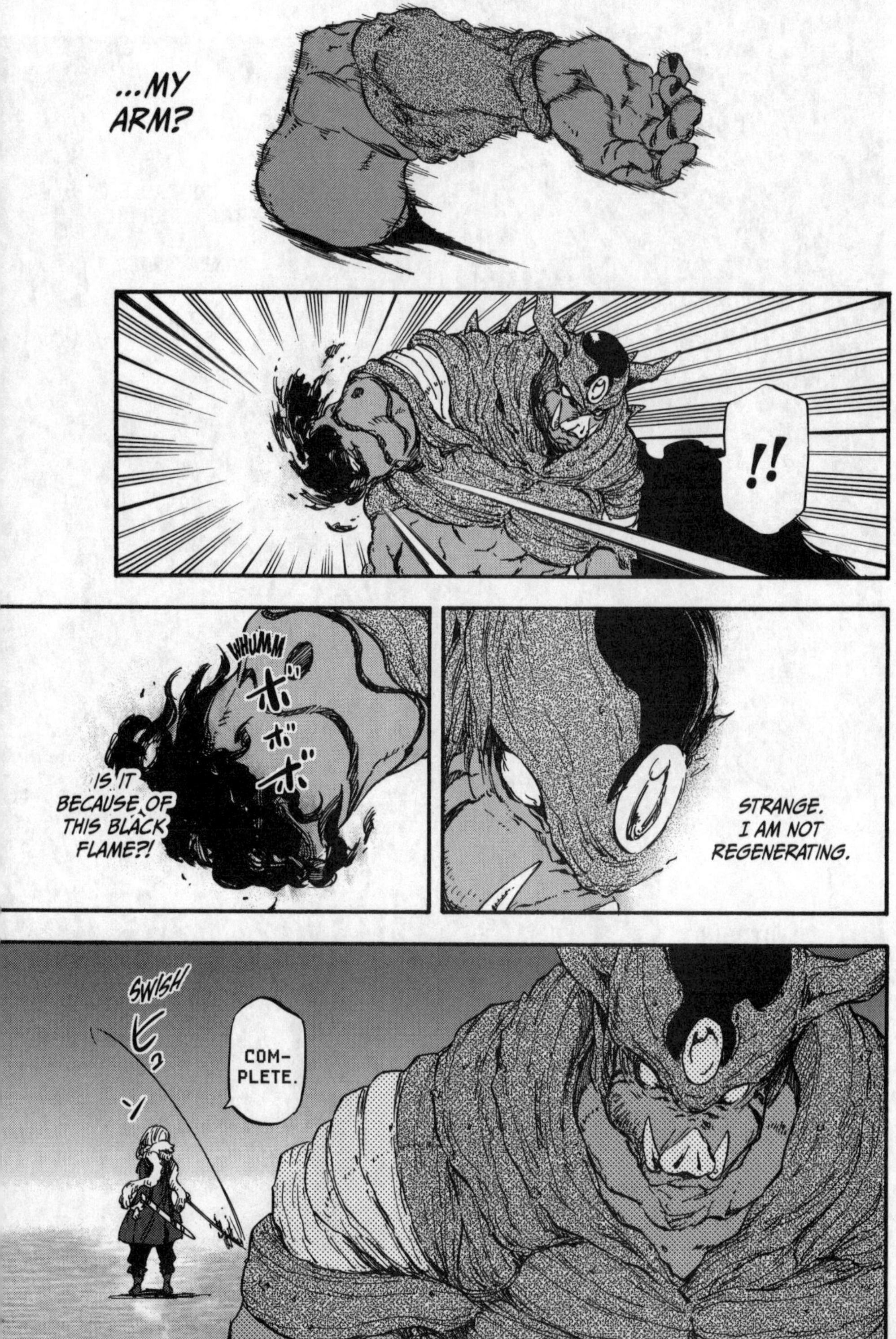

...MY ARM?
!!
STRANGE. I AM NOT REGENERATING.
WHUMM
IS IT BECAUSE OF THIS BLACK FLAME?!
COM-PLETE.
SWISH

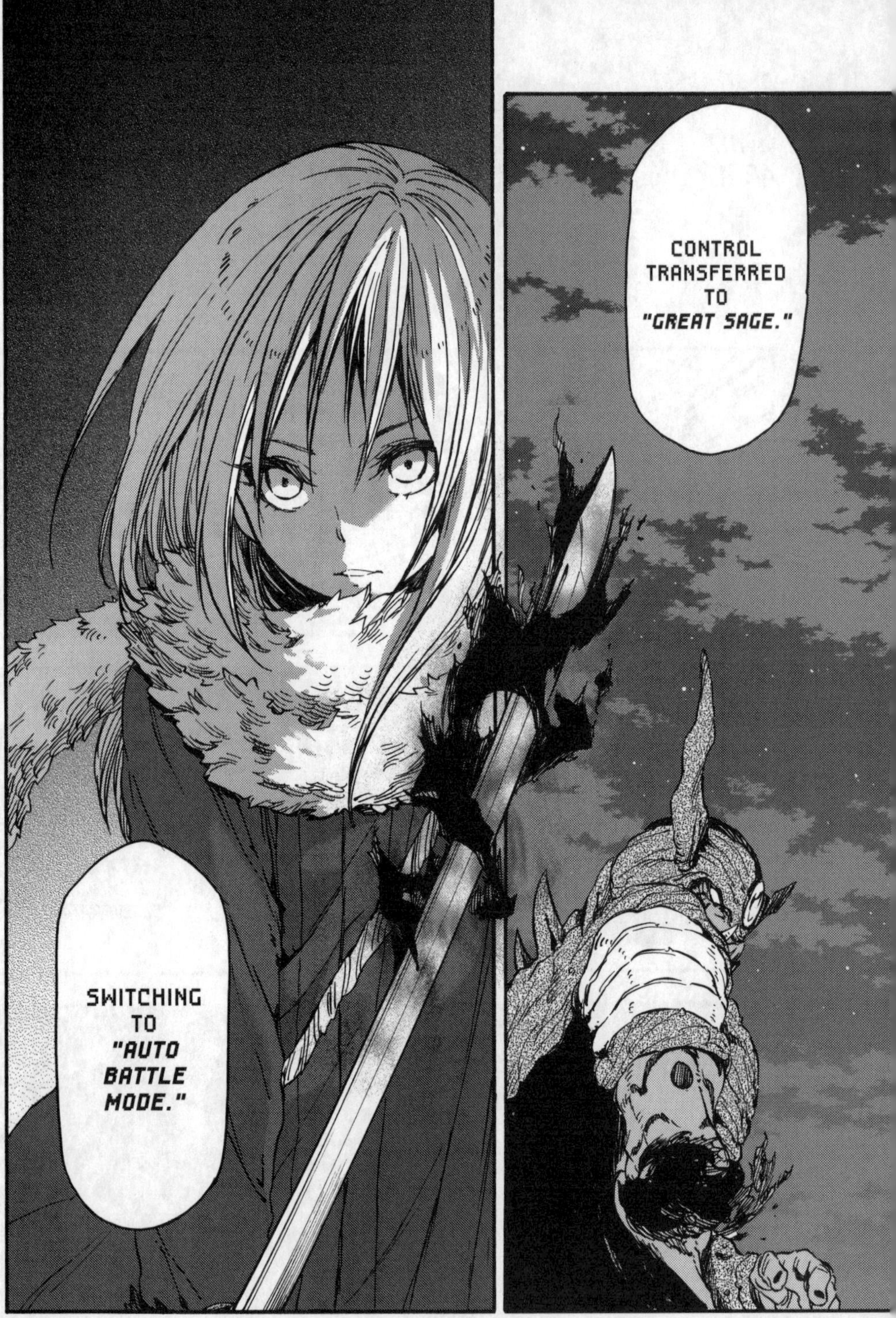
CONTROL TRANSFERRED TO "GREAT SAGE."
SWITCHING TO "AUTO BATTLE MODE."

GOBTA'S HENCHMEN

GOBTSU & GOBTE

Twin brothers, apparently.

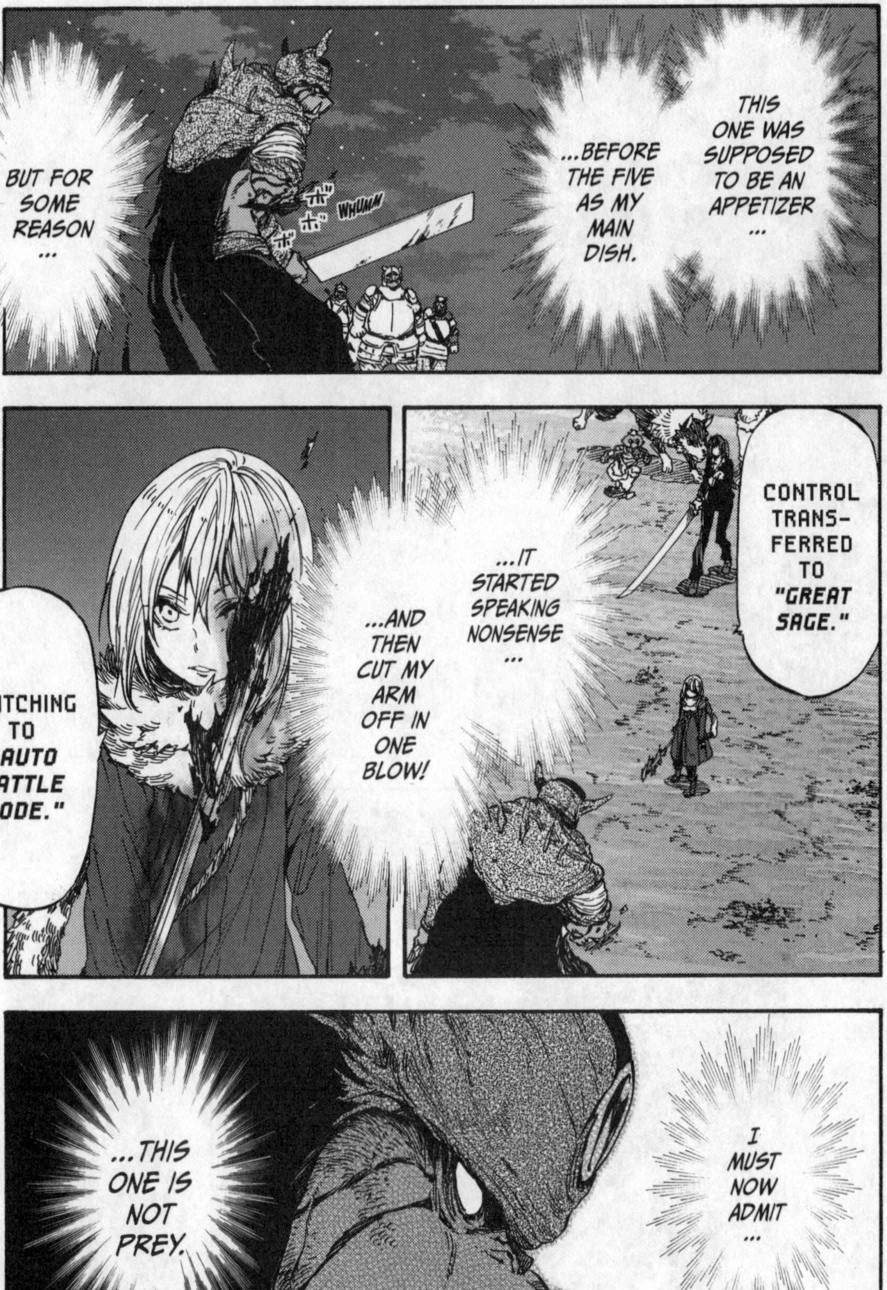
THIS ONE WAS SUPPOSED TO BE AN APPETIZER ...
...BEFORE THE FIVE AS MY MAIN DISH.
BUT FOR SOME REASON ...
ボ ボ ボ
WHUMM
CONTROL TRANS-FERRED TO "GREAT SAGE."
...IT STARTED SPEAKING NONSENSE ...
...AND THEN CUT MY ARM OFF IN ONE BLOW!
SWITCHING TO "AUTO BATTLE MODE."
I MUST NOW ADMIT ...
...THIS ONE IS NOT PREY.

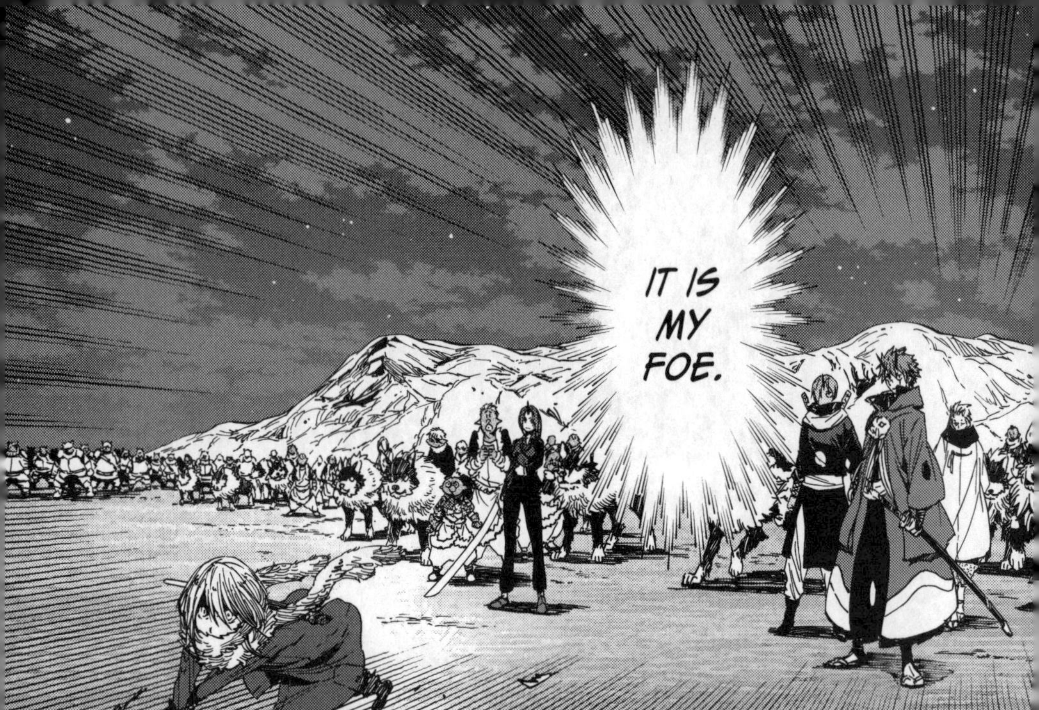
IT IS MY FOE.
CHAPTER 25 That Which Devours All

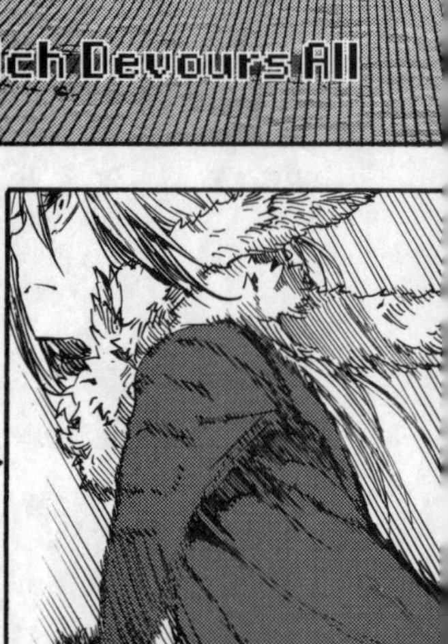

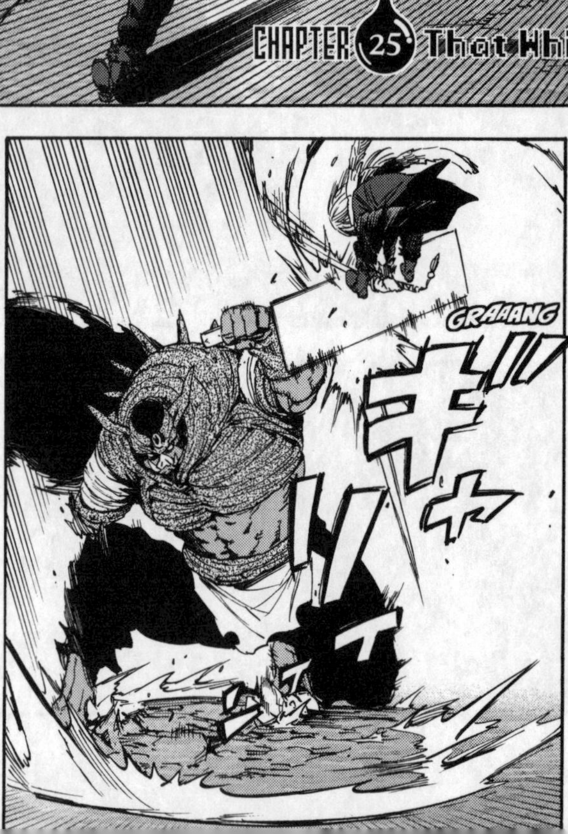
GRAAANG

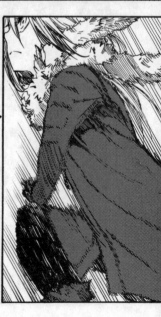

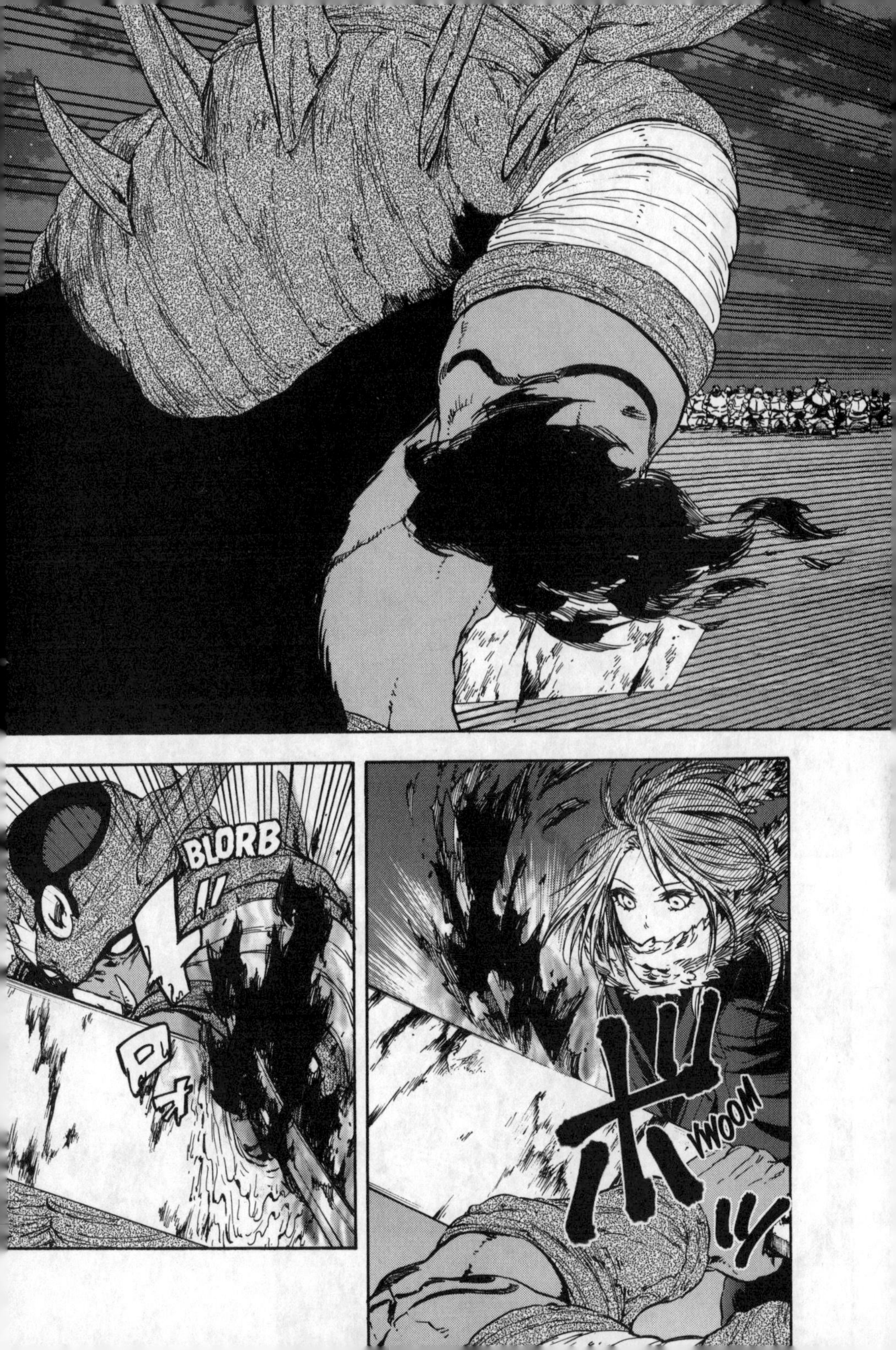
VWOOM
BLORB

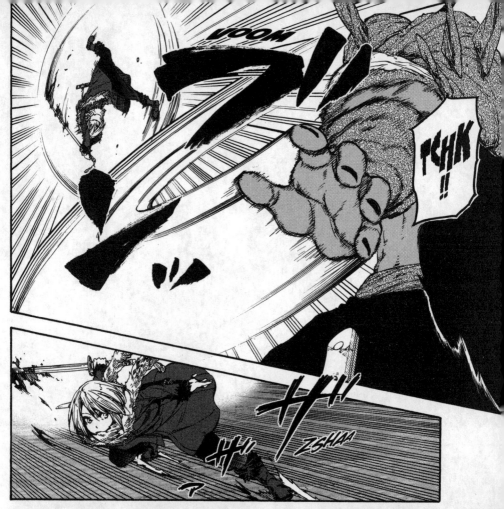

VOOM

TCHK!!

HH!! HH!! ZSHAA

WHY ISN'T THE ORC DISASTER'S ARM REGENERATING ...?

CHAOS EATER!

WHOOSH!

!

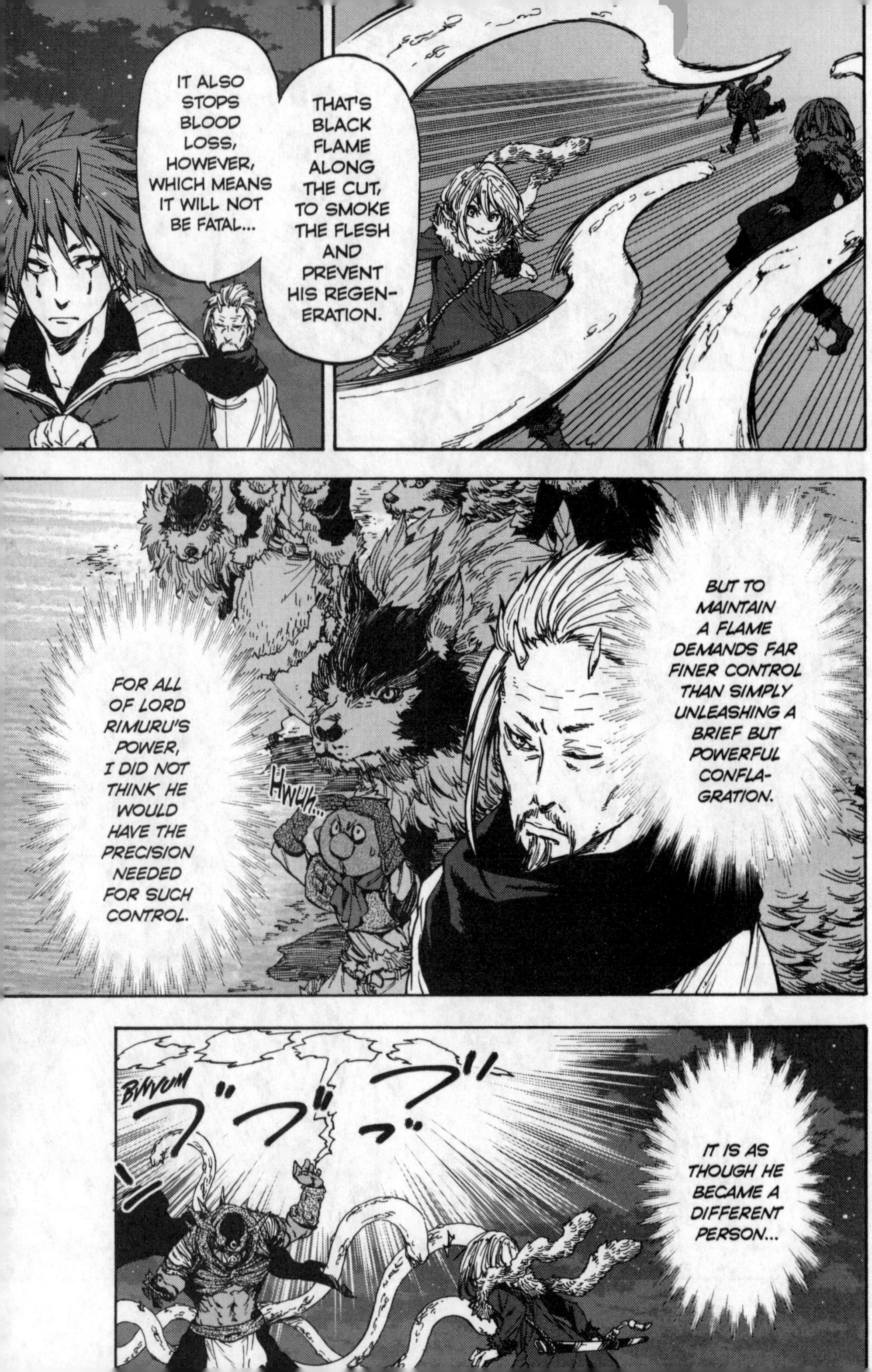
THAT'S BLACK FLAME ALONG THE CUT, TO SMOKE THE FLESH AND PREVENT HIS REGEN-ERATION.
IT ALSO STOPS BLOOD LOSS, HOWEVER, WHICH MEANS IT WILL NOT BE FATAL...
BUT TO MAINTAIN A FLAME DEMANDS FAR FINER CONTROL THAN SIMPLY UNLEASHING A BRIEF BUT POWERFUL CONFLA-GRATION.
HWUH...
FOR ALL OF LORD RIMURU'S POWER, I DID NOT THINK HE WOULD HAVE THE PRECISION NEEDED FOR SUCH CONTROL.
IT IS AS THOUGH HE BECAME A DIFFERENT PERSON...
BVVVUM

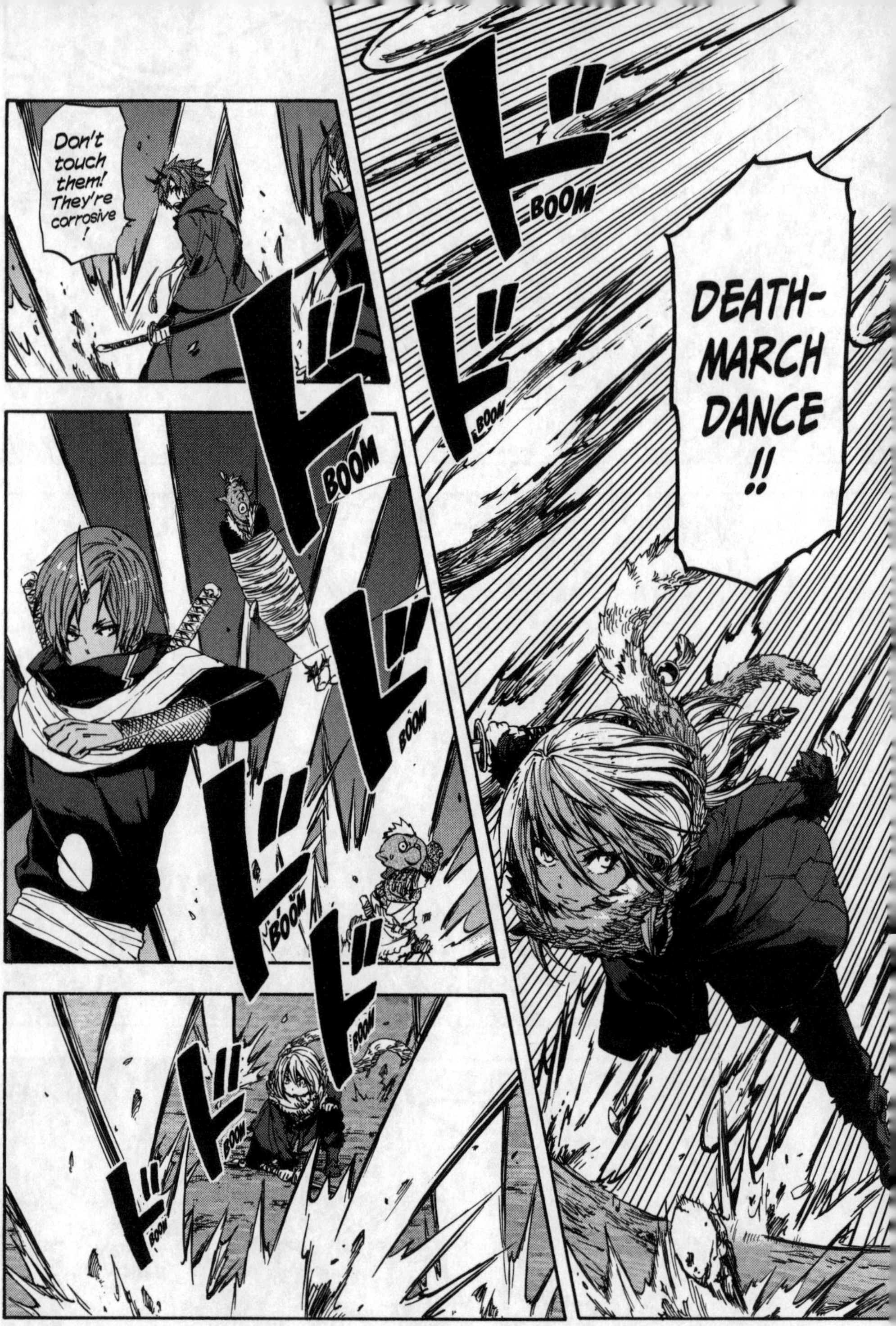
BOOM
BOOM
DEATH-MARCH DANCE!!
Don't touch them! They're corrosive!
BOOM
BOOM
BOOM
BOOM
BOOM
BOOM

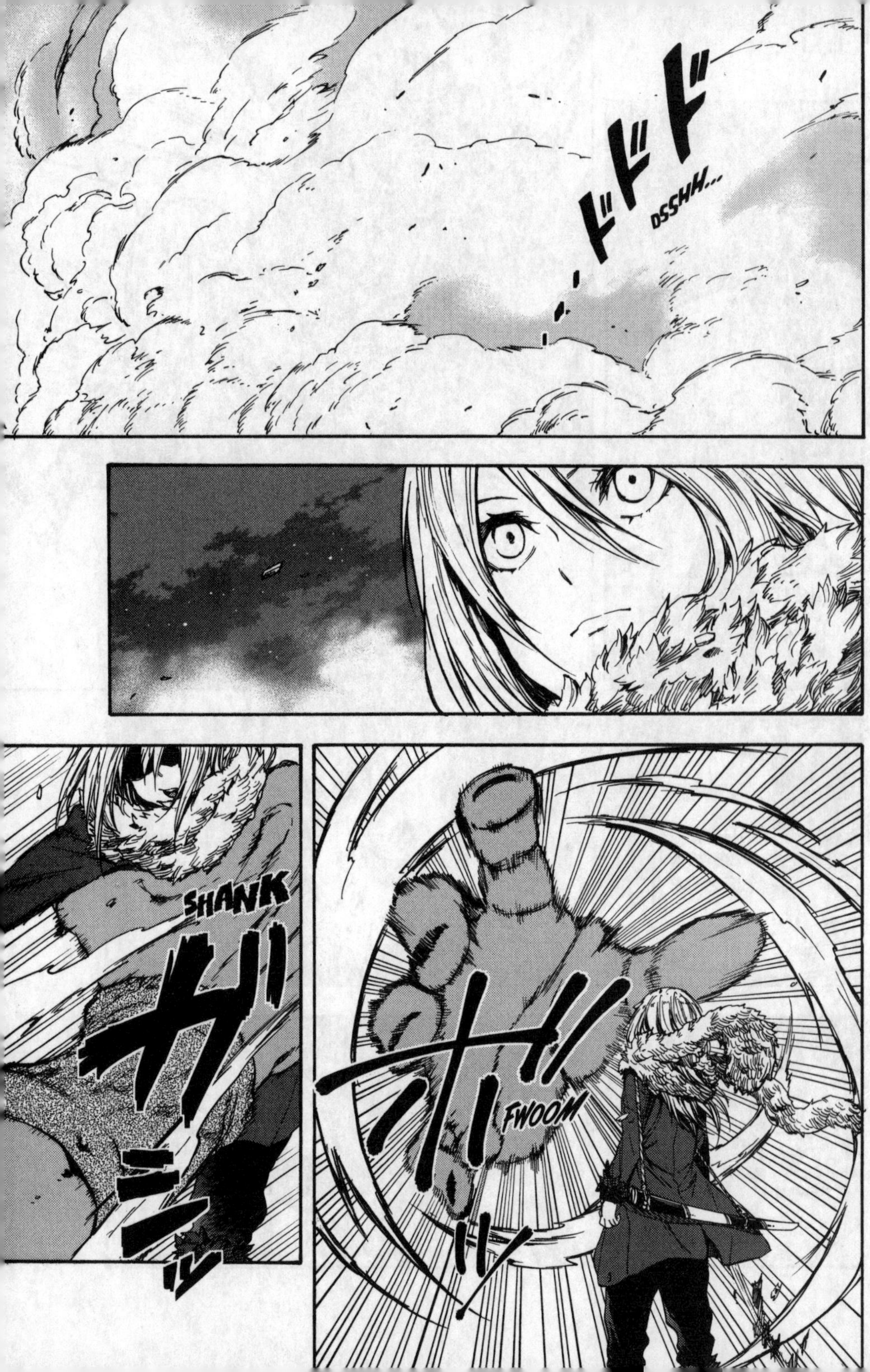
ドドド
DSSHH...
FWOOM
SHANK

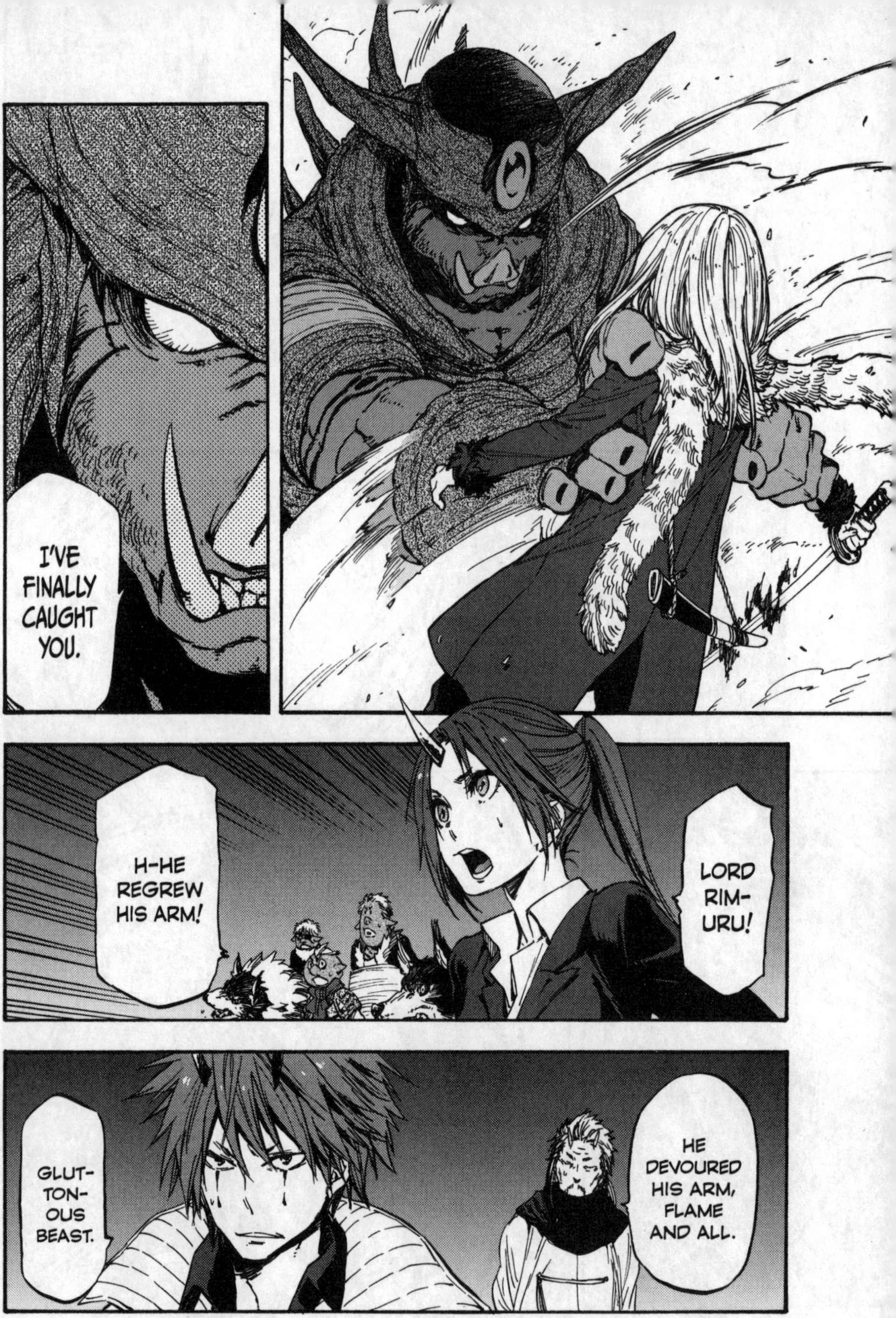
I'VE FINALLY CAUGHT YOU.
LORD RIM-URU!
H-HE REGREW HIS ARM!
HE DEVOURED HIS ARM, FLAME AND ALL.
GLUT-TON-OUS BEAST.

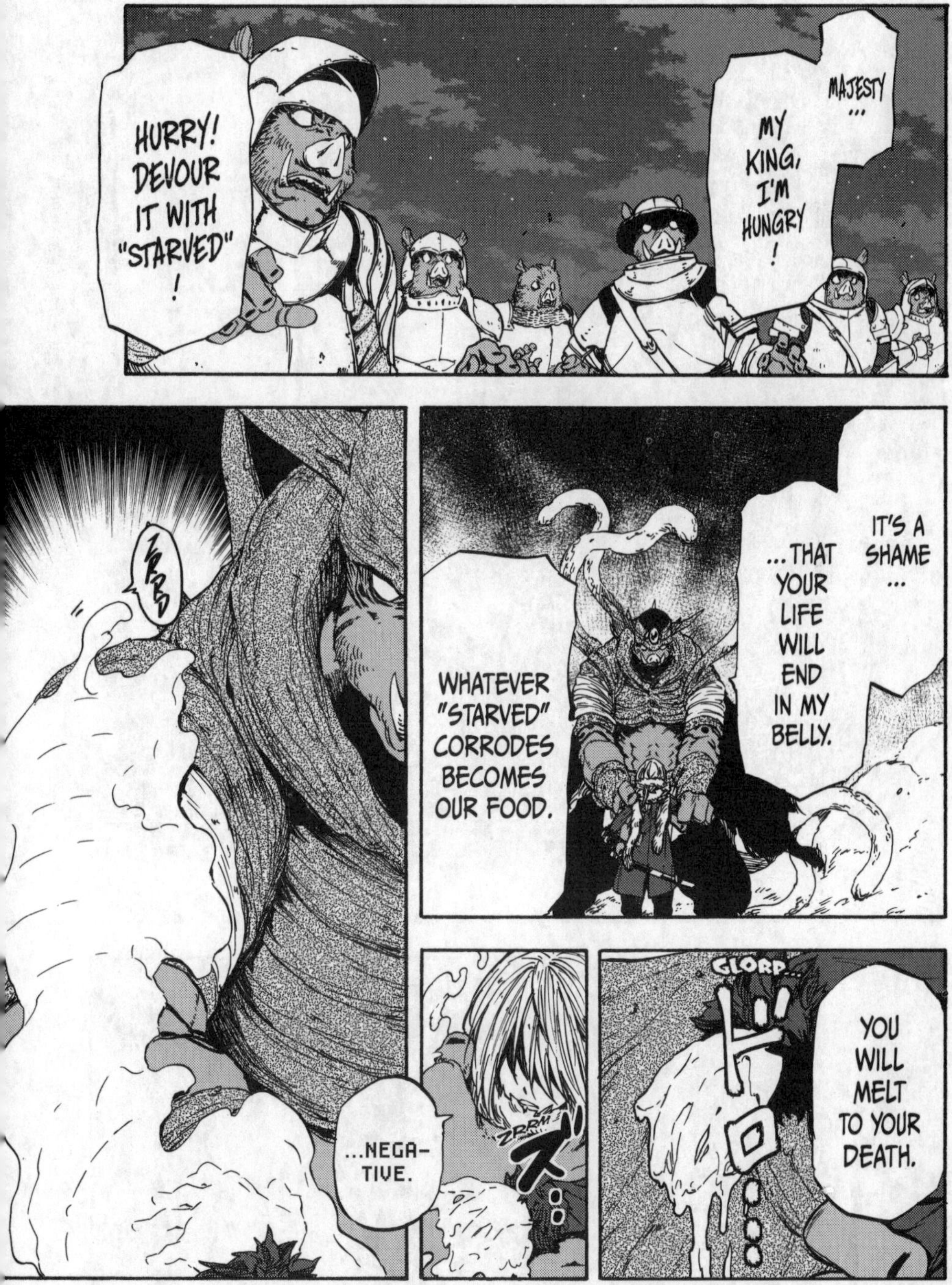
MAJESTY...
MY KING, I'M HUNGRY!
HURRY! DEVOUR IT WITH "STARVED"!
IT'S A SHAME...
...THAT YOUR LIFE WILL END IN MY BELLY.
WHATEVER "STARVED" CORRODES BECOMES OUR FOOD.
GLORP...
YOU WILL MELT TO YOUR DEATH.
ZRRM
...NEGA-TIVE.

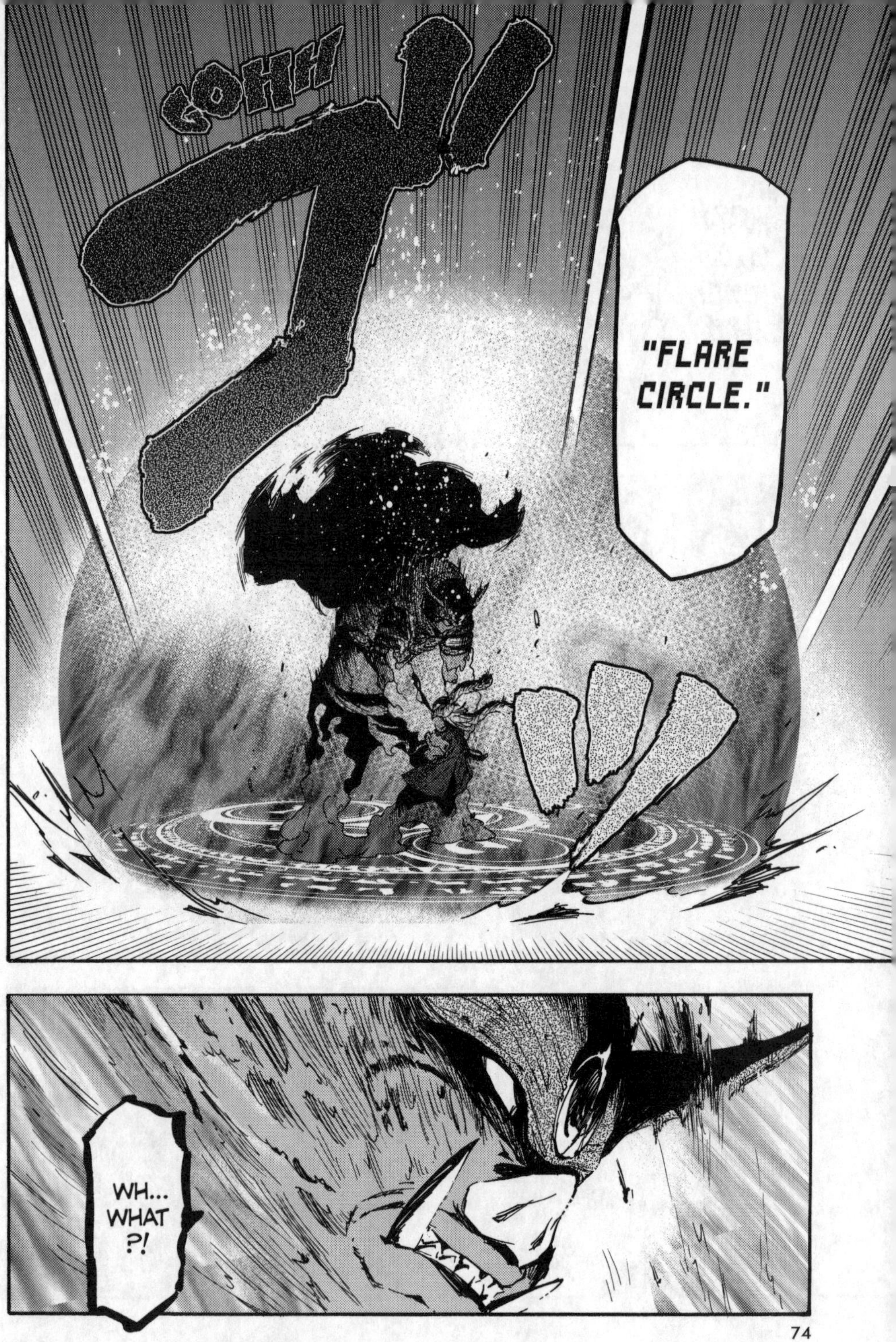
GOHH
"FLARE CIRCLE."
WH... WHAT ?!

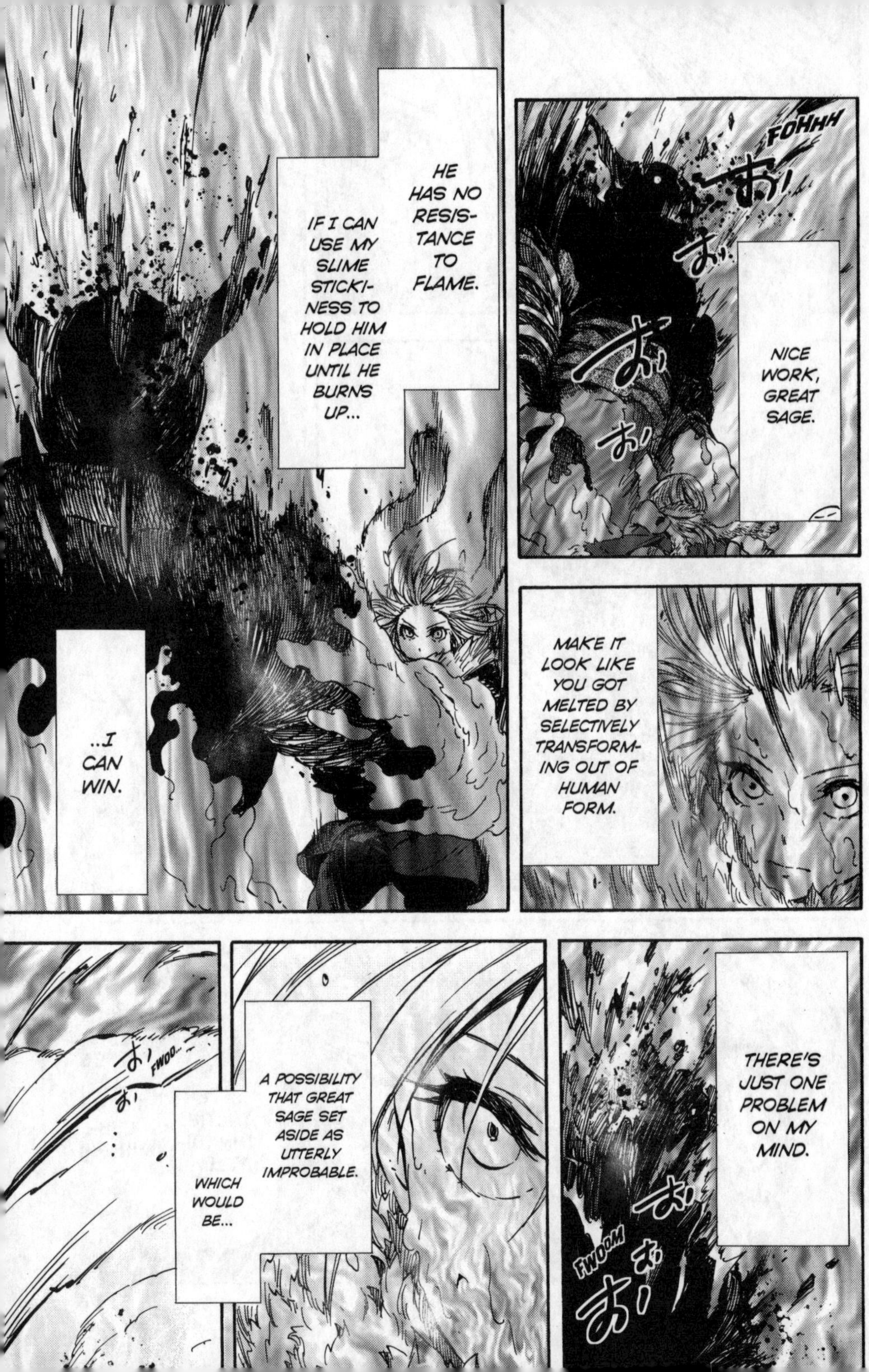
FOHHH
NICE WORK, GREAT SAGE.
MAKE IT LOOK LIKE YOU GOT MELTED BY SELECTIVELY TRANSFORMING OUT OF HUMAN FORM.
HE HAS NO RESISTANCE TO FLAME.
IF I CAN USE MY SLIME STICKINESS TO HOLD HIM IN PLACE UNTIL HE BURNS UP...
...I CAN WIN.
THERE'S JUST ONE PROBLEM ON MY MIND.
FWOOM
A POSSIBILITY THAT GREAT SAGE SET ASIDE AS UTTERLY IMPROBABLE.
FWOO...
WHICH WOULD BE...

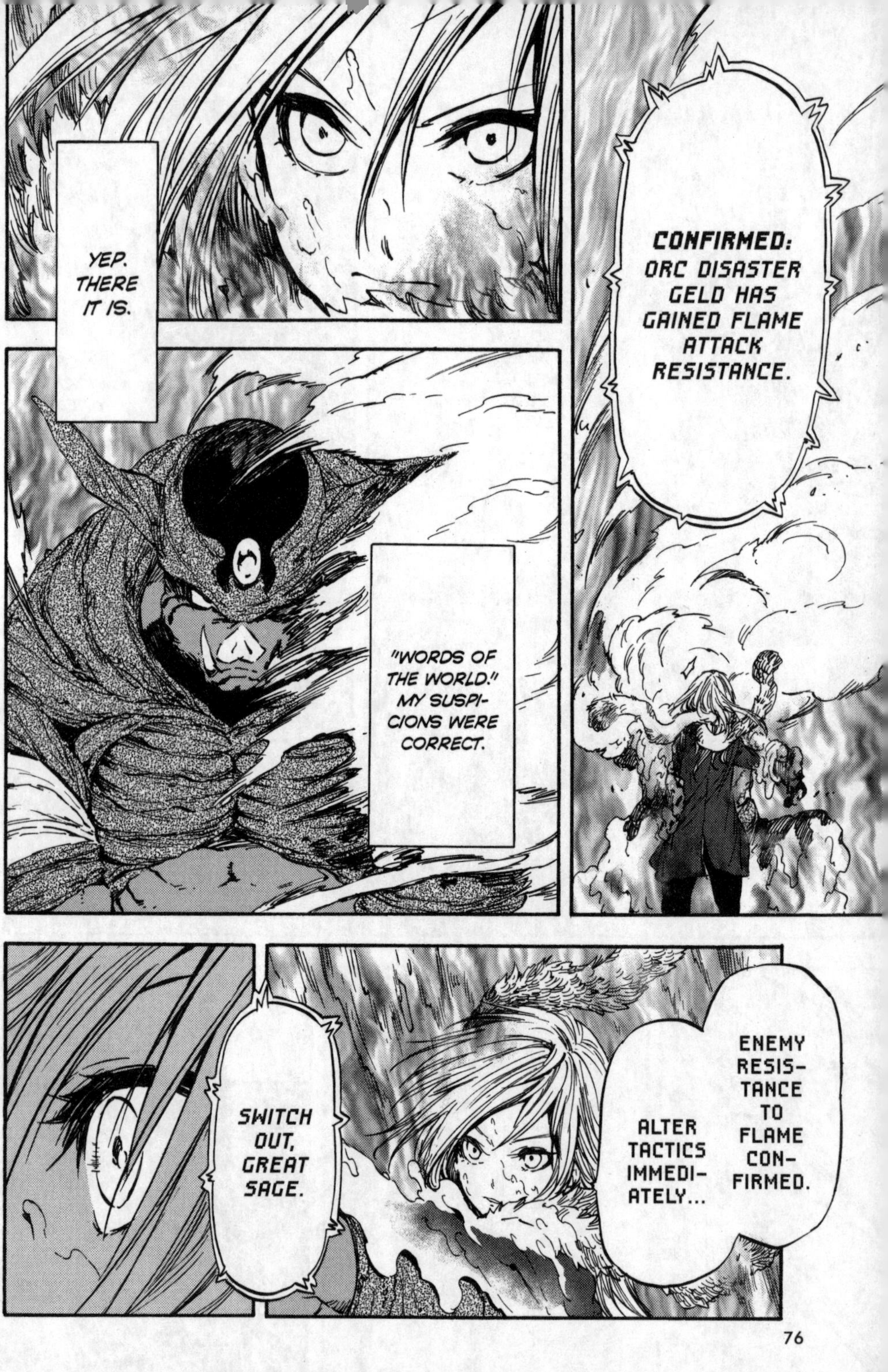
CONFIRMED: ORC DISASTER GELD HAS GAINED FLAME ATTACK RESISTANCE.
YEP. THERE IT IS.
"WORDS OF THE WORLD." MY SUSPICIONS WERE CORRECT.
ENEMY RESISTANCE TO FLAME CONFIRMED.
ALTER TACTICS IMMEDIATELY...
SWITCH OUT, GREAT SAGE.

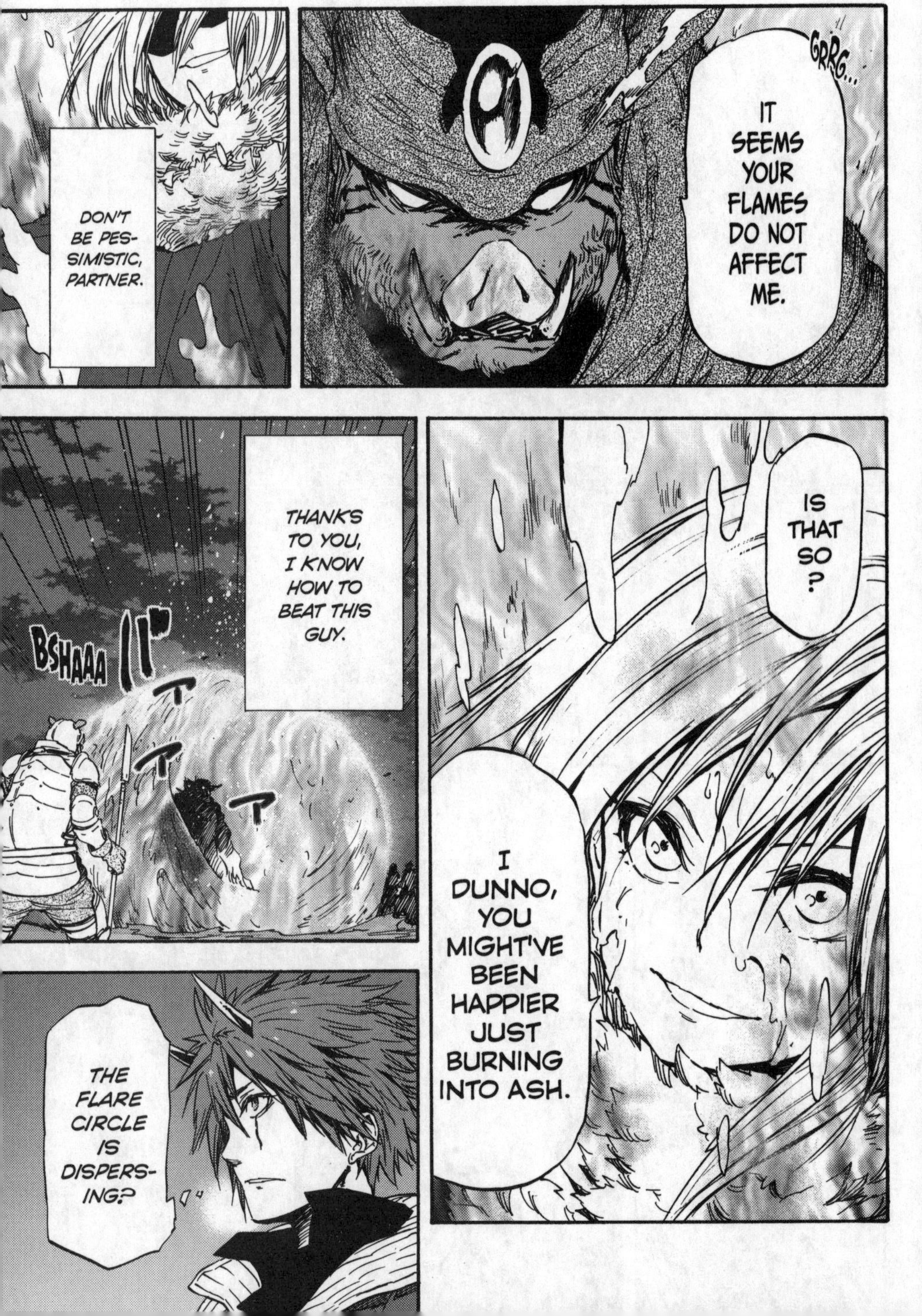
GRRG...
IT SEEMS YOUR FLAMES DO NOT AFFECT ME.
DON'T BE PESSIMISTIC, PARTNER.
IS THAT SO?
I DUNNO, YOU MIGHT'VE BEEN HAPPIER JUST BURNING INTO ASH.
THANKS TO YOU, I KNOW HOW TO BEAT THIS GUY.
BSHAAA
THE FLARE CIRCLE IS DISPERSING?

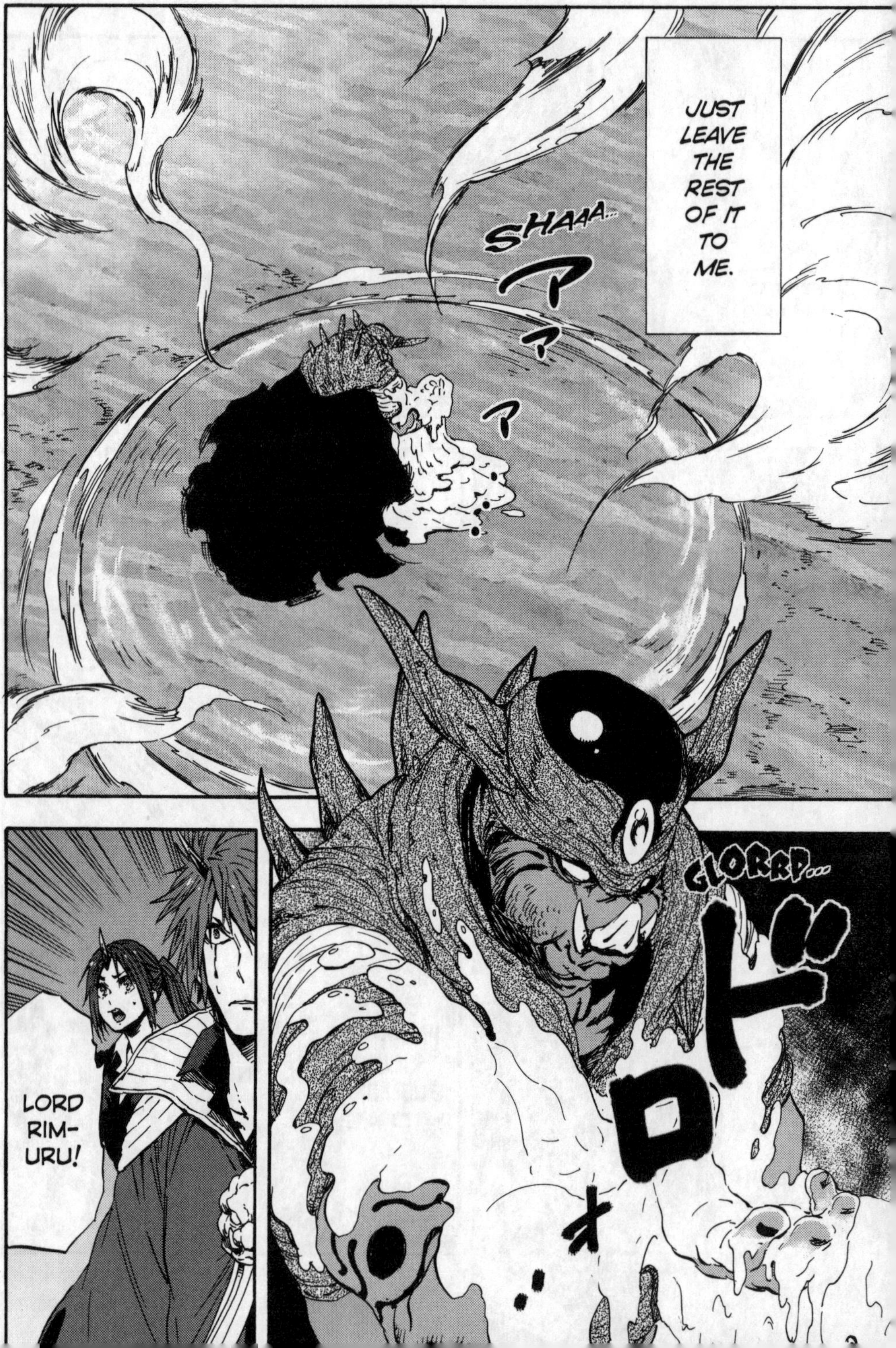
JUST LEAVE THE REST OF IT TO ME.
SHAAA...
アアア
GLORRP...
ドロォ
LORD RIM-URU!

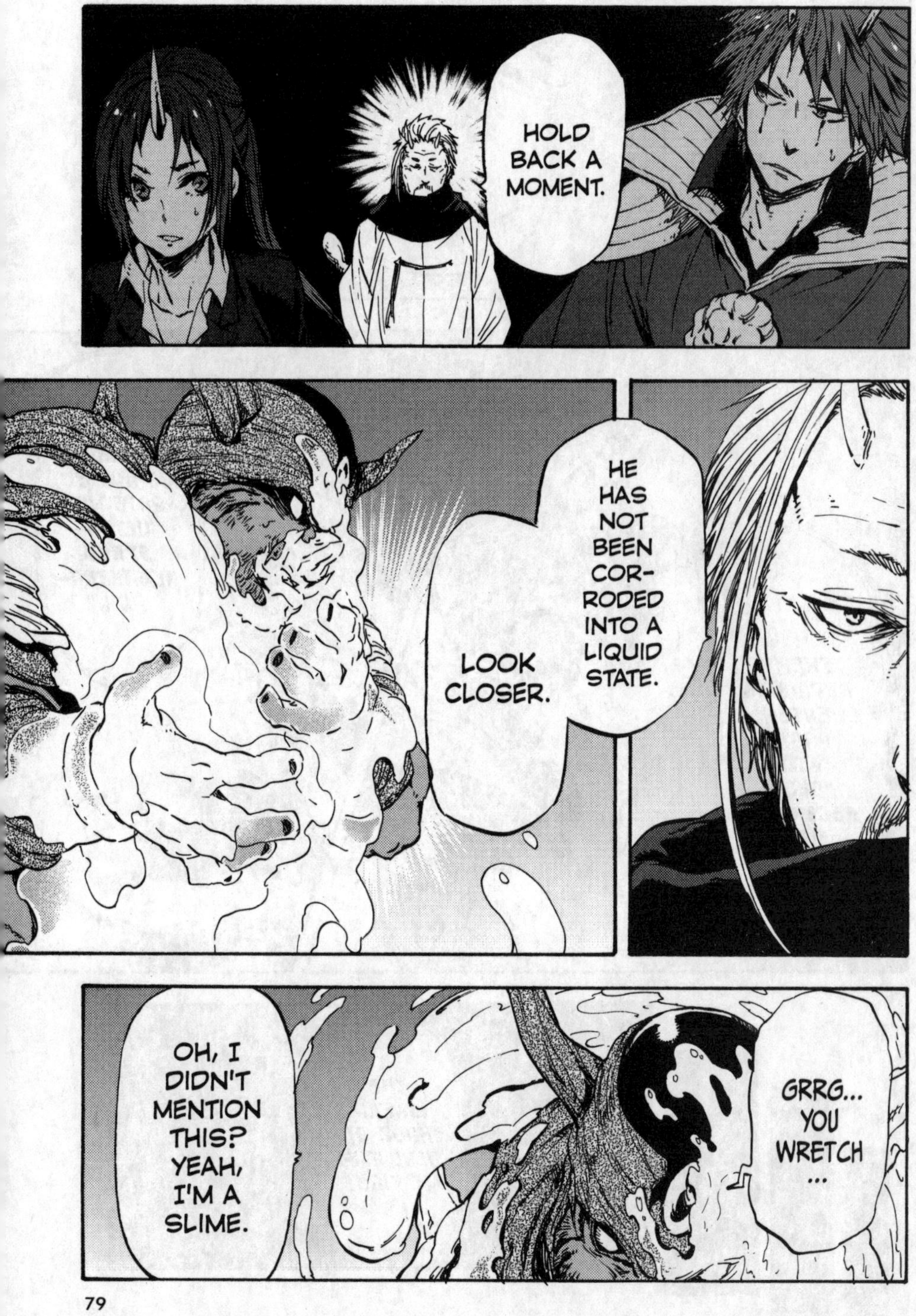
HOLD BACK A MOMENT.
HE HAS NOT BEEN COR- RODED INTO A LIQUID STATE.
LOOK CLOSER.
GRRG... YOU WRETCH ...
OH, I DIDN'T MENTION THIS? YEAH, I'M A SLIME.

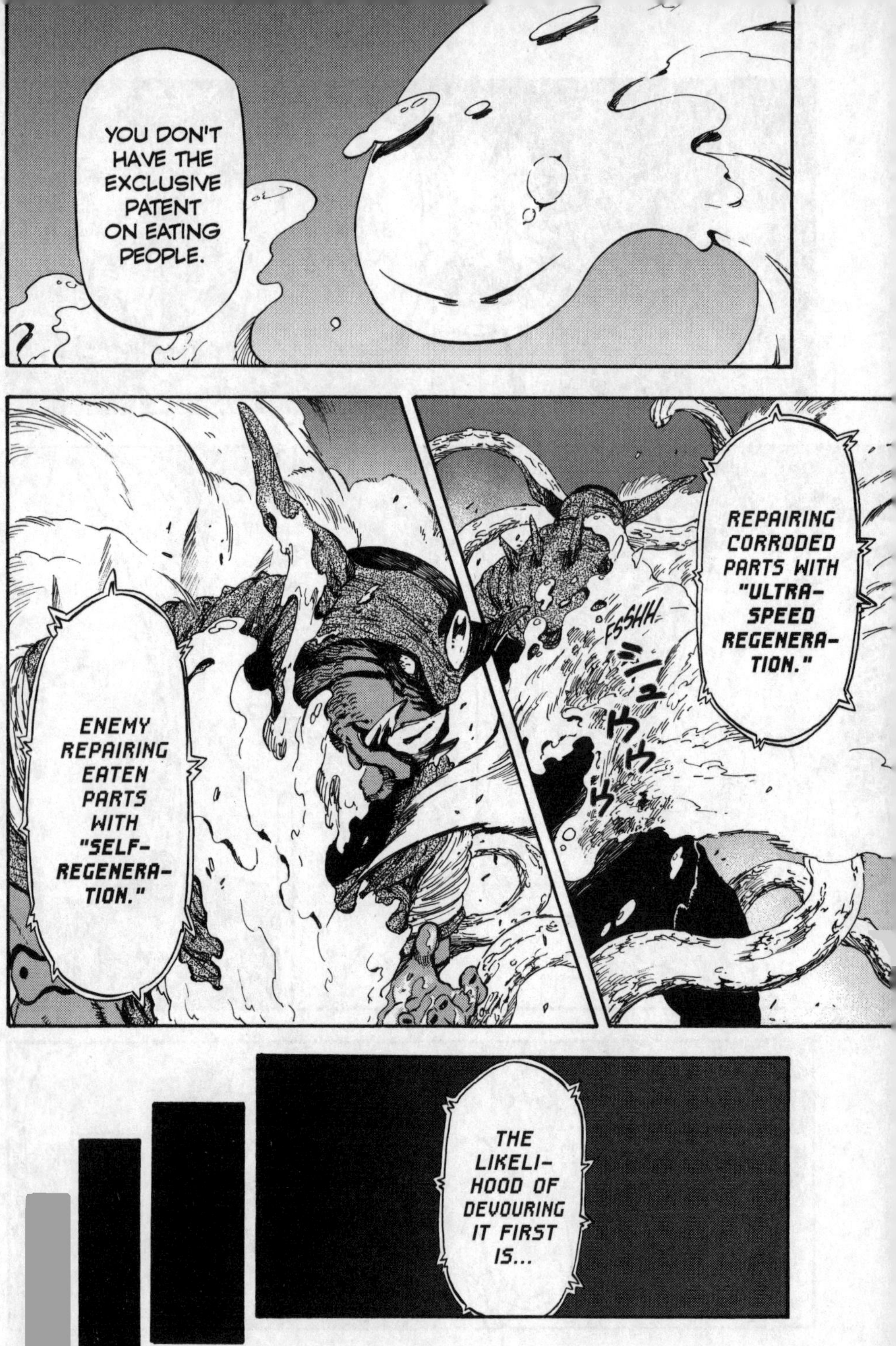
YOU DON'T HAVE THE EXCLUSIVE PATENT ON EATING PEOPLE.
REPAIRING CORRODED PARTS WITH "ULTRA-SPEED REGENERA-TION."
FSSHH
シュウウウ
ENEMY REPAIRING EATEN PARTS WITH "SELF-REGENERA-TION."
THE LIKELI-HOOD OF DEVOURING IT FIRST IS...

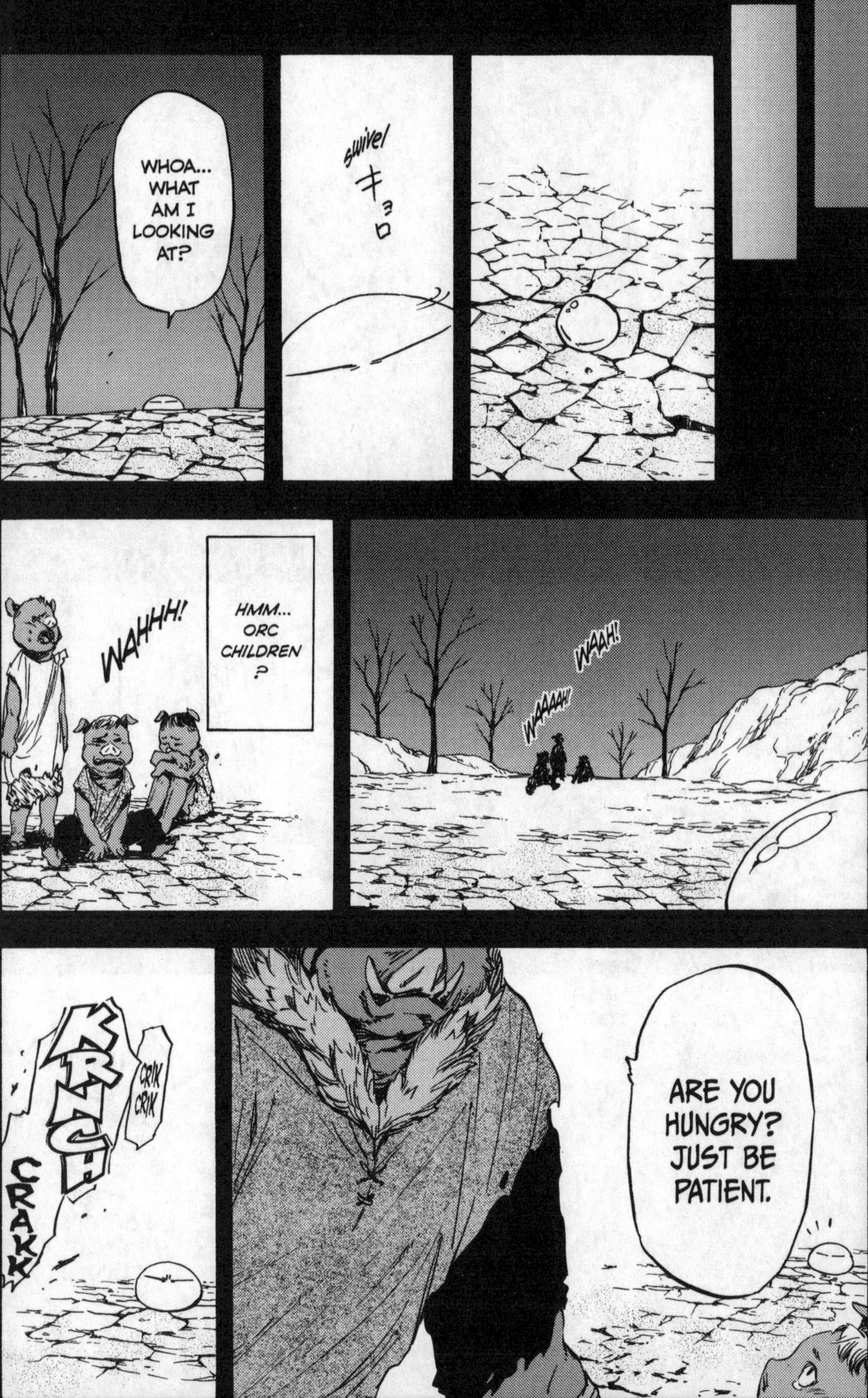
swivel
キョロ
WHOA... WHAT AM I LOOKING AT?
WAAH!
WAAAAH!
HMM... ORC CHILDREN?
WAHHH!
ARE YOU HUNGRY? JUST BE PATIENT.
KRNCH
CRIK CRIK
CRAKK

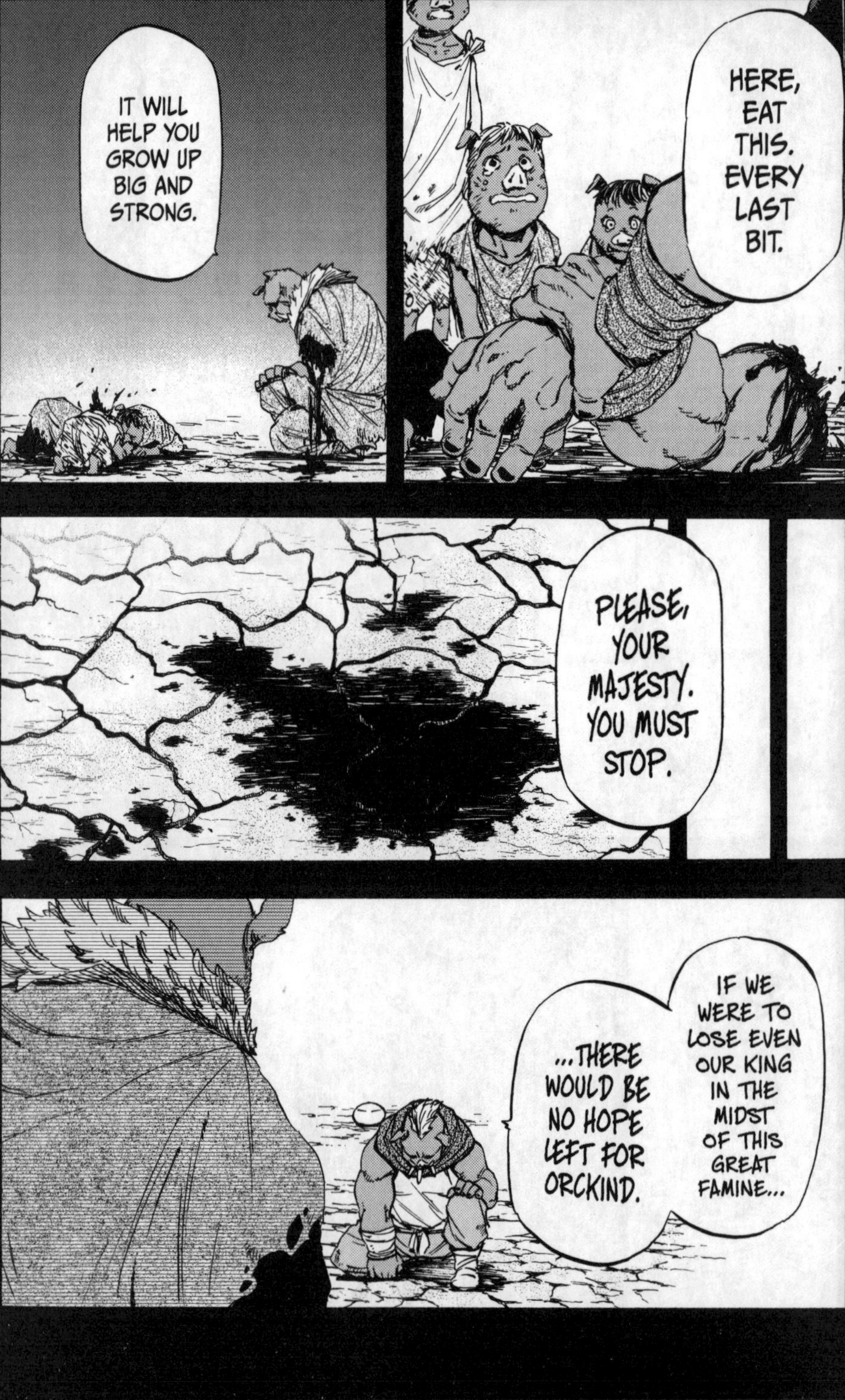
HERE, EAT THIS. EVERY LAST BIT.
IT WILL HELP YOU GROW UP BIG AND STRONG.
PLEASE, YOUR MAJESTY. YOU MUST STOP.
IF WE WERE TO LOSE EVEN OUR KING IN THE MIDST OF THIS GREAT FAMINE...
...THERE WOULD BE NO HOPE LEFT FOR ORCKIND.

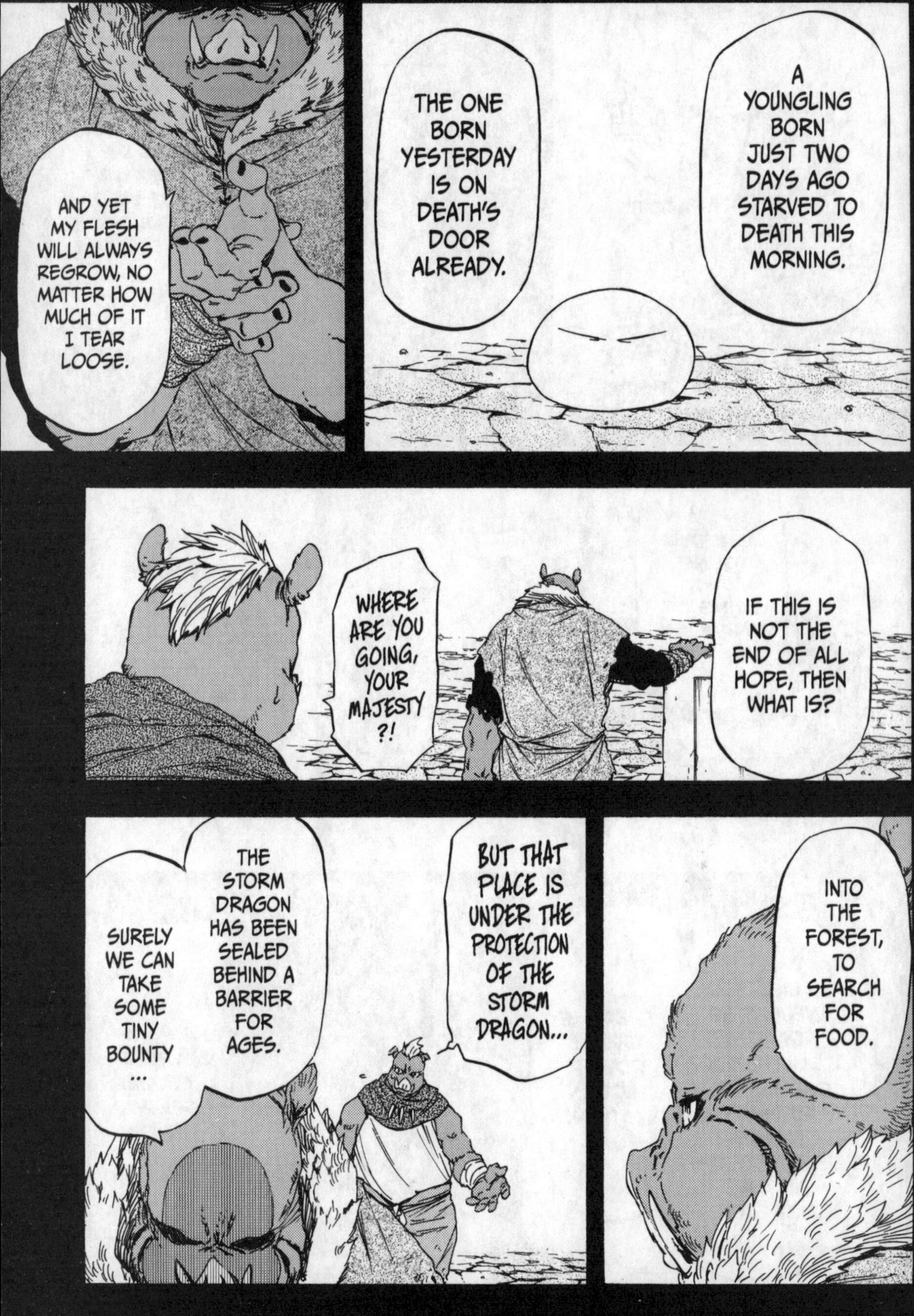
A YOUNGLING BORN JUST TWO DAYS AGO STARVED TO DEATH THIS MORNING.
THE ONE BORN YESTERDAY IS ON DEATH'S DOOR ALREADY.
AND YET MY FLESH WILL ALWAYS REGROW, NO MATTER HOW MUCH OF IT I TEAR LOOSE.
IF THIS IS NOT THE END OF ALL HOPE, THEN WHAT IS?
WHERE ARE YOU GOING, YOUR MAJESTY ?!
INTO THE FOREST, TO SEARCH FOR FOOD.
BUT THAT PLACE IS UNDER THE PROTECTION OF THE STORM DRAGON...
THE STORM DRAGON HAS BEEN SEALED BEHIND A BARRIER FOR AGES.
SURELY WE CAN TAKE SOME TINY BOUNTY ...

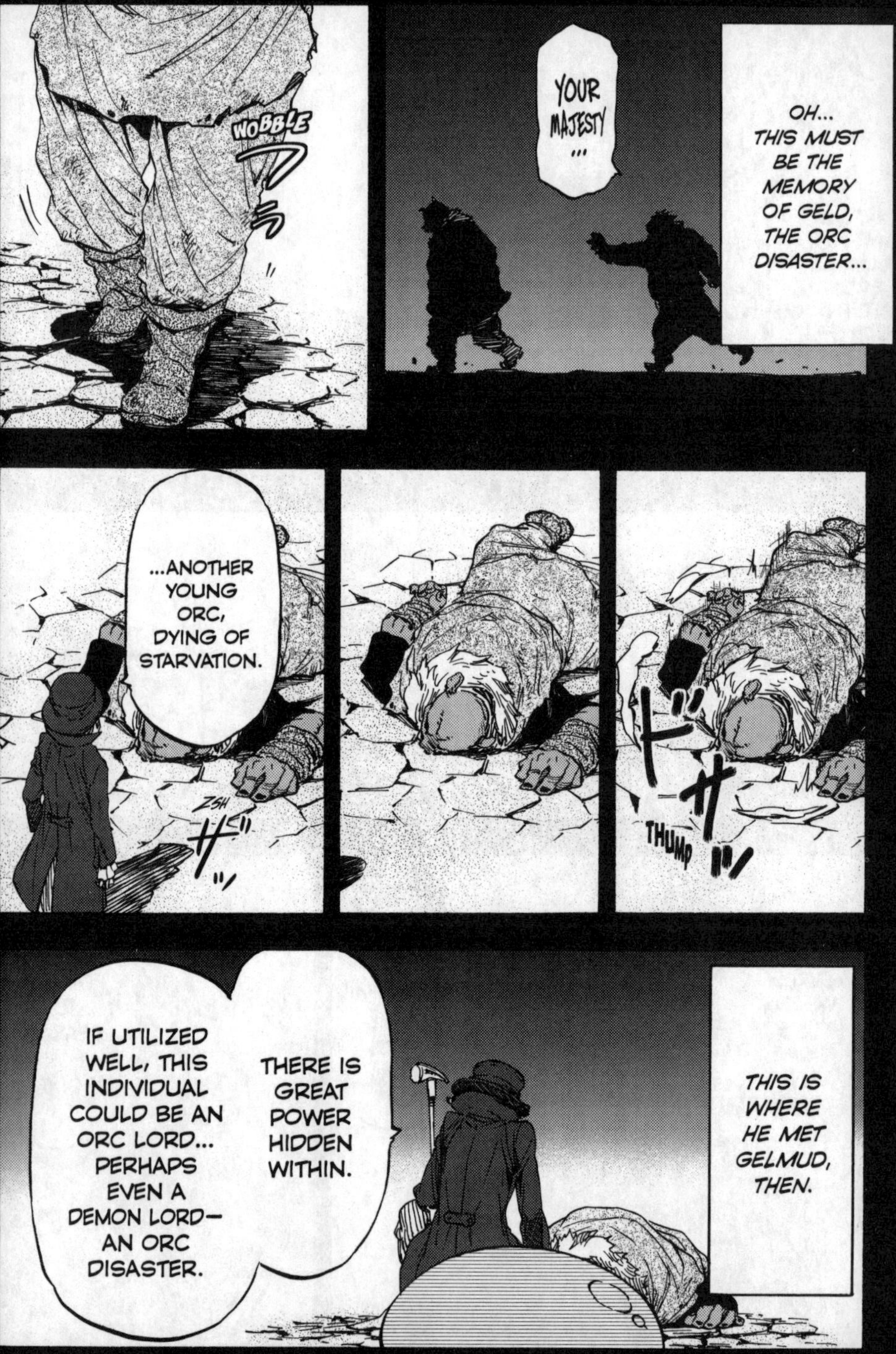
OH... THIS MUST BE THE MEMORY OF GELD, THE ORC DISASTER...
YOUR MAJESTY ...
WOBBLE
THUMP
...ANOTHER YOUNG ORC, DYING OF STARVATION.
ZSH
THIS IS WHERE HE MET GELMUD, THEN.
THERE IS GREAT POWER HIDDEN WITHIN.
IF UTILIZED WELL, THIS INDIVIDUAL COULD BE AN ORC LORD... PERHAPS EVEN A DEMON LORD— AN ORC DISASTER.

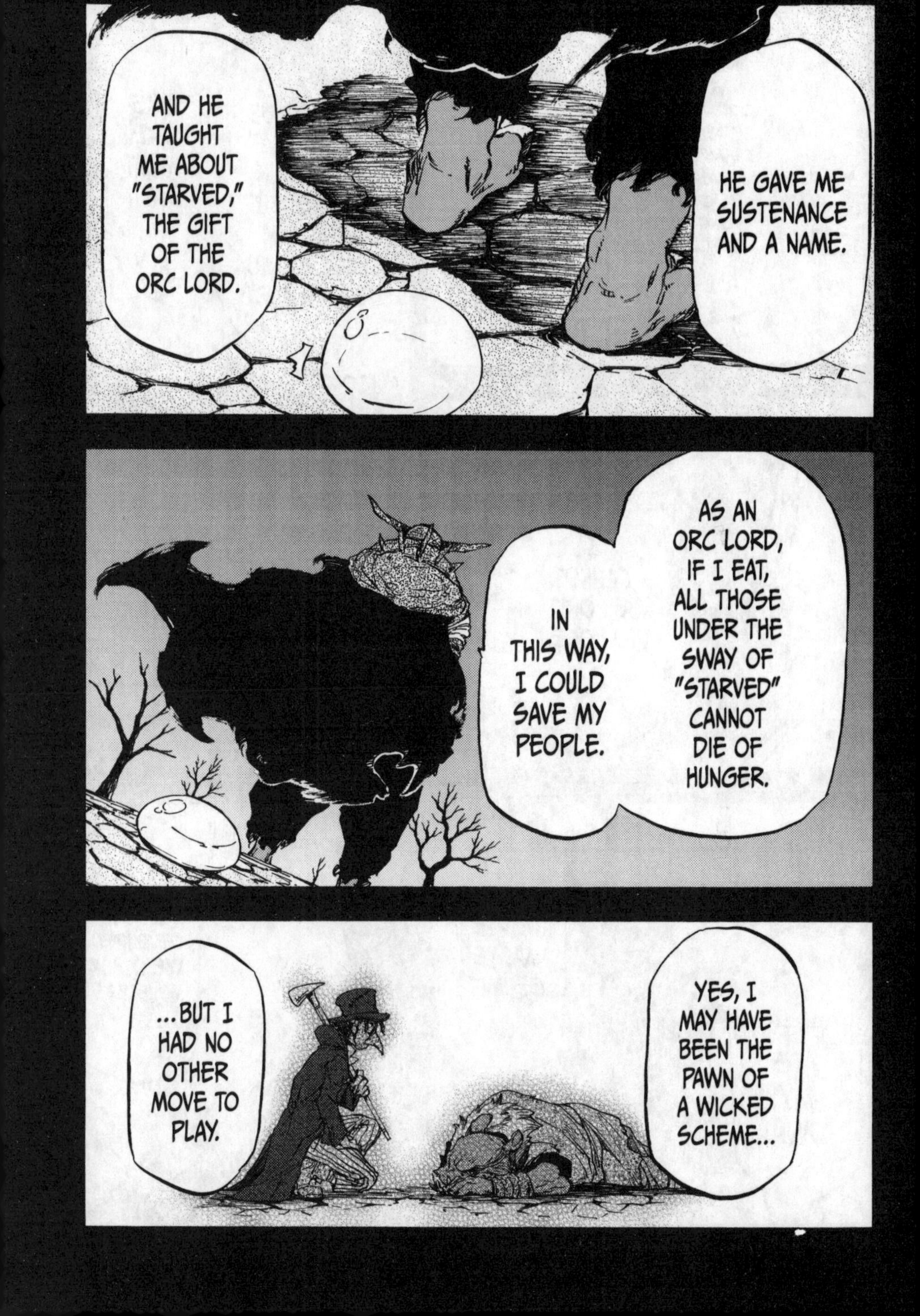
HE GAVE ME SUSTENANCE AND A NAME.
AND HE TAUGHT ME ABOUT "STARVED," THE GIFT OF THE ORC LORD.
AS AN ORC LORD, IF I EAT, ALL THOSE UNDER THE SWAY OF "STARVED" CANNOT DIE OF HUNGER.
IN THIS WAY, I COULD SAVE MY PEOPLE.
YES, I MAY HAVE BEEN THE PAWN OF A WICKED SCHEME...
...BUT I HAD NO OTHER MOVE TO PLAY.

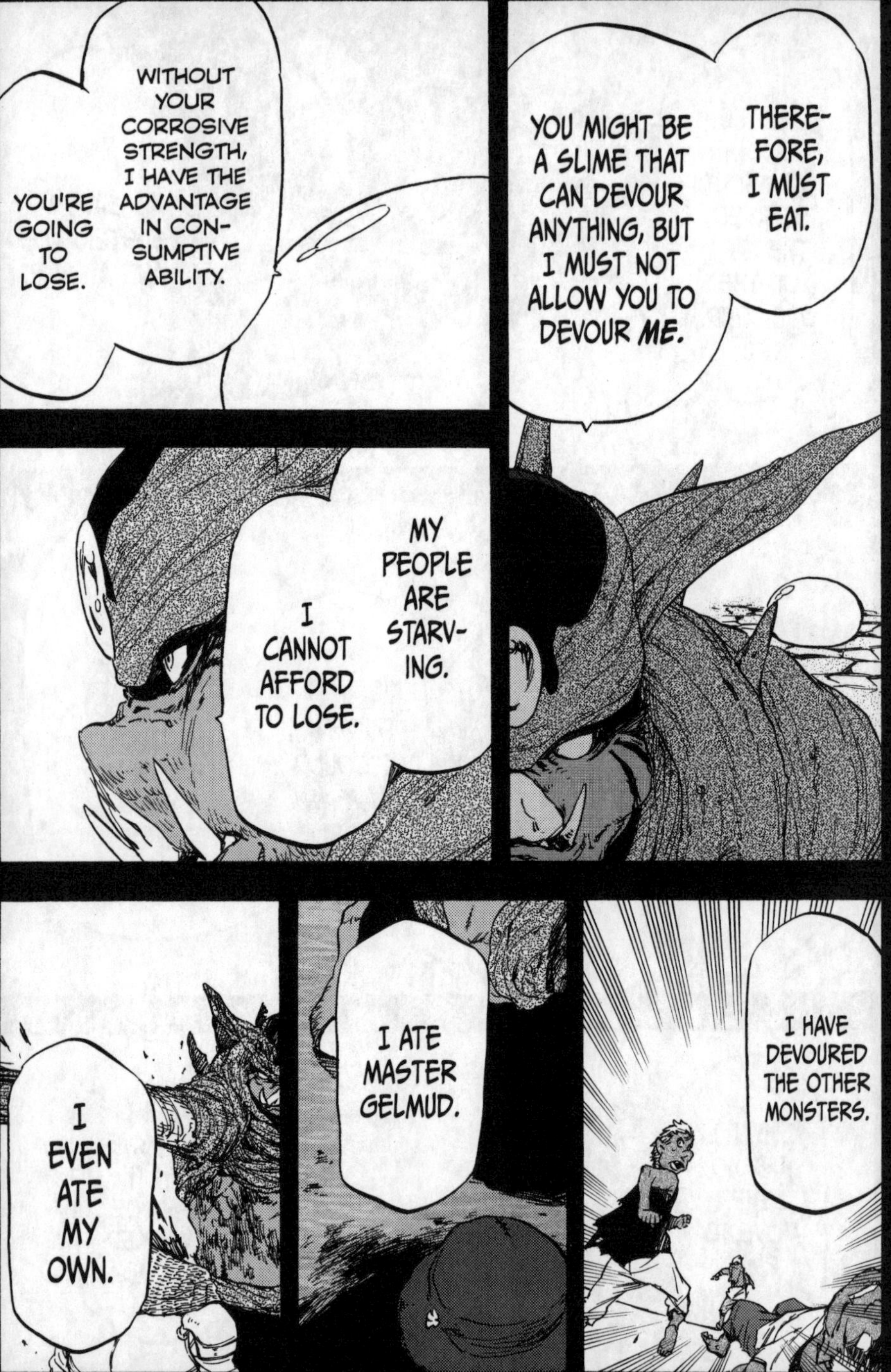
THERE-FORE, I MUST EAT.
YOU MIGHT BE A SLIME THAT CAN DEVOUR ANYTHING, BUT I MUST NOT ALLOW YOU TO DEVOUR ME.
WITHOUT YOUR CORROSIVE STRENGTH, I HAVE THE ADVANTAGE IN CON-SUMPTIVE ABILITY.
YOU'RE GOING TO LOSE.
MY PEOPLE ARE STARV-ING.
I CANNOT AFFORD TO LOSE.
I HAVE DEVOURED THE OTHER MONSTERS.
I ATE MASTER GELMUD.
I EVEN ATE MY OWN.

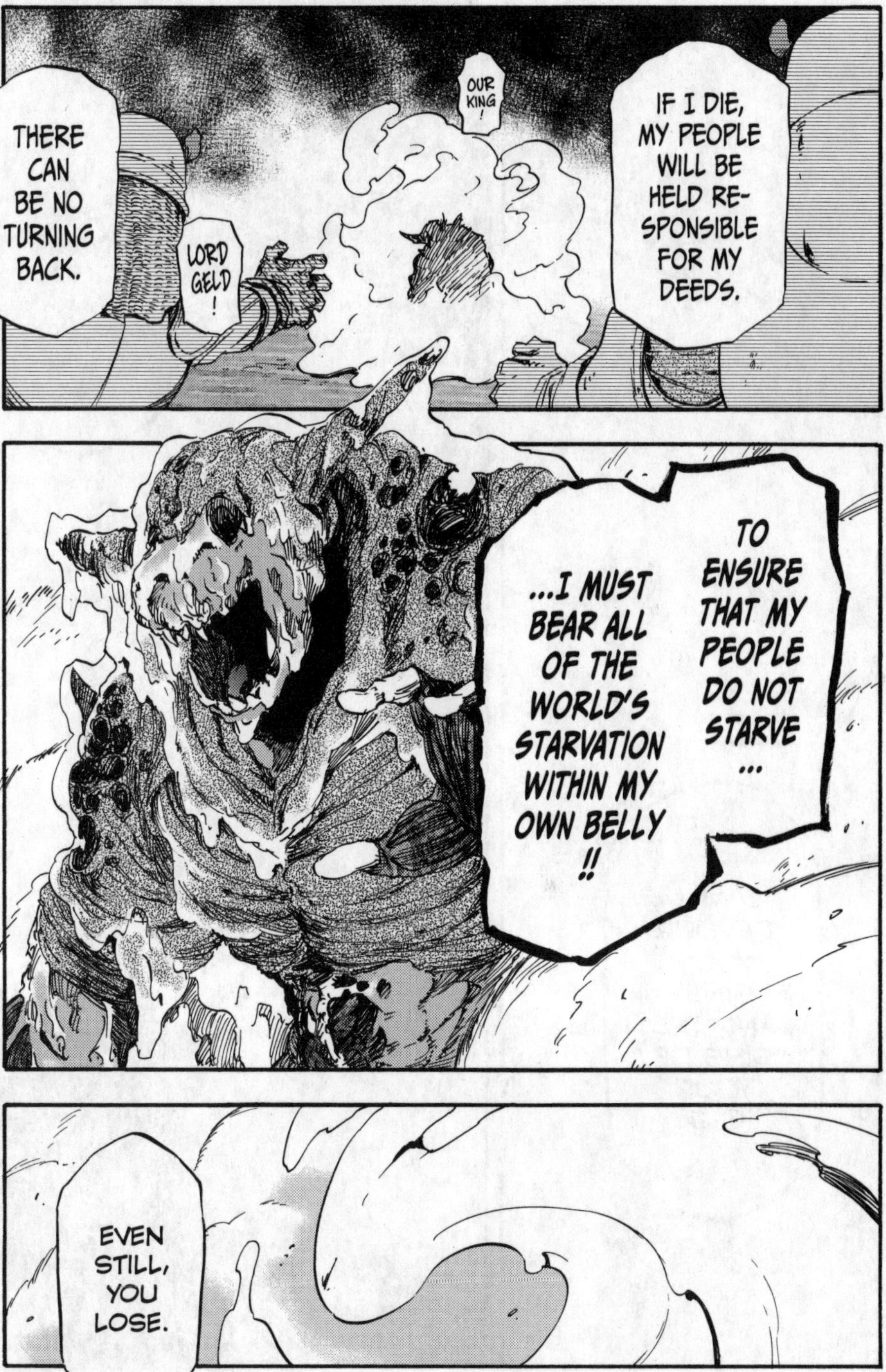
IF I DIE, MY PEOPLE WILL BE HELD RE-SPONSIBLE FOR MY DEEDS.
OUR KING!
THERE CAN BE NO TURNING BACK.
LORD GELD!
TO ENSURE THAT MY PEOPLE DO NOT STARVE...
...I MUST BEAR ALL OF THE WORLD'S STARVATION WITHIN MY OWN BELLY!!
EVEN STILL, YOU LOSE.

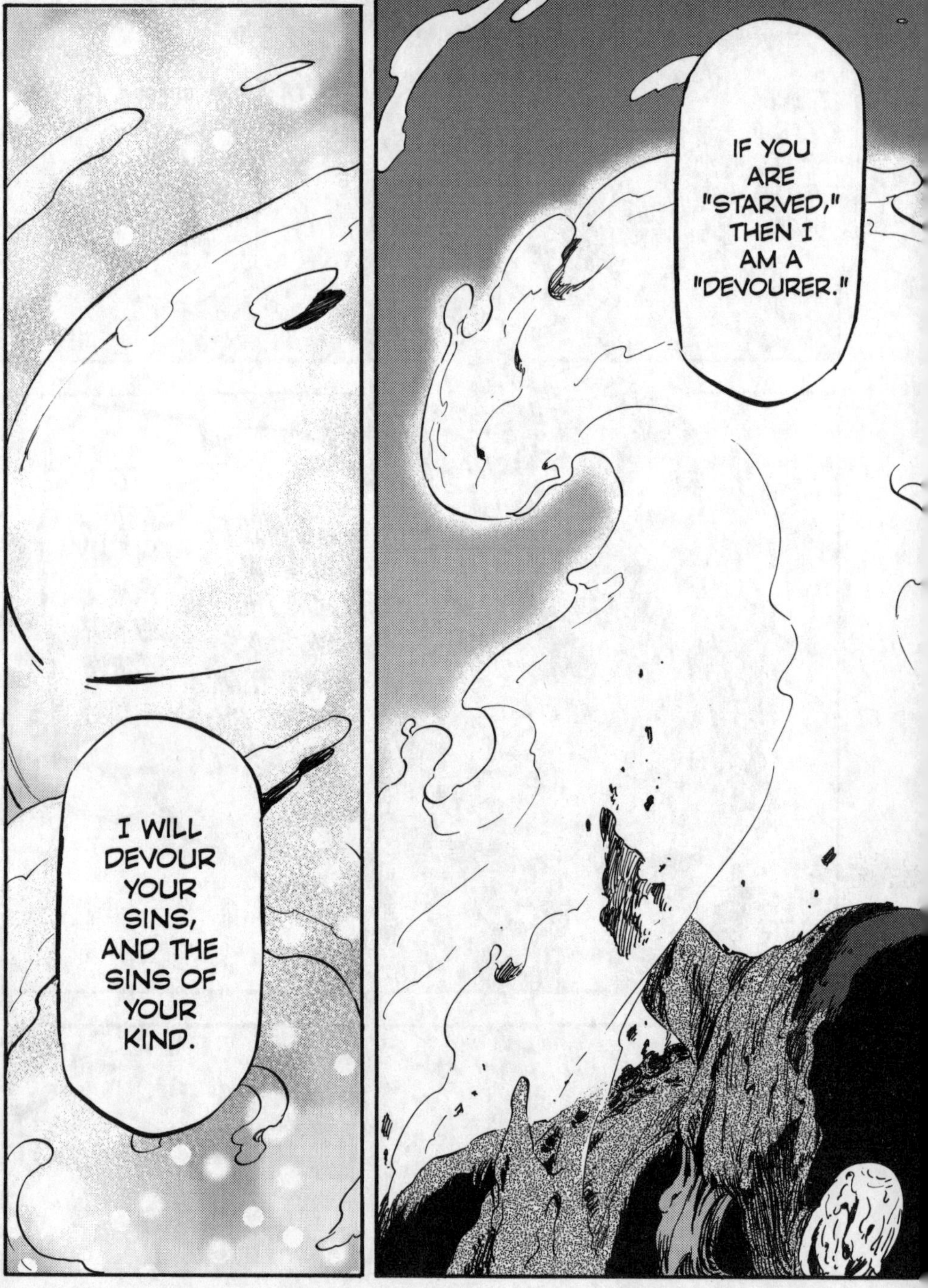
IF YOU ARE "STARVED," THEN I AM A "DEVOURER."
I WILL DEVOUR YOUR SINS, AND THE SINS OF YOUR KIND.

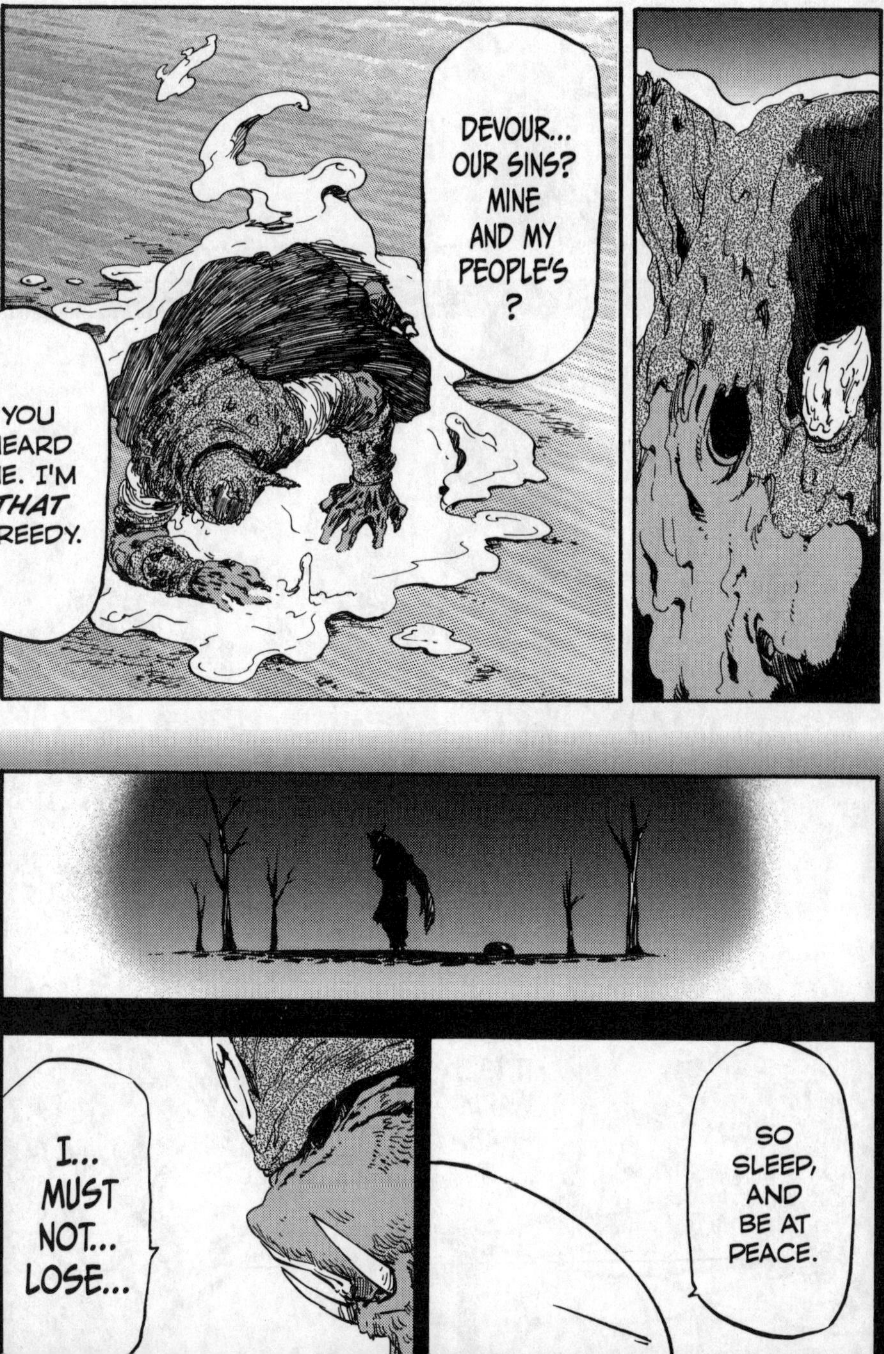
DEVOUR... OUR SINS? MINE AND MY PEOPLE'S ?
YOU HEARD ME. I'M *THAT* GREEDY.
SO SLEEP, AND BE AT PEACE.
I... MUST NOT... LOSE...

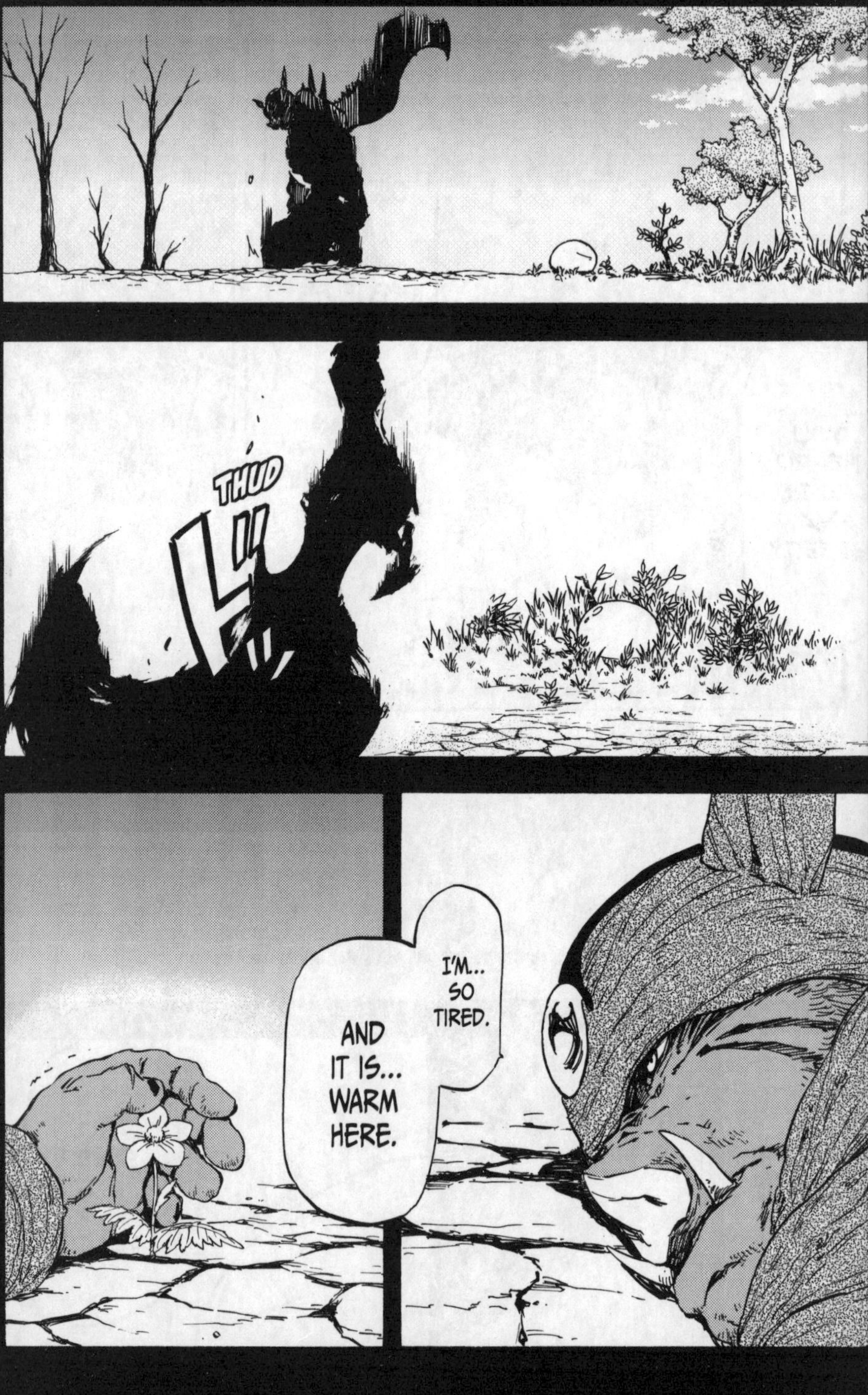
THUD
I'M... SO TIRED.
AND IT IS... WARM HERE.

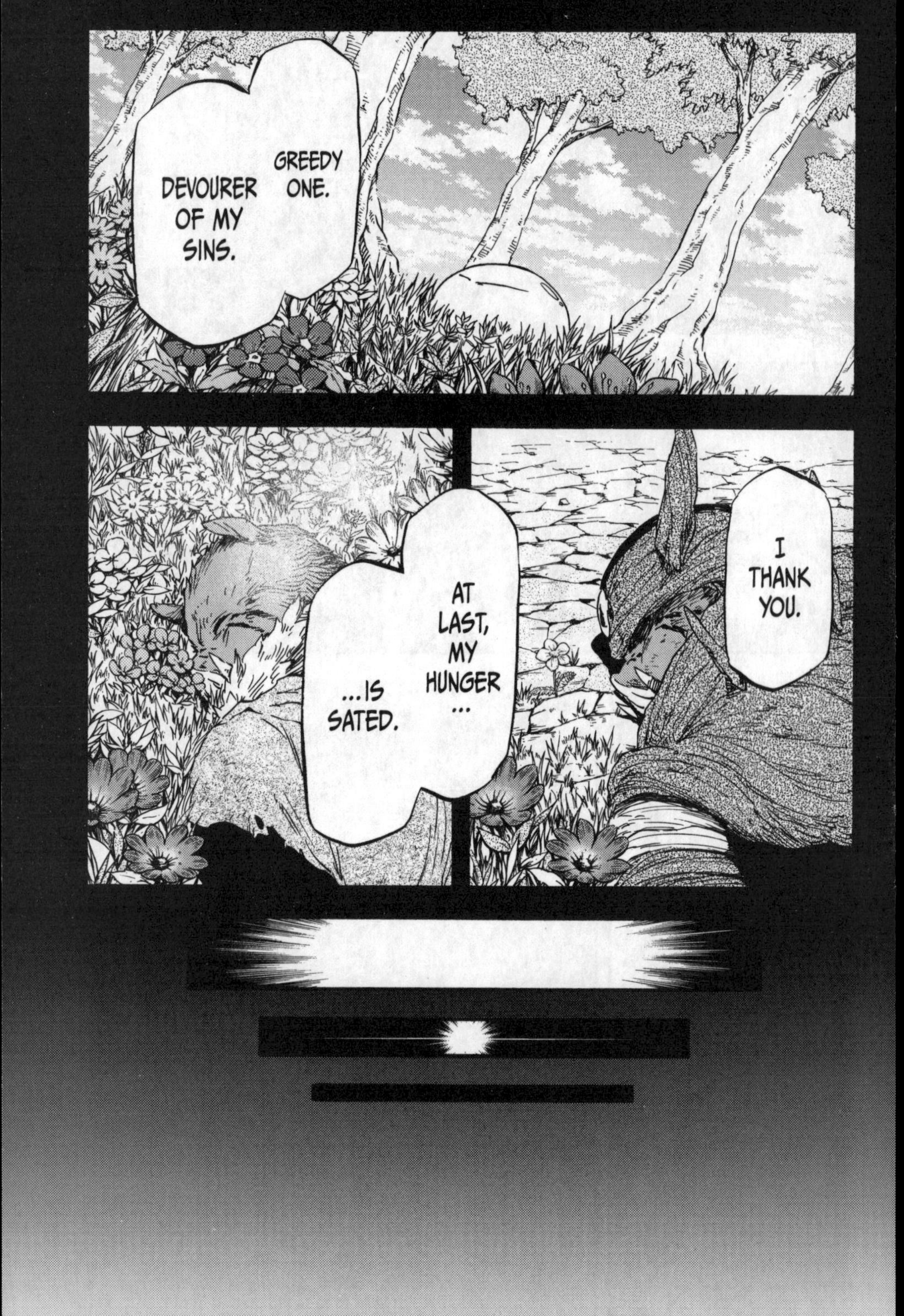
GREEDY ONE.
DEVOURER OF MY SINS.
I THANK YOU.
AT LAST, MY HUNGER...
...IS SATED.

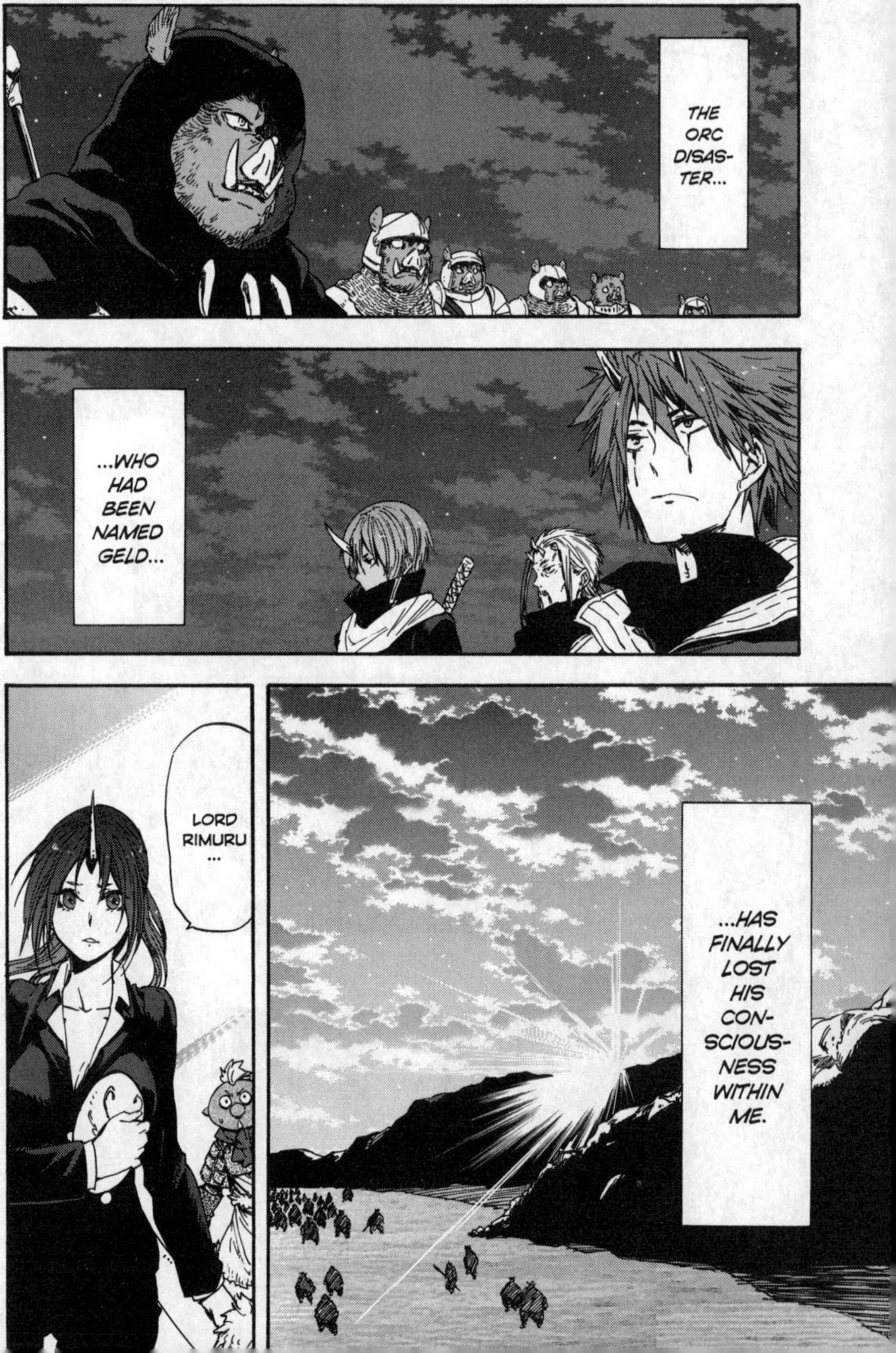
THE ORC DISAS-TER...
...WHO HAD BEEN NAMED GELD...
...HAS FINALLY LOST HIS CON-SCIOUS-NESS WITHIN ME.
LORD RIMURU ...

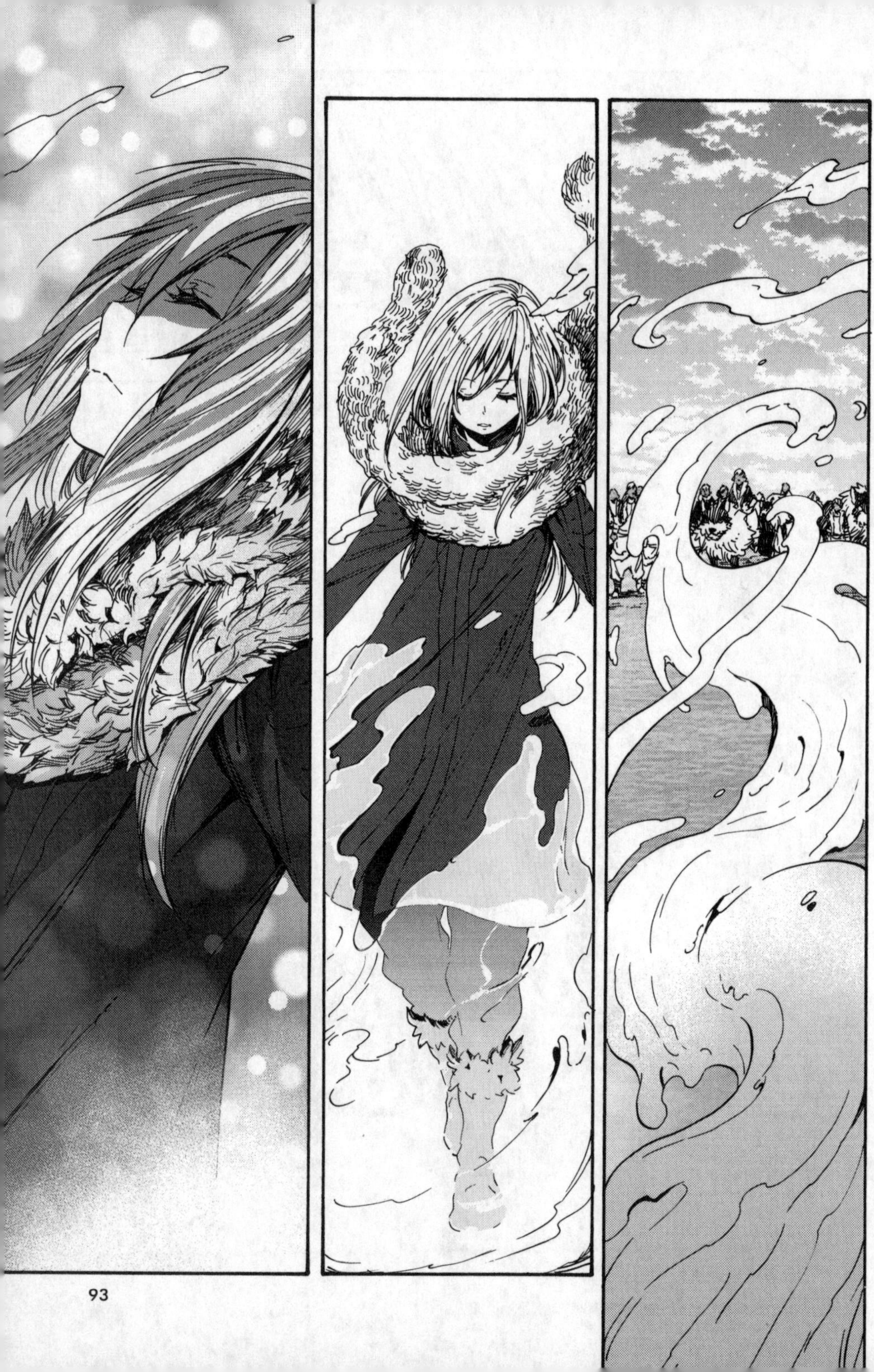

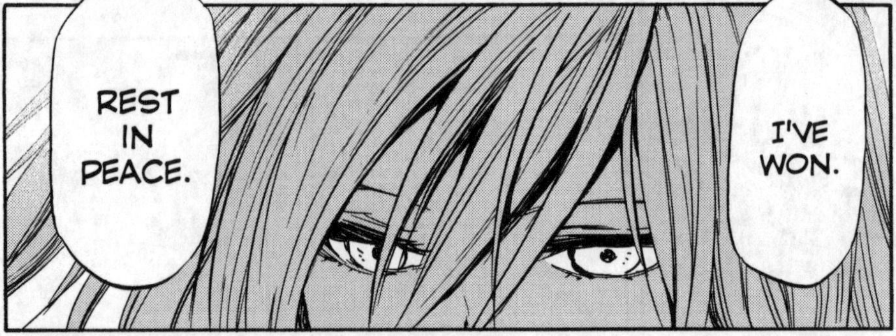
I'VE WON.
REST IN PEACE.
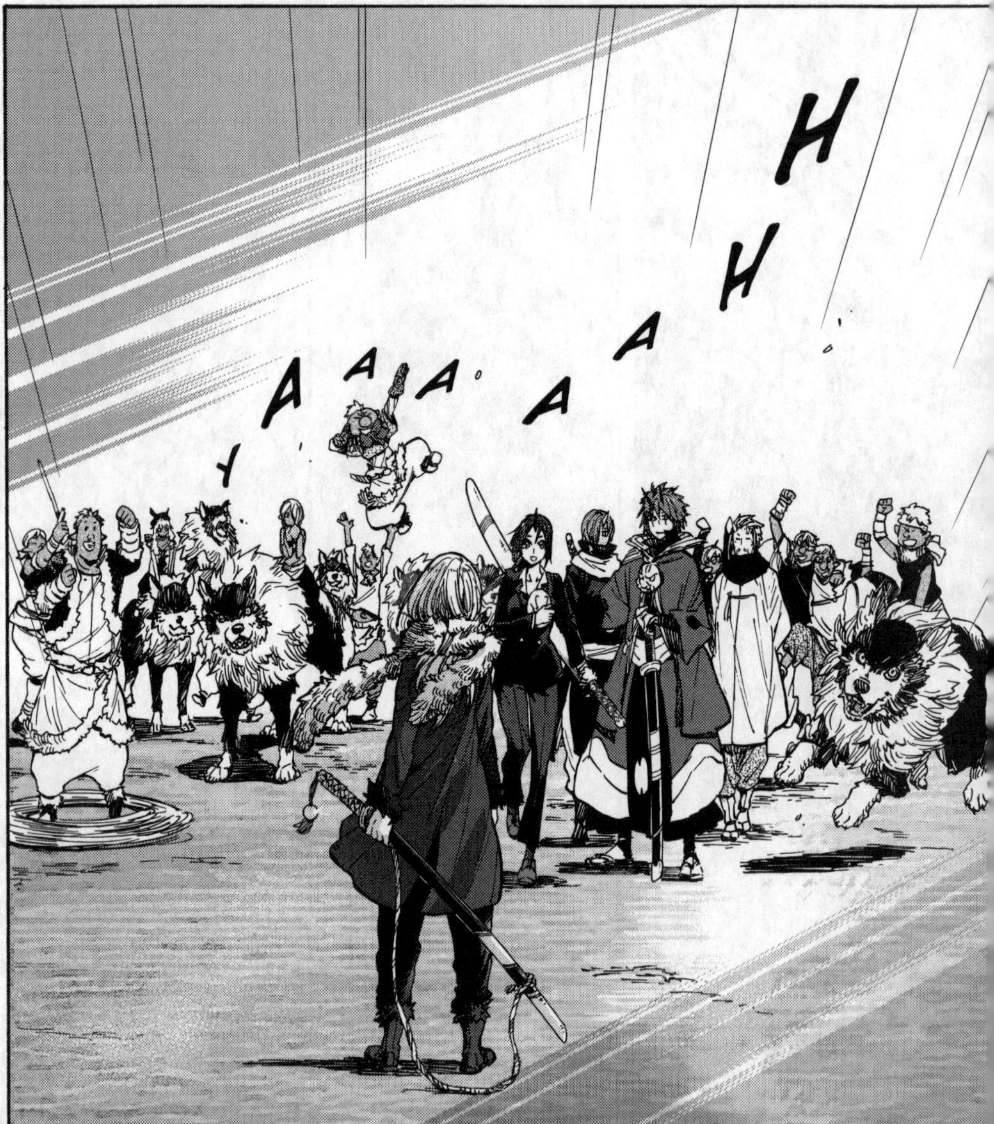
YAAAAAHH

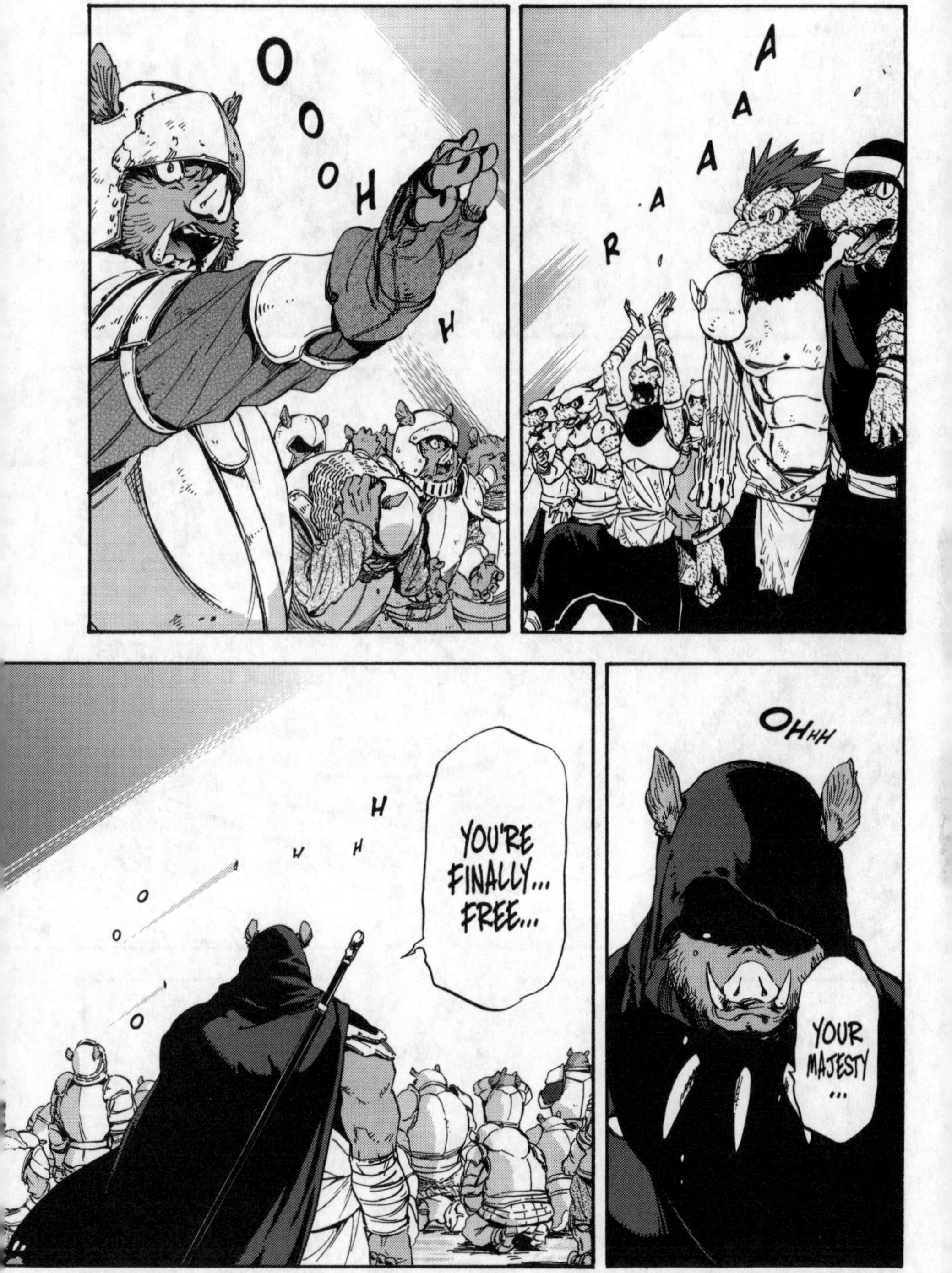
RAAAAA
OOOHH
OHHH
YOUR MAJESTY ...
YOU'RE FINALLY... FREE...
OOOHHH

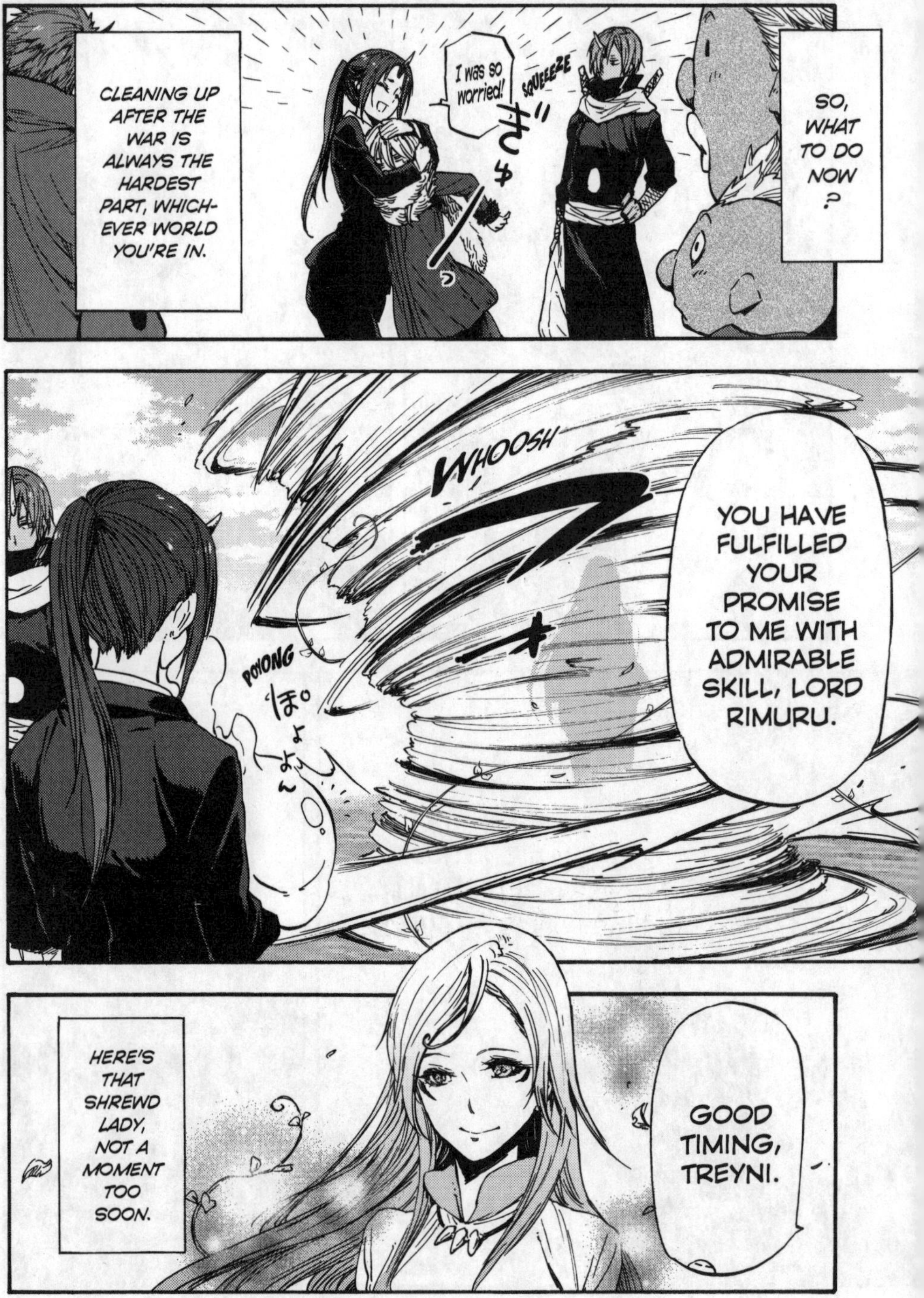
SO, WHAT TO DO NOW?
I was so worried!
SQUEEZE
ぎゅ
CLEANING UP AFTER THE WAR IS ALWAYS THE HARDEST PART, WHICH-EVER WORLD YOU'RE IN.
WHOOSH
YOU HAVE FULFILLED YOUR PROMISE TO ME WITH ADMIRABLE SKILL, LORD RIMURU.
POYONG
ぽよよん
GOOD TIMING, TREYNI.
HERE'S THAT SHREWD LADY, NOT A MOMENT TOO SOON.

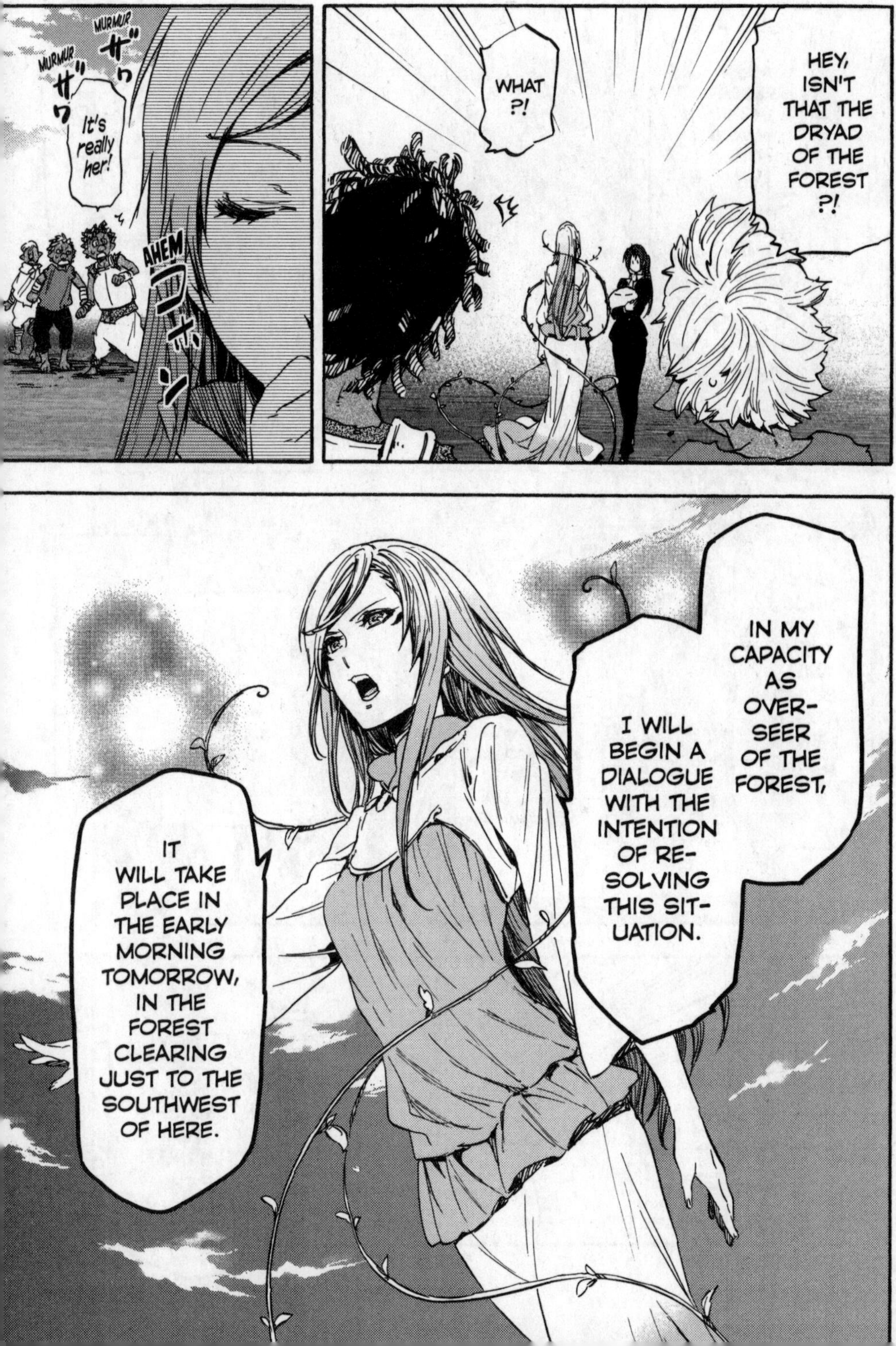

HEY, ISN'T THAT THE DRYAD OF THE FOREST?!
WHAT?!
MURMUR
MURMUR
It's really her!
AHEM
IN MY CAPACITY AS OVER-SEER OF THE FOREST,
I WILL BEGIN A DIALOGUE WITH THE INTENTION OF RE-SOLVING THIS SIT-UATION.
IT WILL TAKE PLACE IN THE EARLY MORNING TOMORROW, IN THE FOREST CLEARING JUST TO THE SOUTHWEST OF HERE.

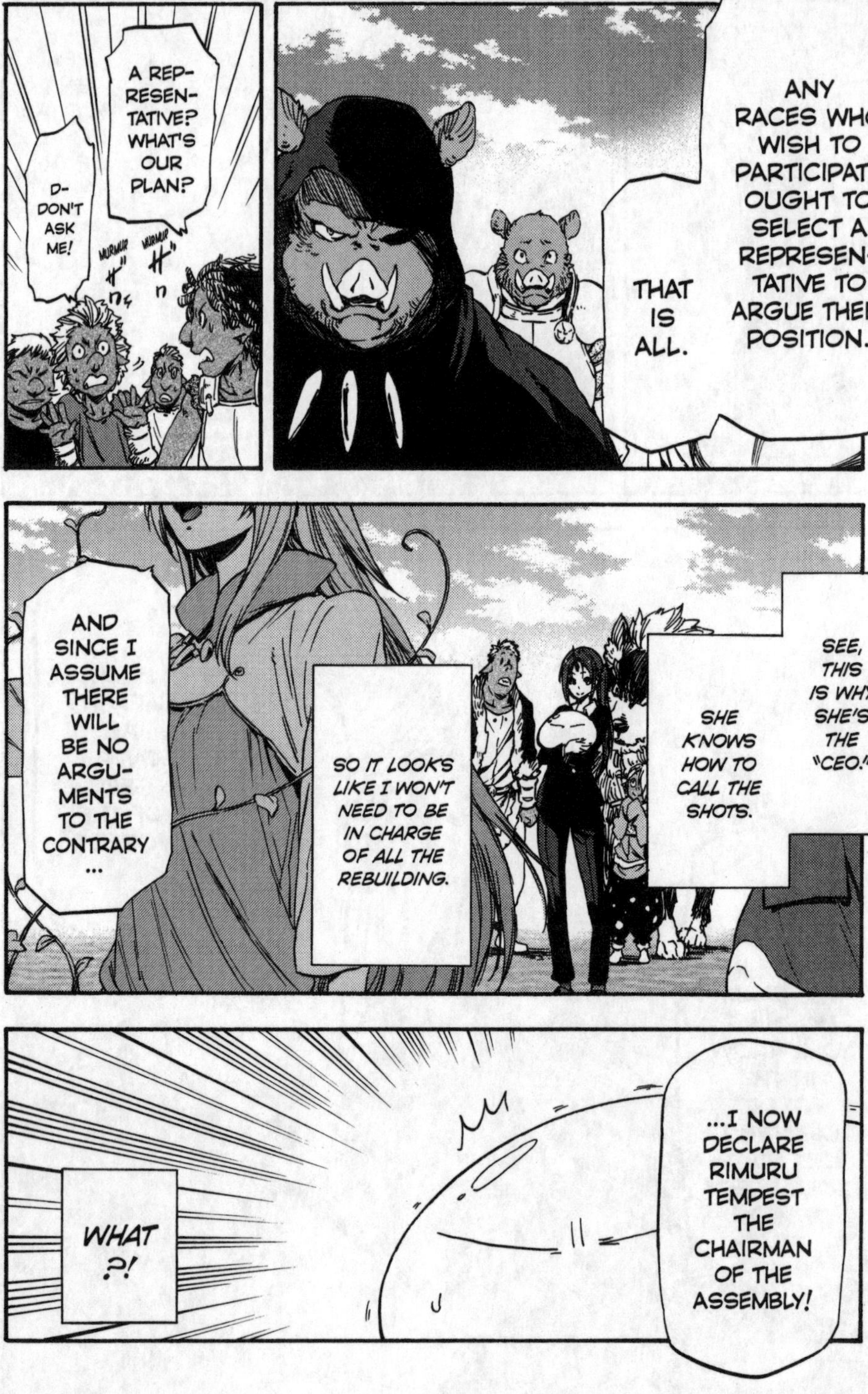
ANY RACES WHO WISH TO PARTICIPATE OUGHT TO SELECT A REPRESENTATIVE TO ARGUE THEIR POSITION.
THAT IS ALL.
A REPRESENTATIVE? WHAT'S OUR PLAN?
MURMUR
MURMUR
D-DON'T ASK ME!
SEE, THIS IS WHY SHE'S THE "CEO."
SHE KNOWS HOW TO CALL THE SHOTS.
SO IT LOOKS LIKE I WON'T NEED TO BE IN CHARGE OF ALL THE REBUILDING.
AND SINCE I ASSUME THERE WILL BE NO ARGUMENTS TO THE CONTRARY...
...I NOW DECLARE RIMURU TEMPEST THE CHAIRMAN OF THE ASSEMBLY!
WHAT?!

In
Memoriam

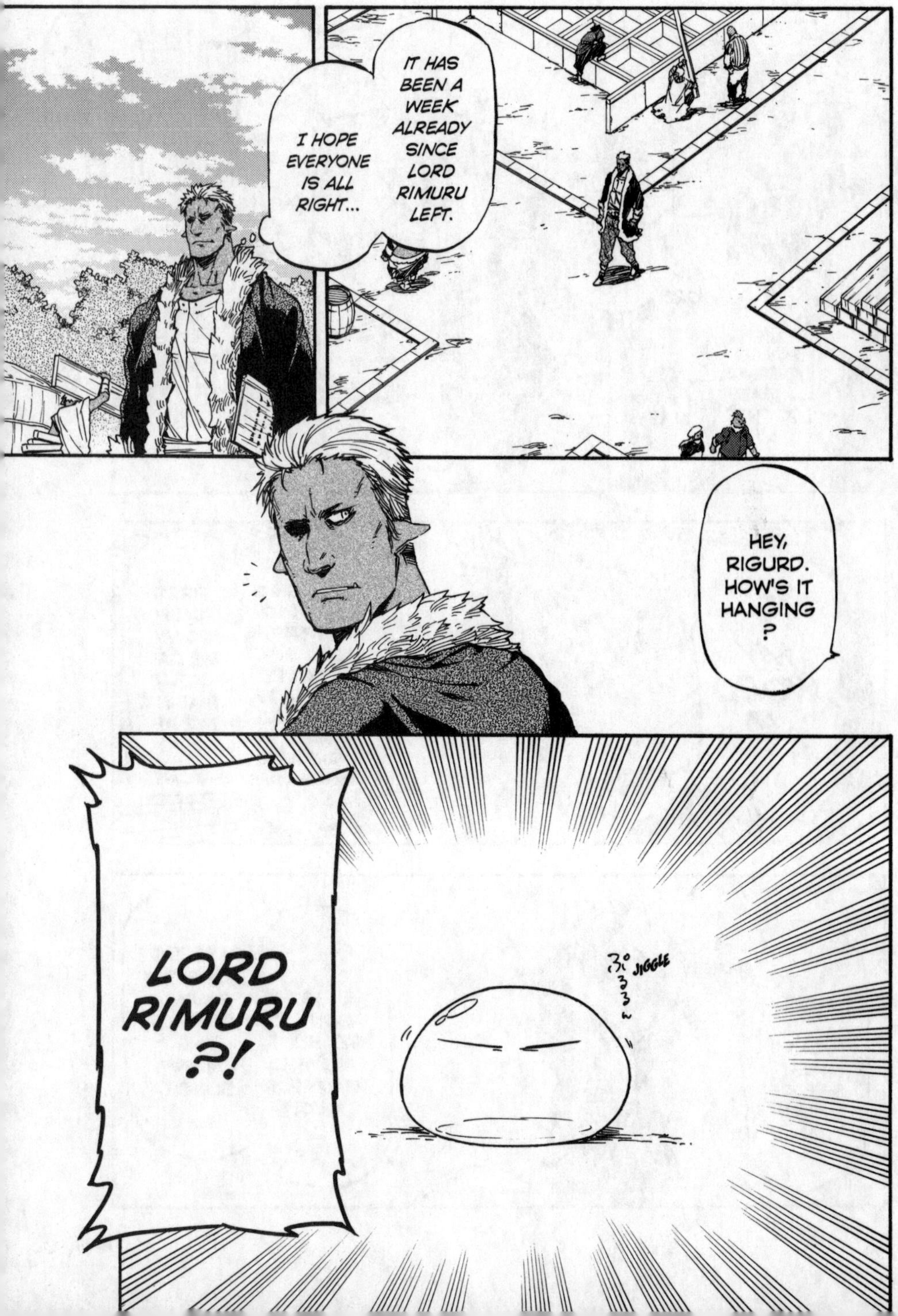
IT HAS BEEN A WEEK ALREADY SINCE LORD RIMURU LEFT.
I HOPE EVERYONE IS ALL RIGHT...
HEY, RIGURD. HOW'S IT HANGING?
ぷるるん
JIGGLE
LORD RIMURU?!

WHEN DID YOU RETURN?!
JUST NOW. SHADOW MOVEMENT.
WHAT ABOUT THE OTHERS?
THEY'RE FINE.
WE ALREADY BEAT THE ORC LORD, SO—
MY WORD!
THEN WE MUST PREPARE A FEAST AT ONCE!!
FIRST, CALM DOWN. WE CAN HOLD THAT IN A MONTH.
I ONLY CAME BACK TO DELIVER THE NEWS, SINCE I FIGURE YOU WERE WORRIED. I HAVE TO LEAVE AGAIN RIGHT AWAY.
MY WORD!!
PASS THE NEWS TO SHUNA, KUROBEI, AND KAIJIN'S BUNCH.
THINGS ARE ABOUT TO GET BUSY. ARE YOU READY FOR THAT?
OF COURSE!!
BUT SURELY YOU CAN REST BEFORE YOU GO...

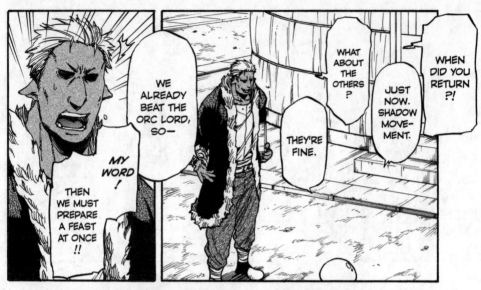

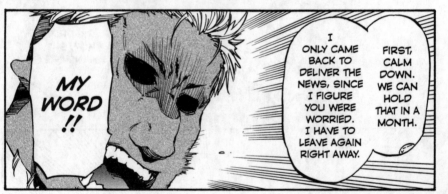

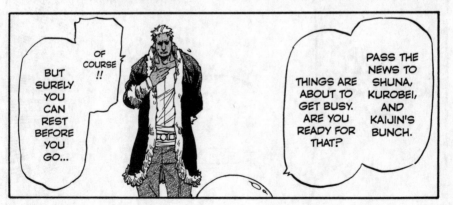

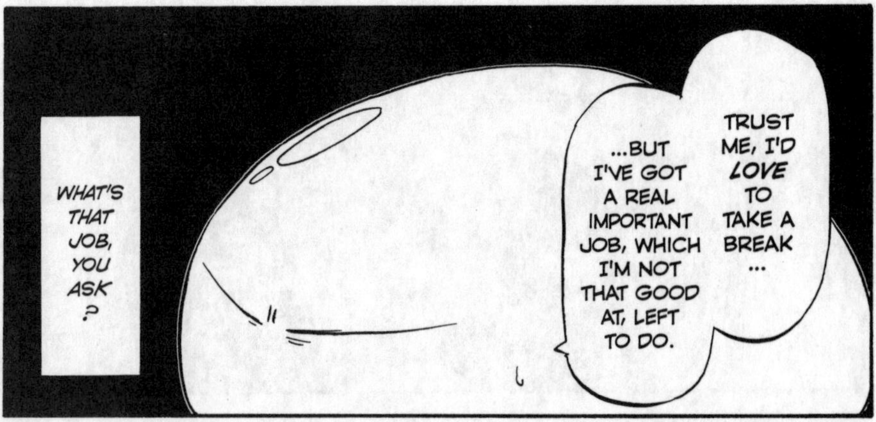
TRUST ME, I'D *LOVE* TO TAKE A BREAK...
...BUT I'VE GOT A REAL IMPORTANT JOB, WHICH I'M NOT THAT GOOD AT, LEFT TO DO.
WHAT'S THAT JOB, YOU ASK?

CHAPTER 26 The Jura Forest Alliance

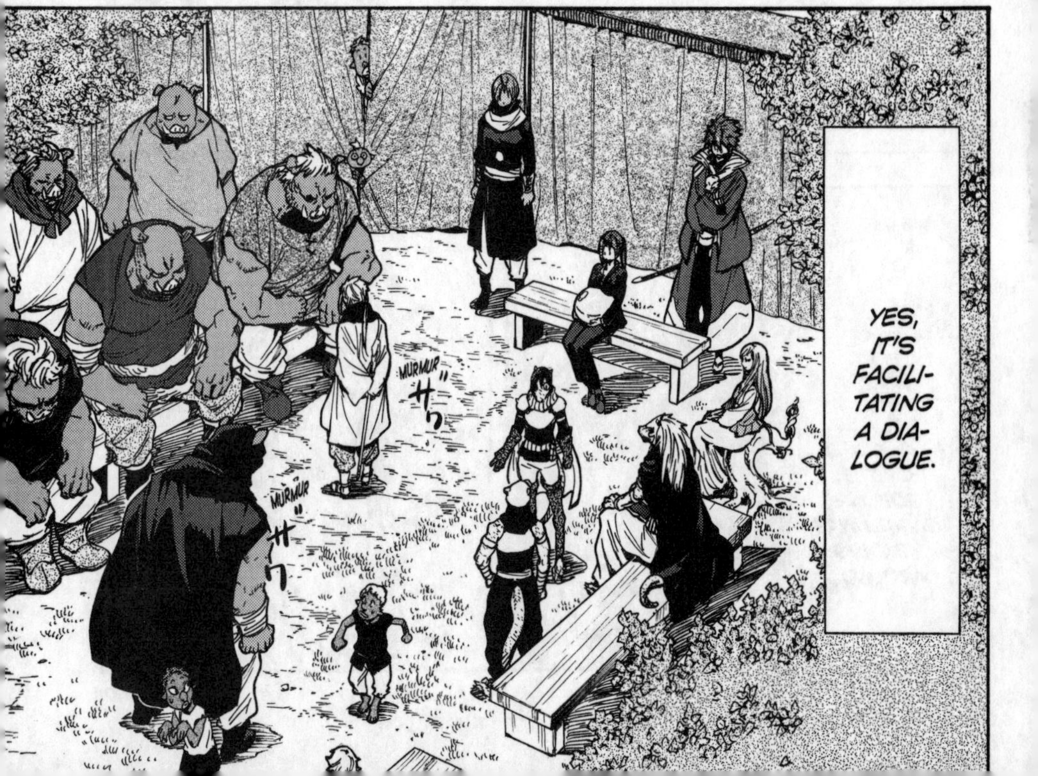
YES, IT'S FACILITATING A DIALOGUE.
MURMUR
MURMUR

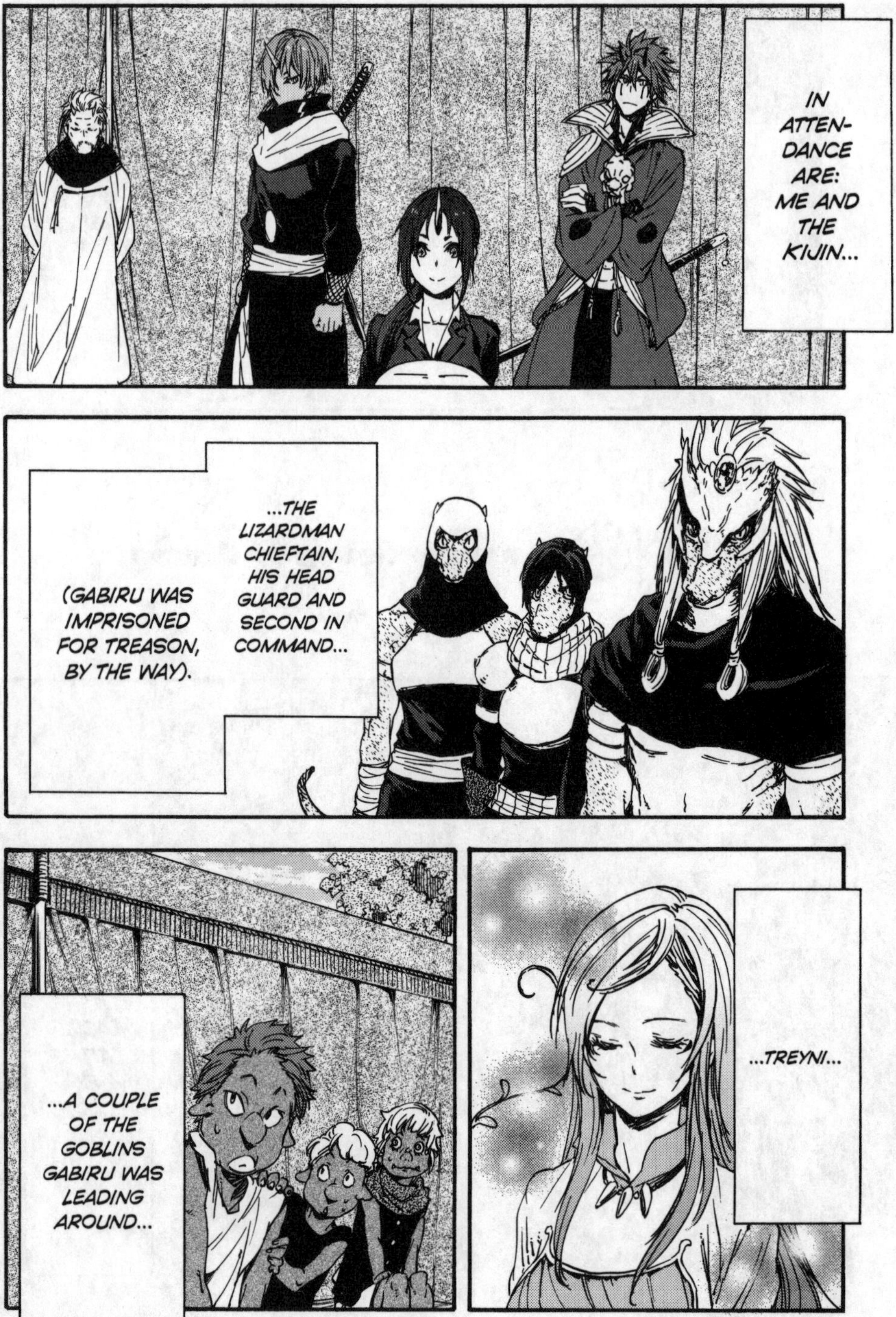
IN ATTENDANCE ARE: ME AND THE KIJIN...
...THE LIZARDMAN CHIEFTAIN, HIS HEAD GUARD AND SECOND IN COMMAND...
(GABIRU WAS IMPRISONED FOR TREASON, BY THE WAY).
...TREYNI...
...A COUPLE OF THE GOBLINS GABIRU WAS LEADING AROUND...

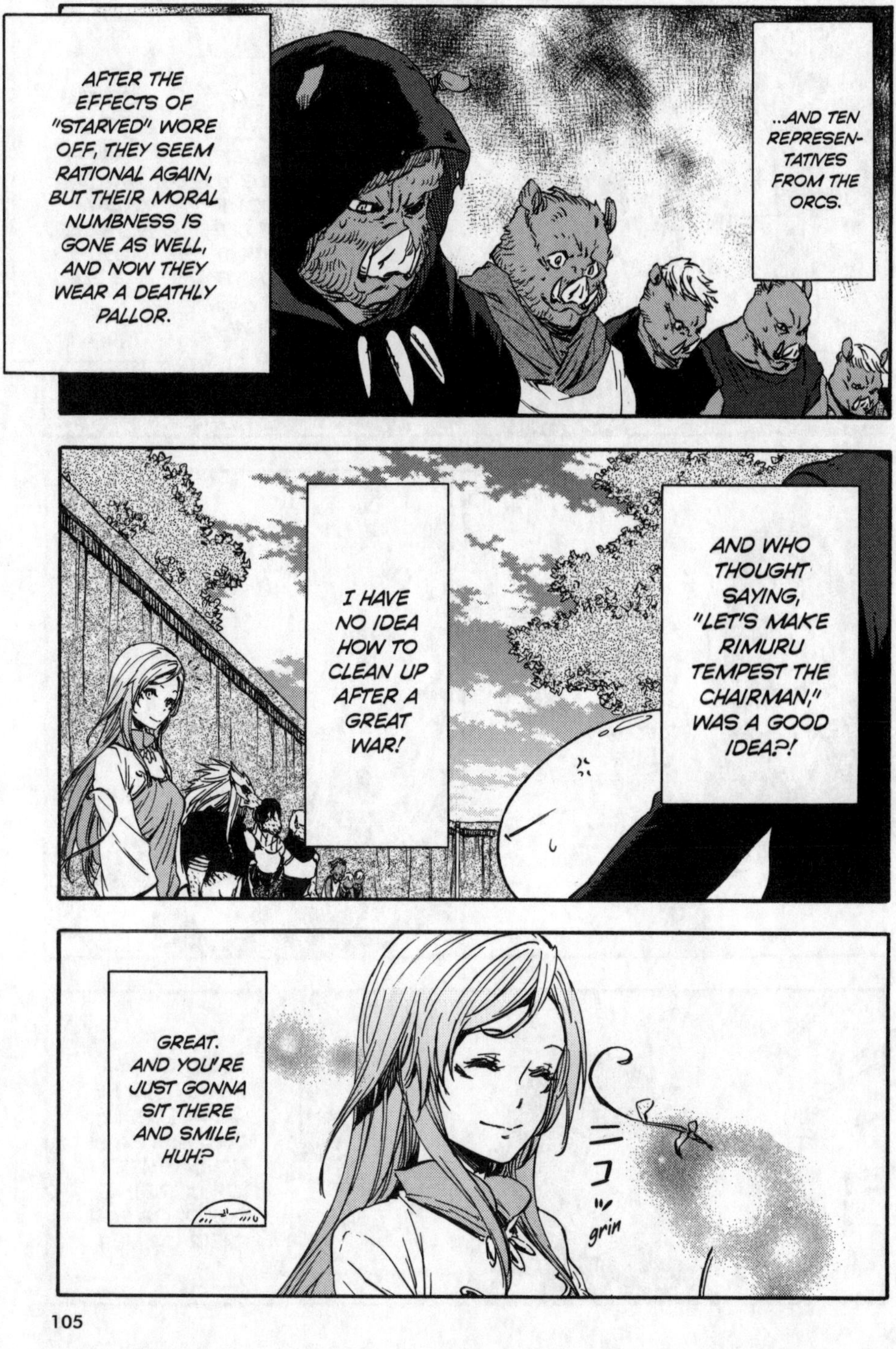
...AND TEN REPRESENTATIVES FROM THE ORCS.
AFTER THE EFFECTS OF "STARVED" WORE OFF, THEY SEEM RATIONAL AGAIN, BUT THEIR MORAL NUMBNESS IS GONE AS WELL, AND NOW THEY WEAR A DEATHLY PALLOR.
AND WHO THOUGHT SAYING, "LET'S MAKE RIMURU TEMPEST THE CHAIRMAN," WAS A GOOD IDEA?!
I HAVE NO IDEA HOW TO CLEAN UP AFTER A GREAT WAR!
grin
GREAT. AND YOU'RE JUST GONNA SIT THERE AND SMILE, HUH?

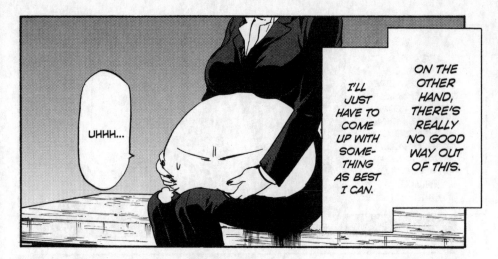

ON THE OTHER HAND, THERE'S REALLY NO GOOD WAY OUT OF THIS.
I'LL JUST HAVE TO COME UP WITH SOME-THING AS BEST I CAN.
UHHH...
THIS IS A FIRST FOR ME. I'M NOT SURE HOW TO PROCEED.
SO I'LL START BY SAYING WHAT I THINK.
THEN I WANT YOU ALL TO DIS-CUSS.
FIRST OF ALL, I WANT TO BE ABSOLUTELY CLEAR: I HAVE NO INTENTION OF JUDGING THE ORCS FOR THEIR CRIMES.
?!

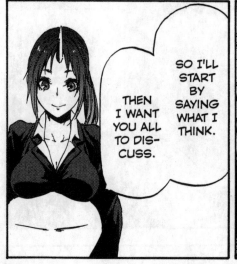

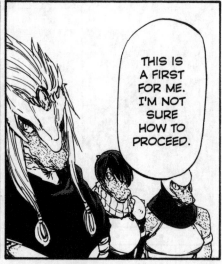

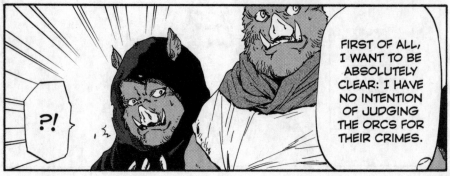

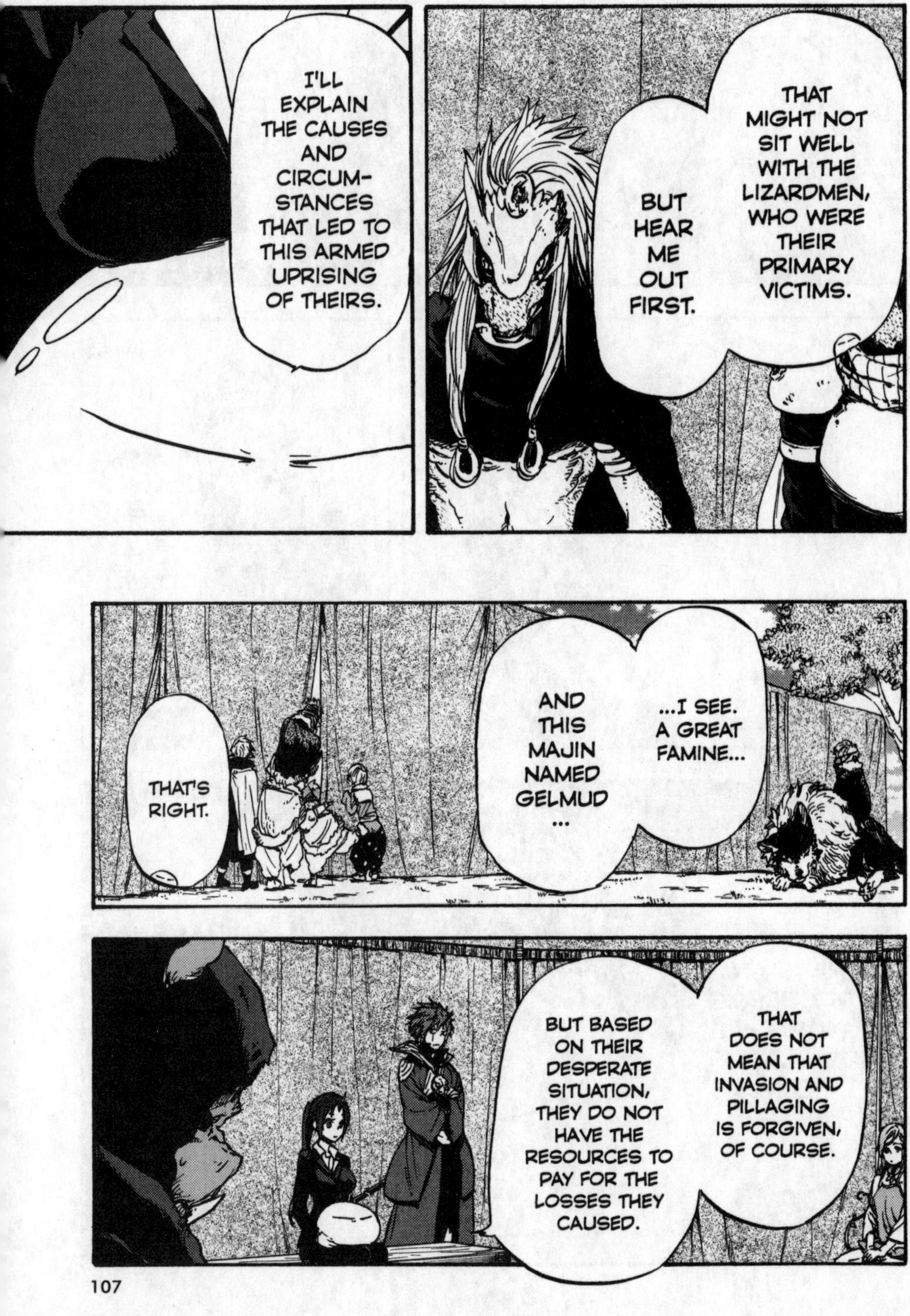
THAT MIGHT NOT SIT WELL WITH THE LIZARDMEN, WHO WERE THEIR PRIMARY VICTIMS.
BUT HEAR ME OUT FIRST.
I'LL EXPLAIN THE CAUSES AND CIRCUMSTANCES THAT LED TO THIS ARMED UPRISING OF THEIRS.
...I SEE. A GREAT FAMINE...
AND THIS MAJIN NAMED GELMUD ...
THAT'S RIGHT.
THAT DOES NOT MEAN THAT INVASION AND PILLAGING IS FORGIVEN, OF COURSE.
BUT BASED ON THEIR DESPERATE SITUATION, THEY DO NOT HAVE THE RESOURCES TO PAY FOR THE LOSSES THEY CAUSED.

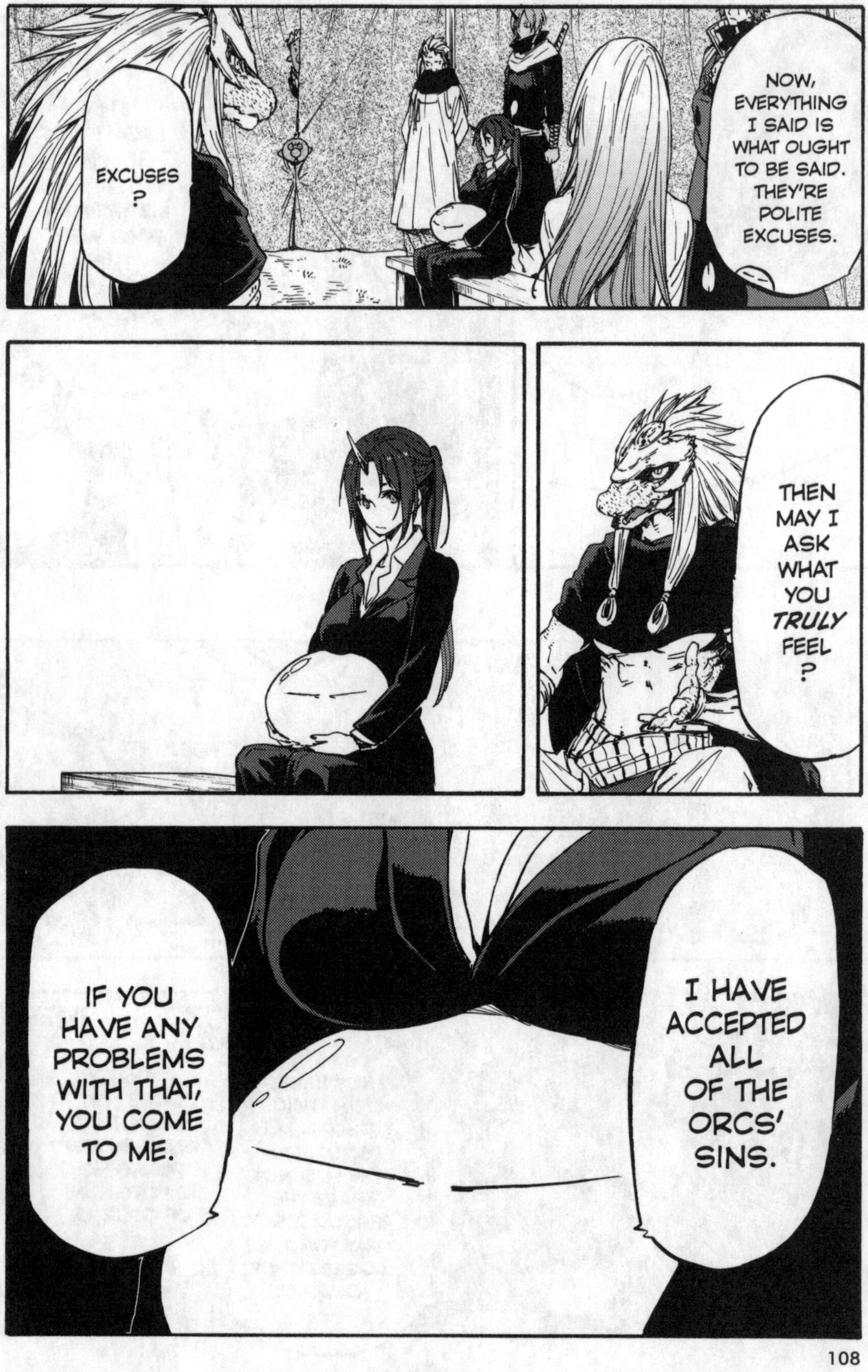
NOW, EVERYTHING I SAID IS WHAT OUGHT TO BE SAID. THEY'RE POLITE EXCUSES.
EXCUSES?
THEN MAY I ASK WHAT YOU *TRULY* FEEL?
I HAVE ACCEPTED ALL OF THE ORCS' SINS.
IF YOU HAVE ANY PROBLEMS WITH THAT, YOU COME TO ME.

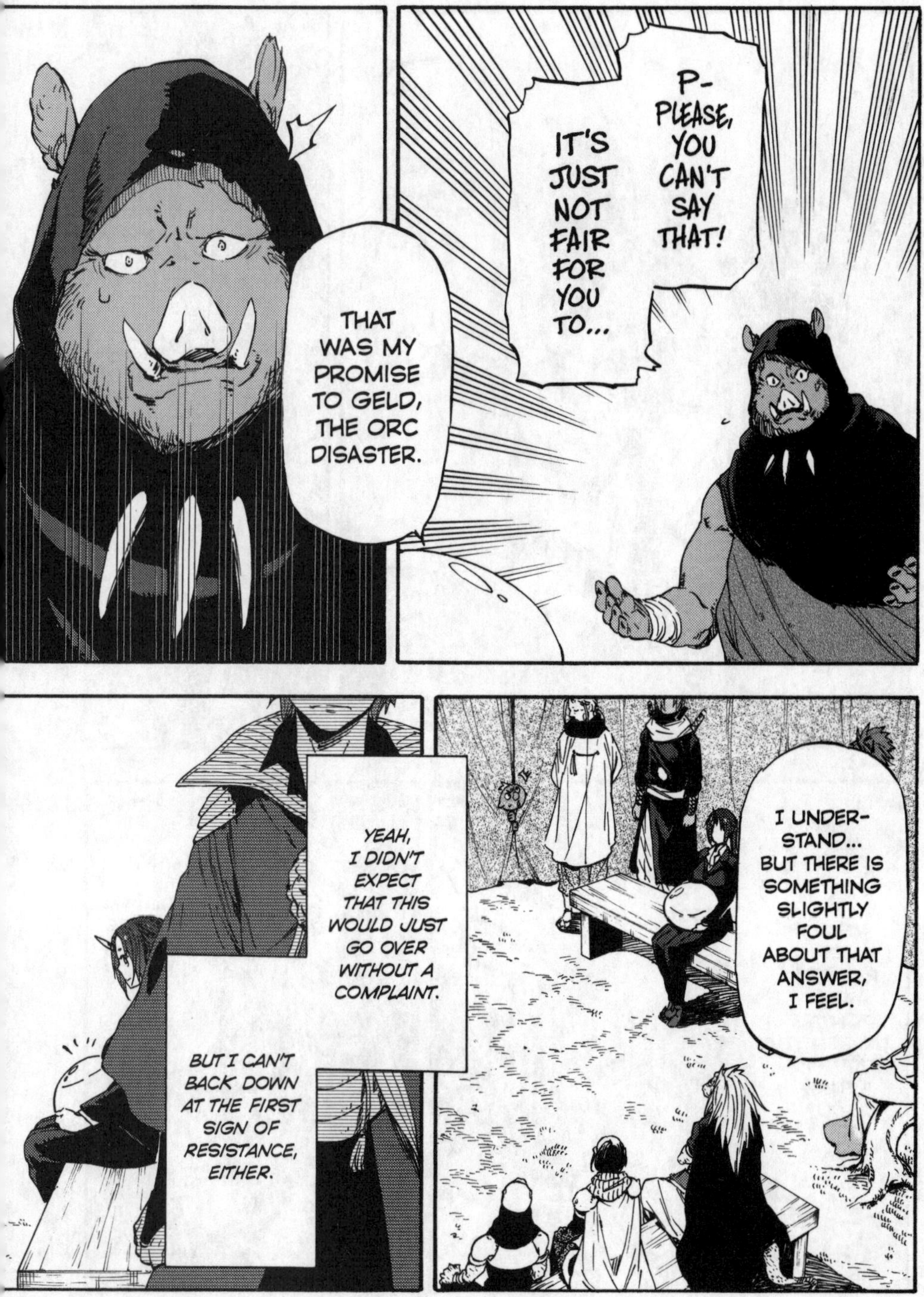
P-PLEASE, YOU CAN'T SAY THAT!
IT'S JUST NOT FAIR FOR YOU TO...
THAT WAS MY PROMISE TO GELD, THE ORC DISASTER.
I UNDERSTAND... BUT THERE IS SOMETHING SLIGHTLY FOUL ABOUT THAT ANSWER, I FEEL.
YEAH, I DIDN'T EXPECT THAT THIS WOULD JUST GO OVER WITHOUT A COMPLAINT.
BUT I CAN'T BACK DOWN AT THE FIRST SIGN OF RESISTANCE, EITHER.

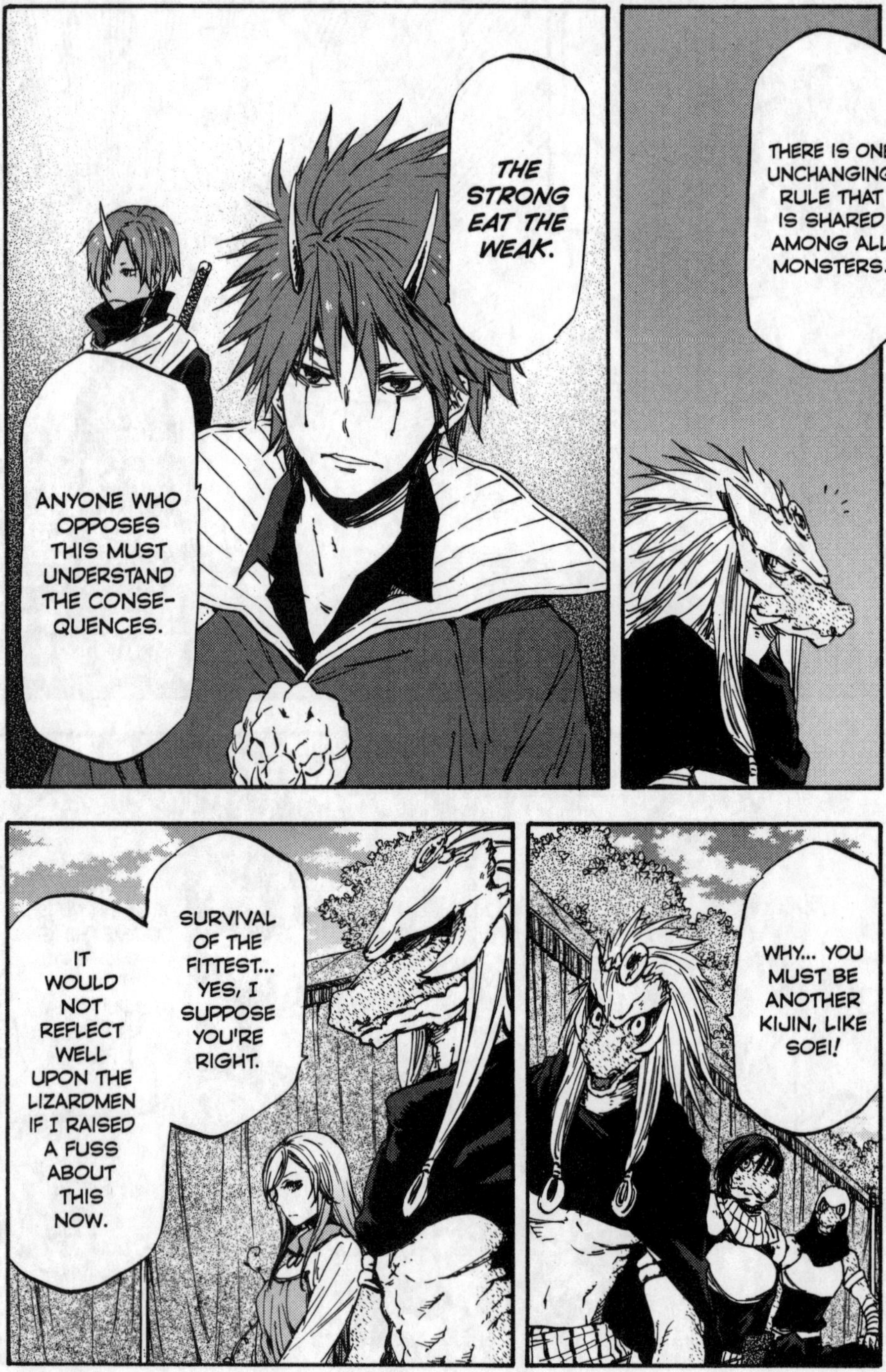
THERE IS ONE UNCHANGING RULE THAT IS SHARED AMONG ALL MONSTERS.
THE STRONG EAT THE WEAK.
ANYONE WHO OPPOSES THIS MUST UNDERSTAND THE CONSE-QUENCES.
WHY... YOU MUST BE ANOTHER KIJIN, LIKE SOEI!
SURVIVAL OF THE FITTEST... YES, I SUPPOSE YOU'RE RIGHT.
IT WOULD NOT REFLECT WELL UPON THE LIZARDMEN IF I RAISED A FUSS ABOUT THIS NOW.

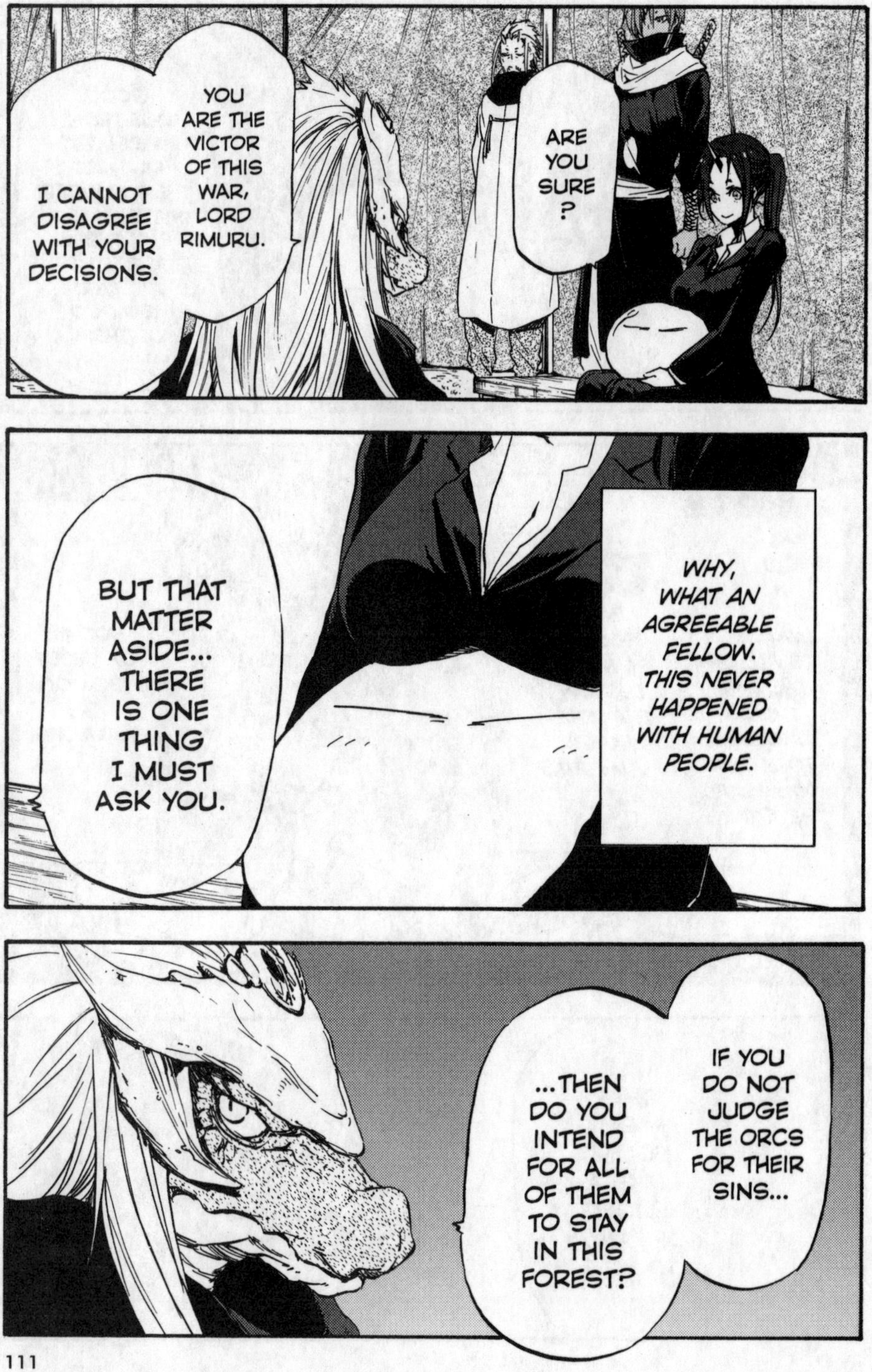
ARE YOU SURE?
YOU ARE THE VICTOR OF THIS WAR, LORD RIMURU.
I CANNOT DISAGREE WITH YOUR DECISIONS.
WHY, WHAT AN AGREEABLE FELLOW. THIS NEVER HAPPENED WITH HUMAN PEOPLE.
BUT THAT MATTER ASIDE... THERE IS ONE THING I MUST ASK YOU.
IF YOU DO NOT JUDGE THE ORCS FOR THEIR SINS...
...THEN DO YOU INTEND FOR ALL OF THEM TO STAY IN THIS FOREST?

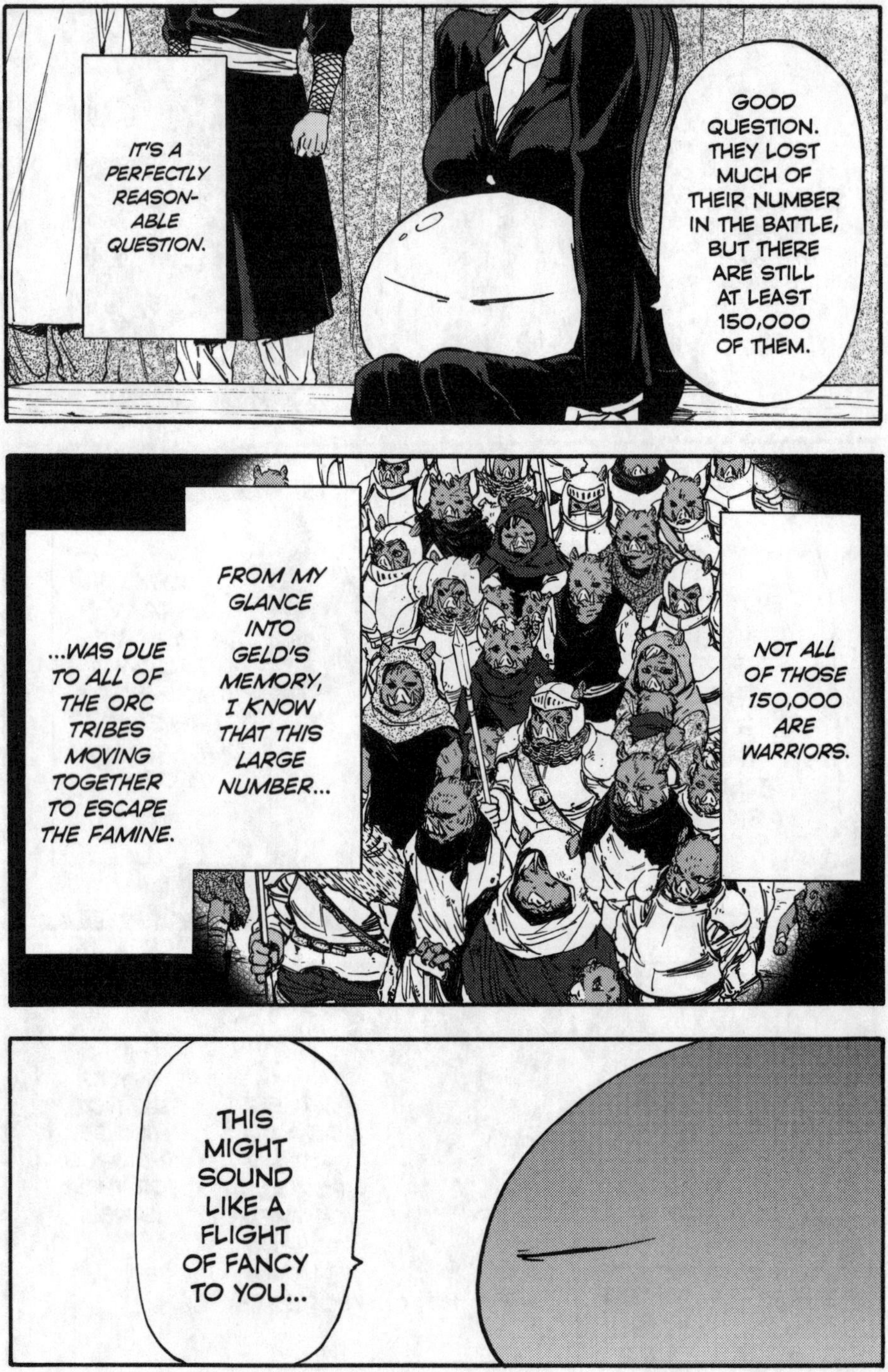
GOOD QUESTION. THEY LOST MUCH OF THEIR NUMBER IN THE BATTLE, BUT THERE ARE STILL AT LEAST 150,000 OF THEM.
IT'S A PERFECTLY REASON-ABLE QUESTION.
NOT ALL OF THOSE 150,000 ARE WARRIORS.
FROM MY GLANCE INTO GELD'S MEMORY, I KNOW THAT THIS LARGE NUMBER...
...WAS DUE TO ALL OF THE ORC TRIBES MOVING TOGETHER TO ESCAPE THE FAMINE.
THIS MIGHT SOUND LIKE A FLIGHT OF FANCY TO YOU...

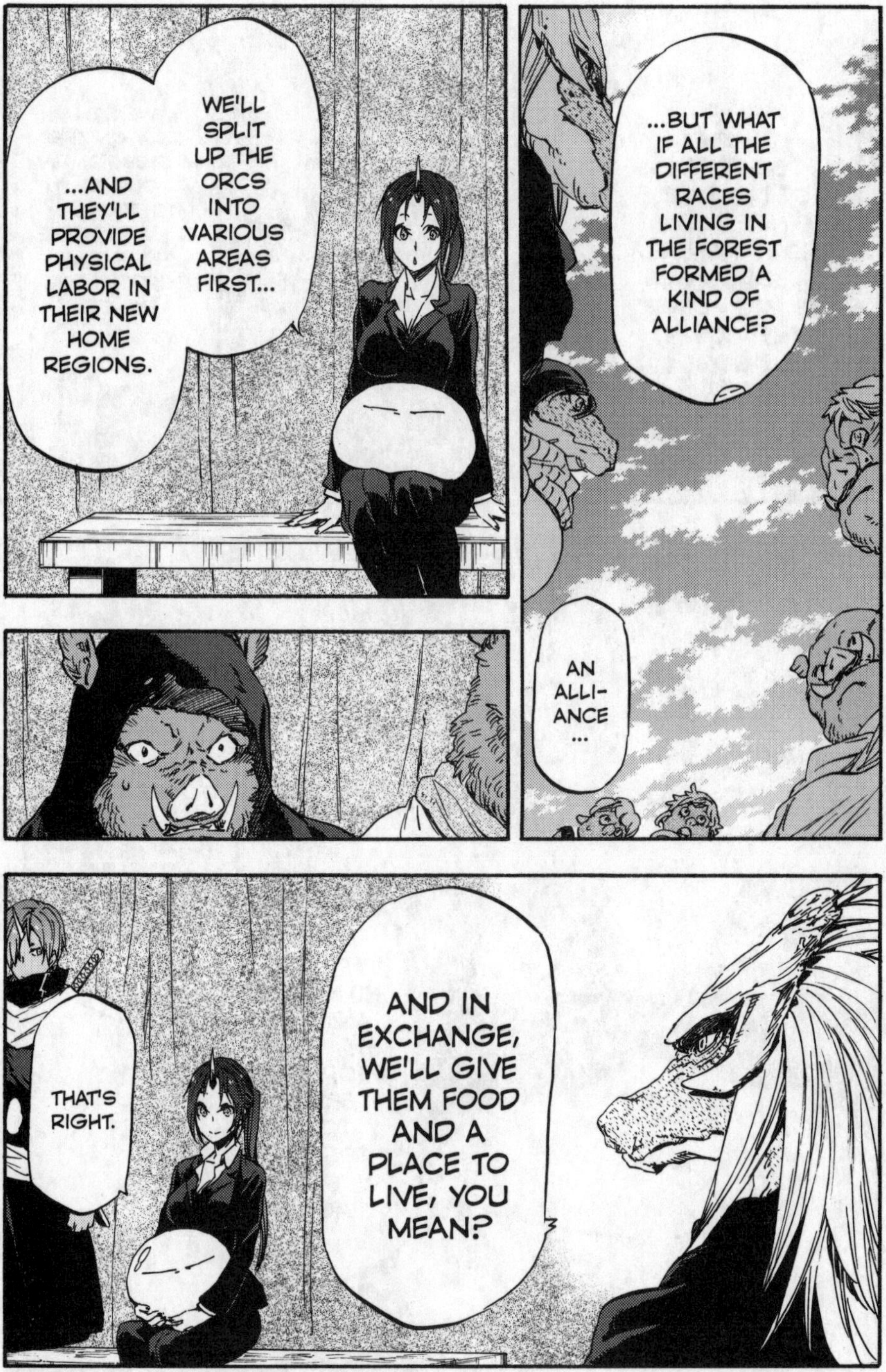
...BUT WHAT IF ALL THE DIFFERENT RACES LIVING IN THE FOREST FORMED A KIND OF ALLIANCE?
AN ALLI-ANCE...
WE'LL SPLIT UP THE ORCS INTO VARIOUS AREAS FIRST...
...AND THEY'LL PROVIDE PHYSICAL LABOR IN THEIR NEW HOME REGIONS.
AND IN EXCHANGE, WE'LL GIVE THEM FOOD AND A PLACE TO LIVE, YOU MEAN?
THAT'S RIGHT.

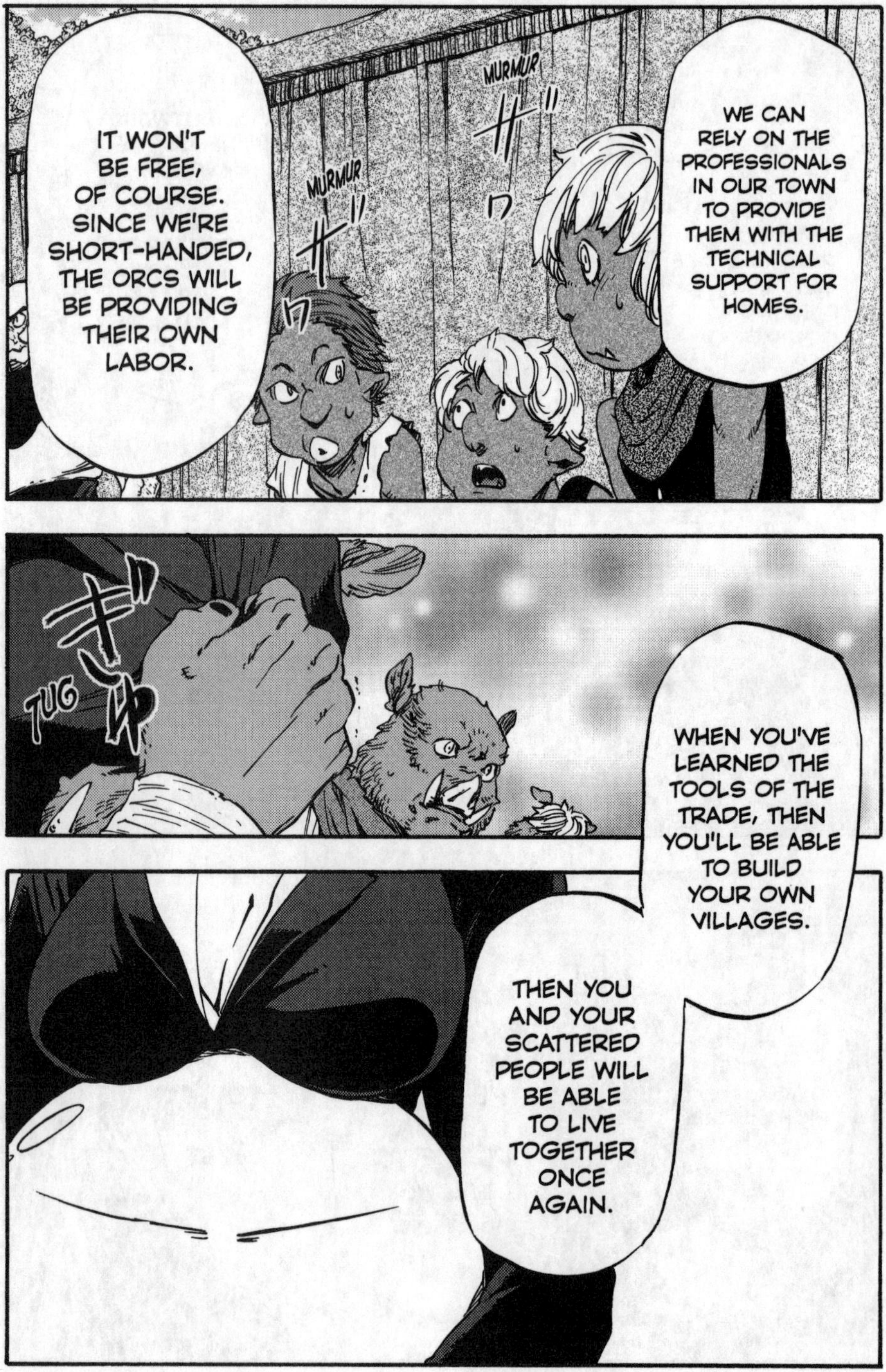
WE CAN RELY ON THE PROFESSIONALS IN OUR TOWN TO PROVIDE THEM WITH THE TECHNICAL SUPPORT FOR HOMES.
MURMUR
MURMUR
IT WON'T BE FREE, OF COURSE. SINCE WE'RE SHORT-HANDED, THE ORCS WILL BE PROVIDING THEIR OWN LABOR.
WHEN YOU'VE LEARNED THE TOOLS OF THE TRADE, THEN YOU'LL BE ABLE TO BUILD YOUR OWN VILLAGES.
TUG
THEN YOU AND YOUR SCATTERED PEOPLE WILL BE ABLE TO LIVE TOGETHER ONCE AGAIN.

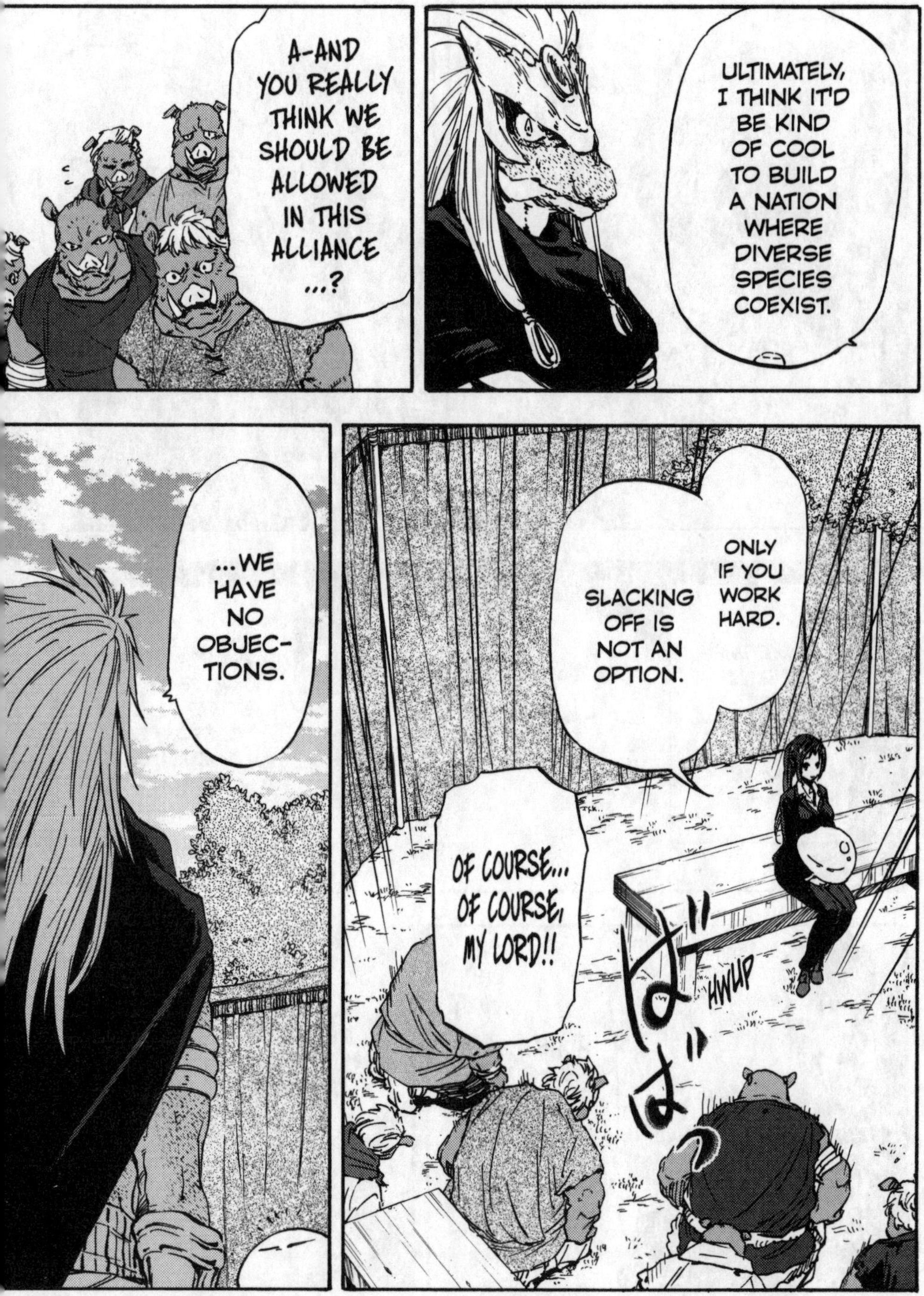
ULTIMATELY, I THINK IT'D BE KIND OF COOL TO BUILD A NATION WHERE DIVERSE SPECIES COEXIST.
A-AND YOU REALLY THINK WE SHOULD BE ALLOWED IN THIS ALLIANCE ...?
ONLY IF YOU WORK HARD.
SLACKING OFF IS NOT AN OPTION.
OF COURSE... OF COURSE, MY LORD!!
ばっ
HWUP
...WE HAVE NO OBJECTIONS.

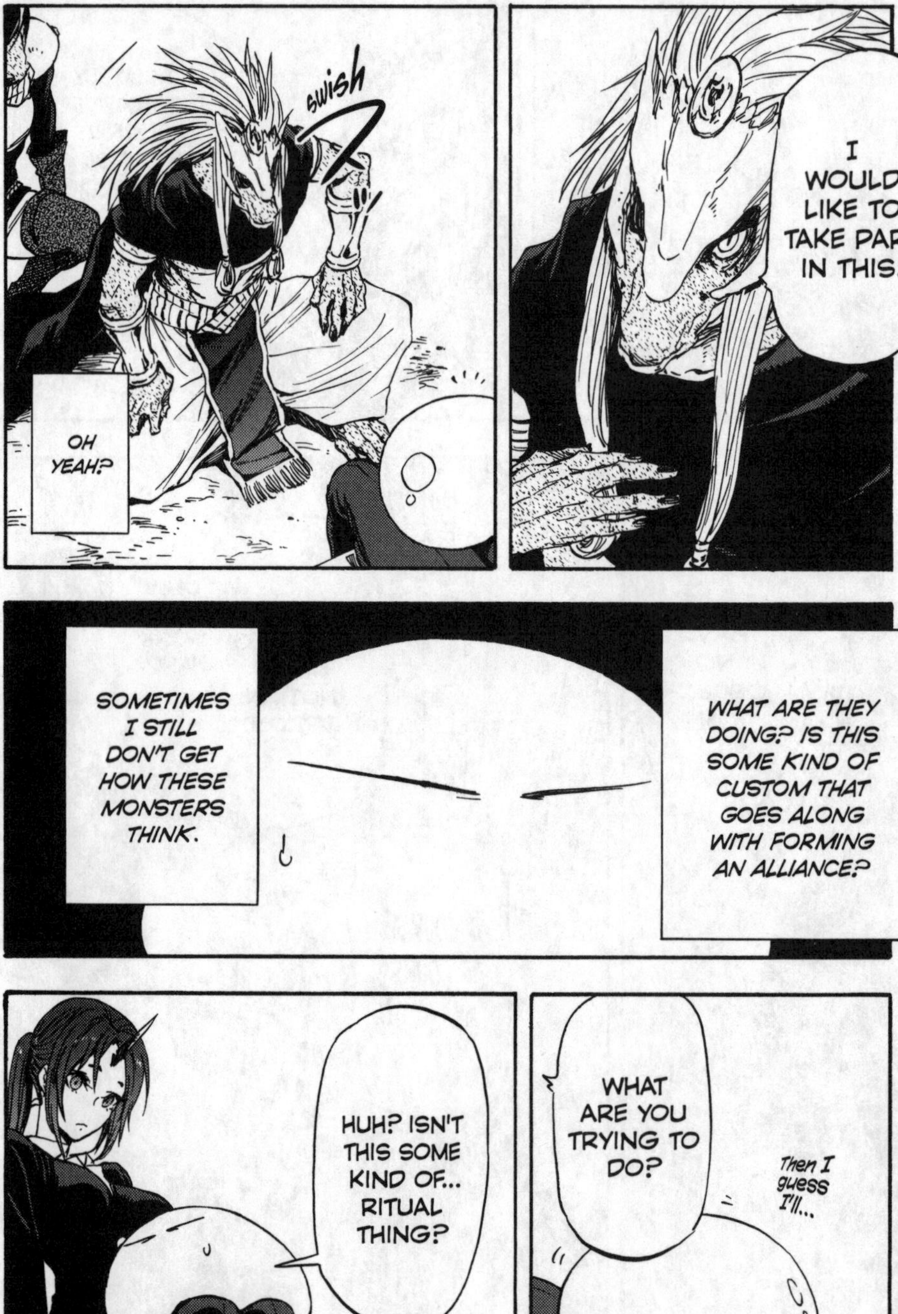
I WOULD LIKE TO TAKE PART IN THIS.
SWISH
OH YEAH?
WHAT ARE THEY DOING? IS THIS SOME KIND OF CUSTOM THAT GOES ALONG WITH FORMING AN ALLIANCE?
SOMETIMES I STILL DON'T GET HOW THESE MONSTERS THINK.
WHAT ARE YOU TRYING TO DO?
Then I guess I'll...
HUH? ISN'T THIS SOME KIND OF... RITUAL THING?

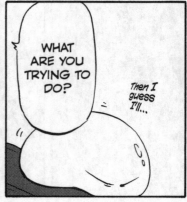

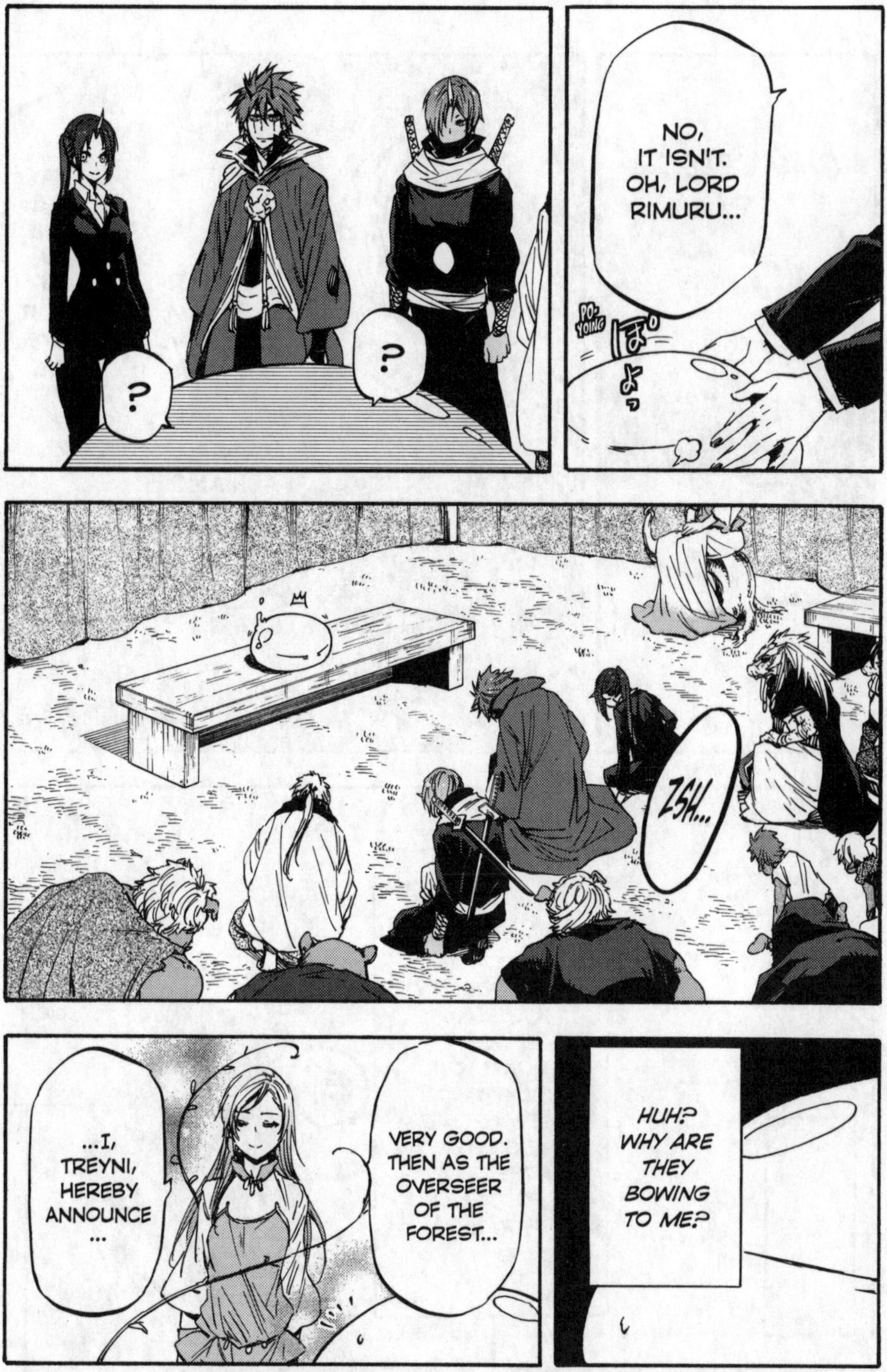
NO, IT ISN'T. OH, LORD RIMURU...
PO-YOING
ぽよっ
?
?
ZSH...
HUH? WHY ARE THEY BOWING TO ME?
VERY GOOD. THEN AS THE OVERSEER OF THE FOREST...
...I, TREYNI, HEREBY ANNOUNCE ...

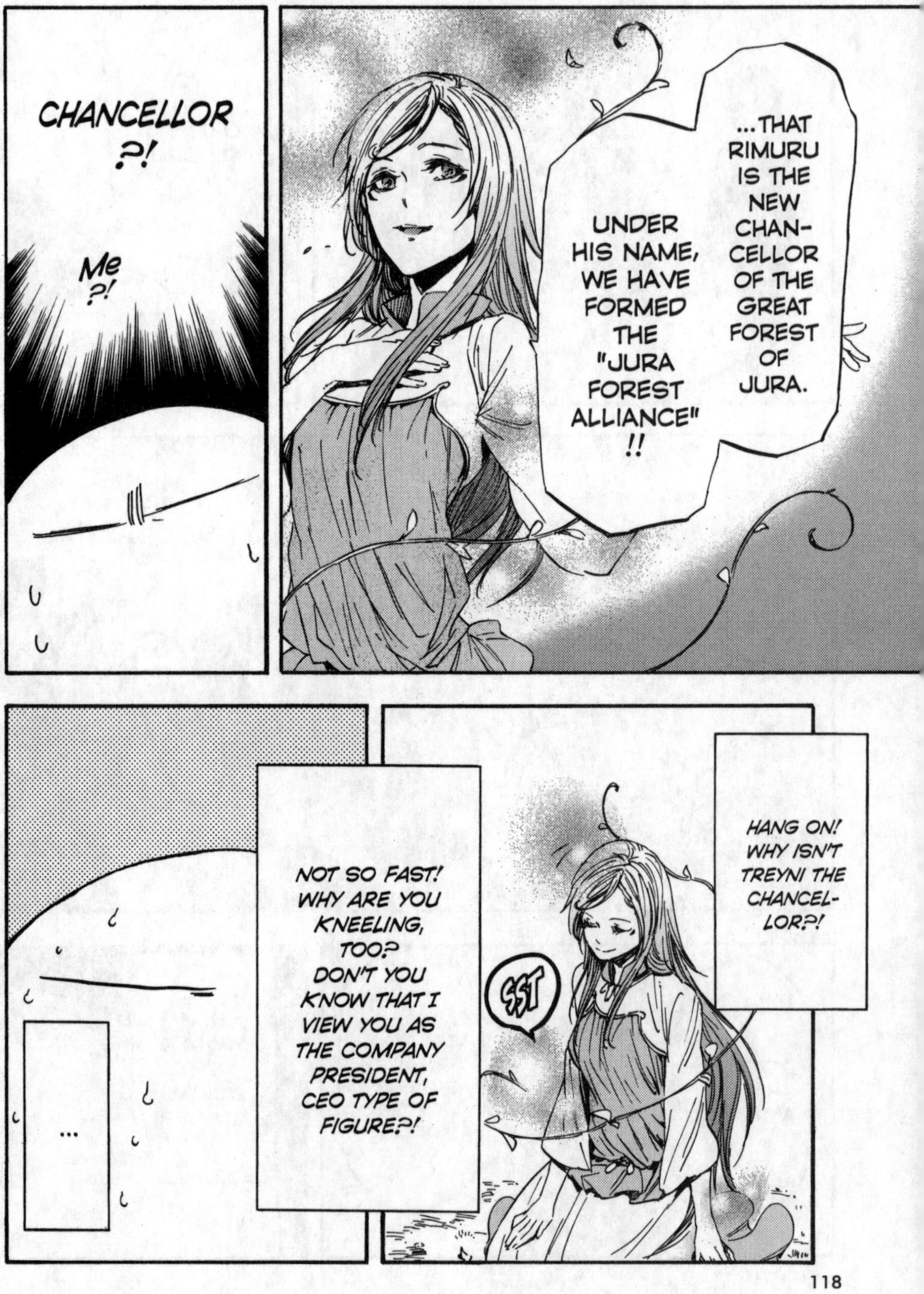
...THAT RIMURU IS THE NEW CHANCELLOR OF THE GREAT FOREST OF JURA.
UNDER HIS NAME, WE HAVE FORMED THE "JURA FOREST ALLIANCE" !!
CHANCELLOR ?!
Me ?!
HANG ON! WHY ISN'T TREYNI THE CHANCELLOR?!
SST
NOT SO FAST! WHY ARE YOU KNEELING, TOO? DON'T YOU KNOW THAT I VIEW YOU AS THE COMPANY PRESIDENT, CEO TYPE OF FIGURE?!
...

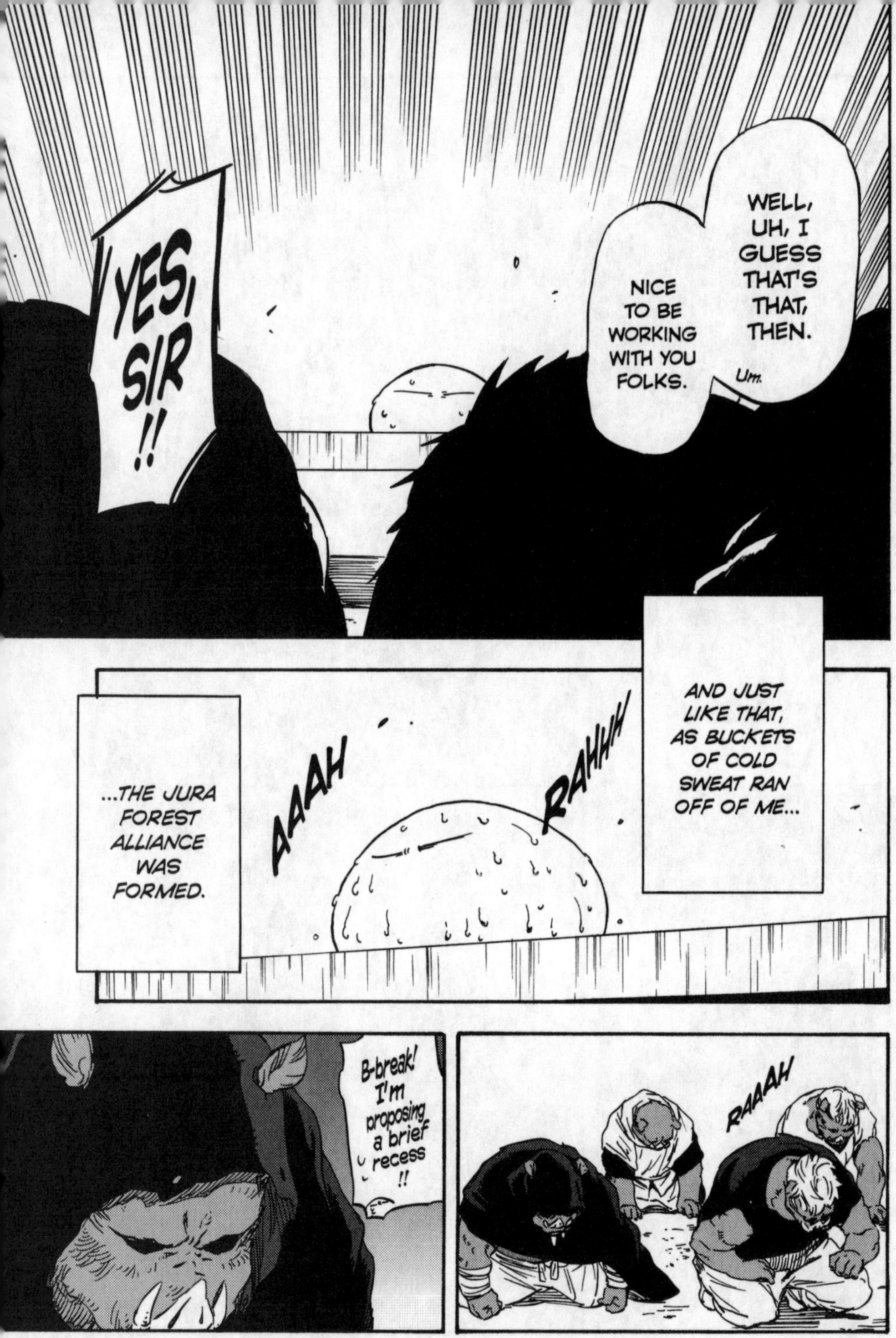
WELL, UH, I GUESS THAT'S THAT, THEN.
Um.
NICE TO BE WORKING WITH YOU FOLKS.
YES, SIR!!
AND JUST LIKE THAT, AS BUCKETS OF COLD SWEAT RAN OFF OF ME...
RAHHH
AAAH
...THE JURA FOREST ALLIANCE WAS FORMED.
RAAAH
B-break! I'm proposing a brief recess!!

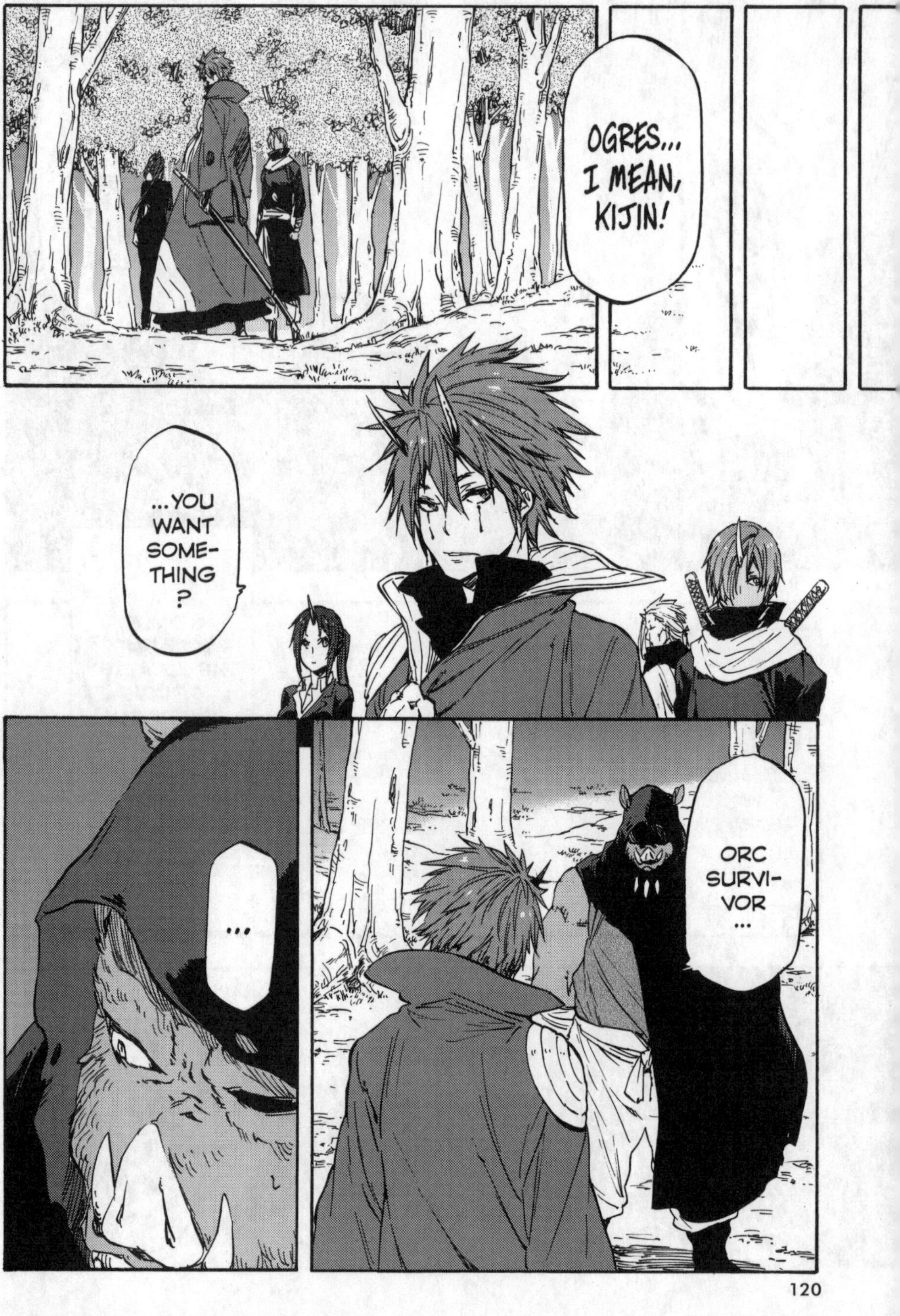
OGRES... I MEAN, KIJIN!
...YOU WANT SOME-THING?
ORC SURVI-VOR...
...

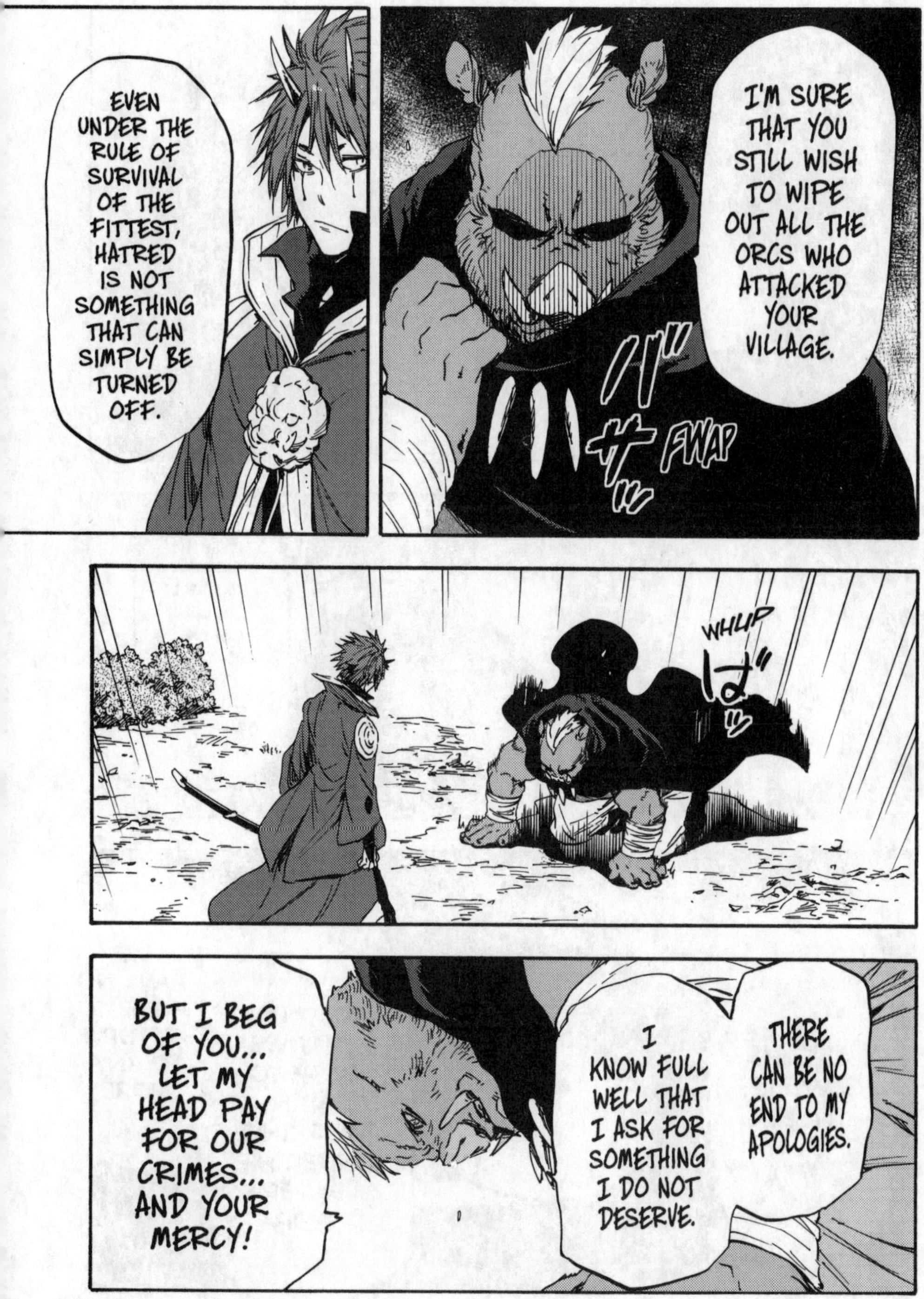
I'M SURE THAT YOU STILL WISH TO WIPE OUT ALL THE ORCS WHO ATTACKED YOUR VILLAGE.
FWAP
EVEN UNDER THE RULE OF SURVIVAL OF THE FITTEST, HATRED IS NOT SOMETHING THAT CAN SIMPLY BE TURNED OFF.
WHUP
THERE CAN BE NO END TO MY APOLOGIES.
I KNOW FULL WELL THAT I ASK FOR SOMETHING I DO NOT DESERVE.
BUT I BEG OF YOU... LET MY HEAD PAY FOR OUR CRIMES... AND YOUR MERCY!

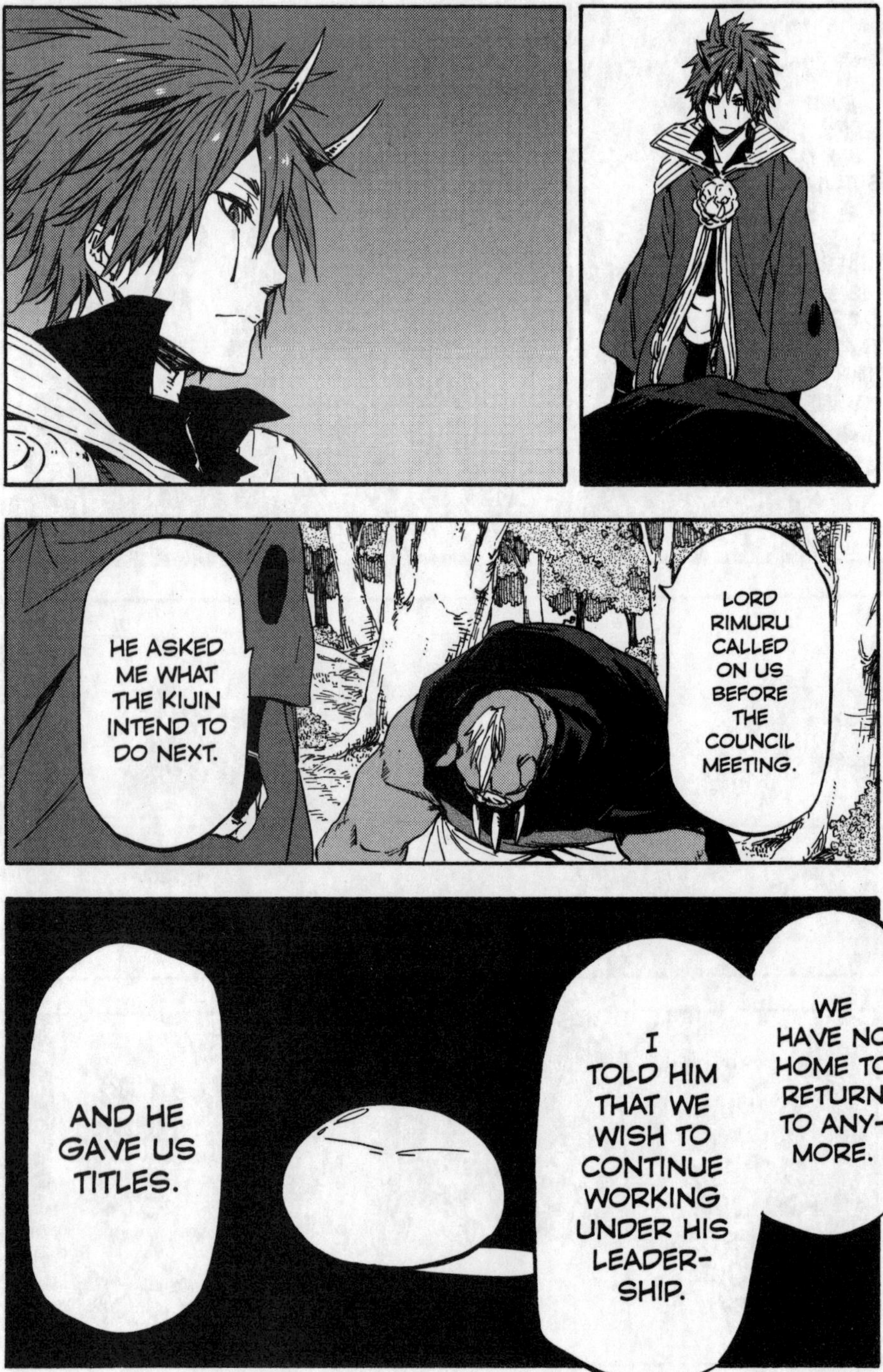
LORD RIMURU CALLED ON US BEFORE THE COUNCIL MEETING.
HE ASKED ME WHAT THE KIJIN INTEND TO DO NEXT.
WE HAVE NO HOME TO RETURN TO ANY-MORE.
I TOLD HIM THAT WE WISH TO CONTINUE WORKING UNDER HIS LEADER-SHIP.
AND HE GAVE US TITLES.

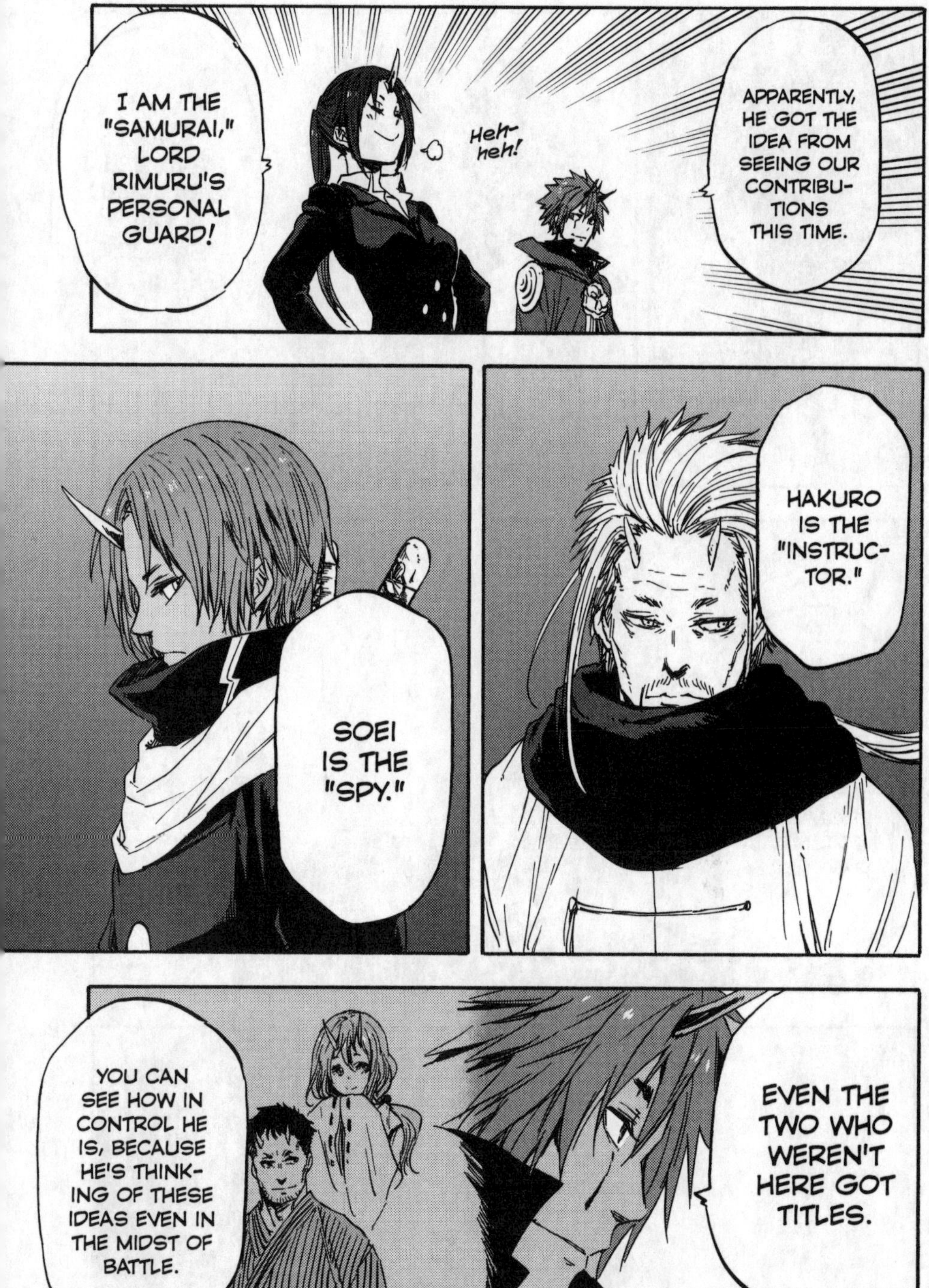
APPARENTLY, HE GOT THE IDEA FROM SEEING OUR CONTRIBUTIONS THIS TIME.
Heh-heh!
I AM THE "SAMURAI," LORD RIMURU'S PERSONAL GUARD!
HAKURO IS THE "INSTRUCTOR."
SOEI IS THE "SPY."
EVEN THE TWO WHO WEREN'T HERE GOT TITLES.
YOU CAN SEE HOW IN CONTROL HE IS, BECAUSE HE'S THINKING OF THESE IDEAS EVEN IN THE MIDST OF BATTLE.

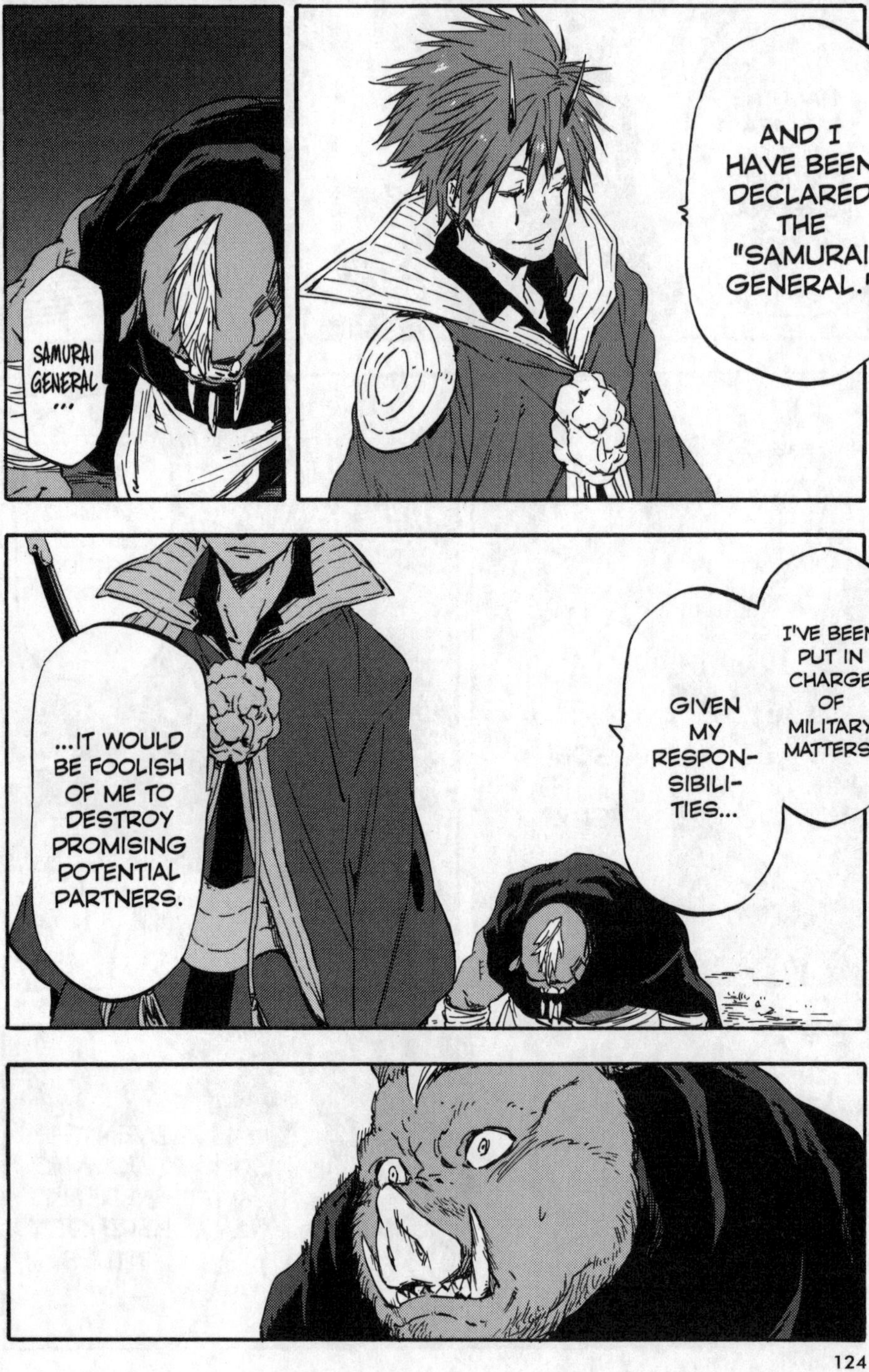
AND I HAVE BEEN DECLARED THE "SAMURAI GENERAL."
SAMURAI GENERAL ...
I'VE BEEN PUT IN CHARGE OF MILITARY MATTERS.
GIVEN MY RESPON-SIBILI-TIES...
...IT WOULD BE FOOLISH OF ME TO DESTROY PROMISING POTENTIAL PARTNERS.

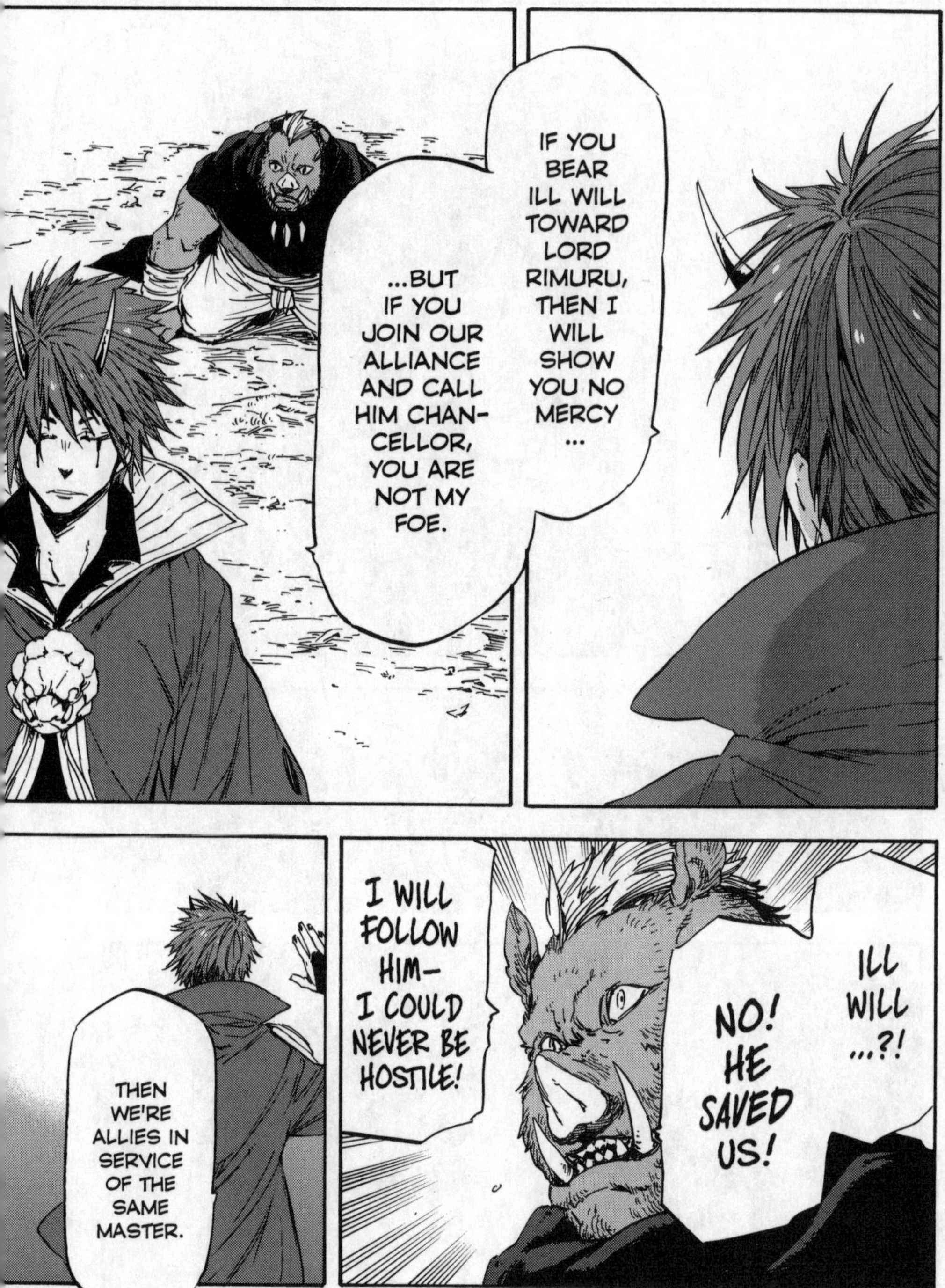
IF YOU BEAR ILL WILL TOWARD LORD RIMURU, THEN I WILL SHOW YOU NO MERCY ...
...BUT IF YOU JOIN OUR ALLIANCE AND CALL HIM CHAN-CELLOR, YOU ARE NOT MY FOE.
ILL WILL ...?!
NO! HE SAVED US!
I WILL FOLLOW HIM— I COULD NEVER BE HOSTILE!
THEN WE'RE ALLIES IN SERVICE OF THE SAME MASTER.

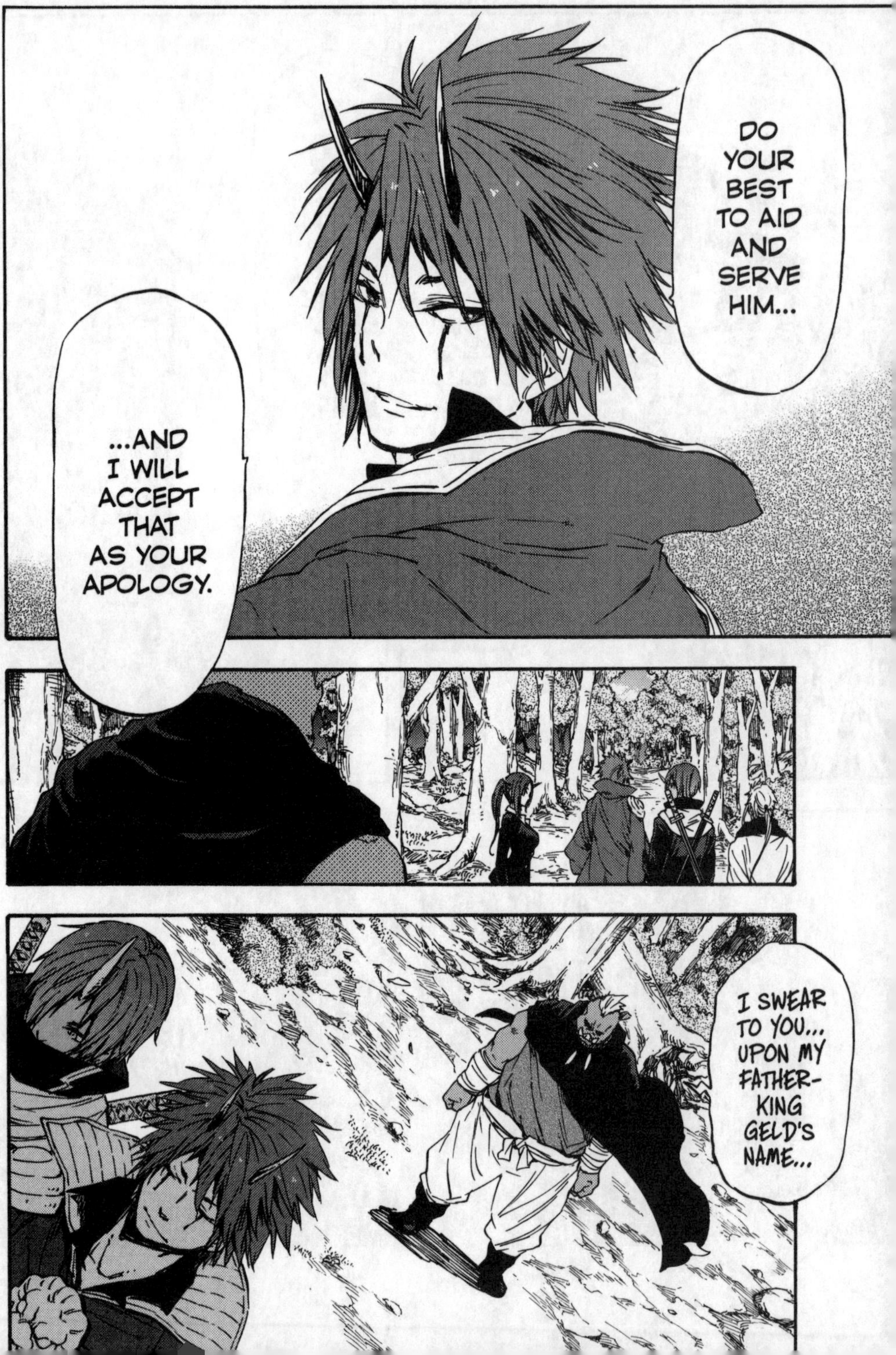
DO YOUR BEST TO AID AND SERVE HIM...
...AND I WILL ACCEPT THAT AS YOUR APOLOGY.
I SWEAR TO YOU... UPON MY FATHER-KING GELD'S NAME...

I just want
to turn into
cold sweat
and evaporate
into nothing.

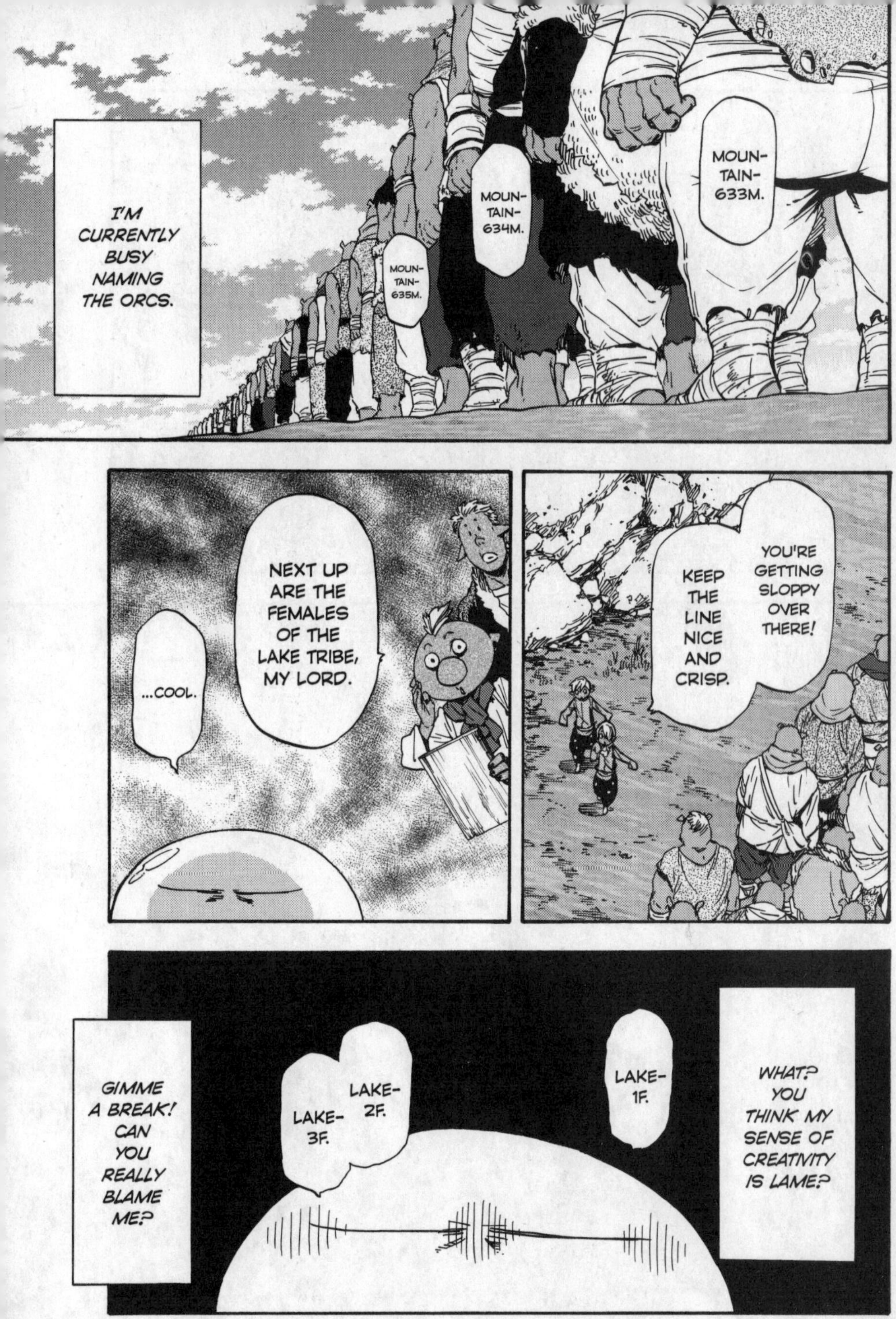

MOUNTAIN-633M.
MOUNTAIN-634M.
MOUNTAIN-635M.
I'M CURRENTLY BUSY NAMING THE ORCS.
YOU'RE GETTING SLOPPY OVER THERE!
KEEP THE LINE NICE AND CRISP.
NEXT UP ARE THE FEMALES OF THE LAKE TRIBE, MY LORD.
...COOL.
WHAT? YOU THINK MY SENSE OF CREATIVITY IS LAME?
LAKE-1F.
LAKE-2F.
LAKE-3F.
GIMME A BREAK! CAN YOU REALLY BLAME ME?

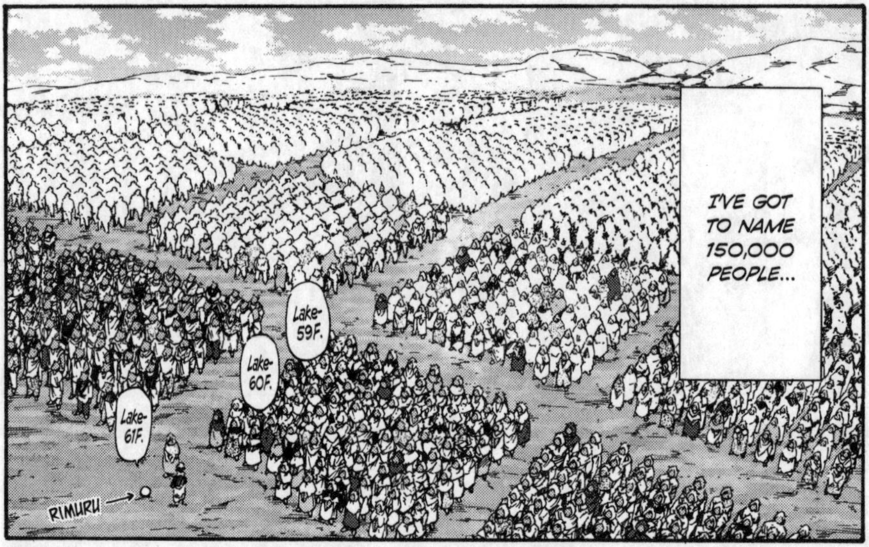
I'VE GOT TO NAME 150,000 PEOPLE...
Lake-59F.
Lake-60F.
Lake-61F.
RIMURU

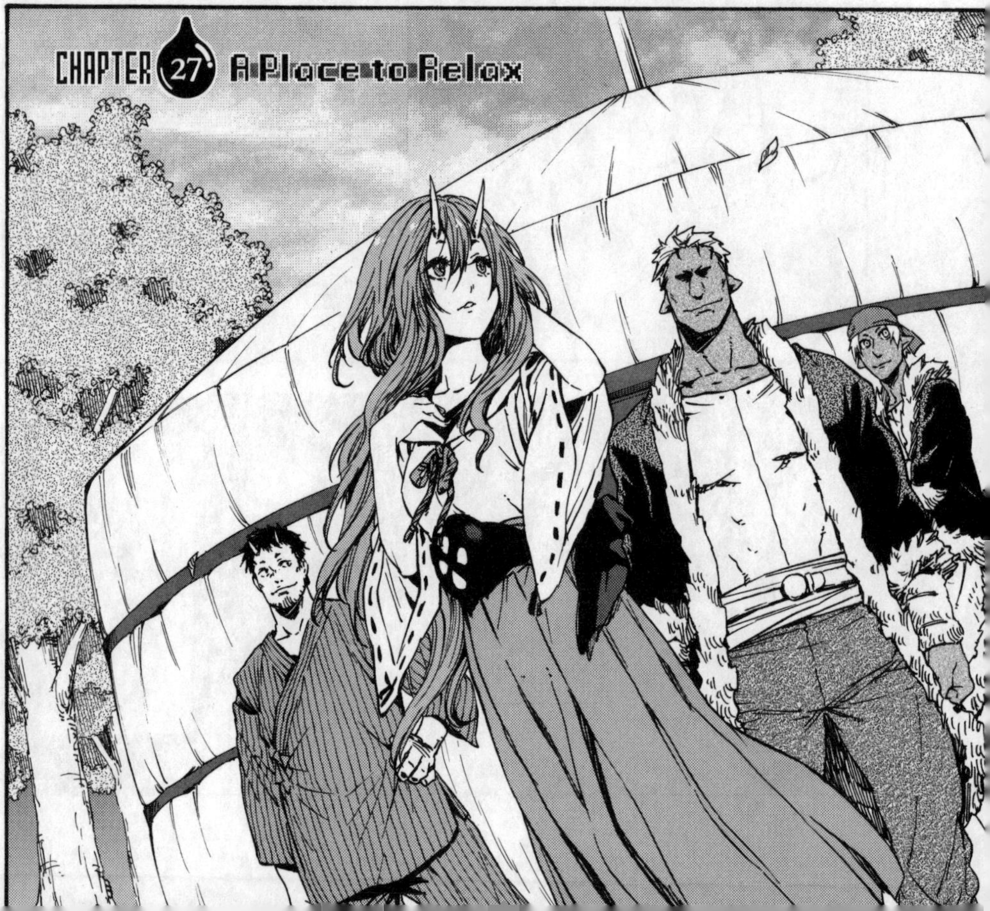
CHAPTER 27 A Place to Relax

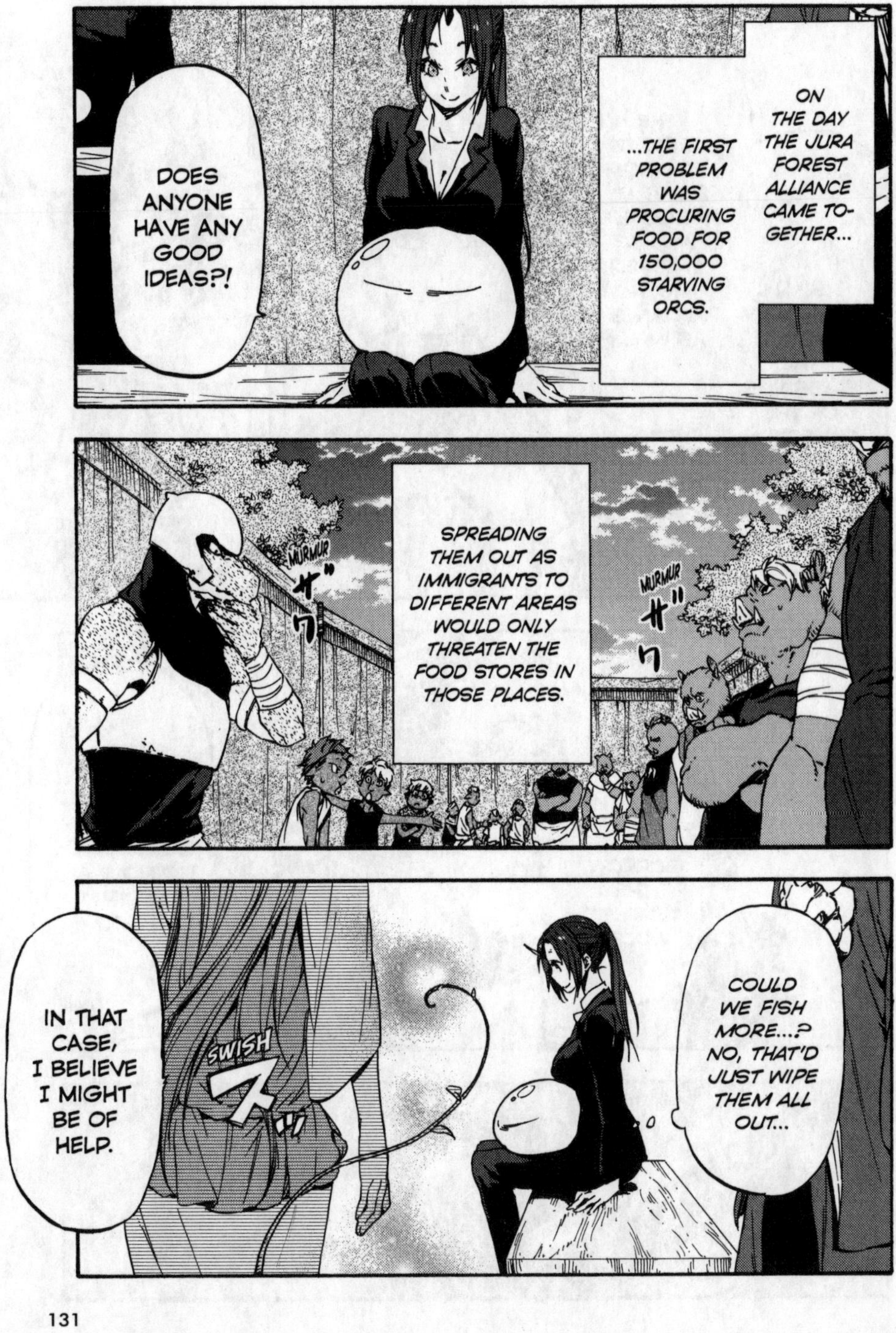
ON THE DAY THE JURA FOREST ALLIANCE CAME TO-GETHER...
...THE FIRST PROBLEM WAS PROCURING FOOD FOR 150,000 STARVING ORCS.
DOES ANYONE HAVE ANY GOOD IDEAS?!
MURMUR
SPREADING THEM OUT AS IMMIGRANTS TO DIFFERENT AREAS WOULD ONLY THREATEN THE FOOD STORES IN THOSE PLACES.
MURMUR
COULD WE FISH MORE...? NO, THAT'D JUST WIPE THEM ALL OUT...
SWISH
IN THAT CASE, I BELIEVE I MIGHT BE OF HELP.

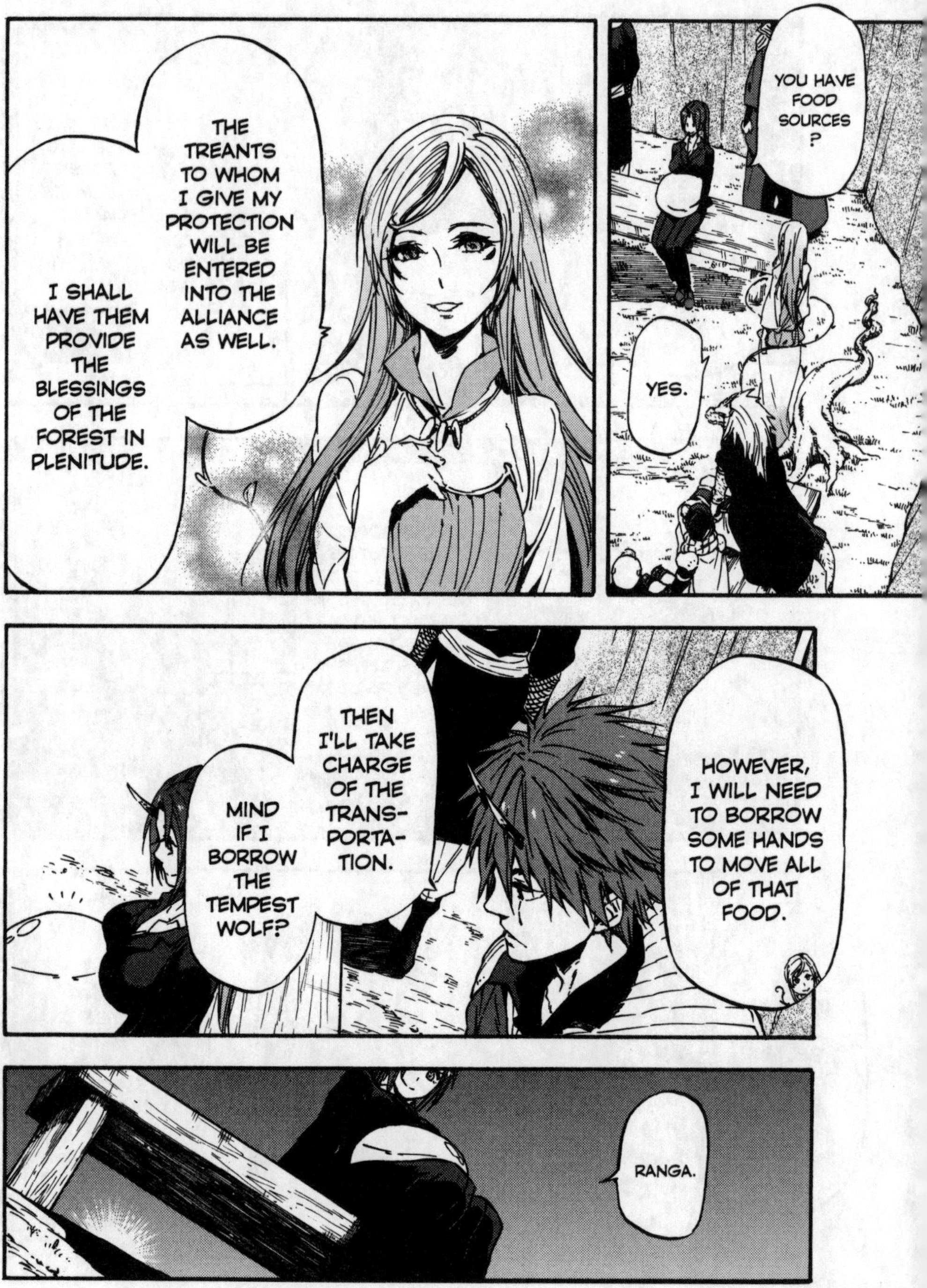
YOU HAVE FOOD SOURCES?
YES.
THE TREANTS TO WHOM I GIVE MY PROTECTION WILL BE ENTERED INTO THE ALLIANCE AS WELL.
I SHALL HAVE THEM PROVIDE THE BLESSINGS OF THE FOREST IN PLENITUDE.
HOWEVER, I WILL NEED TO BORROW SOME HANDS TO MOVE ALL OF THAT FOOD.
THEN I'LL TAKE CHARGE OF THE TRANS-PORTATION.
MIND IF I BORROW THE TEMPEST WOLF?
RANGA.

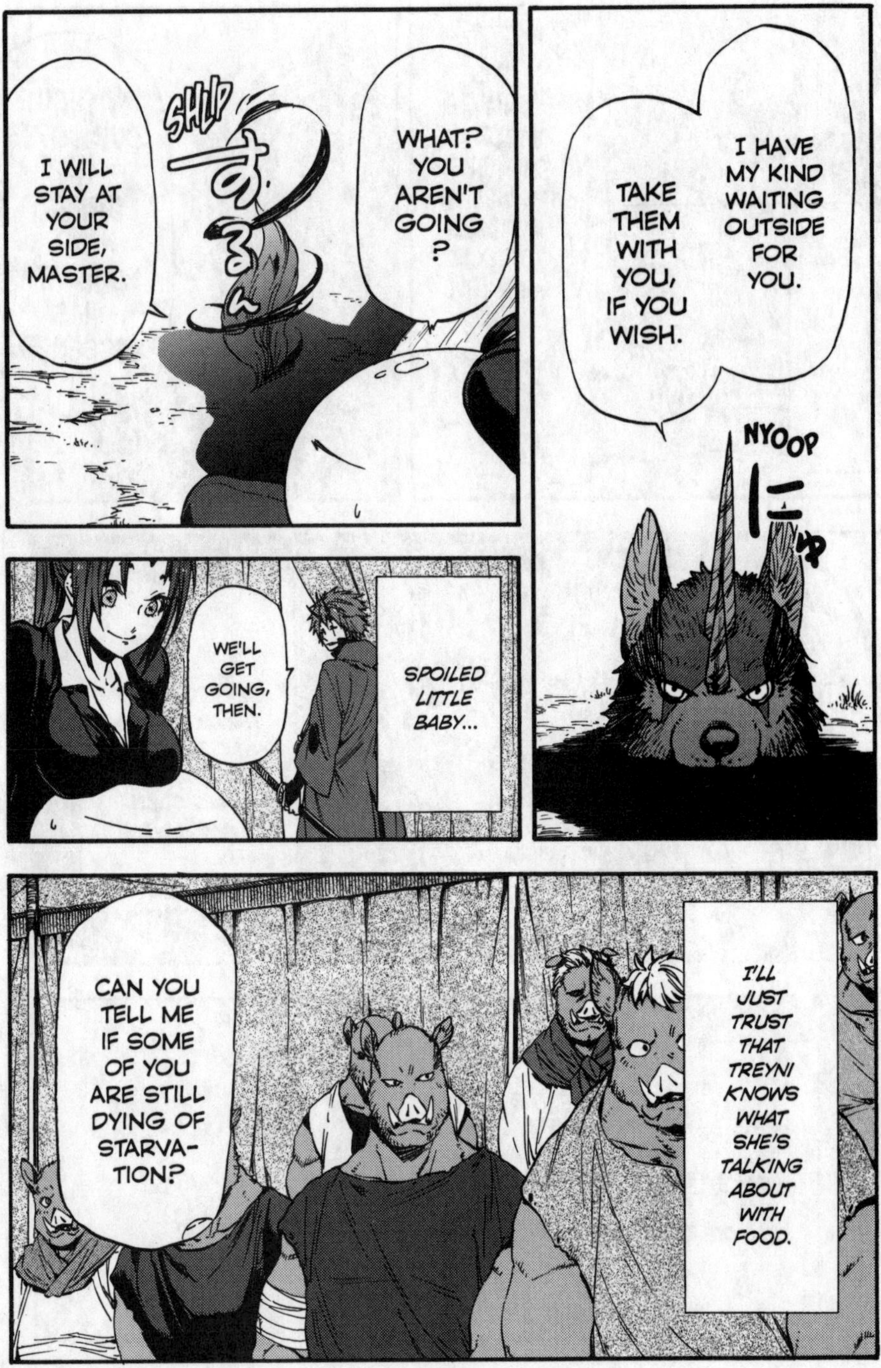
I HAVE MY KIND WAITING OUTSIDE FOR YOU.
TAKE THEM WITH YOU, IF YOU WISH.
NYOOP
WHAT? YOU AREN'T GOING?
SHLIP
I WILL STAY AT YOUR SIDE, MASTER.
SPOILED LITTLE BABY...
WE'LL GET GOING, THEN.
I'LL JUST TRUST THAT TREYNI KNOWS WHAT SHE'S TALKING ABOUT WITH FOOD.
CAN YOU TELL ME IF SOME OF YOU ARE STILL DYING OF STARVATION?

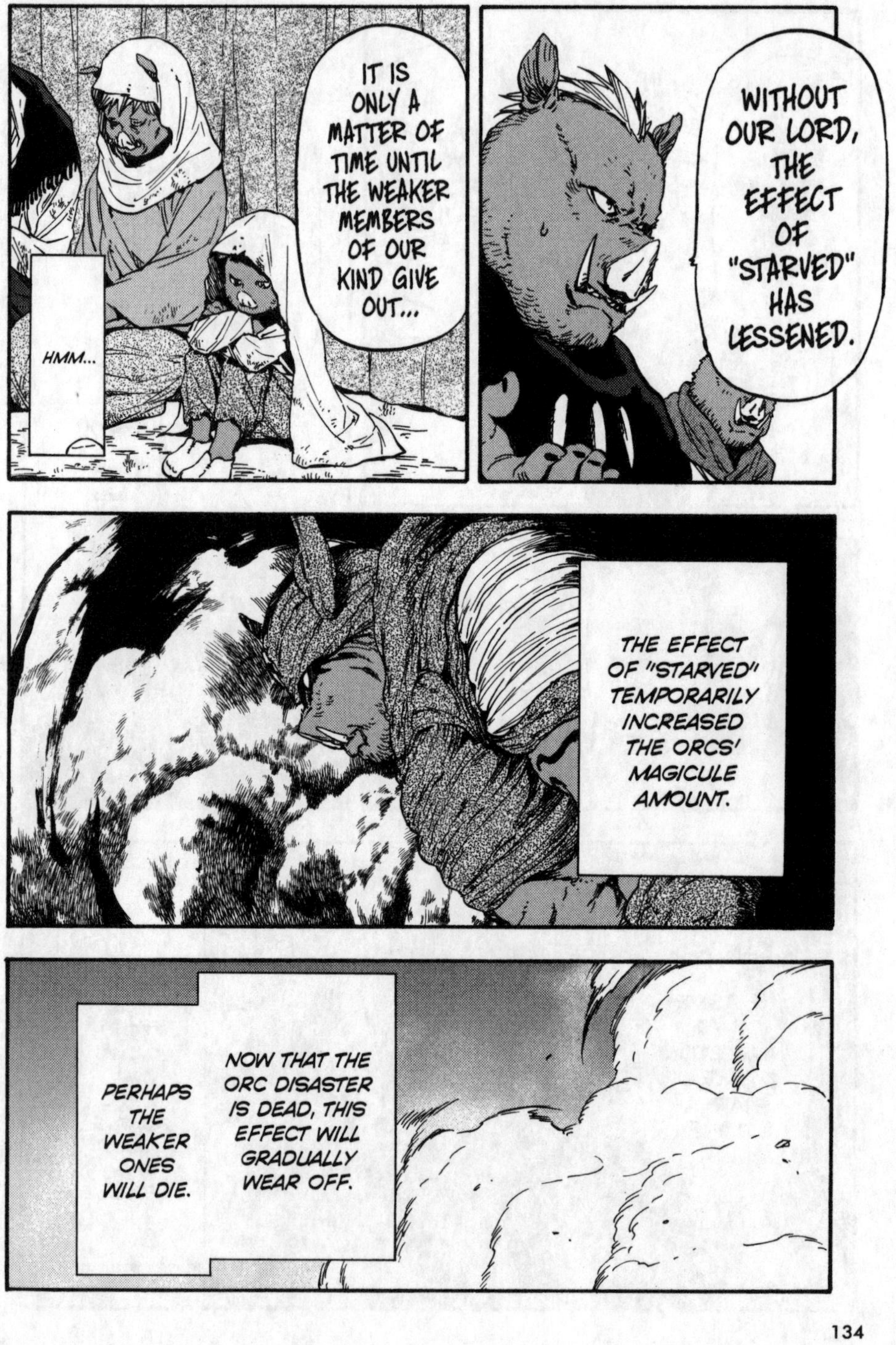
WITHOUT OUR LORD, THE EFFECT OF "STARVED" HAS LESSENED.
IT IS ONLY A MATTER OF TIME UNTIL THE WEAKER MEMBERS OF OUR KIND GIVE OUT...
HMM...
THE EFFECT OF "STARVED" TEMPORARILY INCREASED THE ORCS' MAGICULE AMOUNT.
NOW THAT THE ORC DISASTER IS DEAD, THIS EFFECT WILL GRADUALLY WEAR OFF.
PERHAPS THE WEAKER ONES WILL DIE.

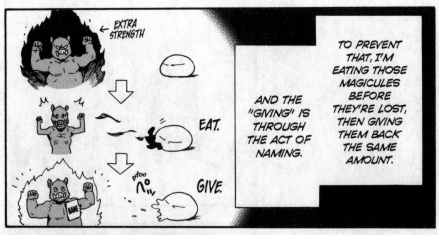

TO PREVENT THAT, I'M EATING THOSE MAGICULES BEFORE THEY'RE LOST, THEN GIVING THEM BACK THE SAME AMOUNT.
AND THE "GIVING" IS THROUGH THE ACT OF NAMING.
EXTRA STRENGTH
EAT.
GIVE.
ptoo
NAME
... NAMES.
NAMES, HUH.
AND THAT LED TO THIS NAME-GIVING HELL.
Deathmarch Dance is starting to work...
NEXT GROUP IS THE LAST ONE, LORD RIMURU.

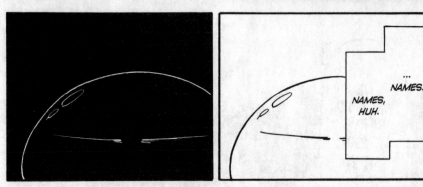

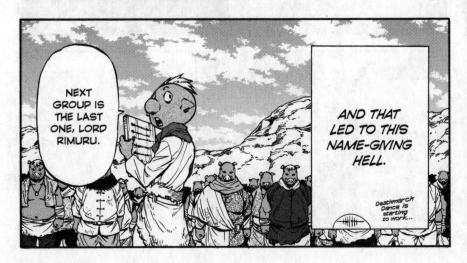

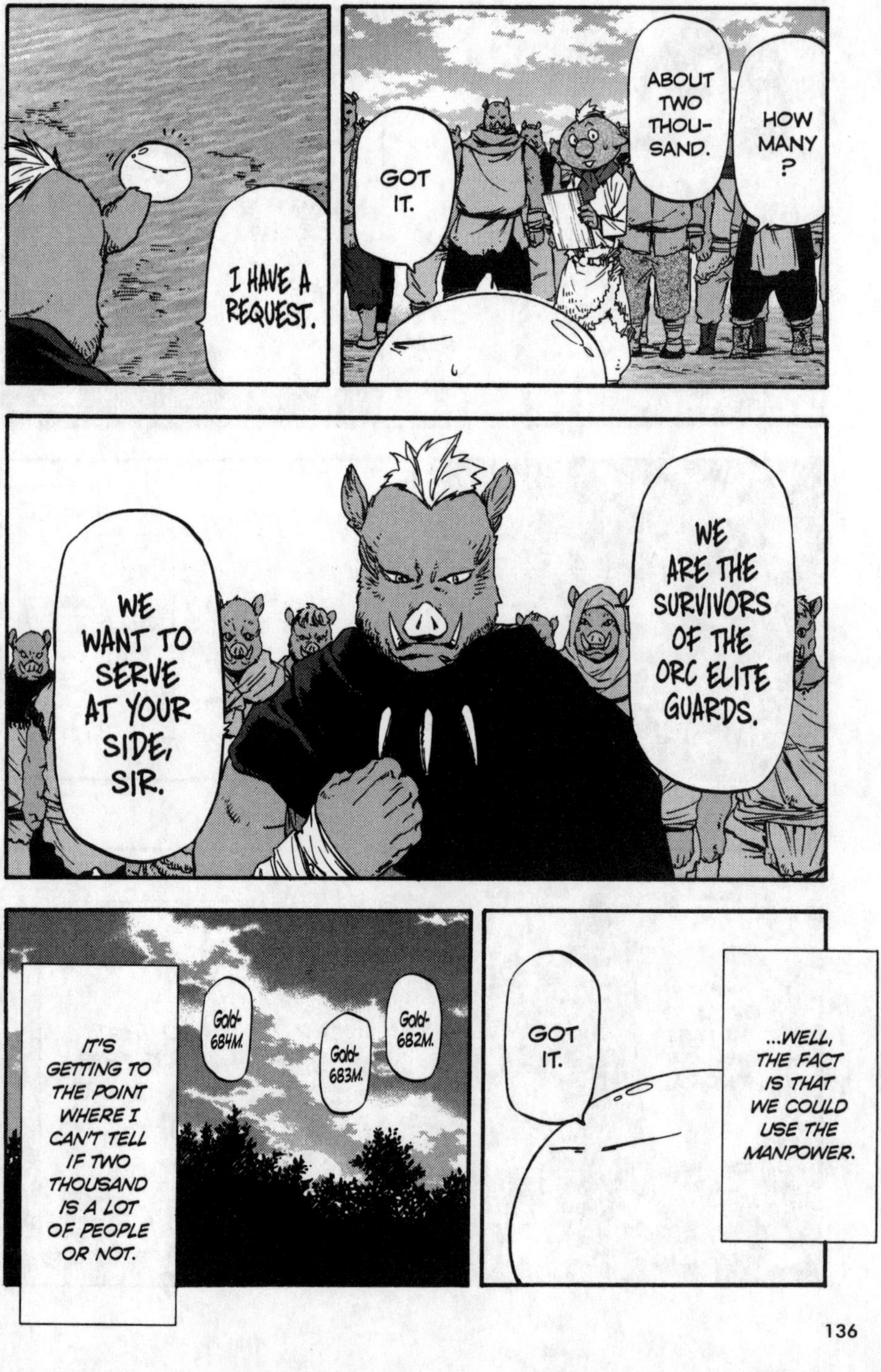
HOW MANY?
ABOUT TWO THOUSAND.
GOT IT.
I HAVE A REQUEST.
WE ARE THE SURVIVORS OF THE ORC ELITE GUARDS.
WE WANT TO SERVE AT YOUR SIDE, SIR.
...WELL, THE FACT IS THAT WE COULD USE THE MANPOWER.
GOT IT.
Gold-682M.
Gold-683M.
Gold-684M.
IT'S GETTING TO THE POINT WHERE I CAN'T TELL IF TWO THOUSAND IS A LOT OF PEOPLE OR NOT.

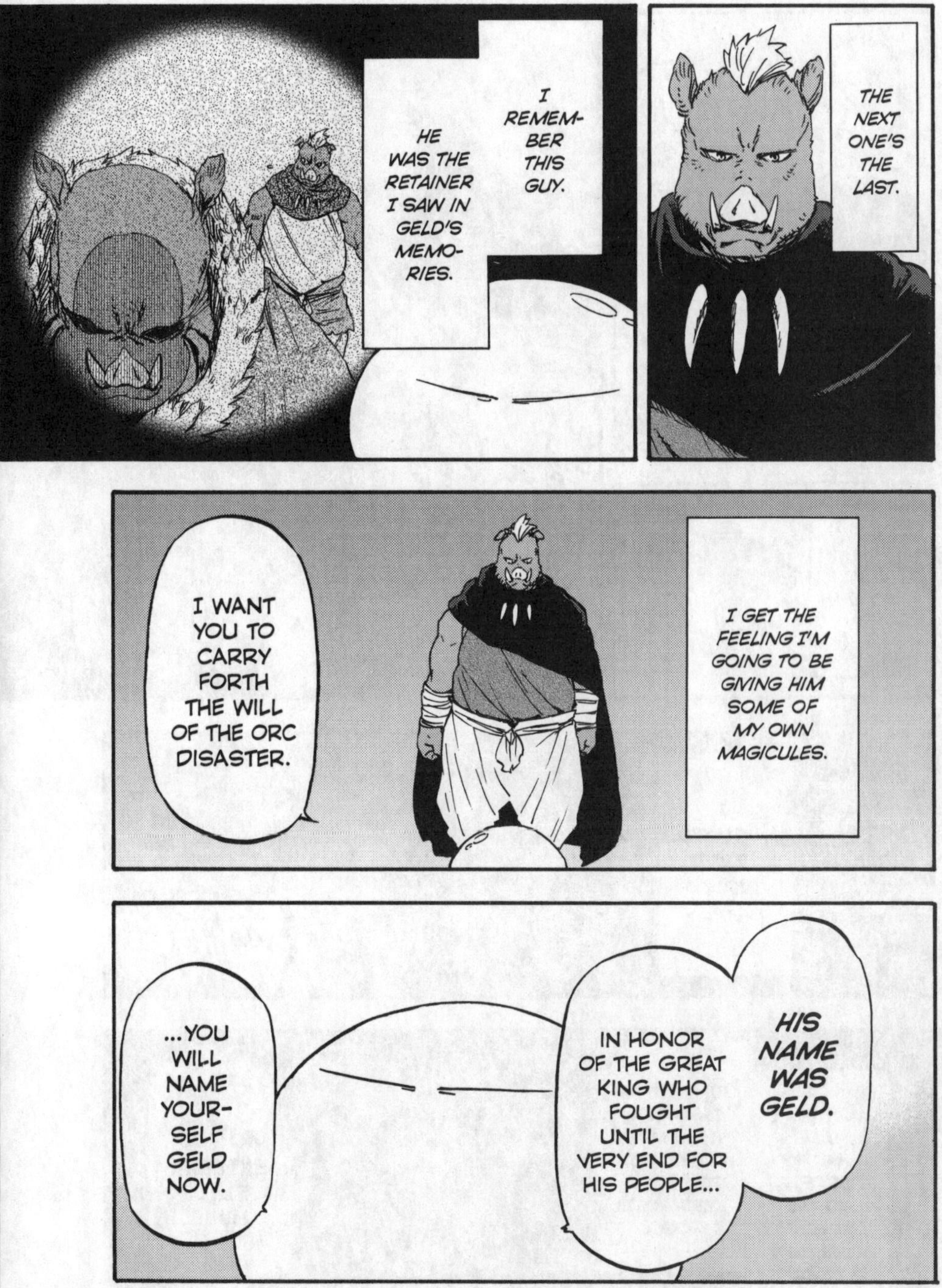
THE NEXT ONE'S THE LAST.
I REMEMBER THIS GUY.
HE WAS THE RETAINER I SAW IN GELD'S MEMORIES.
I GET THE FEELING I'M GOING TO BE GIVING HIM SOME OF MY OWN MAGICULES.
I WANT YOU TO CARRY FORTH THE WILL OF THE ORC DISASTER.
HIS NAME WAS GELD.
IN HONOR OF THE GREAT KING WHO FOUGHT UNTIL THE VERY END FOR HIS PEOPLE...
...YOU WILL NAME YOURSELF GELD NOW.

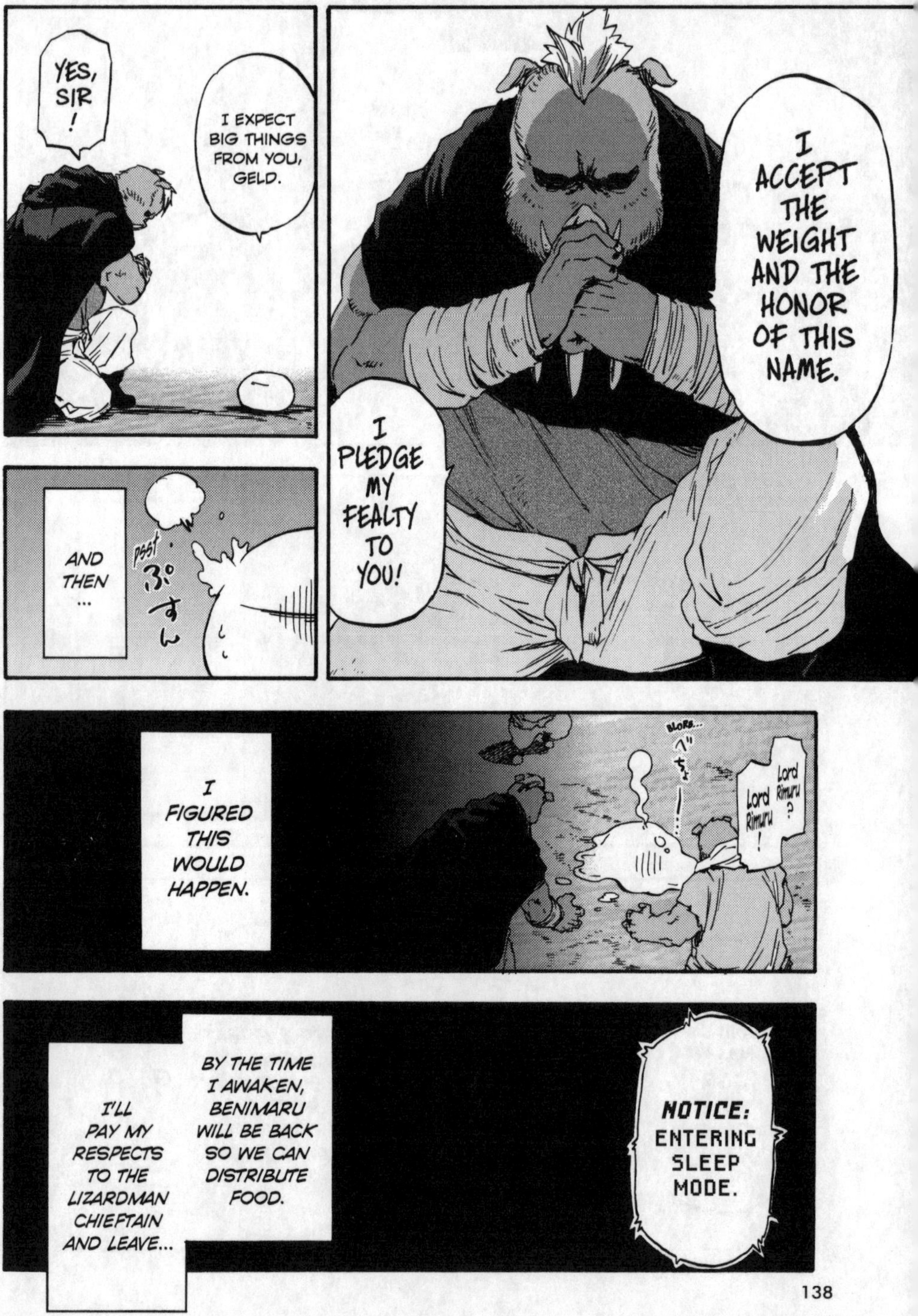
I ACCEPT THE WEIGHT AND THE HONOR OF THIS NAME.
I PLEDGE MY FEALTY TO YOU!
I EXPECT BIG THINGS FROM YOU, GELD.
YES, SIR!
ぷすん
psst
AND THEN...
Lord Rimuru?
Lord Rimuru!
べちょ...
BLORB...
I FIGURED THIS WOULD HAPPEN.
NOTICE: ENTERING SLEEP MODE.
BY THE TIME I AWAKEN, BENIMARU WILL BE BACK SO WE CAN DISTRIBUTE FOOD.
I'LL PAY MY RESPECTS TO THE LIZARDMAN CHIEFTAIN AND LEAVE...

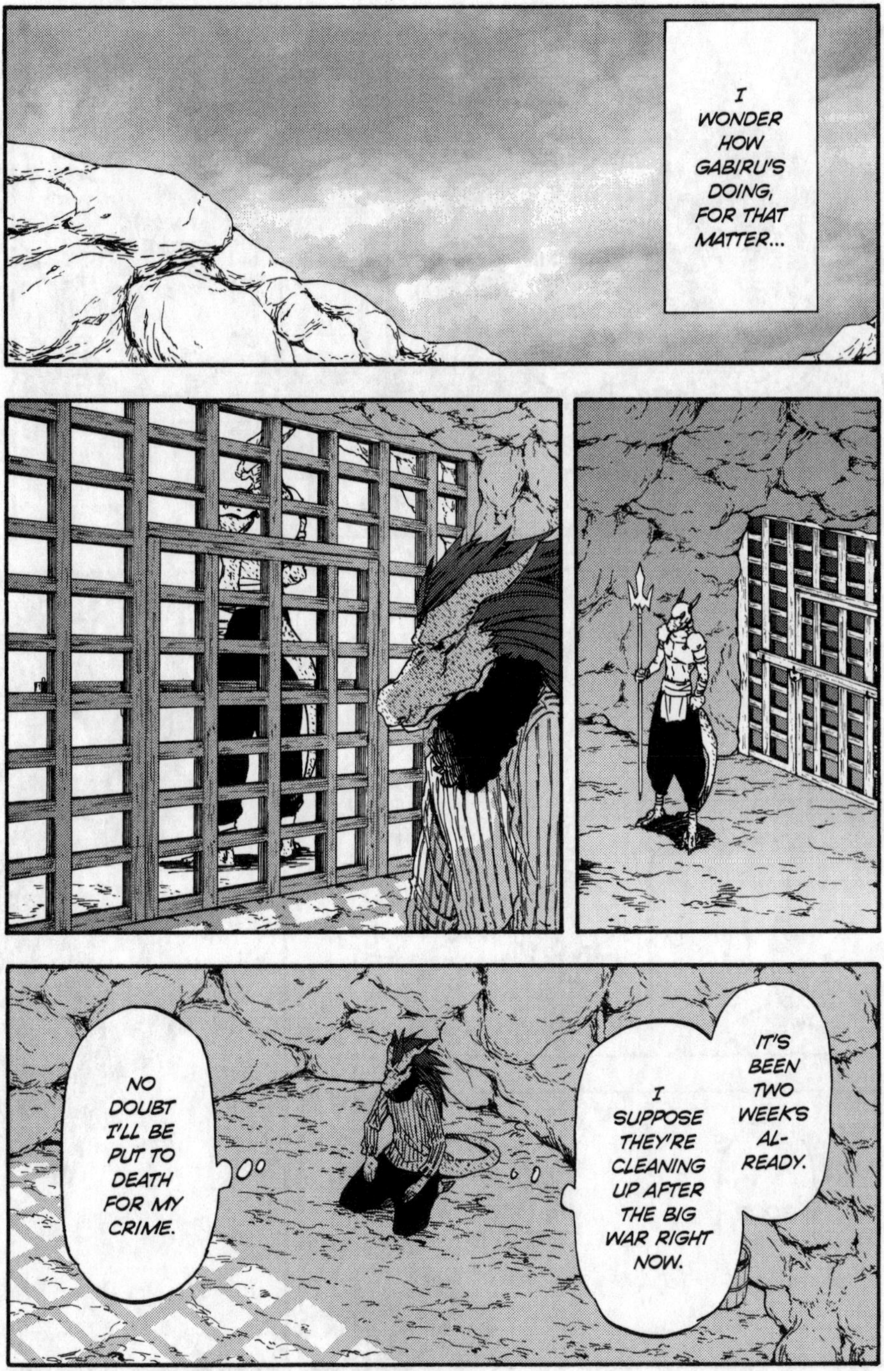
I WONDER HOW GABIRU'S DOING, FOR THAT MATTER...
IT'S BEEN TWO WEEK'S AL-READY.
I SUPPOSE THEY'RE CLEANING UP AFTER THE BIG WAR RIGHT NOW.
NO DOUBT I'LL BE PUT TO DEATH FOR MY CRIME.

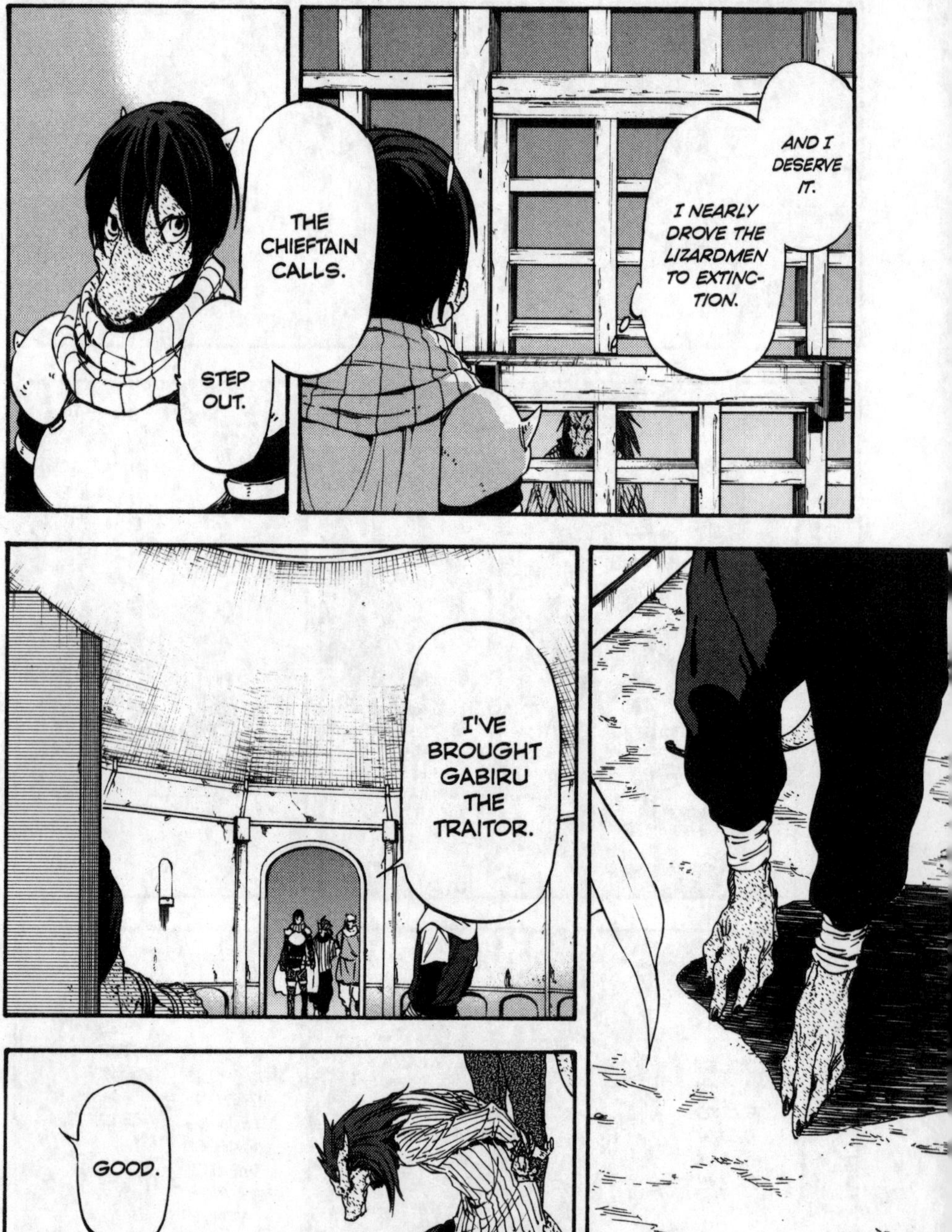
AND I DESERVE IT.
I NEARLY DROVE THE LIZARDMEN TO EXTINCTION.
THE CHIEFTAIN CALLS.
STEP OUT.
I'VE BROUGHT GABIRU THE TRAITOR.
GOOD.

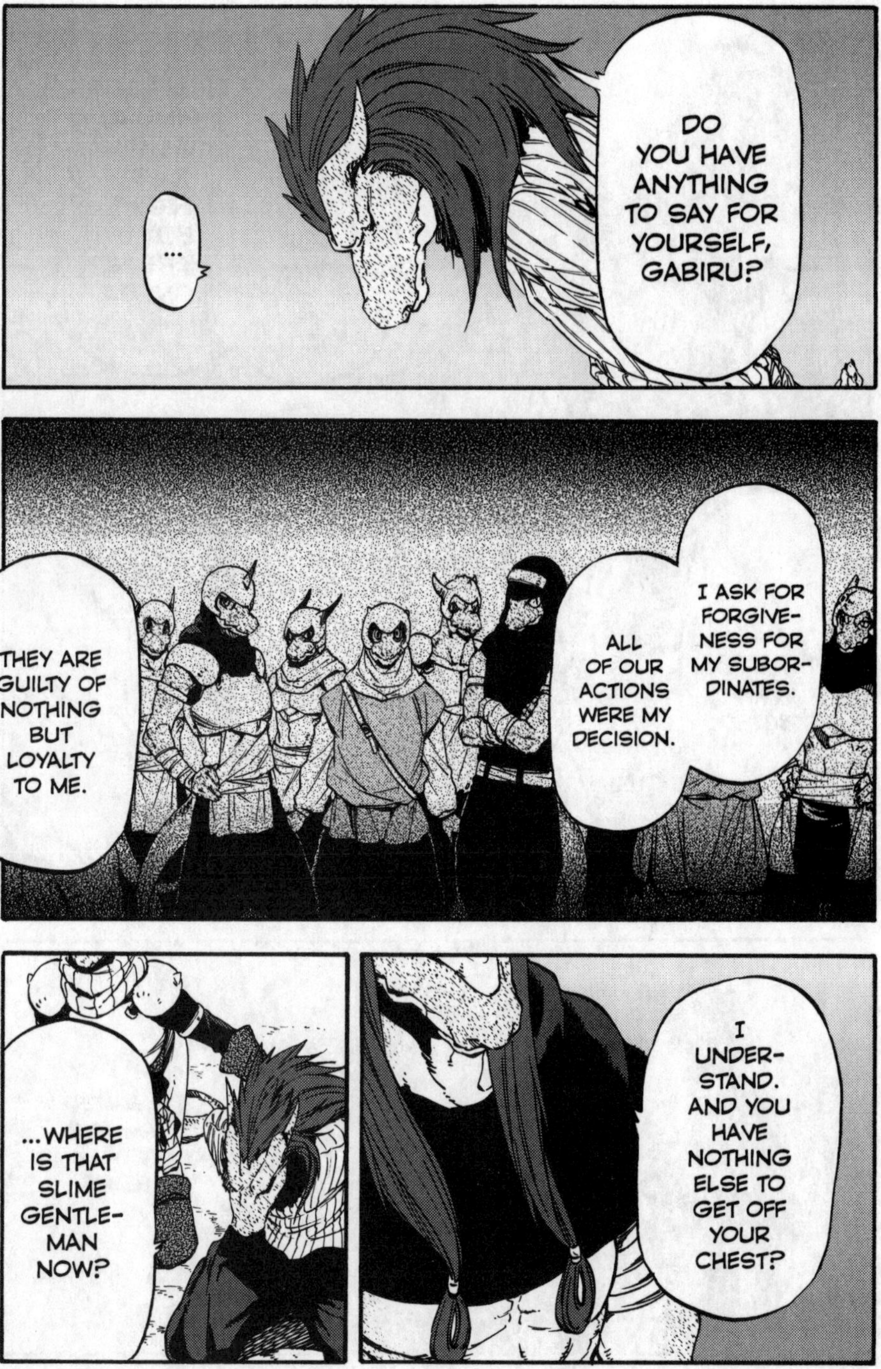
DO YOU HAVE ANYTHING TO SAY FOR YOURSELF, GABIRU?
...
I ASK FOR FORGIVE-NESS FOR MY SUBOR-DINATES.
ALL OF OUR ACTIONS WERE MY DECISION.
THEY ARE GUILTY OF NOTHING BUT LOYALTY TO ME.
I UNDER-STAND. AND YOU HAVE NOTHING ELSE TO GET OFF YOUR CHEST?
...WHERE IS THAT SLIME GENTLE-MAN NOW?

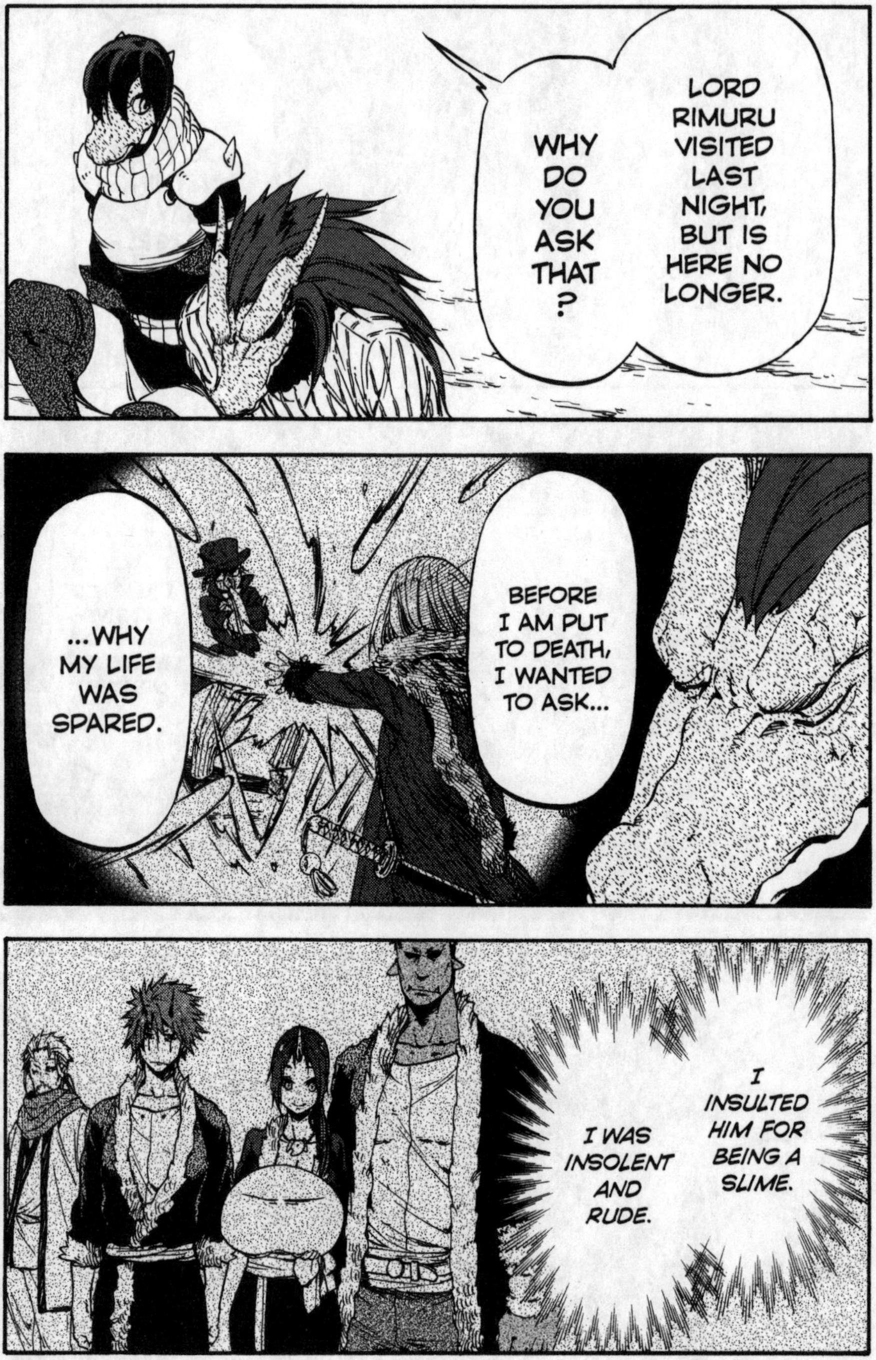
LORD RIMURU VISITED LAST NIGHT, BUT IS HERE NO LONGER.
WHY DO YOU ASK THAT?
BEFORE I AM PUT TO DEATH, I WANTED TO ASK...
...WHY MY LIFE WAS SPARED.
I INSULTED HIM FOR BEING A SLIME.
I WAS INSOLENT AND RUDE.

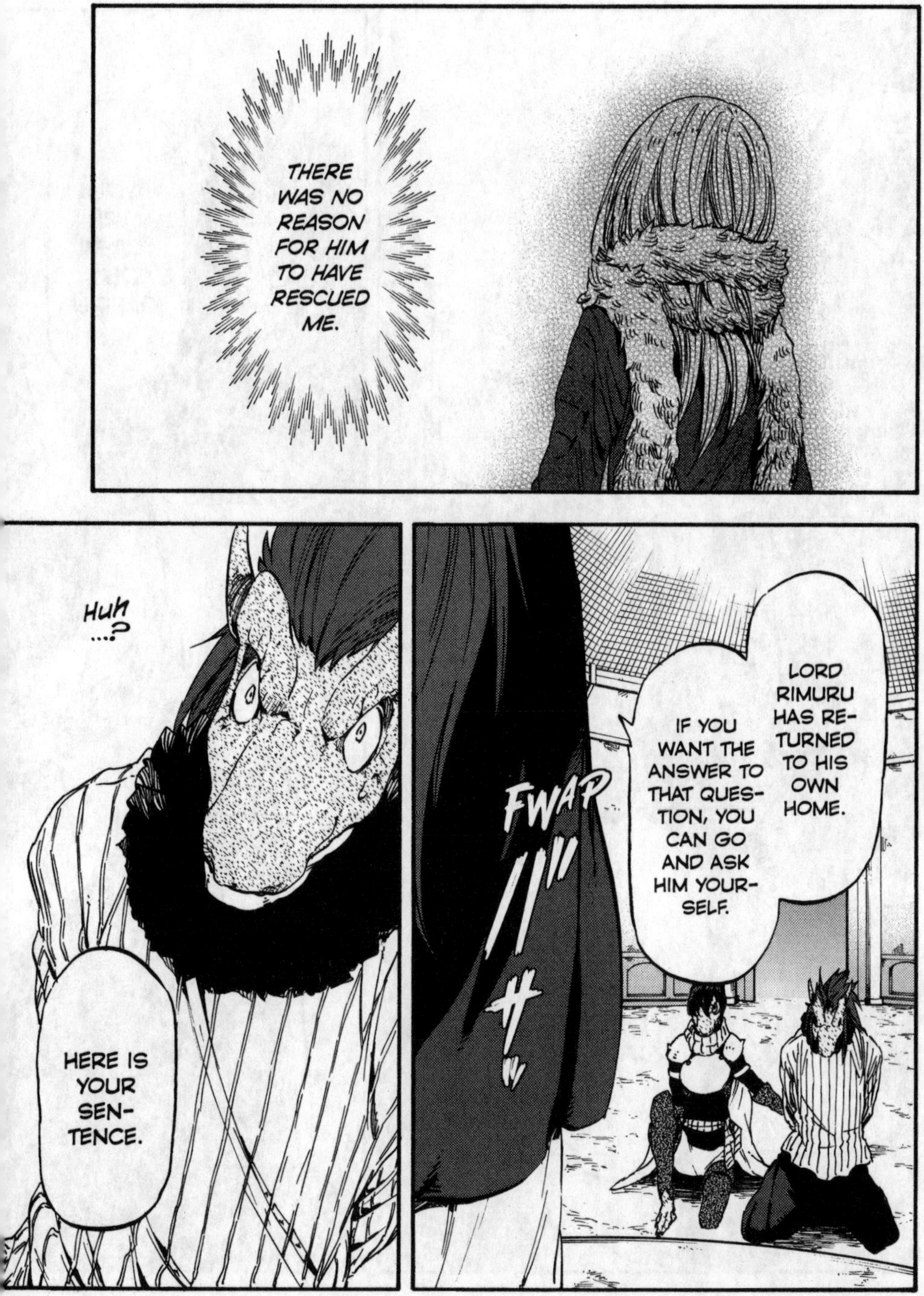
THERE WAS NO REASON FOR HIM TO HAVE RESCUED ME.
LORD RIMURU HAS RETURNED TO HIS OWN HOME.
IF YOU WANT THE ANSWER TO THAT QUESTION, YOU CAN GO AND ASK HIM YOURSELF.
FWAP
Huh ...?
HERE IS YOUR SENTENCE.

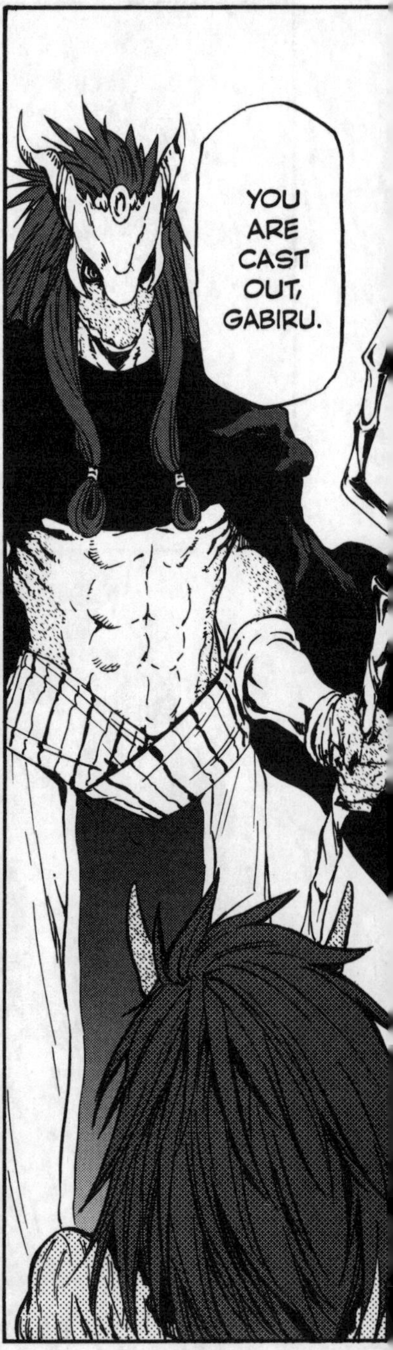
YOU ARE CAST OUT, GABIRU.
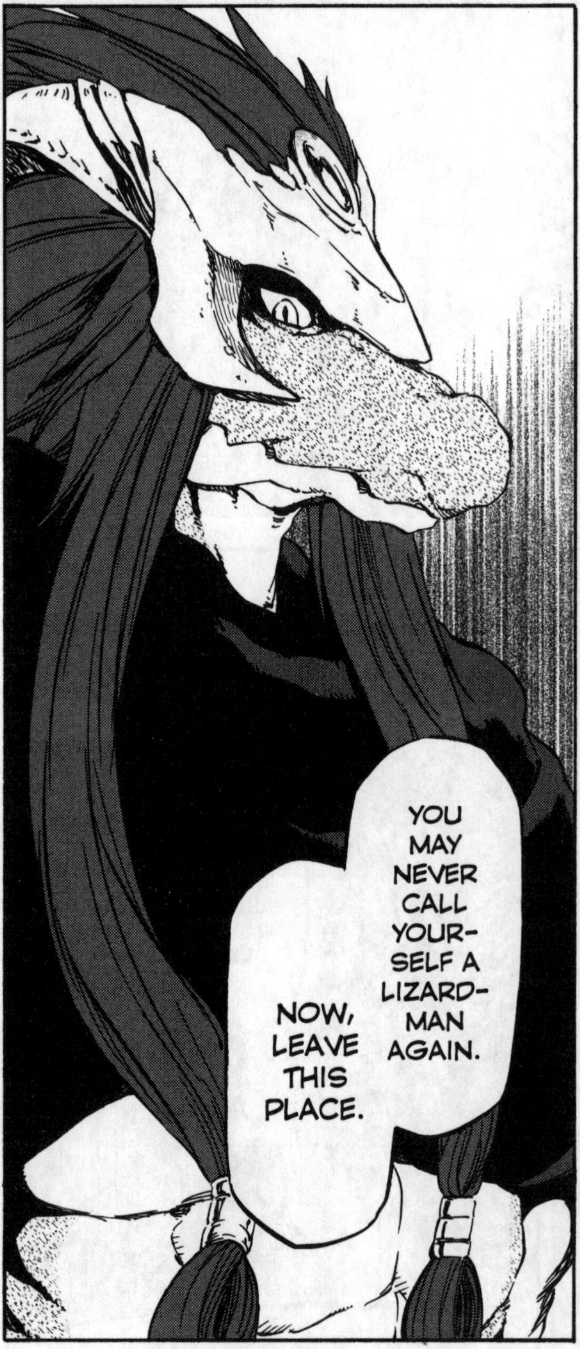
YOU MAY NEVER CALL YOUR-SELF A LIZARD-MAN AGAIN.
NOW, LEAVE THIS PLACE.

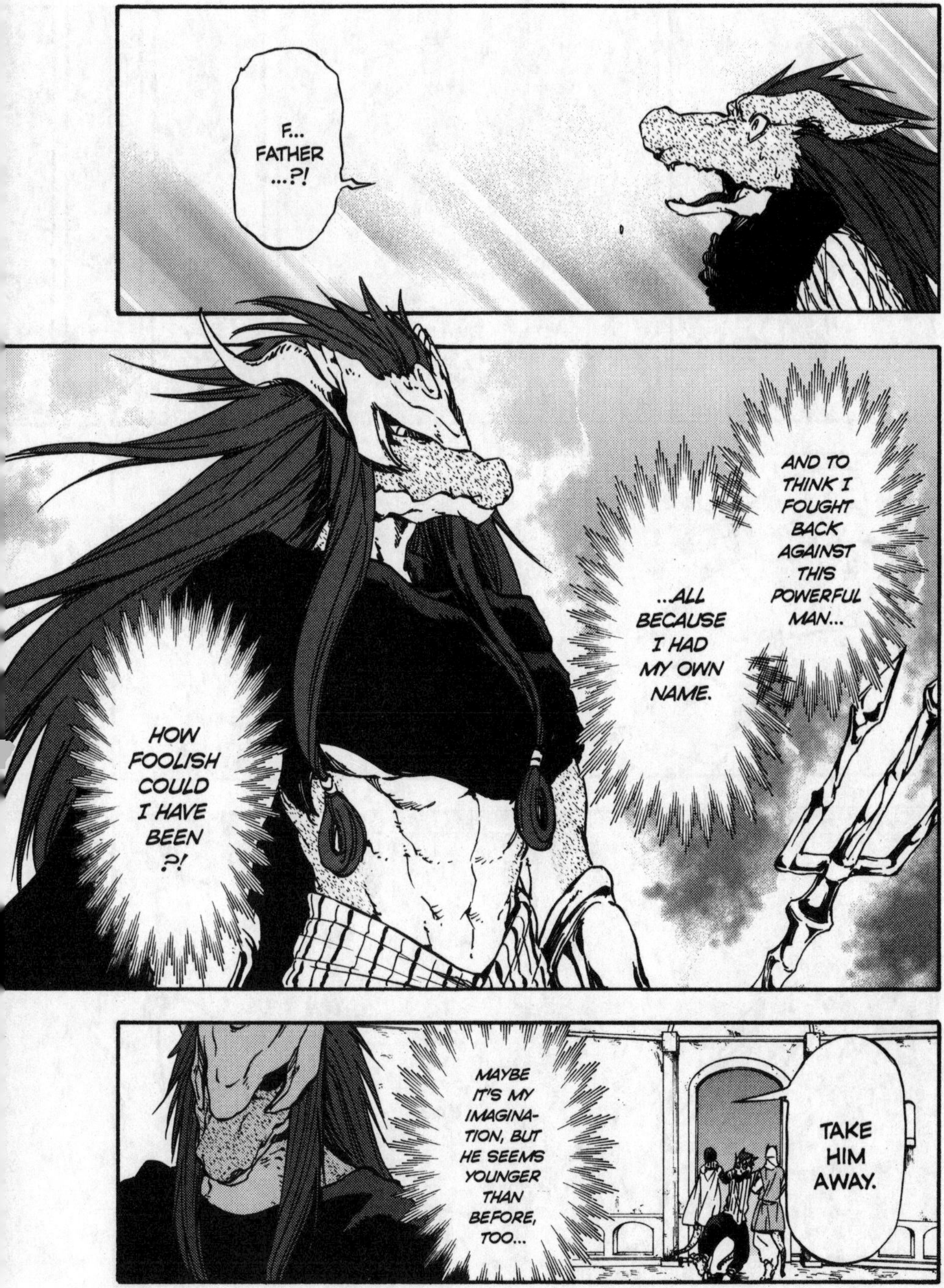
F... FATHER ...?!
AND TO THINK I FOUGHT BACK AGAINST THIS POWERFUL MAN...
...ALL BECAUSE I HAD MY OWN NAME.
HOW FOOLISH COULD I HAVE BEEN ?!
TAKE HIM AWAY.
MAYBE IT'S MY IMAGINA-TION, BUT HE SEEMS YOUNGER THAN BEFORE, TOO...

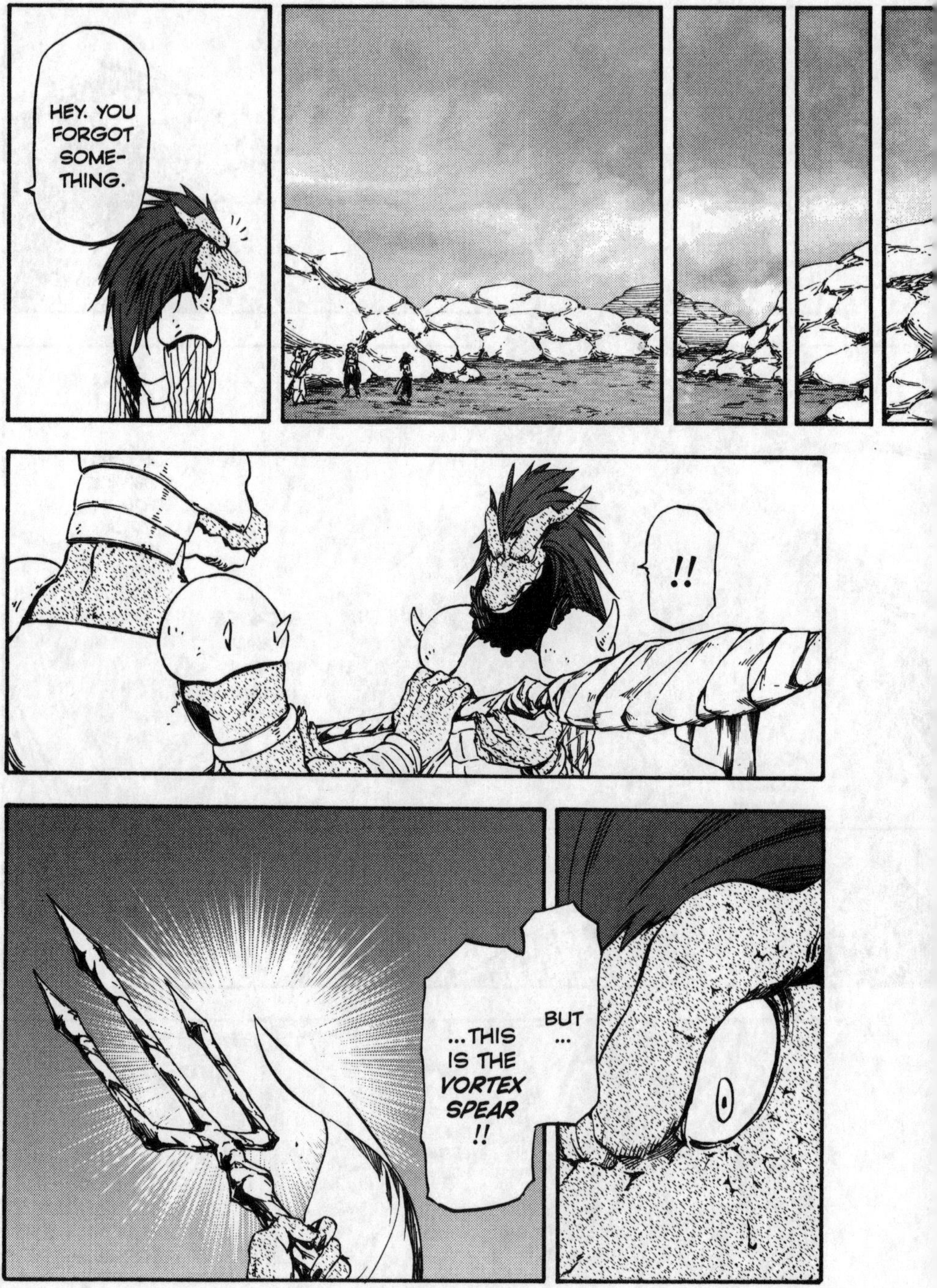

HEY. YOU FORGOT SOME-THING.
!!
BUT ...
...THIS IS THE *VORTEX SPEAR* !!

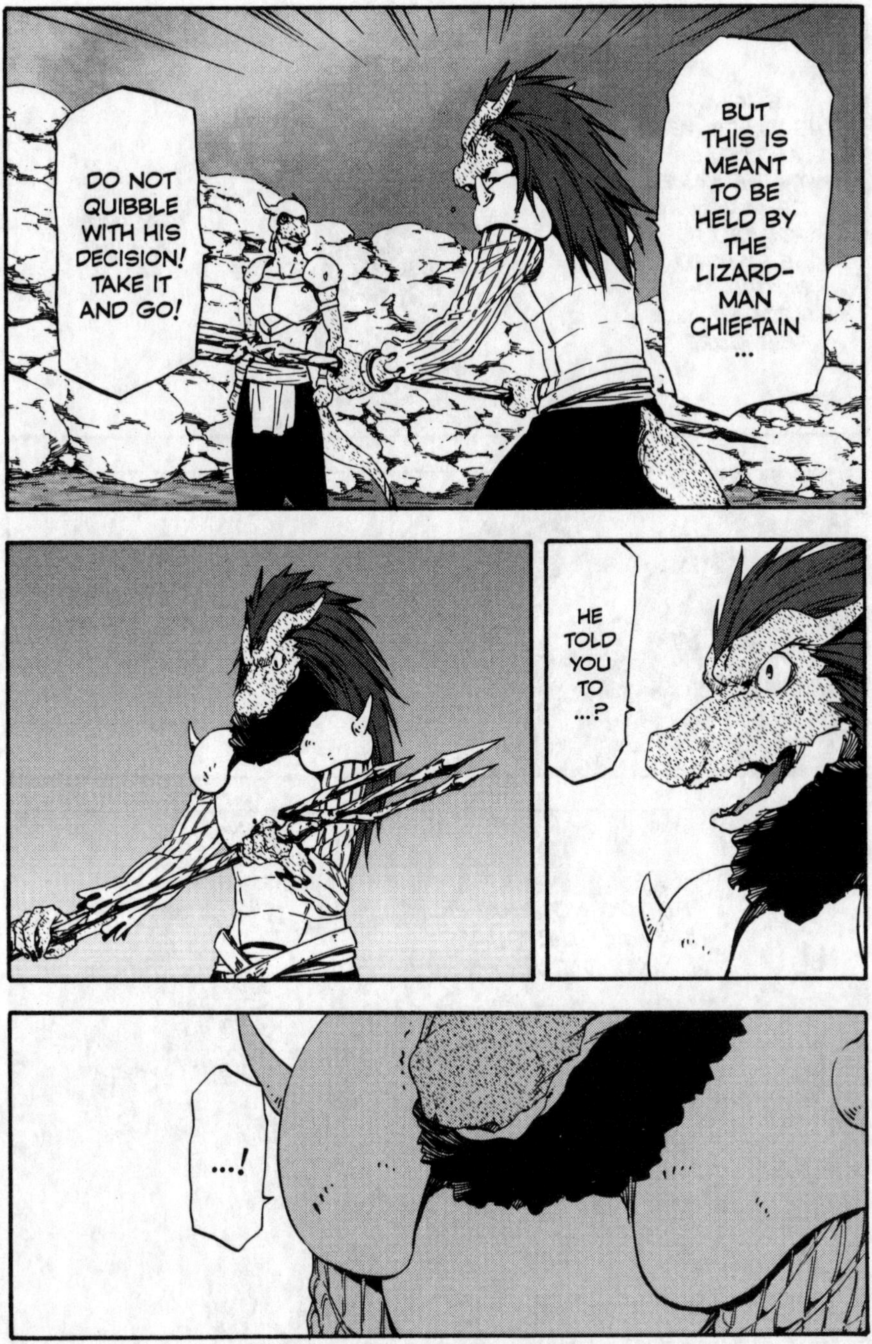
BUT THIS IS MEANT TO BE HELD BY THE LIZARD-MAN CHIEFTAIN ...
DO NOT QUIBBLE WITH HIS DECISION! TAKE IT AND GO!
HE TOLD YOU TO ...?
...!

AS LONG AS I AM ALIVE AND WELL, WITH THE NAME OF "ABIRU" GRANTED TO ME BY LORD RIMURU, THE LIZARDMEN WILL BE SECURE.

GABIRU, MY SON...

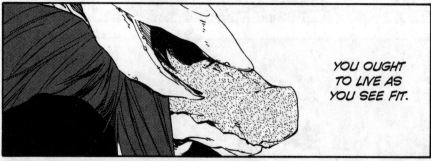

YOU OUGHT TO LIVE AS YOU SEE FIT.

BUT DO NOT TRAFFIC IN HALF-MEASURES AND IDLE WHIMS.

TAKE THIS ADVICE TO HEART.

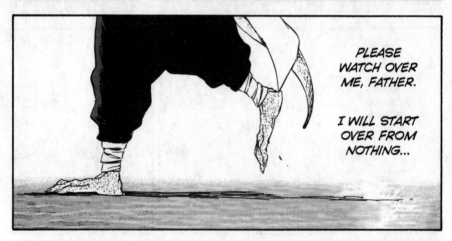

PLEASE WATCH OVER ME, FATHER.

I WILL START OVER FROM NOTHING...

...IN ORDER TO BE A MAN WORTHY OF THIS SPEAR.

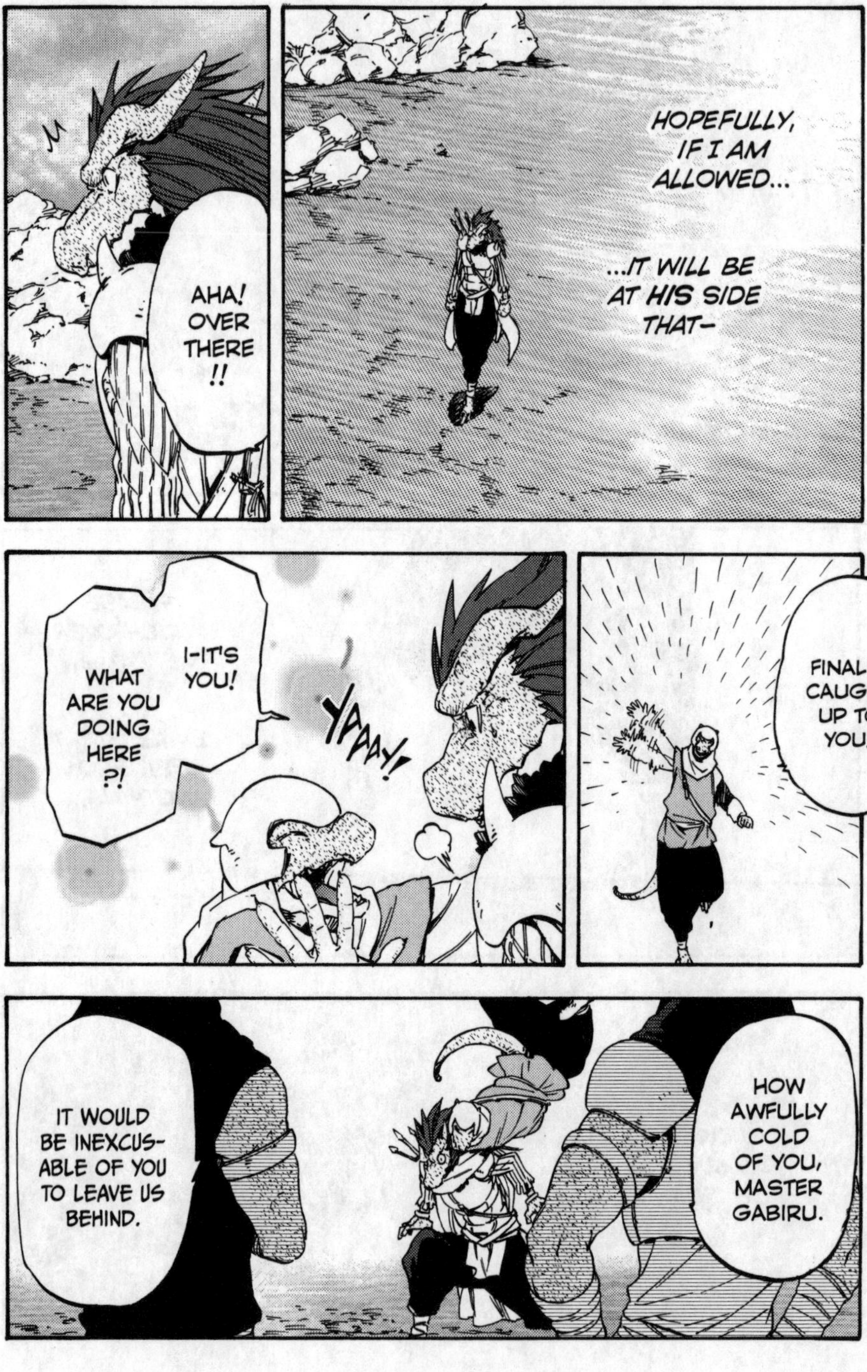
HOPEFULLY, IF I AM ALLOWED...
...IT WILL BE AT HIS SIDE THAT–
AHA! OVER THERE!!
FINALLY CAUGHT UP TO YOU!
YAAAY!
I-IT'S YOU!
WHAT ARE YOU DOING HERE?!
HOW AWFULLY COLD OF YOU, MASTER GABIRU.
IT WOULD BE INEXCUS-ABLE OF YOU TO LEAVE US BEHIND.

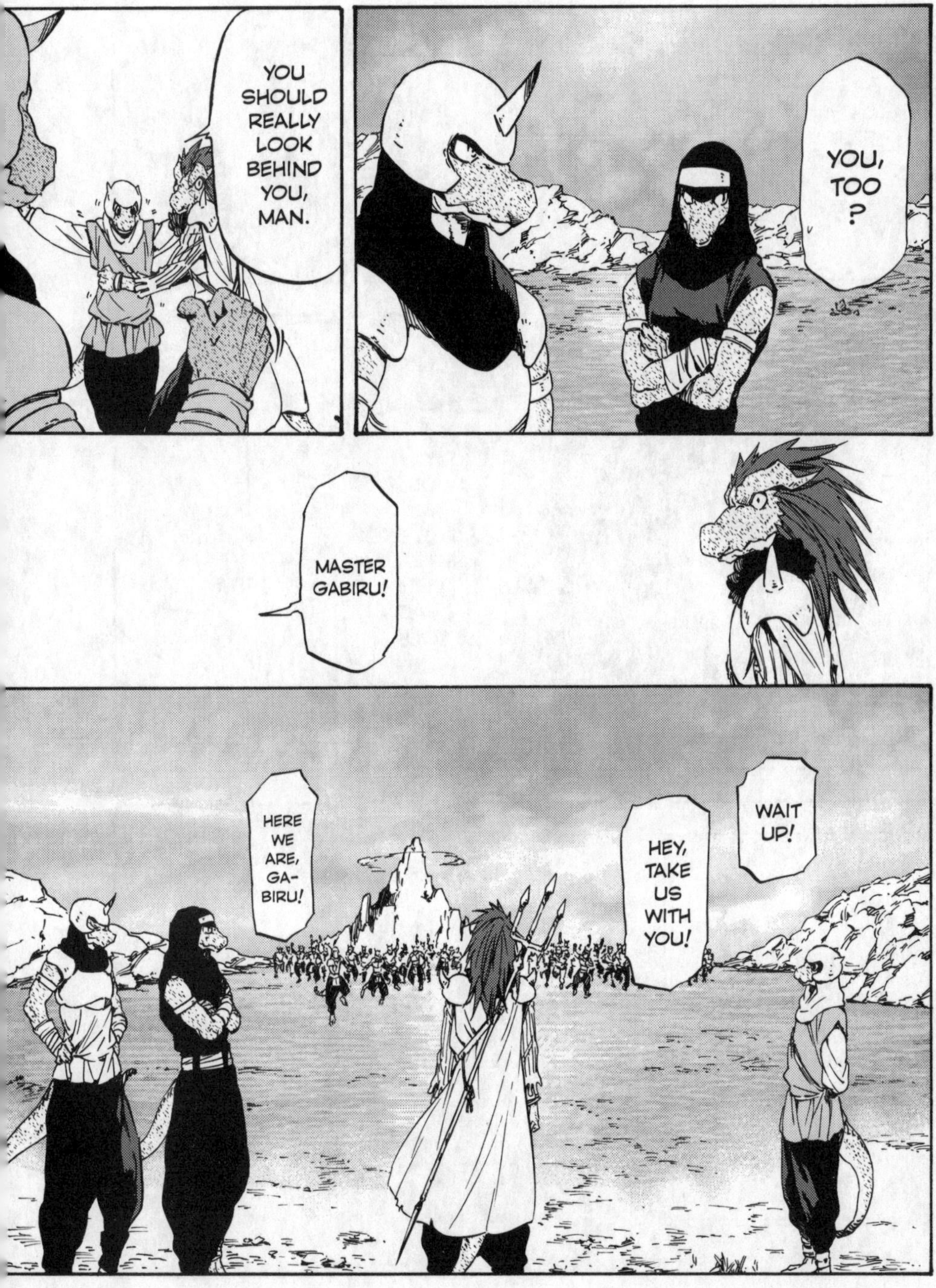
YOU, TOO?
YOU SHOULD REALLY LOOK BEHIND YOU, MAN.
MASTER GABIRU!
WAIT UP!
HEY, TAKE US WITH YOU!
HERE WE ARE, GA-BIRU!

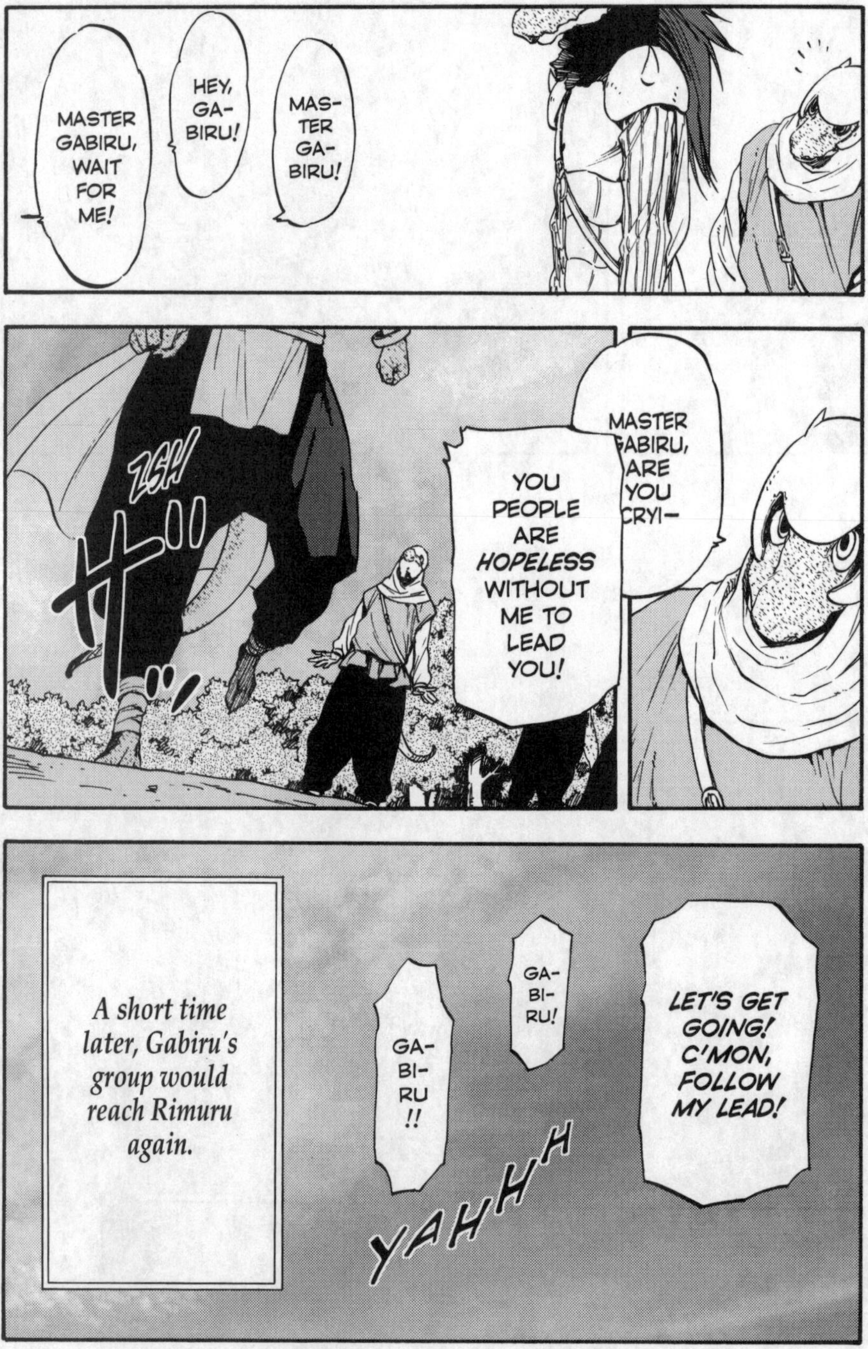
MAS-TER GA-BIRU!
HEY, GA-BIRU!
MASTER GABIRU, WAIT FOR ME!
MASTER GABIRU, ARE YOU CRYI—
YOU PEOPLE ARE *HOPELESS* WITHOUT ME TO LEAD YOU!
ZSH
LET'S GET GOING! C'MON, FOLLOW MY LEAD!
GA-BI-RU!
GA-BI-RU!!
YAHHHH
A short time later, Gabiru's group would reach Rimuru again.

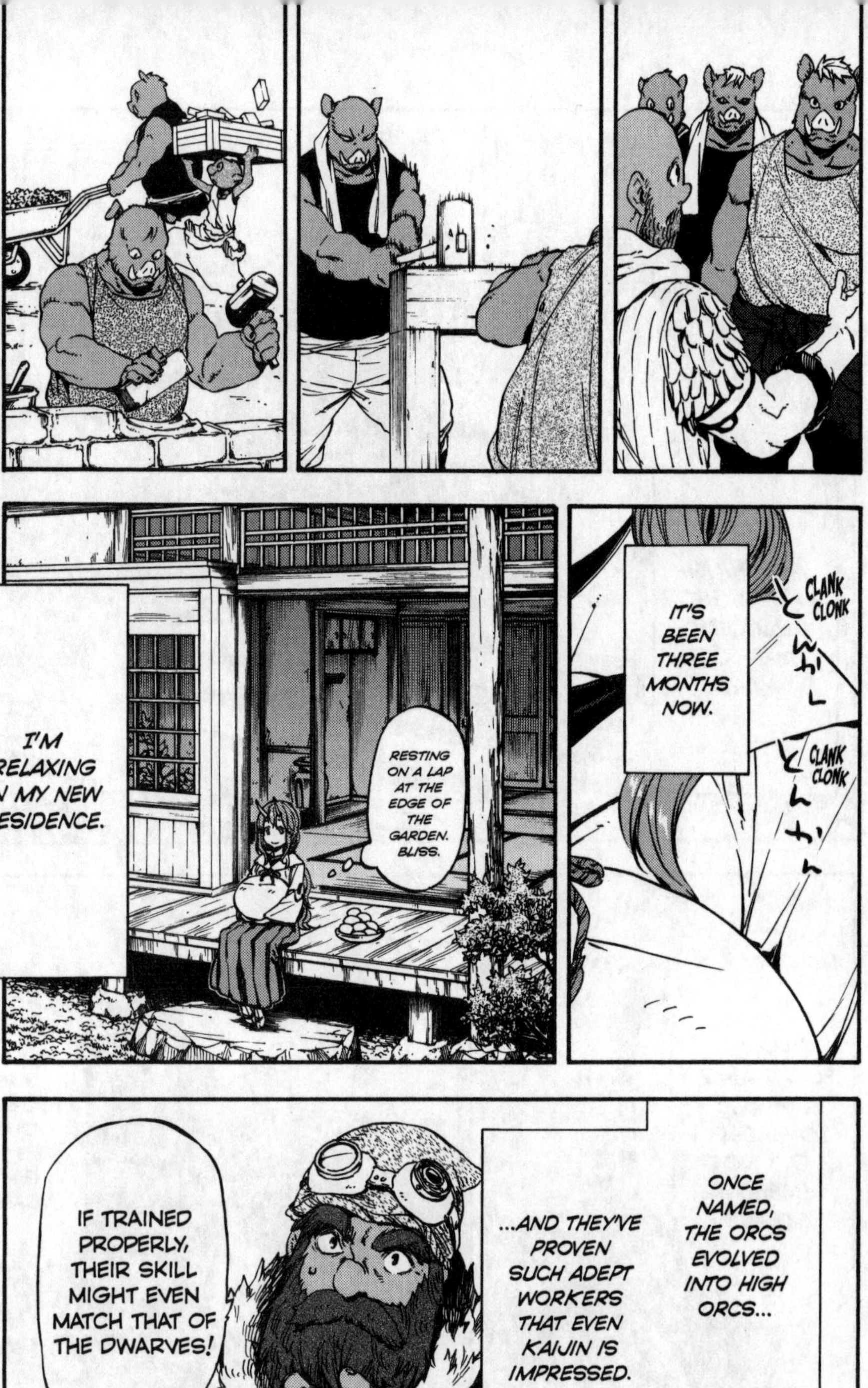
IT'S BEEN THREE MONTHS NOW.
CLANK CLONK
CLANK CLONK
I'M RELAXING IN MY NEW RESIDENCE.
RESTING ON A LAP AT THE EDGE OF THE GARDEN. BLISS.
ONCE NAMED, THE ORCS EVOLVED INTO HIGH ORCS...
...AND THEY'VE PROVEN SUCH ADEPT WORKERS THAT EVEN KAIJIN IS IMPRESSED.
IF TRAINED PROPERLY, THEIR SKILL MIGHT EVEN MATCH THAT OF THE DWARVES!

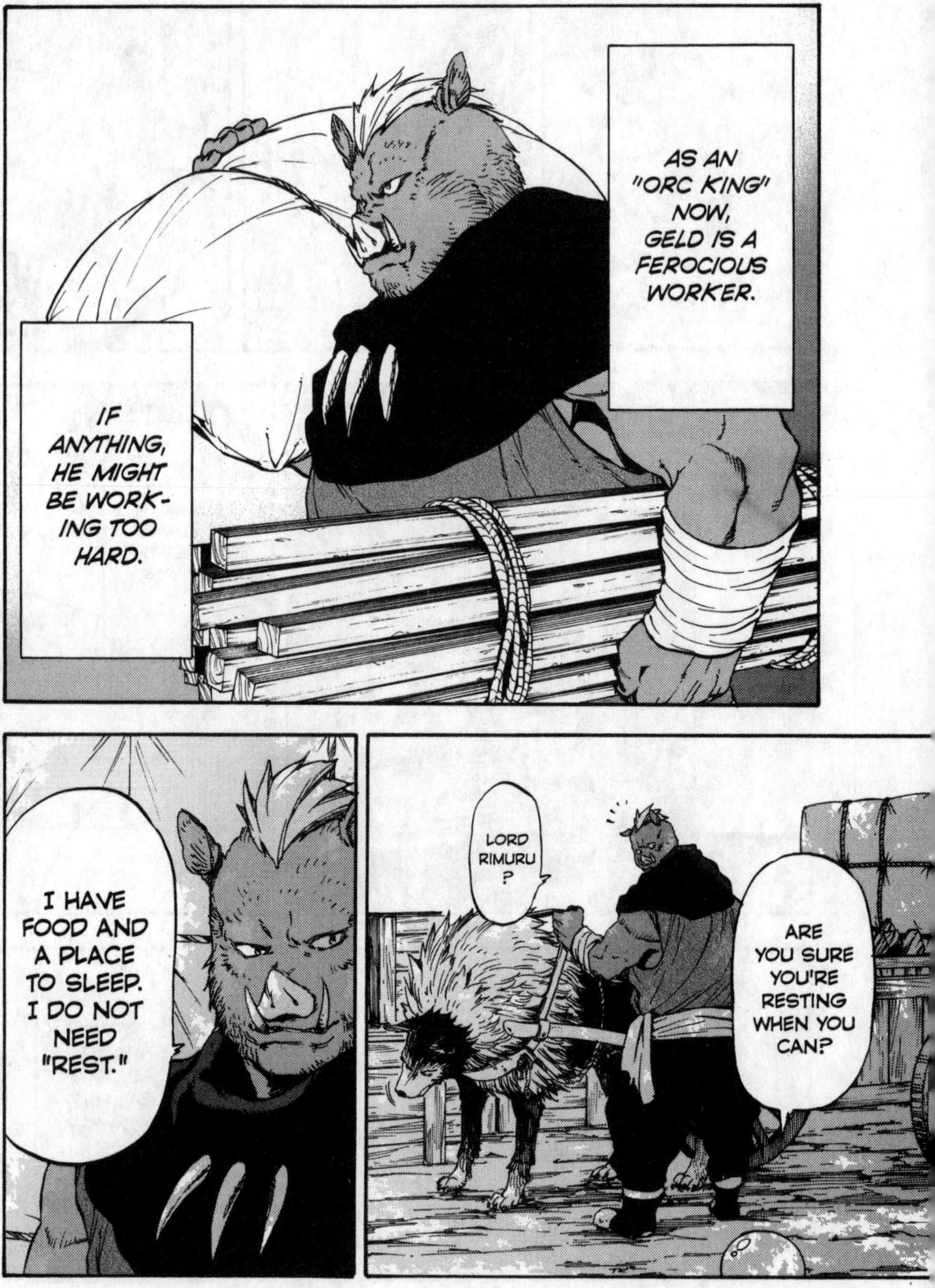
AS AN "ORC KING" NOW, GELD IS A FEROCIOUS WORKER.
IF ANYTHING, HE MIGHT BE WORK-ING TOO HARD.
LORD RIMURU?
ARE YOU SURE YOU'RE RESTING WHEN YOU CAN?
I HAVE FOOD AND A PLACE TO SLEEP. I DO NOT NEED "REST."

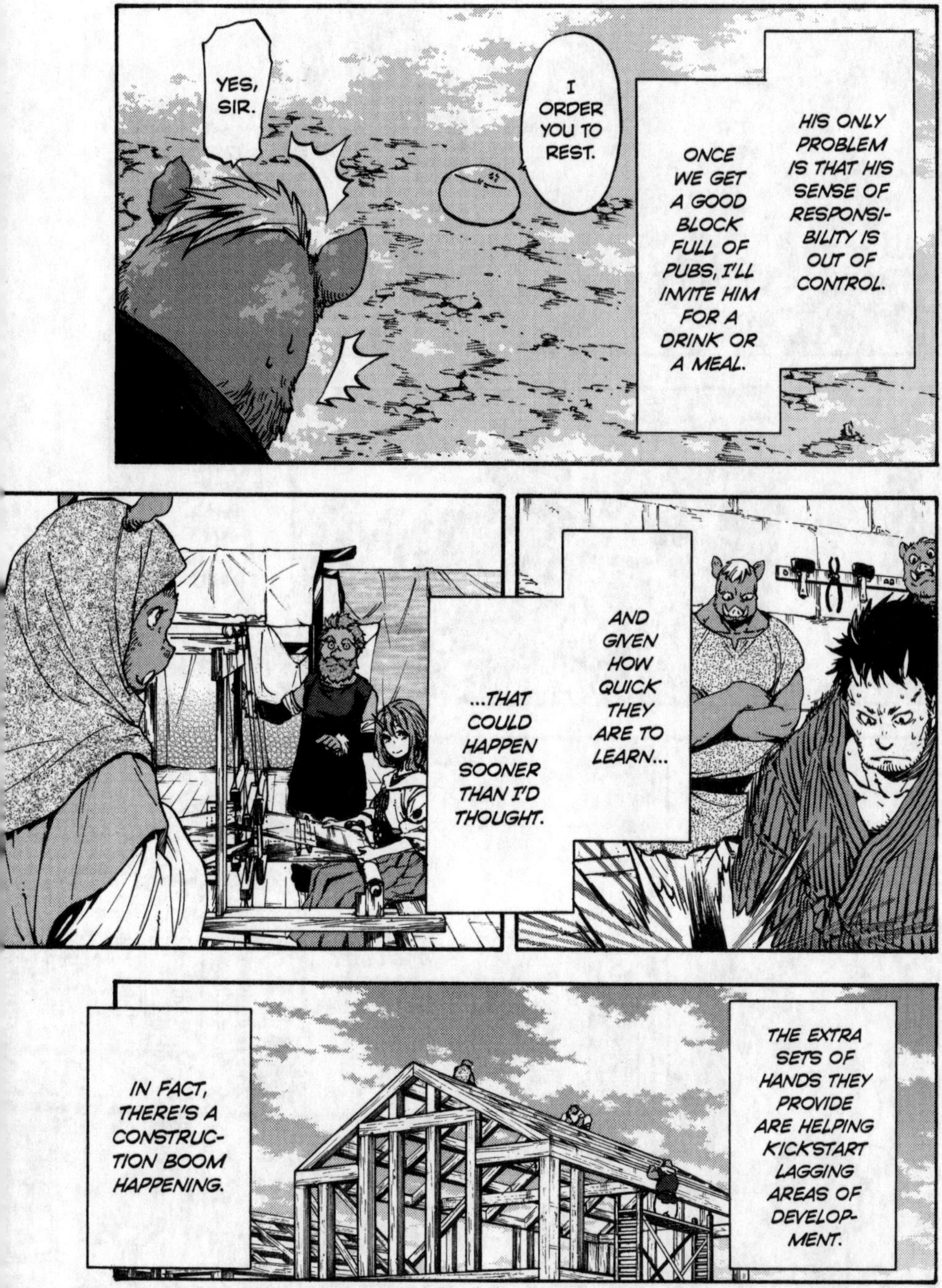
HIS ONLY PROBLEM IS THAT HIS SENSE OF RESPONSIBILITY IS OUT OF CONTROL.
ONCE WE GET A GOOD BLOCK FULL OF PUBS, I'LL INVITE HIM FOR A DRINK OR A MEAL.
I ORDER YOU TO REST.
YES, SIR.
AND GIVEN HOW QUICK THEY ARE TO LEARN...
...THAT COULD HAPPEN SOONER THAN I'D THOUGHT.
THE EXTRA SETS OF HANDS THEY PROVIDE ARE HELPING KICKSTART LAGGING AREAS OF DEVELOPMENT.
IN FACT, THERE'S A CONSTRUCTION BOOM HAPPENING.

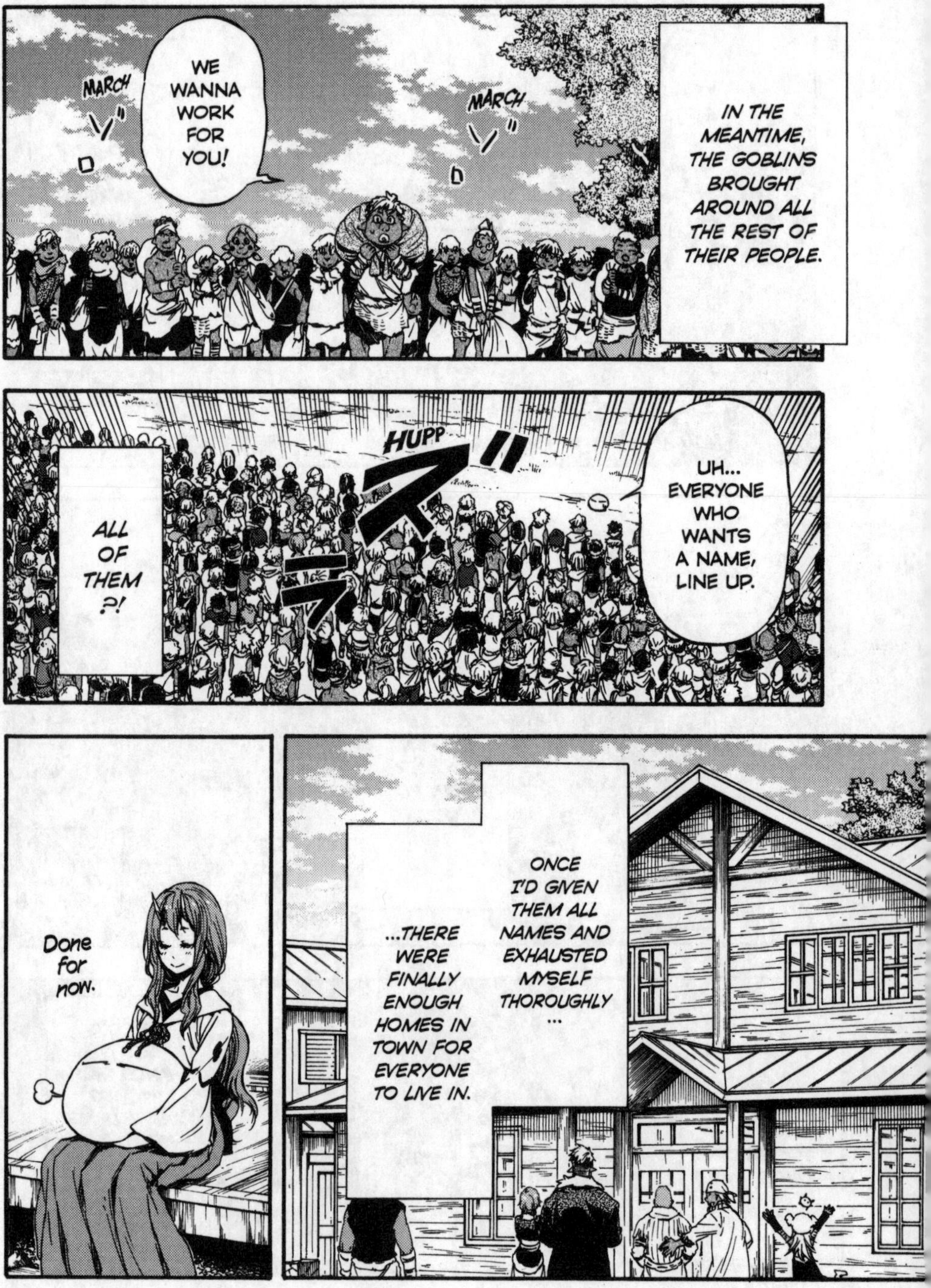

IN THE MEANTIME, THE GOBLINS BROUGHT AROUND ALL THE REST OF THEIR PEOPLE.
MARCH
WE WANNA WORK FOR YOU!
MARCH
UH... EVERYONE WHO WANTS A NAME, LINE UP.
HUPP
ALL OF THEM?!
ONCE I'D GIVEN THEM ALL NAMES AND EXHAUSTED MYSELF THOROUGHLY...
...THERE WERE FINALLY ENOUGH HOMES IN TOWN FOR EVERYONE TO LIVE IN.
Done for now.

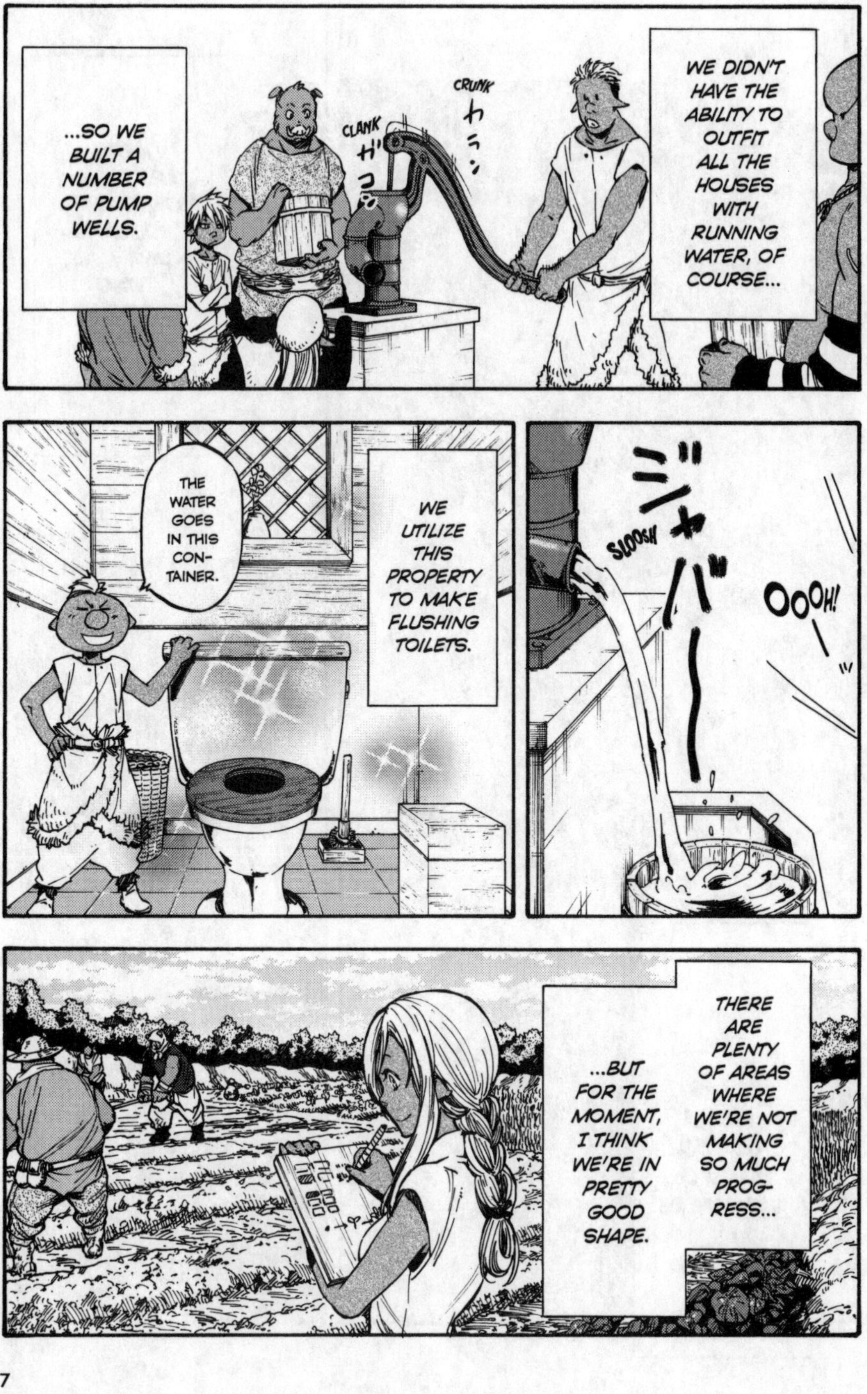
WE DIDN'T HAVE THE ABILITY TO OUTFIT ALL THE HOUSES WITH RUNNING WATER, OF COURSE...
CRUNK
CLANK
...SO WE BUILT A NUMBER OF PUMP WELLS.
ジャバー
SLOOSH
OOOH!
WE UTILIZE THIS PROPERTY TO MAKE FLUSHING TOILETS.
THE WATER GOES IN THIS CON-TAINER.
THERE ARE PLENTY OF AREAS WHERE WE'RE NOT MAKING SO MUCH PROG-RESS...
...BUT FOR THE MOMENT, I THINK WE'RE IN PRETTY GOOD SHAPE.

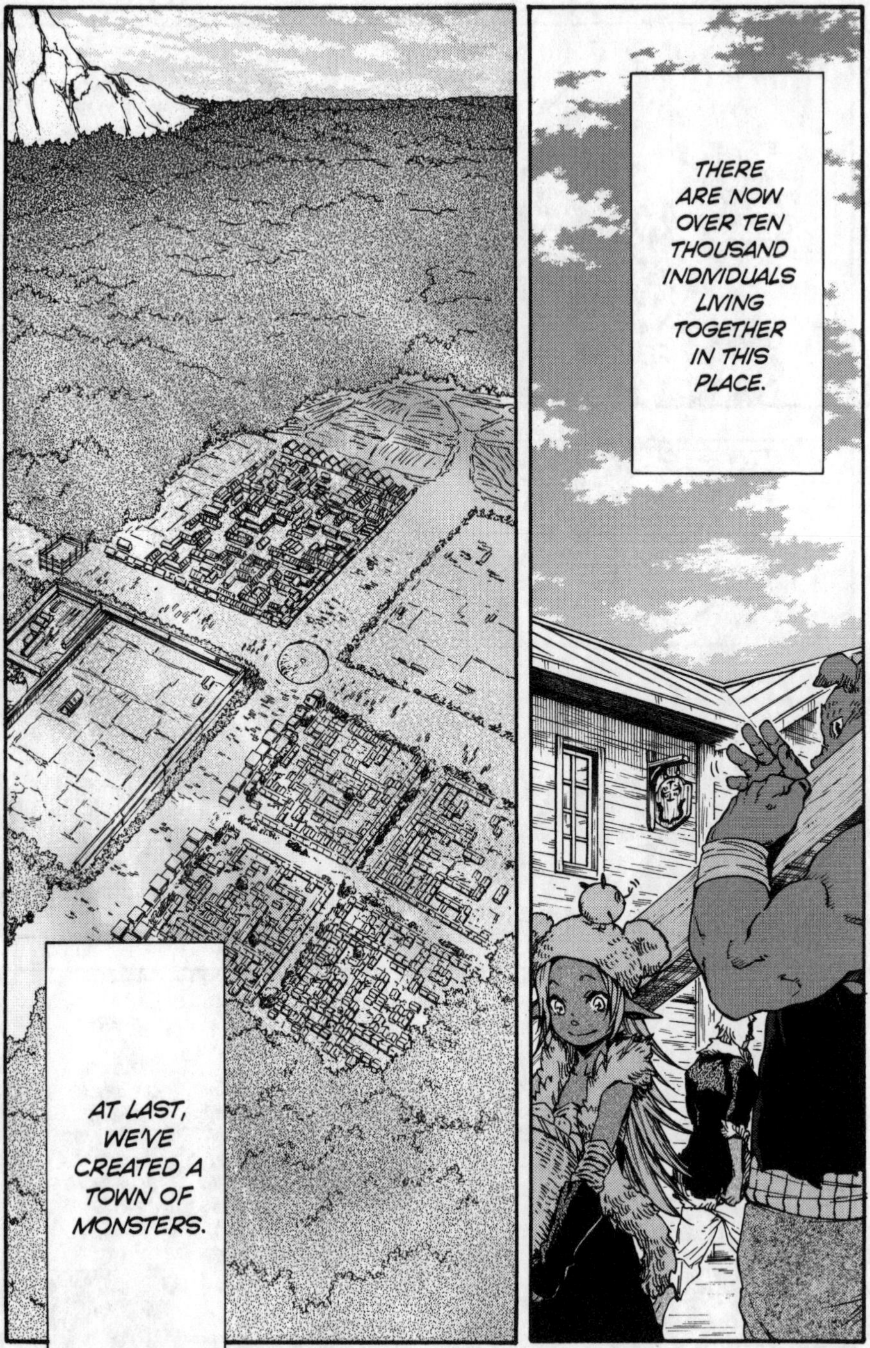
THERE ARE NOW OVER TEN THOUSAND INDIVIDUALS LIVING TOGETHER IN THIS PLACE.
AT LAST, WE'VE CREATED A TOWN OF MONSTERS.

Reincarnate
in Volume 6?

→YES

NO

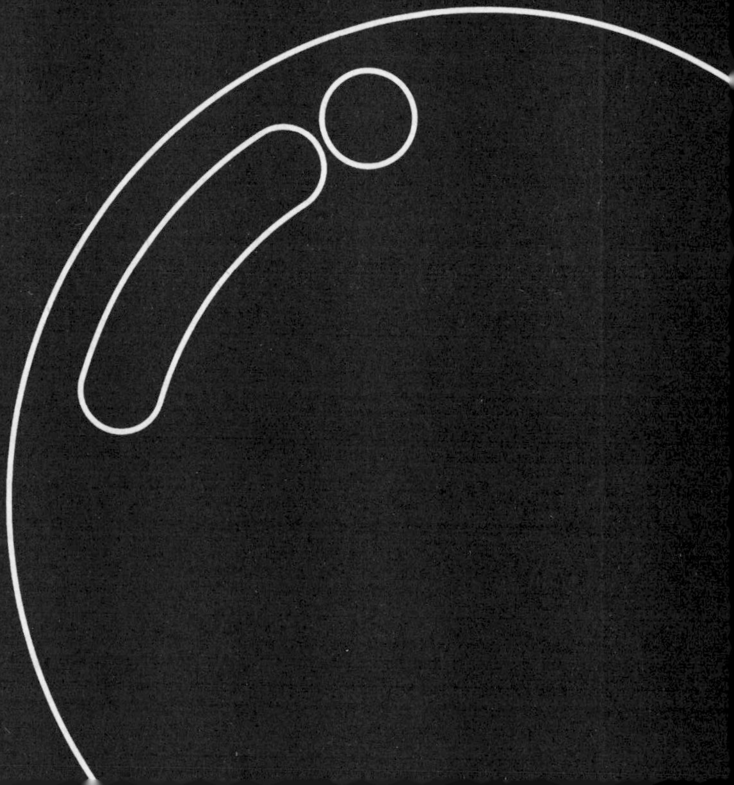

Bonus
Short Story

Veldora's Slime Observation Journal
~FULL STOMACH~

Veldora's Slime Observation Journal
~FULL STOMACH~

◆ORC DISASTER◆

Admittedly, it is starting to get difficult to find titles for these journal entries. Regardless, how is everyone else these days?

I am fine.

"Yes, Master Veldora, but you're still trapped in here…"

Silence.

Do you think I am not aware of my captivity at all times?!

But I suppose this does not matter. What is of more importance now is the fact that Rimuru's battle is entering its climactic stage.

With the help of his kijin companions, Rimuru has laid waste to the greater officers of the orcish horde. The horde itself cannot be ignored, of course, but it is largely toothless as a fighting force now.

The orc lord still remains, but his dullard nature does not inspire much fear, if you ask me.

Before long, however, the situation grows much darker. Now there is some kind of majin wearing a silly mask prancing about the scene.

"What is the meaning of this?!" he screeched at Rimuru. He is panicked and nervous, a sure sign that he is small of heart.

And yet he calls himself "the Great Gelmud." Not to mention that he is explaining all of the details of his plan. What an embarrassing display.

"This majin is no match for Lord Rimuru," said Ifrit, agreeing with me.

However, he is mistaken in one respect, so I corrected him: "Ifrit, fellows like this one are most beneficial, in fact—he will tell you all his secrets before he is destroyed. If we simply killed him right at the start, we would not learn all the facets of this plan he is blabbering about."

"Ah, I see! And that is why Lord Rimuru sits back and observes, rather than taking action?"

"Precisely!" For Rimuru is a clever fellow. Not at all like this fool, Gelmud.

As I expected, he has revealed all sorts of important information. His goal in this campaign is to create a new demon lord in this land.

In my opinion, however, the truly pitiful ones are the orc lord and the lizardman Gabiru. They have been the unwitting tools of such a small-minded, would-be demagogue.

"Ah, yes! I understand! I can see why Gabiru is so worthy of pity, despite his proud, draconic element. Could it be that being named by such a small, petty man has warped his personality?"

Hrm?!

I see. That would certainly line up with the facts. You do me proud as my chief of staff, Ifrit.

"I suppose there is some merit to what you say. In fact, it is exactly what I was thinking," I said happily. Clearly there can be no other reason. If Ifrit had not put that thought together, someone else would have eventually. But enough about that.

"…Gabiru. His timing is excellent."

Surprisingly enough, Gelmud cast an attack spell, Deathmarch Dance, on Gabiru, who might as well be like a son to him. It is a piddling spell, just a few magical projectiles controlled with aura, but even Gelmud's energy is far beyond Gabiru's. A direct hit would surely be fatal.

"It seems he wants to feed Gabiru to the orc lord so that the lord's powers can grow further," Ifrit surmised. "He is wreaking havoc in your territory, Master Veldora. It is unforgivable."

He is correct, of course, but something in that statement caught my attention.

"But Ifrit, were you not wreaking havoc in my forest as well?"

"…Erm, er, was I? I don't seem to recall…"

Is it me, or has this elemental been getting much saucier in recent days? He was perfectly well-behaved at first. I cannot imagine whose behavior has been rubbing off on him.

"You and I are the only ones here, Master Veldora. Sometimes we hear Lord Rimuru's voice, but that is a one-way communication only, through one of his skills."

"That is true. I can read Rimuru's thoughts, but it seems that it requires a considerable amount of effort for Rimuru to make his will known to me. It is not easy for us to communicate, alas."

Of course, I am under no obligation whatsoever to reveal to Ifrit my secret correspondence with Rimuru about playing shogi.

"Yes, which would mean that I am being influenced by…"

"Hrm?! Ah, g-good point. You are under no one's influence. It is my mistake. Indeed, it was all a mistake. *Kwaaaa ha ha ha!*" I laughed, to hide my embarrassment.

Indeed, I was very nearly in danger of promoting the idea that my influence causes others to be rude. That would be impossible.

Best to change the topic. Time to see what is happening outside. This Gelmud will not last long, I suspect.

Rimuru is furious that Gelmud sacrificed Gabiru for his own

ends. Some demon lord or another ordered Gelmud to go around naming monsters in the Jura Forest, we've learned. Now there is no longer any excuse for allowing Gelmud to leave alive.

Hostages are meaningless to a demon lord, and this confession alone has little evidentiary value. He can simply claim that he has no idea what this is about, thus denying the statement is evidence of anything.

It is certainly what I would do, were I to be accused of anything.

Ages ago, when I destroyed the city of the vampiress, I insisted that I had nothing to do with it. And nobody believed me, so it was quite the disaster, really.

"...So...you got what was coming to you?"

"Did I?"

"Yes. It's a surprise to me that you thought anyone would believe you."

Hrm. This is news to me. But not everything goes one's way all the time, and this was long in the past.

"I don't think that saying it happened a long time ago means you weren't in the wrong..."

Ifrit is certainly clinging to this topic, isn't he? He seems upset about it, but if I worry about that, I've lost the argument. More important is the matter of Gelmud.

Rimuru wasn't the only one in a righteous fury. The same could be said of Benimaru, Shion, and Hakuro! The kijin companions bore open rage at Gelmud. It must be because of the sacking of their village.

For his part, Gelmud is a higher majin who performed many namings. If he had not lost so much of his magical energy through that process, he might have found a better outcome for himself. However, the difference between one who manipulates others and those who put themselves on the line for vengeance is vast.

"Th-this can't be happening! H-how can I be trapped like this?!" Gelmud squealed.

He tried to escape, but the entrance of the swift, blue-haired Soei put a stop to that idea. The contest was all but over at this point.

"We've won. *Kwa ha ha ha!*"

Rimuru left Gelmud to the kijin and turned his attention to the orc lord instead. The leader of the orcs was in the thrall of his own power. It was all he had in order to protect his population of two hundred thousand. No wonder it was causing his own consciousness to grow thin.

And yet, it seemed clear that he stands no chance against Rimuru. But what happened next stunned even me.

"H-help me, orc lord! I mean…Geld!!" screeched Gelmud, who abandoned all of his pride as a higher majin and scrambled for his life. But the orc lord's distorted mind responded to his summons in a distorted way. It is hard to believe, but I suppose this is how the namer and the named are bound.

The orc lord attempted to grant Gelmud's wish. With one fell swoop of his meat cleaver, he freed Gelmud's head from his shoulders.

To be honest, I expected this to happen. Naming a monster is, by its nature, a dangerous act. Placing a being stronger than oneself beneath you upsets the order of the strong eating the weak. It was inevitable that this would happen.

Confirmed: the individual Geld is evolving into a Demon Lord seed.

Hmm. That was the "Words of the World." And demon lord seed, you say? That means he is growing into that dreaded being.

Gelmud's ambition was to bring about a new demon lord

in this land. And the surest way to grant this wish was for Gelmud himself to be devoured in order to bring about that evolution.

It was the correct choice. And the orc lord's decisiveness in carrying out that choice is worthy of merit.

...Complete. The individual Geld has evolved into the demon lord "Orc Disaster."

Orc Disaster, eh?

So the orc lord has evolved into the rank of demon lord. One never knows what might happen on the battlefield. He does not appear to be the type of foe that requires great sacrifice to overcome, but who can say?

Frustrated that I could not jump out to take part in the fight, I was forced to stay put and watch the outcome with Ifrit.

◆THE SUBMISSIVE DEMON LORD◆

The Orc Disaster's magical energy is far beyond anything he had before evolving. Now he devours the bodies littering the battlefield to satisfy his raging hunger.

But more importantly, I have made an incredible discovery! Much as a pawn may be promoted in a game of shogi, I feared that the orc lord was about to undergo a similar change. I laughed the feeling off, thinking my powerful imagination was getting away from me, but in retrospect, I might as well have prophesied the evolution of the orc lord in that moment.

"They call that a 'flag,' apparently."

"What?"

"According to Lord Rimuru's wisdom, making knowing statements in the midst of battle is forbidden. Just like how you said, 'We've won, *kwa ha ha ha!*' earlier, Master Veldora. That's called a flag, and it's one of the reasons things turned against us in dramatic fashion."

Could this be? That would mean that I am essentially responsible for this situation.

Well done, me.

No one can accomplish the great and mighty deeds that I bring about. The extent of my incredible capabilities almost frightens me! Even locked behind this damnable seal, my will is capable of affecting the entire world around me.

"Well, if you're happy with that, I'm not going to complain, Master Veldora," Ifrit said. He seemed a bit peeved, but that is surely just my imagination.

As for the battle, by evolving into the Orc Disaster, the orc lord has regained his senses. He knows enough to introduce himself as Geld, and now makes full use of the power that he was barely aware of before.

He will be a fearsome enemy now.

While a demon lord *seed* is merely a step on the way to being a fully-fledged demon lord, it is still a dreadful being far above the average monster or majin. And the first to recognize this change were the battle-hardened kijin.

Shion was the first to strike. Those bountiful breasts of hers are always resting upon Rimuru like a cushion. It drives me mad with jealou—erm, pardon me.

Shion struck at Geld with her tremendous power. Normally, this would be the end of it, but the enemy is now a Disaster-class foe. It will not be as easy as it was before.

Geld took the brunt of her blow without flinching, and emerged superior. I am not surprised. In fact, I relish a good fight.

"You do know that it's not about whether the fight is 'good' or 'bad,' but the fact that if Lord Rimuru dies, you're going to die too…right?"

"Perhaps. But in that case, a new storm dragon will be born elsewhere."

"I see. Well, that's a relief—"

"But while the new dragon shall inherit my memory, it shall not receive my will and personality. My soul will vanish here, while a new soul will inhabit the reborn storm dragon. *Kwaa ha ha ha!*"

"Wait, why are you laughing about that?!" asked the Ifrit.

My point is that he ought to worry more about himself than about me. "It is not such a surprise. I swore an oath to believe in Rimuru. So I can leave all of this to him now. If he fails and proves himself unfit for the task, then that was simply my fate."

"…?! Er, right. That is correct, I suppose. In a sense, it is only because of your whims that I have been granted extra life, Master Veldora. I do wish that I could see Lord Leon once again, but I suppose that will never happen now. It's important to recognize reality for what it is, and accept it."

…He makes such grandiose exaggerations, this fellow.

Still. Though this is not exactly my view, he is correct in the broader sense. There is little need to set him straight. In my case, I merely wish to enjoy my life, but this is not the situation to deliver a speech to that effect.

It would seem that Shion's attack was meant as a distraction to unbalance Geld and allow Hakuro the chance to strike. The elderly fellow's skill with the blade is of the highest caliber. Something in it reminds me of the legendary hero that fought me. It would be weak against the rare creature with Physical Resistance, but his technique alone places him as the strongest of the kijin, in my opinion.

Hakuro struck off Geld's head. *Brilliant!* I thought, but in no time at all, Geld picked up his severed head and stuck it back on.

"I'm telling you, those assumptions are flags..."

Oh! Whoopsy, daisy.

Perhaps my idle thoughts have strengthened Geld yet again. Still, this is not yet the time to panic.

The strongest attack available to the kijin comes from their leader, Benimaru. And Soei did the hard work of immobilizing Geld so that the full brunt of Benimaru's strength can strike true.

Given enough time, Geld should be able to escape Soei's "Sticky Steel Thread," but Benimaru has ample opportunity to unleash his best.

The wide-area conflagration attack: "Hell Flare."

Because he had already used it multiple times, the scale of it was smaller than usual. Still, it was more than powerful enough to burn a single target to a crisp.

"See that, Ifrit?! Not even Geld's incredible regenerative ability can withstand such superheated flames! That hellfire even contains elements of my Black Flame ability, so surely he must be dead now!"

"I told you, you shouldn't say things like—"

Oh! Now Ranga has joined the fray! On Benimaru's orders, he released a "Death Storm." Every last ounce of his magicule energy went into it, with a pinpoint attack against Geld.

"It's over now."

"Well, let's hope so..."

This Ifrit truly cannot keep himself from worrying. There is no way that a newborn demon lord seed could withstand such a furious consecutive assault!

"There, you see, Master Veldora? He's still alive."

"What...?!"

I could not believe my ears and eyes. By expelling all of his energy at once, Geld neutralized the damage, then devoured his own blood and flesh to power his healing ability. Only this mad tactic could allow him to withstand that combination attack.

It would seem that I have underestimated the Orc Disaster and his unique skill, "Starved."

Geld suffered great damage, but eating helps him recover from it. He ate his own followers to heal his wounds. If there is anyone who can hope to defeat Geld at full health...

"Lord Rimuru is stepping forth."

...then it must be you.

Go, Rimuru!

He must be confident, because he spurned Benimaru's help and insisted on facing Geld alone. What will happen now?

With one swipe of the sword, Rimuru severed Geld's right arm. This time, it showed no signs of re-growing. With perfect "Black Flame" control, he covered the wound to prevent Geld's regenerative ability from kicking in. This seems like a promising strategy.

In any case, everything I have is riding upon you.

Go forth, Rimuru, and show us your true power!

Rimuru sprang into action, nimbler than ever before. Surely this is due to my emotional support.

His plan must be to slice Geld into fine pieces, and use "Black Flame" to prevent the Orc Disaster's regeneration. But when did Rimuru get so adept at utilizing his skills? Even the kijin seem amazed.

Sensing that a close positioning was to his disadvantage, Geld switched to employing long-range attacks. This adaptive use of strategy shows him to be far smarter now than in his previous state.

"Deathmarch Dance!!"

Geld is using the same attack as that of the diminutive majin, Gelmud. But in this case, each little magical projectile has the power of the unique skill "Starved" attached. In other words, this "Chaos Eater" intends to devour its targets. Needless to say, the force of the attack is terrible.

"This Orc Disaster Geld is beyond what I imagined…"

"Indeed. He's got even more magical energy than you, Ifrit."

"He does. Nearly twice as much, I imagine."

"Your estimate is accurate. And for your information, I have over a hundred times your energy!"

"I see. But that isn't really very interesting, so…"

What? Ifrit, did you know that you are allowed to express your shock and admiration at this fact? It makes me sad to be dismissed so easily.

"More important, they've caught Lord Rimuru, Master!"

"Whaaaat?!"

I'd been preparing a very good boast, but the situation outside demands attention. Geld's severed arm had regrown, and he grabbed Rimuru with it.

That means Rimuru can no longer take advantage of his superior fleetness. Could this be a moment of life or death?!

"It's a shame that your life will end in my belly. Whatever 'Starved' corrodes becomes our food. You will melt to your death."

"...Negative."

So it's...*not* a moment of life or death?!

If anything, Rimuru's attitude suggests that this was all according to some kind of plan.

"Flare Circle."

Oooh!! Yes, now I see. Rimuru let it appear as though Geld had caught him, but in fact, it was he who was absorbing Geld. By enacting a Flare Circle, he simply ensured that there will be no escape.

"That's one of my better attacks, only more powerful than before," muttered Ifrit, a bit sadly. I can understand that—it hurts a little to see one's own proud technique utilized by others to greater effect.

"That's no surprise. Rimuru simply has more energy than you. But do you really think this is the end?"

"The instantaneous power of Hell Flare is tremendous, but it only lasts a few seconds at best. But Flare Circle will continue until the target is incinerated. No matter how incredible the Orc Disaster's regeneration is, there is little he can do now," Ifrit opined.

But I think differently. What I've learned from this fight is that a battle of historical proportions is completely unpredictable. One cannot know what will happen. I think Rimuru is of the same mind; his expression is tense, with no hint of ease.

Confirmed: Orc Disaster Geld has gained Flame Attack Resistance.

I knew it. I knew this would happen!

"Master Veldora?"

"Do not panic, Ifrit. This is another of your 'flags,' yes? But I presume that Rimuru foresaw this coming as well."

"So you trust Lord Rimuru to handle this?"

"Of course." I trust him far more than any story flag.

"It seems your flames do not affect me," boasted Geld.

"Is that so? I dunno, you might've been happier just burning into ash," said Rimuru, grinning confidently. Of course he has some plan in mind.

Oh! Look at that!!

Rimuru melted and clung to Geld all over. At that point, strength alone cannot pull him loose. This was the meaning behind Rimuru's actions!

"Quite the master stroke. At this point, there is no way for a power-type monster to counteract him."

"I agree," said Ifrit. "With my spiritual body, this would not be a problem, but for those monsters stuck in a material body, this would be impossible to overcome."

Indeed. Power is meaningless in this context. Geld has the ability to eat his foes, but in this situation, it is merely a contest of strength. Each one has regenerative ability, and devouring others is a central part of their power. Whoever can eat the other more quickly will win.

While they might seem evenly matched at a glance, Rimuru is sure to triumph at this point. For one thing, he has such a vast stomach that he was able to swallow me in a single gulp. "Wouldn't that also be a flag?"

"Ifrit, flags are meant to be broken. Victory only comes to those who seize it!"

He had to grimace and agree with me.

I needn't elaborate upon the outcome.

"I've won. Rest in peace," Rimuru announced, a momentous statement in the midst of the now silent battlefield.

◆THE JURA FOREST ALLIANCE◆

After Rimuru devoured Geld, I attempted to reach out to him.

However, Geld's consciousness rejected my call. He claimed that he was satisfied—that he was full.

Geld went to sleep within Rimuru's body, and his soul vanished. In my opinion, it was a brilliant end.

Through Rimuru's heroics, the Great Forest of Jura's crisis was averted. And, as though she had planned it all, Treyni the dryad appeared just then. But of course, she would have been watching it all unfold.

Treyni wanted Rimuru to fight the orc lord to find some weakness in the brute, but then he evolved into the Orc Disaster, only for Rimuru to topple him in that greater form. Surely she could not have calculated that all of this would happen.

But her idea to scoop up the pieces is a credit to her role as manager of the Great Forest of Jura. I was so unconcerned with things of this nature that I'm certain I caused her grief. So I cannot speak with great conviction here, nor do I intend to.

But then Treyni forced the duty of chancellor of the talks

upon Rimuru. She must be plotting something.

Rimuru seems uncomfortable with the idea, and of holding a council for talks. But I am sure he is thinking that if nothing is done here and now, worse consequences will occur later. Such a softhearted goody-two-shoes, he is.

And thus began the council for peace talks.

"First of all, I want to be absolutely clear: I have no intention of judging the orcs for their crimes," said Rimuru. Just as I expected, he is entirely too soft! He must have been thinking of this statement all night.

He even made sure to gain the understanding of the kijin, who bear a deep and reasonable grudge against the orcs. It is both a careful measure to eliminate the roots of hatred, but also a soft and considerate idea that is unbecoming of the truly powerful.

"Master Veldora, perhaps *you* should spend more time think-ing about how to minimize damage to others around you—"

"Silence, child! Even I am still developing as an intelligent being. Why can't you take the long and generous view and overlook my shortcomings?!"

"Umm... So you have a hundred times more energy than me already, and you're still looking forward to growing fur-ther...?"

"But of course. I am always striving to be better."

"Oh...okay..."

Ifrit fell silent for a time, no doubt moved by my inspira-tional example.

As for the council, Rimuru understood the details of the orcs' plight, likely because he read Geld's memories. He explained that the orcs were dying of famine, and only accepting the effect of "Starved" would enable them to survive longer. He also explained that Gelmud had been manipulating this series of events to his benefit.

Moving on to practical answers, he explained that the orcs would not be capable of paying any kind of reparations for their actions. When this was done, Rimuru pointed out that this was all a polite excuse.

"I have accepted all of the orcs' sins. If you have any problems with that, you come to me," he declared. Everyone was stunned.

Only the kijin took it in stride, as they had already heard the idea from Rimuru. To those who were unsettled by it, Rimuru explained, "That was my promise to Geld, the Orc Disaster."

Keeping his promises is one of Rimuru's ironclad rules. So nobody could possibly complain to him about this decision. If there was one thing to be said…

"The strong eat the weak."

It would be what Benimaru just stated. If they had a problem, their only recourse would be to defeat Rimuru. And nobody there could feasibly do that.

The chieftain of the lizardmen, unlike his son, has a calm and collected head on his shoulders. He attempted to understand and accept the entirety of Rimuru's decision. This is the proper way of action for a creature possessing elements of dragonkind.

His question was a very practical one: "If you do not judge the orcs for their sins, then do you intend for all of them to stay in this forest?"

There are over a hundred and fifty thousand orcs remaining. To welcome them all at once would wreak havoc on the forest's food supply. It would lead to unnecessary chaos and squabbling over what little food there is.

It is natural that the leader of a people would be wary of such a situation.

Rimuru replied, "What if all the different races living in the forest formed a kind of alliance?"

Surely knowledge of the orcs' situation led him to this idea, but it is clearly folly. Attempting to shoulder everybody's burdens in search of common ground is noble, but I find it unlikely that all others present would follow his example.

But to my surprise, the actions of all present gave lie to my presumption. They've all been infected by Rimuru's idealism.

You must see reality, people. Such a thing is clearly impossible!

And yet, a part of me couldn't help but be excited. If anyone can do it, perhaps it is Rimuru…

I suppose this sensation was shared by everyone present at this momentous meeting. Did they, like me, find Rimuru's words unrealistic—a wild fancy—and yet worth dreaming for? I imagine that this was the case.

Thus, on this day, the Jura Forest Alliance was formed, with Rimuru as its chancellor.

◆A PLACE TO RELAX◆

I must admire the clever way that Treyni arranged all of this. She very naturally foisted the most annoying and troublesome role upon Rimuru. I must learn from her example.

But Rimuru! When will you ever learn? Now his softhearted ways have got him naming the orcs.

One hundred and fifty thousand orcs! Perhaps even more. They keep coming and coming—I estimate their true number at roughly a hundred and sixty thousand now. He cannot handle such a number with his source of energy alone.

Even if I were to lend my help, I feel this would still be a fool's game.

However, he found a method that reuses each individual's magicule energy instead. The aftereffect of Geld's "Starved" skill put the orcs into a state of magicule over-absorption. Over time, these would descend to the normal level, but Rimuru had the idea to reuse them for the naming process while they were still active.

I could scarcely believe my eyes as I watched the process unfold. Can you really do that? Well, it went off without a hitch.

"I cannot believe it."

"I understand, Master. He has just overturned so much of what we take for granted."

For one thing, if this idea got out, it would make the process of accruing strength so much easier for demon lords.

Instead of risking the danger of naming one's subjects, it is possible to dope them up with extra energy, then name them with that excess value. I suspect the soul bonds are weaker than that of a proper naming ceremony, but in the pursuit of greater military power, this is no real issue.

"...But it is so difficult that even I cannot attempt it."

"Even you, Master Veldora?"

"Indeed. The magicule wavelength differs by individual. Because you cannot simply reuse the magicules, one must absorb them into oneself first. And normally, it is not possible to take in another's energy. Even if it were possible, no more than half of it or so could actually be repurposed for other uses. And yet Rimuru..."

"Is reusing the power with at least ninety...if not a full one-hundred percent efficiency..."

"You see what I mean? I could not do such a thing."

Despite his daft looks, Rimuru often achieves nearly impossible feats with the greatest of ease. As the news of this gets around, more will seek to utilize him to their own ends.

He himself seems totally oblivious to this, and while I doubt that anyone would run about spreading the tale, I do fear that if nothing is done to prevent this possibility, it will one day lead to some catastrophic failure.

It is no easy feat to inspire fear in me. Will your surprises never cease, Rimuru?

On top of that, the last orc was one of the officers of Geld the demon lord. And Rimuru went right ahead and gave that one the name of Geld to carry on!!

"Glarrbbggh!!"

Blast! He took my magicules again!!

Luckily for me, I was ready for this to happen, but I would have appreciated a word of warning first.

Understood. This will be taken into account next time.

Y-you fool! I don't want it "taken into account," I want him to stop naming monsters!

He made quite the miscalculation this time. It hurt a little bit, which is a sign that he took more than his share from my energy.

Sometimes I cannot believe this slime.

But very well. I suppose that I can be magnanimous and forgive him in repayment of all the excitement he provided.

This was the end of the chaos in the Forest of Jura. The various races returned to their home habitats, and peace returned to the woods.
Three months later, Rimuru's village had undergone a dramatic change. Through the naming process, Rimuru had evolved the orcs into high orcs. The resulting increase in

power led to a massive surplus of physical labor.

Thus the residential area expanded and developed at a rapid pace, which brought more and more residents to the area. Excitement flooded into the village, and the thrum of anticipation of a happy future is everywhere.

A place where all monsters can gather: Rimuru's ideals have come to fruition in this remarkable town.

Even I cannot hide my elation. When I am free of this damnable prison, I will build a home in this place, too. Then everyone will praise and compliment me, as I deserve!

I am awaiting this day, Rimuru. My eyes shall not leave your exploits until it happens!

To be reincarnated in Volume 6!

EXTRA ILLUSTRATION

*This was a rejected chapter cover-page design.

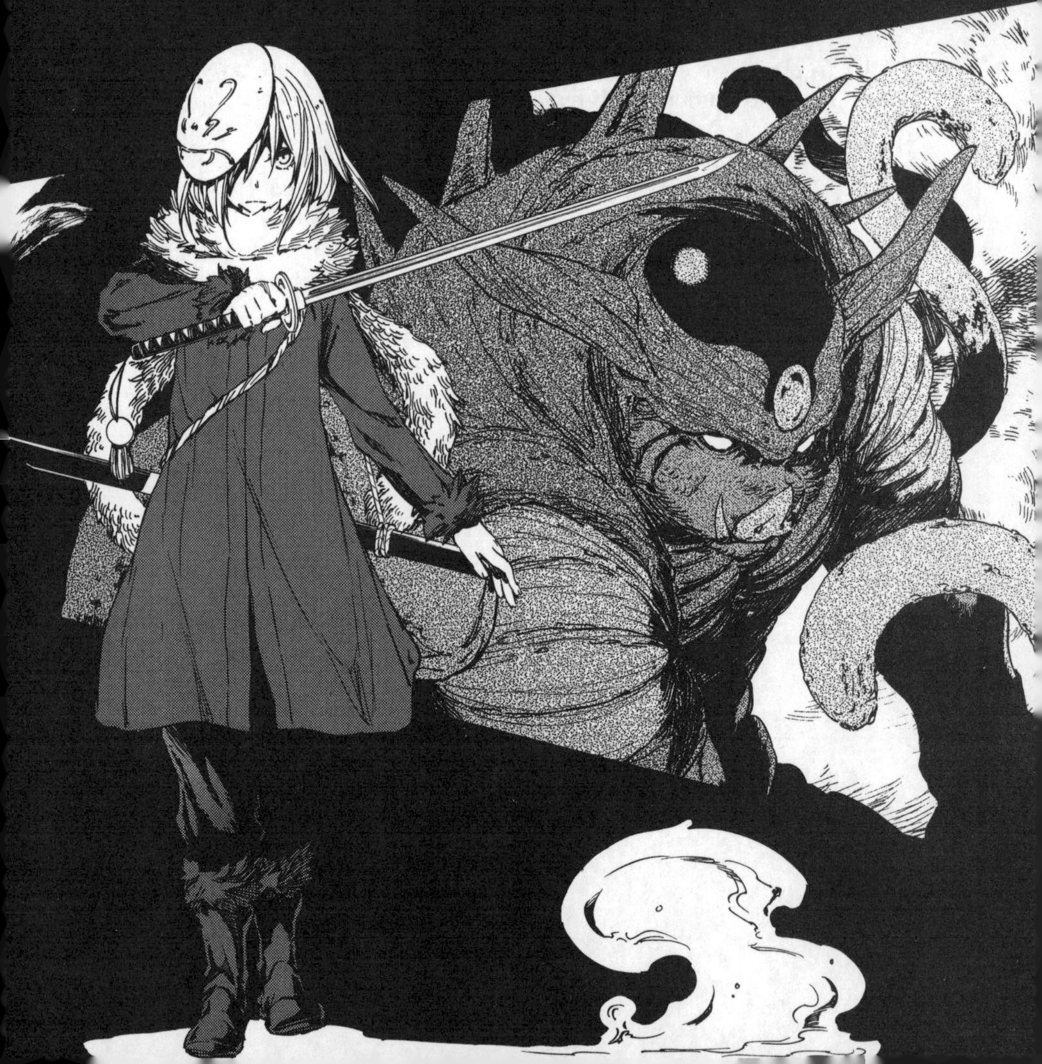

A HUGE FAD IN THE MONSTER KINGDOM

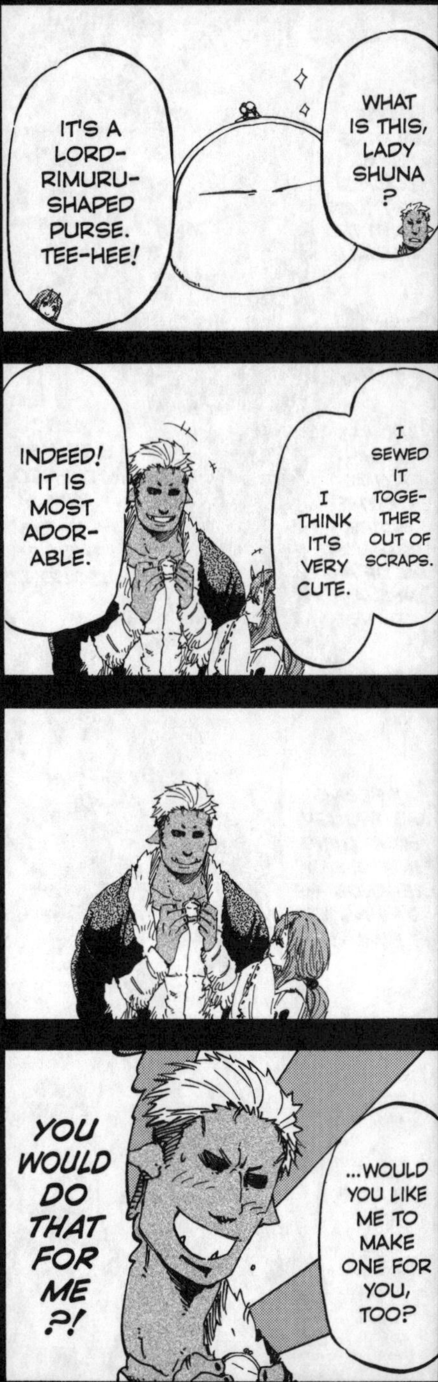
WHAT IS THIS, LADY SHUNA?
IT'S A LORD-RIMURU-SHAPED PURSE. TEE-HEE!
I SEWED IT TOGETHER OUT OF SCRAPS.
I THINK IT'S VERY CUTE.
INDEED! IT IS MOST ADORABLE.
...WOULD YOU LIKE ME TO MAKE ONE FOR YOU, TOO?
YOU WOULD DO THAT FOR ME?!

MOSTLY BENIMARU, SOMETIMES GOBTA

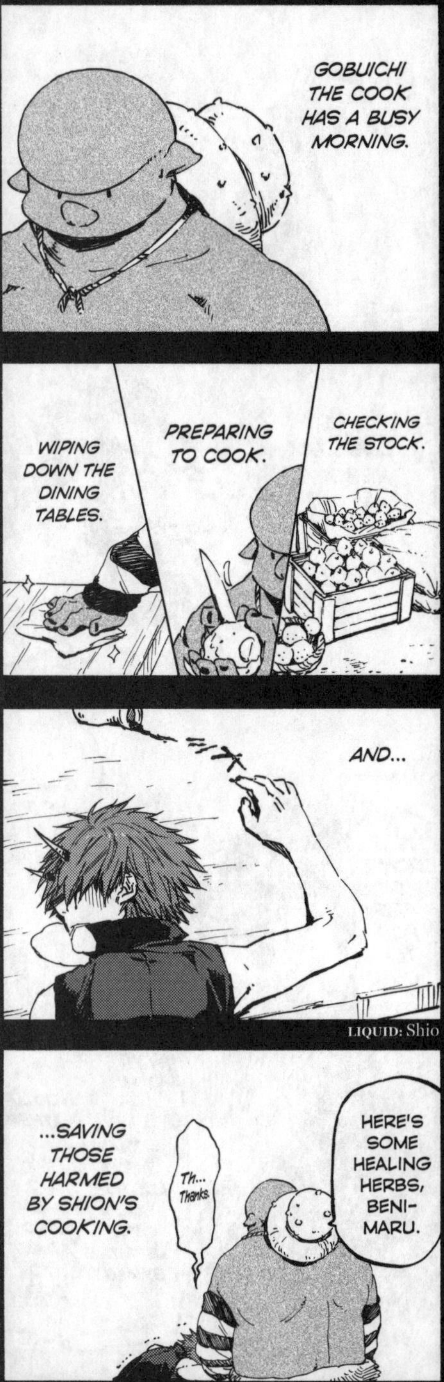
GOBUICHI THE COOK HAS A BUSY MORNING.
CHECKING THE STOCK.
PREPARING TO COOK.
WIPING DOWN THE DINING TABLES.
AND...
LIQUID: Shio
HERE'S SOME HEALING HERBS, BENIMARU.
Th... Thanks.
...SAVING THOSE HARMED BY SHION'S COOKING.

GABIRU THE IDOMITABLE

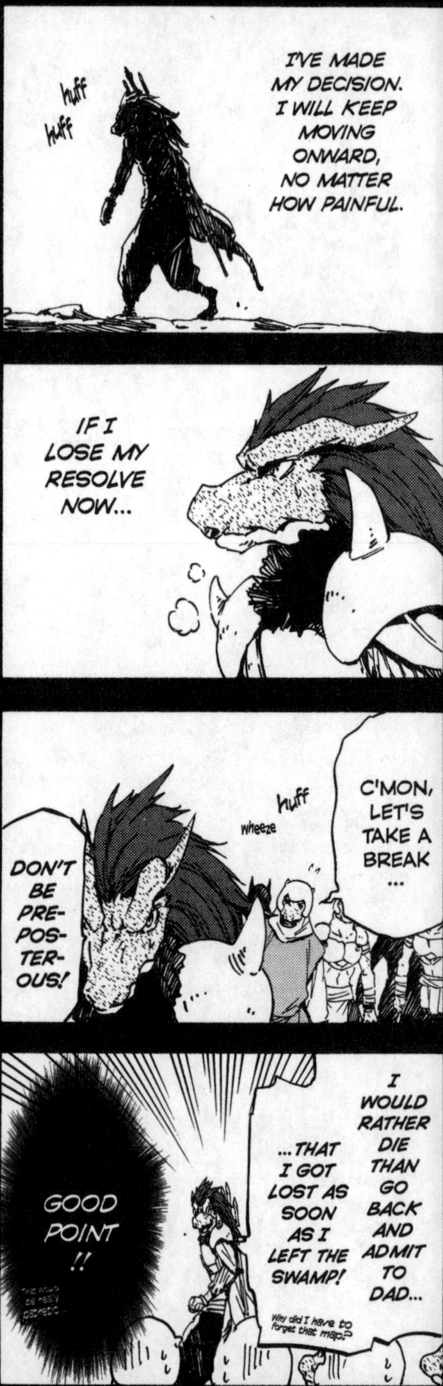
I'VE MADE MY DECISION. I WILL KEEP MOVING ONWARD, NO MATTER HOW PAINFUL.
huff
huff
IF I LOSE MY RESOLVE NOW...
C'MON, LET'S TAKE A BREAK ...
huff
wheeze
DON'T BE PRE-POS-TER-OUS!
I WOULD RATHER DIE THAN GO BACK AND ADMIT TO DAD...
...THAT I GOT LOST AS SOON AS I LEFT THE SWAMP!
Why did I have to forget that map?
GOOD POINT !!

COSMIC TRUTH

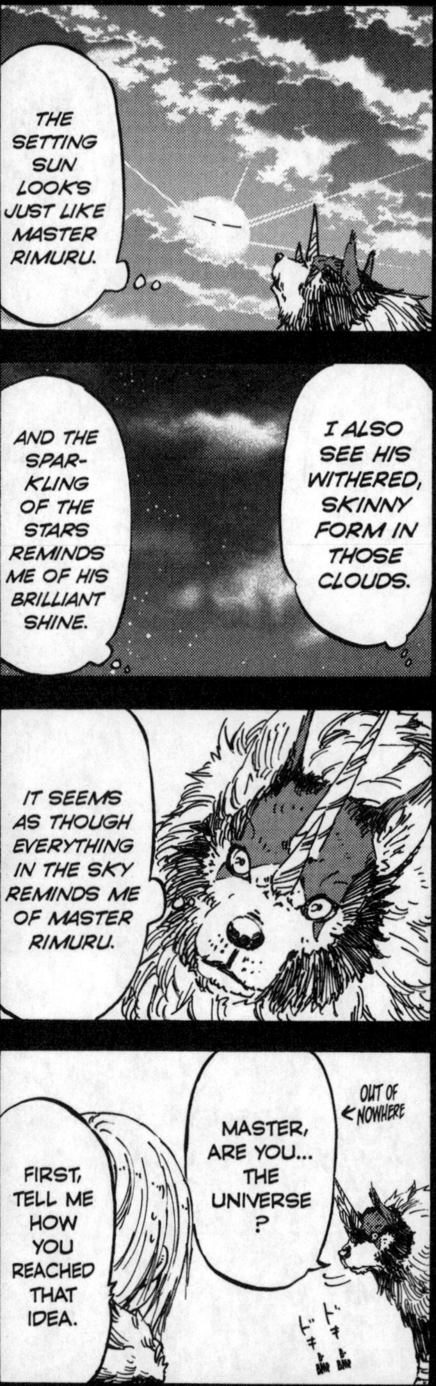
THE SETTING SUN LOOKS JUST LIKE MASTER RIMURU.
I ALSO SEE HIS WITHERED, SKINNY FORM IN THOSE CLOUDS.
AND THE SPAR-KLING OF THE STARS REMINDS ME OF HIS BRILLIANT SHINE.
IT SEEMS AS THOUGH EVERYTHING IN THE SKY REMINDS ME OF MASTER RIMURU.
OUT OF NOWHERE
MASTER, ARE YOU... THE UNIVERSE ?
FIRST, TELL ME HOW YOU REACHED THAT IDEA.
ドキ
ドキ

THE HORN PROBLEM

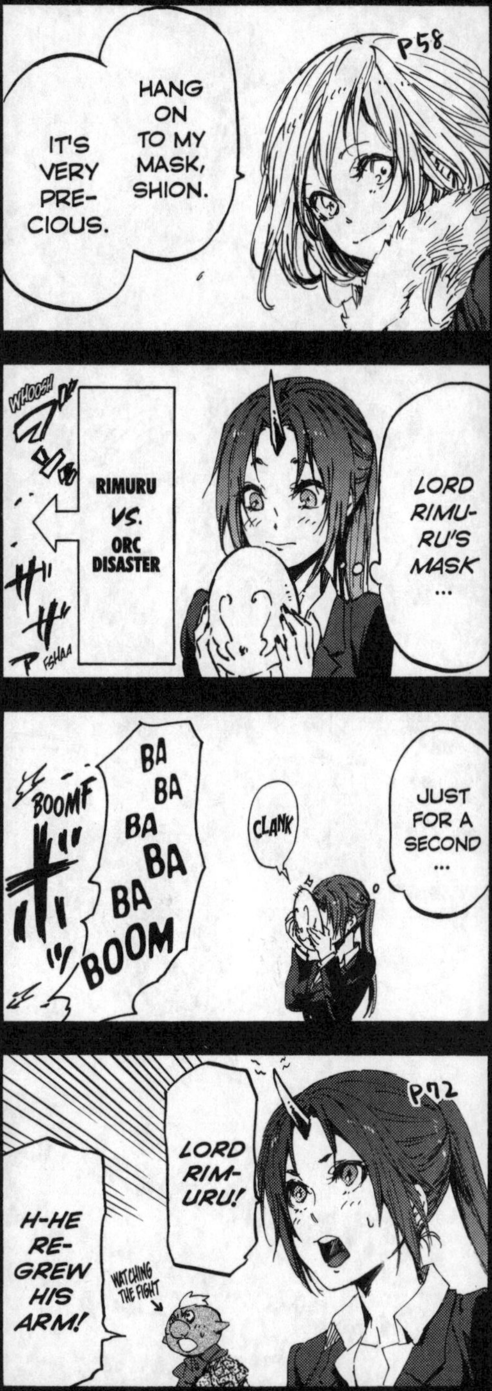
P58
HANG ON TO MY MASK, SHION.
IT'S VERY PRE-CIOUS.
LORD RIMU-RU'S MASK ...
RIMURU VS. ORC DISASTER
WHOOSH
FSHAA
JUST FOR A SECOND ...
CLANK
BA BA BA BA BA BOOM
BOOMF
P72
LORD RIM-URU!
H-HE RE-GREW HIS ARM!
WATCHING THE FIGHT

LIST OF ACKNOWLEDGMENTS

AUTHOR:
Fuse-sensei

CHARACTER DESIGN:
Mitz Vah-sensei

ASSISTANTS:
Muraichi-san
Daiki Haraguchi-san
Masashi Kiritani-sensei
Taku Arao-sensei
Takuya Nishida-sensei

Congrats on getting your own series !!

Everyone at the editorial department

And You!!

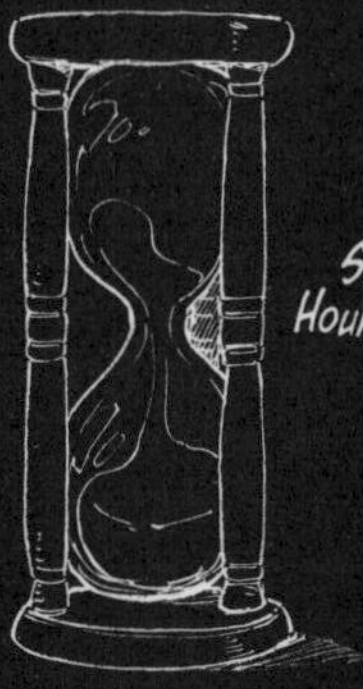
Slime Hourglass

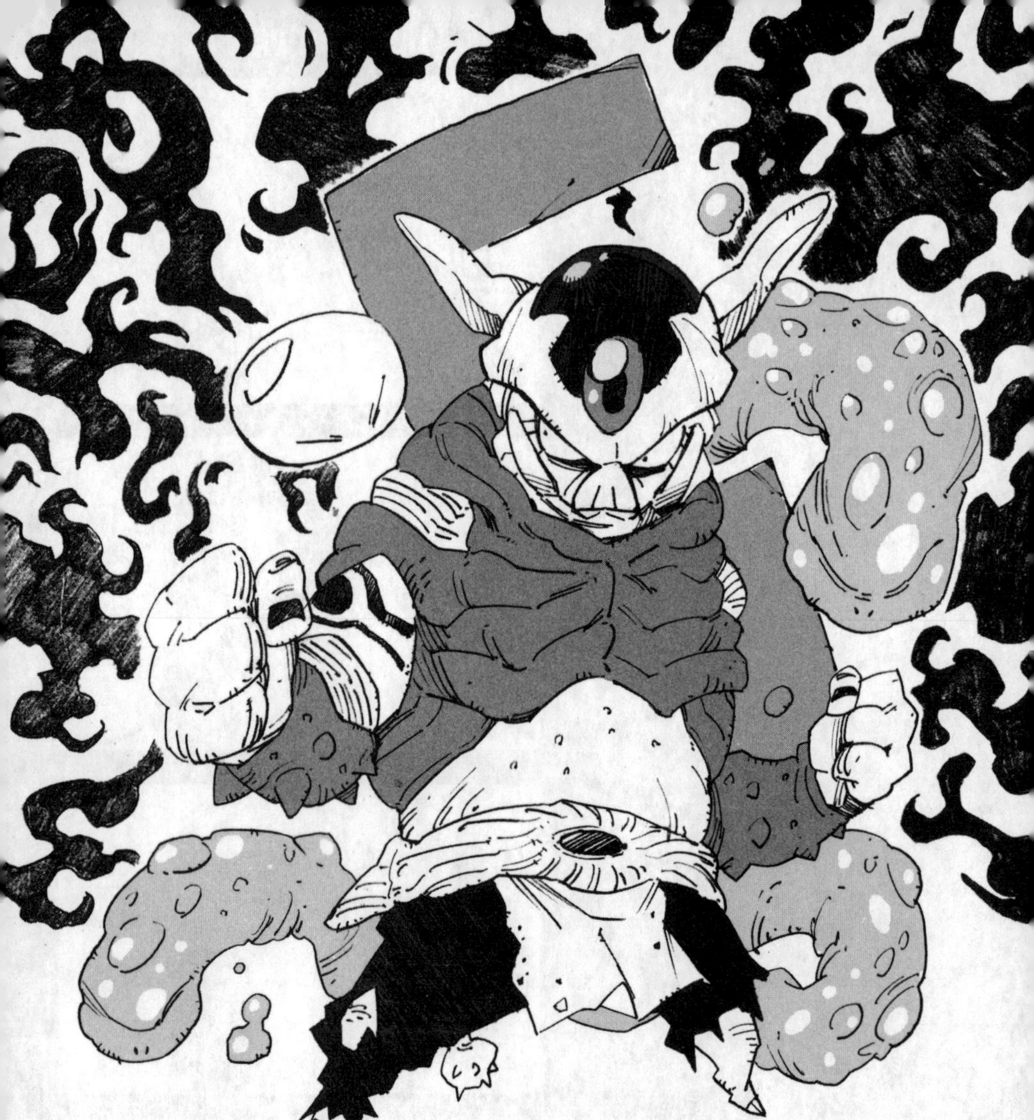

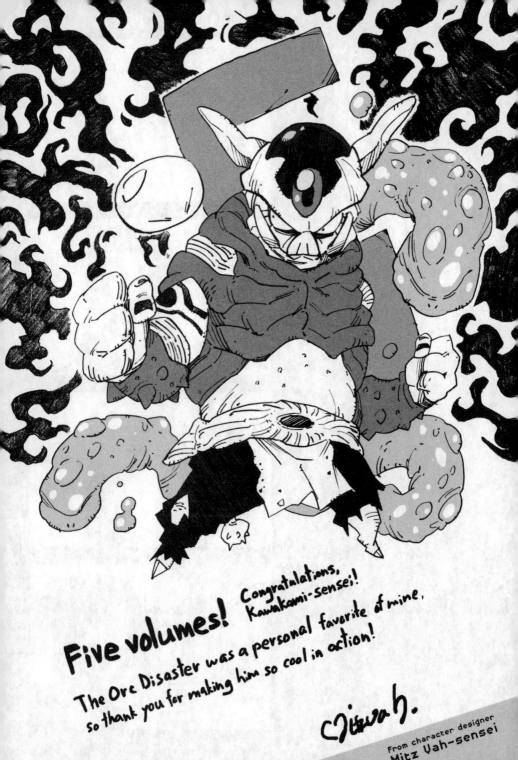

Five volumes! Congratulations, Kawakami-sensei!

The Orc Disaster was a personal favorite of mine, so thank you for making him so cool in action!

Mitz Vah.

From character designer
Mitz Vah-sensei

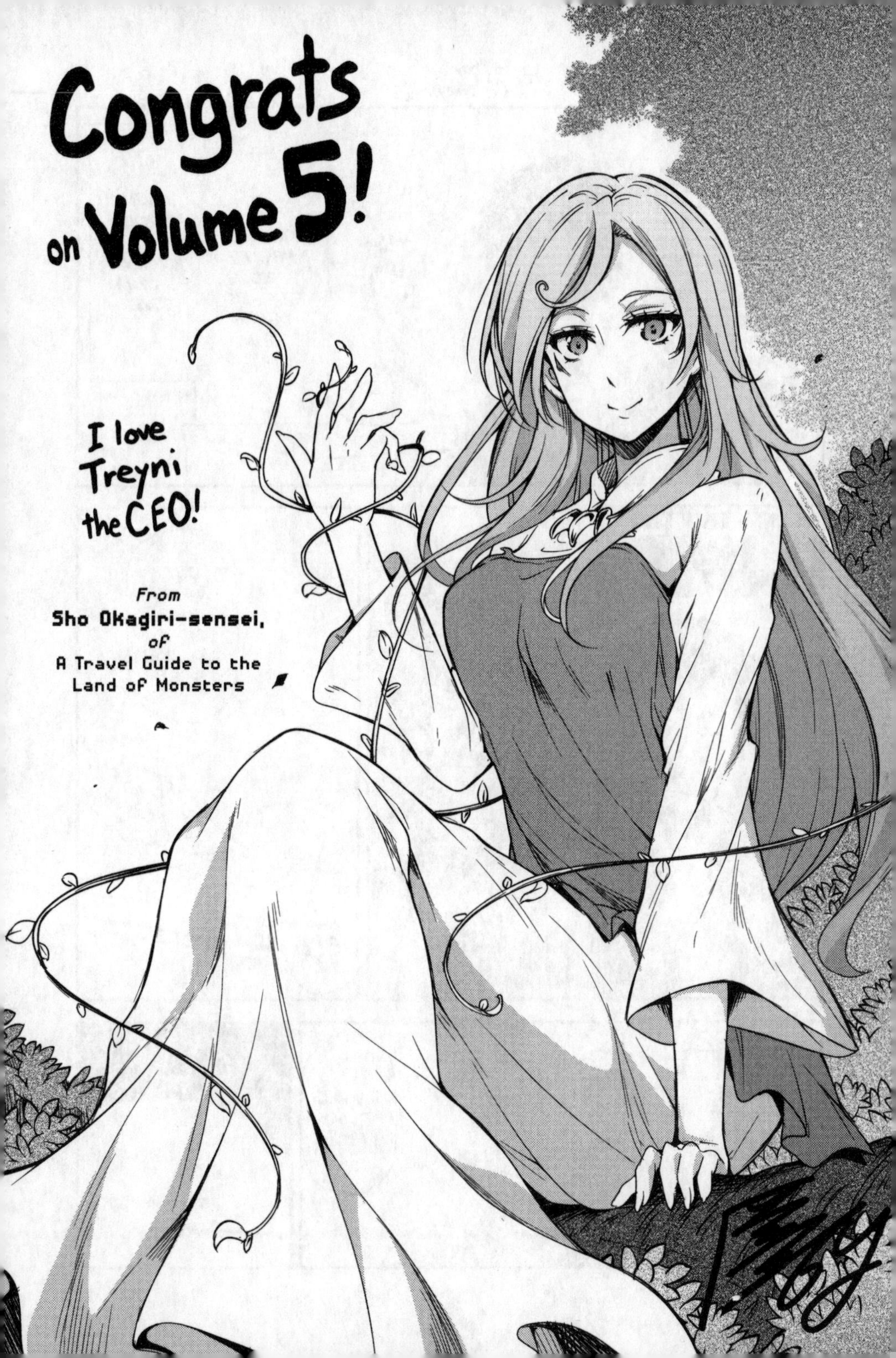
Congrats on Volume 5!
I love Treyni the CEO!
From Sho Okagiri-sensei, of A Travel Guide to the Land of Monsters

Straying Off Course

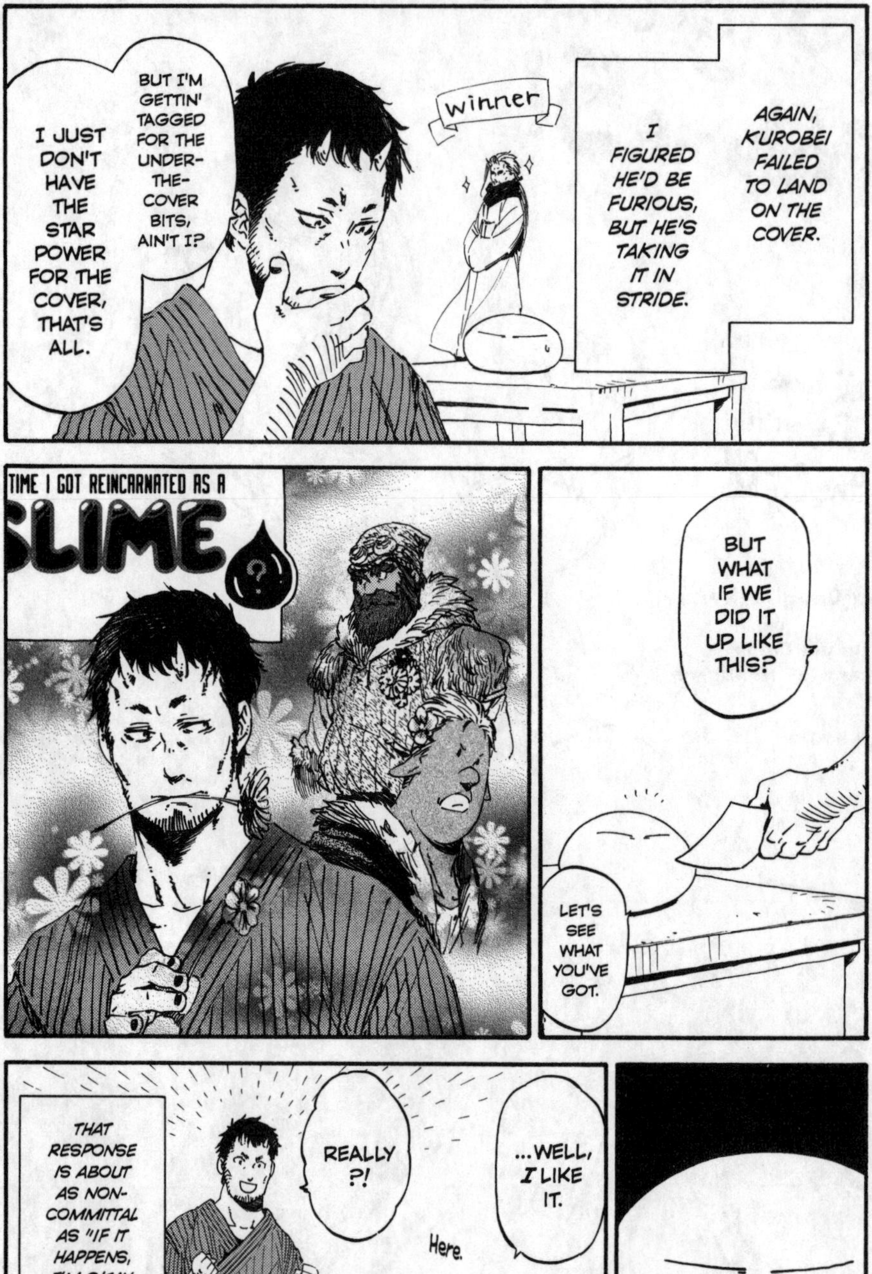
AGAIN, KUROBEI FAILED TO LAND ON THE COVER.
I FIGURED HE'D BE FURIOUS, BUT HE'S TAKING IT IN STRIDE.
Winner
I JUST DON'T HAVE THE STAR POWER FOR THE COVER, THAT'S ALL.
BUT I'M GETTIN' TAGGED FOR THE UNDER-THE-COVER BITS, AIN'T I?
BUT WHAT IF WE DID IT UP LIKE THIS?
LET'S SEE WHAT YOU'VE GOT.
TIME I GOT REINCARNATED AS A
SLIME
?
...WELL, I LIKE IT.
Here.
REALLY ?!
THAT RESPONSE IS ABOUT AS NON-COMMITTAL AS "IF IT HAPPENS, I'M OKAY WITH IT."

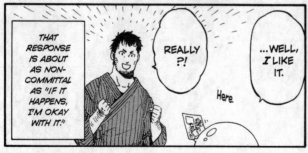

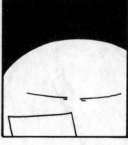

Candy Apple.

Well, the candy part.

TRANSLATION NOTES

HIGH ORCS

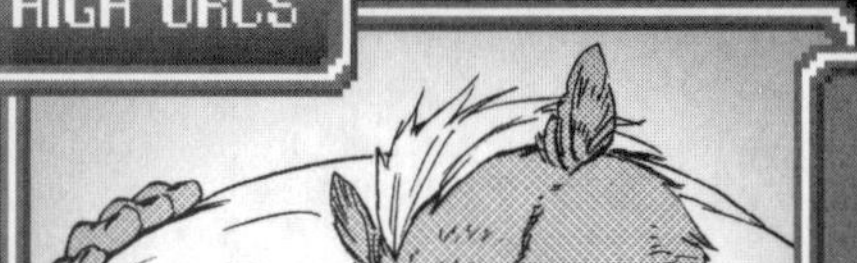

page 153

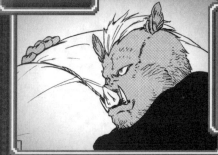

Much like the kijin, who have a different set of *Kanji* from their "ogre" foundation, the orc and high orc terms have their own *Kanji*. The word orc is written as "pig-head clan," while the high orcs are "boar people clan," which again suggests that evolving has brought them a greater human influence. Similarly, orc king is simply written as "boar people king."

That Time I Got Reincarnated as a Slime volume 5 is a work of fiction. Names, characters, places, and incidents are the products of the author's imagination or are used fictitiously. Any resemblance to actual events, locales, or persons, living or dead, is entirely coincidental.

A Kodansha Comics Trade Paperback Original.

Published in the United States by Kodansha Comics,
an imprint of Kodansha USA Publishing, LLC, New York.

Publication rights for this English edition arranged through Kodansha Ltd., Tokyo.

First published in Japan in 2017 by Kodansha Ltd., Tokyo, as *Tensei Shitara Suraimu Datta Ken* volume 5.

ISBN 978-1-63236-639-9

Printed in the United States of America.

www.kodansha.us

7th Printing

Translation: Stephen Paul
Lettering: Evan Hayden
Editing: Ajani Oloye
Kodansha Comics edition cover design: Phil Balsman

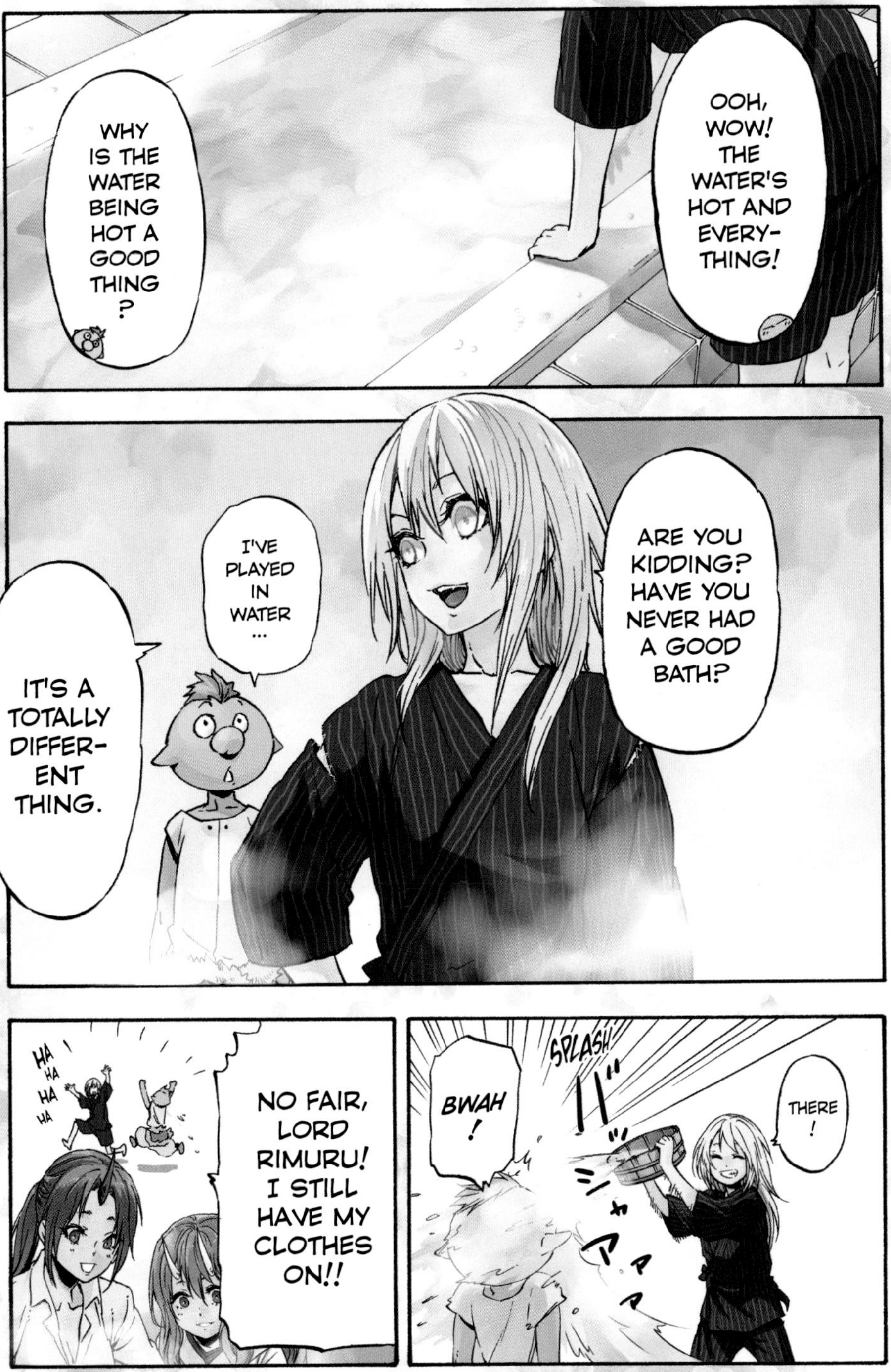
OOH, WOW! THE WATER'S HOT AND EVERY-THING!
WHY IS THE WATER BEING HOT A GOOD THING?
ARE YOU KIDDING? HAVE YOU NEVER HAD A GOOD BATH?
I'VE PLAYED IN WATER ...
IT'S A TOTALLY DIFFER-ENT THING.
THERE!
SPLASH
BWAH!
HA HA HA HA
NO FAIR, LORD RIMURU! I STILL HAVE MY CLOTHES ON!!

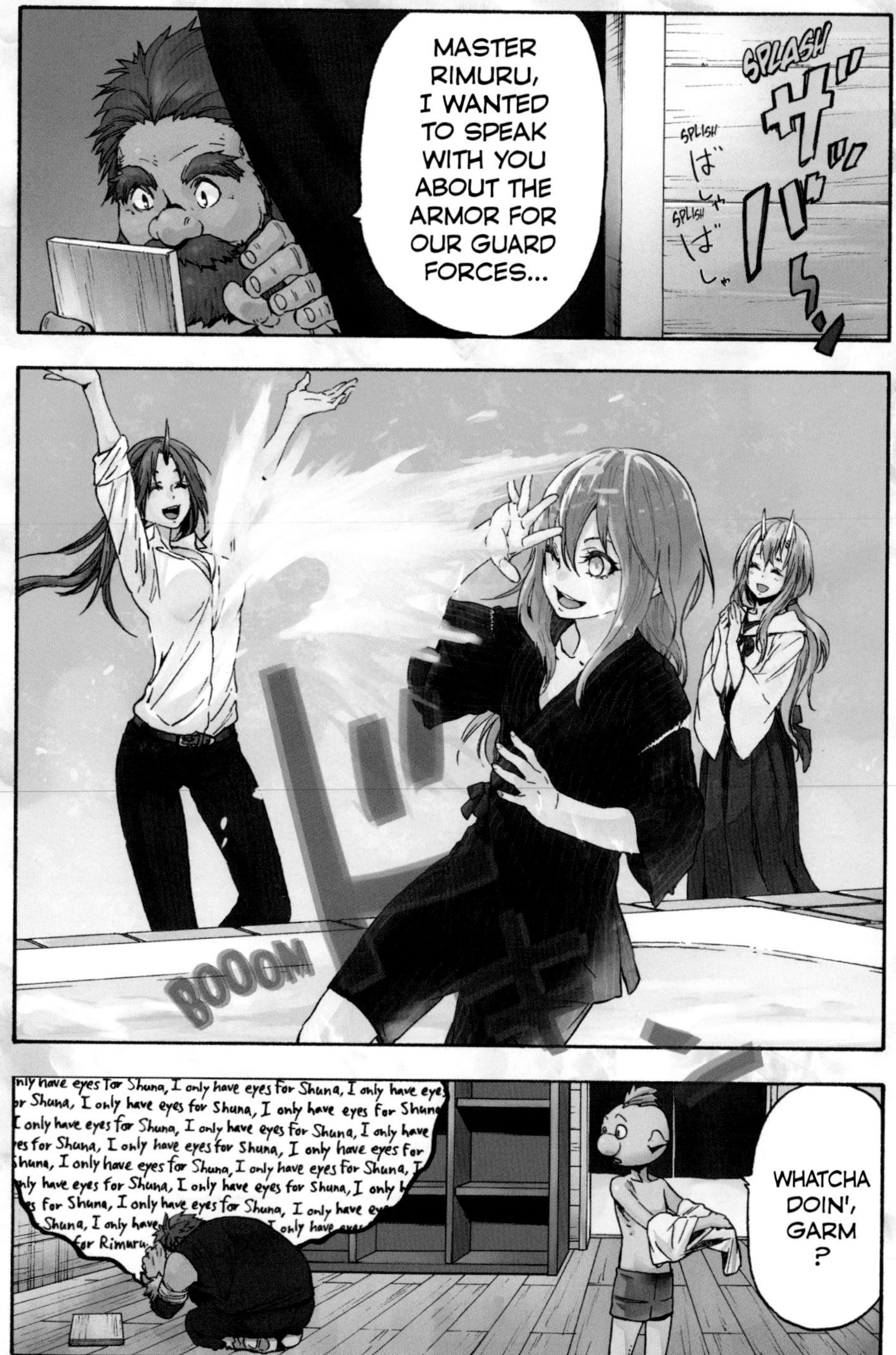
SPLASH
SPLISH
ばしゃ
SPLISH
ばしゃ
MASTER RIMURU, I WANTED TO SPEAK WITH YOU ABOUT THE ARMOR FOR OUR GUARD FORCES...
BOOOM
WHATCHA DOIN', GARM?
nly have eyes for Shuna, I only have eyes for Shuna, I only have eye
r Shuna, I only have eyes for Shuna, I only have eyes for Shun
I only have eyes for Shuna, I only have eyes for Shuna, I only have
es for Shuna, I only have eyes for Shuna, I only have eyes for
huna, I only have eyes for Shuna, I only have eyes for Shuna,
nly have eyes for Shuna, I only have eyes for Shuna, I only
for Shuna, I only have eyes for Shuna, I only have
Shuna, I only have
for Rimuru

CHAPTER 28 Attention on the Town of Monsters

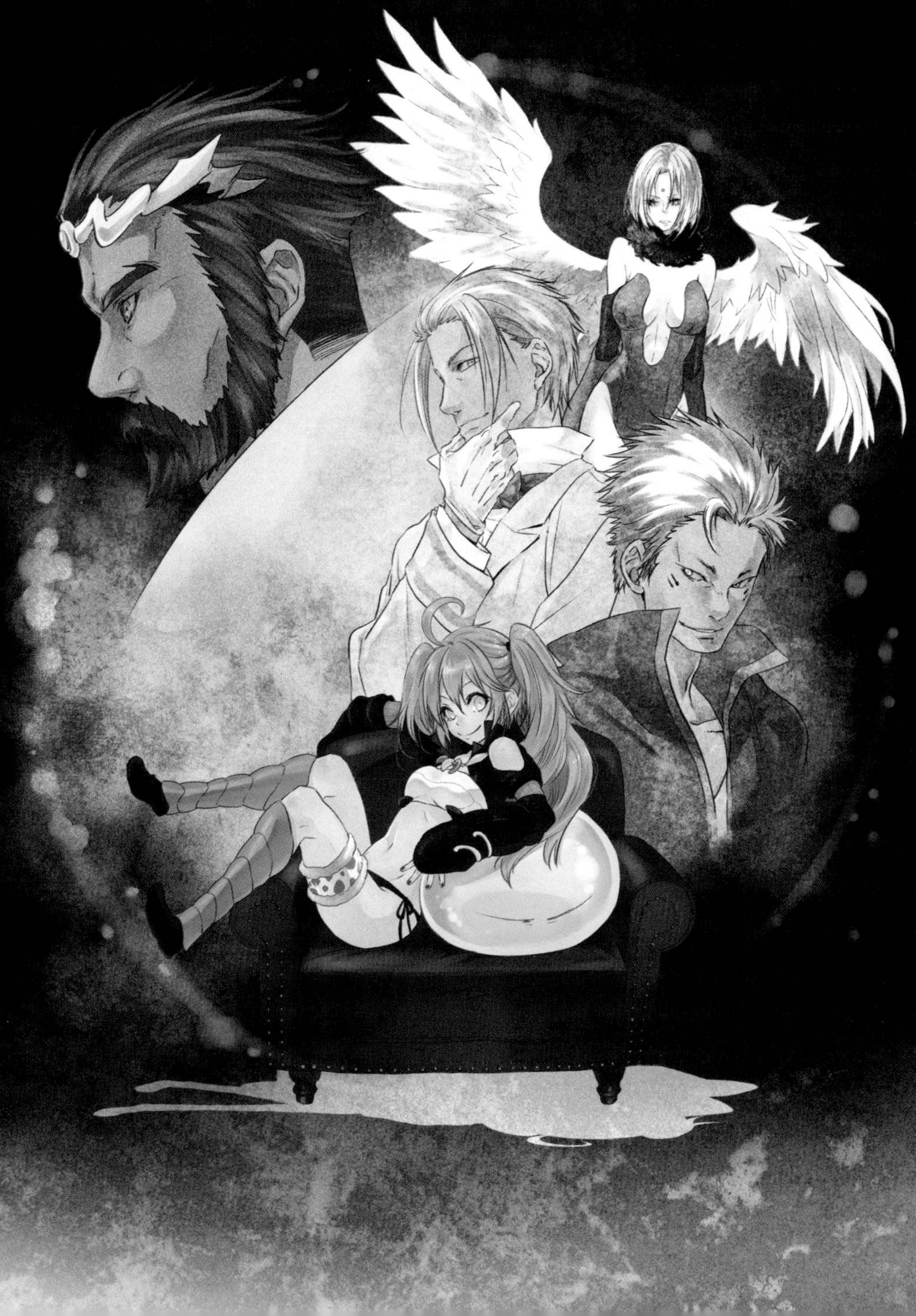

THAT TIME I GOT REINCARNATED AS A

SLIME

6

Author: FUSE

Artist: TAIKI KAWAKAMI

Character design: MITZ VAH

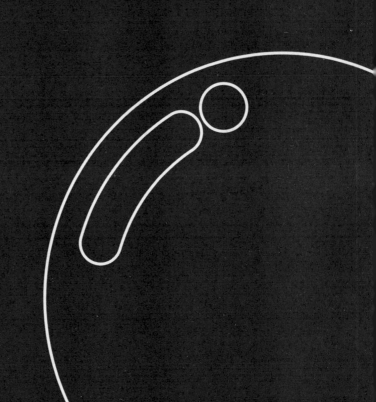

World Map

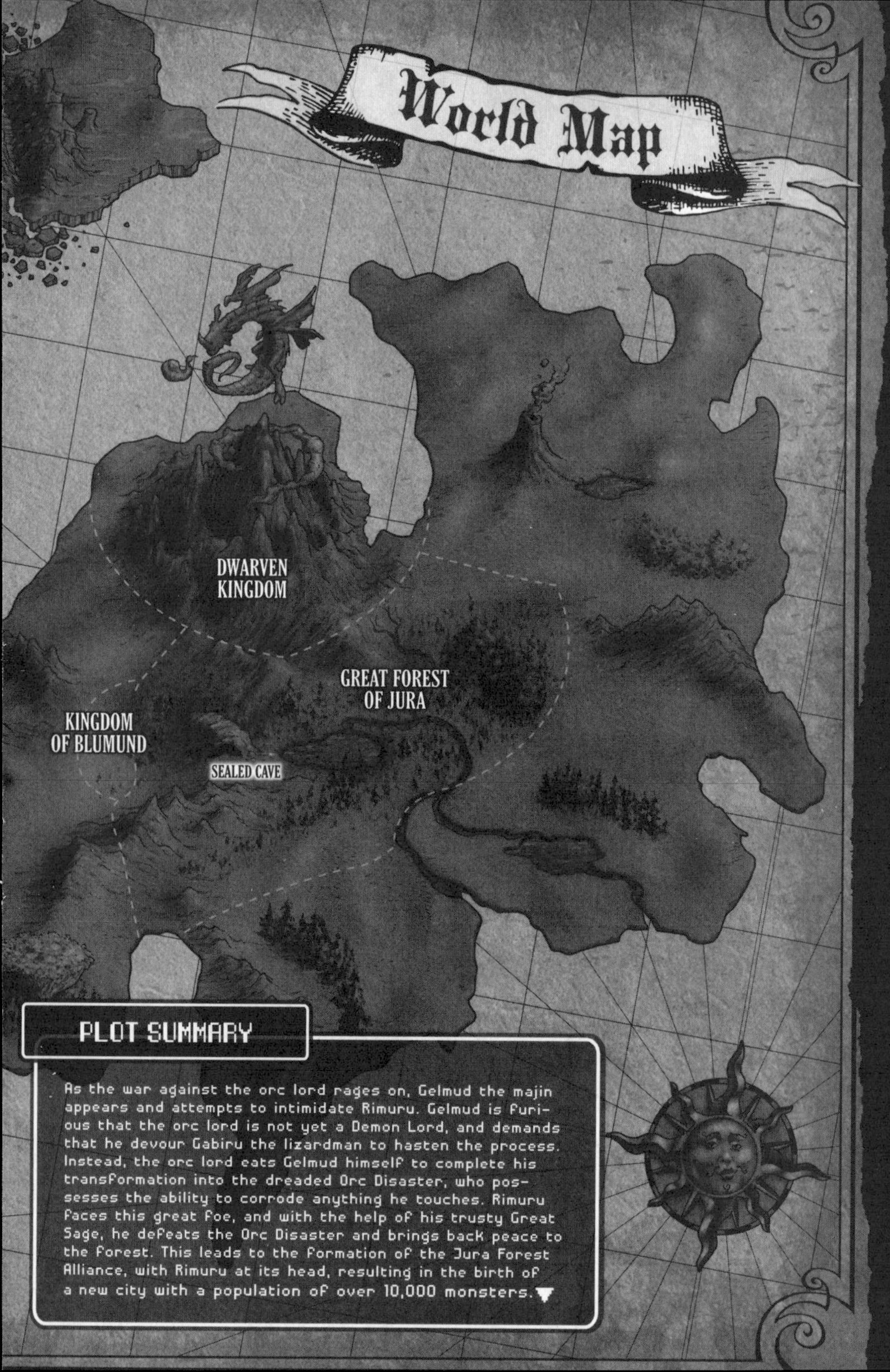
DWARVEN KINGDOM
GREAT FOREST OF JURA
KINGDOM OF BLUMUND
SEALED CAVE

PLOT SUMMARY

As the war against the orc lord rages on, Gelmud the majin appears and attempts to intimidate Rimuru. Gelmud is furious that the orc lord is not yet a Demon Lord, and demands that he devour Gabiru the lizardman to hasten the process. Instead, the orc lord eats Gelmud himself to complete his transformation into the dreaded Orc Disaster, who possesses the ability to corrode anything he touches. Rimuru faces this great foe, and with the help of his trusty Great Sage, he defeats the Orc Disaster and brings back peace to the forest. This leads to the formation of the Jura Forest Alliance, with Rimuru at its head, resulting in the birth of a new city with a population of over 10,000 monsters.

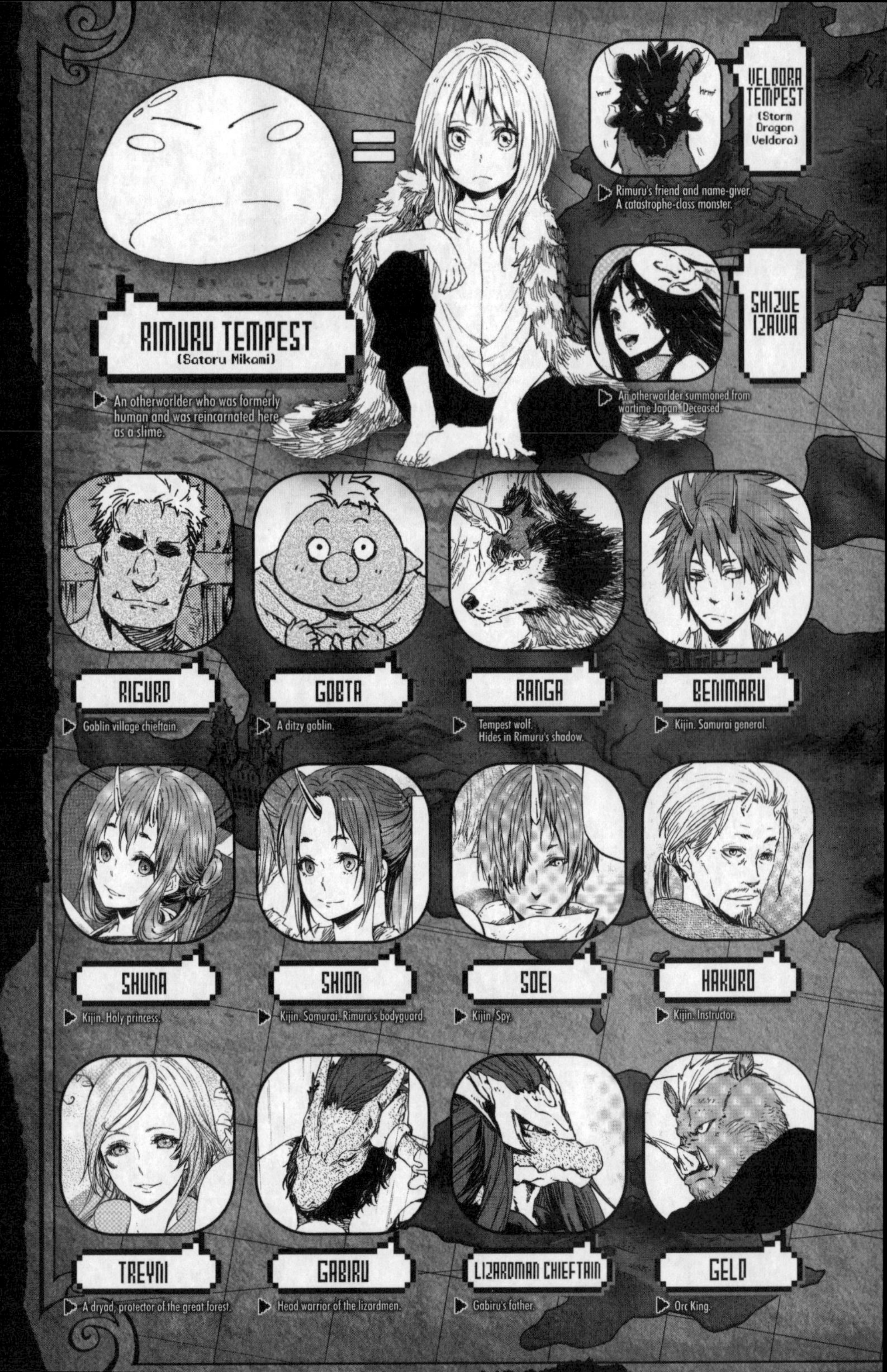

RIMURU TEMPEST
(Satoru Mikami)
An otherworlder who was formerly human and was reincarnated here as a slime.
VELDORA TEMPEST
(Storm Dragon Veldora)
Rimuru's friend and name-giver. A catastrophe-class monster.
SHIZUE IZAWA
An otherworlder summoned from wartime Japan. Deceased.
RIGURD
Goblin village chieftain.
GOBTA
A ditzy goblin.
RANGA
Tempest wolf. Hides in Rimuru's shadow.
BENIMARU
Kijin. Samurai general.
SHUNA
Kijin. Holy princess.
SHION
Kijin. Samurai. Rimuru's bodyguard.
SOEI
Kijin. Spy.
HAKURO
Kijin. Instructor.
TREYNI
A dryad, protector of the great forest.
GABIRU
Head warrior of the lizardmen.
LIZARDMAN CHIEFTAIN
Gabiru's father.
GELD
Orc King.

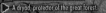

CONTENTS

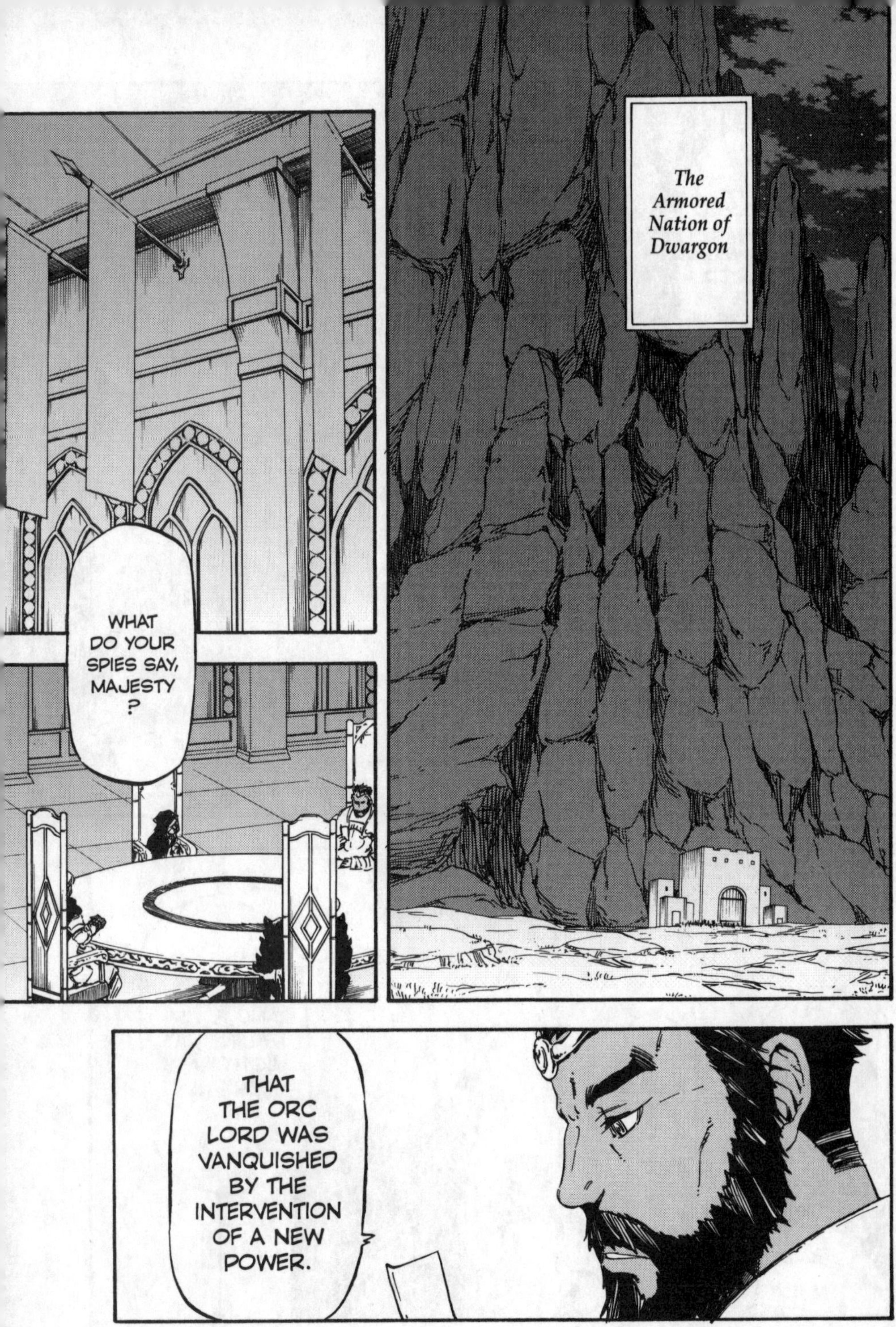
The Armored Nation of Dwargon
WHAT DO YOUR SPIES SAY, MAJESTY?
THAT THE ORC LORD WAS VANQUISHED BY THE INTERVENTION OF A NEW POWER.

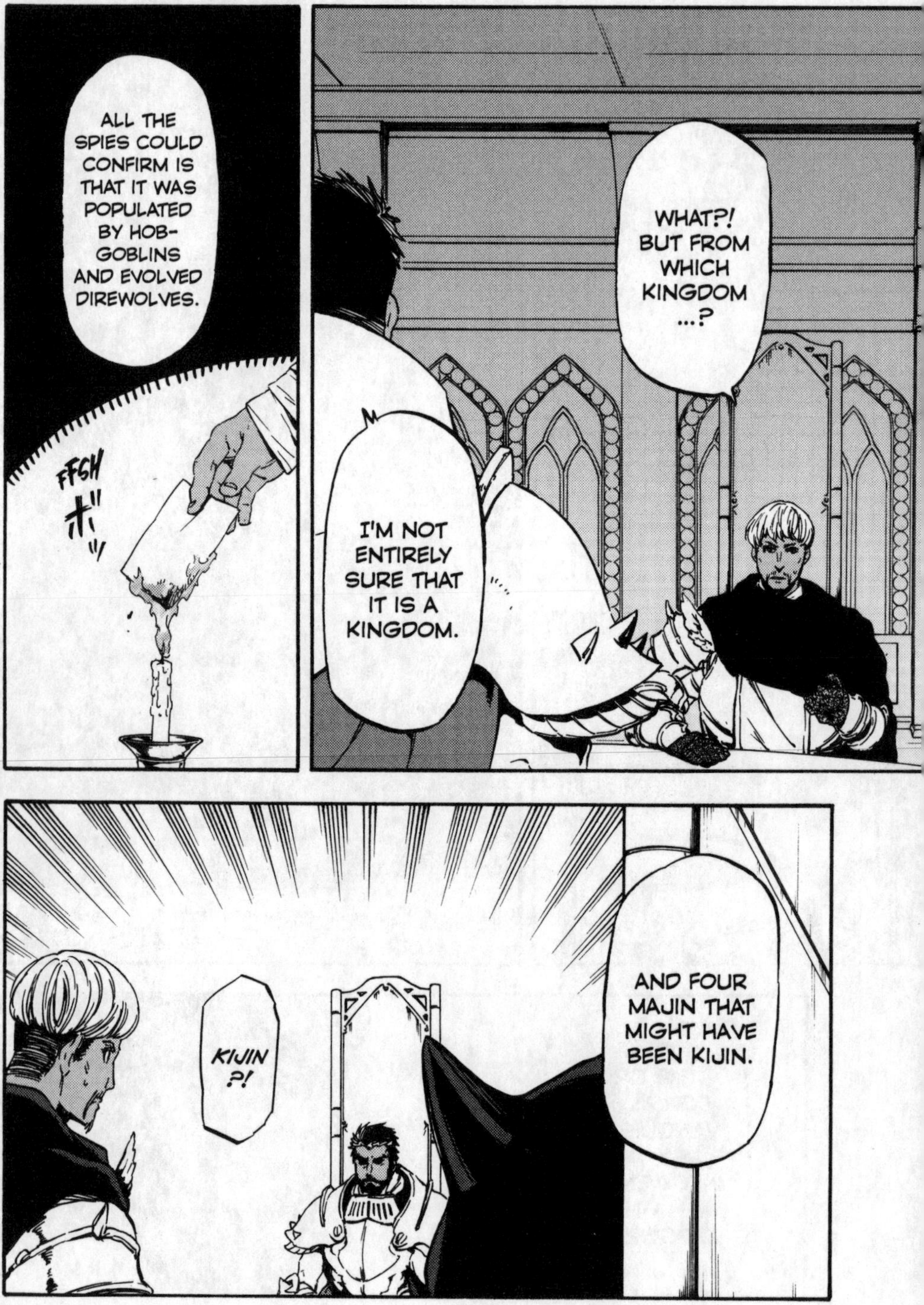

WHAT?! BUT FROM WHICH KINGDOM ...?
I'M NOT ENTIRELY SURE THAT IT IS A KINGDOM.
ALL THE SPIES COULD CONFIRM IS THAT IT WAS POPULATED BY HOB-GOBLINS AND EVOLVED DIREWOLVES.
FFSH
AND FOUR MAJIN THAT MIGHT HAVE BEEN KIJIN.
KIJIN?!

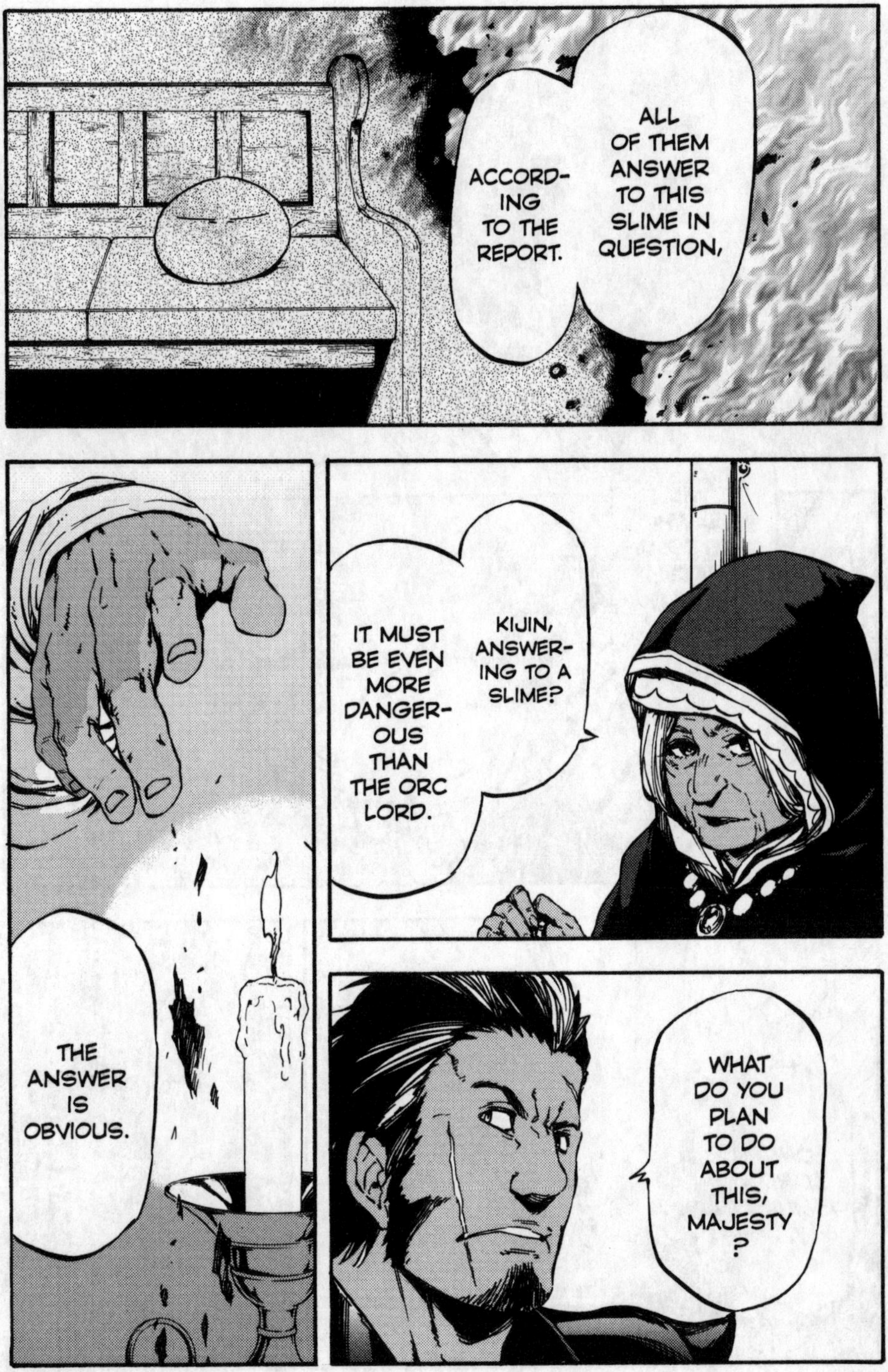
ALL OF THEM ANSWER TO THIS SLIME IN QUESTION,
ACCORDING TO THE REPORT.
KIJIN, ANSWERING TO A SLIME?
IT MUST BE EVEN MORE DANGEROUS THAN THE ORC LORD.
WHAT DO YOU PLAN TO DO ABOUT THIS, MAJESTY?
THE ANSWER IS OBVIOUS.

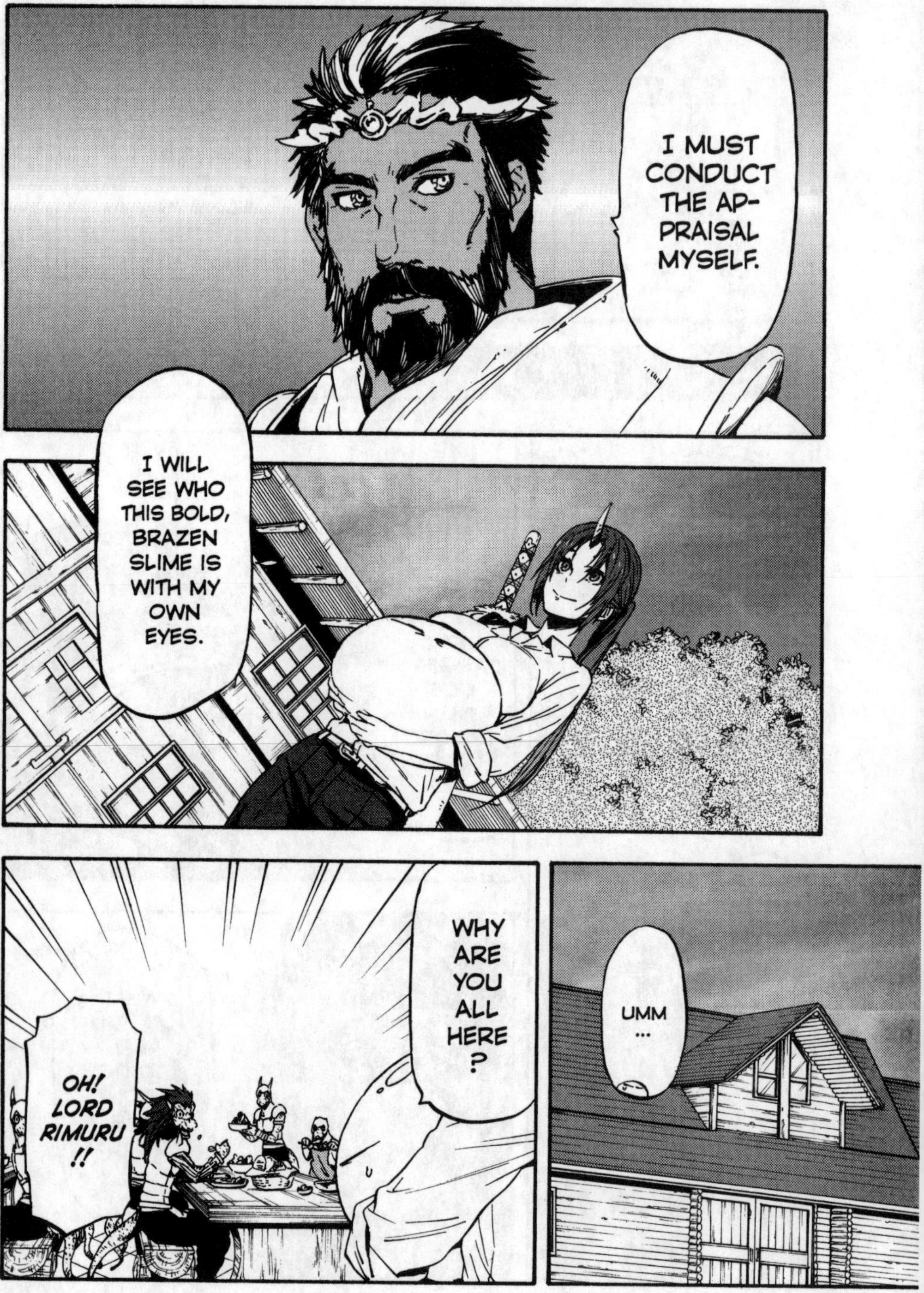
I MUST CONDUCT THE AP-PRAISAL MYSELF.
I WILL SEE WHO THIS BOLD, BRAZEN SLIME IS WITH MY OWN EYES.
UMM ...
WHY ARE YOU ALL HERE?
OH! LORD RIMURU!!

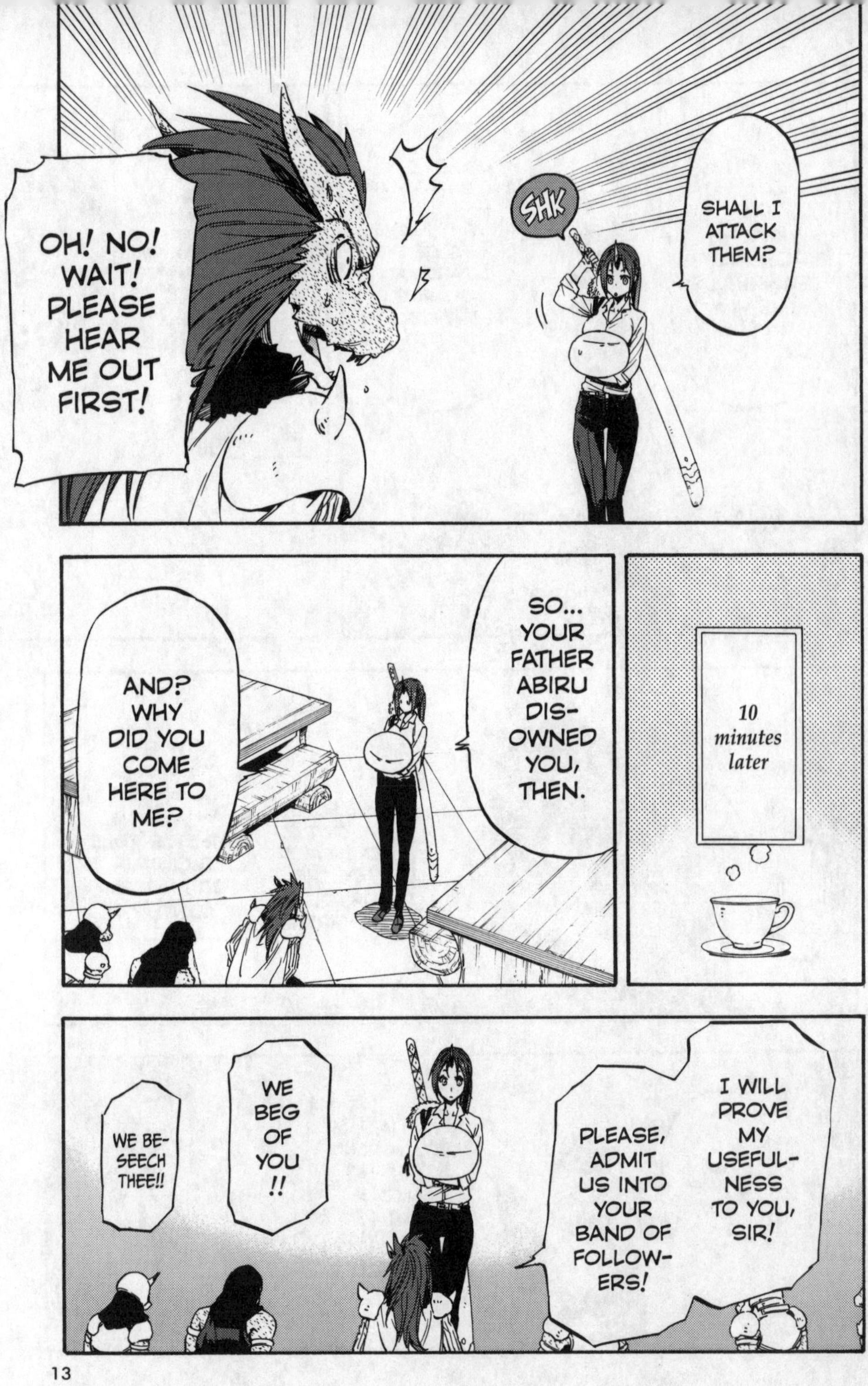
SHALL I ATTACK THEM?
SHK
OH! NO! WAIT! PLEASE HEAR ME OUT FIRST!
10 minutes later
SO... YOUR FATHER ABIRU DISOWNED YOU, THEN.
AND? WHY DID YOU COME HERE TO ME?
I WILL PROVE MY USEFULNESS TO YOU, SIR!
PLEASE, ADMIT US INTO YOUR BAND OF FOLLOWERS!
WE BEG OF YOU!!
WE BESEECH THEE!!

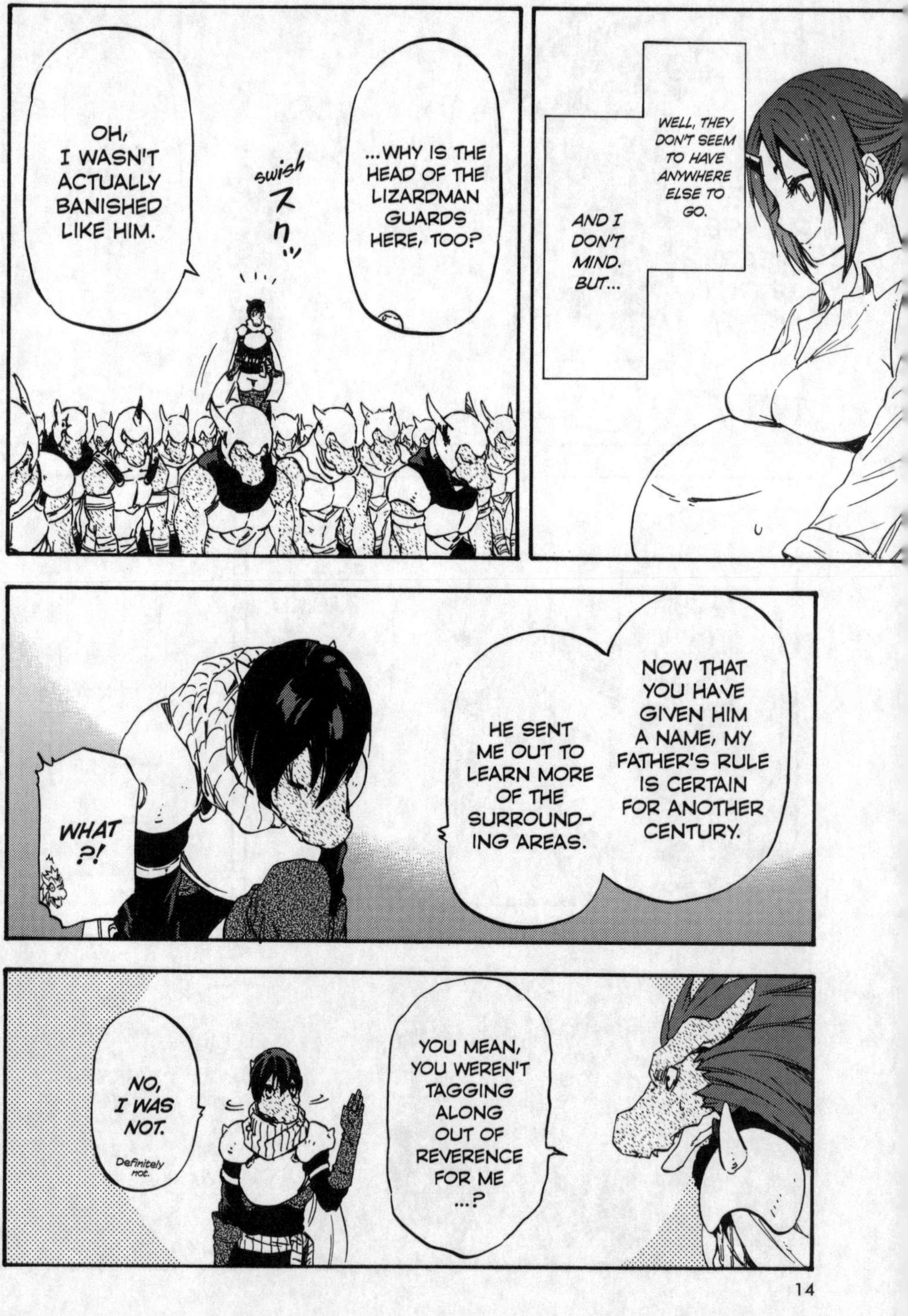
WELL, THEY DON'T SEEM TO HAVE ANYWHERE ELSE TO GO.
AND I DON'T MIND. BUT...
...WHY IS THE HEAD OF THE LIZARDMAN GUARDS HERE, TOO?
swish スッ
OH, I WASN'T ACTUALLY BANISHED LIKE HIM.
NOW THAT YOU HAVE GIVEN HIM A NAME, MY FATHER'S RULE IS CERTAIN FOR ANOTHER CENTURY.
HE SENT ME OUT TO LEARN MORE OF THE SURROUND-ING AREAS.
WHAT?!
YOU MEAN, YOU WEREN'T TAGGING ALONG OUT OF REVERENCE FOR ME ...?
NO, I WAS NOT.
Definitely not.

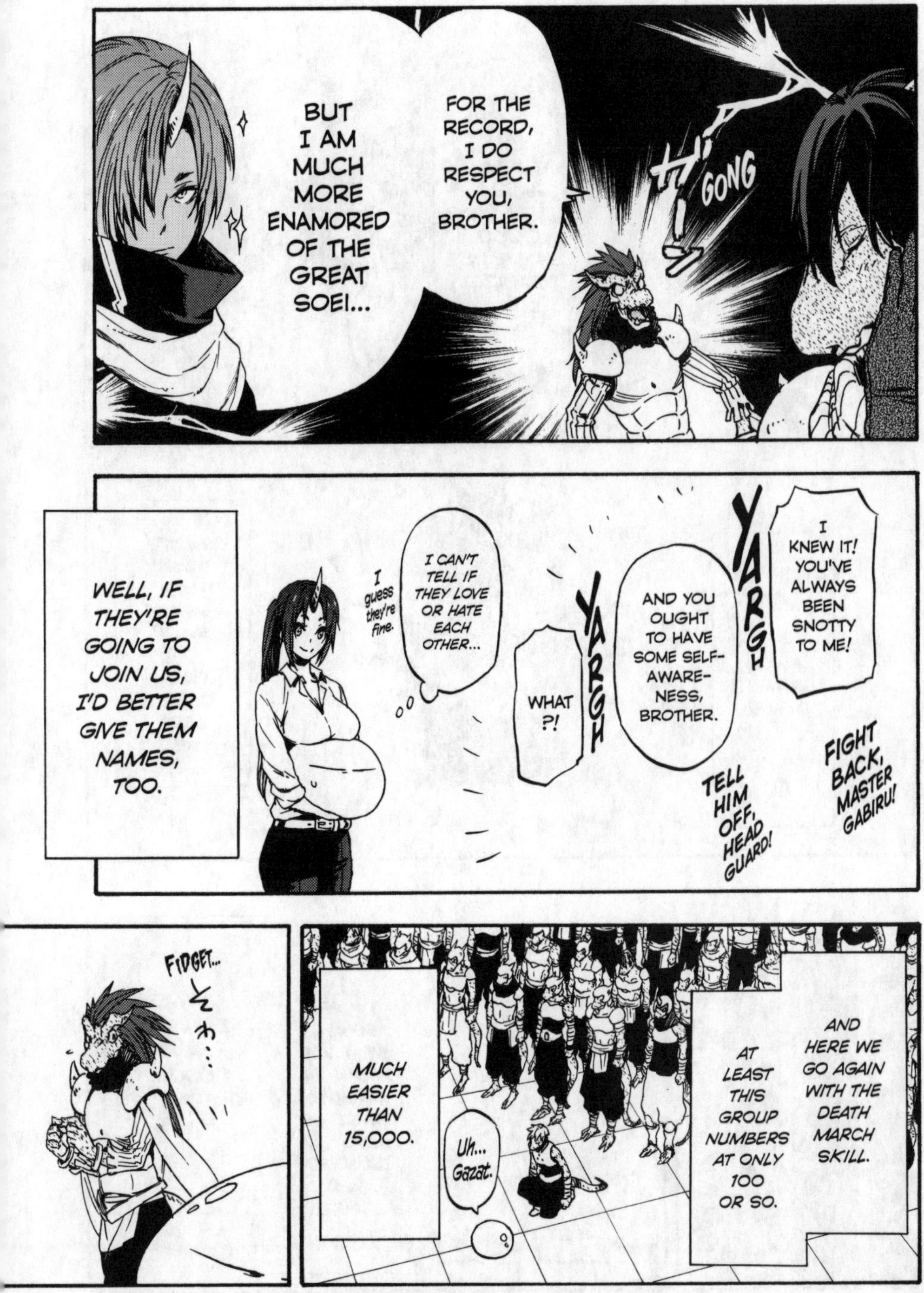
GONG
FOR THE RECORD, I DO RESPECT YOU, BROTHER.
BUT I AM MUCH MORE ENAMORED OF THE GREAT SOEI...
I KNEW IT! YOU'VE ALWAYS BEEN SNOTTY TO ME!
YARGH
FIGHT BACK, MASTER GABIRU!
AND YOU OUGHT TO HAVE SOME SELF-AWARENESS, BROTHER.
YARGH
TELL HIM OFF, HEAD GUARD!
WHAT?!
I CAN'T TELL IF THEY LOVE OR HATE EACH OTHER...
I guess they're fine.
WELL, IF THEY'RE GOING TO JOIN US, I'D BETTER GIVE THEM NAMES, TOO.
AND HERE WE GO AGAIN WITH THE DEATH MARCH SKILL.
AT LEAST THIS GROUP NUMBERS AT ONLY 100 OR SO.
MUCH EASIER THAN 15,000.
Uh... Gazat.
FIDGET...

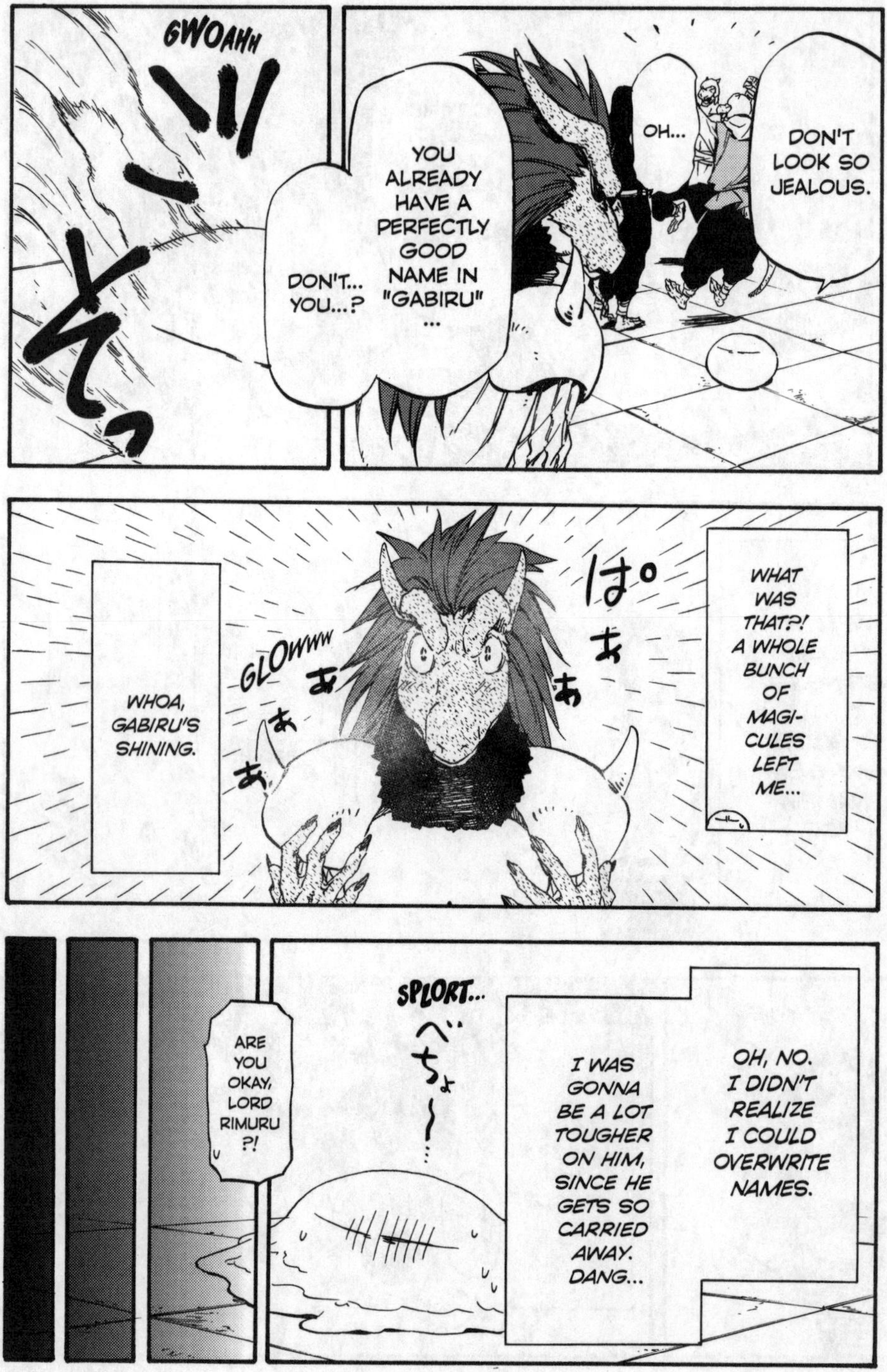
DON'T LOOK SO JEALOUS.
OH...
YOU ALREADY HAVE A PERFECTLY GOOD NAME IN "GABIRU" ...
DON'T... YOU...?
GWOAHH
WHAT WAS THAT?! A WHOLE BUNCH OF MAGI-CULES LEFT ME...
はっ
あ
あ
GLOWWW
あ
あ
あ
WHOA, GABIRU'S SHINING.
OH, NO. I DIDN'T REALIZE I COULD OVERWRITE NAMES.
I WAS GONNA BE A LOT TOUGHER ON HIM, SINCE HE GETS SO CARRIED AWAY. DANG...
SPLORT...
べちょ～…
ARE YOU OKAY, LORD RIMURU ?!

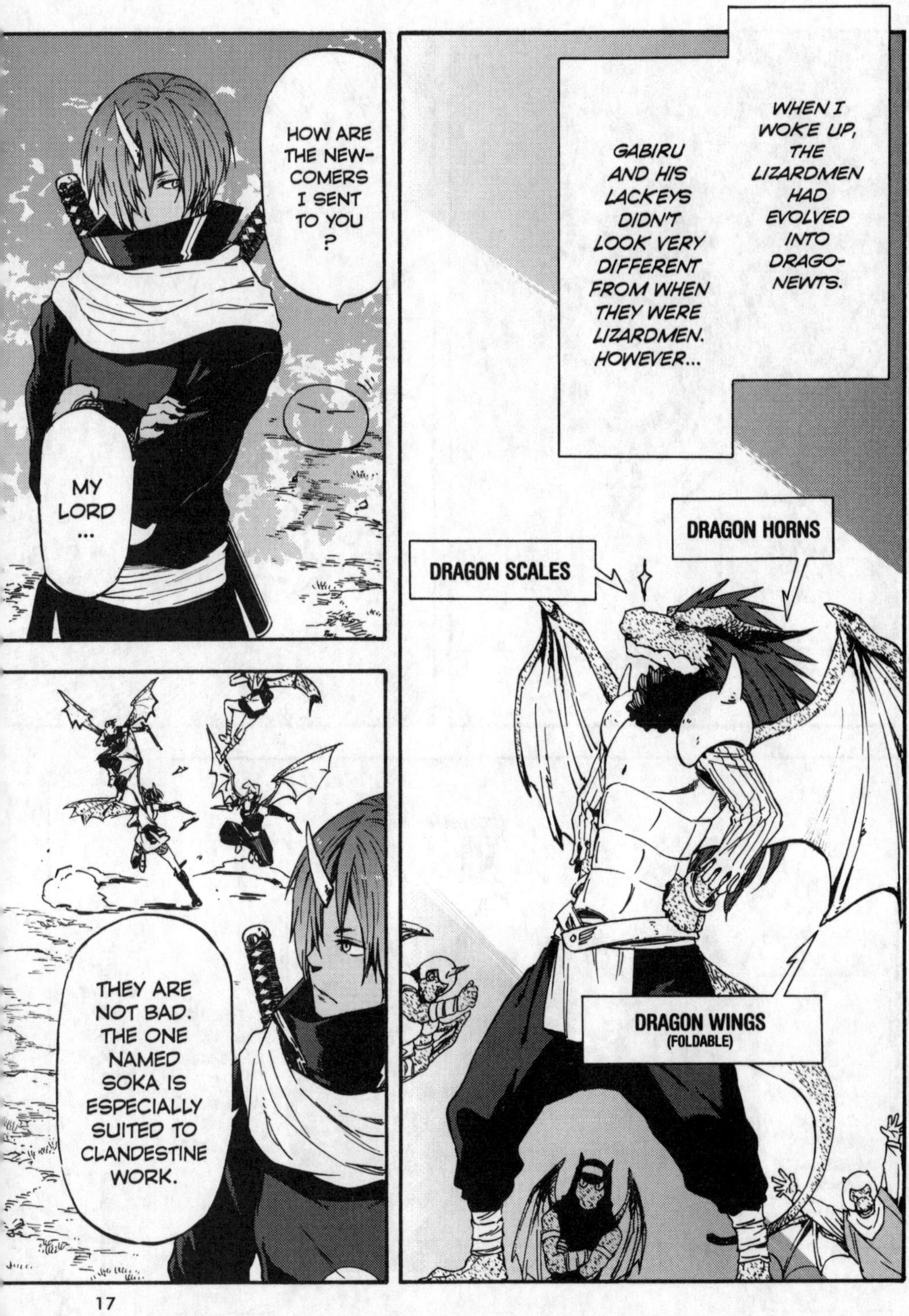
WHEN I WOKE UP, THE LIZARDMEN HAD EVOLVED INTO DRAGONEWTS.
GABIRU AND HIS LACKEYS DIDN'T LOOK VERY DIFFERENT FROM WHEN THEY WERE LIZARDMEN. HOWEVER...
DRAGON HORNS
DRAGON SCALES
DRAGON WINGS (FOLDABLE)
HOW ARE THE NEW-COMERS I SENT TO YOU?
MY LORD...
THEY ARE NOT BAD. THE ONE NAMED SOKA IS ESPECIALLY SUITED TO CLANDESTINE WORK.

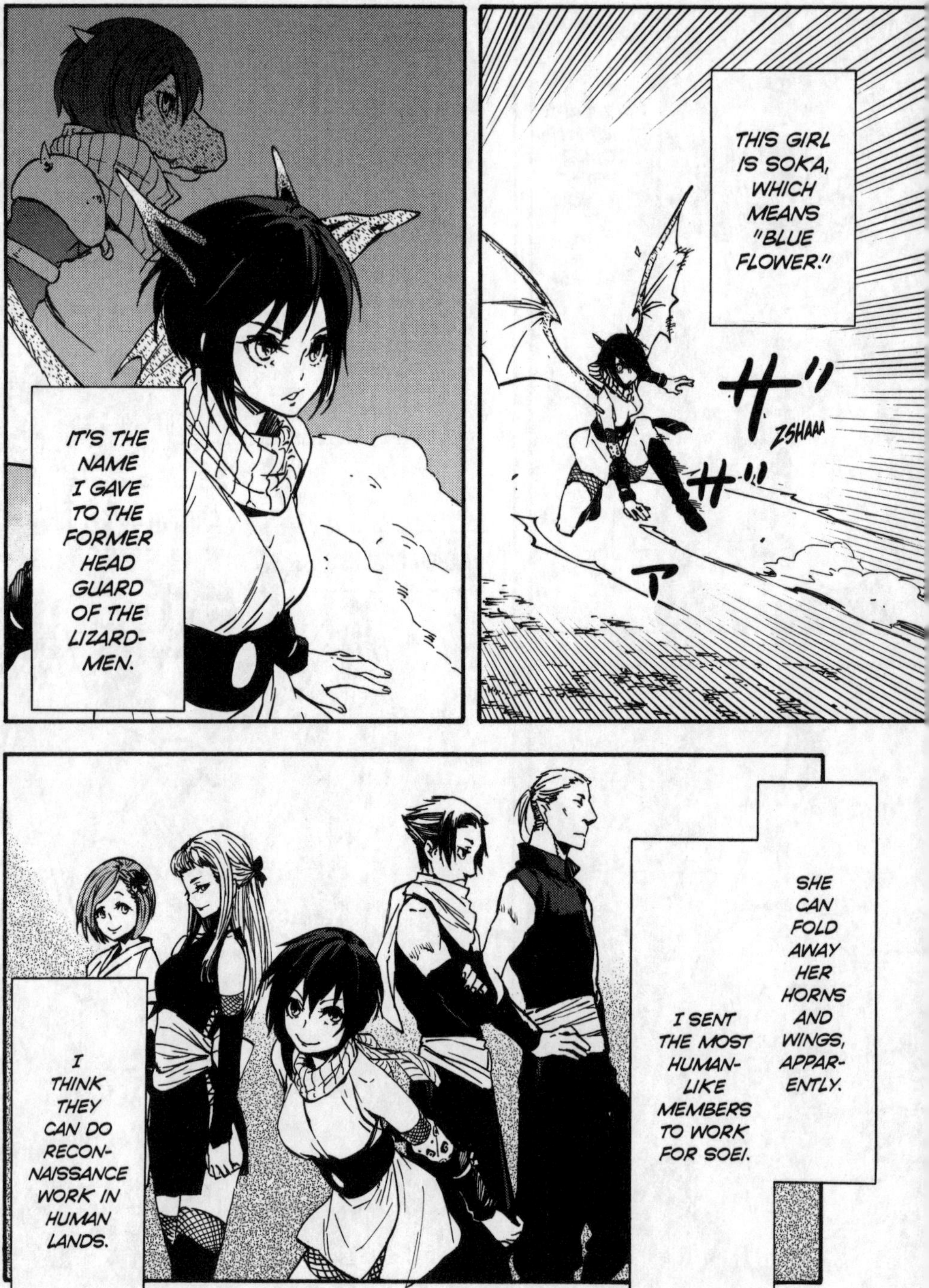
THIS GIRL IS SOKA, WHICH MEANS "BLUE FLOWER."
ZSHAAA
IT'S THE NAME I GAVE TO THE FORMER HEAD GUARD OF THE LIZARD-MEN.
SHE CAN FOLD AWAY HER HORNS AND WINGS, APPAR-ENTLY.
I SENT THE MOST HUMAN-LIKE MEMBERS TO WORK FOR SOEI.
I THINK THEY CAN DO RECON-NAISSANCE WORK IN HUMAN LANDS.

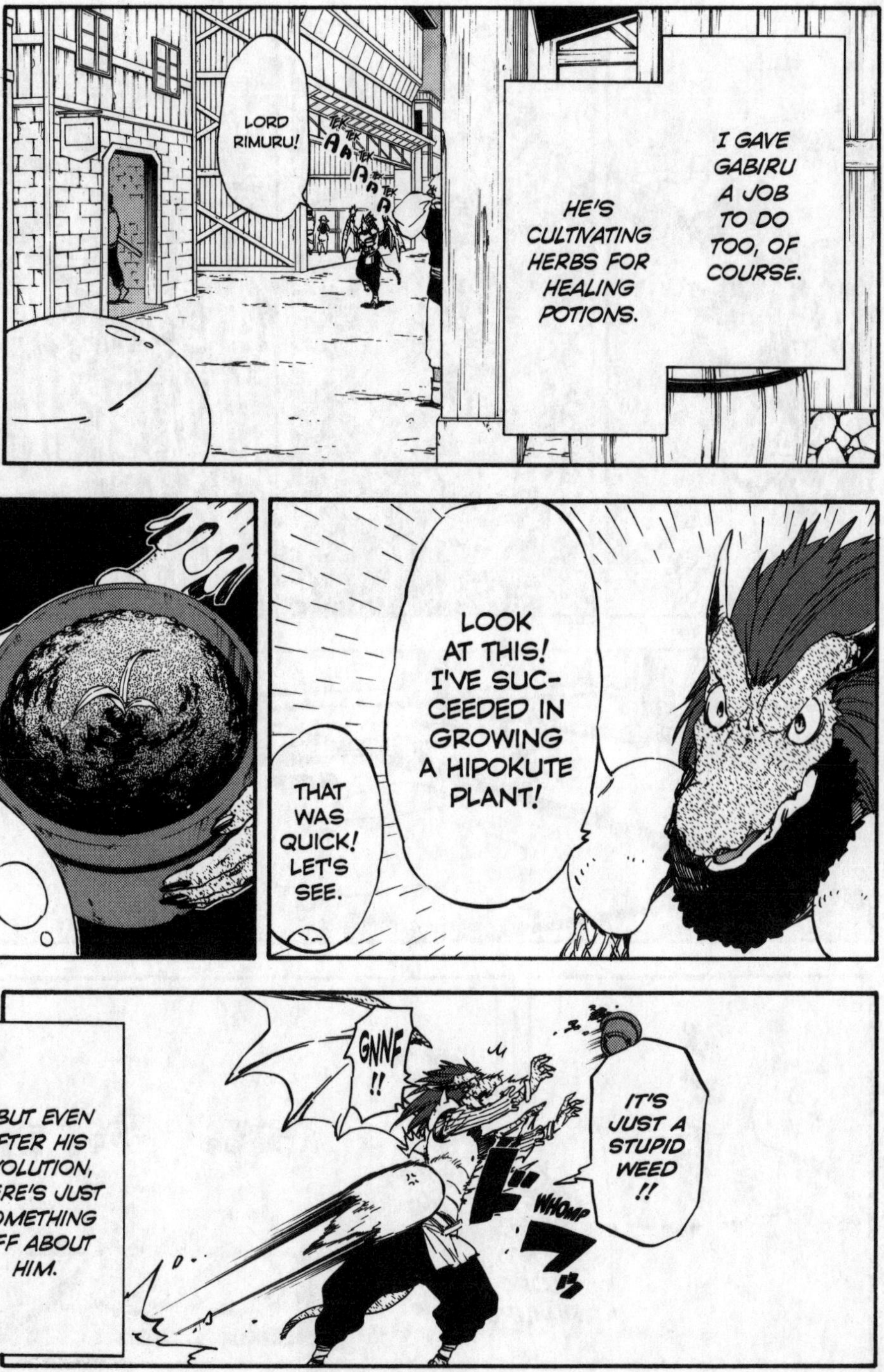
I GAVE GABIRU A JOB TO DO TOO, OF COURSE.
HE'S CULTIVATING HERBS FOR HEALING POTIONS.
LORD RIMURU!
TEK TEK TEK TEK
LOOK AT THIS! I'VE SUC-CEEDED IN GROWING A HIPOKUTE PLANT!
THAT WAS QUICK! LET'S SEE.
IT'S JUST A STUPID WEED!!
WHOMP
GNNF!!
...BUT EVEN AFTER HIS EVOLUTION, THERE'S JUST SOMETHING OFF ABOUT HIM.

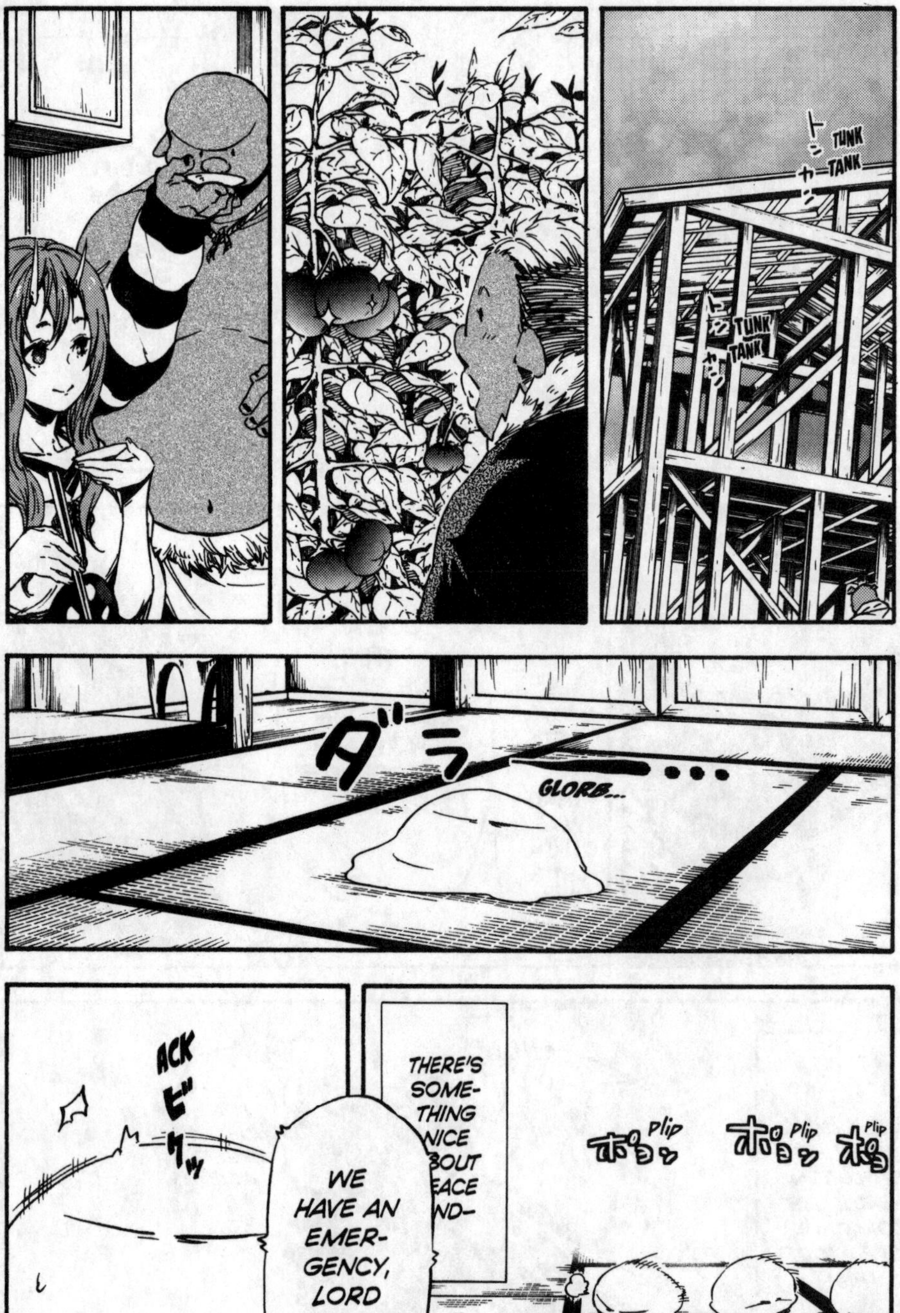
トン TUNK
カン TANK
トン TUNK
カン TANK
ダラ—…
GLORB...
ポヨン Plip
ポヨン Plip
ポヨ Plip
THERE'S SOME-THING NICE BOUT EACE ND-
WE HAVE AN EMER-GENCY, LORD RIMURU.
ACK
ビクッ

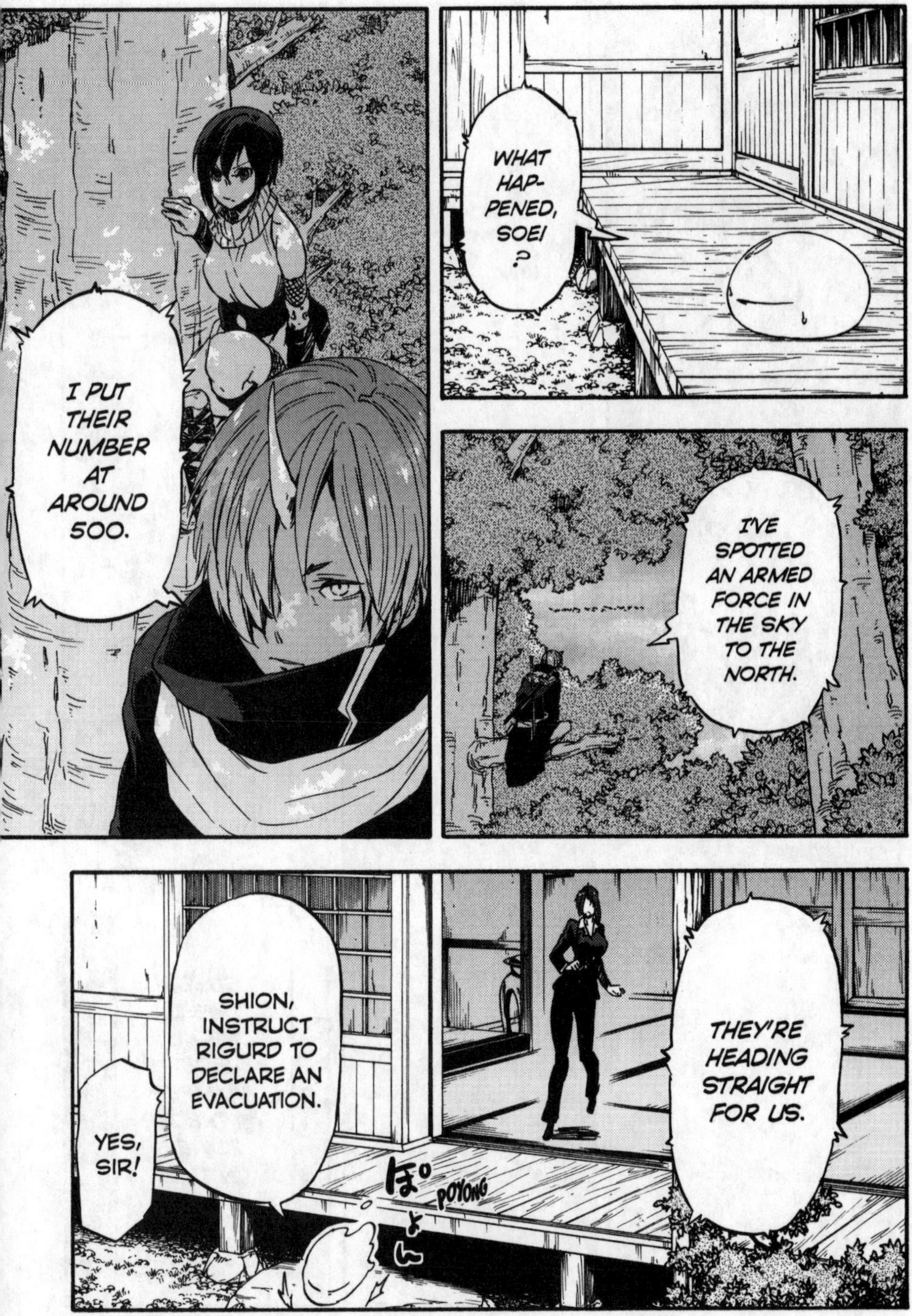
WHAT HAP-PENED, SOEI?
I'VE SPOTTED AN ARMED FORCE IN THE SKY TO THE NORTH.
I PUT THEIR NUMBER AT AROUND 500.
THEY'RE HEADING STRAIGHT FOR US.
SHION, INSTRUCT RIGURD TO DECLARE AN EVACUATION.
YES, SIR!
ぽよん
POYONG

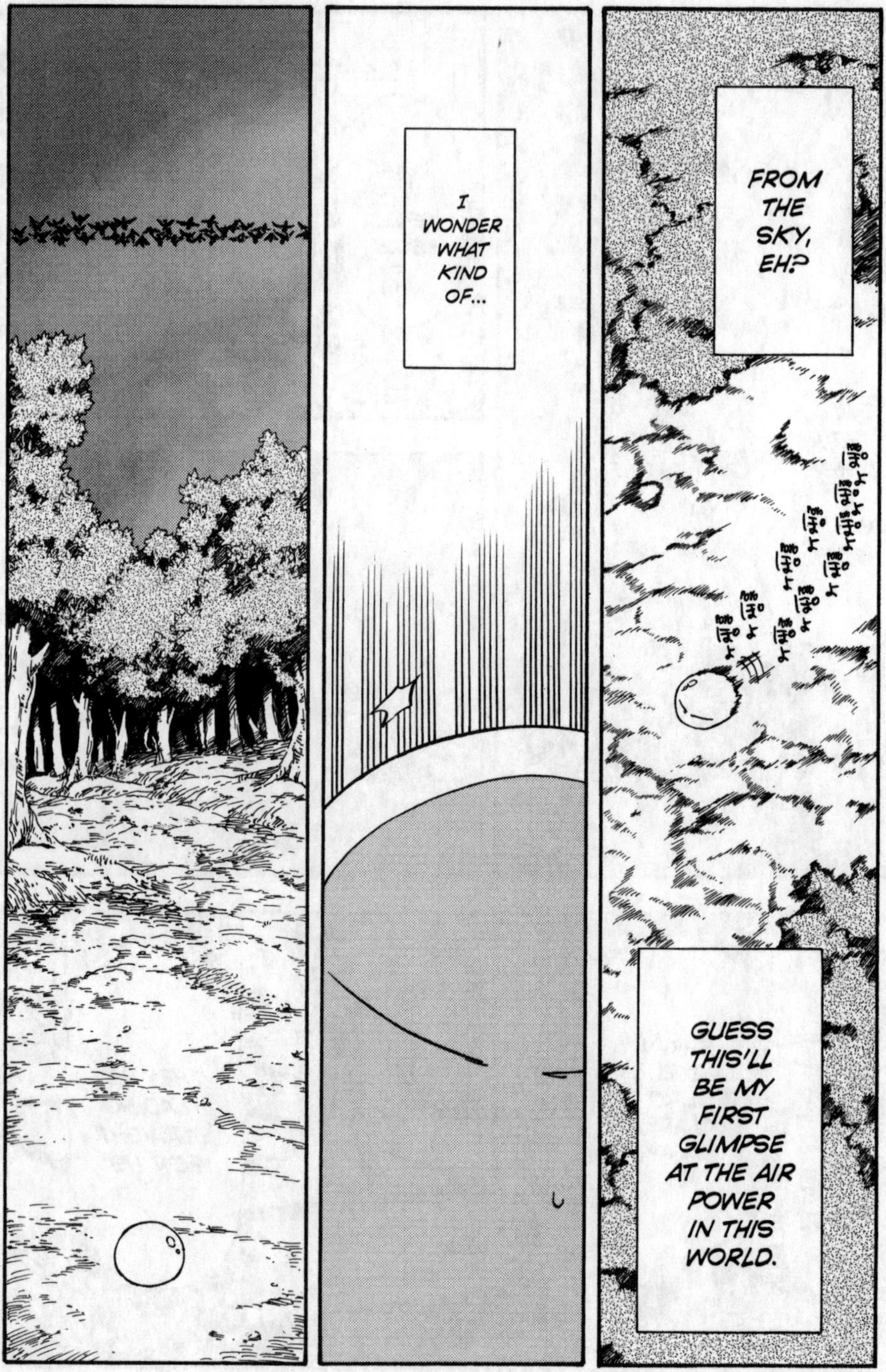
FROM THE SKY, EH?
ぽよ ぽよ ぽよ ぽよ ぽよ ぽよ ぽよ ぽよ ぽよ ぽよ
GUESS THIS'LL BE MY FIRST GLIMPSE AT THE AIR POWER IN THIS WORLD.
I WONDER WHAT KIND OF...

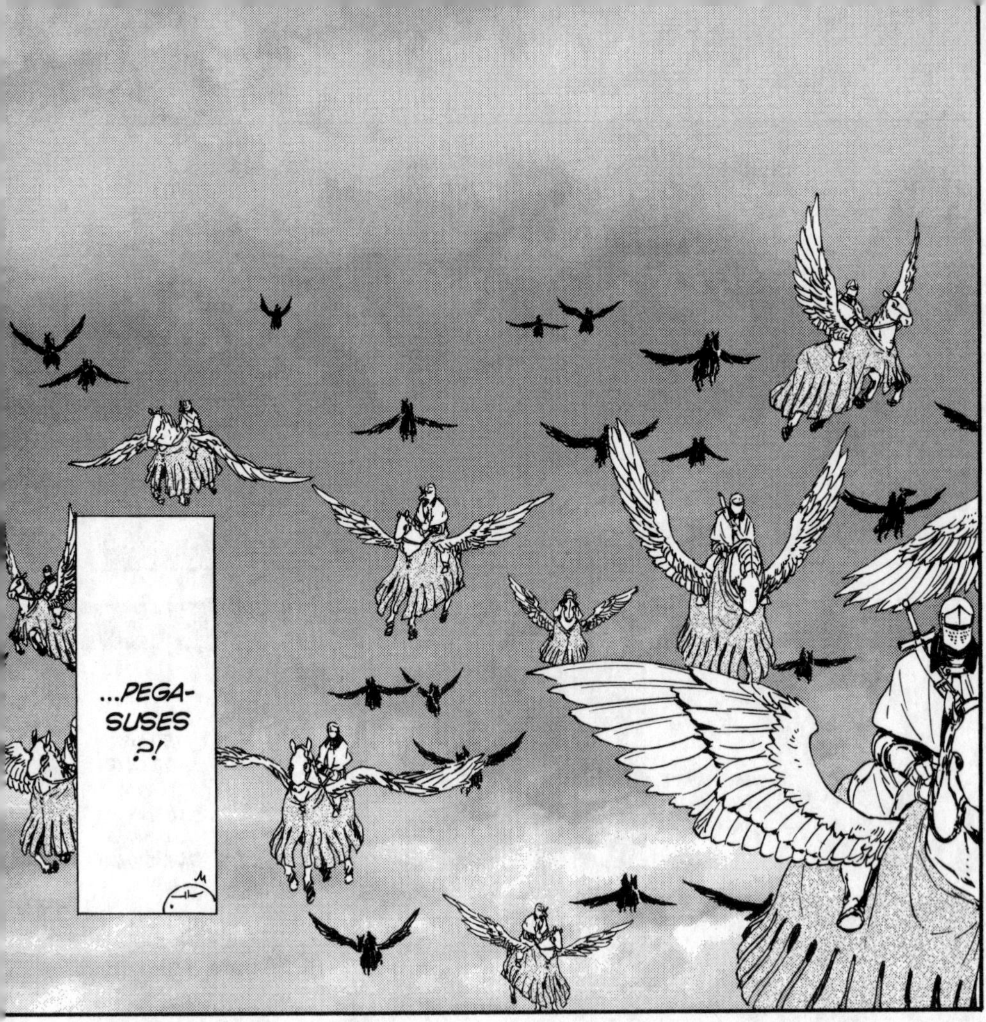
...PEGA-
SUSES
?!

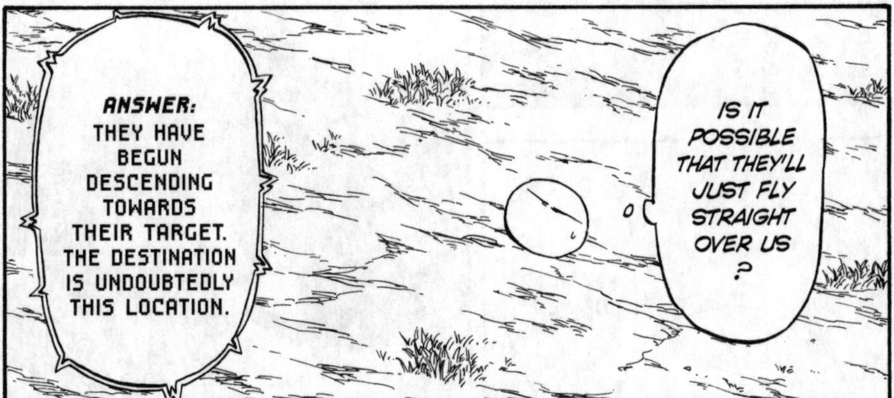
IS IT POSSIBLE THAT THEY'LL JUST FLY STRAIGHT OVER US ?
ANSWER: THEY HAVE BEGUN DESCENDING TOWARDS THEIR TARGET. THE DESTINATION IS UNDOUBTEDLY THIS LOCATION.

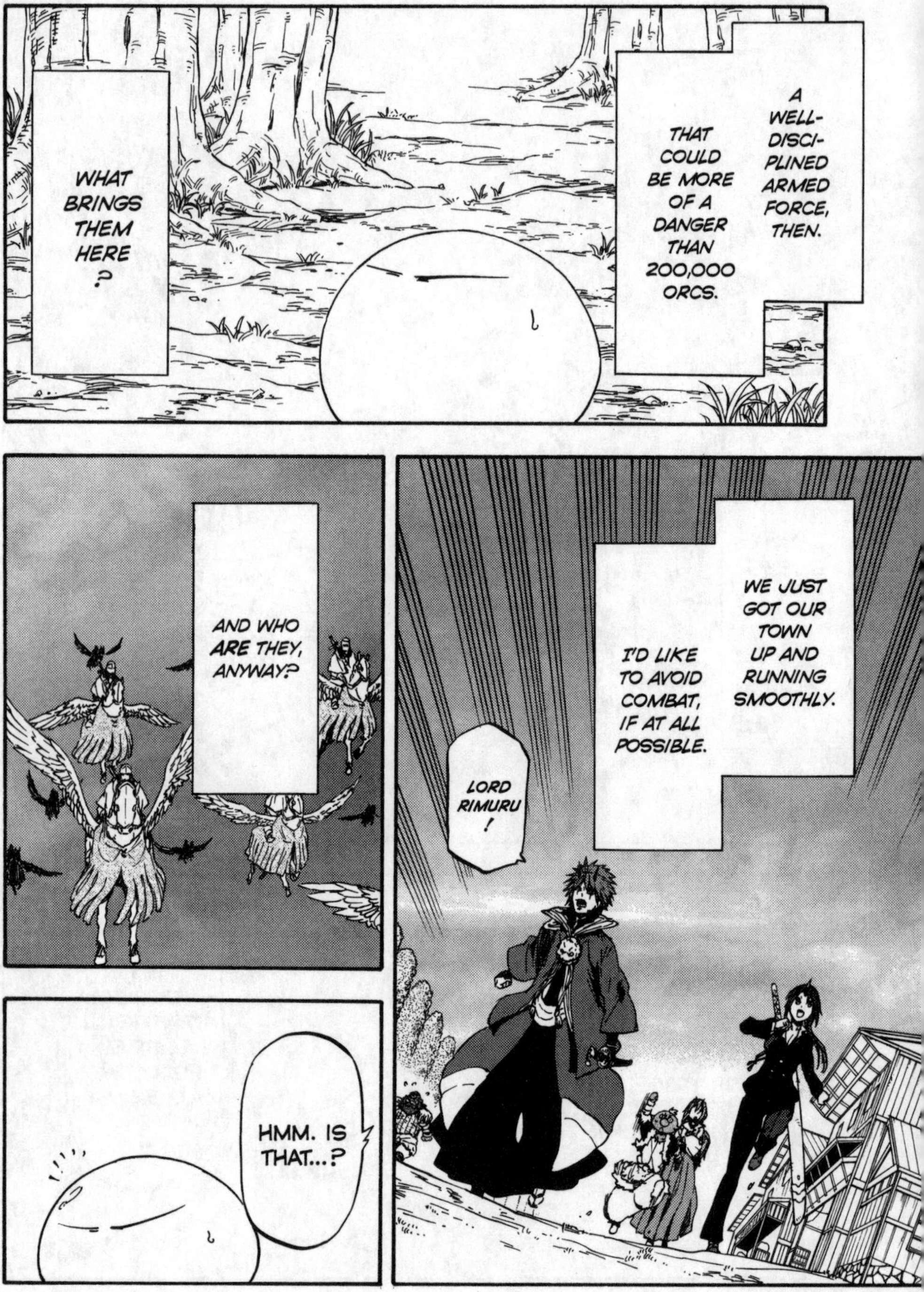
A WELL-DISCIPLINED ARMED FORCE, THEN.
THAT COULD BE MORE OF A DANGER THAN 200,000 ORCS.
WHAT BRINGS THEM HERE?
WE JUST GOT OUR TOWN UP AND RUNNING SMOOTHLY.
I'D LIKE TO AVOID COMBAT, IF AT ALL POSSIBLE.
LORD RIMURU!
AND WHO ARE THEY, ANYWAY?
HMM. IS THAT...?

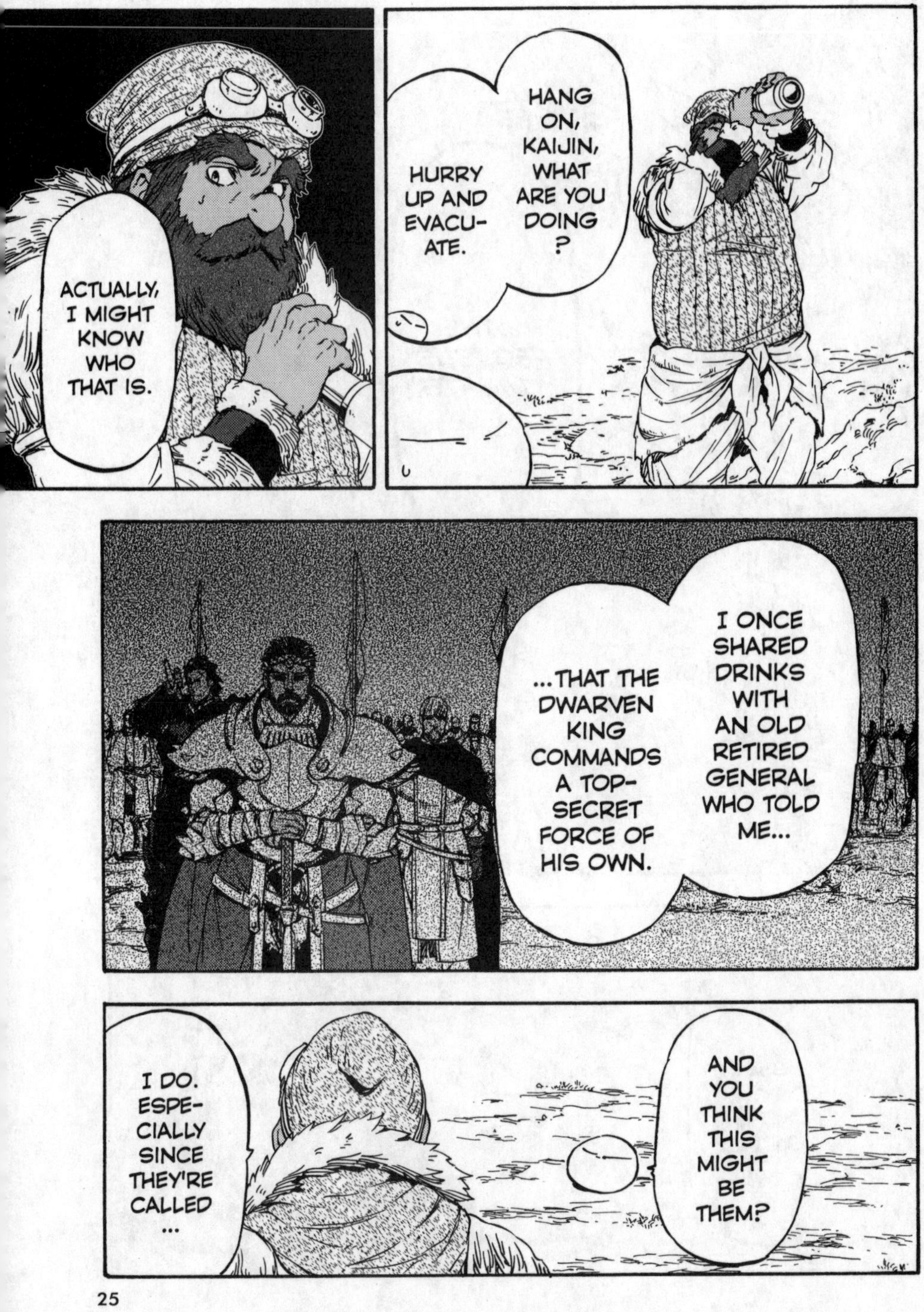
HANG ON, KAIJIN, WHAT ARE YOU DOING ?
HURRY UP AND EVACU-ATE.
ACTUALLY, I MIGHT KNOW WHO THAT IS.
I ONCE SHARED DRINKS WITH AN OLD RETIRED GENERAL WHO TOLD ME...
...THAT THE DWARVEN KING COMMANDS A TOP-SECRET FORCE OF HIS OWN.
AND YOU THINK THIS MIGHT BE THEM?
I DO. ESPE-CIALLY SINCE THEY'RE CALLED ...

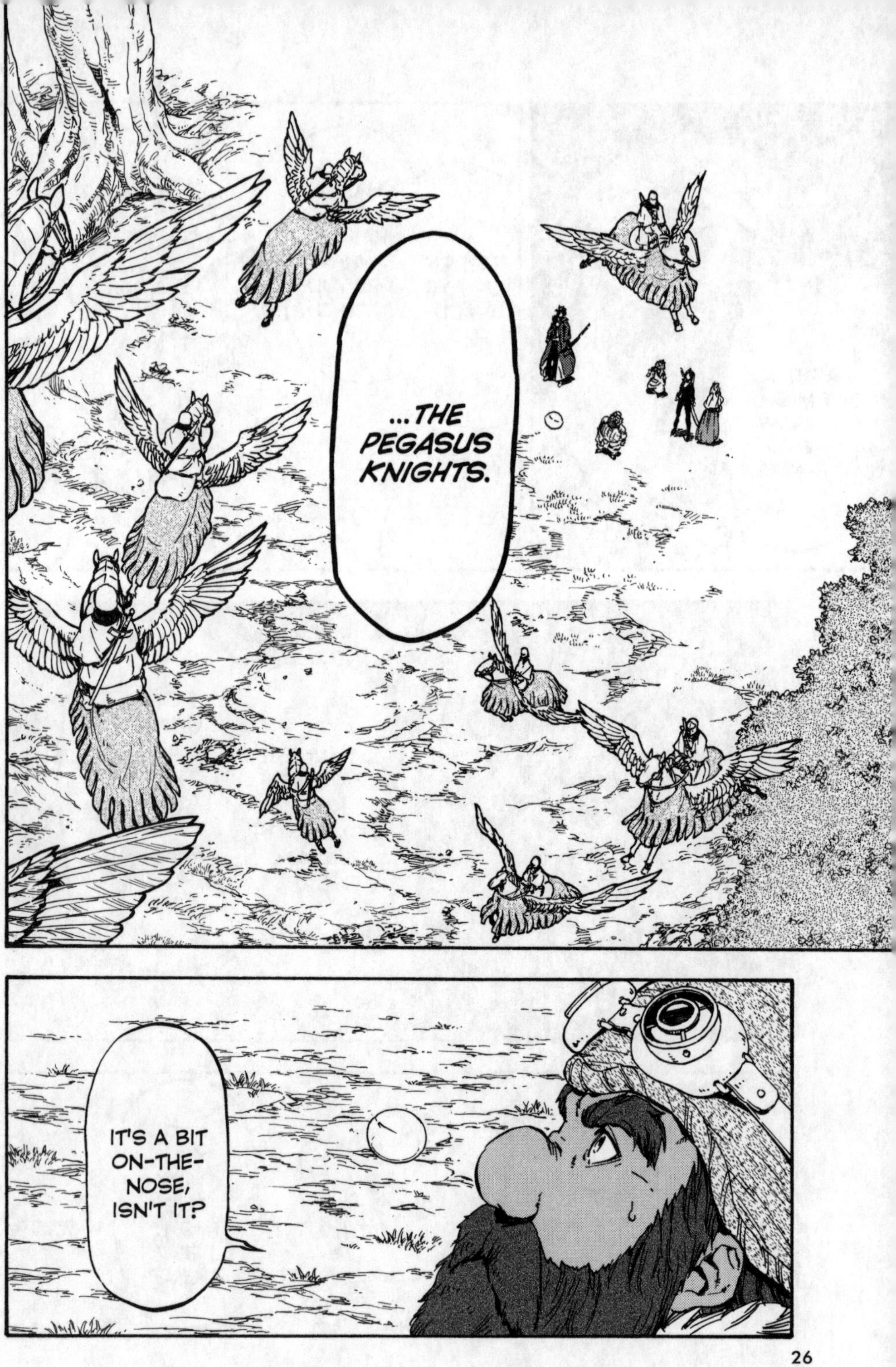
...THE PEGASUS KNIGHTS.
IT'S A BIT ON-THE-NOSE, ISN'T IT?

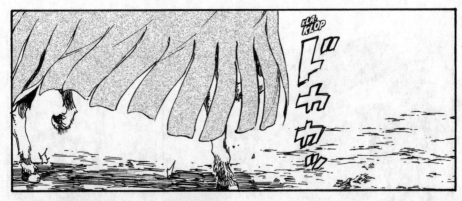

KLA-
KLOP

SWISH

IT IS
GOOD
TO SEE
YOU ARE
WELL...

....!

27

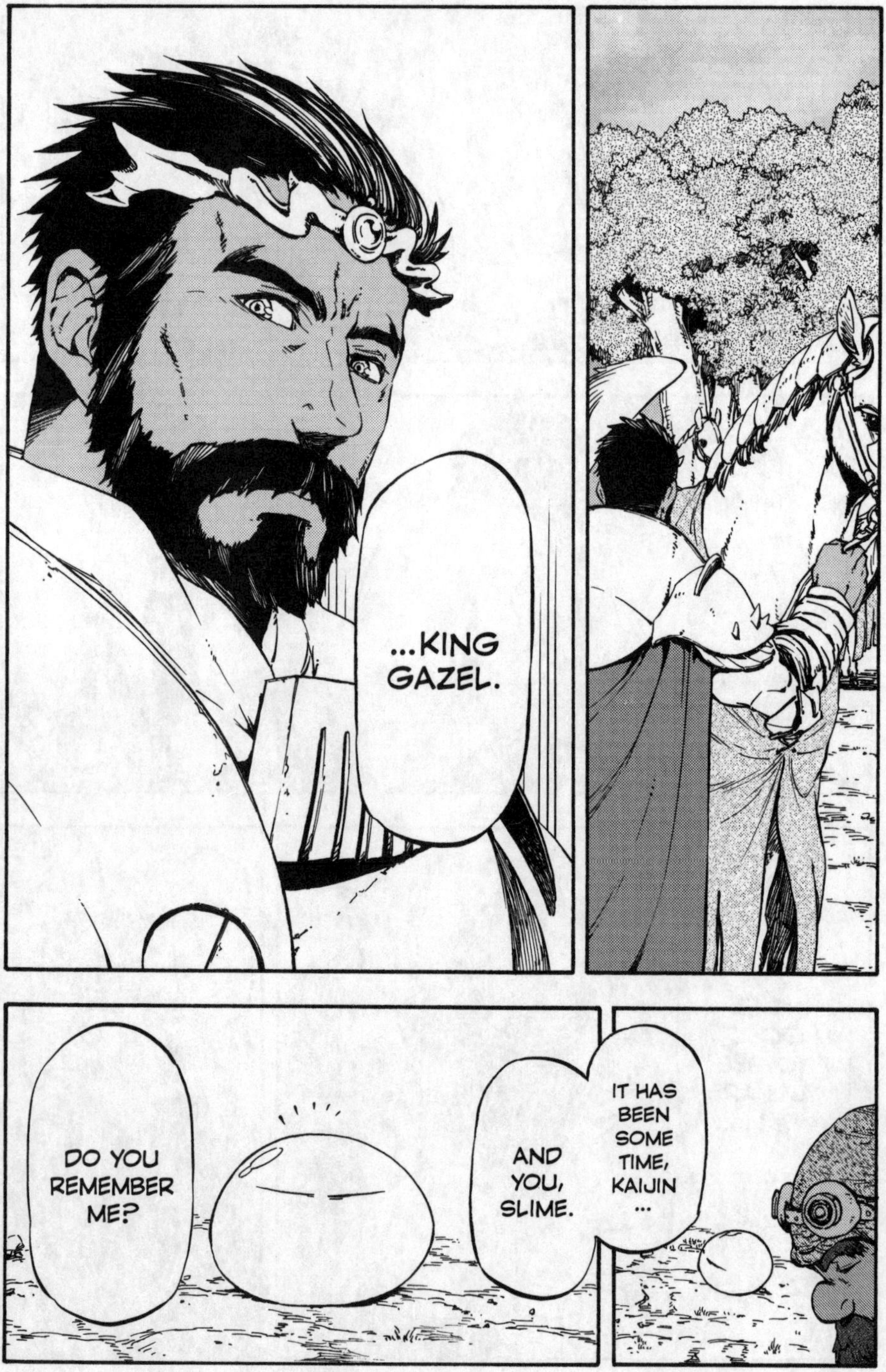
...KING GAZEL.
IT HAS BEEN SOME TIME, KAIJIN...
AND YOU, SLIME.
DO YOU REMEMBER ME?

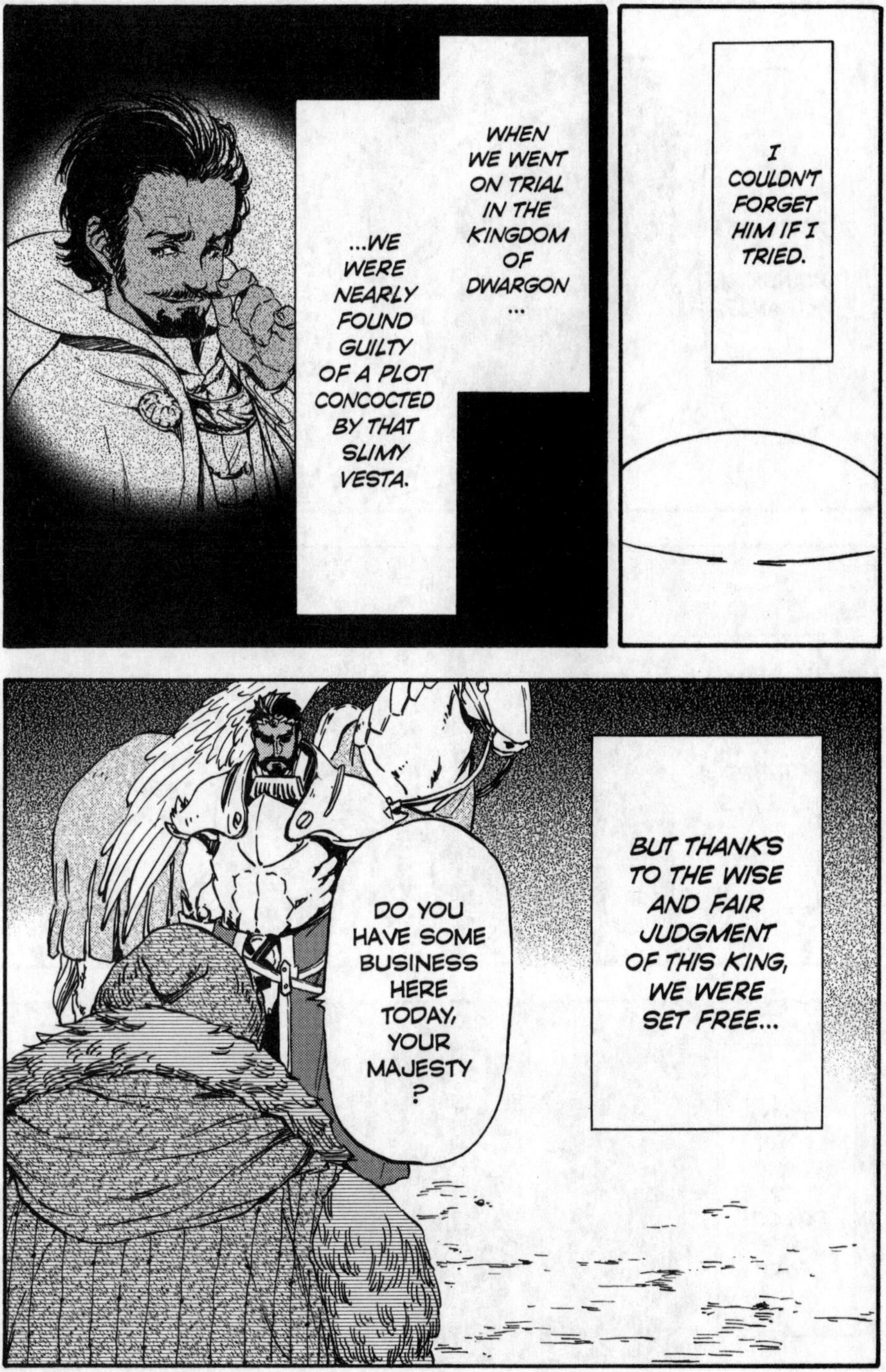
I COULDN'T FORGET HIM IF I TRIED.
WHEN WE WENT ON TRIAL IN THE KINGDOM OF DWARGON...
...WE WERE NEARLY FOUND GUILTY OF A PLOT CONCOCTED BY THAT SLIMY VESTA.
BUT THANKS TO THE WISE AND FAIR JUDGMENT OF THIS KING, WE WERE SET FREE...
DO YOU HAVE SOME BUSINESS HERE TODAY, YOUR MAJESTY?

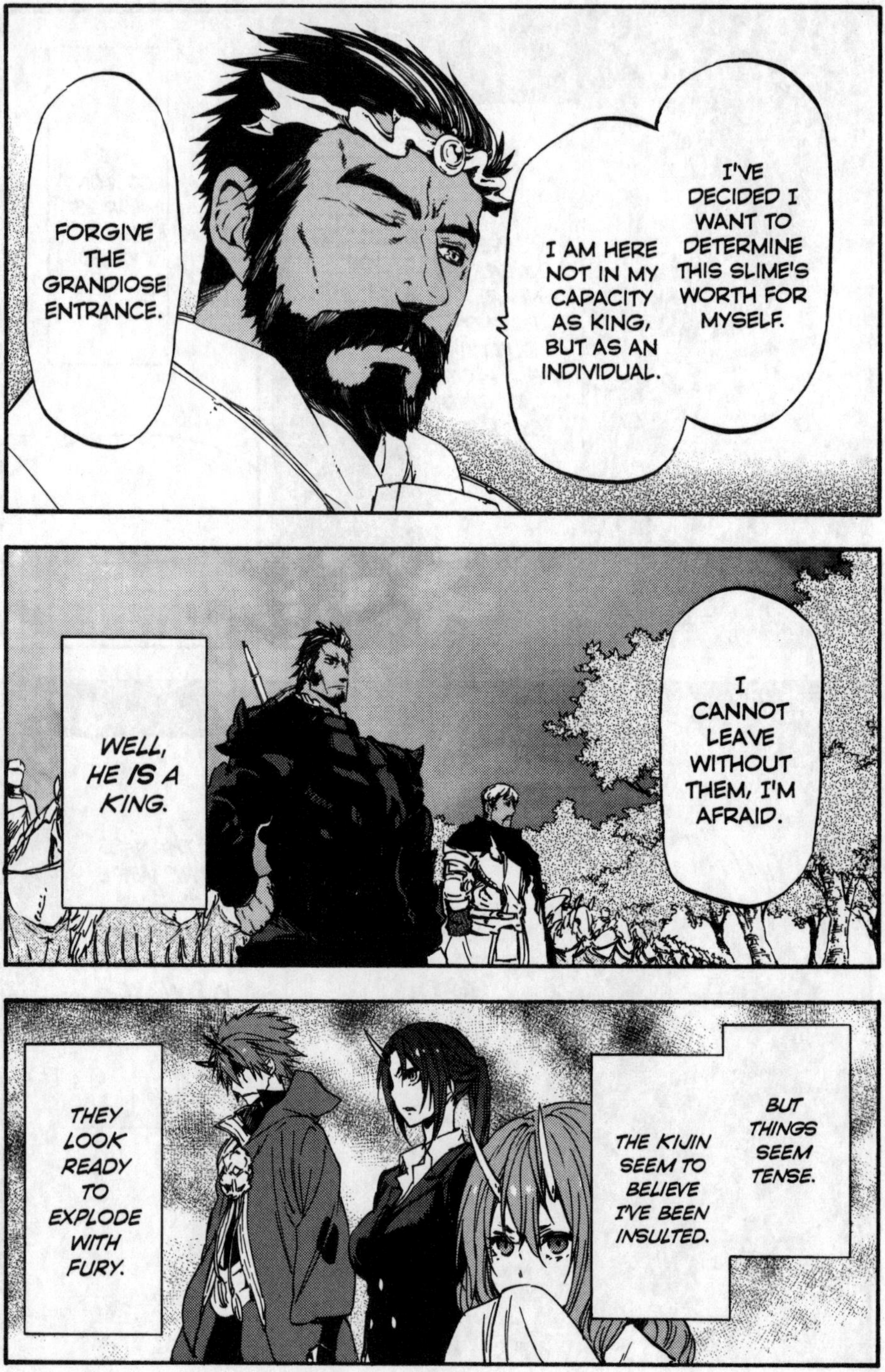
I'VE DECIDED I WANT TO DETERMINE THIS SLIME'S WORTH FOR MYSELF.
I AM HERE NOT IN MY CAPACITY AS KING, BUT AS AN INDIVIDUAL.
FORGIVE THE GRANDIOSE ENTRANCE.
I CANNOT LEAVE WITHOUT THEM, I'M AFRAID.
WELL, HE IS A KING.
BUT THINGS SEEM TENSE.
THE KIJIN SEEM TO BELIEVE I'VE BEEN INSULTED.
THEY LOOK READY TO EXPLODE WITH FURY.

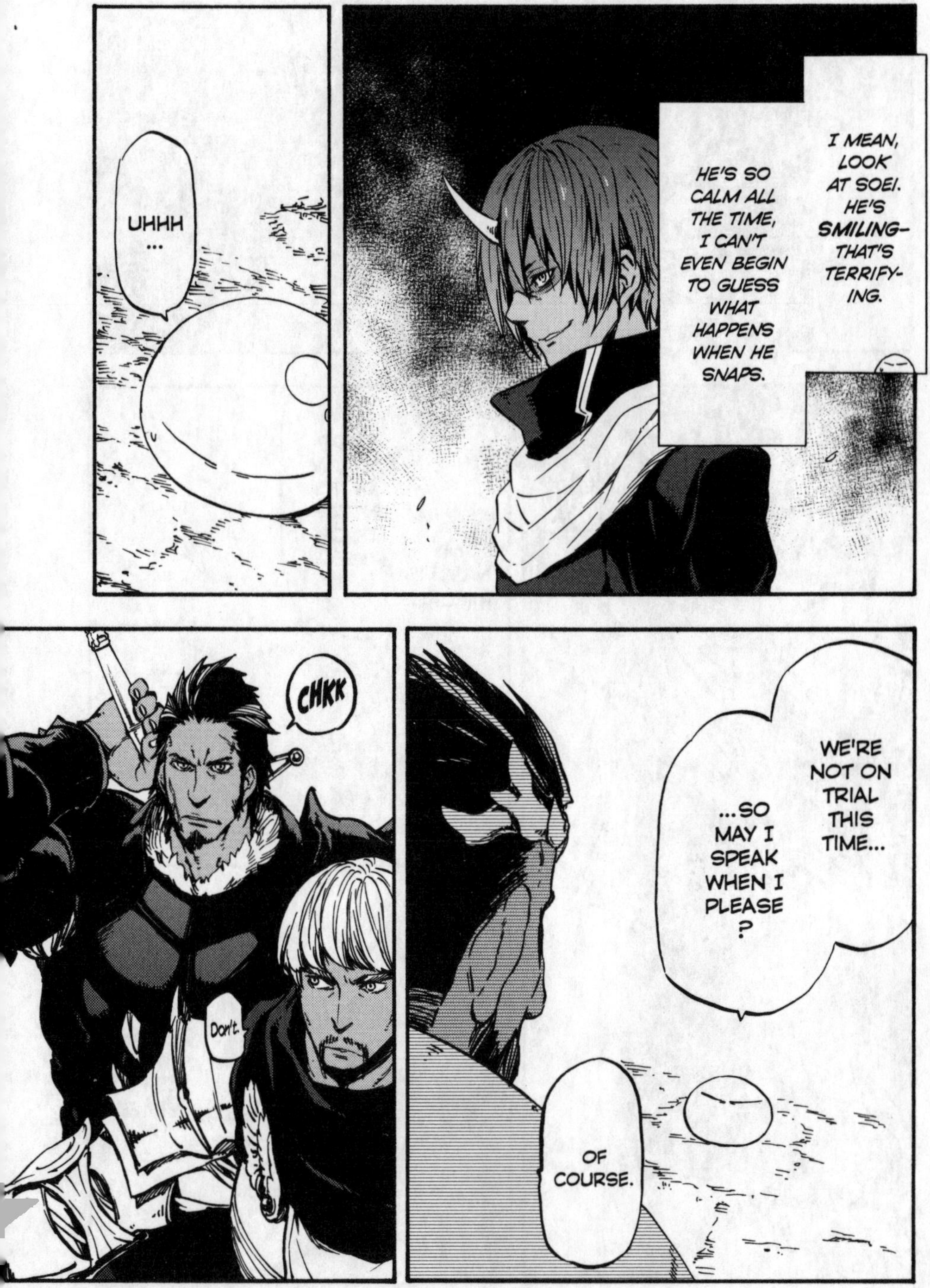
I MEAN, LOOK AT SOEI. HE'S SMILING—THAT'S TERRIFYING.
HE'S SO CALM ALL THE TIME, I CAN'T EVEN BEGIN TO GUESS WHAT HAPPENS WHEN HE SNAPS.
UHHH...
WE'RE NOT ON TRIAL THIS TIME...
...SO MAY I SPEAK WHEN I PLEASE?
OF COURSE.
CHKK
Don't.

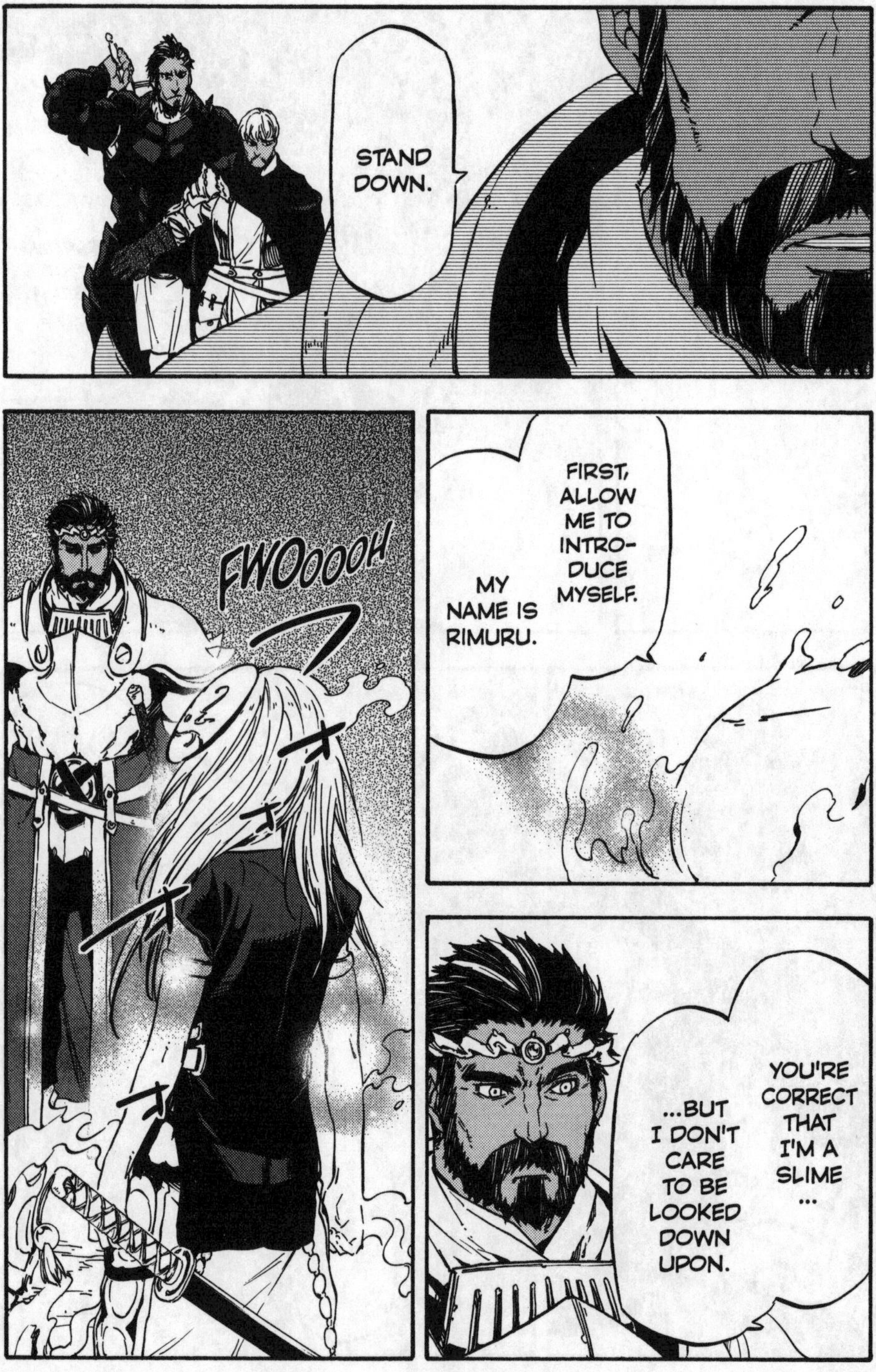
STAND DOWN.
FIRST, ALLOW ME TO INTRO- DUCE MYSELF.
MY NAME IS RIMURU.
YOU'RE CORRECT THAT I'M A SLIME ...
...BUT I DON'T CARE TO BE LOOKED DOWN UPON.
FWOOOOH

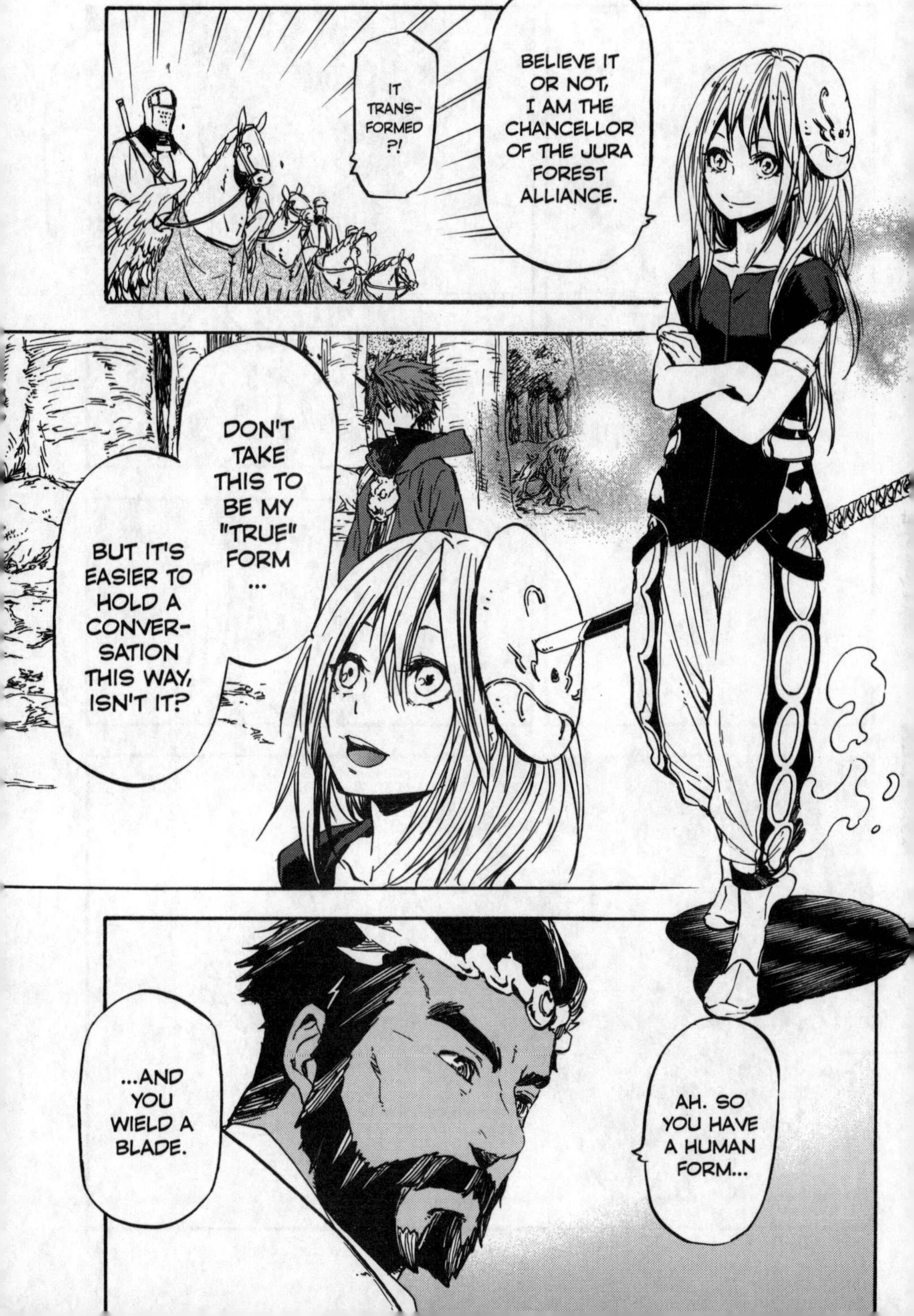
BELIEVE IT OR NOT, I AM THE CHANCELLOR OF THE JURA FOREST ALLIANCE.
IT TRANSFORMED ?!
DON'T TAKE THIS TO BE MY "TRUE" FORM ...
BUT IT'S EASIER TO HOLD A CONVERSATION THIS WAY, ISN'T IT?
AH. SO YOU HAVE A HUMAN FORM...
...AND YOU WIELD A BLADE.

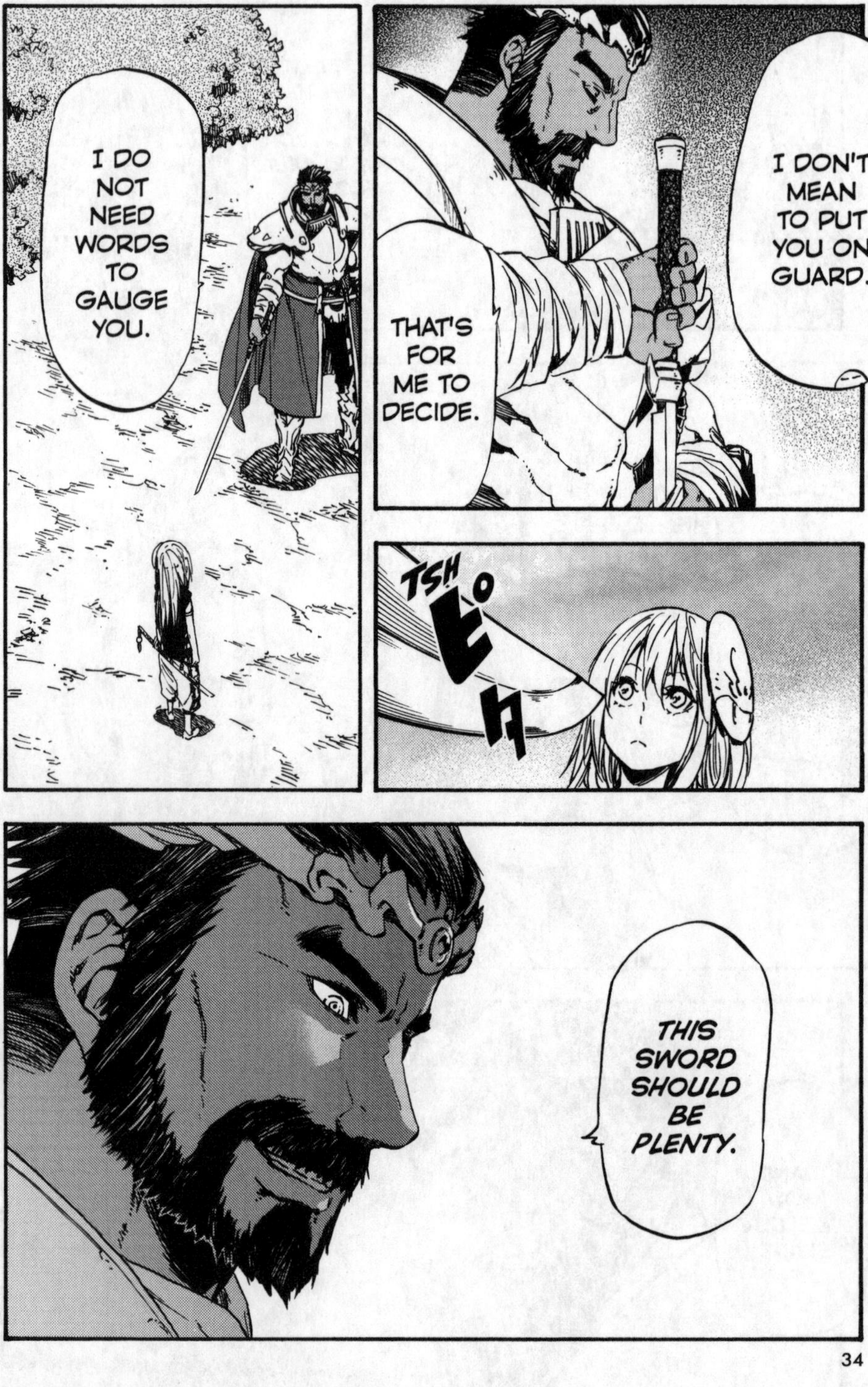
I DON'T MEAN TO PUT YOU ON GUARD.
THAT'S FOR ME TO DECIDE.
TSH
I DO NOT NEED WORDS TO GAUGE YOU.
THIS SWORD SHOULD BE PLENTY.

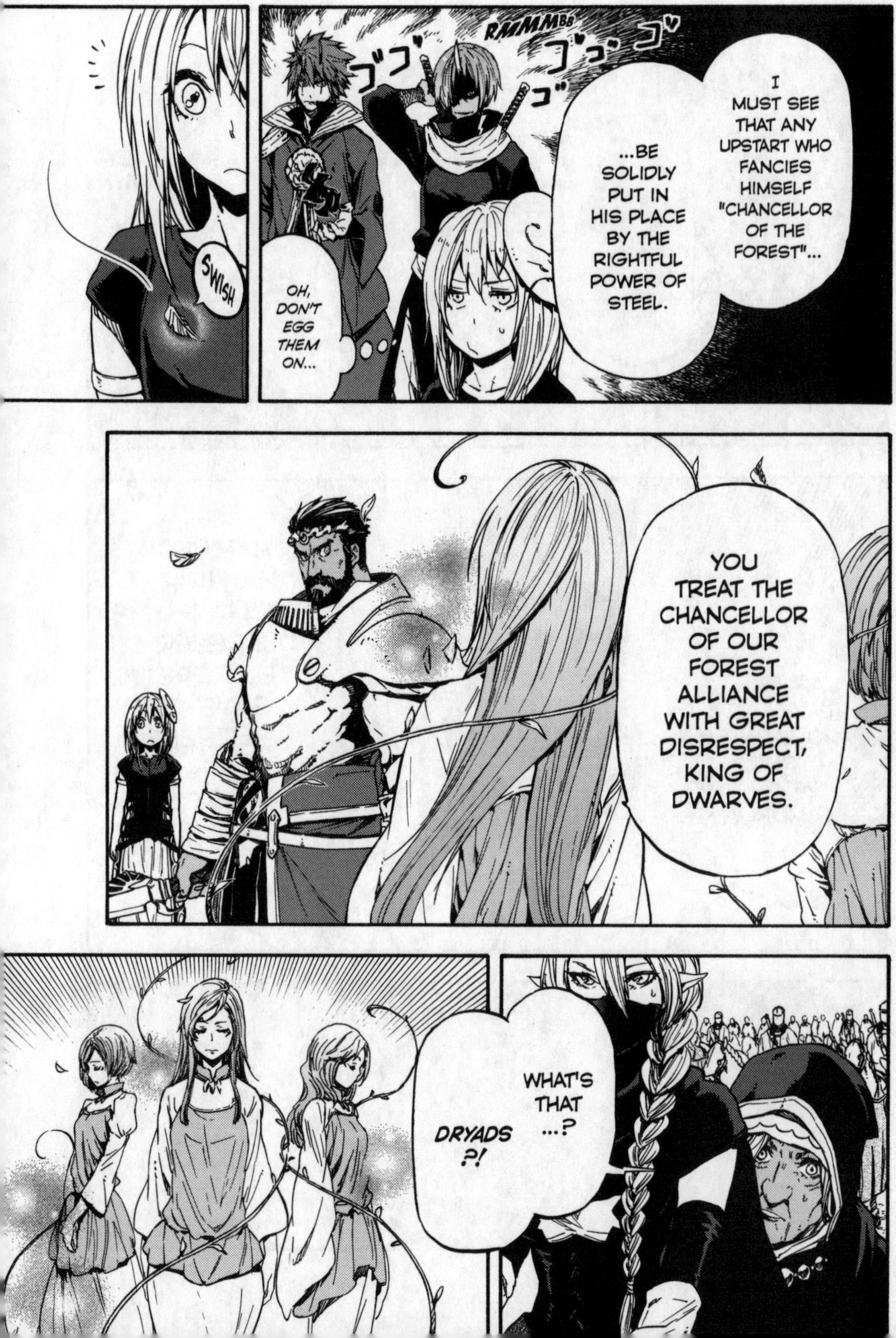
RMMMBB
I MUST SEE THAT ANY UPSTART WHO FANCIES HIMSELF "CHANCELLOR OF THE FOREST"...
...BE SOLIDLY PUT IN HIS PLACE BY THE RIGHTFUL POWER OF STEEL.
OH, DON'T EGG THEM ON...
SWISH
YOU TREAT THE CHANCELLOR OF OUR FOREST ALLIANCE WITH GREAT DISRESPECT, KING OF DWARVES.
WHAT'S THAT ...?
DRYADS ?!

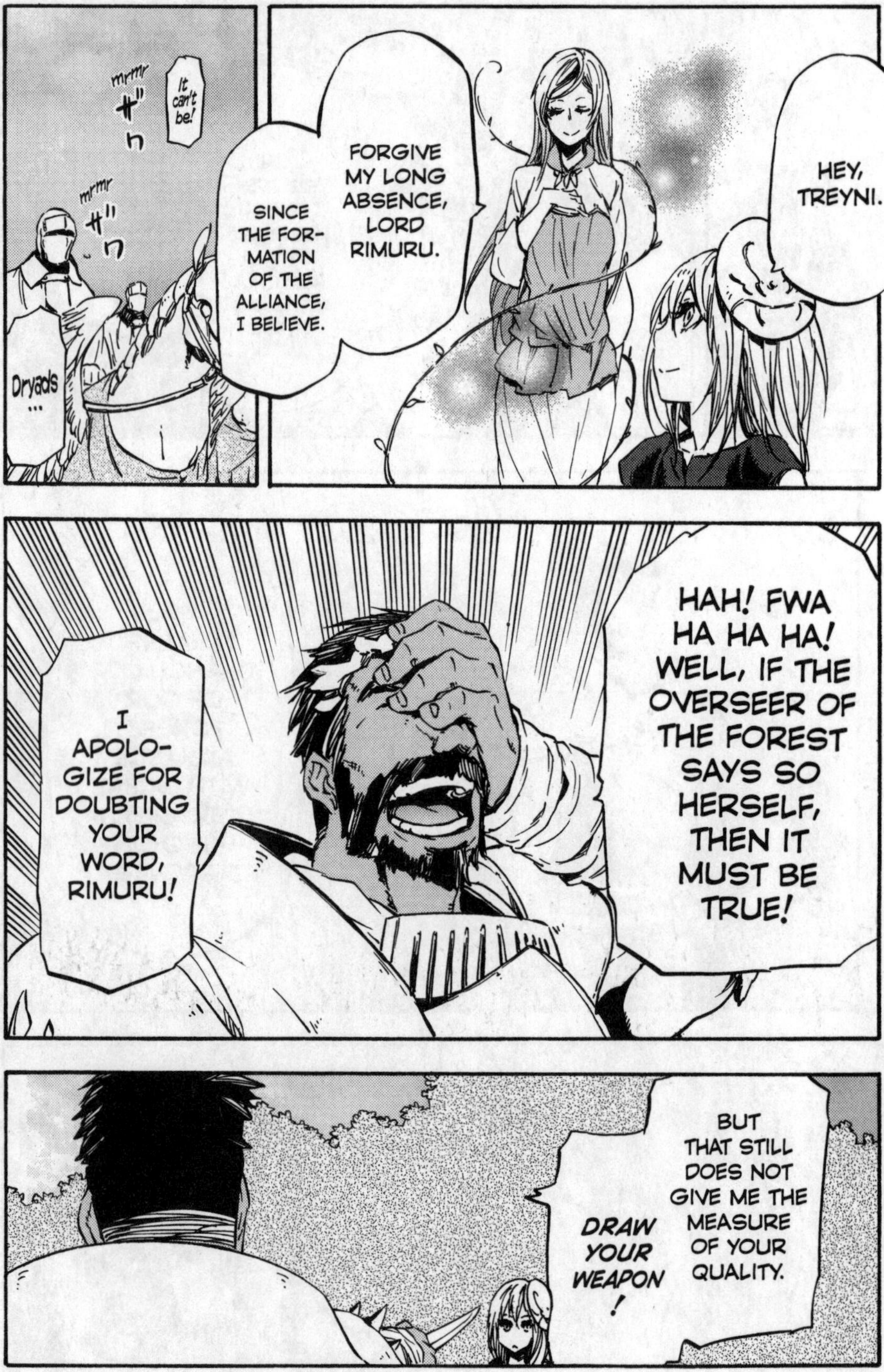
HEY, TREYNI.
FORGIVE MY LONG ABSENCE, LORD RIMURU.
SINCE THE FORMATION OF THE ALLIANCE, I BELIEVE.
mrmr
It can't be!
mrmr
Dryads...
HAH! FWA HA HA HA! WELL, IF THE OVERSEER OF THE FOREST SAYS SO HERSELF, THEN IT MUST BE TRUE!
I APOLOGIZE FOR DOUBTING YOUR WORD, RIMURU!
BUT THAT STILL DOES NOT GIVE ME THE MEASURE OF YOUR QUALITY.
DRAW YOUR WEAPON!

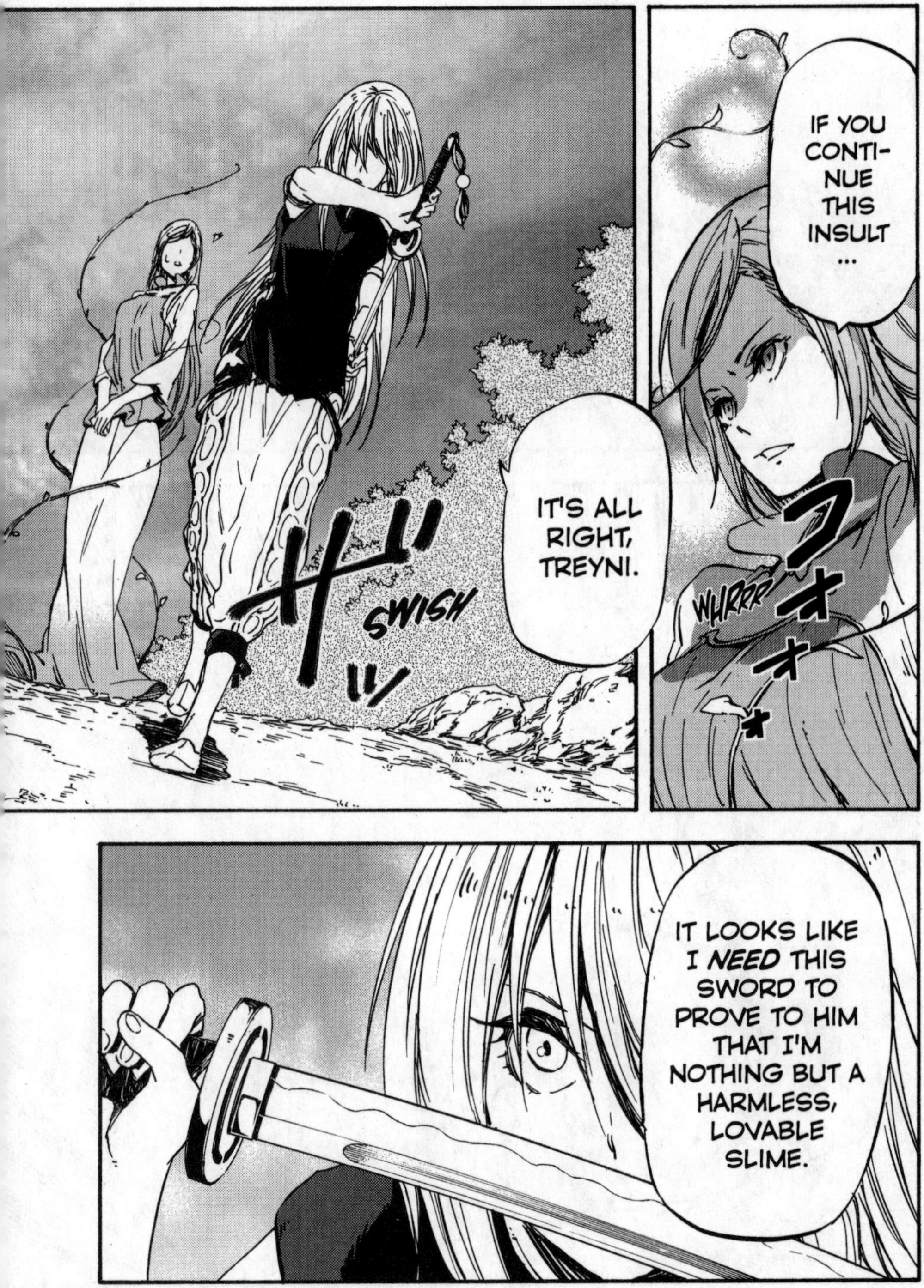
IF YOU CONTI- NUE THIS INSULT ...
フォォォ
WHRRR
IT'S ALL RIGHT, TREYNI.
ザッ
SWISH
IT LOOKS LIKE I *NEED* THIS SWORD TO PROVE TO HIM THAT I'M NOTHING BUT A HARMLESS, LOVABLE SLIME.

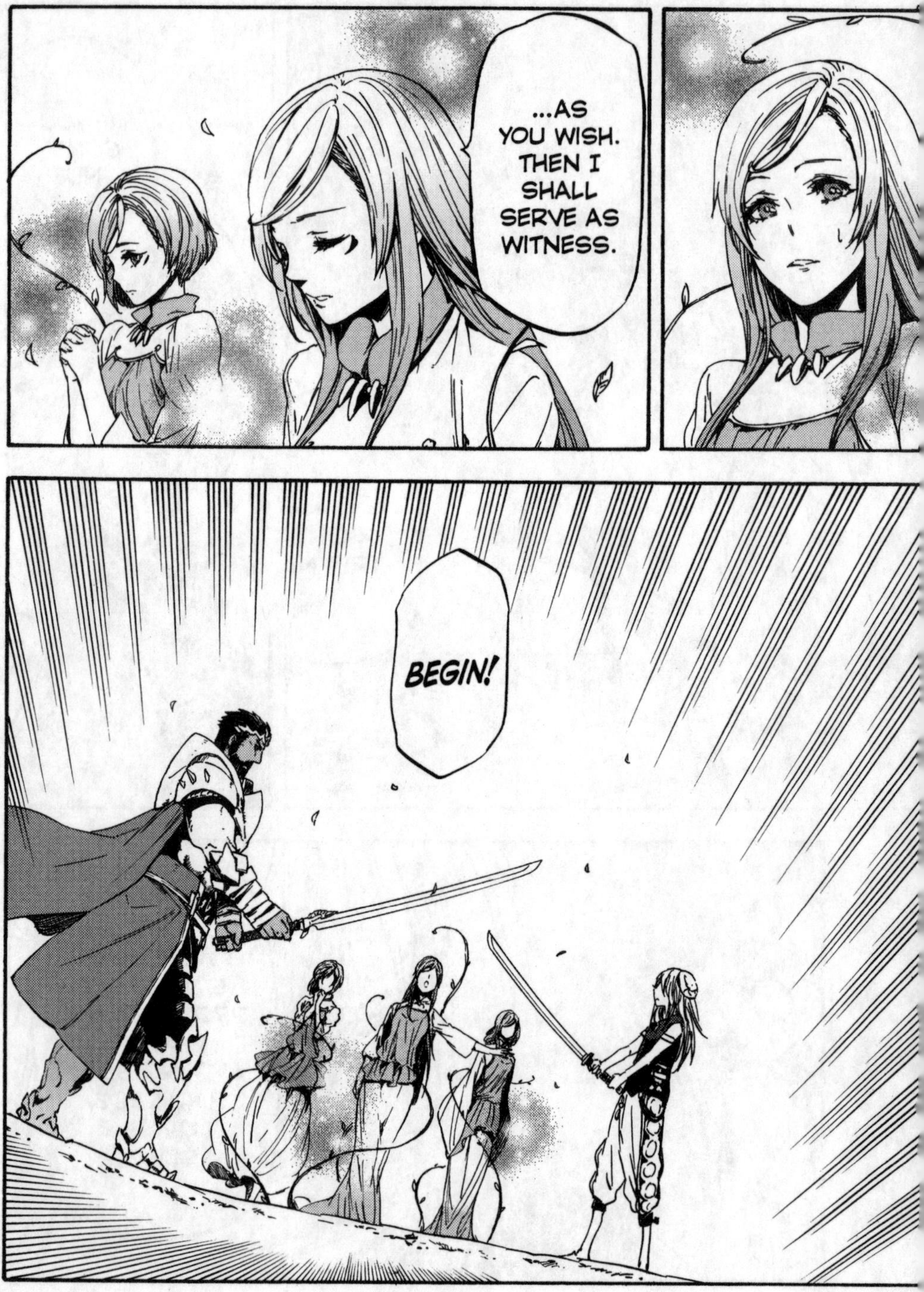
...AS YOU WISH. THEN I SHALL SERVE AS WITNESS.
BEGIN!

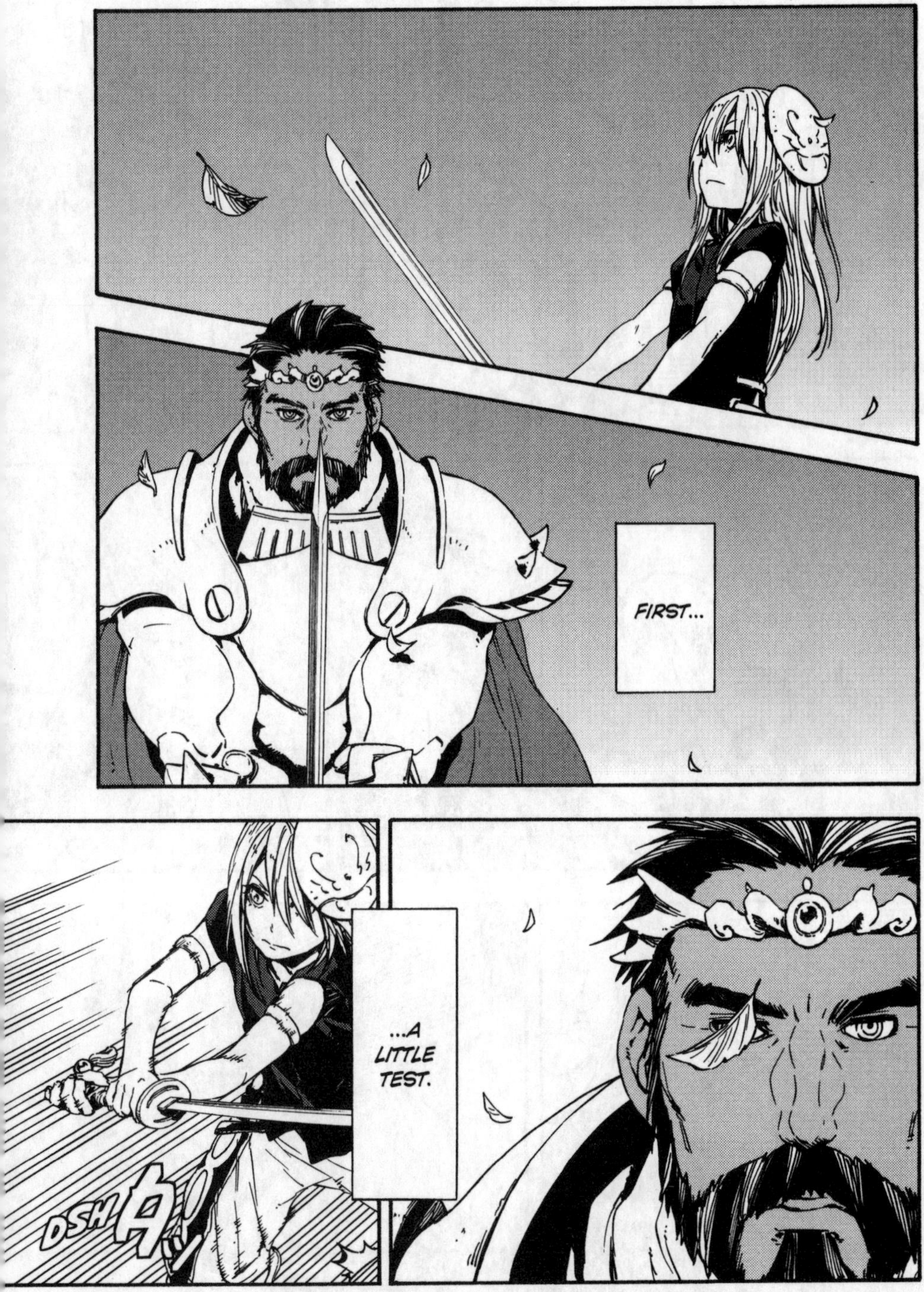
FIRST...
...A LITTLE TEST.
DSH

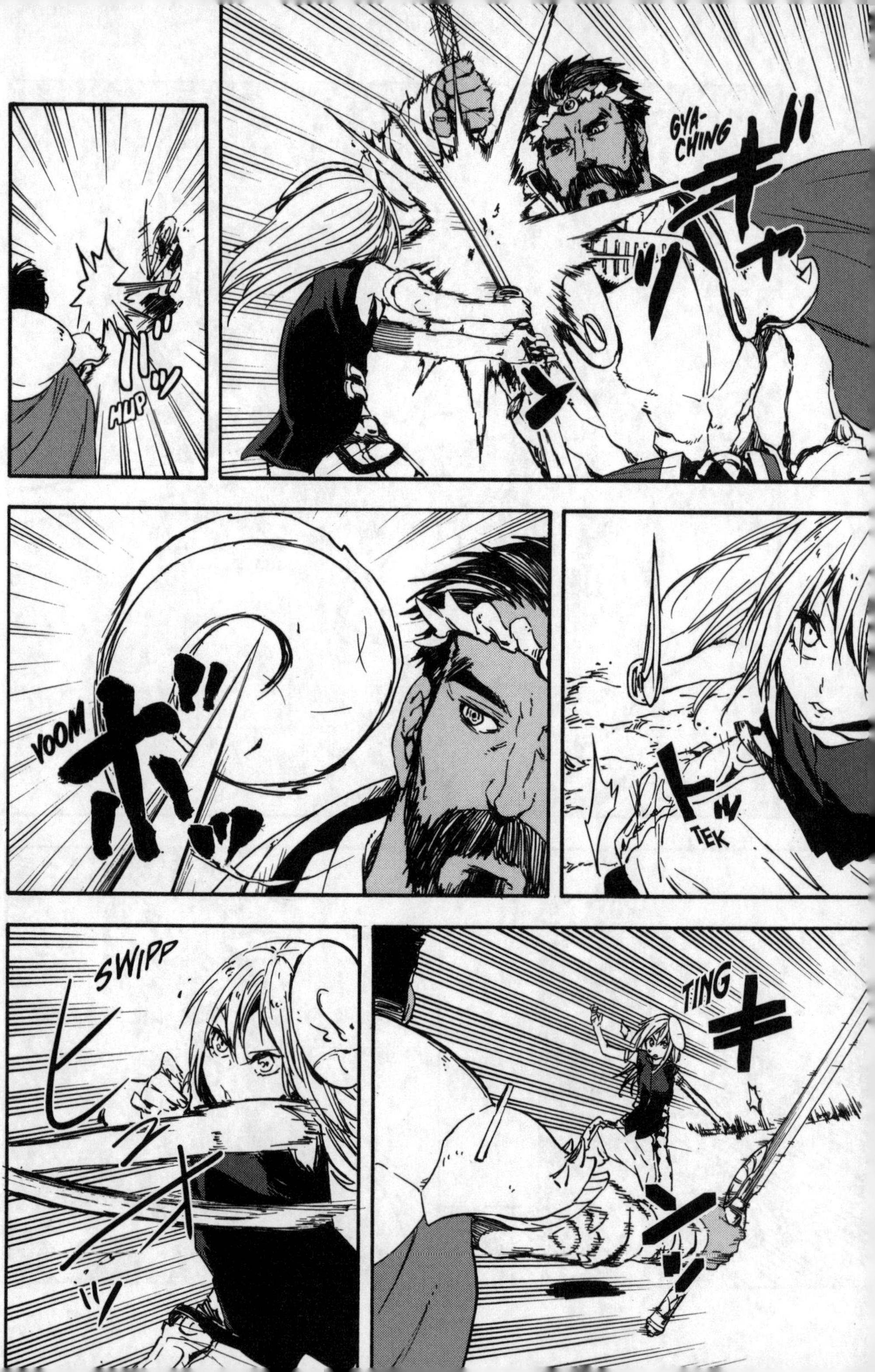
GYA-CHING
HUP
TEK
VOOM
TING
SWIPP

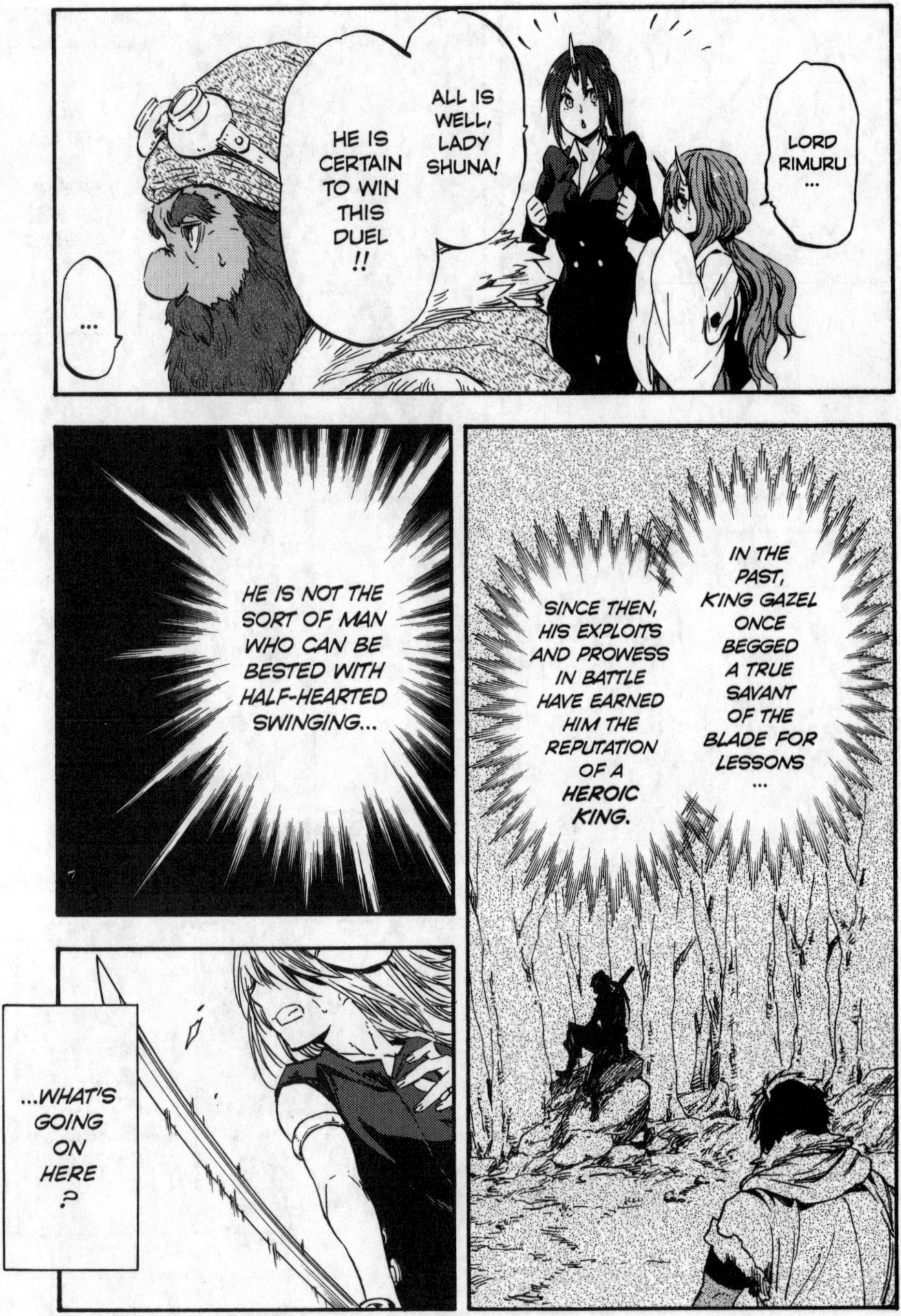

LORD RIMURU ...
ALL IS WELL, LADY SHUNA!
HE IS CERTAIN TO WIN THIS DUEL !!
...
IN THE PAST, KING GAZEL ONCE BEGGED A TRUE SAVANT OF THE BLADE FOR LESSONS ...
SINCE THEN, HIS EXPLOITS AND PROWESS IN BATTLE HAVE EARNED HIM THE REPUTATION OF A HEROIC KING.
HE IS NOT THE SORT OF MAN WHO CAN BE BESTED WITH HALF-HEARTED SWINGING...
...WHAT'S GOING ON HERE ?

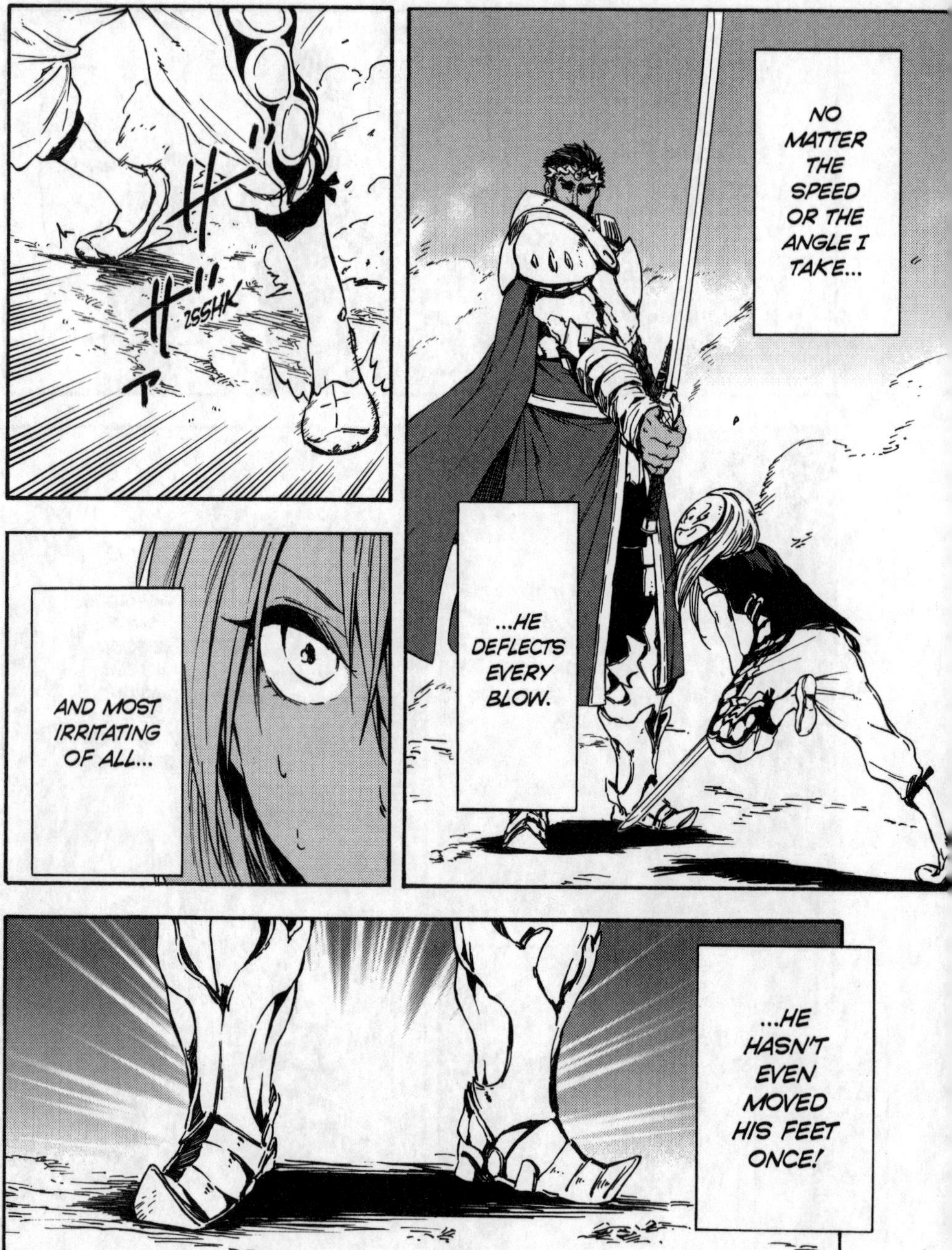
NO MATTER THE SPEED OR THE ANGLE I TAKE...
...HE DEFLECTS EVERY BLOW.
ZSSHK
AND MOST IRRITATING OF ALL...
...HE HASN'T EVEN MOVED HIS FEET ONCE!

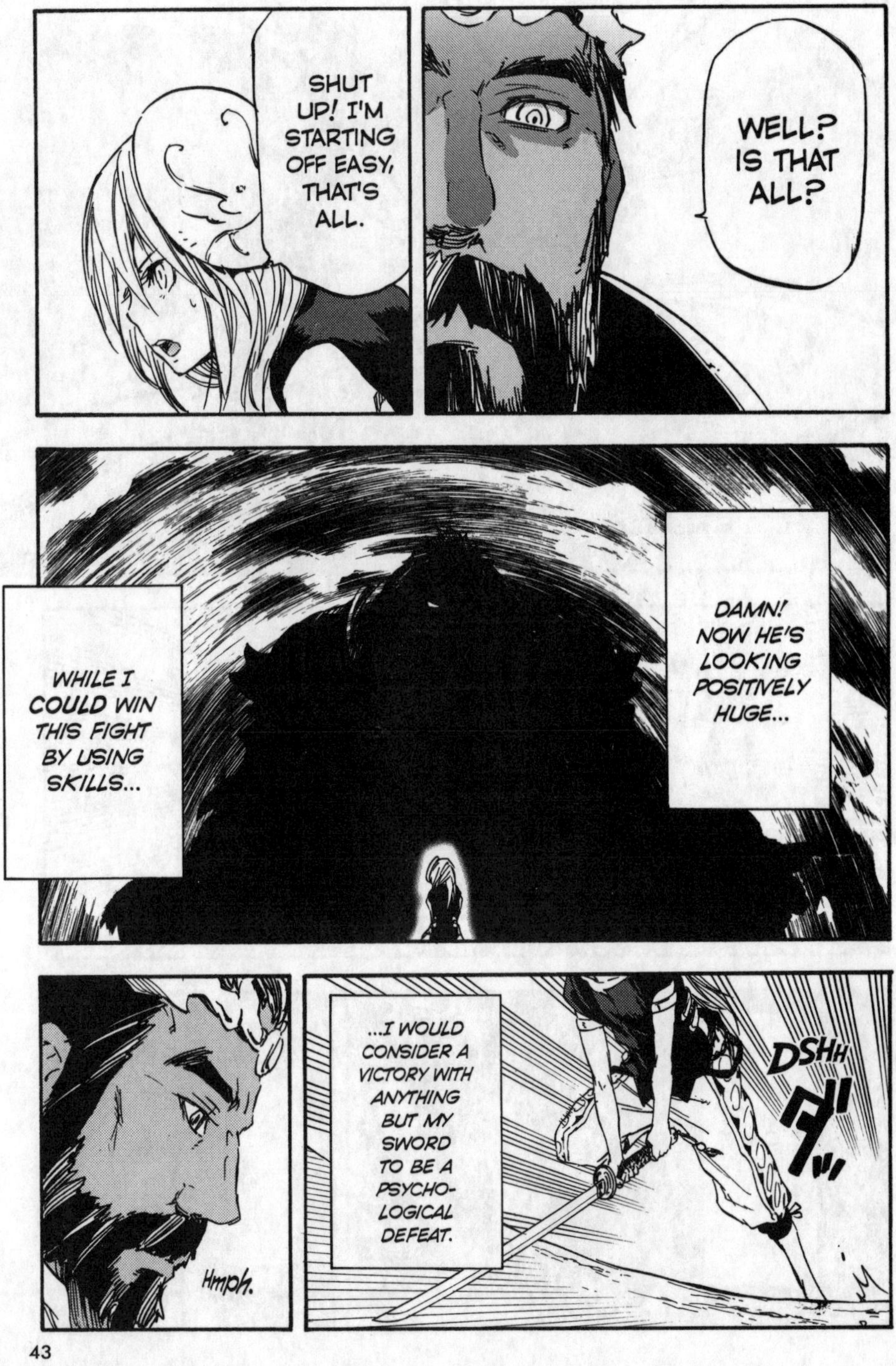

WELL? IS THAT ALL?
SHUT UP! I'M STARTING OFF EASY, THAT'S ALL.
DAMN! NOW HE'S LOOKING POSITIVELY HUGE...
WHILE I COULD WIN THIS FIGHT BY USING SKILLS...
DSHH
ダッ
...I WOULD CONSIDER A VICTORY WITH ANYTHING BUT MY SWORD TO BE A PSYCHOLOGICAL DEFEAT.
Hmph.

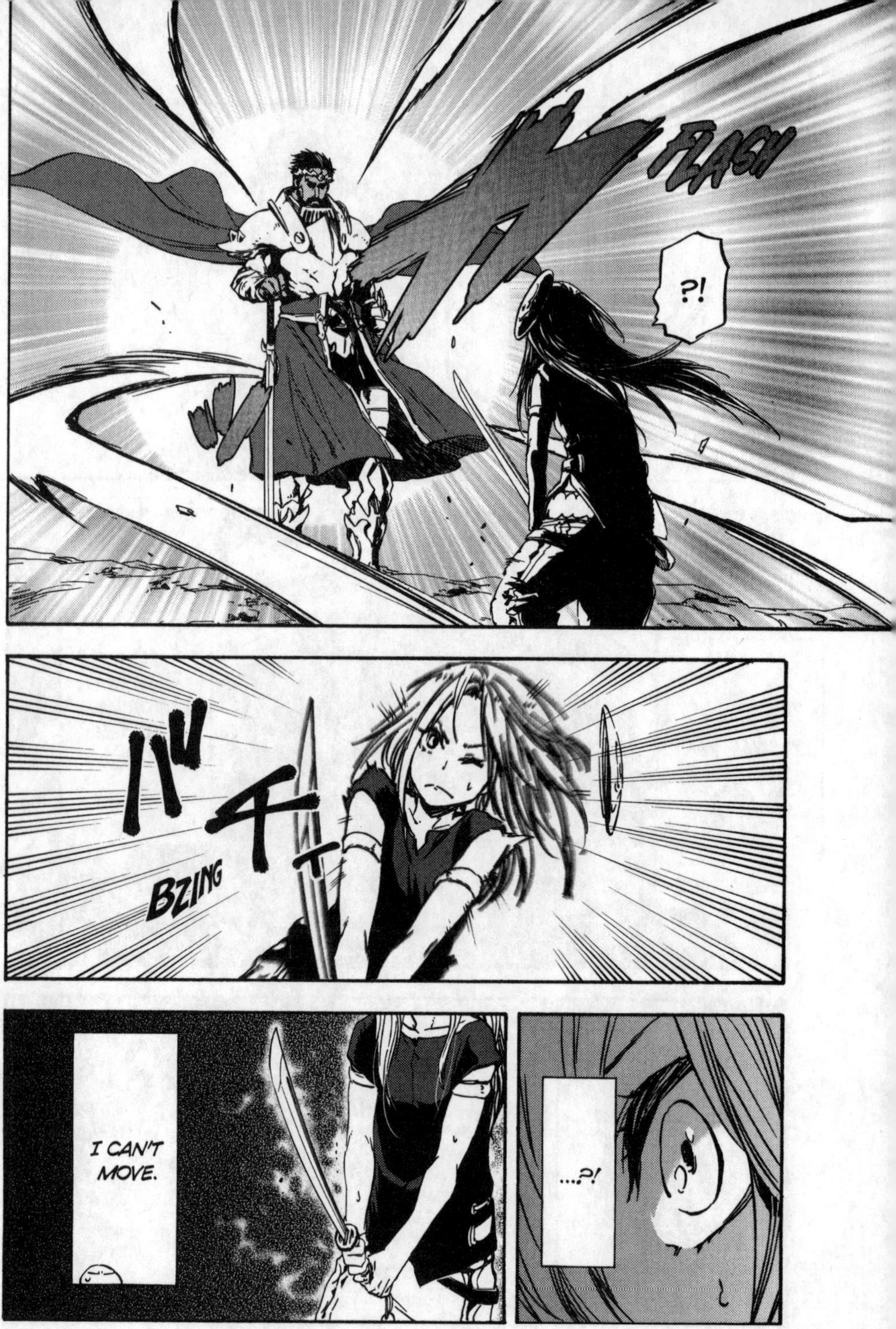
FLASH
?!
BZING
...?!
I CAN'T MOVE.

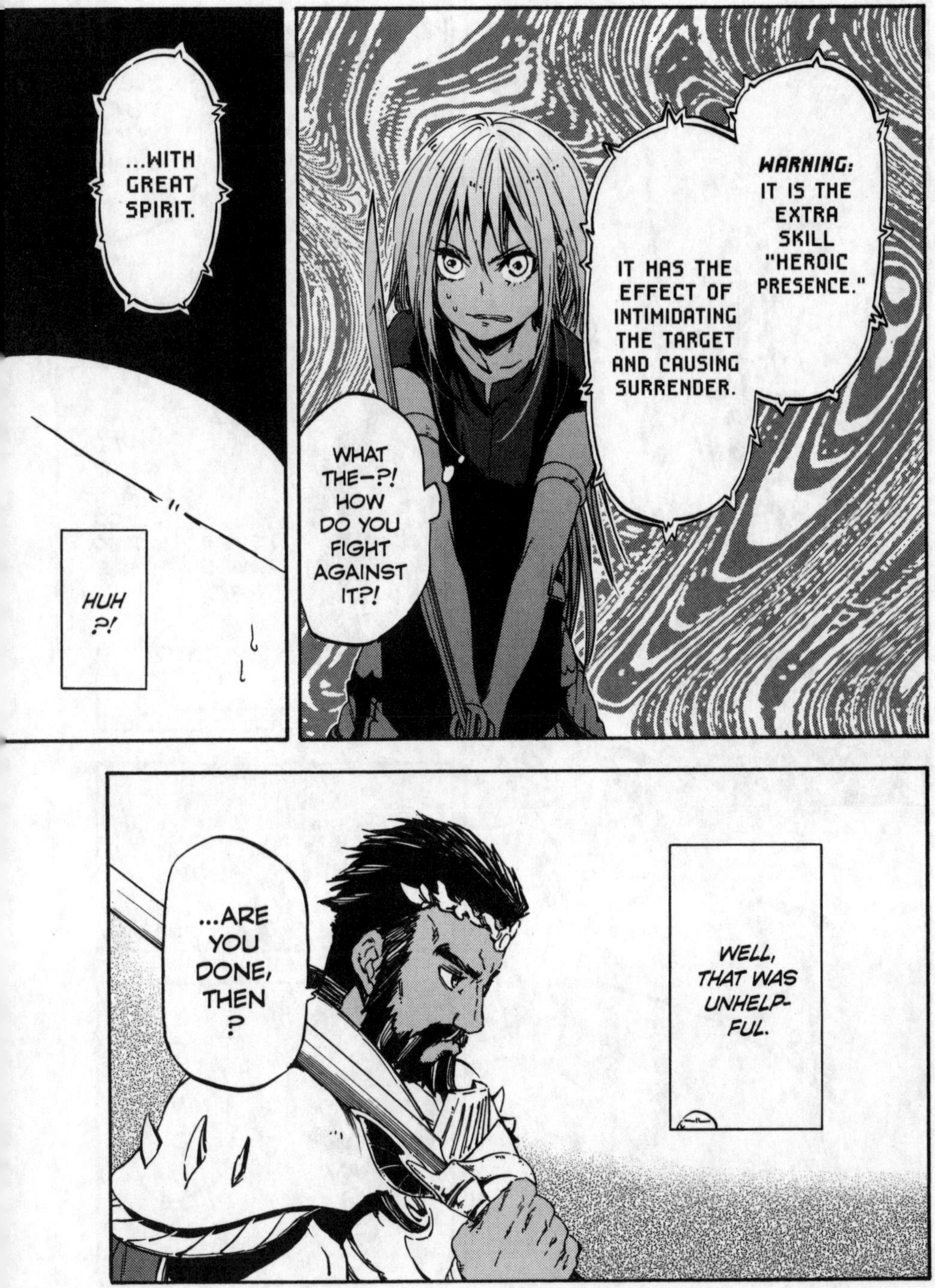
WARNING: IT IS THE EXTRA SKILL "HEROIC PRESENCE."
IT HAS THE EFFECT OF INTIMIDATING THE TARGET AND CAUSING SURRENDER.
WHAT THE-?! HOW DO YOU FIGHT AGAINST IT?!
...WITH GREAT SPIRIT.
HUH ?!
WELL, THAT WAS UNHELP-FUL.
...ARE YOU DONE, THEN ?

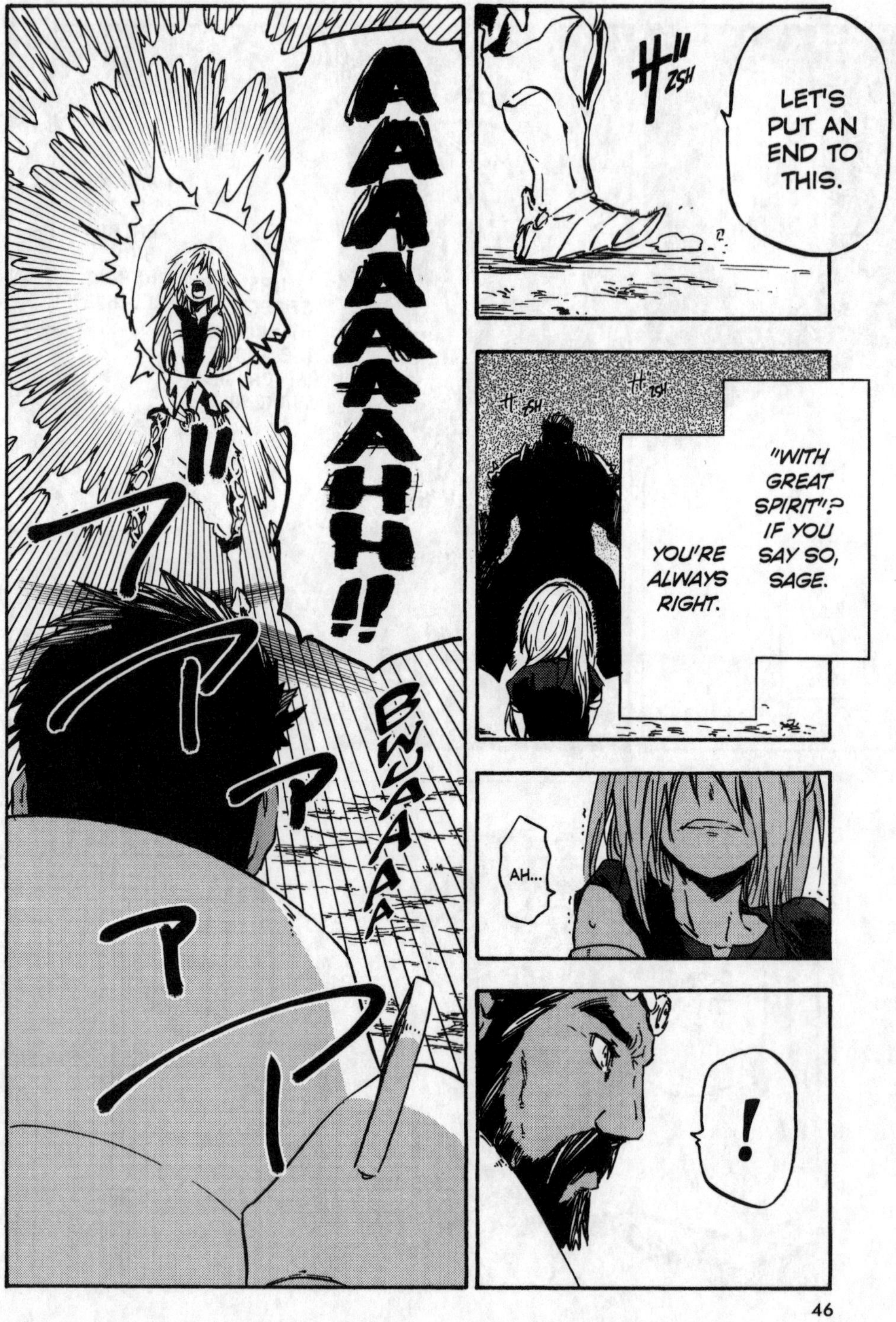
ZSH
LET'S PUT AN END TO THIS.
ZSH
ZSH
"WITH GREAT SPIRIT"? IF YOU SAY SO, SAGE.
YOU'RE ALWAYS RIGHT.
AH...
!
AAAAAAAAHH!!
BWAAAAA

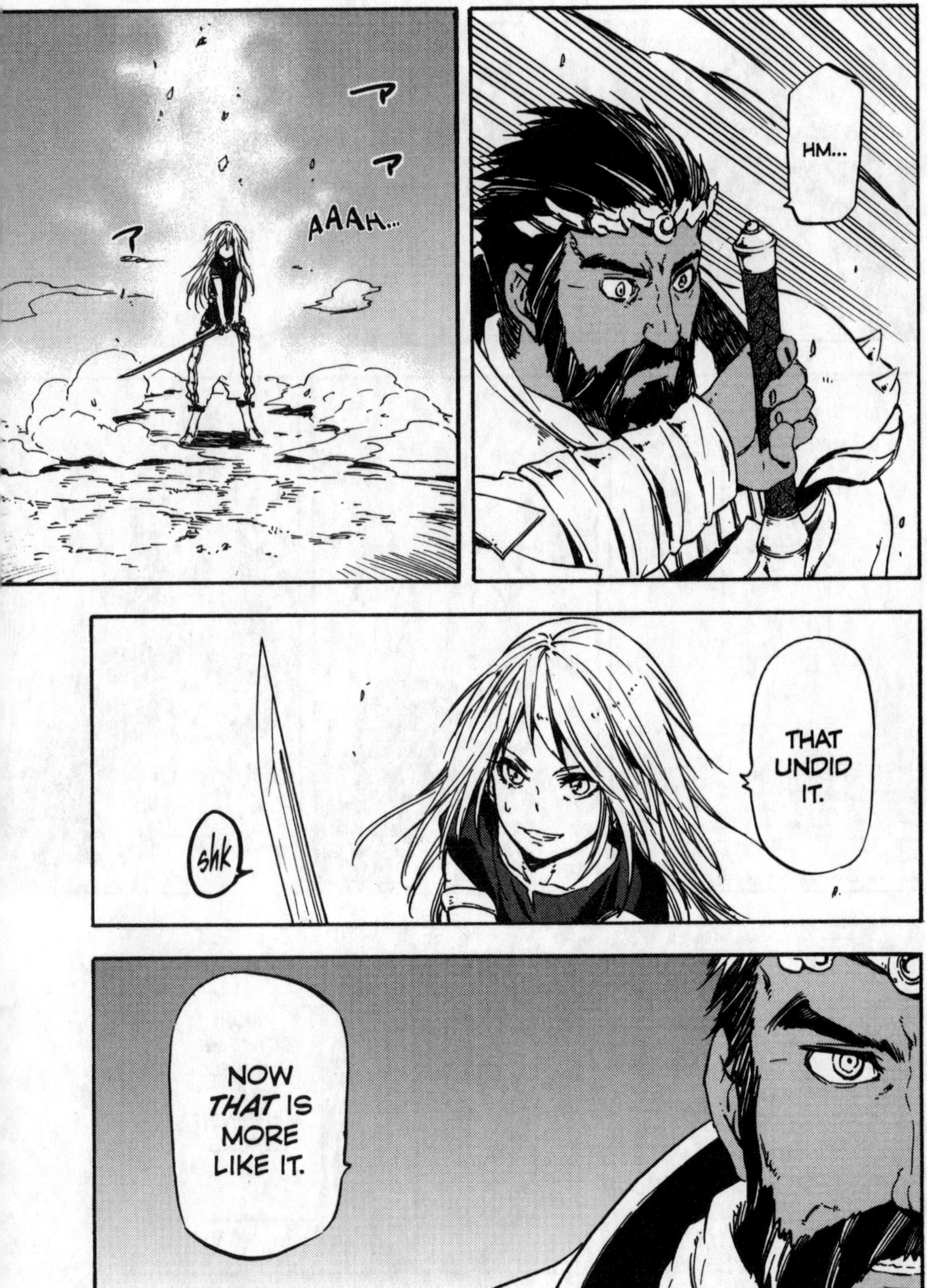
HM...
アアア
AAAH...
THAT UNDID IT.
shk
NOW *THAT* IS MORE LIKE IT.

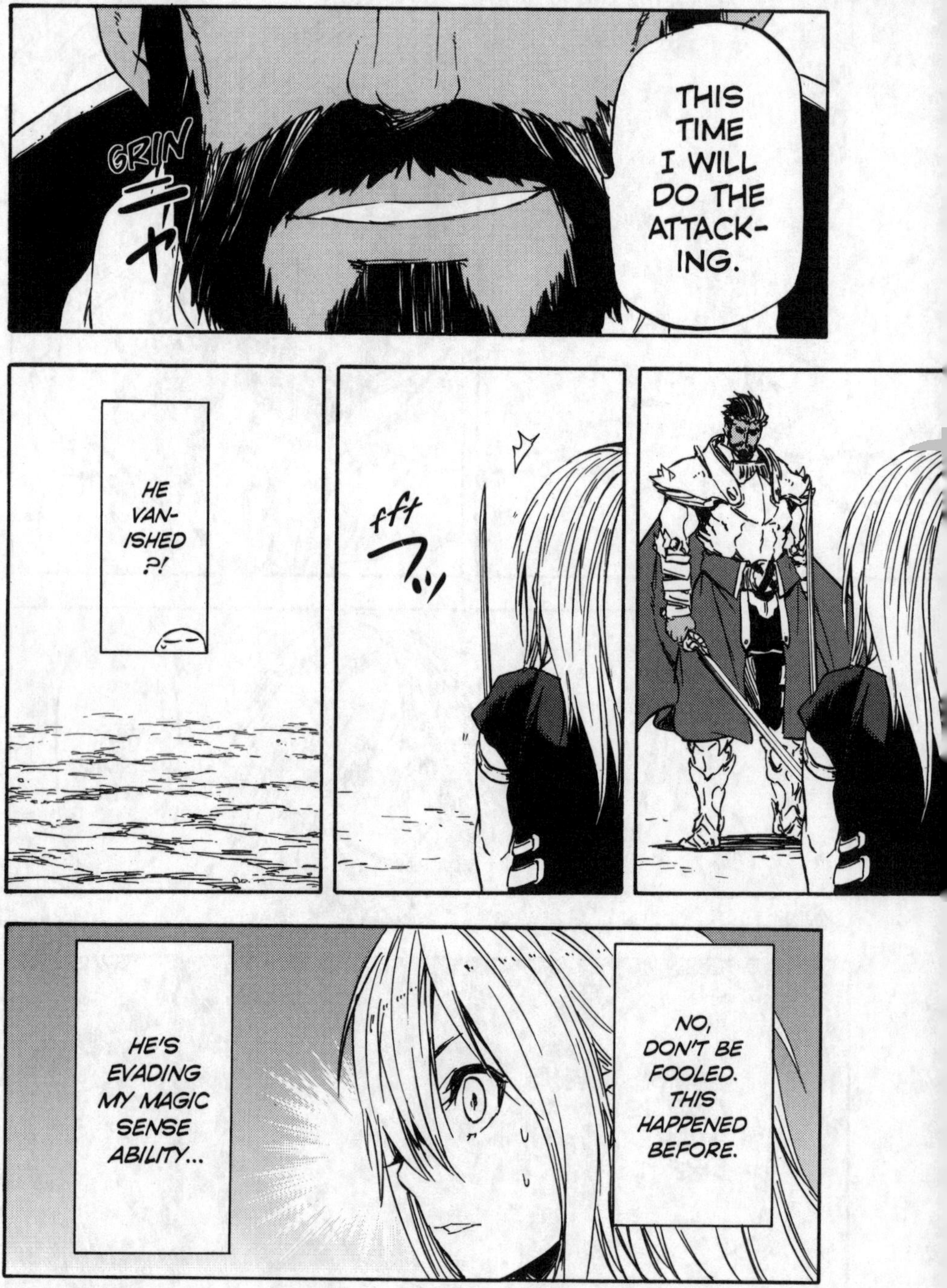
THIS TIME I WILL DO THE ATTACK-ING.
GRIN
fft
HE VAN-ISHED ?!
NO, DON'T BE FOOLED. THIS HAPPENED BEFORE.
HE'S EVADING MY MAGIC SENSE ABILITY...

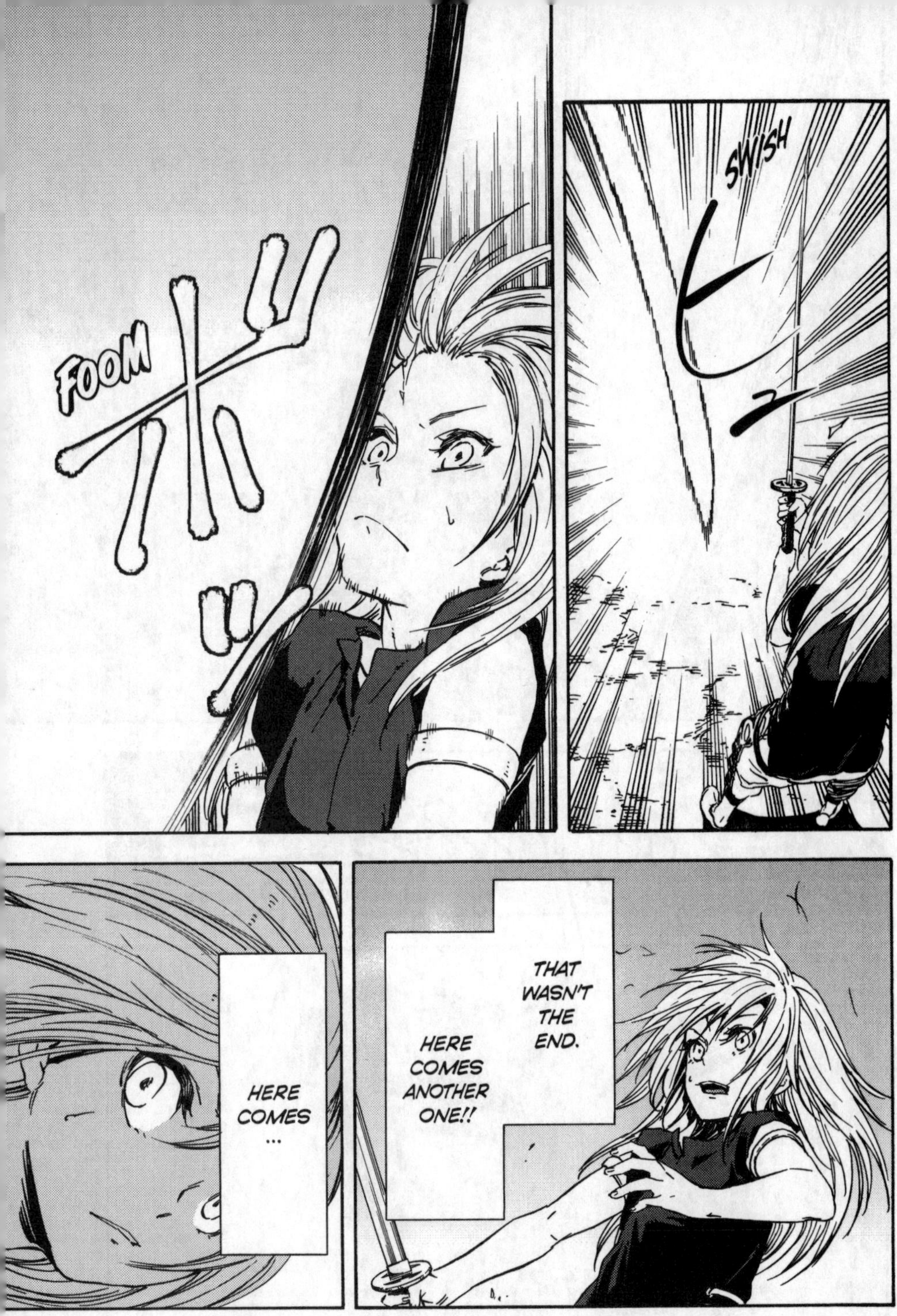
SWISH
FOOM
THAT WASN'T THE END.
HERE COMES ANOTHER ONE!!
HERE COMES ...

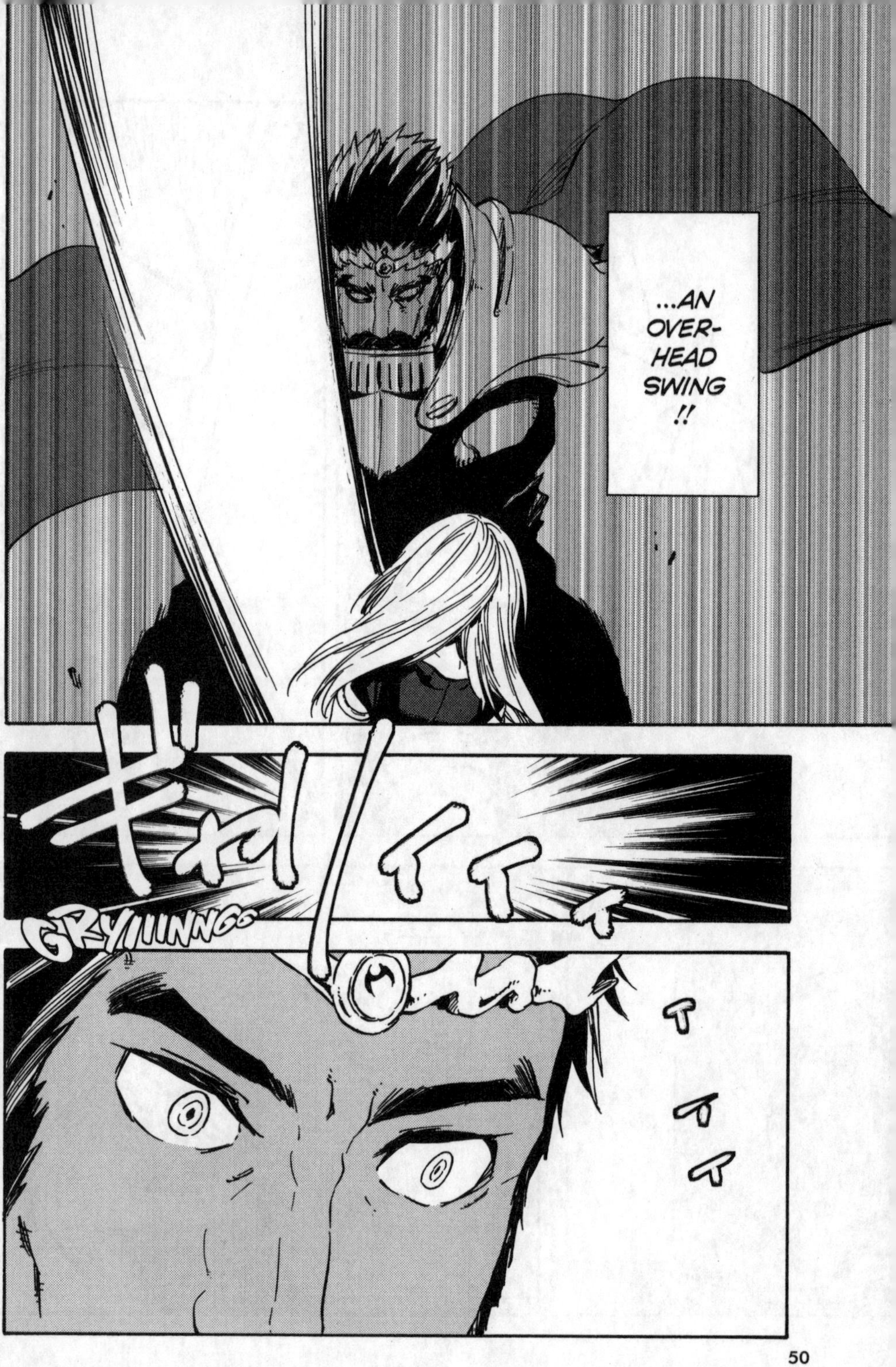
...AN OVER-HEAD SWING !!
GRYIIINNG

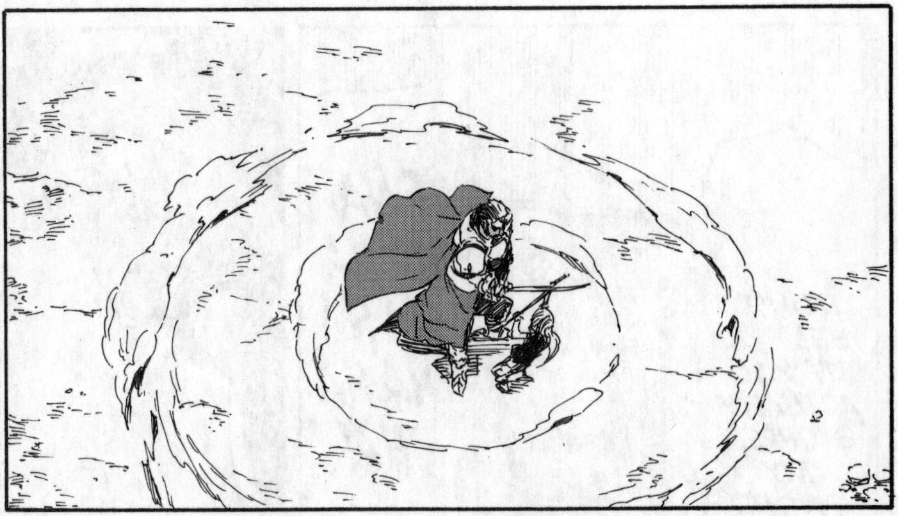

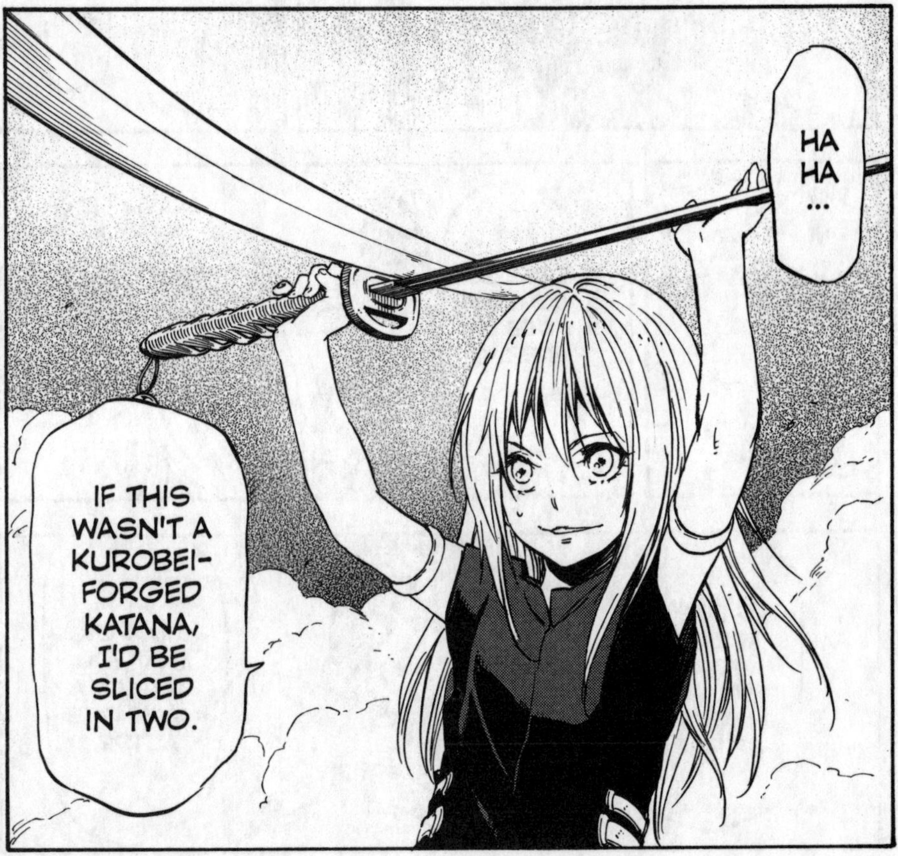
HA HA ...
IF THIS WASN'T A KUROBEI-FORGED KATANA, I'D BE SLICED IN TWO.

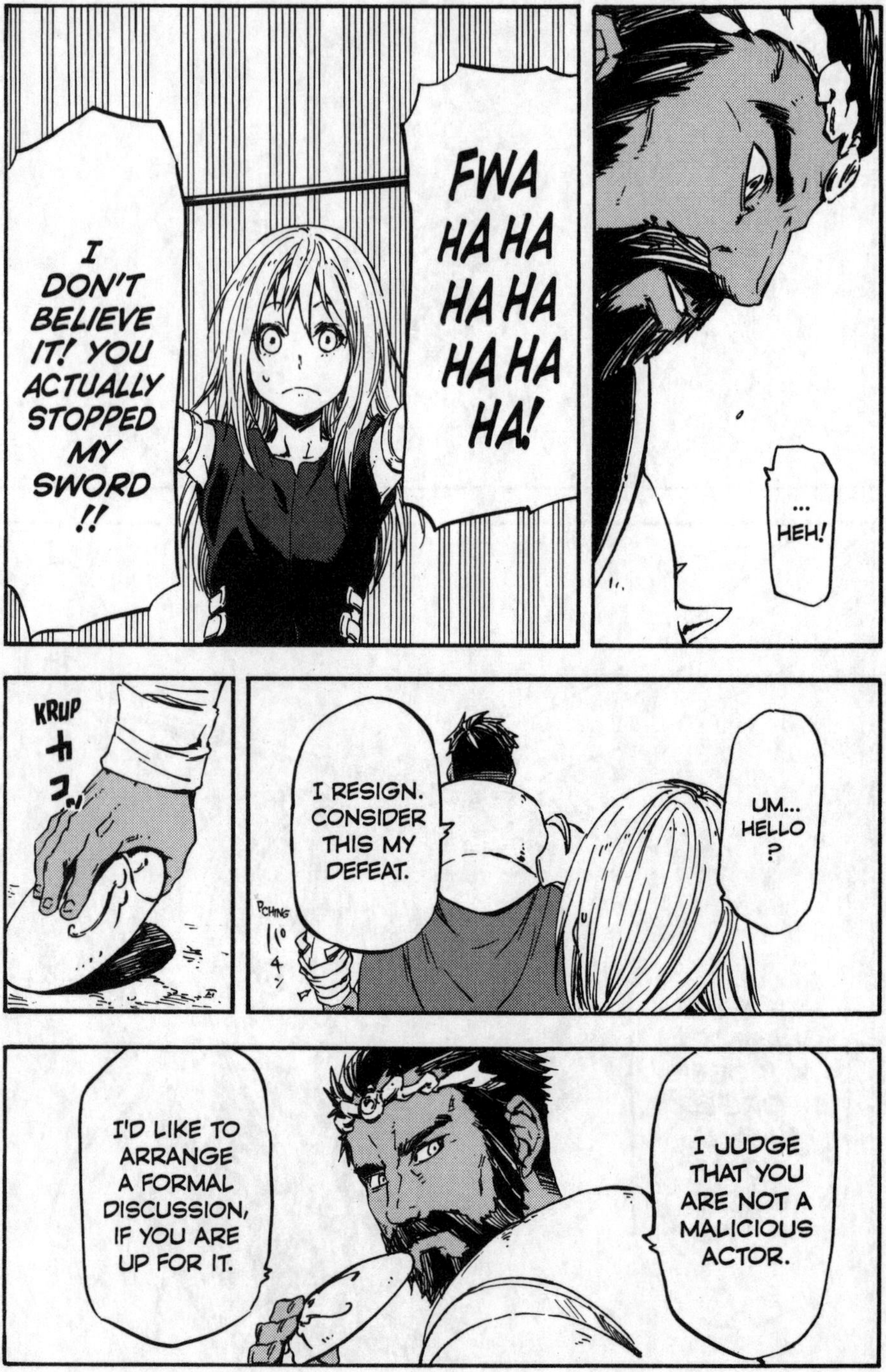

... HEH!
FWA HA HA HA HA HA HA HA!
I DON'T BELIEVE IT! YOU ACTUALLY STOPPED MY SWORD !!
UM... HELLO ?
I RESIGN. CONSIDER THIS MY DEFEAT.
P'CHING
パチン
KRUP
カコッ
I JUDGE THAT YOU ARE NOT A MALICIOUS ACTOR.
I'D LIKE TO ARRANGE A FORMAL DISCUSSION, IF YOU ARE UP FOR IT.

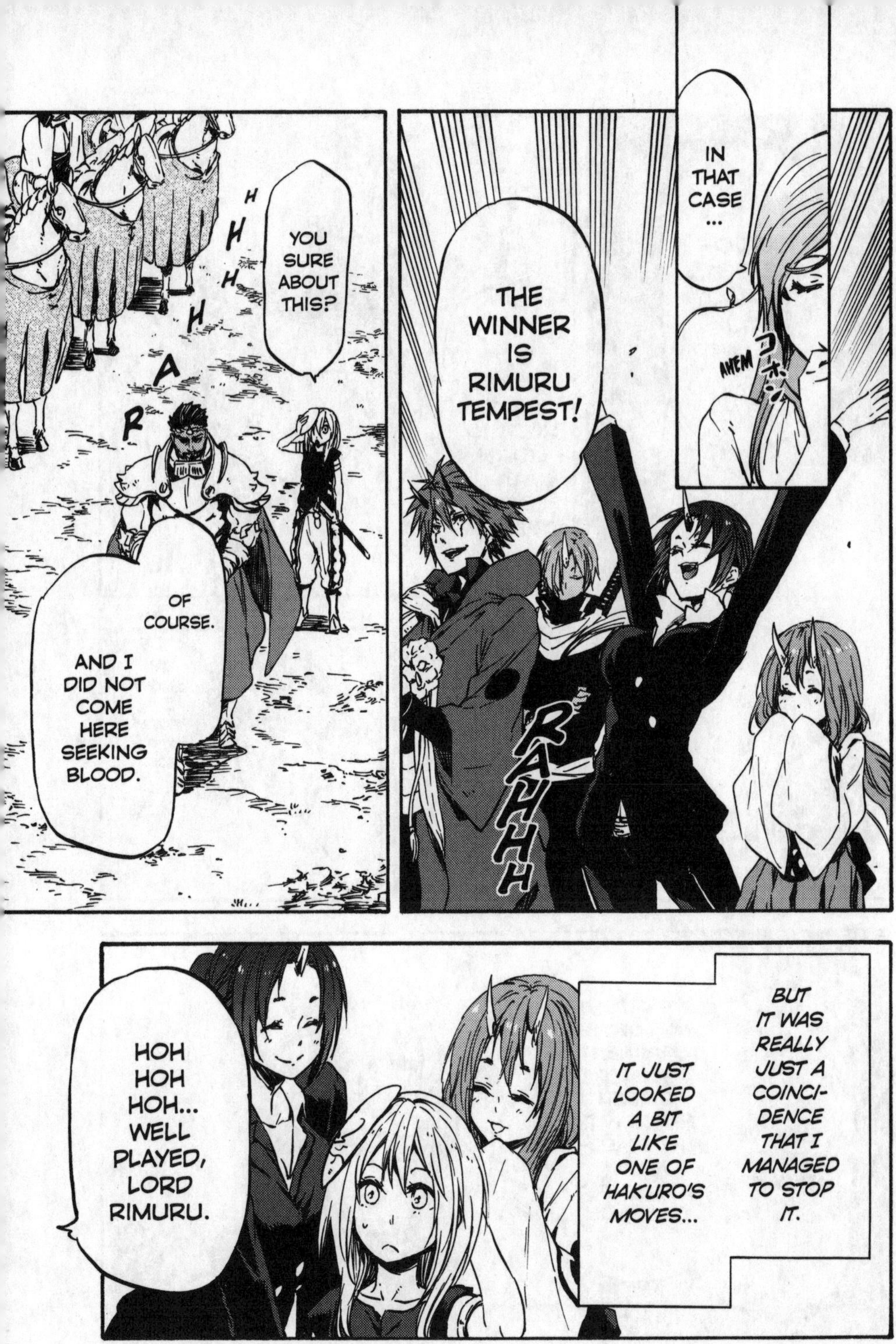
IN THAT CASE ...
AHEM
THE WINNER IS RIMURU TEMPEST!
RAHHHH
RAHHHH
YOU SURE ABOUT THIS?
OF COURSE.
AND I DID NOT COME HERE SEEKING BLOOD.
IT JUST LOOKED A BIT LIKE ONE OF HAKURO'S MOVES...
BUT IT WAS REALLY JUST A COINCI-DENCE THAT I MANAGED TO STOP IT.
HOH HOH HOH... WELL PLAYED, LORD RIMURU.

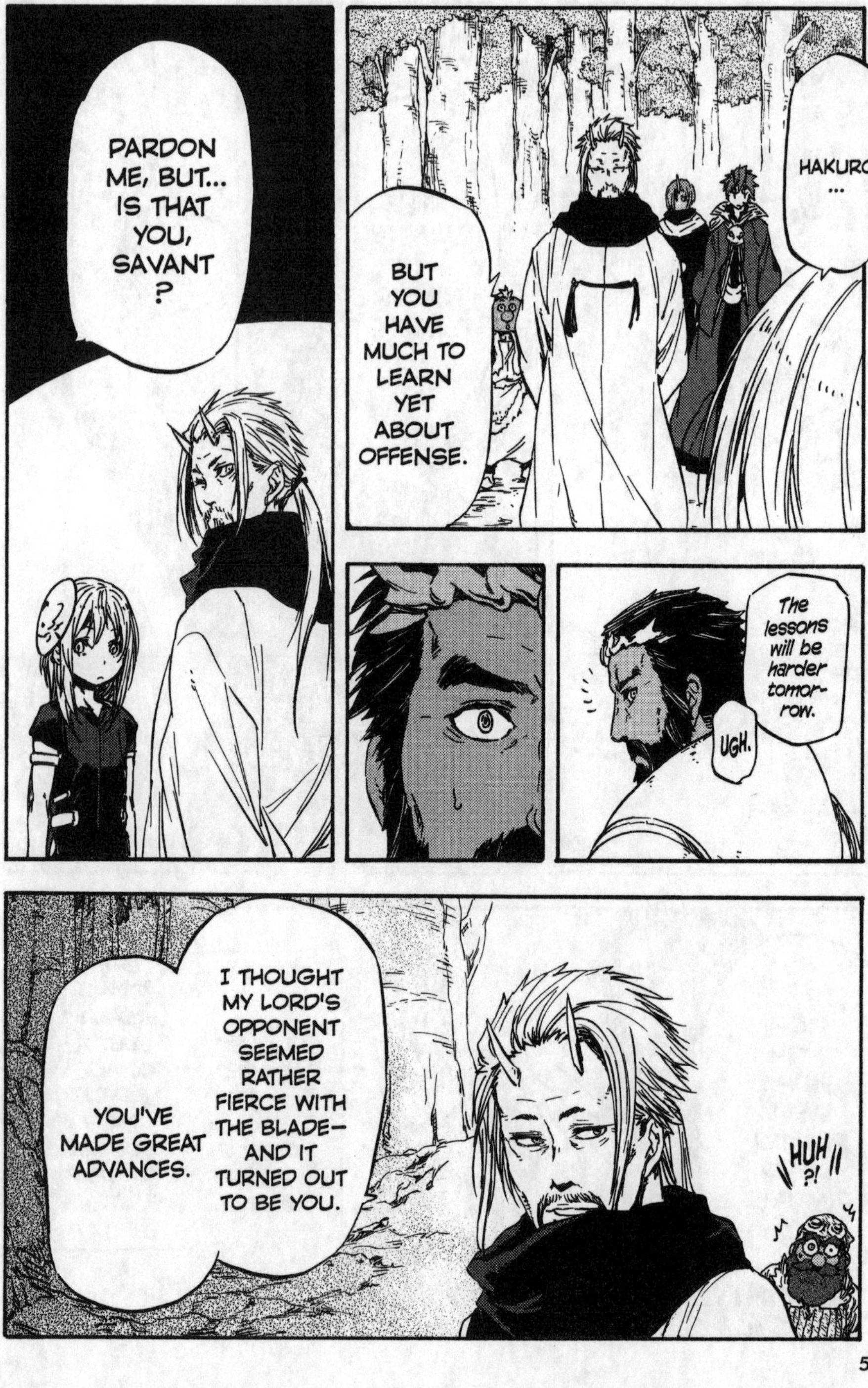
HAKURO ...
BUT YOU HAVE MUCH TO LEARN YET ABOUT OFFENSE.
The lessons will be harder tomorrow.
UGH.
PARDON ME, BUT... IS THAT YOU, SAVANT ?
I THOUGHT MY LORD'S OPPONENT SEEMED RATHER FIERCE WITH THE BLADE— AND IT TURNED OUT TO BE YOU.
YOU'VE MADE GREAT ADVANCES.
HUH ?!

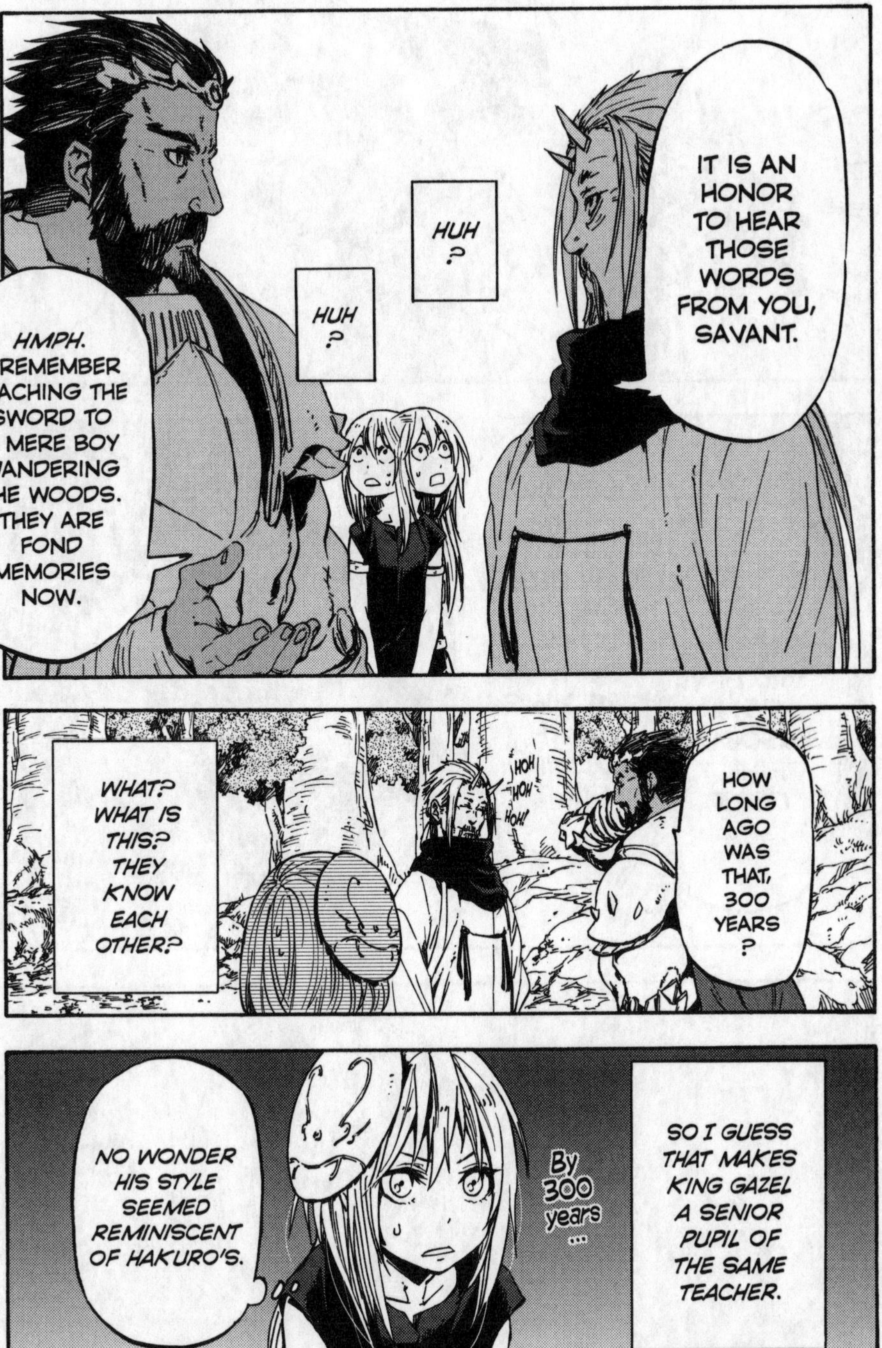
IT IS AN HONOR TO HEAR THOSE WORDS FROM YOU, SAVANT.
HUH?
HUH?
HMPH. I REMEMBER TEACHING THE SWORD TO A MERE BOY WANDERING THE WOODS. THEY ARE FOND MEMORIES NOW.
HOW LONG AGO WAS THAT, 300 YEARS?
HOH HOH HOH!
WHAT? WHAT IS THIS? THEY KNOW EACH OTHER?
SO I GUESS THAT MAKES KING GAZEL A SENIOR PUPIL OF THE SAME TEACHER.
By 300 years...
NO WONDER HIS STYLE SEEMED REMINISCENT OF HAKURO'S.

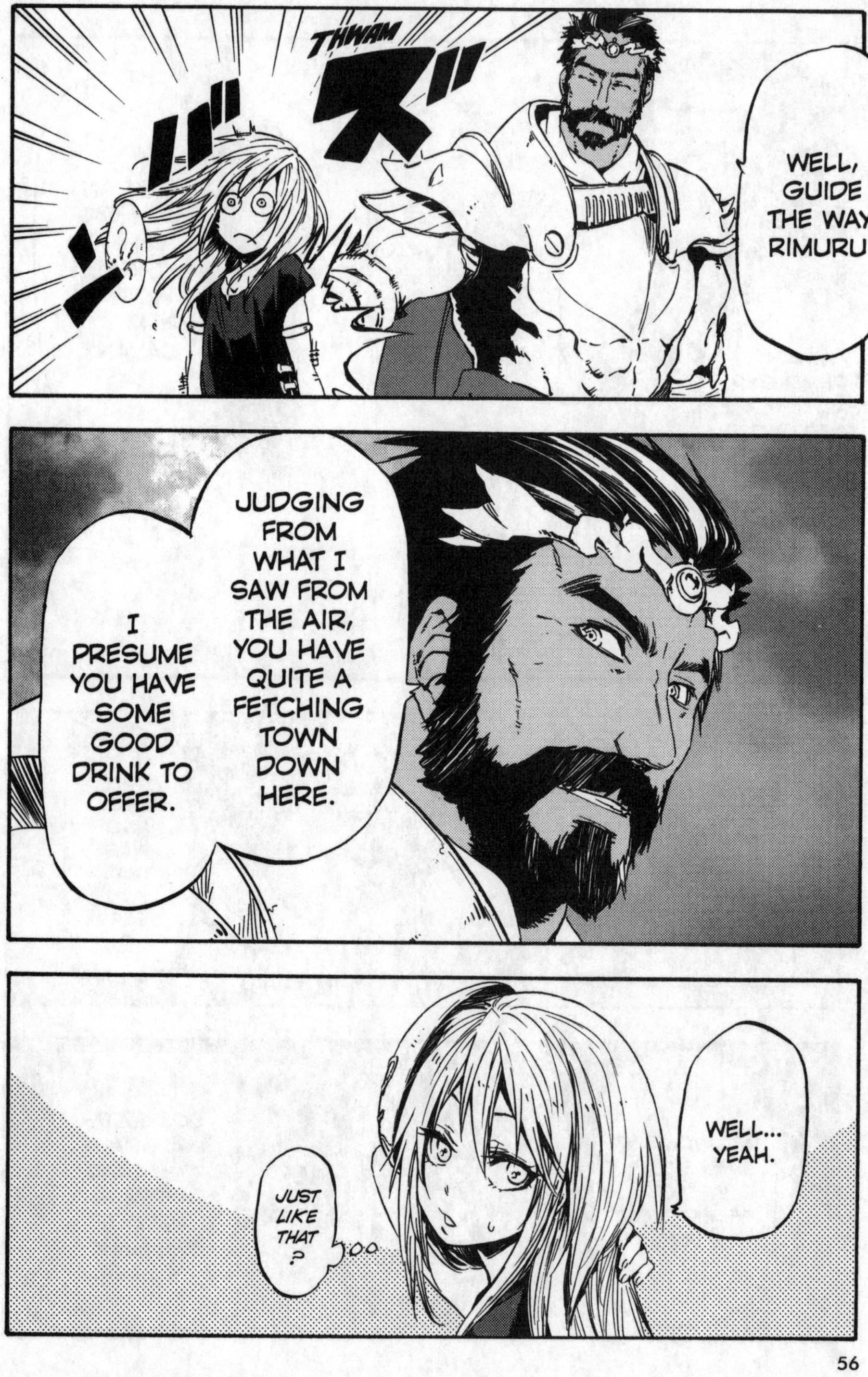
WELL, GUIDE THE WAY, RIMURU.
THWAM
?
JUDGING FROM WHAT I SAW FROM THE AIR, YOU HAVE QUITE A FETCHING TOWN DOWN HERE.
I PRESUME YOU HAVE SOME GOOD DRINK TO OFFER.
WELL... YEAH.
JUST LIKE THAT?

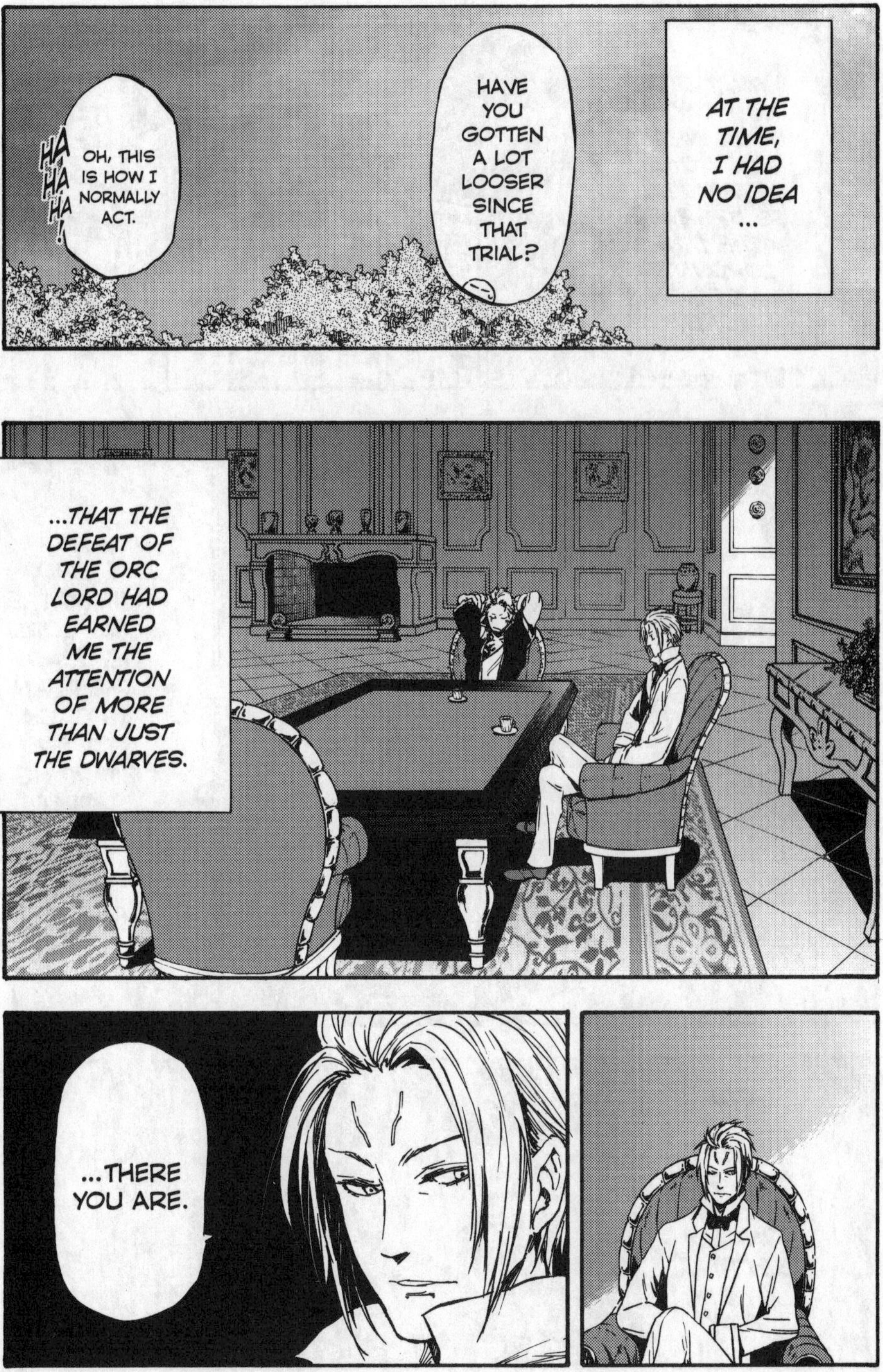
AT THE TIME, I HAD NO IDEA ...
HAVE YOU GOTTEN A LOT LOOSER SINCE THAT TRIAL?
HA HA HA!
OH, THIS IS HOW I NORMALLY ACT.
...THAT THE DEFEAT OF THE ORC LORD HAD EARNED ME THE ATTENTION OF MORE THAN JUST THE DWARVES.
...THERE YOU ARE.

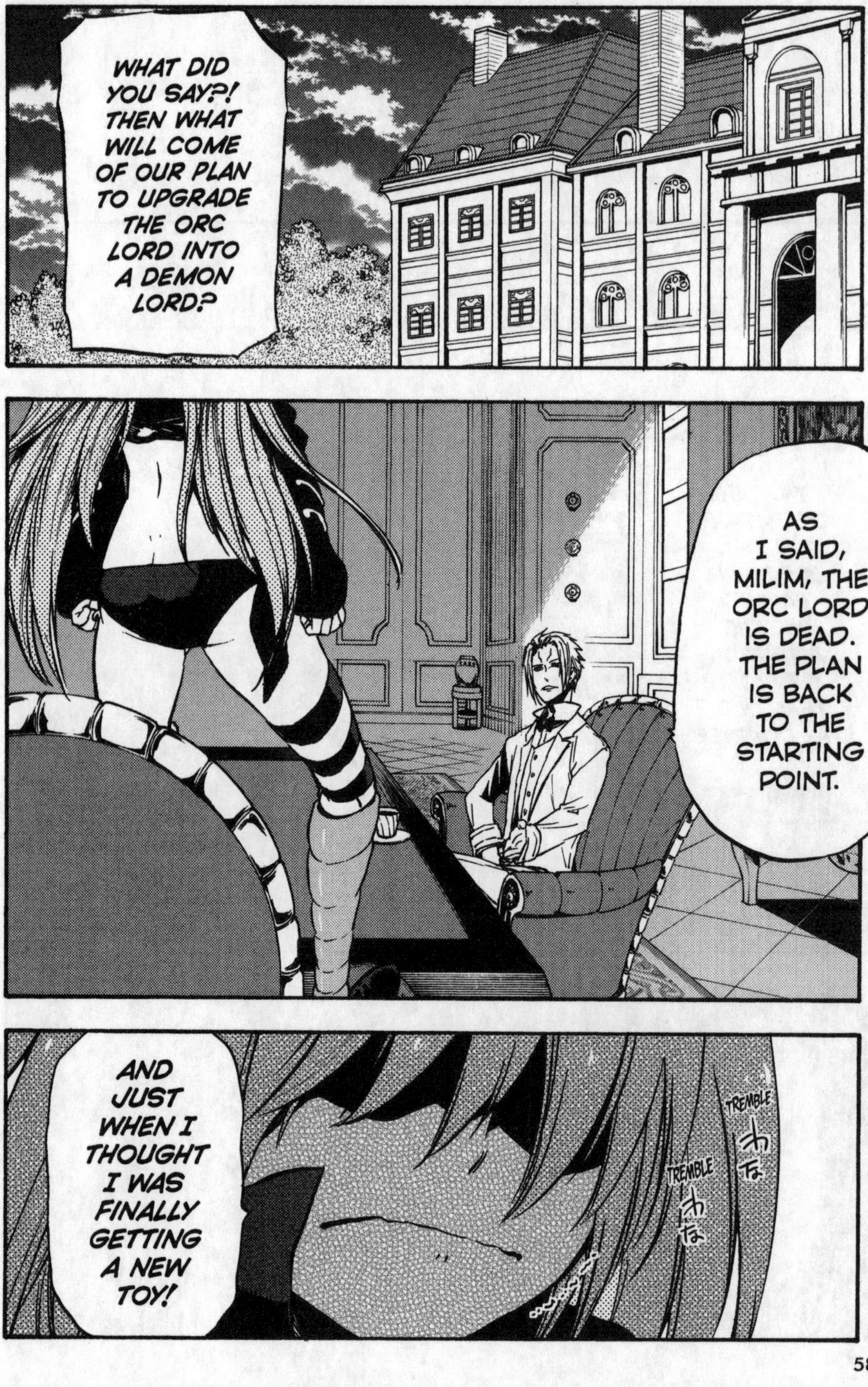
WHAT DID YOU SAY?! THEN WHAT WILL COME OF OUR PLAN TO UPGRADE THE ORC LORD INTO A DEMON LORD?
AS I SAID, MILIM, THE ORC LORD IS DEAD. THE PLAN IS BACK TO THE STARTING POINT.
TREMBLE
TREMBLE
AND JUST WHEN I THOUGHT I WAS FINALLY GETTING A NEW TOY!

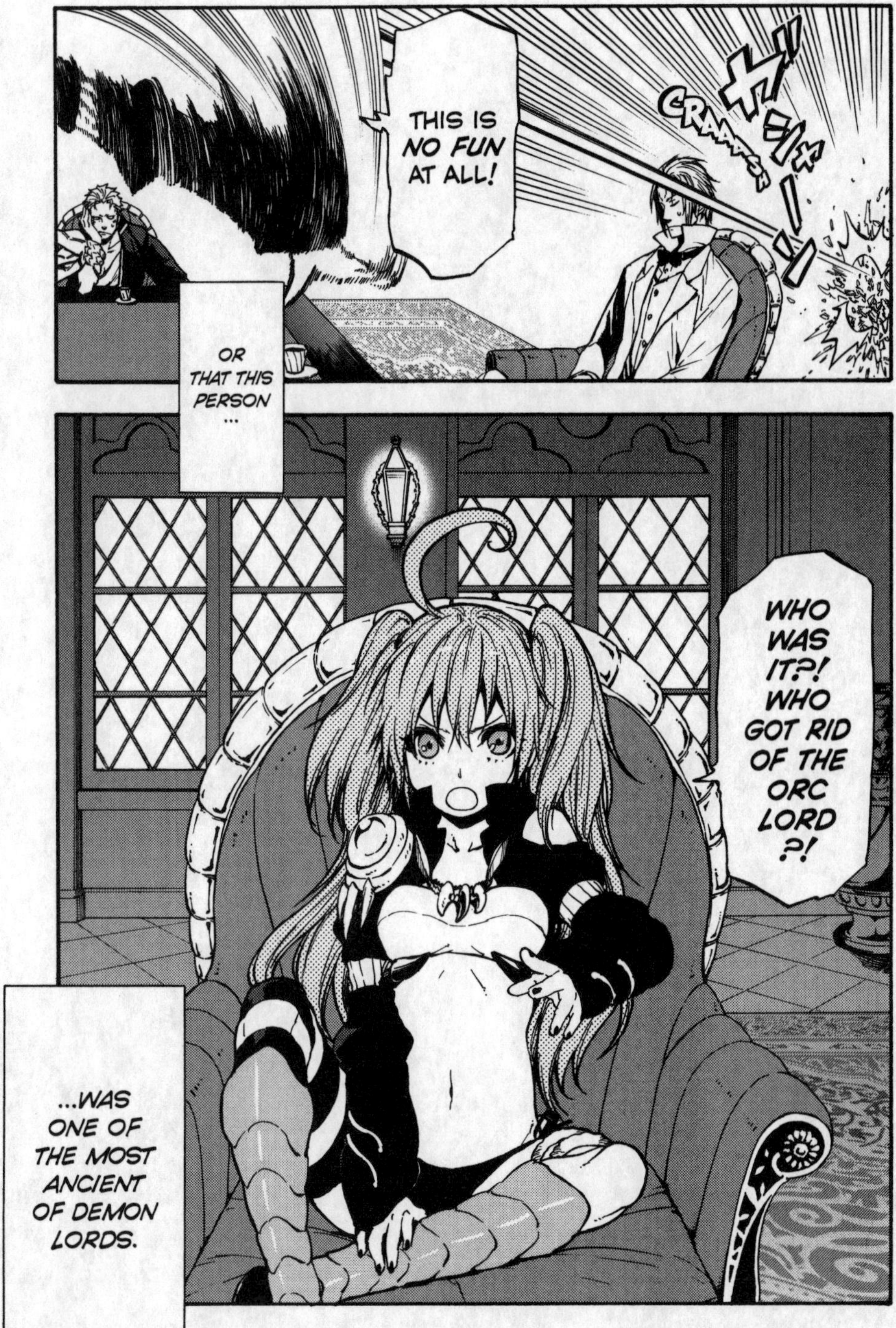
CRAAAASH
THIS IS NO FUN AT ALL!
OR THAT THIS PERSON...
WHO WAS IT?! WHO GOT RID OF THE ORC LORD?!
...WAS ONE OF THE MOST ANCIENT OF DEMON LORDS.

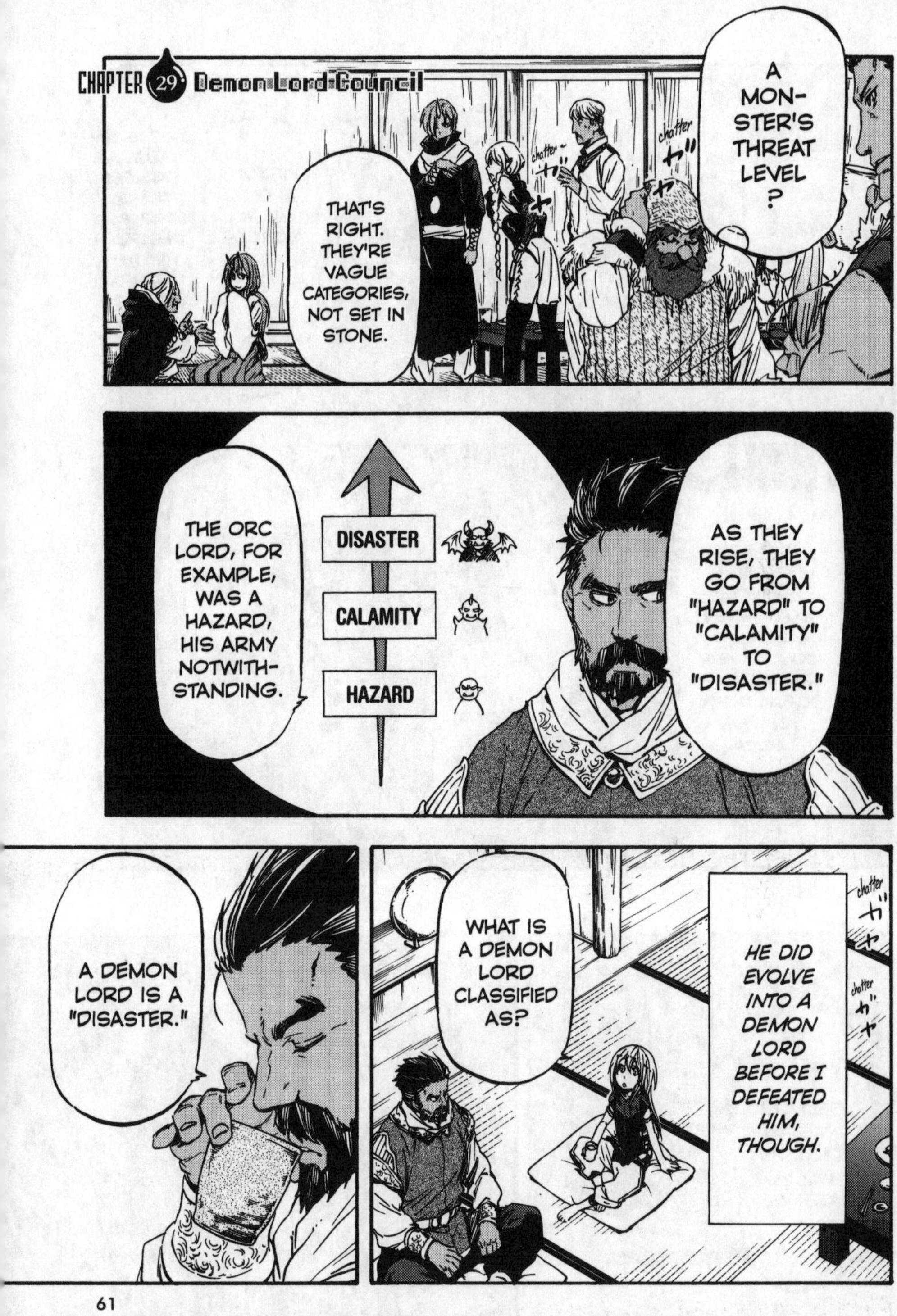
CHAPTER 29 Demon Lord Council
A MON-STER'S THREAT LEVEL?
chatter
chatter
THAT'S RIGHT. THEY'RE VAGUE CATEGORIES, NOT SET IN STONE.
AS THEY RISE, THEY GO FROM "HAZARD" TO "CALAMITY" TO "DISASTER."
DISASTER
CALAMITY
HAZARD
THE ORC LORD, FOR EXAMPLE, WAS A HAZARD, HIS ARMY NOTWITH-STANDING.
chatter
chatter
HE DID EVOLVE INTO A DEMON LORD BEFORE I DEFEATED HIM, THOUGH.
WHAT IS A DEMON LORD CLASSIFIED AS?
A DEMON LORD IS A "DISASTER."

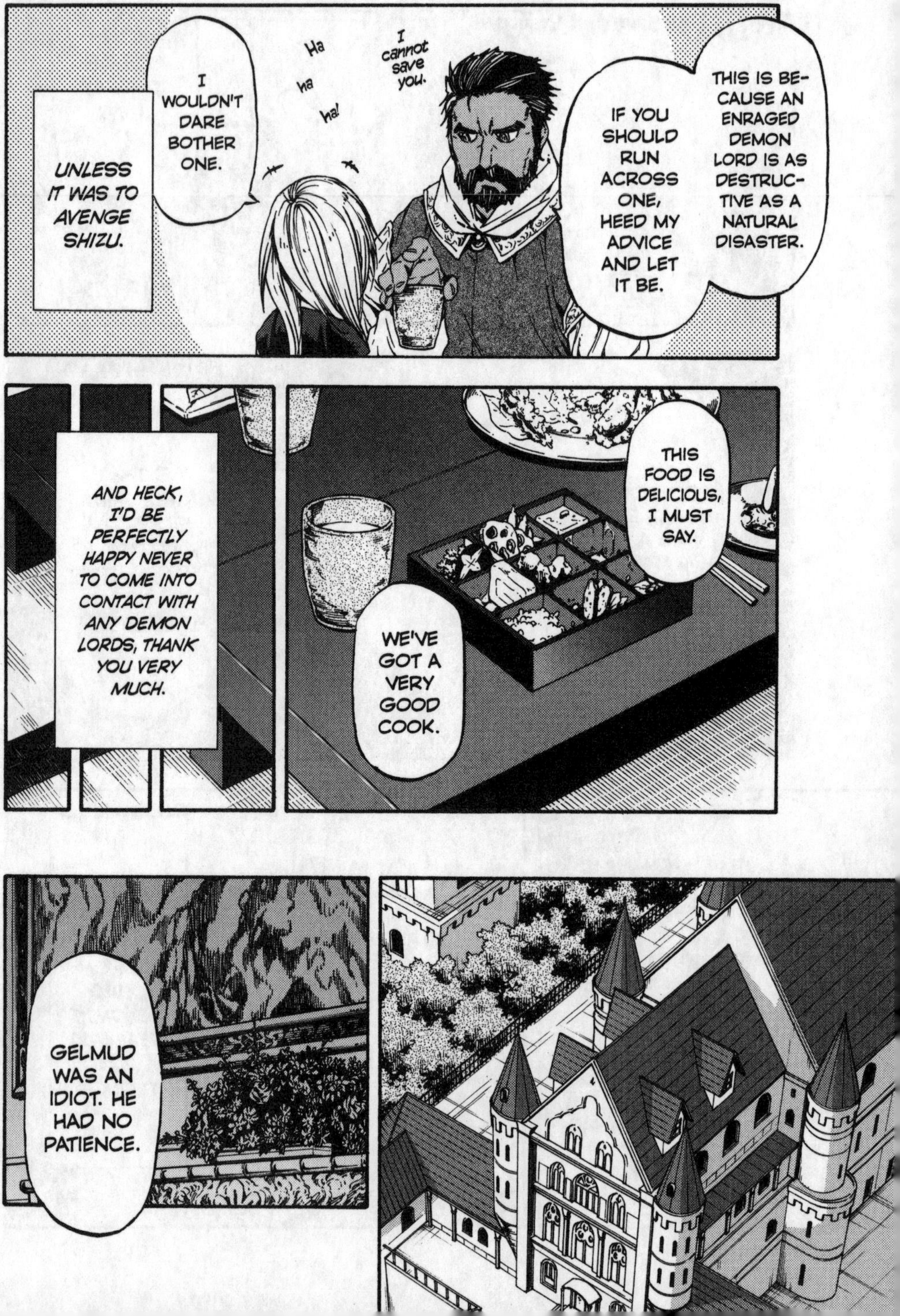
THIS IS BECAUSE AN ENRAGED DEMON LORD IS AS DESTRUCTIVE AS A NATURAL DISASTER.
IF YOU SHOULD RUN ACROSS ONE, HEED MY ADVICE AND LET IT BE.
I cannot save you.
Ha ha ha!
I WOULDN'T DARE BOTHER ONE.
UNLESS IT WAS TO AVENGE SHIZU.
THIS FOOD IS DELICIOUS, I MUST SAY.
WE'VE GOT A VERY GOOD COOK.
AND HECK, I'D BE PERFECTLY HAPPY NEVER TO COME INTO CONTACT WITH ANY DEMON LORDS, THANK YOU VERY MUCH.
GELMUD WAS AN IDIOT. HE HAD NO PATIENCE.

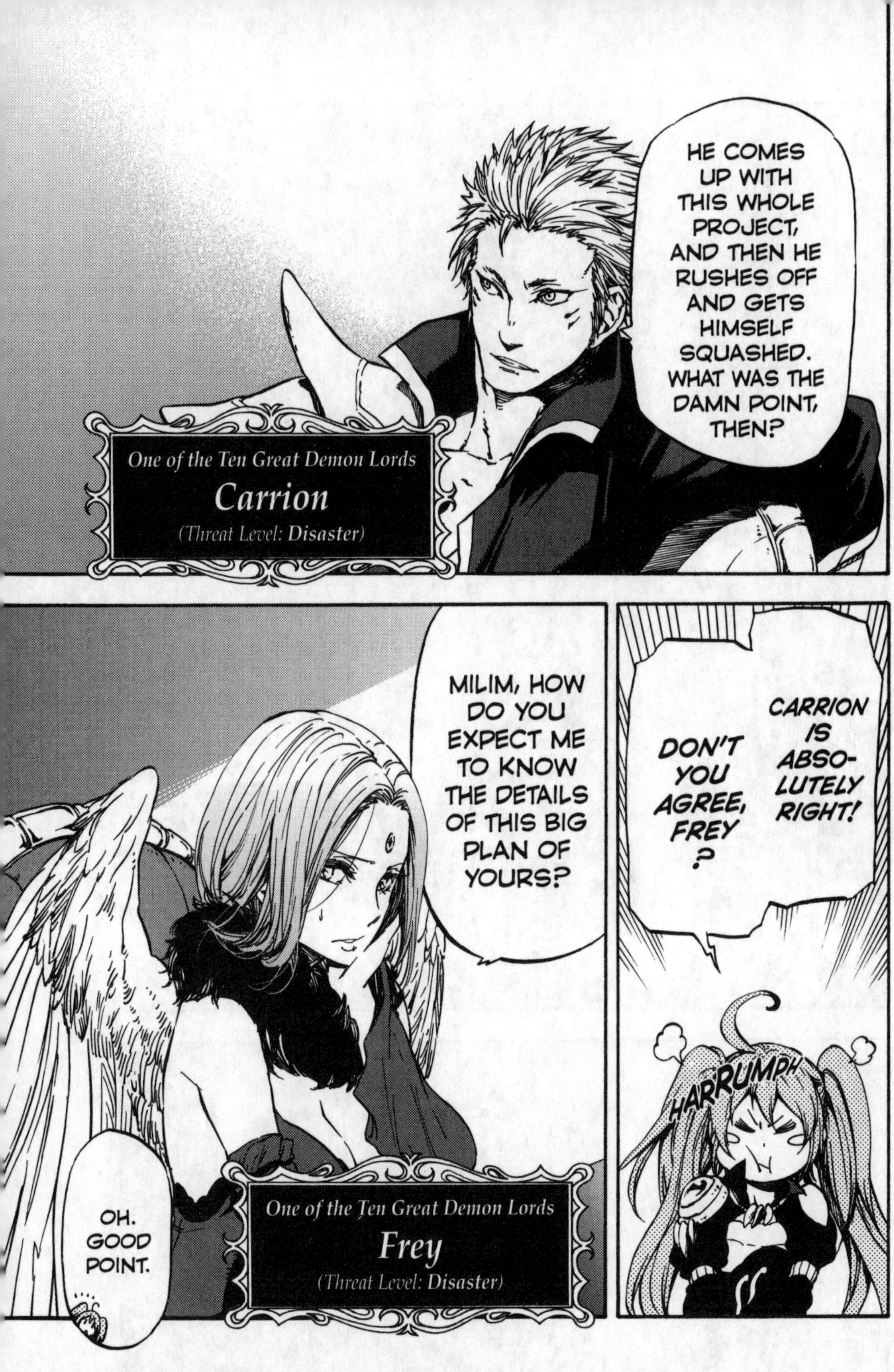
HE COMES UP WITH THIS WHOLE PROJECT, AND THEN HE RUSHES OFF AND GETS HIMSELF SQUASHED. WHAT WAS THE DAMN POINT, THEN?
One of the Ten Great Demon Lords
Carrion
(Threat Level: Disaster)
CARRION IS ABSOLUTELY RIGHT!
DON'T YOU AGREE, FREY?
HARRUMPH
MILIM, HOW DO YOU EXPECT ME TO KNOW THE DETAILS OF THIS BIG PLAN OF YOURS?
One of the Ten Great Demon Lords
Frey
(Threat Level: Disaster)
OH. GOOD POINT.

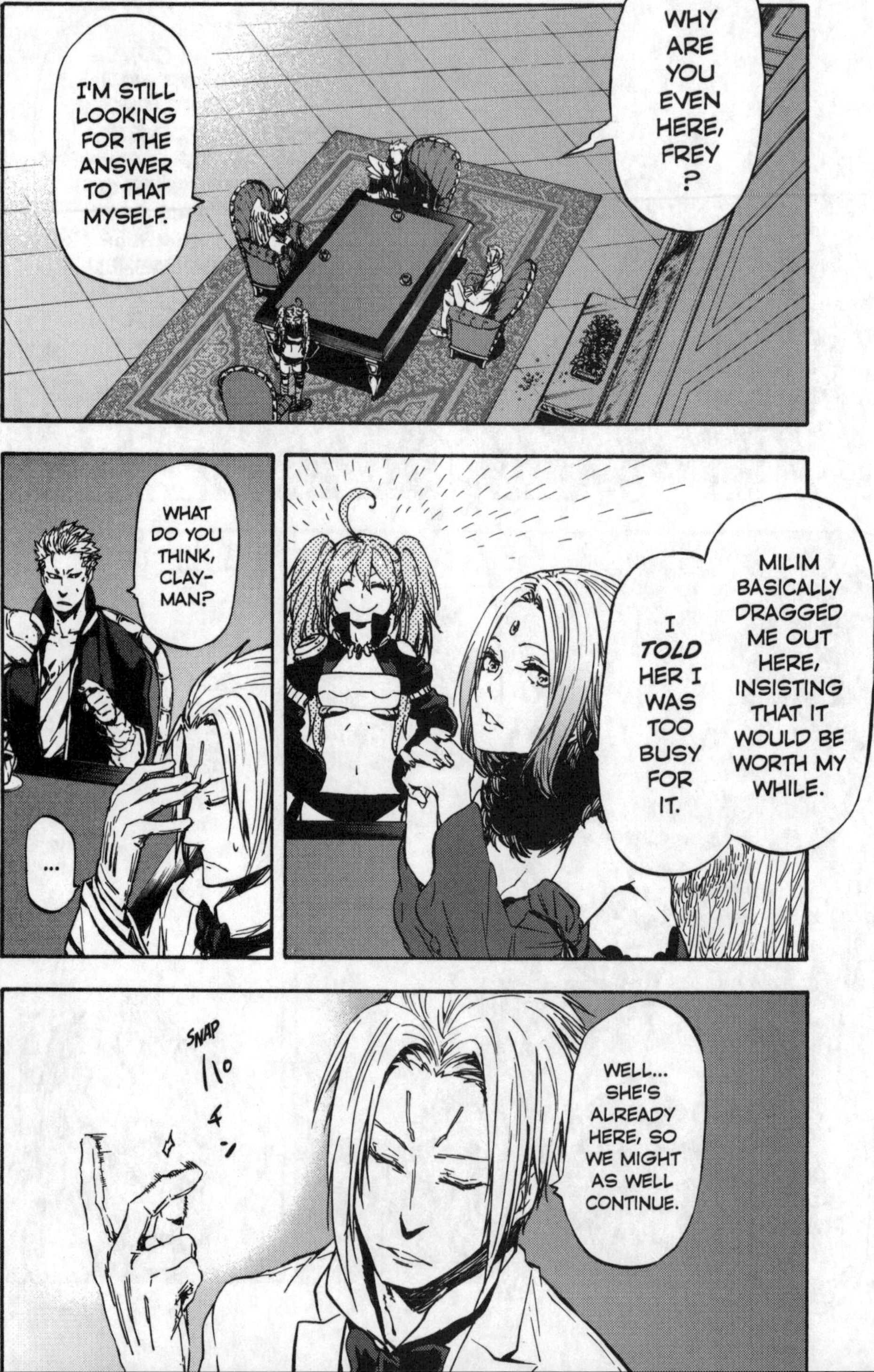
WHY ARE YOU EVEN HERE, FREY?
I'M STILL LOOKING FOR THE ANSWER TO THAT MYSELF.
MILIM BASICALLY DRAGGED ME OUT HERE, INSISTING THAT IT WOULD BE WORTH MY WHILE.
I *TOLD* HER I WAS TOO BUSY FOR IT.
WHAT DO YOU THINK, CLAYMAN?
...
SNAP
WELL... SHE'S ALREADY HERE, SO WE MIGHT AS WELL CONTINUE.

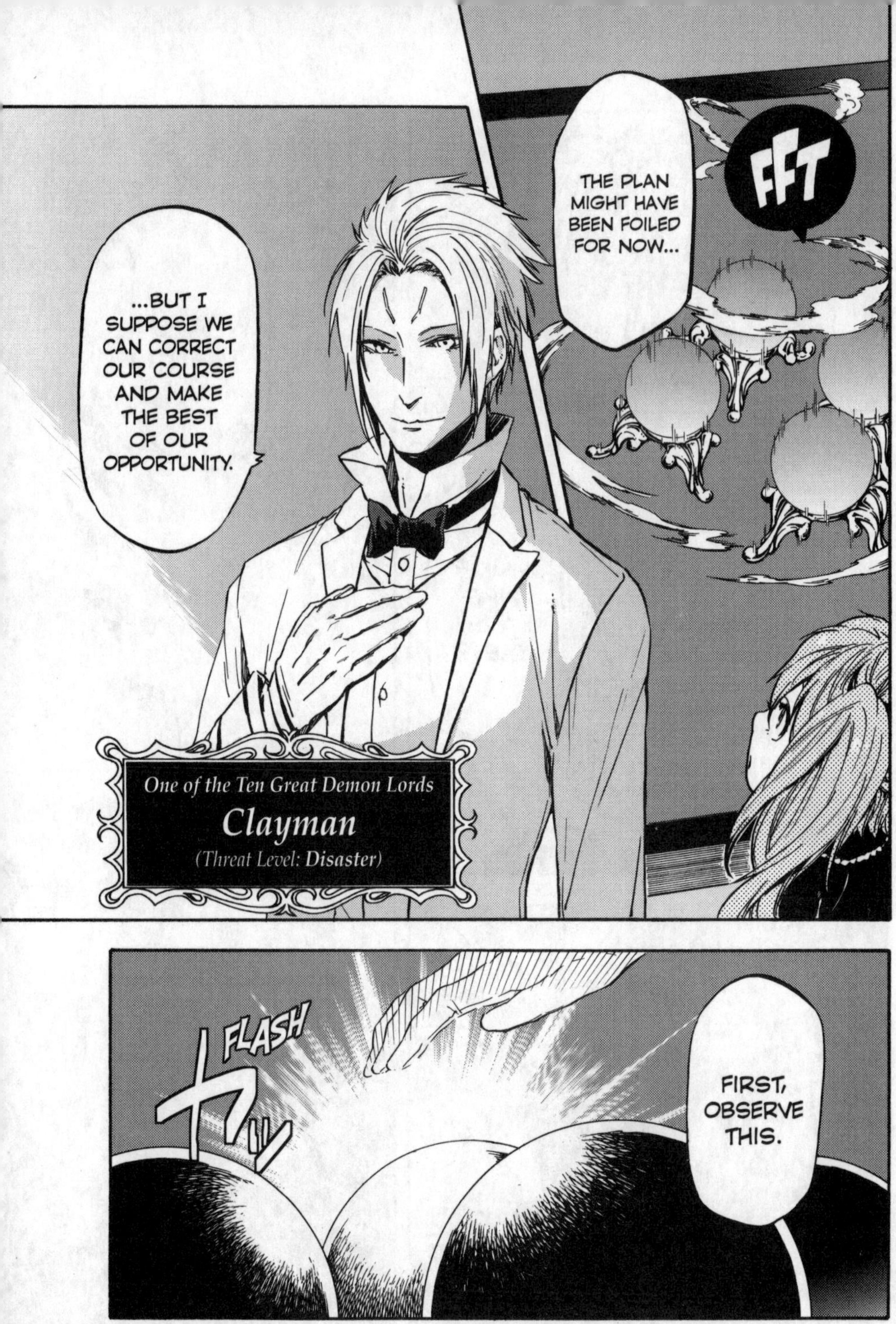
THE PLAN MIGHT HAVE BEEN FOILED FOR NOW...
FFT
...BUT I SUPPOSE WE CAN CORRECT OUR COURSE AND MAKE THE BEST OF OUR OPPORTUNITY.
One of the Ten Great Demon Lords
Clayman
(Threat Level: Disaster)
FIRST, OBSERVE THIS.
FLASH

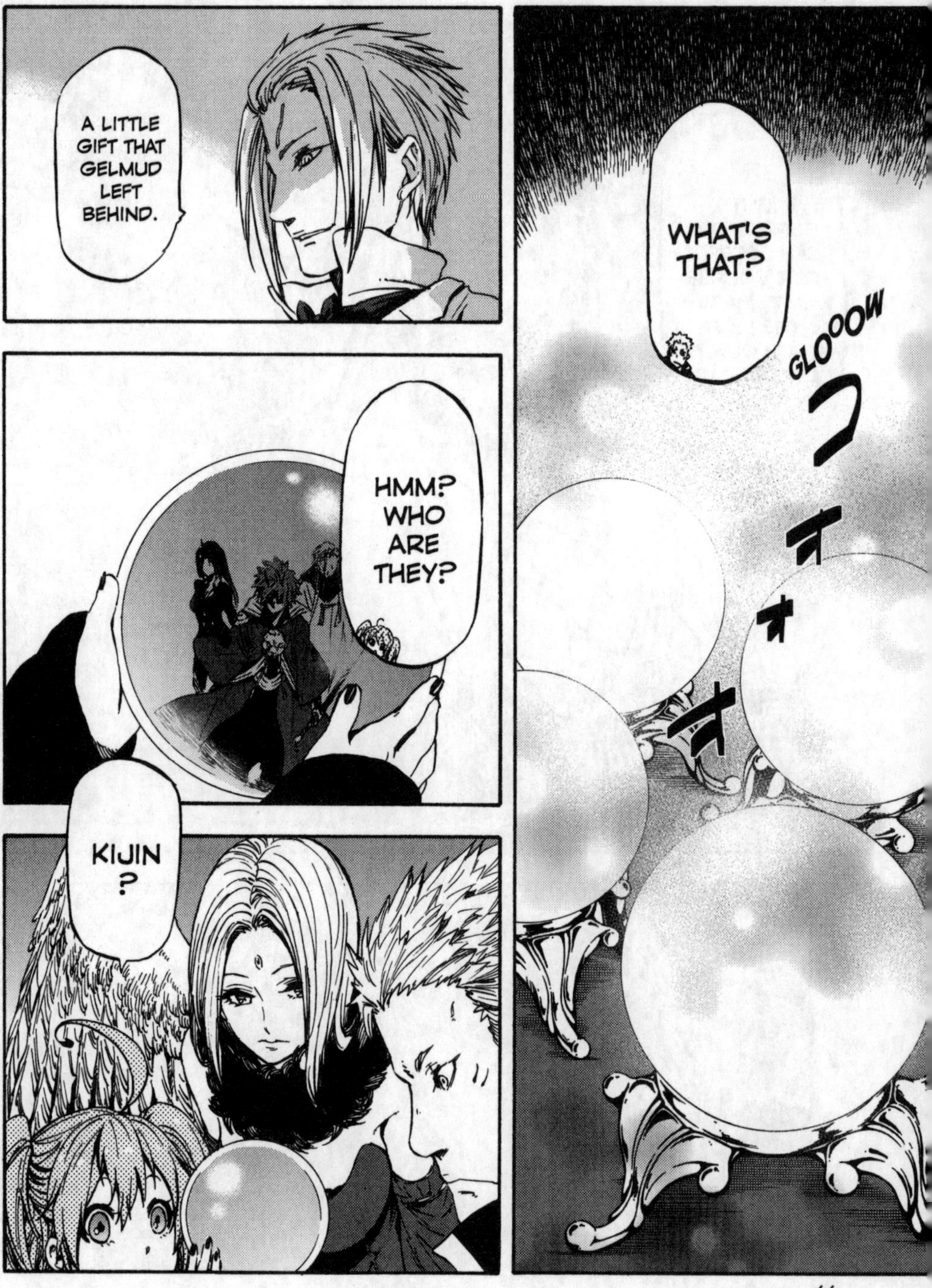
WHAT'S THAT?
GLOOOW
A LITTLE GIFT THAT GELMUD LEFT BEHIND.
HMM? WHO ARE THEY?
KIJIN?

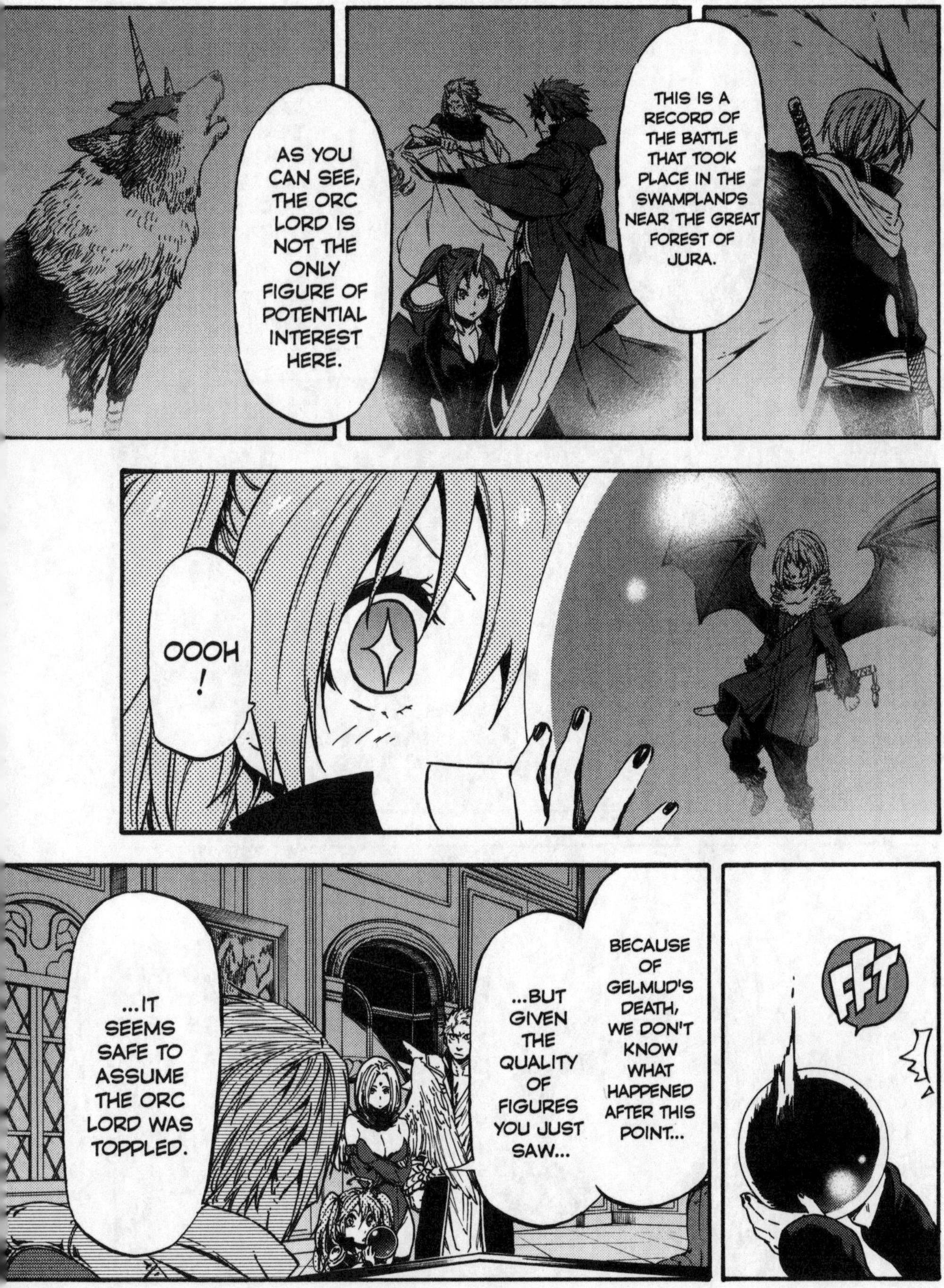
THIS IS A RECORD OF THE BATTLE THAT TOOK PLACE IN THE SWAMPLANDS NEAR THE GREAT FOREST OF JURA.
AS YOU CAN SEE, THE ORC LORD IS NOT THE ONLY FIGURE OF POTENTIAL INTEREST HERE.
OOOH !
FFT
!
BECAUSE OF GELMUD'S DEATH, WE DON'T KNOW WHAT HAPPENED AFTER THIS POINT...
...BUT GIVEN THE QUALITY OF FIGURES YOU JUST SAW...
...IT SEEMS SAFE TO ASSUME THE ORC LORD WAS TOPPLED.

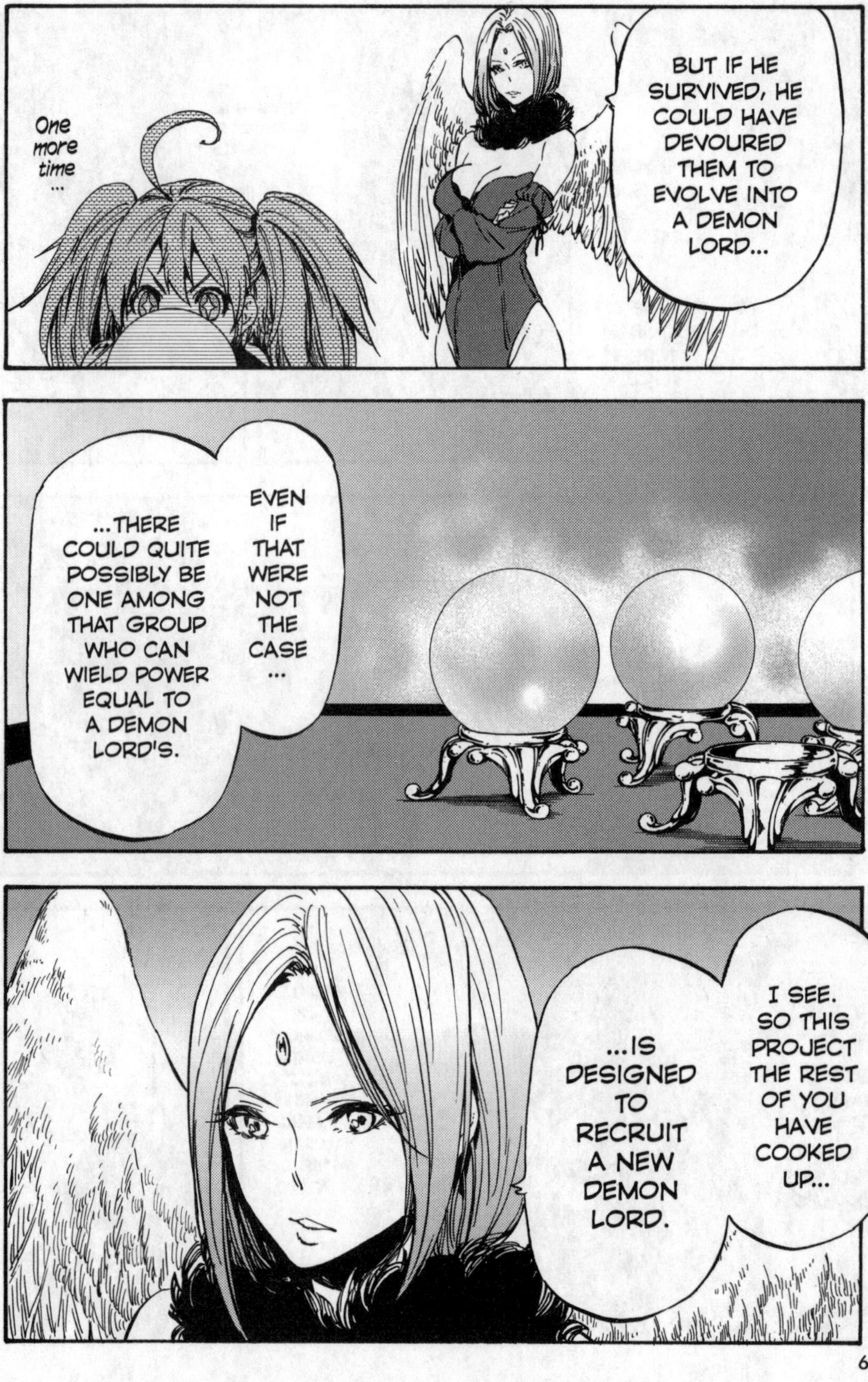
BUT IF HE SURVIVED, HE COULD HAVE DEVOURED THEM TO EVOLVE INTO A DEMON LORD...
One more time ...
EVEN IF THAT WERE NOT THE CASE ...
...THERE COULD QUITE POSSIBLY BE ONE AMONG THAT GROUP WHO CAN WIELD POWER EQUAL TO A DEMON LORD'S.
I SEE. SO THIS PROJECT THE REST OF YOU HAVE COOKED UP...
...IS DESIGNED TO RECRUIT A NEW DEMON LORD.

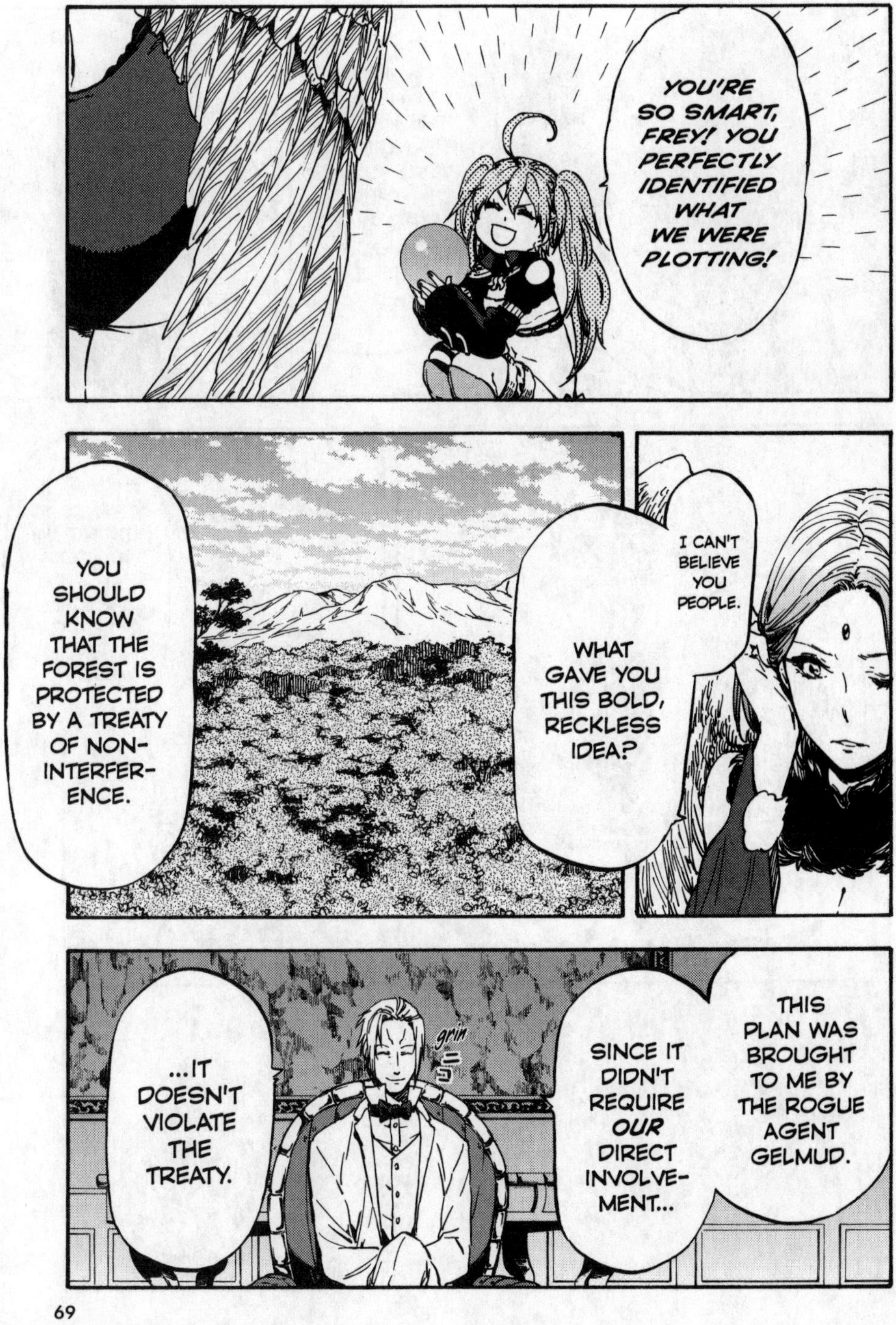
YOU'RE SO SMART, FREY! YOU PERFECTLY IDENTIFIED WHAT WE WERE PLOTTING!
I CAN'T BELIEVE YOU PEOPLE.
WHAT GAVE YOU THIS BOLD, RECKLESS IDEA?
YOU SHOULD KNOW THAT THE FOREST IS PROTECTED BY A TREATY OF NON-INTERFERENCE.
THIS PLAN WAS BROUGHT TO ME BY THE ROGUE AGENT GELMUD.
SINCE IT DIDN'T REQUIRE *OUR* DIRECT INVOLVEMENT...
grin
...IT DOESN'T VIOLATE THE TREATY.

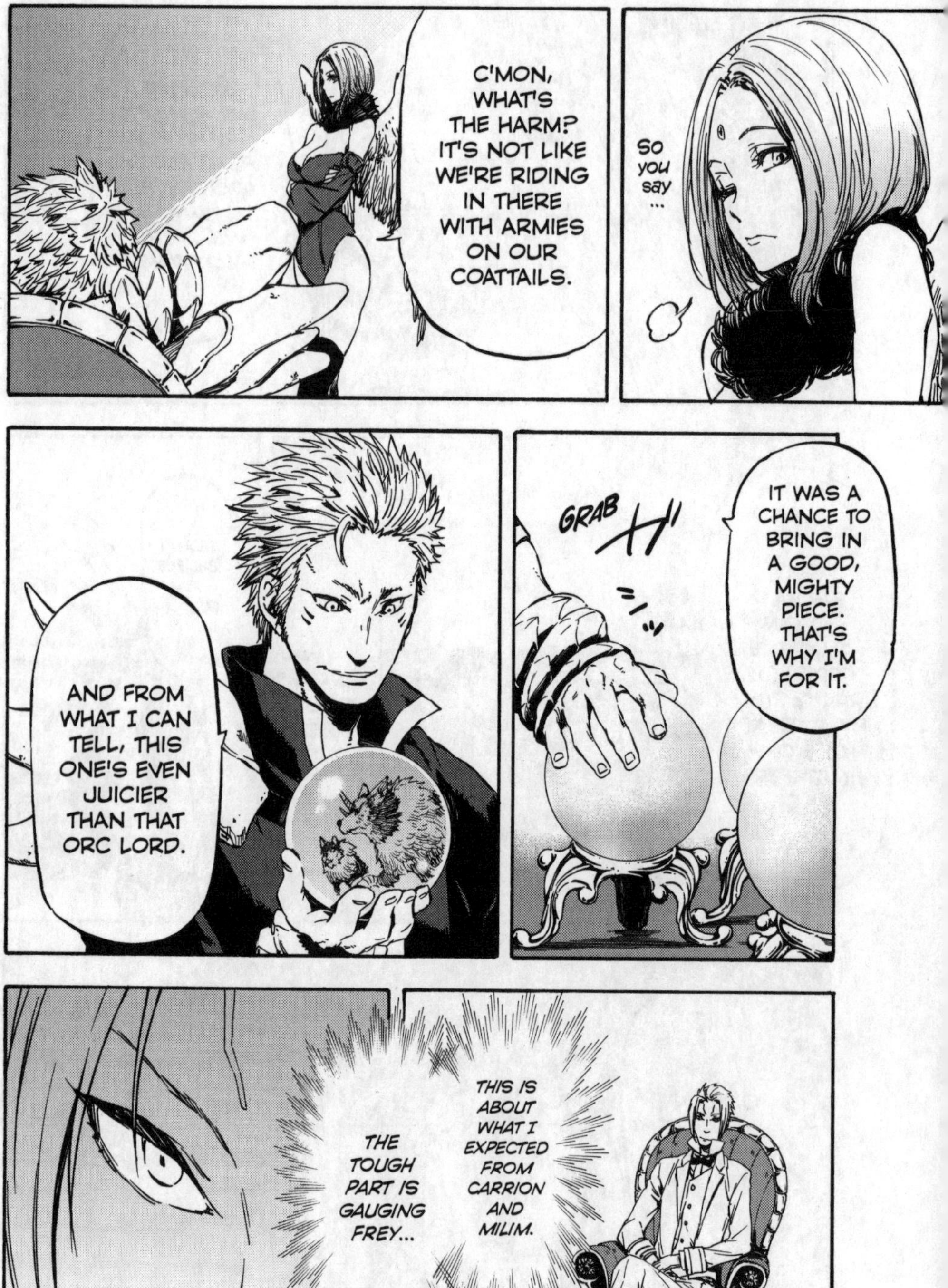
So you say ...
C'MON, WHAT'S THE HARM? IT'S NOT LIKE WE'RE RIDING IN THERE WITH ARMIES ON OUR COATTAILS.
GRAB
IT WAS A CHANCE TO BRING IN A GOOD, MIGHTY PIECE. THAT'S WHY I'M FOR IT.
AND FROM WHAT I CAN TELL, THIS ONE'S EVEN JUICIER THAN THAT ORC LORD.
THIS IS ABOUT WHAT I EXPECTED FROM CARRION AND MILIM.
THE TOUGH PART IS GAUGING FREY...

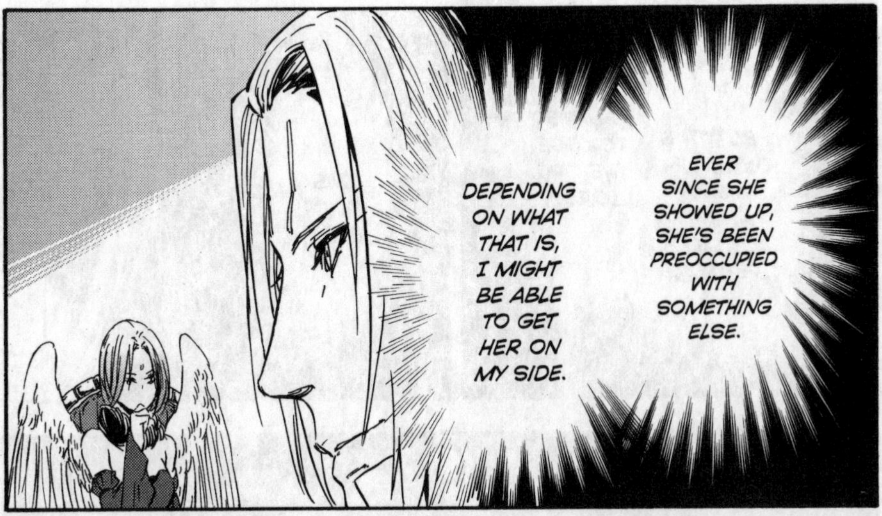
EVER SINCE SHE SHOWED UP, SHE'S BEEN PREOCCUPIED WITH SOMETHING ELSE.
DEPENDING ON WHAT THAT IS, I MIGHT BE ABLE TO GET HER ON MY SIDE.

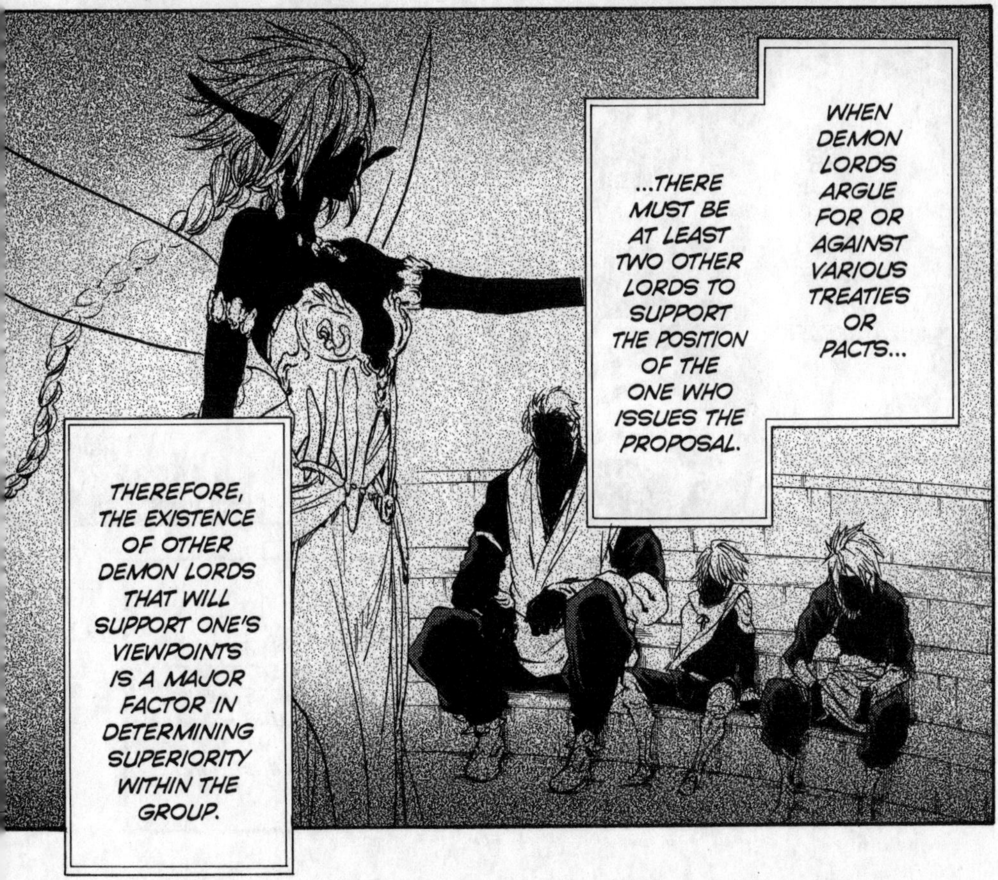
WHEN DEMON LORDS ARGUE FOR OR AGAINST VARIOUS TREATIES OR PACTS...
...THERE MUST BE AT LEAST TWO OTHER LORDS TO SUPPORT THE POSITION OF THE ONE WHO ISSUES THE PROPOSAL.
THEREFORE, THE EXISTENCE OF OTHER DEMON LORDS THAT WILL SUPPORT ONE'S VIEWPOINTS IS A MAJOR FACTOR IN DETERMINING SUPERIORITY WITHIN THE GROUP.

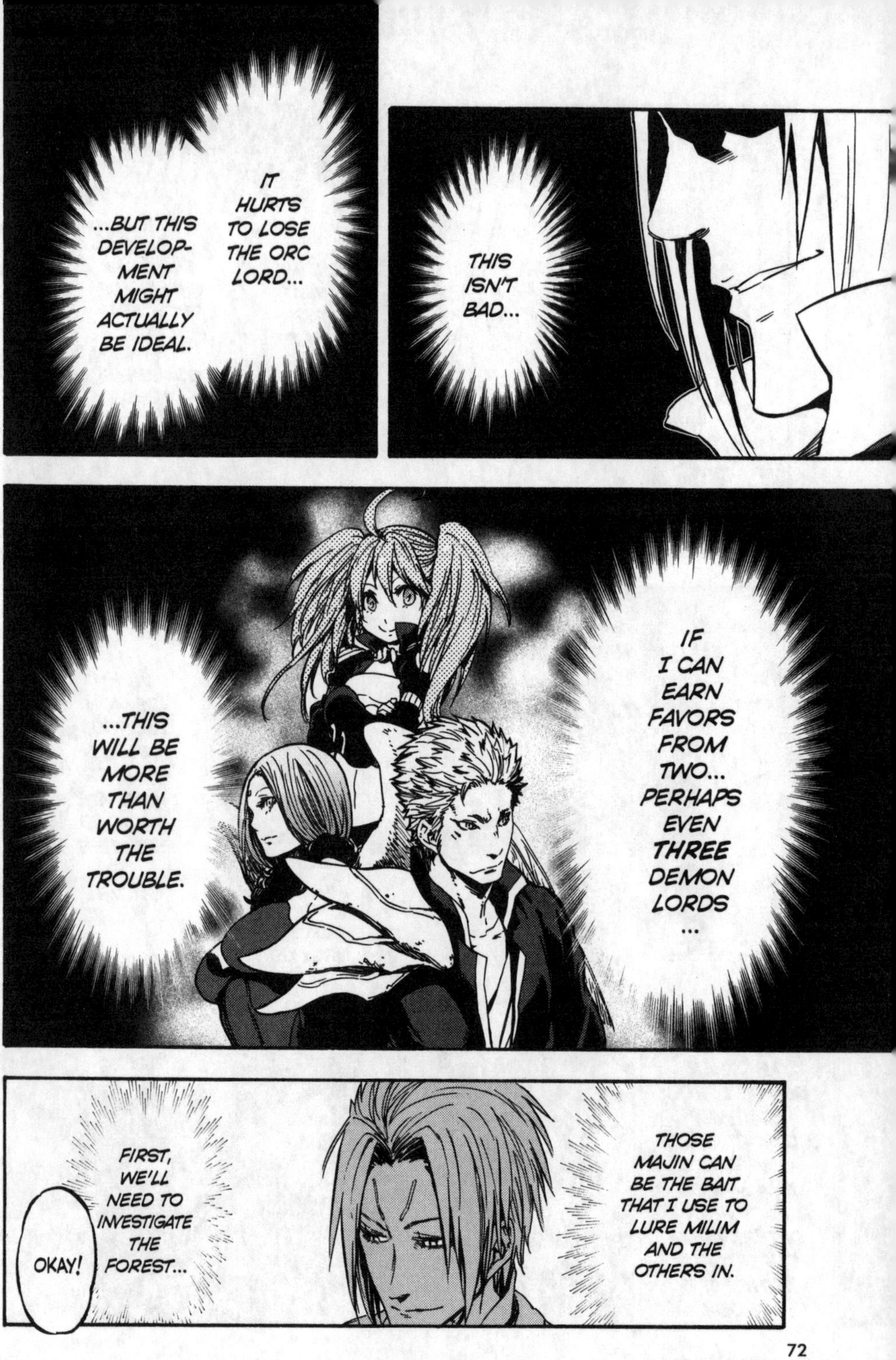
THIS ISN'T BAD...
IT HURTS TO LOSE THE ORC LORD...
...BUT THIS DEVELOP-MENT MIGHT ACTUALLY BE IDEAL.
IF I CAN EARN FAVORS FROM TWO... PERHAPS EVEN THREE DEMON LORDS...
...THIS WILL BE MORE THAN WORTH THE TROUBLE.
THOSE MAJIN CAN BE THE BAIT THAT I USE TO LURE MILIM AND THE OTHERS IN.
FIRST, WE'LL NEED TO INVESTIGATE THE FOREST...
OKAY!

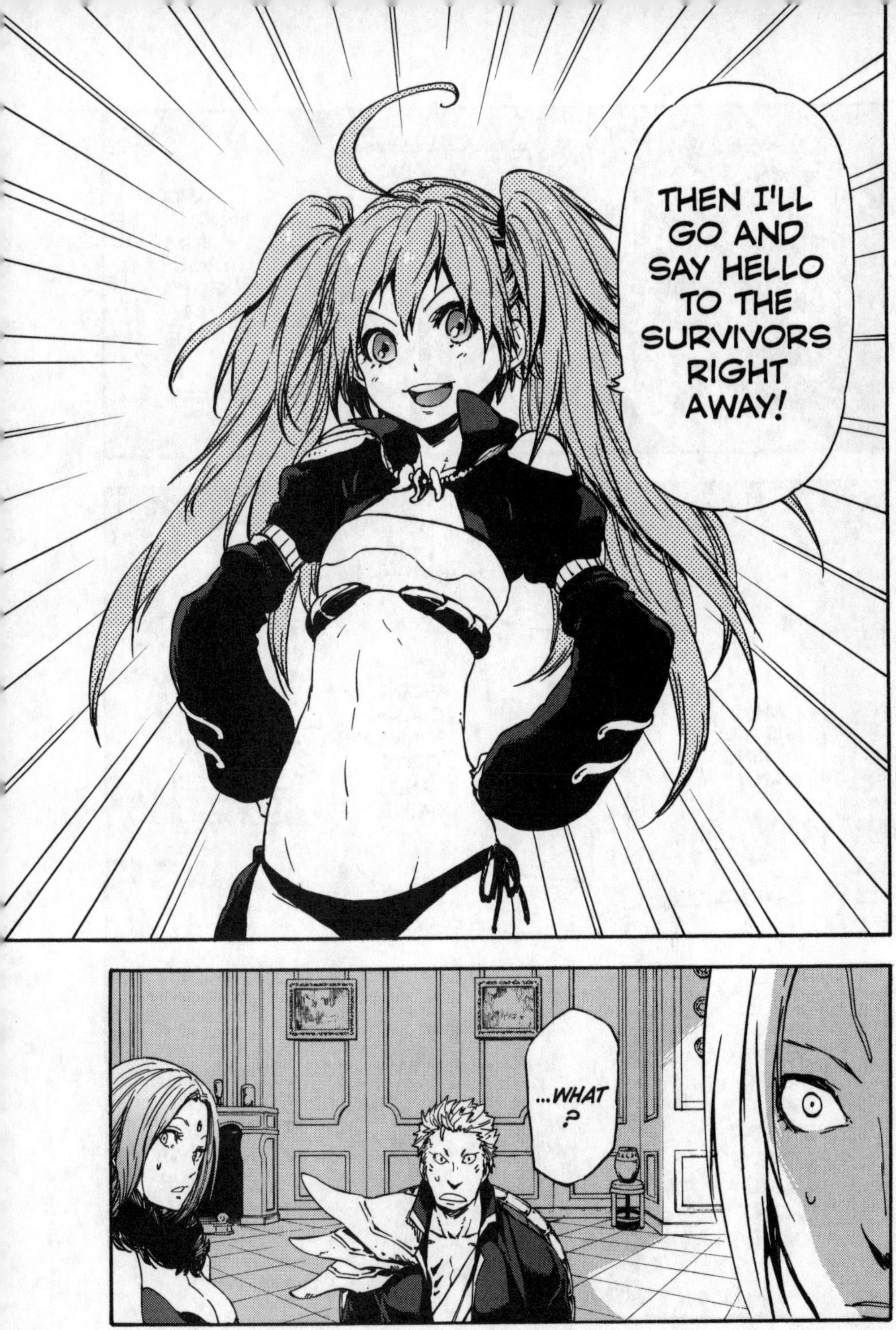
THEN I'LL GO AND SAY HELLO TO THE SURVIVORS RIGHT AWAY!
...WHAT ?

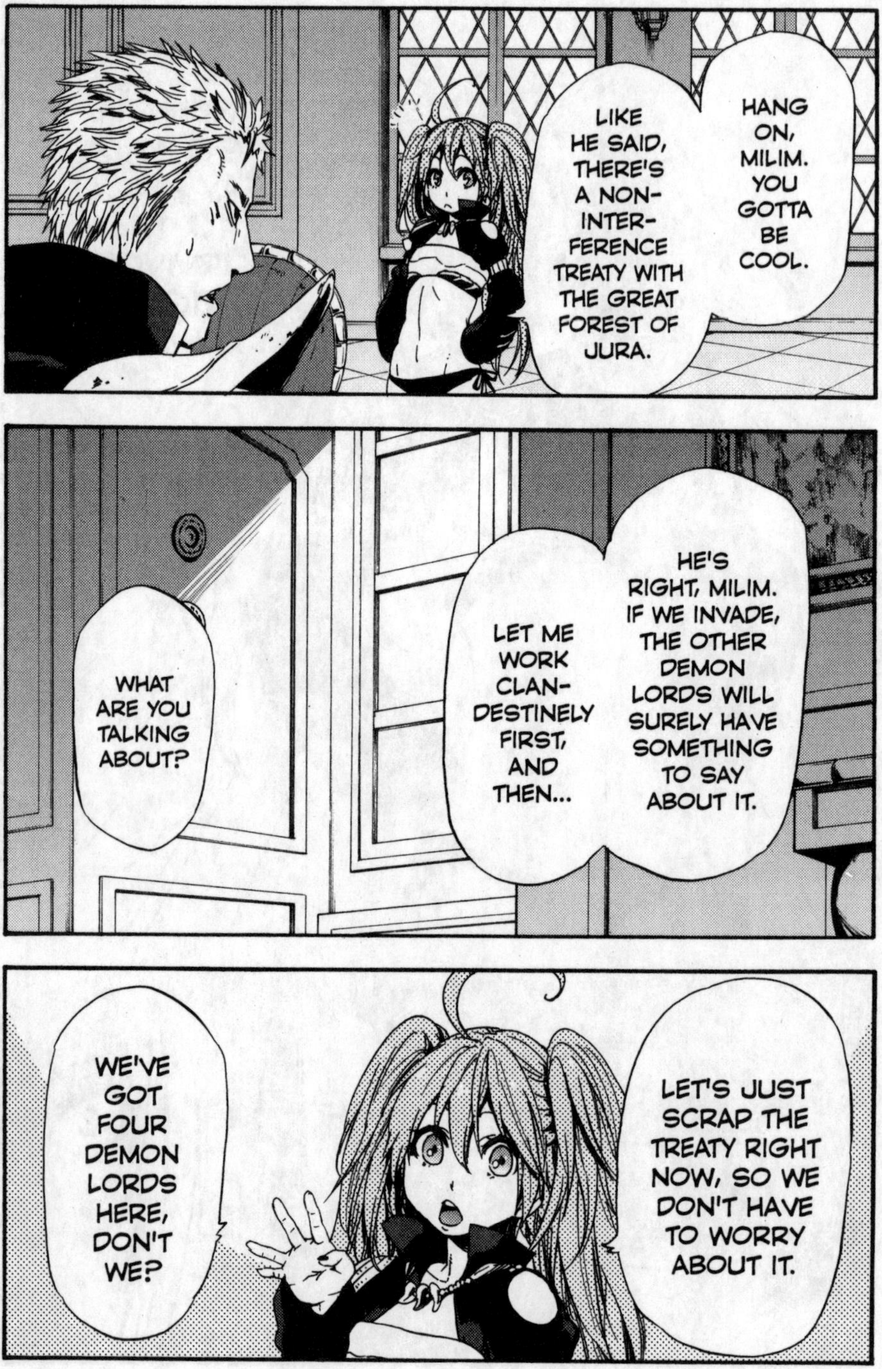
HANG ON, MILIM. YOU GOTTA BE COOL.
LIKE HE SAID, THERE'S A NON-INTERFERENCE TREATY WITH THE GREAT FOREST OF JURA.
HE'S RIGHT, MILIM. IF WE INVADE, THE OTHER DEMON LORDS WILL SURELY HAVE SOMETHING TO SAY ABOUT IT.
LET ME WORK CLANDESTINELY FIRST, AND THEN...
WHAT ARE YOU TALKING ABOUT?
LET'S JUST SCRAP THE TREATY RIGHT NOW, SO WE DON'T HAVE TO WORRY ABOUT IT.
WE'VE GOT FOUR DEMON LORDS HERE, DON'T WE?

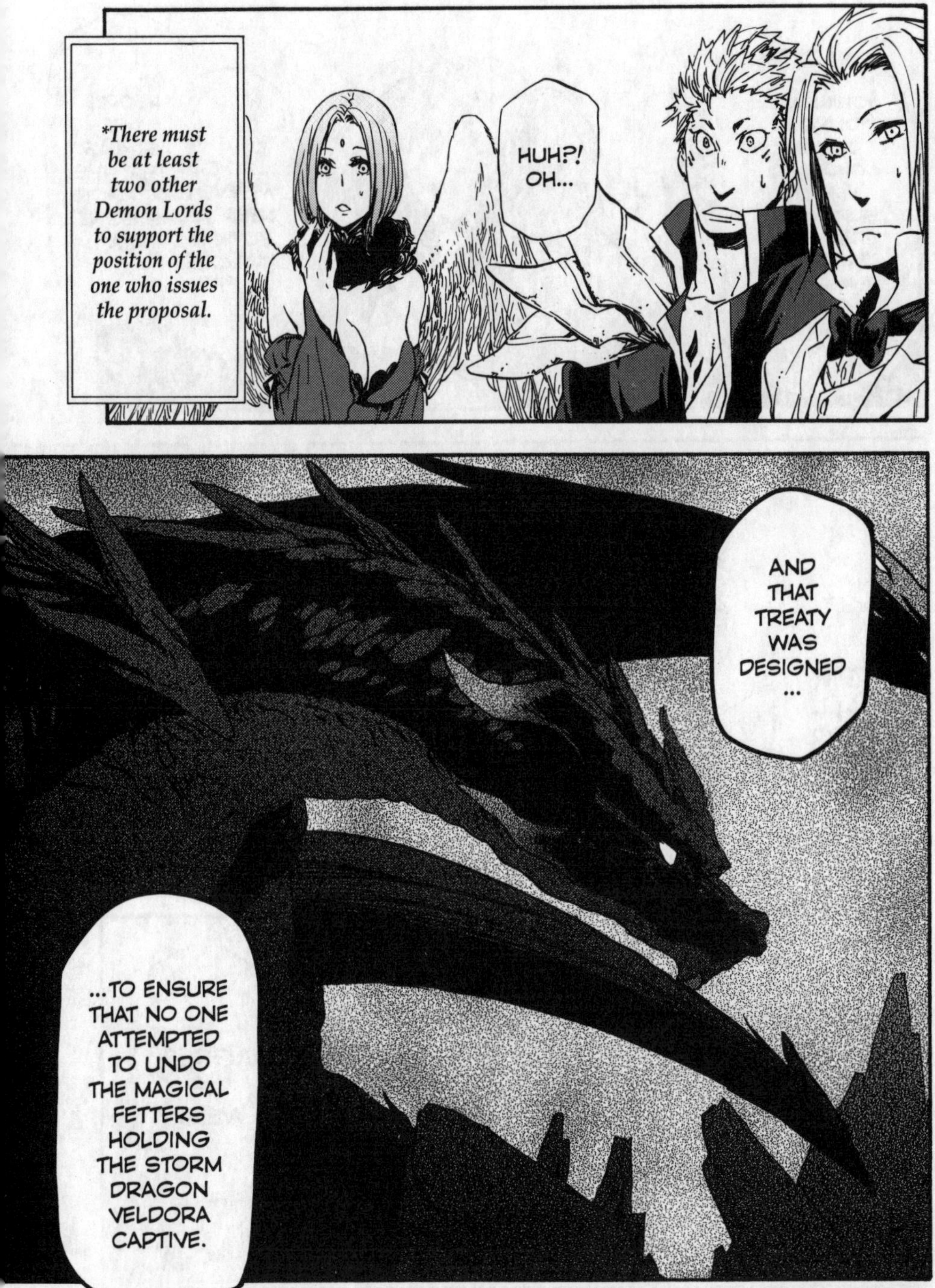
HUH?! OH...
*There must be at least two other Demon Lords to support the position of the one who issues the proposal.
AND THAT TREATY WAS DESIGNED ...
...TO ENSURE THAT NO ONE ATTEMPTED TO UNDO THE MAGICAL FETTERS HOLDING THE STORM DRAGON VELDORA CAPTIVE.

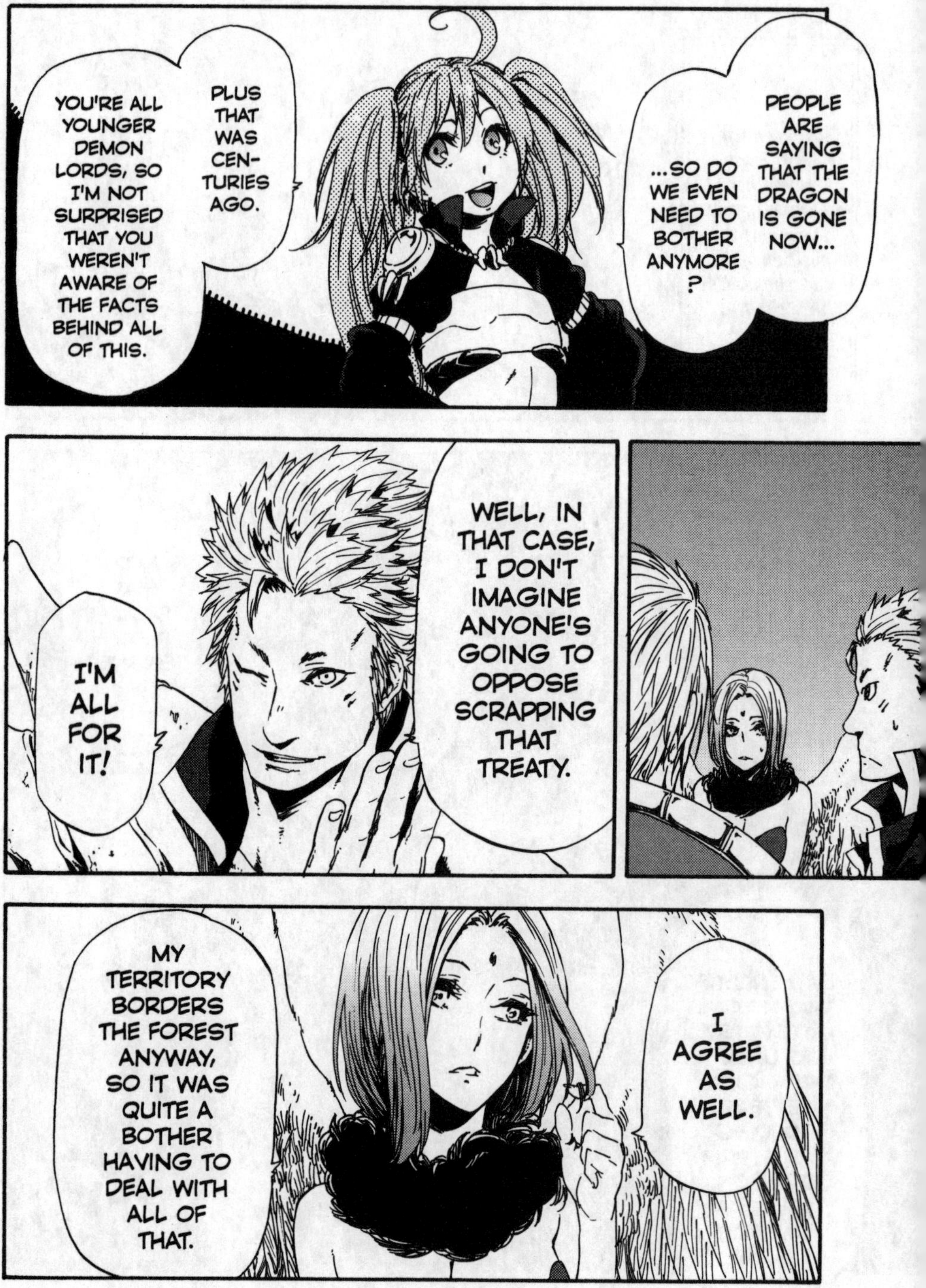
PEOPLE ARE SAYING THAT THE DRAGON IS GONE NOW...
...SO DO WE EVEN NEED TO BOTHER ANYMORE?
PLUS THAT WAS CEN-TURIES AGO.
YOU'RE ALL YOUNGER DEMON LORDS, SO I'M NOT SURPRISED THAT YOU WEREN'T AWARE OF THE FACTS BEHIND ALL OF THIS.
WELL, IN THAT CASE, I DON'T IMAGINE ANYONE'S GOING TO OPPOSE SCRAPPING THAT TREATY.
I'M ALL FOR IT!
I AGREE AS WELL.
MY TERRITORY BORDERS THE FOREST ANYWAY, SO IT WAS QUITE A BOTHER HAVING TO DEAL WITH ALL OF THAT.

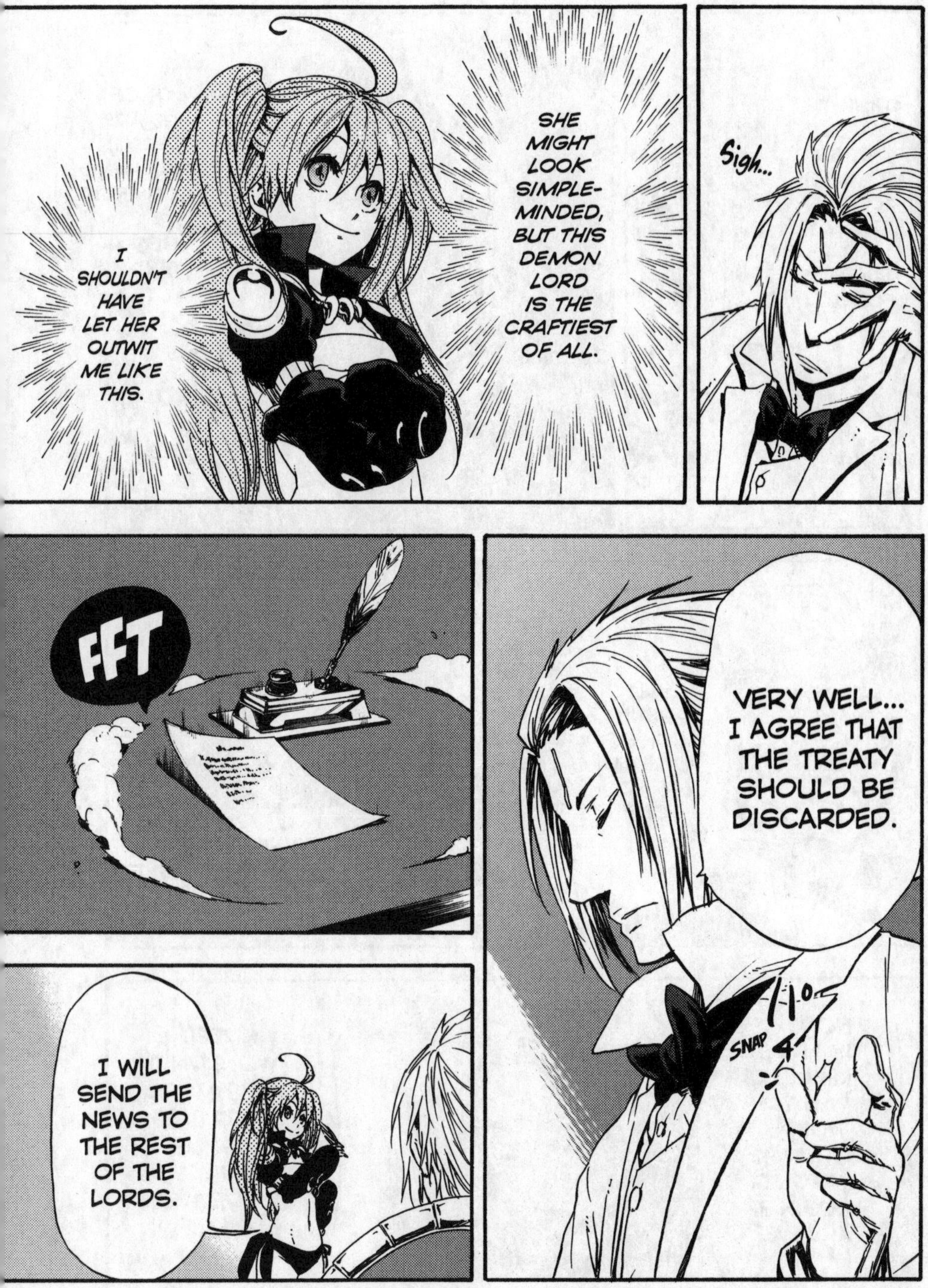
Sigh...
SHE MIGHT LOOK SIMPLE-MINDED, BUT THIS DEMON LORD IS THE CRAFTIEST OF ALL.
I SHOULDN'T HAVE LET HER OUTWIT ME LIKE THIS.
VERY WELL... I AGREE THAT THE TREATY SHOULD BE DISCARDED.
SNAP
FFT
I WILL SEND THE NEWS TO THE REST OF THE LORDS.

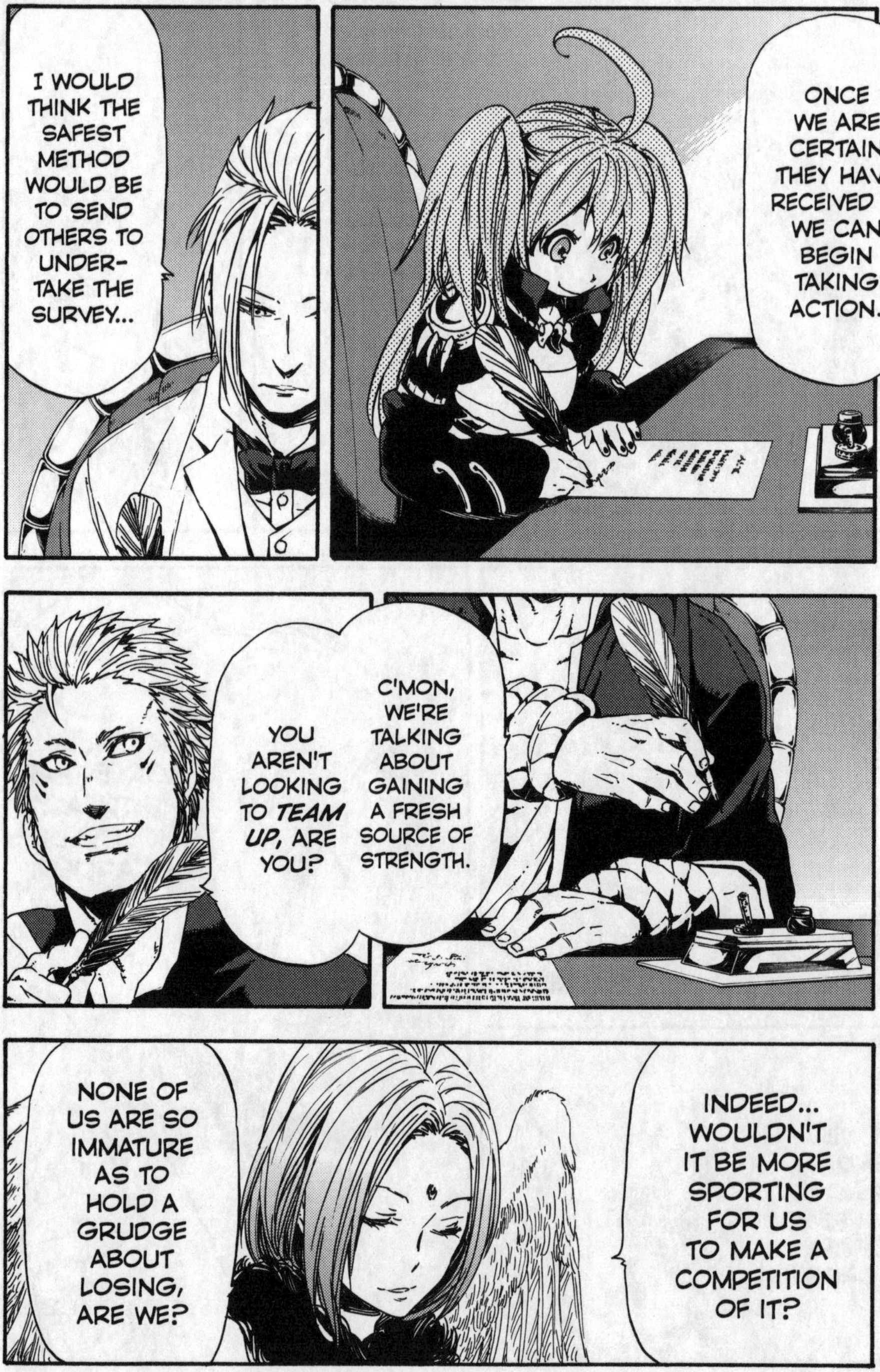
ONCE WE ARE CERTAIN THEY HAVE RECEIVED IT, WE CAN BEGIN TAKING ACTION.
I WOULD THINK THE SAFEST METHOD WOULD BE TO SEND OTHERS TO UNDER-TAKE THE SURVEY...
C'MON, WE'RE TALKING ABOUT GAINING A FRESH SOURCE OF STRENGTH.
YOU AREN'T LOOKING TO *TEAM UP*, ARE YOU?
INDEED... WOULDN'T IT BE MORE SPORTING FOR US TO MAKE A COMPETITION OF IT?
NONE OF US ARE SO IMMATURE AS TO HOLD A GRUDGE ABOUT LOSING, ARE WE?

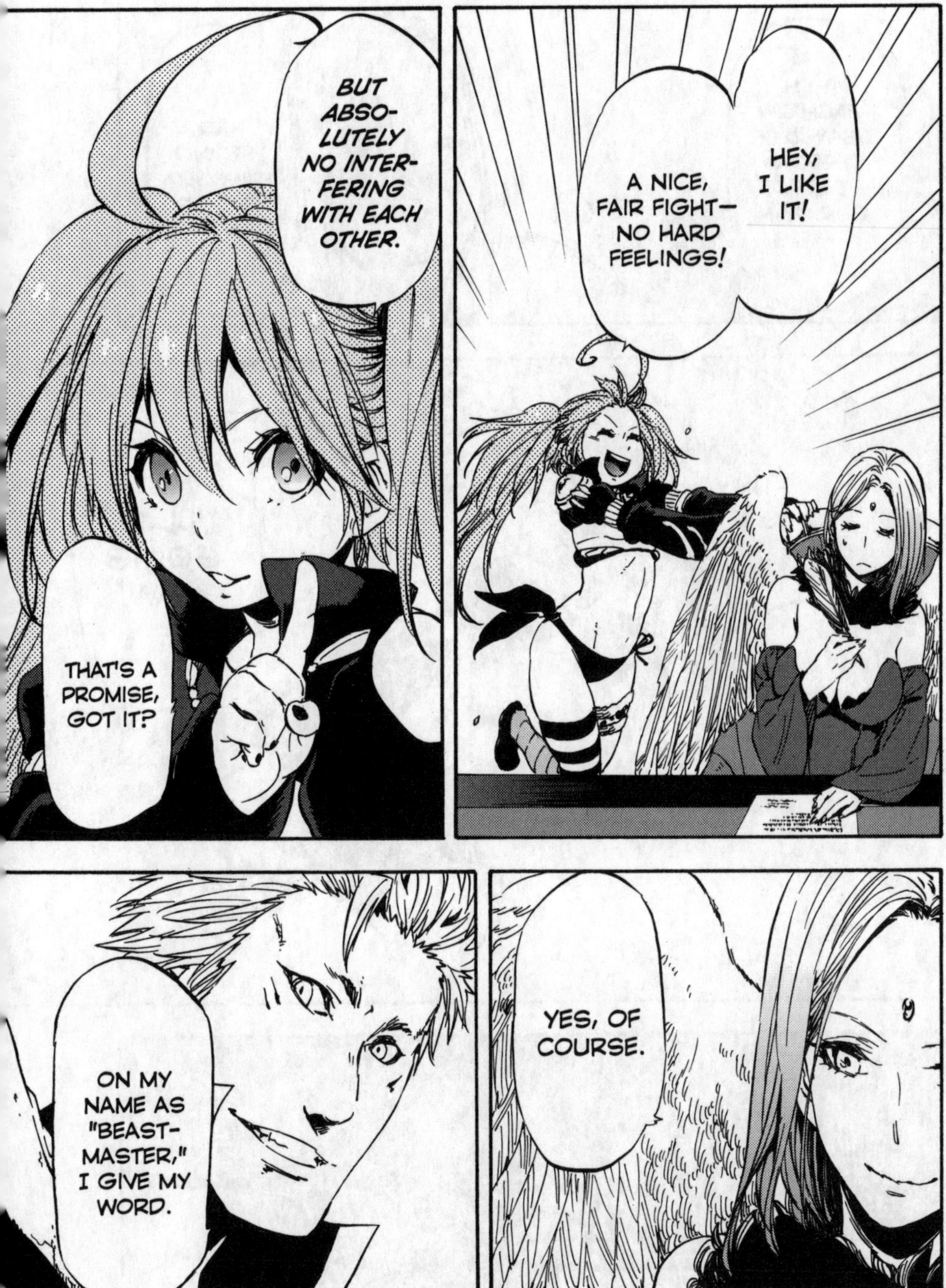
HEY, I LIKE IT!
A NICE, FAIR FIGHT— NO HARD FEELINGS!
BUT ABSO-LUTELY NO INTER-FERING WITH EACH OTHER.
THAT'S A PROMISE, GOT IT?
YES, OF COURSE.
ON MY NAME AS "BEAST-MASTER," I GIVE MY WORD.

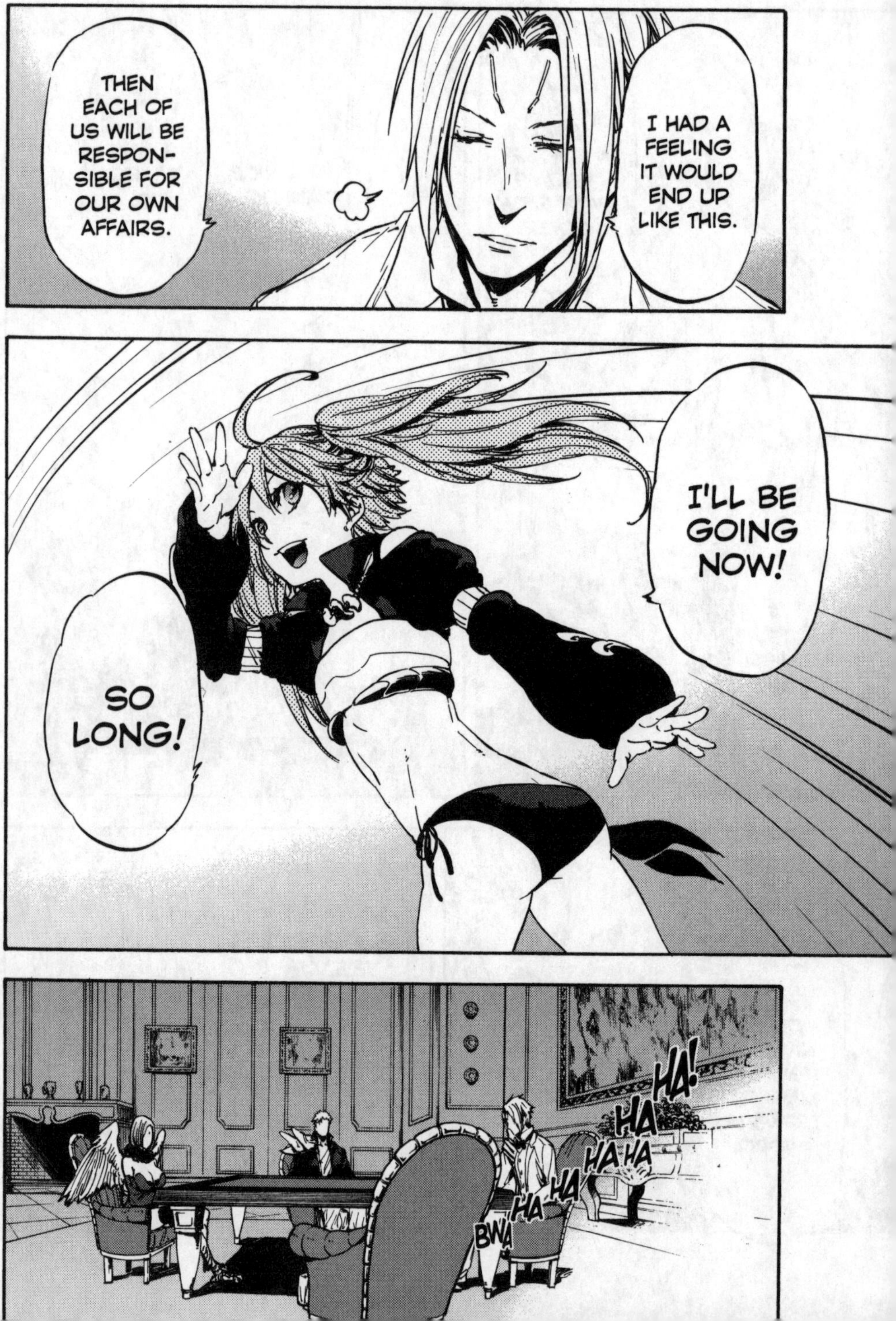
I HAD A FEELING IT WOULD END UP LIKE THIS.
THEN EACH OF US WILL BE RESPONSIBLE FOR OUR OWN AFFAIRS.
I'LL BE GOING NOW!
SO LONG!
BWA HA HA HA HA HA HA!

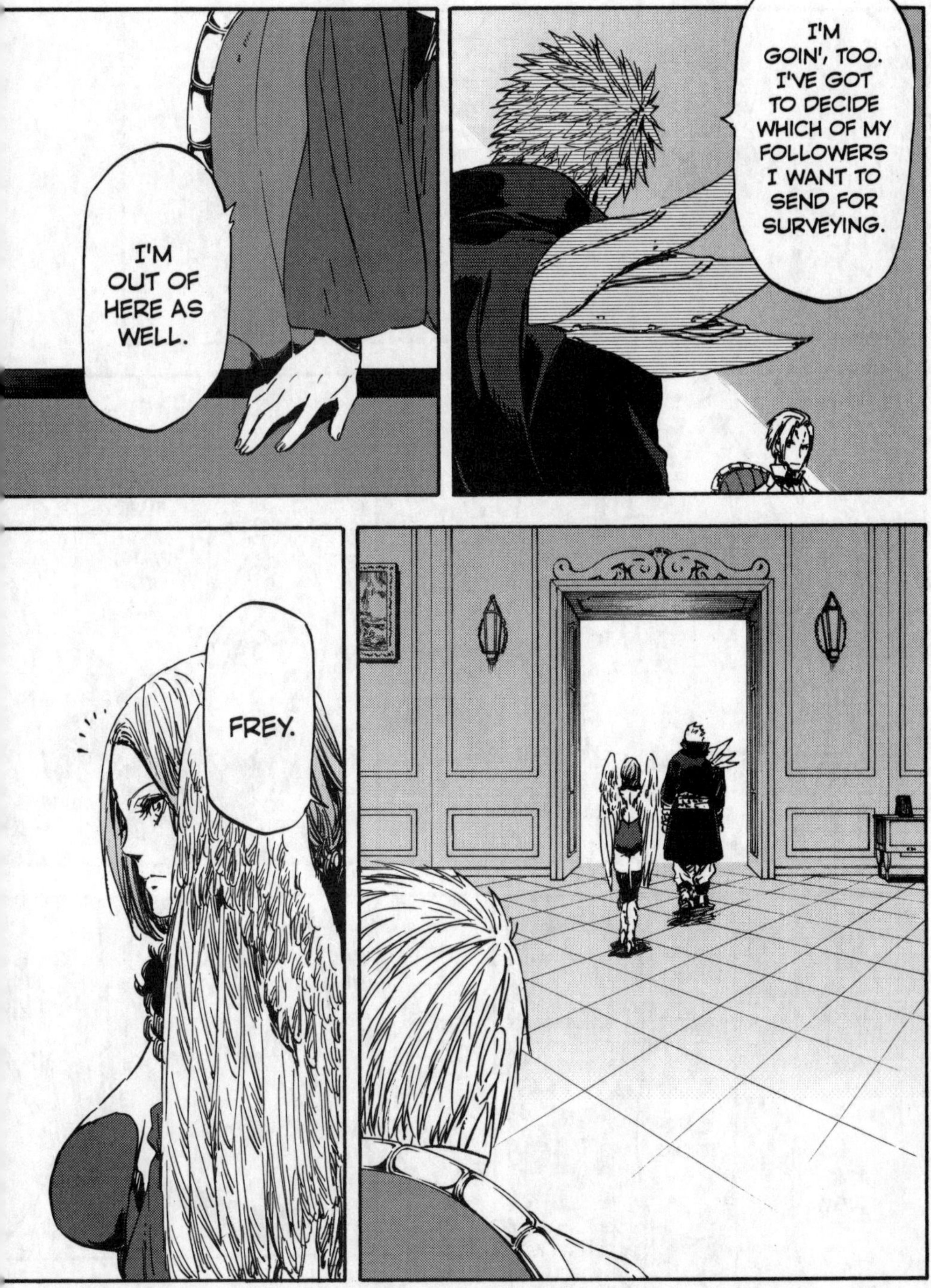
I'M GOIN', TOO. I'VE GOT TO DECIDE WHICH OF MY FOLLOWERS I WANT TO SEND FOR SURVEYING.
I'M OUT OF HERE AS WELL.
FREY.

IF YOU'VE GOT ANY PROBLEMS ON YOUR MIND, I'M MORE THAN WILLING TO HEAR YOU OUT.

THANK YOU.

...I SEE.

spin

ANY-TIME YOU WANT TO TALK.

...

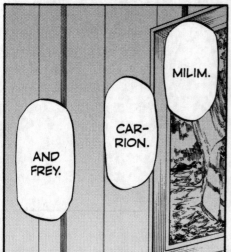

AND FREY.

CAR-RION.

MILIM.

SMIRK

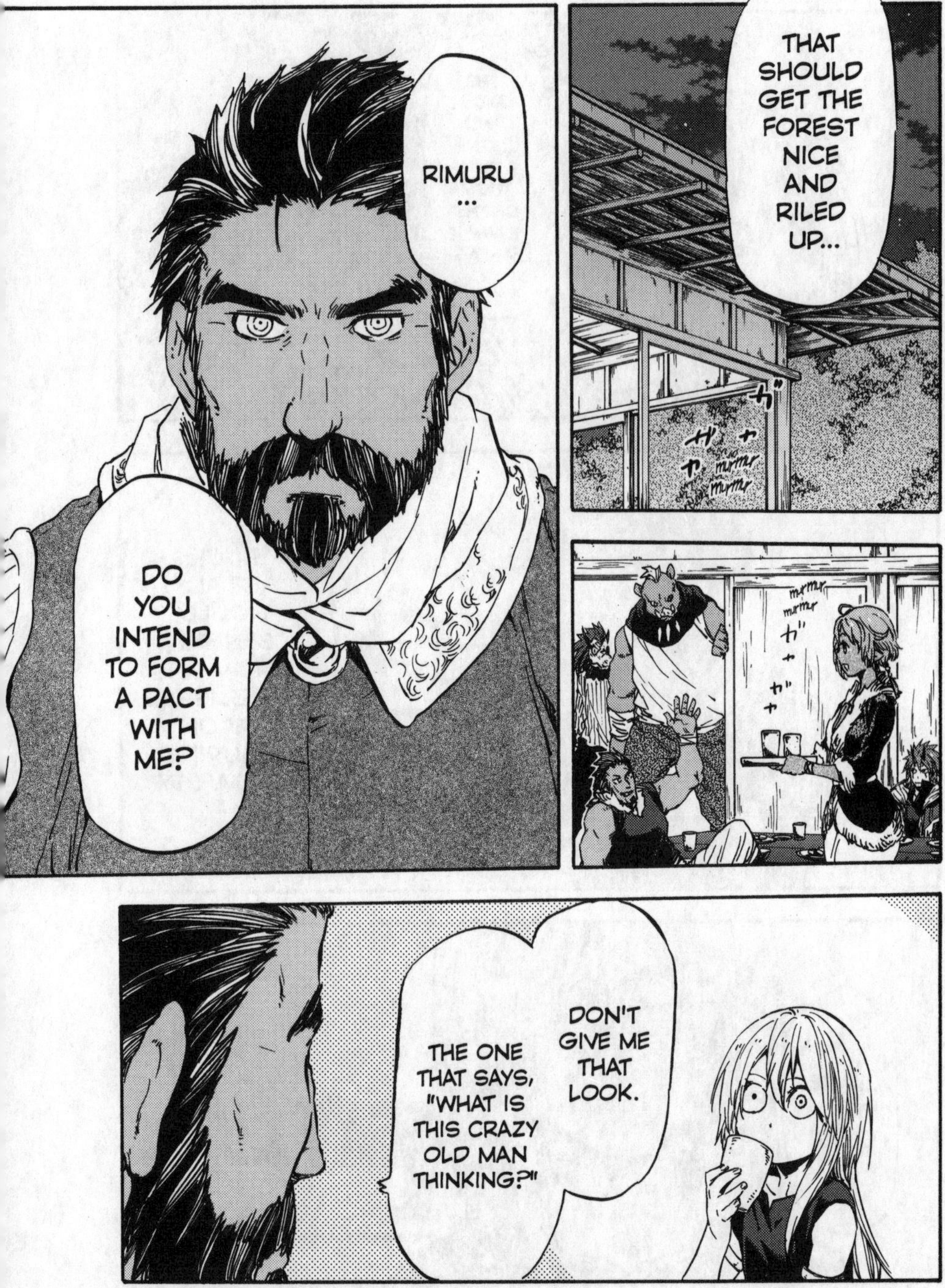
THAT SHOULD GET THE FOREST NICE AND RILED UP...
murmur murmur
murmur murmur
RIMURU ...
DO YOU INTEND TO FORM A PACT WITH ME?
DON'T GIVE ME THAT LOOK.
THE ONE THAT SAYS, "WHAT IS THIS CRAZY OLD MAN THINKING?"

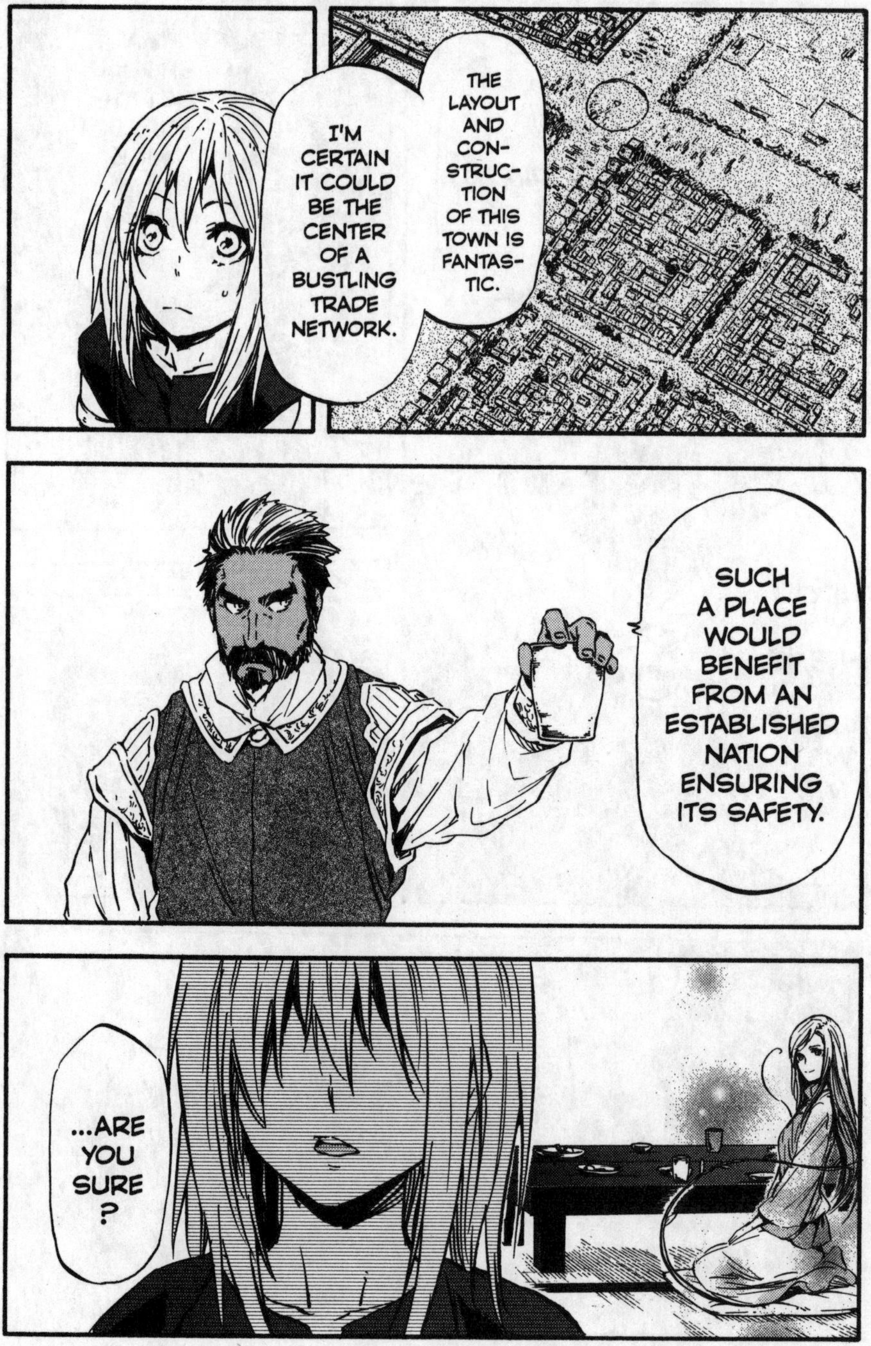
THE LAYOUT AND CONSTRUCTION OF THIS TOWN IS FANTASTIC.
I'M CERTAIN IT COULD BE THE CENTER OF A BUSTLING TRADE NETWORK.
SUCH A PLACE WOULD BENEFIT FROM AN ESTABLISHED NATION ENSURING ITS SAFETY.
...ARE YOU SURE?

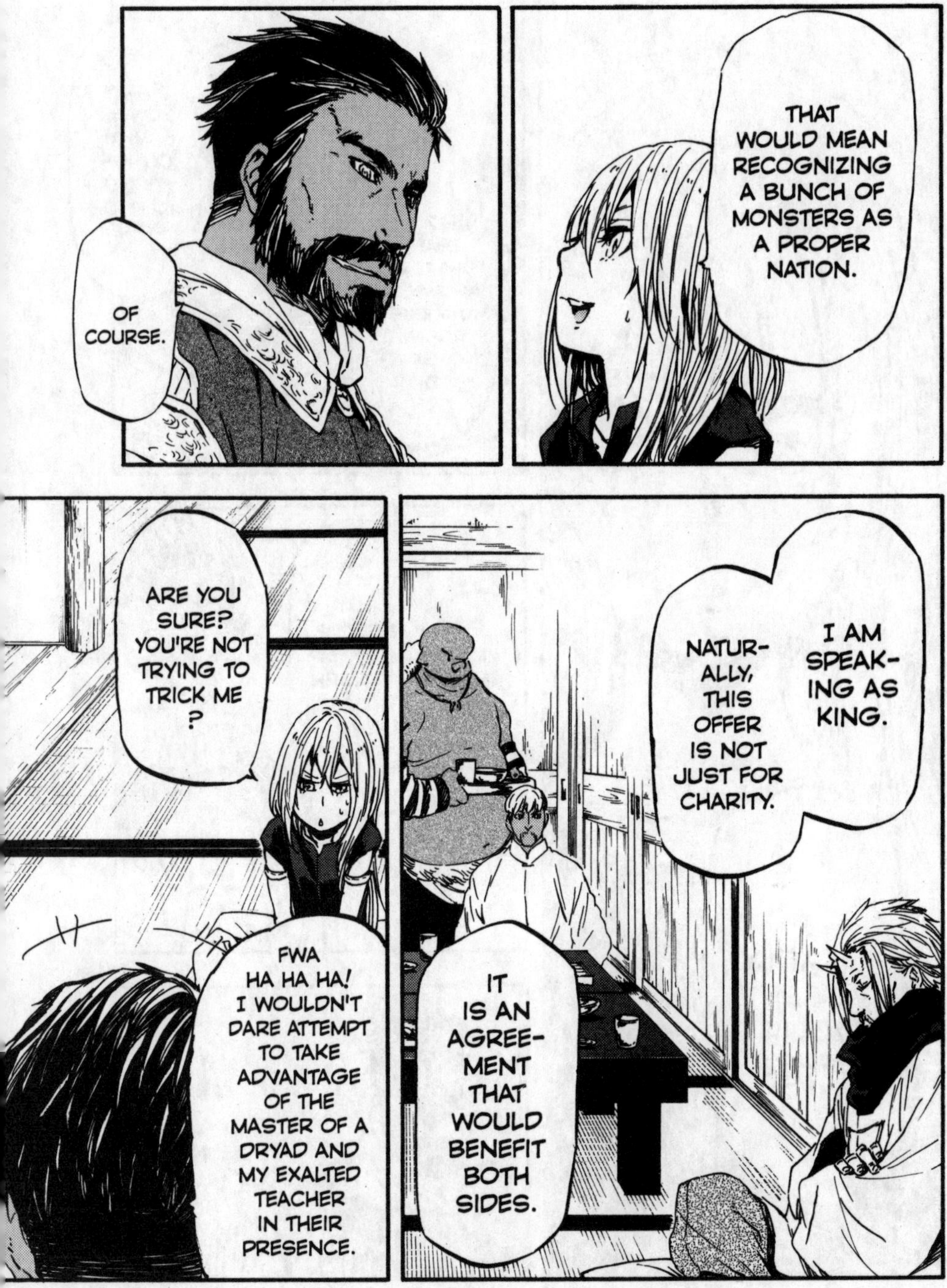
THAT WOULD MEAN RECOGNIZING A BUNCH OF MONSTERS AS A PROPER NATION.
OF COURSE.
I AM SPEAKING AS KING.
NATURALLY, THIS OFFER IS NOT JUST FOR CHARITY.
IT IS AN AGREEMENT THAT WOULD BENEFIT BOTH SIDES.
ARE YOU SURE? YOU'RE NOT TRYING TO TRICK ME?
FWA HA HA HA! I WOULDN'T DARE ATTEMPT TO TAKE ADVANTAGE OF THE MASTER OF A DRYAD AND MY EXALTED TEACHER IN THEIR PRESENCE.

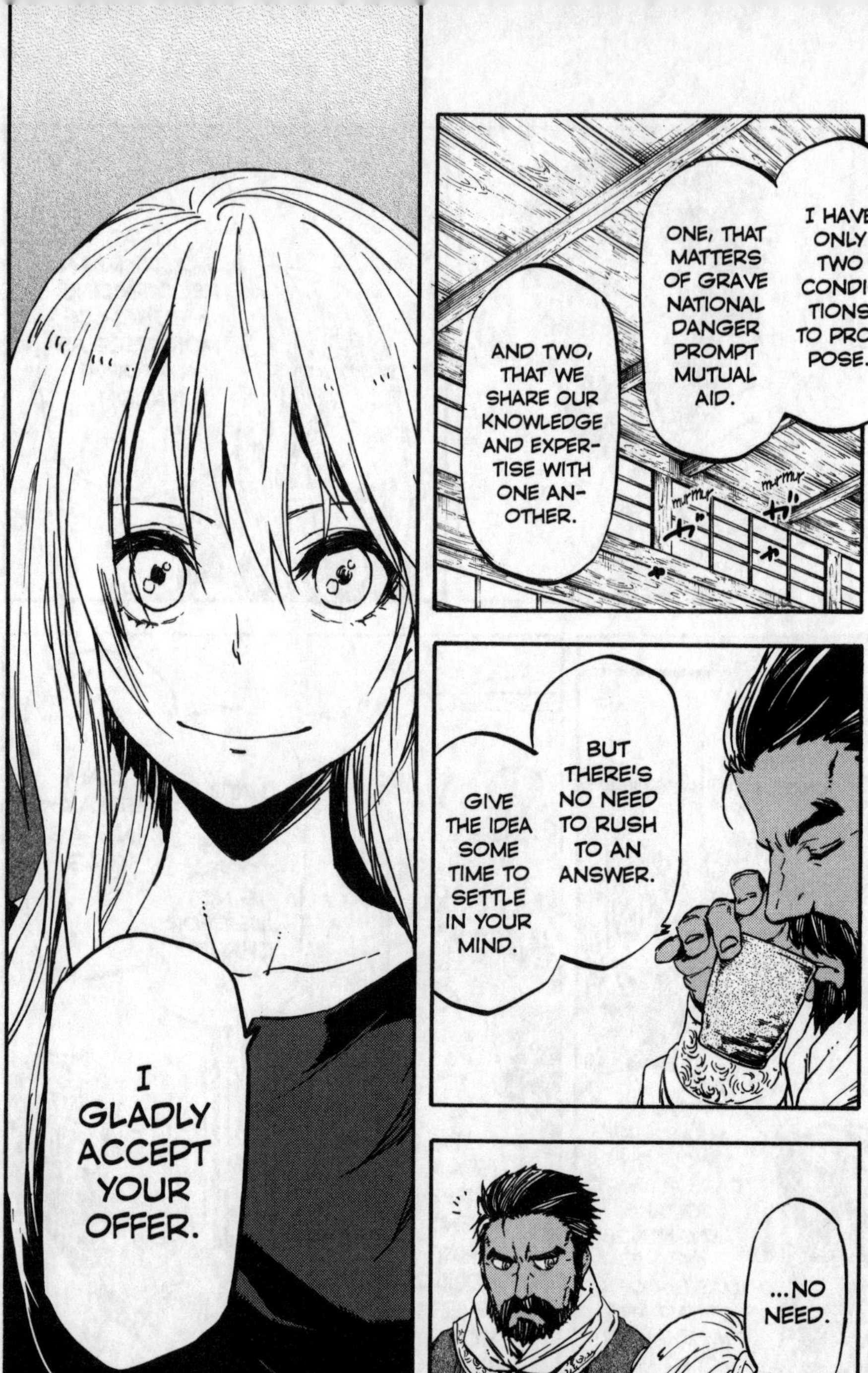
I HAVE ONLY TWO CONDI-TIONS TO PRO-POSE.
ONE, THAT MATTERS OF GRAVE NATIONAL DANGER PROMPT MUTUAL AID.
AND TWO, THAT WE SHARE OUR KNOWLEDGE AND EXPER-TISE WITH ONE AN-OTHER.
murmur
murmur
BUT THERE'S NO NEED TO RUSH TO AN ANSWER.
GIVE THE IDEA SOME TIME TO SETTLE IN YOUR MIND.
...NO NEED.
I GLADLY ACCEPT YOUR OFFER.

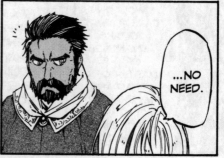

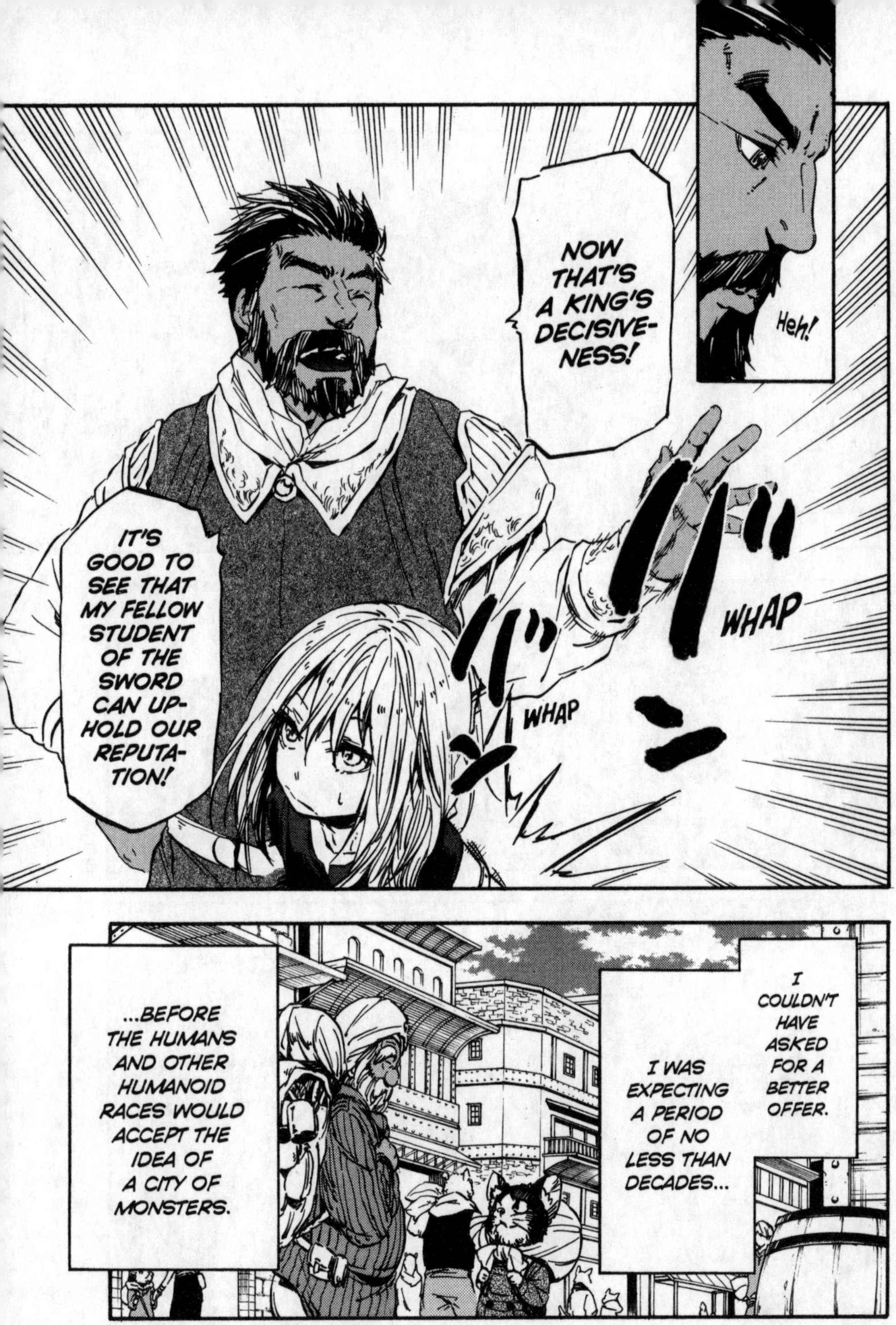
Heh!
NOW THAT'S A KING'S DECISIVENESS!
WHAP
WHAP
IT'S GOOD TO SEE THAT MY FELLOW STUDENT OF THE SWORD CAN UPHOLD OUR REPUTATION!
I COULDN'T HAVE ASKED FOR A BETTER OFFER.
I WAS EXPECTING A PERIOD OF NO LESS THAN DECADES...
...BEFORE THE HUMANS AND OTHER HUMANOID RACES WOULD ACCEPT THE IDEA OF A CITY OF MONSTERS.

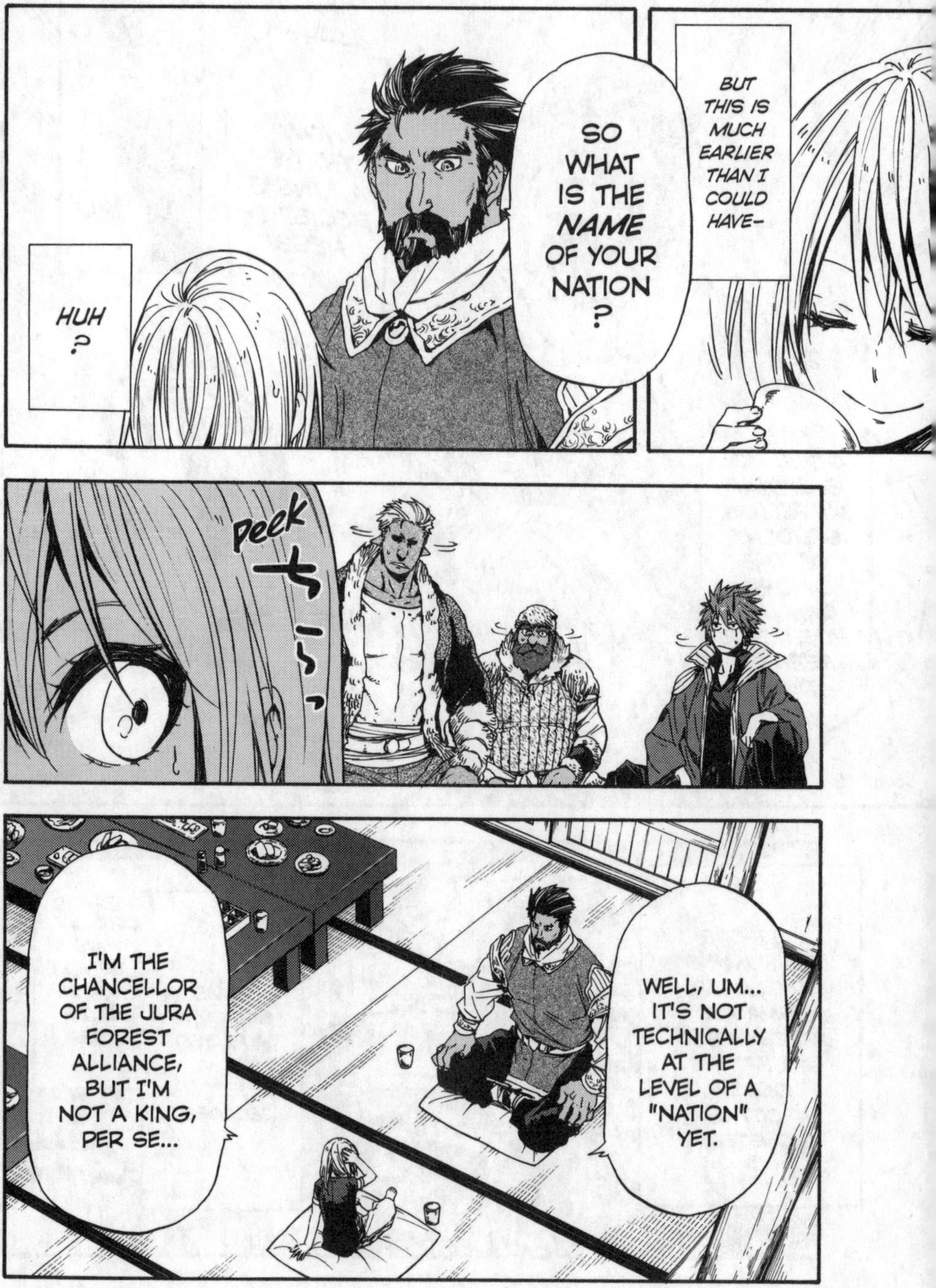
BUT THIS IS MUCH EARLIER THAN I COULD HAVE-
SO WHAT IS THE *NAME* OF YOUR NATION?
HUH?
Peek
WELL, UM... IT'S NOT TECHNICALLY AT THE LEVEL OF A "NATION" YET.
I'M THE CHANCELLOR OF THE JURA FOREST ALLIANCE, BUT I'M NOT A KING, PER SE...

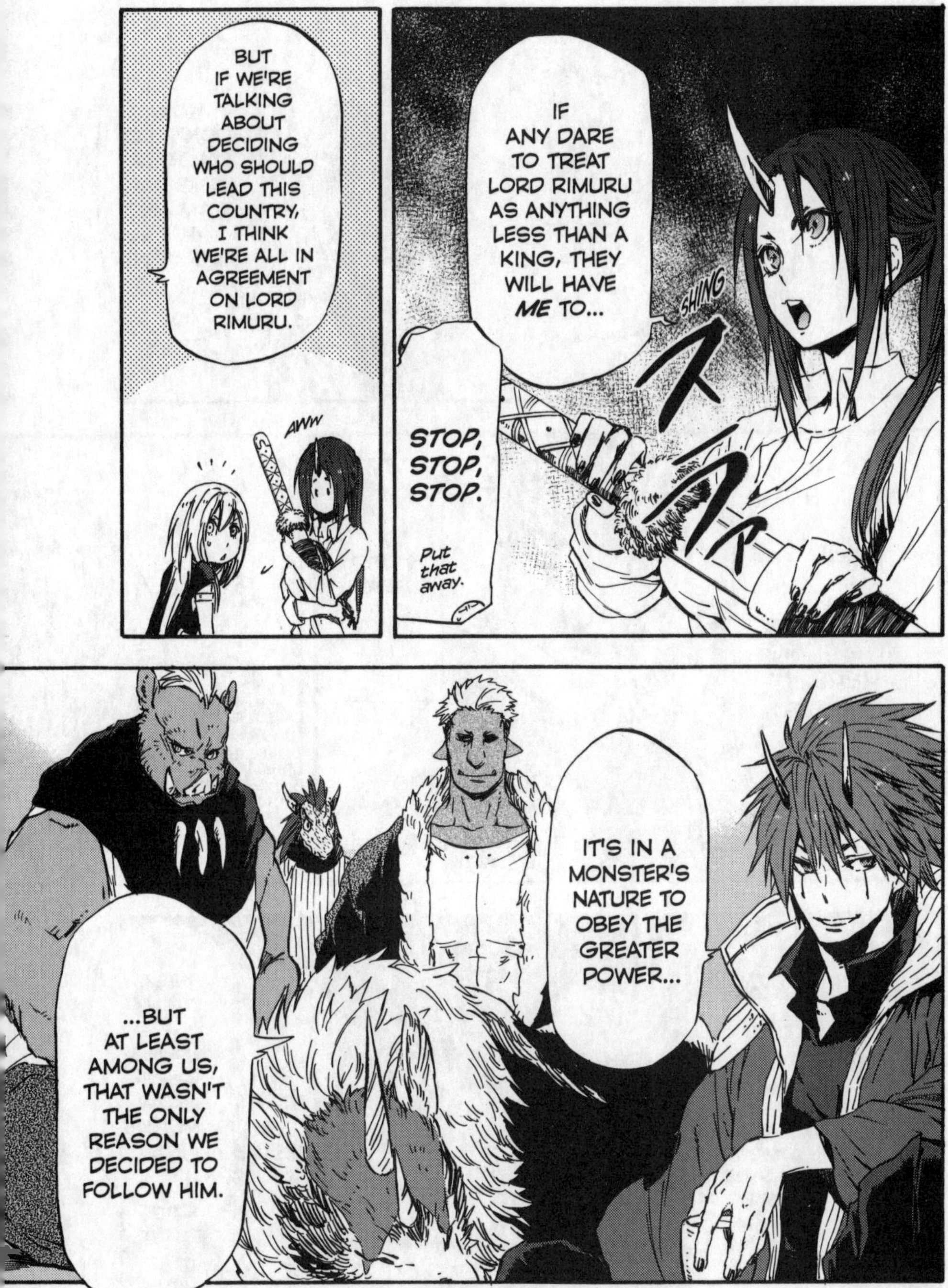
IF ANY DARE TO TREAT LORD RIMURU AS ANYTHING LESS THAN A KING, THEY WILL HAVE *ME* TO...
SHING
STOP, STOP, STOP.
Put that away.
BUT IF WE'RE TALKING ABOUT DECIDING WHO SHOULD LEAD THIS COUNTRY, I THINK WE'RE ALL IN AGREEMENT ON LORD RIMURU.
AWW
IT'S IN A MONSTER'S NATURE TO OBEY THE GREATER POWER...
...BUT AT LEAST AMONG US, THAT WASN'T THE ONLY REASON WE DECIDED TO FOLLOW HIM.

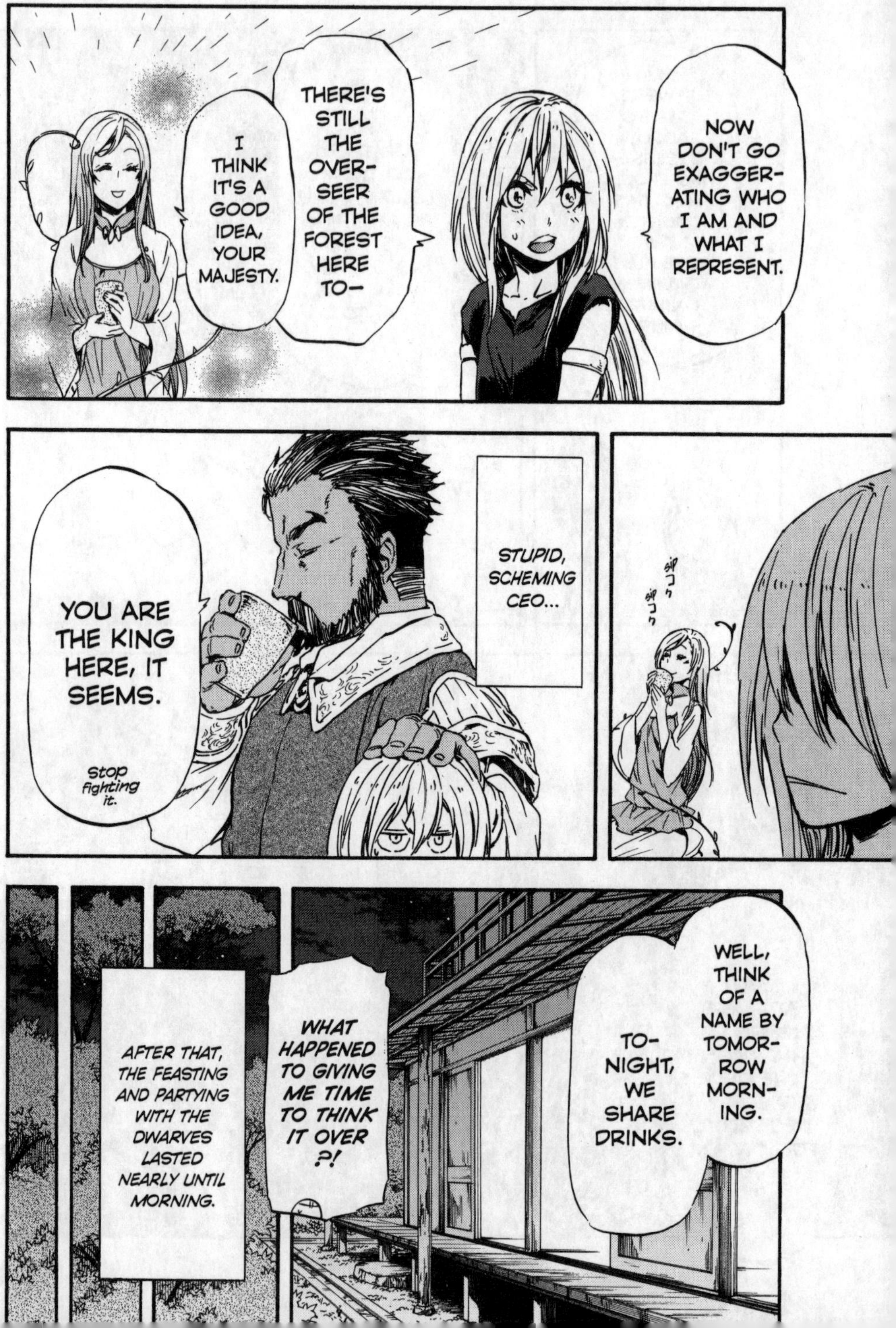
NOW DON'T GO EXAGGER-ATING WHO I AM AND WHAT I REPRESENT.
THERE'S STILL THE OVER-SEER OF THE FOREST HERE TO—
I THINK IT'S A GOOD IDEA, YOUR MAJESTY.
sip
sip
STUPID, SCHEMING CEO...
YOU ARE THE KING HERE, IT SEEMS.
Stop fighting it.
WELL, THINK OF A NAME BY TOMOR-ROW MORN-ING.
TO-NIGHT, WE SHARE DRINKS.
WHAT HAPPENED TO GIVING ME TIME TO THINK IT OVER ?!
AFTER THAT, THE FEASTING AND PARTYING WITH THE DWARVES LASTED NEARLY UNTIL MORNING.

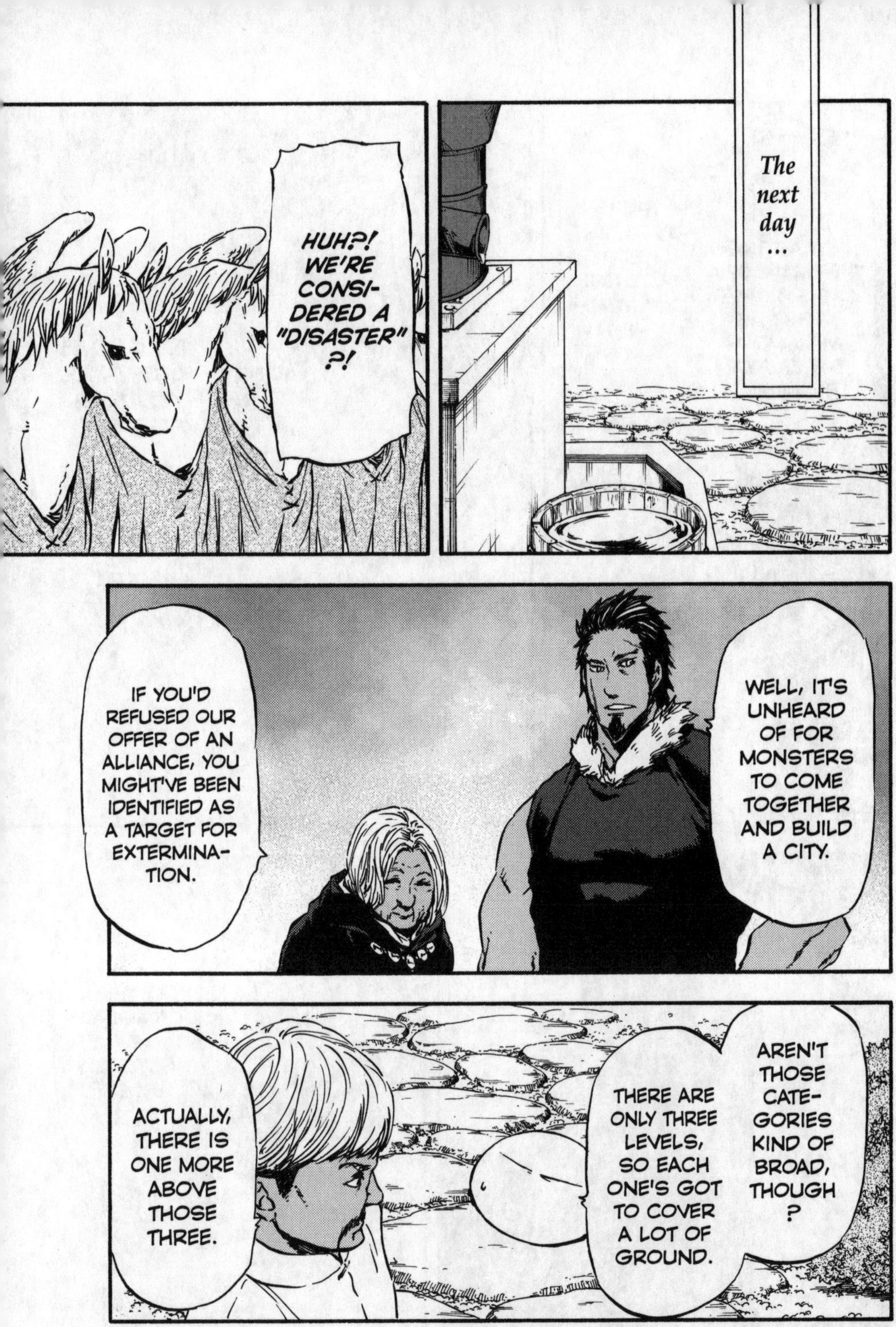
The next day …
HUH?! WE'RE CONSI-DERED A "DISASTER" ?!
WELL, IT'S UNHEARD OF FOR MONSTERS TO COME TOGETHER AND BUILD A CITY.
IF YOU'D REFUSED OUR OFFER OF AN ALLIANCE, YOU MIGHT'VE BEEN IDENTIFIED AS A TARGET FOR EXTERMINA-TION.
AREN'T THOSE CATE-GORIES KIND OF BROAD, THOUGH ?
THERE ARE ONLY THREE LEVELS, SO EACH ONE'S GOT TO COVER A LOT OF GROUND.
ACTUALLY, THERE IS ONE MORE ABOVE THOSE THREE.

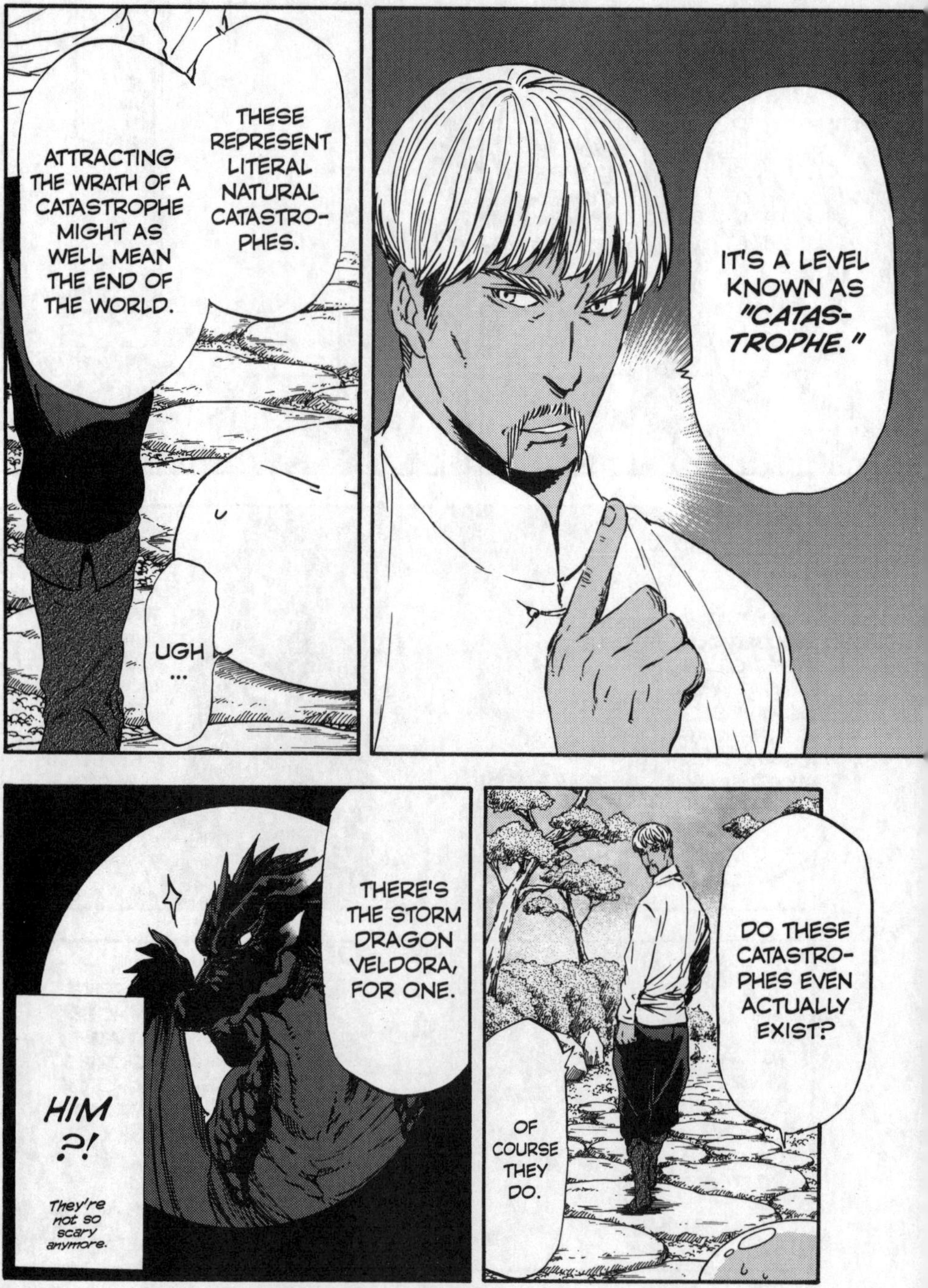
IT'S A LEVEL KNOWN AS "CATASTROPHE."
THESE REPRESENT LITERAL NATURAL CATASTROPHES.
ATTRACTING THE WRATH OF A CATASTROPHE MIGHT AS WELL MEAN THE END OF THE WORLD.
UGH ...
DO THESE CATASTROPHES EVEN ACTUALLY EXIST?
OF COURSE THEY DO.
THERE'S THE STORM DRAGON VELDORA, FOR ONE.
HIM ?!
They're not so scary anymore.

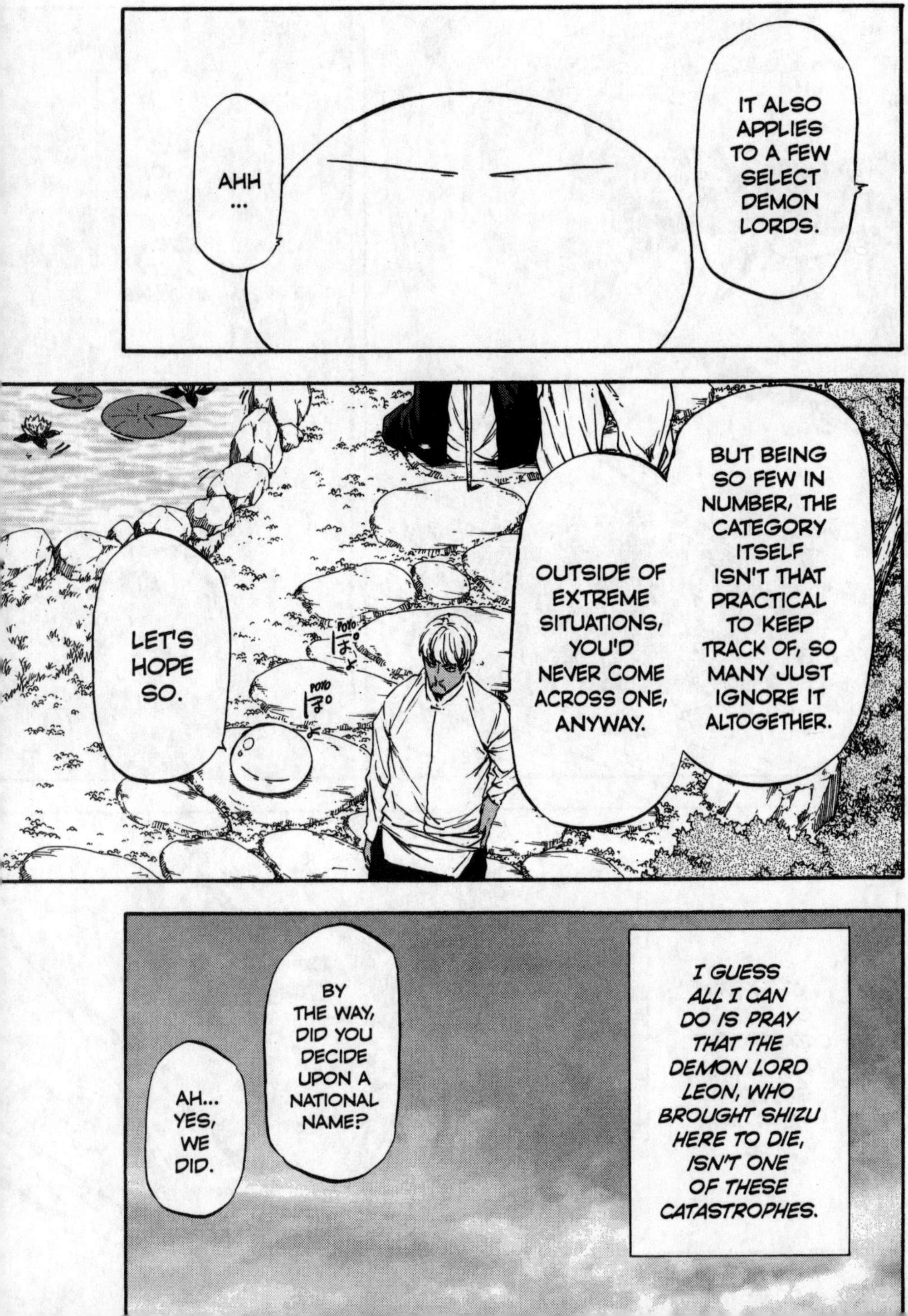
IT ALSO APPLIES TO A FEW SELECT DEMON LORDS.
AHH ...
BUT BEING SO FEW IN NUMBER, THE CATEGORY ITSELF ISN'T THAT PRACTICAL TO KEEP TRACK OF, SO MANY JUST IGNORE IT ALTOGETHER.
OUTSIDE OF EXTREME SITUATIONS, YOU'D NEVER COME ACROSS ONE, ANYWAY.
POYO
POYO
LET'S HOPE SO.
I GUESS ALL I CAN DO IS PRAY THAT THE DEMON LORD LEON, WHO BROUGHT SHIZU HERE TO DIE, ISN'T ONE OF THESE CATASTROPHES.
BY THE WAY, DID YOU DECIDE UPON A NATIONAL NAME?
AH... YES, WE DID.

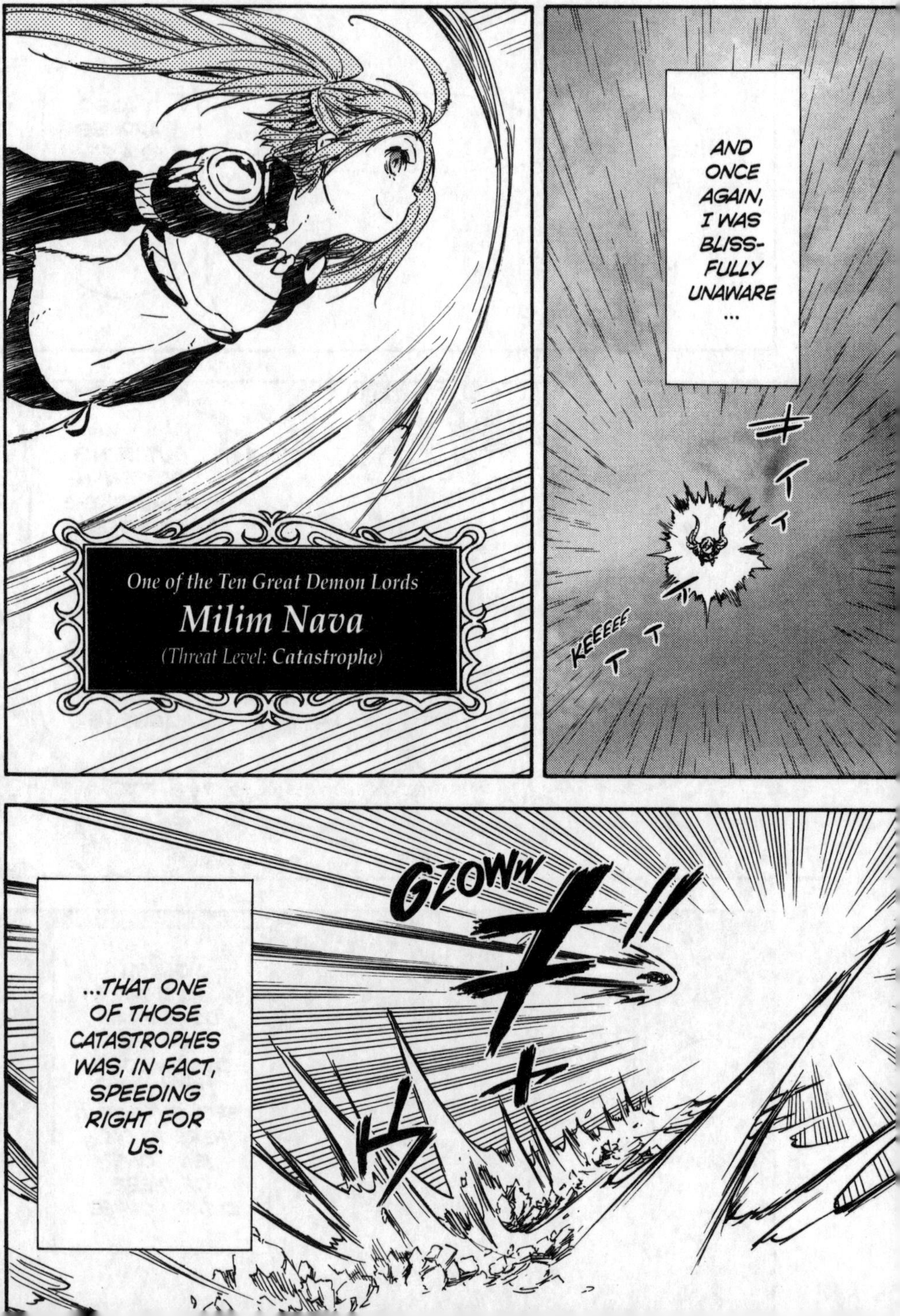
AND ONCE AGAIN, I WAS BLISS-FULLY UNAWARE ...
KEEEEE
One of the Ten Great Demon Lords
Milim Nava
(Threat Level: Catastrophe)
GZOWW
...THAT ONE OF THOSE CATASTROPHES WAS, IN FACT, SPEEDING RIGHT FOR US.

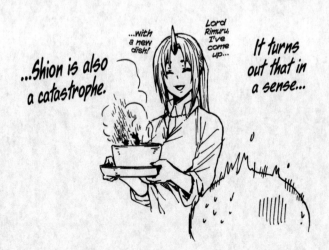

It turns out that in a sense...
Lord Rimuru, I've come up...
...with a new dish!
...Shion is also a catastrophe.

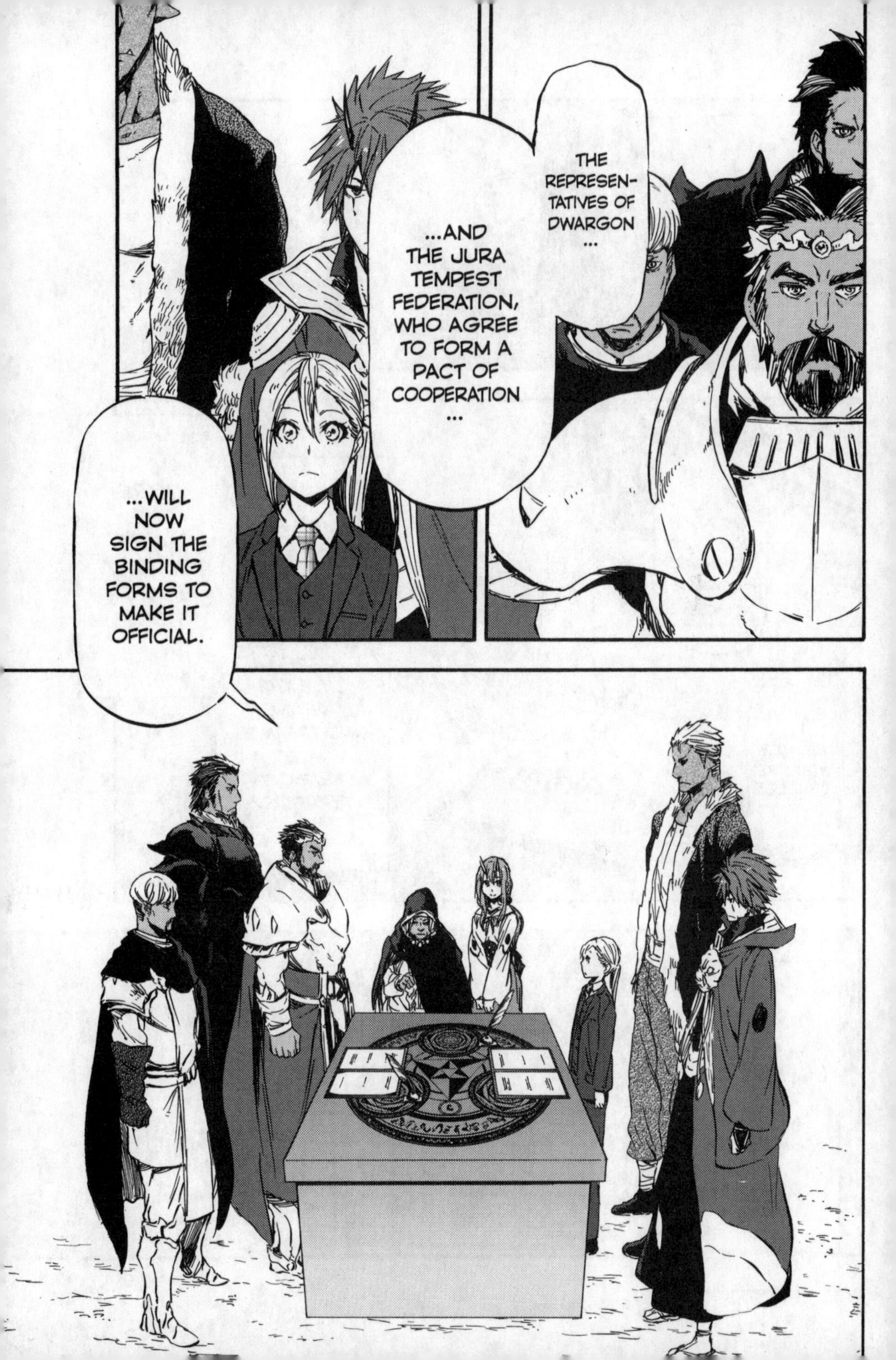
THE REPRESEN-TATIVES OF DWARGON ...
...AND THE JURA TEMPEST FEDERATION, WHO AGREE TO FORM A PACT OF COOPERATION ...
...WILL NOW SIGN THE BINDING FORMS TO MAKE IT OFFICIAL.

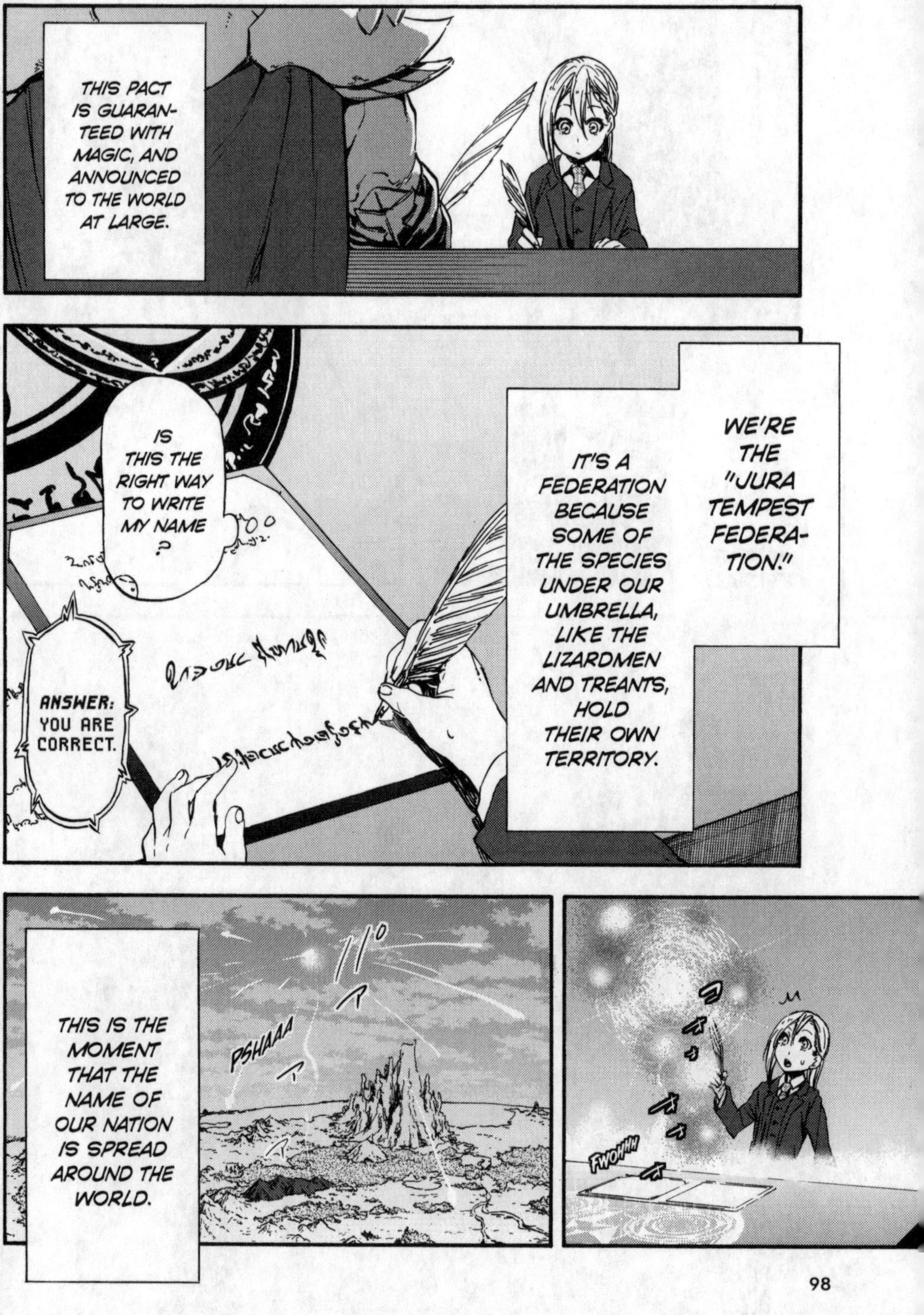
THIS PACT IS GUARANTEED WITH MAGIC, AND ANNOUNCED TO THE WORLD AT LARGE.
WE'RE THE "JURA TEMPEST FEDERATION."
IT'S A FEDERATION BECAUSE SOME OF THE SPECIES UNDER OUR UMBRELLA, LIKE THE LIZARDMEN AND TREANTS, HOLD THEIR OWN TERRITORY.
IS THIS THE RIGHT WAY TO WRITE MY NAME?
ANSWER: YOU ARE CORRECT.
FWOHHH
PSHAAA
THIS IS THE MOMENT THAT THE NAME OF OUR NATION IS SPREAD AROUND THE WORLD.

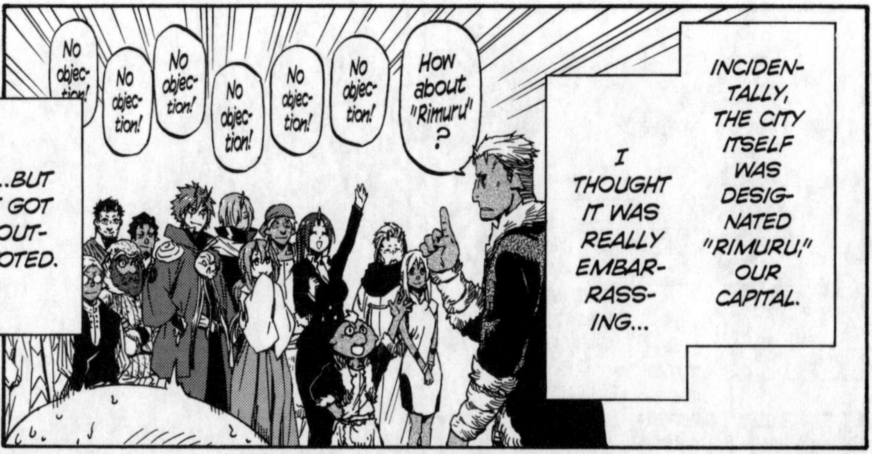
INCIDENTALLY, THE CITY ITSELF WAS DESIGNATED "RIMURU," OUR CAPITAL.
I THOUGHT IT WAS REALLY EMBARRASSING...
How about "Rimuru"?
No objection!
No objection!
No objection!
No objection!
No objection!
No objection!
...BUT I GOT OUTVOTED.

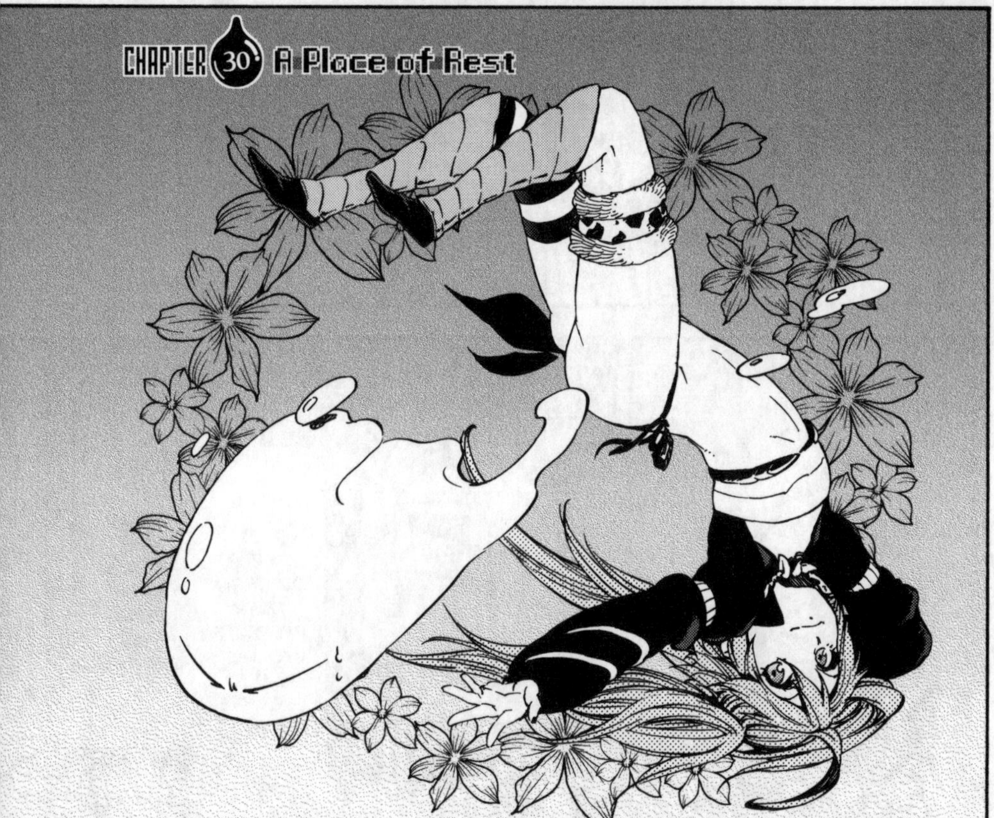
CHAPTER 30 A Place of Rest

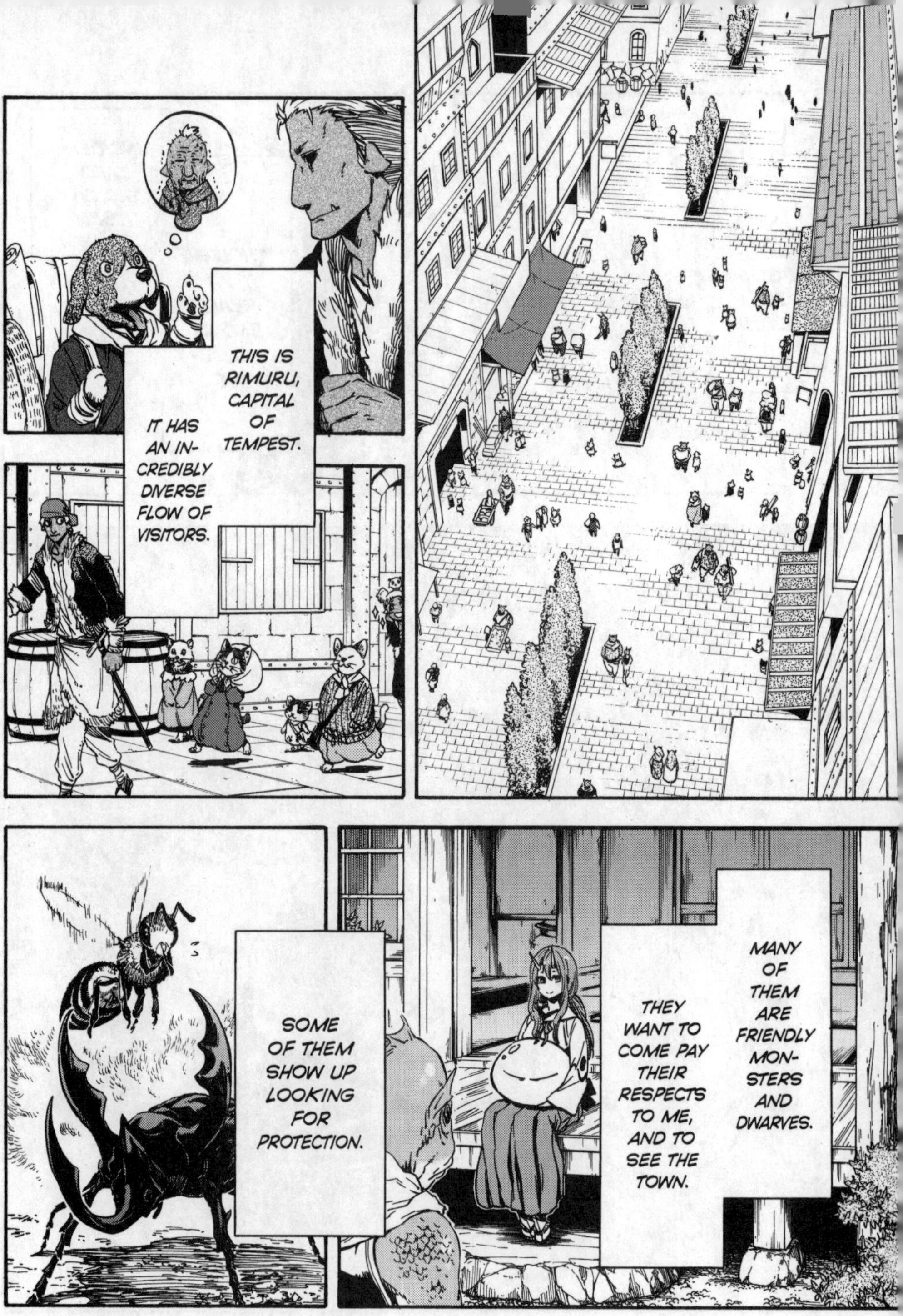
THIS IS RIMURU, CAPITAL OF TEMPEST.
IT HAS AN IN-CREDIBLY DIVERSE FLOW OF VISITORS.
MANY OF THEM ARE FRIENDLY MON-STERS AND DWARVES.
THEY WANT TO COME PAY THEIR RESPECTS TO ME, AND TO SEE THE TOWN.
SOME OF THEM SHOW UP LOOKING FOR PROTECTION.

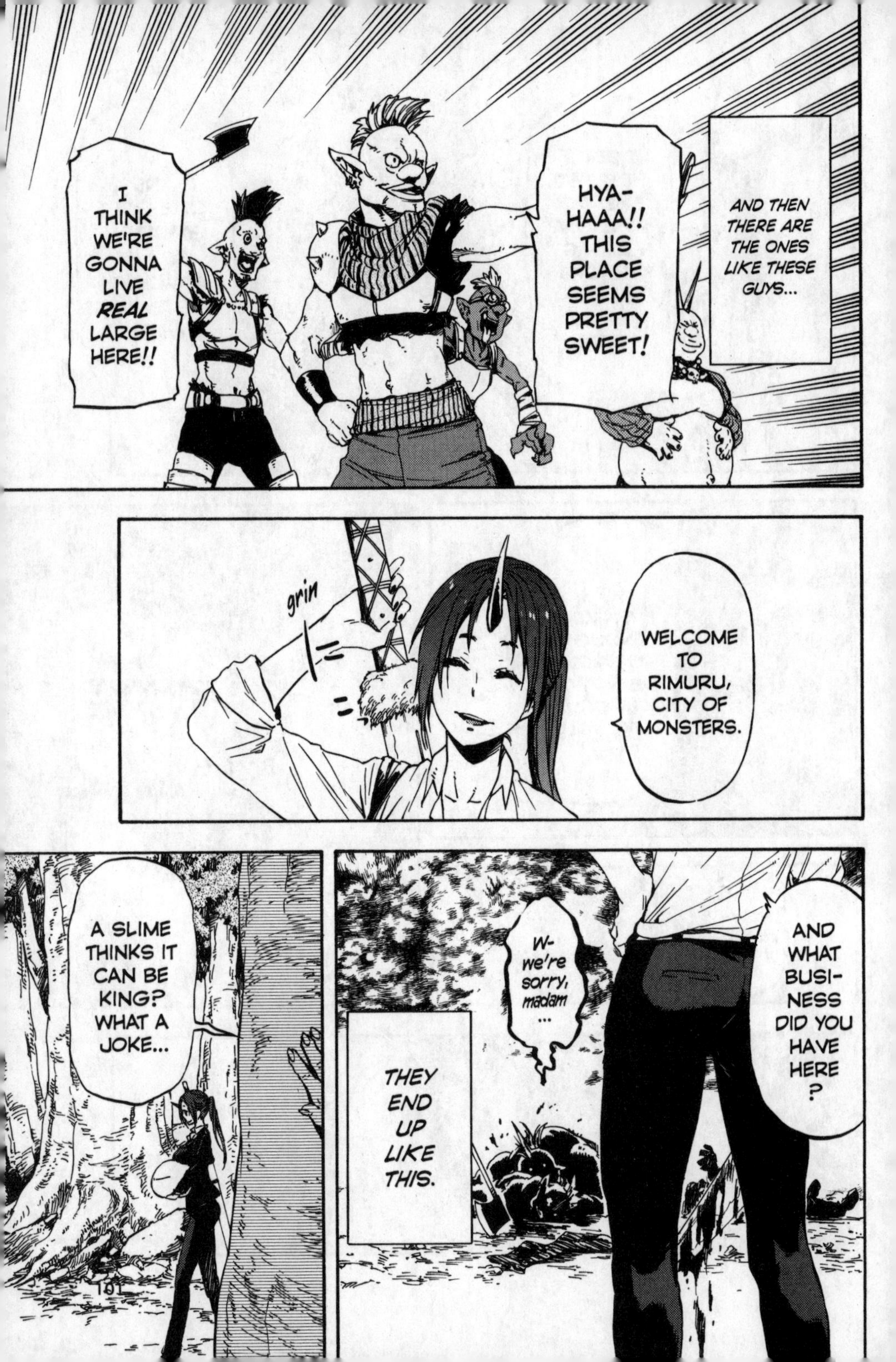
AND THEN THERE ARE THE ONES LIKE THESE GUYS...
HYA-HAAA!! THIS PLACE SEEMS PRETTY SWEET!
I THINK WE'RE GONNA LIVE *REAL* LARGE HERE!!
WELCOME TO RIMURU, CITY OF MONSTERS.
grin
AND WHAT BUSINESS DID YOU HAVE HERE?
W-we're sorry, madam...
THEY END UP LIKE THIS.
A SLIME THINKS IT CAN BE KING? WHAT A JOKE...

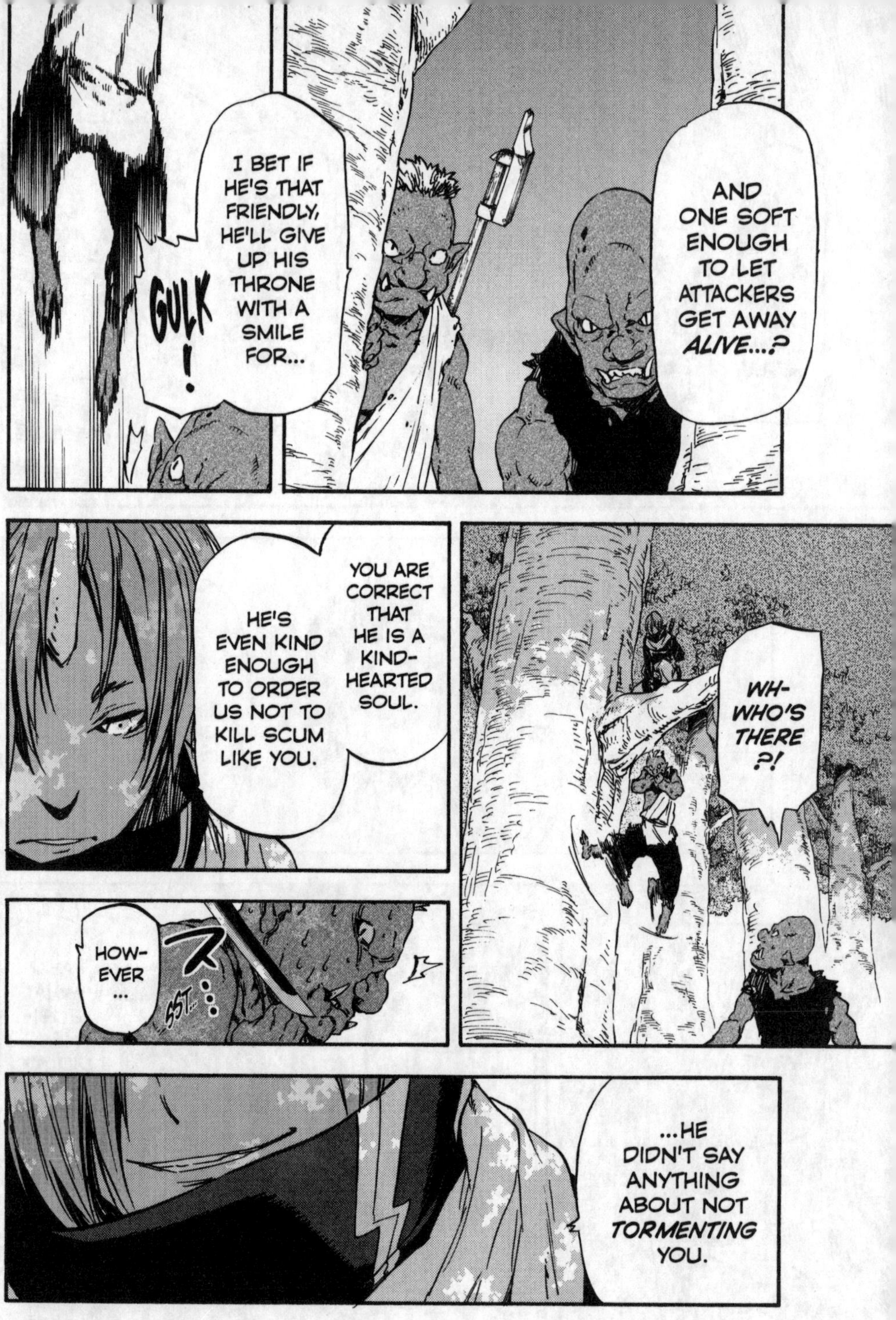
AND ONE SOFT ENOUGH TO LET ATTACKERS GET AWAY *ALIVE*...?
I BET IF HE'S THAT FRIENDLY, HE'LL GIVE UP HIS THRONE WITH A SMILE FOR...
GULK!
WH-WHO'S THERE?!
YOU ARE CORRECT THAT HE IS A KIND-HEARTED SOUL.
HE'S EVEN KIND ENOUGH TO ORDER US NOT TO KILL SCUM LIKE YOU.
HOW-EVER ...
SST...
...HE DIDN'T SAY ANYTHING ABOUT NOT *TORMENTING* YOU.

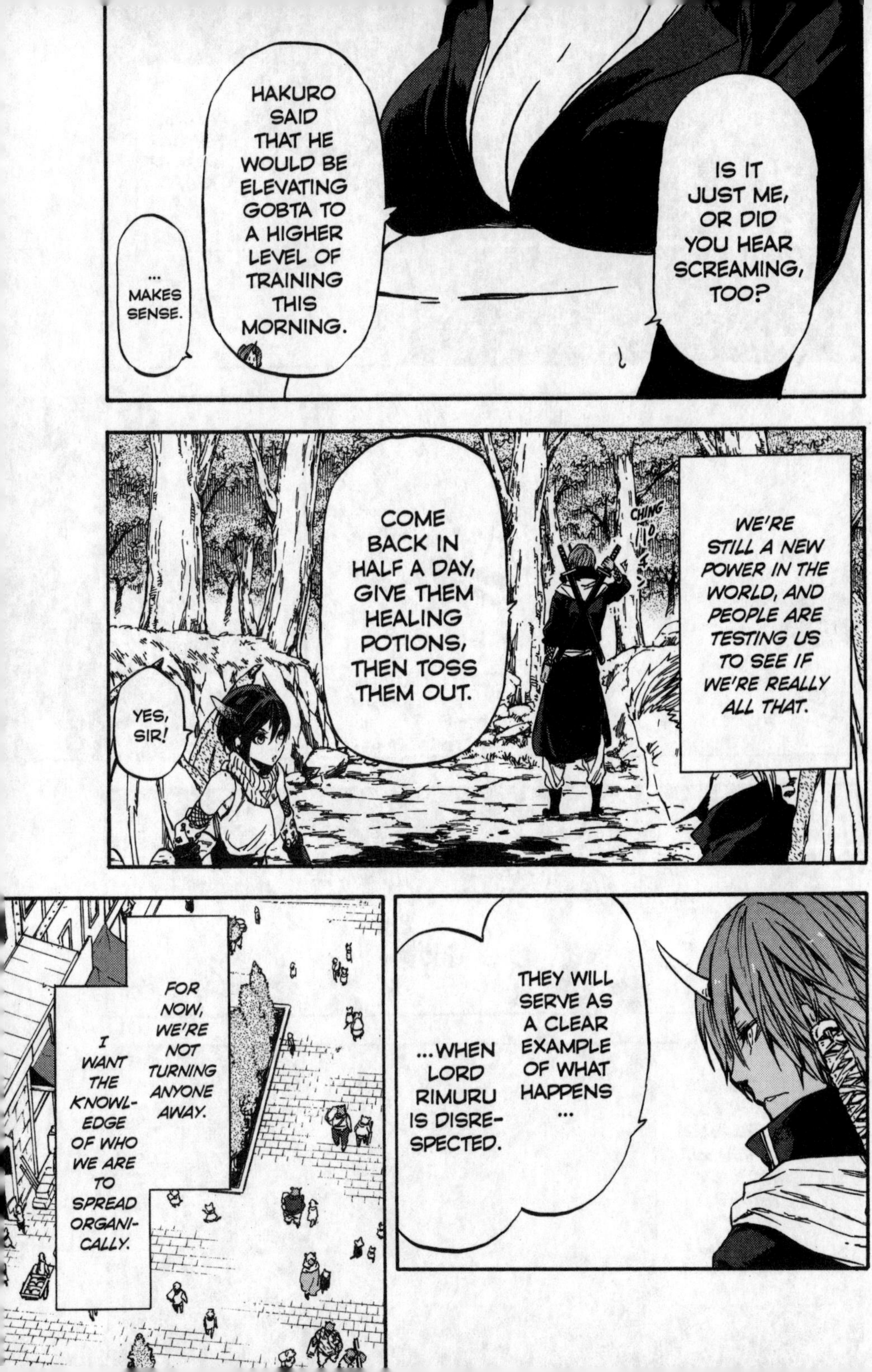
IS IT JUST ME, OR DID YOU HEAR SCREAMING, TOO?
HAKURO SAID THAT HE WOULD BE ELEVATING GOBTA TO A HIGHER LEVEL OF TRAINING THIS MORNING.
... MAKES SENSE.
WE'RE STILL A NEW POWER IN THE WORLD, AND PEOPLE ARE TESTING US TO SEE IF WE'RE REALLY ALL THAT.
CHING
COME BACK IN HALF A DAY, GIVE THEM HEALING POTIONS, THEN TOSS THEM OUT.
YES, SIR!
THEY WILL SERVE AS A CLEAR EXAMPLE OF WHAT HAPPENS ...
...WHEN LORD RIMURU IS DISRESPECTED.
FOR NOW, WE'RE NOT TURNING ANYONE AWAY.
I WANT THE KNOWLEDGE OF WHO WE ARE TO SPREAD ORGANICALLY.

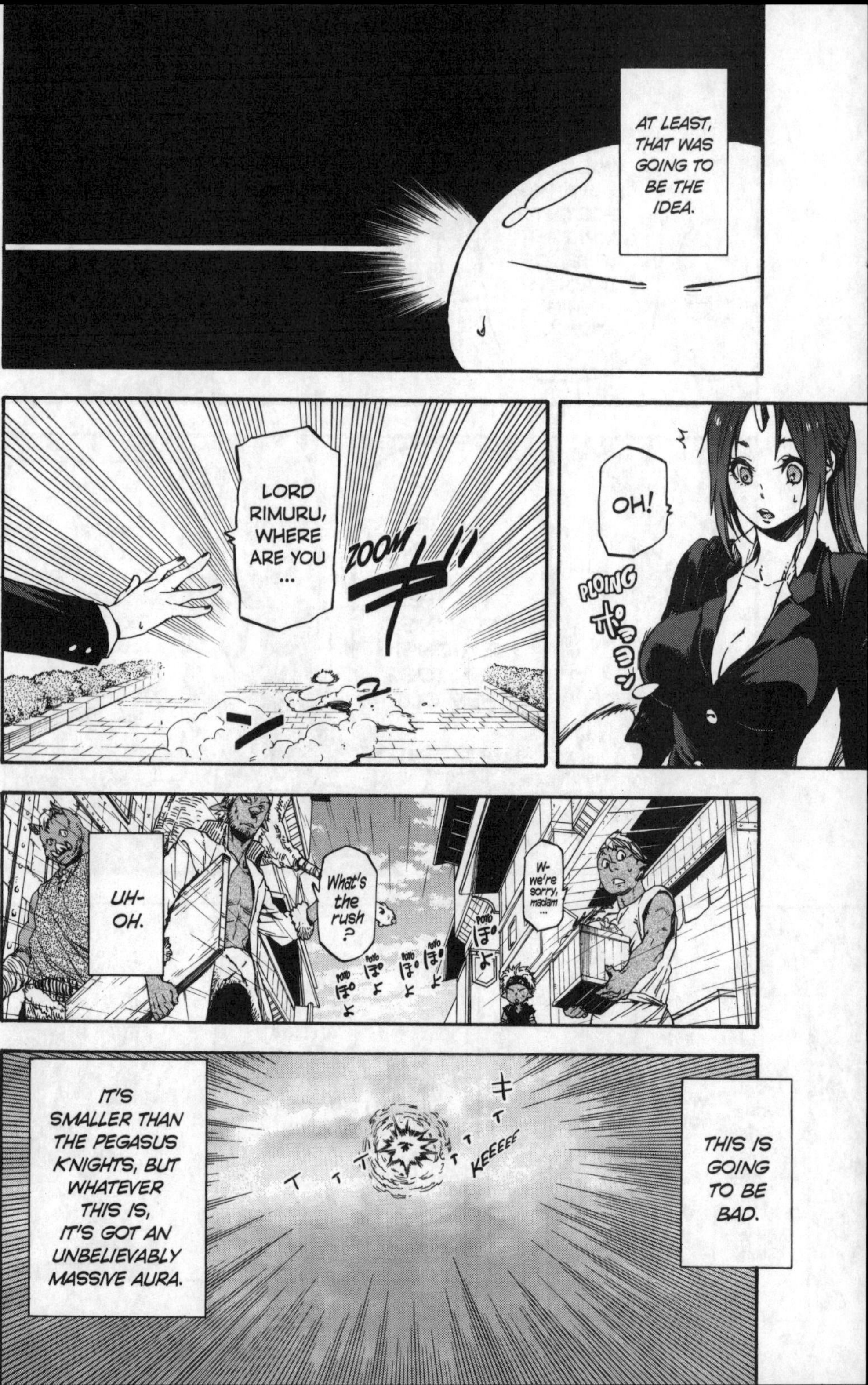
AT LEAST, THAT WAS GOING TO BE THE IDEA.
OH!
PLOING
LORD RIMURU, WHERE ARE YOU ...
ZOOM
W-we're sorry, ma'am ...
POYO
POYO
POYO
POYO
What's the rush?
UH-OH.
THIS IS GOING TO BE BAD.
KEEEEE
IT'S SMALLER THAN THE PEGASUS KNIGHTS, BUT WHATEVER THIS IS, IT'S GOT AN UNBELIEVABLY MASSIVE AURA.

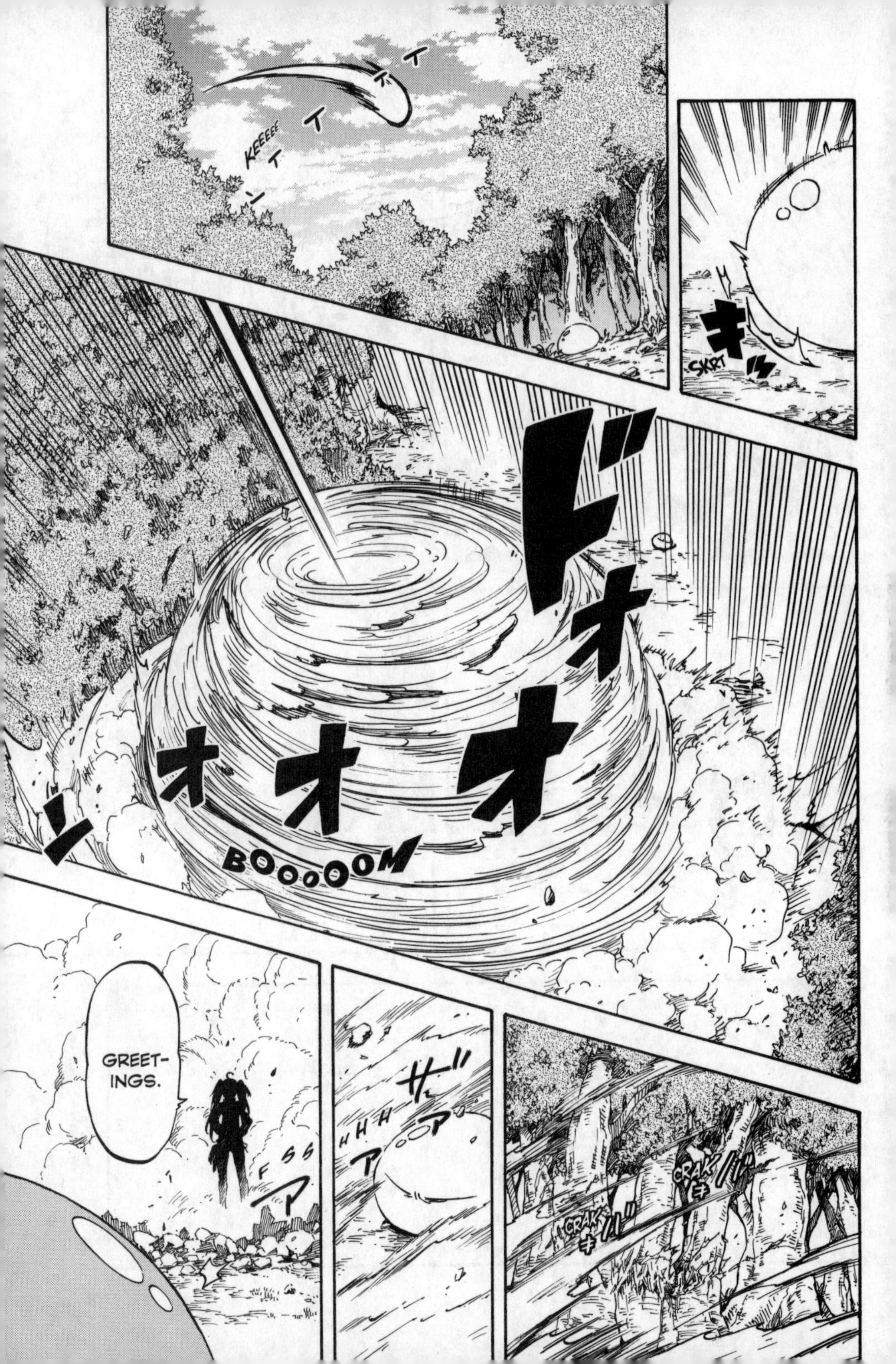
SKRT
KEEEEE
ドォオオオン
BOOOOOM
CRAK
CRAK
HHH
FSS
GREET-
INGS.

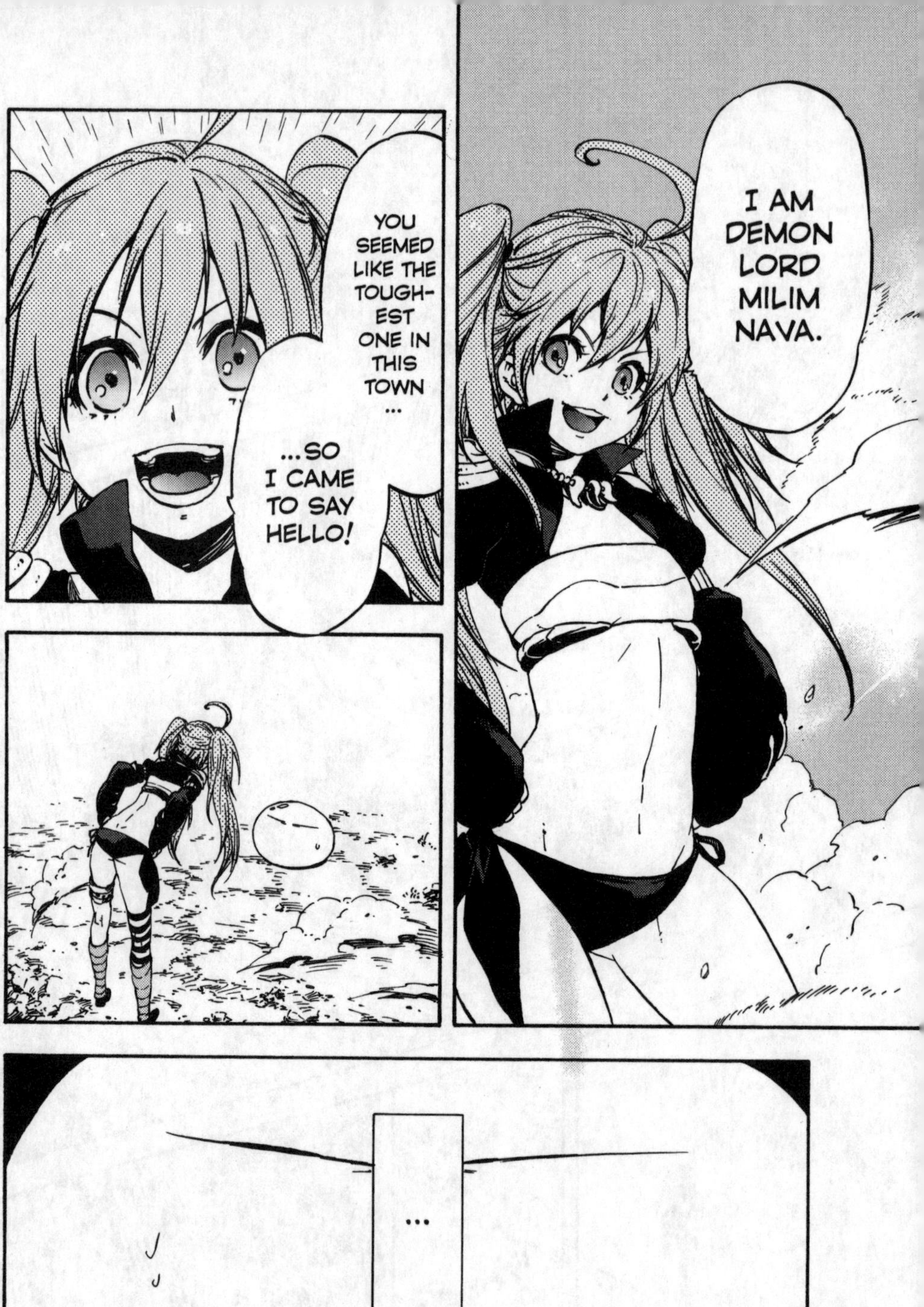
I AM DEMON LORD MILIM NAVA.
YOU SEEMED LIKE THE TOUGH-EST ONE IN THIS TOWN ...
...SO I CAME TO SAY HELLO!
...

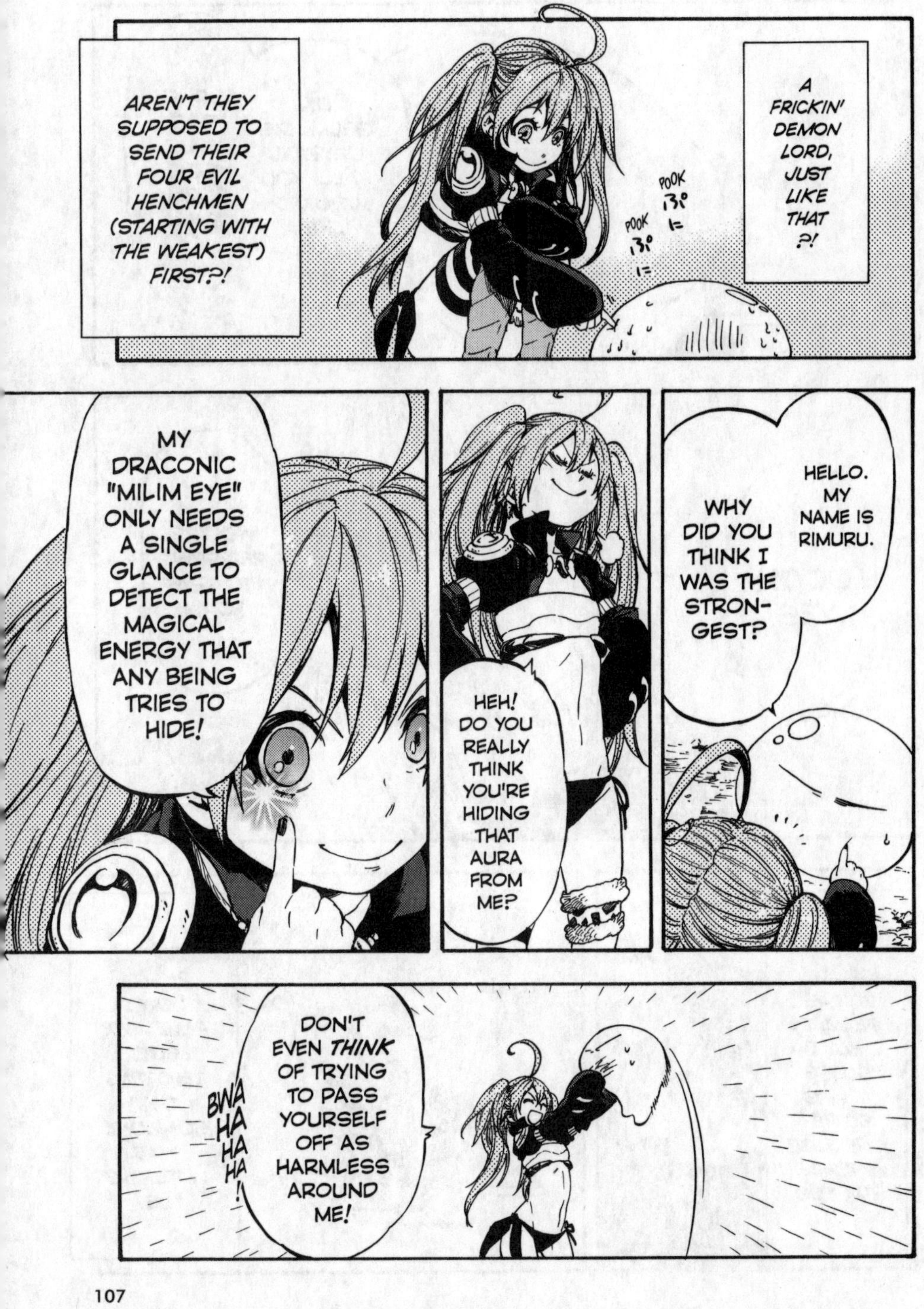
A FRICKIN' DEMON LORD, JUST LIKE THAT?!
POOK
POOK
AREN'T THEY SUPPOSED TO SEND THEIR FOUR EVIL HENCHMEN (STARTING WITH THE WEAKEST) FIRST?!
HELLO. MY NAME IS RIMURU.
WHY DID YOU THINK I WAS THE STRONGEST?
HEH! DO YOU REALLY THINK YOU'RE HIDING THAT AURA FROM ME?
MY DRACONIC "MILIM EYE" ONLY NEEDS A SINGLE GLANCE TO DETECT THE MAGICAL ENERGY THAT ANY BEING TRIES TO HIDE!
DON'T EVEN *THINK* OF TRYING TO PASS YOURSELF OFF AS HARMLESS AROUND ME!
BWA HA HA HA!

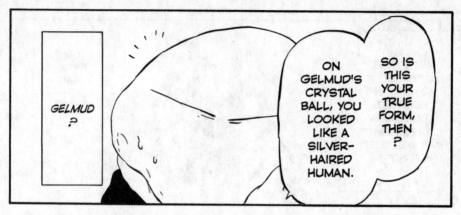

SO IS THIS YOUR TRUE FORM, THEN?
ON GELMUD'S CRYSTAL BALL, YOU LOOKED LIKE A SILVER-HAIRED HUMAN.
GELMUD?
YOU'RE REFERRING TO *THIS* FORM.
FWOHHH
OOOH, YES!
THAT'S RIGHT—NOW I REMEMBER SOEI REPORTING THAT SOMEONE WAS WATCHING US.
Ooooh.
...
Ahhhh.
...HMM?
I JUST ASSUMED IT WAS GELMUD, BUT I GUESS IT WAS SOMEONE ELSE WATCHING HIM, TOO.

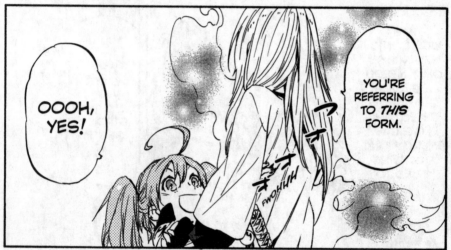

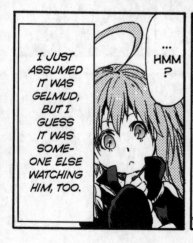

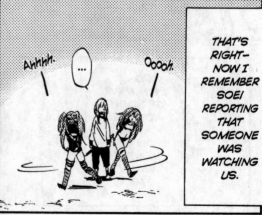

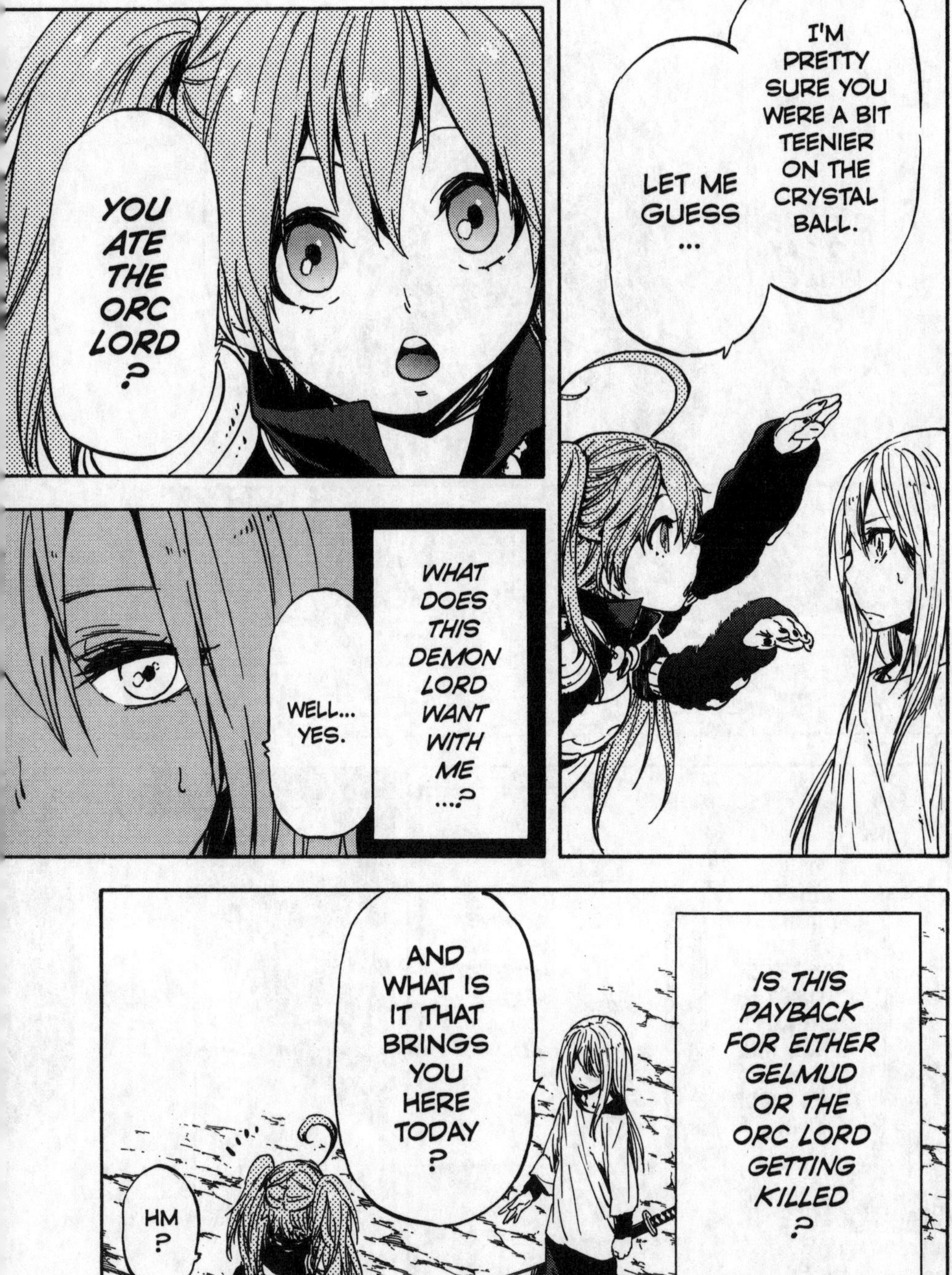
I'M PRETTY SURE YOU WERE A BIT TEENIER ON THE CRYSTAL BALL.
LET ME GUESS ...
YOU ATE THE ORC LORD?
WHAT DOES THIS DEMON LORD WANT WITH ME ...?
WELL... YES.
IS THIS PAYBACK FOR EITHER GELMUD OR THE ORC LORD GETTING KILLED?
AND WHAT IS IT THAT BRINGS YOU HERE TODAY?
HM?

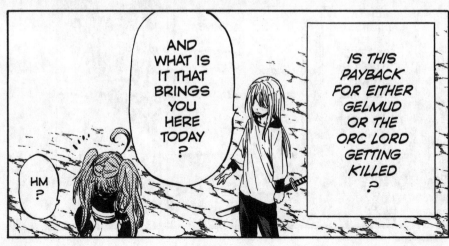

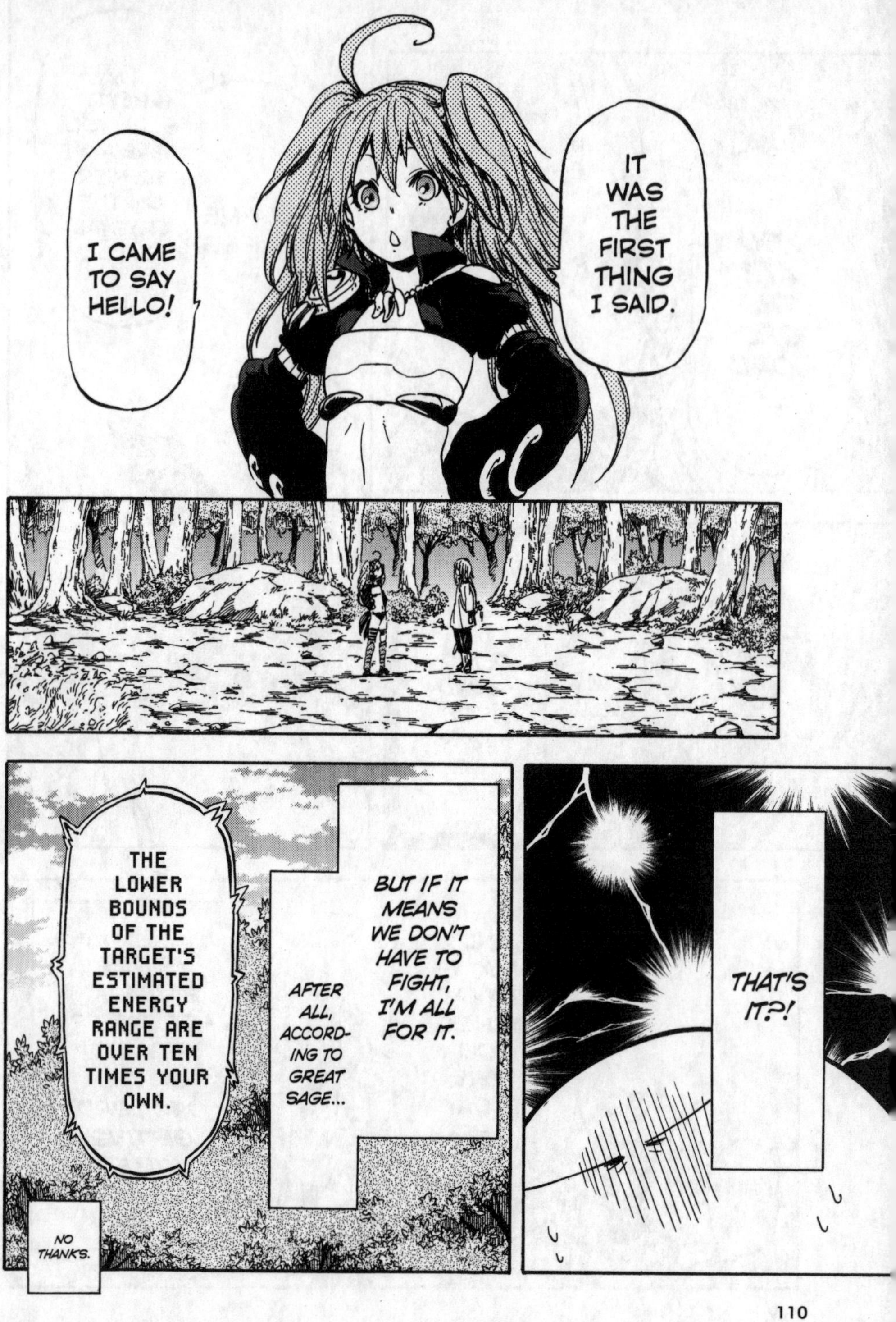
IT WAS THE FIRST THING I SAID.
I CAME TO SAY HELLO!
THAT'S IT?!
BUT IF IT MEANS WE DON'T HAVE TO FIGHT, I'M ALL FOR IT.
AFTER ALL, ACCORDING TO GREAT SAGE...
THE LOWER BOUNDS OF THE TARGET'S ESTIMATED ENERGY RANGE ARE OVER TEN TIMES YOUR OWN.
NO THANKS.

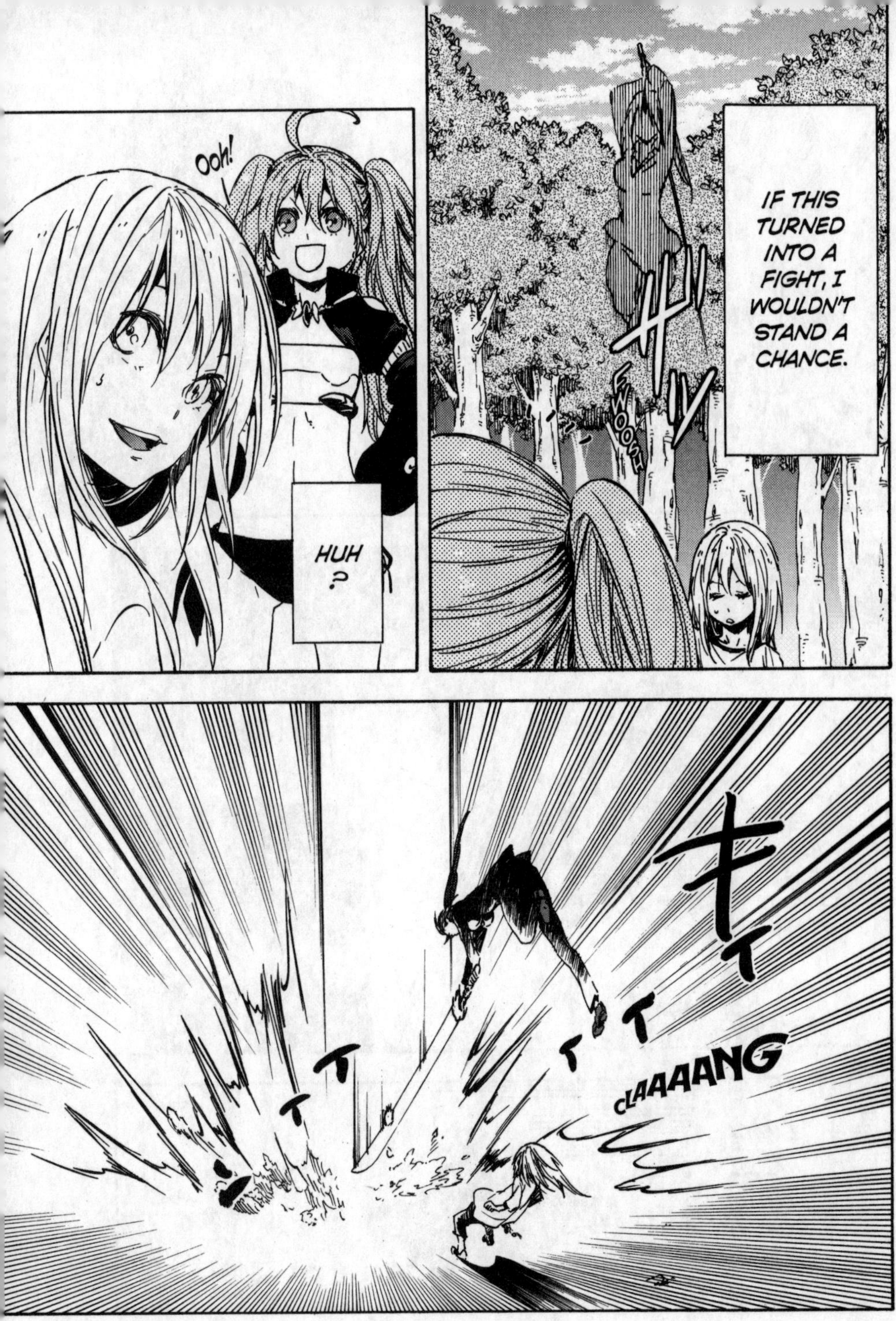
IF THIS TURNED INTO A FIGHT, I WOULDN'T STAND A CHANCE.
WOOSH
Ooh!
HUH?
CLAAAANG

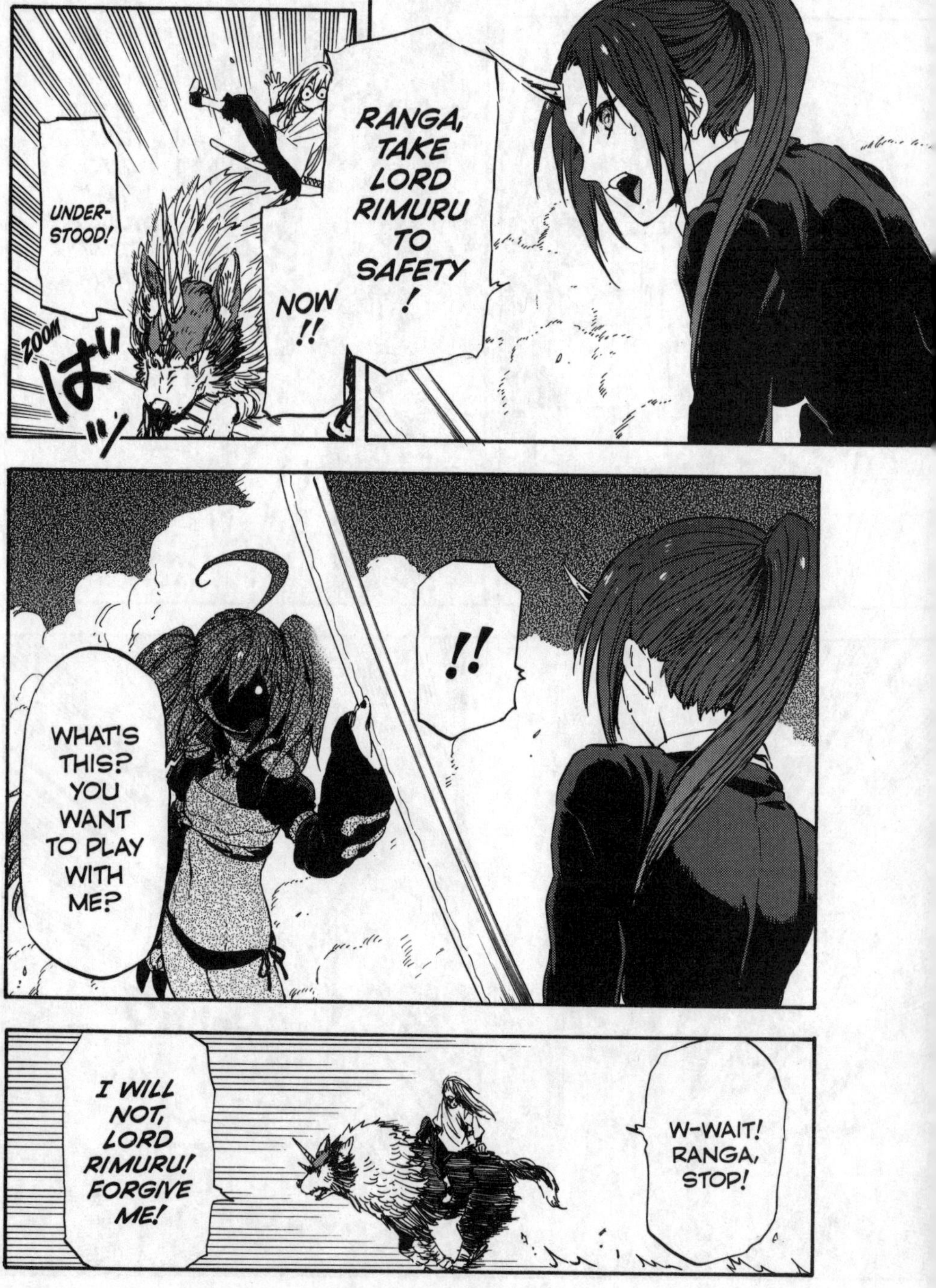
RANGA, TAKE LORD RIMURU TO SAFETY!
NOW!!
UNDER-STOOD!
ZOOM
ばッ
!!
WHAT'S THIS? YOU WANT TO PLAY WITH ME?
W-WAIT! RANGA, STOP!
I WILL NOT, LORD RIMURU! FORGIVE ME!

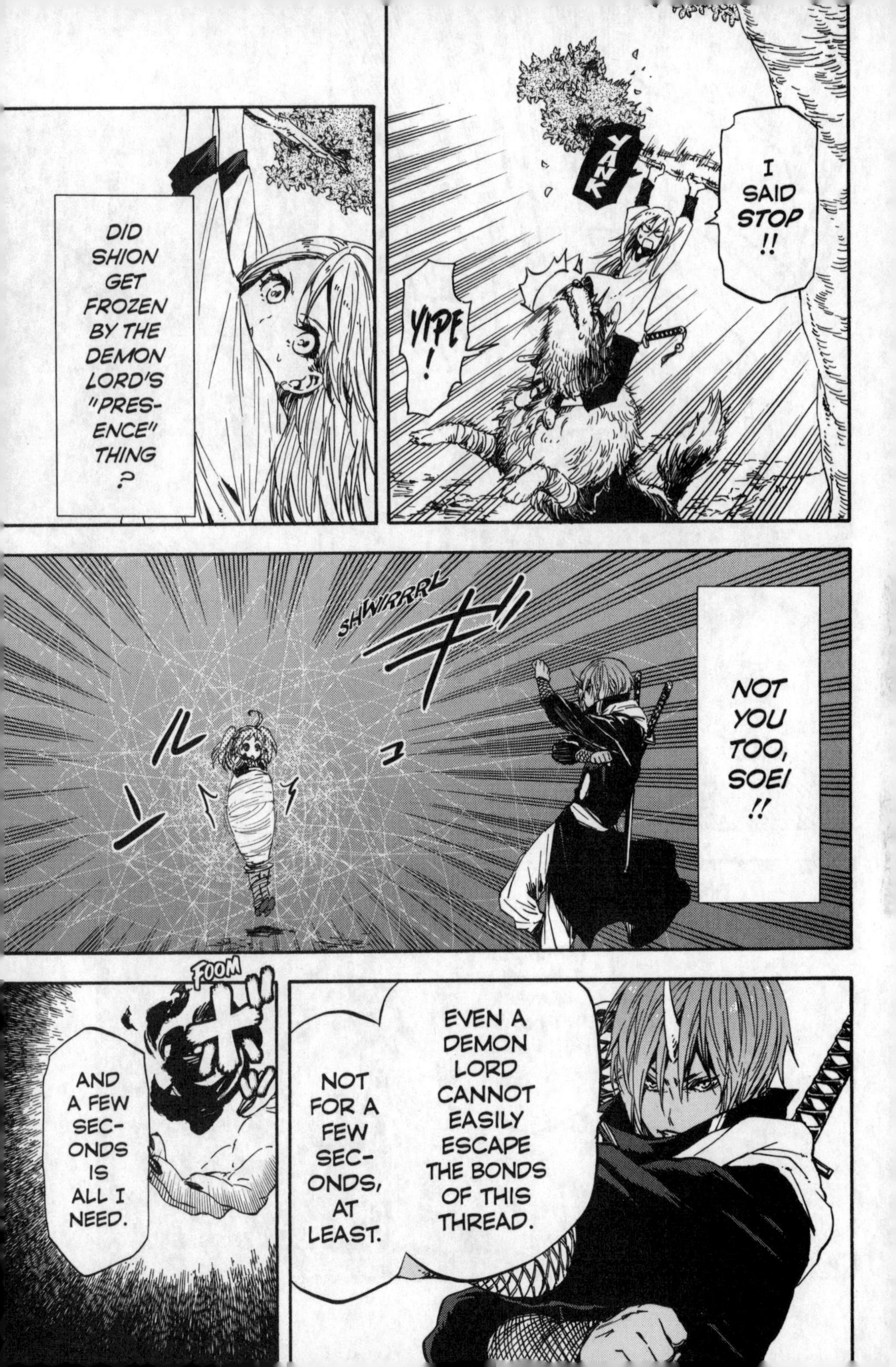
I SAID STOP!!
YANK
YIPE!
DID SHION GET FROZEN BY THE DEMON LORD'S "PRESENCE" THING?
SHWIRRRL
NOT YOU TOO, SOEI!!
EVEN A DEMON LORD CANNOT EASILY ESCAPE THE BONDS OF THIS THREAD.
NOT FOR A FEW SECONDS, AT LEAST.
FOOM
AND A FEW SECONDS IS ALL I NEED.

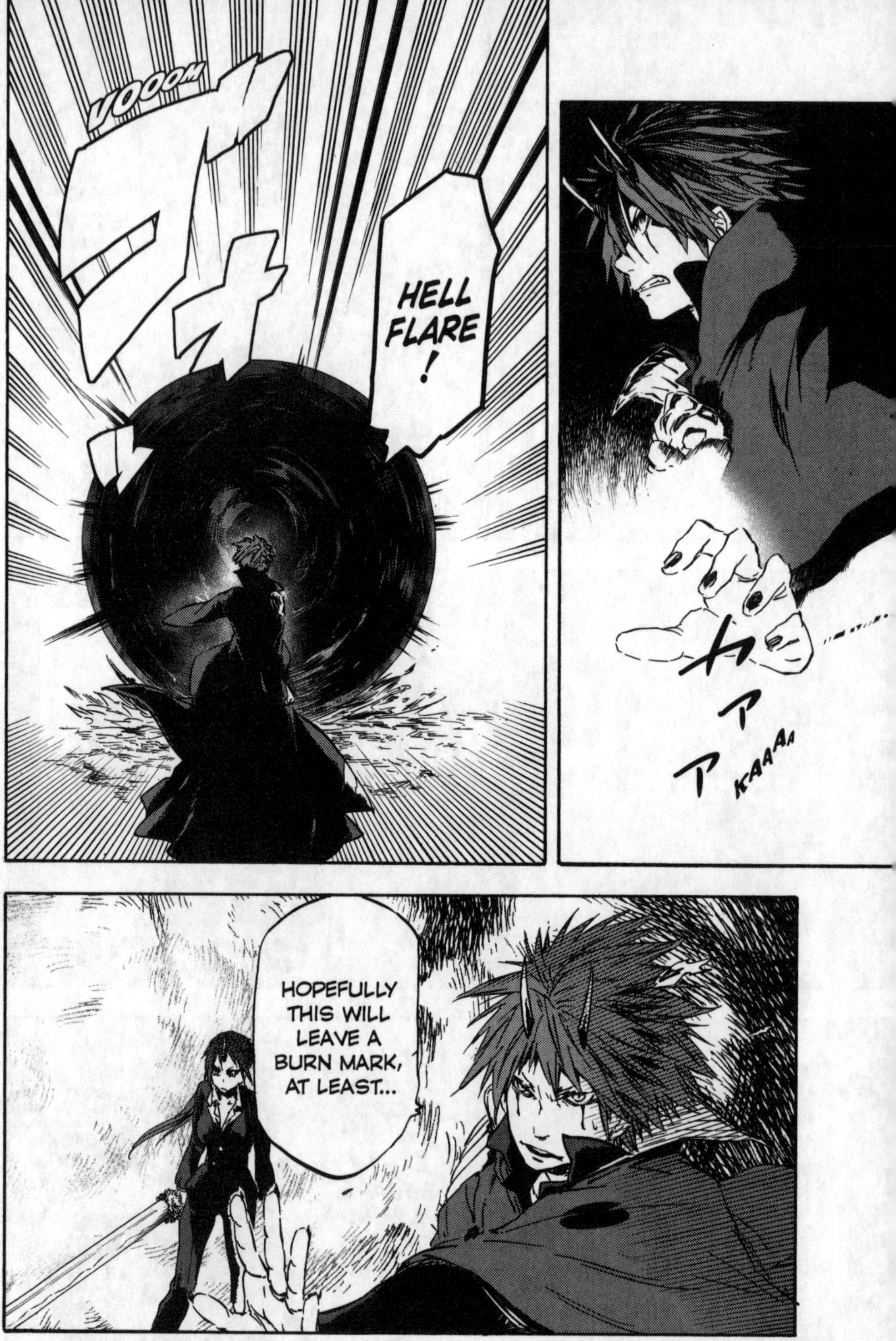
KAAAA
VOOOM
HELL FLARE!
HOPEFULLY THIS WILL LEAVE A BURN MARK, AT LEAST...

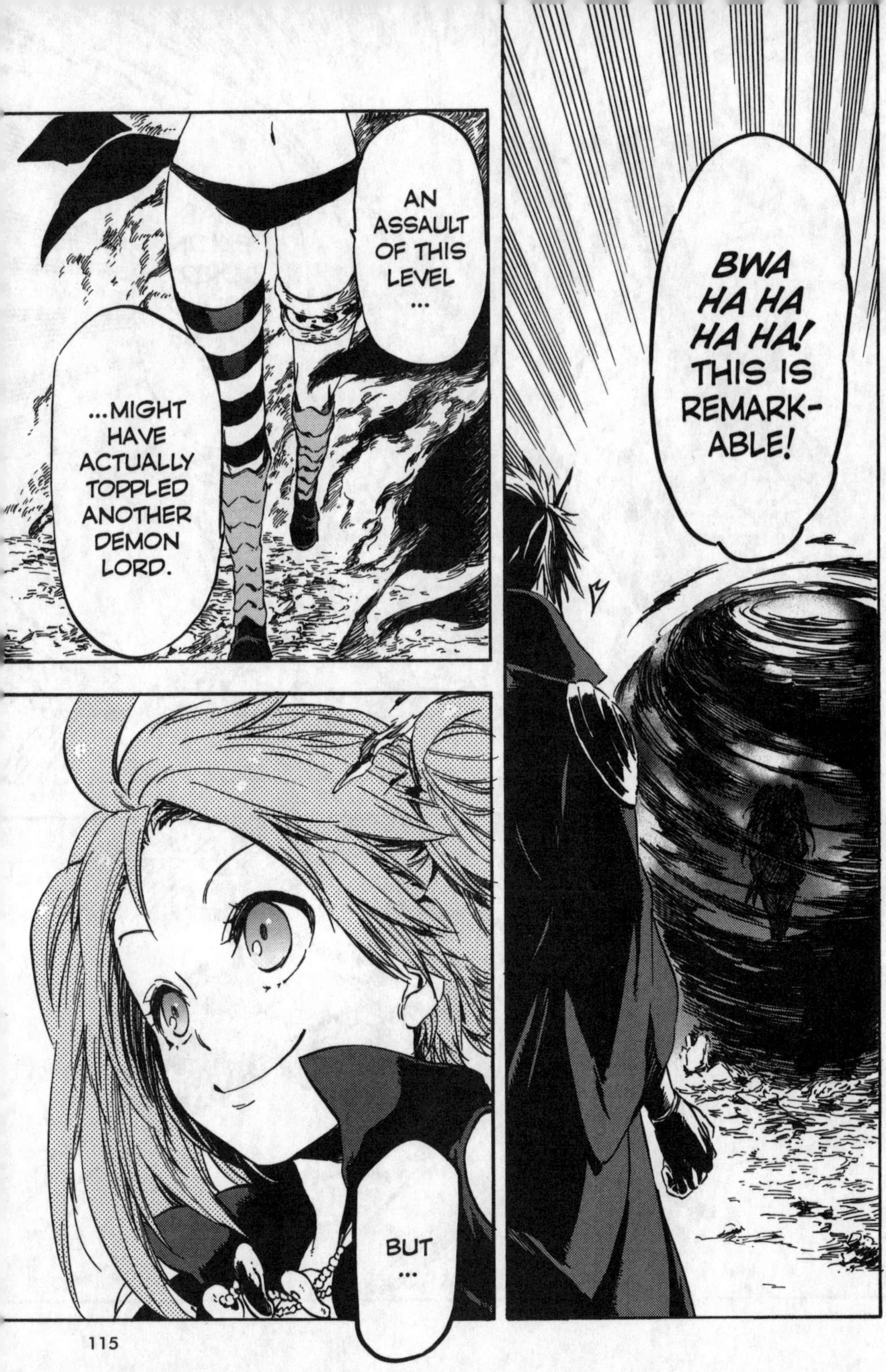
BWA HA HA HA HA! THIS IS REMARK-ABLE!
AN ASSAULT OF THIS LEVEL ...
...MIGHT HAVE ACTUALLY TOPPLED ANOTHER DEMON LORD.
BUT ...

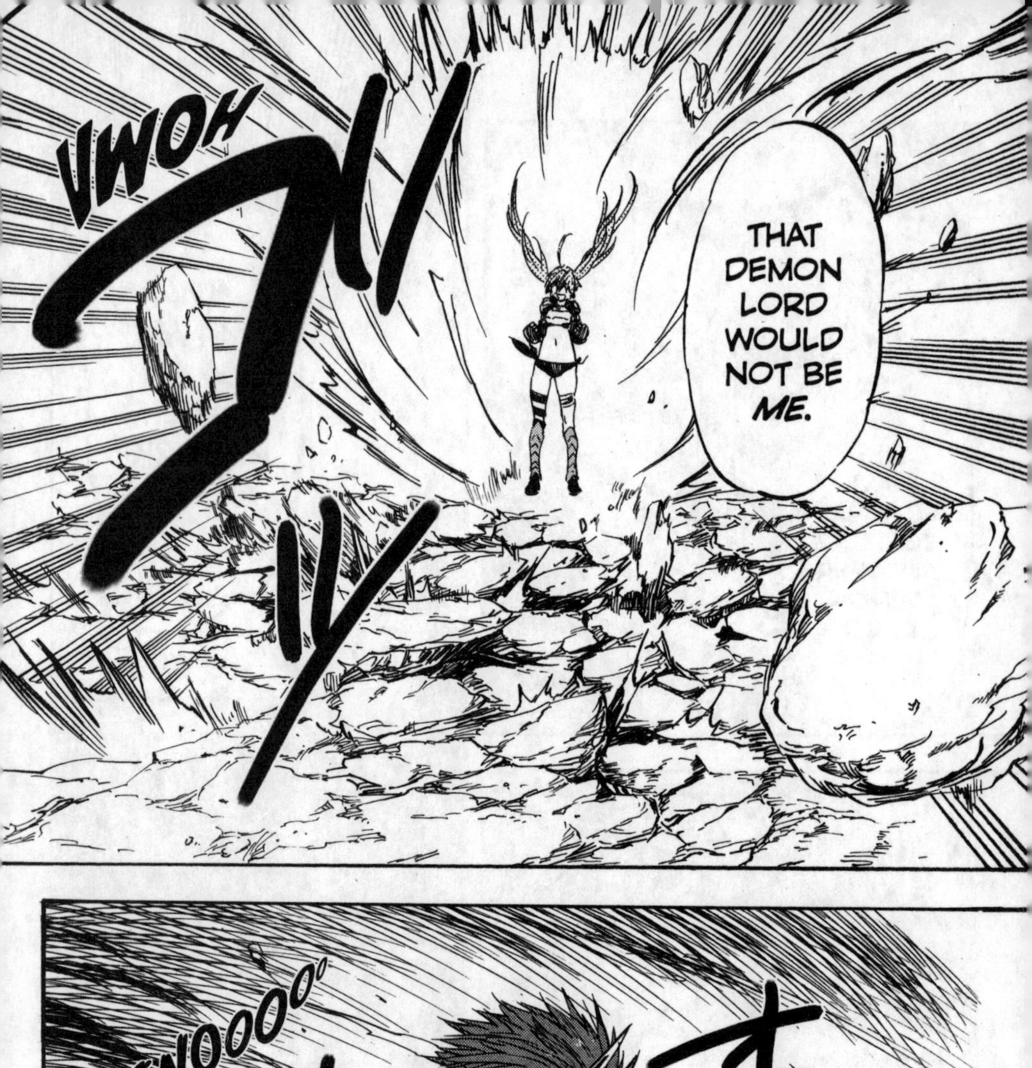
VWOH
THAT DEMON LORD WOULD NOT BE *ME.*

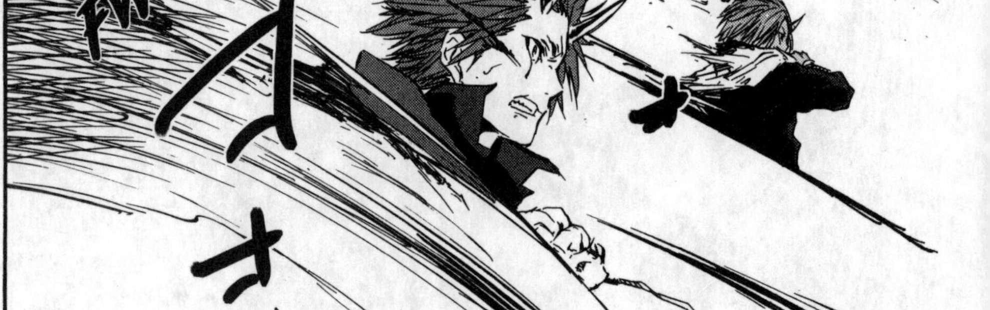
FWOOOOO

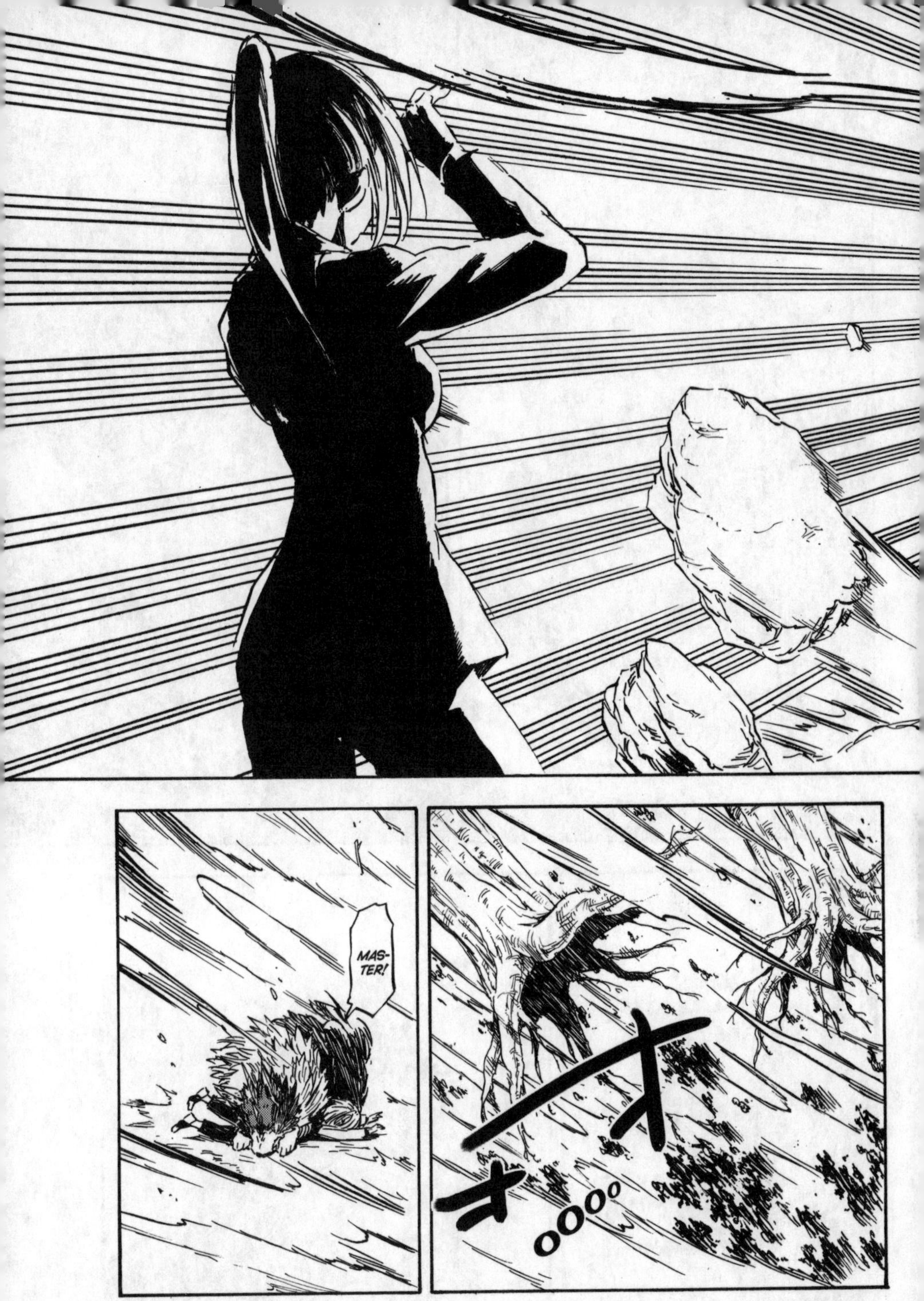
OOOO
MAS-TER!

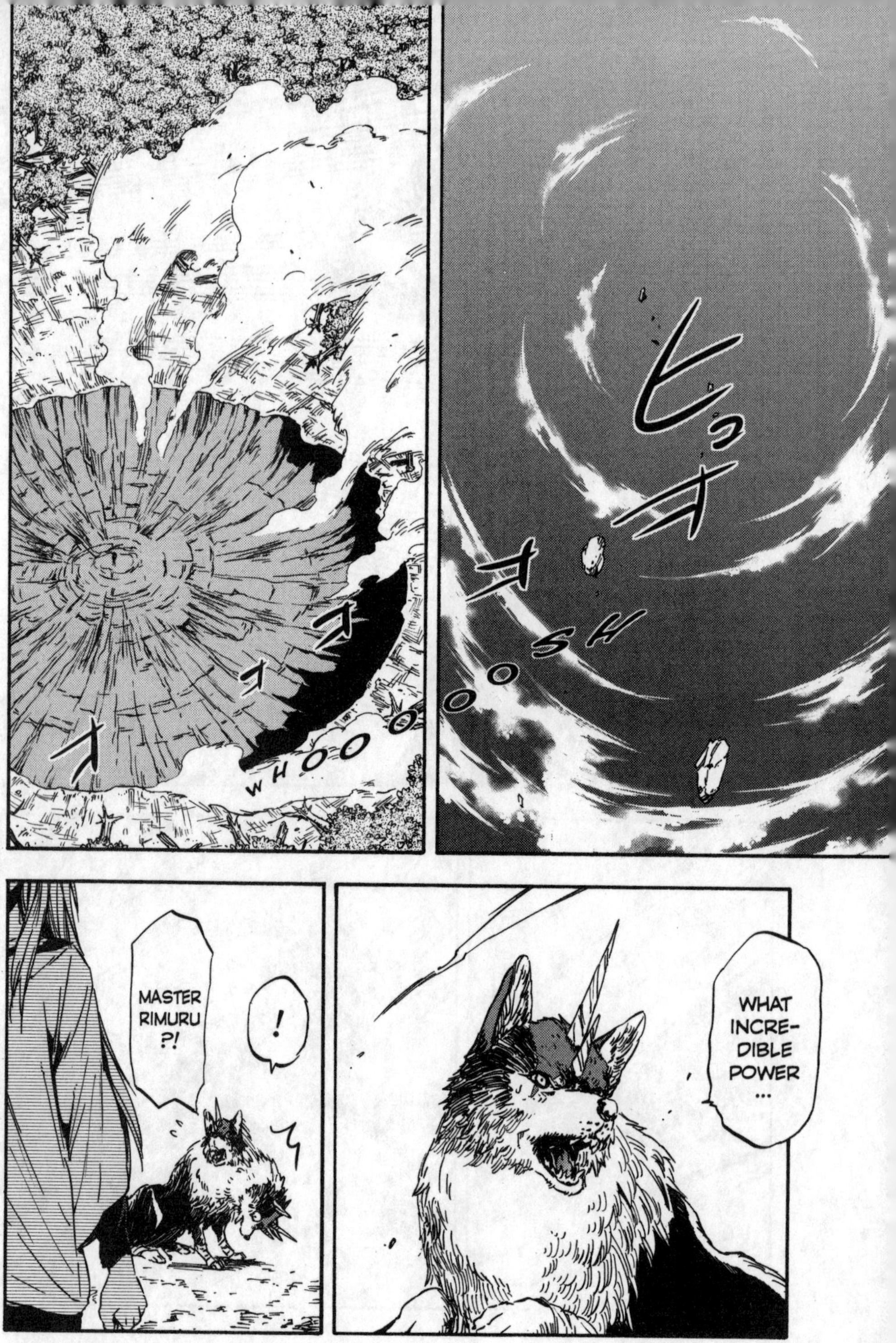
WHOOOOOSH
WHAT INCRE-DIBLE POWER...
!
MASTER RIMURU?!

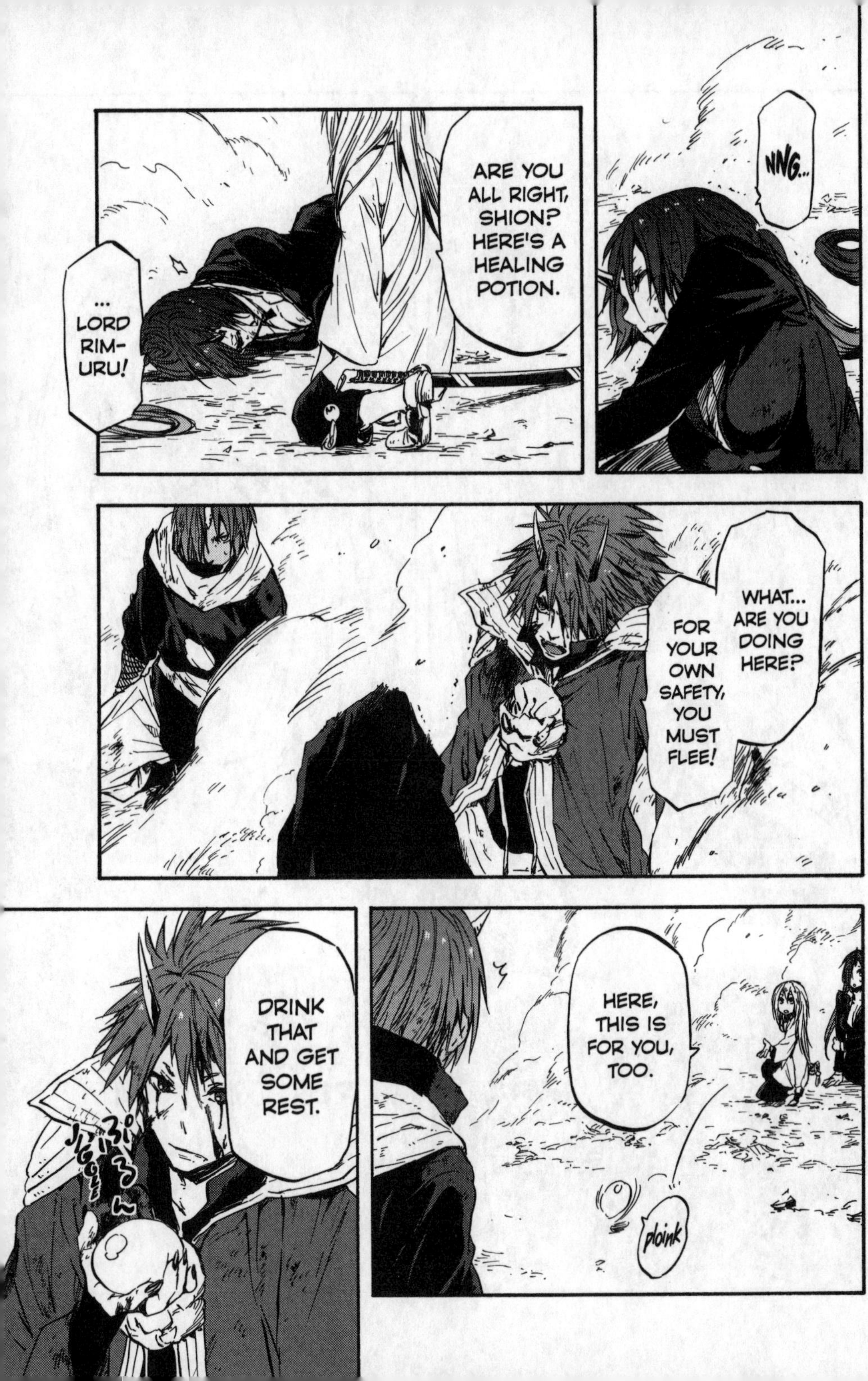
NNG...
ARE YOU ALL RIGHT, SHION? HERE'S A HEALING POTION.
...LORD RIM-URU!
WHAT... ARE YOU DOING HERE?
FOR YOUR OWN SAFETY, YOU MUST FLEE!
HERE, THIS IS FOR YOU, TOO.
ploink
DRINK THAT AND GET SOME REST.
ぷるん
JIGGLE

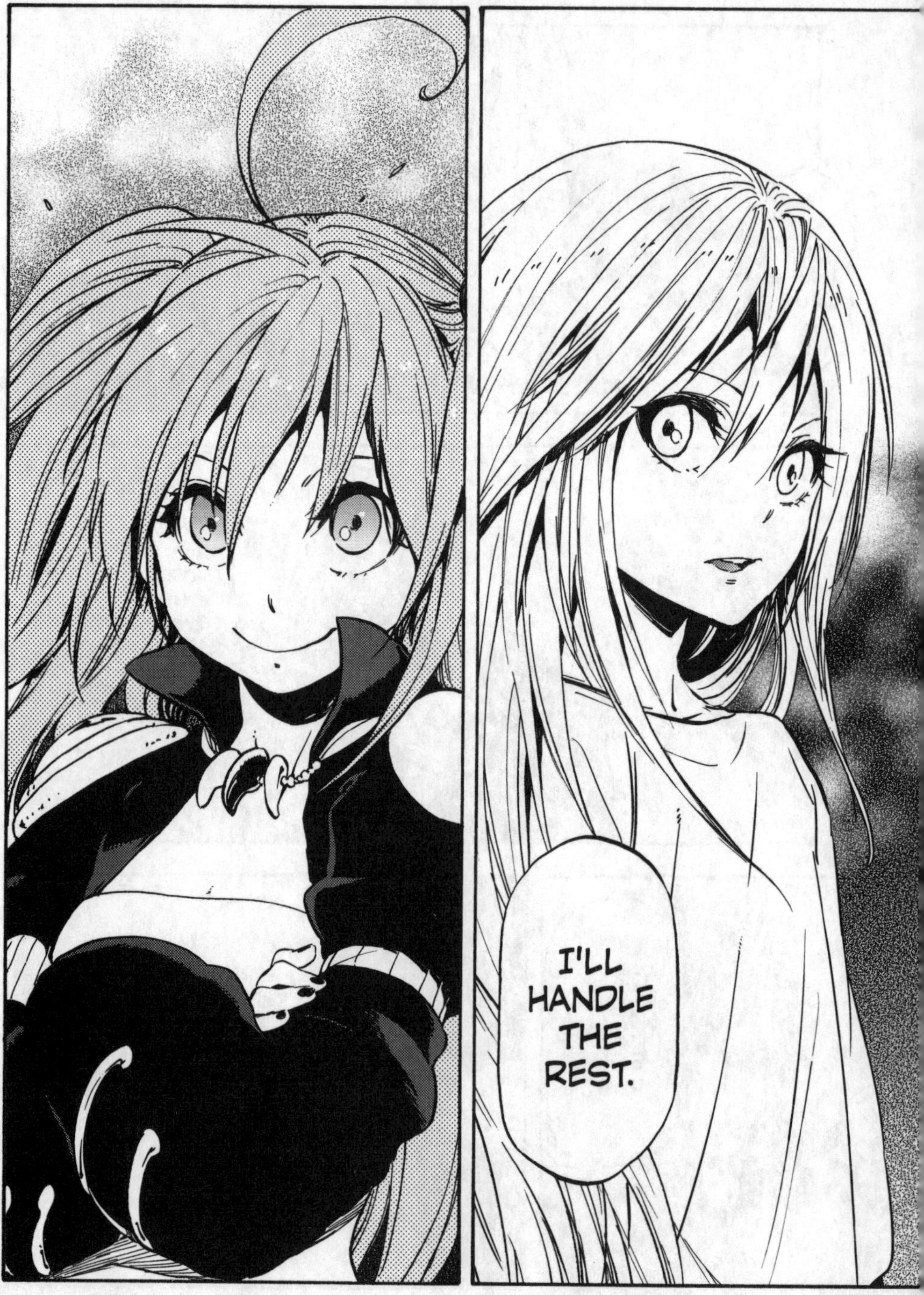
I'LL HANDLE THE REST.

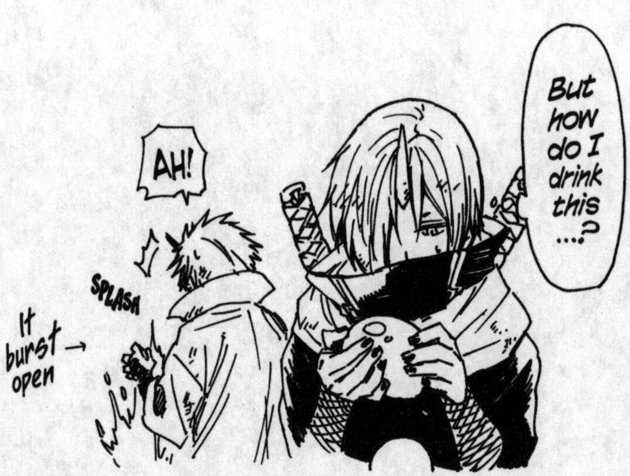
But how do I drink this ...?
AH!
SPLASH
It burst open

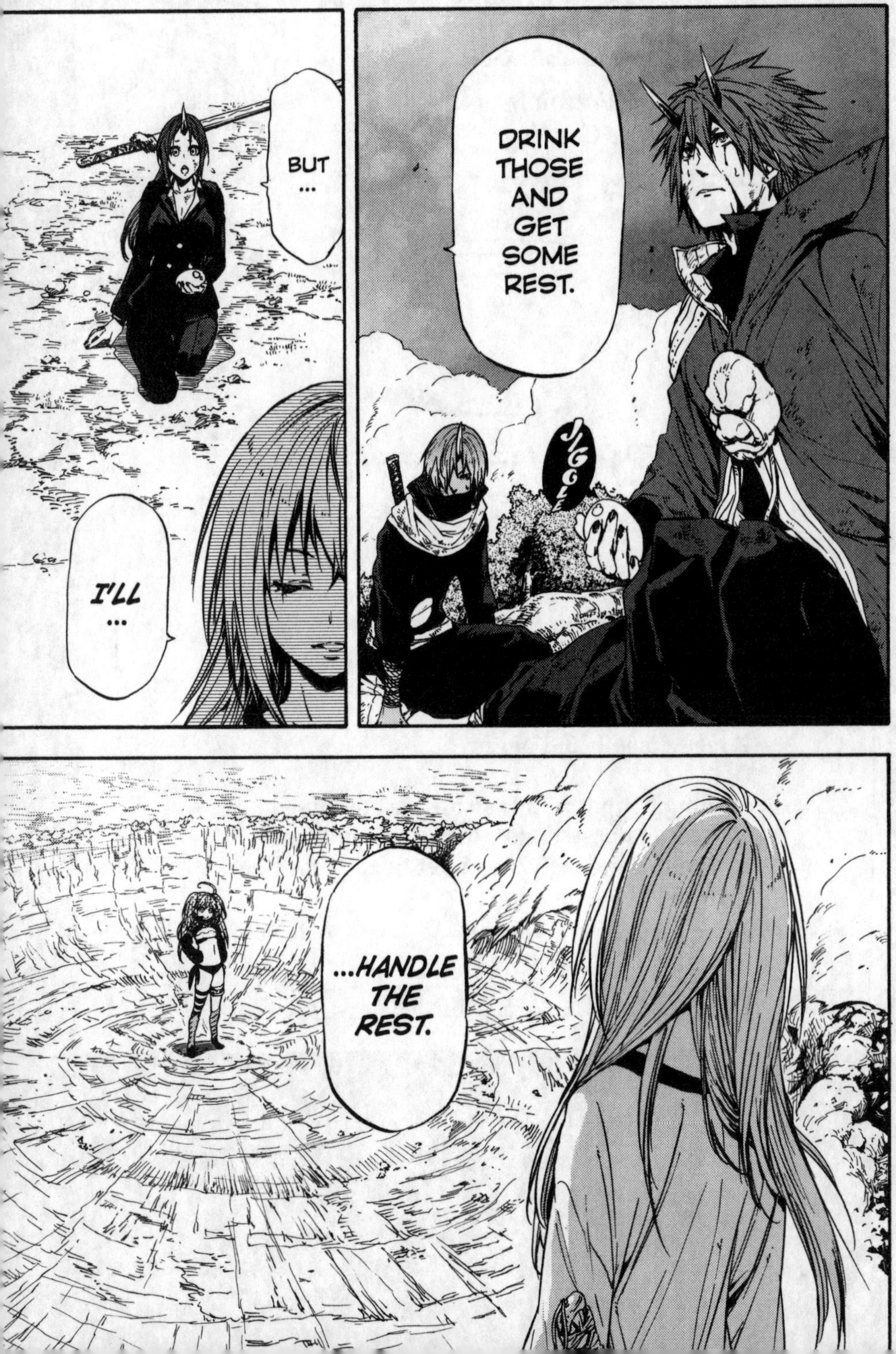
DRINK THOSE AND GET SOME REST.
JIGGLE
BUT ...
I'LL ...
...HANDLE THE REST.

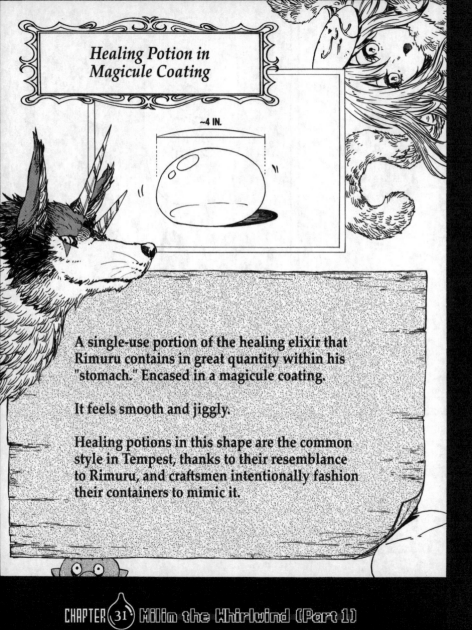

Healing Potion in Magicule Coating

~4 IN.

A single-use portion of the healing elixir that Rimuru contains in great quantity within his "stomach." Encased in a magicule coating.

It feels smooth and jiggly.

Healing potions in this shape are the common style in Tempest, thanks to their resemblance to Rimuru, and craftsmen intentionally fashion their containers to mimic it.

CHAPTER 31 Milim the Whirlwind (Part 1)

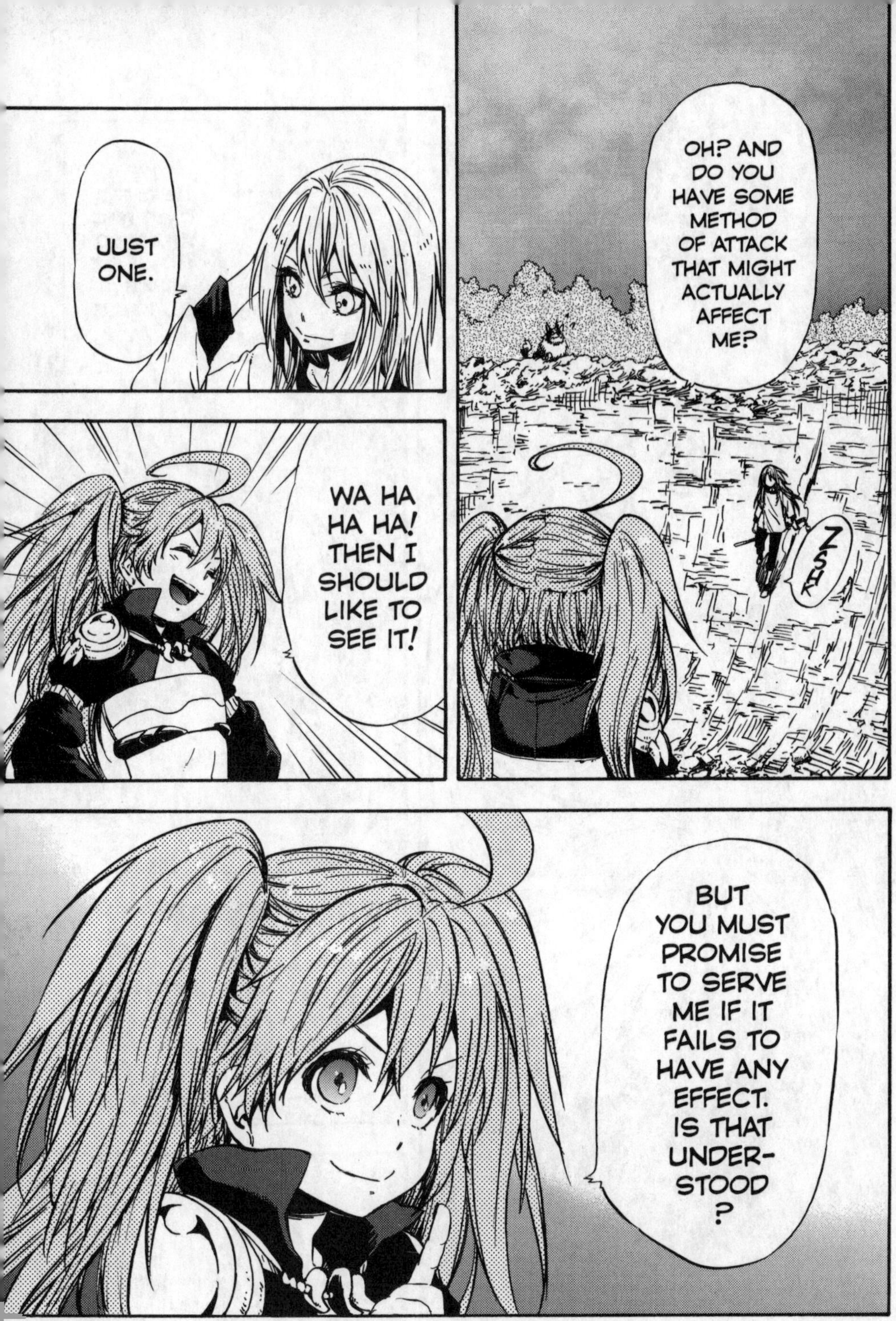
OH? AND DO YOU HAVE SOME METHOD OF ATTACK THAT MIGHT ACTUALLY AFFECT ME?
ZSHK
JUST ONE.
WA HA HA HA! THEN I SHOULD LIKE TO SEE IT!
BUT YOU MUST PROMISE TO SERVE ME IF IT FAILS TO HAVE ANY EFFECT. IS THAT UNDER-STOOD?

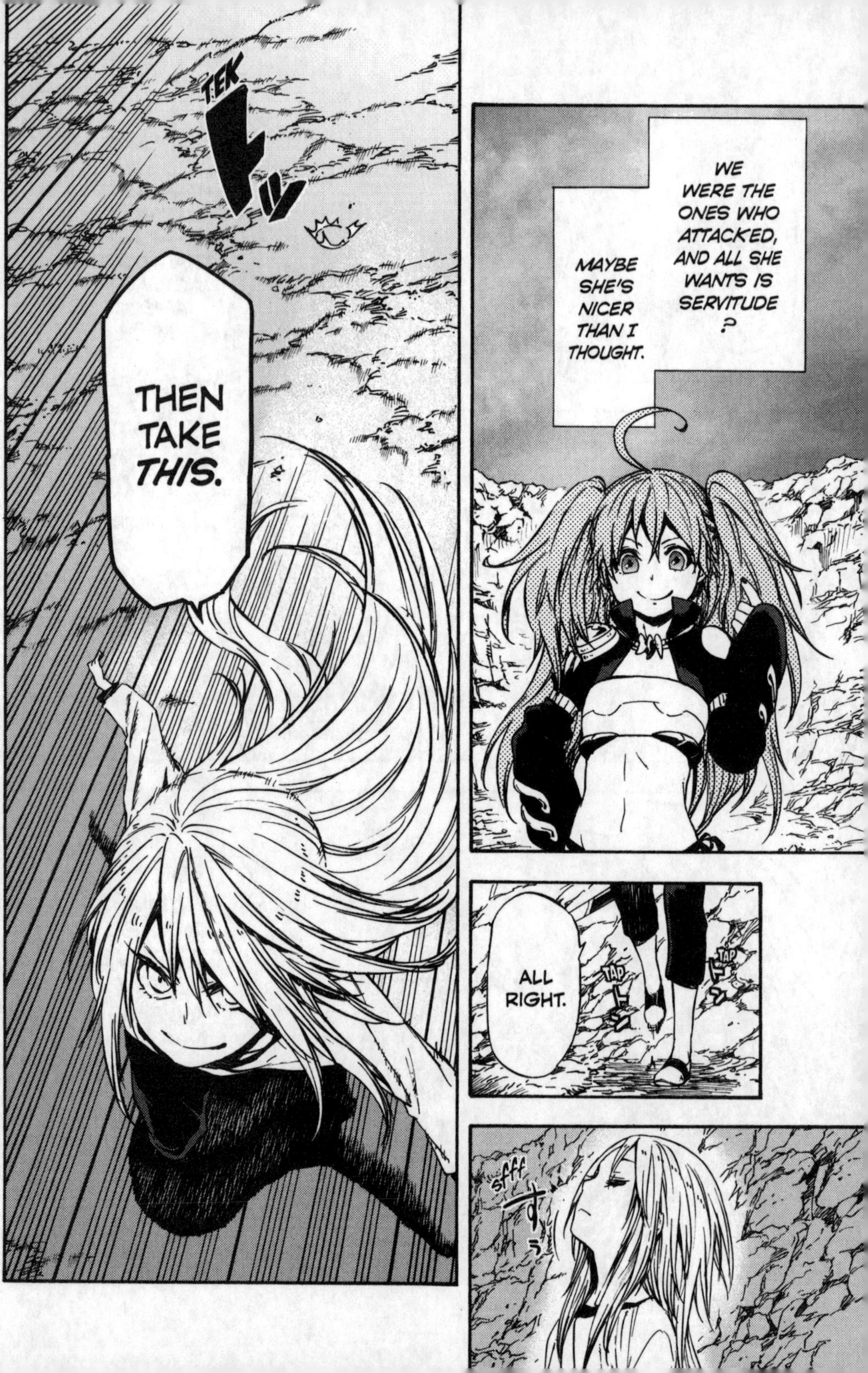
WE WERE THE ONES WHO ATTACKED, AND ALL SHE WANTS IS SERVITUDE?
MAYBE SHE'S NICER THAN I THOUGHT.
TAP
TAP
ALL RIGHT.
sfff
TEK
THEN TAKE THIS.

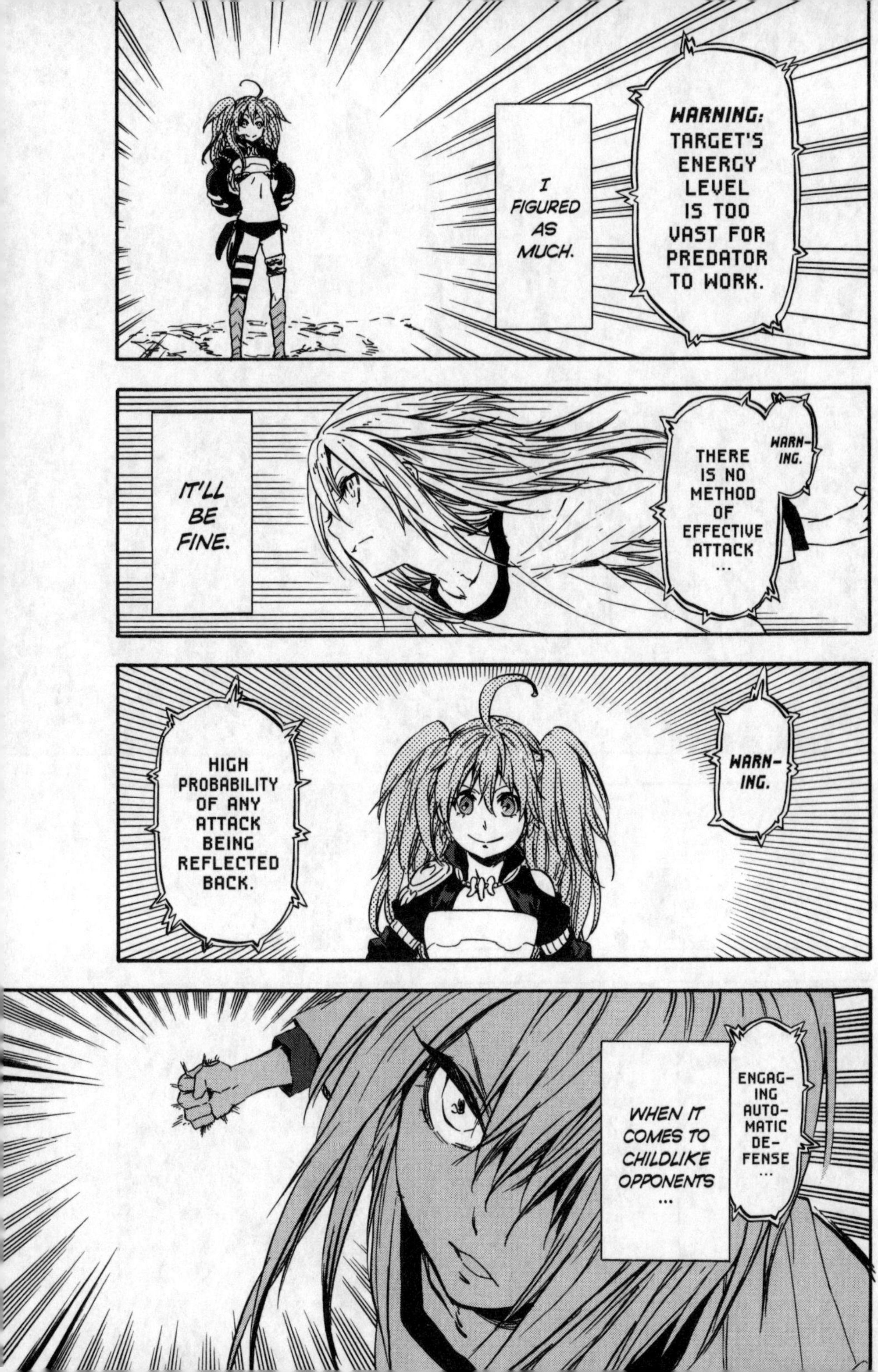
WARNING: TARGET'S ENERGY LEVEL IS TOO VAST FOR PREDATOR TO WORK.
I FIGURED AS MUCH.
WARN-ING.
THERE IS NO METHOD OF EFFECTIVE ATTACK ...
IT'LL BE FINE.
WARN-ING.
HIGH PROBABILITY OF ANY ATTACK BEING REFLECTED BACK.
ENGAG-ING AUTO-MATIC DE-FENSE ...
WHEN IT COMES TO CHILDLIKE OPPONENTS ...

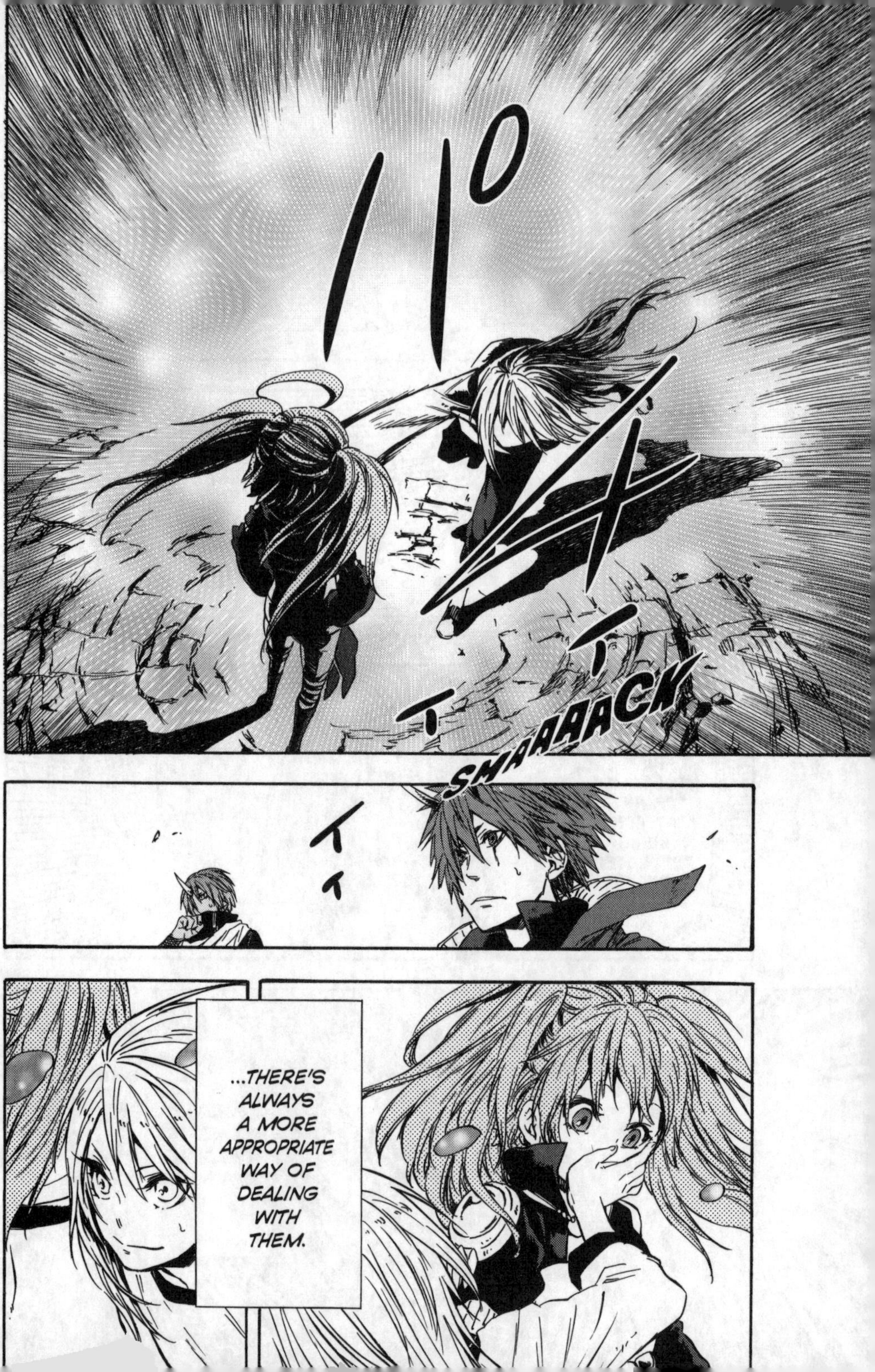
SHAAAACK
...THERE'S ALWAYS A MORE APPROPRIATE WAY OF DEALING WITH THEM.

OBVIOUSLY I DON'T THINK I STAND A CHANCE AGAINST A DEMON LORD IN A NORMAL FIGHT.

SO OUR FATE WILL BE DECIDED...

...BY MILIM'S REACTION AFTER SHE TASTED WHAT I JUST GAVE HER.

lick

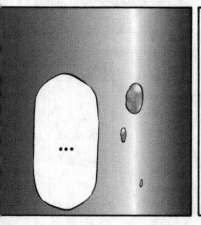

...

129

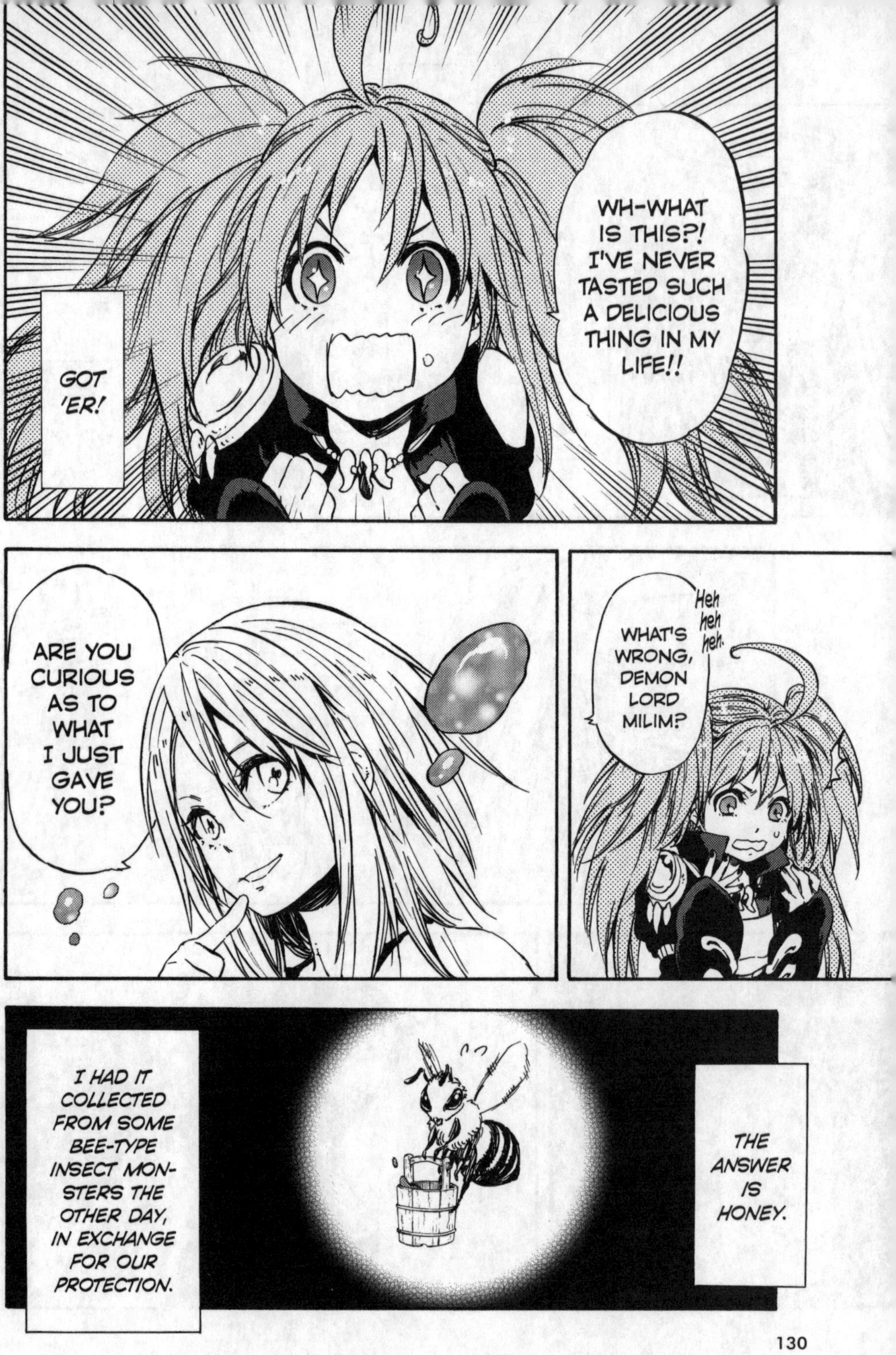
WH-WHAT IS THIS?! I'VE NEVER TASTED SUCH A DELICIOUS THING IN MY LIFE!!
GOT 'ER!
Heh heh heh.
WHAT'S WRONG, DEMON LORD MILIM?
ARE YOU CURIOUS AS TO WHAT I JUST GAVE YOU?
THE ANSWER IS HONEY.
I HAD IT COLLECTED FROM SOME BEE-TYPE INSECT MON-STERS THE OTHER DAY, IN EXCHANGE FOR OUR PROTECTION.

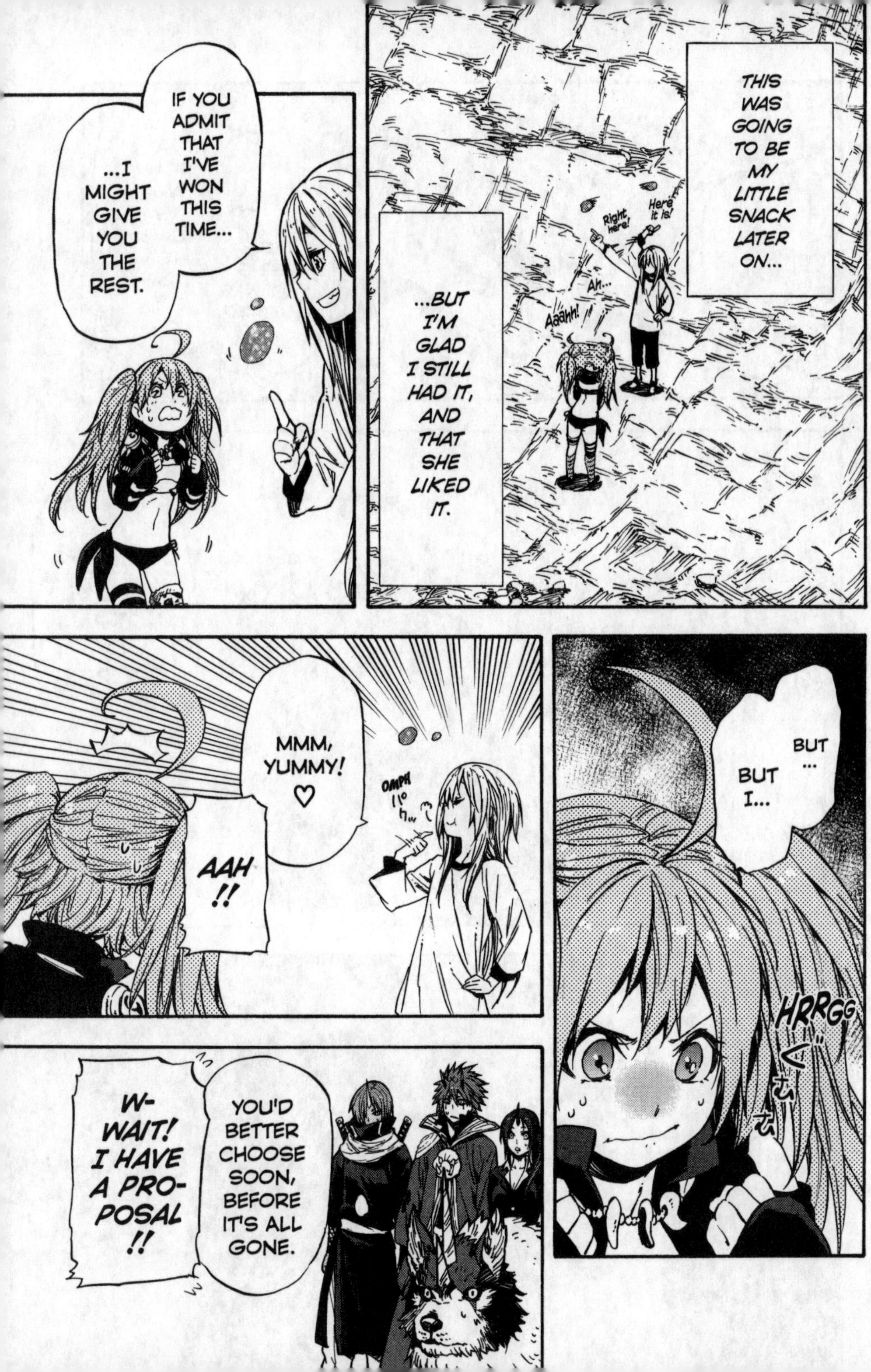
THIS WAS GOING TO BE MY LITTLE SNACK LATER ON...
Here it is!
Right here!
Ah...
Aaahh!
...BUT I'M GLAD I STILL HAD IT, AND THAT SHE LIKED IT.
IF YOU ADMIT THAT I'VE WON THIS TIME...
...I MIGHT GIVE YOU THE REST.
BUT ...
BUT I...
HRRGG
MMM, YUMMY! ♡
OMPH
AAH!!
YOU'D BETTER CHOOSE SOON, BEFORE IT'S ALL GONE.
W-WAIT! I HAVE A PRO-POSAL!!

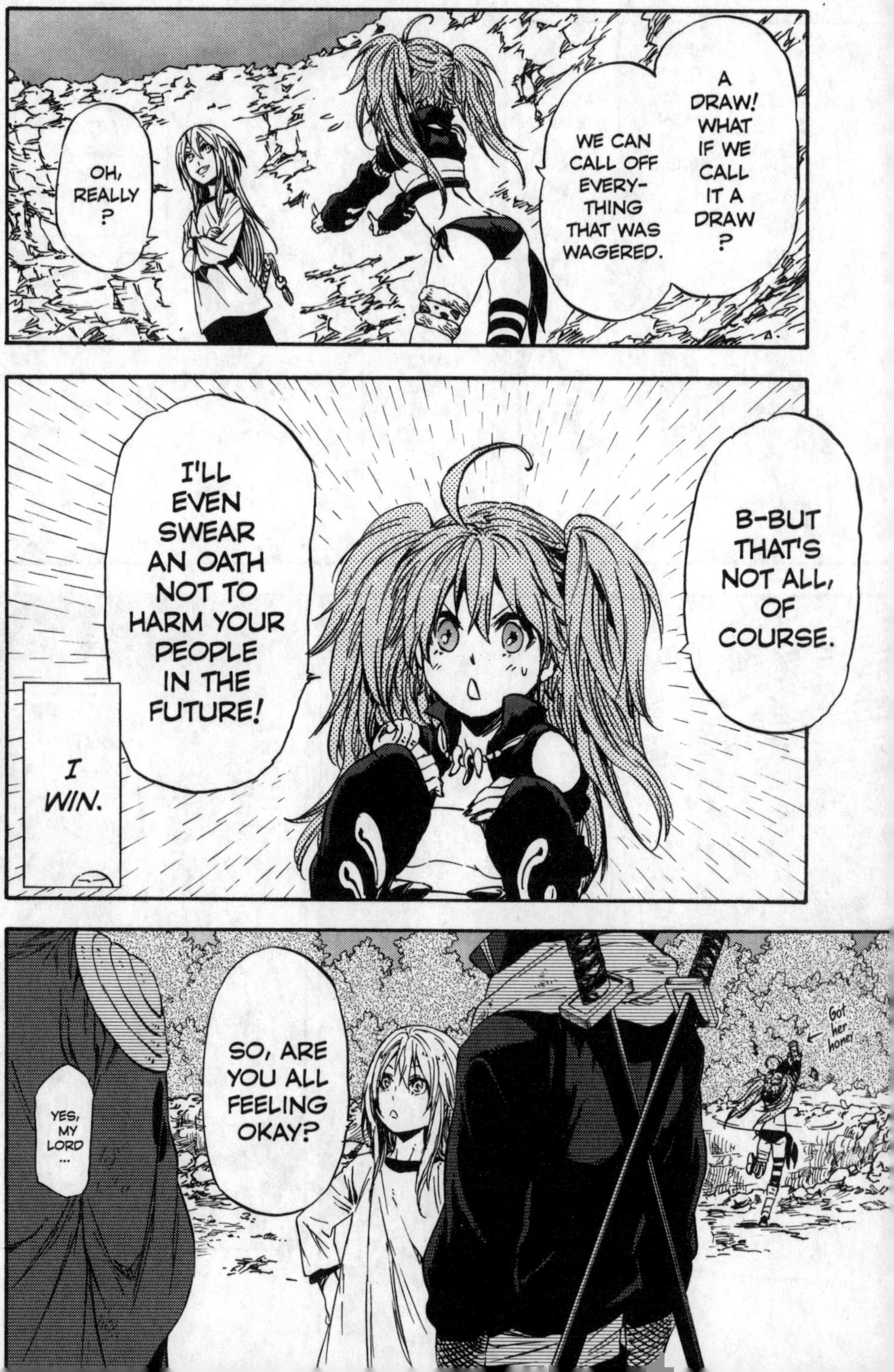
A DRAW! WHAT IF WE CALL IT A DRAW?
WE CAN CALL OFF EVERY-THING THAT WAS WAGERED.
OH, REALLY?
B-BUT THAT'S NOT ALL, OF COURSE.
I'LL EVEN SWEAR AN OATH NOT TO HARM YOUR PEOPLE IN THE FUTURE!
I WIN.
Got her honey
SO, ARE YOU ALL FEELING OKAY?
YES, MY LORD...

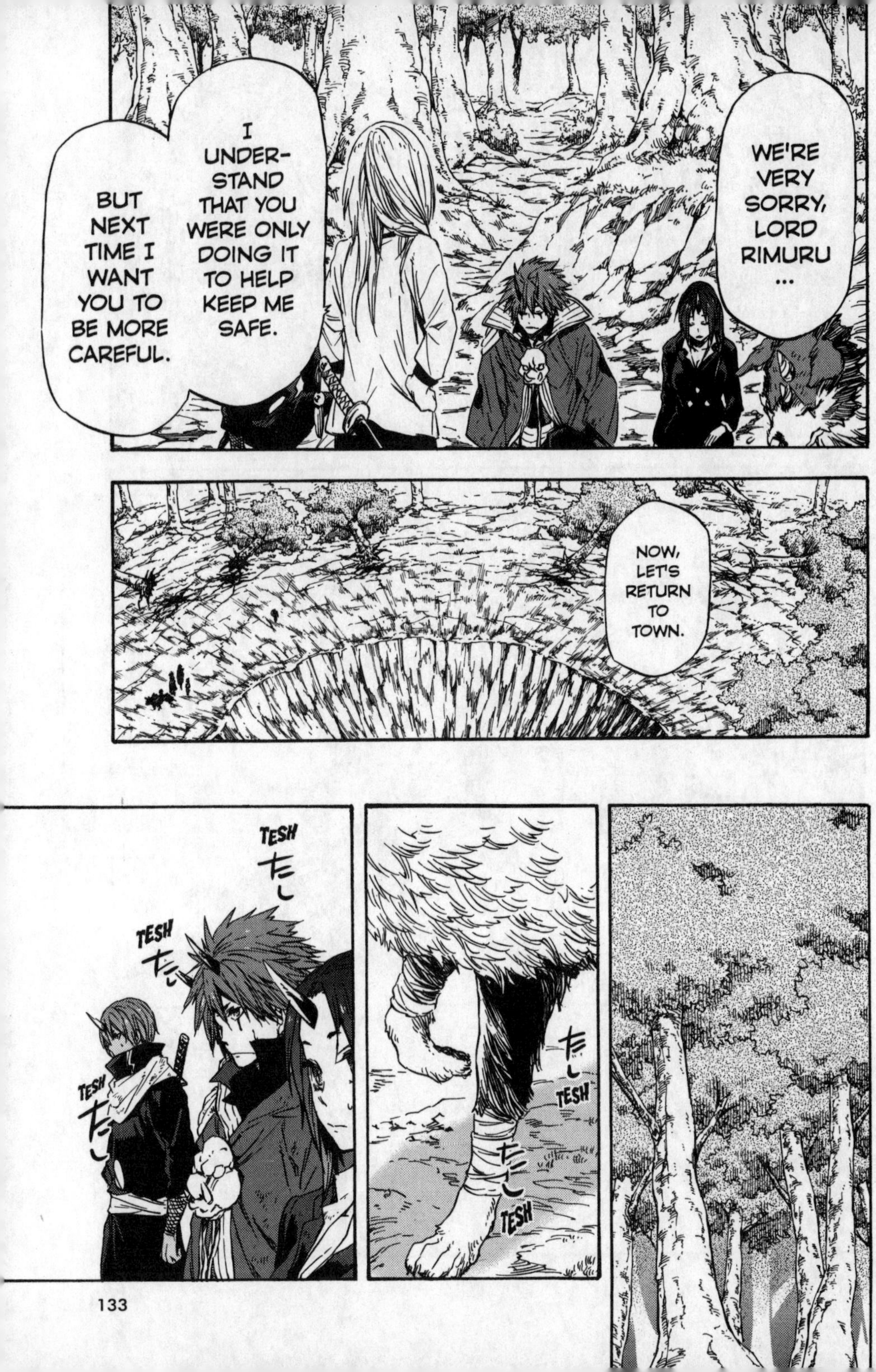
WE'RE VERY SORRY, LORD RIMURU ...
I UNDER-STAND THAT YOU WERE ONLY DOING IT TO HELP KEEP ME SAFE.
BUT NEXT TIME I WANT YOU TO BE MORE CAREFUL.
NOW, LET'S RETURN TO TOWN.
たし TESH
たし TESH
TESH たし
TESH たし
TESH たし

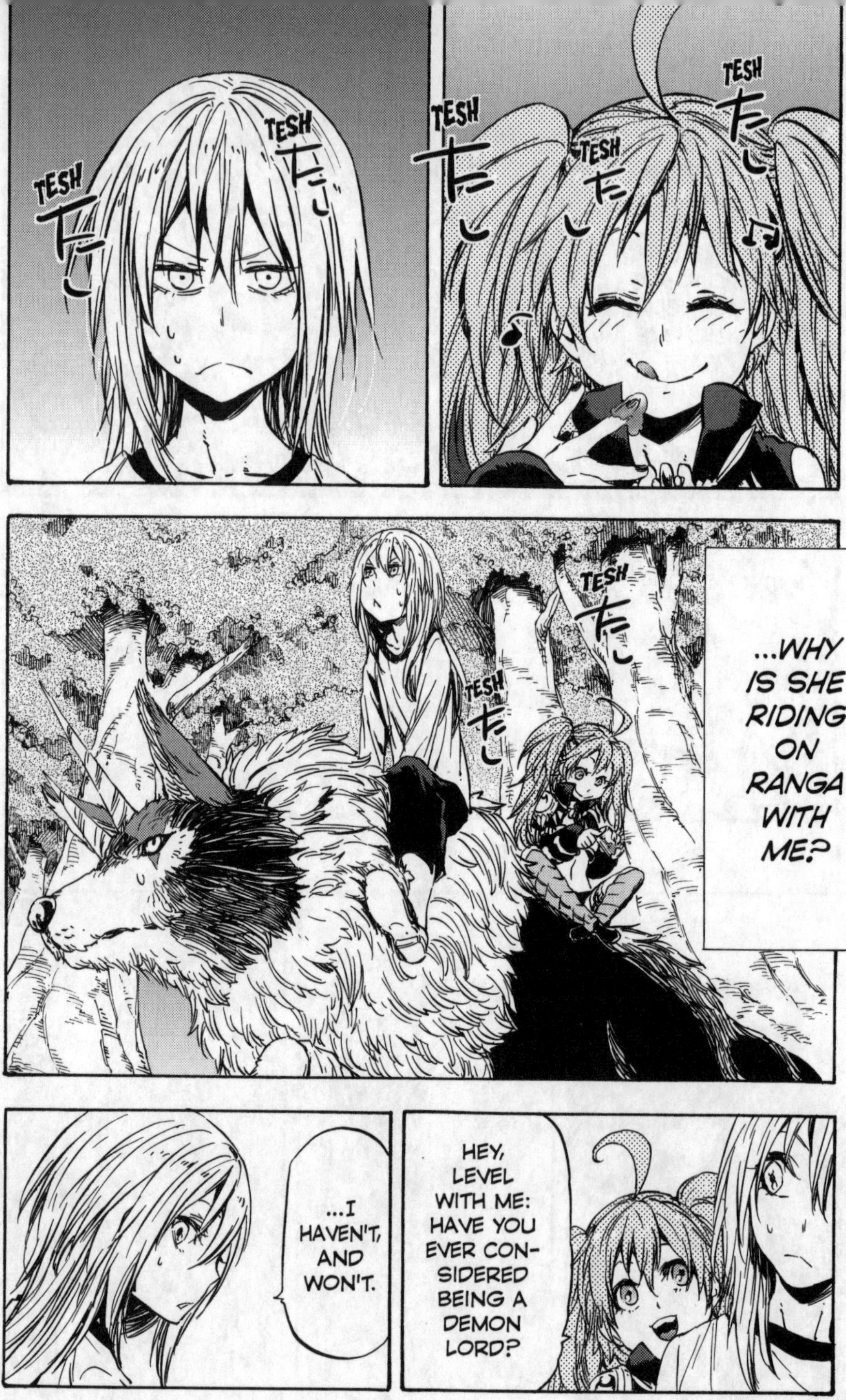
TESH たし
TESH たし
TESH たし
TESH たし
TESH たし
TESH たし
TESH たし
...WHY IS SHE RIDING ON RANGA WITH ME?
HEY, LEVEL WITH ME: HAVE YOU EVER CON-SIDERED BEING A DEMON LORD?
...I HAVEN'T, AND WON'T.

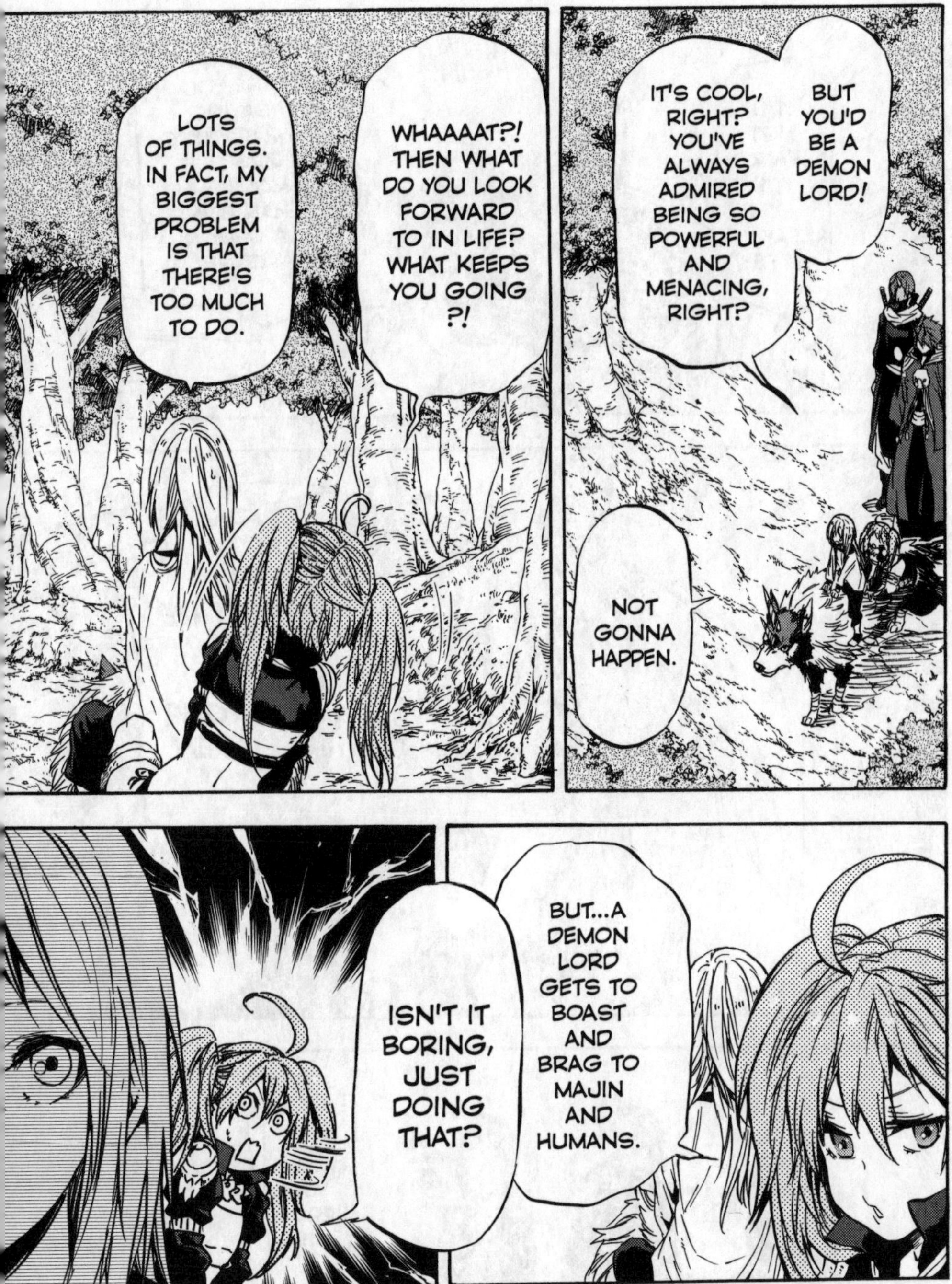
BUT YOU'D BE A DEMON LORD!
IT'S COOL, RIGHT? YOU'VE ALWAYS ADMIRED BEING SO POWERFUL AND MENACING, RIGHT?
NOT GONNA HAPPEN.
WHAAAAT?! THEN WHAT DO YOU LOOK FORWARD TO IN LIFE? WHAT KEEPS YOU GOING?!
LOTS OF THINGS. IN FACT, MY BIGGEST PROBLEM IS THAT THERE'S TOO MUCH TO DO.
BUT...A DEMON LORD GETS TO BOAST AND BRAG TO MAJIN AND HUMANS.
ISN'T IT BORING, JUST DOING THAT?

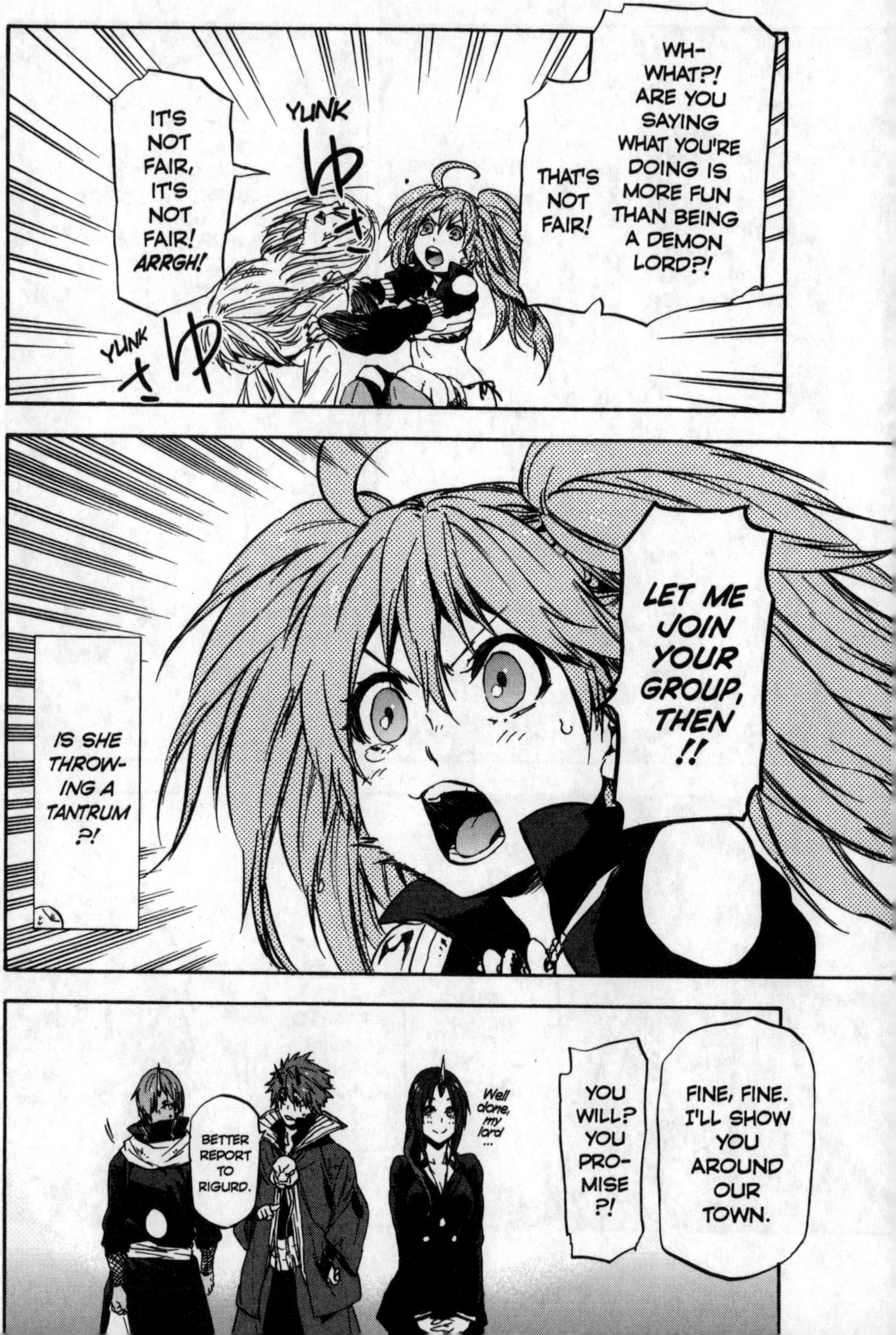
WH- WHAT?! ARE YOU SAYING WHAT YOU'RE DOING IS MORE FUN THAN BEING A DEMON LORD?!
THAT'S NOT FAIR!
YUNK
ゆ
IT'S NOT FAIR, IT'S NOT FAIR! ARRGH!
YUNK
ゆ
LET ME JOIN YOUR GROUP, THEN!!
IS SHE THROWING A TANTRUM?!
FINE, FINE. I'LL SHOW YOU AROUND OUR TOWN.
YOU WILL? YOU PROMISE?!
Well done, my lord...
BETTER REPORT TO RIGURD.

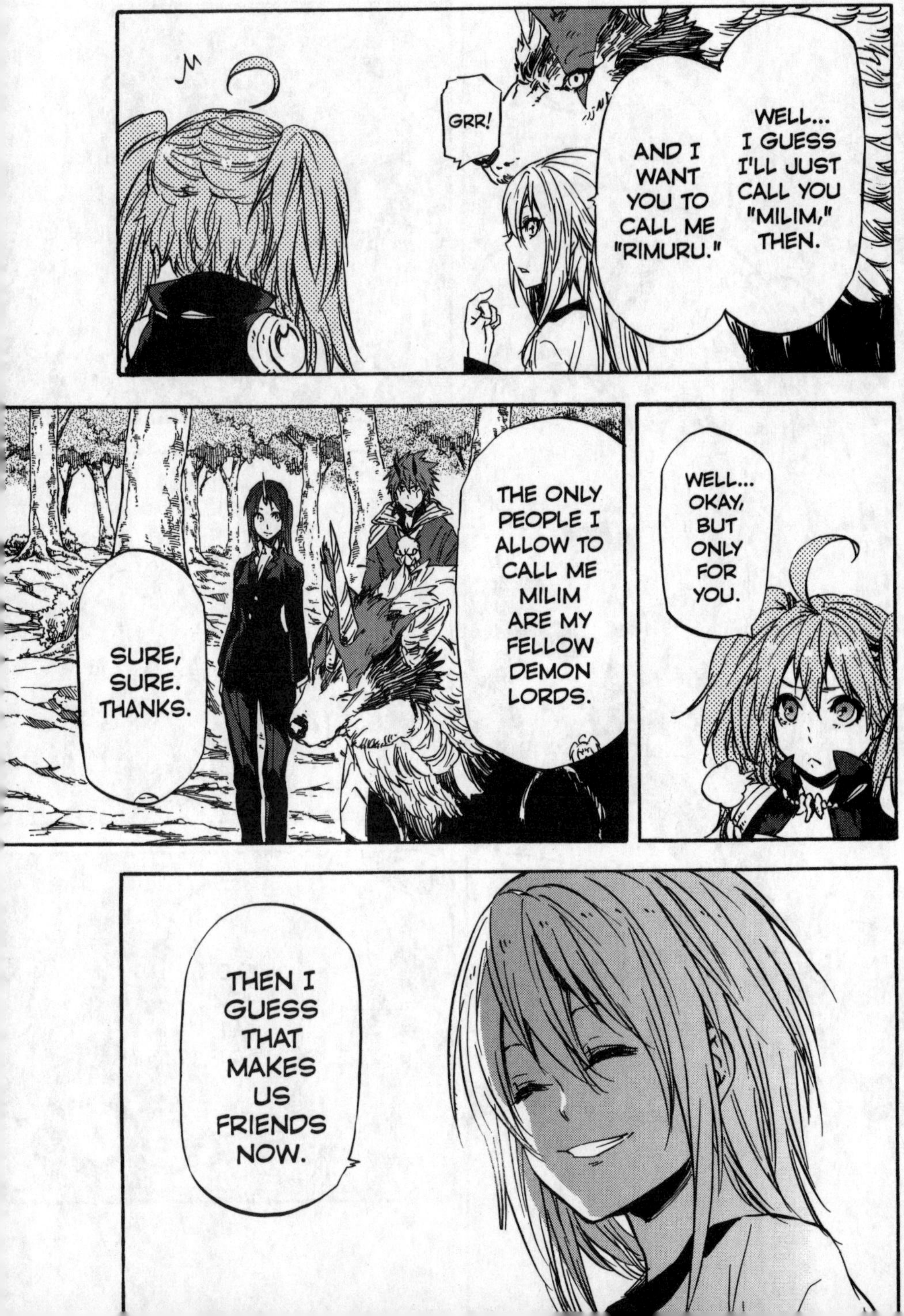
WELL... I GUESS I'LL JUST CALL YOU "MILIM," THEN.
AND I WANT YOU TO CALL ME "RIMURU."
GRR!
WELL... OKAY, BUT ONLY FOR YOU.
THE ONLY PEOPLE I ALLOW TO CALL ME MILIM ARE MY FELLOW DEMON LORDS.
SURE, SURE. THANKS.
THEN I GUESS THAT MAKES US FRIENDS NOW.

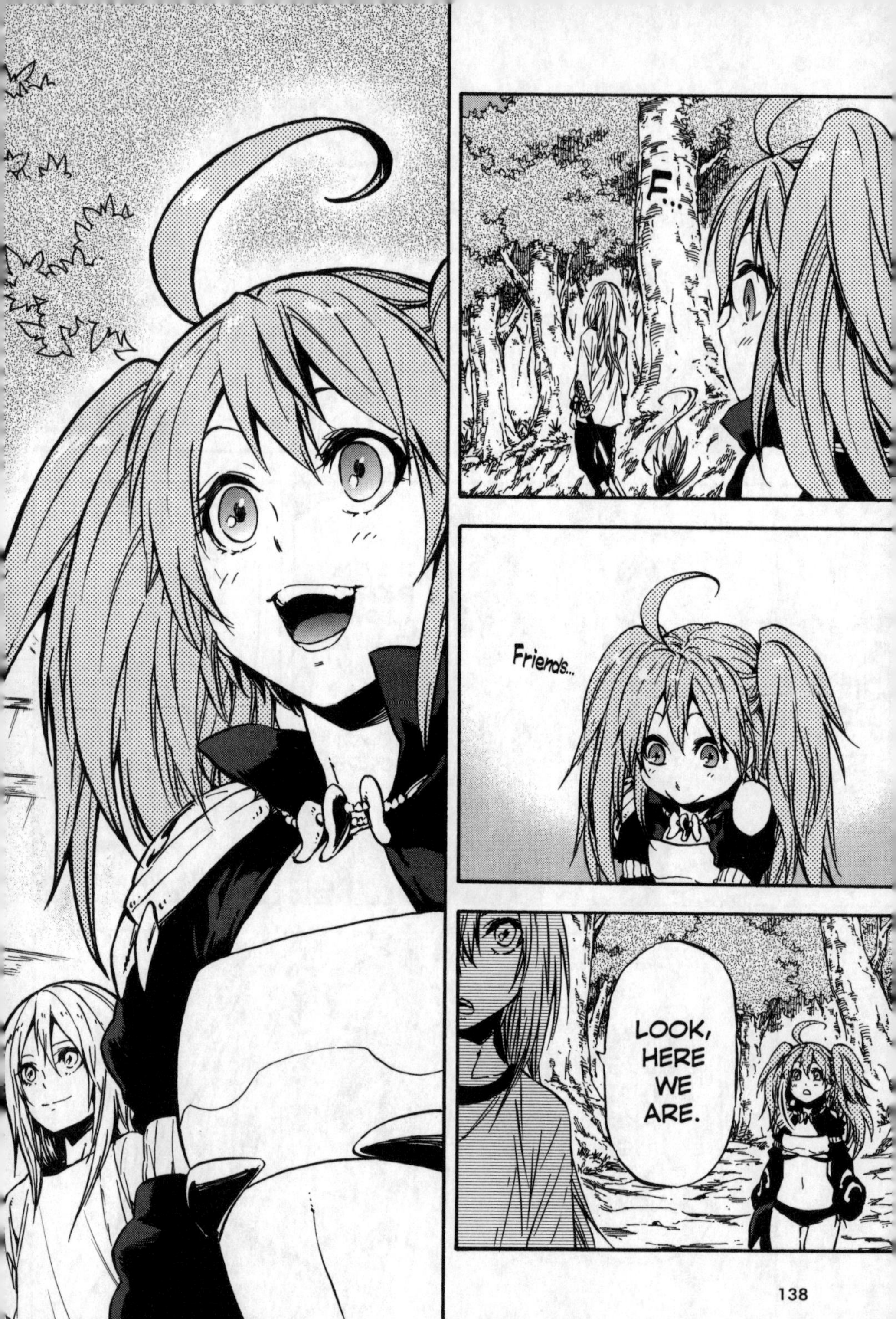
F...
Friends...
LOOK, HERE WE ARE.

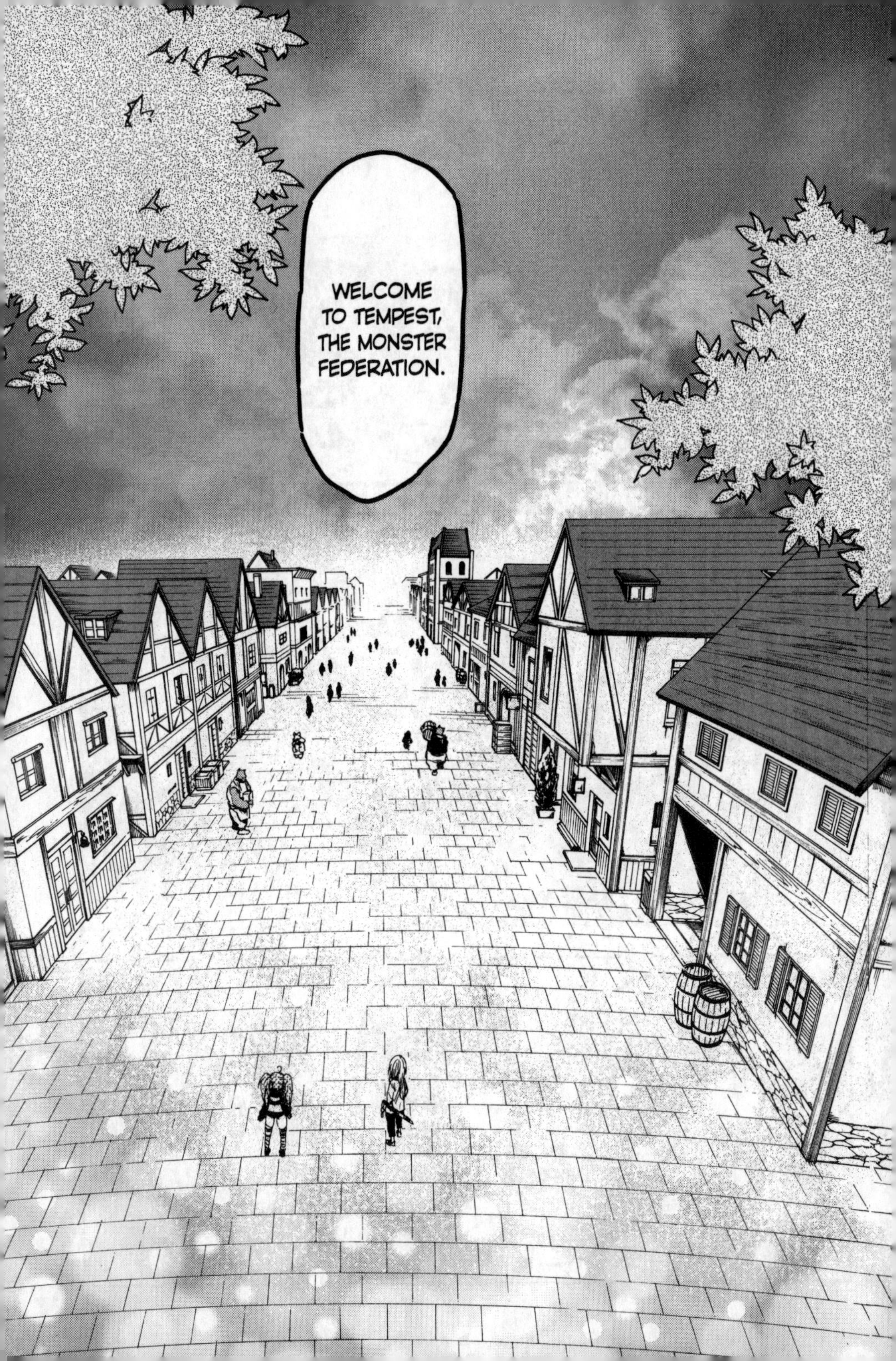
WELCOME TO TEMPEST, THE MONSTER FEDERATION.

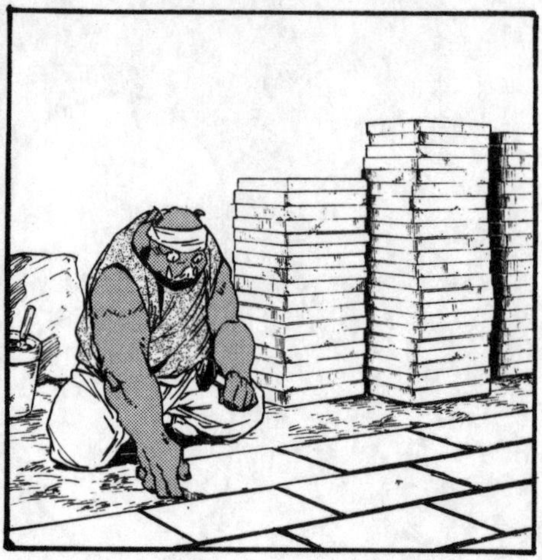

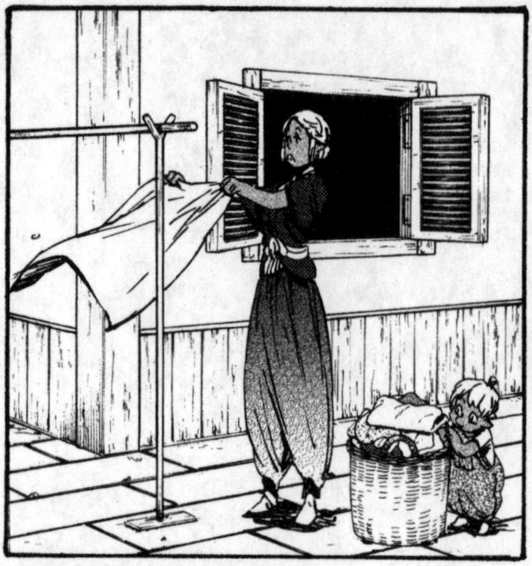

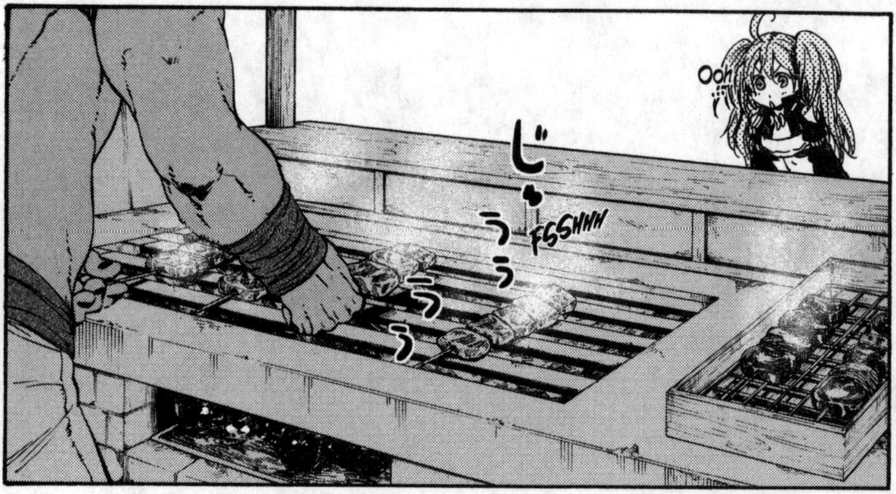
Ooh
じゅううーうう
FSSHHH

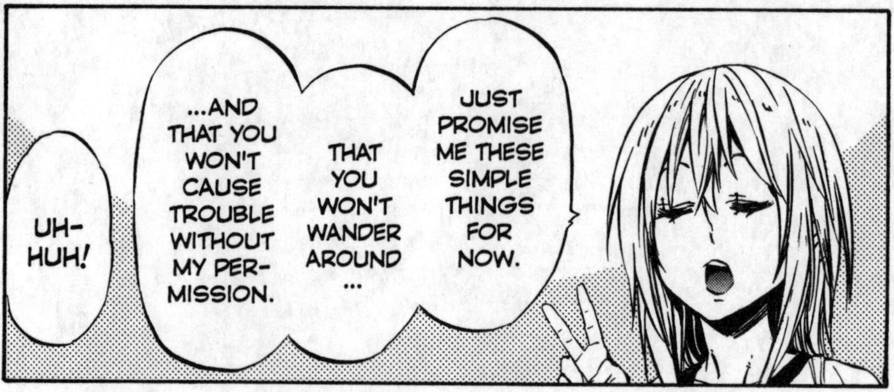
JUST PROMISE ME THESE SIMPLE THINGS FOR NOW.
THAT YOU WON'T WANDER AROUND ...
...AND THAT YOU WON'T CAUSE TROUBLE WITHOUT MY PER-MISSION.
UH-HUH!

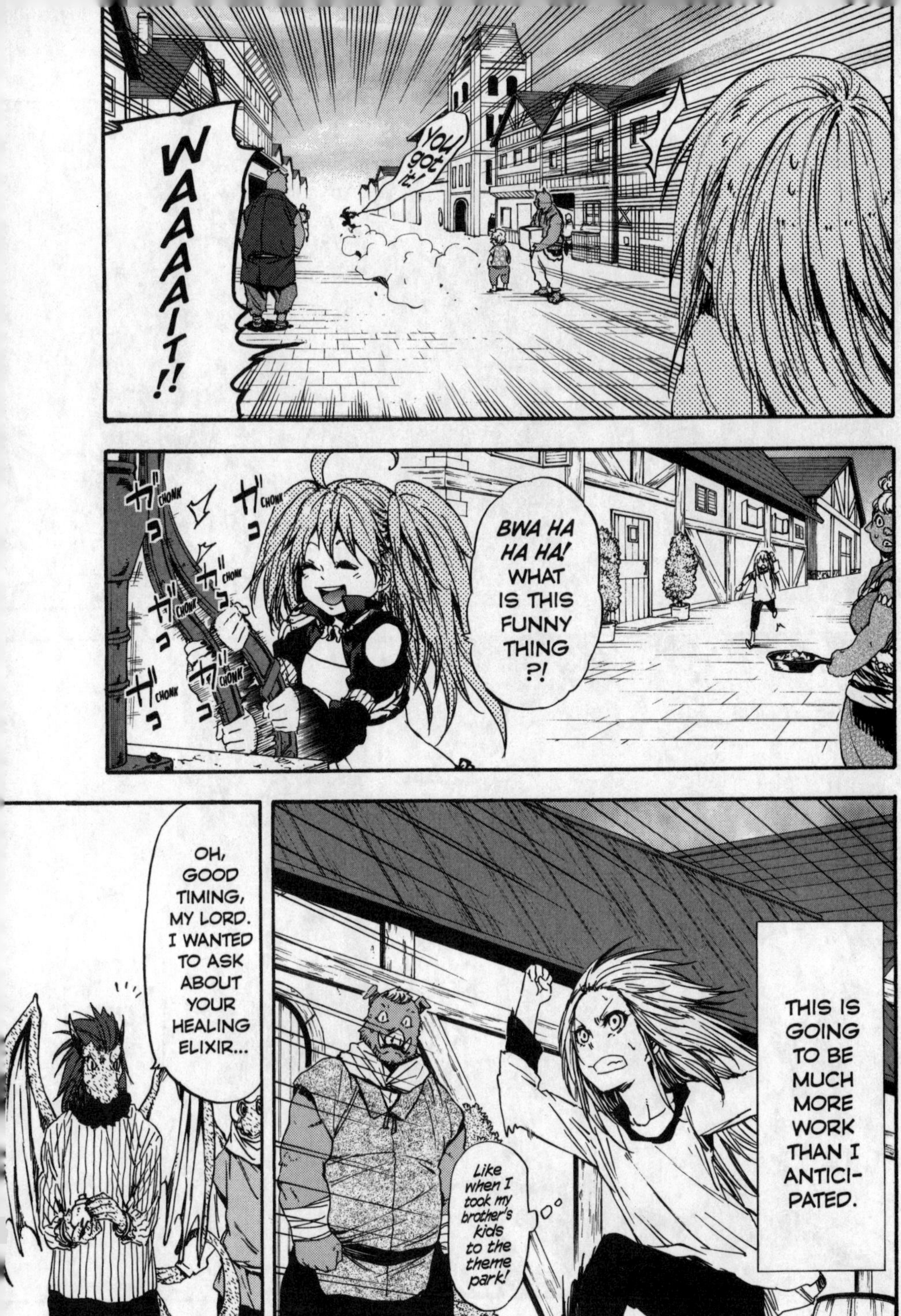
You got it!
WAAAAAIT!!
BWA HA HA HA! WHAT IS THIS FUNNY THING?!
ガッ CHONK
ガッ CHONK
ガッ CHONK
ガッ CHONK
ガッ CHONK
ガッ CHONK
THIS IS GOING TO BE MUCH MORE WORK THAN I ANTICIPATED.
Like when I took my brother's kids to the theme park!
OH, GOOD TIMING, MY LORD. I WANTED TO ASK ABOUT YOUR HEALING ELIXIR...

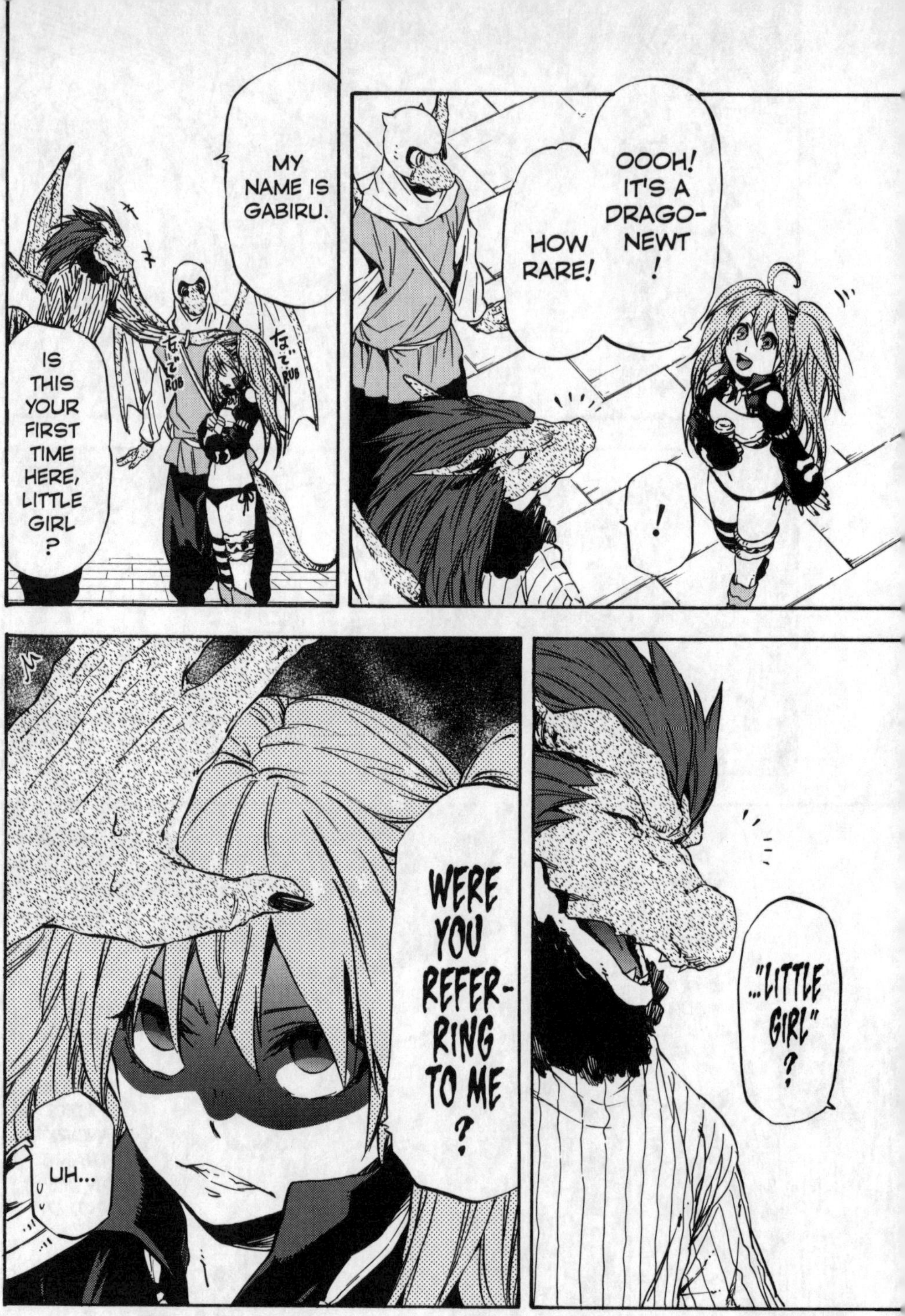

OOOH! IT'S A DRAGO-NEWT!
HOW RARE!
!
MY NAME IS GABIRU.
IS THIS YOUR FIRST TIME HERE, LITTLE GIRL?
なで RUB
なで RUB
..."LITTLE GIRL"?
WERE YOU REFER-RING TO ME?
UH...

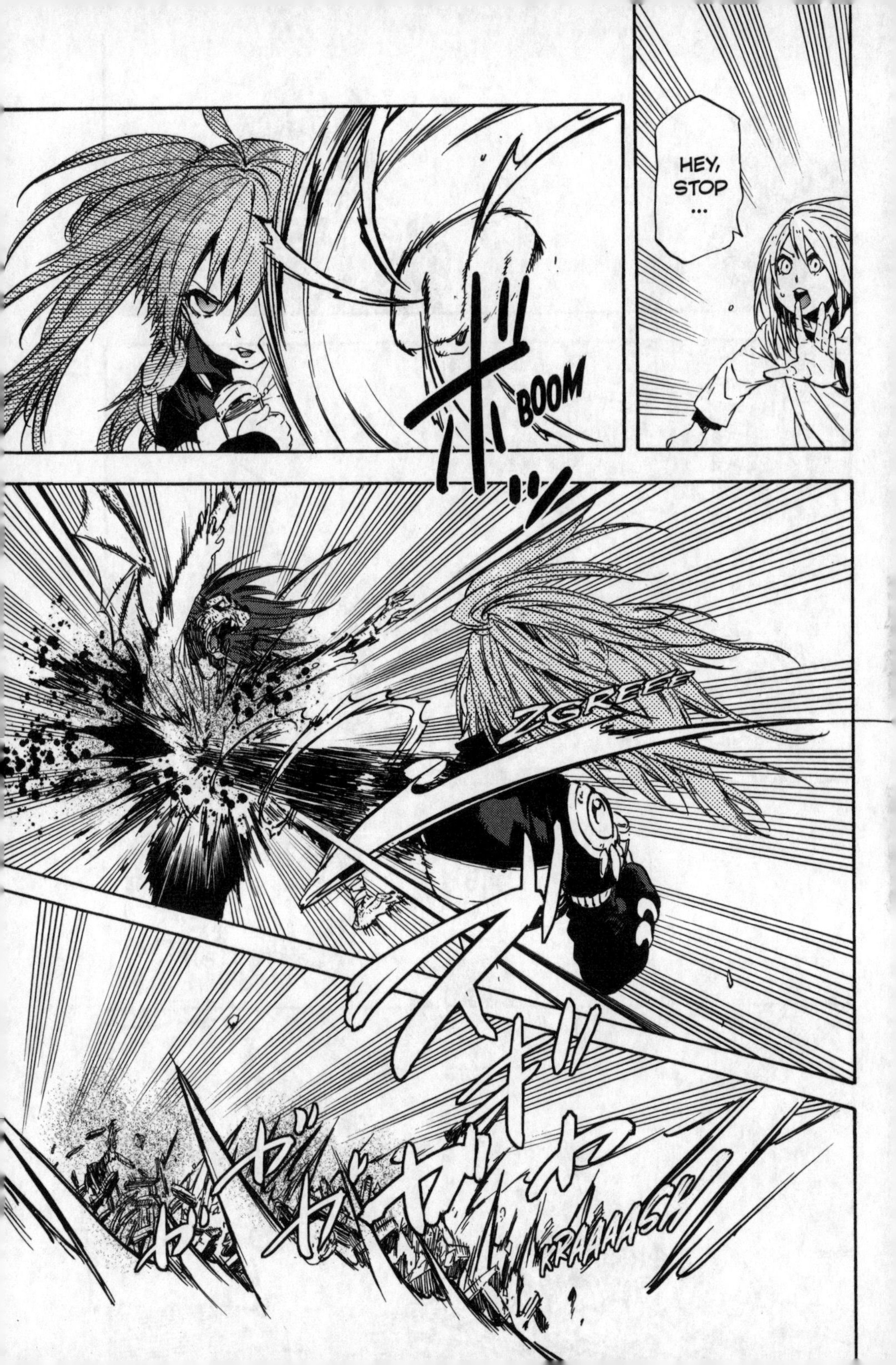
HEY, STOP ...
BOOM
ZGREEE
KRAAAAASH

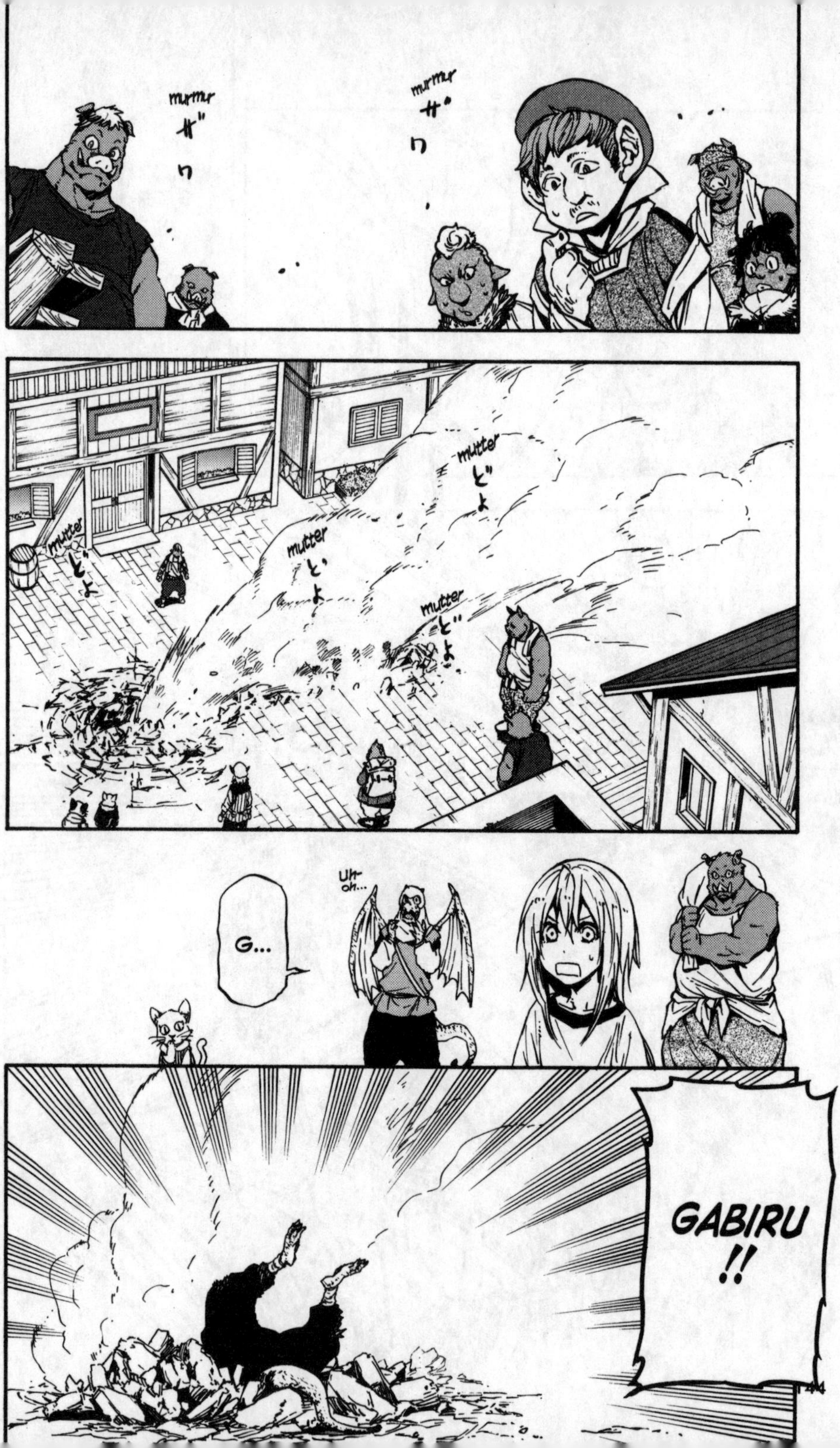
murmur ザワ
murmur ザワ
mutter どよ
mutter どよ
mutter どよ
mutter どよ
Uh-oh...
G...
GABIRU!!

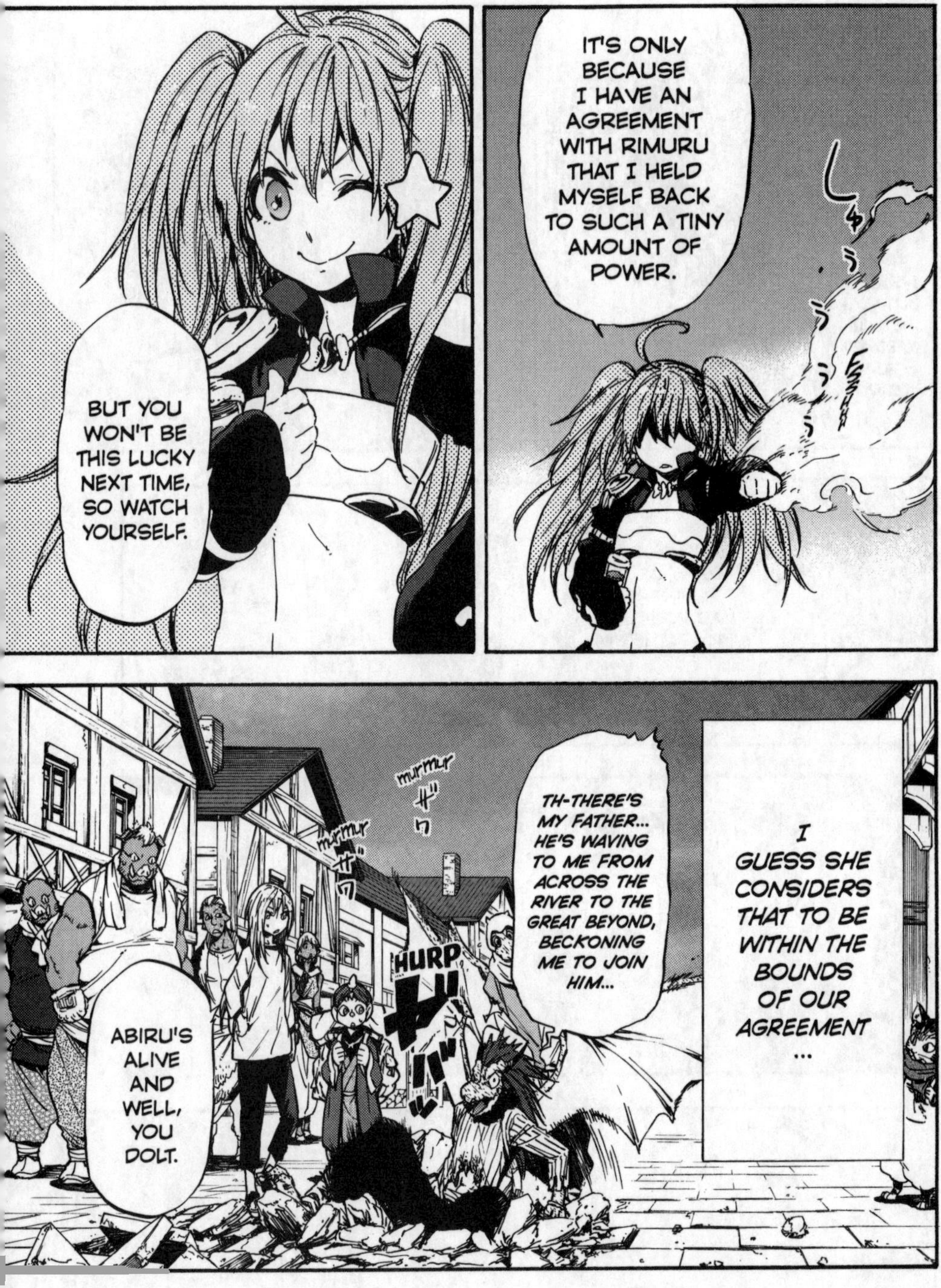
IT'S ONLY BECAUSE I HAVE AN AGREEMENT WITH RIMURU THAT I HELD MYSELF BACK TO SUCH A TINY AMOUNT OF POWER.
BUT YOU WON'T BE THIS LUCKY NEXT TIME, SO WATCH YOURSELF.
I GUESS SHE CONSIDERS THAT TO BE WITHIN THE BOUNDS OF OUR AGREEMENT ...
TH-THERE'S MY FATHER... HE'S WAVING TO ME FROM ACROSS THE RIVER TO THE GREAT BEYOND, BECKONING ME TO JOIN HIM...
HURP
murmur
murmur
ABIRU'S ALIVE AND WELL, YOU DOLT.

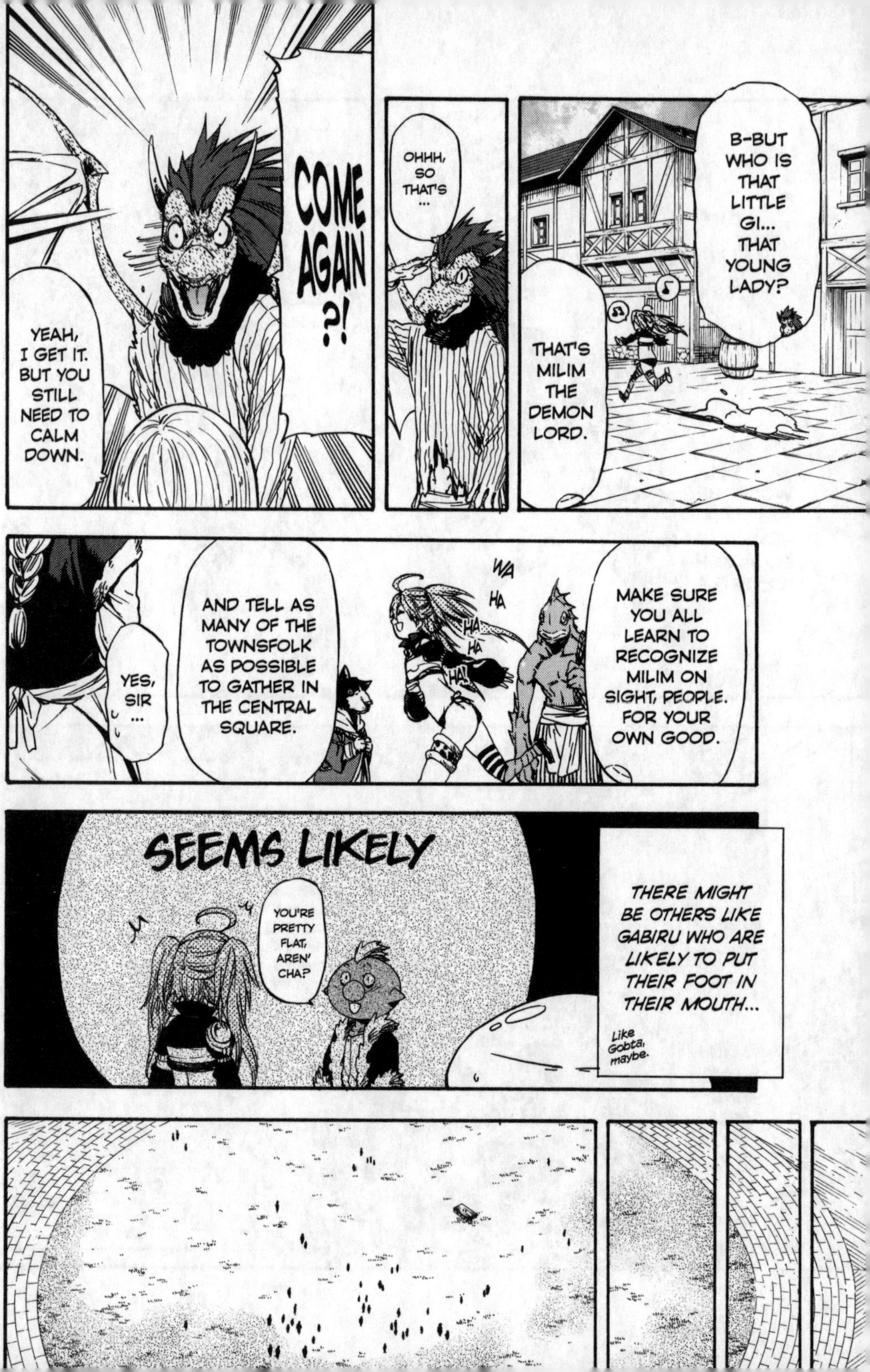
B-BUT WHO IS THAT LITTLE GI... THAT YOUNG LADY?
THAT'S MILIM THE DEMON LORD.
OHHH, SO THAT'S ...
COME AGAIN ?!
YEAH, I GET IT. BUT YOU STILL NEED TO CALM DOWN.
MAKE SURE YOU ALL LEARN TO RECOGNIZE MILIM ON SIGHT, PEOPLE. FOR YOUR OWN GOOD.
WA HA HA HA HA!
AND TELL AS MANY OF THE TOWNSFOLK AS POSSIBLE TO GATHER IN THE CENTRAL SQUARE.
YES, SIR ...
THERE MIGHT BE OTHERS LIKE GABIRU WHO ARE LIKELY TO PUT THEIR FOOT IN THEIR MOUTH...
Like Gobta, maybe.
SEEMS LIKELY
YOU'RE PRETTY FLAT, AREN' CHA?

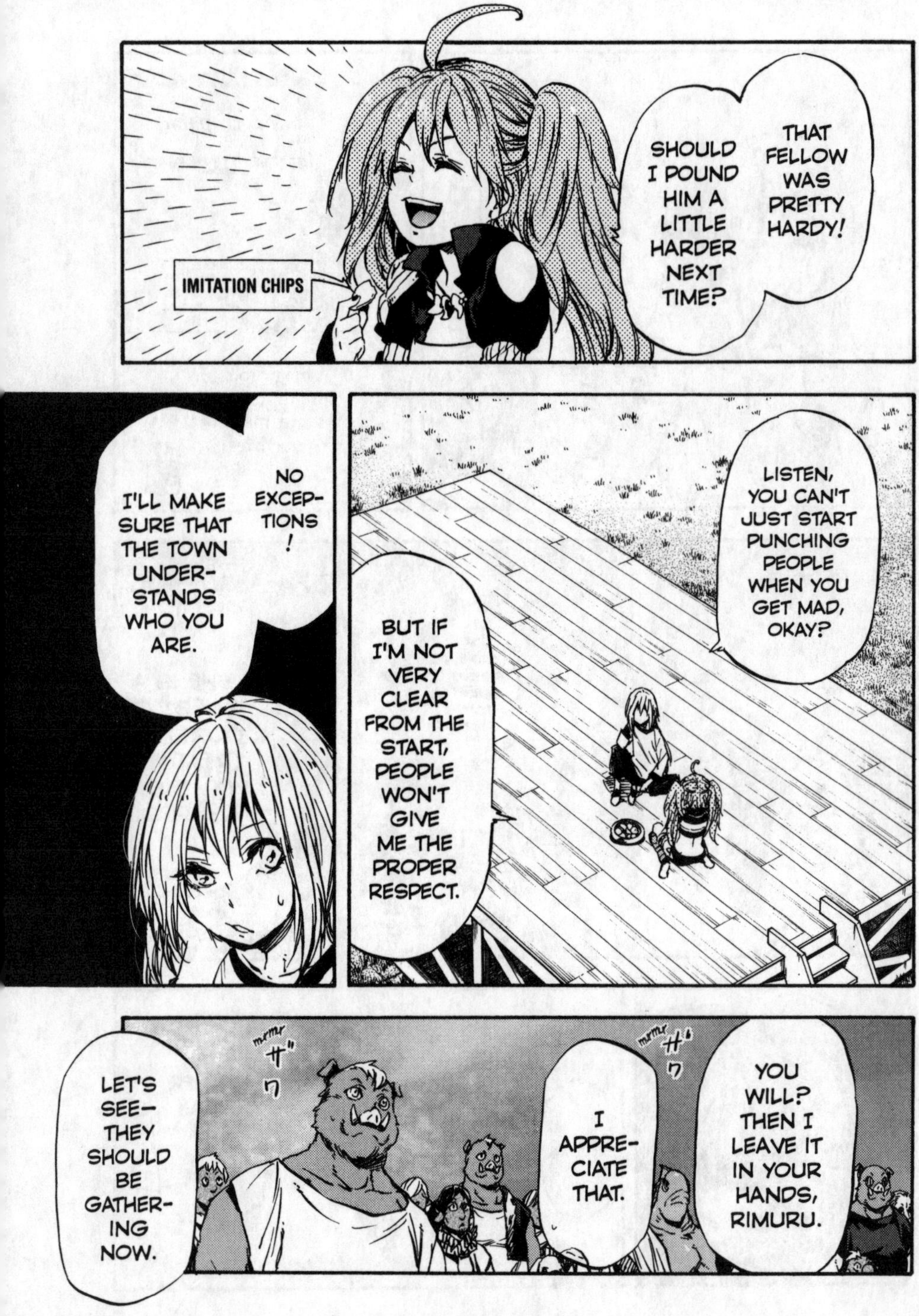
THAT FELLOW WAS PRETTY HARDY!
SHOULD I POUND HIM A LITTLE HARDER NEXT TIME?
IMITATION CHIPS
LISTEN, YOU CAN'T JUST START PUNCHING PEOPLE WHEN YOU GET MAD, OKAY?
BUT IF I'M NOT VERY CLEAR FROM THE START, PEOPLE WON'T GIVE ME THE PROPER RESPECT.
NO EXCEP-TIONS!
I'LL MAKE SURE THAT THE TOWN UNDER-STANDS WHO YOU ARE.
YOU WILL? THEN I LEAVE IT IN YOUR HANDS, RIMURU.
ザワ
I APPRE-CIATE THAT.
ザワ
LET'S SEE—THEY SHOULD BE GATHER-ING NOW.

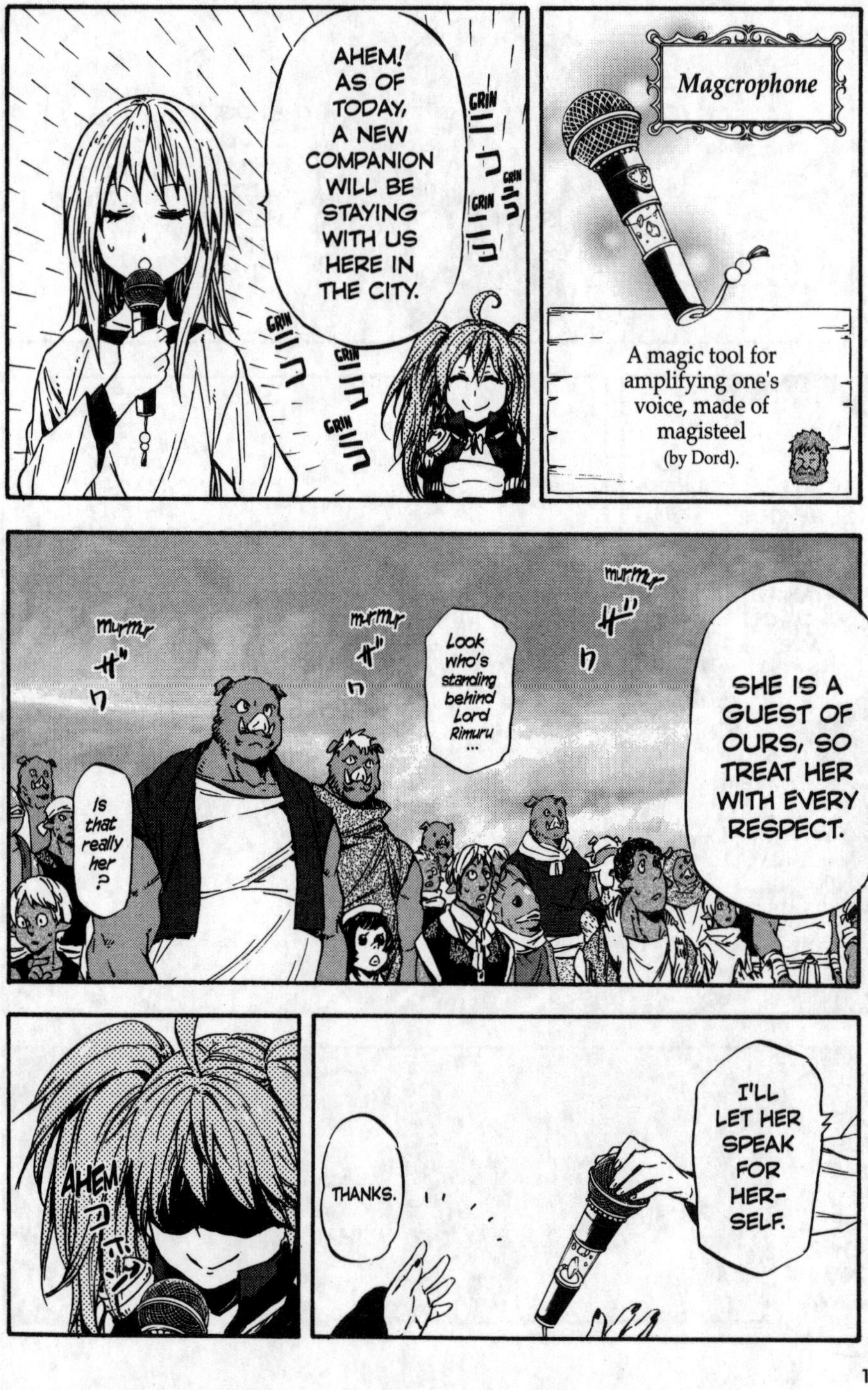
Magcrophone
A magic tool for amplifying one's voice, made of magisteel
(by Dord).
AHEM! AS OF TODAY, A NEW COMPANION WILL BE STAYING WITH US HERE IN THE CITY.
GRIN
GRIN
GRIN
GRIN
GRIN
GRIN
SHE IS A GUEST OF OURS, SO TREAT HER WITH EVERY RESPECT.
murmur
murmur
Look who's standing behind Lord Rimuru...
murmur
Is that really her?
I'LL LET HER SPEAK FOR HER-SELF.
THANKS.
AHEM

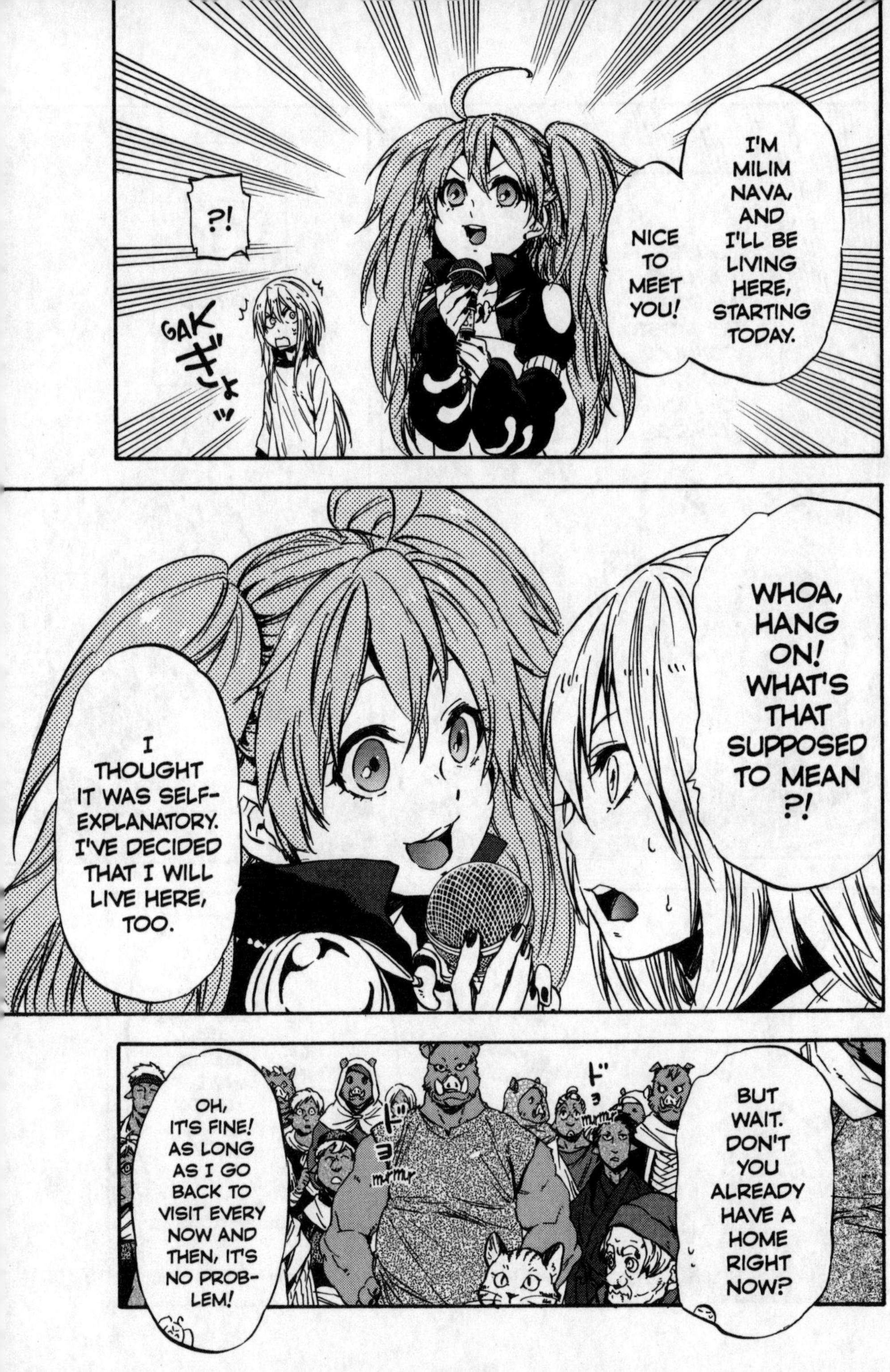
I'M MILIM NAVA, AND I'LL BE LIVING HERE, STARTING TODAY.
NICE TO MEET YOU!
?!
GAK
ぎょッ
WHOA, HANG ON! WHAT'S THAT SUPPOSED TO MEAN ?!
I THOUGHT IT WAS SELF-EXPLANATORY. I'VE DECIDED THAT I WILL LIVE HERE, TOO.
BUT WAIT. DON'T YOU ALREADY HAVE A HOME RIGHT NOW?
OH, IT'S FINE! AS LONG AS I GO BACK TO VISIT EVERY NOW AND THEN, IT'S NO PROB-LEM!

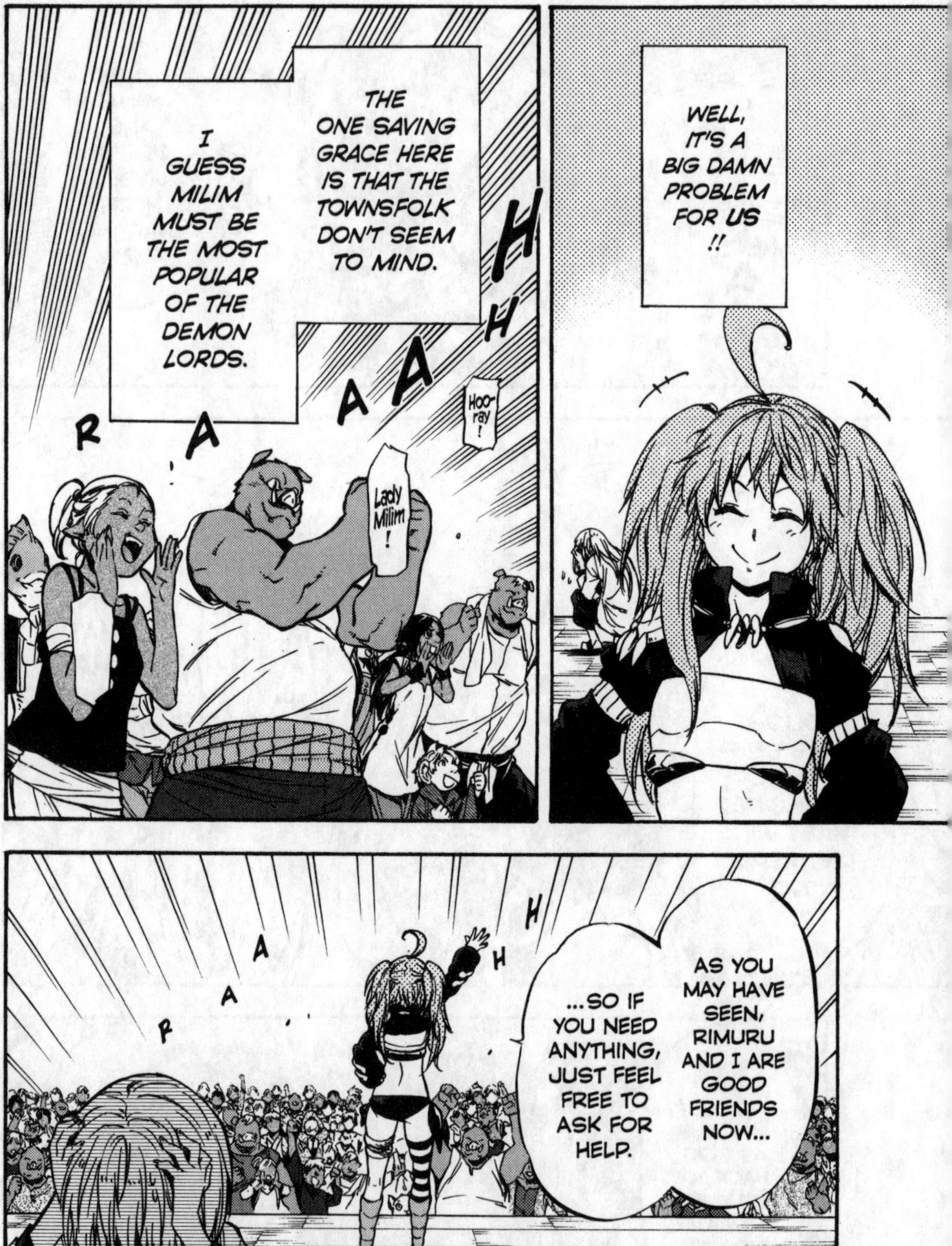
WELL, IT'S A BIG DAMN PROBLEM FOR US !!
THE ONE SAVING GRACE HERE IS THAT THE TOWNSFOLK DON'T SEEM TO MIND.
I GUESS MILIM MUST BE THE MOST POPULAR OF THE DEMON LORDS.
RAAAAHH
Hoo-ray!
Lady Milim!
AS YOU MAY HAVE SEEN, RIMURU AND I ARE GOOD FRIENDS NOW...
...SO IF YOU NEED ANYTHING, JUST FEEL FREE TO ASK FOR HELP.
RAAHH

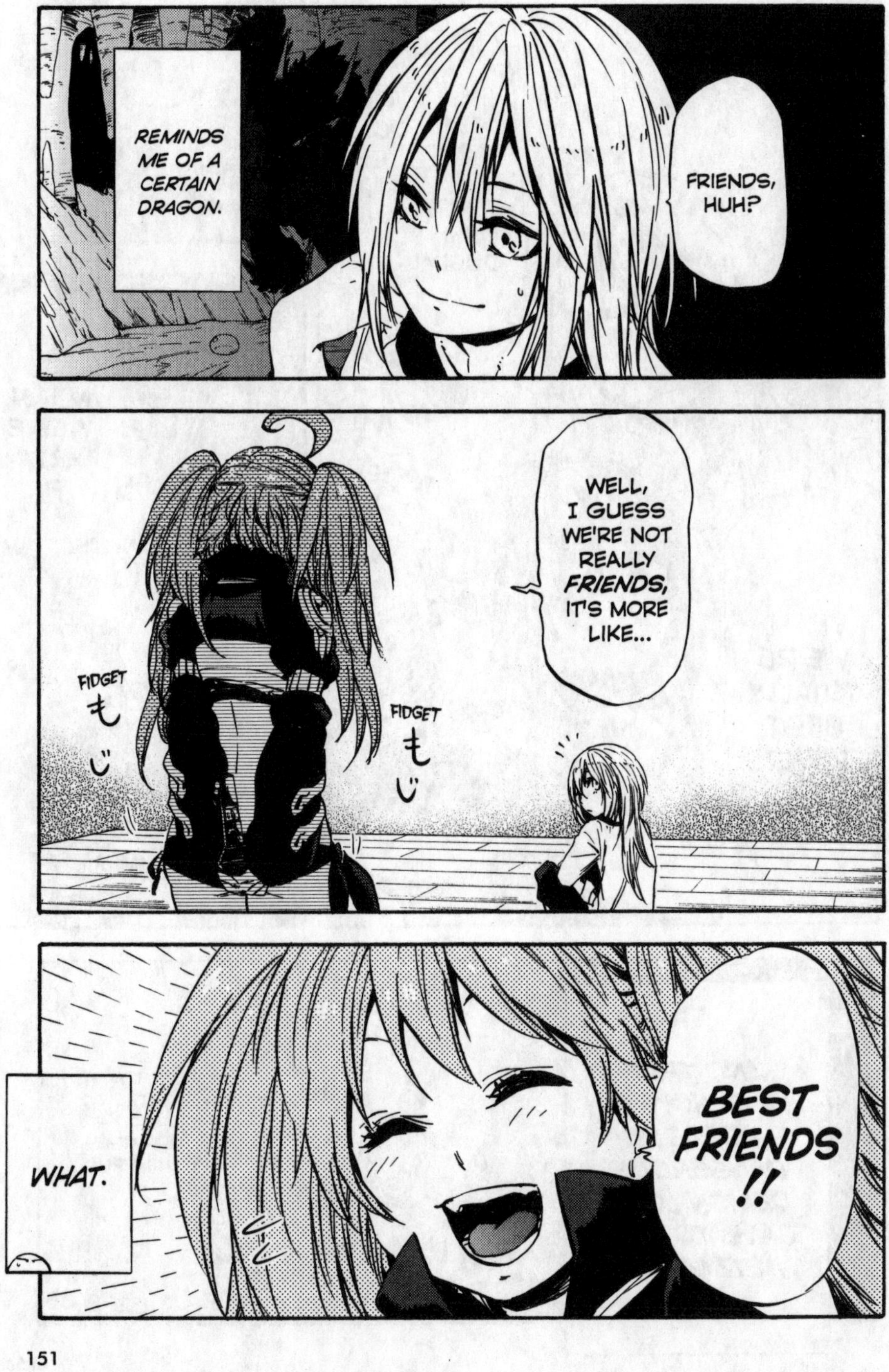
FRIENDS, HUH?
REMINDS ME OF A CERTAIN DRAGON.
WELL, I GUESS WE'RE NOT REALLY FRIENDS, IT'S MORE LIKE...
FIDGET もじ
FIDGET もじ
BEST FRIENDS !!
WHAT.

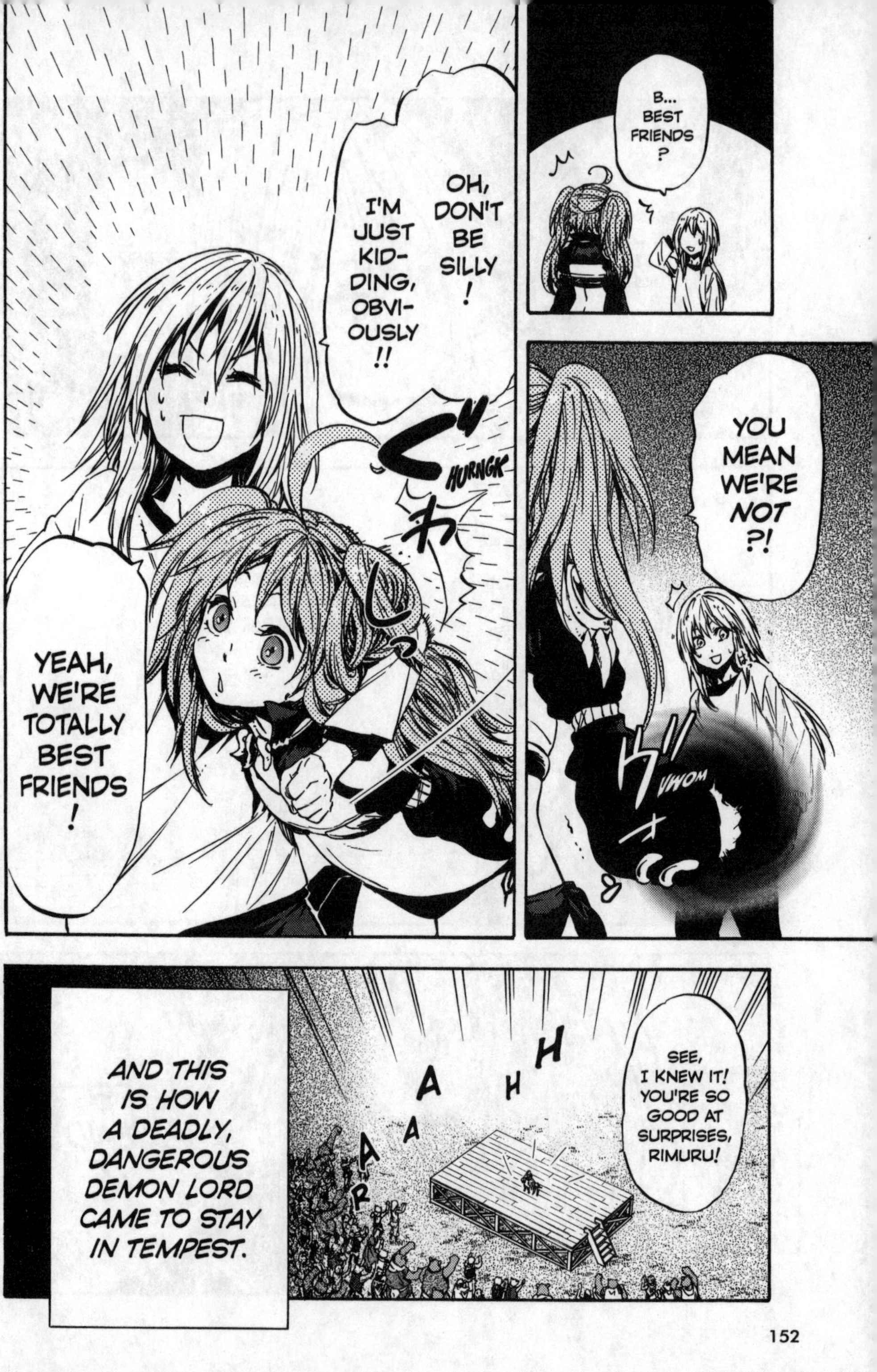
B... BEST FRIENDS?
YOU MEAN WE'RE *NOT*?!
WOM
OH, DON'T BE SILLY!
I'M JUST KIDDING, OBVIOUSLY!!
HURNGK
YEAH, WE'RE TOTALLY BEST FRIENDS!
SEE, I KNEW IT! YOU'RE SO GOOD AT SURPRISES, RIMURU!
RAAAHH
AND THIS IS HOW A DEADLY, DANGEROUS DEMON LORD CAME TO STAY IN TEMPEST.

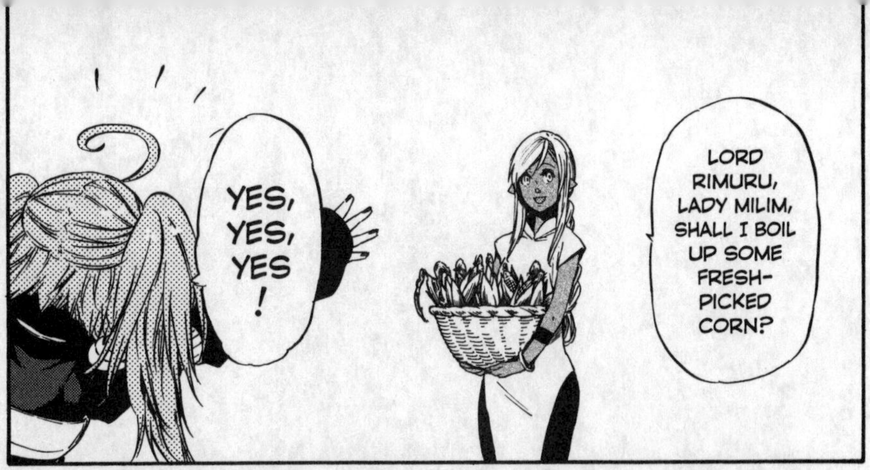
LORD RIMURU, LADY MILIM, SHALL I BOIL UP SOME FRESH-PICKED CORN?
YES, YES, YES!
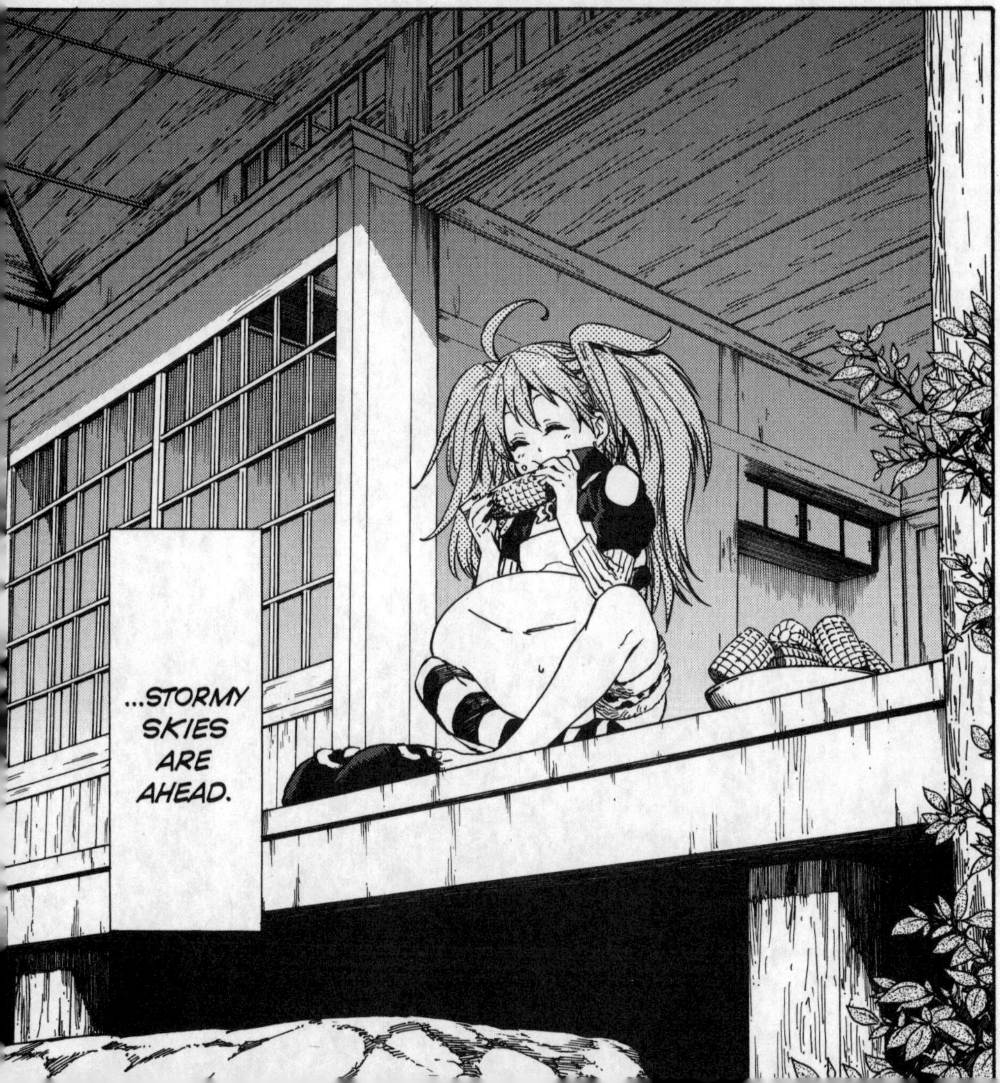
...STORMY SKIES ARE AHEAD.

Reincarnate
in Volume 7?

→YES

NO

Bonus
Short Story

Veldora's Slime Observation Journal
~ENCOUNTER~

Veldora's Slime Observation Journal
~ENCOUNTER~

♦ ATTENTION ON THE TOWN OF MONSTERS ♦

I feel as of late that Ifrit's reverence for me is waning. I am enjoying my peace and quiet.

Now that there is a proper town for monsters to live in, there are many types coming to dwell under Rimuru's command. Even that pompous lizardman Gabiru is here, eating in the dining hall as though he belongs. While Rimuru might be mild-mannered, even he seems annoyed at him.

"Why are you all here?" he asked bluntly.

According to Gabiru's explanation, his father disowned him.

"If you were to ask me, I would say that's likely an excuse," I said.

Rimuru gave the lizardman chieftain the name of Abiru. Thanks to the power this conferred, Abiru turned into a dragonewt. With his control of the tribe firmly in hand, Gabiru must have become a nuisance to him. The fact that Gabiru's sister, the head guard, is also present is surely proof of this. Hence his banishment from—

"Ah, I see. If his son is imprisoned indefinitely for war crimes, there will be no opportunity for him to wipe clean his sins. He must have felt it necessary to banish his son from the territory in order to give him the chance to perform some worthy feats that might restore his honor."

What?! Hrmm. I suppose that is one way to look at it.

Now that I think of it, Abiru the chieftain was a wise and noble fellow, much like me. I suppose it would be natural for him to arrive at an idea like the one Ifrit just laid out. I decided to adopt this opinion for my own.

"You noticed that too, Ifrit?"

"Well, ha ha, I may not have the foresight you do, Master Veldora, but I am studying as hard as I can," Ifrit said, pleased at my praise. He is holding a suspicious-looking tome entitled *Psychology for Dummies: The Wisdom of a Conqueror.*

That looks like one of those difficult textbooks. The kind without pictures. What in the world does Ifrit think he will gain by reading it...?

There was that time that I told Ifrit, "Be my chief of staff," as a joke. In fact, I do believe that he vastly increased his reading time after that point. Perhaps Ifrit really does aspire to be my chief of staff.

It is a pleasing thought. But on the other hand, I must wonder—why would Rimuru have read such a tricky and likely boring book? I have heard stories of this "other world" that he lived in, but it did not seem so wild and dangerous a place as to need this book.

Mysteries still abound around him.

Gabiru's sister is now named Soka, meaning "blue flower." She says that her father sent her out and told her to broaden her horizons.

It would seem that Ifrit's interpretation was correct. Perhaps I ought to learn more about the finer workings of the mind, that my understanding of others' thoughts might deepen.

Then again, only I and Ifrit are here. My only option is to continue observing Rimuru's actions so as to learn from them. With this noble goal in mind, I focused on the slime again.

At the moment, he is giving names to every last one of nearly a hundred new lizardmen. This is clearly a sign of Rimuru's deep generosity.

Gabiru watches with jealousy, but he is already a named monster. There is no point to receiving a name from another—

"Don't look so jealous. You already have a perfectly good name in Gabiru...don't...you...?"

...?!

Something very strange happened then. Foolishly enough, Rimuru actually overwrote the lizardman's name. The surprise of it brought tears to my eyes. It is truly cruel and careless to take another fellow's magical energy out of nowhere like that!

Acknowledgement: Test successful.

Hrrm... It didn't seem to think that Rimuru would actually be successful.

So I guess...I ought to just accept it? Am I being taken advantage of?

Negative. There is no recognition of that state of events.

Oh. Well. That's good...

For one thing, I've never even heard of a name being overwritten. I suppose I shall take the high road and chalk this up to an unforeseeable accident.

So Gabiru is now a dragonewt. There are ways in which an evolution can be affected by personal preference. Some might choose a more humanoid form to be more similar to Rimuru, while others might desire to further accentuate the qualities of their species, like Ranga.

Gabiru must fall into the latter category, as he appears to be an augmented version of his lizardman form. I suppose it also aligns with his desire to be more like his exalted father, as well.

But interestingly, his sister Soka is now a very pretty, human-looking lass. They look entirely different, and yet they are the same species. I'm sure that once they are used to it, they'll be able to change forms between the two at will.

At the end of all of this, Gabiru began answering to Rimuru's orders, while Soei took Soka under his wing. I look forward to their further growth.

The days pass by in peace. The town has visibly grown, and ever greater varieties of food are on display. By raising their own crops, the monsters have expanded their cooking possibilities.

I look forward to the day that I return to power. But for now, I am enjoying other games with the Ifrit, and not just shogi.

I was very curious about these "simulation games" in Rimuru's memory, but sadly they are not accessible to me. Apparently it requires some special contraption, which I was able to recreate the shape of, but which did not actually run.

Instead, we have found the time for cards, *Othello*, and the *Game of Life*. Such card and board games are an entertaining diversion in times of peace.

The problem with peace, however, is that it can be easily and abruptly interrupted. An emergency arose.

"What is happening?"

"It would seem that a group of about five hundred knights are flying in from the north."

"Ahh. Allow me to gauge the strength of these foes."

Hmmm. It is an army of knights riding flying pegasuses. Both mounts and riders are A-minus-rank beings, by my reckoning.

There is also the individual level on top of that. Based on the utter familiarity between each pair, their experience together would put them at a solid A-rank. Five hundred of them in one force is a powerful army, indeed.

One blow of fiery breath from me would utterly annihilate them, of course, but I am speaking in terms of how it would effect a lesser being like Rimuru.

"Five hundred at A-rank level..."

"Indeed. And there are five who stand heads and shoulders above the others. Two of them, in particular, are greater than even you, Ifrit."

"My word!" he said, shocked. I cannot blame him. Despite his appearance, the Ifrit is quite powerful. Given the scope of this force, it is clearly the armed power of an entire nation at work.

But more important than that is the fact that I recognize the aura of the one whose presence stands above all the others. I saw this one when Rimuru dragged me along with him to the Dwarven Kingdom...

"It is good to see you are well, King Gazel," said the crafts-man dwarf Kaijin, taking a knee next to Rimuru.

My memory was correct. This man is the king of the dwarves, a figure indeed more powerful than Rimuru: the hero king Gazel Dwargo.

Rimuru and Gazel, face to face.

The tension is thick in the air, but is there true danger afoot? In their previous meeting, Gazel showed himself to be wise and just, but few of Rimuru's cohorts are aware of that. Several of them bristle with hostility toward Gazel and his knights.

Last time it was in the land of the dwarves, but now we are in our own stronghold. Surely Rimuru knows that there is no reason for him to debase himself before the visiting party. And depending on Gazel's actions, it might even come to blows...

"Do you think Lord Rimuru can win?"

Hmm. Ifrit thinks it will turn into a battle.

"Do not be hasty. Gazel's purpose here is to judge Rimuru's worth."

"His worth? What does that—"

"If Gazel meant to do battle, he would amass his armies and bring his full might to bear. He has met Rimuru before, and must understand the danger he represents."

"I see. So they are not here to fight... But then why *did* King Gazel come to this place?"

That is the question. King Gazel was likely keeping an eye on Rimuru, believing him to be potentially dangerous. After all, Rimuru ended up growing his forces until he was able to vanquish the Orc Lord, and has built a town that continues to expand in scope and power.

A nation cannot simply ignore that situation. In the past, I would have been unable to fathom King Gazel's thoughts. However, now that I have learned much from Rimuru's memory, I understand just how complex and strange a thing a nation can be, and how heavy the responsibility to those who are a part of it.

No matter how Gazel himself feels about it, he has a duty to understand and determine how his kingdom will treat Rimuru and those who have aligned themselves with him.

"Is that the duty of a king?" Ifrit said.

"I don't know. It is how I choose to understand it—but I do not imagine that I am wrong about it."

I do not think Gazel intends to be hostile to Rimuru. But that is no guarantee that he will not attempt something. So I think it likely that he wants to prove that despite their threat, Rimuru's forces and his are capable of mutual understanding.

In other words, this requires negotiations with Rimuru, in a manner that will be clear and open to all.

So what does Gazel plan to do?

Rimuru introduced himself formally, and Gazel answered in kind.

The slime has chosen to undertake this dialogue in human form. This might indeed be a bit more comforting. He is surprisingly rich in expression, so it will be easier for his conversation partner to judge his thoughts this way.

Gazel's reaction to this change was to challenge Rimuru to a swordfight. That idea seemed to come from the sight of the sword hanging from Rimuru's waist, but also from Gazel's own confidence in his blade.

"Is he the one you said was more powerful than me?" Ifrit asked.

"Precisely. I cannot divine his skill with the sword, but even without it, he is stronger than you."

"Meaning it may be unlikely that Lord Rimuru will win?"

"Indeed. Rimuru would win an anything-goes battle with magic and skills, I feel. But as this is a duel and not a fight to the death, he is at the disadvantage."

But now I can see what Gazel wants.

Because Rimuru has accepted the challenge, if he uses any attack other than his sword, it will instantly cause Gazel to lose all faith in him. He would prove himself untrustworthy, and Gazel would no longer seek a dialogue with him.

But does Rimuru see that for himself?

"You treat the chancellor of our forest alliance with great disrespect, King of Dwarves."

It is the trio of dryad sisters. A murmur runs through Gazel's retinue.

"I sense that they are spirits of my class."

"I understand why. Treyni and her sisters are adept at blending in among spirits, as they are very nearly spiritual beings themselves. If they were to summon a higher elemental, its power would likely eclipse your own."

Treyni and her sisters are overseers of the forest, and willing members of the alliance Rimuru propounded. They seem to be angered that Gazel accused their chancellor of being a bragging blowhard.

In my absence, they were the most powerful beings in the forest. Naturally, they pose a considerable threat. Now the gap in strength between the sides has blown apart. If there were to be a battle here, the dwarves would not stand a chance. Gazel surely knows this, but I can see no hesitation in his demeanor. His boldness speaks well of him.

Gazel apologized for insinuating that Rimuru was a liar, but his request for a duel still stands. He had been very direct and consistent in his actions. As his initial proclamation stated, he intends to determine Rimuru's worth, and will not back down from that goal.

"Most impressive. I took him for a small fellow, but his boldness and ambition are quite laudable, in fact. It would seem that I've been overlooking the things which cannot simply be measured in terms of power."

"I agree, Master. I've been learning so many things since Lord Rimuru first defeated me," Ifrit said. We both marveled at our new discoveries.

Meanwhile, Rimuru came to the decision to accept this duel—as I assumed he would. Of course he can sense Gazel's intent, and he himself needs to find a good middle ground between the two sides. If he did not accept the duel, it would cause irreparable harm to any future relationship between their countries.

So with Treyni as witness, the contest was on between Rimuru and Gazel.

Gazel proved himself quite worthy.

"His skill is incredible. Lord Rimuru's sword fighting isn't getting anywhere against him!" Ifrit marveled. Now that he has learned the ways of my Veldora-style Killing Arts, even Ifrit can discern the difference in skill between fighters.

Yes, Gazel is mighty. But if you ask me, he has more to learn.

"Hmph! Compared to the hero I once fought, Gazel's ability is nothing special! All he's doing is imbuing his moves with Heroic Presence, allowing him to sense the movements of his opponent ahead of time."

Still, the very fact that I would use the hero in a comparison to him is proof of Gazel's worth. It is an undeniable truth that in this context, Gazel is more powerful than Rimuru is...

There is not such a large gap in strength and speed, but it's clear that Gazel is several levels higher in terms of skill with the blade. And beyond that, Gazel is much better at wielding his battle spirit.

At this rate, Rimuru will lose. But this is not a bad thing. The real danger is if he uses some skill that is against the rules in an attempt to avoid losing. That would immediately spell the end of the fight.

Meanwhile, Gazel decided to attempt a new test of Rimuru's ability. He intentionally hurled a powerful form of Heroic Presence at our friend, intimidating Rimuru.

This trick would not work without an overwhelming difference in power. If it immobilizes Rimuru, he will have no means of action but to turn to his monster abilities.

The next moment, Rimuru bellowed. "Aaaaaah!!"

Unbelievable. Rimuru broke the spell of Heroic Presence with a simple shout.

"Is that how it's supposed to be broken?"

"Not at all. One is meant to unleash a presence of one's own to cancel it out. It is not the sort of thing that can be overcome just by *yelling!*"

Unbelievable. There is such a thing as being *too* absurd, Rimuru.

Even Gazel cannot help but smirk. And now he realizes that Rimuru plans to fight back solely with his sword.

There is nothing but serious intent in Gazel's eyes. The next sequence will determine the contest.

"He vanished!" said Ifrit, proving that he is incapable of following Gazel's movements.

To be fair, it was impressive. And I recognized that particular technique. As did Rimuru, apparently, for he perfectly timed the incoming blow and blocked it.

The happiest person at this outcome was not actually Rimuru, but Gazel himself. He laughed and announced his defeat in the duel.

This was the correct choice. It was a competition, not a fight to the death, so it was important for one of them to recognize the right moment to step back and give credit for his defeat.

Rimuru upheld the rules and showed that he was worthy of trust. Gazel clearly recognized that there was no need to continue fighting after that point.

It also served as a good way to ease the pressure from Rimuru's comrades. If they protested the outcome of the duel and it started an all-out war, it would be the worst possible outcome.

With Gazel's goal attained, the mood relaxed. It was a victory in strategic terms, at least.

"Observe, Ifrit. Gazel's attitude is what we mean when we speak of the bearing of a king," I explained. Ifrit murmured in admiration.

"There are times when you seem very wise, Master Veldora."

"Seem? I *am* very wise!"

And what does he mean, *there are times?!* It became clear to me that Ifrit was lacking in the proper respect for me—and that would not do.

Gazel's attacks seemed familiar, and it turned out this was because he learned from Hakuro, who is now Rimuru's instructor. Normally, ogres live to about a hundred years, but Hakuro's been around for nearly three centuries. That fact alone should have told me how extraordinary he is.

Hakuro's skill is formidable. He would be classified as weak if judged on magical energy alone, but his ability to fight is nearly unparalleled.

Spiritual beings like Ifrit and I are impervious to physical attacks. But a sword imbued with battle spirit is capable of harming us. This is a unique form of battle arts he calls "spiritual combat." I shall have to incorporate it into my Veldora-style Killing Arts.

Now Ifrit and I are in the midst of training.

"Kwaaaa ha ha ha! How is that, Ifrit?"

"Most impressive, Master Veldora. Your prowess astonishes me every time," Ifrit said, lavishing me with comfortable praise. Yes, this is more like it. I enjoy hearing the cheers and compliments of onlookers.

But there is a problem here.

"Thanks to your guidance, I have grown stronger, too. In the past, I promptly held you back, but now I'm able to stand up to you as a sparring partner for at least a few moments."

"Y-yes, quite. Keep up your hard work..."

My teaching was so effective—too effective, in fact—that Ifrit's growth went beyond my range of expectations. C-could this be...a return of the shogi disaster?! I had a terrible premonition of my natural superiority vanishing into smoke.

"I must admit that you have more promise than I realized. You had only ever used flame attacks before, so I did not foresee how quickly you would successfully combine them with my martial arts."

"I believe that part is thanks to my bodily host, Shizue Izawa. It is because I have the memories of her fighting style that I was able to recreate them for myself."

Angels, demons, and spirits are classified according to the amount of energy they possess. Ifrit is a higher elemental, one of the more powerful of the spirits. He claims that he had no memory before serving Demon Lord Leon. In other words, he is a youngster, not even two hundred years old.

In fact, summoned demons and spirits have no free will at all. They are bound to their summoners, possessing their bodies in order to gain experience. Over time, they may develop their own identity in this manner. Ifrit falls under this category.

These higher creatures are quite powerful on their own, just fighting according to their natural instincts, so it is rare that any bother to train themselves further. In a logical sense, it is accurate that there is no point to practicing bodily battle techniques when one has the ability to control flame. It is this precise reason that I never forced myself to train before now.

So in that sense, the difference in technical level between Ifrit and I is not very large. The Veldora-style Killing Arts are my creation, but if I am careless, I might in fact lose to the fire spirit. Here in Rimuru's metaphysical stomach, it is more the power of imagination than stockpile of magical energy that determines strength.

In Ifrit's case, not only does he have experience from Demon Lord Leon, but also Shizue Izawa after him. He might even be my superior in terms of technique. This is a grave set of circumstances. I must think of a plan to maintain my superiority and the constant flow of plaudits which I so richly deserve…

Just at this moment, Gazel is busy explaining the classifications of threat levels at the feast. An individual Orc Lord is labeled a Hazard, but the Orc Disaster Geld whom Rimuru vanquished was a Calamity, on the same level as the Ifrit. If he continues his personal growth, he will certainly reach the level of Disaster: a Demon Lord.

Now, according to the newly enacted ranks established by the humans, this would put him at Special A-rank. That would take into account not just his energy amount, but also his individual experience level.

In this same way, Gazel's Pegasus Knights receive their rank due to their estimated level being taken into account. They are classified at A-minus simply from their ability to ride a pegasus. So with their unseen level being judged worthy of an entire rank's worth of improvement, that would make them A-rank in total.

Hakuro presents a good example. His energy amount puts him nearly at the status of a Hazard-class threat. But his personal level is tremendous, a good match for the Calamity-class Orc Disaster or Ifrit. Due to their particular characteristics, he could not actually best them in combat, but a comparison of their basic fighting ability would find them roughly equal.

That would mean that going by the standards of humankind, Hakuro would be a Special A-rank being.

On top of that, Rimuru's other companions like Benimaru, Shion, and Soei have enough magical energy to be upper Hazard-class threats. But their individual experience levels are not close to Hakuro's, so I am certain that he would be toughest in a true fight. Perhaps through much future growth, that dynamic might be overturned.

Therefore, my current desire is for greater skill. If I bolster my tremendous energy with experience levels on top of that, my utter superiority will be forever unshakable! In other words, the best way to impress my greatness upon Ifrit is to expend all of that boring, hard effort.

"It seems the time has come for me to truly shine. From this point on, I will dedicate myself to personal improvement more than ever before!" I declared with great conviction.

Ifrit stared at me in admiration. Was he enchanted by my utter cool?

"Ha ha ha. In that case, I must admit that perhaps I should not indulge in your almighty protection either, Master Veldora. I will strive to leave your care and stand on my own."

Ahh, Ifrit has grown much, then. It is true that I was doing much to accommodate him, but I did not expect that he would attempt to strike out on his own. While trapped in Rimuru's stomach, energy scatters and vanishes, absorbed into Rimuru to be his strength. So I have been harboring Ifrit, allowing him to thrive under my protection. I'd figured he would eventually figure it out, and it seems he already has.

"Very well, Ifrit. Then show me that you can support your own bodily structure in here, without my help."

"Ha ha! I'll show you that I can be myself without you, Master Veldora!" Ifrit said, chuckling confidently.

Well, I will not be outdone. I'll strive for an utter, unquestionable victory, *without* using any underhanded tricks this time!

This is how Ifrit started to learn to control his own energy under my tutelage. In the meantime, I refined my own practices, polishing my skills toward my new goal: strength without relying upon magical energy.

Meanwhile, Rimuru and his friends continue their festive gathering. How jealous I am!

I was supposed to be ignoring all distractions and focusing on my training—until I heard a few choice words that I could not overlook.

Not the name of the country. That does not interest me. Not the general classification of Rimuru and his companions as a Disaster-class threat.

No, what was truly important was the mention that I, the great Veldora, am a Catastrophe-class monster, the very highest grade of them all.

Aren't I spectacular?!

"Just brilliant, Master Veldora. I have no choice but to be impressed."
Ahaha. Yes, of course, of course.

Something in Ifrit's delivery seemed a bit monotone to me, but surely that is just my all-powerful imagination playing tricks on me.

I am certain that Rimuru himself was once again blown away by the reality of my my importance. The thought put me into a pleasant mood.

◆ A PLACE OF REST ◆

The name of Rimuru's nation is now the "Jura Tempest Federation." It is a federation because a number of different species are banding together to make up its territory.

I would have preferred the "Glorious Rimuru-Veldora Empire," but the suggestion fell on deaf ears. And really, I would only be bothered by this if I truly cared about the name in the first place. Which I do not.

Since its official ratification, the federation has seen even more visitors to the town than ever before. The Dwarven Kingdom opened its doors to monsters, so I presume some travelers have come from their borders as well.

Not all are well-meaning, and they are truly fools to test Rimuru's patience. He might be on the soft and sympathetic side, but he is certainly no pacifist. He repays every bit of damage that comes his way, and he certainly does not watch quietly as ruffians disturb the peace.

One might be forgiven for not realizing, due to his misleading appearance, that he has quite a Spartan side to him. But even more severe are Rimuru's followers.

They protect their own lands. Only the strong survive in this world, and they are determined to protect their new sanctuary with force if necessary. I understand this feeling now.

If the ignorant should make half-hearted attempts to corrupt this place, they will receive their just punishment. The moment that I am freed from this prison, I too will lend my considerable strength to the protection of this country.

A time of peace settles in again...

Oh? I recognize this aura.

Ifrit and I have been busy with our respective training, but now I sense a familiar presence approaching. I turned my attention towards it and observed a being of incredible energy descending nearby.

The impact left an enormous crater in the ground. Whoever it is, it is clearly a being of great power—if not quite as great as mine.

But, say...isn't that my elder brother's only child?

"Greetings. I am Demon Lord Milim Nava," the visitor said to Rimuru as he approached.

I knew it. I knew it was Milim, although I am not directly acquainted with her.

Milim is not a dragon, strictly speaking. She is a dragonoid—a humanoid species with my brother's blood and power flowing in her veins. She is one of the most powerful Demon Lords among that group, and is famed and feared for her epithet, "The Destroyer."

But why was I avoiding Milim? Was it on my brother's orders? It was so long ago that my memory is foggy. I can't begin to guess why...

Answer: He likely judged that you would be a bad influence upon her.

Hey! Shut up, you! Do not offer your unsolicited guesses!

If you ask me, this is one of Rimuru's biggest drawbacks. You must not offer opinions based on conjecture alone. If anything, based on my just and righteous nature, I would be an ideal model of behavior.

...

Alas, genius is always misunderstood. My fate is to be alone, it would seem. Well, I cannot help that.

"Don't you agree, Ifrit?"

"Agree with what?"

Oops, that is right. Rimuru's words are a one-way communication through a skill, so only I can hear what is directed at me. I decided to play it off and act like it was nothing.

More important at the moment is Milim's arrival.

"Milim the Demon Lord. If she starts hostilities with Rimuru, this town could be blown clean off the map."

"I've never seen her before," Ifrit said. "Is she really such a dreadful figure?"

"But of course. Milim's energy is nearly as great as mine. Even with Rimuru's current strength, he cannot trouble her in the slightest."

"I d-didn't realize she was so powerful..."

"And unlike me, Milim has some knowledge of fighting styles. I hear she is a master with the blade. It is quite un- likely that anyone might catch her unawares."

Nearly as much power as me, plus technique. Perhaps Milim is even stronger than me at this moment.

Hmm. No, I do not think so. I would win if I tried hard enough.

"I see... So unlike you, Master Veldora, she would be a quite formidable foe."

He dares to throw out casual disses at me...?

Oh, by the way, I learned the word "diss" from Rimuru's memory. It is short for "disrespect." It is an unforgiveable insult, but it would be petty to correct him on it. Instead, I merely recorded an insult about Ifrit of my own into my mental journal as a tiny act of revenge, and turned my attention back to Rimuru and Milim.

Milim says that she is here to say hello. Her true purpose is unclear, but any fight between her and us is one that we will lose. Rimuru's attitude is deferential because he knows this as well as I do.

There is such a gap in strength that no trickery can overcome it. Rimuru's best course of action now is to use his most persuasive words to avoid angering her. But I'm sure that he can—

"Ranga, take Lord Rimuru to safety! Now!"

"Understood!"

What? *Huh?!*

I am stunned. And for good reason. With the sharp, high-pitched sound of steel splitting air, Shion leapt at Milim. Without any warning.

"Oh, no! This is not good!"

Shion and the kijin cannot beat Milim. Even if her actions are meant to help Rimuru escape, they will not work.

"But look at what a perfectly executed combination attack she's—"

"You fooool! Those piddling swings will do nothing to Milim!"

First Shion, then Soei and Benimaru brought out their best. They are impressive, to be sure, but only against beings of their own stature, perhaps even against monsters with several times their magical energy.

"An assault of this level might have actually toppled another Demon Lord," Milim said, "but that Demon Lord would not be me."

She is unharmed, for she exists on a truly different scale from her attackers.

Shion, Benimaru and Soei were utterly defeated. Only Rimuru and Ranga remain, but there is nothing left to be done…

"It would seem that we ought to steel ourselves as well," said Ifrit.

"Hmm? What do you mean?"

"I just mean that we are trapped within Lord Rimuru. If he is crushed right here, we will be doomed to share his fate."

…Huh?

Well, yes, that is true, but not so fast. What will happen to us then?

"Dragonkind is ageless and unbeatable, but not immortal. If I die, another me is born somewhere else. But it would be a different Veldora, a different personality…"

My memories will be passed on, but not perfectly. I perished in ancient times before this, but I do not have all of my memories of that era. Things are missing, and I have a way of thinking now that my old self might not have understood.

In other words, I think that I, as I exist now, would cease to be.

"That is very bad!"

"Right…" Ifrit nodded, as though to convey that he'd already been saying as much.

We shared a look, then cradled our heads in our hands. The only hope is that Rimuru runs away to safety somehow…

"I'll handle the rest."

Instead, Rimuru is making clear that he intends to fight. "Well, that's it for us, then," Ifrit lamented.

"Yep," I agreed.

◆ MILIM THE WHIRLWIND ◆

As I watched the fight between Rimuru and Milim, all I could do was pray for a miracle.

"Oh? And do you have some method of attack that might actually affect me?" she taunted.

"Just one."

Well said! Although I'm certain Rimuru is only bluffing...

"But perhaps Lord Rimuru might actually pull this off," Ifrit mused.

"Well, it is impossible for him to win, but he might, in fact, succeed at wiping that confident look off her face, one would hope."

Rimuru is my closest friend and ally, of course. It is hard not to put my hopes on him.

On the other hand, I am a bit surprised to find Milim is more patient than I took her for. Rather than killing Rimuru in the fight, she's ordering him to be her subordinate if she wins.

That is a relief to Ifrit and I. We wait eagerly to see his plan — and there he goes.

Rimuru approaches Milim and hurls something at her face. A simple energy projectile will do nothing to her—even if she made no effort to block it, no damage would result. But surely Rimuru already knows that. So what is his intention?

"...What is this?"

Hrmm? What is wrong with Milim?

"What attack was that...?" asked Ifrit.
"I do not know. I will have to use my Inquirer skill to..."

It would have been a bit of a mad gamble to use that skill now, but it abruptly turned out that I needn't have bothered. Milim's reaction made it clear that he had put some kind of food in her mouth.

I cannot tell if the fact that this desperate ploy worked is a credit to Rimuru's brilliance, or an example of Milim's carelessness...

"What could it have been, that even Lady Milim was taken aback by the taste?"

"Hrrm... We can only view the information from the outside. Without being able to smell or taste it, I cannot begin to guess what it was that Rimuru gave her."

I suppose I ought to have paid more attention to the goings-on outside.

It turns out that the ingredient that Rimuru used to bewitch Milim was a secret stash of honey. Unbelievably enough, he succeeded at seducing the Demon Lord with his sweetened ways.

"H-he actually managed to find equal footing with the great Demon Lord Milim," Ifrit gasped, unable to comprehend what he had just witnessed.

I feel the same way, of course, but more importantly, I am curious about this honey. It was delicious enough that Milim felt the need to shout about it. Surely it must be incredible.

Arrgh, how frustrating this is! I wish to return to my body soon, that I might fill my belly with this so-called delicacy!

And thus I suffered even more damage from this attack than Milim did, afflicted by a hunger that cannot be sated, staring balefully at Rimuru and Milim's bond of peace.

While they may have made peace, Milim shows no sign of leaving anytime soon. In fact, she's now riding on Ranga with Rimuru as though she belongs there. And tasting more of that delectable honey all the while! How infuriating. I feel as though she is simply taunting me now.

"No, I think you might be imagining that..."

"Silence, Ifrit. Help me think of a way to gain taste information from the outside world!" I ordered, but he just sulked and said there was no way to do that.

Well, if I cannot do it, then I suppose there is no way that Ifrit could. But I would think that he could at least make an effort of *trying*. The worst part of this is that I want to complain, but there is no one who will hear me out.

"Hey, level with me: have you ever considered being a Demon Lord?" asked Milim.

"...I haven't, and won't," Rimuru told her.

That makes sense. Only recently have I, too, learned that making threats and intimidating others is not as satisfying as working together and earning their gratitude. The survival of the fittest is still the law of the land, but that is not everything there is to life.

Rimuru did not find Milim's offer appealing because he understands that, of course. And from the looks of her, she does not. In fact, she is carrying on about some great, fascinating secret that Rimuru is keeping from her.

In the course of calming her down, Rimuru managed to become fast friends with Milim somehow.

Friends, eh? I'm happy for you, Milim—and yet, I feel an undeniable sense of frustration.

Let me be clear that he and I are closely allied friends and comrades! I am Rimuru's true number-one friend. When I recover my body, I will need to have a close talk with Milim to make this clear to her.

"That's really childish of you, Master Veldora."

"Silence!"

When did Ifrit get to be so smug and all-knowing?

But I will admit, it feels good to be understood.

Back at the town, Milim raced around with excitement and curiosity.

"Kwaaaa ha ha ha! See how she frolics? Milim really is still a child."

"But she's still far, far older than me..."

He is so stubborn. How set in his way of thinking can Ifrit be? It is not a bad thing to be firm and precise, but I think it would do him good to loosen up. Perhaps I have just the thing to do that.

On the outside, Milim has just declared that she and Rimuru are best friends. I decided to piggyback on that topic.

"Ifrit..."

"What is it?"

"You and I are friends, yes?" I asked. Ifrit looked at me in stunned disbelief.

Was this question a surprise? Well, I have experience with that feeling. I, too, remember how stunned I was when Rimuru asked me, "Would you like to be friends?" And while I didn't think much of it then, I now think I understand how Rimuru must have felt at that moment.

In fact, I didn't realize how nerve-wracking it could be. Now I am filled with a sudden concern: what if he does not say yes?

The wait for his response felt like an eternity.

"...Are you certain?"

That answer put a crinkle onto my lips. I was going to be very cool about it all, but in the big moment, I found myself unable.

"Kwaaa ha ha ha! Do not be bashful. Although I hardly need to tell you that, eh?"

Lately Ifrit has been anything but reserved around me. It was for this precise reason that I asked in the first place. Yes, it was a high-stakes gamble, but it paid off, and now we are friends.

Best of all, it means that Ifrit will have to be nice to me from now on.

"In that case, it's good to be honest about how we feel. So from now on, I will feel more emboldened to point out the ways in which you are less than considerate, Master Veldora."

...Huh?

That's not the response I was expecting!

In the outside world, Rimuru and Milim are laughing and smiling.

But in here, I am cradling my head, expecting disaster. I failed to notice that Ifrit too was smiling a bit bashfully.

To be reincarnated in Volume 7!

GAZEL'S GAZE

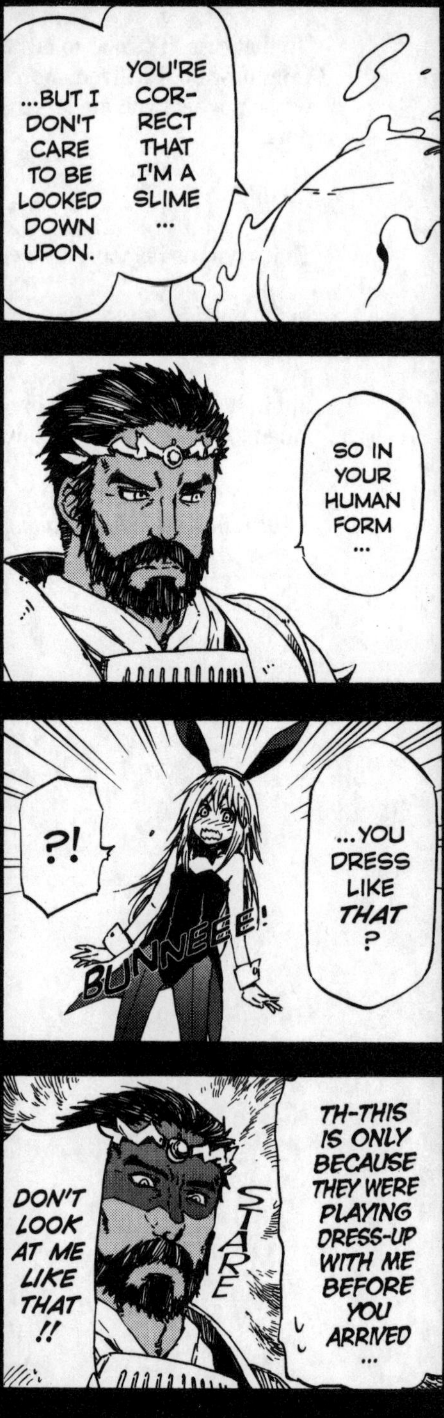
YOU'RE COR-RECT THAT I'M A SLIME ...
...BUT I DON'T CARE TO BE LOOKED DOWN UPON.
SO IN YOUR HUMAN FORM ...
...YOU DRESS LIKE THAT ?
BUNNEEE!
?!
TH-THIS IS ONLY BECAUSE THEY WERE PLAYING DRESS-UP WITH ME BEFORE YOU ARRIVED ...
STARE
DON'T LOOK AT ME LIKE THAT !!

WE NEED COOL BATHS TOO

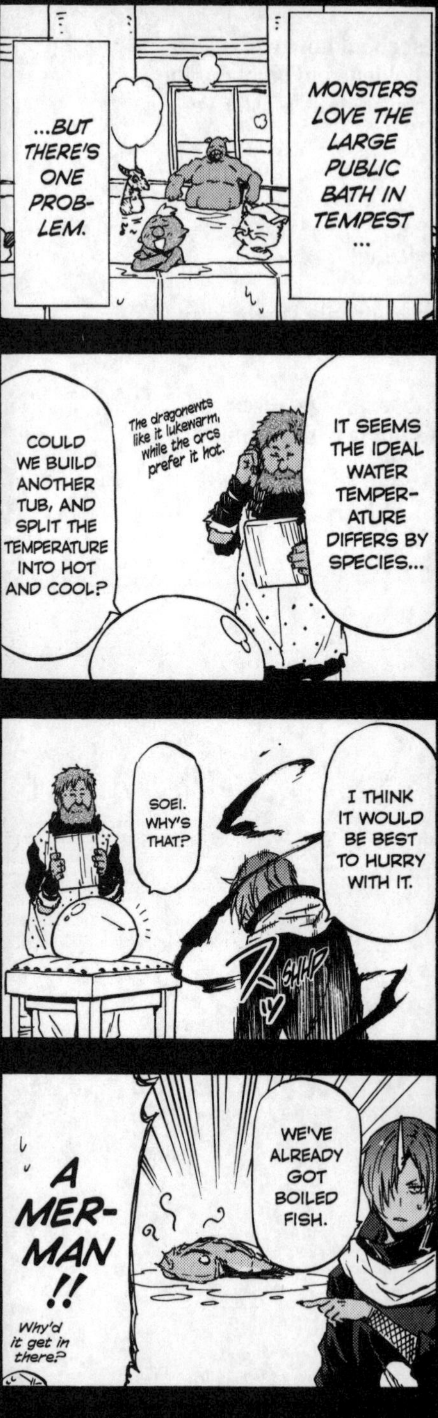
MONSTERS LOVE THE LARGE PUBLIC BATH IN TEMPEST ...
...BUT THERE'S ONE PROB-LEM.
IT SEEMS THE IDEAL WATER TEMPER-ATURE DIFFERS BY SPECIES...
The dragonewts like it lukewarm, while the orcs prefer it hot.
COULD WE BUILD ANOTHER TUB, AND SPLIT THE TEMPERATURE INTO HOT AND COOL?
I THINK IT WOULD BE BEST TO HURRY WITH IT.
SHHP
SOEI. WHY'S THAT?
WE'VE ALREADY GOT BOILED FISH.
A MER-MAN !!
Why'd it get in there?

A CAPABLE WOMAN

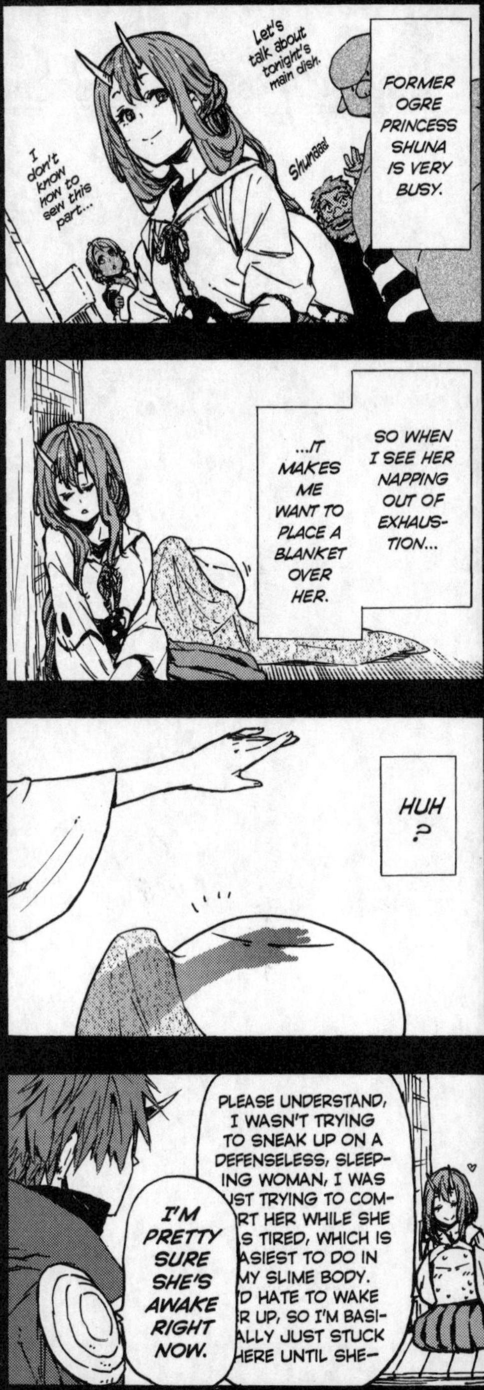

FORMER OGRE PRINCESS SHUNA IS VERY BUSY.
Let's talk about tonight's main dish.
Shunaaa!
I don't know how to sew this part...
SO WHEN I SEE HER NAPPING OUT OF EXHAUSTION...
...IT MAKES ME WANT TO PLACE A BLANKET OVER HER.
HUH?
PLEASE UNDERSTAND, I WASN'T TRYING TO SNEAK UP ON A DEFENSELESS, SLEEPING WOMAN, I WAS UST TRYING TO COM-RT HER WHILE SHE S TIRED, WHICH IS ASIEST TO DO IN MY SLIME BODY. D HATE TO WAKE R UP, SO I'M BASI-ALLY JUST STUCK HERE UNTIL SHE–
I'M PRETTY SURE SHE'S AWAKE RIGHT NOW.

LIST OF ACKNOWLEDGMENTS

AUTHOR:
Fuse-sensei

CHARACTER DESIGN:
Mitz Vah-sensei

ASSISTANTS:
Muraichi-san
Daiki Haraguchi-san
Masashi Kiritani-sensei
Taku Arao-sensei

Everyone at the editorial department

And You!!

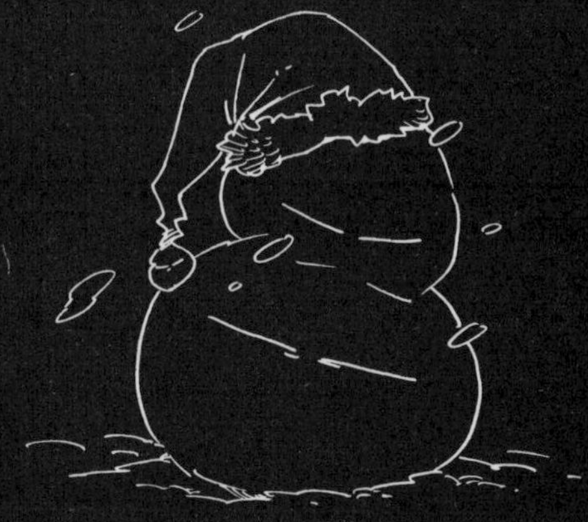

! FROM THE VAULT

Design Sketches Revealed!!

These are rare character pieces done for a pre-series test.

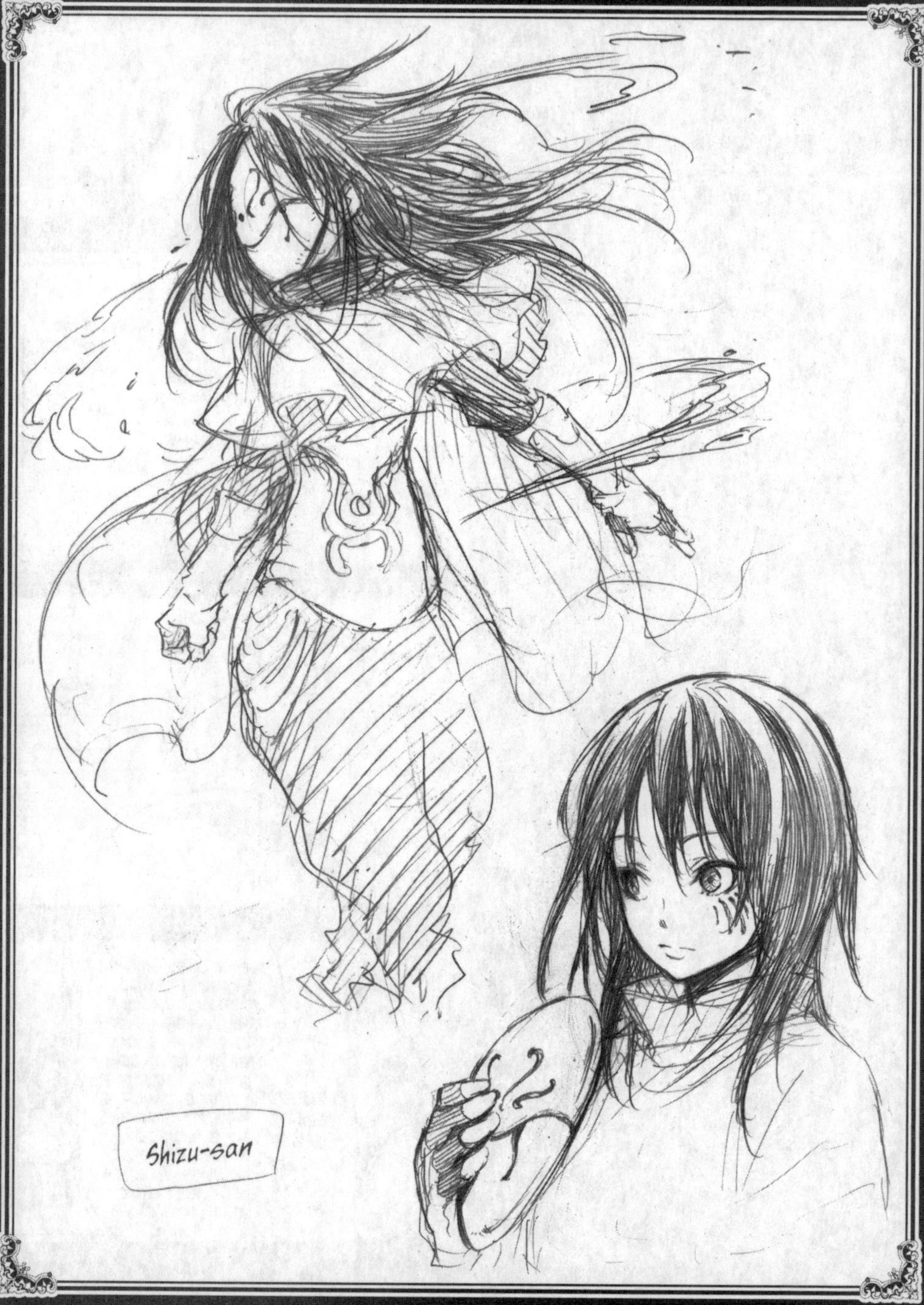
Shizu-san

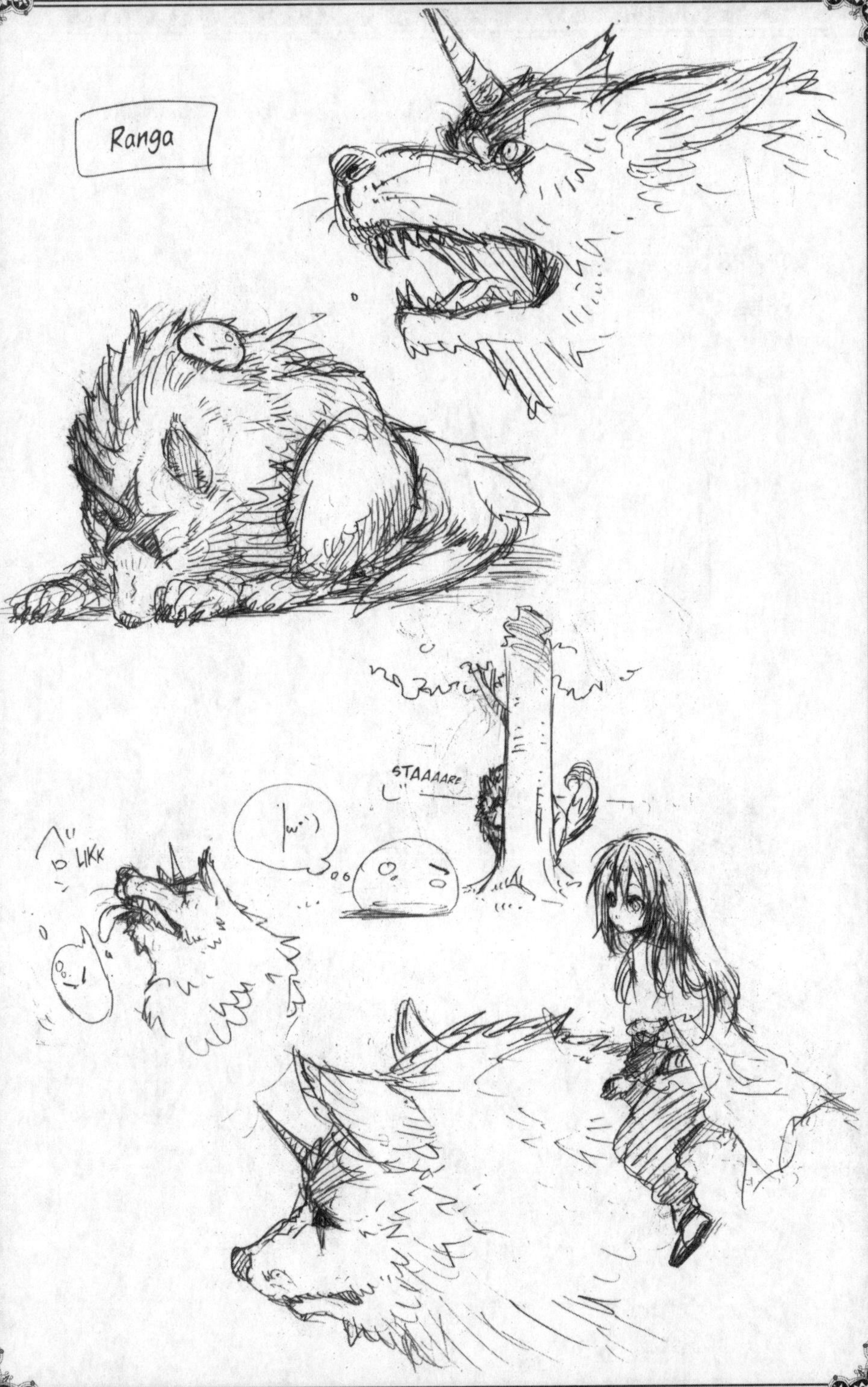
Ranga
STAAAARE
LIKK

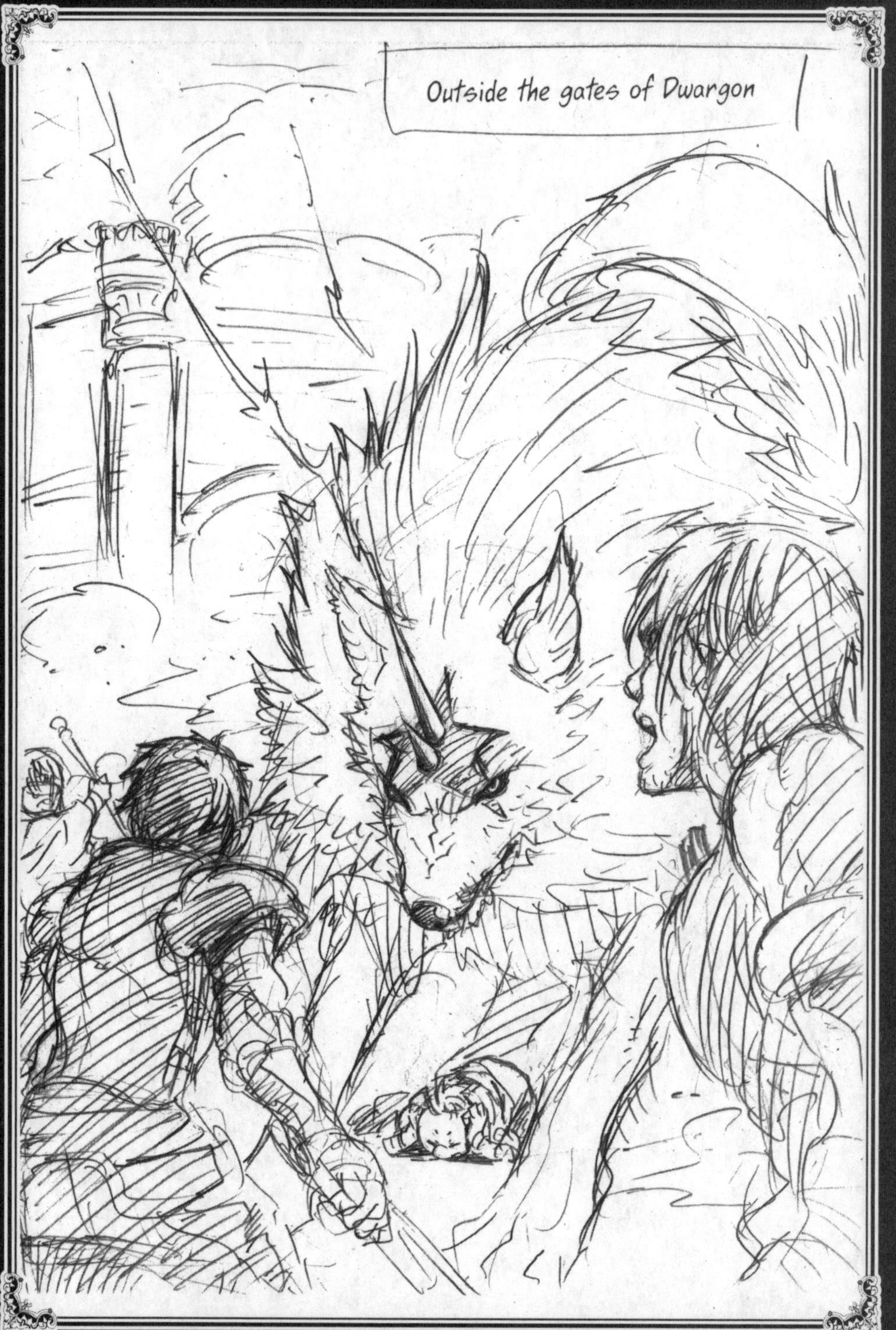
Outside the gates of Dwargon

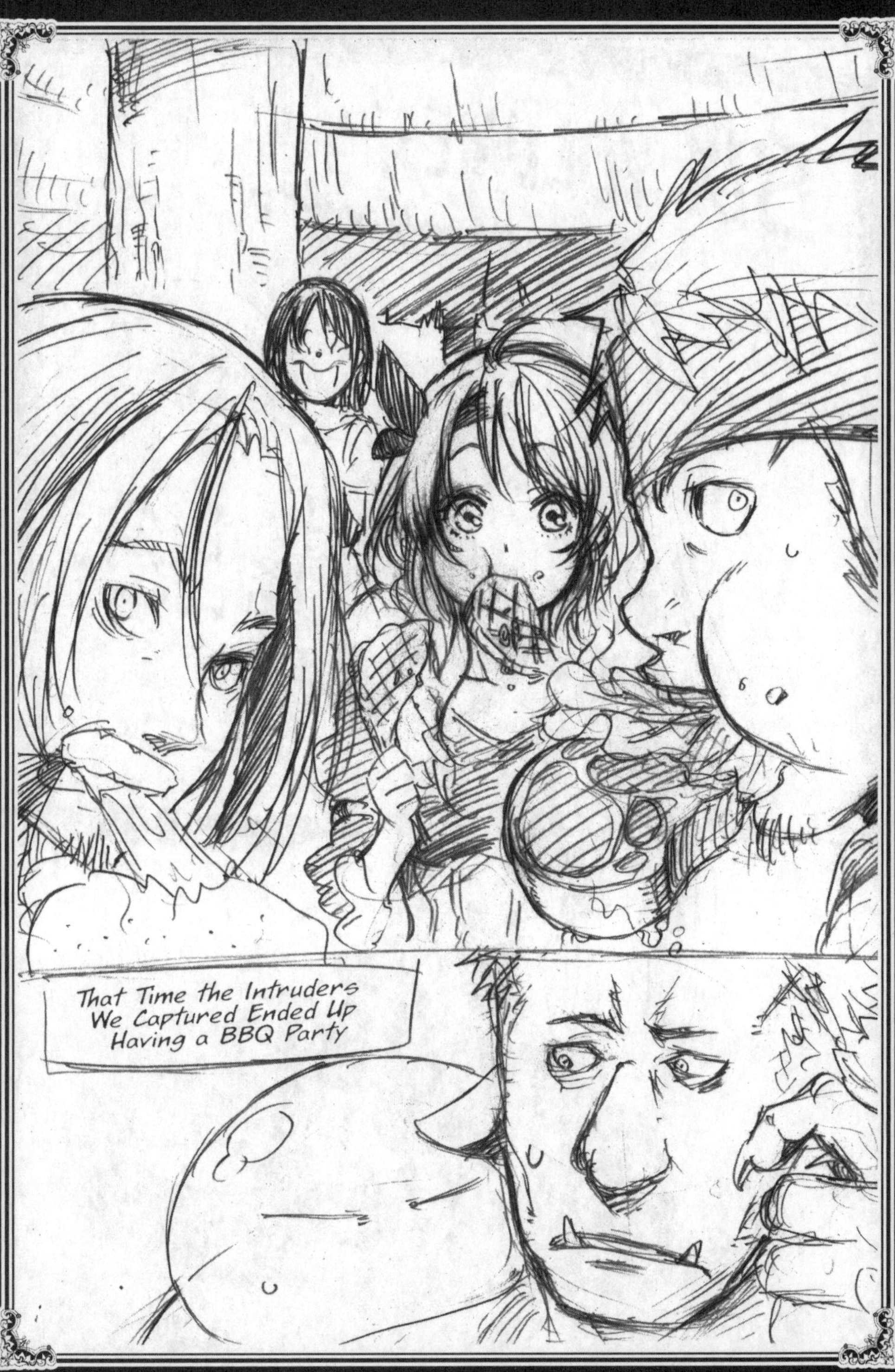
That Time the Intruders We Captured Ended Up Having a BBQ Party

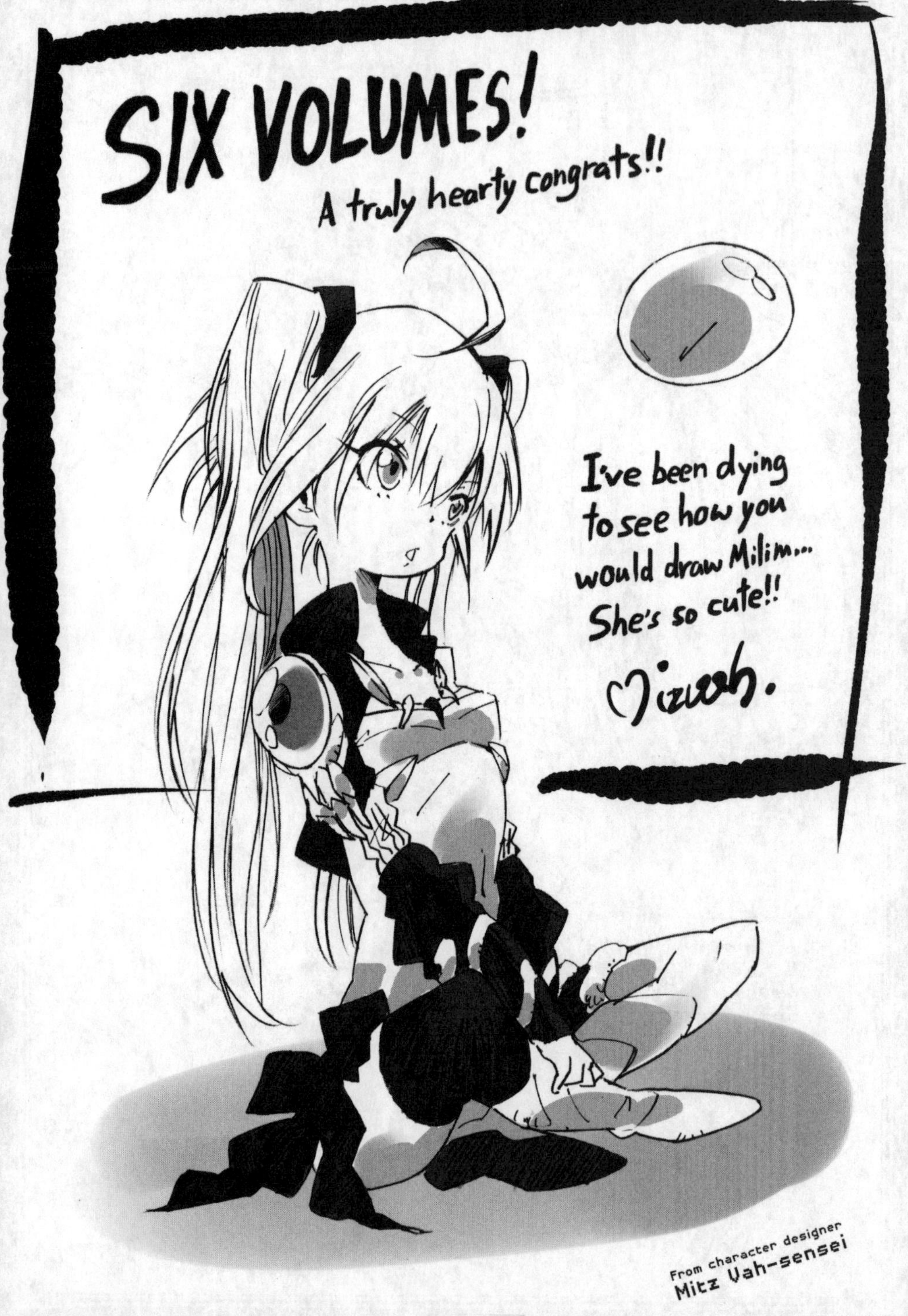
SIX VOLUMES!
A truly hearty congrats!!
I've been dying to see how you would draw Milim... She's so cute!!
Mizuwah.
From character designer
Mitz Vah-sensei

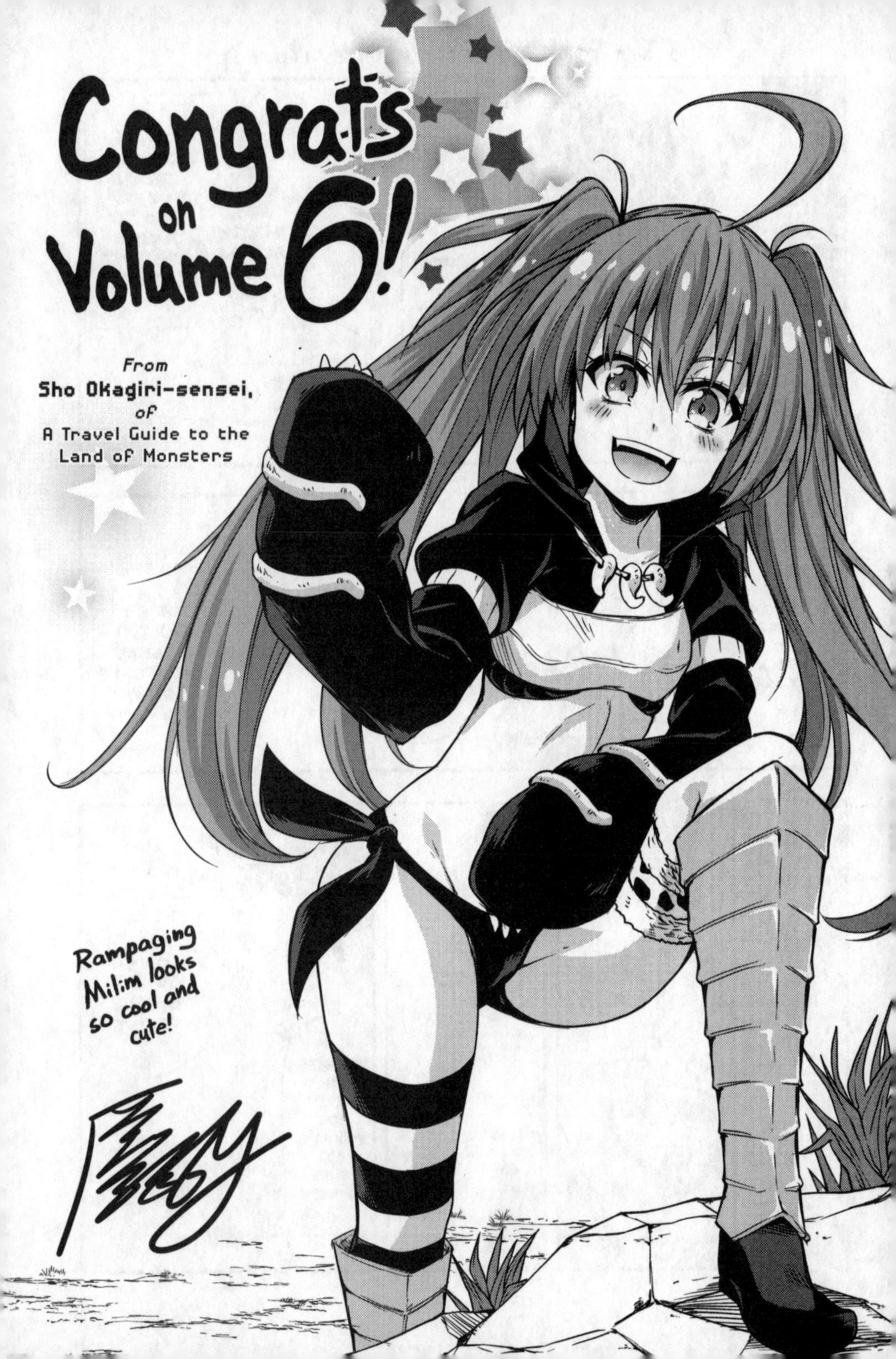
Congrats on Volume 6!
From Sho Okagiri-sensei, of A Travel Guide to the Land of Monsters
Rampaging Milim looks so cool and cute!

If I Turn Traitor, Maybe I Can Get On As an Enemy

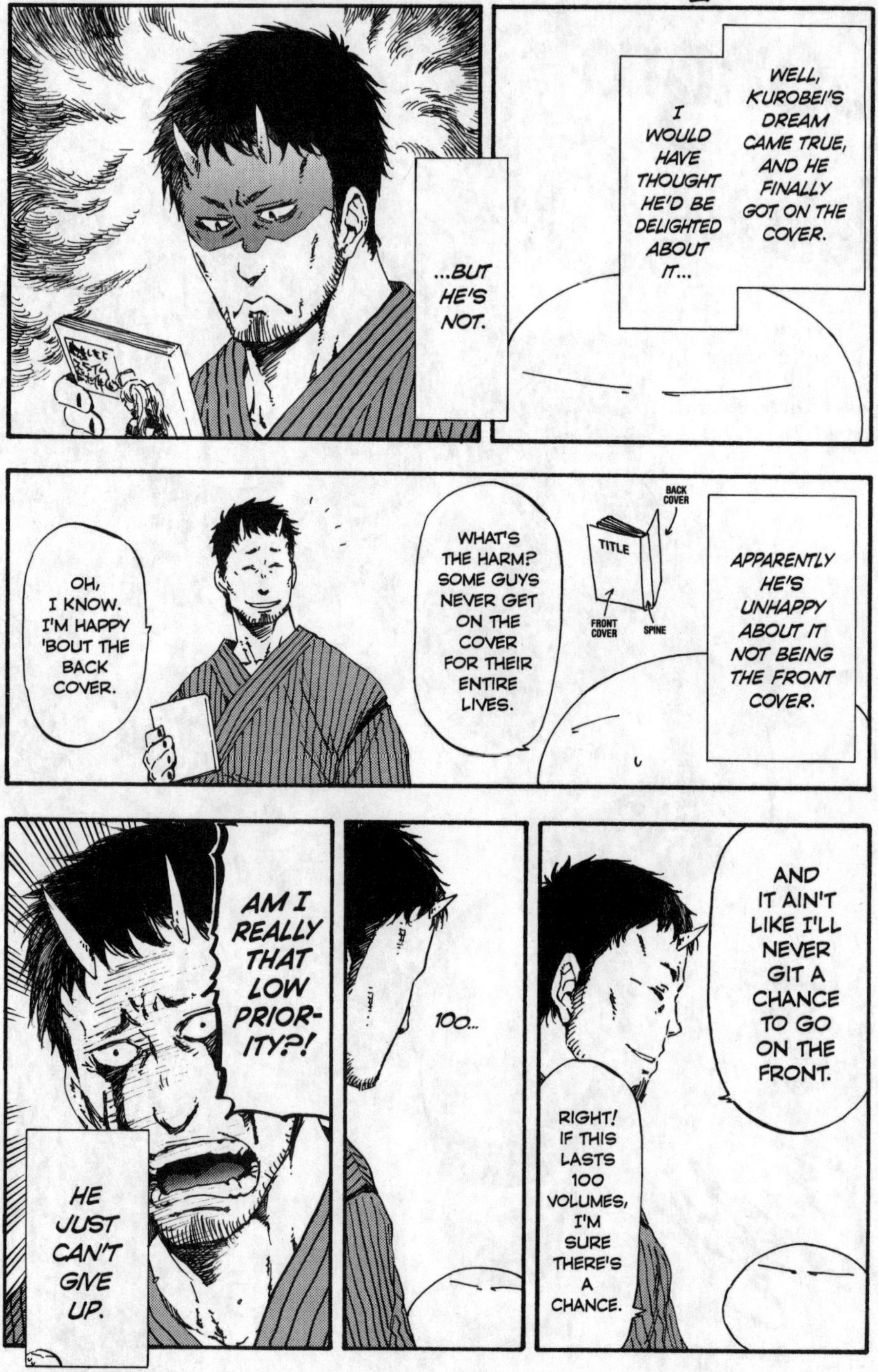
WELL, KUROBEI'S DREAM CAME TRUE, AND HE FINALLY GOT ON THE COVER.
I WOULD HAVE THOUGHT HE'D BE DELIGHTED ABOUT IT...
...BUT HE'S NOT.
APPARENTLY HE'S UNHAPPY ABOUT IT NOT BEING THE FRONT COVER.
BACK COVER
TITLE
FRONT COVER
SPINE
WHAT'S THE HARM? SOME GUYS NEVER GET ON THE COVER FOR THEIR ENTIRE LIVES.
OH, I KNOW. I'M HAPPY 'BOUT THE BACK COVER.
AND IT AIN'T LIKE I'LL NEVER GIT A CHANCE TO GO ON THE FRONT.
RIGHT! IF THIS LASTS 100 VOLUMES, I'M SURE THERE'S A CHANCE.
100...
AM I REALLY THAT LOW PRIORITY?!
HE JUST CAN'T GIVE UP.

Boiled ramen eggs.

Actually, I get the feeling
that the ramen is the
main attraction here.

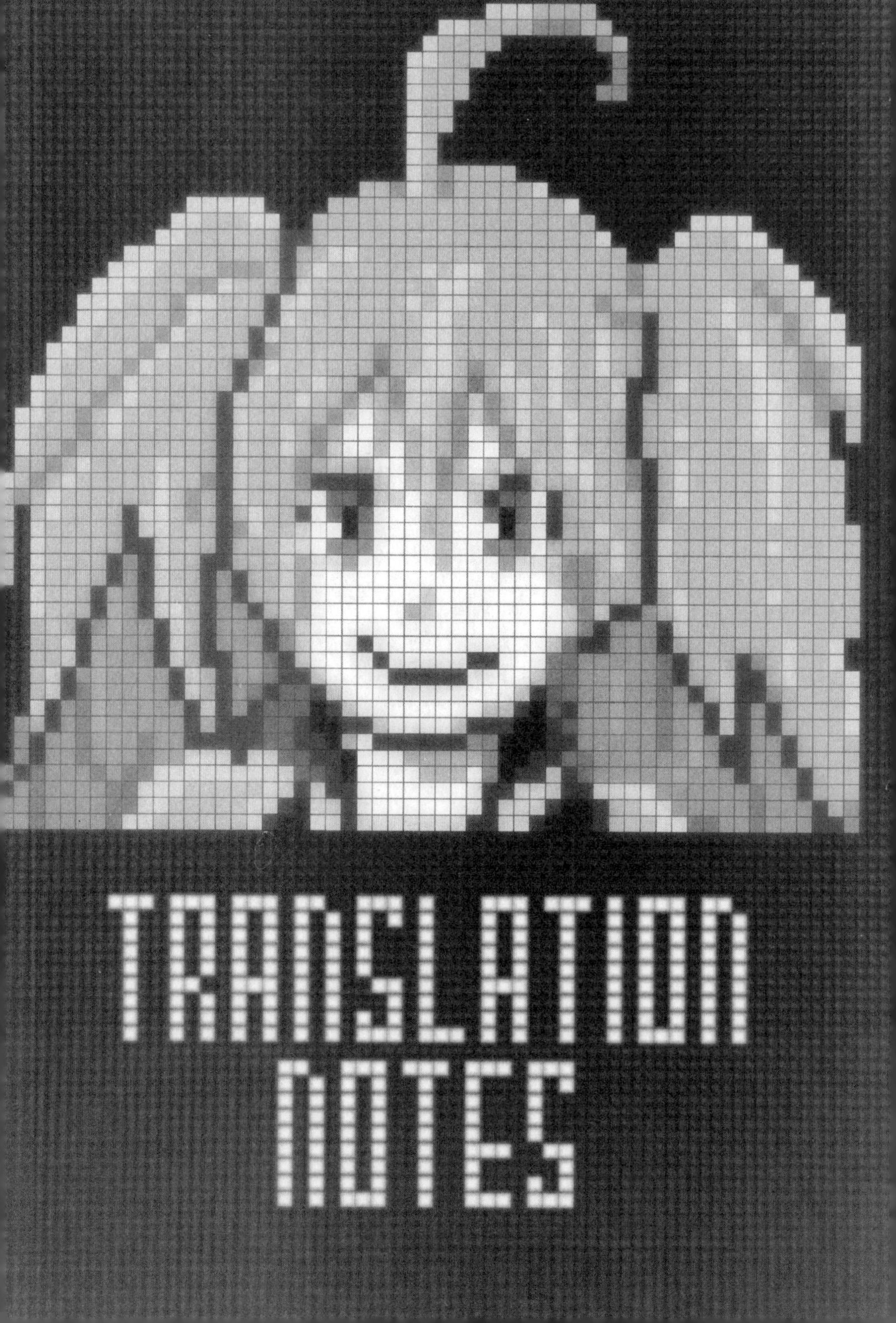

TRANSLATION NOTES

FOUR EVIL HENCHMEN

page 107

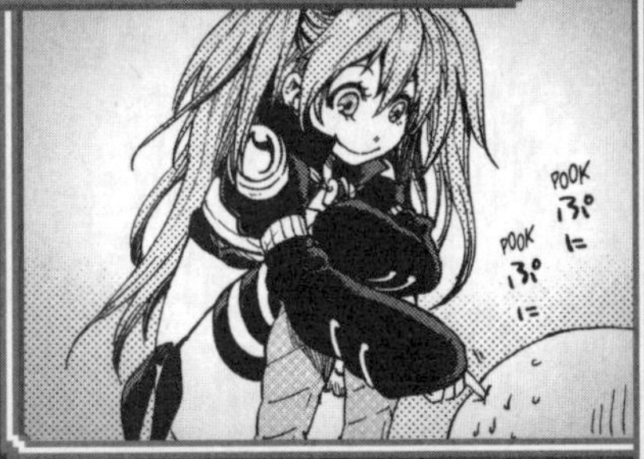
POOK
POOK

The original term used is *shitennô*, or Four Heavenly Kings, which are the gods who preside over the four cardinal directions in Buddhist mythology. In modern Japanese parlance, the term is often used to describe four massive figures in any particular category (often with one "demon lord" standing on their shoulders), particularly in a pop culture sense. It's also a common trope in RPGs, where the big bad guy is introduced with a number of menacing subordinates who come after the player in order of conveniently ascending strength, ensuring that by the time the final villain enters the picture, the party is a high enough level for the challenge.

The Black Museum: The Ghost and the Lady

By Kazuhiro Fujita

Deep in Scotland Yard in London sits an evidence room dedicated to the greatest mysteries of British history. In this "Black Museum" sits a misshapen hunk of lead—two bullets fused together—the key to a wartime encounter between Florence Nightingale, the mother of modern nursing, and a supernatural Man in Grey. This story is unknown to most scholars of history, but a special guest of the museum will tell the tale of The Ghost and the Lady...

Praise for Kazuhiro Fujita's *Ushio and Tora*

"A charming revival that combines a classic look with modern depth and pacing... **Essential viewing both for curmudgeons and new fans alike.**" — Anime News Network

"**GREAT!** The first episode of Ushio and Tora captures the essence of '90s anime." — IGN

KC KODANSHA COMICS

Japan's most powerful spirit medium delves into the ghost world's greatest mysteries!

Story by Kyo Shirodaira, famed author of mystery fiction and creator of *Spiral*, *Blast of Tempest*, and *The Record of a Fallen Vampire*.

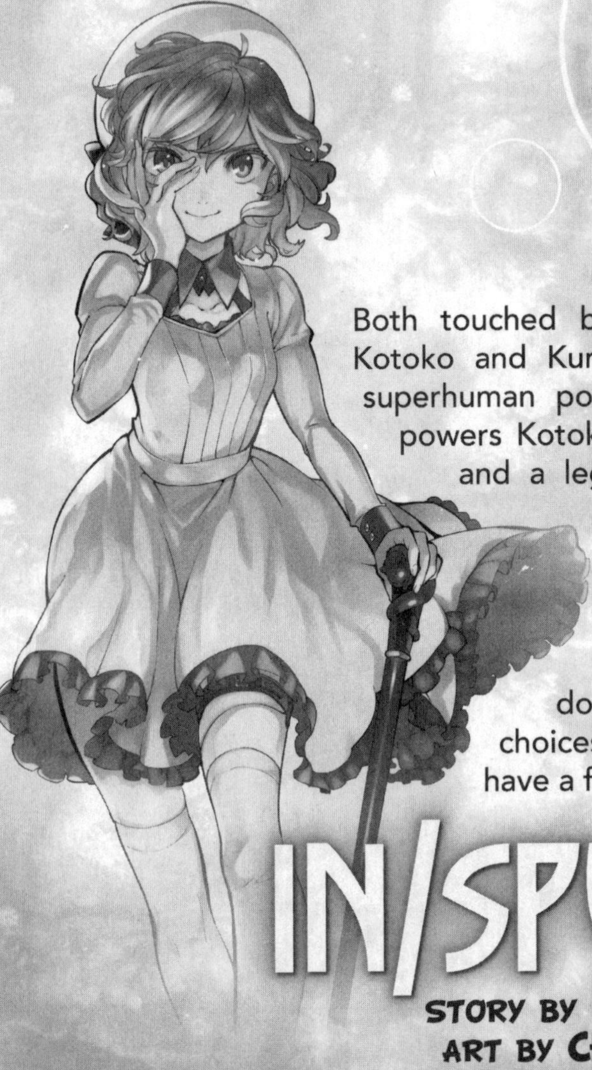

Both touched by spirits called yôkai, Kotoko and Kurô have gained unique superhuman powers. But to gain her powers Kotoko has given up an eye and a leg, and Kurô's personal life is in shambles. So when Kotoko suggests they team up to deal with renegades from the spirit world, Kurô doesn't have many other choices, but Kotoko might just have a few ulterior motives...

IN/SPECTRE

STORY BY KYO SHIRODAIRA
ART BY CHASHIBA KATASE

New action series from Hiroyuki Takei, creator of the classic shonen franchise Shaman King!

In medieval Japan, a bell hanging on the collar is a sign that a cat has a master. Norachiyo's bell hangs from his katana sheath, but he is nonetheless a stray — a ronin. This one-eyed cat samurai travels across a dishonest world, cutting through pretense and deception with his blade.

STRAY CAT SAMURAI

By
Hiroyuki Takei

Having lost his wife, high school teacher Kōhei Inuzuka is doing his best to raise his young daughter Tsumugi as a single father. He's pretty bad at cooking and doesn't have a huge appetite to begin with, but chance brings his little family together with one of his students, the lonely Kotori. The three of them are anything but comfortable in the kitchen, but the healing power of home cooking might just work on their grieving hearts.

"This season's number-one feel-good anime!" —Anime News Network

"A beautifully-drawn story about comfort food and family and grief. Recommended." —Otaku USA Magazine

sweetness & lightning

By Gido Amagakure

KC
KODANSHA
COMICS

That Time I Got Reincarnated as a Slime volume 6 is a work of fiction. Names, characters, places, and incidents are the products of the author's imagination or are used fictitiously. Any resemblance to actual events, locales, or persons, living or dead, is entirely coincidental.

A Kodansha Comics Trade Paperback Original.

Published in the United States by Kodansha Comics,
an imprint of Kodansha USA Publishing, LLC, New York.

Publication rights for this English edition arranged through Kodansha Ltd., Tokyo.

First published in Japan in 2017 by Kodansha Ltd., Tokyo, as *Tensei Shitara Suraimu Datta Ken* volume 6.

ISBN 978-1-63236-640-5

Printed in the United States of America.

www.kodansha.us

7th Printing

Translation: Stephen Paul
Lettering: Evan Hayden
Editing: Ajani Oloye
Kodansha Comics edition cover design: Phil Balsman